2010
ALMANAC

111TH CONGRESS
2ND SESSION

VOLUME LXVI

JAN AUSTIN, EDITOR
JENNIFER RUBIO, PRODUCTION

CQ Roll Call

77 K Street, N.E.
Washington, D.C. 20002

Summary Table of Contents

Appendixes

TABLE OF CONTENTS

CHAPTER 1 — INSIDE CONGRESS

CHAPTER 2 — APPROPRIATIONS

CHAPTER 3 — BANKING & FINANCIAL SERVICES

CHAPTER 4 — BUDGET

CHAPTER 5 — CONGRESSIONAL AFFAIRS

CHAPTER 6 — DEFENSE, INTELLIGENCE & FOREIGN POLICY

CHAPTER 7 — ECONOMIC AFFAIRS

CHAPTER 8 — EMPLOYMENT & LABOR

CHAPTER 9 — HEALTH & EDUCATION

CHAPTER 10 — LEGAL AFFAIRS

CHAPTER 11 — POLITICS

CHAPTER 12 — REGULATORY POLICY, ENERGY & ENVIRONMENT

CHAPTER 13 — SCIENCE & TECHNOLOGY

CHAPTER 14 — TAXES

CHAPTER 15 — TRANSPORTATION & INFRASTRUCTURE

APPENDIXES

Chapter 1

INSIDE CONGRESS

Landmark Health Care Law and Late Flurry of Bills Mark Session

AGAINST CONSIDERABLE ODDS, the second session of the 111th Congress became one of the most productive in decades. On the most prominent issues, lawmakers teetered between a big deal and no deal at all and were buffeted by one surprise after another before finishing with a burst of activity in a lame-duck session.

The first surprise came just three weeks into the session, when Republican Scott P. Brown won a Massachusetts Senate special election to fill the seat of Edward M. Kennedy, who died Aug. 25, 2009.

That reduced the Senate Democratic Caucus to 59 members instead of 60, the bare minimum its leaders had needed to overcome Republican delays on health care and other issues. It also reinforced the confidence of Republicans that there was no harm — and possibly considerable gain — in opposing every element of the ambitious agenda championed by President Obama and the Democrats.

Democrats were nevertheless able to pull out victories in March on the broadest expansion of health care coverage since the creation of Medicare in 1965 and in June on a sweeping rewrite of the way the nation's financial industry was regulated.

But lawmakers got relatively little done in the months that followed, and it looked as if the session would sputter for the rest of the year. Democrats struggled to enact even small pieces of their most high-profile agenda item — job creation and aid to jobless workers. Republicans kept the Senate mired in procedural squabbles, and Democrats punted until after the midterm elections on the year's appropriations bills and on deciding what to do about Bush-era tax cuts from 2001 and 2003 (PL 107-16, PL 108-27) that were due to expire Dec. 31.

The final surprise was the productivity of the lame-duck session usually a relatively low-key affair — particularly in the face of what Obama called the "shellacking" Democrats took in the Nov. 2 elections. Both parties returned from the campaign season to an altered landscape, with Republicans poised to take over the House in 2011 and occupy a greater number of seats in the Senate. Many expected the result to be gridlock.

Instead, during a two-week period leading up to adjournment on Dec. 22, Obama and Republicans struck an agreement on expiring tax rates and unemployment benefits, the Senate ratified a new Strategic Arms Reduction Treaty (New START) with Russia, and lawmakers repealed the "don't ask, don't tell" law that prevented openly gay people from serving in the military.

Congress also cleared a defense authorization bill that had seemed near death only days before and sent the president legislation to give the Food and Drug Administration (FDA) major new authority to regulate food safety.

With their clout reduced as a result of the election, Democrats accepted a short-term appropriations bill that kept the government open through March 4, 2011. The time frame was longer than Republicans wanted, but it still left them an opportunity to put an early stamp on government spending in the new year.

MAKING HISTORY

The health care overhaul and the financial services law were both legacy-making victories for Obama, who had made the hugely ambitious legislation the top domestic priorities for his presidency.

● **Health care.** The House and Senate passed significantly different versions of the bill in the first session — both by margins that seemed to leave little room for compromise. House Democrats were looking for some give and take, although they were not in complete agreement on what they wanted. Some, for example, still pushed for a government-run option for health insurance, while others wanted to strengthen anti-abortion language. But Brown's election removed the possibility of winning another vote on any version of the measure in the Senate, and in the end, House Democrats realized they had no choice but to clear the bill the Senate had passed with great difficulty in December (PL 111-148).

To ease the pain, lawmakers cleared a second bill (PL 111-152) that made modest changes to the overhaul and also contained a major rewrite of federal student loans that made the government the sole provider of the loans and ended the parallel program of federal subsidies to private lenders.

Under the health care overhaul, as modified by the "corrections" bill, about 32 million uninsured Americans were expected to obtain medical insurance coverage, mainly through subsidized private insurance policies or through expanded access to Medicaid, the joint federal-state health program for the poor.

The law required most Americans to have coverage by 2014. Uninsured Americans and small businesses could shop for health plans in state-run marketplaces, and low-income families could get subsidized premiums. The law barred health insurance companies from denying coverage because of pre-existing conditions, allowed parents to keep their children on their policies until age 26, and phased out the "doughnut hole," which required Medicare recipients to pay 100 percent of prescription drug costs above a certain level before costs were again shared between the patient and Medicare.

The cost of the new law — estimated at nearly $1 trillion over 10 years — was offset mainly by applying the Medicare hospital payroll tax to the investment income of the wealthy, placing an excise tax on high-cost insurance plans and reducing payments to Medicare Advantage plans.

Leaders: 111th Congress, 2nd Session

SENATE

President of the Senate: Vice President Joseph R. Biden Jr.
President Pro Tempore: Robert C. Byrd, D-W.Va.[1]

Democrats

Majority Leader . . . . Harry Reid, Nev.
Majority Whip . . . . Richard J. Durbin, Ill.
Caucus Vice Chairman. . . . . Charles E. Schumer, N.Y.
Policy Committee Chairman . . . . . . Byron L. Dorgan, N.D.
Conference Secretary . . . . Patty Murray, Wash.

Steering and Outreach
  Committee Chairwoman . . . . . . Debbie Stabenow, Mich.
Chief Deputy Whip . . . . Barbara Boxer, Calif.
Democratic Senatorial Campaign
  Committee Chairman. . . . . Robert Menendez, N.J.

Republicans

Minority Leader . . . . Mitch McConnell, Ky.
Minority Whip . . . . Jon Kyl, Ariz.
Conference Chairman . . . . Lamar Alexander, Tenn.
Conference Vice Chairwoman . . . . . Lisa Murkowski, Alaska[2]

Policy Committee Chairman . . . . . John Thune, S.D.
Chief Deputy Whip . . . . Richard M. Burr, N.C.
National Republican Senatorial
  Committee Chairman. . . . . John Cornyn, Texas
Counsel & Adviser to the Leader . . Robert F. Bennett, Utah

HOUSE

Speaker of the House: Nancy Pelosi, D-Calif.

Democrats

Majority Leader . . . . Steny H. Hoyer, Md.
Majority Whip . . . . James E. Clyburn, S.C.
Caucus Chairman . . . . John B. Larson, Conn.
Caucus Vice Chairman. . . . . Xavier Becerra, Calif.
Assistant to the Speaker . . . . Chris Van Hollen, Md.
Senior Chief Deputy Whip . . . . John Lewis, Ga.

Democratic Congressional Campaign
  Committee Chairman. . . . . Chris Van Hollen, Md.
Steering and Policy Committee
  Co-Chairwoman. . . . . Rosa DeLauro, Conn.
  Co-Chairman . . . . George Miller, Calif.

Republicans

Minority Leader . . . . John A. Boehner, Ohio
Minority Whip . . . . Eric Cantor, Va.
Conference Chairman . . . . Mike Pence, Ind.
Conference Vice Chairwoman . . . . . Cathy McMorris Rodgers, Wash.

Conference Secretary . . . . John Carter, Texas
Policy Committee Chairman . . . . . Thaddeus McCotter, Mich.
Chief Deputy Whip . . . . Kevin McCarthy, Calif.
National Republican Congressional
  Committee Chairman. . . . . Pete Sessions, Texas

[1] As of April 5, 2010. After the death of Byrd, Daniel K. Inouye of Hawaii assumed the post of Senate president pro tempore.
[2] Murkowski resigned her position after losing the Republican primary and launching a write-in campaign Sept. 17, 2010. She was replaced by John Barrasso of Wyoming on Sept. 22.

Republicans, who sought to block the measure at every step, campaigned on a promise to repeal the law in the next Congress.

● **Financial services.** The overhaul, which altered banking and securities law going back as far as 1933, began in the House, where a version introduced by Financial Services Chairman Barney Frank, D-Mass., passed in December 2009.

In the Senate, Christopher J. Dodd, D-Conn., chairman of the Banking, Housing and Urban Affairs Committee, continued negotiating into early 2010 before introducing a bill that could win approval from his panel. He guided the measure through the Senate virtually unscathed in May, and lawmakers convened a genuine conference committee to resolve differences; it was a method that had come to be used less and less during the decade, as the majority instead traded amended bills back and forth between the chambers until they could agree — or one chamber receded. The conferees reached a compromise in late June.

But Majority Leader Harry Reid, D-Nev., had to hold up further action following the death of the venerable West Virginia Democrat Robert C. Byrd, who had served a half-century in the Senate. Without Byrd's vote, Reid first had to find four Republicans to meet the 60-vote threshold to invoke cloture. The Senate cleared the bill in mid-July (PL 111-203).

The legislation was a response to the financial crisis that began in 2007 and led to the deepest recession since the Great Depression. In an effort to end the "too big to fail" assumption that the government would bail out huge, failing banks, it created an orderly process for tightening restraints on faltering institutions and, in extreme cases, shutting them down before they created a wider crisis.

The law brought derivatives trading under federal regulation for the first time. It created a new consumer protection agency to look out for the interests of consumers and participate when officials examined the state of the economy as a whole.

The Federal Reserve received major new responsibilities, including housing the new consumer agency and playing a central role in bringing risky financial institutions under federal restrictions.

Although the legislation provided direction and set requirements, it remained up to the regulatory agencies to turn it into reality, which was expected to be a lengthy process.

CAUGHT IN THE DOLDRUMS

On many other issues, lawmakers were unable to transcend their partisan disputes. There was little forward movement, particularly during the summer.

● **Jobs agenda.** Even before the health care bill cleared, Democrats from Obama on down were concentrating on job creation as their signature issue in advance of the midterm elections. Some rank-and-file members urged the leadership early in the year to cut their losses on health care and focus instead on jobs bills. Most of the Democratic legislation was aimed at injecting money into the economy to spur growth and employment — either directly, through infrastructure spending and incentives for small business, or indirectly, through tax breaks and unemployment benefits that would give individuals and families more disposable income.

But every effort to pass a big jobs bill was torn apart by disputes over offsetting the costs, and the bills grew and shrank as they moved between the chambers. The result was a piecemeal approach with round after round of temporary extensions and frequent expirations. Federal benefits for the long-term unemployed expired four times during the year; each new extension had to be retroactive.

Democrats generally argued that the tax cuts should be paid for, while extended unemployment benefits were an emergency that did not need to be offset. Republicans argued the opposite, calling tax cuts an extension of existing law, while saying benefits for jobless workers deepened the deficit.

● **Budget.** In an early sign that the appropriations process was in trouble, Democrats made minimal effort to complete a bicameral fiscal 2011 budget resolution. Growing voter concern about the deficit and Republicans' determination to paint the Democrats as deaf to those worries gave the majority little incentive to proceed. Although the annual resolution does not become law, it sets a top-line number for discretionary spending that smooths the way for appropriators to do their job.

The Senate Budget Committee adopted a resolution setting a $1.122 trillion discretionary limit, but the measure never went to the floor and Democrats later floated lower caps. The House committee did not act; instead, the House indirectly adopted a $1.121 trillion discretionary ceiling. No effort was made to resolve the differences.

● **Deficit.** A bipartisan attempt to set up a mechanism to help control the deficit was defeated in the Senate in January. Fiscal conservatives had made their support for a must-pass increase in the debt limit contingent on creating a statutory debt commission and requiring Congress to vote on its recommendations. They ultimately settled for a bipartisan, 18-member commission created by executive order and a promise from Democratic leaders that any proposals gaining 14 votes would be brought to the floor.

The commission presented a set of recommendations in December that called for slashing deficits through a combination of serious spending cuts — including entitlements — and tax increases. A majority of members on the commission backed the plan, but they did not have enough support within the group to send the proposals to Congress. However, the ideas were expected to help shape future debates.

A short-term debt limit bill enacted in February (PL 111-139) increased the Treasury Department's borrowing limit to $14.29 trillion, enough to last into early 2011. Lawmakers attached statutory rules requiring that new legislation that increased existing mandatory spending or cut revenue be offset by other mandatory cuts or tax increases.

● **Appropriations.** Congress cleared a $58.8 billion fiscal 2010 supplemental spending bill in July — primarily for military operations in Afghanistan and Iraq — after two and a half months of debate and negotiations (PL 111-212). House Democratic leaders tried adding billions of dollars in domestic spending to the bill, mainly to avert layoffs of tens of thousands of teachers and other local employees due to local budget cutting. But the domestic money was a non-starter in the Senate, and the House ended up clearing the Senate's narrower bill.

David R. Obey, D-Wis., the retiring chairman of the House Appropriations Committee, had made the teacher funding his chief goal. Lawmakers ended up returning briefly in August to clear a supplemental spending bill for local employees, as well as for federal Medicaid funding to the states (PL 111-226), and a second small measure for border security (PL 111-230).

While it took an extended debate, enactment of the Iraq-Afghanistan supplemental was a foregone conclusion amid war.

The fiscal 2011 appropriations bills were given a much lower priority. Republicans denounced the bills, drafted by Democrats, as too expensive, and Democrats had little appetite for engaging in a fight that Republicans could use against them during the election campaign.

The House passed two of the 12 annual spending bills before the end of the regular session; none of the other House measures got beyond a subcommittee markup. The Senate Appropriations Committee approved 11 of the 12 bills, but none reached the Senate floor.

● **Campaign finance.** House Democrats passed a bill in June aimed at limiting the effect of a January Supreme Court decision that corporations, nonprofits and labor unions had the same free-speech rights as individuals and could use their own treasuries to fund political campaign advertisements. The issue was important enough to Obama that he took the unusual step of criticizing the ruling during his State of the Union address as several justices sat in the front row. As frequently happened, however, the House effort died in the Senate, where Republicans denied Democratic leaders the 60 votes needed to shut off a filibuster.

The House bill would have imposed stricter disclosure rules, required chief executives to appear in their ads and banned election-related spending by companies that received federal aid. The Senate had a similar bill, which sponsors modified in an unsuccessful attempt to woo at least some Republicans.

● **Oil spill.** A massive oil spill in the Gulf of Mexico following the explosion of a Deepwater Horizon oil rig sparked bipartisan sentiment for tougher oil-drilling safety laws. Democrats in both chambers assembled legislation from a flurry of bills, and the House passed legislation in July to overhaul federal regulation of offshore drilling. Among other things, it would have eliminated an existing $75 million cap on a company's liability for economic damages stemming from an oil spill.

Reid scaled back a companion bill twice, but he still was unable to get the votes to pass it in the Senate.

Interest in the legislation declined as lawmakers began fighting over the scope and substance, and the oil spill was eventually controlled and then ended. No legislation was enacted.

A NEW FACE ON THE SUPREME COURT

In a major break in the summer doldrums, the Senate in early August confirmed Obama's choice of Elena Kagan to serve on the Supreme Court, filling the seat vacated by Justice John Paul Stevens, who retired at the end of the 2009-10 session after 35 years on the bench. Kagan, the first woman dean of Harvard Law School and the solicitor general since early 2009, was the second justice Obama chose in two years. Sonia Sotomayor took her place on the bench in 2009

Highlights: 111th Congress, Second Session

CONGRESS DID

- Overhaul the nation's health care system, centering on an expansion of medical insurance coverage.
- Overhaul the regulation of the financial services industry with changes that promised to alter banking and securities law going back as far as 1933.
- Repeal the "don't ask, don't tell" law that prevented openly gay people from serving in the military.
- Confirm Elena Kagan to the Supreme Court.
- Extend 2001 and 2003 individual tax cuts for taxpayers at all income levels.
- Renew the expired tax on estates, with a 35 percent rate and exemption level of $5 million.
- Approve ratification of a new Strategic Arms Reduction Treaty with Russia.
- Fund the operations of the federal government, mostly at fiscal 2010 levels with exceptions, through March 4, 2011.
- Appropriate $33.4 billion for the wars in Iraq and Afghanistan in fiscal 2010 and $157.7 billion in fiscal 2011.
- Extend federal emergency unemployment benefits through Dec. 31, 2011.

- Expand the authority of the Food and Drug Administration to regulate the safety of the food supply.
- Reauthorize intelligence programs for the first time in six years.
- Censure Rep. Charles B. Rangel, D-N.Y., for 11 violations of House rules, the first censure of a representative since 1983.

CONGRESS DID NOT

- Complete any of the 12 regular fiscal 2011 appropriations bills.
- Clear the DREAM Act to provide a path to citizenship for hundreds of thousands of adult children of illegal immigrants.
- Complete legislation to combat global warming by limiting greenhouse gas emissions.
- Provide a multi-year reauthorization for surface transportation programs.
- Provide a multi-year reauthorization for the Federal Aviation Administration.
- Establish a fiscal 2011 budget blueprint for Congress' tax and spending decisions.
- Authorize a program to defend federal computer networks against cyberattacks.
- Clear a campaign finance disclosure bill.

under stiff criticism from many Republicans for what they argued was an activist bent that made the Latina unsuited for the high court.

Kagan was the first court nominee in 39 years with no experience as a judge, a fact that Democrats said would enable her to bring a real-world perspective to the court. Republicans argued that she lacked the background necessary for the high court.

But the nomination attracted far less passion than that of Sotomayor, in part because Kagan carried neither the lengthy judicial paper trail nor the same history of controversial speeches as Sotomayor. Support from several GOP senators also made it virtually impossible for Republicans to get the votes needed to filibuster the nomination.

With Kagan joining Sotomayor and Ruth Bader Ginsburg, the Supreme Court had three women members for the first time.

MOST SEPTEMBER HOPES DASHED

Lawmakers returned from their summer recess on Sept. 13 for three weeks of legislative activity before adjourning to campaign. Democratic leaders began with a high-profile to-do list that included the annual defense authorization bill, immigration legislation, a food safety bill and some of the fiscal 2011 appropriations bills, as well as extending some or all of the Bush-era tax cuts.

But their plans were quickly scuttled by bitter partisanship combined with political nervousness and legislative lethargy brought on by campaign pressures. The chief obstacles came in the Senate, where partisan sparring blocked action on the fiscal 2011 defense authorization bill, particularly because it carried "don't ask, don't tell" repeal language, and on any effort to extend the 2001 and 2003 tax cuts. House Democrats were unwilling to go first on a tax bill, given the Senate's history of burying House-passed legislation.

By late in the month, Senate Democratic leaders had narrowed their agenda to one item: clearing another short-term continuing resolution to carry the government past the election and into the lame-duck session (PL 111-242).

There were a few achievements, particularly in the House, where the

ability to set rules for floor debate gave Democrats more control. Congress cleared the first intelligence authorization bill to be enacted in six years (PL 111-259), after negotiating a compromise with the White House on congressional notification of sensitive intelligence activities. A bill to reauthorize NASA also cleared (PL 111-267), opening the way to more commercial participation in the space program; in that case, the House cleared the Senate bill when it became clear there would not be enough time to settle differences before the end of the session.

The House also cleared a bill to aid small businesses, which were seen as major engines of job creation. The measure (PL 111-240) created a $30 billion fund to encourage lending to small business and provided about $12 billion in tax benefits.

But most of Congress' remaining business was left for the lame-duck session, including fiscal 2011 appropriations, the expiring tax cuts, the defense authorization bill, New START, expiring emergency unemployment benefits, and an impending cut in Medicare doctors' pay that many feared would drive physicians out of serving Medicare beneficiaries.

On Sept. 27, House GOP leaders released a "Pledge to America" campaign manifesto aimed at attracting voters concerned about mounting federal deficit spending and the health care overhaul. Their promises included rolling back government spending from existing levels, repealing major portions of the health care law, permanently extending all the expiring Bush-era tax cuts, overhauling medical liability laws and imposing a net hiring freeze on non-security federal employees.

Democrats had no similar document, and their election prospects looked grim.

GOP GAINS IN NOVEMBER

The Nov. 2 elections reversed the tide that had swept Obama into office and expanded the Democratic majorities in 2008. Republicans — energized by the highly conservative tea party movement — drove the Democrats from power in the House, trimmed

their majority in the Senate and left the president facing the prospect of a far more conservative Congress in a little more than two months.

Republicans gained 62 seats in the House, giving them a majority of 242 members for the 112th Congress, the largest since the 80th Congress in 1947-48. They far outdid their own 53-seat swing in 1994, posting one of the largest House pickups of all time, but fell just shy of the 71 net seats they gained in 1938, the second midterm election in Franklin D. Roosevelt's presidency.

In contrast to the previous two elections, independent voters broke heavily for Republicans. The GOP also benefited from an electorate that was older and less ethnically diverse than in 2008, when millions of young people and African-Americans turned out because Obama was at the top of the ballot. Also different from 2008 was the rise of the tea party movement, a loosely organized amalgam of voters bent on severe spending cuts and smaller government.

The new House freshman class consisted of 87 Republicans to just nine Democrats. Republicans gained six seats in the Senate, bringing them to a total of 47. With a 53-seat caucus, including two independents, Democrats retained control of the chamber, but Republicans gained enough seats to force Democrats to chip off significant GOP support in order to stop a filibuster.

Moreover, big gains at the state level gave Republicans an outsized role in the congressional redistricting process due to be completed in 2012. The GOP ended up with 25 of the 43 governors' seats in states that had more than one U.S. House seat. They also held full control of the legislatures in 21 states that would be redistricting.

LAME DUCK GETS STARTED

Congress convened for one week on Nov. 15, a period that the two parties devoted mainly to organizing for the next Congress.

● **Leadership chosen.** As expected and without opposition, Minority Leader John A. Boehner, R-Ohio, was chosen by his caucus to be the new Speaker of the House in the 112th Congress. His team included Eric Cantor of Virginia as majority leader and Kevin McCarthy of California as majority whip. The choices had to be confirmed by the House in January, which was a formality.

On the Democratic side, Nancy Pelosi of California, the powerful Speaker in the 110th and 111th Congresses, faced a mini-rebellion within her diminished ranks. She was forced to beat back an open challenge by Blue Dog Coalition member Heath Shuler of North Carolina in her bid to return to the minority leader position she held before Democrats took control of the House in 2007. Although she won the caucus nomination handily, 150-43, the fact that the vote even took place indicated the depth of soul-searching among Democrats following the elections.

Pelosi's second-in-command, Majority Leader Steny H. Hoyer of Maryland, was tapped to become minority whip; John B. Larson of Connecticut continued as caucus chairman. A new position, assistant minority leader, was added to keep Majority Whip James E. Clyburn of South Carolina in the mix.

Reid and Mitch McConnell, R-Ky., retained their positions as Senate majority and minority leaders, respectively. Majority Whip Richard J. Durbin, D-Ill., and Minority Whip Jon Kyl, R-Ariz., also kept their positions.

● **Ethics.** On Nov. 18, the Committee on Standards of Official Conduct found 20-term New York Democrat Charles B. Rangel guilty of 11 counts of misconduct in a case that dated to 2008 and included failing to pay taxes, inaccurately reporting his income and improperly

soliciting donations for an education center bearing his name. On Dec. 2, the House censured Rangel, who had been re-elected in November, forcing him to stand in the well as Pelosi read an oral rebuke. It was the first time the House had censured one of its own in 27 years.

GETTING DOWN TO BUSINESS

After a one-week recess for Thanksgiving, lawmakers returned Nov. 29 for a three-and-a-half-week period that ended Dec. 22. Obama stepped in quickly to tamp down what was expected to be a highly partisan session in which agreement on any of the outstanding bills was difficult to imagine.

● **Tax deal.** On Dec. 7, the president broke the longstanding stalemate over taxes, outlining a deal that the White House — principally Vice President Joseph R. Biden Jr. — had negotiated with McConnell and other GOP leaders.

Liberal Democrats were furious that Obama conceded on including the highest income brackets in a two-year extension of the 2001 and 2003 income tax cuts. They also opposed a provision that extended the estate tax with more generous terms than they wanted. Less noticed were the wins Obama scored, most notably the inclusion of a 13-month extension of federal emergency unemployment benefits and an unprecedented one-year reduction in employees' payroll taxes — provisions some economists saw as having the potential to inject significant stimulus money into the economy.

House Democrats were so upset over the concessions — and their exclusion from the negotiations — that they initially prevailed on Pelosi to keep the Obama plan off the floor and instead pass a version that would have let tax breaks for the well-off expire, among other things.

But an overwhelming vote in the Senate for a version that reflected the White House compromise left House Democrats with the choice of clearing the Senate bill or losing the chance to save middle-class taxpayers from stiff hikes in 2010 and to renew expired unemployment benefits. The House cleared the bill on Dec. 17 (PL 111-312).

● **'Don't ask, don't tell.'** The following day, after months of maneuvering, the Senate cleared a House-passed bill (PL 111-321) repealing the 1993 "don't ask, don't tell" provisions that prohibited openly gay people from serving in the military. The repeal gained momentum when it got strong backing from Defense Secretary Robert M. Gates as well as Joint Chiefs Chairman Adm. Mike Mullen and Vice Chairman Gen. James E. Cartwright. The officials cited a Pentagon survey, made public Nov. 30, that found that 70 percent of U.S. military personnel surveyed believed a change in the law would have positive, mixed or no effects.

Gates said he would allow the change only when he was satisfied that all necessary training and education was completed across the military. He had said he did not want the law overturned by the courts, which could require an immediate change and allow little time for the military to prepare.

● **Food safety.** The food safety bill was caught up in a procedural mess over user fees. The Senate had included fees to help pay for the measure — in violation of the House's constitutional prerogative to initiate revenue changes. Supporters doubted that Congress would have time to finish the bill, but lawmakers came up with a workaround, and the House cleared a substitute version with the same content on Dec. 21 (PL 111-353).

● **Continuing appropriations.** Congress faced a Dec. 18 deadline for figuring out how to keep funding flowing to the federal government, a date that was extended to Dec. 21 to give lawmakers more

111th Congress, Second Session: By the Numbers

The second session of the 111th Congress began at noon on Jan. 5, 2010. The House adjourned sine die at 6 p.m. on Dec. 22, 2010. The Senate adjourned sine die at 8:03 p.m. on Dec. 22, 2010. Below are some statistical comparisons of activities in the two chambers over the past decade:

		2010	2009	2008	2007	2006	2005	2004	2003	2002	2001	2000
Days in session	Senate	158	191	184	190	138	159	133	167	149	173	141
	House	127	159	118	164	101	140	110	133	123	142	135
Time in session (hours)	Senate	1,075	1,421	989	1,376	1,028	1,222	1,032	1,454	1,043	1,236	1,018
	House	879	1,247	890	1,478	850	1,067	879	1,015	772	922	1,054
Average length of daily session (hours)	Senate	6.8	7.4	5.4	7.2	7.4	7.7	7.8	8.7	7.0	7.1	7.2
	House	6.9	7.8	7.5	9.0	8.4	7.6	8.0	7.6	6.3	6.5	7.8
Public laws enacted [1]		217	125	285	175	321	161	300	198	269	108	410
Bills and resolutions introduced	Senate	1,506	3,380	1,590	3,033	2,302	2,618	1,318	2,398	1,558	2,212	1,546
	House	3,098	5,691	3,225	6,194	2,451	5,703	2,338	4,616	2,711	4,318	2,701
	Total	**4,604**	**9,071**	**4,815**	**9,227**	**4,753**	**8,321**	**3,656**	**7,014**	**4,269**	**6,530**	**4,247**
Roll calls	Senate	307	397	215	442	279	366	216	459	253	380	298
	House [2]	660	987	688	1,177	541	669	543	675	483	507	600
	House [3]	664	991	690	1,186	543	671	544	677	484	512	603
	Total [3]	**971**	**1,388**	**905**	**1,628**	**822**	**1,037**	**760**	**1,136**	**737**	**892**	**901**
Vetoes		2 [4]	1	4	7 [4]	1	0	0	0	0	0	7 [4]

SOURCE: Congressional Record   [1] Bills signed into law during congressional session   [2] Votes only; excludes quorum calls   [3] Includes quorum calls   [4] Includes pocket vetoes

time to reach a consensus. In a last-ditch effort to push their caucus' priorities on domestic spending, House Democrats passed a long-term continuing resolution that would have kept the discretionary funding level at $1.089 trillion, roughly the 2010 level, for the rest of fiscal 2011. However, it would have shifted money around to provide billions of dollars in extra spending for the Defense Department and favored domestic programs.

The measure stalled in the Senate. An attempt by Appropriations Chairman Daniel K. Inouye, D-Hawaii, and his panel's ranking Republican, Thad Cochran of Mississippi, to win passage of a full-year omnibus package that included all 12 bills was blocked when GOP senators abruptly withdrew their support.

Ultimately, Congress cleared the short-term bill that kept most programs operating at fiscal 2010 levels through March 4, 2011 (PL 111-322), but provided some money for veterans, education, the Pentagon and other programs. The measure was largely a victory for Republicans, although it reflected some compromise: Many House Republicans wanted simply to continue fiscal 2010 funding for the whole year with few or no exceptions.

● **Defense authorization.** The House on Dec. 22 cleared a modified defense authorization bill, which the Senate had passed the previous day (PL 111-383). The measure had been stripped of controversial items, most significantly the "don't ask, don't tell" repeal language and also provisions that would have required the administration to continue funding the development of a second, competing engine for the F-35 Joint Strike Fighter and that would have allowed privately funded abortions in military hospitals. The Senate had rejected cloture on an earlier version of the bill that included the provisions, and lawmakers worried once again that there was not time to finalize the measure. It would have been the first time in 49 years that a defense authorization bill was not enacted.

● **New START.** In the last substantive vote of the year, the Senate approved ratification of New START (Treaty Doc 111-5), an action that had seemed out of reach a week or two earlier, given the rest of the legislation on the Senate's agenda. Ratification was the result of a determined effort by Reid and a tireless White House lobbying campaign led by Biden to win enough Republican support to meet the two-thirds vote threshold for a treaty. Reid had vowed to postpone adjournment if necessary to win the adoption of the treaty, which the administration knew would have less chance in the next Congress. ■

Chapter 2

APPROPRIATIONS

Democrats Make Little Headway on Spending Bills, Instead Pass Four CRs

DEMOCRATS MADE LITTLE effort to move the appropriations process along during the year, with the result being that Congress finished none of the fiscal 2011 spending bills and kept the government operating under a series of bills known as continuing resolutions.

The last of these CRs was enacted Dec. 22 (PL 111-322) and was set to last through March 4, 2011, which promised to give the incoming House Republican majority and the expanded Senate GOP Conference increased input into spending decisions for the remainder of fiscal 2011.

The meltdown began early in the year, when the Democratic majority declined to produce a bicameral budget resolution that would have set spending levels for fiscal 2011 and given the appropriators a common framework for writing the spending bills.

The Senate Budget Committee approved a budget resolution (S Con Res 60) in April that would have set a $1.122 trillion cap on discretionary spending — about $4 billion less than President Obama requested — but the measure went no further. In the absence of action by the House Budget Committee, the House in July indirectly adopted a one-year, $1.121 trillion discretionary spending limit (H Res 1493).

ANNUAL FISCAL 2011 BILLS

As the session progressed, the spending process grew more acrimonious. With growing voter anxiety over deficit spending and midterm elections approaching, Republicans stepped up their attacks on Democrats as big spenders. Democratic leaders made only halting progress on the 12 annual appropriations bills over the summer.

Facing GOP calls to cut spending, Senate Appropriations Chairman Daniel K. Inouye, D-Hawaii, volunteered to set a discretionary cap of $1.114 trillion. But Senate Republicans argued for a $1.108 trillion limit, and Majority Leader Harry Reid, D-Nev., appeared to accept that demand.

In the end, the House passed just two of the regular appropriations bills — one for the Department of Veterans Affairs and military construction, and the other for the departments of Transportation and Housing and Urban Development. None of the other House bills went beyond subcommittee markups. The Senate Appropriations Committee approved all but the Interior measure, but none of the bills reached the floor.

After their resurgence in the November elections, Republicans began calling for a short-term funding measure that would last only into the beginning of 2011, giving them an early opportunity to start cutting spending. Republicans also called for an end to earmarks for individual lawmakers' projects.

In a last-ditch effort to protect their domestic-spending priorities, House Democrats passed a bill (HR 3082) on Dec. 8 that would

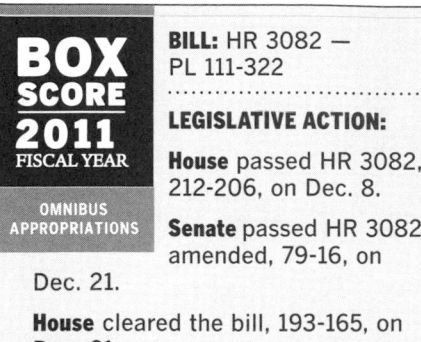

BOX SCORE 2011 FISCAL YEAR

OMNIBUS APPROPRIATIONS

BILL: HR 3082 — PL 111-322

LEGISLATIVE ACTION:

House passed HR 3082, 212-206, on Dec. 8.

Senate passed HR 3082, amended, 79-16, on Dec. 21.

House cleared the bill, 193-165, on Dec. 21.

President signed the bill on Dec. 22.

have kept funding at the fiscal 2010 level of $1.089 trillion through the end of the fiscal year. It would have shifted money around, however, providing billions in additional spending for the Defense Department and for favored domestic programs. The bill passed 212-206 with no GOP support. *(House vote 622, p. H-216)*

The measure stalled in the Senate, and Inouye's attempt to pass a full omnibus package that included all of the spending bills was blocked by Republicans. The package included some $8 billion in earmarks and would have exceeded fiscal 2010 discretionary spending by $18 billion. Inouye had expected to get enough GOP votes to block a filibuster, but Republicans abruptly withdrew their support, dooming the effort.

On Dec. 21, the Senate voted, 79-16, to pass the short-term CR, which froze most programs at fiscal 2010 spending levels, although it included some adjustments. The House cleared the bill, 193-165, later the same day. *(Senate vote 298, p. S-60; House vote 662, p. H-230)*

The final measure included provisions that froze federal nonmilitary pay for two years, as requested by the president; increased the rate of funding for student Pell grants to maintain the existing maximum grant; increased the rate of spending for the Veterans Benefits Administration; and continued higher funding for nuclear weapons labs, a step that was crucial to winning enough support in the Senate to ratify the New START agreement.

It allowed Fannie Mae and Freddie Mac to continue to back high-cost area home mortgages and maintained special pay and benefits for military personnel. It also authorized a Navy plan to buy 20 Littoral Combat Ships from two different contractors, and it extended the authorization for highway and other surface transportation programs through March 4, 2011.

The bill included a $6 billion cut in the budget for the Census Bureau, compared with fiscal 2010 spending, reflecting the fact that the bureau had completed the 2010 census.

Lawmakers had cleared three previous continuing resolutions: The first (PL 111-242), enacted Sept. 30, lasted through Dec. 3. The second (PL 111-290), signed into law Dec. 4, was good through Dec. 18. The third (PL 111-317), enacted Dec. 18, covered just three days and expired Dec. 21.

SUPPLEMENTAL SPENDING BILLS

Congress cleared a $58.8 billion fiscal 2010 supplemental spending bill in July (PL 111-212) that was devoted primarily to paying for operations in Iraq and Afghanistan.

Two smaller supplemental bills provided $600 million to increase patrol activities along the Southwest border (PL 111-230) and $26.1 billion to help state and local governments prevent layoffs of teachers and maintain Medicaid health coverage of the poor (PL 111-226). ■

Appropriations Mileposts
111th Congress — Second Session

Bill	House Action	Senate Action	House Final	Senate Final	President Signed	Story
FY 2011 Continuing Resolutions HR 3082 (PL 111-322); H J Res 105 (PL 111-317); H J Res 101 (PL 111-290); HR 3081 (PL 111-242)			Cleared 12/21/10 Passed 12/17/10 Passed 12/1/10 Cleared 9/30/10	Passed 12/21/10 Cleared 12/17/10 Cleared 12/2/10 Passed 9/29/10	12/22/10 12/18/10 12/4/10 9/30/10	2-3
FY 2011 Agriculture Draft House bill; S 3606	Subcommittee approved draft bill 6/30/10	Committee approved S 3606 7/15/10				2-5
FY 2011 Commerce-Justice-Science Draft House bill; S 3636	Subcommittee approved draft bill 6/29/10	Committee approved S 3636 7/22/10				2-5
FY 2011 Defense Draft House bill; S 3800	Subcommittee approved draft bill 7/27/10	Committee approved S 3800 9/16/10				2-6
FY 2011 Energy-Water Draft House bill; S 3635	Subcommittee approved draft bill 7/15/10	Committee approved S 3635 7/22/10				2-6
FY 2011 Financial Services Draft House bill; S 3677	Subcommittee approved draft bill 7/29/10	Committee approved S 3677 7/29/10				2-7
FY 2011 Homeland Security Draft House bill; S 3607	Subcommittee approved draft bill 6/24/10	Committee approved S 3607 7/15/10				2-7
FY 2011 Interior-Environment Draft House bill	Subcommittee approved draft bill 7/22/10					2-8
FY 2011 Labor-HHS-Education Draft House bill; S 3686	Subcommittee approved draft bill 7/15/10	Committee approved S 3686 7/29/10				2-8
FY 2011 Legislative Branch Draft House bill; S 3799	Subcommittee approved draft bill 7/1/10	Committee approved S 3799 9/16/10				2-9
FY 2011 Military Construction-VA HR 5822; S 3615	Passed HR 5822 7/28/10	Committee approved S 3615 7/15/10				2-9
FY 2011 State-Foreign Operations Draft House bill; S 3676	Subcommittee approved draft bill 6/30/10	Committee approved S 3676 7/29/10				2-9
FY 2011 Transportation-HUD HR 5850; S 3644	Passed HR 5850 7/29/10	Committee approved S 3644 7/22/10				2-10
FY 2010 War Supplemental HR 4899 — PL 111-212	Passed HR 4899, amended, 7/1/10	Passed HR 4899, amended, 5/27/10	Cleared HR 4899 7/27/10	Rejected House amendment 7/1/10	7/29/10	2-15
FY 2010 Border Security Supplemental HR 6080 — PL 111-230			Passed HR 6080 8/10/10	Cleared HR 6080 8/12/10	8/13/10	2-17
FY 2010 Education Supplemental HR 1586 — PL 111-226			Cleared HR 1586 8/10/10	Passed HR 1586, amended, 8/5/10	8/10/10	2-18

Action Aborted on All FY 2011 Bills

CONGRESS COMPLETED NONE OF THE 12 appropriations bills for fiscal 2011, which began on Oct. 1, 2010. To avoid a government shutdown, lawmakers cleared a series of short-term continuing resolutions that froze most government spending at fiscal 2010 levels. The last of these stopgap bills (PL 111-322) was good through March 4, 2011.

The following accounts cover the actions taken on the unfinished individual spending bills during the session.

AGRICULTURE

A FISCAL 2011 SPENDING BILL FOR the Agriculture Department and related agencies was approved by the full Senate Appropriations Committee but did not get beyond the Agriculture Subcommittee in the House. Programs under the bill were funded mostly at fiscal 2010 levels through March 4, 2011, under the continuing resolution signed into law on Dec. 22 (PL 111-322). *(Appropriations overview, p. 2-3)*

The annual Agriculture bill provided discretionary funding for the Women, Infants and Children (WIC) program; some rural conservation accounts; foreign food aid and some farm support programs; and the Food and Drug Administration (FDA). However, most of the funding was mandatory and was allocated under the 2008 farm law (PL 110-146). *(Chart, p. 2-11; farm law, 2008 Almanac, p. 3-3)*

A stand-alone Agriculture spending bill had been enacted only four times in the previous decade.

The chief hurdles for the fiscal 2011 bill, as for many of the year's other spending measures, were the tight overall budget and the brief time for legislating before Congress adjourned for the election. Appropriators in both chambers were working with a cap that kept discretionary spending for the Agriculture bill slightly below the amount enacted for fiscal 2010, forcing them to make tough trade-offs among programs.

The Senate Appropriations Committee approved a $132.1 billion bill (S 3606) by a vote of 17-12 on July 15 that the committee said would provide $10.5 billion more than the fiscal 2010 law. Most of the increase was due to the growth of mandatory spending. The bill included $22.9 billion for discretionary programs, which the panel said was about $600 million below the fiscal 2010 level and close to President Obama's request.

The House Agriculture Subcommittee approved a draft version of the bill by voice vote on June 30 that the panel said would provide $23.1 billion in discretionary spending.

The FDA would have been a winner under both bills, receiving $2.6 billion in the House draft and $2.5 billion in the Senate bill, compared with $2.4 billion in the fiscal 2010 law. Both measures proposed cuts to some popular agriculture conservation programs, drawing fire from agriculture and environmentalist groups.

Citing smaller-than-expected increases in food prices and participation, House appropriators said they would reduce discretionary funding for the WIC food aid program by $125 million from the fiscal 2010 level, to $7.1 billion. The Senate bill proposed freezing the program at the fiscal 2010 level of $7.3 billion; Obama requested $7.6 billion. Both bills would have funded the primary U.S. international food aid program, known as Food for Peace, at the fiscal 2010 level of $1.7 billion.

The House panel said it would fund the Agriculture Department's Food Safety and Inspection Service, the agency responsible for ensuring the safety of meat and poultry, at just more than $1 billion, the level sought by the administration and about $18 million more than in fiscal 2010. Senate appropriators approved $29 million more than the existing level.

Both bills would have eliminated funding for the voluntary National Animal Identification System, for which the administration requested $14 million. House Agriculture Appropriations Chairwoman Rosa DeLauro, D-Conn., complained that $147 million had been spent since 2004, with still no clear plan on how the program would be implemented.

LEGISLATIVE ACTION

▸ House Agriculture Subcommittee approved draft bill by voice vote June 30.

▸ Senate Appropriations Committee approved S 3606 (S Rept 111-221), 17-12, on July 15.

COMMERCE-JUSTICE-SCIENCE

APPROPRIATORS PLANNED TO REDUCE discretionary spending under the fiscal 2011 Commerce-Justice-Science bill — by $3.9 billion in a House draft and $4.3 billion in the Senate version — compared with the previous year. The cuts were more than covered by a proposed $6.1 billion reduction in both bills for the Census Bureau, which had received a boost in fiscal 2010 to carry out the 2010 census.

The bill funded the Commerce and Justice departments, as well as science agencies such as NASA, the National Science Foundation and the National Oceanic and Atmospheric Administration. Versions won approval from the full Senate Appropriations Committee and from the House Commerce-Justice-Science Subcommittee but went no further. *(Chart, p. 2-11)*

Most programs under the bill were funded at fiscal 2010 levels through March 4, 2011, under the continuing resolution signed into law on Dec. 22 (PL 111-322). *(Appropriations overview, p. 2-3)*

Much of the debate on the Commerce-Justice-Science bill centered on the future of NASA. While both measures met President Obama's request of $19 billion for the space agency, they differed on the manned-spaceflight program.

Senate appropriators included money to set the stage for restructuring NASA and investing in commercial spaceflight, which was the direction Obama wanted to take. House appropriators chose to leave the future of NASA's manned spaceflight in the hands of the authorizing committee, withholding $4.3 billion for the program until enactment of a NASA authorization bill, which occurred in October (PL 111-267). The panel took no position on the administration's plan to scrap NASA's Constellation spaceflight program and to replace the space shuttle with commercial carriers. *(NASA, p. 13-3)*

The House draft, which the Commerce-Justice-Science Subcommittee approved by voice vote June 29, totaled about $65.6 billion, with $60.5 billion in discretionary spending, virtually the same as the president's request.

The subcommittee added language to prohibit the use of funds to move detainees held at Guantánamo Bay, Cuba, to the United States or to prepare any facility in the United States to house them.

In a 5-9 party-line vote, the panel rejected an amendment by Jerry Lewis of California, the ranking Republican on the full Appropriations Committee, to reduce the bill's discretionary total by 3.2 percent, applied proportionately to each program. Lewis said his proposal would cut about $2 billion from the measure.

The Senate Appropriations Committee approved a $65.1 billion version of the bill (S 3636), 17-12, on July 22. The measure included $60.1 billion in discretionary funds, $400 million less than in Obama's request and in the House subcommittee's version.

Both bills included roughly $9 billion for the Commerce Department, $30 billion for the Justice Department and $7.4 billion for the National Science Foundation.

LEGISLATIVE ACTION

▸ House Commerce-Justice-Science Subcommittee approved draft bill by voice vote June 29.

▸ Senate Appropriations Committee approved S 3636 (S Rept 111-229), 17-12, on July 22.

DEFENSE

THE ANNUAL DEFENSE SPENDING BILL, typically considered a must-pass measure, was left unfinished along with all the other fiscal 2011 appropriations measures. The bill did not get beyond markups in a House subcommittee and in the full Senate Appropriations Committee. Programs under the bill were funded, mostly at fiscal 2010 levels, through March 4 under the continuing resolution signed into law on Dec. 22 (PL 111-322). (Appropriations overview, p. 2-3)

The bill funded the Defense Department and U.S. intelligence agencies. The House Defense Subcommittee approved its draft of the bill by voice vote July 27, proposing to appropriate $671 billion in fiscal 2011 — $12.2 billion more than enacted for fiscal 2010 but $7.3 billion less than President Obama requested. The Senate committee's version (S 3800), approved 18-12 on Sept. 16, called for only slightly less — $669.9 billion. (Chart, p. 2-11)

Both the House and Senate totals included $157.7 billion for military operations in Iraq and Afghanistan, leaving $513.3 billion and $512.2 billion, respectively, for basic Pentagon accounts. Obama had requested $157.9 billion for the overseas operations. The fiscal 2011 law that authorized the appropriations (PL 111-383) allowed for $158.7 billion. (Defense authorization, p. 6-3)

House appropriators ignored a White House veto threat in approving $450 million for the F-35 Joint Strike Fighter alternative engine, made by General Electric and Rolls-Royce.

Supporters wanted the Pentagon to equip some F-35s with that engine, while powering others with a Pratt & Whitney version. They said competition would mean better engines at lower cost, plus a diminished risk that technical problems would ground all F-35s. Obama and Defense Secretary Robert M. Gates countered that any such benefits were outweighed by the increased cost, and the White House had threatened to veto a measure that included funds for the second engine.

The Senate bill did not include the funds, and the issue became further complicated by the continuing resolution. Because the stopgap bill continued spending at fiscal 2010 levels, it included more than $430 million appropriated that year for research and development for the second engine. However, the expenditure was not authorized in the fiscal 2011 defense authorization law.

Both the House and Senate spending bills included funding for the 1.4 percent military pay raise that Obama recommended. The House

version followed the administration's wishes in omitting funds for additional C-17 transport planes. The subcommittee also approved the full $2 billion that the White House requested for additional training and equipment for Iraqi security forces — a controversial allocation in the view of those in Congress who thought Iraq should be paying more for its own defense. The Senate bill would have cut the request in half, providing $1 billion. (The defense authorization law approved $1.5 billion and required that the Iraqi government pay at least 20 percent of the cost of procuring items or services, other than major military equipment.)

Both bills would have provided $31.5 billion for the Defense Health Program, about $2.2 billion above the fiscal 2010 level; Obama requested $30.9 billion.

LEGISLATIVE ACTION

▸ House Defense Appropriations Subcommittee approved draft bill by voice vote July 27.

▸ Senate Appropriations Committee approved S 3800 (S Rept 111-295), 18-12, on Sept. 16.

ENERGY-WATER

LIKE MOST OF THE FISCAL 2011 appropriations bills, the Energy-Water measure stopped moving once it had been approved in different forms by the full Senate Appropriations Committee and by a House subcommittee. Programs under the bill were funded mostly at fiscal 2010 levels through March 4, 2011, under the continuing resolution signed into law on Dec. 22 (PL 111-322). (Appropriations overview, p. 2-3)

The annual bill covered the Energy Department, the Interior Department's Bureau of Reclamation and hundreds of water projects carried out by the Army Corps of Engineers. For years the bill had drawn broad support from both parties, especially because the politically popular water projects injected funds into districts across the country. But with the practice of setting aside money for specific projects under attack, hundreds of earmarks in the fiscal 2010 law were dropped in the continuing resolution.

Republicans voiced general opposition to the overall spending levels for fiscal 2011, noting, in particular, that the Energy Department had received more than $30 billion in extra funds under the 2009 economic stimulus law (PL 111-5).

The central dispute, however, was over President Obama's decision to shut down the proposed nuclear waste disposal facility at Yucca Mountain in Nevada. Republicans roundly criticized the move, as did some pro-nuclear Democrats. Democratic appropriators in both chambers turned back amendments that would have restored funds to allow the federal licensing process for the facility to continue.

The House Energy-Water Appropriations Subcommittee approved a draft of the bill by voice vote July 15 that would have provided $34.8 billion, about $500 million above the fiscal 2010 level and $1.1 billion less than Obama requested. Virtually all of the funding was discretionary.

The markup was initially delayed because of a dispute over the absence of provisions requested by Obama to support $36 billion in loan guarantees to make it easier for companies to borrow the money needed to build nuclear plants. Under a deal with Chet Edwards, D-Texas, that allowed the markup to proceed, the subcommittee draft included $25 billion each in new loan authority for nuclear power and renewable projects.

The Senate committee approved a $35.1 billion version of the bill

(S 3635) by a vote of 17-12 on July 22. *(Chart, p. 2-12)*

Much of the increase over fiscal 2010 in both bills went to boost funds for nuclear weapons programs — by $526 million in the House draft and $634 million in the Senate committee-approved bill. The continuing resolution retained increased funding for the weapons programs related to the New START agreement. *(New START, p. 6-8)*

Overall, the House proposed $28.1 billion and the Senate $28.3 billion for the Energy Department, including energy programs and nuclear weapons accounts. Both bills included about $5.3 billion for the Corps of Engineers and $1.1 billion for the Bureau of Reclamation.

LEGISLATIVE ACTION

▸ House Energy-Water Subcommittee approved draft bill by voice vote July 15.

▸ Senate Appropriations Committee approved S 3635 (S Rept 111-228), 17-12, on July 22.

FINANCIAL SERVICES

THE FISCAL 2011 FINANCIAL SERVICES spending bill, which contained increased funding for agencies central to implementing the changes enacted in the financial services overhaul law, won approval from the Senate Appropriations Committee and a House Appropriations subcommittee but went no further. Programs under the bill were funded mostly at fiscal 2010 levels through March 4, 2011, under the continuing resolution signed into law on Dec. 22 (PL 111-322). *(Appropriations overview, p. 2-3; financial services overhaul, p. 3-3)*

Democratic leaders had pledged to provide federal regulators with substantial funds to assist them in the task of writing hundreds of new rules needed to implement the financial services overhaul law enacted in July (PL 111-203). But they also faced deep voter anxiety over the amount of money Washington was spending in general.

The House Financial Services Subcommittee approved a draft bill by voice vote on July 29 that would have provided roughly $45.7 billion, $24.5 billion of that for discretionary programs. According to the panel, the discretionary amount was $314 million more than in fiscal 2010, but $757 million less than Obama requested.

The Senate full committee's bill (S 3677), approved 18-12 the same day, was slightly larger at $48.3 billion, with $25.4 billion devoted to discretionary programs. The rest of the money in both bills was mandatory funding, primarily for the Office of Personnel Management to cover pensions and retiree health benefits. *(Chart, p. 2-12)*

Republicans objected to the increase in discretionary spending, but Democrats argued that it was necessary to safeguard the financial system from a repeat of the 2008 crisis that led the country into recession.

Both bills would have given the Securities and Exchange Commission, which had major new responsibilities including writing rules for the derivatives markets, $1.3 billion, a boost of $205 million, or 17 percent, over the existing level. The Senate measure would have increased funding for the Commodity Futures Trading Commission by 70 percent, to $286 million; House funding for the CFTC was in another bill.

The Treasury Department received most of the discretionary funding: $13.8 billion in the House measure and $14 billion in the Senate bill. Virtually all of the funds were for the IRS, which was slated to receive $12.4 billion under the House draft, a $270 million increase over fiscal 2011, and $12.5 billion under the Senate version.

Both bills also included funds for the judiciary ($7.2 billion in both versions) and for the federal payment to the District of Columbia

($759 million and $739 million, respectively).

The two bills also included increases for the Small Business Administration: $1 billion in the House bill, $225 million above fiscal 2010 spending, and $1.1 billion in the Senate bill.

House appropriators included $702 million for the Executive Office of the President, cutting $58 million from Obama's request, mainly by dropping funding that Obama requested for a youth media campaign on drugs. The Senate bill included $795 million for the executive office.

The Senate committee adopted an amendment by voice vote to prohibit brand-name drug companies from paying generic-drug companies to delay introducing cheaper generics into the market. The provision mirrored a bill (S 369) sponsored by Herb Kohl, D-Wis., and approved by the Judiciary Committee in 2009.

Proponents argued that brand-name and generic-drug companies colluded, leading to higher prices for consumers and the federal government. Opponents said the restriction would make it harder for drugmakers to defend their patents. An effort by Arlen Specter, D-Pa., to strike the provision was rejected, 15-15.

Susan Collins of Maine, the top Republican on the Senate Financial Services Appropriations Subcommittee, won voice vote approval to drop a provision that would have required banks and credit unions that offered credit cards to charge the federal government the equivalent of the lowest interchange fee that they provided to their customers. Collins said the provision could harm small community banks and credit unions. Majority Whip Richard J. Durbin, D-Ill., who sponsored the language, argued that credit card issuers charged federal agencies far more than they did commercial businesses, and he promised to continue his fight.

LEGISLATIVE ACTION

▸ House Financial Services Subcommittee approved draft bill by voice vote July 29.

▸ Senate Appropriations Committee approved S 3677 (S Rept 111-238), 18-12, on July 29.

HOMELAND SECURITY

THE ANNUAL HOMELAND SECURITY BILL — often one of the first to reach the president's desk — followed the same path as most of the other fiscal 2011 measures, stalling after being approved by the Senate Appropriations Committee and by a House subcommittee.

Programs under the bill were funded mostly at fiscal 2010 levels through March 4, 2011, under the continuing resolution that was signed into law on Dec. 22 (PL 111-322). *(Appropriations overview, p. 2-3)*

The House Homeland Security Subcommittee approved a draft of the bill by voice vote June 24 that would have provided $45.5 billion for the department (not counting certain fees), of which $43.9 billion was discretionary funding. *(Chart, p. 2-12)*

The Senate version (S 3607), which the full Appropriations Committee approved by a 17-12 vote on July 15, totaled $45.2 billion, with $43.8 billion devoted to discretionary programs. The discretionary amount in both measures was roughly $1 billion more than in the fiscal 2010 law. President Obama requested $43.6 billion.

Funding for most of the department's major components was fairly similar in both bills. Among the biggest differences were funds for the Coast Guard ($10.2 billion in the House draft; $10.4 billion in the Senate bill) and the Federal Emergency Management Agency ($7.6 billion in the House draft; $7.3 billion in the Senate bill).

Both panels proposed $8.1 billion for the Transportation Security

Administration, which was slightly less than requested but about $400 million above fiscal 2010 spending. House Subcommittee Chairman David E. Price, D-N.C., said it was the largest increase proposed for any agency in his bill and that the money was essential to addressing vulnerabilities in the country's aviation security and intelligence sectors.

Both Price and the chairman of the Senate Homeland Security Subcommittee, Frank R. Lautenberg, D-N.J., emphasized the need to continue funding the department's regular operations while keeping an eye on evolving threats. They pointed in particular to a rise in the number of attempted attacks on U.S. soil, such as recent failed airliner and Times Square bombing attempts.

Senate subcommittee ranking Republican George V. Voinovich of Ohio argued that the bill was too costly and said he would try to amend it on the floor. "I bet you I can find over a billion dollars from the Homeland Security budget, and we won't miss it," he said. "I'm willing to bite the bullet and do some things that will make me unhappy."

The House panel adopted, 10-5, an amendment by ranking Republican Harold Rogers of Kentucky to prohibit the transfer of detainees from the prison at Guantánamo Bay, Cuba, to the United States.

LEGISLATIVE ACTION

▸ House Homeland Security Subcommittee approved draft bill by voice vote June 24.

▸ Senate Appropriations Committee approved S 3607 (S Rept 111-222), 17-12, on July 15.

INTERIOR-ENVIRONMENT

LAWMAKERS GOT LESS DONE ON THE Interior-Environment bill than on any of the other 11 fiscal 2011 spending measures. The only action came in the House Interior Appropriations Subcommittee, which approved a draft bill by voice vote on July 22. The process in the Senate did not advance beyond committee hearings.

Programs under the bill were funded mostly at fiscal 2010 levels through March 4, 2011, under the continuing resolution that was signed into law on Dec. 22 (PL 111-322). (Appropriations overview, p. 2-3)

The annual measure funded the Interior Department, the EPA, the Forest Service, the Indian Health Service and agencies such as the Smithsonian Institution and the National Endowments for the Arts and Humanities.

The House bill was also full of policy initiatives, including a temporary ban on new contracts for offshore drilling, approved in the midst of the massive BP oil spill in the Gulf of Mexico, and an increase in funding for climate change research.

While most other fiscal 2011 spending measures had at least a small funding boost, discretionary funding in the House draft was flat at $32.2 billion, the same amount as provided for fiscal 2010 and just slightly less than President Obama requested. (Chart, p. 2-13)

Besides the short-term suspension of drilling contracts along the nation's coasts, the measure included funding for an increase in the number of inspectors for offshore drilling oversight and compliance. It proposed to quadruple, to $40 million, the collection of offshore inspection fees and provide $4 million above the administration's request to study the impact of drilling on marine environments.

The EPA would have gotten $10 billion, about $270 million below the fiscal 2010 level. Had the bill advanced, partisan battles were forecast over provisions to provide about $456 million for climate change adaptation and research efforts, including EPA research, regulatory programs and climate protection grants.

The Interior Department was slated to get $11 billion, virtually the same as in fiscal 2010.

LEGISLATIVE ACTION

▸ House Interior-Environment Subcommittee approved draft bill by voice vote July 22.

LABOR-HHS-EDUCATION

THE BILL FUNDING THE DEPARTMENTS OF Labor, Health and Human Services (HHS), and Education was typically the largest of the appropriations bills and one of the most difficult to pass. A stand-alone version had been enacted only twice in the previous decade — in 2002 and 2006.

Versions of the fiscal 2011 measure won approval in the Senate Appropriations Committee and in the House Labor-HHS-Education Subcommittee but went no further. Programs under the bill were funded mostly at fiscal 2010 levels through March 4, 2011, under the continuing resolution signed into law on Dec. 22 (PL 111-322). (Appropriations overview, p. 2-3)

The Labor-HHS-Education bill funded programs for some of society's most vulnerable citizens — the young and old, the sick and poor — and contained an array of Democratic spending priorities. About three-fourths of the funding, $562.3 billion, was devoted to mandatory spending, much of it for Medicare and Medicaid. (Chart, p. 2-13)

The difference in discretionary funding between the House and Senate versions of the measure was moderate, given the size of the bill. The House subcommittee draft, approved 11-5 on July 15, would have provided $176.4 billion; the Senate committee's bill (S 3686), approved 18-12 on July 29, proposed $169.6 billion.

However, the discretionary amounts were difficult to compare because the panels gave different treatment to a request by President Obama that discretionary funding for Pell grants be made mandatory. In addition, the House panel offered only discretionary numbers for departments and programs, while the Senate amounts included mandatory spending.

Republicans offered 16 amendments during the House subcommittee markup, most intended to cut spending. All were defeated except for a proposal to require federal agencies that spent more than $100 million on research to allow public access to the research information. "At some point we need to get this spending under control," said Todd Tiahrt, R-Kan.

Republicans also sought to put new restrictions on states using funds authorized in the health care overhaul law (PL 111-148, PL 111-152) to pay for abortions. The proposal was rejected, 5-11. "This is not the venue to debate this issue," said David R. Obey, D-Wis., chairman of the subcommittee and the full House Appropriations Committee. (Health care overhaul, p. 9-3)

The Senate committee rejected, 2-18, an amendment by Arlen Specter, D-Pa., to increase funding for the National Institutes of Health by $1 billion. NIH was slated to receive $32 billion under both measures, $1 billion more than in fiscal 2010.

Tom Harkin, D-Iowa, chairman of the Senate Labor-HHS-Education Subcommittee, chided Republicans for voting against the bill on the grounds that it cost too much, given that it included a host of priorities pushed by GOP appropriators and $116 million in Republican-sponsored earmarks. "No Republicans on this committee suggested any specific cuts at all," Harkin said. "They left the tough choices to me."

LEGISLATIVE ACTION

‣ House Labor-HHS-Education Subcommittee approved draft bill, 11-5, on July 15.

‣ Senate Appropriations Committee approved S 3686 (S Rept 111-243), 18-12, on July 29.

LEGISLATIVE BRANCH

THE HOUSE LEGISLATIVE BRANCH Appropriations Subcommittee approved a draft fiscal 2011 bill to fund congressional operations and those of support agencies. The full Senate Appropriations Committee approved a companion bill, but the legislation stopped there. Programs covered by the bill were funded mostly at fiscal 2010 levels through March 4, 2011, under the continuing resolution signed into law on Dec. 22 (PL 111-322). (Appropriations overview, p. 2-3)

The House draft, approved by voice vote July 1, called for a total of $3.6 billion, including $1.4 billion for House operations. By tradition, each chamber included its own operations, plus joint items such as the Capitol Police, the Architect of the Capitol, the Government Accountability Office and the Library of Congress. (Chart, p. 2-13)

The Senate committee bill (S 3799), approved by a vote of 18-12 on Sept. 16, totaled $3.1 billion, including $926 million for the Senate.

The House draft was about $7 million less than the previous year's funding for comparable programs and $337 million less than requested. The Senate's bill was $13 million below fiscal 2010 spending and $436 million less than requested. "Our branch is not exempt from cuts," said Senate Appropriations Chairman Daniel K. Inouye, D-Hawaii.

In a bipartisan decision, the House subcommittee agreed to withhold $20 million from the House Chief Administrative Officer until plans were submitted to improve services, such as the wireless connections for the Capitol Visitor Center. House Chief Administrative Officer Dan Beard resigned just hours after the markup.

The draft House bill included $337 million for the Capitol Police, $9 million above fiscal 2010 funding but $48 million less than requested. The panel denied a request for additional officers, which subcommittee Chairwoman Debbie Wasserman Schultz, D-Fla., said was not adequately justified. The Senate bill included $335 million for the police.

The House subcommittee approved $501 million for the Architect of the Capitol; the Senate bill included $443 million.

LEGISLATIVE ACTION

‣ House subcommittee approved draft bill by voice vote July 1.

‣ Senate Appropriations Committee approved S 3799 (S Rept 111-294), 18-12, on Sept. 16.

MILITARY CONSTRUCTION-VA

THE SPENDING BILL FOR MILITARY construction and the Department of Veterans Affairs (VA) was one of only two fiscal 2011 appropriations bills to pass in the House. (The other was for transportation and housing.) The full Senate Appropriations Committee approved its version of the bill, but the measure did not reach the Senate floor.

Programs under the bill were funded mostly at fiscal 2010 levels through March 4, 2011, under the continuing resolution signed into law on Dec. 22 (PL 111-322). (Appropriations overview, p. 2-3)

The House and Senate bills were nearly identical. The House passed its bill (HR 5822) by a vote of 411-6 on July 28 after the Appropriations Committee approved it by voice vote July 20. (House vote 482, p. H-168)

The Senate Appropriations Committee approved its version of the bill (S 3615), 17-12, on July 15.

Both bills totaled $143.5 billion, with $77.3 billion in discretionary funding — an amount appropriators said was between $600 million and $700 million below comparable fiscal 2010 appropriations and virtually the same as the administration's request.

The totals included $50.6 billion in advance fiscal 2012 funding for several health programs. The appropriations of advance funding began with the fiscal 2010 law (PL 111-117) as a way of giving more predictability and stability to the programs. The rest of the grand total was mandatory spending, virtually all of it for pensions and other benefits administered by the Veterans Benefits Administration. (Chart, p. 2-14)

Overall, the VA would have received $123.2 billion under the House bill and $123.3 billion under the Senate version. Appropriations for the Veterans Health Administration (VHA) would have totaled $51.3 billion under the Senate measure — $50.6 billion for fiscal 2012, plus $710 million in new fiscal 2011 money; the VHA already had $48.2 billion for fiscal 2011 appropriated the previous year. Under the House bill, the health agency would have received $51.2 billion, including $590 million in new fiscal 2011 appropriations.

The VA was trying to reduce a huge backlog of existing veterans' benefits claims and was anticipating a new wave of claims from veterans exposed to Agent Orange, which was widely used to clear jungles in Vietnam. In the fall of 2009, the VA had extended coverage to veterans who developed B-cell leukemia, Parkinson's disease or ischemic heart disease after exposure to the chemical.

The continuing resolution provided funding at an annualized rate of $2.1 billion, an increase of $460 million over fiscal 2010 appropriations, to maintain and expand the number of VA claims processors and reduce processing backlogs.

Both bills proposed $18.7 billion for Defense Department military construction projects, including barracks, family housing and base facilities. Another $1.3 billion was included for military construction for overseas operations.

LEGISLATIVE ACTION

‣ Senate Appropriations Committee approved S 3615 (S Rept 111-226), 17-12, on July 15.

‣ House passed HR 5822 (H Rept 111-559), 411-6, on July 28.

STATE-FOREIGN OPERATIONS

THE BILL THAT COVERED SPENDING for the State Department and U.S. foreign aid in fiscal 2011 stalled after winning approval in a House subcommittee and in the full Senate Appropriations Committee. Programs under the bill were funded mostly at fiscal 2010 levels through March 4, 2011, under the continuing resolution signed into law on Dec. 22 (PL 111-322). (Appropriations overview, p. 2-3)

The House State-Foreign Operations Subcommittee approved a draft bill by voice vote June 30 that would have provided $52.8 billion, $4 billion less than requested but $3.9 billion more than in fiscal 2010. The Senate full committee approved a $54.2 billion bill (S 3676) by a vote of 18-12 on July 29. Virtually all of the funding was discretionary. (Chart, p. 2-14)

The House and Senate measures called for $16.6 billion and $17.5 billion, respectively, for the State Department and related agencies; $23.2 billion and $23.4 billion, respectively, for bilateral aid; and $5.4 billion each for foreign military financing.

Both bills included about $8.2 billion for Global Health and Child Survival programs, about $460 million above fiscal 2010 spending.

Several significant policy issues separated the two bills. In drafting the House bill, subcommittee Chairwoman Nita M. Lowey, D-N.Y, designated no funding for non-humanitarian aid for Afghanistan until the country's government sorted out allegations that vast sums of money had been lost to corruption. The bill included the amount requested for the assistance, but none of the $3.9 billion was designated for Afghanistan. The Senate bill included $2.6 billion for the Afghanistan aid.

House Republicans warned that withholding significant sums could hurt the U.S.-led war effort and the strategy on the ground at a pivotal moment in the conflict.

The subcommittee adopted a handful of GOP amendments, including one by Ander Crenshaw of Florida to prohibit the use of funds to transfer detainees from the U.S. facility in Guantánamo Bay, Cuba, to any other country unless the secretary of State certified that the receiving nation met certain requirements.

The Senate bill included a controversial amendment by Frank R. Lautenberg, D-N.J., that would have codified an Obama administration order repealing the "Mexico City" policy, which barred aid to international organizations that performed or promoted abortions, whether or not they used their own money. It was adopted, 19-11.

"It's time to put aside the politics on women's lives," Lautenberg argued. "Let them make their decisions. Let them make their choices."

Sam Brownback, R-Kan., said he was "very saddened" by the amendment. "It's us funding abortions overseas," he said. "There are a lot of people in the country that find this deeply offensive."

The language had been approved by the committee the previous year but was stripped out before the fiscal 2010 bill (PL 111-117) reached the floor.

LEGISLATIVE ACTION

▶ House State-Foreign Operations Subcommittee approved draft bill by voice vote June 30.

▶ Senate Appropriations Committee approved S 3676 (S Rept 111-237), 18-12, on July 29.

TRANSPORTATION-HUD

THE BILL FOR THE DEPARTMENTS OF Transportation and Housing and Urban Development (HUD) was one of two fiscal 2011 spending measures to pass in the House. (The other was the Military Construction-VA measure.) The Senate Appropriations Committee approved a version of the bill, but the full Senate did not take it up. Programs under the bill were funded mostly at fiscal 2010 levels through March 4, 2011, under the continuing resolution signed into law on Dec. 22 (PL 111-322). (Appropriations overview, p. 2-3)

The House and Senate bills had top-line totals of $126.4 billion and $122.8 billion, respectively. The House bill (HR 5830), passed by a vote of 251-167 on July 29, included $67.4 billion in discretionary spending, $500 million below the fiscal 2010 level and $1.3 billion less than the president requested. (House vote 499, p. H-172; chart, p. 2-14)

The Senate committee bill (S 3644), approved 17-12 on July 22, had a discretionary total of $67.9 billion, which was equal to the amount in the fiscal 2010 law and $838 million less than requested.

Appropriators were still able to exceed President Obama's request for several big-ticket accounts, primarily by omitting $4 billion requested by the president for a National Infrastructure Innovation and Finance Fund within the Transportation Department. They said the administration had not sent Congress a corresponding policy proposal, leaving lawmakers to guess the program's purpose and structure.

The Transportation Department would have gotten $79.4 billion under the House bill, including obligations from the transportation trust funds, and $75.8 billion under the Senate measure. The department had received $75.7 billion in fiscal 2010; Obama requested $77.7 billion for fiscal 2011.

Both measures included $46.6 billion for HUD, about $1 billion more than the administration requested and roughly $525 million above fiscal 2010 spending, while ignoring Obama's call to cut the HOPE VI program, which provided grants to rehabilitate dilapidated public housing.

Appropriators also ignored an administration request to transfer $200 million from the Highway Trust Fund, which was financed mainly by the federal gasoline excise tax, to pay for a new "livable communities" initiative aimed at more closely coordinating spending for transportation and housing programs.

The chief difference between the two bills was the amount each proposed to allocate from the trust funds, particularly for federal highway programs. The House bill would have allowed the Federal Highway Administration (FHA) to use about $45.2 billion from the Highway Trust Fund, $3.1 billion more than it could in fiscal 2010 and $4.1 billion more than Obama requested. The Senate version would have given the FHA access to $41.9 billion, or $3.3 billion less than in the House bill.

The House measure also included $1.4 billion, $400 million more than requested, for investments in high-speed rail, on top of $10.5 billion provided in the 2009 economic stimulus law (PL 111-5). The Senate committee-approved bill proposed spending $1 billion, matching Obama's request.

Democratic appropriators stressed on the House floor that they had come in well below the administration request and the fiscal 2010 enacted level.

"We have still been able to develop a bill that creates jobs through investments in infrastructure and supports families that have been hit the hardest by the foreclosure crisis," said John W. Olver, D-Mass., the chairman of the Transportation-HUD Subcommittee.

But Jerry Lewis of California, ranking Republican on the Appropriations Committee, urged his colleagues to vote against the bill, bemoaning what he called the "majority's agenda of runaway spending, surging taxes and soaring budget deficits."

Democrats rebuffed, 17-35, an attempt by Lewis during the committee markup to automatically adjust the amount that could be obligated from the Highway Trust Fund to prevent the fund from dipping below $4 billion. Appropriations Chairman David R. Obey, D-Wis., dismissed the proposal as a "backdoor way" of cutting $4 billion from highway programs.

In the Senate, Christopher S. Bond of Missouri, the top Republican on the Transportation-HUD Subcommittee, voted against the bill in the full committee markup, taking issue with the discretionary spending allocation for the bill. But Bond praised the panel for rejecting the administration's proposal to create an Office of Livability and for not adding $400 million to the light-rail account as House appropriators had done. "I believe much of what we've achieved in the bill is balanced," he said.

LEGISLATIVE ACTION

▶ Senate Appropriations Committee approved S 3644 (S Rept 111-230), 17-12, on July 22.

▶ House passed HR 5850 (H Rept 111-564), 251-167, on July 29. ■

WHERE THE MONEY GOES — PROPOSED FISCAL 2011 APPROPRIATIONS

(figures are in thousands of dollars of new budget authority)

AGRICULTURE
(House draft; S 3606)

	Fiscal 2010 appropriations	Fiscal 2011 Obama request	House subcommittee approved	Senate committee approved
GRAND TOTAL	$121,570,814	$132,028,200	N/A[1]	$132,053,999
Discretionary total	23,400,640	N/A[1]	$23,100,100	22,928,350
MAIN COMPONENTS				
Farm programs	30,191,573	30,192,013	N/A[1]	30,259,695
Rural development	2,934,309	2,683,073	N/A[1]	2,767,584
Domestic nutrition programs	82,782,603	94,390,725	N/A[1]	94,051,710
Food stamps	58,278,181	68,206,790	N/A[1]	68,209,540
Child nutrition	16,855,829	18,158,393	N/A[1]	18,161,143
Women, Infants and Children	7,252,000	7,603,000	N/A[1]	7,252,000
International food aid	2,089,499	2,168,010	N/A[1]	2,129,010
Food and Drug Administration[2]	2,357,089	2,516,282	2,571,282	2,516,282

[1] Comparable numbers not available.
[2] The FDA is part of the Department of Health and Human Services.

COMMERCE-JUSTICE-SCIENCE
(House draft; S 3636)

	Fiscal 2010 appropriations	Fiscal 2011 Obama request	House subcommittee approved	Senate committee approved
GRAND TOTAL	$68,174,287	$65,418,248	$65,615,563	$65,082,445
Discretionary total	64,415,921	60,538,617	60,535,932	60,139,000
MAIN COMPONENTS				
Commerce Department	14,035,223	8,967,500	8,897,845	8,963,205
Census Bureau	7,324,731	1,266,979	1,237,190	1,244,679
NOAA	4,737,531	5,543,521	5,543,492	5,545,521
Justice Department	28,077,684	29,736,515	30,031,638	29,986,095
FBI	7,898,537	8,264,677	8,203,186	8,264,677
Federal Prison System	6,188,086	6,806,212	6,826,212	6,806,212
State and local law enforcement	3,706,959	3,477,349	N/A*	3,737,285
NASA	18,724,300	19,000,000	19,000,000	19,000,000
National Science Foundation	6,926,510	7,424,400	7,424,400	7,353,400

* Comparable number not available.

DEFENSE
(House draft; S 3800)

	Fiscal 2010 appropriations	Fiscal 2011 Obama request	House subcommittee approved *	Senate committee approved
GRAND TOTAL	$658,706,425	$678,225,185	$670,953,000	$669,871,730
MAIN COMPONENTS				
Operations and maintenance	154,253,711	167,878,542	165,188,000	167,332,004
Military personnel	124,170,847	127,668,630	126,619,000	127,153,296
Procurement	104,397,262	111,189,951	106,331,000	104,765,490
Research, development, test and evaluation	80,537,479	76,130,700	76,681,000	76,193,695
Defense Health Program	29,243,428	30,935,111	31,469,000	31,530,598
Overseas contingency operations	161,034,140	157,935,277	157,682,000	157,680,557

* Subcommittee issued rounded numbers.

SOURCES: House and Senate Appropriations committees

WHERE THE MONEY GOES — PROPOSED FISCAL 2011 APPROPRIATIONS

(figures are in thousands of dollars of new budget authority)

ENERGY-WATER
(House draft; S 3635)

	Fiscal 2010 appropriations	Fiscal 2011 Obama request	House subcommittee approved	Senate subcommittee approved
GRAND TOTAL	$33,978,000	$35,878,274	$34,775,000[1]	$35,073,700
Discretionary total[1]	33,465,000	35,344,000	34,669,000	34,968,000
MAIN COMPONENTS				
Energy Department	27,111,438	29,613,170	28,109,000	28,346,405
Atomic energy defense activities	16,475,226	17,681,003	17,027,000	17,238,910
Nuclear weapons programs	6,384,431	7,008,835	6,910,000	7,018,835
Defense environmental cleanup	5,642,331	5,588,039	5,125,000	5,262,838
Science	4,903,710	5,121,437	4,900,000	5,012,000
Nuclear waste disposal[2]	196,800	0	0	0
Army Corps of Engineers	5,445,000	4,881,000	5,280,000	5,320,000
Interior Department	1,129,720	1,107,701	1,108,000	1,132,719

[1] Rounded numbers.
[2] Includes civilian and defense waste disposal; the latter is also included in the total for atomic energy defense activities.

FINANCIAL SERVICES
(House draft; S 3677)

	Fiscal 2010 appropriations	Fiscal 2011 Obama request	House subcommittee approved	Senate committee approved
GRAND TOTAL	$46,433,993	$48,219,254	N/A[1]	$48,295,857
Discretionary spending[2]	24,186,000	25,256,000	24,500,000	25,400,000
MAIN COMPONENTS				
Treasury Department	13,464,691	13,969,817	N/A[1]	13,951,021
IRS	12,146,123	12,633,270	12,417,600	12,508,243
Executive Office of the President	771,914	760,438	702,100	794,817
Federal Judiciary	6,860,745	7,329,485	7,129,500	7,240,356
Office of Personnel Management	20,378,071	20,833,741	N/A[1]	20,836,387
District of Columbia	752,129	729,673	759,300	738,999

[1] Comparable numbers not available.
[2] Numbers rounded.

HOMELAND SECURITY
(House draft; S 3607)

	Fiscal 2010 appropriations	Fiscal 2011 Obama request	House subcommittee approved	Senate committee approved
GRAND TOTAL	$44,137,241	$45,036,301	$45,540,762	$45,191,136
Discretionary spending	42,775,996	43,635,601	43,890,062	43,790,436
MAIN COMPONENTS				
Customs and Border Protection[1]	10,126,554	9,908,725	9,844,256	10,016,225
Immigration and Customs Enforcement[1]	5,436,952	5,523,800	5,571,628	5,551,162
Transportation Security Administration[2]	7,656,066	8,164,780	8,059,264	8,064,495
Coast Guard	10,140,291	9,867,237	10,158,203	10,400,318
Secret Service	1,482,644	1,571,617	1,581,217	1,575,617
Federal Emergency Management Agency	7,112,468	7,293,450	7,550,460	7,329,070

[1] Totals do not include fees, which increase the amounts available to the bureaus and agencies.
[2] Totals do not include offsetting receipts, which reduce the effect on the deficit.

SOURCES: House and Senate Appropriations committees

WHERE THE MONEY GOES — PROPOSED FISCAL 2011 APPROPRIATIONS

(figures are in thousands of dollars of new budget authority)

INTERIOR-ENVIRONMENT
(House draft)

	Fiscal 2010 appropriations	Fiscal 2011 Obama request[2]	House subcommittee approved[2]
DISCRETIONARY SPENDING[1]	$32,240,000	$32,373,000	$32,240,000
MAIN COMPONENTS			
Interior Department	11,034,000	11,016,000	11,038,000
Bureau of Land Management	1,133,000	1,130,000	1,107,000
Fish and Wildlife Service	1,646,000	1,642,000	1,641,000
National Park Service	2,743,000	2,728,000	2,764,000
Bureau of Indian Affairs	2,619,000	2,566,000	2,578,000
EPA	10,289,000	10,020,000	10,018,000
Forest Service (Agriculture Department)	4,884,000	4,803,000	4,906,000
Indian Health Service (HHS)	4,052,000	4,406,000	4,406,000

[1] Only discretionary figures available; bill includes little mandatory spending.
[2] Rounded numbers.

LABOR-HHS-EDUCATION
(House draft; S 3686)

	Fiscal 2010 appropriations	Fiscal 2011 Obama request	House subcommittee approved	Senate committee approved
GRAND TOTAL	$730,615,742	N/A[1]	N/A[1]	$731,887,000
Discretionary spending[2]	163,727,000	177,922,000	176,412,000[3,4]	169,626,000[3]
MAIN COMPONENTS				
Department of Health and Human Services	610,347,036	577,584,636	N/A[1]	577,890,405
Medicare	214,590,070	229,664,000	N/A[1]	229,664,000
Medicaid state grants	220,962,473	173,143,799	N/A[1]	173,143,799
National Institutes of Health	31,005,201	32,007,237	32,007,237[4]	32,007,237
Children and Family Services	9,313,180	10,312,070	10,356,000[4]	10,359,727
Department of Education	67,362,252	71,033,986	N/A[1]	70,116,915
Pell grants	17,495,000	17,652,000	N/A[1]	17,652,000
Education for the disadvantaged (Title I grants)	14,492,401	14,492,401	14,492,401[4]	14,492,401
Special education grants	11,505,211	11,755,211	11,925,211[4]	11,925,211
Department of Labor	16,588,260	17,255,650	N/A[1]	17,191,215

[1] Comparable numbers not available.
[2] Rounded numbers.
[3] House and Senate totals are not comparable because of their different treatment of President Obama's request that Pell grants be funded from mandatory, rather than discretionary, accounts.
[4] For discretionary spending only.

LEGISLATIVE BRANCH
(House draft; S 3799)

	Fiscal 2010 appropriations	Fiscal 2011 Obama request	House subcommittee approved	Senate committee approved
GRAND TOTAL	$4,656,031[1]	$5,633,000[1]	$3,648,600[2]	$3,136,193[2]
MAIN COMPONENTS				
House of Representatives	1,369,025	1,419,000	1,374,200[3]	0
Senate	926,160	1,042,119	0	926,179
Capitol Police	341,174	385,476	337,200	335,435
Architect of the Capitol	601,586	613,998	501,200	442,611
Library of Congress	643,337	674,785	645,200	643,337
Government Accountability Office	556,849	601,117	560,700	556,849
Government Printing Office	147,461	166,560	147,500	147,461

[1] Numbers reflect combined House and Senate accounts.
[2] House and Senate include only their own spending and that of joint items in their bills.
[3] Rounded numbers.

SOURCES: House and Senate Appropriations committees

WHERE THE MONEY GOES — PROPOSED FISCAL 2011 APPROPRIATIONS

(figures are in thousands of dollars of new budget authority)

MILITARY CONSTRUCTION-VA
(HR 5822; S 3615)

	Fiscal 2010 appropriations	Fiscal 2011 Obama request	House passed	Senate committee approved
GRAND TOTAL	$182,750,300 [1]	$143,531,666 [2]	$143,532,131 [2]	$143,530,131 [2]
MAIN COMPONENTS				
Department of Veterans Affairs	157,790,626 [1]	123,219,865 [2]	123,240,949 [2]	123,270,764 [2]
Veterans Health Administration	93,260,500 [1]	51,200,985 [2]	51,200,985 [2]	51,320,985 [2]
Veterans Benefits Administration	56,734,419	64,013,884	64,013,884	64,013,884
Department of Defense	23,729,950	18,747,368	18,747,368	18,747,368
Military construction	13,466,858	13,825,563	13,725,563	13,825,563
Family housing	2,258,698	1,823,191	1,823,191	1,823,191
Overseas contingency operations	1,398,984	1,257,002	1,257,000	1,257,002

[1] Includes $48,183,000 in advance 2011 appropriations.
[2] Includes $50,610,985 in advance 2012 appropriations.

STATE-FOREIGN OPERATIONS
(House draft; S 3676)

	Fiscal 2010 appropriations	Fiscal 2011 Obama request	House subcommittee approved	Senate committee approved
GRAND TOTAL	$48,922,900	$56,805,543	$52,814,900	$54,214,900
MAIN COMPONENTS				
State Department and related agencies	16,102,108	17,403,708	16,648,050	17,456,011
Administration of foreign affairs	11,181,349	12,533,297	11,841,815	12,638,886
Bilateral economic aid	21,846,232	24,576,242	23,209,210	23,393,850
Global health and child survival	7,779,000	8,513,000	8,250,000	8,239,000
Economic Support Fund	6,337,000	7,811,982	7,020,000	7,157,000
Millennium Challenge Corporation	1,105,000	1,279,700	1,105,000	1,105,000
Foreign military financing	4,195,000	5,473,348	5,446,896	5,435,000
International financial institutions	2,043,670	2,957,176	2,310,000	2,612,750

TRANSPORTATION-HUD
(HR 5850; S 3644)

	Fiscal 2010 appropriations	Fiscal 2011 Obama request	House passed	Senate committee approved
GRAND TOTAL*	$122,142,526	$123,658,007	$126,392,740	$122,817,379
Discretionary spending	67,900,000	68,737,520	67,400,000	67,900,000
MAIN COMPONENTS				
Department of Transportation*	75,699,358	77,701,430	79,367,022	75,766,177
Federal Aviation Administration	15,597,731	16,468,000	16,506,000	16,501,750
Federal Highway Administration	42,049,829	41,099,644	45,181,927	41,888,138
Federal Transit Administration	10,732,752	10,799,534	11,307,422	10,792,296
Amtrak	1,564,625	1,637,000	1,766,500	1,963,000
Department of Housing and Urban Development	46,059,233	45,570,699	46,579,206	46,591,857
Tenant-based rental assistance	18,184,200	19,550,663	19,395,663	19,495,663
Project-based rental assistance	8,551,525	9,382,328	9,382,328	9,382,328
Community planning and development	8,580,500	8,485,100	8,836,600	8,758,435

* Amounts include trust fund obligations.

SOURCES: House and Senate Appropriations committees

Funding for Afghanistan, Iraq Wars

WITH REPUBLICANS TIPPING the balance, the House in July cleared a $58.8 billion fiscal 2010 supplemental spending bill devoted primarily to paying for operations in Iraq and Afghanistan. President Obama signed the legislation on July 29 (HR 4899 — PL 111-212).

Republicans in both chambers generally supported the bill, while House Democrats were sharply divided. Among those voting against the final version was Appropriations Chairman David R. Obey, D-Wis. In floor remarks, Obey told his colleagues he had "the highest respect and appreciation" for U.S. troops but said they are "being let down by the inability of the governments of Afghanistan and in some instances Pakistan to do their parts."

When Obama sent his fiscal 2011 budget to Congress in February, he requested $33 billion in supplemental fiscal 2010 funds, including $30 billion for deployments to Afghanistan and $1 billion to train Iraqi security forces. Subsequent requests for funds for disaster aid, veterans health programs and other purposes brought the total to $64.4 billion.

From the outset, Obey and many other House Democrats wanted to add billions of dollars for domestic needs, particularly to avoid the layoffs of tens of thousands of teachers nationwide at a time when state budgets were stretched thin and funds for the purpose in the 2009 economic stimulus law (PL 111-5) were running dry. Democratic leaders spent several months trying to come up with a package that could win enough votes in the Senate to surmount a filibuster.

A steady stream of negative news about the situation in Afghanistan, including reports of pervasive corruption in the Afghan government as well as criticism of the administration's approach to the war, complicated congressional deliberations.

The Senate passed a bill in May that focused on war spending. After lengthy negotiations among Democrats, the House accepted the Senate's bill but added $22.8 billion, mainly for domestic programs. The Senate decisively rejected the add-ons and sent its original version back to the House. The latest word from the Defense Department was that it would need the funds in mid-August. With members about to leave for the August recess, the House had little choice but to clear the narrower bill, but it did so only with the support of 160 Republicans.

HIGHLIGHTS

The $58.8 billion total for the bill — which was about equal to Obama's amended request — consisted of $45.4 billion in discretionary spending and $13.4 billion in mandatory funds.

The main components were:

● **Defense Department.** $33.4 billion for the Pentagon, which appropriators said included funding for the addition of 30,000 troops in Afghanistan as part of the administration's surge program. Major elements included:

‣ $24.6 billion for operations and maintenance.

‣ $1.8 billion for military personnel.

‣ $4.9 billion for procurement.

BILL: HR 4899 — PL 111-212

....

LEGISLATIVE ACTION:

Senate passed HR 4899, amended (S Rept 111-188), 67-28, on May 27.

House passed HR 4899, amended, in a series of five votes on July 1.

Senate rejected a cloture motion on the House amendment, 46-51, on July 22; 60 votes required.

House cleared HR 4899, 308-114, on July 27.

President signed the bill July 29.

‣ $2.6 billion for the Afghan Security forces and $1 billion for the Iraqi Security forces.

‣ $656 million for military construction.

● **Disaster aid.** $5.1 billion for the Federal Emergency Management Agency (FEMA) to help pay for the costs of previous disasters, including hurricanes Katrina and Rita, the Midwest floods of 2008 and California wildfires.

● **Haiti.** $2.9 billion for aid in response to the Jan. 12 earthquake in Haiti.

● **Oil spill.** $162 million related to the Gulf of Mexico oil spill.

● **Veterans.** $13.4 billion in mandatory funding for the Veterans Affairs Department to cover claims by Vietnam War veterans exposed to the defoliant Agent Orange. The VA had extended coverage in 2009 to veterans who were exposed to Agent Orange and then developed B-cell leukemia, Parkinson's disease or ischemic heart disease, a condition marked by reduced blood supply to the heart.

2010 LEGISLATIVE ACTION
SENATE COMMITTEE

With disagreement among Democrats slowing action in the House, Democratic leaders took the somewhat unorthodox approach of letting Senate appropriators go first. The Senate Appropriations Committee approved the $58.8 billion bill by a vote of 30-0 on May 13 (HR 4899 — S Rept 111-188).

Appropriations Chairman Daniel K. Inouye, D-Hawaii, deliberately kept the measure spare, rejecting bids for school aid and focusing the bill on the wars, veterans and disaster relief. Inouye took a $5.1 billion disaster aid bill that the House had passed in March, stripped out $600 million for summer jobs that also had been in the bill and inserted the funding for the wars and related expenses and for Agent Orange claims.

SENATE FLOOR

The Senate passed the bill, 67-28, on May 27. The key procedural vote took place just hours before passage when the Senate invoked cloture, 69-29, limiting the debate. *(Senate votes 176, p. S-37, and 171, p. S-36)*

Senate Democratic leaders were somewhat defensive about the more modest amount of spending in their bill, compared with what Obey and others in the House were trying to do. "President Obama has drastically scaled down the size of the supplemental and encouraged the defense budgeting process to better incorporate wartime spending, but there is still a dire need for this supplemental," Jack Reed, D-R.I., said at a May 26 news conference seeking to rally support for the measure.

Inouye was able to fend off pressure from his left flank. Sen. Tom Harkin, D-Iowa, had been pressing to include the money to prevent teacher layoffs, but he was unable to assemble the necessary 60 votes.

Republicans offered several amendments, including proposals to

add funds for border security and the prosecution of illegal immigrants, as well as to provide offsets for the bill's cost, but all of them were rejected.

HOUSE COMMITTEE

In a sign of the growing worries about the government's reliance on borrowed money, efforts in the House Appropriations Committee to mark up a more sweeping $84 billion measure ran aground. Obey postponed a scheduled May 27 session, and the markup was never held.

"At some point, they have to be hearing from their constituents that enough is enough," said Jeb Hensarling, R-Texas, a conservative who was serving on a fiscal commission created by Obama to make budget and deficit reduction recommendations. Hensarling's view was echoed by fiscally conservative Democrats. *(Commission, p. 4-11)*

The draft bore the strong stamp of Obey, a progressive set to retire at the end of the 111th Congress, who signaled his intent to spend his final months in the House battling to get more money for schools and other programs he had long supported. Obey's draft included $23 billion for schools.

Before the House markup was postponed, intense negotiations involving both chambers and parties had only seemed to widen the differences among Democrats.

HOUSE FLOOR

The House on July 1 adopted an amendment to the $58.8 billion Senate-passed measure that added $22.8 billion for schools and other Democratic domestic priorities. The decision to add the domestic funding meant postponing further action until mid-July, because the Senate had already adjourned for the July Fourth recess.

Republicans complained that Democrats could easily have gotten the supplemental funds to the Pentagon by July 4 by simply accepting the Senate version.

Under a complicated rule for floor debate, the House amendment was divided into several parts, which gave anti-war Democrats a chance to vote to wind down the U.S. military presence in Afghanistan. At the same time, it allowed fiscal conservatives in the Democratic Blue Dog Coalition to oppose the additional domestic spending without having to vote against the $58.8 billion in the Senate version. The rule, which also automatically approved Democrats' plan for a one-year budget, was adopted, 215-210. The rule had no GOP support and 38 Democratic defectors. *(House vote 428, p. H-150)*

● **Obey amendment.** The House adopted Obey's domestic spending amendment, 239-182, with 15 Democrats and all but three Republicans voting "no." *(House vote 430, p. H-152)*

The amendment included:

▶ $10 billion to enable school districts to avoid laying off teachers for the coming school year. Obey said the funding was fully offset and would help keep 140,000 school employees on the job.

▶ $5 billion to cover a shortfall in Pell grants for low-income college students.

▶ $1 billion for a summer jobs program, a high priority for the Congressional Black Caucus.

▶ $701 million to increase security activities along the U.S.-Mexico border, including the hiring of 1,200 additional Border Patrol agents.

To help offset the added spending, Obey proposed rescinding $800 million in previously appropriated funds for education overhaul programs, including President Obama's signature "Race to the Top"

initiative that provided competitive education grants to states.

The White House issued a statement expressing support for the extra funding for teachers and for Pell grants but warned of a potential veto if the proposed rescissions remained in the final bill. The White House made a similar threat regarding amendments intended to curb military operations in Afghanistan.

A group of 13 senators, led by Evan Bayh, D-Ind., sent a letter to Inouye opposing the proposed rescissions.

● **Anti-war amendments.** Three anti-war amendments were handily defeated, but not before an impassioned debate over the direction of the war and an unusual vote by Speaker Nancy Pelosi, D-Calif., for one of the proposals resisted by the White House.

"The echoes of Vietnam are in this chamber," said Steve Cohen, D-Tenn. "That was a war we couldn't win, and some people wouldn't accept it." Cohen said the money should be spent at home instead.

Jack Kingston, R-Ga., countered: "War is complicated. War does not always go your way.... I think it's very important for us to let the military make these decisions."

During the debate, the House:

▶ Rejected, 25-376, an amendment to strike military funding for Afghanistan from the bill. *(House vote 431, p. H-152)*

▶ Rejected, 100-321, a proposal by Barbara Lee, D-Calif., to limit the use of the military funding for Afghanistan to activities related to withdrawing troops and protecting civilian and military personnel. *(House vote 432, p. H-152)*

▶ Rejected, 162-260, an amendment by Jim McGovern, D-Mass., to require that Obama send Congress a new intelligence estimate on Afghanistan by Jan. 31, 2011, and a plan by April 4, 2011, for redeploying U.S. troops. Funds for Afghanistan could not be spent after July 2011 for any purpose other than beginning a troop drawdown, unless Congress voted otherwise. Pelosi voted for the proposal. *(House vote 433, p. H-152)*

FINAL ACTION

The Senate on July 22 refused to accept the $22.8 billion domestic-spending amendment, paving the way for final action on the bill. By a vote of 46-51, senators rejected a motion to limit debate on the amended House version of the bill. Instead, the Senate agreed by unanimous consent to send its original version back to the House. *(Senate vote 219, p. S-46)*

"While I would have preferred that the Senate take up and pass HR 4899 as further amended by the House, an amendment that addressed several additional critical needs, I understand that we were not going to get 60 votes for that to happen," Inouye said.

As expected, the House accepted the Senate version, clearing it by a vote of 308-114 on July 27. By then, the Pentagon had indicated that it could hold out until early August. *(House vote 474, p. H-166)*

To allow anti-war Democrats another chance to express their concerns, House leaders gave floor time to a resolution (H Con Res 301), sponsored by Dennis J. Kucinich, D-Ohio, that would have directed the president to remove troops from Pakistan within 30 days. The resolution, rejected by a vote of 38-372, invoked the 1973 War Powers Resolution (PL 93-148), which provided that Congress could force the withdrawal of troops fighting abroad if there had been a declaration of war or explicit statutory authorization. The White House had always refused to recognize the act, regardless of who was president, arguing that it was unconstitutional. *(House vote 473, p. H-164)* ■

Border Security Clears During Recess

CONGRESS AGREED IN August to provide $600 million requested by President Obama to increase patrol activities along the Southwest border. President Obama signed the bill into law on Aug. 13 (HR 6080 — PL 111-230).

"Violence on the Mexican side of the border has intensified because of turf battles among murderous transnational criminal organizations competing for drug-, alien- and weapon-trafficking business," said David E. Price, D-N.C., chairman of the House Homeland Security Appropriations Subcommittee. "This funding is urgently needed to counter the pressures our law enforcement agencies in our border communities currently face."

The bill won support from a number of GOP senators, but in the House, Republicans blasted the Democrats for taking a "piecemeal" approach rather than bringing the fiscal 2011 Homeland Security appropriations bill to the floor. Jerry Lewis of California, ranking Republican on the House Appropriations Committee, said his chamber was only considering the bill "to allow the Democratic majority to claim that they care about border security."

2010 LEGISLATIVE ACTION

After an unsuccessful attempt to add border security funds to the fiscal 2010 war supplemental spending bill (PL 111-212), the House passed a separate $701 million border security supplemental spending bill (HR 5875) on July 28.

The cost of the measure, which passed by voice vote, was partially offset with $100 million in rescissions, but the bill included no revenue provisions. Unlike the bill that later became law, it would have required the Defense Department to pay the full costs associated with deploying National Guard troops along the border

---

BOX SCORE 2010 FISCAL YEAR

BORDER SECURITY SUPPLEMENTAL

BILL: HR 6080 — PL 111-230

LEGISLATIVE ACTION:

House passed HR 5875 by voice vote July 28.

Senate passed HR 5875, amended, by unanimous consent Aug. 5.

House passed HR 6080 by voice vote Aug. 10.

Senate cleared HR 6080 by unanimous consent Aug 12.

President signed the bill on Aug. 13.

---

in fiscal 2010 and 2011.

The Senate passed an amended version of the bill by unanimous consent on Aug. 5, shortly before adjourning for a five-week recess. The Senate amendment reduced the bill's total to $600 million and allocated some of the money differently. Most significantly, the costs were fully offset by the addition of a provision to temporarily increase fees paid by companies applying for H-1B and L visas.

The House bristled at the Senate's addition of revenue provisions, which under the Constitution must originate in the House. So, during a one-day session on Aug. 10, the House agreed by voice vote to pass its own identical bill (HR 6080).

The Senate cleared the legislation by unanimous consent in a one-day session Aug. 12.

HIGHLIGHTS

The bill included:

‣ $254 million for Customs and Border Protection, including funds that appropriators said would send 1,500 new patrol agents and two additional unmanned aerial drones to the border to help stem the flow of illegal immigrants and drugs.

‣ $196 million for the Justice Department for increased border-related law enforcement activities.

‣ $80 million for Immigration and Customs Enforcement, including funds for communications equipment.

‣ Increases of $2,000 and $2,500, respectively, in the fees that companies paid when they submitted applications for H-1B and L employee visas.

‣ Rescissions of $100 million in previously enacted spending. ∎

Medicaid, Education Spending Clears

MEMBERS OF THE HOUSE interrupted their August recess to return to Washington and clear a $26.1 billion bill that provided funds to help state and local governments prevent layoffs of teachers and maintain Medicaid health coverage of the poor. President Obama signed the bill into law the day it cleared (HR 1586 — PL 111-226).

Speaker Nancy Pelosi, D-Calif., called the House back into session amid calls from state officials for quick action. New York Gov. David A. Paterson, a Democrat, warned that about 30 states had budgeted on the assumption that the federal funds would arrive.

Republicans criticized the legislation, saying it was essentially a Democratic election year sop to teachers' unions. Democrats disagreed. "There's nothing in this bill that says that anyone has to belong to a union," responded Sen. Tom Harkin, D-Iowa, chairman of the Health, Education, Labor and Pensions Committee.

However, it was not lost on Democrats that the assistance would resonate with many of their constituents.

Republicans also said that one of the prime offsets used to pay for the bill — changes to a number of foreign tax provisions — could harm the economic recovery by imposing new taxes on businesses. Major business groups opposed the tax proposals, saying they would make U.S. companies less competitive abroad. Democrats countered that the changes removed incentives for U.S. companies to locate their operations overseas.

Enactment was a victory, in particular, for liberal Democrat David R. Obey of Wisconsin, chairman of the House Appropriations Committee, who was retiring at the end of the Congress and had made preventing planned teacher layoffs his top priority. The teacher aid was popular among House Democrats, 236 of whom had voted to add it to a war supplemental spending bill in July. The Senate, however, had killed the idea.

Still, many Democrats were unhappy that part of the bill was offset through an $11.9 billion reduction in funds for food stamp benefits and a $1.5 billion reduction in funds for renewable-energy programs.

The bill that Senate Majority Leader Harry Reid, D-Nev., used as a vehicle for the supplemental funding had several previous lives, including as a long-term authorization bill for the Federal Aviation Administration. *(FAA, p. 15-3)*

HIGHLIGHTS

The main provisions of the enacted bill:

● **Teachers.** Appropriated $10 billion for a new Education Jobs Fund. It directed the Education Department to use the funds to provide aid to local school districts to prevent layoffs in elementary and second-

BOX SCORE 2010 FISCAL YEAR

EDUCATION AND MEDICAID SUPPLEMENTAL

BILL: HR 1586 — PL 111-226

LEGISLATIVE ACTION:

Senate passed HR 1586, amended with education and Medicaid provisions, 61-39, on Aug. 5.

House cleared the bill, 247-161, on Aug. 10.

President signed the bill Aug. 10.

ary schools. Under a "maintenance of effort" requirement, states that received aid could not reduce their education funding in fiscal 2011.

● **Medicaid.** Appropriated $16.1 billion over two years to extend for six months, through June 30, 2011, an enhanced federal matching rate for state Medicaid programs. The 2009 economic stimulus law (PL 111-5) authorized the extra funding under the Federal Medical Assistance Percentage, but that provision was set to expire on Dec. 31.

The bill gave states a minimum federal match of 56.2 percent of the cost of their Medicaid programs for the first quarter of fiscal 2011, falling to 53.2 percent in the second quarter and 51.2 percent in the third.

● **Offsets.** Covered the cost of the bill primarily through:

▸ Eliminating a 13.6 percent increase in food stamp benefits that was enacted in the stimulus law, as of March 31, 2014, reducing mandatory spending by $11.9 billion over 10 years.

▸ Clarifying the calculation of rebates that drugmakers were required to provide in order to participate in state Medicaid programs, reducing mandatory spending by $2 billion over 10 years.

▸ Eliminating advance refundability of the earned-income tax credit after Dec. 31, 2010, reducing mandatory spending by $900 million over 10 years.

▸ Rescinding previously appropriated but unspent funds, including $2.3 billion from the economic stimulus law and $2.3 billion from the Defense Department, reducing spending by $2.8 billion over 10 years.

▸ Closing a number of tax loopholes related to the foreign income of U.S.-based multinational corporations, increasing revenue by $9.8 billion over 10 years.

2010 LEGISLATIVE ACTION

SENATE ACTION

The Senate passed the bill Aug. 5 by a vote of 61-39, with Republicans Susan Collins and Olympia J. Snowe of Maine joining all 59 members of the Democratic caucus. Passage was virtually assured after the Senate agreed, 61-38, the previous day to invoke cloture, limiting the length of the debate. *(Senate votes 228, 224, p. S-47)*

HOUSE ACTION

The successful cloture vote in the Senate prompted Pelosi to call the House back. The chamber cleared the measure Aug. 10 by a vote of 247-161. The Democratic majority extolled the measure for saving teachers and emergency personnel from layoffs while Republicans denounced it as a bailout that would do little about long-term economic problems. *(House vote 518, p. H-180)* ∎

Chapter 3

BANKING &
FINANCIAL SERVICES

Historic Financial Overhaul Creates Bureau, Expands Oversight of Banks

IN A MAJOR VICTORY FOR President Obama, Congress in July cleared a sweeping overhaul of the nation's financial regulatory system. The historic legislation promised to alter banking and securities law going back as far as 1933.

Obama signed the bill into law in a ceremony July 21, flanked by members of both chambers who had worked for more than a year to produce the legislation (HR 4173 — PL 111-203). The signing took place in the Ronald Reagan Building and International Trade Center.

The legislation was a response to the financial crisis that began in 2007 and led to the deepest recession since the Great Depression. Work on the bill came in the midst of a weak recovery at a time when voters were fed up with multibillion-dollar bailouts, double-digit unemployment rates and the evaporation of their retirement savings.

The law touched nearly every major piece of 20th century financial regulatory law, from New Deal-era banking and securities acts to the post-savings and loan crisis legislation of the late 1980s and early 1990s.

For the first time, a process was put in place to assess and mitigate the risks of huge financial institutions whose activities or condition could pose a danger to the financial system. The legislation created an orderly process for tightening restraints on faltering institutions and, in extreme cases, shutting down a business that continued to pose a risk despite previous intervention. Lawmakers intended the process to prevent future bailouts and eliminate the assumption that the government would step in to salvage huge companies because they were considered "too big to fail."

The law established a new level of transparency in financial markets, especially in derivatives trading, where complex securities such as currency swaps came under federal regulation for the first time.

A new consumer protection agency was created to look out for the interests of consumers and include them as part of the equation when regulators examined the state of the economy as a whole.

Although the Federal Reserve was put under some new oversight, early attempts to greatly curtail its role were set aside, and the central bank gained major new responsibilities. In addition to retaining its regulation of federally chartered banks, it housed the new consumer agency and was given a central role in bringing risky financial institutions under federal restrictions.

The House passed its version of the bill, sponsored by Financial Services Chairman Barney Frank, D-Mass., on Dec. 11, 2009. The Senate followed suit May 20, 2010, passing a bill sponsored by Christopher J. Dodd, D-Conn., chairman of the Banking, Housing and Urban Affairs Committee. (2009 Almanac, p. 3-5)

Major differences included how to pay the cost of winding down failed financial institutions, where to place the new consumer protec-

---

BOX SCORE

BILL: HR 4173 — PL 111-203

....

LEGISLATIVE ACTION:

Senate passed HR 4173, amended with the text of S 3217 (S Rept 111-176), 59-39, on May 20.

House adopted the conference report (H Rept 111-517), 237-192, on June 30.

Senate cleared the bill, 60-39, on July 15.

President signed the bill July 21.

---

tion bureau, how much new authority to give the Fed and how much to rein it in, and how far to go in regulating derivatives and prohibiting proprietary trading by banks.

House and Senate Democratic negotiators thought they had reached a final agreement on June 25 after two weeks of negotiations, but they had to reconvene to alter the funding mechanism for the overhaul.

They replaced a fund that would have come from fees levied on banks and instead counted on savings from the 2008 bailout program for failing financial institutions and increased deposit insurance fees for large banks. The changes were crucial to securing the 60 votes needed to overcome a Republican filibuster in the Senate.

The House quickly adopted the conference report, but it took Senate leaders until July 15 to assemble the votes to clear the bill.

The Congressional Budget Office (CBO) put the total cost at $26.9 billion over 10 years and said all of it would be offset under the bill.

"To go to the Goldman Sachs, JPMorgan Chases and Blackstones and ask them to make a small contribution is reasonable," Frank said.

HIGHLIGHTS

The following are highlights of the bill. More detailed provisions can be found on p. 3-10.

● **Mitigating systemic risks.** For the first time, a government apparatus was created to identify and monitor companies that had become so large or interconnected that their failure could threaten the entire financial system.

▸ The law created a new Financial Stability Oversight Council made up of existing financial regulators, with the Treasury secretary at the helm, to monitor potential systemwide risks and make recommendations to the Federal Reserve. With a two-thirds majority vote, the council could subject a non-bank company to the Fed's regulatory powers. Also by a two-thirds vote, the council could approve a decision by the Fed to break up a large company that posed a grave threat to the financial system, but only as a last resort.

▸ New rules limited banks' proprietary trading and their ability to invest in hedge funds and private equity funds.

● **Liquidating failed institutions.** An orderly process was created for the Federal Deposit Insurance Corporation (FDIC) to liquidate large failing companies whose collapse would pose a risk to the financial system. The liquidation required the assent of the Treasury secretary, the president and two regulators and could be used only as a last resort if remediation efforts had failed.

▸ Costs of liquidating companies would be covered by the sale of their assets and by assessments on large financial institutions levied by the FDIC.

▸ The law limited the FDIC's authority to guarantee debt of solvent

insured banks. For example, the oversight council was required to approve the guarantee, the Treasury Department had to set a cap on the overall guarantee amount and expedited congressional approval was required.

● **Protecting consumers.** An independent Bureau of Consumer Financial Protection was created within the Federal Reserve system to look out for consumers' interests, with a director appointed by the president and confirmed by the Senate.

▸ The bureau was responsible for enforcing consumer protection laws, as well as consumer regulations for banks and credit unions with assets of more than $10 billion, mortgage-related businesses, payday lenders and others.

▸ The bureau's regulations would generally not pre-empt state laws that provided greater protection for consumers.

● **Federal Reserve powers.** The Fed was a central part of the new regime, albeit with some new restrictions on its powers.

▸ The Federal Reserve was given responsibility for identifying risks and setting heightened standards for financial institutions that were large or interconnected enough that if they faltered, they would pose risks to the financial system as a whole. The Fed could impose increasingly stringent regulations on faltering financial institutions in an effort to help them avoid collapse.

▸ The Federal Reserve also retained its oversight of federally chartered bank holding companies.

▸ The Fed could no longer provide emergency loans for individual institutions, and the Treasury had to approve all Fed emergency lending aimed at the financial system as a whole. The emergency lending authority played a prominent role in enabling the Fed to make emergency loans to rescue American International Group (AIG) and other troubled companies in 2008.

▸ The Government Accountability Office (GAO) was tasked with conducting a one-time audit of all Fed emergency loan programs created during the financial crisis. It also was given the authority to audit future emergency lending and other Fed transactions, with a two-year delay on releasing the results. But conferees declined to open the Fed's most sensitive monetary policy discussions to examination.

● **Regulating derivatives.** The law brought the over-the-counter financial derivatives market under significant government regulation.

▸ Many derivatives had to be traded on exchanges and routed through clearinghouses, with regulators examining trades before they were cleared.

▸ Regulators could impose margin requirements for those derivatives that were not required to go through a clearinghouse. Some exemptions from the new rules were provided for "end users" — companies that used derivatives to hedge business risks.

▸ Banks were required to spin off their riskiest derivatives-trading operations to affiliates.

● **Offsets.** A major source of offsets was a provision to immediately end the Troubled Asset Relief Program (TARP), which was created in 2008 (PL 110-343) to salvage huge failing financial institutions. Another source was higher premium fees for the FDIC's Deposit Insurance Fund for banks with more than $10 billion in assets. CBO estimated that the TARP change would result in $11 billion in savings, while the increased FDIC fees would generate a net $5.7 billion in revenue. *(TARP, 2008 Almanac, p. 7-3)*

● **Other major provisions.** The law also:

▸ Set new federal rules for home mortgages, including requiring lenders to determine whether a borrower could repay a loan and

barring certain incentive payments to mortgage brokers for selling higher-rate loans.

▸ Required hedge funds and private equity advisers to register with the Securities and Exchange Commission (SEC) and to provide information on their portfolios that was necessary to assess systemic risk.

▸ Created a new SEC office focused on credit-rating agencies and required rating agencies to disclose their methodologies. The law created new liability for rating agencies that failed to meet certain investigatory requirements, and it removed many statutory and regulatory references to credit ratings.

▸ Gave shareholders a nonbinding vote on executive pay and on "golden parachutes" for departing executives. The law also gave the SEC authority to grant shareholders proxy access to nominate directors.

▸ Abolished the Office of Thrift Supervision and folded most of the agency's powers into the Office of the Comptroller of the Currency.

▸ Made permanent an increase in federal deposit insurance to $250,000 per account, and increased premiums for FDIC insurance assessed on large depository institutions.

▸ Required the Fed to issue rules that would set limits on the fees banks could charge merchants for debit card transactions that were reasonable and proportional to the cost of processing those transactions.

▸ Required companies that sold products such as mortgage-backed securities to retain at least 5 percent of the credit risk, unless the underlying loans met higher underwriting standards that reduced risk.

2010 LEGISLATIVE ACTION
SENATE COMMITTEE

Dodd cleared the first hurdle March 22, when the Banking Committee approved his bill (S 3217 — S Rept 111-176) on a 13-10 party-line vote. Two days after the markup, Dodd and Frank met with Obama, who had been pressing for action on the bill, and promised to move quickly. *(Highlights of House and Senate bills, p. 3-6)*

"We're going to get a bill done," Dodd said. Despite GOP opposition to the committee bill, some Republicans echoed Dodd's prediction. Judd Gregg, R-N.H., was optimistic that the two parties could work together and said there was a "100 percent" chance that legislation would emerge from the Senate before the end of the year.

Dodd had released his legislation March 15. "There hasn't been financial reform on the scale that I'm proposing this afternoon since the 1930s," he said. He acted after months of bipartisan closed-door discussions that failed to produce a bill. Dodd had held at least two rounds of talks with GOP committee members and negotiated alternately with Richard C. Shelby of Alabama, the ranking Republican on the Banking Committee, and with Bob Corker, R-Tenn. Facing pressure from the White House to move forward, Dodd then focused on panel Democrats to ensure their support.

SENATE FLOOR

The next test for the bill came on the Senate floor. The debate began April 26 and proceeded in fits and starts until May 20, when the Senate passed HR 4173 after inserting the text of S 3217, 59-39. Four Republicans broke with their party to support the bill. They were Olympia J. Snowe and Susan Collins of Maine, Charles E. Grassley of Iowa and Scott P. Brown of Massachusetts. Two Democrats — Russ Feingold of Wisconsin and Maria Cantwell of Washington — voted no. *(Senate vote 162, p. S-35)*

The key vote occurred hours earlier, when the Senate agreed,

60-40, to invoke cloture on the final version of the bill, bringing the prolonged debate to close. Just a day earlier, the Senate had rejected an attempt to limit the debate, 57-42. The critical votes came from Brown, who switched to support cloture, and Arlen Specter, D-Pa., who was absent for the first of the two votes. (Majority Leader Harry Reid, D-Nev., shifted to the "no" side in the first of the two cloture votes to preserve his parliamentary right to move to reconsider at a later point.) *(Senate votes 158, p. S-34, and 160, p. S-35)*

Republicans began their delaying tactics the day Reid first tried to bring the bill up on the floor, sticking together to defeat three cloture motions in as many days. But the Democrats' strategy of using the repeated votes to portray Republicans as opposing a crackdown on Wall Street excesses eventually worked. Republicans called off their filibuster April 28, allowing the Senate to proceed to the bill, but they promised many amendments. *(Senate votes 124, 126, 127, p. S-27)*

To end the filibuster, Democrats agreed to drop a $50 billion resolution fund, financed by fees on big banks, that would have been used to cover the cost of liquidating failed companies. Republicans regarded the change as a victory, although Dodd and Obama had never supported the provision.

Dodd and Shelby were unable to reach a deal on several other issues. The result was a bill that was harder on the industry than might have been expected even a few days before passage.

Despite intense lobbying by the American Bankers Association and others in the financial services industry, Dodd managed to keep the core provisions of the bill mostly intact. During the weeks of floor debate on the bill, the Senate took roll call votes on 28 amendments.

During that time, senators:

● **Resolution fund.** Adopted, 93-5, an amendment by Shelby and Dodd that eliminated the $50 billion resolution fund. Republicans argued that the fund's existence would ensure future bailouts and force healthy banks to pay for the errors of risky institutions. Shelby, who had been negotiating for weeks with Dodd on the amendment, said the change would make it clear "that backdoor bailouts are impossible." *(Senate vote 131, p. S-28)*

Instead, the FDIC would be able to tap a credit line at the Treasury Department to liquidate large companies. The Treasury would be repaid from assets of the failed institution. Creditors of the failing company would have to pay back any funds received in excess of what they would have been awarded in a traditional bankruptcy proceeding in liquidation. If that was insufficient, the FDIC would levy assessments on financial institutions with total consolidated assets of $50 billion or more.

FDIC Chairwoman Sheila C. Bair was a leading backer of the resolution fund but seemed to accept its demise. "When a large and complex institution fails and bankruptcy is not the best option, the FDIC will have the ability to liquidate it in an orderly way and enforce market discipline by making the shareholders and creditors bear the losses," she said.

To underscore that taxpayers would not fund future bailouts, the Senate adopted an amendment by Barbara Boxer, D-Calif., to explicitly prohibit public funding of financial rescues. *(Senate vote 130, p. S-28)*

● **FDIC premiums.**

▸ Adopted, 98-0, an amendment by Jon Tester, D-Mont., to base the premiums that banks paid into the FDIC's Deposit Insurance Fund on the banks' total assets rather than just its deposits. *(Senate vote 132, p. S-29)*

● **Consumer protection agency.**

▸ Rejected, 38-61, an amendment by Shelby that would have drastically scaled back the scope and powers of the consumer protection agency. It would have replaced the agency with a consumer regulator within the FDIC with authority to write new rules for banks and non-banks offering consumer financial services but not to enforce them. *(Senate vote 133, p. S-29)*

Republicans argued that the bill would give the agency unchecked power. They particularly wanted to ensure that financial regulators could intervene if the new agency issued rules that would compromise the safety and soundness of the banks. Dodd responded that he was not willing to weaken consumer protections, "given the enormous abuses we have seen."

▸ Adopted by voice vote an amendment by John D. Rockefeller IV, D-W.Va., and Kay Bailey Hutchison, R-Texas, to allow the Federal Trade Commission (FTC) to retain its authority to write consumer protection rules. As originally drafted, the consumer bureau would have assumed the FTC's authority to police fraud, deception and unfair business practices.

● **Derivatives.**

▸ Rejected, 39-59, an amendment by Saxby Chambliss, R-Ga., to strike the provisions on derivatives and replace them with language that would require more disclosure of swaps and allow the SEC and Commodity Futures Trading Commission (CFTC) to apply some new requirements to swap transactions. *(Senate vote 144, p. S-31)*

Republicans, in particular, wanted to ensure that companies that used derivatives to hedge risk associated with market fluctuations — rather than for trading — would not be subject to the bill's requirements that they clear their trades or place them on a public exchange. The existing legislation had a relatively narrow exemption for such end users.

Republicans and a few Democrats also opposed provisions that would force depository institutions to spin off their lucrative business in derivatives, which were partially blamed for the market meltdown that prompted the legislation. The language was championed by Blanche Lincoln, D-Ark., chairwoman of the Agriculture, Nutrition and Forestry Committee, who was locked in a tough primary race.

The Agriculture Committee approved the stiff provisions in a draft on April 21, and a version was folded into the Dodd bill. Democratic leaders did not want to drop the language out of concern that it would hurt Lincoln's chances, and the calculus continued when she survived a May 18 primary election but was forced into a June runoff. Having failed to minimize the provisions in the Senate, the industry turned their hopes to the conference.

● **Federal Reserve powers.**

▸ Adopted, 96-0, an amendment by Bernard Sanders, I-Vt., to require the GAO to complete an audit of the Federal Reserve within one year and require the central bank to disclose the names of the financial institutions that had gotten emergency financial assistance since December 2007, the amounts, the dates the assistance was provided, the terms of repayment and the "specific rationale" for creating the emergency lending programs. The details would amount to the clearest picture yet of the central bank's lending activities during the 2008-09 financial meltdown. *(Senate vote 137, p. S-30)*

In an effort to gain more votes, Sanders agreed to a number of modifications from Dodd that weakened the amendment. For instance, the amendment explicitly reinforced an existing statute that

Continued on p. 3-8

House and Senate Bills Compared

The following is a comparison of some of the major provisions in the initial House- and Senate-passed versions of the financial regulatory overhaul bill. Major differences included how to pay the cost of liquidating failed institutions, where to locate the new consumer protection agency and how strict to be in banning proprietary trading.

PROVISION	HOUSE VERSION	SENATE VERSION
FINANCIAL STABILITY	A new Financial Stability Oversight Council would monitor the financial services marketplace to identify large, interconnected companies whose distress or failure could pose a risk to the financial system. It could recommend specific regulations for the Federal Reserve to impose on the companies. The council could require the Fed to supervise non-bank financial companies that could pose such risks and recommend heightened standards for them. It could subject systemically important payment, clearing and settlements systems to standards created by the Fed.	A new Financial Stability Oversight Council would monitor the financial system and could determine that a large, interconnected company would pose a systemic risk if it failed. The Treasury, Fed and FDIC could also make such a determination. Such companies could be subject to heightened prudential standards that would increase in stringency if the company continued to pose a "grave" risk. The Fed, acting as agent for the council, would impose the heightened standards. Designation as a systemic risk by the council would make a company a financial holding company subject to supervision by the Fed.
ORDERLY LIQUIDATION AUTHORITY	The Treasury secretary, after certain consultations, could determine that a systemically important company was in default or danger of default. The Federal Deposit Insurance Corporation (FDIC) would be appointed by the Fed to act as receiver for the company. A new, $150 billion Systemic Dissolution Fund would be available to the FDIC to carry out the liquidation. Funding would come from risk-based assessments on large financial institutions. Secured creditors of failing companies would have to take losses of up to 10 percent on claims before they could recoup any losses from the fund.	The Treasury secretary, after certain consultations, could declare a systemically important company to be in default or danger of default. The FDIC would be appointed as receiver for the company. No fund would be set up, and the bill would explicitly bar taxpayer-funded bailouts. The FDIC could tap a credit line at the Treasury if necessary to cover the costs of liquidation. Reimbursement would come from the sale of the firm's assets and, if needed, assessments on large financial institutions. Secured creditors could not receive payments in excess of what they would have won in bankruptcy court.
CONSUMER PROTECTION	A Bureau of Consumer Financial Protection would be created as an independent agency housed in the Fed to protect consumers from unfair, deceptive and abusive acts. It would write rules and combine authority over consumer financial protection held by seven agencies. The Office of the Comptroller of the Currency could pre-empt state consumer financial protection laws only if the state laws discriminated against national banks or were pre-empted by another federal law. State attorneys general could enforce the new law with regard to national banks and federal savings associations. The Fed would be required to limit interchange fees on credit and debit cards. Retailers could not be penalized for offering discounts based on how consumers paid for purchases.	A freestanding Consumer Financial Protection Agency would be created to protect consumers from unfair, deceptive and abusive acts. Rule-making authority of the Fed and other banking agencies under existing laws would be transferred to the agency. Similar language. No similar provision.

NEW CURBS ON THE FED	The Fed (and the FDIC) could no longer provide emergency loans to rescue an individual institution. All emergency loans would have to be approved by the Treasury and be aimed at providing market liquidity.	Similar, although the FDIC could guarantee obligations of solvent financial companies to prevent systemic risk in times of severe economic distress.
	The Government Accountability Office (GAO) would be required to audit all emergency lending provided by the Fed during the financial crisis. It also could audit every aspect of every balance sheet of the Fed and its regional banks. Transcripts of interest rate discussion would be exempt, and publication of information about Fed decisions to intervene in markets would be delayed by 180 days. The bill stated that this was not intended as interference in monetary policy decisions.	The GAO would be required to conduct a one-time audit of emergency actions undertaken by the Fed since the financial crisis began. The Fed would be required to publicly disclose the names of all financial institutions, corporations and foreign central banks that received emergency Fed loans during that period.
DERIVATIVES REGULATION	All over-the-counter derivatives would be regulated by the Securities and Exchange Commission or the Commodity Futures Trading Commission.	Similar language.
	All derivatives would have to be cleared if they were accepted by a clearing agency, and they would have to be executed on an exchange if an exchange accepted them for trading. Uncleared swaps would be subject to margin requirements. All trades would be reported to allow regulators to monitor risks.	Similar language.
	No similar language.	Banks and other depository institutions would have to spin off their derivatives business to keep it separate from federally insured deposits, with a relatively narrow exemption for end users.
PROPRIETARY TRADING	Banks, bank holding companies and other companies that controlled insured deposits would be barred from proprietary trading or investing in hedge funds and private equity funds.	Banks would be barred from most proprietary trading, except for transactions that benefited customers.
OTHER	The Office of Thrift Supervision would be eliminated and its duties taken over by the Office of the Comptroller of the Currency.	Similar language.
	Lenders would be required to make a good-faith effort to verify a borrower's ability to repay a loan before offering a mortgage.	Similar language.
	Credit-rating organizations would be required to register with the SEC, which would review their methodologies and practices annually. The SEC could levy fines on those that failed to meet acceptable internal risk controls. The bill would require the SEC to write rules to increase the disclosure of information.	A new Office of Credit Ratings in the SEC would examine each rating organization annually. The organizations would have to disclose methodologies used for each rating, create and implement an internal controls structure under SEC rules, and report annually to the SEC. Ratings would have to be separate from sales and marketing. Non-compliance with new SEC rules would merit severe penalties.

Continued from p. 3-5
prohibited the GAO from reviewing the central bank's monetary policy or its transactions with foreign central banks.

The amendment was weaker than the House language, which would have allowed monetary policy reviews.

Fed Chairman Ben S. Bernanke wrote a strongly worded letter to Dodd expressing "deep concern" about Sanders' original language, saying the requirements could interfere with the independence of the Fed's monetary policy and damage its credibility in financial markets .

▸ Rejected, 37-62, an attempt by David Vitter, R-La., to go further by removing several existing restrictions on the GAO's authority to examine the Fed. The amendment would have exempted unreleased transcripts and minutes of Federal Reserve and Federal Open Market Committee discussions from the audit and imposed a 180-day delay on the publication of information about Federal Reserve decisions to intervene in markets. *(Senate vote 138, p. S-30)*

● **Credit-rating agencies.**

▸ Adopted, 64-35, an amendment offered by Al Franken, D-Minn., with bipartisan backing, to set up an independent board that would select the rating agency to review certain structured bonds, rather than having the bond issuer select the rater. Lawmakers had blasted the industry for assigning overly optimistic ratings to mortgage-backed securities that had turned sour. *(Senate vote 146, p. S-32)*

● **Pre-emption of state law.**

▸ Rejected, 43-55, a Corker amendment to allow federal pre-emption of state consumer financial protection laws that would interfere with federal law. *(Senate vote 154, p. S-33)*

▸ Adopted, 80-18, an amendment by Thomas R. Carper, D-Del., that would allow for federal pre-emption of state consumer financial protection laws only if the laws would have a discriminatory effect on national banks vs. state-chartered banks. *(Senate vote 155, p. S-33)*

● **Fannie Mae, Freddie Mac.**

▸ Adopted, 63-36, a Dodd amendment to require the Treasury Department to conduct a study on ending the federal conservatorship of mortgage-lending giants Fannie Mae and Freddie Mac that began in September 2008. The amendment required the Treasury to report to Congress by Jan. 31, 2011. *(Senate vote 139, p. S-30; 2008 law, 2008 Almanac, p. 7-9)*

▸ Rejected, 43-56, an amendment by John McCain, R-Ariz., to require the Federal Housing Finance Agency to end the conservatorship of Fannie and Freddie within 30 months of the bill's enactment and dismantle the two companies if they were not financially viable at that point. *(Senate vote 140, p. S-30)*

▸ Rejected an amendment by Michael D. Crapo, R-Idaho, to cap government funding of Fannie Mae and Freddie at $200 billion and place their balance sheets on the federal budget until the end of any federal conservatorship or receivership. The proposal fell after the Senate voted against waiving a point of order. The vote was 47-46, well short of the required 60 votes. The two companies had recently asked for an additional $19 billion from the Treasury. *(Senate vote 151, p. S-33)*

● **Debit card fees.**

▸ Adopted an amendment by Richard J. Durbin, D-Ill., to require the Federal Reserve to promulgate rules for "reasonable and proportional" interchange fees directed primarily at debit card transactions. It also included a prohibition on rules that barred merchants from giving preference to a particular brand of card or from offering a discount for paying in cash. In previous years, the Senate had shied away from voting on language that would restrict the interchange

fees, also known as "swipe fees." But in the anti-industry climate, the Senate easily adopted the amendment, 64-33. *(Senate vote 149, p. S-32)*

CONFERENCE

House and Senate Democratic conferees reached agreement on the bill in the early-morning hours of June 25 after two weeks of negotiations punctuated by an all-night marathon session the final day. The legislation was renamed the Dodd-Frank Act in honor of the bill managers. Afterward, Frank hugged Dodd, who was retiring at year's end, with tears running down his cheeks.

But four days later, Frank was forced to reconvene the conference to scrap plans to cover the cost of the overhaul through fees levied on large financial institutions and hedge funds.

● **Resolution fund.** Under the original conference agreement, the FDIC would have been authorized to raise up to $19 billion over five years for a fund fed by assessments on financial institutions with assets of $50 billion or more and hedge funds that managed more than $10 billion in assets. The proceeds could not have been used for any other purpose, and after 25 years, any unused money would have gone to pay down the national debt.

Democrats dropped the Senate plan after it became clear that several moderate Senate Republicans, including Brown, Snowe and Collins, would not support the conference report if it included the assessment. With the June 28 death of a Senate icon, Democrat Robert C. Byrd of West Virginia, Reid was down to a 58-member caucus. At least two Democrats were talking of opposing the bill, so he could not afford to lose the three GOP votes. *(Byrd, p. 5-7)*

Democrats agreed to replace the bank fees with language by Dodd to free up funds by immediately ending TARP and to authorize the FDIC to increase premium fees for large banks. Democrats rejected an alternative proposed by Gregg that would have used money from the 2009 economic stimulus legislation (PL 111-5) instead.

● **Derivatives holdings.** The chief hurdle to completing the original conference report was Lincoln's proposed ban on depository institutions trading in derivatives.

Under the final compromise, banks were required to divert their riskiest derivatives — those related to commodities, energy, metals, agriculture, equities and below-investment-grade credit default swaps — into a separately capitalized entity walled off from federally insured deposits.

However, they were allowed to keep their business in derivatives tied to interest rate swaps, which represented a huge swath of the market. They also could continue to trade in derivatives related to foreign exchange swaps, credit, gold and silver, investment-grade credit default swaps, and any transaction to hedge risk. The compromise was the work of Lincoln's House counterpart, Agriculture Chairman Collin C. Peterson, D-Minn. House Democrats had warned Lincoln repeatedly that their chamber would not be able to pass the overall legislation if it kept her tougher provision.

The agreement also spared end users from significant requirements that applied to companies that traded in riskier derivatives. But centrist, business-friendly Democrats in the House, along with some Republicans in both chambers, objected that the conference report still did not specifically ban capital requirements on the end users. Chambliss tried to address the issue when the conference reconvened to eliminate the bank fee, offering an amendment to explicitly prevent regulators from creating capital requirements for end users. The amendment was defeated.

Instead, Dodd and Lincoln sent a letter to House lawmakers saying that the legislation would not allow regulators to impose capital requirements on traders who used derivatives only to hedge risk.

● **Volcker rule.** The conferees also struck an eleventh-hour deal on the so-called Volcker rule, which proposed to curb proprietary trading by banks. The final version was not as restrictive as the original Senate provision, which would have completely banned banks from using their own money to buy or sell securities in financial markets to turn a profit. The provision that negotiators accepted gave the regulators less discretion in implementing the Volcker rule, but it loosened the requirements on banks, allowing them to have up to 3 percent of their tangible common equity in a hedge fund or private equity firm.

FINAL ACTION

Frank filed the conference report (H Rept 111-517) on June 29, and the House adopted it the next day. But Reid put off final action until after the July Fourth recess because he still lacked the 60 votes needed to prevent a GOP filibuster.

● **House adopts conference report.** The House adopted the conference report by a vote of 237-192 on June 30, with 14 more supporters — 11 Democrats and three Republicans — than the leadership had been able to muster when the House passed its version in December 2009. *(House vote 413, p. H-146)*

Most Republicans continued to lambast the bill, saying it would stymie job creation and reduce the availability of consumer credit. "It's a job killer," said Jeb Hensarling of Texas. "Once again we have legislation that will make credit . . . less available and more expensive."

The House voted 198-229, along party lines, to reject a motion to recommit the bill that called for the addition of language by Ron Paul, R-Texas, that would have given the GAO significantly expanded audit authority over the Fed, including the ability to monitor some of the central bank's most sensitive monetary policy deliberations. It also would have expanded exemptions from margin requirements for commercial businesses that used financial derivatives to hedge their business risks. *(House vote 412, p. H-144)*

● **Senate clears bill.** Reid finally obtained the last votes he needed on July 12, enabling the Senate to clear the bill, 60-39, on July 15. *(Senate vote 208, p. S-44)*

Reid and Dodd won commitments from Susan Collins, R-Maine, and Maria Cantwell, D-Wash., just before the August recess, but the death of Byrd, plus opposition from Feingold, still left them two votes short.

Facing a significant delay, Dodd worked to keep the pressure on his colleagues. "If we scrap it, we're right back without any of these protections," Dodd said. "It'll be a generation before the Congress comes back to deal with these issues again."

The American Bankers Association and others in the financial services industry redoubled their efforts to defeat the bill. "Congress consistently underestimates the complexity and size of the regulations resulting from new laws," the association's chief executive, Edward L. Yingling, said.

The final commitments came July 11 from Republicans Snowe and Brown, allowing the Senate to clear the bill three days later.

Obama issued a statement the same day saying the bill would provide "the strongest consumer financial protections in history." He also pledged, "There will be no more taxpayer-funded bailouts. Period. If a large financial institution should ever fail, this reform gives us the ability to wind it down without endangering the broader economy. And there will be new rules to make clear that no firm is somehow protected because it is 'too big to fail,' so that we don't have another AIG." ∎

[PROVISIONS]

Details of the Financial Regulations Law

THE FOLLOWING ARE MAJOR provisions of the sweeping financial regulatory overhaul, which was signed into law July 21 (PL 111-203).

SYSTEMIC-RISK REDUCTION
FINANCIAL STABILITY OVERSIGHT COUNCIL

● **Council established.** The law established a Financial Stability Oversight Council, responsible for monitoring and addressing systemwide risks to U.S. financial stability. The council, which was required to meet at least quarterly, was to be funded through the Office of Financial Research created under the law.

The council's membership consisted of federal regulators. The voting members were the Treasury secretary, who was also the chairman; the chairman of the Federal Reserve Board; the comptroller of the Office of the Currency; the director of the Consumer Financial Protection Bureau; the director of the Federal Housing Finance Agency; the chairman of the Securities and Exchange Commission (SEC); the chairman of the Federal Deposit Insurance Corporation (FDIC); the chairman of the Commodity Futures Trading Commission (CFTC); the chairman of the National Credit Union Administration Board; and an independent insurance adviser appointed by the president. Several non-voting members could serve in advisory roles.

● **Authority and duties.** The council was charged with monitoring the financial services market to identify potential threats to the financial stability of the United States. It also was directed to monitor domestic and international regulatory developments and proposals, facilitate information sharing among its member agencies and identify potential regulatory gaps.

If the council determined that a non-bank financial company posed a systemic risk to the country's financial stability, it could vote to require the Fed to supervise and regulate the company and require the company to register with the Fed. Such a decision required a two-thirds majority vote of the council, including an affirmative vote from the chairman. It could also recommend more stringent standards that the Federal Reserve could apply to such financial institutions, including higher risk-based capital, resolution plans, leverage and concentration limits.

OFFICE OF FINANCIAL RESEARCH

● **Office established.** The law created an Office of Financial Research within the Treasury Department, headed by a director appointed by the president and confirmed by the Senate to a six-year term. The office was charged with supporting the council by collecting data and conducting research on potential risks to the U.S. financial system.

● **Funding.** The office was funded through assessments made by the Fed on non-bank financial companies and bank holding companies that had total consolidated assets of at least $50 billion. The provision was to take effect two years after enactment of the bill. In the interim, the Fed would provide funding for the office.

'WINDING DOWN' FAILING INSTITUTIONS

● **'Orderly liquidation.'** The law created an "orderly liquidation" process run by the FDIC for the purpose of "winding down" or dismantling large, failing financial institutions in a manner that minimized the risk to the overall financial system.

This authority could be used only if the Treasury secretary determined — in consultation with the president and based on written recommendations from two other federal regulators — that the financial company was in default or at risk of default, that its failure would seriously damage U.S. financial stability, and that there was no viable private sector alternative. The process was intended for very rare circumstances, with the bankruptcy code continuing to serve as the primary path for winding down a failing institution.

The FDIC could not take an equity interest in or become a shareholder of the financial institution or any subsidiary.

The liquidation process was part of an effort to end the expectation among market participants that certain companies were "too big to fail" and that the government would step in to bail them out.

● **Costs.** The Treasury was the source of the initial funds to cover the upfront costs of winding down a failed institution. The government would then establish a repayment plan and recoup losses first from shareholders and unsecured creditors and, if necessary, from risk-based assessments on financial companies with assets of more than $50 billion. Taxpayers were explicitly protected from losses associated with the use of this authority.

● **Process.** If it was determined that a financial company had to be liquidated, the Treasury secretary would notify the FDIC and the company. If the company's board of directors agreed to the appointment of the FDIC as receiver, the Treasury secretary would make the appointment. If the board did not agree, the secretary would petition the U.S. District Court for the District of Columbia for an order authorizing the appointment of the FDIC as receiver.

Alternatively, the Fed and FDIC could request that the Treasury secretary appoint the FDIC as receiver if they deemed a financial company to be in default or in serious danger of default. The judicial review process still applied.

Under this scenario, the Fed and FDIC would provide the Treasury secretary with a written recommendation that: 1) evaluated whether the financial company was in default or in danger of default; 2) described the effect such a failure would have on U.S. financial stability; 3) recommended steps that should be taken; 4) showed why there were no likely private sector alternatives; 5) showed why bankruptcy was not appropriate; 6) evaluated the effect on creditors, shareholders and counterparties; and 7) described the effect the default would have on low-income, minority or underserved communities.

The secretary also had to consider the cost to the Treasury Department and the possibility that government intervention could increase excessive risk-taking by creditors, shareholders or counterparties due to the belief that the government would limit the downside risk associated with investing in or doing business with a failing institution.

● **Liability and bankruptcy.** The company's board of directors could not be held liable to shareholders or creditors for consenting to the appointment of a receiver. However, the FDIC could hold directors and officers liable for monetary damages in the case of gross negligence. The law expedited federal court consideration of cases

brought by the FDIC against directors, officers, employees and agents of a financial company that was in the process of being liquidated.

If an orderly liquidation was triggered, existing bankruptcy proceedings would be dismissed and new bankruptcy proceedings could not be filed.

● **Claims.** If an orderly liquidation was triggered and the FDIC was made receiver, the law assumed that creditors and shareholders would take losses, and that the management team would be removed. In addition, management, board members and other individuals responsible for the failure would bear financial losses through restitution or other actions. All those that had a right to the claims would be treated in similar fashion, unless the FDIC determined that not doing so would enhance the value of firm assets for sale. Unsecured claims of the United States would have, at a minimum, a higher priority than liabilities of the financial company that counted as regulatory capital.

● **Insurance companies.** Insurance companies that were considered to be covered financial companies were subject to liquidation governed by state law. If the state regulator failed to act, the FDIC had backup authority.

● **Brokers and dealers.** As receiver, the FDIC was directed to appoint the Securities Investor Protection Corporation as the trustee to handle the orderly liquidation of a covered broker or dealer. The determination of claims and the liquidation of assets was administered under the Securities Investor Protection Act (PL 91-598). Brokers or dealers not covered by the act were subject to the applicable bankruptcy laws.

FEDERAL RESERVE
EXPANDED FEDERAL RESERVE POWERS

● **Supervision.** The law gave the Fed formal responsibility — which did not exist under previous law — for identifying, measuring, monitoring and mitigating risks to U.S. financial stability. A company with at least $50 billion in consolidated assets that had recently been classified as a bank holding company and that received financial assistance under the Troubled Asset Relief Program, or TARP (PL 110-343), was automatically subject to Fed supervision and regulation. However, the Fed could not authorize any federal financial assistance.

● **Setting standards.** Under the law, the Fed had the authority — on its own or on the recommendation of the Financial Stability Oversight Council — to establish prudential standards for non-bank financial companies that it supervised and for large bank holding companies, those with total consolidated assets of $50 billion or more. The standards had to be more stringent than those for other financial institutions and could be increasingly restrictive depending on the risk posed by the companies.

● **Remediation.** To limit the chances that an institution in the early stages of trouble would end up failing, the Fed, together with the FDIC and the council, was directed to prescribe restrictions such as limits on capital distributions, acquisitions and asset growth. For a company in the later stages of financial distress, Fed action could include requiring capital restoration plans or capital-raising plans, setting limits on transactions with affiliates, requiring management changes and requiring asset sales.

● **Resolution plan.** Each non-bank financial company supervised by the Fed and each large bank holding company had to report periodically to the Fed, the Financial Stability Oversight Council and the FDIC on its resolution plan — a blueprint for the company's rapid and orderly resolution in the event that it faced material financial distress or failure.

If the Fed and the FDIC jointly determined that a company's resolution plan was not credible and would not facilitate an orderly liquidation under the bankruptcy code, the company would be required to submit a new plan. If the company did not resubmit a satisfactory plan, the Fed, in consultation with the Financial Stability Oversight Council and the FDIC, could impose more stringent regulatory requirements or require the company to divest itself of certain assets or operations.

● **Stress test.** The Fed, in conjunction with other regulators, was charged with conducting semiannual stress tests on large bank holding companies and non-bank financial companies that were under Fed supervision to evaluate whether the individual institutions had the capital, on a total consolidated basis, to absorb losses that could result from adverse economic conditions.

● **Leverage requirements.** The law directed the Fed to require large bank holding companies and non-bank financial companies that it supervised to maintain a debt-to-equity ratio of no more than 15-to-1, if the council determined that the company posed a grave threat to U.S. financial stability and that the requirement was necessary to mitigate the risk.

The computation of capital for purposes of meeting capital requirements had to consider the company's off-balance-sheet activities.

● **Acquisitions.** Unless they provided prior notice to the Fed, large holding companies and non-bank financial companies supervised by the Fed were barred from acquiring or controlling any company that did not engage in banking activities and had $10 billion or more in total consolidated assets. The Fed was directed to take the criteria outlined in the Bank Holding Act (PL 84-511) for acquisitions and mergers into consideration when reviewing the proposed transaction, as well as the level of risk that the acquisition posed to the U.S. financial system.

● **Savings and loans.** The Fed was authorized to set capital reserve levels for savings and loan holding companies and limit asset purchases or sale transactions with company insiders. The central bank was also directed to examine the activities of non-depository subsidiaries of depository holding companies to determine the safety and soundness of the subsidiary's activities.

LIMITS ON FED AUTHORITY

● **Emergency lending restrictions.** The law amended Section 13(3) of the Federal Reserve Act (PL 63-43), which governed the Fed's emergency lending authority. Previously, the Fed could lend to an individual company under "unusual and exigent circumstances," provided that the borrower was unable to secure adequate credit accommodations from other banking institutions. The Fed rarely used this clause until the 2008 crisis in the financial services industry, when it played a central role and loaned money to several institutions, including American International Group (AIG).

The new law prohibited the Fed from providing emergency loans to an individual company. Any lending program had to be approved by the Treasury and be designed to provide liquidity to the system and not to aid a single, failing financial company. Collateral or other security for loans had to be sufficient to protect taxpayers from losses, and the Fed was required to report to Congress within seven days any time it provided lending.

● **Federal Reserve governance.** The law altered the manner in which Federal Reserve bank presidents were elected. The president of each Fed bank would be elected by the directors selected to represent the public

(Class B and Class C directors). Directors representing the member banks (Class A directors) were no longer authorized to vote.

● **GAO audits and congressional reporting requirements.** Within seven days of making an emergency loan, the Fed was required to provide Congress with information that included a justification for issuing the loan; the identity of the loan recipients; the date, amount and form of the assistance; and the material terms of the assistance.

The GAO was directed to conduct a one-time audit of the Fed's emergency lending between December 2007 and the enactment of this law. The audit had to start within 30 days of enactment and be completed within one year, after which the GAO was required to submit a report to Congress.

In a significant departure from previous law, the GAO was authorized to audit future Fed functions, including open-market transactions and discount window advances. But the GAO had to delay its report to Congress and the public to ensure that the information would not have adverse effects on the financial markets.

NEW REGULATION OF FINANCIAL INSTITUTIONS

● **OTS abolished, duties distributed.** The law abolished the Office of Thrift Supervision (OTS) and transferred its functions to: the Office of the Comptroller of the Currency (OCC), which was given responsibility for supervising federal thrifts; the FDIC, which was responsible for supervising state-chartered thrifts; and the Federal Reserve, which was responsible for supervising thrift holding companies. The OTS — a bank regulator that was housed within the Treasury — oversaw savings associations and holding companies that primarily took deposits and loaned them out for residential mortgages.

● **FDIC moratorium.** The law placed a three-year moratorium on the FDIC's ability to approve new applications for deposit insurance for an industrial loan company, credit card bank or trust bank that was owned or controlled by a commercial company. Commercial companies included all affiliates that derived at least 15 percent of their revenue from non-financial activities.

The law temporarily suspended exceptions permitted under the Bank Holding Company Act that allowed commercial companies to own banks. The law required a study of the implications of removing the exceptions before further action was taken.

● **Transparency.** Bank holding companies were required to provide the Fed with information on all company activities, including subsidiary activities, for the purpose of identifying and addressing risks throughout the entire organization. The law removed the so-called Fed-lite provisions under the Gramm-Leach-Bliley Act (PL 106-102), which limited the Fed's ability to obtain information on the activities of bank holding subsidiaries.

● **Coordination by regulators.** The Fed, other federal regulators and state regulators were directed to coordinate as much as possible to reduce duplication in regulatory activities. The law required similar coordination between bank holding company regulators and the primary regulator of a bank holding company's subsidiary. Savings and loan holding companies also were subject to these requirements.

● **Interaffiliate transactions.** The Federal Reserve Act was amended by expanding the list of interaffiliate covered transactions to include credit exposure from a securities borrowing, lending or derivatives transaction. This was an effort to address risks that affiliates could pose to banks when they engaged in risky derivatives transactions and incurred significant losses.

● **Lending limits.** The law tightened national bank lending limits — the percentage of bank capital that could be loaned to a single borrower — by treating credit exposure on derivatives, repurchase agreements and reverse repurchase agreements as extensions of credit. Lending limits, which prevent overexposure to any single borrower and the risk that the borrower would not repay the loan, are considered a key component of bank safety and soundness.

National banks were required to take insider transactions and non-affiliate transactions into account when considering credit exposure. State banks were also subject to the lending limits, although they had a two-year transition period in which to comply.

● **Capital levels.** The Fed and other federal regulators were directed to try to make capital requirements for bank holding companies, savings and loan holding companies and insured depository institutions "countercyclical." The amount of capital that a company was required to maintain would increase in times of economic expansion and decrease in times of economic contraction, consistent with the safety and soundness of the company.

● **Proprietary trading.** The law placed new limits on propriety trading by the largest financial institutions, with exceptions and discretion for regulators. The provision was referred to as the Volcker rule after former Fed Chairman Paul A. Volcker, who advocated such restrictions. The final version was not as restrictive as the original Senate bill, which would have completely banned banks from using their own money to buy or sell securities in financial markets to gain a profit.

With major exceptions, the final bill prohibited insured depository institutions and bank holding companies supervised by the Fed from engaging in proprietary trading or acquiring any ownership interest in a hedge fund or private equity fund.

Non-bank financial companies that were supervised by the Fed and engaged in such activities were subject to additional capital requirements and quantitative limits.

Exceptions to the restrictions on proprietary trading included brokerage activities that involved buying securities with the anticipation that they would be quickly sold to a client, the traditional practice of buying and selling derivatives to hedge risks, and advisory services to a separately capitalized hedge fund.

Big banks were required to reduce their holdings in a hedge fund or private equity fund to no more than 3 percent of the fund's capital, and the holdings had to be "immaterial" to the banking institution. The bank's aggregate holdings in all private equity and hedge funds could not exceed more than 3 percent of the bank's Tier 1 capital.

● **Concentration limits on large companies.** Financial companies were prohibited from merging or consolidating with another company if it would result in the new company having consolidated liabilities that exceeded 10 percent of the total amount of consolidated liabilities for all financial companies. The Financial Stability Oversight Council's recommendation would also be considered in such cases.

Regulators could not approve an application for an interstate merger if the resulting insured depository institution, bank holding company or savings and loan company would control more than 10 percent of the total deposits of insured depository institutions in the United States.

PAYMENT, CLEARING AND SETTLEMENT

● **'Systemically important' utilities.** Generally, financial market utilities were designated as "systemically important" based on the aggregate monetary value of the transactions they processed and the

effect their failure would have on clearing, settlement and payment systems, as well as on counterparties and the U.S. financial system. The designation required a two-thirds vote by the Financial Stability Oversight Council, including an affirmative vote by the chairman.

● **Standards.** In general, the Federal Reserve was authorized to set risk management standards for systemically important financial utilities and the payment, clearing and settlement activities of financial institutions. The CFTC and the SEC also could set standards for the institutions they regulated, but if the council and the Fed determined that the requirements were insufficient, they could impose the standards they determined were needed.

The standards had to address: risk management policies and procedures; margin and collateral requirements; participant or counterparty default policies and procedures; the ability of the institution to complete timely clearing and settlement of financial transactions; and capital and financial resource requirements for designated financial market utilities.

FDIC CHANGES

● **Assessment base.** The law directed the FDIC to change the way it calculated the assessment base used to determine the size of an institution's deposit insurance premiums. The new base was equal to the institution's total assets minus the sum of its tangible equity and long-term unsecured debt. The change would be made unless the FDIC could show that the new calculation would reduce the effectiveness of the risk-based assessment system or increase the risk of loss to the Deposit Insurance Fund.

● **Reserve ratio.** The FDIC was required to take the steps needed to ensure that the reserve ratio of depository institutions reached 1.35 percent of insured deposits, or the comparable percentage of the assessment base, by Sept. 30, 2020. In setting the assessments, the FDIC was directed to offset the effects on insured depository institutions that had total consolidated assets of less than $10 billion.

● **Deposit insurance increase.** The law made permanent an increase in the maximum amount covered by deposit insurance to $250,000 per account. The previous maximum of $100,000 had been temporarily increased to $250,000 through Dec. 31, 2013. The new increase was retroactive to Jan. 1, 2008.

● **Emergency financial stabilization.** The FDIC was authorized to guarantee the debt of solvent insured depository institutions and their holding companies during times of severe economic distress and under specific conditions. The Fed and the FDIC first had to agree, by a two-thirds vote in each agency, that there was a "liquidity event" — a threat to the liquidity of the financial markets. They also had to find that failure to take action would have serious adverse effects on financial stability and that the guarantees were necessary to avoid or mitigate those effects.

The terms and conditions of the short-term FDIC guarantee had to be approved by the Treasury secretary, who, in consultation with the president, would determine the maximum amount of guarantees. Fees for the guarantees had to be set to cover all expected costs. Any losses that occurred would be recouped from the companies that received the guarantees. The program also had to be approved by Congress.

The law prohibited the FDIC from using this systemic-risk authority to establish a widely available debt guarantee program and required the FDIC to become receiver of any insured depository institution that defaulted on its debt guarantee.

The GAO was directed to audit any FDIC debt guarantee program that resulted from a liquidity event.

● **Inclusion of minorities and women.** An Office of Minority and Women Inclusion was to be established in each of several federal agencies, including the Treasury Department, the FDIC, the Fed, the OCC and others. The office would be responsible for ensuring that minorities and women were adequately represented in the various agencies and that the needs and views of minority communities and women were adequately addressed by the agencies.

CONSUMER FINANCIAL PROTECTION BUREAU

● **Bureau established.** The law created a Bureau of Consumer Financial Protection (CFPB) with the authority to ensure that existing consumer protection laws were comprehensive, fair and vigorously enforced. The bureau was established as an independent body within the Federal Reserve, headed by a director appointed by the president and confirmed by the Senate to a five-year term.

● **Covered financial products.** The consumer bureau was charged with overseeing a broad range of retail financial products, including checking accounts, private student loans, credit cards and mortgages.

● **Responsibilities.** The CFPB was responsible for implementing and enforcing federal laws to ensure that markets for consumer financial products and services were fair, transparent and competitive, and that consumers were protected from unfair, deceptive and abusive acts and practices, and from discrimination. Previous law prohibited unfair or deceptive acts or practices, but the addition of abusive acts was designed to ensure that the bureau was empowered to cover instances when providers took unreasonable advantage of consumers.

The consumer bureau was given the authority and accountability to issue rules applicable to all financial institutions, including depository institutions that offered financial products and services to consumers.

It also had examination and enforcement authority over compliance with consumer protection laws by very large banks and non-bank financial institutions, as well as by all insured depository institutions and credit unions with more than $10 billion in assets. The banking regulators retained this authority for insured depository institutions and credit unions with assets of $10 billion or less.

● **Risk factors.** In monitoring for risks, the consumer bureau was directed to consider a variety of factors, including the extent to which the risks that a consumer financial product or service might disproportionately affect traditionally underserved consumers.

● **Independence and funding.** The law made clear that the bureau was meant to operate without interference from the Fed, including in writing rules, issuing orders, appointing or removing employees, and carrying out examinations and enforcement actions.

Funding for the CFPB was independent of the congressional appropriations process, with the goal of increasing the bureau's independence. The Fed was directed to transfer the amount determined by the bureau's director as reasonably necessary for the bureau's annual budget but not to exceed a specified percentage of the Fed's total operating expenses as reported in its 2009 annual report. Funding was capped at 10 percent of the Fed's operating expenses for fiscal 2010, 11 percent for fiscal 2011 and 12 percent for fiscal 2013 and each year thereafter, adjusted for inflation.

● **State laws.** Generally, the bureau's regulations could not pre-empt state laws that provided greater protection for consumers. However, state law could be pre-empted in limited circumstances for national banks, federal savings associations and non-depository institutions. State attorneys general had the power to enforce CFPB regulations,

but they, along with state regulators, had to consult with or notify the bureau and federal financial regulators before initiating such actions. The law generally did not permit a state attorney general to bring a civil action in the name of the state against a national bank or federal savings institution unless it was to enforce a regulation prescribed by the CFPB under a provision of this law or in other limited circumstances.

● **Individuals.** Certain individuals employed at non-depository institutions were also subject to supervision by the consumer bureau, including those that originated or serviced mortgage loans or other consumer financial products. Personal tax advisers, lawyers, insurance professionals under state supervision and others could be exempt under specified circumstances. Others outside the bureau's purview included auto dealers, accountants and real estate brokers.

● **CFPB limitations.** The Financial Stability Oversight Council could set aside a final regulation promulgated by the bureau if, in the view of two-thirds of the council, the regulation would put the safety and soundness of the banking system or the stability of the U.S. financial system at risk.

Also, the law exempted non-financial companies from the CFPB's oversight. For example, dentists, doctors, small retailers and others that simply allowed their customers to pay bills over time were excluded from the bureau's authority.

DERIVATIVES REGULATIONS

The law brought the over-the-counter financial derivatives market under significant government regulation for the first time. Derivatives contracts based on the underlying value of an asset, such as stocks, interest rates, currencies or commodities, were often used by companies to hedge risk. But they could also be used for speculation, which generally involved betting on the price movements of an underlying asset, often without owning that asset and without trying to hedge risk.

One type of derivative, swaps, involved two counterparties that exchanged the benefits of one's security for the benefits of the other's.

REGULATORY AUTHORITY

● **Framework.** The law established a framework for regulating a broad range of participants and products in the over-the-counter derivatives market, requiring that many routine derivatives be routed through clearinghouses and then traded on exchanges. Custom swaps could still be traded over the counter, but they had to be reported to central repositories.

The CFTC and the SEC were authorized to write and enforce rules for the swaps and security-based swaps markets, respectively, and to achieve as much consistency as possible. Swaps are generally based on commodity-oriented assets, while security-based swaps are based on a variety of assets including company securities, interest rates and currencies.

Banking regulators retained exclusive authority to enforce provisions for capital and margin for banks and branches or agencies of foreign banks.

● **'Spin-off' of swap activities.** The law imposed new capital, margin, reporting, record-keeping and business conduct rules for companies that dealt in derivatives, requiring banks to "spin off" their riskiest derivatives trading operations into affiliates.

Banks were allowed to retain operations for interest rate swaps, foreign exchange swaps, and gold and silver swaps, among others, but they were required to move trading in agriculture, uncleared com-

modities, most metals and energy swaps to affiliates.

Depository institutions could be forced to move derivatives trading desks into non-bank affiliates or divest from these activities.

● **Prohibition on federal assistance.** The law prohibited the federal government from providing financial assistance to any swap-based institution. However, there were several exceptions, including for an insured depository institution that had a swap entity affiliate, as long as the depository institution was part of a bank holding company or savings and loan holding company supervised by the Fed. An insured depository institution was also exempt if it limited its swap activities to hedging and similar risk reduction directly related to its depository operations.

MARKET REGULATION

● **Clearinghouses.** All over-the-counter derivatives transactions between dealers and large-market participants had to go through a registered clearinghouse, provided that a clearinghouse accepted the derivative for clearing. The role of the clearinghouse was to examine the particulars of a derivatives contract and, if it accepted the contract for clearing, to guarantee that both sides of the deal would abide by the terms. Clearinghouses were required to submit each swap product or category of swap products to the CFTC or SEC, which would determine whether the transaction needed to be cleared, based on criteria in this law.

● **Exchanges.** A swap that was cleared had to be traded through an exchange, a registered swap execution facility or a foreign swap execution facility. This provision applied to transactions that had been accepted for trading on an exchange and that involved either dealers (companies that buy and sell derivatives for their own accounts) or major market participants (non-dealers who maintain substantial net positions outside of hedging purposes). It did not apply to transactions that were completed before enactment.

Clearing and being traded on an exchange would make many of the details of a derivatives contract, such as pricing, widely available.

● **Exceptions.** The clearing requirements did not apply to a swap product if one of the counterparties was not a financial entity, was using swap products to hedge or mitigate commercial risk, and notified the SEC or CFTC how it generally met the financial obligations associated with entering into non-cleared swap transactions.

An affiliate of a company that qualified for an exception could also qualify for the exception, but only if it used the swap products to hedge commercial risk. The exception did not apply if the affiliate was a swap dealer.

● **Foreign exchange swap products.** The law established regulations for the foreign exchange swap product market, which was valued at roughly $60 trillion and was the second-largest component of the swap market. The Treasury secretary could allow exemptions under certain conditions.

● **Derivatives-clearing organizations.** A derivatives-clearing organization could be exempt from registering to clear swap products if the organization was subject to comparable, comprehensive supervision and regulation by the CFTC or SEC, or by the appropriate government authorities in the home country in the case of a foreign derivative.

● **Uncleared swaps.** Swap products that were not accepted for clearing by any derivatives clearing organization had to be reported to a swap product data repository or, if no repository would accept the swap product, to the CFTC or SEC.

Individuals or businesses engaged in a swap transaction that was not accepted for clearing were required to provide the CFTC or SEC with reports on the swap products they held. They were required to maintain proper books and records and were subject to review by the respective regulator.

Regulators had the authority to impose margin requirements on dealers and major participants for uncleared swaps to ensure that they had adequate financial resources to meet obligations.

In setting margin requirements, regulators could permit the use of non-cash collateral as long as doing so was consistent with preserving the financial integrity of the swaps markets and with preserving the stability of the U.S. financial system.

● **Position limits**. The CFTC and the SEC were to establish limits on the amount of positions, other than true hedge positions, that an individual or business could hold with respect to swap products.

A list of exempt commodities had to be established within 180 days of the date of enactment, and a list of exempt agricultural commodities had to be established within 270 days of enactment.

The SEC and CFTC were also charged, to the maximum extent practicable, with seeking to diminish, eliminate or prevent excessive speculation; deter and prevent market manipulation, squeezes and corners; ensure sufficient market liquidity for hedgers; and ensure that the price discovery function of the underlying market was not disrupted.

REGULATORY IMPROVEMENTS
EXECUTIVE COMPENSATION

● **Shareholder rights.** The law required that shareholders in a public company have a chance at least once every three years to cast a nonbinding advisory vote on executive compensation — a provision known as "say on pay." Brokers who were not beneficial owners of a security were prohibited from voting through company proxies unless the beneficial owner had instructed the broker to vote on his behalf.

The law also provided for shareholder votes on any generous severance package, or "golden parachute," for an outgoing executive in the event of a merger or acquisition. The vote would not overrule a decision by the board of directors, create or imply any change to the board's fiduciary duties, or restrict the ability of shareholders to make proposals for inclusion in proxy materials related to executive compensation.

Federal financial regulators were required to monitor incentive-based payment arrangements larger than $1 billion by financial institutions and prohibit such arrangements if the regulators determined jointly that they could threaten the financial institutions' safety and soundness or could have serious adverse effects on economic conditions or financial stability.

● **Exemptions.** The national securities exchanges or national securities associations could exempt a category of issuers from these requirements, including small issuers that would bear a disproportionate burden under the provision.

● **Conflicts of interest.** The law required a series of steps to prevent potential conflicts of interest by a company's board members. It also expanded disclosure requirements and provided for the potential recovery of compensation in specified circumstances.

Board committees that set compensation policy had to consist only of directors who were independent. Any compensation consultants that were hired also had to be independent.

● **Disclosure.** Companies were required to tell shareholders about the relationship between executive compensation and the company's financial performance, and to have a policy to recover money erroneously paid to executives based on finances that later had to be restated due to an accounting error. They also had to disclose in the annual proxy statement whether employees or members of the board could hedge or offset any decrease in the market value of the equity securities granted.

HEDGE FUND REGISTRATION

● **SEC registration exemptions.** The law eliminated existing exemptions from SEC registration requirements for hedge fund managers and private equity firms — lightly regulated pools of capital with a limited number of investors that often used aggressive trading or investment strategies. The intent was to eliminate a perceived regulatory gap and strengthen record-keeping, examination and disclosure requirements for hedge funds and private equity firms. The law also increased the SEC's ability to take and enforce actions against these firms if necessary. This eliminated the "private adviser" exemption in the Investment Advisers Act of 1940 (PL 76-468).

Under previous law, advisers with fewer than 15 clients were exempt from having to register, and a hedge fund counted as a single client even if it had multiple investors. The new law eliminated this exemption.

Previous law also exempted advisers that had less than $30 million in assets under management. The new law increased that threshold to $100 million. Advisers with less than that amount were the responsibility of the state, allowing the SEC to focus its examination efforts on private funds and improve its performance in catching fraud.

The new law also exempted foreign private advisers, added a limited intrastate exemption and exempted small-business investment companies licensed by the Small Business Administration.

Venture capital firms were exempted from the SEC registration requirement, but they had to maintain records and provide the SEC with reports that were necessary to protect the public interest. Investment advisers of private funds with less than $150 million in assets under management were also exempted.

● **Safeguarding client assets.** Hedge fund advisers were required to submit reports to the SEC describing the assets they had under management, the amount of leverage used, counterparty risk exposure, trading and investment positions, valuation policies, types of assets held, and other information the SEC deemed to be important.

To reduce the possibility of future Ponzi schemes, advisers were required to ensure the safeguarding of client assets over which the adviser had custody. As part of this requirement, the adviser was required to seek verification of assets under custody by an independent public accountant.

INSURANCE
FEDERAL INSURANCE OFFICE

● **Office established.** The law created a Federal Insurance Office within the Treasury Department, with a director who was appointed by the Treasury secretary and also served as an adviser on the new Financial Stability Oversight Council.

● **Power and responsibilities.** The new office was not a federal regulator or supervisor. Its tasks were to monitor all aspects of the insurance industry, make recommendations to the council that certain insurers be designated as non-bank financial institutions subject to Federal Reserve supervision, assist department administration of the Terrorism Risk In-

surance Program, coordinate federal efforts and establish federal policy on prudential aspects of international insurance matters, and consult with states on insurance issues of national importance.

● **Exemptions.** The office was tasked with handling all lines of insurance except crop, health and long-term-care insurance.

● **Pre-emption of state law**. The law placed restrictions on pre-empting state insurance laws. The new Federal Insurance Office was authorized to identify and narrowly pre-empt state insurance laws that were inconsistent with international insurance agreements. However, national insurance regulators could not issue regulations for insurance rates, premium limits, sales and underwriting practices, state antitrust laws, or capital or solvency requirements.

Insurance regulators in an insurer's home state had sole regulatory authority over non-admitted insurance, including the collection and allocation of premium tax obligations. Non-admitted insurance provided coverage for unusual risks and was typically unavailable in the traditional insurance marketplace. The majority of these policies were purchased by sophisticated commercial entities to cover commercial risk, although some individuals also purchased such coverage.

● **Reinsurance market.** The law regulated the reinsurance market, where insurance companies bought insurance to reduce their own risk. If the insurer's home state was accredited by the National Association of Insurance Commissioners or had solvency requirements substantially similar to the association's guidelines, the home state had sole responsibility for regulating the financial solvency of the reinsurer.

ACCESS TO MAINSTREAM FINANCIAL INSTITUTIONS

● **'Underbanked' consumers.** The law included initiatives to encourage the provision of financial products and services that were appropriate and accessible for many individuals who were not fully incorporated into the financial mainstream, including so-called "underbanked" consumers, who relied on non-traditional forms of credit and often were unable to save securely for future needs such as buying a home or paying education expenses.

The law also created a pool of capital to enable community development financial institutions to establish and maintain small-dollar loan programs, creating an alternative to payday or car title loans in local communities.

● **Eligibility and funding.** The Treasury Department was authorized to establish a multi-year program of grants, cooperative agreements, financial agency agreements and similar contracts to promote initiatives to expand access for low- and moderate-income individuals to mainstream financial institutions.

Agencies receiving the Treasury Department grants were required to provide non-federal matching funds equal to 50 percent of the grant.

OFFSETS

● **TARP repayment.** The $700 billion authorized for the TARP was reduced to $475 billion under the law, and no unspent TARP funds could be redirected to new spending. Repayment of TARP funds had to be returned to the Treasury and used to help reduce the deficit. The Treasury could not initiate any new programs under TARP after June 25, 2010. The effect was to end the TARP operation 10 weeks ahead of the scheduled date of Oct. 3, 2010.

The TARP was created in 2008 to stabilize the financial services industry, which was in a tailspin after the collapse of the subprime mortgage market. *(TARP, 2008 Almanac, p. 7-3)*

● **Unused stimulus money.** The law required that funds provided under the 2009 economic stimulus law (PL 111-5) be returned to the Treasury by Dec. 31, 2012, and used to help reduce the federal deficit. The president could waive these requirements if he determined that it was not in the best interest of the nation to rescind a specific unobligated amount. *(Stimulus, 2008 Almanac, 7-17)*

DEBIT CARD FEES

● **Fee limitation.** The law instructed the Federal Reserve to set limits on the amount banks and payment networks could charge merchants for using debit cards and the debit card transaction network. Debit cards were understood to include any card approved for use through a payment card network to debit an account, as well as general-use prepaid cards, but not paper checks. Regulations for the amount of any interchange transaction fee that an issuer could receive or charge for an electronic debit transaction had to be reasonable and proportional to the cost incurred by the issuer with respect to the transaction.

● **Exemptions.** Issuers with less than $10 billion in assets were exempt from the debit card provision. The law also exempted debit cards or general-use prepaid cards provided under a federal, state or local government-administered payment program if the card could be used only to transfer debit funds, monetary value or other assets that had been provided under the government program.

CREDIT-RATING AGENCIES

Credit-rating agencies evaluated the relative risk of default of various securities and debt instruments. Their critical gatekeeper role in the debt market was functionally similar to that of securities analysts, who evaluated the quality of securities in the equity market, and auditors, who reviewed the financial statements of companies.

● **SEC regulation.** The law broadened the SEC's powers to regulate credit-rating agencies, also known as Nationally Recognized Statistical Rating Organizations. A new Office of Credit Ratings was established in the SEC to examine credit-rating agencies at least once a year and make key findings public.

The SEC was authorized to issue new rules requiring the agencies to set up internal controls over the ratings process, establish an independent board of directors, make greater disclosures to the public and investors, and develop universal ratings across asset classes and types of issuers. The SEC was also authorized to de-register a credit-rating agency that provided inaccurate ratings consistently over time.

● **Rating models.** Each credit-rating agency was required to disclose: information about the assumptions underlying its procedures and methodologies; the data it relied on to determine the credit rating; if applicable, how the agency used servicer or remittance reports to conduct surveillance of the credit rating; and information that could be used by investors and other users of credit ratings to better understand ratings in each class issued by the agency.

● **Conflicts of interest.** To address conflicts of interest inherent in the ratings business, the law required rating agencies to prohibit compliance officers from working on ratings, methodologies or sales and to prevent other employees from selling ratings services and rating the securities. A credit agency had to conduct a one-year look-back review when an employee went to work for a company that offered or underwrote a security or money-market instrument subject to a rating by the agency. The look back was to determine whether the employee was giving the company a better rating than it deserved in exchange for future employment. The rating agency also had to report

the employee's new job to the SEC.

● **Reliance on ratings.** To reduce the reliance on ratings, the law required that references to credit ratings be removed from certain regulations, policies and procedures used by federal agencies and that the agencies use a new standard to judge creditworthiness.

● **Investor lawsuits.** The law provided investors with a private right of action to bring suit against a credit-rating agency for a knowing or reckless failure to conduct a reasonable investigation of the facts or to obtain analysis from an independent source.

● **Structured product ratings.** The SEC was directed to establish a system that prohibited issuers of structured financial products from selecting the rating agency that provided the initial credit rating. This practice was common in the rating of various mortgage-related, asset-backed securities and collateralized debt obligations that played a central role in the 2008 crisis. Many of those structured products turned out to have a much poorer credit quality than that designated by a rating agency.

MORTGAGE RULES, PREDATORY LENDING

● **Minimum standards.** The law established minimum national standards for mortgage brokers and institutions, including banks that provided home mortgages. The standards were to be issued as regulations by the consumer protection bureau.

● **Ability to pay.** The standards had to include requirements that a lender or originator of a home loan ensure that a borrower had a reasonable ability to repay the loan at the time the loan was made. The determination had to be based on verified and documented information, including the borrower's credit history, income and other factors.

● **Safe harbor.** Certain low-risk loans, or "qualified mortgages," were exempt from the law's loan standards. A qualified mortgage was a mortgage with a term of 30 years or less, and the lender could not allow the delay of the payment of principal or an increase in the principal balance, among other requirements.

● **Pre-payment penalties.** The law prohibited pre-payment penalties — fees assessed on borrowers for repaying the principal ahead of schedule — for any mortgage that did not meet the standards for a qualified mortgage. When a loan was first made, originators had to offer a version of the loan that did not include a pre-payment penalty.

For mortgages that met the law's underwriting standards, the law limited pre-payment penalties to 3 percent of the outstanding balance in the first year of the loan, 2 percent in the second year and 1 percent in the third year. After the three-year period, no pre-payment penalties could be assessed.

● **Anti-steering.** Lenders were barred from providing any financial incentives, including payments known as "yield spread premiums," to mortgage brokers for steering consumers to loans with higher interest rates. Mortgage originators could not receive payments that varied based on the terms of the loan, other than the amount of the principal.

● **Lender liability.** Mortgage originators that violated their obligations under the act could be sued, with maximum liability per violation of up to three times the total amount of lender fees, plus the consumer's costs including reasonable attorney fees.

● **High-cost home loans.** The Home Ownership and Equity Protection Act of 1994 (PL 103-325) addressed certain deceptive and unfair practices in home equity lending by establishing requirements for certain loans with high interest rates and/or high fees. The law affected refinancing and home equity installment loans that also met the defini-

tion of a high-rate or high-fee loan. The law did not cover loans to buy or build homes, reverse mortgages, or home equity lines of credit.

The new law revised the benchmarks for determining loans subject to the heightened standards under the Home Ownership and Equity Protection Act.

It defined "high-cost home loans" as a primary residence mortgage with an annual interest rate higher than 6.5 percent, or 8.5 percent if the dwelling was personal property and the loan was smaller than $50,000. For a second mortgage or other subordinate loan on the property, a mortgage with an annual percentage rate higher than 8.5 percent qualified as a high-cost mortgage.

● **Balloon payments.** The law barred balloon payments for high-cost mortgages, which included scheduled mortgage payments that were more than twice as large as the average of earlier scheduled payments. It prohibited defaulting on an existing loan that was being refinanced by a high-cost loan. It limited late fees to no more than 4 percent of the amount of payment past due, along with other restrictions. No high-cost loan could accelerate the indebtedness of a loan. No lender could directly or indirectly finance, in connection with any high-cost mortgage, any prepayment fee or penalty payable by the borrower if the lender held the note for the underlying loan.

The provision did not apply if the payment schedule was adjusted to the seasonal or irregular income of the consumer.

● **Housing counseling office.** An Office of Housing Counseling was established in the Department of Housing and Urban Development (HUD) to carry out and coordinate homeownership and rental housing counseling programs. A national public service campaign was established to promote housing counseling with a website and toll-free hotline. The law also authorized funds for counseling grants to HUD-approved groups or agencies.

● **Appraisals.** Lenders could not conclude a high-risk mortgage loan without first getting a written appraisal of the property. Parties to a real estate transaction were prohibited from influencing the independent judgment of an appraiser through collusion, coercion or bribery, among other activities.

● **Appropriations.** The law appropriated funds to make available $1 billion in assistance through an Emergency Homeowners Relief Fund, established by HUD to provide emergency loans to help jobless homeowners make mortgage payments while they were out of work.

The law also provided $1 billion for a third round of funding for the Neighborhood Stabilization Program, through which HUD assisted state and local government efforts to finance the purchase and redevelopment of foreclosed homes and residential properties. In addition, it authorized a HUD-administered grant program to help agencies that provided legal assistance related to homeownership to low- and moderate-income people.

INVESTOR PROTECTION
NEW OVERSIGHT AND RESPONSIBILITIES

● **SEC authority.** The law set new standards for investment advisers and broker-dealers, increased authorized funding for the SEC over the following five years and expanded the commission's authority to set more stringent rules to protect investors. It gave the SEC additional authority to conduct investigations, assess penalties and violations, and impose enforcement actions.

A new Office of Investor Advocate and an ombudsman at the SEC would assist investors in their dealings with the commission. The law also authorized the SEC to impose a fiduciary duty on broker-dealers

and investment advisers to protect retail customers.

● **Whistleblowers.** An investor protection fund was to be established in the Treasury to pay awards to whistleblowers and fund the activities of the SEC inspector general. The law provided incentives and protections for whistleblowers who provided information relating to a violation of the securities laws that led to successful SEC enforcement actions.

● **SIPC.** The law updated statutes related to the Securities Investor Protection Corporation (SIPC) by increasing the minimum assessments on members, raising penalties for fraud and establishing civil and criminal penalties against any person who misrepresented membership in the SIPC. It also increased the limit on the SIPC's borrowing from the Treasury Department from $1 billion to $2.5 billion.

● **Short selling.** The SEC received new authority to increase public reporting of aggregate information on short selling, prohibit manipulative short sales and require that customers be notified that they could choose not to allow their securities to be used in connection with short sales.

● **SEC management.** The law required the completion of several reports assessing the management of the SEC and making recommendations for improvements in areas such as internal supervisory controls, personnel management, financial controls and oversight of national securities associations.

SECURITIZATION

● **Securitization defined.** Securitization involves the process of turning a non-marketable asset into a marketable asset. Different loan-oriented assets — usually corporate loans, mortgages and corporate bonds — are packaged together and then cut up into groups, or "tranches." Bonds are issued from those tranches and are secured by the cash flows generated from the underlying assets. The riskiest tranches pay the highest interest on bonds, which also carry a greater risk of default.

The process was heavily used in the packaging of subprime mortgage loans and had also been used for a variety of purposes on Wall Street and in the corporate world.

● **Securitized assets.** The law required securitizers to retain an economic interest in a material portion of the credit risk for any asset that the securitizer sold or transferred to a third party. In general, firms using securitization were required to retain at least 5 percent of the credit risk. Regulators had discretion to set lower minimums for securitized assets with lower risks. The expectation was that the requirement would force securitizers to focus more on the quality of the underlying assets, thereby reducing excessive risk-taking.

● **Exemptions.** The law provided exemptions for the Farm Credit System and any residential, multifamily or health care facility mortgage loan asset or securitization that was insured or guaranteed by the federal government. Regulators were required to provide total or partial exemptions for municipal securities and for securitizations of assets issued or guaranteed by a federal agency, as long as the exemption was in the public interest and for the protection of investors.

OTHER PROVISIONS

● **Corporate governance.** The law aimed to improve proxy access for shareholders so they had a broader range of candidates to nominate to a company's board of directors. The SEC was directed to consider the burden on small issuers and allowed to issue exemptions from proxy access rules.

● **Municipal securities.** Municipal financial advisers were required to register and be subject to the rules of the Municipal Securities Rulemaking Board. The law reconstituted the board, requiring that a majority of the members be independent of the municipal securities industry. Municipal advisers had a fiduciary duty to municipal entities. The law also created an Office of Municipal Securities within the SEC.

● **Public accounting oversight.** The Public Company Accounting Oversight Board was allowed to examine the auditors of broker-dealers and share information with foreign authorities.

The law authorized portfolio margining — collateral that customers had to post for their holdings — for accounts that held both securities and futures. It also raised the dollar threshold that triggered a full "material loss review" of the Deposit Insurance Fund by federal banking regulators.

Small issuers — those with less than $75 million in market capitalization — were exempt from provisions of the 2002 Sarbanes-Oxley law (PL 107-204) that required external audits of internal controls.

● **SEC match funding.** SEC transaction fee receipts were to be treated as offsetting collections equal to the amount of the annual SEC appropriation. Any excess collections would go to the Treasury Department as general revenue and could not be used to offset any appropriations. The rates had to be reviewed midyear, and if it was determined that they could produce 10 percent more or less in receipts than expected, they would be adjusted.

The law set registration fee targets that were expected to produce $5 billion in revenue over 10 years for the Treasury's general fund.

● **Funds to foreign governments.** The law amended the Bretton Wood Agreement Act (PL 79-171) to require the Treasury secretary to instruct the U.S. executive director of the International Monetary Fund (IMF) to review any IMF proposals that would issue a loan to a country whose public debt was higher than its recent annual gross domestic product or to a country that was not eligible for assistance from the International Development Association. If the review indicated that the loan was not likely to be paid in full, the director would be directed to oppose it.

● **Conflict minerals from the Congo.** All companies that were required to report to the SEC were required to disclose to the agency if minerals extracted during the course of their business operations originated in the Democratic Republic of Congo or adjoining countries. The disclosure report had to describe the measures taken to exercise due diligence on the source and chain of custody of the minerals. The U.S. government was required to develop a strategy to address the illicit minerals trade in the region and a map to address linkages between conflict minerals and armed groups.

● **Mine safety.** The law required mining companies to disclose mine safety violations that were material to investors.

● **Payments for resource extraction.** The law required public disclosure to the SEC of any payment related to the commercial development of oil, natural gas and minerals made to the United States or to a foreign government. ■

Chapter 4

Budget

President Obama's Budget Seeks Freeze on Discretionary Spending

PRESIDENT OBAMA RELEASED a $3.834 trillion fiscal 2011 budget on Feb. 1 that proposed to put the brakes on domestic discretionary spending, but the president left the daunting problem of the nation's rapidly growing debt to a bipartisan commission that he pledged to create. *(Debt commission, p. 4-11)*

Obama offered not to exceed $447 billion per year in each of the following three fiscal years for domestic discretionary programs and then allow the total to grow no faster than the rate of inflation for the next seven years. The White House estimated this would save $250 billion over 10 years. The plan was not an across-the-board cut but rather a flexible freeze — individual departments and agencies could receive more or less funding.

The budget reflected multiple and sometimes conflicting goals. Obama called for reducing the long-term deficit while pumping money into the economy in the short run to promote recovery. He proposed tax cuts for the middle class, as he had promised during his election campaign, while allowing previous tax cuts for the well-to-do to expire at the end of the year, resulting in a sharp increase for those taxpayers.

"When I look at this budget, I strongly agree with the president's budget in the short term," said Kent Conrad, D-N.D., chairman of the Senate Budget Committee. "It is absolutely imperative that we not allow the economy to slip back into recession." But, he said, "I have strong disagreement with the long term."

Republicans said they supported the idea of a freeze in discretionary spending but were quick to point out that the budget would not contain the growth in mandatory spending and said that the discretionary savings would be "puny" in comparison with the deficits being racked up.

On jobs, both sides attacked the president's plan to devote $100 billion to employment-bolstering initiatives. Liberal Democrats said it was not enough, especially considering the country's infrastructure needs, which were potentially a major source of employment. Republicans warned about the public's aversion to more spending. Republicans also argued that a proposal to allow higher taxes on the wealthy would put a damper on job growth and said that Democrats would try another version of the 2009 economic

stimulus bill (PL 111-5) under a different name.

DETAILS OF OBAMA'S BUDGET

Many agencies and programs stood to have their budgets frozen or cut under the budget, but some would still receive increases. In particular, the administration put an emphasis on increased education funding.

● **Discretionary funding.** The White House's Office of Management and Budget (OMB), which prepared the president's budget, put the total request for discretionary spending in fiscal 2011 at $1.415 trillion in outlays ($1.265 trillion in budget authority). The Congressional Budget Office (CBO) issued its annual recalculation of the budget in March based on slightly different economic and technical assumptions. CBO estimated the discretionary request at $1.401 trillion in outlays ($1.269 trillion in budget authority). Congress generally used CBO's estimates , and they are used in the following account as well.

▸ **Defense.** Of the total, $733.1 billion in budget authority was requested for defense, including Defense Department war-related activities and nuclear weapons programs at the Department of Energy. The total consisted of $573.8 billion for base defense funding and about $159 billion for operations in Iraq and Afghanistan. CBO said the total was an increase of $16 billion, or 2 percent above total fiscal 2010 funding.

▸ **Non-defense.** The request included $536.8 billion for non-defense discretionary programs, a drop of $19.4 billion, or 3.5 percent,

Fiscal 2011 Budget Totals Compared

The fiscal 2011 budget that President Obama sent to Congress on Feb. 1 assumed a three-year freeze in non-security discretionary appropriations, some changes in mandatory spending, and a tax increase concentrated on individuals who earned more than $200,000 a year and couples earning more than $250,000. The following is Obama's budget as estimated by the White House's Office of Management and Budget and by the Congressional Budget Office.

Fiscal years, in billions of dollars	ACTUAL 2009	ESTIMATED 2010	PROPOSED 2011	2012	2013	2014	2015	2020
Budget authority								
Obama	$4,077	$3,601	$3,691	$3,722	$3,943	$4,205	$4,447	$5,769
Outlays								
Obama	3,518	3,721	3,834	3,755	3,915	4,161	4,386	5,713
CBO	3,518	3,618	3,802	3,722	3,842	4,065	4,297	5,670
Revenue								
Obama	2,105	2,165	2,567	2,926	3,188	3,455	3,634	4,710
CBO	2,105	2,118	2,460	2,808	3,095	3,341	3,504	4,416
Deficit								
Obama	−1,413	−1,556	−1,267	−828	−727	−706	−752	−1,003
CBO	−1,413	−1,500	−1,342	−914	−747	−724	−793	−1,254
Debt held by the public *as a percentage of GDP*								
Obama	53.0%	63.6%	68.6%	70.8%	71.7%	72.2%	72.9%	77.2%
CBO	53.0%	63.2%	70.1%	73.6%	74.8%	75.7%	77.4%	90.0%

SOURCES: Office of Management and Budget, Congressional Budget Office

Economic Forecasts Compared

Calendar years	2010	2011	2012	2013	2014	2015
Real GDP growth						
Administration	2.7%	3.8%	4.3%	4.2%	4.0%	3.6%
Administration, July 2009	2.0	3.8	4.3	4.3	4.1	3.6
CBO, January	2.2	1.9	4.6	4.8	3.9	2.9
Blue Chip, January	2.8	3.1	—	—	—	—
Inflation (CPI)						
Administration	1.9	1.5	2.0	2.0	2.0	2.0
Administration, July 2009	1.4	1.5	1.9	2.0	2.0	2.0
CBO, January	2.4	1.3	1.2	1.1	1.3	1.7
Blue Chip, January	2.1	2.0	—	—	—	—
Unemployment						
Administration	10.0	9.2	8.2	7.3	6.5	5.9
Administration, July 2009	9.8	8.6	7.7	6.8	5.9	5.6
CBO, January	10.1	9.5	8.0	6.3	5.3	5.1
Blue Chip, January	10.0	9.2	—	—	—	—
Three-month Treasury bills						
Administration	0.4	1.6	3.0	4.0	4.1	4.1
Administration, July 2009	1.3	2.6	3.8	4.0	4.0	4.0
CBO, January	0.2	0.7	1.9	3.0	3.9	4.2
Blue Chip, January	0.4	1.8	—	—	—	—
10-year Treasury notes						
Administration	3.9	4.5	5.0	5.2	5.3	5.3
Administration, July 2009	4.5	4.9	5.2	5.2	5.2	5.2
CBO, January	3.6	3.9	4.2	4.5	4.9	5.2
Blue Chip, January	3.9	4.6	—	—	—	—

This table compares the economic forecast of the Obama administration released Feb. 1, 2010, with the most recent forecasts at the time from the Congressional Budget Office (CBO) and the Blue Chip consensus of private economists, as well as the administration's July 2009 forecast. It projects annual percentage changes in inflation-adjusted gross domestic product (GDP) and the Consumer Price Index (CPI), and annual averages for the unemployment rate and the interest rates on certain Treasury bills and notes. The administration forecast assumed enactment of the president's budget request and as a result was not strictly comparable with the other forecasts.

SOURCES: Office of Management and Budget, Congressional Budget Office, Blue Chip Economic Indicators

from total fiscal 2010 spending.

However, the overall figure included international affairs, which stood to receive a 2.5 percent increase to $58.8 billion under Obama's budget. Appropriations classified as "security-related" accounted for another $14 billion increase over previous funding.

A major factor in Obama's plan to reduce the domestic discretionary budget was a proposal, rejected by Congress in 2009, to shift $18 billion for the Pell grant program from discretionary to mandatory spending. Obama also proposed reducing the budget for the Census Bureau from $7.2 billion in fiscal 2010, when the bureau needed extra funds to complete the decennial census, to $1.3 billion in fiscal 2011.

Among the domestic accounts that stood to get increases above fiscal 2010 spending were those for health programs, slated for a $1.7 billion increase, and energy programs that would be up by $1.1 billion.

Obama proposed cuts for other agencies, including the departments of Agriculture and Housing and Urban Development.

▸ **Supplemental requests.** The budget included a total of $47 billion in supplemental spending requests for fiscal 2010. Most of it, $35 billion, was for military-related activities: $31 billion for military activities and $4 billion for diplomatic operations and foreign aid. Obama also requested $5 billion for disaster relief and almost $5 bil-

lion to settle claims against the government by black farmers and American Indians. (*Lawsuits, p. 10-7*)

● **Mandatory programs.** CBO calculated that the changes to mandatory programs proposed in Obama's budget would increase net mandatory outlays above existing law by $99 billion in fiscal 2011 and $1.853 trillion from 2011 through 2020. Total mandatory spending under the budget would be $2.156 trillion in fiscal 2011 and $25.808 trillion over a decade.

CBO said the biggest anticipated increase came from Obama's health insurance overhaul (PL 111-148, PL 111-152), which the administration at the time estimated would increase mandatory outlays by $6 billion in 2010 and $593 billion over 10 years. (*Health care overhaul, p. 9-3*)

The total was about $150 billion less than the added revenues assumed to result from the legislation.

Proposals to extend or expand various refundable tax credits amounted to a projected 10-year increase in outlays of $401 billion.

While shifting funds for Pell grants from discretionary to mandatory accounts cut discretionary spending under the budget, it boosted mandatory spending by $374 billion over 10 years.

● **Taxes.** The Joint Committee on Taxation (JCT), whose estimates were used by CBO, projected that tax changes proposed in the budget would reduce revenue by $213 billion in fiscal 2011 and $1.439 trillion over 10 years, compared to existing law. The following are some of Obama's major tax proposals with JCT's estimate of the revenue effects.

▸ **2001, 2003 tax cuts.** Obama proposed an extension for middle-class taxpayers of cuts enacted under President George W. Bush in 2001 and 2003 (PL 107-16, PL 108-27). Those lower taxes were due to expire at the end of 2010, and without new legislation, rates would rise to levels set in prior law. The extension was projected to reduce revenues by $95 billion in fiscal 2011 and $2.154 trillion over 10 years. (*2001 Almanac, p. 18-3; 2003 Almanac, p. 17-3*)

Obama wanted to permanently extend the tax rates on income, capital gains and dividends at 2010 levels for married taxpayers' income below $250,000 and single taxpayers' income of less than $200,000. But rates for income above those amounts would rise to the much higher rates set under previous law. Capital gains and dividends would be taxed at 20 percent instead of the 15 percent rate in effect in 2010.

The child tax credit, which was doubled to $1,000 in 2001, would also be extended under the budget.

The president also proposed to revive the estate tax retroactively at 2009 levels with a $3.5 million per-person exemption and a 45 percent top rate. The tax expired at the end of 2009.

▸ **Alternative minimum tax.** To prevent the AMT from reaching millions of additional taxpayers each year, Congress regularly passed a one-year expansion of exemptions under the tax. Obama proposed to make the 2009 exemptions permanent and index them to inflation, at an estimated cost of $66 billion in fiscal 2011 and $577 billion over 10 years.

▸ **Health care legislation.** CBO said the proposal projected to raise the most revenue was Obama's health insurance overhaul. The budget included a placeholder of $743 billion in related revenues over 10 years, although the administration did not provide details.

▸ **Itemized deduction limits.** A proposal to limit, to 28 percent, the rate at which itemized deductions could reduce an individual's tax liability would increase revenues by $7 billion in fiscal 2011 and $289 billion over 10 years.

▸ **Foreign income.** A series of proposed changes to the U.S. system of taxing the international income of multinational corporations was projected to raise revenues by $6 billion in fiscal 2011 and $127 billion over 10 years.

▸ **Bank fee.** A proposed "financial crisis responsibility fee" on the largest banks to recover costs of the financial bailout was projected to raise $8 billion in fiscal 2011 and $90 billion over 10 years.

● **Deficit.** CBO estimated that under Obama's budget, the fiscal 2011 deficit would decline to $1.342 trillion, or 9 percent of the gross domestic product (GDP), from $1.5 trillion, or 10 percent of GDP, in fiscal 2010. Still, the fiscal 2011 deficit would be $346 billion higher than it would with no changes in the law.

Over 10 years, deficits under Obama's polices would total $9.755 trillion, or 5.2 percent of GDP.

ECONOMIC ASSUMPTIONS

The broad economic outlook that provided the underpinning for the budget demonstrated that the administration was counting on an economic rebound, which was essential to its two main election year priorities: reducing the deficit and creating jobs.

The administration's near-term projection for the jobless rate — 9.2 percent in 2011, down from an estimated 10 percent in 2010 — was in line with the most recent estimate from the Blue Chip consensus of private forecasters released in January. Over the longer term, the White House expected unemployment to stay above 6 percent through 2014 before gradually decreasing to 5.2 percent in 2020.

However, White House economists predicted a stronger pace of economic growth in 2011 than either private forecasters or the CBO had, and the administration's inflation estimate was somewhat more favorable than that of the Blue Chip consensus.

The White House forecast that the economy would expand by an inflation-adjusted 3.8 percent in 2011 — faster than the 3.1 percent Blue Chip estimate and the 1.9 percent CBO forecast.

After 2011, the White House projected that the GDP would grow by 4.3 percent in 2012 and that growth would be 4 percent or greater through 2014 before gradually declining to 2.5 percent in 2019.

The average post-World War II expansion rate was roughly 3.3 percent; sustained growth higher than 4 percent had not occurred since the Internet boom of the late 1990s. Then, economic growth and government budget-balancing deals drove the federal budget from deficit into surplus.

The projected rise in growth was a major driver behind the

Fiscal 2010 Deficit Hits $1.3 Trillion

THE FEDERAL GOVERNMENT CHALKED up a $1.293 trillion deficit in fiscal 2010 — the period running from Oct. 1, 2009, to Sept. 30, 2010. The deficit was second only to the all-time record of $1.413 trillion set in fiscal 2009.

The Treasury Department and the Office of Management and Budget released a statement Oct. 15 saying the deficit was 9 percent less than in fiscal 2009, 12 percent less than projected in OMB's midsession review of the budget in July 2010 and 17 percent less than was forecast in President Obama's fiscal 2010 budget.

Viewed another way, the fiscal 2010 total was equal to 8.9 percent of GDP, down from 10 percent in fiscal 2009.

The agencies attributed the decline from OMB's July estimate in large part to lower-than-expected emergency spending on the Troubled Asset Relief Program and on housing finance giants Fannie Mae and Freddie Mac.

The statement said the lower deficit in fiscal 2010, compared with fiscal 2009, was the product of a 2.7 percent increase in net revenues — including higher corporate income tax receipts — and a 5.5 percent reduction in outlays, aside from the two emergency programs.

The statement said the deficit remained high as a result of "the severe economic recession, high unemployment and the financial crisis that were inherited by the current administration."

White House projection that under its budget the deficit would fall significantly.

The White House assumptions did not seem that far off to most economic research outfits, which noted a somewhat more cautious tone from administration economists. "The administration's economic assumptions are more optimistic than our own, but slightly less optimistic than its last budget," said a Feb. 1 analysis released by Goldman Sachs' research arm.

Despite the seeming optimism in the economic forecast, however, administration budget documents conveyed uncertainty about whether the recovery would be as vigorous as the recession was deep and about whether the financial crisis might really be over for good. In the "Analytical Perspectives" that accompanied the budget submission, OMB said its economic growth estimates were slightly lower than the historical average for a post-recession rebound, in part because of the inherent uncertainty of the economic and financial climate. Officials acknowledged that they had been overly optimistic the previous year when they predicted a decline in unemployment that did not materialize. ■

Highlights of the President's Budget Proposal

The following shows major proposals from President Obama's fiscal 2011 budget request by department and major agency. The totals by year are for discretionary programs. The column for regular fiscal 2009 funding includes supplemental appropriations but not the substantial funding provided under the 2009 economic stimulus law (PL 111-5). The stimulus funds are shown in a separate column.

Figures are in billions of dollars

DEPARTMENTS

AGRICULTURE

FY 2009	FY 2009 stimulus	FY 2010 estimate	FY 2011 request
$25.3	$6.9	$27.3	$25.8

- Lower cap on direct farm payments from $40,000 per person to $30,000 per person and reduce over three years adjusted gross income eligibility limits for some subsidies to $250,000 or less for non-agriculture-related income and $500,000 or less for agriculture-related income.
- Reduce funds for the Market Access Program by $166 million over five years. The program aided the promotion of U.S. farm exports.
- Save $8 billion over 10 years by restructuring the federally subsidized crop insurance program.

COMMERCE

FY 2009	FY 2009 stimulus	FY 2010 estimate	FY 2011 request
$9.5	$7.8	$13.8	$8.9

- Provide $1.3 billion for the Census Bureau. Most of the money for the 2010 census was provided in fiscal 2010, making the fiscal 2011 request a reduction of more than 80 percent.
- Provide $2 billion for weather satellites and other systems to monitor changes in climate and global sea levels.

DEFENSE

FY 2009	FY 2009 stimulus	FY 2010 estimate	FY 2011 request
$659.0	$7.4	$693.4	$708.0

- Provide $548.9 billion, a 3 percent increase, for the base Defense Department budget, which did not include overseas contingency funding for operations in Afghanistan and Iraq.
- Eliminate funding for additional Boeing C-17 transport planes and for the alternative engine for the F-35 Joint Strike Fighter.
- Raise basic pay by 1.4 percent.
- Provide $159.3 billion for operations in Iraq and Afghanistan and for Pakistan in fiscal 2011, as well as another $33 billion in fiscal 2010 supplemental funding to pay for Obama's troop buildup in Afghanistan.
- Include a $50 billion per year placeholder figure for future war operations.

EDUCATION

FY 2009	FY 2009 stimulus	FY 2010 estimate	FY 2011 request
$41.4	$81.1	$46.8	$49.7

- Provide $1.4 billion to expand Obama's "Race to the Top" program of competitive grants to states and schools. An additional $950 million would be used for competitive grants to improve teaching.
- Convert the Pell grant program from discretionary to mandatory funding. Set the maximum grant at $5,710, with automatic increases tied to inflation. (To allow comparison, annual amounts do not include Pell grants.)
- Make the federal government the sole originator of student loans, phasing out the role of private lenders and ending their subsidies, saving an estimated $87 billion.

ENERGY

FY 2009	FY 2009 stimulus	FY 2010 estimate	FY 2011 request
$33.9	$36.7	$26.4	$28.4

- Provide $11.2 billion, a jump of almost 14 percent, for activities to maintain a secure and effective stockpile of nuclear weapons.
- Increase funding for energy efficiency and renewable-energy programs by 5 percent, to $2.6 billion.
- Provide $824 million, a 5 percent increase, for nuclear power programs, with a commitment to add $36 billion, for a total of $54.5 billion in fiscal 2011, for loan guarantees for new nuclear power generation.

HEALTH AND HUMAN SERVICES

FY 2009	FY 2009 stimulus	FY 2010 estimate	FY 2011 request
$88.1	$22.4	$84.1	$83.5

- Create a new $2.5 billion emergency fund under the Temporary Assistance for Needy Families program of cash assistance to low-income families.
- Extend higher federal Medicaid funding for six months at a cost of about $25.4 billion to head off state cuts in Medicaid enrollment.
- Provide $6.6 billion, a $1.6 billion increase, for federal assistance for child care.
- Increase funding for the National Institutes of Health by $1 billion, to $32.3 billion, with $6 billion devoted to cancer research.
- Increase funding for Head Start, the early-education program for low-income children, by $1 billion, to $8.2 billion.

HOMELAND SECURITY

FY 2009	FY 2009 stimulus	FY 2010 estimate	FY 2011 request
$42.5	$2.8	$43.3	$43.8

- Provide $734 million to deploy up to 1,000 new full-body scanning machines at airport checkpoints and new explosive-detection equipment for baggage screening.
- Reduce Coast Guard personnel by 1,100 to help pay for upgrading the agency's aging fleet of vessels.

HOUSING AND URBAN DEVELOPMENT

FY 2009	FY 2009 stimulus	FY 2010 estimate	FY 2011 request
$40.1	$13.6	$43.6	$41.6

- Reorganize 13 separate programs to streamline HUD's rental assistance bureaucracy.
- Eliminate funds for HOPE VI, the main source of money for projects to bulldoze and reconstruct public housing.
- Provide $19.6 billion for the Housing Choice Voucher program of rental assistance to very low-income families.

DEPARTMENTS *continued*

INTERIOR

FY 2009	FY 2009 stimulus	FY 2010 estimate	FY 2011 request
$11.3	$3.0	$12.2	$12.0

- Double the inspection fees on oil facilities on the outer continental shelf and create a new fee for onshore oil and gas inspections, generating a combined $30 million.
- Hold most programs relatively flat to accommodate a $39 million decrease from fiscal 2010 for the department but provide increases for the Land and Water Conservation Fund and renewable-energy projects.

JUSTICE

FY 2009	FY 2009 stimulus	FY 2010 estimate	FY 2011 request
$26.2	$4.0	$27.6	$24.1

- Provide $237 million for a maximum-security prison in Illinois to house detainees being held at the U.S. facility at Guantánamo Bay, Cuba, and provide $73 million for costs of trying five alleged conspirators in the Sept. 11 attacks.
- Increase funding for the FBI by 6 percent, to $8.2 billion.

LABOR

FY 2009	FY 2009 stimulus	FY 2010 estimate	FY 2011 request
$12.9	$4.8	$14.3	$14.0

- Plan for a 35 percent reduction, from $126.8 billion to $82.4 billion, in mandatory spending for federal unemployment benefits, reflecting an expectation that the existing extended benefits would not be renewed.
- Require employers that did not offer retirement plans to enroll employees in Individual Retirement Accounts.
- Increase support for training programs that prepared workers for "green" jobs and services.

STATE & OTHER INTERNATIONAL AID

FY 2009	FY 2009 stimulus	FY 2010 estimate	FY 2011 request
$50.0	$0.6	$52.4	$55.8

- Increase foreign assistance, with a majority of the increase going to combat zones.
- Provide $4 billion in assistance for Afghanistan and $3.1 billion for Pakistan for governance, reconstruction and other development activities. Provide $2.6 billion to support ongoing activities in Iraq and prepare the State Department to assume responsibility for key programs previously carried out by the Defense Department.
- Provide $8.5 billion, up from $7.8 billion in fiscal 2010, for programs to improve global maternal and child health and to combat HIV/AIDS, tuberculosis and malaria.

TRANSPORTATION

FY 2009	FY 2009 stimulus	FY 2010 estimate	FY 2011 request
$19.8	$48.1	$21.8	$22.8

- Create a $4 billion infrastructure fund for large-scale transportation projects.
- Provide $1.1 billion for high-speed and intercity passenger rail, in addition to $8 billion in the stimulus law.
- Delay enacting a new surface transportation law into spring 2011.
- Provide $1.3 billion, more than a 30 percent increase, for the Federal Aviation Administration's NextGen air traffic control program, aimed at moving from ground-based radar surveillance to a satellite-based system.

TREASURY

FY 2009	FY 2009 stimulus	FY 2010 estimate	FY 2011 request
$12.6	$0.3	$13.6	$13.9

- Provide $5.9 billion, a 5 percent increase, for IRS enforcement, including hiring 2,000 more people.
- Increase funding for the Securities and Exchange Commission by 12 percent, to $1.3 billion, and for the Commodity Futures Trading Commission by 54 percent, to $261 million.

VETERANS AFFAIRS

FY 2009	FY 2009 stimulus	FY 2010 estimate	FY 2011 request
$47.8	$1.4	$53.1	$57.0

- Increase discretionary appropriations for the Department of Veterans Affairs from $53.1 billion to $57 billion, with much of the funding devoted to veterans' health care.
- Appropriate $53 billion in advance fiscal 2012 funding for veterans' health care, in line with a two-year budget cycle required for those programs under a law enacted in 2009 (PL 111-81).

MAJOR AGENCIES

CORPS OF ENGINEERS

FY 2009	FY 2009 stimulus	FY 2010 estimate	FY 2011 request
$11.9	$4.6	$5.4	$4.9

- Give priority in allocating construction money to dam-safety work, projects that reduced significant risks to human safety and projects that would complete construction during 2011.

EPA

FY 2009	FY 2009 stimulus	FY 2010 estimate	FY 2011 request
$7.7	$7.2	$10.3	$10.0

- Reduce spending for the agency by 3 percent, to $10 billion. However, the EPA received $7.2 billion in extra funds under the stimulus law, and it had not yet spent all of it.
- Allocate $1.3 billion, a 14 percent increase, for grants to states and tribes that implemented environmental programs.

NASA

FY 2009	FY 2009 stimulus	FY 2010 estimate	FY 2011 request
$17.8	$1.0	$18.7	$19.0

- End funding for the Constellation Program, initiated under President George W. Bush to send astronauts back to the moon and on to Mars.
- Provide $6 billion over five years to the commercial space industry to create a new vehicle to carry humans to and from the International Space Station.

NATIONAL SCIENCE FOUNDATION

FY 2009	FY 2009 stimulus	FY 2010 estimate	FY 2011 request
$6.5	$3.0	$6.9	$7.4

- Increase funding for the NSF by 8 percent, to $7.4 billion.
- Create a $766 million, cross-agency research initiative focused on renewable technologies and complex environmental and climate system processes.

Obama's Fiscal 2011 Budget by Department and Agency

Figures in millions of dollars

	BUDGET AUTHORITY			OUTLAYS		
	2009 actual	2010 estimate	2011 estimate	2009 actual	2010 estimate	2011 estimate
Legislative Branch	$4,977	$5,155	$5,633	$4,702	$5,423	$5,579
The Judiciary	6,787	7,170	7,664	6,645	7,159	7,512
Agriculture	127,826	135,520	148,606	114,440	142,016	145,748
Commerce	25,713	13,882	9,108	10,718	16,714	11,500
Defense — military	667,557	696,943	712,270	636,775	692,031	721,285
Education	131,891	61,972	82,278	53,389	106,944	94,261
Energy	68,557	24,561	26,817	23,683	38,278	44,390
Health and Human Services	851,732	881,416	915,475	796,267	868,762	934,426
Homeland Security	46,007	43,580	44,036	51,725	52,903	54,723
Housing and Urban Development	61,810	49,347	48,913	61,019	62,518	53,082
Interior	14,817	12,820	12,065	11,775	12,042	14,045
Justice	32,661	29,704	31,401	27,711	30,333	31,924
Labor	152,821	206,563	117,498	138,157	209,265	116,902
State	27,164	29,854	29,687	21,427	25,726	28,745
Transportation	112,344	78,428	79,176	73,004	90,944	86,665
Treasury	896,975	400,474	560,865	701,775	502,980	593,550
Veterans Affairs	96,929	124,872	121,653	95,457	124,565	124,215
Corps of Engineers	16,587	5,423	4,855	6,842	10,536	6,929
Other Defense — civil programs	57,482	54,517	55,892	57,276	54,317	55,719
EPA	14,754	10,203	9,875	8,070	11,301	11,177
Executive Office of the President	374	434	442	743	715	501
General Services Administration	6,290	554	635	319	1,782	2,279
International Assistance Programs	34,651	35,456	34,130	14,797	23,899	24,343
NASA	18,777	18,710	18,986	19,168	19,123	17,863
National Science Foundation	9,579	6,971	7,522	5,958	7,819	7,647
Office of Personnel Management	74,439	72,931	75,541	72,302	71,603	73,463
Small Business Administration	2,564	5,639	997	2,246	5,978	1,388
Social Security Administration						
On-budget	78,406	84,453	80,876	78,657	85,108	80,933
Off-budget	654,799	686,263	710,847	648,892	683,867	708,620
Other independent agencies						
On-budget	49,841	20,963	17,430	47,635	2,001	31,832
Off-budget	6,578	6,426	4,226	304	6,426	4,226
Allowances	-4	60,500	-1,574	-4	18,750	21,676
Undistributed offsetting receipts	-274,193	-271,127	-283,287	-274,193	-271,127	-283,287
On-budget	(-142,013)	(-137,793)	(-148,634)	(-142,013)	(-137,793)	(-148,634)
Off-budget	(-132,180)	(-133,334)	(-134,653)	(-132,180)	(-133,334)	(-134,653)
TOTALS	$4,077,492	$3,600,577	$3,690,538	$3,517,681	$3,720,701	$3,833,861

NOTES: Budget authority figures for fiscal 2009 and outlay figures for fiscal 2009 and fiscal 2010 include money provided by the 2009 economic stimulus law (PL 111-5). Figures may not add due to rounding.

SOURCE: Office of Management and Budget

Deficit, Election Derail Budget Process

CONGRESS' ANNUAL BUDGET process derailed early in the year in the face of widespread public concern about the deficit and lawmakers' focus on the upcoming November election. As a result, there was no bicameral fiscal 2011 budget resolution.

The Senate Budget Committee approved a five-year budget resolution in April (S Con Res 60) that would have set an upper limit of $1.122 trillion on discretionary spending for fiscal 2011, but the Senate never took it up. Deliberations in the House were complicated by the efforts of some members of the Democratic rank and file and the fiscally conservative Blue Dog Coalition to make what Budget Chairman John M. Spratt Jr., D-S.C., described as cuts to the president's budget that they "could take home and talk about."

Spratt did not bring a fiscal 2011 budget plan before his committee. Instead, House Democratic leaders indirectly won adoption of a scaled-back, one-year $1.121 trillion discretionary spending limit as part of the rule for debate on an unrelated spending bill.

The annual budget resolution outlines Congress' tax and spending policies. It also requires the majority party to show how its policies would affect the deficit over five years — a requirement that made many Democrats uneasy as they looked to the fall election.

Although a budget resolution does not become law, it sets a cap on discretionary spending for the annual appropriations bills that is enforced through House and Senate rules.

The lack of a budget resolution was part of a larger collapse of the budget and appropriations process that ended with none of the regular appropriations bills enacted and government spending largely continued at fiscal 2010 levels through March 4, 2011. *(Appropriations overview, p. 2-3)*

Congress was unable to reach final agreement on the budget in 1998, 2002, 2004 and 2006, but since the modern budget process took effect in 1976, the House always held a floor vote on its own version of the resolution. *(2006 Almanac, p. 3-8; 2004 Almanac, p. 4-9; 2002 Almanac, p. 6-8; 1998 Almanac, p. 6-3)*

Democrats had been highly critical on the three occasions when GOP-controlled Congresses failed to produce a final House-Senate budget. Republicans repaid the favor by lambasting Democrats for not putting forward a five-year fiscal 2011 outline, arguing it was evidence the majority did not have a plan to curtail the deficit.

House Democrats said their one-year approach would restrain spending for fiscal 2011, while a deficit commission established by President Obama developed recommendations for taming the deficit over time. The 18-member commission was due to present its proposals by Dec. 31. *(Debt commission, p. 4-11)*

"We're saying this package is a functional equivalent of a budget resolution," Spratt said.

Progressives, including House Appropriations Chairman David R. Obey, D-Wis., resisted the proposal, which cut from Obama's budget request, but the fiscal hawks prevailed. Obey focused instead on his top priority: providing funding to help states prevent teacher layoffs. *(Domestic supplemental, p. 2-18)*

BOX SCORE

BILLS: S Con Res 60, H Res 1493

LEGISLATIVE ACTION:

Senate Budget Committee approved S Con Res 60, 12-10, on April 22.

House adopted H Res 1493 on July 1 as part of the rule for floor debate on an unrelated fiscal 2010 war supplemental spending bill.

2010 LEGISLATIVE ACTION

SENATE COMMITTEE

The Senate Budget Committee approved a five-year fiscal 2011 budget resolution (S Con Res 60) on April 22 that would have provided up to $1.122 trillion in fiscal 2011 discretionary budget authority, compared with $1.265 trillion in Obama's request. The panel rejected Obama's proposal to reclassify a portion of Pell grant funding as mandatory spending.

The committee approved the measure 12-10, with Russ Feingold, D-Wis., joining all the Republicans in opposition.

Chairman Kent Conrad, D-N.D., said the plan would reduce the deficit from $1.499 trillion, or 9.8 percent of gross domestic product, in fiscal 2010 to $545 billion, or 3 percent of GDP, in fiscal 2015. The resolution called for freezing non-security discretionary spending for three years and assumed that taxes would be cut by $780 billion.

Republicans won a key battle in restricting the use of reconciliation instructions that would have made specific legislation exempt from Senate filibuster rules.

Reflecting the growing unease over the reconciliation process, most recently used to push "corrections" to the health care overhaul to enactment (PL 111-152), seven Democrats joined Republicans to require 60 votes in the Senate to overcome a point of order against reconciliation bills that proposed new spending that exceeded 20 percent of what the relevant authorizing committee was instructed to save. The amendment, by ranking Republican Judd Gregg of New Hampshire, was adopted, 16-6, with Conrad's support.

The committee also:

▶ Adopted, 14-9, an amendment by Lindsey Graham, R-S.C., to end the Treasury's authority to commit unused funds from the 2008 Troubled Asset Relief Program (PL 110-343). Graham said he did not want the funding diverted to other programs. Conrad opposed the amendment, arguing that the program's authority was set to expire in October, and Treasury Secretary Timothy F. Geithner had asked that it not be removed earlier. *(TARP, 2008 Almanac, p. 7-3)*

▶ Adopted, 15-8, a Feingold amendment to require that additional spending for the Iraq and Afghanistan wars be offset over 10 years. "We've paid for absolutely none of it," he said of previous war spending.

▶ Rejected, 10-13, a proposal by Jeff Sessions, R-Ala., to set discretionary spending caps for fiscal 2011 through 2015 and require 67 votes to waive them.

▶ Rejected, 10-13, a proposal by John Cornyn, R-Texas, to rescind $42 billion in unobligated funds from the 2009 economic stimulus law (PL 111-5). *(Stimulus law, 2009 Almanac, p. 7-3)*

▶ Adopted by voice vote, an amendment by Charles E. Grassley, R-Iowa, to assume a delay in tax increases under the health care overhaul (PL 111-148) until 2014, when major portions of that law were due to take effect. Conrad noted that the amendment would have no effect without offsets. *(Health care overhaul, p. 9-3)*

HOUSE FLOOR

House Democratic leaders won adoption of their one-year budget

plan (H Res 1493), which they called a "budget enforcement resolution," without requiring a direct vote. They inserted a provision that automatically adopted the resolution as part of the rule for floor debate on an unrelated fiscal 2010 war supplemental bill (HR 4899). The House adopted the rule (H Res 1500), 215-120, on July 1. *(House vote 428, p. H-150)*

The resolution, which affected only the House, included provisions to:

▸ Set an overall discretionary limit of $1.121 trillion in budget authority for the 12 House fiscal 2011 appropriations bills. The limit was well below the comparable request made by Obama and $1 billion below the amount in the Senate committee's budget resolution.

▸ Allow an additional appropriation of $538 million, which would count against fiscal 2010 limits even if it was spent in fiscal 2011, for "program integrity" initiatives by various agencies to combat waste, fraud and abuse.

▸ Stipulate that any savings that resulted from enactment of recommendations made by the presidential debt commission be used only for deficit reduction. ∎

Federal Borrowing Limit Increased

AMID AN INCREASINGLY acrimonious debate over the government's worsening fiscal condition, congressional Democrats succeeded in clearing a record increase in the statutory ceiling on federal borrowing. The increase was large enough to spare the majority party from having to take another vote on the politically painful issue before the November election.

The joint resolution raised the Treasury Department's borrowing limit to $14.294 trillion, a $1.9 trillion increase above the last ceiling, which was enacted in December 2009. President Obama signed the bill into law Feb. 12 (H J Res 45 — PL 111-139).

Budget-conscious moderates in the House won the inclusion of pay-as-you-go budget rules that required Congress to offset new entitlement spending and tax cuts to avoid increasing the deficit. However, the provisions exempted several major pieces of legislation that were expected during the year. *(Budget enforcement, p. 4-9)*

Senate Democrats won a public pledge from Obama to create a bipartisan commission that would make recommendations on debt reduction. The president made the commitment after the Senate rejected a proposal to create a debt commission by statute. *(Debt commission, p. 4-11)*

The majority party had no choice but to clear some increase in the debt limit. The alternative was a government default, with potentially disastrous consequences for both the United States and global economies. But the vote was politically uncomfortable, especially in the midst of a yawning deficit and an increasingly angry electorate. In line with traditional practice, the minority voted against the increase in both chambers.

Democrats tried to clear a long-term increase in the debt ceiling at the end of 2009, but conflict over the debt commission, favored in the Senate, vs. the pay-as-you-go rules, insisted on by the House, sank the effort. Instead, Congress cleared a short-term bill (PL 111-123), creating the need for a new bill in early 2010. *(2009 Almanac, p. 4-13)*

2010 LEGISLATIVE ACTION
SENATE FLOOR

The Senate passed the debt limit increase (H J Res 45) by a vote of 60-39 along straight party lines Jan. 28. By agreement, 60 votes were

---

BOX SCORE

BILL: H J Res 45 — PL 111-139

LEGISLATIVE ACTION:

Senate passed H J Res 45, amended, 60-39, on Jan. 28.

House adopted a self-executing rule (H Res 1065), 217-212, on Feb. 4, that concurred in the Senate-passed debt ceiling.

House cleared H J Res 45 by concurring, 233-187, on Feb. 4 in a Senate pay-as-you-go amendment.

President signed the measure Feb. 12.

---

required. *(Senate vote 14, p. S-6)*

With no Republican support, Senate Majority Leader Harry Reid, D-Nev., had to secure the votes of Democratic moderates who were unwilling to support a large debt increase without a credible plan to reduce the deficit.

Kent Conrad, D-N.D., chairman of the Budget Committee, and Judd Gregg of New Hampshire, the panel's ranking Republican, attempted to create a bipartisan debt commission, or "fiscal task force," by law. The Senate and House would have been bound to vote on the panel's recommendations — a key point for supporters. But their amendment fell, 53-46, on Jan. 26, seven votes shy of the 60-vote requirement. *(Senate vote 5, p. S-4)*

The following night, Obama pledged in his State of the Union address to create a similar commission by executive order. He issued the order Feb. 18. *(Text of address, p. D-3)*

Because the commission was not created in statute, there was no legal requirement that Congress vote on the panel's recommendations. Conrad and his group waited to accept the plan until they got written assurances from Reid and House Speaker Nancy Pelosi, D-Calif., backed by Vice President Joseph R. Biden Jr., that the recommendations would get floor votes. Pelosi pledged to hold a vote on the recommendations if the Senate passed them first.

In other action during the floor debate, the Senate:

▸ Adopted, 60-40, along party lines, an amendment to write the pay-as-you-go budget rules into law. House leaders had made it clear that support for the commission in their chamber hinged on the pay-as-you-go amendment. *(Senate vote 12, p. S-6)*

The amendment exempted a permanent extension of the middle-class portion of the 2001 and 2003 tax cuts (PL 107-16, PL 108-27); a five-year extension of a provision to block scheduled pay cuts for Medicare doctors; a two-year extension of 2009 estate tax rates and exemptions; and a two-year "patch" to keep the alternative minimum tax from hitting millions more households.

▸ Rejected, 51-49, an amendment by Sam Brownback, R-Kan., to establish a congressional budgetary accountability commission to assess federal agencies and programs and submit legislation to change those that were duplicative or outdated. The legislation would have gotten

expedited action in both chambers. (*Senate vote 10, p. S-5*)

▸ Rejected, 56-44, an amendment by Jeff Sessions, R-Ala., to set discretionary spending caps for five years equal to those for defense and non-defense programs in the fiscal 2010 budget resolution. Sixty votes were required on both. (*Senate vote 11, p. S-5*)

HOUSE FLOOR

The House on Feb. 4 adopted a self-executing rule (H Res 1065) that concurred in the Senate-passed debt ceiling. The vote was

217-212. The House then concurred in the Senate's pay-as-you-go amendment, 233-187, clearing the resolution. (*House votes 46, 48, p. H-20*)

House Democrats could have avoided the unpopular vote if the Senate had not amended the joint resolution. Under House rules, the chamber was deemed to have passed the original version of H J Res 45 on April 29, 2009, when both chambers adopted the conference report on the fiscal 2010 budget resolution (S Con Res 13). ∎

Debt Panel Report Fails to Reach Hill

AN 18-MEMBER DEBT COMMISSION created by President Obama to address the nation's fiscal problems delivered its recommendations on Dec. 3. Although the panel fell short of the votes needed to send its plan to Capitol Hill, leaders from both parties said the proposals would be part of the continuing debate.

The bipartisan commission — formally, the National Commission on Fiscal Responsibility and Reform — was charged with making recommendations to reduce the deficit to about 3 percent of gross domestic product by fiscal 2015, as well as to address the growth of entitlement spending and the need to slow the increase in the debt over the long term.

The commission had little authority on its own to force action. Its power lay in how much the president and party leaders got behind its proposals. Senate Majority Leader Harry Reid, D-Nev., pledged in writing to bring the recommendations to the floor for a vote, and Speaker Nancy Pelosi, D-Calif., promised to hold a vote if the Senate passed them.

The panel was instructed to issue a final report by Dec. 1, but 14 panel members had to support the recommendations before they could be sent to Congress. The chairmen delayed the vote until Dec. 3 in an unsuccessful effort to round up the necessary backing.

Obama established the commission by executive order on Feb. 18. He had pledged to do so in his Jan. 27 State of the Union speech, the day after the Senate rejected an attempt to create a similar panel by statute. Senate moderates made the founding of such a commission a condition of their support for a critical increase in the ceiling on the federal debt. (*Debt limit, p. 4-10; text of speech, p. D-3*)

The commission was led by presidential appointees Erskine Bowles, former chief of staff to President Bill Clinton, and former Sen. Alan K. Simpson, R-Wyo.

Obama appointed four more members, and the rest were named by the House and Senate majority and minority leaders.

▸ Obama named Dave Cote, chief executive of technology firm Honeywell; Ann Fudge, a former chief executive of Young & Rubicam Brands; Alice Rivlin, a former Federal Reserve official and director of the Congressional Budget Office and Office of Management and Budget; and Andy Stern, president of the Service Employees International Union.

▸ Pelosi appointed Democrats John M. Spratt Jr. of South Carolina, chairman of the Budget Committee; Xavier Becerra of California, vice chairman of the Democratic Caucus; and Jan Schakowsky of Illinois.

▸ House Minority Leader John A. Boehner, R-Ohio, appointed Republicans Paul D. Ryan of Wisconsin, Ways and Means ranking

member Dave Camp of Michigan and Jeb Hensarling of Texas.

▸ Reid appointed Democrats Kent Conrad of North Dakota, chairman of the Budget Committee; Finance Chairman Max Baucus of Montana; and Majority Whip Richard J. Durbin of Illinois.

▸ Senate Minority Leader Mitch McConnell, R-Ky., appointed Republicans Judd Gregg of New Hampshire, ranking member of the Budget Committee; Michael D. Crapo of Idaho; and Tom Coburn of Oklahoma.

Eleven members voted for the report. They were: Bowles, Simpson, Spratt, Durbin, Conrad, Crapo, Gregg, Coburn, Rivlin, Cote and Fudge.

HIGHLIGHTS

The following are highlights of the commission proposals:

● **Discretionary spending.**

▸ Cap discretionary spending through 2020, generating savings of $200 billion in 2015 alone.

▸ Adopt immediate discretionary cuts, totaling about $50 billion in 2015, including a reduction of the federal workforce, a three-year freeze on lawmakers' pay, a 15 percent cut in White House and congressional budgets and elimination of all earmarks.

▸ Require equal-share cuts in security and non-security spending.

▸ Require the president to propose annual limits for war spending.

▸ Establish a disaster fund to budget ahead for catastrophes.

▸ Increase the federal gas tax by 15 cents per gallon and dedicate the revenue to the Highway Trust Fund.

● **Comprehensive tax overhaul.**

▸ Reduce the size and number of tax breaks and other tax expenditures, which totaled about $1.1 trillion per year.

▸ Permanently repeal the alternative minimum tax.

▸ Reduce the top individual tax rate to between 23 percent and 29 percent.

▸ Establish a single corporate tax rate between 23 percent and 29 percent.

● **Health care cost containment and savings.**

▸ Develop an improved formula for paying Medicare physicians and fully offset the cost of any annual increase in doctors' reimbursement rates.

▸ Give the Centers for Medicare and Medicaid Services more authority to combat Medicare fraud and waste, resulting in savings of $1 billion in 2015.

▸ Increase cost sharing for Medicare enrollees, saving $10 billion in 2015.

▸ Require health care plans to offer rebates for brand-name drugs in Medicare Part D, reducing anticipated costs by billions in 2015.

▸ Reduce payments to hospitals for medical education, saving $6 billion through 2020.

▸ Require states to take on more responsibility for Medicaid administrative costs, saving $260 million in 2015.

▸ Implement aggressive medical-malpractice changes.

▸ Establish a long-term budget for total health care spending.

● **Mandatory savings.**

▸ Bring civil service and military pensions more in line with standard practices in the private sector, resulting in savings of as much as $70 billion through 2020.

▸ Reduce spending on agriculture subsidies, saving $10 billion through 2020.

▸ Authorize the Pension Benefit Guaranty Corporation to increase premiums to cover budget shortfalls, saving $16 billion through 2020.

▸ Extend the Federal Communications Commission's authority to auction radio spectrum licenses.

● **Social Security changes.**

▸ Gradually transition to a more progressive benefit formula.

▸ Gradually increase the early- and full-retirement ages.

▸ Enhance benefits for the very old and the long-term disabled.

▸ Allow beneficiaries to collect half their benefits at age 62.

▸ Create a hardship exemption for those who cannot work past 62 but who do not qualify for disability benefits.

▸ Gradually increase the portion of wages subject to Social Security tax until it covers 90 percent of wages by 2050. ■

Pay-as-You-Go Provisions Return

STATUTORY PAY-AS-YOU-GO budget rules were enacted for the first time in more than a decade as part of a joint resolution increasing the ceiling on the federal debt. President Obama signed the measure into law Feb. 12 (H J Res 45 — PL 111-139).

The budget provisions, known as "PAY-GO," were attached to the debt measure at the insistence of the House in exchange for an agreement by the Senate to a presidentially appointed commission on the federal debt. *(Debt limit, p. 4-10; debt commission, p. 4-11)*

The statutory rules required that new legislation that changed existing mandatory spending or revenue laws be "budget neutral," meaning that it would not increase the deficit. A report by the Office of Management and Budget (OMB) at the end of each session had to show whether the combination of all such legislation would increase the deficit; if so, the increase had to be offset through sequestration, or automatic across-the-board cuts, in many, but not all, mandatory programs.

The rules did not apply to discretionary spending, which is enacted separately under the annual appropriations bills.

The White House "strongly" supported the pay-as-you-go provisions, as well as the rest of the debt limit legislation.

The pay-as-you-go law was originally enacted in 1990 under the Budget Enforcement Act, part of a huge budget reconciliation bill (PL 101-508). The provisions were extended in 1997 (PL 105-33), but they expired at the end of 2002.

Subsequent efforts to restore pay-as-you-go rules were unsuccessful, mainly because of partisan disagreements over whether to cover both entitlements and taxes or, as Republicans wanted, to apply the rules to taxes only.

Both chambers adopted internal pay-as-you-go rules, but as rules, they had no enforcement mechanism and were regularly waived to pass legislation that had the net effect of increasing the budget deficit.

The House passed a pay-as-you-go bill in 2009 (HR 2920), but the

| BOX SCORE | **BILL:** H J Res 45 — PL 111-139 |

LEGISLATIVE ACTION:

Senate passed H J Res 45, amended, 60-39, on Jan. 28.

House adopted a self-executing rule (H Res 1065), 217-212, on Feb. 4, that concurred in the Senate-passed debt ceiling.

House cleared H J Res 45 by concurring, 233-187, on Feb. 4 in a Senate pay-as-you-go amendment.

President signed the measure Feb. 12.

Senate never acted on it. *(Budget enforcement, 2009 Almanac, p. 4-12)*

HIGHLIGHTS

The following are the main provisions of the pay-as-you-go section of the debt limit law:

● **Estimates.** Legislation with pay-as-you-go implications had to include an estimate by the Congressional Budget Office of the budgetary effect, if one was available.

● **OMB scorecard.** OMB was required to maintain continuously updated scorecards showing the five- and 10-year effects of pay-as-you-go-related legislation brought to the floor during the session.

● **Annual report.** Within 14 days of the end of a session, OMB had to issue a public report on the net effects on the deficit of the year's legislation subject to pay-as-you-go rules.

● **Sequestration.** If OMB determined that the net effect was an increase in the deficit over five or 10 years, the agency would develop a sequestration order that would reduce entitlement and mandatory programs by enough to offset the shortfall. The president would then issue the sequestration order.

A number of programs were exempt from the across-the-board cuts, including Social Security, certain veterans' programs, net interest on the debt, some refundable tax credits and certain low-income and economic recovery programs.

● **Emergency spending.** Items designated as emergency spending were excluded from OMB's pay-as-you go calculations. However, in the Senate, a three-fifths majority was required to waive a point of order against emergency spending in a bill. If the point of order was sustained, the emergency items would be dropped automatically.

● **Exemptions.** The law also effectively made four categories of legislation exempt from the pay-as-you-go requirements through Dec. 31, 2011: a permanent extension of Bush-era middle-class tax

cuts (PL 107-16, PL 108-27); a five-year extension of the so-called Medicare "doc fix" to prevent cuts in Medicare payments to physicians; a two-year extension of the 2009 estate tax exemptions and rates; and a similar two-year reprieve for legislation to keep the alternative minimum tax from hitting millions more households. *(Estate tax, p. 14-7)*

2010 LEGISLATIVE ACTION
SENATE FLOOR

The Senate voted, 60-40, on Jan. 28 to add the statutory pay-as-you-go provisions to the debt limit legislation. Republicans unanimously opposed the amendment, calling it "full of holes." The Senate passed the debt limit bill, 60-39, later the same day. By agreement, 60 votes were required on both votes. *(Senate votes 12, 14, p. S-6)*

Inclusion of the pay-as-you-go language was essential to getting House support for the debt limit. The House in turn accepted a presidentially created bipartisan deficit control commission, a compromise with Senate moderates who opposed the pay-as-you-go provision, especially because it excluded the four pieces of legislation.

Kent Conrad, D-N.D., chairman of the Senate Budget Committee, and ranking Republican Judd Gregg of New Hampshire, had insisted on a statutory commission that had the force of law. But the Senate rejected, 53-46, their attempt to add the commission to the debt limit bill. *(Senate vote 5, p. S-4)*

HOUSE FLOOR

The House on Feb. 4 adopted a self-executing rule (H Res 1065) that concurred in the debt ceiling portion of the Senate-passed bill. Members then concurred in the Senate's pay-as-you-go provisions, 233-187, clearing the joint resolution. *(House vote 48, p. H-20)* ■

Chapter 5

CONGRESSIONAL AFFAIRS

Longtime Ways and Means Chairman Rangel Censured for Ethics Violations

AFTER TWO YEARS OF investigation, an indictment and an aborted trial in which he declined to take part, the once-powerful Democratic Rep. Charles B. Rangel of New York was censured for ethics violations Dec. 2 in a bipartisan vote by his colleagues.

The punishment was the harshest sanction, short of expulsion, for rule-breakers in Congress. Rangel, who had represented Harlem for 40 years, was the 23rd member of Congress to be so judged, and the first in 27 years.

Immediately after the censure vote, the 80-year-old former chairman of the Ways and Means Committee was required to stand in the well of the House while his longtime friend and confidante, Speaker Nancy Pelosi, D-Calif., delivered an oral rebuke.

Six of the violations related specifically to Rangel's efforts to secure donations for an education center in New York bearing his name. Other violations pertained to inaccurate reporting of personal income, failure to pay all his taxes and use of a rent-controlled apartment for office space. The House also found Rangel guilty of breaching the "spirit and letter of the rules of the House" and bringing discredit to the House.

The House had not imposed censure since 1983, when Reps. Gerry E. Studds, D-Mass., and Daniel B. Crane, R-Ill., were both censured for sexual relations with pages. (1983 Almanac, p. 580)

A HOST OF TROUBLES

Rangel's troubles began in July 2008 with news reports about his rent-stabilized apartment in Harlem and inaccurate financial statements. (2008 Almanac, p. 5-5; 2009 Almanac, p. 5-8)

The congressman requested a formal inquiry, and on Feb. 25, 2010, the bipartisan, 10-member ethics committee — officially, the Committee on Standards of Official Conduct — offered its first punishment, admonishing him for improperly accepting Caribbean trips from corporations in 2007 and 2008 in violation of House gift rules.

The ethics committee required Rangel to repay the cost of travel but exonerated five other House Democrats — Bennie Thompson of Mississippi, Yvette D. Clarke of New York, Donald M. Payne of New Jersey, Carolyn Cheeks Kilpatrick of Michigan and Virgin Islands Del. Donna M.C. Christensen — who also participated in the trips but, according to the committee, were unaware of the corporate funding.

A week later, on March 3, Rangel gave up the coveted chairmanship of the Ways and Means Committee amid an expanded investigation into his failure to pay all the taxes on rental income from a villa in the Dominican Republic. Sander M. Levin, D-Mich., succeeded Rangel as chairman.

Rangel stepped down as Republicans were mounting an offensive against him. John Carter of Texas was set to introduce a privileged resolution calling for Rangel to vacate the chairmanship, and many key Democrats had indicated they were prepared to vote with Republicans on the issue.

On July 29, a bipartisan investigatory subcommittee of the Ethics panel approved a 13-count Statement of Alleged Violations. The eth-

ics subcommittee's formal announcement came after lengthy private talks between Rangel's lawyers and the panel's attorneys failed to reach a settlement. (Charges, p. 5-4)

In the absence of a deal, the case was set to move to the trial phase in September. On Aug. 10, the embattled congressman took to the House floor for more than a half-hour to defend himself and appeal for a quick opportunity to clear his name. He told his colleagues that "if I can't get my dignity back here, then fire your best shot on getting rid of me through expulsion."

Democrats decided to postpone the trial until after the November election.

Rangel easily won a 21st term on Nov. 2.

CONVICTION AND CENSURE

Action sped up the week of Nov. 15:

● **Subcommittee approves charges.** On Nov. 15, an adjudicatory subcommittee set up by the ethics panel for Rangel's case approved 13 identical motions for summary judgment, one for each of the 13 charges, determining that there was no dispute with the material fact of each charge.

The subcommittee's approval of the summary charges cut short what many expected to be a several-day "trial," complete with opening and closing statements, live witnesses and hundreds of pieces of evidence. Instead, panel members agreed to move to a closed-door session.

The subcommittee had planned to hold a several-day trial before voting, but Rangel unexpectedly announced at the start of the hearing that he would not participate in the proceedings without a lawyer. Representing himself, he requested that the ethics panel postpone the hearing so he could secure the means to hire an attorney. He said that he had lost his counsel nearly a month before in the face of mounting legal costs of more than $2 million.

The panel met briefly behind closed doors to consider, and ultimately reject, Rangel's request to delay the trial. Subcommittee Chairwoman Zoe Lofgren, D-Calif., said Rangel had repeatedly received guidance from the panel on how to cover his legal costs.

In light of Rangel's decision to let the hearing continue without his participation, Blake Chisam, the staff director and chief counsel for the full committee, recommended the subcommittee waive the trial portion and proceed right to the votes on the charges. He added that Rangel had not contested any of the evidence or witness testimony that the ethics subcommittee told him it would introduce.

"I believe that the congressman, quite frankly, was overzealous in many of the things that he did, and at least sloppy in his personal finances," Chisam said.

● **Rangel found guilty.** The following day, Nov. 16, the adjudicatory subcommittee found Rangel guilty on 11 of the 13 counts, setting the stage for the full ethics committee to decide on sanctions.

Two of the counts were considered so similar that they were combined. The panel voted unanimously to convict Rangel of that combined charge, as well as nine other charges.

The subcommittee voted, 7-1, to find Rangel guilty of violating a

Rangel: Counts And Convictions

ACTING ON RECOMMENDATIONS FROM the Committee on Standards of Official Conduct, the House censured Charles B. Rangel, D-N.Y., on Dec. 2 for 11 violations of House rules. Rangel was originally charged with 13 counts, but an eight-member bipartisan ethics subcommittee narrowed them to 11 after deadlocking on count 3 and merging counts 4 and 5 because they were so similar. The following are the 11 counts on which Rangel was found guilty:

1. Solicitation and Gift Ban Violation. Rangel sought contributions to the Charles B. Rangel Center for Public Service at the City College of New York using congressional resources.

2. Government Code of Ethics Violation. The congressman solicited donations for the center from individuals with whom he had professional relationships.

4 & 5. Violation of Postal and Franking Laws. Rangel solicited center donations using congressional stationery and the frank.

6. House Office Building Commission Regulations Violation. Rangel used congressional office space as the "home base" for seeking funds for the center.

7. Purpose Law and Member's Congressional Handbook Violation. House resources were used to solicit for the center and were paid out of the Member's Representational Allowance.

8. Letterhead Rule Violation. Congressional letterhead was used to solicit donations for the center.

9. Ethics in Government Act and House Rule 26 Violation. Rangel filed incomplete and inaccurate financial disclosure statements.

10. Government Code of Ethics Violation. Rangel accepted use of a rent-controlled residential apartment in New York for office space.

11. Government Code of Ethics Violation. Rental income related to Rangel's Dominican Republic vacation home was unreported.

12. Violation of Code of Conduct — Letter and Spirit of House Rules. Rangel violated "the spirit and letter of the Rules of the House."

13. Violation of Code of Conduct — Conduct Reflecting Discreditably on the House. Rangel violated the rule that a member "shall behave at all times in a manner that shall reflect creditably on the House."

---

broad House rule that "members shall behave at all times in a manner that reflects creditably on the House." Members rejected, 4-4, the remaining charge that Rangel violated a House gift rule.

"None of us were volunteers for this," Lofgren said as she announced the ruling. "We have tried to act with fairness led only by facts and the law and believe we have accomplished that mission."

The congressman, who was not present, said in a statement, "How can anyone have confidence in the decision of the ethics subcommittee when I was deprived of due process rights, right to counsel and was not even in the room? I can only hope that the full committee will treat me more fairly."

Rangel held the record for having been charged with the highest number of counts of misconduct of any other member of the House — former Rep. James A. Traficant, D-Ohio, was expelled from Congress in 2002 on nine counts of ethics violations.

● **Ethics committee recommends censure.** On Nov. 18, the full ethics committee voted, 9-1, to recommend that the House censure the veteran lawmaker.

In the 43-year history of the bipartisan ethics committee, the panel had recommended sanctions against lawmakers 16 times. Four times it recommended expulsion, the most serious sanction; three times it recommended censure, the second-most-severe punishment; and nine times it recommended milder reprimands.

In deciding on punishment, members took into consideration advice from Chisam, who served as the de facto prosecutor against Rangel in these proceedings.

Chisam argued that censure was an appropriate sanction given the severity of Rangel's wrongdoings. "The respondent's course of conduct demonstrated a . . . carelessness over a broad range of issues over a lengthy period of time," Chisam said. "His actions and accumulation of actions . . . brought discredit to the House. His conduct served to undermine public trust in this institution."

Democrat G.K. Butterfield of North Carolina was the only member

to publicly disagree with Chisam's recommendation. "The counsel is a legal scholar . . . if he saw corruption in this case, he would say so," said Butterfield, who was also a colleague of Rangel's in the Congressional Black Caucus.

Rangel returned to the hearing room before the committee went into closed session to deliberate, accompanied by his friend of 50 years and fellow Democrat, John Lewis of Georgia. "I do hope that, no matter what you decide in this sanction, that you might . . . say that this member who was honored to serve with you was not corrupt," Rangel said with emotion. "Put in that report that Charles Rangel never sought any personal gain."

Speaking briefly on his behalf, Lewis told panel members that "Charlie Rangel is a good and decent man . . . [who has] always been a champion for those who have been left out and left behind."

In his opening statement and in answers to questions from lawmakers on the committee, Rangel did not deny his "irresponsible behavior," and apologized for putting his colleagues in the "awkward situation" of having to judge him. He also expressed his frustration that witnesses had not been invited to testify before the committee.

"They would have given an explanation for my faulty behavior," he said. For instance, he said, witnesses would have shown that the City University of New York approached him to lend his name to the public policy center it hoped to establish, not the other way around.

As members sought to parse through the information to determine a verdict, they pushed Chisam to elaborate on whether any of Rangel's ethics violations showed evidence of corruption and personal gain.

Chisam said that the findings suggested there was no indication of either. But some Republican members of the panel had strong words about the need to, nonetheless, impose a harsh punishment.

"A man who wielded one of the most powerful gavels in the land, and was at one time highly regarded by colleagues . . . [is] now showing so little regard for the institution he has claimed to love," said ranking Republican Jo Bonner of Alabama. "The actions, decisions

and behavior of our colleague . . . can no longer reflect either honor or integrity."

● **Rangel censured.** The House voted, 333-79, on Dec. 2 to adopt a resolution (H Res 1737) of censure against Rangel. Although the cen sure resolution did not strip Rangel of any powers in Congress, it did order him to pay unpaid taxes on income received from his property in the Dominican Republic and to provide proof of payment to the Ethics panel. *(House vote 607, p. H-210)*

Lofgren was blunt in her assessment. "We found his actions an accumulation of actions that reflected poorly on the institution of the House and, thereby, brought discredit to the House," she said. Her comments were echoed by Bonner. "It is a sad day for sure," he said. "But now the entire House has a responsibility to join the Ethics committee in rendering your judgment."

Before the vote, Rangel's supporters tried to lighten the sentence to a written reprimand, a sanction that carried less stigma and would not have required Rangel's presence in the chamber after the vote. But the House rejected the proposal, offered by Butterfield, 146-267. *(House vote 606, p. H-210)*

The vote against a lesser sanction split Democrats but was predominantly a party-line affair for Republicans, although three joined Rangel in voting in favor of the reprimand: Peter T. King of New York, Ron Paul of Texas and Don Young of Alaska. Majority Leader Steny H. Hoyer, D-Md., also stood with Rangel by voting yes on the amended resolution, while 105 Democrats voted no. In the censure vote, King and Young joined 77 Democrats in voting no. As was customary for the Speaker, Pelosi did not vote.

Addressing his peers before the vote, Rangel apologized for his actions and again implored members on both sides of the aisle to vote with compassion. "I ask for fairness," he said. "In none of the precedents of the history of this great country has anyone ever suffered the humiliation of a censure when the record is abundantly clear . . . and when . . . counsel on the committee found no evidence at all of corruption."

Two members of the New York delegation, King and Democrat Jerrold Nadler, said neither the substance of the charges nor historical precedent warranted severe punishment. "Why are we departing so significantly from tradition and precedent in the case of Charlie Rangel?" King asked. "Reflect upon not just the lifetime of Charlie Rangel, but more importantly the 220-year history of tradition and precedent of this body."

After Pelosi's reading of the resolution, Rangel addressed his colleagues. "I want to make sure that this body knows it never entered into my mind to enrich myself or do violence" to the integrity of the House, Rangel said. "I know in my heart that . . . I am going to be judged by my life . . . [and] my contributions to society."

Rangel ended his remarks with a line from his autobiography about his good fortune since being wounded in the Korean War: "Compared to where I've been, I haven't had a bad day since," he said. He left the House floor to applause, receiving hugs from some members.

DOWN FROM THE HEIGHTS

Rangel's censure left him in Congress, but drew down the curtain on a historic House career that started in 1971, after the congressman narrowly defeated the legendary but controversial Adam Clayton Powell. As he rose through the ranks, Rangel became a pioneer among blacks in Congress. He was a founder of the Congressional Black Caucus, and in 1974 he became the first African-American to serve on Ways and Means.

The silver-haired, snappily dressed, ever-smiling Rangel was a popular figure, and, until his ethics problems surfaced, a frequent guest on TV interview shows, in part because of his way with a quip.

In 2005, he was asked what he thought of President George W. Bush. "Well," he said, "I think he shatters the myth of white supremacy once and for all." But he could also criticize fellow Democrats. In 1996, when President Bill Clinton signed legislation ending welfare as an entitlement, Rangel wisecracked, "The truth is, the Republicans would throw 2 million people, children, into poverty and my president will only throw 1 million into poverty."

Along with Rep. Pete Stark, D-Calif., Rangel was the longest-serving Ways and Means member in congressional history. Rangel became chairman in 2007 after Democrats took back the House.

Although he was a partisan Democrat and a close friend and supporter of Pelosi, Rangel had a long record of working with GOP members on Ways and Means, both while in the minority and as chairman, to pass bipartisan bills.

In his first term as chairman, during the 110th Congress, he worked with Republicans on legislation providing small-business tax breaks, relief for Hurricane Katrina victims, taxpayer identity protections and a ban on genetic discrimination by health insurers.

He also negotiated a trade framework with the Bush administration that strengthened labor and environmental standards, allowing a free-trade deal with Peru to become law. He paired a minimum-wage increase with tax breaks, which satisfied Republicans. And under Bush and President Obama, he played a key role in economic stimulus packages.

In the 111th Congress, his committee was responsible for finding ways to pay for Democrats' ambitious plans for a health care overhaul. ∎

Waters, Other Ethics Investigations

THE HOUSE ETHICS COMMITTEE announced in August that it would hold a public trial on alleged ethics violations by Maxine Waters, a 10-term Democratic representative from California. The trial was scheduled for late November but was postponed indefinitely after the discovery of undisclosed new evidence.

Waters faced three counts of misconduct based on allegations that she used her spot on the Financial Services Committee to secure federal support for OneUnited Bank, a Los Angeles institution where her husband, Sidney Williams, was a board member from 2004 through 2008 and owned between $250,000 and $500,000 in stock in 2007.

A four-member investigatory subcommittee filed the charges against Waters on July 28. The full bipartisan 10-member ethics committee — formally, the Committee on Standards of Official Conduct — announced Aug. 2 that the subcommittee had found substantial reason to believe Waters violated House rules or federal law, triggering the formation of an adjudicatory subcommittee to hold the trial.

Waters denounced the charges against her in an Aug. 2 statement. "I have not violated any House rules," she said. "Therefore, I simply will not be forced to admit to something I did not do, and instead have chosen to respond to charges . . . in a public hearing. . . . The accusations against me stem from work I have done throughout my decades of public service as an advocate for minority communities and businesses in California and nationally."

The subcommittee reported that when the banking system was on the verge of collapse in September 2008, Waters approached Treasury Secretary Henry M. Paulson Jr. to arrange a meeting between Treasury officials and representatives of the National Bankers Association, a trade group for minority-owned banks. Waters did not attend the meeting.

According to the report, at the meeting, OneUnited executives pressed for federal assistance to compensate for the bank's losses stemming from the federal takeover of Fannie Mae and Freddie Mac. OneUnited subsequently received $12 million through the Troubled Asset Relief Program.

The report said Waters might have violated House rules by having a conflict of interest in pushing the meetings and then allowing monetary compensation through her husband's stock holding to accrue to her interest.

For her part, Waters said she made one phone call on behalf of the bankers association and did not receive any material benefit. "Although I am not convinced that the process for investigating and examining House ethics cases is fair, I welcome the opportunity to show my constituents and the American public that the accusations against me are frivolous and unfounded," she said.

The Waters case stemmed from a probe begun by the outside Office of Congressional Ethics, a bipartisan panel authorized to undertake independent probes of House members and to make recommendations to the House ethics committee for further action. The evidence that the office gathered was turned over to the committee in July 2009.

Speaker Nancy Pelosi, D-Calif., had pushed through creation of the independent panel in 2008, and it continued to draw bipartisan criticism at the Capitol. Lawmakers in both parties charged that it had sown confusion and fear among their ranks, initiated investigations based on weak evidence and sullied the reputations of those facing allegations of wrongdoing, even when they were subsequently cleared.

Longtime advocates for such a board, something states used widely, argued that only an outside body could adequately police congressional ethics.

OTHER INQUIRIES

The House ethics committee also cleared some members of wrongdoing and closed one case. The Senate Select Ethics Committee made no public pronouncements on any cases.

● **PMA Group.** The committee cleared seven House appropriators of having had improper ties to the PMA Group, a since-defunct lobbying firm. At issue was whether the lawmakers exchanged earmarks for campaign contributions from PMA, which closed in 2009 after being raided by the FBI in 2008. The panel found that no member of the Appropriations Committee had earmarked funds to help the firm. The conclusion covered the cases of Reps. Marcy Kaptur, D-Ohio; Norm Dicks, D-Wash.; C.W. Bill Young, R-Fla.; James P. Moran, D-Va.; John P. Murtha, D-Pa., who died Feb. 8; Todd Tiahrt, R-Kan.; and Peter J. Visclosky, D-Ind. Some Republicans said that they would like the panel to reopen the case.

● **Massa.** The ethics panel started, then dropped, an investigation into sexual harassment charges against Eric Massa, D-N.Y., who resigned from the House in March. Although Massa was no longer under the committee's jurisdiction, Republicans repeatedly urged the panel to look into the response of Democratic leaders to the harassment allegations. There were some indications that the panel was pursuing that line of inquiry even after halting the investigation into Massa.

● **Stark.** The panel cleared Pete Stark, D-Calif., of violating House rules after investigating charges that the senior member of the Ways and Means Committee had intentionally filed a false application for a Maryland property tax credit. In its report, the ethics committee sharply criticized the Office of Congressional Ethics, which had concluded that Stark's case was worthy of review. ∎

Byrd, The Quintessential Senator

BY THE MOST OBJECTIVE STANDARD of time served, Robert C. Byrd was a Senate institution: His half-century as a senator — 51 years, five months and 25 days, to be as precise as he would insist — was a record that will be difficult to break.

Byrd died on June 28 at age 92.

By subjective measure, Byrd embodied as much as anyone in American history both the most revered and the most ridiculed characteristics of the institution he loved so passionately: the power of oratory to shape the making of public policy, the influence a single senator could exercise over questions both profound and mundane, and the ability to leverage seniority into largesse for a relative few.

Byrd proudly cultivated his reputation for being among the best in all those things — and, beyond that, for his unrivaled standing as the chief guardian of the Senate's prerogatives and precedents, its reverential historian and the grand master of its arcane rules and venerable procedures.

He was not, and never really set out to be, a legendary force for the remaking of social or foreign policy, although he was particularly influential in determining the fate of the agendas set out by Jimmy Carter in the 1970s (when Byrd was the Democratic majority leader) and by Ronald Reagan in the 1980s (when Byrd served variously as minority leader and majority leader).

His most tangible and personally satisfying legislative achievements came after that, when he turned his attention to the parochial needs of his constituents in West Virginia and delivered a steady and expensive diet of public works projects.

His pursuit of federal money for his home state was remarkably effective and for two decades made him a lightning rod for critics of the congressional spending culture. More than 30 highways, dams, bridges, educational institutions, research facilities and federal agency outposts had been named for the senator even before he died — a roster that seemed sure to grow in the following years.

Byrd, who had a life-size portrait of himself installed in one of his Capitol offices, made no pretense about shunning such gestures of gratitude — undeniably meaningful to someone whose life story might have been penned by Horatio Alger.

"Never having forgotten my roots, I continue to be aware that my highest duty is to West Virginia and to the people of that state who have honored me with public office for more than a half-century," he declared in the exhaustive (at 817 pages) autobiography he published in 2005: "Robert C. Byrd: Child of the Appalachian Coalfields."

It is something of the quintessential American political success story that he triumphed over humble beginnings to win election to more congressional leadership posts than anyone in history. He was Democratic floor leader for a dozen years and Appropriations Committee chairman three times. At his death he was the president pro tempore of the Senate — an honorary post generally awarded to the longest-tenured member of the majority — which placed him third in the line of presidential succession.

But for all his achievements, he never appeared entirely comfortable or gracious in exercising the power he had attained. Even among fellow Democrats, Byrd had a reputation for being imperious, prickly and something of a loner.

His skills as an orator meant he could change hearts and minds with the words he uttered on the Senate floor — but just as often, his speeches were remembered for their grandiloquence and pedantry.

While he revered the Senate's traditions of civility and collegiality and the protection of the minority party's rights, he could be ruthless, vindictive and intensely partisan behind the scenes.

Byrd changed as fundamentally during his six decades in public life as his nation did. He first ran for public office just after World War II as a segregationist, but in 2008 his final presidential endorsement went to an African-American. As Barack Obama prepared to move from his Senate office to the White House in late 2008, he hailed Byrd as "one of the greatest senators of all time."

Byrd broke into the Senate leadership ranks in the 1960s as a conservative insurgent, but in the five years before he died his American Conservative Union approval rating was never above 21 percent. He helped escalate and perpetuate the war in Vietnam, but in his later years there was no more vehement opponent in Congress of the war in Iraq. He began his political career practicing classic rural retail politics, playing "Cripple Creek" and "Rye Whiskey" on his fiddle as he stumped in West Virginia's hills and hollows; at the end of his career his anti-war speeches were getting high marks and decent audiences on YouTube.

Byrd's leftward evolution made no difference to his electoral fortunes, even as his state became somewhat more Republican. Although his health was clearly failing, he won his record ninth Senate term in 2006 with a decisive 64 percent of the vote. (It was his closest race since he first won his Senate seat in 1958.) Byrd was undefeated in 15 consecutive campaigns over more than six decades, starting with his election to the state legislature in 1946, when he was 29, and including elections to three terms in the House in the 1950s.

That political record permitted the senator to boast, as he often did earlier in his career, that "there are four things people believe in in West Virginia: God Almighty; Sears, Roebuck; Carter's Little Liver Pills; and Robert C. Byrd."

MAN OF THE SENATE

His longevity meant that on June 12, 2006, Byrd surpassed Republican Strom Thurmond of South Carolina as the longest-serving senator in history. Three years after that — on Nov. 18, 2009, two days before his 92nd birthday — Byrd marked the 20,774th day he'd been a member of Congress.

That milestone pushed him past Carl T. Hayden, a Democratic congressman and senator from Arizona between 1912 and 1969, as the longest-serving member of Congress. Byrd was a senator for nearly a quarter of the time the Senate had existed. He became a senator before President Obama, as well as 11 of the senators in the 111th Congress, were born. And he served in Congress during the presidencies of 11 of the 43 men who had held the office.

Byrd got to Congress, and stayed there, largely by running on a populist platform of economic and social issues that was heavy on union rights, government benefits, morality, national security, and law and order. After he arrived in the Senate, he quickly allied himself with its Southern power brokers, picking as his mentors conservative Richard B. Russell of Georgia and the more pragmatic Lyndon B. Johnson of Texas, with whom he shared an intense passion for the promises of the New Deal anti-poverty programs of Franklin D. Roosevelt. It was Johnson, majority leader at the time, who escorted Byrd into the chamber for his first swearing-in ceremony in 1959 and fatefully gave him a seat on the Appropriations panel.

That seat, which he never relinquished, was the main reason for his political staying power at home. His unrivaled appetite for earmarking money earned him the derisive sobriquet "King of Pork" in Washington, but it so endeared him to West Virginia's voters that they permitted him the ideological flexibility he needed to advance in the party leadership and become an even more powerful advocate for his state.

"Primarily, he'll be remembered as the No. 1 economic development officer for West Virginia," said Ken Hechler, a Democratic congressman from 1959 through 1976 and West Virginia's secretary of state from 1985 through 2000.

Byrd literally wrote the book on the Senate, publishing a loving and lavish four-volume history between 1988 and 1995 that evolved from an impromptu speech delivered while a granddaughter's fifth-grade class watched from the Senate visitors' gallery in 1980.

Byrd's florid rhetorical style, like the vested suits he favored and the snow-white pompadour of his later years, were reminiscent of an earlier era. Whether he was talking about war and peace, the congressional power of the purse, the co-equality of the legislative and executive branches or the sensual pleasures of the changing seasons, his speeches were sourced in the words of Greek playwrights, Roman warriors, American poets, the Bible and — most frequently — the Constitution, a copy of which he often brandished in a trembling hand.

"Surely no senator needs to reread history," Byrd declared in 2000 while railing against a proposal he viewed as unconstitutional, "in order to remember how much blood and treasure it has cost throughout the long centuries, dating back to the Magna Carta and beyond, to establish the greatest document of its kind that was ever written — the Constitution of the United States."

ABOUT-FACE ON RACE

Byrd cited the Constitution repeatedly as he developed two of his favorite rhetorical themes of the decade before his death: what he regarded as the improper expansion of executive power by George W. Bush and his "colossal blunder" in Iraq. Those tongue-lashings won him a cult following among liberals, many of them too young to remember his passionate efforts in the 1960s to stop civil rights legislation while escalating the military commitment in Southeast Asia.

His evolution on civil rights coincided with his climb in the Democratic Party ranks and the shift in the party's internal balance of power from Southern conservatives to Northern liberals. He joined the Ku Klux Klan when he was 24 and by the 1940s had become a local organizer.

By the time of his first House race he had disassociated himself from the group — he called joining it a youthful indiscretion born of his fear of communism — but he knew he would never make it go away. "The Klan albatross is a mistake which has haunted me throughout my political career, and it will undoubtedly be promi-

nently referred to in my obituaries," he wrote in his autobiography.

He may have renounced the Klan, but his early years in Congress took a decidedly segregationist bent. He was part of the emphatic stand against the Civil Rights Act of 1964. At 7:38 p.m. on June 9, 1964, Byrd began his part of the live filibuster against the bill and did not stop talking for 14 hours and 13 minutes. That marathon included a colloquy with Thurmond, the 1948 segregationist presidential candidate, in which the two heartily agreed that requiring a white masseuse to have a black customer would abrogate the white woman's 13th Amendment right not to be enslaved. Altogether, the filibuster lasted 57 days.

As chairman of the Appropriations Subcommittee on the District of Columbia in the 1960s, Byrd adamantly opposed "home rule" for the overwhelmingly African-American capital, pumped money into welfare investigations and refused to provide federal assistance to unemployed parents of dependent children. He opposed the Voting Rights Act of 1965 and the 1967 confirmation of the first black Supreme Court justice, Thurgood Marshall. In those days he once dismissed the Rev. Martin Luther King Jr. as a "self-serving rabble-rouser."

After the 1966 midterm election, Byrd ousted the much more liberal Joseph S. Clark of Pennsylvania to get on the Senate Democratic leadership ladder as the caucus secretary. But four years later, he sought to position himself in the caucus mainstream — at one point maneuvering to kill an anti-desegregation amendment — as he plotted to move up to majority whip.

Though he continued to oppose busing students as a method of racial integration, he began to support other major civil rights measures in the mid-1970s and did so until he died. He voted for extensions of the Voting Rights Act, pressed for congressional representation for the District of Columbia, backed fair-housing efforts, and voted in 1988 and 1989 to override vetoes of civil rights measures by Reagan and George Bush.

"He had the ability to change, to grow and move from the past," said Rep. John Lewis, the Georgia Democrat who was a leader in the civil rights movement. "I think we have to look at the fact that he got on the right side."

Newly arrived in 2005 as the Senate's only black member, Obama raised money for Byrd's final election campaign and hailed his evolution on race. "He was reflective of his age," Obama said, "and his attitudes now signal an enormous transformation in America."

Another dramatic transformation led Byrd to become the unlikely hero of the modern anti-war movement. His ardent anti-communism led him naturally to be a Cold War defense hawk, and in 1964 he voted with 87 other senators for the Gulf of Tonkin Resolution, essentially giving Johnson broad latitude to prosecute the Vietnam War. As late as 1969, he advocated giving his constituents what he said they wanted — "an honorable conclusion" to the war — not by withdrawing forces but by intensifying the use of military might in an effort to win.

But Byrd came to see his status as the self-described "last man out" on Vietnam as disastrous. "I voted for the Gulf of Tonkin Resolution. I am sorry for that. I am guilty of doing that," he said in 2002 during the debate on authorizing the Iraq War. "But I am not wanting to commit that sin twice, and that is exactly what we are doing here."

LIBERALISM AND LABOR

Cornelius Calvin Sale Jr. was the name the future senator was given when he was born in the furniture and textile town of North Wilkesboro, N.C., on Nov. 20, 1917. Within months, Byrd's mother,

Ada, contracted the influenza that killed more than 50 million people worldwide. She instructed her husband that when she died the infant should be given to her childless sister, Vlurma, and her coal-miner husband, Titus Byrd, in Bluefield, W.Va. Cornelius Sale Sr. stayed with his four older children and did not meet his youngest until the boy, renamed Robert Carlyle Byrd, graduated first in his high school class in 1934.

Byrd was reared by his adoptive parents in the Appalachian coal fields. As a teenager of the Great Depression, he said, he learned firsthand what the federal government could do to help working people and alleviate poverty. "Living in the midst of such circumstances, and realizing with growing anxiety that the time was not far off when Pap would no longer be able to work in the mine, it was with a sense of thankfulness and buoyancy that I watched Franklin Roosevelt's progressive programs unfold, bringing hope and assurance and a feeling of security into the homes of coal miners," he wrote.

The confrontations between coal miners and strikebreakers employed by absentee mine owners in the 1920s left a powerful impression on Byrd, as did the FDR-aided rise of the United Mine Workers of America in the following decade. The first bill he proposed in Congress, the day he took his House seat in January 1953, would have repealed the 1947 Taft-Hartley Act, which restricted the rights granted to organized labor under the watershed National Labor Relations Act of 1935. Through 2006, Byrd had compiled a 78 percent lifetime rating from the AFL-CIO, siding with the pre-eminent labor organization in the nation on 445 votes and opposing it 124 times.

Byrd's reverence for labor was reflected, in a different way, in his own dogged work ethic and lifelong drive for self-improvement. After high school he spent a dozen years pumping gas, bagging groceries, butchering meat and, during World War II, welding naval vessels in Baltimore and Tampa before running for the West Virginia House of Delegates in 1946. In the following years, he worked at the state Capitol, took courses at a handful of colleges and read voraciously while many of his legislative colleagues spent their time socializing.

"I have never in my life had a golf club in my hand. I have never in life hit a tennis ball. I have — believe it or not — never thrown a line over to catch a fish. . . . I don't know how to swim," Byrd once revealed to Sen. George Smathers, according to an oral history the Florida Democrat gave to the Senate Historical Office. "Now there's a fellow who had done nothing but work all of his life," Smathers said. "Have you got to be for a guy like that? I do."

When he came to Washington in 1953, still without an undergraduate degree, Byrd enrolled in American University's law school. A decade later he got his degree at the commencement ceremony at which President John F. Kennedy gave his famous speech on the possibilities for world peace in the Cold War. Byrd became the first person to begin and finish law school while in Congress.

Byrd quickly became known as a creature of the Senate after he arrived in 1959, and his reputation for diligence and meticulousness — and for attending to parochial issues in the Appalachians — allowed him to build a constituency among fellow senators by doing them favors and taking on their chores. As a freshman he presided over the Senate for a record 21 hours and eight minutes consecutively, a totally thankless task in a chamber where the presiding officer has minimal power.

In four years as caucus secretary, Byrd turned the previously unheralded job into a favor factory and spent even more time on the floor, absorbing the chamber's rules, rhythms and folkways. He sent senators congratulatory notes on their birthdays and spread campaign money to his colleagues. All that effort paid off when he decided to mount a stealth campaign for majority whip after the 1970 election. He won, 31-24, over the one-term incumbent, Edward M. Kennedy of Massachusetts, who had never been adept at the job and had become distracted from his congressional obligations after his 1969 car wreck on Chappaquiddick Island in Massachusetts.

LEADER AND FOLLOWER

As whip, Byrd often tended to the mundane but important tasks of leadership in support of his majority leader, Mike Mansfield of Montana. His hand in running the floor schedule and the perquisites he controlled as a senior member of the Rules and Administration Committee further enhanced his standing. And so he was unopposed in moving to the pinnacle of senatorial power when Mansfield retired in 1976. (Hubert H. Humphrey of Minnesota, who had returned to the Senate after serving as vice president, took himself out of the contest in the face of limited support and failing health.) Byrd would be the Democratic floor leader for the next dozen years, half the time when the party was in the majority.

In 1977, when Byrd became majority leader and Carter became president, the senator carefully defined their relationship. "I am the president's friend," he said. "I am not the president's man." In truth, Byrd was a "friend" only in the most formal and professional sense, for he soon came to view Carter as an amateur with little aptitude for the exercise of power. Nonetheless, Byrd repeatedly saved the administration in difficult legislative situations — making sure that Carter knew where the credit belonged.

His most dramatic rescue operation came in 1978, when he saved the Panama Canal transfer treaties through nonstop negotiations with wavering senators, personal diplomacy with Panamanian officials and last-second language changes that finally amassed the votes needed for ratification. Byrd also played an indispensable role in the passage of Carter's energy program, approval of a Middle East arms sales package and approval of the Equal Rights Amendment.

All the while, Byrd refined his mastery of the rules of the Senate as a tool for either getting what he wanted or at least stopping others from getting what they wanted. When he was dissatisfied with the parliamentary status quo, he was capable of dreaming up and imposing procedures of his own — most famously language first enacted in 1985, which is referred to as the "Byrd Rule" in the Senate Manual, that severely restricts the sort of legislative proposal that could advance in the Senate using the expedited procedures for taxing and spending matters known as reconciliation.

But Byrd was at least equally associated with the legendary Rule 22 of the standing rules of the Senate, which governed the ways in which debate could be proscribed and which fostered the chamber's tradition of unfettered debate.

As a practice, early in his career Byrd opposed almost all efforts to invoke cloture, and thereby limit debate, aligning with Southern conservatives to block civil rights legislation. (A two-thirds vote was needed to end a filibuster until 1975, when the Senate dropped its threshold to three-fifths of all senators.) But as majority leader, Byrd sometimes used heavy-handed tactics to kill filibusters. When conservatives employed new methods for delaying action in the Senate, Byrd

used a ruling from Vice President Walter F. Mondale, in his capacity as Senate president, and a bare majority to eliminate the post-cloture filibuster and finish work on 1978 energy legislation.

After his time as floor leader ended, Byrd remained in the self-appointed role of guardian of senatorial power. He was instrumental in reaching the 2005 agreement that preserved a senator's power to mount a filibuster and set an effective 60-vote threshold for the confirmation of federal judges. Tennessee Republican Bill Frist, majority leader at the time, was so intent on advancing Bush's picks for the bench that he was preparing a series of parliamentary moves that could have brought an end to the judicial filibuster.

LEADER TO APPROPRIATOR

As a legislative traffic cop, tactician and parliamentary master Byrd had few rivals, but he exhibited little of the vision that his idol, Johnson, had displayed in beginning to transform domestic policy when he was Senate leader. As a result, despite his longevity, Byrd's name graces few of the hundreds of bills passed during his tenure in the leadership.

Instead, as Republican Sen. Mark O. Hatfield of Oregon said in 1981, Byrd succeeded by adopting the style of a bank manager: "He kept a tab on bills and kept a ledger of what favors he was owed and what favors he owed others."

Given the choice between being liked and respected as majority leader, Byrd wrote later, he chose the latter. But when the Democrats lost control of the Senate in Reagan's 1980 landslide, Byrd found himself in the minority for the first time, and his colleagues began to complain that his style lacked the sophistication needed for the opposition party, especially on television. An effort to oust him came up short in 1984, and another was gaining momentum in 1986 until the Democrats regained the majority — and Byrd was rewarded with a return to the majority leadership.

But his spotlight was fading, and he recognized it. He made a graceful exit two years later, when another challenge to his leadership started brewing just as the chairmanship he had always coveted came open.

"If I live long enough," Byrd had told a newspaper columnist the year he became a senator, "I would like to be chairman of the Senate Appropriations Committee." He got that gavel in 1989 and held it whenever the Democrats were in the majority through the end of 2008. He gave it up under pressure from fellow senators only when it became undeniable that he was too infirm to carry on.

But whether his party was in the majority or the minority over those two decades, Byrd's main objective was constant: to make sure as much federal money as possible was spent in West Virginia. In 2004, for example, the state received $1.83 in federal assistance for every tax dollar it sent to Washington, according to the nonpartisan Tax Foundation.

His departure from party leadership also allowed Byrd to shift from partisan warrior to elder statesman, a role he put to historically important use. As one of the most publicly derisive Democratic critics of President Bill Clinton's affair with White House intern Monica Lewinsky — and as someone legendary not only for guarding senatorial prerogatives but also for promoting propriety in public life — Byrd was central to the prosecution strategy in the 1999 impeachment trial. His support for conviction, Republicans believed, would prompt a wave of other Democrats to follow suit. But the opposite happened: Byrd declared that Clinton's actions did not merit removal from office and proposed dismissing the charges, effectively taking the suspense out of the proceedings even before they began.

Byrd slowed noticeably in his later years. Long afflicted by tremors, he began walking with the aid of two canes and seldom, if ever, appeared in public without an aide close at hand. For his last year, he spent virtually all his time at the Capitol in a wheelchair, but he never lost his ability to move an audience.

Devastated by the loss of his wife, Erma Ora Byrd, after nearly 69 years of marriage, he paid tribute to her on the floor of the Senate in 2006. "Could I have accomplished as much as I have accomplished — whatever that may have been — without her? I think not," he said. "The more important point is that I did it with Erma, and I would not have had it any other way. She was God's greatest gift to me."

David R. Obey, the Wisconsin Democrat who, as chairman of the House Appropriations Committee, grew to know Byrd intimately, summed up his legacy this way: "I can think of no one in the history of the Senate who demonstrated a greater capacity for growth than Robert Byrd. He was unmatched in his recognition of our obligation to the Constitution and to the institution of Congress itself. They really don't make them like him anymore." ■

Congress Loses Two Party Stalwarts

TWO MEN WITH STORIED histories in Congress died in 2010: former Republican Sen. Ted Stevens of Alaska and Democratic Rep. John P. Murtha of Pennsylvania.

SEN. TED STEVENS

Stevens, a pugnacious force in the Senate for four decades and a prodigious source of largesse for his constituents, died Aug. 9 at the age of 86 in an Alaska airplane crash.

Stevens served longer in the Senate than any other Republican before losing his bid for an eighth term in 2008 under the cloud of a corruption conviction that was later thrown out. Long before that career, he fought for statehood for Alaska in the 1950s.

A World War II veteran who earned two Distinguished Flying Crosses piloting transports over China, he was among five killed when a plane owned by Alaska telecommunications company GCI crashed near Dillingham.

Stevens served 40 years until his defeat by Democrat Mark Begich. Along with the late Sen. Robert C. Byrd, D-W.Va., retired Sen. Pete V. Domenici, R-N.M., and others, Stevens personified the Senate's "old bulls" — senior lawmakers fiercely territorial and unapologetic about using their influence for their states and priorities. (*Byrd, p. 5-7*)

Using his famous temper to great effect and wearing his "Incredible Hulk" tie during climactic debates on the floor, Stevens staunchly defended the earmarking process against attacks from John McCain, R-Ariz., and others, contending that lawmakers knew better than bureaucrats where to spend taxpayer dollars. Earmarks increased dramatically during his tenure as chairman of the Senate Appropriations Committee and ultimately sparked a backlash from fiscal conservatives. "I'll take on anyone. They are not waste," Stevens said in a 2004 interview.

In 1984, after eight years of defending congressional perks and enforcing party discipline as Republican whip, the combative lawmaker made a bid to succeed Howard H. Baker Jr. of Tennessee as majority leader. While he outpolled three others, Stevens — a moderate on social issues by his party's standards — lost to Bob Dole of Kansas by three votes on the final ballot.

TOP APPROPRIATOR

Stevens made his biggest mark as an appropriator, joining the panel in 1972 and serving as chairman for much of 1997 to 2005 — except the 18 months that Democrats controlled the chamber in 2001 and 2002. From 2003 to 2007, Stevens was third in line for the presidency as Senate president pro tempore. Stevens forged a lasting friendship with Daniel K. Inouye, D-Hawaii. Both entered the Senate soon after their states were admitted and used the appropriations process to help modernize them. Inouye said in a statement following his friend's death, "Our friendship was a very special one. . . . I have lost my brother."

In 2005, Stevens defended his infamous "bridge to nowhere" earmark, designed to connect the small city of Ketchikan with a sparsely populated island at a cost of $223 million, against an attempt to amend the law and eliminate it. The defeat of the amendment was seen as a sign of lawmakers' unwillingness to end earmarks, including their own.

Under GOP term limits, Stevens gave up the Appropriations gavel in 2005 and became chairman of the Commerce, Science and Transportation Committee, remaining its ranking Republican when Democrats took control of the Senate in 2007.

Stevens also waged a long-running but ultimately unsuccessful battle against environmental groups to open Alaska's Arctic National Wildlife Refuge to oil and gas drilling. At one point in 2005, the Alaskan vowed to visit the constituents of those who voted against him and "tell them what you've done."

Stevens' Senate career ended soon after he was found guilty Oct. 27, 2008, on seven corruption charges of making false statements on financial disclosure forms. Federal prosecutors charged that Stevens failed to disclose that he had netted more than $250,000 from 1999 to 2006 in benefits from an oil services company and its CEO. Begich narrowly defeated Stevens the following week.

In early 2009, however, Attorney General Eric H. Holder Jr. sought to void the conviction, citing the government's failure to provide crucial evidence concerning a key witness's account to the former senator's defense attorneys. A federal judge threw out the conviction. (*Story, 2009 Almanac, p. 5-10*)

Stevens hailed from Indiana and lived in California and elsewhere in the West. After the war, he graduated from Harvard Law School. He moved to Alaska in 1953 to work in a law firm. He later served in the Eisenhower administration's Interior Department, where he advocated for statehood, achieved in 1959.

REP. JOHN P. MURTHA

The old-school style of legislative logrolling lost perhaps its most powerful practitioner when Murtha died Feb. 8 after suffering complications from gallbladder surgery. The 77-year-old Murtha, who was first elected in 1974, died in Arlington, Va., two days after becoming the longest-serving member of the House from his state.

As chairman or ranking member of the House Defense Appropriations Subcommittee for 21 years, Murtha oversaw hundreds of billions of dollars in annual military spending and was often able to speed the Pentagon's annual budget through Congress by giving lawmakers what they wanted back home in return for their votes.

He routinely positioned himself in the last seat on the right in the back row of the chamber, in what became known as Murtha's Corner. Lawmakers would go there to pay tribute if they hoped for favorable consideration of special projects in their districts.

But Murtha's method of doing business — earmarking money for colleagues' projects to advance his own priorities — had already begun losing its luster under the public spotlight as voters came to disdain such practices. More seriously, the Justice Department was taking a look at Murtha's actions, especially his dealings with lobbyists and some other lawmakers.

Murtha wielded his clout unapologetically and was prolific in obtaining federal help for his economically distressed district. In fiscal 2009 alone, he secured $114.5 million for 47 projects in Pennsylvania, according to the watchdog group Taxpayers for Common Sense.

The John Murtha Johnstown-Cambria County Airport in the district's largest municipality — with a population of 22,000 — benefited from tens of millions of dollars in federally funded improvements. Its

only regular commercial service was three round trips daily to Washington Dulles International Airport in Northern Virginia.

AN ADVOCATE FOR THE TROOPS

A burly Marine veteran who won a Bronze Star and two Purple Hearts in Vietnam and then served in the reserve until retiring as a colonel in 1990, Murtha was known for his blunt and salty talk, his passion for military might, and his protectiveness of the Pentagon and its budget.

As he oversaw a steady increase in defense spending, Murtha frequently traveled to war zones and military hospitals to talk to troops and observe conditions. "Generals, they have to talk the party line," he said. "But the troops give me a lot of information about what's going on that I can't get almost anyplace else."

That reputation catapulted Murtha to national prominence when he announced in November 2005 that he was dropping his support for the Iraq War, which he labeled "a flawed policy wrapped in illusion."

The switch made Murtha a darling of the anti-war left, with whom he previously had little in common. An exception was his longtime friendship with liberal Speaker Nancy Pelosi, D-Calif., whose career he helped boost. She returned the favor by backing Murtha for majority leader after Democrats won control of the House in 2006. Pelosi aides said they warned Murtha he would lose, but he pressed ahead. Steny H. Hoyer of Maryland won in a rout, 149-86.

John Patrick "Jack" Murtha Jr. grew up in Mount Pleasant, Pa. His father ran a gas station and car wash. Murtha left college to join the Marines in 1952. After a three-year hitch, he earned an economics degree from the University of Pittsburgh. He was on active duty again in 1966 and 1967 and won a state House seat in 1968. After a special election in early 1974, he became the first Vietnam combat veteran in Congress.

He first gained notoriety in 1980 during the Abscam probe, in which FBI agents posed as wealthy Saudis trying to bribe congressmen to gain admittance to the United States. Murtha was recorded being offered $50,000. "I'm not interested . . . at this point," he said on tape, but if "we do business for a while, maybe I'll be interested, maybe I won't." He then offered to provide names of businesses in his district where the fake Saudis could invest legally to create jobs. Named an unindicted co-conspirator, Murtha testified against two Democratic colleagues. Six members of Congress were convicted of bribery. *(Abscam, 1981 Almanac, p. 388)*

His other brush with trouble began in 2009, when investigators raided the offices of the PMA Group, a since-defunct lobbying firm with ties to Murtha. The firm closed its political action committee amid reports that the FBI was probing possibly illegal contributions.

News stories said federal agents had raided Kuchera Industries, a Johnstown company whose owners hosted a Murtha fundraiser. The stories also said the Justice Department was investigating Concurrent Technologies Corp., a government contractor based in Johnstown that geared up with Murtha earmarks.

In response, Murtha was his blunt self. "If I'm corrupt, it is because I take care of my district," he told the Pittsburgh Post-Gazette. ∎

Chapter 6

DEFENSE, INTELLIGENCE & FOREIGN POLICY

Defense Authorization Survives Setbacks to Reach President's Desk

THE HOUSE CLEARED a stripped-down fiscal 2011 defense authorization bill on the last day of the 111th Congress, two days before Christmas. President Obama signed the measure into law on Jan. 7, 2011 (HR 6523 — PL 111-383). The bill nearly became the first defense authorization in 49 years not to reach the president's desk.

The fiscal 2011 bill authorized $724.6 billion for national security programs, at the departments of Defense and Energy, roughly equal to the president's request for $725.9 billion and about 7 percent more than was authorized under the fiscal 2010 law (PL 111-84). *(2009 Almanac, p. 6-3)*

Although most of the funding could be provided through the appropriations process without an authorization, the bill included some must-pass provisions, such as a 1.4 percent pay raise for military personnel, and it allowed the Armed Services committees to weigh in with policy prescriptions for numerous defense programs. For example, it barred the release into the United States, or the transfer to the United States, of detainees from the U.S. facility at Guantánamo Bay, Cuba, in fiscal 2011.

Of the total authorization, $565.9 billion was considered the base defense budget and $158.7 billion was dedicated to the wars in Afghanistan and Iraq and the general war on terrorism.

There was little disagreement over general funding levels, despite worries about the deficit. The chief stumbling block was language that would have repealed the 1993 law (PL 103-160) known as "don't ask, don't tell," which barred openly gay personnel from serving in the military.

The final version, negotiated by leaders of the House and Senate Armed Services committees, omitted the language on gay servicemembers as well as controversial language on abortions and authorization for an alternative engine for the F-35 Joint Strike Fighter. The bill did not set specific funding levels for particular programs in most cases.

The House passed an initial version of the bill (HR 5136) in May that would have authorized $725.9 billion for defense programs in fiscal 2011, including $159.3 billion specifically for operations in Iraq and Afghanistan. Lawmakers added "don't ask, don't tell" repeal language on the floor. The bill also authorized unrequested funds for the alternative engine for the F-35, a provision that elicited a veto threat from the White House.

The Senate Armed Services Committee approved a companion measure (S 3454), also in May. The bill would have authorized $725.7 billion for defense programs and included a provision to repeal "don't ask, don't tell." That language, and to a lesser degree a provision to allow privately funded abortions in overseas military

BOX SCORE

BILL: HR 6523 — PL 111-383

LEGISLATIVE ACTION:

House passed HR 5136 (H Rept 111-491, Parts 1 and 2), 229-186, on May 28.

Senate rejected cloture on S 3454 (S Rept 111-201), 57-40, on Dec. 9; 60 votes required.

House passed HR 6523, 341-48, on Dec. 17.

Senate passed HR 6523, amended, by unanimous consent Dec. 22.

House cleared the bill by voice vote Dec. 22.

President signed the bill Jan. 7, 2011.

hospitals, effectively prevented the bill from reaching the Senate floor.

After the Senate rejected two attempts to cut off a filibuster, it became clear that the measure could not pass without significant revision. At that point, proponents of a "don't ask, don't tell" repeal, including Sen. Joseph I. Lieberman, I-Conn., introduced stand-alone legislation in both chambers. That bill cleared Dec. 18 (PL 111-321). *(Repeal, p. 6-7)*

In the meantime, the chairmen of the House and Senate Armed Services committees announced that they had reached agreement on a scaled-back fiscal 2011 defense authorization that did not include "don't ask, don't tell" or any other controversial provisions. The measure sailed through Congress, clearing just as the session was about to end.

HIGHLIGHTS

The authorization for the Pentagon's base budget included $168.2 billion for operations and maintenance, $138.5 billion for military personnel costs and $110.4 billion for procurement.

Following are some of the bill's main components:

● **Missile defense.** More than $10 billion was authorized for missile defense programs, $1 billion above the fiscal 2010 level. The bill supported funding for the initial deployment of a national missile defense system based in Alaska and California, as well as the Obama administration's new plan for missile defense in Europe — a largely sea-based system focused on protecting Europe from short- and medium-range Iranian missiles. Obama's strategy replaced President George W. Bush's controversial plan to locate antimissile interceptors and radar facilities in Poland and the Czech Republic.

The committee said it fully supported the president's new approach to missile defense, but it limited the funds for deployment until host countries signed and ratified the necessary agreements. The bill also limited deployment until the Defense secretary certified that the technology was effective, based on successful, realistic flight testing.

The measure also authorized $205 million for Israel's "Iron Dome" antimissile defense system.

It repealed an existing ban on contracting with a foreign government or foreign business for research, development, testing or evaluation related to missile defense.

● **Aircraft.** The base Pentagon authorization for aircraft procurement included $14.7 billion for the Air Force, $18.9 billion for the Navy and $5.9 billion for the Army.

The military's tactical aircraft included three major programs — the F/A-18 Super Hornet, the primary strike aircraft of both the Navy and the Marine Corps; the Air Force's F-22A Raptor, which had ended

Petraeus Takes Over in Afghanistan

ARMY GEN. DAVID H. PETRAEUS WON swift confirmation as the new commander of U.S. forces in Afghanistan, replacing Army Gen. Stanley A. McChrystal, who was forced to step down after Rolling Stone magazine quoted disparaging remarks he had made about the Obama administration.

Petraeus, who was serving as the head of Central Command, had led the troop "surge" in Iraq and wrote the U.S. counterinsurgency operations policy. Senate endorsement was never in doubt because Petraeus was widely respected on Capitol Hill.

The Senate confirmed his nomination, 99-0, on June 30, one day after the Armed Services Committee agreed by voice vote to send it to the floor. *(Senate vote 203, p. S-43)*

In a statement after the Senate vote, President Obama said he was "extremely grateful" for the quick action. "Petraeus' unrivaled experience will ensure we do not miss a beat in our strategy to break the Taliban's momentum and build Afghan capacity," he said.

John McCain of Arizona, ranking Republican on the Armed Services Committee, praised McChrystal's career without discussing his departure. But McCain also praised Petraeus and said Obama's decision to nominate him to succeed McChrystal demonstrated the president's continued commitment to the U.S. mission in Afghanistan. "He has proved that we can win wars," McCain said of Petraeus, "and we need to give him every opportunity."

At the same time, McCain reiterated his opposition to the July 2011 target date Obama had set to begin a withdrawal of U.S. troops from Afghanistan.

Republicans raised the issue repeatedly in Petraeus' June 29 confirmation hearing, saying the deadline sent a mixed message to U.S. allies and enemies alike. They said the president should clearly state that the withdrawal would be based solely on conditions on the ground.

Petraeus, however, left no doubt about his support for the president's plan. He said the withdrawal date helped convey to Afghans the need to take over their own security quickly and build a sustainable government. "As the president has also indicated," the general told the Senate committee, "July 2011 is not a date when we will be rapidly withdrawing our forces and 'switching off the lights and closing the door behind us.'"

But he also acknowledged that the going had been, and was likely to remain, difficult.

Obama announced his nomination of Petraeus on June 23, immediately after relieving McChrystal of his command. "War is bigger than any one man or woman, whether a private, a general or a president," he said.

"The conduct represented in the recently published article does not meet the standard that should be set by a commanding general," Obama said. "It undermines the civilian control of the military that is at the core of our democratic system."

production; and the joint service F-35 Joint Strike Fighter, which had just entered initial production.

The Government Accountability Office (GAO) estimated that the total cost of the three aircraft programs could be well over $400 billion, with annual production costs of $14 billion to $18 billion, before inflation. Continued cost overruns and extended development times had reduced the department's buying power, with the result that the Pentagon planned to replace existing aircraft with about one-third fewer new planes than originally planned.

● **F-35 engine program.** The bill neither endorsed nor prevented additional spending on an alternative engine for the F-35. Congress had continued the second engine, built by Rolls-Royce and General Electric, over the objections of the Pentagon, which argued that the engine being built by Pratt & Whitney was reliable and that the funding was sorely needed elsewhere in the defense budget. Proponents argued that the competition would produce a more cost-effective and reliable engine.

● **Ground Combat Vehicle.** The Ground Combat Vehicle was the Army's proposed replacement for armored fighting vehicles that were part of the Future Combat Systems, a complex, technically challenged and costly system that was canceled in 2009. The bill authorized the administration's request of $461 million for the vehicle, but it withheld some of the funds until the authorizers received requested program documentation.

● **Navy shipbuilding.** The bill authorized $15.7 billion for Navy ship construction and refurbishment.

● **National Guard and Reserve equipment.** The authorizers said severe equipment shortfalls continued across non-deployed National Guard and Reserve units, particularly among items that were critical for dual-use roles of combat operations and domestic emergencies. The bill, therefore, authorized $7.2 billion, $700 million or 10 percent more than requested, for the guard and reserves. The total included funding for aircraft missiles, wheeled and tracked combat vehicles, ammunition, small arms, and tactical radios.

● **Personnel.** The bill set a ceiling of 1.4 million on the number of total active-duty military personnel in fiscal 2011, equal to the president's request and 7,400 above the authorized fiscal 2010 level. The total included 569,400 for the Army, 328,700 for the Navy, 332,200 for the Air Force and 202,100 for the Marine Corps. The limit for the National Guard and Reserve was 856,200. The number of reserve personnel that could be placed on active duty was limited to 78,846, roughly the same as in fiscal 2010.

● **Military pay raise.** Military personnel received a 1.4 percent across-the-board pay raise, equal to the president's request.

● **Defense Health Program.** The bill authorized $31 billion for the Pentagon's defense health care programs, plus an additional $1.4 billion as part of the Iraq-Afghanistan section of the bill.

● **Nuclear weapons programs.** About $17.7 billion was authorized for defense-related activities at the Energy Department. The total included the president's request of $11.2 billion for operating nuclear weapons laboratories and for programs operated by the National Nuclear Security Administration, and $6.5 billion for environmental restoration, waste management and other defense activities, also equal to the request. The National Nuclear Security Administration funding was $1.2 billion more than the fiscal 2010 level, with $624 million of the extra funding to maintain the

existing nuclear stockpile and $551 million for non-proliferation efforts. The stockpile funding was tied to congressional approval of the New Strategic Arms Reduction Treaty, which was ratified the day the defense bill cleared. *(New START, p. 6-8)*

● **Military construction.** The bill authorized $18.2 billion for military construction and family housing projects, including $2.7 billion for base realignment and closure and $1.8 billion for family housing. Additional funds were included in the war funding section of the bill.

● **Overseas contingency operations.** The bill authorized the president's request of $158.7 billion specifically for the wars in Afghanistan and Iraq and the general war on terrorism, although funding authorized elsewhere in the bill could be used to support those operations as well.

The measure also authorized $33.1 billion that had been provided in the fiscal 2010 supplemental appropriations act (PL 111-212) for the surge of additional forces in Afghanistan and in support of relief operations in Haiti in the aftermath of a major earthquake.

The fiscal 2011 total included $114 billion for operations and maintenance, $24.7 billion for procurement and $15.3 billion for personnel.

Among the individual accounts, the bill authorized:

▸ $3.4 billion for Mine Resistant Ambush Protected vehicles.

▸ $3.5 billion to procure and develop countermeasures to prevent improvised explosive device attacks.

▸ $11.6 billion, as requested, for training and equipping Afghanistan's security forces.

▸ $1.5 billion for the Iraqi security forces, $500 million less than requested. The Iraqi government was required to pay at least 20 percent of the cost of procuring items or services, other than major military equipment.

▸ $4 billion in special transfer authority within the overseas contingency account in fiscal 2011.

▸ $506 million for the Commanders' Emergency Response Program, which provided U.S. military commanders in Iraq and Afghanistan with funds for use in small humanitarian and reconstruction projects.

2010 LEGISLATIVE ACTION

HOUSE COMMITTEE

The House Armed Services Committee approved a $725.9 billion authorization bill (HR 5136 — H Rept 111-491, Parts 1 and 2) by a vote of 59-0 on May 19. The panel's six subcommittees had each drafted sections of the measure, which included $159.3 billion to support operations in Afghanistan and Iraq and reflected some differences with the Obama administration over priorities.

As approved by the committee, the bill would have:

▸ Made no changes to the "don't ask, don't tell" policy.

▸ Prohibited the transfer of detainees from Guantánamo to the United States unless the president submitted a comprehensive disposition plan and risk assessment report to Congress. The language by Chairman Ike Skelton, D-Mo., adopted 31-28, replaced a proposal by J. Randy Forbes, R-Va., that would have barred the transfer or release of any detainees into the United States.

▸ Authorized $485 million in fiscal 2011 for an alternative engine for the F-35.

▸ Authorized $11 billion for the F-35 fighter but withheld 25 percent of the funding until the Pentagon certified that all

funds for development and procurement of the fighter's propulsion system had been spent. It also limited the funding to 30 jets, rather than the 42 requested by Obama, until certain conditions were met.

▸ Authorized $500 million to fund eight additional F/A-18 Super Hornet aircraft beyond the 22 that the president requested. The language by Todd Akin, R-Mo., was adopted by voice vote.

▸ Prohibited the Air Force or the Air National Guard from retiring fighter aircraft in fiscal 2011 until the GAO completed a review of the fighter jet inventory, language added by Frank A. LoBiondo, R-N.J., and Gabrielle Giffords, D-Ariz.

▸ Approved a 1.9 percent pay raise for military personnel — half a percentage point more than requested. The Congressional Budget Office estimated the increase would cost an additional $2.4 billion over five years.

▸ Preserved the Pentagon's ability to convert more jobs held by contractors to full-time civilian employee positions. The language, by Jim Langevin, D-R.I., was adopted by voice vote.

HOUSE FLOOR

The House passed the bill, 229-186, on May 28, after agreeing the previous day to add a repeal of "don't ask, don't tell." *(House vote 336, p. H-120)*

The repeal amendment, by Patrick J. Murphy, D-Pa., was adopted 234-194. Reflecting an agreement announced by the Pentagon and the White House, it allowed for implementation only after the Pentagon finished a review of the implications of a repeal and top administration officials certified that it would not hurt readiness. *(House vote 317, p. H-114)*

During the floor action, the House also:

▸ Adopted, 282-131, a procedural motion by Forbes that had the effect of toughening the Guantánamo language to bar the transfer or release of any detainees into the United States. *(House vote 335, p. H-120)*

▸ Rejected, 193-231, an amendment by Chellie Pingree, D-Maine, to strike the $485 million for the second F-35 engine, which she called "a complete waste of money." *(House vote 316, p. H-114)*

▸ Adopted, 218-210, an amendment by Anna G. Eshoo, D-Calif., to allow the GAO to investigate intelligence agencies at the request of congressional committees. The proposal was opposed by the administration. *(House vote 315, p. H-114)*

Hours before the House passed the bill, the White House Office of Management and Budget released a statement saying that Obama's advisers would recommend he veto the bill if it authorized funding for the second F-35 engine. The White House also strongly objected to the limits on procurement of the F-35 jets and warned of a veto if the bill would "seriously disrupt" the program.

SENATE COMMITTEE

The Senate Armed Services Committee approved its version of the bill (S 3454 — S Rept 111-201) by a mostly party-line vote of 18-10 in a closed-door session May 27. The bill totaled $725.7 billion, about $200 million less than in the president's request or the House bill, and included $159.3 billion for operations in Afghanistan and Iraq.

The contentiousness of the measure was underscored May 28 when the panel's ranking Republican, John McCain of Arizona, departed from tradition by not joining Chairman Carl Levin, D-Mich., at a news conference after the markup.

As approved by the committee, the bill would have:

▸ Repealed the "don't ask, don't tell" law. The amendment, by Lieberman — which was identical to the language approved in the House — was adopted 16-12. The amendment prompted warnings from Republicans that they would filibuster the bill on the floor.

▸ Allowed abortions to be performed at military hospitals, if paid for with private money.

▸ Directed the president to send 6,000 National Guard troops to the U.S.-Mexico border. The provision, by McCain, was adopted 15-13 and was strongly opposed by the White House.

▸ Authorized a 1.4 percent across-the-board pay raise for military personnel — the amount requested by the president, but less than the 1.9 percent in the House bill.

▸ Omitted authorization for a second F-35 engine. Levin said he hoped it would be added in conference.

▸ Met Obama's request of $11.5 billion to purchase 42 F-35 jets.

▸ Authorized six additional F/A-18s.

SENATE FLOOR

Chances for clearing the bill — and with it repeal of the "don't ask, don't tell" law — seemed all but lost Dec. 9, when Republicans blocked an attempt to take up the measure. The Senate voted, 57-40, to reject a motion to invoke cloture and end a GOP filibuster. Democrats attracted only one Republican supporter, Susan Collins of Maine, and fell three votes short of the 60 needed. *(Senate vote 270, p. S-55)*

It was the second time Republicans had prevented the Senate from proceeding to the bill. The first cloture motion was defeated, 56-43, on Sept. 21 amid partisan wrangling in advance of the midterm election; Reid voted "no" on procedural grounds to preserve his right to seek another vote later. *(Senate vote 238, p. S-50)*

Prospects for further action were clouded by the limited time remaining on the Senate calendar and a Republican caucus that had stayed nearly united on its vow to hold up all legislation until major tax and spending bills were completed.

COMPROMISE BILL

Considered problematic just two weeks earlier, the defense authorization cleared easily in the final day of the session after leaders agreed on a stripped-down version (HR 6523) that dropped a number of disputed provisions, most notably the "don't ask, don't tell" repeal. The House passed the new version, 341-48, on Dec. 17. The Senate passed it by unanimous consent Dec. 22, after removing a small provision that would have authorized funds for the victims of atrocities committed by the Japanese forces that occupied Guam during World War II. The House cleared the measure by voice vote Dec. 22. *(House vote 650, p. H-226)*

In modifying the bill, the leaders also dropped the provisions requiring that National Guard troops be deployed to the Southwest border and allowing privately funded abortions in military hospitals. Authorization to continue developing a second F-35 engine was also deleted.

However, the bill still contained significant policy provisions. The managers included language similar to that in the House bill to bar the use of authorized fiscal 2011 Pentagon funds to release or transfer to the United States any of the Guantánamo detainees who were not U.S. citizens. Sen. Mark Steven Kirk, R-Ill., had threatened to block the revised bill without the ban.

In signing the bill, the president issued a statement opposing the provision as a "dangerous and unprecedented challenge to critical executive branch authority."

The bill also prohibited the use of funding authorized by the bill to construct or modify facilities in the United States to detain or imprison any of the detainees.

Aides said the requirement that the Iraqi government pay 20 percent of the cost of certain types of equipment could save the U.S. government about $300 million.

The final bill included provisions aimed at strengthening oversight of not only weapons contracts but the acquisition of services such as systems engineering and logistics.

The authorizers took aim at particular initiatives that had experienced trouble. The Pentagon was required to set up a management process to more closely monitor results in the F-35 Joint Strike Fighter program, which had been hit by technical setbacks that created years of delay and billions of dollars in additional costs.

In their managers' statement, the authorizers also said "Congress expects" continued production of F-18 fighter jets in the meantime "to prevent our naval air power from losing significance in our nation's arsenal." ∎

'Don't Ask, Don't Tell' Repeal Clears

AFTER YEARS OF BATTLING and months of legislative maneuvering, gay rights advocates won a landmark victory as Congress cleared legislation repealing the "don't ask, don't tell" law that banned openly gay people from serving in the military. President Obama signed the legislation into law Dec. 22 (HR 2965 — PL 111-321).

"We are not a nation that says, 'Don't ask, don't tell,'" Obama said at a signing ceremony. "We are a nation that says, 'Out of many, we are one.'" In a statement after the bill cleared, Obama said, "By ending 'don't ask, don't tell,' no longer will our nation be denied the service of thousands of patriotic Americans forced to leave the military, despite years of exemplary performance, because they happen to be gay. And no longer will many thousands more be asked to live a lie in order to serve the country they love."

Although the Defense Department was given latitude on how and when to carry out the provisions, the legislation essentially overturned a 1993 law (PL 103-160) that had been the subject of heated political controversy for nearly a generation. Obama had promised to end the 17-year-old law during his presidential campaign, and in his 2010 State of the Union address, he vowed to work with Congress to make that a reality. *(Text, p. D-3; law, 1993 Almanac, p. 454)*

The repeal had strong backing from Defense Secretary Robert M. Gates as well as Joint Chiefs Chairman Adm. Mike Mullen and Vice Chairman Gen. James E. Cartwright. They cited a Pentagon survey, made public Nov. 30, that found that 70 percent of U.S. military personnel surveyed believed a change in the law would have positive, mixed or no effects.

Gates said he would not allow the change until he was satisfied that all necessary training and education was completed across the military. The secretary, in particular, had warned he did not want the law overturned by the courts, which could require an immediate change and allow little time for the military to prepare. Concern that the courts would act before Congress did was heightened by judicial rulings that the existing policy was unconstitutional. Those rulings were under appeal.

The chiefs of the Army, Marine Corps and Air Force were more hesitant. In testimony before the Senate Armed Services Committee on Dec. 3, they expressed varying degrees of concern about the potential effect of the repeal on military morale and readiness, and they agreed that the change should not happen soon.

After the vote clearing the bill, Aubrey Sarvis, the executive director of the Servicemembers Legal Defense Network, an advocacy group, cautioned gay and lesbian servicemembers to continue to abide by the "don't ask, don't tell" limitations until the repeal was implemented. "Even with this historic vote," Sarvis wrote, "servicemembers must continue to serve in silence until repeal is final."

The question of allowing gays and lesbians to serve openly in the U.S. military had been a topic of national debate for almost two decades. The 1993 law became the basis for the military's "don't ask, don't tell" policy. The law itself banned service by military personnel who engaged in homosexual conduct, including declaring their homosexual-

BOX SCORE

BILL: HR 2965 — PL 111-321

LEGISLATIVE ACTION:

House passed HR 2965, 250-175, on Dec. 15.

Senate cleared the bill, 65-31, on Dec. 18.

President signed the bill Dec. 22.

ity or marrying someone of the same sex. It did not address the issue of sexual "orientation" or prohibit commanders from asking about an individual's orientation, although that became part of the Pentagon policy.

HIGHLIGHTS

In overturning the 1993 law, the bill specified that the repeal would take effect only after the president transmitted to the Armed Services committees written certification — signed by the president, Defense secretary and chairman of the Joint Chiefs of Staff — that ending the ban would not harm the military.

The certification had to indicate that the officials had considered the report on the department's review of the existing policy; that the Defense Department had prepared the necessary policy and regulations; and that their implementation would be consistent with standards of military readiness, military effectiveness, unit cohesion, and recruiting and retention of the armed forces. If all conditions were met, then the relevant provision of law would be repealed, effective 60 days after the certification.

Until then, existing law remained in effect.

The measure also stipulated that it could not be construed to require the provision of benefits in violation of the Defense of Marriage Act (PL 104-199), which defined "marriage" as a legal union between one man and one woman as husband and wife, and defined "spouse" as referring only to a person of the opposite sex who was a husband or a wife.

2010 LEGISLATIVE ACTION
DEFENSE AUTHORIZATION

Before passing its version of the 2011 defense authorization bill (HR 5136) on May 28, the House adopted an amendment to repeal the 1993 law, conditional on the Pentagon finishing its review of the implications of a repeal and top administration officials certifying that it would not hurt readiness. The amendment, by Patrick J. Murphy, D-Pa., reflected an agreement backed by the Pentagon and the White House. It was adopted 234-194. *(House vote 317, p. H-114)*

In the Senate, the Armed Services Committee approved a defense bill (S 3454) on May 27 that contained identical repeal language. The language by Joseph I. Lieberman, I-Conn., was adopted 16-12. All but one Democrat, Jim Webb of Virginia, voted for it, while all but one Republican, Susan Collins of Maine, voted "nay."

The bill never reached the Senate floor due to a GOP filibuster sparked by the "don't ask, don't tell" language and other controversial provisions, as well as Republican complaints about a limit on the number of amendments that could be offered. When the second cloture motion on the bill was rejected Dec. 9, it was clear that the repeal language, among other provisions, had to be dropped if the defense authorization was to have a chance of becoming law.

STAND-ALONE BILL

At that point, Lieberman and Collins introduced a stand-alone version of the repeal language; Murphy and Majority Leader Steny H.

Hoyer, D-Md., did the same in the House. With the clock running out on the session, Democratic leaders took a crucial step to shorten the time the Senate would spend on the bill. They inserted the repeal into an unrelated bill (HR 2965) that both chambers had passed in different forms, passed it 250-175 on Dec. 15 and sent the amended measure back to the Senate. Under Senate rules, that prevented a filibuster on a motion to take up the bill. *(House vote 638, p. H-222)*

With all Democrats present and eight Republicans voting yes, the Senate cleared the bill, 65-31, on Dec. 18. The vote came hours after senators voted, 63-33, to limit floor debate. The eight Republicans backing the repeal were Collins and Olympia J. Snowe of Maine, Lisa Murkowski of Alaska, George V. Voinovich of Ohio, Mark Steven Kirk of Illinois, Scott P. Brown of Massachusetts, John Ensign of Nevada and Richard M. Burr of North Carolina. *(Senate votes 281, 279, p. S-57)*

Pivotal backing for the bill in the Senate came from Webb, who said he had received a letter from Gates dated Dec. 17 confirming that his earlier concerns about the repeal's potential effect on unit cohesion could be addressed.

Most of the votes against final passage came from conservative Republicans, some of whom suggested that the time devoted to the vote on "don't ask, don't tell" hurt the chances that they would support

approval of ratification of an arms control treaty with Russia (Treaty Doc 111-5), another item on the Senate's end-of-session agenda. *(Defense authorization, p. 6-3; New START, p. 6-8)*

Obama's 2008 opponent in the presidential race, Senate Armed Services ranking Republican John McCain of Arizona, called the procedural vote to limit floor debate on the repeal measure "a very sad day."

"So here we are about six weeks after an election that repudiated the agenda of the other side," McCain said of the midterm results. "We are jamming or trying to jam major issues through the Senate of the United States because they know they can't get it done beginning next Jan. 5," when the new Congress was set to convene with a GOP-controlled House and a larger force of Republicans in the Senate.

GOP strategist John Ullyot, a former spokesman for the Senate Armed Services panel, suggested that the Republicans who sided with McCain were battling a strong social trend against their viewpoint.

"Republican opposition had a 'going-through-the motions' feel to it, and the tone seemed cranky and outdated," Ullyot said. "We will probably all look back in five years and wonder what the fuss was about and see this as a missed opportunity to move the party to the center on what is likely to be viewed by future generations as a major vote on social policy." ∎

Arms Treaty OK'd at End of Session

DEMOCRATS SCORED THEIR biggest victory of the lame-duck session on the final day of the 111th Congress, when the Senate approved a nuclear arms treaty with Russia that continued the long tradition of bilateral arms accords ratified by the world's two pre-eminent nuclear powers.

Action on the new strategic arms reduction treaty, known as New START (Treaty Doc 111-5), sealed a hard-fought victory for President Obama and proved a stinging rebuke to Republican leaders who sought to block a vote.

Vice President Joseph R. Biden Jr., who led the Obama administration's lobbying effort on the treaty, presided over the Senate for the final ballot.

"This treaty will enhance our leadership to stop the spread of nuclear weapons and seek the peace of a world without them," Obama said at a news conference afterward. "The strong bipartisan vote in the Senate sends a powerful signal to the world that Republicans and Democrats stand together on behalf of our security."

The vote on the "resolution of advice and consent to ratification" followed a tireless White House lobbying effort reinforced by strong Pentagon backing and the support of a veritable who's who of the nation's foreign policy establishment, not to mention the senator long seen as Republicans' unchallenged expert on the subject: Richard G. Lugar of Indiana, the ranking member on the Senate Foreign Relations Committee.

The many high-profile supporters included five former secretaries of State: Colin L. Powell, James A. Baker III, Lawrence S. Eagleburger, George P. Shultz and Henry A. Kissinger.

The intense administration effort and the determination of Senate Majority Leader Harry Reid, D-Nev., to finish the bill before adjourn-

BOX SCORE

BILL: Treaty Doc 111-5

....

LEGISLATIVE ACTION:

Senate approved the resolution of ratification, 71-26, on Dec. 22.

ment helped overcome staunch opposition to a vote before 2011 from Senate Minority Leader Mitch McConnell, R-Ky., and Jon Kyl, R-Ariz., the minority whip and GOP point man on the treaty.

Obama and Russian President Dmitry Medvedev signed the treaty in April 2010 after almost a year of talks. Obama said he deemed it "an important first step forward" in global nonproliferation efforts. But, he added, "it is just one step on a longer journey."

The administration and members of the arms control community regarded the treaty as the sort of modest, straightforward agreement that the White House could get done relatively swiftly before mounting more-ambitious negotiations. There was also broad support for resuming inspection of Russia's nuclear weapons program.

Some arms control advocates even worried that the negotiated cuts to deployed nuclear warheads, which amounted to a 30 percent reduction from the levels of the 2002 Moscow Treaty (approved by the Senate, 95-0, in 2003) were too slight.

Some Republicans, however, maintained that the treaty could have a negative impact on the nation's missile defenses and national security. They also warned that Russia's record on past treaties demonstrates that it should not be trusted.

Kyl had less experience on nuclear issues than Lugar, but he was passionate and determined, and, for most of the debate, the GOP caucus followed his lead. The White House spent months negotiating with him, acceding to his demands for guarantees on funding for modernization of the nation's aging nuclear stockpile and a firm commitment to missile defense.

But when Kyl continued his opposition, maintaining that there was not enough time for sufficient debate, administration officials turned their focus to securing the nine necessary Republican votes, one by one. That strategy was seen initially as a last resort — and possibly futile — but the gamble paid off.

The treaty officially entered into force on Feb. 5, 2011, with the exchange of Instruments of Ratification between Secretary of State Hillary Rodham Clinton and Russian Foreign Minister Sergey Lavrov in Munich.

HIGHLIGHTS

The following are the main provisions of the New START agreement:

- **Limits on nuclear weapons.**
  - ▸ No more than 1,550 deployed warheads per side.
  - ▸ No more than 700 deployed launchers and bombers per side.
  - ▸ No more than 800 nuclear-capable missile launchers and heavy bombers per side.
- **Monitoring and verification.**
  - ▸ Each side allowed to make up to 18 short-notice on-site inspections per year. Regular inspections were part of the START accord that expired in December 2009.
  - ▸ Parties required to exchange data by keeping an extensive database with numbers, types and locations of items limited by the treaty.
  - ▸ Interference with the other side's satellite observations prohibited. The treaty provided for exchange of test data (telemetry) on up to five missile flight tests annually.
- **Ballistic missile defense.**
  - ▸ Conversion of nuclear missile launchers into ballistic missile defense launchers prohibited.
  - ▸ No limit on the number or capabilities of ballistic missile defenses.
- **Other provisions.**
  - ▸ More flexible rules for what had to be done to eliminate a launcher or heavy bomber from the counted supply.
  - ▸ Mobile ICBMs subject to ICBM launcher limits.

2010 LEGISLATIVE ACTION

SENATE COMMITTEE

The Senate Foreign Relations Committee voted 14-4 on Sept. 16 to send the resolution of ratification to the floor. Three Republicans — Lugar, Bob Corker of Tennessee and Johnny Isakson of Georgia — joined all the committee Democrats in support.

Before the vote, the panel gave voice vote approval to a Lugar substitute that added new conditions on how the treaty would be implemented. The language stated that the resolution would not "impose any limitations on the deployment of missile defenses" — a key concern raised by Republicans on the panel.

The amendment also required the president to submit to Congress a plan for dealing with any future resource shortfalls associated with paying for his 10-year, $180 billion plan to modernize the U.S. nuclear weapons stockpile.

By amending the resolution of ratification, the panel was able to include its input on the treaty without reopening negotiations.

Lugar's changes were sufficient to persuade Corker and Isakson to back the treaty, and both Lugar and John Kerry of Massachusetts, chairman of the Foreign Relations Committee, expressed optimism that the accord would win the necessary support from the full Senate.

SENATE FLOOR

Thirteen Republicans joined all 58 members of the Democratic caucus to approve the resolution of ratification in a 71-26 vote on Dec. 22. *(Senate vote 298, p. S-60)*

In a pivotal test, the Senate voted, 67-28, on Dec. 21 to bring debate on the treaty to a close; Democrats had the help of 11 Republicans. The success of the cloture vote started the clock on a potential 30 hours of debate, but with the outcome clear, opponents allowed a final vote the following afternoon. *(Senate vote 292, p. S-59)*

Democrats, led by Kerry, fended off attempts to alter the treaty, which would certainly have killed it.

Before the final vote, the Senate adopted by voice vote two Republican amendments to the resolution.

The first, sponsored by Arizona Republican John McCain, Connecticut independent Joseph I. Lieberman and several others, required the president to certify that the United States did not recognize Russia's argument that the treaty would be viable only when the United States was not building up its missile defenses. The amendment also added language making clear that Congress did not see the treaty's preamble as legally binding.

The other amendment, offered by Kyl, required the president to certify a way forward to fund the facilities that were part of the U.S. nuclear weapons complex.

The president sent a letter to senators Dec. 18 affirming the administration's commitment to the U.S. missile defense program, and another the following week saying he would request the necessary money to fund modernization of the nation's nuclear stockpile.

Lamar Alexander, R-Tenn., cited Obama's letter as a determining factor in his support for New START.

Treaty supporters did lose a few senators thought to have been on the fence. Orrin G. Hatch, R-Utah, and Lindsey Graham, R-S.C., lined up with Kyl. McCain and Mark Steven Kirk, R-Ill., also voted against the resolution. "I don't understand why we can't wait five more weeks to ratify," Graham said.

For the Obama administration, the answer was clear: Ratifying the treaty would have been even more difficult, if not impossible, in the next Congress, when Republicans would control 47 seats and the Democratic Caucus would be reduced to 53 senators, down from 58 senators in the 111th. ■

Long-Delayed Intelligence Bill Clears

AFTER MONTHS OF NEGOTIATIONS — and to the surprise of many — Congress cleared a compromise fiscal 2010 intelligence authorization bill before adjourning for the campaign season. It was the first reauthorization of the nation's intelligence agencies in six years. President Obama signed the measure into law Oct. 7 (HR 2701 — PL 111-259).

Negotiations on the bill had pushed enactment beyond the end of the fiscal year, but members of the House and Senate Intelligence committees persisted, in part to enable Congress to reassert its oversight role of the intelligence community.

Because fiscal 2010 had ended, the measure did not authorize specific funding, but it allowed lawmakers to make policy changes affecting the 16 U.S. intelligence agencies and intelligence-related activities of the U.S. government, including the National Security Agency (NSA), the CIA and the FBI.

The last intelligence bill — which was a major overhaul — had been enacted in 2004 (PL 108-487). Subsequent authorization bills were stymied largely by disagreements between Congress and the George W. Bush administration over attempts to restrict the use by the CIA and other intelligence agencies of certain interrogation procedures, including waterboarding, or simulated drowning. (*2004 Almanac, p. 11-3*)

The main controversy in the 111th Congress concerned the extent to which lawmakers should be briefed on such procedures. The White House had threatened to veto earlier House and Senate versions of the bill over proposed new notification requirements for sensitive spy activities. The White House argued that the provisions would intrude on the executive branch's traditional authority over national security.

The president was required under the National Security Act of 1947 to keep the House and Senate Intelligence committees "fully and currently informed" of intelligence activities. The law enumerated specific procedures for briefings on covert actions, including allowing the president to limit notification to the so-called Gang of Eight — the Democratic and Republican leaders in both chambers, and the chairmen and the ranking members of the House and Senate Intelligence panels — if he determined that such limitations were warranted by extraordinary circumstances affecting vital U.S. interests.

Many lawmakers said the executive branch had overused its ability to limit briefings to the Gang of Eight under Bush, and many argued that Congress could have provided greater oversight of initiatives such as the government's warrantless surveillance program if the entire committee had been notified of them sooner.

The notification controversy was exacerbated by two events in 2009. The first was a partisan fight over exactly when Speaker Nancy Pelosi, D-Calif., had been informed about the use of harsh interrogation techniques such as waterboarding.

The second occurred when CIA Director Leon E. Panetta told the House Intelligence Committee in June that the panel had not been notified about a secret program that began in 2001, reportedly designed to capture or kill leaders of the al Qaeda terrorist network

BOX SCORE	**BILL:** HR 2701 — PL 111-259

LEGISLATIVE ACTION:

House passed HR 2701 (H Rept 111-186), 235-168, on Feb. 26.

Senate passed S 3611 (S Rept 111-223) by unanimous consent Aug. 5.

Senate passed HR 2701, amended, by unanimous consent Sept. 27.

House cleared the bill, 244-181, on Sept. 29.

President signed the bill on Oct. 7.

abroad. (*2009 Almanac, p. 14-3*)

The House Intelligence Committee approved a bill (HR 2701) in June 2009 that would have given the Intelligence committees the authority to set the guidelines on when the executive branch could limit briefings to the Gang of Eight.

Faced with a White House veto threat over this and other provisions, Democratic leaders pulled the measure from the floor schedule.

In September 2009, the Senate passed a version of the legislation (S 1494) that would have allowed the executive branch to continue deciding what briefings to limit to the Gang of Eight. But it would have required that all panel members receive a description of the main features of the intelligence activity or covert action, as well as the reasons for not briefing the full committee.

Both chambers passed revised bills in 2010, but they could not agree on the disclosure requirements, among other things. Most observers believed the bill was dead, but further negotiations produced an agreement, which the Senate passed and the House cleared.

HIGHLIGHTS

The following are major unclassified elements of the bill:

● **Expanded oversight.** The bill repealed the Gang of Eight provision and established in statute that the president was required to brief all members of the Intelligence committees within 180 days of certain intelligence actions. However, it allowed him to limit the briefings if he certified that not disclosing the information was justified by extraordinary circumstances affecting vital U.S. interests.

In such cases, the president had to notify all committee members that a restricted finding had been provided and give them a "general description" of the subject. Within 180 days, all members of the Intelligence committees had to be given access to the finding or notification, unless the president renewed the certification. The president also had to keep a record of members who received the briefing.

The bill required the president to consider a list of criteria in determining whether Congress had to be notified of a covert activity. The criteria included whether the activity involved significant risk of loss of life or of disclosing intelligence sources or methods, was particularly costly or might damage U.S. diplomatic relations if it was disclosed.

The information on a covert activity had to be submitted in writing and include the legal basis under which it was being conducted.

● **GAO review.** The bill required the director of national intelligence (DNI) to issue a directive by May 1, 2011, on access for Government Accountability Office (GAO) personnel to audit certain intelligence agencies. The directive had to be submitted to Congress before it could go into effect.

The House-passed bill would have given the GAO the authority to audit intelligence agencies at the direction of Congress. The White House threatened to veto any measure that included such language.

● **DNI powers.** The bill provided some expansion of the DNI's powers,

including authorization to conduct a review of any "failure or deficiency" by an intelligence agency and recommend corrective or punitive action. The head of any agency that ignored the DNI's recommendation had to notify the Intelligence committees and give the reasons for not complying.

● **Inspector general.** The bill established an office of inspector general for the intelligence community under the DNI. The inspector general was to be appointed by the president and confirmed by the Senate and could be removed only by the president.

● **Contractors.** The DNI was instructed to provide a comprehensive report to the Intelligence and Armed Services committees by Feb. 1, 2011, on the use of contractors, including the guidance given by the individual intelligence agencies on hiring and assignment, and an assessment of the costs of hiring contract personnel compared with that of using government employees.

For major projects such as spy satellites, the DNI was empowered to assess the costs and risks associated with the acquisition and, in the case of significant cost overruns, go so far as to terminate the acquisition.

● **Interrogation techniques.** The bill required the DNI, in coordination with the attorney general and Defense secretary, to submit a report to the Intelligence committees on policies and procedures issued to comply with an executive order released by Obama on Jan. 22, 2009, requiring the intelligence agencies to comply with rules banning cruel, inhuman or degrading treatment of prisoners.

● **Disclosure of covert agents.** The maximum sentence for individuals with authorized access to classified information who intentionally disclosed any information identifying a covert agent was increased from 10 years to 15 years.

● **Cybersecurity.** The bill required the intelligence agencies responsible for cybersecurity programs authorized by presidential findings to report to Congress on the legality of their operations. The DNI was directed to report to Congress within a year with guidelines to improve the capabilities of the intelligence community and law enforcement agencies to protect U.S. cybersecurity.

● **Guantánamo.** The DNI, in consultation with the directors of the CIA and Defense Intelligence Agency, was required to make public an unclassified summary of intelligence relating to recidivism of detainees who were, or had been, held at Guantánamo Bay, Cuba, and an assessment of the likelihood that those detainees would engage in terrorism or communicate with persons in terrorist organizations.

● **Congressional commission.** A Foreign Intelligence and Information Commission was established in Congress to evaluate efforts by the DNI to achieve strategic integration of the often-competing elements of the intelligence community.

2010 LEGISLATIVE ACTION

HOUSE FLOOR

The House on Feb. 26 passed a revised version of its 2009 bill (HR 2701 — H Rept 111-186) that dropped several controversial provisions approved by the Intelligence Committee. The vote was 235-168. *(House vote 73, p. H-30)*

The changes, adopted 246-166 in a manager's amendment, replaced language that would have allowed the Intelligence committees to write guidelines on when the administration could restrict sensitive briefings to the Gang of Eight. Under the amendment, by Intelligence Chairman Silvestre Reyes, D-Texas, the administration could limit the full committees' access, but only if the president certified that the ac-

tion was required by extraordinary circumstances affecting vital U.S. interests. *(House vote 69, p. H-30)*

After 180 days, the DNI would have to report to all members of the Intelligence committees on the subject involved or reissue the certification. All notifications would have to be in writing.

House Democrats spent months negotiating the revised notification language, but the White House renewed its veto threat against both the House and Senate bills. Other provisions that attracted veto warnings included language in both bills that would have authorized the GAO to conduct intelligence and counterintelligence oversight at the direction of Congress.

Reyes' amendment left intact provisions requiring the president to provide the "legal authority" under which an activity was conducted but removed a requirement to include dissenting legal views.

The manager's amendment originally included a 15-year prison sentence for intelligence personnel found to be using cruel, inhuman or degrading interrogation techniques and jail time of up to five years for medical professionals who enabled those interrogations. Reyes supported the provisions but removed them when it became clear they would derail the bill.

The bill included language to prohibit the CIA from hiring contractors to conduct interrogations of detainees and required that the DNI provide a comprehensive report to Congress on the use of contractors.

The House rejected, 186-217, a motion to recommit by Peter Hoekstra of Michigan, the ranking Republican on the Intelligence Committee, that would have, among other things, required the CIA director to make public an unclassified version of briefings to members of Congress on the use of enhanced interrogation techniques. *(House vote 72, p. H-30)*

SENATE FLOOR

In a bid to jump-start the legislation, which had never gone to a formal conference, the Senate passed a new, compromise bill (S 3611 — S Rept 111-223) by unanimous consent on Aug. 5, shortly before leaving for the August recess. Its authors urged the House, which had already adjourned, to clear the measure when it returned briefly for a special session called to clear a state education and Medicaid funding package (HR 1586). *(State aid, p. 2-18)*

The intelligence bill embodied an agreement reached by White House officials and top leaders of the Intelligence committees from both parties. But it lacked changes sought by Pelosi in the congressional notification procedures. Pelosi had backed the notification of all Intelligence committee members of sensitive spy operations.

Instead, the bill proposed several modifications to existing procedures, such as clarifying when the executive branch should notify Congress of a program, including factors such as whether a program risked significant loss of life or expenditure of funds.

The Senate Intelligence Committee had approved the bill, 15-0, in a closed session July 13.

The bill required several reports on the use of contractors, as well as new procedures designed to track cost overruns on major purchases.

It did not include proposed language to prevent the reading of Miranda warnings against self-incrimination to those detained outside the United States.

FINAL ACTION

Despite general expectations that the bill was dead at that point, leaders of the Intelligence committees continued to pursue a

compromise, and on Sept. 27, the Senate adopted an amendment to the House-passed bill (HR 2701) that reflected an agreement reached by Pelosi, the White House and the leaders of the House and Senate Intelligence committees. The Senate adopted the amendment by unanimous consent on Sept. 27. The House agreed, 244-181, on Sept. 29, clearing the bill for the president. *(House vote 558, p. H-194)*

The final dispute in the negotiations was over the notification provisions. Pelosi declared satisfaction with the final language.

Lawmakers also had to resolve the dispute over how much authority the GAO should have to audit spy agencies at the direction of Congress. The new language required the DNI to come up with a directive on GAO access to the intelligence community. ■

Measure Targets Iran's Nuclear Arms

LEGISLATION AIMED AT pressuring Iran to suspend its nuclear weapons program cleared in June. President Obama signed the measure into law July 1 (HR 2194 — PL 111-195).

The bill tightened existing sanctions against multinational companies that assisted Iran in developing its domestic refining capacity and expanded the restrictions to apply to companies that sold refined petroleum products to Tehran.

The measure also increased the number of sanctions available to the president beyond those provided under the 1996 Iran Sanctions Act (PL 104-172). Rep. Brad Sherman, D-Calif., said the best part of the bill was the language on procurement, which required prospective federal contractors to certify that they were not engaging in any sanctionable activity as defined in the bill and levied penalties for a false certification. Sherman was a longtime proponent of tough sanctions against the Iranian regime for its alleged nuclear weapons program.

Advocates said the real impact would depend on the willingness of the Obama administration to enforce the provisions.

House Foreign Affairs Chairman Howard L. Berman, D-Calif., and Senate Banking Chairman Christopher J. Dodd, D-Conn., resisted pressure from the White House to broaden the president's waiver authority, including a blanket exemption for companies based in countries that were participating in other forms of sanctions. Although the final bill did not include the blanket exemptions, it permitted the president to waive sanctions for such companies when a waiver would be in the national interest.

Obama used the 1996 law in the fall of 2009 to impose sanctions on Naftiran, an Iranian oil company based in Switzerland. It was the first time any administration had used the law's sanctions.

Lawmakers began work on the bill in 2009. The House passed a version (HR 2194) in December that focused primarily on companies that did business with Iran's petroleum sector, but it also proposed expanding the sanctions to include financial institutions, adding liquefied natural gas and oil to the items that could not be supplied to Iran and barring civil nuclear cooperation with any country whose citizens provided equipment that aided Iran's nuclear weapons program.

The Senate Banking, Housing and Urban Affairs Committee approved a broader version (S 2799 — S Rept 111-99) in October, but the Senate was preoccupied with overhauling health insurance and did not act on the measure. *(2009 action, 2009 Almanac, p. 12-5)*

BOX SCORE

BILL: HR 2194 — PL 111-195

LEGISLATIVE ACTION:

Senate passed S 2799 (S Rept 111-99) by unanimous consent Jan. 28.

Senate passed HR 2194, amended with the text of S 2799, by unanimous consent March 11.

Senate adopted the conference report on HR 2194 (H Rept 111-512), 99-0, on June 24.

House cleared the bill, 408-8, on June 24.

President signed the bill July 1.

Although the Senate passed the measure in January 2010, final action was delayed at the behest of the administration as it worked with allies to pass a new U.N. Security Council resolution imposing additional multilateral sanctions on Iran; the Security Council passed such a resolution on June 9.

Many Democrats hailed the U.N. sanctions vote as a diplomatic victory for the president that would pave the way for further unilateral sanctions by the EU and the United States. But Republicans generally dismissed the U.N. vote as toothless, pointing out a number of exemptions and loopholes in the sanctions.

Oil experts also said that Iran had plenty of time to take countermeasures to blunt potential sanctions, including expanding its refining capacity, retrofitting cars to run on natural gas and removing subsidies on imported fuel. Another challenge facing both the multilateral and bilateral sanction regimes was that Iran continued to set up new front companies, allowing it to keep one step ahead of whatever new sanctions were imposed.

HIGHLIGHTS

The following are the bill's major provisions:

● **Oil and gas.** The bill amended the Iran Sanctions Act to require the president to impose three or more sanctions if a company knowingly made an investment of $20 million or more in any 12-month period that contributed to Iran's ability to develop its petroleum resources. The sanctions applied to companies that:

▸ Provided goods, services, technology, information or support that would allow Iran to maintain or expand its domestic production of refined petroleum products, including any assistance in the construction, modernization or repair of refineries.

▸ Provided Iran with refined petroleum products or contributed to the country's ability to import refined petroleum resources, including providing ships, vehicles or other means of transportation to deliver the products. The bill expanded the list of petroleum resources to include items such as liquefied natural gas, oil and LNG tankers.

● **New sanctions.** The bill established three new sanctions that could be imposed on companies that did not comply with the law's requirements. The president could bar access to foreign exchanges in the United States, prohibit access to the U.S. banking system and bar property transactions in the United States.

The six existing sanctions were denial of U.S. Export-Import Bank

Gridlock Kills State Department Bill

FOLLOWING A PATTERN THAT HAD BECOME common, Congress left legislation to reauthorize State Department programs unfinished, denying the authorizers a chance to set new policy prescriptions for the department's activities. Funding for existing programs continued flowing at fiscal 2010 levels under a short-term continuing resolution (PL 111-322) that was good through March 4, 2011.

The House passed a two-year version of the reauthorization bill in 2009 (HR 2410 — H Rept 111-136), sponsored by Foreign Affairs Chairman Howard L. Berman, D-Calif.

It would have authorized $20.5 billion in fiscal 2010 and $20.4 billion in fiscal 2011 for State Department programs, the Peace Corps, U.N. peacekeeping dues and other international programs. According to the Congressional Budget Office (CBO), the bulk of the authorization in both years — $18.7 billion and $19.3 billion, respectively — was devoted to State operations and activities and related agencies.

The bill did not include foreign economic or military aid.

The measure would have authorized the hiring of 1,500 new Foreign Service officers and 700 additional staff members at the U.S. Agency for International Development. The number of Peace Corps volunteers would have increased significantly from the existing figure of about 8,000.

Berman said House passage was an important step in his efforts to get Congress "back into exercising its legislative responsibilities" on the foreign policy front.

The Senate Foreign Relations Committee approved its own reauthorization bill (S 2971 — S Rept 111-301) by voice vote on April 27, 2010, marking the first time since 2005 that the panel had considered such an expansive measure. The one-year measure, introduced by Chairman John Kerry, D-Mass., and ranking member Richard G. Lugar, R-Ind., covered only fiscal 2011. By that point, fiscal 2010 appropriations had already been determined. Rather than specifying hard dollar amounts, it authorized "such sums as necessary." CBO estimated the total authorization for fiscal 2011 would come to $20.9 billion, of which $19.2 billion would go to the State Department.

But as a result of gridlock in the Senate, the foreshortened election year schedule and the low priority the leadership gave to the bill, the measure never reached the Senate floor and died at the end of the 111th Congress.

---

loans, denial of licenses for the export of military technology, denial of U.S. bank loans exceeding $10 million in one year, a prohibition on being a primary U.S. government bond dealer, a prohibition on government procurement and a prohibition on allowing a company to import certain items.

● **Increased penalties.** The measure increased criminal penalties on U.S. companies for violating the law, increasing fines to $1 million from $10,000 and jail time to 20 years from 10 years.

● **Federal procurement.** U.S. and foreign firms that violated the law could not enter into procurement contracts with the federal government. This included companies that exported sensitive communications technology to Iran for use in "monitoring, jamming, or other disruption of communications by the people of Iran."

● **Human rights.** The president was required to impose sanctions on human rights violators in Iran.

● **Financial activities.** U.S. banks were forbidden to open or maintain accounts for foreign financial institutions that facilitated transactions by the Islamic Revolutionary Guard Corps or with Iranian entities that were designated under the International Emergency Economic Powers Act (IEEPA) for support of acquisition of weapons of mass destruction or support of terrorism.

Banks were accountable for actions by their foreign subsidiaries.

The president was required to freeze the assets of individuals who had engaged in activities such as terrorism or weapons proliferation under IEEPA sanction.

● **Nuclear cooperation.** The bill prohibited new civil nuclear cooperation agreements with countries that did not take action against individuals or companies that had contributed materially to Iran's nuclear weapons program or Iran's program to produce a nuclear-capable missile.

● **Investigations.** The bill required the president to investigate reports of sanctionable activities and report to Congress, instead of stating that the president "should" conduct such investigations, as under previous law.

2010 LEGISLATIVE ACTION
SENATE FLOOR

The Senate passed its more expansive bill, without amendments, by unanimous consent on Jan. 28. It later inserted the text into HR 2194 and passed that bill by unanimous consent on March 11. The bill included provisions to direct the president to freeze assets of Iranian officials and prohibit the U.S. government from providing contracts to companies that supplied Iran with communications-monitoring technology.

The bill also included provisions to authorize states, local governments and mutual funds to divest from firms investing in Iran's energy sector, and to shield private asset managers from lawsuits over fiduciary duties. It proposed to require the United States to work with Iran's trading partners to prevent the re-export of sensitive dual-use technology to Iran through third countries, and subject those countries to restrictions on exports if they refused U.S. assistance. In addition, it sought to codify the Treasury Department's ban on trade with Iran, with an exception for the export of food, medicine and humanitarian aid and the exchange of information materials.

CONFERENCE/FINAL ACTION

House and Senate negotiators filed a conference report on the bill (H Rept 111-512) on June 23. The Senate adopted the report by a vote of 99-0 the following day, and the House cleared the bill, 408-8, hours later. The final measure followed the contours of the Senate bill. *(Senate vote 199, p. S-42; House vote 394, p. H-138)* ∎

Chapter 7

Economic Affairs

Businesses Get Payroll Tax Breaks, Other Incentives to Create Jobs

THE TOP ITEM ON THE Democrats' legislative agenda for 2010 was tackling the nation's double-digit unemployment. Enactment of a $17.6 billion jobs bill in March was seen as the first victory in that drive. The president signed the bill into law March 18 (HR 2847 — PL 111-147).

But Democrats' hopes that this would provide momentum for other items on their jobs agenda were quickly dashed. The importance assigned to deficit control, along with partisan bickering in the Senate, stymied a number of initiatives. By the end of the year, two other significant pieces of jobs legislation had been enacted: one aimed at preventing widespread teacher reductions and the other to help small business. *(Teacher supplemental, p. 2-18; small business, p. 7-4)*

The centerpiece of the March jobs bill was $13 billion over 10 years in payroll tax relief for employers who hired unemployed workers. The bill also extended expensing rules for small businesses, authorization for highway programs, and the Build America bond program, which was aimed at making it easier for state and local governments to invest in infrastructure and clean-energy projects.

The House passed an initial $154 billion version of the bill, dubbed the Jobs for Main Street Act, in December 2009. But the Senate, which was locked in a debate over health care, was never expected to consider the bill before the end of the session. *(2009 Almanac, p. 7-11)*

The House bill would have provided $48.3 billion for infrastructure projects, $26.7 billion in assistance to state and local governments to preserve public service jobs, and additional assistance to families affected by the recession. It also would have extended unemployment insurance and health insurance subsidies for jobless workers through June at a cost of $53.3 billion, and extended the authorizations for surface transportation and for certain small-business loan programs through the end of fiscal 2010.

The Senate amended the bill in 2010, passing a dramatically reduced, $15 billion version in late February. The House made a few changes in early March, bringing the total to $17.6 billion, and the Senate cleared the bill March 17.

HIGHLIGHTS

The following are highlights of the bill:
- **Payroll tax forgiveness.** Employers were exempted from paying Social Security payroll taxes in 2010 on the wages of unemployed workers hired after Feb. 3 and before Jan. 1, 2011. The newly hired workers could not have been employed for more than 40 hours during the 60-day period prior to their hiring.
- **Business retention credit.** An existing general business tax credit was increased for employers who retained newly hired workers in 2010. The increase was the lesser of $1,000 or 6.2 percent of the wages paid to each worker who was hired at some point during the year and

BOX SCORE	**BILL:** HR 2847 — PL 111-147

LEGISLATIVE ACTION:

Senate passed HR 2847, amended, 70-28, on Feb. 24.

House passed, amended, 217-201, on March 4.

Senate cleared the bill, 68-29, on March 17.

President signed the bill on March 18.

retained for 52 consecutive weeks.
- **Expensing.** Businesses could deduct from taxable income the amount of an investment in the year the investment was made. The measure increased for one year — from $125,000 to $250,000 — the amount that businesses could write off in 2010 for certain investments made in that tax year. Previous law had provided the higher amount for 2008 and 2009 but reverted to $125,000 for 2010. The increase was phased out for property costing more than $800,000 — an increase from the previous threshold of $500,000.
- **Build America bonds.** The bill expanded and made permanent a qualified tax-credit bond initiative, known as the Build America bond program, created under the 2009 stimulus law (PL 111-5). The program gave state and local governments the option of offering tax-credit bonds — which provided federal tax credits to investors instead of interest payments — in lieu of tax-exempt bonds. The purpose was to encourage investment by alleviating the need for the state or local government to make interest payments.

The extension applied to clean renewable-energy bonds, qualified school construction bonds and qualified energy conservation bonds, among others.
- **Surface transportation reauthorization.** Highway, mass transit and road safety programs were extended through Dec. 31. The bill authorized appropriations to be distributed in the same amounts as in fiscal 2009, provided contract authority and extended the authority to spend money from the Highway Trust Fund. The last long-term authorization (PL 109-59) had expired in 2009, and highway, transit and safety programs had been kept alive through a series of short-term extensions. *(Surface transportation, p. 15-4)*

The bill also transferred $19.5 billion from the general fund to the Highway Trust Fund and restored $8.7 billion in contract authority that had been rescinded on Sept. 30, 2009.

2010 LEGISLATIVE ACTION
SENATE FLOOR

The Senate voted, 70-28, on Feb. 24 to amend the 2009 House-passed bill with a smaller $15 billion jobs measure. Majority Leader Harry Reid, D-Nev., pulled the four main provisions from a broader, $85 billion bipartisan draft bill negotiated by Finance Chairman Max Baucus, D-Mont., and the committee's top Republican, Charles E. Grassley of Iowa. *(Senate vote 25, p. S-8)*

Before passage, leaders won a 62-34 vote to waive the chamber's pay-as-you-go budget rules. Judd Gregg, R-N.H., objected particularly to provisions to transfer $19.5 billion from the general fund to the Highway Trust fund. "This isn't so much a jobs bill as it is a debt bill," Gregg said later. *(Senate vote 24, p. S-8)*

Reid's amendment offered tax relief for businesses that hired or

retained workers and proposed to extend surface transportation programs, the Build America bond program and expensing rules for small businesses.

In assembling the amendment, Reid dropped more than $31 billion in tax-cut extensions from the Baucus-Grassley plan, drawing fire from Republicans, who initially withheld their support. That made the critical vote one that enabled Reid to limit debate on the measure and move toward a vote. The Senate agreed, 62-30, to limit members' ability to prolong the debate. *(Senate vote 23, p. S-8)*

The tax provisions that Reid left out would have extended through 2010 a raft of tax breaks that expired at the end of 2009, including the research and development tax credit, tax incentives for the production of biodiesel and a state sales tax deduction for individuals. The cuts would have been partially offset by provisions to limit international tax evasion and curb paper producers' ability to claim a tax credit for making "black liquor," a wood byproduct, bringing in $24 billion.

The Baucus-Grassley compromise also would have extended through the end of May federal unemployment insurance and health insurance subsidies for laid-off workers, temporarily put off a cut in Medicare physicians' payment rates and extended provisions of the counterterrorism law known as the Patriot Act.

A spokesman said Reid pared down the bill after caucus members raised concerns about the makeup of the Baucus-Grassley draft and Republicans were unwilling to agree to moving forward quickly. Liberals objected, in particular, that the business tax breaks were scheduled to last to the end of the year, while benefits for jobless workers' families would last only through May.

HOUSE/FINAL ACTION

The House passed the bill March 4, after making changes negotiated by the Democratic leadership to win over party members who were dissatisfied with the Senate version. The March 4 vote was 217-201. *(House vote 90, p. H-36)*

The changes were aimed at mollifying three groups within the Democratic caucus:

‣ At the insistence of fiscally conservative "Blue Dog" Democrats, the cost of the tax cuts was fully offset. The main change was to a provision that delayed new worldwide interest allocations. The Senate initially proposed a two-year delay, until 2020; the final version delayed them until 2021. The bill also used an accounting gimmick that advanced the deadlines for corporate quarterly estimated tax payments so the revenue fell within the bill's 10-year window.

‣ The revised House bill added language requiring that 10 percent of the funds for certain programs authorized under the bill go to small businesses "controlled by socially and economically disadvantaged individuals."

The change was a nod to members of the Congressional Black Caucus, who were dissatisfied with the size and the focus of the bill. They said it concentrated on business and should do more to help low-income and minority communities that were hit especially hard by the recession.

‣ James L. Oberstar, D-Minn., the chairman of the Transportation and Infrastructure Committee, had held up the bill over objections that the surface transportation extension would fund certain programs based on earmarks in the last long-term surface transportation law. He said that would give 58 percent of the programs' funding to California, Illinois, Louisiana and Washington, and provide no funding to 22 states.

But Oberstar backed off, saying the revised bill would allow certain discretionary funds to be allocated among all states. Hours after the bill cleared, Oberstar won voice vote passage of legislation (HR 4853) to alter the distribution method, but the Senate did not act on the measure.

The Senate cleared the jobs bill by a vote of 68-29 on March 17 after Democrats held off another GOP budgetary challenge. Republicans insisted that even the considerably slimmed-down bill was not deficit-neutral. The Senate voted to waive a budget point of order, raised by Gregg, by a vote of 63-34. *(Senate votes 55, 54, p. S-14)* ∎

Small-Business Assistance Enacted

CONGRESS CLEARED A BILL in September aimed at bolstering small businesses by expanding their access to credit and providing some tax incentives. The aim was to enable small businesses to grow and to hire or retain workers. President Obama signed the measure into law Sept. 27 (HR 5297 — PL 111-240).

During the period between 1990 and 2005, companies with fewer than 500 employees created about two-thirds of jobs, and those with fewer than 50 workers created more than a third of them. But in the aftermath of the financial crisis, small businesses, along with their many supporters in Congress, said that it had become virtually impossible to persuade risk-weary banks to lend to them.

The White House strongly supported the legislation, calling small

BOX SCORE

BILL: HR 5297 — PL 111-240

LEGISLATIVE ACTION:

House passed HR 5297 (H Rept 111-499), 241-182, on June 17.

Senate passed, amended, 61-38, on Sept. 16.

House cleared HR 5297, 237-187, on Sept. 23.

President signed the bill Sept 27.

business the "backbone of the American economy." Obama had called for many of the initiatives in his State of the Union address in January.

The centerpiece of the bill was a $30 billion Small Business Lending Fund designed to help community banks make loans to small businesses, which was combined with tax incentives that were expected to cost $12 billion over 10 years. The tax breaks included an extension of a provision that allowed small businesses to carry back tax credits over five years and excluded proceeds from some small-business stock from capital gains taxes. But the bill also clamped down on businesses that cheated on their taxes. Companies that failed to file returns, for instance, could be fined up to $1.5 million, up from $250,000.

The lending fund emerged as the biggest point of contention, especially in the Senate. Many Republicans called it a smaller version of the $700 billion Troubled Asset Relief Program (TARP) created in 2008 (PL 110-343) to bail out the financial industry. *(2008 Almanac, p. 7-3)*

Democratic leaders ultimately agreed to drop $1.5 billion in agricultural disaster assistance and a revenue-raising offset that had already been used in a state aid measure to win a few GOP votes.

HIGHLIGHTS

The following are major provisions of the bill:

● **Small Business Lending Fund.** The new $30 billion fund was created within the Treasury Department to enable the department to invest in community banks and other small financial institutions with less than $10 billion in risk-based assets, in an effort to expand the availability of credit to small businesses.

▸ The measure authorized the appropriation of whatever sums were necessary to pay the cost of the $30 billion in investment.

▸ As an incentive, interest that the bank owed to the Treasury was tied to how much the bank expanded its small-business lending in the first two years and could go as low as 1 percent. Institutions that did not increase their small-business lending in the first two years could be charged rates of up to 7 percent.

▸ Institutions on the Federal Deposit Insurance Corporation's "problem bank" list were ineligible for the program.

▸ Participating banks were required to repay the capital investment within 10 years. The Treasury had to use any proceeds to pay down the public debt.

● **Small-business credit initiative.** The bill provided $1.5 billion for the creation of a small-business credit initiative to assist states with efforts to increase the amount of capital made available to small businesses by private lenders.

● **Small-business tax incentives.** The $12 billion in tax incentives included the following, with 10-year cost and revenue estimates provided by the Joint Committee on Taxation:

▸ A 100 percent exclusion from taxation of capital gains on certain small-business stock held for five years. The 2009 economic stimulus law (PL 111-5) included a 75 percent exclusion rate for stock acquired between Feb. 17, 2009, and Jan. 1, 2011. (Cost: $518 million)

▸ A provision that allowed certain small businesses to carry back unused general business tax credits to offset taxes paid over the previous five years. Ordinarily, the carryback period was one year. (Cost: $107 million)

▸ A provision that allowed small businesses to use the general business credit to offset liability under the alternative minimum tax in 2010. (Cost: $977 million)

▸ A one-year extension of a "bonus depreciation" provision from the economic stimulus law. The extension allowed small businesses to immediately write off 50 percent of the cost of new equipment placed in service in 2010. (Cost: $5.5 billion)

▸ A temporary increase in the amount businesses could deduct for certain capital expenditures in the year the expenditures were made. The maximum deduction in 2010 and 2011 was $500,000, up from $250,000, and was phased out once the expenditures exceeded $2 million, up from $800,000. The definition of property eligible for the deduction was also expanded. (Cost: $2.2 billion)

▸ A deduction in 2010 for health insurance costs in computing self-employment taxes. (Cost $1.9 billion)

● **Revenue-raisers.** The Joint Tax Committee estimated that revenue-raising tax changes would bring in $14.5 billion over 10 years, more than paying for the tax breaks. The bill included provisions to:

▸ Make it easier for the IRS to seize property from certain federal contractors to pay the contractors' tax liability. (Revenue: $1.1 billion)

▸ Allow distributions from certain retirement accounts to be rolled over to Roth IRAs; the distributions would be treated as gross income. Taxes on Roth accounts were paid up front, rather than being deferred. (Revenue: $5.1 billion)

▸ Require taxpayers who received rental income to file informational returns to the IRS on payments made to service providers such as plumbers. (Revenue: $2.5 billion)

2010 LEGISLATIVE ACTION
HOUSE FLOOR

The House passed its version of the bill by a vote of 241-182 on June 17. The Financial Services Committee had approved the measure (HR 5297 — H Rept 111-499), 42-23, on May 19. *(House vote 375, p. H-132)*

In addition to establishing a $30 billion lending fund, the bill would have created a $2 billion state small-business credit initiative and a $1 billion Small Business Administration program for investments in "early stage" businesses.

The measure included $3.6 billion in tax breaks over 11 years, provided in a separate bill (HR 5486) that the House passed, 247-170, on June 15. The tax measure was automatically incorporated into the lending bill under a rule for floor debate that covered both pieces of legislation. *(House vote 363, p. H-130)*

The main tax benefit was a one-year, 100 percent exclusion from capital gains taxes for profits on certain small-business stock. The provision would have cost $2 billion more than the final version, because it would have applied to stock purchased after March 15, rather than after the date of enactment, as in the final bill. The House tax bill included $7.1 billion in offsets over 11 years from changes to the inheritance tax and the cellulosic biofuel tax credit.

SENATE FLOOR

With the help of two departing Republican lawmakers, the Senate passed an amended version of the bill, 61-38, on Sept. 16. Before passage, the Senate voted, also by 61-38, to invoke cloture, ending a GOP filibuster that had delayed the legislation for weeks. *(Senate votes 237, 236, p. S-49)*

The president took a dig at Senate Republicans who obstructed passage. "It should not have taken this long to pass this bill. At a time when small-business owners are still struggling to make payroll and they're still holding off hiring, we put together a plan that would give them some tax relief and make it easier for them to take out loans," the president said on Sept. 15 in anticipation of Senate passage.

The critical vote took place two days earlier, when the Senate voted, 61-37, to invoke cloture on a substitute amendment by Finance Chairman Max Baucus, D-Mont., that contained the substance of the final bill. *(Senate vote 233, p. S-48)*

The partisan maneuvering had been going on since July. Democrats had wanted to pass the bill by the August recess, but Republicans complained that they were not given a fair chance to get votes on their amendments. Minority Leader Mitch McConnell, R-Ky., sought an agreement, which was not forthcoming, that would have allowed eight amendments, including votes on the estate tax, nuclear energy loan guarantees and border security.

Baucus and Louisiana Democrat Mary L. Landrieu, chairwoman of

the Small Business and Entrepreneurship panel, filed several versions of the measure before securing the support of George LeMieux, R-Fla., and George V. Voinovich, R-Ohio, to overcome the procedural hurdles to pass the bill. In all, the Senate took six cloture votes before managing to pass the measure.

During the debate on the bill, the Senate also:

▶ Rejected, 46-52, a motion to invoke cloture on an amendment by Mike Johanns, R-Neb., that would have repealed a requirement in the health care overhaul (PL 111-148, PL 111-152) that, beginning in 2012, businesses file informational reports to the IRS for each vendor to whom they paid more than $600 in a tax year. To cover the cost of dropping the tax compliance provision, Johanns would have cut $19.2 billion from the cost of the health care law by limiting the reach of its individual mandate and reducing funding for preventive-care programs. Many Democrats who supported repealing the "1099 provision," named for the associated IRS form, rejected the proposed offset. Sixty votes are required for cloture. *(Senate vote 231, p. S-48)*

▶ Rejected, 56-42, a motion to invoke cloture on an amendment by Bill Nelson, D-Fla., to exempt businesses with fewer than 25 employees from the requirement and raise the reporting threshold to $5,000 for companies required to file. Nelson proposed covering the $10.1 billion cost of his amendment by preventing the largest oil companies from using a 6 percent tax deduction designed to aid domestic manufacturing. *(Senate vote 232, p. S-48)*

FINAL ACTION

Rather than making changes that were likely to sidetrack the bill in the Senate, the House chose to accept the Senate's version and cleared the bill, 237-187, on Sept. 23. *(House vote 539, p. H-188)*

Though House leaders expressed some disappointment with the Senate package, it was clear that sending an altered version back to the Senate would have doomed the legislation. Instead, they emphasized the need for the legislation and said it would be critical in any effort to spur job creation. ∎

House Passes China Currency Bill

LEGISLATION TO GIVE THE Commerce Department new tools to pressure China's government into revising its currency practices passed with strong bipartisan support in the House but was not taken up in the Senate.

The bill, which passed 348-79 on Sept. 29, was an effort to address the trade imbalances between the United States and China. *(House vote 554, p. H-194)*

The Ways and Means Committee had approved the bill by voice vote on Sept. 24 (HR 2378 — H Rept 111-646).

Most experts agreed that the Chinese government maintained its currency, the yuan, at an artificially low value to keep Chinese exports cheap and imports expensive.

Congressional criticism had been muted because of China's role as the U.S. government's most important creditor. But slow economic recovery and continued high unemployment made China a target for congressional ire and demands for economic retaliation through tariffs or other measures.

Dave Camp of Michigan, the top Republican on the Ways and Means Committee, said the legislation "sends a clear signal to China that Congress' patience is running out." He added, "This legislation also sends an important signal to the administration: It's time to produce results."

The bill would have barred the Commerce Department from using a longstanding rule that made it difficult to define an undervalued currency as an illegal export subsidy that could lead to economic sanctions. Its stated purpose was "to clarify that countervailing duties may

be imposed to address subsidies relating to a fundamentally undervalued currency of any foreign country." Countervailing duties are levied by governments on certain imports to offset the price advantage that the import's producer gained from government subsidies.

In essence, it would have changed the law so that Commerce could not dismiss a claim just because non-exporters in a foreign country also received the same subsidy. The department was to retain the power to make the final decision on whether to impose countervailing duties.

Sponsor Tim Ryan, D-Ohio, said the bill would strengthen the nation's manufacturing base and stimulate the economy without adding to the deficit. Although the bill attracted support from most Republicans, some GOP lawmakers said it would not reduce the trade deficit but would raise prices for consumers.

The bill had strong backing from labor unions. The Economic Policy Institute estimated that the growth in the U.S. trade deficit with China had caused the loss or displacement of 2.4 million U.S. jobs, mostly from the manufacturing sector, from 2001 to 2008.

But the U.S. business community was split. Small and midsize U.S.-based manufacturers, which faced intense competition from Chinese imports, were the primary members of the business community pushing for the currency legislation.

But the National Retail Federation, whose members brought in huge quantities of goods from China, opposed the legislation. Many corporations and business groups also worried that the bill would invite Chinese retaliation. ∎

Chapter 8

Employment & Labor

Federal Unemployment Benefits Extended After Yearlong Conflict

CONGRESS KEPT A PROGRAM of emergency federal benefits for jobless workers alive through the end of 2011 as part of a year-end bargain between Republicans and President Obama that was primarily over tax cuts. The extension cleared as part of the tax package, which Obama signed into law Dec. 17 (HR 4853 — PL 111-312).

The extended benefits were available to the long-term unemployed who had exhausted the regular 26-week program run by each state and overseen by the Labor Department. The federal government paid 100 percent of the cost of the extra assistance.

The year-end bill was the fourth short-term renewal of the federal benefits to be enacted in 2010. Each of the first three was the culmination of a prolonged legislative battle that led to the expiration of the benefits and required that the new short-term extension be retroactive. In addition to covering all of 2011, the last bill was retroactive to Nov. 30, when the previous short-term law expired.

While Republicans were careful to express support for extending unemployment benefits, they argued that the cost should be offset and accused Democrats of recklessly adding to the national debt.

Democrats countered that the benefits should qualify as emergency spending, not subject to statutory pay-as-you-go requirements, because such a large number of workers were unemployed and in need of help. They blasted Republicans for insensitivity to the unemployed.

A similar federal program had been enacted during the economic downturn in 2002 and 2003, but Congress allowed the benefits to expire after that (PL 107-147, PL 108-1, PL 108-26). *(2002 Almanac, p. 12-6; 2003 Almanac, p. 12-5)*

A new initiative began in 2008 as the meltdown in the financial markets and the accompanying economic downturn drove up unemployment rates, and it was extended through a series of laws. *(2008 Almanac, p. 9-11)*

▶ The new program was kicked off in a supplemental spending bill enacted in June 2008 (PL 110-252). The law made laid-off workers who had run through their 26 weeks of state benefits eligible for an additional 13 weeks of federal benefits through March 31, 2009.

▶ With national unemployment rates rising to 6.2 percent, Congress cleared a bill in October 2008 (PL 110-449) that increased the 13 weeks of federal benefits to 20 weeks and added another 13 weeks for workers in states with a jobless rate of 6 percent or higher.

▶ The economic stimulus law (PL 111-5) enacted in February 2009 extended the benefits through Dec. 31, 2009, and provided an extra $25 per week. *(2009 Almanac, p. 9-3)*

▶ In response to the continuing rise in unemployment, which reached 10.1 percent in October 2009, Congress enhanced the stimulus provisions in November by adding 14 more weeks of benefits for all states (PL 111-92). It added another four weeks for states with unemployment rates of 4 percent or more and six weeks more for

---

BOX SCORE

BILL: HR 4853 — PL 111-312

....

LEGISLATIVE ACTION:

Senate passed HR 4853, including unemployment provisions, 81-19, on Dec. 15.

House cleared the bill, 277-148, on Dec. 17.

President signed the bill on Dec. 17.

---

states where unemployment had reached an 8.5 percent rate. The measure did not extend the expiration date in the stimulus.

▶ With the benefits scheduled to expire before members returned in January, Congress in December extended the provisions to Feb. 28, 2010, as part of the fiscal 2010 Defense appropriations bill (PL 111-118).

2010 LEGISLATIVE ACTION
EXTENSION TO APRIL 5

Congress cleared a bill (HR 4691– PL 111-144) in March 2010 that kept the federal unemployment provisions, including the extra $25 per week, in place for one more month, through April 5, and made them retroactive to Feb. 28.

The House passed the short-term bill by voice vote Feb. 25, but when the measure reached the Senate, Jim Bunning, R-Ky., insisted that it be paid for with funds from the 2009 stimulus law. Bunning

---

COBRA Coverage Subsidy Expires

CONGRESS EXTENDED A SPECIAL HEALTH insurance subsidy for jobless workers through May in bills that extended federal unemployment benefits and other social safety net programs. But with the electorate in an anti-deficit mood shared by many within their own caucus, House Democratic leaders dropped a further extension in July. The subsidy ended May 31.

The subsidy had been available since February 2009 for people who got their medical insurance under COBRA, the Consolidated Omnibus Budget Reconciliation Act of 1985 (PL 99-272). COBRA permitted unemployed workers to stay on their former health plans for 18 months as long as they paid all of the premium. But the cost was high, typically about $1,000 a month for a family.

With unemployment hovering around 8 percent, Congress provided a temporary 65 percent premium subsidy, good through Dec. 31, 2009, as part of the 2009 economic stimulus law (PL 111-5). *(Stimulus, 2009 Almanac, p. 7-3)*

Lawmakers extended it through Feb. 28, 2010, as part of the fiscal 2010 Defense appropriations law (PL 111-118).

Two extensions enacted in 2010 continued the subsidy, first through March 31 (PL 111-144), then through May 31 (PL 111-157), after which it died.

Wage Parity Bill Languishes in Senate

EFFORTS BY DEMOCRATS to advance legislation intended to give women and men comparable wages foundered in the Senate.

The measure, which the House passed in early 2009, would have amended the 1938 Fair Labor Standards Act (PL 75-718) to make it easier to file sex discrimination cases over wage claims. It would have put the legal onus on employers to prove that pay discrepancies between women and men doing the same jobs were the result of non-discriminatory business necessities.

The bill also included provisions to allow workers to collect both compensatory and punitive damages in the event of a successful lawsuit, and it would have effectively removed the existing caps on such damages. It also would have prohibited retaliation by employers against employees who shared salary information with their colleagues.

After passing its bill, the House combined it with another measure, known as the Lilly Ledbetter Act, written to reverse a 2007 Supreme Court decision that prevented workers from suing for wage discrimination years after the discrimination initially occurred. The Senate did not act on the combined bill and instead passed a much narrower measure that focused only on the Ledbetter provisions. That bill cleared in January 2009 (PL 111-2). (2009 Almanac, p. 9-4)

On Nov. 17, 2010, the Senate rejected an attempt by Majority Leader Harry Reid, D-Nev., to limit debate on proceeding to the Senate version of the parity bill (S 3772). The motion to invoke cloture was rejected, 58-41, short of the 60 votes required. (Senate vote 249, p. S-51)

---

engaged in a one-man filibuster undeterred by warnings from Democrats that millions of Americans hardest hit by the recession would stop receiving unemployment checks if the bill was not finished by the end of February.

"The simple fact of the matter is that this is an emergency situation and should be treated as such," said Majority Whip Richard J. Durbin, D-Ill. But Bunning, who was not running for re-election, held firm. "I'm going to object every time, because you won't pay for this, and you propose never to pay for it," he said.

Bunning relented March 2, after accepting an offer from Democratic leaders for a vote on a proposal to pay for the bill by curbing paper manufacturers' ability to claim tax breaks for a wood byproduct called "black liquor." The amendment was defeated, 43-53, on a procedural vote. (Senate vote 31, p. S-9)

The Senate cleared the bill, 78-19, and Obama signed it into law the same day. (Senate vote 32, p. S-9)

EXTENSION TO JUNE 2

The next unemployment extension (HR 4851 — PL 111-157) cleared April 15, 10 days after the previous provisions had expired. The bill extended the benefits, including the $25-per-week increase, through June 2 and was retroactive to April 5. It also extended a number of other programs, such as health insurance assistance for unemployed workers and a delay in rate cuts to Medicare doctors, known as the "doc fix." (COBRA, p. 8-3; Medicare payments, p. 9-15)

The short-term measure was intended to buy time for lawmakers to reach a deal on a larger bill (HR 4213) that would have extended the programs until the end of 2010. Democrats presented the bill as part of their "jobs agenda."

The House passed a one-month version of HR 4851 by voice vote March 17. The Senate passed an amended bill, 59-38, on April 15 after nearly a week of debate. (Senate vote 117, p. S-25)

Senate Democrats rebuffed several GOP efforts to pay for the bill, including three amendments by Tom Coburn of Oklahoma, who argued that the measure should not add to the deficit. Senate Finance Chairman Max Baucus, D-Mont., insisted it was not the time to demand offsets for spending on safety net and other essential programs.

The key procedural votes came April 12 and April 14. In the first, the Senate voted, 60-34, to limit debate on proceeding to the bill. Two days later, senators voted, 60-40, to waive a point of order that the plan violated pay-as-you-go rules. Four Republicans voted with the Democratic majority both times. (Senate votes 109, 112, p. S-24)

Obama signed the bill the day it cleared.

EXTENSION TO NOV. 30

With emotions raw on both sides after five months of wrangling, Congress cleared the next extension July 21, keeping the federal program alive through Nov. 30 and making it retroactive to June 2. This time the legislation did not include the $25-per-week increase. Obama signed it into law July 22 (HR 4213 — PL 111-205).

The bill had expanded and contracted as it moved back and forth between chambers, but it ended up focusing exclusively on the unemployment benefits. The original version, which the House had passed in December 2009, was devoted to extending expiring or expired tax provision. (Tax extenders, p. 14-5)

The process that led to enactment of the bill was particularly agonizing:

▶ On March 10, the Senate passed an expanded version of the bill that included a provision to keep federal unemployment benefits flowing through Dec. 31. Other provisions would have delayed the cut in physicians' Medicare reimbursement rates, provided temporary aid to states struggling to cover Medicaid costs and extended some small-business loan and satellite TV programs. It also included more than $30 billion in tax break extensions. Offsets covered the tax provisions but not the rest of the package.

The bill, which had become the main front in the Democrats' jobs agenda, passed 62-36 after Majority Leader Harry Reid, D-Nev., twice mustered more than the 60 votes needed to limit debate. The motions to invoke cloture — first on the substance of the bill, offered as an amendment, and then on the bill itself — were adopted 66-34 and 66-33. (Senate votes 48, 46, 47, p. S-12)

▶ To eke out the necessary votes, Democratic leaders had to scale back what had grown to a $200 billion package during negotiations between Baucus and House Ways and Means Chairman Sander M. Levin, D-Mich.

Major changes cut the price tag to $113 billion, moving just enough

moderate Democrats to win a majority. The House approved the provisions 215-204 on May 28; a separate vote was taken on the doc fix, sending the bill back to the Senate. The proposed extension of jobless benefits was shortened by a month, lasting through Nov. 30. *(House vote 324, p. H-116)*

▸ The bill stalled for weeks in the Senate, where Reid repeatedly failed to garner the 60 votes needed to invoke cloture and limit debate. Democrats had found offsets for everything but the unemployment provisions. Reid ultimately pulled the bill from the floor June 24 after a cloture motion fell, 57-41. He lambasted Republicans, saying that they had abused the process and that the ball was now in their court. *(Senate vote 200, p. S-42)*

▸ Senate Democrats tried a new tack, combining a simple extension of the federal unemployment benefits through Nov. 30 with provisions to allow more homebuyers to qualify for a popular tax credit by extending the deadline for closing on a home purchase from June 30 to Sept. 30.

But Reid fell one vote short of the 60 needed to limit debate. The June 30 tally was 58-38, after Reid switched to "no" to preserve his ability to try again. The Senate then cleared a bill containing only the homebuyer credit (HR 5623). *(Senate vote 204, p. S-43)*

Republicans continued to demand offsets. "My concern is that the Democrats are more interested in having this issue to demagogue for political gamesmanship than they are in simply passing the benefits extension," George V. Voinovich, R-Ohio, said.

Democrats, by contrast, said Congress had routinely extended benefits without offsets during times of high unemployment. "This is an obligation to stand up and help people who need the help," said Jack Reed, D-R.I.

▸ Senate Democrats eventually pared the legislation to contain only the unemployment provisions and dropped the extra $25 per week, a move that attracted the support of moderate Maine Republicans Olympia J. Snowe and Susan Collins. One Senate Democrat, Ben Nelson of Nebraska, opposed the extension of benefits because the cost was not offset. Democrats still had to wait until Carte P. Goodwin, Robert C. Byrd's Democratic successor, was sworn in July 21, giving Reid the votes he needed to win a 60-40 cloture vote on July 20. The following day, the Senate passed the amended bill, 59-39. *(Senate votes 209, p. S-44, and 215, p. S-45)*

Recognizing that it was the only way to get the unemployment extension through the Senate, House Democrats won a 272-152 vote on July 22 to clear the bill, with the support of 270 Democrats and 29 Republicans. *(House vote 463, p. H-162)*

EXTENSION TO DEC. 31, 2011

One of the agreements that Obama secured from Republicans as part of the major year-end tax package was the 13-month extension of the federal benefits, retroactive to Nov. 30 (HR 4853 — PL 111-312).

The unemployment benefits were widely popular, but enactment was contingent on acceptance of the overall package by both chambers. The Senate passed the bill, 81-19, on Dec. 15, and the House cleared it, 277-148, on Dec. 17 with the support of 138 Republicans. *(Senate vote 276, p. S-56; House vote 647, p. H-226; estate tax, p. 14-7)* ∎

Chapter 9

HEALTH &
EDUCATION

Health Care Overhaul Makes History For Obama, Democratic Congress

THE BROADEST EXPANSION of health care coverage since the creation of Medicare in 1965 became law in March, culminating nine months of dogged work by President Obama and Democratic leaders in Congress. Obama, who had staked his presidency on the outcome, signed the legislation on March 23, two days after the House cleared it in a rare Sunday evening vote (HR 3590 — PL 111-148).

A hundred years after Theodore Roosevelt first proposed national health care, Obama, who had delayed a trip to Asia to be on hand, stressed the significance of the day. "Today, after almost a century of trying; today, after over a year of debate; today, after all the votes have been tallied, health insurance reform becomes law in the United States of America," he said.

John D. Dingell, D-Mich., the dean of the House, sat next to the president at the White House signing ceremony. Dingell's father, who was a congressman in the 1930s, was the first federal lawmaker to introduce a bill calling for universal health insurance. Several subsequent overhaul efforts — from a bid by President Harry S. Truman in the 1940s to President Bill Clinton's attempt in 1994 — were unsuccessful. *(Clinton plan, 1994 Almanac, p. 319)*

The final legislation was the same as the bill the Senate had passed, with great difficulty, in December 2009. Reluctant House Democrats were persuaded to clear it rather than negotiating a compromise that was certain to stall in the Senate. The price for the Democrats' support was a second bill with modest changes that brought some provisions closer to those in the version the House had passed in November 2009. Among other things, it increased subsidies to help uninsured individuals buy health coverage and increased certain taxes and fees to help pay for the expanded coverage. It also removed an embarrassing provision added in 2009 that helped secure the support of Ben Nelson, D-Neb., by providing special Medicaid funding for his state. Obama signed the second bill March 30 (HR 4872 — PL 111-152).

Under the health care overhaul, as modified by the corrections bill, roughly 32 million uninsured Americans were expected to obtain health insurance coverage, mainly through subsidized private insurance policies or through expanded access to Medicaid, the joint federal-state health program for the poor.

The law required most Americans to have health coverage by 2014. States were required to create "American Health Benefit Exchanges," or marketplaces, where uninsured individuals, families and small businesses could shop for health plans. Families with incomes up to 400 percent of the federal poverty level could get federal subsidies to help pay for premiums and out-of-pocket expenses. Employers with 50 or more workers were required to pay fees to help cover the cost to the government of employees who received subsidized coverage

BOX SCORE

BILL: HR 3590 — PL 111-148; HR 4872 — PL 111-152

LEGISLATIVE ACTION:

House cleared HR 3590, 219-212, on March 21.

President signed HR 3590 on March 23.

House passed HR 4872, 220-211, on March 21.

Senate passed HR 4872, amended, 56-43, on March 25.

House cleared HR 4872, 220-207, on March 25.

President signed HR 4872 on March 30.

through an exchange.

The law barred health insurance companies from denying coverage because of preexisting conditions, allowed parents to keep their children on their policies until age 26, and phased out the "doughnut hole," which required Medicare recipients to bear 100 percent of prescription drug costs above a certain level before costs were again shared between the patient and Medicare.

The cost of the combined bills — nearly $1 trillion over 10 years — was offset mainly by a new Medicare hospital payroll tax on investment income of the wealthy, an excise tax on high-cost insurance plans and reductions in Medicare payment rates. *(Provisions, p. 9-6)*

The legislation was entirely the work of Democrats. Republican leaders sought to block the bill at every stage, arguing that the vast majority of Americans rejected the makeover. No Republican voted for the final bill in either chamber. As a result, virtually all of the wooing, cajoling and bargaining took place within the Democratic Caucus.

That had largely been the story of the legislation from its beginnings in early 2009. Speaker Nancy Pelosi, D-Calif., and her leadership team managed to win House passage of a painstakingly negotiated overhaul bill by a vote of 220-215 on Nov. 7. Majority Leader Harry Reid, D-Nev., kept the Senate in session for 25 straight days while he adjusted the Senate version to secure the votes of all 60 members of his caucus, the number needed to overcome a GOP filibuster. The vote to invoke cloture was 60-39; the bill passed Dec. 24 by the same margin. *(Health care, 2009 Almanac, p. 13-3)*

The only significant effort to write a bipartisan version took place in the summer of 2009 in informal negotiations among three Democrats and three Republicans on the Senate Finance Committee. Although the effort ultimately failed, the Senate bill reflected many of the compromises worked out in the talks and came closer than the House version to satisfying moderates.

Given the narrow margins of victory and the extensive bargaining that had gone into both bills, the notion of finding a compromise that could satisfy both chambers seemed nearly out of reach at the end of 2009.

Democrats' options narrowed further on Jan. 19, 2010, when Republican Scott P. Brown was elected to the seat that had been held by Sen. Edward M. Kennedy, D-Mass., until his death in August 2009. Brown replaced Democrat Paul G. Kirk Jr., who had occupied the seat on an interim basis, leaving Reid one vote short of the crucial 60-vote majority. *(Kennedy, 2009 Almanac, p. 5-3)*

After appearing on the brink of defeat several times, Democrats ultimately succeeded by having the House clear the Senate-passed bill, then pass a separate "corrections" bill that was sent to the Senate for final action. The plan worked because Democrats used reconciliation

procedures, which limited amendments to the corrections bill and barred a filibuster, enabling the leadership to avoid the need for 60 votes and pass the measure with a simple majority. The fiscal 2010 budget resolution had made the reconciliation rules available for health care legislation. (*Budget resolution, 2009 Almanac, p. 4-9*)

Leaders also used the reconciliation package for another longtime Democratic goal: an overhaul of the student loan program. The provisions made the federal government the sole originator of the loans, which Democrats argued was less costly to taxpayers than subsidizing private student loans. (*Student loans, p. 9-16*)

HIGHLIGHTS

The following are highlights of the health care overhaul as passed by the Senate, amended by the corrections bill, cleared by the House and signed into law:

● **Exchanges.** Unlike the House-passed bill, the final measure created a system of state-run exchanges where uninsured people could purchase health insurance coverage. The House version would have created a single national exchange run by a new federal agency.

● **'Public option.'** Liberal Democrats in both chambers avidly supported the inclusion of a government-run insurance plan, or "public option," to compete with private plans in the exchanges. The House-passed bill included a public option, and Obama supported it, saying the competition was crucial to driving down insurance costs. But virtually all Republicans and some moderate Democrats rejected the idea, arguing that a government-sponsored plan would have unfair advantages over private competitors and that it would bring government bureaucrats into private health care decisions. Some warned that it was the first step toward "socialized medicine." Although many Senate Democrats favored a public option, they recognized that it would not pass in their chamber.

The final bill required the Office of Personnel Management to contract with insurers to offer at least two multistate plans in each exchange. At least one plan had to be offered by a nonprofit group.

● **Subsidies.** House Democrats had to settle for lower subsidies than they wanted for insurance purchased in the exchanges by low- and moderate-income individuals and families. The subsidies — which took the form of refundable tax credits — limited the portion of household income that a family had to spend on premiums and out-of-pocket expenses for those earning 133 percent to 400 percent of the federal poverty level. (Those earning less generally qualified for Medicaid.)

However, the reconciliation bill made the subsidies more generous than they would have been under the Senate-passed version.

● **Abortion.** The law restated the existing statute that barred the use of federal funds to cover abortions except to end pregnancies that resulted from rape or incest or that endangered the woman's life. Insurance plans that participated in an exchange and offered additional abortion coverage had to create separate accounts for premium payments for the abortion services. To get the additional coverage, an enrollee had to make two premium payments: one for regular benefits and one for the abortion services. The law did not pre-empt state abortion laws, and states could prohibit plans in their exchange from offering abortion coverage.

The House bill contained stricter abortion language, which Pelosi was forced to accept in 2009 as the price for getting critical votes from Democratic abortion foes. The House-passed measure would have barred the use of public funds to pay for abortions or for any health insurance plan that covered abortion in any program created by the bill. Plans offered on the exchanges could have included abortion coverage, but they would not have been eligible for government subsidies. To get abortion coverage, enrollees who received tax credits would have had to purchase separate, supplemental policies with their own money. Plans that offered abortion coverage on the exchange would have had to offer an identical plan that did not include the coverage.

● **Individual mandate.** The new law required that most Americans obtain basic health coverage by 2014 or pay a tax penalty that would be phased in over three years. The House bill would have set the penalty at 2.5 percent of household income above the tax filing threshold (at the time, $18,700 for a family). The original Senate-passed bill would have set a fine of $750 per year, up to a maximum of 2 percent of a family's income. The fee in the final, amended bill was $695 per year up to a maximum of 2.5 percent of household income.

● **Employer mandate.** Unlike the House bill, the new law did not include a "play or pay" provision, which would have required employers with payrolls of $500,000 and above to offer health insurance or pay a penalty of up to 8 percent of their payroll. Instead, the final bill as modified required employers to pay a fee if they had employees who got subsidized insurance through an exchange; the fee was higher than in the original Senate-passed bill.

● **'Doughnut hole.'** Like the House-passed version, the final bill, as amended by the corrections measure, phased out the gap in Medicare Part D prescription drug coverage over 10 years. It also provided a $500 reduction in the gap in 2010. The Senate bill would have provided only a one-time $500 reduction.

● **Revenue.** In accepting the Senate bill, the House had to give up the chief source of revenue proposed in its legislation: a surtax on the income of top earners. Instead, the final bill included a modified version of a Senate provision that imposed an excise tax on insurers of high-cost employer-sponsored health plans, a cost that was likely to be passed on to the company and the employee.

Labor leaders and many House Democrats opposed this tax on so-called Cadillac plans as unfair, saying it would hit workers in high-risk professions and union members who had negotiated generous benefits, often in lieu of higher wages.

The House proposal would have raised about twice as much revenue, but the Congressional Budget Office (CBO) said the Senate's excise tax would encourage consumers and employers to seek out lower-cost plans and eventually drive down health care costs.

The corrections bill scaled back the Senate-passed provision somewhat, delaying the effective date until 2018, rather than 2013. It also raised the threshold at which the tax would apply to $10,200 a year for individual health coverage and $27,500 for family coverage, up from $8,500 and $23,000 in the original Senate-passed bill.

Congress' Joint Committee on Taxation projected that the modified tax would raise $32 billion over 10 years, down from the $148.9 billion estimated for the original Senate provision.

The reconciliation bill made up for the drop in revenue by expanding a Senate provision that increased the 1.45 percent Medicare payroll tax for hospital insurance by 0.9 percent for income above $200,000 for individuals and $250,000 for couples. The reconciliation bill added a 3.8 percent excise hospital insurance tax on investment income that exceeded those levels. The Joint Tax Committee estimated the 10-year revenue at $210.2 billion, up from $86.8 billion in the earlier Senate bill.

● **Medicaid.** The new law expanded eligibility under state Medicaid programs to all individuals under age 65, including parents and

childless adults, with household incomes up to 133 percent of the federal poverty level, while keeping in place the Children's Health Insurance Program (CHIP). The House bill called for expanding Medicaid eligibility to those with household incomes up to 150 percent of the poverty level, while doing away with CHIP and shifting those children and families into health insurance exchanges or Medicaid. Under previous law, close to half of poor Americans did not have Medicaid coverage.

● **Deficit.** CBO estimated that the combined health care overhaul and corrections legislation would reduce the deficit by a net $143 billion in the first decade after enactment. The projected reduction came largely through lowering anticipated Medicare costs by slowing the growth of payments to health care providers — mainly hospitals — and slashing payments to insurers who participated in the Medicare Advantage program. Under Medicare Advantage, an option strongly favored by Republicans, individuals who were eligible for Medicare could get their insurance from private companies rather than the federal government. Many Democrats contended that Medicare Advantage overpaid insurers for work the government could do just as well.

Hospitals were more or less accepting of their lot in the bill, but insurers strongly opposed the cuts.

2010 LEGISLATIVE ACTION
NEGOTIATIONS

When Democrats began talking about a final bill in January 2010, Pelosi and other House Democratic leaders insisted they would not simply accept the Senate-passed version. They hoped to negotiate a compromise, attach it to the Senate bill and send it to the other chamber to be cleared. But the math in the Senate ultimately made that impossible.

With Brown's victory, making changes that would require another Senate vote on the overhaul became a non-starter, and hopes for completing the overhaul began to fade. Democrats appeared rattled, with some talking of declaring the bill dead and going back to the drawing board to find a compromise that could win at least some GOP support. Others advocated clearing the Senate bill with a subsequent bill to amend it, breaking out and clearing pieces that had bipartisan support, or dropping the issue and turning instead to job creation, which many rank-and-file Democrats said was a higher priority with midyear elections looming.

But Obama never seemed to consider backing away from his ambitious overhaul plan. He released a new proposal on Feb. 22 — essentially what a conference report might look like if lawmakers were able to write one — with compromises on key features of the House- and Senate-passed bills. Three days later, he held a televised health care forum that he said would give Republicans one more chance to join in completing the legislation. Predictably, each side reiterated its talking points, with Democrats calling Republicans obstinate and GOP leaders urging Obama to scrap his plan.

"Our view, with all respect, is that this is a car that can't be recalled or fixed and that we ought to start over," said Sen. Lamar Alexander, R-Tenn.

Having demonstrated that Republicans had no interest in the legislation, Obama gave up his longtime pledge to have a final health bill worked out in the open. Instead, he backed Democratic leaders' plan to bring the long battle to a climactic vote on the House floor without GOP support and to use reconciliation procedures to ease the process in the Senate.

"We cannot have another yearlong debate about this," Obama said.

"The question that I'm going to ask myself, and I ask of all of you, is: Is there enough serious effort that in a month's time or a few weeks' time or six weeks' time we could actually resolve something? And if we can't, then I think we've got to go ahead and make some decisions, and then that's what elections are for."

Democratic leaders set in motion a timetable to get the overhaul to Obama by March 26, the start of Congress' spring recess, and Obama undertook a personal campaign to persuade wavering lawmakers from different groups within the Democratic Caucus.

HOUSE FLOOR ACTION

Despite Obama's personal lobbying, House Democrats still remained wary of the Senate bill. Pelosi worked to limit defections among several factions, including liberals who were still unhappy over the lack of a public option, felt the subsidies for low-income families were insufficient and opposed the tax on high-cost plans. Anti-abortion Democrats threatened to vote against the bill if it did not include the stronger House language on abortion. Republicans added to Pelosi's headaches by urging moderates who voted for the original House bill to break with Obama, warning them they could pay a steep political price if they did not.

But on Sunday, March 21, Democratic leaders won a 219-212 vote to clear the Senate-passed health care overhaul, unchanged. *(House vote 165, p. H-60)*

Shortly afterward, the House passed the reconciliation bill (HR 4872), which carried modifications to the new health care law, by a vote of 220-211. A GOP motion to require the Budget Committee to report the bill back immediately after restoring the House language on abortion failed, 199-232. *(House vote 166, 167, pp. H-60, H-62)*

Many House Democrats were nervous about clearing the overhaul before the Senate had signed off on the modifications. But the Senate parliamentarian ruled that a reconciliation bill could only change existing law, which left Democrats no choice but to send the overhaul to Obama first and trust that the Senate would clear the corrections measure.

Minority Leader John A. Boehner, R-Ohio, accused the Democrats of recklessly disregarding the will of the American people, who, he said, rejected the majority's ideas. "We have failed to listen to America, and we have failed to reflect the will of our constituents," he said. His voice rising, Boehner warned the Democratic majority: "In a democracy you can only ignore the will of the people for so long."

"Shame on each and every one of you who substitutes your will and your desires above those of your fellow countrymen," he added.

Democratic leaders, however, suggested that history was on their side when it came to social welfare legislation.

Alluding to other landmark pieces of legislation, Majority Leader Steny H. Hoyer, D-Md., said the attacks of Republicans and other opponents were as wrong as GOP attacks on Social Security and Medicare, enacted in 1935 and 1965. "Those slurs were false in 1935; they were false in 1965; and, ladies and gentlemen of this House, they are false in 2010," he said. He added, "This bill will stand in the same company — for the misguided outrage of its opposition and for its lasting accomplishment for the American people."

A group of anti-abortion Democrats, led by Bart Stupak of Michigan, dropped their threats to try to scuttle the legislation only after Obama promised to issue an executive order stating that nothing in the health care overhaul would permit public funding of abortions. Obama issued the order March 24, but it did not satisfy some abortion foes. Stupak was among 10 or so House Democrats who received

threats after voting for the overhaul, and House leaders from both parties spoke out against the behavior. Pelosi warned members to take care that the rhetoric they used during floor debate did not inflame those who would use violence. Boehner said that "threats and violence should not be part of a political debate."

SENATE FLOOR ACTION

The Senate passed the reconciliation bill by a vote of 56-43 on March 25, with three Democrats and all Republicans senators opposed. Before passing the bill, the chamber spent most of three days on a series of 41 GOP amendments. *(Senate vote 105, p. S-23)*

When the time for final passage arrived, Reid held a moment of silence in memory of Kennedy, who had fought for almost half a century in the Senate to provide universal health care. The chamber was so quiet that the whir of computers and electronic devices on

the dais could be heard, as could the ambient noise outside the chamber.

Senators then cast their votes from their desks, a practice reserved for important occasions, with Vice President Joseph R. Biden Jr. holding the gavel in his role as president of the Senate.

Although Republicans won no significant changes to the bill, two minor provisions were dropped after the Senate parliamentarian ruled they were not germane. As a result, the measure was sent back to the House, which cleared it, 220-207, in the early evening of March 25. *(House vote 194, p. H-70)*

Congress' work was done. The massive health care overhaul would henceforth be in the hands of federal agencies such as the Center for Medicare and Medicaid Services and the Office of Personnel Management, as well as the states, which would be called on to turn the myriad details of the new law into concrete rules and programs. ∎

[PROVISIONS]

Health Care Overhaul's Key Provisions

THE FOLLOWING ARE THE MAIN PROVISIONS of the landmark health care overhaul legislation that President Obama signed into law March 23 (PL 111-148), as amended by the reconciliation law (PL 111-152).

EXPANSION OF COVERAGE
EXCHANGES

● **State-run exchanges.** States were required to create "American Health Benefit Exchanges" by 2014 that offered a choice of health insurance plans to qualifying individuals and small businesses. The exchanges could be administered by either a governmental agency or a nonprofit entity established by the state. The law provided federal funding for states to create the exchanges but required that the exchanges be financially self-sustaining by 2015.

The law required that, if a state did not create an exchange by Jan. 1, 2014, the Department of Health and Human Services (HHS) create and operate one, either directly or through an agreement with a not-for-profit organization.

Health plans offered through the exchanges had to meet a number of requirements, including offering a "sufficient choice of providers," serving medically underserved communities, and meeting certain clinical access and quality standards. The details of the requirements were to be finalized in rulemaking by HHS.

The Office of Personnel Management was directed to contract with health insurers so that at least two multistate plans were offered in each new state health insurance exchange. Insurers had to provide both individual and employer health plans, and one of the two in each exchange had to be run by a nonprofit organization. Also, each exchange had to have one plan that did not offer coverage of abortion services beyond the specifications of the Hyde amendment, which barred federal funding for abortion except in cases of rape or incest or when the pregnancy threatened the life of the woman.

Two or more states could enter into an agreement to operate multi-

state or regional exchanges, as long as HHS approved the arrangement and the exchanges covered a "distinct geographic area."

In addition, the law created a new Consumer Operated and Oriented Plan (CO-OP) program intended to encourage the development of nonprofit entities to provide health insurance coverage. The measure appropriated $6 billion for loans and grants to help finance the CO-OP program, which had to be awarded by July 1, 2013.

● **Eligibility for exchanges.** Citizens and legal residents who were not incarcerated could obtain coverage through the new health insurance exchanges. Starting in 2014, employers with 100 or fewer employees could purchase coverage through the new state exchanges. Businesses with more than 100 employees could purchase health insurance through the exchanges beginning in 2017.

Individuals who applied for coverage in a state exchange had to be screened for eligibility for Medicaid, the federal-state health insurance program for low-income and disabled people, or for the federal-state Children's Health Insurance Program (CHIP) and be enrolled if eligible. Children who met income eligibility guidelines for CHIP but were unable to enroll because a state with budget constraints had frozen enrollment could receive tax credits to help pay premiums for health insurance through an exchange. Effective in fiscal 2016, states would have the option of transitioning CHIP-eligible children into a health insurance exchange, instead of CHIP, as long as HHS approved the transition.

● **'Essential benefits package.'** All qualified health benefits plans offered in the exchanges were required to provide coverage that met or exceeded the standards of an "essential benefits package." At a minimum, the essential benefits had to include outpatient services; emergency services; hospitalization; maternity and newborn care; mental health services, including behavioral health treatment; prescription drugs; laboratory services; preventive and wellness services; chronic disease management; rehabilitative services; and pediatric services, including dental and vision care.

● **Benefit structure.** The new law created five tiers of health benefits to be offered in the health insurance exchanges. The Bronze Plan, which was the minimum level of health coverage available through the exchanges, covered 60 percent of the costs of the medical benefits provided. The Silver Plan covered 70 percent. The Gold Plan covered 80 percent. The Platinum Plan, which was the most generous health insurance coverage available through the exchanges, covered 90 percent of the costs of medical benefits. Finally, a Catastrophic Plan would be available to individuals age 30 or younger who were exempt from the law's requirement to purchase health insurance; it would cover only medically catastrophic events, such as injuries suffered in a major car accident, with the maximum amount of cost-sharing permitted under the law. The Catastrophic Plan was not available to employers.

● **'Basic Health Plan.'** States could create a "Basic Health Plan" that provided coverage to uninsured individuals with annual household incomes of 133 percent to 200 percent of the federal poverty level. The states would have to contract with private insurers to provide at least the essential benefits package.

● **Tax credits for lower-income households.** Tax credits for part of the cost of premiums were available, starting in 2014, for those with household incomes of 100 percent to 400 percent of the federal poverty level (an annual income of $22,050 to $88,200 for a family of four, at the time). Within each income bracket, the tax credits would be determined on a sliding scale that limited the costs families had to pay for health insurance premiums to a percentage of their income, as follows:

▸ Households with incomes of 133 percent to 150 percent of the federal poverty level would pay 3 percent to 4 percent of their incomes for premiums.

▸ Those with incomes of 150 percent to 200 percent of the federal poverty level would pay 4 percent to 6.3 percent of their incomes.

▸ Those with incomes of 200 percent to 250 percent of the federal poverty level would pay 6.3 percent to 8.05 percent of their incomes.

▸ Those with incomes of 250 percent to 300 percent of the federal poverty level would pay 8.05 percent to 9.5 percent of their incomes.

▸ Those with incomes of 300 percent to 400 percent of the federal poverty level would pay 9.5 percent of their incomes for premiums.

Starting in 2015, the premium tax credits were to be adjusted to reflect year-to-year premium growth in the health plans.

The credits would be reduced if any member of a household was residing in the United States illegally. For example, if four people were supported by one income, and one family member was an illegal immigrant, the family income would be counted as supporting only three people.

The Congressional Budget Office projected that in 2015, the average federal premium tax credit would be $5,200 per household.

● **Limit on out-of-pocket costs.** The percentage of a plan's cost that a low-income household would pay out of pocket was limited to:

▸ 6 percent for households with incomes of 100 percent to 150 percent of the federal poverty level.

▸ 13 percent for households with incomes of 150 percent to 200 percent of the federal poverty level.

▸ 27 percent for households with incomes of 200 percent to 250 percent of the federal poverty level.

▸ 30 percent for households with incomes of 250 percent to 400 percent of the federal poverty level.

● **Tax credits for small businesses.** Starting in 2010, employers with 25 or fewer employees and annual average wages of less than $50,000 were eligible for new tax credits phased in over the course of several years. In tax years 2010 through 2013, qualifying small employers could receive a tax credit of 35 percent of the employer contribution to health insurance premiums, as long as the employer contributed at least 50 percent of the total premium costs. In tax years 2014 and after, the law provided a tax credit of 50 percent for qualified employers for the first two years in which they purchased health insurance through a state exchange, as long as they contributed at least 50 percent of the total premium costs.

Tax-exempt small businesses, such as religious organizations, that met all the other requirements were eligible for tax credits of up to 35 percent of their contributions to employees' premiums.

● **Abortion coverage.** Health plans in a state exchange that covered abortion services beyond those allowed under the Hyde amendment were required to segregate payments for abortion coverage into separate accounts for those enrollees who received premium tax credits. To get the abortion coverage, an enrollee had to make two premium payments: one for regular benefits and one for abortion services. The enrollee could not receive federal tax credits for the premium for abortion services.

The law did not pre-empt state laws pertaining to abortion services, and states could choose to prohibit coverage of such services in the exchange. Health insurers in an exchange could not discriminate against health providers who were unwilling to provide abortion services or to refer patients to providers who did offer such services.

● **Temporary high-risk pool.** Within 90 days of enactment, HHS was required to create a temporary, national high-risk insurance pool program to provide health care benefits to individuals who had pre-existing conditions, until the health insurance exchanges created by the law were functioning in 2014. States that already had their own high-risk pools were required to continue operating them.

To be eligible for the high-risk pool, an individual could not be eligible for Medicare, Medicaid or an employer-based plan, and could not have had insurance during the six-month period before applying. Illegal immigrants could not get coverage through the pool. The law appropriated $5 billion to pay claims and cover administrative costs of the high-risk pool that exceeded the premiums that were collected. If the funding in a given fiscal year was insufficient, HHS could make necessary adjustments.

INDIVIDUAL AND EMPLOYER REQUIREMENTS

● **Individual mandate.** Starting in 2014, all citizens and legal residents were required to have "minimum essential coverage," defined as employer-sponsored coverage; government programs including Medicare, Medicaid or CHIP; or coverage obtained through the new health insurance exchanges.

Those exempted from the requirements included illegal immigrants; individuals who were incarcerated; individuals who could not afford coverage, defined as those whose contributions to the cost of insurance were greater than 8 percent of their household incomes; individuals with household incomes of less than 100 percent of the federal poverty level ($10,830 per year for an individual or $22,050 for a family of four, at the time), although people at this income level were entitled to coverage under Medicaid; members of American Indian tribes; individuals who were uninsured for a period of less than three continuous months; individuals for whom obtaining

health insurance would create a "hardship," as determined by HHS; and those who belonged to certain religious groups with tenets that included conscientious objection to private or public insurance.

• **Individual penalties.** Beginning in 2014, individuals who were required to obtain health insurance coverage and did not do so were subject to a flat penalty tax. The tax was to be phased in over three years, reaching a maximum in 2016 of $695 per year for each individual who did not have health insurance for more than three months in a given year. The penalty per household could not exceed 2.5 percent of household income.

• **Employer penalties.** The law did not require employers to offer health insurance benefits. But starting in 2014, employers with more than 50 workers that did not offer insurance, and that had at least one employee who received a federal premium tax credit to purchase insurance through an exchange, would be required to pay a $2,000 fee for each full-time employee, excluding the first 30 workers.

Employers with more than 50 workers that did offer health insurance benefits would be required to pay the lesser of $3,000 for each employee who received a premium credit or $2,000 per full-time employee, excluding the first 30 employees.

• **Employer vouchers.** Starting in 2014, employers that offered health benefits had to offer vouchers to purchase insurance in the exchanges for low- and moderate-income employees who would have difficulty paying for the employer's health plan. Specifically, employers were required to offer vouchers to employees with incomes of up to 400 percent of the federal poverty level whose contribution to employer-sponsored insurance would constitute from 8 percent to 9.8 percent of their income.

• **Automatic enrollment in employer health plans.** Employers with more than 200 employees were required to automatically enroll new, full-time employees in a health insurance plan (if one was offered) and to maintain the coverage each year unless an employee opted out. The law required employers to provide adequate notice so that employees could choose to opt out. This provision did not supersede any state law regarding automatic enrollment that was at least as stringent.

MEDICAID EXPANSION

• **Medicaid eligibility.** The law expanded eligibility under state Medicaid programs to all individuals with household incomes of up to 133 percent of the federal poverty level, effective in 2014. State Medicaid programs were required to cover qualified individuals who previously did not have to be covered, including those under age 65, those who were not disabled and adults without dependent children. The law prohibited states from changing their Medicaid programs in a way that set more restrictive standards, methodologies or procedures than those that were in effect on the date of enactment — a so-called maintenance-of-effort requirement — through Dec. 31, 2013.

• **Federal matching funds for Medicaid.** The federal government was required to cover 100 percent of the state's cost of covering newly eligible people, including parents and childless adults, from 2014 through 2016. The percentage would drop to 95 percent in 2017, 94 percent in 2018, 93 percent in 2019, and 90 percent in 2020 and beyond. States that previously provided coverage to childless adults at 100 percent of the federal poverty level who continued to be enrolled in Medicaid would receive the same federal funding as states that did not previously provide such coverage.

• **Increased matching funds for Louisiana.** Starting in 2011, the law provided an increase in federal Medicaid matching funds for Louisiana for continuing recovery efforts from major disasters, including Hurricane Katrina.

• **Medicaid income eligibility rules.** Starting in 2014, the law required all states to use a uniform method to determine eligibility for Medicaid based on a household's modified gross income. States would no longer be permitted to disregard income or deduct certain types of income when determining eligibility, as many states did. However, states could continue to disregard or deduct income for applicants who were elderly, blind or disabled. The law also prohibited states from imposing an asset test when determining eligibility for Medicaid, as many states did in the case of parents.

• **Federal matching funds for U.S. territories.** The law provided an increase estimated at $7.3 billion for federal matching payments for Medicaid programs in the five U.S. territories in the period of fiscal 2014 through 2019 and increased caps on federal funding in the territories. It earmarked $925 million of the funds for Puerto Rico.

• **Medicaid reimbursements for primary care.** Medicaid reimbursements for primary care services were increased in 2013 and 2014 to 100 percent of the Medicare payment rates for such services.

CHILDREN'S HEALTH INSURANCE PROGRAM

• **Federal matching funds.** Starting in fiscal 2014, states were to receive an increase of 23 percentage points in their federal matching funds for CHIP, to a cap of 100 percent of the cost of a state's program. This provision effectively increased the minimum federal match for CHIP programs to 88 percent from the previous 65 percent, meaning that states would have to fund, at most, 12 percent of the cost of their programs.

• **Eligibility rules.** States could not change their programs in a way that imposed more restrictive standards, methodologies or procedures than were in effect June 16, 2009, through Sept. 30, 2019.

• **Exchanges.** Children who met income eligibility guidelines for CHIP but were unable to enroll because a state had frozen enrollment due to budget constraints were eligible for premium tax credits to obtain health insurance through the new exchanges starting in 2014. Children who received subsidized coverage through the exchange were not eligible for coverage under CHIP. Children in an exchange could not switch to CHIP if the state reopened enrollment. Starting in fiscal 2016, states could transition children who were eligible for CHIP to receive coverage through one of the new health insurance exchanges instead, as long as HHS approved the transition.

NEW HEALTH INSURANCE REGULATIONS

• **Pre-existing conditions.** Starting in 2014, health insurers who offered group or individual coverage were prohibited from denying coverage because a potential enrollee had a pre-existing condition. The law immediately prohibited insurers from denying coverage to children with pre-existing conditions. Specifically, when determining eligibility for coverage, health insurers could not take into account health status, claims history, physical or mental medical conditions, genetic information, disability, or other factors determined by HHS.

• **Protection against coverage rescission.** Starting in September 2010 (six months after enactment), health insurers were prohibited from rescinding group or individual coverage, unless there was clear

and convincing evidence of fraud or intentional misrepresentation by an enrollee. If insurers did rescind coverage, they had to provide adequate prior notice to the affected enrollees.

● **Coverage of young adults.** Starting in September 2010, health insurers who offered dependent coverage were required to continue coverage of children on their parents' plans, at the parents' discretion, until the children turned 26. Group health plans that were operating before enactment had to cover these adult children only if the children did not have an offer of employer-sponsored insurance.

● **Lifetime spending limits.** Starting in September 2010, health insurers were prohibited from setting lifetime limits on the dollar value of health care provided to an enrollee. Starting in 2014, insurers were barred from setting annual spending limits. Before 2014, insurers could set "reasonable" annual spending limits only if approved by the federal government.

● **Limit on deductibles.** The law limited deductibles in employer-sponsored health plans in the small-group markets to $2,000 per year for individual coverage and $4,000 per year for family coverage, starting in 2014. These deductibles could be increased only if such an increase was offset through an amount "reasonably available" to an employee through a flexible spending arrangement.

● **Coverage of preventive care.** The law required health insurers to cover certain preventive-care services without requiring any cost-sharing — meaning co-payments, co-insurance or deductibles — by enrollees in individual or group plans. The services that had to be covered included vaccinations and screenings recommended by federal agencies. The law specifically stated that the recommendations issued in November 2009 by the federal Preventive Service Task Force on breast cancer screening and mammography did not apply, and that insurers, therefore, had to provide mammograms more frequently than called for in the guidelines. The task force had stated that women younger than 50 with no family history of breast cancer did not need to undergo mammograms, and that women 50 and older needed mammograms only once every two years. Previous guidelines had called for annual mammograms for women 40 and older.

● **Premium reporting.** Health insurers who offered coverage in the small- and large-group markets had to publicly report the percentage of premiums they spent for specific services, such as reimbursement for clinical services, efforts to promote quality of care and administrative costs. Insurers were required to provide rebates to enrollees if the medical loss ratio — the portion of the premium that was spent on medical services as opposed to administrative expenses — for a given year was below 85 percent for large-group plans and 80 percent for small-group and individual-market plans. The provision was intended to limit insurers' administrative costs to 15 percent for large groups and 20 percent for small-group and individual coverage. The rebates began in 2011 and were in effect only until the health insurance exchanges were fully established.

● **Review of premium increases.** Beginning in 2010, HHS was required to create a process, in conjunction with states, to review premium increases by health insurers. Health insurers had to submit a justification for any premium increase before implementing it and place the information prominently on their websites. HHS was required to ensure public disclosure of the information. Starting in 2014, states were required to monitor premium increases inside and outside their insurance exchanges. States that met certain requirements could receive grants to assist them in reviewing and approving premium increases, where allowed by state law.

CHANGES IN PUBLIC PROGRAMS
MEDICARE

● **Payment advisory commission.** The law created an Independent Payment Advisory Board to draft legislative proposals to slow the growth rate in Medicare spending if spending exceeded a certain target rate. The Centers for Medicare and Medicaid Services (CMS) was required to project, on April 15, 2013, whether Medicare spending would exceed the projected growth in the Consumer Price Index that year. If so, the new 15-member board had to meet and submit recommendations to Congress and the president on how to slow Medicare's growth. The recommendations would be due Jan. 15, 2014. Beginning in January 2018, recommendations would be required if the growth in Medicare spending was projected to exceed gross domestic product growth by more than 1 percent.

Board recommendations could include a reduction in reimbursements to Medicare Advantage plans or to prescription drug plans, or proposals to restructure Medicare payment mechanisms generally. Under Medicare Advantage, individuals who were eligible for Medicare got their insurance from private companies rather than the federal government. The board's targeted savings rate was 0.5 percent of projected total Medicare spending in 2015, 1 percent in 2016, 1.25 percent in 2017, and 1.5 percent in 2018 and beyond. The target rate could be less than the specified levels if so recommended by the chief actuary of CMS. The board recommendations could not include rationing care, changing benefits, changing eligibility rules or requiring cost sharing, such as premiums and co-payments.

Once the commission submitted recommendations, Congress would have to consider the legislative proposals. If Congress did not act on a proposal by Aug. 15 of the year it was submitted, CMS would be required to implement the commission's proposal.

● **Medicare drug benefit.** The new law phased out the gap in Medicare drug coverage, known as the "doughnut hole," over 10 years. Under previous law, after beneficiaries met their deductible for the year, the government covered 75 percent of their drug costs up to a set dollar amount. After that, the beneficiary entered the doughnut hole and was responsible for 100 percent of the costs up to a second dollar amount, known as the catastrophic threshold. The federal government was responsible for 95 percent of any remaining costs above the catastrophic limit for the rest of the year.

Under the new law, beneficiaries who fell into the doughnut hole in 2010 were eligible for a one-time $250 rebate. Starting in 2011, beneficiaries who fell into the coverage gap were eligible for a 50 percent discount on brand-name drugs. The discount would increase to 75 percent by 2020, with the government paying the rest of the cost of the drugs.

● **Medicare Advantage payments.** Effective in 2011, the law froze federal payments to Medicare Advantage and then reformulated payments according to local costs. Under the new, phased-in formula, payments were to be allocated based on geographic variability of Medicare spending. Payments would start at 95 percent of traditional fee-for-service Medicare payments in areas that were in the top quartile of Medicare spending, and increase to 115 percent in areas in the lowest quartile. Starting in 2014, the amount that Medicare Advantage plans could spend on administrative costs was capped at 15 percent of the amount collected from premiums. If a plan spent more than that, it would be required to pay HHS a fine equal to the amount of funds spent on administrative costs that exceeded the cap.

● **'Market basket updates.'** The law reduced the "market basket updates" used to determine the reimbursement for certain services by Medicare providers. Generally, market baskets are used to adjust payments annually, based on projected changes in indexes used to measure how much more or less it would cost to buy the same goods and services that year. The new law incorporated adjustments based on gains in productivity into several market baskets used under Part A that did not previously incorporate such provisions. The "productivity adjustments" were to be phased in during different years for different types of providers and would affect inpatient hospitals, long-term care hospitals, inpatient rehabilitation facilities, psychiatric hospitals and outpatient hospitals. The formula was expected to reduce anticipated mandatory spending by an estimated $156.6 billion over 10 years.

● **Disproportionate-share payments.** The law reduced Medicare disproportionate-share hospital payments, federal payments to hospitals that treat a disproportionate share of low-income patients. Starting in fiscal 2014, the payments were reduced by 75 percent, and then they increased based on both the percentage of the population that was uninsured in the area served by the hospital and the percentage of the hospital's care that went to uninsured patients.

● **Additional Medicare hospital payments.** A total of $400 million was set aside from the Federal Hospital Trust Fund to cover additional Medicare payments in fiscal 2011 and 2012 to hospitals located in counties that were in the lowest quartile of per-capita Medicare spending for Part A and Part B (hospital services and physician services, respectively).

● **Center for Medicare and Medicaid Innovation.** The law created a new Center for Medicare and Medicaid Innovation as part of CMS and provided $15 million over 10 years for the center. The new center was directed to evaluate "innovative payment and service delivery models" that would reduce costs without negatively affecting the quality of care or the scope of benefits provided to enrollees. Models to be explored included: payment structured around patient-centered medical homes; contracting directly with groups of providers for care coordination; using comprehensive care plans for geriatric care; creating community-based health teams to support medical homes; and promoting greater access to outpatient services when possible.

● **Physician-owned hospitals.** Effective in 2011, new physician-owned hospitals generally were prohibited from receiving Medicare reimbursements for patients who were referred by physicians with investment interests in the hospital. The law prohibited physician-owned hospitals from expanding, although hospitals could apply to the federal government to be exempted from the ban. The law permitted physician self-referrals to hospitals only if the hospital met certain criteria, including public disclosure of the financial interests of referring physicians and agreements with physicians governing investment in the hospitals.

● **Medicare Part B premiums.** The new law froze the income levels used to calculate premiums for Medicare Part B (physician services) in 2011 through 2019 at levels set for 2010. Medicare Part B premiums were calculated based on income levels, and beneficiaries paid premiums based on their annual income two years before the coverage year.

● **Reimbursement for hospital-acquired infections.** Starting in fiscal 2015, reimbursements would be reduced by 1 percent for certain hospital-acquired conditions, to be determined by HHS.

● **Reimbursement for preventable readmission.** A hospital's reimbursement rates would be reduced for what were considered to be preventable readmissions of Medicare beneficiaries. The provision was intended to give hospitals and health care providers incentives to allow for adequate medical follow-up to prevent multiple hospital readmissions for patients with chronic conditions. Starting in fiscal 2012, CMS would reduce payments by specified percentages, depending on the billing code, for preventable hospital readmissions. CMS was tasked with determining the number of hospital readmissions for a given condition that would be considered excessive and thus subject to reduced reimbursements. Within two years of enactment, a new CMS program would aid hospitals in reducing excessive readmissions.

● **Accountable Care Organizations.** Starting in 2012, qualified health care providers were allowed to form groups, or Accountable Care Organizations, that were eligible for federal payments if they met certain quality standards. Eligibility criteria included having a leadership and administrative structure in place; demonstrating a willingness to take responsibility for the overall quality and cost of care of Medicare beneficiaries who were assigned to the group; and agreeing to contract with CMS for at least three years. The groups were required to submit data allowing CMS to evaluate the quality of care being provided.

MEDICAID COST SAVINGS

● **Medicaid disproportionate-share payments.** Federal matching Medicaid disproportionate-share payments — additional reimbursements for hospitals that served a disproportionate share of low-income individuals — would be reduced by $14.1 billion over the period of fiscal 2014 through 2019.

● **Medicaid prescription drug rebates.** The law increased the rebate that Medicaid programs received for brand-name drugs by 23.1 percent starting in 2010. The discount included Medicaid managed-care plans run by private insurers. The law increased the Medicaid drug rebate for generic drugs to 13 percent of the average manufacturer price.

● **Acquired conditions.** Effective July 1, 2011, the law prohibited federal funding to state Medicaid programs for certain acquired health care conditions, with the specific list up to HHS.

● **Premium assistance.** Starting in 2014, states were required to provide premium assistance to anyone eligible for Medicaid who had employer-sponsored coverage available if doing so was cost-effective for the state. The employer would have to contribute at least 40 percent of the cost of the health insurance premium. Under previous law, it was optional for states to provide premium assistance for employer-sponsored coverage for children and parents who were eligible for Medicaid, if it was cost effective for the state.

OTHER HEALTH CARE PROVISIONS

● **Long-term care.** The law established a new national voluntary insurance program called Community Living Assistance Service and Support (CLASS) to assist adults with functional limitations in purchasing community living assistance services. It also established an infrastructure to address national needs, alleviate burdens on family caregivers and address institutional bias.

HHS was required to develop at least three actuarially sound benefit plans as alternatives for designation as the CLASS Independence Benefit Plan. The premiums established in the first and subsequent year had to be based on actuarial analysis of the 75-year costs to ensure solvency for that 75-year period. Such plans would have to provide for payment of a cash benefit with an average of at least $50 per day

varying based on functional ability. The benefit would have to be paid either daily or weekly and could not be subject to lifetime or aggregate limits.

Once set, a monthly premium generally would remain the same as long as an individual was enrolled. The law provided exceptions to guarantee the program's solvency, but premium increases in those cases would not apply to those age 65 or older or to those who had paid premiums for at least 20 years.

Those age 18 or older who received qualifying taxable wages and were actively employed were eligible for the program as long as they were not patients in a hospital, nursing home, care facility or institution for mental diseases and were not receiving Medicaid.

● **Comparative-effectiveness research.** The law created a nonprofit Patient-Centered Outcomes Research Institute to identify research priorities and conduct research to compare the effectiveness of medical treatments and technologies. The new institution replaced the Federal Coordinating Council that was created under the economic stimulus law (PL 111-5). The purpose of the institute was to assist patients, clinicians, purchasers and policy makers in making informed health decisions. The law appropriated $210 million for the institute in fiscal 2010 through 2012, and $150 million in each of fiscal years 2013 through 2019.

● **Biologic drug patents.** The law created a process for the Food and Drug Administration (FDA) to receive and approve applications for biological products that were either similar to, or interchangeable with, a so-called reference product — a biological product that had already been approved. Biologic drugs were a new technology in which drug manufacturers used living cells to produce drug technology; previously, the FDA lacked statutory authority to approve generic versions of biologic drugs, known as biosimilars.

The law provided exclusivity for the first interchangeable product for certain periods and stipulated that a biosimilar product application could not be approved until 12 years after the date the reference product was first approved. It provided for an additional six months for reference products that had demonstrated benefits from pediatric studies. The FDA had to require labeling and packaging that uniquely identified the biosimilar product.

● **Community health centers.** Funding was increased for community health centers that provided primary care services in areas where economic, geographic or cultural barriers limited access to primary care. The law appropriated $1 billion in fiscal 2011, $1.2 billion in fiscal 2012, $1.5 billion in fiscal 2013, $2.2 billion in fiscal 2014 and $3.6 billion in fiscal 2015.

● **Medical malpractice.** A new five-year demonstration program allowed states to evaluate alternatives to the existing medical liability tort system. HHS could award grants to states that developed pilot programs that allowed for the resolution of medical malpractice disputes and promoted a reduction of medical errors by encouraging the collection and analysis of relevant data. For instance, a state could propose a "no fault" dispute resolution process, in which all victims of certain errors would be compensated equally and health care providers would not be held at fault. States had to identify funding sources for any victim compensation. In addition, states were required to identify a "scope of jurisdiction" for the alternative system they were testing and notify patients who fell within that scope. The jurisdiction could be a geographic area, a health care system, a specific group of health care providers or a specific specialization within medical practice.

● **Restaurant menu labeling.** Chain restaurants and food vending machines with more than 20 outlets were required to list nutritional information for each available item, including the caloric content of each standard item, and provide an easily understood statement regarding the daily recommended intake of calories. Calorie labeling had to be placed near menu boards, drive-through window menus and vending machines. The Agriculture Department was required to issue regulations regarding this provision within one year of enactment.

● **American Indian health.** The law permanently reauthorized the Indian Health Care Improvement Act, which governed the provision of health care to American Indians and Alaska Natives through the HHS Indian Health Service. The law authorized programs aimed at increasing the recruitment and retention of health care professionals; expanded mental and behavioral health programs to address issues such as fetal alcohol spectrum disorders, child sexual abuse and domestic violence; and authorized long-term care services. It required the Indian Health Service budget to account for medical inflation rates and population growth to address underfunding issues.

● **Sex education.** The law provided grants of at least $250,000 per year for each state to conduct "Personal Responsibility Education Programs" to educate teenagers about "both abstinence and contraception for the prevention of pregnancy and sexually transmitted infections, including HIV/AIDS," as well as other life topics such as financial literacy and career skills.

● **Health insurance overhaul implementation fund.** The law appropriated $1 billion to HHS for the administrative costs of implementing the law's provisions.

REVENUE PROVISIONS
MAJOR REVENUE-RAISERS

● **Excise tax on health plans.** The law established a 40 percent excise tax on high-cost insurance plans offered by employers. The tax, which would become effective in 2018, applied to the cost of premiums for medical coverage above designated thresholds: $10,200 for individuals and $27,500 for families. If medical costs rose faster than expected between 2010 and 2018, as measured by a formula set out in the law, the 2018 thresholds would be adjusted accordingly. The starting thresholds would increase from 2018 to 2019 by the Consumer Price Index plus 1 percent, and by the Consumer Price Index after that.

Several specified groups of taxpayers would get adjusted thresholds in an attempt to ensure that the tax targeted the highest-cost benefits. Thresholds would be increased to the extent that the age and gender characteristics of a company's workforce required higher premiums than would a more typical pool of employees. Thresholds would also be increased by an additional $1,650 for individuals and $3,450 for families for retirees who were not eligible for Medicare and for workers in high-risk professions, such as law enforcement, mining, construction, agriculture and fishing.

Generally, the tax was to be paid by the insurance company or by the plan administrator for self-insured companies. The threshold amount was the sum of premiums and contributions to flexible spending arrangements, health savings accounts and other similar mechanisms. Dental and vision benefits did not count toward the total.

The tax was expected to raise $32 billion in 2010 through 2019, the window set under the budget resolution, but because the tax did not begin until 2018, it was expected to bring in much more after that.

● **Additional hospital insurance tax.** Effective in 2013, the law created a second tax bracket in the payroll levy used to finance Medicare. In addition to paying the existing 1.45 percent employee share of the

Medicare tax, employees were required to pay an extra 0.9 percent on wages and self-employment income above $200,000 for individuals, and above $250,000 for married couples.

Also starting in 2013, individuals with adjusted gross income over $200,000 and married couples with adjusted gross income over $250,000 had to pay a new 3.8 percent Medicare tax on unearned income. That included capital gains, interest, dividends, annuities, royalties and rents, along with passive business investments. Active business income from sole proprietorships, S corporations and partnerships was not subject to the tax. The tax applied to all of an individual's unearned income, but only to the extent that the total adjusted gross income exceeded the threshold. For example, an individual with $150,000 in unearned income out of a total of $250,000 in adjusted gross income would pay taxes on $50,000 of the unearned income — the amount by which adjusted gross income exceeded the $200,000 threshold.

Together, the two provisions were expected to raise $210.2 billion over 10 years.

● **Pharmaceutical industry fee.** The prescription drug industry as a whole was responsible for paying an annual fee, beginning with a total of $2.5 billion in 2011. The amount rose to $2.8 billion for 2012 and 2013; $3 billion for 2014, 2015 and 2016; $4 billion for 2017; $4.1 billion for 2018; and $2.8 billion beyond that. The government would divide the fees among pharmaceutical companies based on the value of the drugs they sold to certain government health care programs.

The fees were expected to raise $27 billion over 10 years.

● **Medical device tax.** A new 2.3 percent excise tax on medical devices, effective in 2013, applied to a wide range of devices, particularly those used in hospitals and doctors' offices. The tax did not apply to eyeglasses, contact lenses and hearing aids; other items manufactured and sold at retail stores for individual use could also be exempted.

The tax was expected to generate $20 billion over 10 years.

● **Health insurance industry fee.** Starting in 2014, health insurance providers were required to pay an annual industrywide fee. The total annual fee was to begin at $8 billion in 2014, then rise to $11.3 billion for 2015 and 2016, $13.9 billion for 2017 and $14.3 billion for 2018. After that, the total would increase by the same percentage as health care premiums. The annual total would be divided among health insurers according to market share, based on each company's premiums as a percentage of those of the overall health insurance industry. The law provided a break for certain not-for-profit insurers and did not include any government entities or self-insuring employers.

The fees were projected to raise $60.1 billion over 10 years.

SMALLER HEALTH REVENUE-RAISERS

● **Health spending account limits.** Starting in 2011, people with health flexible spending arrangements, health savings accounts, health reimbursement accounts and Archer medical savings accounts could not use the pretax money to pay for over-the-counter medication unless it was prescribed by a doctor. The provision was expected to raise $5 billion over 10 years.

● **Penalties on nonmedical expenses.** The law increased, from 10 percent to 20 percent, the tax penalty for people who used tax-advantaged health savings accounts and Archer medical savings accounts for non-health purposes, generating an estimated $1.4 billion over 10 years.

● **Flexible spending caps.** A statutory cap of $2,500 was placed on the amount of pretax dollars that a worker could set aside in a health flexible spending arrangement. The cap took effect in 2013, with annual adjustments after that based on the Consumer Price Index. The change was expected to generate $13 billion.

● **Charitable hospitals.** Nonprofit hospitals had to meet a new set of requirements to keep their tax exemptions. They had to conduct regular community health needs assessments and tell the IRS how they met the needs. They also had to establish written, publicized criteria for providing financial assistance to patients, and the law placed limits on their collections processes and fees.

● **Part D deduction elimination.** A deduction that businesses received for providing prescription drug plans for their retirees was repealed. Previously, companies could get federal subsidies for offering the plans without counting the subsidies as income, then deduct the full cost of the plans, including the value of the subsidies. The change allowed companies to continue excluding subsidies from income but prohibited them from also deducting the subsidies. It was expected to generate $4.5 billion.

● **Itemized deduction.** The law raised the threshold above which taxpayers could deduct medical expenses from 7.5 percent of adjusted gross income to 10 percent. The provision took effect in 2013, but for the first four years it did not apply to taxpayers who were age 65 and older or had a spouse in that age group. It was expected to raise $15.2 billion over 10 years.

● **Executive compensation deductions.** Health insurance companies faced new limits on their ability to deduct the compensation of their executives. The cap was $1 million for most companies, but it was $500,000 for health insurers. The provision took effect for payments made starting in 2013 for services provided anytime after 2009. Unlike most companies, health insurers were required to count any performance-based compensation and commissions toward the cap, and the limitation applied to all employees, directors and consultants, not just a small group of executives. It was projected to raise $600 million over 10 years.

● **Blue Cross and Blue Shield.** Blue Cross and Blue Shield health insurance plans had new restrictions starting in 2010. To keep a special 25 percent deduction for certain claims and an exception from the 20 percent reduction in deductions for certain premiums that for-profit companies faced, the Blue Cross and Blue Shield plans were required to have a medical loss ratio of at least 85 percent. The provision was expected to raise $400 million over 10 years.

● **Tanning tax.** A new 10 percent tax on indoor tanning services took effect in July 2010 and was expected to raise $2.7 billion over 10 years.

NON-HEALTH REVENUE PROVISIONS

● **'Black liquor.'** The law prevented paper companies from claiming a $1.01-per-gallon cellulosic biofuel tax credit for a manufacturing byproduct known as "black liquor." The substance was often used as fuel in the manufacturing process. The change was credited with raising $23.6 billion over 10 years.

● **'Economic substance.'** The doctrine of "economic substance" that governed certain tax cases was put into statute. Under the legislation, business transactions had to have a substantial economic or business purpose and not be executed for tax purposes alone to qualify for tax benefits. Companies engaging in such transactions faced penalties of 20 percent to 40 percent if their maneuvers were disallowed. The change was expected to raise $4.5 billion over 10 years.

● **Information reporting.** A provision aimed at increasing tax com-

pliance required that, effective in 2012, businesses report to the IRS aggregate payments to a single provider of goods or services if the payments totaled $600 or more in a calendar year. This expanded a previous requirement that similar payments to individuals be reported, and it included penalties for failure to file. The law was expected to generate $17.1 billion over 10 years.

● **Corporate estimated taxes.** Corporations faced a timing shift in their quarterly estimated taxes that affected revenue in 2014 only.

OTHER REVENUE-RELATED PROVISIONS

● **Adoption credit.** The law increased the maximum tax credit for adopting children by $1,000, to $13,170. The credit was made refundable, and the scheduled date for the expiration of the credit was delayed from the end of 2010 to the end of 2011. The exclusion for employer-provided adoption assistance underwent a similar change. The provision was expected to cost $1.2 billion over 10 years.

● **W-2 reporting.** Starting in 2011, employers had to report the cost of their employees' health coverage on their annual W-2 form.

● **Therapeutic discovery projects.** Small companies could get a 50 percent tax credit for certain investments for medical research. Projects had to be certified, address medical needs that were not being met, reduce long-term health care costs or make a major advance in cancer treatment. The provision took effect for expenses made starting in 2009 and expired at the end of 2010. It was expected to cost $900 million over 10 years.

● **Veterans' health study.** By the end of 2012, the Secretary of Veterans Affairs was required to produce a study on whether the fees and taxes on insurers, prescription drug manufacturers and medical device makers were having an effect on the cost of veterans' medical care and access to drugs and devices.

● **Indian tribal governments exclusion.** People receiving health care provided by the Indian Health Service or an American Indian tribe could exclude the value of those benefits from income.

● **Simple cafeteria plans for small businesses.** Beginning in 2011, the law made it easier for small businesses to set up cafeteria plans for employee benefits. ■

Child Nutrition Legislation Cleared

THE HOUSE CLEARED a Senate child nutrition bill in early December after House Democrats spent weeks rallying support, overcoming objections to funding offsets and fending off a last-minute Republican attempt to derail the measure. President Obama signed the measure into law on Dec. 13 (S 3307 — PL 111-296).

The bill boosted mandatory spending on child nutrition programs by $4.5 billion over 10 years and, for the first time, gave the Agriculture Department the authority to set nutrition standards for foods sold in school vending machines, a la carte lines and snack stores.

It also authorized the first increase in meal reimbursements to schools since 1973. The higher payment was tied to schools meeting new nutrition standards that promoted more fresh foods on school menus.

The legislation reauthorized school lunch, school breakfast and after-school feeding programs, and the Special Supplemental Nutrition Program for Women, Infants and Children (WIC), among others, through 2015. The programs had been operating under short-term extensions, the last of which was set to expire Dec. 3 under a continuing resolution (PL 111-242) enacted Sept. 30.

Participation in meal programs was expected to increase under a pilot program that allowed school districts to qualify low-income children for federally subsidized free and reduced-price meals using Medicaid enrollment information. Children could already qualify for subsidized meals if they received other forms of public assistance.

The cost was offset in part by moving up the end date for a temporary boost in food stamp benefits that was enacted in the 2009 stimulus law (PL 111-5), a plan that drew significant Democratic opposition.

BOX SCORE

BILL: S 3307 — PL 111-296

LEGISLATIVE ACTION:

House Education and Labor Committee approved HR 5504, 32-13, on July 15.

Senate passed S 3307 (S Rept 111-178) by unanimous consent on Aug. 5.

House cleared S 3307, 264-157, on Dec. 2.

President signed the bill on Dec. 13.

Some lawmakers also criticized a requirement that school districts put more non-federal money into their meal accounts. State and school leaders said this would mean higher lunch fees for students who paid full price for their meals.

The White House issued a statement expressing strong support for the bill, although the new spending was less than half the $10 billion the administration had requested.

Final House action on the bill was aided in part by an administration pledge to congressional leaders that it would help see that the food stamp program — officially the Supplemental Nutrition Assistance Program, or SNAP — received the necessary funding.

2010 LEGISLATIVE ACTION
SENATE COMMITTEE

The Senate Agriculture, Nutrition and Forestry Committee on March 24 gave voice vote approval to the $4.5 billion bill (S 3307 — S Rept 111-178), despite some concerns over how to pay for it.

Senators from both parties applauded the increase proposed in the bill, which was sponsored by committee Chairwoman Blanche Lincoln, D-Ark. But they raised repeated concerns over the decision to pay for the boost in part by cutting $2.2 billion over 10 years from the Environmental Quality Incentives Program (EQIP), a popular federal program that paid farmers to adopt conservation practices.

Lincoln called the program "critically important" and said she would work with other senators to identify alternate ways to pay for the bill. A coalition of environmental groups sent a letter to the committee March 23, urging senators to find offsets, stressing that the proposed

reduction would cut the baseline amount for conservation funds, which would result in lower conservation funding in the next farm bill.

The committee rejected, 10-11, an amendment by Saxby Chambliss of Georgia, the panel's ranking Republican, that would have paid for the nutrition increase by instead cutting funds from the Conservation Stewardship Program, a separate Agriculture Department conservation program that he said had far fewer applicants.

The committee adopted a manager's package of amendments by voice vote, as well as:

▸ A proposal by John Thune, R-S.D., to ensure that funds in the bill were spent to research child hunger, obesity and Type 2 diabetes on Indian reservations.

▸ An amendment by Sherrod Brown, D-Ohio, to establish an organic-food school pilot program.

▸ Another Brown amendment to provide competitive grants to state agencies for summer food service programs.

▸ A plan by Debbie Stabenow, D-Mich., to require a study of best practices of states participating in a federal after-school supper program.

HOUSE COMMITTEE

The House Education and Labor panel voted 32-13 on July 15 to approve a version of the legislation (HR 5504) that would have increased funding for school breakfast, lunch and other nutrition programs by $8 billion over a decade without offsets.

Republicans insisted that the new spending be paid for. Chairman George Miller, D-Calif., promised to work out offsets before the measure reached the floor.

Amendments adopted during the markup included:

▸ A manager's amendment by Miller, adopted 31-14, that reconciled some of the discrepancies between the House and Senate bills, including adding a provision that would provide for a nationwide expansion of an after-school meal program that existed in 13 states and the District of Columbia.

The amendment also added language to require the Agriculture Department to contract for an independent review of new ingredients in foods to be available for WIC.

▸ An amendment by Joe Courtney, D-Conn., adopted by voice vote, to require the Agriculture Department to purchase low-fat cheeses for the school breakfast and lunch programs. The need to help children stave off obesity had come into sharper focus as a result of a campaign spearheaded by first lady Michelle Obama that emphasized exercise and healthy foods.

SENATE FLOOR

The Senate passed its bipartisan bill by unanimous consent on Aug. 5. It was seen as a victory for Lincoln, who was locked in a tough re-election battle.

Lincoln had warned that not acting before the August recess could endanger key policy changes to school lunch, school breakfast, after-school meals and other nutrition programs, which were due to expire on Sept. 30.

Before the bill came to the floor, Lincoln and Chambliss reached an agreement that avoided tapping EQIP and instead offset the new spending with an early end to the boost in monthly food stamp benefits included in the stimulus package.

Advocacy groups opposed paying for the child nutrition bill with food stamp funds. "The bill, if enacted, will do far more harm than good," said Jim Weill, president of the Food Research and Action Center, who said the food stamp cuts would "increase hunger in America."

HOUSE FLOOR

House Democratic leaders had to overcome several obstacles before winning a 264-157 vote to clear the Senate bill on Dec. 2. (House vote 603, p. H-210)

Republicans were careful to express support for reauthorizing school meal programs, but they argued that the bill constituted an overreach by the federal government and complained that in clearing the Senate bill, Democrats were eliminating chances for House input.

Democratic leaders had to pull the bill from the floor temporarily Dec. 1 after John Kline of Minnesota, ranking Republican on the Education and Labor Committee, introduced a motion to recommit the measure that seemed likely to succeed. Kline's motion would have dropped a provision that set a minimum price for paid school lunches and replaced it with language to bar institutions from receiving certain federal food funding if they had convicted sex offenders on staff or did not run background checks on child care staff.

Kline cited a bipartisan letter written by the National Governors Association earlier in the year saying the bill "would establish a federal mandate for every paid meal in every school in the country for the first time ever" and "destabilize" fair market prices for school meals.

To give members of their caucus political cover to vote against the motion, Democratic leaders brought a newly introduced bill (HR 6469) to the floor containing the background check language.

The House passed that measure, 416-3, on Dec. 2 and then rejected Kline's motion on the child nutrition bill, 200-221. (House votes 601, p. H-208, and 602, H-210)

Majority Leader Steny H. Hoyer, D-Md., dismissed those charges. "The real purpose of this motion to recommit was to delay this bipartisan bill from being signed into law," he charged. Any change would have sent the bill back to the Senate, where it was expected to die, given the short time left on the legislative calendar.

While Democrats came together to clear the legislation, conflict over the food stamp provisions had stalled the measure. More than 100 liberal lawmakers signed a letter in August calling on Speaker Nancy Pelosi, D-Calif., not to bring the bill to the floor with the offset.

But Democratic leaders stressed that this was their best chance to clear the bill, which would be unlikely to be taken up by the Republican-controlled House in the next Congress. And the White House weighed in with its promise to seek more money for the program.

"Quite frankly, if I did not believe that commitment to restore SNAP funding was real, I would have had a hard time voting for the underlying legislation," said Jim McGovern, D-Mass., co-author of the food stamp letter and co-chairman of the House Hunger Caucus and the Congressional Hunger Center. ∎

Doctors' Medicare Pay Cut Averted

DOCTORS WERE SPARED a 25 percent cut in Medicare reimbursement rates in 2011 under a bill cleared late in the session. President Obama signed the measure into law Dec. 15 (HR 4994 – PL 111-309).

The costs of the bipartisan, one-year bill were offset mainly by recouping more money from consumers who received excessive insurance subsidies under the new health care overhaul law (PL 111-148, PL 111-152).

The bill was the fifth so-called "doc fix" enacted during the congressional session. Taken together, the first four bills enabled doctors to avoid a 21.1 percent reduction in 2010.

Each of the bills covered only a few months because the costs of a longer-term solution were unacceptable to many members at a time of widespread concern over the soaring federal deficit. Even the short-term bills were so difficult to pass that three of them were signed after the previous law had expired and were retroactive.

The delays resulted largely from the fact that the issue became entangled in ongoing fighting over broader Democratic "jobs" bills, including the issue of offsetting the costs. A pay-as-you-go law enacted in February (PL 111-139) explicitly exempted legislation preventing the doctors' pay cut through 2011. However, Republicans still objected strongly to allowing a pay fix that added to the deficit.

The reimbursement issue grew out of the 1997 Balanced Budget Act (PL 105-33), which created a statutory cost control formula for calculating annual adjustments in the fees paid to physicians for their services to Medicare patients. Beginning in 2002, the formula necessitated annual reductions in fee rates. Concerned that fewer doctors would be willing to see Medicare patients, lawmakers regularly passed legislation to prevent the scheduled cuts. As a result, none of the reductions had taken place. *(1997 Almanac, p. 2-47)*

In November 2009, the House passed a bill (HR 3961) that would have blocked the scheduled 21.2 percent fee reduction in 2010 and instead increased doctors' pay by about 1.2 percent. Beginning in 2011, it would have replaced the cost control formula with a method closely tied to inflation, eliminating the need for the annual fixes. *(2009 action, 2009 Almanac, p. 13-17)*

The Congressional Budget Office estimated that the bill would have required $209.6 billion in additional spending in fiscal years 2010 through 2019. Democrats said the spending was already taking place year by year as Congress canceled the scheduled cuts, and that replacing a broken law, rather than blocking it one year at a time, was not something that required offsets.

Republicans did not agree. They argued that the larger reimbursements would require vast new spending that would add to the deficit unless it was offset, and they succeeded in blocking a companion bill in the Senate.

At the end of the 2009 session, Congress attached language to the fiscal 2010 Defense appropriations bill (PL 111-118) that delayed

---

BOX SCORE

BILL: HR 4994 – PL 111-309

....

LEGISLATIVE ACTION:

Senate passed HR 4994, amended, by unanimous consent on Dec. 8.

House cleared the bill, 409-2, on Dec. 9.

President signed the bill on Dec. 15.

---

the scheduled 21.2 percent pay cut for 2010 through Feb. 28. *(Appropriations, p. 2-6)*

2010 LEGISLATIVE ACTION

In the absence of a longer-term solution, Congress kept the 2010 pay cuts at bay through a series of four short-term extensions of the provision enacted in December 2009. The fifth bill delayed cuts through 2011.

EXTENSION TO MARCH 31

Unable to get Senate agreement on a large package of spending and tax-cut extensions, lawmakers cleared a quick one-month Medicare reimbursement bill in March that blocked the pay cut through March 31. It also extended federal unemployment benefits and a few other urgent expiring programs. President Obama signed the measure on March 2 (HR 4691 – PL 111-144).

The House passed the short-term bill, which included no offsets, by voice vote Feb. 25. But when the bill came to the Senate, Jim Bunning, R-Ky., mounted a one-man filibuster, insisting that Congress pay for the measure with unspent funds from the 2009 economic stimulus law (PL 111-5). As a result of the delay, Congress missed the Feb. 28 cutoff date. Bunning relented on March 2, after getting a vote on a proposed offset; he lost 43-53 on a procedural vote. *(Senate vote 31, p. S-9)*

The Senate then cleared the retroactive bill, 78-19. *(Senate vote 32, p. S-9)*

EXTENSION TO MAY 31

Continued partisan wrangling in the Senate led to another brief lapse in the Medicare reimbursement provisions as well as in several other programs. Democrats and Republicans left in late March for their spring recess deadlocked over the bill, which was not signed until April 15 (HR 4851 – PL 111-157). The measure delayed the Medicare rate cut for two more months, through May 31. Again, it was retroactive.

Other programs covered by the bill included federal unemployment insurance, health insurance premium subsidies for jobless workers, flood insurance and small-business loan guarantees.

The House passed the bill by voice vote March 17, but several Senate Republicans, led by Tom Coburn of Oklahoma, refused to allow a vote in that chamber unless the bill's cost was fully offset.

After returning from the recess, Senate Democratic leaders tried again, rebuffing several amendments to pay for the bill. The Senate passed a slightly amended version of the bill by a vote of 59-38 on April 15, and the House cleared it, 289-112, later the same day. *(Senate vote 117, p. S-25; House vote 211, p. H-76)*

EXTENSION TO NOV. 30

After more efforts by Senate Democrats to pass a bill that would renew a number of expired tax provisions and social safety-net programs, including the Medicare doc fix, the leadership pulled the measure and passed a stand-alone bill that postponed the deep cut in Medicare payments to physicians through Nov. 30. Obama signed the retroactive

bill on June 25 (HR 3962 — PL 111-192).

The Senate had passed the measure by unanimous consent on June 18, and the House cleared it, 417-1, on June 24. *(House vote 393, H-138)*

In response to calls from Senate moderates, the $6.4 billion cost of the bill was fully offset. It included provisions requiring certain pension plans to make extra contributions if they offered compensation in excess of $1 million to any employee, paid unusually high dividends, or engaged in extraordinary stock buybacks. The provision was estimated to raise about $2.1 billion over 10 years. The bill also prohibited health care providers from submitting separate claims for certain outpatient services, saving an estimated $4.2 billion over 10 years.

EXTENSION TO DEC. 31

Lawmakers postponed the rate cut for the remainder of the year with a bill enacted Nov. 30 (HR 5712 — PL 111-286). The Senate passed the bill by unanimous consent on Nov. 18. The House cleared it by voice vote Nov. 29.

The cost was estimated at $1 billion over 10 years, and although the price tag was exempt under the pay-as-you-go law, deficit concerns had reached a point that only a fully funded bill was able to advance. The costs were offset by codifying a new Centers for Medicare and Medicaid Services policy that reduced Medicare payments for multiple therapy services provided to patients in one day.

2011 EXTENSION

As part of wrapping up the legislative year, lawmakers cleared a bill that blocked what would have been a 25 percent rate cut for the whole of 2011. The estimated cost was $14.9 billion over 10 years.

The legislation also extended several expiring Medicare programs, including protections for rural doctors and hospitals, adding $4.6 billion to the price tag.

The extensions were paid for mainly by changing a part of the health care overhaul that provided tax credits to help people with incomes between 100 percent and 400 percent of the federal poverty rate buy health insurance, beginning in 2014. Under the original law, recipients were required to pay back part of the subsidy — up to $250 for an individual or $400 for families — if they misstated their income or their income increased during the year. The bill replaced the repayment schedule with a sliding-scale structure, requiring smaller repayments at lower incomes and dramatically increasing the maximum amount for high earners.

It was the first time Congress had significantly altered a provision of the overhaul.

The measure was the result of a bipartisan compromise reached by Senate Finance Chairman Max Baucus, D-Mont., and the panel's ranking Republican, Charles E. Grassley of Iowa. ∎

Student Loan Measure Moves Quietly

THE MOST DRAMATIC CHANGE to federal student loan programs in a decade was enacted in tandem with President Obama's overhaul of the health insurance system. The intensity of the health care debate overshadowed the student loan provisions, which were included in a "corrections" bill that made limited changes to the health care overhaul. President Obama signed the measure into law March 30 (HR 4872 — PL 111-152).

The bill made the federal government the sole provider of student loans, cutting out the role of private companies as middlemen. Previously, the government had two programs: one that provided direct loans and another that guaranteed loans by private lenders.

Eliminating the federal guarantees and subsidies that had enabled private lenders to keep interest rates low was expected to save about $61 billion in mandatory spending over 10 years, according to the Congressional Budget Office (CBO). About 70 percent of the savings, or $42 billion, was dedicated to increased funding for Pell grants and other federal education programs. Another $10 billion was set aside for deficit reduction, and $9 billion went to help offset costs of the health care overhaul.

The measure provided about 45 percent less funding for education programs than a stand-alone student loan bill that the House had passed in 2009 (HR 3221). CBO estimated that the earlier House-

BOX SCORE

BILL: HR 4872 — PL 111-152

LEGISLATIVE ACTION:

House passed HR 4872, 220-211, on March 21.

Senate passed HR 4872, amended, 56-43, on March 25.

House cleared the bill, 220-207, on March 25.

President signed the bill on March 30.

passed bill would have reduced federal spending on student loans by $87 billion, of which $77 billion was directed to education programs. Since that time, however, CBO had reduced the projected net savings as more colleges and universities voluntarily enrolled in the federal lending program and costs associated with higher student eligibility and enrollment rose.

Also, under the earlier bill, all the net savings were used for education programs.

Among other things, the enacted measure did not include $8 billion that the earlier House-passed bill would have devoted to competitive grants for early-childhood education, and it eliminated $7 billion for a program to improve graduation rates and upgrade facilities at two-year colleges. *(House bill, 2009 Almanac, p. 8-3)*

Technically, the measure was a budget reconciliation bill, which gave it protection from filibusters in the Senate, sparing Democratic leaders from having to obtain the 60 votes needed to overcome GOP delaying tactics. The use of the protective rules for the bill was sanctioned under the fiscal 2010 budget resolution (S Con Res 13), which called for reconciliation legislation that changed health care law and saved at least $1 billion from education programs.

The reconciliation bill was devoted primarily to modest changes to the health care package aimed at mollifying House Democrats who had to swallow the Senate-passed version of the health care bill, giving

up many of their own priorities. *(Health care, p. 9-3)*

While some Democratic senators balked at including the student loan provisions in the reconciliation bill, the plan provided needed offsets for the health care overhaul and was seen as attracting votes for that legislation in the House.

The Federal Family Education Loan Program, which provided federal guarantees for private student loans, was created in 1965 (PL 89-329) under President Lyndon B. Johnson. The Direct Loan program was a later addition, established in 1993 (PL 103-66) under President Bill Clinton to provide federal student loans directly to borrowers.

Democrats and Republicans had argued for years over which was the better approach. Democrats said direct loans were more reliable and efficient and saved billions of dollars that could better be used to expand programs for low-income students. Republicans called that a job-killing government takeover of a private industry.

Since taking majority control of Congress in 2007, the Democrats had been chipping away at the private student loan program. A 2007 law (PL 110-84) cut interest rates on subsidized student loans in half over four years. A 2008 law (PL 110-227) reauthorizing the 1965 Higher Education Act placed several new restrictions on private lenders. Another 2008 law (PL 110-350) temporarily allowed the government to buy private student loans and take other actions to ensure that students could still get college loans despite a freeze in the nation's credit markets. *(2007 Almanac, p. 8-3; 2008 Almanac, p. 9-10)*

HIGHLIGHTS

The following are major education provisions in the bill:

- **Direct loans.** The legislation eliminated federal guarantees for private student loans under the Federal Family Education Loan Program as of July 1, 2010, and made the Direct Loan program administered by the Department of Education the sole provider of the loans. Private lenders could continue servicing the loans under a competitive bidding system.

- **Pell grants.** The bill increased funding for the federal Pell grant program, the largest source of federal grants to low-income students attending college or other postsecondary programs. It provided permanent mandatory budget authority, which was meant to supplement discretionary Pell grant funding and bring the maximum Pell grant award up to an annual level specified in the law.

Overall, CBO estimated that the bill would increase mandatory spending for the Pell grant program by $36.1 billion over 10 years.

- **Loan repayment.** Income-based student loan payments were capped for new borrowers after July 1, 2014, at 10 percent of the borrower's net income, after adjustments for basic living costs, with the remaining balances forgiven after 20 years of repayment.

- **Minority-serving institutions.** The measure extended through 2019 a program that provided $255 million per year in mandatory funding for historically black colleges and universities and minority-serving institutions.

- **Community colleges.** Community colleges were provided $500 million annually for fiscal years 2011 through 2014 to develop and improve educational or career training programs.

- **Low-income students.** The bill provided a total of $750 million in fiscal years 2010 to 2014 for state grants to increase the number of low-income students prepared to enter and succeed in college and to manage their student loans.

2010 LEGISLATIVE ACTION

Shortly after the House cleared the health care overhaul in a rare Sunday session March 21, it turned to the reconciliation bill, passing it by a vote of 220-211. The debate was a continuation of the months-long disputes over health care and made virtually no reference to the education provisions. *(House vote 167, p. H-62)*

The Senate passed the reconciliation bill by a vote of 56-43 on March 25, after spending most of three days on a series of GOP amendments and adopting two minor changes. *(Senate vote 105, p. S-23)*

That sent the bill back to the House, which cleared it, 220-207, in the early evening of March 25. *(House vote 194, p. H-70)*

Although some Republican senators had vowed to impede the legislation with questions about whether portions of it truly constituted budget-related changes governed by the reconciliation rules, their appeals to the Senate parliamentarian were mainly in vain. The Senate dropped two minor education provisions after the parliamentarian ruled that they were out of order because they did not affect either mandatory spending or federal revenues. The changes had little effect on the bill but forced it back to the House to be cleared.

One of the provisions would have authorized the Education Department to provide additional mandatory funding in fiscal 2010 and subsequent fiscal years to cover the increased federal Pell grant amounts under the bill. The underlying bill, however, still appropriated additional Pell grant funds and indexed the funding to inflation.

The other excised provision would have eliminated a requirement in existing law that the Education Department reduce Pell grant funding across the board if it was insufficient in a given year to provide the maximum grant level specified by law. The underlying bill effectively eliminated the requirement anyway by stipulating that a Pell grant awarded in a given year could not be smaller than the grant awarded the previous year. ∎

Chapter 10

LEGAL AFFAIRS

Elena Kagan Confirmed, Putting Three Women on Supreme Court

THE SENATE ON AUG. 5 confirmed Elena Kagan to serve as the 112th Supreme Court justice, filling the seat vacated by Justice John Paul Stevens, who retired at the end of the 2009-10 session after 35 years on the bench. She was sworn in two days later. *(Stevens, p. 10-4)*

The second member of the high court to be appointed by President Obama, Kagan joined Ruth Bader Ginsburg and Sonia Sotomayor to bring the number of women on the court to three for the first time in U.S. history. The only other woman to serve on the Supreme Court was Sandra Day O'Connor, who retired at the beginning of 2006. *(O'Connor, 2005 Almanac, p. 14-7)*

Kagan's nomination, which Obama announced at a White House ceremony May 10, attracted far less passion in either party than that of Sotomayor, Obama's first Supreme Court pick and the first Hispanic female justice. Kagan, whose only judicial experience was as a clerk for Justice Thurgood Marshall, carried neither the lengthy judicial paper trail nor the same history of controversial speeches as Sotomayor. *(Sotomayor, 2009 Almanac, p. 15-3)*

Because she was replacing the liberal Stevens, Kagan was not expected to alter the court's ideological balance. And a unified Democratic Caucus joined by several GOP senators made a filibuster virtually impossible to sustain. So, despite some fiery floor speeches, Republicans showed little appetite for a serious fight.

In announcing the nomination, Obama said Kagan was "widely regarded as one of the nation's foremost legal minds. She's an acclaimed legal scholar with a rich understanding of constitutional law. She is a former White House aide with a lifelong commitment to public service and a firm grasp of the nexus and boundaries between our three branches of government." Obama also praised what he described as "her openness to a broad array of viewpoints; her habit, to borrow a phrase from Justice Stevens, 'of understanding before disagreeing;' her fair-mindedness and skill as a consensus builder."

In talking of Kagan's personal background, Obama noted that she was a granddaughter of immigrants, that her mother and brothers became public schoolteachers and that her father was a tenants' rights lawyer.

"Someone as gifted as Elena could easily have settled into a comfortable life in a corporate law practice," Obama said. "Instead, she chose a life of service."

At the time of her nomination, the 50-year-old New York native was the solicitor general, heading the office that represented the federal government in cases before the Supreme Court. The Senate confirmed her to that position, 61-31, in 2009.

Kagan's professional background set her apart from her eight would-be colleagues, a fact that drew both praise and criticism. She was the first court nominee in 39 years with no experience as a judge; the other eight had all joined the court from seats on the federal circuit courts of appeals. Before becoming solicitor general, Kagan had limited experience as a practicing lawyer; she worked as an associate White House counsel in the Clinton administration and as an associate at a Washington law firm. President Clinton had tapped her for an appellate court seat in 1999, but GOP senators blocked her confirmation.

Kagan had served on the faculty at the University of Chicago Law School and then at Harvard Law School before becoming that institution's first woman dean. She also had been on Clinton's Domestic Policy Council.

Democrats argued that Kagan would bring a much-needed real-world perspective to the court about how public policy was actually made. Supporters also cited her work while dean of Harvard Law as evidence that the nominee was a savvy pragmatist who had a history of building goodwill with conservatives, and who therefore stood a good chance of building consensus on a fractured Supreme Court.

Senate Majority Leader Harry Reid, D-Nev., said he was "particularly pleased President Obama has chosen a nominee from outside the judicial monastery."

Most Republicans cast Kagan's résumé in a very different light. They portrayed her as an elitist who graduated from Princeton, Oxford and Harvard; worked in two Democratic administrations; and served on an advisory board to the investment bank Goldman Sachs.

"It strikes me that if a nominee does not have judicial experience, they should have substantial litigation experience," said Senate Minority Leader Mitch McConnell, R-Ky. "Ms. Kagan has neither."

"Elena Kagan may well be the nominee with the least amount of relevant experience for the job in the last five decades or more," said Ed Whelan, president of the conservative-leaning Ethics and Public

---

ELENA KAGAN

Residence: Cambridge, Mass.

Born: April 28, 1960, in Manhattan's Stuyvesant Town neighborhood

Family: Single

Religion: Jewish

Education: Graduated Hunter College High School, 1977; A.B. summa cum laude (history), Princeton U., 1981; M.Phil., Oxford U., 1983; J.D. magna cum laude, Harvard U., 1986

Career: Clerk for Judge Abner J. Mikva, U.S. Court of Appeals for the District of Columbia Circuit, 1986-87; clerk for Supreme Court Justice Thurgood Marshall, 1987-88; staff member, Dukakis for President, 1988; associate, Williams & Connolly in Washington, 1989-91; faculty of the University of Chicago Law School, 1991-97; special counsel, Senate Judiciary Committee, 1993; associate White House counsel and Domestic Policy Council deputy director, 1995-99; nominated by President Bill Clinton in June 1999 to be a judge on the D.C. Circuit (no confirmation hearing was held); faculty of Harvard Law School, 1999-2009 (dean, 2003-09); nominated by President Obama in January 2009 to be solicitor general and confirmed by the Senate, 61-31, in March 2009.

Stevens Retires From High Court

JUSTICE JOHN PAUL STEVENS RETIRED from the Supreme Court on June 29, after 35 terms on the bench. He announced his planned departure April 9, just days before his 90th birthday, giving President Obama time to get a new justice in place before the next court term began Oct. 1.

The Senate on Aug. 5 confirmed Elena Kagan to replace Stevens. (*Kagan, p. 10-3*)

Stevens' departure represented a generational and demographic shift. He was the court's only military veteran, having served in World War II helping to decipher secret Japanese codes, and its sole Protestant, serving alongside six Catholic and two Jewish justices.

Although named by Republican President Gerald Ford, Stevens ended up as the senior member of the court's liberal bloc, after Republican presidents Ronald Reagan, George Bush and George W. Bush named several justices who were more conservative.

During Stevens' early years on the court, he was "the unpredictable justice — the justice who would often take his own approach in a brilliant, thoughtful way," according to Erwin Chemerinsky, law school dean at the University of California at Irvine. Over time, however, as he became more identified with the liberals, Chemerinsky added, Stevens "became much more the consensus builder."

Stevens put his stamp on an array of federal laws, from criminal justice to the limits of executive power in wartime. In recent years, he had used increasingly sharp language to voice concern about the court's conservative drift, most recently in January in a decision easing restrictions on corporate campaign financing.

"Essentially, five justices were unhappy with the limited nature of the case before us, so they changed the case to give themselves an opportunity to change the law," Stevens wrote in a stinging 90-page dissent.

Stevens had been the senior associate justice since 1994, which allowed him to assign the opinions in any case on which he found himself on the opposite side of the chief justice. He sometimes used that power to assign himself an opinion, as he did in *Hamdan v. Rumsfeld*, a seminal 2006 case on executive power that voided George W. Bush's military commissions for suspected terrorists detained at Guantánamo Bay, Cuba, and led to a new legal framework (PL 109-366) for trying terrorist suspects. (*Tribunals, 2006 Almanac, p. 5-9*)

In that case, Stevens wrote perhaps his most significant majority opinion. "Common Article 3 [of the Geneva Conventions] obviously tolerates a great degree of flexibility in trying individuals captured during armed conflict; its requirements are general ones, crafted to accommodate a wide variety of legal systems," Stevens wrote. "But requirements they are nonetheless. The commission that the president has convened to try Hamdan does not meet those requirements."

Policy Center. "The fact that she hasn't been a judge is something that reinforces the concerns both sides have. She's in many respects a cipher."

Patrick J. Leahy, D-Vt., chairman of the Senate Judiciary Committee, cited Louis D. Brandeis, Felix Frankfurter, Hugo L. Black and William H. Rehnquist as evidence that "some of the greatest justices in American history" had never been federal judges.

Judicial experience was, indeed, a relatively new litmus test for Supreme Court nominees. Half a century before, the court was populated with justices who included a former governor, senator, attorney general and even chairman of the Securities and Exchange Commission. As late as 1971, President Richard Nixon filled two open seats with non-judges: Lewis F. Powell, a corporate lawyer, and Rehnquist, a Justice Department official.

The GOP critique was softened somewhat by one of the court's leading conservatives, Justice Antonin Scalia, who declared himself "happy to see" that his potential new colleague was not a sitting judge.

Republicans also cited memos that Kagan had written for Marshall in 1987 and 1988 and some of the 170,000 pages of documents from her time in the Clinton administration to warn that she was a political activist who would approach cases not as an impartial jurist but as a strategist seeking a generally liberal outcome. They argued that she could be a rubber stamp for Obama administration policies, including the recently enacted health care overhaul, which was already being challenged in court. (*Health care, p. 9-3*)

Tom Coburn, R-Okla., announced his opposition to Kagan's confirmation in a posting on the National Review's website. "With Kagan on the court," he wrote, "the chances are slim that the Supreme Court will rein in Congress and throw away years of expansive precedents that have nearly destroyed the Constitution."

2010 LEGISLATIVE ACTION
SENATE COMMITTEE

The Senate Judiciary Committee approved Kagan's nomination by a vote of 13-6 on July 20. Lindsey Graham of South Carolina was the only Republican to break party ranks and join the panel's 12 Democrats in support of the nominee.

"I'm going to vote for her because I believe the last election had consequences, and this president chose someone who was qualified, who has the experience and knowledge to serve on this court, who is in the mainstream of liberal judicial philosophy and understands the difference between being a liberal judge and being a politician," Graham said.

But other Republicans expressed their concerns that Kagan would be an activist liberal force.

During her confirmation hearings, which ran from June 28 to June 30, Kagan was adept and often witty at addressing the many legal topics thrown her way. But, as had become the custom in such hearings, she also sidestepped most controversial subjects, such as abortion and what legal protections should be afforded terrorism suspects, saying those issues might come before the court.

Pointing to the high standard for confirmation hearings that Kagan had set out in a 1995 law review article — where she lamented that the process had become a "vapid and hollow charade" — Republicans insisted that the burden was on the nominee to provide candid

answers. But they also made it clear they would be skeptical about any assurances Kagan might provide. "Broad affirmations of 'fidelity to law' during these hearings will not settle the question," said Alabama's Jeff Sessions, the ranking member on the Judiciary panel. "Indeed, it is easy to pledge fidelity to a law when you believe you can change its meaning later, if you become a judge."

In her opening statement, Kagan alluded to GOP concerns about judicial activism. She said jurists must be "properly deferential to the decisions of the American people and their elected representatives."

"The Supreme Court, of course, has the responsibility of ensuring that our government never oversteps its proper bounds or violates the rights of individuals," she said. "But the court must also recognize the limits on itself and respect the choices made by the American people."

Part of the questioning addressed an issue that had come up repeatedly since Kagan's nomination: her role in denying military recruiters access to the career services office while she was dean of Harvard Law.

In the late 1970s, the law school adopted a policy requiring prospective employers to sign a statement that they did not discriminate on the basis of sexual orientation or other criteria. Because the military followed a policy prohibiting service by openly gay individuals, it was barred from using the career services office for recruiting.

In 2002, when the George W. Bush administration threatened to cut off funding to the university under the Solomon amendment, a provision of law that denied federal funds to schools that disallowed military recruiters, Kagan's predecessor as dean agreed to allow the recruiters to use the career services office.

Kagan continued that policy when she was named dean in 2003. But in 2004, after a federal appeals court ruled the Solomon amendment unconstitutional, she reinstated the ban for several months, lifting it when federal officials again warned they would cut off funding to the university.

While the ban was in place, she said, the military was permitted to recruit through a student veterans' group. Sessions said Kagan's assertion that military recruiters continued to have access through the group was "unconnected to reality" and concluded that she "mishandled" the matter.

"I did believe that it was an equally effective substitute," Kagan said

later when Orrin G. Hatch, R-Utah, pursued the issue.

Leahy read from a letter from a 2006 Harvard Law School graduate serving with the Army Reserve in Afghanistan, who wrote: "To attack Ms. Kagan for a principled position she took as a law school dean that had no practical effect on military recruitment looks, from where I stand, like a political distraction."

Democrats, for their part, had little success getting Kagan to advance their accusation of pro-business activism by conservative justices led by Chief Justice John G. Roberts Jr. She repeatedly demurred when asked to characterize recent decisions by the court as activist.

SENATE FLOOR

In its last vote before adjourning for the August recess, the Senate confirmed Kagan, 63-37, on Aug. 5, with the support of five Republicans who had already announced their plans to back the nominee. With the outcome clear, the three days of floor debate leading up to the vote often lacked energy. *(Senate vote 229, p. S-47)*

The five Republicans, all of whom had voted for Sotomayor, were Graham, Richard G. Lugar of Indiana, Susan Collins and Olympia J. Snowe of Maine, and Judd Gregg of New Hampshire. Three other Republicans seen as potential supporters — George V. Voinovich of Ohio, Christopher S. Bond of Missouri and Scott P. Brown of Massachusetts — cited Kagan's lack of judicial experience and their concern about the direction of the court in siding against her.

On the Democratic side, the only surprise leading up to the debate was an announcement by Ben Nelson of Nebraska that he would vote against Kagan. Nelson became the first Democrat to vote against his own president's Supreme Court nominee since Abe Fortas' failed elevation to chief justice in 1968. *(Fortas, 1968 Almanac, p. 531)*

Senators from both parties largely repeated the arguments they had laid out two weeks earlier in the committee.

"I believe she does not have the gifts and the qualities of mind or temperament that one must have to be a justice," Sessions said. "And worse still, she possesses a judicial philosophy that does not properly value discipline, restraint and rigorous intellectual honesty."

"I believe the American people have a sense of her impressive knowledge of the law, her good humor and her judicial philosophy," Leahy said. "In her testimony, she made clear she'll base her approach on deciding cases on the law and the Constitution — not on politics, not on [an] ideological agenda." ■

Terrorism Law Extended One Year

DEMOCRATS POSTPONED efforts to modify three provisions of existing law that gave the FBI special authority to investigate suspected terrorists. Instead, Congress cleared a one-year extension without changes, good through Feb. 28, 2011. President Obama signed the bill Feb. 27 (HR 3961 — PL 111-141).

The affected provisions permitted federal law enforcement authorities to seek a court order for "any tangible thing" related to a terrorism investigation, to conduct surveillance on suspects who communicated on multiple devices and to conduct surveillance of "lone wolf" terrorists who were not connected to any terrorist group.

The first two provisions were enacted in the 2001 anti-terrorism law known as the Patriot Act (PL 107-56), which was written after the Sept. 11 attacks, and were among 16 portions of that law that were set to expire after four years absent a reauthorization. The lone-wolf provision was enacted in a 2004 overhaul of the intelligence community (PL 108-458) and was written to sunset at the same time as the other two. *(2001 Almanac, p. 14-3; 2004 Almanac, p. 11-3)*

A pair of laws enacted in 2006 (PL 109-177; PL 109-178) made 14 of the 16 expiring provisions permanent, but left the other two and the lone-wolf provision temporary, with an expiration at the end of 2009. *(2006 Almanac, p. 16-9)*

The Justice Department called on Congress to reauthorize the provisions without major changes. The House and Senate Judiciary committees reported bills in 2009 (HR 3845, S 1692) that proposed modest new restrictions on government powers, but neither chamber acted on the bills. Instead, Congress cleared a two-month extension in December, as part of the fiscal 2010 Defense appropriations bill (PL 111-118). *(2009 Almanac, p. 15-7)*

HIGHLIGHTS

The following are details of the three provisions that were extended:

● **Business records.** The first gave the FBI expanded authority to gain access to items such as business and library records. The provision was one of the focal points of criticism of the Patriot Act, uniting liberals and libertarians, who said it was too broadly written and could allow the government to access a virtually unlimited range of records.

Under prior law, court orders requested under the Foreign Intelligence Surveillance Act (FISA) for access to business records had to state that there were "specific and articulable facts giving reason to believe that the person to whom the records pertain [was] a foreign power or an agent of a foreign power." The law limited the records to those of hotels, motels, car and truck rental agencies, and storage rental facilities.

The anti-terrorism law modified requirements for a FISA court order to include "any tangible things," including library or bookstore records, regardless of the business or individual holding the item, as long as law enforcement officials asserted that the records were sought in an effort to obtain foreign intelligence or in a terrorism investigation. The application had to include a "statement of facts" proving that the information sought was "relevant" to the investigation.

The Justice Department said in a September 2009 letter that the FISA

BOX SCORE

BILL: HR 3961 — PL 111-141

LEGISLATIVE ACTION:

Senate passed by voice vote Feb. 24.

House cleared, 315-97, on Feb. 25.

President signed the bill Feb. 27.

court had issued about 220 orders to produce business records from 2004 to 2007.

The 2006 law specified that libraries operating in traditional roles, including allowing patrons access to the Internet, were not subject to the searches, unless they were acting as Internet providers. Critics tried unsuccessfully to get language that would have required the FBI to tie a proposed search directly to a terrorist suspect or a case of espionage.

● **'Roving' wiretaps.** The second provision enabled federal law enforcement officials to pursue terrorists who used multiple devices, or who repeatedly changed cell phone numbers or carriers in order to thwart surveillance efforts under FISA. The law permitted authorities to obtain multipoint or "roving" wiretaps rather than having to file multiple applications to continue an investigation.

The application did not have to include specific information on the location of the wiretap or the names of third parties who would be involved in assisting authorities with setting it up. The court orders applied to the person or persons and not a particular device. If the location of surveillance was unknown at the time of a court order, investigators were required to notify the court within 10 days of the start of surveillance at any new location, a deadline that could be extended to up to 60 days.

The Justice Department said the provision had "proven an important intelligence-gathering tool in a small but significant subset of FISA electronic surveillance orders." The 2009 letter noted that the government could get the authority only if it provided specific information that the surveillance target might engage in countersurveillance activities.

● **Lone-wolf provision.** The 2004 law allowed federal law enforcement officials to seek warrants from the FISA court to conduct surveillance on suspected individuals or "targets" who were engaging in international terrorism activities or preparation for such activities but could not be connected to specific terrorist groups or foreign nations. The provision applied only if the target was not a U.S. citizen, legal immigrant or resident.

Before 2004, national security officials had to show a court that a target was an agent of a foreign power or acting on behalf of a foreign power. A Justice Department official stated in 2009 that the department had never filed a FISA application using this provision but that it wanted the authority renewed because situations could arise in which it would be the only avenue for surveillance.

2010 LEGISLATIVE ACTION

The Senate passed the one-year extension of the anti-terrorism provisions by voice vote on Feb. 24, after Democrats were unable to pass a short-term extension bill that also included a wide range of other federal programs, such as unemployment insurance and Medicare physician payments. After the Senate passed the one-year bill, Judiciary Chairman Patrick J. Leahy, D-Vt., said he would have "preferred to add oversight and judicial review" language but that some GOP senators objected. *(Unemployment benefits, p. 8-3; doctors' pay, p. 9-15)*

The House cleared the bill, 315-97, on Feb. 25. *(House vote 67, p. H-28)* ■

Measure Pays for Legal Settlements

CONGRESS CLEARED LEGISLATION during the lame-duck session to pay for two federal legal settlements resolving decades-long challenges against the government by black farmers and by American Indians.

President Obama signed the measure into law Dec. 8 (HR 4783 – PL 111-291).

The bill approved a settlement in *Cobell v. Salazar*, a long-running class-action lawsuit in which plaintiffs alleged that the Interior Department had mismanaged billions of dollars in grazing land, gas, oil and other royalties owed to thousands of American Indians.

It also appropriated funds for a settlement in a class-action suit, *Pigford v. Glickman*, in which African-American farmers alleged that the Agriculture Department had exhibited racial bias in allocating farm loans and services.

After Congress missed a December 2009 deadline set by plaintiffs in the *Cobell* case, the two settlements were joined in the same legislation. The House included approval for the settlements in broader bills that provided supplementary war funding (PL 111-212) and extended unemployment benefits (PL 111-205), but the provisions were dropped in the Senate before the bills were enacted.

Although there was broad accord on the basic issues, Sen. Tom Coburn, R-Okla., blocked efforts to pass legislation in the weeks before the midterm elections, citing concerns about the bill's potential fiscal impact. An earlier effort to approve the accords was blocked by Sen. John Barrasso, R-Wyo., who sought to limit lawyers' fees in the *Cobell* case.

Then, just before the Thanksgiving recess, the Senate passed a stand-alone bill to approve the two deals, as well as settlements dealing with American Indian water rights sought by Jon Kyl, R-Ariz.

The cost of the measure was offset with provisions to reduce erroneous payments of unemployment benefits, extend customs users fees and rescind $562 million from the Women, Infants and Children program. The offsets satisfied Coburn that the bill would be budget-neutral. The House easily cleared the bill, which also extended funding through fiscal 2011 for the Temporary Assistance for Needy Families (TANF) program.

HIGHLIGHTS

The key elements of the bill:

● **American Indians.** Approved a December 2009 settlement reached by the Obama administration in the *Cobell v. Salazar* case and authorized $3.4 billion to implement the deal.

BOX SCORE

BILL: HR 4783 — PL 111-291

....

LEGISLATIVE ACTION:

Senate passed HR 4783, amended, by unanimous consent Nov. 19.

House cleared the bill, 256-152, on Nov. 30.

President signed the bill Dec. 8.

The royalty dispute stemmed from an 1887 law that distributed parcels of land to individual American Indians but did not allow them to control how the land was used. Instead, the properties were placed into trust accounts. The lead plaintiff in the lawsuit, Elouise Cobell, contended that the account holders were cheated out of their share of the revenue the government received for leasing the land.

The funding included $1.4 billion to pay approximately 500,000 plaintiffs, and $2 billion to consolidate land holdings where the presence of multiple heirs had complicated the management of accounts.

Money for the settlement came out of the Judgment Fund maintained by the Treasury Department, meaning that no further appropriation of funding was necessary.

● **Black farmers.** Appropriated $1.15 billion to implement a settlement reached in what had come to be called Pigford II.

Under a settlement of the *Pigford v. Glickman* suit, approved by a federal district court judge in 1999, African-Americans who farmed from 1981 through 1996 and who filed a complaint against the department by July 1, 1997, were eligible to seek monetary compensation from the government. The settlement was widely criticized because it left out tens of thousands of African-American farmers who filed claims later than the 1997 cutoff date.

The 2008 farm law (PL 110-246) authorized $100 million for the settlement of these claims. However, the law was inadequate to deal with the huge number of black farmers who filed claims.

In February 2010, the administration announced a settlement of the Pigford II claims and requested $1.15 billion to implement it.

● **TANF.** Extended TANF through Sept. 30, 2011, at fiscal 2010 levels. The bill also provided a six-month extension for a supplemental TANF grant program for states with high population growth or historically below-average welfare grants. The bill did not revive a TANF emergency fund, enacted as part of the 2009 economic stimulus law (PL 111-5), that enabled states to place adults with private employers and youth in summer jobs programs.

2010 LEGISLATIVE ACTION

The Senate passed the provisions by unanimous consent with little fanfare, as a substitute amendment to an unrelated House-passed bill (HR 4783). The House cleared the bill, 256-152, on Nov. 30. *(House vote 584, p. H-204)* ■

Chapter 11

POLITICS

GOP Wave Yields Control of House, Greater Numbers in the Senate

AFTER DISASTROUS PERFORMANCES IN the previous two congressional elections, Republicans bounced back in force in 2010, picking up a historic 63 seats to regain control of the House and significantly narrowing the Democratic majority in the Senate.

It was the greatest net gain of House seats for a party since 1938, when the GOP won back 72 seats in what had been an increasingly lopsided Democratic chamber during the first six years of Franklin D. Roosevelt's presidency. Indeed, with many fewer seats to defend in 2010 than in 1938 — 255 vs. 334 — the Democrats' poor performance in 2010 may have been even more striking.

The 2010 Republican tidal wave cut a wide swath, upending long-term incumbents such as moderate Democrat James L. Oberstar, a 34-year veteran from northern Minnesota, as well as dozens from marginal districts who owed their seats in part to the Democratic tides in the previous two election cycles. In the Senate, Republicans gained a net of six seats, knocking out incumbent Democrats Russ Feingold of Wisconsin and Blanche Lincoln of Arkansas while picking up open seats in Illinois, Indiana, North Dakota and Pennsylvania. *(House, p. 11-6; Senate, p. 11-10)*

GOP gains were most striking in the South and Midwest, but the party also picked up seats in the Northeast and West, where it had lost considerable ground in the previous two elections. After the 2008 elections, Republican House membership from New England had dwindled to zero. But in 2010, the party recaptured both of New Hampshire's seats and more than tripled what had been nominal representation in Pennsylvania and New York.

The rapid swing in 2010 was the result of a potent coalescence of forces: a stagnant economy that made independent voters fearful and dissatisfied, the sudden emergence of a movement of ideologically driven conservative activists, a broad sense that the federal government was overreaching under the Democrats, and a shift in the demographics of those who came out to vote.

A REVERSAL IN FORTUNES

Indications of a possible GOP surge — steadily decreasing support in polls for the president, the Democratic Congress and their agenda — stirred slowly during the first year of the Obama administration but then exploded in January 2010, when Republican Scott P. Brown won a special Senate election in heavily Democratic Massachusetts to replace the late Sen. Edward M. Kennedy. At the outset of the campaign Brown was given almost no chance, but he capitalized on a bubbling discontent in the electorate about recent passage by both congressional chambers of health care legislation.

By late summer, opinion polls were showing pronounced momentum for Republican candidates across the country. The surge was most noticeable among independent voters, whose nearly 2-to-1 support had swept in Democrats in 2006 and 2008 but who had dramatically shifted to the Republican side by a similar margin by mid-2010.

A late-campaign assessment of each of the 37 races for the Senate and of the contests for all 435 House seats revealed just how successful the Republicans were at reversing the dynamic of the previous two campaign cycles. In 2006 and 2008, it was the Democrats who managed to expand the playing field of winnable races and force the Republican Party into a mostly defensive posture. In 2010, the Republicans instead went on the offensive, with the Democrats struggling to hold on to seats.

The results underscored just how far and fast the political pendulum had swung back in the GOP's favor. It took the Democrats two elections to pick up a net of 51 House seats; it took the Republicans just one to wipe out that gain and add even more.

In the Senate, where only one-third of the seats are at stake every two years, the competitive imbalance was not as overwhelming, although the net pickup of six for the GOP was comparable to the gains for Democrats in both 2006 and 2008.

IT'S THE ECONOMY

Partisan and nonpartisan observers alike agreed that the nation's economic troubles were the starting point for any discussion of the Democrats' election year struggles.

"This is all because the economy is genuinely bad, and Democrats have overpromised and underdelivered, in the view of most voters," said Larry J. Sabato, director of the University of Virginia's Center for Politics, shortly before the election. "People know what they see, and they use midterm elections to send their public officials a message. This is a classic message-sending, checks-and-balances election generated by a deeply dissatisfied public."

Or, as expressed by Darrell West, director of governance studies at the Brookings Institution, "It is difficult to get voters to believe your agenda is effective when there is nearly double-digit unemployment."

Most strikingly, the disappointment over the economy helped move independents to the Republican column in droves.

The summer of 2010 "was not the summer of economic recovery," said G. Evans Witt, CEO of Princeton Survey Research Associates. "That on-the-ground reality is viewed as an Obama policy failure by the voters, rightly or wrongly."

TOO MUCH, TOO FAST?

Many also cited the unpopularity of the legislative record of the 111th Congress for the drubbing the voters gave the Democrats.

Obama and congressional Democrats, led by Majority Leader Harry Reid, D-Nev., in the Senate and Speaker Nancy Pelosi, D-Calif., in the House, moved quickly at the start of the Congress to leverage what they saw as significant political capital coming off Obama's historic victory to implement an ambitious policy agenda. With the nation reeling from a deep recession, sparked by a near collapse of the nation's financial sector, most Americans said they had faith in a new leader whose campaign had been built on inspirational themes of hope and change. Polls showed he had the approval of about two-thirds of the American people.

Early in the first session, Democrats won enactment of a $787 billion economic stimulus measure (PL 111-5) aimed at halting the

recessionary spiral and putting the nation on the road to recovery. Then Obama and congressional Democrats embarked on what turned into a tortuous but successful effort to enact a historic overhaul of the health insurance system (PL 111-148, PL 111-152), fulfilling a campaign promise to provide medical coverage to the uninsured.

Democrats pushed a bill through the House that would have imposed a highly controversial "cap and trade" plan to limit industrial greenhouse gas emissions. They also enacted an overhaul of the regulation of the financial services industry, which had been blamed for its key role in instigating the recession (PL 111-203).

For the incumbent party, a distaste among the electorate for that much lawmaking in such a short time proved difficult to overcome.

"You know, it's very interesting. What I hear all across my state are three words: 'Enough is enough,' " Sen. Kent Conrad, D-N.D., said upon reflection after what Obama called the party's "shellacking." "When you put together TARP [Troubled Asset Relief Program], of course, which was done under the Bush administration, but it sort of all runs into the same reaction by people, and you add stimulus, and the auto bailout, and the health care bill, it just struck people that there was too much coming from the federal government, and so people wanted to make a change," said Conrad.

"With comprehensive legislation, it is easy to scare people and make them think the worst about the new policies," West said. "Republicans have done an outstanding job playing to their base and winning over independents at the same time."

In West's view, Democrats took big political risks pushing ahead with a sweeping policy agenda, especially the health care bill that dominated the congressional agenda for months, at a time while voters were fixated on the high unemployment rate.

GROWTH OF THE TEA PARTY

From the outset of Obama's presidency, a number of conservatives and people fearful of Democratic control in Washington billed the new president as "socialist" and leftist. They were dismayed as well by the kind of Republicanism that had come into favor under George W. Bush. And they inserted themselves energetically into the campaign.

On their own, in prosperous times, such ideologues probably would not have gotten as far. Their rhetoric was extreme, their candidates often inexperienced. In less tumultuous years, many would have been dismissed as part of an unelectable fringe. But with the economy flat, people favored by the new activists emerged, sometimes from obscurity, to become unorthodox major-party candidates.

From this confluence of circumstances arose the potential for a wave of change and two phenomena that were certain to endure as indelible symbols of this moment: Sarah Palin and the tea party.

Often using the online platforms of Facebook and Twitter, Palin figuratively roamed the nation dropping endorsements in Republican primaries, sometimes transforming also-rans into contenders. Having emerged as a political force as the 2008 Republican vice presidential nominee, the former Alaska governor established herself as the leader of a wave of charged-up conservative women proudly wearing the "Mama Grizzly" label she bestowed on them.

At the same time, a segment of strong-

ly conservative voters — who would have opposed what they considered Obama's activist government agenda no matter what anyone else thought — fashioned themselves in the same light as the yeoman patriots who fought British tyranny during the Revolutionary era, fueling the rapid rise of a populist tea party movement and candidates who came to be called tea party favorites.

GOP congressional contenders who rode the support of tea party activists to primary victories over Republican establishment favorites included some of the most prominent of the year's Senate candidates, although their record on Election Day was spotty. Tea party-backed candidates were not able to knock off Reid in Nevada or Michael Bennet in Colorado and lost a colorful race in Delaware, but Republican Rand Paul easily bested his Democratic opponent in Kentucky.

THE INDEPENDENTS

For all the talk of disaffected Democrats and angry tea partiers, self-described independent voters still played the role of inadvertent power brokers. They remained the untamed, unpredictable — and often decisive — factor in determining who would control the White House and Congress, an important lesson that was not lost on party strategists looking toward future elections.

Constituting more than a quarter of voters, this constituency included millions of Americans who seemed perpetually angry about the perceived failures of the government in Washington and were deeply distrustful of both parties. The tendency of independent voters to rage against the machine, whoever the incumbent machine happened to be at the moment, could be clearly seen in exit poll results, as published by CNN.

In 2008, independent voters favored Democratic House candidates by 51 percent to 43 percent, making common cause with the energized liberal activists who set out to punish the Republican Party for what they regarded as the Bush administration's failures. But in 2010, independents swung over to join with the conservative activists who lashed back against Obama's policy agenda, giving Republican House candidates a whopping 56 percent to 38 percent advantage over Democrats.

The prominence of this frustrated but relatively non-ideological amalgamation of voters in tipping national elections meant both parties faced the prospect of navigating a minefield of difficult strategic and tactical decisions over the following two years.

THE AGE FACTOR

One of the Democrats' signal successes in 2008 was in turning out the youngest cohort of voters, ages 18-24, in greater numbers than usual, in large part because younger voters harbored antipathy

Independent Vote

In the House elections, independents veered to the right in 2010, making the difference for the Republican Party.

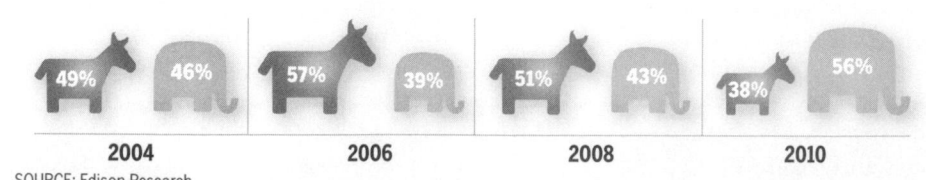

2004	2006	2008	2010
49% / 46%	57% / 39%	51% / 43%	38% / 56%

SOURCE: Edison Research

toward Bush and were inspired by Obama's messages of hope and change and by his bid to become the nation's first African-American president.

Yet many reverted to their non-voting habits in 2010. The 2008 exit polls showed 10 percent of the total electorate was made up of 18- to 24-year-olds who split 62 percent to 35 percent in favor of Obama; that group was nearly as Democratic-leaning in 2010 (58 percent to 39 percent) but was only half as large as a percentage of all voters.

The change gave more clout to the oldest voters, ages 65 and over, who were 15 percent of all voters in 2008 and 23 percent in 2010. That made their big swing — from a slight Democratic edge of 49 percent to 48 percent in 2008 to a daunting 59-38 edge in favor of Republicans in 2010 — a major factor in the GOP's gains.

"I think the Republicans did a very good job of positioning themselves on policy to the 2010 electorate, knowing that the elderly were going to be out in force in a midterm election," said Michael McDonald, a leading expert on voter turnout who taught political science at George Mason University in Virginia.

Despite suggestions by some Republicans that an "enthusiasm gap" favoring their party would result in record-shattering turnout for a midterm election, McDonald calculated that voter participation was 41.5 percent of eligible voting-age citizens, an uptick of just 1 percentage point over the Democrats' congressional upsurge year of 2006, and well below the 61.6 percent turnout for the 2008 election.

That made turnout in the 2010 voting a third lower than that two years earlier — in other words, a typical midterm election year, although one with an unusually profound partisan effect.

LOOKING AHEAD

Despite the electoral setback, Democrats still found themselves in a stronger position than was the case early in the decade, when they were shut out of power in both chambers as well as the White House.

That reality underscored the fact that 2010 was just the latest skirmish in a long-running but seemingly futile battle between Democrats and Republicans for lasting majority-party status, one that was certain to be ratcheted up in the 2012 election, when Obama would defend the Democrats' hold on the White House.

Democrats would have to reconnect with those independent voters who turned against them because they believed the party failed to focus hard enough on boosting the stagnant economy and getting the jobless back to work, or who said the Democrats overreached with an activist government agenda.

But they had to do so without further alienating a liberal Democratic base that already was contending that Obama and his party allies in Congress failed to push hard enough to institute a new progressive era in Washington.

Republican leaders faced at least as daunting a challenge in deciding what face to show to the public in the run-up to the 2012 elections. They were certain to be confronted by loud demands from their fired-up activist wing to follow through on campaign promises to deeply reduce the size and cost of the federal government, ease regulation of business, try to repeal the health care law and carry out other top items on the conservative agenda. But they had to do so without planting their flag too far to the right and leaving the impression that they were trying to shove their agenda down the throats of more moderate Republicans and the opposition instead of pursuing workable compromises.

"While there's no doubt many more people self-identify as conservative, people are pragmatic. They go for what works," Norman J. Ornstein, a resident fellow at the American Enterprise Institute, said.

Although the vast majority of Republicans in the huge House Class of 2010 ran on strongly conservative platforms, many of them won in districts that under normal circumstances had highly competitive elections or even leaned Democratic: The number of Republicans elected in districts that favored Obama over GOP opponent John McCain jumped from 34 prior to the elections to at least 59 in the 112th Congress.

That was similar to the situation faced by the Democrats after their big gains in 2006 and 2008, when many of their "majority making" candidates won in districts that normally leaned Republican.

The level of risk faced by members representing swing districts could not have been illustrated more clearly: Of the 48 races in which Democratic candidates represented districts carried in 2008 by McCain, only 12 were successfully defended by the incumbent party.

Just how little consensus existed on key policy issues was again made clear in the exit polls. On the health care law, 31 percent of respondents said it should be expanded and 16 percent said it should be left alone, for a total of 47 percent, a virtual tie with the 48 percent of respondents who said it should be repealed — even though the same electorate leaned strongly Republican in its candidate voting behavior. Notably, among those who wanted to keep the new law, nearly a third said they voted for Republican House candidates.

When asked whether 2001 and 2003 Bush-era tax cuts should be extended beyond their expiration date on Dec. 31, 2010, just more than half the respondents — including a substantial number who said they voted Republican — expressed reservations. Of the 37 percent of respondents who said the cuts should be extended only for those with annual incomes below $250,000, a third were GOP voters. Of the 15 percent who said none of the cuts should be extended, nearly a quarter were Republican voters.

The demographics of the exit-poll respondents also suggest that Republicans, unless they broadly popularized their agenda prior to the 2012 campaigns, would face an electorate very different from and more disposed toward Democrats than the one that showed up for the 2010 midterms. Young people, who polls showed had generally stuck to their Democratic-leaning ways even though they voted at a lower rate in the midterms, were likely to make up a larger share of the electorate in 2012, giving Obama and congressional Democrats a better chance. ∎

Record Wins Hand House to GOP

DISCONTENTED VOTERS slammed House Democrats with historic losses on Nov. 2, washing away all the gains and more that the party had made over the previous two election cycles and giving Republicans a majority for the first time since 2006.

Few targeted Democrats were safe from the GOP wave, and Republicans also pulled off several long-shot surprises. In the "shellacking," as President Obama described it the day after, Democrats also lost more than a dozen seats that demographics suggested had slipped from their grasp for at least the next cycle in 2012, when the president also faced re-election.

Needing 39 seats to seize the gavel from House Speaker Nancy Pelosi, D-Calif., the GOP achieved a net gain of 62 seats.

Their majority of 242 members in the 112th Congress was the largest since the 80th Congress in 1947-48. Republicans far outdid their own 52-seat swing in 1994, posting one of the largest House swings of all time. They fell shy of the 71 net seats they gained in 1938, the second midterm election in Franklin D. Roosevelt's presidency.

In contrast to the previous two elections, independent voters broke heavily for Republicans, who also benefited from an electorate that was older and less ethnically diverse than voters were in 2008.

Exit polls, for example, found that the turnout of African-Americans as a percentage of all those voting was down from historic highs two years before. That also was true of voters ages 18 to 29. According to CNN exit polls, black voters made up 10 percent of the voting population, down from 13 percent in 2008. After making up 18 percent of the voters in 2008, young voters accounted for just 11 percent of votes in 2010. Voters 65 and older made up 23 percent of those going to the polls, up from 16 percent in 2008.

In addition, men strongly favored the GOP, while women, who had tilted toward Democrats in recent years, evenly split their allegiance.

House Minority Leader John A. Boehner of Ohio, the Speaker-in-waiting for the new Congress, repeatedly fought back tears when facing a rowdy crowd in Washington while delivering his victory speech on election night. "For far too long, Washington has been doing what's best for Washington and not what's best for the American people. And tonight that begins to change," he said. "This is not a time for celebration. This is a time to roll up our sleeves and go to work."

DEMOCRATIC LOSSES

The long list of Democratic losses included several party stalwarts.

Three committee chairmen fell: John M. Spratt Jr. of South Carolina, head of the Budget Committee; Armed Services Chairman Ike Skelton of Missouri; and 18-term Rep. James L. Oberstar of Minnesota, who headed the Transportation and Infrastructure Committee. In a sign of the surprising strength of the Republican wave, until the last few days of the campaign, Oberstar was not thought to be in

THE HOUSE

	111th Congress		112th Congress
Democrats	255	Republicans	242
Republicans	178	Democrats	193
Vacant on Nov. 2 *	2		

* Seats had been held by Eric Massa, D-N.Y. and Mark Souder, R-Ind.

DEMOCRATS

Net loss	-62
Freshmen	9
Incumbents re-elected	184
Incumbents defeated	54

REPUBLICANS

Net gain	+62
Freshmen	87
Incumbents re-elected	155
Incumbents defeated	4

trouble in his bid to retain his Duluth-based seat against GOP challenger Chip Cravaack, a Navy veteran and retired airline pilot.

Democratic losses were particularly large in several big states, including Ohio, Pennsylvania, New York and Florida, where a total of 18 incumbents lost. Prominent among the casualties were first- and second-term Democrats who represented suburban swing districts. But the damage was not limited to high-profile states. Republicans captured the at-large seats in both Dakotas as well as both seats in New Hampshire.

Party turnovers in favor of Democrats were few and far between. Democrats captured just three seats: a victory for the open Delaware seat and the ouster of two Republican incumbents, Reps. Charles K. Djou of Hawaii and Anh "Joseph" Cao of Louisiana.

There was little doubt that dozens of districts in states such as Ohio, Pennsylvania, Florida and New York would continue to be competitive in 2012 and beyond. Independent voters, many of them in suburban areas in the Midwest and Mountain West, had backed Democrats up and down the ballot in 2006 and 2008. But they swung heavily toward Republicans in 2010. Those areas were likely to be decisive in the next presidential cycle as well.

Among the 62 seats Republicans won, there also were 15 or more staunchly conservative districts where Democrats were unlikely to make competitive races again anytime soon.

Democrats suffered heavy House losses in the South and the coal-rich Ohio River Valley — two areas where down-ballot Democrats on the ticket in 2012 would have to run well ahead of Obama, who performed weakly there in 2008, to compete.

Moreover, big gains at the state level gave Republicans an outsized role in the congressional redistricting process due to be completed in 2012. The GOP ended up with 25 of the 43 governors' seats in states that had more than one U.S. House seat. They also held full control of the legislatures in 21 congressional redistricting states. *(States, p. 11-18)*

Beyond the redistricting issue, by the day after the election, some Republican leaders were already viewing the results as the beginning of a new realignment of the American political system. Ed Gillespie, a longtime Republican strategist, said that the elections would go down as bringing "broader and deeper" changes to American politics than even the historic 1994 election. "I believe it's pretty long-lasting. I think there's a chord that's been struck," Gillespie said. "I do think that 2012 will be a very defining moment for the country, and voters will see it that way."

But as Democrats spent the day after the election trying to put their losses in perspective, some suggested that a seesaw electorate could change its mind again sooner than Gillespie expected.

"I've been through enough of these now where I'm reminding my staff today that in 2008, they were talking about the Republican Party being dead. In 2004, they were talking about a permanent Republican majority," North Carolina Democratic Party Executive Director

Andrew Whalen said. "These things are cyclical, and what the map looks like today, it's not going to look like in 2012."

Democratic pollster John Anzalone said the only real conclusion one could take was that the congressional battleground was huge and either party could take advantage of it in any given election. "I think we're now in a period of politics where over 100 seats are swing or targetable, and those don't go away just because the Republicans won one year and the Democrats won the previous cycle," Anzalone said.

The GOP wave that washed over the electoral map began early on election night with the surprise early defeat of Democrat Rick Boucher, a 14-term veteran who represented a coal-mining district in southwestern Virginia. Despite the district's conservative bent, the moderate Boucher had won with easy margins in recent years; in 2008, he faced no Republican opposition.

By the time the GOP wave had swept away 11-term Democrat Gene Taylor of Mississippi, well past midnight, it had officially hit tsunami proportions. Both Boucher and Taylor had survived the 1994 elections and had routinely been re-elected with ease and remained popular even as their districts proved to be reliable Republican strongholds when it came to other state and federal offices. Once they lost, it was hard to see how Democrats would be competitive again in their southern Mississippi and southwestern Virginia districts. Republican insiders believed Democrats lost 15 or more seats that fit into the category of being permanently off the board.

"One of our major strategies from the beginning was to target the reddest seats, regardless of how popular the Democrat incumbent was," said GOP strategist Brad Todd, who helped craft House Republicans' strategy through his work with the National Republican Congressional Committee.

Todd offered several reasons the GOP believed that strategy could work. "One, we expected a polarized national election where Republicans would have a better chance the redder the district," he said. "And two, we felt it would help build a lasting majority if we elected Republicans in districts that wanted to elect Republicans for the long term."

Democrats lost a pair of open seats in Arkansas that Democrats Marion Berry and Vic Snyder won two years after the 1994 GOP wave. Republicans also captured two open seats and defeated a Democratic incumbent in Tennessee, a state that had swung increasingly Republican in recent years.

With the seats flipped, Republican strategists expressed confidence they would be able to keep all five pickups and perhaps even strengthen them through the redistricting process to ensure they remained in the GOP column. The same could also be said for the GOP pickup in Spratt's conservative district in South Carolina.

In Texas, where Republicans knocked off 10-term Democrat Chet Edwards in a seat that gave Republican John McCain one of his largest margins of victory in the 2008 presidential election, Republicans did not appear to need any extra help to hold the seat.

Democrats also saw Jim Marshall lose a conservative seat in Georgia. The party also lost control of the open seat in Louisiana that Democrat Charlie Melancon left open to run for the Senate; his district had trended decidedly Republican in recent years.

Several junior members of the fiscally conservative House Blue Dog Coalition also lost despite their right-leaning voting records during their short time on Capitol Hill. They included Travis Childers of Mississippi, Frank Kratovil Jr. of Maryland, Bobby Bright of Alabama and Walt Minnick of Idaho.

Bernie Pinsonat, an independent pollster with Southern Media & Opinion Research, said one reason Democrats were likely to have a particularly hard time winning back their losses in many of those districts was that the national party had lost touch with a large part of America.

"Most of the things that Democrats are pushing nationally are truly disliked by Southern voters," Pinsonat said. "We don't like big government. We don't like taxes. Unions don't have a foothold of any consequence. . . . The national Democratic Party is winning on the coast with those messages, but in the heartland, and especially in the South, their constituencies and the people that they kowtow to are not popular."

The rise of the conservative tea party movement certainly embodied that sentiment and provided an outlet for voter anger. Pinsonat painted a bleak picture for what that meant for Democrats in the cycles to come. "I don't have anything to throw out as even a bone to give them hope," he said. "I don't have anything in my polls that says 'if you do this, you'll do better.' "

But Anzalone said that the only real conclusion one could take from the 2010 cycle was that the congressional battleground could continue to be large, and that either party could take advantage of it in a given election.

Anzalone dismissed talk that Democrats had lost certain seats forever. "Voters are fickle mistresses, and they have a more difficult appetite to satiate than it was 10 and 20 years ago," he said. "Do I think that we're going to have a wholesale resurgence two years from now in the Deep South? No. Do I think these seats are lost forever? No. As long as we have good candidates and a decent breeze at our back . . . we're going to see some of these seats in play." ∎

New House Members in the 112th Congress

Alabama 2	Martha Roby, R	Defeated Rep. Bobby Bright, D
Alabama 5	Mo Brooks, R	Defeated Steve Raby, D, after defeating Rep. Parker Griffith in the primary
Alabama 7	Terri A. Sewell, D	Defeated Don Chamberlain, R, to succeed Artur Davis, who ran for governor
Arizona 1	Paul Gosar, R	Defeated Rep. Ann Kirkpatrick, D
Arizona 3	Ben Quayle, R	Defeated Jon Hulburd, D, to succeed John Shadegg, R, who retired
Arizona 5	David Schweikert, R	Defeated Rep. Harry E. Mitchell, D
Arkansas 1	Rick Crawford, R	Defeated Chad Causey, D, to succeed Marion Berry, D, who retired
Arkansas 2	Tim Griffin, R	Defeated Joyce Elliott, D, to succeed Vic Snyder, D, who retired
Arkansas 3	Steve Womack, R	Defeated David Whitaker, D, to succeed John Boozman, R, who ran for Senate
California 19	Jeff Denham, R	Defeated Loraine Goodwin, D, to succeed George Radanovich, R, who retired
California 33	Karen Bass, D	Defeated James Andion, R, to succeed Diane Watson, D, who retired
Colorado 3	Scott Tipton, R	Defeated Rep. John Salazar, D
Colorado 4	Cory Gardner, R	Defeated Rep. Betsy Markey, D
Delaware AL	John Carney, D	Defeated Glen Urquhart, R, to succeed Michael N. Castle, R, who ran for Senate
Florida 2	Steve Southerland II, R	Defeated Rep. Allen Boyd, D
Florida 5	Rich Nugent, R	Defeated Jim Piccillo, D, to succeed Ginny Brown-Waite, R, who retired
Florida 8	Daniel Webster, R	Defeated Rep. Alan Grayson, D
Florida 12	Dennis A. Ross, R	Defeated Lori Edwards, D, to succeed Adam H. Putnam, R, who retired
Florida 17	Frederica S. Wilson, D	Defeated Roderick Vereen, I, to succeed Kendrick B. Meek, D, who ran for Senate
Florida 22	Allen B. West, R	Defeated Rep. Ron Klein, D
Florida 24	Sandy Adams, R	Defeated Rep. Suzanne M. Kosmas, D
Florida 25	David Rivera, R	Defeated Joe Garcia, D, to succeed Mario Diaz-Balart, R
Georgia 7	Rob Woodall, R	Defeated Doug Heckman, D, to succeed John Linder, R, who retired
Georgia 8	Austin Scott, R	Defeated Rep. Jim Marshall, D
Hawaii 1	Colleen Hanabusa, D	Defeated Rep. Charles K. Djou, R
Idaho 1	Raúl R. Labrador, R	Defeated Rep. Walt Minnick, D
Illinois 8	Joe Walsh, R	Defeated Rep. Melissa Bean, D
Illinois 10	Robert Dold, R	Defeated Dan Seals, D, to succeed Mark Steven Kirk, R, who ran for Senate
Illinois 11	Adam Kinzinger, R	Defeated Rep. Debbie Halvorson, D
Illinois 14	Randy Hultgren, R	Defeated Rep. Bill Foster, D
Illinois 17	Bobby Schilling, R	Defeated Rep. Phil Hare, D
Indiana 3	Marlin Stutzman, R	Defeated Tom Hayhurst, D, to fill a vacancy
Indiana 4	Todd Rokita, R	Defeated David Sanders, D, to succeed Steve Buyer, R, who retired
Indiana 8	Larry Bucshon, R	Defeated Trent Van Haaften, D, to succeed Brad Ellsworth, D, who ran for Senate
Indiana 9	Todd Young, R	Defeated Rep. Baron P. Hill, D
Kansas 1	Tim Huelskamp, R	Defeated Alan Jilka, D, to succeed Jerry Moran, R, who ran for Senate
Kansas 3	Kevin Yoder, R	Defeated Stephene Moore, D, to succeed Dennis Moore, D, who retired
Kansas 4	Mike Pompeo, R	Defeated Raj Goyle, D, to succeed Todd Tiahrt, R, who ran for Senate
Louisiana 2	Cedric L. Richmond, D	Defeated Rep. Anh "Joseph" Cao, R
Louisiana 3	Jeff Landry, R	Defeated Ravi Sangisetty, D, to succeed Charlie Melancon, D, who ran for Senate
Maryland 1	Andy Harris, R	Defeated Rep. Frank Kratovil Jr., D
Massachusetts 10	William Keating, D	Defeated Jeff Perry, R, to succeed Bill Delahunt, D, who retired
Michigan 1	Dan Benishek, R	Defeated Gary McDowell, D, to succeed Bart Stupak, D, who retired
Michigan 2	Bill Huizenga, R	Defeated Fred Johnson, D, to succeed Peter Hoekstra, R, who retired
Michigan 3	Justin Amash, R	Defeated Pat Miles, D, to succeed Vernon J. Ehlers, R, who retired
Michigan 7	Tim Walberg, R	Defeated Rep. Mark Schauer, D
Michigan 13	Hansen Clarke, D	Defeated John Hauler, R, after defeating Rep. Carolyn Cheeks Kilpatrick in the primary

Mississippi 1	Alan Nunnelee, R	Defeated Rep. Travis W. Childers, D
Mississippi 4	Steven M. Palazzo, R	Defeated Rep. Gene Taylor, D
Missouri 4	Vicky Hartzler, R	Defeated Rep. Ike Skelton, D
Missouri 7	Billy Long, R	Defeated Scott Eckersley, D, to succeed Roy Blunt, R, who ran for Senate
Nevada 3	Joe Heck, R	Defeated Rep. Dina Titus, D
New Hampshire 1	Frank Guinta, R	Defeated Rep. Carol Shea-Porter, D
New Hampshire 2	Charles Bass, R	Defeated Ann McLane Kuster, D, to succeed Paul W. Hodes, who ran for Senate
New Jersey 3	Jon Runyan, R	Defeated Rep. John Adler, D
New Mexico 2	Steve Pearce, R	Defeated Rep. Harry Teague, D
New York 13	Michael G. Grimm, R	Defeated Rep. Michael E. McMahon, D
New York 19	Nan Hayworth, R	Defeated Rep. John Hall, D
New York 20	Chris Gibson, R	Defeated Rep. Scott Murphy, D
New York 24	Richard Hanna, R	Defeated Rep. Michael Arcuri, D
New York 25	Ann Marie Buerkle, R	Defeated Rep. Dan Maffei, D
New York 29	Tom Reed, R	Defeated Matt Zeller, D, to fill a vacancy
North Carolina 2	Renee Ellmers, R	Defeated Rep. Bob Etheridge, D
North Dakota AL	Rick Berg, R	Defeated Rep. Earl Pomeroy, D
Ohio 1	Steve Chabot, R	Defeated Rep. Steve Driehaus, D
Ohio 6	Bill Johnson, R	Defeated Rep. Charlie Wilson, D
Ohio 15	Steve Stivers, R	Defeated Rep. Mary Jo Kilroy, D
Ohio 16	James B. Renacci, R	Defeated Rep. John Boccieri, D
Ohio 18	Bob Gibbs, R	Defeated Rep. Zack Space, D
Oklahoma 5	James Lankford, R	Defeated Billy Coyle, D, to succeed Mary Fallin, R, who ran for governor
Pennsylvania 3	Mike Kelly, R	Defeated Rep. Kathy Dahlkemper, D
Pennsylvania 7	Patrick Meehan, R	Defeated Bryan Lentz, D, to succeed Joe Sestak, D, who ran for Senate
Pennsylvania 8	Michael G. Fitzpatrick, R	Defeated Rep. Patrick J. Murphy, D
Pennsylvania 10	Tom Marino, R	Defeated Rep. Christopher Carney, D
Pennsylvania 11	Lou Barletta, R	Defeated Rep. Paul E. Kanjorski, D
Rhode Island 1	David Cicilline, D	Defeated John Loughlin, R, to succeed Patrick J. Kennedy, D, who retired
South Carolina 1	Tim Scott, R	Defeated Ben Frasier, D, to succeed Henry E. Brown Jr., who retired
South Carolina 3	Jeff Duncan, R	Defeated Jane Dyer, D, to succeed J. Gresham Barrett, R, who ran for governor
South Carolina 4	Trey Gowdy, R	Defeated Paul Corden, D, after defeating Bob Inglis in the primary
South Carolina 5	Mick Mulvaney, R	Defeated Rep. John M. Spratt Jr., D
South Dakota AL	Kristi Noem, R	Defeated Rep. Stephanie Herseth Sandlin, D
Tennessee 3	Chuck Fleischmann, R	Defeated John Wolfe Jr., D, to succeed Zach Wamp, R, who ran for governor
Tennessee 4	Scott DesJarlais, R	Defeated Rep. Lincoln Davis, D
Tennessee 6	Diane Black, R	Defeated Brett Carter, D, to succeed Bart Gordon, D, who retired
Tennessee 8	Stephen Fincher, R	Defeated Roy Herron, D, to suceed John Tanner, D, who retired
Texas 17	Bill Flores, R	Defeated Rep. Chet Edwards, D
Texas 23	Francisco "Quico" Canseco, R	Defeated Rep. Ciro D. Rodriguez, D
Texas 27	Blake Farenthold, R	Defeated Rep. Solomon P. Ortiz, D
Virginia 2	Scott Rigell, R	Defeated Rep. Glenn Nye, D
Virginia 5	Robert Hurt, R	Defeated Rep. Tom Perriello, D
Virginia 9	Morgan Griffith, R	Defeated Rep. Rick Boucher, D
Washington 3	Jaime Herrera Beutler, R	Defeated Denny Heck, D, to succeed Brian Baird, D, who retired
West Virginia 1	David B. McKinley, R	Defeated Mike Oliverio, D, to succeed Alan B. Mollohan, D, who lost the primary
Wisconsin 7	Sean P. Duffy, R	Defeated Julie Lassa, D, to succeed David R. Obey, D, who retired
Wisconsin 8	Reid Ribble, R	Defeated Rep. Steve Kagen, D

Democrats Relieved to Keep Majority

EVEN AS THEIR PARTY colleagues in the House went down in droves on election night, Democratic senators were able to breathe a sigh of relief by late in the evening, retaining control of the chamber as the party held on in several key Western battlegrounds.

It was a bittersweet victory, at best: The loss of six elections trimmed the Democratic caucus numbers substantially, from 59 to 53 seats.

Still, the overwhelming feeling among Senate Democrats was one of relief, especially when their leader, Harry Reid of Nevada, managed to pull out a victory in his own re-election race despite abysmal poll ratings and a concerted campaign by conservative activists to unseat him.

"Almost any time you win one you're not supposed to, it gives a boost," Sen. Ben Nelson of Nebraska said shortly after Reid's victory was secure. His glass-half-full view summarized an election cycle that brought the Democratic Party from the heights to its knees in the course of 24 months.

But despite coming up short, Republicans buoyed by their greater numbers also took great satisfaction in the results.

Days after the election, in fact, Senate Minority Leader Mitch McConnell, R-Ky., fired a warning shot about the next election cycle. "Our friends on the other side can change now and work with us to address the issues that are important to the American people, that we all understood," he said. "Or further change, obviously, can happen in 2012."

The wildly shifting storylines of the 2010 Senate elections saw the rise and impact of the conservative tea party movement, a set of colorful players, dramatic shifts and opportunities lost — and a flood of outside spending that made it, by any measure, the most expensive midterm election yet. But the conservative uprising that energized the party for 18 months — and led to the largest House gains in the post-war era — also saddled the GOP with a few Senate candidates who could not win.

RACE FOR THE MAJORITY

The marquee races generally involved conservative Republicans taking on establishment Democrats and, in some cases, their own party in primaries. Their record was mixed.

▸ Nevada's Sharron Angle, a former GOP state representative, ran an extraordinarily well-financed challenge to Reid, losing in the end by 5 percentage points.

▸ Alaska's Joe Miller, a Republican lawyer, scored a stunning upset over incumbent Lisa Murkowski in the GOP primary. But she came back to mount a write-in campaign that returned her to the Senate for the 112th. Democrat Scott McAdams, a small-town mayor, trailed far behind both.

▸ Colorado's Ken Buck, a rural county Republican district attorney, defeated former Lt. Gov. Jane Norton for the right to challenge appointed Democrat Michael Bennet but ended up falling short by about 2 points. Bennet had been appointed to his seat in January 2009

THE SENATE			
111th Congress		112th Congress	
Democrats	57	Democrats	51
Republicans	41	Republicans	47
Independents	2	Independents	2

DEMOCRATS	
Net loss	-6
Freshmen	3
Incumbents re-elected	13
Incumbents defeated	3

REPUBLICANS	
Net gain	+6
Freshmen	13
Incumbents re-elected	24
Incumbents defeated	1

after fellow Democrat Ken Salazar agreed to become President Obama's Interior secretary,

▸ Kentucky's Rand Paul, an eye doctor and son of libertarian icon Rep. Ron Paul, R-Texas, easily bested Democratic state Attorney General Jack Conway after trouncing Secretary of State Trey Grayson in the GOP primary.

▸ Delaware's Christine O'Donnell slipped past heavy primary favorite Michael N. Castle, a GOP moderate who had held Delaware's only House seat for 18 years, before losing by almost 20 points to Democrat Chris Coons, a county commissioner who had been given virtually no chance of beating Castle.

None of those standard-bearers ran anything approaching a flawless campaign. Angle made several highly publicized gaffes, including one toward the end of the campaign when she told a group of Hispanic students that some of them looked "a little more Asian to me." Paul caused a stir by questioning whether the Civil Rights Act should govern business practices and by proposing that Medicare beneficiaries be subject to a $2,000 deductible as a way of trimming the deficit.

Buck took flak for describing homosexuality as a lifestyle choice and was plagued by recollections of an incident when, as a prosecutor, he told a woman alleging rape that a jury might conclude that she had "buyer's remorse" after consenting to sex.

Miller and O'Donnell both were sidetracked by questions about their personal finances — although O'Donnell's bigger problem was widespread circulation of video clips in which she discussed religion, sex, the occult and other aspects of her personal life. One campaign ad featured her assuring voters, "I am not a witch."

Yet it was symbolic of how toxic the year's political atmosphere had turned for the Democrats that among all of those one-time long-shot candidates, only O'Donnell was a clear underdog on Election Day. All the rest remained highly competitive with their general election opponents. Had Buck and Angle won, Republicans would have ended up with 49 seats, tantalizingly close to a majority.

But the contest for the Senate majority involved many more races than those targeted by the tea party. Ultimately, it came down to a handful of key states where Democrats protected prominent Senate candidates who suddenly looked vulnerable, including Reid in Nevada, Bennet in Colorado, incumbent Barbara Boxer in California and Gov. Joe Manchin III in West Virginia.

Republicans succeeded in knocking off two incumbents and flipped four open seats held by Democrats, while not a single incumbent Republican seat turned over. In Wisconsin, three-term Democrat Russ Feingold fell to Republican businessman Ron Johnson by about 5 points, and in Arkansas, Blanche Lincoln, a two-term incumbent, suffered a 21-point defeat at the hands of Republican Rep. John Boozman. Republicans claimed open Democratic seats in Pennsylvania, Illinois, North Dakota and Indiana.

Although it was not the historic upset that changed the face of the

New Senators in the 112th Congress

Arkansas	John Boozman, R	Defeated Sen. Blanche Lincoln, D
Connecticut	Richard Blumenthal, D	Defeated Linda McMahon, R, to succeed Christopher J. Dodd, D, who retired
Delaware	Chris Coons, D	Defeated Christine O'Donnell, R, to succeed Ted Kaufman, D, who retired
Florida	Marco Rubio, R	Defeated Kendrick B. Meek, D, to succeed George LeMieux, R, who retired
Illinois	Mark Steven Kirk, R	Defeated Alexi Giannoulias, D, to succeed Roland W. Burris, D, who retired
Indiana	Dan Coats, R	Defeated Brad Ellsworth, D, to succeed Evan Bayh, D, who retired
Kansas	Jerry Moran, R	Defeated Lisa Johnston, D, to succeed Sam Brownback, R, who ran for governor
Kentucky	Rand Paul, R	Defeated Jack Conway, D, to succeed Jim Bunning, R, who retired
Missouri	Roy Blunt, R	Defeated Robin Carnahan, D, to succeed Christopher S. Bond, R, who retired
New Hampshire	Kelly Ayotte, R	Defeated Rep. Paul W. Hodes, D, to succeed Judd Gregg, R, who retired
North Dakota	John Hoeven, R	Defeated Tracy Potter, D, to succeed Byron L. Dorgan, D, who retired
Ohio	Rob Portman, R	Defeated Lee Fisher, D, to succeed George V. Voinovich, R, who retired
Pennsylvania	Patrick J. Toomey, R	Defeated Rep. Joe Sestak, D, to succeed Arlen Specter, D, who lost in the primary
Utah	Mike Lee, R	Defeated Sam Granato, D, to succeed Robert F. Bennett, R, who was not renominated
West Virginia	Joe Manchin III, D	Defeated John Raese, R, to succeed Carte P. Goodwin, D, who retired
Wisconsin	Ron Johnson, R	Defeated Sen. Russ Feingold, D

House, the Republican Senate performance was an important shift that reflected public unhappiness with the Democrats.

"When voters are dissatisfied with the party in power, the wave of public protest is like a hurricane that washes away everything in its path," said Ron Faucheux, president of the Clarus public opinion research firm in Washington.

The views expressed by many of the GOP candidates on fiscal issues, and in most cases on hot-button social issues, might in ordinary years have facilitated Democratic efforts to brand their opponents as out of the mainstream. Even in the highly charged political environment of 2010, national Republican strategists had serious doubts about the electability of some of the tea party favorites and so pushed to secure the nomination of alternatives, all veteran party insiders who presented milder demeanors to the public.

In doing so, they demonstrated that the factions within their nascent coalition were not necessarily on the same page. Those who associated themselves with the tea party demanded absolute fealty to the conservative principles they identified with the Republican Party.

That ultimately posed a potential conflict with a large segment of independent voters who, while leaning Republican in November, also by and large wanted the parties to stop bickering and work out effective solutions to the nation's problems.

Still, Republicans stoked the sense of populist rebellion with rhetoric verging at times on the apocalyptic.

In one example, Ohio Republican John A. Boehner, who was elevated to the House Speakership when his party took control, said that the fight over health care was "Armageddon."

In another, Newt Gingrich, who had spearheaded the last GOP takeover in 1994 and then served four years as Speaker, endorsed the view, espoused by conservative writer Dinesh D'Souza, that the president's world view reflects the "Kenyan anti-colonial" fervor of his father.

And South Carolina's Jim DeMint said during the campaign that he'd rather be in a Republican Senate minority made up entirely of conservative true believers than in a majority made of "mushy" moderates. DeMint saw his star rise as several long-shot conservatives he'd endorsed won their GOP primaries.

But many Democrats viewed the high pitch of Republican rhetoric

as their own saving grace, cutting their losses in the Senate if not the House. In an effort to spur a counter-reaction among their own voting base — and close an "enthusiasm gap" with Republican voters that appeared consistently in public opinion polls through the election cycle — Democrats from the president on down branded the Republicans of 2010 as extremists.

TEA PARTY EFFECT

Some analysts concluded that, by insisting in key states on nominating extremely conservative Republicans, the tea party movement quashed the party's chance to take the Senate majority. Others insisted the conservative uprising created the environment that made it possible to make big gains in the first place.

By most accounts, the tea party came to life in early 2009, a year before Democrats' Senate outlook began to darken with the January 2010 special election of Republican Scott P. Brown in Massachusetts to take the seat held for almost all of the past 57 years in the heavily Democratic state by John F. Kennedy (1953-60) and his brother Edward M. Kennedy (1962-2009).

There were at least two elements to the tea party: the intentionally loosely knit grass-roots movements in each state and organized national groups such as the Tea Party Express. The former opened an enthusiasm gap between the parties in virtually every state, even in places where Democrats held a widespread registration advantage, such as Pennsylvania and Illinois. The latter group operated much like a political party, funneling financial resources, paid media and get-out-the-vote operations to like-minded candidates in Nevada, Alaska, Colorado and Delaware. The formalized tea party groups had spokespersons and media-savvy leaders who ultimately became the faces of the anti-establishment movement.

On the morning after the election, top Republican strategist Carl Forti said tea party candidates' "deficiencies" might have cost the party multiple Senate seats. He would not say whether those shortcomings cost Republicans control of the chamber, "but we did leave seats on the table, definitely," he said.

"I think that it's easier for that kind of movement to have an effect on a House race where there's less people voting," Forti said. But in Senate races, he said, "there's so much money being spent on both

sides, there's so much scrutiny on the candidates, that the deficiencies of candidates become more glaringly clear at a statewide level."

Looking at the map, Delaware and Nevada led the list of opportunities lost. O'Donnell's primary win over Castle in Delaware allowed Democrat Coons to suddenly become the favorite to win a seat once thought to be an easy victory for Republicans. Castle, a moderate former governor who had won statewide for decades, had consistently polled far ahead of Coons in theoretical match-ups.

In Nevada, the Tea Party Express fueled Angle's candidacy in pursuit of its goal of knocking off Reid.

Forti served as the political director for American Crossroads and as advocacy director for Crossroads GPS — independent fundraising groups affiliated with GOP strategist Karl Rove that together spent $3.5 million on the Nevada race.

"We were the only group that advertised all summer," Forti said. "We've been on [television] since the week after the primary, driving Harry's negatives and trying to keep that race competitive, trying to keep her in it." He continued: "She didn't win. In the end, what that race and others show you is that candidates matter. Outside groups can only have so much influence."

The same was true in Colorado, where millions in outside money failed to push tea party favorite Buck past the incumbent Bennet.

Tea Party Express spokesman Levi Russell acknowledged some disappointments, stressing that his organization was not always engaged in battle with just one party.

"There were a few races where tea party candidates came up short, including Senate races in Delaware and Nevada," he said. "In those races, the tea party candidates had to battle both the Republican and Democrat political establishments during their quests for election victory, and this is exactly as it should be."

"The biggest victory might be the fact that the impact of the tea party movement was so strong that everyone — even many Democrats — started adopting the messaging and positions of the tea party movement," Russell added. "There weren't all that many candidates running on the platform defending tax-spend-bailout policies or big-government excess, such as 'Obamacare.'"

Shortly after the election, Democratic Sen. Sheldon Whitehouse of Rhode Island said that his colleagues understood that they would have to adapt.

"The facts are that the Republicans control the House of Representatives, and we will have a slim and far-from-filibuster-proof majority, so the terrain has changed," he said. "Traditional Democrats will have some different expectations now. We can't just cross our arms and stand in the corner in a huff." ∎

Republicans Break Losing Streak

ELEVEN SPECIAL ELECTIONS WERE HELD in 2010, yielding six victories for the Republicans and five for the Democrats, signaling a breakthrough for the GOP, which did not win any special elections in 2009. Republicans won two Senate elections and four House races. Democrats won three Senate contests and two House races. Six of the special elections were held Nov. 2 — coinciding with the general midterm elections. In addition to serving in the lame-duck session, three winning candidates — one in the Senate and two in the House — were also elected to full terms.

UPSET IN MASSACHUSETTS

Republican Scott P. Brown pulled off one of the biggest political upsets in recent history on Jan. 19, when he defeated Democrat Martha Coakley in Massachusetts' hotly contested race to fill the Senate seat of Edward M. Kennedy, who died in August 2009. Brown took 52 percent of the vote to Coakley's 47 percent. *(Kennedy obituary, 2009 Almanac, p. 5-3)*

The outcome, unthinkable only weeks before, prompted deep soul-searching among Democrats and stripped them of the 60-seat supermajority that had enabled them to thwart numerous GOP filibuster threats in the Senate.

Brown replaced Paul G. Kirk Jr., a longtime Democratic Party insider and Kennedy ally, who was appointed by Gov. Deval Patrick in September 2009 to serve until the special election. Kirk was not a candidate.

Not even a last-minute visit from President Obama could stanch the surge of momentum for Brown, a previously little-known state senator. Democrats had any number of explanations for how they managed to let the seat slip from their grasp, but the failure essentially boiled down to a poorly run campaign combined with a political environment that was more toxic than they expected.

"Had she or her campaign taken Brown seriously from the get-go," said a Massachusetts-based Democratic strategist, "then [he] would have never gotten the lift that [he] needed to reach critical mass."

Brown reinforced his image with folksy TV spots featuring President John F. Kennedy morphing into Brown, and Brown driving his truck around the state and shaking hands with voters.

Brown also turned the campaign focus to health care, touting his role as the potential 41st vote against the Democrats' pending overhaul bill, a piece of legislation that had become unpopular even in liberal-leaning Massachusetts (PL 111-148, PL 111-152). *(Health care overhaul, p. 9-3)*

Brown denied, however, that he planned to go to Washington purely to put the brakes on Obama's agenda, and he spoke warmly both of Obama, who carried the state by 26 points in 2008, and Massachusetts' senior senator, Democrat John Kerry. Brown also vowed to maintain his independence, emphasizing dialogue and transparency over partisanship.

OTHER SENATE RACES
DELAWARE

Democratic New Castle County Executive Chris Coons easily beat archconservative tea party activist Christine O'Donnell on Nov. 2 to serve the remainder of the full term of Joseph R. Biden Jr., who left to become vice president; the term was due to end in January 2015.

Ted Kaufman had been appointed temporarily to fill the seat until the general election. Coons won with 56.6 percent of the vote to O'Donnell's 40 percent.

The election was initially considered an easy GOP pickup. But Coons' victory was essentially guaranteed after O'Donnell defeated moderate Michael N. Castle for the GOP nomination. Castle had been the state's sole House member since 1993 and governor for eight years before that. O'Donnell received a great deal of unfavorable press attention about her troubled personal finances, her castigation of masturbation and, most of all, her previous dabblings in the occult. A major TV advertisement in which she declared "I'm not a witch" was a clear sign her candidacy was in trouble. Even her own party did not endorse her fall campaign.

Coons was the rarest type of freshman entering the Senate — an avowed liberal who believed government could and should do more and who was expected to be a reliable backer of most Democratic policies.

While the White House hoped to move a series of trade agreements, Coons sided with organized labor and other liberal constituencies in demanding protections for the environment and workers.

ILLINOIS

Republican Rep. Mark Steven Kirk, who had charted a path of fiscal conservatism and social moderation during five terms in the House, won a special election Nov. 2 to take a Senate seat being vacated by Democrat Roland W. Burris for the rest of the 111th Congress. On the same day, Kirk also won a new six-year term. In both cases, he prevailed over Democrat Alexi Giannoulias, besting his opponent by 47.3 percent to 46.3 percent in the special election and 48 percent to 46.4 percent in the general election.

Kirk, a centrist, had trouble during the campaign allaying distrust among conservative tea party activists and also faced a series of difficult questions about apparent résumé inflation.

A self-described "national security hawk," Kirk had taken part in training missions in Afghanistan as a Navy reservist in 2008. He pushed to boost the rewards for information on international terrorists, including Osama bin Laden, and opposed moving prisoners from Guantánamo Bay, Cuba, to detention facilities in the United States. He served on three Appropriations subcommittees in the House, including the Homeland Security panel.

He pushed for fiscal restraint, an end to earmarking and a balanced budget. He supported making the Bush-era tax cuts permanent, repealing the estate tax and doubling the child tax credit.

Burris had been appointed by Democratic Gov. Rod R. Blagojevich to hold Barack Obama's seat until the election. That was before Blagojevich was arrested and expelled from office on charges that included trying to sell the appointment. Burris' high disapproval ratings precluded him from running in November.

NEW YORK

Democrat Kirsten Gillibrand easily won a Nov. 2 special election as New York's junior senator after being temporarily appointed to the job by New York Democratic Gov. David A. Paterson in January 2009. Her temporary appointment was to replace Hillary Rodham Clinton,

who left to become secretary of State.

Gillibrand's 2010 Senate race was a cakewalk after every potential high-profile Republican opponent declined to run. She defeated GOP former Rep. Joseph DioGuardi in the special election, besting him by 62.9 percent to 35.1 percent, to hold the seat for the remainder of Clinton's term, set to expire in January 2013.

Gillibrand's 2009 appointment had been somewhat of a surprise. The initial front-runner had been Caroline Kennedy, the daughter of the late president, but she withdrew her name after questions arose about her lack of political experience and lackluster performance in TV appearances. In tapping Gillibrand, Paterson also passed over more widely known prospects such as then-state Attorney General Andrew M. Cuomo, who was elected governor on Nov. 2.

WEST VIRGINIA

Democratic Gov. Joe Manchin III became the first newly elected senator from West Virginia in a quarter of a century after winning a Nov. 2 special election to finish the term of Democrat Robert C. Byrd, who died June 28.

Manchin easily prevailed over Republican John Raese, winning 53.5 percent of the vote to Raese's 43.4 percent.

As governor, a post he had held since 2005, Manchin enjoyed approval ratings that were consistently around 70 percent. Prior to being elected governor, he served as secretary of state and in both houses of the West Virginia Legislature. He worked in several family-owned businesses before entering politics.

Considered a moderate, he campaigned at a distance from the White House, promising not to "rubber stamp" Obama's policies.

Carte P. Goodwin, a young, well-connected Democratic lawyer, had been appointed by Manchin to hold the seat temporarily until the special election. *(Byrd obituary, p. 5-7)*

Goodwin's appointment on July 16 to what amounted to an unusually glamorous temp job had been anxiously awaited by Senate leaders because it restored the Democratic caucus in the Senate to 59 seats, against the Republicans' 41. At age 39, Goodwin had been by far the youngest member of the Senate, supplanting 41-year-old George LeMieux of Florida, himself an appointed placeholder.

HOUSE SPECIAL ELECTIONS
FLORIDA 19

Democratic state Sen. Ted Deutch cruised to victory April 13 in a special election to fill the seat of former Democratic Rep. Robert Wexler in Florida's overwhelmingly Democratic 19th District. Wexler left Congress to head the nonprofit Center for Middle East Peace and Economic Cooperation.

Deutch prevailed over Republican Edward J. Lynch in the special election by 62.1 percent to 35.2 percent. Deutch went on to best Lynch in the general election, taking 62.6 percent to Lynch's 37.3 percent for a full term in the 112th Congress.

Lynch had hoped to pull off an upset by attempting to make his campaign a referendum on the new health care overhaul legislation, but the Democratic bent of the district, which gave Obama 66 percent of the vote in 2008, proved too strong for Lynch to overcome.

Deutch earned Wexler's endorsement along with those of other local, state and national Democratic leaders, including former President Bill Clinton, who traveled to Florida to host a fundraiser. As was the case with Wexler, the liberal Deutch was expected to be a generally reliable vote for the majority.

GEORGIA 9

Republican state Rep. Tom Graves won a special-election runoff in Georgia's 9th District on June 8, besting former state Sen. Lee Hawkins by nearly 13 percentage points to serve out the unexpired term of GOP Rep. Nathan Deal, who gave up his House seat to focus on his bid for governor. Graves was unopposed in the November general election for a full term.

A groundswell of support from tea party activists and socially conservative Republicans propelled Graves to victory. Saying "the No. 1 issue is out-of-control spending," Graves supported lower taxes, repeal of the Democrats' health care overhaul and stronger enforcement of immigration laws.

He opposed earmarks and called for a constitutional amendment permitting line-item vetoes to excise "pork" from appropriations measures. He also supported a balanced-budget amendment to the Constitution and supported replacing the income tax with a nationwide sales tax.

Graves joined the anti-tax group Club for Growth's "Repeal It!" pledge to fight to undo the federal health care overhaul. He proposed, instead, to offer tax breaks on insurance for individuals. He also won the backing of the Minuteman Project, a California-based group fighting illegal immigration.

Formerly an owner of a landscaping company, Graves operated as a commercial property developer, an enterprise that raised questions toward the end of the special-election campaign when it was reported that a bank had sued his company for non-payment of a loan. Graves filed a counterclaim.

Graves won endorsements from House Republican Conference Chairman Mike Pence of Indiana, House Minority Whip Eric Cantor of Virginia and Rep. Paul D. Ryan, R-Wis.

HAWAII 1

Republican Charles K. Djou, a Honolulu city councilman, won a May 22 race for a seat that had been held by Democratic Rep. Neil Abercrombie, who resigned in February to run for governor in a race that he won.

Djou's victory was the first time in the 111th Congress that Republicans had won a House special election, a victory doubly satisfying to the party as it came in heavily Democratic Hawaii in the district where Obama was born.

Djou was subsequently defeated 53.2 percent to 46.8 percent by Democratic Senate President Colleen Hanabusa in the general election.

He won in May in part because of the nature of the special election, which allowed more than one candidate from each party on the ballot. The top Republican in the race, Djou took 39.8 percent, ahead of two well-known Democrats, Hanabusa, with 31 percent, and former Rep. Ed Case (2003-07), with 28 percent.

Djou adhered to the fiscal conservative pillars of lower taxes and less government. He said he planned to push for a balanced-budget constitutional amendment and to work to lower the debt.

Opposition to the $787 billion stimulus package (PL 111-5) and health care overhaul won Djou an endorsement from national tea party activists. Case and Hanabusa backed the legislation.

In a rare point of agreement with Obama, Djou said "the president has struck it right in Iraq and Afghanistan." A month after the Sept. 11 terrorist attacks, Djou joined the Army Reserve as a judge advocate general.

INDIANA 3

GOP state Sen. Marlin Stutzman simultaneously won election Nov. 2 to fill a vacancy created by the resignation of Republican Mark Souder and to serve a full term in the House. Stutzman rolled over Democrat Thomas Hayhurst in both contests, taking 62.8 percent of the vote to Hayhurst's 33 percent in the regular election.

A fourth-generation farmer, Stutzman was elected to the state House in 2002 and to the state Senate in 2008. He tried to advance earlier in the year, getting some tea party movement backing but losing the GOP primary for the state's open Senate seat to Dan Coats. His second chance for a seat in Congress came just two weeks later, when Souder resigned May 21 after admitting an affair with an aide.

NEW YORK 29

Republican Tom Reed brought a conservative voice to Washington for a district that had not had a representative in the House since March 2010, when Democrat Eric Massa, who had been in Congress just 14 months, resigned after being accused of sexually harassing male staff members. Reed handily beat Democrat Matthew Zeller in a Nov. 2 special election to finish out the term and bested him by 56.5 percent to 43.3 percent in the general election for a full two-year term.

Reed's previous political experience was limited to a two-year term as mayor of the small city of Corning. But GOP strategists had been touting him as a top prospect since July 2009, when he decided to run in a district that took in the largely rural Southern Tier region and parts of suburban Rochester. He became the prohibitive favorite after the incumbent freshman resigned amid a wave of stories about inappropriate behavior with his staff. The Democrats were so thrown off by the turn of events that they could never recruit a viable candidate to take his place, even though Obama got 48 percent of the district's vote in the 2008 presidential race.

PENNSYLVANIA 12

Democrat Mark Critz won a May 18 special election in southwestern Pennsylvania to replace John P. Murtha, who died Feb. 8. As a district aide to the 19-term veteran, Critz had coordinated the distribution of hundreds of millions of dollars in federal funding that Murtha directed home from his perch as an Appropriations Committee member and chairman of its Defense Subcommittee. *(Murtha obituary, p. 5-11)*

But Critz convinced voters that he was no Murtha clone, defeating GOP businessman Tim Burns on May 18 by a little less than 8 percentage points. Critz held the seat in a rematch with Burns in the November midterm election in which he won 50.8 percent to 49.2 percent.

Although his former boss had voted for it, Critz campaigned against the health care overhaul, arguing that the law should be changed but not repealed. Like Burns, he also spoke against legislation aimed at reducing greenhouse gas emissions, legislation that Murtha had supported. He focused on investment in "clean coal" technologies and pledged to support incentives for companies that created local factory and mill jobs. Critz emphasized the importance of transportation projects and defense industry jobs — many of which had been funded by earmarks set aside by Murtha — to attracting new business to western Pennsylvania's flagging industrial region.

Burns tried to tie Critz to Democratic leaders, stressing Murtha's close relationship with House Speaker Nancy Pelosi, D-Calif. But Critz responded, saying in an ad, "I'm pro-life and pro-gun. That's not liberal." Attempts to implicate Critz in an ethics probe of Murtha also fell flat.

Critz was aided by campaigners such as Vice President Biden and former President Bill Clinton, although Obama's unpopularity in the region kept him out of ads and off the stump. ∎

Departing Members of the 111th Congress

RETIRING SENATORS (6 D, 5 R)	ELECTED	SUCCESSOR
Evan Bayh, D-Ind.	1998	Dan Coats (R)
Christopher S. Bond, R-Mo.	1986	Roy Blunt (R)
Jim Bunning, R-Ky.	1998	Rand Paul (R)
Roland W. Burris, D-Ill.	2009[1]	Mark Steven Kirk (R)[2]
Christopher J. Dodd, D-Conn.	1980	Richard Blumenthal (D)
Byron L. Dorgan, D-N.D.	1992	John Hoeven (R)
Carte P. Goodwin, D-W.Va.	2010[1]	Joe Manchin III, (D)[2]
Judd Gregg, R-N.H.	1992	Kelly Ayotte (R)
Ted Kaufman, D-Del.	2009[1]	Chris Coons (D)[2]
George LeMieux, R-Fla.	2009[1]	Marco Rubio (R)
George V. Voinovich, R-Ohio	1998	Rob Portman (R)

RESIGNED SENATORS (5 D, 1 R)	RESIGNED	SUCCESSOR
Barack Obama, D-Ill.	Nov. 16, 2008	Roland W. Burris (D)[1] *sworn in Jan. 15, 2009*
Joseph R. Biden Jr., D-Del.	Jan. 15, 2009	Ted Kaufman (D)[1] *sworn in Jan. 16, 2009*
Ken Salazar, D-Colo.	Jan. 20, 2009	Michael Bennet (D)[1] *sworn in Jan. 22, 2009*
Hillary Rodham Clinton, D-N.Y.	Jan. 21, 2009	Kirsten Gillibrand (D)[1] *sworn in Jan. 27, 2009*
Mel Martinez, R-Fla.	Sept. 9, 2009	George LeMieux (R)[1] *sworn in Sept. 10, 2009*
Paul G. Kirk Jr., D-Mass.	Feb. 4, 2010	Scott P. Brown (R) *Jan. 19, 2010, special election*

RETIRING HOUSE MEMBERS (11 D, 8 R)	ELECTED	SUCCESSOR
Brian Baird, D-Wash. (3)	1998	Jaime Herrera (R)
Marion Berry, D-Ark. (1)	1996	Rick Crawford (R)
Henry E. Brown Jr., R-S.C. (1)	2000	Tim Scott (R)
Ginny Brown-Waite, R-Fla. (5)	2002	Richard Nugent (R)
Steve Buyer, R-Ind. (4)	1992	Todd Rokita (R)
Lincoln Diaz-Balart, R-Fla. (21)	1992	Mario Diaz-Balart (R)
Bill Delahunt, D-Mass. (10)	1996	William Keating (D)
Vernon J. Ehlers, R-Mich. (3)	1993	Justin Amash (R)
Bart Gordon, D-Tenn. (6)	1984	Diane Black (R)
Patrick J. Kennedy, D-R.I. (1)	1994	David Cicilline (D)
John Linder, R-Ga. (7)	1992	Rob Woodall (R)
Dennis Moore, D-Kan. (3)	1998	Kevin Yoder (R)
David R. Obey, D-Wis. (7)	1969	Sean P. Duffy (R)
George Radanovich, R-Calif. (19)	1994	Jeff Denham (R)
John Shadegg, R-Ariz. (3)	1994	Ben Quayle (R)
Vic Snyder, D-Ark. (2)	1996	Tim Griffin (R)
Bart Stupak, D-Mich. (1)	1992	Dan Benishek (R)
John Tanner, D-Tenn. (8)	1988	Stephen Fincher (R)
Diane Watson, D-Calif. (33)	2001	Karen Bass (D)

RESIGNED HOUSE MEMBERS (7 D, 3 R)	RESIGNED	SUCCESSOR
Rahm Emanuel, D-Ill. (5)	Jan. 2, 2009	Mike Quigley (D) *April 7, 2009, special election*
Kirsten Gillibrand, D-N.Y. (20)	Jan. 26, 2009	Scott Murphy (D) *March 31, 2009, special election*
Hilda L. Solis, D-Calif. (32)	Feb. 24, 2009	Judy Chu (D) *July 14, 2009, special election*
Ellen O. Tauscher, D-Calif. (10)	June 26, 2009	John Garamendi (D) *Nov. 3, 2009, special election*
John M. McHugh, R-N.Y. (23)	Sept. 21, 2009	Bill Owens (D) *Nov. 3, 2009, special election*
Robert Wexler, D-Fla. (19)	Jan. 3, 2010	Ted Deutch (D) *April 13, 2010, special election*
Neil Abercrombie, D-Hawaii (1)	Feb. 28, 2010	Charles K. Djou (R) *May 22, 2010, special election*
Eric Massa, D-N.Y. (29)	March 8, 2010	Tom Reed (R) *Nov. 2, 2010, special election*
Nathan Deal, R-Ga. (9)	March 21, 2010	Tom Graves (R) *June 8, 2010, special election*
Mark Souder, R-Ind. (3)	May 21, 2010	Marlin Stutzman (R) *Nov. 2, 2010, special election*

DECEASED SENATORS (2 D)	DIED	SUCCESSOR
Edward M. Kennedy, D-Mass.	Aug. 25, 2009	Paul G. Kirk Jr. (D)[1] *sworn in Sept. 25, 2009*
Robert C. Byrd, D-W.Va.	June 28, 2010	Carte P. Goodwin (D)[1] *sworn in July 20, 2010*

DECEASED HOUSE MEMBER (1 D)	DIED	SUCCESSOR
John P. Murtha, D-Pa.	Feb. 8, 2010	Mark Critz (D) *May 18 special election*

NOTES:

[1] Appointed to Senate seat

[2] Won Nov. 2 special election

[3] Did not serve 2005-07

HOUSE MEMBERS DEFEATED IN GENERAL ELECTION (51 D, 2 R)

	ELECTED	WINNER
John Adler, D-N.J. (3)	2008	Jon Runyan (R)
Michael Arcuri, D-N.Y. (24)	2006	Richard Hanna (R)
Melissa Bean, D-Ill. (8)	2004	Joe Walsh (R)
John Boccieri, D-Ohio (16)	2008	Jim Renacci (R)
Rick Boucher, D-Va. (9)	1982	Morgan Griffith (R)
Allen Boyd, D-Fla. (2)	1996	Steve Southerland (R)
Bobby Bright, D-Ala. (2)	2008	Martha Roby (R)
Anh "Joseph" Cao, R-La. (2)	2008	Cedric Richmond (D)
Christopher Carney, D-Pa. (10)	2006	Tom Marino (R)
Travis W. Childers, D-Miss. (1)	2008	Alan Nunnelee (R)
Kathy Dahlkemper, D-Pa. (3)	2008	Mike Kelly (R)
Lincoln Davis, D-Tenn. (4)	2002	Scott DesJarlais (R)
Charles K. Djou, R-Hawaii (1)	2010	Colleen Hanabusa (D)
Steve Driehaus, D-Ohio (1)	2008	Steve Chabot (R)
Chet Edwards, D-Texas (17)	1990	Bill Flores (R)
Bob Etheridge, D-N.C. (2)	1996	Renee Ellmers (R)
Bill Foster, D-Ill. (14)	2008	Randy Hultgren (R)
Alan Grayson, D-Fla. (8)	2008	Daniel Webster (R)
John Hall, D-N.Y. (19)	2006	Nan Hayworth (R)
Debbie Halvorson, D-Ill. (11)	2008	Adam Kinzinger (R)
Phil Hare, D-Ill. (17)	2006	Bobby Schilling (R)
Stephanie Herseth Sandlin, D-S.D. (AL)	2004	Kristi Noem (R)
Baron P. Hill, D-Ind. (9)	1998 [3]	Todd Young (R)
Steve Kagen, D-Wis. (8)	2006	Reid Ribble (R)
Paul E. Kanjorski, D-Pa. (11)	1984	Lou Barletta (R)
Mary Jo Kilroy, D-Ohio (15)	2008	Steve Stivers (R)
Ann Kirkpatrick, D-Ariz. (1)	2008	Paul Gosar (R)
Ron Klein, D-Fla. (22)	2006	Allen West (R)
Suzanne M. Kosmas, D-Fla. (24)	2008	Sandy Adams (R)
Frank Kratovil Jr., D-Md. (1)	2008	Andy Harris (R)
Dan Maffei, D-N.Y. (25)	2008	Ann Marie Buerkle (R)
Betsy Markey, D-Colo. (4)	2008	Cory Gardner (R)
Jim Marshall, D-Ga. (8)	2002	Austin Scott (R)
Michael E. McMahon, D-N.Y. (13)	2008	Michael Grimm (R)
Walt Minnick, D-Idaho (1)	2008	Rául R. Labrador (R)
Harry E. Mitchell, D-Ariz. (5)	2006	David Schweikert (R)
Patrick J. Murphy, D-Pa. (8)	2006	Michael G. Fitzpatrick (R)
Scott Murphy, D-N.Y. (20)	2009	Chris Gibson (R)
Glenn Nye, D-Va. (2)	2008	Scott Rigell (R)
James L. Oberstar, D-Minn. (8)	1974	Chip Cravaack (R)
Tom Perriello, D-Va. (5)	2008	Robert Hurt (R)
Earl Pomeroy, D-N.D. (AL)	1992	Rick Berg (R)
Ciro D. Rodriguez, D-Texas (23)	1997 [3]	Francisco "Quico" Canseco (R)
John Salazar, D-Colo. (3)	2004	Scott Tipton (R)
Mark Schauer, D-Mich. (7)	2008	Tim Walberg (R)
Carol Shea-Porter, D-N.H. (1)	2006	Frank Guinta (R)
Ike Skelton, D-Mo. (4)	1976	Vicky Hartzler (R)
Zack Space, D-Ohio (18)	2006	Bob Gibbs (R)
John M. Spratt Jr., D-S.C. (5)	1982	Mick Mulvaney (R)
Gene Taylor, D-Miss. (4)	1989	Steven Palazzo (R)
Harry Teague, D-N.M. (2)	2008	Steve Pearce (R)
Dina Titus, D-Nev. (3)	2008	Joe Heck (R)
Charlie Wilson, D-Ohio (6)	2006	Bill Johnson (R)

SENATORS DEFEATED IN GENERAL ELECTION (2 D)

	ELECTED	WINNER
Russ Feingold, D-Wis.	1992	Ron Johnson (R)
Blanche Lincoln, D-Ark.	1998	John Boozman (R)

SENATOR WHO SOUGHT OTHER OFFICE (1 R)

	ELECTED	SOUGHT / RESULT
Sam Brownback, R-Kan.	1996	Governor / Won

HOUSE MEMBERS WHO SOUGHT OTHER OFFICE (6 D, 11 R)

	ELECTED	SOUGHT / RESULT
J. Gresham Barrett, R-S.C. (3)	2002	Governor / Lost primary
Roy Blunt, R-Mo. (7)	1996	Senate / Won
John Boozman, R-Ark. (3)	2001	Senate / Won
Michael N. Castle, R-Del. (AL)	1992	Senate / Lost primary
Artur Davis, D-Ala. (7)	2002	Governor / Lost primary
Brad Ellsworth, D-Ind. (8)	2006	Senate / Lost
Mary Fallin, R-Okla. (5)	2006	Governor / Won
Paul W. Hodes, D-N.H. (2)	2006	Senate / Lost
Peter Hoekstra, R-Mich. (2)	1992	Governor / Lost primary
Mark Steven Kirk, R-Ill. (10)	2000	Senate / Won
Kendrick B. Meek, D-Fla. (17)	2002	Senate / Lost
Charlie Melancon, D-La. (3)	2004	Senate / Lost
Jerry Moran, R-Kan. (1)	1996	Senate / Won
Adam H. Putnam, R-Fla. (12)	2000	State agriculture commissioner / Won
Joe Sestak, D-Pa. (7)	2006	Senate / Lost
Todd Tiahrt, R-Kan. (4)	1994	Senate / Lost primary
Zach Wamp, R-Tenn. (3)	1994	Governor / Lost primary

SENATORS DENIED RENOMINATION (1 D, 1 R)

	ELECTED
Robert F. Bennett, R-Utah	1992
Arlen Specter, D-Pa.	1980

HOUSE MEMBERS DENIED RENOMINATION (2 D, 2 R)

	ELECTED
Parker Griffith, R-Ala. (5)	2008
Bob Inglis, R-S.C. (4)	2004
Carolyn Cheeks Kilpatrick, D-Mich. (13)	1996
Alan B. Mollohan, D-W.Va. (1)	1982

State Gains Foster Future GOP Hopes

THE REPUBLICAN SURGE of 2010 put the GOP in control of redrawing congressional maps for close to half of the seats in the House.

"2010 will go down as a defining political election that will shape the national political landscape for at least the next 10 years," Tim Storey, elections specialist with the National Conference of State Legislatures (NCSL), said in a statement. He said Republicans were "in the best position for both congressional and state legislative line-drawing" than at any time in "the modern era of redistricting."

The 2010 elections produced a well-timed comeback for Republicans, who had lost offices up and down the ballot in the 2006 and 2008 elections.

There were 37 contests for governors' seats in 2010. Of these, 18 switched party control, and Republicans were winners in 12 of the races, for a net gain of six seats. That gave the GOP 29 governors' seats for 2011, to 20 for the Democrats and one held by an independent.

Republicans also strengthened their position in state legislatures, equally important in the redistricting process following the 2010 census. The GOP gained roughly 680 state legislative seats, according to an analysis by the bipartisan NCSL.

That was the largest gain by either party since 1966, surpassing the Democratic gains in the post-Watergate election of 1974, and the largest number of legislative seats Republicans had held since the Great Depression.

GOVERNORSHIPS

Still, after being significantly outspent in a toxic political climate, Democrats could have faced much worse losses. They scored a big takeover in California, the most populous state, where Democrat Jerry Brown won to succeed term-limited Republican Arnold Schwarzenegger. The GOP held on to seats in the next-biggest states, Texas and Florida, but Democrats maintained the seat in New York.

The GOP was practically handed four of the governorships. Democratic governors were term-limited out of office in four strongly Republican states — Kansas, Oklahoma, Tennessee and Wyoming — where Barack Obama failed to crack 42 percent for president in 2008. Republican candidates won those seats easily.

Republicans added to their number in a Rust Belt rout that gave them open Democratic seats in Michigan, Wisconsin and Pennsylvania while also defeating incumbent Democrats Ted Strickland in Ohio and Chet Culver in Iowa.

Even in the face of Ohio's high unemployment figures, Strickland was competitive in his race until the end and lost to Republican John R. Kasich by just 2 percentage points. Democrats spent millions of dollars in advertising trying to demonize Kasich for his direct connections to Wall Street as a managing director for the since-defunct Lehman

THE GOVERNORS

	Before 2010 Election		2010 Election	
Democrats		26	Democrats	20
Republicans		23	Republicans	29
Independent		1	Independent	1

DEMOCRATS

Net loss	-6
Freshmen	8
Incumbents re-elected	11
Incumbents defeated	2

REPUBLICANS

Net gain	+6
Freshmen	17
Incumbents re-elected	10
Incumbents defeated	0

Brothers Holdings Inc. and to Washington as a former House Budget Committee chairman.

According to exit polls, a third of Ohio voters primarily blamed Wall Street for their state's economic problems, but those voters went for Kasich 49 percent to 47 percent. "Sometimes people have all the information on the candidates and still vote for the other guy," said Nathan Daschle, the executive director of the Democratic Governors Association.

Twenty-six men and women were set to replace incumbent governors in 2011, but like Kasich, many of them were not political newcomers.

Republican Sen. Sam Brownback was elected governor in Kansas, and House GOP veterans Mary Fallin and Nathan Deal won in Oklahoma and Georgia, respectively. Deal had resigned his House seat earlier in the year to focus on his gubernatorial run, and Georgia's strong Republican leanings helped him weather ethics questions raised after his departure and defeat former Gov. Roy Barnes, a Democrat who was not exactly a fresh face either.

Former Maryland Republican Gov. Bob Ehrlich lost his re-election bid as well. But former governors Terry Branstad of Iowa, a Republican, and John Kitzhaber of Oregon, a Democrat, won comeback bids after serving previous terms and leaving office.

Kitzhaber was first elected in 1994, fighting an earlier GOP wave, and left office as a popular governor after two terms. In 2010, he narrowly squeaked out a victory against former professional basketball player Chris Dudley, a first-time candidate with a thin track record for Democrats to attack. Iowa's Branstad won by a 10 percentage point margin over Democrat incumbent Culver, who had the misfortune of serving his one term during a major economic downturn.

In California, where a long economic boom had gone bust, voters turned to former Gov. Brown, who had last led the state in 1983 and made three bids for the Democratic presidential nomination. This time he defeated Meg Whitman, the former chief executive of eBay, who broke records by spending $144 million of her own money to boost her chances on the Republican ticket.

Democrats also were able to offset some of their losses in the Midwest by taking back traditionally Democratic strongholds such as Hawaii, where another familiar face, longtime Democratic Rep. Neil Abercrombie, won the governorship.

Indeed, Republicans failed to meet their own expectations on election night. "If we don't have at least 30, I'll be disappointed," Mississippi Gov. Haley Barbour, who was also chairman of the Republican Governors Association, said the day before the election.

The disappointment could be traced to the Northeast, where several GOP hopes did not materialize. Democrat Dan Malloy won to succeed retired Republican M. Jodi Rell in Connecticut. Republicans were unable to knock off Democratic Gov. Deval Patrick of Massachusetts despite his mediocre job approval numbers, and lost open governorships in Vermont and Rhode Island. Former Sen. Lincoln Chafee, previously a liberal-leaning Republican, won his state as an independent.

Republicans picked up the governorship in Maine, where Waterville Mayor Paul LePage, backed by tea party movement conservatives, won with less than 40 percent as two more-liberal candidates divided the Democratic and independent vote. Independent Eliot Cutler surged ahead of Democratic nominee Libby Mitchell in the race's final weeks and nearly pulled off a victory.

Third-party candidates were also significant factors in Massachusetts, Minnesota, Colorado and Illinois, although only Rhode Island's Chafee was victorious.

In Illinois, former Democratic nominee for lieutenant governor Scott Lee Cohen ran as an independent, but he got only 4 percent of the vote; the Green Party candidate got 3 percent; and Gov. Pat Quinn scraped by GOP legislator Bill Brady — a major disappointment for the Republican Party. Voters had consistently given Quinn poor marks for the job he had done since succeeding disgraced former Gov. Rod R. Blagojevich, who was expelled from office in January 2009.

Colorado was another big disappointment for Republicans. As Democratic Gov. Bill Ritter Jr.'s job ratings sank, GOP prospects brightened. But after Ritter decided not to run for re-election, Democrats turned to popular Denver Mayor John Hickenlooper.

Republicans, meanwhile, became mired in a messy primary and nominated Dan Maes over former Rep. Scott McInnis. Former GOP Rep. Tom Tancredo deemed Maes unelectable and ran at the last minute on the conservative American Constitution Party line. Maes tanked, Tancredo became the de facto GOP nominee, and the division was enough for the Republican Governors Association to walk away from the opportunity.

ON THEIR WAY UP

Republicans did elevate some potential rising stars for the party.

South Carolina elected Nikki R. Haley, the first female Indian-American governor and second Indian-American governor after Louisiana's Bobby Jindal, also a Republican.

In New Mexico, voters turned to former Dona Ana County prosecutor Susana Martinez, a Hispanic woman. She was one of several law-and-order Republican candidates to win gubernatorial bids, along with former U.S. Attorney Matt Mead in Wyoming and former U.S. District Judge Brian Sandoval in Nevada, who defeated Rory Reid, Senate Democratic leader Harry Reid's son.

In Michigan, wealthy Republican businessman Rick Snyder got attention for his creative television ads, which portrayed him as "one tough nerd." His impressive outsider campaign carried him through a competitive primary and an easier general election to take over a recession-buffeted state that had been elusive for the GOP.

In Florida, another wealthy businessman, Rick Scott, came out of nowhere to knock off state Attorney General Bill McCollum in the primary and narrowly defeat the Democratic nominee, state Chief Financial Officer Alex Sink, in the general election.

Scott's victory was something of a surprise: He was forced to resign in 1997 as head of a health care company that became involved in what was then the largest Medicare fraud case ever. The company ultimately pleaded guilty to 14 felonies and paid more than $2 billion to the government and private plaintiffs. Scott's opponents seized on the issue and drove up his negative ratings, but in the end, his outsider message resonated with enough voters.

According to strategists on both sides of the aisle, the Florida gubernatorial race was a prime example of how the sins of an outsider candidate were less damaging than a perceived connection to the political establishment.

CONTROL OF STATE LEGISLATURES

While Republicans did not deliver a knockout blow in gubernatorial races, their decisive victories at the state level had potential long-term consequences for the Democrats.

For months, Democratic strategists privately expressed concern that the party had the expertise and resources to stem the GOP tide in some federal races, but there was not enough attention on races further down the ballot. Their prediction came true on Nov. 2.

Republicans picked up 21 state chambers, then flipped another, the Louisiana Senate, in a February 2011 special election. That gave the GOP control of, or a tie in, 61 out of 99 legislative chambers in the country (including Nebraska's nominally nonpartisan unicameral legislature, which was mostly Republican).

More importantly, Republicans achieved total control over legislatures in 26 states, up from 15 before the election, including some key redistricting states. In 22 of those states they also controlled the governorship.

"Of the 18 states that are going to gain or lose seats in reapportionment, Republicans now have majorities in 10 of those states," said Ed Gillespie, chairman of the Republican State Leadership Committee.

Every one of the 43 states with more than one House district would redraw its congressional map, even if it did not gain or lose a seat in the House reapportionment that accompanied the December 2010 release of the year's national population census.

"If you are a political party, you never want to have a really bad election," said veteran political handicapper Charlie Cook of the Cook Political Report. "But if you're going to have one, you really don't want to have it in a year that ends in a zero."

EYE ON REDISTRICTING

The state-level gains and their effect in boosting the GOP's clout in redistricting promised to have implications that could extend for the next decade.

Republicans were particularly excited about their gains in the Great Lakes states of Wisconsin, Michigan, Ohio and Pennsylvania, all of which would have GOP majorities in both chambers and a Republican governor.

In Ohio, Republicans picked up not only the governorship but also the state House from Democrats, and they already had control of the state Senate. With five Republican pickups in the state's 2010 U.S. House elections and the state losing two seats to reapportionment, the state-level gains were sure to be felt as a new map was drawn.

"It's much better to have Dennis Kucinich's seat in danger of being carved out than John Boehner's," said Gillespie, referring respectively to the liberal Cleveland Democrat and the new GOP Speaker-in-waiting.

Democrats were as concerned as Gillespie was jubilant about the ramifications of the realignment. Texas Democrat Matt Angle, founder of the Lone Star Project, said Republicans will "gerrymander districts" if they can and could put federally mandated Voting Rights Act districts at risk. The Lone Star Project was a Democratic group focused on influencing the redistricting process in Texas, a state that ended up gaining four seats through reapportionment.

"The timing could not have been worse for a sweep by Republicans," Angle added. ∎

State Delegations in the 112th Congress

Italics indicate new member.
Democrats   **Republicans**   Independents

Alabama
SENATE
Richard C. Shelby
Jeff Sessions
HOUSE
1 **Jo Bonner**
2 *Martha Roby*
3 **Mike D. Rogers**
4 **Robert B. Aderholt**
5 *Mo Brooks*
6 **Spencer Bachus**
7 *Terri A. Sewell*

Alaska
SENATE
Lisa Murkowski
Mark Begich
HOUSE
AL **Don Young**

Arizona
SENATE
John McCain
Jon Kyl
HOUSE
1 *Paul Gosar*
2 **Trent Franks**
3 *Ben Quayle*
4 Ed Pastor
5 *David Schweikert*
6 **Jeff Flake**
7 Raúl M. Grijalva
8 Gabrielle Giffords

Arkansas
SENATE
Mark Pryor
John Boozman
HOUSE
1 *Rick Crawford*
2 *Tim Griffin*
3 *Steve Womack*
4 Mike Ross

California
SENATE
Dianne Feinstein
Barbara Boxer
HOUSE
1 Mike Thompson
2 **Wally Herger**
3 **Dan Lungren**
4 **Tom McClintock**
5 Doris Matsui
6 Lynn Woolsey
7 George Miller
8 Nancy Pelosi
9 Barbara Lee
10 John Garamendi
11 Jerry McNerney
12 Jackie Speier
13 Pete Stark
14 Anna G. Eshoo
15 Michael M. Honda
16 Zoe Lofgren
17 Sam Farr
18 Dennis Cardoza
19 *Jeff Denham*
20 Jim Costa
21 **Devin Nunes**
22 **Kevin McCarthy**
23 Lois Capps
24 **Elton Gallegly**
25 **Howard P. "Buck" McKeon**
26 **David Dreier**
27 Brad Sherman
28 Howard L. Berman
29 Adam B. Schiff
30 Henry A. Waxman
31 Xavier Becerra
32 Judy Chu
33 *Karen Bass*
34 Lucille Roybal-Allard
35 Maxine Waters
36 Jane Harman
37 Laura Richardson
38 Grace F. Napolitano
39 Linda T. Sánchez
40 **Ed Royce**
41 **Jerry Lewis**
42 **Gary G. Miller**
43 Joe Baca
44 **Ken Calvert**
45 **Mary Bono Mack**
46 **Dana Rohrabacher**
47 Loretta Sanchez
48 **John Campbell**
49 **Darrell Issa**
50 **Brian P. Bilbray**
51 Bob Filner
52 **Duncan Hunter**
53 Susan A. Davis

Colorado
SENATE
Mark Udall
Michael Bennet
HOUSE
1 Diana DeGette
2 Jared Polis
3 *Scott Tipton*
4 *Cory Gardner*
5 **Doug Lamborn**
6 **Mike Coffman**
7 Ed Perlmutter

Connecticut
SENATE
Joseph I. Lieberman
Richard Blumenthal
HOUSE
1 John B. Larson
2 Joe Courtney
3 Rosa DeLauro
4 Jim Himes
5 Christopher S. Murphy

Delaware
SENATE
Thomas R. Carper
Chris Coons
HOUSE
AL *John Carney*

Florida
SENATE
Bill Nelson
Marco Rubio
HOUSE
1 **Jeff Miller**
2 *Steve Southerland II*
3 Corrine Brown
4 **Ander Crenshaw**
5 *Rich Nugent*
6 **Cliff Stearns**
7 **John L. Mica**
8 *Daniel Webster*
9 **Gus Bilirakis**
10 **C.W. Bill Young**
11 Kathy Castor
12 *Dennis A. Ross*
13 **Vern Buchanan**
14 **Connie Mack**
15 **Bill Posey**
16 **Tom Rooney**
17 *Frederica S. Wilson*
18 **Ileana Ros-Lehtinen**
19 Ted Deutch
20 Debbie Wasserman Schultz
21 **Mario Diaz-Balart**
22 *Allen B. West*
23 Alcee L. Hastings
24 *Sandy Adams*
25 *David Rivera*

Georgia
SENATE
Saxby Chambliss
Johnny Isakson
HOUSE
1 **Jack Kingston**
2 Sanford D. Bishop Jr.
3 **Lynn Westmoreland**
4 Hank Johnson
5 John Lewis
6 **Tom Price**
7 *Rob Woodall*
8 *Austin Scott*
9 **Tom Graves**
10 **Paul Broun**
11 **Phil Gingrey**
12 John Barrow
13 David Scott

Hawaii
SENATE
Daniel K. Inouye
Daniel K. Akaka
HOUSE
1 *Colleen Hanabusa*
2 Mazie K. Hirono

Idaho
SENATE
Michael D. Crapo
Jim Risch
HOUSE
1 *Raúl R. Labrador*
2 **Mike Simpson**

Illinois
SENATE
Richard J. Durbin
Mark Steven Kirk
HOUSE
1 Bobby L. Rush
2 Jesse L. Jackson Jr.
3 Daniel Lipinski
4 Luis V. Gutierrez
5 Mike Quigley
6 **Peter Roskam**
7 Danny K. Davis
8 *Joe Walsh*
9 Jan Schakowsky
10 *Robert Dold*
11 *Adam Kinzinger*
12 Jerry F. Costello
13 **Judy Biggert**
14 *Randy Hultgren*
15 **Timothy V. Johnson**
16 **Donald Manzullo**
17 *Bobby Schilling*
18 **Aaron Schock**
19 **John Shimkus**

Indiana
SENATE
Richard G. Lugar
Dan Coats
HOUSE
1 Peter J. Visclosky
2 Joe Donnelly
3 *Marlin Stutzman*
4 *Todd Rokita*

5   **Dan Burton**
6   **Mike Pence**
7   André Carson
8   *Larry Bucshon*
9   *Todd Young*

Iowa
SENATE
   Charles E. Grassley
   Tom Harkin
HOUSE
1   Bruce Braley
2   Dave Loebsack
3   Leonard L. Boswell
4   **Tom Latham**
5   **Steve King**

Kansas
SENATE
   Pat Roberts
   Jerry Moran
HOUSE
1   *Tim Huelskamp*
2   **Lynn Jenkins**
3   *Kevin Yoder*
4   *Mike Pompeo*

Kentucky
SENATE
   Mitch McConnell
   Rand Paul
HOUSE
1   **Ed Whitfield**
2   **Brett Guthrie**
3   John Yarmuth
4   **Geoff Davis**
5   **Harold Rogers**
6   Ben Chandler

Louisiana
SENATE
   Mary L. Landrieu
   David Vitter
HOUSE
1   **Steve Scalise**
2   *Cedric L. Richmond*
3   *Jeff Landry*
4   **John Fleming**
5   **Rodney Alexander**
6   **Bill Cassidy**
7   **Charles Boustany Jr.**

Maine
SENATE
   Olympia J. Snowe
   Susan Collins
HOUSE
1   Chellie Pingree
2   Michael H. Michaud

Maryland
SENATE
   Barbara A. Mikulski
   Benjamin L. Cardin
HOUSE
1   *Andy Harris*

2   C.A. Dutch Ruppersberger
3   John Sarbanes
4   Donna Edwards
5   Steny H. Hoyer
6   **Roscoe G. Bartlett**
7   Elijah E. Cummings
8   Chris Van Hollen

Massachusetts
SENATE
   John Kerry
   Scott P. Brown
HOUSE
1   John W. Olver
2   Richard E. Neal
3   Jim McGovern
4   Barney Frank
5   Niki Tsongas
6   John F. Tierney
7   Edward J. Markey
8   Michael E. Capuano
9   Stephen F. Lynch
10   *William Keating*

Michigan
SENATE
   Carl Levin
   Debbie Stabenow
HOUSE
1   *Dan Benishek*
2   *Bill Huizenga*
3   *Justin Amash*
4   **Dave Camp**
5   Dale E. Kildee
6   **Fred Upton**
7   *Tim Walberg*
8   **Mike Rogers**
9   Gary Peters
10   **Candice S. Miller**
11   **Thaddeus McCotter**
12   Sander M. Levin
13   *Hansen Clarke*
14   John Conyers Jr.
15   John D. Dingell

Minnesota
SENATE
   Amy Klobuchar
   Al Franken
HOUSE
1   Tim Walz
2   **John Kline**
3   **Erik Paulsen**
4   Betty McCollum
5   Keith Ellison
6   **Michele Bachmann**
7   Collin C. Peterson
8   *Chip Cravaack*

Mississippi
SENATE
   Thad Cochran
   Roger Wicker
HOUSE
1   *Alan Nunnelee*
2   Bennie Thompson

3   **Gregg Harper**
4   *Steven M. Palazzzo*

Missouri
SENATE
   Claire McCaskill
   Roy Blunt
HOUSE
1   William Lacy Clay
2   **Todd Akin**
3   Russ Carnahan
4   *Vicky Hartzler*
5   Emanuel Cleaver II
6   **Sam Graves**
7   *Billy Long*
8   **Jo Ann Emerson**
9   **Blaine Luetkemeyer**

Montana
SENATE
   Max Baucus
   Jon Tester
HOUSE
AL   **Denny Rehberg**

Nebraska
SENATE
   Ben Nelson
   Mike Johanns
HOUSE
1   **Jeff Fortenberry**
2   **Lee Terry**
3   **Adrian Smith**

Nevada
SENATE
   Harry Reid
   John Ensign
HOUSE
1   Shelley Berkley
2   **Dean Heller**
3   *Joe Heck*

New Hampshire
SENATE
   Jeanne Shaheen
   Kelly Ayotte
HOUSE
1   *Frank Guinta*
2   *Charles Bass*

New Jersey
SENATE
   Frank R. Lautenberg
   Robert Menendez
HOUSE
1   Robert E. Andrews
2   **Frank A. LoBiondo**
3   *Jon Runyan*
4   **Christopher H. Smith**
5   **Scott Garrett**
6   Frank Pallone Jr.
7   **Leonard Lance**
8   Bill Pascrell Jr.
9   Steven R. Rothman
10   Donald M. Payne

11   **Rodney Frelinghuysen**
12   Rush D. Holt
13   Albio Sires

New Mexico
SENATE
   Jeff Bingaman
   Tom Udall
HOUSE
1   Martin Heinrich
2   *Steve Pearce*
3   Ben Ray Luján

New York
SENATE
   Charles E. Schumer
   Kirsten Gillibrand
HOUSE
1   Timothy H. Bishop
2   Steve Israel
3   **Peter T. King**
4   Carolyn McCarthy
5   Gary L. Ackerman
6   Gregory W. Meeks
7   Joseph Crowley
8   Jerrold Nadler
9   Anthony Weiner
10   Edolphus Towns
11   Yvette D. Clarke
12   Nydia M. Velázquez
13   *Michael G. Grimm*
14   Carolyn B. Maloney
15   Charles B. Rangel
16   José E. Serrano
17   Eliot L. Engel
18   Nita M. Lowey
19   *Nan Hayworth*
20   *Chris Gibson*
21   Paul Tonko
22   Maurice D. Hinchey
23   Bill Owens
24   *Richard Hanna*
25   *Ann Marie Buerkle*
26   **Christopher Lee**
27   Brian Higgins
28   Louise M. Slaughter
29   *Tom Reed*

North Carolina
SENATE
   Richard M. Burr
   Kay Hagan
HOUSE
1   G.K. Butterfield
2   *Renee Ellmers*
3   **Walter B. Jones**
4   David E. Price
5   **Virginia Foxx**
6   **Howard Coble**
7   Mike McIntyre
8   Larry Kissell
9   **Sue Myrick**
10   **Patrick T. McHenry**
11   Heath Shuler
12   Melvin Watt
13   Brad Miller

North Dakota

SENATE
Kent Conrad
John Hoeven

HOUSE
AL *Rick Berg*

Ohio

SENATE
Sherrod Brown
Rob Portman

HOUSE
1 *Steve Chabot*
2 *Jean Schmidt*
3 *Michael R. Turner*
4 *Jim Jordan*
5 *Bob Latta*
6 *Bill Johnson*
7 *Steve Austria*
8 *John A. Boehner*
9 Marcy Kaptur
10 Dennis J. Kucinich
11 Marcia L. Fudge
12 *Pat Tiberi*
13 Betty Sutton
14 *Steven C. LaTourette*
15 *Steve Stivers*
16 *James B. Renacci*
17 Tim Ryan
18 *Bob Gibbs*

Oklahoma

SENATE
James M. Inhofe
Tom Coburn

HOUSE
1 *John Sullivan*
2 Dan Boren
3 *Frank D. Lucas*
4 *Tom Cole*
5 *James Lankford*

Oregon

SENATE
Ron Wyden
Jeff Merkley

HOUSE
1 David Wu
2 *Greg Walden*
3 Earl Blumenauer
4 Peter A. DeFazio
5 Kurt Schrader

Pennsylvania

SENATE
Bob Casey
Patrick J. Toomey

HOUSE
1 Robert A. Brady
2 Chaka Fattah
3 *Mike Kelly*
4 Jason Altmire
5 *Glenn Thompson*
6 Jim Gerlach
7 *Patrick Meehan*
8 *Michael G. Fitzpatrick*
9 *Bill Shuster*
10 *Tom Marino*
11 *Lou Barletta*
12 Mark Critz
13 Allyson Y. Schwartz
14 Mike Doyle
15 *Charlie Dent*
16 *Joe Pitts*
17 Tim Holden
18 *Tim Murphy*
19 *Todd R. Platts*

Rhode Island

SENATE
Jack Reed
Sheldon Whitehouse

HOUSE
1 *David Cicilline*
2 Jim Langevin

South Carolina

SENATE
Lindsey Graham
Jim DeMint

HOUSE
1 *Tim Scott*
2 *Joe Wilson*
3 *Jeff Duncan*
4 *Trey Gowdy*
5 *Mick Mulvaney*
6 James E. Clyburn

South Dakota

SENATE
Tim Johnson
John Thune

HOUSE
AL *Kristi Noem*

Tennessee

SENATE
Lamar Alexander
Bob Corker

HOUSE
1 *Phil Roe*
2 *John J. "Jimmy" Duncan Jr.*
3 *Chuck Fleischmann*
4 *Scott DesJarlais*
5 Jim Cooper
6 *Diane Black*
7 *Marsha Blackburn*
8 *Stephen Fincher*
9 Steve Cohen

Texas

SENATE
Kay Bailey Hutchison
John Cornyn

HOUSE
1 *Louie Gohmert*
2 *Ted Poe*
3 *Sam Johnson*
4 *Ralph M. Hall*
5 *Jeb Hensarling*
6 *Joe L. Barton*
7 *John Culberson*
8 *Kevin Brady*
9 Al Green
10 *Michael McCaul*
11 *K. Michael Conaway*
12 *Kay Granger*
13 *William M. "Mac" Thornberry*
14 *Ron Paul*
15 Rubén Hinojosa
16 Silvestre Reyes
17 *Bill Flores*
18 Sheila Jackson Lee
19 *Randy Neugebauer*
20 Charlie Gonzalez
21 *Lamar Smith*
22 *Pete Olson*
23 *Francisco "Quico" Canseco*
24 *Kenny Marchant*
25 Lloyd Doggett
26 *Michael C. Burgess*
27 *Blake Farenthold*
28 Henry Cuellar
29 Gene Green
30 Eddie Bernice Johnson
31 *John Carter*
32 *Pete Sessions*

Utah

SENATE
Orrin G. Hatch
Mike Lee

HOUSE
1 *Rob Bishop*
2 Jim Matheson
3 *Jason Chaffetz*

Vermont

SENATE
Patrick J. Leahy
Bernard Sanders

HOUSE
AL Peter Welch

Virginia

SENATE
Jim Webb
Mark Warner

HOUSE
1 *Rob Wittman*
2 *Scott Rigell*
3 Robert C. Scott
4 *J. Randy Forbes*
5 *Robert Hurt*
6 *Robert W. Goodlatte*
7 *Eric Cantor*
8 James P. Moran
9 *Morgan Griffith*
10 *Frank R. Wolf*
11 Gerald E. Connolly

Washington

SENATE
Patty Murray
Maria Cantwell

HOUSE
1 Jay Inslee
2 Rick Larsen
3 *Jaime Herrera Beutler*
4 *Doc Hastings*
5 *Cathy McMorris Rodgers*
6 Norm Dicks
7 Jim McDermott
8 *Dave Reichert*
9 Adam Smith

West Virginia

SENATE
John D. Rockefeller IV
Joe Manchin III

HOUSE
1 *David B. McKinley*
2 *Shelley Moore Capito*
3 Nick J. Rahall II

Wisconsin

SENATE
Herb Kohl
Ron Johnson

HOUSE
1 *Paul D. Ryan*
2 Tammy Baldwin
3 Ron Kind
4 Gwen Moore
5 *F. James Sensenbrenner Jr.*
6 *Tom Petri*
7 *Sean P. Duffy*
8 *Reid Ribble*

Wyoming

SENATE
Michael B. Enzi
John Barrasso

HOUSE
AL *Cynthia M. Lummis*

Delegates

AMERICAN SAMOA
Eni F.H. Faleomavaega

DISTRICT OF COLUMBIA
Eleanor Holmes Norton

GUAM
Madeleine Z. Bordallo

NORTHERN MARIANA ISLANDS
Gregorio Kilili Camacho Sablan

PUERTO RICO
Pedro R. Pierluisi

VIRGIN ISLANDS
Donna M.C. Christensen

Gubernatorial, Senate and House Election Results

	Votes	Percent
Alabama		
GOVERNOR		
Robert Bentley (R)	860,472	57.6
Ron Sparks (D)	625,710	41.9
SENATE		
Richard C. Shelby (R)	968,181	65.2
William G. Barnes (D)	515,619	34.7
HOUSE		
1 **Jo Bonner (R)**	129,063	82.6
David Walter (CNSTP)	26,357	16.9
write-ins (WRI)	861	.6
2 **Martha Roby (R)** *	111,645	51.0
Bobby Bright (D)	106,865	48.8
write-ins (WRI)	518	.2
3 **Mike D. Rogers (R)**	117,736	59.4
Steve Segrest (D)	80,204	40.5
write-ins (WRI)	199	.1
4 **Robert B. Aderholt (R)**	167,714	98.8
write-ins (WRI)	2,007	1.2
5 **Mo Brooks (R)** *	131,109	57.9
Steve Raby (D)	95,192	42.1
write-in (WRI)		.0
6 **Spencer Bachus (R)**	205,288	98.0
write-ins (WRI)	4,076	1.9
7 **Terri A. Sewell (D)** *	136,696	72.4
Don Chamberlain (R)	51,890	27.5
write-in (WRI)	138	.1
Alaska		
GOVERNOR		
Sean Parnell (R)	151,318	59.1
Ethan Berkowitz (D)	96,519	37.7
Don R. Wright (AKI)	4,775	1.9
Billy Toien (LIBERT)	2,682	1.0
SENATE		
Lisa Murkowski (WRI)	101,091	39.2
Joe Miller (R)	90,839	35.3
Scott T. McAdams (D)	60,045	23.3
Frederick D. "David" Haase (LIBERT)	1,459	.6
Tim Carter (UNA)	927	.4
Ted Gianoutsos (UNA)	458	.2

	Votes	Percent
HOUSE		
AL **Don Young (R)**	175,384	69.0
Harry T. Crawford Jr. (D)	77,606	30.5
write-ins (WRI)	1,345	.5
Arizona		
GOVERNOR		
Jan Brewer (R)	938,934	54.3
Terry Goddard (D)	733,935	42.5
Barry J. Hess II (LIBERT)	38,722	2.2
Larry Gist (GREEN)	16,128	.9
SENATE		
John McCain (R)	1,005,615	58.9
Rodney Glassman (D)	592,011	34.6
David F. Nolan (LIBERT)	80,097	4.7
Jerry Joslyn (GREEN)	24,603	1.4
Ian Gilyeat (WRI)	5,938	.3
Loyd Ellis (WRI)	160	.0
Santos Chavez (WRI)	39	.0
Sydney Dudikoff (WRI)	14	.0
Ray J. Caplette (WRI)	7	.0
HOUSE		
1 **Paul Gosar (R)** *	112,816	49.7
Ann Kirkpatrick (D)	99,233	43.7
Nicole Patti (LIBERT)	14,869	6.6
2 **Trent Franks (R)**	173,173	64.9
John Thrasher (D)	82,891	31.1
Powell Gammill (LIBERT)	10,820	4.0
William Crum (WRI)	8	.0
Mark Rankin (WRI)	2	.0
3 **Ben Quayle (R)** *	108,689	58.9
Jon Hulburd (D)	62,120	33.6
Michael Shoen (LIBERT)	10,478	5.7
Leonard Clark (GREEN)	3,294	1.8
4 **Ed Pastor (D)**	61,524	66.9
Janet Contreras (R)	25,300	27.5
Joe Cobb (LIBERT)	2,718	3.0
Rebecca DeWitt (GREEN)	2,365	2.6
5 **David Schweikert (R)** *	110,374	52.0
Harry E. Mitchell (D)	91,749	43.2
Nick Coons (LIBERT)	10,127	4.8

	Votes	Percent
6 **Jeff Flake (R)**	165,649	66.4
Rebecca Schneider (D)	72,615	29.1
Darell Tapp (LIBERT)	7,712	3.1
Richard Grayson (GREEN)	3,407	1.4
7 **Raúl M. Grijalva (D)**	79,935	50.2
Ruth McClung (R)	70,385	44.2
Harley Meyer (I)	4,506	2.8
George Keane (LIBERT)	4,318	2.7
8 **Gabrielle Giffords (D)**	138,280	48.8
Jesse Kelly (R)	134,124	47.3
Steven Stoltz (LIBERT)	11,174	3.9
Arkansas		
GOVERNOR		
Mike Beebe (D)	503,336	64.4
Jim Keet (R)	262,784	33.6
Jim Lendall (GREEN)	14,513	1.9
SENATE		
John Boozman (R) *	451,618	57.9
Blanche Lincoln (D)	288,156	36.9
Trevor Drown (I)	25,234	3.2
John Laney Gray III (GREEN)	14,430	1.8
Stephan "Troublemaker" Hercher (WRI)	519	.1
HOUSE		
1 **Rick Crawford (R)** *	93,224	51.8
Chad Causey (D)	78,267	43.5
Ken Adler (GREEN)	8,320	4.6
Mickey Vernon Higgins (WRI)	205	.1
2 **Tim Griffin (R)** *	122,091	57.9
Joyce Elliott (D)	80,687	38.3
Lance Levi (I)	4,421	2.1
Lewis Kennedy (GREEN)	3,599	1.7
Danial Suits (WRI)	54	.0
3 **Steve Womack (R)** *	148,581	72.4
David Whitaker (D)	56,542	27.6
4 **Mike Ross (D)**	102,479	57.5
Beth Anne Rankin (R)	71,526	40.2
Josh Drake (GREEN)	4,129	2.3

Abbreviation for Party Designations

AC	– American Constitution	GRP	– Green Populist	R	– Republican
AKI	– Alaskan Independence	GTP	– Green Tea Patriots	REF	– Reform
ALP	– American Labor Party	I	– Independent	RTH	– Rent Is Too High
AMI	– American Independent	IA	– Independent American	S	– Socialist
ANO	– Action No Talk Party	IGREEN	– Independent Green	TEA	– Tea Party
ARM	– American Renaissance Movement	INDC	– Independence	TFC	– Time For Change
BLU	– Blue Enigma	IRFM	- Independent Reform	TVH	– Truth Vision Hope
CFL	– Connecticut for Lieberman	LIBERT	– Libertarian	UC	– United Citizens
CNSTP	– Constitution	MOUNT	– Mountain	UNA	– Unaffiliated
D	– Democratic	NL	– Natural Law	USTAX	- U.S. Taxpayers
DAC	– Defend American Constitution	NPA	– No Party Affiliation	WFM	– Working Families
FE	– Free Energy	PFP	– Peace and Freedom	YCA	– Your Country Again
GBS	– Gravity Buoyancy Solution	PRO	– Progressive	X	– Not Applicable
GREEN	– Green	PTF	– Party Free		

California

	Votes	Percent
GOVERNOR		
Jerry Brown (D)	5,428,458	53.8
Meg Whitman (R)	4,127,371	40.9
Chelene Nightingale (AMI)	166,308	1.6
Dale Ogden (LIBERT)	150,898	1.5
Laura Wells (GREEN)	129,231	1.3
Carlos Alvarez (PFP)	92,856	.9
SENATE		
Barbara Boxer (D)	5,218,441	52.2
Carly Fiorina (R)	4,217,366	42.2
Gail K. Lightfoot (LIBERT)	175,242	1.8
Marsha Feinland (PFP)	135,093	1.4
Duane Roberts (GREEN)	128,510	1.3
Edward C. Noonan (AMI)	125,441	1.2
HOUSE		
1 Mike Thompson (D)	147,307	62.8
Loren Hanks (R)	72,803	31.0
Carol Wolman (GREEN)	8,486	3.6
Mike Rodrigues (LIBERT)	5,996	2.6
2 Wally Herger (R)	130,837	57.1
Jim Reed (D)	98,092	42.8
write-in (WRI)	11	.0
3 Dan Lungren (R)	131,169	50.1
Ami Bera (D)	113,128	43.2
Jerry L. Leidecker (AMI)	6,577	2.5
Douglas Arthur Tuma (LIBERT)	6,275	2.4
Michael Roskey (PFP)	4,789	1.8
4 Tom McClintock (R)	186,397	61.3
Clint Curtis (D)	95,653	31.4
Benjamin "Ben" Emery (GREEN)	22,179	7.3
5 Doris Matsui (D)	124,220	72.0
Paul A. Smith (R)	43,577	25.3
Gerald Allen Frink (PFP)	4,594	2.7
write-in (WRI)	19	.0
6 Lynn Woolsey (D)	172,216	65.9
Jim Judd (R)	77,361	29.6
Eugene E. Ruyle (PFP)	5,915	2.3
Joel Smolen (LIBERT)	5,660	2.2
7 George Miller (D)	122,435	68.3
Rick Tubbs (R)	56,764	31.7
8 Nancy Pelosi (D)	167,957	80.1
John Dennis (R)	31,711	15.1
Gloria E. La Riva (PFP)	5,161	2.5
Philip Berg (LIBERT)	4,843	2.3
write-in (WRI)	24	.0
9 Barbara Lee (D)	180,400	84.3
Gerald Hashimoto (R)	23,054	10.8
Dave Heller (GREEN)	4,848	2.3
James Eyer (LIBERT)	4,113	1.9
Larry Allen (PFP)	1,670	.8
10 John Garamendi (D)	137,578	58.8
Gary Clift (R)	88,512	37.9
Jeremy Cloward (GREEN)	7,716	3.3
11 Jerry McNerney (D)	115,361	48.0
David Harmer (R)	112,703	46.9
David Christensen (AMI)	12,439	5.2
12 Jackie Speier (D)	152,044	75.6
Mike Moloney (R)	44,475	22.1
Mark Paul Williams (LIBERT)	4,611	2.3
write-in (WRI)	32	.0

	Votes	Percent
13 Pete Stark (D)	118,278	72.0
Forest Baker (R)	45,575	27.7
write-in (WRI)	525	.3
14 Anna G. Eshoo (D)	151,217	69.1
Dave Chapman (R)	60,917	27.8
Paul Lazaga (LIBERT)	6,735	3.1
15 Michael M. Honda (D)	126,147	67.6
Scott Kirkland (R)	60,468	32.4
16 Zoe Lofgren (D)	105,841	67.8
Daniel Sahagun (R)	37,913	24.3
Edward Gonzalez (LIBERT)	12,304	7.9
17 Sam Farr (D)	118,734	66.6
Jeff Taylor (R)	53,176	29.8
Eric Petersen (GREEN)	3,397	1.9
Mary V. Larkin (LIBERT)	2,742	1.5
write-in (WRI)	90	.0
18 Dennis Cardoza (D)	72,853	58.5
Michael Clare Berryhill Sr. (R)	51,716	41.5
19 Jeff Denham (R)*	128,394	64.6
Loraine Goodwin (D)	69,912	35.1
write-in (WRI)	596	.3
20 Jim Costa (D)	46,247	51.7
Andy Vidak (R)	43,197	48.3
21 Devin Nunes (R)	135,979	100.0
22 Kevin McCarthy (R)	173,490	98.8
John Uebersax (WRI)	2,173	1.2
23 Lois Capps (D)	111,768	57.8
Tom Watson (R)	72,744	37.6
John V. Hager (I)	5,625	2.9
Darrell M. Stafford (LIBERT)	3,326	1.7
24 Elton Gallegly (R)	144,055	59.9
Timothy J. Allison (D)	96,279	40.1
25 Howard P. "Buck" McKeon (R)	118,308	61.8
Jackie Conaway (D)	73,028	38.2
26 David Dreier (R)	112,774	54.1
Russ Warner (D)	76,093	36.5
David L. Miller (AMI)	12,784	6.1
Randall Weissbuch (LIBERT)	6,696	3.2
27 Brad Sherman (D)	102,927	65.2
Mark Reed (R)	55,056	34.8
28 Howard L. Berman (D)	88,385	69.5
Merlin Froyd (R)	28,493	22.4
Carlos A. Rodriguez (LIBERT)	10,229	8.0
29 Adam B. Schiff (D)	104,374	64.8
John P. Colbert (R)	51,534	32.0
William P. Cushing (LIBERT)	5,218	3.2
30 Henry A. Waxman (D)	153,663	64.6
Charles E. Wilkerson (R)	75,948	31.9
Erich D. Miller (LIBERT)	5,021	2.1
Richard R. Castaldo (PFP)	3,115	1.3
31 Xavier Becerra (D)	76,363	83.8
Stephen C. Smith (R)	14,740	16.2
write-in (WRI)	3	.0
32 Judy Chu (D)	77,759	71.0
Edward "Ed" Schmerling (R)	31,697	29.0
33 Karen Bass (D)*	131,990	86.1
James L. Andion (R)	21,342	13.9
write-in (WRI)	1	.0
34 Lucille Roybal-Allard (D)	69,382	77.2
Wayne Miller (R)	20,457	22.8

	Votes	Percent
35 Maxine Waters (D)	98,131	79.3
K. Bruce Brown (R)	25,561	20.7
write-in (WRI)	2	.0
36 Jane Harman (D)	114,489	59.6
Mattie Fein (R)	66,706	34.7
Herb Peters (LIBERT)	10,840	5.6
37 Laura Richardson (D)	85,799	68.4
Star Parker (R)	29,159	23.2
Nicholas Dibs (I)	10,560	8.4
38 Grace F. Napolitano (D)	85,459	73.4
Robert Vaughn (R)	30,883	26.5
39 Linda T. Sánchez (D)	81,590	63.3
Larry S. Andre (R)	42,037	32.6
John Smith (AMI)	5,334	4.1
40 Ed Royce (R)	119,455	66.8
Christina Avalos (D)	59,400	33.2
41 Jerry Lewis (R)	127,857	63.2
Pat Meagher (D)	74,394	36.8
write-in (WRI)	35	.0
42 Gary G. Miller (R)	127,161	62.2
Michael Williamson (D)	65,122	31.9
Mark Lambert (LIBERT)	12,115	5.9
43 Joe Baca (D)	70,026	65.5
Scott Folkens (R)	36,890	34.5
44 Ken Calvert (R)	107,482	55.6
Bill Hedrick (D)	85,784	44.4
45 Mary Bono Mack (R)	106,472	51.5
Steve Pougnet (D)	87,141	42.1
Bill Lussenheide (AMI)	13,188	6.4
46 Dana Rohrabacher (R)	139,822	62.2
Ken Arnold (D)	84,940	37.8
write-in (WRI)	20	.0
47 Loretta Sanchez (D)	50,832	53.0
Van Tran (R)	37,679	39.3
Cecilia "Ceci" Iglesias (I)	7,443	7.8
48 John Campbell (R)	145,481	59.9
Beth Krom (D)	88,465	36.4
Mike Binkley (LIBERT)	8,773	3.6
49 Darrell Issa (R)	119,088	62.8
Howard Katz (D)	59,714	31.5
Dion Clark (AMI)	6,585	3.5
Mike Paster (LIBERT)	4,290	2.3
50 Brian P. Bilbray (R)	142,247	56.6
Francine Busby (D)	97,818	39.0
Lars Grossmith (LIBERT)	5,546	2.2
Miriam E. Clark (PFP)	5,470	2.2
51 Bob Filner (D)	86,423	60.0
Nick Popaditch (R)	57,488	39.9
write-in (WRI)	5	.0
52 Duncan Hunter (R)	139,460	63.1
Ray Lutz (D)	70,870	32.1
Michael Benoit (LIBERT)	10,732	4.8
53 Susan A. Davis (D)	104,800	62.3
Michael Crimmins (R)	57,230	34.0
Paul Dekker (LIBERT)	6,298	3.7

Colorado

	Votes	Percent
GOVERNOR		
John W. Hickenlooper (D)	912,005	51.0
Tom Tancredo (AC)	651,232	36.4
Dan Maes (R)	199,034	11.1
Jaimes Brown (LIBERT)	13,314	.7
Jason Clark (I)	8,576	.5
Paul Fiorino (I)	3,483	.2
SENATE		
Michael Bennet (D)	851,590	48.0
Ken Buck (R)	822,731	46.4
Bob Kinsey (GREEN)	38,768	2.2
Maclyn "Mac" Stringer (LIBERT)	22,589	1.3
Jason Napolitano (IRFM)	19,415	1.1
Charley Miller (UNA)	11,330	.6
J. Moromisato (UNA)	5,767	.3
HOUSE		
1 Diana DeGette (D)	140,073	67.4
Mike Fallon (R)	59,747	28.8
Gary Swing (GREEN)	2,923	1.4
Clint Jones (LIBERT)	2,867	1.4
Chris Styskal (AC)	2,141	1.0
2 Jared Polis (D)	148,720	57.4
Stephen Bailey (R)	98,171	37.9
Jenna Goss (AC)	7,080	2.7
Curtis Harris (LIBERT)	5,056	2.0
write-in (WRI)	7	.0
3 Scott Tipton (R)*	129,257	50.1
John Salazar (D)	118,048	45.8
Gregory Gilman (LIBERT)	5,678	2.2
Jake Segrest (UNA)	4,982	1.9
write-ins (WRI)	34	.0
4 Cory Gardner (R)*	138,634	52.5
Betsy Markey (D)	109,249	41.4
Doug Aden (AC)	12,312	4.7
Ken "Wasko" Waszkiewicz (UNA)	3,986	1.5
5 Doug Lamborn (R)	152,829	65.8
Kevin Bradley (D)	68,039	29.3
Brian "Barron X" Scott (AC)	5,886	2.5
Jerell Klaver (LIBERT)	5,680	2.4
6 Mike Coffman (R)	217,368	65.7
John Flerlage (D)	104,104	31.5
Rob McNealy (LIBERT)	9,466	2.9
write-in (WRI)	5	.0
7 Ed Perlmutter (D)	112,667	53.4
Ryan Frazier (R)	88,026	41.8
Buck Bailey (LIBERT)	10,117	4.8

Connecticut

	Votes	Percent
GOVERNOR		
Dannel P. Malloy (D)	567,278	49.5
Tom Foley (R)	560,874	49.0
Thomas Marsh (I)	17,629	1.5
SENATE		
Richard Blumenthal (D, WFM)*	636,040	55.2
Linda McMahon (R)	498,341	43.2
Warren B. Mosler (I)	11,275	1.0
John Mertens (CFL)	6,735	.6

	Votes	Percent
HOUSE		
1 John B. Larson (D)	138,440	61.2
Ann Brickley (R)	84,076	37.2
Kenneth J. Krayeske (GREEN)	2,564	1.1
Christopher J. Hutchinson (X)	955	.4
write-in (WRI)	3	.0
2 Joe Courtney (D)	147,748	59.9
Janet Peckinpaugh (R)	95,671	38.8
G. Scott Deshefy (GREEN)	3,344	1.4
write-ins (WRI)	46	.0
3 Rosa DeLauro (D)	143,565	65.1
Jerry Labriola Jr. (R)	74,107	33.6
Charles A. Pillsbury (GREEN)	2,984	1.4
write-in (WRI)	5	.0
4 Jim Himes (D)	115,351	53.1
Dan Debicella (R)	102,030	46.9
write-in (WRI)	10	.0
5 Christopher S. Murphy (D)	122,879	54.1
Sam Caligiuri (R, I)	104,402	45.9
write-ins (WRI)	22	.0

Delaware

	Votes	Percent
SENATE		
Chris Coons (D)*	174,012	56.6
Christine O'Donnell (R)	123,053	40.0
Glenn A. Miller (I)	8,201	2.7
James W. Rash Jr. (LIBERT)	2,101	.7
Maurice F. Bourgeois (WRI)		.0
Samtra Devard (WRI)		.0
HOUSE		
AL John Carney (D)*	173,543	56.8
Glen Urquhart (R)	125,442	41.0
Earl R. Lofland (I)	3,704	1.2
Brent A. Wangen (LIBERT)	1,986	.6
Jeffrey Brown (BLU)	961	.3

Florida

	Votes	Percent
GOVERNOR		
Rick Scott (R)	2,619,335	48.9
Alex Sink (D)	2,557,785	47.7
Peter Allen (I)	123,831	2.3
C. C. Reed (NPA)	18,842	.4
Michael E. Arth (NPA)	18,644	.3
Daniel Imperato (NPA)	13,690	.3
Farid Khavari (NPA)	7,487	.1
Josue Larose (WRI)	121	.0
SENATE		
Marco Rubio (R)*	2,645,743	48.9
Charlie Crist (I)	1,607,549	29.7
Kendrick B. Meek (D)	1,092,936	20.2
Alexander Andrew Snitker (LIBERT)	24,850	.5
Sue Askeland (NPA)	15,340	.3
Rick Tyler (NPA)	7,397	.1
Bernie DeCastro (CNSTP)	4,792	.1
Lewis Jerome Armstrong (NPA)	4,443	.1
Bobbie Bean (NPA)	4,301	.1
Bruce Ray Riggs (NPA)	3,647	.1
Piotr Blass (WRI)	47	.0
Richard Lock (WRI)	18	.0
Belinda Gail Quarterman-Noah (WRI)	18	.0
George Drake (WRI)	13	.0
Robert Monroe (WRI)	6	.0
Howard Knepper (WRI)	4	.0
Carol Ann Joyce LaRosa (WRI)	2	.0

	Votes	Percent
HOUSE		
1 Jeff Miller (R)	170,821	80.0
Joe Cantrell (NPA)	23,250	10.9
John Krause (NPA)	18,253	8.5
Jim Bryan (WRI)	1,202	.6
2 Steve Southerland II (R)*	136,371	53.6
Allen Boyd (D)	105,211	41.4
Paul C. McKain (NPA)	7,135	2.8
Dianne Berryhill (NPA)	5,705	2.2
Ray Netherwood (WRI)	16	.0
3 Corrine Brown (D)	94,744	63.0
Michael "Mike" Yost (R)	50,932	33.9
Terry Martin-Back (NPA)	4,625	3.1
4 Ander Crenshaw (R)	178,238	77.2
Troy Dwayne Stanley (NPA)	52,540	22.8
Deborah Katz Pueschel (D)	40	.0
Gary Koniz (WRI)	27	.0
5 Rich Nugent (R)*	208,815	67.4
James Jim Piccillo (D)	100,858	32.6
6 Cliff Stearns (R)	179,349	71.5
Steve Schonberg (NPA)	71,632	28.5
7 John L. Mica (R)	185,470	69.0
Heather Beaven (D)	83,206	31.0
8 Daniel Webster (R)*	123,586	56.1
Alan Grayson (D)	84,167	38.2
Peg Dunmire (TEA)	8,337	3.8
George L. Metcalfe (NPA)	4,143	1.9
Steven Gerritzen (WRI)	11	.0
9 Gus Bilirakis (R)	165,433	71.4
Anita de Palma (D)	66,158	28.6
10 C.W. Bill Young (R)	137,943	65.9
Charlie Justice (D)	71,313	34.1
11 Kathy Castor (D)	91,328	59.6
Mike Prendergast (R)	61,817	40.4
12 Dennis A. Ross (R)*	102,704	48.1
Lori Edwards (D)	87,769	41.1
Randy Wilkinson (TEA)	22,857	10.7
13 Vern Buchanan (R)	183,811	68.9
James T. Golden (D)	83,123	31.1
14 Connie Mack (R)	188,341	68.6
James Lloyd Roach (D)	74,525	27.1
William "Maverick" St. Claire (NPA)	11,825	4.3
15 Bill Posey (R)	157,079	64.7
Shannon Roberts (D)	85,595	35.3
16 Tom Rooney (R)	162,285	66.8
Jim Horn (D)	80,327	33.1
William Dean (WRI)	151	.1
17 Frederica S. Wilson (D)*	106,361	86.2
Roderick D. Vereen (NPA)	17,009	13.8
18 Ileana Ros-Lehtinen (R)	102,360	68.9
Rolando A. Banciella (D)	46,235	31.1
19 Ted Deutch (D)	132,098	62.6
Joe Budd (R)	78,733	37.3
Stan Smilan (D)	228	.1
20 Debbie Wasserman Schultz (D)	100,787	60.1
Karen Harrington (R)	63,845	38.1
Stanley Blumenthal (NPA)	1,663	1.0
Robert "Bob" Kunst (D)	1,272	.8
Clayton Schock (WRI)	3	.0
21 Mario Diaz-Balart (R)		●

	Votes	Percent
22 Allen B. West (R)*	118,890	54.4
Ron Klein (D)	99,804	45.6
23 Alcee L. Hastings (D)	100,066	79.1
Bernard Sansaricq (R)	26,414	20.9
24 Sandy Adams (R)*	146,129	59.6
Suzanne M. Kosmas (D)	98,787	40.3
Nicholas Ruiz (WRI)	115	.0
25 David Rivera (R)*	74,859	52.1
Joe Garcia (D)	61,138	42.6
Roly Arrojo (TEA)	4,312	3.0
Craig Porter (FWP)	3,244	2.3

Georgia
GOVERNOR

	Votes	Percent
Nathan Deal (R)	1,365,832	53.0
Roy Barnes (D)	1,107,011	43.0
John H. Monds (LIBERT)	103,194	4.0

SENATE

	Votes	Percent
Johnny Isakson (R)	1,489,904	58.3
Michael "Mike" Thurmond (D)	996,516	39.0
Chuck Donovan (LIBERT)	68,750	2.7

HOUSE

	Votes	Percent
1 Jack Kingston (R)	117,270	71.6
Oscar L. Harris II (D)	46,449	28.4
2 Sanford D. Bishop Jr. (D)	86,520	51.4
Mike Keown (R)	81,673	48.6
3 Lynn Westmoreland (R)	168,304	69.5
Frank Saunders (D)	73,932	30.5
write-in (WRI)	3	.0
4 Hank Johnson (D)	131,760	74.7
Lisbeth "Liz" Carter (R)	44,707	25.3
5 John Lewis (D)	130,782	73.7
Fenn Little (R)	46,622	26.3
6 Tom Price (R)	198,100	99.9
write-in (WRI)	188	.1
7 Rob Woodall (R)*	160,898	67.1
Doug Heckman (D)	78,996	32.9
8 Austin Scott (R)*	102,770	52.7
Jim Marshall (D)	92,250	47.3
9 Tom Graves (R)	173,512	100.0
10 Paul Broun (R)	138,062	67.4
Russell Edwards (D)	66,905	32.6
11 Phil Gingrey (R)	163,515	100.0
12 John Barrow (D)	92,459	56.6
Raymond McKinney (R)	70,938	43.4
13 David Scott (D)	140,294	69.4
Mike Crane (R)	61,771	30.6

Hawaii
GOVERNOR

	Votes	Percent
Neil Abercrombie (D)	222,724	58.2
Duke Aiona (R)	157,311	41.1
Daniel H. Cunningham (FE)	1,265	.3
Thomas Pollard (NPA)	1,263	.3

SENATE

	Votes	Percent
Daniel K. Inouye (D)	277,228	74.8
Cam Cavasso (R)	79,939	21.6
Jim Brewer (NPA)	7,762	2.1
Lloyd Jeffrey Mallan (LIBERT)	2,957	.8
Jeff Jarrett (NPA)	2,697	.7

HOUSE

	Votes	Percent
1 Colleen Hanabusa (D)*	94,140	53.2
Charles K. Djou (R)	82,723	46.8
2 Mazie K. Hirono (D)	132,290	72.2
John W. Willoughby (R)	46,404	25.3
Pat Brock (LIBERT)	3,254	1.8
Andrew Vsevolod Von Sonn (NPA)	1,310	.7

Idaho
GOVERNOR

	Votes	Percent
C. L. "Butch" Otter (R)	267,483	59.1
Keith Allred (D)	148,680	32.8
Jana Kemp (I)	26,655	5.9
Ted Dunlap (LIBERT)	5,867	1.3
Pro-Life (I)	3,850	.8

SENATE

	Votes	Percent
Michael D. Crapo (R)	319,953	71.2
P. Tom Sullivan (D)	112,057	24.9
Randy Lynn Bergquist (CNSTP)	17,429	3.9

HOUSE

	Votes	Percent
1 Raúl R. Labrador (R)*	126,231	51.0
Walt Minnick (D)	102,135	41.3
Dave Olson (D)	14,365	5.8
Mike Washburn (LIBERT)	4,696	1.9
2 Mike Simpson (R)	137,468	68.8
Mike Crawford (D)	48,749	24.4
Brian Schad (I)	13,500	6.8

Illinois
GOVERNOR

	Votes	Percent
Pat Quinn (D)	1,745,219	46.8
Bill Brady (R)	1,713,385	45.9
Scott Lee Cohen (I)	135,705	3.6
Rich Whitney (GREEN)	100,756	2.7
Lex Green (LIBERT)	34,681	.9

SENATE

	Votes	Percent
Mark Steven Kirk (R)*	1,778,698	48.0
Alexi Giannoulias (D)	1,719,478	46.4
LeAlan M. Jones (GREEN)	117,914	3.2
Mike Labno (LIBERT)	87,247	2.4

HOUSE

	Votes	Percent
1 Bobby L. Rush (D)	148,170	80.4
Raymond G. Wardingley (R)	29,253	15.9
Jeff Adams (D)	6,963	3.8
2 Jesse L. Jackson Jr. (D)	150,666	80.5
Isaac C. Hayes (R)	25,883	13.8
Anthony W. Williams (GREEN)	10,564	5.6
3 Daniel Lipinski (D)	116,120	69.7
Michael A. Bendas (R)	40,479	24.3
Laurel Lambert Schmidt (GREEN)	10,028	6.0
4 Luis V. Gutierrez (D)	63,273	77.4
Israel Vasquez (R)	11,711	14.3
Robert J. Burns (GREEN)	6,808	8.3
5 Mike Quigley (D)	108,360	70.6
David Ratowitz (R)	38,935	25.4
Matt Reichel (GREEN)	6,140	4.0
6 Peter Roskam (R)	114,456	63.6
Benjamin S. Lowe (D)	65,379	36.4
7 Danny K. Davis (D)	149,846	81.5
Mark M. Weiman (R)	29,575	16.1
Clarence Desmond Clemons (D)	4,428	2.4
8 Joe Walsh (R)*	98,115	48.5
Melissa Bean (D)	97,825	48.3
Bill Scheuer (GREEN)	6,495	3.2

	Votes	Percent
9 Jan Schakowsky (D)	117,553	66.3
Joel Barry Pollak (R)	55,182	31.1
Simon Ribeiro (GREEN)	4,472	2.5
10 Robert Dold (R)*	109,941	51.1
Dan Seals (D)	105,290	48.9
write-in (WRI)	1	.0
11 Adam Kinzinger (R)*	129,108	57.3
Debbie Halvorson (D)	96,019	42.6
12 Jerry F. Costello (D)	121,272	59.8
Teri Newman (R)	74,046	36.5
Rodger W. Jennings (GREEN)	7,387	3.6
13 Judy Biggert (R)	152,132	63.8
Scott Harper (D)	86,281	36.2
14 Randy Hultgren (R)*	112,369	51.3
Bill Foster (D)	98,645	45.0
Daniel J. Kairis (GREEN)	7,949	3.6
write-in (WRI)	50	.0
15 Timothy V. Johnson (R)	136,915	64.3
David Gill (D)	75,948	35.7
16 Donald Manzullo (R)	138,299	65.0
George W. Gaulrapp (D)	66,037	31.0
Terry G. Campbell (GREEN)	8,425	4.0
17 Bobby Schilling (R)*	104,583	52.6
Phil Hare (D)	85,454	43.0
Roger K. Davis (GREEN)	8,861	4.5
18 Aaron Schock (R)	152,868	69.1
Deirdre "DK" Hirner (D)	57,046	25.8
Sheldon Schafer (GREEN)	11,256	5.1
19 John Shimkus (R)	166,166	71.2
Tim Bagwell (D)	67,132	28.8

Indiana
SENATE

	Votes	Percent
Dan Coats (R)	952,116	54.6
Brad Ellsworth (D)	697,775	40.0
Rebecca Sink-Burris (LIBERT)	94,330	5.4

HOUSE

	Votes	Percent
1 Peter J. Visclosky (D)	99,387	58.6
Mark Leyva (R)	65,558	38.6
Jon Morris (LIBERT)	4,762	2.8
2 Joe Donnelly (D)	91,341	48.2
Jackie Walorski (R)	88,803	46.8
Mark Vogel (D)	9,447	5.0
3 Marlin Stutzman (R)*	116,140	62.8
Thomas Hayhurst (D)	61,267	33.1
Scott Wise (D)	7,631	4.1
write-ins (WRI)	11	.0
4 Todd Rokita (R)*	138,732	68.6
David Sanders (D)	53,167	26.3
John Duncan (LIBERT)	10,423	5.2
5 Dan Burton (R)	146,899	62.1
Tim Crawford (D)	60,024	25.4
Richard Reid (LIBERT)	18,266	7.7
Jesse C. Trueblood (I)	11,218	4.7
6 Mike Pence (R)	126,027	66.6
Barry A. Welsh (D)	56,647	29.9
T.J. Thompson (LIBERT)	6,635	3.5
7 André Carson (D)	86,011	58.9
Marvin B. Scott (R)	55,213	37.8
Dav Wilson (LIBERT)	4,815	3.3

		Votes	Percent
8	Larry Bucshon (R) *	117,259	57.5
	Trent Van Haaften (D)	76,265	37.4
	John Cunningham (LIBERT)	10,240	5.0
9	Todd Young (R) *	118,040	52.3
	Baron P. Hill (D)	95,353	42.3
	Greg Knott (LIBERT)	12,070	5.4
	write-in (WRI)	69	.0

Iowa

GOVERNOR

	Votes	Percent
Terry E. Branstad (R)	589,828	52.9
Chet Culver (D)	481,590	43.2
Jonathan Narcisse (X)	20,747	1.9
Eric Cooper (LIBERT)	14,293	1.3
Gregory James Hughes (X)	3,846	.3
David Rosenfeld (SW)	2,730	.2

SENATE

	Votes	Percent
Charles E. Grassley (R)	718,215	64.4
Roxanne Conlin (D)	371,686	33.3
John Heiderscheit (LIBERT)	25,290	2.3

HOUSE

		Votes	Percent
1	Bruce Braley (D)	104,428	49.5
	Benjamin Lange (R)	100,219	47.5
	Rob J. Petsche (LIBERT)	4,087	1.9
	Jason A. Faulkner (I)	2,092	1.0
	write-ins (WRI)	76	.0
2	Dave Loebsack (D)	115,839	51.0
	Mariannette Miller-Meeks (R)	104,319	45.9
	Gary Sicard (LIBERT)	4,356	1.9
	Jon Tack (CNSTP)	2,463	1.1
	write-ins (WRI)	198	.1
3	Leonard L. Boswell (D)	122,147	50.7
	Brad Zaun (R)	111,925	46.5
	Rebecca Williamson (SW)	6,258	2.6
	write-ins (WRI)	426	.2
4	Tom Latham (R)	152,588	65.6
	Bill Maske (D)	74,300	32.0
	Dan Lensing (I)	5,499	2.4
	write-ins (WRI)	132	.1
5	Steve King (R)	128,363	65.7
	Matthew Campbell (D)	63,160	32.4
	Martin James Monroe (I)	3,622	1.9
	write-ins (WRI)	94	.0

Kansas

GOVERNOR

	Votes	Percent
Sam Brownback (R)	530,760	63.3
Tom Holland (D)	270,166	32.2
Andrew Gray (LIBERT)	22,460	2.7
Ken Cannon (REF)	15,397	1.8

SENATE

	Votes	Percent
Jerry Moran (R) *	587,175	70.1
Lisa Johnston (D)	220,971	26.4
Michael Wm. Dann (LIBERT)	17,922	2.1
Joe Bellis (D)	11,624	1.4

HOUSE

		Votes	Percent
1	Tim Huelskamp (R) *	142,281	73.8
	Alan Jilka (D)	44,068	22.8
	Jack Warner (D)	6,537	3.4
2	Lynn Jenkins (R)	130,034	63.1
	Cheryl Hudspeth (D)	66,588	32.3
	Robert Garrard (D)	9,353	4.5

		Votes	Percent
3	Kevin Yoder (R) *	136,246	58.4
	Stephene Moore (D)	90,193	38.7
	Jasmin Talbert (LIBERT)	6,846	2.9
4	Mike Pompeo (R) *	119,575	58.8
	Raj Goyle (D)	74,143	36.4
	Susan G. Ducey (D)	5,041	2.5
	Shawn Smith (LIBERT)	4,624	2.3

Kentucky

SENATE

	Votes	Percent
Rand Paul (R) *	755,411	55.7
Jack Conway (D)	599,843	44.2

HOUSE

		Votes	Percent
1	Edward Whitfield (R)	153,519	71.2
	Charles Kendall Hatchett (D)	61,960	28.8
2	Brett Guthrie (R)	155,906	67.9
	Ed Marksberry (D)	73,749	32.1
3	John Yarmuth (D)	139,940	54.7
	Todd Lally (R)	112,627	44.0
	Edward Martin (D)	2,029	.8
	Michael D. Hansen (I)	1,334	.5
4	Geoff Davis (R)	151,774	69.5
	John William Waltz (D)	66,675	30.5
5	Harold Rogers (R)	151,019	77.4
	Jim Holbert (D)	44,034	22.6
6	Ben Chandler (D)	119,812	50.1
	Andy Barr (R)	119,165	49.8
	write-ins (WRI)	247	.1

Louisiana

SENATE

	Votes	Percent
David Vitter (R)	715,415	56.6
Charlie Melancon (D)	476,572	37.7
Randall Todd Hayes (LIBERT)	13,957	1.1
Michael Karlton Brown (NPA)	9,973	.8
Michael Lane Spears (I)	9,190	.7
Ernest D. Wooton (I)	8,167	.6
R.A. "Skip" Galan (NPA)	7,474	.6
William R. McShan (REF)	5,879	.5
William Robert "Bob" Lang Jr. (I)	5,734	.4
Milton Gordon (NPA)	4,810	.4
Thomas G. LaFargue (I)	4,043	.3
Sam Houston Melton Jr. (NPA)	3,780	.3

HOUSE

		Votes	Percent
1	Steve Scalise (R)	157,182	78.5
	Myron Katz (D)	38,416	19.2
	Arden Wells (I)	4,578	2.3
2	Cedric L. Richmond (D) *	83,705	64.6
	Anh "Joseph" Cao (R)	43,378	33.5
	Anthony Marquize (NPA)	1,876	1.4
	Jack Radosta (NPA)	645	.5
3	Jeff Landry (R) *	108,963	63.8
	Ravi Sangisetty (D)	61,914	36.2
4	John Fleming (R)	105,223	62.3
	David Melville (D)	54,609	32.4
	Artis "Doc" Cash (I)	8,962	5.3
5	Rodney Alexander (R)	122,033	78.6
	Tom Gibbs (NPA)	33,279	21.4
6	Bill Cassidy (R)	138,607	65.6
	Merritt E. McDonald Sr. (D)	72,577	34.4
7	Charles Boustany Jr. (R)		●

Maine

GOVERNOR

	Votes	Percent
Paul R. LePage (R)	218,065	38.1
Eliot Cutler (I)	208,270	36.4
Libby Mitchell (D)	109,387	19.1
Shawn Moody (I)	28,756	5.0
Kevin Scott (I)	5,664	1.0

HOUSE

		Votes	Percent
1	Chellie Pingree (D)	169,114	56.8
	Dean Scontras (R)	128,501	43.2
	write-ins (WRI)	42	.0
2	Michael H. Michaud (D)	147,042	55.1
	Jason J. Levesque (R)	119,669	44.9

Maryland

GOVERNOR

	Votes	Percent
Martin O'Malley (D)	1,044,961	56.2
Robert L. Ehrlich Jr. (R)	776,319	41.8
Susan J. Gaztanaga (LIBERT)	14,137	.8
Maria Allwine (GREEN)	11,825	.6
Eric Delano Knowles (CNSTP)	8,612	.5
Ralph Jaffe (WRI)	319	.0
Corrogan R. Vaughn (WRI)	179	.0

SENATE

	Votes	Percent
Barbara A. Mikulski (D)	1,140,531	62.2
Eric Wargotz (R)	655,666	35.8
Kenniss Henry (GREEN)	20,717	1.1
Richard Shawver (CNSTP)	14,746	.8
Claud L. Asbury (WRI)	204	.0
Donald Kaplan (WRI)	110	.0
James T. Lynch Jr. (WRI)	84	.0
Lih Young (WRI)	80	.0

HOUSE

		Votes	Percent
1	Andy Harris (R) *	155,118	54.1
	Frank Kratovil Jr. (D)	120,400	42.0
	Richard Davis (LIBERT)	10,876	3.8
	write-ins (WRI)	242	.1
	Jack Wilson (NPA)	158	.1
	Michael Kennedy (WRI)	18	.0
2	C.A. Dutch Ruppersberger (D)	134,133	64.2
	Marcelo Cardarelli (R)	69,523	33.3
	Lorenzo Gaztanaga (LIBERT)	5,090	2.4
	write-ins (WRI)	158	.1
3	John Sarbanes (D)	147,448	61.1
	Jim Wilhelm (R)	86,947	36.0
	Jerry McKinley (LIBERT)	5,212	2.2
	Alain Lareau (CNSTP)	1,634	.7
	write-ins (WRI)	188	.1
4	Donna Edwards (D)	160,228	83.4
	Robert Broadus (R)	31,467	16.4
	write-ins (WRI)	325	.2
5	Steny H. Hoyer (D)	155,110	64.3
	Charles J. Lollar (R)	83,575	34.6
	H. Gavin Shickle (LIBERT)	2,578	1.1
	write-ins (WRI)	120	.0
6	Roscoe G. Bartlett (R)	148,820	61.4
	Andrew James Duck (D)	80,455	33.2
	Dan Massey (LIBERT)	6,816	2.8
	Michael Shannon Reed (CNSTP)	5,907	2.4
	write-ins (WRI)	191	.1

		Votes	Percent
7	Elijah E. Cummings (D)	152,669	75.2
	Frank Mirabile Jr. (R)	46,375	22.8
	Scott Spencer (LIBERT)	3,814	1.9
	write-ins (WRI)	135	.1
	Fred Dickson (WRI)	55	.0
	Ray Bly (WRI)	20	.0
8	Chris Van Hollen (D)	153,613	73.3
	Michael Lee Philips (R)	52,421	25.0
	Mark Grannis (LIBERT)	2,713	1.3
	Fred Nordhorn (CNSTP)	696	.3
	write-ins (WRI)	224	.1

Massachusetts

GOVERNOR

	Votes	Percent
Deval Patrick (D)	1,112,283	48.4
Charlie Baker (R)	964,866	42.0
Tim Cahill (I)	184,395	8.0
Jill Stein (GREEN)	32,895	1.4

HOUSE

		Votes	Percent
1	John W. Olver (D)	128,011	60.0
	William J. Gunn (R)	74,418	34.9
	Michael Engel (I)	10,880	5.1
	write-ins (WRI)	55	.0
2	Richard E. Neal (D)	122,751	57.3
	Tom Wesley (R)	91,209	42.6
	write-ins (WRI)	164	.1
3	Jim McGovern (D)	122,708	56.5
	Marty Lamb (R)	85,124	39.2
	Patrick Barron (I)	9,388	4.3
	write-ins (WRI)	132	.1
4	Barney Frank (D)	126,194	53.9
	Sean Bielat (R)	101,517	43.4
	Susan Allen (D)	3,445	1.5
	Donald M. Jordan (I)	2,873	1.2
	write-ins (WRI)	98	.0
5	Niki Tsongas (D)	122,858	54.8
	Jon Golnik (R)	94,646	42.2
	Dale E. Brown (I)	4,387	2.0
	Robert M. Clark (I)	1,991	.9
	write-ins (WRI)	147	.1
6	John F. Tierney (D)	142,732	56.8
	Bill John Hudak Jr. (R)	107,930	43.0
	write-ins (WRI)	419	.2
7	Edward J. Markey (D)	145,696	66.4
	Gerry Dembrowski (R)	73,467	33.5
	write-ins (WRI)	194	.1
8	Michael E. Capuano (D)	134,974	98.0
	write-ins (WRI)	2,686	2.0
9	Stephen F. Lynch (D)	157,071	68.3
	Vernon Harrison (R)	59,965	26.1
	Phil Dunkelbarger (I)	12,572	5.5
	write-ins (WRI)	356	.2
10	William Keating (D)*	132,743	46.9
	Jeff Perry (R)	120,029	42.4
	Maryanne Lewis (I)	16,705	5.9
	James Sheets (I)	10,445	3.7
	Joe Van Nes (I)	3,084	1.1
	write-ins (WRI)	191	.1

Michigan

GOVERNOR

	Votes	Percent
Rick Snyder (R)	1,874,834	58.1
Virg Bernero (D)	1,287,320	39.9
Ken Proctor (LIBERT)	22,390	.7
Stacey Mathia (USTAX)	20,818	.6
Harley G. Mikkelson (GREEN)	20,699	.6

HOUSE

		Votes	Percent
1	Dan Benishek (R)*	120,523	51.9
	Gary McDowell (D)	94,824	40.9
	Glenn Wilson (I)	7,847	3.4
	Patrick Lambert (USTAX)	4,200	1.8
	Keith Shelton (LIBERT)	2,571	1.1
	Ellis Boal (GREEN)	2,072	.9
2	Bill Huizenga (R)*	148,864	65.3
	Fred Johnson (D)	72,118	31.6
	Joseph Gillotte (LIBERT)	2,701	1.2
	Ronald E. Graeser (USTAX)	2,379	1.0
	Lloyd Clarke (GREEN)	2,016	.9
3	Justin Amash (R)*	133,714	59.7
	Pat Miles (D)	83,953	37.5
	James Rogers (LIBERT)	2,677	1.2
	Ted Gerrard (USTAX)	2,144	1.0
	Charlie Shick (GREEN)	1,575	.7
4	Dave Camp (R)	148,531	66.2
	Jerry M. Campbell (D)	68,458	30.5
	John Emerick (USTAX)	3,861	1.7
	Clint Foster (LIBERT)	3,504	1.6
5	Dale E. Kildee (D)	107,286	53.0
	John Kupiec (R)	89,680	44.3
	Matthew de Heus (GREEN)	2,649	1.3
	Michael J. Moon (LIBERT)	2,648	1.3
6	Fred Upton (R)	123,142	62.0
	Don Cooney (D)	66,729	33.6
	Melvin D. Valkner (USTAX)	3,672	1.8
	Fred Strand (LIBERT)	3,369	1.7
	Pat Foster (GREEN)	1,784	.9
7	Tim Walberg (R)*	113,185	50.2
	Mark Schauer (D)	102,402	45.4
	Scott Eugene Aughney (USTAX)	3,705	1.6
	Greg Merle (LIBERT)	3,239	1.4
	Richard Wunsch (GREEN)	3,117	1.4
	write-in (WRI)	21	.0
8	Mike Rogers (R)	156,931	64.1
	Lance Enderle (D)	84,069	34.3
	Bhagwan Dashairya (LIBERT)	3,881	1.6
	write-ins (WRI)	13	.0
9	Gary Peters (D)	125,730	49.8
	Rocky Raczkowski (R)	119,325	47.2
	Adam Goodman (LIBERT)	2,601	1.0
	Douglas Campbell (GREEN)	2,484	1.0
	Bob Gray (NPA)	1,866	.7
	Matthew Kuofie (NPA)	644	.2
10	Candice S. Miller (R)	168,364	72.0
	Henry Yanez (D)	58,530	25.0
	Claude Beavers (LIBERT)	3,750	1.6
	Candace R. Caveny (GREEN)	3,286	1.4
11	Thaddeus McCotter (R)	141,224	59.3
	Natalie Mosher (D)	91,710	38.5
	John Tatar (LIBERT)	5,353	2.2

		Votes	Percent
12	Sander M. Levin (D)	124,671	61.1
	Don Volaric (R)	71,372	35.0
	Julia Williams (GREEN)	3,038	1.5
	Leonard Schwartz (LIBERT)	2,342	1.1
	Les Townsend (USTAX)	2,285	1.1
	Alan Jacquemotte (I)	409	.2
13	Hansen Clarke (D)*	100,885	79.4
	John Hauler (R)	23,462	18.5
	George L. Corsetti (GREEN)	1,032	.8
	Duane Montgomery (NPA)	881	.7
	Heidi Peterson (LIBERT)	815	.6
	write-ins (WRI)	1	.0
14	John Conyers Jr. (D)	115,511	76.8
	Don Ukrainec (R)	29,902	19.9
	Marc J. Sosnowski (USTAX)	3,206	2.1
	Richard J. Secula (LIBERT)	1,859	1.2
15	John D. Dingell (D)	118,336	56.8
	Rob Steele (R)	83,488	40.1
	Aimee Smith (GREEN)	2,686	1.3
	Kerry Lee Morgan (LIBERT)	1,969	.9
	Matthew Furman (USTAX)	1,821	.9
	write-in (WRI)	9	.0

Minnesota

GOVERNOR

	Votes	Percent
Mark Dayton (D)	919,232	43.6
Tom Emmer (R)	910,462	43.2
Tom Horner (INDC)	251,487	11.9
Chris Wright (GR)	7,516	.4
Farheen Hakeem (GREEN)	6,188	.3
Ken Pentel (EDP)	6,180	.3
Linda S. Eno (RES)	4,092	.2

HOUSE

		Votes	Percent
1	Tim Walz (D)	122,365	49.3
	Randy Demmer (R)	109,242	44.0
	Steven Wilson (INDC)	13,242	5.3
	Lars Johnson (PTF)	3,054	1.2
	write-ins (WRI)	102	.0
2	John Kline (R)	181,341	63.3
	Shelley Madore (D)	104,809	36.6
	write-ins (WRI)	303	.1
3	Erik Paulsen (R)	161,177	58.8
	Jim Meffert (D)	100,240	36.6
	Jon Oleson (INDC)	12,508	4.6
	write-ins (WRI)	167	.1
4	Betty McCollum (D)	136,746	59.1
	Teresa Collett (R)	80,141	34.6
	Steve Carlson (INDC)	14,207	6.1
	write-ins (WRI)	332	.1
5	Keith Ellison (D)	154,833	67.7
	Joel Demos (R)	55,222	24.1
	Lynne Torgerson (I)	8,548	3.7
	Tom Schrunk (INDC)	7,446	3.3
	Michael Cavlan (IDP)	2,468	1.1
	write-ins (WRI)	229	.1
6	Michele Bachmann (R)	159,476	52.5
	Tarryl Clark (D)	120,846	39.8
	Bob Anderson (INDC)	17,698	5.8
	Aubrey Immelman (I)	5,490	1.8
	write-ins (WRI)	181	.1

		Votes	Percent
7	Collin C. Peterson (D)	133,096	55.2
	Lee Byberg (R)	90,652	37.6
	Gene Waldorf (I)	9,317	3.9
	Glen Menze (INDC)	7,839	3.2
	write-ins (WRI)	193	.1
8	Chip Cravaack (R)*	133,490	48.2
	James L. Oberstar (D)	129,091	46.6
	Tim Olson (INDC)	11,876	4.3
	Richard "George" Burton (CNSTP)	2,492	.9
	write-ins (WRI)	132	.0

Mississippi

HOUSE

		Votes	Percent
1	Alan Nunnelee (R)*	121,074	55.3
	Travis W. Childers (D)	89,388	40.8
	Wally Pang (I)	2,180	1.0
	Les Green (I)	2,020	.9
	A.G. Baddley (I)	1,882	.9
	Gail Giaramita (CNSTP)	1,235	.6
	Rick Hoskins (I)	478	.2
	Harold M. Taylor (LIBERT)	447	.2
	Barbara Dale Washer (REF)	389	.2
2	Bennie Thompson (D)	105,327	61.5
	William "Bill" Marcy (R)	64,499	37.6
	Ashley Norwood (REF)	1,530	.9
3	Gregg Harper (R)	132,393	68.0
	Joel L. Gill (D)	60,737	31.2
	Tracella Lou O'Hara Hill (REF)	1,586	.8
4	Steven M. Palazzo (R)*	105,613	51.9
	Gene Taylor (D)	95,243	46.8
	Kenneth "Tim" Hampton (LIBERT)	1,741	.9
	Anna Jewel Revies (REF)	787	.4

Missouri

SENATE

		Votes	Percent
	Roy Blunt (R)*	1,054,160	54.2
	Robin Carnahan (D)	789,736	40.6
	Jonathan Dine (LIBERT)	58,663	3.0
	Jerry Beck (CNSTP)	41,309	2.1
	Frazier Glenn Miller (WRI)	7	.0
	Jeff Wirick (WRI)	4	.0
	Richie L. Wolfe (WRI)	2	.0
	Mark Memoly (WRI)	1	.0

HOUSE

		Votes	Percent
1	William Lacy Clay (D)	135,907	73.6
	Robyn Hamlin (R)	43,649	23.6
	Julie Stone (LIBERT)	5,223	2.8
2	Todd Akin (R)	180,481	67.9
	Arthur Lieber (D)	77,467	29.2
	Steve Mosbacher (LIBERT)	7,677	2.9
	Patrick M. Cannon (WRI)	7	.0
3	Russ Carnahan (D)	99,398	48.9
	Ed Martin (R)	94,757	46.7
	Steven R. Hedrick (LIBERT)	5,772	2.8
	Nicholas J. Ivanovich (CNSTP)	3,155	1.6
	Brian Wallner (WRI)	3	.0
4	Vicky Hartzler (R)*	113,489	50.4
	Ike Skelton (D)	101,532	45.1
	Jason Michael Braun (LIBERT)	6,123	2.7
	Greg Cowan (CNSTP)	3,912	1.7
5	Emanuel Cleaver II (D)	102,076	53.3
	Jacob Turk (R)	84,578	44.2
	Randall D. "Randy" Langkraehr (LIBERT)	3,077	1.6
	Dave Lay (CNSTP)	1,692	.9

		Votes	Percent
6	Sam Graves (R)	154,103	69.4
	Clint Hylton (D)	67,762	30.5
	Kyle Yarber (WRI)	47	.0
7	Billy Long (R)*	141,010	63.4
	Scott Eckersley (D)	67,545	30.4
	Kevin Craig (LIBERT)	13,866	6.2
	Nicholas Ivan Ladendorf (WRI)	10	.0
8	Jo Ann Emerson (R)	128,499	65.6
	Tommy Sowers (D)	56,377	28.8
	Larry Bill (I)	7,193	3.7
	Rick Vandeven (LIBERT)	3,930	2.0
9	Blaine Luetkemeyer (R)	162,724	77.4
	Christopher W. Dwyer (LIBERT)	46,817	22.3
	Jeff Reed (WRI)	748	.4
	Ron Burrus (WRI)	69	.0

Montana

HOUSE

		Votes	Percent
AL	Denny Rehberg (R)	217,696	60.4
	Dennis McDonald (D)	121,954	33.8
	Mike Fellows (LIBERT)	20,691	5.7

Nebraska

GOVERNOR

		Votes	Percent
	Dave Heineman (R)	360,645	73.9
	Mike Meister (D)	127,343	26.1

HOUSE

		Votes	Percent
1	Jeff Fortenberry (R)	116,871	71.3
	Ivy Harper (D)	47,106	28.7
2	Lee Terry (R)	93,840	60.8
	Tom White (D)	60,486	39.2
3	Adrian Smith (R)	117,275	70.1
	Rebekah Davis (D)	29,932	17.9
	Dan Hill (I)	20,036	12.0

Nevada

GOVERNOR

		Votes	Percent
	Brian Sandoval (R)	382,350	53.4
	Rory Reid (D)	298,171	41.6
	Eugene Disimone (I)	6,403	.9
	Floyd Fitzgibbons (IA)	5,049	.7
	Arthur Lampitt (LIBERT)	4,672	.6
	David Curtis (GREEN)	4,437	.6
	Aaron Honig (I)	3,216	.4

SENATE

		Votes	Percent
	Harry Reid (D)	362,785	50.3
	Sharron Angle (R)	321,361	44.5
	Scott Ashjian (TEA)	5,811	.8
	Michael L. Haines (I)	4,261	.6
	Tim Fasano (IA)	3,185	.4
	Jesse Holland (I)	3,175	.4
	Jeffrey C. Reeves (I)	2,510	.3
	Wil Stand (I)	2,119	.3

HOUSE

		Votes	Percent
1	Shelley Berkley (D)	103,246	61.7
	Kenneth Wegner (R)	58,995	35.3
	Jonathan Hansen (IA)	2,847	1.7
	Edward G. Klapproth (LIBERT)	2,118	1.3
2	Dean Heller (R)	169,458	63.3
	Nancy Price (D)	87,421	32.7
	Russell Best (IA)	10,829	4.0

		Votes	Percent
3	Joe Heck (R)*	128,916	48.1
	Dina Titus (D)	127,168	47.5
	Barry Michaels (I)	6,473	2.4
	Joseph P. Silvestri (LIBERT)	4,026	1.5
	Scott David Narter (IA)	1,291	.5

New Hampshire

GOVERNOR

		Votes	Percent
	John Lynch (D)	240,346	52.6
	John A. Stephen (R)	205,616	45.0
	John Babiarz (LIBERT)	10,089	2.2

SENATE

		Votes	Percent
	Kelly Ayotte (R)*	273,218	60.0
	Paul W. Hodes (D)	167,545	36.8
	Chris Booth (I)	9,194	2.0
	Ken Blevens (LIBERT)	4,753	1.0

HOUSE

		Votes	Percent
1	Frank Guinta (R)*	121,655	54.0
	Carol Shea-Porter (D)	95,503	42.4
	Philip Hodson (LIBERT)	7,966	3.5
	write-ins (WRI)	299	.1
2	Charles Bass (R)*	108,610	48.3
	Ann McLane Kuster (D)	105,060	46.8
	Tim vanBlommesteyn (I)	6,197	2.8
	Howard L. Wilson (LIBERT)	4,796	2.1

New Jersey

HOUSE

		Votes	Percent
1	Robert E. Andrews (D)	106,334	63.2
	Dale M. Glading (R)	58,562	34.8
	Mark Heacock (GREEN)	1,593	.9
	Margaret M. Chapman (TFC)	1,257	.7
	Nicky Petrutz (DAC)	521	.3
2	Frank A. LoBiondo (R)	109,460	65.5
	Gary Stein (D)	51,690	30.9
	Peter F. Boyce (CNSTP)	4,120	2.5
	Mark Lovett (I)	1,123	.7
	Vitov Valdes-Munoz (ALP)	727	.4
3	Jon Runyan (R)*	110,215	50.0
	John Adler (D)	104,252	47.3
	Peter DeStefano (TEA)	3,284	1.5
	Russ Conger (LIBERT)	1,445	.7
	Lawrence J. Donahue (YCA)	1,113	.5
4	Christopher H. Smith (R)	129,752	69.4
	Howard Kleinhendler (D)	52,118	27.9
	Joseph A. Siano (LIBERT)	2,912	1.6
	Steven Welzer (GREEN)	1,574	.8
	David R. Meiswinkle (ARM)	582	.3
5	Scott Garrett (R)	124,030	64.9
	Tod Theise (D)	62,634	32.8
	Ed Fanning (GREEN)	2,347	1.2
	Mark D. Quick (FA)	1,646	.9
	James Douglas Radigan (BD)	336	.2
6	Frank Pallone Jr. (D)	81,933	54.7
	Anna C. Little (R)	65,413	43.7
	Jack Freudenheim (I)	1,299	.9
	Karen Anne Zaletel (GTP)	1,017	.7
7	Leonard Lance (R)	105,084	59.4
	Ed Potosnak (D)	71,902	40.6
8	Bill Pascrell Jr. (D)	88,478	62.7
	Roland Straten (R)	51,023	36.1
	Raymond Giangrasso (I)	1,707	1.2

		Votes	Percent
9	**Steven R. Rothman (D)**	83,564	60.7
	Michael Agosta (R)	52,082	37.8
	Patricia Alessandrini (GREEN)	1,980	1.4
10	**Donald M. Payne (D)**	95,299	85.2
	Michael J. Alonso (R)	14,357	12.8
	Robert Louis Toussaint (ANO)	1,141	1.0
	Joanne Miller (AOC)	1,080	1.0
11	**Rodney Frelinghuysen (R)**	122,149	67.2
	Douglas Herbert (D)	55,472	30.5
	Jim Gawron (LIBERT)	4,179	2.3
12	**Rush D. Holt (D)**	108,214	53.0
	Scott Sipprelle (R)	93,634	45.9
	Kenneth J. Cody (TVH)	2,154	1.1
13	**Albio Sires (D)**	62,840	74.1
	Henrietta Dwyer (R)	19,538	23.0
	Anthony Zanowic (IA)	1,508	1.8
	Maximo Gomez Nacer (GBS)	910	1.1

New Mexico

GOVERNOR

	Votes	Percent
Susana Martinez (R)	320,871	53.3
Diane Denish (D)	279,888	46.5

HOUSE

		Votes	Percent
1	**Martin Heinrich (D)**	112,010	51.8
	Jon Barela (R)	104,215	48.2
2	**Steve Pearce (R)***	94,053	55.4
	Harry Teague (D)	75,708	44.6
3	**Ben Ray Luján (D)**	120,048	57.0
	Tom Mullins (R)	90,617	43.0

New York

GOVERNOR

	Votes	Percent
Andrew M. Cuomo (D)	2,911,616	62.5
Carl P. Paladino (R)	1,548,101	33.2
Howie Hawkins (GRP)	59,928	1.3
Warren Redlich (LIBERT)	48,386	1.0
Jimmy McMillan (D)	41,131	.9
Charles Barron (I)	24,572	.5
Kristin Davis (I)	20,429	.4

SENATE

	Votes	Percent
Charles E. Schumer (D)	3,047,775	66.3
Jay Townsend (R)	1,480,337	32.2
Colia Clark (GREEN)	42,341	.9
Randy Credico (LIBERT)	24,869	.5
Kirsten Gillibrand (D)	2,837,589	62.9
Joseph J. DioGuardi (R)	1,582,603	35.1
Cecile A. Lawrence (GREEN)	35,487	.8
John Clifton (LIBERT)	18,414	.4
Joseph Huff (RTH)	17,018	.4
Vivia Morgan (I)	11,785	.3
Bruce Blakeman (I)	4,516	.1

HOUSE

		Votes	Percent
1	**Timothy H. Bishop (D)**	98,316	50.1
	Randy Altschuler (R)	97,723	49.8
	write-ins (WRI)	125	.1
2	**Steve Israel (D)**	94,594	56.3
	John Gomez (R)	72,029	42.9
	Anthony Tolda (CNSTP)	1,256	.7
	write-ins (WRI)	30	.0
3	**Peter T. King (R)**	131,674	71.9
	Howard A. Kudler (D)	51,346	28.0
	write-ins (WRI)	67	.0

		Votes	Percent
4	**Carolyn McCarthy (D)**	94,483	53.6
	Fran Becker (R)	81,718	46.4
	write-ins (WRI)	52	.0
5	**Gary L. Ackerman (D)**	72,239	63.0
	James Milano (R)	41,493	36.2
	Elizabeth Berney (I)	798	.7
	write-ins (WRI)	53	.0
6	**Gregory W. Meeks (D)**	85,096	87.7
	Asher Taub (R)	11,826	12.2
	write-ins (WRI)	72	.1
7	**Joseph Crowley (D)**	71,247	80.5
	Ken Reynolds (R)	16,145	18.2
	Anthony Gronowicz (GREEN)	1,038	1.2
	write-ins (WRI)	41	.0
8	**Jerrold Nadler (D)**	88,758	73.4
	Susan Kone (R)	31,996	26.5
	write-ins (WRI)	93	.1
9	**Anthony Weiner (D)**	67,011	60.8
	Bob Turner (R)	43,129	39.1
	write-ins (WRI)	65	.1
10	**Edolphus Towns (D)**	95,485	91.1
	Diana Muniz (R)	7,419	7.1
	Ernest Johnson (C)	1,853	1.8
	write-ins (WRI)	82	.1
11	**Yvette D. Clarke (D)**	104,297	90.5
	Hugh C. Carr (R)	10,858	9.4
	write-ins (WRI)	44	.0
12	**Nydia M. Velázquez (D)**	68,624	93.8
	Alice Gaffney (C)	4,482	6.1
	write-ins (WRI)	59	.1
13	**Michael G. Grimm (R)***	65,024	51.3
	Michael E. McMahon (D)	60,773	47.9
	Tom Venditteli (LIBERT)	929	.7
	write-ins (WRI)	72	.1
14	**Carolyn B. Maloney (D)**	107,327	75.0
	Ryan Brumberg (R)	32,065	22.4
	Tim Healy (C)	1,891	1.3
	Dino LaVerghetta (R)	1,617	1.1
	write-ins (WRI)	142	.1
15	**Charles B. Rangel (D)**	91,225	80.2
	Michel Faulkner (R)	11,754	10.3
	Craig Schley (INDC)	7,803	6.9
	Roger Calero (SW)	2,647	2.3
	write-ins (WRI)	257	.2
16	**Jose E. Serrano (D)**	61,642	95.7
	Frank DellaValle (R)	2,758	4.3
	write-ins (WRI)	38	.1
17	**Eliot L. Engel (D)**	95,346	72.8
	Anthony Mele (R)	29,792	22.8
	York Kleinhandler (R)	5,661	4.3
	write-ins (WRI)	82	.1
18	**Nita M. Lowey (D)**	104,836	63.4
	Jim Russell (R)	60,513	36.6
	write-ins (WRI)	67	.0
19	**Nan Hayworth (R)***	109,956	52.6
	John Hall (D)	98,766	47.2
	write-ins (WRI)	516	.2
20	**Chris Gibson (R)***	130,178	54.8
	Scott Murphy (D)	107,075	45.1
	write-ins (WRI)	87	.0

		Votes	Percent
21	**Paul Tonko (D)**	124,889	59.2
	Theodore J. Danz Jr. (R)	85,752	40.7
	write-ins (WRI)	150	.1
22	**Maurice D. Hinchey (D)**	98,661	52.6
	George K. Phillips (R)	88,687	47.3
	write-ins (WRI)	73	.0
23	**Bill Owens (D)**	82,232	47.5
	Matt Doheny (R)	80,237	46.4
	Doug Hoffman (C)	10,507	6.1
	write-ins (WRI)	115	.1
24	**Richard Hanna (R)***	101,599	53.0
	Michael Arcuri (D)	89,809	46.8
	write-ins (WRI)	292	.2
25	**Ann Marie Buerkle (R)***	104,602	50.1
	Dan Maffei (D)	103,954	49.8
	write-ins (WRI)	178	.1
26	**Christopher Lee (R)**	151,449	73.6
	Philip A. Fedele (D)	54,307	26.4
	write-ins (WRI)	49	.0
27	**Brian Higgins (D)**	119,085	60.9
	Leonard A. Roberto (R)	76,320	39.1
	write-ins (WRI)	10	.0
28	**Louise M. Slaughter (D)**	102,514	64.9
	Jill A. Rowland (R)	55,392	35.1
	write-ins (WRI)	41	.0
29	**Tom Reed (R)***	112,314	56.5
	Matthew Zeller (D)	86,099	43.3
	write-ins (WRI)	527	.3

North Carolina

SENATE

	Votes	Percent
Richard M. Burr (R)	1,458,046	54.8
Elaine Marshall (D)	1,145,074	43.0
Mike Beitler (LIBERT)	55,687	2.1

HOUSE

		Votes	Percent
1	**G.K. Butterfield (D)**	103,294	59.3
	Ashley Woolard (R)	70,867	40.7
2	**Renee Ellmers (R)***	93,876	49.5
	Bob Etheridge (D)	92,393	48.7
	Tom Rose (LIBERT)	3,505	1.8
3	**Walter B. Jones (R)**	143,225	71.9
	Johnny Rouse (D)	51,317	25.7
	Darryl Holloman (LIBERT)	4,762	2.4
4	**David E. Price (D)**	155,384	57.2
	William "B.J." Lawson (R)	116,448	42.8
5	**Virginia Foxx (R)**	140,525	65.9
	Billy Kennedy (D)	72,762	34.1
6	**Howard Coble (R)**	156,252	75.2
	Sam Turner (D)	51,507	24.8
7	**Mike McIntyre (D)**	113,957	53.7
	Ilario Pantano (R)	98,328	46.3
8	**Larry Kissell (D)**	88,776	53.0
	Harold Johnson (R)	73,129	43.7
	Thomas Hill (LIBERT)	5,098	3.0
	Anthony W. Graves (WRI)	439	.3
9	**Sue Myrick (R)**	158,790	69.0
	Jeff Doctor (D)	71,450	31.0
10	**Patrick T. McHenry (R)**	130,813	71.2
	Jeff Gregory (D)	52,972	28.8
11	**Heath Shuler (D)**	131,225	54.3
	Jeff Miller (R)	110,246	45.7

	Votes	Percent
12 Melvin Watt (D)	103,495	63.9
Greg Dority (R)	55,315	34.1
Lon Cecil (LIBERT)	3,197	2.0
13 Brad Miller (D)	116,103	55.5
William Randall (R)	93,099	44.5

North Dakota

SENATE
	Votes	Percent
John Hoeven (R)*	181,689	76.1
Tracy Potter (D)	52,955	22.2
Keith J. Hanson (LIBERT)	3,890	1.6

HOUSE
	Votes	Percent
AL Rick Berg (R)*	129,802	54.7
Earl Pomeroy (D)	106,542	44.9
write-ins (WRI)	793	.3

Ohio

GOVERNOR
	Votes	Percent
John R. Kasich (R)	1,889,180	49.0
Ted Strickland (D)	1,812,047	47.0
Ken Matesz (LIBERT)	92,116	2.4
Dennis Spisak (GREEN)	58,475	1.5

SENATE
	Votes	Percent
Rob Portman (R)*	2,168,736	56.8
Lee Fisher (D)	1,503,286	39.4
Eric Deaton (CNSTP)	65,856	1.7
Michael L. Pryce (I)	50,100	1.3
Daniel LaBotz (S)	26,454	.7
Arthur T. Sullivan (WRI)	648	.0

HOUSE
	Votes	Percent
1 Steve Chabot (R)*	103,770	51.5
Steve Driehaus (D)	92,672	46.0
Jim Berns (LIBERT)	3,076	1.5
Rich Stevenson (GREEN)	2,000	1.0
2 Jean Schmidt (R)	139,027	58.4
Surya Yalamanchili (D)	82,431	34.7
Marc Johnston (LIBERT)	16,259	6.8
Randy Lee Conover (WRI)	128	.0
3 Michael R. Turner (R)	152,629	68.1
Joe Roberts (D)	71,455	31.9
4 Jim Jordan (R)	146,029	71.5
Doug Litt (D)	50,533	24.7
Donald Charles Kissick (LIBERT)	7,708	3.8
5 Bob Latta (R)	140,703	67.8
Caleb Finkenbiner (D)	54,919	26.5
Brian L. Smith (LIBERT)	11,831	5.7
6 Bill Johnson (R)*	103,170	50.2
Charlie Wilson (D)	92,823	45.2
Richard E. Cadle (CNSTP)	5,077	2.5
Martin J. Elsass (LIBERT)	4,505	2.2
7 Steve Austria (R)	135,721	62.2
William R. Conner (D)	70,400	32.2
John D. Anderson (LIBERT)	9,381	4.3
David W. Easton (CNSTP)	2,811	1.3
8 John A. Boehner (R)	142,731	65.6
Justin A. Coussoule (D)	65,883	30.3
David A. Harlow (LIBERT)	5,121	2.4
James J. Condit Jr. (CNSTP)	3,701	1.7
9 Marcy Kaptur (D)	121,819	59.4
Rich Iott (R)	83,423	40.6
10 Dennis J. Kucinich (D)	101,340	53.0
Peter Corrigan (R)	83,807	43.9
Jeff Goggins (LIBERT)	5,874	3.1

	Votes	Percent
11 Marcia L. Fudge (D)	139,684	82.9
Thomas Pekarek (R)	28,752	17.1
12 Pat Tiberi (R)	150,163	55.8
Paula Brooks (D)	110,307	41.0
Travis M. Irvine (LIBERT)	8,710	3.2
13 Betty Sutton (D)	118,806	55.7
Tom Ganley (R)	94,367	44.3
14 Steven C. LaTourette (R)	149,878	64.9
Bill O'Neill (D)	72,604	31.4
John M. Jelenic (LIBERT)	8,383	3.6
15 Steve Stivers (R)*	119,471	54.2
Mary Jo Kilroy (D)	91,077	41.3
William J. Kammerer (LIBERT)	6,116	2.8
David Ryon (CNSTP)	3,887	1.8
Bill Buckel (WRI)	45	.0
16 James B. Renacci (R)*	114,652	52.1
John Boccieri (D)	90,833	41.3
Jeffrey J. Blevins (LIBERT)	14,585	6.6
Robert L. Ross (WRI)	67	.0
17 Tim Ryan (D)	102,758	53.9
Jim Graham (R)	57,352	30.1
James A. Traficant Jr. (I)	30,556	16.0
18 Bob Gibbs (R)*	107,426	53.9
Zack Space (D)	80,756	40.5
Lindsey Sutton (CNSTP)	11,246	5.6
Mark Pitrone (WRI)	20	.0

Oklahoma

GOVERNOR
	Votes	Percent
Mary Fallin (R)	625,506	60.4
Jari Askins (D)	409,261	39.6

SENATE
	Votes	Percent
Tom Coburn (R)	718,482	70.6
Jim Rogers (D)	265,814	26.1
Stephen P. Wallace (I)	25,048	2.5
Ronald F. Dwyer (I)	7,807	.8

HOUSE
	Votes	Percent
1 John Sullivan (R)	151,173	76.8
Angelia O'Dell (I)	45,656	23.2
2 Dan Boren (D)	108,203	56.5
Charles Thompson (R)	83,226	43.5
3 Frank D. Lucas (R)	161,927	78.0
Frankie Robbins (D)	45,689	22.0
4 Tom Cole (R)		●
5 James Lankford (R)*	123,236	62.5
Billy Coyle (D)	68,074	34.5
Clark Duffe (LIBERT)	3,067	1.6
Dave White (I)	2,728	1.4

Oregon

GOVERNOR
	Votes	Percent
John Kitzhaber (D)	716,525	49.3
Chris Dudley (R)	694,287	47.8
Greg Kord (CNSTP)	20,475	1.4
Wes Wagner (LIBERT)	19,048	1.3

SENATE
	Votes	Percent
Ron Wyden (D)	825,507	57.2
Jim Huffman (R)	566,199	39.2
Bruce Cronk (WFM)	18,940	1.3
Marc Delphine (LIBERT)	16,028	1.1
Rick Staggenborg (PRO)	14,466	1.0

HOUSE
	Votes	Percent
1 David Wu (D)	160,357	54.7
Rob Cornilles (R)	122,858	41.9
Donald H. LaMunyon (CNSTP)	3,855	1.3
Chris Henry (PACGRN)	2,955	1.0
H. Joe Tabor (LIBERT)	2,492	.8
write-ins (WRI)	392	.1
2 Greg Walden (R)	206,245	73.9
Joyce B. Segers (D)	72,173	25.9
write-ins (WRI)	619	.2
3 Earl Blumenauer (D)	193,104	70.0
Delia Lopez (R)	67,714	24.6
Jeffrey T. Lawrence (LIBERT)	8,380	3.0
Michael Meo (PACGRN)	6,197	2.2
write-ins (WRI)	407	.2
4 Peter A. DeFazio (D)	162,416	54.5
Art Robinson (R)	129,877	43.6
Mike Beilstein (PACGRN)	5,215	1.8
write-ins (WRI)	544	.2
5 Kurt Schrader (D)	145,319	51.2
Scott Bruun (R)	130,313	46.0
Chris Lugo (PACGRN)	7,557	2.7
write-ins (WRI)	367	.1

Pennsylvania

GOVERNOR
	Votes	Percent
Tom Corbett (R)	2,172,763	54.5
Dan Onorato (D)	1,814,788	45.5

SENATE
	Votes	Percent
Patrick J. Toomey (R)*	2,028,945	51.0
Joe Sestak (D)	1,948,716	49.0

HOUSE
	Votes	Percent
1 Robert A. Brady (D)	149,944	100.0
2 Chaka Fattah (D)	182,800	89.3
Rick Hellberg (R)	21,907	10.7
3 Mike Kelly (R)*	111,909	55.7
Kathy Dahlkemper (D)	88,924	44.3
4 Jason Altmire (D)	120,827	50.8
Keith Rothfus (R)	116,958	49.2
5 Glenn Thompson (R)	127,427	68.7
Michael Pipe (D)	52,375	28.2
Vernon L. Etzel (LIBERT)	5,710	3.1
6 Jim Gerlach (R)	133,770	57.1
Manan Trivedi (D)	100,493	42.9
7 Patrick Meehan (R)	137,825	54.9
Bryan Lentz (D)	110,314	44.0
Jim Schneller (I)	2,708	1.1
8 Michael G. Fitzpatrick (R)*	130,759	53.5
Patrick J. Murphy (D)	113,547	46.5
9 Bill Shuster (R)	141,904	73.1
Tom Conners (D)	52,322	26.9
10 Tom Marino (R)*	110,599	55.2
Christopher Carney (D)	89,846	44.8
11 Lou Barletta (R)*	102,179	54.7
Paul E. Kanjorski (D)	84,618	45.3
12 Mark Critz (D)	94,056	50.8
Tim Burns (R)	91,170	49.2
13 Allyson Y. Schwartz (D)	118,710	56.3
Dee Adcock (R)	91,987	43.7
14 Mike Doyle (D)	122,073	68.8
Melissa Haluszczak (R)	49,997	28.2
Ed Bortz (GREEN)	5,400	3.0

		Votes	Percent
15	**Charlie Dent (R)**	**109,534**	53.5
	John Callahan (D)	79,766	39.0
	Jake Towne (I)	15,248	7.4
16	**Joe Pitts (R)**	**134,113**	65.4
	Lois K. Herr (D)	70,994	34.6
17	**Tim Holden (D)**	**118,486**	55.5
	Dave Argall (R)	95,000	44.5
18	**Tim Murphy (R)**	**161,888**	67.3
	Dan Connolly (D)	78,558	32.7
19	**Todd R. Platts (R)**	**165,219**	71.9
	Ryan S. Sanders (D)	53,549	23.3
	Joshua A. Monighan (I)	10,988	4.8

Rhode Island

GOVERNOR

	Votes	Percent
Lincoln Chafee (I)	**123,571**	36.1
John F. Robitaille (R)	114,911	33.6
Frank T. Caprio (D)	78,896	23.0
Kenneth J. Block (MDE)	22,146	6.5
Joseph M. Lusi (I)	1,091	.3
Todd Giroux (I)	882	.3
Ronald Algieri (I)	793	.2

HOUSE

		Votes	Percent
1	**David Cicilline (D)***	**81,269**	50.6
	John Loughlin (R)	71,542	44.6
	Kenneth A. Capalbo (I)	6,424	4.0
	Gregory Raposa (I)	1,334	.8
2	**Jim Langevin (D)**	**104,442**	59.9
	Mark Zaccaria (R)	55,409	31.8
	John O. Matson (I)	14,584	8.4

South Carolina

GOVERNOR

	Votes	Percent
Nikki R. Haley (R)	**690,525**	51.4
Vincent Sheheen (D)	630,534	46.9
Morgan Bruce Reeves (GREEN)	20,114	1.5

SENATE

	Votes	Percent
Jim DeMint (R)	**810,771**	61.5
Alvin M. Greene (D)	364,598	27.6
Tom Clements (GREEN)	121,472	9.2

HOUSE

		Votes	Percent
1	**Tim Scott (R)***	**152,755**	65.4
	Ben Frasier (D)	67,008	28.7
	Rob Groce (WFM)	4,148	1.8
	Robert Dobbs (GREEN)	3,369	1.4
	Keith Blandford (LIBERT)	2,750	1.2
	Jimmy Wood (INDC)	2,489	1.1
	M.E. "Mac" McCullough (UC)	1,013	.4
	write-ins (WRI)	163	.1
2	**Joe Wilson (R)**	**138,861**	53.5
	Rob Miller (D)	113,625	43.8
	Eddie McCain (LIBERT)	4,228	1.6
	Marc Beaman (CNSTP)	2,856	1.1
	write-ins (WRI)	102	.0
3	**Jeff Duncan (R)***	**126,235**	62.5
	Jane Dyer (D)	73,095	36.2
	John Dalen (CNSTP)	2,682	1.3
	write-ins (WRI)	96	.0
4	**Trey Gowdy (R)***	**137,586**	63.4
	Paul Corden (D)	62,438	28.8
	Dave Edwards (CNSTP)	11,059	5.1
	Rick Mahler (LIBERT)	3,010	1.4
	C. Faye Walters (GREEN)	2,564	1.2
	write-ins (WRI)	181	.1

		Votes	Percent
5	**Mick Mulvaney (R)***	**125,834**	55.1
	John M. Spratt Jr. (D)	102,296	44.8
	write-ins (WRI)	156	.1
6	**James E. Clyburn (D)**	**125,459**	62.9
	Jim Pratt (R)	72,661	36.4
	Nammu Y. Muhammad (GREEN)	1,389	.7
	write-ins (WRI)	81	.0

South Dakota

GOVERNOR

	Votes	Percent
Dennis Daugaard (R)	**195,046**	61.5
Scott Heidepriem (D)	122,037	38.5

SENATE

	Votes	Percent
John Thune (R)	**227,947**	100.0

HOUSE

		Votes	Percent
AL	**Kristi Noem (R)***	**153,703**	48.1
	Stephanie Herseth Sandlin (D)	146,589	45.9
	B. Thomas Marking (I)	19,134	6.0

Tennessee

GOVERNOR

	Votes	Percent
Bill Haslam (R)	**1,041,545**	65.0
Mike McWherter (D)	529,851	33.1
Carl Two Feathers Whitaker (I)	6,536	.4
Brandon Dodds (I)	4,728	.3
Bayron Binkley (I)	4,663	.3
June Griffin (I)	2,587	.2
Linda Kay Perry (I)	2,057	.1
Howard M. Switzer (I)	1,887	.1
Samuel David Duck (I)	1,755	.1
Thomas Smith II (I)	1,207	.1
Toni K. Hall (I)	993	.1
David Gatchell (I)	859	.0
Boyce T. McCall (I)	828	.0
James Reesor (I)	809	.0
Mike Knois (I)	600	.0
Donald Ray McFolin (I)	583	.0

HOUSE

		Votes	Percent
1	**Phil Roe (R)**	**123,006**	80.8
	Michael Edward Clark (D)	26,045	17.1
	Kermit E. Steck (I)	3,110	2.0
2	**John J. "Jimmy" Duncan Jr. (R)**	**141,796**	81.8
	Dave Hancock (D)	25,400	14.6
	Joseph R. Leinweber Jr. (I)	2,497	1.4
	D. H. "Andy" Andrew (I)	1,993	1.1
	Greg Samples (I)	1,185	.7
	H. James Headings (I)	509	.3
3	**Chuck Fleischmann (R)***	**92,032**	56.8
	John Wolfe Jr. (D)	45,387	28.0
	Savas T. Kyriakidis (I)	17,077	10.5
	Mark DeVol (I)	5,773	3.6
	Don Barkman (I)	811	.5
	Gregory C. Goodwin (I)	380	.2
	Robert Humphries (I)	380	.2
	Mo Kiah (I)	216	.1
4	**Scott DesJarlais (R)***	**103,969**	57.1
	Lincoln Davis (D)	70,254	38.6
	Paul H. Curtis (I)	3,178	1.7
	Gerald York (I)	2,159	1.2
	James Anthony Gray (I)	1,714	.9
	Richard S. Johnson (I)	917	.5

		Votes	Percent
5	**Jim Cooper (D)**	**99,162**	56.2
	David Hall (R)	74,204	42.1
	Stephen W. Collings (I)	584	.3
	John "Big John" Smith (I)	533	.3
	Jackie Miller (I)	444	.2
	John P. Miglietta (I)	396	.2
	Bill Crook (I)	391	.2
	James G. Whitfield II (I)	333	.2
	Joe D. Moore Jr. (I)	159	.1
	Clark Taylor (I)	156	.1
6	**Diane Black (R)***	**128,517**	67.3
	Brett Carter (D)	56,145	29.4
	Jim Boyd (I)	2,157	1.1
	David Purcell (I)	1,296	.7
	Tommy N. Hay (I)	1,270	.7
	Brandon E. Gore (I)	1,103	.6
	Stephen R. Sprague (I)	596	.3
7	**Marsha Blackburn (R)**	**158,916**	72.4
	Greg Rabidoux (D)	54,347	24.8
	J.W. "Bill" Stone (I)	6,320	2.9
8	**Stephen Fincher (R)***	**98,759**	59.0
	Roy Herron (D)	64,960	38.8
	Donn Janes (I)	2,440	1.5
	Mark J. Rawles (I)	1,237	.7
	write-in (WRI)	9	.0
9	**Steve Cohen (D)**	**99,827**	74.0
	Charlotte Bergmann (R)	33,879	25.1
	Sandra Sullivan (I)	673	.5
	Perry Steele (I)	528	.4

Texas

GOVERNOR

	Votes	Percent
Rick Perry (R)	**2,737,481**	55.0
William H. "Bill" White (D)	2,106,395	42.3
Kathie Glass (LIBERT)	109,211	2.2
Deb Shafto (GREEN)	19,516	.4

HOUSE

		Votes	Percent
1	**Louie Gohmert (R)**	**129,398**	89.7
	Charles Parkes (LIBERT)	14,811	10.3
2	**Ted Poe (R)**	**130,020**	88.6
	David W. Smith (LIBERT)	16,711	11.4
3	**Sam Johnson (R)**	**101,180**	66.3
	John Lingenfelder (D)	47,848	31.3
	Christopher J. Claytor (LIBERT)	3,602	2.4
	Harry Pierce (WRI)	22	.0
4	**Ralph M. Hall (R)**	**136,338**	73.2
	VaLinda Hathcox (D)	40,975	22.0
	Jim Prindle (LIBERT)	4,729	2.5
	Shane Shepard (I)	4,244	2.3
5	**Jeb Hensarling (R)**	**106,742**	70.5
	Tom Berry (D)	41,649	27.5
	Ken Ashby (LIBERT)	2,958	2.0
6	**Joe L. Barton (R)**	**107,140**	65.9
	David E. Cozad (D)	50,717	31.2
	Byron Severns (LIBERT)	4,700	2.9
7	**John Culberson (R)**	**143,655**	81.
	Bob Townsend (LIBERT)	31,704	18.
	Lissa Squiers (WRI)	1,019	.
8	**Kevin Brady (R)**	**161,417**	80.3
	Kent Hargett (D)	34,694	17.2
	Bruce West (LIBERT)	4,988	2.5

		Votes	Percent
9	Al Green (D)	80,107	75.7
	Steve Mueller (R)	24,201	22.9
	Michael W. Hope (LIBERT)	1,459	1.4
10	Michael McCaul (R)	144,980	64.7
	Ted Ankrum (D)	74,086	33.0
	Jeremiah Perkins (LIBERT)	5,105	2.3
11	K. Michael Conaway (R)	125,581	80.8
	James Quillian (D)	23,989	15.4
	James A. Powell (LIBERT)	4,321	2.8
	Jim Howe (GREEN)	1,449	.9
12	Kay Granger (R)	109,882	71.9
	Tracey Smith (D)	38,434	25.1
	Matthew Solodow (LIBERT)	4,601	3.0
13	William M. "Mac" Thornberry (R)	113,201	87.0
	Keith Dyer (I)	11,192	8.6
	John T. Burwell (LIBERT)	5,650	4.3
14	Ron Paul (R)	140,623	76.0
	Robert Pruett (D)	44,431	24.0
15	Rubén Hinojosa (D)	53,546	55.7
	Eddie Zamora (R)	39,964	41.6
	Aaron I. Cohn (LIBERT)	2,570	2.7
16	Silvestre Reyes (D)	49,301	58.1
	Tim Besco (R)	31,051	36.6
	Bill Collins (LIBERT)	4,319	5.1
	Tim Collins (WRI)	221	.3
17	Bill Flores (R) *	106,696	61.8
	Chet Edwards (D)	63,138	36.6
	Richard B. Kelly (LIBERT)	2,808	1.6
18	Sheila Jackson Lee (D)	85,108	70.2
	John Faulk (R)	33,067	27.3
	Mike Taylor (LIBERT)	3,118	2.6
	Charles B. Meyer (WRI)	28	.0
19	Randy Neugebauer (R)	106,059	77.8
	Andy Wilson (D)	25,984	19.1
	Richard "Chip" Peterson (LIBERT)	4,315	3.2
20	Charlie Gonzalez (D)	58,645	63.6
	Clayton Trotter (R)	31,757	34.4
	Michael Idrogo (LIBERT)	1,783	1.9
21	Lamar Smith (R)	162,924	68.9
	Lainey Melnick (D)	65,927	27.9
	James Arthur Strohm (LIBERT)	7,694	3.2
22	Pete Olson (R)	140,537	67.5
	Kesha Rogers (D)	62,082	29.8
	Steven Susman (LIBERT)	5,538	2.7
	Johnny Williams (WRI)	66	.0
23	Francisco "Quico" Canseco (R) *	74,853	49.4
	Ciro D. Rodriguez (D)	67,348	44.4
	Craig T. Stephens (I)	5,432	3.6
	Martin Nitschke (LIBERT)	2,482	1.6
	Ed Scharf (GREEN)	1,419	.9
24	Kenny Marchant (R)	100,078	81.6
	David Sparks (LIBERT)	22,609	18.4
25	Lloyd Doggett (D)	99,967	52.8
	Donna Campbell (R)	84,849	44.8
	Jim Stutsman (LIBERT)	4,431	2.3
26	Michael C. Burgess (R)	120,984	67.0
	Neil L. Durrance (D)	55,385	30.7
	Mark Boler (LIBERT)	4,062	2.2
27	Blake Farenthold (R) *	51,001	47.8
	Solomon P. Ortiz (D)	50,226	47.1
	Edward C. Mishou (LIBERT)	5,372	5.0

		Votes	Percent
28	Henry Cuellar (D)	62,773	56.3
	Bryan Underwood (R)	46,740	42.0
	Stephen Kaat (LIBERT)	1,889	1.7
29	Gene Green (D)	43,257	64.6
	Roy Morales (R)	22,825	34.1
	Brad Walters (LIBERT)	866	1.3
30	Eddie Bernice Johnson (D)	86,322	75.7
	Stephen E. Broden (R)	24,668	21.6
	J.B. Oswalt (LIBERT)	2,988	2.6
31	John Carter (R)	126,384	82.5
	Bill Oliver (LIBERT)	26,735	17.5
32	Pete Sessions (R)	79,433	62.6
	Grier Raggio (D)	44,258	34.9
	John Jay Myers (LIBERT)	3,178	2.5

Utah

GOVERNOR

	Votes	Percent
Gary R. Herbert (R)	412,151	64.1
Peter Corroon (D)	205,246	31.9
Farley Anderson (I)	13,038	2.0
Andrew McCullough (LIBERT)	12,871	2.0

SENATE

	Votes	Percent
Mike Lee (R) *	390,179	61.6
Sam F. Granato (D)	207,685	32.8
Scott N. Bradley (CNSTP)	35,937	5.7
Brian E. Kamerath (WRI)	20	.0
Cody Judy (WRI)	2	.0

HOUSE

		Votes	Percent
1	Rob Bishop (R)	135,247	69.2
	Morgan E. Bowen (D)	46,765	23.9
	Kirk D. Pearson (CNSTP)	9,143	4.7
	Jared Paul Stratton (LIBERT)	4,307	2.2
2	Jim Matheson (D)	127,151	50.5
	Morgan Philpot (R)	116,001	46.1
	Randall Hinton (CNSTP)	4,578	1.8
	Dave Glissmeyer (UNA)	2,391	.9
	Wayne L. Hill (UNA)	1,726	.7
3	Jason Chaffetz (R)	139,721	72.3
	Karen Hyer (D)	44,320	22.9
	Douglas Sligting (CNSTP)	4,596	2.4
	Jake Shannon (LIBERT)	2,945	1.5
	Joseph L. Puente (UNA)	1,604	.8

Vermont

GOVERNOR

	Votes	Percent
Peter Shumlin (D)	119,543	49.5
Brian E. Dubie (R)	115,212	47.7
Dennis Steele (I)	1,917	.8
Cris Ericson (M)	1,819	.8
Dan Feliciano (I)	1,341	.6
Em Peyton (I)	684	.3
Ben Mitchell (LU)	429	.2

SENATE

	Votes	Percent
Patrick J. Leahy (D)	151,281	64.3
Len Britton (R)	72,699	30.9
Daniel Freilich (I)	3,544	1.5
Cris Ericson (USM)	2,731	1.2
Stephen J. Cain (I)	2,356	1.0
Peter Diamondstone (S)	1,433	.6
Johenry Nunes (I)	1,021	.4

HOUSE

		Votes	Percent
AL	Peter Welch (D)	154,006	64.6
	Paul D. Beaudry (R)	76,403	32.0
	Gus Jaccaci (I)	4,704	2.0
	Jane Newton (S)	3,222	1.4
	write-ins (WRI)	186	.1

Virginia

HOUSE

		Votes	Percent
1	Rob Wittman (R)	135,564	63.9
	Krystal M. Ball (D)	73,824	34.8
	G. Gail "for Rail" Parker (IGREEN)	2,544	1.2
	write-ins (WRI)	304	.1
2	Scott Rigell (R)	88,340	53.1
	Glenn Nye (D)	70,591	42.4
	Kenny E. Golden (I)	7,194	4.3
	write-ins (WRI)	164	.1
3	Robert C. Scott (D)	114,754	70.0
	C.L. "Chuck" Smith Jr. (R)	44,553	27.2
	James J. Quigley (LIBERT)	2,383	1.4
	John D. Kelly (I)	2,039	1.2
	write-ins (WRI)	171	.1
4	J. Randy Forbes (R)	123,659	62.3
	Wynne V.E. LeGrow (D)	74,298	37.4
	write-ins (WRI)	432	.2
5	Robert Hurt (R) *	119,560	50.8
	Tom Perriello (D)	110,562	47.0
	Jeffrey A. Clark (I)	4,992	2.1
	write-ins (WRI)	185	.1
6	Robert W. Goodlatte (R)	127,487	76.3
	Jeffrey W. Vanke (I)	21,649	13.0
	Stuart M. Bain (LIBERT)	15,309	9.2
	write-ins (WRI)	2,709	1.6
7	Eric Cantor (R)	138,209	59.2
	Rick E. Waugh Jr. (D)	79,616	34.1
	Floyd C. Bayne (IGREEN)	15,164	6.5
	write-ins (WRI)	413	.2
8	James P. Moran (D)	116,404	61.0
	J. Patrick Murray (R)	71,145	37.3
	J. Ron Fisher (IGREEN)	2,707	1.4
	write-ins (WRI)	492	.3
9	Morgan Griffith (R) *	95,726	51.2
	Rick Boucher (D)	86,743	46.4
	Jeremiah D. Heaton (I)	4,282	2.3
	write-ins (WRI)	166	.1
10	Frank R. Wolf (R)	131,116	62.9
	Jeffrey R. Barnett (D)	72,604	34.8
	William B. Redpath (LIBERT)	4,607	2.2
	write-ins (WRI)	229	.1
11	Gerald E. Connolly (D)	111,720	49.2
	Keith Fimian (R)	110,739	48.8
	Christopher F. DeCarlo (I)	1,846	.8
	David L. Dotson (LIBERT)	1,382	.6
	David William Gillis Jr. (IGREEN)	959	.4
	write-ins (WRI)	305	.1

Washington

SENATE

	Votes	Percent
Patty Murray (D)	1,314,930	52.4
Dino Rossi (R)	1,196,164	47.6

HOUSE

		Votes	Percent
1	Jay Inslee (D)	172,642	57.7
	James Watkins (R)	126,737	42.3

2	Rick Larsen (D)	155,241	51.1
	John Koster (R)	148,722	48.9
3	Jaime Herrera Beutler (R)*	152,799	53.0
	Denny Heck (D)	135,654	47.0
4	Doc Hastings (R)	156,726	67.6
	Jay Clough (D)	74,973	32.4
5	Cathy McMorris Rodgers (R)	177,235	63.7
	Daryl Romeyn (D)	101,146	36.3
6	Norm Dicks (D)	151,873	58.0
	Doug Cloud (R)	109,800	42.0
7	Jim McDermott (D)	232,649	83.0
	Bob Jeffers-Schroder (I)	47,741	17.0
8	Dave Reichert (R)	161,296	52.0
	Suzan DelBene (D)	148,581	48.0
9	Adam Smith (D)	123,743	54.8
	Richard "Dick" Muri (R)	101,851	45.1

West Virginia

SENATE

Joe Manchin III (D)*		283,358	53.5
John Raese (R)		230,013	43.4
Jesse Johnson (MOUNT)		10,152	1.9
Jeff Becker (CNSTP)		6,425	1.2

HOUSE

1	David B. McKinley (R)*	90,660	50.4
	Mike Oliverio (D)	89,220	49.6
2	Shelley Moore Capito (R)	126,814	68.5
	Virginia Lynch Graf (D)	55,001	29.7
	Phil Hudok (CNSTP)	3,431	1.8

3	Nick J. Rahall II (D)	83,636	56.0
	Elliott E. "Spike" Maynard (R)	65,611	44.0

Wisconsin

GOVERNOR

Scott Walker (R)	1,128,941	52.2
Tom Barrett (D)	1,004,303	46.5
Jim Langer (I)	10,608	.5
James James (CS)	8,273	.4
Terry Virgil (LIBERT)	6,790	.3

SENATE

Ron Johnson (R)*	1,125,999	51.9
Russ Feingold (D)	1,020,958	47.0
Rob Taylor (CNSTP)	23,473	1.1

HOUSE

1	Paul D. Ryan (R)	179,819	68.2
	John Heckenlively (D)	79,363	30.1
	Joseph Kexel (LIBERT)	4,311	1.6
	write-ins (WRI)	134	.0
2	Tammy Baldwin (D)	191,164	61.8
	Chad Lee (R)	118,099	38.2
	write-ins (WRI)	197	.1
3	Ron Kind (D)	126,380	50.3
	Dan Kapanke (R)	116,838	46.5
	Michael Krsiean (I)	8,001	3.2
	write-ins (WRI)	121	.0
4	Gwen Moore (D)	143,559	69.0
	Dan Sebring (R)	61,543	29.6
	Eddie Ahmad Ayyash (I)	2,802	1.3
	write-ins (WRI)	199	.1

5	F. James Sensenbrenner Jr. (R)	229,642	69.3
	Todd P. Kolosso (D)	90,634	27.4
	Robert R. Raymond (I)	10,813	3.3
	write-ins (WRI)	169	.0
6	Tom Petri (R)	183,271	70.7
	Joseph C. Kallas (D)	75,926	29.3
	write-ins (WRI)	170	.1
7	Sean P. Duffy (R)*	132,551	52.1
	Julie Lassa (D)	113,018	44.4
	Gary Kauther (I)	8,397	3.3
	write-ins (WRI)	423	.2
8	Reid Ribble (R)*	143,998	54.8
	Steve Kagen (D)	118,646	45.1
	write-ins (WRI)	294	.1

Wyoming

GOVERNOR

Matt Mead (R)	123,780	65.7
Leslie Petersen (D)	43,240	22.9
Mike Wheeler (LIBERT)	5,362	2.8

HOUSE

AL	Cynthia M. Lummis (R)	131,661	70.4
	David Wendt (D)	45,768	24.5
	John V. Love (LIBERT)	9,253	4.9
	write-ins (WRI)	287	.2

Campaign Finance Measure Stalls

DEMOCRATS TRIED WITHOUT success to limit the impact of a Supreme Court ruling that opened the door for corporations and labor unions to directly fund campaign advertising. The House passed a bill that would have required increased financial disclosure and disclaimers, but Republicans blocked a similar measure in the Senate.

The legislation was a response to a Jan. 21 Supreme Court ruling that struck down laws that prevented corporations, unions and certain other interest groups, including so-called 527 political advocacy groups, from spending their own funds for advertising that called for the election or defeat of a candidate.

The court decided 5-4 in *Citizens United v. Federal Election Commission* that those laws violated the right to free speech under the First Amendment, effectively ruling that corporations had the same free-speech rights as individuals.

The decision applied to advertising expenditures that were not coordinated with a political campaign. Corporations were still barred from contributing directly to a campaign.

Democrats warned that the ruling could allow wealthy businesses to buy elections by pouring money into campaign ads and drowning out the voices of less well-funded grass-roots groups. President Obama took the controversial step of chiding the Supreme Court justices for the decision as they sat before him during his State of the Union address.

But from the start, a large coalition of business groups, led by the U.S. Chamber of Commerce, opposed the legislation as an infringement on the right of free speech, and they had strong Republican backing.

2010 LEGISLATIVE ACTION

HOUSE COMMITTEE

The House Administration Committee approved its bill (HR 5175 — H Rept 111-492, Part 1) by voice vote on May 20.

The measure, drafted by Chris Van Hollen, D-Md., would have created new disclaimer requirements, including a "stand by your ad" provision under which individuals or groups funding an ad would have to identify themselves. Organizations would have been required to provide the identities of donors who gave at least $600 in a year for campaign-related activities. The bill required that chief executives appear in ads funded by their organizations and included a ban on election-related spending by companies that received federal aid or had significant foreign ownership or large government contracts.

Obama said he supported the legislation because it would "shine an unprecedented light on corporate spending in political campaigns so that the American people can clearly see who is trying to influence campaigns for public office."

During the markup, the committee:

▶ Adopted by voice vote an amendment by Zoe Lofgren, D-Calif., to exempt from the ban businesses whose government contracts were less than $1 million. "The concern we have is about large corporations having undue influence," she said.

▶ Rejected 3-5, along party lines, an amendment by the panel's rank-

ing Republican, Dan Lungren of California, to prohibit labor unions that had representational contracts with the government from making election expenditures. The amendment was part of an unsuccessful effort by Republicans to apply the election-financing prohibitions to labor unions in the same fashion that they would apply to corporations. "We have to do this to avoid it being ruled unconstitutional on its face," Lungren argued.

HOUSE FLOOR

The House passed a modified version of the bill on June 24, after extensive prodding by Democratic leaders. The 219-206 vote came after the House adopted a rule for floor debate that created a controversial carve-out exempting the National Rifle Association (NRA) and certain other tax-exempt nonprofit organizations from the bill's reporting and disclaimer requirements. *(House vote 391, p. H-138)*

Several interest groups — including the National Rifle Association, the National Right to Life Committee and the U.S. Chamber of Commerce — had raised concerns over the committee-approved version of the bill, arguing that the reporting and disclaimer provisions were too onerous.

In response, lawmakers announced plans June 14 to exempt nonprofit tax-exempt groups with more than 1 million dues-paying members in the United States that had been in existence for at least 10 years and received no more than 15 percent of their funding from corporations or unions.

The NRA accepted the provision, but progressive Democrats and members of the Congressional Black Caucus — along with groups such as the Brady Campaign to Prevent Gun Violence and the U.S. Public Interest Research Group — objected, saying there should not be exemptions for special interest groups. Fiscally conservative Blue Dog Democrats supported the NRA exemption but voiced concern about taking a politically difficult vote on a bill that might never be considered in the Senate.

Most Republicans continued to oppose the measure, as did a coalition of hundreds of groups, including the U.S. Chamber of Commerce, the National Association of Manufacturers and Planned Parenthood Federation of America.

As House leaders worked to garner votes, Senate Majority Leader Harry Reid, D-Nev., and Sen. Charles E. Schumer, D-N.Y., sent a letter to Speaker Nancy Pelosi, D-Calif., pledging that the Senate would consider the legislation soon, "so it can be signed by the president in time to take effect for the 2010 elections." Schumer was the sponsor of a companion bill.

A new agreement was released June 23 that reduced the threshold for the exemption to organizations with more than 500,000 dues-paying members, which included the Sierra Club among other groups. That change was included in the rule.

During the floor debate, the House:

▶ Adopted, 274-152, an amendment by Patrick J. Murphy, D-Pa., to require sponsors of political advertisements to disclose their locations. *(House vote 389, p. H-136)*

▸ Adopted by voice vote an amendment by Dennis J. Kucinich, D-Ohio, to clarify that the provisions of the bill would apply to companies with federal leases to drill for oil and gas in the outer continental shelf.

▸ Rejected, 57-369, an amendment by Steve King, R-Iowa, that would have exempted contributions made beginning in 2009 from the existing law on federal campaign contributions. *(House vote 388, p. H-136)*

▸ Rejected, 208-217, a motion by Lungren to send the bill back to committee with instructions to add language that would have banned contributions by lobbyists whose clients included individuals or governments that repeatedly supported acts of international terrorism. It also would have prohibited the use of campaign funds for political robocalls to those on the national "do not call" list. *(House vote 390, p. H-138)*

SENATE FLOOR

The Senate voted 57-41 on July 27 to reject an effort to end a GOP filibuster on a motion to proceed to Schumer's bill (S 3628). No Republicans backed the cloture motion, which needed 60 votes. All Democrats voted for it except Reid, who voted no to have the option of again calling up the bill. *(Senate vote 220, p. S-46)*

Like the House bill, Schumer's measure sought to promote transparency by requiring chief executives to appear in ads funded by their organizations. It also would have banned election-related spending by companies that received federal aid, those with large government contracts or those with more than 20 percent foreign ownership.

Schumer made several changes to the bill in an unsuccessful effort to defuse GOP arguments that it would give unions an unfair advantage and to try to win over either of Maine's two Republican senators, Olympia J. Snowe and Susan Collins.

He removed a provision that would have required businesses, unions and other groups to disclose transfers of $10,000 or more to, from or between their affiliates. He also struck two provisions that

were in the House version: one to prevent oil and gas companies that drilled in the outer continental shelf from funding political advertisements, and another to require organizations to disclose their location in TV and radio ads.

But Republicans remained unified in opposing the bill. Minority Leader Mitch McConnell of Kentucky called it a "monstrosity" whose sole purpose was to give Democrats an election year advantage.

Schumer said he would "keep fighting and fighting" for passage, but when Reid tried to proceed to the bill again in September, Republicans united once again to defeat a motion to invoke cloture. The 59-39 vote effectively rendered the legislation dead. *(Senate vote 240, p. S-50)*

Republicans stuck together in part because of concerns about protecting the rights of the minority party to offer amendments to legislation on the floor, although Schumer said that if the bill reached the floor, Democrats would amend it to make it effective in 2011 and would "welcome Republican amendments."

During lengthy debate Sept. 22, Democrats again criticized the Supreme Court for its decision in *Citizens United v. Federal Election Commission.*

Speaking at a fundraiser that same day, Obama pressed Democratic donors to support the party to counter independent expenditure groups backing GOP candidates.

"None of them will disclose who is paying for these ads. They are spending tens of millions of dollars against Democratic candidates without telling the American people where that flood of money is coming from," he said.

Republicans were not convinced. "There are many concerns I have with this legislation," Snowe said in a statement, "including the continued unequal treatment of unions and corporations, and I continue to believe this bill would not withstand constitutional scrutiny due to the overly burdensome federal mandates it would impose upon free speech." ∎

Chapter 12

REGULATORY POLICY, ENERGY & ENVIRONMENT

FDA Regulatory Powers Expanded Under Food Safety Legislation

THE FOOD AND DRUG Administration gained major new authority to regulate food products under a food safety bill that the House cleared Dec. 21. President Obama backed the measure and signed it into law Jan. 4, 2011 (HR 2751 — PL 111-353).

The bill gave the FDA the power to order mandatory food recalls, create a better system to track food and trace sources of foodborne illnesses, inspect food facilities on the basis of risk, and step up oversight of imported foods. The agency was also authorized to collect fees to pay for the cost of the new regulations.

The measure was aimed primarily at fruit and vegetable growers, domestic food processors and manufacturers, and food importers. The Agriculture Department still had the authority to regulate meat, poultry and egg products. There were exemptions in the bill for small farms and businesses.

The total cost of the bill was estimated at $1.4 billion over fiscal 2011-15.

There was broad, bipartisan accord in both chambers that the FDA needed more effective tools to regulate food safety, following a string of high-profile recalls of contaminated products including spinach and peanuts, but there were disagreements over issues such as the cost and the potential effect on small-scale producers and facilities.

The House passed food safety legislation in July 2009 (HR 2749), and the Senate Health, Education, Labor and Pensions (HELP) Committee marked up a separate version in November 2009 (S 510). *(2009 Almanac, p. 17-3)*

Among the chief differences was House language, not included in the Senate measure, that would have allowed the FDA to enforce civil and criminal penalties on food producers and distributors and given the agency subpoena powers in investigating the outbreak of foodborne illness.

The House bill also included quarantine authority, which would have allowed the FDA to limit the movement of food products within a state. And it called for the agency to do a study on whether bisphenol A (BPA), a chemical widely used in food and beverage containers, posed a health risk to infants, young children and pregnant women. If it found that a risk existed for any of those groups, the FDA would have been required to propose rules to modify or phase out use of the chemical.

The Senate measure, which was virtually identical to the final bill, contained provisions not in the House version that allowed the FDA to create new regulations governing the sanitary transportation of food products and to set standards for decontamination and disposal after a food emergency. It also created a program for the FDA to help foreign governments enhance their own food safety regulations.

BOX SCORE

BILL: HR 2751 — PL 111-353

LEGISLATIVE ACTION:

Senate passed S 510, 73-25, on Nov. 30.

Senate passed HR 2751, amended, by unanimous consent Dec. 19.

House cleared HR 2751, 215-144, on Dec. 21.

President signed the bill Jan. 4, 2011.

The Senate passed S 510 in November 2010 but quickly ran into a constitutional challenge over the inclusion of fees, which must originate in the House. The two chambers ultimately passed and cleared an identical bill with a House bill number.

HIGHLIGHTS

The following are major provisions of the food safety bill:

DOMESTIC FOOD PRODUCTION

● **Records.** The bill expanded the FDA's access to the records of food manufacturers, processors and distributors where the agency had reason to believe that a suspect ingredient would cause harm or could contaminate other food handled in the same facility.

● **Registration.** Food production facilities were required to register with the FDA every two years, provide contact information for any foreign partner facilities and allow FDA inspections.

● **Prevention.** Owners and operators of facilities were required to develop preventive-action plans that were available to the FDA and to identify and act to minimize any "reasonably foreseeable" hazards. The plan also had to outline the corrective actions they would take if the preventive measures failed.

● **Safe produce.** New FDA rules would govern the safe production and harvest of fruits and vegetables grown as commodities. The rules had to include minimum standards for soil amendments, hygiene, packaging, temperature controls, animal encroachment and water, as well as hazards that might occur naturally or be introduced. The bill directed the Department of Health and Human Services (HHS) to coordinate with the Agriculture Department in making the new rules.

● **Tracking food.** The FDA was authorized to create a new product-tracking system to gather the information that would be necessary in the event of an outbreak of foodborne illness or the distribution of adulterated food products. The bill also established pilot projects to determine, and report to Congress within 18 months, effective methods of rapidly identifying recipients of potentially contaminated food products.

● **Stepped-up inspections.** The bill authorized the FDA to step up its inspections of "high risk" domestic food facilities, requiring such inspections at least once in the five-year period following enactment and at least once every three years after that. Facilities designated as "low risk" had to be inspected once in the seven-year period following enactment and once every five years thereafter.

● **Mandatory recalls.** The FDA was authorized to issue mandatory recalls of products already on the market that would cause serious health problems or death, if a food facility failed to voluntarily recall the product. The agency also could order a facility to stop producing, distributing, holding or selling an adulterated or

hazardous food product if a request to take voluntary action was ignored.

FOOD IMPORTS AND FOREIGN FACILITIES

● **FDA inspection.** The measure required HHS to arrange with foreign governments to provide for FDA inspection of food export production facilities, with a special emphasis on facilities that produced high-risk products identified by the FDA or the Agriculture Department. If a foreign government or facility manager refused to allow the inspections, the FDA had the authority to prevent its products from entering the United States.

The FDA was required to inspect at least 600 registered foreign food export facilities in the first year after enactment. The number doubled every year for five years after that.

● **FDA offices.** The bill required HHS to consult with the departments of State and Homeland Security to establish FDA offices abroad to help expand the regulatory and enforcement capacity of foreign governments with regard to their domestic food industries.

● **Supplier verification.** U.S. importers were required to establish a risk-based supplier verification system that ensured that imported food was not adulterated or misbranded. The FDA could deny U.S. entry to food products from any importer that refused to create such a verification program.

● **Voluntary program.** A new voluntary program would be created to expedite the review and importation of food products from qualified importers. Importers whose products came from certified production facilities and met FDA standards could participate.

● **Third-party certification.** The bill directed the FDA to create a system for recognizing foreign government agencies and other third parties to inspect and certify food production facilities.

● **'Port shopping.'** The FDA was instructed to notify the Department of Homeland Security and U.S. Customs if an imported food product was turned back at a U.S. port, with the goal of preventing entry at another port, a practice referred to as "port shopping."

USER FEES

● **Fee authority.** The FDA was authorized to collect fees to cover 100 percent of the cost of implementing the provisions in the new law. Fees were limited to $25 million per year.

● **User fees.** The agency was authorized to collect fees from domestic facilities subject to reinspection or recalls.

● **Import fees.** Fees would also be paid by importers participating in the voluntary qualified importer program and by those subject to reinspection.

2010 LEGISLATIVE ACTION
SENATE FLOOR

The Senate passed its bill (S 510) by a vote of 73-25 on Nov. 30, after months of work by Tom Harkin, D-Iowa, chairman of the Health, Education, Labor and Pensions (HELP) Committee, and the panel's ranking Republican, Michael B. Enzi of Wyoming. *(Senate vote 257, p. S-52)*

Harkin, a Midwestern progressive who sought tougher food regulation, and Enzi, a conservative pro-business Westerner, negotiated with fellow senators on a variety of issues. They reached an agreement with John McCain, R-Ariz., and the supplements industry to allow the FDA to go after harmful products without changing existing regulations that treated dietary supplements as food. However, they were unable to reach agreement with Dianne Feinstein, D-Calif., who wanted to ban BPA, a proposal they feared would prompt a filibuster.

In a key compromise, they added language by Jon Tester, D-Mont., that exempted small-scale farm and food-processing operations that sold directly to consumers within a 275-mile area and averaged less than $500,000 in annual sales. The FDA could withdraw an exemption if a farm or a facility was involved in an outbreak of a foodborne illness.

Tester had insisted that the legislation's costly new rules would drive small-scale farmers and processors out of business and kill the local-food movement. A broad business coalition that included the Grocery Manufacturers of America and the U.S. Chamber of Commerce backed the bill despite the provisions.

When the bill finally reached the floor, it easily survived two cloture votes, 74-25 and 69-26. *(Senate votes 250, p. S-51, and 252, p. S-52)*

FINAL ACTION

Just when the bill appeared ready to clear, it was stopped dead in its tracks. The House Ways and Means Committee flagged the fees and several other provisions as unconstitutional because they related to revenue and therefore had to originate in the House. The House could have adopted a resolution "blue slipping" the bill, sending it back to the HELP Committee to remedy the problem. Although the Senate had passed the bill by a comfortable margin, sending a new version back to that chamber would have allowed opponents to renew delaying tactics that had held up the bill for months before the successful cloture votes.

The House tried attaching the measure to a long-term continuing resolution (HR 3082), but the Senate dropped the House provisions. In the end, Senate leaders used an earlier House revenue-related bill as a shell, inserted the text of S 510, and passed the measure (HR 2751) by unanimous consent Dec. 19. The House cleared the bill, 215-144, on Dec. 21. *(House vote 661, p. H-230)* ■

Flood Insurance Changes Not Settled

FEDERAL FLOOD INSURANCE was extended to Sept. 30, 2011, giving negotiators another year to try to work out a long-term authorization. The House passed a long-term flood insurance bill in July, but Gulf Coast lawmakers wanted to expand the program to cover wind damage as well.

The National Flood Insurance Program had received several short-term extensions since the last long-term reauthorization (PL 108-264) expired in September 2008. The House and Senate each passed versions of a long-term bill in the 110th Congress, but disagreements over whether the government should offer "multi-peril" policies that covered wind as well as flood damage helped sink the legislation. (*2008 Almanac, p. 3-13; 2007 Almanac, p. 16-4*)

The flood insurance program was created in 1968 (PL 90-448), in response to increasing federal government spending for disaster relief following a series of hurricanes that caused severe flooding in the 1960s. The program was supported by premium revenue until 2005, when Hurricanes Katrina, Rita and Wilma devastated New Orleans and other parts of the Gulf Coast and put the program nearly $20 billion in the red, money that it still owed the Treasury.

The Federal Emergency Management Agency (FEMA) administered the program and issued the rate maps that designated flood hazard areas, defined as those projected to have at least a 1 percent chance of flooding in any given year. These maps ultimately determined where government flood insurance was provided as well as the insurance rates.

Proponents of adding wind coverage, including some Gulf Coast Republicans, said private insurers had refused to pay claims when property damage was caused by both wind and flood events, leaving the government to pay for the damages through disaster aid.

Gulf Coast senators blocked a flood insurance bill in the Senate in 2007 because it did not include such "multi-peril" coverage.

The Obama administration, along with the U.S. Chamber of Commerce and other business groups, opposed the change, saying that wind insurance was widely available both in the private market and through state insurance plans. They said adding it would increase the debt of an already-overburdened federal program. A number of environmental groups said it would encourage people to build in fragile coastal areas.

BOX SCORE

BILL: HR 5114

LEGISLATIVE ACTION:

House passed HR 5114 (H Rept 111-495), 329-90, on July 15.

per year, rather than 10 percent, as allowed under existing law.

▸ Delay for five years a requirement that homeowners living in newly designated Special Flood Hazard Areas purchase flood insurance.

▸ Phase out subsidies for commercial and second homes built before 1974, the point at which flood insurance rate maps went into effect and premium subsidies were provided for property already in the flood zones. The phaseout would also apply to principal residences sold after enactment of the bill. It would not apply to multi-family rental properties or rentals that were a tenant's primary residence.

▸ Create a premium payment installation plan for low-income families, which would include families with an income level at or below 200 percent of the poverty level or that had no employed adult member.

▸ Authorize $250 million over five years for a new competitive grant program for local government agencies that conducted education and outreach to encourage homeowners to purchase flood insurance.

Several lawmakers expressed frustration with a program they viewed as subsidizing reckless behavior. Jeb Hensarling, R-Texas, argued that constituents in districts like his, where flooding was not a major risk, ended up picking up the tab for others.

Gene Taylor, D-Miss., questioned why an amendment he submitted to the Rules Committee to create an option for property owners to buy both wind and flood coverage was not made in order. Taylor's Gulf Coast home had been destroyed in Hurricane Katrina, and he later sued his insurance company for denying his wind-damage claim. Majority Leader Steny H. Hoyer, D-Md., announced that a bill (HR 1264) sponsored by Taylor containing similar provisions would be brought to the floor. (The measure was marked up but went no further.)

During the debate, the House:

▸ Adopted by voice vote an amendment by Adam H. Putnam, R-Fla., to require FEMA to report annually on use of the funds for the creation of the education and outreach program and the effectiveness of the grants.

▸ Rejected, 191-229, a motion by Hensarling to recommit the bill to the Financial Services Committee with instructions that it be reported back immediately without the education provisions. (*House vote 446, p. H-156*)

2010 LEGISLATIVE ACTION

HOUSE FLOOR

The House passed its bill by a lopsided 329-90 vote on July 15. The measure would have reauthorized the National Flood Insurance Program through fiscal 2015. (*House vote 447, p. H-156*)

The House Financial Services Committee had approved the measure (HR 5114 — H Rept 111-495) by voice vote April 27.

The House bill included provisions to:

▸ Increase the maximum coverage limit for flood insurance policies to $335,000 for residences, up from $250,000; $135,000 for the contents of a home, up from $100,000; and $670,000 for commercial property, up from $500,000.

▸ Allow flood insurance premiums to increase by up to 20 percent

SHORT-TERM EXTENSION

The federal flood insurance program was extended to Sept. 30, 2011, after the House agreed to allow another year for negotiations.

The Senate passed the bill by unanimous consent Sept. 21 and the House cleared it two days later by voice vote. President Obama signed the measure Sept. 30 (S 3814 — PL 111-250).

The previous short-term extension (PL 111-196) had kept the plan going through Sept. 30. Senate Democrats Mary L. Landrieu of Louisiana and Bill Nelson of Florida urged expedited passage of the new extension in order to avoid disrupting the program. Existing policies would have remained in effect during a lapse, but providers could not underwrite new policies, causing delays in real estate transactions when flood insurance was a condition of obtaining a mortgage. ■

Support for Oil-Drilling Bills Fades

INITIALLY THERE WAS BROAD bipartisan support for addressing some of the safety and regulatory issues exposed by the April 20 explosion of a Deepwater Horizon oil rig that allowed oil to pour into the Gulf of Mexico for months. But that sentiment yielded to bickering over both the scope and substance of the legislation.

The House passed a bill to overhaul the regulation of offshore drilling, but partisan divisions and policy disputes within the Democratic Caucus stalled action in the Senate.

The issue faded after the hole was plugged temporarily in July and permanently in September, and the legislation died at the end of the Congress.

Both the House-passed bill and a version developed by Senate Majority Leader Harry Reid, D-Nev., focused on overhauling federal management of the outer continental shelf to address numerous legal, regulatory and safety issues highlighted by the gulf spill. Both measures incorporated provisions from a flurry of bills that followed the explosion of the Deepwater Horizon rig.

Republicans in both chambers protested that Democrats were using the crisis to push what GOP members called overly broad bills that included provisions unrelated to the spill.

2010 LEGISLATIVE ACTION
HOUSE FLOOR

The House on July 30 passed a comprehensive offshore-drilling bill (HR 3534) by a largely party-line vote of 209-193, after Democratic leaders allowed caucus members from oil- and gas-producing states a vote on an amendment to ease a temporary moratorium on new deep-water drilling that the Obama administration had put in place in the aftermath of the explosion. *(House vote 513, p. H-178)*

Minutes before passage, the House adopted, 216-195, an amendment by Louisiana Democrat Charlie Melancon to exempt drillers from the moratorium if they demonstrated compliance with new safety requirements issued by the Interior Department. *(House vote 511, p. H-178)*

As many as 30 "oil patch" Democrats had signaled that they would oppose the bill because of concerns about the moratorium, which was thrown out by a federal court in June. The administration later issued a revised ban, sparking intense criticism from Republicans and industry-friendly Democrats, who said the job losses and other economic effects of the pause outweighed the risks from a second oil spill. (The administration lifted the moratorium in October, saying that new regulations had reduced the risks.)

On other amendments, the House:

▸ Adopted, 399-8, a proposal by Harry Teague, D-N.M., to allow companies to meet stringent new financial requirements for obtaining federal leases by pooling their resources. The approach was similar to a proposal under discussion in the Senate to allow the industry to collectively share the unlimited liability for economic damages

---

BOX SCORE	BILL: HR 3534
	LEGISLATIVE ACTION:

House passed HR 3534 (H Rept 111-575, Parts 1 and 2), 209-193, on July 30.

---

that companies would face under both the House and Senate drilling overhauls. *(House vote 509, p. H-176)*

The unlimited-liability provision sparked considerable opposition from the industry, Republicans and some Democrats, but the House Rules Committee did not allow votes on amendments that would have removed or altered the language in the House bill.

▸ Rejected, 166-239, a motion by Bill Cassidy, R-La., to return the bill to the Natural Resources Committee with instructions that it be reported back immediately with an amendment that would provide for termination of the moratorium. *(House vote 512, p. H-178)*

Key provisions in the bill would have:

▸ Repealed the existing $75 million cap on liability for offshore oil spills.

▸ Abolished the Minerals Management Service, the Interior Department's main offshore-drilling regulator, and assigned its duties to three new regulatory and leasing agencies. The management service had been plagued by scandals in recent years, and congressional investigations reported that the agency was mismanaged.

▸ Created numerous safety regulations for offshore oil and gas development leases, including features designed to prevent well blowouts.

▸ Required all vessels engaged in oil drilling in the U.S. Exclusive Economic Zone to register in the United States.

▸ Repealed a law that had provided "royalty relief" for certain oil and natural gas producers. The bill would have barred issuing new leases to companies that held oil and gas leases on which no royalties were paid unless the company renegotiated the leases to include royalty payments. It also would have prohibited the transfer or sale of such leases, unless the leases were similarly renegotiated.

▸ Created annual conservation fees for all oil and natural gas leases located on federal lands.

SENATE DEBATE

After failing to reach agreement with Republicans to stage test votes on competing energy bills, Reid put off until after the August recess his effort to bring his offshore-drilling overhaul and energy bill (S 3663) to the floor.

Reid had scaled back the bill twice in an effort to win approval before the recess. First to be jettisoned was a cap on greenhouse gas emissions. Next was a renewable-energy standard that had broader support among Democrats but still raised regional issues.

The legislation eventually included provisions from an offshore-drilling overhaul that had won bipartisan support in committee, as well as modest proposals to promote electric and natural gas vehicles, energy efficiency retrofits for homes, and increased funding for the federal Land and Water Conservation Fund.

But Reid could not satisfy everyone. A provision to eliminate the $75 million liability cap was more than Republicans, along with a handful of oil-friendly Democrats, were willing to accept. Lifting the cap entirely, they argued, would force independent producers out of the business.

Climate Legislation Shelved for Year

THE HOUSE PASSED A COMPREHENSIVE energy and climate bill in June 2009, but companion legislation stalled in the Senate over Republican opposition and intense skepticism from a handful of Democrats.

The centerpieces of the House bill were a cap-and-trade system for reducing greenhouse gas emissions and a first-time federal renewable-energy standard, both longtime goals of environmentalists and their congressional allies. To get the bill through, leaders also assured vulnerable members that the Senate would follow suit and vote on a similar measure. The lack of Senate action left some rank-and-file Democrats disgruntled.

The Senate Environment and Public Works Committee approved S 1733, a bill that was modeled closely after the House measure, in November 2009. However, Republicans boycotted the markup, and the legislation never advanced. *(2009 Almanac, p. 10-3)*

Despite more than 18 months of negotiations among industry, environmentalists and senators from both parties, designed to reach a grand bargain to link caps on emissions to incentives to expand nuclear energy and offshore drilling, supporters never came close to the 60 votes necessary to move such a bill past a filibuster in the Senate.

Sens. John Kerry, D-Mass.; Joseph I. Lieberman, I-Conn.; and Lindsey Graham, R-S.C., led an effort that targeted a handful of moderate Republicans, while working to address the concerns of Democrats who represented Midwestern manufacturers and coal-producing states.

With oil gushing into the Gulf of Mexico following the April 2010 explosion of an offshore-drilling rig, supporters of carbon caps saw the spill as a new opportunity to push for an overhaul. Just as the talks appeared to be on the verge of a breakthrough, however, Graham walked away, saying he was angry over indications that Democratic leaders wanted to move immigration legislation first. That deprived Kerry and Lieberman of their pivotal GOP partner, and the talks collapsed.

Unlike the economywide cap-and-trade model of the House-passed bill (HR 2454), the Senate plan took a sector-by-sector approach, addressing emissions by the utility, manufacturing and transportation sectors in distinct ways.

Meanwhile, a growing chorus of Democrats wanted to see a federal renewable-energy standard return to the mix, requiring utilities to generate an increasing percentage of electricity from renewable sources, such as wind and energy.

John Kerry, D-Mass., and Joseph I. Lieberman, I-Conn., had pressed to include mandatory limits on greenhouse gas emissions, and a vocal group of liberals still wanted carbon controls. But the pair's climate push sparked not only opposition from Republicans but also grumbling from moderate Democrats from coal-dependent and manufacturing states, who wanted Reid to advance a narrower bill focused on the spill.

Reid never found a formula that would yield the 60 votes he needed to limit debate. That, plus the short period left before the end of the regular session, precluded further consideration of the bill. ∎

SCIENCE & TECHNOLOGY

Bill Restructures NASA Programs, Boosts Commercial Spaceflight

CONGRESS SENT President Obama a three-year NASA authorization bill at the end of September after months of negotiations over the administration's plan to restructure the agency's manned spaceflight program. Obama signed the measure into law Oct. 11 (S 3729 — PL 111-267).

The bill authorized $58.4 billion for the National Aeronautics and Space Administration (NASA) for fiscal 2011 through 2013. It directed NASA to retain its shuttle-related workforce through fiscal 2011, but it also authorized the agency to foster the development of commercial capabilities in keeping with the administration's push to shift the U.S. human spaceflight program toward commercial carriers.

The measure directed NASA to contract with the National Academies in fiscal 2012 to conduct a study of the U.S. human spaceflight program.

Obama initially provoked hostility in Congress when he sought to end NASA's Constellation human spaceflight program and foster commercial carriers instead. The Constellation program was begun as part of President George W. Bush's plans to send astronauts to the space station, then to the moon and ultimately to Mars and beyond.

The Senate passed a modified version of the president's proposal in August that included another shuttle flight beyond what had already been authorized and plans for NASA to develop some spacecraft. It also supported a call by the president to extend the station's use from 2015 through at least 2020.

The House Science and Technology Committee had approved a bill earlier in the year that would have authorized significantly less for commercial development programs, but the House cleared the Senate version when it became clear there would not be enough time to settle the differences before the end of the session.

"For the sake of providing a degree of certainty, stability and clarity to the NASA workforce," said Bart Gordon, D-Tenn., chairman of the House Science and Technology Committee, "I felt it was better to consider a flawed bill than no bill at all as a new fiscal year begins."

The last reauthorization, a one-year law, had been enacted in 2008 (PL 110-422).

Obama laid out his proposal for NASA as part of his fiscal 2011 budget, following the receipt of a report on the future of manned spaceflight from an independent committee that he had established in 2009. The panel, known as the Augustine Committee, concluded that the Constellation program — which consisted of the *Ares* launch vehicles, the *Orion* crew vehicle and systems needed to explore the moon's surface by 2020 — had little chance of success under existing budget conditions.

The committee also noted that NASA had siphoned funding from other important programs, such as robotic exploration and technology development, in an effort to keep the elements of the exploration program on track. In light of the International Space Station's value for research and international collaboration, the panel said the administration should consider extending the life of the space station beyond 2015.

Obama's plan, released in February, proposed a number of controversial changes, including canceling the Constellation program and making significant investments in the commercial space industry to develop a vehicle to transport crew to the space station.

Citing the findings of the Augustine Committee, Obama called for aggressive investments in research and technology development, and for restoring funds for Earth sciences. He sought a hiatus until 2015 in NASA's vehicle, launch and launch-related activities and a decrease in the singular focus on the moon as a destination for exploration. He also agreed with the panel on extending the space station until at least 2020.

Following heavy public criticism, the president adjusted his plan in April. He proposed that NASA develop a new heavy-lift rocket and a crew rescue vehicle for astronauts on the space station based on the crew capsule that had been under development in the Constellation program.

The existing shuttle program had been scheduled to end after early 2011, making international partners dependent on Russia to service the space station during the five years before a new U.S. vehicle was expected to be ready.

HIGHLIGHTS

The following are some of the bill's main provisions:

● **Authorization.** The bill authorized $19 billion in fiscal 2011, $19.5 billion in fiscal 2012 and $20 billion in fiscal 2013. The amounts were equal to those requested by Obama.

● **Policy.** The legislation reiterated previous congressional prescriptions that NASA have a balanced and adequately funded portfolio of programs in human spaceflight and exploration, aeronautics research and development, and scientific research.

It also directed NASA to focus on designing and building elements of the manned space program within the amount budgeted rather than focusing on increasing performance, which the committee said would be "a fundamental change from NASA's recent history with the Constellation program and a number of previous NASA launch initiatives."

● **Human spaceflight.** The bill directed NASA to develop a new space launch system and continue work on a multipurpose crew vehicle as a follow-on to the shuttle and Constellation programs. The committee said that the legislation would provide a "government-owned and -operated capability" to support exploration missions and activities, and crew and cargo delivery to the space station "as a backup, if necessary, to commercially developed" vehicles.

BOX SCORE

BILL: S 3729 — PL 111-267

LEGISLATIVE ACTION:

Senate passed S 3729 (S Rept 111-278), amended, by unanimous consent Aug. 5.

House cleared the bill, 304-118, on Sept. 29.

President signed the bill Oct. 11.

The measure included:

‣ $8.9 billion for the space station through fiscal 2013 and authority, with international partners, to support full utilization of the space station through at least 2020.

‣ $1.6 billion in fiscal 2011 to support space shuttle flight operations and allow one additional shuttle flight, which the Senate committee said could be essential to ensure the space station's sustainability.

‣ $6.9 billion toward development of a heavy-lift rocket, beginning in fiscal 2011, sooner than Obama had proposed, with a goal of having the core capabilities operational in 2016. NASA was directed to try to make use of existing assets and capabilities from the shuttle and Constellation programs.

‣ $3.9 billion over three years for a multipurpose crew vehicle that would be fully operational in 2016 and would make use of concept, designs, prototypes and other materials developed for the *Orion* project.

‣ $1.6 billion for commercial development of space systems for manned crews and cargo.

● **Other priorities.** The authorization also included:

‣ $4.8 billion over three years for Earth sciences.

‣ $11 billion over three years for space science.

‣ $1.8 billion for aeronautics.

‣ $1.4 billion for space technology.

2010 LEGISLATIVE ACTION
HOUSE COMMITTEE

The House Science and Technology Committee approved a $58.4 billion NASA bill (HR 5781 — H Rept 111-576) by voice vote July 22.

The bill directed NASA to restructure its space exploration program to include a government-owned, government-operated crew transportation system as well as the development of a heavy-lift launch vehicle. It required that the program use work already done on vehicles such as *Orion* and *Ares I*, and it called for NASA to phase in a new crew transportation system by the end of 2015 to minimize the coming gap in human spaceflight.

The bill hewed less closely than the Senate version to the administration's plan, including less for the transition to commercial carriers. The bill would have authorized $50 million in fiscal 2011 for crew development and $14 million for a cargo demonstration program, plus another $100 million for a new loan guarantee program for commercial carriers. The Senate bill, which had been marked up a few days earlier, included $300 million for commercial cargo development and $312 million for commercial crew development and related studies.

An amendment by Suzanne M. Kosmas, D-Fla., to increase funding for crew development to $312 million and funding for commercial cargo to $300 million was rejected by voice vote. But the House panel brought its bill closer to the Senate measure by approving, also by voice vote, a Kosmas amendment to add another flight for the retiring space shuttle fleet.

SENATE COMMITTEE

The Senate Commerce, Science and Transportation Committee gave voice vote approval July 15 to a bill (S 3729 — S Rept 111-278) that had been worked out by a bipartisan group of senators in negotiations with the White House.

The measure preserved some rocket and capsule development at NASA but also authorized funding for the transition to commercial carriers. "We reached a sensible center . . . what I like to call the third way for NASA," said John D. Rockefeller IV, D-W.Va., the panel's chairman.

In its report accompanying the bill, the committee explained the priority it placed on using elements of the Constellation program. It noted that NASA had already invested about $9 billion in the Constellation program and said that to cancel it outright would risk the loss of design and hardware, and could cost $2.5 billion in contract termination fees. Instead, it said, the committee's bill directed NASA "to maximize the use of recent investments and existing capabilities while still enabling the agency to develop substantial new technologies, commercial and international partnerships, and innovative approaches to meet its overall goal of ensuring long-term human presence and expansion in space."

An administration official said the measure contained "the critical elements necessary for achieving the president's vision for NASA."

SENATE FLOOR

The Senate passed the bill by unanimous consent Aug. 5, shortly before leaving for the August recess. Kay Bailey Hutchison of Texas, the top Republican on the Commerce, Science and Transportation Committee, called it "a critical milestone that will boost America's human spaceflight program" and encouraged her House colleagues to act on the bill. The House had not passed its bill. But with bipartisan backing and the administration's support, the Senate measure appeared likely to become the vehicle for setting a new direction for NASA.

HOUSE FLOOR/FINAL ACTION

With only a few weeks left before the new fiscal year began Oct. 1, the House-Senate split on the pace of the proposed transition to commercial carriers remained unresolved. At that point, the question seemed likely to be settled by the appropriators in a stopgap funding measure that would not address policy changes.

But after weeks of negotiations between the House and Senate authorizers, the House accepted the Senate bill and cleared it by a vote of 304-118 on Sept. 29. *(House vote 561, p. H-196)*

Dissenters in the House still questioned bipartisan arguments that the bill would preserve NASA's human spaceflight activities and protect jobs. Gabrielle Giffords, D-Ariz., chairwoman of the House Science panel's Space and Aeronautics Subcommittee, called the jobs argument a "red herring" and noted that the funding would actually be set by subsequent appropriations. She argued that the measure would authorize funds for companies that had not yet proven their ability to develop spacecraft to transport crew and cargo. ■

Science, Technology Funds Extended

THE HOUSE CLEARED a three-year authorization of the primary federal science, technology, engineering and mathematics programs, after House Democrats were unable to advance a broader five-year measure. President Obama signed the science bill into law Jan. 4, 2011 (HR 5116 — PL 111-358).

The bill reauthorized a 2007 law (PL 110-69) known as the America COMPETES Act, which was designed to improve U.S. economic competitiveness by providing funding for innovation and education.

Specifically, the measure authorized $45.2 billion over three years for research programs at the National Science Foundation, the National Institute of Standards and Technology and the Energy Department, and for education and training in the so-called STEM fields of science, technology, engineering and mathematics.

The authorized spending was still subject to annual appropriations, which fell short of the authorization level.

Despite strong support for the underlying substance of the legislation, it took three tries and an unusual procedural device for House Democrats to circumvent Republican objections and pass the bill.

The Senate took its turn, reducing the time frame from five years in the House-passed bill to three years and adjusting some spending levels. The bill's supporters were anxious to get the measure to the president's desk before the end of the year out of concern that Republicans' greater clout in the next Congress would mean cutbacks in spending on science. As a result, the House accepted the Senate bill.

The bill authorized:

● **National Science Foundation.** $23.5 billion for the NSF, an independent federal agency that was the major source of federal funding for math and science research in colleges and universities. The bill included provisions directing the NSF to:

▸ Create a program to award competitive grants to support fundamental research in colleges and universities leading to transformative advances in manufacturing technologies, processes and enterprises, including research in nanotechnology, robotics, and advanced sensing and control techniques.

▸ Award grants to strengthen and expand scientific and technical education and training in advanced manufacturing, with the goal of helping to ensure a well-trained manufacturing workforce.

▸ Establish a National Center for Science and Engineering Statistics within the NSF to serve as a federal clearinghouse for the collection, interpretation, analysis and dissemination of objective data on science, engineering, technology, and research and development.

● **National Institute of Standards and Technology.** $2.9 billion over three years for NIST, an agency in the Commerce Department created to promote U.S. competitiveness by working with private industry to develop and apply technology, standards and measurements.

● **Energy Department.**

▸ $16.9 billion over three years for programs in the department's Office of Science, including basic energy science, advanced

---

BOX SCORE

BILL: HR 5116 — PL 111-358

....

LEGISLATIVE ACTION:

House passed HR 5116 (H Rept 111-478, Part 1), 262-150, on May 28.

Senate passed HR 5116, amended, by unanimous consent, on Dec. 17.

House cleared the bill, 228-130, on Dec. 21.

President signed the bill on Jan. 4, 2011.

---

scientific computing and fusion energy research. The Office of Science was the largest supporter of basic research in the physical sciences in the country, providing more than 40 percent of total funding for such research.

▸ $918 million over three years for the department's Advanced Research Projects Agency (ARPA-E), which was designed to fund projects that would reduce dependence on foreign energy imports, reduce energy consumption and improve energy efficiency in all sectors of the economy.

● **Education Department.**

▸ $225 million over three years for a program of competitive grants to help schools increase the number of teachers and students participating in international baccalaureate or advanced-placement courses in high-need schools.

▸ $12 million over three years for the Teachers for a Competitive Tomorrow program directed to programs for bachelor's and master's degrees in the STEM fields or in critical foreign languages.

● **Commerce Department.** Authorizations including $300 million over three years to award grants for the development of feasibility studies and plans for the construction of new science parks, or the renovation or expansion of existing parks. An additional $21 million over three years was authorized to enable the department to guarantee up to 80 percent of a loan used to finance the construction, expansion or renovation of science parks.

2010 LEGISLATIVE ACTION
HOUSE FLOOR

The House passed a five-year, $85.6 billion science programs reauthorization bill by a vote of 262-150 on May 28, after Democrats employed a rarely used parliamentary procedure to circumvent GOP maneuvering that had tripped up the measure on two previous attempts.

The chamber's Science and Technology Committee had approved the bill (HR 5116 — H Rept 111-478, Part 1) on April 28. Republicans objected mainly to the authorization levels, which they said were too high. The panel rejected several GOP amendments that would have reduced the authorization levels, while adopting an amendment by Bart Gordon, D-Tenn., chairman of the Science and Technology Committee, to reduce authorizations across the board by about 10 percent.

The bill appeared headed for passage in mid-May when it was abruptly pulled from the House floor after Republicans successfully offered a motion to recommit. The motion required that the bill be revised to freeze the authorizations at fiscal 2010 levels for most programs, that the length be reduced from five years to three years and that the authorization for the ARPA-E program be deleted.

The motion also included language prohibiting the use of funds to pay the salaries of government employees who were disciplined for viewing pornography on their work computers. That provision was

hard to oppose, and the motion was adopted, 292-126, on May 13. *(House vote 270, p. H-98)*

Republicans stymied a second effort on May 19 — this one to pass a pared-back, three-year version of the bill (HR 5325) — by denying the leadership the two-thirds majority needed for passage under a procedure known as suspension of the rules. The vote was 261-148, 12 votes short. The $48 billion amended version retained the anti-pornography language. *(House vote 277, p. H-100)*

On May 28, Gordon brought the five-year version of HR 5116 back to the floor and employed a parliamentary procedure known as "dividing the question" to force nine votes on the GOP motion to recommit, allowing members to vote on each of the items separately.

Lawmakers supported the anti-pornography language by a vote of 409-0, while rejecting, 181-234, a provision that would have reduced the authorization's length by two years. They also turned down amendments that would have struck from the bill a new manufacturing loan guarantee program and new multidisciplinary energy technology research centers, known as energy innovation hubs. The chamber also voted, 348-68, to prevent schools from receiving grants under the bill if they did not allow military recruiters on their campuses. *(House votes 329, 331 and 330, pp. H-118, H-120)*

SENATE FLOOR/FINAL ACTION

The Senate passed an amended version of the House bill by unanimous consent Dec. 17, and the House cleared it, 228-130, on Dec. 21. *(House vote 659, p. H-230)*

The revised measure covered three years instead of five and carried a reduced price tag of $45.2 billion. It included language barring salary payments for employees convicted of a criminal offense involving pornography. It also required the Government Accountability Office to study the programs funded under the bill and report to Congress by spring 2013.

Several provisions in the House-passed version were dropped, including the authorization for energy innovation hubs. On the other hand, the bill addressed agencies not in the earlier House version. For example, it included policy provisions related to NASA and the National Oceanic and Atmospheric Administration, and it authorized funds for certain Education Department programs.

The Senate Commerce, Science and Transportation Committee had approved a three-year bill (S 3605 — S Rept 111-363) on July 22 that would have authorized funding for the NSF and NIST but not the Energy or Education department programs.

While acknowledging that concessions were made "in light of the economic environment," Gordon said the bill preserved the intent of the original legislation. ∎

Chapter 14

TAXES

White House, Lawmakers Agree on Extension of Bush-Era Tax Cuts

WITH LESS THAN a week to go before the end of the Congress, lawmakers cleared an $857.8 billion tax and unemployment benefits package that extended George W. Bush-era tax cuts for all Americans for two years. President Obama signed the bill into law Dec. 17 (HR 4853 — PL 111-312).

The legislation reflected a deal that Obama had reached with Republican leaders in early December.

Most Democrats, particularly those in the House, were sharply critical of the agreement, saying Obama had capitulated to Republicans. They were especially angry that the deal extended tax breaks for the wealthy and revived the estate tax on the GOP's more-generous terms.

But Obama also got concessions: most significantly a 13-month extension of federal emergency unemployment benefits, a year-long reduction in employees' Social Security payroll taxes and other items that, together, were expected to give the economy a $180 billion boost over the following year.

At a signing ceremony for the bill, he praised leaders from both parties and called the legislation "a substantial victory for middle-class families across the country." He continued, "They're the ones hit hardest by the recession we've endured. They're the ones who need relief right now. And that's what is at the heart of this bill."

The bill did not include spending cuts or tax increases to pay for any of the provisions.

What drove the two sides into a deal was the looming Dec. 31 expiration of the 2001 and 2003 tax cuts (PL 107-16, PL 108-27). If nothing was done, income tax rates for everyone would have risen on Jan. 31 to the higher levels of 2001.

Democrats, including Obama, had long called for extending the tax breaks on income, capital gains and dividends only for individuals making less than $200,000 a year and families making less than $250,000 — and letting tax rates for wealthier Americans rise. But Republicans insisted the tax cuts should be made permanent for all income levels. They also had blocked efforts to extend unemployment benefits past Nov. 30 without corresponding cuts in other spending. (*Unemployment, p. 8-3; 2001 tax law, 2001 Almanac, p. 18-3; 2003 tax law, 2003 Almanac, p. 17-3*)

Democrats had been divided all year over what to do about the expiring tax cuts. Their leaders in both chambers had refused to vote — or undertake any serious debate — on an extension of the cuts before the midterm elections, leaving Obama with little leverage in November when Republicans won the House and made significant gains in the Senate for the next Congress.

After the election, the White House and a small bipartisan group of lawmakers began negotiations aimed at striking a deal.

BOX SCORE

BILL: HR 4853 — PL 111-312

LEGISLATIVE ACTION:

House passed HR 4853, 234-188, on Dec. 2.

Senate passed the bill, amended, 81-19, on Dec. 15.

House cleared HR 4853, 277-148, on Dec. 17.

President signed HR 4853 on Dec. 17.

But with Republicans refusing to settle for anything less than a full extension of all the tax cuts, House Democrats staged a largely symbolic vote, passing a version of the bill that would have made only the middle-income cuts permanent. Even Democratic leaders in the House acknowledged that the proposal could not get enough votes in the Senate.

Seeking a quick end to the standoff, Obama announced Dec. 6 that he had struck a deal with Senate Republicans. Liberal Democrats in the House erupted in anger, lambasting both the deal and the fact that they had been excluded from the negotiations. But an overwhelming vote for the measure in the Senate, and the impending expiration date, left the House with little choice. The chamber cleared the bill, with 112 Democrats voting no.

HIGHLIGHTS

The following are highlights of the tax and unemployment bill. In some cases, part of the cost is counted as outlays rather than lost revenue:

● **Individual tax cuts.** The bill extended provisions of the 2001 and 2003 tax laws for all income levels for 2011 and 2012 at a cost of $407.6 billion over 10 years — more than 45 percent of the bill's total price tag.

The extensions included:

▸ Lower marginal income tax rates, including continuation of the 10 percent bracket created under the 2001 law, as well as the retention of the reduced 25 percent, 28 percent, 33 percent and 35 percent brackets. (Estimated cost: $186.8 billion over 10 years.)

▸ The maximum child tax credit of $1,000, as well as provisions that expanded eligibility for the refundable portion. (Estimated cost: $71.7 billion over 10 years.)

▸ Relief from the so-called marriage penalty through an increase in the standard deduction for married couples filing jointly. (Estimated cost: $17.9 billion over 10 years.)

▸ Simplified rules and expanded eligibility for the earned-income tax credit and provisions that increased the income range at which the credit phased out for married couples. (Estimated cost: $8.9 billion over 10 years.)

● **Dividends and capital gains.** The two-year extension of individual tax cuts included the maximum rate of 15 percent on capital gains and dividends and the 0 percent rate for the two lowest brackets. (Estimated combined cost: $53.2 billion over 10 years.)

● **Alternative minimum tax (AMT).** A two-year "patch" increased the amount of income that was exempt from the AMT and allowed various non-refundable personal credits to be claimed against the tax. The exemption was set at $47,450 for individuals and $72,450

for couples filing jointly in 2010, increasing to $48,450 and $74,540, respectively, in 2011. The purpose was to prevent an estimated 25 million additional taxpayers from falling under the AMT, which was created to prevent wealthy taxpayers from escaping taxes. (Estimated cost: $136.7 billion over 10 years.)

● **Estate tax.** The estate tax, which lapsed at the end of 2009, was reinstated for two years at a 35 percent top rate for estates worth more than $5 million. The top rate in 2009 was 45 percent with a $3.5 million exemption. Without congressional action, the tax would have reverted to the pre-2001 level, with a 55 percent top rate and $1 million exemption. (Estimated cost: $68.1 billion over 10 years.) *(Estate tax, p. 14-7)*

● **'Tax extenders.'** The bill extended a number of expired tax provisions through fiscal 2011 at a total 10-year cost of $55.3 billion. They included the research and experimentation credit, a deduction for state and local sales taxes in lieu of state income taxes, an above-the-line deduction for qualified education expenses, temporary expensing rules for small businesses, and tax incentives for biodiesel and renewable diesel fuel. *(Tax extenders, p. 14-5)*

● **Unemployment insurance.** The bill extended, through the end of 2011, emergency federal unemployment insurance benefits for jobless workers who had exhausted their state benefits. The extension was retroactive to Nov. 30, the last time the benefits, which could provide as much as 99 weeks of assistance in some states, had expired. (Estimated cost: $56.5 billion over 10 years.)

● **Investment incentives.** In 2011, small businesses were allowed to deduct the full cost of investments in plants and equipment in the year the items were placed in service, rather than depreciating the cost over time. For 2012, they could write off up to 50 percent in the first year. (Estimated cost: $20.9 billion over 10 years.)

● **Payroll tax reduction.** Employees' half of the payroll tax was reduced to 4.2 percent from 6.2 percent in 2011. The employer's half was unchanged. Self-employed individuals were subject to a rate of 10.4 percent instead of 12.4 percent. (Estimated cost: $111.7 billion over 10 years.)

2010 LEGISLATIVE ACTION
HOUSE FLOOR

The House voted, 234-188, largely along partisan lines Dec. 2 in favor of a measure (HR 4853) to permanently extend the 2001 and 2003 Bush tax cuts for income up to $200,000 for individuals and $250,000 for couples filing jointly. Income above those levels would have been taxed at higher, 2001 rates beginning Jan. 1, 2011. *(House vote 604, p. H-210)*

Majority Leader Steny H. Hoyer, D-Md., acknowledged that the House-passed bill would not be the final product but would serve as the vehicle for a compromise being negotiated in the Senate. Twenty Democrats voted against the measure, while three Republicans supported it.

"We know that the White House has its own view, but this will be critically important as we move this issue forward," Hoyer said. He suggested that an extension of the tax breaks on higher incomes could be tied to legislation to extend jobless insurance benefits.

House Ways and Means ranking Republican Dave Camp of Michigan was more blunt, saying the Democrats' tax bill would not "see the light of day" in the Senate. "Let's face it. This bill is as misguided as it is futile," Camp said.

While the White House welcomed the House vote and reaffirmed Obama's position that extending the middle-class breaks "is the most important thing we can do for our economy right now," the administration acknowledged that the GOP would block any proposal that did not also include a multi-year extension of high-income tax cuts.

Four days later, Obama announced the agreement with GOP leaders. Liberal anger over the deal bubbled over Dec. 9, when a united bloc of House Democrats won approval of a nonbinding resolution calling on Speaker Nancy Pelosi, D-Calif., to keep the Obama-brokered package off the floor.

Obama criticized Democratic opposition to his plan. "I know there's some people in my own party and in the other party who would rather prolong this battle, even if we can't reach a compromise. But I'm not willing to let working families across this country become collateral damage for political warfare here in Washington. And I'm not willing to let our economy slip backwards just as we're pulling ourselves out of this devastating recession."

On Dec. 10, Obama brought former President Bill Clinton to the White House press room to pitch the legislation at a news conference, where he spoke at length.

SENATE FLOOR

The Senate adopted the Obama tax deal in a bipartisan vote of 81-19 on Dec. 15. The chamber had been expected to pass the bill, which was brought to the floor by Majority Leader Harry Reid, D-Nev., and Minority Leader Mitch McConnell, R-Ky. But the overwhelming vote was something of a surprise and added strong momentum for the House to clear the measure unchanged. *(Senate vote 276, p. S-56)*

McConnell warned that the deal was non-negotiable. "This agreement is not subject to being reopened," he said.

"This bill is not perfect," Reid said, "but it gives the middle class the boost they so desperately need."

The bill was only slightly changed from the original agreement. In an effort to end the standoff between House Democrats and the White House, leaders had included several renewable-energy incentives, including an extension of a popular renewable-energy grant program and an extension of ethanol subsidies.

The key vote came Dec. 13, when the Senate agreed 83-15, well above the 60 votes needed, to invoke cloture, thereby limiting debate on the bill. *(Senate vote 272, p. S-56)*

The Senate already had demonstrated that excluding the wealthy from the income tax extension was a non-starter. In a Saturday session on Dec. 4, senators rejected, 53-36, a motion to limit debate on a proposal offered by Finance Chairman Max Baucus, D-Mont., that would have made the income tax cuts permanent for individuals earning less than $200,000 and couples making less than $250,000. It would have reinstated the estate tax at 2009 levels and extended unemployment insurance benefits, as well as extending a slew of expiring tax provisions. *(Senate vote 258, p. S-53)*

The Senate also rejected cloture, 53-37, on an amendment by Charles E. Schumer, D-N.Y., that would have permanently extended the tax cuts on income under $1 million. *(Senate vote 259, p. S-53)*

Before passing the bill, the Senate rejected three last-minute efforts by opponents to get votes on what would have been bill-killing amendments.

Senators rejected, 47-52, an attempt by Tom Coburn, R-Okla., to get a vote on trimming $156 billion from the deficit. It turned down, 37-63, a proposal by Jim DeMint, R-S.C., to make the tax rate extensions permanent. Bernard Sanders, I-Vt., who spoke for hours against the measure Dec. 10, proposed to allow the top tax rates to rise in 2011, along with other changes. The Senate rejected Sanders' motion, 43-57. *(Senate votes 273, 274 and 275, p. S-56)*

FINAL ACTION

The House cleared the bill, 277-148, on Dec. 17, just after midnight, with the vote following a last-gasp attempt by liberals to derail the package. *(House vote 647, p. H-226)*

The session was expected to be marked by the swift — if grudging — clearing of the legislation, but many liberal Democrats refused to go down without a fight. Their policy and procedural objections created a chaotic atmosphere that forced the party's leaders to shift the voting well into the night.

Having surrendered on trying to pare the income tax cuts to apply only to the lower and middle classes, upset liberals turned their attention instead to the estate tax. Ultimately, the leadership allowed only one amendment, a proposal by Earl Pomeroy, D-N.D., to set a 45 percent tax rate on estates worth more than $3.5 million for individuals and $7 million for couples. The amendment was defeated, 194-233. *(House vote 646, p. H-224)*

Had the amendment been adopted, the altered bill would have re-turned to the Senate, where it was certain to have been rejected in light of the delicate negotiations on the issue that had brought Republicans and a smattering of conservative Democrats on board.

Before the vote on the amendment, Pelosi took to the floor to denounce the GOP estate tax rate for the wealthy. "Members will have to make up their minds as to how we go forward on the bill," she said, "but I hope that all of them in their consideration of it will vote for the Pomeroy amendment, which addresses the most egregious — with stiff competition, mind you, in this bill — the most egregious provision when it comes to fairness, reducing the deficit, and not creating jobs."

All of the yes votes on the amendment came from Democrats. The few dozen party members who voted no seemed to have come to the same conclusion as their colleagues in the Senate — that the bill included plenty of provisions that they supported, such as the 13-month extension of expanded jobless benefits and the AMT "patch," and that the clock was not on their side. ■

Tax Extenders Clear in Lame Duck

AFTER TRYING IN VAIN for months, law-makers cleared legislation during the lame-duck session that extended several dozen popular tax breaks that had expired at the end of 2009. The provisions became law as part of a large tax package that President Obama negotiated with Republican leaders in December. Obama signed the measure Dec. 17 (HR 4853 — PL 111-312).

The centerpiece of the bill was the continuation of 2001 and 2003 tax cuts enacted under President George W. Bush, but the measure also included a number of other items, among them a long list of so-called tax extenders — tax breaks that Congress usually renewed a year or two at a time. *(Tax package, p. 14-3)*

Lawmakers had considered a variety of proposals during the year to renew the extenders, but disagreements over what else to include in the legislation and how to pay for it doomed the efforts until the end of the year. The final bill had no offsets.

The House passed a version of the bill (HR 4213) in December 2009 that would have extended more than 40 expiring tax provisions at an estimated cost of $31 billion over 10 years. The bill would have been fully offset, mainly through a proposed change in the treatment of "carried interest" that had relatively little support in the Senate. *(2009 Almanac, p. 18-5)*

The bill grew significantly in the Senate, where it was packaged in March 2010 with extensions of a number of federal safety-net programs. House leaders generally agreed with the bill but made a few changes. By the time the bill arrived back in the Senate, Republicans were demanding offsets for unemployment and state aid provisions. Several attempts to pare back the bill failed, and Democrats eventually jettisoned the extenders and other provisions and cleared the bill with only the unemployment extension. *(Unemployment, p. 8-3)*

BOX SCORE

BILL: HR 4853 — PL 111-312

LEGISLATIVE ACTION:

Senate passed HR 4213, amended, 62-36, on March 10.

House passed HR 4213, amended, 215-204 and 245-171, on May 28.

House passed HR 4853, 234-188, on Dec. 2.

Senate passed HR 4853, amended, 81-19, on Dec. 15.

House cleared HR 4853, 277-148, on Dec. 17.

President signed HR 4853 on Dec. 17.

The extenders were finally rescued in the larger tax package.

HIGHLIGHTS

The business, energy and individual extenders renewed for fiscal 2010 and 2011 were expected to cost $55.3 billion over 10 years. Temporary investment incentives added $21.8 billion. The provisions included:

● **Business extensions.**

▸ The research and development tax credit, which generally covered 20 percent of a business' qualified research costs above a certain level. (Estimated cost: $13.3 billion over 10 years.)

▸ A provision that allowed restaurants and retail businesses to recover the costs of improvements over an accelerated, 15-year period. (Estimated cost: $3.6 billion over 10 years.)

▸ A provision that allowed financial service companies to defer U.S. taxes on income earned overseas from active financing operations until the income was transferred to the United States. (Estimated cost: $9.2 billion over 10 years.)

● **Energy extensions.**

▸ A production tax credit for biodiesel and biomass diesel, as well as a 10-cents-per-gallon credit for small agri-biodiesel producers. (Estimated cost: $2 billion over 10 years.)

▸ Tax credits for alcohol fuels and fuel mixtures. (Estimated cost: $4.9 billion over 10 years.)

● **Individual extensions.**

▸ Deduction of individual state and local sales taxes in lieu of itemized deductions for state and local income taxes. (Estimated cost: $5.5 billion over 10 years.)

▸ Deduction for qualified tuition and other education expenses. (Estimated cost: $1.2 billion over 10 years.)

▶ An above-the-line deduction for teachers' out-of-pocket classroom expenses. (Estimated cost: $390 million over 10 years.)

● **Investment incentives.**

▶ A full deduction for small businesses in 2011 for the cost of investments in plants and equipment in the year the items were placed in service, rather than depreciating the cost over time. For 2012, they could write off up to 50 percent in the first year. (Estimated cost: $20.9 billion over 10 years.)

2010 LEGISLATIVE ACTION
SENATE FLOOR

The Senate passed a greatly expanded version of the 2009 House bill (HR 4213) on March 10, after eight days of debate. The measure, which passed by a vote of 62-36, had a price tag in excess of $100 billion. (*Senate vote 48, p. S-12*)

Before passage, Majority Leader Harry Reid, D-Nev., twice mustered more than the 60 votes needed to halt a GOP filibuster. The motions to invoke cloture — first on the substance of the Senate amendment and then on the bill itself — were adopted 66-34 and 66-33. (*Senate votes 46 and 47, p. S-12*)

Like the original House bill, the measure would have provided about $31 billion in tax break extensions, including the research and development credit, the deduction for teachers' out-of-pocket expenses and incentives for producing biofuels. It also would have extended tax breaks for people affected by natural disasters, favorable tax treatment for farm equipment and tax incentives for investment in economically distressed areas.

In addition to the tax breaks, the bill would have extended federal unemployment benefits and health insurance subsidies for jobless workers, as well as flood insurance and small-business programs. Other provisions would have extended an adjustment for Medicare doctors' payment, given states a temporary increase in federal Medicaid payments and reauthorized satellite TV law. (*Small-business assistance, p. 7-4; physician payment rates, p. 9-15; flood insurance, p. 12-5*)

The Senate version of the bill grew out of a bipartisan package of tax breaks and longer-term economic safety-net extensions assembled by Finance Chairman Max Baucus, D-Mont., and the panel's ranking Republican, Charles E. Grassley of Iowa, although Grassley dropped his support because some of the extensions were for a longer period than he wanted.

The bill was modified from the original Baucus-Grassley proposal after rank-and-file Democrats complained that the earlier version would have extended tax breaks for companies by one year but extended federal unemployment benefits and health insurance subsidies for only three months.

Most of the extended tax breaks were offset with revenue-raisers, but the other provisions were not. The main offset was a curb on paper manufacturers' ability to claim a tax credit for a byproduct called "black liquor." Most paper companies never expected to claim the credit, but the fact that it was on the books meant that the Joint Committee on Taxation counted the proposed change as raising $21.7 billion over 10 years.

During the floor debate, the Senate:

▶ Rejected a bid to cap discretionary spending for four years beginning in fiscal 2011 at the levels in the fiscal 2010 budget resolution (S Con Res 13). The proposal by Jeff Sessions, R-Ala., and Claire McCaskill, D-Mo., fell 59-41, one vote shy of the 60 votes needed to overcome a budget point of order. (*Senate vote 42, p. S-11*)

▶ Rejected a proposal by Scott P. Brown, R-Mass., for a six-month cut in payroll taxes, paid for with unobligated funds from the 2009 economic stimulus law (PL 111-5). The amendment was defeated, 44-56, on a budget point of order. (*Senate vote 40, p. S-11*)

▶ Rejected, 22-78, on another point of order, a proposal by Richard M. Burr, R-N.C., to provide a national tax holiday paid for with stimulus funds. (*Senate vote 41, p. S-11*)

▶ Rejected an amendment by Patty Murray, D-Wash., to authorize a $1.3 billion, six-month extension of the emergency fund of the Temporary Assistance to Needy Families program. It also would have provided $1.3 billion for a summer jobs program for young people. The amendment fell, 55-45, on a procedural motion that required 60 votes. (*Senate vote 45, p. S-12*)

HOUSE FLOOR

With the electorate in an anti-deficit mood shared by many within their own party's caucus, House Democratic leaders were forced to sharply scale back their ambitions for the package, eking out enough votes on May 28 to send a smaller, $113 billion version of the bill back to the Senate.

The House passed the bill by adopting two amendments. Members agreed to tax-cut and social-spending extensions by a vote of 215-204, and adopted the change to Medicare doctor payments, 245-171. (*House votes 324, p. H-116, and 325, p. H-118*)

To get the necessary votes, House leaders trimmed what had swollen to a $200 billion package, unveiled the week before by Baucus and House Ways and Means Chairman Sander M. Levin, D-Mich. The cuts came from the social safety-net extensions. The tax proposals were offset, but the extensions of Medicare payment rates and unemployment benefits were not.

The bill included new revenue-raisers, in part to replace the "black liquor" provision, which had been used to help pay for the new health care overhaul (PL 111-148, PL 111-152). (*Health care overhaul, p. 9-3*)

The most controversial revenue generator was a proposed change in the tax treatment of "carried interest" earned by real estate investors, venture capitalists and private equity fund managers. Under the bill, 50 percent of carried-interest earnings, which were taxed as capital gains under existing law, would have been taxed at the higher rate applicable to ordinary income until 2013, when 75 percent would be taxed at the higher rate. Republicans argued that the provision would discourage long-term investment, particularly in startup companies.

Other offsets included changes designed to limit corporations' ability to use foreign tax credits and new limits on the ability of small professional-service companies structured as S corporations to avoid the self-employment taxes that they would pay if their earnings were treated as wages instead of profits.

In response to the massive, ongoing oil leak caused by the April explosion of a Deepwater Horizon oil rig in the Gulf of Mexico, the revised bill proposed to increase the per-barrel tax for the Oil Spill Liability Trust Fund from 8 cents to 34 cents. (*Oil spill, p. 12-6*)

SENATE FLOOR

Despite an appeal from the president and the new, pared-back House proposal, Senate Democrats were unable to break a deadlock over the bill. Reid pulled the measure from the floor June 24 after failing to garner 60 votes for a motion to invoke cloture, which would have ended a

GOP filibuster. The vote was 57-41. *(Senate vote 200, p. S-42)*

"This process has been abused," Reid charged after the vote, saying the ball was now in Republicans' court.

Minority Leader Mitch McConnell, R-Ky., dismissed the new proposal, as he had previous versions, calling it the "deficit extenders bill." Democrats "will not pass a bill unless it adds to the deficit," McConnell charged.

Reid and Baucus had begun by shopping a $140 billion version of the bill, but in a test vote June 16, the Senate refused, 45-52, to waive a procedural objection to the leadership plan. Twelve members of the Democratic Caucus voted "no." *(Senate vote 190, p. S-40)*

Hours later, Baucus released a $118 billion version, which won additional support from Democrats but still left the leaders short of the 60 votes they needed. The Senate rejected a cloture motion, 56-40, on June 17. *(Senate vote 194, p. S-41)*

Baucus continued modifying provisions to woo a handful of moderates, but none of them budged.

Reid ultimately stripped the bill of all but the unemployment provisions. The Senate passed it, 59-39, on July 20; the House cleared it, 272-152, two days later, and it was signed hours after that (HR 4213 — PL 111-157). *(Senate vote 215, p. S-45; House vote 423, p. H-148)*

FINAL ACTION

Although the Senate action appeared to end hopes of passing the extensions, most of the provisions were revived and became law at the end of the year, thanks to the impending expiration of the Bush-era income tax breaks. The inclusion of the tax extenders in the package was relatively noncontroversial. The debate focused largely on other issues, especially on whether the income tax cuts should be extended for higher-income taxpayers.

The Senate passed the package, 81-19, on Dec. 15. The House cleared the measure, 277-148, on Dec. 17. *(Senate vote 276, p. S-56; House vote 647, p. H-226)* ■

Congress Resuscitates Estate Tax

CONGRESS REVIVED THE estate tax for two years as part of a year-end package that centered on an extension of expiring income tax cuts and unemployment benefits. President Obama signed the bill into law Dec. 17 (HR 4853 — PL 111-312).

The bill restored the tax for 2011 and 2012 at a top rate of 35 percent of the value of estates in excess of $5 million per spouse. It also set a 35 percent tax rate on gifts of $1 million or more given before death in 2010 and unified the gift tax with the estate tax in 2011.

The 2001 tax law, enacted under President George W. Bush, gradually phased out the estate tax until it vanished for one year in 2010. However, the 2001 law (PL 107-16) was due to expire Dec. 31. After that, the tax was set to reappear at the 55 percent top rate that had been in effect prior to 2001, with a per-person exemption of $1 million. *(2001 law, 2001 Almanac, p. 18-3)*

Most Democrats and virtually all Republicans opposed that outcome, but they had long been at odds over how to avoid it. Republicans railed year after year against what they called the "death tax" and tried repeatedly to make the repeal permanent.

The House passed a bill (HR 4154) at the end of 2009 that would have preserved the tax at 2009 levels, with a top rate of 45 percent and an exemption for the first $3.5 million in the value of an estate. *(House bill, 2009 Almanac, p. 18-3)*

The legislation languished in the Senate through most of 2010 because of a standoff within the Democratic Caucus. Most in the party preferred to pass something similar to the House bill. But others, including Blanche Lincoln of Arkansas, wanted lower rates and a larger exemption. She and Republican Jon Kyl of Arizona worked out a compromise that would have set the top rate at 35 percent and applied

BOX SCORE

BILL: HR 4853 — PL 111-312

LEGISLATIVE ACTION:

House passed HR 4853, 234-188, on Dec. 2.

Senate passed HR 4853, amended, 81-19, on Dec. 15.

House cleared HR 4853, 277-148, on Dec. 17.

President signed HR 4853 on Dec. 17.

it to the value of estates in excess of $5 million per person.

The plan stalled when Senate leaders decided to hold off on addressing all the expiring Bush-era tax cuts, including lower income tax rates, until after the November election. Senators remained deadlocked after the election, and with the clock ticking and lower income tax rates about to expire, Obama negotiated an $857.8 billion tax and unemployment benefits package with Republican leaders.

Liberal House Democrats were furious — first, that the plan included the Lincoln-Kyl compromise on the estate tax when Obama and most Democrats had long advocated letting the rate rise and the threshold decline; second, that the deal, announced on Dec. 6, extended lower tax rates for the wealthy; and third, that they had been shut out of the negotiations.

On Dec. 9, a solid bloc of House Democrats approved a nonbinding resolution calling on Speaker Nancy Pelosi, D-Calif., not to bring the package to the floor.

But after a surprisingly lopsided 81-19 Senate vote for the bill — and a vow from the GOP that a change in the estate tax provision would kill the deal — House Democrats had little choice. The leadership allowed only one floor amendment, a proposal by Earl Pomeroy, D-N.D. Similar to the provision in the House's 2009 bill, the amendment would have set a 45 percent rate on individuals' estates worth more than $3.5 million and couples' estates worth more than $7 million. The amendment, which Pelosi urged her caucus to back, was defeated 194-233; all of the support came from Democrats. *(Senate vote 276, p. S-56; House vote 646, p. H-224)*

The House then cleared the bill, 277-148, after midnight Dec. 17, with 112 Democrats voting nay. *(House vote 647, p. H-226)* ■

Chapter 15

Transportation & Infrastructure

FAA Multi-Year Bill Remains Elusive; Short-Term Extension Clears

LAWMAKERS CAME CLOSE to a final deal on a Federal Aviation Administration (FAA) reauthorization bill before the August recess. But several last-minute disputes once again sidetracked the long-stalled bill, and Congress left for the year with the agency operating on a short-term extension (HR 6473 —PL 111-329) good through March 11, 2011.

The FAA had been operating under a string of temporary extensions since the last full reauthorization of aviation programs and the taxes and fees that fed the aviation trust fund (PL 108-176) expired at the end of fiscal 2007. *(Last reauthorization, 2003 Almanac, p. 20-3)*

The Senate passed a two-year version of the new reauthorization bill in March, amended to reflect a version approved by a Senate committee in 2009. The House took up the bill and passed it, after substituting language from a three-year FAA authorization measure and a pilot training bill, both of which it had passed in 2009. *(2009 action, 2009 Almanac, p. 19-3)*

There was no formal conference, but transportation committee members from both chambers negotiated informally without reaching a final agreement. At the end of the regular session, Senate Majority Leader Harry Reid, D-Nev., used the unfinished bill as a vehicle to enact other, unrelated provisions increasing Medicaid assistance to states and appropriating supplemental funds to avoid teacher layoffs (PL 111-226). *(Supplemental, p. 2-18)*

The key stumbling blocks in the negotiations included differences over raising the maximum excise tax on passenger tickets, expanding long-distance flights to and from Reagan Washington National Airport, curtailing antitrust immunity for airline alliances and changing the treatment of express carriers such as FedEx under labor laws.

With primary responsibility over civil aviation, the FAA included in its portfolio safety regulation, air traffic management, making grants to airports through the Airport Improvement Program and subsidizing services at small airports. While many FAA programs could continue without a reauthorization in place, the Airport Improvement Program and aviation trust fund revenue collection required an authorization bill.

2010 LEGISLATIVE ACTION
SENATE FLOOR

The Senate passed HR 1586, which had originally been a tax bill, by a vote of 93-0 on March 22, after inserting provisions similar to a bill (S 1451) approved by the Commerce, Science and Transportation Committee in 2009. The Senate-passed bill provided for a total FAA authorization of $34.5 billion for fiscal 2010 and 2011. *(Senate vote 61, p. S-16)*

Among its hundreds of provisions, the bill included language to:

BOX SCORE	**BILLS:** HR 1586; HR 6473 — PL 111-329

LEGISLATIVE ACTION:

Senate passed HR 1586, amended, 93-0, on March 22.

House passed HR 1586, amended with the text of HR 915 and HR 3371, 276-145, on March 25.

House passed HR 6473 by voice vote on Dec. 2.

Senate cleared HR 6473 by unanimous consent on Dec. 18.

President signed HR 6473 on Dec. 22.

▸ Establish a pilot program that would allow up to six airports to collect passenger ticket fees with no statutory limit.

▸ Increase the excise tax on non-commercial aviation jet fuel to 35.9 cents per gallon from the existing 21.8 cents as a way to help fund the modernization of the air traffic control system through the Next Generation Air Transport System, or NextGen.

A special account created within the airport and airway trust fund would provide $400 million per year to fund NextGen implementation, with the funds coming from the jet fuel tax.

The bill contained numerous provisions aimed at strengthening the organizational structure and accelerating the pace of implementing the NextGen program.

▸ Require pilots hired by the airlines to have 800 hours of flight experience. Under existing law, captains had to have 1,500 hours, while first officers needed 250 hours.

▸ Require the FAA to establish a centralized database to make pilots' performance histories more accessible to the airlines. Pilots unions strongly opposed the idea, saying it could hurt pilots' careers. The House bill contained similar provisions.

▸ Require the FAA to make random, unannounced, on-site inspections of regional air carriers annually. The House bill would have required the Transportation Department to review FAA oversight of air carriers.

▸ Provide for a wide range of passenger rights, including limits to waiting time on the tarmac. However, most of the provisions were limited to studies, reviews, disclosure or notification. The FAA implemented some of them by rulemaking.

▸ Establish an Aviation Safety Whistleblower Investigation Office within the FAA. The House bill had a similar provision.

Before passing the bill, the Senate rejected a number of unrelated amendments that were intended to call attention to the government's overall fiscal situation. The Senate:

▸ Rejected, 56-40, on a procedural motion, an amendment by Jeff Sessions, R-Ala., and Claire McCaskill, D-Mo., that would have imposed discretionary spending limits for three years beginning in fiscal 2011. Another, by Arkansas Democrat Mark Pryor, would have imposed discretionary spending limits based on the cap in the president's fiscal 2011 budget. It was defeated, 27-70, also on a procedural motion. Sixty votes were needed to waive budget points of order against both amendments. *(Senate votes 57, 58, p. S-15)*

▸ Rejected, 41-56, an amendment by James M. Inhofe, R-Okla., to limit non-security-related spending. *(Senate vote 59, p. S-15)*

▸ Rejected, 26-70, an amendment by John McCain, R-Ariz., to bar earmarks in years when there was a federal deficit. *(Senate vote 60, p. S-15)*

No Progress on Surface Transportation Bill

THE LACK OF BROAD agreement on a new revenue source for infrastructure spending stymied hopes for a new surface transportation bill and left highway and other surface transportation programs operating under a short-term extension of the last full reauthorization.

The only surface transportation measure introduced in the 111th Congress was a House draft bill, which did not see action after a Transportation and Infrastructure subcommittee marked it up in 2009. No draft was introduced in the Senate. (House draft, 2009 Almanac, p. 19-5)

The House draft would have authorized $337.4 billion for highways, $99.8 billion for public transit, $12.6 billion for highway and motor carrier safety and $50 billion for high-speed rail over six years. It did not include any revenue mechanisms, which would have had to be written by the House Ways and Means Committee.

Once the Obama administration signaled that it would not endorse a motor fuels tax increase in the midst of a struggling economy, the House draft was effectively mothballed, and the Senate never took up legislation of its own. Instead, substantive policy discussions revolved around how long the existing law should be extended to give lawmakers more time to figure out how to pay for the next bill.

The White House released a set of principles intended to inform the writing of the next surface transportation bill, but the document did not contain any proposals about how to raise revenue to help fund a multi-year bill and backstop the flagging Highway Trust Fund.

The last full reauthorization, enacted in 2005 and known as SAFETEA-LU, expired Sept. 30, 2009. Congress extended the law through the end of 2010 as part of a jobs bill (PL 111-147). The last short-term extension of the year was enacted as part of a continuing appropriations measure (PL 111-312) that was good through March 4, 2011. (Appropriations overview, p. 2-3)

HOUSE FLOOR

The House passed HR 1586 by a vote of 276-145 on March 25 after substituting the text of its 2009 reauthorization bill (HR 915). The measure would have authorized $53.5 billion for FAA programs in fiscal years 2010 through 2012. The rule for floor debate incorporated a separate bill (HR 3371) aimed at setting stricter safety standards for pilots in the wake of a series of accidents by regional carriers. (House vote 190, p. H-68)

The bill included provisions to:

▶ Increase the maximum passenger fee that airports could tack onto the price of a ticket to $7 per ticket from $4.50 per ticket under existing law. The commercial carriers argued against any change that would raise fare prices beyond the amounts they set.

▶ Increase the excise tax on general aviation jet fuel to 35.9 cents per gallon, as in the Senate bill, but the House measure also proposed to increase the tax on general aviation gasoline from 19.3 cents a gallon to 24.1 cents per gallon.

▶ Require that every pilot in an airline cockpit have an Airline Transport Pilot certificate, which required, among other things, 1,500 hours of flight time. The mandate was stiffer than that in the House bill, but it allowed certain classroom training to count under the requirement. The bill also included many other training requirements.

▶ Establish a centralized database of pilot records with more extensive information than under the Senate plan.

▶ Allow an additional 12 slots at Ronald Reagan Washington National Airport, 10 of them for flights beyond a 1,250-mile perimeter. The 10 would replace existing short-haul slots. Existing law limited to 24 the number of flights per day that could go beyond the perimeter. The Senate had no similar provision.

In the longstanding dispute over expanding long-distance flights to and from Reagan Airport, lawmakers from Western states sought more direct flights home from the airport, a little more than four miles from the Capitol, as opposed to Dulles International Airport, which was about 26 miles away. But lawmakers from Virginia and Maryland, whose constituents feared that an expansion — especially of long-distance flights — would mean more noise and disruption, fought the addition of flights.

▶ Change labor laws for express carriers such as FedEx, making it easier for the company's workers to unionize, a change strongly backed by the company's chief rival, UPS. Under existing law, UPS was treated as a trucking company and was covered by the 1935 National Labor Relations Act (PL 74-198), which allowed employees to organize locally. By contrast, FedEx was considered an express carrier, which put it under the 1926 Railway Labor Act (PL 69-257). The act allowed workers to organize only nationally, a more difficult task.

UPS argued that the existing law gave FedEx an unfair competitive advantage. The Teamsters union and the AFL-CIO's Transportation Trades Department also supported the change, but FedEx was adamantly opposed. The two Republican senators from FedEx's home state of Tennessee, Lamar Alexander and Bob Corker, threatened to block any bill that would alter the labor laws affecting the company, and Corker did hold up the legislation for a time in the Senate.

▶ Repeal the antitrust immunity granted to certain airline alliances. The alliances generally involved several U.S. and international airlines, and enabled them to collaborate on prices and schedules. The House bill would have ended the antitrust status within three years, after which an alliance would have to reapply for the status under new terms written by the Transportation Department. The Senate bill did not address the issue.

Participating airlines opposed the plan, arguing that the ability to assist passengers in booking between airlines on international flights made them more competitive. They said the proposed sunset was unwarranted government intrusion and could bite substantially into their profits on international routes. But advocates said the antitrust protection hurt competition among airlines and could enable an alliance to obtain a monopoly on certain routes.

▶ Bar Congress from considering legislation that used less than 90 percent of the revenue in the aviation trust fund annually. Existing law required that all of the funds be spent each year. The Senate bill continued the 100 percent requirement.

▶ Make numerous changes, many of them similar to those in the House version, to the organization of NextGen, including strengthening the role of the director. ■

Appendix A

CONGRESS AND ITS MEMBERS

Glossary of Congressional Terms

Act — The term for legislation once it has passed both chambers of Congress and has been signed by the president or passed over his veto, thus becoming law. Also used in parliamentary terminology for a bill that has been passed by one house and engrossed. *(Also see engrossed bill.)*

Adjournment sine die — Adjournment without a fixed day for reconvening; literally, "adjournment without a day." Usually used to connote the final adjournment of a session of Congress. A session can continue until noon Jan. 3 of the following year, when, under the 20th Amendment to the Constitution, it automatically terminates. Both chambers must agree to a concurrent resolution for either chamber to adjourn for more than three days.

Adjournment to a day certain — Adjournment under a motion or resolution that fixes the next time of meeting. Under the Constitution, neither chamber can adjourn for more than three days without the concurrence of the other. A session of Congress is not ended by adjournment to a day certain.

Amendment — A proposal by a member of Congress to alter the language, provisions or stipulations in a bill or in another amendment. An amendment usually is printed, debated and voted upon in the same manner as a bill.

Amendment in the nature of a substitute — Usually an amendment that seeks to replace the entire text of a bill by striking out everything after the enacting clause and inserting a new version of the bill. An amendment in the nature of a substitute can also refer to an amendment that replaces a large portion of the text of a bill.

Appeal — A member's challenge of a ruling or decision made by the presiding officer of the chamber. A senator can appeal to members of the Senate to override the decision. If carried by a majority vote, the appeal nullifies the chair's ruling. In the House, the decision of the Speaker traditionally has been final; seldom are there successful appeals to the members to reverse the Speaker's stand. To appeal a ruling is considered an attack on the Speaker.

Appropriations bill — A bill that gives legal authority to spend or obligate money from the Treasury. The Constitution disallows money to be drawn from the Treasury "but in Consequence of Appropriations made by Law."

By congressional custom, an appropriations bill originates in the House. It is not supposed to be considered by the full House or Senate until a related measure authorizing the funding is enacted. An appropriations bill grants the actual budget authority approved by the authorization bill, though not necessarily the full amount permissible under the authorization.

If the 12 regular appropriations bills are not enacted by the start of the fiscal year, Congress must pass a stopgap spending bill or the departments and agencies covered by the unfinished bills must shut down.

About half of all budget authority, notably that for Social Security and interest on the federal debt, does not require annual appropriations; those programs exist under permanent appropriations. *(Also see authorization bill, budget authority, budget process and supplemental appropriations bill.)*

Authorization bill — Basic, substantive legislation that establishes or continues the legal operation of a federal program or agency either indefinitely or for a specific period of time, or which sanctions a particular type of obligation or expenditure. Under the rules of both chambers, appropriations for a program or agency may not be considered until the program has been authorized, although this requirement is often waived. An authorization sets the maximum amount of funds that can be given to a program or agency, although sometimes it merely authorizes "such sums as may be necessary." *(Also see backdoor spending authority.)*

Backdoor spending authority — Budget authority provided in legislation outside the normal appropriations process. The most common forms of backdoor spending are borrowing authority, contract authority, entitlements and loan guarantees that commit the government to payments of principal and interest on loans made by banks or other private lenders. Loan guarantees result in actual outlays only when there is a default by the borrower.

In some cases, such as interest on the public debt, a permanent appropriation is provided that becomes available without further action by Congress.

Bills — Most legislative proposals before Congress are in the form of bills and are designated according to the chamber in which they originate — HR in the House of Representatives or S in the Senate — and by a number assigned in the order in which they are introduced during the two-year period of a congressional term.

"Public bills" address general questions and become public laws if they are cleared by Congress and signed by the president. "Private bills" deal with individual matters, such as claims against the government, immigration and naturalization cases, or land titles, and become private laws if cleared and signed. *(Also see private bill, resolution.)*

Bills introduced — In both the House and Senate, any number of members may join in introducing a single bill or resolution. The first member listed is the sponsor of the bill, and all subsequent members listed are cosponsors.

Many bills are committee bills and are introduced under the name of the chairman of the committee or subcommittee. All appropriations bills fall into this category. A committee frequently holds hearings on a number of related bills and may agree to one of them or to an entirely new bill. *(Also see clean bill.)*

Bills referred — After a bill is introduced, it is referred to the committee or committees that have jurisdiction over the subject with which the bill is concerned. Under the standing rules of the House and Senate, bills are referred by the Speaker in the House and by the presiding officer in the Senate. In practice, the House and Senate parliamentarians act for these officials and refer the vast majority of bills. *(Also see discharge a committee.)*

Borrowing authority — Statutory authority that permits a federal agency to incur obligations and make payments for specified purposes with borrowed money.

Budget — The document sent to Congress by the president early each year estimating government revenue and expenditures for the ensuing fiscal year.

Budget Act — The common name for the Congressional Budget and Impoundment Control Act of 1974, which established the current budget process and created the Congressional Budget Office. The act also put limits on presidential authority to spend appropriated money. It has undergone several major revisions since 1974. *(Also see budget process.)*

Budget authority — Authority for federal agencies to enter into obligations that result in immediate or future outlays. The basic forms of budget authority are appropriations, contract authority and borrowing authority. Budget authority may be classified by (1) the period of availability (one-year, multiple-year or without a time limitation), (2) the timing of congressional action (current or permanent) or (3) the manner of determining the amount available (definite or indefinite). *(Also see appropriations bill, outlays.)*

Budget process — The annual budget process was created by the Congressional Budget and Impoundment Control Act of 1974, with a timetable that was modified in 1990. Under the law, the president must submit his proposed budget by the first Monday in February. Congress is supposed to complete an annual budget resolution by April 15, setting guidelines for congressional action on spending and tax measures. *(Also see pay-as-you-go rules.)*

Budget resolution — A concurrent resolution that is adopted by both chambers of Congress and sets a strict ceiling on discretionary budget authority, along with nonbinding recommendations about how the spending should be allocated. The budget resolution may also contain "reconciliation instructions" requiring authorizing and tax-writing committees to propose changes in existing law to meet deficit reduction goals. If more than one committee is involved, the Budget Committee in each chamber bundles those proposals, without change, into a reconciliation bill and sends it to the floor. The budget resolution is a congressional document and is not sent to the president. *(Also see reconciliation.)*

By request — A phrase used when a senator or representative introduces a bill at the request of an executive agency or private organization but does not necessarily endorse the legislation.

Calendar — An agenda or list of business awaiting possible action by each chamber. The House uses four legislative calendars. They are the Discharge, House, Private and Union calendars. *(Also see individual calendar listings.)*

In the Senate, all legislative matters reported from committee go on one calendar. They are listed there in the order in which committees report them or the Senate places them on the calendar, but they may be called up out of order by the majority leader, either by obtaining unanimous consent of the Senate or by a motion to call up a bill. The Senate also has one non-legislative calendar, which is used for treaties and nominations. *(Also see Executive Calendar.)*

Call of the calendar — Senate bills that are not brought up for debate by a motion, unanimous consent or a unanimous consent agreement are brought before the Senate for action when the calendar listing them is "called." Bills must be called in the order listed. Measures considered by this method usually are non-controversial, and debate on the bill and any proposed amendments is limited to five minutes for each senator.

Chamber — The meeting place for the membership of either the House or the Senate; also the membership of the House or Senate meeting as such.

Chief administrative officer — An elected officer of the House who, under House rules, has operational and functional responsibility for matters assigned by the House Administration Committee. The office of the chief administrative officer was established under a 1995 change to House rules and replaced the office of director of non-legislative and financial services.

Clean bill — Frequently after a committee has finished a major revision of a bill, one of the committee members, usually the chairman, will assemble the changes and what is left of the original bill into a new measure and introduce it as a "clean bill." The revised measure, which is given a new number, is referred back to the committee, which reports it to the floor for consideration. This often is a time saver, as committee-recommended changes in a clean bill do not have to be considered and voted on by the chamber. Reporting a clean bill also protects committee amendments that could be subject to points of order concerning germaneness.

Clerk of the House — An officer of the House of Representatives who supervises its records and legislative business.

Cloture — The process by which a filibuster can be ended in the Senate other than by unanimous consent. A motion for cloture can apply to any measure before the Senate, including a proposal to change the chamber's rules. To end a filibuster, the cloture motion must obtain the votes of three-fifths of the entire Senate membership (60 if there are no vacancies), except when the filibuster is against a proposal to amend the standing rules of the Senate; then a two-thirds vote of senators present and voting is required.

The cloture request is put to a roll call vote one hour after the Senate meets on the second day following introduction of the motion. If approved, cloture limits each senator to one hour of debate. The bill or amendment in question comes to a final vote after 30 hours of consideration, including debate time and the time it takes to conduct roll calls, quorum calls and other procedural motions. *(Also see filibuster.)*

Committee — A division of the House or Senate that prepares legislation for action by the parent chamber or makes investigations as directed by the parent chamber.

There are several types of committees. Most standing committees are divided into subcommittees, which study legislation, hold hearings and report bills, with or without amendments, to the full committee. Only the full committee can report legislation for action by the House or Senate. *(Also see standing, oversight, and select or special committees.)*

Committee of the Whole — The working title of what is formally "The Committee of the Whole House [of Representatives] on the State of the Union." The membership is composed of all House members sitting as a committee. Any 100 members who are present on the floor of the chamber to consider legislation constitute a quorum of the committee.

Technically, the Committee of the Whole considers only bills directly or indirectly appropriating money, authorizing appropriations, or involving taxes or charges on the public. Because the Committee of the Whole need number only 100 representatives, a quorum is more readily attained and legislative business is expedited. Before 1971, members' positions were not individually recorded on votes taken in the Committee of the Whole. Under a rules change in the 110th Congress, delegates are permitted to vote.

When the full House resolves itself into the Committee of the Whole, it replaces the Speaker with a "chairman." A measure is debated and amendments may be proposed, with votes on amendments as needed. (Also see five-minute rule.)

When the committee completes its work on the measure, it dissolves itself by "rising." The Speaker returns, and the chairman of the Committee of the Whole reports to the House that the committee's work has been completed. At this time, members may demand a roll call vote on any amendment adopted in the Committee of the Whole. The final vote is on passage of the legislation. (Also see delegate.)

Committee veto — A requirement added to a few statutes directing that certain policy directives by an executive department or agency be reviewed by certain congressional committees before they are implemented. Under common practice, the government department or agency and the committees involved are expected to reach a consensus before the directives are carried out.

Concurrent resolution — A concurrent resolution, designated H Con Res or S Con Res, must be adopted by both chambers, but it is not sent to the president for approval and, therefore, does not have the force of law. A concurrent resolution, for example, is used to fix the time for adjournment of a Congress. It is also used to express the sense of Congress on a foreign policy or domestic issue. The annual budget resolution is a concurrent resolution.

Conference — A meeting between representatives of the House and the Senate to reconcile differences between the two chambers on provisions of a bill. House conferees are appointed by the Speaker; Senate conferees are appointed by the presiding officer of the Senate.

A majority of the conferees for each chamber must agree on a compromise, reflected in a "conference report," before the final bill can go back to both chambers for approval. When the conference report goes to the floor, it is difficult to amend. If it is not approved by both chambers, the bill may go back to conference under certain situations, or a new conference may be convened. Many rules and informal practices govern the conduct of conference committees.

Bills that are passed by both chambers do not have to be sent to conference. Either chamber may "concur" with the other's amendments, completing action on the legislation, or they may further amend the measure and send it back to the other chamber. Sometimes leaders of the committees of jurisdiction work out an informal compromise instead of having a formal conference. (Also see custody of the papers.)

Confirmations — (See nominations.)

Congressional Record — The daily printed account of proceedings in both the House and Senate chambers, showing substantially verbatim debate and statements and a record of floor action. Highlights of legislative and committee action are given in a Daily Digest section of the Record, and members are entitled to have their extraneous remarks printed in an appendix known as "Extension of Remarks." Members may edit and revise remarks made on the floor during debate.

The Congressional Record provides a way to distinguish remarks spoken on the floor of the House and Senate from undelivered speeches. In the Senate, all speeches, articles and other matter that members insert in the Record without actually reading them on the floor are set off by large black dots, or bullets. However, a loophole allows a member to avoid the bulleting if he or she delivers any portion of the speech in person. In the House, undelivered speeches and other material are printed in a distinctive typeface. The record is also available in electronic form. (Also see Journal.)

Congressional terms of office — Terms normally begin on Jan. 3 of the year following a general election. Terms are two years for representatives and six years for senators. Representatives elected in special elections are sworn in for the remainder of a term. Under most state laws, a person may be appointed to fill a Senate vacancy and serve until a successor is elected; the successor serves until the end of the term applying to the vacant seat.

Continuing resolution — A joint resolution, cleared by Congress and signed by the president, to provide new budget authority for federal agencies and programs whose regular appropriations bills have not been enacted. Also known as CRs or continuing appropriations, continuing resolutions are used to keep agencies operating when, as often happens, Congress does not finish the regular appropriations process by the start of the new fiscal year.

The CR usually specifies a maximum rate at which an agency may incur obligations, based on the rate of the prior year, the president's budget request, or an appropriations bill passed by either or both chambers of Congress but not yet enacted.

A CR can be a short-term measure that funds programs temporarily until the regular appropriations bill is enacted, or it can carry spending for the balance of the fiscal year in lieu of the unfinished appropriations bills.

Contract authority — Budget authority contained in an authorization bill that permits the federal government to enter into contracts or other obligations for future payments from funds not yet appropriated by Congress. The assumption is that funds will be provided in a subsequent appropriations act. (Also see budget authority.)

Correcting recorded votes — Rules prohibit members from changing their votes after the result has been announced. Occasionally, however, a member may announce hours, days or months after a vote has been taken that he or she was "incorrectly recorded." In the Senate, a request to change one's vote almost always receives unanimous consent, as long as it does not change the outcome. In the House, members are prohibited from changing votes if they were tallied by the electronic voting system.

Cosponsor — (See bills introduced.)

Current services estimates — Estimated budget authority and outlays for federal programs and operations for the forthcoming fiscal year based on continuation of existing levels of service without policy changes but with adjustments for inflation and for demographic changes that affect programs. These estimates, accompanied by the underlying economic and policy assumptions upon which they are based, are transmitted by the president to Congress when the budget is submitted.

Custody of the papers — To reconcile differences between the House and Senate versions of a bill, a conference may be arranged. The chamber with "custody of the papers" — the engrossed bill, engrossed amendments, messages of transmittal — is the only body empowered to request the conference. By custom, the chamber that asks for a conference is the last to act on the conference report.

Custody of the papers sometimes is manipulated to ensure that a particular chamber acts either first or last on the conference report. *(Also see conference.)*

Deferral — Executive branch action to defer, or delay, the spending of appropriated money. The 1974 Congressional Budget and Impoundment Control Act requires a special message from the president to Congress reporting a proposed deferral of spending. Deferrals may not extend beyond the end of the fiscal year in which the message is transmitted. A federal district court in 1986 struck down the president's authority to defer spending for policy reasons; the ruling was upheld by a federal appeals court in 1987. Congress can prohibit proposed deferrals by enacting a law doing so; most often, cancellations of proposed deferrals are included in appropriations bills. *(Also see rescission.)*

Delegate — A non-voting official representing the District of Columbia, Guam, American Samoa, the U.S. Virgin Islands, the Northern Mariana Islands or Puerto Rico in the House. The first five serve two-year terms. Puerto Rico's non-voting representative is known as a resident commissioner and serves a four-year term. The delegates cannot vote in the full House but are permitted to vote in committees and can introduce and cosponsor legislation. Under a House rule in place in 1993 and 1994, and restored in 2007, delegates are permitted to vote in the Committee of the Whole, in which the House considers appropriations, authorization and tax bills for amendment. If the votes of the delegates are decisive on any vote in the Committee of the Whole, the amendment is automatically voted on again in the full House, where the delegates cannot vote.

Dilatory motion — A motion made for the purpose of killing time and preventing action on a bill or amendment. House rules outlaw dilatory motions, but enforcement is largely within the discretion of the Speaker or chairman of the Committee of the Whole. The Senate does not have a rule barring dilatory motions except under cloture.

Discharge a committee — Occasionally, attempts are made to relieve a committee of jurisdiction over a bill that is before it. This is attempted more often in the House than in the Senate, and the procedure rarely is successful.

In the House, if a committee does not report a bill within 30 days after the measure is referred to it, any member may file a discharge motion. Once offered, the motion is treated as a petition needing the signatures of a majority of members (218 if there are no vacancies).

After the required signatures have been obtained, there is a delay of seven days.

Thereafter, on the second and fourth Mondays of each month, except during the last six days of a session, any member who has signed the petition must be recognized, if he or she so desires, to move that the committee be discharged. Debate on the motion to discharge is limited to 20 minutes. If the motion is carried, consideration of the bill becomes a matter of high privilege.

If a resolution to consider a bill is held up in the Rules Committee for more than seven legislative days, any member may enter a motion to discharge the committee. The motion is handled like any other discharge petition in the House. Occasionally, to expedite non-controversial legislative business, a committee is discharged by unanimous consent of the House, and a petition is not required. In 1993, the signatures on pending discharge petitions — previously kept secret — were made a matter of public record. *(For Senate procedure, see discharge resolution.)*

Discharge Calendar — The House calendar to which motions to discharge committees are referred when they have the required number of signatures (218) and are awaiting floor action. *(Also see calendar.)*

Discharge petition — *(See discharge a committee.)*

Discharge resolution — In the Senate, a special motion that any senator may introduce to relieve a committee from consideration of a bill before it. The resolution can be called up for Senate approval or disapproval in the same manner as any other Senate business. *(For House procedure, see discharge a committee.)*

Discretionary spending — Budget authority provided through appropriations bills in amounts determined by Congress. *(Also see mandatory spending.)*

Direct spending — *(See mandatory spending.)*

Division of a question for voting — A practice that is more common in the Senate but also used in the House whereby a member may demand a division of an amendment or a motion for purposes of voting. When the amendment or motion lends itself to such a division, the individual parts are voted on separately.

Emergency spending — Spending that the president and Congress have designated as an emergency requirement. Emergency spending is not subject to limits on discretionary spending set in the budget resolution or to pay-as-you-go rules. The designation is intended for unanticipated items that are not included in the budget for a fiscal year, such as spending to respond to disasters. However, most of the appropriations for the Iraq War have been designated as emergency spending.

Enacting clause — Key phrase in bills beginning, "Be it enacted by the Senate and House of Representatives." A successful motion to strike it from legislation kills the measure.

Engrossed bill — The final copy of a bill as passed by one chamber, with the text as amended by floor action and certified by the clerk of the House or the secretary of the Senate.

Enrolled bill — The final copy of a bill that has been passed in identical form by both chambers. It is certified by an officer of the chamber of origin (clerk of the House or secretary of the Senate) and then sent on for the signatures of the House Speaker, the Senate president pro tempore and the president of the United States. An enrolled bill is printed on parchment.

Entitlement — A program that guarantees payments to anyone who meets the eligibility criteria set in law. Examples include Social Security, Medicare, Medicaid and food stamps. (Also see mandatory spending.)

Executive Calendar — A non-legislative calendar in the Senate that lists presidential documents such as treaties and nominations. (Also see calendar.)

Executive document — A document, usually a treaty, sent to the Senate by the president for consideration or approval. Executive documents are referred to committee in the same manner as other measures. Unlike legislative documents, treaties do not die at the end of a Congress but remain "live" proposals until acted on by the Senate or withdrawn by the president.

Executive session — A meeting of a Senate or House committee (or occasionally of either chamber) that only its members may attend. Witnesses regularly appear at committee meetings in executive session — for example, Defense Department officials during presentations of classified defense information. Other members of Congress may be invited, but the public and news media are not allowed to attend.

Filibuster — A time-delaying tactic associated with the Senate and used by a minority in an effort to prevent a vote on a bill, amendment or motion that probably would prevail if voted upon directly. The most common method is to take advantage of the Senate's rules permitting unlimited debate, but other forms of parliamentary maneuvering may be used.

The stricter rules of the House make filibusters more difficult, but delaying tactics are employed occasionally through various procedural devices allowed by House rules. (Also see cloture.)

Fiscal year — Financial operations of the government are carried out in a 12-month fiscal year, beginning Oct. 1 and ending Sept. 30. The fiscal year carries the date of the calendar year in which it ends. (From fiscal 1844 to fiscal 1976, the fiscal year began July 1 and ended the following June 30.)

Five-minute rule — A debate-limiting rule of the House that is invoked when the House sits as the Committee of the Whole. Under the rule, a member offering an amendment and a member opposing it are each allowed to speak for five minutes. Debate is then closed. In practice, amendments regularly are debated for more than 10 minutes, with members gaining the floor by offering pro forma amendments or obtaining unanimous consent to speak longer than five minutes. (Also see Committee of the Whole, hour rule, strike out the last word.)

Floor manager — A member who has the task of steering legislation through floor debate and amendment to a final vote in the House or the Senate. Floor managers usually are chairmen or ranking members of the committee that reported the bill. Managers are responsible for apportioning the debate time granted to supporters of the bill. The ranking minority member of the committee normally apportions time for the minority party's participation in the debate.

Frank — A member's facsimile signature, which is used on envelopes in lieu of stamps for the member's official outgoing mail. The "franking privilege" is the right to send mail postage-free.

Germane — Pertaining to the subject matter of the measure at hand. All House amendments must be germane to the bill being considered. The Senate requires that amendments be germane when they are proposed to general appropriations bills or to bills being considered once cloture has been invoked or, frequently, when the Senate is proceeding under a unanimous consent agreement placing a time limit on consideration of a bill. The 1974 Budget Act also requires that amendments to concurrent budget resolutions be germane.

In the House, floor debate must be germane, and the first three hours of debate each day in the Senate must be germane to the pending business. (Also see cloture.)

Gramm-Rudman-Hollings Deficit Reduction Act — (See sequester.)

Grandfather clause — A provision that exempts people or other entities already engaged in an activity from new rules or legislation affecting that activity.

Hearings — Committee sessions for taking testimony from witnesses. At hearings on legislation, witnesses usually include specialists, government officials, and spokesmen for individuals or entities affected by the bill or bills under study. Hearings related to special investigations bring forth a variety of witnesses. Committees sometimes use their subpoena power to summon reluctant witnesses. The public and news media may attend open hearings but are barred from closed, or "executive," hearings. The vast majority of hearings are open to the public. (Also see executive session.)

Hold-harmless clause — A provision added to legislation to ensure that recipients of federal funds do not receive less in a future year than they did in the current year if a new formula for allocating funds authorized in the legislation would result in a reduction to the recipients. This clause has been used most often to soften the impact of sudden reductions in federal grants.

Hopper — A box on the House clerk's desk into which members deposit bills and resolutions to introduce them.

Hour rule — A provision in the rules of the House that permits one hour of debate time for each member on amendments debated in the House of Representatives sitting as the House. Therefore, the House normally amends bills while sitting as the Committee of the Whole, where the five-minute rule on amendments operates.

House as in the Committee of the Whole — A procedure that can be used to expedite consideration of certain measures such as continuing resolutions and, when there is debate, private bills. The procedure can be invoked only with the unanimous consent of the House or a rule from the Rules Committee and has procedural elements of both the House sitting as the House of Representatives, such as the Speaker

presiding and the previous question motion being in order, and the House sitting as the Committee of the Whole, with the five-minute rule being in order. *(Also see Committee of the Whole.)*

House Calendar — A listing for action by the House of public bills and resolutions that do not directly or indirectly appropriate money or raise revenue. *(Also see calendar.)*

Immunity — The constitutional privilege of members of Congress to make verbal statements on the floor and in committee for which they cannot be sued or arrested for slander or libel. Also, freedom from arrest while traveling to or from sessions of Congress or on official business. Members in this status may be arrested only for treason, felonies or a breach of the peace, as defined by congressional manuals.

Joint committee — A committee composed of a specified number of members of both the House and Senate. A joint committee may be investigative or research-oriented, an example of the latter being the Joint Economic Committee. Others have housekeeping duties; examples include the joint committees on Printing and the Library of Congress.

Joint resolution — Like a bill, a joint resolution, designated H J Res or S J Res, requires the approval of both chambers and generally the signature of the president and has the force of law if approved. There is no practical difference between a bill and a joint resolution. A joint resolution generally is used to address a limited matter such as a single appropriation.

Joint resolutions are also used to propose amendments to the Constitution. In that case, they require a two-thirds majority in both chambers. They do not require a presidential signature, but they must be ratified by three-fourths of the states to become a part of the Constitution. *(Also see concurrent resolution, resolution.)*

Journal — The official record of the proceedings of the House and Senate. The Journal records the actions taken in each chamber, but, unlike the Congressional Record, it does not include the substantially verbatim report of speeches, debates, statements and the like.

Law — An act of Congress that has been signed by the president or passed, over his veto, by Congress. Public bills, when signed, become public laws and are cited by the letters PL and a hyphenated number. The number before the hyphen corresponds to the Congress, and the one or more digits after the hyphen refer to the numerical sequence in which the president signed the bills during that Congress. Private bills, when signed, become private laws. *(Also see bills, private bill.)*

Legislative day — The "day" extending from the time either chamber meets after an adjournment until the time it next adjourns. Because the House normally adjourns from day to day, legislative days and calendar days usually coincide. But in the Senate, a legislative day may, and frequently does, extend over several calendar days. *(Also see recess.)*

Line-item veto — Presidential authority to strike individual items from appropriations bills, which presidents since Ulysses S. Grant have sought. Congress gave the president a form of the power in 1996 (PL 104-130), but this "enhanced rescission authority" was struck down by the Supreme Court in 1998 as unconstitutional because it allowed the president to change laws on his own.

Loan guarantees — Loans to third parties for which the federal government guarantees the repayment of principal or interest, in whole or in part, to the lender in the event of default.

Lobby — A group seeking to influence the passage or defeat of legislation. Originally the term referred to people frequenting the lobbies or corridors of legislative chambers to speak to lawmakers.

The definition of a lobby and the activity of lobbying is a matter of differing interpretation. By some definitions, lobbying is limited to direct attempts to influence lawmakers through personal interviews and persuasion. Under other definitions, lobbying includes attempts at indirect, or grass-roots, influence, such as persuading members of a group to write or visit their district's representative and state's senators or attempting to create a climate of opinion favorable to a desired legislative goal.

The right to attempt to influence legislation is based on the First Amendment to the Constitution, which says Congress shall make no law abridging the right of the people "to petition the government for a redress of grievances."

Majority leader — The floor leader for the majority party in each chamber. In the Senate, in consultation with the minority leader, the majority leader directs the legislative schedule for the chamber. This person is also the party's spokesman and chief strategist. In the House, the majority leader is second to the Speaker in the majority party's leadership and serves as the party's legislative strategist. *(Also see Speaker, whip.)*

Mandatory spending — Budget authority and outlays provided under laws other than appropriations acts. Mandatory spending, also known as direct spending, includes entitlement funding and payment of interest on the public debt. *(Also see entitlement.)*

Manual — The official handbook in each chamber prescribing in detail its organization, procedures and operations.

Marking up a bill — Going through the contents of a piece of legislation in committee or subcommittee to, for example, consider the provisions, act on amendments to provisions and proposed revisions to the language, and insert new sections and phraseology. If the bill is extensively amended, the committee's version may be introduced as a separate (or "clean") bill, with a new number, before being considered by the full House or Senate. *(Also see clean bill.)*

Minority leader — The floor leader for the minority party in each chamber.

Morning hour — The time set aside at the beginning of each legislative day for the consideration of regular, routine business. The "hour" is of indefinite duration in the House, where it is rarely used. In the Senate, it is the first two hours of a session following an adjournment, as distinguished from a recess. The morning hour can be terminated earlier if the morning business has been completed.

Business includes such matters as messages from the president, communications from the heads of departments, messages from the House, the presentation of petitions, reports of standing and select committees, and the introduction of bills and resolutions.

During the first hour of the morning hour in the Senate, no motion to proceed to the consideration of any bill on the calendar is in order

except by unanimous consent. During the second hour, motions can be made but must be decided without debate. Senate committees may meet while the Senate conducts the morning hour.

Motion — In the House or Senate chamber, a request by a member to institute any one of a wide array of parliamentary actions. He or she "moves" for a certain procedure, such as the consideration of a measure. The precedence of motions, and whether they are debatable, is set forth in the House and Senate rules.

Nominations — Presidential appointments to office subject to Senate confirmation. Although most nominations win quick Senate approval, some are controversial and become the topic of hearings and debate. Sometimes senators object to appointees for patronage reasons — for example, when a nomination to a local federal job is made without consulting the senators of the state concerned. In some situations a senator may object that the nominee is "personally obnoxious" to him. Usually other senators join in blocking such appointments out of courtesy to their colleagues. (*Also see senatorial courtesy.*)

One-minute speeches — Addresses by House members at the beginning of a legislative day. The speeches may cover any subject but are limited to one minute's duration.

Outlays — Actual spending that flows from the liquidation of budget authority. Outlays associated with appropriations bills and other legislation are estimates of future spending made by the Congressional Budget Office (CBO) and the White House's Office of Management and Budget (OMB). CBO's estimates govern bills for the purpose of congressional floor debate, while OMB's numbers govern when it comes to determining whether legislation exceeds spending caps.

Outlays in a given fiscal year may result from budget authority provided in the current year or in previous years. (*Also see budget authority, budget process.*)

Override a veto — If the president vetoes a bill and sends it back to Congress with his objections, Congress may try to override his veto and enact the bill into law. Neither chamber is required to attempt to override a veto. The override of a veto requires a recorded vote with a two-thirds majority of those present and voting in each chamber. The question put to each chamber is: "Shall the bill pass, the objections of the president to the contrary notwithstanding?" (*Also see pocket veto, veto.*)

Oversight committee — A congressional committee or designated subcommittee that is charged with general oversight of one or more federal agencies' programs and activities. Usually, the oversight panel for a particular agency is also the authorizing committee for that agency's programs and operations.

Pair — A voluntary, informal arrangement that two lawmakers, usually on opposite sides of an issue, make on recorded votes. In many cases, the result is to subtract a vote from each side, with no effect on the outcome.

Pairs are not authorized in the rules of either chamber, are not counted in tabulating the final result and have no official standing. However, paired members are identified in the Congressional Record, along with their positions on such votes, if known. A member who expects to be absent for a vote can pair with a member who plans to vote, with the latter agreeing to withhold his or her vote.

There are three types of pairs:

(1) A live pair involves a member who is present for a vote and another who is absent. The member in attendance votes and then withdraws the vote, announcing that he or she has a live pair with colleague "X" and stating how the two members would have voted, one in favor, the other opposed. A live pair may affect the outcome of a closely contested vote, since it subtracts one "yea" or one "nay" from the final tally. A live pair may cover one or several specific issues.

(2) A general pair, widely used in the House, does not entail any arrangement between two members and does not affect the vote. Members who expect to be absent notify the clerk that they wish to make a general pair. Each member then is paired with another desiring a pair, and their names are listed in the Congressional Record. The member may or may not be paired with another taking the opposite position, and no indication of how the members would have voted is given.

(3) A specific pair is similar to a general pair, except that the opposing stands of the two members are identified and printed in the Congressional Record.

Pay-as-you-go (PAYGO) rules — House rules for the 110th and 111th Congresses specify that it is out of order to consider any legislation, including conference reports, that contains tax provisions or new or expanded entitlement programs that have the net effect of increasing the deficit or reducing the surplus. The restriction applies to the current year and the following five years, as well as the current year and the following 10 years.

Beginning with the fiscal 2008 budget resolution, Senate rules have conformed with the House rule.

Petition — A request or plea sent to one or both chambers from an organization or private citizens' group seeking support for particular legislation or favorable consideration of a matter not yet receiving congressional attention. Petitions are referred to appropriate committees. In the House, a petition signed by a majority of members (218) can discharge a bill from a committee. (*Also see discharge a committee.*)

Pocket veto — The act of the president in withholding his approval of a bill after Congress has adjourned. When Congress is in session, a bill becomes law without the president's signature if he does not act upon it within 10 days, excluding Sundays, from the time he receives it. But if Congress adjourns sine die within that 10-day period, the bill, if unsigned, will die even if the president does not formally veto it.

The Supreme Court in 1986 agreed to decide whether the president could pocket veto a bill during recesses and between sessions of the same Congress or only between Congresses. The justices in 1987 declared the case moot, however, because the bill in question was invalid once the case reached the court. The House has treated pocket vetoes between sessions as regular vetoes. (*Also see adjournment sine die, veto.*)

Point of order — An objection raised by a member that the chamber is departing from rules governing its conduct of business. The objector cites the rule violated, with the chair sustaining his or her objection if correctly made. The chair restores order by suspending proceedings of the chamber until it conforms to the prescribed "order of business."

Both chambers have procedures for overcoming a point of order, either by vote or — as is most common in the House — by including

language in the rule for floor consideration that waives a point of order against a given bill. *(Also see rules.)*

President of the Senate — Under the Constitution, the vice president of the United States presides over the Senate. In his absence, the president pro tempore, or a senator designated by the president pro tempore, presides over the chamber.

President pro tempore — The chief officer of the Senate in the absence of the vice president — literally, but loosely, the president for a time. The president pro tempore is elected by his fellow senators. Recent practice has been to elect the senator of the majority party with the longest period of continuous service. The president pro tempore is third in the line of presidential succession, after the vice president and the Speaker of the House.

Previous question — A motion for the previous question, when carried, has the effect of cutting off further debate, preventing the offering of further amendments and forcing a vote on the pending matter. In the House, a motion for the previous question is not permitted in the Committee of the Whole, unless a rule governing debate provides otherwise. The motion for the previous question is not in order in the Senate.

Printed amendment — Some House rules guarantee five minutes of floor debate in support and five minutes in opposition, and no other debate time, on amendments printed in the Congressional Record at least one day prior to the amendment's consideration in the Committee of the Whole.

In the Senate, while amendments may be submitted for printing, they have no parliamentary standing or status. An amendment submitted for printing in the Senate, however, may be called up by any senator.

Private bill — A bill dealing with individual matters, such as claims against the government, immigration or land titles. If two members officially object to consideration of a private bill that is before the chamber, it is recommitted to committee. The backers still have recourse, however. The measure can be put into an omnibus claims bill — several private bills rolled into one. As with any bill, no part of an omnibus claims bill may be deleted without a vote. When the private bill goes back to the House floor in this form, it can be deleted from the omnibus bill only by majority vote.

Private Calendar — The House calendar for private bills. The Private Calendar must be called on the first Tuesday of each month, and the Speaker may call it on the third Tuesday of each month as well. *(Also see calendar, private bill.)*

Privileged questions — The order in which bills, motions and other legislative measures are considered on the floor of the Senate and House is governed by strict priorities. A motion to table, for instance, is more privileged than a motion to recommit. Thus, if a member moves to recommit a bill to committee for further consideration, another member can supersede the first action by moving to table it, and a vote will occur on the motion to table (or kill) before the motion to recommit. A motion to adjourn is considered "of the highest privilege" and must be considered before virtually any other motion.

Pro forma amendment — *(See strike out the last word.)*

Pro forma session — A meeting of the House and Senate during which no legislative business is conducted. The sessions are held to satisfy a provision of the Constitution that prohibits either chamber from adjourning for more than three days without the permission of the other chamber. When the House or Senate recesses or adjourns for more than three days, both chambers adopt concurrent resolutions providing for the recess or adjournment. Also, the Senate sometimes holds pro forma sessions during recess periods to prevent the president from making recess appointments.

Public laws — *(See law.)*

Questions of privilege — These are matters affecting members of Congress individually or collectively. Matters affecting the rights, safety, dignity and integrity of proceedings of the House or Senate as a whole are questions of privilege in both chambers.

Questions involving individual members are called questions of "personal privilege." A member rising to ask a question of personal privilege is given precedence over almost all other proceedings. For instance, if a member feels that he or she has been improperly impugned in comments by another member, he or she can immediately demand to be heard on the floor on a question of personal privilege. An annotation in the House rules points out that the privilege rests primarily on the Constitution, which gives members a conditional immunity from arrest and an unconditional freedom to speak in the House.

In 1993, the House changed its rules to allow the Speaker to delay for two legislative days the floor consideration of a resolution raising a question of the privileges of the House unless it is offered by the majority leader or minority leader.

Quorum — The number of members whose presence is necessary for the transaction of business. In the Senate and House, it is a majority of the membership. In the Committee of the Whole, a quorum is 100. If a point of order is made that a quorum is not present, the only business that is in order is either a motion to adjourn or a motion to direct the sergeant at arms to request the attendance of absentees. In practice, however, both chambers conduct much of their business without a quorum present. *(Also see Committee of the Whole.)*

Quorum call — Procedures used in the House and Senate to establish that a quorum is present. In the House, quorum calls are usually conducted using the electronic voting system, and no roll call is recorded. In the Senate, quorum calls are usually conducted by calling the roll of senators. The House and Senate conduct annual quorum calls at the beginning of each session of Congress. The Senate also uses quorum calls when no senators are speaking on the floor.

Reading of bills — Traditional parliamentary procedure required bills to be read three times before they were passed. This custom is of little modern significance. Normally a bill is considered to have its first reading when it is introduced and printed, by title, in the Congressional Record. In the House, a bill's second reading comes when floor consideration begins. (The actual reading of a bill is most likely to occur at this point if at all.) The second reading in the Senate is supposed to occur on the legislative day after the measure is introduced, but before it is referred to committee. The third reading (again,

usually by title) takes place when floor action has been completed on amendments.

Recess — A recess, as distinguished from adjournment, does not end a legislative day and, therefore, does not interrupt unfinished business. The House usually adjourns from day to day. The Senate often recesses, thus meeting on the same legislative day for several calendar days or even weeks at a time. The rules in each chamber set forth certain matters to be taken up and disposed of at the beginning of each legislative day.

Recognition — The power of recognition of a member is lodged in the Speaker of the House and the presiding officer of the Senate. The presiding officer names the member to speak first when two or more members simultaneously request recognition. The order of recognition is governed by precedents and tradition for many situations. In the Senate, for instance, the majority leader has the right to be recognized first.

Recommit — A motion to return a bill or joint resolution to committee after the measure has been debated on the floor. In the House, the right to offer a motion to recommit is guaranteed to the minority leader or someone he or she designates, and there must be an opponent.

Under a 2009 House rules change, a motion to recommit with instructions must direct a committee to report the bill back "forthwith" — that is, immediately. Previously, the motion could include the term "promptly," which did not require that the bill be returned to the floor and instead required full committee action.

Reconciliation — The 1974 Budget Act created a reconciliation procedure for bringing existing tax and spending laws into conformity with ceilings set in the congressional budget resolution. Under the procedure, the budget resolution sets specific deficit reduction targets and instructs tax-writing and authorizing committees to propose changes in existing law to meet those targets. If more than one committee is involved, the Budget committees consolidate the recommendations, without change, into an omnibus reconciliation bill, which then must be considered and approved by both chambers of Congress.

Special rules in the Senate limit debate on a reconciliation bill to 20 hours and bar extraneous or non-germane amendments. *(Also see budget resolution, sequester.)*

Reconsider a vote — Until it is disposed of, a motion to reconsider the vote by which an action was taken has the effect of putting the action in abeyance. In the Senate, the motion can be made only by a member who voted on the prevailing side of the original question or by a member who did not vote at all. In the House, it can be made only by a member on the prevailing side.

A common practice in the Senate after close votes on an issue is a motion to reconsider, followed by a motion to table the motion to reconsider. On this motion to table, senators vote as they voted on the original question, which allows the motion to table to prevail, assuming there are no switches. That closes the matter, and further motions to reconsider are not entertained.

In the House, as a routine precaution, a motion to reconsider usually is made every time a measure is passed. Such a motion almost always is tabled immediately, thus shutting off the possibility of future reconsideration except by unanimous consent.

Motions to reconsider must be entered in the Senate within the next two days the Senate is in session after the original vote has been taken. In the House, they must be entered either on the same day or the next succeeding day that the House is in session. Sometimes on a close vote, a member — in the Senate, often the majority leader — will switch his or her vote to be eligible to offer a motion to reconsider.

Recorded vote — A vote upon which each member's stand is individually made known. In the Senate, this is accomplished through a roll call of the entire membership, to which each senator on the floor must answer "yea," "nay" or "present." Since January 1973, the House has used an electronic voting system for recorded votes, including "yea" and "nay" votes formerly taken by roll calls.

When not required by the Constitution, a recorded vote can be obtained on questions in the House on the demand of one-fifth (44 members) of a quorum or one-fourth (25) of a quorum in the Committee of the Whole. Recorded votes are required in the House for appropriations, budget and tax bills. *(Also see "yeas" and "nays.")*

Report — Both a verb and a noun as a congressional term. A committee that has been examining a bill referred to it by the parent chamber "reports" its findings and recommendations to the chamber when it completes consideration and returns the measure. The process is called "reporting" a bill. In some cases, a bill is reported without a written report.

A "report" is the document setting forth the committee's explanation of its action. Senate and House reports are numbered separately and are designated S Rept or H Rept. When a committee report is not unanimous, the dissenting committee members may file a statement of their views, called minority or dissenting views and referred to as a minority report. Members in disagreement with some provisions of a bill may file additional or supplementary views. Sometimes a bill or resolution is reported without a committee recommendation.

Legislative committees occasionally submit adverse reports. However, when a committee is opposed to a bill, it usually does not report the bill at all. Some laws require that committee reports — favorable or adverse — be filed.

Rescission — Cancellation of budget authority that was previously appropriated but has not yet been spent.

Resolution — A "simple" resolution, designated H Res or S Res, deals with matters entirely within the prerogatives of a single chamber. It requires neither adoption by the other chamber nor approval by the president, and it does not have the force of law. Most resolutions deal with the rules or procedures of one chamber. They are also used to express the sentiments of a single chamber, such as condolences to the family of a deceased member, or to comment on foreign policy or executive business. A simple resolution is the vehicle for a "rule" from the House Rules Committee. *(Also see concurrent and joint resolutions, rules.)*

Rider — An amendment, usually not germane, that its sponsor hopes to get through more easily by including it in other legislation. A rider becomes law if the bill to which it is attached is enacted. Amendments providing legislative directives in appropriations bills are examples of riders, although technically legislation is barred from appropriations bills.

The House, unlike the Senate, has a strict germaneness rule; thus,

riders usually are Senate devices to get legislation enacted quickly or to bypass lengthy House consideration and, possibly, opposition.

Rules — Each chamber has a body of rules and precedents that govern the conduct of business. These rules deal with issues such as duties of officers, the order of business, admission to the floor, parliamentary procedures on handling amendments and voting, and jurisdictions of committees.

The House re-adopts its rules, usually with some changes, at the beginning of each Congress. Senate rules carry over from one Congress to the next.

In the House, a rule may also be a resolution reported by the Rules Committee to govern the handling of a particular bill on the floor. The committee may report a rule, also called a special order, in the form of a simple resolution. If the House adopts the resolution, the temporary rule becomes as valid as any standing rule and lapses only after action has been completed on the measure to which it pertains.

The rule sets the time limit on general debate. It may also waive points of order against provisions of the bill in question such as non-germane language or against certain amendments expected on the floor. It may even forbid all amendments or all amendments except those proposed by the legislative committee that handled the bill. In this instance, it is known as a "closed" rule, as opposed to an "open" rule, which puts no limitation on floor amendments, thus leaving the bill completely open to alteration by the adoption of germane amendments. *(Also see point of order.)*

Secretary of the Senate — Chief administrative officer of the Senate, responsible for overseeing the duties of Senate employees, educating Senate pages, administering oaths, overseeing the registration of lobbyists and handling other tasks necessary for the continuing operation of the Senate. *(Also see Clerk of the House.)*

Select or special committee — A committee set up for a special purpose and, usually, for a limited time by resolution of either the House or Senate. Most special committees are investigative and lack legislative authority: Legislation is not referred to them, and they cannot report bills to their parent chambers. Each chamber has a Select Committee on Intelligence.

Senatorial courtesy — A general practice with no written rule — sometimes referred to as "the courtesy of the Senate" — applied to consideration of executive nominations. Generally, it means that nominees from a state are not to be confirmed unless they have been approved by the senators of the president's party of that state, with other senators following their colleagues' lead in the attitude they take toward consideration of such nominations. *(Also see nominations.)*

Sequester — Automatic, across-the-board spending cuts. Under the 1985 Gramm-Rudman-Hollings anti-deficit law, modified in 1987, a year-end sequester was triggered if the deficit exceeded a pre-set maximum. The Budget Enforcement Act of 1990, updated in 1993 and 1997, effectively replaced that procedure through fiscal 2002.

Sine die — *(See adjournment sine die.)*

Speaker — The presiding officer of the House of Representatives, selected by the majority party's caucus and formally elected by the whole House. While both parties nominate candidates, choice by the majority party is tantamount to election. The Speaker is second in the line of presidential succession, after the vice president.

Special session — A session of Congress after it has adjourned sine die, completing its regular session. Special sessions are convened by the president.

Spending authority — The 1974 Budget Act defines spending authority as borrowing authority, contract authority and entitlement authority for which budget authority is not provided in advance by appropriations acts.

Sponsor — *(See bills introduced.)*

Standing committees — Committees that are permanently established by House and Senate rules. The standing committees of the House were reorganized in 1974, with some changes in jurisdictions and titles made when Republicans took control of the House in 1995. House Democrats changed the names of five committees in 2007. The last major realignment of Senate committees was in 1977. The standing committees are legislative committees: Legislation may be referred to them, and they may report bills and resolutions to their parent chambers.

Standing vote — A non-recorded vote used in both the House and Senate. (A standing vote is also called a division vote.) Members in favor of a proposal stand and are counted by the presiding officer. Then members opposed stand and are counted. There is no record of how individual members voted.

Statutes at large — A chronological arrangement of the laws enacted in each session of Congress. Though indexed, the laws are not arranged by subject matter, and there is no indication of how they changed previously enacted laws. *(Also see law, U.S. Code.)*

Strike from the Record — A member of the House who is offended by remarks made on the House floor may move that the offending words be "taken down" for the Speaker's cognizance and then expunged from the debate as published in the Congressional Record.

Strike out the last word — A motion whereby a House member is entitled to speak for five minutes on an amendment then being debated by the chamber. A member gains recognition from the chair by moving to "strike out the last word" of the amendment or section of the bill under consideration. The motion is pro forma, requires no vote and does not change the amendment being debated. *(Also see five-minute rule.)*

Substitute — A motion, amendment or entire bill introduced in place of the pending legislative business. Adoption of the substitute supplants the original text. The substitute may also be amended. *(Also see amendment in the nature of a substitute.)*

Supplemental appropriations bill — Legislation appropriating funds after the regular annual appropriations bill for a federal department or agency has been enacted. In the past, supplemental appropriations bills often arrived about halfway through the fiscal year to pay for urgent needs, such as relief from natural disasters, that Congress

and the president did not anticipate (or may not have wanted to fund). President George W. Bush used emergency supplementals to pay for the wars in Iraq and Afghanistan.

Suspend the rules — A time-saving procedure for passing bills in the House. The wording of the motion, which may be made by any member recognized by the Speaker, is "I move to suspend the rules and pass the bill." A favorable vote by two-thirds of those present is required for passage. Debate is limited to 40 minutes, and no amendments from the floor are permitted. If a two-thirds favorable vote is not attained, the bill may be considered later under regular procedures. The suspension procedure is in order every Monday, Tuesday and Wednesday, and it is intended to be reserved for non-controversial bills. It also may be used to concur in Senate amendments, adopt conference reports and agree to resolutions.

Table a bill — Motions to table, or to "lay on the table," are used to block or kill amendments or other parliamentary questions. When approved, a tabling motion is considered the final disposition of that issue. One of the most widely used parliamentary procedures, the motion to table is not debatable, and adoption requires a simple majority vote.

In the Senate, however, different language sometimes is used. The motion may be worded to let a bill "lie on the table," perhaps for subsequent "picking up." This motion is more flexible, keeping the bill pending for later action, if desired. Tabling motions on amendments are effective debate-ending devices in the Senate.

Treaties — Executive proposals — in the form of resolutions of ratification — that must be submitted to the Senate for approval by two-thirds of the senators present. Treaties are normally sent to the Foreign Relations Committee for scrutiny before the Senate takes action. Foreign Relations has jurisdiction over all treaties, regardless of the subject matter. Treaties are read three times and debated on the floor in much the same manner as legislative proposals. After approval by the Senate, treaties are formally ratified by the president.

Trust funds — Funds collected and used by the federal government for carrying out specific purposes and programs according to terms of a trust agreement or statute such as the Social Security and unemployment compensation trust funds. Such funds are administered by the government in a fiduciary capacity and are not available for the general purposes of the government.

Unanimous consent — A procedure used to expedite floor action. Proceedings of the House or Senate and action on legislation often take place upon the unanimous consent of the chamber, whether or not a rule of the chamber is being violated. It is frequently used in a routine fashion, such as by a senator requesting the unanimous consent of the Senate to have specified members of his or her staff present on the floor during debate on a specific amendment. A single member's objection blocks a unanimous consent request.

Unanimous consent agreement — A device used in the Senate to expedite legislation. Much of the Senate's legislative business, dealing with both minor and controversial issues, is conducted through unanimous consent or unanimous consent agreements. On major legislation, such agreements usually are printed and transmitted to all senators in ad-

vance of floor debate. Once agreed to, they are binding on all members unless the Senate, by unanimous consent, agrees to modify them. An agreement may list the order in which various bills are to be considered; specify the length of time for debate on bills and contested amendments and when they are to be voted upon; and, frequently, require that all amendments introduced be germane to the bill under consideration.

In this regard, unanimous consent agreements are similar to the "rules" issued by the House Rules Committee for bills pending in the House. The House rarely sets conditions for floor debate under unanimous consent.

Union Calendar — Bills that directly or indirectly appropriate money or raise revenue are placed on this House calendar according to the date they are reported from committee. (Also see calendar.)

U.S. Code — A consolidation and codification of the general and permanent laws of the United States arranged by subject under 50 titles, the first six dealing with general or political subjects, and the other 44 alphabetically arranged from agriculture to war. The U.S. Code is updated annually, and a new set of bound volumes is published every six years. (Also see law, statutes at large.)

Veto — Disapproval by the president of a bill or joint resolution (other than one proposing an amendment to the Constitution). When Congress is in session, the president must veto a bill within 10 days, excluding Sundays, after he has received it; otherwise, it becomes law without his signature. When the president vetoes a bill, he returns it to the chamber of origin along with a message stating his objections. (Also see pocket veto, override a veto.)

Voice vote — In either the House or Senate, members answer "aye" or "no" in chorus, and the presiding officer decides the result. The term is also used loosely to indicate action by unanimous consent or without objection. (Also see "yeas" and "nays.")

Whip — In effect, the assistant majority or minority leader, in either the House or Senate. His or her job is to help marshal votes in support of party strategy and legislation.

Without objection — Used in lieu of a vote on non-controversial motions, amendments or bills that may be passed in either chamber if no member voices an objection.

"Yeas" and "nays" — The Constitution requires that "yea" and "nay" votes be taken and recorded when requested by one-fifth of the members present. In the House, the Speaker determines whether one-fifth of the members present requested a vote. In the Senate, practice requires only 11 members. The Constitution requires the yeas and nays on a veto override attempt. (Also see recorded vote.)

Yielding — When a member has been recognized to speak, no other member may speak unless he or she obtains permission from the member recognized. This permission is called yielding and usually is requested in the form, "Will the gentleman (or gentlelady) yield to me?" While this activity occasionally is seen in the Senate, the Senate has no rule or practice to parcel out time. In the House, the floor manager of a bill usually apportions debate time by yielding specific amounts of time to members who have requested it. ■

Members of the 111th Congress, 2nd Session . . .

(As of Dec. 22, 2010, when the Senate adjourned sine die.)

REPRESENTATIVES
D 255, R 179
1 vacancy

— A —

Ackerman, Gary L., D-N.Y. (5)
Aderholt, Robert B., R-Ala. (4)
Adler, John, D-N.J. (3)
Akin, Todd, R-Mo. (2)
Alexander, Rodney, R-La. (5)
Altmire, Jason, D-Pa. (4)
Andrews, Robert E., D-N.J. (1)
Arcuri, Michael, D-N.Y. (24)
Austria, Steve, R-Ohio (7)

— B —

Baca, Joe, D-Calif. (43)
Bachmann, Michele, R-Minn. (6)
Bachus, Spencer, R-Ala. (6)
Baird, Brian, D-Wash. (3)
Baldwin, Tammy, D-Wis. (2)
Barrett, J. Gresham, R-S.C. (3)
Barrow, John, D-Ga. (12)
Bartlett, Roscoe G., R-Md. (6)
Barton, Joe L., R-Texas (6)
Bean, Melissa, D-Ill. (8)
Becerra, Xavier, D-Calif. (31)
Berkley, Shelley, D-Nev. (1)
Berman, Howard L., D-Calif. (28)
Berry, Marion, D-Ark. (1)
Biggert, Judy, R-Ill. (13)
Bilbray, Brian P., R-Calif. (50)
Bilirakis, Gus, R-Fla. (9)
Bishop, Rob, R-Utah (1)
Bishop, Sanford D. Jr., D-Ga. (2)
Bishop, Timothy H., D-N.Y. (1)
Blackburn, Marsha, R-Tenn. (7)
Blumenauer, Earl, D-Ore. (3)
Blunt, Roy, R-Mo. (7)
Boccieri, John, D-Ohio (16)
Boehner, John A., R-Ohio (8)
Bonner, Jo, R-Ala. (1)
Bono Mack, Mary, R-Calif. (45)
Boozman, John, R-Ark. (3)
Boren, Dan, D-Okla. (2)
Boswell, Leonard L., D-Iowa (3)
Boucher, Rick, D-Va. (9)
Boustany, Charles Jr., R-La. (7)
Boyd, Allen, D-Fla. (2)
Brady, Kevin, R-Texas (8)
Brady, Robert A., D-Pa. (1)
Braley, Bruce, D-Iowa (1)
Bright, Bobby, D-Ala. (2)
Broun, Paul, R-Ga. (10)
Brown, Corrine, D-Fla. (3)
Brown, Henry E. Jr., R-S.C. (1)
Brown-Waite, Ginny, R-Fla. (5)
Buchanan, Vern, R-Fla. (13)
Burgess, Michael C., R-Texas (26)
Burton, Dan, R-Ind. (5)
Butterfield, G.K., D-N.C. (1)
Buyer, Steve, R-Ind. (4)

— C —

Calvert, Ken, R-Calif. (44)
Camp, Dave, R-Mich. (4)
Campbell, John, R-Calif. (48)
Cantor, Eric, R-Va. (7)
Cao, Anh "Joseph," R-La. (2)
Capito, Shelley Moore, R-W.Va. (2)
Capps, Lois, D-Calif. (23)
Capuano, Michael E., D-Mass. (8)
Cardoza, Dennis, D-Calif. (18)
Carnahan, Russ, D-Mo. (3)
Carney, Christopher, D-Pa. (10)
Carson, André, D-Ind. (7)
Carter, John, R-Texas (31)
Cassidy, Bill, R-La. (6)
Castle, Michael N., R-Del. (AL)
Castor, Kathy, D-Fla. (11)
Chaffetz, Jason, R-Utah (3)
Chandler, Ben, D-Ky. (6)
Childers, Travis W., D-Miss. (1)

Chu, Judy, D-Calif. (32)
Clarke, Yvette D., D-N.Y. (11)
Clay, William Lacy, D-Mo. (1)
Cleaver, Emanuel II, D-Mo. (5)
Clyburn, James E., D-S.C. (6)
Coble, Howard, R-N.C. (6)
Coffman, Mike, R-Colo. (6)
Cohen, Steve, D-Tenn. (9)
Cole, Tom, R-Okla. (4)
Conaway, K. Michael, R-Texas (11)
Connolly, Gerald E., D-Va. (11)
Conyers, John Jr., D-Mich. (14)
Cooper, Jim, D-Tenn. (5)
Costa, Jim, D-Calif. (20)
Costello, Jerry F., D-Ill. (12)
Courtney, Joe, D-Conn. (2)
Crenshaw, Ander, R-Fla. (4)
Critz, Mark, D-Pa. (12)
Crowley, Joseph, D-N.Y. (7)
Cuellar, Henry, D-Texas (28)
Culberson, John, R-Texas (7)
Cummings, Elijah E., D-Md. (7)

— D —

Dahlkemper, Kathy, D-Pa. (3)
Davis, Artur, D-Ala. (7)
Davis, Danny K., D-Ill. (7)
Davis, Geoff, R-Ky. (4)
Davis, Lincoln, D-Tenn. (4)
Davis, Susan A., D-Calif. (53)
DeFazio, Peter A., D-Ore. (4)
DeGette, Diana, D-Colo. (1)
Delahunt, Bill, D-Mass. (10)
DeLauro, Rosa, D-Conn. (3)
Dent, Charlie, R-Pa. (15)
Deutch, Ted, D-Fla. (19)
Diaz-Balart, Lincoln, R-Fla. (21)
Diaz-Balart, Mario, R-Fla. (25)
Dicks, Norm, D-Wash. (6)
Dingell, John D., D-Mich. (15)
Djou, Charles K., R-Hawaii (1)
Doggett, Lloyd, D-Texas (25)
Donnelly, Joe, D-Ind. (2)
Doyle, Mike, D-Pa. (14)
Dreier, David, R-Calif. (26)
Driehaus, Steve, D-Ohio (1)
Duncan, John J. "Jimmy" Jr., R-Tenn. (2)

— E, F —

Edwards, Chet, D-Texas (17)
Edwards, Donna, D-Md. (4)
Ehlers, Vernon J., R-Mich. (3)
Ellison, Keith, D-Minn. (5)
Ellsworth, Brad, D-Ind. (8)
Emerson, Jo Ann, R-Mo. (8)
Engel, Eliot L., D-N.Y. (17)
Eshoo, Anna G., D-Calif. (14)
Etheridge, Bob, D-N.C. (2)
Fallin, Mary, R-Okla. (5)
Farr, Sam, D-Calif. (17)
Fattah, Chaka, D-Pa. (2)
Filner, Bob, D-Calif. (51)
Flake, Jeff, R-Ariz. (6)
Fleming, John, R-La. (4)
Forbes, J. Randy, R-Va. (4)
Fortenberry, Jeff, R-Neb. (1)
Foster, Bill, D-Ill. (14)
Foxx, Virginia, R-N.C. (5)
Frank, Barney, D-Mass. (4)
Franks, Trent, R-Ariz. (2)
Frelinghuysen, Rodney, R-N.J. (11)
Fudge, Marcia L., D-Ohio (11)

— G —

Gallegly, Elton, R-Calif. (24)
Garamendi, John, D-Calif. (10)
Garrett, Scott, R-N.J. (5)
Gerlach, Jim, R-Pa. (6)
Giffords, Gabrielle, D-Ariz. (8)
Gingrey, Phil, R-Ga. (11)
Gohmert, Louie, R-Texas (1)
Gonzalez, Charlie, D-Texas (20)
Goodlatte, Robert W., R-Va. (6)
Gordon, Bart, D-Tenn. (6)
Granger, Kay, R-Texas (12)
Graves, Sam, R-Mo. (6)
Graves, Tom, R-Ga. (9)
Grayson, Alan, D-Fla. (8)

Green, Al, D-Texas (9)
Green, Gene, D-Texas (29)
Griffith, Parker, R-Ala. (5)
Grijalva, Raúl M., D-Ariz. (7)
Guthrie, Brett, R-Ky. (2)
Gutierrez, Luis V., D-Ill. (4)

— H —

Hall, John, D-N.Y. (19)
Hall, Ralph M., R-Texas (4)
Halvorson, Debbie, D-Ill. (11)
Hare, Phil, D-Ill. (17)
Harman, Jane, D-Calif. (36)
Harper, Gregg, R-Miss. (3)
Hastings, Alcee L., D-Fla. (23)
Hastings, Doc, R-Wash. (4)
Heinrich, Martin, D-N.M. (1)
Heller, Dean, R-Nev. (2)
Hensarling, Jeb, R-Texas (5)
Herger, Wally, R-Calif. (2)
Herseth Sandlin, Stephanie, D-S.D. (AL)
Higgins, Brian, D-N.Y. (27)
Hill, Baron P., D-Ind. (9)
Himes, Jim, D-Conn. (4)
Hinchey, Maurice D., D-N.Y. (22)
Hinojosa, Rubén, D-Texas (15)
Hirono, Mazie K., D-Hawaii (2)
Hodes, Paul W., D-N.H. (2)
Hoekstra, Peter, R-Mich. (2)
Holden, Tim, D-Pa. (17)
Holt, Rush D., D-N.J. (12)
Honda, Michael M., D-Calif. (15)
Hoyer, Steny H., D-Md. (5)
Hunter, Duncan, R-Calif. (52)

— I, J —

Inglis, Bob, R-S.C. (4)
Inslee, Jay, D-Wash. (1)
Israel, Steve, D-N.Y. (2)
Issa, Darrell, R-Calif. (49)
Jackson, Jesse L. Jr., D-Ill. (2)
Jackson Lee, Sheila, D-Texas (18)
Jenkins, Lynn, R-Kan. (2)
Johnson, Eddie Bernice, D-Texas (30)
Johnson, Hank, D-Ga. (4)
Johnson, Sam, R-Texas (3)
Johnson, Timothy V., R-Ill. (15)
Jones, Walter B., R-N.C. (3)
Jordan, Jim, R-Ohio (4)

— K —

Kagen, Steve, D-Wis. (8)
Kanjorski, Paul E., D-Pa. (11)
Kaptur, Marcy, D-Ohio (9)
Kennedy, Patrick J., D-R.I. (1)
Kildee, Dale E., D-Mich. (5)
Kilpatrick, Carolyn Cheeks, D-Mich. (13)
Kilroy, Mary Jo, D-Ohio (15)
Kind, Ron, D-Wis. (3)
King, Peter T., R-N.Y. (3)
King, Steve, R-Iowa (5)
Kingston, Jack, R-Ga. (1)
Kirkpatrick, Ann, D-Ariz. (1)
Kissell, Larry, D-N.C. (8)
Klein, Ron, D-Fla. (22)
Kline, John, R-Minn. (2)
Kosmas, Suzanne M., D-Fla. (24)
Kratovil, Frank Jr., D-Md. (1)
Kucinich, Dennis J., D-Ohio (10)

— L —

Lamborn, Doug, R-Colo. (5)
Lance, Leonard, R-N.J. (7)
Langevin, Jim, D-R.I. (2)
Larsen, Rick, D-Wash. (2)
Larson, John B., D-Conn. (1)
Latham, Tom, R-Iowa (4)
LaTourette, Steven C., R-Ohio (14)
Latta, Bob, R-Ohio (5)
Lee, Barbara, D-Calif. (9)
Lee, Christopher, R-N.Y. (26)
Levin, Sander M., D-Mich. (12)
Lewis, Jerry, R-Calif. (41)
Lewis, John, D-Ga. (5)
Linder, John, R-Ga. (7)
Lipinski, Daniel, D-Ill. (3)
LoBiondo, Frank A., R-N.J. (2)
Loebsack, Dave, D-Iowa (2)

Lofgren, Zoe, D-Calif. (16)
Lowey, Nita M., D-N.Y. (18)
Lucas, Frank D., R-Okla. (3)
Luetkemeyer, Blaine, R-Mo. (9)
Luján, Ben Ray, D-N.M. (3)
Lummis, Cynthia M., R-Wyo. (AL)
Lungren, Dan, R-Calif. (3)
Lynch, Stephen F., D-Mass. (9)

— M —

Mack, Connie, R-Fla. (14)
Maffei, Dan, D-N.Y. (25)
Maloney, Carolyn B., D-N.Y. (14)
Manzullo, Donald, R-Ill. (16)
Marchant, Kenny, R-Texas (24)
Markey, Betsy, D-Colo. (4)
Markey, Edward J., D-Mass. (7)
Marshall, Jim, D-Ga. (8)
Matheson, Jim, D-Utah (2)
Matsui, Doris, D-Calif. (5)
McCarthy, Carolyn, D-N.Y. (4)
McCarthy, Kevin, R-Calif. (22)
McCaul, Michael, R-Texas (10)
McClintock, Tom, R-Calif. (4)
McCollum, Betty, D-Minn. (4)
McCotter, Thaddeus, R-Mich. (11)
McDermott, Jim, D-Wash. (7)
McGovern, Jim, D-Mass. (3)
McHenry, Patrick T., R-N.C. (10)
McIntyre, Mike, D-N.C. (7)
McKeon, Howard P. "Buck," R-Calif. (25)
McMahon, Michael E., D-N.Y. (13)
McMorris Rodgers, Cathy, R-Wash. (5)
McNerney, Jerry, D-Calif. (11)
Meek, Kendrick B., D-Fla. (17)
Meeks, Gregory W., D-N.Y. (6)
Melancon, Charlie, D-La. (3)
Mica, John L., R-Fla. (7)
Michaud, Michael H., D-Maine (2)
Miller, Brad, D-N.C. (13)
Miller, Candice S., R-Mich. (10)
Miller, Gary G., R-Calif. (42)
Miller, George, D-Calif. (7)
Miller, Jeff, R-Fla. (1)
Minnick, Walt, D-Idaho (1)
Mitchell, Harry E., D-Ariz. (5)
Mollohan, Alan B., D-W.Va. (1)
Moore, Dennis, D-Kan. (3)
Moore, Gwen, D-Wis. (4)
Moran, James P., D-Va. (8)
Moran, Jerry, R-Kan. (1)
Murphy, Christopher S., D-Conn. (5)
Murphy, Patrick J., D-Pa. (8)
Murphy, Scott, D-N.Y. (20)
Murphy, Tim, R-Pa. (18)
Myrick, Sue, R-N.C. (9)

— N, O —

Nadler, Jerrold, D-N.Y. (8)
Napolitano, Grace F., D-Calif. (38)
Neal, Richard E., D-Mass. (2)
Neugebauer, Randy, R-Texas (19)
Nunes, Devin, R-Calif. (21)
Nye, Glenn, D-Va. (2)
Oberstar, James L., D-Minn. (8)
Obey, David R., D-Wis. (7)
Olson, Pete, R-Texas (22)
Olver, John W., D-Mass. (1)
Ortiz, Solomon P., D-Texas (27)
Owens, Bill, D-N.Y. (23)

— P —

Pallone, Frank Jr., D-N.J. (6)
Pascrell, Bill Jr., D-N.J. (8)
Pastor, Ed, D-Ariz. (4)
Paul, Ron, R-Texas (14)
Paulsen, Erik, R-Minn. (3)
Payne, Donald M., D-N.J. (10)
Pelosi, Nancy, D-Calif. (8)
Pence, Mike, R-Ind. (6)
Perlmutter, Ed, D-Colo. (7)
Perriello, Tom, D-Va. (5)
Peters, Gary, D-Mich. (9)
Peterson, Collin C., D-Minn. (7)
Petri, Tom, R-Wis. (6)
Pingree, Chellie, D-Maine (1)
Pitts, Joe, R-Pa. (16)
Platts, Todd R., R-Pa. (19)

... Governors, Supreme Court, Executive Branch

Poe, Ted, R-Texas (2)
Polis, Jared, D-Colo. (2)
Pomeroy, Earl, D-N.D. (AL)
Posey, Bill, R-Fla. (15)
Price, David E., D-N.C. (4)
Price, Tom, R-Ga. (6)
Putnam, Adam H., R-Fla. (12)

— Q, R —

Quigley, Mike, D-Ill. (5)
Radanovich, George, R-Calif. (19)
Rahall, Nick J. II, D-W.Va. (3)
Rangel, Charles B., D-N.Y. (15)
Reed, Tom, R-N.Y. (29)
Rehberg, Denny, R-Mont. (AL)
Reichert, Dave, R-Wash. (8)
Reyes, Silvestre, D-Texas (16)
Richardson, Laura , D-Calif. (37)
Rodriguez, Ciro D., D-Texas (23)
Roe, Phil, R-Tenn. (1)
Rogers, Harold, R-Ky. (5)
Rogers, Mike D., R-Ala. (3)
Rogers, Mike, R-Mich. (8)
Rohrabacher, Dana, R-Calif. (46)
Rooney, Tom, R-Fla. (16)
Ros-Lehtinen, Ileana, R-Fla. (18)
Roskam, Peter, R-Ill. (6)
Ross, Mike, D-Ark. (4)
Rothman, Steven R., D-N.J. (9)
Roybal-Allard, Lucille, D-Calif. (34)
Royce, Ed, R-Calif. (40)
Ruppersberger, C.A. Dutch, D-Md. (2)
Rush, Bobby L., D-Ill. (1)
Ryan, Paul D., R-Wis. (1)
Ryan, Tim, D-Ohio (17)

— S —

Salazar, John, D-Colo. (3)
Sánchez, Linda T., D-Calif. (39)
Sanchez, Loretta, D-Calif. (47)
Sarbanes, John, D-Md. (3)
Scalise, Steve, R-La. (1)
Schakowsky, Jan, D-Ill. (9)
Schauer, Mark, D-Mich. (7)
Schiff, Adam B., D-Calif. (29)
Schmidt, Jean, R-Ohio (2)
Schock, Aaron, R-Ill. (18)
Schrader, Kurt, D-Ore. (5)
Schwartz, Allyson Y., D-Pa. (13)
Scott, David, D-Ga. (13)
Scott, Robert C., D-Va. (3)
Sensenbrenner, F. James Jr., R-Wis. (5)
Serrano, José E., D-N.Y. (16)
Sessions, Pete, R-Texas (32)
Sestak, Joe, D-Pa. (7)
Shadegg, John, R-Ariz. (3)
Shea-Porter, Carol, D-N.H. (1)
Sherman, Brad, D-Calif. (27)
Shimkus, John, R-Ill. (19)
Shuler, Heath, D-N.C. (11)
Shuster, Bill, R-Pa. (9)
Simpson, Mike, R-Idaho (2)
Sires, Albio, D-N.J. (13)
Skelton, Ike, D-Mo. (4)
Slaughter, Louise M., D-N.Y. (28)
Smith, Adam, D-Wash. (9)
Smith, Adrian, R-Neb. (3)
Smith, Christopher H., R-N.J. (4)
Smith, Lamar, R-Texas (21)
Snyder, Vic, D-Ark. (2)
Space, Zack, D-Ohio (18)
Speier, Jackie, D-Calif. (12)
Spratt, John M. Jr., D-S.C. (5)
Stark, Pete, D-Calif. (13)
Stearns, Cliff, R-Fla. (6)
Stupak, Bart, D-Mich. (1)
Stutzman, Marlin, R-Ind. (3)
Sullivan, John, R-Okla. (1)
Sutton, Betty, D-Ohio (13)

— T —

Tanner, John, D-Tenn. (8)
Taylor, Gene, D-Miss. (4)
Teague, Harry, D-N.M. (2)
Terry, Lee, R-Neb. (2)
Thompson, Bennie, D-Miss. (2)
Thompson, Glenn, R-Pa. (5)
Thompson, Mike, D-Calif. (1)

Thornberry, William M. "Mac," R-Texas (13)
Tiahrt, Todd, R-Kan. (4)
Tiberi, Pat, R-Ohio (12)
Tierney, John F., D-Mass. (6)
Titus, Dina, D-Nev. (3)
Tonko, Paul, D-N.Y. (21)
Towns, Edolphus, D-N.Y. (10)
Tsongas, Niki, D-Mass. (5)
Turner, Michael R., R-Ohio (3)

— U, V —

Upton, Fred, R-Mich. (6)
Van Hollen, Chris, D-Md. (8)
Velázquez, Nydia M., D-N.Y. (12)
Visclosky, Peter J., D-Ind. (1)

— W —

Walden, Greg, R-Ore. (2)
Walz, Tim, D-Minn. (1)
Wamp, Zach, R-Tenn. (3)
Wasserman Schultz, Debbie, D-Fla. (20)
Waters, Maxine, D-Calif. (35)
Watson, Diane, D-Calif. (33)
Watt, Melvin, D-N.C. (12)
Waxman, Henry A., D-Calif. (30)
Weiner, Anthony, D-N.Y. (9)
Welch, Peter, D-Vt. (AL)
Westmoreland, Lynn, R-Ga. (3)
Whitfield, Edward, R-Ky. (1)
Wilson, Charlie, D-Ohio (6)
Wilson, Joe, R-S.C. (2)
Wittman, Rob, R-Va. (1)
Wolf, Frank R., R-Va. (10)
Woolsey, Lynn, D-Calif. (6)
Wu, David, D-Ore. (1)

— X, Y, Z —

Yarmuth, John, D-Ky. (3)
Young, C.W. Bill, R-Fla. (10)
Young, Don, R-Alaska (AL)

DELEGATES
D 6

Bordallo, Madeleine Z., D-Guam
Christensen, Donna M.C., D-V.I.
Faleomavaega, Eni F.H., D-A.S.
Norton, Eleanor Holmes, D-D.C.
Pierluisi, Pedro R., D-P.R.
Sablan, Gregorio Kilili Camacho, D-N. Marianas

SENATORS
D 56, R 42, I 2

Akaka, Daniel K., D-Hawaii
Alexander, Lamar, R-Tenn.
Barrasso, John, R-Wyo.
Baucus, Max, D-Mont.
Bayh, Evan, D-Ind.
Begich, Mark, D-Alaska
Bennet, Michael, D-Colo.
Bennett, Robert F., R-Utah
Bingaman, Jeff, D-N.M.
Bond, Christopher S., R-Mo.
Boxer, Barbara, D-Calif.
Brown, Scott P., R-Mass.
Brown, Sherrod, D-Ohio
Brownback, Sam, R-Kan.
Bunning, Jim, R-Ky.
Burr, Richard M., R-N.C.
Cantwell, Maria, D-Wash.
Cardin, Benjamin L., D-Md.
Carper, Thomas R., D-Del.
Casey, Bob, D-Pa.
Chambliss, Saxby, R-Ga.
Coburn, Tom, R-Okla.
Cochran, Thad, R-Miss.
Collins, Susan, R-Maine
Coons, Chris, D-Del.
Conrad, Kent, D-N.D.
Corker, Bob, R-Tenn.
Cornyn, John, R-Texas
Crapo, Michael D., R-Idaho
DeMint, Jim, R-S.C.
Dodd, Christopher J., D-Conn.
Dorgan, Byron L., D-N.D.
Durbin, Richard J., D-Ill.

Ensign, John, R-Nev.
Enzi, Michael B., R-Wyo.
Feingold, Russ, D-Wis.
Feinstein, Dianne, D-Calif.
Franken, Al, D-Minn.
Gillibrand, Kirsten, D-N.Y.
Graham, Lindsey, R-S.C.
Grassley, Charles E., R-Iowa
Gregg, Judd, R-N.H.
Hagan, Kay, D-N.C.
Harkin, Tom, D-Iowa
Hatch, Orrin G., R-Utah
Hutchison, Kay Bailey, R-Texas
Inhofe, James M., R-Okla.
Inouye, Daniel K., D-Hawaii
Isakson, Johnny, R-Ga.
Johanns, Mike, R-Neb.
Johnson, Tim, D-S.D.
Kerry, John, D-Mass.
Kirk, Mark Steven, R-Ill.
Klobuchar, Amy, D-Minn.
Kohl, Herb, D-Wis.
Kyl, Jon, R-Ariz.
Landrieu, Mary L., D-La.
Lautenberg, Frank R., D-N.J.
Leahy, Patrick J., D-Vt.
LeMieux, George, R-Fla.
Levin, Carl, D-Mich.
Lieberman, Joseph I., I-Conn.
Lincoln, Blanche, D-Ark.
Lugar, Richard G., R-Ind.
Manchin, Joe III, D-W.Va.
McCain, John, R-Ariz.
McCaskill, Claire, D-Mo.
McConnell, Mitch, R-Ky.
Menendez, Robert, D-N.J.
Merkley, Jeff, D-Ore.
Mikulski, Barbara A., D-Md.
Murkowski, Lisa, R-Alaska
Murray, Patty, D-Wash.
Nelson, Ben, D-Neb.
Nelson, Bill, D-Fla.
Pryor, Mark, D-Ark.
Reed, Jack, D-R.I.
Reid, Harry, D-Nev.
Risch, Jim, R-Idaho
Roberts, Pat, R-Kan.
Rockefeller, John D. IV, D-W.Va.
Sanders, Bernard, I-Vt.
Schumer, Charles E., D-N.Y.
Sessions, Jeff, R-Ala.
Shaheen, Jeanne, D-N.H.
Shelby, Richard C., R-Ala.
Snowe, Olympia J., R-Maine
Specter, Arlen, D-Pa.
Stabenow, Debbie, D-Mich.
Tester, Jon, D-Mont.
Thune, John, R-S.D.
Udall, Mark, D-Colo.
Udall, Tom, D-N.M.
Vitter, David, R-La.
Voinovich, George V., R-Ohio
Warner, Mark, D-Va.
Webb, Jim, D-Va.
Whitehouse, Sheldon, D-R.I.
Wicker, Roger, R-Miss.
Wyden, Ron, D-Ore.

GOVERNORS
D 26, R 23, I 1

Ala. — Bob Riley, R
Alaska — Sean Parnell, R
Ariz. — Jan Brewer, R
Ark. — Mike Beebe, D
Calif. — Arnold Schwarzenegger, R
Colo. — Bill Ritter Jr., D
Conn. — M. Jodi Rell, R
Del. — Jack Markell, D
Fla. — Charlie Crist, I
Ga. — Sonny Perdue, R
Hawaii — Linda Lingle, R
Idaho — C.L. "Butch" Otter, R
Ill. — Pat Quinn, D
Ind. — Mitch Daniels, R
Iowa — Chet Culver, D
Kan. — Mark Parkinson, D
Ky. — Steven L. Beshear, D
La. — Bobby Jindal, R

Maine — John Baldacci, D
Md. — Martin O'Malley, D
Mass. — Deval Patrick, D
Mich. — Jennifer M. Granholm, D
Minn. — Tim Pawlenty, R
Miss. — Haley Barbour, R
Mo. — Jay Nixon, D
Mont. — Brian Schweitzer, D
Neb. — Dave Heineman, R
Nev. — Jim Gibbons, R
N.H. — John Lynch, D
N.J. — Chris Christie, R
N.M. — Bill Richardson, D
N.Y. — David A. Paterson, D
N.C. — Bev Perdue, D
N.D. — John Hoeven, R
Ohio — Ted Strickland, D
Okla. — Brad Henry, D
Ore. — Theodore R. Kulongoski, D
Pa. — Edward G. Rendell, D
R.I. — Donald L. Carcieri, R
S.C. — Mark Sanford, R
S.D. — Michael Rounds, R
Tenn. — Phil Bredesen, D
Texas — Rick Perry, R
Utah — Gary R. Herbert, R
Vt. — Jim Douglas, R
Va. — Bob McDonnell, R
Wash. — Christine Gregoire, D
W.Va. — Earl Ray Tomblin, D
Wis. — James E. Doyle, D
Wyo. — Dave Freudenthal, D

SUPREME COURT

Roberts, John G. Jr. — Md., Chief Justice
Alito, Samuel A. Jr. — N.J.
Breyer, Stephen G. — Mass.
Ginsburg, Ruth Bader — N.Y.
Kagan, Elena — N.Y.
Kennedy, Anthony M. — Calif.
Scalia, Antonin — Va.
Sotomayor, Sonia — N.Y.
Thomas, Clarence — Ga.

EXECUTIVE BRANCH

Obama, Barack — President
Biden, Joseph R. Jr. — Vice President

DEPARTMENT SECRETARIES

Chu, Steven — Energy
Clinton, Hillary Rodham — State
Donovan, Shaun — Housing and Urban Development
Duncan, Arne — Education
Gates, Robert M. — Defense
Geithner, Timothy F. — Treasury
Holder, Eric H. Jr. — Attorney General
LaHood, Ray —Transportation
Locke, Gary — Commerce
Napolitano, Janet — Homeland Security
Salazar, Ken — Interior
Sebelius, Kathleen — Health and Human Services
Shinseki, Eric — Veterans Affairs
Solis, Hilda L. — Labor
Vilsack, Tom — Agriculture

OTHER EXECUTIVE BRANCH OFFICERS

Blair, Dennis C. — Director of National Intelligence
Browner, Carol M. — Coordinator of Energy and Climate Policy
Kirk, Ron — U.S. Trade Representative
Jackson, Lisa P. — EPA Administrator
Jones, James L. — Assistant to the President for National Security Affairs
Mullen, Adm. Mike — Chairman, Joint Chiefs of Staff
Orszag, Peter R. — Director, Office of Management and Budget
Panetta, Leon E. — CIA Director
Rice, Susan E. — U.N. Ambassador
Summers, Lawrence H. — Director, National Economic Council
Vacant — White House Chief of Staff

Appendix B

VOTE STUDIES

Legislative Success for Obama Came With Political Challenge

PRESIDENTIAL LEADERSHIP IS ABOUT many things: the ability to communicate, the power of persuasion and the need to bring people together, to name a few. But it's also about adapting to change. For all of their power, presidents do not get to choose their circumstances. They just get to choose how they react.

It was a lesson that Barack Obama was learning, whether he liked it or not. Take the tax deal that the president struck with Republicans following his party's drubbing in November's election.

After two years of accomplishing his goals by negotiating only with Democrats, he found himself with little leverage to allow decade-old tax cuts for the wealthy to expire. So he switched gears and made a deal with newly ascendant Republicans to prevent a big tax increase on all Americans from taking effect Jan. 1, 2011 — and also secured priorities of his own, including a reduction in the Social Security tax paid by employees and an extension of benefits for the long-term unemployed.

The deal infuriated the liberal base of his party at the same time as it was hailed by many as a political masterstroke. Obama appeared almost uncomfortable with his own power play. At a Dec. 7 news conference, he awkwardly complained about the concessions that Republicans had forced him to make, and he railed against "sanctimonious" liberals in his own party while simultaneously defending the deal.

This was the discomfort of a president in the midst of change, and as Obama looked toward the second half of his term under radically altered circumstances — a Republican takeover of the House as a result of the November elections and diminished Democratic control in the Senate — he faced little choice but to adapt, or face an aimless drift.

How convincingly he adapted seemed crucial to both his political survival over the following two years and his ability to lead. Lawmakers — not to mention voters — expect a president to set the agenda even when the other party controls part or all of Congress. The challenge for Obama was adjusting his governing style to deal with a Republican Party torn between sharing the governing responsibility and defeating him, and Democrats wary about where he may take them.

In 2010, Obama won 85.8 percent of the votes on which he took a clearly stated position, according to Congressional Quarterly's annual study of voting patterns. That was less successful than his historic numbers in 2009, when he had a 96.7 percent success rate, the best tally since CQ began these voting pattern studies in 1953.

But his 2010 rate was the 10th-highest on record and the fourth-highest for a president in his second year. And the number did not capture the sheer size of the legislation enacted during his second year: the tax deal, in addition to overhauls of the health care system and financial regulations, not to mention student loans, food safety, a strategic weapons treaty with Russia and a repeal of the ban on openly gay people serving in the military.

Yet these legislative victories — all priorities the administration pushed for much of the year — didn't win him much favor with voters. "Leadership is more than getting a lot of bills through Congress," noted Julian Zelizer, a presidential historian at Princeton University.

How the tax cut compromise was viewed by the public would not be known until the 2012 election, at least, but it looked like it might be a pivot point in Obama's evolution.

As such, his dealing on taxes drew an inevitable comparison with President Bill Clinton after the Republican takeover of Congress in the 1994 election — particularly after Obama trotted out the former president to help sell the deal. But selling a tax cut to the public, and to lawmakers, was easy compared with Obama's other goals. And

CQ Vote Study Guide

Congressional Quarterly has conducted studies analyzing the voting behavior of members of Congress since 1945.

The three principal vote studies currently produced by CQ — presidential support, party unity and voting participation — have been conducted in a consistent manner since 1953. This is how the studies are carried out:

Selecting votes CQ bases its vote studies on all floor votes on which members were asked to vote "yea" or "nay." In 2010, there were 660 such roll call votes in the House and 299 in the Senate. The House total excludes quorum calls (there were four in 2010) because they require only that members vote "present."

The House total does include votes on procedural matters, including votes to approve the Journal (six in 2010). The Senate total includes votes to instruct the sergeant at arms to request members' presence in the chamber (five in 2010).

The presidential support and party unity studies are based on votes selected from the total according to the criteria described on pages B-7 and B-17.

Individual scores Members' scores in the accompanying charts are based only on the votes each member actually cast. This makes individual support and opposition scores add up to 100 percent. The same method is used to identify the leading scorers on pages B-5 and B-15.

Overall scores For consistency with previous years, calculations of average scores by chamber, party and region are based on all eligible "yea" or "nay" votes, whether or not all members participated. As a result, the failure of one or more lawmakers to participate in a roll call vote reduces average support and opposition scores. Therefore, chamber and party averages are not strictly comparable with individual member scores. (Methodology, 1987 Almanac, p. 22-C)

Rounding Scores in the tables for the full House and Senate membership are rounded to the nearest percentage point, although rounding is not used to increase any score to 100 percent or to reduce any score to zero. Scores for party and chamber support and opposition leaders are reported to one decimal point to rank them more precisely.

How Often the President Won

For the second straight year, President Obama was highly successful on roll call votes on which he took a clear position. His success rate of 85.8 percent, though down from his record-setting performance in 2009, was the 10th-highest of all time and the fourth-highest for the second year of any presidency. The data combines House and Senate figures.

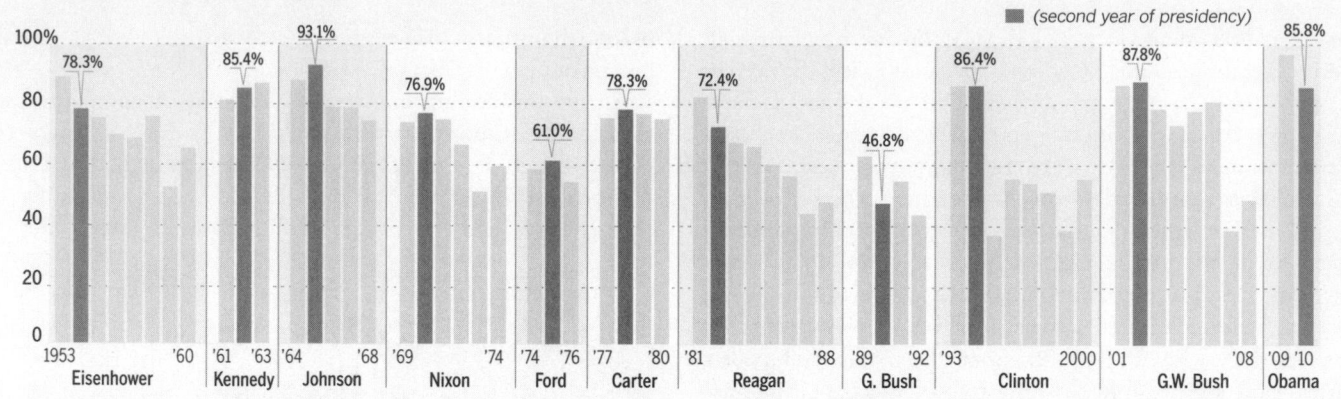

while the tax bill was ultimately a legislative victory, it had roots in his inability to build an early consensus behind his position.

"What is going to be fascinating to watch with the president is whether he is as adept as Clinton at making the quick kind of mental calculations to be able to simultaneously get some things that he wants to in terms of accomplishments, while also in effect discouraging any kind of, let's say, progressive uprising in the party," said Bill Lacy, a former aide in the Reagan White House and GOP operative who was the director of the Robert J. Dole Institute of Politics in Kansas.

GOP OPPOSITION, PRESIDENTIAL OPPORTUNITY?

Democrats often maligned Obama's ability to communicate a clear stance on issues such as the economy and health care and to distinguish the party's position from that of Republicans — a striking phenomenon for a man who rose to power in part on the strength of his oratorical skills. To liberals, the tax cut deal constituted yet another failure in this regard.

Yet while the outcome of the November election may have reflected weaknesses in Obama's approach, it might have made such situations easier to manage in the future: With Republicans taking the House, the White House would have a foil.

"The White House and the Senate are going to be in the business of responding to very conservative proposals from the House of Representatives. That is not necessarily a disadvantage," said William Galston, a former domestic policy adviser to Clinton and a senior fellow at the Brookings Institution.

In fact, while Obama got relatively little help from Republicans in 2010, he did better on average among GOP lawmakers in both chambers than Clinton did in most of the six years that Republicans controlled Congress during his presidency.

On Obama's biggest victories in 2010 — the votes on overhauling the health care system and tightening the regulation of Wall Street — he continued his general approach of setting broad goals, then letting his Democratic allies in Congress take the reins.

That often meant seeking to pick off just enough Republicans to win a 60-vote supermajority in the Senate. It was especially necessary once Massachusetts elected Republican Scott P. Brown in January to

the Senate seat long held by Edward M. Kennedy, depriving Democrats of their ability to overcome filibusters without GOP help.

While Obama's strategy worked in some cases — such as with an initial job creation bill that won Brown's support — it often fell short. Republican senators repeatedly rejected Democratic proposals to extend expired tax provisions and enact new stimulus spending.

So in December, Democrats staged votes in both chambers on their preferred tax strategy — extending tax cuts only for the middle class and letting those for the wealthy lapse — even though they knew their legislation had no chance of becoming law. To Rep. Roy Blunt, R-Mo., it was emblematic of the White House's preference to defer to Democratic leaders in Congress to accomplish its goals, no matter what damage it did to Obama politically. "They still don't have the process under control," Blunt said in late November, before the tax deal was announced. After two years of ramming through bill after bill, the president still didn't grasp "how to get everyone on your side willing to head in the direction you're trying to go," Blunt said.

Many Republicans were well aware that the more they cooperated with the president, the better he looked. It was no coincidence that some Republicans began to signal their opposition to the New START arms reduction accord with Russia just as Obama was winning high-profile deals on taxes and repealing the ban on gays and lesbians serving in the U.S. military. In that case, Obama won on START — not by cooperation, but by holding the line — an indication that on certain issues, he could pursue a strategy akin to that of Truman, who ran against a "Do-Nothing Congress" in 1948.

From a statistical perspective, a closer look at the breakdown of the midnight House vote on the Obama tax compromise Dec. 17 illustrated the dynamics the president would face in the House in 2011.

Tea party activists disavowed the deal, and Speaker-in-waiting John A. Boehner of Ohio remained quiet about the whole process. One out of five of the Republicans who voted — mainly die-hard conservatives such as Michele Bachmann of Minnesota and Joe Wilson of South Carolina — voted no on the bill. That group stood

FOR MORE INFORMATION	
Top scorers	B-5
Background	B-7
Vote lists	B-8
Senators' scores	B-9
House members' scores	B-10

Leading Scorers: Presidential Support

Support indicates those who voted in 2010 most often for President Obama's position, when it was clearly known. **Opposition** shows those who voted most often against his position. Lawmakers who left office or who missed half or more of the votes are not listed. Scores are reported to one decimal point only here; those with identical scores are listed alphabetically. *(Complete scores, p. B-9)*

SENATE

SUPPORT

Democrats		Republicans	
Carper, Del.	100.0%	Collins, Maine	68.8%
Conrad, N.D.	100.0	Snowe, Maine	65.6
Durbin, Ill.	100.0	Voinovich, Ohio*	61.7
Johnson, S.D.	100.0	Brown, Mass.	60.7
Kerry, Mass.	100.0	Murkowski, Alaska	60.0
Klobuchar, Minn.	100.0	Lugar, Ind.	54.7
Kohl, Wis.	100.0	Alexander, Tenn.	51.6
Menendez, N.J.	100.0	Gregg, N.H.*	49.0
Schumer, N.Y.	100.0	Johanns, Neb.	48.4
Shaheen, N.H.	100.0	LeMieux, Fla.*	48.3
18 senators	98.4	Bond, Mo.*	47.3
		2 senators	46.9

OPPOSITION

Democrats		Republicans	
Nelson, Neb.	25.0%	Roberts, Kan.	71.4%
Feingold, Wis.*	12.7	DeMint, S.C.	70.7
Lincoln, Ark.*	9.8	Hutchison, Texas	70.0
Pryor, Ark.	8.1	Coburn, Okla.	66.7
Wyden, Ore.	5.3	Thune, S.D.	66.7
Cantwell, Wash.	4.8	Ensign, Nev.	66.1
Hagan, N.C.	4.8	Brownback, Kan.*	65.4
Harkin, Iowa	4.8	Bunning, Ky.*	64.9
Merkley, Ore.	4.8	Crapo, Idaho	63.9
Udall, Colo.	4.8	Vitter, La.	62.7
Webb, Va.	4.7	Barrasso, Wyo.	62.5
Bayh, Ind.*	3.6	Risch, Idaho	62.5

HOUSE

SUPPORT

Democrats		Republicans	
Capps, Calif.	97.6%	Cao, La.*	69.0%
Dicks, Wash.	97.6	Castle, Del.*	61.9
Hare, Ill.*	97.6	Murphy, Pa.	52.4
Hoyer, Md.	97.6	Djou, Hawaii*	51.7
Levin, Mich.	97.6	Jones, N.C.	51.3
Schiff, Calif.	97.6	Ehlers, Mich.*	48.7
Sherman, Calif.	97.6	Ros-Lehtinen, Fla.	46.3
Berman, Calif.	97.5	LaTourette, Ohio	43.9
Himes, Conn.	97.5	Diaz-Balart, L., Fla.*	43.6
Deutch, Fla.	96.8	Dent, Pa.	42.9
19 members	95.2	Gerlach, Pa.	42.9
		Platts, Pa.	42.9
		Posey, Fla.	42.9
		Diaz-Balart, M., Fla.	40.5
		LoBiondo, N.J.	40.5
		Smith, N.J.	40.5
		Bilbray, Calif.	39.5
		2 members	39.0

OPPOSITION

Democrats		Republicans	
Taylor, Miss.*	56.1%	Moran, Kan.*	81.8%
Bright, Ala.*	48.8	Campbell, Calif.	81.6
Minnick, Idaho*	38.1	Flake, Ariz.	80.5
McIntyre, N.C.	35.7	Akin, Mo.	80.0
Childers, Miss.*	35.0	Chaffetz, Utah	78.6
Cooper, Tenn.	34.1	Franks, Ariz.	78.6
Berry, Ark.*	33.3	Lamborn, Colo.	78.6
Nye, Va.*	33.3	Hoekstra, Mich.*	78.3
Marshall, Ga.*	32.5	Broun, Ga.	78.0
Boren, Okla.	32.4	Duncan, Tenn.	78.0
Critz, Pa.	31.0	Jordan, Ohio	78.0
Peterson, Minn.	31.0	King, Iowa	78.0
Shuler, N.C.	28.9	Boehner, Ohio	77.5
Herseth Sandlin, S.D.*	28.6	Ryan, Wis.	76.3
Tanner, Tenn.*	28.2	7 members	76.2
Boucher, Va.*	27.5		
3 members	26.2		

Defeated for re-election, retired or elected to other office.

o grow in number and influence within the GOP caucus when the conservative freshman class arrived Jan. 5, 2011, and it seemed less likely to entertain compromise on much of anything with Obama.

BRINGING ALONG DEMOCRATS

The numbers also warranted caution on the Democratic side. Part of the president's success in the 111th Congress stemmed from a high degree of unity among Democrats. It meant prodding — and sometimes dragging along — reluctant members of his own party.

The 112 House Democrats who opposed the tax deal included not only hard-core liberals but also a number of Democrats toward the middle, such as Kentucky's John Yarmuth, Washington's Adam Smith and Maryland's Chris Van Hollen, a leadership negotiator on the tax question.

The tax vote showed that if Obama moved to meet Republicans halfway, he could face even more difficulties in holding onto Democrats.

A switch in control of the House also inevitably meant that the president's party lost a number of moderates and lawmakers from swing districts, leaving a smaller caucus dominated by the

Share of Presidential Positions Stays Low

The House held 42 roll call votes in 2010 on which President Obama took a clear position, and the Senate held 64. In recent years, the frequency of presidential support votes has been generally declining. As a share of all House votes, the figure fell to 6.4 percent, the second-lowest since 1953. The percentage of Senate presidential support votes rose a bit in 2010, to 21.4 percent.

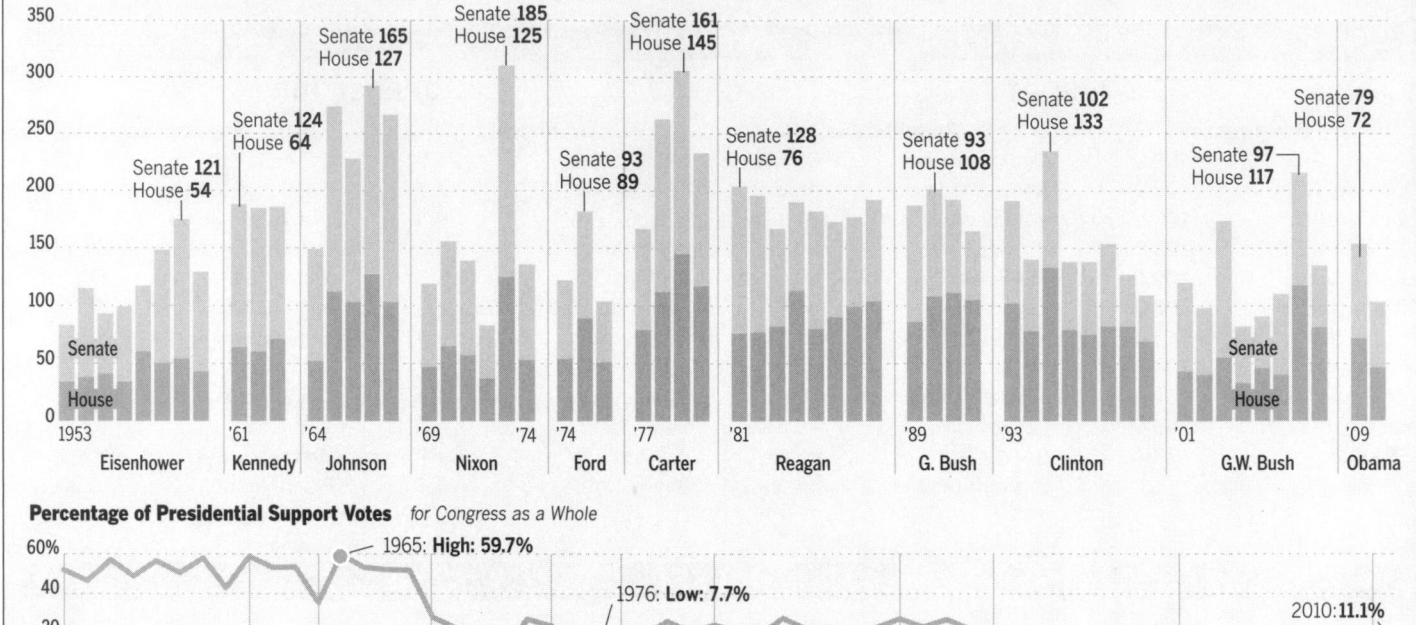

most liberal or conservative members from safe districts — even as the president tried to reach independents critical to a national election.

"It's harder dealing with the survivors in the party," noted Connecticut Democrat Christopher J. Dodd, who was retiring from the Senate after 30 years. "Their base is different than your base."

That, of course, was exactly the situation in which Obama found himself after the tax deal. House Democrats, who had repeatedly stuck their necks out for the president over the previous two years, were furious at having been cut out of the loop. "It's tough for the party who shares the affiliation with the president," Dodd said.

The question was how much Obama would be able to accom-plish with Boehner, and not Nancy Pelosi, D-Calif., holding the Speaker's gavel — and how many Democrats in both chambers would be there for him when he compromised with Republicans. That's not a dynamic he had faced previously: The degree of opposition shown by House Democrats to a president from their party was the second-lowest in the history of CQ's vote studies. Only 2009 was lower.

Veteran House Democrats insisted that the tax compromise was a function of the looming end-of-the-year expiration date that came with the 2001 and 2003 tax cuts — not a blueprint for Obama's legislative strategy moving forward. "I think we're in a unique situation with the tax bill. I think it's much too early to predict anything beyond what had to happen because of the Dec. 31 deadline," said Massachusetts Democrat Edward J. Markey. ■

Winning Votes

Obama didn't enjoy quite the overwhelming success in Congress in 2010 that he had in 2009. But on roll call votes where he got involved, he still did well by historical standards, winning record support from Senate Democrats.

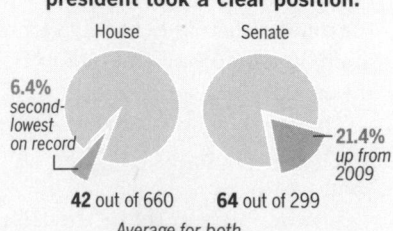

Share of votes on which the president took a clear position:

House
6.4% second-lowest on record
42 out of 660

Senate
21.4% up from 2009
64 out of 299

Average for both chambers: 11.1%

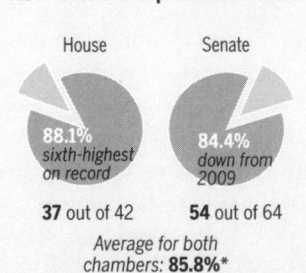

How often the president won:

House
88.1% sixth-highest on record
37 out of 42

Senate
84.4% down from 2009
54 out of 64

Average for both chambers: 85.8%*

*down from a record of 96.7% in 2009

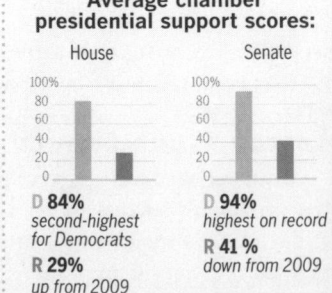

Average chamber presidential support scores:

House
D 84% second-highest for Democrats
R 29% up from 2009

Senate
D 94% highest on record
R 41% down from 2009

Presidential Support Background

Congressional Quarterly's editors select presidential support votes each year based on clear statements by the president or authorized spokesmen. **Support** scores show the percentage of roll call votes on which members of Congress voted in agreement with the president's position. **Success** shows the percentage of the selected votes on which the president prevailed.

Presidential Success by Issues

Economic affairs includes votes on taxes, trade, and omnibus and some supplemental spending bills, which may fund both domestic and defense/foreign policy programs. **Confirmation** votes in the Senate are included only in the chamber's overall scores.

	Defense/Foreign Policy		Domestic		Economic Affairs		Overall	
	2010	2009	2010	2009	2010	2009	2010	2009
House	75.0%	85.7%	100.0%	97.6%	86.7%	93.8%	88.1%	94.4%
Senate	100.0	93.8	55.6	100.0	73.7	100.0	84.4	98.7
Congress	80.0	90.0	83.3	98.4	79.4	96.2	85.8	96.7

House Average Presidential Support Scores

	DEMOCRATS	REPUBLICANS		DEMOCRATS	REPUBLICANS		DEMOCRATS	REPUBLICANS		DEMOCRATS	REPUBLICANS		DEMOCRATS	REPUBLICANS
Eisenhower, R			**Johnson, D**			**Ford, R**			1986	25%	65%	1999	73%	23%
1954	44%	71%	1964	74%	38%	1974	41%	51%	1987	24	62	2000	73	27
1955	53	60	1965	74	41	1975	38	63	1988	25	57			
1956	52	72	1966	63	37	1976	32	63				**G.W. Bush, R**		
1957	49	54	1967	69	46				**G. Bush, R**			2001	31	86
1958	44	67	1968	64	51	**Carter, D**			1989	36	69	2002	32	82
1959	40	68				1977	63	42	1990	25	63	2003	26	89
1960	44	59	**Nixon, R**			1978	60	36	1991	34	72	2004	30	80
			1969	48	57	1979	64	34	1992	25	71	2005	24	81
Kennedy, D			1970	53	66	1980	63	40				2006	31	85
1961	73	37	1971	47	72				**Clinton, D**			2007	7	72
1962	72	42	1972	47	64	**Reagan, R**			1993	77	39	2008	16	64
1963	72	32	1973	35	62	1981	42	68	1994	75	47			
			1974	46	65	1982	39	64	1995	75	22	**Obama, D**		
						1983	28	70	1996	74	38	2009	90	26
						1984	34	60	1997	71	30	2010	84	29
						1985	30	67	1998	74	26			

Senate Average Presidential Support Scores

	DEMOCRATS	REPUBLICANS		DEMOCRATS	REPUBLICANS		DEMOCRATS	REPUBLICANS		DEMOCRATS	REPUBLICANS		DEMOCRATS	REPUBLICANS
Eisenhower, R			**Johnson, D**			**Ford, R**			1986	37%	78%	1999	84%	34%
1954	38%	73%	1964	61%	45%	1974	39%	55%	1987	36	64	2000	89	46
1955	56	72	1965	64	48	1975	47	68	1988	47	68			
1956	39	72	1966	57	43	1976	39	62				**G.W. Bush, R**		
1957	51	69	1967	61	53				**G. Bush, R**			2001	66	94
1958	44	67	1968	48	47	**Carter, D**			1989	55	82	2002	71	89
1959	38	72				1977	70	52	1990	38	70	2003	48	94
1960	43	66	**Nixon, R**			1978	66	41	1991	41	83	2004	60	91
			1969	47	66	1979	68	47	1992	32	73	2005	38	86
Kennedy, D			1970	45	60	1980	62	45				2006	51	85
1961	65	36	1971	40	64				**Clinton, D**			2007	37	78
1962	63	39	1972	44	66	**Reagan, R**			1993	87	29	2008	34	70
1963	63	44	1973	37	61	1981	49	80	1994	86	42			
			1974	39	57	1982	43	74	1995	81	29	**Obama, D**		
						1983	42	73	1996	83	37	2009	92	50
						1984	41	76	1997	85	60	2010	94	41
						1985	35	75	1998	82	41			

2010 Presidential Position Votes

The following is a list of the 42 House and 64 Senate roll call votes in 2010 on which the president took a clear position, based on his statements or those of authorized spokesmen. A victory is a vote on which the president's position prevailed.

HOUSE

Defense and Foreign Policy

VOTE DESCRIPTION
NUMBER

9 Victories

98	Troop withdrawal
230	Weapons acquisitions
317	Military service
431	War funding
432	Troop withdrawal
473	Troop withdrawal
474	Defense spending
482	Defense spending
638	Military service

3 Defeats

316	Weapons acquisitions
335	Detainee policy
336	Defense policy

Domestic Policy

VOTE DESCRIPTION
NUMBER

15 Victories

2	Executive powers
64	Health care
165	Health care
167	Health care
194	Health care
255	Climate change
362	Health care
391	Campaign finance
492	Domestic spending
499	Domestic spending
506	Oil drilling
512	Oil drilling
603	Social policy
625	Immigration
626	Entitlements

Economic Affairs and Trade

VOTE DESCRIPTION
NUMBER

13 Victories

46	Debt limit
48	Budget policy
90	Tax extensions
186	Economic stimulus
211	Economic stimulus
375	Economic stimulus
413	Financial regulation
463	Economic stimulus
518	Economic stimulus
539	Economic stimulus
573	Foreclosure policy
604	Tax extensions
647	Tax extensions

2 Defeats

579	Economic stimulus
611	Economic stimulus

House Success Score

Victories	37
Defeats	5
Total	42
Success rate	**88.1%**

SENATE

Defense and Foreign Policy

VOTE DESCRIPTION
NUMBER

3 Victories

176	Defense spending
281	Military service
298	Foreign policy

Domestic Policy

VOTE DESCRIPTION
NUMBER

5 Victories

105	Health care
184	Climate change
239	Workplace issues
244	Health care
257	Food regulation

4 Defeats

220	Campaign finance
240	Campaign finance
249	Workplace issues
278	Immigration

Economic Affairs and Trade

VOTE DESCRIPTION
NUMBER

14 Victories

2	Financial industry bailout
14	Debt limit
25	Economic stimulus
48	Tax extensions
55	Economic stimulus
117	Tax extensions
133	Financial regulation
162	Financial regulation
208	Financial regulation
215	Economic stimulus
226	Tax extensions
228	Economic stimulus
237	Economic stimulus
276	Tax extensions

5 Defeats

5	Debt policy
45	Tax extensions
221	Economic stimulus
258	Tax extensions
267	Economic stimulus

Nominations

VOTE DESCRIPTION
NUMBER

32 Victories

1	Beverly Baldwin Martin	203	David H. Petraeus
3	Rosanna Malouf Peterson	205	Sharon Johnson Coleman
16	Ben S. Bernanke	229	Elena Kagan
18	M. Patricia Smith	230	Jane Branstetter Stranch
20	Martha N. Johnson	280	Ellen Lipton Hollander
21	Joseph A. Greenaway Jr.	284	Raymond Joseph Lohier Jr.
30	Barbara Milano Keenan	290	Benita Y. Pearson
43	William M. Conley	291	William Joseph Martinez
56	Rogeriee Thompson	299	Mary Helen Murguia
119	Lael Brainard		
120	Marisa J. Demeo		
121	Christopher H. Schroeder		
122	Thomas I. Vanaskie		
123	Denny Chin		
128	Gloria M. Navarro		
129	Nancy D. Freudenthal		
177	Audrey Goldstein Fleissig		
178	Lucy Haeran Koh		
185	Tanya Walton Pratt		
186	Brian Anthony Jackson		
195	Mark A. Goldsmith		
196	Marc T. Treadwell		
201	Gary Scott Feinerman		

1 Defeat

22	Craig Becker (*cloture*)

Senate Success Score

Victories	54
Defeats	10
Total	64
Success rate	**84.4%**
Success rate, minus nominations	**71.0%**

IN THE SENATE | By Vote Number

1. Presidential Support Score. Percentage of recorded votes cast in 2010 on which President Obama took a position and on which the senator voted "yea" or "nay" in agreement with the president's position. Failure to vote does not lower an individual's score.

2. Presidential Opposition Score. Percentage of recorded votes cast in 2010 on which President Obama took a position and on which the senator voted "yea" or "nay" in disagreement with the president's position. Failure to vote does not lower an individual's score.

3. Participation in Presidential Support Votes. Percentage of the recorded Senate votes in 2010 on which President Obama took a position and for which the senator was eligible and present and voted "yea" or "nay." There were a total of 64 such recorded votes.

	1	2	3		1	2	3
ALABAMA				**MONTANA**			
Shelby	41	59	98	Baucus	97	3	98
Sessions	40	60	97	Tester	97	3	100
ALASKA				**NEBRASKA**			
Murkowski	60	40	86	Nelson	75	25	100
Begich	97	3	98	**Johanns**	48	52	97
ARIZONA				**NEVADA**			
McCain	39	61	100	Reid	97	3	100
Kyl	40	60	98	**Ensign**	34	66	92
ARKANSAS				**NEW HAMPSHIRE**			
Lincoln	90	10	95	**Gregg**	49	51	77
Pryor	92	8	97	Shaheen	100	0	97
CALIFORNIA				**NEW JERSEY**			
Feinstein	98	2	100	Lautenberg	97	3	98
Boxer	98	2	98	Menendez	100	0	100
COLORADO				**NEW MEXICO**			
Udall	95	5	97	Bingaman	98	2	100
Bennet	98	2	100	Udall	97	3	100
CONNECTICUT				**NEW YORK**			
Dodd	98	2	100	Schumer	100	0	100
Lieberman	97	3	98	Gillibrand	98	2	97
DELAWARE				**NORTH CAROLINA**			
Carper	100	0	100	**Burr**	43	57	95
Kaufman[1]	98	2	98	Hagan	95	5	97
Coons[1]	100	0	100	**NORTH DAKOTA**			
FLORIDA				Conrad	100	0	100
Nelson	98	2	95	Dorgan	97	3	98
LeMieux	48	52	94	**OHIO**			
GEORGIA				**Voinovich**	62	38	94
Chambliss	42	58	97	Brown	98	2	100
Isakson	42	58	94	**OKLAHOMA**			
HAWAII				**Inhofe**	39	61	95
Inouye	98	2	92	**Coburn**	33	67	98
Akaka	98	2	100	**OREGON**			
IDAHO				Wyden	95	5	89
Crapo	36	64	95	Merkley	95	5	98
Risch	37	63	100	**PENNSYLVANIA**			
ILLINOIS				Specter	97	3	97
Durbin	100	0	98	Casey	98	2	98
Burris[2]	98	2	100	**RHODE ISLAND**			
Kirk[2]	45	55	92	Reed	98	2	100
INDIANA				Whitehouse	97	3	100
Lugar	55	45	100	**SOUTH CAROLINA**			
Bayh	96	4	86	**Graham**	47	53	97
IOWA				**DeMint**	29	71	91
Grassley	42	58	100	**SOUTH DAKOTA**			
Harkin	95	5	98	Johnson	100	0	98
KANSAS				**Thune**	33	67	94
Brownback	35	65	81	**TENNESSEE**			
Roberts	29	71	87	**Alexander**	52	48	97
KENTUCKY				**Corker**	47	53	100
McConnell	41	59	100	**TEXAS**			
Bunning	35	65	89	**Hutchison**	30	70	78
LOUISIANA				**Cornyn**	38	62	98
Landrieu	98	2	94	**UTAH**			
Vitter	37	63	80	**Hatch**	46	54	92
MAINE				**Bennett**	41	59	77
Snowe	66	34	100	**VERMONT**			
Collins	69	31	100	Leahy	98	2	100
MARYLAND				*Sanders*	95	5	95
Mikulski	98	2	95	**VIRGINIA**			
Cardin	98	2	100	Webb	95	5	100
MASSACHUSETTS				Warner	97	3	97
Kerry	100	0	98	**WASHINGTON**			
Kirk[3]	87	13	100	Murray	98	2	98
Brown[3]	61	39	100	Cantwell	95	5	98
MICHIGAN				**WEST VIRGINIA**			
Levin	98	2	100	Byrd[4]	94	6	44
Stabenow	98	2	97	Rockefeller	97	3	100
MINNESOTA				Goodwin[4]	100	0	100
Klobuchar	100	0	98	Manchin[4]	90	10	77
Franken	98	2	100	**WISCONSIN**			
MISSISSIPPI				Kohl	100	0	98
Cochran	47	53	100	Feingold	87	13	98
Wicker	41	59	100	**WYOMING**			
MISSOURI				**Enzi**	42	58	97
Bond	47	53	86	**Barrasso**	37	63	100
McCaskill	98	2	92				

KEY   **Republicans**   Democrats   *Independents*

[1] Sen. Chris Coons, D-Del., was sworn in Nov. 15 to replace Democrat Ted Kaufman, appointed Jan. 15, 2009, to temporarily fill the vacancy created by Democrat Joseph R. Biden Jr., who resigned to become vice president. The first vote for which Coons was eligible was vote 249; the last vote for which Kaufman was eligible was vote 248.

[2] Sen. Mark Steven Kirk, R-Ill., was sworn in Nov. 29 to replace Democrat Roland W. Burris, who was appointed Dec. 30, 2008, to temporarily fill the vacancy created by Democrat Barack Obama, who resigned to become president. The first vote for which Kirk was eligible was vote 252; the last vote for which Burris was eligible was vote 251.

[3] Sen. Scott P. Brown, R-Mass., was sworn in Feb. 4 to replace Democrat Paul G. Kirk Jr., who was appointed Sept. 24, 2009, to temporarily fill the vacancy created by Democrat Edward M. Kennedy, who died Aug. 25, 2009. The first vote for which Brown was eligible was vote 21; the last vote for which Kirk was eligible was vote 20.

[4] Sen. Joe Manchin III, D-W.Va., was sworn in Nov. 15 to replace Democrat Carte P. Goodwin, who was appointed July 16 to temporarily fill the vacancy created by Democrat Robert C. Byrd, who died June 28. The first vote for which Manchin was eligible was vote 249. Goodwin was eligible for votes 209 through 248. The last vote for which Byrd was eligible was vote 200.

IN THE HOUSE | By Vote Number

1. Presidential Support. Percentage of recorded votes cast in 2010 on which President Obama took a position and on which the member voted "yea" or "nay" in agreement with the president's position. Failure to vote does not lower an individual's score.

2. Presidential Opposition. Percentage of recorded votes cast in 2010 on which President Obama took a position and on which the member voted "yea" or "nay" in disagreement with the president's position. Failure to vote does not lower an individual's score.

3. Participation in Presidential Support Votes. Percentage of the recorded votes in 2010 on which President Obama took a position and for which the member was eligible and present and voted "yea" or "nay." There were a total of 42 such recorded votes.

		1	2	3
ALABAMA				
1	**Bonner**	29	71	98
2	Bright	51	49	98
3	**Rogers**	26	74	100
4	**Aderholt**	29	71	100
5	**Griffith**	30	70	79
6	**Bachus**	32	68	98
7	Davis	87	13	74
ALASKA				
AL	**Young**	38	62	88
ARIZONA				
1	Kirkpatrick	80	20	95
2	**Franks**	21	79	100
3	**Shadegg**	29	71	90
4	Pastor	90	10	98
5	Mitchell	76	24	100
6	**Flake**	20	80	98
7	Grijalva	80	20	98
8	Giffords	88	12	100
ARKANSAS				
1	Berry	67	33	71
2	Snyder	95	5	98
3	**Boozman**	30	70	95
4	Ross	74	26	100
CALIFORNIA				
1	Thompson	88	12	98
2	**Herger**	29	71	100
3	**Lungren**	27	73	98
4	**McClintock**	29	71	100
5	Matsui	90	10	100
6	Woolsey	89	11	88
7	Miller, George	88	12	98
8	Pelosi[1]	95	5	52
9	Lee	85	15	98
10	Garamendi	83	17	100
11	McNerney	86	14	100
12	Speier	87	13	95
13	Stark	85	15	95
14	Eshoo	93	7	98
15	Honda	90	10	98
16	Lofgren	90	10	98
17	Farr	86	14	100
18	Cardoza	95	5	95
19	**Radanovich**	25	75	57
20	Costa	93	7	98
21	**Nunes**	27	73	95
22	**McCarthy**	30	70	88
23	Capps	98	2	98
24	**Gallegly**	29	71	90
25	**McKeon**	26	74	100
26	**Dreier**	31	69	100
27	Sherman	98	2	100
28	Berman	97	3	95
29	Schiff	98	2	98
30	Waxman	95	5	95
31	Becerra	90	10	100
32	Chu	88	12	98
33	Watson	87	13	76
34	Roybal-Allard	93	7	100
35	Waters	78	22	88
36	Harman	95	5	95
37	Richardson	83	17	100
38	Napolitano	83	17	100
39	Sánchez, Linda	85	15	95
40	**Royce**	26	74	100
41	**Lewis**	27	73	98
42	**Miller, Gary**	29	71	98
43	Baca	93	7	100
44	**Calvert**	27	73	98
45	**Bono Mack**	31	69	100
46	**Rohrabacher**	24	76	100
47	Sanchez, Loretta	86	14	100
48	**Campbell**	18	82	90
49	**Issa**	29	71	98
50	**Bilbray**	39	61	90
51	Filner	80	20	95
52	**Hunter**	26	74	100
53	Davis	95	5	100

		1	2	3
COLORADO				
1	DeGette	92	8	93
2	Polis	81	19	100
3	Salazar	93	7	100
4	Markey	88	12	100
5	**Lamborn**	21	79	100
6	**Coffman**	29	71	100
7	Perlmutter	95	5	98
CONNECTICUT				
1	Larson	88	12	100
2	Courtney	95	5	100
3	DeLauro	90	10	100
4	Himes	97	3	95
5	Murphy	90	10	100
DELAWARE				
AL	**Castle**	62	38	100
FLORIDA				
1	**Miller**	33	67	95
2	Boyd	78	22	88
3	Brown	87	13	93
4	**Crenshaw**	34	66	98
5	**Brown-Waite**	37	63	83
6	**Stearns**	33	67	100
7	**Mica**	29	71	100
8	Grayson	83	17	95
9	**Bilirakis**	33	67	100
10	**Young**	32	68	67
11	Castor	93	8	95
12	**Putnam**	36	64	93
13	**Buchanan**	39	61	98
14	**Mack**	29	71	100
15	**Posey**	43	57	100
16	**Rooney**	32	68	98
17	Meek	94	6	79
18	**Ros-Lehtinen**	46	54	98
19	Deutch[2]	97	3	97
20	Wasserman Schultz	95	5	93
21	**Diaz-Balart, L.**	44	56	93
22	Klein	93	7	98
23	Hastings	83	17	83
24	Kosmas	90	10	98
25	**Diaz-Balart, M.**	40	60	100
GEORGIA				
1	**Kingston**	26	74	100
2	Bishop	90	10	100
3	**Westmoreland**	27	73	98
4	Johnson	90	10	98
5	Lewis	83	17	95
6	**Price**	26	74	100
7	**Linder**	24	76	79
8	Marshall	67	33	95
9	**Deal**[3]	17	83	75
9	**Graves**[3]	24	76	100
10	**Broun**	22	78	98
11	**Gingrey**	25	75	95
12	Barrow	83	17	98
13	Scott	95	5	100
HAWAII				
1	Abercrombie[4]	100	0	75
1	**Djou**[4]	52	48	100
2	Hirono	93	7	98
IDAHO				
1	Minnick	62	38	100
2	**Simpson**	29	71	100
ILLINOIS				
1	Rush	83	17	98
2	Jackson	79	21	100
3	Lipinski	86	14	100
4	Gutierrez	82	18	90
5	Quigley	88	12	100
6	**Roskam**	29	71	98
7	Davis	83	17	100
8	Bean	90	10	98
9	Schakowsky	88	12	98
10	Kirk[5]	41	59	91
11	Halvorson	90	10	98
12	Costello	79	21	100
13	**Biggert**	38	62	100
14	Foster	90	10	98
15	**Johnson**	29	71	100

[1] The Speaker votes only at her discretion.

[2] Rep. Ted Deutch, D-Fla., was sworn in April 15 to fill the seat vacated by the Jan. 3 resignation of Democrat Robert Wexler. The first vote for which Deutch was eligible was vote 205; Wexler was not eligible for any presidential support votes in 2010.

[3] Rep. Tom Graves, R-Ga., was sworn in June 14 to fill the seat vacated by Republican Nathan Deal, who resigned March 21 to run for governor. The first vote for which Graves was eligible was vote 356; the last vote for which Deal was eligible was vote 168.

[4] Rep. Charles K. Djou, R-Hawaii, was sworn in May 25 to fill the seat vacated by Democrat Neil Abercrombie, who resigned Feb. 28 to run for governor. The first vote for which Djou was eligible was vote 296; the last vote for which Abercrombie was eligible was vote 74.

[5] Rep. Mark Steven Kirk, R-Ill., resigned Nov. 29 to assume the Senate seat he won in a Nov. 2 special election. The last vote for which Kirk was eligible was vote 580.

[6] Rep. Marlin Stutzman, R-Ind., was sworn in Nov. 16 to fill the vacancy created by the May 21 resignation of Republican Mark Souder. The first vote for which Stutzman was eligible was vote 571; the last vote for which Souder was eligible was vote 290.

[7] Rep. Tom Reed, R-N.Y., was sworn in Nov. 18 to fill the vacancy created by the March 8 resignation of Democrat Eric Massa. The first vote for which Reed was eligible was vote 580; the last vote for which Massa was eligible was vote 91.

[8] Rep. Mark Critz, D-Pa., was sworn in May 20 to fill the seat vacated by the Feb. 8 death of Democrat John P. Murtha. The first vote for which Critz was eligible was vote 286; the last vote for which Murtha was eligible was vote 48.

KEY   **Republicans**   Democrats

	1	2	3
16 Manzullo	36	64	100
17 Hare	98	2	100
18 Schock	33	67	100
19 Shimkus	31	69	100
INDIANA			
1 Visclosky	83	17	98
2 Donnelly	76	24	100
3 Souder[6]	23	77	100
3 Stutzman[6]	25	75	89
4 Buyer	31	69	86
5 Burton	26	74	100
6 Pence	25	75	95
7 Carson	93	8	95
8 Ellsworth	86	14	100
9 Hill	86	14	100
IOWA			
1 Braley	93	7	98
2 Loebsack	95	5	100
3 Boswell	93	7	100
4 Latham	29	71	100
5 King	22	78	98
KANSAS			
1 Moran	18	82	79
2 Jenkins	26	74	100
3 Moore	93	7	100
4 Tiahrt	26	74	74
KENTUCKY			
1 Whitfield	39	61	98
2 Guthrie	29	71	98
3 Yarmuth	90	10	98
4 Davis	31	69	83
5 Rogers	26	74	100
6 Chandler	78	22	98
LOUISIANA			
1 Scalise	31	69	100
2 Cao	69	31	100
3 Melancon	86	14	88
4 Fleming	24	76	100
5 Alexander	26	74	100
6 Cassidy	35	65	95
7 Boustany	33	67	95
MAINE			
1 Pingree	83	17	95
2 Michaud	88	12	100
MARYLAND			
1 Kratovil	81	19	100
2 Ruppersberger	93	7	98
3 Sarbanes	95	5	100
4 Edwards	77	23	95
5 Hoyer	98	2	100
6 Bartlett	27	73	98
7 Cummings	90	10	100
8 Van Hollen	95	5	100
MASSACHUSETTS			
1 Olver	90	10	100
2 Neal	88	12	100
3 McGovern	85	15	98
4 Frank	85	15	98
5 Tsongas	88	12	100
6 Tierney	83	17	100
7 Markey	86	14	100
8 Capuano	85	15	98
9 Lynch	88	12	98
10 Delahunt	87	13	74
MICHIGAN			
1 Stupak	85	15	93
2 Hoekstra	22	78	55
3 Ehlers	49	51	93
4 Camp	37	63	98
5 Kildee	95	5	100
6 Upton	36	64	100
7 Schauer	88	12	100
8 Rogers	35	65	95
9 Peters	83	17	100
10 Miller	31	69	100
11 McCotter	34	66	98
12 Levin	98	2	98
13 Kilpatrick	83	17	83
14 Conyers	92	8	88
15 Dingell	95	5	98
MINNESOTA			
1 Walz	95	5	100
2 Kline	27	73	98
3 Paulsen	33	67	100
4 McCollum	90	10	98

	1	2	3
5 Ellison	83	17	100
6 Bachmann	26	74	90
7 Peterson	69	31	100
8 Oberstar	93	7	100
MISSISSIPPI			
1 Childers	65	35	95
2 Thompson	83	17	100
3 Harper	26	74	100
4 Taylor	44	56	98
MISSOURI			
1 Clay	80	20	98
2 Akin	20	80	83
3 Carnahan	93	7	100
4 Skelton	76	24	98
5 Cleaver	81	19	100
6 Graves	28	72	86
7 Blunt	29	71	83
8 Emerson	33	67	100
9 Luetkemeyer	29	71	98
MONTANA			
AL Rehberg	26	74	100
NEBRASKA			
1 Fortenberry	29	71	100
2 Terry	29	71	98
3 Smith	26	74	100
NEVADA			
1 Berkley	95	5	100
2 Heller	33	67	95
3 Titus	88	12	100
NEW HAMPSHIRE			
1 Shea-Porter	88	12	98
2 Hodes	90	10	95
NEW JERSEY			
1 Andrews	93	7	98
2 LoBiondo	40	60	100
3 Adler	81	19	100
4 Smith	40	60	100
5 Garrett	24	76	100
6 Pallone	93	7	98
7 Lance	31	69	100
8 Pascrell	95	5	100
9 Rothman	95	5	98
10 Payne	83	17	98
11 Frelinghuysen	29	71	100
12 Holt	90	10	100
13 Sires	86	14	100
NEW MEXICO			
1 Heinrich	95	5	100
2 Teague	80	20	98
3 Luján	95	5	100
NEW YORK			
1 Bishop	95	5	100
2 Israel	93	7	100
3 King	33	67	93
4 McCarthy	93	8	95
5 Ackerman	93	7	95
6 Meeks	95	5	95
7 Crowley	87	13	95
8 Nadler	86	14	100
9 Weiner	86	14	100
10 Towns	83	17	98
11 Clarke	76	24	100
12 Velázquez	79	21	100
13 McMahon	80	20	98
14 Maloney	87	13	95
15 Rangel	85	15	95
16 Serrano	81	19	100
17 Engel	90	10	100
18 Lowey	95	5	100
19 Hall	95	5	98
20 Murphy	83	17	100
21 Tonko	86	14	100
22 Hinchey	90	10	98
23 Owens	83	17	100
24 Arcuri	83	17	98
25 Maffei	79	21	100
26 Lee	31	69	100
27 Higgins	90	10	98
28 Slaughter	89	11	88
29 Massa[7]	75	25	80
29 Reed[7]	29	71	100
NORTH CAROLINA			
1 Butterfield	90	10	100
2 Etheridge	90	10	100
3 Jones	51	49	93
4 Price	95	5	100

	1	2	3
5 Foxx	26	74	100
6 Coble	27	73	98
7 McIntyre	64	36	100
8 Kissell	81	19	100
9 Myrick	27	73	98
10 McHenry	29	71	100
11 Shuler	71	29	90
12 Watt	90	10	98
13 Miller	90	10	100
NORTH DAKOTA			
AL Pomeroy	83	17	100
OHIO			
1 Driehaus	88	12	100
2 Schmidt	24	76	100
3 Turner	36	64	100
4 Jordan	22	78	98
5 Latta	25	75	95
6 Wilson	90	10	100
7 Austria	29	71	100
8 Boehner	23	77	95
9 Kaptur	86	14	100
10 Kucinich	83	17	100
11 Fudge	83	17	98
12 Tiberi	33	67	100
13 Sutton	93	7	100
14 LaTourette	44	56	98
15 Kilroy	93	7	100
16 Boccieri	88	12	100
17 Ryan	93	7	100
18 Space	76	24	98
OKLAHOMA			
1 Sullivan	26	74	100
2 Boren	68	32	88
3 Lucas	26	74	100
4 Cole	29	71	100
5 Fallin	28	72	69
OREGON			
1 Wu	87	13	95
2 Walden	33	67	100
3 Blumenauer	88	12	98
4 DeFazio	85	15	95
5 Schrader	78	22	98
PENNSYLVANIA			
1 Brady	95	5	100
2 Fattah	95	5	98
3 Dahlkemper	80	20	98
4 Altmire	83	17	100
5 Thompson	31	69	93
6 Gerlach	43	57	100
7 Sestak	95	5	100
8 Murphy, P.	90	10	98
9 Shuster	27	73	98
10 Carney	84	16	90
11 Kanjorski	86	14	100
12 Murtha[8]	69	31	100
12 Critz[8]	100	0	33
13 Schwartz	95	5	95
14 Doyle	90	10	98
15 Dent	43	57	100
16 Pitts	25	75	95
17 Holden	81	19	100
18 Murphy, T.	52	48	100
19 Platts	43	57	100
RHODE ISLAND			
1 Kennedy	92	8	90
2 Langevin	93	7	100
SOUTH CAROLINA			
1 Brown	30	70	79
2 Wilson	24	76	100
3 Barrett	27	73	71
4 Inglis	30	70	95
5 Spratt	90	10	100
6 Clyburn	93	8	95
SOUTH DAKOTA			
AL Herseth Sandlin	71	29	100
TENNESSEE			
1 Roe	31	69	100
2 Duncan	22	78	98
3 Wamp	35	65	95
4 Davis	75	25	95
5 Cooper	66	34	98
6 Gordon	95	5	95
7 Blackburn	32	68	98
8 Tanner	72	28	93
9 Cohen	89	11	90

	1	2	3
TEXAS			
1 Gohmert	29	71	98
2 Poe	24	76	98
3 Johnson, S.	25	75	95
4 Hall	29	71	100
5 Hensarling	29	71	100
6 Barton	29	71	98
7 Culberson	26	74	100
8 Brady	26	74	100
9 Green, A.	95	5	100
10 McCaul	26	74	100
11 Conaway	26	74	100
12 Granger	30	70	88
13 Thornberry	26	74	100
14 Paul	24	76	100
15 Hinojosa	90	10	98
16 Reyes	93	7	100
17 Edwards	74	26	100
18 Jackson Lee	84	16	90
19 Neugebauer	30	70	95
20 Gonzalez	95	5	98
21 Smith	26	74	100
22 Olson	26	74	100
23 Rodriguez	90	10	95
24 Marchant	26	74	81
25 Doggett	86	14	100
26 Burgess	31	69	100
27 Ortiz	83	17	98
28 Cuellar	90	10	100
29 Green, G.	88	12	100
30 Johnson, E.	90	10	95
31 Carter	26	74	100
32 Sessions	26	74	100
UTAH			
1 Bishop	26	74	100
2 Matheson	74	26	100
3 Chaffetz	21	79	100
VERMONT			
AL Welch	83	17	100
VIRGINIA			
1 Wittman	31	69	100
2 Nye	67	33	100
3 Scott	86	14	100
4 Forbes	26	74	100
5 Perriello	86	14	100
6 Goodlatte	26	74	100
7 Cantor	27	73	98
8 Moran	85	15	98
9 Boucher	73	27	95
10 Wolf	29	71	100
11 Connolly	93	7	100
WASHINGTON			
1 Inslee	88	12	100
2 Larsen	95	5	100
3 Baird	78	22	98
4 Hastings	27	73	98
5 McMorris Rodgers	28	72	86
6 Dicks	98	2	100
7 McDermott	88	12	98
8 Reichert	38	62	93
9 Smith	90	10	100
WEST VIRGINIA			
1 Mollohan	95	5	95
2 Capito	36	64	93
3 Rahall	88	12	98
WISCONSIN			
1 Ryan	24	76	90
2 Baldwin	85	15	98
3 Kind	87	13	95
4 Moore	87	13	93
5 Sensenbrenner	24	76	100
6 Petri	38	62	100
7 Obey	90	10	98
8 Kagen	87	13	95
WYOMING			
AL Lummis	26	74	100
DELEGATES			
Faleomavaega (A.S.)	100	0	100
Norton (D.C.)	67	33	100
Bordallo (Guam)	67	33	100
Sablan (N. Marianas)	100	0	33
Pierluisi (P.R.)	100	0	33
Christensen (V.I.)	100	0	100

Partisanship Shows Staying Power

IN PUBLIC OPINION SURVEYS, VOTERS OFTEN said they wanted parties and politicians to work together. But in real life, voters turned around and rewarded the ones who did just the opposite.

The lesson was not lost on members of Congress. They had been increasingly partisan for decades, and according to Congressional Quarterly's annual analysis of roll call votes, they were even more partisan in the 111th Congress.

The divisions between the parties on Capitol Hill — and consequently the degree of party unity displayed — were at or near record levels in 2010.

The November election results suggested that the gap could get greater. Of the 50 House Democrats most likely to cross party lines in 2010, 30 lost their re-election bids. Two of the House Republicans most likely to oppose their fellow caucus members were also defeated at the polls. And three moderate Democrats lost their Senate races. Voters were apparently unimpressed with the role played by lawmakers from both parties who sought to find a middle path and who in the process helped Democrats achieve their legislative triumphs.

This trend toward polarization began in the early 1990s, was given a boost in the Republican takeover of Congress after the 1994 elections and accelerated in the past decade. Given the outcome at the polls in November, it was easy to see how 2011 might easily perpetuate this pattern, or even make it more pronounced.

"There's a lot of bad blood that's accumulated, and it will be very difficult to get anything done with that level of distrust," said Steven Schier, a political science professor at Carleton College in Minnesota who specializes in Congress.

CLEAR IN THE NUMBERS

Since 1953, CQ has specifically looked at roll call votes in which the majority of Republicans voted one way and a majority of Democrats voted the other, as a means of evaluating the level of party unity and polarization in Washington.

The high degree of partisanship shown by the study for 2010 came as no surprise. While partisanship can sometimes lead to gridlock, it can also produce legislative achievement when one side has the numbers to get its way. For the most, Democrats in 2010 had more than sufficient numbers in the House and not quite a bare minimum to deflect threatened filibusters in the Senate. As a consequence, they were able to complete the comprehensive and controversial health care overhaul with no Republican help and pass an equally sweeping overhaul of financial regulations with very few GOP votes.

In telling fashion, almost four out of every five Senate roll call votes — 78.6 percent — split the parties. That was the highest percentage of party unity votes in the study's 58 years. With 59 members in their caucus, and the need for just 60 to prevent filibusters, Democrats won on vote after vote. Their victory rate of 83.4 percent was the sixth-highest ever, though down from the record 92.3 percent set in 2009, when the party caucus held 59, then 60 Senate seats.

Democrats Dominate In Both Chambers

Although Democrats in the House and Senate were victorious less often in 2010 than the year before on roll call votes that divided the two parties, their success rates remained historically high. The House Democrats' 89.4 percent success rate was the fifth-highest in the history of the study. The Senate Democrats' 83.4 percent success rate was the sixth-highest ever.

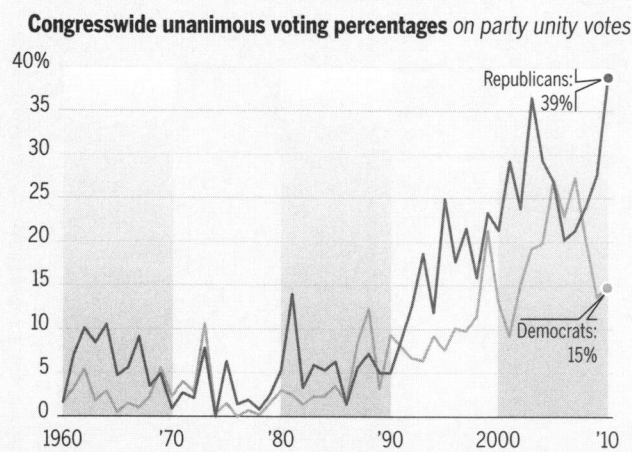

Congresswide unanimous voting percentages *on party unity votes*

Republicans: 39%

Democrats: 15%

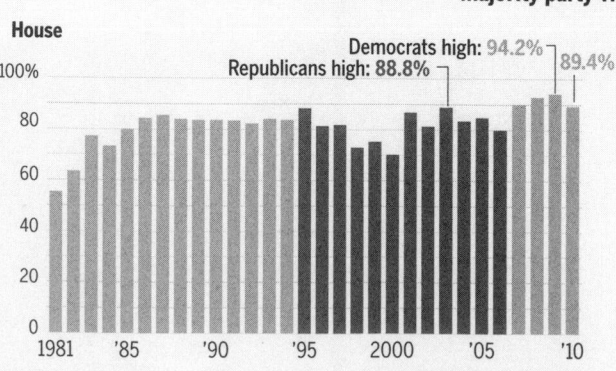

Majority party victory percentages *on party unity votes*

House

Democrats high: 94.2% — 89.4%
Republicans high: 88.8%

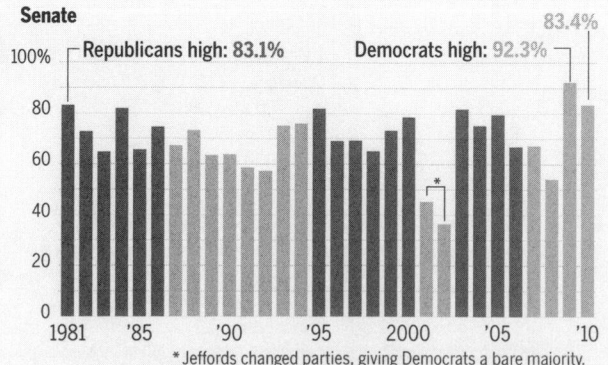

Senate

Republicans high: 83.1% Democrats high: 92.3% — 83.4%

* Jeffords changed parties, giving Democrats a bare majority.

Republicans were almost as unified in opposition. The average Republican senator voted with the GOP caucus majority 89 percent of the time on party unity votes. More significantly, perhaps, Republicans stood together without dissent on roughly one out of every two votes that split the parties, yielding an all-time high for unanimous voting in the chamber.

Senate Republicans often perceived to be moderates were more loyal than usual. The three Republicans most likely to buck their party all were more loyal in 2010 than they'd been since Democrats seized the chamber in 2007. Susan Collins of Maine voted with her caucus 69 percent of the time, up from a more typical 48 percent in 2009. Her Maine colleague Olympia J. Snowe saw her party unity score rise to 73 percent in 2010, up from 49 percent the previous year. And Ohio's George V. Voinovich, even as he planned to retire at the end of 2010, was more loyal to his caucus, voting with his side 68 percent of the time, up from 58 percent in 2009.

In the Senate, Majority Leader Harry Reid, D-Nev., worked to hold his fellow caucus members together. On average, Senate Democrats voted together a record 91 percent of the time. Were it not for a few outliers, such as Ben Nelson of Nebraska, who voted with his caucus only half the time, the average support score would have been even higher. Half of the Senate Democrats had party unity scores higher than 97 percent.

In the House, which tackled many more non-controversial issues as it waited for the Senate to move on the big debates of the year, only four out of every 10 votes split the parties. But when those votes came up, House Speaker Nancy Pelosi, D-Calif., demanded, and got, unity from her party's caucus. The average Democrat voted with the caucus 89 percent of the time, close to a record. As in the Senate, a few outliers whose defections didn't cost the party many victories held down the average. Half of the House Democrats also had party unity scores higher than 97 percent.

House Republicans were almost as unified in opposition as their Senate colleagues. The average House GOP lawmaker supported the caucus on 88 percent of party unity votes. The number of occasions on which not a single member defected to the other side underscored the point, as House Republicans also set a record for unanimity: 35 percent of party unity votes.

Given the Democrats' big majority in the chamber, GOP unity didn't matter much. Democrats won 89.4 percent of the votes that split the parties in the House, their fifth-highest success score in the history of the study.

From the health care overhaul signed by President Obama in March to the financial regulatory law enacted in July, the year was marked by Democratic victories won by the power of their numbers.

Cases where a split in the Democratic Caucus handed Republicans a victory were few and peripheral to the main debates, such as when Republican Rep. J. Randy Forbes of Virginia moved in May to send the defense authorization bill back to committee with instructions to add an amendment barring the transfer of detainees held at Guantánamo Bay, Cuba, to the United States for trial. Half of the House Democrats bolted to side with an almost-unanimous GOP caucus in favor of the motion.

That same month in the Senate, Collins was able to sway 19 Democrats and independent Joseph I. Lieberman of Connecticut to support an amendment to emergency spending legislation to prevent the EPA from enforcing rules that required contractors to adopt safe practices when dealing with lead paint. But these were not the major legislative debates of the year.

Party unity votes that split both caucuses to yield a GOP victory were even rarer. One occurred in May, when the House rejected an amendment by Democrat Chellie Pingree of Maine that would have removed spending to develop a new engine for the F-35 fighter jet from the annual defense authorization bill. Democrats voted 136-115 in favor of the amendment. Republicans voted 57-116 in opposition, and they prevailed. While a rare victory for the GOP, it was a big one because it also constituted an even rarer defeat for Obama on a vote where he had staked out a clear position. Obama, who had a record year of successes on floor votes in 2009 and did almost as well in 2010, relied mostly on support from Democrats. CQ's parallel study of presidential support votes showed he benefited considerably from the high degree of Democratic Party unity. *(Presidential support, p. B-3)*

The biggest victories for Republicans came in the Senate, where they were able to exploit procedural rules that often required a supermajority of 60 votes to do business. Democrats' inability to muster sufficient votes to overcome that hurdle forced them to abandon a public health insurance option in the health care overhaul and to forgo an independent consumer financial protection agency as part of the financial services regulatory overhaul. It also prevented consideration of an immigration bill in the final days of the session.

Democratic disunity on certain issues, such as a broad measure to address climate change, meant that Senate party leaders never brought them to the floor for a vote.

VOTING FOR PARTISANSHIP

After the 2010 election, Obama said the American people did not vote for "unyielding partisanship."

But in a sense, they did. The ranks of House Democratic moderates were thinned in dramatic fashion. Many had won in GOP-leaning districts in 2006 amid widespread voter frustration directed at President

---

All Together

Postwar partisanship remained near all-time highs in 2010. In the Senate, a record percentage of votes divided the parties, and Democrats voted together at a record rate. Republicans in both chambers stuck together more than in 2009.

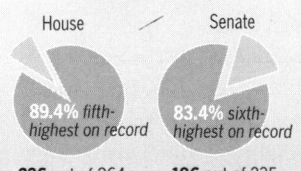

Frequency of party unity votes:

House — 40.0% lowest since 1982 — 264 out of 660

Senate — 78.6% highest on record — 235 out of 299

Average for both chambers: **52.0%**

How often the Democrats won:

House — 89.4% fifth-highest on record — 236 out of 264

Senate — 83.4% sixth-highest on record — 196 out of 235

Average for both chambers: **86.6%**

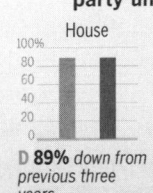

Average chamber party unity scores:

House — D **89%** down from previous three years — R **88%** highest since 2006

Senate — D **91%** highest on record (matching 2009) — R **89%** highest since 2004

GOP Loyalty Rises Toward Democrats' Level

Party unity stayed high in 2010. Republicans in both chambers voted with their colleagues more often than the year before on roll calls where the parties divided. Senate Democrats matched the record 91 percent support they scored the previous year. And although House Democrats saw their unity score decline, it remained higher than that of the chamber's Republicans.

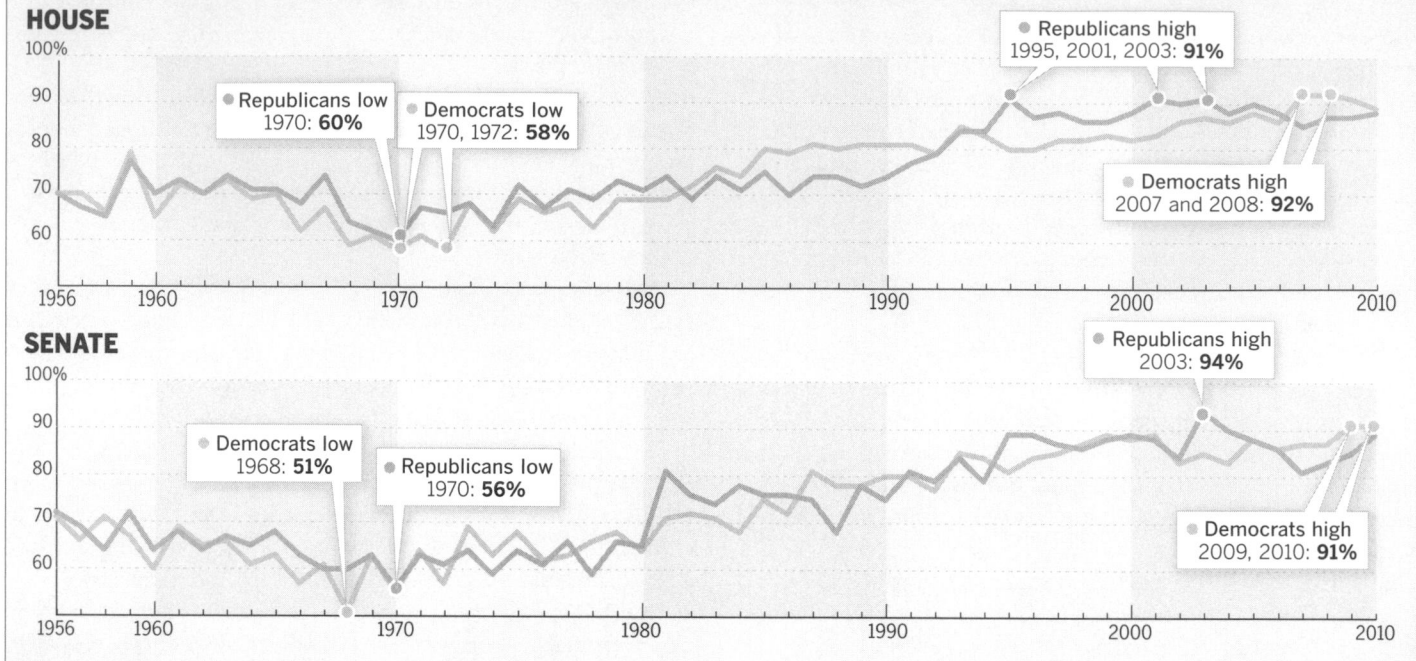

George W. Bush and congressional Republicans. Others were elected in 2008, riding on Obama's coattails.

Only 13 of the 34 House Democrats who voted against final passage of Obama's health care overhaul were re-elected. Of those leaving, 17 lost their re-election campaigns, two retired and two lost bids for higher office.

The three House seats that Republicans lost were all previously held by moderates. Louisiana Rep. Anh "Joseph" Cao, for example, was the Republican most likely to vote against his party's wishes. Rep. Michael N. Castle of Delaware, who lost a primary bid to run for Senate, was third, and Charles K. Djou of Hawaii was sixth.

Meanwhile, the small moderate caucus in the Senate became smaller. Of the five Republicans and five Democrats most likely to cross party lines in 2010, four were not coming back, having either retired or lost re-election bids. One who survived almost didn't; Republican Sen. Lisa Murkowski of Alaska was denied her party's nomination and had to win re-election as a write-in candidate.

The replacements for the ousted moderates were expected to make for a more partisan environment in the Senate. Take the Indiana seat previously held by Evan Bayh, who retired at the end of 2010. He was one of the Democrats most willing to buck the party line. By contrast, his replacement, Dan Coats, compiled a loyal Republican voting record during a previous stint in the Senate in the 1990s.

The same could be said about John Boozman, the Arkansas Republican who defeated Sen. Democrat Blanche Lincoln. During four terms in the House, Boozman was a consistent ally of his caucus colleagues. In 2010, he voted with fellow Republicans 96 percent of the time on party unity votes. By contrast, Lincoln was the third-most-likely Democrat to cross party lines in 2010, voting with Republicans three times out of every 10.

In the House, the election results were much the same, with conservative Republicans such as Raúl R. Labrador of Idaho and Martha Roby of Alabama taking seats previously held by moderate Democrats Walt Minnick and Bobby Bright.

Given that overall trend, the victories of a few moderate Republicans, such as Charles Bass of New Hampshire, hardly seemed significant enough to alter the House GOP's strongly conservative makeup.

While swing voters say they want the parties to work together, politicians aren't often willing to offend their hard-line supporters to make deals, said Richard Fleisher, a political science professor at Fordham University in New York. "When politicians say, 'The public wants us to work together,' what they mean by that is, 'You should accept my policy positions and cave in on your own,'" he said. "Neither side means: 'Let's both make compromises and achieve some position in the middle.'"

SIGNS OF BIPARTISANSHIP?

Still, enactment of a law conditionally ending the "don't ask, don't tell" policy on gays in the military and approval of ratification of a nuclear arms treaty with Russia during the lame-duck session were cited by some as indicating that bipartisanship was a possibility in the 112th Congress. Leaders of both parties said to expect it, pointing to Obama's year-end deal to extend tax cuts and unemployment benefits as evidence that they could and would work together.

"I think we all agree there's no particular reason why we can't find areas of agreement and do some important things for the

Leading Scorers: Party Unity

Support indicates those who voted most often with a majority of their party against a majority of the other party in 2009. **Opposition** shows those who voted most often against their party's majority. Lawmakers who left office or who missed half or more of the votes are not listed. Scores are reported to one decimal point only; those with identical scores are listed alphabetically. *(Complete scores, p. B-19)*

SENATE

SUPPORT

Democrats		Republicans	
Leahy, Vt.	100.0%	Brownback, Kan.*	99.5%
Schumer, N.Y.	99.6	Cornyn, Texas	99.1
Whitehouse, R.I.	99.6	Thune, S.D.	99.1
Brown, Ohio	99.1	DeMint, S.C.	98.7
Cardin, Md.	99.1	Hutchison, Texas	98.6
Durbin, Ill.	99.1	Roberts, Kan.	98.6
Franken, Minn.	99.1	Barrasso, Wyo.	98.3
Gillibrand, N.Y.	99.1	Coburn, Okla.	98.3
Levin, Mich.	99.1	McCain, Ariz.	98.3
Casey, Pa.	98.7	McConnell, Ky.	97.9
Mikulski, Md.	98.7	3 senators	97.8
Stabenow, Mich.	98.7		

OPPOSITION

Democrats		Republicans	
Nelson, Neb.	46.4%	Voinovich, Ohio*	31.7%
Bayh, Ind.*	31.9	Collins, Maine	31.5
Lincoln, Ark.*	27.7	Snowe, Maine	27.2
Feingold, Wis.*	17.4	Brown, Mass.	22.0
McCaskill, Mo.	15.4	Murkowski, Alaska	17.4
Webb, Va.	15.2	Lugar, Ind.	15.9
Pryor, Ark.	14.7	Gregg, N.H.*	13.4
Bennet, Colo.	13.2	Bond, Mo.*	13.0
Hagan, N.C.	12.1	Alexander, Tenn.	12.5
Tester, Mont.	10.8	Bennett, Utah*	10.6
Nelson, Fla.	10.5	Cochran, Miss.	10.6
Warner, Va.	10.4	LeMieux, Fla.*	9.1

HOUSE

SUPPORT

Democrats		Republicans	
Capps, Calif.	100.0%	Boehner, Ohio	99.6%
Lewis, Ga.	100.0	Conaway, Texas	99.6
Matsui, Calif.	100.0	Foxx, N.C.	99.6
Slaughter, N.Y.	100.0	Franks, Ariz.	99.6
Van Hollen, Md.	100.0	Lamborn, Colo.	99.6
15 members	99.6	Latta, Ohio	99.6
		Neugebauer, Texas	99.6
		Price, Ga.	99.6
		Royce, Calif.	99.6
		Barrett, S.C.*	99.3
		Graves, Ga.	99.3
		8 members	99.2

OPPOSITION

Democrats		Republicans	
Bright, Ala.*	67.2%	Cao, La.*	35.3%
Taylor, Miss.*	58.0	Ehlers, Mich.*	30.4
Minnick, Idaho*	56.2	Castle, Del.*	29.3
Mitchell, Ariz.*	53.2	Jones, N.C.	28.3
Childers, Miss.*	46.6	Dent, Pa.	24.3
Nye, Va.*	44.7	Djou, Hawaii*	23.7
Shuler, N.C.	40.0	Reichert, Wash.	20.4
Giffords, Ariz.	39.8	LaTourette, Ohio	20.2
Kratovil, Md.*	34.7	Johnson, Ill.	19.9
Kirkpatrick, Ariz.*	33.5	Murphy, Pa.	19.3
Adler, N.J.*	31.0	Young, Alaska	18.8
Boren, Okla.	30.6	Gerlach, Pa.	17.2
McIntyre, N.C.	30.5	Diaz-Balart, L., Fla.*	16.7
Herseth Sandlin, S.D.*	29.4	Smith, N.J.	15.6
Marshall, Ga.*	28.0	Platts, Pa.	15.3
Donnelly, Ind.	27.4	Ros-Lehtinen, Fla.	14.8
Hill, Ind.*	26.4	Capito, W.Va.	14.0
Ellsworth, Ind.*	23.6	LoBiondo, N.J.	14.0

Defeated for re-election, retired or elected to other office.

Frequency of Party Unity Votes Declines

The number of roll call votes during 2010 in which a majority of Democrats opposed a majority of Republicans declined from 2009, not only because there were fewer votes overall, but also because the frequency of such party unity votes fell off significantly in the House. Congresswide, the percentage of roll calls that were party unity votes fell to 52 percent, the lowest since 2004.

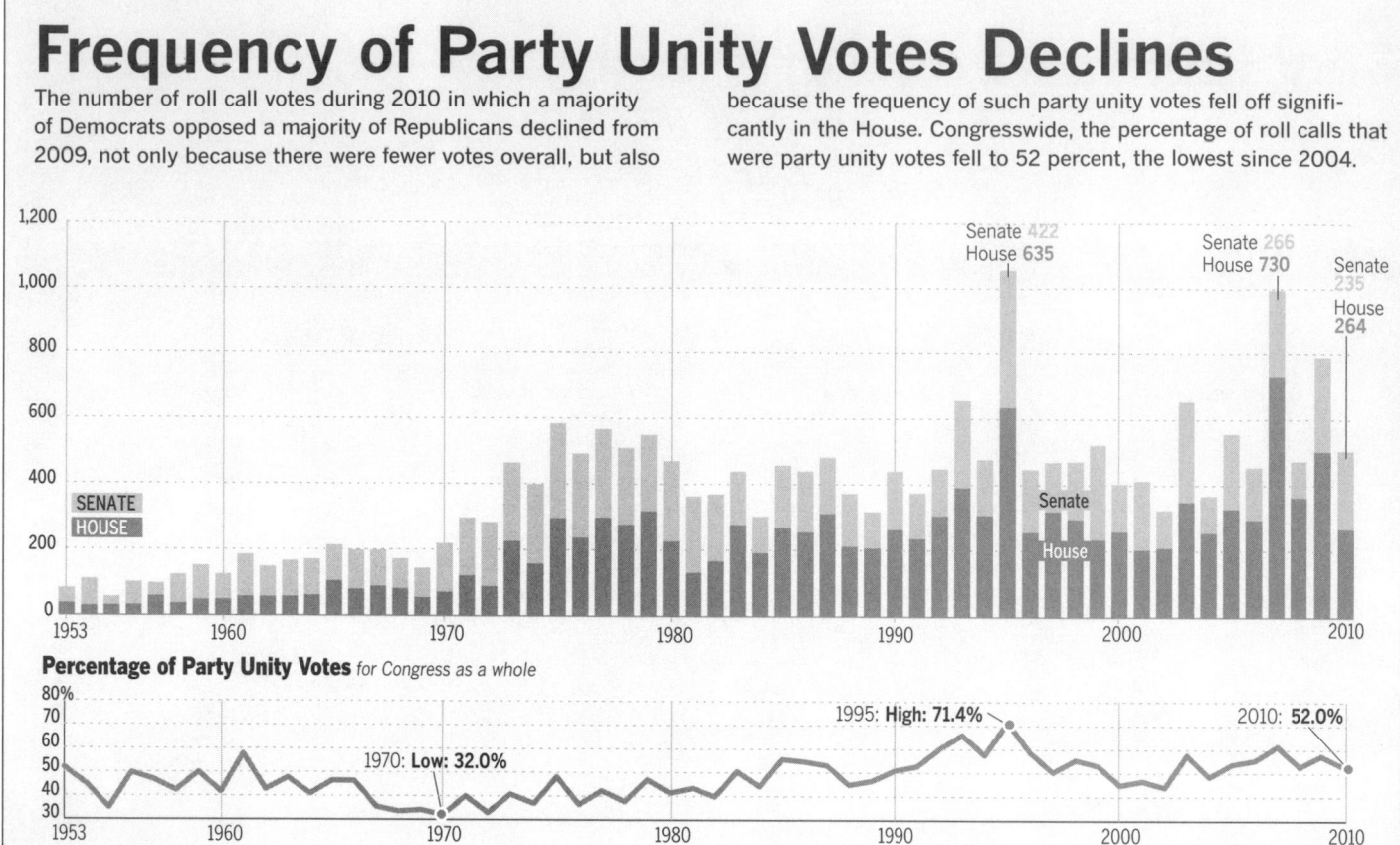

Percentage of Party Unity Votes *for Congress as a whole*

American people over the next two years," said Mitch McConnell of Kentucky, the Senate's Republican leader, in a November news conference. Indeed, McConnell said doomsday scenarios of partisan gridlock did not square with history. It's "important to remember that some of these periods when you have divided government have been quite productive," he said, citing deals cut by President Bill Clinton in the 1990s on welfare programs, balanced budgets and trade.

House Minority Leader John A. Boehner of Ohio echoed those sentiments. "The more time that we do spend together, we can find the common ground," he said. Boehner said he had been studying the lessons of 1995, when Republicans were blamed for an appropriations impasse that shut down government agencies and helped Clinton win re-election the following year.

Others said the bipartisanship shown on the tax deal might not set any precedent for the next Congress. "It's what we call an ends-against-the-middle vote," said Jon R. Bond, a professor at Texas A&M University, noting that the opponents of the compromise tended to be the most liberal Democrats and the most conservative Republicans.

In neither the House nor the Senate did the votes on the tax bill divide the parties. Majorities of each party backed it, so it did not register as a party unity vote.

Bond said such votes were infrequent given the partisanship and typically occurred under just the sort of unusual circumstances that existed at the end of 2010: keen pressure on both parties to extend middle-class tax cuts, combined with the awareness on the part of Democrats that Republicans might be less willing to bargain in 2011 after they assumed control of the House. Bond said he wasn't confident that the dynamic would appear again soon: "It's only going to get more partisan." ∎

Party Unity Background

Roll call votes used for the party unity study are those on which a majority of voting Democrats opposed a majority of voting Republicans. **Support** indicates the percentage of the time that members voted in agreement with the majority of their party on such party unity votes. **Opposition** indicates the percentage of the time that members voted against the majority of their party. In calculations of average scores by party and chamber, a member's failure to vote lowers the score for the group. The tables below also show the number of party unity votes on which each party was **victorious** and the number of instances in which either party voted **unanimously**.

Average Party Unity Scores by Chamber

		SUPPORT		OPPOSITION	
		2010	2009	2010	2009
HOUSE	Democrats	89%	91%	7%	6%
	Republicans	88	87	6	10
SENATE	Democrats	91	91	6	6
	Republicans	89	85	7	13
CONGRESS	Democrats	89	91	7	6
	Republicans	88	87	6	11

Victories in Party Unity Votes

	HOUSE		SENATE		CONGRESS	
YEAR	DEMOCRATS	REPUBLICANS	DEMOCRATS	REPUBLICANS	DEMOCRATS	REPUBLICANS
2010	236	28	196	39	432	67
2009	473	29	264	22	737	51
2008	342	25	60	51	402	76
2007	658	72	179	87	837	159
2006	59	236	53	107	112	343
2005	50	278	47	182	97	460
2004	42	213	28	85	70	298
2003	39	310	56	250	95	560
2002	39	170	42	73	81	243
2001	27	177	95	115	122	292
2000	77	182	31	114	108	296
1999	58	177	77	211	135	388
1998	80	216	61	114	141	330
1997	58	261	46	104	104	365
1996	48	208	59	132	107	340
1995	74	561	77	345	151	906
1994	257	50	129	41	386	91

Unanimous Voting by Parties

	HOUSE		SENATE		CONGRESS	
YEAR	DEMOCRATS	REPUBLICANS	DEMOCRATS	REPUBLICANS	DEMOCRATS	REPUBLICANS
2010	10	91	67	106	77	197
2009	29	144	79	74	108	218
2008	66	96	30	19	96	115
2007	170	177	102	35	272	212
2006	70	62	34	30	104	92
2005	82	91	69	59	151	150
2004	70	77	3	31	73	108
2003	94	109	32	130	126	239
2002	37	54	12	23	49	77
2001	1	66	37	55	38	121
2000	1	67	52	19	53	86
1999	11	59	100	63	111	122
1998	8	42	46	33	54	75
1997	11	63	35	38	46	101
1996	10	32	35	47	45	79
1995	17	159	63	104	80	263
1994	7	38	37	19	44	57

Party Unity History

The left section of the table below shows how frequently during roll call votes a majority of Democrats aligned against a majority of Republicans. The center and right sections show the average party unity support score for each party in each chamber.

YEAR	Frequency of Unity Votes		House Average Scores		Senate Average Scores	
	HOUSE	SENATE	DEMOCRATS	REPUBLICANS	DEMOCRATS	REPUBLICANS
2010	40.0%	78.6%	89%	88%	91%	89%
2009	50.9	72.0	91	87	91	85
2008	53.3	51.6	92	87	87	83
2007	62.0	60.2	92	85	87	81
2006	54.5	57.3	86	88	86	86
2005	49.0	62.6	88	90	88	88
2004	47.0	52.3	86	88	83	90
2003	51.7	66.7	87	91	85	94
2002	43.3	45.5	86	90	83	84
2001	40.2	55.3	83	91	89	88
2000	43.2	48.7	82	88	88	89
1999	47.3	62.8	83	86	89	88
1998	55.5	55.7	82	86	87	86
1997	50.4	50.3	82	88	85	87
1996	56.4	62.4	80	87	84	89
1995	73.2	68.8	80	91	81	89
1994	61.8	51.7	83	84	84	79
1993	65.5	67.1	85	84	85	84
1992	64.5	53.0	79	79	77	79
1991	55.1	49.3	81	77	80	81
1990	49.1	54.3	81	74	80	75
1989	56.3	35.3	81	72	78	78
1988	47.0	42.5	80	74	78	68
1987	63.7	40.7	81	74	81	75
1986	56.5	52.3	79	70	72	76
1985	61.0	49.6	80	75	75	76
1984	47.1	40.0	74	71	68	78
1983	55.6	43.7	76	74	71	74
1982	36.4	43.4	72	69	72	76
1981	37.4	47.8	69	74	71	81
1980	37.6	45.8	69	71	64	65
1979	47.3	46.7	69	73	68	66
1978	33.2	45.2	63	69	66	59
1977	42.2	42.4	68	71	63	66
1976	35.9	37.2	66	67	62	61
1975	48.4	47.8	69	72	68	64
1974	29.4	44.3	62	63	63	59
1973	41.8	39.9	68	68	69	64
1972	27.1	36.5	58	66	57	61
1971	37.8	41.6	61	67	64	63
1970	27.1	35.2	58	60	55	56
1969	31.1	36.3	61	62	63	63
1968	35.2	32.0	59	64	51	60
1967	36.3	34.6	67	74	61	60
1966	41.5	50.2	62	68	57	63
1965	52.2	41.9	70	71	63	68
1964	54.9	35.7	69	71	61	65
1963	48.7	47.2	73	74	66	67
1962	46.0	41.1	70	70	65	64
1961	50.0	62.3	72	73	69	68
1960	52.7	36.7	65	70	60	64
1959	55.2	47.9	79	77	67	72
1958	39.8	43.5	66	65	71	64
1957	59.0	35.5	70	67	66	69
1956	43.8	53.1	70	70	71	72
1955	40.8	29.9				
1954	38.2	48.0				

Tallying Party Unity Votes

In the House in 2010, the two parties aligned against each other on just 264 of 660 roll call votes, or 40 percent of the time — the lowest frequency of unity votes since 1982. In the Senate, the parties opposed each other on 235 of 299 roll calls, or 78.6 percent of the time — the highest ever. A list of roll call votes that pitted majorities of the two parties against each other is available upon request from Congressional Quarterly.

Calculations of average scores by chamber and party are based on all eligible "yea" or "nay" votes, whether or not all members participated. Under this methodology, average support and opposition scores are reduced when members choose not to vote. Because individual member scores are based on the number of votes cast, party and chamber averages are not strictly comparable to individual member scores. (Complete member scores, p. B-19.)

Also, in the member score tables, Sens. Joseph I. Lieberman, I-Conn., and Bernard Sanders, I-Vt., are treated as if they are Democrats when calculating their support and opposition scores. However, Lieberman's and Sanders' votes were not used to determine which roll calls were party unity votes, and they are not included in the Democratic Party averages for the Senate.

SENATE

1. Party Unity. Percentage of recorded party unity votes in 2010 on which a senator voted "yea" or "nay" in agreement with a majority of his or her party. (Party unity votes are those on which a majority of voting Democrats opposed a majority of voting Republicans.) Percentages are based on votes cast; thus, failure to vote does not lower a member's score.

2. Party Opposition. Percentage of recorded party unity votes in 2010 on which a senator voted "yea" or "nay" in disagreement with a majority of his or her party. Percentages are based on votes cast; thus, failure to vote does not lower a member's score.

3. Participation in Party Unity Votes. Percentage of the Senate party unity votes in 2010 for which a senator was eligible and present and voted "yea" or "nay." There were a total of 235 such recorded votes.

	1	2	3		1	2	3
ALABAMA				**MONTANA**			
Shelby	96	4	98	Baucus	93	7	99
Sessions	98	2	98	Tester	89	11	99
ALASKA				**NEBRASKA**			
Murkowski	83	17	91	Nelson	54	46	100
Begich	93	7	97	**Johanns**	93	7	98
ARIZONA				**NEVADA**			
McCain	98	2	99	Reid	95	5	100
Kyl	97	3	98	**Ensign**	95	5	98
ARKANSAS				**NEW HAMPSHIRE**			
Lincoln	72	28	94	**Gregg**	87	13	89
Pryor	85	15	99	Shaheen	94	6	98
CALIFORNIA				**NEW JERSEY**			
Feinstein	97	3	100	Lautenberg	99	1	94
Boxer	97	3	98	Menendez	97	3	98
COLORADO				**NEW MEXICO**			
Udall	90	10	99	Bingaman	97	3	100
Bennet	87	13	100	Udall	98	2	99
CONNECTICUT				**NEW YORK**			
Dodd	96	4	99	Schumer	99	1	99
Lieberman	87	13	97	Gillibrand	99	1	99
DELAWARE				**NORTH CAROLINA**			
Carper	95	5	99	**Burr**	96	4	97
Kaufman [1]	98	2	98	Hagan	88	12	98
Coons [1]	100	0	100	**NORTH DAKOTA**			
FLORIDA				Conrad	94	6	99
Nelson	89	11	97	Dorgan	97	3	99
LeMieux	91	9	99	**OHIO**			
GEORGIA				**Voinovich**	68	32	94
Chambliss	98	2	94	Brown	99	1	100
Isakson	93	7	76	**OKLAHOMA**			
HAWAII				**Inhofe**	96	4	97
Inouye	98	2	99	**Coburn**	98	2	99
Akaka	98	2	99	**OREGON**			
IDAHO				Wyden	95	5	95
Crapo	98	2	98	Merkley	97	3	99
Risch	98	2	99	**PENNSYLVANIA**			
ILLINOIS				Specter	97	3	96
Durbin	99	1	100	Casey	99	1	100
Burris [2]	99	1	100	**RHODE ISLAND**			
Kirk [2]	76	24	97	Reed	98	2	100
INDIANA				Whitehouse	99	1	99
Lugar	84	16	99	**SOUTH CAROLINA**			
Bayh	68	32	89	**Graham**	95	5	98
IOWA				**DeMint**	99	1	95
Grassley	93	7	100	**SOUTH DAKOTA**			
Harkin	98	2	99	Johnson	98	2	99
KANSAS				**Thune**	99	1	99
Brownback	99	1	89	**TENNESSEE**			
Roberts	99	1	93	**Alexander**	87	13	99
KENTUCKY				**Corker**	91	9	100
McConnell	98	2	100	**TEXAS**			
Bunning	98	2	94	**Hutchison**	99	1	88
LOUISIANA				**Cornyn**	99	1	98
Landrieu	93	7	99	**UTAH**			
Vitter	94	6	91	**Hatch**	97	3	97
MAINE				**Bennett**	89	11	89
Snowe	73	27	100	**VERMONT**			
Collins	69	31	100	Leahy	100	0	98
MARYLAND				*Sanders*	99	1	99
Mikulski	99	1	96	**VIRGINIA**			
Cardin	99	1	100	Webb	85	15	98
MASSACHUSETTS				Warner	90	10	94
Kerry	97	3	99	**WASHINGTON**			
Kirk [3]	92	8	100	Murray	97	3	98
Brown [3]	78	22	100	Cantwell	92	8	99
MICHIGAN				**WEST VIRGINIA**			
Levin	99	1	99	Byrd [4]	94	6	40
Stabenow	99	1	99	Rockefeller	97	3	95
MINNESOTA				Goodwin [4]	100	0	100
Klobuchar	90	10	99	Manchin [4]	88	12	89
Franken	99	1	100	**WISCONSIN**			
MISSISSIPPI				Kohl	94	6	99
Cochran	89	11	100	Feingold	83	17	100
Wicker	96	4	98	**WYOMING**			
MISSOURI				**Enzi**	97	3	97
Bond	87	13	85	**Barrasso**	98	2	100
McCaskill	85	15	97				

KEY **Republicans** Democrats *Independents*

[1] Sen. Chris Coons, D-Del., was sworn in Nov. 15 to replace Democrat Ted Kaufman, appointed on Jan. 15, 2009, to temporarily fill the vacancy created by Democrat Joseph R. Biden Jr., who resigned to become vice president. The first vote for which Coons was eligible was vote 249; the last vote for which Kaufman was eligible was vote 248.

[2] Sen. Mark Steven Kirk, R-Ill., was sworn in Nov. 29 to replace Democrat Roland W. Burris, who was appointed on Dec. 30, 2008, to temporarily fill the vacancy created by Democrat Barack Obama, who resigned to become president. The first vote for which Kirk was eligible was vote 252; the last vote for which Burris was eligible was vote 251.

[3] Sen. Scott P. Brown, R-Mass., was sworn in Feb. 4 to replace Democrat Paul G. Kirk Jr., who appointed Sept. 24, 2009, to temporarily fill the vacancy created by Democrat Edward M. Kennedy, who died Aug. 25, 2009. The first vote for which Brown was eligible was vote 21; the last vote for which Kirk was eligible was vote 20.

[4] Sen. Joe Manchin III, D-W.Va., was sworn in Nov. 15 to replace Democrat Carte P. Goodwin, who was appointed July 16 to temporarily fill the vacancy created by Democrat Robert C. Byrd, who died June 28. The first vote for which Manchin was eligible was vote 249. Goodwin was eligible for votes 209 through 248. The last vote for which Byrd was eligible was vote 200.

HOUSE

1. **Party Unity.** Percentage of recorded party unity votes in 2010 on which a member voted "yea" or "nay" in agreement with a majority of his or her party. (Party unity votes are those on which a majority of voting Democrats opposed a majority of voting Republicans.) Percentages are based on votes cast; thus, failure to vote does not lower a member's score.

2. **Party Opposition.** Percentage of recorded party unity votes in 2010 on which a member voted "yea" or "nay" in disagreement with a majority of his or her party. Percentages are based on votes cast; thus, failure to vote does not lower a member's score.

3. **Participation in Party Unity Votes.** Percentage of the House party unity votes in 2010 for which a member was eligible and present, and voted "yea" or "nay." There were a total of 264 such recorded votes.

[1] The Speaker votes only at her discretion.

[2] Rep. Ted Deutch, D-Fla., was sworn in April 15 to fill the seat vacated by the Jan. 3 resignation of Democrat Robert Wexler. The first vote for which Deutch was eligible was vote 205; Wexler was not eligible for any party unity votes in 2010.

[3] Rep. Tom Graves, R-Ga., was sworn in June 14 to fill the seat vacated by Republican Nathan Deal, who resigned March 21 to run for governor. The first vote for which Graves was eligible was vote 356; the last vote for which Deal was eligible was vote 168.

[4] Rep. Charles K. Djou, R-Hawaii, was sworn in May 25 to fill the seat vacated by Democrat Neil Abercrombie, who resigned Feb. 28 to run for governor. The first vote for which Djou was eligible was vote 296; the last vote for which Abercrombie was eligible was vote 74.

[5] Rep. Mark Steven Kirk, R-Ill., resigned Nov. 29 to assume the Senate seat he won in a Nov. 2 special election. The last vote for which Kirk was eligible was vote 580.

[6] Rep. Marlin Stutzman, R-Ind., was sworn in Nov. 16 to fill the vacancy created by the May 21 resignation of Republican Mark Souder. The first vote for which Stutzman was eligible was vote 571; the last vote for which Souder was eligible was vote 290.

[7] Rep. Tom Reed, R-N.Y., was sworn in Nov. 18 to fill the vacancy created by the March 8 resignation of Democrat Eric Massa. The first vote for which Reed was eligible was vote 580; the last vote for which Massa was eligible was vote 91.

[8] Rep. Mark Critz, D-Pa., was sworn in May 20 to fill the seat vacated by the Feb. 8 death of Democrat John P. Murtha. The first vote for which Critz was eligible was vote 286; the last vote for which Murtha was eligible was vote 48.

	1	2	3
ALABAMA			
1 **Bonner**	94	6	92
2 Bright	33	67	92
3 **Rogers**	95	5	99
4 **Aderholt**	95	5	98
5 **Griffith**	96	4	81
6 **Bachus**	95	5	97
7 Davis	88	12	61
ALASKA			
AL **Young**	81	19	84
ARIZONA			
1 Kirkpatrick	67	33	95
2 **Franks**	99	1	99
3 **Shadegg**	98	2	86
4 Pastor	98	2	95
5 Mitchell	47	53	95
6 **Flake**	97	3	98
7 Grijalva	96	4	96
8 Giffords	60	40	98
ARKANSAS			
1 Berry	88	12	81
2 Snyder	97	3	98
3 **Boozman**	96	4	97
4 Ross	84	16	98
CALIFORNIA			
1 Thompson	97	3	99
2 **Herger**	99	1	99
3 **Lungren**	93	7	98
4 **McClintock**	95	5	100
5 Matsui	100	0	99
6 Woolsey	98	2	91
7 Miller, George	99	1	98
8 Pelosi [1]	100	0	18
9 Lee	98	2	97
10 Garamendi	99	1	94
11 McNerney	91	9	98
12 Speier	99	1	89
13 Stark	97	3	84
14 Eshoo	99	1	95
15 Honda	97	3	93
16 Lofgren	98	2	91
17 Farr	99	1	98
18 Cardoza	93	7	93
19 **Radanovich**	96	4	57
20 Costa	86	14	98
21 **Nunes**	99	1	91
22 **McCarthy**	97	3	89
23 Capps	100	0	97
24 **Gallegly**	97	3	92
25 **McKeon**	96	4	98
26 **Dreier**	97	3	100
27 Sherman	97	3	99
28 Berman	99	1	96
29 Schiff	99	1	99
30 Waxman	99	1	93
31 Becerra	98	2	97
32 Chu	99	1	97
33 Watson	98	2	86
34 Roybal-Allard	98	2	99
35 Waters	97	3	88
36 Harman	98	2	96
37 Richardson	96	4	96
38 Napolitano	98	2	95
39 Sánchez, Linda	99	1	94
40 **Royce**	99	1	99
41 Lewis	96	4	97
42 **Miller, Gary**	98	2	90
43 Baca	98	2	95
44 **Calvert**	96	4	93
45 **Bono Mack**	90	10	97
46 **Rohrabacher**	97	3	98
47 Sanchez, Loretta	99	1	95
48 **Campbell**	95	5	89
49 **Issa**	95	5	98
50 **Bilbray**	88	12	92
51 Filner	96	4	97
52 **Hunter**	98	2	99
53 Davis	98	2	98

	1	2	3
COLORADO			
1 DeGette	99	1	90
2 Polis	97	3	99
3 Salazar	92	8	94
4 Markey	87	13	98
5 **Lamborn**	99	1	99
6 **Coffman**	95	5	99
7 Perlmutter	98	2	95
CONNECTICUT			
1 Larson	99	1	99
2 Courtney	96	4	99
3 DeLauro	99	1	99
4 Himes	88	12	94
5 Murphy	97	3	99
DELAWARE			
AL **Castle**	71	29	99
FLORIDA			
1 **Miller**	98	2	95
2 Boyd	89	11	90
3 Brown	98	2	96
4 **Crenshaw**	92	8	94
5 **Brown-Waite**	91	9	80
6 **Stearns**	98	2	99
7 **Mica**	97	3	99
8 Grayson	97	3	98
9 **Bilirakis**	92	8	98
10 **Young**	90	10	67
11 Castor	99	1	95
12 **Putnam**	92	8	91
13 **Buchanan**	89	11	96
14 **Mack**	97	3	95
15 **Posey**	89	11	100
16 **Rooney**	95	5	98
17 Meek	98	2	87
18 **Ros-Lehtinen**	85	15	89
19 Deutch [2]	98	2	92
20 Wasserman Schultz	99	1	92
21 **Diaz-Balart, L.**	83	17	89
22 Klein	96	4	98
23 Hastings	99	1	85
24 Kosmas	90	10	97
25 **Diaz-Balart, M.**	87	13	97
GEORGIA			
1 **Kingston**	97	3	99
2 Bishop	96	4	95
3 **Westmoreland**	99	1	96
4 Johnson	98	2	93
5 Lewis	100	0	97
6 **Price**	99	1	98
7 **Linder**	97	3	85
8 Marshall	72	28	96
9 **Deal** [3]	100	0	49
9 **Graves** [3]	99	1	100
10 **Broun**	99	1	98
11 **Gingrey**	99	1	96
12 Barrow	91	9	98
13 Scott	98	2	99
HAWAII			
1 Abercrombie [4]	100	0	60
1 **Djou** [4]	76	24	95
2 Hirono	99	1	99
IDAHO			
1 Minnick	44	56	98
2 **Simpson**	90	10	98
ILLINOIS			
1 Rush	96	4	89
2 Jackson	98	2	99
3 Lipinski	88	12	96
4 Gutierrez	95	5	83
5 Quigley	95	5	97
6 **Roskam**	98	2	95
7 Davis	96	4	91
8 Bean	85	15	97
9 Schakowsky	98	2	98
10 Kirk [5]	77	23	89
11 Halvorson	88	12	98
12 Costello	90	10	93
13 **Biggert**	87	13	99
14 Foster	89	11	99
15 Johnson	80	20	99

KEY   **Republicans**   Democrats

	1	2	3
16 Manzullo	95	5	98
17 Hare	99	1	98
18 Schock	93	7	94
19 Shimkus	96	4	98
INDIANA			
1 Visclosky	95	5	98
2 Donnelly	73	27	99
3 Souder[6]	99	1	87
3 Stutzman[6]	100	0	95
4 Buyer	97	3	73
5 Burton	98	2	96
6 Pence	99	1	93
7 Carson	99	1	98
8 Ellsworth	76	24	95
9 Hill	74	26	96
IOWA			
1 Braley	98	2	97
2 Loebsack	97	3	99
3 Boswell	97	3	98
4 Latham	90	10	97
5 King	98	2	99
KANSAS			
1 Moran	99	1	80
2 Jenkins	97	3	100
3 Moore	98	2	97
4 Tiahrt	98	2	78
KENTUCKY			
1 Whitfield	90	10	96
2 Guthrie	96	4	98
3 Yarmuth	99	1	96
4 Davis	99	1	87
5 Rogers	97	3	99
6 Chandler	89	11	97
LOUISIANA			
1 Scalise	97	3	99
2 Cao	65	35	96
3 Melancon	85	15	83
4 Fleming	98	2	99
5 Alexander	97	3	95
6 Cassidy	92	8	99
7 Boustany	96	4	95
MAINE			
1 Pingree	99	1	94
2 Michaud	91	9	100
MARYLAND			
1 Kratovil	65	35	99
2 Ruppersberger	97	3	96
3 Sarbanes	99	1	98
4 Edwards	98	2	99
5 Hoyer	99	1	98
6 Bartlett	95	5	99
7 Cummings	99	1	98
8 Van Hollen	100	0	97
MASSACHUSETTS			
1 Olver	99	1	99
2 Neal	99	1	97
3 McGovern	99	1	99
4 Frank	98	2	97
5 Tsongas	99	1	98
6 Tierney	99	1	97
7 Markey	99	1	98
8 Capuano	98	2	96
9 Lynch	95	5	94
10 Delahunt	99	1	73
MICHIGAN			
1 Stupak	95	5	92
2 Hoekstra	99	1	46
3 Ehlers	70	30	99
4 Camp	96	4	95
5 Kildee	99	1	100
6 Upton	94	6	100
7 Schauer	91	9	100
8 Rogers	94	6	95
9 Peters	83	17	99
10 Miller	94	6	99
11 McCotter	91	9	98
12 Levin	99	1	99
13 Kilpatrick	96	4	77
14 Conyers	99	1	94
15 Dingell	99	1	97
MINNESOTA			
1 Walz	97	3	99
2 Kline	94	6	99
3 Paulsen	89	11	99
4 McCollum	98	2	97

	1	2	3
5 Ellison	97	3	95
6 Bachmann	98	2	94
7 Peterson	81	19	99
8 Oberstar	99	1	97
MISSISSIPPI			
1 Childers	53	47	95
2 Thompson	98	2	99
3 Harper	97	3	99
4 Taylor	42	58	95
MISSOURI			
1 Clay	97	3	92
2 Akin	99	1	87
3 Carnahan	98	2	99
4 Skelton	87	13	99
5 Cleaver	98	2	95
6 Graves	95	5	89
7 Blunt	96	4	76
8 Emerson	94	6	98
9 Luetkemeyer	96	4	98
MONTANA			
AL Rehberg	95	5	99
NEBRASKA			
1 Fortenberry	87	13	96
2 Terry	92	8	98
3 Smith	97	3	100
NEVADA			
1 Berkley	98	2	96
2 Heller	92	8	95
3 Titus	92	8	99
NEW HAMPSHIRE			
1 Shea-Porter	97	3	98
2 Hodes	88	12	86
NEW JERSEY			
1 Andrews	98	2	94
2 LoBiondo	86	14	100
3 Adler	69	31	98
4 Smith	84	16	99
5 Garrett	97	3	98
6 Pallone	99	1	98
7 Lance	91	9	100
8 Pascrell	99	1	99
9 Rothman	99	1	97
10 Payne	97	3	95
11 Frelinghuysen	91	9	100
12 Holt	99	1	99
13 Sires	98	2	94
NEW MEXICO			
1 Heinrich	97	3	100
2 Teague	86	14	95
3 Luján	99	1	99
NEW YORK			
1 Bishop	96	4	98
2 Israel	98	2	99
3 King	89	11	93
4 McCarthy	96	4	93
5 Ackerman	99	1	91
6 Meeks	99	1	92
7 Crowley	99	1	98
8 Nadler	98	2	96
9 Weiner	96	4	98
10 Towns	97	3	94
11 Clarke	98	2	98
12 Velázquez	96	4	97
13 McMahon	80	20	95
14 Maloney	98	2	97
15 Rangel	98	2	98
16 Serrano	99	1	98
17 Engel	99	1	96
18 Lowey	98	2	98
19 Hall	98	2	97
20 Murphy	78	22	96
21 Tonko	97	3	99
22 Hinchey	99	1	95
23 Owens	83	17	98
24 Arcuri	84	16	97
25 Maffei	93	7	98
26 Lee	90	10	98
27 Higgins	98	2	94
28 Slaughter	100	0	96
29 Massa[7]	92	8	80
29 Reed[7]	92	8	100
NORTH CAROLINA			
1 Butterfield	98	2	94
2 Etheridge	95	5	99
3 Jones	72	28	88
4 Price	99	1	99

	1	2	3
5 Foxx	99	1	99
6 Coble	97	3	95
7 McIntyre	70	30	97
8 Kissell	93	7	99
9 Myrick	98	2	96
10 McHenry	98	2	96
11 Shuler	60	40	89
12 Watt	95	5	98
13 Miller	99	1	99
NORTH DAKOTA			
AL Pomeroy	94	6	97
OHIO			
1 Driehaus	89	11	100
2 Schmidt	98	2	99
3 Turner	89	11	98
4 Jordan	99	1	98
5 Latta	99	1	96
6 Wilson	96	4	95
7 Austria	96	4	100
8 Boehner	99	1	95
9 Kaptur	95	5	97
10 Kucinich	92	8	100
11 Fudge	98	2	99
12 Tiberi	91	9	99
13 Sutton	98	2	97
14 LaTourette	80	20	96
15 Kilroy	95	5	97
16 Boccieri	86	14	99
17 Ryan	98	2	98
18 Space	80	20	95
OKLAHOMA			
1 Sullivan	98	2	96
2 Boren	69	31	89
3 Lucas	96	4	99
4 Cole	89	11	97
5 Fallin	97	3	66
OREGON			
1 Wu	91	9	95
2 Walden	93	7	98
3 Blumenauer	98	2	95
4 DeFazio	95	5	93
5 Schrader	94	6	94
PENNSYLVANIA			
1 Brady	99	1	95
2 Fattah	99	1	98
3 Dahlkemper	85	15	97
4 Altmire	77	23	100
5 Thompson	93	7	98
6 Gerlach	83	17	99
7 Sestak	94	6	99
8 Murphy, P.	93	7	94
9 Shuster	98	2	98
10 Carney	80	20	89
11 Kanjorski	95	5	99
12 Murtha[8]	88	12	100
12 Critz[8]	89	11	64
13 Schwartz	98	2	96
14 Doyle	99	1	95
15 Dent	76	24	98
16 Pitts	86	14	98
17 Holden	85	15	99
18 Murphy, T.	81	19	98
19 Platts	85	15	99
RHODE ISLAND			
1 Kennedy	99	1	89
2 Langevin	97	3	98
SOUTH CAROLINA			
1 Brown	97	3	81
2 Wilson	97	3	99
3 Barrett	99	1	56
4 Inglis	97	3	98
5 Spratt	97	3	98
6 Clyburn	99	1	98
SOUTH DAKOTA			
AL Herseth Sandlin	71	29	97
TENNESSEE			
1 Roe	97	3	99
2 Duncan	96	4	98
3 Wamp	94	6	48
4 Davis	89	11	90
5 Cooper	81	19	99
6 Gordon	98	2	91
7 Blackburn	98	2	95
8 Tanner	89	11	91
9 Cohen	98	2	93

	1	2	3
TEXAS			
1 Gohmert	95	5	91
2 Poe	99	1	96
3 Johnson, S.	99	1	93
4 Hall	95	5	97
5 Hensarling	99	1	99
6 Barton	97	3	93
7 Culberson	97	3	89
8 Brady	97	3	98
9 Green, A.	98	2	99
10 McCaul	95	5	98
11 Conaway	99	1	97
12 Granger	96	4	87
13 Thornberry	99	1	99
14 Paul	91	9	93
15 Hinojosa	97	3	84
16 Reyes	98	2	91
17 Edwards	87	13	98
18 Jackson Lee	99	1	94
19 Neugebauer	99	1	96
20 Gonzalez	98	2	97
21 Smith	96	4	98
22 Olson	98	2	97
23 Rodriguez	97	3	94
24 Marchant	99	1	83
25 Doggett	95	5	99
26 Burgess	96	4	91
27 Ortiz	93	7	98
28 Cuellar	97	3	95
29 Green, G.	99	1	91
30 Johnson, E.	98	2	97
31 Carter	99	1	99
32 Sessions	99	1	99
UTAH			
1 Bishop	97	3	95
2 Matheson	82	18	99
3 Chaffetz	93	7	98
VERMONT			
AL Welch	96	4	96
VIRGINIA			
1 Wittman	90	10	98
2 Nye	55	45	100
3 Scott	97	3	100
4 Forbes	94	6	99
5 Perriello	80	20	100
6 Goodlatte	95	5	100
7 Cantor	98	2	96
8 Moran	97	3	97
9 Boucher	88	12	92
10 Wolf	89	11	100
11 Connolly	90	10	98
WASHINGTON			
1 Inslee	99	1	98
2 Larsen	98	2	100
3 Baird	91	9	94
4 Hastings	98	2	96
5 McMorris Rodgers	97	3	86
6 Dicks	98	2	99
7 McDermott	99	1	99
8 Reichert	80	20	93
9 Smith	96	4	95
WEST VIRGINIA			
1 Mollohan	97	3	91
2 Capito	86	14	98
3 Rahall	94	6	98
WISCONSIN			
1 Ryan	98	2	91
2 Baldwin	99	1	99
3 Kind	95	5	97
4 Moore	96	4	91
5 Sensenbrenner	98	2	99
6 Petri	94	6	99
7 Obey	98	2	96
8 Kagen	99	1	94
WYOMING			
AL Lummis	95	5	99
DELEGATES			
Faleomavaega (A.S.)	100	0	62
Norton (D.C.)	97	3	94
Bordallo (Guam)	97	3	97
Sablan (N. Marianas)	98	2	82
Pierluisi (P.R.)	100	0	82
Christensen (V.I.)	93	7	85

Lawmakers' Attendance Down

AT ABOUT 5:30 ON THE EVENING OF DEC. 22, the bells rang in the House to summon lawmakers for the very last roll call vote of the second session of the 111th Congress. The issue at hand was a bill to provide assistance to first-responders who were still suffering from exposure to toxic dust and debris at Ground Zero after the Sept. 11 terrorist attacks a decade ago. And while it wasn't the most controversial vote of the year, it did carry a measure of ideological baggage.

What was notable about the vote wasn't the outcome, which was an expected win for its Democratic sponsors. Rather, it was the number of lawmakers who skipped out — a whopping 168. That figure was extraordinary, first because it was so large in relation to the significance of the vote and second because it reflected a trend in the House in 2010 that was out of the ordinary. Lawmakers simply didn't show up as often as they had in the recent past to perform their No. 1 duty: to vote.

Lawmakers were called to the House chamber 664 times last year: four times for quorum calls, for which they are asked only to record their presence, and 660 times to cast "yea" or "nay" votes. Although that was an unremarkable number of roll calls — the House voted 987 times in 2009 — an average of 25 House members were absent every time, up from 17 the year before. Whether that was a function of a fractious election year in which 61 lawmakers were unseated or whether some other factors were in play, attendance was plainly off.

Overall, House lawmakers cast votes 94.2 percent of the time during the session, the lowest level of participation for the chamber since 2004 and below the 20-year average of 95.5 percent. Still, more than half of all House members voted at least 96 percent of the time.

Senators were summoned to vote 299 times in 2010, a bit less often than average. As is typical in a chamber where cooperation — even when it appears forced — is an intrinsic element of the mores, participation in roll calls was higher than in the House. Despite an aggressive lame-duck agenda that kept Congress busy almost until Christmas and required seven votes on the last weekend of the session, senators mostly managed to show up, participating on average in 96.6 percent of the roll calls, barely down from their 97 percent performance the year before and about on par for the past two decades.

More than half of the senators made at least 98 percent of the year's votes, although ailing lawmakers lowered the average. Robert C. Byrd of West Virginia, who died in June at 92 as the oldest senator and longest-serving lawmaker in U.S. history, made just 39 percent of his votes. (Byrd, p. 5-7)

Perfect attendance was about the same as in 2009. Seven House members and 15 senators cast every possible vote. Sen. Charles E. Grassley of Iowa, perfect since 1993, had yet another year in which he declined to sit one out. Four senators and two House members who either departed before the year ended or came in midyear also scored 100 percent, voting every time they could. ■

Lawmakers Missed Floor Votes More Often in 2010

This past year marked a decline for lawmaker participation in roll call votes in both chambers, a pattern consistent with election years. The average House member voted roughly 94 percent of the time, the lowest midterm rate in almost two decades. The average senator voted less than 97 percent of the time, close to what has been typical in that chamber since about 1990. Overall, median congressional voting participation has been marginally lower in the most recent decade than it was in the 1990s.

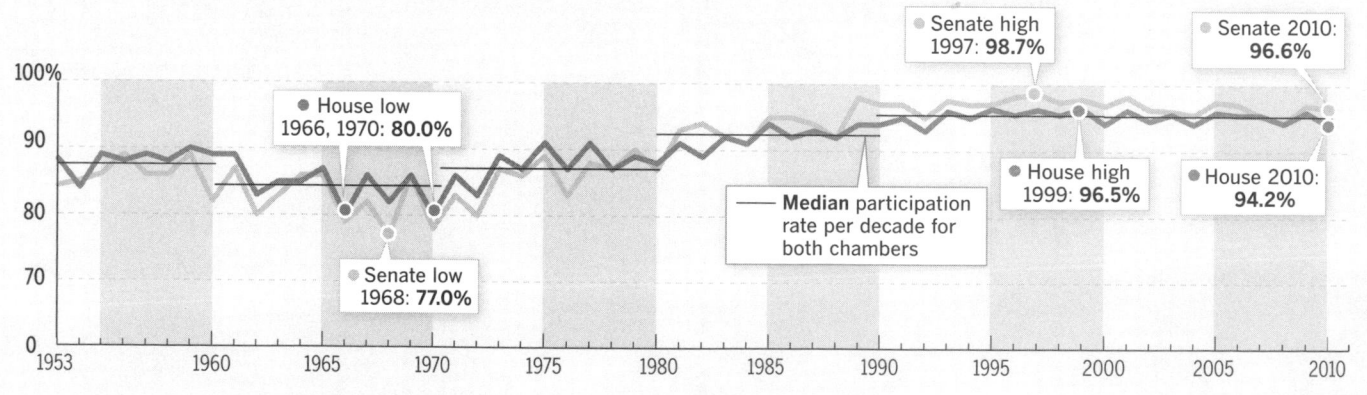

Voting Participation History

These tables show the number of roll call votes in each chamber and in Congress as a whole since 1953 and the frequency with which lawmakers on average cast "yea" or "nay" votes. Participation in floor votes had held close to 95 percent since the mid-1990s.

	House		Senate		Congress as a Whole	
YEAR	ROLL CALLS	RATE	ROLL CALLS	RATE	ROLL CALLS	RATE
2010	660	94.2%	299	96.6%	959	94.4%
2009	987	96.0	397	97.0	1,384	96.1
2008	688	94.3	215	94.3	903	94.3
2007	1,177	95.5	442	95.0	1,619	95.4
2006	541	95.5	279	97.1	820	95.7
2005	669	95.9	366	97.4	1,035	96.1
2004	543	94.1	216	95.5	759	94.2
2003	675	95.6	459	96.1	1,134	95.7
2002	483	94.6	253	96.3	736	94.8
2001	507	96.2	380	98.2	887	96.5
2000	600	94.1	298	96.9	898	94.4
1999	609	96.5	374	97.9	983	96.6
1998	533	95.5	314	97.4	847	95.7
1997	633	96.3	298	98.7	931	96.5
1996	454	95.5	306	98.2	760	95.8
1995	867	96.4	613	97.1	1,480	96.5
1994	497	95.0	329	97.0	826	95.0
1993	597	96.0	395	97.6	992	96.0
1992	473	93.0	270	95.0	743	93.4
1991	428	95.0	280	97.0	708	95.0
1990	536	94.0	326	97.0	862	95.0
1989	368	94.0	312	98.0	680	95.0
1988	451	92.0	379	92.0	830	92.0
1987	488	93.0	420	94.0	908	93.0
1986	451	92.0	354	95.0	805	93.0
1985	439	94.0	381	95.0	820	94.0
1984	408	91.0	275	91.0	683	91.0
1983	498	92.0	371	92.0	869	92.0
1982	459	89.0	465	94.0	924	90.0
1981	353	91.0	483	93.0	836	92.0
1980	604	88.0	531	87.0	1,135	87.0
1979	672	89.0	497	90.0	1,169	89.0
1978	834	87.0	516	87.0	1,350	87.0
1977	706	91.0	635	88.0	1,341	90.0
1976	661	87.0	688	83.0	1,349	86.0
1975	612	91.0	602	89.0	1,214	91.0
1974	537	87.0	544	86.0	1,081	87.0
1973	541	89.0	594	87.0	1,135	89.0
1972	329	83.0	532	80.0	861	82.0
1971	320	86.0	423	83.0	743	85.0
1970	266	80.0	418	78.0	684	79.0
1969	177	86.0	245	86.0	422	86.0
1968	233	82.0	281	77.0	514	80.0
1967	245	86.0	315	82.0	560	85.0
1966	193	80.0	235	79.0	428	79.0
1965	201	87.0	258	86.0	459	87.0
1964	113	85.0	305	86.0	418	85.0
1963	119	85.0	229	83.0	348	84.0
1962	124	83.0	224	80.0	348	82.0
1961	116	89.0	204	87.0	320	88.0
1960	93	89.0	207	82.0	300	87.0
1959	87	90.0	215	89.0	302	89.0
1958	93	88.0	200	86.0	293	87.0
1957	100	89.0	107	86.0	207	88.0
1956	73	88.0	130	89.0	203	88.0
1955	76	89.0	87	86.0	163	88.0
1954	76	84.0	171	85.0	247	84.0

Perfect Records Of Attendance

As is typical in an election year, voting participation declined in 2010. And while participation in the Senate was higher than it was in 2008, a year in which many lawmakers campaigned for president, the House figures roughly matched for both years. The count of those with perfect attendance on roll call votes was about the same as in 2009. Seven House members and 15 senators cast a "yea" or a "nay" on every recorded vote.

Perfect Attendance, House

Democrats

Jason Altmire of Pennsylvania
Dale E. Kildee of Michigan
Michael H. Michaud of Maine

Republicans

Lynn Jenkins of Kansas
Leonard Lance of New Jersey
Frank A. LoBiondo of New Jersey
Fred Upton of Michigan

Perfect Attendance, Senate

Democrats

Michael Bennet of Colorado
Sherrod Brown of Ohio
Benjamin L. Cardin of Maryland
Dianne Feinstein of California
Al Franken of Minnesota
Ben Nelson of Nebraska
Jack Reed of Rhode Island
Harry Reid of Nevada

Republicans

John Barrasso of Wyoming
Thad Cochran of Mississippi
Susan Collins of Maine
Bob Corker of Tennessee
Charles E. Grassley of Iowa
Mitch McConnell of Kentucky
Olympia J. Snowe of Maine

(Two other House members and four other senators had perfect attendance but weren't eligible for all votes in 2010.)

HOUSE

1. Voting Participation. Percentage of recorded votes in 2010 on which a representative was eligible and present, and voted "yea" or "nay." There were a total of 660 such recorded votes. Quorum calls, although they are included in the House list of recorded roll calls, are not counted as votes because lawmakers are only asked to respond "present." There were four recorded quorum calls in 2010.

2. Voting Participation (without Journal votes). Percentage of recorded votes in 2010 on which a representative was eligible and present, and voted "yea" or "nay." There were a total of 654 such recorded votes in this version of the study. Six votes on motions to approve the House Journal were excluded.

Absences because of illness. Congressional Quarterly no longer designates members who missed votes because of illness. In the past, notations to that effect were based on official statements published in the Congressional Record, but these were found to be inconsistently used.

Rounding. Scores are rounded to the nearest percentage point, except that no scores are rounded up to 100 percent. Members with a 100 percent score participated in all recorded votes for which they were eligible.

[1] The Speaker votes only at her discretion.

[2] Rep. Ted Deutch, D-Fla., was sworn in April 15 to fill the seat vacated by the Jan. 3 resignation of Democrat Robert Wexler. The first vote for which Deutch was eligible was vote 205; Wexler was not eligible for any votes in 2010.

[3] Rep. Tom Graves, R-Ga., was sworn in June 14 to fill the seat vacated by Republican Nathan Deal, who resigned March 21 to run for governor. The first vote for which Graves was eligible was vote 356; the last vote for which Deal was eligible was vote 168.

[4] Rep. Charles K. Djou, R-Hawaii, was sworn in May 25 to fill the seat vacated by Democrat Neil Abercrombie, who resigned Feb. 28 to run for governor. The first vote for which Djou was eligible was vote 296; the last vote for which Abercrombie was eligible was vote 74.

[5] Rep. Mark Steven Kirk, R-Ill., resigned Nov. 29 to assume the Senate seat he won in a Nov. 2 special election. The last vote for which Kirk was eligible was vote 580.

[6] Rep. Marlin Stutzman, R-Ind., was sworn in Nov. 16 to fill the vacancy created by the May 21 resignation of Republican Mark Souder. The first vote for which Stutzman was eligible was vote 571; the last vote for which Souder was eligible was vote 290.

[7] Rep. Tom Reed, R-N.Y., was sworn in Nov. 18 to fill the vacancy created by the March 8 resignation of Democrat Eric Massa. The first vote for which Reed was eligible was vote 580; the last vote for which Massa was eligible was vote 91.

[8] Rep. Mark Critz, D-Pa., was sworn in May 20 to fill the seat vacated by the Feb. 8 death of Democrat John P. Murtha. The first vote for which Critz was eligible was vote 286; the last vote for which Murtha was eligible was vote 48.

		1	2
ALABAMA			
1	**Bonner**	91	91
2	Bright	94	94
3	**Rogers**	99	99
4	**Aderholt**	98	99
5	**Griffith**	81	81
6	**Bachus**	95	95
7	Davis	52	53
ALASKA			
AL	**Young**	86	86
ARIZONA			
1	Kirkpatrick	93	94
2	**Franks**	99	99
3	**Shadegg**	90	90
4	Pastor	97	97
5	Mitchell	98	98
6	**Flake**	96	96
7	Grijalva	88	89
8	Giffords	97	97
ARKANSAS			
1	Berry	81	81
2	Snyder	99	99
3	**Boozman**	95	95
4	Ross	99	99
CALIFORNIA			
1	Thompson	98	98
2	**Herger**	98	98
3	**Lungren**	99	99
4	**McClintock**	99	99
5	Matsui	99	99
6	Woolsey	88	89
7	Miller, George	96	96
8	Pelosi [1]	9	9
9	Lee	95	94
10	Garamendi	91	91
11	McNerney	98	98
12	Speier	87	87
13	Stark	82	81
14	Eshoo	95	95
15	Honda	94	94
16	Lofgren	91	91
17	Farr	97	97
18	Cardoza	91	91
19	**Radanovich**	60	59
20	Costa	95	95
21	**Nunes**	94	94
22	**McCarthy**	93	93
23	Capps	96	96
24	**Gallegly**	93	93
25	**McKeon**	97	97
26	**Dreier**	99	99
27	Sherman	98	98
28	Berman	95	95
29	Schiff	99	99
30	Waxman	94	94
31	Becerra	96	96
32	Chu	97	97
33	Watson	89	89
34	Roybal-Allard	99	99
35	Waters	85	85
36	Harman	93	93
37	Richardson	96	96
38	Napolitano	96	96
39	Sánchez, Linda	90	90
40	**Royce**	99	99
41	**Lewis**	96	96
42	**Miller, Gary**	93	93
43	Baca	97	97
44	**Calvert**	95	95
45	**Bono Mack**	97	97
46	**Rohrabacher**	94	94
47	Sanchez, Loretta	94	94
48	**Campbell**	88	88
49	**Issa**	97	97
50	**Bilbray**	90	90
51	Filner	97	97
52	**Hunter**	99	99
53	Davis	98	98

		1	2
COLORADO			
1	DeGette	92	92
2	Polis	98	98
3	Salazar	94	94
4	Markey	96	96
5	**Lamborn**	98	98
6	**Coffman**	99	99
7	Perlmutter	96	96
CONNECTICUT			
1	Larson	97	97
2	Courtney	99	99
3	DeLauro	99	99
4	Himes	96	96
5	Murphy	99	99
DELAWARE			
AL	**Castle**	99	99
FLORIDA			
1	**Miller**	95	95
2	Boyd	91	91
3	Brown	93	93
4	**Crenshaw**	93	93
5	**Brown-Waite**	82	81
6	**Stearns**	99	99
7	**Mica**	99	99
8	Grayson	97	96
9	**Bilirakis**	98	98
10	**Young**	66	66
11	Castor	95	94
12	**Putnam**	83	83
13	**Buchanan**	97	97
14	**Mack**	93	93
15	**Posey**	99	99
16	**Rooney**	99	99
17	Meek	85	85
18	**Ros-Lehtinen**	91	91
19	Deutch [2]	92	92
20	Wasserman Schultz	94	94
21	**Diaz-Balart, L.**	90	90
22	Klein	97	97
23	Hastings	88	88
24	Kosmas	98	98
25	**Diaz-Balart, M.**	95	95
GEORGIA			
1	**Kingston**	98	98
2	Bishop	95	94
3	**Westmoreland**	96	96
4	Johnson	93	93
5	Lewis	95	95
6	**Price**	94	94
7	**Linder**	87	87
8	Marshall	97	97
9	**Deal** [3]	34	34
9	**Graves** [3]	100	100
10	**Broun**	98	98
11	**Gingrey**	94	94
12	Barrow	97	97
13	Scott	98	98
HAWAII			
1	Abercrombie [4]	67	67
1	**Djou** [4]	96	96
2	Hirono	99	99
IDAHO			
1	**Minnick**	97	97
2	**Simpson**	94	94
ILLINOIS			
1	Rush	83	83
2	Jackson	99	99
3	Lipinski	95	95
4	Gutierrez	77	77
5	Quigley	95	95
6	**Roskam**	96	96
7	Davis	89	89
8	Bean	96	96
9	Schakowsky	98	98
10	Kirk [5]	81	81
11	Halvorson	99	99
12	Costello	94	94
13	**Biggert**	99	99
14	Foster	99	99
15	**Johnson**	96	96

KEY   **Republicans**   Democrats

	1	2
16 Manzullo	96	96
17 Hare	99	99
18 Schock	95	96
19 Shimkus	98	98
INDIANA		
1 Visclosky	97	97
2 Donnelly	99	99
3 **Souder**[6]	80	80
3 **Stutzman**[6]	96	96
4 **Buyer**	75	76
5 **Burton**	96	96
6 **Pence**	93	93
7 Carson	98	98
8 Ellsworth	92	92
9 Hill	97	97
IOWA		
1 Braley	96	96
2 Loebsack	98	98
3 Boswell	98	98
4 **Latham**	98	98
5 **King**	98	98
KANSAS		
1 **Moran**	81	81
2 **Jenkins**	100	100
3 Moore	96	96
4 **Tiahrt**	80	80
KENTUCKY		
1 **Whitfield**	97	97
2 **Guthrie**	99	99
3 Yarmuth	97	97
4 **Davis**	92	92
5 **Rogers**	98	98
6 Chandler	97	96
LOUISIANA		
1 **Scalise**	98	98
2 **Cao**	94	94
3 Melancon	85	85
4 **Fleming**	98	98
5 **Alexander**	94	94
6 **Cassidy**	97	97
7 **Boustany**	97	96
MAINE		
1 Pingree	95	95
2 Michaud	100	100
MARYLAND		
1 Kratovil	99	99
2 Ruppersberger	94	94
3 Sarbanes	98	98
4 Edwards	99	99
5 Hoyer	99	99
6 **Bartlett**	99	99
7 Cummings	96	96
8 Van Hollen	98	98
MASSACHUSETTS		
1 Olver	98	98
2 Neal	96	96
3 McGovern	99	99
4 Frank	95	95
5 Tsongas	96	96
6 Tierney	95	95
7 Markey	97	97
8 Capuano	95	95
9 Lynch	94	94
10 Delahunt	72	72
MICHIGAN		
1 Stupak	92	92
2 **Hoekstra**	41	41
3 **Ehlers**	95	95
4 **Camp**	95	95
5 Kildee	100	100
6 **Upton**	100	100
7 Schauer	99	99
8 **Rogers**	96	96
9 Peters	99	99
10 **Miller**	99	99
11 **McCotter**	99	99
12 Levin	99	99
13 Kilpatrick	79	79
14 Conyers	88	88
15 Dingell	96	96
MINNESOTA		
1 Walz	99	99
2 **Kline**	99	99
3 **Paulsen**	99	99
4 McCollum	98	98

	1	2
5 Ellison	95	95
6 **Bachmann**	95	95
7 Peterson	98	98
8 Oberstar	94	94
MISSISSIPPI		
1 Childers	95	95
2 Thompson	98	98
3 **Harper**	98	98
4 Taylor	93	93
MISSOURI		
1 Clay	93	93
2 **Akin**	90	89
3 Carnahan	97	97
4 Skelton	98	98
5 Cleaver	95	94
6 **Graves**	87	87
7 **Blunt**	73	73
8 **Emerson**	98	98
9 **Luetkemeyer**	99	99
MONTANA		
AL **Rehberg**	98	98
NEBRASKA		
1 **Fortenberry**	94	94
2 **Terry**	97	97
3 **Smith**	99	99
NEVADA		
1 Berkley	97	97
2 **Heller**	96	96
3 Titus	99	99
NEW HAMPSHIRE		
1 Shea-Porter	96	96
2 Hodes	83	83
NEW JERSEY		
1 Andrews	94	94
2 **LoBiondo**	100	100
3 Adler	98	98
4 **Smith**	99	99
5 **Garrett**	98	98
6 Pallone	99	99
7 **Lance**	100	100
8 Pascrell	97	97
9 Rothman	97	97
10 Payne	92	92
11 **Frelinghuysen**	99	99
12 Holt	99	99
13 Sires	94	94
NEW MEXICO		
1 **Heinrich**	99	99
2 Teague	94	94
3 Luján	99	99
NEW YORK		
1 Bishop	95	95
2 Israel	98	98
3 **King**	94	94
4 McCarthy	93	93
5 Ackerman	90	90
6 Meeks	93	93
7 Crowley	97	97
8 Nadler	96	96
9 Weiner	98	98
10 Towns	91	91
11 Clarke	98	98
12 Velázquez	95	95
13 McMahon	95	95
14 Maloney	95	95
15 Rangel	95	95
16 Serrano	98	98
17 Engel	93	93
18 Lowey	98	98
19 Hall	94	94
20 Murphy	97	97
21 Tonko	99	99
22 Hinchey	93	94
23 Owens	97	97
24 Arcuri	95	95
25 Maffei	97	97
26 Lee	97	96
27 Higgins	93	93
28 Slaughter	93	93
29 Massa[7]	73	73
29 **Reed**[7]	100	100
NORTH CAROLINA		
1 Butterfield	91	91
2 Etheridge	99	99
3 **Jones**	93	93
4 Price	99	99

	1	2
5 **Foxx**	99	99
6 **Coble**	96	96
7 McIntyre	98	98
8 Kissell	98	98
9 **Myrick**	95	95
10 **McHenry**	96	96
11 Shuler	92	92
12 Watt	99	99
13 Miller	98	98
NORTH DAKOTA		
AL Pomeroy	96	96
OHIO		
1 Driehaus	99	99
2 **Schmidt**	99	99
3 **Turner**	98	98
4 **Jordan**	97	96
5 **Latta**	98	98
6 Wilson	96	96
7 **Austria**	98	98
8 **Boehner**	88	88
9 Kaptur	96	96
10 Kucinich	99	99
11 Fudge	98	98
12 **Tiberi**	98	98
13 Sutton	97	97
14 **LaTourette**	95	96
15 Kilroy	98	98
16 Boccieri	97	97
17 Ryan	96	96
18 Space	93	93
OKLAHOMA		
1 **Sullivan**	95	95
2 Boren	91	91
3 **Lucas**	98	98
4 **Cole**	96	96
5 **Fallin**	60	60
OREGON		
1 Wu	95	95
2 **Walden**	97	97
3 Blumenauer	96	96
4 DeFazio	91	91
5 Schrader	92	92
PENNSYLVANIA		
1 Brady	95	95
2 Fattah	98	98
3 Dahlkemper	96	96
4 Altmire	100	100
5 **Thompson**	98	98
6 **Gerlach**	97	97
7 Sestak	98	98
8 Murphy, P.	95	94
9 **Shuster**	96	96
10 Carney	90	89
11 Kanjorski	99	99
12 Murtha[8]	99	99
12 Critz[8]	51	51
13 Schwartz	97	97
14 Doyle	95	95
15 **Dent**	97	97
16 **Pitts**	97	97
17 Holden	96	96
18 **Murphy, T.**	98	98
19 **Platts**	95	95
RHODE ISLAND		
1 Kennedy	88	88
2 Langevin	97	97
SOUTH CAROLINA		
1 **Brown**	83	83
2 **Wilson**	98	98
3 **Barrett**	47	47
4 **Inglis**	88	88
5 Spratt	98	98
6 Clyburn	97	97
SOUTH DAKOTA		
AL Herseth Sandlin	97	97
TENNESSEE		
1 **Roe**	99	99
2 **Duncan**	99	99
3 **Wamp**	47	46
4 Davis	91	91
5 Cooper	99	99
6 Gordon	88	88
7 **Blackburn**	95	95
8 Tanner	92	92
9 Cohen	92	92

	1	2
TEXAS		
1 **Gohmert**	87	88
2 **Poe**	95	96
3 **Johnson, S.**	94	94
4 **Hall**	97	97
5 **Hensarling**	99	99
6 **Barton**	94	94
7 **Culberson**	90	90
8 **Brady**	96	96
9 Green, A.	99	99
10 **McCaul**	96	96
11 **Conaway**	97	97
12 **Granger**	87	87
13 **Thornberry**	99	99
14 **Paul**	93	93
15 Hinojosa	83	83
16 Reyes	91	91
17 Edwards	95	95
18 Jackson Lee	91	91
19 **Neugebauer**	97	97
20 Gonzalez	97	97
21 **Smith**	98	98
22 **Olson**	96	96
23 Rodriguez	93	94
24 **Marchant**	84	84
25 Doggett	99	99
26 **Burgess**	97	97
27 Ortiz	91	91
28 Cuellar	98	98
29 Green, G.	95	95
30 Johnson, E.	90	90
31 **Carter**	95	96
32 **Sessions**	97	97
UTAH		
1 **Bishop**	93	94
2 Matheson	97	97
3 **Chaffetz**	97	97
VERMONT		
AL Welch	94	94
VIRGINIA		
1 **Wittman**	98	98
2 Nye	99	99
3 Scott	98	98
4 **Forbes**	98	98
5 Perriello	99	99
6 **Goodlatte**	99	99
7 **Cantor**	96	96
8 Moran	93	94
9 Boucher	92	92
10 **Wolf**	99	99
11 Connolly	98	98
WASHINGTON		
1 Inslee	98	98
2 Larsen	99	99
3 Baird	93	93
4 **Hastings**	95	95
5 **McMorris Rodgers**	87	87
6 Dicks	96	96
7 McDermott	98	98
8 **Reichert**	94	94
9 Smith	95	95
WEST VIRGINIA		
1 Mollohan	90	89
2 **Capito**	96	96
3 Rahall	98	98
WISCONSIN		
1 **Ryan**	92	92
2 Baldwin	99	99
3 Kind	97	97
4 Moore	90	90
5 **Sensenbrenner**	99	99
6 **Petri**	98	98
7 Obey	96	96
8 Kagen	95	95
WYOMING		
AL **Lummis**	98	98
DELEGATES		
Faleomavaega (A.S.)	66	66
Norton (D.C.)	93	93
Bordallo (Guam)	97	97
Sablan (N. Marianas)	85	85
Pierluisi (P.R.)	82	82
Christensen (V.I.)	78	78

SENATE

1. Voting Participation.
Percentage of recorded votes in 2010 on which a senator was eligible and present, and voted "yea" or "nay." There were a total of 299 such recorded votes.

2. Voting Participation (without motions to instruct).
Percentage of recorded votes in 2010 on which a senator was eligible and present, and voted "yea" or "nay." There were a total of 294 recorded votes in this version of the study. Five votes to instruct the sergeant at arms to request the attendance of absent senators were excluded.

Absences because of illness. Congressional Quarterly no longer designates members who missed votes because of illness. In the past, notations to that effect were based on official statements published in the Congressional Record, but these were found to be inconsistently used.

Rounding. Scores are rounded to the nearest percentage point, except that no scores are rounded up to 100 percent. Senators with a 100 percent score participated in all recorded votes for which they were eligible.

State / Senator	1	2		State / Senator	1	2
ALABAMA				**MONTANA**		
Shelby	98	98		Baucus	99	99
Sessions	98	98		Tester	99	99
ALASKA				**NEBRASKA**		
Murkowski	90	90		Nelson	100	100
Begich	97	97		Johanns	99	99
ARIZONA				**NEVADA**		
McCain	99	99		Reid	100	100
Kyl	98	99		Ensign	98	98
ARKANSAS				**NEW HAMPSHIRE**		
Lincoln	91	91		Gregg	88	88
Pryor	99	99		Shaheen	97	98
CALIFORNIA				**NEW JERSEY**		
Feinstein	100	100		Lautenberg	95	95
Boxer	98	98		Menendez	99	99
COLORADO				**NEW MEXICO**		
Udall	99	99		Bingaman	99	99
Bennet	100	100		Udall	99	99
CONNECTICUT				**NEW YORK**		
Dodd	97	97		Schumer	99	99
Lieberman	98	98		Gillibrand	99	99
DELAWARE				**NORTH CAROLINA**		
Carper	99	99		Burr	97	97
Kaufman [1]	98	98		Hagan	98	99
Coons [1]	98	98		**NORTH DAKOTA**		
FLORIDA				Conrad	99	99
Nelson	96	97		Dorgan	99	99
LeMieux	97	97		**OHIO**		
GEORGIA				Voinovich	94	95
Chambliss	94	94		Brown	100	100
Isakson	80	80		**OKLAHOMA**		
HAWAII				Inhofe	96	97
Inouye	98	98		Coburn	98	98
Akaka	99	99		**OREGON**		
IDAHO				Wyden	93	93
Crapo	97	98		Merkley	99	99
Risch	99	99		**PENNSYLVANIA**		
ILLINOIS				Specter	95	95
Durbin	99	99		Casey	99	99
Burris [2]	100	100		**RHODE ISLAND**		
Kirk [2]	83	83		Reed	100	100
INDIANA				Whitehouse	99	99
Lugar	99	99		**SOUTH CAROLINA**		
Bayh	89	90		Graham	98	98
IOWA				DeMint	94	95
Grassley	100	100		**SOUTH DAKOTA**		
Harkin	98	98		Johnson	99	99
KANSAS				Thune	98	99
Brownback	86	86		**TENNESSEE**		
Roberts	92	92		Alexander	98	98
KENTUCKY				Corker	100	100
McConnell	100	100		**TEXAS**		
Bunning	94	95		Hutchison	86	87
LOUISIANA				Cornyn	98	99
Landrieu	98	98		**UTAH**		
Vitter	90	90		Hatch	97	97
MAINE				Bennett	85	86
Snowe	100	100		**VERMONT**		
Collins	100	100		Leahy	99	99
MARYLAND				*Sanders*	98	98
Mikulski	96	97		**VIRGINIA**		
Cardin	100	100		Webb	97	98
MASSACHUSETTS				Warner	93	93
Kerry	98	99		**WASHINGTON**		
Kirk [3]	100	100		Murray	98	99
Brown [3]	100	100		Cantwell	99	99
MICHIGAN				**WEST VIRGINIA**		
Levin	99	99		Byrd [4]	39	40
Stabenow	99	99		Rockefeller	96	96
MINNESOTA				Goodwin [4]	100	100
Klobuchar	99	99		Manchin [4]	90	90
Franken	100	100		**WISCONSIN**		
MISSISSIPPI				Kohl	99	99
Cochran	100	100		Feingold	99	99
Wicker	98	99		**WYOMING**		
MISSOURI				Enzi	98	99
Bond	86	86		Barrasso	100	100
McCaskill	96	96				

KEY   Republicans   Democrats   *Independents*

[1] Sen. Chris Coons, D-Del., was sworn in Nov. 15 to replace Democrat Ted Kaufman, appointed Jan. 15, 2009, to temporarily fill the vacancy created by Democrat Joseph R. Biden Jr., who resigned to become vice president. The first vote for which Coons was eligible was vote 249; the last vote for which Kaufman was eligible was vote 248.

[2] Sen. Mark Steven Kirk, R-Ill., was sworn in Nov. 29 to replace Democrat Roland W. Burris, who was appointed on Dec. 30, 2008, to temporarily fill the vacancy created by Democrat Barack Obama, who resigned to become president. The first vote for which Kirk was eligible was vote 252; the last vote for which Burris was eligible was vote 251.

[3] Sen. Scott P. Brown, R-Mass., was sworn in Feb. 4 to replace Democrat Paul G. Kirk Jr., who was appointed Sept. 24, 2009, to temporarily fill the vacancy created by Democrat Edward M. Kennedy, who died Aug. 25, 2009. The first vote for which Brown was eligible was vote 21; the last vote for which Kirk was eligible was vote 20.

[4] Sen. Joe Manchin III, D-W.Va., was sworn in Nov. 15 to replace Democrat Carte P. Goodwin, who was appointed July 16 to temporarily fill the vacancy created by Democrat Robert C. Byrd, who died June 28. The first vote for which Manchin was eligible was vote 249. Goodwin was eligible for votes 209 through 248. The last vote for which Byrd was eligible was vote 200.

Appendix C

KEY VOTES

A Show of Force, Then Finesse as Democrats' Majorities Are Shaken

WATCHING THE LAME-DUCK session of the 111th Congress, it almost seemed as though lawmakers had saved their intensity for last, that all they really needed was the ticking clock and the true deadline of an impending sine die adjournment to push through some major initiatives. There was nothing lame about it: a big treaty with Russia, a big tax deal and a conditional repeal of the "don't ask, don't tell" policy barring openly gay people from serving in the military.

One might wonder whether the preceding 10 months were even necessary, given the vast difference between the flurry of activity that took place after Thanksgiving and the relatively inert status of legislation in the months beforehand.

The larger picture, of course, was more complicated than that. Earlier in the year, there were major legislative initiatives: the big health care bill that Democratic leaders pushed through in March and the financial regulations overhaul that they cleared during the summer.

The difference was the way the majority Democrats had to maneuver to get these things through. With both health care and financial regulations, the method was brute force. The votes were partisan, and the margins were tight. Republicans for the most part opposed these initiatives, and the partisan nature of the votes showed it.

Then came a campaign, an election, a president who acknowledged his party's "shellacking" and a sense that the status quo would no longer do.

And by year's end, Democrats were able to stage a string of successes, including a deal between President Obama and Republicans to extend income and estate tax cuts, conditional repeal of the ban on gays in the military and approval of ratification of a nuclear arms treaty with Russia. All three votes came with the help of Republicans.

On the tax legislation, Democrats, especially liberals, were furious that the president cut a deal with Republicans in which everyone, including those with high incomes, would see their Bush-era tax cuts extended. But the deal also included sweeteners for Democrats, including a yearlong extension of extra unemployment benefits that Republicans hadn't wanted. Few, if anyone, liked all of it: the essence of compromise.

One common theme in both the pre- and post-election votes was the degree to which presidential power was at stake. Obama got his way on many of the votes that Congressional Quarterly's editors chose as key for 2010, starting with the Democrats' successful bid to enact a health care overhaul.

In the early part of the year, though, it took a determined majority to do it. In January, his health care overhaul, already hanging by a

How CQ Picks Key Votes

Since its founding in 1945, Congressional Quarterly has selected a series of key votes for both the House and Senate on major issues of the year.

A vote is judged to be key by the extent to which it represents:

- a matter of major controversy.
- a matter of presidential or political power.
- a matter of potentially great impact on the nation and lives of Americans.

For each group of related votes in each chamber on an issue, one key vote is usually chosen — one that, in the opinion of CQ editors, was the most important in determining the outcome of the issue for the year or that best reflected the views of the individual members on that issue.

thread as the House and Senate pondered a conference to fix differences in the bills passed at the end of 2009, was further threatened. Republican Scott P. Brown captured the Massachusetts Senate seat long held by the late Edward M. Kennedy, trimming the Democratic majority to 59. In the highly partisan Senate, 60 "ayes" were needed to advance most legislation, and Brown, whose election was seen largely as a referendum on health care, joined all 40 other Republicans as a definite "nay."

Democrats went back to the drawing board. They devised a plan in which the House would vote to clear the Senate version and then fashion a bill under a process called reconciliation to address their concerns about the Senate bill. Because reconciliation measures are not subject to delaying tactics in the Senate, a bare majority can move such legislation. The Senate passed the bill with no GOP support and three Democrats against it; in the House, dozens of generally conservative Democrats defected.

But the Brown election had a more sweeping, even psychological, effect on Republicans as they anticipated echoes of Brown's victory in the November election. Standing firm against the Obama agenda apparently was paying off with voters, and the way in which the overhaul was enacted only made activists more livid. Adding to Democrats' headaches, the summertime death of Robert C. Byrd, D-W.Va., stalled other items on the party's agenda until the governor chose a replacement.

So it went for Senate Democrats for the middle part of the year, the main exception being the clearing of a historic overhaul of banking regulations — also a priority for Obama — that required the votes of Brown and Maine's two moderate Republican senators, Olympia J. Snowe and Susan Collins.

In addition, the Senate approved Obama nominees for two vital positions: Elena Kagan as an associate Supreme Court justice and Ben S. Bernanke for another four-year term as Federal Reserve chairman. But in both cases there was significant opposition — fierce partisanship in the case of Kagan and, with Bernanke, anger from both sides of the political spectrum about the Fed's role in the recent economic meltdown.

In the lame-duck session, though, Senate Republicans were able to use their levers of power on some Democratic bills they simply wanted to put on ice. They blocked debate on a limited House-passed immigration bill that would have allowed eventual citizenship for some young undocumented residents who went to college or entered the military. The vote was a rebuke of sorts of Senate Majority Leader Harry Reid, D-Nev., who had championed broader legislation to no avail throughout a year in which he faced re-election in a state where immigration is an important issue. Also dead in the water was a

House-passed bill designed to limit corporate campaign contributions. Efforts to overcome a Senate filibuster on the issue were rejected several times, although Democrats on Sept. 23 managed to muster 59 votes to advance the measure.

Although partisan divides shaped the votes on those lame-duck issues, two other key Senate votes in the final week came down to factors such as individual preference or persuasion that eclipsed party loyalty, while another key vote showed that reports of the death of bipartisanship, albeit at legislative gunpoint, might have been premature:

The chamber approved ratification of a nuclear treaty with Russia. Holding the balance of power on a vote that required a two-thirds majority were 13 Republicans who — heeding either heavy White House lobbying, the advice of a bipartisan group of former secretaries of state or the arguments of pro-treaty GOP colleagues such as Richard G. Lugar of Indiana — went against a determined party leadership.

For the first time devoid of any connection with other legislation, a repeal of the ban on gays in the military was reduced to a simple bill. In that sense, it became a conscience vote. Ultimately, eight Senate Republicans joined their Democratic colleagues in voting for repeal, including two conservatives never expected to be listed in the "yea" column: Richard M. Burr of North Carolina and John Ensign of Nevada.

The vote to limit debate on the tax-cut extensions deal, as well as the bill itself, won overwhelming support from both parties in the Senate, as Republicans stood by their bargain with the president, while Democrats, who perhaps for the first time in the 111th Congress felt they were being asked to back a bill they strongly opposed, voted with Obama, but without enthusiasm. But Democrats were in a bind: They knew it was the best deal they could get before the session expired.

On the following pages are backgrounds and explanations for each of the 28 votes — 15 in the House and 13 in the Senate — that Congressional Quarterly editors chose as key among the recorded votes of 2010.

SENATE VOTES

5 Debt Limit and Fiscal Task Force

Defeat of an amendment to a measure to increase the debt limit. The amendment would have established a bipartisan task force to address long-term debt and the deficit.

Senate Budget Chairman Kent Conrad, D-N.D., and ranking member Judd Gregg, R-N.H., began pushing for a vote on their proposal to create a debt commission late in the first session of the 111th Congress, and a compromise worked out just before the Senate adjourned in December 2009 gave them almost a month to find bipartisan support for their plan.

But many from both parties were uneasy about a provision that would have required Congress to hold straight up-or-down votes — without amendments — on any recommendation supported by a supermajority on the proposed panel. The amendment became a key test of whether lawmakers would commit to such a vote. In the end, they showed an unwillingness to force themselves to go on the record for or against a yet-to-be-determined deficit-cutting plan.

They made that call even as they were preparing to agree that the nation's statutory debt limit would have to be raised by $1.9 trillion to $14.294 trillion.

Eleven months later, an 18-member bipartisan debt commission created by President Obama released recommendations to cut domestic and defense spending by hundreds of billions of dollars, overhaul the tax system by lowering rates and eliminating popular deductions, raise the retirement age for Social Security and make other changes in entitlement programs.

In a compromise with Conrad and Gregg, Democratic leaders in the House and Senate had agreed informally to hold votes on the panel's plan if 14 of the 18 members endorsed it. But the commission vote on the recommendations was three shy of that threshold, and lawmakers never had to record a position on those proposals.

SENATE REJECTED the Conrad, D-N.D., amendment to H J Res 45 (PL 111-139) on Jan. 26, **53-46:** R 16-23; D 36-22; I 1-1. By unanimous consent, the Senate agreed to raise the majority requirement for adoption of the amendment to 60 votes. *(Senate vote 5, p. C-15; debt commission, p. 4-11)*

16 Confirmation of Ben S. Bernanke

Confirmation of Ben S. Bernanke for a second four-year term as chairman of the Federal Reserve.

The first time Bernanke was nominated to be Fed chairman, the Senate confirmed him by a unanimous consent agreement and without a roll call. But four years later, senators saw a chance to use this vote to express their frustrations with the Obama administration over the state of the economy and the cost of keeping the financial system functioning.

Although the Senate ultimately confirmed Bernanke for a second term, 30 senators voted "no." It was the most votes ever cast against a nominee for Fed chairman and almost double the 16 "no" votes recorded against Paul A. Volcker in 1983, when he was up for a second term after pushing interest rates into double digits to combat a serious inflation threat.

The bipartisan group of senators who objected to Bernanke's second term — 11 Democrats, 18 Republicans and one independent — foreshadowed the difficulty the Fed would face later in the year as Congress debated reining in the central bank's powers as part of an overhaul of financial services regulations. Yet, just as with Bernanke's confirmation, lawmakers ultimately opted to leave the Fed's authority intact and in some ways enhanced it by year's end.

Bernanke had led the central bank in pumping trillions of dollars into banks and other threatened enterprises and had pressed for enactment of the $700 billion bailout fund in 2008. Time magazine named him "Man of the Year" for 2009.

But Bernanke was attacked by lawmakers from the left for

having ignored the needs of middle-class and poor Americans and for having spent money shoring up Wall Street, while those on the right objected to the scope of the Fed's intervention in markets and financial institutions. The central bank was singled out by lawmakers at both ends of the ideological spectrum for having contributed to the financial crisis.

Obama had announced his intention to keep Bernanke at the Fed in August 2009, five months before the chairman's term was up, as a way to reassure skittish investors who were fearful of a change in monetary policy. But the Senate Banking Committee did not act on the nomination until mid-December, and the fact that seven lawmakers — one Democrat and six Republicans — voted against sending it to the floor was a sign that confirmation would not be simple.

As the nomination headed for a vote in late January, the White House stepped up its lobbying and portrayed the vote as a test of the nation's financial stability. Senate leaders assured lawmakers they would have other opportunities down the road to express their anger and to insist upon greater transparency and accountability at the Fed.

SENATE CONFIRMED Bernanke on Jan. 28, **70-30:** R 22-18; D 47-11; I 1-1. (Senate vote 16, p. C-15; financial regulation key vote, p. C-6)

105 Health Care Reconciliation

Passage of a budget reconciliation bill that modified an earlier health care overhaul and revised federal student loan programs.

The vote on the reconciliation bill (HR 4872 — PL 111-152) served as the final piece of the complex legislative puzzle that was the historic health care overhaul. It was essentially a way to make good on promises offered to liberal Democrats in the House who supported the underlying bill but who wanted more generous subsidies for the uninsured.

The bill made numerous changes to the underlying health care bill (HR 3590 — PL 111-148) that the Senate had passed Dec. 24, 2009. It increased subsidies to help uninsured people buy health coverage beginning in 2014 and boosted certain taxes and fees to help pay for the expanded coverage. It also made the federal government the sole originator of college student loans and increased the maximum Pell grant for low-income students.

The vote on the "sidecar" bill served two purposes: It gave members who thought the subsidies in the underlying bill were too low an opportunity to expand them, and it allowed senators to reaffirm their support for the overhaul itself.

The bill was part of a delicate deal put together by Democratic leaders and the White House. Many House Democrats had been reluctant to support the Senate bill, demanding leaders' assurances that they would push the second measure through Congress.

Democratic leaders gave those assurances, then chose to use a fast-track budget reconciliation process, which does not require 60 votes in the Senate, to move the companion bill. Had the reconciliation bill been defeated in the Senate, the deal almost certainly would have disintegrated. The Senate passed it, 56-43.

Three senators did join Republicans in voting against final passage of the secondary legislation, even though they had supported the underlying bill: Ben Nelson of Nebraska and Mark Pryor and Blanche Lincoln of Arkansas.

During the debate, Republicans did everything they could to disrupt the process. Senate leaders had to navigate through a lengthy "vote-a-rama" in which Republicans offered unlimited amendments after the end of debate time. The GOP strategy was to win the war on public opinion and make Democrats take politically tough votes.

Democrats defeated amendment after amendment, hoping to avoid having to send the bill back to the House for one last vote. But their hopes were dashed when the Senate parliamentarian upheld a GOP challenge to two minor provisions dealing with higher education grants. The House then passed the secondary bill.

SENATE PASSED HR 4872 (PL 111-152) on March 25, **56-43:** R 0-40; D 54-3; I 2-0. (Senate vote 105, p. C-15; House vote 165, p. C-18; health care overhaul, p. 9-3)

181 Discretionary Spending Caps

Rejection of a motion to place a spending cap on appropriations.

Although Jeff Sessions, R-Ala., and Claire McCaskill, D-Mo., never mustered the 60 votes necessary to win adoption of an amendment to limit government spending, their efforts helped shape the appropriations debate in Congress.

The Senate voted four times from January to June on their joint offering, which would have capped spending at $1.108 trillion annually through fiscal 2014.

The 57-41 vote on June 9 was the high-water mark of their effort. Still, 16 Democrats bucked their leadership. McCaskill said she considered it a victory that so many of her Democratic colleagues "withstood the pressure of leadership trying to convince people to jump ship."

Despite the votes to reject it, Minority Leader Mitch McConnell, R-Ky., gave the Sessions-McCaskill proposal a prominent role in the debate on fiscal 2011 spending. He and other Republicans announced at a Senate Appropriations Committee markup in July that they would not vote for any bill that spent more than the Sessions-McCaskill number.

Senate Appropriations Chairman Daniel K. Inouye, D-Hawaii, pushed for a $1.114 trillion cap, but he eventually relented and began writing spending bills that would come in under the $1.108 trillion limit.

SENATE REJECTED the motion to waive the Budget Act on the Sessions, R-Ala., amendment to HR 4213 (PL 111-205) on June 9, **57-41:** R 40-0; D 16-40; I 1-1. Three-fifths of the total Senate (60) is required to waive the Budget Act. (Senate vote 181, p. C-15; appropriations overview, p. 2-3)

184 Greenhouse Gas Regulation

Rejection of a disapproval resolution that would have stripped the EPA of its authority to regulate greenhouse gases under the federal Clean Air Act.

Although the vote on Alaska Republican Lisa Murkowski's resolution to rein in the EPA was unsuccessful, it marked a shift by environmentalists and their political allies from offense to defense in the fight over controlling greenhouse gases.

Murkowski's resolution was filed under the Congressional Review Act (PL 104-121), which allowed lawmakers to cast an up-or-down vote on an agency's regulations before they took effect. It would have negated EPA's so-called endangerment finding: a determination that greenhouse gas emissions posed a public health threat. That finding, which stemmed from a 2007 Supreme Court decision, triggered a requirement for the agency to regulate emissions.

For months, President Obama held out the prospect of EPA regulation of greenhouse gas emissions to pressure Congress to enact a "cap and trade" law that would restrict overall emissions of carbon dioxide and other gases that contribute to global warming and would establish a market for trading government-issued pollution allowances. The House had passed a cap-and-trade bill in June 2009, but efforts to assemble a bipartisan bill in the Senate fell apart in the spring of 2010. That meant EPA regulation was no longer a fallback plan for the administration, but rather an imminent reality.

On the eve of the vote, the outcome was uncertain. Solid Republican support was expected, but the positions of several moderate Democrats who could swing the vote was unknown. Ultimately, just six Democrats voted with a unanimous GOP caucus in favor of the resolution.

Even if the resolution had succeeded in the Senate, it was unlikely to get through the House, and if it did, it faced a certain presidential veto. Still, Senate adoption would have been a symbolic setback for the administration.

SENATE REJECTED a motion to proceed on S J Res 26 on June 10, **47-53:** R 41-0; D 6-51; I 0-2. *(Senate vote 184, p. C-16; climate change, p. 12-7)*

208 Financial Regulatory Overhaul

Clearing an overhaul of federal regulation of the financial services industry.

The Senate's final action on this bill put into law the greatest changes in financial regulation since the Great Depression and gave President Obama his second major legislative accomplishment, coming three months after his health care overhaul cleared.

The legislation granted financial industry regulators broad new authority and created agencies to oversee consumer lending and to determine whether changing financial conditions were a threat to the economy. The Federal Deposit Insurance Corporation was given new powers to take over and wind down huge financial companies on the verge of collapse. Trading in derivatives, the complex instruments that brought down the likes of insurance giant American International Group Inc., came under close regulatory scrutiny, mostly for the first time.

The vote on a House-Senate conference report on the bill (HR 4173) showed a united Democratic Caucus in favor of setting new standards for industry. Republicans, on the other hand, were fairly consistent in their stance that the bill gave the government too much power and could damage an already-weak economy.

In the early germination of the Senate bill, Banking Chairman Christopher J. Dodd, D-Conn., had hoped to reach an agreement with his panel's ranking member, Alabama Republican Richard C. Shelby. Talks broke down over expanding consumer protections and government powers to dismantle failed financial institutions.

The White House pushed Democrats to take a hard line on consumer protections, urging the creation of a powerful new regulator that could restrict or ban financial products it deemed abusive or predatory. Administration officials also demanded tough regulations

for the over-the-counter financial derivatives market.

The House passed its version of the bill in December 2009 with no Republican support; only three GOP House members backed the conference report. But in the final Senate vote, Democrats won the support of three New England Republicans: Scott P. Brown of Massachusetts and Susan Collins and Olympia J. Snowe of Maine. It took only a simple majority in the Senate to adopt a conference report, so their votes were not critical to clearing the bill. But their backing was crucial earlier in the day on two procedural votes requiring 60 "ayes."

Democrat Russ Feingold of Wisconsin, concerned that the legislation did not go far enough in regulating the banks, voted with the minority on the procedural votes as well as on clearing the package. That defection, plus the vacancy left by the June death of Democrat Robert C. Byrd of West Virginia, left no room to spare for supporters.

SENATE CLEARED HR 4173 (PL 111-203) by adopting a conference report on the bill July 15, **60-39:** R 3-38; D 55-1; I 2-0. *(Senate vote 208, p. C-16; House vote 413, p. C-20; financial regulatory overhaul, p. 3-3)*

228 Medicaid and Education Assistance

Passage of a bill to provide state and local funds to avert layoffs of teachers and other public employees and to extend increased Medicaid reimbursements for states.

One of the great divides of 2010 was between those who believed in more government spending to foster economic recovery and those who felt government was spending enough already. That bright line was clear in a Senate vote in August on a domestic spending bill that provided $10 billion to avert teacher layoffs and $16.1 billion to extend increased Medicaid reimbursements to states for six months.

Democrats, who had to rely on the votes of Maine Republicans Susan Collins and Olympia J. Snowe to obtain cloture on the bill, said the measure would boost the economy and protect vulnerable state and local government jobs. Most Republicans criticized it as an election year gambit by Democrats to assuage teachers' unions, among their biggest campaign supporters.

The Senate previously had turned back the education funding when the House attached it to a $58.8 billion fiscal 2010 supplemental appropriations measure to pay for the wars in Afghanistan and Iraq, as well as other priorities (PL 111-212).

The effort to pass the stand-alone bill was led by Majority Leader Harry Reid, D-Nev., and Patty Murray, D-Wash., who faced difficult re-election challenges.

Offsets to pay for the bill — a potpourri of spending rescissions and revenue-raisers — drew criticism from a number of sources. Republicans disliked provisions that targeted use of foreign tax credits by multinational corporations. Supporters of the food stamp program opposed reductions starting in 2014 to extra benefits that had been provided under the 2009 economic stimulus package (PL 111-5). In addition, the bill rescinded $1.5 billion in stimulus funds for an Energy Department program backed by many Democrats, including House Speaker Nancy Pelosi, D-Calif.

SENATE PASSED, through a motion to concur with an amendment, HR 1586 (PL 111-226) on Aug. 5, **61-39:** R 2-39; D 57-0; I 2-0. *(Senate vote 228, p. C-16; House vote 518, p. C-22; education and Medicaid supplemental, p. 2-18)*

229 Confirmation of Elena Kagan

Confirmation of Elena Kagan as an associate justice of the Supreme Court.

With this vote, the Senate gave Solicitor General Elena Kagan a lifetime seat on the Supreme Court, replacing Associate Justice John Paul Stevens.

Five Republicans supported her confirmation, but that was four fewer than President Obama's first nominee to the high court, Sonia Sotomayor, had received a year earlier, demonstrating an increasing reluctance among senators to back nominees selected by presidents of the opposing party.

There was little doubt about the outcome of the vote, given the sizable Democratic majority and Kagan's competent and occasionally humorous performance before the Senate Judiciary Committee. Any concerns about possible drama on the Senate floor were eliminated on the last day of Kagan's testimony, when Republicans conceded that her confirmation was all but inevitable and said a filibuster would be unrealistic.

Jeff Sessions of Alabama, the top Republican on the committee, led the charge against Kagan, citing her lack of prior experience as a judge and her work history as a lawyer and domestic policy adviser in Bill Clinton's White House.

In the days before the vote, five Republicans who had voted for Sotomayor announced plans to vote for Kagan. The first was Lindsey Graham of South Carolina, the only one of the seven Republicans on the Judiciary Committee to support her. He was joined by four who also had voted the previous year for Kagan's nomination to be solicitor general: Richard G. Lugar of Indiana; Susan Collins and Olympia J. Snowe of Maine; and Judd Gregg of New Hampshire, who was retiring.

That left three other potential Republican supporters: George V. Voinovich of Ohio and Christopher S. Bond of Missouri, two senior lawmakers who also were retiring at the end of 2010 and had voted for Sotomayor but opposed Kagan as solicitor general; and Scott P. Brown of Massachusetts, who had spoken well of Kagan following a private meeting after her nomination. But all three came out against Kagan.

On the Democratic side, the only surprise came the week before the vote, when Ben Nelson of Nebraska announced that he intended to vote against Kagan. He became the first Democrat to vote against a nominee of his president's own party since Abe Fortas' failed elevation to chief justice in 1968.

SENATE CONFIRMED Kagan on Aug. 5, **63-37**: R 5-36; D 56-1; I 2-0. *(Senate vote 229, p. C-16; Kagan confirmation, p. 10-3)*

240 Campaign Finance Disclosure

Refusal to invoke cloture to proceed to a bill that would have broadened campaign finance disclosure and reporting.

Senate Democratic leaders could not invoke cloture on a far-reaching campaign finance disclosure bill backed by the White House, as Republicans stood firm in opposition for the second time in two months to effectively kill the measure. The bill (S 3628) was a response to a Supreme Court decision handed down eight months earlier.

In *Citizens United v. Federal Election Commission*, the court held that

corporations had the same free-speech rights as individuals and could spend their own funds to influence elections. The decision was sharply criticized by Democrats, including President Obama, who charged that the 5-4 majority had sided with "powerful interests" over average Americans and that it would unleash a flood of donations aimed at swaying elections.

The measure, which would have set new disclosure requirements and spending limits on foreign companies or those receiving federal assistance, first reached the Senate floor in July, one month after the House passed its version (HR 5175). Republicans united against the bill, which they said unconstitutionally impinged on free speech and gave preferential treatment to unions.

In the first vote, after Democrats fell short of the 60 supporters needed to stop debate, Majority Leader Harry Reid, D-Nev., changed his vote to "nay" in order to leave open the possibility of reconsideration. In an effort to attract the single Republican vote they needed the second time around, sponsors proposed amending the measure to delay implementation until January 2011.

But that was not enough to win over any of the three New England Republicans identified as the most likely GOP supporters: Susan Collins and Olympia J. Snowe of Maine, and Scott P. Brown of Massachusetts.

SENATE REJECTED a motion to invoke cloture to proceed to S 3628 on Sept. 23, **59-39**: R 0-39; D 57-0; I 2-0. Three-fifths of the total Senate (60) is required to invoke cloture. *(Senate vote 240, p. C-16; House vote 391, p. C-20; campaign finance, p. 11-3)*

272 Tax-Cut Extensions

Successful cloture motion that allowed a vote on passage of a bill to extend income tax cuts for two years and set a new rate and threshold for estate taxes.

When President Obama announced Dec. 6 that he had reached a compromise with Republicans to extend 2001 and 2003 George W. Bush-era tax cuts — including those for the wealthiest Americans — many congressional Democrats were openly angry. The most vocal resentment came from House Democrats, especially from the liberal wing of the party.

So the next day, Obama dispatched Vice President Joseph R. Biden Jr. to the Hill — not to the House, but to his old stomping ground, the Senate, even though reaction there had been much more restrained.

Less than a week later, the Senate gave such overwhelming support to a bill to enact Obama's proposal that the House had little choice but to go along with it. In a Senate where the search for 60 votes dominated strategy all year on almost any piece of legislation or nomination, the 83-15 vote to advance the president's initiative essentially signaled that the deal had been sealed, and House Democrats would look irresponsible if they chose to fight back.

Immediately after the Senate agreed to invoke cloture and limit debate on the bill (HR 4853), talk in the House shifted from a demand by Democrats to not bring up the measure to how it could reach the floor, possibly with changes to its estate tax provisions. The Senate's slightly narrower 81-19 vote to pass the bill two days later all but ensured that the measure could not be changed.

When the House took up the bill Dec. 16, Democrats in that chamber had to settle for a separate, guaranteed-to-fail vote on an amendment to increase the estate tax rate for upper-income people

(rejected 194-233), before clearing the bill 10 days after Obama asked for it.

The plan extends the expiring 2001 and 2003 tax rates (PL 107-16, PL 108-27) for two years for all taxpayers and revives the estate tax at a rate of 35 percent on estates worth more than $5 million for individuals. It also extends unemployment benefits for 13 months.

Republicans got the extension of the tax cut for those making more than $200,000 a year, as well as their preferred levels on the estate tax. For Democrats, the proposal contained the emergency unemployment benefits and a one-year rate cut in the payroll tax for Social Security, as well as an extension of tax cuts for the middle class.

The nine Democrats who voted against cloture generally were among the most liberal senators, such as Russ Feingold of Wisconsin and Sherrod Brown of Ohio. The five Republicans who opposed the bill in that vote were among the most conservative, including Tom Coburn of Oklahoma and Jim DeMint of South Carolina.

SENATE AGREED to invoke cloture on a motion to limit debate on HR 4853 (PL 111-312) on Dec. 13, **83-15:** R 37-5; D 45-9; I 1-1. *(Senate vote 272, p. C-17; House vote 647, p. C-24; income tax cut extensions, p. 14-3)*

278 Immigration Policy

Refusal to invoke cloture to limit debate on a bill that would have allowed legal status for some undocumented children of illegal immigrants.

Immigration policy at the end of the 111th Congress was left largely where it had been at the beginning: in a state of uncertainty. Nothing captured that situation better than the end-of-the-session Senate vote to reject cloture on the bill known as the DREAM Act.

The legislation was drafted narrowly to provide a path for legal status for adults younger than 30 who were brought illegally to the United States before turning 16. Those who met the age eligibility and finished two years of college or military service would be eligible to apply for permanent residency and ultimately for citizenship.

The 55-41 vote demonstrated that a majority of senators wanted to move on the legislation. But it did not meet the 60-vote threshold needed to invoke cloture. The vote showed that Senate conservatives from both parties were reluctant to go ahead with piecemeal legislation in the absence of a more comprehensive overhaul of immigration policy that included tougher measures to enforce border protection and limit amnesty.

Some opponents said that whatever its merits — and there was debate even about that — the legislation just was not enough given the severity of the immigration situation.

SENATE REJECTED a motion to invoke cloture on HR 5281 on Dec. 18, **55-41**: R 3-36; D 50-5; I 2-0. Three-fifths of the total Senate (60) is required to invoke cloture. *(Senate vote 278, p. C-17; House vote 625, p. C-24)*

281 'Don't Ask, Don't Tell' Repeal

Clearing a repeal of the law banning openly gay people from serving in the military.

The Senate vote was a significant victory for President Obama, who had fought to repeal the ban.

The president had argued that asking servicemen and women who put their lives on the line to lie about who they are was anathema to the honor and integrity embodied by the uniformed services. A number of GOP senators argued against repeal, saying a time of war was the wrong moment to introduce such a change into an already-stressed force. But an internal Pentagon study released in early December on how to implement the change appeared to swing enough Republican votes to secure passage.

Repeal of the 1993 law (PL 103-160) was always expected to face its greatest challenge in the Senate. But the effort gathered strong momentum after Adm. Mike Mullen, chairman of the Joint Chiefs of Staff, spoke passionately before the Senate Armed Services Committee early in the year about the necessity of such a change. After Defense Secretary Robert M. Gates launched a study on how to implement the change, Democrat Carl Levin of Michigan, chairman of the Armed Services panel, indicated he would incorporate repeal language into the fiscal 2011 defense authorization bill.

In September, Senate Republicans blocked consideration of the authorization bill, primarily because of the repeal language. As a result, Joseph I. Lieberman, I-Conn., and Susan Collins, R-Maine, quickly filed a stand-alone repeal bill. Rep. Patrick J. Murphy, D-Pa., and House Majority Leader Steny H. Hoyer, D-Md., filed a similar measure, which the House passed Dec. 15.

The House bill was sent to the Senate in the form of a message, enabling Majority Leader Harry Reid, D-Nev., to bring it up without a procedural vote that would have required 60 votes. At that point, a few Republican senators indicated they had been swayed by the results of the internal study.

Others, such as John McCain of Arizona and Lindsey Graham of South Carolina, continued to oppose the measure. Graham called the bill a partisan measure that "poisoned the water."

Undeterred, pro-repeal senators on Dec. 18 cleared a major procedural hurdle, invoking cloture by a 63-33 vote.

SENATE CLEARED, through a motion to concur, HR 2965 (PL 111-321) on Dec. 18, **65-31:** R 8-31; D 55-0; I 2-0. *(Senate vote 281, p. C-17; House vote 317, p. C-18; "don't ask, don't tell" repeal, p. 6-7)*

298 New START Ratification

Approval of ratification of a strategic arms reduction treaty with Russia.

In its last major vote of the 111th Congress, the Senate handed President Obama an important victory when 13 Republicans joined all 58 members of the Democratic caucus in voting to approve ratification of the newest arms accord with Russia, known as New START (Treaty Doc 111-5).

Although the treaty did not earn the resounding support that past bilateral arms treaties enjoyed in the Senate, Democrats secured more than enough GOP support to reach the two-thirds vote threshold necessary to approve ratification.

Entering the final week of the lame-duck session, it remained uncertain whether the Senate would approve ratification of New START. Democrats needed at least nine Republicans to guarantee ratification, but only four had publicly confirmed their support, and the Senate's two top Republicans — Minority Leader Mitch McConnell of Kentucky and Minority Whip Jon Kyl of Arizona — announced they would vote against ratification.

It soon became clear, however, that the Obama administration was making headway with its weeks-long lobbying push. After a closed Senate session on the treaty during the afternoon of Dec. 20, a series of support statements from Republicans brought to 10 the number of GOP senators prepared to approve ratification of New START.

In the end, Republicans Thad Cochran of Mississippi, Judd Gregg of New Hampshire and Mike Johanns of Nebraska joined them in voting yes.

As notable as the Republican supporters were those in opposition, especially Kyl, John McCain of Arizona and Lindsey Graham of South Carolina, in addition to McConnell.

The administration spent more than a year wooing Kyl, the GOP's

point man on the treaty, and was stunned when he announced in November that he did not believe there would be sufficient time in the lame-duck session for a proper debate on New START. Kyl's stance was initially seen as the death knell for a vote on the accord in 2010, but Democrats' persistent and ultimately successful effort to peel off Republicans without his blessing left Kyl with weakened authority.

SENATE ADOPTED the resolution of ratification of Treaty Doc 111-5 on Dec. 22, **71-26:** R 13-26; D 56-0; I 2-0. A two-thirds majority of those present and voting (65 in this case) is required for adoption of resolutions of ratification. *(Senate vote 298, p. C-17; New START, p. 6-8)*

HOUSE VOTES

165 Health Care Overhaul

Clearing a bill to overhaul health care insurance coverage by requiring most individuals to buy insurance, requiring employers with more than 50 workers to provide coverage and creating state-run marketplaces for consumers to buy insurance. It also placed new taxes on drug and medical-device makers and prohibited insurance companies from denying care to people with pre-existing conditions.

The overhaul represented the largest rewrite of federal health policy since the enactment of Medicare in 1965. It was the product of negotiations between the House and Senate over the previous nine months, but those talks were mostly among Democrats; some wanted more-generous subsidies to help people buy insurance, and others were concerned that the measure would cost the government too much.

As such, the 219-212 vote was a reflection of members' views on the size and role of government in the American health care system. No Republicans voted for the legislation (HR 3590 — PL 111-148) and 34 Democrats, mostly moderates and members of the fiscally conservative Blue Dog Coalition, joined all 178 Republicans in voting against the bill.

During the floor debate, Republicans characterized the measure as one that expanded government's role to the point of socialized medicine. They criticized the requirement that employers provide insurance as a "job killer." Democrats argued that it was necessary to prevent insurance companies from discriminating against people with pre-existing conditions and to get uninsured Americans coverage they needed.

Conservative Democrats departed from the majority of their caucus based on cost considerations. Some members of the party, led by Bart Stupak of Michigan, wanted the legislation to prohibit the use of federal funds to cover abortions. They agreed to vote for the bill only after President Obama issued an executive order stating that no federal funds would go to abortions.

Given the Democratic defections, the vote was a measure of the abilities of Speaker Nancy Pelosi, D-Calif., and her leadership team to persuade wavering members to get on board.

For some liberal Democrats, the vote was a difficult one. They had hoped that a more-liberal health care bill passed in November 2009 would be blended with one passed by the Senate on Dec. 24 of that year. But when the Democrats lost a Senate seat with the election of Massachusetts Republican Scott P. Brown, it became clear that the Senate measure would have to be the operative one.

The measure offered less-generous subsidies to help individuals buy insurance than many Democrats wanted, and it contained a number of special provisions criticized as sweetheart deals designed to win senators' votes.

To allay members' concerns and remove many of the special deals, the Democratic leadership developed a companion reconciliation bill (HR 4872 — PL 111-152) that they said would improve the Senate bill. They hoped to vote on that bill first and spare their members a direct vote on the Senate measure, but they had to scrap the idea after the Senate parliamentarian objected. House Democrats acquiesced and took up the reconciliation bill second. It passed, 220-211.

HOUSE CLEARED HR 3590 (PL 111-148) on March 21, **219-212:** R 0-178; D 219-34. *(House vote 165, p. C-18; Senate vote 105, p. C-15; health care overhaul, p. 9-3)*

316 Funding for F-35 Alternative Engine

Defeat of an amendment to the fiscal 2011 defense authorization bill to strike funding for the F-35 Joint Strike Fighter alternative engine.

Members of Congress tend to protect their prerogative over defense funding, often benefiting manufacturing plants in their districts and keeping them in control of the largest slice of federal spending.

Nowhere was that protective impulse clearer than on the May 27 vote to defeat an amendment to the defense authorization bill that would have struck funding for General Electric's alternative engine for the F-35 Joint Strike Fighter, despite repeated veto threats from President Obama. Congress had funded the alternative engine for 14 years.

Obama and Defense Secretary Robert M. Gates argued that spending an additional $2.9 billion to complete development of the F136 engine program over the next six years was unnecessary. GE and its proponents disputed the $2.9 billion figure, saying they believed it could be about $1 billion less. But Gates, armed with internal Pentagon studies, argued that competition probably would not save enough to offset development costs. Given the significant budget shortfalls the Defense Department faced in a tough budget climate, Gates

argued that the money would be better spent elsewhere.

But proponents of a second engine to complement and compete with the base Pratt & Whitney-built F135 engine — armed with a Government Accountability Office study — said a second engine would save enough over the life of the program to pay for itself. They also argued, as did the internal Pentagon studies and the GAO, that there were non-monetary benefits to having a competitive engine, such as improved contractor responsiveness and engine reliability.

The House Armed Services Committee proposed authorizing $485 million for alternative-engine development and included language to prohibit the Pentagon from spending 25 percent of its F-35 budget until all alternative-engine funds had been obligated.

On the day the House turned back the amendment to drop the funding, the White House threatened a veto.

The House vote took on even greater significance when, on the same day, the Senate Armed Services Committee reported a defense authorization bill that heeded the president's veto threat and did not include the funding authorization.

In July, the House Defense Appropriations Subcommittee included $450 million for the alternative engine in deference to the House vote in May. Funding for the engine was left out of a Senate Appropriations Committee draft in September. With time running out on the session, Congress cleared a trimmed-down defense authorization that neither endorsed nor blocked spending for the alternative engine. A continuing resolution cleared in December funded the program at the fiscal 2010 level until early March. Congress had appropriated $465 million for the F136 engine in fiscal 2010, $35 million of which was for procurement.

HOUSE REJECTED the Pingree, D-Maine, amendment to HR 5136 on May 27, **193-231**: R 57-116; D 136-115. *(House vote 316, p. C-18; defense authorization, p. 6-3)*

317 Repeal of 'Don't Ask, Don't Tell' Policy

Adoption of an amendment to the 2011 defense authorization bill to repeal the law that banned openly gay people from serving in the military.

The House's May 27 vote in favor of repeal represented a landmark decision by lawmakers after years of debate within the military and the nation about the "don't ask, don't tell" policy. It was the first point at which lawmakers had a chance to register their position on an issue that was ultimately resolved when Congress cleared a bill to end the law.

Adoption of the amendment was the initial House attempt to repeal the 1993 law (PL 103-160) that barred openly gay people from serving in the military, and forbade their commanders to ask about sexual orientation. Many of those who voted in May against repealing the law did so because they were opposed to openly gay people serving in the military. But others voted "nay" for a different reason: They were undecided, or at least wanted to first hear the results of a Pentagon review of the matter that did not come until Dec. 1, a full six months after the House vote.

Indeed, until just days before the spring vote, the Pentagon's most senior civilian and uniformed leaders had argued that Congress should not pass legislation to delete or alter the Clinton-era law until the Pentagon completed its review. But on May 24, the White House, Pentagon and congressional advocates of the repeal agreed on the provision that later was incorporated into the House and Senate

defense authorization bills.

What enabled the compromise was language added to the amendment stipulating that the repeal would not occur before completion of the Pentagon review, nor before the White House and Defense Department certified that repeal would not harm the military.

With those caveats in place, Defense Secretary Robert M. Gates and Adm. Mike Mullen, chairman of the Joint Chiefs of Staff, said they were comfortable with Congress legislating on the matter.

But the service chiefs remained opposed to congressional action ahead of the review's completion, and their views were often cited by Republicans and conservative Democrats who voted against the repeal provision during the House vote. Indeed, several of the chiefs continued to oppose repeal into December, after the review was completed, but at that time the focus of their concerns became the possible fallout among troops in combat.

HOUSE ADOPTED the Murphy, D-Pa., amendment to HR 5136 on May 27, **234-194**: R 5-168; D 229-26. *(House vote 317, p. C-18; Senate vote 281, p. C-17; "don't ask, don't tell," p. 6-7)*

335 Guantánamo Base Closing

Adoption of a motion to bar the transfer or release of any military detainees held at Guantánamo Bay, Cuba, to the United States.

With a significant number of Democrats joining Republicans, the House sent a strong signal of opposition to President Obama's plans to close the detention facility at Guantánamo Bay.

While the vote was on a procedural issue — a motion to recommit the defense authorization bill to committee — the meaning was big: The House was trying to bar the Obama administration from funding the transfer or release of Guantánamo detainees into the United States. The language was included in the final agreement on the defense authorization bill.

Closing the facility had been one of the top national security priorities of the Obama administration, which argued that Guantánamo served as a recruitment tool for terrorist organizations. But Congress had grown leery of alternatives favored by the president and had stymied his Guantánamo agenda.

In 2009, Congress cleared language to forbid closing the Guantánamo prison before the administration provided Congress with a plan for doing so. But by and large that year, Democrats turned away the most restrictive GOP amendments on Guantánamo, such as an effort to bar the use of funds to build or modify a facility to hold the detainees in the United States.

Since then, a number of prominent terrorism cases helped swing some Democrats against Obama's Guantánamo plans, which included a mixture of U.S.-based trials, transfer to foreign countries and the placement of remaining detainees in a U.S. prison. The November 2009 Fort Hood, Texas, shooting; the attempted Dec. 25, 2009, airline bombing; and the failed May 2010 Times Square bombing raised new concerns about domestic terrorism threats and the wisdom of trying or holding terrorism suspects on U.S. soil. In the vote, 114 Democrats joined 168 Republicans to support the motion.

HOUSE AGREED to a motion to recommit HR 5136 on May 28, **282-131**: R 168-1; D 114-130. *(House vote 335, p. C-18; defense authorization, p. 6-3)*

391 Campaign Finance Disclosure

Passage of a bill to broaden campaign finance disclosure and reporting requirements.

After a 5-4 Supreme Court ruling in January in *Citizens United v. Federal Election Commission*, which held that corporations had the same free-speech rights as individuals and could spend corporate money to sway election campaigns, Democrats mobilized to develop a legislative response.

A few days after the ruling, President Obama made an unusually direct criticism of the decision during his State of the Union address — as several justices sat in the audience — saying it had been wrongly decided in favor of "powerful interests."

Congressional Democrats voiced the same populist critique in introducing this bill to tighten disclosure rules on campaign advertising by corporations, unions and other independent groups and to prohibit foreign-controlled corporations or corporations receiving government assistance from making expenditures in political campaigns.

Republicans strongly opposed the measure, which they said would unconstitutionally curb free-speech rights and was designed mostly to improve Democrats' prospects in the midterm elections.

In seeking a majority to back the bill, Democrats angered advocacy groups and liberal lawmakers by amending the bill to exempt the National Rifle Association from certain disclosure requirements. An endorsement from Obama and assurances from Senate Democratic leaders that they would bring up the measure despite an almost-certain filibuster helped soften liberal opposition and ensure passage.

The House vote, it turned out, was the high-water mark for the measure, which died in the Senate.

HOUSE PASSED HR 5175 on June 24, **219-206:** R 2-170; D 217-36. *(House vote 391, p. C-20; Senate vote 240, p. C-16; campaign finance, p. 11-35)*

413 Financial Regulatory Overhaul

Adoption of the conference report on financial regulatory overhaul.

Having used their majority to push through a major remake of the health care system in early 2010, Democrats forged ahead in their efforts on another major sector of the economy: financial services.

The House had passed a financial regulation bill at the end of 2009. After Senate passage of its bill in May 2010, a conference committee produced an agreement (H Rept 111-517) in the next two months. The key vote in the House was thus on adoption of the conference report in late June.

Even though the House had already passed the underlying bill, partisan tensions had worsened in the intervening six months, partly because of the nature of the debate and votes on health care. Meanwhile, the economy was showing very few signs of improving, and conservatives, fueled by the sensation of the tea party movement, were gaining steam in their arguments that less, not more, government intervention in the economy was the best approach. Republicans seized on that theme when the bill came to the floor.

The result was a mostly party-line vote on an issue — banking regulation — that had historically been developed in a more bipartisan way.

Conferees made some changes to the underlying bill, but the overall intent was the same: to create new regulatory mechanisms to deal with the risks posed by large financial companies, establish a new federal agency to oversee consumer financial products, and force most banks and other financial institutions to hold more capital to protect against future upheaval. The measure also provided a process for the orderly dissolution of failing financial institutions that posed a threat to the economy, brought the derivatives market under significant federal regulation for the first time, and gave company shareholders and regulators greater say on executive-pay packages.

The conference report did win 14 more supporters — 11 Democrats and three Republicans — than the December House-passed version.

HOUSE ADOPTED the conference report on HR 4173 (PL 111-203) on June 30, **237-192:** R 3-173; D 234-19. *(House vote 413, p. C-20; Senate vote 208, p. C-16; financial regulatory overhaul, p. 3-3)*

432 Funding for Afghanistan War

Rejection of an amendment to the fiscal 2010 supplemental spending bill to force withdrawal of U.S. troops from Afghanistan.

President Obama's request for $33.5 billion in supplemental funding to support his Afghanistan surge strategy split House Democrats into two camps. It became clear just how deeply divided the party was in the early summer, when 93 Democrats voted in favor of an amendment that instead would have used supplemental spending to pay for the withdrawal of U.S. troops.

That proposal was rejected, 100-321, but the vote demonstrated to administration officials that they needed significant House GOP support for the new strategy, which was set to place 30,000 additional U.S. forces in Afghanistan to blunt and roll back Taliban gains.

On July 27, the House voted, 308-114, to clear the spending measure and support the president's strategy, but only 148 of 250 Democrats supported the measure, while 160 of 172 Republicans backed the bill.

House Democrats were Obama's most avid supporters throughout the early part of his presidency, but the war-spending votes challenged party unity. The divide became most apparent when Missouri Democrat Ike Skelton, chairman of the Armed Services Committee, rose on the House floor to bitterly oppose the amendment.

In a statement issued the day of the debate, the White House warned of a veto if the amendment prevailed.

Californian Jerry Lewis, ranking Republican on the House Appropriations Committee, led the opposition to the amendment. He cited the veto threat and said, "Indeed, it is time for us to recognize that the war on terror is very real. The challenge in Afghanistan is supported by the president because he recognizes it's very real, and it's one of the bases of operation for their activities."

HOUSE REJECTED a motion to concur in the Senate amendments to HR 4899 with a Barbara Lee, D-Calif., amendment July 1, **100-321:** R 7-164; D 93-157. *(House vote 432, p. C-20; war supplemental, p. 2-15)*

474   Supplemental Appropriations

Clearing a bill to provide $58.8 billion in emergency spending to fund the nation's war efforts.

Senate appropriators won an interchamber pingpong match with this measure, insisting that the bill stick mostly to its intended purpose of ensuring that the wars in Iraq and Afghanistan were funded through the rest of the fiscal year. The House had amended the bill with an extra $22.8 billion in domestic-spending provisions, but the Senate refused to allow the measure to grow.

With the August recess approaching — and the chance to return home to campaign for the midterm elections — House Democratic leaders conceded defeat and scheduled another vote on the Senate's original work, this time under suspension of the rules, avoiding any further attempts to amend it.

The 308-114 vote showed that the appetite for attaching as many projects as possible onto a critical spending bill had diminished as the tea party cry for reducing the deficit grew louder. More than 100 Democrats — including Appropriations Chairman David R. Obey, D-Wis. — voted in protest against the leadership's handling of the measure. Overwhelming Republican support ended up making the difference in clearing the bill.

Obey's dogged persistence did pay off eventually, as another measure (PL 111-226) passed in August to provide $10 billion for schools and Medicaid assistance for states.

HOUSE CLEARED, through a motion to concur, HR 4899 (PL 111-212) on July 27, **308-114:** R 160-12; D 148-102. The bill was considered under suspension of the rules, thereby requiring a two-thirds majority of those present and voting (282 in this case) for passage. *(House vote 474, p. C-20; war supplemental, p. 2-15)*

513   Offshore Oil Drilling Regulations

Passage of a bill to revamp federal oversight of offshore drilling and lift the $75 million cap on liability for offshore oil spills.

Congressional hearings after the April 20 explosion of the Deepwater Horizon drilling rig in the Gulf of Mexico exposed serious weaknesses in the regulation of offshore drilling and shortcomings by the agency that was supposed to be policing operations. The disaster killed 11 workers and caused the worst oil spill in U.S. history.

Congress' main legislative response came in the House, which passed a bill designed to split the duties of the troubled Minerals Management Service among three agencies, establish new safety requirements for offshore oil and gas development and lift the $75 million cap on liability for a spill.

House leaders took the bill to the floor just before the August recess, as the magnitude of the spill was sinking in with an angry public and weeks before oil giant BP was able to cap the ruptured well. But while bipartisan sentiment for a tough legislative response initially ran high, by the eve of the vote, prospects for passage were in doubt.

Stubbornly high national unemployment was compounded in the Gulf region by the spill, which crippled both the energy and fishing industries. As many as 30 "oil patch" Democrats threatened to join Republicans in opposing the bill over concerns about the Obama administration's temporary ban on new deep-water drilling.

But enough Democrats were kept on board with an amendment by Democrats Charlie Melancon of Louisiana and Travis W. Childers of Mississippi to exempt drillers from the moratorium if they demonstrate compliance with new Interior Department safety requirements. The House also adopted an amendment to let companies pool their resources to meet tough new financial requirements under the bill for obtaining federal leases. Democrats dropped unrelated environmental provisions.

The concessions did not satisfy Republicans — who also complained that the bill was loaded with provisions unrelated to the spill — but it allowed Democrats to pass the bill with just 16 votes to spare. All but two Republicans voted against passage, but only 39 Democrats defected.

However, the Senate never took up the House bill or its own companion legislation (S 3663), so the offshore drilling overhaul did not become law.

HOUSE PASSED HR 3534 on July 30, **209-193:** R 2-154; D 207-39. *(House vote 513, p. C-22; oil spill, p. 12-6)*

518   Medicaid and Education Assistance

Clearing a bill aimed at preventing layoffs of teachers and other public employees and boosting Medicaid reimbursement to states.

The vote to clear a scaled-back bill (HR 1586) that provided $10 billion to create or retain education-related jobs and $16.1 billion to extend increased Medicaid aid to states represented a small victory for Democratic leaders, who for months had been unable to deliver on promises of more ambitious help.

After intense lobbying from governors, states, teachers and public employees unions, Democrats generally voted for the legislation despite concerns about some of the offsets, including an $11.9 billion cut from increased food stamps benefits starting in April 2014 and a $1.5 billion reduction in appropriated funds for an Energy Department renewable-energy program.

Republicans objected to another round of government spending and characterized the bill as a political payoff to unions.

House Appropriations Chairman David R. Obey, D-Wis., who championed the measure, criticized Senate Republicans for delays in moving it forward. The Senate had previously turned back the $10 billion in education funding, which Obey had attached to a $58.8 billion fiscal 2010 supplemental appropriations measure to fund the wars in Afghanistan and Iraq (PL 111-212).

HOUSE CLEARED, by agreeing to a motion to concur, HR 1586 (PL 111-226) on Aug. 10, **247-161:** R 2-158; D 245-3. *(House vote 518, p. C-22; Senate vote 228, p. C-16; education and Medicaid supplemental, p. 2-15)*

554   Chinese Currency Valuation

Passage of a bill designed to encourage China to raise the value of its currency by giving the Commerce Department power to impose duties on products deemed to be unfairly subsidized by Chinese currency policy.

Taken just before lawmakers left town for the final campaign stretch, this unexpectedly bipartisan House vote demonstrated a deep level of public and congressional unease with China's trade

practices, and to some degree with the inability of the White House to remedy the situation.

The vote came amid growing frustration with China's refusal to allow its currency, the yuan, to appreciate against the dollar — a tactic that Beijing had long used to help its exporters — in the face of complaints from the Obama administration. To some observers, the vote strengthened the White House's hand in currency negotiations with Beijing, reflecting the longstanding good-cop bad-cop dynamics of the issue, with Congress applying public pressure while the administration toed a more diplomatic line.

With the election approaching, rank-and-file Democrats made clear that they wanted an opportunity to vote on the legislation, and the Ways and Means Committee quickly revised an earlier version of the bill, addressing concerns that it would violate World Trade Organization rules. Some lawmakers viewed the vote as a signal to China to stop undervaluing the yuan; others used it to voice frustration with the administration's approach.

The bill split the business community. Many large corporations worried it would spark a trade war with China, while many small and midsize manufacturers backed it.

Despite opposition from GOP leaders, the bill won the support of 99 Republicans, a majority of the caucus, including Dave Camp of Michigan, the ranking member of Ways and Means. Organized labor strongly backed the bill, and only a handful of generally pro-business Democrats voted no.

Despite strong bipartisan support for currency legislation in the Senate, the issue cooled somewhat after the election. A packed lame-duck calendar thwarted efforts to schedule a vote on the issue.

HOUSE PASSED HR 2378 on Sept. 29, **348-79:** R 99-74; D 249-5. *(House vote 554, p. C-22; China currency, p. 7-6)*

558 Intelligence Authorization

Clearing the fiscal 2010 intelligence authorization bill.

This vote sent legislation to President Obama that became the first intelligence authorization law in six years. The measure required the executive branch to more broadly disclose information to Congress about the most sensitive intelligence activities. It also re-established the main legislative method by which the House and Senate Select Intelligence panels exerted authority over spy agencies.

Although there was some question of how effective the legislation would be in compelling administration disclosures about its intelligence operations, the new set of rules gave the congressional Intelligence committees a potential lever they did not have before. Under previous law, only the "Gang of Eight" — made up of party leaders in both chambers and on the two Intelligence committees — received briefings on findings in covert actions.

The new rules required that the entire membership of the Intelligence panels receive notification when a Gang of Eight briefing occurred, along with a general description of the subject. The Obama administration threatened to veto earlier proposals in both the House and Senate bills but reached a compromise on language with committee leaders. House Speaker Nancy Pelosi, D-Calif., pressed for and won additional concessions from the White House, although the final bill language did not go as far as she wanted.

Many in Congress, and many outside experts, pointed out that the lack of adequate information about the actions of spy agencies meant the Intelligence committees were unable to conduct proper oversight. Inadequate oversight had been blamed for allowing some of the George W. Bush administration's controversial intelligence operations to go forward. Also, without a legislative vehicle, the Intelligence committees had little ability to curtail spy agency activities with which they disagreed.

Although the Senate moved the bill to the House by voice vote, House Republicans were less enthusiastic than their Senate counterparts. The bill excluded several House GOP proposals included in earlier versions of the legislation, such as a provision to forbid officials from reading Miranda rights to terrorism suspects.

HOUSE CLEARED, through a motion to concur, HR 2701 on Sept. 29, **244-181:** R 1-172; D 243-9. *(House vote 558, p. C-22; intelligence authorization, p. 6-10)*

561 NASA Authorization

Clearing a reauthorization of NASA programs and changes to the federal focus on manned space missions.

The vote in the House was a test of President Obama's ability to win congressional backing for his proposal to make fundamental changes to the government's approach to manned spaceflight.

The president proposed ending the agency's manned spaceflight program, known as Constellation, which was begun during the George W. Bush administration to develop vehicles to send astronauts to the moon and Mars. Instead, Obama sought to emphasize development of commercial carriers for both astronauts and cargo, in a departure from the approach to space exploration that NASA had followed since the Mercury flights of the 1960s.

The House and Senate authorizing committees approved legislation that differed from Obama's proposal. The White House worked closely with the Senate, so that chamber's bill, which was passed by voice vote in early August, hewed more closely to Obama's proposal than did the House version. The Senate bill authorized significantly more funding to support the development of commercial space transportation systems, although it added one more shuttle flight than previously authorized in an attempt to mollify skeptics of the new approach.

With the two chambers unable to resolve their differences, Senate Democrats persuaded their House counterparts to vote on the Senate-passed bill so the space agency would have some direction from Congress as fiscal 2011 began.

On the day of the vote, Florida Democrat Bill Nelson, the lead senator in the effort, spent a lot of time on the House floor and in the corridors near the chamber lobbying his counterparts to vote to clear the Senate bill. Nelson had reason to worry: 64 Democrats joined 54 Republicans in voting against the bill, which House Democratic leaders brought to the floor under suspension of the rules, meaning that it required a two-thirds majority of those voting to pass.

HOUSE CLEARED S 3729 (PL 111-267) on Sept. 29, **304-118:** R 119-54; D 185-64. The bill was considered under suspension of the rules, thereby requiring a two-thirds majority of those present and voting (282 in this case) for passage. *(House vote 561, p. C-24; NASA authorization, p. 13-3)*

625 Immigration Policy

Passage of a bill to allow legal status for some undocumented children of illegal immigrants.

Although the legislation was stripped down from a more ambitious proposal to overhaul federal immigration policy, so as to strengthen its prospects in the Senate, passage made it the first significant immigration-related bill to advance in the House in several years.

The measure, known as the DREAM Act, would have applied to adults younger than 30 who immigrated illegally to the United States before turning 16 and who had been in the country for at least five years. It would have granted conditional legal status — and after 10 years, permanent residency — to qualifying young adults who completed at least two years of college or military service. Under the bill, those permanent residents would have been eligible to apply for naturalization after three years.

The bill would have imposed application fees and required individuals applying for permanent status to pay any outstanding federal tax liability. It also would have required applicants to undergo background and medical checks and to submit biometric information.

The nearly party-line vote reflected the deep partisan divisions over immigration policy in general and the bill specifically.

Even though Democrats won the vote, in the end it was for naught, as the Senate rejected cloture on the bill in the last few days of the 111th Congress.

HOUSE PASSED, through a motion to concur with an amendment, HR 5281 on Dec. 8, **216-198:** R 8-160; D 208-38. *(House vote 625, p. C-24; Senate vote 278, p. C-17)*

647 Tax-Cut Extensions

Clearing legislation extending income tax cuts for two years and setting a new rate and threshold for estate taxes.

The evolution of the tax-cut legislation and the subsequent votes on it were a measure of the degree to which lawmakers had come to accept the post-election political dynamics. Many did, but some, particularly House liberals, did not.

The deal came about after the White House, recognizing Republican ascendancy, negotiated directly with Senate Republicans. Liberal Democrats in both chambers were left out of the talks, making them as angry about the process as they were about the substance.

In the resulting deal, Democrats were asked to give up their hopes for an end to the tax cuts for the wealthiest Americans and to swallow a reinstatement of the estate tax at GOP-preferred rates of 35 percent on estates of more than $5 million.

Republicans, on the other hand, were being asked to agree with their leaders on several concessions to the White House, including a one-year payroll tax cut and a 13-month extension of federal unemployment benefits. Neither of those provisions was offset, as many Republicans had demanded.

For members in the liberal and conservative wings of their respective parties, the vote was a reflection of their willingness to move away from their ideological base and come to the center.

Some did not go quietly. Liberals in the House erupted in anger over the deal, and Democrats even approved a caucus resolution Dec. 9 disapproving of it, threatening to scuttle the package when it eventually came to the floor for a final vote.

They focused their anger on the estate tax provisions and the extension of lower income tax rates for wealthy taxpayers. Democrats wanted a higher rate — 45 percent — that would cover estates worth more than $3.5 million for individuals and $7 million for couples.

But an overwhelming vote in favor of the agreement in the Senate — and the clock ticking down to the end of the year — left liberals with little room to maneuver.

The Senate passed the package overwhelmingly Dec. 15. The House cleared the measure Dec. 17, just after midnight, ending a frenzied month of post-election bargaining and averting a substantial rise in tax rates that would have taken effect Jan. 1.

The final $857 billion package remained largely unchanged from the initial compromise.

HOUSE CLEARED, through a motion to concur, HR 4853 (PL 111-312) on Dec. 17, **277-148:** R 138-36; D 139-112. *(House vote 647, p. C-24; Senate vote 272, p. C-17; income tax cut extensions, p. 14-3)* ∎

IN THE SENATE | By Vote Number

5. **H J Res 45. Debt Limit Increase/Fiscal Task Force.** Conrad, D-N.D., amendment to the Baucus, D-Mont., substitute amendment. The Conrad amendment would establish a bipartisan fiscal task force with the authority to propose debt and deficit reduction policies. The task force would transmit proposals in legislative language. The proposals would be considered under expedited floor procedure, could not be amended and would require a three-fifths majority vote in both chambers. Congress would have to consider any proposal supported by 14 of the panel's 18 members. Rejected 53-46: D 36-22; R 16-23; I 1-1. (By unanimous consent, the Senate agreed to raise the majority requirement for adoption of the Conrad amendment to 60 votes.) A "yea" was a vote in support of the president's position. Jan. 26, 2010. *(Story, p. C-4)*

16. **Bernanke Nomination/Confirmation.** Confirmation of President Obama's nomination of Ben S. Bernanke of New Jersey to be chairman of the Board of Governors of the Federal Reserve System. Confirmed 70-30: D 47-11; R 22-18; I 1-1. A "yea" was a vote in support of the president's position. Jan. 28, 2010. *(Story, p. C-4)*

105. **HR 4872. Health Care Reconciliation/Passage.** Passage of the bill that would make changes to the 2010 health care overhaul law, revise student loan programs and include revenue-raising provisions. It would increase federal subsidies to help low- and moderate-income families purchase coverage through new health insurance exchanges, phase out the coverage gap for Medicare prescription drug enrollees and adjust the federal matching funds for Medicaid. It would delay a tax on high-cost health plans and reduce the reach of the tax, and it would modify a Medicare payroll tax for high-income taxpayers. The federal government would cover 100 percent of the cost of coverage for newly eligible Medicaid recipients in all states from 2014 to 2016. The bill also would make the federal government the sole originator of federal student loans and direct the savings generated to education programs, including Pell grants. Passed 56-43: D 54-3; R 0-40; I 2-0. A "yea" was a vote in support of the president's position. March 25, 2010. *(Story, p. C-5)*

181. **HR 4213. Tax Extensions/Spending Caps.** Sessions, R-Ala., motion to waive the Budget Act and budget resolutions with respect to the Baucus, D-Mont., point of order against the Sessions amendment to the Baucus substitute amendment. The Sessions amendment would establish discretionary spending limits for fiscal years 2011, 2012 and 2013 equal to the levels for defense and non-defense spending in the fiscal 2010 budget resolution. It would also limit spending on overseas deployments and related operations. Points of order against emergency spending designations could be waived by a three-fifths majority vote in the Senate; two-thirds would be required to waive other restrictions. Motion rejected 57-41: D 16-40; R 40-0; I 1-1. A three-fifths majority vote (60) of the total Senate is required to waive the Budget Act. (Subsequently, the chair upheld the point of order, and the amendment fell.) June 9, 2010. *(Story, p. C-5)*

	5	16	105	181
ALABAMA				
Shelby	N	N	N	Y
Sessions	N	N	N	Y
ALASKA				
Murkowski	?	Y	N	Y
Begich	Y	N	Y	Y
ARIZONA				
McCain	N	N	N	Y
Kyl	N	Y	N	Y
ARKANSAS				
Lincoln	Y	Y	N	Y
Pryor	Y	Y	N	N
CALIFORNIA				
Feinstein	Y	Y	Y	N
Boxer	Y	N	Y	N
COLORADO				
Udall	Y	Y	Y	Y
Bennet	Y	Y	Y	Y
CONNECTICUT				
Dodd	N	Y	Y	N
Lieberman	Y	Y	Y	Y
DELAWARE				
Carper	Y	Y	Y	Y
Kaufman	Y	N	Y	N
FLORIDA				
Nelson	Y	Y	Y	N
LeMieux	Y	N	N	Y
GEORGIA				
Chambliss	Y	Y	N	Y
Isakson	Y	Y	?	Y
HAWAII				
Inouye	N	Y	Y	N
Akaka	N	Y	Y	N
IDAHO				
Crapo	N	N	N	Y
Risch	N	N	N	Y
ILLINOIS				
Durbin	Y	Y	Y	N
Burris	N	Y	Y	N
INDIANA				
Lugar	Y	Y	N	Y
Bayh	Y	Y	Y	Y
IOWA				
Grassley	N	N	N	Y
Harkin	N	N	Y	N
KANSAS				
Brownback	N	N	N	Y
Roberts	N	N	N	?
KENTUCKY				
McConnell	N	Y	N	Y
Bunning	N	N	N	Y
LOUISIANA				
Landrieu	Y	Y	Y	N
Vitter	Y	N	N	Y
MAINE				
Snowe	N	Y	N	Y
Collins	Y	Y	N	Y
MARYLAND				
Mikulski	N	Y	Y	N
Cardin	N	Y	Y	N
MASSACHUSETTS				
Kerry	Y	Y	Y	N
Kirk*	N	Y		
Brown*			N	Y
MICHIGAN				
Levin	Y	Y	Y	N
Stabenow	N	Y	Y	N
MINNESOTA				
Klobuchar	Y	Y	Y	Y
Franken	Y	N	Y	N
MISSISSIPPI				
Cochran	N	Y	N	Y
Wicker	Y	N	N	Y
MISSOURI				
Bond	Y	Y	N	Y
McCaskill	Y	Y	Y	Y

	5	16	105	181
MONTANA				
Baucus	N	Y	Y	N
Tester	Y	Y	Y	N
NEBRASKA				
Nelson	Y	Y	N	Y
Johanns	Y	Y	N	Y
NEVADA				
Reid	Y	Y	Y	N
Ensign	N	N	N	Y
NEW HAMPSHIRE				
Gregg	Y	Y	N	Y
Shaheen	Y	Y	Y	Y
NEW JERSEY				
Lautenberg	N	Y	Y	N
Menendez	Y	Y	Y	N
NEW MEXICO				
Bingaman	Y	Y	Y	N
Udall	N	Y	Y	N
NEW YORK				
Schumer	Y	Y	Y	N
Gillibrand	Y	Y	Y	N
NORTH CAROLINA				
Burr	N	Y	N	Y
Hagan	Y	Y	Y	Y
NORTH DAKOTA				
Conrad	Y	Y	Y	N
Dorgan	Y	N	Y	N
OHIO				
Voinovich	Y	Y	N	Y
Brown	N	Y	Y	N
OKLAHOMA				
Inhofe	N	N	N	Y
Coburn	N	Y	N	Y
OREGON				
Wyden	Y	Y	Y	N
Merkley	N	N	Y	N
PENNSYLVANIA				
Specter	N	N	Y	N
Casey	N	Y	Y	Y
RHODE ISLAND				
Reed	N	Y	Y	N
Whitehouse	N	N	Y	N
SOUTH CAROLINA				
Graham	Y	Y	N	Y
DeMint	N	N	N	Y
SOUTH DAKOTA				
Johnson	Y	Y	Y	N
Thune	N	N	N	Y
TENNESSEE				
Alexander	Y	Y	N	Y
Corker	Y	Y	N	Y
TEXAS				
Hutchison	N	N	N	Y
Cornyn	Y	N	N	Y
UTAH				
Hatch	N	Y	N	Y
Bennett	N	Y	N	Y
VERMONT				
Leahy	Y	Y	Y	N
Sanders	N	N	Y	N
VIRGINIA				
Webb	Y	Y	Y	Y
Warner	Y	Y	Y	Y
WASHINGTON				
Murray	N	Y	Y	N
Cantwell	N	N	Y	N
WEST VIRGINIA				
Byrd	N	Y	Y	?
Rockefeller	N	Y	Y	N
WISCONSIN				
Kohl	Y	Y	Y	N
Feingold	Y	N	Y	N
WYOMING				
Enzi	Y	Y	N	Y
Barrasso	N	Y	N	Y

KEY	**Republicans**	Democrats	*Independents*
Y Voted for (yea)	X Paired against	C Voted "present" to avoid possible conflict of interest
# Paired for	– Announced against	
+ Announced for	P Voted "present"	? Did not vote or otherwise make a position known
N Voted against (nay)		

* Sen. Scott P. Brown, R-Mass., was sworn in Feb. 4 to replace Democrat Paul G. Kirk Jr., who was appointed Sept. 24, 2009, to temporarily fill the vacancy created by Democrat Edward M. Kennedy, who died Aug. 25, 2009. The first vote for which Brown was eligible was vote 21; the last vote for which Kirk was eligible was vote 20.

IN THE SENATE | By Vote Number

184. S J Res 26. Greenhouse Gas Regulation/Motion to Proceed.
Murkowski, R-Alaska, motion to proceed to consideration of a joint resolution that would provide for congressional disapproval of an EPA endangerment finding that greenhouse gases qualify as dangerous pollutants under the Clean Air Act. Motion rejected 47-53: D 6-51; R 41-0; I 0-2. A "nay" was a vote in support of the president's position. June 10, 2010. (Story, p. C-5)

208. HR 4173. Financial Regulatory Overhaul/Conference Report.
Adoption of the conference report on the bill that would overhaul the regulation of the financial services industry. The measure would create new regulatory mechanisms to assess risks posed by very large financial institutions and facilitate the orderly dissolution of failing businesses that pose a threat to the economy. It would create a new federal agency to oversee consumer financial products, bring the derivatives market under significant federal regulation for the first time, and give company shareholders and regulators greater say on executive-pay packages. The costs would be offset by terminating the Troubled Asset Relief Program and increasing deposit insurance premiums paid by some banks. Adopted (thus cleared for the president) 60-39: D 55-1; R 3-38; I 2-0. A "yea" was a vote in support of the president's position. July 15, 2010. (Story, p. C-6)

228. HR 1586. Medicaid and Education Assistance/Motion to Concur.
Reid, D-Nev., motion to concur in the House amendment to the Senate amendment with the further Murray, D-Wash., substitute amendment that would provide $16.1 billion to extend increased Medicaid assistance to states and $10 billion in funding for states to create or retain teachers' jobs. The costs would be offset by changing foreign tax provisions, ending increased food stamp benefits beginning in April 2014 and rescinding previously enacted spending. Motion agreed to 61-39: D 57-0; R 2-39; I 2-0. A "yea" was a vote in support of the president's position. Aug. 5, 2010. (Story, p. C-6)

229. Kagan Nomination/Confirmation.
Confirmation of President Obama's nomination of Elena Kagan of Massachusetts to be an associate justice of the U.S. Supreme Court. Confirmed 63-37: D 56-1; R 5-36; I 2-0. A "yea" was a vote in support of the president's position. Aug. 5, 2010. (Story, p. C-7)

240. S 3628. Campaign Finance Disclosure/Cloture.
Motion to invoke cloture (thus limiting debate) on the motion to proceed to the bill that would require corporations and unions to disclose in their campaign advertising the chief donors who paid for the ad. Motion rejected 59-39: D 57-0; R 0-39; I 2-0. Three-fifths of the total Senate (60) is required to invoke cloture. (Previously, a Reid, D-Nev., motion to reconsider was adopted by unanimous consent.) A "yea" was a vote in support of the president's position. Sept. 23, 2010. (Story, p. C-7)

	184	208	228	229	240
ALABAMA					
Shelby	Y	N	N	N	N
Sessions	Y	N	N	N	N
ALASKA					
Murkowski	Y	N	N	N	?
Begich	N	Y	Y	Y	Y
ARIZONA					
McCain	Y	N	N	N	N
Kyl	Y	N	N	N	N
ARKANSAS					
Lincoln	Y	Y	Y	Y	Y
Pryor	Y	Y	Y	Y	Y
CALIFORNIA					
Feinstein	N	Y	Y	Y	Y
Boxer	N	Y	Y	Y	Y
COLORADO					
Udall	N	Y	Y	Y	Y
Bennet	N	Y	Y	Y	Y
CONNECTICUT					
Dodd	N	Y	Y	Y	Y
Lieberman	N	Y	Y	Y	Y
DELAWARE					
Carper	N	Y	Y	Y	Y
Kaufman	N	Y	Y	Y	Y
FLORIDA					
Nelson	N	Y	Y	Y	Y
LeMieux	Y	N	N	N	N
GEORGIA					
Chambliss	Y	N	N	N	N
Isakson	Y	N	N	N	N
HAWAII					
Inouye	N	Y	Y	Y	Y
Akaka	N	Y	Y	Y	Y
IDAHO					
Crapo	Y	N	N	N	N
Risch	Y	N	N	N	N
ILLINOIS					
Durbin	N	Y	Y	Y	Y
Burris	N	Y	Y	Y	Y
INDIANA					
Lugar	Y	N	N	Y	N
Bayh	Y	Y	Y	Y	Y
IOWA					
Grassley	Y	N	N	N	N
Harkin	N	Y	Y	Y	Y
KANSAS					
Brownback	Y	N	N	N	N
Roberts	Y	N	N	N	N
KENTUCKY					
McConnell	Y	N	N	N	N
Bunning	Y	N	N	N	N
LOUISIANA					
Landrieu	Y	Y	Y	Y	Y
Vitter	Y	N	N	N	N
MAINE					
Snowe	Y	Y	Y	N	N
Collins	Y	Y	Y	Y	N
MARYLAND					
Mikulski	N	Y	Y	Y	Y
Cardin	N	Y	Y	Y	Y
MASSACHUSETTS					
Kerry	N	Y	Y	Y	Y
Brown	Y	N	N	N	N
MICHIGAN					
Levin	N	Y	Y	Y	Y
Stabenow	N	Y	Y	Y	Y
MINNESOTA					
Klobuchar	N	Y	Y	Y	Y
Franken	N	Y	Y	Y	Y
MISSISSIPPI					
Cochran	Y	N	N	N	N
Wicker	Y	N	N	N	N
MISSOURI					
Bond	Y	N	N	N	N
McCaskill	N	Y	Y	Y	Y

	184	208	228	229	240
MONTANA					
Baucus	N	Y	Y	Y	Y
Tester	N	Y	Y	Y	Y
NEBRASKA					
Nelson	Y	Y	Y	N	Y
Johanns	Y	N	N	N	N
NEVADA					
Reid	N	Y	Y	Y	Y
Ensign	Y	N	N	N	N
NEW HAMPSHIRE					
Gregg	Y	N	N	Y	N
Shaheen	N	Y	Y	Y	Y
NEW JERSEY					
Lautenberg	N	Y	Y	Y	Y
Menendez	N	Y	Y	Y	Y
NEW MEXICO					
Bingaman	N	Y	Y	Y	Y
Udall	N	Y	Y	Y	Y
NEW YORK					
Schumer	N	Y	Y	Y	Y
Gillibrand	N	Y	Y	Y	Y
NORTH CAROLINA					
Burr	Y	N	N	N	N
Hagan	N	Y	Y	Y	Y
NORTH DAKOTA					
Conrad	N	Y	Y	Y	Y
Dorgan	N	Y	Y	Y	Y
OHIO					
Voinovich	Y	N	N	N	N
Brown	N	Y	Y	Y	Y
OKLAHOMA					
Inhofe	Y	N	N	N	N
Coburn	Y	N	N	N	N
OREGON					
Wyden	N	Y	Y	Y	Y
Merkley	N	Y	Y	Y	Y
PENNSYLVANIA					
Specter	N	Y	Y	Y	Y
Casey	N	Y	Y	Y	Y
RHODE ISLAND					
Reed	N	Y	Y	Y	Y
Whitehouse	N	Y	Y	Y	Y
SOUTH CAROLINA					
Graham	Y	N	N	Y	N
DeMint	Y	N	N	N	N
SOUTH DAKOTA					
Johnson	N	Y	Y	Y	Y
Thune	Y	N	N	N	N
TENNESSEE					
Alexander	Y	N	N	N	N
Corker	Y	N	N	N	N
TEXAS					
Hutchison	Y	N	N	N	?
Cornyn	Y	N	N	N	N
UTAH					
Hatch	Y	N	N	N	N
Bennett	Y	N	N	N	N
VERMONT					
Leahy	N	Y	Y	Y	Y
Sanders	N	Y	Y	Y	Y
VIRGINIA					
Webb	N	Y	Y	Y	Y
Warner	N	Y	Y	Y	Y
WASHINGTON					
Murray	N	Y	Y	Y	Y
Cantwell	N	Y	Y	Y	Y
WEST VIRGINIA					
Byrd*	N				
Rockefeller	Y	Y	Y	Y	Y
Goodwin*			Y	Y	Y
WISCONSIN					
Kohl	N	Y	Y	Y	Y
Feingold	N	N	Y	Y	Y
WYOMING					
Enzi	Y	N	N	N	N
Barrasso	Y	N	N	N	N

KEY Republicans Democrats *Independents*

Y Voted for (yea)	X Paired against	C Voted "present" to avoid possible conflict of interest
# Paired for	− Announced against	
+ Announced for	P Voted "present"	? Did not vote or otherwise make a position known
N Voted against (nay)		

*Sen. Carte P. Goodwin, D-W.Va., was appointed July 16 to temporarily fill the vacancy created by Democrat Robert C. Byrd, who died June 28. The last vote for which Byrd was eligible was vote 200; the first vote for which Goodwin was eligible was vote 209.

IN THE SENATE | By Vote Number

272. **HR 4853. Tax Rates Extensions/Cloture.** Motion to invoke cloture (thus limiting debate) on the Reid, D-Nev., motion to concur in the House amendment to the Senate amendment with a further Reid and McConnell, R-Ky., substitute amendment that would extend the 2001 and 2003 tax cuts for all taxpayers for two years, as well as reinstitute the estate tax at a 35 percent rate on the value of estates in excess of $5 million. It also would continue expanded unemployment insurance benefits for 13 months. Motion agreed to 83-15: D 45-9; R 37-5; I 1-1. Three-fifths of the total Senate (60) is required to invoke cloture. Dec. 13, 2010. (*Story, p. C-7*)

278. **HR 5281. Immigration Policy Revisions/Cloture.** Motion to invoke cloture (thus limiting debate) on the Reid, D-Nev., motion to concur in the House amendment to the third Senate amendment to the bill. The House amendment would allow the Homeland Security Department to grant conditional non-immigrant status to the undocumented children of illegal immigrants if they meet certain requirements, including having been in the United States continuously for more than five years, having been younger than 16 when they entered the country, and having been admitted to a U.S. college or university or enlisted in the military. The individual would have to pay a $525 application surcharge and a subsequent fee and could be eligible to apply for legal permanent status after 10 years. Motion rejected 55-41: D 50-5; R 3-36; I 2-0. Three-fifths of the total Senate (60) is required to invoke cloture. A "yea" was a vote in support of the president's position. Dec. 18, 2010. (*Story, p. C-8*)

281. **HR 2965. 'Don't Ask, Don't Tell' Policy Repeal/Motion to Concur.** Reid, D-Nev., motion to concur in the Senate amendment to the bill with a House amendment that would allow for the repeal of the "don't ask, don't tell" policy, which prohibits military service by openly gay men and women, after certain requirements are met, including the submission of a written certification, signed by the president, the secretary of Defense and the chairman of the Joint Chiefs of Staff, that the repeal is consistent with military readiness and effectiveness and that they have considered the recommendations of the Comprehensive Review Working Group and prepared the necessary policies and regulations to implement the repeal. Motion agreed to, thus clearing the bill for the president, 65-31: D 55-0; R 8-31; I 2-0. A "yea" was a vote in support of the president's position. Dec. 18, 2010. (*Story, p. C-8*)

298. **Treaty Doc 111-5. New START Agreement/Adoption.** Adoption of the resolution of ratification for the New Strategic Arms Reduction Treaty (START) with Russia. The treaty would restrict each country to a maximum of 1,550 deployed nuclear warheads, a cut of about 30 percent. The resolution of ratification would state that the April 2010 unilateral statement by Russia on missile defense does not impose any legal obligation on the United States. Adopted (thus consenting to ratification) 71-26: D 56-0; R 13-26; I 2-0. A two-thirds majority of those present and voting (65 in this case) is required for adoption of resolutions of ratification. A "yea" was a vote in support of the president's position. Dec. 22, 2010. (*Story, p. C-8*)

	272	278	281	298			272	278	281	298
ALABAMA						**MONTANA**				
Shelby	Y	N	N	N		Baucus	Y	N	Y	Y
Sessions	N	N	N	N		Tester	Y	N	Y	Y
ALASKA						**NEBRASKA**				
Murkowski	Y	Y	Y	Y		Nelson	Y	N	Y	Y
Begich	Y	Y	Y	Y		Johanns	Y	N	N	Y
ARIZONA						**NEVADA**				
McCain	Y	N	N	N		Reid	Y	Y	Y	Y
Kyl	Y	N	N	N		Ensign	N	N	Y	N
ARKANSAS						**NEW HAMPSHIRE**				
Lincoln	Y	Y	Y	Y		Gregg	Y	?	?	Y
Pryor	Y	N	Y	Y		Shaheen	Y	Y	Y	Y
CALIFORNIA						**NEW JERSEY**				
Feinstein	Y	Y	Y	Y		Lautenberg	N	Y	Y	Y
Boxer	Y	Y	Y	Y		Menendez	Y	Y	Y	Y
COLORADO						**NEW MEXICO**				
Udall	N	Y	Y	Y		Bingaman	N	Y	Y	Y
Bennet	Y	Y	Y	Y		Udall	Y	Y	Y	Y
CONNECTICUT						**NEW YORK**				
Dodd	Y	Y	Y	Y		Schumer	Y	Y	Y	Y
Lieberman	Y	Y	Y	Y		Gillibrand	N	Y	Y	Y
DELAWARE						**NORTH CAROLINA**				
Carper	Y	Y	Y	Y		Burr	Y	N	Y	N
Coons¹	Y	Y	Y	Y		Hagan	N	N	Y	Y
FLORIDA						**NORTH DAKOTA**				
Nelson	Y	Y	Y	Y		Conrad	Y	Y	Y	Y
LeMieux	Y	N	N	N		Dorgan	Y	Y	Y	Y
GEORGIA						**OHIO**				
Chambliss	Y	N	N	N		Voinovich	N	N	Y	Y
Isakson	Y	N	N	Y		Brown	N	Y	Y	Y
HAWAII						**OKLAHOMA**				
Inouye	Y	Y	Y	Y		Inhofe	Y	N	N	N
Akaka	Y	Y	Y	Y		Coburn	N	N	N	N
IDAHO						**OREGON**				
Crapo	Y	N	N	N		Wyden	?	Y	Y	Y
Risch	Y	N	N	N		Merkley	?	Y	Y	Y
ILLINOIS						**PENNSYLVANIA**				
Durbin	Y	Y	Y	Y		Specter	Y	Y	Y	Y
Kirk	Y	N	Y	N		Casey	Y	Y	Y	Y
INDIANA						**RHODE ISLAND**				
Lugar	Y	Y	N	Y		Reed	Y	Y	Y	Y
Bayh	Y	Y	Y	Y		Whitehouse	Y	Y	Y	Y
IOWA						**SOUTH CAROLINA**				
Grassley	Y	N	N	N		Graham	Y	N	N	N
Harkin	Y	Y	Y	Y		DeMint	N	N	N	N
KANSAS						**SOUTH DAKOTA**				
Brownback	Y	N	N	?		Johnson	Y	Y	Y	Y
Roberts	Y	N	N	N		Thune	Y	N	N	N
KENTUCKY						**TENNESSEE**				
McConnell	Y	N	N	N		Alexander	Y	N	N	Y
Bunning	Y	–	–	?		Corker	Y	N	N	Y
LOUISIANA						**TEXAS**				
Landrieu	Y	Y	Y	Y		Hutchison	Y	N	N	N
Vitter	Y	N	N	N		Cornyn	Y	N	N	N
MAINE						**UTAH**				
Snowe	Y	N	Y	Y		Hatch	Y	–	–	N
Collins	Y	N	Y	Y		Bennett	Y	N	N	Y
MARYLAND						**VERMONT**				
Mikulski	Y	Y	Y	Y		Leahy	N	Y	Y	Y
Cardin	Y	Y	Y	Y		*Sanders*	N	Y	Y	Y
MASSACHUSETTS						**VIRGINIA**				
Kerry	Y	Y	Y	Y		Webb	Y	Y	Y	Y
Brown	Y	N	Y	Y		Warner	Y	Y	Y	Y
MICHIGAN						**WASHINGTON**				
Levin	N	Y	Y	Y		Murray	Y	Y	Y	Y
Stabenow	Y	Y	Y	Y		Cantwell	Y	Y	Y	Y
MINNESOTA						**WEST VIRGINIA**				
Klobuchar	Y	Y	Y	Y		Rockefeller	Y	Y	Y	Y
Franken	Y	Y	Y	Y		Manchin²	Y	–	?	Y
MISSISSIPPI						**WISCONSIN**				
Cochran	Y	N	N	Y		Kohl	Y	Y	Y	Y
Wicker	Y	N	N	N		Feingold	N	Y	Y	Y
MISSOURI						**WYOMING**				
Bond	Y	N	N	?		Enzi	Y	N	N	N
McCaskill	Y	Y	Y	Y		Barrasso	Y	N	N	N

KEY	**Republicans**	Democrats	*Independents*			
Y	Voted for (yea)		**X** Paired against		**C**	Voted "present" to avoid possible conflict of interest
#	Paired for		**–** Announced against			
+	Announced for		**P** Voted "present"		**?**	Did not vote or otherwise make a position known
N	Voted against (nay)					

¹ Sen. Chris Coons, D-Del., was sworn in Nov. 15 to replace fellow Democrat Ted Kaufman, appointed Jan. 15, 2009, to temporarily fill the vacancy created by Democrat Joseph R. Biden Jr., who resigned to become vice president. The first vote for which Coons was eligible was vote 249; the last vote for which Kaufman was eligible was vote 248.

² Sen. Joe Manchin III, D-W.Va., was sworn in Nov. 15 to replace fellow Democrat Carte P. Goodwin, who was appointed July 16 to temporarily fill the vacancy created by Democrat Robert C. Byrd, who died June 28. The first vote for which Manchin was eligible was vote 249. Goodwin was eligible for votes 209 through 248. The last vote for which Byrd was eligible was vote 200.

IN THE HOUSE | By Vote Number

165. **HR 3590. Health Care Overhaul/Motion to Concur.** Spratt, D-S.C., motion to concur in the Senate amendment to the bill that would overhaul the nation's health insurance system and would require most individuals to buy health insurance by 2014. It would create a system of private insurance plans supervised by the Office of Personnel Management and create state-run marketplaces for purchasing health insurance. Those who do not obtain coverage would be subject to an excise tax, with exceptions. Employers with more than 50 workers would have to provide coverage or pay a fine if any employee gets a subsidized plan on the exchange. Certain small businesses would get tax credits for providing coverage, and those with low incomes, excluding illegal immigrants, could get subsidies. It would bar the use of federal funds to pay for abortions in the new programs, except in the cases of rape or incest or if the woman's life is in danger. Insurance companies could not deny coverage based on pre-existing medical conditions beginning in 2014 and could not drop coverage of people who become ill. It would expand eligibility for Medicaid and would shrink Medicare's so-called doughnut hole. Motion agreed to, thus clearing the bill for the president, 219-212: D 219-34; R 0-178. A "yea" was a vote in support of the president's position. March 21, 2010. *(Story, p. C-9)*

316. **HR 5136. Fiscal 2011 Defense Authorization/F-35 Alternative Engine.** Pingree, D-Maine, amendment that would strike funds authorized for the F-35 alternative-engine program. Rejected in Committee of the Whole 193-231: D 136-115; R 57-116. A "yea" was a vote in support of the president's position. May 27, 2010. *(Story, p. C-9)*

317. **HR 5136. Fiscal 2011 Defense Authorization/'Don't Ask, Don't Tell' Policy Repeal.** Murphy, D-Pa., amendment that would repeal the "don't ask, don't tell" policy on military service by openly gay men and women after receipt of Pentagon recommendations on how to implement a repeal. It would take effect 60 days after certification by the Defense secretary, chairman of the Joint Chiefs and the president that the repeal is consistent with the standards of military readiness, military effectiveness, unit cohesion and recruiting. Adopted in Committee of the Whole 234-194: D 229-26; R 5-168. A "yea" was a vote in support of the president's position. May 27, 2010. *(Story, p. C-10)*

335. **HR 5136. Fiscal 2011 Defense Authorization/Recommit.** Forbes, R-Va., motion to recommit the bill to the Armed Services Committee with instructions that it be reported back immediately with an amendment that would prohibit the use of funds authorized in the bill to transfer or release individuals detained at the U.S. facility at Guantánamo Bay, Cuba, into the United States or its territories. Motion agreed to 282-131: D 114-130; R 168-1. A "nay" was a vote in support of the president's position. May 28, 2010. *(Story, p. C-10)*

	165	316	317	335
ALABAMA				
1 Bonner	N	N	N	Y
2 Bright	N	N	N	Y
3 Rogers	N	N	N	Y
4 Aderholt	N	N	N	Y
5 Griffith	N	Y	N	Y
6 Bachus	N	N	N	Y
7 Davis	N	?	?	?
ALASKA				
AL Young	N	N	N	Y
ARIZONA				
1 Kirkpatrick	Y	Y	Y	Y
2 Franks	N	N	N	Y
3 Shadegg	N	Y	N	Y
4 Pastor	Y	Y	Y	N
5 Mitchell	Y	Y	Y	Y
6 Flake	N	Y	N	Y
7 Grijalva	Y	Y	Y	N
8 Giffords	Y	Y	Y	Y
ARKANSAS				
1 Berry	N	Y	N	N
2 Snyder	Y	N	Y	N
3 Boozman	N	N	N	Y
4 Ross	N	Y	N	Y
CALIFORNIA				
1 Thompson	Y	Y	Y	N
2 Herger	N	Y	N	Y
3 Lungren	N	N	N	Y
4 McClintock	N	Y	N	Y
5 Matsui	Y	Y	Y	N
6 Woolsey	Y	P	Y	N
7 Miller, George	Y	Y	Y	N
8 Pelosi[1]	Y		Y	
9 Lee	Y	Y	Y	N
10 Garamendi	Y	N	Y	Y
11 McNerney	Y	N	Y	N
12 Speier	Y	Y	Y	N
13 Stark	Y	Y	Y	N
14 Eshoo	Y	Y	Y	N
15 Honda	Y	Y	Y	N
16 Lofgren	Y	Y	Y	N
17 Farr	Y	Y	Y	N
18 Cardoza	Y	Y	Y	Y
19 Radanovich	N	N	N	Y
20 Costa	Y	Y	Y	N
21 Nunes	N	N	N	Y
22 McCarthy	N	N	N	Y
23 Capps	Y	Y	Y	N
24 Gallegly	N	N	N	Y
25 McKeon	N	N	N	Y
26 Dreier	N	N	N	Y
27 Sherman	Y	Y	Y	N
28 Berman	Y	Y	Y	?
29 Schiff	Y	Y	Y	N
30 Waxman	Y	Y	Y	N
31 Becerra	Y	Y	Y	N
32 Chu	Y	N	Y	N
33 Watson	Y	N	Y	N
34 Roybal-Allard	Y	N	Y	N
35 Waters	Y	P	Y	N
36 Harman	Y	Y	Y	N
37 Richardson	Y	N	Y	N
38 Napolitano	Y	Y	Y	N
39 Sánchez, Linda	Y	Y	Y	N
40 Royce	N	N	N	Y
41 Lewis	N	N	N	Y
42 Miller, Gary	N	N	N	Y
43 Baca	Y	N	Y	Y
44 Calvert	N	N	N	Y
45 Bono Mack	N	N	N	Y
46 Rohrabacher	N	N	N	Y
47 Sanchez, Loretta	Y	N	Y	N
48 Campbell	N	Y	N	Y
49 Issa	N	N	N	Y
50 Bilbray	N	N	N	Y
51 Filner	Y	Y	Y	N
52 Hunter	N	N	N	Y
53 Davis	Y	N	Y	N

	165	316	317	335
COLORADO				
1 DeGette	Y	Y	Y	N
2 Polis	Y	Y	Y	N
3 Salazar	Y	Y	Y	N
4 Markey	Y	Y	Y	Y
5 Lamborn	N	N	N	Y
6 Coffman	N	Y	N	Y
7 Perlmutter	Y	Y	Y	N
CONNECTICUT				
1 Larson	Y	Y	Y	N
2 Courtney	Y	Y	Y	Y
3 DeLauro	Y	Y	Y	N
4 Himes	Y	Y	Y	N
5 Murphy	Y	Y	Y	N
DELAWARE				
AL Castle	N	N	N	Y
FLORIDA				
1 Miller	N	Y	N	Y
2 Boyd	Y	Y	Y	Y
3 Brown	Y	Y	Y	Y
4 Crenshaw	N	N	N	Y
5 Brown-Waite	N	?	?	?
6 Stearns	N	Y	N	Y
7 Mica	N	Y	N	Y
8 Grayson	Y	Y	Y	Y
9 Bilirakis	N	N	N	Y
10 Young	N	N	N	Y
11 Castor	Y	Y	Y	N
12 Putnam	N	N	N	Y
13 Buchanan	N	Y	N	Y
14 Mack	N	Y	N	Y
15 Posey	N	Y	N	Y
16 Rooney	N	Y	N	Y
17 Meek	Y	Y	Y	N
18 Ros-Lehtinen	N	N	N	Y
19 Deutch[2]		Y	Y	N
20 Wasserman Schultz	Y	N	Y	N
21 Diaz-Balart, L.	N	N	N	Y
22 Klein	Y	Y	Y	Y
23 Hastings	Y	?	?	?
24 Kosmas	Y	Y	Y	Y
25 Diaz-Balart, M.	N	N	N	Y
GEORGIA				
1 Kingston	N	N	N	Y
2 Bishop	Y	Y	N	Y
3 Westmoreland	N	Y	N	Y
4 Johnson	Y	Y	Y	Y
5 Lewis	Y	Y	Y	N
6 Price	N	N	N	Y
7 Linder	N	Y	N	?
8 Marshall	N	N	N	Y
9 Vacant				
10 Broun	N	Y	N	Y
11 Gingrey	N	Y	N	Y
12 Barrow	N	Y	Y	Y
13 Scott	Y	N	Y	N
HAWAII				
1 Djou[3]		N	Y	Y
2 Hirono	Y	Y	Y	N
IDAHO				
1 Minnick	N	Y	Y	Y
2 Simpson	N	N	N	Y
ILLINOIS				
1 Rush	Y	Y	Y	N
2 Jackson	Y	Y	Y	Y
3 Lipinski	N	N	N	Y
4 Gutierrez	Y	N	Y	N
5 Quigley	Y	Y	Y	N
6 Roskam	N	N	N	Y
7 Davis	Y	Y	Y	N
8 Bean	Y	Y	Y	Y
9 Schakowsky	Y	N	Y	N
10 Kirk	N	Y	N	Y
11 Halvorson	Y	N	Y	Y
12 Costello	N	N	N	Y
13 Biggert	N	N	Y	N
14 Foster	Y	N	Y	Y
15 Johnson	N	Y	N	Y

[1] The Speaker votes only at her discretion.

[2] Rep. Ted Deutch, D-Fla., was sworn in April 15 to fill the seat vacated by the Jan. 3 resignation of Democrat Robert Wexler. The first vote for which Deutch was eligible was vote 205; Wexler was not eligible for any votes in 2010.

[3] Rep. Charles K. Djou, R-Hawaii, was sworn in May 25 to fill the seat vacated by Democrat Neil Abercrombie, who resigned Feb. 28 to run for governor. The first vote for which Djou was eligible was vote 296; the last vote for which Abercrombie was eligible was vote 74.

[4] Rep. Mark Souder, R-Ind., resigned May 21. The last vote for which he was eligible was vote 290.

[5] Rep. Eric Massa, D-N.Y., resigned March 8. The last vote for which he was eligible was vote 91.

[6] Rep. Mark Critz, D-Pa., was sworn in May 20 to fill the seat vacated by the Feb. 8 death of fellow Democrat John P. Murtha, D-Pa. The first vote for which Critz was eligible was vote 286; the last vote for which Murtha was eligible was vote 48.

KEY	**Republicans**	Democrats	
Y Voted for (yea)		X Paired against	C Voted "present" to avoid possible conflict of interest
# Paired for		– Announced against	
+ Announced for		P Voted "present"	? Did not vote or otherwise make a position known
N Voted against (nay)			

	165	316	317	335
16 Manzullo	N	N	N	Y
17 Hare	Y	Y	Y	N
18 Schock	N	N	N	Y
19 Shimkus	N	N	N	Y
INDIANA				
1 Visclosky	Y	N	Y	Y
3 Souder⁴	N			
2 Donnelly	Y	N	N	Y
4 Buyer	N	N	N	Y
5 Burton	N	N	N	Y
6 Pence	N	N	N	Y
7 Carson	Y	N	Y	Y
8 Ellsworth	Y	N	Y	Y
9 Hill	Y	N	Y	Y
IOWA				
1 Braley	Y	Y	Y	N
2 Loebsack	Y	N	Y	Y
3 Boswell	Y	N	Y	Y
4 Latham	N	N	N	Y
5 King	N	N	N	Y
KANSAS				
1 Moran	N	Y	N	Y
2 Jenkins	N	Y	N	Y
3 Moore	Y	N	Y	Y
4 Tiahrt	N	Y	N	Y
KENTUCKY				
1 Whitfield	N	N	N	Y
2 Guthrie	N	N	N	Y
3 Yarmuth	Y	N	Y	N
4 Davis	N	–	–	+
5 Rogers	N	N	N	Y
6 Chandler	N	N	Y	Y
LOUISIANA				
1 Scalise	N	N	N	Y
2 Cao	N	N	Y	Y
3 Melancon	N	?	?	?
4 Fleming	N	N	N	Y
5 Alexander	N	N	N	Y
6 Cassidy	N	Y	N	Y
7 Boustany	N	Y	N	Y
MAINE				
1 Pingree	Y	Y	Y	N
2 Michaud	Y	Y	Y	N
MARYLAND				
1 Kratovil	N	Y	Y	Y
2 Ruppersberger	Y	N	Y	Y
3 Sarbanes	Y	N	Y	Y
4 Edwards	Y	Y	Y	Y
5 Hoyer	Y	Y	Y	Y
6 Bartlett	N	N	N	Y
7 Cummings	Y	Y	Y	Y
8 Van Hollen	Y	Y	Y	Y
MASSACHUSETTS				
1 Olver	Y	Y	Y	N
2 Neal	Y	Y	Y	N
3 McGovern	Y	N	Y	N
4 Frank	Y	N	Y	N
5 Tsongas	Y	N	Y	N
6 Tierney	Y	N	Y	N
7 Markey	Y	N	Y	N
8 Capuano	Y	N	Y	N
9 Lynch	N	N	Y	Y
10 Delahunt	Y	N	Y	?
MICHIGAN				
1 Stupak	Y	Y	Y	–
2 Hoekstra	N	Y	N	Y
3 Ehlers	N	N	N	Y
4 Camp	N	Y	N	Y
5 Kildee	Y	N	Y	Y
6 Upton	N	Y	N	Y
7 Schauer	Y	N	Y	Y
8 Rogers	N	N	N	Y
9 Peters	Y	N	Y	Y
10 Miller	N	N	N	Y
11 McCotter	N	N	N	Y
12 Levin	Y	N	Y	Y
13 Kilpatrick	Y	N	Y	N
14 Conyers	Y	N	Y	N
15 Dingell	Y	N	Y	N
MINNESOTA				
1 Walz	Y	Y	Y	Y
2 Kline	N	N	N	Y
3 Paulsen	N	Y	N	Y
4 McCollum	Y	Y	Y	N

	165	316	317	335
5 Ellison	Y	Y	Y	N
6 Bachmann	N	N	N	Y
7 Peterson	N	Y	N	Y
8 Oberstar	Y	Y	Y	N
MISSISSIPPI				
1 Childers	N	N	N	Y
2 Thompson	Y	N	Y	N
3 Harper	N	N	N	Y
4 Taylor	N	N	N	Y
MISSOURI				
1 Clay	Y	N	Y	N
2 Akin	N	N	N	Y
3 Carnahan	Y	Y	Y	Y
4 Skelton	N	N	N	Y
5 Cleaver	Y	N	Y	N
6 Graves	N	–	–	+
7 Blunt	N	N	N	Y
8 Emerson	N	N	N	Y
9 Luetkemeyer	N	N	N	Y
MONTANA				
AL Rehberg	N	Y	N	Y
NEBRASKA				
1 Fortenberry	N	N	N	Y
2 Terry	N	N	N	Y
3 Smith	N	N	N	Y
NEVADA				
1 Berkley	Y	Y	Y	Y
2 Heller	N	N	N	Y
3 Titus	Y	Y	Y	Y
NEW HAMPSHIRE				
1 Shea-Porter	Y	N	Y	Y
2 Hodes	Y	Y	Y	Y
NEW JERSEY				
1 Andrews	Y	N	Y	Y
2 LoBiondo	N	N	N	Y
3 Adler	N	N	Y	Y
4 Smith	N	N	N	Y
5 Garrett	N	Y	N	Y
6 Pallone	Y	Y	Y	N
7 Lance	N	Y	N	Y
8 Pascrell	Y	Y	Y	N
9 Rothman	Y	N	Y	N
10 Payne	Y	N	Y	N
11 Frelinghuysen	N	N	N	Y
12 Holt	Y	Y	Y	N
13 Sires	Y	N	Y	Y
NEW MEXICO				
1 Heinrich	Y	Y	Y	N
2 Teague	N	Y	Y	Y
3 Luján	Y	Y	Y	N
NEW YORK				
1 Bishop	Y	Y	Y	Y
2 Israel	Y	N	Y	N
3 King	N	Y	N	?
4 McCarthy	Y	N	Y	N
5 Ackerman	Y	N	Y	?
6 Meeks	Y	Y	Y	N
7 Crowley	Y	N	Y	N
8 Nadler	Y	Y	Y	N
9 Weiner	Y	N	Y	N
10 Towns	Y	Y	Y	N
11 Clarke	Y	N	Y	N
12 Velázquez	Y	N	Y	N
13 McMahon	N	N	Y	Y
14 Maloney	Y	Y	Y	N
15 Rangel	Y	N	Y	N
16 Serrano	Y	N	Y	N
17 Engel	Y	N	Y	Y
18 Lowey	Y	Y	Y	Y
19 Hall	Y	Y	Y	Y
20 Murphy	Y	N	Y	Y
21 Tonko	Y	N	Y	Y
22 Hinchey	Y	Y	Y	N
23 Owens	Y	Y	Y	Y
24 Arcuri	N	N	Y	Y
25 Maffei	Y	N	Y	Y
26 Lee	N	Y	N	Y
27 Higgins	Y	N	Y	Y
28 Slaughter	Y	P	Y	?
29 Vacant⁵				
NORTH CAROLINA				
1 Butterfield	Y	N	Y	N
2 Etheridge	Y	N	N	Y
3 Jones	N	Y	N	?
4 Price	Y	N	Y	N

	165	316	317	335
5 Foxx	N	N	N	Y
6 Coble	N	N	N	Y
7 McIntyre	N	N	N	Y
8 Kissell	N	N	Y	Y
9 Myrick	N	N	N	Y
10 McHenry	N	N	N	Y
11 Shuler	N	N	N	?
12 Watt	Y	Y	Y	Y
13 Miller	Y	N	Y	Y
NORTH DAKOTA				
AL Pomeroy	Y	N	N	Y
OHIO				
1 Driehaus	Y	N	Y	Y
2 Schmidt	N	N	N	Y
3 Turner	N	N	N	Y
4 Jordan	N	N	N	Y
5 Latta	N	N	N	+
6 Wilson	Y	N	Y	Y
7 Austria	N	N	N	Y
8 Boehner	N	N	N	Y
9 Kaptur	Y	N	Y	N
10 Kucinich	Y	N	Y	N
11 Fudge	Y	N	Y	N
12 Tiberi	N	N	N	Y
13 Sutton	Y	N	Y	Y
14 LaTourette	N	N	N	Y
15 Kilroy	Y	N	Y	N
16 Boccieri	Y	N	Y	Y
17 Ryan	Y	N	Y	Y
18 Space	N	N	Y	Y
OKLAHOMA				
1 Sullivan	N	Y	N	Y
2 Boren	N	+	–	+
3 Lucas	N	N	N	Y
4 Cole	N	Y	N	Y
5 Fallin	N	N	N	Y
OREGON				
1 Wu	Y	Y	Y	N
2 Walden	N	Y	N	Y
3 Blumenauer	Y	Y	Y	N
4 DeFazio	Y	Y	Y	N
5 Schrader	Y	Y	Y	Y
PENNSYLVANIA				
1 Brady	Y	N	Y	N
2 Fattah	Y	N	Y	N
3 Dahlkemper	Y	N	Y	Y
4 Altmire	N	Y	Y	Y
5 Thompson	N	Y	N	Y
6 Gerlach	N	N	N	Y
7 Sestak	Y	N	Y	N
8 Murphy, P.	Y	Y	Y	N
9 Shuster	N	N	N	Y
10 Carney	Y	N	Y	N
11 Kanjorski	Y	N	Y	Y
12 Critz⁶	N	N	Y	Y
13 Schwartz	Y	Y	Y	Y
14 Doyle	Y	Y	Y	N
15 Dent	N	Y	N	Y
16 Pitts	N	N	N	Y
17 Holden	N	Y	Y	Y
18 Murphy, T.	N	N	N	?
19 Platts	N	N	N	Y
RHODE ISLAND				
1 Kennedy	Y	N	Y	N
2 Langevin	Y	N	Y	Y
SOUTH CAROLINA				
1 Brown	N	N	N	Y
2 Wilson	N	N	N	Y
3 Barrett	N	N	N	Y
4 Inglis	N	N	N	Y
5 Spratt	Y	N	N	Y
6 Clyburn	Y	N	Y	N
SOUTH DAKOTA				
AL Herseth Sandlin	N	Y	Y	Y
TENNESSEE				
1 Roe	N	Y	N	Y
2 Duncan	N	Y	N	Y
3 Wamp	N	Y	N	Y
4 Davis	N	Y	N	Y
5 Cooper	Y	Y	Y	Y
6 Gordon	Y	N	Y	Y
7 Blackburn	N	N	N	Y
8 Tanner	N	Y	N	Y
9 Cohen	Y	Y	Y	N

	165	316	317	335
TEXAS				
1 Gohmert	N	Y	N	Y
2 Poe	N	N	N	Y
3 Johnson, S.	N	Y	N	Y
4 Hall	N	N	N	Y
5 Hensarling	N	Y	N	Y
6 Barton	N	Y	N	Y
7 Culberson	N	N	N	Y
8 Brady	N	Y	N	Y
9 Green, A.	Y	Y	Y	N
10 McCaul	N	N	N	Y
11 Conaway	N	N	N	Y
12 Granger	N	Y	N	Y
13 Thornberry	N	N	N	Y
14 Paul	N	Y	N	Y
15 Hinojosa	Y	N	Y	Y
16 Reyes	Y	Y	Y	Y
17 Edwards	N	N	Y	Y
18 Jackson Lee	Y	Y	Y	N
19 Neugebauer	N	Y	N	Y
20 Gonzalez	Y	Y	Y	Y
21 Smith	N	N	N	Y
22 Olson	N	N	N	Y
23 Rodriguez	Y	N	Y	Y
24 Marchant	N	N	N	Y
25 Doggett	Y	Y	Y	N
26 Burgess	N	Y	N	Y
27 Ortiz	Y	Y	Y	Y
28 Cuellar	Y	Y	Y	Y
29 Green, G.	Y	N	Y	Y
30 Johnson, E.	Y	Y	Y	Y
31 Carter	N	N	N	Y
32 Sessions	N	N	N	Y
UTAH				
1 Bishop	N	N	N	Y
2 Matheson	N	N	Y	Y
3 Chaffetz	N	Y	N	Y
VERMONT				
AL Welch	Y	N	Y	N
VIRGINIA				
1 Wittman	N	N	N	Y
2 Nye	N	N	Y	Y
3 Scott	Y	N	Y	N
4 Forbes	N	N	N	Y
5 Perriello	Y	Y	Y	Y
6 Goodlatte	N	N	N	Y
7 Cantor	N	N	N	Y
8 Moran	Y	N	Y	N
9 Boucher	N	N	N	Y
10 Wolf	N	N	N	Y
11 Connolly	Y	N	Y	Y
WASHINGTON				
1 Inslee	Y	Y	Y	N
2 Larsen	Y	N	Y	N
3 Baird	Y	Y	Y	N
4 Hastings	N	N	N	Y
5 McMorris Rodgers	N	N	N	Y
6 Dicks	Y	Y	Y	N
7 McDermott	Y	Y	Y	N
8 Reichert	N	N	N	Y
9 Smith	Y	N	Y	N
WEST VIRGINIA				
1 Mollohan	Y	N	Y	N
2 Capito	N	Y	N	Y
3 Rahall	Y	Y	N	Y
WISCONSIN				
1 Ryan	N	+	–	+
2 Baldwin	Y	Y	Y	N
3 Kind	Y	Y	Y	N
4 Moore	Y	Y	Y	N
5 Sensenbrenner	N	Y	N	Y
6 Petri	N	Y	N	Y
7 Obey	Y	Y	Y	N
8 Kagen	Y	Y	Y	N
WYOMING				
AL Lummis	N	N	N	Y
DELEGATES				
Faleomavaega (A.S.)		Y		Y
Norton (D.C.)		N		Y
Bordallo (Guam)		N		Y
Sablan (N. Marianas)		?		?
Pierluisi (P.R.)		?		?
Christensen (V.I.)		Y		Y

IN THE HOUSE | By Vote Number

391. **HR 5175. Campaign Finance Disclosure/Passage.** Passage of the bill that would establish new reporting requirements for corporations, unions and other interest groups for campaign-related activities. It would prohibit corporations that are foreign-controlled or have received a specified amount of government assistance from making expenditures in political campaigns. As amended, it would exempt from some identification disclosure rules certain charitable organizations as well as organizations that are at least 10 years old, have at least 500,000 dues-paying members, have members in each state and receive no more than 15 percent of their funding from corporations and unions. Passed 219-206: D 217-36; R 2-170. A "yea" was a vote in support of the president's position. June 24, 2010. *(Story, p. C-11)*

413. **HR 4173. Financial Regulatory Overhaul/Conference Report.** Adoption of the conference report on the bill that would overhaul the regulation of the financial services industry. The measure would create a new regulatory mechanism to assess risks posed by very large financial institutions and facilitate the orderly dissolution of failing firms that pose a threat to the economy. It would create a new federal agency to oversee consumer financial products, bring the derivatives market under significant federal regulation for the first time and give company shareholders and regulators greater say on executive-pay packages. The costs would be offset by terminating the Troubled Asset Relief Program and increasing deposit insurance premiums paid by some banks. Adopted (thus sent to the Senate) 237-192: D 234-19; R 3-173. A "yea" was a vote in support of the president's position. June 30, 2010. *(Story, p. C-11)*

432. **HR 4899. Supplemental Appropriations/Motion to Concur.** Fourth portion of the divided question on the Obey, D-Wis., motion to concur in the Senate amendments to the bill with House amendments. The fourth portion consists of a Lee, D-Calif., amendment that would limit the use of military funding for Afghanistan to activities relating to the safe withdrawal of U.S. troops and protection of civilian and military personnel in the country. Motion rejected 100-321: D 93-157; R 7-164. A "nay" was a vote in support of the president's position. July 1, 2010. *(Story, p. C-11)*

474. **HR 4899. Supplemental Appropriations/Passage.** Obey, D-Wis., motion to suspend the rules, recede from the House amendment to the Senate amendment and concur in the Senate amendment to the bill that would provide $58.8 billion in supplemental funds for fiscal 2010. That total includes $33.5 billion for the Defense Department for the addition of 30,000 troops in Afghanistan, $3.6 billion for Afghan and Iraqi security forces, and $4.9 billion for Defense Department procurement. It would provide $162 million in funds related to the oil spill in the Gulf of Mexico. It would also provide $5.1 billion for the Federal Emergency Management Agency to pay for costs of past disasters and $13.4 billion in mandatory funds to compensate Vietnam War veterans exposed to Agent Orange. Motion agreed to (thus clearing the bill for the president), 308-114: D 148-102; R 160-12. A two-thirds majority of those present and voting (282 in this case) is required for passage under suspension of the rules. A "yea" was a vote in support of the president's position. July 27, 2010. *(Story, p. C-12)*

[1] The Speaker votes only at her discretion.

[2] Rep. Tom Graves, R-Ga., was sworn in June 14 to fill the seat vacated by Republican Nathan Deal, who resigned March 21 to run for governor. The first vote for which Graves was eligible was vote 356; the last vote for which Deal was eligible was vote 168.

	391	413	432	474
ALABAMA				
1 **Bonner**	N	N	N	Y
2 Bright	N	N	N	Y
3 **Rogers**	N	N	N	Y
4 **Aderholt**	N	N	N	Y
5 **Griffith**	N	N	?	Y
6 **Bachus**	N	N	N	Y
7 Davis	Y	Y	N	Y
ALASKA				
AL **Young**	N	?	?	Y
ARIZONA				
1 Kirkpatrick	Y	N	N	Y
2 **Franks**	N	N	N	Y
3 **Shadegg**	N	N	N	Y
4 Pastor	Y	Y	Y	Y
5 Mitchell	N	N	N	Y
6 **Flake**	N	N	N	N
7 Grijalva	Y	Y	Y	N
8 Giffords	Y	Y	N	Y
ARKANSAS				
1 Berry	Y	N	N	Y
2 Snyder	Y	Y	N	Y
3 **Boozman**	N	N	N	Y
4 Ross	Y	N	N	Y
CALIFORNIA				
1 Thompson	Y	Y	N	N
2 **Herger**	N	N	N	Y
3 **Lungren**	N	N	N	Y
4 **McClintock**	N	N	N	Y
5 Matsui	Y	Y	Y	N
6 Woolsey	Y	+	+	N
7 Miller, George	Y	Y	Y	N
8 Pelosi [1]	Y	Y		
9 Lee	Y	Y	Y	N
10 Garamendi	Y	Y	Y	N
11 McNerney	Y	Y	N	Y
12 Speier	Y	Y	Y	N
13 Stark	Y	Y	Y	N
14 Eshoo	Y	Y	N	N
15 Honda	Y	Y	Y	N
16 Lofgren	Y	Y	Y	N
17 Farr	Y	Y	Y	N
18 Cardoza	Y	Y	N	Y
19 **Radanovich**	N	N	?	Y
20 Costa	Y	Y	N	Y
21 **Nunes**	N	N	N	Y
22 **McCarthy**	N	N	N	Y
23 Capps	Y	Y	N	Y
24 **Gallegly**	N	N	N	Y
25 **McKeon**	N	N	N	Y
26 **Dreier**	N	N	N	Y
27 Sherman	Y	Y	N	Y
28 Berman	Y	Y	N	Y
29 Schiff	Y	Y	N	Y
30 Waxman	Y	Y	Y	N
31 Becerra	Y	Y	Y	N
32 Chu	Y	Y	Y	N
33 Watson	Y	Y	?	?
34 Roybal-Allard	Y	Y	N	Y
35 Waters	N	Y	Y	N
36 Harman	Y	Y	Y	Y
37 Richardson	Y	Y	Y	N
38 Napolitano	Y	Y	Y	N
39 Sánchez, Linda	Y	Y	Y	N
40 **Royce**	N	N	N	Y
41 **Lewis**	N	N	N	Y
42 **Miller, Gary**	N	N	N	Y
43 Baca	Y	Y	N	Y
44 **Calvert**	N	N	N	Y
45 **Bono Mack**	N	N	N	Y
46 **Rohrabacher**	N	N	Y	N
47 Sanchez, Loretta	Y	Y	Y	N
48 **Campbell**	N	N	Y	N
49 **Issa**	N	N	N	Y
50 **Bilbray**	N	N	N	Y
51 Filner	Y	Y	Y	N
52 **Hunter**	N	Y	N	Y
53 Davis	Y	Y	N	Y

	391	413	432	474
COLORADO				
1 DeGette	Y	Y	Y	Y
2 Polis	Y	Y	N	Y
3 Salazar	Y	Y	N	Y
4 Markey	Y	Y	N	Y
5 **Lamborn**	N	N	N	Y
6 **Coffman**	N	N	N	Y
7 Perlmutter	Y	Y	N	Y
CONNECTICUT				
1 Larson	Y	Y	Y	N
2 Courtney	Y	Y	N	Y
3 DeLauro	Y	Y	Y	N
4 Himes	Y	Y	N	Y
5 Murphy	Y	Y	N	N
DELAWARE				
AL **Castle**	Y	Y	N	Y
FLORIDA				
1 **Miller**	N	N	N	Y
2 Boyd	Y	Y	N	Y
3 Brown	Y	Y	N	N
4 **Crenshaw**	N	N	N	Y
5 **Brown-Waite**	N	N	N	Y
6 **Stearns**	N	N	N	Y
7 **Mica**	N	N	N	Y
8 Grayson	Y	Y	Y	–
9 **Bilirakis**	N	N	N	Y
10 **Young**	N	N	N	?
11 Castor	Y	Y	N	N
12 **Putnam**	N	N	N	Y
13 **Buchanan**	N	N	N	Y
14 **Mack**	N	N	N	Y
15 **Posey**	N	N	N	Y
16 **Rooney**	N	N	N	Y
17 Meek	Y	Y	N	?
18 **Ros-Lehtinen**	N	N	N	Y
19 Deutch	Y	Y	N	N
20 Wasserman Schultz	Y	Y	N	Y
21 **Diaz-Balart, L.**	N	N	N	Y
22 Klein	Y	Y	N	Y
23 Hastings	N	Y	Y	N
24 Kosmas	Y	Y	N	Y
25 **Diaz-Balart, M.**	N	N	N	Y
GEORGIA				
1 **Kingston**	N	N	N	Y
2 Bishop	N	Y	N	Y
3 **Westmoreland**	N	N	N	Y
4 Johnson	Y	Y	N	N
5 Lewis	Y	Y	Y	N
6 **Price**	N	N	N	Y
7 **Linder**	N	N	N	Y
8 Marshall	N	Y	N	Y
9 **Graves** [2]	N	N	N	Y
10 **Broun**	N	N	N	N
11 **Gingrey**	N	N	N	Y
12 Barrow	N	Y	N	Y
13 Scott	Y	Y	N	Y
HAWAII				
1 **Djou**	N	N	N	Y
2 Hirono	Y	Y	Y	N
IDAHO				
1 Minnick	N	Y	N	Y
2 **Simpson**	N	N	N	Y
ILLINOIS				
1 Rush	N	Y	Y	N
2 Jackson	Y	Y	Y	N
3 Lipinski	Y	Y	N	Y
4 Gutierrez	Y	Y	Y	N
5 Quigley	Y	Y	Y	N
6 **Roskam**	N	N	N	Y
7 Davis	N	Y	Y	N
8 Bean	N	Y	N	Y
9 Schakowsky	Y	Y	Y	N
10 **Kirk**	N	N	N	Y
11 Halvorson	Y	Y	N	Y
12 Costello	Y	Y	Y	N
13 **Biggert**	N	N	N	Y
14 Foster	Y	Y	N	Y
15 **Johnson**	N	N	Y	N

KEY   **Republicans**   Democrats

Y Voted for (yea)	X Paired against	C Voted "present" to avoid possible conflict of interest
# Paired for	– Announced against	
+ Announced for	P Voted "present"	? Did not vote or otherwise make a position known
N Voted against (nay)		

	391	413	432	474
16 Manzullo	N	N	N	Y
17 Hare	Y	Y	N	Y
18 Schock	N	N	N	Y
19 Shimkus	N	N	N	Y
INDIANA				
1 Visclosky	+	Y	N	Y
2 Donnelly	N	Y	N	Y
3 Vacant				
4 Buyer	N	N	N	Y
5 Burton	N	N	N	Y
6 Pence	–	N	N	Y
7 Carson	Y	Y	N	?
8 Ellsworth	Y	Y	N	Y
9 Hill	N	Y	N	Y
IOWA				
1 Braley	Y	Y	N	Y
2 Loebsack	Y	Y	N	Y
3 Boswell	Y	Y	N	Y
4 Latham	N	N	N	Y
5 King	N	N	N	Y
KANSAS				
1 Moran	N	N	N	?
2 Jenkins	N	N	N	Y
3 Moore	Y	Y	N	Y
4 Tiahrt	N	N	N	?
KENTUCKY				
1 Whitfield	N	N	N	Y
2 Guthrie	N	N	N	Y
3 Yarmuth	Y	Y	Y	Y
4 Davis	N	N	N	Y
5 Rogers	N	N	N	Y
6 Chandler	Y	N	N	Y
LOUISIANA				
1 Scalise	N	N	N	Y
2 Cao	Y	Y	N	Y
3 Melancon	Y	Y	N	Y
4 Fleming	N	N	N	Y
5 Alexander	N	N	N	Y
6 Cassidy	N	N	N	Y
7 Boustany	N	N	N	Y
MAINE				
1 Pingree	Y	Y	Y	N
2 Michaud	Y	Y	Y	N
MARYLAND				
1 Kratovil	N	Y	N	Y
2 Ruppersberger	Y	Y	N	Y
3 Sarbanes	Y	Y	N	Y
4 Edwards	N	Y	Y	N
5 Hoyer	Y	Y	N	Y
6 Bartlett	N	N	N	Y
7 Cummings	Y	Y	Y	N
8 Van Hollen	Y	Y	N	Y
MASSACHUSETTS				
1 Olver	Y	Y	Y	N
2 Neal	Y	Y	Y	N
3 McGovern	Y	Y	Y	N
4 Frank	Y	Y	Y	N
5 Tsongas	Y	Y	Y	N
6 Tierney	Y	Y	Y	N
7 Markey	Y	Y	Y	N
8 Capuano	Y	Y	Y	N
9 Lynch	Y	Y	N	Y
10 Delahunt	Y	Y	Y	N
MICHIGAN				
1 Stupak	Y	Y	Y	N
2 Hoekstra	?	N	?	Y
3 Ehlers	N	N	N	N
4 Camp	N	N	N	Y
5 Kildee	Y	Y	N	Y
6 Upton	N	N	N	Y
7 Schauer	Y	Y	N	Y
8 Rogers	N	N	N	Y
9 Peters	Y	Y	N	Y
10 Miller	N	N	N	Y
11 McCotter	N	N	N	Y
12 Levin	Y	Y	N	Y
13 Kilpatrick	N	Y	N	Y
14 Conyers	Y	Y	?	N
15 Dingell	Y	Y	N	Y
MINNESOTA				
1 Walz	Y	Y	N	Y
2 Kline	N	N	N	Y
3 Paulsen	N	N	N	Y
4 McCollum	Y	Y	Y	N
5 Ellison	Y	Y	Y	N
6 Bachmann	N	N	N	Y
7 Peterson	N	Y	N	Y
8 Oberstar	Y	Y	Y	N
MISSISSIPPI				
1 Childers	N	N	N	Y
2 Thompson	N	Y	Y	N
3 Harper	N	N	N	Y
4 Taylor	N	?	N	Y
MISSOURI				
1 Clay	Y	Y	Y	N
2 Akin	N	N	N	+
3 Carnahan	Y	Y	N	Y
4 Skelton	Y	N	N	Y
5 Cleaver	Y	Y	Y	N
6 Graves	N	N	N	+
7 Blunt	?	N	N	Y
8 Emerson	N	N	N	Y
9 Luetkemeyer	N	N	N	Y
MONTANA				
AL Rehberg	N	N	N	Y
NEBRASKA				
1 Fortenberry	N	N	N	Y
2 Terry	N	N	N	Y
3 Smith	N	N	N	Y
NEVADA				
1 Berkley	Y	Y	N	Y
2 Heller	N	N	N	+
3 Titus	Y	Y	N	Y
NEW HAMPSHIRE				
1 Shea-Porter	Y	Y	N	N
2 Hodes	Y	Y	N	Y
NEW JERSEY				
1 Andrews	Y	Y	N	Y
2 LoBiondo	N	N	N	Y
3 Adler	Y	Y	N	Y
4 Smith	N	N	N	Y
5 Garrett	N	N	N	Y
6 Pallone	Y	Y	Y	N
7 Lance	N	N	N	Y
8 Pascrell	Y	Y	N	Y
9 Rothman	?	Y	N	Y
10 Payne	N	Y	Y	N
11 Frelinghuysen	N	N	N	Y
12 Holt	Y	Y	N	Y
13 Sires	Y	Y	Y	Y
NEW MEXICO				
1 Heinrich	Y	Y	N	Y
2 Teague	Y	Y	N	Y
3 Luján	Y	Y	N	Y
NEW YORK				
1 Bishop	Y	Y	N	Y
2 Israel	Y	Y	N	Y
3 King	N	N	N	Y
4 McCarthy	N	Y	N	Y
5 Ackerman	Y	Y	N	Y
6 Meeks	Y	Y	N	N
7 Crowley	Y	Y	Y	N
8 Nadler	Y	Y	Y	N
9 Weiner	Y	Y	Y	N
10 Towns	Y	Y	Y	N
11 Clarke	N	Y	N	Y
12 Velázquez	Y	Y	Y	N
13 McMahon	Y	Y	N	Y
14 Maloney	Y	Y	N	Y
15 Rangel	Y	Y	Y	N
16 Serrano	Y	Y	Y	N
17 Engel	Y	Y	N	Y
18 Lowey	Y	Y	N	Y
19 Hall	Y	Y	N	Y
20 Murphy	Y	Y	N	Y
21 Tonko	Y	Y	Y	N
22 Hinchey	Y	Y	Y	N
23 Owens	N	N	N	Y
24 Arcuri	Y	Y	N	Y
25 Maffei	Y	Y	N	Y
26 Lee	N	N	N	Y
27 Higgins	Y	Y	N	Y
28 Slaughter	Y	Y	Y	N
29 Vacant				
NORTH CAROLINA				
1 Butterfield	N	Y	N	Y
2 Etheridge	Y	Y	N	Y
3 Jones	N	Y	Y	Y
4 Price	Y	Y	N	Y
5 Foxx	N	N	N	Y
6 Coble	N	N	N	Y
7 McIntyre	N	N	N	Y
8 Kissell	Y	Y	N	Y
9 Myrick	N	N	N	Y
10 McHenry	N	N	N	Y
11 Shuler	Y	Y	N	Y
12 Watt	N	Y	Y	N
13 Miller	Y	Y	N	Y
NORTH DAKOTA				
AL Pomeroy	Y	Y	N	Y
OHIO				
1 Driehaus	Y	Y	N	Y
2 Schmidt	N	N	N	Y
3 Turner	N	N	N	Y
4 Jordan	N	N	N	Y
5 Latta	N	N	N	Y
6 Wilson	Y	Y	N	Y
7 Austria	N	N	N	Y
8 Boehner	N	N	N	Y
9 Kaptur	Y	N	N	N
10 Kucinich	Y	Y	Y	N
11 Fudge	N	Y	Y	N
12 Tiberi	N	N	N	Y
13 Sutton	Y	N	N	Y
14 LaTourette	N	N	N	Y
15 Kilroy	Y	Y	N	Y
16 Boccieri	Y	Y	N	Y
17 Ryan	Y	Y	N	Y
18 Space	Y	Y	N	Y
OKLAHOMA				
1 Sullivan	N	N	N	Y
2 Boren	N	N	N	Y
3 Lucas	N	N	N	Y
4 Cole	N	N	N	Y
5 Fallin	N	N	N	Y
OREGON				
1 Wu	Y	Y	N	N
2 Walden	N	N	N	Y
3 Blumenauer	Y	Y	Y	N
4 DeFazio	Y	Y	Y	N
5 Schrader	Y	Y	Y	N
PENNSYLVANIA				
1 Brady	Y	Y	N	Y
2 Fattah	Y	Y	N	N
3 Dahlkemper	N	Y	N	Y
4 Altmire	Y	Y	N	Y
5 Thompson	N	N	N	Y
6 Gerlach	N	N	N	Y
7 Sestak	Y	Y	N	Y
8 Murphy, P.	Y	Y	N	Y
9 Shuster	N	N	N	Y
10 Carney	Y	Y	N	Y
11 Kanjorski	Y	Y	N	Y
12 Critz	N	N	N	Y
13 Schwartz	Y	Y	N	Y
14 Doyle	Y	Y	N	Y
15 Dent	N	N	N	Y
16 Pitts	N	N	N	Y
17 Holden	N	Y	N	Y
18 Murphy, T.	N	N	N	Y
19 Platts	N	N	N	Y
RHODE ISLAND				
1 Kennedy	Y	Y	Y	Y
2 Langevin	Y	Y	N	Y
SOUTH CAROLINA				
1 Brown	?	N	N	Y
2 Wilson	N	N	N	Y
3 Barrett	?	N	N	Y
4 Inglis	N	N	N	Y
5 Spratt	Y	Y	N	Y
6 Clyburn	Y	Y	N	Y
SOUTH DAKOTA				
AL Herseth Sandlin	N	Y	N	Y
TENNESSEE				
1 Roe	N	N	N	Y
2 Duncan	N	Y	Y	N
3 Wamp	?	?	?	Y
4 Davis	N	N	N	Y
5 Cooper	Y	N	N	Y
6 Gordon	Y	Y	N	Y
7 Blackburn	N	N	N	Y
8 Tanner	Y	Y	N	Y
9 Cohen	Y	Y	N	Y
TEXAS				
1 Gohmert	N	N	N	Y
2 Poe	N	N	N	Y
3 Johnson, S.	N	N	?	Y
4 Hall	N	N	N	Y
5 Hensarling	N	N	N	Y
6 Barton	N	N	N	Y
7 Culberson	N	N	N	Y
8 Brady	N	N	N	Y
9 Green, A.	Y	Y	N	Y
10 McCaul	N	N	N	Y
11 Conaway	N	N	N	Y
12 Granger	N	N	N	Y
13 Thornberry	N	N	N	Y
14 Paul	N	N	Y	N
15 Hinojosa	Y	Y	Y	Y
16 Reyes	Y	Y	N	Y
17 Edwards	N	N	N	Y
18 Jackson Lee	Y	Y	Y	Y
19 Neugebauer	N	N	N	Y
20 Gonzalez	Y	Y	N	Y
21 Smith	N	N	N	Y
22 Olson	N	N	N	Y
23 Rodriguez	Y	Y	?	Y
24 Marchant	N	N	N	Y
25 Doggett	Y	Y	N	N
26 Burgess	N	N	N	Y
27 Ortiz	Y	Y	N	Y
28 Cuellar	Y	Y	N	Y
29 Green, G.	Y	Y	N	Y
30 Johnson, E.	Y	Y	N	N
31 Carter	N	N	N	Y
32 Sessions	N	N	N	N
UTAH				
1 Bishop	N	N	N	Y
2 Matheson	Y	Y	N	Y
3 Chaffetz	N	Y	Y	N
VERMONT				
AL Welch	Y	Y	Y	N
VIRGINIA				
1 Wittman	N	N	N	Y
2 Nye	N	Y	N	Y
3 Scott	Y	Y	Y	N
4 Forbes	N	N	N	Y
5 Perriello	Y	Y	N	Y
6 Goodlatte	N	N	N	Y
7 Cantor	N	N	N	Y
8 Moran	Y	Y	N	Y
9 Boucher	Y	Y	N	Y
10 Wolf	N	N	N	Y
11 Connolly	Y	Y	N	Y
WASHINGTON				
1 Inslee	Y	Y	Y	N
2 Larsen	Y	Y	N	Y
3 Baird	Y	Y	N	Y
4 Hastings	N	N	N	Y
5 McMorris Rodgers	N	N	N	Y
6 Dicks	Y	Y	N	Y
7 McDermott	Y	Y	Y	N
8 Reichert	N	N	N	Y
9 Smith	Y	Y	N	Y
WEST VIRGINIA				
1 Mollohan	Y	Y	N	Y
2 Capito	N	N	?	Y
3 Rahall	Y	Y	N	Y
WISCONSIN				
1 Ryan	N	N	N	Y
2 Baldwin	Y	Y	Y	N
3 Kind	Y	Y	N	Y
4 Moore	Y	Y	Y	N
5 Sensenbrenner	N	N	N	Y
6 Petri	N	N	N	Y
7 Obey	Y	Y	N	Y
8 Kagen	Y	Y	N	N
WYOMING				
AL Lummis	N	N	N	Y
DELEGATES				
Faleomavaega (A.S.)				
Norton (D.C.)				
Bordallo (Guam)				
Sablan (N. Marianas)				
Pierluisi (P.R.)				
Christensen (V.I.)				

IN THE HOUSE | By Vote Number

513. **HR 3534. Offshore Drilling Regulation Overhaul/Passage.**
Passage of the bill that would repeal the current $75 million cap on liability for offshore oil spills. It also would abolish the agency formerly known as the Minerals Management Service in the Interior Department and assign its responsibilities to three new agencies in the department. It would create numerous new safety regulations for leases for offshore oil and gas development, including features designed to prevent well blowouts, and it would require some holders of leases to renegotiate royalty payments disputed by industry. As amended it would prevent oil companies from shifting oil spill cleanup costs to taxpayers in the event one of its subsidiaries goes bankrupt. Passed 209-193: D 207-39; R 2-154. July 30, 2010. *(Story, p. C-12)*

518. **HR 1586. Medicaid and Education Assistance/Motion to Concur.** Obey, D-Wis., motion to concur in the Senate amendment to the House amendment to the Senate amendment to the bill that would provide $16.1 billion to extend increased Medicaid assistance to states and $10 billion in funding for states to create or retain teachers' jobs. The costs would be offset by changing foreign tax provisions, ending increased food stamp benefits beginning in April 2014 and rescinding previously enacted spending. Motion agreed to (thus clearing the bill for the president) 247-161: D 245-3; R 2-158. A "yea" was a vote in support of the president's position. Aug. 10, 2010. *(Story, p. C-12)*

554. **HR 2378. U.S. Trade Currency Policy/Passage.** Passage of the bill that would permit the Commerce Department to impose countervailing duties on imported goods if it finds that a foreign government has undervalued its currency. Passed 348-79: D 249-5; R 99-74. Sept. 29, 2010. *(Story, p. C-12)*

558. **HR 2701. Fiscal 2010 Intelligence Authorization/Motion to Concur.** Reyes, D-Texas, motion to concur in the Senate amendment to the bill that would authorize intelligence programs for fiscal 2010. The bill would expand disclosure requirements and congressional oversight of intelligence agencies and require the director of national intelligence to allow access for GAO personnel to audit certain intelligence agencies. Motion agreed to, thus clearing the bill for the president, 244-181: D 243-9; R 1-172. Sept. 29, 2010. *(Story, p. C-13)*

	513	518	554	558
ALABAMA				
1 **Bonner**	N	N	Y	N
2 Bright	N	N	Y	Y
3 **Rogers**	N	N	Y	N
4 **Aderholt**	N	N	Y	N
5 **Griffith**	?	N	Y	N
6 **Bachus**	N	N	Y	N
7 Davis	N	Y	Y	Y
ALASKA				
AL **Young**	N	?	Y	N
ARIZONA				
1 Kirkpatrick	N	Y	Y	Y
2 **Franks**	N	N	N	N
3 **Shadegg**	?	N	N	N
4 Pastor	Y	Y	Y	Y
5 Mitchell	N	Y	N	Y
6 **Flake**	N	N	N	N
7 Grijalva	Y	Y	Y	Y
8 Giffords	Y	Y	Y	Y
ARKANSAS				
1 Berry	?	?	Y	Y
2 Snyder	Y	?	N	Y
3 **Boozman**	N	N	Y	N
4 Ross	N	Y	Y	Y
CALIFORNIA				
1 Thompson	Y	Y	Y	Y
2 **Herger**	N	N	N	N
3 **Lungren**	N	?	Y	N
4 **McClintock**	N	N	N	N
5 Matsui	Y	Y	Y	Y
6 Woolsey	Y	Y	Y	Y
7 Miller, George	Y	Y	Y	Y
8 Pelosi*	Y	Y	Y	
9 Lee	Y	Y	Y	N
10 Garamendi	Y	Y	Y	Y
11 McNerney	Y	Y	Y	Y
12 Speier	Y	?	Y	Y
13 Stark	Y	Y	Y	N
14 Eshoo	Y	Y	Y	Y
15 Honda	Y	Y	Y	Y
16 Lofgren	Y	Y	Y	Y
17 Farr	Y	Y	Y	Y
18 Cardoza	Y	Y	Y	Y
19 **Radanovich**	?	?	?	?
20 Costa	N	Y	Y	Y
21 **Nunes**	?	N	N	N
22 **McCarthy**	?	N	N	N
23 Capps	Y	Y	Y	Y
24 **Gallegly**	N	N	Y	N
25 **McKeon**	?	N	Y	N
26 **Dreier**	N	N	N	N
27 Sherman	Y	Y	Y	Y
28 Berman	Y	Y	Y	Y
29 Schiff	Y	Y	Y	Y
30 Waxman	Y	Y	Y	N
31 Becerra	Y	Y	Y	Y
32 Chu	Y	Y	Y	Y
33 Watson	?	Y	Y	Y
34 Roybal-Allard	Y	Y	Y	Y
35 Waters	Y	Y	Y	Y
36 Harman	Y	Y	Y	Y
37 Richardson	Y	Y	Y	?
38 Napolitano	Y	Y	Y	Y
39 Sánchez, Linda	Y	Y	Y	Y
40 **Royce**	N	N	Y	N
41 **Lewis**	N	N	N	N
42 **Miller, Gary**	P	?	N	N
43 Baca	Y	Y	N	Y
44 **Calvert**	N	N	Y	N
45 **Bono Mack**	N	N	N	N
46 **Rohrabacher**	N	N	Y	N
47 Sanchez, Loretta	Y	Y	Y	Y
48 **Campbell**	?	N	N	N
49 **Issa**	N	N	N	N
50 **Bilbray**	N	N	Y	N
51 Filner	Y	Y	Y	Y
52 **Hunter**	N	N	N	N
53 Davis	Y	Y	Y	Y

	513	518	554	558
COLORADO				
1 DeGette	Y	?	Y	Y
2 Polis	Y	Y	N	Y
3 Salazar	N	Y	Y	Y
4 Markey	Y	Y	Y	Y
5 **Lamborn**	N	N	N	N
6 **Coffman**	N	N	Y	N
7 Perlmutter	?	Y	Y	Y
CONNECTICUT				
1 Larson	Y	Y	Y	Y
2 Courtney	Y	Y	Y	Y
3 DeLauro	Y	Y	Y	Y
4 Himes	+	Y	Y	Y
5 Murphy	Y	Y	Y	Y
DELAWARE				
AL **Castle**	N	Y	Y	N
FLORIDA				
1 **Miller**	N	N	Y	N
2 Boyd	Y	Y	Y	Y
3 Brown	Y	Y	Y	Y
4 **Crenshaw**	N	N	Y	N
5 **Brown-Waite**	N	N	Y	N
6 **Stearns**	N	N	Y	N
7 **Mica**	N	N	Y	N
8 Grayson	Y	Y	Y	Y
9 **Bilirakis**	N	N	Y	N
10 **Young**	?	?	?	?
11 Castor	Y	Y	Y	Y
12 **Putnam**	N	N	Y	N
13 **Buchanan**	N	?	N	N
14 **Mack**	N	N	N	N
15 **Posey**	N	N	Y	N
16 **Rooney**	N	?	Y	N
17 Meek	Y	?	Y	Y
18 **Ros-Lehtinen**	N	N	Y	N
19 Deutch	Y	Y	Y	Y
20 Wasserman Schultz	Y	Y	Y	Y
21 **Diaz-Balart, L.**	N	?	Y	N
22 Klein	Y	Y	Y	Y
23 Hastings	Y	Y	Y	Y
24 Kosmas	Y	Y	Y	Y
25 **Diaz-Balart, M.**	N	N	Y	N
GEORGIA				
1 **Kingston**	N	N	N	N
2 Bishop	Y	Y	Y	Y
3 **Westmoreland**	N	N	N	N
4 Johnson	Y	Y	Y	Y
5 Lewis	Y	Y	Y	Y
6 **Price**	N	N	N	N
7 **Linder**	?	?	N	N
8 Marshall	N	Y	Y	Y
9 **Graves**	N	N	N	N
10 **Broun**	N	?	N	N
11 **Gingrey**	N	?	Y	N
12 Barrow	N	Y	Y	Y
13 Scott	Y	Y	Y	Y
HAWAII				
1 **Djou**	N	N	N	N
2 Hirono	Y	Y	Y	Y
IDAHO				
1 Minnick	Y	Y	Y	Y
2 **Simpson**	N	N	Y	N
ILLINOIS				
1 Rush	Y	Y	Y	Y
2 Jackson	Y	Y	Y	Y
3 Lipinski	Y	Y	Y	Y
4 Gutierrez	Y	Y	Y	Y
5 Quigley	Y	Y	Y	Y
6 **Roskam**	N	?	Y	N
7 Davis	Y	Y	Y	Y
8 Bean	Y	Y	Y	Y
9 Schakowsky	Y	Y	Y	Y
10 **Kirk**	N	N	Y	N
11 Halvorson	N	Y	Y	Y
12 Costello	Y	Y	Y	Y
13 **Biggert**	N	N	Y	N
14 Foster	Y	Y	Y	Y
15 **Johnson**	Y	N	Y	N

KEY   **Republicans**   Democrats

Y Voted for (yea)	**X** Paired against	**C** Voted "present" to avoid possible conflict of interest
# Paired for	**–** Announced against	
+ Announced for	**P** Voted "present"	**?** Did not vote or otherwise make a position known
N Voted against (nay)		

* The Speaker votes only at her discretion.

	513	518	554	558
16 Manzullo	N	N	Y	N
17 Hare	Y	Y	Y	Y
18 Schock	N	N	Y	N
19 Shimkus	N	N	Y	N
INDIANA				
1 Visclosky	Y	Y	Y	Y
2 Donnelly	N	Y	Y	Y
3 Vacant				
4 Buyer	?	N	?	N
5 Burton	N	N	Y	N
6 Pence	N	N	N	N
7 Carson	Y	Y	Y	Y
8 Ellsworth	N	Y	Y	Y
9 Hill	Y	Y	Y	Y
IOWA				
1 Braley	Y	Y	Y	Y
2 Loebsack	Y	Y	Y	Y
3 Boswell	Y	Y	Y	Y
4 Latham	N	N	N	N
5 King	N	N	N	N
KANSAS				
1 Moran	?	N	Y	N
2 Jenkins	N	N	N	N
3 Moore	Y	Y	Y	Y
4 Tiahrt	?	N	N	N
KENTUCKY				
1 Whitfield	N	N	Y	N
2 Guthrie	N	N	Y	N
3 Yarmuth	Y	Y	Y	Y
4 Davis	–	N	Y	N
5 Rogers	N	N	Y	N
6 Chandler	Y	Y	Y	Y
LOUISIANA				
1 Scalise	N	N	N	N
2 Cao	N	Y	Y	N
3 Melancon	Y	Y	Y	Y
4 Fleming	N	N	N	N
5 Alexander	N	N	Y	N
6 Cassidy	N	N	Y	N
7 Boustany	N	?	N	N
MAINE				
1 Pingree	Y	Y	Y	Y
2 Michaud	Y	Y	Y	Y
MARYLAND				
1 Kratovil	Y	Y	Y	Y
2 Ruppersberger	Y	Y	Y	Y
3 Sarbanes	Y	Y	Y	Y
4 Edwards	Y	Y	Y	Y
5 Hoyer	Y	Y	Y	Y
6 Bartlett	N	N	N	N
7 Cummings	Y	Y	Y	Y
8 Van Hollen	Y	Y	Y	Y
MASSACHUSETTS				
1 Olver	Y	Y	Y	Y
2 Neal	Y	Y	Y	Y
3 McGovern	Y	Y	Y	Y
4 Frank	Y	Y	Y	Y
5 Tsongas	Y	Y	Y	Y
6 Tierney	Y	Y	Y	Y
7 Markey	Y	Y	Y	Y
8 Capuano	Y	Y	Y	N
9 Lynch	Y	Y	Y	Y
10 Delahunt	?	Y	?	?
MICHIGAN				
1 Stupak	Y	Y	Y	Y
2 Hoekstra	?	N	Y	N
3 Ehlers	Y	N	Y	N
4 Camp	N	N	Y	N
5 Kildee	Y	Y	Y	Y
6 Upton	N	N	Y	N
7 Schauer	Y	Y	Y	Y
8 Rogers	?	N	Y	N
9 Peters	Y	Y	Y	Y
10 Miller	N	N	Y	N
11 McCotter	N	N	Y	N
12 Levin	Y	Y	Y	Y
13 Kilpatrick	+	Y	Y	Y
14 Conyers	Y	Y	Y	Y
15 Dingell	Y	Y	Y	Y
MINNESOTA				
1 Walz	Y	Y	Y	Y
2 Kline	N	N	N	N
3 Paulsen	N	N	Y	N
4 McCollum	Y	Y	Y	Y

	513	518	554	558
5 Ellison	Y	Y	Y	Y
6 Bachmann	N	N	N	N
7 Peterson	N	Y	Y	Y
8 Oberstar	Y	Y	Y	Y
MISSISSIPPI				
1 Childers	N	Y	Y	Y
2 Thompson	Y	Y	Y	Y
3 Harper	N	N	Y	N
4 Taylor	Y	N	Y	Y
MISSOURI				
1 Clay	Y	Y	Y	Y
2 Akin	–	N	Y	N
3 Carnahan	Y	Y	Y	Y
4 Skelton	N	Y	Y	Y
5 Cleaver	Y	Y	Y	Y
6 Graves	N	N	Y	?
7 Blunt	?	?	?	?
8 Emerson	N	N	Y	N
9 Luetkemeyer	N	N	Y	N
MONTANA				
AL Rehberg	N	N	Y	N
NEBRASKA				
1 Fortenberry	N	N	Y	N
2 Terry	N	N	Y	N
3 Smith	N	N	N	N
NEVADA				
1 Berkley	Y	Y	Y	Y
2 Heller	N	N	N	N
3 Titus	N	Y	Y	Y
NEW HAMPSHIRE				
1 Shea-Porter	Y	Y	Y	Y
2 Hodes	Y	Y	Y	Y
NEW JERSEY				
1 Andrews	Y	Y	Y	Y
2 LoBiondo	N	N	Y	N
3 Adler	Y	Y	Y	Y
4 Smith	N	N	Y	N
5 Garrett	N	N	N	N
6 Pallone	Y	Y	Y	Y
7 Lance	N	N	N	N
8 Pascrell	Y	Y	Y	Y
9 Rothman	Y	Y	Y	Y
10 Payne	Y	Y	Y	Y
11 Frelinghuysen	N	N	N	N
12 Holt	Y	Y	Y	Y
13 Sires	Y	Y	Y	Y
NEW MEXICO				
1 Heinrich	Y	Y	Y	Y
2 Teague	N	Y	Y	Y
3 Luján	Y	Y	Y	Y
NEW YORK				
1 Bishop	Y	Y	Y	Y
2 Israel	Y	Y	Y	Y
3 King	N	N	N	N
4 McCarthy	Y	Y	Y	Y
5 Ackerman	Y	Y	Y	Y
6 Meeks	Y	Y	Y	Y
7 Crowley	Y	Y	Y	Y
8 Nadler	Y	Y	Y	Y
9 Weiner	Y	Y	Y	Y
10 Towns	Y	Y	Y	Y
11 Clarke	Y	Y	Y	Y
12 Velázquez	Y	Y	Y	Y
13 McMahon	N	Y	Y	Y
14 Maloney	Y	Y	Y	Y
15 Rangel	Y	Y	Y	Y
16 Serrano	Y	Y	Y	Y
17 Engel	Y	Y	Y	Y
18 Lowey	Y	Y	Y	Y
19 Hall	Y	Y	Y	Y
20 Murphy	Y	Y	Y	Y
21 Tonko	Y	Y	Y	Y
22 Hinchey	Y	Y	Y	Y
23 Owens	Y	Y	Y	Y
24 Arcuri	Y	Y	Y	Y
25 Maffei	Y	Y	Y	Y
26 Lee	N	N	Y	N
27 Higgins	Y	Y	Y	Y
28 Slaughter	Y	Y	Y	Y
29 Vacant				
NORTH CAROLINA				
1 Butterfield	Y	Y	Y	Y
2 Etheridge	Y	Y	Y	Y
3 Jones	N	?	Y	N
4 Price	Y	Y	Y	Y

	513	518	554	558
5 Foxx	N	N	Y	N
6 Coble	N	N	Y	N
7 McIntyre	Y	Y	Y	Y
8 Kissell	Y	Y	Y	Y
9 Myrick	N	N	Y	N
10 McHenry	N	N	Y	N
11 Shuler	Y	Y	Y	Y
12 Watt	Y	Y	Y	Y
13 Miller	Y	Y	Y	Y
NORTH DAKOTA				
AL Pomeroy	N	Y	Y	Y
OHIO				
1 Driehaus	Y	Y	Y	Y
2 Schmidt	N	N	N	N
3 Turner	N	N	Y	N
4 Jordan	N	N	N	N
5 Latta	N	N	N	N
6 Wilson	N	N	Y	N
7 Austria	N	N	Y	N
8 Boehner	N	N	N	N
9 Kaptur	Y	Y	Y	Y
10 Kucinich	Y	Y	Y	Y
11 Fudge	Y	Y	Y	Y
12 Tiberi	N	N	Y	N
13 Sutton	Y	Y	Y	Y
14 LaTourette	N	?	Y	N
15 Kilroy	Y	Y	Y	Y
16 Boccieri	N	Y	Y	N
17 Ryan	Y	Y	Y	Y
18 Space	N	Y	Y	Y
OKLAHOMA				
1 Sullivan	N	N	N	N
2 Boren	N	Y	Y	Y
3 Lucas	N	N	Y	N
4 Cole	N	N	Y	N
5 Fallin	N	N	?	?
OREGON				
1 Wu	Y	Y	Y	N
2 Walden	N	N	N	N
3 Blumenauer	Y	Y	Y	Y
4 DeFazio	Y	Y	Y	Y
5 Schrader	Y	Y	Y	Y
PENNSYLVANIA				
1 Brady	Y	Y	Y	Y
2 Fattah	Y	Y	Y	Y
3 Dahlkemper	Y	Y	Y	Y
4 Altmire	Y	Y	Y	Y
5 Thompson	N	N	Y	N
6 Gerlach	N	N	Y	N
7 Sestak	Y	Y	Y	Y
8 Murphy, P.	Y	Y	Y	Y
9 Shuster	N	N	Y	N
10 Carney	?	Y	Y	N
11 Kanjorski	Y	Y	Y	Y
12 Critz	Y	Y	Y	Y
13 Schwartz	Y	Y	Y	Y
14 Doyle	Y	Y	Y	Y
15 Dent	N	N	Y	N
16 Pitts	N	N	Y	N
17 Holden	N	Y	Y	N
18 Murphy, T.	N	N	Y	N
19 Platts	N	N	Y	N
RHODE ISLAND				
1 Kennedy	Y	Y	Y	Y
2 Langevin	Y	Y	Y	Y
SOUTH CAROLINA				
1 Brown	?	N	Y	N
2 Wilson	N	N	Y	N
3 Barrett	–	N	Y	N
4 Inglis	N	N	Y	N
5 Spratt	Y	Y	Y	Y
6 Clyburn	Y	Y	Y	Y
SOUTH DAKOTA				
AL Herseth Sandlin	N	Y	Y	Y
TENNESSEE				
1 Roe	N	N	Y	N
2 Duncan	N	N	Y	N
3 Wamp	?	?	Y	N
4 Davis	N	Y	Y	Y
5 Cooper	N	N	Y	Y
6 Gordon	Y	Y	Y	Y
7 Blackburn	N	N	N	N
8 Tanner	N	?	Y	Y
9 Cohen	Y	Y	Y	Y

	513	518	554	558
TEXAS				
1 Gohmert	N	N	N	N
2 Poe	N	N	N	N
3 Johnson, S.	?	N	N	N
4 Hall	N	N	N	N
5 Hensarling	N	N	N	N
6 Barton	N	N	N	N
7 Culberson	N	N	N	N
8 Brady	N	N	N	N
9 Green, A.	Y	Y	Y	Y
10 McCaul	N	N	N	N
11 Conaway	N	N	N	N
12 Granger	N	N	N	N
13 Thornberry	N	N	N	N
14 Paul	N	N	N	N
15 Hinojosa	N	?	Y	Y
16 Reyes	?	Y	Y	Y
17 Edwards	N	Y	Y	Y
18 Jackson Lee	N	Y	Y	Y
19 Neugebauer	N	?	N	N
20 Gonzalez	N	Y	Y	Y
21 Smith	N	N	N	N
22 Olson	N	N	N	N
23 Rodriguez	N	Y	Y	Y
24 Marchant	N	N	N	N
25 Doggett	Y	Y	Y	Y
26 Burgess	N	N	N	N
27 Ortiz	N	Y	Y	Y
28 Cuellar	N	Y	N	Y
29 Green, G.	N	Y	Y	Y
30 Johnson, E.	Y	Y	Y	Y
31 Carter	N	N	N	N
32 Sessions	N	N	N	N
UTAH				
1 Bishop	N	N	Y	N
2 Matheson	N	Y	Y	Y
3 Chaffetz	N	N	N	N
VERMONT				
AL Welch	Y	Y	Y	N
VIRGINIA				
1 Wittman	N	N	Y	N
2 Nye	N	Y	Y	Y
3 Scott	Y	Y	Y	Y
4 Forbes	N	N	Y	N
5 Perriello	N	Y	Y	Y
6 Goodlatte	N	N	Y	N
7 Cantor	N	N	N	N
8 Moran	Y	Y	Y	Y
9 Boucher	N	Y	Y	Y
10 Wolf	N	N	Y	N
11 Connolly	Y	Y	Y	Y
WASHINGTON				
1 Inslee	Y	Y	Y	Y
2 Larsen	Y	Y	N	Y
3 Baird	Y	Y	Y	Y
4 Hastings	N	N	N	N
5 McMorris Rodgers	N	N	N	N
6 Dicks	Y	Y	Y	Y
7 McDermott	Y	Y	Y	Y
8 Reichert	N	N	N	N
9 Smith	Y	Y	Y	Y
WEST VIRGINIA				
1 Mollohan	Y	Y	Y	Y
2 Capito	N	N	Y	N
3 Rahall	Y	Y	Y	Y
WISCONSIN				
1 Ryan	N	N	N	N
2 Baldwin	Y	Y	Y	Y
3 Kind	Y	Y	Y	Y
4 Moore	Y	Y	Y	Y
5 Sensenbrenner	N	N	N	N
6 Petri	N	N	Y	N
7 Obey	?	Y	Y	Y
8 Kagen	Y	Y	Y	Y
WYOMING				
AL Lummis	N	N	N	N
DELEGATES				
Faleomavaega (A.S.)				
Norton (D.C.)				
Bordallo (Guam)				
Sablan (N. Marianas)				
Pierluisi (P.R.)				
Christensen (V.I.)				

IN THE HOUSE | By Vote Number

561. **S 3729. NASA Reauthorization/Passage.** Gordon, D-Tenn., motion to suspend the rules and pass the bill that would authorize $58.4 billion for NASA in fiscal 2011 through 2013, including $1.6 billion for commercial crew and cargo systems development, $6.9 billion for a NASA space launch system, $3.9 billion for a crew vehicle and $1.6 billion for space shuttle flight operations. It would allow for one additional shuttle flight, support using the International Space Station through at least 2020 and authorize $8.9 billion for the station. Motion agreed to, thus clearing the bill for the president, 304-118: D 185-64; R 119-54. A two-thirds majority of those present and voting (282 in this case) is required for passage under suspension of the rules. Sept. 29, 2010. *(Story, p. C-13)*

625. **HR 5281. Immigration Policy Revisions/Motion to Concur.** Conyers, D-Mich., motion to concur in Senate amendments to the bill with a House amendment that would add language to allow the Homeland Security Department to grant conditional non-immigrant status to the undocumented children of illegal immigrants if they meet certain requirements, including having been in the United States continuously for more than five years, been younger than 16 when they entered the country and been admitted to a U.S. college or university or enlisted in the military. The individuals would have to pay a $525 application surcharge and a subsequent fee and could be eligible to apply for legal permanent status after 10 years. Motion agreed to, thus sent to the Senate, 216-198: D 208-38; R 8-160. A "yea" was a vote in support of the president's position. Dec. 8, 2010. *(Story, p. C-14)*

647. **HR 4853. Tax Rates Extensions/Motion to Concur.** Levin, D-Mich., motion to concur in the Senate amendment to the House amendment to the Senate amendment to the bill that would extend the 2001- and 2003-enacted tax cuts for all taxpayers for two years and revive the lapsed estate tax, setting the tax rate at 35 percent on the value of estates in excess of $5 million for 2011 and 2012. It would also continue expanded unemployment insurance benefits for 13 months and cut the employee portion of the Social Security tax by 2 percentage points. Motion agreed to, thus clearing the bill for the president, 277-148: D 139-112; R 138-36. A "yea" was a vote in support of the president's position. Dec. 17, 2010 (in the session that began in the Congressional Record dated Dec. 16, 2010). *(Story, p. C-14)*

[1] The Speaker votes only at her discretion.

[2] Rep. Mark Steven Kirk, R-Ill., resigned Nov. 29 to assume the Senate seat he won in a Nov. 2 special election. The last vote for which Kirk was eligible was vote 580.

[3] Rep. Marlin Stutzman, R-Ind., was sworn in Nov. 16 to fill the vacancy created by the May 21 resignation of Republican Mark Souder. The first vote for which Stutzman was eligible was vote 571; the last vote for which Souder was eligible was vote 290.

[4] Rep. Tom Reed, R-N.Y., was sworn in Nov. 18 to fill the vacancy created by the March 8 resignation of Democrat Eric Massa. The first vote for which Reed was eligible was vote 580; the last vote for which Massa was eligible was vote 91.

	561	625	647
ALABAMA			
1 **Bonner**	Y	N	Y
2 Bright	Y	N	Y
3 **Rogers**	Y	N	N
4 **Aderholt**	Y	N	Y
5 **Griffith**	Y	?	Y
6 **Bachus**	Y	N	Y
7 Davis	Y	Y	Y
ALASKA			
AL **Young**	N	N	Y
ARIZONA			
1 Kirkpatrick	Y	?	Y
2 **Franks**	Y	N	N
3 **Shadegg**	Y	N	N
4 Pastor	Y	Y	Y
5 Mitchell	Y	Y	Y
6 **Flake**	N	N	N
7 Grijalva	N	Y	N
8 Giffords	N	Y	Y
ARKANSAS			
1 Berry	N	?	?
2 Snyder	N	Y	Y
3 **Boozman**	Y	N	Y
4 Ross	Y	N	Y
CALIFORNIA			
1 Thompson	Y	Y	N
2 **Herger**	N	N	Y
3 **Lungren**	Y	N	Y
4 **McClintock**	Y	N	Y
5 Matsui	Y	Y	N
6 Woolsey	N	Y	N
7 Miller, George	Y	Y	N
8 Pelosi [1]		Y	
9 Lee	N	Y	N
10 Garamendi	Y	Y	N
11 McNerney	Y	Y	Y
12 Speier	Y	Y	N
13 Stark	N	Y	N
14 Eshoo	Y	Y	N
15 Honda	Y	Y	N
16 Lofgren	Y	Y	N
17 Farr	Y	Y	N
18 Cardoza	Y	Y	Y
19 **Radanovich**	?	?	Y
20 Costa	Y	Y	Y
21 **Nunes**	Y	N	Y
22 **McCarthy**	Y	N	Y
23 Capps	Y	Y	N
24 **Gallegly**	Y	N	Y
25 **McKeon**	Y	N	Y
26 **Dreier**	Y	N	Y
27 Sherman	Y	Y	Y
28 Berman	N	Y	Y
29 Schiff	Y	?	Y
30 Waxman	N	Y	Y
31 Becerra	Y	Y	N
32 Chu	Y	N	N
33 Watson	Y	Y	N
34 Roybal-Allard	Y	Y	N
35 Waters	Y	Y	N
36 Harman	Y	Y	Y
37 Richardson	?	Y	Y
38 Napolitano	Y	Y	N
39 Sánchez, Linda	Y	Y	N
40 **Royce**	Y	N	Y
41 **Lewis**	Y	N	Y
42 **Miller, Gary**	Y	N	Y
43 Baca	Y	Y	Y
44 **Calvert**	Y	N	Y
45 **Bono Mack**	Y	N	Y
46 **Rohrabacher**	Y	N	Y
47 Sanchez, Loretta	Y	Y	N
48 **Campbell**	Y	N	N
49 **Issa**	Y	N	Y
50 **Bilbray**	N	?	Y
51 Filner	Y	Y	N
52 **Hunter**	Y	N	Y
53 Davis	Y	Y	Y

	561	625	647
COLORADO			
1 DeGette	Y	Y	N
2 Polis	Y	Y	Y
3 Salazar	Y	Y	Y
4 Markey	Y	Y	Y
5 **Lamborn**	Y	N	N
6 **Coffman**	Y	N	Y
7 Perlmutter	Y	Y	N
CONNECTICUT			
1 Larson	Y	Y	N
2 Courtney	N	Y	Y
3 DeLauro	Y	Y	N
4 Himes	Y	Y	Y
5 Murphy	Y	Y	N
DELAWARE			
AL **Castle**	N	Y	Y
FLORIDA			
1 **Miller**	Y	N	Y
2 Boyd	Y	Y	N
3 Brown	Y	Y	Y
4 **Crenshaw**	Y	N	Y
5 **Brown-Waite**	Y	N	Y
6 **Stearns**	Y	N	Y
7 **Mica**	Y	N	Y
8 Grayson	Y	Y	N
9 **Bilirakis**	Y	N	Y
10 **Young**	?	N	?
11 Castor	Y	Y	Y
12 **Putnam**	Y	N	Y
13 **Buchanan**	Y	N	Y
14 **Mack**	N	N	N
15 **Posey**	Y	N	Y
16 **Rooney**	Y	N	Y
17 Meek	Y	Y	Y
18 **Ros-Lehtinen**	Y	Y	Y
19 Deutch	Y	Y	Y
20 Wasserman Schultz	Y	Y	Y
21 **Diaz-Balart, L.**	Y	Y	Y
22 Klein	Y	Y	Y
23 Hastings	Y	Y	Y
24 Kosmas	Y	Y	Y
25 **Diaz-Balart, M.**	Y	Y	Y
GEORGIA			
1 **Kingston**	N	N	N
2 Bishop	Y	Y	Y
3 **Westmoreland**	N	N	N
4 Johnson	Y	Y	Y
5 Lewis	N	Y	N
6 **Price**	N	N	Y
7 **Linder**	Y	N	N
8 Marshall	Y	?	Y
9 **Graves**	N	N	N
10 **Broun**	Y	N	N
11 **Gingrey**	Y	?	Y
12 Barrow	N	N	Y
13 Scott	Y	Y	Y
HAWAII			
1 **Djou**	Y	Y	Y
2 Hirono	N	Y	N
IDAHO			
1 Minnick	Y	Y	Y
2 **Simpson**	N	N	N
ILLINOIS			
1 Rush	Y	Y	N
2 Jackson	N	Y	N
3 Lipinski	Y	N	Y
4 Gutierrez	Y	Y	Y
5 Quigley	Y	Y	Y
6 **Roskam**	N	N	Y
7 Davis	Y	Y	Y
8 Bean	N	Y	Y
9 Schakowsky	Y	Y	Y
10 Kirk [2]		Y	
Vacant [2]			
11 Halvorson	Y	Y	Y
12 Costello	Y	N	N
13 **Biggert**	Y	N	Y
14 Foster	Y	Y	Y
15 **Johnson**	N	N	Y

KEY **Republicans** Democrats

Y Voted for (yea)	X Paired against
# Paired for	– Announced against
+ Announced for	P Voted "present"
N Voted against (nay)	

C Voted "present" to avoid possible conflict of interest

? Did not vote or otherwise make a position known

	561	625	647
16 Manzullo	Y	N	Y
17 Hare	Y	Y	Y
18 Schock	Y	N	Y
19 Shimkus	N	N	Y
INDIANA			
1 Visclosky	N	N	N
2 Donnelly	Y	N	Y
3 Stutzman[3]		–	Y
4 Buyer	Y	?	Y
5 Burton	Y	N	Y
6 Pence	Y	N	N
7 Carson	Y	Y	Y
8 Ellsworth	Y	N	Y
9 Hill	N	Y	Y
IOWA			
1 Braley	Y	Y	N
2 Loebsack	Y	Y	Y
3 Boswell	N	Y	Y
4 Latham	Y	N	Y
5 King	Y	N	N
KANSAS			
1 Moran	Y	N	N
2 Jenkins	Y	N	Y
3 Moore	Y	Y	Y
4 Tiahrt	Y	N	Y
KENTUCKY			
1 Whitfield	Y	N	Y
2 Guthrie	Y	N	Y
3 Yarmuth	N	Y	N
4 Davis	Y	N	Y
5 Rogers	Y	N	Y
6 Chandler	N	N	Y
LOUISIANA			
1 Scalise	Y	N	Y
2 Cao	Y	Y	Y
3 Melancon	Y	Y	N
4 Fleming	Y	N	N
5 Alexander	Y	N	Y
6 Cassidy	Y	N	Y
7 Boustany	Y	N	Y
MAINE			
1 Pingree	N	Y	N
2 Michaud	N	Y	N
MARYLAND			
1 Kratovil	Y	N	Y
2 Ruppersberger	Y	Y	Y
3 Sarbanes	Y	Y	Y
4 Edwards	N	Y	N
5 Hoyer	Y	Y	Y
6 Bartlett	Y	N	Y
7 Cummings	Y	Y	Y
8 Van Hollen	Y	Y	Y
MASSACHUSETTS			
1 Olver	Y	Y	N
2 Neal	Y	Y	N
3 McGovern	N	Y	N
4 Frank	N	Y	N
5 Tsongas	Y	Y	N
6 Tierney	N	Y	N
7 Markey	Y	Y	N
8 Capuano	N	Y	N
9 Lynch	N	Y	N
10 Delahunt	?	?	Y
MICHIGAN			
1 Stupak	Y	N	N
2 Hoekstra	N	N	N
3 Ehlers	N	Y	Y
4 Camp	N	N	Y
5 Kildee	Y	Y	Y
6 Upton	N	N	Y
7 Schauer	Y	Y	Y
8 Rogers	N	N	Y
9 Peters	Y	Y	Y
10 Miller	N	N	Y
11 McCotter	N	N	N
12 Levin	Y	Y	Y
13 Kilpatrick	Y	?	N
14 Conyers	N	Y	N
15 Dingell	Y	Y	Y
MINNESOTA			
1 Walz	N	Y	Y
2 Kline	Y	N	Y
3 Paulsen	N	N	Y
4 McCollum	Y	Y	Y

	561	625	647
5 Ellison	Y	Y	N
6 Bachmann	Y	N	N
7 Peterson	Y	N	Y
8 Oberstar	N	Y	Y
MISSISSIPPI			
1 Childers	N	N	Y
2 Thompson	N	Y	N
3 Harper	Y	N	Y
4 Taylor	Y	N	N
MISSOURI			
1 Clay	N	Y	Y
2 Akin	Y	N	Y
3 Carnahan	Y	Y	Y
4 Skelton	Y	Y	Y
5 Cleaver	Y	Y	N
6 Graves	?	N	Y
7 Blunt	?	?	Y
8 Emerson	N	N	Y
9 Luetkemeyer	Y	N	Y
MONTANA			
AL Rehberg	Y	N	N
NEBRASKA			
1 Fortenberry	Y	N	N
2 Terry	N	N	Y
3 Smith	Y	N	Y
NEVADA			
1 Berkley	Y	Y	Y
2 Heller	N	N	N
3 Titus	Y	Y	Y
NEW HAMPSHIRE			
1 Shea-Porter	N	Y	N
2 Hodes	N	Y	Y
NEW JERSEY			
1 Andrews	N	Y	Y
2 LoBiondo	Y	N	Y
3 Adler	N	Y	Y
4 Smith	Y	N	Y
5 Garrett	N	N	N
6 Pallone	Y	Y	Y
7 Lance	N	N	Y
8 Pascrell	Y	Y	Y
9 Rothman	Y	Y	Y
10 Payne	N	Y	N
11 Frelinghuysen	N	N	Y
12 Holt	N	Y	N
13 Sires	Y	Y	Y
NEW MEXICO			
1 Heinrich	Y	Y	N
2 Teague	Y	Y	Y
3 Luján	Y	Y	N
NEW YORK			
1 Bishop	Y	Y	Y
2 Israel	N	Y	Y
3 King	Y	N	Y
4 McCarthy	Y	Y	+
5 Ackerman	Y	Y	N
6 Meeks	Y	Y	Y
7 Crowley	N	Y	Y
8 Nadler	Y	Y	N
9 Weiner	Y	Y	N
10 Towns	Y	Y	N
11 Clarke	N	Y	N
12 Velázquez	Y	Y	N
13 McMahon	+	Y	Y
14 Maloney	Y	Y	N
15 Rangel	Y	Y	N
16 Serrano	Y	Y	N
17 Engel	Y	Y	N
18 Lowey	Y	Y	Y
19 Hall	Y	Y	Y
20 Murphy	Y	Y	Y
21 Tonko	Y	Y	N
22 Hinchey	N	Y	N
23 Owens	N	N	Y
24 Arcuri	Y	N	Y
25 Maffei	N	Y	Y
26 Lee	Y	N	Y
27 Higgins	Y	Y	N
28 Slaughter	Y	Y	N
29 Reed[4]		N	Y
NORTH CAROLINA			
1 Butterfield	N	Y	N
2 Etheridge	?	Y	Y
3 Jones	N	N	Y
4 Price	Y	Y	Y

	561	625	647
5 Foxx	Y	N	N
6 Coble	N	N	Y
7 McIntyre	Y	N	Y
8 Kissell	Y	N	Y
9 Myrick	N	N	Y
10 McHenry	Y	N	Y
11 Shuler	Y	N	Y
12 Watt	N	Y	Y
13 Miller	N	Y	N
NORTH DAKOTA			
AL Pomeroy	Y	Y	N
OHIO			
1 Driehaus	Y	Y	Y
2 Schmidt	N	N	N
3 Turner	N	N	Y
4 Jordan	N	N	N
5 Latta	N	N	Y
6 Wilson	N	N	Y
7 Austria	N	N	Y
8 Boehner	N	N	Y
9 Kaptur	Y	N	N
10 Kucinich	N	Y	Y
11 Fudge	Y	Y	N
12 Tiberi	N	N	Y
13 Sutton	Y	Y	Y
14 LaTourette	N	N	Y
15 Kilroy	N	Y	N
16 Boccieri	Y	N	Y
17 Ryan	Y	Y	Y
18 Space	Y	N	Y
OKLAHOMA			
1 Sullivan	N	N	N
2 Boren	Y	N	Y
3 Lucas	Y	N	Y
4 Cole	Y	N	Y
5 Fallin	?	?	Y
OREGON			
1 Wu	N	?	N
2 Walden	N	N	Y
3 Blumenauer	Y	Y	N
4 DeFazio	N	Y	N
5 Schrader	Y	N	N
PENNSYLVANIA			
1 Brady	Y	Y	Y
2 Fattah	Y	Y	Y
3 Dahlkemper	N	N	N
4 Altmire	Y	N	Y
5 Thompson	Y	N	Y
6 Gerlach	Y	Y	Y
7 Sestak	Y	Y	Y
8 Murphy, P.	Y	Y	Y
9 Shuster	N	N	Y
10 Carney	Y	Y	Y
11 Kanjorski	Y	N	Y
12 Critz	Y	N	Y
13 Schwartz	Y	Y	Y
14 Doyle	Y	Y	Y
15 Dent	Y	N	Y
16 Pitts	Y	N	Y
17 Holden	Y	N	Y
18 Murphy, T.	Y	N	Y
19 Platts	Y	N	Y
RHODE ISLAND			
1 Kennedy	Y	Y	Y
2 Langevin	Y	Y	Y
SOUTH CAROLINA			
1 Brown	Y	N	?
2 Wilson	N	N	N
3 Barrett	N	N	Y
4 Inglis	N	Y	Y
5 Spratt	Y	Y	Y
6 Clyburn	Y	Y	N
SOUTH DAKOTA			
AL Herseth Sandlin	Y	Y	Y
TENNESSEE			
1 Roe	Y	N	Y
2 Duncan	N	N	Y
3 Wamp	Y	N	?
4 Davis	Y	Y	Y
5 Cooper	Y	Y	N
6 Gordon	Y	Y	Y
7 Blackburn	N	N	Y
8 Tanner	N	Y	N
9 Cohen	N	+	N

	561	625	647
TEXAS			
1 Gohmert	Y	N	N
2 Poe	Y	N	N
3 Johnson, S.	Y	N	Y
4 Hall	Y	N	Y
5 Hensarling	N	N	Y
6 Barton	Y	N	N
7 Culberson	Y	N	Y
8 Brady	Y	N	Y
9 Green, A.	Y	Y	Y
10 McCaul	Y	N	Y
11 Conaway	Y	N	Y
12 Granger	Y	–	+
13 Thornberry	Y	N	Y
14 Paul	N	N	Y
15 Hinojosa	?	Y	Y
16 Reyes	Y	Y	N
17 Edwards	Y	N	Y
18 Jackson Lee	Y	Y	N
19 Neugebauer	Y	N	Y
20 Gonzalez	Y	Y	Y
21 Smith	Y	N	Y
22 Olson	Y	N	Y
23 Rodriguez	Y	Y	N
24 Marchant	Y	–	–
25 Doggett	Y	Y	Y
26 Burgess	Y	N	N
27 Ortiz	Y	Y	Y
28 Cuellar	Y	Y	Y
29 Green, G.	Y	Y	Y
30 Johnson, E.	Y	Y	?
31 Carter	Y	N	Y
32 Sessions	Y	N	Y
UTAH			
1 Bishop	Y	N	Y
2 Matheson	Y	N	Y
3 Chaffetz	Y	N	N
VERMONT			
AL Welch	Y	Y	N
VIRGINIA			
1 Wittman	Y	N	Y
2 Nye	Y	N	Y
3 Scott	Y	Y	N
4 Forbes	Y	N	Y
5 Perriello	Y	Y	Y
6 Goodlatte	N	N	Y
7 Cantor	Y	N	Y
8 Moran	Y	N	Y
9 Boucher	Y	N	Y
10 Wolf	Y	N	Y
11 Connolly	Y	Y	Y
WASHINGTON			
1 Inslee	Y	Y	N
2 Larsen	Y	Y	Y
3 Baird	N	N	N
4 Hastings	Y	N	Y
5 McMorris Rodgers	Y	–	Y
6 Dicks	Y	Y	Y
7 McDermott	N	Y	N
8 Reichert	Y	N	Y
9 Smith	N	Y	N
WEST VIRGINIA			
1 Mollohan	Y	?	Y
2 Capito	Y	N	Y
3 Rahall	Y	N	Y
WISCONSIN			
1 Ryan	N	N	Y
2 Baldwin	N	Y	N
3 Kind	Y	Y	N
4 Moore	N	Y	N
5 Sensenbrenner	N	N	Y
6 Petri	Y	Y	N
7 Obey	Y	Y	N
8 Kagen	N	Y	N
WYOMING			
AL Lummis	N	N	Y
DELEGATES			
Faleomavaega (A.S.)			
Norton (D.C.)			
Bordallo (Guam)			
Sablan (N. Marianas)			
Pierluisi (P.R.)			
Christensen (V.I.)			

Appendix D

TEXTS

Obama Outlines Plans for Economy, Praises American Spirit of Resilience

The following is the White House transcript of President Obama's State of the Union address, delivered to a joint session of Congress on Jan. 27, 2010.

MADAME SPEAKER, VICE President Biden, members of Congress, distinguished guests, and fellow Americans:

Our Constitution declares that from time to time, the President shall give to Congress information about the state of our union. For 220 years, our leaders have fulfilled this duty. They've done so during periods of prosperity and tranquility. And they've done so in the midst of war and depression; at moments of great strife and great struggle.

It's tempting to look back on these moments and assume that our progress was inevitable — that America was always destined to succeed. But when the Union was turned back at Bull Run, and the Allies first landed at Omaha Beach, victory was very much in doubt. When the market crashed on Black Tuesday, and civil rights marchers were beaten on Bloody Sunday, the future was anything but certain. These were the times that tested the courage of our convictions, and the strength of our union. And despite all our divisions and disagreements, our hesitations and our fears, America prevailed because we chose to move forward as one nation, as one people.

Again, we are tested. And again, we must answer history's call.

One year ago, I took office amid two wars, an economy rocked by a severe recession, a financial system on the verge of collapse, and a government deeply in debt. Experts from across the political spectrum warned that if we did not act, we might face a second depression. So we acted — immediately and aggressively. And one year later, the worst of the storm has passed.

But the devastation remains. One in 10 Americans still cannot find work. Many businesses have shuttered. Home values have declined. Small towns and rural communities have been hit especially hard. And for those who'd already known poverty, life has become that much harder.

This recession has also compounded the burdens that America's families have been dealing with for decades — the burden of working harder and longer for less, of being unable to save enough to retire or help kids with college.

So I know the anxieties that are out there right now. They're not new. These struggles are the reason I ran for president. These struggles are what I've witnessed for years in places like Elkhart, Ind., Galesburg, Ill. I hear about them in the letters that I read each night. The toughest to read are those written by children — asking why they have to move from their home, asking when their mom or dad will be able to go back to work.

For these Americans and so many others, change has not come fast enough. Some are frustrated; some are angry. They don't understand why it seems like bad behavior on Wall Street is rewarded, but hard work on Main Street isn't; or why Washington has been unable or unwilling to solve any of our problems. They're tired of the partisanship and the shouting and the pettiness. They know we can't afford it. Not now.

So we face big and difficult challenges. And what the American people hope — what they deserve — is for all of us, Democrats and Republicans, to work through our differences, to overcome the numbing weight of our politics. For while the people who sent us here have different backgrounds, different stories, different beliefs, the anxieties they face are the same. The aspirations they hold are shared: a job that pays the bills; a chance to get ahead; most of all, the ability to give their children a better life.

You know what else they share? They share a stubborn resilience in the face of adversity. After one of the most difficult years in our history, they remain busy building cars and teaching kids, starting businesses and going back to school. They're coaching Little League and helping their neighbors. One woman wrote to me and said, "We are strained but hopeful, struggling but encouraged."

It's because of this spirit — this great decency and great strength — that I have never been more hopeful about America's future than I am tonight. Despite our hardships, our union is strong. We do not give up. We do not quit. We do not allow fear or division to break our spirit. In this new decade, it's time the American people get a government that matches their decency, that embodies their strength.

And tonight, tonight I'd like to talk about how together we can deliver on that promise.

REVIVING THE ECONOMY

It begins with our economy.

Our most urgent task upon taking office was to shore up the same banks that helped cause this crisis. It was not easy to do. And if there's one thing that has unified Democrats and Republicans, and everybody in between, it's that we all hated the bank bailout. I hated it — I hated it. You hated it. It was about as popular as a root canal.

But when I ran for president, I promised I wouldn't just do what was popular — I would do what was necessary. And if we had allowed the meltdown of the financial system, unemployment might be double what it is today. More businesses would certainly have closed. More homes would have surely been lost.

So I supported the last administration's efforts to create the financial rescue program. And when we took that program over, we made it more transparent and more accountable. And as a result, the markets are now stabilized, and we've recovered most of the money we spent on the banks. Most, but not all.

To recover the rest, I've proposed a fee on the biggest banks. Now, I know Wall Street isn't keen on this idea. But if these firms can afford to hand out big bonuses again, they can afford a modest fee to pay back the taxpayers who rescued them in their time of need.

Now, as we stabilized the financial system, we also took steps to get our economy growing again, save as many jobs as possible and help Americans who had become unemployed.

That's why we extended or increased unemployment benefits for more than 18 million Americans, made health insurance 65 percent cheaper for families who get their

coverage through COBRA, and passed 25 different tax cuts.

Now, let me repeat: We cut taxes. We cut taxes for 95 percent of working families. We cut taxes for small businesses. We cut taxes for first-time homebuyers. We cut taxes for parents trying to care for their children. We cut taxes for 8 million Americans paying for college.

I thought I'd get some applause on that one.

As a result, millions of Americans had more to spend on gas and food and other necessities, all of which helped businesses keep more workers. And we haven't raised income taxes by a single dime on a single person. Not a single dime.

Because of the steps we took, there are about 2 million Americans working right now who would otherwise be unemployed. Two hundred thousand work in construction and clean energy; 300,000 are teachers and other education workers. Tens of thousands are cops, firefighters, correctional officers, first-responders. And we're on track to add another 1½ million jobs to this total by the end of the year.

The plan that has made all of this possible, from the tax cuts to the jobs, is the Recovery Act. That's right — the Recovery Act, also known as the stimulus bill. Economists on the left and the right say this bill has helped save jobs and avert disaster. But you don't have to take their word for it. Talk to the small business in Phoenix that will triple its workforce because of the Recovery Act. Talk to the window manufacturer in Philadelphia who said he used to be skeptical about the Recovery Act, until he had to add two more work shifts just because of the business it created. Talk to the single teacher raising two kids who was told by her principal in the last week of school that because of the Recovery Act, she wouldn't be laid off after all.

There are stories like this all across America. And after two years of recession, the economy is growing again. Retirement funds have started to gain back some of their value. Businesses are beginning to invest again, and slowly some are starting to hire again.

But I realize that for every success story, there are other stories, of men and women who wake up with the anguish of not knowing where their next paycheck will come from; who send out résumés week after week and hear nothing in response. That is why jobs must be our number one focus in 2010, and that's why I'm calling for a new jobs bill tonight.

Now, the true engine of job creation in this country will always be America's businesses. But government can create the conditions necessary for businesses to expand and hire more workers.

SMALL BUSINESSES

We should start where most new jobs do — in small businesses, companies that begin when — companies that begin when an entrepreneur — when an entrepreneur takes a chance on a dream, or a worker decides it's time she became her own boss. Through sheer grit and determination, these companies have weathered the recession and they're ready to grow. But when you talk to small-business owners in places like Allentown, Pa., or Elyria, Ohio, you find out that even though banks on Wall Street are lending again, they're mostly lending to bigger companies. Financing remains difficult for small-business owners across the country, even those that are making a profit.

So tonight, I'm proposing that we take $30 billion of the money Wall Street banks have repaid and use it to help community banks give small businesses the credit they need to stay afloat. I'm also proposing a new small-business tax credit — one that will go to over 1 million small businesses who hire new workers or raise wages. While we're at it, let's also eliminate all capital gains taxes on small-business investment, and provide a tax incentive for all large businesses and all small businesses to invest in new plants and equipment.

Next, we can put Americans to work today building the infrastructure of tomorrow. From the first railroads to the Interstate Highway System, our nation has always been built to compete. There's no reason Europe or China should have the fastest trains, or the new factories that manufacture clean-energy products.

Tomorrow, I'll visit Tampa, Fla., where workers will soon break ground on a new high-speed railroad funded by the Recovery Act. There are projects like that all across this country that will create jobs and help move our nation's goods, services and information.

We should put more Americans to work building clean-energy facilities and give rebates to Americans who make their homes more energy efficient, which supports clean-energy jobs. And to encourage these and other businesses to stay within our borders, it is time to finally slash the tax breaks for companies that ship our jobs overseas, and give those tax breaks to companies that create jobs right here in the United States of America.

Now, the House has passed a jobs bill that includes some of these steps. As the first order of business this year, I urge the Senate to do the same, and I know they will. They will. People are out of work. They're hurting. They need our help. And I want a jobs bill on my desk without delay.

But the truth is, these steps won't make up for the 7 million jobs that we've lost over the last two years. The only way to move to full employment is to lay a new foundation for long-term economic growth, and finally address the problems that America's families have confronted for years.

We can't afford another so-called economic "expansion" like the one from the last decade — what some call the "lost decade" — where jobs grew more slowly than during any prior expansion; where the income of the average American household declined while the cost of health care and tuition reached record highs; where prosperity was built on a housing bubble and financial speculation.

FINANCIAL REGULATIONS

From the day I took office, I've been told that addressing our larger challenges is too ambitious; such an effort would be too contentious. I've been told that our political system is too gridlocked and that we should just put things on hold for a while.

For those who make these claims, I have one simple question: How long should we wait? How long should America put its future on hold?

You see, Washington has been telling us to wait for decades, even as the problems have grown worse. Meanwhile, China is not waiting to revamp its economy. Germany is not waiting. India is not waiting. These nations — they're not standing still. These nations aren't playing for second place. They're putting more emphasis on math and science. They're rebuilding their infrastructure. They're making serious investments in clean energy because they want those jobs. Well, I do not accept second place for the United States of America.

As hard as it may be, as uncomfortable and contentious as the debates may become, it's time to get serious about fixing the problems that are hampering our growth.

Now, one place to start is serious financial reform. Look, I am not interested in punishing banks. I'm interested in protecting our economy. A strong, healthy financial

market makes it possible for businesses to access credit and create new jobs. It channels the savings of families into investments that raise incomes. But that can only happen if we guard against the same recklessness that nearly brought down our entire economy.

We need to make sure consumers and middle-class families have the information they need to make financial decisions. We can't allow financial institutions, including those that take your deposits, to take risks that threaten the whole economy.

Now, the House has already passed financial reform with many of these changes. And the lobbyists are trying to kill it. But we cannot let them win this fight. And if the bill that ends up on my desk does not meet the test of real reform, I will send it back until we get it right. We've got to get it right.

Next, we need to encourage American innovation. Last year, we made the largest investment in basic research funding in history — an investment that could lead to the world's cheapest solar cells or treatment that kills cancer cells but leaves healthy ones untouched. And no area is more ripe for such innovation than energy. You can see the results of last year's investments in clean energy — in the North Carolina company that will create 1,200 jobs nationwide helping to make advanced batteries; or in the California business that will put a thousand people to work making solar panels.

But to create more of these clean-energy jobs, we need more production, more efficiency, more incentives. And that means building a new generation of safe, clean nuclear power plants in this country. It means making tough decisions about opening new offshore areas for oil and gas development. It means continued investment in advanced biofuels and clean-coal technologies. And, yes, it means passing a comprehensive energy and climate bill with incentives that will finally make clean energy the profitable kind of energy in America.

I am grateful to the House for passing such a bill last year. And this year I'm eager to help advance the bipartisan effort in the Senate.

I know there have been questions about whether we can afford such changes in a tough economy. I know that there are those who disagree with the overwhelming scientific evidence on climate change. But here's the thing — even if you doubt the evidence, — providing incentives for energy efficiency and clean energy are the right thing to do for our future, because the nation that leads the clean-

energy economy will be the nation that leads the global economy. And America must be that nation.

Third, we need to export more of our goods, because the more products we make and sell to other countries, the more jobs we support right here in America. So tonight, we set a new goal: We will double our exports over the next five years, an increase that will support 2 million jobs in America. To help meet this goal, we're launching a National Export Initiative that will help farmers and small businesses increase their exports, and reform export controls consistent with national security.

We have to seek new markets aggressively, just as our competitors are. If America sits on the sidelines while other nations sign trade deals, we will lose the chance to create jobs on our shores. But realizing those benefits also means enforcing those agreements so our trading partners play by the rules. And that's why we'll continue to shape a Doha trade agreement that opens global markets, and why we will strengthen our trade relations in Asia and with key partners like South Korea and Panama and Colombia.

Fourth, we need to invest in the skills and education of our people.

EDUCATIONAL SUCCESS

Now, this year, we've broken through the stalemate between left and right by launching a national competition to improve our schools. And the idea here is simple: Instead of rewarding failure, we only reward success. Instead of funding the status quo, we only invest in reform — reform that raises student achievement, inspires students to excel in math and science, and turns around failing schools that steal the future of too many young Americans, from rural communities to the inner city. In the 21st century, the best anti-poverty program around is a world-class education. And in this country, the success of our children cannot depend more on where they live than on their potential.

When we renew the Elementary and Secondary Education Act, we will work with Congress to expand these reforms to all 50 states. Still, in this economy, a high school diploma no longer guarantees a good job. That's why I urge the Senate to follow the House and pass a bill that will revitalize our community colleges, which are a career pathway to the children of so many working families.

To make college more affordable, this bill will finally end the unwarranted taxpayer subsidies that go to banks for student loans.

Instead, let's take that money and give families a $10,000 tax credit for four years of college and increase Pell grants. And let's tell another 1 million students that when they graduate, they will be required to pay only 10 percent of their income on student loans, and all of their debt will be forgiven after 20 years — and forgiven after 10 years if they choose a career in public service, because in the United States of America, no one should go broke because they chose to go to college.

And by the way, it's time for colleges and universities to get serious about cutting their own costs, because they, too, have a responsibility to help solve this problem.

Now, the price of college tuition is just one of the burdens facing the middle class. That's why last year I asked Vice President Biden to chair a task force on middle-class families. That's why we're nearly doubling the child care tax credit, and making it easier to save for retirement by giving access to every worker a retirement account and expanding the tax credit for those who start a nest egg. That's why we're working to lift the value of a family's single largest investment — their home. The steps we took last year to shore up the housing market have allowed millions of Americans to take out new loans and save an average of $1,500 on mortgage payments.

This year, we will step up refinancing so that homeowners can move into more affordable mortgages. And it is precisely to relieve the burden on middle-class families that we still need health insurance reform. Yes, we do.

Now, let's clear a few things up. I didn't choose to tackle this issue to get some legislative victory under my belt. And by now it should be fairly obvious that I didn't take on health care because it was good politics. I took on health care because of the stories I've heard from Americans with pre-existing conditions whose lives depend on getting coverage; patients who've been denied coverage; families — even those with insurance — who are just one illness away from financial ruin.

After nearly a century of trying — Democratic administrations, Republican administrations — we are closer than ever to bringing more security to the lives of so many Americans. The approach we've taken would protect every American from the worst practices of the insurance industry. It would give small businesses and uninsured Americans a chance to choose an affordable health care plan in a competitive market. It would require every insurance plan to cover preventive care.

And by the way, I want to acknowledge our first lady, Michelle Obama, who this year is creating a national movement to tackle the epidemic of childhood obesity and make kids healthier. Thank you. She gets embarrassed.

Our approach would preserve the right of Americans who have insurance to keep their doctor and their plan. It would reduce costs and premiums for millions of families and businesses. And according to the Congressional Budget Office — the independent organization that both parties have cited as the official scorekeeper for Congress — our approach would bring down the deficit by as much as $1 trillion over the next two decades.

Still, this is a complex issue, and the longer it was debated, the more skeptical people became. I take my share of the blame for not explaining it more clearly to the American people. And I know that with all the lobbying and horse-trading, the process left most Americans wondering, "What's in it for me?"

But I also know this problem is not going away. By the time I'm finished speaking tonight, more Americans will have lost their health insurance. Millions will lose it this year. Our deficit will grow. Premiums will go up. Patients will be denied the care they need. Small-business owners will continue to drop coverage altogether. I will not walk away from these Americans, and neither should the people in this chamber.

So, as temperatures cool, I want everyone to take another look at the plan we've proposed. There's a reason why many doctors, nurses, and health care experts who know our system best consider this approach a vast improvement over the status quo. But if anyone from either party has a better approach that will bring down premiums, bring down the deficit, cover the uninsured, strengthen Medicare for seniors and stop insurance company abuses, let me know. Let me know. Let me know. I'm eager to see it.

Here's what I ask Congress, though: Don't walk away from reform. Not now. Not when we are so close. Let us find a way to come together and finish the job for the American people. Let's get it done. Let's get it done.

FACING THE DEBT

Now, even as health care reform would reduce our deficit, it's not enough to dig us out of a massive fiscal hole in which we find ourselves. It's a challenge that makes all others that much harder to solve, and one that's been subject to a lot of political posturing. So let me

start the discussion of government spending by setting the record straight.

At the beginning of the last decade, the year 2000, America had a budget surplus of over $200 billion. By the time I took office, we had a one-year deficit of over $1 trillion and projected deficits of $8 trillion over the next decade. Most of this was the result of not paying for two wars, two tax cuts and an expensive prescription drug program. On top of that, the effects of the recession put a $3 trillion hole in our budget. All this was before I walked in the door.

Now — just stating the facts. Now, if we had taken office in ordinary times, I would have liked nothing more than to start bringing down the deficit. But we took office amid a crisis. And our efforts to prevent a second depression have added another $1 trillion to our national debt. That, too, is a fact.

I'm absolutely convinced that was the right thing to do. But families across the country are tightening their belts and making tough decisions. The federal government should do the same. So tonight, I'm proposing specific steps to pay for the trillion dollars that it took to rescue the economy last year.

Starting in 2011, we are prepared to freeze government spending for three years. Spending related to our national security, Medicare, Medicaid and Social Security will not be affected. But all other discretionary government programs will. Like any cash-strapped family, we will work within a budget to invest in what we need and sacrifice what we don't. And if I have to enforce this discipline by veto, I will.

We will continue to go through the budget, line by line, page by page, to eliminate programs that we can't afford and don't work. We've already identified $20 billion in savings for next year. To help working families, we'll extend our middle-class tax cuts. But at a time of record deficits, we will not continue tax cuts for oil companies, for investment fund managers, and for those making over $250,000 a year. We just can't afford it.

Now, even after paying for what we spent on my watch, we'll still face the massive deficit we had when I took office. More importantly, the cost of Medicare, Medicaid and Social Security will continue to skyrocket. That's why I've called for a bipartisan fiscal commission, modeled on a proposal by Republican Judd Gregg and Democrat Kent Conrad. This can't be one of those Washington gimmicks that lets us pretend we solved a problem. The commission will have to provide a specific set of solutions by a certain deadline.

Now, yesterday the Senate blocked a bill that would have created this commission. So I'll issue an executive order that will allow us to go forward, because I refuse to pass this problem on to another generation of Americans. And when the vote comes tomorrow, the Senate should restore the pay-as-you-go law that was a big reason for why we had record surpluses in the 1990s.

Now, I know that some in my own party will argue that we can't address the deficit or freeze government spending when so many are still hurting. And I agree — which is why this freeze won't take effect until next year, when the economy is stronger. That's how budgeting works. But understand — understand, if we don't take meaningful steps to rein in our debt, it could damage our markets, increase the cost of borrowing, and jeopardize our recovery — all of which would have an even worse effect on our job growth and family incomes.

From some on the right, I expect we'll hear a different argument — that if we just make fewer investments in our people, extend tax cuts including those for the wealthier Americans, eliminate more regulations, maintain the status quo on health care, our deficits will go away. The problem is, that's what we did for eight years. That's what helped us into this crisis. It's what helped lead to these deficits. We can't do it again.

Rather than fight the same tired battles that have dominated Washington for decades, it's time to try something new. Let's invest in our people without leaving them a mountain of debt. Let's meet our responsibility to the citizens who sent us here. Let's try common sense. A novel concept.

'A DEFICIT OF TRUST'

To do that, we have to recognize that we face more than a deficit of dollars right now. We face a deficit of trust — deep and corrosive doubts about how Washington works that have been growing for years. To close that credibility gap we have to take action on both ends of Pennsylvania Avenue — to end the outsized influence of lobbyists; to do our work openly; to give our people the government they deserve.

That's what I came to Washington to do. That's why — for the first time in history — my administration posts our White House visitors online. That's why we've excluded lobbyists from policy-making jobs or seats on federal boards and commissions.

But we can't stop there. It's time to require

lobbyists to disclose each contact they make on behalf of a client with my administration or with Congress. It's time to put strict limits on the contributions that lobbyists give to candidates for federal office.

With all due deference to separation of powers, last week the Supreme Court reversed a century of law that I believe will open the floodgates for special interests — including foreign corporations — to spend without limit in our elections. I don't think American elections should be bankrolled by America's most powerful interests, or worse, by foreign entities. They should be decided by the American people. And I'd urge Democrats and Republicans to pass a bill that helps to correct some of these problems.

I'm also calling on Congress to continue down the path of earmark reform. Democrats and Republicans. Democrats and Republicans. You've trimmed some of this spending; you've embraced some meaningful change. But restoring the public trust demands more. For example, some members of Congress post some earmark requests online. Tonight, I'm calling on Congress to publish all earmark requests on a single website before there's a vote, so that the American people can see how their money is being spent.

Of course, none of these reforms will even happen if we don't also reform how we work with one another. Now, I'm not naïve. I never thought that the mere fact of my election would usher in peace and harmony and some post-partisan era. I knew that both parties have fed divisions that are deeply entrenched. And on some issues, there are simply philosophical differences that will always cause us to part ways. These disagreements, about the role of government in our lives, about our national priorities and our national security, they've been taking place for over 200 years. They're the very essence of our democracy.

CHANGING POLITICS

But what frustrates the American people is a Washington where every day is Election Day. We can't wage a perpetual campaign where the only goal is to see who can get the most embarrassing headlines about the other side — a belief that if you lose, I win. Neither party should delay or obstruct every single bill just because they can. The confirmation of — I'm speaking to both parties now — the confirmation of well-qualified public servants shouldn't be held hostage to the pet projects or grudges of a few individual senators.

Washington may think that saying any-thing about the other side, no matter how false, no matter how malicious, is just part of the game. But it's precisely such politics that has stopped either party from helping the American people. Worse yet, it's sowing further division among our citizens, further distrust in our government.

So, no, I will not give up on trying to change the tone of our politics. I know it's an election year. And after last week, it's clear that campaign fever has come even earlier than usual. But we still need to govern.

To Democrats, I would remind you that we still have the largest majority in decades, and the people expect us to solve problems, not run for the hills. And if the Republican leadership is going to insist that 60 votes in the Senate are required to do any business at all in this town — a supermajority — then the responsibility to govern is now yours as well. Just saying no to everything may be good short-term politics, but it's not leadership. We were sent here to serve our citizens, not our ambitions. So let's show the American people that we can do it together.

This week, I'll be addressing a meeting of the House Republicans. I'd like to begin monthly meetings with both Democratic and Republican leadership. I know you can't wait.

IRAQ AND AFGHANISTAN WARS

Throughout our history, no issue has united this country more than our security. Sadly, some of the unity we felt after 9/11 has dissipated. We can argue all we want about who's to blame for this, but I'm not interested in relitigating the past. I know that all of us love this country. All of us are committed to its defense. So let's put aside the schoolyard taunts about who's tough. Let's reject the false choice between protecting our people and upholding our values. Let's leave behind the fear and division, and do what it takes to defend our nation and forge a more hopeful future — for America and for the world.

That's the work we began last year. Since the day I took office, we've renewed our focus on the terrorists who threaten our nation. We've made substantial investments in our homeland security and disrupted plots that threatened to take American lives. We are filling unacceptable gaps revealed by the failed Christmas attack with better airline security and swifter action on our intelligence. We've prohibited torture and strengthened partnerships from the Pacific to South Asia to the Arabian Peninsula. And in the past year,

hundreds of al Qaeda's fighters and affiliates, including many senior leaders, have been captured or killed — far more than in 2008.

And in Afghanistan, we're increasing our troops and training Afghan security forces so they can begin to take the lead in July of 2011, and our troops can begin to come home. We will reward good governance, work to reduce corruption, and support the rights of all Afghans — men and women alike. We're joined by allies and partners who have increased their own commitments and who will come together tomorrow in London to reaffirm our common purpose. There will be difficult days ahead. But I am absolutely confident we will succeed.

As we take the fight to al Qaeda, we are responsibly leaving Iraq to its people. As a candidate, I promised that I would end this war, and that is what I am doing as president. We will have all of our combat troops out of Iraq by the end of this August. We will support the Iraqi government — we will support the Iraqi government as they hold elections, and we will continue to partner with the Iraqi people to promote regional peace and prosperity. But make no mistake: This war is ending, and all of our troops are coming home.

Tonight, all of our men and women in uniform — in Iraq, in Afghanistan, and around the world — they have to know that we — that they have our respect, our gratitude, our full support. And just as they must have the resources they need in war, we all have a responsibility to support them when they come home. That's why we made the largest increase in investments for veterans in decades last year. That's why we're building a 21st century VA. And that's why Michelle has joined with Jill Biden to forge a national commitment to support military families.

NUCLEAR THREATS

Now, even as we prosecute two wars, we're also confronting perhaps the greatest danger to the American people — the threat of nuclear weapons. I've embraced the vision of John F. Kennedy and Ronald Reagan through a strategy that reverses the spread of these weapons and seeks a world without them. To reduce our stockpiles and launchers, while ensuring our deterrent, the United States and Russia are completing negotiations on the farthest-reaching arms control treaty in nearly two decades. And at April's Nuclear Security Summit, we will bring 44 nations together here in Washington, D.C., behind a clear goal: securing all vulnerable nuclear materials around

the world in four years, so that they never fall into the hands of terrorists.

Now, these diplomatic efforts have also strengthened our hand in dealing with those nations that insist on violating international agreements in pursuit of nuclear weapons. That's why North Korea now faces increased isolation and stronger sanctions — sanctions that are being vigorously enforced. That's why the international community is more united and the Islamic Republic of Iran is more isolated. And as Iran's leaders continue to ignore their obligations, there should be no doubt: They, too, will face growing consequences. That is a promise.

That's the leadership that we are providing — engagement that advances the common security and prosperity of all people. We're working through the G-20 to sustain a lasting global recovery. We're working with Muslim communities around the world to promote science and education and innovation. We have gone from a bystander to a leader in the fight against climate change. We're helping developing countries to feed themselves, and continuing the fight against HIV/AIDS. And we are launching a new initiative that will give us the capacity to respond faster and more effectively to bioterrorism or an infectious disease — a plan that will counter threats at home and strengthen public health abroad.

As we have for over 60 years, America takes these actions because our destiny is connected to those beyond our shores. But we also do it because it is right. That's why, as we meet here tonight, over 10,000 Americans are working with many nations to help the people of Haiti recover and rebuild. That's why we stand with the girl who yearns to go to school in Afghanistan; why we support the human rights of the women marching through the streets of Iran; why we advocate for the young man denied a job by corruption in Guinea. For America must always stand on the side of freedom and human dignity. Always.

EQUAL RIGHTS

Abroad, America's greatest source of strength has always been our ideals. The same is true at home. We find unity in our incredible diversity, drawing on the promise enshrined in our Constitution: the notion that we're all created equal; that no matter who you are or what you look like, if you abide by the law you should be protected by it; if you adhere to our common values you should be treated no different than anyone else.

We must continually renew this promise.

My administration has a Civil Rights Division that is once again prosecuting civil rights violations and employment discrimination. We finally strengthened our laws to protect against crimes driven by hate. This year, I will work with Congress and our military to finally repeal the law that denies gay Americans the right to serve the country they love because of who they are. It's the right thing to do.

We're going to crack down on violations of equal-pay laws — so that women get equal pay for an equal day's work. And we should continue the work of fixing our broken immigration system — to secure our borders and enforce our laws, and ensure that everyone who plays by the rules can contribute to our economy and enrich our nation.

A SPIRIT OF OPTIMISM

In the end, it's our ideals, our values that built America — values that allowed us to forge a nation made up of immigrants from every corner of the globe, values that drive our citizens still. Every day, Americans meet their responsibilities to their families and their employers. Time and again, they lend a hand to their neighbors and give back to their country. They take pride in their labor and are generous in spirit. These aren't Republican values or Democratic values that they're living by, business values or labor values. They're American values.

Unfortunately, too many of our citizens have lost faith that our biggest institutions — our corporations, our media, and, yes, our government — still reflect these same values. Each of these institutions are full of honorable men and women doing important work that helps our country prosper. But each time a CEO rewards himself for failure, or a banker puts the rest of us at risk for his own selfish gain, people's doubts grow. Each time lobbyists game the system or politicians tear each other down instead of lifting this country up, we lose faith. The more that TV pundits reduce serious debates to silly arguments, big issues into sound bites, our citizens turn away.

No wonder there's so much cynicism out there. No wonder there's so much disappointment.

I campaigned on the promise of change — change we can believe in, the slogan went. And right now, I know there are many Americans who aren't sure if they still believe we can change — or that I can deliver it.

But remember this — I never suggested that change would be easy, or that I could do it alone. Democracy in a nation of 300 million people can be noisy and messy and compli-

cated. And when you try to do big things and make big changes, it stirs passions and controversy. That's just how it is.

Those of us in public office can respond to this reality by playing it safe and avoid telling hard truths and pointing fingers. We can do what's necessary to keep our poll numbers high and get through the next election instead of doing what's best for the next generation.

But I also know this: If people had made that decision 50 years ago, or 100 years ago, or 200 years ago, we wouldn't be here tonight. The only reason we are here is because generations of Americans were unafraid to do what was hard; to do what was needed even when success was uncertain; to do what it took to keep the dream of this nation alive for their children and their grandchildren.

Our administration has had some political setbacks this year, and some of them were deserved. But I wake up every day knowing that they are nothing compared to the setbacks that families all across this country have faced this year. And what keeps me going — what keeps me fighting — is that despite all these setbacks, that spirit of determination and optimism, that fundamental decency that has always been at the core of the American people, that lives on.

It lives on in the struggling small-business owner who wrote to me of his company, "None of us," he said, ". . . are willing to consider, even slightly, that we might fail."

It lives on in the woman who said that even though she and her neighbors have felt the pain of recession, "We are strong. We are resilient. We are American."

It lives on in the 8-year-old boy in Louisiana who just sent me his allowance and asked if I would give it to the people of Haiti.

And it lives on in all the Americans who've dropped everything to go someplace they've never been and pull people they've never known from the rubble, prompting chants of "U.S.A.! U.S.A.! U.S.A!" when another life was saved.

The spirit that has sustained this nation for more than two centuries lives on in you, its people. We have finished a difficult year. We have come through a difficult decade. But a new year has come. A new decade stretches before us. We don't quit. I don't quit. Let's seize this moment — to start anew, to carry the dream forward, and to strengthen our union once more.

Thank you. God bless you. And God bless the United States of America. ■

GOP: Government Doing Too Much

The following is the CQ Transcriptions transcript of the Republican response to the State of the Union address, delivered by Virginia Gov. Bob McDonnell on Jan. 27, 2010.

THANK YOU VERY MUCH. Thank you.

Good evening. I'm Bob McDonnell. Eleven days ago, I was honored to be sworn in as the 71st governor of Virginia. I'm standing in the historic House Chamber of Virginia's Capitol, a building designed by Virginia's second governor, Thomas Jefferson.

It's not easy to follow the president of the United States. And my 18-year-old twin boys have added pressure to me tonight by giving me exactly 10 minutes to finish before they leave to go watch "SportsCenter."

I'm joined by fellow Virginians to share a Republican perspective on how to best address the challenges facing our nation today.

We were encouraged to hear President Obama speak this evening about the need to create jobs. All Americans should have the opportunity to find and keep meaningful work, and the dignity that comes with it.

ECONOMIC GROWTH

Many — many of us here tonight — and many of you watching — have family or friends who have lost their jobs. In fact, one in 10 Americans is unemployed. That is unacceptable.

Here in Virginia, we've faced our highest unemployment rate in more than 25 years, and bringing new jobs and more opportunities to our citizens is the top priority of my administration.

Good government policy should spur economic growth and strengthen the private sector's ability to create new jobs.

We must enact policies that promote entrepreneurship and innovation so America can better compete with the world. What government should not do is pile on more taxation, regulation and litigation that kill jobs and hurt the middle class.

It was Thomas Jefferson who called for "a wise and frugal government which shall leave men free to regulate their own pursuits of industry and shall not take from the mouth of labor the bread it has earned." He was right.

Today, the federal government is simply trying to do too much. Last year, we were told that massive new federal spending would create more jobs immediately and hold unemployment below 8 percent.

In the past year, more than 3 million people have lost their jobs, and yet the Democratic Congress continues deficit spending, adding to the bureaucracy, and increasing the national debt on our children and our grandchildren.

The amount of debt is on pace to double in five years and triple in 10. The federal debt is now over $100,000 per household. This is simply unsustainable.

LIMITED GOVERNMENT

The president's partial freeze announced tonight on discretionary spending is a laudable step, but a small one. The circumstances of our time demand that we reconsider and restore the proper limited role of government at every level.

Without reform, the excessive growth of government threatens our very liberty and our prosperity.

In recent months, the American people have made clear that they want government leaders to listen and then act on the issues most important to them. We want results, not rhetoric. We want cooperation, not partisanship.

There is much common ground. All Americans agree that we need health — health care system that is affordable, accessible and high quality. But most Americans do not want to turn over the best medical care system in the world to the federal government.

Republicans in Congress have offered legislation to reform health care, without shifting Medicaid costs to the states, without cutting Medicare, and without raising your taxes.

And we will do that by implementing common-sense reforms, like letting families and businesses buy health insurance policies across state lines and ending frivolous lawsuits against doctors and hospitals that drive up the cost of your health care.

And our solutions aren't 1,000-page bills that no one has fully read, after being crafted behind closed doors with special interests. In fact, many of our proposals are available online at solutions.gop.gov, and we welcome your ideas on Facebook and Twitter.

All Americans agree that this nation must become more energy independent and secure. We are blessed here in America with vast natural resources, and we must use them all.

Advances in technology can unleash more natural gas, nuclear, wind, coal — alternative energy that will lower your utility bills.

Here in Virginia, we have the opportunity to become the first state on the East Coast to explore for and produce oil and natural gas offshore.

But this administration's policies are delaying offshore production, hindering nuclear energy expansion and seeking to impose job-killing cap-and-trade energy taxes. Now is the time to adopt innovative energy policies that create jobs and lower energy prices.

All Americans agree that a young person needs a world-class education to compete in the global economy. As a young kid, my dad told me, "Son, if you want a good job, you need a good education." Dad was right, and that's even more true today.

The president and I agree on expanding the number of high-quality charter schools and rewarding teachers for excellent performance. More school choices for parents and students mean more accountability and greater achievement.

A child's educational opportunity should be determined by her intellect and work ethic, not by her ZIP code.

TERRORISM DETAINEES

All Americans agree that we must maintain a strong national defense. The courage and success of our armed forces is allowing us to draw down troop levels in Iraq as that government is increasingly able to step up.

My oldest daughter, Jeanine, was an Army platoon leader in Iraq, so I am personally grateful for the service and sacrifice of all our men and women in uniform, and a grateful nation thanks them.

We applaud President Obama's decision to deploy 30,000 more troops to Afghanistan. We agree that victory there is imperative for national security.

But we have serious concerns over the recent steps the administration has taken regarding suspected terrorists. Americans were shocked on Christmas Day to learn of the attempted bombing of a flight to Detroit. This foreign terror suspect was given the

same legal rights as a U.S. citizen and immediately stopped providing critical intelligence.

As Sen.-elect Scott Brown has said, we should be spending taxpayer dollars to defeat terrorists, not to protect them.

Here at home, government must help foster a society in which all our people can use their God-given talents and liberty to pursue the great American dream. Republicans know that government cannot guarantee individual outcomes, but we strongly believe that it must guarantee equality of opportunity for all.

That opportunity exists best in a democracy which promotes free enterprise, economic growth, strong families and individual achievement.

Many Americans are concerned about this administration's effort to exert greater control over car companies, banks, energy and health care, but over-regulating employers won't create more employment; overtaxing investors won't foster more investment.

Top-down, one-size-fits-all decision-making should not replace the personal choices of free people in a free market, nor undermine the proper role of state and local governments in our system of federalism. As our founders clearly stated, and we governors clearly understand, government closest to the people governs best.

'CARING AMERICANS'

And no government program can ever replace the actions of caring Americans freely choosing to help one another. The Scriptures say, "To whom much is given, much will be required." As the most generous and prosperous nation on Earth, it is heartwarming to see Americans giving much time and money to the people of Haiti.

Thank you for your ongoing compassion. Some people say they're afraid that America is no longer the great land of promise that she has always been. They should not be.

America will always blaze the trail of opportunity and prosperity. America will — must always be a land where liberty and property are valued and respected and innocent human life is protected.

Government should have this clear goal: Where opportunity is absent, we must create it. Where opportunity is limited, we must expand it. Where opportunity is unequal, we must make it open to everyone.

Our founders pledged their lives, their fortunes and their sacred honor to create this great nation. Now we should pledge as Democrats, Republicans and independents — Americans all — to work together to leave this nation an ever better place than we found it.

God bless you, and God bless this great land of America. Thank you very much. ∎

Notary Bill Gets Presidential Veto

The following is the text of President Obama's Dec. 30 memorandum of disapproval on HR 3808, a bill regarding court recognition of notarized statements. The president vetoed the bill because of concerns about proper oversight.

MEMORANDUM OF DISAPPROVAL

It is necessary to have further deliberations about the possible unintended impact of H.R. 3808, the "Interstate Recognition of Notarizations Act of 2010," on consumer protections, including those for mortgages, before the bill can be finalized. Accordingly, I am withholding my approval of this bill. (The Pocket Veto Case, 279 U.S. 655 (1929)).

The authors of this bill no doubt had the best intentions in mind when trying to remove impediments to interstate commerce. My Administration will work with them and other leaders in Congress to explore the best ways to achieve this goal going forward.

To leave no doubt that the bill is being vetoed, in addition to withholding my signature, I am returning H.R. 3808 to the Clerk of the House of Representatives, along with this Memorandum of Disapproval.

BARACK OBAMA
THE WHITE HOUSE
October 8, 2010

Appendix E

PUBLIC LAWS

Laws Enacted in the Second Session Of the 111th Congress

Public Laws 111-1 through 111-125, enacted in the first session of the 111th Congress, were published in the previous edition of the CQ Almanac. (2009 Almanac, p. E-3)

■ **PL 111-126** (HR 4462) Accelerate the income tax benefits for charitable cash contributions for the relief of victims of the earthquake in Haiti. Introduced by RANGEL, D-N.Y., on Jan. 19, 2010. House passed, under suspension of the rules, Jan. 20. Senate passed Jan. 21. President signed Jan. 22, 2010.

■ **PL 111-127** (S 2949) Amend Section 1113 of the Social Security Act to provide authority for increased fiscal 2010 payments for temporary assistance to U.S. citizens returned from foreign countries and to provide necessary funding to avoid shortfalls in the Medicare cost-sharing program for low-income qualifying individuals. Introduced by BAUCUS, D-Mont., on Jan. 25, 2010. Senate passed Jan. 25. House passed, under suspension of the rules, Jan. 26. President signed Jan. 27, 2010.

■ **PL 111-128** (HR 1817) Designate the facility of the U.S. Postal Service located at 116 N. West St. in Somerville, Tenn., as the "John S. Wilder Post Office Building." Introduced by BLACKBURN, R-Tenn., on March 31, 2009. House passed, under suspension of the rules, June 4. Senate Homeland Security and Governmental Affairs reported Dec. 17 (no written report). Senate passed Dec. 21. President signed Jan. 29, 2010.

■ **PL 111-129** (HR 2877) Designate the facility of the U.S. Postal Service located at 76 Brookside Ave. in Chester, N.Y., as the "1st Lt. Louis Allen Post Office." Introduced by HALL, D-N.Y., on June 15, 2009. House passed, under suspension of the rules, Oct. 13. Senate Homeland Security and Governmental Affairs reported Dec. 17 (no written report). Senate passed Dec. 21. President signed Jan. 29, 2010.

■ **PL 111-130** (HR 3072) Designate the facility of the U.S. Postal Service located at 9810 Halls Ferry Road in St. Louis as the "Coach Jodie Bailey Post Office Building." Introduced by CLAY, D-Mo., on June 26, 2009. House passed, under suspension of the rules, July 29. Senate Homeland Security and Governmental Affairs reported Dec. 17 (no written report). Senate passed Dec. 21. President signed Jan. 29, 2010.

■ **PL 111-131** (HR 3319) Designate the facility of the U.S. Postal Service located at 440 S. Gulling St. in Portola, Calif., as the "Army Spc. Jeremiah Paul McCleery Post Office Building." Introduced by MCCLINTOCK, R-Calif., July 23, 2009. House passed, under suspension of the rules, Oct. 20. Senate Homeland Security and Governmental Affairs reported Dec. 17 (no written report). Senate passed Dec. 21. President signed Jan. 29, 2010.

■ **PL 111-132** (HR 3539) Designate the facility of the U.S. Postal Service located at 427 Harrison Ave. in Harrison, N.J., as the "Patricia D. McGinty Juhl Post Office Building." Introduced by SIRES, D-N.J., on Sept. 8, 2009. House passed, under suspension of the rules, Nov. 16. Senate Homeland Security and Governmental Affairs reported Dec. 17 (no written report). Senate passed Dec. 21. President signed Jan. 29, 2010.

■ **PL 111-133** (HR 3667) Designate the facility of the U.S. Postal Service located at 16555 Springs St. in White Springs, Fla., as the "Clyde L. Hillhouse Post Office Building." Introduced by CRENSHAW, R-Fla., on Sept. 29, 2009. House passed, under suspension of the rules, Dec. 1. Senate Homeland Security and Governmental Affairs reported Dec. 17 (no written report). Senate passed Dec. 21. President signed Jan. 29, 2010.

■ **PL 111-134** (HR 3767) Designate the facility of the U.S. Postal Service located at 170 N. Main St. in Smithfield, Utah, as the "W. Hazen Hillyard Post Office Building." Introduced by BISHOP, R-Utah, on Oct. 8, 2009. House passed, under suspension of the rules, Nov. 16. Senate Homeland Security and Governmental Affairs reported Dec. 17 (no written report). Senate passed Dec. 21. President signed Jan. 29, 2010.

■ **PL 111-135** (HR 3788) Designate the facility of the U.S. Postal Service located at 3900 Darrow Road in Stow, Ohio, as the "Cpl. Joseph A. Tomci Post Office Building." Introduced by LATOURETTE, R-Ohio, on Oct. 13, 2009. House passed, under suspension of the rules, Nov. 6. Senate Homeland Security and Governmental Affairs reported Dec. 17 (no written report). Senate passed Dec. 21. President signed Jan. 29, 2010.

■ **PL 111-136** (HR 4508) Provide for an additional temporary extension of programs under the Small Business Act and the Small Business Investment Act of 1958. Introduced by VELÁZQUEZ, D-N.Y., on Jan. 26, 2010. House passed, under suspension of the rules, Jan. 27. Senate passed Jan. 28. President signed Jan. 29, 2010.

■ **PL 111-137** (HR 1377) Amend Title 38 of the U.S. Code to expand veteran eligibility for reimbursement by the Department of Veterans Affairs for emergency treatment furnished in a non-department facility, introduced by FILNER, D-Calif., on March 6, 2009. House Veterans' Affairs reported, amended, March 26 (H Rept 111-55). House passed, under suspension of the rules, March 30. Senate Veterans' Affairs discharged Dec. 18. Senate passed Dec. 18. President signed Feb. 1, 2010.

■ **PL 111-138** (S 692) Provide that claims of the United States to certain documents relating to Franklin Delano Roosevelt shall be treated as waived and relinquished in certain circumstances. Introduced by SCHUMER, D-N.Y., on March 25, 2009. Senate Homeland Security and Governmental Affairs reported Oct. 5 (S Rept 111-87). Senate passed Oct. 14. House passed, under suspension of the rules, Jan. 13, 2010. President signed Feb. 1, 2010.

■ **PL 111-139** (H J Res 45) Increase the statutory limit on the public debt. Introduced April 29, 2009. House passed April 29. Senate Finance discharged. Senate passed, amended, Jan. 28, 2010. House adopted Senate amendments Feb. 4. President signed Feb. 12, 2010.

■ **PL 111-140** (HR 730) Strengthen efforts by the Department of Homeland Security to develop nuclear forensics capabilities to permit attribution of the source of nuclear material. Introduced by SCHIFF, D-Calif., on Jan. 27, 2009. House passed, under suspension of the rules, March 24. Senate Homeland Security and Governmental Affairs reported Dec. 17 (no written report). Senate passed, amended, Dec. 23. House agreed to Senate amendment, under suspension of the rules, Jan. 21, 2010. President signed Feb. 16, 2010.

■ **PL 111-141** (HR 3961) Extend expiring provisions of the USA Patriot Improvement and Reauthorization Act of 2005 and the Intelligence Reform and Terrorism Prevention Act of 2004 until Feb. 28, 2011. Introduced by DINGELL, D-Mich., on Oct. 29, 2009. House passed Nov. 19. Senate passed, amended, Feb. 24, 2010. House agreed to Senate amendments Feb. 25. President signed Feb. 27, 2010.

■ **PL 111-142** (HR 4532) Provide for permanent extension of the attorney-fee-withholding procedures under Title II of the Social Security Act to Title XVI of the act, and provide for permanent extension of such procedures under Titles II and XVI of the act to qualified non-attorney representatives. Introduced by TANNER, D-Tenn., on Jan. 27, 2010. House passed, under suspension of the rules, Feb. 4. Senate passed Feb. 22. President signed Feb. 27, 2010.

■ **PL 111-143** (S 2950) Extend the pilot program for volunteer groups to obtain criminal history background checks. Introduced by SCHUMER, D-N.Y., on Jan. 25, 2010. Senate passed Jan. 25. House passed, under suspension of the rules, Feb. 4. President signed March 1, 2010.

■ **PL 111-144** (HR 4691) Provide a temporary extension of extended federal unemployment payments, federal insurance subsidies to jobless workers and other programs. Introduced by RANGEL, D-N.Y., on Feb. 25, 2010. House passed, under suspension of the rules, Feb. 25. Senate passed March 2. President signed March 2, 2010.

■ **PL 111-145** (HR 1299) Make technical corrections to the laws affecting certain administrative authorities of the U.S. Capitol Police. Introduced by BRADY, D-Pa., on March 4, 2009. House Administration reported March 30 (H Rept 111-66). House passed, under suspension of the rules, March 31. Senate Rules and Administration discharged. Senate passed, amended, Oct. 29. House agreed to Senate amendment, with an amendment, Nov. 16. Senate agreed to House amendment to Senate amendment Feb. 25, 2010. President signed March 4, 2010.

■ **PL 111-146** (S 2968) Make certain technical and conforming amendments to the Lanham Act. Introduced by LEAHY, D-Vt., on Jan. 28, 2010. Senate passed Jan. 28. House passed, under suspension of the rules, March 3. President signed March 17, 2010.

■ **PL 111-147** (HR 2847) Provide incentives for hiring and retaining employees and extend certain surface transportation programs. Introduced by MOLLOHAN, D-W.Va., on June 12, 2009. House Appropriations reported June 12 (H Rept 111-149). House passed June 18. Senate Appropriations reported, amended, June 25 (S Rept 111-34). Senate passed, amended, Nov. 5. House agreed to Senate amendment, with an amendment, Dec. 16. Senate agreed to House amendment to Senate amendment, with an amendment, Feb. 24, 2010. House agreed to Senate amendment to House amendment, with an amendment, March 4. Senate agreed to House amendment to Senate amendment to House amendment to Senate amendment March 17. President signed March 18, 2010.

■ **PL 111-148** (HR 3590) Patient Protection and Affordable Care Act. Introduced by RANGEL, D-N.Y., on Sept. 17, 2009. House passed, under suspension of the rules, Oct. 8. Senate passed, amended, Dec. 24. House agreed to Senate amendments March 21, 2010. President signed March 23, 2010.

■ **PL 111-149** (HR 3433) Amend the North American Wetlands Conservation Act to establish requirements regarding payment of the non-federal share of the costs of wetlands conservation projects in Canada funded under that act. Introduced by WITTMAN, R-Va., on July 30, 2009. House Natural Resources reported Oct. 9 (H Rept 111-296). House passed, under suspension of the rules, Oct. 13. Senate Environment and Public Works reported March 5, 2010 (S Rept 111-158). Senate passed March 9. President signed March 25, 2010.

■ **PL 111-150** (HR 4938) Permit the use of previously appropriated funds to extend the Small Business Loan Guarantee Program. Introduced by SERRANO, D-N.Y., on March 25, 2010. House passed, under suspension of the rules, March 25. Senate passed March 25. President signed March 26, 2010.

■ **PL 111-151** (S 3186) Reauthorize the Satellite Home Viewer Extension and Reauthorization Act of 2004 through April 30, 2010. Introduced by ROCKEFELLER, D-W.Va., on March 25, 2010. Senate passed March 25. House passed March 25. President signed March 26, 2010.

■ **PL 111-152** (HR 4872) Provide for reconciliation pursuant to Title II of the concurrent resolution on the fiscal 2010 budget (S Con Res 13). Introduced by SPRATT, D-S.C., on March 17, 2010. House Budget reported March 17 (H Rept 111-443). House passed March 21. Senate passed, amended, March 25. House agreed to Senate amendments March 25. President signed March 30, 2010.

■ **PL 111-153** (HR 4957) Extend the funding and expenditure authority of the Airport and Airway Trust Fund, and extend authorizations for the airport improvement program. Introduced by RICHARDSON, D-Calif., on March 25, 2010. House Transportation discharged. House Ways and Means discharged. House passed March 25. Senate passed March 26. President signed March 31, 2010.

■ **PL 111-154** (S 1147) Prevent tobacco smuggling and ensure the collection of all tobacco taxes. Introduced by KOHL, D-Wis., on May 21, 2009. Senate Judiciary reported, amended, Nov. 19 (no written report). Senate passed, amended, March 11, 2010. House passed, under suspension of the rules, March 17. President signed March 31, 2010.

■ **PL 111-155** (HR 4621) Protect the integrity of the constitutionally mandated U.S. census and prohibit deceptive mail practices that attempt to exploit the decennial census. Introduced by MALONEY, D-N.Y., on Feb. 9, 2010. House passed, amended, under suspension of the rules, March 10. Senate Homeland Security and Governmental affairs discharged. Senate passed March 26. President signed April 7, 2010.

■ **PL 111-156** (H J Res 80) Recognize and honor the Blinded Veterans Association on its 65th anniversary of representing blinded veterans and their families. Introduced by HALVORSON, D-Ill., on March 4, 2010. House passed, under suspension of the rules, March 23. Senate passed March 26. President signed April 7, 2010.

■ **PL 111-157** (HR 4851) Provide a temporary extension of federal unemployment benefits, COBRA subsidies and other programs. Introduced by LEVIN, D-Mich., on March 16, 2010. House passed, amended, under suspension of the rules, March 17. Senate passed, amended, April 15. House agreed to Senate amendment, April 15. President signed April 15, 2010.

■ **PL 111-158** (HR 4573) Urge the secretary of the Treasury to instruct the U.S. executive directors at the International Monetary Fund, the World Bank, the Inter-American Development Bank, and other multilateral development institutions to seek the cancellation of Haiti's debts to such institutions. Introduced by WATERS, D-Calif., Feb. 2, 2010. House passed, amended, under suspension of the rules, March 10. Senate passed, amended, March 26. House agreed to Senate amendments, under suspension of the rules, April 14. President signed April 26, 2010.

■ **PL 111-159** (HR 4887) Amend the Internal Revenue Code of 1986 to ensure that health coverage provided by the Department of Defense is treated as minimal essential coverage. Introduced by SKELTON, D-Mo., on March 19, 2010. House passed, amended, under suspension of the rules, March 20. Senate Finance discharged. Senate passed April 12. President signed April 26, 2010.

■ **PL 111-160** (S J Res 25) Grant the consent and approval of Congress to amendments made by the State of Maryland, the Commonwealth of Virginia, and the District of Columbia to the Washington Metropolitan Area Transit Regulation Compact. Introduced by CARDIN, D-Md., on Dec. 24, 2009. Senate Judiciary discharged. Senate passed Jan. 21, 2010. House passed, under suspension of the rules, April 14. President signed April 26, 2010.

■ **PL 111-161** (HR 5147) Extend the funding and expenditure authority of the Airport and Airway Trust Fund and extend authorizations for the airport improvement program. Introduced by OBERSTAR, D-Minn., on April 27, 2010. House passed, under suspension of the rules, April 28. Senate passed April 28. President signed April 30, 2010.

■ **PL 111-162** (S 3253) Provide for an additional temporary extension of programs under the Small Business Act and the Small Business Investment Act of 1958. Introduced by LANDRIEU, D-La., on April 22, 2010. Senate passed April 22. House passed, under suspension of the rules, April 27. President signed April 30, 2010.

■ **PL 111-163** (S 1963) Amend Title 38, U.S. Code, to provide assistance to the caregivers of veterans and improve the provision of health care to veterans. Introduced by AKAKA, D-Hawaii, on Oct. 28, 2009. Senate passed Nov. 19. House passed, amended, under suspension of the rules, April 21, 2010. Senate agreed to House amendment April 22. President signed May 5, 2010.

■ **PL 111-164** (HR 4360) Designate the Department of Veterans Affairs blind rehabilitation center in Long Beach, Calif., as the "Major Charles Robert Soltes Jr., O.D. Department of Veterans Affairs Blind Rehabilitation Center." Introduced by CAMPBELL, R-Calif., on Dec. 16, 2009. House passed, under suspension of the rules, March 25, 2010. Senate Veterans' Affairs discharged. Senate passed April 19. President signed May 7, 2010.

■ **PL 111-165** (HR 5146) Provide that members of Congress shall not receive a cost-of-living adjustment in pay for fiscal 2011. Introduced by MITCHELL, D-Ariz., on April 27, 2010. House passed, under suspension of the rules, April 27. Senate passed April 28. President signed May 14, 2010.

■ **PL 111-166** (HR 3714) Amend the Foreign Assistance Act of 1961 to include information in the Annual Country Reports on Human Rights Practices about press freedom in foreign countries. Introduced by SCHIFF, D-Calif., on Oct. 1, 2009. House passed, amended, under suspension of the rules, Dec. 16. Senate Foreign Relations discharged. Senate passed April 29, 2010. President signed May 17, 2010.

■ **PL 111-167** (HR 1121) Authorize a land exchange to acquire lands for the Blue Ridge Parkway from the town of Blowing Rock, N.C. Introduced by FOXX, R-Va., on Feb. 23, 2009. House Natural Resources reported, amended, July 24 (H Rept 111-227). House passed, amended, under suspension of the rules, July 27. Senate Energy and Natural Resources reported March 2, 2010 (S Rept 111-147). Senate passed May 7. President signed May 24, 2010.

■ **PL 111-168** (HR 1442) Provide for the sale of the federal government's reversionary interest in approximately 60 acres of land in Salt Lake City originally conveyed to the Mount Olivet Cemetery Association under the Act of January 23, 1909. Introduced by MATHESON, D-Utah, on March 11, 2009. House Natural Resources reported, amended, July 10 (H Rept 111-198). House passed, amended, under suspension of the rules, July 16. Senate Energy and Natural Resources reported March 2, 2010 (S Rept 111-150). Senate passed May 7. President signed May 24, 2010.

■ **PL 111-169** (HR 2802) Provide for an extension of the legislative authority of the Adams Memorial Foundation to establish a commemorative work honoring President John Adams. Introduced by DELAHUNT, D- Mass., on June 10, 2009. House Natural Resources reported, amended, Sept. 21 (H Rept 111-261). House passed, amended, under suspension of the rules, Sept. 22. Senate Energy and Natural Resources reported March 2, 2010 (S Rept 111-155). Senate passed May 7. President signed May 24, 2010.

■ **PL 111-170** (HR 5148) Amend Title 39, U.S. Code, to clarify the instances in which the term "census" may appear on mailable matter.

Introduced by ISSA, R-Calif., on April 27, 2010. House passed, under suspension of the rules, April 28. Senate Homeland Security and Governmental Affairs discharged. Senate passed May 5. President signed May 24, 2010.

■ **PL 111-171** (HR 5160) Extend the Caribbean Basin Economic Recovery Act and provide customs support services to Haiti. Introduced by RANGEL, D-N.Y., on April 28, 2010. House passed, amended, under suspension of the rules, May 5. Senate passed May 6. President signed May 24, 2010.

■ **PL 111-172** (S 1067) Support stabilization and lasting peace in northern Uganda and areas affected by the Lord's Resistance Army. Introduced by FEINGOLD, D-Wis., on May 19, 2009. Senate Foreign Relations reported, amended, Dec. 15 (S Rept 111-108). Senate passed, amended, March 10, 2010. House passed, under suspension of the rules, May 12. President signed May 24, 2010.

■ **PL 111-173** (HR 5014) Clarify the definition of health care provided by the secretary of Veterans Affairs that constitutes minimum essential coverage. Introduced by FILNER, D-Calif., on April 14, 2010. House passed, amended, under suspension of the rules, May 12. Senate passed May 18. President signed May 27, 2010.

■ **PL 111-174** (S 1782) Provide improvements for the operations of the federal courts. Introduced by WHITEHOUSE, D-R.I., on Oct. 14, 2009. Senate Judiciary discharged. Senate passed March 16, 2010. House passed, under suspension of the rules, May 18. President signed May 27, 2010.

■ **PL 111-175** (S 3333) Extend the statutory license for secondary transmissions of television broadcast signals under Title 17, U.S. Code. Introduced by LEAHY, D-Vt., on May 7, 2010. Senate passed May 7. House passed, under suspension of the rules, May 12. President signed May 27, 2010.

■ **PL 111-176** (HR 5128) Designate the U.S. Department of Interior Building in Washington, D.C., as the "Stewart Lee Udall Department of the Interior Building." Introduced by HEINRICH, D-N.M., on April 22, 2010. House Transportation reported, amended, May 18 (H Rept 111-485). House passed, amended, under suspension of the rules, May 20. Senate passed May 25. President signed June 8, 2010.

■ **PL 111-177** (HR 5139) Extend immunities provided in the International Organizations Immunities Act to the Office of the High Representative and the International Civilian Office in Kosovo. Introduced by BERMAN, D-Calif., on April 26, 2010. House passed, amended, under suspension of the rules, May 19. Senate passed May 20. President signed June 8, 2010.

■ **PL 111-178** (HR 2711) Provide transportation of the dependents, remains, and effects of certain federal employees who die as a result of injuries sustained in the performance of official duties. Introduced by ROGERS, R-Mich., on June 4, 2009. House Oversight and Government Reform reported, amended, Sept. 29 (H Rept 111-274). House passed, amended, under suspension of the rules, Dec. 8. Senate Homeland Security and Governmental Affairs reported Dec. 17 (no written report). Senate passed, amended, May 14, 2010. House

agreed to Senate amendments, under suspension of the rules, May 25. President signed June 9, 2010.

■ **PL 111-179** (HR 3250) Designate the facility of the U.S. Postal Service located at 1210 West Main St. in Riverhead, N.Y., as the "Private First Class Garfield M. Langhorn Post Office Building." Introduced by BISHOP, D-N.Y., on July 17, 2009. House passed, under suspension of the rules, Jan. 21, 2010. Senate Homeland Security and Governmental Affairs reported May 18 (no written report). Senate passed May 25. President signed June 9, 2010.

■ **PL 111-180** (HR 3634) Designate the facility of the U.S. Postal Service located at 109 Main St. in Swifton, Ark., as the "George Kell Post Office." Introduced by BERRY, D-Ark., on Sept. 23, 2009. House passed, under suspension of the rules, Dec. 2. Senate Homeland Security and Governmental Affairs reported May 18, 2010 (no written report). Senate passed May 25. President signed June 9, 2010.

■ **PL 111-181** (HR 3892) Designate the facility of the U.S. Postal Service located at 101 West Highway 64 Bypass in Roper, N.C., as the "E.V. Wilkins Post Office." Introduced by BUTTERFIELD, D-N.C., on Oct. 21, 2009. House passed, under suspension of the rules, Jan. 13, 2010. Senate Homeland Security and Governmental Affairs reported May 18 (no written report). Senate passed May 25. President signed June 9, 2010.

■ **PL 111-182** (HR 4017) Designate the facility of the U.S. Postal Service located at 43 Maple Ave. in Shrewsbury, Mass., as the "Ann Marie Blute Post Office." Introduced by MCGOVERN, D-Mass., on Nov. 4, 2009. House passed, under suspension of the rules, Dec. 10. Senate Homeland Security and Governmental Affairs reported May 18, 2010 (no written report). Senate passed May 25. President signed June 9, 2010.

■ **PL 111-183** (HR 4095) Designate the facility of the U.S. Postal Service located at 9727 Antioch Road in Overland Park, Kan., as the "Congresswoman Jan Meyers Post Office Building." Introduced by MOORE, D-Kan., on Nov. 17, 2009. House passed, under suspension of the rules, Jan. 20, 2010. Senate Homeland Security and Governmental Affairs reported May 18 (no written report). Senate passed May 25. President signed June 9, 2010.

■ **PL 111-184** (HR 4139) Designate the facility of the U.S. Postal Service located at 7464 Highway 503 in Hickory, Miss., as the "Sgt. Matthew L. Ingram Post Office." Introduced by HARPER, R-Miss., on Nov. 19, 2009. House passed, under suspension of the rules, Jan. 13, 2010. Senate Homeland Security and Governmental Affairs reported May 18 (no written report). Senate passed May 25. President signed June 9, 2010.

■ **PL 111-185** (HR 4214) Designate the facility of the U.S. Postal Service located at 45300 Portola Ave. in Palm Desert, Calif., as the "Roy Wilson Post Office." Introduced by BONO MACK, R-Calif., on Dec. 7, 2009. House passed, under suspension of the rules, March 18, 2010. Senate Homeland Security and Governmental Affairs reported May 18 (no written report). Senate passed May 25. President signed June 9, 2010.

■ **PL 111-186** (HR 4238) Designate the facility of the U.S. Postal Service located at 930 39th Ave. in Greeley, Colo., as the "W.D. Farr Post Office Building." Introduced by MARKEY, D-Colo., on Dec. 8, 2009. House passed, under suspension of the rules, Feb. 22, 2010. Senate Homeland Security and Governmental Affairs reported May 18 (no written report). Senate passed May 25. President signed June 9, 2010.

■ **PL 111-187** (HR 4425) Designate the facility of the U.S. Postal Service located at 2-116th St. in North Troy, N.Y., as the "Martin G. 'Marty' Mahar Post Office." Introduced by TONKO, D-N.Y., on Jan. 12, 2010. House passed, under suspension of the rules, Feb. 22. Senate Homeland Security and Governmental Affairs reported May 18 (no written report). Senate passed May 25. President signed June 9, 2010.

■ **PL 111-188** (HR 4547) Designate the facility of the U.S. Postal Service located at 119 Station Road in Cheyney, Pa., as the "Capt. Luther H. Smith, U.S. Army Air Forces Post Office." Introduced by SESTAK, D-Pa., on Jan. 27, 2010. House passed, under suspension of the rules, March 9. Senate Homeland Security and Governmental Affairs reported May 18 (no written report). Senate passed May 25. President signed June 9, 2010.

■ **PL 111-189** (HR 4628) Designate the facility of the U.S. Postal Service located at 216 Westwood Ave. in Westwood, N.J., as the "Sgt. Christopher R. Hrbek Post Office Building." Introduced by GARRETT, R-N.J., on Feb. 22, 2010. House passed, under suspension of the rules, March 16. Senate Homeland Security and Governmental Affairs reported May 18 (no written report). Senate passed May 25. President signed June 9, 2010.

■ **PL 111-190** (HR 5330) Extend certain provisions of the Antitrust Criminal Penalty Enhancement and Reform Act of 2004. Introduced by JOHNSON, D-Ga., on May 18, 2010. House passed, amended, under suspension of the rules, May 24. Senate passed May 27. President signed June 9, 2010.

■ **PL 111-191** (S 3473) Amend the Oil Pollution Act of 1990 to authorize advances from the Oil Spill Liability Trust Fund for the Deepwater Horizon oil spill. Introduced by REID, D-Nev., on June 9, 2010. Senate passed June 9. House passed, under suspension of the rules, June 10. President signed June 15, 2010.

■ **PL 111-192** (HR 3962) Prevent a Medicare payment cut to physicians and provide a payment increase in 2010. Introduced by DINGELL, D-Mich., on Oct. 29, 2009. House passed, amended, Nov. 7. Senate passed, amended, June 18, 2010. House agreed to Senate amendments to the House amendment, under suspension of the rules, June 24. President signed June 25, 2010.

■ **PL 111-193** (HR 3951) Designate the facility of the U.S. Postal Service located at 2000 Louisiana Ave. in New Orleans as the "Roy Rondeno Sr. Post Office Building." Introduced by CAO, R-La., on Oct. 28, 2009. House passed, under suspension of the rules, Dec. 9. Senate Homeland Security and Governmental Affairs reported June 14, 2010 (no written report). Senate passed June 15. President signed June 28, 2010.

■ **PL 111-194** (S J Res 33) Provide for the reconsideration and revision of the proposed constitution of the U.S. Virgin Islands to correct provisions inconsistent with the U.S. Constitution and federal law. Introduced by BINGAMAN, D-N.M., on June 17, 2010. Senate passed June 17. House passed, under suspension of the rules, June 29. President signed June 30, 2010.

■ **PL 111-195** (HR 2194) Amend the Iran Sanctions Act of 1996 to enhance U.S. diplomatic efforts with respect to Iran by expanding economic sanctions against Iran. Introduced by BERMAN, D-Calif., on April 30, 2009. House Foreign Affairs reported, amended, Nov. 19 (H Rept 111-342, Part 1). House Financial Services discharged. House Oversight and Government Reform discharged. House Ways and Means discharged. House passed, amended, under suspension of the rules, Dec. 15. Senate Banking, Housing, and Urban Affairs discharged. Senate passed, amended, March 11, 2010. Conference report filed in the House on June 23 (H Rept 111-512). Senate agreed to conference report June 24. House agreed to conference report, under suspension of the rules, June 24. President signed July 1, 2010.

■ **PL 111-196** (HR 5569) Extend the National Flood Insurance Program until Sept. 30, 2010. Introduced by WATERS, D-Calif., on June 22, 2010. House passed, under suspension of the rules, June 23. Senate passed June 30. President signed July 2, 2010.

■ **PL 111-197** (HR 5611) Amend the Internal Revenue Code of 1986 to extend the funding and expenditure authority of the Airport and Airway Trust Fund, and amend Title 49, U.S. Code, to extend authorizations for the airport improvement program. Introduced by LEVIN, D-Mich., on June 28, 2010. House passed, under suspension of the rules, June 29. Senate passed June 30. President signed July 2, 2010.

■ **PL 111-198** (HR 5623) Amend the Internal Revenue Code of 1986 to extend the homebuyer tax credit to homes purchased by Oct. 1, 2010. Introduced by DAHLKEMPER, D-Pa., on June 29, 2010. House passed, amended, under suspension of the rules, June 29. Senate passed June 30. President signed July 2, 2010.

■ **PL 111-199** (S 1660) Amend the Toxic Substances Control Act to reduce the emissions of formaldehyde from composite wood products. Introduced by KLOBUCHAR, D-Minn., on Sept. 10, 2009. Senate Environment and Public Works reported, amended, April 19, 2010 (S Rept 111-169). Senate passed, amended, June 14. House passed, under suspension of the rules, June 23. President signed July 7, 2010.

■ **PL 111-200** (S 2865) Reauthorize the Congressional Award Act. Introduced by LIEBERMAN I-Conn., on Dec. 10, 2009. Senate Homeland Security and Governmental Affairs reported March 15, 2010 (S Rept 111-163). Senate passed March 17. House passed, under suspension of the rules, June 23. President signed July 7, 2010.

■ **PL 111-201** (S J Res 32) Recognize the 60th anniversary of the outbreak of the Korean War and reaffirm the United States-Korea alliance. Introduced by BURR, R-N.C., on June 16, 2010. Senate passed June 16. House passed, under suspension of the rules, June 23. President signed July 7, 2010.

■ **PL 111-202** (S 3104) Permanently authorize Radio Free Asia. Introduced by LUGAR, R-Ind., on March 11, 2010. Senate Foreign Relations reported, amended, June 22 (S Rept 111-214). Senate passed, amended, June 25. House passed, under suspension of the rules, June 30. President signed July 13, 2010.

■ **PL 111-203** (HR 4173) Provide for financial regulatory reform, protect consumers and investors, enhance federal understanding of insurance issues, and regulate the over-the-counter derivatives markets. Introduced by FRANK, D-Mass., on Dec. 2, 2009. House passed, amended, Dec. 11. Senate Banking, Housing and Urban Affairs discharged. Senate passed, amended, May 20, 2010. Conference report filed in the House on June 29 (H Rept 111-517). House agreed to conference report June 30. Senate agreed to conference report July 15. President signed July 21, 2010.

■ **PL 111-204** (S 1508) Amend the Improper Payments Information Act of 2002 to reduce improper payments by federal agencies. Introduced by CARPER, D-Del., on July 23, 2009. Senate Homeland Security and Governmental Affairs reported, amended, June 15, 2010 (no written report). Senate passed, amended, June 23. House passed, under suspension of the rules, July 14. President signed July 22, 2010.

■ **PL 111-205** (HR 4213) Amend the Internal Revenue Code of 1986 to extend certain expiring provisions. Introduced by RANGEL, D-N.Y., on Dec. 7, 2009. House passed Dec. 9. Senate Finance discharged. Senate passed, amended, March 10, 2010. House agreed to Senate amendment, with amendments, May 28. Senate agreed to House amendment to Senate amendment, with amendment, July 1. House agreed to Senate amendment to House amendment to Senate amendment July 22. President signed July 22, 2010.

■ **PL 111-206** (HR 689) Exchange administrative jurisdiction of certain federal lands between the Forest Service and the Bureau of Land Management. Introduced by HERGER, R-Calif., on Jan. 26, 2009. House Natural Resources reported, amended, May 14 (H Rept 111-108). House passed, amended, under suspension of the rules, June 2. Senate Energy and Natural Resources reported, amended, March 2, 2010 (S Rept 111-145). Senate passed, amended, May 7. House agreed to Senate amendment, under suspension of the rules, July 13. President signed July 27, 2010.

■ **PL 111-207** (HR 3360) Amend Title 46, U.S. Code, to establish requirements to ensure the security and safety of passengers and crew on cruise vessels. Introduced by MATSUI, D-Calif., on July 28, 2009. House Transportation and Infrastructure reported Nov. 7 (H Rept 111-332). House passed, amended, under suspension of the rules, Nov. 17. Senate passed, amended, June 10, 2010. House agreed to Senate amendment, under suspension of the rules, June 30. President signed July 27, 2010.

■ **PL 111-208** (HR 4840) Designate the facility of the U.S. Postal Service located at 1981 Cleveland Ave. in Columbus, Ohio, as the "Clarence D. Lumpkin Post Office." Introduced by TIBERI, R-Ohio, on March 12, 2010. House passed, under suspension of the rules, March 21. Senate Homeland Security and Governmental Affairs reported, amended, May 18 (no written report). Senate passed,

amended, May 25. House agreed to Senate amendment, under suspension of the rules, July 14. President signed July 27, 2010.

■ **PL 111-209** (HR 5502) Amend the effective date of the gift card provisions of the Credit Card Accountability Responsibility and Disclosure Act of 2009. Introduced by MAFFEI, D-N.Y., on June 10, 2010. House passed, under suspension of the rules, June 14. Senate Banking, Housing and Urban Affairs discharged. Senate passed July 13. President signed July 27, 2010.

■ **PL 111-210** (H J Res 83) Approve the renewal of import restrictions contained in the Burmese Freedom and Democracy Act of 2003. Introduced by CROWLEY, D-N.Y., on May 11, 2010. House passed, amended, under suspension of the rules, July 14. Senate passed July 22. President signed July 27, 2010.

■ **PL 111-211** (HR 725) Protect American Indian arts and crafts through the improvement of applicable criminal proceedings. Introduced by PASTOR, D-Ariz., on Jan. 27, 2009. House Natural Resources reported Jan. 15, 2010 (H Rept 111-397, Part 1). House Judiciary discharged. House passed, amended, under suspension of the rules, Jan. 19. Senate passed, amended, June 23. House agreed to Senate amendment, under suspension of the rules, July 21. President signed July 29, 2010.

■ **PL 111-212** (HR 4899) Make emergency supplemental appropriations for operations in Iraq and Afghanistan and for other purposes for the fiscal year ending Sept. 30, 2010. Introduced by OBEY, D-Wis., on March 21, 2010. House passed March 24. Senate Appropriations reported, amended, May 14 (S Rept 111-188). Senate passed, amended, May 27. House agreed to Senate amendment, with amendments July 1. Senate disagreed to House amendment to Senate amendment July 22. House receded and concurred in Senate amendment, under suspension of the rules, July 27. President signed July 29, 2010.

■ **PL 111-213** (HR 5610) Provide a technical adjustment with respect to funding for independent living centers under the Rehabilitation Act of 1973. Introduced by MILLER, D-Calif., on June 28, 2010. House passed, amended, under suspension of the rules, June 30. Senate Health, Education, Labor and Pensions discharged. Senate passed, amended, July 27. House agreed to Senate amendment, under suspension of the rules, July 28. President signed July 29, 2010.

■ **PL 111-214** (HR 5849) Provide for an additional temporary extension of programs under the Small Business Act and the Small Business Investment Act of 1958. Introduced by VELÁZQUEZ, D-N.Y., on July 26, 2010. House passed, under suspension of the rules, July 27. Senate passed July 27. President signed July 30, 2010.

■ **PL 111-215** (S 3372) Modify the date on which the EPA administrator and applicable states may require permits for discharges from certain vessels. Introduced by BOXER, D-Calif., on May 13, 2010. Senate Environment and Public Works reported June 18 (S Rept 111-209). Senate passed July 14. House passed, under suspension of the rules, July 29. President signed July 30, 2010.

■ **PL 111-216** (HR 5900) Amend the Internal Revenue Code of 1986 to extend the funding and expenditure authority of the Airport and

Airway Trust Fund; amend Title 49, U.S. Code, to extend airport improvement program project grant authority; and improve airline safety. Introduced by OBERSTAR, D-Minn., on July 28, 2010. House passed, under suspension of the rules, July 29. Senate passed July 30. President signed Aug. 1, 2010.

■ **PL 111-217** (HR 4861) Designate the facility of the U.S. Postal Service located at 1343 West Irving Park Road in Chicago as the "Steve Goodman Post Office Building." Introduced by QUIGLEY, D-Ill., on March 16, 2010. House passed, under suspension of the rules, April 26. Senate Homeland Security and Governmental Affairs reported June 29 (no written report). Senate passed July 14. President signed Aug. 3, 2010.

■ **PL 111-218** (HR 5051) Designate the facility of the U.S. Postal Service located at 23 Genesee St. in Hornell, N.Y., as the "Zachary Smith Post Office Building." Introduced by CROWLEY, D-N.Y., on April 15, 2010. House passed, under suspension of the rules, May 11. Senate Homeland Security and Governmental Affairs reported June 29 (no written report). Senate passed July 14. President signed Aug. 3, 2010.

■ **PL 111-219** (HR 5099) Designate the facility of the U.S. Postal Service located at 15 South Main St. in Sharon, Mass., as the "Michael C. Rothberg Post Office." Introduced by FRANK, D-Mass., on April 21, 2010. House passed, under suspension of the rules, May 19. Senate Homeland Security and Governmental Affairs reported June 29 (no written report). Senate passed July 14. President signed Aug. 3, 2010.

■ **PL 111-220** (S 1789) Reduce the disparity in sentencing guidelines between powder and crack cocaine for federal drug offenses. Introduced by DURBIN, D-Ill., on Oct. 15, 2009. Senate Judiciary reported, amended, March 15, 2010 (no written report). Senate passed, amended, March 17. House passed, under suspension of the rules, July 28. President signed Aug. 3, 2010.

■ **PL 111-221** (HR 4684) Require the secretary of the Treasury to strike medals in commemoration of the 10th anniversary of the Sept. 11, 2001, terrorist attacks and the establishment of the National September 11 Memorial & Museum at the World Trade Center. Introduced by NADLER, D-N.Y., on Feb. 24, 2010. House passed, amended, under suspension of the rules, July 20. Senate passed July 22. President signed Aug. 6, 2010.

■ **PL 111-222** (S 1053) Amend the National Law Enforcement Museum Act to delay the termination date. Introduced by MURKOWSKI, R-Alaska, on May 14, 2009. Senate Energy and Natural Resources reported March 2, 2010 (S Rept 111-137). Senate passed May 7. House passed, under suspension of the rules, July 21. President signed Aug. 6, 2010.

■ **PL 111-223** (HR 2765) Amend Title 28, U.S. Code, to prohibit recognition and enforcement of foreign defamation judgments and certain foreign judgments against the providers of interactive computer services. Introduced by COHEN, D-Tenn., on June 9, 2009. House Judiciary reported June 15 (H Rept 111-154). House passed, amended, under suspension of the rules, June 15. Senate Judiciary reported, amended, July 14, 2010 (S Rept 111-224). Senate passed,

amended, July 19. House agreed to Senate amendment, under suspension of the rules, July 27. President signed Aug. 10, 2010.

■ **PL 111-224** (HR 5874) Make supplemental appropriations for the U.S. Patent and Trademark Office for the fiscal year ending Sept. 30, 2010. Introduced by MOLLOHAN, D-W.Va., on July 27, 2010. House passed, under suspension of the rules, July 28. Senate passed July 29. President signed Aug. 10, 2010.

■ **PL 111-225** (S 1749) Amend Title 18, U.S. Code, to prohibit the possession or use of cell phones and similar wireless devices by federal prisoners. Introduced by FEINSTEIN, D-Calif., on Oct. 5, 2009. Senate Judiciary reported, amended, Feb. 2, 2010 (no written report). Senate passed, amended, April 13. House passed, amended, under suspension of the rules, July 20. Senate agreed to House amendment July 28. President signed Aug. 10, 2010.

■ **PL 111-226** (HR 1586) To provide Medicaid and education funding for states and localities. Introduced by RANGEL, D-N.Y., as tax bill on March 18, 2009. House passed, under suspension of the rules, March 19. Senate passed, amended, as Federal Aviation Administration authorization, March 22, 2010. House agreed to Senate amendment, with amendment, March 25. Senate agreed to House amendment to Senate amendment, with amendment, as state Medicaid and education funding Aug. 5. House agreed to Senate amendment to House amendment to Senate amendment Aug. 10. President signed Aug. 10, 2010.

■ **PL 111-227** (HR 4380) Amend the Harmonized Tariff Schedule of the United States to modify temporarily certain rates of duty. Introduced by LEVIN, D-Mich., on Dec. 16, 2009. House passed, amended, under suspension of the rules, July 21, 2010. Senate passed July 27. President signed Aug. 11, 2010.

■ **PL 111-228** (HR 5872) Provide adequate commitment authority for fiscal year 2010 for guaranteed loans that are obligations of the General and Special Risk Insurance Funds of the Department of Housing and Urban Development. Introduced by FRANK, D-Mass., on July 27, 2010. House passed, amended, under suspension of the rules, July 28. Senate Banking, Housing and Urban Affairs discharged. Senate passed Aug. 4. President signed Aug. 11, 2010.

■ **PL 111-229** (HR 5981) Increase the flexibility of the secretary of Housing and Urban Development on the amount of premiums charged for FHA single-family housing mortgage insurance. Introduced by FRANK, D-Mass., on July 30, 2010. House passed, under suspension of the rules, July 30. Senate Banking, Housing and Urban Affairs discharged. Senate passed Aug. 4. President signed Aug. 11, 2010.

■ **PL 111-230** (HR 6080) Make emergency supplemental appropriations for border security for the fiscal year ending Sept. 30, 2010. Introduced by PRICE, D-N.C., on Aug. 9, 2010. House passed, under suspension of the rules, Aug. 10. Senate passed Aug. 12. President signed Aug. 13, 2010.

■ **PL 111-231** (HR 511) Authorize the secretary of Agriculture to terminate certain easements held by the secretary on land owned by

the village of Caseyville, Ill., and terminate associated contractual arrangements with the village. Introduced by COSTELLO, D-Ill., on Jan. 14, 2009. House Agriculture reported Sept. 10 (II Rept 111-253). House passed, under suspension of the rules, Sept. 15. Senate Agriculture, Nutrition, and Forestry reported Dec. 16 (no written report). Senate passed Aug. 5, 2010. President signed Aug. 16, 2010.

■ **PL 111-232** (HR 2097) Require the secretary of the Treasury to mint coins in commemoration of the bicentennial of the writing of "The Star-Spangled Banner." Introduced by RUPPERSBERGER, D-Md., on April 23, 2009. House passed, under suspension of the rules, Sept. 9. Senate Banking, Housing and Urban Affairs discharged. Senate passed Aug. 2, 2010. President signed Aug. 16, 2010.

■ **PL 111-233** (HR 3509) Reauthorize state agricultural mediation programs under Title V of the Agricultural Credit Act of 1987. Introduced by PETERSON, D-Minn., on July 31, 2009. House passed, under suspension of the rules, March 18, 2010. Senate Agriculture, Nutrition, and Forestry discharged. Senate passed Aug. 5. President signed Aug. 16, 2010.

■ **PL 111-234** (HR 4275) Designate the annex building under construction for the Elbert P. Tuttle U.S. Court of Appeals Building in Atlanta as the "John C. Godbold Federal Building." Introduced by LEWIS, D-Ga., on Dec. 10, 2009. House Transportation and Infrastructure reported, amended, March 18, 2010 (H Rept 111-444). House passed, amended, under suspension of the rules, April 14. Senate Environment and Public Works reported June 15 (no written report). Senate passed Aug. 5. President signed Aug. 16, 2010.

■ **PL 111-235** (HR 5278) Designate the facility of the U.S. Postal Service located at 405 West Second St. in Dixon, Ill., as the "President Ronald W. Reagan Post Office Building." Introduced by FOSTER, D-Ill., on May 12, 2010. House passed, under suspension of the rules, June 9. Senate Homeland Security and Governmental Affairs reported July 28 (no written report). Senate passed July 30. President signed Aug. 16, 2010.

■ **PL 111-236** (HR 5395) Designate the facility of the U.S. Postal Service located at 151 North Maitland Ave. in Maitland, Fla., as the "Paula Hawkins Post Office Building." Introduced by MICA, R-Fla., on May 25, 2010. House passed, under suspension of the rules, June 30. Senate Homeland Security and Governmental Affairs reported July 28 (no written report). Senate passed July 30. President signed Aug. 16, 2010.

■ **PL 111-237** (HR 5552) Amend the Internal Revenue Code of 1986 to require that the manufacturers' excise tax on recreational equipment be paid quarterly and provide for the assessment by the secretary of the Treasury of certain criminal restitution. Introduced by KIND, D-Wis., on June 17, 2010. House passed, amended, under suspension of the rules, June 29. Senate passed Aug. 5. President signed Aug. 16, 2010.

■ **PL 111-238** (HR 6102) Amend the National Defense Authorization Act for fiscal year 2010 to extend the authority of the secretary of the Navy to enter into multi-year contracts for F/A-18E, F/A-18F and EA-18G aircraft. Introduced by TAYLOR, D-Miss., on Aug. 10,

2010. House passed, under suspension of the rules, Sept. 14. Senate passed Sept. 16. President signed Sept. 27, 2010.

■ **PL 111-239** (S 3656) Amend the Agricultural Marketing Act of 1946 to improve the reporting on sales of livestock and dairy products. Introduced by LINCOLN, D-Ark., on July 27, 2010. Senate Agriculture, Nutrition and Forestry reported Aug. 5 (no written report). Senate passed Aug. 5. House passed, under suspension of the rules, Sept. 15. President signed Sept. 27, 2010.

■ **PL 111-240** (HR 5297) Create the Small Business Lending Fund to increase the availability of credit for small businesses and amend the Internal Revenue Code of 1986 to provide tax incentives for small-business job creation. Introduced by FRANK, D-Mass., on May 13, 2010. House Financial Services reported, amended, May 27 (H Rept 111-499). House passed, amended, June 17. Senate passed, amended, Sept. 16. House agreed to Senate amendment Sept. 23. President signed Sept. 27, 2010.

■ **PL 111-241** (HR 1454) Provide for the issuance of a multinational species conservation funds semipostal stamp. Introduced by BROWN, R-S.C., on March 12, 2009. House Natural Resources reported, amended, Dec. 7 (H Rept 111-358, Part 1). House Oversight and Government Reform discharged. House passed, amended, under suspension of the rules, Dec. 7. Senate Homeland Security and Governmental Affairs reported, amended, July 27, 2010 (S Rept 111-234). Senate passed, amended, July 29. House agreed to Senate amendment, under suspension of the rules, Sept. 22. President signed Sept. 30, 2010.

■ **PL 111-242** (HR 3081) Make continuing appropriations for fiscal year 2011. Introduced by LOWEY, D-N.Y., on June 26, 2009, as fiscal 2010 Foreign Operations bill. House Appropriations reported June 26 (H Rept 111-187). House passed, amended, July 9. Senate passed, amended, as continuing resolution, Sept. 29, 2010. House agreed to Senate amendment Sept. 30. President signed Sept. 30, 2010.

■ **PL 111-243** (HR 3562) Designate the federally occupied building at 1220 Echelon Parkway in Jackson, Miss., as the "James Chaney, Andrew Goodman, Michael Schwerner and Roy K. Moore Federal Building." Introduced by THOMPSON, D-Miss., on Sept. 14, 2009. House Transportation and Infrastructure reported, amended, Feb. 22, 2010 (H Rept 111-414). House passed, amended, under suspension of the rules, March 24. Senate Environment and Public Works reported, amended, July 26 (no written report). Senate passed, amended, Aug. 5. House agreed to Senate amendment, under suspension of the rules, Sept. 16. President signed Sept. 30, 2010.

■ **PL 111-244** (HR 3940) Clarify the availability of existing funds for political status education in the territory of Guam. Introduced by BORDALLO, D-Guam, on Oct. 27, 2009. House Natural Resources reported, amended, Dec. 7 (H Rept 111-357). House passed, amended, under suspension of the rules, Dec. 7. Senate Energy and Natural Resources discharged. Senate passed, amended, Sept. 28, 2010. House agreed to Senate amendment, under suspension of the rules, Sept. 30. President signed Sept. 30, 2010.

■ **PL 111-245** (HR 3978) Amend the Homeland Security Act of 2002 to authorize the secretary of Homeland Security to accept

and use gifts for otherwise authorized activities of the Center for Domestic Preparedness that are related to preparedness for a response to terrorism. Introduced by ROGERS, R-Ala., on Nov. 2, 2009. House Homeland Security reported Dec. 15 (H Rept 111-376). House passed, under suspension of the rules, Dec. 15. Senate Homeland Security and Governmental Affairs reported, amended, Aug. 2, 2010 (no written report). Senate passed, amended, Aug. 5. House agreed to Senate amendment, under suspension of the rules, Sept. 15. President signed Sept. 30, 2010.

■ **PL 111-246** (HR 4505) Enable the secretary of Veterans Affairs to allow state homes to furnish nursing-home care to parents who had at least one child die while serving in the Armed Forces. Introduced by THORNBERRY, R-Texas, on Jan. 26, 2010. House passed, under suspension of the rules, June 30. Senate Veterans' Affairs discharged. Senate passed Sept. 20. President signed Sept. 30, 2010.

■ **PL 111-247** (HR 4667) Increase, effective Dec. 1, 2010, the rates of compensation for veterans with service-connected disabilities and the rates of dependency and indemnity compensation for the survivors of certain disabled veterans. Introduced by PERRI-ELLO, D-Va., on Feb. 23, 2010. House Veterans' Affairs reported March 22 (H Rept 111-452). House passed, under suspension of the rules, March 22. Senate Veterans' Affairs discharged. Senate passed Sept. 22. President signed Sept. 30, 2010.

■ **PL 111-248** (HR 5682) Improve the operation of certain facilities and programs of the House of Representatives. Introduced by BRADY, D-Pa., on July 1, 2010. House Administration reported July 27 (H Rept 111-569). House passed, amended, under suspension of the rules, July 27. Senate Rules and Administration discharged. Senate passed Sept. 22. President signed Sept. 30, 2010.

■ **PL 111-249** (HR 6190) Amend the Internal Revenue Code of 1986 to extend the funding and expenditure authority of the Airport and Airway Trust Fund and amend Title 49, U.S. Code, to extend the airport improvement program. Introduced by LEVIN, D-Mich., on Sept. 23, 2010. House passed, under suspension of the rules, Sept. 23. Senate passed Sept. 24. President signed Sept. 30, 2010.

■ **PL 111-250** (S 3814) Extend the National Flood Insurance Program until Sept. 30, 2011. Introduced by VITTER, R-La., on Sept. 21, 2010. Senate passed Sept. 21. House passed, under suspension of the rules, Sept. 23. President signed Sept. 30, 2010.

■ **PL 111-251** (S 3839) Provide for an additional temporary extension of programs under the Small Business Act and the Small Business Investment Act of 1958. Introduced by LANDRIEU, D-La., on Sept. 24, 2010. Senate passed Sept. 24. House passed, under suspension of the rules, Sept. 28. President signed Sept. 30, 2010.

■ **PL 111-252** (HR 1517) Allow certain U.S. Customs and Border Protection employees who serve under an overseas limited appointment for at least two years, and whose service is rated fully successful or higher throughout that time, to be converted to a permanent appointment in the competitive service. Introduced by ENGEL, D-N.Y., on March 16, 2009. House Homeland Security reported, amended, Dec. 14 (H Rept 111-373, Part 1). House Oversight and Government Reform discharged. House passed, amended, under suspension of the rules, Dec. 15. Senate Homeland Security and Governmental Affairs reported, amended, Aug. 5, 2010 (S Rept 111-248). Senate passed, amended, Aug. 5. House agreed to Senate amendment, under suspension of the rules, Sept. 23. President signed Oct. 5, 2010.

■ **PL 111-253** (S 846) Award a congressional gold medal to Dr. Muhammad Yunus in recognition of his contributions to the fight against global poverty. Introduced by DURBIN, D-Ill., on April 21, 2009. Senate Banking, Housing and Urban Affairs discharged. Senate passed Oct. 13. House passed, under suspension of the rules, Sept. 23, 2010. President signed Oct. 5, 2010.

■ **PL 111-254** (S 1055) Grant the congressional gold medal, collectively, to the 100th Infantry Battalion and the 442nd Regimental Combat Team, U.S. Army, in recognition of their dedicated service during World War II. Introduced by BOXER, D-Calif., on May 14, 2009. Senate Banking, Housing and Urban Affairs discharged. Senate passed, amended, Aug. 2, 2010. House passed, under suspension of the rules, Sept. 23. President signed Oct. 5, 2010.

■ **PL 111-255** (S 1674) Provide for an exclusion under the Supplemental Security Income program and the Medicaid program for compensation provided to individuals who participate in clinical trials for rare diseases or conditions. Introduced by WYDEN, D-Ore., on Sept. 15, 2009. Senate Finance discharged. Senate passed Aug. 5, 2010. House passed, under suspension of the rules, Sept. 23. President signed Oct. 5, 2010.

■ **PL 111-256** (S 2781) Change references in federal law from "mental retardation" to "intellectual disability" and change references from a "mentally retarded" individual to an individual with an "intellectual disability." Introduced by MIKULSKI, D-Md., on Nov. 17, 2009. Senate Health, Education, Labor and Pensions reported, amended, Aug. 3, 2010 (S Rept 111-244). Senate passed, amended, Aug. 5. House passed, under suspension of the rules, Sept. 22. President signed Oct. 5, 2010.

■ **PL 111-257** (S 3717) Amend the Securities Exchange Act of 1934, the Investment Company Act of 1940 and the Investment Advisers Act of 1940 to provide for certain disclosures under Section 552, Title 5, U.S. Code (commonly referred to as the Freedom of Information Act). Introduced by LEAHY, D-Vt., on Aug. 5, 2010. Senate Judiciary reported Sept. 16 (no written report). Senate passed Sept. 21. House passed, under suspension of the rules, Sept. 23. President signed Oct. 5, 2010.

■ **PL 111-258** (HR 553) Require the secretary of Homeland Security to develop a strategy to prevent the overclassification of homeland security and other information and to promote the sharing of unclassified homeland security and other information. Introduced by HARMAN, D-Calif., on Jan. 15, 2009. House passed, under suspension of the rules, Feb. 3. Senate Homeland Security and Governmental Affairs reported, amended, May 27, 2010. (S Rept 111-200). Senate passed, amended, Sept. 27. House agreed to Senate amendment, under suspension of the rules, Sept. 28. President signed Oct. 7, 2010.

■ **PL 111-259** (HR 2701) Authorize appropriations for fiscal year 2010 for intelligence and intelligence-related activities of the U.S. government, the Community Management Account and the Central Intelligence Agency Retirement and Disability System. Introduced by REYES, D-Texas, on June 4, 2009. House Select Intelligence reported, amended, June 26 (H Rept 111-186). House passed, amended, Feb. 26, 2010. Senate passed, amended, Sept. 27. House agreed to Senate amendment Sept. 29. President signed Oct. 7, 2010.

■ **PL 111-260** (S 3304) Increase the access of persons with disabilities to modern communications. Introduced by PRYOR, D-Ark., on May 4, 2010. Senate Commerce, Science and Transportation reported, amended, Aug. 3 (no written report). Senate passed, amended, Aug. 5. House passed, under suspension of the rules, Sept. 28. President signed Oct. 8, 2010.

■ **PL 111-261** (HR 714) Authorize the secretary of the Interior to lease certain lands in the Virgin Islands National Park. Introduced by CHRISTENSEN, D-V.I., on Jan. 27, 2009. House passed, under suspension of the rules, Feb. 23. Senate Energy and Natural Resources reported, amended, March 2, 2010 (S Rept 111-146). Senate passed, amended, May 13. House agreed to Senate amendment, under suspension of the rules, Sept. 28. President signed Oct. 8, 2010.

■ **PL 111-262** (HR 1177) Require the secretary of the Treasury to mint coins in recognition of five U.S. Army five-star generals: George Marshall, Douglas MacArthur, Dwight D. Eisenhower, Henry "Hap" Arnold and Omar Bradley, all alumni of the U.S. Army Command and General Staff College, Fort Leavenworth, Kan., to coincide with the celebration of the 132nd Anniversary of the founding of the U.S. Army Command and General Staff College. Introduced by MOORE, D-Kan., on Feb. 25, 2009. House passed, amended, under suspension of the rules, May 20, 2010. Senate Banking, Housing and Urban Affairs discharged. Senate passed Sept. 28. President signed Oct. 8, 2010.

■ **PL 111-263** (S 2868) Provide increased access to the federal supply schedule of the General Services Administration to the American Red Cross, other qualified organizations, and state and local governments. Introduced by LIEBERMAN, I-Conn., on Dec. 10, 2009. Senate Homeland Security and Governmental Affairs reported May 17, 2010 (S Rept 111-192). Senate passed May 24. House Oversight and Government Reform reported, amended, Sept. 14 (H Rept 111-587). House passed, amended, under suspension of the rules, Sept. 15. Senate agreed to House amendment Sept. 27. President signed Oct. 8, 2010.

■ **PL 111-264** (S 3751) Amend the Stem Cell Therapeutic and Research Act of 2005 to revise the National Cord Blood Inventory Program. Introduced by HATCH, R-Utah, on Aug. 5, 2010. Senate Health, Education, Labor and Pensions reported, amended, Sept. 23 (no written report). Senate passed Sept. 28. House passed, under suspension of the rules, Sept. 30. President signed Oct. 8, 2010.

■ **PL 111-265** (S 3828) Make technical corrections in the 21st Century Communications and Video Accessibility Act of 2010 and the amendments made by that act. Introduced by PRYOR, D-Ark., on Sept. 22, 2010. Senate passed Sept. 22. House passed, under suspension of the rules, Sept. 28. President signed Oct. 8, 2010.

■ **PL 111-266** (S 3847) Implement certain defense trade cooperation treaties. Introduced by KERRY, D-Mass., on Sept. 27, 2010. Senate passed Sept. 27. House passed, under suspension of the rules, Sept. 28. President signed Oct. 8, 2010.

■ **PL 111-267** (S 3729) Authorize the programs of the National Aeronautics and Space Administration for fiscal years 2011 through 2013. Introduced by ROCKEFELLER, D-W.Va., on Aug. 5, 2010. Senate Commerce, Science and Transportation reported Aug. 5 (S Rept 111-278). Senate passed, amended, Aug. 5. House passed, under suspension of the rules, Sept. 29. President signed Oct. 11, 2010.

■ **PL 111-268** (HR 2923) Enhance the ability to combat methamphetamine. Introduced by GORDON, D-Tenn., on June 17, 2009. House Energy and Commerce reported Sept. 22, 2010 (H Rept 111-615, Part 1). House Judiciary discharged. House passed, amended, under suspension of the rules, Sept. 22. Senate passed Sept. 27. President signed Oct. 12, 2010.

■ **PL 111-269** (HR 3553) Exclude from consideration as income under the Native American Housing Assistance and Self-Determination Act of 1996 amounts received by a family from the Department of Veterans Affairs for service-related disabilities of a member of the family. Introduced by KIRKPATRICK, D-Ariz., on Sept. 10, 2009. House passed, under suspension of the rules, April 20, 2010. Senate Indian Affairs reported Sept. 22 (S Rept 111-299). Senate passed Sept. 27. President signed Oct. 12, 2010.

■ **PL 111-270** (HR 3689) Provide for an extension of the legislative authority of the Vietnam Veterans Memorial Fund Inc. to establish a Vietnam Veterans Memorial visitor center. Introduced by RAHALL, D-W.Va., on Oct. 1, 2009. House passed, under suspension of the rules, Oct. 13. Senate Energy and Natural Resources reported May 24, 2010 (S Rept 111-198). Senate passed Sept. 28. President signed Oct. 12, 2010.

■ **PL 111-271** (HR 3980) Provide for identifying and eliminating redundant reporting requirements and developing meaningful performance metrics for homeland security preparedness grants. Introduced by CUELLAR, D-Texas, on Nov. 2, 2009. House Homeland Security reported Dec. 1 (H Rept 111-346). House passed, amended, under suspension of the rules, Dec. 2. Senate Homeland Security and Governmental Affairs reported, amended, Sept. 16, 2010 (S Rept 111-291). Senate passed, amended, Sept. 22. House agreed to Senate amendment, under suspension of the rules, Sept. 28. President signed Oct. 12, 2010.

■ **PL 111-272** (S 1132) Amend Title 18, U.S. Code, to improve the provisions relating to the carrying of concealed weapons by law enforcement officers. Introduced by LEAHY, D-Vt., on May 21, 2009. Senate Judiciary reported, amended, March 11, 2010 (S Rept 111-233). Senate passed, amended, May 13. House passed, under suspension of the rules, Sept. 29. President signed Oct. 12, 2010.

■ **PL 111-273** (S 3397) Amend the Controlled Substances Act to provide for take-back disposal of controlled substances in certain instances. Introduced by KLOBUCHAR, D-Minn., on May 24, 2010.

Senate Judiciary reported, amended, July 29 (no written report). Senate passed, amended, Aug. 3. House passed, amended, under suspension of the rules, Sept. 29. Senate agreed to House amendment Sept. 29. President signed Oct. 12, 2010.

■ **PL 111-274** (HR 946) Enhance citizen access to government information and services by establishing that government documents issued to the public must be written in language the public can understand and use. Introduced by BRALEY, D-Iowa, on Feb. 10, 2009. House Oversight and Government Reform reported, amended, March 11, 2010 (H Rept 111-432). House passed, amended, under suspension of the rules, March 17. Senate passed, amended, Sept. 27. House agreed to Senate amendment, under suspension of the rules, Sept. 29. President signed Oct. 13, 2010.

■ **PL 111-275** (HR 3219) Amend Title 38, U.S. Code, to make certain improvements in the laws administered by the secretary of Veterans Affairs relating to insurance and health care. Introduced by FILNER, D-Calif., on July 15, 2009. House Veterans' Affairs reported July 23 (H Rept 111-223). Passed House, amended, under suspension of the rules, July 27. Senate Veterans' Affairs discharged. Senate passed, amended, Sept. 28, 2010. House agreed to Senate amendment, under suspension of the rules, Sept. 29. President signed Oct. 13, 2010.

■ **PL 111-276** (HR 4543) Designate the facility of the U.S. Postal Service located at 4285 Payne Ave. in San Jose, Calif., as the "Anthony J. Cortese Post Office Building." Introduced by LOFGREN, D-Calif., on Jan. 27, 2010. House passed, under suspension of the rules, April 26. Senate Homeland Security and Governmental Affairs reported Sept. 29 (no written report). Senate passed Sept. 29. President signed Oct. 13, 2010.

■ **PL 111-277** (HR 5341) Designate the facility of the U.S. Postal Service located at 100 Orndorf Drive in Brighton, Mich., as the "Joyce Rogers Post Office Building." Introduced by DINGELL, D-Mich., on May 19, 2010. House passed, under suspension of the rules, July 22. Senate Homeland Security and Governmental Affairs reported Sept. 29 (no written report). Senate passed Sept. 29. President signed Oct. 13, 2010.

■ **PL 111-278** (HR 5390) Designate the facility of the U.S. Postal Service located at 13301 Smith Road in Cleveland as the "David John Donafee Post Office Building." Introduced by KUCINICH, D-Ohio, on May 25, 2010. House passed, under suspension of the rules, July 14. Senate Homeland Security and Governmental Affairs reported Sept. 29 (no written report). Senate passed Sept. 29. President signed Oct. 13, 2010.

■ **PL 111-279** (HR 5450) Designate the facility of the U.S. Postal Service located at 3894 Crenshaw Blvd. in Los Angeles as the "Tom Bradley Post Office Building." Introduced by WATSON, D-Calif., on May 27, 2010. House passed, under suspension of the rules, July 14, 2010. Senate Homeland Security and Governmental Affairs reported Sept. 29 (no written report). Senate passed Sept. 29. President signed Oct. 13, 2010.

■ **PL 111-280** (HR 6200) Amend Part A of Title XI of the Social Security Act to provide for a one-year extension of the authoriza-

tions for the Work Incentives Planning and Assistance program and the Protection and Advocacy for Beneficiaries of Social Security program. Introduced by POMEROY, D-N.D., on Sept. 23, 2010. House passed, under suspension of the rules, Sept. 28. Senate passed Sept. 29. President signed Oct. 13, 2010.

■ **PL 111-281** (HR 3619) Authorize appropriations for the Coast Guard for fiscal year 2011. Introduced by OBERSTAR, D-Minn., on Sept. 22, 2009. House Transportation and Infrastructure reported, amended, Oct. 16 (H Rept 111-303, Part 1). House Homeland Security discharged. House passed, amended, Oct. 23. Senate passed, amended, May 7, 2010. House agreed to Senate amendment, with amendment, Sept. 28. Senate agreed to House amendment to Senate amendment, with amendment, Sept. 29. House agreed to Senate amendment to House amendment to Senate amendment Sept. 30. President signed Oct. 15, 2010.

■ **PL 111-282** (S 1510) Transfer statutory entitlements to pay and hours of work authorized by the District of Columbia Code for current members of the U.S. Secret Service Uniformed Division to the U.S. Code. Introduced by LIEBERMAN, I-Conn., on July 23, 2009. Senate Homeland Security and Governmental Affairs reported Oct. 5 (S Rept 111-86). Senate passed Oct. 13. House passed, amended, under suspension of the rules, June 28, 2010. Senate agreed to House amendment, with amendment, Sept. 27. House agreed to Senate amendment to House amendment Sept. 30. President signed Oct. 15, 2010.

■ **PL 111-283** (S 3196) Amend the Presidential Transition Act of 1963 to provide that certain transition services shall be available to eligible candidates before the general election. Introduced by KAUFMAN, D-Del., on April 13, 2010. Senate Homeland Security and Governmental Affairs reported Aug. 2 (S Rept 111-239). Senate passed, amended, Sept. 24. House passed, under suspension of the rules, Sept. 30. President signed Oct. 15, 2010.

■ **PL 111-284** (S 3802) Designate a mountain and icefield in the state of Alaska as "Mount Stevens" and the "Ted Stevens Icefield," respectively. Introduced by MURKOWSKI, R-Alaska, on Sept. 20, 2010. Senate Energy and Natural Resources discharged. Senate passed, amended, Sept. 27. House Natural Resources discharged. House passed Sept. 30. President signed Oct. 18, 2010.

■ **PL 111-285** (S 3774) Extend the deadline for Social Services Block Grant expenditure of supplemental funds appropriated following disasters occurring in 2008. Introduced by CORNYN, R-Texas, on Sept. 14, 2010. Senate passed, amended, Sept. 29. House passed, under suspension of the rules, Nov. 18. President signed Nov. 24, 2010.

■ **PL 111-286** (HR 5712) Provide for certain clarifications and extensions under Medicare, Medicaid and the Children's Health Insurance Program. Introduced by LEVIN, D-Mich., on July 13, 2010. House passed, under suspension of the rules, Aug. 14. Senate passed, amended, Nov. 29. House agreed to Senate amendments, under suspension of the rules, Nov. 29. President signed Nov. 30, 2010.

■ **PL 111-287** (S 1376) Restore immunization and sibling age exemptions for children adopted by U.S. citizens under the Hague Convention on Intercountry Adoption to allow their admission into

the United States. Introduced by KLOBUCHAR, D-Minn., on June 25, 2009. Senate Judiciary reported, amended, July 14, 2010 (S Rept 111-220). Senate passed, amended, July 21. House passed, under suspension of the rules, Nov. 15. President signed Nov. 30, 2010.

■ **PL 111-288** (S 3567) Designate the facility of the U.S. Postal Service located at 100 Broadway in Lynbrook, N.Y., as the "Navy Corpsman Jeffrey L. Wiener Post Office Building." Introduced by SCHUMER, D-N.Y., on July 12, 2010. Senate Homeland and Governmental Affairs reported July 28 (no written report). Senate passed July 30. House passed, under suspension of the rules, Nov 16. President signed Nov. 30, 2010.

■ **PL 111-289** (S J Res 40) Appoint the day for the convening of the first session of the 112th Congress. Introduced by REID, D-Nev., on Nov. 15, 2010. Senate passed Nov. 15. House passed Nov. 17. President signed Nov. 30, 2010.

■ **PL 111-290** (H J Res 101) Making further continuing appropriations for fiscal year 2011. Introduced by OBEY, D-Wis., on Nov. 30, 2010. House passed Dec. 1. Senate passed Dec. 2. President signed Dec. 4, 2010.

■ **PL 111-291** (HR 4783) Provide for final settlement of claims against the government regarding the allocation of farm loans and services and by American Indians regarding government-run trust funds. Introduced by LEVIN, D-Mich., on March 9, 2010, to accelerate the income tax benefits for charitable cash contributions for victims of the earthquake in Chile, and to extend the period from which such contributions for victims of the earthquake in Haiti could be accelerated. House passed, under suspension of the rules, March 10. Senate passed, amended, Nov. 19. House agreed to Senate amendments, Nov. 30. President signed Dec. 8, 2010.

■ **PL 111-292** (HR 1722) Develop a program that allows employees at executive branch agencies to telework at least 20 percent of the hours worked in every two administrative workweeks. Introduced by SARBANES, D-Md., on March 25, 2009. House Oversight and Government Reform reported, amended, May 4, 2010 (H Rept 111-474). House passed, amended, July 14. Senate passed, with an amendment, Sept. 29. House agreed to Senate amendment Nov. 18. President signed Dec. 9, 2011.

■ **PL 111-293** (HR 5283) Provide for adjustment of status for certain Haitian orphans paroled into the United States after the earthquake of Jan. 12, 2010. Introduced by FORTENBERRY, R-Neb., on May 12, 2010. House passed, amended, under suspension of the rules, July 20. Senate passed, with an amendment, Aug. 4. House agreed to Senate amendment, under suspension of the rules, Dec. 1. President signed Dec. 9, 2010.

■ **PL 111-294** (HR 5566) Amend Title 18, U.S. Code, to prohibit interstate commerce in animal "crush" videos. Introduced by GALLEGLY, R-Calif., on June 22, 2010. House Judiciary reported July 19 (H Rept 111-549). House passed, under suspension of the rules, July 21. Senate passed, with an amendment, Sept. 28. House agreed to the Senate amendment, with an amendment, Nov. 15. Senate agreed to House amendment Nov. 19. President signed Dec. 9, 2010.

■ **PL 111-295** (S 3689) Clarify, improve and correct the laws relating to copyrights. Introduced by LEAHY, D-Vt., on Aug. 2, 2010. Senate passed Aug. 2. House passed, amended, Nov. 15. Senate agreed to House amendments, under suspension of the rules, Nov. 19. President signed Dec. 9, 2010.

■ **PL 111-296** (S 3307) Reauthorize child nutrition programs. Introduced by LINCOLN, D-Ark., on May 5, 2010. Senate Agriculture, Nutrition and Forestry reported (S Rept 111-178). Senate passed Aug. 5. House passed Dec. 2. President signed Dec. 13, 2010.

■ **PL 111-297** (HR 4387) Designate the federal building located at 100 North Palafox St. in Pensacola, Fla., as the "Winston E. Arnow Federal Building." Introduced by MILLER, R-Fla., on Dec. 16, 2009. House Transportation reported Sept. 20, 2010 (H Rept 111-610). House passed, under suspension of the rules, Sept. 28. Senate Environment and Public Works reported Nov. 30 (no written report). Senate passed Dec. 1. President signed Dec. 14, 2010.

■ **PL 111-298** (HR 5651) Designate the federal building and U.S. courthouse located at 515 9th St. in Rapid City, S.D., as the "Andrew W. Bogue Federal Building and United States Courthouse." Introduced by HERSETH SANDLIN, D-S.D., on June 30, 2010. House Transportation and Infrastructure reported Sept. 14 (H Rept 111-590). House passed, under suspension of the rules, Sept. 15. Senate Environment and Public Works reported Nov. 30 (no written report). Senate passed Dec. 1. President signed Dec. 14, 2010.

■ **PL 111-299** (HR 5706) Designate the building occupied by the Government Printing Office located at 31451 East United Ave. in Pueblo, Colo., as the "Frank Evans Government Printing Office Building." Introduced by SALAZAR, D-Colo., on July 1, 2010. House Transportation and Infrastructure reported, amended, Sept. 14 (H Rept 111-591). House passed, under suspension of the rules, Sept. 15. Senate Environment and Public Works reported Nov. 30 (no written report). Senate passed Dec. 1. President signed Dec. 14, 2010.

■ **PL 111-300** (HR 5758) Designate the facility of the U.S. Postal Service located at 2 Government Center in Fall River, Mass., as the "Sgt. Robert Barrett Post Office Building." Introduced by FRANK, D-Mass., on July 15, 2010. House passed, under suspension of the rules, Nov. 17. Senate Homeland Security and Governmental Affairs reported Dec. 1 (no written report). Senate passed Dec. 2. President signed Dec. 14, 2010.

■ **PL 111-301** (HR 5773) Designate the federal building located at 6401 Security Blvd. in Baltimore as the "Robert M. Ball Federal Building." Introduced by CUMMINGS, D-Md., on July 19, 2010. House Transportation and Infrastructure reported, amended, Sept. 14 (H Rept 111-592). House passed, under suspension of the rules, Sept 15. Senate Environment and Public Works reported Nov. 30 (no written report). Senate passed Dec. 1. President signed Dec. 14, 2010.

■ **PL 111-302** (HR 6162) Provide research and development authority for alternative coinage materials to the secretary of the Treasury, increase congressional oversight over coin production and ensure the continuity of certain numismatic items. Introduced by WATT,

D-N.C., on Sept. 22, 2010. House passed Sept. 29. Senate passed Nov. 30. President signed Dec. 14, 2010.

■ **PL 111-303** (HR 6166) Authorize the production of palladium bullion coins to provide affordable opportunities for investments in precious metals. Introduced by REHBERG, R-Mont., on Sept. 22, 2010. House passed Sept. 29. Senate passed Nov. 30. President signed Dec. 14, 2010.

■ **PL 111-304** (HR 6237) Designate the facility of the U.S. Postal Service located at 1351 2nd St. in Napa, Calif., the "Tom Kongsgaard Post Office Building." Introduced by THOMPSON, D-Calif., on Sept. 28, 2010. House passed, amended, under suspension of the rules, Nov. 16. Senate Homeland Security and Governmental Affairs reported Dec. 1 (no written report). Senate passed Dec. 2. President signed Dec. 14, 2010.

■ **PL 111-305** (HR 6387) Designate the facility of the U.S. Postal Service located at 337 West Clark St. in Eureka, Calif., as the "Sam Sacco Post Office Building." Introduced by THOMPSON, D-Calif., on Sept. 29, 2010. House passed, amended, under suspension of the rules, Nov. 16. Senate Homeland Security and Governmental Affairs reported Dec. 1 (no written report). Senate passed Dec. 2. President signed Dec. 14, 2010.

■ **PL 111-306** (S 1338) Require English language programs for foreign students entering the United States to study English be accredited by an agency recognized by the Education secretary. Introduced by CARPER, D-Del., on June 24, 2009. Senate passed Sept. 27, 2010. House passed, under suspension of the rules, Dec. 1. President signed Dec. 14, 2010.

■ **PL 111-307** (S 1421) Amend Section 42, Title 18 of the U.S. Code to prohibit the importation and shipment of certain species of carp. Introduced by LEVIN, D-Mich., on July 9, 2009. Senate Environment and Public Works reported May 5, 2010 (S Rept 111-181). Senate passed Nov. 17. House passed, under suspension of the rules, Dec. 1. President signed Dec. 14, 2010.

■ **PL 111-308** (S 3250) Provide for the training of federal building personnel. Introduced by CARPER, D-Del., on April 22, 2010. Senate Environment and Public Works reported June 21 (S Rept 111-212). Senate passed July 20. House passed, under suspension of the rules, Dec. 1. President signed Dec. 14, 2010.

■ **PL 111-309** (HR 4994) Extend certain expiring provisions of the Medicare and Medicaid programs. Introduced by LEWIS, D-Ga., on April 13, 2010, as a bill to revise certain tax provisions. House passed, amended, under suspension of the rules, April 14. Senate passed, amended, Dec. 8. House agreed to Senate amendments, under suspension of the rules, Dec. 9. President signed Dec. 15, 2010.

■ **PL 111-310** (HR 6118) Designate the facility of the U.S. Postal Service located at 2 Massachusetts Ave. NE in Washington, D.C., as the "Dorothy I. Height Post Office." Introduced by NORTON, D-D.C., on Sept. 14, 2010. House passed, amended, under suspension of the rules, Sept. 30. Senate Homeland Security reported Dec. 1 (no written report). Senate passed Dec. 2. President signed Dec. 15, 2010.

■ **PL 111-311** (S 2847) Regulate the audio volume of commercials. Introduced by WHITEHOUSE, D-R.I., on Dec. 8, 2009. Senate Commerce, Science, and Transportation reported, amended, Sept. 28, 2010 (no written report). Senate passed, with an amendment, Sept. 29. House passed, under suspension of the rules, Dec. 2. President signed Dec. 15, 2010.

■ **PL 111-312** (HR 4853) Extend tax cuts, investment incentives and unemployment insurance, revive the estate tax and cut the employee portion of the Social Security tax. Introduced by OBERSTAR, D-Minn., on March 16, 2010, as a bill to extend Federal Aviation Administration programs. House passed, under suspension of the rules, March 17. Senate passed, amended, Sept. 23. House agreed to Senate amendments, amended, Dec. 2. Senate agreed to House amendments, amended, Dec. 15. House agreed to Senate amendments, Dec. 16. President signed Dec. 17, 2010.

■ **PL 111-313** (HR 2480) Improve the accuracy of fur product labeling. Introduced by MORAN, D-Va., on May 19, 2009. House Energy and Commerce reported, amended, July 27, 2010 (H Rept 111-571). House passed, under suspension of the rules, July 28. Senate passed Dec. 7. President signed Dec. 18, 2010.

■ **PL 111-314** (HR 3237) Codify certain existing laws relating to national and commercial space programs as Title 51, U.S. Code, "National and Commercial Space Programs." Introduced by CONYERS, D-Mich., on July 16, 2009. House Judiciary reported Nov. 2 (H Rept 111-325). House passed, under suspension of the rules, Jan. 13, 2010. Senate Judiciary reported May 10 (no written report). Senate passed Dec. 3. President signed Dec. 18, 2010.

■ **PL 111-315** (HR 6184) Amend the Water Resources Development Act of 2000 to extend and modify the program allowing the secretary of the Army to accept and expend funds contributed by non-federal public entities to expedite the evaluation of permits. Introduced by LARSEN, D-Wash., on Sept. 22, 2010. House passed, amended, under suspension of the rules, Dec. 1. Senate passed Dec. 7. President signed Dec. 18, 2010.

■ **PL 111-316** (HR 6399) Improve certain administrative operations of the Office of the Architect of the Capitol. Introduced by BRADY, D-Pa., on Nov. 15, 2010. House passed, under suspension of the rules, Nov. 16. Senate passed Dec. 4. President signed Dec. 18, 2010.

■ **PL 111-317** (H J Res 105) Make further continuing appropriations for fiscal year 2011. Introduced by OBEY, D-Wis., on Dec. 17, 2010. House passed Dec. 17. Senate passed Dec. 17. President signed Dec. 18, 2010.

■ **PL 111-318** (S 3789) Limit access to Social Security account numbers. Introduced by FEINSTEIN, D-Calif., on Sept. 15, 2010. Senate passed Sept. 28. House passed, under suspension of the rules, Dec. 8. President signed Dec. 18, 2010.

■ **PL 111-319** (S 3987) Amend the Fair Credit Reporting Act with respect to the applicability of identity theft guidelines to creditors. Introduced by THUNE, R-S.D., on Nov. 30, 2010. Senate passed Nov. 30. House passed, under suspension of the rules, Dec. 7. President signed Dec. 18, 2010.

■ **PL 111-320** (S 3817) Reauthorize and amend the Child Abuse Prevention and Treatment Act, the Family Violence Prevention and Services Act, the Child Abuse Prevention and Treatment and Adoption Reform Act of 1978, and the Abandoned Infants Assistance Act of 1988. Introduced by DODD, D-Conn., on Sept. 22, 2010. Senate Health, Education, Labor and Pensions reported Dec. 2 (no written report). Senate passed, amended, Dec. 3. House passed, with an amendment, under suspension of the rules, Dec. 8. Senate agreed to House amendment Dec. 10. President signed Dec. 20, 2010.

■ **PL 111-321** (HR 2965) Repeal the statutory elements of the military's "don't ask don't tell" policy. Introduced by ALTMIRE, D-Pa., on June 19, 2009, as a bill to enhance small-business research and innovation. House Small Business reported, amended, June 26 (H Rept 111-190, Part 1). House Science and Technology reported, amended, July 7 (H Rept 111-190, Part 2). House passed July 8. Senate passed, with an amendment, July 13. House agreed to Senate amendment, with an amendment, Dec. 15, 2010. Senate agreed to the House amendment, Dec. 18. President signed Dec. 22, 2010.

■ **PL 111-322** (HR 3082) Make further continuing appropriations for fiscal year 2011 and extend surface transportation programs. Introduced by EDWARDS, D-Texas, on June 26, 2009, as a bill to provide appropriations for military construction, the Department of Veterans Affairs, and related agencies for the fiscal year ending Sept. 30, 2010. House Appropriations reported June 26 (H Rept 111-188). House passed July 10. Senate passed, with an amendment, Nov. 17. House agreed to Senate amendment, with an amendment, Dec. 8, 2010. Senate agreed to the House amendment, with an amendment, Dec. 21. House agreed to Senate amendment Dec. 21. President signed Dec. 22, 2010.

■ **PL 111-323** (HR 1061) Place certain land into trust for the Hoh Indian Tribe. Introduced by DICKS, D-Wash., on Feb. 13, 2009. House Natural Resources reported, amended, Oct. 21 (H Rept 111-306). House passed, under suspension of the rules, June 8, 2010. Senate passed, amended, Sept. 29. House agreed to Senate amendments, under suspension of the rules, Dec. 14. President signed Dec. 22, 2010.

■ **PL 111-324** (HR 2941) Reauthorize and enhance Johanna's Law to increase public awareness and knowledge with respect to gynecologic cancers. Introduced by DELAURO, D-Conn., on June 18, 2009. House Energy and Commerce reported, amended, Sept. 28, 2010 (H Rept 111-635). House passed, under suspension of the rules, Sept. 30. Senate Health, Education, Labor and Pensions reported, amended, Dec. 6 (no written report). Senate passed, amended, Dec. 10. House agreed to Senate amendment, under suspension of the rules, Dec. 16. President signed Dec. 22, 2010.

■ **PL 111-325** (HR 4337) Amend the Internal Revenue Code of 1986 to modify certain rules applicable to regulated investment companies. Introduced by RANGEL, D-N.Y., on Dec. 16, 2009. House passed, amended, under suspension of the rules, Sept. 28, 2010. Senate passed, with an amendment, Dec. 8. House agreed to Senate amendment, under suspension of the rules, Dec. 15. President signed Dec. 22, 2010.

■ **PL 111-326** (HR 5591) Designate the airport traffic control tower located at Spokane International Airport in Spokane, Wash., as

the "Ray Daves Airport Traffic Control Tower." Introduced by MCMORRIS RODGERS, R-Wash., on June 24, 2010. House Transportation and Infrastructure reported, amended, Sept. 20 (H Rept 111-611). House passed, under suspension of the rules, Sept. 28. Senate passed Dec. 9. President signed Dec. 22, 2010.

■ **PL 111-327** (HR 6198) Amend Title 11 of the U.S. Code to make technical corrections to bankruptcy law. Introduced by CONYERS, D-Mich., on Sept. 23, 2010. House passed, amended, under suspension of the rules, Sept. 28. Senate passed, with an amendment, Nov. 19. House agreed to the Senate amendment, under suspension of the rules, Dec. 16. President signed Dec. 22, 2010.

■ **PL 111-328** (HR 6278) Amend the National Children's Island Act of 1995 to expand allowable uses for Kingman and Heritage islands by the District of Columbia. Introduced by NORTON, D-D.C., on Sept. 29, 2010. House passed, under suspension of the rules, Nov. 16. Senate passed Dec. 13. President signed Dec. 22.

■ **PL 111-329** (HR 6473) Amend the Internal Revenue Code of 1986 to extend the funding and expenditure authority of the Airport and Airway Trust Fund and to amend Title 49, U.S. Code, to extend the airport improvement program. Introduced by OBERSTAR, D-Minn., on Dec. 2, 2010. House passed, under suspension of the rules, Dec. 2. Senate passed Dec. 18. President signed Dec. 22, 2010.

■ **PL 111-330** (HR 6516) Make technical corrections to provisions of law enacted by the Coast Guard Authorization Act of 2010. Introduced by OBERSTAR, D-Minn., on Dec. 13, 2010. House passed, under suspension of the rules, Dec. 14. Senate passed Dec. 15. President signed Dec. 22, 2010.

■ **PL 111-331** (S 30) Amend the Communications Act of 1934 to prohibit manipulation of caller identification information. Introduced by NELSON, D-Fla., on Jan. 7, 2009. Senate Commerce, Science and Transportation reported Nov. 2 (S Rept 111-96). Senate passed, amended, Feb. 23, 2010. House passed, under suspension of the rules, Dec. 15. President signed Dec. 22, 2010.

■ **PL 111-332** (S 1275) Establish a National Foundation on Physical Fitness and Sports to carry out activities to support and supplement the mission of the President's Council on Physical Fitness and Sports. Introduced by WARNER, D-Va., on June 16, 2009. Senate Health, Education, Labor and Pensions reported, amended, Dec. 7, 2010 (no written report). Senate passed Dec. 9. House passed, under suspension of the rules, Dec. 14. President signed Dec. 22, 2010.

■ **PL 111-333** (S 1405) Redesignate the Longfellow National Historic Site in Cambridge, Mass., as the "Longfellow House-Washington's Headquarters National Historic Site." Introduced by KENNEDY, D-Mass., on July 7, 2009. Senate Energy and Natural Resources reported March 2, 2010 (S Rept 111-141). Senate passed May 7. House passed, under suspension of the rules, Dec. 14. President signed Dec. 22, 2010.

■ **PL 111-334** (S 1448) Amend the Act of August 9, 1955, to authorize the Coquille Indian Tribe; the Confederated Tribes of Siletz Indians; the Confederated Tribes of the Coos, Lower Umpqua and Siuslaw; the

Klamath Tribes; and the Burns Paiute Tribe to obtain 99-year lease authority for trust land. Introduced by MERKLEY, D-Ore., on July 14, 2009. Senate Indian Affairs reported Aug. 3, 2010 (S Rept 111-245). Senate passed Sept. 22. House passed, under suspension of the rules, Dec. 14. President signed Dec. 22, 2010.

■ **PL 111-335** (S 1609) Authorize a single fisheries cooperative for the Bering Sea Aleutian Islands longline catcher processor subsector. Introduced by CANTWELL, D-Wash., on Aug. 6, 2009. Senate Commerce, Science and Transportation reported Aug. 5, 2010 (S Rept 111-250). Senate passed Nov. 18. House passed, under suspension of the rules, Dec. 14. President signed Dec. 22, 2010.

■ **PL 111-336** (S 2906) Amend the Act of August 9, 1955, to modify a provision relating to leases involving certain Indian tribes. Introduced by CANTWELL, D-Wash., on Dec. 18, 2009. Senate Indian Affairs reported, amended, Aug. 3, 2010 (S Rept 111-246). Senate passed Sept. 22. House passed, under suspension of the rules, Dec. 14. President signed Dec. 22, 2010.

■ **PL 111-337** (S 3199) Amend the Public Health Service Act regarding early detection, diagnosis and treatment of hearing loss. Introduced by SNOWE, R-Maine, on April 14, 2010. Senate Health, Education, Labor and Pensions reported, amended, Dec. 6 (no written report). Senate passed Dec. 7. House passed, under suspension of the rules, Dec. 15. President signed Dec. 22, 2010.

■ **PL 111-338** (S 3794) Amend Chapter 5, Title 40 of the U.S. Code to include organizations whose memberships comprise "substantially veterans" as recipient organizations for the donation of federal surplus personal property through state agencies. Introduced by LEAHY, D-Vt., on Sept. 16, 2010. Senate Homeland Security and Governmental Affairs reported, amended, Sept. 29 (no written report). Senate passed Sept. 29. House passed, under suspension of the rules, Dec. 14. President signed Dec. 22, 2010.

■ **PL 111-339** (S 3860) Require reports on the management of Arlington National Cemetery. Introduced by McCASKILL, D-Mo., on Sept. 28, 2010. Senate passed Dec. 4. House passed, under suspension of the rules, Dec. 16. President signed Dec. 22, 2010.

■ **PL 111-340** (S 3984) Amend and extend the Museum and Library Services Act. Introduced by REED, D-R.I., on Nov. 29, 2010. Senate Health, Education, Labor and Pensions reported Dec. 3 (no written report). Senate passed Dec. 7. House passed, under suspension of the rules, Dec. 14. President signed Dec. 22, 2010.

■ **PL 111-341** (S 3998) Extend the Child Safety Pilot Program. Introduced by SCHUMER, D-N.Y., on Dec. 1, 2010. Senate passed Dec. 1. House passed, under suspension of the rules, Dec. 8. President signed Dec. 22, 2010.

■ **PL 111-342** (S 4005) Amend Title 28 of the U.S. Code to prevent the proceeds or instrumentalities of foreign crime located in the United States from being shielded from foreign forfeiture proceedings. Introduced by WHITEHOUSE, D-R.I. on Dec. 2, 2010. Senate passed Dec. 15. House passed, under suspension of the rules, Dec. 16. President signed Dec. 22, 2010.

■ **PL 111-343** (HR 6398) Require the Federal Deposit Insurance Corporation to fully insure interest on Lawyers Trust Accounts. Introduced by DOGGETT, D-Texas, on Nov. 15, 2010. House passed, amended, under suspension of the rules, Nov. 30. Senate passed Dec. 22. President signed Dec. 29, 2010.

■ **PL 111-344** (HR 6517) Extend Trade Adjustment Assistance and certain trade preference programs and amend the Harmonized Tariff Schedule of the United States to modify temporarily certain rates of duty. Introduced by LEVIN, D-Mich., on Dec. 13, 2010. House passed, amended, under suspension of the rules, Dec. 15. Senate passed, with an amendment, Dec. 22. House agreed to the Senate amendment Dec. 22. President signed Dec. 29, 2010.

■ **PL 111-345** (S 3386) Protect consumers from certain aggressive sales tactics on the Internet. Introduced by ROCKEFELLER, D-W.Va., on May 19, 2010. Senate Commerce, Science and Transportation reported, amended, Aug. 2 (S Rept 111-240). Senate passed, amended, Nov. 30. House passed, under suspension of the rules, Dec. 15. President signed Dec. 29, 2010.

■ **PL 111-346** (S 4058) Extend certain expiring provisions that provide enhanced protections for servicemembers relating to mortgages and mortgage foreclosure. Introduced by KERRY, D-Mass., on Dec. 22, 2010. Senate passed Dec. 22. House passed Dec. 22. President signed Dec. 29, 2010.

■ **PL 111-347** (HR 847) Amend the Public Health Service Act to extend and improve protections and services to individuals directly affected by the Sept. 11, 2001, terrorist attack in New York City. Introduced by MALONEY, D-N.Y., on Feb. 4, 2009. House Energy and Commerce reported, amended, July 22, 2010 (H Rept 111-560, Part 1). House Judiciary reported, amended, July 22 (H Rept 111-560, Part 2). House passed Sept. 29. Senate passed, amended, Dec. 22. House agreed to Senate amendment Dec. 22. President signed Jan. 2, 2011.

■ **PL 111-348** (HR 81) Amend the High Seas Driftnet Fishing Moratorium Protection Act and the Magnuson-Stevens Fishery Conservation and Management Act to improve the conservation of sharks. Introduced by BORDALLO, D-Guam, on Jan. 6, 2009. House passed, under suspension of the rules, March 2. Senate passed, amended, Dec. 20, 2010. House agreed to Senate amendment, under suspension of the rules, Dec. 21. President signed Jan. 4, 2011.

■ **PL 111-349** (HR 628) Establish a pilot program in certain U.S. district courts to encourage enhancement of expertise in patent cases among district judges. Introduced by ISSA, R-Calif., on Jan. 22, 2009. House passed, under suspension of the rules, March 17. Senate passed, amended, Dec. 13, 2010. House agreed to Senate amendment, under suspension of the rules, Dec. 17. President signed Jan. 4, 2011.

■ **PL 111-350** (HR 1107) Enact certain laws relating to public contracts as Title 41, U.S. Code, "Public Contracts." Introduced by CONYERS, D-Mich., on Feb. 23, 2009. House Judiciary reported March 23 (H Rept 111-42). House passed, under suspension of the rules, May 6. Senate passed, amended, Dec. 2, 2010. House agreed to Senate amendments, under suspension of the rules, Dec. 17. President signed Jan. 4, 2011.

■ **PL 111-351** (HR 1746) Amend the Robert T. Stafford Disaster Relief and Emergency Assistance Act to reauthorize the pre-disaster mitigation program of the Federal Emergency Management Agency. Introduced by OBERSTAR, D-Minn., on March 26, 2009. House Transportation and Infrastructure reported April 23 (H Rept 111-83). House passed, under suspension of the rules, April 27. Senate passed, amended, Dec. 20, 2010. House agreed to Senate amendment, under suspension of the rules, Dec. 21. President signed Jan. 4, 2011.

■ **PL 111-352** (HR 2142) Require quarterly performance assessments of government programs for the purpose of assessing agency performance and improvement, and establish agency performance improvement officers and the Performance Improvement Council. Introduced by CUELLAR, D-Texas, on April 28, 2009. House Oversight and Government Reform reported June 14, 2010 (H Rept 111-504). House passed, under suspension of the rules, June 16. Senate Homeland Security and Governmental Affairs reported, amended, Dec. 16 (S Rept 111-372). Senate passed, amended, Dec. 16. House agreed to Senate amendment Dec. 21. President signed Jan. 4, 2011.

■ **PL 111-353** (HR 2751) Amend the Federal Food, Drug, and Cosmetic Act with respect to the safety of the food supply. Introduced by SUTTON, D-Ohio, on June 8, 2009, as a bill to accelerate motor fuel savings nationwide and provide incentives to registered owners of high-polluting automobiles to replace them with new fuel efficient and less-polluting cars. House passed, under suspension of the rules, June 9. Senate passed, amended, Dec. 19, 2010. House agreed to Senate amendments Dec. 21. President signed Jan. 4, 2011.

■ **PL 111-354** (HR 4445) Amend Public Law 95-232 to repeal a restriction on treating certain lands held in trust for American Indian pueblos in New Mexico as Indian country. Introduced by HEINRICH, D-N.M., on Jan. 13, 2010. House Natural Resources reported, amended, June 28 (H Rept 111-515). House passed, under suspension of the rules, June 30. Senate Indian Affairs reported Dec. 20 (S Rept 111-379). Senate passed Dec. 21. President signed Jan. 4, 2011.

■ **PL 111-355** (HR 4602) Designate the facility of the U.S. Postal Service located at 1332 Sharon Copley Road in Sharon Center, Ohio, as the "Emil Bolas Post Office." Introduced by BOCCIERI, D-Ohio, on Feb. 4, 2010. House passed, under suspension of the rules, Sept. 30. Senate passed Dec. 16. President signed Jan. 4, 2011.

■ **PL 111-356** (HR 4748) Amend the Office of National Drug Control Policy Reauthorization Act of 2006 to require a northern-border counternarcotics strategy. Introduced by OWENS, D-N.Y., on March 3, 2010. House passed, under suspension of the rules, July 27. Senate passed, amended, Dec. 20. House agreed to Senate amendment, under suspension of the rules, Dec. 21. President signed Jan. 4, 2011.

■ **PL 111-357** (HR 4973) Amend the Fish and Wildlife Act of 1956 to reauthorize volunteer programs and community partnerships for national wildlife refuges. Introduced by KRATOVIL, D-Md., on March 25, 2010. House Natural Resources reported, amended, July 13 (H Rept 111-531). House passed, under suspension of the rules, July 13. Senate Environment and Public Works reported Dec. 14 (S Rept 111-366). Senate passed Dec. 17. President signed Jan. 4, 2011.

■ **PL 111-358** (HR 5116) Invest in innovation through research and development to improve U.S. competitiveness. Introduced by GORDON, D-Tenn., on April 22, 2010. House Science and Technology reported, amended, May 7 (H Rept 111-478). House passed May 28. Senate passed, amended, Dec. 17. House agreed to Senate amendment Dec. 21. President signed Jan. 4, 2011.

■ **PL 111-359** (HR 5133) Designate the facility of the U.S. Postal Service located at 331 First St. in Carlstadt, N.J., as the "Staff Sgt. Frank T. Carvill and Lance Cpl. Michael A. Schwarz Post Office Building." Introduced by ROTHMAN, D-N.J., on April 22, 2010. House passed, under suspension of the rules, June 9. Senate passed Dec. 16. President signed Jan. 4, 2011.

■ **PL 111-360** (HR 5470) Exempt from certain energy efficiency standards under the Energy Policy and Conservation Act external power supplies for certain security or life-safety alarms and surveillance system components. Introduced by PALLONE, D-N.J., on May 28, 2010. House passed, under suspension of the rules, Dec. 8. Senate passed Dec. 21. President signed Jan. 4, 2011.

■ **PL 111-361** (HR 5605) Designate the facility of the U.S. Postal Service located at 47 East Fayette St. in Uniontown, Pa., as the "George C. Marshall Post Office." Introduced by CRITZ, D-Pa., on June 25, 2010. House passed, under suspension of the rules, Sept. 30. Senate passed Dec. 16. President signed Jan. 4, 2011.

■ **PL 111-362** (HR 5606) Designate the facility of the U.S. Postal Service located at 47 South Seventh St. in Indiana, Pa., as the "James M. 'Jimmy' Stewart Post Office Building." Introduced by CRITZ, D-Pa., on June 25, 2010. House passed, under suspension of the rules, Sept. 30. Senate passed Dec. 16. President signed Jan. 4, 2011.

■ **PL 111-363** (HR 5655) Designate the Little River Branch facility of the U.S. Postal Service located at 140 Northeast 84th St. in Miami as the "Jesse J. McCrary Jr. Post Office." Introduced by MEEK, D-Fla., on June 30, 2010. House passed, under suspension of the rules, Nov. 16. Senate passed Dec. 16. President signed Jan. 4, 2011.

■ **PL 111-364** (HR 5809) Amend the Energy Policy Act of 2005 to reauthorize and modify provisions relating to the diesel emissions reduction program. Introduced by INSLEE, D-Wash., on July 21, 2010. House Energy and Commerce reported, amended, Sept. 22 (H Rept 111-618). House passed, under suspension of the rules, Sept. 22. Senate passed, amended, Dec. 16. House agreed to Senate amendments, under suspension of the rules, Dec. 21. President signed Jan. 4, 2011.

■ **PL 111-365** (HR 5877) Designate the facility of the U.S. Postal Service located at 655 Centre St. in Jamaica Plain, Mass., as the "Lance Cpl. Alexander Scott Arredondo, U.S. Marine Corps Post Office Building." Introduced by CAPUANO, D-Mass., on July 27, 2010. House passed, under suspension of the rules, Nov. 29. Senate passed Dec. 16. President signed Jan. 4, 2011.

■ **PL 111-366** (HR 5901) Amend the Internal Revenue Code of 1986 to authorize the tax court to appoint employees. Introduced by CROWLEY, D-N.Y., on July 28, 2010. House passed, under suspension

of the rules, July 30. Senate passed, amended, Dec. 17. House agreed to Senate amendments Dec. 22. President signed Jan. 4, 2011.

■ **PL 111-367** (IIR 6392) Designate the facility of the U.S. Postal Service located at 5003 Westfields Blvd. in Centreville, Va., as the "Col. George Juskalian Post Office Building." Introduced by WOLF, R-Va., on Sept. 29, 2010. House passed, under suspension of the rules, Nov. 29. Senate passed Dec. 16. President signed Jan. 4, 2011.

■ **PL 111-368** (HR 6400) Designate the facility of the U.S. Postal Service located at 111 North Sixth St. in St. Louis as the "Earl Wilson Jr. Post Office." Introduced by CLAY, D-Mo., on Nov. 15, 2010. House passed, under suspension of the rules, Dec. 7. Senate passed Dec. 16. President signed Jan. 4, 2011.

■ **PL 111-369** (HR 6412) Amend Title 28, U.S. Code, to require the attorney general to share criminal records with state sentencing commissions. Introduced by SCOTT, D-Va., on Nov. 16, 2010. House passed, under suspension of the rules, Dec. 9. Senate passed Dec. 20. President signed Jan. 4, 2011.

■ **PL 111-370** (HR 6510) Direct the administrator of general services to convey a parcel of real property in Houston to the Military Museum of Texas. Introduced by JACKSON LEE, D-Texas, on Dec. 9, 2010. House passed, under suspension of the rules, Dec. 14. Senate passed Dec. 18. President signed Jan. 4, 2011.

■ **PL 111-371** (HR 6533) Implement the recommendations of the Federal Communications Commission report to Congress regarding low-power FM service. Introduced by DOYLE, D-Pa., on Dec. 16, 2010. House passed, under suspension of the rules, Dec. 17. Senate passed Dec. 18. President signed Jan. 4, 2011.

■ **PL 111-372** (S 118) Amend Section 202 of the Housing Act of 1959 to improve the program for supportive housing for the elderly. Introduced by KOHL, D-Wis., on Jan. 6, 2009. Senate Banking, Housing and Urban Affairs reported, amended, Nov. 30, 2010 (no written report). Senate passed Dec. 18. House passed, under suspension of the rules, Dec. 21. President signed Jan. 4, 2011.

■ **PL 111-373** (S 841) Direct the secretary of Transportation to study and establish a motor vehicle safety standard that provides for a means of alerting blind and other pedestrians of motor vehicle operation. Introduced by KERRY, D-Mass., on April 21, 2009. Senate passed, amended, Dec. 9, 2010. House passed, under suspension of the rules, Dec. 16. President signed Jan. 4, 2011.

■ **PL 111-374** (S 1481) Amend Section 811 of the Cranston-Gonzalez National Affordable Housing Act to improve the program for supportive housing for persons with disabilities. Introduced by MENENDEZ, D-N.J., on July 21, 2009. Senate Banking, Housing and Urban Affairs reported, amended, Dec. 14, 2010 (no written report). Senate passed Dec. 17. House passed, under suspension of the rules, Dec. 21. President signed Jan. 4, 2011.

■ **PL 111-375** (S 3036) Establish the National Alzheimer's Project. Introduced by BAYH, D-Ind., on Feb. 24, 2010. Senate Health, Education, Labor and Pensions reported, amended, Dec. 6 (no written

report). Senate passed, amended, Dec. 8. House passed, under suspension of the rules, Dec. 15. President signed Jan. 4, 2011.

■ **PL 111-376** (S 3243) Require U.S. Customs and Border Protection to administer polygraph examinations to all applicants for law enforcement positions with the agency and to require it to initiate all periodic background reinvestigations of certain law enforcement personnel. Introduced by PRYOR, D-Ark., on April 21, 2010. Senate Homeland Security and Governmental Affairs reported, amended, Sept. 27 (S Rept 111-338). Senate passed, amended, Sept. 28. House passed, under suspension of the rules, Dec. 21. President signed Jan. 4, 2011.

■ **PL 111-377** (S 3447) Amend Title 38, U.S. Code, to improve educational assistance for veterans who served in the Armed Forces after Sept. 11, 2001. Introduced by AKAKA, D-Hawaii, on May 27, 2010. Senate Veterans' Affairs reported, amended, Oct. 26 (S Rept 111-346). Senate passed Dec. 13. House passed, under suspension of the rules, Dec. 16. President signed Jan. 4, 2011.

■ **PL 111-378** (S 3481) Amend the Federal Water Pollution Control Act to clarify federal responsibility for stormwater pollution. Introduced by CARDIN, D-Md., on June 10, 2010. Senate Environment and Public Works reported Dec. 17 (no written report). Senate passed, amended, Dec. 21. House passed, under suspension of the rules, Dec. 22. President signed Jan. 4, 2011.

■ **PL 111-379** (S 3592) Designate the facility of the U.S. Postal Service located at 100 Commerce Drive in Tyrone, Ga., as the "1st Lt. Robert Wilson Collins Post Office Building." Introduced by CHAMBLISS, R-Ga., on July 15, 2010. Senate passed Dec. 16. House passed, under suspension of the rules, Dec. 21. President signed Jan. 4, 2011.

■ **PL 111-380** (S 3874) Amend the Safe Drinking Water Act to reduce lead in drinking water. Introduced by BOXER, D-Calif., on Sept. 29, 2010. Senate Environment and Public Works reported Dec. 16 (no written report). Senate passed Dec. 16. House passed, under suspension of the rules, Dec. 17. President signed Jan. 4, 2011.

■ **PL 111-381** (S 3903) Authorize leases of up to 99 years for lands held in trust for Ohkay Owingeh Pueblo. Introduced by UDALL, D-N.M., on Sept. 29, 2010. Senate Indian Affairs reported, amended, Dec. 16 (S Rept 111-371). Senate passed Dec. 21. House passed Dec. 22. President signed Jan. 4, 2011.

■ **PL 111-382** (S 4036) Clarify the National Credit Union Administration authority to make stabilization fund expenditures without borrowing from the Treasury. Introduced by DODD, D-Conn., on Dec. 16, 2010. Senate passed Dec. 16. House passed Dec. 22. President signed Jan. 4, 2011.

■ **PL 111-383** (HR 6523) Authorize appropriations for fiscal year 2011 for military activities of the Department of Defense, for military construction and for defense activities of the Energy Department. Introduced by SKELTON, D-Mo., on Dec. 15, 2010. House passed, under suspension of the rules, Dec. 17. Senate passed, amended, Dec. 22. House agreed to Senate amendment Dec. 22. President signed Jan. 7, 2011. ■

Appendix H

HOUSE ROLL CALL VOTES

House Roll Call Index
By Bill Number

HOUSE BILLS

H Con Res 126, H-158
H Con Res 227, H-28
H Con Res 238, H-30
H Con Res 242, H-130
H Con Res 244, H-54
H Con Res 248, H-38, H-40
H Con Res 249, H-40
H Con Res 257, H-64
H Con Res 268, H-94
H Con Res 278, H-106
H Con Res 282, H-110
H Con Res 284, H-142
H Con Res 285, H-136
H Con Res 288, H-134
H Con Res 290, H-150
H Con Res 293, H-144
H Con Res 301, H-164
H Con Res 308, H-168
H Con Res 321, H-192
H Con Res 323, H-206
H Con Res 328, H-198
H Con Res 332, H-200
H Con Res 336, H-226
H Con Res 454, H-158
H J Res 45, H-20
H J Res 64, H-4
H J Res 80, H-64
H J Res 101, H-206
H J Res 105, H-228
H Res 267, H-44
H Res 311, H-46
H Res 362, H-36
H Res 403, H-102
H Res 518, H-122
H Res 546, H-134
H Res 584, H-108
H Res 605, H-46
H Res 699, H-34
H Res 716, H-198
H Res 747, H-32
H Res 771, H-204
H Res 860, H-4
H Res 900, H-58
H Res 901, H-14
H Res 917, H-66
H Res 925, H-60
H Res 935, H-38
H Res 944, H-26
H Res 957, H-14
H Res 989, H-122
H Res 990, H-10
H Res 991, H-6
H Res 1002, H-4
H Res 1003, H-10
H Res 1004, H-6

H Res 1011, H-10
H Res 1014, H-14
H Res 1015, H-6
H Res 1021, H-8
H Res 1022, H-18
H Res 1024, H-10
H Res 1027, H-54
H Res 1031, H-40, H-42
H Res 1039, H-24
H Res 1040, H-56
H Res 1041, H-72
H Res 1042, H-72
H Res 1043, H-14
H Res 1044, H-16
H Res 1046, H-24
H Res 1052, H-182
H Res 1059, H-22
H Res 1062, H-74
H Res 1066, H-22
H Res 1069, H-38
H Res 1072, H-32
H Res 1074, H-26
H Res 1075, H-58
H Res 1079, H-36
H Res 1085, H-28
H Res 1086, H-34
H Res 1088, H-38
H Res 1089, H-46
H Res 1096, H-32
H Res 1097, H-32
H Res 1099, H-62
H Res 1103, H-82
H Res 1104, H-78
H Res 1107, H-42
H Res 1111, H-34
H Res 1119, H-62
H Res 1125, H-70
H Res 1127, H-34
H Res 1128, H-46
H Res 1131, H-82
H Res 1132, H-90
H Res 1133, H-54
H Res 1141, H-48
H Res 1144, H-40
H Res 1145, H-44
H Res 1161, H-110
H Res 1163, H-44
H Res 1164, H-42
H Res 1167, H-46
H Res 1169, H-110
H Res 1170, H-44
H Res 1172, H-108
H Res 1173, H-50
H Res 1174, H-56
H Res 1178, H-122
H Res 1184, H-46
H Res 1186, H-64

H Res 1189, H-108
H Res 1190, H-48, H-50
H Res 1193, H-50
H Res 1194, H-50
H Res 1213, H-90
H Res 1215, H-70
H Res 1216, H-78
H Res 1217, H-206
H Res 1219, H-158
H Res 1220, H-68
H Res 1222, H-72
H Res 1228, H-146
H Res 1236, H-72
H Res 1242, H-76
H Res 1244, H-140
H Res 1246, H-74
H Res 1249, H-74
H Res 1255, H-76
H Res 1256, H-102
H Res 1257, H-78
H Res 1258, H-106
H Res 1264, H-212
H Res 1270, H-80
H Res 1271, H-78
H Res 1272, H-90
H Res 1287, H-80
H Res 1292, H-102
H Res 1294, H-94
H Res 1295, H-92
H Res 1299, H-94
H Res 1301, H-90
H Res 1307, H-90
H Res 1313, H-210
H Res 1316, H-110
H Res 1320, H-90
H Res 1321, H-148
H Res 1322, H-130
H Res 1326, H-194
H Res 1327, H-100
H Res 1328, H-94
H Res 1330, H-124
H Res 1336, H-104
H Res 1337, H-98
H Res 1338, H-98
H Res 1347, H-108
H Res 1361, H-104
H Res 1362, H-102
H Res 1363, H-104
H Res 1364, H-102
H Res 1366, H-164
H Res 1368, H-128
H Res 1369, H-134
H Res 1372, H-110
H Res 1377, H-226
H Res 1382, H-106
H Res 1383, H-128
H Res 1385, H-110

H Res 1388, H-136
H Res 1389, H-128
H Res 1391, H-116
H Res 1402, H-214
H Res 1404, H-110
H Res 1405, H-148
H Res 1407, H-134
H Res 1409, H-128
H Res 1411, H-160
H Res 1412, H-148
H Res 1414, H-130
H Res 1422, H-130
H Res 1424, H-122
H Res 1428, H-200
H Res 1429, H-132
H Res 1430, H-206
H Res 1434, H-134
H Res 1439, H-140
H Res 1446, H-142
H Res 1460, H-146
H Res 1462, H-152
H Res 1464, H-138
H Res 1472, H-158
H Res 1475, H-198
H Res 1491, H-158
H Res 1504, H-164
H Res 1513, H-160
H Res 1516, H-158
H Res 1522, H-182
H Res 1531, H-214
H Res 1540, H-212
H Res 1543, H-166
H Res 1558, H-174
H Res 1566, H-174
H Res 1571, H-182
H Res 1576, H-208
H Res 1585, H-204
H Res 1598, H-208
H Res 1610, H-182
H Res 1613, H-184
H Res 1638, H-208
H Res 1642, H-212
H Res 1704, H-214
H Res 1713, H-198
H Res 1715, H-200
H Res 1717, H-212
H Res 1724, H-208
H Res 1735, H-206
H Res 1737, H-210
H Res 1740, H-204
H Res 1743, H-222
H Res 1746, H-216
H Res 1752, H-214
H Res 1759, H-220
H Res 1761, H-222
H Res 1771, H-228
HR 512, H-196

HR 628, H-226
HR 725, H-160
HR 730, H-8
HR 847, H-170, H-192, H-230
HR 946, H-48, H-196
HR 1017, H-106
HR 1020, H-12
HR 1024, H-10
HR 1061, H-122
HR 1065, H-6, H-8
HR 1107, H-226
HR 1264, H-162
HR 1320, H-164
HR 1325, H-100
HR 1469, H-162
HR 1514, H-100
HR 1554, H-144
HR 1558, H-174
HR 1586, H-68, H-180
HR 1612, H-52, H-54, H-56
HR 1722, H-92, H-154, H-156, H-202
HR 1745, H-190
HR 1879, H-66
HR 2039, H-182
HR 2142, H-228, H-230
HR 2194, H-80, H-138
HR 2288, H-100
HR 2314, H-22, H-24, H-26
HR 2340, H-146
HR 2378, H-192, H-194
HR 2499, H-84, H-86, H-88
HR 2701, H-28, H-30, H-192, H-194
HR 2711, H-108
HR 2751, H-230
HR 2788, H-52
HR 2847, H-36
HR 2864, H-154
HR 2965, H-222
HR 3040, H-170
HR 3081, H-196
HR 3082, H-214, H-216, H-230
HR 3101, H-164
HR 3125, H-74
HR 3199, H-190
HR 3254, H-6
HR 3342, H-6, H-8
HR 3421, H-194
HR 3470, H-186
HR 3509, H-50
HR 3534, H-174, H-176, H-178
HR 3538, H-6

HR 3542, H-50
HR 3562, H-184
HR 3590, H-58, H-60
HR 3644, H-52
HR 3650, H-38, H-44
HR 3671, H-52
HR 3685, H-192
HR 3726, H-6, H-10, H-12
HR 3808, H-200
HR 3820, H-32
HR 3885, H-108
HR 3892, H-4
HR 3940, H-196
HR 3954, H-48
HR 3961, H-28
HR 3962, H-138
HR 3976, H-64
HR 3993, H-136
HR 4003, H-54
HR 4061, H-14, H-16, H-18
HR 4072, H-194
HR 4098, H-66
HR 4173, H-124, H-142, H-144, H-146
HR 4213, H-116, H-118, H-142, H-144, H-160, H-162
HR 4214, H-48
HR 4238, H-22
HR 4247, H-32
HR 4307, H-142
HR 4360, H-70
HR 4380, H-160
HR 4395, H-54
HR 4425, H-22
HR 4438, H-154
HR 4445, H-146
HR 4474, H-10, H-12
HR 4495, H-14
HR 4501, H-216
HR 4505, H-144
HR 4506, H-44
HR 4508, H-12
HR 4532, H-20
HR 4543, H-82
HR 4592, H-64
HR 4614, H-100
HR 4621, H-38
HR 4626, H-26, H-28
HR 4628, H-46
HR 4667, H-62
HR 4692, H-166
HR 4715, H-74, H-76
HR 4748, H-166

HR 4773, H-154
HR 4783, H-204
HR 4785, H-184
HR 4810, H-62
HR 4823, H-188
HR 4825, H-48
HR 4840, H-56
HR 4849, H-64, H-66
HR 4851, H-76
HR 4853, H-208, H-210, H-224, H-226
HR 4855, H-128
HR 4861, H-82
HR 4872, H-60, H-62, H-70
HR 4887, H-56
HR 4899, H-66, H-68, H-150, H-152, H-166
HR 4994, H-72, H-218
HR 5013, H-84
HR 5014, H-94
HR 5017, H-82
HR 5019, H-90, H-92
HR 5072, H-122, H-124, H-126
HR 5099, H-102
HR 5110, H-188
HR 5114, H-156
HR 5116, H-94, H-96, H-98, H-118, H-120, H-230
HR 5128, H-104
HR 5131, H-186
HR 5133, H-124
HR 5136, H-112, H-114, H-120
HR 5145, H-106
HR 5146, H-82
HR 5175, H-136, H-138
HR 5278, H-124
HR 5281, H-216, H-218
HR 5297, H-128, H-130, H-132, H-186, H-188
HR 5307, H-188
HR 5325, H-100
HR 5327, H-102
HR 5330, H-106
HR 5341, H-162
HR 5366, H-182
HR 5395, H-142
HR 5414, H-154, H-174
HR 5446, H-220
HR 5481, H-134
HR 5486, H-128, H-130
HR 5502, H-128
HR 5510, H-228
HR 5551, H-134

HR 5552, H-140
HR 5566, H-160
HR 5604, H-158
HR 5609, H-150
HR 5618, H-140, H-146, H-148
HR 5623, H-140
HR 5710, H-190
HR 5730, H-164
HR 5756, H-190
HR 5758, H-200
HR 5822, H-166, H-168
HR 5827, H-166
HR 5850, H-168, H-170, H-172
HR 5851, H-174, H-176
HR 5873, H-182
HR 5877, H-204
HR 5893, H-168
HR 5901, H-174
HR 5982, H-178
HR 5987, H-212
HR 5993, H-194
HR 6160, H-194
HR 6205, H-220
HR 6400, H-212
HR 6412, H-218
HR 6419, H-202
HR 6469, H-208
HR 6495, H-214
HR 6510, H-220
HR 6523, H-226
HR 6540, H-228
HR 6547, H-230

SENATE BILLS

S 841, H-222
S 987, H-224
S 1147, H-48
S 1405, H-220
S 1508, H-156
S 1963, H-78
S 3167, H-220
S 3307, H-204, H-206, H-210
S 3447, H-224
S 3473, H-126
S 3689, H-198
S 3729, H-196
S 3774, H-202
S 3860, H-222
S 3874, H-228
S 3998, H-218
S Con Res 72, H-220

IN THE HOUSE | By Vote Number

1. Procedural Matter/Quorum Call.[1] A quorum was present with 373 members responding (61 members did not respond). Jan. 12, 2010.

2. H J Res 64. Short-Term Continuing Appropriations/Veto Override. Passage, over President Obama's Dec. 30, 2009, veto, of the joint resolution that would provide continuing appropriations until Dec. 23, 2009, for all federal departments and agencies whose fiscal 2010 appropriations bills have not been enacted. Rejected 143-245: D 3-223; R 140-22. A two-thirds majority of those present and voting (259 in this case for the House) of both chambers is required to override a veto. A "nay" was a vote in support of the president's position. Jan. 13, 2010.

3. H Res 1002. Tribute to Martin Luther King Jr./Adoption. Kildee, D-Mich., motion to suspend the rules and adopt the resolution that would encourage individuals to pay tribute to the life and work of Dr. Martin Luther King Jr. through community service projects on Martin Luther King Jr. Day. Motion agreed to 379-0: D 223-0; R 156-0. A two-thirds majority of those present and voting (253 in this case) is required for adoption under suspension of the rules. Jan. 13, 2010.

4. H Res 860. Illinois Outdoor Initiative/Adoption. Kildee, D-Mich., motion to suspend the rules and adopt the resolution that would support the "Leave No Child Inside" initiative of the Chicago Wilderness regional alliance, a program aimed at increasing outdoor activities for children. Motion agreed to 369-1: D 218-0; R 151-1. A two-thirds majority of those present and voting (247 in this case) is required for adoption under suspension of the rules. Jan. 13, 2010.

5. HR 3892. E.V. Wilkins Post Office/Passage. Lynch, D-Mass., motion to suspend the rules and pass the bill that would designate a post office in Roper, N.C., as the "E.V. Wilkins Post Office." Motion agreed to 356-1: D 205-0; R 151-1. A two-thirds majority of those present and voting (238 in this case) is required for passage under suspension of the rules. Jan. 13, 2010.

	2	3	4	5
ALABAMA				
1 **Bonner**	Y	Y	Y	Y
2 Bright	N	Y	Y	Y
3 **Rogers**	Y	Y	Y	Y
4 **Aderholt**	Y	Y	Y	Y
5 **Griffith**	Y	Y	Y	Y
6 **Bachus**	Y	Y	Y	Y
7 Davis	?	?	?	?
ALASKA				
AL **Young**	N	Y	Y	Y
ARIZONA				
1 Kirkpatrick	N	Y	Y	Y
2 **Franks**	Y	Y	Y	Y
3 **Shadegg**	Y	Y	Y	Y
4 Pastor	N	Y	Y	Y
5 Mitchell	N	Y	Y	Y
6 **Flake**	Y	Y	Y	Y
7 Grijalva	?	?	?	?
8 Giffords	N	Y	Y	Y
ARKANSAS				
1 Berry	?	?	?	?
2 Snyder	N	Y	Y	?
3 **Boozman**	Y	Y	Y	Y
4 Ross	N	Y	?	?
CALIFORNIA				
1 Thompson	N	Y	Y	Y
2 **Herger**	Y	Y	Y	Y
3 **Lungren**	Y	Y	Y	Y
4 **McClintock**	N	Y	Y	Y
5 Matsui	N	Y	Y	Y
6 Woolsey	N	Y	Y	Y
7 Miller, George	N	Y	?	?
8 Pelosi				
9 Lee	N	Y	Y	Y
10 Garamendi	N	Y	Y	?
11 McNerney	N	Y	Y	Y
12 Speier	N	Y	?	Y
13 Stark	N	Y	Y	Y
14 Eshoo	N	Y	Y	Y
15 Honda	N	Y	Y	Y
16 Lofgren	N	Y	Y	Y
17 Farr	N	Y	Y	Y
18 Cardoza	?	?	?	?
19 **Radanovich**	?	?	?	?
20 Costa	?	?	?	?
21 **Nunes**	Y	Y	Y	Y
22 **McCarthy**	Y	Y	Y	Y
23 Capps	N	Y	Y	Y
24 **Gallegly**	?	?	?	?
25 **McKeon**	Y	Y	Y	Y
26 **Dreier**	Y	Y	Y	Y
27 Sherman	N	Y	Y	Y
28 Berman	?	?	?	?
29 Schiff	N	Y	Y	Y
30 Waxman	?	?	?	?
31 Becerra	N	Y	+	Y
32 Chu	N	Y	Y	Y
33 Watson	N	Y	Y	Y
34 Roybal-Allard	N	Y	Y	Y
35 Waters	?	?	?	?
36 Harman	?	?	?	?
37 Richardson	N	Y	Y	Y
38 Napolitano	N	Y	Y	?
39 Sánchez, Linda	N	Y	Y	Y
40 **Royce**	Y	Y	Y	Y
41 **Lewis**	?	?	?	?
42 **Miller, Gary**	N	Y	Y	Y
43 Baca	N	Y	Y	Y
44 **Calvert**	?	?	?	?
45 **Bono Mack**	Y	Y	Y	Y
46 **Rohrabacher**	Y	Y	Y	Y
47 Sanchez, Loretta	N	Y	Y	Y
48 **Campbell**	?	?	?	?
49 **Issa**	Y	Y	Y	Y
50 **Bilbray**	?	?	?	?
51 Filner	Y	Y	Y	Y
52 **Hunter**	Y	Y	Y	Y
53 Davis	N	Y	Y	Y

	2	3	4	5
COLORADO				
1 DeGette	N	Y	Y	?
2 Polis	N	Y	Y	Y
3 Salazar	N	Y	Y	Y
4 Markey	N	Y	Y	Y
5 **Lamborn**	Y	Y	Y	Y
6 **Coffman**	Y	Y	Y	Y
7 Perlmutter	N	Y	Y	Y
CONNECTICUT				
1 Larson	N	Y	Y	Y
2 Courtney	N	Y	Y	Y
3 DeLauro	N	Y	Y	Y
4 Himes	N	Y	Y	Y
5 Murphy	N	Y	Y	Y
DELAWARE				
AL **Castle**	N	Y	Y	Y
FLORIDA				
1 **Miller**	Y	Y	?	Y
2 Boyd	?	?	?	?
3 Brown	N	Y	Y	Y
4 **Crenshaw**	?	?	?	?
5 **Brown-Waite**	Y	Y	Y	Y
6 **Stearns**	Y	Y	Y	Y
7 **Mica**	Y	Y	Y	Y
8 Grayson	N	Y	Y	Y
9 **Bilirakis**	Y	Y	Y	Y
10 **Young**	N	Y	Y	Y
11 Castor	N	Y	Y	?
12 **Putnam**	Y	Y	Y	Y
13 **Buchanan**	Y	Y	Y	Y
14 **Mack**	Y	Y	Y	Y
15 **Posey**	N	Y	Y	Y
16 **Rooney**	Y	Y	Y	Y
17 Meek	N	Y	Y	Y
18 **Ros-Lehtinen**	?	?	?	?
19 Vacant[2]				
20 Wasserman Schultz	N	Y	Y	Y
21 **Diaz-Balart, L.**	Y	Y	Y	Y
22 Klein	N	Y	Y	Y
23 Hastings	?	?	?	?
24 Kosmas	N	Y	Y	Y
25 **Diaz-Balart, M.**	Y	Y	Y	Y
GEORGIA				
1 **Kingston**	Y	Y	Y	Y
2 Bishop	N	Y	Y	Y
3 **Westmoreland**	Y	Y	Y	Y
4 Johnson	N	Y	Y	?
5 Lewis	?	?	?	?
6 **Price**	N	Y	Y	Y
7 **Linder**	Y	Y	Y	Y
8 Marshall	N	Y	Y	Y
9 **Deal**	?	?	?	?
10 **Broun**	N	Y	Y	Y
11 **Gingrey**	Y	Y	Y	Y
12 Barrow	–	+	+	+
13 Scott	N	Y	Y	Y
HAWAII				
1 Abercrombie	?	?	?	?
2 Hirono	N	Y	Y	Y
IDAHO				
1 Minnick	N	Y	Y	Y
2 **Simpson**	N	Y	Y	Y
ILLINOIS				
1 Rush	N	Y	Y	Y
2 Jackson	N	Y	Y	Y
3 Lipinski	N	Y	Y	Y
4 Gutierrez	–	+	+	+
5 Quigley	N	Y	Y	?
6 **Roskam**	Y	Y	Y	Y
7 Davis	N	Y	Y	Y
8 Bean	N	Y	Y	Y
9 Schakowsky	N	Y	Y	Y
10 **Kirk**	?	?	?	?
11 Halvorson	N	Y	Y	Y
12 Costello	N	Y	Y	Y
13 **Biggert**	Y	Y	Y	Y
14 Foster	N	Y	Y	Y
15 **Johnson**	N	Y	Y	Y

KEY	**Republicans**	Democrats		
Y	Voted for (yea)	X Paired against	C	Voted "present" to avoid possible conflict of interest
#	Paired for	– Announced against		
+	Announced for	P Voted "present"	?	Did not vote or otherwise make a position known
N	Voted against (nay)			

[1] CQ does not include quorum calls in its vote charts.

[2] Rep. Robert Wexler, D-Fla., resigned Jan. 3. He was not eligible for any votes in 2010.

	2	3	4	5
16 Manzullo	N	Y	Y	Y
17 Hare	N	Y	Y	Y
18 Schock	Y	Y	Y	Y
19 Shimkus	Y	Y	Y	Y
INDIANA				
1 Visclosky	N	Y	Y	Y
2 Donnelly	N	Y	Y	Y
3 Souder	Y	Y	Y	Y
4 Buyer	N	Y	Y	Y
5 Burton	Y	Y	Y	Y
6 Pence	Y	Y	Y	Y
7 Carson	N	Y	Y	Y
8 Ellsworth	N	Y	Y	Y
9 Hill	N	Y	Y	Y
IOWA				
1 Braley	N	Y	Y	Y
2 Loebsack	N	Y	Y	Y
3 Boswell	N	Y	Y	Y
4 Latham	Y	Y	Y	Y
5 King	N	Y	?	Y
KANSAS				
1 Moran	Y	Y	Y	Y
2 Jenkins	Y	Y	Y	Y
3 Moore	N	Y	Y	Y
4 Tiahrt	Y	Y	Y	Y
KENTUCKY				
1 Whitfield	Y	Y	Y	Y
2 Guthrie	Y	Y	Y	Y
3 Yarmuth	N	Y	Y	Y
4 Davis	Y	Y	Y	Y
5 Rogers	Y	Y	Y	Y
6 Chandler	?	?	?	?
LOUISIANA				
1 Scalise	Y	Y	Y	Y
2 Cao	N	Y	Y	Y
3 Melancon	N	Y	Y	?
4 Fleming	Y	Y	Y	Y
5 Alexander	Y	Y	Y	?
6 Cassidy	Y	Y	Y	Y
7 Boustany	?	?	?	?
MAINE				
1 Pingree	?	Y	Y	Y
2 Michaud	N	Y	Y	Y
MARYLAND				
1 Kratovil	N	Y	Y	Y
2 Ruppersberger	N	Y	Y	Y
3 Sarbanes	N	Y	Y	Y
4 Edwards	N	Y	Y	Y
5 Hoyer	N	Y	Y	?
6 Bartlett	Y	Y	Y	Y
7 Cummings	N	Y	Y	Y
8 Van Hollen	N	Y	Y	Y
MASSACHUSETTS				
1 Olver	N	Y	Y	Y
2 Neal	N	Y	Y	Y
3 McGovern	N	Y	Y	?
4 Frank	?	?	?	?
5 Tsongas	N	Y	Y	Y
6 Tierney	N	Y	Y	Y
7 Markey	N	Y	Y	Y
8 Capuano	N	Y	Y	Y
9 Lynch	N	Y	Y	Y
10 Delahunt	N	?	?	?
MICHIGAN				
1 Stupak	N	Y	Y	Y
2 Hoekstra	Y	Y	Y	Y
3 Ehlers	?	?	?	?
4 Camp	Y	Y	Y	Y
5 Kildee	N	Y	Y	Y
6 Upton	Y	Y	Y	Y
7 Schauer	N	Y	Y	Y
8 Rogers	Y	Y	Y	Y
9 Peters	N	Y	Y	Y
10 Miller	Y	Y	Y	Y
11 McCotter	Y	Y	Y	?
12 Levin	N	Y	Y	Y
13 Kilpatrick	N	Y	Y	Y
14 Conyers	N	Y	Y	Y
15 Dingell	N	Y	Y	Y
MINNESOTA				
1 Walz	N	Y	Y	Y
2 Kline	Y	Y	Y	Y
3 Paulsen	Y	Y	Y	Y
4 McCollum	N	Y	Y	Y

	2	3	4	5
5 Ellison	N	Y	Y	Y
6 Bachmann	Y	Y	Y	Y
7 Peterson	N	Y	Y	Y
8 Oberstar	N	Y	Y	?
MISSISSIPPI				
1 Childers	N	Y	Y	Y
2 Thompson	N	Y	Y	Y
3 Harper	Y	Y	Y	Y
4 Taylor	Y	Y	Y	Y
MISSOURI				
1 Clay	N	Y	Y	Y
2 Akin	Y	Y	Y	Y
3 Carnahan	N	Y	Y	Y
4 Skelton	N	Y	Y	Y
5 Cleaver	N	Y	Y	Y
6 Graves	N	Y	Y	Y
7 Blunt	Y	Y	Y	Y
8 Emerson	Y	Y	Y	Y
9 Luetkemeyer	Y	Y	Y	Y
MONTANA				
AL Rehberg	Y	Y	Y	Y
NEBRASKA				
1 Fortenberry	Y	Y	Y	Y
2 Terry	Y	Y	Y	Y
3 Smith	Y	Y	Y	Y
NEVADA				
1 Berkley	N	Y	Y	Y
2 Heller	Y	Y	Y	Y
3 Titus	N	Y	Y	Y
NEW HAMPSHIRE				
1 Shea-Porter	N	Y	Y	Y
2 Hodes	N	Y	Y	Y
NEW JERSEY				
1 Andrews	N	Y	Y	?
2 LoBiondo	Y	Y	Y	Y
3 Adler	N	Y	Y	Y
4 Smith	Y	Y	Y	Y
5 Garrett	Y	Y	Y	Y
6 Pallone	N	Y	Y	Y
7 Lance	Y	Y	Y	Y
8 Pascrell	N	Y	Y	Y
9 Rothman	N	Y	Y	?
10 Payne	N	Y	Y	Y
11 Frelinghuysen	Y	Y	Y	Y
12 Holt	N	Y	Y	Y
13 Sires	N	Y	Y	Y
NEW MEXICO				
1 Heinrich	N	Y	Y	Y
2 Teague	N	Y	Y	Y
3 Luján	N	Y	Y	Y
NEW YORK				
1 Bishop	N	Y	Y	Y
2 Israel	N	Y	Y	Y
3 King	Y	Y	Y	Y
4 McCarthy	N	Y	Y	Y
5 Ackerman	N	Y	Y	Y
6 Meeks	?	?	?	?
7 Crowley	N	Y	Y	Y
8 Nadler	N	Y	Y	Y
9 Weiner	N	Y	?	Y
10 Towns	N	Y	Y	Y
11 Clarke	N	Y	Y	Y
12 Velázquez	N	Y	Y	Y
13 McMahon	N	Y	Y	Y
14 Maloney	N	Y	Y	Y
15 Rangel	?	?	?	?
16 Serrano	N	Y	Y	Y
17 Engel	N	Y	Y	Y
18 Lowey	N	Y	Y	Y
19 Hall	N	Y	Y	Y
20 Murphy	N	Y	Y	Y
21 Tonko	N	Y	Y	Y
22 Hinchey	N	Y	Y	Y
23 Owens	N	Y	Y	Y
24 Arcuri	N	?	?	?
25 Maffei	N	Y	Y	Y
26 Lee	Y	Y	Y	Y
27 Higgins	?	?	?	?
28 Slaughter	N	Y	Y	Y
29 Massa	N	Y	Y	Y
NORTH CAROLINA				
1 Butterfield	N	Y	Y	Y
2 Etheridge	N	Y	Y	Y
3 Jones	N	Y	Y	Y
4 Price	N	Y	Y	Y

	2	3	4	5
5 Foxx	N	Y	Y	Y
6 Coble	Y	Y	Y	Y
7 McIntyre	N	Y	Y	Y
8 Kissell	N	Y	Y	Y
9 Myrick	Y	Y	Y	Y
10 McHenry	Y	Y	Y	Y
11 Shuler	?	?	?	?
12 Watt	N	Y	Y	Y
13 Miller	N	Y	?	Y
NORTH DAKOTA				
AL Pomeroy	N	Y	Y	Y
OHIO				
1 Driehaus	N	Y	Y	
2 Schmidt	Y	Y	Y	Y
3 Turner	Y	Y	Y	Y
4 Jordan	Y	Y	Y	Y
5 Latta	Y	Y	Y	Y
6 Wilson	N	Y	Y	Y
7 Austria	Y	Y	Y	Y
8 Boehner	Y	Y	Y	Y
9 Kaptur	N	Y	Y	Y
10 Kucinich	N	Y	Y	Y
11 Fudge	N	Y	Y	Y
12 Tiberi	N	Y	Y	Y
13 Sutton	N	Y	Y	Y
14 LaTourette	Y	Y	Y	Y
15 Kilroy	N	Y	Y	Y
16 Boccieri	N	Y	Y	+
17 Ryan	N	Y	Y	Y
18 Space	N	Y	Y	?
OKLAHOMA				
1 Sullivan	Y	Y	Y	Y
2 Boren	N	Y	Y	Y
3 Lucas	Y	?	?	?
4 Cole	Y	Y	Y	Y
5 Fallin	Y	Y	Y	Y
OREGON				
1 Wu	N	Y	Y	Y
2 Walden	Y	Y	Y	Y
3 Blumenauer	N	Y	Y	Y
4 DeFazio	N	?	Y	Y
5 Schrader	N	Y	Y	Y
PENNSYLVANIA				
1 Brady	N	Y	Y	Y
2 Fattah	N	Y	Y	Y
3 Dahlkemper	N	Y	Y	Y
4 Altmire	N	Y	Y	Y
5 Thompson	P	Y	Y	Y
6 Gerlach	Y	Y	Y	Y
7 Sestak	N	Y	Y	Y
8 Murphy, P.	N	Y	Y	Y
9 Shuster	?	?	?	?
10 Carney	Y	Y	Y	Y
11 Kanjorski	N	Y	Y	Y
12 Murtha	N	Y	Y	Y
13 Schwartz	−	Y	Y	Y
14 Doyle	N	?	?	?
15 Dent	Y	Y	Y	Y
16 Pitts	Y	Y	Y	Y
17 Holden	N	Y	Y	Y
18 Murphy, T.	N	Y	Y	Y
19 Platts	Y	Y	Y	Y
RHODE ISLAND				
1 Kennedy	N	Y	Y	Y
2 Langevin	N	Y	Y	Y
SOUTH CAROLINA				
1 Brown	Y	Y	Y	Y
2 Wilson	Y	Y	Y	Y
3 Barrett	Y	Y	Y	Y
4 Inglis	Y	Y	Y	Y
5 Spratt	N	Y	Y	Y
6 Clyburn	?	?	?	?
SOUTH DAKOTA				
AL Herseth Sandlin	N	Y	Y	Y
TENNESSEE				
1 Roe	Y	Y	Y	Y
2 Duncan	N	Y	Y	Y
3 Wamp	?	?	?	?
4 Davis	N	Y	Y	Y
5 Cooper	N	Y	Y	Y
6 Gordon	N	Y	Y	?
7 Blackburn	Y	Y	Y	Y
8 Tanner	?	?	?	?
9 Cohen	N	Y	Y	Y

	2	3	4	5
TEXAS				
1 Gohmert	Y	Y	?	Y
2 Poe	?	?	?	?
3 Johnson, S.	Y	Y	Y	Y
4 Hall	Y	?	?	?
5 Hensarling	Y	Y	Y	Y
6 Barton	Y	?	?	?
7 Culberson	Y	Y	Y	Y
8 Brady	Y	Y	Y	Y
9 Green, A.	N	Y	Y	Y
10 McCaul	Y	Y	Y	Y
11 Conaway	Y	Y	Y	Y
12 Granger	N	Y	Y	Y
13 Thornberry	Y	Y	Y	Y
14 Paul	N	Y	N	N
15 Hinojosa	N	Y	Y	Y
16 Reyes	N	Y	Y	Y
17 Edwards	N	Y	Y	Y
18 Jackson Lee	N	Y	Y	Y
19 Neugebauer	Y	Y	Y	Y
20 Gonzalez	N	Y	Y	Y
21 Smith	Y	Y	Y	Y
22 Olson	Y	Y	Y	Y
23 Rodriguez	N	Y	Y	Y
24 Marchant	Y	?	?	?
25 Doggett	N	Y	Y	Y
26 Burgess	Y	?	?	?
27 Ortiz	N	Y	Y	Y
28 Cuellar	N	Y	Y	Y
29 Green, G.	N	Y	Y	Y
30 Johnson, E.	?	?	?	?
31 Carter	Y	?	?	?
32 Sessions	Y	Y	Y	Y
UTAH				
1 Bishop	Y	Y	?	Y
2 Matheson	N	Y	Y	Y
3 Chaffetz	Y	Y	Y	?
VERMONT				
AL Welch	N	Y	Y	Y
VIRGINIA				
1 Wittman	Y	Y	Y	Y
2 Nye	N	Y	Y	Y
3 Scott	N	Y	Y	Y
4 Forbes	Y	Y	Y	Y
5 Perriello	N	Y	Y	Y
6 Goodlatte	Y	Y	Y	Y
7 Cantor	Y	Y	Y	?
8 Moran	N	Y	Y	Y
9 Boucher	N	Y	Y	Y
10 Wolf	Y	Y	Y	Y
11 Connolly	N	?	?	?
WASHINGTON				
1 Inslee	N	Y	Y	Y
2 Larsen	N	Y	Y	Y
3 Baird	N	Y	Y	Y
4 Hastings	Y	?	?	?
5 McMorris Rodgers	Y	Y	Y	Y
6 Dicks	N	Y	Y	Y
7 McDermott	N	Y	Y	Y
8 Reichert	Y	Y	Y	Y
9 Smith	N	Y	Y	Y
WEST VIRGINIA				
1 Mollohan	N	Y	Y	Y
2 Capito	Y	Y	Y	Y
3 Rahall	?	?	?	?
WISCONSIN				
1 Ryan	Y	Y	Y	Y
2 Baldwin	N	Y	Y	Y
3 Kind	?	?	?	?
4 Moore	?	?	?	?
5 Sensenbrenner	Y	Y	Y	Y
6 Petri	Y	Y	Y	Y
7 Obey	N	Y	Y	Y
8 Kagen	N	Y	Y	Y
WYOMING				
AL Lummis	Y	Y	Y	Y
DELEGATES				
Faleomavaega (A.S.)				
Norton (D.C.)				
Bordallo (Guam)				
Sablan (N. Marianas)				
Pierluisi (P.R.)				
Christensen (V.I.)				

IN THE HOUSE | By Vote Number

6. **H Res 1004. Tribute to Northwestern University School of Medicine/Adoption.** Hirono, D-Hawaii, motion to suspend the rules and adopt the resolution that would commend the Northwestern University Feinberg School of Medicine on its 150th anniversary. Motion agreed to 397-0: D 233-0; R 164-0. A two-thirds vote (265 votes in this case) is required for adoption under suspension of the rules. Jan. 19, 2010.

7. **H Res 1015. Tribute to Penn State Women's Volleyball/ Adoption.** Hirono, D-Hawaii, motion to suspend the rules and adopt the resolution that would commend the Pennsylvania State University women's volleyball team on winning the 2009 NCAA Division I national championship. Motion agreed to 396-0: D 233-0; R 163-0. A two-thirds majority (264 votes in this case) is required for adoption under suspension of the rules. Jan. 19, 2010.

8. **H Res 991. Tribute to University of Virginia Men's Soccer/ Adoption.** Hirono, D-Hawaii, motion to suspend the rules and adopt the resolution that would commend the University of Virginia men's soccer team for winning the 2009 NCAA Division I national championship. Motion agreed to 398-0: D 234-0; R 164-0. A two-thirds majority (266 votes in this case) is required for adoption under suspension of the rules. Jan. 19, 2010.

9. **HR 1065, HR 3254, HR 3342. Indian Tribe Water Settlements/ Previous Question.** McGovern, D-Mass., motion to order the previous question (thus ending debate and possibility of amendment) on adoption of the rule (H Res 1017) to provide for House floor consideration of three bills that would approve water claims settlements between the government and American Indian tribes in Arizona and New Mexico. Motion agreed to 239-175: D 239-8; R 0-167. (Subsequently, the rule was adopted by voice vote.) Jan. 20, 2010.

10. **HR 3726. Castle Nugent National Historic Site/Passage.** Bordallo, D-Guam, motion to suspend the rules and pass the bill that would establish the Castle Nugent National Historic Site in St. Croix, V.I. Motion rejected 241-173: D 241-4; R 0-169. A two-thirds majority (276 in this case) is required for passage under suspension of the rules. Jan. 20, 2010.

11. **HR 3538. Idaho Wilderness Water Facilities/Passage.** Bordallo, D-Guam, motion to suspend the rules and pass the bill that would authorize the continued use of water facilities located on National Forest System land in north central Idaho. Motion rejected 225-191: D 61-187; R 164-4. A two-thirds majority (278 votes in this case) is required for passage under suspension of the rules. Jan. 20, 2010.

	6	7	8	9	10	11
ALABAMA						
1 **Bonner**	?	?	?	?	?	?
2 Bright	Y	Y	Y	Y	N	Y
3 **Rogers**	Y	Y	Y	N	N	Y
4 **Aderholt**	Y	Y	Y	N	N	Y
5 **Griffith**	Y	Y	Y	N	N	Y
6 **Bachus**	Y	Y	Y	N	N	Y
7 Davis	?	?	?	?	?	?
ALASKA						
AL **Young**	?	?	?	?	?	?
ARIZONA						
1 Kirkpatrick	Y	Y	Y	Y	Y	Y
2 **Franks**	Y	Y	Y	N	N	Y
3 **Shadegg**	Y	Y	Y	N	N	Y
4 Pastor	Y	Y	Y	Y	Y	N
5 Mitchell	Y	Y	Y	N	N	Y
6 **Flake**	Y	Y	Y	N	N	Y
7 Grijalva	?	?	?	Y	Y	N
8 Giffords	Y	Y	Y	Y	Y	Y
ARKANSAS						
1 Berry	Y	Y	Y	Y	Y	N
2 Snyder	Y	Y	Y	Y	Y	N
3 **Boozman**	Y	Y	Y	N	N	Y
4 Ross	Y	Y	Y	Y	Y	N
CALIFORNIA						
1 Thompson	Y	Y	Y	Y	Y	N
2 **Herger**	Y	Y	Y	N	N	Y
3 **Lungren**	Y	Y	Y	N	N	Y
4 **McClintock**	Y	Y	Y	N	N	Y
5 Matsui	Y	Y	Y	Y	Y	N
6 Woolsey	+	Y	Y	Y	Y	N
7 Miller, George	Y	Y	Y	Y	Y	Y
8 Pelosi				?		
9 Lee	Y	Y	Y	Y	Y	N
10 Garamendi	Y	Y	Y	Y	Y	N
11 McNerney	Y	Y	Y	Y	Y	N
12 Speier	Y	Y	Y	Y	Y	Y
13 Stark	Y	Y	Y	?	?	Y
14 Eshoo	Y	Y	Y	Y	Y	N
15 Honda	Y	Y	Y	Y	Y	N
16 Lofgren	Y	Y	Y	?	Y	N
17 Farr	Y	Y	Y	Y	Y	N
18 Cardoza	Y	Y	Y	Y	Y	N
19 **Radanovich**	?	?	?	?	?	?
20 Costa	Y	Y	Y	Y	Y	N
21 **Nunes**	Y	Y	Y	N	N	Y
22 **McCarthy**	Y	Y	Y	N	N	Y
23 Capps	Y	Y	Y	Y	Y	N
24 **Gallegly**	Y	Y	Y	N	N	Y
25 **McKeon**	Y	Y	Y	N	N	Y
26 **Dreier**	Y	Y	Y	N	N	Y
27 Sherman	Y	Y	Y	Y	Y	Y
28 Berman	Y	Y	Y	Y	Y	N
29 Schiff	Y	Y	Y	Y	Y	N
30 Waxman	Y	Y	Y	Y	Y	N
31 Becerra	Y	Y	Y	Y	Y	N
32 Chu	Y	Y	Y	Y	Y	N
33 Watson	Y	Y	Y	Y	Y	N
34 Roybal-Allard	Y	Y	Y	Y	Y	N
35 Waters	Y	Y	Y	Y	Y	N
36 Harman	Y	Y	Y	Y	Y	N
37 Richardson	Y	Y	Y	Y	Y	Y
38 Napolitano	Y	Y	Y	Y	Y	N
39 Sánchez, Linda	Y	Y	Y	Y	Y	N
40 **Royce**	Y	Y	Y	N	N	Y
41 **Lewis**	?	?	?	?	?	?
42 **Miller, Gary**	Y	Y	Y	N	N	Y
43 Baca	Y	Y	Y	Y	Y	N
44 **Calvert**	Y	Y	Y	N	N	Y
45 **Bono Mack**	Y	Y	Y	N	N	Y
46 **Rohrabacher**	?	?	?	N	N	Y
47 Sanchez, Loretta	Y	Y	Y	Y	Y	N
48 **Campbell**	Y	Y	Y	N	N	Y
49 **Issa**	Y	Y	Y	N	N	Y
50 **Bilbray**	?	?	?	N	N	Y
51 Filner	Y	Y	Y	Y	Y	N
52 **Hunter**	Y	Y	Y	N	N	Y
53 Davis	Y	Y	Y	Y	Y	N

	6	7	8	9	10	11
COLORADO						
1 DeGette	Y	Y	Y	Y	Y	N
2 Polis	Y	Y	Y	Y	Y	N
3 Salazar	Y	Y	Y	Y	Y	Y
4 Markey	Y	Y	Y	Y	Y	N
5 **Lamborn**	Y	Y	Y	N	N	Y
6 **Coffman**	Y	Y	Y	N	N	Y
7 Perlmutter	?	?	?	Y	Y	N
CONNECTICUT						
1 Larson	Y	Y	Y	Y	Y	N
2 Courtney	Y	Y	Y	Y	Y	N
3 DeLauro	Y	Y	Y	Y	Y	N
4 Himes	Y	Y	Y	Y	Y	Y
5 Murphy	Y	Y	Y	Y	Y	N
DELAWARE						
AL **Castle**	Y	Y	Y	N	N	Y
FLORIDA						
1 **Miller**	Y	Y	Y	N	N	Y
2 Boyd	Y	Y	Y	Y	Y	N
3 Brown	?	?	?	Y	Y	N
4 **Crenshaw**	?	?	?	?	?	?
5 **Brown-Waite**	Y	Y	Y	N	N	Y
6 **Stearns**	Y	Y	Y	N	N	Y
7 **Mica**	Y	Y	Y	N	N	Y
8 Grayson	Y	Y	Y	Y	Y	N
9 **Bilirakis**	Y	Y	Y	N	N	Y
10 **Young**	Y	Y	Y	N	N	Y
11 Castor	Y	Y	Y	Y	Y	N
12 **Putnam**	Y	Y	Y	N	N	Y
13 **Buchanan**	Y	Y	Y	N	N	Y
14 **Mack**	Y	Y	Y	N	N	Y
15 **Posey**	Y	Y	Y	N	N	Y
16 **Rooney**	Y	Y	Y	N	N	Y
17 Meek	Y	Y	Y	Y	Y	N
18 **Ros-Lehtinen**	Y	Y	Y	?	N	Y
19 Vacant						
20 Wasserman Schultz	Y	Y	Y	Y	Y	N
21 **Diaz-Balart, L.**	Y	?	Y	N	N	Y
22 Klein	Y	Y	Y	Y	Y	N
23 Hastings	Y	Y	Y	Y	Y	N
24 Kosmas	Y	Y	Y	Y	Y	Y
25 **Diaz-Balart, M.**	Y	Y	Y	N	N	Y
GEORGIA						
1 **Kingston**	Y	Y	Y	N	N	Y
2 Bishop	Y	Y	Y	Y	Y	N
3 **Westmoreland**	Y	Y	Y	N	N	?
4 Johnson	Y	Y	Y	Y	Y	N
5 Lewis	Y	Y	Y	Y	Y	N
6 **Price**	Y	Y	Y	N	N	Y
7 **Linder**	Y	Y	Y	N	N	Y
8 Marshall	Y	Y	Y	Y	Y	N
9 **Deal**	?	?	?	N	N	Y
10 **Broun**	Y	Y	Y	N	N	Y
11 **Gingrey**	Y	Y	Y	N	N	Y
12 Barrow	Y	Y	Y	Y	Y	N
13 Scott	Y	Y	Y	Y	Y	N
HAWAII						
1 Abercrombie	Y	Y	Y	?	?	?
2 Hirono	Y	Y	Y	Y	Y	N
IDAHO						
1 Minnick	Y	Y	Y	N	Y	Y
2 **Simpson**	Y	Y	Y	N	N	Y
ILLINOIS						
1 Rush	?	?	?	Y	Y	N
2 Jackson	Y	Y	Y	Y	Y	N
3 Lipinski	Y	Y	Y	Y	Y	Y
4 Gutierrez	+	+	+	Y	Y	N
5 Quigley	Y	Y	Y	Y	Y	N
6 **Roskam**	Y	Y	Y	N	N	Y
7 Davis	Y	Y	Y	Y	Y	N
8 Bean	Y	Y	Y	Y	Y	N
9 Schakowsky	Y	Y	Y	Y	Y	N
10 **Kirk**	Y	Y	Y	N	N	Y
11 Halvorson	Y	Y	Y	Y	Y	N
12 Costello	Y	Y	Y	Y	Y	N
13 **Biggert**	Y	Y	Y	N	N	Y
14 Foster	Y	Y	Y	Y	Y	N
15 **Johnson**	Y	Y	Y	N	N	Y

KEY **Republicans** Democrats

Y Voted for (yea)	X Paired against	C Voted "present" to avoid possible conflict of interest
# Paired for	– Announced against	
+ Announced for	P Voted "present"	? Did not vote or otherwise make a position known
N Voted against (nay)		

	6	7	8	9	10	11
16 **Manzullo**	Y	Y	Y	N	N	Y
17 Hare	Y	Y	Y	Y	?	N
18 **Schock**	Y	Y	Y	N	N	Y
19 **Shimkus**	Y	Y	Y	N	N	Y
INDIANA						
1 Visclosky	Y	Y	Y	Y	Y	Y
2 Donnelly	Y	Y	Y	N	Y	Y
3 **Souder**	Y	Y	Y	N	N	Y
4 **Buyer**	?	?	?	N	N	Y
5 **Burton**	Y	Y	Y	N	N	Y
6 **Pence**	Y	Y	Y	N	N	Y
7 Carson	Y	Y	Y	Y	Y	N
8 Ellsworth	Y	Y	Y	Y	Y	Y
9 Hill	Y	Y	Y	N	Y	N
IOWA						
1 Braley	Y	Y	Y	Y	Y	N
2 Loebsack	Y	Y	Y	Y	Y	Y
3 Boswell	Y	Y	Y	Y	Y	N
4 **Latham**	Y	Y	Y	N	N	Y
5 **King**	Y	Y	Y	N	N	Y
KANSAS						
1 **Moran**	Y	Y	Y	N	N	Y
2 **Jenkins**	Y	Y	Y	N	N	Y
3 Moore	Y	Y	Y	Y	Y	Y
4 **Tiahrt**	?	?	?	N	N	Y
KENTUCKY						
1 **Whitfield**	Y	Y	Y	N	N	Y
2 **Guthrie**	Y	Y	Y	N	N	Y
3 Yarmuth	Y	Y	Y	Y	Y	N
4 **Davis**	Y	Y	Y	N	N	Y
5 **Rogers**	Y	Y	Y	N	N	Y
6 Chandler	Y	Y	Y	Y	Y	N
LOUISIANA						
1 **Scalise**	Y	Y	Y	N	N	Y
2 **Cao**	Y	Y	Y	N	N	Y
3 Melancon	Y	Y	Y	Y	Y	N
4 **Fleming**	Y	Y	Y	N	N	Y
5 **Alexander**	?	?	?	N	N	Y
6 **Cassidy**	Y	Y	Y	N	N	Y
7 **Boustany**	Y	Y	Y	N	N	Y
MAINE						
1 Pingree	Y	Y	Y	Y	Y	N
2 Michaud	Y	Y	Y	Y	Y	Y
MARYLAND						
1 Kratovil	Y	Y	Y	N	Y	Y
2 Ruppersberger	Y	Y	Y	Y	Y	N
3 Sarbanes	Y	Y	Y	Y	Y	N
4 Edwards	Y	Y	Y	Y	Y	N
5 Hoyer	Y	Y	Y	Y	Y	N
6 **Bartlett**	Y	Y	Y	N	N	Y
7 Cummings	Y	Y	Y	Y	Y	N
8 Van Hollen	Y	Y	Y	Y	Y	N
MASSACHUSETTS						
1 Olver	Y	Y	Y	Y	Y	N
2 Neal	Y	Y	Y	Y	Y	N
3 McGovern	Y	Y	Y	Y	Y	N
4 Frank	Y	Y	Y	Y	Y	N
5 Tsongas	?	?	?	Y	Y	N
6 Tierney	Y	Y	Y	Y	Y	N
7 Markey	?	?	?	Y	Y	N
8 Capuano	Y	Y	Y	Y	Y	N
9 Lynch	Y	Y	Y	Y	Y	N
10 Delahunt	Y	Y	Y	Y	Y	N
MICHIGAN						
1 Stupak	Y	Y	Y	Y	Y	N
2 **Hoekstra**	?	?	?	?	?	?
3 **Ehlers**	Y	Y	Y	N	N	Y
4 **Camp**	Y	Y	Y	N	N	Y
5 Kildee	Y	Y	Y	Y	Y	N
6 **Upton**	Y	Y	Y	N	N	Y
7 Schauer	Y	Y	Y	Y	Y	N
8 **Rogers**	Y	Y	Y	N	N	Y
9 Peters	Y	Y	Y	Y	Y	N
10 **Miller**	Y	Y	Y	N	N	Y
11 **McCotter**	Y	Y	Y	N	N	Y
12 Levin	Y	Y	Y	Y	Y	N
13 Kilpatrick	Y	Y	Y	Y	Y	N
14 Conyers	Y	Y	Y	Y	Y	N
15 Dingell	Y	Y	Y	Y	Y	N
MINNESOTA						
1 Walz	Y	Y	Y	Y	Y	N
2 **Kline**	Y	Y	Y	N	N	Y
3 **Paulsen**	Y	Y	Y	N	N	Y
4 McCollum	Y	Y	Y	Y	Y	N

	6	7	8	9	10	11
5 Ellison	Y	Y	Y	Y	Y	N
6 **Bachmann**	Y	Y	Y	N	N	Y
7 Peterson	Y	Y	Y	Y	Y	N
8 Oberstar	?	P	P	Y	Y	N
MISSISSIPPI						
1 Childers	Y	Y	Y	Y	Y	Y
2 Thompson	Y	Y	Y	Y	Y	N
3 **Harper**	Y	Y	Y	N	N	Y
4 Taylor	Y	Y	Y	N	Y	Y
MISSOURI						
1 Clay	Y	Y	Y	Y	Y	N
2 **Akin**	Y	Y	Y	N	?	?
3 Carnahan	Y	Y	Y	Y	Y	N
4 Skelton	Y	Y	Y	Y	Y	N
5 Cleaver	Y	Y	Y	?	?	?
6 **Graves**	Y	Y	Y	N	N	Y
7 **Blunt**	Y	Y	Y	N	N	Y
8 **Emerson**	Y	Y	Y	N	N	Y
9 **Luetkemeyer**	Y	Y	Y	N	N	Y
MONTANA						
AL **Rehberg**	Y	Y	Y	N	N	Y
NEBRASKA						
1 **Fortenberry**	Y	Y	Y	N	N	Y
2 **Terry**	Y	Y	Y	N	N	Y
3 **Smith**	Y	Y	Y	N	N	Y
NEVADA						
1 Berkley	Y	Y	Y	Y	Y	Y
2 **Heller**	Y	Y	Y	N	N	Y
3 Titus	Y	Y	Y	Y	Y	Y
NEW HAMPSHIRE						
1 Shea-Porter	Y	Y	Y	Y	Y	N
2 Hodes	Y	Y	Y	Y	Y	Y
NEW JERSEY						
1 Andrews	Y	Y	Y	Y	Y	N
2 **LoBiondo**	Y	Y	Y	N	N	Y
3 Adler	Y	Y	Y	Y	Y	N
4 **Smith**	Y	Y	Y	N	N	Y
5 **Garrett**	Y	Y	Y	N	N	Y
6 Pallone	Y	Y	Y	Y	Y	N
7 **Lance**	Y	Y	Y	N	N	Y
8 Pascrell	Y	Y	Y	Y	Y	Y
9 Rothman	Y	Y	Y	Y	Y	N
10 Payne	Y	Y	Y	Y	Y	N
11 **Frelinghuysen**	Y	Y	Y	N	N	Y
12 Holt	Y	Y	Y	Y	Y	N
13 Sires	Y	Y	Y	Y	Y	N
NEW MEXICO						
1 Heinrich	Y	Y	Y	Y	Y	N
2 Teague	?	?	?	Y	Y	N
3 Luján	Y	Y	Y	Y	Y	N
NEW YORK						
1 Bishop	Y	Y	Y	Y	Y	N
2 Israel	Y	Y	Y	Y	Y	N
3 **King**	Y	Y	Y	N	N	Y
4 McCarthy	Y	Y	Y	Y	Y	N
5 Ackerman	Y	Y	Y	Y	Y	N
6 Meeks	Y	Y	Y	Y	Y	Y
7 Crowley	Y	Y	Y	Y	Y	N
8 Nadler	Y	Y	Y	Y	Y	N
9 Weiner	Y	Y	Y	Y	Y	N
10 Towns	Y	Y	Y	Y	Y	N
11 Clarke	Y	Y	Y	Y	Y	N
12 Velázquez	Y	Y	Y	Y	Y	N
13 McMahon	Y	Y	Y	Y	Y	N
14 Maloney	+	+	+	Y	Y	N
15 Rangel	Y	Y	Y	Y	Y	N
16 Serrano	Y	Y	Y	Y	Y	N
17 Engel	Y	Y	Y	Y	Y	N
18 Lowey	Y	Y	Y	Y	Y	Y
19 Hall	Y	Y	Y	Y	Y	N
20 Murphy	Y	Y	Y	Y	N	Y
21 Tonko	Y	Y	Y	Y	Y	N
22 Hinchey	Y	Y	Y	Y	Y	Y
23 Owens	Y	Y	Y	Y	N	N
24 Arcuri	Y	Y	Y	Y	Y	Y
25 Maffei	Y	Y	Y	Y	Y	N
26 **Lee**	Y	Y	Y	N	N	Y
27 Higgins	+	+	+	Y	Y	N
28 Slaughter	Y	Y	Y	Y	Y	N
29 Massa	Y	Y	Y	Y	Y	Y
NORTH CAROLINA						
1 Butterfield	Y	Y	Y	Y	Y	N
2 Etheridge	Y	Y	Y	Y	Y	N
3 **Jones**	Y	Y	Y	N	N	Y
4 Price	Y	Y	Y	Y	Y	N

	6	7	8	9	10	11
5 **Foxx**	Y	Y	Y	N	N	Y
6 **Coble**	Y	Y	Y	N	N	Y
7 McIntyre	Y	Y	Y	Y	Y	Y
8 Kissell	?	?	?	Y	Y	Y
9 **Myrick**	Y	Y	Y	N	N	Y
10 **McHenry**	Y	Y	Y	N	N	Y
11 Shuler	Y	Y	Y	N	Y	Y
12 Watt	Y	Y	Y	Y	Y	N
13 Miller	Y	Y	Y	Y	Y	Y
NORTH DAKOTA						
AL Pomeroy	Y	Y	Y	Y	Y	Y
OHIO						
1 Driehaus	Y	Y	Y	Y	Y	Y
2 **Schmidt**	Y	Y	Y	N	N	Y
3 **Turner**	Y	Y	Y	N	N	Y
4 **Jordan**	Y	Y	Y	N	N	Y
5 **Latta**	Y	Y	Y	N	N	Y
6 Wilson	Y	Y	Y	Y	?	Y
7 **Austria**	Y	Y	Y	N	N	Y
8 **Boehner**	Y	Y	Y	–	N	Y
9 Kaptur	Y	Y	Y	Y	Y	N
10 Kucinich	Y	Y	Y	Y	Y	Y
11 Fudge	Y	Y	Y	Y	Y	N
12 **Tiberi**	Y	Y	Y	N	N	Y
13 Sutton	Y	Y	Y	Y	Y	N
14 **LaTourette**	Y	Y	Y	N	N	Y
15 Kilroy	Y	Y	Y	Y	Y	N
16 Boccieri	Y	Y	P	Y	Y	Y
17 Ryan	Y	Y	Y	Y	Y	N
18 Space	Y	Y	Y	Y	?	Y
OKLAHOMA						
1 **Sullivan**	Y	Y	Y	N	N	Y
2 Boren	Y	Y	Y	Y	Y	N
3 **Lucas**	Y	Y	Y	N	N	Y
4 **Cole**	Y	Y	Y	N	N	Y
5 **Fallin**	Y	Y	Y	N	N	Y
OREGON						
1 Wu	Y	Y	Y	Y	Y	N
2 **Walden**	Y	Y	Y	N	N	Y
3 Blumenauer	?	Y	Y	Y	Y	N
4 DeFazio	Y	Y	Y	Y	Y	N
5 Schrader	?	?	?	Y	Y	Y
PENNSYLVANIA						
1 Brady	Y	Y	Y	Y	Y	N
2 Fattah	Y	Y	Y	Y	Y	N
3 Dahlkemper	Y	Y	Y	Y	Y	N
4 Altmire	Y	Y	Y	N	Y	Y
5 **Thompson**	Y	Y	Y	N	N	Y
6 **Gerlach**	Y	Y	Y	N	N	Y
7 Sestak	Y	Y	Y	Y	Y	Y
8 Murphy, P.	?	?	?	?	?	?
9 **Shuster**	Y	Y	Y	N	N	Y
10 Carney	Y	Y	Y	Y	Y	Y
11 Kanjorski	Y	Y	Y	Y	Y	N
12 Murtha	Y	Y	Y	Y	Y	Y
13 Schwartz	Y	Y	Y	Y	Y	N
14 Doyle	Y	Y	Y	Y	Y	N
15 **Dent**	Y	Y	Y	N	N	Y
16 **Pitts**	Y	Y	Y	N	N	Y
17 Holden	Y	Y	Y	Y	Y	N
18 **Murphy, T.**	Y	Y	Y	N	N	Y
19 **Platts**	Y	Y	Y	N	N	Y
RHODE ISLAND						
1 Kennedy	Y	?	Y	Y	Y	N
2 Langevin	Y	Y	Y	Y	Y	N
SOUTH CAROLINA						
1 **Brown**	Y	Y	Y	N	N	Y
2 **Wilson**	Y	Y	Y	N	N	N
3 **Barrett**	+	+	+	?	?	?
4 **Inglis**	Y	Y	Y	?	N	Y
5 Spratt	Y	Y	Y	Y	Y	N
6 Clyburn	Y	Y	Y	Y	Y	N
SOUTH DAKOTA						
AL Herseth Sandlin	Y	Y	Y	Y	Y	N
TENNESSEE						
1 **Roe**	Y	Y	Y	N	N	Y
2 **Duncan**	Y	Y	Y	N	N	Y
3 **Wamp**	Y	Y	Y	N	N	Y
4 Davis	Y	Y	Y	Y	Y	N
5 Cooper	Y	Y	Y	Y	Y	N
6 Gordon	Y	Y	Y	Y	Y	N
7 **Blackburn**	Y	Y	Y	N	N	Y
8 Tanner	Y	Y	Y	Y	Y	Y
9 Cohen	Y	Y	Y	Y	Y	Y

	6	7	8	9	10	11
TEXAS						
1 **Gohmert**	Y	Y	Y	N	N	Y
2 **Poe**	Y	Y	Y	N	N	Y
3 **Johnson, S.**	Y	Y	Y	N	N	Y
4 **Hall**	Y	Y	Y	N	N	Y
5 **Hensarling**	Y	Y	Y	N	N	Y
6 **Barton**	Y	Y	Y	N	N	Y
7 **Culberson**	Y	Y	Y	?	?	?
8 **Brady**	Y	Y	Y	N	N	N
9 Green, A.	Y	Y	Y	Y	Y	N
10 **McCaul**	Y	Y	Y	N	N	Y
11 **Conaway**	Y	Y	Y	N	N	Y
12 **Granger**	Y	Y	Y	N	N	Y
13 **Thornberry**	Y	Y	Y	N	N	Y
14 **Paul**	Y	Y	Y	N	N	N
15 Hinojosa	?	?	?	?	?	?
16 Reyes	?	?	?	Y	Y	N
17 Edwards	?	?	?	Y	Y	N
18 Jackson Lee	Y	Y	Y	Y	Y	N
19 **Neugebauer**	Y	Y	Y	N	N	Y
20 Gonzalez	Y	Y	Y	Y	Y	Y
21 **Smith**	Y	Y	Y	N	N	Y
22 **Olson**	Y	Y	Y	N	N	Y
23 Rodriguez	Y	Y	Y	Y	Y	N
24 **Marchant**	Y	Y	Y	N	N	Y
25 Doggett	Y	Y	Y	Y	Y	N
26 **Burgess**	Y	Y	Y	N	N	Y
27 Ortiz	Y	Y	Y	Y	Y	N
28 Cuellar	Y	Y	Y	Y	Y	Y
29 Green, G.	Y	Y	Y	Y	Y	N
30 Johnson, E.	?	?	?	?	?	?
31 **Carter**	Y	Y	Y	N	N	Y
32 **Sessions**	Y	Y	Y	N	N	Y
UTAH						
1 **Bishop**	Y	Y	Y	N	N	Y
2 Matheson	Y	Y	Y	Y	Y	N
3 **Chaffetz**	Y	Y	Y	N	N	Y
VERMONT						
AL Welch	Y	Y	Y	Y	Y	N
VIRGINIA						
1 **Wittman**	Y	Y	Y	N	N	Y
2 Nye	Y	Y	Y	Y	Y	Y
3 Scott	Y	Y	Y	Y	Y	N
4 **Forbes**	Y	Y	Y	N	N	Y
5 Perriello	Y	Y	Y	Y	Y	N
6 **Goodlatte**	Y	Y	Y	N	N	Y
7 **Cantor**	Y	Y	Y	N	N	Y
8 Moran	?	?	?	Y	Y	Y
9 Boucher	Y	Y	Y	Y	Y	Y
10 **Wolf**	Y	Y	Y	N	N	Y
11 Connolly	Y	Y	Y	Y	Y	N
WASHINGTON						
1 Inslee	Y	Y	Y	Y	Y	N
2 Larsen	Y	Y	Y	Y	Y	Y
3 Baird	Y	Y	Y	Y	Y	N
4 **Hastings**	Y	Y	Y	N	N	Y
5 **McMorris Rodgers**	Y	Y	Y	N	N	Y
6 Dicks	Y	Y	Y	Y	Y	Y
7 McDermott	Y	?	Y	Y	Y	N
8 **Reichert**	Y	Y	Y	N	N	Y
9 Smith	Y	Y	Y	Y	Y	N
WEST VIRGINIA						
1 Mollohan	Y	Y	Y	Y	Y	N
2 **Capito**	?	?	?	N	N	Y
3 Rahall	Y	Y	Y	Y	Y	N
WISCONSIN						
1 **Ryan**	Y	Y	Y	N	N	Y
2 Baldwin	Y	Y	Y	Y	Y	N
3 Kind	Y	Y	Y	Y	Y	N
4 Moore	Y	Y	Y	Y	Y	N
5 **Sensenbrenner**	Y	Y	Y	N	N	Y
6 **Petri**	Y	Y	Y	N	N	Y
7 Obey	Y	Y	Y	Y	Y	N
8 Kagen	Y	Y	Y	Y	Y	N
WYOMING						
AL **Lummis**	Y	Y	Y	N	N	Y
DELEGATES						
Faleomavaega (A.S.)						
Norton (D.C.)						
Bordallo (Guam)						
Sablan (N. Marianas)						
Pierluisi (P.R.)						
Christensen (V.I.)						

IN THE HOUSE | By Vote Number

12. **HR 3254. Taos Pueblo Water Settlement/Passage.** Passage of the bill that would ratify a water rights settlement between American Indian tribes in Taos Pueblo, N.M., and local governments. It would also authorize $121 million through fiscal 2016 for water infrastructure projects and expenses related to water use in Taos Pueblo. Passed 254-158: D 240-5; R 14-153. Jan. 21, 2010.

13. **HR 3342. Aamodt Litigation Water Settlement/Passage.** Passage of the bill that would ratify a water rights settlement between the Nambe, Pojoaque, San Ildefonso and Tesuque Pueblos; the state of New Mexico; Santa Fe county; and the federal government. It would also authorize $106.4 million through fiscal 2022 to construct Pueblo water systems and $10.4 million for the Interior Department to assist the Pueblos in acquiring water rights and systems. Passed 249-153: D 234-4; R 15-149. Jan. 21, 2010.

14. **HR 1065. White Mountain Apache Tribe Water Settlement/ Passage.** Passage of the bill that would ratify a water-rights settlement between the White Mountain Apache Tribe, the state of Arizona, several local governments and the federal government. It would also authorize $126 million for the Bureau of Reclamation to construct a water system for the White Mountain Apache Tribe and area governments, and $114 million for the Treasury Department to create a fund to protect area water structures. Passed 262-147: D 243-4; R 19-143. Jan. 21, 2010.

15. **H Res 1021. Haiti Earthquake Condolences/Adoption.** Lee, D-Calif., motion to suspend the rules and adopt the resolution that would express condolences and sympathy for the loss of life and the damage in Haiti caused by the earthquake Jan. 12, 2010, and express solidarity with Haitians, Haitian-Americans and all those who have been affected by the tragedy. It also would urge those who hold debt against Haiti to suspend further debt payments and cancel all remaining debt. Motion agreed to 411-1: D 246-0; R 165-1. A two-thirds majority of those present and voting (275 in this case) is required for adoption under suspension of the rules. Jan. 21, 2010.

16. **HR 730. Nuclear Forensics and Attribution Capabilities/ Passage.** Clarke, D-N.Y., motion to suspend the rules and concur in the Senate amendment to the bill that would direct the Homeland Security Department's Domestic Nuclear Detection Office to develop a five-year plan for improving nuclear forensic and attribution capabilities. Motion agreed to 397-10: D 242-1; R 155-9. A two-thirds majority of those present and voting (272 in this case) is required for passage under suspension of the rules. Jan. 21, 2010.

	12	13	14	15	16
ALABAMA					
1 **Bonner**	?	?	?	?	?
2 Bright	N	N	?	Y	Y
3 **Rogers**	N	N	N	Y	Y
4 **Aderholt**	N	N	N	Y	Y
5 **Griffith**	N	N	N	Y	Y
6 **Bachus**	N	N	N	Y	Y
7 Davis	?	?	?	?	?
ALASKA					
AL **Young**	?	?	?	?	?
ARIZONA					
1 Kirkpatrick	Y	Y	Y	Y	Y
2 **Franks**	N	N	Y	Y	Y
3 **Shadegg**	N	N	Y	Y	Y
4 Pastor	Y	Y	Y	Y	Y
5 Mitchell	Y	Y	Y	Y	Y
6 **Flake**	Y	Y	Y	Y	N
7 Grijalva	Y	?	Y	Y	Y
8 Giffords	Y	Y	Y	Y	Y
ARKANSAS					
1 Berry	Y	Y	Y	Y	Y
2 Snyder	Y	Y	Y	Y	Y
3 **Boozman**	N	N	N	Y	Y
4 Ross	Y	Y	Y	Y	Y
CALIFORNIA					
1 Thompson	Y	Y	Y	Y	Y
2 **Herger**	N	N	N	Y	Y
3 **Lungren**	Y	Y	Y	Y	Y
4 **McClintock**	N	N	N	Y	Y
5 Matsui	Y	Y	Y	Y	Y
6 Woolsey	Y	Y	Y	Y	Y
7 Miller, George	?	?	Y	Y	Y
8 Pelosi					
9 Lee	Y	Y	Y	Y	Y
10 Garamendi	Y	Y	Y	Y	Y
11 McNerney	Y	Y	Y	Y	Y
12 Speier	Y	Y	Y	Y	Y
13 Stark	Y	Y	Y	Y	Y
14 Eshoo	Y	Y	Y	Y	Y
15 Honda	Y	Y	Y	Y	Y
16 Lofgren	Y	Y	Y	Y	Y
17 Farr	Y	Y	Y	Y	Y
18 Cardoza	Y	Y	Y	Y	Y
19 **Radanovich**	?	?	?	?	?
20 Costa	Y	Y	Y	Y	Y
21 **Nunes**	N	N	N	Y	Y
22 **McCarthy**	N	N	N	Y	Y
23 Capps	Y	Y	Y	Y	Y
24 **Gallegly**	N	N	N	Y	Y
25 **McKeon**	Y	Y	Y	Y	Y
26 **Dreier**	N	N	N	Y	Y
27 Sherman	Y	Y	Y	Y	Y
28 Berman	Y	Y	Y	Y	Y
29 Schiff	Y	Y	Y	Y	Y
30 Waxman	Y	Y	Y	Y	Y
31 Becerra	Y	Y	Y	Y	Y
32 Chu	Y	Y	Y	Y	Y
33 Watson	Y	?	Y	Y	Y
34 Roybal-Allard	Y	Y	Y	Y	Y
35 Waters	Y	Y	Y	Y	?
36 Harman	Y	Y	Y	Y	Y
37 Richardson	Y	Y	Y	Y	Y
38 Napolitano	Y	?	Y	Y	Y
39 Sánchez, Linda	Y	Y	Y	Y	N
40 **Royce**	N	?	N	Y	Y
41 **Lewis**	?	?	?	?	?
42 **Miller, Gary**	N	N	N	Y	Y
43 Baca	Y	Y	Y	Y	Y
44 **Calvert**	Y	Y	Y	Y	Y
45 **Bono Mack**	Y	Y	Y	Y	Y
46 **Rohrabacher**	N	N	N	Y	Y
47 Sanchez, Loretta	Y	Y	Y	Y	Y
48 **Campbell**	N	N	N	Y	Y
49 **Issa**	N	Y	Y	Y	Y
50 **Bilbray**	N	N	?	Y	Y
51 Filner	Y	Y	Y	Y	Y
52 **Hunter**	N	N	N	Y	Y
53 Davis	Y	Y	Y	Y	Y

	12	13	14	15	16
COLORADO					
1 DeGette	Y	Y	Y	Y	Y
2 Polis	Y	Y	Y	Y	Y
3 Salazar	Y	Y	Y	Y	Y
4 Markey	Y	Y	Y	Y	Y
5 **Lamborn**	N	N	N	Y	Y
6 **Coffman**	N	N	N	Y	Y
7 Perlmutter	Y	Y	Y	Y	Y
CONNECTICUT					
1 Larson	Y	Y	Y	Y	Y
2 Courtney	Y	Y	Y	Y	Y
3 DeLauro	Y	Y	Y	Y	Y
4 Himes	Y	Y	Y	Y	Y
5 Murphy	Y	Y	Y	Y	Y
DELAWARE					
AL **Castle**	N	N	N	Y	Y
FLORIDA					
1 **Miller**	N	N	N	Y	Y
2 Boyd	Y	Y	Y	Y	Y
3 Brown	Y	Y	Y	Y	Y
4 **Crenshaw**	?	?	?	?	?
5 **Brown-Waite**	N	N	N	Y	Y
6 **Stearns**	N	N	N	Y	Y
7 **Mica**	N	N	N	Y	Y
8 Grayson	Y	Y	Y	Y	Y
9 **Bilirakis**	N	N	N	Y	Y
10 **Young**	N	N	N	Y	Y
11 Castor	Y	Y	Y	Y	Y
12 **Putnam**	N	N	N	Y	Y
13 **Buchanan**	N	N	N	Y	Y
14 **Mack**	N	N	N	Y	Y
15 **Posey**	N	N	N	Y	Y
16 **Rooney**	N	N	N	Y	Y
17 Meek	Y	Y	Y	Y	Y
18 **Ros-Lehtinen**	?	?	?	?	?
19 Vacant					
20 Wasserman Schultz	Y	Y	Y	Y	Y
21 **Diaz-Balart, L.**	Y	Y	Y	Y	Y
22 Klein	Y	Y	Y	Y	Y
23 Hastings	Y	Y	Y	Y	Y
24 Kosmas	Y	Y	Y	Y	Y
25 **Diaz-Balart, M.**	N	N	N	Y	Y
GEORGIA					
1 **Kingston**	N	?	N	Y	Y
2 Bishop	?	?	?	?	?
3 **Westmoreland**	N	N	N	Y	Y
4 Johnson	?	Y	Y	Y	Y
5 Lewis	Y	Y	Y	Y	Y
6 **Price**	N	N	N	Y	Y
7 **Linder**	N	N	N	Y	Y
8 Marshall	Y	Y	Y	Y	Y
9 **Deal**	?	?	?	?	?
10 **Broun**	N	N	N	Y	N
11 **Gingrey**	N	N	N	Y	Y
12 Barrow	Y	Y	Y	Y	Y
13 Scott	Y	Y	Y	Y	Y
HAWAII					
1 Abercrombie	Y	Y	Y	?	?
2 Hirono	Y	Y	Y	Y	Y
IDAHO					
1 Minnick	Y	Y	Y	Y	Y
2 **Simpson**	Y	Y	Y	Y	Y
ILLINOIS					
1 Rush	Y	Y	Y	Y	Y
2 Jackson	Y	Y	Y	Y	Y
3 Lipinski	Y	Y	Y	Y	Y
4 Gutierrez	Y	?	Y	Y	Y
5 Quigley	Y	Y	Y	Y	Y
6 **Roskam**	N	N	N	Y	Y
7 Davis	Y	Y	Y	Y	Y
8 Bean	N	N	Y	Y	Y
9 Schakowsky	Y	Y	Y	Y	Y
10 **Kirk**	N	N	N	Y	Y
11 Halvorson	Y	+	Y	Y	Y
12 Costello	Y	Y	Y	Y	Y
13 **Biggert**	N	N	N	Y	Y
14 Foster	Y	Y	Y	Y	Y
15 **Johnson**	N	N	N	Y	Y

KEY **Republicans**   Democrats

Y	Voted for (yea)	X	Paired against	C Voted "present" to avoid possible conflict of interest
#	Paired for	–	Announced against	
+	Announced for	P	Voted "present"	? Did not vote or otherwise make a position known
N	Voted against (nay)			

	12	13	14	15	16
16 **Manzullo**	N	N	N	Y	Y
17 Hare	Y	Y	Y	Y	Y
18 **Schock**	N	N	N	Y	Y
19 **Shimkus**	N	N	N	Y	Y
INDIANA					
1 Visclosky	Y	Y	Y	Y	Y
2 Donnelly	Y	Y	Y	Y	Y
3 **Souder**	N	N	N	Y	Y
4 **Buyer**	N	N	N	Y	Y
5 **Burton**	N	N	N	Y	Y
6 **Pence**	N	N	N	Y	Y
7 Carson	Y	Y	Y	Y	Y
8 Ellsworth	Y	Y	Y	Y	Y
9 Hill	Y	Y	Y	Y	Y
IOWA					
1 Braley	Y	Y	Y	Y	?
2 Loebsack	Y	Y	Y	Y	Y
3 Boswell	Y	Y	Y	Y	Y
4 **Latham**	N	N	N	Y	Y
5 **King**	N	N	N	Y	Y
KANSAS					
1 **Moran**	N	N	N	Y	Y
2 **Jenkins**	N	N	N	Y	Y
3 Moore	Y	Y	Y	Y	Y
4 **Tiahrt**	N	N	N	Y	Y
KENTUCKY					
1 **Whitfield**	N	N	N	Y	Y
2 **Guthrie**	N	N	N	Y	Y
3 Yarmuth	Y	Y	Y	Y	Y
4 **Davis**	N	N	?	Y	Y
5 **Rogers**	N	N	N	Y	Y
6 Chandler	Y	Y	Y	Y	Y
LOUISIANA					
1 **Scalise**	N	N	N	Y	Y
2 **Cao**	N	N	Y	Y	Y
3 Melancon	Y	Y	Y	Y	Y
4 **Fleming**	N	N	N	Y	Y
5 **Alexander**	N	N	N	Y	Y
6 **Cassidy**	N	N	N	Y	Y
7 **Boustany**	?	?	?	?	?
MAINE					
1 Pingree	Y	Y	Y	Y	Y
2 Michaud	Y	Y	Y	Y	Y
MARYLAND					
1 Kratovil	Y	Y	Y	Y	Y
2 Ruppersberger	Y	Y	Y	Y	Y
3 Sarbanes	Y	Y	Y	Y	Y
4 Edwards	Y	Y	Y	Y	Y
5 Hoyer	Y	Y	Y	Y	Y
6 **Bartlett**	N	N	N	Y	Y
7 Cummings	Y	Y	Y	?	Y
8 Van Hollen	Y	Y	Y	Y	Y
MASSACHUSETTS					
1 Olver	Y	Y	Y	Y	Y
2 Neal	Y	Y	Y	Y	Y
3 McGovern	Y	Y	Y	Y	Y
4 Frank	?	?	Y	Y	Y
5 Tsongas	Y	Y	Y	Y	Y
6 Tierney	Y	Y	Y	Y	Y
7 Markey	Y	Y	Y	Y	Y
8 Capuano	Y	Y	Y	Y	Y
9 Lynch	Y	Y	Y	Y	Y
10 Delahunt	Y	Y	Y	Y	Y
MICHIGAN					
1 Stupak	Y	Y	Y	Y	Y
2 **Hoekstra**	N	N	N	Y	Y
3 **Ehlers**	Y	Y	Y	Y	Y
4 **Camp**	N	N	N	Y	Y
5 Kildee	Y	Y	Y	Y	Y
6 **Upton**	N	N	N	Y	Y
7 Schauer	Y	Y	Y	Y	Y
8 **Rogers**	N	N	N	Y	Y
9 Peters	Y	Y	Y	Y	Y
10 **Miller**	N	N	N	Y	Y
11 **McCotter**	Y	Y	Y	Y	Y
12 Levin	Y	Y	Y	Y	Y
13 Kilpatrick	Y	Y	Y	Y	Y
14 Conyers	Y	Y	Y	Y	Y
15 Dingell	Y	Y	Y	Y	Y
MINNESOTA					
1 Walz	Y	Y	Y	Y	Y
2 **Kline**	N	N	N	Y	Y
3 **Paulsen**	N	N	N	Y	Y
4 McCollum	Y	Y	Y	Y	Y

	12	13	14	15	16
5 Ellison	Y	?	Y	Y	Y
6 **Bachmann**	N	N	N	Y	Y
7 Peterson	Y	Y	Y	Y	Y
8 Oberstar	Y	Y	Y	Y	Y
MISSISSIPPI					
1 Childers	Y	Y	Y	Y	Y
2 Thompson	Y	Y	Y	Y	Y
3 **Harper**	N	N	N	Y	Y
4 Taylor	Y	Y	Y	Y	Y
MISSOURI					
1 Clay	Y	Y	Y	Y	Y
2 **Akin**	N	N	N	Y	Y
3 Carnahan	Y	Y	Y	Y	Y
4 Skelton	N	?	N	Y	Y
5 Cleaver	?	?	?	?	?
6 **Graves**	N	N	N	Y	Y
7 **Blunt**	N	N	N	Y	Y
8 **Emerson**	N	N	N	Y	Y
9 **Luetkemeyer**	N	N	N	Y	Y
MONTANA					
AL **Rehberg**	N	N	N	Y	Y
NEBRASKA					
1 **Fortenberry**	Y	Y	Y	Y	Y
2 **Terry**	N	N	N	Y	?
3 **Smith**	N	N	N	Y	Y
NEVADA					
1 Berkley	Y	Y	Y	Y	Y
2 **Heller**	N	N	N	Y	Y
3 Titus	Y	Y	Y	Y	Y
NEW HAMPSHIRE					
1 Shea-Porter	Y	Y	Y	Y	Y
2 Hodes	Y	Y	Y	Y	Y
NEW JERSEY					
1 Andrews	Y	Y	Y	Y	Y
2 **LoBiondo**	N	N	N	Y	Y
3 Adler	Y	Y	Y	Y	Y
4 **Smith**	N	N	N	Y	Y
5 **Garrett**	N	N	N	Y	Y
6 Pallone	Y	Y	Y	Y	Y
7 **Lance**	N	N	N	Y	Y
8 Pascrell	Y	Y	Y	Y	Y
9 Rothman	Y	Y	Y	Y	Y
10 Payne	Y	Y	Y	Y	Y
11 **Frelinghuysen**	N	N	N	Y	Y
12 Holt	Y	Y	Y	Y	Y
13 Sires	Y	Y	Y	Y	Y
NEW MEXICO					
1 Heinrich	Y	Y	Y	Y	Y
2 Teague	Y	Y	Y	Y	Y
3 Luján	Y	Y	Y	Y	Y
NEW YORK					
1 Bishop	Y	Y	Y	Y	Y
2 Israel	Y	Y	Y	Y	Y
3 **King**	N	N	N	Y	Y
4 McCarthy	Y	Y	Y	Y	Y
5 Ackerman	Y	Y	Y	Y	Y
6 Meeks	Y	Y	Y	Y	Y
7 Crowley	Y	Y	Y	Y	Y
8 Nadler	Y	Y	Y	Y	Y
9 Weiner	Y	Y	Y	Y	Y
10 Towns	Y	Y	Y	Y	Y
11 Clarke	Y	Y	Y	Y	Y
12 Velázquez	Y	Y	Y	Y	Y
13 McMahon	Y	Y	Y	Y	?
14 Maloney	Y	Y	Y	Y	Y
15 Rangel	Y	Y	Y	Y	Y
16 Serrano	Y	Y	Y	Y	?
17 Engel	Y	?	Y	Y	Y
18 Lowey	Y	Y	Y	Y	Y
19 Hall	Y	Y	Y	Y	Y
20 Murphy	Y	Y	Y	Y	Y
21 Tonko	Y	Y	Y	Y	Y
22 Hinchey	Y	Y	Y	Y	Y
23 Owens	Y	Y	Y	Y	Y
24 Arcuri	Y	Y	Y	Y	Y
25 Maffei	Y	Y	Y	Y	Y
26 **Lee**	N	N	N	Y	Y
27 Higgins	Y	Y	Y	Y	Y
28 Slaughter	Y	Y	Y	Y	Y
29 Massa	Y	Y	Y	Y	Y
NORTH CAROLINA					
1 Butterfield	?	?	?	?	?
2 Etheridge	Y	Y	Y	Y	Y
3 **Jones**	N	N	Y	Y	Y
4 Price	Y	Y	Y	Y	Y

	12	13	14	15	16
5 **Foxx**	N	N	N	Y	Y
6 **Coble**	N	N	N	Y	N
7 McIntyre	Y	Y	Y	Y	Y
8 Kissell	Y	Y	Y	Y	Y
9 **Myrick**	N	N	N	Y	Y
10 **McHenry**	N	N	N	Y	Y
11 Shuler	Y	Y	Y	Y	Y
12 Watt	Y	Y	Y	Y	Y
13 Miller	Y	Y	Y	Y	Y
NORTH DAKOTA					
AL Pomeroy	Y	Y	Y	Y	Y
OHIO					
1 Driehaus	Y	Y	Y	Y	Y
2 **Schmidt**	N	N	N	Y	Y
3 **Turner**	N	N	N	Y	Y
4 **Jordan**	N	N	N	Y	Y
5 **Latta**	N	N	N	Y	Y
6 Wilson	Y	Y	Y	Y	Y
7 **Austria**	N	N	N	Y	Y
8 **Boehner**	N	N	N	Y	Y
9 Kaptur	Y	Y	Y	Y	Y
10 Kucinich	Y	Y	Y	Y	Y
11 Fudge	Y	Y	Y	Y	Y
12 **Tiberi**	N	N	N	Y	Y
13 Sutton	Y	Y	Y	Y	Y
14 **LaTourette**	Y	Y	Y	Y	Y
15 Kilroy	Y	Y	Y	Y	Y
16 Boccieri	Y	Y	Y	Y	Y
17 Ryan	Y	Y	Y	Y	Y
18 Space	Y	Y	Y	Y	Y
OKLAHOMA					
1 **Sullivan**	N	N	N	Y	Y
2 Boren	Y	Y	Y	Y	Y
3 **Lucas**	N	N	N	Y	Y
4 **Cole**	Y	Y	Y	Y	Y
5 **Fallin**	N	–	N	Y	Y
OREGON					
1 Wu	Y	Y	Y	Y	Y
2 **Walden**	N	N	N	Y	Y
3 Blumenauer	Y	Y	Y	Y	Y
4 DeFazio	Y	Y	Y	Y	Y
5 Schrader	Y	Y	Y	Y	Y
PENNSYLVANIA					
1 Brady	?	?	?	?	?
2 Fattah	Y	Y	Y	Y	Y
3 Dahlkemper	Y	Y	Y	Y	Y
4 Altmire	N	N	Y	Y	Y
5 **Thompson**	N	N	N	Y	Y
6 **Gerlach**	N	N	N	Y	Y
7 Sestak	Y	Y	Y	Y	Y
8 Murphy, P.	Y	Y	Y	Y	Y
9 **Shuster**	N	N	N	Y	Y
10 Carney	N	N	N	Y	Y
11 Kanjorski	Y	Y	Y	Y	Y
12 Murtha	Y	Y	Y	Y	Y
13 Schwartz	Y	Y	Y	Y	Y
14 Doyle	Y	Y	Y	Y	Y
15 **Dent**	N	N	N	Y	Y
16 **Pitts**	N	N	N	Y	Y
17 Holden	Y	Y	Y	Y	Y
18 **Murphy, T.**	Y	Y	Y	Y	Y
19 **Platts**	N	N	N	Y	Y
RHODE ISLAND					
1 Kennedy	Y	Y	Y	Y	Y
2 Langevin	Y	Y	Y	Y	Y
SOUTH CAROLINA					
1 **Brown**	N	N	N	Y	Y
2 **Wilson**	N	N	N	Y	Y
3 **Barrett**	?	?	?	?	?
4 **Inglis**	N	N	N	Y	Y
5 Spratt	Y	Y	Y	Y	Y
6 Clyburn	Y	Y	Y	Y	Y
SOUTH DAKOTA					
AL Herseth Sandlin	Y	Y	Y	Y	Y
TENNESSEE					
1 **Roe**	N	N	N	Y	Y
2 **Duncan**	N	N	?	Y	N
3 **Wamp**	?	?	?	?	?
4 Davis	Y	Y	Y	Y	Y
5 Cooper	Y	Y	Y	Y	Y
6 Gordon	Y	Y	Y	Y	Y
7 **Blackburn**	N	N	N	Y	Y
8 Tanner	Y	Y	Y	Y	Y
9 Cohen	Y	Y	Y	Y	Y

	12	13	14	15	16
TEXAS					
1 **Gohmert**	N	N	N	Y	N
2 **Poe**	N	N	N	Y	Y
3 **Johnson, S.**	N	N	N	Y	Y
4 **Hall**	N	N	N	Y	Y
5 **Hensarling**	N	N	?	Y	?
6 **Barton**	N	N	N	Y	Y
7 **Culberson**	?	?	?	?	?
8 **Brady**	N	N	?	Y	Y
9 Green, A.	Y	Y	Y	Y	Y
10 **McCaul**	N	N	N	Y	?
11 **Conaway**	N	N	N	Y	Y
12 **Granger**	N	N	N	Y	Y
13 **Thornberry**	N	N	N	Y	Y
14 **Paul**	N	N	N	N	N
15 **Hinojosa**	?	?	?	?	?
16 Reyes	Y	Y	Y	Y	Y
17 Edwards	Y	Y	Y	Y	Y
18 Jackson Lee	Y	Y	Y	Y	Y
19 **Neugebauer**	N	N	N	Y	Y
20 Gonzalez	Y	Y	Y	Y	Y
21 **Smith**	N	N	N	Y	Y
22 **Olson**	N	N	N	Y	Y
23 Rodriguez	Y	Y	Y	Y	Y
24 **Marchant**	N	N	N	Y	Y
25 Doggett	Y	Y	Y	Y	Y
26 **Burgess**	N	N	N	Y	Y
27 Ortiz	Y	Y	Y	Y	Y
28 Cuellar	Y	Y	Y	Y	Y
29 Green, G.	Y	Y	Y	Y	Y
30 Johnson, E.	?	?	?	?	?
31 **Carter**	N	N	N	Y	Y
32 **Sessions**	N	N	N	Y	Y
UTAH					
1 **Bishop**	N	N	N	Y	Y
2 Matheson	Y	Y	Y	Y	Y
3 **Chaffetz**	N	N	N	Y	Y
VERMONT					
AL Welch	Y	Y	Y	Y	Y
VIRGINIA					
1 **Wittman**	N	N	N	Y	Y
2 Nye	Y	Y	Y	Y	Y
3 Scott	Y	Y	Y	Y	Y
4 **Forbes**	N	N	N	Y	Y
5 Perriello	Y	Y	Y	Y	Y
6 **Goodlatte**	N	N	N	Y	Y
7 **Cantor**	N	N	N	Y	Y
8 Moran	Y	Y	Y	Y	Y
9 Boucher	Y	Y	Y	Y	Y
10 **Wolf**	N	N	N	Y	Y
11 Connolly	Y	Y	Y	Y	Y
WASHINGTON					
1 Inslee	Y	Y	Y	Y	Y
2 Larsen	Y	Y	Y	Y	Y
3 Baird	Y	Y	Y	Y	Y
4 **Hastings**	N	N	N	Y	Y
5 **McMorris Rodgers**	N	N	N	Y	Y
6 Dicks	Y	Y	Y	Y	Y
7 McDermott	Y	Y	Y	Y	Y
8 **Reichert**	N	N	N	Y	Y
9 Smith	Y	Y	Y	Y	Y
WEST VIRGINIA					
1 Mollohan	Y	Y	Y	Y	Y
2 **Capito**	N	N	N	Y	Y
3 Rahall	Y	Y	Y	Y	Y
WISCONSIN					
1 **Ryan**	N	N	N	Y	Y
2 Baldwin	Y	Y	Y	Y	Y
3 Kind	Y	Y	Y	Y	Y
4 Moore	Y	Y	Y	Y	Y
5 **Sensenbrenner**	N	N	N	Y	N
6 **Petri**	N	N	N	Y	N
7 Obey	Y	Y	Y	Y	Y
8 Kagen	Y	Y	Y	Y	Y
WYOMING					
AL **Lummis**	N	N	N	Y	N
DELEGATES					
Faleomavaega (A.S.)					
Norton (D.C.)					
Bordallo (Guam)					
Sablan (N. Marianas)					
Pierluisi (P.R.)					
Christensen (V.I.)					

IN THE HOUSE | By Vote Number

17. **H Res 990. National Mentoring Month/Adoption.** Woolsey, D-Calif., motion to suspend the rules and adopt the resolution that would support the designation of National Mentoring Month and recognize the contributions of adults and students already volunteering as mentors. Motion agreed to 398-0: D 236-0; R 162-0. A two-thirds majority of those present and voting (266 in this case) is required for adoption under suspension of the rules. Jan. 26, 2010.

18. **H Res 1011. Cervical Health Awareness Month/Adoption.** Pallone, D-N.J., motion to suspend the rules and adopt the resolution that would support the goals of Cervical Health Awareness Month and recognize the importance of detecting cervical cancer during its earliest stages. Motion agreed to 400-0: D 239-0; R 161-0. A two-thirds majority of those present and voting (267 in this case) is required for adoption under suspension of the rules. Jan. 26, 2010.

19. **H Res 1003. National Influenza Vaccination Week/Adoption.** Pallone, D-N.J., motion to suspend the rules and adopt the resolution that would support the designation of National Influenza Vaccination Week and encourage citizens to get vaccinated. Motion agreed to 398-2: D 237-1; R 161-1. A two-thirds majority of those present and voting (267 in this case) is required for adoption under suspension of the rules. Jan. 26, 2010.

20. **HR 3726, HR 4474. Virgin Islands and Idaho Lands Bills/Rule.** Adoption of the rule (H Res 1038) to provide for House floor consideration of the measures that would establish the Castle Nugent National Historic Site in St. Croix, V.I., and authorize certain water facilities in Idaho wilderness areas. Adopted 234-174: D 232-8; R 2-166. Jan. 27, 2010.

21. **H Res 1024. Poverty in America Awareness Month/Adoption.** McDermott, D-Wash., motion to suspend the rules and adopt the resolution that would support the designation of Poverty in America Awareness Month and state that poverty eradication should be a goal for the people and government of the United States. Motion agreed to 387-18: D 242-0; R 145-18. A two-thirds majority of those present and voting (270 in this case) is required for adoption under suspension of the rules. Jan. 27, 2010.

	17	18	19	20	21
ALABAMA					
1 Bonner	Y	Y	Y	N	Y
2 Bright	Y	Y	Y	Y	Y
3 Rogers	Y	Y	Y	N	Y
4 Aderholt	Y	Y	Y	N	Y
5 Griffith	Y	Y	Y	N	Y
6 Bachus	Y	Y	Y	N	Y
7 Davis	?	?	?	?	?
ALASKA					
AL Young	Y	Y	Y	N	Y
ARIZONA					
1 Kirkpatrick	Y	Y	Y	Y	Y
2 Franks	Y	Y	Y	N	N
3 Shadegg	Y	Y	Y	N	Y
4 Pastor	Y	Y	Y	Y	Y
5 Mitchell	Y	Y	Y	N	Y
6 Flake	Y	Y	Y	N	N
7 Grijalva	?	?	?	Y	Y
8 Giffords	Y	Y	Y	N	Y
ARKANSAS					
1 Berry	Y	Y	Y	Y	Y
2 Snyder	Y	Y	Y	Y	Y
3 Boozman	Y	Y	Y	N	Y
4 Ross	Y	Y	Y	Y	Y
CALIFORNIA					
1 Thompson	Y	Y	Y	Y	Y
2 Herger	Y	Y	N	N	Y
3 Lungren	Y	Y	Y	N	Y
4 McClintock	Y	Y	Y	N	N
5 Matsui	Y	Y	Y	Y	Y
6 Woolsey	Y	Y	Y	Y	Y
7 Miller, George	Y	Y	Y	Y	Y
8 Pelosi					
9 Lee	Y	Y	Y	Y	Y
10 Garamendi	Y	Y	Y	Y	Y
11 McNerney	Y	Y	Y	Y	Y
12 Speier	?	?	?	?	?
13 Stark	Y	Y	Y	Y	Y
14 Eshoo	Y	Y	Y	Y	Y
15 Honda	Y	Y	Y	Y	Y
16 Lofgren	Y	Y	Y	Y	Y
17 Farr	Y	Y	Y	Y	Y
18 Cardoza	Y	Y	Y	Y	Y
19 Radanovich	Y	Y	Y	?	?
20 Costa	Y	Y	Y	Y	Y
21 Nunes	Y	Y	N	N	Y
22 McCarthy	Y	Y	Y	N	Y
23 Capps	Y	Y	Y	Y	Y
24 Gallegly	Y	Y	Y	N	Y
25 McKeon	Y	Y	Y	N	Y
26 Dreier	Y	Y	Y	N	Y
27 Sherman	Y	Y	Y	Y	Y
28 Berman	Y	Y	Y	Y	Y
29 Schiff	Y	Y	Y	Y	Y
30 Waxman	Y	Y	Y	?	Y
31 Becerra	Y	Y	Y	Y	Y
32 Chu	Y	Y	Y	Y	Y
33 Watson	Y	Y	Y	Y	Y
34 Roybal-Allard	Y	Y	Y	Y	Y
35 Waters	?	?	?	?	?
36 Harman	Y	Y	Y	Y	Y
37 Richardson	Y	Y	Y	Y	Y
38 Napolitano	Y	Y	Y	Y	Y
39 Sánchez, Linda	Y	Y	Y	Y	Y
40 Royce	Y	Y	Y	N	Y
41 Lewis	Y	Y	Y	N	Y
42 Miller, Gary	Y	Y	Y	N	Y
43 Baca	Y	Y	Y	Y	Y
44 Calvert	Y	Y	Y	N	Y
45 Bono Mack	Y	Y	Y	N	Y
46 Rohrabacher	Y	Y	Y	N	Y
47 Sanchez, Loretta	Y	Y	Y	Y	Y
48 Campbell	Y	Y	Y	N	Y
49 Issa	Y	Y	Y	N	?
50 Bilbray	Y	Y	Y	Y	Y
51 Filner	Y	Y	Y	Y	Y
52 Hunter	Y	Y	Y	N	Y
53 Davis	Y	Y	Y	Y	Y

	17	18	19	20	21
COLORADO					
1 DeGette	Y	Y	Y	Y	Y
2 Polis	Y	Y	N	Y	Y
3 Salazar	Y	Y	Y	Y	Y
4 Markey	Y	Y	Y	Y	Y
5 Lamborn	Y	Y	Y	N	Y
6 Coffman	Y	Y	Y	N	Y
7 Perlmutter	Y	Y	Y	Y	Y
CONNECTICUT					
1 Larson	Y	Y	Y	Y	Y
2 Courtney	Y	Y	Y	Y	Y
3 DeLauro	Y	Y	Y	Y	Y
4 Himes	Y	Y	Y	Y	Y
5 Murphy	Y	Y	Y	Y	Y
DELAWARE					
AL Castle	Y	Y	Y	N	Y
FLORIDA					
1 Miller	?	?	?	N	Y
2 Boyd	Y	Y	Y	Y	Y
3 Brown	Y	Y	Y	Y	Y
4 Crenshaw	?	?	?	?	?
5 Brown-Waite	Y	Y	Y	N	Y
6 Stearns	Y	Y	Y	N	Y
7 Mica	Y	Y	Y	N	Y
8 Grayson	Y	Y	Y	Y	Y
9 Bilirakis	Y	Y	Y	N	Y
10 Young	Y	Y	Y	N	Y
11 Castor	Y	Y	Y	?	Y
12 Putnam	?	?	?	N	Y
13 Buchanan	Y	Y	Y	N	Y
14 Mack	Y	Y	N	N	Y
15 Posey	Y	Y	Y	N	Y
16 Rooney	Y	Y	Y	N	Y
17 Meek	Y	Y	Y	Y	Y
18 Ros-Lehtinen	Y	Y	Y	N	Y
19 Vacant					
20 Wasserman Schultz	Y	Y	Y	Y	Y
21 Diaz-Balart, L.	Y	Y	Y	N	Y
22 Klein	Y	Y	Y	Y	Y
23 Hastings	Y	Y	Y	Y	Y
24 Kosmas	Y	Y	Y	Y	Y
25 Diaz-Balart, M.	Y	Y	Y	N	Y
GEORGIA					
1 Kingston	Y	Y	Y	N	N
2 Bishop	?	?	?	?	?
3 Westmoreland	Y	Y	Y	N	N
4 Johnson	Y	Y	Y	Y	Y
5 Lewis	Y	Y	Y	Y	Y
6 Price	Y	Y	Y	N	N
7 Linder	Y	Y	Y	N	Y
8 Marshall	Y	Y	Y	Y	Y
9 Deal	?	?	?	?	?
10 Broun	Y	Y	Y	N	N
11 Gingrey	Y	Y	Y	N	?
12 Barrow	Y	Y	Y	Y	Y
13 Scott	Y	Y	Y	Y	Y
HAWAII					
1 Abercrombie	Y	Y	Y	+	+
2 Hirono	Y	Y	Y	Y	Y
IDAHO					
1 Minnick	Y	Y	Y	Y	Y
2 Simpson	Y	Y	Y	Y	Y
ILLINOIS					
1 Rush	Y	Y	Y	Y	Y
2 Jackson	Y	Y	Y	Y	Y
3 Lipinski	Y	Y	Y	Y	Y
4 Gutierrez	+	+	+	Y	Y
5 Quigley	Y	Y	Y	Y	Y
6 Roskam	Y	Y	Y	N	Y
7 Davis	Y	Y	Y	Y	Y
8 Bean	Y	Y	Y	Y	Y
9 Schakowsky	Y	Y	Y	Y	Y
10 Kirk	Y	Y	Y	N	Y
11 Halvorson	Y	Y	Y	Y	Y
12 Costello	Y	Y	Y	Y	Y
13 Biggert	Y	Y	Y	N	Y
14 Foster	Y	Y	Y	Y	Y
15 Johnson	Y	Y	Y	N	Y

KEY   **Republicans**   Democrats

Y Voted for (yea)	X Paired against	C Voted "present" to avoid possible conflict of interest
# Paired for	– Announced against	
+ Announced for	P Voted "present"	? Did not vote or otherwise make a position known
N Voted against (nay)		

	17	18	19	20	21
16 **Manzullo**	Y	Y	Y	N	Y
17 **Hare**	Y	Y	Y	N	Y
18 **Schock**	Y	Y	Y	N	Y
19 **Shimkus**	Y	Y	Y	N	Y
INDIANA					
1 Visclosky	Y	Y	Y	Y	Y
2 Donnelly	Y	Y	Y	N	Y
3 **Souder**	Y	Y	Y	N	Y
4 **Buyer**	Y	Y	Y	N	Y
5 **Burton**	Y	Y	Y	N	N
6 **Pence**	Y	Y	Y	N	N
7 Carson	Y	Y	Y	Y	Y
8 Ellsworth	Y	Y	Y	Y	Y
9 Hill	Y	Y	Y	N	Y
IOWA					
1 Braley	Y	Y	Y	Y	Y
2 Loebsack	Y	Y	Y	Y	Y
3 Boswell	Y	Y	Y	Y	Y
4 **Latham**	Y	Y	Y	N	Y
5 **King**	?	?	?	N	Y
KANSAS					
1 **Moran**	Y	Y	Y	?	?
2 **Jenkins**	Y	Y	Y	N	Y
3 Moore	Y	Y	Y	N	Y
4 **Tiahrt**	Y	Y	Y	N	Y
KENTUCKY					
1 **Whitfield**	Y	Y	Y	N	Y
2 **Guthrie**	Y	Y	Y	N	Y
3 Yarmuth	?	Y	Y	Y	Y
4 **Davis**	Y	Y	Y	N	Y
5 **Rogers**	Y	Y	Y	N	Y
6 Chandler	Y	Y	Y	Y	Y
LOUISIANA					
1 **Scalise**	Y	Y	Y	N	N
2 **Cao**	Y	Y	Y	N	Y
3 Melancon	Y	Y	Y	Y	Y
4 **Fleming**	Y	Y	Y	N	Y
5 **Alexander**	?	?	?	N	Y
6 **Cassidy**	Y	Y	Y	N	Y
7 **Boustany**	Y	Y	Y	N	Y
MAINE					
1 Pingree	Y	Y	Y	Y	Y
2 Michaud	Y	Y	Y	Y	Y
MARYLAND					
1 Kratovil	Y	Y	Y	Y	Y
2 Ruppersberger	Y	Y	Y	Y	Y
3 Sarbanes	Y	Y	Y	Y	Y
4 Edwards	Y	Y	Y	Y	Y
5 Hoyer	Y	Y	Y	Y	Y
6 **Bartlett**	Y	Y	Y	N	Y
7 Cummings	Y	Y	Y	Y	Y
8 Van Hollen	Y	Y	Y	Y	Y
MASSACHUSETTS					
1 Olver	Y	Y	Y	Y	Y
2 Neal	Y	Y	Y	Y	Y
3 McGovern	Y	Y	Y	Y	Y
4 Frank	?	?	?	?	?
5 Tsongas	Y	Y	Y	Y	Y
6 Tierney	Y	Y	Y	Y	Y
7 Markey	Y	Y	Y	?	Y
8 Capuano	Y	Y	Y	Y	Y
9 Lynch	Y	Y	Y	Y	Y
10 Delahunt	?	?	?	Y	Y
MICHIGAN					
1 Stupak	Y	Y	Y	Y	Y
2 **Hoekstra**	?	?	?	N	Y
3 **Ehlers**	Y	Y	Y	N	Y
4 **Camp**	Y	Y	Y	N	Y
5 Kildee	Y	Y	Y	Y	Y
6 **Upton**	Y	Y	Y	N	Y
7 Schauer	Y	Y	Y	Y	Y
8 **Rogers**	Y	Y	Y	N	Y
9 Peters	Y	Y	Y	N	Y
10 **Miller**	Y	Y	Y	N	Y
11 **McCotter**	Y	Y	Y	Y	Y
12 Levin	Y	Y	Y	Y	Y
13 Kilpatrick	Y	Y	Y	Y	Y
14 Conyers	?	Y	Y	Y	Y
15 Dingell	Y	Y	Y	Y	Y
MINNESOTA					
1 Walz	+	+	+	Y	Y
2 **Kline**	Y	Y	Y	N	Y
3 **Paulsen**	?	?	?	N	Y
4 McCollum	Y	Y	Y	Y	Y

	17	18	19	20	21
5 Ellison	?	?	?	Y	Y
6 **Bachmann**	+	+	+	N	Y
7 Peterson	Y	Y	Y	N	Y
8 Oberstar	Y	Y	Y	Y	Y
MISSISSIPPI					
1 Childers	Y	Y	Y	Y	Y
2 Thompson	Y	Y	Y	Y	Y
3 **Harper**	Y	Y	Y	N	Y
4 Taylor	Y	Y	Y	N	Y
MISSOURI					
1 Clay	Y	Y	Y	Y	Y
2 **Akin**	+	+	+	N	Y
3 Carnahan	Y	Y	Y	Y	Y
4 Skelton	Y	Y	Y	Y	Y
5 Cleaver	Y	Y	Y	Y	Y
6 **Graves**	Y	Y	Y	N	Y
7 **Blunt**	Y	Y	Y	N	?
8 **Emerson**	Y	Y	Y	N	Y
9 **Luetkemeyer**	Y	Y	Y	N	Y
MONTANA					
AL **Rehberg**	?	?	?	N	Y
NEBRASKA					
1 **Fortenberry**	Y	Y	Y	N	Y
2 **Terry**	Y	Y	Y	N	Y
3 **Smith**	Y	Y	Y	N	?
NEVADA					
1 Berkley	Y	Y	Y	Y	Y
2 **Heller**	Y	Y	Y	N	Y
3 Titus	Y	Y	Y	Y	Y
NEW HAMPSHIRE					
1 Shea-Porter	Y	Y	Y	Y	Y
2 Hodes	Y	Y	Y	Y	Y
NEW JERSEY					
1 Andrews	Y	Y	Y	Y	Y
2 **LoBiondo**	+	+	+	N	Y
3 Adler	Y	Y	Y	Y	Y
4 **Smith**	Y	Y	Y	N	Y
5 **Garrett**	?	Y	Y	N	Y
6 Pallone	Y	Y	Y	Y	Y
7 **Lance**	Y	Y	Y	N	Y
8 Pascrell	Y	Y	Y	Y	Y
9 Rothman	Y	Y	Y	Y	Y
10 Payne	Y	Y	Y	Y	Y
11 **Frelinghuysen**	Y	Y	Y	N	Y
12 Holt	Y	Y	Y	Y	Y
13 Sires	Y	Y	Y	Y	Y
NEW MEXICO					
1 Heinrich	Y	Y	Y	Y	Y
2 Teague	Y	Y	Y	Y	Y
3 Luján	Y	Y	Y	Y	Y
NEW YORK					
1 Bishop	Y	Y	Y	Y	Y
2 Israel	Y	Y	Y	Y	Y
3 **King**	Y	Y	Y	N	Y
4 McCarthy	Y	Y	Y	Y	Y
5 Ackerman	Y	Y	Y	Y	Y
6 Meeks	Y	Y	Y	Y	Y
7 Crowley	Y	Y	Y	Y	Y
8 Nadler	Y	Y	Y	Y	Y
9 Weiner	Y	Y	Y	Y	Y
10 Towns	?	Y	Y	Y	Y
11 Clarke	Y	Y	Y	Y	Y
12 Velázquez	Y	Y	Y	Y	Y
13 McMahon	Y	Y	Y	Y	Y
14 Maloney	Y	Y	Y	Y	Y
15 Rangel	Y	Y	Y	Y	Y
16 Serrano	Y	Y	Y	Y	Y
17 Engel	Y	Y	Y	Y	Y
18 Lowey	Y	Y	Y	Y	Y
19 Hall	Y	Y	Y	Y	Y
20 Murphy	Y	Y	Y	N	Y
21 Tonko	Y	Y	Y	Y	Y
22 Hinchey	Y	Y	Y	Y	Y
23 Owens	Y	Y	Y	Y	Y
24 Arcuri	Y	Y	Y	Y	Y
25 Maffei	Y	Y	Y	Y	Y
26 **Lee**	Y	Y	Y	N	Y
27 Higgins	Y	Y	Y	Y	Y
28 Slaughter	Y	Y	Y	Y	Y
29 Massa	Y	Y	Y	Y	Y
NORTH CAROLINA					
1 Butterfield	Y	Y	Y	Y	?
2 Etheridge	Y	Y	Y	Y	Y
3 **Jones**	Y	Y	Y	N	Y
4 Price	Y	Y	Y	Y	Y

	17	18	19	20	21
5 **Foxx**	Y	Y	Y	N	N
6 **Coble**	Y	Y	Y	N	?
7 McIntyre	Y	Y	Y	Y	Y
8 Kissell	Y	Y	Y	Y	Y
9 **Myrick**	Y	Y	Y	N	Y
10 **McHenry**	Y	Y	Y	?	Y
11 Shuler	Y	Y	Y	Y	Y
12 Watt	Y	Y	Y	Y	Y
13 Miller	Y	Y	Y	Y	Y
NORTH DAKOTA					
AL Pomeroy	Y	Y	Y	Y	Y
OHIO					
1 Driehaus	Y	Y	Y	Y	Y
2 **Schmidt**	Y	Y	Y	N	Y
3 **Turner**	?	?	?	N	Y
4 **Jordan**	Y	Y	Y	N	?
5 **Latta**	Y	Y	Y	N	Y
6 Wilson	Y	Y	Y	Y	Y
7 **Austria**	Y	Y	Y	N	Y
8 **Boehner**	Y	Y	Y	N	Y
9 Kaptur	Y	Y	Y	Y	Y
10 Kucinich	Y	Y	Y	Y	Y
11 Fudge	Y	Y	Y	Y	Y
12 **Tiberi**	Y	Y	Y	N	Y
13 Sutton	Y	Y	Y	Y	Y
14 **LaTourette**	Y	?	Y	N	Y
15 Kilroy	Y	Y	Y	?	Y
16 Boccieri	?	?	?	Y	Y
17 Ryan	?	?	?	Y	Y
18 Space	Y	Y	Y	Y	Y
OKLAHOMA					
1 **Sullivan**	Y	Y	Y	N	Y
2 Boren	Y	Y	Y	Y	Y
3 **Lucas**	Y	Y	Y	?	?
4 **Cole**	Y	Y	Y	N	Y
5 **Fallin**	Y	Y	Y	N	Y
OREGON					
1 Wu	Y	Y	Y	Y	Y
2 **Walden**	Y	Y	Y	N	Y
3 Blumenauer	Y	Y	Y	Y	Y
4 DeFazio	Y	Y	Y	Y	Y
5 Schrader	Y	Y	Y	Y	Y
PENNSYLVANIA					
1 Brady	Y	Y	Y	Y	Y
2 Fattah	Y	Y	Y	Y	Y
3 Dahlkemper	Y	Y	Y	Y	Y
4 Altmire	Y	Y	Y	Y	Y
5 **Thompson**	Y	Y	Y	N	Y
6 **Gerlach**	?	?	?	N	Y
7 Sestak	Y	Y	Y	Y	Y
8 Murphy, P.	Y	Y	Y	Y	Y
9 **Shuster**	Y	Y	Y	N	Y
10 Carney	Y	Y	Y	Y	Y
11 Kanjorski	Y	Y	Y	Y	Y
12 Murtha	Y	Y	Y	Y	Y
13 Schwartz	Y	Y	Y	Y	Y
14 Doyle	Y	Y	Y	Y	Y
15 **Dent**	Y	Y	Y	N	Y
16 **Pitts**	Y	Y	Y	N	Y
17 Holden	Y	Y	Y	Y	Y
18 **Murphy, T.**	Y	Y	Y	N	Y
19 **Platts**	Y	Y	Y	N	Y
RHODE ISLAND					
1 Kennedy	Y	Y	?	?	?
2 Langevin	Y	Y	Y	?	Y
SOUTH CAROLINA					
1 **Brown**	Y	Y	Y	N	Y
2 **Wilson**	Y	Y	Y	N	Y
3 **Barrett**	+	+	+	?	?
4 **Inglis**	Y	Y	Y	N	Y
5 Spratt	Y	Y	Y	Y	Y
6 Clyburn	Y	Y	Y	Y	Y
SOUTH DAKOTA					
AL Herseth Sandlin	Y	Y	Y	Y	Y
TENNESSEE					
1 **Roe**	Y	Y	Y	N	Y
2 **Duncan**	Y	Y	Y	N	Y
3 **Wamp**	?	?	?	?	?
4 Davis	Y	Y	Y	Y	Y
5 Cooper	Y	Y	Y	Y	Y
6 Gordon	Y	Y	Y	Y	Y
7 **Blackburn**	Y	Y	Y	N	Y
8 Tanner	Y	Y	Y	Y	Y
9 Cohen	Y	Y	Y	Y	Y

	17	18	19	20	21
TEXAS					
1 **Gohmert**	Y	Y	Y	N	?
2 **Poe**	Y	Y	Y	N	N
3 **Johnson, S.**	Y	Y	Y	N	Y
4 **Hall**	Y	Y	Y	N	Y
5 **Hensarling**	Y	Y	Y	N	N
6 **Barton**	Y	?	Y	?	?
7 **Culberson**	Y	Y	Y	N	Y
8 **Brady**	Y	Y	Y	N	Y
9 Green, A.	Y	Y	Y	Y	Y
10 **McCaul**	Y	Y	Y	N	Y
11 **Conaway**	Y	Y	Y	N	N
12 **Granger**	Y	Y	Y	N	Y
13 **Thornberry**	Y	Y	Y	N	Y
14 **Paul**	Y	Y	N	N	Y
15 Hinojosa	Y	Y	Y	Y	Y
16 Reyes	Y	Y	Y	Y	Y
17 Edwards	Y	Y	Y	?	?
18 Jackson Lee	Y	Y	Y	Y	Y
19 **Neugebauer**	Y	Y	Y	N	Y
20 Gonzalez	Y	Y	Y	Y	Y
21 **Smith**	Y	Y	Y	Y	Y
22 **Olson**	Y	Y	Y	N	Y
23 Rodriguez	Y	Y	Y	Y	Y
24 **Marchant**	Y	Y	Y	N	N
25 Doggett	Y	Y	Y	Y	Y
26 **Burgess**	Y	Y	Y	N	N
27 Ortiz	+	+	+	+	+
28 Cuellar	Y	Y	Y	Y	Y
29 Green, G.	Y	Y	Y	Y	Y
30 Johnson, E.	?	?	?	?	?
31 **Carter**	Y	Y	Y	N	N
32 **Sessions**	Y	Y	Y	N	Y
UTAH					
1 **Bishop**	Y	Y	Y	N	Y
2 **Matheson**	Y	Y	Y	Y	Y
3 **Chaffetz**	Y	Y	Y	N	Y
VERMONT					
AL Welch	Y	Y	Y	Y	?
VIRGINIA					
1 **Wittman**	Y	Y	Y	N	Y
2 Nye	Y	Y	Y	Y	Y
3 Scott	Y	Y	Y	Y	Y
4 **Forbes**	Y	Y	Y	N	Y
5 Perriello	Y	Y	Y	Y	Y
6 **Goodlatte**	Y	Y	Y	N	Y
7 **Cantor**	Y	Y	Y	N	Y
8 **Moran**	?	?	?	?	?
9 Boucher	Y	Y	Y	Y	Y
10 **Wolf**	Y	Y	Y	N	Y
11 Connolly	Y	Y	Y	Y	Y
WASHINGTON					
1 Inslee	Y	Y	Y	Y	Y
2 Larsen	Y	Y	Y	Y	Y
3 Baird	Y	Y	Y	Y	Y
4 **Hastings**	Y	Y	Y	N	Y
5 **McMorris Rodgers**	Y	Y	Y	?	Y
6 Dicks	Y	Y	Y	Y	Y
7 McDermott	Y	Y	Y	Y	Y
8 **Reichert**	Y	Y	Y	N	Y
9 Smith	Y	Y	Y	Y	Y
WEST VIRGINIA					
1 Mollohan	Y	Y	Y	Y	Y
2 **Capito**	Y	Y	Y	N	Y
3 Rahall	Y	Y	Y	Y	Y
WISCONSIN					
1 **Ryan**	Y	Y	Y	N	Y
2 Baldwin	Y	Y	Y	Y	Y
3 Kind	+	+	+	Y	Y
4 Moore	Y	Y	Y	Y	Y
5 **Sensenbrenner**	Y	Y	Y	N	Y
6 **Petri**	Y	Y	Y	N	Y
7 Obey	Y	Y	Y	Y	Y
8 Kagen	Y	Y	Y	Y	Y
WYOMING					
AL **Lummis**	Y	Y	Y	N	N
DELEGATES					
Faleomavaega (A.S.)					
Norton (D.C.)					
Bordallo (Guam)					
Sablan (N. Marianas)					
Pierluisi (P.R.)					
Christensen (V.I.)					

IN THE HOUSE | By Vote Number

22. **HR 4474. Idaho Wilderness Water Facilities/Passage.** Passage of the bill that would authorize the continued use of water facilities located on National Forest System land in north-central Idaho. It would also require owners to maintain the facilities. Passed 415-0: D 245-0; R 170-0. Jan. 27, 2010.

23. **HR 3726. Castle Nugent National Historic Site/Passage.** Passage of the bill that would establish a Castle Nugent national historic site in St. Croix, V.I. It would also authorize the Interior Department to purchase land for the site with appropriated funds. Passed 240-175: D 240-4; R 0-171. Jan. 27, 2010.

24. **HR 4508. Small Business Administration Programs Extension/ Passage.** Velázquez, D-N.Y., motion to suspend the rules and pass the bill that would extend Small Business Administration programs until April 30, 2010. Motion agreed to 410-4: D 245-0; R 165-4. A two-thirds majority of those present and voting (276 in this case) is required for passage under suspension of the rules. Jan. 27, 2010.

25. **H Res 1020. Rocky Mountain National Park Anniversary/ Adoption.** Christensen, D-V.I., motion to suspend the rules and adopt the resolution that would mark the 95th anniversary of the signing of the Rocky Mountain National Park Act, which created the park. Motion agreed to 408-0: D 241-0; R 167-0. A two-thirds majority of those present and voting (272 in this case) is required for adoption under suspension of the rules. Jan. 27, 2010.

	22	23	24	25
ALABAMA				
1 **Bonner**	Y	N	Y	Y
2 **Bright**	Y	N	Y	Y
3 **Rogers**	Y	N	Y	Y
4 **Aderholt**	Y	N	Y	Y
5 **Griffith**	?	N	Y	Y
6 **Bachus**	Y	N	Y	Y
7 Davis	?	?	?	?
ALASKA				
AL **Young**	Y	N	Y	Y
ARIZONA				
1 Kirkpatrick	Y	Y	Y	Y
2 **Franks**	Y	N	Y	Y
3 **Shadegg**	Y	N	Y	Y
4 Pastor	Y	Y	Y	Y
5 Mitchell	Y	N	Y	Y
6 **Flake**	Y	N	N	Y
7 Grijalva	Y	Y	Y	Y
8 Giffords	Y	Y	Y	Y
ARKANSAS				
1 Berry	Y	Y	Y	Y
2 Snyder	Y	Y	Y	Y
3 **Boozman**	Y	N	Y	Y
4 Ross	Y	Y	Y	Y
CALIFORNIA				
1 Thompson	Y	Y	Y	Y
2 **Herger**	Y	N	Y	Y
3 **Lungren**	Y	N	Y	Y
4 **McClintock**	Y	N	N	Y
5 Matsui	Y	Y	Y	Y
6 Woolsey	Y	Y	Y	Y
7 Miller, George	Y	Y	Y	Y
8 Pelosi				
9 Lee	Y	Y	Y	Y
10 Garamendi	Y	Y	Y	Y
11 McNerney	Y	Y	Y	Y
12 Speier	?	?	?	?
13 Stark	Y	Y	Y	Y
14 Eshoo	Y	Y	Y	Y
15 Honda	Y	Y	Y	Y
16 Lofgren	Y	Y	Y	Y
17 Farr	Y	Y	Y	Y
18 Cardoza	Y	Y	Y	Y
19 **Radanovich**	Y	N	Y	Y
20 Costa	Y	Y	Y	Y
21 **Nunes**	Y	N	Y	Y
22 **McCarthy**	Y	N	Y	Y
23 Capps	Y	Y	Y	Y
24 **Gallegly**	Y	N	Y	Y
25 **McKeon**	Y	N	Y	Y
26 **Dreier**	Y	N	Y	Y
27 Sherman	Y	Y	Y	Y
28 Berman	Y	Y	Y	Y
29 Schiff	Y	Y	Y	Y
30 Waxman	Y	Y	Y	Y
31 Becerra	Y	Y	Y	Y
32 Chu	Y	Y	Y	Y
33 Watson	Y	Y	Y	Y
34 Roybal-Allard	Y	Y	Y	Y
35 Waters	?	?	?	?
36 Harman	Y	Y	Y	Y
37 Richardson	Y	Y	Y	Y
38 Napolitano	Y	Y	Y	Y
39 Sánchez, Linda	Y	Y	Y	Y
40 **Royce**	Y	N	Y	Y
41 **Lewis**	Y	N	Y	Y
42 **Miller, Gary**	Y	N	Y	Y
43 Baca	Y	Y	Y	Y
44 **Calvert**	Y	N	Y	Y
45 **Bono Mack**	Y	N	Y	Y
46 **Rohrabacher**	Y	N	Y	Y
47 Sanchez, Loretta	Y	Y	Y	Y
48 **Campbell**	Y	N	Y	Y
49 **Issa**	Y	N	Y	Y
50 **Bilbray**	Y	N	Y	Y
51 Filner	Y	Y	Y	Y
52 **Hunter**	Y	N	Y	Y
53 Davis	Y	Y	Y	Y

	22	23	24	25
COLORADO				
1 DeGette	Y	Y	Y	Y
2 Polis	Y	Y	Y	Y
3 Salazar	Y	Y	Y	Y
4 Markey	Y	Y	Y	Y
5 **Lamborn**	Y	N	Y	Y
6 **Coffman**	Y	N	Y	Y
7 Perlmutter	Y	Y	Y	Y
CONNECTICUT				
1 Larson	Y	Y	Y	Y
2 Courtney	Y	Y	Y	Y
3 DeLauro	Y	Y	Y	Y
4 Himes	Y	Y	Y	Y
5 Murphy	Y	Y	Y	Y
DELAWARE				
AL **Castle**	Y	N	Y	Y
FLORIDA				
1 **Miller**	Y	N	Y	Y
2 Boyd	Y	Y	Y	Y
3 Brown	Y	Y	Y	Y
4 **Crenshaw**	?	?	?	?
5 **Brown-Waite**	Y	N	Y	Y
6 **Stearns**	Y	N	Y	Y
7 **Mica**	Y	N	Y	Y
8 Grayson	Y	Y	Y	Y
9 **Bilirakis**	Y	N	Y	Y
10 **Young**	Y	N	Y	Y
11 Castor	Y	Y	Y	Y
12 **Putnam**	Y	N	Y	Y
13 **Buchanan**	Y	N	Y	Y
14 **Mack**	Y	N	Y	Y
15 **Posey**	Y	N	Y	Y
16 **Rooney**	Y	N	Y	Y
17 Meek	Y	Y	Y	?
18 **Ros-Lehtinen**	Y	N	Y	Y
19 Vacant				
20 Wasserman Schultz	Y	Y	Y	Y
21 **Diaz-Balart, L.**	Y	N	Y	Y
22 Klein	Y	Y	Y	Y
23 Hastings	Y	Y	Y	Y
24 Kosmas	Y	Y	Y	Y
25 **Diaz-Balart, M.**	Y	N	Y	Y
GEORGIA				
1 **Kingston**	Y	N	Y	Y
2 Bishop	?	?	?	?
3 **Westmoreland**	Y	N	Y	Y
4 Johnson	?	?	?	?
5 Lewis	Y	Y	Y	Y
6 **Price**	Y	N	Y	Y
7 **Linder**	Y	N	Y	Y
8 Marshall	Y	Y	Y	Y
9 **Deal**	?	?	?	?
10 **Broun**	Y	N	N	Y
11 **Gingrey**	Y	N	Y	Y
12 Barrow	Y	Y	Y	Y
13 Scott	Y	Y	Y	Y
HAWAII				
1 Abercrombie	+	+	+	+
2 Hirono	Y	Y	Y	Y
IDAHO				
1 Minnick	Y	Y	Y	Y
2 **Simpson**	Y	N	?	Y
ILLINOIS				
1 Rush	Y	Y	Y	Y
2 Jackson	Y	Y	Y	Y
3 Lipinski	Y	Y	Y	Y
4 Gutierrez	Y	Y	Y	Y
5 Quigley	Y	Y	Y	Y
6 **Roskam**	Y	N	Y	Y
7 Davis	Y	Y	Y	Y
8 Bean	Y	Y	Y	Y
9 Schakowsky	Y	Y	Y	Y
10 **Kirk**	Y	N	Y	Y
11 Halvorson	Y	Y	Y	Y
12 Costello	Y	Y	Y	Y
13 **Biggert**	Y	N	Y	Y
14 Foster	Y	Y	?	Y
15 Johnson	Y	N	Y	Y

KEY	Republicans	Democrats		
Y	Voted for (yea)	X	Paired against	C Voted "present" to avoid possible conflict of interest
#	Paired for	–	Announced against	
+	Announced for	P	Voted "present"	? Did not vote or otherwise make a position known
N	Voted against (nay)			

	22	23	24	25
16 Manzullo	Y	N	Y	Y
17 Hare	Y	Y	Y	Y
18 Schock	?	?	?	?
19 Shimkus	Y	N	Y	Y
INDIANA				
1 Visclosky	Y	Y	Y	Y
2 Donnelly	Y	Y	Y	Y
3 Souder	Y	N	Y	Y
4 Buyer	Y	N	Y	Y
5 Burton	Y	N	Y	Y
6 Pence	Y	N	Y	Y
7 Carson	Y	Y	Y	Y
8 Ellsworth	Y	Y	Y	Y
9 Hill	Y	Y	Y	Y
IOWA				
1 Braley	Y	Y	Y	Y
2 Loebsack	Y	Y	Y	Y
3 Boswell	Y	Y	Y	Y
4 Latham	Y	N	Y	Y
5 King	Y	N	Y	?
KANSAS				
1 Moran	?	?	?	?
2 Jenkins	Y	N	Y	Y
3 Moore	Y	Y	Y	?
4 Tiahrt	Y	N	Y	Y
KENTUCKY				
1 Whitfield	Y	N	Y	Y
2 Guthrie	Y	N	Y	Y
3 Yarmuth	Y	Y	Y	Y
4 Davis	Y	N	Y	Y
5 Rogers	Y	N	Y	Y
6 Chandler	Y	Y	Y	Y
LOUISIANA				
1 Scalise	Y	N	Y	Y
2 Cao	Y	N	Y	Y
3 Melancon	Y	Y	Y	Y
4 Fleming	Y	N	Y	Y
5 Alexander	Y	N	Y	Y
6 Cassidy	Y	N	?	Y
7 Boustany	Y	N	Y	Y
MAINE				
1 Pingree	Y	Y	Y	Y
2 Michaud	Y	Y	Y	Y
MARYLAND				
1 Kratovil	Y	Y	Y	Y
2 Ruppersberger	Y	Y	Y	Y
3 Sarbanes	Y	Y	Y	Y
4 Edwards	Y	Y	Y	Y
5 Hoyer	Y	Y	Y	Y
6 Bartlett	Y	N	Y	Y
7 Cummings	Y	Y	Y	Y
8 Van Hollen	Y	Y	Y	Y
MASSACHUSETTS				
1 Olver	Y	Y	Y	Y
2 Neal	Y	Y	Y	Y
3 McGovern	Y	Y	Y	Y
4 Frank	?	?	?	?
5 Tsongas	Y	Y	Y	Y
6 Tierney	Y	Y	Y	Y
7 Markey	Y	Y	Y	Y
8 Capuano	Y	Y	Y	Y
9 Lynch	Y	Y	Y	Y
10 Delahunt	Y	Y	Y	Y
MICHIGAN				
1 Stupak	Y	Y	Y	Y
2 Hoekstra	Y	N	Y	Y
3 Ehlers	Y	N	Y	Y
4 Camp	Y	N	Y	Y
5 Kildee	Y	Y	Y	Y
6 Upton	Y	N	Y	Y
7 Schauer	Y	Y	Y	Y
8 Rogers	Y	N	Y	Y
9 Peters	Y	Y	Y	Y
10 Miller	Y	N	Y	Y
11 McCotter	Y	N	Y	Y
12 Levin	Y	Y	Y	Y
13 Kilpatrick	Y	Y	Y	Y
14 Conyers	Y	Y	Y	Y
15 Dingell	Y	Y	Y	Y
MINNESOTA				
1 Walz	Y	?	Y	Y
2 Kline	Y	N	Y	Y
3 Paulsen	Y	N	Y	Y
4 McCollum	Y	Y	Y	Y

	22	23	24	25
5 Ellison	Y	Y	Y	Y
6 Bachmann	Y	N	Y	Y
7 Peterson	Y	Y	Y	Y
8 Oberstar	Y	Y	Y	Y
MISSISSIPPI				
1 Childers	Y	Y	Y	Y
2 Thompson	Y	Y	Y	Y
3 Harper	Y	N	Y	Y
4 Taylor	Y	Y	Y	Y
MISSOURI				
1 Clay	Y	Y	Y	Y
2 Akin	Y	N	Y	Y
3 Carnahan	Y	Y	Y	Y
4 Skelton	Y	Y	Y	Y
5 Cleaver	Y	Y	Y	Y
6 Graves	Y	N	Y	Y
7 Blunt	Y	N	Y	?
8 Emerson	Y	N	Y	Y
9 Luetkemeyer	Y	N	Y	Y
MONTANA				
AL Rehberg	Y	N	Y	Y
NEBRASKA				
1 Fortenberry	Y	N	Y	?
2 Terry	Y	N	Y	Y
3 Smith	Y	N	Y	Y
NEVADA				
1 Berkley	Y	Y	Y	Y
2 Heller	Y	N	Y	Y
3 Titus	Y	Y	Y	Y
NEW HAMPSHIRE				
1 Shea-Porter	Y	Y	Y	Y
2 Hodes	Y	Y	Y	Y
NEW JERSEY				
1 Andrews	Y	Y	Y	Y
2 LoBiondo	Y	N	Y	Y
3 Adler	Y	Y	Y	Y
4 Smith	Y	N	Y	Y
5 Garrett	Y	N	Y	Y
6 Pallone	Y	Y	Y	Y
7 Lance	Y	N	Y	Y
8 Pascrell	Y	Y	Y	Y
9 Rothman	Y	Y	Y	Y
10 Payne	Y	Y	Y	Y
11 Frelinghuysen	Y	N	Y	Y
12 Holt	Y	Y	Y	Y
13 Sires	Y	Y	Y	Y
NEW MEXICO				
1 Heinrich	Y	Y	Y	Y
2 Teague	Y	Y	Y	Y
3 Luján	Y	Y	Y	Y
NEW YORK				
1 Bishop	Y	Y	Y	Y
2 Israel	Y	Y	Y	Y
3 King	Y	N	Y	Y
4 McCarthy	Y	Y	Y	Y
5 Ackerman	Y	Y	Y	Y
6 Meeks	Y	Y	Y	Y
7 Crowley	Y	Y	Y	Y
8 Nadler	Y	Y	Y	Y
9 Weiner	Y	Y	Y	Y
10 Towns	Y	Y	Y	Y
11 Clarke	Y	Y	Y	Y
12 Velázquez	Y	Y	Y	Y
13 McMahon	Y	Y	Y	Y
14 Maloney	Y	Y	Y	Y
15 Rangel	Y	Y	Y	Y
16 Serrano	Y	Y	Y	Y
17 Engel	Y	Y	Y	Y
18 Lowey	Y	Y	Y	Y
19 Hall	Y	Y	Y	Y
20 Murphy	Y	N	Y	Y
21 Tonko	Y	Y	Y	Y
22 Hinchey	Y	Y	Y	Y
23 Owens	Y	N	Y	Y
24 Arcuri	Y	Y	Y	Y
25 Maffei	Y	Y	Y	Y
26 Lee	Y	N	Y	Y
27 Higgins	Y	Y	Y	?
28 Slaughter	Y	Y	Y	Y
29 Massa	Y	Y	Y	Y
NORTH CAROLINA				
1 Butterfield	Y	Y	Y	Y
2 Etheridge	Y	Y	Y	Y
3 Jones	Y	N	Y	Y
4 Price	Y	Y	Y	Y

	22	23	24	25
5 Foxx	Y	N	Y	Y
6 Coble	?	?	?	?
7 McIntyre	Y	Y	Y	Y
8 Kissell	Y	Y	Y	Y
9 Myrick	Y	N	Y	Y
10 McHenry	Y	N	Y	Y
11 Shuler	Y	Y	Y	Y
12 Watt	Y	Y	Y	Y
13 Miller	Y	Y	Y	Y
NORTH DAKOTA				
AL Pomeroy	Y	Y	Y	Y
OHIO				
1 Driehaus	Y	Y	Y	Y
2 Schmidt	Y	N	Y	Y
3 Turner	Y	N	Y	Y
4 Jordan	Y	N	Y	Y
5 Latta	Y	N	Y	Y
6 Wilson	Y	Y	Y	Y
7 Austria	Y	N	Y	Y
8 Boehner	Y	N	Y	Y
9 Kaptur	Y	Y	Y	Y
10 Kucinich	Y	Y	Y	Y
11 Fudge	Y	Y	Y	Y
12 Tiberi	Y	N	Y	Y
13 Sutton	?	Y	Y	Y
14 LaTourette	Y	N	Y	Y
15 Kilroy	Y	Y	Y	Y
16 Boccieri	Y	Y	Y	Y
17 Ryan	Y	Y	Y	Y
18 Space	Y	Y	Y	Y
OKLAHOMA				
1 Sullivan	Y	N	Y	Y
2 Boren	Y	Y	Y	Y
3 Lucas	Y	N	Y	Y
4 Cole	Y	N	Y	Y
5 Fallin	Y	N	Y	Y
OREGON				
1 Wu	Y	Y	Y	Y
2 Walden	Y	N	Y	Y
3 Blumenauer	Y	Y	Y	Y
4 DeFazio	Y	Y	Y	Y
5 Schrader	Y	Y	Y	Y
PENNSYLVANIA				
1 Brady	Y	Y	Y	Y
2 Fattah	Y	Y	Y	Y
3 Dahlkemper	Y	Y	Y	Y
4 Altmire	Y	Y	Y	Y
5 Thompson	Y	N	Y	Y
6 Gerlach	Y	N	Y	Y
7 Sestak	Y	Y	Y	Y
8 Murphy, P.	Y	Y	Y	Y
9 Shuster	Y	N	Y	Y
10 Carney	Y	Y	Y	Y
11 Kanjorski	Y	Y	Y	Y
12 Murtha	Y	Y	Y	Y
13 Schwartz	Y	Y	Y	Y
14 Doyle	Y	Y	Y	Y
15 Dent	Y	N	Y	Y
16 Pitts	Y	N	Y	Y
17 Holden	Y	Y	Y	Y
18 Murphy, T.	Y	N	Y	Y
19 Platts	Y	N	Y	Y
RHODE ISLAND				
1 Kennedy	Y	Y	Y	Y
2 Langevin	Y	Y	Y	Y
SOUTH CAROLINA				
1 Brown	Y	N	Y	Y
2 Wilson	Y	N	Y	Y
3 Barrett	?	?	?	?
4 Inglis	Y	N	Y	Y
5 Spratt	Y	Y	Y	Y
6 Clyburn	Y	Y	Y	Y
SOUTH DAKOTA				
AL Herseth Sandlin	Y	Y	Y	Y
TENNESSEE				
1 Roe	Y	N	Y	Y
2 Duncan	Y	N	Y	Y
3 Wamp	?	?	?	?
4 Davis	Y	Y	Y	Y
5 Cooper	Y	Y	Y	Y
6 Gordon	Y	Y	Y	?
7 Blackburn	Y	N	Y	Y
8 Tanner	Y	Y	Y	Y
9 Cohen	Y	Y	Y	Y

	22	23	24	25
TEXAS				
1 Gohmert	Y	N	Y	Y
2 Poe	Y	N	Y	Y
3 Johnson, S.	Y	N	Y	Y
4 Hall	Y	N	Y	Y
5 Hensarling	Y	N	Y	Y
6 Barton	Y	N	Y	Y
7 Culberson	Y	N	Y	Y
8 Brady	Y	N	Y	Y
9 Green, A.	Y	Y	Y	Y
10 McCaul	Y	N	Y	Y
11 Conaway	Y	N	Y	Y
12 Granger	Y	N	Y	Y
13 Thornberry	Y	N	Y	Y
14 Paul	Y	N	N	Y
15 Hinojosa	Y	Y	Y	Y
16 Reyes	Y	Y	Y	Y
17 Edwards	Y	Y	Y	Y
18 Jackson Lee	Y	Y	Y	Y
19 Neugebauer	Y	N	Y	Y
20 Gonzalez	Y	Y	Y	Y
21 Smith	Y	N	Y	Y
22 Olson	Y	N	Y	Y
23 Rodriguez	Y	Y	Y	Y
24 Marchant	Y	N	Y	Y
25 Doggett	Y	Y	Y	Y
26 Burgess	Y	N	Y	Y
27 Ortiz	+	+	+	+
28 Cuellar	Y	Y	Y	Y
29 Green, G.	Y	Y	Y	Y
30 Johnson, E.	?	?	?	?
31 Carter	Y	N	Y	Y
32 Sessions	Y	N	Y	Y
UTAH				
1 Bishop	Y	N	Y	Y
2 Matheson	Y	Y	Y	Y
3 Chaffetz	Y	N	Y	Y
VERMONT				
AL Welch	Y	?	?	?
VIRGINIA				
1 Wittman	Y	N	Y	Y
2 Nye	Y	Y	Y	Y
3 Scott	Y	Y	Y	Y
4 Forbes	Y	N	Y	Y
5 Perriello	Y	Y	Y	Y
6 Goodlatte	Y	N	Y	Y
7 Cantor	Y	N	Y	Y
8 Moran	Y	Y	Y	Y
9 Boucher	Y	Y	Y	Y
10 Wolf	Y	N	Y	Y
11 Connolly	Y	Y	Y	Y
WASHINGTON				
1 Inslee	Y	Y	Y	Y
2 Larsen	Y	Y	Y	Y
3 Baird	Y	Y	Y	Y
4 Hastings	Y	N	Y	Y
5 McMorris Rodgers	Y	N	Y	Y
6 Dicks	Y	Y	Y	Y
7 McDermott	Y	Y	Y	Y
8 Reichert	Y	N	Y	Y
9 Smith	Y	Y	Y	Y
WEST VIRGINIA				
1 Mollohan	Y	Y	Y	Y
2 Capito	Y	N	Y	Y
3 Rahall	Y	Y	Y	Y
WISCONSIN				
1 Ryan	Y	N	Y	Y
2 Baldwin	Y	Y	Y	Y
3 Kind	Y	Y	Y	Y
4 Moore	Y	?	Y	Y
5 Sensenbrenner	Y	N	Y	Y
6 Petri	Y	N	Y	Y
7 Obey	Y	Y	Y	Y
8 Kagen	Y	Y	Y	Y
WYOMING				
AL Lummis	Y	N	Y	Y
DELEGATES				
Faleomavaega (A.S.)				
Norton (D.C.)				
Bordallo (Guam)				
Sablan (N. Marianas)				
Pierluisi (P.R.)				
Christensen (V.I.)				

IN THE HOUSE | By Vote Number

26. **HR 4495. Jim Kolbe Post Office/Passage.** Towns, D-N.Y., motion to suspend the rules and pass the bill that would designate a post office in Patagonia, Ariz., as the "Jim Kolbe Post Office." Motion agreed to 390-0: D 229-0; R 161-0. A two-thirds majority of those present and voting (260 in this case) is required for passage under suspension of the rules. Feb. 2, 2010.

27. **H Res 957. Tribute to Jimmie Johnson/Adoption.** Towns, D-N.Y., motion to suspend the rules and adopt the resolution that would recognize the achievements of Jimmie Kenneth Johnson, the 2009 NASCAR Sprint Cup champion, and his driving team. Motion agreed to 391-1: D 230-1; R 161-0. A two-thirds majority of those present and voting (262 in this case) is required for adoption under suspension of the rules. Feb. 2, 2010.

28. **H Res 1014. North American Inclusion Month/Adoption.** Towns, D-N.Y., motion to suspend the rules and adopt the resolution that would recognize and support the goals of North American Inclusion Month. Motion agreed to 389-0: D 229-0; R 160-0. A two-thirds majority of those present and voting (260 in this case) is required for adoption under suspension of the rules. Feb. 2, 2010.

29. **HR 4061. Cybersecurity Programs/Previous Question.** Arcuri, D-N.Y., motion to order the previous question (thus ending debate and possibility of amendment) on adoption of the rule (H Res 1051) to provide for House floor consideration of the bill that would reauthorize and expand programs intended to strengthen the security of federal computers and websites. Motion agreed to 238-175: D 238-5; R 0-170. Feb. 3, 2010.

30. **HR 4061. Cybersecurity Programs/Rule.** Adoption of the rule (H Res 1051) to provide for House floor consideration of the bill that would reauthorize and expand programs intended to strengthen the security of federal computers and websites. Adopted 237-176: D 237-7; R 0-169. Feb. 3, 2010.

31. **H Res 1043. Tribute to Brescia University/Adoption.** Fudge, D-Ohio, motion to suspend the rules and adopt the resolution that would recognize Brescia University's 60th anniversary as an institution of higher education and commend the university for service to the community of Owensboro, Ky. Motion agreed to 418-0: D 247-0; R 171-0. A two-thirds majority of those present and voting (279 in this case) is required for adoption under suspension of the rules. Feb. 3, 2010.

32. **H Res 901. Anniversary of New Orleans School Integration/Adoption.** Fudge, D-Ohio, motion to suspend the rules and adopt the resolution that would recognize the 49th anniversary of the first day of integrated schools in New Orleans. Motion agreed to 416-0: D 245-0; R 171-0. A two-thirds majority of those present and voting (278 in this case) is required for adoption under suspension of the rules. Feb. 3, 2010.

	26	27	28	29	30	31	32
ALABAMA							
1 Bonner	Y	Y	Y	N	N	Y	Y
2 Bright	Y	Y	Y	Y	Y	Y	Y
3 Rogers	Y	Y	Y	N	N	Y	Y
4 Aderholt	Y	Y	Y	N	N	Y	Y
5 Griffith	Y	Y	Y	N	N	Y	Y
6 Bachus	Y	Y	Y	N	N	Y	Y
7 Davis	?	?	?	?	?	Y	Y
ALASKA							
AL Young	Y	Y	Y	N	N	Y	Y
ARIZONA							
1 Kirkpatrick	?	?	?	?	?	?	?
2 Franks	Y	Y	Y	N	N	Y	Y
3 Shadegg	Y	Y	Y	N	N	Y	Y
4 Pastor	Y	Y	Y	Y	Y	Y	Y
5 Mitchell	Y	Y	Y	Y	Y	Y	Y
6 Flake	Y	Y	Y	N	N	Y	Y
7 Grijalva	?	?	?	Y	Y	Y	Y
8 Giffords	Y	Y	Y	N	N	Y	Y
ARKANSAS							
1 Berry	Y	Y	Y	Y	Y	Y	Y
2 Snyder	Y	Y	Y	Y	Y	Y	Y
3 Boozman	Y	Y	Y	N	N	Y	Y
4 Ross	Y	Y	Y	Y	Y	Y	Y
CALIFORNIA							
1 Thompson	Y	Y	Y	Y	Y	Y	Y
2 Herger	Y	Y	Y	N	N	Y	Y
3 Lungren	Y	Y	Y	N	N	Y	Y
4 McClintock	Y	Y	Y	N	N	Y	Y
5 Matsui	Y	Y	Y	Y	Y	Y	Y
6 Woolsey	Y	Y	Y	Y	Y	Y	Y
7 Miller, George	Y	Y	Y	Y	Y	Y	Y
8 Pelosi							
9 Lee	Y	Y	Y	Y	Y	Y	Y
10 Garamendi	Y	Y	Y	Y	Y	Y	Y
11 McNerney	Y	Y	Y	Y	Y	Y	Y
12 Speier	Y	Y	Y	Y	Y	Y	Y
13 Stark	?	?	?	Y	Y	Y	Y
14 Eshoo	Y	Y	Y	Y	Y	Y	Y
15 Honda	Y	Y	Y	Y	Y	Y	Y
16 Lofgren	Y	Y	Y	Y	Y	Y	Y
17 Farr	Y	Y	Y	Y	Y	Y	Y
18 Cardoza	Y	Y	Y	Y	Y	Y	Y
19 Radanovich	?	?	?	?	?	?	?
20 Costa	?	?	?	Y	Y	Y	Y
21 Nunes	Y	Y	Y	N	N	Y	Y
22 McCarthy	Y	Y	Y	N	N	Y	Y
23 Capps	Y	Y	Y	Y	Y	Y	Y
24 Gallegly	Y	Y	Y	N	N	Y	Y
25 McKeon	Y	Y	Y	N	N	Y	Y
26 Dreier	Y	Y	Y	N	N	Y	Y
27 Sherman	Y	Y	Y	Y	Y	Y	Y
28 Berman	Y	Y	Y	Y	Y	Y	Y
29 Schiff	Y	Y	Y	Y	Y	Y	Y
30 Waxman	Y	Y	Y	Y	Y	Y	Y
31 Becerra	Y	Y	Y	Y	Y	Y	Y
32 Chu	Y	Y	Y	Y	Y	Y	Y
33 Watson	Y	Y	Y	Y	Y	Y	Y
34 Roybal-Allard	Y	Y	Y	Y	Y	Y	Y
35 Waters	?	?	?	Y	Y	Y	Y
36 Harman	Y	Y	Y	Y	Y	Y	Y
37 Richardson	Y	Y	Y	Y	Y	Y	Y
38 Napolitano	Y	Y	Y	Y	Y	Y	Y
39 Sánchez, Linda	?	?	?	?	?	?	?
40 Royce	Y	Y	Y	N	N	Y	Y
41 Lewis	Y	Y	Y	N	N	Y	Y
42 Miller, Gary	Y	Y	Y	N	N	Y	Y
43 Baca	Y	Y	Y	Y	Y	Y	Y
44 Calvert	Y	Y	Y	N	N	Y	Y
45 Bono Mack	Y	Y	Y	N	N	Y	Y
46 Rohrabacher	?	?	?	N	N	Y	Y
47 Sanchez, Loretta	Y	Y	Y	Y	Y	Y	Y
48 Campbell	Y	Y	Y	N	N	Y	Y
49 Issa	Y	Y	Y	N	N	Y	Y
50 Bilbray	Y	Y	Y	N	N	Y	Y
51 Filner	Y	Y	Y	Y	Y	Y	Y
52 Hunter	Y	Y	Y	N	N	Y	Y
53 Davis	Y	Y	Y	Y	Y	Y	Y

	26	27	28	29	30	31	32
COLORADO							
1 DeGette	Y	Y	Y	Y	Y	Y	Y
2 Polis	Y	Y	Y	Y	Y	Y	Y
3 Salazar	Y	Y	Y	Y	Y	Y	Y
4 Markey	Y	Y	Y	Y	Y	Y	Y
5 Lamborn	Y	Y	Y	N	N	Y	Y
6 Coffman	Y	Y	Y	N	N	Y	Y
7 Perlmutter	Y	Y	Y	Y	Y	Y	Y
CONNECTICUT							
1 Larson	+	+	+	Y	Y	Y	Y
2 Courtney	Y	Y	Y	Y	Y	Y	Y
3 DeLauro	Y	Y	Y	Y	Y	Y	Y
4 Himes	Y	Y	Y	Y	Y	Y	Y
5 Murphy	Y	Y	Y	Y	Y	Y	Y
DELAWARE							
AL Castle	Y	Y	Y	N	N	Y	Y
FLORIDA							
1 Miller	Y	Y	Y	N	N	Y	Y
2 Boyd	?	?	?	Y	Y	Y	Y
3 Brown	Y	Y	Y	Y	Y	Y	Y
4 Crenshaw	Y	Y	Y	N	N	Y	Y
5 Brown-Waite	Y	Y	Y	N	N	Y	Y
6 Stearns	Y	Y	Y	N	N	Y	Y
7 Mica	Y	Y	Y	N	N	Y	Y
8 Grayson	Y	Y	Y	Y	Y	Y	Y
9 Bilirakis	Y	Y	Y	N	N	Y	Y
10 Young	?	?	?	?	?	?	?
11 Castor	Y	Y	Y	Y	Y	Y	Y
12 Putnam	Y	Y	Y	N	N	Y	Y
13 Buchanan	Y	Y	Y	N	N	Y	Y
14 Mack	Y	Y	Y	N	N	Y	Y
15 Posey	Y	Y	Y	N	N	Y	Y
16 Rooney	Y	Y	Y	N	N	Y	Y
17 Meek	Y	Y	Y	Y	Y	Y	Y
18 Ros-Lehtinen	Y	Y	Y	N	N	Y	Y
19 Vacant							
20 Wasserman Schultz	Y	Y	?	Y	Y	Y	Y
21 Diaz-Balart, L.	Y	Y	Y	N	N	Y	Y
22 Klein	Y	Y	Y	Y	Y	Y	Y
23 Hastings	Y	Y	Y	Y	Y	Y	Y
24 Kosmas	Y	Y	Y	Y	Y	Y	Y
25 Diaz-Balart, M.	Y	Y	Y	N	N	Y	Y
GEORGIA							
1 Kingston	Y	Y	Y	N	N	Y	Y
2 Bishop	Y	Y	Y	Y	Y	Y	Y
3 Westmoreland	Y	Y	Y	N	N	Y	Y
4 Johnson	Y	Y	Y	Y	Y	Y	Y
5 Lewis	Y	Y	Y	Y	Y	Y	Y
6 Price	Y	Y	Y	N	N	Y	Y
7 Linder	Y	Y	Y	N	N	Y	Y
8 Marshall	Y	Y	Y	Y	Y	Y	Y
9 Deal	?	?	?	?	?	?	?
10 Broun	Y	Y	Y	N	N	Y	Y
11 Gingrey	Y	Y	Y	N	N	Y	Y
12 Barrow	Y	Y	Y	Y	Y	Y	Y
13 Scott	Y	Y	Y	Y	Y	Y	Y
HAWAII							
1 Abercrombie	Y	Y	Y	?	Y	Y	Y
2 Hirono	Y	Y	Y	Y	Y	Y	Y
IDAHO							
1 Minnick	Y	Y	Y	N	N	Y	Y
2 Simpson	Y	Y	Y	N	N	Y	Y
ILLINOIS							
1 Rush	?	?	?	?	?	?	?
2 Jackson	Y	Y	Y	Y	Y	Y	Y
3 Lipinski	?	?	?	Y	Y	Y	Y
4 Gutierrez	+	+	+	+	+	+	+
5 Quigley	Y	Y	Y	Y	Y	Y	Y
6 Roskam	Y	Y	Y	N	N	Y	Y
7 Davis	?	?	?	?	?	Y	Y
8 Bean	Y	Y	Y	Y	Y	Y	Y
9 Schakowsky	?	?	?	Y	Y	Y	Y
10 Kirk	?	?	?	?	?	?	?
11 Halvorson	Y	Y	Y	Y	Y	Y	Y
12 Costello	Y	Y	Y	Y	Y	Y	Y
13 Biggert	Y	Y	Y	N	N	Y	Y
14 Foster	Y	Y	Y	Y	Y	Y	Y
15 Johnson	Y	Y	Y	N	N	Y	Y

KEY

	26	27	28	29	30	31	32
16 **Manzullo**	Y	Y	Y	N	N	Y	Y
17 Hare	Y	Y	Y	Y	Y	Y	Y
18 **Schock**	Y	Y	Y	N	N	Y	Y
19 **Shimkus**	?	?	?	N	N	Y	Y
INDIANA							
1 Visclosky	Y	Y	Y	Y	Y	Y	Y
2 Donnelly	Y	Y	Y	Y	N	Y	Y
3 **Souder**	?	?	?	?	?	?	?
4 **Buyer**	Y	Y	Y	N	N	Y	Y
5 **Burton**	Y	Y	Y	N	N	Y	Y
6 **Pence**	Y	Y	Y	N	N	Y	Y
7 Carson	Y	Y	Y	Y	Y	Y	Y
8 Ellsworth	Y	Y	Y	Y	Y	Y	Y
9 Hill	Y	Y	Y	N	N	Y	Y
IOWA							
1 Braley	Y	Y	Y	Y	Y	Y	Y
2 Loebsack	?	?	?	Y	Y	Y	Y
3 Boswell	Y	Y	Y	Y	Y	Y	Y
4 **Latham**	Y	Y	Y	N	N	Y	Y
5 **King**	Y	Y	Y	N	N	Y	Y
KANSAS							
1 **Moran**	?	?	?	N	N	Y	Y
2 **Jenkins**	Y	Y	Y	N	N	Y	Y
3 Moore	Y	Y	Y	Y	Y	Y	Y
4 **Tiahrt**	?	?	?	N	N	Y	Y
KENTUCKY							
1 **Whitfield**	Y	Y	Y	N	N	Y	Y
2 **Guthrie**	Y	Y	Y	N	N	Y	Y
3 Yarmuth	Y	Y	Y	Y	Y	Y	Y
4 **Davis**	Y	Y	Y	N	N	Y	Y
5 **Rogers**	Y	Y	Y	N	N	Y	Y
6 Chandler	Y	Y	Y	Y	Y	Y	Y
LOUISIANA							
1 **Scalise**	Y	Y	Y	N	N	Y	Y
2 **Cao**	Y	Y	Y	N	N	Y	Y
3 Melancon	?	Y	Y	Y	Y	Y	Y
4 **Fleming**	Y	Y	Y	N	N	Y	Y
5 **Alexander**	Y	Y	Y	N	N	Y	Y
6 **Cassidy**	?	?	?	N	N	Y	Y
7 **Boustany**	Y	Y	Y	N	N	Y	Y
MAINE							
1 Pingree	Y	Y	Y	Y	Y	Y	Y
2 Michaud	Y	Y	Y	Y	Y	Y	Y
MARYLAND							
1 Kratovil	Y	Y	Y	Y	Y	Y	Y
2 Ruppersberger	Y	Y	Y	Y	Y	Y	Y
3 Sarbanes	Y	Y	Y	Y	Y	Y	Y
4 Edwards	Y	Y	Y	Y	Y	Y	Y
5 Hoyer	Y	Y	Y	Y	Y	Y	Y
6 **Bartlett**	Y	Y	Y	N	N	Y	Y
7 Cummings	Y	Y	Y	Y	Y	Y	Y
8 Van Hollen	Y	Y	Y	Y	Y	Y	Y
MASSACHUSETTS							
1 Olver	Y	Y	Y	Y	Y	Y	Y
2 Neal	Y	Y	Y	Y	Y	Y	Y
3 McGovern	Y	Y	Y	Y	Y	Y	Y
4 Frank	Y	Y	Y	Y	Y	Y	Y
5 Tsongas	Y	Y	Y	Y	Y	Y	Y
6 Tierney	Y	Y	Y	Y	Y	Y	Y
7 Markey	Y	Y	Y	Y	Y	Y	Y
8 Capuano	Y	Y	Y	Y	Y	Y	Y
9 Lynch	Y	Y	Y	Y	Y	Y	Y
10 Delahunt	Y	Y	Y	Y	Y	Y	Y
MICHIGAN							
1 Stupak	Y	Y	Y	Y	Y	Y	Y
2 **Hoekstra**	?	?	?	N	?	Y	Y
3 **Ehlers**	?	?	?	N	N	Y	Y
4 **Camp**	Y	Y	?	N	N	Y	Y
5 Kildee	Y	Y	Y	Y	Y	Y	Y
6 **Upton**	Y	Y	Y	N	N	Y	Y
7 Schauer	Y	Y	Y	Y	Y	Y	Y
8 **Rogers**	Y	Y	Y	N	N	Y	Y
9 Peters	Y	Y	Y	Y	Y	Y	Y
10 **Miller**	Y	Y	Y	N	N	Y	Y
11 **McCotter**	Y	Y	Y	N	N	Y	Y
12 Levin	Y	Y	Y	Y	Y	Y	Y
13 Kilpatrick	Y	Y	Y	Y	Y	Y	Y
14 Conyers	Y	Y	Y	Y	Y	Y	Y
15 Dingell	Y	Y	Y	Y	Y	Y	Y
MINNESOTA							
1 Walz	Y	Y	Y	Y	Y	Y	Y
2 **Kline**	Y	Y	Y	N	N	Y	Y
3 **Paulsen**	?	?	?	N	N	Y	Y
4 McCollum	Y	Y	Y	Y	Y	Y	Y
5 Ellison	?	?	?	Y	Y	Y	Y
6 **Bachmann**	Y	Y	Y	N	?	Y	Y
7 Peterson	Y	Y	Y	Y	Y	Y	Y
8 Oberstar	Y	Y	Y	Y	Y	Y	Y
MISSISSIPPI							
1 Childers	Y	Y	Y	N	N	Y	Y
2 Thompson	Y	Y	Y	Y	Y	Y	Y
3 **Harper**	Y	Y	Y	N	N	Y	Y
4 Taylor	Y	Y	Y	N	N	Y	Y
MISSOURI							
1 Clay	Y	Y	Y	Y	Y	Y	Y
2 **Akin**	Y	Y	Y	N	N	Y	Y
3 Carnahan	Y	Y	Y	Y	Y	Y	Y
4 Skelton	Y	Y	Y	Y	Y	Y	Y
5 Cleaver	Y	Y	?	Y	Y	Y	?
6 **Graves**	Y	Y	Y	N	N	Y	Y
7 **Blunt**	Y	Y	Y	N	N	Y	Y
8 **Emerson**	?	?	?	N	N	Y	Y
9 **Luetkemeyer**	Y	Y	Y	N	N	Y	Y
MONTANA							
AL **Rehberg**	Y	Y	Y	N	N	Y	Y
NEBRASKA							
1 **Fortenberry**	Y	Y	Y	N	N	Y	Y
2 **Terry**	Y	Y	Y	N	N	Y	Y
3 **Smith**	Y	Y	Y	N	N	Y	Y
NEVADA							
1 Berkley	Y	Y	Y	Y	Y	Y	Y
2 **Heller**	Y	Y	Y	N	N	Y	Y
3 Titus	Y	Y	Y	Y	Y	Y	Y
NEW HAMPSHIRE							
1 Shea-Porter	Y	Y	Y	Y	Y	Y	Y
2 Hodes	Y	Y	Y	Y	Y	Y	Y
NEW JERSEY							
1 Andrews	Y	Y	Y	Y	Y	Y	Y
2 **LoBiondo**	Y	Y	Y	N	N	Y	Y
3 Adler	Y	Y	Y	Y	Y	Y	Y
4 **Smith**	Y	Y	Y	N	N	Y	Y
5 **Garrett**	?	?	?	?	N	Y	Y
6 Pallone	Y	Y	Y	Y	Y	Y	Y
7 **Lance**	Y	Y	Y	N	N	Y	Y
8 Pascrell	Y	Y	Y	Y	Y	Y	Y
9 Rothman	Y	Y	Y	Y	Y	Y	Y
10 Payne	Y	Y	Y	Y	Y	Y	Y
11 **Frelinghuysen**	Y	Y	Y	N	N	Y	Y
12 Holt	Y	Y	Y	Y	Y	Y	Y
13 Sires	Y	Y	Y	Y	Y	Y	Y
NEW MEXICO							
1 Heinrich	Y	Y	Y	Y	Y	Y	Y
2 Teague	Y	Y	Y	Y	Y	Y	Y
3 Luján	Y	Y	Y	Y	Y	Y	Y
NEW YORK							
1 Bishop	Y	Y	Y	Y	Y	Y	Y
2 Israel	Y	Y	Y	Y	Y	Y	Y
3 **King**	Y	Y	Y	N	N	Y	Y
4 McCarthy	Y	Y	Y	Y	Y	Y	Y
5 Ackerman	Y	Y	Y	Y	Y	Y	Y
6 Meeks	Y	Y	Y	Y	Y	Y	Y
7 Crowley	Y	Y	Y	Y	Y	Y	Y
8 Nadler	Y	Y	Y	Y	Y	Y	Y
9 Weiner	Y	Y	Y	Y	Y	Y	Y
10 Towns	Y	Y	Y	Y	Y	Y	Y
11 Clarke	Y	Y	Y	Y	Y	Y	Y
12 Velázquez	Y	Y	Y	Y	Y	Y	Y
13 McMahon	Y	Y	Y	Y	Y	Y	Y
14 Maloney	Y	Y	Y	Y	Y	Y	Y
15 Rangel	Y	Y	Y	Y	Y	Y	Y
16 Serrano	Y	Y	Y	?	Y	Y	Y
17 Engel	?	?	Y	Y	Y	Y	Y
18 Lowey	Y	Y	Y	Y	Y	Y	Y
19 Hall	?	?	?	Y	Y	Y	Y
20 Murphy	Y	Y	Y	Y	Y	Y	Y
21 Tonko	Y	Y	Y	Y	Y	Y	Y
22 Hinchey	Y	Y	Y	Y	Y	Y	Y
23 Owens	Y	Y	Y	Y	Y	Y	Y
24 Arcuri	Y	Y	Y	Y	Y	Y	Y
25 Maffei	Y	Y	Y	Y	Y	Y	Y
26 **Lee**	Y	Y	Y	N	N	Y	Y
27 Higgins	Y	Y	Y	Y	Y	Y	?
28 Slaughter	Y	Y	Y	Y	Y	Y	Y
29 Massa	?	?	?	?	?	?	?
NORTH CAROLINA							
1 Butterfield	Y	Y	Y	Y	Y	Y	Y
2 Etheridge	Y	Y	Y	Y	Y	Y	Y
3 **Jones**	Y	Y	Y	N	N	Y	Y
4 Price	Y	Y	Y	Y	Y	Y	Y
5 **Foxx**	Y	Y	Y	N	N	Y	Y
6 **Coble**	Y	Y	Y	N	N	Y	Y
7 McIntyre	Y	Y	Y	Y	Y	Y	Y
8 Kissell	Y	Y	Y	Y	Y	Y	Y
9 **Myrick**	Y	Y	Y	N	N	Y	Y
10 **McHenry**	Y	Y	Y	N	N	Y	Y
11 Shuler	Y	Y	Y	Y	N	Y	Y
12 Watt	Y	Y	Y	Y	Y	Y	Y
13 Miller	Y	Y	Y	Y	Y	Y	Y
NORTH DAKOTA							
AL Pomeroy	Y	Y	Y	Y	Y	Y	Y
OHIO							
1 Driehaus	Y	Y	Y	Y	Y	Y	Y
2 **Schmidt**	Y	Y	Y	N	N	Y	Y
3 **Turner**	Y	Y	Y	N	N	Y	Y
4 **Jordan**	Y	Y	Y	N	N	Y	Y
5 **Latta**	Y	Y	Y	N	N	Y	Y
6 Wilson	Y	Y	Y	Y	Y	Y	Y
7 **Austria**	Y	Y	Y	N	N	Y	Y
8 **Boehner**	Y	Y	Y	N	N	Y	Y
9 Kaptur	Y	Y	Y	Y	Y	Y	Y
10 Kucinich	Y	Y	Y	Y	Y	Y	Y
11 Fudge	Y	Y	Y	Y	Y	Y	Y
12 **Tiberi**	Y	Y	Y	N	N	Y	Y
13 Sutton	Y	Y	Y	Y	Y	Y	Y
14 **LaTourette**	Y	Y	Y	N	N	Y	Y
15 Kilroy	Y	Y	Y	Y	Y	Y	Y
16 Boccieri	Y	Y	Y	Y	Y	Y	Y
17 Ryan	Y	Y	Y	Y	Y	Y	Y
18 Space	Y	Y	Y	Y	Y	Y	Y
OKLAHOMA							
1 **Sullivan**	Y	Y	Y	N	N	Y	Y
2 Boren	Y	Y	Y	Y	Y	Y	Y
3 **Lucas**	Y	Y	Y	N	N	Y	Y
4 **Cole**	Y	Y	Y	N	N	Y	Y
5 **Fallin**	Y	Y	Y	N	N	Y	Y
OREGON							
1 Wu	Y	Y	Y	Y	Y	Y	Y
2 **Walden**	Y	Y	Y	N	N	Y	Y
3 Blumenauer	Y	Y	Y	Y	Y	Y	Y
4 DeFazio	Y	Y	?	Y	Y	Y	Y
5 Schrader	Y	N	Y	Y	Y	Y	Y
PENNSYLVANIA							
1 Brady	Y	Y	Y	Y	Y	Y	Y
2 Fattah	Y	Y	Y	Y	Y	Y	Y
3 Dahlkemper	Y	Y	Y	Y	Y	Y	Y
4 Altmire	Y	Y	Y	Y	Y	Y	Y
5 **Thompson**	Y	Y	Y	N	N	Y	Y
6 **Gerlach**	Y	Y	Y	N	N	Y	Y
7 Sestak	Y	Y	Y	Y	Y	Y	Y
8 Murphy, P.	Y	Y	Y	Y	Y	Y	Y
9 **Shuster**	Y	Y	Y	N	N	Y	Y
10 Carney	+	+	+	Y	Y	Y	Y
11 Kanjorski	Y	Y	Y	Y	Y	Y	Y
12 Murtha	?	?	?	?	?	?	?
13 Schwartz	Y	Y	Y	Y	Y	Y	Y
14 Doyle	?	?	?	Y	Y	Y	Y
15 **Dent**	Y	Y	Y	N	N	Y	Y
16 **Pitts**	Y	Y	Y	N	N	Y	Y
17 Holden	Y	Y	Y	Y	Y	Y	Y
18 **Murphy, T.**	Y	Y	Y	N	N	Y	Y
19 **Platts**	Y	Y	Y	N	N	Y	Y
RHODE ISLAND							
1 Kennedy	Y	Y	Y	Y	Y	Y	Y
2 Langevin	Y	Y	Y	Y	Y	Y	Y
SOUTH CAROLINA							
1 **Brown**	Y	Y	Y	N	N	Y	Y
2 **Wilson**	Y	Y	Y	N	N	Y	Y
3 **Barrett**	?	?	?	?	?	?	?
4 **Inglis**	Y	Y	Y	N	N	Y	Y
5 Spratt	Y	Y	Y	Y	Y	Y	Y
6 Clyburn	Y	Y	Y	Y	Y	Y	Y
SOUTH DAKOTA							
AL Herseth Sandlin	Y	Y	Y	Y	Y	Y	Y
TENNESSEE							
1 **Roe**	Y	Y	Y	N	N	Y	Y
2 **Duncan**	Y	Y	Y	N	N	Y	Y
3 **Wamp**	Y	Y	Y	N	N	Y	Y
4 Davis	Y	Y	Y	Y	Y	Y	Y
5 Cooper	Y	Y	Y	Y	Y	Y	Y
6 Gordon	Y	Y	Y	Y	Y	Y	Y
7 **Blackburn**	Y	Y	Y	N	N	Y	Y
8 Tanner	Y	Y	Y	Y	Y	Y	Y
9 Cohen	Y	Y	Y	Y	Y	Y	Y
TEXAS							
1 **Gohmert**	Y	Y	Y	N	N	Y	Y
2 **Poe**	Y	Y	Y	N	N	Y	Y
3 **Johnson, S.**	Y	Y	Y	N	N	Y	Y
4 **Hall**	Y	Y	Y	N	N	Y	Y
5 **Hensarling**	Y	Y	Y	N	N	Y	Y
6 **Barton**	Y	Y	Y	N	N	Y	Y
7 **Culberson**	Y	Y	Y	?	?	?	?
8 **Brady**	?	?	?	N	N	Y	Y
9 Green, A.	Y	Y	Y	Y	Y	Y	Y
10 **McCaul**	Y	Y	Y	N	N	Y	Y
11 **Conaway**	Y	Y	Y	N	N	Y	Y
12 **Granger**	Y	Y	Y	N	N	Y	Y
13 **Thornberry**	Y	Y	Y	N	N	Y	Y
14 **Paul**	Y	Y	Y	N	N	Y	Y
15 Hinojosa	Y	Y	Y	Y	Y	Y	Y
16 Reyes	Y	Y	Y	Y	?	Y	Y
17 Edwards	Y	Y	Y	Y	Y	Y	Y
18 Jackson Lee	Y	Y	Y	Y	Y	Y	Y
19 **Neugebauer**	Y	Y	Y	N	N	Y	Y
20 Gonzalez	Y	Y	Y	Y	Y	Y	Y
21 **Smith**	Y	Y	Y	N	N	Y	Y
22 **Olson**	Y	Y	Y	N	N	Y	Y
23 Rodriguez	Y	Y	Y	Y	Y	Y	Y
24 **Marchant**	Y	Y	Y	N	N	Y	Y
25 Doggett	Y	Y	Y	Y	Y	Y	Y
26 **Burgess**	Y	Y	Y	N	N	Y	Y
27 Ortiz	Y	Y	Y	Y	Y	Y	Y
28 Cuellar	Y	Y	Y	Y	Y	Y	Y
29 Green, G.	Y	Y	Y	Y	Y	Y	Y
30 Johnson, E.	Y	Y	Y	?	?	?	?
31 **Carter**	Y	Y	Y	N	N	Y	Y
32 **Sessions**	Y	Y	Y	N	N	Y	Y
UTAH							
1 **Bishop**	Y	Y	Y	N	N	Y	Y
2 Matheson	Y	Y	Y	Y	Y	Y	Y
3 **Chaffetz**	Y	Y	Y	N	N	Y	Y
VERMONT							
AL Welch	?	Y	Y	Y	Y	Y	Y
VIRGINIA							
1 **Wittman**	Y	Y	Y	N	N	Y	Y
2 Nye	Y	Y	Y	Y	Y	Y	Y
3 Scott	Y	Y	Y	Y	Y	Y	Y
4 **Forbes**	Y	Y	Y	N	N	Y	Y
5 Perriello	Y	Y	Y	Y	Y	Y	Y
6 **Goodlatte**	Y	Y	Y	N	N	Y	Y
7 **Cantor**	Y	Y	Y	N	N	Y	Y
8 Moran	Y	Y	Y	Y	Y	Y	Y
9 Boucher	Y	Y	Y	Y	Y	Y	Y
10 **Wolf**	Y	Y	Y	N	N	Y	Y
11 Connolly	Y	Y	Y	Y	Y	Y	Y
WASHINGTON							
1 Inslee	Y	Y	Y	Y	Y	Y	Y
2 Larsen	Y	Y	Y	Y	Y	Y	Y
3 Baird	Y	Y	Y	Y	Y	Y	Y
4 **Hastings**	Y	Y	Y	N	N	Y	Y
5 **McMorris Rodgers**	Y	Y	Y	N	N	Y	Y
6 Dicks	Y	Y	Y	Y	Y	Y	Y
7 McDermott	Y	Y	Y	Y	Y	Y	Y
8 **Reichert**	Y	Y	Y	N	N	Y	Y
9 Smith	?	?	?	?	?	?	?
WEST VIRGINIA							
1 Mollohan	Y	Y	Y	Y	Y	Y	Y
2 **Capito**	Y	Y	Y	N	N	Y	Y
3 Rahall	Y	Y	Y	Y	Y	Y	Y
WISCONSIN							
1 **Ryan**	Y	Y	Y	N	N	Y	Y
2 Baldwin	Y	Y	Y	Y	Y	Y	Y
3 Kind	Y	Y	Y	Y	Y	Y	Y
4 Moore	Y	Y	Y	Y	Y	Y	Y
5 **Sensenbrenner**	Y	Y	Y	N	N	Y	Y
6 **Petri**	Y	Y	Y	N	N	Y	Y
7 Obey	Y	Y	Y	Y	Y	Y	Y
8 Kagen	?	+	+	Y	Y	Y	Y
WYOMING							
AL **Lummis**	Y	Y	Y	N	N	Y	Y
DELEGATES							
Faleomavaega (A.S.)							
Norton (D.C.)							
Bordallo (Guam)							
Sablan (N. Marianas)							
Pierluisi (P.R.)							
Christensen (V.I.)							

IN THE HOUSE | By Vote Number

33. **H Res 1044. Anniversary of Auschwitz Liberation/Adoption.**
Klein, D-Fla., motion to suspend the rules and adopt the resolution that would commemorate the 65th anniversary of the liberation of the Nazi death camp at Auschwitz. It also would honor the victims of Auschwitz and other Nazi concentration and extermination camps. Motion agreed to 414-0: D 243-0; R 171-0. A two-thirds majority of those present and voting (276 in this case) is required for adoption under suspension of the rules. Feb. 3, 2010.

34. **HR 4061. Cybersecurity Programs/Minority Representation.**
Hastings, D-Fla., amendment that would require that a cybersecurity workforce assessment describe how programs are engaging minority communities. It also would include minority-serving institutions in the Cybersecurity University-Industry Task Force. Adopted in Committee of the Whole 417-5: D 249-0; R 168-5. Feb. 3, 2010.

35. **HR 4061. Cybersecurity Programs/Earmark Ban.** Flake, R-Ariz., amendment that would prohibit the earmarking of funds authorized for grants in the bill. Adopted in Committee of the Whole 396-31: D 225-28; R 171-3. Feb. 3, 2010.

36. **HR 4061. Cybersecurity Programs/Grant Collaboration.**
Dahlkemper, D-Pa., amendment that would allow for collaboration among community colleges, universities and Manufacturing Extension Partnership Centers for the Computer and Network Security Capacity Building Grants. Adopted in Committee of the Whole 419-3: D 249-0; R 170-3. Feb. 3, 2010.

37. **HR 4061. Cybersecurity Programs/Education and Training Programs.** Cuellar, D-Texas, amendment that would require the cybersecurity strategic research and development plan to determine how all levels of cybersecurity education and training programs can be improved. Adopted in Committee of the Whole 416-4: D 247-0; R 169-4. Feb. 3, 2010.

38. **HR 4061. Cybersecurity Programs/Youth Education.**
Connolly, D-Va., amendment that would clarify that cybersecurity education include children and young adults. Adopted in Committee of the Whole 417-4: D 249-0; R 168-4. Feb. 3, 2010.

39. **HR 4061. Cybersecurity Programs/Veteran Status.** Halvorson, D-Ill., amendment that would require that veteran status be considered as one of the criteria for selection for the Federal Cyber Scholarship for Service Program. Adopted in Committee of the Whole 424-0: D 253-0; R 171-0. Feb. 4, 2010.

	33	34	35	36	37	38	39
ALABAMA							
1 Bonner	Y	Y	Y	Y	Y	Y	Y
2 Bright	Y	Y	Y	Y	Y	Y	Y
3 Rogers	Y	Y	Y	Y	Y	Y	Y
4 Aderholt	Y	Y	Y	Y	Y	Y	?
5 Griffith	Y	Y	Y	Y	Y	Y	Y
6 Bachus	Y	Y	Y	Y	Y	Y	Y
7 Davis	Y	Y	Y	Y	Y	Y	Y
ALASKA							
AL Young	Y	Y	N	Y	Y	Y	Y
ARIZONA							
1 Kirkpatrick	?	?	?	?	?	?	Y
2 Franks	Y	Y	Y	Y	Y	Y	Y
3 Shadegg	Y	Y	Y	Y	Y	Y	Y
4 Pastor	Y	Y	Y	Y	Y	Y	Y
5 Mitchell	Y	Y	Y	Y	Y	Y	Y
6 Flake	Y	Y	Y	N	N	N	Y
7 Grijalva	Y	Y	N	Y	Y	Y	Y
8 Giffords	Y	Y	Y	Y	Y	Y	Y
ARKANSAS							
1 Berry	Y	Y	N	Y	Y	Y	Y
2 Snyder	Y	Y	Y	Y	Y	Y	Y
3 Boozman	Y	Y	Y	Y	Y	Y	?
4 Ross	Y	Y	Y	Y	Y	Y	Y
CALIFORNIA							
1 Thompson	Y	Y	Y	Y	Y	Y	Y
2 Herger	Y	Y	Y	Y	Y	Y	Y
3 Lungren	Y	Y	Y	Y	Y	Y	Y
4 McClintock	Y	N	Y	N	N	N	Y
5 Matsui	?	Y	Y	Y	Y	Y	Y
6 Woolsey	Y	?	N	Y	Y	Y	Y
7 Miller, George	Y	Y	Y	Y	Y	Y	Y
8 Pelosi							
9 Lee	Y	Y	N	Y	Y	Y	Y
10 Garamendi	Y	Y	Y	?	Y	Y	Y
11 McNerney	Y	Y	Y	Y	Y	Y	Y
12 Speier	Y	Y	Y	Y	Y	?	Y
13 Stark	Y	Y	Y	Y	Y	Y	Y
14 Eshoo	Y	Y	Y	Y	Y	Y	Y
15 Honda	Y	Y	Y	Y	Y	Y	Y
16 Lofgren	Y	Y	Y	Y	Y	Y	Y
17 Farr	Y	Y	Y	Y	Y	Y	Y
18 Cardoza	Y	Y	Y	Y	Y	Y	Y
19 Radanovich	?	?	?	?	?	?	?
20 Costa	Y	Y	Y	Y	Y	Y	Y
21 Nunes	Y	Y	Y	Y	Y	Y	Y
22 McCarthy	Y	Y	Y	Y	Y	Y	Y
23 Capps	Y	Y	Y	Y	Y	Y	Y
24 Gallegly	Y	Y	Y	Y	Y	Y	Y
25 McKeon	Y	Y	Y	Y	Y	Y	Y
26 Dreier	Y	Y	Y	Y	Y	Y	Y
27 Sherman	Y	Y	N	Y	Y	Y	Y
28 Berman	Y	Y	N	Y	Y	Y	Y
29 Schiff	Y	Y	Y	Y	Y	Y	Y
30 Waxman	Y	Y	Y	Y	Y	Y	Y
31 Becerra	Y	Y	Y	Y	Y	Y	Y
32 Chu	Y	Y	Y	Y	Y	Y	Y
33 Watson	Y	Y	N	Y	Y	Y	Y
34 Roybal-Allard	Y	Y	Y	Y	Y	Y	Y
35 Waters	Y	Y	N	Y	Y	Y	Y
36 Harman	Y	Y	Y	Y	Y	Y	Y
37 Richardson	Y	Y	Y	Y	Y	Y	Y
38 Napolitano	Y	Y	Y	Y	?	Y	Y
39 Sánchez, Linda	?	?	?	?	?	?	Y
40 Royce	Y	Y	Y	Y	Y	Y	Y
41 Lewis	Y	Y	Y	Y	Y	Y	Y
42 Miller, Gary	Y	Y	Y	Y	Y	Y	Y
43 Baca	Y	Y	Y	Y	Y	Y	Y
44 Calvert	Y	Y	Y	Y	Y	Y	Y
45 Bono Mack	Y	Y	Y	Y	Y	Y	Y
46 Rohrabacher	Y	Y	Y	Y	Y	Y	Y
47 Sanchez, Loretta	Y	Y	Y	Y	Y	Y	Y
48 Campbell	Y	Y	Y	Y	Y	Y	Y
49 Issa	Y	Y	Y	Y	Y	Y	Y
50 Bilbray	Y	Y	Y	Y	Y	Y	Y
51 Filner	Y	Y	N	Y	Y	Y	Y
52 Hunter	Y	Y	Y	Y	Y	Y	Y
53 Davis	Y	Y	Y	Y	Y	Y	Y

	33	34	35	36	37	38	39
COLORADO							
1 DeGette	Y	Y	Y	Y	Y	Y	Y
2 Polis	Y	Y	Y	Y	Y	Y	Y
3 Salazar	Y	Y	Y	Y	Y	Y	Y
4 Markey	Y	Y	Y	Y	Y	Y	Y
5 Lamborn	Y	Y	Y	Y	Y	Y	Y
6 Coffman	Y	Y	Y	Y	Y	Y	Y
7 Perlmutter	Y	Y	Y	Y	Y	Y	Y
CONNECTICUT							
1 Larson	?	Y	Y	Y	Y	Y	Y
2 Courtney	Y	Y	Y	Y	Y	Y	Y
3 DeLauro	Y	Y	Y	Y	Y	Y	Y
4 Himes	Y	Y	Y	Y	Y	Y	Y
5 Murphy	Y	Y	Y	?	Y	Y	Y
DELAWARE							
AL Castle	Y	Y	Y	Y	Y	Y	Y
FLORIDA							
1 Miller	Y	Y	Y	Y	Y	Y	Y
2 Boyd	Y	Y	Y	Y	Y	Y	Y
3 Brown	Y	Y	N	Y	Y	Y	?
4 Crenshaw	Y	Y	Y	Y	Y	Y	Y
5 Brown-Waite	Y	Y	Y	Y	Y	Y	Y
6 Stearns	Y	Y	Y	Y	Y	Y	Y
7 Mica	Y	Y	Y	Y	Y	Y	Y
8 Grayson	Y	Y	Y	Y	Y	Y	Y
9 Bilirakis	Y	Y	Y	Y	Y	Y	Y
10 Young	?	?	?	?	?	?	?
11 Castor	Y	Y	Y	Y	Y	?	Y
12 Putnam	Y	Y	Y	Y	Y	Y	Y
13 Buchanan	Y	Y	Y	Y	Y	Y	Y
14 Mack	Y	N	Y	Y	Y	Y	Y
15 Posey	Y	Y	Y	Y	Y	Y	Y
16 Rooney	Y	Y	Y	Y	Y	Y	Y
17 Meek	Y	Y	Y	Y	Y	Y	Y
18 Ros-Lehtinen	Y	Y	Y	Y	Y	Y	Y
19 Vacant							
20 Wasserman Schultz	Y	Y	Y	Y	Y	Y	Y
21 Diaz-Balart, L.	Y	Y	Y	Y	Y	Y	Y
22 Klein	Y	Y	Y	Y	Y	Y	Y
23 Hastings	Y	Y	N	Y	Y	?	?
24 Kosmas	Y	Y	Y	Y	Y	Y	Y
25 Diaz-Balart, M.	Y	Y	Y	Y	Y	Y	Y
GEORGIA							
1 Kingston	Y	Y	Y	Y	Y	Y	Y
2 Bishop	Y	Y	Y	Y	Y	Y	Y
3 Westmoreland	Y	Y	Y	Y	Y	Y	Y
4 Johnson	Y	Y	Y	Y	Y	Y	Y
5 Lewis	Y	Y	Y	Y	?	Y	Y
6 Price	Y	Y	Y	Y	Y	Y	Y
7 Linder	Y	Y	Y	Y	Y	Y	Y
8 Marshall	Y	Y	Y	Y	Y	Y	Y
9 Deal	?	Y	Y	Y	Y	Y	Y
10 Broun	Y	N	Y	N	N	N	Y
11 Gingrey	Y	Y	Y	?	Y	Y	Y
12 Barrow	Y	Y	Y	Y	Y	Y	Y
13 Scott	Y	Y	Y	Y	Y	Y	Y
HAWAII							
1 Abercrombie	Y	Y	Y	Y	Y	Y	?
2 Hirono	Y	Y	Y	Y	Y	Y	Y
IDAHO							
1 Minnick	Y	Y	Y	Y	Y	Y	Y
2 Simpson	Y	Y	Y	Y	Y	Y	Y
ILLINOIS							
1 Rush	?	?	?	?	?	?	Y
2 Jackson	Y	Y	Y	Y	Y	Y	Y
3 Lipinski	Y	Y	Y	Y	Y	Y	Y
4 Gutierrez	+	+	+	+	+	+	?
5 Quigley	Y	Y	Y	Y	Y	Y	Y
6 Roskam	Y	Y	Y	Y	Y	Y	Y
7 Davis	Y	Y	Y	Y	Y	Y	Y
8 Bean	Y	Y	Y	Y	Y	Y	Y
9 Schakowsky	Y	Y	Y	Y	Y	Y	Y
10 Kirk	?	?	?	?	?	?	Y
11 Halvorson	Y	Y	Y	Y	Y	Y	Y
12 Costello	Y	Y	Y	Y	Y	Y	Y
13 Biggert	Y	Y	Y	Y	Y	Y	Y
14 Foster	Y	Y	Y	?	Y	Y	Y
15 Johnson	Y	Y	Y	Y	Y	Y	Y

KEY	Republicans		Democrats			
Y	Voted for (yea)		X	Paired against	C	Voted "present" to avoid possible conflict of interest
#	Paired for		–	Announced against		
+	Announced for		P	Voted "present"	?	Did not vote or otherwise make a position known
N	Voted against (nay)					

	33	34	35	36	37	38	39
16 **Manzullo**	Y	Y	Y	Y	Y	Y	Y
17 Hare	Y	Y	Y	Y	Y	Y	Y
18 **Schock**	Y	Y	Y	Y	Y	Y	Y
19 **Shimkus**	Y	Y	Y	Y	Y	Y	Y
INDIANA							
1 Visclosky	Y	Y	Y	Y	Y	Y	Y
2 Donnelly	Y	Y	Y	Y	Y	Y	Y
3 **Souder**	?	Y	Y	Y	Y	Y	Y
4 **Buyer**	Y	Y	Y	Y	Y	Y	Y
5 **Burton**	Y	Y	Y	Y	Y	Y	Y
6 **Pence**	Y	Y	Y	Y	Y	Y	Y
7 Carson	Y	Y	Y	Y	Y	Y	Y
8 Ellsworth	Y	Y	Y	Y	Y	Y	Y
9 Hill	Y	Y	Y	Y	Y	Y	Y
IOWA							
1 Braley	Y	Y	Y	Y	Y	Y	Y
2 Loebsack	Y	Y	Y	Y	Y	Y	Y
3 Boswell	Y	Y	Y	Y	Y	Y	Y
4 **Latham**	Y	Y	Y	Y	Y	Y	Y
5 **King**	Y	Y	Y	Y	Y	?	Y
KANSAS							
1 **Moran**	Y	Y	Y	Y	Y	Y	Y
2 **Jenkins**	Y	Y	Y	Y	Y	Y	Y
3 Moore	Y	Y	Y	Y	Y	Y	Y
4 **Tiahrt**	Y	Y	Y	Y	Y	Y	Y
KENTUCKY							
1 **Whitfield**	Y	Y	Y	Y	Y	Y	Y
2 **Guthrie**	Y	Y	Y	Y	Y	Y	Y
3 Yarmuth	Y	Y	Y	Y	Y	Y	Y
4 **Davis**	Y	Y	Y	Y	Y	Y	Y
5 **Rogers**	Y	Y	Y	Y	Y	Y	Y
6 Chandler	Y	Y	Y	Y	Y	Y	Y
LOUISIANA							
1 **Scalise**	Y	Y	Y	Y	Y	Y	Y
2 **Cao**	Y	Y	Y	Y	Y	Y	Y
3 Melancon	Y	Y	Y	Y	Y	Y	Y
4 **Fleming**	Y	Y	Y	Y	Y	Y	Y
5 **Alexander**	Y	Y	Y	Y	Y	Y	Y
6 **Cassidy**	Y	Y	Y	Y	Y	Y	Y
7 **Boustany**	Y	Y	Y	Y	Y	Y	Y
MAINE							
1 Pingree	Y	Y	Y	Y	Y	Y	Y
2 Michaud	Y	Y	Y	Y	Y	Y	Y
MARYLAND							
1 Kratovil	Y	Y	Y	Y	Y	Y	Y
2 Ruppersberger	Y	Y	N	Y	Y	Y	?
3 Sarbanes	Y	Y	Y	Y	Y	Y	Y
4 Edwards	Y	Y	N	Y	Y	Y	Y
5 Hoyer	Y	Y	Y	Y	Y	Y	Y
6 **Bartlett**	Y	Y	Y	Y	Y	Y	Y
7 Cummings	Y	Y	Y	Y	Y	Y	Y
8 Van Hollen	Y	Y	Y	Y	Y	Y	Y
MASSACHUSETTS							
1 Olver	Y	Y	Y	Y	Y	Y	Y
2 Neal	Y	Y	Y	Y	Y	Y	Y
3 McGovern	Y	Y	Y	Y	Y	Y	Y
4 Frank	Y	Y	Y	Y	Y	Y	Y
5 Tsongas	Y	Y	Y	Y	?	Y	Y
6 Tierney	Y	Y	Y	Y	Y	Y	Y
7 Markey	Y	Y	Y	Y	Y	Y	Y
8 Capuano	Y	Y	Y	Y	Y	Y	Y
9 Lynch	Y	Y	Y	Y	Y	Y	Y
10 Delahunt	Y	Y	Y	Y	Y	Y	Y
MICHIGAN							
1 Stupak	Y	Y	Y	Y	Y	Y	Y
2 **Hoekstra**	Y	Y	Y	Y	Y	Y	Y
3 **Ehlers**	Y	Y	Y	Y	Y	Y	Y
4 **Camp**	Y	Y	Y	Y	Y	Y	Y
5 Kildee	Y	Y	Y	Y	Y	Y	Y
6 **Upton**	Y	Y	Y	Y	Y	Y	Y
7 Schauer	Y	Y	Y	Y	Y	Y	Y
8 **Rogers**	Y	Y	Y	Y	Y	Y	Y
9 Peters	Y	Y	Y	Y	Y	Y	Y
10 **Miller**	Y	Y	Y	Y	Y	Y	Y
11 **McCotter**	Y	Y	Y	Y	Y	Y	Y
12 Levin	Y	Y	Y	Y	Y	Y	Y
13 Kilpatrick	Y	Y	Y	Y	Y	Y	Y
14 Conyers	Y	Y	N	Y	Y	Y	Y
15 Dingell	Y	Y	Y	Y	Y	Y	Y
MINNESOTA							
1 Walz	Y	Y	Y	Y	Y	Y	Y
2 **Kline**	Y	Y	Y	Y	Y	Y	Y
3 **Paulsen**	Y	Y	Y	Y	Y	Y	Y
4 McCollum	Y	Y	Y	Y	Y	Y	Y

	33	34	35	36	37	38	39
5 Ellison	Y	Y	Y	Y	Y	Y	Y
6 **Bachmann**	Y	Y	Y	Y	Y	Y	Y
7 Peterson	Y	Y	Y	Y	Y	Y	Y
8 Oberstar	Y	Y	Y	Y	Y	Y	Y
MISSISSIPPI							
1 Childers	Y	Y	Y	Y	Y	Y	Y
2 Thompson	Y	Y	Y	Y	Y	Y	Y
3 **Harper**	Y	Y	Y	Y	Y	Y	Y
4 Taylor	Y	Y	Y	Y	Y	Y	Y
MISSOURI							
1 Clay	Y	Y	Y	Y	Y	Y	Y
2 **Akin**	Y	Y	Y	Y	Y	Y	Y
3 Carnahan	Y	Y	Y	Y	Y	Y	Y
4 Skelton	Y	Y	Y	Y	Y	Y	Y
5 Cleaver	Y	Y	Y	Y	Y	Y	Y
6 **Graves**	Y	Y	Y	Y	Y	Y	Y
7 **Blunt**	Y	Y	Y	Y	Y	Y	Y
8 **Emerson**	Y	Y	Y	Y	Y	Y	Y
9 **Luetkemeyer**	Y	Y	Y	Y	Y	Y	Y
MONTANA							
AL **Rehberg**	Y	Y	Y	Y	Y	Y	Y
NEBRASKA							
1 **Fortenberry**	Y	Y	Y	Y	Y	Y	Y
2 **Terry**	Y	Y	Y	Y	Y	Y	Y
3 **Smith**	Y	Y	Y	Y	Y	Y	Y
NEVADA							
1 Berkley	Y	Y	Y	Y	Y	Y	Y
2 **Heller**	Y	Y	Y	Y	Y	Y	Y
3 Titus	Y	Y	Y	Y	Y	Y	Y
NEW HAMPSHIRE							
1 Shea-Porter	Y	Y	Y	Y	Y	Y	Y
2 Hodes	Y	Y	Y	Y	Y	Y	Y
NEW JERSEY							
1 Andrews	Y	Y	Y	Y	Y	Y	Y
2 **LoBiondo**	Y	Y	Y	Y	Y	Y	Y
3 Adler	Y	Y	Y	Y	Y	Y	Y
4 **Smith**	Y	Y	Y	Y	Y	Y	Y
5 **Garrett**	Y	Y	Y	Y	Y	Y	Y
6 Pallone	Y	Y	Y	Y	Y	Y	Y
7 **Lance**	Y	Y	Y	Y	Y	Y	Y
8 Pascrell	Y	Y	Y	Y	Y	Y	Y
9 Rothman	Y	Y	N	Y	Y	Y	Y
10 Payne	Y	Y	N	Y	Y	Y	Y
11 **Frelinghuysen**	Y	Y	Y	Y	Y	Y	Y
12 Holt	Y	Y	Y	Y	Y	Y	Y
13 Sires	Y	Y	Y	Y	Y	Y	Y
NEW MEXICO							
1 Heinrich	Y	Y	Y	Y	Y	Y	Y
2 Teague	Y	Y	Y	Y	Y	Y	Y
3 Luján	Y	Y	Y	Y	Y	Y	Y
NEW YORK							
1 Bishop	Y	Y	Y	Y	Y	Y	Y
2 Israel	Y	Y	Y	Y	Y	Y	Y
3 **King**	Y	Y	Y	Y	Y	Y	Y
4 McCarthy	Y	Y	Y	Y	Y	Y	Y
5 Ackerman	Y	Y	Y	Y	Y	Y	Y
6 Meeks	Y	Y	Y	Y	Y	Y	Y
7 Crowley	Y	Y	N	Y	Y	Y	Y
8 Nadler	Y	?	N	Y	Y	Y	Y
9 Weiner	Y	Y	Y	Y	Y	Y	Y
10 Towns	Y	Y	Y	Y	Y	Y	Y
11 Clarke	Y	Y	N	Y	Y	Y	Y
12 Velázquez	Y	Y	Y	Y	Y	Y	Y
13 McMahon	Y	Y	Y	Y	Y	Y	Y
14 Maloney	Y	Y	Y	Y	Y	Y	Y
15 Rangel	Y	Y	Y	Y	?	Y	Y
16 Serrano	Y	Y	Y	Y	Y	Y	Y
17 Engel	Y	Y	Y	Y	Y	Y	?
18 Lowey	Y	Y	Y	Y	Y	Y	Y
19 Hall	Y	Y	N	Y	Y	Y	Y
20 Murphy	Y	Y	Y	Y	Y	Y	Y
21 Tonko	Y	+	Y	Y	Y	Y	Y
22 Hinchey	Y	Y	Y	Y	Y	Y	Y
23 Owens	Y	Y	Y	Y	Y	Y	Y
24 Arcuri	Y	Y	Y	Y	Y	Y	Y
25 Maffei	Y	Y	Y	Y	Y	Y	Y
26 **Lee**	Y	Y	Y	Y	Y	Y	Y
27 Higgins	Y	Y	Y	Y	Y	Y	Y
28 Slaughter	Y	Y	Y	?	?	?	Y
29 Massa	?	?	?	?	?	?	Y
NORTH CAROLINA							
1 Butterfield	Y	Y	Y	Y	Y	Y	Y
2 Etheridge	Y	Y	Y	Y	Y	Y	Y
3 **Jones**	Y	Y	N	Y	Y	Y	Y
4 Price	Y	Y	Y	Y	Y	Y	Y

	33	34	35	36	37	38	39
5 **Foxx**	Y	Y	Y	Y	Y	Y	Y
6 **Coble**	Y	Y	Y	Y	Y	Y	Y
7 McIntyre	Y	Y	Y	Y	Y	Y	Y
8 Kissell	Y	Y	Y	Y	Y	Y	Y
9 **Myrick**	Y	Y	Y	Y	Y	Y	Y
10 **McHenry**	Y	Y	Y	Y	Y	Y	Y
11 Shuler	Y	Y	Y	Y	Y	Y	Y
12 Watt	Y	Y	N	Y	Y	Y	Y
13 Miller	Y	Y	Y	Y	Y	?	Y
NORTH DAKOTA							
AL Pomeroy	Y	Y	Y	Y	Y	Y	Y
OHIO							
1 Driehaus	Y	Y	Y	Y	Y	Y	Y
2 **Schmidt**	Y	Y	Y	Y	Y	Y	Y
3 **Turner**	Y	Y	Y	Y	Y	Y	Y
4 **Jordan**	Y	Y	Y	Y	Y	Y	Y
5 **Latta**	Y	Y	Y	Y	Y	Y	Y
6 Wilson	Y	Y	Y	Y	Y	Y	Y
7 **Austria**	Y	Y	Y	Y	Y	Y	Y
8 **Boehner**	Y	Y	Y	?	Y	Y	Y
9 Kaptur	Y	Y	Y	Y	Y	Y	Y
10 Kucinich	Y	Y	N	Y	Y	Y	Y
11 Fudge	Y	Y	N	Y	Y	Y	Y
12 **Tiberi**	Y	Y	Y	Y	Y	Y	Y
13 Sutton	Y	Y	Y	Y	Y	Y	Y
14 **LaTourette**	Y	Y	Y	Y	Y	Y	Y
15 Kilroy	Y	Y	Y	Y	Y	Y	Y
16 Boccieri	Y	Y	Y	Y	Y	Y	Y
17 Ryan	?	?	N	Y	Y	Y	Y
18 Space	Y	Y	Y	Y	Y	Y	Y
OKLAHOMA							
1 **Sullivan**	Y	Y	Y	Y	Y	Y	Y
2 Boren	Y	Y	Y	Y	Y	Y	Y
3 **Lucas**	Y	Y	Y	Y	Y	Y	Y
4 **Cole**	Y	Y	Y	Y	Y	Y	Y
5 **Fallin**	Y	Y	Y	Y	Y	Y	Y
OREGON							
1 Wu	Y	Y	Y	Y	Y	Y	Y
2 **Walden**	Y	Y	Y	Y	Y	Y	Y
3 Blumenauer	Y	Y	Y	Y	Y	Y	Y
4 DeFazio	Y	Y	Y	Y	Y	Y	Y
5 Schrader	Y	Y	Y	Y	Y	Y	Y
PENNSYLVANIA							
1 Brady	Y	Y	Y	Y	Y	Y	Y
2 Fattah	Y	Y	Y	Y	Y	Y	Y
3 Dahlkemper	Y	Y	Y	Y	Y	Y	Y
4 Altmire	Y	Y	Y	Y	Y	Y	Y
5 **Thompson**	Y	Y	Y	Y	Y	Y	?
6 **Gerlach**	Y	Y	Y	Y	Y	Y	Y
7 Sestak	Y	Y	Y	Y	Y	Y	Y
8 Murphy, P.	Y	Y	Y	Y	Y	Y	Y
9 **Shuster**	Y	Y	Y	Y	Y	Y	Y
10 Carney	Y	Y	Y	Y	Y	Y	Y
11 Kanjorski	Y	Y	Y	Y	Y	Y	Y
12 Murtha	?	?	?	?	?	?	?
13 Schwartz	Y	Y	Y	Y	Y	Y	Y
14 Doyle	Y	Y	Y	Y	Y	Y	Y
15 **Dent**	Y	Y	Y	Y	Y	Y	Y
16 **Pitts**	Y	Y	Y	Y	Y	Y	Y
17 Holden	Y	Y	Y	Y	Y	Y	Y
18 **Murphy, T.**	Y	Y	Y	Y	Y	Y	Y
19 **Platts**	Y	Y	Y	Y	Y	Y	?
RHODE ISLAND							
1 Kennedy	Y	Y	N	Y	Y	Y	Y
2 Langevin	Y	Y	Y	Y	Y	Y	Y
SOUTH CAROLINA							
1 **Brown**	Y	Y	Y	Y	Y	Y	Y
2 **Wilson**	Y	Y	Y	Y	Y	?	Y
3 **Barrett**	?	?	?	?	?	?	?
4 **Inglis**	Y	Y	Y	Y	Y	Y	Y
5 Spratt	Y	Y	Y	Y	Y	Y	Y
6 Clyburn	Y	Y	N	Y	Y	Y	Y
SOUTH DAKOTA							
AL Herseth Sandlin	Y	Y	Y	Y	Y	Y	Y
TENNESSEE							
1 **Roe**	Y	Y	Y	Y	Y	Y	Y
2 **Duncan**	Y	Y	Y	Y	Y	Y	Y
3 **Wamp**	Y	Y	Y	Y	Y	Y	Y
4 Davis	Y	Y	Y	Y	Y	Y	Y
5 Cooper	Y	Y	Y	Y	Y	Y	Y
6 Gordon	Y	Y	Y	Y	Y	Y	Y
7 **Blackburn**	Y	Y	Y	Y	Y	Y	Y
8 Tanner	Y	Y	Y	Y	Y	Y	Y
9 Cohen	Y	Y	Y	Y	Y	Y	Y

	33	34	35	36	37	38	39
TEXAS							
1 **Gohmert**	Y	?	Y	Y	Y	Y	Y
2 **Poe**	Y	N	Y	Y	Y	Y	Y
3 **Johnson, S.**	Y	Y	Y	Y	Y	Y	Y
4 **Hall**	Y	Y	Y	Y	Y	Y	Y
5 **Hensarling**	Y	Y	Y	Y	Y	Y	Y
6 **Barton**	Y	Y	Y	Y	Y	Y	Y
7 **Culberson**	?	Y	Y	Y	Y	Y	Y
8 **Brady**	Y	Y	Y	Y	Y	Y	Y
9 Green, A.	Y	Y	Y	Y	Y	Y	Y
10 **McCaul**	Y	Y	Y	Y	Y	Y	Y
11 **Conaway**	Y	Y	Y	Y	Y	Y	Y
12 **Granger**	Y	Y	Y	Y	Y	Y	Y
13 **Thornberry**	Y	Y	Y	Y	Y	Y	Y
14 **Paul**	Y	N	N	N	N	N	Y
15 Hinojosa	Y	Y	Y	Y	Y	Y	Y
16 Reyes	Y	Y	Y	Y	Y	Y	Y
17 Edwards	Y	Y	Y	Y	Y	Y	?
18 Jackson Lee	Y	Y	Y	Y	Y	Y	Y
19 **Neugebauer**	Y	Y	Y	Y	Y	Y	Y
20 Gonzalez	Y	Y	Y	Y	Y	Y	Y
21 **Smith**	Y	Y	Y	Y	Y	Y	Y
22 **Olson**	Y	Y	Y	Y	Y	Y	Y
23 Rodriguez	Y	Y	Y	Y	Y	Y	Y
24 **Marchant**	Y	Y	Y	Y	Y	Y	Y
25 Doggett	Y	Y	Y	Y	Y	Y	Y
26 **Burgess**	Y	Y	Y	Y	Y	Y	Y
27 Ortiz	Y	Y	Y	Y	Y	Y	Y
28 Cuellar	Y	Y	Y	Y	Y	Y	Y
29 Green, G.	Y	Y	Y	Y	Y	Y	Y
30 Johnson, E.	?	?	?	?	?	?	?
31 **Carter**	Y	Y	Y	Y	Y	Y	Y
32 **Sessions**	Y	Y	Y	Y	Y	Y	Y
UTAH							
1 **Bishop**	Y	Y	Y	Y	Y	Y	Y
2 Matheson	Y	Y	Y	Y	Y	Y	Y
3 **Chaffetz**	Y	Y	Y	Y	Y	Y	Y
VERMONT							
AL Welch	Y	Y	Y	Y	Y	Y	Y
VIRGINIA							
1 **Wittman**	Y	Y	Y	Y	Y	Y	Y
2 Nye	Y	Y	Y	Y	Y	Y	Y
3 Scott	Y	Y	Y	Y	Y	Y	Y
4 **Forbes**	Y	Y	Y	Y	Y	Y	Y
5 Perriello	Y	Y	Y	Y	Y	Y	Y
6 **Goodlatte**	Y	Y	Y	Y	Y	Y	Y
7 **Cantor**	Y	Y	Y	Y	Y	Y	Y
8 Moran	Y	Y	Y	Y	Y	Y	Y
9 Boucher	?	Y	Y	Y	Y	Y	Y
10 **Wolf**	Y	Y	Y	Y	Y	Y	Y
11 Connolly	Y	Y	Y	Y	Y	Y	Y
WASHINGTON							
1 Inslee	Y	Y	Y	Y	Y	Y	Y
2 Larsen	Y	Y	Y	Y	Y	Y	Y
3 Baird	Y	Y	Y	Y	Y	Y	Y
4 **Hastings**	Y	Y	Y	Y	Y	Y	Y
5 **McMorris Rodgers**	Y	Y	Y	Y	Y	Y	Y
6 Dicks	Y	Y	Y	Y	Y	Y	Y
7 McDermott	Y	Y	Y	Y	Y	Y	Y
8 **Reichert**	Y	Y	Y	Y	Y	Y	Y
9 Smith	?	Y	Y	Y	Y	Y	Y
WEST VIRGINIA							
1 Mollohan	Y	Y	Y	Y	Y	Y	Y
2 **Capito**	Y	Y	Y	Y	Y	Y	Y
3 Rahall	Y	Y	N	Y	Y	Y	Y
WISCONSIN							
1 **Ryan**	Y	Y	Y	Y	Y	Y	Y
2 Baldwin	Y	Y	Y	Y	Y	Y	Y
3 Kind	Y	Y	Y	Y	Y	Y	Y
4 Moore	Y	Y	N	Y	Y	Y	Y
5 **Sensenbrenner**	Y	Y	Y	Y	Y	Y	Y
6 **Petri**	Y	Y	Y	Y	Y	Y	Y
7 Obey	Y	Y	Y	Y	Y	Y	Y
8 Kagen	Y	Y	Y	Y	Y	Y	Y
WYOMING							
AL **Lummis**	Y	Y	Y	Y	Y	Y	Y
DELEGATES							
Faleomavaega (A.S.)		Y	Y	Y	Y	Y	Y
Norton (D.C.)		Y	Y	Y	?	Y	Y
Bordallo (Guam)		Y	Y	Y	Y	Y	Y
Sablan (N. Marianas)		Y	Y	Y	Y	Y	Y
Pierluisi (P.R.)		Y	Y	Y	Y	Y	Y
Christensen (V.I.)		?	?	?	?	?	Y

IN THE HOUSE | By Vote Number

40. HR 4061. Cybersecurity Programs/Student Recruitment. Kilroy, D-Ohio, amendment that would require the Federal Cyber Scholarship for Service program to support outreach activities to recruit students in secondary schools and two-year institutions into cybersecurity-related fields. Adopted in Committee of the Whole 419-4: D 254-0; R 165-4. Feb. 4, 2010.

41. HR 4061. Cybersecurity Programs/Secure Software Design. Kissell, D-N.C., amendment that would require the Computer and Network Security Capacity Building Grants mission statement to reiterate the importance of teaching about secure software design. Adopted in Committee of the Whole 423-6: D 255-0; R 168-6. Feb. 4, 2010.

42. HR 4061. Cybersecurity Programs/Sensitive Information. Owens, D-N.Y., amendment that would require the Cybersecurity Strategic Research and Development plan to address technologies to secure sensitive information shared among federal agencies. Adopted in Committee of the Whole 430-0: D 257-0; R 173-0. Feb. 4, 2010.

43. HR 4061. Cybersecurity Programs/Passage. Passage of the bill that would reauthorize and expand cybersecurity research programs at the National Science Foundation and the National Institute of Standards and Technology. It also would establish a cybersecurity scholarship program, require certain agencies to develop strategic cybersecurity research plans and establish a university-industry task force to explore public-private research partnerships. It would authorize $109 million for scholarships and $395 million for research through fiscal 2014. Passed 422-5: D 253-0; R 169-5. Feb. 4, 2010.

44. H Res 1022. Tribute to Medgar Evers/Adoption. Johnson, D-Ga., motion to suspend the rules and adopt the resolution that would honor the life and sacrifice of civil rights leader Medgar Evers and congratulate the Navy for naming a naval supply ship after Evers. Motion agreed to 426-0: D 253-0; R 173-0. A two-thirds majority of those present and voting (284 in this case) is required for adoption under suspension of the rules. Feb. 4, 2010.

	40	41	42	43	44
ALABAMA					
1 Bonner	Y	Y	Y	Y	Y
2 Bright	Y	Y	Y	Y	Y
3 Rogers	Y	Y	Y	Y	Y
4 Aderholt	Y	Y	Y	Y	Y
5 Griffith	Y	Y	Y	Y	Y
6 Bachus	Y	Y	Y	Y	Y
7 Davis	Y	Y	Y	Y	Y
ALASKA					
AL Young	Y	Y	Y	Y	Y
ARIZONA					
1 Kirkpatrick	Y	Y	Y	Y	Y
2 Franks	Y	Y	Y	Y	Y
3 Shadegg	Y	Y	Y	Y	Y
4 Pastor	Y	Y	Y	Y	Y
5 Mitchell	Y	Y	Y	Y	Y
6 Flake	N	N	Y	N	Y
7 Grijalva	Y	Y	Y	Y	Y
8 Giffords	Y	Y	Y	Y	Y
ARKANSAS					
1 Berry	Y	Y	Y	Y	Y
2 Snyder	Y	Y	Y	Y	Y
3 Boozman	Y	Y	Y	Y	Y
4 Ross	Y	Y	Y	Y	Y
CALIFORNIA					
1 Thompson	Y	Y	Y	Y	Y
2 Herger	Y	Y	Y	Y	Y
3 Lungren	Y	Y	Y	Y	Y
4 McClintock	N	N	Y	Y	Y
5 Matsui	Y	Y	Y	Y	Y
6 Woolsey	Y	Y	Y	Y	Y
7 Miller, George	Y	Y	Y	Y	Y
8 Pelosi					
9 Lee	Y	Y	Y	Y	Y
10 Garamendi	Y	Y	Y	Y	Y
11 McNerney	Y	Y	Y	Y	Y
12 Speier	Y	Y	Y	Y	Y
13 Stark	Y	Y	Y	Y	Y
14 Eshoo	Y	Y	Y	Y	Y
15 Honda	Y	Y	Y	Y	Y
16 Lofgren	Y	Y	Y	Y	Y
17 Farr	Y	Y	Y	Y	Y
18 Cardoza	Y	Y	Y	Y	Y
19 Radanovich	?	?	?	?	?
20 Costa	Y	Y	Y	Y	Y
21 Nunes	Y	Y	Y	Y	Y
22 McCarthy	Y	Y	Y	Y	Y
23 Capps	Y	Y	Y	Y	Y
24 Gallegly	Y	Y	Y	Y	Y
25 McKeon	Y	Y	Y	Y	Y
26 Dreier	Y	Y	Y	Y	Y
27 Sherman	Y	Y	Y	Y	Y
28 Berman	Y	Y	Y	Y	Y
29 Schiff	Y	Y	Y	Y	Y
30 Waxman	Y	Y	Y	Y	Y
31 Becerra	Y	Y	Y	Y	Y
32 Chu	Y	Y	Y	Y	Y
33 Watson	Y	Y	Y	Y	Y
34 Roybal-Allard	Y	Y	Y	Y	Y
35 Waters	Y	Y	Y	Y	Y
36 Harman	Y	Y	Y	Y	Y
37 Richardson	Y	Y	Y	Y	Y
38 Napolitano	Y	Y	Y	Y	Y
39 Sánchez, Linda	Y	Y	Y	Y	Y
40 Royce	Y	Y	Y	Y	Y
41 Lewis	Y	N	Y	Y	Y
42 Miller, Gary	Y	Y	Y	Y	Y
43 Baca	Y	Y	Y	Y	Y
44 Calvert	Y	Y	Y	Y	Y
45 Bono Mack	Y	Y	Y	Y	Y
46 Rohrabacher	Y	Y	Y	Y	Y
47 Sanchez, Loretta	Y	Y	Y	Y	Y
48 Campbell	Y	N	Y	Y	Y
49 Issa	Y	Y	Y	Y	Y
50 Bilbray	Y	Y	Y	Y	Y
51 Filner	Y	Y	Y	Y	Y
52 Hunter	Y	Y	Y	Y	Y
53 Davis	Y	Y	Y	Y	Y

	40	41	42	43	44
COLORADO					
1 DeGette	Y	Y	Y	Y	Y
2 Polis	Y	Y	Y	Y	Y
3 Salazar	Y	Y	Y	Y	Y
4 Markey	Y	Y	Y	Y	Y
5 Lamborn	Y	Y	Y	Y	Y
6 Coffman	Y	Y	Y	Y	Y
7 Perlmutter	Y	Y	Y	Y	Y
CONNECTICUT					
1 Larson	Y	Y	Y	Y	Y
2 Courtney	Y	Y	Y	Y	Y
3 DeLauro	Y	Y	Y	Y	Y
4 Himes	Y	Y	Y	Y	Y
5 Murphy	Y	Y	Y	Y	Y
DELAWARE					
AL Castle	Y	Y	Y	Y	Y
FLORIDA					
1 Miller	Y	Y	Y	Y	Y
2 Boyd	Y	Y	Y	Y	Y
3 Brown	?	?	?	Y	Y
4 Crenshaw	Y	Y	Y	Y	Y
5 Brown-Waite	Y	Y	Y	Y	Y
6 Stearns	Y	Y	Y	Y	Y
7 Mica	Y	Y	Y	Y	Y
8 Grayson	Y	Y	Y	Y	Y
9 Bilirakis	Y	Y	Y	Y	Y
10 Young	?	?	?	?	?
11 Castor	Y	Y	Y	Y	Y
12 Putnam	Y	Y	Y	Y	Y
13 Buchanan	Y	Y	Y	Y	Y
14 Mack	Y	Y	Y	Y	Y
15 Posey	Y	Y	Y	Y	Y
16 Rooney	Y	Y	Y	Y	Y
17 Meek	Y	Y	Y	Y	Y
18 Ros-Lehtinen	Y	Y	Y	Y	Y
19 Vacant					
20 Wasserman Schultz	Y	Y	Y	Y	Y
21 Diaz-Balart, L.	?	Y	Y	Y	Y
22 Klein	Y	Y	Y	Y	Y
23 Hastings	Y	Y	Y	Y	Y
24 Kosmas	Y	Y	Y	Y	Y
25 Diaz-Balart, M.	Y	Y	Y	Y	Y
GEORGIA					
1 Kingston	Y	Y	Y	Y	Y
2 Bishop	Y	Y	Y	Y	Y
3 Westmoreland	Y	Y	Y	Y	Y
4 Johnson	Y	Y	Y	Y	Y
5 Lewis	Y	Y	Y	Y	Y
6 Price	Y	Y	Y	Y	Y
7 Linder	Y	Y	Y	Y	Y
8 Marshall	Y	Y	Y	Y	Y
9 Deal	?	Y	Y	Y	Y
10 Broun	N	N	Y	N	Y
11 Gingrey	Y	Y	Y	Y	Y
12 Barrow	Y	Y	Y	Y	Y
13 Scott	Y	Y	Y	Y	Y
HAWAII					
1 Abercrombie	Y	Y	Y	Y	Y
2 Hirono	Y	Y	Y	Y	Y
IDAHO					
1 Minnick	Y	Y	Y	Y	Y
2 Simpson	Y	Y	Y	Y	Y
ILLINOIS					
1 Rush	Y	Y	Y	Y	Y
2 Jackson	Y	Y	Y	Y	Y
3 Lipinski	Y	Y	Y	Y	Y
4 Gutierrez	?	?	?	?	?
5 Quigley	Y	Y	Y	Y	Y
6 Roskam	Y	Y	Y	Y	Y
7 Davis	Y	Y	Y	Y	Y
8 Bean	Y	Y	Y	Y	Y
9 Schakowsky	Y	Y	Y	Y	Y
10 Kirk	Y	Y	Y	Y	Y
11 Halvorson	Y	Y	Y	Y	Y
12 Costello	Y	Y	Y	Y	Y
13 Biggert	Y	Y	Y	Y	Y
14 Foster	Y	Y	Y	Y	Y
15 Johnson	Y	Y	Y	Y	Y

KEY	Republicans	Democrats	
Y Voted for (yea)		X Paired against	C Voted "present" to avoid possible conflict of interest
# Paired for		– Announced against	
+ Announced for		P Voted "present"	? Did not vote or otherwise make a position known
N Voted against (nay)			

	40	41	42	43	44
16 Manzullo	Y	Y	Y	Y	Y
17 Hare	Y	Y	Y	Y	Y
18 Schock	Y	Y	Y	Y	Y
19 Shimkus	Y	Y	Y	Y	Y
INDIANA					
1 Visclosky	Y	Y	Y	Y	Y
2 Donnelly	Y	Y	Y	Y	Y
3 Souder	Y	Y	Y	Y	Y
4 Buyer	Y	Y	Y	Y	Y
5 Burton	Y	Y	Y	Y	Y
6 Pence	Y	Y	Y	Y	Y
7 Carson	Y	Y	Y	Y	Y
8 Ellsworth	Y	?	Y	Y	Y
9 Hill	Y	Y	Y	Y	Y
IOWA					
1 Braley	Y	Y	Y	Y	Y
2 Loebsack	Y	Y	Y	Y	Y
3 Boswell	Y	Y	Y	Y	Y
4 Latham	Y	Y	Y	Y	Y
5 King	Y	Y	Y	Y	Y
KANSAS					
1 Moran	Y	Y	Y	Y	Y
2 Jenkins	Y	Y	Y	Y	Y
3 Moore	Y	Y	Y	Y	Y
4 Tiahrt	Y	Y	Y	Y	Y
KENTUCKY					
1 Whitfield	Y	Y	Y	Y	Y
2 Guthrie	Y	Y	Y	Y	Y
3 Yarmuth	Y	Y	Y	Y	Y
4 Davis	?	Y	Y	Y	Y
5 Rogers	Y	Y	Y	Y	Y
6 Chandler	Y	Y	Y	Y	Y
LOUISIANA					
1 Scalise	Y	Y	Y	Y	Y
2 Cao	Y	Y	Y	Y	Y
3 Melancon	Y	Y	Y	Y	Y
4 Fleming	Y	Y	Y	Y	Y
5 Alexander	Y	Y	Y	Y	Y
6 Cassidy	Y	Y	?	Y	Y
7 Boustany	Y	Y	Y	Y	Y
MAINE					
1 Pingree	Y	Y	Y	Y	Y
2 Michaud	Y	Y	Y	Y	Y
MARYLAND					
1 Kratovil	Y	Y	Y	Y	Y
2 Ruppersberger	?	Y	Y	Y	Y
3 Sarbanes	Y	Y	Y	Y	Y
4 Edwards	Y	Y	Y	Y	Y
5 Hoyer	Y	Y	Y	Y	Y
6 Bartlett	Y	Y	Y	Y	Y
7 Cummings	Y	Y	Y	Y	Y
8 Van Hollen	Y	Y	Y	Y	Y
MASSACHUSETTS					
1 Olver	Y	Y	Y	Y	Y
2 Neal	Y	Y	Y	Y	Y
3 McGovern	Y	Y	Y	Y	Y
4 Frank	Y	Y	Y	Y	Y
5 Tsongas	Y	Y	Y	Y	Y
6 Tierney	Y	Y	Y	Y	Y
7 Markey	Y	Y	Y	Y	Y
8 Capuano	Y	Y	Y	Y	Y
9 Lynch	Y	Y	Y	Y	Y
10 Delahunt	Y	Y	Y	Y	Y
MICHIGAN					
1 Stupak	Y	Y	Y	Y	Y
2 Hoekstra	Y	Y	Y	Y	Y
3 Ehlers	Y	Y	Y	Y	Y
4 Camp	Y	Y	Y	Y	Y
5 Kildee	Y	Y	Y	Y	Y
6 Upton	Y	Y	Y	Y	Y
7 Schauer	Y	Y	Y	Y	Y
8 Rogers	Y	Y	Y	Y	Y
9 Peters	Y	Y	Y	Y	Y
10 Miller	Y	Y	Y	Y	Y
11 McCotter	Y	Y	Y	Y	Y
12 Levin	Y	Y	Y	Y	Y
13 Kilpatrick	Y	Y	Y	Y	Y
14 Conyers	Y	Y	Y	Y	Y
15 Dingell	Y	Y	Y	Y	Y
MINNESOTA					
1 Walz	Y	Y	Y	Y	Y
2 Kline	Y	Y	Y	Y	Y
3 Paulsen	Y	Y	Y	Y	Y
4 McCollum	Y	Y	Y	Y	Y

	40	41	42	43	44
5 Ellison	Y	Y	Y	Y	Y
6 Bachmann	Y	Y	Y	Y	Y
7 Peterson	Y	Y	Y	Y	Y
8 Oberstar	Y	Y	Y	Y	Y
MISSISSIPPI					
1 Childers	Y	Y	Y	Y	Y
2 Thompson	Y	Y	Y	Y	Y
3 Harper	Y	Y	Y	Y	Y
4 Taylor	Y	Y	Y	Y	Y
MISSOURI					
1 Clay	Y	Y	Y	Y	Y
2 Akin	Y	Y	Y	Y	Y
3 Carnahan	Y	Y	Y	Y	Y
4 Skelton	Y	Y	Y	Y	Y
5 Cleaver	Y	Y	Y	Y	Y
6 Graves	Y	Y	Y	Y	Y
7 Blunt	Y	Y	Y	Y	Y
8 Emerson	Y	Y	Y	Y	Y
9 Luetkemeyer	Y	Y	Y	Y	Y
MONTANA					
AL Rehberg	Y	Y	Y	Y	Y
NEBRASKA					
1 Fortenberry	Y	Y	Y	Y	Y
2 Terry	Y	Y	Y	Y	Y
3 Smith	Y	Y	Y	Y	Y
NEVADA					
1 Berkley	Y	Y	Y	Y	Y
2 Heller	Y	Y	Y	Y	Y
3 Titus	Y	Y	Y	Y	Y
NEW HAMPSHIRE					
1 Shea-Porter	Y	Y	Y	Y	Y
2 Hodes	Y	Y	Y	Y	Y
NEW JERSEY					
1 Andrews	Y	Y	Y	Y	Y
2 LoBiondo	Y	Y	Y	Y	Y
3 Adler	Y	Y	Y	Y	Y
4 Smith	Y	Y	Y	Y	Y
5 Garrett	Y	Y	Y	Y	Y
6 Pallone	Y	Y	Y	Y	Y
7 Lance	Y	Y	Y	Y	Y
8 Pascrell	Y	Y	Y	Y	Y
9 Rothman	Y	Y	Y	Y	Y
10 Payne	Y	Y	Y	Y	Y
11 Frelinghuysen	Y	Y	Y	Y	Y
12 Holt	Y	Y	Y	Y	Y
13 Sires	Y	Y	Y	Y	Y
NEW MEXICO					
1 Heinrich	Y	Y	Y	Y	Y
2 Teague	Y	Y	Y	Y	Y
3 Luján	Y	Y	Y	Y	Y
NEW YORK					
1 Bishop	Y	Y	Y	Y	Y
2 Israel	Y	Y	Y	Y	Y
3 King	Y	Y	Y	Y	Y
4 McCarthy	Y	Y	Y	Y	Y
5 Ackerman	Y	Y	Y	Y	Y
6 Meeks	Y	Y	Y	Y	Y
7 Crowley	Y	Y	Y	Y	Y
8 Nadler	Y	Y	Y	Y	Y
9 Weiner	Y	Y	Y	Y	Y
10 Towns	Y	Y	Y	Y	Y
11 Clarke	Y	Y	Y	Y	Y
12 Velázquez	Y	Y	Y	Y	Y
13 McMahon	Y	Y	Y	Y	Y
14 Maloney	Y	Y	Y	Y	Y
15 Rangel	Y	Y	Y	Y	Y
16 Serrano	Y	Y	Y	Y	Y
17 Engel	?	?	?	Y	Y
18 Lowey	Y	Y	Y	Y	Y
19 Hall	Y	Y	Y	Y	Y
20 Murphy	Y	Y	Y	Y	Y
21 Tonko	Y	Y	Y	Y	Y
22 Hinchey	Y	Y	Y	Y	Y
23 Owens	Y	Y	Y	Y	Y
24 Arcuri	Y	Y	Y	Y	Y
25 Maffei	Y	Y	Y	Y	Y
26 Lee	Y	Y	Y	Y	Y
27 Higgins	Y	Y	Y	Y	Y
28 Slaughter	Y	Y	Y	Y	Y
29 Massa	Y	Y	Y	Y	Y
NORTH CAROLINA					
1 Butterfield	Y	Y	Y	Y	Y
2 Etheridge	Y	Y	Y	Y	Y
3 Jones	Y	Y	Y	Y	Y
4 Price	Y	Y	Y	Y	Y

	40	41	42	43	44
5 Foxx	Y	Y	Y	Y	Y
6 Coble	Y	Y	Y	Y	Y
7 McIntyre	Y	Y	Y	Y	Y
8 Kissell	Y	Y	Y	Y	Y
9 Myrick	Y	Y	Y	Y	Y
10 McHenry	Y	Y	Y	Y	Y
11 Shuler	Y	Y	Y	Y	Y
12 Watt	Y	Y	Y	Y	Y
13 Miller	Y	Y	Y	Y	Y
NORTH DAKOTA					
AL Pomeroy	Y	Y	Y	Y	Y
OHIO					
1 Driehaus	Y	Y	Y	Y	Y
2 Schmidt	Y	Y	Y	Y	Y
3 Turner	Y	Y	Y	Y	Y
4 Jordan	Y	Y	Y	Y	Y
5 Latta	Y	Y	Y	Y	Y
6 Wilson	Y	Y	Y	Y	Y
7 Austria	Y	Y	Y	Y	Y
8 Boehner	Y	Y	Y	Y	Y
9 Kaptur	Y	Y	Y	Y	Y
10 Kucinich	Y	Y	Y	Y	Y
11 Fudge	Y	Y	Y	Y	Y
12 Tiberi	Y	Y	Y	Y	Y
13 Sutton	Y	Y	Y	Y	Y
14 LaTourette	Y	Y	Y	Y	Y
15 Kilroy	Y	Y	Y	Y	Y
16 Boccieri	Y	Y	Y	Y	Y
17 Ryan	Y	Y	Y	Y	Y
18 Space	Y	Y	Y	Y	Y
OKLAHOMA					
1 Sullivan	Y	Y	Y	Y	Y
2 Boren	Y	Y	Y	Y	Y
3 Lucas	Y	Y	Y	Y	Y
4 Cole	Y	Y	Y	Y	?
5 Fallin	Y	Y	Y	Y	Y
OREGON					
1 Wu	Y	Y	Y	Y	Y
2 Walden	Y	Y	Y	Y	Y
3 Blumenauer	Y	Y	Y	Y	Y
4 DeFazio	Y	Y	Y	Y	Y
5 Schrader	Y	Y	Y	Y	Y
PENNSYLVANIA					
1 Brady	Y	Y	Y	Y	Y
2 Fattah	Y	Y	Y	Y	Y
3 Dahlkemper	Y	Y	Y	Y	Y
4 Altmire	Y	Y	Y	Y	Y
5 Thompson	?	?	?	?	?
6 Gerlach	Y	Y	Y	Y	Y
7 Sestak	Y	Y	Y	Y	Y
8 Murphy, P.	Y	Y	Y	Y	Y
9 Shuster	Y	Y	Y	Y	Y
10 Carney	Y	Y	Y	Y	Y
11 Kanjorski	Y	Y	Y	Y	Y
12 Murtha	?	?	?	?	?
13 Schwartz	Y	Y	Y	Y	Y
14 Doyle	Y	Y	Y	Y	Y
15 Dent	Y	Y	Y	Y	Y
16 Pitts	Y	Y	Y	Y	Y
17 Holden	Y	Y	Y	Y	Y
18 Murphy, T.	Y	Y	Y	Y	Y
19 Platts	?	Y	Y	Y	Y
RHODE ISLAND					
1 Kennedy	Y	Y	Y	Y	Y
2 Langevin	Y	Y	Y	Y	Y
SOUTH CAROLINA					
1 Brown	Y	Y	Y	Y	Y
2 Wilson	Y	Y	Y	Y	Y
3 Barrett	?	?	?	?	Y
4 Inglis	Y	Y	Y	Y	Y
5 Spratt	Y	Y	Y	Y	Y
6 Clyburn	Y	Y	Y	Y	Y
SOUTH DAKOTA					
AL Herseth Sandlin	Y	Y	Y	Y	Y
TENNESSEE					
1 Roe	Y	Y	Y	Y	Y
2 Duncan	Y	Y	Y	Y	Y
3 Wamp	Y	Y	Y	Y	Y
4 Davis	Y	Y	Y	Y	Y
5 Cooper	Y	Y	Y	Y	Y
6 Gordon	Y	Y	Y	Y	Y
7 Blackburn	Y	Y	Y	Y	Y
8 Tanner	Y	Y	Y	Y	Y
9 Cohen	Y	Y	Y	Y	Y

	40	41	42	43	44
TEXAS					
1 Gohmert	Y	Y	Y	N	Y
2 Poe	Y	Y	Y	Y	Y
3 Johnson, S.	Y	Y	Y	Y	Y
4 Hall	Y	Y	Y	Y	Y
5 Hensarling	Y	Y	Y	Y	Y
6 Barton	Y	Y	Y	Y	Y
7 Culberson	Y	Y	Y	Y	Y
8 Brady	Y	Y	Y	Y	Y
9 Green, A.	Y	Y	Y	Y	Y
10 McCaul	Y	Y	Y	Y	Y
11 Conaway	Y	Y	Y	Y	Y
12 Granger	Y	Y	Y	Y	Y
13 Thornberry	Y	Y	Y	Y	Y
14 Paul	N	N	Y	N	Y
15 Hinojosa	?	Y	Y	Y	Y
16 Reyes	Y	Y	Y	Y	Y
17 Edwards	Y	Y	Y	Y	Y
18 Jackson Lee	Y	Y	Y	Y	Y
19 Neugebauer	Y	Y	Y	Y	Y
20 Gonzalez	Y	Y	Y	Y	Y
21 Smith	Y	Y	Y	Y	Y
22 Olson	Y	Y	Y	Y	Y
23 Rodriguez	Y	Y	Y	Y	Y
24 Marchant	Y	Y	Y	Y	Y
25 Doggett	Y	Y	Y	Y	Y
26 Burgess	Y	Y	Y	Y	Y
27 Ortiz	Y	Y	Y	Y	Y
28 Cuellar	Y	Y	Y	Y	Y
29 Green, G.	Y	Y	Y	Y	Y
30 Johnson, E.	?	?	Y	Y	Y
31 Carter	Y	Y	Y	Y	Y
32 Sessions		Y	Y	Y	Y
UTAH					
1 Bishop	Y	Y	Y	Y	Y
2 Matheson	Y	Y	Y	Y	Y
3 Chaffetz	Y	Y	Y	Y	Y
VERMONT					
AL Welch	Y	Y	Y	Y	Y
VIRGINIA					
1 Wittman	Y	Y	Y	Y	Y
2 Nye	Y	Y	Y	Y	Y
3 Scott	Y	Y	Y	Y	Y
4 Forbes	Y	Y	Y	Y	Y
5 Perriello	Y	Y	Y	Y	Y
6 Goodlatte	Y	Y	Y	Y	Y
7 Cantor	?	Y	Y	Y	Y
8 Moran	Y	Y	Y	Y	Y
9 Boucher	Y	Y	Y	Y	Y
10 Wolf	Y	Y	Y	Y	?
11 Connolly	Y	Y	Y	Y	Y
WASHINGTON					
1 Inslee	Y	Y	Y	Y	Y
2 Larsen	Y	Y	Y	Y	Y
3 Baird	Y	Y	Y	Y	Y
4 Hastings	Y	Y	Y	Y	Y
5 McMorris Rodgers	Y	Y	Y	Y	Y
6 Dicks	Y	Y	Y	Y	Y
7 McDermott	Y	Y	Y	Y	Y
8 Reichert	Y	Y	Y	Y	Y
9 Smith	Y	Y	Y	Y	Y
WEST VIRGINIA					
1 Mollohan	Y	Y	Y	Y	Y
2 Capito	Y	Y	Y	Y	Y
3 Rahall	Y	Y	Y	Y	Y
WISCONSIN					
1 Ryan	Y	Y	Y	Y	Y
2 Baldwin	Y	Y	Y	Y	Y
3 Kind	Y	Y	Y	Y	Y
4 Moore	Y	Y	Y	Y	Y
5 Sensenbrenner	Y	Y	Y	N	Y
6 Petri	Y	Y	Y	Y	Y
7 Obey	Y	Y	Y	Y	Y
8 Kagen	Y	Y	Y	Y	Y
WYOMING					
AL Lummis	Y	Y	Y	Y	Y
DELEGATES					
Faleomavaega (A.S.)	Y	Y	Y		
Norton (D.C.)	Y	Y	Y		
Bordallo (Guam)	Y	Y	Y		
Sablan (N. Marianas)	Y	Y	Y		
Pierluisi (P.R.)	Y	Y	Y		
Christensen (V.I.)	Y	Y	Y		

IN THE HOUSE | By Vote Number

45. H J Res 45. Debt Limit Increase/Previous Question.
McGovern, D-Mass., motion to order the previous question (thus ending debate and possibility of amendment) on adoption of the rule (H Res 1065) that would provide for House floor consideration of the Senate amendment to the joint resolution that would increase the statutory debt limit by $1.9 trillion and enact pay-as-you-go budget enforcement rules. Motion agreed to 233-195: D 233-20; R 0-175. Feb. 4, 2010.

46. H J Res 45. Debt Limit Increase/Rule.
Adoption of the rule (H Res 1065) that would provide for House floor consideration of the Senate amendment to the joint resolution that would increase the statutory debt limit by $1.9 trillion and enact pay-as-you-go budget enforcement rules. The rule contains self-executing language that would provide for the automatic adoption of the debt limit portion of the measure and would require a separate vote on the pay-as-you-go provisions. Adopted 217-212: D 217-37; R 0-175. A "yea" was a vote in support of the president's position. Feb. 4, 2010.

47. HR 4532. Social Security Attorney Fees/Passage.
Tanner, D-Tenn., motion to suspend the rules and pass the bill that would make permanent a Social Security Administration program that allows the use of a portion of awarded past-due benefits to pay representatives of plaintiffs claiming Social Security or Supplemental Security Income benefits. It also would allow the Social Security Administration to charge fees to cover the cost of vetting non-attorney representatives. Motion agreed to 412-6: D 247-0; R 165-6. A two-thirds majority of those present and voting (279 in this case) is required for passage under suspension of the rules. Feb. 4, 2010.

48. H J Res 45. Debt Limit Increase/Motion to Concur.
Division II of the Hoyer, D-Md., motion to concur in the Senate amendment to the joint resolution that would increase the debt limit by $1.9 trillion and add pay-as-you-go budget rules into law. The portion of the Senate amendment covered by the division would establish a statutory requirement that new tax and mandatory spending legislation be budget-neutral, enforced by automatic across-the-board spending cuts in non-exempt programs if the pay-as-you-go tally at the end of the year shows a deficit. It would exempt measures to extend certain tax cuts scheduled to expire in 2010 and treat the alternative minimum tax exemption as though it had been extended beyond Dec. 31, 2009. Motion agreed to, thus clearing the bill for the president, 233-187: D 233-15; R 0-172. Division I of the motion to concur, which covered language to increase the debt limit, was considered adopted pursuant to the rule. A "yea" was a vote in support of the president's position. Feb. 4, 2010.

	45	46	47	48
ALABAMA				
1 Bonner	N	N	Y	N
2 Bright	N	N	Y	N
3 Rogers	N	N	Y	N
4 Aderholt	N	N	Y	N
5 Griffith	N	N	Y	N
6 Bachus	N	N	Y	N
7 Davis	Y	Y	Y	Y
ALASKA				
AL Young	N	N	Y	N
ARIZONA				
1 Kirkpatrick	Y	N	Y	Y
2 Franks	N	N	Y	N
3 Shadegg	N	N	Y	N
4 Pastor	Y	Y	Y	N
5 Mitchell	N	N	Y	N
6 Flake	N	N	Y	N
7 Grijalva	Y	Y	Y	Y
8 Giffords	N	N	Y	Y
ARKANSAS				
1 Berry	Y	Y	Y	Y
2 Snyder	Y	Y	Y	Y
3 Boozman	N	N	Y	N
4 Ross	Y	Y	Y	Y
CALIFORNIA				
1 Thompson	Y	Y	Y	Y
2 Herger	N	N	Y	N
3 Lungren	N	N	Y	N
4 McClintock	N	N	N	N
5 Matsui	Y	Y	Y	Y
6 Woolsey	Y	Y	Y	Y
7 Miller, George	Y	Y	Y	Y
8 Pelosi		Y		Y
9 Lee	Y	Y	Y	Y
10 Garamendi	Y	Y	Y	Y
11 McNerney	Y	Y	Y	N
12 Speier	Y	Y	Y	Y
13 Stark	Y	Y	Y	?
14 Eshoo	Y	Y	Y	Y
15 Honda	Y	Y	Y	Y
16 Lofgren	Y	Y	Y	Y
17 Farr	Y	Y	Y	Y
18 Cardoza	Y	Y	Y	Y
19 Radanovich	?	?	?	?
20 Costa	Y	Y	Y	Y
21 Nunes	N	N	Y	N
22 McCarthy	N	N	Y	N
23 Capps	Y	Y	Y	Y
24 Gallegly	N	N	Y	N
25 McKeon	N	N	Y	N
26 Dreier	N	N	Y	N
27 Sherman	Y	Y	Y	Y
28 Berman	Y	Y	?	Y
29 Schiff	Y	Y	Y	Y
30 Waxman	Y	Y	Y	Y
31 Becerra	Y	Y	Y	Y
32 Chu	Y	Y	Y	Y
33 Watson	Y	Y	Y	Y
34 Roybal-Allard	Y	Y	Y	Y
35 Waters	Y	Y	Y	N
36 Harman	Y	Y	Y	Y
37 Richardson	Y	Y	Y	Y
38 Napolitano	Y	Y	Y	Y
39 Sánchez, Linda	Y	Y	Y	Y
40 Royce	N	N	Y	N
41 Lewis	N	N	Y	N
42 Miller, Gary	N	N	Y	N
43 Baca	Y	Y	Y	Y
44 Calvert	N	N	Y	N
45 Bono Mack	N	N	Y	N
46 Rohrabacher	N	N	Y	N
47 Sanchez, Loretta	Y	Y	Y	Y
48 Campbell	N	N	N	N
49 Issa	N	N	Y	N
50 Bilbray	N	N	Y	N
51 Filner	Y	Y	Y	N
52 Hunter	N	N	Y	N
53 Davis	Y	Y	Y	Y

	45	46	47	48
COLORADO				
1 DeGette	Y	Y	Y	Y
2 Polis	Y	Y	Y	Y
3 Salazar	Y	Y	Y	Y
4 Markey	Y	N	Y	Y
5 Lamborn	N	N	Y	N
6 Coffman	N	N	N	N
7 Perlmutter	Y	Y	Y	Y
CONNECTICUT				
1 Larson	Y	Y	Y	Y
2 Courtney	Y	Y	Y	Y
3 DeLauro	Y	Y	Y	Y
4 Himes	Y	Y	Y	Y
5 Murphy	Y	Y	Y	Y
DELAWARE				
AL Castle	N	N	Y	N
FLORIDA				
1 Miller	N	N	Y	N
2 Boyd	Y	Y	Y	Y
3 Brown	Y	Y	Y	Y
4 Crenshaw	N	N	Y	N
5 Brown-Waite	N	N	Y	N
6 Stearns	N	N	Y	N
7 Mica	N	N	Y	N
8 Grayson	Y	N	Y	Y
9 Bilirakis	N	N	Y	N
10 Young	?	?	?	?
11 Castor	Y	Y	Y	Y
12 Putnam	N	N	Y	N
13 Buchanan	N	N	Y	N
14 Mack	N	N	Y	N
15 Posey	N	N	Y	N
16 Rooney	N	N	Y	N
17 Meek	Y	Y	Y	Y
18 Ros-Lehtinen	N	N	Y	N
19 Vacant				
20 Wasserman Schultz	Y	Y	Y	Y
21 Diaz-Balart, L.	N	N	Y	N
22 Klein	Y	Y	Y	Y
23 Hastings	Y	Y	Y	Y
24 Kosmas	N	N	Y	N
25 Diaz-Balart, M.	N	N	Y	N
GEORGIA				
1 Kingston	N	N	Y	N
2 Bishop	Y	Y	Y	Y
3 Westmoreland	N	N	Y	N
4 Johnson	Y	Y	Y	Y
5 Lewis	Y	Y	Y	Y
6 Price	N	N	Y	N
7 Linder	N	N	?	?
8 Marshall	Y	Y	Y	Y
9 Deal	N	N	Y	N
10 Broun	N	N	Y	N
11 Gingrey	N	N	Y	N
12 Barrow	Y	Y	Y	Y
13 Scott	Y	Y	Y	Y
HAWAII				
1 Abercrombie	Y	Y	?	Y
2 Hirono	Y	Y	Y	Y
IDAHO				
1 Minnick	N	N	Y	N
2 Simpson	N	N	Y	N
ILLINOIS				
1 Rush	Y	Y	?	Y
2 Jackson	Y	Y	Y	Y
3 Lipinski	Y	Y	Y	Y
4 Gutierrez	?	?	?	?
5 Quigley	Y	Y	Y	Y
6 Roskam	N	N	Y	N
7 Davis	Y	Y	?	Y
8 Bean	Y	Y	Y	Y
9 Schakowsky	Y	Y	Y	Y
10 Kirk	N	N	Y	N
11 Halvorson	Y	Y	Y	Y
12 Costello	Y	Y	Y	Y
13 Biggert	N	N	Y	N
14 Foster	Y	Y	Y	Y
15 Johnson	N	N	Y	N

KEY   Republicans   Democrats

Y Voted for (yea)	X Paired against	C Voted "present" to avoid possible conflict of interest
# Paired for	– Announced against	
+ Announced for	P Voted "present"	? Did not vote or otherwise make a position known
N Voted against (nay)		

Member	45	46	47	48
16 Manzullo	N	N	Y	N
17 Hare	Y	Y	Y	Y
18 Schock	N	N	Y	N
19 Shimkus	N	N	Y	N
INDIANA				
1 Visclosky	Y	Y	Y	Y
2 Donnelly	Y	N	Y	Y
3 Souder	N	N	Y	N
4 Buyer	N	N	Y	N
5 Burton	N	N	Y	N
6 Pence	N	N	Y	N
7 Carson	Y	Y	Y	Y
8 Ellsworth	N	N	Y	Y
9 Hill	Y	Y	Y	Y
IOWA				
1 Braley	Y	Y	Y	Y
2 Loebsack	Y	Y	Y	Y
3 Boswell	Y	Y	Y	Y
4 Latham	N	N	Y	N
5 King	N	N	N	N
KANSAS				
1 Moran	N	N	Y	N
2 Jenkins	N	N	Y	N
3 Moore	Y	Y	Y	Y
4 Tiahrt	N	N	Y	N
KENTUCKY				
1 Whitfield	N	N	Y	N
2 Guthrie	N	N	Y	N
3 Yarmuth	Y	Y	Y	Y
4 Davis	N	N	Y	N
5 Rogers	N	N	Y	N
6 Chandler	Y	Y	Y	Y
LOUISIANA				
1 Scalise	N	N	Y	N
2 Cao	N	N	Y	N
3 Melancon	Y	N	Y	Y
4 Fleming	N	N	Y	N
5 Alexander	N	N	Y	N
6 Cassidy	N	N	Y	?
7 Boustany	N	N	Y	N
MAINE				
1 Pingree	Y	Y	Y	Y
2 Michaud	Y	Y	Y	Y
MARYLAND				
1 Kratovil	N	N	Y	Y
2 Ruppersberger	Y	Y	Y	Y
3 Sarbanes	Y	Y	Y	Y
4 Edwards	Y	Y	Y	Y
5 Hoyer	Y	Y	Y	Y
6 Bartlett	N	N	Y	N
7 Cummings	Y	Y	Y	Y
8 Van Hollen	Y	Y	Y	Y
MASSACHUSETTS				
1 Olver	Y	Y	Y	Y
2 Neal	Y	Y	Y	Y
3 McGovern	Y	Y	Y	Y
4 Frank	Y	Y	Y	Y
5 Tsongas	Y	Y	Y	Y
6 Tierney	Y	Y	Y	Y
7 Markey	Y	Y	Y	Y
8 Capuano	Y	Y	Y	Y
9 Lynch	Y	Y	Y	Y
10 Delahunt	Y	Y	Y	Y
MICHIGAN				
1 Stupak	Y	Y	?	?
2 Hoekstra	N	N	Y	N
3 Ehlers	N	N	Y	?
4 Camp	N	N	Y	N
5 Kildee	Y	Y	Y	Y
6 Upton	N	N	Y	N
7 Schauer	N	N	Y	Y
8 Rogers	N	N	?	N
9 Peters	Y	N	Y	N
10 Miller	N	N	Y	N
11 McCotter	N	N	Y	N
12 Levin	Y	Y	Y	Y
13 Kilpatrick	Y	Y	Y	Y
14 Conyers	Y	Y	Y	Y
15 Dingell	Y	Y	Y	Y
MINNESOTA				
1 Walz	Y	Y	Y	Y
2 Kline	N	N	Y	N
3 Paulsen	N	N	Y	N
4 McCollum	Y	Y	Y	Y
5 Ellison	Y	Y	Y	Y
6 Bachmann	N	N	Y	N
7 Peterson	Y	Y	Y	Y
8 Oberstar	Y	Y	Y	Y
MISSISSIPPI				
1 Childers	N	N	Y	Y
2 Thompson	Y	Y	Y	Y
3 Harper	N	N	Y	N
4 Taylor	N	N	Y	N
MISSOURI				
1 Clay	Y	Y	?	?
2 Akin	N	N	Y	N
3 Carnahan	Y	Y	Y	Y
4 Skelton	Y	Y	Y	Y
5 Cleaver	Y	Y	Y	Y
6 Graves	N	N	Y	N
7 Blunt	N	N	Y	N
8 Emerson	N	N	Y	N
9 Luetkemeyer	N	N	Y	N
MONTANA				
AL Rehberg	N	N	Y	N
NEBRASKA				
1 Fortenberry	N	N	Y	N
2 Terry	N	N	Y	N
3 Smith	N	N	Y	N
NEVADA				
1 Berkley	Y	Y	Y	Y
2 Heller	N	N	Y	N
3 Titus	Y	N	Y	Y
NEW HAMPSHIRE				
1 Shea-Porter	Y	Y	Y	Y
2 Hodes	Y	N	Y	Y
NEW JERSEY				
1 Andrews	Y	Y	Y	Y
2 LoBiondo	N	N	Y	N
3 Adler	Y	N	Y	Y
4 Smith	N	N	Y	N
5 Garrett	N	N	Y	N
6 Pallone	Y	Y	Y	Y
7 Lance	N	N	Y	N
8 Pascrell	Y	Y	Y	Y
9 Rothman	Y	Y	Y	Y
10 Payne	Y	Y	Y	Y
11 Frelinghuysen	N	N	Y	N
12 Holt	Y	Y	Y	Y
13 Sires	Y	Y	Y	Y
NEW MEXICO				
1 Heinrich	Y	Y	Y	Y
2 Teague	N	N	Y	Y
3 Luján	Y	Y	Y	Y
NEW YORK				
1 Bishop	Y	Y	Y	Y
2 Israel	Y	Y	Y	Y
3 King	N	N	Y	N
4 McCarthy	Y	Y	Y	Y
5 Ackerman	Y	Y	Y	Y
6 Meeks	Y	Y	Y	?
7 Crowley	Y	Y	Y	Y
8 Nadler	Y	Y	Y	Y
9 Weiner	Y	Y	Y	N
10 Towns	Y	Y	Y	Y
11 Clarke	Y	Y	Y	Y
12 Velázquez	Y	Y	Y	Y
13 McMahon	Y	N	Y	Y
14 Maloney	Y	Y	Y	Y
15 Rangel	Y	Y	Y	Y
16 Serrano	Y	Y	Y	Y
17 Engel	Y	Y	Y	Y
18 Lowey	Y	Y	Y	Y
19 Hall	Y	Y	Y	Y
20 Murphy	Y	N	Y	Y
21 Tonko	Y	Y	Y	Y
22 Hinchey	Y	Y	Y	Y
23 Owens	Y	N	Y	Y
24 Arcuri	Y	N	Y	Y
25 Maffei	Y	N	Y	N
26 Lee	N	N	Y	N
27 Higgins	Y	Y	Y	Y
28 Slaughter	Y	Y	Y	Y
29 Massa	Y	N	Y	Y
NORTH CAROLINA				
1 Butterfield	Y	Y	Y	Y
2 Etheridge	Y	Y	Y	Y
3 Jones	N	N	Y	N
4 Price	Y	Y	Y	Y
5 Foxx	N	N	Y	N
6 Coble	N	N	Y	N
7 McIntyre	N	N	Y	N
8 Kissell	Y	N	Y	Y
9 Myrick	N	N	Y	N
10 McHenry	N	N	Y	N
11 Shuler	Y	Y	Y	Y
12 Watt	Y	Y	Y	Y
13 Miller	Y	Y	Y	Y
NORTH DAKOTA				
AL Pomeroy	Y	Y	Y	Y
OHIO				
1 Driehaus	N	N	Y	Y
2 Schmidt	N	N	Y	N
3 Turner	N	N	Y	N
4 Jordan	N	N	Y	N
5 Latta	N	N	Y	N
6 Wilson	Y	Y	Y	Y
7 Austria	N	N	Y	N
8 Boehner	N	N	?	N
9 Kaptur	Y	Y	Y	Y
10 Kucinich	N	Y	Y	Y
11 Fudge	Y	Y	Y	Y
12 Tiberi	N	N	Y	N
13 Sutton	Y	Y	Y	Y
14 LaTourette	N	N	Y	N
15 Kilroy	Y	Y	Y	Y
16 Boccieri	N	N	Y	N
17 Ryan	Y	Y	Y	Y
18 Space	Y	N	Y	Y
OKLAHOMA				
1 Sullivan	N	N	Y	N
2 Boren	Y	Y	Y	Y
3 Lucas	N	N	Y	N
4 Cole	N	N	Y	N
5 Fallin	N	N	Y	N
OREGON				
1 Wu	Y	N	Y	Y
2 Walden	N	N	Y	N
3 Blumenauer	Y	Y	Y	Y
4 DeFazio	Y	Y	Y	Y
5 Schrader	Y	Y	Y	Y
PENNSYLVANIA				
1 Brady	Y	Y	Y	Y
2 Fattah	Y	Y	Y	Y
3 Dahlkemper	N	N	Y	Y
4 Altmire	Y	N	Y	Y
5 Thompson	?	?	?	?
6 Gerlach	N	N	Y	N
7 Sestak	Y	Y	Y	Y
8 Murphy, P.	N	N	Y	Y
9 Shuster	N	N	Y	N
10 Carney	N	N	Y	Y
11 Kanjorski	Y	Y	Y	Y
12 Murtha	?	?	?	?
13 Schwartz	Y	Y	Y	Y
14 Doyle	Y	Y	Y	Y
15 Dent	N	N	Y	N
16 Pitts	N	N	Y	N
17 Holden	Y	Y	Y	Y
18 Murphy, T.	N	N	Y	N
19 Platts	N	N	Y	N
RHODE ISLAND				
1 Kennedy	Y	Y	Y	Y
2 Langevin	Y	Y	Y	Y
SOUTH CAROLINA				
1 Brown	N	N	Y	N
2 Wilson	N	N	Y	N
3 Barrett	N	N	Y	N
4 Inglis	N	N	Y	N
5 Spratt	Y	Y	Y	Y
6 Clyburn	Y	Y	Y	Y
SOUTH DAKOTA				
AL Herseth Sandlin	Y	Y	Y	Y
TENNESSEE				
1 Roe	N	N	Y	N
2 Duncan	N	N	Y	N
3 Wamp	N	N	Y	N
4 Davis	Y	Y	Y	?
5 Cooper	Y	Y	Y	Y
6 Gordon	Y	Y	Y	Y
7 Blackburn	N	N	Y	N
8 Tanner	Y	Y	Y	Y
9 Cohen	Y	Y	Y	Y
TEXAS				
1 Gohmert	N	N	N	N
2 Poe	N	N	Y	N
3 Johnson, S.	N	N	Y	N
4 Hall	N	N	Y	N
5 Hensarling	N	N	Y	N
6 Barton	N	N	Y	N
7 Culberson	N	N	?	N
8 Brady	N	N	Y	N
9 Green, A.	Y	Y	Y	Y
10 McCaul	N	N	Y	N
11 Conaway	N	N	Y	N
12 Granger	N	N	Y	N
13 Thornberry	N	N	Y	N
14 Paul	N	N	Y	N
15 Hinojosa	Y	Y	Y	Y
16 Reyes	Y	Y	Y	Y
17 Edwards	Y	Y	Y	Y
18 Jackson Lee	Y	Y	Y	Y
19 Neugebauer	N	N	Y	N
20 Gonzalez	Y	Y	Y	Y
21 Smith	N	N	Y	N
22 Olson	N	N	Y	N
23 Rodriguez	Y	Y	Y	Y
24 Marchant	N	N	Y	N
25 Doggett	Y	Y	Y	Y
26 Burgess	N	N	Y	N
27 Ortiz	Y	Y	Y	Y
28 Cuellar	Y	Y	Y	Y
29 Green, G.	Y	Y	Y	Y
30 Johnson, E.	Y	Y	Y	Y
31 Carter	N	N	Y	N
32 Sessions	N	N	Y	N
UTAH				
1 Bishop	N	N	Y	N
2 Matheson	Y	Y	Y	Y
3 Chaffetz	N	N	Y	N
VERMONT				
AL Welch	Y	Y	Y	Y
VIRGINIA				
1 Wittman	N	N	Y	N
2 Nye	N	N	Y	N
3 Scott	Y	Y	Y	Y
4 Forbes	N	N	Y	N
5 Perriello	Y	Y	Y	Y
6 Goodlatte	N	N	Y	N
7 Cantor	N	N	Y	N
8 Moran	Y	Y	Y	Y
9 Boucher	Y	Y	Y	Y
10 Wolf	N	N	Y	N
11 Connolly	Y	Y	Y	Y
WASHINGTON				
1 Inslee	Y	Y	Y	Y
2 Larsen	Y	Y	Y	Y
3 Baird	Y	Y	Y	Y
4 Hastings	N	N	Y	N
5 McMorris Rodgers	N	N	Y	N
6 Dicks	Y	Y	Y	Y
7 McDermott	Y	Y	Y	Y
8 Reichert	N	N	Y	N
9 Smith	Y	Y	Y	Y
WEST VIRGINIA				
1 Mollohan	Y	Y	Y	Y
2 Capito	N	N	Y	N
3 Rahall	Y	Y	Y	Y
WISCONSIN				
1 Ryan	N	N	Y	N
2 Baldwin	Y	Y	Y	Y
3 Kind	Y	Y	Y	Y
4 Moore	Y	Y	Y	?
5 Sensenbrenner	N	N	Y	N
6 Petri	N	N	Y	N
7 Obey	Y	Y	Y	Y
8 Kagen	Y	Y	Y	Y
WYOMING				
AL Lummis	N	N	N	N
DELEGATES				
Faleomavaega (A.S.)				
Norton (D.C.)				
Bordallo (Guam)				
Sablan (N. Marianas)				
Pierluisi (P.R.)				
Christensen (V.I.)				

IN THE HOUSE | By Vote Number

49. **HR 4425. Marty Mahar Post Office/Passage.** Lynch, D-Mass., motion to suspend the rules and pass the bill that would designate a post office in North Troy, N.Y., as the "Martin G. 'Marty' Mahar Post Office." Motion agreed to 330-0: D 193-0; R 137-0. A two-thirds majority of those present and voting (220 in this case) is required for passage under suspension of the rules. Feb. 22, 2010.

50. **HR 4238. W.D. Farr Post Office/Passage.** Lynch, D-Mass., motion to suspend the rules and pass the bill that would designate a post office in Greeley, Colo., as the "W.D. Farr Post Office Building." Motion agreed to 331-0: D 194-0; R 137-0. A two-thirds majority of those present and voting (221 in this case) is required for passage under suspension of the rules. Feb. 22, 2010.

51. **HR 2314. Native Hawaiian Sovereignty/Rule.** Adoption of the rule (H Res 1083) to provide for House floor consideration of the bill that would formally recognize Native Hawaiians as a distinct indigenous group and outline a process for establishing a Native Hawaiian governing entity. Adopted 238-165: D 235-3; R 3-162. Feb. 23, 2010.

52. **H Res 1066. Tribute to Haiti Earthquake Responders/Adoption.** Skelton, D-Mo., motion to suspend the rules and adopt the resolution that would recognize the U.S. armed forces, local first-responders and other members of Operation Unified Response for their efforts to help the Haitian people and with the evacuation of U.S. citizens affected by the earthquake in Haiti. Motion agreed to 406-0: D 240-0; R 166-0. A two-thirds majority of those present and voting (271 in this case) is required for adoption under suspension of the rules. Feb. 23, 2010.

53. **H Res 1059. Tribute to Rescue Workers in Haiti/Adoption.** McMahon, D-N.Y., motion to suspend the rules and adopt the resolution that would recognize the United States Agency for International Development and the U.S. Foreign Disaster Assistance Office-supported urban search-and-rescue teams and congratulate rescue workers for lives saved after the earthquake in Haiti. Motion agreed to 406-0: D 241-0; R 165-0. A two-thirds majority of those present and voting (271 in this case) is required for adoption under suspension of the rules. Feb. 23, 2010.

	49	50	51	52	53
ALABAMA					
1 **Bonner**	Y	Y	N	Y	Y
2 Bright	Y	Y	Y	Y	Y
3 **Rogers**	Y	Y	N	Y	Y
4 **Aderholt**	Y	Y	N	Y	Y
5 Griffith	Y	Y	N	Y	Y
6 **Bachus**	Y	Y	N	Y	Y
7 Davis	?	?	Y	Y	Y
ALASKA					
AL **Young**	?	?	Y	Y	Y
ARIZONA					
1 Kirkpatrick	Y	Y	Y	Y	Y
2 **Franks**	Y	Y	N	Y	Y
3 **Shadegg**	Y	Y	N	Y	Y
4 Pastor	Y	Y	Y	Y	Y
5 Mitchell	Y	Y	Y	Y	Y
6 **Flake**	Y	Y	N	Y	Y
7 Grijalva	?	?	?	Y	Y
8 Giffords	+	+	Y	Y	Y
ARKANSAS					
1 Berry	?	?	Y	Y	Y
2 Snyder	Y	Y	Y	Y	Y
3 **Boozman**	Y	Y	N	Y	Y
4 Ross	Y	Y	Y	Y	Y
CALIFORNIA					
1 Thompson	Y	Y	Y	Y	Y
2 **Herger**	Y	Y	N	Y	Y
3 **Lungren**	Y	Y	N	Y	Y
4 **McClintock**	Y	Y	N	Y	Y
5 Matsui	Y	Y	Y	Y	Y
6 Woolsey	Y	Y	Y	Y	Y
7 Miller, George	Y	Y	Y	Y	Y
8 Pelosi					
9 Lee	Y	Y	Y	Y	Y
10 Garamendi	Y	Y	?	?	?
11 McNerney	?	?	Y	Y	Y
12 Speier	Y	Y	?	Y	Y
13 Stark	?	?	?	?	?
14 Eshoo	Y	Y	Y	Y	Y
15 Honda	Y	Y	Y	Y	Y
16 Lofgren	Y	Y	Y	Y	Y
17 Farr	Y	Y	Y	Y	Y
18 Cardoza	Y	Y	Y	Y	Y
19 **Radanovich**	?	?	?	?	?
20 Costa	Y	Y	Y	Y	Y
21 **Nunes**	Y	Y	N	Y	Y
22 **McCarthy**	Y	Y	N	Y	Y
23 Capps	Y	Y	+	+	+
24 **Gallegly**	Y	Y	N	Y	Y
25 **McKeon**	Y	Y	N	Y	Y
26 **Dreier**	?	?	N	Y	Y
27 Sherman	?	?	Y	Y	Y
28 Berman	Y	Y	Y	Y	Y
29 Schiff	Y	Y	Y	Y	Y
30 Waxman	Y	Y	Y	Y	Y
31 Becerra	Y	Y	Y	Y	Y
32 Chu	Y	Y	Y	Y	Y
33 Watson	?	Y	Y	Y	Y
34 Roybal-Allard	Y	Y	Y	Y	Y
35 Waters	Y	Y	Y	Y	Y
36 Harman	?	?	Y	Y	Y
37 Richardson	Y	Y	Y	Y	Y
38 Napolitano	Y	Y	Y	Y	Y
39 Sánchez, Linda	Y	Y	Y	Y	Y
40 **Royce**	Y	Y	N	Y	Y
41 **Lewis**	Y	Y	N	Y	Y
42 **Miller, Gary**	Y	Y	N	Y	Y
43 Baca	Y	Y	Y	Y	Y
44 **Calvert**	?	?	N	Y	Y
45 **Bono Mack**	?	?	?	?	?
46 **Rohrabacher**	?	?	N	Y	Y
47 Sanchez, Loretta	?	?	Y	Y	Y
48 **Campbell**	?	?	N	Y	Y
49 **Issa**	Y	Y	N	Y	Y
50 **Bilbray**	Y	Y	N	Y	Y
51 Filner	?	?	Y	Y	Y
52 **Hunter**	Y	Y	N	Y	Y
53 Davis	Y	Y	?	Y	Y

	49	50	51	52	53
COLORADO					
1 DeGette	Y	Y	Y	Y	Y
2 Polis	Y	Y	Y	Y	Y
3 Salazar	?	?	Y	Y	Y
4 Markey	Y	Y	Y	Y	Y
5 **Lamborn**	Y	Y	N	Y	Y
6 **Coffman**	Y	Y	N	Y	Y
7 Perlmutter	Y	Y	Y	Y	Y
CONNECTICUT					
1 Larson	Y	Y	Y	Y	Y
2 Courtney	Y	Y	Y	Y	Y
3 DeLauro	Y	Y	Y	Y	Y
4 Himes	Y	Y	N	Y	Y
5 Murphy	Y	Y	Y	Y	Y
DELAWARE					
AL **Castle**	Y	Y	N	Y	Y
FLORIDA					
1 **Miller**	Y	Y	N	Y	Y
2 Boyd	Y	Y	Y	Y	Y
3 Brown	Y	Y	Y	Y	Y
4 **Crenshaw**	Y	Y	N	Y	Y
5 **Brown-Waite**	Y	Y	N	Y	Y
6 **Stearns**	Y	Y	N	Y	Y
7 **Mica**	Y	Y	N	Y	Y
8 Grayson	Y	Y	Y	Y	Y
9 **Bilirakis**	Y	Y	N	Y	Y
10 **Young**	Y	Y	N	Y	Y
11 Castor	Y	Y	Y	Y	Y
12 **Putnam**	Y	Y	N	Y	Y
13 **Buchanan**	Y	Y	N	Y	Y
14 **Mack**	?	?	?	?	?
15 **Posey**	Y	Y	N	Y	Y
16 **Rooney**	Y	Y	N	Y	Y
17 Meek	?	?	Y	Y	Y
18 **Ros-Lehtinen**	?	?	?	Y	Y
19 Vacant					
20 Wasserman Schultz	Y	Y	Y	Y	Y
21 **Diaz-Balart, L.**	Y	Y	N	Y	Y
22 Klein	Y	Y	Y	Y	Y
23 Hastings	Y	Y	Y	Y	Y
24 Kosmas	Y	Y	Y	Y	Y
25 **Diaz-Balart, M.**	Y	Y	N	Y	Y
GEORGIA					
1 **Kingston**	Y	Y	N	Y	Y
2 Bishop	Y	Y	Y	Y	Y
3 **Westmoreland**	?	?	Y	Y	Y
4 Johnson	Y	Y	?	Y	Y
5 Lewis	Y	Y	Y	Y	Y
6 **Price**	?	?	?	?	?
7 **Linder**	Y	Y	N	Y	Y
8 Marshall	Y	Y	Y	Y	Y
9 **Deal**	?	?	N	Y	Y
10 **Broun**	Y	Y	N	Y	Y
11 **Gingrey**	?	?	N	Y	Y
12 Barrow	+	+	Y	Y	Y
13 Scott	Y	Y	Y	Y	Y
HAWAII					
1 Abercrombie	Y	Y	Y	Y	Y
2 Hirono	Y	Y	Y	Y	Y
IDAHO					
1 Minnick	Y	Y	N	Y	Y
2 **Simpson**	Y	Y	N	Y	Y
ILLINOIS					
1 Rush	?	?	Y	Y	Y
2 Jackson	Y	Y	Y	Y	Y
3 Lipinski	?	?	Y	Y	Y
4 Gutierrez	+	+	Y	Y	Y
5 Quigley	Y	Y	Y	Y	Y
6 **Roskam**	?	Y	N	Y	Y
7 Davis	Y	Y	Y	Y	Y
8 Bean	?	?	Y	Y	Y
9 Schakowsky	Y	Y	Y	Y	Y
10 **Kirk**	?	?	N	Y	Y
11 Halvorson	Y	Y	Y	Y	Y
12 Costello	?	?	?	?	?
13 **Biggert**	+	+	N	Y	Y
14 Foster	Y	Y	Y	Y	Y
15 **Johnson**	+	+	N	Y	Y

KEY	**Republicans**	Democrats
Y	Voted for (yea)	X Paired against	C Voted "present" to avoid possible conflict of interest
#	Paired for	– Announced against	
+	Announced for	P Voted "present"	? Did not vote or otherwise make a position known
N	Voted against (nay)		

* Rep. John P. Murtha, D-Pa., died Feb. 8, 2010. The last vote for which he was eligible was vote 48.

Member	49	50	51	52	53
16 Manzullo	Y	Y	N	Y	Y
17 Hare	Y	Y	Y	Y	Y
18 Schock	Y	Y	N	Y	Y
19 Shimkus	Y	Y	N	Y	Y
INDIANA					
1 Visclosky	Y	Y	Y	Y	Y
2 Donnelly	Y	Y	Y	Y	Y
3 Souder	Y	Y	N	Y	Y
4 Buyer	Y	Y	N	Y	Y
5 Burton	Y	Y	N	Y	Y
6 Pence	Y	Y	N	Y	Y
7 Carson	Y	Y	Y	Y	Y
8 Ellsworth	Y	Y	Y	Y	Y
9 Hill	Y	Y	Y	Y	Y
IOWA					
1 Braley	?	?	Y	Y	Y
2 Loebsack	?	?	Y	Y	Y
3 Boswell	Y	Y	Y	Y	Y
4 Latham	Y	Y	Y	Y	Y
5 King	Y	Y	N	Y	Y
KANSAS					
1 Moran	?	?	?	?	?
2 Jenkins	Y	Y	N	Y	Y
3 Moore	+	+	Y	Y	?
4 Tiahrt	Y	Y	N	Y	Y
KENTUCKY					
1 Whitfield	Y	Y	Y	Y	Y
2 Guthrie	Y	Y	N	Y	Y
3 Yarmuth	Y	Y	Y	Y	Y
4 Davis	Y	Y	N	Y	Y
5 Rogers	Y	Y	N	Y	Y
6 Chandler	Y	Y	Y	Y	Y
LOUISIANA					
1 Scalise	?	?	N	Y	Y
2 Cao	Y	Y	Y	Y	Y
3 Melancon	?	?	Y	Y	Y
4 Fleming	Y	Y	N	Y	Y
5 Alexander	Y	Y	N	Y	Y
6 Cassidy	Y	Y	N	Y	Y
7 Boustany	Y	Y	N	Y	Y
MAINE					
1 Pingree	Y	Y	Y	Y	Y
2 Michaud	Y	Y	Y	Y	Y
MARYLAND					
1 Kratovil	Y	Y	Y	Y	Y
2 Ruppersberger	Y	Y	Y	Y	Y
3 Sarbanes	Y	Y	Y	Y	Y
4 Edwards	Y	Y	Y	Y	Y
5 Hoyer	Y	Y	Y	Y	Y
6 Bartlett	Y	Y	N	Y	Y
7 Cummings	Y	Y	Y	Y	Y
8 Van Hollen	Y	Y	Y	Y	Y
MASSACHUSETTS					
1 Olver	Y	Y	Y	Y	Y
2 Neal	?	?	Y	Y	Y
3 McGovern	Y	?	Y	Y	Y
4 Frank	Y	Y	Y	Y	Y
5 Tsongas	Y	Y	Y	Y	Y
6 Tierney	Y	Y	Y	Y	Y
7 Markey	Y	Y	Y	Y	Y
8 Capuano	Y	Y	Y	Y	Y
9 Lynch	Y	Y	Y	Y	Y
10 Delahunt	?	?	Y	Y	Y
MICHIGAN					
1 Stupak	Y	Y	Y	Y	Y
2 Hoekstra	?	?	?	?	?
3 Ehlers	?	?	N	Y	Y
4 Camp	?	?	N	Y	Y
5 Kildee	Y	Y	Y	Y	Y
6 Upton	Y	Y	N	Y	Y
7 Schauer	Y	Y	Y	Y	Y
8 Rogers	Y	Y	N	Y	Y
9 Peters	Y	Y	Y	Y	Y
10 Miller	?	?	N	Y	Y
11 McCotter	Y	Y	Y	Y	Y
12 Levin	Y	Y	Y	Y	Y
13 Kilpatrick	?	?	Y	Y	Y
14 Conyers	?	?	Y	Y	Y
15 Dingell	Y	Y	Y	Y	Y
MINNESOTA					
1 Walz	Y	Y	Y	Y	Y
2 Kline	Y	Y	N	Y	Y
3 Paulsen	Y	Y	N	Y	Y
4 McCollum	?	?	Y	Y	Y
5 Ellison	Y	Y	Y	Y	Y
6 Bachmann	Y	Y	N	Y	Y
7 Peterson	Y	Y	Y	Y	Y
8 Oberstar	Y	Y	Y	Y	Y
MISSISSIPPI					
1 Childers	?	?	Y	Y	Y
2 Thompson	?	?	Y	Y	Y
3 Harper	Y	Y	N	Y	Y
4 Taylor	Y	Y	Y	Y	Y
MISSOURI					
1 Clay	Y	Y	Y	Y	Y
2 Akin	Y	Y	N	Y	Y
3 Carnahan	?	?	?	?	?
4 Skelton	Y	Y	Y	Y	Y
5 Cleaver	?	?	Y	Y	Y
6 Graves	?	?	N	Y	Y
7 Blunt	Y	Y	?	?	?
8 Emerson	Y	Y	N	Y	Y
9 Luetkemeyer	Y	Y	N	Y	Y
MONTANA					
AL Rehberg	Y	Y	N	Y	Y
NEBRASKA					
1 Fortenberry	?	?	N	Y	Y
2 Terry	Y	Y	N	Y	Y
3 Smith	Y	Y	N	Y	Y
NEVADA					
1 Berkley	Y	Y	Y	Y	Y
2 Heller	Y	Y	N	Y	Y
3 Titus	?	?	Y	Y	Y
NEW HAMPSHIRE					
1 Shea-Porter	Y	Y	Y	Y	Y
2 Hodes	?	?	?	?	?
NEW JERSEY					
1 Andrews	Y	Y	?	?	?
2 LoBiondo	Y	Y	N	Y	Y
3 Adler	Y	Y	Y	Y	Y
4 Smith	Y	Y	N	Y	Y
5 Garrett	Y	Y	N	Y	Y
6 Pallone	Y	Y	Y	Y	Y
7 Lance	Y	Y	Y	Y	Y
8 Pascrell	+	+	Y	Y	Y
9 Rothman	Y	Y	Y	Y	Y
10 Payne	Y	Y	?	?	?
11 Frelinghuysen	Y	Y	N	Y	Y
12 Holt	Y	Y	Y	Y	Y
13 Sires	?	?	?	?	?
NEW MEXICO					
1 Heinrich	Y	Y	Y	Y	Y
2 Teague	?	?	Y	Y	Y
3 Luján	Y	Y	Y	Y	Y
NEW YORK					
1 Bishop	Y	Y	Y	Y	Y
2 Israel	Y	Y	Y	Y	Y
3 King	Y	Y	N	Y	Y
4 McCarthy	Y	Y	Y	Y	Y
5 Ackerman	?	?	Y	Y	Y
6 Meeks	Y	Y	Y	Y	Y
7 Crowley	Y	Y	Y	Y	Y
8 Nadler	Y	Y	Y	Y	Y
9 Weiner	Y	Y	Y	Y	Y
10 Towns	Y	Y	Y	Y	Y
11 Clarke	Y	Y	Y	Y	Y
12 Velázquez	?	?	Y	Y	Y
13 McMahon	Y	Y	Y	Y	Y
14 Maloney	Y	Y	Y	Y	Y
15 Rangel	Y	Y	Y	Y	Y
16 Serrano	Y	Y	Y	Y	Y
17 Engel	?	?	Y	Y	Y
18 Lowey	Y	Y	Y	Y	Y
19 Hall	Y	Y	Y	Y	Y
20 Murphy	Y	Y	Y	Y	Y
21 Tonko	Y	Y	Y	Y	Y
22 Hinchey	Y	Y	Y	Y	Y
23 Owens	Y	Y	Y	?	Y
24 Arcuri	Y	Y	Y	Y	Y
25 Maffei	?	?	Y	Y	Y
26 Lee	Y	Y	N	Y	Y
27 Higgins	?	?	Y	Y	Y
28 Slaughter	Y	Y	Y	Y	Y
29 Massa	Y	Y	Y	Y	Y
NORTH CAROLINA					
1 Butterfield	Y	Y	Y	Y	Y
2 Etheridge	+	+	Y	Y	Y
3 Jones	Y	Y	N	Y	Y
4 Price	Y	Y	Y	Y	Y
5 Foxx	Y	Y	N	Y	Y
6 Coble	Y	Y	N	Y	Y
7 McIntyre	?	?	Y	Y	Y
8 Kissell	?	?	Y	Y	Y
9 Myrick	Y	Y	N	Y	Y
10 McHenry	Y	Y	N	Y	Y
11 Shuler	Y	Y	N	Y	Y
12 Watt	Y	Y	Y	Y	Y
13 Miller	?	?	Y	Y	Y
NORTH DAKOTA					
AL Pomeroy	?	?	Y	Y	Y
OHIO					
1 Driehaus	Y	Y	Y	Y	Y
2 Schmidt	Y	Y	N	Y	Y
3 Turner	Y	Y	N	Y	Y
4 Jordan	+	+	N	Y	Y
5 Latta	Y	Y	N	Y	Y
6 Wilson	?	?	?	?	?
7 Austria	?	?	N	Y	Y
8 Boehner	Y	Y	N	Y	Y
9 Kaptur	?	?	Y	Y	Y
10 Kucinich	Y	Y	Y	Y	Y
11 Fudge	Y	Y	Y	Y	Y
12 Tiberi	Y	Y	N	Y	Y
13 Sutton	Y	Y	Y	Y	Y
14 LaTourette	Y	Y	N	Y	Y
15 Kilroy	Y	Y	Y	Y	Y
16 Boccieri	?	?	Y	Y	Y
17 Ryan	?	?	?	?	?
18 Space	Y	Y	Y	Y	Y
OKLAHOMA					
1 Sullivan	Y	?	N	Y	Y
2 Boren	?	?	Y	Y	Y
3 Lucas	Y	Y	N	Y	Y
4 Cole	Y	Y	N	Y	Y
5 Fallin	?	?	N	Y	Y
OREGON					
1 Wu	Y	Y	Y	Y	Y
2 Walden	Y	Y	N	Y	Y
3 Blumenauer	Y	Y	Y	Y	Y
4 DeFazio	?	?	Y	Y	Y
5 Schrader	?	?	Y	Y	Y
PENNSYLVANIA					
1 Brady	Y	Y	Y	Y	Y
2 Fattah	Y	Y	Y	Y	Y
3 Dahlkemper	Y	Y	Y	Y	Y
4 Altmire	Y	Y	Y	Y	Y
5 Thompson	Y	Y	N	Y	Y
6 Gerlach	Y	Y	N	Y	Y
7 Sestak	Y	Y	Y	Y	Y
8 Murphy, P.	?	?	Y	Y	Y
9 Shuster	Y	?	N	Y	Y
10 Carney	Y	Y	Y	Y	Y
11 Kanjorski	Y	Y	Y	Y	Y
12 Vacant*					
13 Schwartz	Y	Y	Y	Y	Y
14 Doyle	Y	Y	Y	Y	Y
15 Dent	+	+	N	Y	Y
16 Pitts	Y	Y	N	Y	Y
17 Holden	Y	Y	Y	Y	Y
18 Murphy, T.	Y	Y	N	Y	Y
19 Platts	?	?	N	Y	Y
RHODE ISLAND					
1 Kennedy	Y	Y	Y	Y	Y
2 Langevin	Y	Y	Y	Y	Y
SOUTH CAROLINA					
1 Brown	Y	Y	N	Y	Y
2 Wilson	Y	Y	N	Y	Y
3 Barrett	?	?	?	?	?
4 Inglis	?	?	N	Y	Y
5 Spratt	Y	Y	Y	Y	Y
6 Clyburn	Y	Y	Y	Y	Y
SOUTH DAKOTA					
AL Herseth Sandlin	Y	Y	Y	Y	Y
TENNESSEE					
1 Roe	Y	Y	N	Y	Y
2 Duncan	Y	Y	N	Y	Y
3 Wamp	?	?	?	?	?
4 Davis	Y	Y	Y	Y	Y
5 Cooper	Y	Y	Y	Y	Y
6 Gordon	Y	Y	Y	Y	Y
7 Blackburn	?	Y	N	Y	Y
8 Tanner	Y	Y	Y	Y	Y
9 Cohen	Y	Y	Y	Y	Y
TEXAS					
1 Gohmert	Y	Y	N	Y	Y
2 Poe	+	+	N	Y	Y
3 Johnson, S.	Y	Y	N	Y	Y
4 Hall	Y	Y	N	Y	Y
5 Hensarling	Y	Y	N	Y	Y
6 Barton	?	?	N	Y	Y
7 Culberson	?	?	?	?	?
8 Brady	Y	Y	N	Y	Y
9 Green, A.	Y	Y	Y	Y	Y
10 McCaul	Y	Y	N	Y	Y
11 Conaway	Y	Y	N	Y	Y
12 Granger	Y	Y	N	Y	Y
13 Thornberry	Y	Y	N	Y	Y
14 Paul	Y	Y	N	?	Y
15 Hinojosa	Y	Y	?	?	?
16 Reyes	Y	Y	Y	Y	Y
17 Edwards	Y	Y	Y	Y	Y
18 Jackson Lee	Y	Y	Y	Y	Y
19 Neugebauer	+	+	N	Y	Y
20 Gonzalez	Y	Y	Y	Y	Y
21 Smith	Y	Y	N	Y	Y
22 Olson	Y	Y	N	Y	Y
23 Rodriguez	Y	Y	Y	Y	Y
24 Marchant	Y	Y	N	Y	Y
25 Doggett	Y	Y	Y	Y	Y
26 Burgess	Y	Y	N	Y	Y
27 Ortiz	Y	Y	Y	Y	Y
28 Cuellar	+	+	Y	Y	Y
29 Green, G.	Y	Y	Y	Y	Y
30 Johnson, E.	Y	Y	Y	Y	Y
31 Carter	Y	Y	N	Y	Y
32 Sessions	?	?	N	Y	Y
UTAH					
1 Bishop	Y	Y	N	Y	Y
2 Matheson	Y	Y	N	Y	Y
3 Chaffetz	Y	Y	N	Y	?
VERMONT					
AL Welch	Y	Y	Y	Y	Y
VIRGINIA					
1 Wittman	Y	Y	N	Y	Y
2 Nye	Y	Y	N	Y	Y
3 Scott	Y	Y	Y	Y	Y
4 Forbes	Y	Y	N	Y	Y
5 Perriello	Y	Y	Y	Y	Y
6 Goodlatte	Y	Y	N	Y	Y
7 Cantor	Y	Y	?	Y	Y
8 Moran	?	?	Y	Y	Y
9 Boucher	?	?	Y	Y	Y
10 Wolf	Y	Y	N	Y	Y
11 Connolly	Y	Y	Y	Y	Y
WASHINGTON					
1 Inslee	Y	Y	Y	Y	Y
2 Larsen	?	?	Y	Y	Y
3 Baird	Y	Y	Y	Y	Y
4 Hastings	?	?	N	Y	Y
5 McMorris Rodgers	Y	Y	N	Y	Y
6 Dicks	Y	Y	Y	Y	Y
7 McDermott	Y	Y	Y	Y	Y
8 Reichert	?	?	?	?	?
9 Smith	+	+	Y	Y	Y
WEST VIRGINIA					
1 Mollohan	Y	Y	Y	Y	Y
2 Capito	Y	Y	N	Y	Y
3 Rahall	Y	Y	Y	Y	Y
WISCONSIN					
1 Ryan	Y	Y	N	Y	Y
2 Baldwin	Y	Y	Y	Y	Y
3 Kind	Y	Y	Y	Y	Y
4 Moore	?	?	?	Y	Y
5 Sensenbrenner	Y	Y	N	Y	Y
6 Petri	Y	Y	N	Y	Y
7 Obey	Y	Y	Y	Y	Y
8 Kagen	Y	Y	Y	Y	Y
WYOMING					
AL Lummis	Y	Y	N	Y	Y
DELEGATES					
Faleomavaega (A.S.)					
Norton (D.C.)					
Bordallo (Guam)					
Sablan (N. Marianas)					
Pierluisi (P.R.)					
Christensen (V.I.)					

IN THE HOUSE | By Vote Number

54. **H Res 1039. American Heart Month/Adoption.** Lynch, D-Mass., motion to suspend the rules and adopt the resolution that would support the goals of American Heart Month and National Wear Red Day. Motion agreed to 408-0: D 242-0; R 166-0. A two-thirds majority of those present and voting (272 in this case) is required for adoption under suspension of the rules. Feb. 23, 2010.

55. **H Res 1046. Black History Month/Adoption.** Lynch, D-Mass., motion to suspend the rules and adopt the resolution that would recognize the significance of Black History Month and the contributions of African-Americans in American history. Motion agreed to 402-0: D 237-0; R 165-0. A two-thirds majority of those present and voting (268 in this case) is required for adoption under suspension of the rules. Feb. 23, 2010.

56. **HR 2314. Native Hawaiian Sovereignty/Hawaii Voter Approval.** Hastings, R-Wash., amendment to the Abercrombie, D-Hawaii, substitute amendment. The Hastings amendment would require Hawaii voters to approve native Hawaiian governing entity documents before federal recognition is given. The substitute would formally recognize native Hawaiians as a distinct indigenous group and outline a process for establishing a native Hawaiian governing entity. Rejected 163-241: D 1-236; R 162-5. Feb. 23, 2010.

57. **HR 2314. Native Hawaiian Sovereignty/Equal Protection Clause.** Flake, R-Ariz., amendment to the Abercrombie, D-Hawaii, substitute amendment. The Flake amendment would clarify that nothing in the bill could be interpreted to exempt a new native Hawaiian governing authority from complying with the Equal Protection Clause of the 14th Amendment of the U.S. Constitution. Rejected 177-233: D 18-225; R 159-8. Feb. 23, 2010.

58. **HR 2314. Native Hawaiian Sovereignty/Substitute.** Abercrombie, D-Hawaii, substitute amendment that would formally recognize native Hawaiians as a distinct indigenous group and outline a process for establishing a native Hawaiian governing entity. It would clarify that the United States would not take land into trust. It would also clarify that the government entity would not receive U.S. government land transfers, would not be immune to state or federal lawsuits and would not pre-empt federal or state jurisdiction over individual native Hawaiians or their property. Adopted 245-164: D 239-4; R 6-160. Feb. 23, 2010.

	54	55	56	57	58
ALABAMA					
1 Bonner	Y	Y	Y	Y	N
2 Bright	Y	Y	Y	Y	N
3 Rogers	Y	Y	Y	Y	N
4 Aderholt	Y	Y	Y	Y	N
5 Griffith	Y	Y	Y	Y	N
6 Bachus	Y	Y	Y	Y	N
7 Davis	Y	Y	N	N	Y
ALASKA					
AL Young	Y	Y	N	N	Y
ARIZONA					
1 Kirkpatrick	Y	Y	N	N	Y
2 Franks	Y	Y	Y	Y	N
3 Shadegg	Y	Y	Y	Y	N
4 Pastor	Y	Y	N	N	Y
5 Mitchell	Y	Y	N	N	Y
6 Flake	Y	Y	Y	Y	N
7 Grijalva	Y	Y	N	N	Y
8 Giffords	Y	Y	N	Y	Y
ARKANSAS					
1 Berry	Y	Y	N	N	Y
2 Snyder	Y	Y	N	N	Y
3 Boozman	Y	Y	Y	Y	N
4 Ross	Y	Y	N	N	Y
CALIFORNIA					
1 Thompson	Y	Y	N	N	Y
2 Herger	Y	Y	Y	Y	N
3 Lungren	Y	Y	Y	Y	N
4 McClintock	Y	Y	Y	Y	N
5 Matsui	Y	Y	N	N	Y
6 Woolsey	Y	Y	N	N	Y
7 Miller, George	Y	?	N	N	Y
8 Pelosi					
9 Lee	Y	Y	N	N	Y
10 Garamendi	?	Y	N	N	Y
11 McNerney	Y	Y	N	N	Y
12 Speier	Y	Y	N	N	Y
13 Stark	?	?	?	?	?
14 Eshoo	Y	Y	N	N	Y
15 Honda	Y	Y	N	N	Y
16 Lofgren	Y	Y	N	N	Y
17 Farr	Y	Y	N	N	Y
18 Cardoza	Y	Y	N	N	Y
19 Radanovich	?	?	?	?	?
20 Costa	Y	Y	N	N	Y
21 Nunes	Y	Y	Y	Y	N
22 McCarthy	Y	Y	Y	Y	N
23 Capps	+	+	N	N	Y
24 Gallegly	Y	Y	Y	Y	N
25 McKeon	Y	Y	Y	Y	N
26 Dreier	Y	Y	Y	Y	N
27 Sherman	Y	Y	N	N	Y
28 Berman	Y	Y	?	?	?
29 Schiff	Y	Y	N	N	Y
30 Waxman	Y	?	N	N	Y
31 Becerra	Y	Y	N	N	Y
32 Chu	Y	Y	N	N	Y
33 Watson	Y	Y	N	N	Y
34 Roybal-Allard	Y	Y	N	N	Y
35 Waters	Y	Y	N	N	Y
36 Harman	Y	Y	N	N	Y
37 Richardson	Y	Y	?	N	Y
38 Napolitano	Y	Y	N	N	Y
39 Sánchez, Linda	Y	Y	N	N	Y
40 Royce	Y	Y	Y	Y	N
41 Lewis	Y	Y	Y	Y	N
42 Miller, Gary	Y	Y	Y	Y	N
43 Baca	Y	Y	N	N	Y
44 Calvert	Y	Y	Y	Y	N
45 Bono Mack	?	?	?	?	?
46 Rohrabacher	Y	Y	Y	Y	N
47 Sanchez, Loretta	Y	Y	N	N	Y
48 Campbell	Y	Y	Y	Y	N
49 Issa	Y	Y	Y	Y	N
50 Bilbray	Y	Y	Y	Y	N
51 Filner	Y	Y	N	N	Y
52 Hunter	Y	Y	Y	Y	N
53 Davis	Y	Y	N	N	Y

	54	55	56	57	58
COLORADO					
1 DeGette	Y	Y	N	N	Y
2 Polis	Y	Y	N	Y	Y
3 Salazar	Y	Y	N	N	Y
4 Markey	Y	Y	?	N	Y
5 Lamborn	Y	Y	Y	Y	N
6 Coffman	Y	Y	Y	Y	N
7 Perlmutter	Y	Y	?	Y	Y
CONNECTICUT					
1 Larson	Y	Y	N	N	Y
2 Courtney	Y	Y	N	N	Y
3 DeLauro	Y	Y	N	N	Y
4 Himes	Y	Y	N	N	Y
5 Murphy	Y	Y	N	N	Y
DELAWARE					
AL Castle	Y	Y	N	N	N
FLORIDA					
1 Miller	Y	Y	Y	Y	N
2 Boyd	Y	Y	N	N	Y
3 Brown	Y	Y	N	N	Y
4 Crenshaw	Y	Y	Y	Y	N
5 Brown-Waite	Y	Y	Y	Y	N
6 Stearns	Y	Y	Y	Y	N
7 Mica	Y	Y	Y	Y	N
8 Grayson	Y	Y	N	N	Y
9 Bilirakis	Y	Y	Y	Y	N
10 Young	Y	Y	Y	Y	N
11 Castor	Y	Y	N	N	Y
12 Putnam	Y	Y	Y	Y	N
13 Buchanan	Y	Y	Y	Y	N
14 Mack	?	?	?	?	?
15 Posey	Y	Y	Y	Y	N
16 Rooney	Y	Y	Y	Y	N
17 Meek	Y	?	N	N	Y
18 Ros-Lehtinen	Y	?	?	?	Y
19 Vacant					
20 Wasserman Schultz	Y	Y	N	N	?
21 Diaz-Balart, L.	Y	Y	Y	Y	N
22 Klein	Y	Y	N	N	Y
23 Hastings	Y	Y	N	N	Y
24 Kosmas	Y	Y	N	Y	Y
25 Diaz-Balart, M.	Y	Y	Y	Y	N
GEORGIA					
1 Kingston	Y	Y	Y	Y	N
2 Bishop	Y	Y	N	N	Y
3 Westmoreland	Y	Y	Y	Y	N
4 Johnson	Y	Y	?	N	Y
5 Lewis	Y	Y	N	N	Y
6 Price	?	?	Y	Y	N
7 Linder	Y	?	Y	Y	N
8 Marshall	Y	Y	N	N	Y
9 Deal	Y	Y	Y	Y	N
10 Broun	Y	Y	Y	Y	N
11 Gingrey	Y	Y	Y	Y	N
12 Barrow	Y	Y	N	N	Y
13 Scott	Y	Y	N	N	Y
HAWAII					
1 Abercrombie	Y	Y	N	N	Y
2 Hirono	Y	Y	N	N	Y
IDAHO					
1 Minnick	Y	?	N	Y	Y
2 Simpson	Y	Y	Y	Y	N
ILLINOIS					
1 Rush	Y	Y	N	N	Y
2 Jackson	Y	Y	N	N	Y
3 Lipinski	Y	Y	N	N	Y
4 Gutierrez	Y	Y	N	N	Y
5 Quigley	Y	Y	N	N	Y
6 Roskam	Y	Y	Y	Y	N
7 Davis	Y	Y	N	N	Y
8 Bean	Y	Y	N	N	Y
9 Schakowsky	Y	Y	N	N	Y
10 Kirk	Y	Y	Y	Y	N
11 Halvorson	Y	Y	N	Y	Y
12 Costello	?	?	?	?	?
13 Biggert	Y	Y	Y	Y	N
14 Foster	Y	Y	N	Y	Y
15 Johnson	Y	Y	Y	Y	N

KEY	**Republicans**	Democrats		
Y Voted for (yea)		X Paired against		C Voted "present" to avoid possible conflict of interest
# Paired for		– Announced against		
+ Announced for		P Voted "present"		? Did not vote or otherwise make a position known
N Voted against (nay)				

	54	55	56	57	58
16 Manzullo	Y	Y	Y	Y	N
17 Hare	Y	Y	N	N	Y
18 Schock	Y	Y	Y	Y	N
19 Shimkus	Y	Y	Y	Y	N
INDIANA					
1 Visclosky	Y	Y	N	N	Y
2 Donnelly	Y	Y	N	N	Y
3 Souder	Y	Y	Y	Y	N
4 Buyer	Y	Y	Y	Y	N
5 Burton	Y	Y	Y	Y	N
6 Pence	Y	Y	Y	Y	N
7 Carson	Y	Y	N	N	Y
8 Ellsworth	Y	Y	N	N	Y
9 Hill	Y	Y	N	N	Y
IOWA					
1 Braley	Y	Y	N	N	Y
2 Loebsack	Y	Y	N	N	Y
3 Boswell	Y	Y	N	N	Y
4 Latham	Y	Y	Y	Y	N
5 King	Y	Y	Y	Y	N
KANSAS					
1 Moran	?	?	Y	Y	?
2 Jenkins	Y	Y	Y	Y	N
3 Moore	Y	Y	N	N	Y
4 Tiahrt	Y	?	Y	Y	N
KENTUCKY					
1 Whitfield	Y	Y	Y	Y	Y
2 Guthrie	Y	Y	Y	Y	N
3 Yarmuth	Y	Y	N	N	Y
4 Davis	Y	Y	Y	Y	N
5 Rogers	Y	Y	Y	Y	N
6 Chandler	Y	Y	N	N	Y
LOUISIANA					
1 Scalise	Y	Y	Y	Y	N
2 Cao	Y	Y	N	N	Y
3 Melancon	Y	Y	N	N	Y
4 Fleming	Y	Y	Y	Y	N
5 Alexander	Y	Y	Y	Y	N
6 Cassidy	Y	Y	Y	Y	N
7 Boustany	Y	Y	Y	Y	N
MAINE					
1 Pingree	Y	Y	N	N	Y
2 Michaud	Y	Y	N	N	Y
MARYLAND					
1 Kratovil	Y	Y	N	Y	Y
2 Ruppersberger	Y	Y	N	N	Y
3 Sarbanes	Y	Y	N	N	Y
4 Edwards	Y	Y	N	N	Y
5 Hoyer	Y	Y	N	N	Y
6 Bartlett	Y	Y	Y	Y	N
7 Cummings	Y	Y	N	N	Y
8 Van Hollen	Y	Y	N	N	Y
MASSACHUSETTS					
1 Olver	Y	Y	N	N	Y
2 Neal	Y	Y	N	N	Y
3 McGovern	Y	Y	N	N	Y
4 Frank	Y	Y	N	N	Y
5 Tsongas	Y	Y	N	N	Y
6 Tierney	Y	Y	N	N	Y
7 Markey	Y	Y	N	N	Y
8 Capuano	Y	Y	N	N	Y
9 Lynch	Y	Y	N	N	Y
10 Delahunt	Y	Y	?	?	?
MICHIGAN					
1 Stupak	Y	Y	N	N	Y
2 Hoekstra	?	?	?	?	?
3 Ehlers	Y	Y	Y	Y	Y
4 Camp	Y	Y	Y	Y	N
5 Kildee	Y	Y	N	N	Y
6 Upton	Y	Y	Y	Y	N
7 Schauer	Y	Y	N	N	Y
8 Rogers	Y	Y	N	N	Y
9 Peters	Y	Y	N	N	Y
10 Miller	Y	Y	Y	Y	N
11 McCotter	Y	Y	N	N	Y
12 Levin	Y	Y	N	N	Y
13 Kilpatrick	Y	Y	N	N	Y
14 Conyers	Y	Y	N	N	Y
15 Dingell	Y	Y	?	?	?
MINNESOTA					
1 Walz	Y	Y	N	N	Y
2 Kline	Y	Y	Y	Y	N
3 Paulsen	Y	Y	Y	Y	N
4 McCollum	Y	Y	N	N	Y

	54	55	56	57	58
5 Ellison	Y	Y	N	Y	Y
6 Bachmann	Y	Y	Y	Y	N
7 Peterson	Y	Y	N	N	Y
8 Oberstar	Y	Y	N	N	Y
MISSISSIPPI					
1 Childers	Y	Y	N	N	Y
2 Thompson	Y	Y	N	N	Y
3 Harper	Y	Y	Y	Y	N
4 Taylor	Y	Y	N	Y	Y
MISSOURI					
1 Clay	Y	Y	N	N	Y
2 Akin	Y	Y	Y	Y	N
3 Carnahan	?	?	N	N	Y
4 Skelton	Y	Y	N	N	Y
5 Cleaver	Y	Y	N	N	Y
6 Graves	Y	Y	Y	Y	N
7 Blunt	?	?	?	?	?
8 Emerson	Y	Y	Y	Y	N
9 Luetkemeyer	Y	Y	Y	Y	N
MONTANA					
AL Rehberg	Y	Y	Y	Y	N
NEBRASKA					
1 Fortenberry	Y	Y	Y	Y	N
2 Terry	Y	Y	Y	Y	N
3 Smith	Y	Y	Y	Y	N
NEVADA					
1 Berkley	Y	Y	N	N	Y
2 Heller	Y	Y	Y	Y	N
3 Titus	Y	Y	N	N	Y
NEW HAMPSHIRE					
1 Shea-Porter	Y	Y	N	?	Y
2 Hodes	?	?	N	N	Y
NEW JERSEY					
1 Andrews	?	?	?	?	?
2 LoBiondo	Y	Y	Y	Y	N
3 Adler	Y	Y	N	Y	Y
4 Smith	Y	Y	N	Y	Y
5 Garrett	Y	Y	Y	Y	N
6 Pallone	Y	Y	N	N	Y
7 Lance	Y	Y	Y	Y	N
8 Pascrell	Y	Y	N	N	Y
9 Rothman	Y	Y	N	N	Y
10 Payne	?	?	?	?	?
11 Frelinghuysen	Y	Y	Y	Y	N
12 Holt	Y	Y	N	N	Y
13 Sires	?	?	?	?	?
NEW MEXICO					
1 Heinrich	Y	Y	N	N	Y
2 Teague	Y	Y	N	N	Y
3 Luján	Y	Y	N	N	Y
NEW YORK					
1 Bishop	Y	Y	N	N	Y
2 Israel	Y	Y	N	N	Y
3 King	Y	Y	Y	Y	N
4 McCarthy	Y	Y	N	N	Y
5 Ackerman	Y	Y	N	N	Y
6 Meeks	Y	Y	N	N	Y
7 Crowley	Y	Y	N	N	Y
8 Nadler	Y	+	N	N	Y
9 Weiner	Y	Y	N	N	Y
10 Towns	Y	Y	N	N	Y
11 Clarke	Y	Y	N	N	Y
12 Velázquez	Y	Y	N	N	Y
13 McMahon	Y	Y	?	Y	N
14 Maloney	Y	Y	N	N	Y
15 Rangel	Y	Y	N	N	Y
16 Serrano	Y	Y	N	N	Y
17 Engel	Y	Y	N	N	Y
18 Lowey	Y	Y	?	N	Y
19 Hall	Y	Y	N	N	Y
20 Murphy	Y	Y	N	N	Y
21 Tonko	Y	Y	N	N	Y
22 Hinchey	Y	Y	N	N	Y
23 Owens	Y	Y	N	N	Y
24 Arcuri	Y	Y	N	Y	Y
25 Maffei	Y	Y	N	N	Y
26 Lee	Y	Y	Y	Y	N
27 Higgins	Y	Y	N	N	Y
28 Slaughter	Y	Y	N	N	Y
29 Massa	Y	Y	N	N	Y
NORTH CAROLINA					
1 Butterfield	Y	Y	N	N	Y
2 Etheridge	Y	Y	N	N	Y
3 Jones	Y	Y	N	N	N
4 Price	Y	Y	N	N	Y

	54	55	56	57	58
5 Foxx	Y	Y	Y	Y	N
6 Coble	Y	Y	Y	Y	N
7 McIntyre	Y	Y	N	N	Y
8 Kissell	Y	Y	N	N	Y
9 Myrick	Y	Y	Y	Y	N
10 McHenry	Y	Y	Y	Y	N
12 Shuler	Y	Y	N	N	Y
13 Watt	Y	Y	N	N	Y
14 Miller	Y	Y	N	N	Y
NORTH DAKOTA					
AL Pomeroy	Y	Y	N	N	Y
OHIO					
1 Driehaus	Y	Y	N	N	Y
2 Schmidt	Y	Y	Y	Y	N
3 Turner	Y	Y	?	?	?
4 Jordan	Y	Y	Y	Y	N
5 Latta	Y	Y	Y	Y	N
6 Wilson	?	?	N	N	Y
7 Austria	Y	Y	Y	Y	N
8 Boehner	Y	Y	Y	Y	N
9 Kaptur	Y	Y	N	N	Y
10 Kucinich	Y	Y	N	N	Y
11 Fudge	Y	Y	N	N	Y
12 Tiberi	Y	Y	Y	Y	N
13 Sutton	Y	Y	N	N	Y
14 LaTourette	Y	Y	Y	Y	N
15 Kilroy	Y	Y	N	N	Y
16 Boccieri	Y	Y	N	N	Y
17 Ryan	?	?	N	N	Y
18 Space	Y	?	N	N	Y
OKLAHOMA					
1 Sullivan	Y	Y	Y	Y	N
2 Boren	Y	Y	N	N	Y
3 Lucas	Y	Y	Y	Y	N
4 Cole	Y	Y	N	N	Y
5 Fallin	Y	Y	Y	Y	N
OREGON					
1 Wu	Y	Y	N	Y	Y
2 Walden	Y	Y	Y	Y	N
3 Blumenauer	Y	Y	N	N	Y
4 DeFazio	Y	Y	N	N	Y
5 Schrader	Y	Y	N	N	Y
PENNSYLVANIA					
1 Brady	Y	Y	N	N	Y
2 Fattah	Y	Y	N	N	Y
3 Dahlkemper	Y	Y	N	N	Y
4 Altmire	Y	Y	N	N	Y
5 Thompson	Y	Y	Y	Y	N
6 Gerlach	Y	Y	Y	Y	N
7 Sestak	Y	Y	N	N	Y
8 Murphy, P.	Y	Y	N	N	Y
9 Shuster	Y	Y	Y	Y	N
10 Carney	Y	Y	N	N	Y
11 Kanjorski	Y	Y	N	N	Y
12 Vacant					
13 Schwartz	Y	Y	N	N	Y
14 Doyle	Y	Y	N	N	Y
15 Dent	Y	Y	Y	Y	N
16 Pitts	Y	Y	Y	Y	N
17 Holden	Y	Y	N	N	Y
18 Murphy, T.	Y	Y	N	Y	N
19 Platts	Y	Y	Y	Y	N
RHODE ISLAND					
1 Kennedy	Y	Y	N	N	Y
2 Langevin	Y	Y	N	N	Y
SOUTH CAROLINA					
1 Brown	Y	Y	Y	Y	N
2 Wilson	Y	Y	Y	Y	N
3 Barrett	?	?	?	?	?
4 Inglis	Y	Y	Y	Y	N
5 Spratt	Y	Y	N	N	Y
6 Clyburn	Y	Y	N	N	Y
SOUTH DAKOTA					
AL Herseth Sandlin	Y	Y	N	N	Y
TENNESSEE					
1 Roe	Y	Y	Y	Y	N
2 Duncan	Y	Y	Y	Y	N
3 Wamp	?	?	?	?	?
4 Davis	Y	Y	N	N	Y
5 Cooper	Y	Y	N	N	Y
6 Gordon	Y	Y	?	?	?
7 Blackburn	Y	Y	Y	Y	N
8 Tanner	Y	Y	N	N	Y
9 Cohen	Y	Y	N	N	Y

	54	55	56	57	58
TEXAS					
1 Gohmert	Y	Y	Y	Y	N
2 Poe	Y	Y	Y	Y	N
3 Johnson, S.	Y	Y	Y	Y	N
4 Hall	Y	Y	Y	Y	N
5 Hensarling	Y	Y	Y	Y	N
6 Barton	Y	Y	Y	Y	N
7 Culberson	?	?	?	?	?
8 Brady	Y	Y	Y	Y	N
9 Green, A.	Y	Y	N	N	Y
10 McCaul	Y	Y	Y	Y	N
11 Conaway	Y	Y	Y	Y	N
12 Granger	Y	Y	Y	Y	N
13 Thornberry	Y	Y	Y	Y	N
14 Paul	?	Y	Y	N	N
15 Hinojosa	?	?	?	?	?
16 Reyes	Y	Y	N	N	Y
17 Edwards	Y	Y	N	N	Y
18 Jackson Lee	Y	Y	N	N	Y
19 Neugebauer	Y	Y	Y	Y	N
20 Gonzalez	Y	Y	N	N	Y
21 Smith	Y	Y	Y	Y	N
22 Olson	Y	Y	Y	Y	N
23 Rodriguez	Y	Y	N	N	Y
24 Marchant	Y	Y	Y	Y	N
25 Doggett	Y	Y	N	N	Y
26 Burgess	Y	Y	Y	Y	N
27 Ortiz	Y	Y	N	N	Y
28 Cuellar	Y	Y	N	N	Y
29 Green, G.	Y	Y	N	N	Y
30 Johnson, E.	Y	Y	N	N	Y
31 Carter	Y	Y	Y	Y	N
32 Sessions	Y	Y	Y	Y	N
UTAH					
1 Bishop	Y	Y	Y	Y	N
2 Matheson	Y	Y	N	N	Y
3 Chaffetz	Y	Y	Y	Y	N
VERMONT					
AL Welch	Y	Y	N	N	Y
VIRGINIA					
1 Wittman	Y	Y	Y	Y	N
2 Nye	Y	Y	N	N	Y
3 Scott	Y	Y	N	N	Y
4 Forbes	Y	Y	Y	Y	N
5 Perriello	Y	Y	N	N	Y
6 Goodlatte	Y	Y	Y	Y	N
7 Cantor	Y	Y	Y	Y	N
8 Moran	Y	Y	N	N	Y
9 Boucher	Y	Y	N	N	Y
10 Wolf	Y	Y	Y	Y	N
11 Connolly	Y	Y	N	N	Y
WASHINGTON					
1 Inslee	Y	Y	N	N	Y
2 Larsen	Y	Y	N	N	Y
3 Baird	Y	Y	N	N	Y
4 Hastings	Y	Y	Y	Y	N
5 McMorris Rodgers	Y	Y	Y	Y	N
6 Dicks	Y	Y	N	N	Y
7 McDermott	Y	Y	N	N	Y
8 Reichert	?	?	?	?	?
9 Smith	Y	Y	N	N	Y
WEST VIRGINIA					
1 Mollohan	Y	Y	N	N	Y
2 Capito	Y	Y	Y	Y	N
3 Rahall	Y	Y	N	N	Y
WISCONSIN					
1 Ryan	Y	Y	Y	Y	N
2 Baldwin	Y	Y	N	N	Y
3 Kind	Y	Y	N	N	Y
4 Moore	Y	Y	?	N	Y
5 Sensenbrenner	Y	Y	Y	Y	N
6 Petri	Y	Y	Y	Y	N
7 Obey	Y	Y	N	N	Y
8 Kagen	Y	Y	N	N	Y
WYOMING					
AL Lummis	Y	Y	Y	Y	N
DELEGATES					
Faleomavaega (A.S.)					
Norton (D.C.)					
Bordallo (Guam)					
Sablan (N. Marianas)					
Pierluisi (P.R.)					
Christensen (V.I.)					

IN THE HOUSE | By Vote Number

59. **HR 2314. Native Hawaiian Sovereignty/Passage.** Passage of the bill that would formally recognize Native Hawaiians as a distinct indigenous group and outline a process for establishing a Native Hawaiian governing entity that would enter into negotiations with state and federal governments. Federal recognition would be extended to the governing body after the Interior Department certified documents and the election of governing officers. The bill would prohibit the native government from conducting gaming activities and would stipulate that American Indian trade law would not apply to lands or land transfers in Hawaii. Passed 245-164: D 239-4; R 6-160. Feb. 23, 2010.

60. **HR 4626. Health Insurer Antitrust Exemption Repeal/Rule.** Adoption of the rule (H Res 1098) to provide for House floor consideration of the bill that would repeal health insurers' exemption from federal antitrust laws. Adopted 238-181: D 238-10; R 0-171. Feb. 24, 2010.

61. **H Res 1074. Tribute to Miep Gies/Adoption.** McMahon, D-N.Y., motion to suspend the rules and adopt the resolution that would recognize Miep Gies' effort to hide and provide for the Frank family in Nazi-occupied Holland and commend her for preserving the diary of Anne Frank. Motion agreed to 421-0: D 249-0; R 172-0. A two-thirds majority of those present and voting (281 in this case) is required for adoption under suspension of the rules. Feb. 24, 2010.

62. **H Res 944. Iraqi Religious and Ethnic Minorities/Adoption.** McMahon, D-N.Y., motion to suspend the rules and adopt the resolution that would state the House's concern for Iraqi religious and ethnic minorities and would urge the Iraqi government to ensure that the upcoming national elections in Iraq are safe and fair so that all citizens can participate. Motion agreed to 415-3: D 248-0; R 167-3. A two-thirds majority of those present and voting (279 in this case) is required for adoption under suspension of the rules. Feb. 24, 2010.

63. **HR 4626. Health Insurer Antitrust Exemption Repeal/Recommit.** Smith, R-Texas, motion to recommit the bill to the House Judiciary Committee with instructions that it be immediately reported back with an amendment that would allow health insurers to collect and distribute data on claims paid, in addition to requiring a Government Accountability Office report on the impact of the legislation. Motion rejected 170-249: D 5-246; R 165-3. Feb. 24, 2010.

	59	60	61	62	63
ALABAMA					
1 **Bonner**	N	N	Y	Y	Y
2 Bright	N	N	Y	Y	Y
3 **Rogers**	N	N	Y	Y	Y
4 **Aderholt**	N	N	Y	Y	Y
5 **Griffith**	N	N	Y	Y	Y
6 **Bachus**	N	N	Y	Y	Y
7 Davis	Y	Y	Y	Y	N
ALASKA					
AL **Young**	Y	N	Y	Y	Y
ARIZONA					
1 Kirkpatrick	Y	Y	Y	Y	N
2 **Franks**	N	N	Y	Y	Y
3 **Shadegg**	N	N	Y	Y	Y
4 Pastor	Y	Y	Y	Y	N
5 Mitchell	Y	N	Y	Y	N
6 **Flake**	N	N	Y	N	Y
7 Grijalva	Y	Y	Y	Y	N
8 Giffords	N	N	Y	Y	N
ARKANSAS					
1 Berry	Y	Y	Y	Y	N
2 Snyder	Y	Y	Y	Y	N
3 **Boozman**	N	N	Y	Y	Y
4 Ross	Y	Y	Y	Y	N
CALIFORNIA					
1 Thompson	Y	Y	Y	Y	N
2 **Herger**	N	N	Y	Y	Y
3 **Lungren**	N	N	Y	Y	Y
4 **McClintock**	N	N	Y	Y	N
5 Matsui	Y	Y	Y	Y	N
6 Woolsey	Y	Y	Y	Y	N
7 Miller, George	Y	Y	Y	Y	N
8 Pelosi					
9 Lee	Y	Y	Y	Y	N
10 Garamendi	Y	Y	Y	Y	N
11 McNerney	Y	Y	Y	Y	N
12 Speier	Y	Y	Y	Y	N
13 Stark	?	?	?	?	?
14 Eshoo	Y	Y	Y	Y	N
15 Honda	Y	Y	Y	Y	N
16 Lofgren	Y	Y	Y	Y	N
17 Farr	Y	Y	Y	Y	N
18 Cardoza	Y	Y	Y	Y	N
19 **Radanovich**	?	?	?	?	?
20 Costa	Y	Y	Y	Y	N
21 **Nunes**	N	N	Y	Y	Y
22 **McCarthy**	N	N	Y	Y	Y
23 Capps	Y	Y	Y	Y	N
24 **Gallegly**	N	N	Y	Y	Y
25 **McKeon**	N	N	Y	Y	Y
26 **Dreier**	N	N	Y	Y	Y
27 Sherman	Y	Y	Y	Y	N
28 Berman	?	Y	Y	Y	N
29 Schiff	Y	Y	Y	Y	N
30 Waxman	Y	Y	Y	Y	N
31 Becerra	Y	Y	Y	Y	N
32 Chu	Y	Y	Y	Y	N
33 Watson	Y	Y	Y	Y	N
34 Roybal-Allard	Y	Y	Y	Y	N
35 Waters	Y	Y	Y	Y	N
36 Harman	Y	Y	Y	Y	N
37 Richardson	Y	Y	Y	Y	N
38 Napolitano	Y	Y	Y	Y	N
39 Sánchez, Linda	Y	Y	Y	Y	N
40 **Royce**	N	N	Y	Y	Y
41 **Lewis**	N	N	Y	Y	Y
42 **Miller, Gary**	N	N	Y	Y	Y
43 Baca	Y	Y	Y	Y	N
44 **Calvert**	N	N	Y	Y	Y
45 **Bono Mack**	?	N	Y	Y	Y
46 **Rohrabacher**	N	N	Y	Y	Y
47 Sanchez, Loretta	Y	Y	Y	Y	N
48 **Campbell**	N	N	Y	Y	Y
49 **Issa**	N	N	Y	Y	Y
50 **Bilbray**	N	N	Y	Y	Y
51 Filner	Y	Y	Y	Y	N
52 **Hunter**	N	N	Y	Y	Y
53 Davis	Y	Y	Y	Y	N

	59	60	61	62	63
COLORADO					
1 DeGette	Y	Y	Y	Y	N
2 Polis	Y	Y	Y	Y	N
3 Salazar	Y	Y	Y	Y	N
4 Markey	Y	Y	Y	Y	N
5 **Lamborn**	N	N	Y	Y	Y
6 **Coffman**	N	N	Y	Y	Y
7 Perlmutter	Y	Y	Y	Y	N
CONNECTICUT					
1 Larson	Y	Y	Y	Y	N
2 Courtney	Y	Y	Y	Y	N
3 DeLauro	Y	Y	Y	Y	N
4 Himes	N	Y	Y	Y	N
5 Murphy	Y	Y	Y	?	N
DELAWARE					
AL **Castle**	N	N	Y	Y	Y
FLORIDA					
1 **Miller**	N	N	Y	Y	Y
2 Boyd	Y	Y	Y	Y	N
3 Brown	Y	Y	Y	Y	N
4 **Crenshaw**	N	N	Y	Y	Y
5 **Brown-Waite**	N	N	Y	Y	Y
6 **Stearns**	N	N	Y	Y	Y
7 **Mica**	N	N	Y	Y	Y
8 Grayson	Y	Y	Y	Y	N
9 **Bilirakis**	N	N	Y	Y	Y
10 **Young**	N	N	Y	Y	Y
11 Castor	Y	Y	Y	Y	N
12 **Putnam**	N	N	Y	Y	Y
13 **Buchanan**	N	N	Y	Y	Y
14 **Mack**	?	N	Y	Y	Y
15 **Posey**	N	N	Y	Y	Y
16 **Rooney**	N	N	Y	Y	Y
17 Meek	Y	Y	Y	Y	N
18 **Ros-Lehtinen**	?	N	Y	Y	Y
19 Vacant					
20 Wasserman Schultz	Y	Y	Y	Y	N
21 **Diaz-Balart, L.**	N	N	Y	Y	Y
22 Klein	Y	Y	Y	Y	N
23 Hastings	Y	Y	Y	Y	N
24 Kosmas	Y	Y	Y	Y	N
25 **Diaz-Balart, M.**	N	N	Y	Y	Y
GEORGIA					
1 **Kingston**	N	N	Y	Y	Y
2 Bishop	Y	Y	Y	Y	N
3 **Westmoreland**	N	N	Y	?	Y
4 Johnson	Y	Y	Y	Y	N
5 Lewis	Y	Y	Y	Y	N
6 **Price**	N	N	Y	Y	Y
7 **Linder**	N	N	Y	Y	Y
8 Marshall	Y	Y	Y	Y	N
9 **Deal**	N	N	Y	Y	Y
10 **Broun**	N	N	Y	N	Y
11 **Gingrey**	N	N	Y	Y	Y
12 Barrow	Y	Y	Y	Y	N
13 Scott	Y	Y	Y	Y	N
HAWAII					
1 Abercrombie	Y	Y	Y	Y	N
2 Hirono	Y	Y	Y	Y	N
IDAHO					
1 Minnick	Y	N	Y	Y	N
2 **Simpson**	N	N	Y	Y	Y
ILLINOIS					
1 Rush	Y	Y	Y	Y	N
2 Jackson	Y	Y	Y	Y	N
3 Lipinski	Y	Y	Y	Y	N
4 Gutierrez	Y	Y	Y	Y	N
5 Quigley	Y	Y	Y	Y	N
6 **Roskam**	N	N	Y	Y	Y
7 Davis	Y	Y	Y	Y	N
8 Bean	Y	Y	Y	Y	N
9 Schakowsky	Y	Y	Y	Y	N
10 **Kirk**	N	N	Y	Y	Y
11 Halvorson	Y	Y	Y	Y	N
12 Costello	?	Y	Y	Y	N
13 **Biggert**	N	N	Y	Y	Y
14 Foster	Y	Y	Y	Y	N
15 **Johnson**	N	N	Y	Y	Y

KEY   **Republicans**   Democrats

Y Voted for (yea)	X Paired against C Voted "present" to avoid possible conflict of interest
# Paired for	– Announced against
+ Announced for	P Voted "present" ? Did not vote or otherwise make a position known
N Voted against (nay)	

	59	60	61	62	63
16 Manzullo	N	N	Y	Y	Y
17 Hare	Y	Y	Y	Y	N
18 Schock	N	N	Y	Y	?
19 Shimkus	N	N	Y	Y	Y
INDIANA					
1 Visclosky	Y	Y	Y	Y	N
2 Donnelly	Y	Y	Y	Y	N
3 Souder	N	N	Y	Y	Y
4 Buyer	N	?	Y	Y	?
5 Burton	N	N	Y	Y	Y
6 Pence	N	N	Y	Y	Y
7 Carson	Y	Y	Y	Y	N
8 Ellsworth	Y	N	Y	Y	N
9 Hill	Y	N	Y	Y	N
IOWA					
1 Braley	Y	Y	Y	Y	N
2 Loebsack	Y	Y	Y	Y	N
3 Boswell	Y	Y	Y	Y	N
4 Latham	N	N	Y	Y	Y
5 King	N	N	Y	Y	Y
KANSAS					
1 Moran	N	N	Y	Y	Y
2 Jenkins	N	N	Y	Y	Y
3 Moore	Y	Y	Y	Y	N
4 Tiahrt	N	N	Y	Y	Y
KENTUCKY					
1 Whitfield	N	N	Y	Y	Y
2 Guthrie	N	N	Y	Y	Y
3 Yarmuth	Y	Y	Y	Y	N
4 Davis	N	N	Y	Y	?
5 Rogers	N	N	Y	Y	Y
6 Chandler	Y	Y	Y	Y	N
LOUISIANA					
1 Scalise	N	N	Y	Y	Y
2 Cao	Y	N	Y	Y	N
3 Melancon	Y	Y	Y	Y	N
4 Fleming	N	N	Y	Y	Y
5 Alexander	N	N	Y	Y	Y
6 Cassidy	N	N	Y	Y	Y
7 Boustany	N	N	Y	Y	Y
MAINE					
1 Pingree	Y	Y	Y	Y	N
2 Michaud	Y	Y	Y	Y	N
MARYLAND					
1 Kratovil	Y	Y	Y	Y	N
2 Ruppersberger	Y	Y	Y	Y	N
3 Sarbanes	Y	Y	Y	Y	N
4 Edwards	Y	Y	Y	Y	N
5 Hoyer	Y	Y	Y	Y	N
6 Bartlett	N	N	Y	Y	Y
7 Cummings	Y	Y	Y	Y	N
8 Van Hollen	Y	Y	Y	Y	N
MASSACHUSETTS					
1 Olver	Y	Y	Y	Y	N
2 Neal	Y	Y	Y	Y	N
3 McGovern	Y	Y	Y	Y	N
4 Frank	Y	Y	Y	Y	N
5 Tsongas	Y	Y	Y	Y	N
6 Tierney	Y	Y	Y	Y	N
7 Markey	Y	Y	Y	Y	N
8 Capuano	Y	Y	Y	Y	N
9 Lynch	Y	Y	Y	Y	N
10 Delahunt	?	Y	Y	Y	N
MICHIGAN					
1 Stupak	Y	Y	Y	Y	N
2 Hoekstra	?	?	?	?	?
3 Ehlers	Y	N	Y	Y	N
4 Camp	N	N	Y	Y	N
5 Kildee	Y	Y	Y	Y	N
6 Upton	N	N	Y	Y	N
7 Schauer	Y	Y	Y	Y	N
8 Rogers	N	N	Y	Y	Y
9 Peters	Y	Y	Y	Y	N
10 Miller	N	N	Y	Y	Y
11 McCotter	N	N	Y	Y	Y
12 Levin	Y	Y	Y	Y	N
13 Kilpatrick	Y	Y	Y	Y	N
14 Conyers	Y	Y	Y	Y	N
15 Dingell	?	?	?	?	?
MINNESOTA					
1 Walz	Y	Y	Y	Y	N
2 Kline	N	N	Y	Y	Y
3 Paulsen	N	N	Y	Y	Y
4 McCollum	Y	Y	Y	Y	N

	59	60	61	62	63
5 Ellison	Y	Y	Y	Y	N
6 Bachmann	N	N	Y	Y	Y
7 Peterson	Y	N	Y	Y	N
8 Oberstar	Y	Y	Y	Y	N
MISSISSIPPI					
1 Childers	Y	N	Y	Y	N
2 Thompson	Y	Y	Y	Y	N
3 Harper	N	N	Y	Y	Y
4 Taylor	Y	Y	Y	Y	N
MISSOURI					
1 Clay	Y	?	?	?	N
2 Akin	N	N	Y	Y	Y
3 Carnahan	Y	Y	Y	Y	N
4 Skelton	Y	Y	Y	Y	N
5 Cleaver	Y	Y	Y	Y	N
6 Graves	N	N	Y	Y	Y
7 Blunt	?	?	?	?	?
8 Emerson	N	N	Y	Y	Y
9 Luetkemeyer	N	N	Y	Y	Y
MONTANA					
AL Rehberg	N	N	Y	Y	Y
NEBRASKA					
1 Fortenberry	N	N	Y	Y	Y
2 Terry	N	N	Y	Y	Y
3 Smith	N	N	Y	Y	Y
NEVADA					
1 Berkley	Y	Y	Y	Y	N
2 Heller	N	N	Y	Y	Y
3 Titus	Y	Y	Y	Y	N
NEW HAMPSHIRE					
1 Shea-Porter	Y	Y	Y	Y	N
2 Hodes	Y	Y	Y	Y	N
NEW JERSEY					
1 Andrews	?	Y	Y	Y	N
2 LoBiondo	N	N	Y	Y	Y
3 Adler	Y	Y	Y	Y	Y
4 Smith	N	N	Y	Y	Y
5 Garrett	N	N	Y	Y	Y
6 Pallone	Y	Y	Y	Y	N
7 Lance	N	N	Y	Y	Y
8 Pascrell	Y	Y	Y	Y	N
9 Rothman	Y	Y	?	Y	N
10 Payne	?	Y	Y	Y	N
11 Frelinghuysen	N	N	Y	Y	Y
12 Holt	Y	Y	Y	Y	N
13 Sires	?	Y	Y	Y	N
NEW MEXICO					
1 Heinrich	Y	Y	Y	Y	N
2 Teague	Y	Y	Y	Y	Y
3 Luján	Y	Y	Y	Y	N
NEW YORK					
1 Bishop	Y	Y	Y	Y	N
2 Israel	Y	Y	Y	Y	N
3 King	N	N	Y	Y	Y
4 McCarthy	Y	Y	Y	Y	N
5 Ackerman	Y	Y	Y	Y	N
6 Meeks	Y	Y	Y	Y	N
7 Crowley	Y	Y	Y	Y	N
8 Nadler	Y	Y	Y	Y	N
9 Weiner	Y	Y	Y	Y	N
10 Towns	Y	Y	Y	Y	N
11 Clarke	Y	Y	Y	Y	N
12 Velázquez	Y	Y	Y	Y	N
13 McMahon	N	Y	Y	Y	N
14 Maloney	Y	Y	Y	Y	?
15 Rangel	Y	Y	Y	Y	N
16 Serrano	Y	Y	Y	Y	N
17 Engel	Y	Y	Y	Y	N
18 Lowey	Y	Y	Y	Y	N
19 Hall	Y	Y	Y	Y	N
20 Murphy	Y	N	Y	Y	N
21 Tonko	Y	Y	Y	Y	N
22 Hinchey	Y	Y	Y	Y	N
23 Owens	Y	Y	Y	Y	N
24 Arcuri	Y	Y	Y	Y	N
25 Maffei	Y	Y	Y	Y	N
26 Lee	N	N	Y	Y	Y
27 Higgins	Y	?	Y	Y	N
28 Slaughter	Y	Y	Y	Y	N
29 Massa	Y	Y	Y	Y	N
NORTH CAROLINA					
1 Butterfield	Y	Y	Y	Y	N
2 Etheridge	Y	Y	Y	Y	N
3 Jones	Y	N	Y	Y	N
4 Price	Y	Y	Y	Y	N

	59	60	61	62	63
5 Foxx	N	N	Y	Y	Y
6 Coble	N	N	Y	Y	Y
7 McIntyre	Y	Y	Y	Y	N
8 Kissell	Y	N	Y	Y	N
9 Myrick	N	N	Y	Y	Y
10 McHenry	N	N	Y	Y	Y
11 Shuler	Y	N	Y	Y	N
12 Watt	Y	Y	Y	Y	N
13 Miller	?	Y	Y	?	N
NORTH DAKOTA					
AL Pomeroy	Y	Y	Y	Y	N
OHIO					
1 Driehaus	Y	Y	Y	Y	N
2 Schmidt	N	N	Y	Y	Y
3 Turner	?	N	Y	Y	Y
4 Jordan	N	N	Y	Y	Y
5 Latta	N	N	Y	Y	Y
6 Wilson	Y	Y	Y	Y	N
7 Austria	N	N	Y	Y	Y
8 Boehner	N	N	Y	Y	Y
9 Kaptur	Y	Y	Y	Y	N
10 Kucinich	Y	Y	Y	Y	N
11 Fudge	Y	Y	Y	Y	N
12 Tiberi	N	N	Y	Y	Y
13 Sutton	Y	Y	Y	Y	N
14 LaTourette	N	N	Y	Y	Y
15 Kilroy	Y	Y	Y	Y	N
16 Boccieri	Y	Y	Y	Y	N
17 Ryan	Y	Y	Y	Y	N
18 Space	Y	Y	Y	Y	N
OKLAHOMA					
1 Sullivan	N	N	Y	Y	Y
2 Boren	Y	Y	Y	Y	N
3 Lucas	N	N	Y	Y	Y
4 Cole	Y	N	Y	Y	Y
5 Fallin	N	N	Y	Y	Y
OREGON					
1 Wu	Y	Y	Y	Y	N
2 Walden	N	N	Y	Y	Y
3 Blumenauer	Y	Y	Y	Y	N
4 DeFazio	Y	Y	Y	Y	N
5 Schrader	Y	Y	Y	Y	N
PENNSYLVANIA					
1 Brady	Y	Y	Y	Y	N
2 Fattah	Y	Y	Y	Y	N
3 Dahlkemper	Y	N	Y	Y	N
4 Altmire	Y	Y	Y	Y	N
5 Thompson	N	N	Y	Y	Y
6 Gerlach	N	N	Y	Y	Y
7 Sestak	Y	Y	Y	Y	N
8 Murphy, P.	Y	Y	Y	Y	N
9 Shuster	N	N	Y	Y	Y
10 Carney	Y	Y	Y	Y	N
11 Kanjorski	Y	Y	Y	Y	N
12 Vacant					
13 Schwartz	Y	Y	Y	Y	N
14 Doyle	Y	Y	Y	Y	N
15 Dent	N	N	Y	Y	Y
16 Pitts	N	?	?	?	?
17 Holden	Y	Y	Y	Y	N
18 Murphy, T.	Y	N	Y	Y	Y
19 Platts	N	N	Y	Y	Y
RHODE ISLAND					
1 Kennedy	Y	Y	Y	Y	N
2 Langevin	Y	Y	Y	Y	N
SOUTH CAROLINA					
1 Brown	N	N	Y	Y	Y
2 Wilson	N	N	Y	Y	Y
3 Barrett	?	?	?	?	?
4 Inglis	N	N	Y	Y	Y
5 Spratt	Y	?	Y	Y	N
6 Clyburn	Y	Y	Y	Y	N
SOUTH DAKOTA					
AL Herseth Sandlin	Y	Y	Y	Y	N
TENNESSEE					
1 Roe	N	N	Y	Y	Y
2 Duncan	N	N	Y	Y	Y
3 Wamp	?	N	Y	Y	Y
4 Davis	Y	Y	Y	Y	N
5 Cooper	Y	Y	Y	Y	N
6 Gordon	?	Y	Y	Y	N
7 Blackburn	N	N	Y	Y	Y
8 Tanner	Y	Y	Y	Y	N
9 Cohen	Y	Y	Y	Y	N

	59	60	61	62	63
TEXAS					
1 Gohmert	N	N	Y	Y	Y
2 Poe	N	N	Y	Y	Y
3 Johnson, S.	N	N	Y	Y	Y
4 Hall	N	N	Y	Y	Y
5 Hensarling	N	N	Y	Y	Y
6 Barton	N	N	Y	Y	Y
7 Culberson	?	N	Y	Y	Y
8 Brady	N	N	Y	Y	Y
9 Green, A.	Y	Y	Y	Y	N
10 McCaul	N	N	Y	Y	Y
11 Conaway	N	N	Y	Y	Y
12 Granger	N	N	Y	Y	Y
13 Thornberry	N	N	Y	Y	Y
14 Paul	N	N	Y	N	Y
15 Hinojosa	?	Y	Y	Y	N
16 Reyes	Y	Y	Y	Y	N
17 Edwards	Y	Y	Y	Y	N
18 Jackson Lee	Y	Y	Y	Y	N
19 Neugebauer	N	N	Y	Y	Y
20 Gonzalez	Y	Y	Y	Y	N
21 Smith	N	N	Y	Y	Y
22 Olson	N	N	Y	Y	Y
23 Rodriguez	Y	Y	Y	Y	N
24 Marchant	N	N	Y	Y	Y
25 Doggett	Y	Y	Y	Y	N
26 Burgess	N	N	Y	Y	Y
27 Ortiz	Y	Y	Y	Y	N
28 Cuellar	Y	Y	Y	Y	N
29 Green, G.	Y	Y	Y	Y	N
30 Johnson, E.	Y	Y	Y	Y	N
31 Carter	N	N	Y	Y	Y
32 Sessions	N	N	Y	Y	Y
UTAH					
1 Bishop	?	N	Y	Y	Y
2 Matheson	Y	Y	Y	Y	N
3 Chaffetz	N	N	Y	Y	Y
VERMONT					
AL Welch	Y	Y	?	?	N
VIRGINIA					
1 Wittman	N	N	Y	Y	Y
2 Nye	Y	Y	Y	Y	N
3 Scott	Y	Y	Y	Y	N
4 Forbes	N	N	Y	Y	Y
5 Perriello	Y	Y	Y	Y	N
6 Goodlatte	N	N	Y	Y	Y
7 Cantor	N	N	Y	Y	Y
8 Moran	Y	Y	Y	Y	N
9 Boucher	Y	Y	Y	Y	N
10 Wolf	N	N	Y	Y	Y
11 Connolly	Y	Y	Y	Y	N
WASHINGTON					
1 Inslee	Y	Y	Y	Y	N
2 Larsen	Y	Y	Y	Y	N
3 Baird	Y	Y	Y	Y	N
4 Hastings	N	N	Y	Y	Y
5 McMorris Rodgers	N	N	Y	?	Y
6 Dicks	Y	Y	Y	Y	N
7 McDermott	Y	Y	Y	Y	N
8 Reichert	?	?	?	?	?
9 Smith	Y	Y	Y	Y	N
WEST VIRGINIA					
1 Mollohan	Y	Y	Y	Y	N
2 Capito	N	N	Y	Y	Y
3 Rahall	Y	Y	Y	Y	N
WISCONSIN					
1 Ryan	N	N	Y	Y	Y
2 Baldwin	Y	Y	Y	Y	N
3 Kind	Y	Y	Y	Y	N
4 Moore	Y	?	Y	Y	N
5 Sensenbrenner	N	N	Y	Y	Y
6 Petri	N	N	Y	Y	Y
7 Obey	Y	Y	Y	Y	N
8 Kagen	Y	Y	Y	Y	N
WYOMING					
AL Lummis	N	N	Y	Y	Y
DELEGATES					
Faleomavaega (A.S.)					
Norton (D.C.)					
Bordallo (Guam)					
Sablan (N. Marianas)					
Pierluisi (P.R.)					
Christensen (V.I.)					

IN THE HOUSE | By Vote Number

64. **HR 4626. Health Insurer Antitrust Exemption Repeal/Passage.** Passage of the bill that would repeal health insurers' exemption from federal antitrust laws. It also would prohibit insurers from sharing data on claims paid. Passed 406-19: D 253-0; R 153-19. A "yea" was a vote in support of the president's position. Feb. 24, 2010.

65. **H Res 1085. National African-American History Month/Adoption.** Brown, D-Fla., motion to suspend the rules and adopt the resolution that would support the goals of National African-American History Month and honor African-American contributions to transportation and infrastructure. Motion agreed to 419-0: D 249-0; R 170-0. A two-thirds majority of those present and voting (280 in this case) is required for adoption under suspension of the rules. Feb. 24, 2010.

66. **HR 2701. Fiscal 2010 Intelligence Authorization/Rule.** Adoption of the rule (H Res 1105) to provide for House floor consideration of the bill that would authorize classified amounts in fiscal 2010 for 16 U.S. intelligence activities and agencies, including the CIA, Office of the Director of National Intelligence and National Security Agency. It also would permit the Speaker to entertain motions to suspend the rules at any time and waive the two-thirds majority vote requirement for same-day consideration of resolutions reported from the Rules Committee through the legislative day of Feb. 26, 2010. Adopted 237-176: D 237-10; R 0-166. Feb. 25, 2010.

67. **HR 3961. 'Patriot Act' Extensions/Motion to Concur.** Conyers, D-Mich., motion to concur in the Senate amendments to the bill that would extend until Feb. 28, 2011, three provisions of the anti-terrorism law known as the Patriot Act. The provisions allow the government to request access to "any tangible thing" it says is related to a terrorism investigation, to seek court orders for "roving" wiretaps on suspects who use multiple devices or modes of communication, and to allow federal law enforcement officials to seek warrants to conduct surveillance of "lone wolf" foreign terrorist suspects who may not be connected to a terrorist group. Motion agreed to, thus clearing the bill for the president, 315-97: D 162-87; R 153-10. Feb. 25, 2010.

68. **H Con Res 227. National Urban Crimes Awareness Week/Adoption.** Scott, D-Va., motion to suspend the rules and adopt the concurrent resolution that would support the goals and ideals of National Urban Crimes Awareness Week. Motion agreed to 411-0: D 248-0; R 163-0. A two-thirds majority of those present and voting (274 in this case) is required for adoption under suspension of the rules. Feb. 25, 2010.

		64	65	66	67	68
ALABAMA						
1	Bonner	Y	Y	N	Y	Y
2	Bright	Y	Y	N	Y	Y
3	Rogers	Y	Y	N	Y	Y
4	Aderholt	Y	Y	N	Y	Y
5	Griffith	Y	Y	N	Y	Y
6	Bachus	Y	Y	N	Y	Y
7	Davis	Y	?	Y	Y	Y
ALASKA						
AL	Young	Y	Y	N	N	Y
ARIZONA						
1	Kirkpatrick	Y	Y	Y	Y	Y
2	Franks	N	Y	N	Y	Y
3	Shadegg	Y	Y	N	Y	Y
4	Pastor	Y	Y	N	Y	Y
5	Mitchell	Y	Y	N	Y	Y
6	Flake	Y	Y	N	Y	Y
7	Grijalva	Y	Y	Y	N	Y
8	Giffords	Y	Y	Y	Y	Y
ARKANSAS						
1	Berry	Y	Y	Y	Y	Y
2	Snyder	Y	Y	Y	Y	Y
3	Boozman	Y	Y	N	Y	Y
4	Ross	Y	Y	Y	Y	Y
CALIFORNIA						
1	Thompson	Y	Y	Y	N	Y
2	Herger	Y	Y	N	Y	Y
3	Lungren	Y	Y	N	Y	Y
4	McClintock	Y	Y	N	Y	Y
5	Matsui	Y	Y	Y	N	Y
6	Woolsey	Y	Y	Y	N	Y
7	Miller, George	Y	?	Y	N	Y
8	Pelosi	Y				
9	Lee	Y	Y	Y	N	Y
10	Garamendi	Y	Y	Y	Y	Y
11	McNerney	Y	Y	Y	Y	Y
12	Speier	Y	Y	Y	N	Y
13	Stark	?	?	?	?	?
14	Eshoo	Y	Y	Y	Y	Y
15	Honda	Y	Y	Y	N	Y
16	Lofgren	Y	Y	Y	Y	Y
17	Farr	Y	Y	Y	N	Y
18	Cardoza	Y	?	?	Y	Y
19	Radanovich	?	?	?	?	?
20	Costa	Y	Y	Y	Y	Y
21	Nunes	Y	Y	N	Y	Y
22	McCarthy	Y	Y	N	Y	Y
23	Capps	Y	Y	Y	?	?
24	Gallegly	Y	Y	N	Y	Y
25	McKeon	Y	Y	N	Y	Y
26	Dreier	Y	Y	N	Y	Y
27	Sherman	Y	Y	Y	N	Y
28	Berman	Y	Y	Y	N	Y
29	Schiff	Y	Y	Y	Y	Y
30	Waxman	Y	Y	Y	N	Y
31	Becerra	Y	Y	Y	N	Y
32	Chu	Y	Y	Y	N	Y
33	Watson	Y	Y	Y	Y	Y
34	Roybal-Allard	Y	Y	Y	Y	Y
35	Waters	Y	Y	Y	N	Y
36	Harman	Y	Y	Y	N	Y
37	Richardson	Y	Y	Y	N	Y
38	Napolitano	Y	Y	Y	Y	Y
39	Sánchez, Linda	Y	Y	Y	N	Y
40	Royce	Y	Y	N	Y	Y
41	Lewis	Y	Y	N	Y	Y
42	Miller, Gary	Y	Y	N	Y	Y
43	Baca	Y	Y	Y	Y	Y
44	Calvert	Y	Y	N	Y	Y
45	Bono Mack	Y	Y	N	Y	Y
46	Rohrabacher	Y	Y	N	Y	Y
47	Sanchez, Loretta	Y	Y	Y	N	Y
48	Campbell	Y	Y	N	Y	Y
49	Issa	Y	Y	N	Y	Y
50	Bilbray	Y	Y	N	Y	Y
51	Filner	Y	Y	Y	N	Y
52	Hunter	Y	Y	N	Y	Y
53	Davis	Y	Y	Y	Y	Y
COLORADO						
1	DeGette	Y	Y	Y	Y	Y
2	Polis	Y	Y	Y	N	Y
3	Salazar	Y	Y	Y	Y	Y
4	Markey	Y	Y	Y	Y	Y
5	Lamborn	N	Y	N	Y	Y
6	Coffman	Y	Y	N	Y	Y
7	Perlmutter	Y	Y	Y	Y	Y
CONNECTICUT						
1	Larson	Y	Y	Y	N	Y
2	Courtney	Y	Y	Y	Y	Y
3	DeLauro	Y	Y	Y	Y	Y
4	Himes	Y	Y	Y	Y	Y
5	Murphy	Y	Y	Y	Y	Y
DELAWARE						
AL	Castle	Y	Y	N	Y	Y
FLORIDA						
1	Miller	Y	Y	N	Y	Y
2	Boyd	Y	Y	Y	Y	Y
3	Brown	Y	Y	Y	Y	Y
4	Crenshaw	Y	Y	N	Y	Y
5	Brown-Waite	Y	Y	N	Y	Y
6	Stearns	Y	Y	N	Y	Y
7	Mica	Y	Y	N	Y	Y
8	Grayson	Y	Y	Y	Y	Y
9	Bilirakis	Y	Y	N	Y	Y
10	Young	Y	Y	N	Y	Y
11	Castor	Y	Y	Y	Y	Y
12	Putnam	Y	Y	N	Y	Y
13	Buchanan	Y	Y	N	Y	Y
14	Mack	Y	Y	N	?	?
15	Posey	Y	Y	N	Y	Y
16	Rooney	Y	Y	N	Y	Y
17	Meek	Y	Y	Y	Y	Y
18	Ros-Lehtinen	Y	Y	?	Y	Y
19	Vacant					
20	Wasserman Schultz	Y	Y	Y	Y	Y
21	Diaz-Balart, L.	Y	Y	N	Y	Y
22	Klein	Y	Y	Y	Y	Y
23	Hastings	Y	Y	Y	N	Y
24	Kosmas	Y	Y	Y	Y	Y
25	Diaz-Balart, M.	Y	Y	N	Y	Y
GEORGIA						
1	Kingston	Y	Y	N	Y	Y
2	Bishop	Y	Y	Y	Y	Y
3	Westmoreland	N	Y	?	?	?
4	Johnson	Y	Y	Y	N	Y
5	Lewis	Y	Y	Y	N	Y
6	Price	N	Y	?	?	?
7	Linder	N	?	N	Y	Y
8	Marshall	Y	Y	Y	Y	Y
9	Deal	Y	Y	N	?	?
10	Broun	N	Y	N	Y	Y
11	Gingrey	Y	Y	?	?	?
12	Barrow	Y	Y	Y	Y	Y
13	Scott	Y	Y	Y	Y	Y
HAWAII						
1	Abercrombie	Y	Y	Y	N	Y
2	Hirono	Y	Y	Y	N	Y
IDAHO						
1	Minnick	Y	Y	N	N	Y
2	Simpson	Y	Y	N	Y	Y
ILLINOIS						
1	Rush	Y	Y	Y	Y	Y
2	Jackson	Y	Y	Y	Y	Y
3	Lipinski	Y	Y	Y	Y	Y
4	Gutierrez	Y	Y	Y	Y	Y
5	Quigley	Y	Y	Y	Y	Y
6	Roskam	Y	Y	N	Y	Y
7	Davis	Y	Y	Y	Y	Y
8	Bean	Y	Y	Y	Y	Y
9	Schakowsky	Y	Y	Y	N	Y
10	Kirk	Y	Y	N	Y	Y
11	Halvorson	Y	Y	N	Y	Y
12	Costello	Y	Y	Y	N	Y
13	Biggert	Y	Y	N	Y	Y
14	Foster	Y	Y	Y	Y	Y
15	Johnson	Y	Y	N	N	Y

KEY   Republicans   Democrats

Y Voted for (yea)	X Paired against	C Voted "present" to avoid possible conflict of interest
# Paired for	– Announced against	
+ Announced for	P Voted "present"	? Did not vote or otherwise make a position known
N Voted against (nay)		

	64	65	66	67	68
16 Manzullo	Y	Y	N	Y	Y
17 Hare	Y	Y	Y	N	Y
18 Schock	Y	Y	N	Y	Y
19 Shimkus	Y	Y	?	Y	Y
INDIANA					
1 Visclosky	Y	Y	Y	N	Y
2 Donnelly	Y	Y	N	Y	Y
3 Souder	Y	Y	N	Y	Y
4 Buyer	N	Y	N	Y	Y
5 Burton	Y	Y	N	Y	Y
6 Pence	Y	Y	?	Y	Y
7 Carson	Y	Y	Y	Y	Y
8 Ellsworth	Y	Y	N	Y	Y
9 Hill	Y	Y	N	Y	Y
IOWA					
1 Braley	Y	Y	Y	N	Y
2 Loebsack	Y	Y	Y	N	Y
3 Boswell	Y	Y	Y	Y	Y
4 Latham	Y	Y	N	Y	Y
5 King	N	Y	N	Y	Y
KANSAS					
1 Moran	N	Y	N	Y	Y
2 Jenkins	N	Y	N	Y	Y
3 Moore	Y	Y	Y	Y	Y
4 Tiahrt	N	Y	N	Y	Y
KENTUCKY					
1 Whitfield	Y	Y	N	Y	Y
2 Guthrie	Y	Y	N	Y	Y
3 Yarmuth	Y	Y	Y	Y	Y
4 Davis	Y	Y	N	Y	Y
5 Rogers	Y	Y	N	Y	Y
6 Chandler	Y	Y	Y	Y	Y
LOUISIANA					
1 Scalise	Y	Y	N	Y	Y
2 Cao	Y	Y	N	Y	Y
3 Melancon	Y	Y	Y	Y	Y
4 Fleming	Y	Y	N	Y	Y
5 Alexander	Y	Y	N	Y	Y
6 Cassidy	Y	Y	N	Y	Y
7 Boustany	Y	Y	N	Y	Y
MAINE					
1 Pingree	Y	Y	Y	N	Y
2 Michaud	Y	Y	Y	N	Y
MARYLAND					
1 Kratovil	Y	Y	N	Y	Y
2 Ruppersberger	Y	Y	Y	Y	Y
3 Sarbanes	Y	Y	Y	N	Y
4 Edwards	Y	Y	Y	Y	Y
5 Hoyer	Y	Y	Y	Y	Y
6 Bartlett	Y	Y	N	N	Y
7 Cummings	Y	Y	Y	N	Y
8 Van Hollen	Y	Y	Y	Y	Y
MASSACHUSETTS					
1 Olver	Y	Y	Y	N	Y
2 Neal	Y	Y	Y	N	Y
3 McGovern	Y	Y	Y	N	Y
4 Frank	Y	Y	Y	N	Y
5 Tsongas	Y	Y	Y	Y	?
6 Tierney	Y	Y	Y	N	Y
7 Markey	Y	Y	Y	N	Y
8 Capuano	Y	Y	Y	N	Y
9 Lynch	Y	Y	Y	N	Y
10 Delahunt	Y	Y	Y	Y	Y
MICHIGAN					
1 Stupak	Y	Y	Y	?	?
2 Hoekstra	?	?	N	Y	Y
3 Ehlers	Y	Y	N	N	Y
4 Camp	Y	Y	Y	N	Y
5 Kildee	Y	Y	Y	N	Y
6 Upton	Y	Y	N	Y	Y
7 Schauer	Y	Y	Y	N	Y
8 Rogers	Y	Y	N	Y	Y
9 Peters	Y	Y	Y	N	Y
10 Miller	Y	Y	N	Y	Y
11 McCotter	Y	Y	N	Y	Y
12 Levin	Y	Y	Y	N	Y
13 Kilpatrick	Y	Y	Y	N	Y
14 Conyers	Y	Y	Y	N	Y
15 Dingell	?	?	Y	Y	N
MINNESOTA					
1 Walz	Y	Y	Y	N	Y
2 Kline	Y	Y	N	Y	Y
3 Paulsen	Y	Y	N	Y	Y
4 McCollum	Y	Y	Y	N	Y

	64	65	66	67	68
5 Ellison	Y	Y	Y	N	Y
6 Bachmann	Y	Y	N	Y	Y
7 Peterson	Y	Y	Y	Y	Y
8 Oberstar	Y	Y	Y	N	Y
MISSISSIPPI					
1 Childers	Y	Y	Y	Y	Y
2 Thompson	Y	Y	Y	Y	Y
3 Harper	Y	Y	N	Y	Y
4 Taylor	Y	Y	Y	Y	Y
MISSOURI					
1 Clay	Y	Y	Y	Y	Y
2 Akin	N	Y	N	Y	Y
3 Carnahan	Y	Y	Y	Y	Y
4 Skelton	Y	Y	Y	Y	Y
5 Cleaver	Y	Y	Y	N	Y
6 Graves	Y	Y	N	Y	Y
7 Blunt	?	?	N	Y	Y
8 Emerson	Y	Y	N	Y	Y
9 Luetkemeyer	Y	Y	N	Y	Y
MONTANA					
AL Rehberg	Y	Y	N	Y	Y
NEBRASKA					
1 Fortenberry	Y	Y	N	Y	Y
2 Terry	Y	Y	N	Y	Y
3 Smith	Y	Y	N	Y	Y
NEVADA					
1 Berkley	Y	Y	Y	Y	Y
2 Heller	Y	Y	N	N	Y
3 Titus	Y	Y	Y	Y	Y
NEW HAMPSHIRE					
1 Shea-Porter	Y	Y	Y	N	Y
2 Hodes	Y	Y	Y	N	Y
NEW JERSEY					
1 Andrews	Y	Y	Y	Y	Y
2 LoBiondo	Y	Y	N	Y	Y
3 Adler	Y	Y	Y	Y	Y
4 Smith	Y	Y	N	Y	Y
5 Garrett	N	Y	N	Y	Y
6 Pallone	Y	Y	Y	N	Y
7 Lance	Y	Y	N	Y	Y
8 Pascrell	Y	Y	Y	Y	Y
9 Rothman	Y	Y	Y	N	Y
10 Payne	Y	Y	Y	N	Y
11 Frelinghuysen	Y	Y	N	Y	Y
12 Holt	Y	Y	Y	N	Y
13 Sires	Y	Y	Y	Y	Y
NEW MEXICO					
1 Heinrich	Y	Y	Y	Y	Y
2 Teague	Y	Y	Y	Y	Y
3 Luján	Y	Y	Y	N	Y
NEW YORK					
1 Bishop	Y	Y	?	?	?
2 Israel	Y	Y	Y	N	Y
3 King	Y	Y	N	Y	Y
4 McCarthy	Y	Y	Y	Y	Y
5 Ackerman	Y	Y	Y	Y	Y
6 Meeks	Y	Y	Y	N	Y
7 Crowley	Y	Y	Y	N	Y
8 Nadler	Y	Y	Y	N	Y
9 Weiner	Y	Y	Y	N	Y
10 Towns	Y	Y	?	N	Y
11 Clarke	Y	Y	Y	N	Y
12 Velázquez	Y	Y	Y	N	Y
13 McMahon	Y	Y	Y	N	Y
14 Maloney	Y	Y	Y	N	Y
15 Rangel	Y	Y	Y	N	Y
16 Serrano	Y	Y	Y	N	Y
17 Engel	Y	Y	Y	N	Y
18 Lowey	Y	Y	Y	N	Y
19 Hall	Y	Y	Y	N	Y
20 Murphy	Y	Y	Y	Y	Y
21 Tonko	Y	Y	Y	N	Y
22 Hinchey	Y	Y	Y	N	Y
23 Owens	Y	Y	Y	Y	Y
24 Arcuri	Y	Y	Y	Y	Y
25 Maffei	Y	Y	Y	N	Y
26 Lee	Y	Y	N	Y	Y
27 Higgins	Y	Y	Y	Y	Y
28 Slaughter	Y	Y	Y	N	Y
29 Massa	Y	Y	Y	Y	Y
NORTH CAROLINA					
1 Butterfield	Y	Y	Y	Y	Y
2 Etheridge	Y	Y	Y	Y	Y
3 Jones	Y	Y	N	N	Y
4 Price	Y	Y	Y	N	Y

	64	65	66	67	68
5 Foxx	Y	Y	N	Y	Y
6 Coble	Y	Y	N	Y	Y
7 McIntyre	Y	Y	Y	Y	Y
8 Kissell	Y	Y	Y	Y	Y
9 Myrick	Y	Y	N	?	?
10 McHenry	Y	Y	N	Y	Y
11 Shuler	Y	Y	N	Y	Y
12 Watt	Y	Y	N	Y	Y
13 Miller	Y	Y	Y	Y	Y
NORTH DAKOTA					
AL Pomeroy	Y	Y	Y	Y	Y
OHIO					
1 Driehaus	Y	Y	Y	Y	Y
2 Schmidt	Y	Y	N	Y	Y
3 Turner	Y	Y	N	Y	Y
4 Jordan	N	Y	N	Y	Y
5 Latta	Y	Y	N	Y	Y
6 Wilson	Y	Y	N	Y	Y
7 Austria	Y	Y	N	Y	Y
8 Boehner	N	Y	N	Y	Y
9 Kaptur	Y	Y	Y	Y	Y
10 Kucinich	Y	Y	N	N	Y
11 Fudge	Y	Y	Y	N	Y
12 Tiberi	Y	Y	N	Y	Y
13 Sutton	Y	Y	Y	N	Y
14 LaTourette	Y	Y	N	Y	Y
15 Kilroy	Y	Y	Y	Y	Y
16 Boccieri	Y	Y	Y	N	Y
17 Ryan	Y	Y	Y	N	Y
18 Space	Y	Y	Y	Y	Y
OKLAHOMA					
1 Sullivan	Y	Y	N	?	?
2 Boren	Y	Y	Y	Y	Y
3 Lucas	Y	Y	N	Y	Y
4 Cole	Y	Y	N	Y	Y
5 Fallin	Y	Y	N	?	?
OREGON					
1 Wu	Y	Y	Y	N	Y
2 Walden	Y	Y	N	Y	Y
3 Blumenauer	Y	Y	Y	N	Y
4 DeFazio	Y	Y	Y	N	Y
5 Schrader	Y	Y	Y	Y	Y
PENNSYLVANIA					
1 Brady	Y	Y	Y	Y	Y
2 Fattah	Y	Y	Y	Y	Y
3 Dahlkemper	Y	Y	N	Y	Y
4 Altmire	Y	Y	N	Y	Y
5 Thompson	Y	Y	N	Y	Y
6 Gerlach	Y	Y	N	Y	Y
7 Sestak	Y	Y	N	Y	Y
8 Murphy, P.	Y	Y	N	Y	Y
9 Shuster	Y	Y	N	Y	Y
10 Carney	Y	Y	Y	Y	Y
11 Kanjorski	Y	Y	Y	Y	Y
12 Vacant					
13 Schwartz	Y	Y	Y	Y	Y
14 Doyle	Y	Y	Y	Y	Y
15 Dent	Y	Y	N	?	?
16 Pitts	?	?	?	?	?
17 Holden	Y	Y	Y	Y	Y
18 Murphy, T.	Y	Y	N	Y	Y
19 Platts	Y	Y	N	Y	Y
RHODE ISLAND					
1 Kennedy	Y	Y	?	Y	Y
2 Langevin	Y	Y	Y	Y	Y
SOUTH CAROLINA					
1 Brown	Y	Y	N	Y	Y
2 Wilson	Y	Y	?	?	?
3 Barrett	?	?	?	?	?
4 Inglis	Y	Y	N	Y	Y
5 Spratt	Y	Y	Y	Y	Y
6 Clyburn	Y	Y	Y	Y	Y
SOUTH DAKOTA					
AL Herseth Sandlin	Y	Y	Y	Y	Y
TENNESSEE					
1 Roe	Y	Y	N	Y	Y
2 Duncan	Y	Y	N	N	Y
3 Wamp	Y	Y	N	Y	Y
4 Davis	Y	Y	N	Y	Y
5 Cooper	Y	Y	Y	Y	Y
6 Gordon	Y	Y	Y	N	Y
7 Blackburn	Y	Y	N	Y	Y
8 Tanner	Y	Y	N	Y	Y
9 Cohen	Y	Y	Y	Y	Y

	64	65	66	67	68
TEXAS					
1 Gohmert	Y	Y	N	Y	Y
2 Poe	Y	Y	N	Y	Y
3 Johnson, S.	Y	Y	N	Y	Y
4 Hall	Y	Y	?	?	?
5 Hensarling	Y	Y	N	Y	Y
6 Barton	Y	Y	N	Y	Y
7 Culberson	Y	?	N	Y	Y
8 Brady	N	Y	N	Y	Y
9 Green, A.	Y	Y	Y	N	Y
10 McCaul	Y	Y	N	Y	Y
11 Conaway	Y	Y	N	Y	Y
12 Granger	Y	Y	N	Y	Y
13 Thornberry	Y	Y	N	Y	Y
14 Paul	N	Y	N	N	Y
15 Hinojosa	Y	Y	Y	Y	Y
16 Reyes	Y	Y	Y	Y	Y
17 Edwards	Y	Y	Y	Y	Y
18 Jackson Lee	Y	Y	Y	Y	Y
19 Neugebauer	Y	Y	N	Y	Y
20 Gonzalez	Y	Y	Y	Y	Y
21 Smith	Y	Y	N	Y	Y
22 Olson	Y	Y	N	Y	Y
23 Rodriguez	Y	Y	Y	Y	Y
24 Marchant	Y	Y	N	Y	Y
25 Doggett	Y	Y	Y	N	Y
26 Burgess	Y	Y	N	Y	Y
27 Ortiz	Y	Y	Y	Y	Y
28 Cuellar	Y	Y	Y	Y	Y
29 Green, G.	Y	Y	Y	Y	Y
30 Johnson, E.	Y	Y	?	Y	Y
31 Carter	Y	Y	N	Y	Y
32 Sessions	Y	Y	N	Y	Y
UTAH					
1 Bishop	Y	Y	N	N	Y
2 Matheson	Y	Y	Y	Y	Y
3 Chaffetz	Y	Y	N	N	Y
VERMONT					
AL Welch	Y	Y	Y	N	Y
VIRGINIA					
1 Wittman	Y	Y	N	Y	Y
2 Nye	Y	Y	Y	Y	Y
3 Scott	Y	Y	Y	N	Y
4 Forbes	Y	Y	N	Y	Y
5 Perriello	Y	Y	N	Y	Y
6 Goodlatte	Y	Y	N	Y	Y
7 Cantor	Y	Y	N	Y	Y
8 Moran	Y	Y	Y	Y	Y
9 Boucher	Y	Y	?	?	?
10 Wolf	Y	Y	N	Y	Y
11 Connolly	Y	Y	Y	Y	Y
WASHINGTON					
1 Inslee	Y	Y	Y	N	Y
2 Larsen	Y	Y	Y	N	Y
3 Baird	Y	Y	Y	Y	Y
4 Hastings	Y	Y	N	Y	Y
5 McMorris Rodgers	Y	Y	N	Y	Y
6 Dicks	Y	Y	Y	Y	Y
7 McDermott	Y	Y	Y	N	Y
8 Reichert	?	?	?	?	?
9 Smith	Y	Y	Y	Y	Y
WEST VIRGINIA					
1 Mollohan	Y	Y	Y	Y	Y
2 Capito	Y	Y	N	Y	Y
3 Rahall	Y	Y	Y	Y	Y
WISCONSIN					
1 Ryan	N	Y	N	Y	Y
2 Baldwin	Y	Y	Y	N	Y
3 Kind	Y	Y	Y	N	Y
4 Moore	Y	Y	Y	N	Y
5 Sensenbrenner	N	Y	N	Y	Y
6 Petri	Y	Y	N	Y	Y
7 Obey	Y	Y	Y	Y	Y
8 Kagen	Y	Y	Y	N	Y
WYOMING					
AL Lummis	Y	Y	N	Y	Y
DELEGATES					
Faleomavaega (A.S.)					
Norton (D.C.)					
Bordallo (Guam)					
Sablan (N. Marianas)					
Pierluisi (P.R.)					
Christensen (V.I.)					

IN THE HOUSE | By Vote Number

69. HR 2701. Fiscal 2010 Intelligence Authorization/Manager's Amendment. Reyes, D-Texas, manager's amendment that would allow the executive branch to limit congressional intelligence committees' access to sensitive intelligence if the administration submits certification that the action meets "extraordinary circumstances affecting vital interests of the United States." It also would make other changes, including allowing congressional committees to request Government Accountability Office reports on intelligence issues and requiring the FBI director to consult with the secretary of State to review extraterritorial jurisdiction in U.S. law. Adopted in Committee of the Whole 246-166: D 245-4; R 1-162. Feb. 26, 2010.

70. HR 2701. Fiscal 2010 Intelligence Authorization/National Intelligence Diversity. Hastings, D-Fla., amendment that would require the director of national intelligence to submit a report on plans to increase diversity in the intelligence community. Adopted in Committee of the Whole 401-11: D 249-0; R 152-11. Feb. 26, 2010.

71. HR 2701. Fiscal 2010 Intelligence Authorization/Report on Attempted Dec. 25 Airline Attack. Schauer, D-Mich., amendment that would require the director of national intelligence to submit a report to Congress on the attempted terrorist attack on Northwest Flight 253 and intelligence community efforts to prevent failures to share information. Adopted in Committee of the Whole 410-1: D 248-1; R 162-0. Feb. 26, 2010.

72. HR 2701. Fiscal 2010 Intelligence Authorization/Recommit. Hoekstra, R-Mich., motion to recommit the bill to the Permanent Select Committee on Intelligence with instructions that it be immediately reported back with an amendment that would require the CIA inspector general to investigate any members' objection to covert action and the corresponding CIA response, and direct the CIA director to release unclassified memos on congressional briefings about interrogations involving torture. It also would require the national intelligence director to coordinate the interrogation of high-value detainees and approve the reading of Miranda rights to these detainees. Motion rejected 186-217: D 28-217; R 158-0. Feb. 26, 2010.

73. HR 2701. Fiscal 2010 Intelligence Authorization/Passage. Passage of the bill that would authorize classified amounts in fiscal 2010 for 16 intelligence agencies, including the director of national intelligence, the CIA and the National Security Agency, and for intelligence activities of the Defense Department, the FBI, the Homeland Security Department and other agencies. It would allow the transfer of Guantánamo Bay detainees to the United States, but delay the transfer for 120 days after the president submits a report to Congress. As amended, it would allow the executive branch to limit congressional intelligence committees' access to sensitive intelligence if the administration submits certification that the action meets "extraordinary circumstances affecting vital interests of the United States." Passed 235-168: D 234-9; R 1-159. Feb. 26, 2010.

74. H Con Res 238. Recognition of Black Veterans/Adoption. Filner, D-Calif., motion to suspend the rules and adopt the concurrent resolution that would recognize the sacrifices of black veterans and the difficulties they faced at home after serving in the military. Motion agreed to 383-0: D 236-0; R 147-0. A two-thirds majority of those present and voting (256 in this case) is required for adoption under suspension of the rules. Feb. 26, 2010.

	69	70	71	72	73	74
ALABAMA						
1 Bonner	N	Y	Y	Y	N	Y
2 Bright	Y	Y	+	Y	Y	Y
3 Rogers	N	Y	Y	Y	N	Y
4 Aderholt	N	Y	Y	Y	N	Y
5 Griffith	N	Y	Y	Y	N	Y
6 Bachus	N	Y	Y	?	N	Y
7 Davis	Y	Y	Y	N	?	?
ALASKA						
AL Young	N	N	Y	Y	N	Y
ARIZONA						
1 Kirkpatrick	Y	Y	Y	Y	Y	Y
2 Franks	N	N	Y	Y	N	Y
3 Shadegg	N	Y	Y	Y	N	Y
4 Pastor	Y	Y	Y	N	Y	Y
5 Mitchell	Y	Y	Y	Y	Y	Y
6 Flake	N	Y	Y	Y	N	Y
7 Grijalva	Y	Y	Y	N	Y	?
8 Giffords	Y	Y	Y	Y	Y	Y
ARKANSAS						
1 Berry	Y	Y	Y	N	Y	Y
2 Snyder	Y	Y	Y	N	Y	Y
3 Boozman	N	Y	Y	Y	N	Y
4 Ross	Y	Y	Y	N	Y	Y
CALIFORNIA						
1 Thompson	Y	Y	Y	N	Y	Y
2 Herger	N	Y	Y	Y	N	?
3 Lungren	N	N	Y	Y	N	Y
4 McClintock	N	N	Y	Y	N	Y
5 Matsui	Y	Y	Y	N	Y	Y
6 Woolsey	Y	Y	N	N	N	Y
7 Miller, George	Y	Y	Y	N	Y	Y
8 Pelosi						
9 Lee	Y	Y	Y	N	N	Y
10 Garamendi	Y	Y	Y	N	Y	Y
11 McNerney	Y	Y	Y	Y	Y	Y
12 Speier	Y	Y	Y	N	Y	Y
13 Stark	?	?	?	?	?	?
14 Eshoo	Y	Y	Y	N	Y	Y
15 Honda	Y	Y	Y	N	Y	Y
16 Lofgren	Y	Y	Y	N	Y	Y
17 Farr	Y	Y	Y	N	Y	Y
18 Cardoza	Y	Y	Y	N	Y	Y
19 Radanovich	?	?	?	?	?	?
20 Costa	Y	Y	Y	N	Y	Y
21 Nunes	N	Y	Y	Y	N	Y
22 McCarthy	N	Y	Y	Y	N	Y
23 Capps	+	+	+	–	+	+
24 Gallegly	N	Y	Y	Y	N	?
25 McKeon	N	Y	Y	Y	N	Y
26 Dreier	N	Y	Y	Y	N	Y
27 Sherman	Y	Y	Y	N	Y	Y
28 Berman	Y	Y	Y	N	Y	Y
29 Schiff	Y	Y	Y	N	Y	Y
30 Waxman	Y	Y	Y	N	Y	Y
31 Becerra	Y	Y	Y	N	Y	Y
32 Chu	Y	Y	Y	N	Y	Y
33 Watson	Y	Y	Y	N	Y	Y
34 Roybal-Allard	Y	Y	Y	N	Y	Y
35 Waters	N	Y	Y	N	Y	Y
36 Harman	Y	Y	Y	N	Y	Y
37 Richardson	Y	Y	Y	N	Y	Y
38 Napolitano	Y	Y	Y	N	Y	Y
39 Sánchez, Linda	Y	Y	Y	N	Y	Y
40 Royce	N	N	Y	Y	N	Y
41 Lewis	N	Y	Y	Y	N	Y
42 Miller, Gary	N	N	Y	Y	N	Y
43 Baca	Y	Y	Y	N	Y	?
44 Calvert	N	Y	Y	Y	N	?
45 Bono Mack	N	Y	Y	Y	N	Y
46 Rohrabacher	N	N	Y	Y	N	Y
47 Sanchez, Loretta	Y	Y	Y	N	Y	Y
48 Campbell	N	N	Y	Y	N	Y
49 Issa	N	Y	Y	Y	N	Y
50 Bilbray	N	Y	Y	Y	N	Y
51 Filner	N	Y	Y	N	N	Y
52 Hunter	N	Y	Y	Y	N	Y
53 Davis	Y	Y	Y	N	Y	Y

	69	70	71	72	73	74
COLORADO						
1 DeGette	Y	Y	Y	N	Y	Y
2 Polis	Y	Y	Y	N	Y	Y
3 Salazar	Y	Y	Y	N	Y	Y
4 Markey	Y	Y	Y	N	Y	Y
5 Lamborn	N	Y	Y	Y	N	Y
6 Coffman	N	Y	Y	Y	N	Y
7 Perlmutter	Y	Y	Y	N	Y	Y
CONNECTICUT						
1 Larson	Y	Y	Y	N	Y	?
2 Courtney	Y	Y	Y	N	Y	Y
3 DeLauro	Y	Y	Y	N	Y	Y
4 Himes	Y	Y	Y	N	Y	Y
5 Murphy	Y	Y	Y	N	Y	Y
DELAWARE						
AL Castle	N	Y	Y	Y	N	Y
FLORIDA						
1 Miller	N	Y	Y	Y	N	Y
2 Boyd	Y	Y	Y	N	Y	Y
3 Brown	Y	Y	Y	N	Y	Y
4 Crenshaw	N	Y	Y	Y	N	Y
5 Brown-Waite	N	Y	Y	Y	N	Y
6 Stearns	N	Y	Y	Y	N	Y
7 Mica	N	Y	Y	Y	N	Y
8 Grayson	Y	Y	Y	N	Y	Y
9 Bilirakis	N	Y	Y	Y	N	Y
10 Young	N	Y	Y	Y	N	Y
11 Castor	Y	Y	Y	N	Y	Y
12 Putnam	N	Y	Y	Y	N	Y
13 Buchanan	N	Y	Y	Y	N	Y
14 Mack	?	?	?	?	?	?
15 Posey	N	Y	Y	Y	N	Y
16 Rooney	N	Y	Y	Y	N	Y
17 Meek	Y	Y	Y	N	Y	Y
18 Ros-Lehtinen	N	Y	Y	Y	N	Y
19 Vacant						
20 Wasserman Schultz	Y	Y	Y	N	Y	Y
21 Diaz-Balart, L.	N	Y	Y	Y	N	Y
22 Klein	Y	Y	Y	N	Y	Y
23 Hastings	Y	Y	Y	N	Y	Y
24 Kosmas	Y	Y	Y	N	Y	Y
25 Diaz-Balart, M.	N	Y	Y	Y	N	Y
GEORGIA						
1 Kingston	N	Y	Y	Y	N	Y
2 Bishop	Y	Y	Y	N	Y	Y
3 Westmoreland	–	+	+	+	–	+
4 Johnson	?	Y	Y	N	Y	Y
5 Lewis	Y	Y	Y	N	Y	Y
6 Price	N	Y	Y	?	N	Y
7 Linder	N	Y	Y	Y	N	?
8 Marshall	Y	Y	Y	Y	Y	Y
9 Deal	?	?	?	?	?	?
10 Broun	N	N	Y	Y	N	Y
11 Gingrey	N	Y	Y	Y	N	Y
12 Barrow	Y	Y	Y	Y	Y	Y
13 Scott	Y	Y	Y	N	Y	Y
HAWAII						
1 Abercrombie	?	?	?	?	?	?
2 Hirono	Y	Y	Y	N	Y	Y
IDAHO						
1 Minnick	Y	Y	Y	Y	Y	Y
2 Simpson	N	Y	Y	Y	N	Y
ILLINOIS						
1 Rush	Y	Y	Y	N	Y	Y
2 Jackson	Y	Y	Y	N	Y	Y
3 Lipinski	Y	Y	Y	N	Y	Y
4 Gutierrez	Y	Y	Y	N	Y	Y
5 Quigley	Y	Y	Y	N	Y	Y
6 Roskam	N	Y	Y	Y	N	Y
7 Davis	Y	Y	Y	N	Y	Y
8 Bean	Y	Y	Y	N	Y	Y
9 Schakowsky	Y	Y	Y	N	Y	Y
10 Kirk	N	Y	Y	Y	N	Y
11 Halvorson	Y	Y	Y	Y	Y	Y
12 Costello	N	Y	Y	N	Y	Y
13 Biggert	N	Y	Y	Y	N	Y
14 Foster	Y	Y	Y	Y	Y	Y
15 Johnson	N	Y	Y	Y	N	Y

KEY | Republicans | Democrats

Y Voted for (yea)	X Paired against	C Voted "present" to avoid possible conflict of interest
# Paired for	– Announced against	
+ Announced for	P Voted "present"	? Did not vote or otherwise make a position known
N Voted against (nay)		

	69	70	71	72	73	74
16 **Manzullo**	N	Y	Y	Y	N	Y
17 Hare	Y	Y	Y	N	Y	Y
18 **Schock**	N	Y	Y	Y	N	Y
19 **Shimkus**	N	Y	Y	Y	N	Y
INDIANA						
1 Visclosky	Y	Y	Y	N	Y	Y
2 Donnelly	Y	Y	Y	Y	Y	Y
3 **Souder**	N	Y	Y	Y	N	Y
4 **Buyer**	N	Y	Y	Y	N	Y
5 **Burton**	N	Y	Y	Y	N	Y
6 **Pence**	N	Y	Y	Y	N	Y
7 Carson	Y	Y	Y	N	Y	Y
8 Ellsworth	Y	Y	Y	N	Y	Y
9 Hill	Y	Y	Y	N	Y	Y
IOWA						
1 Braley	Y	Y	Y	N	Y	Y
2 Loebsack	Y	Y	Y	N	Y	Y
3 Boswell	Y	Y	Y	N	Y	Y
4 **Latham**	N	Y	Y	Y	N	Y
5 **King**	N	N	Y	Y	N	Y
KANSAS						
1 **Moran**	?	?	?	+	–	?
2 **Jenkins**	N	Y	Y	Y	N	Y
3 Moore	Y	Y	Y	N	Y	Y
4 **Tiahrt**	N	Y	Y	Y	N	Y
KENTUCKY						
1 **Whitfield**	N	Y	Y	Y	N	?
2 **Guthrie**	N	Y	Y	Y	N	Y
3 Yarmuth	Y	Y	Y	N	Y	Y
4 **Davis**	N	Y	Y	Y	N	Y
5 **Rogers**	N	Y	Y	Y	N	Y
6 Chandler	Y	Y	Y	N	Y	Y
LOUISIANA						
1 **Scalise**	?	?	?	?	?	?
2 **Cao**	Y	Y	Y	Y	Y	Y
3 Melancon	Y	Y	Y	Y	Y	Y
4 **Fleming**	N	Y	Y	Y	N	Y
5 **Alexander**	N	Y	Y	Y	N	Y
6 **Cassidy**	N	Y	Y	Y	N	Y
7 **Boustany**	N	Y	Y	Y	N	?
MAINE						
1 Pingree	Y	Y	Y	N	Y	Y
2 Michaud	Y	Y	Y	N	Y	Y
MARYLAND						
1 Kratovil	Y	Y	Y	N	Y	Y
2 Ruppersberger	Y	Y	Y	N	Y	Y
3 Sarbanes	Y	Y	Y	N	Y	Y
4 Edwards	Y	Y	Y	N	Y	Y
5 Hoyer	Y	Y	Y	N	Y	Y
6 **Bartlett**	N	Y	Y	Y	N	Y
7 Cummings	Y	Y	Y	N	Y	Y
8 Van Hollen	Y	Y	Y	N	Y	Y
MASSACHUSETTS						
1 Olver	Y	?	Y	N	Y	Y
2 Neal	Y	Y	Y	N	Y	Y
3 McGovern	Y	Y	Y	N	Y	Y
4 Frank	Y	Y	Y	N	Y	Y
5 Tsongas	Y	Y	Y	N	Y	Y
6 Tierney	Y	Y	Y	N	Y	Y
7 Markey	Y	Y	Y	N	Y	Y
8 Capuano	Y	Y	Y	N	Y	Y
9 Lynch	Y	Y	Y	N	?	Y
10 Delahunt	Y	Y	Y	N	Y	Y
MICHIGAN						
1 Stupak	+	+	+	–	+	+
2 **Hoekstra**	N	Y	Y	Y	N	?
3 **Ehlers**	N	Y	Y	Y	N	Y
4 **Camp**	N	Y	Y	Y	N	Y
5 Kildee	Y	Y	Y	N	Y	Y
6 **Upton**	N	Y	Y	Y	N	Y
7 Schauer	Y	Y	Y	N	Y	Y
8 **Rogers**	N	Y	Y	Y	N	Y
9 Peters	Y	Y	Y	Y	Y	Y
10 **Miller**	N	Y	Y	Y	N	Y
11 **McCotter**	N	Y	Y	Y	N	Y
12 Levin	Y	Y	Y	N	Y	Y
13 Kilpatrick	Y	Y	Y	N	Y	Y
14 Conyers	Y	Y	Y	N	Y	Y
15 Dingell	Y	Y	Y	N	Y	?
MINNESOTA						
1 Walz	Y	Y	Y	N	Y	Y
2 **Kline**	N	Y	Y	Y	N	Y
3 **Paulsen**	N	Y	Y	Y	N	Y
4 McCollum	Y	Y	Y	N	Y	Y

	69	70	71	72	73	74
5 Ellison	Y	Y	Y	N	Y	Y
6 **Bachmann**	N	Y	Y	Y	N	Y
7 Peterson	Y	Y	Y	N	Y	Y
8 Oberstar	Y	Y	Y	N	Y	Y
MISSISSIPPI						
1 Childers	Y	Y	Y	Y	Y	Y
2 Thompson	Y	Y	Y	N	Y	Y
3 **Harper**	N	Y	Y	Y	N	Y
4 Taylor	Y	Y	Y	Y	Y	Y
MISSOURI						
1 Clay	Y	Y	Y	N	Y	Y
2 **Akin**	N	N	Y	Y	N	Y
3 Carnahan	Y	Y	Y	N	Y	Y
4 Skelton	Y	Y	Y	N	Y	Y
5 Cleaver	Y	Y	Y	N	Y	Y
6 **Graves**	N	Y	Y	Y	N	Y
7 **Blunt**	N	Y	Y	?	?	?
8 **Emerson**	N	Y	Y	Y	N	Y
9 **Luetkemeyer**	N	Y	Y	Y	N	Y
MONTANA						
AL **Rehberg**	N	Y	Y	Y	N	Y
NEBRASKA						
1 **Fortenberry**	N	Y	Y	Y	N	Y
2 **Terry**	N	Y	Y	Y	N	Y
3 **Smith**	N	Y	Y	Y	N	Y
NEVADA						
1 Berkley	Y	Y	Y	N	Y	Y
2 **Heller**	N	Y	Y	Y	N	Y
3 Titus	Y	Y	Y	N	Y	Y
NEW HAMPSHIRE						
1 Shea-Porter	Y	Y	Y	N	Y	Y
2 Hodes	Y	Y	Y	N	Y	Y
NEW JERSEY						
1 Andrews	Y	Y	Y	N	Y	Y
2 **LoBiondo**	N	Y	Y	Y	N	Y
3 Adler	Y	Y	Y	Y	Y	Y
4 **Smith**	N	Y	Y	Y	N	Y
5 **Garrett**	N	Y	Y	Y	N	Y
6 Pallone	Y	Y	Y	N	Y	Y
7 **Lance**	N	Y	Y	Y	N	Y
8 Pascrell	Y	Y	Y	N	Y	?
9 Rothman	Y	Y	Y	N	Y	Y
10 Payne	Y	Y	Y	N	N	Y
11 **Frelinghuysen**	N	Y	Y	Y	N	Y
12 Holt	Y	Y	Y	N	Y	Y
13 Sires	Y	Y	Y	N	Y	Y
NEW MEXICO						
1 Heinrich	Y	Y	Y	N	Y	Y
2 Teague	Y	Y	Y	Y	Y	Y
3 Luján	Y	Y	Y	N	Y	Y
NEW YORK						
1 Bishop	+	+	–	+	+	?
2 Israel	Y	Y	Y	N	Y	Y
3 **King**	–	+	+	+	–	+
4 McCarthy	Y	Y	Y	N	Y	Y
5 Ackerman	?	?	?	?	?	?
6 Meeks	Y	Y	Y	N	Y	Y
7 Crowley	Y	Y	Y	N	Y	Y
8 Nadler	Y	Y	Y	N	Y	Y
9 Weiner	Y	Y	Y	N	Y	Y
10 Towns	Y	Y	Y	N	Y	Y
11 Clarke	Y	Y	Y	N	Y	Y
12 Velázquez	Y	Y	Y	N	Y	Y
13 McMahon	Y	Y	Y	Y	Y	Y
14 Maloney	Y	Y	Y	N	Y	Y
15 Rangel	Y	Y	Y	N	Y	?
16 Serrano	Y	Y	Y	N	Y	Y
17 Engel	Y	Y	Y	N	Y	Y
18 Lowey	Y	Y	Y	N	Y	Y
19 Hall	Y	Y	Y	N	Y	Y
20 Murphy	Y	Y	Y	N	Y	Y
21 Tonko	Y	Y	Y	N	Y	Y
22 Hinchey	Y	Y	Y	N	Y	Y
23 Owens	Y	Y	Y	Y	Y	?
24 Arcuri	Y	Y	Y	Y	Y	Y
25 Maffei	Y	Y	Y	N	Y	Y
26 **Lee**	N	Y	Y	Y	N	Y
27 Higgins	Y	Y	Y	N	Y	Y
28 Slaughter	Y	Y	Y	N	Y	Y
29 Massa	Y	Y	Y	N	Y	Y
NORTH CAROLINA						
1 Butterfield	Y	Y	Y	N	Y	Y
2 Etheridge	Y	Y	Y	N	Y	Y
3 **Jones**	N	Y	Y	Y	N	Y
4 Price	Y	Y	Y	N	Y	Y

	69	70	71	72	73	74
5 **Foxx**	N	Y	Y	Y	N	Y
6 **Coble**	N	Y	Y	Y	N	Y
7 McIntyre	Y	Y	Y	N	Y	Y
8 Kissell	Y	Y	Y	N	Y	Y
9 **Myrick**	N	Y	Y	Y	N	Y
10 **McHenry**	N	Y	Y	Y	N	Y
11 Shuler	Y	Y	Y	N	Y	Y
12 Watt	Y	Y	Y	N	Y	Y
13 Miller	Y	Y	Y	N	Y	Y
NORTH DAKOTA						
AL Pomeroy	Y	Y	Y	Y	Y	Y
OHIO						
1 Driehaus	Y	Y	Y	N	Y	Y
2 **Schmidt**	N	Y	Y	Y	N	Y
3 **Turner**	N	Y	Y	Y	N	Y
4 **Jordan**	N	Y	Y	Y	N	?
5 **Latta**	N	Y	Y	Y	N	Y
6 Wilson	Y	Y	Y	N	Y	Y
7 **Austria**	N	Y	Y	Y	N	Y
8 **Boehner**	?	?	?	?	?	?
9 Kaptur	Y	Y	Y	N	Y	Y
10 Kucinich	N	Y	Y	N	N	Y
11 Fudge	Y	Y	Y	N	Y	Y
12 **Tiberi**	N	Y	Y	Y	N	Y
13 Sutton	Y	Y	Y	N	Y	Y
14 **LaTourette**	N	Y	Y	Y	N	Y
15 Kilroy	Y	Y	Y	N	Y	Y
16 Boccieri	Y	Y	Y	N	Y	Y
17 Ryan	Y	Y	Y	N	Y	Y
18 Space	Y	Y	Y	Y	N	Y
OKLAHOMA						
1 **Sullivan**	?	?	?	?	?	?
2 Boren	Y	Y	Y	Y	Y	Y
3 **Lucas**	N	Y	Y	Y	N	Y
4 **Cole**	N	Y	Y	Y	N	+
5 **Fallin**	?	?	?	?	?	?
OREGON						
1 Wu	Y	Y	Y	N	Y	Y
2 **Walden**	N	Y	Y	Y	N	Y
3 Blumenauer	Y	Y	Y	N	Y	Y
4 DeFazio	Y	Y	Y	N	Y	Y
5 Schrader	Y	Y	Y	N	Y	Y
PENNSYLVANIA						
1 Brady	Y	Y	Y	N	Y	Y
2 Fattah	Y	Y	Y	N	Y	Y
3 Dahlkemper	Y	Y	Y	Y	Y	Y
4 Altmire	Y	Y	Y	Y	Y	Y
5 **Thompson**	N	Y	Y	Y	N	Y
6 **Gerlach**	N	Y	Y	Y	N	Y
7 Sestak	Y	Y	Y	N	Y	Y
8 Murphy, P.	Y	Y	Y	N	Y	Y
9 **Shuster**	N	Y	Y	Y	N	Y
10 Carney	Y	Y	Y	N	Y	Y
11 Kanjorski	Y	Y	Y	N	Y	Y
12 Vacant						
13 Schwartz	Y	Y	Y	N	Y	Y
14 Doyle	Y	Y	Y	N	Y	?
15 **Dent**	–	+	+	+	–	+
16 **Pitts**	N	Y	Y	Y	N	Y
17 Holden	Y	Y	Y	N	Y	Y
18 **Murphy, T.**	N	Y	Y	Y	N	?
19 **Platts**	N	Y	Y	Y	N	Y
RHODE ISLAND						
1 Kennedy	Y	Y	Y	N	Y	Y
2 Langevin	Y	Y	Y	N	Y	Y
SOUTH CAROLINA						
1 **Brown**	N	Y	Y	Y	N	Y
2 **Wilson**	N	Y	Y	Y	N	Y
3 **Barrett**	–	+	+	+	–	+
4 **Inglis**	N	Y	Y	Y	N	Y
5 Spratt	Y	Y	Y	N	Y	Y
6 Clyburn	Y	Y	Y	N	Y	Y
SOUTH DAKOTA						
AL Herseth Sandlin	Y	Y	Y	Y	N	Y
TENNESSEE						
1 **Roe**	N	Y	Y	Y	N	Y
2 **Duncan**	N	Y	Y	Y	N	Y
3 **Wamp**	N	Y	Y	Y	N	Y
4 Davis	Y	Y	Y	N	Y	Y
5 Cooper	Y	Y	Y	N	Y	Y
6 Gordon	Y	Y	Y	N	Y	Y
7 **Blackburn**	N	Y	?	?	?	?
8 Tanner	?	?	?	?	?	?
9 Cohen	Y	Y	Y	N	Y	Y

	69	70	71	72	73	74
TEXAS						
1 **Gohmert**	N	Y	Y	Y	N	?
2 **Poe**	N	Y	Y	Y	N	Y
3 **Johnson, S.**	N	Y	Y	Y	N	Y
4 **Hall**	?	?	?	?	?	?
5 **Hensarling**	N	Y	Y	Y	N	Y
6 **Barton**	N	Y	Y	?	?	?
7 **Culberson**	N	Y	Y	Y	N	Y
8 **Brady**	N	Y	Y	Y	N	Y
9 Green, A.	Y	Y	Y	N	Y	Y
10 **McCaul**	N	Y	Y	Y	N	Y
11 **Conaway**	N	Y	Y	Y	N	Y
12 **Granger**	N	Y	Y	Y	N	Y
13 **Thornberry**	N	Y	Y	Y	N	Y
14 **Paul**	?	?	?	?	?	?
15 Hinojosa	Y	Y	Y	N	Y	Y
16 Reyes	Y	Y	Y	N	Y	Y
17 Edwards	Y	Y	Y	N	Y	Y
18 Jackson Lee	Y	Y	Y	N	Y	Y
19 **Neugebauer**	N	Y	Y	Y	N	Y
20 Gonzalez	Y	Y	Y	N	Y	Y
21 **Smith**	N	Y	Y	Y	N	Y
22 **Olson**	N	Y	Y	Y	N	Y
23 Rodriguez	Y	Y	Y	N	Y	Y
24 **Marchant**	N	Y	Y	Y	N	Y
25 Doggett	Y	Y	Y	N	Y	Y
26 **Burgess**	N	Y	Y	Y	N	Y
27 Ortiz	Y	Y	Y	N	Y	Y
28 Cuellar	Y	Y	Y	N	Y	Y
29 Green, G.	Y	Y	Y	N	Y	Y
30 Johnson, E.	Y	Y	Y	N	Y	Y
31 **Carter**	N	Y	Y	Y	N	?
32 **Sessions**	N	Y	Y	Y	N	Y
UTAH						
1 **Bishop**	N	Y	Y	Y	N	Y
2 Matheson	Y	Y	Y	N	Y	Y
3 **Chaffetz**	N	Y	Y	Y	N	Y
VERMONT						
AL Welch	Y	Y	Y	N	Y	Y
VIRGINIA						
1 **Wittman**	N	Y	Y	Y	N	Y
2 Nye	Y	Y	Y	Y	Y	Y
3 Scott	Y	Y	Y	N	Y	Y
4 **Forbes**	N	Y	Y	Y	N	Y
5 Perriello	Y	Y	Y	N	Y	Y
6 **Goodlatte**	N	Y	Y	Y	N	Y
7 **Cantor**	N	Y	Y	Y	N	Y
8 Moran	Y	Y	Y	N	Y	Y
9 Boucher	?	?	?	?	?	?
10 **Wolf**	N	Y	Y	Y	N	Y
11 Connolly	Y	Y	Y	N	Y	Y
WASHINGTON						
1 Inslee	?	?	?	?	?	?
2 Larsen	Y	Y	Y	N	Y	Y
3 Baird	Y	Y	Y	N	Y	Y
4 **Hastings**	N	Y	Y	Y	N	Y
5 **McMorris Rodgers**	N	Y	Y	Y	N	Y
6 Dicks	Y	Y	Y	N	Y	Y
7 McDermott	Y	Y	Y	N	N	Y
8 **Reichert**	–	+	+	+	–	+
9 Smith	Y	Y	Y	N	Y	Y
WEST VIRGINIA						
1 Mollohan	Y	Y	Y	N	Y	Y
2 **Capito**	N	Y	Y	Y	N	Y
3 Rahall	Y	Y	Y	N	Y	Y
WISCONSIN						
1 **Ryan**	N	Y	Y	Y	N	?
2 Baldwin	Y	Y	Y	N	Y	Y
3 Kind	Y	Y	Y	N	Y	Y
4 Moore	Y	Y	Y	N	Y	Y
5 **Sensenbrenner**	N	Y	Y	Y	N	Y
6 **Petri**	N	Y	Y	Y	N	Y
7 Obey	Y	Y	Y	N	Y	Y
8 Kagen	Y	Y	Y	N	Y	Y
WYOMING						
AL **Lummis**	N	Y	Y	Y	N	Y
DELEGATES						
Faleomavaega (A.S.)	Y	Y	Y			
Norton (D.C.)	Y	Y	Y			
Bordallo (Guam)	Y	Y	Y			
Sablan (N. Marianas)	Y	Y	Y			
Pierluisi (P.R.)	?	?	?			
Christensen (V.I.)	Y	Y	Y			

IN THE HOUSE | By Vote Number

75. H Res 1072. Louisiana State University 150th Anniversary/ Adoption. Courtney, D-Conn., motion to suspend the rules and adopt the resolution that would recognize the 150th anniversary of Louisiana State University. Motion agreed to 383-0: D 227-0; R 156-0. A two-thirds majority of those present and voting (256 in this case) is required for adoption under suspension of the rules. March 2, 2010.

76. HR 3820. Earthquake and Windstorm Research/Passage. Wu, D-Ore., motion to suspend the rules and pass the bill that would authorize $872 million through fiscal 2014 for programs that coordinate federal agency research on reducing the damage caused by earthquakes and windstorms. Motion agreed to 335-50: D 227-2; R 108-48. A two-thirds majority of those present and voting (257 in this case) is required for passage under suspension of the rules. March 2, 2010.

77. H Res 1097. National Engineers Week/Adoption. Wu, D-Ore., motion to suspend the rules and adopt the resolution that would support National Engineers Week and state the chamber's commitment to ensuring that engineers can continue to innovate. Motion agreed to 382-0: D 228-0; R 154-0. A two-thirds majority of those present and voting (255 in this case) is required for adoption under the suspension of the rules. March 2, 2010.

78. HR 4247. Federal Standards for School Punishments/Rule. Adoption of the rule (H Res 1126) to provide for House floor consideration of the bill that would set minimum federal standards for the use of seclusion and restraint in schools receiving federal funds. It also would permit the Speaker to entertain motions to suspend the rules at any time and waive the two-thirds majority vote requirement for same-day consideration of resolutions reported from the Rules Committee through the legislative day of March 4, 2010. Adopted 228-184: D 228-14; R 0-170. March 3, 2010.

79. H Res 747. Tribute to the West Point Military Academy/ Adoption. Marshall, D-Ga., motion to suspend the rules and adopt the resolution that would congratulate the U.S. Military Academy at West Point for being named as America's best college for 2009 by Forbes magazine. Motion agreed to 416-0: D 246-0; R 170-0. A two-thirds majority of those present and voting (278 in this case) is required for adoption under suspension of the rules. March 3, 2010.

80. H Res 1096. Encouraging Census Participation/Adoption. Lynch, D-Mass., motion to suspend the rules and adopt the resolution that would encourage individuals in the United States to participate in the 2010 census to ensure an accurate and complete count. It also would support the designation of Census Awareness Month. Motion agreed to 409-1: D 246-0; R 163-1. A two-thirds majority of those present and voting (274 in this case) is required for adoption under suspension of the rules. March 3, 2010.

	75	76	77	78	79	80
ALABAMA						
1 Bonner	Y	Y	Y	N	Y	Y
2 Bright	Y	Y	Y	N	Y	Y
3 Rogers	Y	Y	Y	N	Y	Y
4 Aderholt	Y	Y	Y	N	Y	Y
5 Griffith	Y	Y	Y	N	Y	Y
6 Bachus	Y	Y	Y	N	Y	Y
7 Davis	?	?	?	?	?	?
ALASKA						
AL Young	Y	N	Y	N	Y	Y
ARIZONA						
1 Kirkpatrick	Y	N	Y	N	Y	Y
2 Franks	Y	N	Y	N	Y	Y
3 Shadegg	Y	Y	Y	N	Y	Y
4 Pastor	Y	Y	Y	Y	Y	Y
5 Mitchell	Y	Y	Y	N	Y	Y
6 Flake	Y	N	Y	N	Y	Y
7 Grijalva	?	?	?	Y	Y	Y
8 Giffords	Y	Y	Y	N	Y	Y
ARKANSAS						
1 Berry	Y	Y	Y	Y	Y	Y
2 Snyder	Y	Y	Y	Y	Y	Y
3 Boozman	Y	Y	Y	N	Y	Y
4 Ross	Y	Y	Y	Y	Y	Y
CALIFORNIA						
1 Thompson	Y	Y	Y	Y	Y	Y
2 Herger	Y	Y	Y	N	Y	Y
3 Lungren	Y	Y	Y	N	Y	Y
4 McClintock	Y	Y	Y	N	Y	Y
5 Matsui	Y	Y	Y	Y	Y	Y
6 Woolsey	Y	Y	Y	Y	Y	Y
7 Miller, George	Y	Y	Y	Y	Y	Y
8 Pelosi						
9 Lee	Y	Y	Y	Y	Y	Y
10 Garamendi	?	?	?	?	?	?
11 McNerney	Y	Y	Y	Y	Y	Y
12 Speier	Y	Y	Y	Y	Y	Y
13 Stark	?	?	?	Y	Y	Y
14 Eshoo	Y	Y	Y	+	Y	Y
15 Honda	Y	Y	Y	Y	Y	Y
16 Lofgren	Y	Y	Y	Y	Y	Y
17 Farr	Y	Y	Y	Y	Y	Y
18 Cardoza	Y	Y	Y	Y	Y	Y
19 Radanovich	Y	Y	Y	N	Y	Y
20 Costa	Y	Y	Y	Y	Y	Y
21 Nunes	Y	N	Y	N	Y	Y
22 McCarthy	Y	Y	Y	N	Y	Y
23 Capps	Y	Y	Y	Y	Y	Y
24 Gallegly	Y	Y	Y	N	Y	Y
25 McKeon	Y	Y	Y	N	Y	Y
26 Dreier	Y	Y	Y	N	Y	Y
27 Sherman	Y	Y	Y	Y	Y	Y
28 Berman	Y	Y	Y	Y	Y	Y
29 Schiff	Y	Y	Y	Y	Y	Y
30 Waxman	Y	Y	Y	Y	Y	Y
31 Becerra	Y	Y	Y	Y	Y	Y
32 Chu	Y	Y	Y	Y	Y	Y
33 Watson	Y	Y	Y	Y	Y	Y
34 Roybal-Allard	Y	Y	Y	Y	Y	Y
35 Waters	Y	Y	Y	Y	Y	Y
36 Harman	Y	Y	Y	Y	Y	Y
37 Richardson	Y	Y	Y	Y	Y	Y
38 Napolitano	Y	Y	Y	?	Y	Y
39 Sánchez, Linda	Y	Y	Y	Y	Y	Y
40 Royce	Y	Y	Y	N	Y	Y
41 Lewis	Y	Y	Y	N	Y	Y
42 Miller, Gary	Y	Y	Y	N	Y	Y
43 Baca	Y	Y	Y	Y	Y	Y
44 Calvert	Y	Y	Y	N	Y	Y
45 Bono Mack	Y	Y	Y	N	Y	Y
46 Rohrabacher	Y	Y	Y	N	Y	Y
47 Sanchez, Loretta	Y	Y	Y	Y	Y	Y
48 Campbell	?	?	?	?	?	?
49 Issa	Y	Y	Y	N	Y	Y
50 Bilbray	Y	Y	Y	N	Y	?
51 Filner	Y	Y	Y	Y	Y	Y
52 Hunter	Y	Y	Y	N	Y	Y
53 Davis	Y	Y	Y	Y	Y	Y

	75	76	77	78	79	80
COLORADO						
1 DeGette	Y	Y	Y	Y	Y	Y
2 Polis	Y	Y	Y	Y	Y	Y
3 Salazar	Y	Y	Y	Y	Y	Y
4 Markey	Y	Y	Y	Y	Y	Y
5 Lamborn	Y	N	Y	N	Y	Y
6 Coffman	Y	N	Y	N	Y	Y
7 Perlmutter	Y	Y	Y	Y	Y	Y
CONNECTICUT						
1 Larson	Y	Y	Y	Y	Y	Y
2 Courtney	Y	Y	Y	Y	Y	Y
3 DeLauro	Y	Y	Y	Y	Y	Y
4 Himes	Y	Y	Y	Y	Y	Y
5 Murphy	Y	Y	Y	Y	Y	Y
DELAWARE						
AL Castle	Y	N	Y	N	Y	Y
FLORIDA						
1 Miller	Y	N	Y	N	Y	Y
2 Boyd	Y	Y	Y	Y	Y	Y
3 Brown	?	?	?	Y	Y	Y
4 Crenshaw	Y	N	Y	N	Y	Y
5 Brown-Waite	Y	Y	Y	N	Y	?
6 Stearns	Y	N	Y	N	Y	Y
7 Mica	Y	N	Y	N	Y	Y
8 Grayson	+	+	+	Y	Y	Y
9 Bilirakis	Y	Y	Y	N	Y	Y
10 Young	Y	Y	Y	N	Y	Y
11 Castor	Y	Y	Y	Y	Y	Y
12 Putnam	+	−	+	N	Y	Y
13 Buchanan	Y	Y	Y	N	Y	Y
14 Mack	Y	Y	Y	N	Y	Y
15 Posey	Y	Y	Y	N	Y	Y
16 Rooney	Y	N	Y	N	Y	Y
17 Meek	Y	Y	Y	Y	Y	Y
18 Ros-Lehtinen	Y	Y	Y	N	Y	Y
19 Vacant						
20 Wasserman Schultz	Y	Y	Y	?	?	?
21 Diaz-Balart, L.	Y	Y	Y	N	Y	Y
22 Klein	Y	Y	Y	Y	Y	Y
23 Hastings	Y	Y	Y	Y	Y	Y
24 Kosmas	Y	Y	Y	Y	Y	Y
25 Diaz-Balart, M.	Y	Y	Y	N	Y	Y
GEORGIA						
1 Kingston	Y	N	Y	N	Y	?
2 Bishop	Y	Y	Y	Y	Y	Y
3 Westmoreland	Y	N	Y	N	Y	Y
4 Johnson	Y	Y	Y	Y	Y	Y
5 Lewis	Y	Y	Y	Y	Y	Y
6 Price	Y	Y	Y	N	Y	Y
7 Linder	Y	Y	Y	N	Y	?
8 Marshall	Y	Y	Y	Y	Y	Y
9 Deal	?	?	?	?	?	?
10 Broun	Y	N	Y	N	Y	Y
11 Gingrey	Y	Y	Y	N	Y	Y
12 Barrow	Y	Y	Y	Y	Y	Y
13 Scott	Y	Y	Y	Y	Y	Y
HAWAII						
1 Vacant*						
2 Hirono	Y	Y	Y	Y	Y	Y
IDAHO						
1 Minnick	Y	Y	Y	Y	Y	Y
2 Simpson	Y	Y	Y	N	Y	Y
ILLINOIS						
1 Rush	?	?	?	Y	Y	Y
2 Jackson	?	?	?	Y	Y	Y
3 Lipinski	Y	Y	Y	Y	Y	Y
4 Gutierrez	?	+	+	Y	Y	Y
5 Quigley	Y	Y	Y	Y	Y	Y
6 Roskam	Y	Y	Y	N	Y	Y
7 Davis	Y	Y	Y	Y	Y	Y
8 Bean	Y	Y	Y	Y	Y	Y
9 Schakowsky	Y	Y	Y	Y	Y	Y
10 Kirk	Y	Y	Y	N	Y	Y
11 Halvorson	Y	Y	Y	Y	Y	Y
12 Costello	?	?	?	Y	Y	Y
13 Biggert	Y	Y	Y	N	Y	Y
14 Foster	Y	Y	Y	Y	Y	Y
15 Johnson	Y	N	Y	N	Y	Y

KEY **Republicans** Democrats

Y Voted for (yea)	X Paired against	C Voted "present" to avoid possible conflict of interest
# Paired for	− Announced against	
+ Announced for	P Voted "present"	? Did not vote or otherwise make a position known
N Voted against (nay)		

* Rep. Neil Abercrombie, D-Hawaii, resigned Feb. 28, 2010. The last vote for which he was eligible was vote 74.

	75	76	77	78	79	80
16 **Manzullo**	Y	N	Y	N	Y	Y
17 Hare	Y	Y	Y	Y	Y	Y
18 **Schock**	Y	Y	Y	N	Y	Y
19 **Shimkus**	Y	N	Y	N	Y	Y
INDIANA						
1 Visclosky	Y	Y	Y	Y	Y	Y
2 Donnelly	Y	Y	Y	N	Y	Y
3 **Souder**	Y	N	Y	N	Y	Y
4 **Buyer**	?	?	?	N	Y	Y
5 **Burton**	Y	N	Y	N	Y	Y
6 **Pence**	Y	N	Y	N	Y	Y
7 Carson	Y	Y	Y	Y	Y	Y
8 Ellsworth	Y	Y	Y	N	Y	Y
9 Hill	Y	Y	Y	N	Y	Y
IOWA						
1 Braley	Y	Y	Y	Y	Y	Y
2 Loebsack	Y	Y	Y	Y	Y	Y
3 Boswell	Y	Y	Y	Y	Y	Y
4 **Latham**	Y	Y	Y	N	Y	Y
5 **King**	Y	N	Y	N	Y	Y
KANSAS						
1 **Moran**	Y	Y	Y	N	Y	Y
2 **Jenkins**	Y	Y	Y	N	Y	Y
3 Moore	Y	Y	Y	Y	Y	Y
4 **Tiahrt**	Y	Y	Y	N	Y	Y
KENTUCKY						
1 **Whitfield**	Y	Y	Y	N	Y	Y
2 **Guthrie**	Y	Y	Y	N	Y	Y
3 Yarmuth	Y	Y	Y	Y	Y	Y
4 **Davis**	Y	Y	Y	N	Y	Y
5 **Rogers**	Y	Y	Y	N	Y	Y
6 Chandler	Y	Y	Y	Y	Y	Y
LOUISIANA						
1 **Scalise**	Y	Y	Y	N	Y	Y
2 **Cao**	Y	Y	Y	N	Y	Y
3 Melancon	Y	Y	Y	Y	Y	Y
4 **Fleming**	Y	Y	Y	N	Y	Y
5 **Alexander**	Y	Y	Y	N	Y	Y
6 **Cassidy**	?	?	?	N	Y	Y
7 **Boustany**	Y	Y	Y	N	Y	Y
MAINE						
1 Pingree	Y	Y	Y	Y	Y	Y
2 Michaud	Y	Y	Y	Y	Y	Y
MARYLAND						
1 Kratovil	Y	Y	Y	N	Y	Y
2 Ruppersberger	Y	Y	Y	Y	Y	Y
3 Sarbanes	Y	Y	Y	Y	Y	Y
4 Edwards	Y	Y	Y	Y	Y	Y
5 Hoyer	Y	Y	Y	Y	Y	Y
6 **Bartlett**	Y	Y	Y	N	Y	Y
7 Cummings	Y	Y	Y	Y	Y	Y
8 Van Hollen	Y	Y	Y	Y	Y	Y
MASSACHUSETTS						
1 Olver	Y	Y	Y	Y	Y	Y
2 Neal	Y	Y	Y	Y	Y	Y
3 McGovern	Y	Y	Y	Y	Y	Y
4 Frank	Y	Y	Y	Y	Y	Y
5 Tsongas	Y	Y	Y	Y	Y	Y
6 Tierney	Y	Y	Y	Y	Y	Y
7 Markey	Y	Y	Y	Y	Y	Y
8 Capuano	Y	Y	Y	Y	Y	Y
9 Lynch	Y	Y	Y	Y	Y	Y
10 Delahunt	Y	Y	Y	Y	Y	Y
MICHIGAN						
1 Stupak	Y	Y	Y	Y	Y	Y
2 **Hoekstra**	?	?	?	?	?	?
3 **Ehlers**	Y	Y	Y	N	Y	Y
4 **Camp**	?	?	?	N	Y	Y
5 Kildee	Y	Y	Y	Y	Y	Y
6 **Upton**	Y	Y	Y	N	Y	Y
7 Schauer	Y	Y	Y	Y	Y	Y
8 **Rogers**	Y	Y	Y	N	Y	Y
9 Peters	Y	Y	Y	Y	Y	Y
10 **Miller**	Y	N	Y	N	Y	Y
11 **McCotter**	Y	Y	Y	N	Y	Y
12 Levin	Y	Y	Y	Y	Y	Y
13 Kilpatrick	Y	Y	Y	Y	Y	Y
14 Conyers	Y	Y	Y	Y	Y	Y
15 Dingell	Y	Y	Y	Y	Y	Y
MINNESOTA						
1 Walz	Y	Y	Y	Y	Y	Y
2 **Kline**	Y	Y	Y	N	Y	Y
3 **Paulsen**	Y	Y	Y	N	Y	Y
4 McCollum	Y	Y	Y	Y	Y	Y

	75	76	77	78	79	80
5 Ellison	Y	Y	Y	+	Y	Y
6 **Bachmann**	Y	Y	Y	N	Y	Y
7 Peterson	Y	Y	Y	Y	Y	Y
8 Oberstar	Y	Y	Y	Y	Y	Y
MISSISSIPPI						
1 Childers	Y	Y	Y	N	Y	Y
2 Thompson	Y	Y	Y	Y	Y	Y
3 **Harper**	Y	Y	Y	N	Y	Y
4 Taylor	?	?	?	N	Y	Y
MISSOURI						
1 Clay	Y	Y	Y	Y	Y	Y
2 **Akin**	Y	Y	Y	N	Y	Y
3 Carnahan	Y	Y	Y	Y	Y	Y
4 Skelton	Y	Y	Y	Y	Y	Y
5 Cleaver	Y	Y	Y	Y	Y	Y
6 **Graves**	Y	Y	Y	N	Y	Y
7 **Blunt**	Y	Y	Y	N	Y	Y
8 **Emerson**	Y	Y	?	N	Y	Y
9 **Luetkemeyer**	Y	Y	Y	N	Y	Y
MONTANA						
AL **Rehberg**	?	?	?	N	Y	Y
NEBRASKA						
1 **Fortenberry**	Y	Y	Y	N	Y	Y
2 **Terry**	Y	Y	Y	N	Y	Y
3 **Smith**	Y	Y	Y	N	Y	Y
NEVADA						
1 Berkley	Y	Y	Y	Y	Y	Y
2 **Heller**	Y	Y	Y	N	Y	Y
3 Titus	Y	Y	Y	Y	Y	Y
NEW HAMPSHIRE						
1 Shea-Porter	Y	Y	Y	Y	Y	Y
2 Hodes	Y	Y	Y	Y	Y	Y
NEW JERSEY						
1 Andrews	Y	Y	Y	Y	Y	Y
2 **LoBiondo**	Y	Y	Y	N	Y	Y
3 Adler	Y	Y	Y	Y	Y	Y
4 **Smith**	Y	Y	Y	N	Y	Y
5 **Garrett**	Y	N	Y	N	Y	Y
6 Pallone	Y	Y	Y	Y	Y	Y
7 **Lance**	Y	Y	Y	N	Y	Y
8 Pascrell	Y	Y	Y	Y	Y	Y
9 Rothman	Y	Y	Y	Y	Y	Y
10 Payne	Y	Y	Y	Y	Y	Y
11 **Frelinghuysen**	Y	Y	Y	N	Y	Y
12 Holt	Y	Y	Y	Y	Y	Y
13 Sires	Y	Y	Y	Y	Y	Y
NEW MEXICO						
1 Heinrich	Y	Y	Y	Y	Y	Y
2 Teague	Y	Y	Y	Y	Y	Y
3 Luján	Y	Y	Y	Y	Y	Y
NEW YORK						
1 Bishop	Y	Y	Y	Y	Y	Y
2 Israel	Y	Y	Y	Y	Y	Y
3 **King**	Y	Y	Y	N	Y	Y
4 McCarthy	Y	Y	Y	Y	Y	Y
5 Ackerman	Y	Y	Y	Y	Y	Y
6 Meeks	Y	Y	Y	Y	Y	Y
7 Crowley	Y	Y	Y	Y	Y	Y
8 Nadler	Y	Y	Y	Y	Y	Y
9 Weiner	Y	Y	Y	Y	Y	Y
10 Towns	Y	Y	Y	Y	Y	Y
11 Clarke	?	Y	Y	Y	Y	Y
12 Velázquez	Y	Y	Y	Y	Y	Y
13 McMahon	+	+	+	+	Y	Y
14 Maloney	Y	Y	Y	Y	Y	Y
15 Rangel	Y	Y	Y	Y	Y	Y
16 Serrano	Y	Y	Y	?	Y	Y
17 Engel	?	Y	Y	Y	Y	Y
18 Lowey	Y	Y	Y	Y	Y	Y
19 Hall	Y	Y	Y	Y	Y	Y
20 Murphy	Y	Y	Y	N	Y	Y
21 Tonko	Y	Y	Y	Y	Y	Y
22 Hinchey	Y	Y	Y	Y	Y	Y
23 Owens	Y	N	Y	Y	Y	Y
24 Arcuri	Y	Y	Y	Y	Y	Y
25 Maffei	Y	Y	Y	Y	Y	Y
26 **Lee**	Y	Y	Y	N	Y	Y
27 Higgins	Y	Y	Y	Y	Y	Y
28 Slaughter	Y	Y	Y	Y	Y	Y
29 Massa	Y	Y	Y	Y	Y	Y
NORTH CAROLINA						
1 Butterfield	?	?	?	Y	?	Y
2 Etheridge	Y	Y	Y	Y	Y	Y
3 **Jones**	Y	N	Y	N	Y	Y
4 Price	Y	Y	Y	Y	Y	Y

	75	76	77	78	79	80
5 **Foxx**	Y	N	Y	N	Y	Y
6 **Coble**	Y	N	Y	N	Y	Y
7 McIntyre	Y	Y	Y	Y	Y	Y
8 Kissell	Y	Y	Y	Y	Y	Y
9 **Myrick**	Y	Y	Y	N	Y	Y
10 **McHenry**	Y	Y	Y	N	Y	Y
11 Shuler	Y	Y	Y	N	Y	Y
12 Watt	Y	Y	Y	Y	Y	Y
13 Miller	Y	Y	Y	Y	Y	Y
NORTH DAKOTA						
AL Pomeroy	Y	Y	Y	Y	Y	?
OHIO						
1 Driehaus	Y	Y	Y	N	Y	Y
2 **Schmidt**	Y	N	Y	N	Y	Y
3 **Turner**	Y	Y	Y	?	?	?
4 **Jordan**	Y	N	Y	N	Y	Y
5 **Latta**	Y	N	Y	N	Y	Y
6 Wilson	Y	Y	Y	Y	Y	Y
7 **Austria**	?	?	?	N	Y	Y
8 **Boehner**	Y	Y	Y	N	Y	Y
9 Kaptur	Y	Y	Y	Y	Y	Y
10 Kucinich	Y	Y	Y	Y	Y	Y
11 Fudge	Y	Y	Y	Y	Y	Y
12 **Tiberi**	Y	Y	Y	N	Y	Y
13 Sutton	Y	Y	Y	Y	Y	Y
14 **LaTourette**	Y	Y	Y	N	Y	Y
15 Kilroy	Y	Y	Y	Y	Y	Y
16 Boccieri	Y	Y	Y	Y	Y	Y
17 Ryan	Y	Y	Y	Y	Y	Y
18 Space	Y	Y	Y	Y	Y	Y
OKLAHOMA						
1 **Sullivan**	?	?	?	?	?	?
2 Boren	Y	Y	Y	Y	Y	Y
3 **Lucas**	Y	Y	Y	N	Y	Y
4 **Cole**	Y	Y	Y	N	Y	Y
5 **Fallin**	?	?	?	?	?	?
OREGON						
1 Wu	Y	Y	Y	Y	Y	Y
2 **Walden**	Y	Y	Y	N	Y	Y
3 Blumenauer	Y	Y	Y	Y	Y	Y
4 DeFazio	Y	Y	Y	Y	Y	Y
5 Schrader	Y	Y	Y	Y	Y	Y
PENNSYLVANIA						
1 Brady	Y	Y	Y	Y	Y	Y
2 Fattah	Y	Y	Y	Y	Y	Y
3 Dahlkemper	?	?	?	?	?	?
4 Altmire	Y	Y	Y	Y	Y	Y
5 **Thompson**	Y	Y	Y	N	Y	Y
6 **Gerlach**	Y	Y	Y	N	Y	Y
7 Sestak	Y	Y	Y	Y	Y	Y
8 Murphy, P.	Y	Y	Y	Y	Y	Y
9 **Shuster**	Y	Y	Y	N	Y	Y
10 Carney	Y	Y	Y	Y	Y	Y
11 Kanjorski	Y	Y	Y	Y	Y	Y
12 Vacant						
13 Schwartz	?	?	?	Y	Y	Y
14 Doyle	Y	Y	Y	Y	Y	Y
15 **Dent**	Y	Y	Y	N	Y	Y
16 **Pitts**	Y	Y	Y	N	Y	Y
17 Holden	Y	Y	Y	Y	Y	Y
18 **Murphy, T.**	Y	Y	Y	N	Y	Y
19 **Platts**	Y	N	Y	N	Y	Y
RHODE ISLAND						
1 Kennedy	Y	Y	Y	Y	Y	Y
2 Langevin	Y	Y	Y	Y	Y	Y
SOUTH CAROLINA						
1 **Brown**	?	?	?	N	Y	Y
2 **Wilson**	Y	Y	Y	N	Y	Y
3 **Barrett**	?	?	?	?	?	?
4 **Inglis**	?	?	?	N	Y	Y
5 Spratt	Y	Y	Y	Y	Y	Y
6 Clyburn	Y	Y	Y	Y	Y	Y
SOUTH DAKOTA						
AL Herseth Sandlin	Y	Y	Y	N	Y	Y
TENNESSEE						
1 **Roe**	Y	Y	Y	N	Y	Y
2 **Duncan**	Y	N	Y	N	Y	Y
3 **Wamp**	?	?	?	?	?	?
4 Davis	Y	Y	Y	Y	Y	Y
5 Cooper	Y	Y	Y	Y	Y	Y
6 Gordon	?	?	?	Y	Y	Y
7 **Blackburn**	Y	Y	Y	N	Y	Y
8 Tanner	?	?	?	Y	Y	Y
9 Cohen	?	?	?	Y	Y	Y

	75	76	77	78	79	80
TEXAS						
1 **Gohmert**	Y	N	Y	N	Y	?
2 **Poe**	Y	N	Y	N	Y	Y
3 **Johnson, S.**	Y	N	?	N	Y	Y
4 **Hall**	?	?	?	N	Y	Y
5 **Hensarling**	Y	N	Y	N	Y	Y
6 **Barton**	Y	N	Y	N	Y	Y
7 **Culberson**	Y	N	Y	N	Y	Y
8 **Brady**	?	?	?	N	Y	Y
9 Green, A.	Y	Y	Y	Y	Y	Y
10 **McCaul**	?	?	?	N	Y	Y
11 **Conaway**	Y	N	Y	N	Y	Y
12 **Granger**	?	?	?	N	Y	Y
13 **Thornberry**	Y	Y	Y	N	Y	Y
14 **Paul**	Y	N	Y	N	Y	N
15 Hinojosa	?	?	?	?	?	?
16 Reyes	?	?	?	Y	Y	Y
17 Edwards	Y	Y	?	Y	Y	Y
18 Jackson Lee	?	?	?	?	?	?
19 **Neugebauer**	Y	N	Y	N	Y	Y
20 Gonzalez	Y	Y	Y	Y	Y	Y
21 **Smith**	?	?	?	N	Y	Y
22 **Olson**	Y	Y	Y	N	Y	Y
23 Rodriguez	?	?	?	Y	Y	Y
24 **Marchant**	?	?	?	N	Y	Y
25 Doggett	Y	Y	Y	Y	Y	Y
26 **Burgess**	?	?	?	N	Y	Y
27 Ortiz	Y	Y	Y	Y	Y	Y
28 Cuellar	Y	Y	Y	Y	Y	Y
29 Green, G.	+	+	+	Y	Y	Y
30 Johnson, E.	Y	Y	Y	Y	Y	Y
31 **Carter**	Y	Y	Y	N	Y	Y
32 **Sessions**	Y	Y	Y	N	Y	Y
UTAH						
1 **Bishop**	Y	N	Y	N	Y	P
2 Matheson	Y	Y	Y	Y	Y	Y
3 **Chaffetz**	Y	N	Y	N	Y	Y
VERMONT						
AL Welch	Y	Y	Y	Y	Y	Y
VIRGINIA						
1 **Wittman**	Y	Y	Y	N	Y	Y
2 Nye	Y	Y	Y	Y	Y	Y
3 Scott	Y	Y	Y	Y	Y	Y
4 **Forbes**	Y	Y	Y	N	Y	Y
5 Perriello	Y	Y	Y	Y	Y	Y
6 **Goodlatte**	Y	N	Y	N	Y	Y
7 **Cantor**	Y	Y	Y	N	Y	Y
8 Moran	Y	Y	Y	Y	Y	Y
9 Boucher	Y	Y	Y	Y	Y	Y
10 **Wolf**	Y	Y	Y	N	Y	Y
11 Connolly	Y	Y	Y	Y	Y	Y
WASHINGTON						
1 Inslee	Y	Y	Y	Y	Y	Y
2 Larsen	Y	Y	Y	Y	Y	Y
3 Baird	Y	Y	Y	Y	Y	Y
4 **Hastings**	Y	N	Y	N	Y	Y
5 **McMorris Rodgers**	Y	Y	Y	N	Y	Y
6 Dicks	Y	Y	Y	Y	Y	Y
7 McDermott	Y	Y	Y	Y	Y	Y
8 **Reichert**	Y	Y	Y	N	Y	Y
9 Smith	Y	Y	Y	Y	Y	Y
WEST VIRGINIA						
1 Mollohan	?	?	?	N	Y	Y
2 **Capito**	Y	Y	Y	N	Y	Y
3 Rahall	Y	Y	Y	Y	Y	Y
WISCONSIN						
1 **Ryan**	Y	N	Y	N	Y	Y
2 Baldwin	Y	Y	Y	Y	Y	Y
3 Kind	Y	Y	Y	Y	Y	Y
4 Moore	Y	Y	Y	Y	Y	Y
5 **Sensenbrenner**	Y	Y	Y	N	Y	Y
6 **Petri**	Y	N	Y	N	Y	Y
7 Obey	Y	Y	Y	Y	Y	Y
8 Kagen	Y	Y	Y	Y	Y	Y
WYOMING						
AL **Lummis**	Y	N	Y	N	Y	Y
DELEGATES						
Faleomavaega (A.S.)						
Norton (D.C.)						
Bordallo (Guam)						
Sablan (N. Marianas)						
Pierluisi (P.R.)						
Christensen (V.I.)						

IN THE HOUSE | By Vote Number

81. **HR 4247. Federal Standards for School Punishments/Grant Awards and Earmark Ban.** Flake, R-Ariz., amendment that would require the Education secretary to submit an explanation to Congress if grants authorized by the bill are not awarded competitively. It also would bar the use of funds for congressionally directed spending. Adopted 391-24: D 223-23; R 168-1. March 3, 2010.

82. **HR 4247. Federal Standards for School Punishments/Passage.** Passage of the bill that would set minimum federal standards for the use of seclusion and restraint in schools receiving federal funds. It would allow schools to use restraints on students in cases when there is immediate danger to the student or others. States would be required to submit a plan within two years to prove their policies and procedures meet federal standards. Passed 262-153: D 238-8; R 24-145. March 3, 2010.

83. **H Res 1127. IRS Suicide Plane Attack Condemnation/Adoption.** Lewis, D-Ga., motion to suspend the rules and adopt the resolution that would condemn the Feb. 18, 2010, suicide plane attack against IRS employees in a federal building in Austin, Texas. It also would honor Vernon Hunter, a victim of the crash, and commend IRS employees for their dedication and public service. Motion agreed to 408-2: D 242-0; R 166-2. A two-thirds majority of those present and voting (274 in this case) is required for adoption under suspension of the rules. March 3, 2010.

84. **H Res 699. Tribute to 139th Airlift Wing/Adoption.** Marshall, D-Ga., motion to suspend the rules and adopt the resolution that would recognize and commend the service and sacrifice of the members of the Air Force's 139th Airlift Wing and their families. Motion agreed to 421-0: D 246-0; R 175-0. A two-thirds majority of those present and voting (281 in this case) is required for adoption under suspension of the rules. March 4, 2010.

85. **H Res 1086. 2010 Census Participation/Adoption.** Baca, D-Calif., motion to suspend the rules and adopt the resolution that would recognize the significance of the 2010 Census and encourage full participation in the process. Motion agreed to 415-1: D 243-0; R 172-1. A two-thirds majority of those present and voting (278 in this case) is required for adoption under suspension of the rules. March 4, 2010.

86. **H Res 1111. Read Across America Day/Adoption.** Courtney, D-Conn., motion to suspend the rules and adopt the resolution that would honor the 13th anniversary of Read Across America Day. It also would recognize Theodor Geisel, also known as Dr. Seuss, for encouraging children to read. Motion agreed to 414-0: D 241-0; R 173-0. A two-thirds majority of those present and voting (276 in this case) is required for adoption under suspension of the rules. March 4, 2010.

	81	82	83	84	85	86
ALABAMA						
1 **Bonner**	Y	N	Y	Y	Y	Y
2 Bright	Y	Y	Y	Y	Y	Y
3 **Rogers**	Y	N	Y	Y	Y	Y
4 **Aderholt**	Y	N	Y	Y	Y	Y
5 **Griffith**	Y	N	Y	Y	Y	Y
6 **Bachus**	Y	N	Y	Y	Y	Y
7 Davis	?	?	?	Y	Y	Y
ALASKA						
AL **Young**	Y	N	N	Y	Y	Y
ARIZONA						
1 Kirkpatrick	Y	N	Y	Y	Y	Y
2 **Franks**	Y	N	Y	Y	Y	Y
3 **Shadegg**	Y	N	Y	Y	Y	Y
4 Pastor	Y	Y	Y	Y	Y	Y
5 Mitchell	Y	N	Y	Y	Y	Y
6 **Flake**	Y	N	Y	Y	Y	Y
7 Grijalva	N	Y	Y	Y	Y	Y
8 Giffords	Y	Y	Y	Y	Y	Y
ARKANSAS						
1 Berry	Y	Y	Y	Y	Y	Y
2 Snyder	Y	Y	Y	Y	Y	Y
3 **Boozman**	Y	N	Y	Y	Y	Y
4 Ross	Y	Y	Y	Y	Y	Y
CALIFORNIA						
1 Thompson	Y	Y	Y	Y	Y	Y
2 **Herger**	Y	N	Y	Y	Y	Y
3 **Lungren**	Y	N	Y	Y	Y	Y
4 **McClintock**	Y	N	Y	Y	Y	Y
5 Matsui	Y	Y	Y	Y	Y	Y
6 Woolsey	N	Y	Y	Y	Y	Y
7 Miller, George	Y	Y	Y	Y	Y	Y
8 Pelosi						
9 Lee	N	Y	Y	Y	Y	Y
10 Garamendi	?	?	?	Y	Y	Y
11 McNerney	Y	Y	Y	Y	Y	Y
12 Speier	Y	Y	Y	Y	Y	Y
13 Stark	Y	Y	Y	Y	Y	Y
14 Eshoo	Y	Y	Y	Y	Y	Y
15 Honda	Y	Y	Y	Y	Y	Y
16 Lofgren	Y	Y	Y	Y	Y	Y
17 Farr	Y	Y	Y	Y	Y	Y
18 Cardoza	Y	Y	Y	Y	Y	Y
19 **Radanovich**	?	?	?	Y	Y	Y
20 Costa	Y	Y	Y	Y	Y	Y
21 **Nunes**	Y	N	Y	Y	Y	Y
22 **McCarthy**	Y	N	Y	Y	Y	Y
23 Capps	Y	Y	Y	Y	Y	Y
24 **Gallegly**	Y	N	Y	Y	Y	Y
25 **McKeon**	Y	N	Y	Y	Y	Y
26 **Dreier**	Y	N	Y	Y	Y	Y
27 Sherman	Y	Y	Y	Y	Y	Y
28 Berman	Y	Y	Y	Y	Y	Y
29 Schiff	Y	Y	Y	Y	Y	Y
30 Waxman	Y	Y	Y	Y	Y	Y
31 Becerra	Y	Y	Y	Y	Y	Y
32 Chu	Y	Y	Y	Y	Y	Y
33 Watson	Y	Y	Y	Y	Y	Y
34 Roybal-Allard	Y	Y	Y	Y	Y	Y
35 Waters	N	Y	Y	Y	Y	Y
36 Harman	Y	Y	Y	Y	Y	Y
37 Richardson	Y	Y	Y	Y	Y	Y
38 Napolitano	Y	Y	Y	Y	Y	Y
39 Sánchez, Linda	Y	Y	Y	Y	Y	Y
40 **Royce**	Y	N	Y	Y	Y	Y
41 **Lewis**	Y	N	Y	Y	Y	Y
42 **Miller, Gary**	Y	N	Y	Y	Y	Y
43 Baca	Y	Y	Y	Y	Y	Y
44 **Calvert**	Y	N	Y	Y	Y	Y
45 **Bono Mack**	Y	N	Y	Y	Y	Y
46 **Rohrabacher**	Y	N	Y	Y	Y	Y
47 Sanchez, Loretta	Y	Y	Y	Y	Y	Y
48 **Campbell**	?	?	?	?	?	?
49 **Issa**	Y	N	Y	Y	Y	Y
50 **Bilbray**	Y	N	Y	Y	Y	Y
51 Filner	Y	Y	Y	Y	Y	Y
52 **Hunter**	Y	N	Y	Y	Y	Y
53 Davis	Y	Y	Y	Y	Y	Y

	81	82	83	84	85	86
COLORADO						
1 DeGette	Y	Y	Y	Y	Y	Y
2 Polis	Y	Y	Y	Y	Y	Y
3 Salazar	Y	Y	Y	Y	Y	Y
4 Markey	Y	N	Y	Y	Y	Y
5 **Lamborn**	Y	N	Y	Y	Y	Y
6 **Coffman**	Y	N	Y	Y	Y	Y
7 Perlmutter	Y	N	Y	Y	Y	Y
CONNECTICUT						
1 Larson	Y	Y	Y	Y	Y	Y
2 Courtney	Y	Y	Y	Y	Y	Y
3 DeLauro	Y	Y	Y	Y	Y	Y
4 Himes	Y	Y	Y	Y	Y	Y
5 Murphy	Y	Y	Y	Y	Y	Y
DELAWARE						
AL **Castle**	Y	Y	Y	Y	Y	Y
FLORIDA						
1 **Miller**	Y	N	Y	Y	Y	Y
2 Boyd	Y	Y	Y	Y	Y	Y
3 Brown	N	Y	Y	Y	Y	Y
4 **Crenshaw**	Y	N	Y	Y	Y	Y
5 **Brown-Waite**	Y	N	Y	Y	Y	Y
6 **Stearns**	Y	N	Y	Y	Y	Y
7 **Mica**	Y	N	Y	Y	Y	Y
8 Grayson	Y	Y	Y	Y	+	?
9 **Bilirakis**	Y	N	Y	Y	Y	Y
10 **Young**	Y	N	Y	Y	Y	Y
11 Castor	Y	Y	Y	Y	Y	Y
12 **Putnam**	Y	N	Y	Y	Y	Y
13 **Buchanan**	Y	N	Y	Y	Y	+
14 **Mack**	Y	N	Y	Y	Y	Y
15 **Posey**	Y	N	Y	Y	Y	Y
16 **Rooney**	Y	Y	Y	Y	Y	Y
17 Meek	Y	Y	Y	Y	Y	Y
18 **Ros-Lehtinen**	Y	Y	Y	Y	Y	Y
19 Vacant						
20 Wasserman Schultz	?	?	?	Y	Y	Y
21 **Diaz-Balart, L.**	Y	Y	Y	Y	Y	Y
22 Klein	Y	Y	Y	Y	Y	Y
23 Hastings	N	Y	Y	Y	Y	Y
24 Kosmas	Y	Y	Y	Y	Y	Y
25 **Diaz-Balart, M.**	Y	Y	Y	Y	Y	Y
GEORGIA						
1 **Kingston**	Y	N	Y	Y	Y	Y
2 Bishop	Y	Y	Y	Y	Y	?
3 **Westmoreland**	Y	N	Y	Y	Y	Y
4 Johnson	Y	Y	Y	Y	Y	Y
5 Lewis	N	Y	Y	Y	Y	Y
6 **Price**	Y	N	Y	Y	Y	Y
7 **Linder**	Y	N	Y	Y	Y	Y
8 Marshall	Y	N	Y	Y	Y	Y
9 **Deal**	?	?	?	Y	Y	Y
10 **Broun**	Y	N	Y	Y	Y	Y
11 **Gingrey**	Y	N	Y	Y	Y	Y
12 Barrow	Y	Y	Y	Y	Y	Y
13 Scott	N	Y	Y	Y	Y	Y
HAWAII						
1 Vacant						
2 Hirono	Y	Y	Y	Y	Y	Y
IDAHO						
1 Minnick	Y	Y	Y	Y	Y	Y
2 **Simpson**	Y	N	Y	Y	Y	Y
ILLINOIS						
1 Rush	N	Y	Y	Y	Y	Y
2 Jackson	Y	Y	Y	Y	Y	Y
3 Lipinski	Y	Y	Y	Y	Y	Y
4 Gutierrez	Y	Y	Y	Y	Y	Y
5 Quigley	Y	Y	Y	Y	Y	Y
6 **Roskam**	Y	N	Y	Y	Y	Y
7 Davis	N	Y	Y	Y	Y	Y
8 Bean	Y	Y	Y	Y	Y	?
9 Schakowsky	Y	Y	Y	Y	Y	Y
10 **Kirk**	Y	Y	Y	Y	Y	Y
11 Halvorson	Y	Y	Y	Y	Y	Y
12 Costello	Y	Y	Y	Y	Y	Y
13 **Biggert**	Y	Y	Y	Y	Y	Y
14 Foster	Y	Y	Y	Y	Y	Y
15 **Johnson**	Y	Y	Y	Y	Y	Y

KEY	**Republicans**	Democrats	
Y Voted for (yea)		X Paired against	C Voted "present" to avoid possible conflict of interest
# Paired for		– Announced against	
+ Announced for		P Voted "present"	? Did not vote or otherwise make a position known
N Voted against (nay)			

	81	82	83	84	85	86
16 **Manzullo**	Y	N	Y	Y	Y	Y
17 Hare	Y	Y	Y	Y	Y	Y
18 **Schock**	Y	Y	Y	Y	Y	Y
19 **Shimkus**	Y	N	Y	Y	Y	Y
INDIANA						
1 Visclosky	Y	Y	Y	Y	Y	Y
2 Donnelly	Y	Y	Y	Y	Y	Y
3 **Souder**	Y	N	Y	Y	Y	Y
4 **Buyer**	Y	N	Y	Y	Y	Y
5 **Burton**	Y	N	Y	Y	Y	Y
6 **Pence**	Y	N	Y	Y	Y	Y
7 Carson	Y	Y	?	Y	Y	Y
8 Ellsworth	Y	Y	Y	Y	Y	Y
9 Hill	Y	Y	Y	Y	Y	Y
IOWA						
1 Braley	Y	Y	Y	Y	Y	Y
2 Loebsack	Y	Y	Y	Y	Y	Y
3 Boswell	Y	Y	Y	Y	Y	Y
4 **Latham**	Y	N	Y	Y	Y	Y
5 **King**	Y	N	Y	Y	Y	Y
KANSAS						
1 **Moran**	Y	N	Y	Y	Y	Y
2 **Jenkins**	Y	N	Y	Y	Y	Y
3 Moore	Y	Y	Y	Y	?	Y
4 **Tiahrt**	Y	N	Y	Y	Y	Y
KENTUCKY						
1 **Whitfield**	Y	N	Y	Y	Y	Y
2 **Guthrie**	Y	N	Y	Y	Y	Y
3 Yarmuth	Y	Y	Y	Y	Y	Y
4 **Davis**	Y	N	Y	Y	Y	Y
5 **Rogers**	Y	N	Y	Y	Y	Y
6 Chandler	Y	Y	Y	Y	Y	Y
LOUISIANA						
1 **Scalise**	Y	N	Y	Y	Y	Y
2 **Cao**	Y	Y	Y	Y	Y	Y
3 Melancon	Y	Y	Y	Y	Y	Y
4 **Fleming**	Y	N	Y	Y	Y	Y
5 **Alexander**	Y	N	Y	Y	Y	Y
6 **Cassidy**	Y	N	Y	Y	Y	Y
7 **Boustany**	Y	N	Y	Y	Y	Y
MAINE						
1 Pingree	Y	Y	?	Y	Y	Y
2 Michaud	Y	Y	Y	Y	Y	Y
MARYLAND						
1 Kratovil	Y	Y	Y	Y	Y	Y
2 Ruppersberger	Y	Y	Y	Y	Y	Y
3 Sarbanes	Y	Y	Y	Y	Y	Y
4 Edwards	N	Y	Y	Y	Y	Y
5 Hoyer	Y	Y	Y	Y	Y	Y
6 **Bartlett**	Y	N	Y	Y	Y	Y
7 Cummings	Y	Y	Y	Y	Y	Y
8 Van Hollen	Y	Y	Y	Y	Y	Y
MASSACHUSETTS						
1 Olver	Y	Y	Y	Y	Y	Y
2 Neal	Y	Y	Y	Y	Y	Y
3 McGovern	Y	Y	Y	Y	Y	Y
4 Frank	Y	Y	Y	Y	Y	Y
5 Tsongas	Y	Y	Y	?	?	Y
6 Tierney	Y	Y	Y	Y	Y	Y
7 Markey	Y	Y	+	Y	Y	Y
8 Capuano	Y	Y	Y	Y	Y	Y
9 Lynch	Y	Y	Y	Y	Y	Y
10 Delahunt	Y	Y	Y	?	?	?
MICHIGAN						
1 Stupak	Y	Y	Y	Y	Y	Y
2 **Hoekstra**	?	?	?	?	?	?
3 **Ehlers**	Y	Y	Y	Y	Y	Y
4 **Camp**	Y	N	Y	Y	Y	Y
5 Kildee	Y	Y	Y	Y	Y	Y
6 **Upton**	Y	N	Y	Y	Y	Y
7 Schauer	Y	Y	Y	Y	Y	Y
8 **Rogers**	Y	N	Y	Y	Y	Y
9 Peters	Y	Y	Y	Y	Y	Y
10 **Miller**	Y	N	Y	Y	Y	Y
11 **McCotter**	Y	N	Y	Y	Y	Y
12 Levin	Y	Y	Y	Y	Y	Y
13 Kilpatrick	N	Y	Y	Y	Y	Y
14 Conyers	N	Y	Y	Y	Y	Y
15 Dingell	Y	Y	Y	Y	Y	Y
MINNESOTA						
1 Walz	Y	Y	Y	Y	Y	Y
2 **Kline**	Y	N	Y	Y	Y	Y
3 **Paulsen**	Y	N	Y	Y	Y	Y
4 McCollum	Y	Y	Y	Y	Y	Y

	81	82	83	84	85	86
5 Ellison	Y	Y	Y	Y	Y	Y
6 **Bachmann**	Y	N	Y	Y	Y	Y
7 Peterson	Y	Y	Y	Y	Y	Y
8 Oberstar	N	Y	Y	Y	Y	Y
MISSISSIPPI						
1 Childers	Y	Y	Y	Y	Y	Y
2 Thompson	Y	Y	Y	Y	Y	Y
3 **Harper**	Y	Y	Y	Y	Y	Y
4 Taylor	Y	N	Y	Y	Y	Y
MISSOURI						
1 Clay	Y	Y	Y	?	Y	Y
2 **Akin**	Y	N	Y	Y	Y	Y
3 Carnahan	Y	Y	Y	?	?	?
4 Skelton	Y	Y	Y	Y	Y	Y
5 Cleaver	N	Y	Y	Y	Y	Y
6 **Graves**	Y	N	Y	Y	Y	Y
7 **Blunt**	Y	N	Y	Y	Y	Y
8 **Emerson**	Y	N	Y	Y	Y	Y
9 **Luetkemeyer**	Y	N	Y	Y	Y	Y
MONTANA						
AL **Rehberg**	Y	N	Y	Y	Y	Y
NEBRASKA						
1 **Fortenberry**	Y	N	Y	Y	Y	Y
2 **Terry**	Y	N	Y	Y	Y	Y
3 **Smith**	Y	N	Y	Y	Y	Y
NEVADA						
1 Berkley	Y	Y	Y	Y	?	?
2 **Heller**	Y	N	Y	Y	Y	Y
3 Titus	Y	Y	Y	Y	?	?
NEW HAMPSHIRE						
1 Shea-Porter	Y	Y	Y	Y	Y	Y
2 Hodes	Y	Y	Y	Y	Y	Y
NEW JERSEY						
1 Andrews	Y	Y	Y	Y	Y	Y
2 **LoBiondo**	Y	Y	Y	Y	Y	Y
3 Adler	Y	Y	Y	Y	Y	Y
4 **Smith**	Y	Y	Y	Y	Y	Y
5 **Garrett**	Y	N	Y	Y	Y	Y
6 Pallone	Y	Y	Y	Y	Y	Y
7 **Lance**	Y	Y	Y	Y	Y	Y
8 Pascrell	Y	Y	?	Y	Y	Y
9 Rothman	Y	Y	Y	Y	Y	Y
10 Payne	Y	Y	Y	Y	Y	Y
11 **Frelinghuysen**	Y	Y	Y	Y	Y	Y
12 Holt	Y	Y	Y	Y	Y	Y
13 Sires	Y	Y	Y	Y	Y	Y
NEW MEXICO						
1 Heinrich	Y	Y	Y	Y	Y	Y
2 Teague	Y	Y	Y	Y	Y	Y
3 Luján	Y	Y	Y	Y	Y	Y
NEW YORK						
1 Bishop	Y	Y	Y	Y	Y	Y
2 Israel	Y	Y	Y	Y	Y	Y
3 **King**	Y	Y	Y	Y	Y	Y
4 McCarthy	Y	Y	Y	Y	Y	Y
5 Ackerman	Y	Y	Y	Y	Y	Y
6 Meeks	Y	Y	Y	Y	Y	Y
7 Crowley	Y	Y	Y	Y	Y	?
8 Nadler	Y	Y	Y	Y	Y	Y
9 Weiner	Y	Y	Y	Y	Y	Y
10 Towns	Y	Y	Y	Y	Y	Y
11 Clarke	N	Y	Y	Y	Y	Y
12 Velázquez	Y	Y	Y	Y	Y	Y
13 McMahon	Y	Y	Y	Y	Y	Y
14 Maloney	Y	Y	Y	Y	Y	Y
15 Rangel	Y	Y	Y	Y	Y	Y
16 Serrano	Y	Y	Y	Y	Y	Y
17 Engel	Y	Y	Y	Y	Y	Y
18 Lowey	Y	Y	Y	Y	Y	Y
19 Hall	Y	Y	Y	Y	Y	Y
20 Murphy	Y	Y	Y	Y	Y	Y
21 Tonko	Y	Y	Y	Y	Y	Y
22 Hinchey	Y	Y	Y	Y	Y	Y
23 Owens	Y	Y	Y	Y	Y	Y
24 Arcuri	Y	Y	Y	Y	Y	Y
25 Maffei	Y	Y	Y	Y	Y	Y
26 **Lee**	Y	Y	Y	Y	Y	Y
27 Higgins	Y	Y	Y	Y	Y	Y
28 Slaughter	Y	Y	Y	Y	Y	Y
29 Massa	?	?	?	?	?	?
NORTH CAROLINA						
1 Butterfield	Y	Y	Y	Y	Y	?
2 Etheridge	Y	Y	Y	Y	Y	Y
3 **Jones**	Y	N	Y	Y	Y	Y
4 Price	Y	Y	Y	Y	Y	Y

	81	82	83	84	85	86
5 **Foxx**	Y	N	Y	Y	Y	Y
6 **Coble**	Y	N	Y	Y	Y	Y
7 McIntyre	Y	Y	Y	Y	Y	Y
8 Kissell	Y	Y	Y	Y	Y	Y
9 **Myrick**	Y	N	Y	Y	Y	Y
10 **McHenry**	Y	N	Y	Y	Y	Y
11 Shuler	Y	Y	Y	Y	Y	Y
12 Watt	N	Y	Y	Y	Y	Y
13 Miller	Y	Y	Y	Y	Y	Y
NORTH DAKOTA						
AL Pomeroy	Y	Y	Y	Y	Y	Y
OHIO						
1 Driehaus	Y	N	Y	Y	Y	Y
2 **Schmidt**	Y	N	Y	Y	Y	Y
3 **Turner**	?	?	?	Y	Y	Y
4 **Jordan**	Y	N	Y	Y	Y	Y
5 **Latta**	Y	N	Y	Y	Y	Y
6 Wilson	Y	Y	Y	Y	Y	Y
7 **Austria**	Y	N	Y	Y	Y	Y
8 **Boehner**	Y	N	Y	Y	Y	Y
9 Kaptur	Y	Y	Y	Y	Y	Y
10 Kucinich	N	Y	Y	Y	Y	Y
11 Fudge	N	Y	Y	Y	Y	Y
12 **Tiberi**	Y	N	Y	Y	Y	Y
13 Sutton	Y	Y	Y	Y	Y	Y
14 **LaTourette**	Y	N	Y	Y	Y	Y
15 Kilroy	Y	Y	Y	Y	Y	Y
16 Boccieri	Y	Y	Y	?	Y	Y
17 Ryan	Y	Y	Y	Y	Y	Y
18 Space	Y	Y	Y	Y	Y	Y
OKLAHOMA						
1 **Sullivan**	?	?	?	Y	Y	Y
2 Boren	Y	Y	Y	Y	Y	Y
3 **Lucas**	Y	N	Y	Y	Y	Y
4 **Cole**	Y	N	Y	Y	Y	Y
5 **Fallin**	?	?	?	?	?	?
OREGON						
1 Wu	Y	Y	Y	Y	Y	Y
2 **Walden**	Y	N	Y	Y	Y	Y
3 Blumenauer	Y	Y	Y	Y	Y	Y
4 DeFazio	Y	Y	Y	Y	Y	Y
5 Schrader	Y	N	Y	Y	Y	Y
PENNSYLVANIA						
1 Brady	Y	Y	Y	Y	Y	Y
2 Fattah	Y	Y	Y	Y	Y	Y
3 Dahlkemper	?	?	?	?	?	?
4 Altmire	Y	Y	Y	Y	Y	Y
5 **Thompson**	Y	N	Y	Y	Y	Y
6 **Gerlach**	Y	Y	Y	Y	Y	Y
7 Sestak	Y	Y	Y	Y	Y	Y
8 Murphy, P.	Y	Y	Y	Y	Y	Y
9 **Shuster**	Y	N	Y	Y	Y	Y
10 Carney	Y	Y	Y	Y	Y	Y
11 Kanjorski	Y	Y	Y	Y	Y	Y
12 Vacant						
13 Schwartz	Y	Y	Y	Y	Y	Y
14 Doyle	Y	Y	Y	Y	Y	Y
15 **Dent**	Y	Y	Y	Y	Y	Y
16 **Pitts**	Y	N	Y	Y	Y	Y
17 Holden	Y	Y	Y	Y	Y	Y
18 **Murphy, T.**	Y	Y	Y	Y	Y	Y
19 **Platts**	Y	Y	Y	Y	Y	Y
RHODE ISLAND						
1 Kennedy	Y	Y	Y	Y	Y	Y
2 Langevin	Y	Y	Y	Y	Y	Y
SOUTH CAROLINA						
1 **Brown**	Y	N	Y	Y	Y	Y
2 **Wilson**	Y	Y	Y	Y	Y	Y
3 **Barrett**	?	?	?	Y	Y	Y
4 **Inglis**	Y	N	Y	Y	Y	Y
5 Spratt	Y	Y	Y	Y	Y	Y
6 Clyburn	N	Y	Y	Y	Y	Y
SOUTH DAKOTA						
AL Herseth Sandlin	Y	Y	Y	Y	Y	Y
TENNESSEE						
1 **Roe**	Y	N	Y	Y	Y	Y
2 **Duncan**	Y	N	Y	Y	Y	Y
3 **Wamp**	?	?	?	Y	Y	Y
4 Davis	Y	Y	Y	Y	Y	Y
5 Cooper	Y	Y	Y	Y	Y	Y
6 Gordon	Y	Y	Y	Y	Y	Y
7 **Blackburn**	Y	N	Y	Y	Y	Y
8 Tanner	Y	Y	Y	Y	Y	Y
9 Cohen	N	Y	Y	Y	Y	Y

	81	82	83	84	85	86
TEXAS						
1 **Gohmert**	Y	N	Y	Y	?	Y
2 **Poe**	Y	N	Y	Y	Y	Y
3 **Johnson, S.**	Y	N	Y	Y	Y	Y
4 **Hall**	Y	N	Y	Y	Y	Y
5 **Hensarling**	Y	N	Y	Y	Y	Y
6 **Barton**	Y	N	Y	Y	Y	?
7 **Culberson**	Y	N	Y	Y	Y	Y
8 **Brady**	Y	N	Y	Y	Y	Y
9 Green, A.	Y	Y	Y	Y	Y	Y
10 **McCaul**	Y	N	Y	Y	Y	Y
11 **Conaway**	Y	N	Y	Y	Y	Y
12 **Granger**	Y	N	Y	Y	Y	Y
13 **Thornberry**	Y	N	Y	Y	Y	Y
14 **Paul**	N	N	N	Y	N	Y
15 Hinojosa	?	?	?	Y	Y	Y
16 Reyes	Y	Y	Y	Y	Y	Y
17 Edwards	Y	Y	Y	Y	Y	Y
18 Jackson Lee	?	?	?	Y	Y	Y
19 **Neugebauer**	Y	N	Y	Y	Y	Y
20 Gonzalez	Y	Y	Y	Y	Y	Y
21 **Smith**	Y	N	Y	Y	Y	Y
22 **Olson**	Y	N	Y	Y	Y	Y
23 Rodriguez	Y	Y	Y	Y	Y	Y
24 **Marchant**	Y	N	Y	Y	Y	Y
25 Doggett	Y	Y	Y	Y	Y	Y
26 **Burgess**	Y	N	Y	Y	Y	Y
27 Ortiz	Y	Y	Y	Y	Y	Y
28 Cuellar	Y	Y	Y	Y	Y	Y
29 Green, G.	Y	Y	Y	Y	Y	Y
30 Johnson, E.	N	Y	Y	Y	Y	Y
31 **Carter**	Y	N	Y	Y	Y	Y
32 **Sessions**	Y	N	Y	Y	Y	Y
UTAH						
1 **Bishop**	Y	N	Y	Y	P	Y
2 Matheson	Y	Y	Y	Y	Y	Y
3 **Chaffetz**	Y	N	Y	Y	Y	Y
VERMONT						
AL Welch	Y	Y	Y	Y	Y	Y
VIRGINIA						
1 **Wittman**	Y	N	Y	Y	Y	Y
2 Nye	Y	Y	Y	Y	Y	Y
3 Scott	Y	Y	Y	Y	Y	Y
4 **Forbes**	Y	N	Y	Y	Y	Y
5 Perriello	Y	Y	Y	Y	Y	Y
6 **Goodlatte**	Y	N	Y	Y	Y	Y
7 **Cantor**	Y	N	Y	Y	Y	Y
8 Moran	Y	Y	Y	Y	?	Y
9 Boucher	Y	Y	Y	Y	Y	Y
10 **Wolf**	Y	N	Y	Y	Y	Y
11 Connolly	Y	Y	Y	Y	Y	?
WASHINGTON						
1 Inslee	Y	Y	Y	Y	Y	Y
2 Larsen	Y	Y	Y	Y	Y	Y
3 Baird	Y	Y	Y	Y	Y	Y
4 **Hastings**	Y	N	?	Y	Y	Y
5 **McMorris Rodgers**	Y	Y	Y	Y	Y	Y
6 Dicks	Y	Y	Y	Y	Y	Y
7 McDermott	Y	Y	Y	Y	Y	Y
8 **Reichert**	Y	Y	Y	Y	Y	Y
9 Smith	Y	Y	Y	Y	Y	Y
WEST VIRGINIA						
1 Mollohan	Y	Y	Y	Y	Y	Y
2 **Capito**	Y	N	Y	Y	Y	Y
3 Rahall	Y	Y	Y	Y	Y	Y
WISCONSIN						
1 **Ryan**	Y	N	Y	Y	Y	Y
2 Baldwin	Y	Y	Y	Y	Y	Y
3 Kind	Y	Y	Y	Y	Y	Y
4 Moore	N	Y	Y	Y	Y	Y
5 **Sensenbrenner**	Y	N	Y	Y	Y	Y
6 **Petri**	Y	N	Y	Y	Y	Y
7 Obey	Y	Y	Y	Y	Y	Y
8 Kagen	Y	Y	Y	Y	Y	Y
WYOMING						
AL **Lummis**	Y	N	Y	Y	Y	Y
DELEGATES						
Faleomavaega (A.S.)						
Norton (D.C.)						
Bordallo (Guam)						
Sablan (N. Marianas)						
Pierluisi (P.R.)						
Christensen (V.I.)						

IN THE HOUSE | By Vote Number

87. **HR 2847. Business Tax Exemptions and Highway Extensions/ Previous Question.** Matsui, D-Calif., motion to order the previous question (thus ending debate and possibility of amendment) on adoption of the rule (H Res 1137) to provide for House floor consideration of the Senate amendment to the bill that would provide payroll tax exemptions for employers who hire new workers, extend the Highway Trust Fund and the Build America Bonds program, and extend increased expense deductions for small businesses. Motion agreed to 236-184: D 236-13; R 0-171. March 4, 2010.

88. **HR 2847. Business Tax Exemptions and Highway Extensions/ Rule.** Adoption of the rule (H Res 1137) to provide for House floor consideration of the Senate amendment to the bill that would provide payroll tax exemptions for employers who hire new workers, extend the Highway Trust Fund and the Build America Bonds program, and extend increased expense deductions for small businesses. Adopted 212-209: D 212-38; R 0-171. March 4, 2010.

89. **H Res 362. National School Lunch Program/Adoption.** Courtney, D-Conn., motion to suspend the rules and adopt the resolution that would support the goals of the National School Lunch Program. Motion agreed to 403-13: D 248-0; R 155-13. A two-thirds majority of those present and voting (278 in this case) is required for adoption under suspension of the rules. March 4, 2010.

90. **HR 2847. Business Tax Exemptions and Highway Extensions/ Motion to Concur.** Etheridge, D-N.C., motion to concur in the Senate amendment to the House amendment to the Senate amendment with an additional House amendment. The additional House amendment would change the payment structure for certain tax-credit bond programs and would delay by one more year the effective date of new interest allocation rules for multinational companies. The measure would exempt employers from Social Security payroll taxes for certain new hires made in 2010. It also would expand the Build American Bonds program and would extend the Highway Trust Fund and certain transportation safety programs through Dec. 31, 2010. It also would extend through 2010 the ability of small businesses to deduct $250,000 of qualified property purchases from income taxes in the year of purchase. Motion agreed to 217-201: D 211-35; R 6-166. A "yea" was a vote in support of the president's position. March 4, 2010.

91. **H Res 1079. Tribute to New Orleans Saints/Adoption.** Melancon, D-La., motion to suspend the rules and adopt the resolution that would congratulate the New Orleans Saints' coaches and players, and the members of the "Who Dat" Nation, for winning Super Bowl XLIV. Motion agreed to 375-1: D 217-0; R 158-1. A two-thirds majority of those present and voting (253 in this case) is required for adoption under suspension of the rules. March 4, 2010.

	87	88	89	90	91
ALABAMA					
1 **Bonner**	N	N	Y	N	Y
2 **Bright**	N	N	Y	Y	Y
3 **Rogers**	N	N	Y	N	Y
4 **Aderholt**	N	N	Y	N	Y
5 **Griffith**	N	N	Y	N	Y
6 **Bachus**	N	N	Y	N	Y
7 Davis	Y	Y	Y	Y	?
ALASKA					
AL **Young**	N	N	Y	Y	Y
ARIZONA					
1 Kirkpatrick	Y	N	Y	N	Y
2 **Franks**	N	N	Y	N	Y
3 **Shadegg**	N	N	N	N	Y
4 Pastor	Y	Y	Y	N	Y
5 Mitchell	N	N	Y	N	Y
6 **Flake**	N	N	N	N	Y
7 Grijalva	Y	Y	Y	N	?
8 Giffords	Y	Y	Y	Y	Y
ARKANSAS					
1 Berry	Y	Y	Y	Y	Y
2 Snyder	Y	Y	Y	Y	Y
3 **Boozman**	N	N	Y	N	Y
4 Ross	Y	Y	Y	Y	Y
CALIFORNIA					
1 Thompson	Y	Y	Y	Y	Y
2 **Herger**	N	N	Y	N	Y
3 **Lungren**	N	N	Y	N	Y
4 **McClintock**	N	N	N	N	Y
5 Matsui	Y	Y	Y	Y	Y
6 Woolsey	Y	Y	Y	Y	Y
7 Miller, George	Y	Y	Y	Y	?
8 Pelosi		Y		Y	Y
9 Lee	Y	N	Y	N	Y
10 Garamendi	Y	Y	Y	Y	?
11 McNerney	Y	Y	Y	Y	Y
12 Speier	Y	Y	Y	Y	Y
13 Stark	Y	Y	Y	Y	Y
14 Eshoo	?	?	?	?	?
15 Honda	Y	Y	Y	Y	Y
16 Lofgren	Y	Y	Y	Y	Y
17 Farr	Y	Y	Y	Y	?
18 Cardoza	Y	Y	Y	Y	Y
19 **Radanovich**	N	N	Y	N	?
20 Costa	Y	Y	Y	Y	Y
21 **Nunes**	N	N	Y	N	Y
22 **McCarthy**	N	N	Y	N	?
23 Capps	Y	Y	Y	–	Y
24 **Gallegly**	N	N	Y	N	Y
25 **McKeon**	N	N	Y	N	?
26 **Dreier**	N	N	Y	N	Y
27 Sherman	Y	Y	Y	Y	?
28 Berman	Y	Y	Y	Y	Y
29 Schiff	Y	Y	Y	Y	Y
30 Waxman	Y	Y	Y	Y	Y
31 Becerra	Y	Y	Y	Y	Y
32 Chu	Y	Y	Y	Y	Y
33 Watson	N	N	Y	Y	Y
34 Roybal-Allard	Y	Y	Y	Y	Y
35 Waters	N	N	Y	N	Y
36 Harman	Y	Y	Y	Y	Y
37 Richardson	Y	N	Y	N	Y
38 Napolitano	Y	Y	Y	Y	Y
39 Sánchez, Linda	Y	Y	Y	Y	Y
40 **Royce**	N	N	Y	N	Y
41 **Lewis**	N	N	Y	N	Y
42 **Miller, Gary**	N	N	Y	N	Y
43 Baca	Y	Y	Y	N	Y
44 **Calvert**	N	N	Y	N	Y
45 **Bono Mack**	N	N	Y	N	Y
46 **Rohrabacher**	N	N	Y	N	Y
47 Sanchez, Loretta	Y	Y	Y	Y	?
48 **Campbell**	?	?	?	?	?
49 **Issa**	N	N	Y	N	Y
50 **Bilbray**	N	N	Y	N	Y
51 Filner	Y	Y	Y	Y	Y
52 **Hunter**	N	N	Y	N	Y
53 Davis	Y	Y	Y	Y	Y

	87	88	89	90	91
COLORADO					
1 DeGette	Y	Y	Y	Y	Y
2 Polis	Y	Y	Y	N	Y
3 Salazar	Y	Y	Y	Y	Y
4 Markey	Y	Y	Y	Y	Y
5 **Lamborn**	N	N	N	N	Y
6 **Coffman**	N	N	Y	N	Y
7 Perlmutter	Y	Y	Y	Y	Y
CONNECTICUT					
1 Larson	Y	Y	Y	Y	Y
2 Courtney	Y	Y	Y	Y	Y
3 DeLauro	?	Y	Y	Y	Y
4 Himes	Y	Y	Y	Y	Y
5 Murphy	Y	Y	Y	Y	Y
DELAWARE					
AL **Castle**	N	N	Y	N	Y
FLORIDA					
1 **Miller**	N	N	Y	N	Y
2 Boyd	Y	Y	Y	Y	?
3 Brown	N	N	Y	N	Y
4 **Crenshaw**	N	N	Y	N	Y
5 **Brown-Waite**	N	N	Y	N	Y
6 **Stearns**	N	N	Y	N	Y
7 **Mica**	N	N	Y	N	Y
8 Grayson	Y	Y	Y	Y	Y
9 **Bilirakis**	N	N	Y	N	Y
10 **Young**	N	N	Y	N	Y
11 Castor	Y	Y	Y	Y	Y
12 **Putnam**	N	N	Y	N	Y
13 **Buchanan**	N	N	Y	N	Y
14 **Mack**	N	N	Y	N	Y
15 **Posey**	N	N	Y	N	Y
16 **Rooney**	N	N	Y	N	Y
17 Meek	Y	Y	Y	Y	Y
18 **Ros-Lehtinen**	N	N	Y	N	?
19 Vacant					
20 Wasserman Schultz	Y	Y	Y	Y	Y
21 **Diaz-Balart, L.**	N	N	Y	N	?
22 Klein	Y	Y	Y	Y	Y
23 Hastings	Y	Y	Y	N	Y
24 Kosmas	Y	Y	Y	Y	Y
25 **Diaz-Balart, M.**	N	N	Y	N	Y
GEORGIA					
1 **Kingston**	N	N	Y	N	Y
2 Bishop	Y	Y	Y	Y	Y
3 **Westmoreland**	N	N	Y	N	Y
4 Johnson	Y	Y	Y	Y	Y
5 Lewis	Y	Y	Y	Y	Y
6 **Price**	N	N	Y	N	Y
7 **Linder**	?	?	?	?	?
8 Marshall	Y	Y	Y	Y	P
9 **Deal**	N	N	Y	N	?
10 **Broun**	N	N	N	N	Y
11 **Gingrey**	N	N	Y	N	Y
12 Barrow	Y	Y	Y	Y	Y
13 Scott	Y	Y	Y	Y	Y
HAWAII					
1 Vacant					
2 Hirono	Y	Y	Y	Y	Y
IDAHO					
1 Minnick	N	N	Y	Y	Y
2 **Simpson**	N	N	?	N	Y
ILLINOIS					
1 Rush	Y	N	Y	N	Y
2 Jackson	Y	N	Y	N	Y
3 Lipinski	Y	Y	Y	Y	Y
4 Gutierrez	Y	Y	?	Y	?
5 Quigley	Y	N	Y	Y	Y
6 **Roskam**	N	N	Y	N	?
7 Davis	Y	N	Y	N	Y
8 Bean	Y	Y	Y	–	Y
9 Schakowsky	Y	Y	Y	Y	Y
10 **Kirk**	N	N	Y	N	Y
11 Halvorson	Y	Y	Y	Y	Y
12 Costello	Y	Y	Y	Y	Y
13 **Biggert**	N	N	Y	N	Y
14 Foster	Y	–	Y	Y	Y
15 **Johnson**	N	N	Y	N	N

KEY   **Republicans**   Democrats

Y Voted for (yea)	X Paired against	C Voted "present" to avoid possible conflict of interest
# Paired for	– Announced against	
+ Announced for	P Voted "present"	? Did not vote or otherwise make a position known
N Voted against (nay)		

Member	87	88	89	90	91
16 Manzullo	N	N	Y	N	Y
17 Hare	Y	Y	Y	Y	Y
18 Schock	N	N	Y	N	Y.
19 Shimkus	N	N	Y	N	Y
INDIANA					
1 Visclosky	Y	Y	Y	N	Y
2 Donnelly	Y	Y	Y	Y	Y
3 Souder	N	N	Y	N	Y
4 Buyer	?	?	?	N	?
5 Burton	N	N	Y	N	Y
6 Pence	N	N	Y	N	Y
7 Carson	Y	Y	Y	N	Y
8 Ellsworth	Y	Y	Y	Y	Y
9 Hill	Y	Y	Y	Y	?
IOWA					
1 Braley	Y	Y	Y	Y	Y
2 Loebsack	Y	Y	Y	Y	Y
3 Boswell	Y	Y	Y	Y	Y
4 Latham	N	N	Y	N	Y
5 King	N	N	Y	N	Y
KANSAS					
1 Moran	N	N	Y	N	Y
2 Jenkins	N	N	Y	N	Y
3 Moore	Y	Y	Y	Y	Y
4 Tiahrt	?	?	?	?	?
KENTUCKY					
1 Whitfield	N	N	Y	N	Y
2 Guthrie	N	N	Y	N	Y
3 Yarmuth	Y	Y	Y	Y	Y
4 Davis	N	N	Y	N	Y
5 Rogers	N	N	Y	N	Y
6 Chandler	Y	Y	Y	Y	Y
LOUISIANA					
1 Scalise	N	N	Y	N	Y
2 Cao	N	N	Y	Y	Y
3 Melancon	Y	Y	Y	Y	Y
4 Fleming	N	N	Y	N	Y
5 Alexander	N	N	Y	N	Y
6 Cassidy	N	N	Y	N	Y
7 Boustany	N	N	Y	N	Y
MAINE					
1 Pingree	Y	Y	Y	Y	Y
2 Michaud	Y	Y	Y	Y	Y
MARYLAND					
1 Kratovil	N	N	Y	Y	Y
2 Ruppersberger	Y	Y	Y	Y	Y
3 Sarbanes	Y	Y	Y	Y	Y
4 Edwards	Y	N	Y	N	Y
5 Hoyer	Y	Y	Y	Y	Y
6 Bartlett	N	N	Y	N	Y
7 Cummings	Y	N	Y	Y	Y
8 Van Hollen	Y	Y	Y	Y	Y
MASSACHUSETTS					
1 Olver	Y	Y	Y	Y	Y
2 Neal	Y	Y	Y	Y	Y
3 McGovern	Y	Y	Y	Y	Y
4 Frank	Y	Y	Y	Y	Y
5 Tsongas	Y	Y	Y	Y	Y
6 Tierney	Y	Y	Y	Y	Y
7 Markey	Y	Y	Y	Y	Y
8 Capuano	Y	Y	Y	Y	Y
9 Lynch	Y	Y	Y	Y	Y
10 Delahunt	Y	Y	Y	Y	Y
MICHIGAN					
1 Stupak	Y	Y	Y	Y	Y
2 Hoekstra	?	?	?	?	?
3 Ehlers	N	N	Y	N	Y
4 Camp	N	N	Y	Y	?
5 Kildee	Y	Y	Y	Y	Y
6 Upton	N	N	Y	N	Y
7 Schauer	Y	Y	Y	Y	Y
8 Rogers	N	N	Y	N	Y
9 Peters	Y	Y	Y	N	Y
10 Miller	N	N	Y	N	Y
11 McCotter	N	N	Y	N	Y
12 Levin	Y	Y	Y	Y	Y
13 Kilpatrick	Y	Y	Y	N	Y
14 Conyers	Y	Y	Y	N	Y
15 Dingell	Y	Y	Y	Y	Y
MINNESOTA					
1 Walz	Y	Y	Y	Y	Y
2 Kline	N	N	Y	N	Y
3 Paulsen	N	N	Y	N	Y
4 McCollum	Y	Y	Y	Y	Y
5 Ellison	Y	Y	Y	Y	Y
6 Bachmann	N	N	Y	N	Y
7 Peterson	Y	Y	Y	Y	Y
8 Oberstar	Y	Y	Y	Y	P
MISSISSIPPI					
1 Childers	N	Y	Y	Y	Y
2 Thompson	Y	N	Y	N	?
3 Harper	N	N	Y	N	Y
4 Taylor	N	N	Y	Y	Y
MISSOURI					
1 Clay	Y	N	Y	N	Y
2 Akin	N	N	N	N	Y
3 Carnahan	Y	Y	Y	Y	Y
4 Skelton	Y	Y	Y	Y	Y
5 Cleaver	Y	N	Y	N	?
6 Graves	N	N	Y	N	Y
7 Blunt	N	N	Y	N	Y
8 Emerson	N	N	Y	N	Y
9 Luetkemeyer	N	N	Y	N	Y
MONTANA					
AL Rehberg	N	N	Y	N	Y
NEBRASKA					
1 Fortenberry	N	N	Y	N	Y
2 Terry	N	N	Y	N	Y
3 Smith	N	N	Y	N	Y
NEVADA					
1 Berkley	Y	Y	Y	Y	Y
2 Heller	N	N	Y	N	Y
3 Titus	Y	Y	Y	Y	Y
NEW HAMPSHIRE					
1 Shea-Porter	Y	Y	Y	Y	Y
2 Hodes	Y	Y	Y	Y	Y
NEW JERSEY					
1 Andrews	Y	Y	Y	Y	Y
2 LoBiondo	N	N	Y	N	Y
3 Adler	Y	Y	Y	Y	Y
4 Smith	N	N	Y	N	Y
5 Garrett	N	N	N	N	Y
6 Pallone	Y	Y	Y	Y	Y
7 Lance	N	N	Y	N	Y
8 Pascrell	Y	Y	Y	Y	?
9 Rothman	Y	Y	Y	Y	Y
10 Payne	Y	N	Y	N	Y
11 Frelinghuysen	N	N	Y	N	Y
12 Holt	Y	Y	Y	Y	Y
13 Sires	Y	Y	Y	Y	Y
NEW MEXICO					
1 Heinrich	Y	Y	Y	Y	Y
2 Teague	N	Y	Y	Y	Y
3 Luján	Y	Y	Y	Y	Y
NEW YORK					
1 Bishop	Y	Y	Y	Y	Y
2 Israel	Y	Y	Y	Y	Y
3 King	N	N	Y	N	Y
4 McCarthy	Y	Y	Y	Y	?
5 Ackerman	Y	Y	Y	Y	?
6 Meeks	Y	N	Y	Y	?
7 Crowley	Y	Y	Y	?	Y
8 Nadler	Y	Y	Y	Y	?
9 Weiner	Y	Y	Y	Y	Y
10 Towns	Y	N	Y	N	Y
11 Clarke	Y	N	Y	N	Y
12 Velázquez	Y	Y	Y	Y	?
13 McMahon	Y	Y	Y	Y	?
14 Maloney	Y	Y	Y	Y	Y
15 Rangel	Y	Y	Y	Y	?
16 Serrano	Y	Y	Y	Y	Y
17 Engel	Y	Y	Y	Y	Y
18 Lowey	Y	Y	Y	Y	Y
19 Hall	Y	Y	Y	Y	Y
20 Murphy	Y	N	Y	Y	?
21 Tonko	Y	Y	Y	Y	Y
22 Hinchey	Y	Y	Y	Y	Y
23 Owens	Y	Y	Y	Y	Y
24 Arcuri	Y	Y	Y	N	Y
25 Maffei	Y	Y	Y	Y	Y
26 Lee	N	N	Y	N	Y
27 Higgins	Y	Y	Y	Y	Y
28 Slaughter	Y	Y	Y	Y	?
29 Massa	?	?	?	?	?
NORTH CAROLINA					
1 Butterfield	Y	N	Y	Y	Y
2 Etheridge	Y	Y	Y	Y	Y
3 Jones	N	N	Y	N	Y
4 Price	Y	Y	Y	Y	Y
5 Foxx	N	N	N	N	Y
6 Coble	N	N	Y	N	Y
7 McIntyre	Y	Y	Y	Y	Y
8 Kissell	Y	Y	Y	Y	Y
9 Myrick	N	N	Y	N	Y
10 McHenry	N	N	Y	N	Y
11 Shuler	N	Y	Y	Y	Y
12 Watt	Y	N	Y	N	Y
13 Miller	Y	Y	Y	Y	Y
NORTH DAKOTA					
AL Pomeroy	Y	Y	Y	Y	Y
OHIO					
1 Driehaus	N	N	Y	N	Y
2 Schmidt	N	N	Y	N	Y
3 Turner	N	N	Y	N	Y
4 Jordan	?	?	?	?	?
5 Latta	N	N	Y	N	Y
6 Wilson	Y	Y	Y	Y	Y
7 Austria	N	N	Y	N	Y
8 Boehner	N	N	Y	N	Y
9 Kaptur	Y	Y	Y	Y	Y
10 Kucinich	Y	Y	Y	N	Y
11 Fudge	Y	N	Y	N	Y
12 Tiberi	N	N	Y	N	Y
13 Sutton	Y	Y	Y	Y	Y
14 LaTourette	N	N	Y	N	Y
15 Kilroy	Y	Y	Y	Y	Y
16 Boccieri	Y	Y	Y	Y	Y
17 Ryan	Y	Y	Y	Y	Y
18 Space	Y	N	Y	Y	Y
OKLAHOMA					
1 Sullivan	N	N	Y	N	Y
2 Boren	Y	Y	Y	Y	?
3 Lucas	N	N	Y	N	Y
4 Cole	N	N	Y	N	Y
5 Fallin	?	?	?	?	?
OREGON					
1 Wu	Y	Y	Y	Y	Y
2 Walden	N	N	Y	N	Y
3 Blumenauer	Y	Y	?	Y	?
4 DeFazio	Y	Y	Y	Y	?
5 Schrader	Y	Y	Y	N	Y
PENNSYLVANIA					
1 Brady	Y	Y	Y	Y	Y
2 Fattah	Y	Y	Y	Y	Y
3 Dahlkemper	?	?	?	?	?
4 Altmire	Y	Y	Y	Y	Y
5 Thompson	N	N	Y	N	Y
6 Gerlach	N	N	Y	N	Y
7 Sestak	Y	Y	Y	Y	Y
8 Murphy, P.	Y	Y	Y	Y	Y
9 Shuster	N	N	Y	N	Y
10 Carney	Y	Y	Y	Y	Y
11 Kanjorski	Y	Y	Y	Y	Y
12 Vacant					
13 Schwartz	Y	Y	Y	+	Y
14 Doyle	Y	Y	Y	Y	?
15 Dent	N	N	Y	N	Y
16 Pitts	N	N	Y	N	?
17 Holden	Y	Y	Y	Y	?
18 Murphy, T.	N	N	Y	N	Y
19 Platts	N	N	Y	N	Y
RHODE ISLAND					
1 Kennedy	Y	Y	Y	Y	Y
2 Langevin	Y	Y	Y	Y	Y
SOUTH CAROLINA					
1 Brown	N	N	Y	N	Y
2 Wilson	N	N	Y	N	Y
3 Barrett	N	N	Y	N	Y
4 Inglis	N	N	Y	N	Y
5 Spratt	Y	Y	Y	Y	Y
6 Clyburn	Y	Y	Y	Y	Y
SOUTH DAKOTA					
AL Herseth Sandlin	Y	Y	Y	Y	Y
TENNESSEE					
1 Roe	N	N	Y	N	Y
2 Duncan	N	N	Y	Y	Y
3 Wamp	N	N	Y	Y	Y
4 Davis	Y	Y	Y	Y	Y
5 Cooper	Y	Y	Y	Y	Y
6 Gordon	Y	Y	Y	Y	Y
7 Blackburn	N	N	Y	N	Y
8 Tanner	Y	Y	Y	Y	Y
9 Cohen	Y	Y	Y	Y	Y
TEXAS					
1 Gohmert	N	N	?	N	Y
2 Poe	N	N	N	N	Y
3 Johnson, S.	N	N	Y	N	Y
4 Hall	N	N	Y	N	Y
5 Hensarling	N	N	Y	N	Y
6 Barton	N	N	Y	N	Y
7 Culberson	N	N	Y	N	Y
8 Brady	N	N	Y	N	Y
9 Green, A.	Y	N	Y	N	Y
10 McCaul	N	N	Y	N	Y
11 Conaway	N	N	Y	N	Y
12 Granger	N	N	Y	N	Y
13 Thornberry	N	N	Y	N	Y
14 Paul	N	N	N	N	Y
15 Hinojosa	Y	Y	Y	Y	Y
16 Reyes	Y	Y	Y	Y	Y
17 Edwards	Y	Y	Y	Y	?
18 Jackson Lee	Y	N	Y	N	Y
19 Neugebauer	N	N	?	N	Y
20 Gonzalez	Y	Y	Y	Y	Y
21 Smith	N	N	Y	N	Y
22 Olson	N	N	Y	N	Y
23 Rodriguez	Y	Y	Y	Y	Y
24 Marchant	N	N	Y	N	Y
25 Doggett	Y	Y	Y	N	?
26 Burgess	N	N	Y	N	Y
27 Ortiz	Y	Y	Y	Y	Y
28 Cuellar	Y	Y	Y	Y	Y
29 Green, G.	Y	Y	Y	Y	Y
30 Johnson, E.	Y	N	Y	N	Y
31 Carter	N	N	Y	N	Y
32 Sessions	N	N	Y	N	Y
UTAH					
1 Bishop	N	N	Y	N	Y
2 Matheson	Y	Y	Y	Y	Y
3 Chaffetz	N	N	N	N	?
VERMONT					
AL Welch	Y	Y	Y	Y	P
VIRGINIA					
1 Wittman	N	N	Y	N	Y
2 Nye	Y	Y	Y	Y	Y
3 Scott	Y	N	Y	N	Y
4 Forbes	N	N	Y	N	Y
5 Perriello	Y	Y	Y	Y	Y
6 Goodlatte	N	N	Y	N	Y
7 Cantor	N	N	Y	N	Y
8 Moran	Y	Y	Y	Y	Y
9 Boucher	Y	Y	Y	Y	Y
10 Wolf	N	N	Y	N	Y
11 Connolly	Y	Y	Y	Y	Y
WASHINGTON					
1 Inslee	Y	Y	Y	Y	Y
2 Larsen	Y	Y	Y	Y	Y
3 Baird	Y	Y	Y	Y	Y
4 Hastings	N	N	Y	N	?
5 McMorris Rodgers	N	N	Y	N	Y
6 Dicks	Y	Y	Y	Y	Y
7 McDermott	Y	Y	Y	Y	Y
8 Reichert	N	N	Y	N	Y
9 Smith	Y	Y	Y	Y	?
WEST VIRGINIA					
1 Mollohan	Y	Y	Y	Y	Y
2 Capito	N	N	Y	N	Y
3 Rahall	Y	Y	Y	Y	Y
WISCONSIN					
1 Ryan	N	N	Y	N	Y
2 Baldwin	Y	Y	Y	Y	Y
3 Kind	Y	Y	Y	+	Y
4 Moore	Y	Y	Y	N	Y
5 Sensenbrenner	N	N	N	N	Y
6 Petri	N	N	Y	N	Y
7 Obey	Y	Y	Y	Y	Y
8 Kagen	Y	Y	Y	Y	Y
WYOMING					
AL Lummis	N	N	N	N	Y
DELEGATES					
Faleomavaega (A.S.)					
Norton (D.C.)					
Bordallo (Guam)					
Sablan (N. Marianas)					
Pierluisi (P.R.)					
Christensen (V.I.)					

IN THE HOUSE | By Vote Number

92. **HR 3650. Algal Bloom Reduction Program/Passage.** Baird, D-Wash., motion to suspend the rules and pass the bill that would establish a National Harmful Algal Bloom and Hypoxia Program to develop a strategy to reduce marine and freshwater algal blooms. It would authorize $41 million over five years for the program. Motion rejected 263-142: D 231-7; R 32-135. A two-thirds majority of those present and voting (270 in this case) is required for passage under suspension of the rules. March 9, 2010.

93. **H Res 1069. Tribute to Physics Nobel Prize Winners/Adoption.** Baird, D-Wash., motion to suspend the rules and adopt the resolution that would congratulate Willard S. Boyle and George E. Smith for being awarded the Nobel Prize in physics and recognize Bell Laboratories in Murray Hill, N.J., as a leader in scientific research and innovation. Motion agreed to 402-0: D 236-0; R 166-0. A two-thirds majority of those present and voting (268 in this case) is required for adoption under suspension of the rules. March 9, 2010.

94. **H Res 935. Tribute to National Medal of Technology and Innovation Winners/Adoption.** Baird, D-Wash., motion to suspend the rules and adopt the resolution that would congratulate John E. Warnock, Charles M. Geschke, Forrest M. Bird, Esther Sans Takeuchi and IBM Corp. for receiving the 2008 National Medal of Technology and Innovation. Motion agreed to 402-0: D 238-0; R 164-0. A two-thirds majority of those present and voting (268 in this case) is required for adoption under suspension of the rules. March 9, 2010.

95. **H Con Res 248. Afghanistan Troop Withdrawal/Rule.** Adoption of the rule (H Res 1146) to provide for House floor consideration of the concurrent resolution that would direct the president to remove U.S. troops from Afghanistan. Adopted 225-195: D 220-28; R 5-167. March 10, 2010.

96. **H Res 1088. East Africa Albinism/Adoption.** Connolly, D-Va., motion to suspend the rules and adopt the resolution that would condemn the murder and mutilation of people with albinism in East Africa and urge the governments of Tanzania and Burundi to prosecute and convict the perpetrators of such crimes. Motion agreed to 418-1: D 247-0; R 171-1. A two-thirds majority of those present and voting (280 in this case) is required for adoption under suspension of the rules. March 10, 2010.

97. **HR 4621. 'Census' Mail Requirements/Passage.** Clay, D-Mo., motion to suspend the rules and pass the bill that would require mail marked "census" to include the name and address of the sender. It also would require non-government mail marked "census" to provide a disclaimer that the mail is not from or affiliated with the federal government. Motion agreed to 416-0: D 246-0; R 170-0. A two-thirds majority of those present and voting (278 in this case) is required for passage under suspension of the rules. March 10, 2010.

	92	93	94	95	96	97
ALABAMA						
1 Bonner	N	Y	Y	N	Y	Y
2 Bright	N	Y	Y	N	Y	Y
3 Rogers	N	Y	Y	N	Y	Y
4 Aderholt	N	Y	Y	N	Y	Y
5 Griffith	N	Y	Y	N	Y	Y
6 Bachus	N	Y	Y	N	Y	Y
7 Davis	?	?	?	?	?	?
ALASKA						
AL Young	N	Y	Y	N	Y	Y
ARIZONA						
1 Kirkpatrick	N	Y	Y	N	Y	Y
2 Franks	N	Y	Y	N	Y	Y
3 Shadegg	N	Y	Y	N	Y	Y
4 Pastor	Y	Y	Y	Y	Y	Y
5 Mitchell	Y	Y	Y	Y	Y	Y
6 Flake	N	Y	Y	N	Y	Y
7 Grijalva	?	?	?	Y	Y	Y
8 Giffords	Y	Y	Y	N	Y	Y
ARKANSAS						
1 Berry	Y	Y	Y	Y	Y	Y
2 Snyder	Y	Y	Y	Y	Y	Y
3 Boozman	N	Y	Y	N	Y	Y
4 Ross	Y	Y	Y	Y	Y	Y
CALIFORNIA						
1 Thompson	Y	Y	Y	Y	Y	Y
2 Herger	N	Y	Y	N	Y	Y
3 Lungren	N	Y	Y	N	Y	Y
4 McClintock	N	Y	Y	N	Y	Y
5 Matsui	Y	Y	Y	Y	Y	?
6 Woolsey	+	+	+	Y	Y	Y
7 Miller, George	Y	Y	Y	Y	Y	Y
8 Pelosi						
9 Lee	Y	Y	Y	Y	Y	Y
10 Garamendi	Y	Y	Y	Y	Y	Y
11 McNerney	Y	Y	Y	Y	Y	Y
12 Speier	Y	Y	Y	Y	Y	Y
13 Stark	Y	Y	Y	Y	Y	Y
14 Eshoo	Y	Y	Y	Y	Y	Y
15 Honda	Y	Y	Y	Y	Y	Y
16 Lofgren	Y	Y	Y	Y	Y	Y
17 Farr	Y	Y	Y	Y	Y	Y
18 Cardoza	Y	Y	Y	N	Y	Y
19 Radanovich	N	Y	Y	N	Y	Y
20 Costa	Y	Y	Y	Y	Y	Y
21 Nunes	N	Y	Y	N	Y	Y
22 McCarthy	N	Y	Y	N	Y	Y
23 Capps	Y	Y	Y	Y	+	Y
24 Gallegly	N	Y	Y	N	Y	Y
25 McKeon	N	Y	Y	N	Y	Y
26 Dreier	N	Y	Y	N	Y	Y
27 Sherman	Y	Y	Y	Y	Y	Y
28 Berman	Y	Y	?	Y	Y	Y
29 Schiff	Y	Y	Y	Y	Y	Y
30 Waxman	Y	Y	Y	Y	Y	Y
31 Becerra	Y	?	Y	Y	?	Y
32 Chu	Y	Y	Y	Y	Y	Y
33 Watson	Y	Y	Y	Y	Y	Y
34 Roybal-Allard	Y	Y	Y	Y	Y	Y
35 Waters	Y	Y	Y	Y	Y	Y
36 Harman	Y	Y	Y	Y	Y	Y
37 Richardson	Y	Y	Y	Y	Y	Y
38 Napolitano	Y	Y	Y	Y	Y	Y
39 Sánchez, Linda	Y	Y	Y	Y	Y	Y
40 Royce	N	Y	Y	N	Y	Y
41 Lewis	N	Y	Y	N	Y	Y
42 Miller, Gary	N	Y	Y	N	Y	Y
43 Baca	Y	Y	Y	Y	Y	Y
44 Calvert	N	Y	Y	N	Y	Y
45 Bono Mack	Y	Y	Y	N	Y	Y
46 Rohrabacher	Y	Y	Y	N	Y	Y
47 Sanchez, Loretta	Y	Y	Y	Y	Y	Y
48 Campbell	N	Y	Y	Y	Y	Y
49 Issa	N	Y	Y	N	Y	Y
50 Bilbray	N	Y	Y	N	Y	Y
51 Filner	Y	Y	Y	Y	Y	Y
52 Hunter	N	Y	Y	N	Y	Y
53 Davis	Y	Y	Y	Y	Y	Y

	92	93	94	95	96	97
COLORADO						
1 DeGette	Y	Y	Y	Y	Y	Y
2 Polis	Y	Y	Y	Y	Y	Y
3 Salazar	Y	Y	Y	N	Y	Y
4 Markey	Y	Y	Y	Y	Y	Y
5 Lamborn	N	Y	Y	N	Y	Y
6 Coffman	N	Y	Y	N	Y	Y
7 Perlmutter	?	?	?	Y	Y	Y
CONNECTICUT						
1 Larson	Y	Y	Y	Y	Y	Y
2 Courtney	Y	Y	Y	Y	Y	Y
3 DeLauro	Y	Y	Y	Y	Y	Y
4 Himes	Y	Y	Y	N	Y	Y
5 Murphy	Y	Y	Y	Y	Y	Y
DELAWARE						
AL Castle	N	Y	Y	N	Y	Y
FLORIDA						
1 Miller	N	Y	Y	N	Y	Y
2 Boyd	Y	Y	Y	Y	Y	Y
3 Brown	Y	Y	Y	Y	Y	Y
4 Crenshaw	N	Y	Y	N	Y	Y
5 Brown-Waite	Y	Y	Y	N	Y	Y
6 Stearns	N	Y	Y	N	Y	Y
7 Mica	N	Y	Y	N	Y	Y
8 Grayson	Y	Y	Y	Y	Y	Y
9 Bilirakis	Y	Y	Y	N	Y	Y
10 Young	?	?	?	?	?	?
11 Castor	Y	Y	Y	Y	Y	Y
12 Putnam	Y	Y	Y	N	Y	Y
13 Buchanan	Y	Y	Y	N	Y	Y
14 Mack	Y	Y	Y	N	Y	Y
15 Posey	Y	Y	Y	N	Y	Y
16 Rooney	Y	Y	Y	N	Y	Y
17 Meek	Y	Y	Y	Y	Y	Y
18 Ros-Lehtinen	Y	Y	Y	Y	Y	Y
19 Vacant						
20 Wasserman Schultz	Y	Y	Y	Y	Y	Y
21 Diaz-Balart, L.	Y	Y	Y	N	Y	Y
22 Klein	Y	Y	Y	Y	Y	Y
23 Hastings	Y	Y	Y	Y	Y	Y
24 Kosmas	Y	Y	Y	N	Y	Y
25 Diaz-Balart, M.	Y	Y	Y	N	Y	Y
GEORGIA						
1 Kingston	N	Y	Y	N	Y	Y
2 Bishop	Y	Y	Y	Y	Y	Y
3 Westmoreland	N	Y	Y	N	Y	Y
4 Johnson	Y	Y	Y	Y	Y	Y
5 Lewis	Y	Y	Y	Y	Y	Y
6 Price	N	Y	Y	N	Y	Y
7 Linder	N	Y	Y	N	Y	Y
8 Marshall	N	Y	Y	Y	Y	Y
9 Deal	?	?	?	?	?	?
10 Broun	N	Y	Y	N	Y	Y
11 Gingrey	N	Y	Y	N	Y	Y
12 Barrow	Y	Y	Y	N	Y	Y
13 Scott	Y	Y	Y	Y	Y	Y
HAWAII						
1 Vacant						
2 Hirono	Y	Y	Y	Y	Y	Y
IDAHO						
1 Minnick	Y	Y	Y	Y	Y	Y
2 Simpson	N	Y	Y	N	Y	Y
ILLINOIS						
1 Rush	Y	Y	Y	Y	Y	Y
2 Jackson	Y	Y	Y	Y	Y	Y
3 Lipinski	Y	Y	Y	Y	Y	Y
4 Gutierrez	+	+	+	Y	Y	Y
5 Quigley	Y	?	?	Y	Y	Y
6 Roskam	N	Y	Y	N	Y	?
7 Davis	Y	Y	Y	Y	Y	Y
8 Bean	Y	Y	Y	Y	Y	Y
9 Schakowsky	Y	Y	Y	Y	Y	?
10 Kirk	?	?	?	N	Y	Y
11 Halvorson	Y	Y	Y	N	Y	Y
12 Costello	Y	Y	Y	Y	Y	Y
13 Biggert	Y	Y	Y	N	Y	Y
14 Foster	Y	Y	Y	Y	Y	Y
15 Johnson	N	Y	Y	Y	Y	Y

KEY	**Republicans**	Democrats		
Y Voted for (yea)		X Paired against		C Voted "present" to avoid possible conflict of interest
# Paired for		− Announced against		
+ Announced for		P Voted "present"		? Did not vote or otherwise make a position known
N Voted against (nay)				

* Rep. Eric Massa, D-N.Y., resigned March 8, 2010. The last vote for which he was eligible was vote 91.

	92	93	94	95	96	97
16 **Manzullo**	N	?	?	N	Y	Y
17 Hare	Y	Y	Y	Y	Y	Y
18 **Schock**	N	Y	Y	N	Y	Y
19 **Shimkus**	N	Y	Y	N	Y	Y
INDIANA						
1 Visclosky	Y	Y	Y	Y	Y	Y
2 Donnelly	Y	Y	Y	N	Y	Y
3 **Souder**	N	Y	Y	N	Y	Y
4 **Buyer**	N	Y	Y	N	Y	Y
5 **Burton**	N	Y	Y	N	Y	Y
6 **Pence**	N	Y	Y	N	Y	Y
7 Carson	Y	Y	Y	Y	Y	Y
8 Ellsworth	Y	Y	Y	Y	Y	Y
9 Hill	Y	Y	Y	Y	Y	Y
IOWA						
1 Braley	Y	Y	Y	Y	Y	Y
2 Loebsack	Y	Y	Y	Y	Y	Y
3 Boswell	Y	Y	Y	Y	Y	?
4 **Latham**	N	Y	Y	N	Y	Y
5 **King**	N	Y	Y	N	Y	Y
KANSAS						
1 **Moran**	N	Y	Y	N	Y	Y
2 **Jenkins**	N	Y	Y	N	Y	Y
3 Moore	Y	Y	Y	Y	Y	Y
4 **Tiahrt**	N	Y	Y	N	Y	Y
KENTUCKY						
1 **Whitfield**	N	Y	Y	N	Y	Y
2 **Guthrie**	N	Y	Y	N	Y	Y
3 Yarmuth	Y	Y	Y	Y	Y	Y
4 **Davis**	N	Y	Y	N	Y	Y
5 **Rogers**	N	Y	Y	N	Y	Y
6 Chandler	Y	Y	Y	Y	Y	Y
LOUISIANA						
1 **Scalise**	Y	Y	Y	N	Y	Y
2 **Cao**	Y	Y	Y	N	Y	Y
3 Melancon	Y	Y	Y	Y	Y	Y
4 **Fleming**	Y	Y	Y	N	Y	Y
5 **Alexander**	Y	Y	Y	N	Y	Y
6 **Cassidy**	Y	Y	Y	N	Y	Y
7 **Boustany**	Y	Y	Y	N	Y	Y
MAINE						
1 Pingree	Y	Y	Y	Y	Y	Y
2 Michaud	Y	Y	Y	Y	Y	Y
MARYLAND						
1 Kratovil	Y	Y	Y	N	Y	Y
2 Ruppersberger	Y	Y	Y	Y	Y	Y
3 Sarbanes	Y	Y	Y	Y	Y	Y
4 Edwards	Y	Y	Y	Y	Y	Y
5 Hoyer	Y	Y	Y	Y	Y	Y
6 **Bartlett**	N	Y	Y	N	Y	?
7 Cummings	Y	Y	Y	Y	Y	Y
8 Van Hollen	Y	Y	Y	Y	Y	Y
MASSACHUSETTS						
1 Olver	Y	Y	Y	Y	Y	Y
2 Neal	Y	Y	Y	Y	Y	Y
3 McGovern	Y	Y	Y	Y	Y	Y
4 Frank	Y	Y	Y	Y	Y	Y
5 Tsongas	Y	Y	Y	Y	Y	Y
6 Tierney	Y	Y	Y	Y	Y	Y
7 Markey	Y	Y	Y	Y	Y	Y
8 Capuano	Y	Y	Y	Y	Y	Y
9 Lynch	Y	Y	Y	Y	Y	Y
10 Delahunt	Y	Y	Y	Y	Y	Y
MICHIGAN						
1 Stupak	Y	Y	Y	Y	Y	Y
2 **Hoekstra**	?	?	?	?	?	?
3 **Ehlers**	Y	Y	Y	N	Y	Y
4 **Camp**	?	?	?	?	?	?
5 Kildee	Y	Y	Y	Y	Y	Y
6 **Upton**	N	Y	Y	N	Y	Y
7 Schauer	Y	Y	Y	Y	Y	Y
8 **Rogers**	N	Y	Y	N	Y	Y
9 Peters	Y	Y	Y	Y	Y	Y
10 **Miller**	N	Y	Y	N	Y	Y
11 **McCotter**	N	Y	Y	N	Y	Y
12 Levin	Y	Y	Y	Y	Y	Y
13 Kilpatrick	?	?	?	Y	Y	Y
14 Conyers	+	+	+	+	?	+
15 Dingell	Y	Y	Y	Y	Y	Y
MINNESOTA						
1 Walz	Y	Y	Y	Y	Y	Y
2 **Kline**	N	Y	Y	N	Y	Y
3 **Paulsen**	N	Y	Y	N	Y	Y
4 McCollum	Y	Y	Y	Y	Y	Y

	92	93	94	95	96	97
5 Ellison	Y	Y	Y	Y	Y	Y
6 **Bachmann**	N	Y	Y	N	Y	Y
7 Peterson	Y	Y	Y	Y	Y	?
8 Oberstar	Y	Y	Y	Y	Y	Y
MISSISSIPPI						
1 Childers	N	Y	Y	N	Y	Y
2 Thompson	Y	Y	Y	Y	Y	Y
3 **Harper**	N	Y	Y	N	Y	Y
4 Taylor	Y	Y	Y	N	Y	Y
MISSOURI						
1 Clay	Y	Y	Y	Y	Y	Y
2 **Akin**	N	Y	Y	N	Y	Y
3 Carnahan	Y	Y	Y	Y	Y	Y
4 Skelton	Y	Y	Y	N	Y	Y
5 Cleaver	Y	Y	Y	Y	Y	Y
6 **Graves**	N	Y	Y	N	Y	Y
7 **Blunt**	?	?	?	N	Y	Y
8 **Emerson**	N	Y	Y	N	Y	Y
9 **Luetkemeyer**	N	Y	Y	N	Y	Y
MONTANA						
AL **Rehberg**	N	Y	Y	N	Y	Y
NEBRASKA						
1 **Fortenberry**	Y	Y	Y	N	Y	Y
2 **Terry**	N	Y	?	N	Y	Y
3 **Smith**	Y	Y	Y	N	Y	Y
NEVADA						
1 Berkley	Y	Y	Y	Y	Y	Y
2 **Heller**	N	Y	Y	N	Y	Y
3 Titus	?	Y	Y	Y	Y	Y
NEW HAMPSHIRE						
1 Shea-Porter	Y	Y	Y	Y	Y	Y
2 Hodes	Y	Y	Y	Y	Y	Y
NEW JERSEY						
1 Andrews	Y	Y	Y	Y	Y	Y
2 **LoBiondo**	Y	Y	Y	N	Y	Y
3 Adler	Y	Y	Y	Y	Y	Y
4 **Smith**	Y	Y	Y	N	Y	Y
5 **Garrett**	N	Y	Y	N	Y	Y
6 Pallone	Y	Y	Y	Y	Y	Y
7 **Lance**	N	Y	Y	N	Y	Y
8 Pascrell	Y	Y	Y	Y	Y	Y
9 Rothman	Y	Y	Y	Y	Y	Y
10 Payne	Y	Y	Y	Y	Y	Y
11 **Frelinghuysen**	N	Y	Y	N	Y	Y
12 Holt	Y	Y	Y	Y	Y	Y
13 Sires	Y	Y	Y	Y	Y	Y
NEW MEXICO						
1 Heinrich	Y	Y	Y	Y	Y	Y
2 Teague	Y	Y	Y	N	Y	Y
3 Luján	Y	Y	Y	Y	Y	Y
NEW YORK						
1 Bishop	Y	Y	Y	Y	Y	Y
2 Israel	Y	Y	Y	Y	Y	Y
3 **King**	N	Y	Y	N	Y	Y
4 McCarthy	Y	Y	Y	Y	Y	Y
5 Ackerman	Y	Y	Y	Y	Y	Y
6 Meeks	Y	Y	Y	Y	Y	Y
7 Crowley	Y	Y	Y	Y	Y	Y
8 Nadler	?	?	?	Y	Y	Y
9 Weiner	Y	Y	Y	Y	Y	Y
10 Towns	Y	Y	Y	Y	Y	Y
11 Clarke	Y	Y	Y	Y	Y	Y
12 Velázquez	Y	Y	Y	Y	Y	Y
13 McMahon	Y	Y	Y	Y	Y	Y
14 Maloney	Y	Y	Y	Y	Y	Y
15 Rangel	Y	Y	Y	Y	Y	Y
16 Serrano	Y	?	Y	Y	Y	Y
17 Engel	?	?	?	Y	Y	Y
18 Lowey	Y	Y	Y	Y	Y	Y
19 Hall	Y	Y	Y	Y	Y	Y
20 Murphy	Y	Y	Y	Y	Y	Y
21 Tonko	Y	Y	Y	Y	Y	Y
22 Hinchey	Y	Y	Y	Y	Y	Y
23 Owens	N	Y	Y	Y	Y	Y
24 Arcuri	Y	Y	Y	N	Y	Y
25 Maffei	Y	Y	Y	Y	?	Y
26 **Lee**	N	Y	Y	N	Y	Y
27 Higgins	Y	Y	Y	Y	Y	Y
28 Slaughter	Y	Y	Y	Y	Y	Y
29 Vacant*						
NORTH CAROLINA						
1 Butterfield	Y	Y	Y	Y	Y	Y
2 Etheridge	Y	Y	Y	Y	Y	Y
3 **Jones**	Y	Y	Y	Y	Y	Y
4 Price	Y	Y	Y	Y	Y	Y

	92	93	94	95	96	97
5 **Foxx**	N	Y	Y	N	Y	Y
6 **Coble**	N	Y	Y	N	Y	Y
7 McIntyre	Y	?	Y	N	Y	Y
8 Kissell	Y	Y	Y	N	Y	Y
9 **Myrick**	N	Y	Y	N	Y	Y
10 **McHenry**	N	Y	Y	N	Y	Y
11 Shuler	Y	Y	Y	N	Y	Y
12 Watt	Y	Y	Y	Y	Y	Y
13 Miller	Y	Y	Y	Y	Y	Y
NORTH DAKOTA						
AL Pomeroy	Y	Y	Y	Y	Y	Y
OHIO						
1 Driehaus	Y	Y	Y	Y	Y	Y
2 **Schmidt**	N	Y	Y	N	Y	Y
3 **Turner**	N	Y	Y	N	Y	Y
4 **Jordan**	+	+	+	N	Y	Y
5 **Latta**	N	Y	Y	N	Y	Y
6 Wilson	Y	Y	Y	Y	Y	Y
7 **Austria**	N	Y	Y	N	Y	Y
8 **Boehner**	N	Y	Y	N	Y	Y
9 Kaptur	Y	Y	Y	Y	Y	Y
10 Kucinich	Y	Y	Y	Y	Y	Y
11 Fudge	Y	Y	Y	Y	Y	Y
12 **Tiberi**	N	Y	Y	N	Y	Y
13 Sutton	Y	Y	Y	Y	Y	Y
14 **LaTourette**	Y	Y	Y	N	Y	Y
15 Kilroy	Y	Y	Y	Y	Y	Y
16 Boccieri	Y	Y	Y	N	Y	Y
17 Ryan	?	?	?	Y	Y	Y
18 Space	?	Y	Y	N	Y	Y
OKLAHOMA						
1 **Sullivan**	N	Y	Y	N	Y	Y
2 Boren	N	Y	Y	N	Y	Y
3 **Lucas**	N	Y	Y	N	Y	Y
4 **Cole**	N	Y	Y	N	Y	Y
5 **Fallin**	?	?	?	N	Y	Y
OREGON						
1 Wu	Y	Y	Y	N	Y	Y
2 **Walden**	N	Y	Y	N	Y	Y
3 Blumenauer	Y	Y	Y	Y	Y	Y
4 DeFazio	Y	Y	Y	Y	Y	Y
5 Schrader	Y	Y	Y	Y	Y	Y
PENNSYLVANIA						
1 Brady	Y	Y	Y	Y	Y	Y
2 Fattah	Y	Y	Y	Y	Y	Y
3 Dahlkemper	?	?	?	N	Y	Y
4 Altmire	N	Y	Y	N	Y	Y
5 **Thompson**	N	Y	Y	N	Y	Y
6 **Gerlach**	N	Y	Y	N	Y	Y
7 Sestak	Y	Y	Y	Y	Y	Y
8 Murphy, P.	Y	Y	Y	Y	Y	Y
9 **Shuster**	N	Y	Y	N	Y	Y
10 Carney	Y	Y	Y	Y	Y	Y
11 Kanjorski	Y	Y	Y	Y	Y	Y
12 Vacant						
13 Schwartz	Y	Y	Y	Y	Y	Y
14 Doyle	Y	Y	Y	Y	Y	Y
15 **Dent**	N	Y	Y	N	Y	Y
16 **Pitts**	N	Y	Y	N	Y	Y
17 Holden	Y	Y	Y	Y	Y	Y
18 **Murphy, T.**	N	Y	Y	N	Y	Y
19 **Platts**	N	Y	Y	N	Y	Y
RHODE ISLAND						
1 Kennedy	?	?	?	?	Y	Y
2 Langevin	Y	Y	Y	Y	Y	Y
SOUTH CAROLINA						
1 **Brown**	N	Y	Y	N	Y	Y
2 **Wilson**	N	Y	Y	N	Y	Y
3 **Barrett**	?	?	?	?	?	?
4 **Inglis**	N	Y	Y	N	Y	Y
5 Spratt	Y	Y	Y	Y	Y	Y
6 Clyburn	Y	Y	Y	Y	Y	Y
SOUTH DAKOTA						
AL Herseth Sandlin	Y	Y	Y	Y	Y	Y
TENNESSEE						
1 **Roe**	N	Y	Y	N	Y	Y
2 **Duncan**	N	Y	Y	Y	Y	Y
3 **Wamp**	?	?	?	?	?	?
4 Davis	Y	Y	Y	N	Y	Y
5 Cooper	Y	Y	Y	Y	Y	Y
6 Gordon	Y	Y	Y	Y	Y	Y
7 **Blackburn**	N	Y	Y	N	Y	Y
8 Tanner	Y	Y	Y	Y	Y	Y
9 Cohen	Y	Y	Y	Y	Y	Y

	92	93	94	95	96	97
TEXAS						
1 **Gohmert**	Y	Y	?	N	Y	Y
2 **Poe**	N	Y	Y	N	Y	Y
3 **Johnson, S.**	N	Y	Y	N	Y	Y
4 **Hall**	N	Y	Y	N	Y	Y
5 **Hensarling**	N	Y	Y	N	Y	Y
6 **Barton**	N	Y	Y	N	Y	Y
7 **Culberson**	N	Y	Y	N	Y	Y
8 **Brady**	N	Y	Y	N	Y	Y
9 Green, A.	Y	Y	Y	Y	Y	Y
10 **McCaul**	N	Y	Y	N	Y	Y
11 **Conaway**	N	Y	Y	N	Y	Y
12 **Granger**	N	Y	Y	N	Y	Y
13 **Thornberry**	N	Y	Y	N	Y	Y
14 **Paul**	N	Y	Y	Y	N	Y
15 Hinojosa	Y	Y	Y	Y	Y	Y
16 Reyes	Y	Y	Y	Y	Y	Y
17 Edwards	Y	Y	Y	Y	Y	Y
18 Jackson Lee	Y	Y	Y	Y	Y	Y
19 **Neugebauer**	N	Y	Y	N	Y	Y
20 Gonzalez	Y	Y	Y	Y	Y	Y
21 **Smith**	N	Y	Y	N	Y	Y
22 **Olson**	N	Y	Y	N	Y	Y
23 Rodriguez	Y	Y	Y	Y	Y	Y
24 **Marchant**	N	Y	Y	N	Y	Y
25 Doggett	Y	Y	Y	Y	Y	Y
26 **Burgess**	N	Y	Y	N	Y	Y
27 Ortiz	Y	Y	Y	Y	Y	Y
28 Cuellar	Y	Y	Y	Y	Y	Y
29 Green, G.	Y	Y	Y	Y	Y	Y
30 Johnson, E.	Y	Y	Y	Y	Y	Y
31 **Carter**	N	Y	Y	N	Y	Y
32 **Sessions**	N	Y	Y	N	Y	Y
UTAH						
1 **Bishop**	N	Y	Y	N	Y	Y
2 Matheson	Y	Y	Y	Y	Y	Y
3 **Chaffetz**	N	Y	Y	N	Y	Y
VERMONT						
AL Welch	Y	Y	Y	Y	Y	Y
VIRGINIA						
1 **Wittman**	Y	Y	Y	N	Y	Y
2 Nye	Y	Y	Y	N	Y	Y
3 Scott	Y	Y	Y	Y	Y	Y
4 **Forbes**	?	?	?	N	Y	Y
5 Perriello	Y	Y	Y	Y	Y	Y
6 **Goodlatte**	N	Y	Y	N	Y	Y
7 **Cantor**	N	Y	Y	N	Y	Y
8 Moran	Y	Y	Y	Y	Y	Y
9 Boucher	Y	Y	Y	Y	Y	Y
10 **Wolf**	N	Y	Y	N	Y	Y
11 Connolly	Y	Y	Y	Y	Y	Y
WASHINGTON						
1 Inslee	Y	Y	Y	+	Y	Y
2 Larsen	Y	Y	Y	Y	Y	Y
3 Baird	Y	Y	Y	Y	Y	Y
4 **Hastings**	N	Y	Y	N	Y	Y
5 **McMorris Rodgers**	N	Y	Y	N	Y	Y
6 Dicks	Y	Y	Y	Y	Y	Y
7 McDermott	Y	Y	Y	Y	Y	Y
8 **Reichert**	Y	Y	Y	N	Y	Y
9 Smith	Y	Y	Y	Y	Y	Y
WEST VIRGINIA						
1 Mollohan	Y	Y	Y	Y	Y	Y
2 **Capito**	Y	Y	Y	N	Y	Y
3 Rahall	Y	Y	Y	Y	Y	Y
WISCONSIN						
1 **Ryan**	Y	Y	Y	N	Y	Y
2 Baldwin	Y	Y	Y	Y	Y	Y
3 Kind	Y	Y	Y	Y	Y	Y
4 Moore	Y	Y	Y	Y	Y	Y
5 **Sensenbrenner**	N	Y	Y	N	Y	Y
6 **Petri**	N	Y	Y	N	Y	Y
7 Obey	Y	Y	Y	Y	Y	Y
8 Kagen	Y	Y	Y	Y	Y	Y
WYOMING						
AL **Lummis**	N	Y	Y	N	Y	Y
DELEGATES						
Faleomavaega (A.S.)						
Norton (D.C.)						
Bordallo (Guam)						
Sablan (N. Marianas)						
Pierluisi (P.R.)						
Christensen (V.I.)						

IN THE HOUSE | By Vote Number

98. **H Con Res 248. Afghanistan Troop Withdrawal/Adoption.** Adoption of the concurrent resolution that would direct the president to remove U.S. forces from Afghanistan within 30 days of adoption, or by Dec. 31 if the president determined that a withdrawal could not be accomplished safely within 30 days. Rejected 65-356: D 60-189; R 5-167. A "nay" was a vote in support of the president's position. March 10, 2010.

99. **H Con Res 249. Bloody Sunday 45th Anniversary/Adoption.** Cohen, D-Tenn., motion to suspend the rules and adopt the concurrent resolution that would commemorate the 45th anniversary of Bloody Sunday and the enactment of the Voting Rights Act of 1965. Motion agreed to 409-0: D 242-0; R 167-0. A two-thirds majority of those present and voting (273 in this case) is required for adoption under suspension of the rules. March 10, 2010.

100. **H Res 1144. Chile Earthquake Victims/Adoption.** Connolly, D-Va., motion to suspend the rules and adopt the resolution that would acknowledge the loss of life and physical damage caused by the Feb. 27, 2010, earthquake in Chile. It also would urge the president to continue to support the Chilean government as it assesses relief and recovery needs. Motion agreed to 404-1: D 239-0; R 165-1. A two-thirds majority of those present and voting (270 in this case) is required for adoption under suspension of the rules. March 10, 2010.

101. **Procedural Matter/Quorum Call.** * A quorum was present with 405 members responding (26 members did not respond). March 11, 2010.

102. **H Res 1031. Impeachment of Judge Porteous/Improper Relationships with Lawyers.** Adoption of Article I of the resolution, which would impeach Judge G. Thomas Porteous Jr. of the U.S. District Court for the Eastern District of Louisiana for receiving money from lawyers involved in *Lifemark Hospitals of La. Inc. v. Liljeberg Enterprises*, a 1996-2000 case that Porteous oversaw. Adopted 412-0: D 242-0; R 170-0. March 11, 2010.

103. **H Res 1031. Impeachment of Judge Porteous/Bondsmen Bribery Charges.** Adoption of Article II of the resolution, which would impeach Judge G. Thomas Porteous Jr. of the U.S. District Court for the Eastern District of Louisiana for accepting items of value from bail bondsman Louis M. Marcotte III and his sister Lori Marcotte in exchange for taking official actions that benefited the Marcottes, including setting, reducing and splitting bonds as requested by the Marcottes, and improperly setting aside or expunging felony convictions for two Marcotte employees. Adopted 410-0: D 245-0; R 165-0. March 11, 2010.

	98	99	100	102	103
ALABAMA					
1 **Bonner**	N	Y	Y	Y	Y
2 **Bright**	N	Y	Y	Y	Y
3 **Rogers**	N	Y	Y	Y	Y
4 **Aderholt**	N	Y	Y	Y	Y
5 **Griffith**	N	Y	Y	Y	?
6 **Bachus**	N	Y	Y	Y	Y
7 Davis	?	?	?	?	?
ALASKA					
AL **Young**	N	Y	Y	Y	Y
ARIZONA					
1 **Kirkpatrick**	N	Y	Y	Y	Y
2 **Franks**	N	Y	Y	Y	Y
3 **Shadegg**	N	Y	Y	Y	Y
4 Pastor	N	Y	Y	Y	Y
5 Mitchell	N	Y	Y	Y	Y
6 **Flake**	N	Y	Y	Y	Y
7 Grijalva	Y	?	?	Y	Y
8 Giffords	N	Y	Y	Y	Y
ARKANSAS					
1 Berry	N	Y	Y	Y	Y
2 Snyder	N	Y	Y	Y	Y
3 **Boozman**	N	Y	Y	Y	Y
4 Ross	N	Y	Y	Y	Y
CALIFORNIA					
1 Thompson	N	Y	Y	Y	Y
2 **Herger**	N	Y	Y	Y	Y
3 **Lungren**	N	Y	Y	Y	Y
4 **McClintock**	N	Y	Y	Y	Y
5 Matsui	N	Y	Y	Y	Y
6 Woolsey	Y	Y	Y	Y	?
7 Miller, George	Y	Y	Y	Y	?
8 Pelosi					
9 Lee	Y	Y	Y	Y	Y
10 Garamendi	N	Y	Y	Y	Y
11 McNerney	N	Y	Y	Y	Y
12 Speier	Y	Y	Y	Y	Y
13 Stark	Y	Y	Y	Y	Y
14 Eshoo	N	Y	Y	Y	Y
15 Honda	N	Y	Y	Y	Y
16 Lofgren	N	Y	Y	Y	Y
17 Farr	Y	?	Y	Y	Y
18 Cardoza	N	Y	?	Y	Y
19 **Radanovich**	N	Y	Y	Y	Y
20 Costa	N	Y	Y	Y	Y
21 **Nunes**	N	Y	Y	Y	Y
22 **McCarthy**	N	Y	Y	Y	Y
23 Capps	N	Y	Y	Y	Y
24 **Gallegly**	N	Y	Y	Y	Y
25 **McKeon**	N	Y	Y	Y	Y
26 **Dreier**	N	Y	Y	Y	Y
27 Sherman	N	Y	Y	Y	Y
28 Berman	N	Y	Y	Y	Y
29 Schiff	N	Y	Y	Y	Y
30 Waxman	N	Y	Y	Y	Y
31 Becerra	N	Y	Y	Y	Y
32 Chu	Y	Y	Y	Y	Y
33 Watson	Y	Y	Y	Y	Y
34 Roybal-Allard	N	Y	Y	Y	Y
35 Waters	Y	Y	Y	Y	Y
36 Harman	N	Y	?	Y	Y
37 Richardson	Y	Y	Y	?	Y
38 Napolitano	Y	Y	Y	Y	Y
39 Sánchez, Linda	Y	Y	Y	Y	Y
40 **Royce**	N	Y	Y	Y	Y
41 **Lewis**	N	Y	?	Y	Y
42 **Miller, Gary**	N	Y	Y	Y	Y
43 Baca	N	Y	Y	Y	Y
44 **Calvert**	N	Y	Y	Y	Y
45 **Bono Mack**	N	Y	Y	Y	Y
46 **Rohrabacher**	N	Y	Y	Y	Y
47 Sanchez, Loretta	Y	Y	Y	Y	Y
48 **Campbell**	Y	Y	Y	Y	Y
49 **Issa**	N	Y	Y	Y	Y
50 **Bilbray**	N	Y	Y	Y	?
51 Filner	Y	Y	Y	Y	Y
52 **Hunter**	N	Y	Y	Y	?
53 Davis	N	Y	Y	+	Y

	98	99	100	102	103
COLORADO					
1 DeGette	N	Y	Y	Y	Y
2 Polis	Y	?	Y	Y	Y
3 Salazar	N	Y	Y	Y	Y
4 Markey	N	Y	Y	Y	Y
5 **Lamborn**	N	Y	Y	Y	Y
6 **Coffman**	N	Y	Y	Y	Y
7 Perlmutter	N	Y	Y	Y	Y
CONNECTICUT					
1 Larson	Y	+	Y	+	+
2 Courtney	N	Y	Y	Y	Y
3 DeLauro	N	Y	Y	Y	Y
4 Himes	N	Y	Y	Y	Y
5 Murphy	N	Y	Y	Y	Y
DELAWARE					
AL **Castle**	N	Y	Y	Y	Y
FLORIDA					
1 **Miller**	N	Y	Y	Y	Y
2 Boyd	N	Y	Y	Y	Y
3 Brown	N	Y	Y	Y	Y
4 **Crenshaw**	N	Y	Y	Y	Y
5 **Brown-Waite**	N	Y	Y	Y	?
6 **Stearns**	N	Y	Y	Y	Y
7 **Mica**	N	Y	Y	Y	Y
8 Grayson	Y	Y	Y	Y	Y
9 **Bilirakis**	N	Y	Y	+	Y
10 **Young**	?	?	?	?	?
11 Castor	N	Y	Y	Y	Y
12 **Putnam**	N	Y	Y	Y	Y
13 **Buchanan**	N	Y	Y	Y	Y
14 **Mack**	N	Y	Y	Y	Y
15 **Posey**	N	Y	Y	Y	Y
16 **Rooney**	N	Y	Y	Y	Y
17 Meek	N	Y	Y	Y	Y
18 **Ros-Lehtinen**	N	Y	Y	Y	?
19 Vacant					
20 Wasserman Schultz	-	Y	Y	Y	Y
21 **Diaz-Balart, L.**	?	?	?	?	?
22 Klein	N	Y	Y	Y	Y
23 Hastings	Y	Y	Y	Y	Y
24 Kosmas	N	Y	Y	Y	Y
25 **Diaz-Balart, M.**	N	Y	Y	Y	+
GEORGIA					
1 **Kingston**	N	Y	Y	Y	Y
2 Bishop	N	Y	Y	Y	Y
3 **Westmoreland**	N	Y	Y	Y	Y
4 Johnson	N	Y	Y	Y	Y
5 Lewis	Y	Y	Y	Y	Y
6 **Price**	N	Y	Y	Y	Y
7 **Linder**	N	Y	Y	Y	Y
8 Marshall	N	Y	Y	Y	Y
9 **Deal**	?	?	?	?	?
10 **Broun**	N	Y	Y	Y	Y
11 **Gingrey**	N	Y	Y	Y	Y
12 Barrow	N	Y	Y	Y	Y
13 Scott	N	Y	Y	Y	Y
HAWAII					
1 Vacant					
2 Hirono	N	Y	Y	Y	Y
IDAHO					
1 Minnick	N	Y	Y	Y	Y
2 **Simpson**	N	Y	Y	Y	Y
ILLINOIS					
1 Rush	N	Y	Y	Y	Y
2 Jackson	Y	Y	Y	Y	Y
3 Lipinski	N	Y	Y	Y	Y
4 Gutierrez	Y	Y	Y	Y	Y
5 Quigley	Y	Y	Y	Y	Y
6 **Roskam**	N	Y	?	Y	Y
7 Davis	Y	Y	Y	Y	Y
8 Bean	N	Y	Y	Y	Y
9 Schakowsky	Y	Y	Y	+	Y
10 **Kirk**	N	Y	Y	Y	Y
11 Halvorson	N	Y	Y	Y	Y
12 Costello	N	Y	Y	Y	Y
13 **Biggert**	N	Y	Y	Y	Y
14 Foster	N	Y	Y	Y	Y
15 **Johnson**	Y	Y	Y	Y	Y

KEY **Republicans**   Democrats

Y Voted for (yea)	X Paired against
# Paired for	– Announced against
+ Announced for	P Voted "present"
N Voted against (nay)	

C Voted "present" to avoid possible conflict of interest

? Did not vote or otherwise make a position known

*CQ does not include quorum calls in its vote charts.

	98	99	100	102	103
16 Manzullo	N	Y	Y	Y	Y
17 Hare	N	Y	Y	Y	Y
18 Schock	N	Y	Y	Y	Y
19 Shimkus	N	Y	Y	Y	Y
INDIANA					
1 Visclosky	N	Y	Y	Y	Y
2 Donnelly	N	Y	Y	Y	Y
3 **Souder**	N	Y	Y	Y	Y
4 **Buyer**	N	Y	Y	?	?
5 **Burton**	N	?	Y	Y	Y
6 **Pence**	N	Y	Y	Y	Y
7 Carson	N	Y	Y	Y	Y
8 Ellsworth	N	Y	Y	Y	Y
9 Hill	N	Y	Y	Y	Y
IOWA					
1 Braley	N	Y	Y	Y	Y
2 Loebsack	N	Y	Y	Y	Y
3 Boswell	N	Y	Y	Y	Y
4 **Latham**	N	Y	Y	Y	Y
5 **King**	N	Y	Y	Y	Y
KANSAS					
1 **Moran**	N	Y	Y	Y	Y
2 **Jenkins**	N	Y	Y	Y	Y
3 Moore	N	Y	Y	Y	Y
4 **Tiahrt**	N	Y	Y	Y	Y
KENTUCKY					
1 **Whitfield**	N	Y	Y	Y	Y
2 **Guthrie**	N	Y	Y	Y	Y
3 Yarmuth	N	Y	Y	Y	Y
4 **Davis**	N	Y	Y	Y	Y
5 **Rogers**	N	Y	Y	Y	Y
6 Chandler	N	Y	Y	Y	Y
LOUISIANA					
1 **Scalise**	N	Y	Y	Y	Y
2 **Cao**	N	Y	Y	Y	Y
3 Melancon	N	Y	?	Y	Y
4 **Fleming**	N	Y	Y	Y	Y
5 **Alexander**	N	Y	Y	Y	Y
6 **Cassidy**	N	Y	Y	Y	Y
7 **Boustany**	N	Y	Y	Y	Y
MAINE					
1 Pingree	Y	Y	Y	Y	Y
2 Michaud	Y	Y	Y	Y	Y
MARYLAND					
1 Kratovil	N	Y	Y	Y	Y
2 Ruppersberger	N	Y	Y	Y	Y
3 Sarbanes	N	Y	Y	Y	Y
4 Edwards	Y	Y	Y	Y	Y
5 Hoyer	N	Y	Y	Y	Y
6 **Bartlett**	N	Y	Y	Y	Y
7 Cummings	N	Y	Y	Y	Y
8 Van Hollen	N	Y	Y	Y	Y
MASSACHUSETTS					
1 Olver	Y	Y	Y	Y	Y
2 Neal	Y	Y	Y	Y	Y
3 McGovern	Y	Y	Y	Y	Y
4 Frank	Y	Y	Y	Y	Y
5 Tsongas	Y	Y	Y	Y	Y
6 Tierney	Y	Y	Y	Y	Y
7 Markey	Y	Y	Y	Y	Y
8 Capuano	Y	Y	Y	Y	Y
9 Lynch	N	Y	Y	Y	Y
10 Delahunt	N	Y	?	Y	Y
MICHIGAN					
1 Stupak	Y	Y	Y	Y	Y
2 **Hoekstra**	?	?	?	?	?
3 **Ehlers**	N	Y	Y	Y	Y
4 **Camp**	?	?	?	?	?
5 Kildee	N	Y	Y	Y	Y
6 **Upton**	N	Y	Y	Y	Y
7 Schauer	N	Y	Y	Y	Y
8 **Rogers**	N	Y	Y	Y	Y
9 Peters	N	Y	Y	Y	Y
10 **Miller**	N	Y	Y	Y	Y
11 **McCotter**	N	Y	Y	Y	Y
12 Levin	N	Y	Y	Y	Y
13 Kilpatrick	N	Y	Y	Y	Y
14 Conyers	+	+	+	Y	Y
15 Dingell	N	Y	Y	Y	Y
MINNESOTA					
1 Walz	N	Y	Y	Y	Y
2 **Kline**	N	?	?	Y	Y
3 **Paulsen**	N	Y	Y	Y	Y
4 McCollum	N	Y	Y	Y	Y

	98	99	100	102	103
5 Ellison	Y	Y	Y	Y	Y
6 **Bachmann**	N	Y	Y	Y	Y
7 Peterson	N	Y	Y	Y	Y
8 Oberstar	N	Y	Y	Y	Y
MISSISSIPPI					
1 Childers	N	Y	Y	Y	Y
2 Thompson	N	Y	Y	Y	Y
3 **Harper**	N	Y	Y	Y	Y
4 Taylor	N	Y	Y	Y	Y
MISSOURI					
1 Clay	Y	Y	Y	Y	Y
2 **Akin**	N	Y	?	Y	Y
3 Carnahan	N	Y	Y	Y	Y
4 Skelton	N	Y	Y	Y	Y
5 Cleaver	Y	Y	Y	Y	Y
6 **Graves**	N	Y	Y	Y	Y
7 **Blunt**	N	?	?	Y	Y
8 **Emerson**	N	Y	Y	Y	Y
9 **Luetkemeyer**	N	Y	Y	Y	Y
MONTANA					
AL **Rehberg**	N	Y	Y	Y	Y
NEBRASKA					
1 **Fortenberry**	N	Y	Y	Y	Y
2 **Terry**	N	Y	Y	Y	Y
3 **Smith**	N	Y	Y	Y	Y
NEVADA					
1 Berkley	N	Y	Y	Y	Y
2 **Heller**	N	Y	Y	Y	Y
3 Titus	N	Y	Y	Y	Y
NEW HAMPSHIRE					
1 Shea-Porter	N	Y	Y	Y	Y
2 Hodes	N	?	?	Y	Y
NEW JERSEY					
1 Andrews	N	Y	Y	Y	Y
2 **LoBiondo**	N	Y	Y	Y	Y
3 Adler	N	Y	Y	Y	Y
4 **Smith**	N	Y	Y	Y	Y
5 **Garrett**	N	Y	Y	Y	Y
6 Pallone	N	Y	Y	Y	Y
7 **Lance**	N	Y	Y	Y	Y
8 Pascrell	N	Y	Y	Y	Y
9 Rothman	N	Y	Y	Y	Y
10 Payne	Y	Y	Y	Y	Y
11 **Frelinghuysen**	N	Y	Y	Y	Y
12 Holt	N	Y	Y	Y	Y
13 Sires	N	Y	Y	Y	Y
NEW MEXICO					
1 Heinrich	N	Y	Y	Y	Y
2 Teague	N	Y	Y	Y	Y
3 Luján	N	Y	Y	Y	Y
NEW YORK					
1 Bishop	N	Y	Y	Y	Y
2 Israel	N	Y	Y	Y	Y
3 **King**	N	Y	Y	Y	Y
4 McCarthy	N	Y	?	Y	Y
5 Ackerman	N	Y	Y	Y	Y
6 Meeks	N	Y	Y	Y	Y
7 Crowley	Y	Y	Y	Y	Y
8 Nadler	Y	Y	?	Y	Y
9 Weiner	N	Y	Y	Y	Y
10 Towns	Y	Y	Y	?	?
11 Clarke	Y	Y	Y	Y	Y
12 Velázquez	Y	Y	?	Y	Y
13 McMahon	N	Y	Y	Y	Y
14 Maloney	Y	Y	Y	Y	Y
15 Rangel	Y	Y	Y	Y	Y
16 Serrano	Y	Y	Y	Y	Y
17 Engel	N	Y	Y	Y	Y
18 Lowey	N	Y	Y	?	Y
19 Hall	N	Y	Y	Y	Y
20 Murphy	N	Y	Y	+	Y
21 Tonko	N	Y	Y	+	Y
22 Hinchey	N	Y	Y	Y	Y
23 Owens	N	Y	Y	Y	Y
24 Arcuri	N	Y	Y	Y	Y
25 Maffei	Y	Y	Y	Y	Y
26 **Lee**	N	?	?	Y	Y
27 Higgins	N	Y	Y	Y	Y
28 Slaughter	N	Y	Y	Y	Y
29 Vacant					
NORTH CAROLINA					
1 Butterfield	N	Y	Y	Y	?
2 Etheridge	N	Y	Y	Y	Y
3 **Jones**	Y	Y	Y	Y	Y
4 Price	N	Y	Y	Y	Y

	98	99	100	102	103
5 **Foxx**	N	Y	Y	Y	Y
6 **Coble**	N	Y	Y	Y	Y
7 McIntyre	N	Y	Y	Y	Y
8 Kissell	N	Y	Y	Y	Y
9 **Myrick**	N	Y	Y	Y	Y
10 **McHenry**	N	Y	Y	Y	Y
11 Shuler	N	Y	Y	Y	Y
12 Watt	N	Y	Y	Y	Y
13 Miller	N	Y	Y	Y	Y
NORTH DAKOTA					
AL Pomeroy	N	Y	Y	Y	Y
OHIO					
1 Driehaus	N	Y	Y	Y	Y
2 **Schmidt**	N	Y	Y	Y	Y
3 **Turner**	N	Y	Y	Y	Y
4 **Jordan**	N	Y	Y	Y	Y
5 **Latta**	N	Y	Y	Y	Y
6 Wilson	N	Y	Y	Y	Y
7 **Austria**	N	Y	Y	Y	Y
8 **Boehner**	N	Y	Y	?	Y
9 Kaptur	N	Y	?	Y	Y
10 Kucinich	Y	Y	Y	Y	Y
11 Fudge	N	Y	Y	Y	Y
12 **Tiberi**	N	Y	Y	Y	Y
13 Sutton	N	Y	Y	Y	Y
14 **LaTourette**	N	?	Y	Y	Y
15 Kilroy	N	Y	Y	Y	Y
16 Boccieri	N	Y	Y	Y	Y
17 Ryan	N	Y	Y	Y	Y
18 Space	N	Y	Y	Y	Y
OKLAHOMA					
1 **Sullivan**	N	Y	Y	Y	Y
2 Boren	N	Y	Y	Y	Y
3 **Lucas**	N	Y	Y	Y	Y
4 **Cole**	N	Y	Y	Y	Y
5 **Fallin**	N	Y	Y	Y	Y
OREGON					
1 Wu	N	Y	Y	Y	Y
2 **Walden**	N	Y	Y	Y	Y
3 Blumenauer	N	Y	Y	Y	Y
4 DeFazio	Y	Y	Y	Y	Y
5 Schrader	N	Y	Y	Y	Y
PENNSYLVANIA					
1 Brady	N	Y	Y	Y	Y
2 Fattah	N	Y	Y	Y	Y
3 Dahlkemper	N	Y	Y	Y	Y
4 Altmire	N	Y	Y	Y	Y
5 **Thompson**	N	Y	Y	Y	Y
6 **Gerlach**	N	Y	Y	Y	Y
7 Sestak	N	Y	Y	Y	Y
8 Murphy, P.	N	Y	Y	Y	Y
9 **Shuster**	N	Y	Y	Y	?
10 Carney	N	Y	Y	Y	Y
11 Kanjorski	N	Y	Y	Y	Y
12 Vacant					
13 Schwartz	N	Y	Y	Y	Y
14 Doyle	Y	Y	Y	Y	Y
15 **Dent**	N	Y	Y	Y	Y
16 **Pitts**	N	Y	Y	Y	Y
17 Holden	N	Y	Y	Y	Y
18 **Murphy, T.**	N	Y	Y	Y	Y
19 **Platts**	N	Y	Y	Y	Y
RHODE ISLAND					
1 Kennedy	N	Y	Y	Y	Y
2 Langevin	N	Y	Y	Y	Y
SOUTH CAROLINA					
1 **Brown**	N	Y	Y	?	?
2 **Wilson**	N	Y	Y	Y	Y
3 **Barrett**	?	?	?	Y	Y
4 **Inglis**	N	Y	Y	Y	Y
5 Spratt	N	Y	Y	Y	Y
6 Clyburn	N	Y	Y	Y	Y
SOUTH DAKOTA					
AL Herseth Sandlin	N	Y	Y	Y	Y
TENNESSEE					
1 **Roe**	N	Y	Y	Y	Y
2 **Duncan**	Y	Y	Y	Y	Y
3 **Wamp**	N	Y	Y	Y	Y
4 Davis	N	Y	Y	Y	Y
5 Cooper	N	Y	Y	Y	Y
6 Gordon	N	?	?	Y	Y
7 **Blackburn**	N	Y	Y	Y	Y
8 Tanner	N	Y	Y	Y	Y
9 Cohen	N	Y	Y	Y	Y

	98	99	100	102	103
TEXAS					
1 **Gohmert**	N	Y	Y	Y	Y
2 **Poe**	N	Y	Y	Y	Y
3 **Johnson, S.**	N	Y	Y	Y	Y
4 **Hall**	N	Y	Y	Y	Y
5 **Hensarling**	N	Y	Y	Y	Y
6 **Barton**	N	Y	Y	Y	Y
7 **Culberson**	N	Y	Y	Y	Y
8 **Brady**	N	Y	Y	Y	Y
9 Green, A.	N	Y	Y	Y	Y
10 **McCaul**	N	Y	Y	Y	Y
11 **Conaway**	N	Y	Y	Y	Y
12 **Granger**	N	Y	Y	Y	Y
13 **Thornberry**	N	Y	Y	Y	Y
14 **Paul**	Y	Y	N	Y	Y
15 Hinojosa	N	Y	Y	Y	Y
16 Reyes	N	Y	Y	Y	Y
17 Edwards	N	?	Y	Y	Y
18 Jackson Lee	Y	Y	Y	?	Y
19 **Neugebauer**	N	Y	Y	Y	Y
20 Gonzalez	N	Y	Y	Y	Y
21 **Smith**	N	Y	Y	Y	Y
22 **Olson**	N	Y	Y	Y	Y
23 Rodriguez	N	Y	Y	Y	Y
24 **Marchant**	N	Y	Y	Y	Y
25 Doggett	N	Y	Y	Y	Y
26 **Burgess**	N	Y	Y	Y	Y
27 Ortiz	N	Y	Y	Y	Y
28 Cuellar	N	Y	Y	Y	Y
29 Green, G.	N	Y	Y	Y	Y
30 Johnson, E.	Y	Y	Y	Y	Y
31 **Carter**	N	Y	Y	Y	Y
32 **Sessions**	N	Y	Y	Y	Y
UTAH					
1 **Bishop**	N	Y	Y	Y	Y
2 Matheson	N	Y	Y	Y	Y
3 **Chaffetz**	N	Y	Y	Y	Y
VERMONT					
AL Welch	Y	Y	Y	Y	Y
VIRGINIA					
1 **Wittman**	N	Y	Y	Y	Y
2 Nye	N	Y	Y	Y	Y
3 Scott	N	Y	Y	Y	Y
4 **Forbes**	N	Y	Y	Y	Y
5 Perriello	N	Y	Y	Y	Y
6 **Goodlatte**	N	Y	Y	Y	Y
7 **Cantor**	N	Y	Y	Y	Y
8 Moran	N	Y	Y	Y	Y
9 Boucher	N	Y	Y	Y	Y
10 **Wolf**	N	Y	Y	Y	Y
11 Connolly	N	Y	Y	Y	Y
WASHINGTON					
1 Inslee	N	Y	Y	Y	Y
2 Larsen	N	Y	Y	Y	Y
3 Baird	N	Y	Y	Y	Y
4 **Hastings**	N	Y	Y	Y	Y
5 **McMorris Rodgers**	N	Y	Y	Y	Y
6 Dicks	N	?	?	Y	Y
7 McDermott	Y	Y	Y	Y	Y
8 **Reichert**	N	Y	Y	Y	Y
9 Smith	N	Y	Y	Y	Y
WEST VIRGINIA					
1 Mollohan	N	Y	Y	Y	Y
2 **Capito**	N	Y	Y	Y	Y
3 Rahall	N	Y	Y	Y	Y
WISCONSIN					
1 **Ryan**	N	Y	Y	Y	Y
2 Baldwin	Y	Y	Y	Y	?
3 Kind	N	Y	Y	Y	Y
4 Moore	N	Y	Y	Y	Y
5 **Sensenbrenner**	N	Y	Y	Y	Y
6 **Petri**	N	Y	Y	Y	Y
7 Obey	Y	Y	Y	Y	Y
8 Kagen	Y	Y	Y	Y	Y
WYOMING					
AL **Lummis**	N	Y	Y	Y	Y
DELEGATES					
Faleomavaega (A.S.)					
Norton (D.C.)					
Bordallo (Guam)					
Sablan (N. Marianas)					
Pierluisi (P.R.)					
Christensen (V.I.)					

IN THE HOUSE | By Vote Number

104. H Res 1031. Impeachment of Judge Porteous/False Statements on Bankruptcy Filing. Adoption of Article III of the resolution, which would impeach Judge G. Thomas Porteous Jr. of the U.S. District Court for the Eastern District of Louisiana for making false statements and representations under penalty of perjury related to his personal bankruptcy filing and repeatedly violating a court order in his bankruptcy case. Adopted 416-0: D 246-0; R 170-0. March 11, 2010.

105. H Res 1031. Impeachment of Judge Porteous/False Statements in Confirmation Process. Adoption of Article IV of the resolution, which would impeach Judge G. Thomas Porteous Jr. of the U.S. District Court for the Eastern District of Louisiana for making false statements about his past to both the Senate and the FBI during his Senate confirmation process. Adopted 423-0: D 251-0; R 172-0. March 11, 2010.

106. H Res 1164. Reporting of Massa Allegations/Previous Question. Clyburn, D-S.C., motion to order the previous question (thus ending debate and possibility of amendment) on the Clyburn motion to refer the Boehner, R-Ohio, privileged resolution to the Committee on Standards of Official Conduct. The Boehner resolution would require the committee to investigate if House Democratic leaders and their staff knew of allegations of misconduct against former Rep. Eric Massa, D-N.Y., before March 3, 2010. Motion agreed to 404-2: D 244-0; R 160-2. March 11, 2010.

107. Res 1164. Reporting of Massa Allegations/Motion to Refer. Clyburn, D-S.C., motion to refer the Boehner, R-Ohio, privileged resolution to the Committee on Standards of Official Conduct. Motion agreed to 402-1: D 240-1; R 162-0. March 11, 2010.

108. H Res 1107. Greek Independence Anniversary/Adoption. Connolly, D-Va., motion to suspend the rules and adopt the resolution that would congratulate the people of Greece on the 189th anniversary of the country's independence and express support for the principles of democratic governance of Greece. Motion agreed to 414-0: D 247-0; R 167-0. A two-thirds majority of those present and voting (276 in this case) is required for adoption under suspension of the rules. March 11, 2010.

	104	105	106	107	108
ALABAMA					
1 Bonner	Y	Y	P	P	Y
2 Bright	Y	Y	Y	Y	Y
3 Rogers	Y	Y	Y	Y	Y
4 Aderholt	Y	Y	Y	Y	Y
5 Griffith	?	?	?	?	?
6 Bachus	Y	Y	Y	Y	Y
7 Davis	?	?	?	?	?
ALASKA					
AL Young	Y	Y	Y	?	Y
ARIZONA					
1 Kirkpatrick	Y	Y	Y	Y	Y
2 Franks	Y	Y	Y	Y	Y
3 Shadegg	Y	Y	Y	Y	Y
4 Pastor	Y	Y	Y	Y	Y
5 Mitchell	Y	Y	Y	?	Y
6 Flake	Y	Y	Y	Y	Y
7 Grijalva	Y	Y	Y	Y	Y
8 Giffords	Y	Y	Y	Y	Y
ARKANSAS					
1 Berry	Y	Y	Y	?	Y
2 Snyder	Y	Y	Y	Y	Y
3 Boozman	Y	Y	Y	Y	Y
4 Ross	Y	Y	Y	Y	Y
CALIFORNIA					
1 Thompson	Y	Y	Y	Y	Y
2 Herger	Y	Y	Y	Y	Y
3 Lungren	Y	Y	Y	Y	Y
4 McClintock	Y	Y	Y	Y	Y
5 Matsui	Y	Y	Y	Y	Y
6 Woolsey	?	Y	Y	Y	Y
7 Miller, George	?	Y	Y	Y	Y
8 Pelosi					
9 Lee	Y	Y	Y	Y	Y
10 Garamendi	Y	Y	P	Y	Y
11 McNerney	Y	Y	Y	Y	Y
12 Speier	?	Y	Y	?	?
13 Stark	Y	Y	Y	Y	Y
14 Eshoo	Y	Y	Y	?	Y
15 Honda	Y	Y	Y	Y	Y
16 Lofgren	Y	Y	P	P	Y
17 Farr	Y	Y	Y	Y	Y
18 Cardoza	Y	Y	Y	Y	Y
19 Radanovich	Y	Y	Y	Y	Y
20 Costa	Y	Y	Y	Y	Y
21 Nunes	Y	Y	Y	Y	Y
22 McCarthy	Y	Y	Y	Y	Y
23 Capps	Y	Y	Y	Y	Y
24 Gallegly	Y	Y	Y	Y	Y
25 McKeon	Y	Y	Y	Y	Y
26 Dreier	Y	Y	Y	Y	Y
27 Sherman	Y	Y	Y	Y	Y
28 Berman	Y	Y	Y	Y	Y
29 Schiff	Y	Y	Y	Y	Y
30 Waxman	Y	Y	Y	Y	Y
31 Becerra	Y	Y	Y	Y	Y
32 Chu	Y	Y	Y	Y	Y
33 Watson	Y	Y	Y	Y	Y
34 Roybal-Allard	Y	Y	Y	Y	Y
35 Waters	Y	Y	Y	Y	?
36 Harman	Y	Y	Y	Y	Y
37 Richardson	Y	Y	Y	Y	Y
38 Napolitano	Y	Y	Y	Y	Y
39 Sánchez, Linda	Y	Y	Y	Y	Y
40 Royce	Y	Y	Y	Y	Y
41 Lewis	Y	Y	Y	Y	Y
42 Miller, Gary	Y	Y	Y	Y	Y
43 Baca	Y	Y	Y	Y	Y
44 Calvert	Y	Y	Y	Y	Y
45 Bono Mack	Y	Y	Y	Y	Y
46 Rohrabacher	Y	Y	N	Y	Y
47 Sanchez, Loretta	Y	Y	Y	Y	Y
48 Campbell	Y	Y	Y	Y	Y
49 Issa	Y	Y	Y	Y	Y
50 Bilbray	Y	Y	Y	Y	Y
51 Filner	Y	Y	Y	Y	Y
52 Hunter	Y	Y	Y	Y	Y
53 Davis	Y	Y	Y	Y	Y

	104	105	106	107	108
COLORADO					
1 DeGette	Y	Y	Y	Y	Y
2 Polis	Y	Y	Y	Y	Y
3 Salazar	Y	Y	Y	Y	Y
4 Markey	Y	Y	Y	Y	Y
5 Lamborn	Y	Y	Y	Y	Y
6 Coffman	Y	Y	Y	Y	Y
7 Perlmutter	Y	Y	Y	Y	Y
CONNECTICUT					
1 Larson	+	Y	Y	Y	Y
2 Courtney	Y	Y	Y	Y	Y
3 DeLauro	Y	Y	Y	Y	Y
4 Himes	Y	Y	Y	Y	Y
5 Murphy	Y	Y	Y	Y	Y
DELAWARE					
AL Castle	Y	Y	Y	Y	Y
FLORIDA					
1 Miller	Y	Y	Y	Y	Y
2 Boyd	Y	Y	Y	Y	Y
3 Brown	Y	Y	Y	Y	Y
4 Crenshaw	Y	Y	Y	Y	Y
5 Brown-Waite	Y	Y	Y	Y	Y
6 Stearns	Y	Y	Y	Y	Y
7 Mica	Y	Y	Y	Y	Y
8 Grayson	Y	Y	Y	Y	Y
9 Bilirakis	Y	Y	Y	Y	Y
10 Young	?	?	?	?	?
11 Castor	Y	Y	P	P	Y
12 Putnam	Y	Y	Y	Y	Y
13 Buchanan	Y	Y	Y	Y	Y
14 Mack	Y	Y	Y	Y	Y
15 Posey	Y	Y	Y	Y	Y
16 Rooney	Y	Y	Y	Y	Y
17 Meek	Y	Y	Y	Y	Y
18 Ros-Lehtinen	Y	Y	Y	Y	Y
19 Vacant					
20 Wasserman Schultz	Y	Y	Y	Y	Y
21 Diaz-Balart, L.	?	?	?	?	?
22 Klein	Y	Y	Y	Y	Y
23 Hastings	Y	Y	Y	Y	Y
24 Kosmas	Y	Y	Y	Y	Y
25 Diaz-Balart, M.	Y	Y	Y	Y	Y
GEORGIA					
1 Kingston	Y	Y	Y	Y	Y
2 Bishop	Y	Y	Y	Y	Y
3 Westmoreland	Y	Y	P	P	Y
4 Johnson	Y	Y	Y	Y	Y
5 Lewis	Y	Y	Y	Y	Y
6 Price	Y	Y	Y	Y	Y
7 Linder	Y	Y	Y	Y	?
8 Marshall	Y	Y	Y	Y	Y
9 Deal	?	?	?	?	?
10 Broun	Y	Y	Y	Y	Y
11 Gingrey	Y	Y	Y	Y	Y
12 Barrow	Y	Y	Y	Y	Y
13 Scott	Y	Y	Y	Y	Y
HAWAII					
1 Vacant					
2 Hirono	Y	Y	Y	Y	Y
IDAHO					
1 Minnick	Y	Y	Y	Y	Y
2 Simpson	Y	Y	P	P	Y
ILLINOIS					
1 Rush	Y	Y	Y	Y	Y
2 Jackson	Y	Y	Y	Y	Y
3 Lipinski	Y	Y	Y	Y	Y
4 Gutierrez	Y	Y	Y	Y	Y
5 Quigley	Y	Y	Y	Y	Y
6 Roskam	Y	Y	Y	Y	Y
7 Davis	Y	Y	Y	Y	Y
8 Bean	Y	Y	Y	Y	Y
9 Schakowsky	Y	Y	Y	Y	Y
10 Kirk	Y	Y	Y	Y	Y
11 Halvorson	Y	Y	Y	Y	Y
12 Costello	Y	Y	Y	Y	Y
13 Biggert	Y	Y	Y	Y	Y
14 Foster	Y	Y	Y	Y	Y
15 Johnson	Y	Y	N	Y	Y

KEY

Republicans	Democrats	
Y Voted for (yea)	**X** Paired against	**C** Voted "present" to avoid possible conflict of interest
# Paired for	**–** Announced against	
+ Announced for	**P** Voted "present"	**?** Did not vote or otherwise make a position known
N Voted against (nay)		

	104	105	106	107	108
16 Manzullo	Y	Y	Y	Y	Y
17 Hare	Y	Y	Y	Y	Y
18 Schock	Y	Y	Y	Y	Y
19 Shimkus	Y	Y	Y	Y	Y
INDIANA					
1 Visclosky	Y	Y	Y	Y	Y
2 Donnelly	Y	Y	Y	Y	Y
3 Souder	Y	Y	Y	Y	Y
4 Buyer	?	?	?	?	?
5 Burton	Y	Y	Y	Y	Y
6 Pence	Y	Y	Y	Y	?
7 Carson	Y	Y	Y	Y	Y
8 Ellsworth	Y	Y	Y	Y	Y
9 Hill	Y	Y	Y	Y	Y
IOWA					
1 Braley	Y	Y	Y	Y	Y
2 Loebsack	Y	Y	Y	Y	Y
3 Boswell	Y	Y	Y	Y	Y
4 Latham	Y	Y	Y	Y	Y
5 King	Y	Y	Y	Y	Y
KANSAS					
1 Moran	Y	Y	Y	Y	Y
2 Jenkins	Y	Y	Y	Y	Y
3 Moore	Y	Y	Y	Y	Y
4 Tiahrt	Y	Y	Y	Y	Y
KENTUCKY					
1 Whitfield	Y	Y	Y	Y	Y
2 Guthrie	Y	Y	Y	Y	Y
3 Yarmuth	Y	Y	Y	Y	Y
4 Davis	Y	Y	Y	Y	Y
5 Rogers	Y	Y	Y	Y	Y
6 Chandler	Y	Y	P	P	Y
LOUISIANA					
1 Scalise	Y	Y	Y	Y	Y
2 Cao	Y	Y	Y	Y	Y
3 Melancon	Y	Y	Y	Y	Y
4 Fleming	Y	Y	Y	Y	Y
5 Alexander	Y	Y	Y	Y	Y
6 Cassidy	Y	Y	Y	Y	Y
7 Boustany	Y	Y	Y	Y	Y
MAINE					
1 Pingree	Y	Y	Y	Y	Y
2 Michaud	Y	Y	Y	Y	Y
MARYLAND					
1 Kratovil	Y	Y	Y	Y	Y
2 Ruppersberger	Y	Y	Y	Y	Y
3 Sarbanes	Y	Y	Y	Y	Y
4 Edwards	Y	Y	Y	Y	Y
5 Hoyer	Y	Y	Y	Y	Y
6 Bartlett	Y	Y	Y	Y	Y
7 Cummings	Y	Y	Y	Y	Y
8 Van Hollen	Y	Y	Y	Y	Y
MASSACHUSETTS					
1 Olver	Y	Y	Y	Y	Y
2 Neal	Y	Y	Y	Y	Y
3 McGovern	Y	Y	Y	Y	Y
4 Frank	Y	Y	Y	Y	Y
5 Tsongas	Y	Y	Y	Y	Y
6 Tierney	Y	Y	Y	Y	Y
7 Markey	Y	Y	Y	Y	Y
8 Capuano	Y	Y	Y	Y	Y
9 Lynch	Y	Y	Y	Y	Y
10 Delahunt	Y	Y	Y	Y	Y
MICHIGAN					
1 Stupak	Y	Y	Y	Y	Y
2 Hoekstra	?	?	?	?	?
3 Ehlers	Y	Y	Y	Y	Y
4 Camp	Y	Y	Y	Y	Y
5 Kildee	Y	Y	Y	Y	Y
6 Upton	Y	Y	Y	Y	Y
7 Schauer	Y	Y	Y	Y	Y
8 Rogers	Y	Y	Y	Y	Y
9 Peters	Y	Y	Y	Y	Y
10 Miller	Y	Y	Y	Y	Y
11 McCotter	Y	Y	Y	Y	Y
12 Levin	Y	Y	Y	Y	Y
13 Kilpatrick	Y	Y	Y	Y	Y
14 Conyers	Y	Y	Y	Y	?
15 Dingell	Y	Y	Y	Y	Y
MINNESOTA					
1 Walz	Y	Y	Y	Y	Y
2 Kline	Y	Y	Y	Y	Y
3 Paulsen	Y	Y	Y	Y	Y
4 McCollum	Y	Y	Y	Y	Y

	104	105	106	107	108
5 Ellison	Y	Y	Y	Y	Y
6 Bachmann	Y	Y	Y	Y	Y
7 Peterson	Y	Y	Y	Y	Y
8 Oberstar	Y	Y	Y	Y	Y
MISSISSIPPI					
1 Childers	Y	Y	Y	Y	Y
2 Thompson	Y	Y	Y	Y	Y
3 Harper	Y	Y	P	P	Y
4 Taylor	Y	Y	Y	Y	Y
MISSOURI					
1 Clay	Y	Y	Y	Y	Y
2 Akin	Y	Y	?	Y	Y
3 Carnahan	Y	Y	Y	Y	Y
4 Skelton	Y	Y	Y	Y	Y
5 Cleaver	Y	Y	Y	Y	Y
6 Graves	Y	Y	Y	Y	Y
7 Blunt	Y	Y	Y	Y	Y
8 Emerson	Y	Y	Y	Y	Y
9 Luetkemeyer	Y	Y	Y	Y	Y
MONTANA					
AL Rehberg	Y	Y	Y	Y	Y
NEBRASKA					
1 Fortenberry	Y	Y	Y	Y	Y
2 Terry	Y	Y	Y	Y	Y
3 Smith	Y	Y	Y	Y	Y
NEVADA					
1 Berkley	Y	Y	Y	Y	Y
2 Heller	Y	Y	Y	Y	Y
3 Titus	Y	Y	Y	Y	Y
NEW HAMPSHIRE					
1 Shea-Porter	Y	Y	Y	Y	Y
2 Hodes	Y	Y	Y	Y	Y
NEW JERSEY					
1 Andrews	Y	Y	Y	Y	Y
2 LoBiondo	Y	Y	Y	Y	Y
3 Adler	Y	Y	Y	Y	Y
4 Smith	Y	Y	Y	Y	Y
5 Garrett	Y	Y	Y	Y	Y
6 Pallone	Y	Y	Y	Y	Y
7 Lance	Y	Y	Y	Y	Y
8 Pascrell	Y	Y	Y	Y	Y
9 Rothman	Y	Y	Y	Y	Y
10 Payne	Y	Y	Y	Y	Y
11 Frelinghuysen	Y	Y	Y	Y	Y
12 Holt	Y	Y	Y	Y	Y
13 Sires	Y	Y	Y	Y	Y
NEW MEXICO					
1 Heinrich	Y	Y	Y	Y	Y
2 Teague	Y	Y	Y	Y	Y
3 Luján	Y	Y	Y	Y	Y
NEW YORK					
1 Bishop	Y	Y	Y	Y	Y
2 Israel	Y	Y	Y	Y	Y
3 King	Y	Y	Y	Y	Y
4 McCarthy	Y	Y	Y	Y	Y
5 Ackerman	Y	Y	Y	Y	Y
6 Meeks	Y	Y	Y	Y	Y
7 Crowley	Y	Y	Y	Y	Y
8 Nadler	Y	Y	Y	Y	Y
9 Weiner	Y	Y	Y	Y	Y
10 Towns	Y	Y	Y	Y	Y
11 Clarke	Y	Y	Y	Y	Y
12 Velázquez	Y	Y	Y	Y	Y
13 McMahon	Y	Y	Y	Y	Y
14 Maloney	Y	Y	Y	Y	Y
15 Rangel	?	Y	Y	Y	Y
16 Serrano	Y	Y	Y	Y	Y
17 Engel	Y	Y	Y	Y	Y
18 Lowey	Y	Y	Y	Y	Y
19 Hall	Y	Y	Y	Y	Y
20 Murphy	Y	Y	Y	Y	Y
21 Tonko	Y	Y	Y	Y	Y
22 Hinchey	Y	Y	Y	Y	Y
23 Owens	Y	Y	Y	Y	Y
24 Arcuri	Y	Y	Y	Y	Y
25 Maffei	Y	Y	Y	Y	Y
26 Lee	Y	Y	Y	Y	Y
27 Higgins	Y	Y	Y	Y	Y
28 Slaughter	Y	Y	Y	Y	Y
29 Vacant					
NORTH CAROLINA					
1 Butterfield	Y	Y	P	P	Y
2 Etheridge	Y	Y	Y	Y	Y
3 Jones	Y	Y	Y	Y	Y
4 Price	Y	Y	Y	Y	Y

	104	105	106	107	108
5 Foxx	Y	Y	Y	Y	Y
6 Coble	Y	Y	Y	Y	Y
7 McIntyre	Y	Y	Y	Y	Y
8 Kissell	Y	Y	Y	Y	Y
9 Myrick	Y	Y	P	P	Y
10 McHenry	Y	Y	Y	Y	Y
11 Shuler	Y	Y	Y	Y	Y
12 Watt	Y	Y	Y	Y	Y
13 Miller	Y	Y	Y	Y	Y
NORTH DAKOTA					
AL Pomeroy	Y	Y	Y	Y	Y
OHIO					
1 Driehaus	Y	Y	Y	Y	Y
2 Schmidt	Y	Y	Y	Y	Y
3 Turner	Y	Y	Y	Y	Y
4 Jordan	Y	Y	Y	Y	Y
5 Latta	Y	Y	Y	Y	Y
6 Wilson	Y	Y	Y	Y	Y
7 Austria	Y	Y	Y	Y	Y
8 Boehner	Y	Y	Y	Y	Y
9 Kaptur	Y	Y	Y	Y	Y
10 Kucinich	Y	Y	Y	Y	Y
11 Fudge	Y	Y	Y	Y	Y
12 Tiberi	Y	Y	Y	Y	Y
13 Sutton	Y	Y	Y	Y	Y
14 LaTourette	Y	Y	Y	Y	Y
15 Kilroy	Y	Y	Y	Y	Y
16 Boccieri	Y	Y	Y	Y	Y
17 Ryan	Y	Y	?	Y	Y
18 Space	Y	Y	Y	Y	Y
OKLAHOMA					
1 Sullivan	Y	Y	Y	Y	Y
2 Boren	Y	Y	Y	Y	Y
3 Lucas	Y	Y	Y	Y	Y
4 Cole	Y	Y	Y	Y	Y
5 Fallin	Y	Y	Y	Y	Y
OREGON					
1 Wu	Y	Y	Y	Y	Y
2 Walden	Y	Y	P	P	Y
3 Blumenauer	Y	Y	Y	Y	Y
4 DeFazio	Y	Y	Y	Y	Y
5 Schrader	Y	Y	Y	Y	Y
PENNSYLVANIA					
1 Brady	Y	Y	Y	Y	Y
2 Fattah	Y	Y	Y	N	Y
3 Dahlkemper	Y	Y	Y	Y	Y
4 Altmire	Y	Y	Y	Y	Y
5 Thompson	Y	Y	Y	Y	Y
6 Gerlach	Y	Y	Y	Y	Y
7 Sestak	Y	Y	Y	Y	Y
8 Murphy, P.	Y	Y	Y	Y	Y
9 Shuster	Y	Y	Y	Y	Y
10 Carney	Y	Y	Y	Y	Y
11 Kanjorski	Y	Y	Y	Y	Y
12 Vacant					
13 Schwartz	Y	Y	Y	Y	Y
14 Doyle	Y	Y	Y	Y	Y
15 Dent	Y	Y	P	P	Y
16 Pitts	Y	Y	Y	Y	Y
17 Holden	Y	Y	Y	Y	Y
18 Murphy, T.	Y	Y	Y	Y	?
19 Platts	Y	Y	Y	Y	Y
RHODE ISLAND					
1 Kennedy	Y	Y	Y	Y	Y
2 Langevin	Y	Y	Y	Y	Y
SOUTH CAROLINA					
1 Brown	?	Y	Y	Y	Y
2 Wilson	Y	Y	Y	Y	Y
3 Barrett	Y	Y	Y	Y	Y
4 Inglis	Y	Y	Y	Y	Y
5 Spratt	Y	Y	Y	Y	Y
6 Clyburn	Y	Y	Y	Y	Y
SOUTH DAKOTA					
AL Herseth Sandlin	Y	Y	Y	Y	?
TENNESSEE					
1 Roe	Y	Y	Y	Y	Y
2 Duncan	Y	Y	Y	Y	Y
3 Wamp	Y	Y	Y	Y	Y
4 Davis	Y	Y	Y	Y	Y
5 Cooper	Y	Y	Y	Y	Y
6 Gordon	Y	Y	Y	Y	Y
7 Blackburn	Y	Y	Y	Y	Y
8 Tanner	Y	Y	Y	Y	Y
9 Cohen	Y	Y	Y	Y	Y

	104	105	106	107	108
TEXAS					
1 Gohmert	Y	Y	Y	Y	P
2 Poe	Y	Y	Y	Y	Y
3 Johnson, S.	Y	Y	Y	Y	Y
4 Hall	Y	Y	Y	Y	Y
5 Hensarling	Y	Y	Y	Y	Y
6 Barton	Y	Y	Y	Y	Y
7 Culberson	Y	Y	Y	Y	Y
8 Brady	Y	Y	Y	Y	Y
9 Green, A.	Y	Y	Y	Y	Y
10 McCaul	Y	Y	P	P	Y
11 Conaway	Y	Y	P	P	Y
12 Granger	Y	Y	Y	Y	Y
13 Thornberry	Y	Y	Y	Y	Y
14 Paul	Y	Y	Y	Y	?
15 Hinojosa	Y	Y	Y	Y	Y
16 Reyes	Y	Y	Y	Y	Y
17 Edwards	Y	Y	Y	Y	Y
18 Jackson Lee	Y	Y	Y	Y	Y
19 Neugebauer	Y	Y	Y	Y	Y
20 Gonzalez	Y	Y	Y	Y	Y
21 Smith	Y	Y	Y	Y	Y
22 Olson	Y	Y	Y	Y	Y
23 Rodriguez	Y	Y	Y	Y	Y
24 Marchant	Y	Y	Y	Y	Y
25 Doggett	Y	Y	Y	Y	Y
26 Burgess	Y	Y	Y	Y	Y
27 Ortiz	Y	Y	Y	Y	Y
28 Cuellar	Y	Y	Y	Y	Y
29 Green, G.	Y	Y	Y	Y	Y
30 Johnson, E.	Y	Y	Y	Y	Y
31 Carter	Y	Y	Y	Y	Y
32 Sessions	Y	Y	Y	Y	Y
UTAH					
1 Bishop	?	Y	Y	Y	Y
2 Matheson	Y	Y	Y	Y	Y
3 Chaffetz	Y	Y	Y	Y	Y
VERMONT					
AL Welch	Y	Y	P	P	Y
VIRGINIA					
1 Wittman	Y	Y	Y	Y	Y
2 Nye	Y	Y	Y	Y	Y
3 Scott	Y	Y	Y	Y	Y
4 Forbes	Y	Y	Y	Y	Y
5 Perriello	Y	Y	Y	Y	Y
6 Goodlatte	Y	Y	Y	Y	Y
7 Cantor	Y	Y	Y	Y	Y
8 Moran	Y	Y	Y	Y	Y
9 Boucher	Y	Y	Y	Y	Y
10 Wolf	Y	Y	Y	Y	Y
11 Connolly	Y	Y	Y	Y	Y
WASHINGTON					
1 Inslee	Y	Y	Y	Y	Y
2 Larsen	Y	Y	Y	Y	Y
3 Baird	Y	Y	Y	Y	Y
4 Hastings	Y	Y	P	P	Y
5 McMorris Rodgers	Y	Y	Y	Y	Y
6 Dicks	Y	Y	Y	Y	Y
7 McDermott	Y	Y	Y	Y	Y
8 Reichert	Y	Y	Y	Y	Y
9 Smith	Y	Y	Y	Y	Y
WEST VIRGINIA					
1 Mollohan	Y	Y	Y	Y	Y
2 Capito	Y	Y	Y	Y	Y
3 Rahall	Y	Y	Y	Y	Y
WISCONSIN					
1 Ryan	Y	Y	Y	Y	Y
2 Baldwin	Y	Y	Y	Y	Y
3 Kind	Y	Y	Y	Y	Y
4 Moore	Y	Y	Y	Y	Y
5 Sensenbrenner	Y	Y	Y	Y	Y
6 Petri	Y	Y	Y	Y	Y
7 Obey	Y	Y	Y	Y	Y
8 Kagen	Y	Y	Y	Y	Y
WYOMING					
AL Lummis	Y	Y	Y	Y	Y
DELEGATES					
Faleomavaega (A.S.)					
Norton (D.C.)					
Bordallo (Guam)					
Sablan (N. Marianas)					
Pierluisi (P.R.)					
Christensen (V.I.)					

IN THE HOUSE | By Vote Number

109. **HR 3650. Algal Bloom Reduction Program/Passage.** Passage of the bill that would establish a National Harmful Algal Bloom and Hypoxia Program to develop a strategy to reduce marine and freshwater algal blooms. It would authorize $41 million annually from fiscal 2011 through fiscal 2015 for the program. Passed 251-103: D 213-5; R 38-98. March 12, 2010.

110. **Procedural Motion/Journal.** Approval of the House Journal of Thursday, March 11, 2010. Approved 203-144: D 186-29; R 17-115. March 12, 2010.

111. **HR 4506. Federal Bankruptcy Judgeships/Passage.** Cohen, D-Tenn., motion to suspend the rules and pass the bill that would authorize 13 new federal bankruptcy judgeships, make permanent 22 temporary positions and extend the authorization of two temporary judgeships for at least five years. The cost of employing the judges would be offset by an increase in bankruptcy filing fees. Motion agreed to 345-5: D 216-1; R 129-4. A two-thirds majority of those present and voting (234 in this case) is required for passage under suspension of the rules. March 12, 2010.

112. **H Res 1145. Tribute to University of Arizona/Adoption.** Hirono, D-Hawaii, motion to suspend the rules and adopt the resolution that would recognize the University of Arizona's 125th anniversary and congratulate the university for its dedication to higher education. Motion agreed to 392-0: D 235-0; R 157-0. A two-thirds majority of those present and voting (262 in this case) is required for adoption under suspension of the rules. March 15, 2010.

113. **H Res 1170. Voice of Democracy Scholarships/Adoption.** Hirono, D-Hawaii, motion to suspend the rules and adopt the resolution that would congratulate the winners of the Voice of Democracy national scholarship program. Motion agreed to 384-0: D 230-0; R 154-0. A two-thirds majority of those present and voting (256 in this case) is required for adoption under suspension of the rules. March 15, 2010.

114. **H Res 1163. Tribute to Washington State University Honors College/Adoption.** Hirono, D-Hawaii, motion to suspend the rules and adopt the resolution that would recognize the 50th anniversary of Washington State University Honors College. Motion agreed to 389-0: D 234-0; R 155-0. A two-thirds majority of those present and voting (260 in this case) is required for adoption under suspension of the rules. March 15, 2010.

115. **H Res 267. Significance of Nowruz/Adoption.** Lynch, D-Mass., motion to suspend the rules and adopt the resolution that would recognize the cultural and historical significance of Nowruz, which marks the traditional Iranian New Year. It also would express appreciation for the contributions of Iranian-Americans to the United States. Motion agreed to 384-2: D 232-0; R 152-2. A two-thirds majority of those present and voting (258 in this case) is required for adoption under suspension of the rules. March 15, 2010.

	109	110	111	112	113	114	115
ALABAMA							
1 **Bonner**	N	N	Y	?	?	?	?
2 Bright	N	N	N	Y	Y	Y	Y
3 **Rogers**	N	N	Y	Y	Y	Y	Y
4 **Aderholt**	N	N	Y	Y	Y	Y	Y
5 **Griffith**	N	N	Y	Y	Y	Y	Y
6 **Bachus**	N	N	Y	Y	Y	Y	Y
7 Davis	?	?	?	Y	Y	Y	?
ALASKA							
AL **Young**	N	N	Y	Y	Y	Y	Y
ARIZONA							
1 Kirkpatrick	N	N	Y	Y	Y	Y	Y
2 **Franks**	N	N	Y	Y	Y	Y	Y
3 **Shadegg**	N	N	Y	?	?	?	?
4 Pastor	Y	?	?	Y	Y	Y	Y
5 Mitchell	Y	N	Y	Y	Y	Y	Y
6 **Flake**	?	?	?	?	?	?	?
7 Grijalva	?	?	?	?	?	?	?
8 Giffords	Y	N	Y	Y	Y	Y	Y
ARKANSAS							
1 Berry	Y	Y	Y	Y	Y	Y	Y
2 Snyder	Y	Y	Y	Y	Y	Y	Y
3 **Boozman**	Y	N	Y	?	?	?	?
4 Ross	Y	Y	Y	Y	Y	Y	Y
CALIFORNIA							
1 Thompson	+	?	+	Y	Y	Y	Y
2 **Herger**	N	N	Y	Y	Y	Y	Y
3 **Lungren**	N	N	Y	Y	Y	Y	Y
4 **McClintock**	N	Y	Y	?	?	?	?
5 Matsui	Y	Y	Y	Y	Y	Y	Y
6 Woolsey	Y	Y	?	Y	Y	Y	Y
7 Miller, George	Y	Y	Y	Y	Y	Y	Y
8 Pelosi							
9 Lee	Y	Y	Y	Y	Y	Y	Y
10 Garamendi	Y	Y	Y	?	?	Y	?
11 McNerney	Y	Y	Y	Y	Y	Y	Y
12 Speier	?	?	?	?	?	?	?
13 Stark	Y	Y	Y	Y	Y	Y	Y
14 Eshoo	Y	Y	Y	Y	Y	Y	Y
15 Honda	Y	Y	Y	Y	Y	Y	Y
16 Lofgren	?	?	?	Y	Y	Y	Y
17 Farr	Y	Y	Y	Y	Y	Y	Y
18 Cardoza	Y	N	Y	Y	Y	Y	Y
19 **Radanovich**	N	N	Y	Y	Y	Y	Y
20 Costa	Y	N	Y	Y	Y	Y	Y
21 **Nunes**	N	N	Y	Y	Y	Y	Y
22 **McCarthy**	N	N	Y	Y	Y	Y	Y
23 Capps	Y	Y	Y	Y	Y	Y	Y
24 **Gallegly**	?	?	?	Y	Y	Y	Y
25 **McKeon**	N	N	Y	Y	Y	Y	Y
26 **Dreier**	N	N	Y	Y	Y	Y	Y
27 Sherman	Y	Y	Y	Y	Y	Y	Y
28 Berman	Y	?	?	Y	Y	Y	Y
29 Schiff	Y	Y	Y	Y	Y	Y	Y
30 Waxman	Y	Y	Y	Y	Y	Y	Y
31 Becerra	Y	Y	Y	Y	Y	Y	Y
32 Chu	Y	Y	Y	Y	Y	Y	Y
33 Watson	Y	Y	Y	Y	Y	Y	Y
34 Roybal-Allard	Y	Y	Y	Y	Y	Y	Y
35 Waters	Y	Y	Y	?	?	?	?
36 Harman	Y	Y	Y	Y	Y	Y	Y
37 Richardson	Y	Y	Y	Y	Y	Y	Y
38 Napolitano	+	?	+	Y	Y	Y	Y
39 Sánchez, Linda	Y	Y	Y	Y	Y	Y	Y
40 **Royce**	N	N	Y	Y	Y	Y	Y
41 **Lewis**	N	N	Y	Y	Y	Y	Y
42 **Miller, Gary**	?	?	?	Y	Y	Y	Y
43 **Baca**	?	?	?	Y	Y	Y	Y
44 **Calvert**	?	?	?	Y	Y	Y	Y
45 **Bono Mack**	Y	N	Y	Y	Y	Y	Y
46 **Rohrabacher**	?	?	?	Y	Y	Y	Y
47 Sanchez, Loretta	Y	Y	Y	Y	Y	Y	Y
48 **Campbell**	?	?	?	Y	Y	Y	Y
49 **Issa**	?	?	?	Y	Y	Y	Y
50 **Bilbray**	Y	N	Y	Y	Y	Y	Y
51 Filner	Y	Y	Y	Y	Y	Y	Y
52 **Hunter**	N	N	Y	Y	Y	Y	Y
53 Davis	Y	Y	Y	Y	Y	Y	Y

	109	110	111	112	113	114	115
COLORADO							
1 DeGette	Y	Y	Y	Y	Y	Y	Y
2 Polis	Y	Y	Y	Y	Y	Y	Y
3 Salazar	Y	Y	Y	Y	Y	Y	Y
4 Markey	Y	N	Y	Y	Y	Y	Y
5 **Lamborn**	N	N	Y	Y	Y	Y	Y
6 **Coffman**	N	N	Y	Y	Y	Y	Y
7 Perlmutter	Y	Y	Y	Y	Y	Y	Y
CONNECTICUT							
1 Larson	Y	Y	Y	Y	Y	Y	Y
2 Courtney	Y	Y	Y	Y	Y	Y	Y
3 DeLauro	Y	Y	Y	Y	Y	Y	Y
4 Himes	Y	N	Y	Y	Y	Y	Y
5 Murphy	?	?	?	Y	Y	Y	Y
DELAWARE							
AL Castle	Y	Y	Y	Y	Y	Y	Y
FLORIDA							
1 **Miller**	N	N	Y	Y	Y	Y	N
2 Boyd	Y	Y	Y	Y	Y	Y	Y
3 Brown	Y	Y	Y	Y	Y	Y	Y
4 **Crenshaw**	Y	N	Y	?	?	?	?
5 **Brown-Waite**	Y	Y	N	?	?	?	?
6 **Stearns**	N	N	Y	Y	Y	Y	Y
7 **Mica**	N	N	Y	Y	Y	Y	Y
8 Grayson	Y	Y	Y	Y	Y	Y	Y
9 **Bilirakis**	Y	N	Y	Y	Y	Y	Y
10 **Young**	?	?	?	?	?	?	?
11 Castor	Y	Y	Y	Y	Y	Y	Y
12 **Putnam**	Y	N	Y	?	?	?	?
13 **Buchanan**	?	?	?	?	?	?	?
14 **Mack**	Y	N	Y	Y	Y	Y	Y
15 **Posey**	Y	Y	Y	Y	Y	Y	N
16 **Rooney**	Y	Y	Y	Y	Y	Y	Y
17 Meek	Y	Y	Y	Y	Y	Y	Y
18 **Ros-Lehtinen**	?	?	?	?	?	?	?
19 Vacant							
20 Wasserman Schultz	Y	Y	Y	Y	Y	Y	Y
21 **Diaz-Balart, L.**	?	?	?	?	?	?	?
22 Klein	Y	Y	Y	Y	Y	Y	Y
23 Hastings	Y	Y	Y	Y	Y	Y	Y
24 Kosmas	Y	Y	Y	Y	Y	Y	Y
25 **Diaz-Balart, M.**	?	?	?	Y	Y	Y	Y
GEORGIA							
1 **Kingston**	N	N	Y	Y	Y	Y	Y
2 Bishop	Y	Y	Y	Y	Y	Y	Y
3 **Westmoreland**	N	N	N	Y	Y	Y	Y
4 Johnson	Y	Y	Y	Y	Y	Y	Y
5 Lewis	Y	Y	Y	Y	Y	Y	Y
6 **Price**	N	N	Y	Y	Y	Y	Y
7 **Linder**	N	?	?	Y	Y	Y	Y
8 **Marshall**	?	?	?	Y	Y	Y	Y
9 **Deal**	?	?	?	?	?	?	?
10 **Broun**	N	N	N	Y	Y	Y	Y
11 **Gingrey**	?	?	?	?	?	?	?
12 **Barrow**	Y	Y	Y	Y	Y	Y	Y
13 Scott	Y	Y	Y	Y	Y	Y	Y
HAWAII							
1 Vacant							
2 Hirono	Y	Y	Y	Y	Y	Y	Y
IDAHO							
1 Minnick	Y	N	Y	Y	Y	Y	Y
2 **Simpson**	N	?	Y	Y	Y	Y	Y
ILLINOIS							
1 Rush	?	Y	Y	?	?	?	?
2 Jackson	Y	Y	Y	Y	Y	Y	Y
3 Lipinski	Y	Y	Y	Y	Y	Y	Y
4 Gutierrez	Y	?	Y	?	+	?	?
5 Quigley	Y	Y	Y	?	?	?	?
6 **Roskam**	?	?	Y	Y	Y	Y	Y
7 Davis	Y	Y	Y	?	?	?	?
8 Bean	Y	Y	Y	?	?	?	?
9 Schakowsky	Y	Y	Y	Y	Y	Y	Y
10 **Kirk**	?	?	?	Y	Y	Y	Y
11 Halvorson	Y	Y	Y	Y	Y	Y	Y
12 Costello	?	?	?	Y	Y	Y	Y
13 **Biggert**	Y	N	Y	Y	Y	Y	Y
14 Foster	Y	Y	Y	Y	Y	Y	Y
15 Johnson	Y	Y	Y	+	+	+	+

KEY   **Republicans**   Democrats

Y	Voted for (yea)	X	Paired against
#	Paired for	–	Announced against
+	Announced for	P	Voted "present"
N	Voted against (nay)	C	Voted "present" to avoid possible conflict of interest
		?	Did not vote or otherwise make a position known

	109	110	111	112	113	114	115
16 **Manzullo**	N	N	Y	Y	Y	Y	Y
17 Hare	Y	Y	Y	Y	Y	Y	Y
18 **Schock**	?	?	?	Y	Y	Y	Y
19 **Shimkus**	?	?	?	Y	Y	Y	Y
INDIANA							
1 Visclosky	Y	Y	Y	Y	Y	Y	Y
2 Donnelly	Y	N	Y	Y	Y	Y	Y
3 **Souder**	N	N	Y	?	?	?	?
4 **Buyer**	?	?	?	Y	Y	Y	?
5 **Burton**	N	N	Y	Y	Y	Y	Y
6 **Pence**	?	?	?	+	+	+	+
7 Carson	Y	Y	Y	Y	Y	Y	Y
8 Ellsworth	Y	N	Y	Y	Y	Y	Y
9 Hill	?	?	?	Y	Y	Y	Y
IOWA							
1 Braley	Y	Y	Y	?	+	?	?
2 Loebsack	?	?	?	Y	Y	Y	Y
3 Boswell	?	?	?	Y	Y	Y	Y
4 **Latham**	N	Y	Y	Y	Y	Y	Y
5 **King**	N	N	Y	Y	Y	Y	Y
KANSAS							
1 **Moran**	?	?	?	Y	Y	Y	Y
2 **Jenkins**	N	N	Y	Y	Y	Y	Y
3 Moore	Y	Y	Y	Y	Y	Y	Y
4 **Tiahrt**	N	N	Y	Y	Y	Y	Y
KENTUCKY							
1 **Whitfield**	N	N	Y	Y	Y	Y	Y
2 **Guthrie**	N	N	Y	Y	Y	Y	Y
3 Yarmuth	Y	Y	Y	Y	Y	Y	Y
4 **Davis**	N	N	Y	Y	?	Y	Y
5 **Rogers**	?	?	?	?	?	?	?
6 Chandler	Y	N	Y	Y	Y	Y	Y
LOUISIANA							
1 **Scalise**	Y	N	Y	Y	Y	Y	Y
2 **Cao**	?	?	?	Y	Y	Y	Y
3 Melancon	Y	N	Y	Y	Y	Y	Y
4 **Fleming**	Y	N	Y	Y	Y	Y	Y
5 **Alexander**	?	?	?	Y	Y	Y	Y
6 **Cassidy**	Y	N	Y	Y	Y	Y	Y
7 **Boustany**	Y	N	Y	Y	Y	Y	Y
MAINE							
1 Pingree	Y	Y	Y	Y	Y	Y	Y
2 Michaud	Y	Y	Y	Y	Y	Y	Y
MARYLAND							
1 Kratovil	Y	N	Y	Y	Y	Y	Y
2 Ruppersberger	Y	Y	Y	Y	Y	Y	Y
3 Sarbanes	Y	Y	Y	Y	Y	Y	Y
4 Edwards	Y	Y	Y	Y	Y	Y	Y
5 Hoyer	Y	Y	Y	Y	Y	Y	Y
6 **Bartlett**	N	N	Y	Y	Y	Y	Y
7 Cummings	Y	Y	Y	Y	Y	Y	Y
8 Van Hollen	Y	Y	Y	Y	Y	Y	Y
MASSACHUSETTS							
1 Olver	Y	Y	Y	Y	Y	Y	Y
2 Neal	Y	Y	Y	Y	Y	Y	Y
3 McGovern	Y	Y	Y	Y	Y	Y	Y
4 Frank	?	?	?	Y	Y	Y	Y
5 Tsongas	Y	Y	Y	Y	Y	Y	Y
6 Tierney	Y	Y	Y	Y	Y	Y	Y
7 Markey	Y	Y	Y	Y	Y	Y	Y
8 Capuano	Y	Y	Y	Y	Y	Y	Y
9 Lynch	Y	Y	Y	Y	Y	Y	Y
10 Delahunt	?	?	?	Y	Y	Y	Y
MICHIGAN							
1 Stupak	Y	Y	Y	Y	Y	Y	Y
2 **Hoekstra**	?	?	?	?	?	?	?
3 **Ehlers**	Y	N	Y	Y	Y	Y	Y
4 **Camp**	N	N	Y	Y	Y	Y	Y
5 Kildee	Y	Y	Y	Y	Y	Y	Y
6 **Upton**	N	N	Y	Y	Y	Y	Y
7 Schauer	Y	Y	Y	Y	Y	?	Y
8 **Rogers**	N	N	Y	Y	Y	Y	?
9 Peters	Y	N	Y	Y	Y	Y	Y
10 **Miller**	N	N	Y	Y	Y	Y	Y
11 **McCotter**	Y	N	Y	Y	Y	Y	Y
12 Levin	Y	Y	Y	Y	Y	Y	Y
13 Kilpatrick	+	?	?	Y	Y	Y	Y
14 Conyers	Y	Y	Y	Y	Y	Y	Y
15 Dingell	Y	Y	Y	Y	Y	Y	Y
MINNESOTA							
1 Walz	Y	Y	Y	Y	Y	Y	Y
2 **Kline**	Y	N	Y	Y	Y	Y	Y
3 **Paulsen**	Y	Y	Y	Y	Y	Y	Y
4 McCollum	Y	Y	Y	Y	Y	Y	Y
5 Ellison	Y	Y	Y	Y	Y	Y	Y
6 **Bachmann**	N	Y	Y	Y	Y	Y	Y
7 Peterson	Y	N	Y	Y	Y	Y	Y
8 Oberstar	Y	Y	Y	Y	Y	Y	Y
MISSISSIPPI							
1 Childers	?	?	?	Y	Y	Y	Y
2 Thompson	Y	Y	Y	Y	Y	Y	Y
3 **Harper**	N	N	Y	Y	Y	Y	Y
4 Taylor	Y	N	Y	Y	Y	Y	Y
MISSOURI							
1 Clay	?	?	?	Y	Y	Y	Y
2 **Akin**	N	N	Y	Y	Y	Y	Y
3 Carnahan	Y	Y	Y	Y	Y	Y	Y
4 Skelton	Y	Y	Y	Y	Y	Y	Y
5 Cleaver	Y	Y	Y	Y	Y	Y	Y
6 **Graves**	N	N	Y	Y	Y	Y	Y
7 **Blunt**	?	?	?	?	?	?	?
8 **Emerson**	N	N	Y	Y	Y	Y	Y
9 **Luetkemeyer**	N	Y	Y	Y	Y	Y	Y
MONTANA							
AL **Rehberg**	Y	N	Y	Y	Y	Y	Y
NEBRASKA							
1 **Fortenberry**	Y	Y	Y	Y	Y	Y	Y
2 **Terry**	?	?	?	Y	Y	Y	Y
3 **Smith**	Y	N	Y	Y	+	Y	Y
NEVADA							
1 Berkley	Y	Y	Y	Y	Y	Y	Y
2 **Heller**	+	?	+	Y	Y	Y	Y
3 Titus	Y	Y	Y	Y	Y	Y	Y
NEW HAMPSHIRE							
1 Shea-Porter	Y	Y	Y	?	?	?	?
2 Hodes	Y	Y	Y	Y	Y	Y	Y
NEW JERSEY							
1 Andrews	Y	Y	Y	Y	Y	Y	Y
2 **LoBiondo**	Y	N	Y	Y	Y	Y	Y
3 Adler	Y	N	Y	Y	Y	Y	Y
4 **Smith**	Y	N	Y	Y	Y	Y	Y
5 **Garrett**	N	N	Y	Y	Y	Y	Y
6 Pallone	Y	Y	Y	Y	Y	Y	Y
7 **Lance**	N	N	Y	Y	Y	Y	Y
8 Pascrell	Y	Y	Y	?	?	?	?
9 Rothman	Y	Y	Y	Y	Y	Y	Y
10 Payne	Y	Y	Y	Y	Y	Y	?
11 **Frelinghuysen**	N	N	Y	Y	Y	Y	Y
12 Holt	Y	Y	Y	Y	Y	Y	Y
13 Sires	?	?	?	Y	Y	Y	Y
NEW MEXICO							
1 Heinrich	Y	Y	Y	Y	?	Y	Y
2 Teague	Y	Y	Y	Y	Y	Y	Y
3 Luján	?	?	?	Y	Y	Y	Y
NEW YORK							
1 Bishop	Y	Y	Y	Y	?	Y	Y
2 Israel	Y	Y	Y	Y	Y	Y	Y
3 **King**	N	N	Y	Y	Y	Y	Y
4 McCarthy	Y	Y	Y	Y	Y	Y	Y
5 Ackerman	?	?	?	Y	Y	Y	Y
6 Meeks	Y	Y	Y	Y	Y	Y	Y
7 Crowley	Y	Y	Y	Y	Y	Y	Y
8 Nadler	Y	?	Y	Y	Y	Y	Y
9 Weiner	Y	Y	Y	Y	Y	Y	Y
10 Towns	Y	Y	Y	Y	Y	Y	Y
11 Clarke	Y	Y	Y	Y	Y	Y	Y
12 Velázquez	Y	Y	Y	Y	Y	Y	Y
13 McMahon	Y	Y	Y	Y	Y	Y	Y
14 Maloney	?	?	?	Y	Y	Y	Y
15 Rangel	Y	Y	Y	Y	Y	Y	Y
16 Serrano	Y	Y	Y	Y	Y	Y	Y
17 Engel	Y	Y	Y	Y	Y	Y	Y
18 Lowey	Y	Y	Y	Y	Y	Y	Y
19 Hall	Y	Y	Y	Y	Y	Y	Y
20 Murphy	?	?	?	Y	Y	Y	Y
21 Tonko	Y	Y	Y	Y	Y	Y	Y
22 Hinchey	Y	Y	Y	Y	Y	Y	Y
23 Owens	N	Y	Y	Y	?	Y	Y
24 Arcuri	Y	N	Y	Y	Y	Y	Y
25 Maffei	Y	Y	Y	Y	Y	Y	Y
26 **Lee**	N	N	Y	Y	Y	Y	Y
27 Higgins	?	?	?	Y	Y	Y	Y
28 Slaughter	Y	Y	Y	Y	Y	Y	Y
29 Vacant							
NORTH CAROLINA							
1 Butterfield	Y	Y	Y	?	?	?	?
2 Etheridge	Y	Y	Y	Y	Y	Y	Y
3 **Jones**	?	?	?	Y	+	Y	Y
4 Price	Y	Y	Y	Y	Y	Y	Y
5 **Foxx**	N	N	Y	Y	Y	Y	Y
6 **Coble**	N	N	Y	Y	Y	Y	Y
7 McIntyre	Y	Y	Y	Y	Y	Y	Y
8 Kissell	Y	N	Y	Y	Y	Y	Y
9 **Myrick**	N	N	Y	Y	Y	Y	Y
10 **McHenry**	N	N	Y	Y	Y	Y	Y
11 Shuler	Y	N	Y	Y	Y	Y	Y
12 Watt	Y	Y	Y	Y	Y	Y	Y
13 Miller	Y	Y	Y	Y	Y	Y	Y
NORTH DAKOTA							
AL Pomeroy	?	?	?	Y	Y	Y	Y
OHIO							
1 Driehaus	Y	Y	Y	Y	Y	Y	Y
2 **Schmidt**	N	N	Y	Y	Y	Y	Y
3 **Turner**	N	N	Y	Y	Y	Y	Y
4 **Jordan**	N	N	Y	Y	Y	Y	Y
5 **Latta**	N	N	Y	Y	Y	Y	Y
6 Wilson	Y	Y	Y	Y	Y	Y	Y
7 **Austria**	N	N	Y	Y	Y	Y	Y
8 **Boehner**	N	N	Y	Y	Y	Y	Y
9 Kaptur	?	?	?	Y	Y	Y	Y
10 Kucinich	Y	Y	Y	Y	Y	Y	Y
11 Fudge	Y	Y	Y	Y	Y	Y	Y
12 **Tiberi**	N	Y	Y	Y	Y	Y	Y
13 Sutton	Y	?	Y	Y	Y	Y	Y
14 **LaTourette**	?	?	?	Y	Y	Y	Y
15 Kilroy	Y	Y	Y	Y	Y	Y	Y
16 Boccieri	Y	N	Y	Y	Y	Y	Y
17 Ryan	Y	Y	Y	Y	Y	Y	Y
18 Space	Y	Y	Y	Y	Y	Y	Y
OKLAHOMA							
1 **Sullivan**	N	N	Y	Y	Y	Y	Y
2 Boren	N	N	Y	Y	Y	Y	Y
3 **Lucas**	Y	N	Y	Y	Y	Y	Y
4 **Cole**	Y	N	Y	Y	Y	Y	Y
5 **Fallin**	Y	N	Y	?	?	?	?
OREGON							
1 Wu	Y	Y	Y	Y	Y	Y	Y
2 **Walden**	?	?	?	Y	Y	Y	Y
3 Blumenauer	Y	Y	Y	Y	Y	Y	Y
4 DeFazio	?	?	?	Y	Y	Y	Y
5 Schrader	Y	Y	Y	?	?	?	?
PENNSYLVANIA							
1 Brady	Y	Y	Y	Y	Y	Y	Y
2 Fattah	Y	Y	Y	Y	Y	Y	Y
3 Dahlkemper	Y	N	Y	Y	Y	Y	Y
4 Altmire	N	N	Y	Y	Y	Y	Y
5 **Thompson**	N	N	Y	Y	Y	Y	Y
6 **Gerlach**	Y	N	Y	Y	Y	Y	Y
7 Sestak	Y	Y	Y	Y	Y	Y	Y
8 Murphy, P.	Y	Y	Y	Y	Y	Y	Y
9 **Shuster**	N	N	Y	Y	Y	Y	Y
10 Carney	Y	N	Y	Y	?	Y	Y
11 Kanjorski	Y	Y	Y	Y	Y	Y	Y
12 Vacant							
13 Schwartz	Y	Y	Y	Y	Y	Y	Y
14 Doyle	Y	Y	Y	Y	?	Y	Y
15 **Dent**	Y	Y	Y	Y	Y	Y	Y
16 **Pitts**	N	N	Y	Y	Y	Y	Y
17 Holden	Y	Y	Y	Y	Y	Y	Y
18 **Murphy, T.**	+	?	+	Y	Y	Y	Y
19 **Platts**	Y	N	Y	Y	Y	Y	Y
RHODE ISLAND							
1 Kennedy	Y	Y	Y	Y	Y	Y	Y
2 Langevin	Y	Y	Y	Y	Y	Y	Y
SOUTH CAROLINA							
1 **Brown**	?	?	?	Y	Y	Y	Y
2 **Wilson**	N	N	Y	Y	Y	Y	Y
3 **Barrett**	N	N	Y	?	?	?	?
4 **Inglis**	N	N	Y	Y	Y	?	Y
5 Spratt	Y	Y	Y	Y	Y	Y	Y
6 Clyburn	Y	Y	Y	Y	Y	Y	Y
SOUTH DAKOTA							
AL Herseth Sandlin	Y	Y	Y	Y	Y	Y	Y
TENNESSEE							
1 **Roe**	N	Y	Y	Y	Y	Y	Y
2 **Duncan**	N	N	N	Y	Y	Y	Y
3 **Wamp**	?	?	?	?	?	?	?
4 Davis	Y	Y	Y	Y	Y	Y	Y
5 Cooper	Y	Y	Y	Y	Y	Y	Y
6 Gordon	Y	Y	Y	Y	Y	Y	Y
7 **Blackburn**	N	N	Y	Y	Y	?	Y
8 Tanner	Y	Y	Y	Y	Y	Y	Y
9 Cohen	Y	Y	Y	Y	Y	Y	Y
TEXAS							
1 **Gohmert**	Y	P	Y	Y	Y	Y	?
2 **Poe**	N	N	Y	Y	Y	Y	Y
3 **Johnson, S.**	?	?	?	Y	Y	Y	Y
4 **Hall**	N	N	Y	Y	Y	Y	Y
5 **Hensarling**	N	N	?	Y	Y	Y	Y
6 **Barton**	?	?	?	Y	Y	Y	Y
7 **Culberson**	N	N	Y	Y	Y	Y	Y
8 **Brady**	N	N	Y	Y	Y	Y	Y
9 Green, A.	Y	Y	Y	Y	Y	Y	Y
10 **McCaul**	N	N	Y	Y	Y	Y	Y
11 **Conaway**	N	N	Y	Y	Y	?	Y
12 **Granger**	N	N	Y	Y	Y	Y	Y
13 **Thornberry**	N	N	Y	Y	Y	Y	Y
14 **Paul**	?	?	?	Y	Y	Y	Y
15 Hinojosa	Y	Y	Y	Y	Y	Y	Y
16 Reyes	?	?	?	Y	Y	Y	Y
17 Edwards	Y	Y	Y	Y	Y	Y	Y
18 Jackson Lee	Y	Y	Y	Y	Y	Y	Y
19 **Neugebauer**	N	N	Y	Y	Y	Y	Y
20 Gonzalez	Y	Y	Y	Y	Y	Y	Y
21 **Smith**	N	N	Y	Y	Y	Y	Y
22 **Olson**	N	N	Y	Y	Y	Y	Y
23 Rodriguez	?	?	?	Y	Y	Y	Y
24 **Marchant**	?	?	?	Y	Y	Y	Y
25 Doggett	Y	Y	Y	Y	Y	Y	Y
26 **Burgess**	?	?	?	Y	Y	Y	Y
27 Ortiz	Y	Y	Y	Y	Y	Y	Y
28 Cuellar	Y	Y	Y	Y	Y	Y	Y
29 Green, G.	Y	Y	Y	Y	Y	Y	Y
30 Johnson, E.	Y	Y	Y	Y	Y	Y	Y
31 **Carter**	?	?	?	Y	Y	Y	Y
32 **Sessions**	N	N	Y	Y	Y	Y	Y
UTAH							
1 **Bishop**	?	?	?	Y	Y	Y	Y
2 Matheson	Y	Y	Y	Y	Y	Y	Y
3 **Chaffetz**	?	?	?	Y	Y	Y	Y
VERMONT							
AL Welch	Y	Y	Y	Y	Y	Y	Y
VIRGINIA							
1 **Wittman**	Y	N	Y	Y	Y	Y	Y
2 Nye	Y	N	Y	Y	Y	Y	Y
3 Scott	Y	Y	Y	Y	Y	Y	Y
4 **Forbes**	N	Y	Y	Y	Y	Y	Y
5 Perriello	Y	N	Y	Y	Y	Y	Y
6 **Goodlatte**	N	Y	Y	Y	Y	Y	Y
7 **Cantor**	N	N	Y	Y	Y	Y	Y
8 Moran	Y	Y	Y	?	?	?	?
9 Boucher	Y	Y	Y	?	?	?	?
10 **Wolf**	N	N	Y	Y	Y	Y	Y
11 Connolly	Y	N	Y	Y	Y	Y	Y
WASHINGTON							
1 Inslee	Y	Y	Y	Y	Y	Y	Y
2 Larsen	Y	Y	Y	Y	Y	Y	Y
3 Baird	Y	Y	Y	Y	Y	Y	Y
4 **Hastings**	N	N	Y	Y	Y	Y	Y
5 **McMorris Rodgers**	N	N	Y	Y	Y	Y	Y
6 Dicks	Y	Y	Y	Y	Y	Y	Y
7 McDermott	Y	Y	Y	Y	Y	Y	Y
8 **Reichert**	Y	N	Y	Y	Y	Y	Y
9 Smith	+	?	+	?	?	?	?
WEST VIRGINIA							
1 Mollohan	Y	Y	Y	Y	Y	Y	Y
2 **Capito**	Y	Y	Y	Y	Y	Y	Y
3 Rahall	Y	Y	Y	Y	Y	Y	Y
WISCONSIN							
1 **Ryan**	Y	?	Y	Y	Y	Y	Y
2 Baldwin	Y	Y	Y	Y	Y	Y	Y
3 Kind	Y	Y	Y	Y	Y	Y	Y
4 Moore	Y	?	?	Y	Y	Y	Y
5 **Sensenbrenner**	N	N	Y	Y	Y	Y	Y
6 **Petri**	Y	N	Y	Y	Y	Y	Y
7 Obey	Y	Y	Y	Y	Y	Y	Y
8 Kagen	?	?	?	?	?	?	?
WYOMING							
AL **Lummis**	N	N	Y	Y	Y	Y	Y
DELEGATES							
Faleomavaega (A.S.)							
Norton (D.C.)							
Bordallo (Guam)							
Sablan (N. Marianas)							
Pierluisi (P.R.)							
Christensen (V.I.)							

IN THE HOUSE | By Vote Number

116. **HR 4628. Hrbek Post Office/Passage.** Lynch, D-Mass., motion to suspend the rules and pass the bill that would designate a post office in Westwood, N.J., as the "Sgt. Christopher R. Hrbek Post Office Building." Motion agreed to 416-0: D 246-0; R 170-0. A two-thirds majority of those present and voting (278 in this case) is required for passage under suspension of the rules. March 16, 2010.

117. **H Res 311. Red Cross Month/Adoption.** Watson, D-Calif., motion to suspend the rules and adopt the resolution that would support the goals and ideals of Red Cross Month and recognize the contributions of American National Red Cross volunteers. Motion agreed to 417-0: D 245-0; R 172-0. A two-thirds majority of those present and voting (278 in this case) is required for adoption under suspension of the rules. March 16, 2010.

118. **H Res 605. Falun Gong Persecution/Adoption.** Watson, D-Calif., motion to suspend the rules and adopt the resolution that would urge the Chinese government to cease persecution of Falun Gong practitioners. Motion agreed to 412-1: D 245-0; R 167-1. A two-thirds majority of those present and voting (276 in this case) is required for adoption under suspension of the rules. March 16, 2010.

119. **H Res 1128. Tribute to 2010 Winter Olympics/Adoption.** Watson, D-Calif., motion to suspend the rules and adopt the resolution that would congratulate Canada, Team USA, the athletes of the world and the city of Vancouver, British Columbia, for the 2010 Winter Olympics. Motion agreed to 420-0: D 249-0; R 171-0. A two-thirds majority of those present and voting (280 in this case) is required for adoption under suspension of the rules. March 16, 2010.

120. **H Res 1089. Tribute to Augustana College/Adoption.** Shea-Porter, D-N.H., motion to suspend the rules and adopt the resolution that would recognize the 150th anniversary of Augustana College in Illinois. Motion agreed to 421-0: D 247-0; R 174-0. A two-thirds majority of those present and voting (281 in this case) is required for adoption under suspension of the rules. March 17, 2010.

121. **H Res 1167. Recognizing Social Workers/Adoption.** Shea-Porter, D-N.H., motion to suspend the rules and adopt the resolution that would support the goals of Professional Social Work Month and World Social Work Day. Motion agreed to 419-0: D 246-0; R 173-0. A two-thirds majority of those present and voting (280 in this case) is required for adoption under suspension of the rules. March 17, 2010.

122. **H Res 1184. Tribute to University of Maryland Men's Basketball Team/Adoption.** Shea-Porter, D-N.H., motion to suspend the rules and adopt the resolution that would recognize the 2009-10 University of Maryland men's basketball team. Motion agreed to 279-132: D 237-2; R 42-130. A two-thirds majority of those present and voting (274 in this case) is required for adoption under suspension of the rules. March 17, 2010.

	116	117	118	119	120	121	122
ALABAMA							
1 Bonner	Y	Y	Y	Y	Y	Y	Y
2 Bright	Y	Y	Y	Y	Y	?	Y
3 Rogers	Y	Y	Y	Y	Y	Y	N
4 Aderholt	Y	Y	Y	Y	Y	Y	N
5 Griffith	Y	+	+	Y	Y	Y	N
6 Bachus	Y	Y	Y	Y	Y	Y	N
7 Davis	Y	Y	Y	Y	Y	Y	Y
ALASKA							
AL Young	Y	Y	Y	Y	Y	Y	N
ARIZONA							
1 Kirkpatrick	Y	Y	Y	Y	Y	Y	
2 Franks	Y	Y	Y	Y	Y	Y	N
3 Shadegg	Y	Y	Y	Y	Y	Y	N
4 Pastor	Y	Y	Y	Y	Y	Y	Y
5 Mitchell	Y	Y	Y	Y	Y	Y	Y
6 Flake	Y	Y	Y	Y	Y	Y	N
7 Grijalva	Y	Y	Y	Y	Y	Y	?
8 Giffords	Y	Y	Y	Y	Y	Y	Y
ARKANSAS							
1 Berry	Y	Y	Y	Y	Y	Y	Y
2 Snyder	Y	Y	Y	Y	Y	Y	Y
3 Boozman	Y	Y	Y	Y	Y	Y	N
4 Ross	Y	Y	Y	Y	Y	Y	Y
CALIFORNIA							
1 Thompson	Y	Y	Y	Y	Y	Y	Y
2 Herger	Y	Y	Y	Y	Y	Y	N
3 Lungren	Y	Y	Y	Y	Y	Y	N
4 McClintock	Y	Y	Y	Y	Y	Y	N
5 Matsui	Y	Y	Y	Y	Y	Y	Y
6 Woolsey	Y	Y	Y	Y	Y	Y	Y
7 Miller, George	?	Y	Y	Y	Y	Y	Y
8 Pelosi							
9 Lee	Y	Y	Y	Y	Y	Y	Y
10 Garamendi	Y	Y	Y	Y	Y	Y	Y
11 McNerney	Y	Y	Y	Y	Y	Y	Y
12 Speier	Y	Y	Y	Y	Y	Y	Y
13 Stark	?	?	?	?	?	?	?
14 Eshoo	Y	Y	Y	Y	Y	Y	Y
15 Honda	Y	Y	Y	Y	Y	Y	Y
16 Lofgren	Y	Y	Y	Y	Y	Y	Y
17 Farr	Y	Y	Y	Y	Y	Y	Y
18 Cardoza	Y	Y	Y	Y	Y	Y	Y
19 Radanovich	Y	Y	Y	Y	Y	Y	Y
20 Costa	Y	Y	Y	Y	Y	Y	Y
21 Nunes	Y	Y	Y	Y	Y	Y	N
22 McCarthy	Y	Y	Y	Y	Y	Y	N
23 Capps	Y	Y	Y	Y	Y	Y	Y
24 Gallegly	Y	Y	Y	Y	Y	Y	N
25 McKeon	Y	Y	Y	Y	Y	Y	N
26 Dreier	Y	Y	Y	Y	Y	Y	N
27 Sherman	Y	Y	Y	Y	Y	Y	Y
28 Berman	Y	Y	Y	Y	Y	Y	Y
29 Schiff	Y	Y	Y	Y	Y	Y	Y
30 Waxman	Y	Y	Y	Y	Y	Y	?
31 Becerra	Y	Y	Y	Y	Y	Y	Y
32 Chu	Y	Y	?	Y	Y	Y	Y
33 Watson	Y	Y	Y	Y	Y	Y	Y
34 Roybal-Allard	Y	Y	Y	Y	Y	Y	Y
35 Waters	Y	Y	Y	Y	Y	Y	Y
36 Harman	Y	Y	Y	Y	Y	Y	Y
37 Richardson	Y	Y	Y	Y	Y	Y	Y
38 Napolitano	Y	Y	Y	Y	Y	Y	Y
39 Sánchez, Linda	Y	Y	Y	Y	Y	Y	Y
40 Royce	Y	Y	Y	Y	Y	Y	N
41 Lewis	Y	Y	Y	Y	Y	Y	N
42 Miller, Gary	Y	Y	Y	Y	Y	Y	N
43 Baca	Y	Y	Y	Y	Y	Y	Y
44 Calvert	Y	Y	Y	Y	Y	Y	N
45 Bono Mack	Y	Y	Y	Y	Y	Y	N
46 Rohrabacher	Y	Y	Y	Y	Y	Y	N
47 Sanchez, Loretta	Y	?	Y	Y	Y	Y	Y
48 Campbell	Y	Y	Y	Y	Y	Y	N
49 Issa	Y	Y	Y	Y	Y	Y	N
50 Bilbray	Y	Y	Y	Y	Y	Y	N
51 Filner	Y	Y	Y	Y	Y	Y	Y
52 Hunter	Y	Y	Y	Y	Y	Y	N
53 Davis	Y	Y	Y	Y	Y	Y	Y

	116	117	118	119	120	121	122
COLORADO							
1 DeGette	Y	Y	Y	Y	Y	Y	Y
2 Polis	Y	Y	Y	Y	Y	Y	Y
3 Salazar	Y	Y	Y	Y	Y	Y	Y
4 Markey	Y	Y	Y	Y	Y	?	Y
5 Lamborn	Y	Y	Y	Y	Y	Y	Y
6 Coffman	Y	Y	Y	Y	Y	Y	N
7 Perlmutter	Y	Y	Y	Y	Y	Y	
CONNECTICUT							
1 Larson	Y	Y	Y	Y	Y	Y	Y
2 Courtney	Y	Y	Y	Y	Y	Y	Y
3 DeLauro	Y	Y	Y	Y	Y	Y	Y
4 Himes	Y	Y	?	Y	Y	Y	Y
5 Murphy	Y	Y	Y	Y	Y	Y	Y
DELAWARE							
AL Castle	Y	Y	Y	Y	Y	Y	Y
FLORIDA							
1 Miller	Y	Y	Y	Y	Y	Y	N
2 Boyd	Y	Y	Y	Y	Y	Y	Y
3 Brown	Y	Y	Y	Y	Y	Y	Y
4 Crenshaw	Y	Y	Y	Y	Y	Y	Y
5 Brown-Waite	Y	Y	Y	Y	Y	Y	N
6 Stearns	Y	Y	Y	Y	Y	Y	N
7 Mica	Y	Y	Y	Y	Y	Y	N
8 Grayson	Y	Y	Y	Y	Y	Y	Y
9 Bilirakis	Y	Y	Y	Y	Y	Y	N
10 Young	?	?	?	?	?	?	?
11 Castor	Y	Y	Y	Y	Y	Y	Y
12 Putnam	?	?	?	?	Y	Y	Y
13 Buchanan	Y	Y	Y	Y	Y	Y	N
14 Mack	Y	Y	Y	Y	Y	Y	N
15 Posey	Y	Y	Y	Y	Y	Y	N
16 Rooney	Y	Y	Y	Y	Y	Y	N
17 Meek	Y	Y	Y	Y	Y	Y	Y
18 Ros-Lehtinen	Y	Y	Y	Y	Y	Y	N
19 Vacant							
20 Wasserman Schultz	Y	Y	Y	Y	Y	Y	Y
21 Diaz-Balart, L.	Y	Y	Y	Y	Y	Y	N
22 Klein	Y	Y	Y	Y	Y	Y	Y
23 Hastings	Y	Y	Y	Y	Y	Y	Y
24 Kosmas	Y	Y	Y	Y	Y	Y	Y
25 Diaz-Balart, M.	Y	Y	Y	Y	Y	Y	N
GEORGIA							
1 Kingston	Y	Y	Y	Y	Y	Y	N
2 Bishop	Y	Y	Y	Y	Y	Y	Y
3 Westmoreland	Y	Y	Y	Y	Y	Y	N
4 Johnson	Y	Y	Y	Y	Y	Y	Y
5 Lewis	Y	Y	Y	Y	Y	Y	Y
6 Price	Y	Y	Y	Y	Y	Y	N
7 Linder	Y	Y	Y	Y	Y	Y	N
8 Marshall	Y	Y	Y	Y	Y	Y	P
9 Deal	?	?	?	?	?	?	?
10 Broun	?	Y	Y	Y	Y	Y	N
11 Gingrey	Y	Y	Y	Y	Y	Y	N
12 Barrow	Y	Y	Y	Y	Y	Y	Y
13 Scott	?	Y	Y	Y	Y	Y	Y
HAWAII							
1 Vacant							
2 Hirono	Y	Y	Y	Y	Y	Y	Y
IDAHO							
1 Minnick	Y	Y	Y	Y	Y	Y	Y
2 Simpson	Y	Y	Y	Y	Y	Y	N
ILLINOIS							
1 Rush	Y	?	Y	Y	Y	Y	Y
2 Jackson	Y	Y	Y	Y	Y	Y	Y
3 Lipinski	Y	Y	Y	Y	Y	Y	Y
4 Gutierrez	Y	Y	Y	Y	Y	Y	Y
5 Quigley	Y	Y	Y	Y	Y	Y	Y
6 Roskam	Y	Y	Y	Y	Y	Y	Y
7 Davis	?	Y	Y	Y	Y	Y	Y
8 Bean	Y	Y	Y	Y	Y	Y	Y
9 Schakowsky	Y	Y	Y	Y	Y	Y	Y
10 Kirk	Y	Y	Y	Y	Y	Y	Y
11 Halvorson	Y	Y	Y	Y	Y	Y	Y
12 Costello	Y	Y	Y	Y	Y	Y	Y
13 Biggert	Y	Y	Y	Y	Y	Y	N
14 Foster	Y	Y	Y	Y	Y	Y	Y
15 Johnson	Y	Y	Y	Y	Y	Y	N

KEY **Republicans** Democrats

Y Voted for (yea)	X Paired against	C Voted "present" to avoid possible conflict of interest
# Paired for	− Announced against	
+ Announced for	P Voted "present"	? Did not vote or otherwise make a position known
N Voted against (nay)		

	116	117	118	119	120	121	122
16 **Manzullo**	Y	Y	Y	Y	Y	Y	N
17 Hare	Y	Y	Y	Y	Y	Y	Y
18 **Schock**	Y	Y	Y	Y	Y	Y	N
19 **Shimkus**	Y	Y	Y	Y	Y	Y	N
INDIANA							
1 Visclosky	Y	Y	Y	Y	Y	Y	Y
2 Donnelly	Y	Y	Y	Y	Y	Y	Y
3 **Souder**	Y	Y	Y	Y	Y	Y	N
4 **Buyer**	Y	Y	?	Y	Y	Y	N
5 **Burton**	Y	Y	Y	Y	Y	Y	N
6 **Pence**	Y	Y	Y	Y	Y	Y	?
7 Carson	Y	Y	Y	Y	Y	Y	Y
8 Ellsworth	Y	Y	Y	Y	Y	Y	Y
9 Hill	Y	Y	Y	Y	Y	Y	Y
IOWA							
1 Braley	Y	Y	Y	Y	Y	Y	Y
2 Loebsack	Y	Y	Y	Y	Y	Y	Y
3 Boswell	Y	Y	Y	Y	Y	Y	Y
4 **Latham**	Y	Y	Y	Y	Y	Y	Y
5 **King**	Y	Y	Y	Y	Y	Y	N
KANSAS							
1 **Moran**	Y	Y	Y	Y	Y	Y	N
2 **Jenkins**	Y	Y	Y	Y	Y	Y	N
3 Moore	Y	Y	Y	Y	Y	Y	Y
4 **Tiahrt**	Y	Y	Y	Y	Y	Y	N
KENTUCKY							
1 **Whitfield**	Y	Y	Y	Y	Y	Y	N
2 **Guthrie**	Y	Y	Y	Y	Y	Y	N
3 Yarmuth	Y	Y	Y	Y	Y	Y	Y
4 **Davis**	Y	Y	Y	Y	Y	Y	N
5 **Rogers**	Y	Y	Y	Y	Y	Y	N
6 Chandler	Y	Y	?	Y	Y	Y	P
LOUISIANA							
1 **Scalise**	Y	Y	Y	Y	Y	Y	N
2 **Cao**	Y	Y	Y	Y	Y	Y	Y
3 Melancon	Y	Y	Y	Y	Y	Y	Y
4 **Fleming**	Y	Y	Y	Y	Y	Y	N
5 **Alexander**	Y	Y	Y	Y	Y	Y	Y
6 **Cassidy**	Y	Y	Y	Y	Y	Y	N
7 **Boustany**	Y	Y	Y	Y	Y	Y	N
MAINE							
1 Pingree	Y	Y	Y	Y	Y	Y	Y
2 Michaud	Y	Y	Y	Y	Y	Y	Y
MARYLAND							
1 Kratovil	Y	Y	Y	Y	Y	Y	Y
2 Ruppersberger	Y	Y	Y	Y	Y	Y	Y
3 Sarbanes	Y	Y	Y	Y	Y	Y	Y
4 Edwards	Y	Y	Y	Y	Y	Y	Y
5 Hoyer	Y	Y	Y	Y	Y	Y	Y
6 **Bartlett**	Y	Y	Y	Y	Y	Y	Y
7 Cummings	Y	Y	Y	Y	Y	Y	Y
8 Van Hollen	Y	Y	Y	Y	Y	Y	Y
MASSACHUSETTS							
1 Olver	Y	Y	Y	Y	Y	Y	Y
2 Neal	Y	Y	Y	Y	Y	Y	Y
3 McGovern	Y	Y	Y	Y	Y	Y	Y
4 Frank	Y	Y	Y	Y	Y	Y	Y
5 Tsongas	Y	?	Y	Y	Y	Y	Y
6 Tierney	Y	Y	Y	Y	Y	Y	Y
7 Markey	Y	Y	Y	Y	Y	Y	Y
8 Capuano	Y	Y	Y	Y	Y	Y	Y
9 Lynch	Y	Y	Y	Y	Y	Y	Y
10 Delahunt	Y	Y	Y	Y	Y	Y	Y
MICHIGAN							
1 Stupak	Y	Y	Y	Y	Y	Y	Y
2 **Hoekstra**	?	Y	Y	Y	Y	Y	N
3 **Ehlers**	Y	Y	Y	Y	Y	Y	N
4 **Camp**	Y	Y	Y	Y	Y	Y	N
5 Kildee	Y	Y	Y	Y	Y	Y	Y
6 **Upton**	Y	Y	Y	Y	Y	Y	N
7 Schauer	Y	Y	Y	Y	Y	Y	Y
8 **Rogers**	Y	Y	Y	Y	Y	Y	N
9 Peters	Y	Y	Y	Y	Y	Y	Y
10 **Miller**	Y	Y	Y	Y	Y	Y	N
11 **McCotter**	Y	Y	Y	Y	Y	Y	N
12 Levin	Y	Y	Y	Y	Y	Y	Y
13 Kilpatrick	Y	Y	Y	Y	Y	Y	Y
14 Conyers	Y	Y	Y	Y	Y	Y	Y
15 Dingell	Y	Y	Y	Y	Y	Y	Y
MINNESOTA							
1 Walz	Y	Y	Y	Y	Y	Y	Y
2 **Kline**	Y	Y	Y	Y	Y	Y	N
3 **Paulsen**	Y	Y	Y	Y	Y	Y	N
4 McCollum	Y	Y	Y	Y	Y	Y	Y
5 Ellison	Y	Y	Y	Y	Y	Y	Y
6 **Bachmann**	Y	Y	Y	Y	Y	Y	N
7 Peterson	Y	Y	Y	Y	Y	Y	Y
8 Oberstar	Y	Y	Y	Y	Y	Y	P
MISSISSIPPI							
1 Childers	Y	Y	Y	Y	Y	Y	Y
2 Thompson	Y	Y	Y	Y	Y	Y	Y
3 **Harper**	Y	Y	Y	Y	Y	Y	N
4 Taylor	Y	Y	Y	Y	Y	Y	Y
MISSOURI							
1 Clay	Y	Y	Y	Y	Y	Y	Y
2 **Akin**	Y	Y	Y	Y	Y	Y	N
3 Carnahan	Y	Y	Y	Y	Y	Y	Y
4 Skelton	Y	Y	Y	Y	Y	Y	Y
5 Cleaver	Y	Y	Y	Y	Y	Y	Y
6 **Graves**	Y	Y	?	Y	Y	Y	Y
7 **Blunt**	Y	Y	Y	Y	Y	Y	Y
8 **Emerson**	Y	Y	Y	Y	Y	Y	Y
9 **Luetkemeyer**	Y	Y	Y	Y	Y	Y	N
MONTANA							
AL **Rehberg**	Y	Y	Y	Y	Y	Y	Y
NEBRASKA							
1 **Fortenberry**	Y	Y	Y	Y	Y	Y	N
2 **Terry**	Y	Y	Y	Y	Y	Y	Y
3 **Smith**	Y	Y	Y	Y	Y	Y	N
NEVADA							
1 Berkley	Y	Y	Y	Y	Y	Y	Y
2 **Heller**	Y	Y	Y	Y	Y	Y	N
3 Titus	Y	Y	Y	Y	Y	Y	Y
NEW HAMPSHIRE							
1 Shea-Porter	Y	Y	Y	Y	Y	Y	Y
2 Hodes	Y	Y	Y	Y	Y	Y	Y
NEW JERSEY							
1 Andrews	Y	Y	Y	Y	Y	Y	Y
2 **LoBiondo**	Y	Y	Y	Y	Y	Y	Y
3 Adler	Y	Y	Y	Y	Y	Y	Y
4 **Smith**	Y	Y	Y	Y	Y	Y	Y
5 **Garrett**	Y	Y	Y	Y	Y	Y	Y
6 Pallone	Y	Y	Y	Y	Y	Y	Y
7 **Lance**	Y	Y	Y	Y	Y	Y	N
8 Pascrell	Y	Y	Y	Y	Y	Y	Y
9 Rothman	Y	Y	Y	Y	Y	Y	Y
10 Payne	Y	Y	Y	Y	Y	Y	Y
11 **Frelinghuysen**	Y	Y	Y	Y	Y	Y	N
12 Holt	Y	Y	Y	Y	Y	Y	Y
13 Sires	Y	Y	Y	Y	Y	Y	Y
NEW MEXICO							
1 Heinrich	Y	Y	Y	Y	Y	Y	Y
2 Teague	Y	?	Y	Y	Y	Y	Y
3 Luján	Y	Y	Y	Y	Y	Y	Y
NEW YORK							
1 Bishop	Y	Y	Y	Y	Y	Y	Y
2 Israel	Y	Y	Y	Y	Y	Y	Y
3 **King**	Y	Y	Y	Y	Y	Y	N
4 McCarthy	Y	Y	Y	Y	Y	Y	Y
5 Ackerman	Y	Y	Y	Y	Y	Y	Y
6 Meeks	Y	Y	Y	Y	Y	Y	Y
7 Crowley	Y	Y	Y	Y	Y	Y	Y
8 Nadler	Y	Y	Y	Y	Y	Y	Y
9 Weiner	Y	Y	Y	Y	Y	Y	Y
10 Towns	Y	Y	Y	Y	Y	Y	Y
11 Clarke	Y	Y	Y	Y	Y	Y	Y
12 Velázquez	Y	Y	Y	Y	Y	Y	Y
13 McMahon	Y	Y	Y	Y	Y	Y	Y
14 Maloney	Y	Y	Y	Y	Y	Y	Y
15 Rangel	Y	Y	Y	Y	Y	Y	Y
16 Serrano	Y	Y	Y	Y	Y	Y	Y
17 Engel	Y	Y	Y	Y	?	?	?
18 Lowey	Y	Y	Y	Y	Y	Y	Y
19 Hall	?	?	?	?	Y	Y	Y
20 Murphy	Y	Y	Y	Y	Y	Y	Y
21 Tonko	Y	Y	Y	Y	Y	Y	Y
22 Hinchey	Y	Y	Y	Y	Y	Y	Y
23 Owens	Y	Y	Y	Y	Y	Y	Y
24 Arcuri	Y	Y	Y	Y	Y	Y	Y
25 Maffei	Y	Y	Y	Y	Y	Y	Y
26 **Lee**	Y	Y	Y	Y	Y	Y	N
27 Higgins	Y	Y	Y	Y	Y	Y	Y
28 Slaughter	Y	Y	Y	Y	Y	Y	Y
29 Vacant							
NORTH CAROLINA							
1 Butterfield	Y	?	Y	Y	Y	Y	Y
2 Etheridge	Y	Y	Y	Y	Y	Y	Y
3 **Jones**	Y	Y	Y	Y	Y	Y	Y
4 Price	Y	Y	Y	Y	Y	Y	Y
5 **Foxx**	Y	Y	Y	Y	Y	Y	N
6 **Coble**	Y	Y	Y	Y	Y	Y	Y
7 McIntyre	Y	Y	?	Y	Y	Y	Y
8 Kissell	Y	Y	Y	Y	Y	Y	Y
9 **Myrick**	Y	Y	Y	Y	Y	Y	Y
10 **McHenry**	Y	Y	Y	Y	Y	Y	N
11 Shuler	Y	Y	Y	Y	Y	Y	Y
12 Watt	Y	Y	Y	Y	Y	Y	Y
13 Miller	Y	Y	Y	Y	Y	Y	Y
NORTH DAKOTA							
AL Pomeroy	Y	Y	Y	Y	Y	Y	Y
OHIO							
1 Driehaus	Y	Y	Y	Y	Y	Y	Y
2 **Schmidt**	Y	Y	Y	Y	Y	Y	Y
3 **Turner**	Y	Y	Y	Y	Y	Y	N
4 **Jordan**	Y	Y	Y	Y	Y	Y	N
5 **Latta**	Y	Y	Y	Y	Y	Y	N
6 Wilson	Y	Y	Y	Y	Y	Y	Y
7 **Austria**	Y	Y	Y	Y	Y	Y	N
8 **Boehner**	Y	Y	Y	Y	Y	Y	N
9 Kaptur	?	Y	Y	Y	Y	Y	Y
10 Kucinich	Y	Y	Y	Y	Y	Y	Y
11 Fudge	Y	Y	Y	Y	Y	Y	Y
12 **Tiberi**	Y	Y	Y	Y	Y	Y	N
13 Sutton	Y	Y	Y	Y	Y	Y	Y
14 **LaTourette**	Y	Y	Y	Y	Y	Y	Y
15 Kilroy	Y	Y	Y	Y	Y	Y	Y
16 Boccieri	Y	Y	Y	Y	Y	Y	Y
17 Ryan	Y	Y	Y	Y	Y	Y	Y
18 Space	Y	Y	Y	Y	Y	Y	Y
OKLAHOMA							
1 **Sullivan**	Y	Y	Y	Y	Y	Y	N
2 Boren	Y	Y	Y	Y	Y	Y	Y
3 **Lucas**	Y	Y	Y	Y	Y	Y	N
4 **Cole**	Y	Y	Y	Y	Y	Y	N
5 **Fallin**	Y	Y	Y	Y	Y	Y	N
OREGON							
1 Wu	Y	Y	Y	Y	Y	Y	Y
2 **Walden**	Y	Y	Y	Y	Y	Y	N
3 Blumenauer	Y	Y	Y	Y	Y	Y	Y
4 DeFazio	Y	Y	Y	Y	Y	Y	P
5 Schrader	Y	?	?	?	?	?	?
PENNSYLVANIA							
1 Brady	Y	Y	Y	Y	Y	Y	Y
2 Fattah	Y	Y	Y	Y	Y	Y	Y
3 Dahlkemper	Y	Y	Y	Y	Y	Y	Y
4 Altmire	Y	Y	Y	Y	Y	Y	N
5 **Thompson**	Y	Y	Y	Y	Y	Y	Y
6 **Gerlach**	Y	Y	Y	Y	Y	Y	Y
7 Sestak	Y	Y	Y	Y	Y	Y	Y
8 Murphy, P.	Y	Y	Y	Y	Y	Y	Y
9 **Shuster**	Y	Y	Y	Y	Y	Y	N
10 Carney	Y	Y	Y	Y	Y	Y	Y
11 Kanjorski	Y	Y	Y	Y	Y	Y	Y
12 Vacant							
13 Schwartz	Y	Y	Y	Y	Y	Y	Y
14 Doyle	Y	Y	Y	Y	Y	Y	?
15 **Dent**	Y	Y	Y	Y	Y	Y	Y
16 **Pitts**	Y	Y	Y	Y	Y	Y	Y
17 Holden	Y	Y	Y	Y	Y	Y	Y
18 **Murphy, T.**	Y	Y	Y	Y	Y	Y	Y
19 **Platts**	Y	Y	Y	Y	Y	Y	Y
RHODE ISLAND							
1 Kennedy	Y	Y	Y	Y	Y	Y	Y
2 Langevin	Y	Y	Y	Y	Y	Y	Y
SOUTH CAROLINA							
1 **Brown**	Y	Y	Y	Y	?	?	?
2 **Wilson**	Y	Y	Y	Y	Y	Y	Y
3 **Barrett**	?	?	?	?	?	?	?
4 **Inglis**	Y	Y	Y	Y	Y	Y	N
5 Spratt	Y	Y	Y	Y	Y	Y	Y
6 Clyburn	Y	Y	Y	Y	Y	Y	Y
SOUTH DAKOTA							
AL Herseth Sandlin	Y	Y	Y	Y	Y	Y	Y
TENNESSEE							
1 **Roe**	Y	Y	Y	Y	Y	Y	N
2 **Duncan**	Y	Y	Y	Y	Y	Y	N
3 **Wamp**	?	?	?	?	Y	Y	N
4 Davis	Y	Y	Y	Y	Y	Y	Y
5 Cooper	Y	Y	Y	Y	Y	Y	Y
6 Gordon	Y	Y	Y	Y	Y	Y	Y
7 **Blackburn**	Y	Y	Y	Y	Y	Y	N
8 Tanner	Y	Y	Y	Y	Y	Y	Y
9 Cohen	Y	Y	Y	Y	Y	Y	Y
TEXAS							
1 **Gohmert**	Y	Y	?	?	Y	?	N
2 **Poe**	Y	Y	Y	Y	Y	Y	N
3 **Johnson, S.**	Y	Y	Y	Y	Y	Y	N
4 **Hall**	Y	Y	Y	Y	Y	Y	Y
5 **Hensarling**	Y	Y	Y	Y	Y	Y	N
6 **Barton**	Y	Y	Y	Y	Y	Y	Y
7 **Culberson**	Y	Y	Y	Y	Y	Y	Y
8 **Brady**	Y	Y	Y	Y	Y	Y	N
9 Green, A.	Y	Y	Y	Y	Y	Y	Y
10 **McCaul**	Y	Y	Y	Y	Y	Y	Y
11 **Conaway**	Y	Y	Y	Y	Y	Y	N
12 **Granger**	Y	Y	Y	Y	Y	Y	N
13 **Thornberry**	Y	Y	Y	Y	Y	Y	N
14 **Paul**	Y	Y	N	Y	Y	Y	N
15 Hinojosa	Y	Y	Y	Y	Y	Y	Y
16 Reyes	Y	Y	Y	Y	Y	Y	Y
17 Edwards	Y	Y	Y	Y	Y	Y	Y
18 Jackson Lee	Y	Y	Y	Y	Y	Y	Y
19 **Neugebauer**	Y	Y	Y	Y	Y	Y	N
20 Gonzalez	Y	Y	Y	Y	Y	Y	Y
21 **Smith**	Y	Y	Y	Y	Y	Y	N
22 **Olson**	?	Y	Y	Y	Y	Y	N
23 Rodriguez	Y	Y	Y	Y	Y	Y	Y
24 **Marchant**	Y	Y	?	Y	Y	Y	N
25 Doggett	Y	Y	Y	Y	Y	Y	Y
26 **Burgess**	Y	Y	Y	Y	Y	Y	N
27 Ortiz	Y	Y	Y	Y	Y	Y	Y
28 Cuellar	Y	Y	Y	Y	?	?	?
29 Green, G.	Y	Y	Y	Y	Y	Y	P
30 Johnson, E.	Y	Y	Y	Y	Y	Y	Y
31 **Carter**	Y	Y	Y	Y	Y	Y	N
32 **Sessions**	Y	Y	Y	Y	Y	Y	N
UTAH							
1 **Bishop**	Y	Y	Y	Y	Y	Y	N
2 Matheson	Y	Y	Y	Y	Y	Y	Y
3 **Chaffetz**	Y	Y	Y	Y	Y	Y	N
VERMONT							
AL Welch	Y	Y	Y	Y	Y	Y	Y
VIRGINIA							
1 **Wittman**	Y	Y	Y	Y	Y	Y	Y
2 Nye	Y	Y	Y	Y	Y	Y	Y
3 Scott	Y	Y	Y	Y	Y	Y	Y
4 **Forbes**	Y	Y	Y	Y	Y	Y	N
5 Perriello	Y	Y	Y	Y	?	Y	Y
6 **Goodlatte**	Y	Y	Y	Y	Y	Y	Y
7 **Cantor**	Y	Y	Y	Y	Y	Y	?
8 Moran	Y	Y	Y	Y	Y	Y	Y
9 Boucher	Y	Y	Y	Y	Y	Y	Y
10 **Wolf**	Y	Y	Y	Y	Y	Y	Y
11 Connolly	Y	Y	Y	Y	Y	Y	Y
WASHINGTON							
1 Inslee	Y	Y	Y	Y	Y	Y	Y
2 Larsen	Y	Y	Y	Y	Y	Y	Y
3 Baird	Y	Y	Y	Y	Y	Y	Y
4 **Hastings**	Y	Y	Y	?	Y	Y	N
5 **McMorris Rodgers**	Y	Y	Y	Y	Y	Y	N
6 Dicks	Y	Y	Y	Y	Y	Y	Y
7 McDermott	Y	Y	Y	Y	Y	Y	Y
8 **Reichert**	Y	Y	Y	Y	Y	Y	Y
9 Smith	Y	Y	Y	Y	Y	Y	Y
WEST VIRGINIA							
1 Mollohan	Y	Y	Y	Y	Y	Y	Y
2 **Capito**	Y	Y	Y	Y	Y	Y	Y
3 Rahall	Y	Y	Y	Y	Y	Y	N
WISCONSIN							
1 **Ryan**	Y	Y	Y	Y	Y	Y	N
2 Baldwin	Y	Y	Y	Y	Y	Y	Y
3 Kind	Y	Y	Y	Y	Y	Y	Y
4 Moore	Y	Y	Y	Y	Y	Y	Y
5 **Sensenbrenner**	Y	Y	Y	Y	Y	Y	N
6 **Petri**	Y	Y	Y	Y	Y	Y	N
7 Obey	Y	Y	Y	Y	Y	Y	Y
8 Kagen	Y	Y	Y	Y	Y	Y	P
WYOMING							
AL **Lummis**	Y	Y	Y	Y	Y	Y	N
DELEGATES							
Faleomavaega (A.S.)							
Norton (D.C.)							
Bordallo (Guam)							
Sablan (N. Marianas)							
Pierluisi (P.R.)							
Christensen (V.I.)							

IN THE HOUSE | By Vote Number

123. **H Res 1141. Tribute to Justice O'Connor/Adoption.** Cohen, D-Tenn., motion to suspend the rules and adopt the resolution that would recognize the achievements and career of Supreme Court Justice Sandra Day O'Connor. Motion agreed to 416-0: D 245-0; R 171-0. A two-thirds majority of those present and voting (278 in this case) is required for adoption under suspension of the rules. March 17, 2010.

124. **S 1147. Tobacco Shipping Requirements/Passage.** Cohen, D-Tenn., motion to suspend the rules and pass the bill that would require companies selling or shipping tobacco products to verify that recipients are of legal age and prohibit shipments of tobacco products over 10 pounds. It also would require firms selling or shipping tobacco products to register with the Justice Department. Motion agreed to, thus clearing the bill for the president, 387-25: D 237-5; R 150-20. A two-thirds majority of those present and voting (275 in this case) is required for passage under suspension of the rules. March 17, 2010.

125. **HR 3954. Florida Land Transfers/Passage.** Baca, D-Calif., motion to suspend the rules and pass the bill that would authorize the Agriculture Department to transfer 114 acres in Leon County, Fla., to the state of Florida. It also would allow the U.S. Forest Service to make an equivalent transfer within the Ocala and Apalachicola national forests in Florida. Motion agreed to 418-1: D 247-0; R 171-1. A two-thirds majority of those present and voting (280 in this case) is required for passage under suspension of the rules. March 17, 2010.

126. **HR 946. Plain Language in Government Communications/ Passage.** Clay, D-Mo., motion to suspend the rules and pass the bill that would require the federal government to use plain language in all communications that explain how to comply with federal requirements or obtain government benefits or services. Motion agreed to 386-33: D 247-0; R 139-33. A two-thirds majority of those present and voting (280 in this case) is required for passage under suspension of the rules. March 17, 2010.

127. **HR 4825. Unused Member Office Funds/Passage.** Brady, D-Pa., motion to suspend the rules and pass the bill that would direct unused funds from House members' office accounts at the end of each fiscal year to the Treasury Department for deficit reduction. Motion agreed to 413-1: D 242-1; R 171-0. A two-thirds majority of those present and voting (276 in this case) is required for passage under suspension of the rules. March 17, 2010.

128. **HR 4214. Roy Wilson Post Office/Passage.** Clay, D-Mo., motion to suspend the rules and pass the bill that would designate a post office in Palm Desert, Calif., as the "Roy Wilson Post Office." Motion agreed to 419-0: D 246-0; R 173-0. A two-thirds majority of those present and voting (280 in this case) is required for passage under suspension of the rules. March 18, 2010.

129. **H Res 1190. Suspension Motions/Previous Question.** McGovern, D-Mass., motion to order the previous question (thus ending debate and possibility of amendment) on adoption of the rule (H Res 1190) that would permit the Speaker to entertain motions to suspend the rules through the calendar day of March 21. Motion agreed to 222-203: D 222-28; R 0-175. March 18, 2010.

	123	124	125	126	127	128	129
ALABAMA							
1 **Bonner**	Y	Y	Y	Y	Y	Y	N
2 Bright	Y	Y	Y	Y	Y	Y	N
3 **Rogers**	Y	Y	Y	Y	Y	Y	N
4 **Aderholt**	Y	Y	Y	Y	Y	Y	N
5 **Griffith**	Y	Y	Y	Y	Y	Y	N
6 **Bachus**	Y	Y	Y	Y	Y	Y	N
7 Davis	Y	Y	Y	Y	Y	Y	N
ALASKA							
AL **Young**	Y	N	Y	N	Y	Y	N
ARIZONA							
1 Kirkpatrick	Y	Y	Y	Y	Y	Y	Y
2 **Franks**	Y	Y	Y	Y	Y	Y	N
3 **Shadegg**	Y	N	Y	Y	Y	Y	N
4 Pastor	Y	Y	Y	Y	Y	Y	Y
5 Mitchell	Y	Y	Y	Y	Y	Y	N
6 **Flake**	Y	N	Y	N	Y	Y	N
7 Grijalva	Y	Y	Y	Y	Y	Y	Y
8 Giffords	Y	Y	Y	Y	Y	Y	N
ARKANSAS							
1 Berry	Y	Y	Y	Y	Y	Y	Y
2 Snyder	Y	Y	Y	Y	Y	Y	Y
3 **Boozman**	Y	Y	Y	Y	Y	Y	N
4 Ross	Y	Y	Y	Y	Y	Y	Y
CALIFORNIA							
1 Thompson	Y	Y	Y	Y	Y	Y	Y
2 **Herger**	Y	Y	Y	Y	Y	Y	N
3 **Lungren**	Y	Y	Y	Y	Y	Y	N
4 **McClintock**	Y	N	Y	N	Y	Y	N
5 Matsui	Y	Y	Y	Y	Y	Y	Y
6 Woolsey	Y	Y	Y	Y	Y	Y	Y
7 Miller, George	Y	Y	Y	Y	Y	Y	Y
8 Pelosi							Y
9 Lee	Y	Y	Y	Y	Y	Y	Y
10 Garamendi	Y	Y	Y	?	Y	Y	Y
11 McNerney	Y	Y	Y	Y	Y	Y	N
12 Speier	Y	Y	Y	Y	Y	Y	Y
13 Stark	?	?	?	?	?	?	?
14 Eshoo	Y	Y	Y	Y	Y	Y	Y
15 Honda	Y	Y	Y	Y	Y	Y	Y
16 Lofgren	Y	Y	Y	Y	Y	?	?
17 Farr	Y	Y	Y	Y	Y	Y	Y
18 Cardoza	Y	Y	Y	Y	Y	Y	Y
19 **Radanovich**	Y	Y	Y	Y	Y	Y	N
20 Costa	Y	Y	Y	Y	Y	?	Y
21 **Nunes**	Y	Y	Y	N	Y	Y	N
22 **McCarthy**	Y	Y	Y	Y	Y	Y	N
23 Capps	Y	Y	Y	Y	Y	Y	Y
24 **Gallegly**	Y	Y	Y	Y	Y	Y	N
25 **McKeon**	Y	Y	Y	Y	Y	Y	N
26 **Dreier**	Y	Y	Y	N	Y	Y	N
27 Sherman	Y	Y	Y	Y	Y	Y	Y
28 Berman	Y	Y	Y	Y	Y	Y	Y
29 Schiff	Y	Y	Y	Y	Y	Y	Y
30 Waxman	Y	Y	Y	Y	Y	Y	Y
31 Becerra	Y	Y	Y	Y	Y	Y	Y
32 Chu	Y	Y	Y	Y	Y	Y	Y
33 Watson	Y	Y	Y	Y	Y	Y	Y
34 Roybal-Allard	Y	Y	Y	Y	Y	Y	Y
35 Waters	Y	Y	Y	Y	Y	Y	Y
36 Harman	Y	Y	Y	Y	Y	Y	Y
37 Richardson	Y	Y	Y	Y	Y	Y	Y
38 Napolitano	Y	Y	Y	Y	Y	Y	Y
39 Sánchez, Linda	Y	Y	Y	Y	Y	Y	Y
40 **Royce**	Y	Y	Y	N	Y	Y	N
41 **Lewis**	?	Y	Y	N	Y	Y	N
42 **Miller, Gary**	Y	N	Y	Y	Y	Y	N
43 Baca	Y	Y	Y	Y	Y	Y	Y
44 **Calvert**	Y	Y	Y	N	Y	Y	N
45 **Bono Mack**	Y	Y	Y	Y	Y	Y	N
46 **Rohrabacher**	Y	N	Y	Y	Y	Y	N
47 Sanchez, Loretta	Y	Y	Y	Y	Y	Y	Y
48 **Campbell**	Y	N	Y	N	Y	Y	N
49 **Issa**	Y	?	Y	Y	Y	Y	N
50 **Bilbray**	Y	Y	Y	Y	Y	Y	N
51 Filner	Y	Y	Y	Y	Y	Y	Y
52 **Hunter**	Y	Y	Y	Y	Y	N	N
53 Davis	Y	Y	Y	Y	Y	Y	Y
COLORADO							
1 DeGette	Y	Y	Y	Y	Y	Y	Y
2 Polis	Y	Y	Y	Y	Y	Y	Y
3 Salazar	Y	Y	Y	Y	Y	Y	Y
4 Markey	Y	Y	Y	Y	Y	Y	Y
5 **Lamborn**	Y	Y	Y	N	Y	Y	N
6 **Coffman**	Y	Y	Y	Y	Y	Y	N
7 Perlmutter	Y	Y	Y	Y	Y	Y	Y
CONNECTICUT							
1 Larson	Y	+	Y	Y	Y	Y	Y
2 Courtney	Y	Y	Y	Y	Y	Y	Y
3 DeLauro	?	Y	Y	Y	Y	Y	Y
4 Himes	Y	Y	Y	Y	Y	Y	Y
5 Murphy	Y	Y	Y	Y	Y	Y	Y
DELAWARE							
AL **Castle**	Y	Y	Y	Y	Y	Y	Y
FLORIDA							
1 **Miller**	Y	N	Y	Y	Y	Y	N
2 Boyd	Y	Y	Y	Y	Y	Y	Y
3 Brown	Y	Y	Y	Y	Y	Y	Y
4 **Crenshaw**	Y	Y	Y	Y	Y	Y	N
5 **Brown-Waite**	Y	Y	Y	Y	Y	Y	N
6 **Stearns**	Y	Y	Y	Y	Y	Y	N
7 **Mica**	Y	Y	Y	Y	Y	Y	N
8 Grayson	?	?	Y	Y	Y	Y	Y
9 **Bilirakis**	Y	Y	Y	Y	Y	Y	N
10 **Young**	?	?	?	?	?	?	Y
11 Castor	Y	Y	Y	Y	Y	Y	Y
12 **Putnam**	Y	Y	Y	Y	Y	Y	N
13 **Buchanan**	Y	Y	Y	Y	Y	Y	N
14 **Mack**	Y	Y	Y	Y	Y	Y	N
15 **Posey**	Y	Y	Y	Y	Y	?	N
16 **Rooney**	Y	N	Y	N	Y	Y	N
17 Meek	Y	Y	Y	Y	Y	Y	Y
18 **Ros-Lehtinen**	Y	Y	Y	Y	Y	Y	N
19 Vacant							
20 Wasserman Schultz	Y	Y	Y	Y	Y	Y	Y
21 **Diaz-Balart, L.**	Y	Y	Y	Y	Y	Y	N
22 Klein	Y	Y	Y	Y	Y	Y	Y
23 Hastings	Y	Y	Y	Y	Y	Y	Y
24 Kosmas	Y	Y	Y	Y	Y	Y	N
25 **Diaz-Balart, M.**	Y	Y	Y	Y	Y	Y	N
GEORGIA							
1 **Kingston**	Y	N	Y	N	Y	Y	N
2 Bishop	Y	Y	Y	Y	Y	Y	Y
3 **Westmoreland**	Y	N	Y	Y	Y	?	?
4 Johnson	Y	?	Y	Y	Y	Y	Y
5 Lewis	Y	Y	Y	Y	Y	Y	Y
6 **Price**	Y	Y	Y	Y	Y	Y	N
7 **Linder**	Y	Y	Y	Y	Y	Y	N
8 Marshall	Y	Y	Y	Y	Y	Y	Y
9 **Deal**	?	?	?	?	?	?	N
10 **Broun**	Y	N	Y	N	Y	Y	N
11 **Gingrey**	Y	Y	Y	Y	Y	Y	N
12 Barrow	Y	Y	Y	Y	Y	Y	Y
13 Scott	Y	Y	Y	Y	Y	Y	Y
HAWAII							
1 Vacant							
2 Hirono	Y	Y	Y	Y	Y	Y	Y
IDAHO							
1 Minnick	Y	Y	Y	Y	Y	Y	N
2 **Simpson**	Y	Y	Y	Y	Y	Y	N
ILLINOIS							
1 Rush	Y	Y	Y	Y	Y	Y	Y
2 Jackson	Y	Y	Y	Y	Y	Y	Y
3 Lipinski	Y	Y	Y	Y	Y	Y	N
4 Gutierrez	Y	Y	Y	Y	Y	Y	Y
5 Quigley	Y	Y	Y	Y	Y	Y	Y
6 **Roskam**	Y	Y	Y	Y	Y	Y	N
7 Davis	Y	Y	Y	Y	Y	Y	Y
8 Bean	Y	Y	Y	Y	Y	Y	Y
9 Schakowsky	Y	Y	Y	Y	Y	Y	Y
10 **Kirk**	Y	Y	Y	Y	Y	Y	N
11 Halvorson	Y	N	Y	Y	Y	Y	Y
12 Costello	Y	Y	Y	Y	Y	Y	N
13 **Biggert**	Y	Y	Y	Y	Y	Y	N
14 Foster	Y	Y	Y	Y	Y	Y	Y
15 **Johnson**	Y	Y	Y	Y	Y	Y	N

KEY   **Republicans**   Democrats

Y Voted for (yea)	**X** Paired against	**C** Voted "present" to avoid possible conflict of interest
# Paired for	**–** Announced against	
+ Announced for	**P** Voted "present"	**?** Did not vote or otherwise make a position known
N Voted against (nay)		

	123	124	125	126	127	128	129
16 **Manzullo**	Y	Y	Y	N	Y	Y	N
17 Hare	Y	Y	Y	Y	Y	Y	Y
18 **Schock**	Y	Y	Y	Y	Y	Y	N
19 **Shimkus**	Y	Y	Y	Y	Y	Y	N
INDIANA							
1 Visclosky	Y	Y	Y	Y	Y	Y	Y
2 Donnelly	Y	Y	Y	Y	Y	Y	Y
3 **Souder**	Y	Y	Y	Y	Y	Y	N
4 **Buyer**	Y	Y	Y	Y	?	?	N
5 **Burton**	Y	Y	Y	N	Y	Y	N
6 **Pence**	Y	Y	Y	?	Y	Y	N
7 Carson	Y	Y	Y	Y	Y	Y	Y
8 Ellsworth	Y	N	Y	Y	Y	Y	Y
9 Hill	Y	Y	Y	Y	Y	Y	Y
IOWA							
1 Braley	Y	Y	Y	Y	Y	Y	Y
2 Loebsack	Y	Y	Y	Y	Y	Y	Y
3 Boswell	Y	Y	Y	Y	Y	Y	Y
4 **Latham**	Y	Y	Y	Y	Y	Y	N
5 **King**	Y	Y	Y	Y	Y	Y	N
KANSAS							
1 **Moran**	Y	Y	Y	Y	Y	Y	N
2 **Jenkins**	Y	Y	Y	N	Y	Y	N
3 Moore	Y	Y	Y	Y	Y	Y	Y
4 **Tiahrt**	Y	Y	Y	N	Y	Y	N
KENTUCKY							
1 **Whitfield**	Y	N	N	N	Y	Y	N
2 **Guthrie**	Y	Y	Y	Y	Y	Y	N
3 Yarmuth	Y	Y	Y	Y	Y	Y	Y
4 **Davis**	Y	Y	Y	Y	Y	Y	N
5 **Rogers**	Y	Y	Y	Y	Y	Y	N
6 Chandler	Y	Y	Y	Y	Y	Y	Y
LOUISIANA							
1 **Scalise**	Y	Y	Y	Y	Y	Y	N
2 **Cao**	Y	Y	Y	Y	Y	Y	N
3 Melancon	Y	Y	Y	Y	Y	Y	N
4 **Fleming**	Y	Y	Y	Y	Y	Y	N
5 **Alexander**	Y	Y	Y	Y	Y	Y	N
6 **Cassidy**	Y	Y	Y	Y	Y	Y	N
7 **Boustany**	Y	Y	Y	Y	Y	Y	N
MAINE							
1 Pingree	Y	Y	Y	Y	Y	Y	Y
2 Michaud	Y	Y	Y	Y	Y	Y	N
MARYLAND							
1 Kratovil	Y	Y	Y	Y	Y	Y	N
2 Ruppersberger	Y	Y	Y	Y	Y	Y	Y
3 Sarbanes	Y	Y	Y	Y	Y	Y	Y
4 Edwards	Y	Y	Y	Y	Y	Y	Y
5 Hoyer	Y	Y	Y	Y	Y	Y	Y
6 **Bartlett**	Y	Y	Y	N	Y	Y	N
7 Cummings	Y	Y	Y	Y	Y	Y	Y
8 Van Hollen	Y	Y	Y	Y	Y	Y	Y
MASSACHUSETTS							
1 Olver	Y	Y	Y	Y	Y	Y	Y
2 Neal	Y	Y	Y	Y	Y	Y	Y
3 McGovern	Y	Y	Y	Y	Y	Y	Y
4 Frank	Y	Y	Y	Y	Y	Y	Y
5 Tsongas	Y	Y	Y	Y	Y	Y	Y
6 Tierney	Y	Y	Y	Y	?	Y	Y
7 Markey	Y	Y	Y	Y	Y	Y	Y
8 Capuano	Y	Y	Y	Y	Y	Y	Y
9 Lynch	Y	Y	Y	Y	Y	Y	Y
10 Delahunt	?	?	?	?	?	Y	Y
MICHIGAN							
1 Stupak	Y	Y	Y	Y	Y	Y	N
2 **Hoekstra**	Y	Y	Y	Y	Y	?	?
3 **Ehlers**	Y	Y	Y	Y	Y	Y	N
4 **Camp**	Y	Y	Y	Y	Y	Y	N
5 Kildee	Y	Y	Y	Y	Y	Y	Y
6 **Upton**	Y	Y	Y	Y	Y	Y	N
7 Schauer	Y	Y	Y	Y	Y	Y	Y
8 **Rogers**	Y	Y	Y	Y	Y	Y	N
9 Peters	Y	Y	Y	Y	Y	Y	Y
10 **Miller**	Y	Y	Y	Y	Y	Y	N
11 **McCotter**	Y	Y	Y	Y	Y	Y	N
12 Levin	Y	Y	Y	Y	Y	Y	Y
13 Kilpatrick	Y	Y	Y	Y	Y	Y	Y
14 Conyers	Y	Y	Y	Y	Y	Y	Y
15 Dingell	Y	Y	?	?	?	Y	Y
MINNESOTA							
1 Walz	Y	Y	Y	Y	Y	Y	Y
2 **Kline**	Y	Y	Y	Y	Y	Y	N
3 **Paulsen**	Y	Y	Y	Y	Y	Y	N
4 McCollum	Y	Y	Y	Y	Y	Y	Y

	123	124	125	126	127	128	129
5 Ellison	Y	Y	Y	Y	Y	Y	Y
6 **Bachmann**	Y	Y	Y	Y	Y	Y	N
7 Peterson	Y	Y	Y	Y	Y	Y	Y
8 Oberstar	Y	Y	Y	Y	Y	Y	Y
MISSISSIPPI							
1 Childers	Y	Y	Y	Y	Y	Y	N
2 Thompson	Y	Y	Y	Y	Y	Y	Y
3 **Harper**	Y	Y	Y	Y	Y	Y	N
4 Taylor	Y	Y	Y	Y	Y	Y	N
MISSOURI							
1 Clay	Y	Y	Y	Y	Y	Y	Y
2 **Akin**	Y	Y	Y	N	Y	Y	N
3 Carnahan	Y	Y	Y	Y	Y	Y	Y
4 Skelton	Y	Y	Y	Y	Y	Y	Y
5 Cleaver	Y	Y	Y	Y	Y	Y	Y
6 **Graves**	Y	Y	Y	Y	Y	Y	N
7 **Blunt**	Y	Y	Y	Y	Y	Y	N
8 **Emerson**	Y	Y	Y	Y	Y	Y	N
9 **Luetkemeyer**	Y	Y	Y	Y	Y	Y	N
MONTANA							
AL **Rehberg**	Y	Y	Y	Y	Y	Y	N
NEBRASKA							
1 **Fortenberry**	?	Y	Y	Y	Y	Y	N
2 **Terry**	Y	Y	Y	Y	Y	Y	N
3 **Smith**	Y	Y	Y	N	Y	Y	N
NEVADA							
1 Berkley	Y	?	Y	Y	Y	Y	Y
2 **Heller**	Y	Y	Y	Y	Y	Y	N
3 Titus	Y	Y	Y	Y	Y	Y	Y
NEW HAMPSHIRE							
1 Shea-Porter	Y	Y	Y	Y	Y	Y	Y
2 Hodes	Y	Y	Y	Y	Y	Y	Y
NEW JERSEY							
1 Andrews	Y	Y	Y	Y	Y	Y	Y
2 **LoBiondo**	Y	Y	Y	Y	Y	Y	N
3 Adler	Y	Y	Y	Y	Y	Y	N
4 **Smith**	Y	Y	Y	Y	Y	Y	N
5 **Garrett**	Y	N	Y	N	Y	Y	N
6 Pallone	Y	Y	Y	Y	Y	Y	Y
7 **Lance**	Y	Y	Y	Y	Y	Y	N
8 Pascrell	Y	Y	Y	Y	Y	Y	Y
9 Rothman	Y	Y	Y	Y	Y	Y	Y
10 Payne	Y	Y	Y	Y	Y	Y	Y
11 **Frelinghuysen**	Y	Y	Y	Y	Y	Y	N
12 Holt	Y	Y	Y	Y	Y	Y	Y
13 Sires	Y	Y	Y	Y	Y	Y	Y
NEW MEXICO							
1 Heinrich	Y	Y	Y	Y	Y	Y	Y
2 Teague	Y	Y	Y	Y	Y	Y	N
3 Luján	Y	Y	Y	Y	Y	Y	Y
NEW YORK							
1 Bishop	Y	Y	Y	Y	Y	Y	Y
2 Israel	Y	Y	Y	Y	Y	Y	Y
3 **King**	Y	Y	Y	Y	Y	Y	N
4 McCarthy	?	Y	Y	Y	Y	Y	Y
5 Ackerman	Y	Y	Y	Y	Y	?	?
6 Meeks	Y	Y	Y	Y	Y	Y	Y
7 Crowley	Y	Y	Y	Y	Y	Y	Y
8 Nadler	Y	Y	Y	Y	N	Y	Y
9 Weiner	Y	Y	Y	Y	Y	Y	Y
10 Towns	Y	Y	Y	Y	Y	Y	Y
11 Clarke	Y	Y	Y	Y	Y	Y	Y
12 Velázquez	Y	Y	Y	Y	Y	Y	Y
13 McMahon	Y	Y	Y	Y	Y	Y	Y
14 Maloney	Y	Y	Y	Y	Y	Y	Y
15 Rangel	Y	Y	Y	Y	Y	Y	Y
16 Serrano	Y	Y	Y	Y	Y	Y	Y
17 Engel	Y	Y	Y	Y	Y	Y	Y
18 Lowey	Y	Y	Y	Y	Y	Y	Y
19 Hall	Y	Y	Y	Y	Y	?	Y
20 Murphy	Y	Y	Y	Y	Y	Y	Y
21 Tonko	Y	Y	Y	Y	Y	Y	Y
22 Hinchey	Y	Y	Y	Y	Y	Y	Y
23 Owens	Y	Y	Y	Y	?	Y	Y
24 Arcuri	Y	Y	Y	Y	Y	Y	N
25 Maffei	Y	Y	Y	Y	Y	Y	Y
26 **Lee**	Y	Y	Y	Y	Y	Y	N
27 Higgins	Y	Y	Y	Y	Y	Y	Y
28 Slaughter	Y	?	?	?	?	Y	Y
29 Vacant							
NORTH CAROLINA							
1 Butterfield	Y	Y	Y	Y	Y	Y	Y
2 Etheridge	Y	Y	Y	Y	Y	Y	Y
3 **Jones**	Y	Y	Y	Y	Y	Y	N
4 Price	Y	Y	Y	Y	Y	Y	Y

	123	124	125	126	127	128	129
5 **Foxx**	Y	Y	Y	Y	Y	Y	N
6 **Coble**	Y	Y	Y	Y	Y	Y	N
7 McIntyre	Y	Y	Y	Y	Y	Y	N
8 Kissell	Y	Y	Y	Y	Y	Y	Y
9 **Myrick**	Y	Y	Y	Y	Y	Y	N
10 **McHenry**	Y	Y	Y	Y	Y	Y	N
11 Shuler	Y	Y	Y	Y	Y	Y	N
12 Watt	Y	Y	Y	Y	Y	Y	Y
13 Miller	Y	Y	Y	Y	Y	Y	Y
NORTH DAKOTA							
AL Pomeroy	Y	Y	Y	Y	Y	Y	Y
OHIO							
1 Driehaus	Y	Y	Y	Y	Y	Y	Y
2 **Schmidt**	Y	?	Y	Y	Y	Y	N
3 **Turner**	Y	Y	Y	Y	Y	Y	N
4 **Jordan**	Y	Y	Y	N	Y	Y	N
5 **Latta**	Y	Y	Y	Y	Y	Y	N
6 Wilson	Y	Y	Y	Y	Y	Y	Y
7 **Austria**	Y	Y	Y	Y	Y	Y	N
8 **Boehner**	Y	Y	Y	Y	Y	Y	N
9 Kaptur	Y	Y	Y	Y	Y	Y	Y
10 Kucinich	Y	Y	Y	Y	Y	Y	Y
11 Fudge	Y	Y	Y	Y	Y	Y	Y
12 **Tiberi**	Y	Y	Y	Y	Y	Y	N
13 Sutton	Y	Y	Y	Y	Y	Y	Y
14 **LaTourette**	Y	Y	Y	Y	Y	Y	N
15 Kilroy	Y	Y	Y	Y	Y	Y	Y
16 Boccieri	Y	Y	Y	Y	Y	Y	Y
17 Ryan	Y	Y	Y	Y	Y	Y	Y
18 Space	?	?	?	?	?	Y	Y
OKLAHOMA							
1 **Sullivan**	Y	Y	Y	Y	Y	Y	N
2 Boren	Y	N	Y	Y	Y	Y	N
3 **Lucas**	Y	Y	Y	Y	Y	Y	N
4 **Cole**	Y	Y	Y	Y	Y	Y	N
5 **Fallin**	Y	Y	Y	Y	Y	Y	N
OREGON							
1 Wu	Y	Y	Y	Y	Y	Y	Y
2 **Walden**	Y	Y	Y	Y	Y	Y	N
3 Blumenauer	Y	Y	Y	Y	Y	Y	Y
4 DeFazio	Y	Y	Y	Y	Y	Y	Y
5 Schrader	Y	Y	Y	Y	Y	Y	Y
PENNSYLVANIA							
1 Brady	Y	Y	Y	Y	Y	Y	Y
2 Fattah	Y	Y	Y	Y	Y	Y	Y
3 Dahlkemper	Y	Y	Y	Y	Y	Y	N
4 Altmire	Y	Y	Y	Y	Y	Y	Y
5 **Thompson**	Y	Y	Y	Y	Y	Y	N
6 **Gerlach**	Y	Y	Y	Y	Y	Y	N
7 Sestak	Y	Y	Y	Y	Y	Y	Y
8 Murphy, P.	Y	Y	Y	Y	Y	Y	Y
9 **Shuster**	Y	Y	Y	Y	Y	Y	N
10 Carney	Y	Y	Y	Y	Y	Y	N
11 Kanjorski	Y	Y	Y	Y	Y	Y	Y
12 Vacant							
13 Schwartz	Y	Y	Y	Y	Y	Y	Y
14 Doyle	Y	Y	Y	Y	Y	Y	Y
15 **Dent**	Y	Y	Y	Y	Y	Y	N
16 **Pitts**	Y	Y	Y	Y	Y	Y	N
17 Holden	Y	Y	Y	Y	Y	Y	N
18 **Murphy, T.**	Y	Y	Y	Y	Y	Y	N
19 **Platts**	Y	Y	Y	Y	Y	Y	N
RHODE ISLAND							
1 Kennedy	Y	Y	Y	Y	Y	Y	Y
2 Langevin	Y	Y	Y	Y	Y	Y	Y
SOUTH CAROLINA							
1 **Brown**	?	?	?	?	?	Y	N
2 **Wilson**	Y	Y	Y	Y	Y	Y	N
3 **Barrett**	?	?	?	?	?	Y	N
4 **Inglis**	Y	Y	Y	Y	Y	Y	N
5 Spratt	Y	Y	Y	Y	Y	Y	Y
6 Clyburn	Y	Y	Y	Y	Y	Y	Y
SOUTH DAKOTA							
AL Herseth Sandlin	Y	N	Y	Y	Y	Y	N
TENNESSEE							
1 **Roe**	Y	Y	Y	Y	Y	Y	N
2 **Duncan**	Y	N	Y	Y	Y	Y	N
3 **Wamp**	Y	Y	Y	Y	Y	Y	N
4 Davis	Y	Y	Y	Y	Y	Y	Y
5 Cooper	Y	Y	Y	Y	Y	Y	N
6 Gordon	Y	Y	Y	Y	Y	Y	Y
7 **Blackburn**	Y	?	?	N	Y	Y	N
8 Tanner	Y	Y	Y	Y	Y	Y	Y
9 Cohen	Y	Y	Y	Y	Y	Y	Y

	123	124	125	126	127	128	129
TEXAS							
1 **Gohmert**	Y	Y	Y	N	Y	Y	N
2 **Poe**	Y	Y	Y	N	Y	Y	N
3 **Johnson, S.**	Y	Y	Y	Y	Y	Y	N
4 **Hall**	Y	Y	Y	Y	Y	Y	N
5 **Hensarling**	Y	Y	Y	Y	Y	Y	N
6 **Barton**	Y	Y	Y	Y	Y	Y	N
7 **Culberson**	Y	Y	Y	Y	Y	Y	N
8 **Brady**	Y	Y	Y	Y	Y	Y	N
9 Green, A.	Y	Y	Y	Y	Y	Y	Y
10 **McCaul**	Y	Y	Y	Y	Y	Y	N
11 **Conaway**	Y	Y	Y	Y	Y	Y	N
12 **Granger**	Y	Y	Y	Y	Y	Y	N
13 **Thornberry**	Y	Y	Y	Y	Y	Y	N
14 **Paul**	Y	N	Y	N	Y	Y	N
15 Hinojosa	Y	Y	Y	Y	Y	Y	Y
16 Reyes	Y	Y	Y	Y	Y	Y	Y
17 Edwards	Y	Y	Y	Y	Y	Y	Y
18 Jackson Lee	Y	Y	Y	Y	Y	Y	Y
19 **Neugebauer**	Y	Y	Y	Y	Y	Y	N
20 Gonzalez	Y	Y	Y	Y	Y	Y	Y
21 **Smith**	Y	Y	Y	Y	Y	Y	N
22 **Olson**	Y	Y	Y	Y	Y	Y	N
23 Rodriguez	Y	Y	Y	Y	Y	Y	Y
24 **Marchant**	Y	Y	Y	N	Y	Y	N
25 Doggett	Y	Y	Y	Y	Y	Y	Y
26 **Burgess**	Y	Y	Y	N	Y	Y	N
27 Ortiz	Y	Y	Y	Y	Y	Y	Y
28 Cuellar	Y	Y	Y	Y	Y	Y	Y
29 Green, G.	Y	Y	Y	Y	Y	Y	Y
30 Johnson, E.	Y	Y	Y	Y	Y	Y	Y
31 **Carter**	Y	N	Y	Y	Y	Y	N
32 **Sessions**	Y	Y	Y	Y	Y	Y	N
UTAH							
1 **Bishop**	Y	Y	Y	Y	Y	Y	N
2 Matheson	Y	Y	Y	Y	Y	Y	Y
3 **Chaffetz**	Y	Y	Y	N	Y	Y	N
VERMONT							
AL Welch	Y	Y	Y	Y	Y	Y	Y
VIRGINIA							
1 **Wittman**	Y	Y	Y	Y	Y	Y	N
2 Nye	Y	Y	Y	Y	Y	Y	N
3 Scott	Y	Y	Y	Y	Y	Y	Y
4 **Forbes**	Y	Y	Y	Y	Y	Y	N
5 Perriello	Y	Y	Y	Y	Y	Y	N
6 **Goodlatte**	Y	Y	Y	Y	Y	Y	N
7 **Cantor**	Y	Y	Y	Y	Y	Y	N
8 Moran	Y	Y	Y	Y	Y	Y	Y
9 Boucher	Y	Y	Y	Y	Y	Y	Y
10 **Wolf**	Y	Y	Y	Y	Y	Y	N
11 Connolly	Y	Y	Y	Y	Y	Y	Y
WASHINGTON							
1 Inslee	Y	Y	Y	Y	Y	Y	Y
2 Larsen	?	?	Y	Y	?	Y	Y
3 Baird	Y	Y	Y	Y	Y	Y	Y
4 **Hastings**	Y	Y	Y	Y	Y	?	?
5 **McMorris Rodgers**	Y	Y	Y	Y	Y	Y	N
6 Dicks	Y	N	Y	Y	Y	Y	Y
7 McDermott	Y	Y	Y	Y	Y	Y	Y
8 **Reichert**	Y	Y	Y	Y	Y	Y	N
9 Smith	Y	Y	Y	Y	Y	Y	Y
WEST VIRGINIA							
1 Mollohan	Y	Y	Y	Y	Y	Y	Y
2 **Capito**	?	?	?	?	?	?	N
3 Rahall	Y	Y	Y	Y	Y	Y	Y
WISCONSIN							
1 **Ryan**	Y	Y	Y	Y	Y	Y	N
2 Baldwin	Y	Y	Y	Y	Y	Y	Y
3 Kind	Y	Y	Y	Y	Y	Y	Y
4 Moore	Y	?	Y	Y	Y	Y	Y
5 **Sensenbrenner**	Y	N	Y	N	Y	Y	N
6 **Petri**	Y	N	Y	N	Y	Y	N
7 Obey	Y	Y	Y	Y	Y	Y	Y
8 Kagen	Y	Y	Y	Y	Y	Y	Y
WYOMING							
AL **Lummis**	Y	N	Y	N	Y	Y	N
DELEGATES							
Faleomavaega (A.S.)							
Norton (D.C.)							
Bordallo (Guam)							
Sablan (N. Marianas)							
Pierluisi (P.R.)							
Christensen (V.I.)							

IN THE HOUSE | By Vote Number

130. **H Res 1190. Suspension Motions/Rule.** Adoption of the rule that would permit the Speaker to entertain motions to suspend the rules through the calendar day of March 21. Adopted 232-187: D 231-16; R 1-171. March 18, 2010.

131. **H Res 1193. PMA Group Investigation/Motion to Refer.** McGovern, D-Mass., motion to refer the Flake, R-Ariz., privileged resolution to the Committee on Official Standards and Conduct. The resolution would require the Committee on Official Standards and Conduct to issue a report detailing the number of people interviewed, subpoenas issued and documents reviewed in the panel's investigation of members' dealings with the PMA Group. Motion agreed to 397-0: D 238-0; R 159-0. March 18, 2010.

132. **H Res 1194. Disapproval of Democratic Leadership/Motion to Table.** Hoyer, D-Md., motion to table (kill) the Cantor, R-Va., privileged resolution. The Cantor resolution would express the House's disapproval of the Democratic leadership for allegedly abandoning their duties of office. Motion agreed to 232-181: D 232-10; R 0-171. March 18, 2010.

133. **HR 3542. State Flags at the Capitol/Passage.** Brady, D-Pa., motion to suspend the rules and pass the bill that would require the Architect of the Capitol to fly the flag of each state over the U.S. Capitol building on the anniversary of the state's admission to the United States. Motion agreed to 408-0: D 239-0; R 169-0. A two-thirds majority of those present and voting (272 in this case) is required for passage under suspension of the rules. March 18, 2010.

134. **HR 3509. Agricultural Loan Mediation/Passage.** Baca, D-Calif., motion to suspend the rules and pass the bill that would extend the authorization of $7.5 million each year from fiscal 2011 to fiscal 2015 for grants to fund state programs that mediate loan disputes between agricultural producers and their creditors. Motion agreed to 382-26: D 235-3; R 147-23. A two-thirds majority of those present and voting (272 in this case) is required for passage under suspension of the rules. March 18, 2010.

135. **H Res 1173. Tribute to the Vermont Long Trail/Adoption.** Bordallo, D-Guam, motion to suspend the rules and adopt the resolution that would recognize the 100th anniversary of Vermont's Long Trail, the oldest long-distance hiking trail in the United States. Motion agreed to 409-1: D 241-0; R 168-1. A two-thirds majority of those present and voting (274 in this case) is required for adoption under suspension of the rules. March 18, 2010.

	130	131	132	133	134	135
ALABAMA						
1 **Bonner**	N	P	N	Y	Y	Y
2 Bright	Y	Y	Y	Y	Y	Y
3 **Rogers**	N	Y	N	Y	Y	Y
4 **Aderholt**	N	Y	N	Y	Y	Y
5 **Griffith**	N	Y	N	Y	Y	Y
6 **Bachus**	N	Y	N	Y	Y	Y
7 Davis	N	Y	Y	Y	Y	Y
ALASKA						
AL **Young**	N	Y	N	Y	Y	N
ARIZONA						
1 Kirkpatrick	N	Y	Y	Y	Y	Y
2 **Franks**	N	Y	N	Y	N	Y
3 **Shadegg**	N	Y	N	Y	N	Y
4 Pastor	Y	Y	Y	Y	Y	Y
5 Mitchell	N	Y	N	Y	N	Y
6 **Flake**	N	Y	N	Y	N	Y
7 Grijalva	Y	?	Y	Y	Y	Y
8 Giffords	Y	Y	N	Y	Y	Y
ARKANSAS						
1 Berry	Y	Y	Y	Y	Y	Y
2 Snyder	Y	Y	Y	Y	Y	Y
3 **Boozman**	N	Y	N	Y	Y	Y
4 Ross	Y	Y	Y	Y	Y	Y
CALIFORNIA						
1 Thompson	Y	Y	Y	Y	Y	Y
2 **Herger**	N	Y	N	Y	Y	Y
3 **Lungren**	N	Y	N	Y	Y	Y
4 **McClintock**	N	Y	N	Y	Y	Y
5 Matsui	Y	Y	Y	Y	Y	Y
6 Woolsey	Y	Y	Y	Y	Y	Y
7 Miller, George	Y	Y	Y	Y	Y	Y
8 Pelosi			?			
9 Lee	Y	Y	Y	Y	Y	Y
10 Garamendi	Y	Y	Y	Y	Y	Y
11 McNerney	Y	Y	Y	Y	?	?
12 Speier	Y	Y	Y	Y	Y	Y
13 Stark	?	?	?	?	?	?
14 Eshoo	?	Y	Y	Y	Y	Y
15 Honda	Y	Y	Y	Y	Y	Y
16 Lofgren	?	?	?	?	?	?
17 Farr	Y	Y	Y	Y	Y	Y
18 Cardoza	Y	Y	Y	Y	Y	Y
19 **Radanovich**	N	?	?	?	?	?
20 Costa	N	Y	Y	Y	Y	Y
21 **Nunes**	N	Y	N	Y	Y	Y
22 **McCarthy**	N	Y	N	Y	Y	Y
23 Capps	Y	Y	Y	Y	Y	Y
24 **Gallegly**	N	Y	N	Y	Y	Y
25 **McKeon**	N	Y	N	Y	Y	Y
26 **Dreier**	N	Y	N	Y	Y	Y
27 Sherman	Y	Y	Y	Y	Y	Y
28 Berman	Y	Y	Y	Y	Y	Y
29 Schiff	Y	Y	Y	+	Y	Y
30 Waxman	Y	Y	Y	Y	Y	Y
31 Becerra	Y	Y	?	Y	Y	Y
32 Chu	Y	Y	Y	Y	Y	Y
33 Watson	Y	Y	Y	Y	Y	Y
34 Roybal-Allard	Y	Y	Y	Y	Y	Y
35 Waters	Y	Y	Y	Y	Y	Y
36 Harman	Y	Y	Y	Y	Y	Y
37 Richardson	Y	Y	Y	Y	Y	Y
38 Napolitano	Y	Y	Y	Y	Y	Y
39 Sánchez, Linda	Y	?	?	?	?	?
40 **Royce**	N	Y	N	Y	N	Y
41 **Lewis**	N	Y	N	Y	Y	Y
42 **Miller, Gary**	N	Y	N	Y	Y	Y
43 Baca	Y	Y	Y	Y	Y	Y
44 **Calvert**	N	Y	N	Y	Y	Y
45 **Bono Mack**	N	Y	N	Y	Y	Y
46 **Rohrabacher**	N	Y	N	Y	N	Y
47 Sanchez, Loretta	Y	Y	Y	Y	Y	Y
48 **Campbell**	N	Y	N	Y	Y	Y
49 **Issa**	N	Y	N	Y	Y	Y
50 **Bilbray**	N	Y	N	Y	Y	Y
51 Filner	Y	Y	Y	Y	Y	Y
52 **Hunter**	N	Y	N	Y	Y	Y
53 Davis	Y	Y	Y	Y	Y	Y

	130	131	132	133	134	135
COLORADO						
1 DeGette	Y	Y	Y	Y	Y	Y
2 Polis	Y	Y	Y	Y	Y	Y
3 Salazar	Y	Y	Y	Y	Y	Y
4 Markey	Y	Y	Y	Y	Y	Y
5 **Lamborn**	N	Y	N	Y	N	Y
6 **Coffman**	N	Y	N	Y	Y	Y
7 Perlmutter	Y	Y	Y	Y	Y	Y
CONNECTICUT						
1 Larson	Y	Y	Y	Y	Y	Y
2 Courtney	Y	Y	Y	Y	Y	Y
3 DeLauro	Y	Y	Y	Y	Y	Y
4 Himes	Y	Y	Y	Y	Y	Y
5 Murphy	Y	Y	Y	Y	Y	Y
DELAWARE						
AL **Castle**	N	Y	N	Y	Y	Y
FLORIDA						
1 **Miller**	N	Y	N	Y	Y	Y
2 Boyd	Y	Y	Y	Y	?	?
3 Brown	Y	Y	Y	Y	Y	Y
4 **Crenshaw**	N	Y	N	Y	Y	Y
5 **Brown-Waite**	N	Y	N	Y	Y	Y
6 **Stearns**	N	Y	N	Y	N	Y
7 **Mica**	N	Y	N	Y	Y	Y
8 Grayson	Y	Y	Y	Y	Y	Y
9 Bilirakis	N	Y	N	Y	Y	Y
10 **Young**	N	Y	N	Y	Y	Y
11 Castor	Y	P	Y	Y	Y	Y
12 **Putnam**	N	Y	N	Y	Y	Y
13 **Buchanan**	N	Y	N	Y	Y	Y
14 **Mack**	N	Y	N	Y	Y	Y
15 **Posey**	N	Y	N	Y	Y	Y
16 **Rooney**	N	Y	N	Y	Y	Y
17 Meek	Y	Y	Y	Y	Y	Y
18 **Ros-Lehtinen**	N	Y	N	Y	Y	Y
19 Vacant						
20 Wasserman Schultz	Y	Y	Y	Y	Y	Y
21 **Diaz-Balart, L.**	N	P	N	Y	Y	Y
22 Klein	Y	Y	Y	Y	Y	Y
23 Hastings	Y	Y	Y	Y	Y	Y
24 Kosmas	Y	?	Y	Y	Y	Y
25 **Diaz-Balart, M.**	?	Y	N	Y	Y	Y
GEORGIA						
1 **Kingston**	N	Y	N	Y	Y	Y
2 Bishop	Y	Y	Y	Y	Y	Y
3 **Westmoreland**	?	?	?	?	?	?
4 Johnson	Y	Y	Y	Y	Y	Y
5 Lewis	Y	Y	Y	Y	Y	Y
6 **Price**	N	Y	N	Y	N	Y
7 **Linder**	N	Y	N	Y	Y	Y
8 Marshall	Y	Y	Y	Y	Y	Y
9 **Deal**	N	?	?	?	?	?
10 **Broun**	N	Y	N	Y	N	Y
11 **Gingrey**	N	Y	N	Y	Y	Y
12 Barrow	Y	Y	Y	Y	Y	Y
13 Scott	Y	Y	Y	Y	Y	Y
HAWAII						
1 Vacant						
2 Hirono	Y	Y	Y	Y	Y	Y
IDAHO						
1 Minnick	N	Y	N	Y	Y	Y
2 **Simpson**	N	P	N	Y	Y	Y
ILLINOIS						
1 Rush	Y	?	Y	Y	Y	?
2 Jackson	Y	Y	Y	Y	Y	Y
3 Lipinski	N	Y	Y	Y	Y	Y
4 Gutierrez	Y	Y	Y	Y	Y	Y
5 Quigley	N	Y	Y	Y	Y	Y
6 **Roskam**	N	Y	N	Y	Y	Y
7 Davis	Y	Y	Y	?	Y	Y
8 Bean	Y	Y	Y	Y	N	Y
9 Schakowsky	Y	Y	Y	Y	Y	Y
10 **Kirk**	N	Y	N	Y	Y	Y
11 Halvorson	Y	Y	Y	Y	Y	Y
12 Costello	N	Y	Y	Y	Y	Y
13 **Biggert**	N	Y	N	Y	Y	Y
14 Foster	Y	Y	Y	Y	Y	Y
15 **Johnson**	N	Y	N	Y	Y	Y

KEY | Republicans | Democrats

Y	Voted for (yea)	X	Paired against	C	Voted "present" to avoid possible conflict of interest
#	Paired for	–	Announced against		
+	Announced for	P	Voted "present"	?	Did not vote or otherwise make a position known
N	Voted against (nay)				

	130	131	132	133	134	135
16 **Manzullo**	N	Y	N	Y	N	Y
17 Hare	Y	Y	Y	Y	Y	Y
18 **Schock**	N	Y	N	Y	Y	Y
19 **Shimkus**	N	Y	N	Y	Y	Y
INDIANA						
1 Visclosky	Y	Y	Y	Y	Y	Y
2 Donnelly	Y	Y	Y	Y	Y	Y
3 **Souder**	N	Y	N	Y	Y	Y
4 **Buyer**	N	Y	N	Y	Y	Y
5 **Burton**	N	Y	N	Y	Y	Y
6 **Pence**	N	Y	N	Y	Y	Y
7 Carson	Y	Y	Y	Y	Y	Y
8 Ellsworth	Y	Y	?	Y	Y	Y
9 Hill	Y	Y	Y	Y	Y	Y
IOWA						
1 Braley	Y	Y	Y	Y	Y	Y
2 Loebsack	Y	Y	Y	Y	Y	Y
3 Boswell	Y	Y	Y	Y	Y	Y
4 **Latham**	N	P	N	Y	Y	Y
5 **King**	N	Y	?	?	Y	Y
KANSAS						
1 **Moran**	N	Y	N	Y	Y	Y
2 **Jenkins**	N	Y	N	Y	Y	Y
3 Moore	Y	Y	Y	Y	Y	Y
4 **Tiahrt**	N	Y	N	Y	Y	Y
KENTUCKY						
1 **Whitfield**	N	Y	N	Y	Y	?
2 **Guthrie**	N	Y	N	Y	Y	Y
3 Yarmuth	Y	Y	Y	Y	Y	Y
4 **Davis**	N	Y	N	Y	Y	Y
5 **Rogers**	N	Y	N	Y	Y	Y
6 Chandler	Y	P	Y	Y	Y	Y
LOUISIANA						
1 **Scalise**	N	Y	N	Y	Y	Y
2 **Cao**	N	?	N	Y	Y	Y
3 Melancon	N	Y	Y	Y	Y	Y
4 **Fleming**	N	Y	N	Y	Y	Y
5 **Alexander**	N	Y	N	Y	Y	Y
6 **Cassidy**	N	Y	N	Y	Y	Y
7 **Boustany**	N	Y	N	Y	Y	Y
MAINE						
1 Pingree	Y	Y	Y	Y	Y	Y
2 Michaud	Y	Y	Y	Y	Y	Y
MARYLAND						
1 Kratovil	Y	Y	Y	Y	Y	Y
2 Ruppersberger	Y	Y	Y	Y	Y	Y
3 Sarbanes	Y	Y	Y	Y	Y	Y
4 Edwards	Y	Y	Y	Y	Y	Y
5 Hoyer	Y	Y	Y	Y	Y	Y
6 **Bartlett**	N	Y	N	Y	Y	Y
7 Cummings	Y	?	?	?	?	?
8 Van Hollen	Y	Y	Y	Y	Y	Y
MASSACHUSETTS						
1 Olver	Y	Y	Y	Y	Y	Y
2 Neal	Y	Y	Y	Y	Y	Y
3 McGovern	Y	Y	Y	Y	Y	Y
4 Frank	Y	Y	Y	Y	Y	Y
5 Tsongas	Y	Y	Y	Y	Y	Y
6 Tierney	Y	Y	Y	Y	Y	Y
7 Markey	Y	Y	Y	Y	Y	Y
8 Capuano	Y	Y	Y	Y	Y	Y
9 Lynch	Y	Y	Y	Y	Y	Y
10 Delahunt	Y	Y	Y	Y	Y	Y
MICHIGAN						
1 Stupak	Y	Y	Y	Y	Y	Y
2 **Hoekstra**	?	?	?	?	?	?
3 **Ehlers**	?	Y	N	Y	Y	Y
4 **Camp**	N	Y	N	Y	Y	Y
5 Kildee	Y	Y	Y	Y	Y	Y
6 **Upton**	N	Y	N	Y	Y	Y
7 Schauer	Y	Y	Y	Y	Y	Y
8 **Rogers**	N	Y	N	Y	?	Y
9 Peters	Y	Y	Y	Y	N	Y
10 **Miller**	N	Y	N	Y	Y	Y
11 **McCotter**	N	Y	N	Y	Y	Y
12 Levin	Y	Y	Y	Y	Y	Y
13 Kilpatrick	Y	Y	Y	Y	Y	Y
14 Conyers	Y	Y	Y	Y	Y	Y
15 Dingell	Y	Y	Y	Y	Y	Y
MINNESOTA						
1 Walz	Y	Y	Y	Y	Y	Y
2 **Kline**	N	Y	N	Y	Y	Y
3 **Paulsen**	N	Y	N	Y	Y	Y
4 McCollum	Y	Y	Y	Y	Y	Y

	130	131	132	133	134	135
5 Ellison	Y	Y	Y	Y	Y	Y
6 **Bachmann**	N	Y	N	Y	Y	Y
7 Peterson	Y	Y	Y	Y	Y	Y
8 Oberstar	Y	Y	Y	Y	Y	Y
MISSISSIPPI						
1 Childers	N	Y	N	Y	Y	Y
2 Thompson	Y	Y	Y	Y	Y	Y
3 **Harper**	N	P	N	Y	Y	Y
4 Taylor	N	Y	N	Y	Y	Y
MISSOURI						
1 Clay	Y	Y	Y	Y	Y	Y
2 **Akin**	N	Y	N	Y	N	Y
3 Carnahan	Y	Y	Y	Y	Y	Y
4 Skelton	Y	Y	Y	Y	Y	Y
5 Cleaver	Y	Y	Y	Y	Y	Y
6 **Graves**	N	Y	N	Y	Y	Y
7 **Blunt**	N	Y	N	Y	Y	Y
8 **Emerson**	N	Y	N	Y	Y	Y
9 **Luetkemeyer**	N	Y	N	Y	Y	Y
MONTANA						
AL **Rehberg**	N	Y	N	Y	Y	Y
NEBRASKA						
1 **Fortenberry**	N	Y	N	Y	Y	Y
2 **Terry**	N	Y	N	Y	Y	Y
3 **Smith**	N	Y	N	Y	Y	?
NEVADA						
1 Berkley	Y	Y	Y	Y	Y	Y
2 **Heller**	N	Y	N	Y	Y	Y
3 Titus	Y	Y	Y	Y	Y	Y
NEW HAMPSHIRE						
1 Shea-Porter	Y	Y	Y	Y	Y	Y
2 Hodes	Y	Y	Y	Y	Y	Y
NEW JERSEY						
1 Andrews	Y	Y	Y	Y	Y	Y
2 **LoBiondo**	N	Y	N	Y	Y	Y
3 Adler	Y	Y	Y	Y	Y	Y
4 **Smith**	N	Y	N	Y	Y	Y
5 **Garrett**	N	Y	N	Y	N	Y
6 Pallone	Y	Y	Y	Y	Y	Y
7 **Lance**	N	Y	N	Y	Y	Y
8 Pascrell	Y	Y	Y	Y	Y	Y
9 Rothman	Y	Y	Y	Y	Y	Y
10 Payne	Y	Y	Y	Y	Y	Y
11 **Frelinghuysen**	N	Y	N	Y	Y	Y
12 Holt	Y	Y	Y	Y	Y	Y
13 Sires	Y	Y	Y	Y	Y	Y
NEW MEXICO						
1 Heinrich	Y	Y	Y	Y	Y	Y
2 Teague	Y	Y	Y	Y	?	Y
3 Luján	Y	Y	Y	Y	Y	Y
NEW YORK						
1 Bishop	Y	?	?	?	?	?
2 Israel	Y	Y	Y	Y	Y	Y
3 **King**	N	Y	N	Y	Y	Y
4 McCarthy	Y	Y	Y	Y	Y	Y
5 Ackerman	?	?	?	?	?	?
6 Meeks	Y	Y	Y	Y	Y	Y
7 Crowley	Y	Y	Y	Y	Y	Y
8 Nadler	Y	Y	Y	Y	Y	Y
9 Weiner	Y	Y	Y	Y	Y	Y
10 Towns	Y	Y	Y	Y	Y	Y
11 Clarke	Y	Y	Y	Y	Y	Y
12 Velázquez	Y	Y	Y	Y	Y	Y
13 McMahon	Y	Y	Y	Y	Y	Y
14 Maloney	Y	Y	Y	Y	Y	Y
15 Rangel	Y	Y	Y	Y	Y	Y
16 Serrano	Y	Y	Y	Y	Y	Y
17 Engel	Y	Y	Y	Y	Y	Y
18 Lowey	Y	Y	Y	Y	Y	Y
19 Hall	Y	Y	Y	Y	Y	Y
20 Murphy	Y	Y	Y	Y	Y	Y
21 Tonko	Y	Y	Y	Y	Y	Y
22 Hinchey	Y	Y	Y	Y	Y	Y
23 Owens	Y	Y	Y	Y	Y	Y
24 Arcuri	Y	Y	Y	Y	Y	?
25 Maffei	Y	Y	Y	Y	Y	Y
26 **Lee**	N	Y	N	Y	Y	Y
27 Higgins	Y	Y	Y	Y	Y	Y
28 Slaughter	Y	Y	Y	Y	Y	Y
29 Vacant						
NORTH CAROLINA						
1 Butterfield	Y	P	Y	Y	Y	Y
2 Etheridge	Y	Y	Y	Y	Y	Y
3 **Jones**	N	Y	N	Y	Y	Y
4 Price	Y	Y	Y	Y	Y	Y

	130	131	132	133	134	135
5 **Foxx**	N	Y	N	Y	N	Y
6 **Coble**	N	Y	N	Y	Y	Y
7 McIntyre	N	Y	N	Y	Y	Y
8 Kissell	Y	Y	N	Y	Y	Y
9 **Myrick**	N	Y	N	Y	N	Y
10 **McHenry**	N	Y	N	Y	Y	Y
11 Shuler	N	Y	N	Y	Y	Y
12 Watt	Y	Y	Y	Y	Y	Y
13 Miller	Y	Y	Y	Y	Y	Y
NORTH DAKOTA						
AL Pomeroy	Y	Y	Y	Y	Y	Y
OHIO						
1 Driehaus	Y	Y	Y	Y	Y	Y
2 **Schmidt**	N	Y	N	Y	Y	Y
3 **Turner**	N	Y	N	Y	Y	Y
4 **Jordan**	N	Y	N	Y	N	Y
5 **Latta**	N	Y	N	Y	Y	Y
6 Wilson	Y	Y	Y	Y	Y	Y
7 **Austria**	N	Y	N	Y	Y	Y
8 **Boehner**	N	Y	N	?	?	Y
9 Kaptur	Y	?	Y	?	?	Y
10 Kucinich	Y	Y	Y	Y	Y	Y
11 Fudge	Y	Y	Y	Y	Y	Y
12 **Tiberi**	N	Y	N	Y	Y	Y
13 Sutton	Y	Y	Y	Y	Y	Y
14 **LaTourette**	N	Y	N	Y	Y	Y
15 Kilroy	Y	Y	Y	Y	Y	Y
16 Boccieri	Y	Y	Y	Y	Y	Y
17 Ryan	Y	Y	Y	Y	Y	Y
18 Space	Y	Y	Y	Y	Y	Y
OKLAHOMA						
1 **Sullivan**	N	?	N	Y	Y	Y
2 Boren	N	Y	N	Y	Y	Y
3 **Lucas**	N	Y	N	Y	Y	Y
4 **Cole**	N	Y	N	Y	Y	Y
5 **Fallin**	N	Y	N	+	Y	Y
OREGON						
1 Wu	Y	Y	?	Y	Y	Y
2 **Walden**	N	P	N	Y	Y	Y
3 Blumenauer	Y	Y	Y	Y	Y	Y
4 DeFazio	Y	Y	Y	Y	Y	Y
5 Schrader	Y	Y	Y	Y	Y	Y
PENNSYLVANIA						
1 Brady	Y	Y	Y	Y	Y	Y
2 Fattah	Y	Y	Y	Y	Y	Y
3 Dahlkemper	Y	Y	Y	Y	Y	Y
4 Altmire	Y	Y	Y	Y	Y	Y
5 **Thompson**	N	Y	N	Y	Y	Y
6 **Gerlach**	N	Y	N	Y	Y	Y
7 Sestak	Y	Y	Y	Y	Y	Y
8 Murphy, P.	Y	Y	Y	Y	Y	Y
9 **Shuster**	N	Y	N	Y	Y	Y
10 Carney	Y	Y	Y	Y	Y	Y
11 Kanjorski	?	Y	Y	Y	Y	Y
12 Vacant						
13 Schwartz	Y	Y	Y	Y	Y	Y
14 Doyle	Y	Y	Y	Y	Y	Y
15 **Dent**	N	P	N	Y	Y	Y
16 **Pitts**	N	Y	N	Y	Y	Y
17 Holden	Y	Y	Y	Y	Y	Y
18 **Murphy, T.**	N	Y	N	Y	Y	Y
19 **Platts**	N	Y	N	Y	Y	Y
RHODE ISLAND						
1 Kennedy	Y	Y	Y	Y	Y	Y
2 Langevin	Y	Y	Y	Y	Y	Y
SOUTH CAROLINA						
1 **Brown**	N	Y	N	Y	Y	Y
2 **Wilson**	N	Y	N	Y	Y	Y
3 **Barrett**	N	?	?	?	?	?
4 **Inglis**	N	Y	N	Y	N	Y
5 Spratt	Y	Y	Y	Y	Y	Y
6 Clyburn	Y	Y	Y	Y	Y	Y
SOUTH DAKOTA						
AL Herseth Sandlin	N	Y	Y	Y	Y	Y
TENNESSEE						
1 **Roe**	N	Y	N	Y	Y	Y
2 **Duncan**	N	Y	N	Y	N	Y
3 **Wamp**	N	Y	N	Y	Y	Y
4 Davis	Y	?	?	?	?	?
5 Cooper	Y	Y	Y	Y	Y	Y
6 Gordon	Y	Y	Y	?	Y	Y
7 **Blackburn**	N	Y	N	Y	Y	Y
8 Tanner	Y	Y	Y	Y	Y	Y
9 Cohen	Y	Y	Y	Y	Y	Y

	130	131	132	133	134	135
TEXAS						
1 **Gohmert**	N	Y	N	Y	N	Y
2 **Poe**	N	Y	N	Y	Y	Y
3 **Johnson, S.**	N	Y	N	Y	Y	?
4 **Hall**	N	Y	N	Y	Y	Y
5 **Hensarling**	N	Y	N	Y	N	Y
6 **Barton**	N	Y	N	Y	Y	Y
7 **Culberson**	N	Y	N	Y	Y	Y
8 **Brady**	N	Y	N	Y	Y	Y
9 Green, A.	Y	Y	Y	Y	Y	Y
10 **McCaul**	N	P	N	Y	Y	Y
11 **Conaway**	N	P	N	Y	Y	Y
12 **Granger**	N	Y	N	Y	Y	Y
13 **Thornberry**	N	Y	N	Y	Y	Y
14 **Paul**	N	Y	N	Y	N	Y
15 Hinojosa	Y	Y	Y	Y	Y	Y
16 Reyes	Y	Y	Y	Y	Y	Y
17 Edwards	Y	Y	Y	Y	Y	Y
18 Jackson Lee	Y	Y	Y	Y	Y	Y
19 **Neugebauer**	N	Y	N	Y	Y	Y
20 Gonzalez	Y	Y	Y	Y	Y	Y
21 **Smith**	N	Y	N	Y	Y	Y
22 **Olson**	N	Y	N	Y	Y	Y
23 Rodriguez	Y	Y	Y	Y	Y	Y
24 **Marchant**	N	Y	N	Y	Y	Y
25 Doggett	Y	Y	Y	Y	Y	Y
26 **Burgess**	N	?	N	Y	Y	Y
27 Ortiz	Y	Y	Y	Y	Y	Y
28 Cuellar	Y	Y	Y	Y	Y	Y
29 Green, G.	Y	Y	Y	Y	Y	Y
30 Johnson, E.	Y	Y	Y	Y	Y	Y
31 **Carter**	N	Y	N	Y	Y	Y
32 **Sessions**	N	Y	N	Y	Y	Y
UTAH						
1 **Bishop**	N	?	N	Y	Y	Y
2 Matheson	Y	Y	Y	Y	Y	Y
3 **Chaffetz**	N	Y	N	Y	N	Y
VERMONT						
AL Welch	Y	Y	Y	?	?	Y
VIRGINIA						
1 **Wittman**	N	Y	N	Y	Y	Y
2 Nye	Y	Y	Y	Y	Y	Y
3 Scott	Y	Y	Y	Y	Y	Y
4 **Forbes**	N	Y	N	Y	Y	Y
5 Perriello	N	Y	N	Y	Y	Y
6 **Goodlatte**	N	Y	N	Y	Y	Y
7 **Cantor**	N	Y	N	Y	N	Y
8 Moran	Y	Y	Y	Y	Y	Y
9 Boucher	Y	Y	Y	Y	Y	Y
10 **Wolf**	N	Y	N	Y	Y	Y
11 Connolly	Y	Y	Y	Y	Y	Y
WASHINGTON						
1 Inslee	Y	Y	Y	Y	Y	Y
2 Larsen	Y	Y	Y	Y	Y	Y
3 Baird	Y	Y	Y	Y	Y	Y
4 **Hastings**	?	?	?	?	?	?
5 **McMorris Rodgers**	?	Y	N	Y	Y	Y
6 Dicks	Y	Y	Y	Y	?	Y
7 McDermott	Y	Y	Y	?	Y	Y
8 **Reichert**	Y	Y	N	Y	Y	Y
9 Smith	Y	Y	Y	Y	Y	Y
WEST VIRGINIA						
1 Mollohan	Y	Y	Y	Y	Y	Y
2 **Capito**	N	Y	N	Y	Y	Y
3 Rahall	Y	Y	Y	Y	Y	Y
WISCONSIN						
1 **Ryan**	N	Y	N	Y	Y	Y
2 Baldwin	Y	Y	Y	Y	Y	Y
3 Kind	Y	Y	Y	Y	?	Y
4 Moore	Y	Y	Y	Y	Y	Y
5 **Sensenbrenner**	N	Y	N	Y	N	Y
6 **Petri**	N	Y	N	Y	Y	Y
7 Obey	Y	Y	Y	Y	Y	Y
8 Kagen	Y	Y	Y	Y	Y	Y
WYOMING						
AL **Lummis**	N	Y	N	Y	Y	Y
DELEGATES						
Faleomavaega (A.S.)						
Norton (D.C.)						
Bordallo (Guam)						
Sablan (N. Marianas)						
Pierluisi (P.R.)						
Christensen (V.I.)						

IN THE HOUSE | By Vote Number

136. **HR 3644, HR 1612. Water Education and Conservation Programs/Rule.** Adoption of the rule (H Res 1192) to provide for House floor consideration of bills that would authorize two federal grant programs for water education and expand federal agency land conservation programs. Adopted 236-171: D 235-6; R 1-165. March 19, 2010.

137. **HR 3671. Upper Mississippi River Basin/Passage.** Bordallo, D-Guam, motion to suspend the rules and pass the bill that would authorize $6 million per year for a program to monitor the environmental quality of the Upper Mississippi River Basin. Motion agreed to 289-121: D 240-4; R 49-117. A two-thirds majority of those present and voting (274 in this case) is required for passage under suspension of the rules. March 19, 2010.

138. **HR 2788. Distinguished Flying Cross National Memorial/Passage.** Bordallo, D-Guam, motion to suspend the rules and pass the bill that would designate a memorial under development in Riverside, Calif., as the Distinguished Flying Cross National Memorial. Motion agreed to 410-0: D 244-0; R 166-0. A two-thirds majority of those present and voting (274 in this case) is required for passage under suspension of the rules. March 19, 2010.

139. **HR 3644. Water Education Programs/Earmark Ban.** Flake, R-Ariz., amendment to the Capps, D-Calif., substitute amendment. The Flake amendment would prohibit the earmarking of funds appropriated under the bill. The substitute would authorize $65 million in fiscal 2011 through 2015 for the Bay-Watershed Education and Training Program and $81 million over the same period for the Environmental Literacy Grant Program. Adopted 376-37: D 207-36; R 169-1. March 19, 2010.

140. **HR 3644. Water Education Programs/Substitute.** Capps, D-Calif., substitute amendment that would authorize $65 million in fiscal 2011 through 2015 for the Bay-Watershed Education and Training Program and $81 million over the same period for the Environmental Literacy Grant Program.. Adopted 233-178: D 229-11; R 4-167. March 19, 2010.

141. **HR 3644. Water Education Programs/Recommit.** Chaffetz, R-Utah, motion to recommit the bill to the Natural Resources Committee with instructions that it be immediately reported back with an amendment that would require the Environmental Literacy Grant Program to provide financial assistance to examine the effects of natural gas and oil seeps on oceans, beaches, air quality and the coast environment, and the possibility of mitigating those impacts through resources and energy development. It would change the authorization levels to $12 million for the environmental program and $10 million for the Bay-Watershed Education and Training Program. Motion rejected 200-215: D 31-215; R 169-0. March 19, 2010.

142. **HR 3644. Water Education Programs/Passage.** Passage of the bill that would reauthorize two National Oceanic and Atmospheric Administration programs. It would authorize $65 million in fiscal 2011 through 2015 for the Bay-Watershed Education and Training Program and $81 million over the same period for the Environmental Literacy Grant Program. Passed 244-170: D 236-9; R 8-161. March 19, 2010.

	136	137	138	139	140	141	142
ALABAMA							
1 **Bonner**	N	Y	Y	Y	N	Y	N
2 Bright	Y	N	Y	Y	N	Y	N
3 **Rogers**	N	N	Y	Y	N	Y	N
4 **Aderholt**	N	N	Y	Y	N	Y	N
5 **Griffith**	N	Y	Y	Y	N	Y	N
6 **Bachus**	N	Y	Y	Y	N	Y	N
7 Davis	Y	Y	Y	Y	Y	N	Y
ALASKA							
AL **Young**	?	?	?	Y	N	Y	N
ARIZONA							
1 Kirkpatrick	Y	Y	Y	Y	Y	N	Y
2 **Franks**	N	N	Y	Y	N	Y	N
3 **Shadegg**	N	N	Y	Y	N	Y	N
4 Pastor	Y	Y	Y	Y	Y	N	Y
5 Mitchell	N	N	Y	Y	N	Y	N
6 **Flake**	Y	Y	Y	Y	N	Y	N
7 Grijalva	Y	Y	Y	N	Y	N	Y
8 Giffords	N	Y	Y	Y	N	Y	N
ARKANSAS							
1 Berry	Y	Y	Y	N	Y	N	Y
2 Snyder	Y	Y	Y	Y	Y	N	Y
3 **Boozman**	N	N	Y	Y	N	Y	N
4 Ross	Y	Y	Y	Y	Y	N	Y
CALIFORNIA							
1 Thompson	Y	Y	Y	Y	Y	N	Y
2 **Herger**	N	N	Y	Y	N	Y	N
3 **Lungren**	N	N	Y	Y	N	Y	N
4 **McClintock**	N	N	Y	Y	N	Y	N
5 Matsui	Y	Y	Y	Y	Y	N	Y
6 Woolsey	Y	Y	Y	N	Y	N	Y
7 Miller, George	Y	Y	Y	Y	Y	N	Y
8 Pelosi							
9 Lee	Y	Y	Y	N	Y	N	Y
10 Garamendi	?	?	?	Y	Y	N	Y
11 McNerney	Y	Y	Y	Y	Y	N	Y
12 Speier	Y	Y	Y	Y	Y	N	Y
13 Stark	?	?	?	?	?	?	?
14 Eshoo	Y	Y	Y	Y	Y	N	Y
15 Honda	Y	Y	Y	?	?	N	Y
16 Lofgren	+	+	+	+	+	–	+
17 Farr	Y	Y	Y	N	Y	N	Y
18 Cardoza	Y	Y	Y	Y	Y	Y	Y
19 **Radanovich**	N	N	Y	Y	N	Y	N
20 Costa	Y	Y	Y	?	Y	N	Y
21 **Nunes**	N	N	Y	N	?	?	?
22 **McCarthy**	N	N	Y	Y	N	Y	N
23 Capps	Y	Y	Y	Y	Y	N	Y
24 **Gallegly**	N	N	Y	Y	N	Y	N
25 **McKeon**	N	N	Y	Y	N	Y	N
26 **Dreier**	N	N	Y	Y	N	Y	N
27 Sherman	Y	Y	Y	N	Y	N	Y
28 Berman	Y	Y	Y	Y	Y	N	Y
29 Schiff	Y	Y	Y	Y	Y	N	Y
30 Waxman	Y	Y	Y	Y	Y	N	Y
31 Becerra	Y	Y	Y	Y	Y	N	Y
32 Chu	Y	Y	Y	Y	Y	N	Y
33 Watson	Y	Y	Y	N	Y	N	Y
34 Roybal-Allard	Y	Y	Y	N	Y	N	Y
35 Waters	Y	Y	Y	N	Y	N	Y
36 Harman	Y	Y	Y	Y	Y	N	Y
37 Richardson	Y	Y	Y	Y	Y	N	Y
38 Napolitano	Y	Y	Y	Y	N	Y	Y
39 Sánchez, Linda	Y	Y	Y	Y	Y	N	Y
40 **Royce**	N	N	Y	Y	N	Y	N
41 **Lewis**	N	N	Y	Y	N	Y	N
42 **Miller, Gary**	N	N	Y	Y	N	Y	N
43 Baca	Y	Y	Y	Y	Y	N	Y
44 **Calvert**	N	N	Y	Y	N	Y	N
45 **Bono Mack**	N	N	Y	Y	N	Y	N
46 **Rohrabacher**	N	N	Y	Y	N	Y	N
47 Sanchez, Loretta	Y	Y	Y	Y	Y	N	Y
48 **Campbell**	N	N	Y	Y	N	Y	N
49 **Issa**	N	N	Y	Y	N	Y	N
50 **Bilbray**	N	N	Y	Y	N	Y	N
51 Filner	Y	Y	Y	N	Y	N	Y
52 **Hunter**	N	N	Y	Y	N	Y	N
53 Davis	Y	Y	Y	Y	Y	N	Y

	136	137	138	139	140	141	142
COLORADO							
1 DeGette	Y	Y	Y	Y	Y	N	Y
2 Polis	Y	Y	Y	Y	Y	N	Y
3 Salazar	Y	Y	Y	Y	Y	N	Y
4 Markey	Y	Y	Y	Y	Y	N	Y
5 **Lamborn**	N	N	Y	Y	N	Y	N
6 **Coffman**	N	N	Y	Y	N	Y	N
7 Perlmutter	Y	Y	Y	Y	Y	N	N
CONNECTICUT							
1 Larson	Y	Y	Y	Y	Y	N	Y
2 Courtney	Y	Y	Y	Y	Y	N	Y
3 DeLauro	Y	Y	Y	Y	Y	N	Y
4 Himes	Y	Y	Y	Y	Y	Y	Y
5 Murphy	Y	Y	Y	Y	Y	N	Y
DELAWARE							
AL **Castle**	N	N	Y	Y	N	Y	Y
FLORIDA							
1 **Miller**	N	N	Y	Y	N	Y	N
2 Boyd	Y	Y	Y	Y	Y	N	Y
3 Brown	Y	Y	Y	N	Y	N	Y
4 **Crenshaw**	N	N	Y	Y	N	Y	N
5 **Brown-Waite**	N	N	Y	Y	N	Y	N
6 **Stearns**	N	N	Y	Y	N	Y	N
7 **Mica**	N	N	Y	Y	N	Y	N
8 Grayson	Y	Y	Y	Y	Y	N	Y
9 **Bilirakis**	N	N	Y	Y	N	Y	N
10 **Young**	?	?	?	Y	N	Y	N
11 Castor	Y	Y	Y	Y	Y	N	Y
12 **Putnam**	N	N	Y	Y	N	Y	N
13 **Buchanan**	N	N	Y	Y	N	Y	?
14 **Mack**	N	N	Y	Y	N	Y	N
15 **Posey**	N	N	Y	Y	N	Y	N
16 **Rooney**	N	N	Y	Y	N	Y	N
17 Meek	Y	Y	Y	Y	Y	N	Y
18 **Ros-Lehtinen**	?	?	?	?	?	?	?
19 Vacant							
20 Wasserman Schultz	Y	Y	Y	Y	Y	N	Y
21 **Diaz-Balart, L.**	N	N	Y	Y	N	Y	N
22 Klein	Y	Y	Y	Y	Y	N	Y
23 Hastings	Y	Y	Y	Y	Y	N	Y
24 Kosmas	Y	Y	Y	Y	Y	N	Y
25 **Diaz-Balart, M.**	N	N	Y	Y	N	Y	N
GEORGIA							
1 **Kingston**	N	N	Y	Y	N	Y	N
2 Bishop	Y	Y	Y	N	Y	N	Y
3 **Westmoreland**	N	N	Y	Y	N	Y	N
4 Johnson	Y	Y	Y	Y	Y	N	Y
5 Lewis	Y	Y	Y	Y	Y	N	Y
6 **Price**	N	N	Y	Y	N	Y	N
7 **Linder**	N	N	Y	Y	N	Y	N
8 Marshall	Y	Y	Y	Y	?	N	Y
9 **Deal**	?	?	?	?	?	?	?
10 **Broun**	N	N	Y	Y	N	Y	N
11 **Gingrey**	N	N	Y	Y	N	Y	N
12 Barrow	Y	Y	Y	Y	Y	Y	Y
13 Scott	Y	Y	Y	Y	Y	N	Y
HAWAII							
1 Vacant							
2 Hirono	Y	Y	Y	Y	Y	N	Y
IDAHO							
1 Minnick	Y	Y	Y	Y	Y	Y	Y
2 **Simpson**	N	N	Y	Y	N	Y	N
ILLINOIS							
1 Rush	Y	Y	Y	Y	Y	N	Y
2 Jackson	Y	Y	Y	N	Y	N	Y
3 Lipinski	Y	Y	Y	Y	Y	N	Y
4 Gutierrez	?	?	?	?	?	?	?
5 Quigley	Y	Y	Y	Y	Y	N	Y
6 **Roskam**	N	?	Y	Y	N	Y	N
7 Davis	Y	Y	Y	N	Y	N	Y
8 Bean	Y	Y	Y	Y	Y	N	N
9 Schakowsky	Y	Y	Y	Y	Y	N	Y
10 **Kirk**	N	Y	Y	Y	N	Y	N
11 Halvorson	Y	Y	Y	Y	Y	N	Y
12 Costello	Y	Y	Y	Y	Y	N	Y
13 **Biggert**	N	Y	Y	N	Y	N	Y
14 Foster	Y	Y	Y	Y	Y	N	Y
15 **Johnson**	N	Y	Y	Y	N	Y	N

	136	137	138	139	140	141	142
16 **Manzullo**	N	Y	Y	Y	N	Y	N
17 Hare	Y	Y	Y	Y	Y	N	Y
18 **Schock**	N	Y	Y	Y	N	Y	N
19 **Shimkus**	N	Y	Y	Y	N	Y	N
INDIANA							
1 Visclosky	Y	Y	Y	Y	Y	N	Y
2 Donnelly	Y	Y	Y	Y	Y	Y	Y
3 **Souder**	?	?	?	Y	N	Y	N
4 **Buyer**	?	?	?	?	?	?	?
5 **Burton**	N	N	Y	Y	N	Y	N
6 **Pence**	N	N	Y	Y	N	?	N
7 Carson	Y	Y	Y	Y	Y	N	Y
8 Ellsworth	Y	Y	Y	Y	N	Y	Y
9 Hill	N	Y	Y	Y	Y	Y	Y
IOWA							
1 Braley	Y	Y	Y	Y	Y	N	Y
2 Loebsack	Y	Y	Y	Y	Y	N	Y
3 Boswell	Y	Y	Y	Y	Y	N	Y
4 **Latham**	N	Y	Y	Y	N	Y	N
5 **King**	N	Y	Y	Y	N	Y	N
KANSAS							
1 **Moran**	N	N	Y	Y	N	Y	N
2 **Jenkins**	N	N	Y	Y	N	Y	N
3 Moore	Y	Y	Y	Y	Y	N	Y
4 **Tiahrt**	N	N	Y	Y	N	Y	N
KENTUCKY							
1 **Whitfield**	N	Y	Y	Y	N	Y	N
2 **Guthrie**	N	N	Y	Y	N	Y	N
3 Yarmuth	Y	Y	Y	Y	Y	N	Y
4 **Davis**	N	N	Y	Y	N	Y	N
5 **Rogers**	N	N	Y	Y	N	Y	N
6 Chandler	Y	Y	Y	Y	Y	N	Y
LOUISIANA							
1 **Scalise**	N	Y	Y	Y	N	Y	N
2 **Cao**	N	Y	Y	Y	Y	Y	Y
3 Melancon	Y	Y	Y	Y	Y	Y	Y
4 **Fleming**	N	Y	Y	Y	N	Y	N
5 **Alexander**	N	Y	Y	Y	N	Y	N
6 **Cassidy**	N	Y	Y	Y	Y	Y	Y
7 **Boustany**	N	Y	Y	Y	N	Y	N
MAINE							
1 Pingree	Y	Y	Y	Y	Y	N	Y
2 Michaud	Y	Y	Y	Y	Y	N	Y
MARYLAND							
1 Kratovil	Y	Y	Y	Y	Y	N	Y
2 Ruppersberger	Y	Y	Y	Y	Y	N	Y
3 Sarbanes	Y	Y	Y	Y	Y	N	Y
4 Edwards	Y	Y	Y	N	Y	N	Y
5 Hoyer	Y	Y	Y	Y	Y	N	Y
6 **Bartlett**	N	N	Y	Y	N	Y	N
7 Cummings	?	Y	Y	N	Y	N	Y
8 Van Hollen	Y	Y	Y	Y	Y	N	Y
MASSACHUSETTS							
1 Olver	Y	Y	?	Y	Y	N	Y
2 Neal	Y	Y	Y	Y	Y	N	Y
3 McGovern	Y	Y	Y	Y	Y	N	Y
4 Frank	Y	Y	Y	Y	Y	N	Y
5 Tsongas	Y	Y	Y	Y	Y	N	Y
6 Tierney	Y	Y	Y	Y	Y	N	Y
7 Markey	Y	Y	Y	Y	Y	N	Y
8 Capuano	Y	Y	Y	Y	Y	N	Y
9 Lynch	?	Y	Y	Y	Y	N	Y
10 Delahunt	Y	Y	Y	Y	Y	N	Y
MICHIGAN							
1 Stupak	Y	Y	Y	Y	Y	N	Y
2 **Hoekstra**	?	?	?	?	?	?	?
3 **Ehlers**	Y	Y	Y	Y	Y	Y	Y
4 **Camp**	N	N	Y	Y	N	Y	N
5 Kildee	Y	Y	Y	N	Y	N	Y
6 **Upton**	N	N	Y	Y	N	Y	N
7 Schauer	Y	Y	Y	Y	Y	Y	Y
8 **Rogers**	N	Y	Y	Y	N	Y	N
9 Peters	Y	Y	Y	Y	Y	Y	Y
10 **Miller**	N	N	Y	Y	N	Y	N
11 **McCotter**	N	N	Y	Y	N	Y	N
12 Levin	Y	Y	Y	Y	Y	N	Y
13 Kilpatrick	Y	Y	Y	N	Y	N	Y
14 Conyers	Y	Y	Y	N	Y	N	Y
15 Dingell	Y	Y	Y	Y	Y	N	Y
MINNESOTA							
1 Walz	Y	Y	Y	Y	Y	N	Y
2 **Kline**	N	Y	Y	Y	N	Y	N
3 **Paulsen**	N	Y	Y	Y	N	Y	N
4 McCollum	Y	Y	Y	Y	Y	N	Y

	136	137	138	139	140	141	142
5 Ellison	Y	Y	Y	Y	+	N	Y
6 **Bachmann**	N	Y	Y	Y	N	Y	N
7 Peterson	Y	Y	Y	Y	Y	N	Y
8 Oberstar	Y	Y	Y	Y	Y	N	Y
MISSISSIPPI							
1 Childers	N	Y	Y	Y	Y	Y	Y
2 Thompson	Y	Y	Y	N	Y	N	Y
3 **Harper**	N	N	Y	Y	N	Y	N
4 Taylor	N	Y	Y	Y	Y	Y	Y
MISSOURI							
1 Clay	?	?	?	Y	Y	N	Y
2 **Akin**	N	N	Y	Y	N	Y	N
3 Carnahan	Y	Y	Y	Y	Y	N	Y
4 Skelton	Y	N	Y	Y	Y	N	Y
5 Cleaver	Y	Y	Y	Y	Y	N	Y
6 **Graves**	N	Y	Y	Y	N	Y	N
7 **Blunt**	?	?	?	?	?	?	?
8 **Emerson**	?	?	?	Y	N	Y	N
9 **Luetkemeyer**	N	N	Y	Y	N	Y	N
MONTANA							
AL **Rehberg**	N	N	Y	Y	N	Y	N
NEBRASKA							
1 **Fortenberry**	?	?	?	?	–	+	–
2 **Terry**	N	N	Y	Y	N	Y	N
3 **Smith**	N	Y	Y	Y	N	Y	N
NEVADA							
1 Berkley	Y	Y	Y	Y	Y	N	Y
2 **Heller**	N	N	Y	Y	N	Y	N
3 Titus	Y	Y	Y	Y	Y	N	Y
NEW HAMPSHIRE							
1 Shea-Porter	Y	Y	Y	Y	Y	N	Y
2 Hodes	Y	Y	Y	Y	Y	Y	Y
NEW JERSEY							
1 Andrews	Y	Y	Y	Y	Y	N	Y
2 **LoBiondo**	N	Y	Y	Y	N	Y	N
3 Adler	Y	Y	Y	Y	Y	Y	Y
4 **Smith**	N	Y	Y	Y	N	Y	N
5 **Garrett**	N	N	Y	Y	N	Y	N
6 Pallone	Y	Y	Y	Y	Y	N	Y
7 **Lance**	N	Y	Y	Y	N	Y	N
8 Pascrell	Y	Y	Y	N	Y	N	Y
9 Rothman	Y	Y	Y	Y	Y	N	Y
10 Payne	Y	Y	Y	N	Y	N	Y
11 **Frelinghuysen**	N	N	Y	Y	N	Y	N
12 Holt	Y	Y	Y	Y	Y	N	Y
13 Sires	Y	Y	Y	Y	Y	N	Y
NEW MEXICO							
1 Heinrich	Y	Y	Y	Y	Y	N	Y
2 Teague	Y	Y	Y	Y	N	Y	Y
3 Luján	Y	Y	Y	Y	Y	N	Y
NEW YORK							
1 Bishop	Y	Y	Y	Y	Y	N	Y
2 Israel	Y	Y	Y	Y	Y	N	Y
3 **King**	N	N	Y	Y	N	Y	N
4 McCarthy	Y	Y	Y	Y	Y	N	Y
5 Ackerman	?	?	?	?	?	?	?
6 Meeks	Y	Y	Y	Y	Y	N	Y
7 Crowley	Y	Y	Y	?	?	N	Y
8 Nadler	Y	Y	Y	N	Y	N	Y
9 Weiner	?	?	Y	Y	Y	N	Y
10 Towns	Y	Y	Y	N	Y	N	Y
11 Clarke	Y	Y	Y	N	Y	N	Y
12 Velázquez	Y	Y	Y	Y	Y	N	Y
13 McMahon	Y	Y	Y	Y	Y	Y	Y
14 Maloney	Y	Y	Y	Y	Y	N	Y
15 Rangel	Y	Y	Y	Y	Y	N	Y
16 Serrano	Y	Y	Y	Y	Y	N	Y
17 Engel	Y	Y	Y	Y	?	N	Y
18 Lowey	Y	Y	Y	Y	Y	N	Y
19 Hall	Y	Y	Y	Y	Y	N	Y
20 Murphy	Y	Y	Y	Y	N	N	N
21 Tonko	Y	Y	Y	Y	Y	N	Y
22 Hinchey	Y	Y	Y	N	Y	N	Y
23 Owens	Y	N	Y	Y	N	N	N
24 Arcuri	Y	Y	Y	Y	N	Y	Y
25 Maffei	Y	Y	Y	Y	Y	N	Y
26 **Lee**	?	?	?	Y	N	Y	N
27 Higgins	Y	Y	Y	Y	Y	N	Y
28 Slaughter	Y	Y	Y	Y	Y	N	Y
29 Vacant							
NORTH CAROLINA							
1 Butterfield	Y	Y	Y	N	Y	N	Y
2 Etheridge	Y	Y	Y	Y	Y	N	Y
3 **Jones**	N	Y	Y	Y	N	Y	N
4 Price	Y	Y	Y	Y	Y	N	Y

	136	137	138	139	140	141	142
5 **Foxx**	N	N	Y	Y	N	Y	N
6 **Coble**	N	N	Y	Y	N	Y	N
7 McIntyre	Y	Y	Y	Y	Y	N	Y
8 Kissell	Y	Y	Y	Y	Y	N	Y
9 **Myrick**	N	N	Y	Y	N	Y	N
10 **McHenry**	N	N	Y	Y	N	Y	N
11 Shuler	N	Y	Y	Y	Y	Y	Y
12 Watt	Y	Y	Y	N	Y	N	Y
13 Miller	Y	Y	Y	Y	Y	N	Y
NORTH DAKOTA							
AL Pomeroy	Y	Y	Y	Y	Y	N	Y
OHIO							
1 Driehaus	Y	Y	Y	Y	Y	N	Y
2 **Schmidt**	N	N	Y	Y	N	Y	N
3 **Turner**	N	Y	Y	Y	N	Y	N
4 **Jordan**	N	N	Y	Y	N	Y	N
5 **Latta**	N	N	Y	Y	N	Y	N
6 Wilson	Y	Y	Y	Y	Y	N	Y
7 **Austria**	N	N	Y	Y	N	Y	N
8 **Boehner**	N	N	Y	Y	N	Y	N
9 Kaptur	?	Y	Y	Y	Y	N	Y
10 Kucinich	Y	Y	Y	N	Y	N	Y
11 Fudge	Y	Y	Y	N	Y	N	Y
12 **Tiberi**	N	Y	Y	Y	N	Y	N
13 Sutton	Y	Y	Y	Y	Y	N	Y
14 **LaTourette**	N	Y	Y	Y	N	Y	Y
15 Kilroy	Y	Y	Y	Y	Y	N	Y
16 Boccieri	Y	Y	Y	Y	Y	Y	Y
17 Ryan	Y	Y	Y	Y	Y	N	Y
18 Space	Y	Y	Y	Y	Y	Y	Y
OKLAHOMA							
1 **Sullivan**	N	N	Y	Y	N	Y	N
2 Boren	Y	Y	Y	Y	Y	N	Y
3 **Lucas**	N	Y	Y	Y	N	Y	N
4 **Cole**	N	Y	Y	Y	N	Y	N
5 **Fallin**	N	N	Y	Y	N	Y	N
OREGON							
1 Wu	Y	Y	Y	Y	Y	N	Y
2 **Walden**	N	N	Y	Y	N	Y	N
3 Blumenauer	Y	Y	Y	Y	Y	N	Y
4 DeFazio	Y	Y	Y	Y	Y	N	Y
5 Schrader	Y	Y	Y	Y	Y	N	?
PENNSYLVANIA							
1 Brady	Y	Y	Y	Y	Y	N	Y
2 Fattah	Y	Y	Y	Y	Y	N	Y
3 Dahlkemper	Y	Y	Y	Y	Y	Y	Y
4 Altmire	Y	Y	Y	Y	N	Y	Y
5 **Thompson**	N	N	Y	P	N	Y	N
6 **Gerlach**	N	Y	Y	Y	N	Y	N
7 Sestak	Y	Y	Y	Y	Y	N	Y
8 Murphy, P.	Y	Y	Y	Y	Y	N	N
9 **Shuster**	N	N	Y	Y	N	Y	N
10 Carney	Y	Y	Y	Y	N	Y	Y
11 Kanjorski	Y	Y	Y	Y	Y	N	Y
12 Vacant							
13 Schwartz	Y	Y	Y	Y	Y	N	Y
14 Doyle	Y	Y	Y	Y	Y	N	Y
15 **Dent**	N	Y	Y	Y	N	Y	N
16 **Pitts**	N	Y	Y	Y	N	Y	N
17 Holden	Y	Y	Y	Y	Y	N	Y
18 **Murphy, T.**	N	N	Y	Y	N	Y	N
19 **Platts**	N	N	Y	Y	N	Y	N
RHODE ISLAND							
1 Kennedy	Y	Y	Y	N	Y	N	Y
2 Langevin	Y	Y	Y	Y	Y	N	Y
SOUTH CAROLINA							
1 **Brown**	N	N	Y	Y	N	Y	N
2 **Wilson**	N	N	Y	Y	N	Y	N
3 **Barrett**	N	N	Y	Y	N	Y	N
4 **Inglis**	N	N	Y	Y	N	Y	N
5 Spratt	Y	Y	Y	Y	Y	N	Y
6 Clyburn	Y	Y	Y	N	Y	N	Y
SOUTH DAKOTA							
AL Herseth Sandlin	Y	Y	Y	Y	Y	N	Y
TENNESSEE							
1 **Roe**	N	N	Y	Y	N	Y	N
2 **Duncan**	N	N	?	Y	N	Y	N
3 **Wamp**	N	Y	Y	Y	?	?	?
4 Davis	?	?	?	?	?	?	?
5 Cooper	Y	Y	Y	Y	Y	N	Y
6 Gordon	Y	Y	Y	Y	Y	N	Y
7 **Blackburn**	N	N	Y	Y	N	Y	N
8 Tanner	Y	Y	Y	Y	Y	N	Y
9 Cohen	Y	Y	Y	Y	Y	N	Y

	136	137	138	139	140	141	142
TEXAS							
1 **Gohmert**	N	N	Y	Y	N	Y	N
2 **Poe**	N	N	Y	Y	N	Y	N
3 **Johnson, S.**	N	N	Y	Y	N	Y	N
4 **Hall**	N	N	Y	Y	N	Y	N
5 **Hensarling**	N	N	Y	Y	N	Y	N
6 **Barton**	N	N	Y	Y	N	Y	N
7 **Culberson**	N	N	Y	Y	N	Y	N
8 **Brady**	N	N	Y	Y	N	Y	N
9 Green, A.	Y	Y	Y	Y	Y	N	Y
10 **McCaul**	N	N	Y	Y	N	Y	N
11 **Conaway**	N	N	Y	Y	N	Y	N
12 **Granger**	N	Y	Y	Y	N	Y	N
13 **Thornberry**	N	N	Y	Y	N	Y	N
14 **Paul**	N	N	Y	N	N	Y	N
15 Hinojosa	Y	Y	Y	Y	Y	N	Y
16 Reyes	Y	Y	Y	Y	Y	N	Y
17 Edwards	Y	Y	Y	Y	Y	N	Y
18 Jackson Lee	Y	Y	Y	Y	Y	N	Y
19 **Neugebauer**	N	N	Y	Y	N	Y	N
20 Gonzalez	Y	Y	Y	Y	Y	N	Y
21 **Smith**	N	N	Y	Y	N	Y	N
22 **Olson**	N	N	Y	Y	N	Y	N
23 Rodriguez	Y	Y	Y	Y	Y	N	Y
24 **Marchant**	N	N	Y	Y	N	Y	N
25 Doggett	Y	Y	Y	Y	Y	N	Y
26 **Burgess**	N	N	Y	Y	N	Y	N
27 Ortiz	Y	Y	Y	Y	Y	N	Y
28 Cuellar	Y	Y	Y	Y	Y	N	Y
29 Green, G.	Y	Y	Y	Y	Y	N	Y
30 Johnson, E.	Y	Y	Y	N	Y	N	Y
31 **Carter**	?	N	Y	Y	N	Y	N
32 **Sessions**	N	N	Y	Y	N	Y	N
UTAH							
1 **Bishop**	N	Y	Y	Y	N	Y	N
2 Matheson	Y	Y	Y	Y	Y	N	Y
3 **Chaffetz**	N	Y	Y	Y	N	Y	N
VERMONT							
AL Welch	Y	Y	Y	Y	Y	N	Y
VIRGINIA							
1 **Wittman**	N	Y	Y	Y	N	Y	N
2 Nye	Y	Y	Y	Y	Y	Y	Y
3 Scott	Y	Y	Y	Y	Y	N	Y
4 **Forbes**	N	N	Y	Y	N	Y	N
5 Perriello	Y	Y	Y	Y	Y	Y	Y
6 **Goodlatte**	N	N	Y	Y	N	Y	N
7 **Cantor**	N	N	Y	Y	N	Y	N
8 Moran	Y	Y	Y	Y	Y	N	Y
9 Boucher	Y	Y	Y	Y	Y	N	Y
10 **Wolf**	N	N	Y	Y	N	Y	N
11 Connolly	Y	Y	Y	?	?	?	?
WASHINGTON							
1 Inslee	Y	Y	Y	Y	Y	N	Y
2 Larsen	Y	Y	Y	Y	Y	N	Y
3 Baird	Y	Y	Y	Y	Y	N	Y
4 **Hastings**	N	Y	Y	Y	N	Y	N
5 **McMorris Rodgers**	N	Y	Y	Y	N	Y	N
6 Dicks	Y	Y	Y	Y	Y	N	Y
7 McDermott	Y	Y	Y	N	Y	N	Y
8 **Reichert**	N	Y	Y	Y	N	Y	Y
9 Smith	Y	Y	Y	Y	Y	N	Y
WEST VIRGINIA							
1 Mollohan	Y	Y	Y	Y	Y	N	Y
2 **Capito**	N	Y	Y	Y	N	Y	N
3 Rahall	Y	Y	Y	N	Y	N	Y
WISCONSIN							
1 **Ryan**	N	Y	Y	Y	N	Y	N
2 Baldwin	Y	Y	Y	Y	Y	N	Y
3 Kind	Y	Y	Y	Y	Y	N	Y
4 Moore	Y	Y	Y	N	Y	N	Y
5 **Sensenbrenner**	N	N	Y	Y	N	Y	N
6 **Petri**	N	Y	Y	Y	N	Y	N
7 Obey	Y	Y	Y	Y	?	N	Y
8 Kagen	Y	Y	Y	Y	Y	N	Y
WYOMING							
AL **Lummis**	N	Y	Y	Y	N	Y	N
DELEGATES							
Faleomavaega (A.S.)							
Norton (D.C.)							
Bordallo (Guam)							
Sablan (N. Marianas)							
Pierluisi (P.R.)							
Christensen (V.I.)							

IN THE HOUSE | By Vote Number

143. **HR 4003. Hudson River Valley Study/Passage.** Bordallo, D-Guam, motion to suspend the rules and pass the bill that would authorize the Interior secretary to issue a study on the feasibility of designating the Hudson River Valley in New York as a national park. Motion agreed to 293-115: D 243-1; R 50-114. A two-thirds majority of those present and voting (272 in this case) is required for passage under suspension of the rules. March 19, 2010.

144. **HR 4395. Gettysburg National Military Park Expansion/ Passage.** Bordallo, D-Guam, motion to suspend the rules and pass the bill that would expand the Gettysburg National Military Park by adding land known as the Gettysburg Train Station and land located along Plum Run in Cumberland Township, Pa. Motion agreed to 372-31: D 234-4; R 138-27. A two-thirds majority of those present and voting (269 in this case) is required for passage under suspension of the rules. March 19, 2010.

145. **H Res 1133. African-American Scientific Achievement/ Adoption.** Johnson, D-Texas, motion to suspend the rules and adopt the resolution that would recognize African-Americans who have overcome significant obstacles to enhance innovation and competitiveness in science and would encourage federal investment in programs to reduce the achievement gap of African-Americans and other minorities. Motion agreed to 399-0: D 235-0; R 164-0. A two-thirds majority of those present and voting (266 in this case) is required for adoption under suspension of the rules. March 19, 2010.

146. **H Res 1027. Mariana Trench Exploration/Adoption.** Johnson, D-Texas, motion to suspend the rules and adopt the resolution that would recognize the 50th anniversary of the dive to the Challenger Deep in the Mariana Trench, the achievements of Capt. Don Walsh and Jacques Piccard, and the need to continue exploring the trench to lead to scientific discoveries. Motion agreed to 398-2: D 235-0; R 163-2. A two-thirds majority of those present and voting (267 in this case) is required for adoption under suspension of the rules. March 19, 2010.

147. **H Con Res 244. Long-Term Care Physician Day/Adoption.** Speier, D-Calif., motion to suspend the rules and adopt the concurrent resolution that would support the designation of a national day of recognition for physicians who provide long-term care. Motion agreed to 395-0: D 232-0; R 163-0. A two-thirds majority of those present and voting (264 in this case) is required for adoption under suspension of the rules. March 19, 2010.

148. **HR 1612. Land Conservation Workers Program/Restricting Funding.** Bishop, R-Utah, amendment that would retain the existing authorization level of $12 million per fiscal year for a federal land conservation program. It also would authorize the program for five years. Adopted 227-180: D 56-179; R 171-1. March 20, 2010.

149. **HR 1612. Land Conservation Workers Program/Housing in Tribal Areas.** Cole, R-Okla., amendment that would allow federal agencies to work with tribal governments to provide temporary housing to federal land conservation program workers. Adopted 402-0: D 232-0; R 170-0. March 20, 2010.

	143	144	145	146	147	148	149
ALABAMA							
1 Bonner	Y	Y	Y	Y	Y	Y	Y
2 Bright	N	N	Y	Y	Y	Y	Y
3 Rogers	N	Y	Y	Y	Y	Y	Y
4 Aderholt	N	Y	Y	Y	Y	Y	Y
5 Griffith	N	Y	Y	Y	Y	Y	Y
6 Bachus	N	Y	Y	Y	Y	Y	Y
7 Davis	Y	Y	Y	?	Y	Y	Y
ALASKA							
AL Young	N	N	Y	N	Y	Y	Y
ARIZONA							
1 Kirkpatrick	Y	Y	Y	Y	Y	N	Y
2 Franks	N	N	Y	Y	Y	Y	Y
3 Shadegg	N	N	Y	Y	Y	Y	Y
4 Pastor	Y	Y	Y	Y	Y	N	+
5 Mitchell	Y	N	Y	Y	Y	N	Y
6 Flake	N	N	Y	Y	Y	Y	Y
7 Grijalva	Y	Y	Y	Y	Y	N	Y
8 Giffords	Y	Y	Y	Y	Y	N	Y
ARKANSAS							
1 Berry	Y	Y	Y	Y	Y	N	Y
2 Snyder	Y	Y	Y	Y	Y	N	Y
3 Boozman	N	Y	Y	Y	Y	Y	Y
4 Ross	Y	Y	Y	Y	Y	N	Y
CALIFORNIA							
1 Thompson	Y	Y	Y	Y	Y	N	Y
2 Herger	N	Y	Y	Y	Y	Y	Y
3 Lungren	N	Y	Y	Y	Y	Y	Y
4 McClintock	N	Y	Y	Y	Y	Y	Y
5 Matsui	Y	Y	Y	Y	Y	N	Y
6 Woolsey	Y	Y	Y	Y	Y	N	Y
7 Miller, George	Y	Y	Y	Y	Y	N	Y
8 Pelosi							
9 Lee	Y	Y	Y	Y	Y	N	Y
10 Garamendi	Y	Y	Y	Y	Y	N	?
11 McNerney	Y	Y	Y	Y	Y	N	Y
12 Speier	Y	Y	Y	Y	Y	N	Y
13 Stark	?	?	?	?	?	?	?
14 Eshoo	Y	Y	Y	Y	Y	N	Y
15 Honda	Y	Y	Y	Y	Y	N	Y
16 Lofgren	+	+	+	+	+	−	+
17 Farr	Y	Y	Y	Y	Y	N	Y
18 Cardoza	?	Y	Y	Y	?	Y	Y
19 Radanovich	N	?	?	?	?	Y	Y
20 Costa	Y	Y	Y	Y	Y	N	Y
21 Nunes	?	N	Y	Y	Y	Y	Y
22 McCarthy	N	Y	Y	?	Y	Y	Y
23 Capps	Y	Y	Y	Y	Y	N	Y
24 Gallegly	N	Y	Y	Y	Y	Y	Y
25 McKeon	N	Y	Y	Y	Y	Y	Y
26 Dreier	N	Y	Y	Y	Y	Y	Y
27 Sherman	Y	Y	Y	Y	Y	N	Y
28 Berman	Y	Y	Y	Y	Y	N	Y
29 Schiff	Y	Y	Y	Y	Y	N	Y
30 Waxman	Y	Y	Y	Y	Y	N	Y
31 Becerra	Y	Y	Y	Y	Y	N	Y
32 Chu	Y	Y	Y	Y	Y	N	Y
33 Watson	Y	Y	Y	Y	Y	N	Y
34 Roybal-Allard	Y	Y	Y	Y	Y	N	Y
35 Waters	Y	Y	Y	Y	?	?	?
36 Harman	Y	Y	Y	Y	Y	N	Y
37 Richardson	Y	Y	Y	Y	Y	?	?
38 Napolitano	Y	Y	Y	Y	Y	N	Y
39 Sánchez, Linda	Y	Y	Y	Y	Y	N	Y
40 Royce	N	N	Y	Y	Y	Y	Y
41 Lewis	Y	N	Y	Y	Y	Y	Y
42 Miller, Gary	N	Y	Y	Y	Y	Y	Y
43 Baca	Y	Y	Y	Y	Y	N	Y
44 Calvert	N	Y	Y	Y	Y	Y	Y
45 Bono Mack	N	Y	Y	Y	Y	Y	Y
46 Rohrabacher	N	N	Y	Y	Y	Y	Y
47 Sanchez, Loretta	Y	Y	Y	Y	Y	?	?
48 Campbell	N	Y	Y	Y	Y	Y	Y
49 Issa	N	N	Y	Y	Y	Y	Y
50 Bilbray	N	Y	Y	Y	Y	Y	Y
51 Filner	Y	Y	Y	Y	Y	N	Y
52 Hunter	N	Y	Y	Y	Y	Y	Y
53 Davis	Y	Y	Y	Y	Y	N	Y

	143	144	145	146	147	148	149
COLORADO							
1 DeGette	Y	Y	Y	Y	?	N	Y
2 Polis	Y	Y	Y	Y	Y	N	Y
3 Salazar	Y	Y	Y	Y	Y	N	Y
4 Markey	Y	Y	Y	Y	Y	Y	Y
5 Lamborn	?	N	Y	Y	Y	Y	Y
6 Coffman	N	Y	Y	Y	Y	Y	Y
7 Perlmutter	Y	Y	Y	Y	Y	N	Y
CONNECTICUT							
1 Larson	Y	Y	Y	Y	Y	N	Y
2 Courtney	Y	Y	Y	Y	Y	Y	Y
3 DeLauro	Y	Y	Y	Y	Y	N	Y
4 Himes	Y	Y	Y	Y	Y	N	Y
5 Murphy	Y	Y	Y	Y	Y	Y	Y
DELAWARE							
AL Castle	Y	Y	Y	Y	Y	Y	Y
FLORIDA							
1 Miller	N	Y	Y	Y	Y	Y	Y
2 Boyd	Y	Y	Y	Y	Y	N	Y
3 Brown	Y	Y	Y	Y	Y	N	Y
4 Crenshaw	?	?	?	?	?	Y	Y
5 Brown-Waite	N	Y	Y	Y	Y	Y	Y
6 Stearns	N	N	Y	Y	Y	Y	Y
7 Mica	N	Y	Y	Y	Y	Y	Y
8 Grayson	Y	Y	Y	Y	Y	N	Y
9 Bilirakis	Y	Y	Y	Y	Y	Y	Y
10 Young	Y	Y	Y	Y	Y	Y	Y
11 Castor	Y	Y	Y	Y	Y	N	Y
12 Putnam	N	Y	Y	Y	Y	Y	Y
13 Buchanan	Y	Y	Y	Y	Y	Y	Y
14 Mack	N	Y	Y	Y	Y	Y	Y
15 Posey	N	Y	Y	Y	Y	Y	Y
16 Rooney	N	Y	Y	Y	Y	Y	Y
17 Meek	Y	Y	Y	Y	Y	N	Y
18 Ros-Lehtinen	?	?	?	?	?	Y	Y
19 Vacant							
20 Wasserman Schultz	Y	Y	Y	Y	Y	N	Y
21 Diaz-Balart, L.	Y	Y	Y	Y	Y	Y	Y
22 Klein	Y	Y	Y	Y	Y	N	Y
23 Hastings	Y	Y	Y	Y	Y	N	Y
24 Kosmas	Y	Y	Y	Y	Y	N	Y
25 Diaz-Balart, M.	Y	Y	Y	Y	Y	Y	Y
GEORGIA							
1 Kingston	N	N	Y	Y	Y	Y	Y
2 Bishop	Y	Y	Y	Y	Y	N	Y
3 Westmoreland	N	N	Y	Y	Y	Y	Y
4 Johnson	Y	Y	Y	Y	Y	N	Y
5 Lewis	Y	Y	Y	Y	Y	N	Y
6 Price	N	Y	Y	Y	Y	Y	Y
7 Linder	N	Y	Y	Y	Y	Y	Y
8 Marshall	Y	N	Y	Y	Y	N	Y
9 Deal	?	?	?	?	?	?	?
10 Broun	N	N	Y	Y	Y	Y	Y
11 Gingrey	N	N	Y	Y	Y	?	Y
12 Barrow	Y	Y	Y	Y	Y	N	Y
13 Scott	Y	Y	Y	Y	Y	N	Y
HAWAII							
1 Vacant							
2 Hirono	Y	Y	Y	Y	Y	N	Y
IDAHO							
1 Minnick	Y	Y	?	Y	Y	Y	Y
2 Simpson	N	Y	Y	Y	Y	Y	Y
ILLINOIS							
1 Rush	Y	Y	Y	Y	Y	N	Y
2 Jackson	Y	Y	Y	Y	Y	N	Y
3 Lipinski	Y	Y	Y	Y	Y	N	Y
4 Gutierrez	?	?	?	?	?	N	Y
5 Quigley	Y	?	Y	Y	Y	N	Y
6 Roskam	N	Y	Y	Y	Y	Y	Y
7 Davis	Y	Y	Y	Y	Y	N	Y
8 Bean	Y	Y	Y	Y	Y	N	Y
9 Schakowsky	Y	Y	Y	Y	Y	N	Y
10 Kirk	?	Y	Y	Y	Y	Y	Y
11 Halvorson	Y	Y	Y	Y	Y	N	Y
12 Costello	Y	Y	Y	Y	Y	N	Y
13 Biggert	Y	Y	Y	Y	Y	Y	Y
14 Foster	Y	Y	Y	Y	Y	N	Y
15 Johnson	Y	Y	Y	Y	Y	Y	Y

KEY **Republicans** Democrats

Y Voted for (yea)	X Paired against
# Paired for	− Announced against
+ Announced for	P Voted "present"
N Voted against (nay)	C Voted "present" to avoid possible conflict of interest
	? Did not vote or otherwise make a position known

	143	144	145	146	147	148	149
16 **Manzullo**	N	Y	Y	Y	Y	Y	Y
17 Hare	Y	Y	Y	Y	Y	N	Y
18 **Schock**	N	Y	Y	Y	Y	Y	Y
19 **Shimkus**	N	Y	Y	Y	Y	Y	Y
INDIANA							
1 Visclosky	Y	Y	Y	Y	Y	N	Y
2 Donnelly	Y	Y	Y	Y	Y	Y	Y
3 **Souder**	N	Y	Y	Y	Y	Y	Y
4 **Buyer**	?	?	?	?	?	?	Y
5 **Burton**	N	N	Y	Y	Y	Y	Y
6 **Pence**	N	+	+	+	+	Y	Y
7 Carson	Y	Y	Y	Y	Y	N	Y
8 Ellsworth	Y	N	Y	Y	Y	Y	Y
9 Hill	Y	Y	Y	Y	Y	Y	Y
IOWA							
1 Braley	Y	Y	Y	Y	Y	N	Y
2 Loebsack	Y	Y	Y	Y	Y	N	Y
3 Boswell	Y	Y	Y	Y	Y	N	Y
4 **Latham**	N	Y	Y	Y	Y	Y	Y
5 **King**	N	Y	Y	Y	Y	Y	Y
KANSAS							
1 **Moran**	N	Y	Y	Y	Y	Y	Y
2 **Jenkins**	Y	Y	Y	Y	Y	Y	Y
3 Moore	Y	Y	Y	Y	Y	N	Y
4 **Tiahrt**	N	N	Y	Y	Y	Y	Y
KENTUCKY							
1 **Whitfield**	Y	Y	Y	Y	Y	Y	Y
2 **Guthrie**	Y	Y	Y	Y	Y	Y	Y
3 Yarmuth	Y	Y	Y	Y	Y	N	Y
4 **Davis**	N	Y	Y	Y	Y	Y	Y
5 **Rogers**	N	Y	Y	Y	Y	Y	Y
6 Chandler	Y	Y	Y	Y	Y	N	Y
LOUISIANA							
1 **Scalise**	N	?	?	?	?	Y	Y
2 **Cao**	Y	Y	?	Y	Y	Y	Y
3 Melancon	Y	Y	Y	Y	Y	N	Y
4 **Fleming**	N	Y	Y	Y	Y	Y	Y
5 **Alexander**	Y	Y	Y	Y	Y	Y	Y
6 **Cassidy**	Y	Y	Y	Y	Y	Y	Y
7 **Boustany**	Y	Y	Y	Y	Y	Y	Y
MAINE							
1 Pingree	Y	Y	Y	Y	Y	N	Y
2 Michaud	Y	Y	Y	Y	Y	N	Y
MARYLAND							
1 Kratovil	Y	Y	Y	Y	Y	N	Y
2 Ruppersberger	Y	Y	Y	Y	Y	Y	Y
3 Sarbanes	Y	Y	Y	Y	Y	?	?
4 Edwards	Y	Y	Y	Y	Y	N	Y
5 Hoyer	Y	Y	Y	Y	Y	N	Y
6 **Bartlett**	N	Y	Y	Y	Y	Y	Y
7 Cummings	Y	Y	Y	Y	Y	N	Y
8 Van Hollen	Y	Y	Y	Y	Y	N	Y
MASSACHUSETTS							
1 Olver	Y	Y	Y	Y	Y	N	Y
2 Neal	Y	Y	Y	Y	Y	N	Y
3 McGovern	Y	Y	Y	Y	Y	N	Y
4 Frank	Y	Y	Y	Y	Y	N	Y
5 Tsongas	Y	Y	Y	Y	Y	N	Y
6 Tierney	Y	Y	Y	Y	Y	N	Y
7 Markey	Y	Y	Y	Y	Y	N	Y
8 Capuano	Y	Y	Y	Y	Y	N	Y
9 Lynch	Y	Y	Y	Y	Y	Y	Y
10 Delahunt	Y	Y	Y	Y	Y	N	Y
MICHIGAN							
1 Stupak	Y	Y	Y	Y	Y	N	Y
2 **Hoekstra**	?	?	?	?	?	?	?
3 **Ehlers**	Y	Y	Y	Y	Y	N	Y
4 **Camp**	N	Y	Y	Y	Y	Y	Y
5 Kildee	Y	Y	Y	Y	Y	N	Y
6 **Upton**	N	Y	Y	Y	Y	Y	Y
7 Schauer	Y	Y	Y	Y	Y	Y	Y
8 **Rogers**	Y	Y	Y	Y	Y	Y	Y
9 Peters	Y	Y	Y	Y	Y	Y	Y
10 **Miller**	N	Y	Y	Y	Y	Y	Y
11 **McCotter**	Y	Y	Y	Y	Y	Y	Y
12 Levin	Y	Y	Y	Y	Y	N	Y
13 Kilpatrick	Y	Y	Y	Y	Y	N	Y
14 Conyers	Y	Y	Y	Y	Y	N	Y
15 Dingell	Y	Y	Y	Y	Y	N	Y
MINNESOTA							
1 Walz	Y	Y	Y	Y	Y	Y	Y
2 **Kline**	Y	Y	Y	Y	Y	Y	Y
3 **Paulsen**	Y	Y	Y	Y	Y	Y	Y
4 McCollum	Y	Y	Y	Y	Y	N	Y

	143	144	145	146	147	148	149
5 Ellison	Y	Y	Y	Y	Y	–	+
6 **Bachmann**	N	Y	Y	Y	Y	Y	Y
7 Peterson	Y	Y	Y	Y	Y	Y	Y
8 Oberstar	Y	Y	Y	?	Y	N	Y
MISSISSIPPI							
1 Childers	Y	Y	Y	Y	Y	Y	Y
2 Thompson	Y	Y	Y	Y	Y	N	Y
3 **Harper**	Y	Y	Y	Y	Y	Y	Y
4 Taylor	Y	Y	Y	Y	Y	Y	Y
MISSOURI							
1 Clay	Y	?	?	?	?	N	Y
2 **Akin**	N	Y	Y	Y	Y	Y	Y
3 Carnahan	Y	Y	Y	Y	Y	Y	Y
4 Skelton	Y	Y	Y	Y	Y	Y	Y
5 Cleaver	Y	Y	Y	Y	Y	N	Y
6 **Graves**	N	Y	Y	Y	Y	Y	Y
7 **Blunt**	?	?	?	?	?	?	?
8 **Emerson**	N	Y	Y	Y	Y	Y	Y
9 **Luetkemeyer**	Y	Y	Y	Y	Y	Y	Y
MONTANA							
AL **Rehberg**	Y	Y	Y	Y	Y	Y	Y
NEBRASKA							
1 **Fortenberry**	+	+	+	+	+	+	+
2 **Terry**	N	Y	Y	Y	Y	Y	Y
3 **Smith**	Y	Y	Y	Y	Y	Y	Y
NEVADA							
1 Berkley	Y	Y	Y	Y	Y	N	Y
2 **Heller**	N	Y	Y	Y	Y	Y	Y
3 Titus	Y	Y	Y	Y	Y	Y	Y
NEW HAMPSHIRE							
1 Shea-Porter	Y	Y	Y	Y	Y	N	Y
2 Hodes	Y	Y	Y	Y	Y	Y	Y
NEW JERSEY							
1 Andrews	Y	Y	Y	Y	Y	Y	?
2 **LoBiondo**	Y	Y	Y	Y	Y	Y	Y
3 Adler	Y	Y	Y	Y	Y	Y	Y
4 **Smith**	Y	Y	Y	Y	Y	Y	Y
5 **Garrett**	N	Y	Y	Y	Y	Y	Y
6 Pallone	Y	Y	Y	Y	Y	N	Y
7 **Lance**	Y	Y	Y	Y	Y	Y	Y
8 Pascrell	Y	Y	Y	Y	Y	N	Y
9 Rothman	Y	Y	Y	Y	Y	N	Y
10 Payne	Y	Y	Y	Y	Y	?	?
11 **Frelinghuysen**	Y	Y	Y	Y	Y	Y	Y
12 Holt	Y	Y	Y	Y	Y	?	?
13 Sires	Y	Y	Y	Y	Y	N	Y
NEW MEXICO							
1 Heinrich	Y	Y	Y	Y	Y	N	Y
2 Teague	Y	Y	Y	Y	Y	N	Y
3 Luján	Y	Y	Y	Y	Y	N	Y
NEW YORK							
1 Bishop	Y	+	+	+	+	N	Y
2 Israel	Y	?	?	?	?	N	Y
3 **King**	Y	Y	Y	Y	Y	Y	Y
4 McCarthy	Y	Y	Y	Y	Y	N	Y
5 Ackerman	?	?	?	?	?	?	?
6 Meeks	Y	Y	Y	Y	Y	?	?
7 Crowley	Y	Y	Y	Y	Y	N	Y
8 Nadler	Y	Y	Y	Y	Y	–	–
9 Weiner	Y	Y	Y	Y	Y	Y	Y
10 Towns	Y	Y	Y	Y	Y	?	?
11 Clarke	Y	Y	Y	Y	Y	N	Y
12 Velázquez	Y	Y	Y	Y	Y	N	Y
13 McMahon	Y	Y	Y	Y	?	Y	Y
14 Maloney	Y	Y	Y	Y	Y	N	Y
15 Rangel	Y	Y	Y	Y	Y	N	Y
16 Serrano	Y	Y	Y	Y	Y	N	Y
17 Engel	Y	Y	Y	Y	Y	?	Y
18 Lowey	Y	Y	Y	Y	Y	N	Y
19 Hall	Y	Y	Y	Y	Y	N	Y
20 Murphy	Y	?	Y	Y	Y	Y	Y
21 Tonko	Y	Y	Y	Y	Y	N	Y
22 Hinchey	Y	?	?	?	?	?	?
23 Owens	Y	Y	Y	Y	Y	Y	Y
24 Arcuri	Y	Y	Y	Y	Y	Y	Y
25 Maffei	Y	Y	Y	Y	Y	Y	Y
26 **Lee**	Y	Y	Y	Y	Y	Y	Y
27 Higgins	Y	Y	Y	Y	Y	N	Y
28 Slaughter	Y	Y	Y	Y	Y	N	Y
29 Vacant							
NORTH CAROLINA							
1 Butterfield	Y	Y	Y	Y	?	N	Y
2 Etheridge	Y	Y	Y	Y	Y	N	Y
3 **Jones**	Y	Y	Y	Y	Y	Y	Y
4 Price	Y	Y	Y	Y	Y	N	Y

	143	144	145	146	147	148	149
5 **Foxx**	N	Y	Y	Y	Y	Y	Y
6 **Coble**	N	N	Y	Y	Y	Y	Y
7 McIntyre	Y	Y	Y	Y	Y	Y	Y
8 Kissell	Y	Y	Y	Y	Y	N	Y
9 **Myrick**	N	N	Y	Y	Y	Y	Y
10 **McHenry**	N	Y	Y	Y	Y	Y	Y
11 Shuler	Y	Y	Y	Y	Y	N	Y
12 Watt	Y	Y	Y	Y	Y	N	Y
13 Miller	Y	Y	Y	Y	Y	N	Y
NORTH DAKOTA							
AL Pomeroy	Y	Y	Y	Y	Y	Y	Y
OHIO							
1 Driehaus	Y	Y	Y	Y	Y	Y	Y
2 **Schmidt**	Y	Y	Y	Y	Y	Y	Y
3 **Turner**	Y	Y	Y	Y	Y	Y	Y
4 **Jordan**	N	Y	Y	Y	Y	Y	Y
5 **Latta**	N	Y	Y	Y	Y	Y	Y
6 Wilson	Y	Y	Y	Y	Y	N	Y
7 **Austria**	Y	Y	Y	Y	Y	Y	Y
8 **Boehner**	N	Y	Y	Y	?	Y	Y
9 Kaptur	Y	Y	Y	Y	Y	N	?
10 Kucinich	Y	Y	Y	Y	Y	N	Y
11 Fudge	Y	Y	Y	Y	Y	N	Y
12 **Tiberi**	Y	Y	Y	Y	Y	Y	Y
13 Sutton	Y	Y	Y	Y	Y	N	Y
14 **LaTourette**	?	Y	Y	Y	Y	?	?
15 Kilroy	Y	Y	Y	Y	Y	Y	Y
16 Boccieri	Y	Y	Y	Y	Y	Y	Y
17 Ryan	Y	Y	Y	Y	Y	N	Y
18 Space	Y	Y	?	?	?	Y	Y
OKLAHOMA							
1 **Sullivan**	N	Y	Y	Y	Y	Y	Y
2 Boren	Y	Y	Y	Y	Y	Y	Y
3 **Lucas**	Y	Y	Y	Y	Y	Y	Y
4 **Cole**	Y	Y	Y	Y	Y	Y	Y
5 **Fallin**	N	Y	Y	Y	Y	Y	Y
OREGON							
1 Wu	Y	Y	Y	Y	Y	N	Y
2 **Walden**	N	Y	Y	Y	Y	Y	Y
3 Blumenauer	Y	Y	Y	Y	Y	N	Y
4 DeFazio	Y	Y	Y	Y	Y	N	Y
5 Schrader	Y	Y	Y	Y	Y	N	Y
PENNSYLVANIA							
1 Brady	Y	Y	Y	Y	Y	N	Y
2 Fattah	Y	Y	Y	Y	Y	N	Y
3 Dahlkemper	Y	Y	Y	Y	Y	N	Y
4 Altmire	Y	Y	Y	Y	Y	Y	Y
5 **Thompson**	N	Y	Y	Y	Y	Y	Y
6 **Gerlach**	Y	Y	Y	Y	Y	Y	Y
7 Sestak	Y	Y	Y	Y	Y	N	Y
8 Murphy, P.	Y	Y	Y	Y	Y	N	Y
9 **Shuster**	N	Y	Y	Y	Y	Y	Y
10 Carney	Y	Y	Y	Y	Y	Y	Y
11 Kanjorski	Y	Y	Y	Y	Y	N	Y
12 Vacant							
13 Schwartz	Y	Y	Y	Y	Y	Y	Y
14 Doyle	Y	Y	Y	Y	Y	N	Y
15 **Dent**	Y	Y	Y	Y	Y	Y	Y
16 **Pitts**	N	Y	Y	Y	Y	Y	Y
17 Holden	Y	?	?	?	?	?	?
18 **Murphy, T.**	N	+	+	+	+	Y	Y
19 **Platts**	N	Y	Y	Y	Y	Y	Y
RHODE ISLAND							
1 Kennedy	Y	Y	Y	Y	Y	N	Y
2 Langevin	Y	Y	Y	Y	Y	N	Y
SOUTH CAROLINA							
1 **Brown**	Y	Y	Y	Y	Y	Y	Y
2 **Wilson**	N	Y	Y	Y	Y	Y	Y
3 **Barrett**	N	Y	Y	Y	Y	Y	Y
4 **Inglis**	N	Y	Y	Y	Y	Y	Y
5 Spratt	Y	Y	Y	Y	Y	N	Y
6 Clyburn	Y	Y	Y	Y	Y	N	Y
SOUTH DAKOTA							
AL Herseth Sandlin	Y	Y	Y	Y	Y	Y	Y
TENNESSEE							
1 **Roe**	N	Y	Y	Y	Y	Y	Y
2 **Duncan**	N	N	Y	Y	Y	Y	Y
3 **Wamp**	?	?	?	?	?	Y	Y
4 Davis	?	?	?	?	?	N	Y
5 Cooper	Y	Y	Y	Y	Y	N	Y
6 Gordon	Y	Y	Y	Y	Y	Y	Y
7 **Blackburn**	N	Y	Y	Y	Y	Y	Y
8 Tanner	Y	Y	Y	Y	Y	N	Y
9 Cohen	Y	Y	Y	Y	Y	N	Y

	143	144	145	146	147	148	149
TEXAS							
1 **Gohmert**	N	Y	?	Y	Y	Y	?
2 **Poe**	N	N	Y	Y	Y	Y	Y
3 **Johnson, S.**	N	Y	Y	Y	Y	Y	Y
4 **Hall**	Y	Y	Y	Y	Y	Y	Y
5 **Hensarling**	N	Y	Y	Y	Y	Y	Y
6 **Barton**	N	Y	Y	Y	Y	Y	Y
7 **Culberson**	N	Y	Y	Y	Y	Y	Y
8 **Brady**	Y	Y	Y	Y	Y	Y	Y
9 Green, A.	Y	Y	Y	Y	Y	N	Y
10 **McCaul**	N	Y	Y	Y	Y	Y	Y
11 **Conaway**	N	N	Y	Y	Y	Y	Y
12 **Granger**	N	Y	Y	Y	Y	Y	Y
13 **Thornberry**	N	Y	Y	Y	Y	Y	Y
14 **Paul**	N	N	Y	N	Y	Y	Y
15 Hinojosa	Y	Y	Y	Y	Y	N	Y
16 Reyes	Y	Y	Y	Y	Y	N	Y
17 Edwards	Y	Y	Y	Y	Y	N	Y
18 Jackson Lee	Y	Y	Y	Y	Y	N	Y
19 **Neugebauer**	N	N	Y	Y	Y	Y	Y
20 Gonzalez	Y	Y	Y	Y	Y	N	Y
21 **Smith**	N	Y	Y	Y	Y	Y	Y
22 **Olson**	N	Y	Y	Y	Y	Y	Y
23 Rodriguez	Y	Y	Y	Y	Y	N	Y
24 **Marchant**	N	Y	Y	Y	Y	Y	Y
25 Doggett	Y	Y	Y	Y	Y	N	Y
26 **Burgess**	N	Y	Y	Y	Y	Y	Y
27 Ortiz	Y	Y	Y	Y	Y	N	Y
28 Cuellar	Y	Y	Y	Y	Y	N	Y
29 Green, G.	Y	+	+	+	+	?	+
30 Johnson, E.	Y	Y	Y	Y	Y	N	Y
31 **Carter**	N	Y	Y	Y	?	Y	Y
32 **Sessions**	N	N	Y	Y	Y	Y	Y
UTAH							
1 **Bishop**	Y	?	Y	Y	Y	Y	Y
2 Matheson	Y	Y	Y	Y	Y	N	Y
3 **Chaffetz**	?	Y	Y	Y	Y	Y	Y
VERMONT							
AL Welch	Y	Y	Y	Y	Y	Y	Y
VIRGINIA							
1 **Wittman**	Y	Y	Y	Y	Y	Y	Y
2 Nye	Y	Y	Y	Y	Y	Y	Y
3 Scott	Y	Y	Y	Y	Y	N	Y
4 **Forbes**	Y	Y	Y	Y	Y	Y	Y
5 Perriello	Y	Y	Y	Y	Y	Y	Y
6 **Goodlatte**	N	Y	Y	Y	Y	Y	Y
7 **Cantor**	N	Y	Y	Y	Y	Y	?
8 Moran	Y	Y	Y	Y	Y	N	Y
9 Boucher	Y	Y	Y	Y	Y	Y	Y
10 **Wolf**	N	Y	Y	Y	Y	Y	Y
11 Connolly	?	Y	Y	Y	Y	N	Y
WASHINGTON							
1 Inslee	Y	Y	Y	Y	Y	N	Y
2 Larsen	Y	Y	Y	Y	Y	N	Y
3 Baird	Y	Y	?	?	?	N	Y
4 **Hastings**	Y	Y	Y	Y	Y	Y	Y
5 **McMorris Rodgers**	Y	Y	Y	Y	Y	Y	Y
6 Dicks	?	?	?	?	?	N	Y
7 McDermott	Y	Y	Y	Y	Y	N	Y
8 **Reichert**	Y	Y	Y	Y	Y	Y	Y
9 Smith	Y	Y	Y	Y	Y	Y	Y
WEST VIRGINIA							
1 Mollohan	Y	Y	Y	Y	Y	N	Y
2 **Capito**	Y	Y	Y	Y	Y	Y	Y
3 Rahall	Y	Y	Y	Y	Y	N	Y
WISCONSIN							
1 **Ryan**	?	Y	Y	Y	Y	Y	Y
2 Baldwin	Y	Y	Y	Y	Y	N	Y
3 Kind	Y	Y	Y	Y	Y	N	Y
4 Moore	Y	?	?	?	?	N	Y
5 **Sensenbrenner**	N	N	Y	Y	Y	Y	Y
6 **Petri**	N	N	Y	Y	Y	Y	Y
7 Obey	Y	Y	Y	Y	Y	N	Y
8 Kagen	Y	Y	Y	Y	Y	N	Y
WYOMING							
AL **Lummis**	N	Y	Y	Y	Y	Y	Y
DELEGATES							
Faleomavaega (A.S.)							
Norton (D.C.)							
Bordallo (Guam)							
Sablan (N. Marianas)							
Pierluisi (P.R.)							
Christensen (V.I.)							

IN THE HOUSE | By Vote Number

150. **HR 1612. Land Conservation Workers Program/Recommit.**
Lummis, R-Wyo., motion to recommit the bill to the Natural Resources Committee with instructions that it be immediately reported back with an amendment that would require 75 percent of federal land conservation program funding be directed to forest restoration projects. Adults participating in the program would have to undergo a criminal background check. Motion agreed to 387-21: D 215-21; R 172-0. March 20, 2010.

151. **HR 1612. Land Conservation Workers Program/Passage.**
Passage of the bill that would expand a public land conservation volunteer program for youth to all Interior Department agencies and the National Oceanic and Atmospheric Administration. As amended, it would authorize $12 million per year through fiscal 2015 for the program and require that 75 percent of funding be used for forest restoration projects. Passed 288-116: D 230-2; R 58-114. March 20, 2010.

152. **HR 4887. Military Health Plan Qualification/Passage.** Levin, D-Mich., motion to suspend the rules and pass the bill that would clarify that military health programs qualify as minimum coverage under the individual insurance mandate contained in Senate-passed health care overhaul legislation. Motion agreed to 403-0: D 232-0; R 171-0. A two-thirds majority of those present and voting (269 in this case) is required for passage under suspension of the rules. March 20, 2010.

153. **Procedural Motion/Journal.** Approval of the House Journal of Friday, March 19, 2010. Approved 211-186: D 198-30; R 13-156. March 20, 2010.

154. **H Res 1040. Tribute to Donald Harington/Adoption.** Speier, D-Calif., motion to suspend the rules and adopt the resolution that would recognize Donald Harington for his contributions to literature in the United States. Motion agreed to 399-0: D 232-0; R 167-0. A two-thirds majority of those present and voting (266 in this case) is required for adoption under suspension of the rules. March 20, 2010.

155. **HR 4840. Clarence D. Lumpkin Post Office/Passage.** Speier, D-Calif., motion to suspend the rules and pass the bill that would designate a post office in Columbus, Ohio, as the "Clarence D. Lumpkin Post Office." Motion agreed to 420-0: D 243-0; R 177-0. A two-thirds majority of those present and voting (280 in this case) is required for passage under suspension of the rules. March 21, 2010.

156. **H Res 1174. National Women's History Month/Adoption.** Speier, D-Calif., motion to suspend the rules and adopt the resolution that would support the goals and ideals of National Women's History Month in March 2010 and recognize the women and organizations in the United States that have fought for and continue to promote the teaching of women's history. Motion agreed to 420-0: D 245-0; R 175-0. A two-thirds majority of those present and voting (280 in this case) is required for adoption under suspension of the rules. March 21, 2010.

	150	151	152	153	154	155	156
ALABAMA							
1 **Bonner**	Y	N	Y	N	Y	Y	Y
2 Bright	Y	N	Y	N	Y	Y	Y
3 **Rogers**	Y	N	Y	N	Y	Y	Y
4 **Aderholt**	Y	N	Y	N	Y	Y	Y
5 **Griffith**	Y	N	Y	N	Y	Y	Y
6 **Bachus**	Y	N	Y	N	?	Y	Y
7 Davis	Y	Y	Y	?	?	?	?
ALASKA							
AL **Young**	Y	N	Y	N	Y	Y	Y
ARIZONA							
1 **Kirkpatrick**	Y	Y	Y	Y	Y	?	?
2 **Franks**	Y	N	Y	N	Y	Y	Y
3 **Shadegg**	Y	N	Y	N	Y	Y	Y
4 Pastor	Y	Y	Y	Y	Y	Y	Y
5 Mitchell	Y	Y	Y	N	Y	Y	Y
6 **Flake**	Y	N	Y	N	Y	Y	Y
7 Grijalva	N	Y	?	?	?	Y	Y
8 Giffords	Y	Y	Y	Y	Y	Y	Y
ARKANSAS							
1 Berry	Y	Y	Y	Y	Y	Y	Y
2 Snyder	Y	Y	Y	Y	Y	Y	Y
3 **Boozman**	Y	N	Y	N	Y	Y	Y
4 Ross	Y	Y	Y	Y	Y	Y	Y
CALIFORNIA							
1 Thompson	Y	Y	Y	N	Y	Y	Y
2 **Herger**	Y	N	Y	N	Y	Y	Y
3 **Lungren**	Y	Y	Y	N	Y	Y	Y
4 **McClintock**	Y	N	Y	Y	Y	Y	Y
5 Matsui	Y	Y	Y	Y	Y	Y	Y
6 Woolsey	N	Y	Y	Y	Y	Y	Y
7 Miller, George	Y	Y	Y	Y	Y	Y	Y
8 Pelosi							
9 Lee	N	Y	Y	Y	Y	Y	Y
10 Garamendi	Y	Y	Y	Y	Y	Y	Y
11 McNerney	Y	Y	Y	Y	Y	Y	Y
12 Speier	Y	Y	Y	Y	Y	Y	Y
13 Stark	?	?	?	?	?	Y	Y
14 Eshoo	Y	Y	Y	Y	Y	Y	Y
15 Honda	N	Y	Y	Y	Y	Y	Y
16 Lofgren	+	+	+	+	?	Y	Y
17 Farr	Y	Y	Y	Y	Y	Y	Y
18 Cardoza	Y	Y	Y	?	Y	Y	Y
19 **Radanovich**	Y	N	Y	N	Y	Y	Y
20 Costa	Y	Y	Y	Y	Y	Y	Y
21 **Nunes**	Y	Y	Y	N	Y	Y	Y
22 **McCarthy**	Y	Y	Y	N	Y	Y	Y
23 Capps	N	Y	Y	Y	Y	Y	Y
24 **Gallegly**	Y	N	Y	N	Y	Y	Y
25 **McKeon**	Y	Y	Y	N	Y	Y	Y
26 **Dreier**	Y	Y	Y	N	Y	Y	Y
27 Sherman	Y	Y	Y	Y	Y	Y	Y
28 Berman	Y	Y	Y	Y	Y	Y	Y
29 Schiff	Y	Y	Y	Y	Y	Y	Y
30 Waxman	N	Y	Y	Y	Y	Y	?
31 Becerra	Y	Y	Y	Y	Y	Y	Y
32 Chu	N	Y	Y	Y	Y	Y	Y
33 Watson	N	Y	Y	Y	Y	Y	Y
34 Roybal-Allard	Y	Y	Y	Y	Y	Y	Y
35 Waters	?	?	Y	N	?	Y	Y
36 Harman	N	Y	Y	Y	Y	Y	Y
37 Richardson	?	?	?	?	?	Y	Y
38 Napolitano	N	Y	Y	Y	?	Y	Y
39 Sánchez, Linda	N	Y	Y	Y	Y	Y	Y
40 **Royce**	Y	N	Y	N	Y	Y	Y
41 **Lewis**	Y	N	Y	N	Y	Y	Y
42 **Miller, Gary**	Y	N	Y	N	Y	Y	Y
43 Baca	Y	Y	Y	Y	Y	Y	Y
44 **Calvert**	Y	Y	Y	N	Y	Y	Y
45 **Bono Mack**	Y	Y	Y	N	Y	Y	Y
46 **Rohrabacher**	Y	N	Y	N	Y	Y	Y
47 Sanchez, Loretta	?	?	?	?	?	Y	Y
48 **Campbell**	Y	N	Y	N	Y	Y	Y
49 **Issa**	Y	N	Y	N	Y	Y	Y
50 **Bilbray**	Y	Y	Y	N	Y	Y	?
51 Filner	Y	Y	Y	Y	Y	Y	Y
52 **Hunter**	Y	N	Y	N	Y	Y	Y
53 Davis	Y	Y	Y	Y	Y	Y	Y

	150	151	152	153	154	155	156
COLORADO							
1 DeGette	Y	?	Y	Y	Y	Y	Y
2 Polis	Y	Y	Y	Y	Y	Y	Y
3 Salazar	Y	?	Y	Y	Y	Y	Y
4 Markey	Y	Y	Y	N	Y	Y	Y
5 **Lamborn**	Y	N	Y	N	Y	Y	Y
6 **Coffman**	Y	Y	Y	N	Y	Y	Y
7 Perlmutter	Y	Y	Y	?	Y	Y	Y
CONNECTICUT							
1 Larson	Y	Y	Y	Y	Y	Y	Y
2 Courtney	Y	Y	Y	Y	Y	Y	Y
3 DeLauro	Y	Y	Y	Y	Y	Y	Y
4 Himes	Y	Y	Y	N	Y	Y	Y
5 Murphy	Y	Y	Y	Y	Y	Y	Y
DELAWARE							
AL **Castle**	Y	Y	Y	Y	Y	Y	Y
FLORIDA							
1 **Miller**	Y	N	Y	N	Y	Y	Y
2 Boyd	Y	Y	Y	Y	Y	Y	Y
3 Brown	Y	Y	Y	Y	Y	Y	Y
4 **Crenshaw**	Y	N	Y	N	Y	Y	Y
5 **Brown-Waite**	Y	N	Y	N	Y	Y	Y
6 **Stearns**	Y	N	Y	N	Y	Y	Y
7 **Mica**	Y	N	Y	N	Y	Y	Y
8 Grayson	Y	Y	Y	Y	Y	Y	Y
9 **Bilirakis**	Y	Y	Y	N	Y	Y	Y
10 **Young**	Y	Y	Y	N	?	Y	Y
11 Castor	Y	Y	Y	Y	Y	Y	Y
12 **Putnam**	Y	Y	Y	N	Y	Y	Y
13 **Buchanan**	Y	Y	Y	N	Y	Y	Y
14 **Mack**	Y	N	Y	N	Y	Y	Y
15 **Posey**	Y	N	Y	N	Y	Y	Y
16 **Rooney**	Y	Y	Y	N	Y	Y	Y
17 Meek	Y	Y	Y	Y	Y	Y	Y
18 **Ros-Lehtinen**	Y	Y	Y	N	Y	Y	Y
19 Vacant							
20 Wasserman Schultz	Y	Y	Y	?	Y	Y	Y
21 **Diaz-Balart, L.**	Y	Y	Y	N	Y	Y	Y
22 Klein	Y	Y	Y	Y	Y	Y	Y
23 Hastings	Y	Y	Y	N	Y	Y	Y
24 Kosmas	Y	Y	Y	Y	Y	Y	Y
25 **Diaz-Balart, M.**	Y	Y	Y	N	Y	Y	Y
GEORGIA							
1 **Kingston**	Y	N	Y	N	Y	Y	Y
2 Bishop	Y	?	Y	Y	Y	Y	Y
3 **Westmoreland**	Y	N	Y	N	Y	Y	Y
4 Johnson	Y	Y	Y	Y	Y	Y	Y
5 Lewis	Y	Y	Y	Y	Y	Y	Y
6 **Price**	Y	N	Y	N	Y	Y	Y
7 **Linder**	Y	N	Y	N	Y	Y	Y
8 Marshall	Y	Y	Y	Y	Y	Y	Y
9 **Deal**	?	?	?	?	?	Y	Y
10 **Broun**	Y	N	Y	N	Y	Y	Y
11 **Gingrey**	Y	N	Y	N	Y	Y	Y
12 Barrow	Y	Y	Y	Y	Y	Y	Y
13 Scott	Y	Y	Y	Y	Y	Y	Y
HAWAII							
1 Vacant							
2 Hirono	Y	Y	Y	Y	Y	Y	Y
IDAHO							
1 Minnick	Y	Y	Y	N	Y	Y	Y
2 **Simpson**	Y	Y	?	?	?	Y	Y
ILLINOIS							
1 Rush	Y	Y	Y	Y	Y	Y	Y
2 Jackson	Y	Y	Y	Y	Y	Y	Y
3 Lipinski	Y	Y	Y	Y	Y	Y	Y
4 Gutierrez	Y	Y	Y	Y	Y	+	?
5 Quigley	Y	Y	Y	Y	Y	Y	Y
6 **Roskam**	Y	N	Y	?	?	Y	Y
7 Davis	Y	Y	Y	Y	Y	Y	Y
8 Bean	Y	Y	Y	Y	Y	Y	Y
9 Schakowsky	Y	Y	Y	Y	Y	Y	Y
10 **Kirk**	Y	Y	Y	N	Y	Y	Y
11 Halvorson	Y	Y	Y	N	Y	Y	Y
12 Costello	Y	Y	Y	Y	Y	Y	Y
13 **Biggert**	Y	Y	Y	N	Y	Y	Y
14 Foster	Y	Y	Y	Y	Y	Y	Y
15 **Johnson**	Y	Y	Y	Y	Y	Y	Y

KEY **Republicans**   Democrats

Y Voted for (yea)	X Paired against	C Voted "present" to avoid possible conflict of interest
# Paired for	– Announced against	
+ Announced for	P Voted "present"	? Did not vote or otherwise make a position known
N Voted against (nay)		

	150	151	152	153	154	155	156
16 **Manzullo**	Y	N	Y	N	Y	Y	Y
17 Hare	Y	Y	Y	?	Y	Y	Y
18 **Schock**	Y	N	Y	N	Y	Y	Y
19 **Shimkus**	Y	Y	Y	N	Y	Y	Y
INDIANA							
1 Visclosky	Y	Y	Y	Y	Y	Y	Y
2 Donnelly	Y	Y	Y	Y	Y	Y	Y
3 **Souder**	Y	N	Y	N	Y	Y	Y
4 **Buyer**	Y	N	Y	N	?	Y	Y
5 **Burton**	Y	N	Y	N	Y	Y	Y
6 **Pence**	Y	N	Y	N	Y	Y	Y
7 Carson	Y	Y	Y	Y	Y	Y	Y
8 Ellsworth	Y	Y	Y	N	Y	Y	Y
9 Hill	Y	Y	Y	Y	Y	Y	Y
IOWA							
1 Braley	Y	Y	Y	Y	Y	Y	Y
2 Loebsack	Y	Y	Y	Y	Y	Y	Y
3 Boswell	Y	Y	Y	Y	Y	Y	Y
4 **Latham**	Y	Y	Y	N	Y	Y	Y
5 **King**	Y	N	Y	N	Y	Y	Y
KANSAS							
1 **Moran**	Y	N	Y	N	Y	Y	Y
2 **Jenkins**	Y	N	Y	N	Y	Y	Y
3 Moore	Y	Y	Y	Y	Y	Y	Y
4 **Tiahrt**	Y	N	Y	N	Y	Y	Y
KENTUCKY							
1 **Whitfield**	Y	N	Y	N	Y	Y	Y
2 **Guthrie**	Y	N	Y	N	Y	Y	Y
3 Yarmuth	Y	Y	Y	Y	Y	Y	Y
4 **Davis**	Y	N	Y	N	Y	Y	Y
5 **Rogers**	Y	N	Y	N	Y	Y	Y
6 Chandler	Y	Y	Y	Y	Y	Y	Y
LOUISIANA							
1 **Scalise**	Y	N	Y	N	Y	Y	Y
2 **Cao**	Y	Y	Y	N	Y	Y	Y
3 Melancon	Y	Y	Y	N	Y	Y	Y
4 **Fleming**	Y	N	Y	N	Y	Y	Y
5 **Alexander**	Y	N	Y	N	Y	Y	Y
6 **Cassidy**	Y	N	Y	N	Y	Y	Y
7 **Boustany**	Y	N	Y	N	Y	Y	Y
MAINE							
1 Pingree	Y	Y	Y	?	Y	Y	Y
2 Michaud	Y	Y	Y	Y	Y	Y	Y
MARYLAND							
1 Kratovil	Y	Y	Y	N	Y	Y	Y
2 Ruppersberger	Y	Y	Y	Y	?	Y	Y
3 Sarbanes	?	?	?	?	?	Y	Y
4 Edwards	Y	Y	Y	Y	Y	Y	Y
5 Hoyer	Y	Y	Y	Y	Y	Y	Y
6 **Bartlett**	Y	N	Y	N	Y	Y	Y
7 Cummings	Y	Y	Y	Y	Y	Y	Y
8 Van Hollen	Y	Y	Y	Y	Y	Y	Y
MASSACHUSETTS							
1 Olver	Y	Y	Y	Y	Y	Y	Y
2 Neal	Y	Y	Y	Y	Y	Y	Y
3 McGovern	Y	Y	Y	Y	Y	Y	Y
4 Frank	Y	Y	Y	Y	Y	Y	Y
5 Tsongas	Y	Y	Y	Y	Y	Y	Y
6 Tierney	Y	Y	Y	Y	Y	Y	Y
7 Markey	Y	Y	?	Y	Y	Y	Y
8 Capuano	Y	Y	Y	Y	Y	Y	Y
9 Lynch	Y	Y	Y	Y	Y	Y	Y
10 Delahunt	Y	Y	Y	Y	Y	Y	Y
MICHIGAN							
1 Stupak	Y	Y	Y	N	Y	Y	Y
2 **Hoekstra**	?	?	?	?	?	Y	Y
3 **Ehlers**	Y	Y	Y	N	Y	Y	Y
4 **Camp**	Y	Y	Y	N	Y	Y	Y
5 Kildee	Y	Y	Y	Y	Y	Y	Y
6 **Upton**	Y	Y	Y	N	Y	Y	Y
7 Schauer	Y	Y	Y	Y	Y	Y	Y
8 **Rogers**	Y	Y	Y	N	Y	Y	Y
9 Peters	Y	N	Y	N	Y	Y	Y
10 **Miller**	Y	N	Y	N	Y	Y	Y
11 **McCotter**	Y	Y	Y	N	Y	Y	Y
12 Levin	Y	Y	Y	Y	Y	Y	Y
13 Kilpatrick	N	Y	Y	Y	Y	Y	Y
14 Conyers	N	Y	Y	Y	Y	?	Y
15 Dingell	N	Y	Y	Y	Y	Y	Y
MINNESOTA							
1 Walz	Y	Y	Y	Y	Y	Y	Y
2 **Kline**	Y	N	Y	N	Y	Y	Y
3 **Paulsen**	Y	Y	Y	Y	Y	Y	Y
4 McCollum	Y	Y	Y	Y	Y	Y	Y

	150	151	152	153	154	155	156
5 Ellison	–	+	+	+	+	Y	Y
6 **Bachmann**	Y	N	Y	Y	Y	Y	Y
7 Peterson	Y	Y	Y	N	Y	Y	Y
8 Oberstar	Y	Y	Y	Y	Y	Y	Y
MISSISSIPPI							
1 Childers	Y	Y	Y	N	Y	Y	Y
2 Thompson	Y	Y	Y	Y	Y	Y	Y
3 **Harper**	Y	N	Y	Y	Y	Y	Y
4 Taylor	Y	Y	Y	Y	Y	Y	Y
MISSOURI							
1 Clay	Y	Y	?	?	?	Y	Y
2 **Akin**	Y	N	Y	N	Y	Y	Y
3 Carnahan	Y	Y	Y	Y	Y	Y	Y
4 Skelton	Y	Y	Y	Y	Y	Y	Y
5 Cleaver	Y	Y	Y	Y	Y	Y	Y
6 **Graves**	Y	N	Y	Y	Y	Y	Y
7 **Blunt**	?	?	?	?	?	Y	Y
8 **Emerson**	Y	N	Y	N	Y	Y	Y
9 **Luetkemeyer**	Y	N	Y	Y	Y	Y	Y
MONTANA							
AL **Rehberg**	Y	Y	Y	N	Y	Y	Y
NEBRASKA							
1 **Fortenberry**	+	+	+	–	+	Y	Y
2 **Terry**	Y	Y	Y	N	Y	Y	Y
3 **Smith**	Y	N	Y	N	Y	Y	Y
NEVADA							
1 Berkley	Y	Y	Y	Y	Y	Y	Y
2 **Heller**	Y	Y	Y	Y	Y	Y	Y
3 Titus	Y	Y	Y	Y	Y	Y	Y
NEW HAMPSHIRE							
1 Shea-Porter	Y	Y	Y	Y	Y	Y	Y
2 Hodes	Y	Y	Y	Y	Y	Y	Y
NEW JERSEY							
1 Andrews	Y	Y	Y	Y	Y	Y	Y
2 **LoBiondo**	Y	Y	Y	N	Y	Y	Y
3 Adler	Y	Y	Y	N	Y	Y	Y
4 **Smith**	Y	Y	Y	N	Y	Y	Y
5 **Garrett**	Y	N	Y	N	Y	Y	Y
6 Pallone	Y	Y	Y	Y	Y	Y	Y
7 **Lance**	Y	Y	Y	N	Y	Y	Y
8 Pascrell	N	Y	Y	Y	Y	Y	Y
9 Rothman	Y	Y	Y	Y	Y	Y	Y
10 Payne	?	?	?	?	?	Y	Y
11 **Frelinghuysen**	Y	Y	Y	N	Y	Y	Y
12 Holt	?	?	?	?	?	Y	Y
13 Sires	Y	Y	Y	Y	Y	?	?
NEW MEXICO							
1 Heinrich	Y	Y	Y	Y	Y	Y	Y
2 Teague	Y	Y	Y	Y	Y	Y	Y
3 Luján	Y	Y	Y	Y	Y	Y	Y
NEW YORK							
1 Bishop	Y	Y	Y	Y	Y	Y	Y
2 Israel	Y	Y	Y	Y	Y	Y	Y
3 **King**	Y	Y	Y	N	Y	Y	Y
4 McCarthy	Y	Y	Y	Y	Y	Y	Y
5 Ackerman	?	?	Y	Y	Y	Y	Y
6 Meeks	?	?	?	?	?	Y	Y
7 Crowley	Y	Y	Y	Y	Y	Y	Y
8 Nadler	?	+	+	+	+	Y	Y
9 Weiner	Y	Y	Y	Y	Y	Y	Y
10 Towns	?	?	?	?	?	?	?
11 Clarke	Y	?	Y	Y	Y	Y	Y
12 Velázquez	Y	Y	Y	Y	Y	Y	Y
13 McMahon	Y	Y	Y	Y	Y	Y	Y
14 Maloney	Y	Y	Y	Y	Y	Y	Y
15 Rangel	Y	Y	Y	Y	Y	?	Y
16 Serrano	Y	Y	Y	Y	Y	Y	Y
17 Engel	Y	Y	Y	Y	Y	Y	Y
18 Lowey	Y	Y	Y	Y	Y	Y	Y
19 Hall	Y	Y	Y	Y	Y	Y	Y
20 Murphy	Y	Y	Y	N	Y	Y	Y
21 Tonko	Y	Y	Y	Y	Y	Y	Y
22 Hinchey	?	?	?	?	?	?	?
23 Owens	Y	Y	Y	Y	Y	Y	Y
24 Arcuri	Y	Y	Y	N	Y	Y	Y
25 Maffei	Y	Y	Y	Y	Y	Y	Y
26 **Lee**	Y	N	Y	N	Y	?	Y
27 Higgins	Y	Y	Y	Y	Y	Y	Y
28 Slaughter	Y	Y	Y	Y	Y	Y	Y
29 Vacant							
NORTH CAROLINA							
1 Butterfield	Y	Y	Y	Y	Y	Y	Y
2 Etheridge	Y	Y	Y	N	Y	Y	Y
3 **Jones**	Y	Y	Y	Y	Y	Y	Y
4 Price	Y	Y	Y	Y	Y	Y	Y

	150	151	152	153	154	155	156
5 **Foxx**	Y	N	Y	N	Y	Y	Y
6 **Coble**	Y	N	Y	N	Y	Y	Y
7 McIntyre	Y	Y	Y	Y	Y	Y	Y
8 Kissell	Y	Y	Y	Y	Y	Y	Y
9 **Myrick**	Y	N	Y	N	Y	Y	Y
10 **McHenry**	Y	N	Y	N	Y	Y	Y
11 Shuler	Y	Y	Y	?	Y	Y	Y
12 Watt	N	Y	Y	Y	Y	Y	Y
13 Miller	Y	Y	Y	Y	Y	Y	Y
NORTH DAKOTA							
AL Pomeroy	Y	Y	Y	Y	Y	Y	Y
OHIO							
1 Driehaus	Y	Y	Y	Y	Y	Y	Y
2 **Schmidt**	Y	N	Y	N	Y	Y	Y
3 **Turner**	Y	Y	Y	N	Y	Y	Y
4 **Jordan**	Y	N	Y	N	Y	Y	Y
5 **Latta**	Y	N	Y	N	Y	Y	Y
6 Wilson	Y	Y	Y	Y	Y	Y	Y
7 **Austria**	Y	N	Y	N	Y	Y	Y
8 **Boehner**	Y	N	Y	N	Y	Y	Y
9 Kaptur	Y	Y	Y	Y	Y	Y	Y
10 Kucinich	Y	Y	Y	Y	Y	Y	Y
11 Fudge	Y	Y	Y	Y	Y	Y	Y
12 **Tiberi**	Y	Y	Y	N	Y	Y	Y
13 Sutton	Y	Y	Y	Y	Y	Y	Y
14 **LaTourette**	?	?	?	?	?	Y	?
15 Kilroy	Y	?	Y	Y	Y	Y	Y
16 Boccieri	Y	Y	Y	?	Y	Y	Y
17 Ryan	Y	Y	Y	Y	Y	Y	Y
18 Space	Y	Y	Y	Y	Y	Y	Y
OKLAHOMA							
1 **Sullivan**	Y	N	Y	N	Y	Y	Y
2 Boren	Y	Y	Y	N	Y	Y	Y
3 **Lucas**	Y	N	Y	N	Y	Y	Y
4 **Cole**	Y	Y	Y	N	Y	Y	Y
5 **Fallin**	Y	N	Y	N	Y	Y	Y
OREGON							
1 Wu	Y	Y	Y	Y	Y	Y	Y
2 **Walden**	Y	Y	Y	N	Y	Y	Y
3 Blumenauer	N	Y	?	Y	Y	Y	Y
4 DeFazio	Y	Y	Y	Y	Y	Y	Y
5 Schrader	Y	Y	Y	Y	Y	Y	Y
PENNSYLVANIA							
1 Brady	Y	Y	Y	Y	Y	Y	Y
2 Fattah	Y	Y	Y	Y	Y	Y	Y
3 Dahlkemper	Y	Y	Y	N	Y	Y	Y
4 Altmire	Y	Y	Y	N	Y	Y	Y
5 **Thompson**	Y	Y	Y	N	Y	Y	Y
6 **Gerlach**	Y	Y	Y	N	Y	Y	Y
7 Sestak	Y	Y	Y	Y	Y	Y	Y
8 Murphy, P.	Y	Y	Y	Y	Y	Y	Y
9 **Shuster**	Y	N	Y	N	Y	Y	Y
10 Carney	Y	Y	Y	N	Y	Y	Y
11 Kanjorski	Y	Y	Y	Y	Y	Y	Y
12 Vacant							
13 Schwartz	Y	Y	Y	Y	Y	Y	Y
14 Doyle	Y	Y	Y	Y	Y	Y	Y
15 **Dent**	Y	Y	Y	Y	Y	Y	Y
16 **Pitts**	Y	N	Y	N	Y	Y	Y
17 Holden	?	?	?	?	?	Y	Y
18 **Murphy, T.**	Y	N	Y	N	Y	Y	Y
19 **Platts**	Y	Y	Y	N	Y	Y	Y
RHODE ISLAND							
1 Kennedy	Y	Y	Y	Y	Y	Y	Y
2 Langevin	Y	Y	Y	Y	Y	?	Y
SOUTH CAROLINA							
1 **Brown**	Y	N	Y	N	Y	Y	Y
2 **Wilson**	Y	N	Y	N	Y	Y	Y
3 **Barrett**	Y	N	Y	N	Y	Y	Y
4 **Inglis**	Y	N	Y	N	Y	Y	Y
5 Spratt	Y	Y	Y	Y	Y	Y	Y
6 Clyburn	Y	Y	Y	Y	Y	Y	Y
SOUTH DAKOTA							
AL Herseth Sandlin	Y	Y	Y	N	Y	Y	Y
TENNESSEE							
1 **Roe**	Y	N	Y	N	Y	Y	Y
2 **Duncan**	Y	N	Y	N	Y	Y	Y
3 **Wamp**	Y	N	Y	N	Y	Y	Y
4 Davis	Y	Y	Y	Y	Y	Y	Y
5 Cooper	Y	Y	Y	Y	Y	Y	Y
6 Gordon	Y	Y	Y	Y	Y	Y	Y
7 **Blackburn**	Y	N	Y	N	Y	Y	Y
8 Tanner	Y	Y	Y	Y	Y	Y	Y
9 Cohen	Y	Y	Y	Y	Y	Y	Y

	150	151	152	153	154	155	156
TEXAS							
1 **Gohmert**	?	?	Y	?	?	Y	Y
2 **Poe**	Y	N	Y	N	Y	Y	Y
3 **Johnson, S.**	Y	N	Y	N	Y	Y	Y
4 **Hall**	Y	N	?	N	Y	Y	Y
5 **Hensarling**	Y	N	Y	N	Y	Y	Y
6 **Barton**	Y	N	Y	N	Y	Y	Y
7 **Culberson**	Y	N	Y	N	Y	Y	Y
8 **Brady**	Y	Y	Y	N	Y	Y	Y
9 Green, A.	Y	Y	Y	Y	Y	Y	Y
10 **McCaul**	Y	N	Y	N	Y	Y	Y
11 **Conaway**	Y	N	Y	N	Y	Y	Y
12 **Granger**	Y	N	Y	N	Y	Y	Y
13 **Thornberry**	Y	N	Y	N	Y	Y	Y
14 **Paul**	Y	N	Y	N	Y	Y	Y
15 Hinojosa	Y	Y	Y	Y	Y	Y	Y
16 Reyes	N	Y	Y	Y	Y	Y	Y
17 Edwards	Y	Y	Y	Y	Y	Y	Y
18 Jackson Lee	Y	Y	Y	Y	Y	Y	Y
19 **Neugebauer**	Y	N	Y	N	Y	Y	Y
20 Gonzalez	Y	Y	Y	Y	Y	Y	Y
21 **Smith**	Y	N	Y	N	Y	Y	?
22 **Olson**	Y	N	Y	N	Y	Y	Y
23 Rodriguez	Y	Y	Y	Y	Y	Y	Y
24 **Marchant**	Y	N	Y	N	Y	Y	Y
25 Doggett	Y	Y	Y	Y	Y	Y	Y
26 **Burgess**	Y	Y	Y	N	Y	Y	Y
27 Ortiz	Y	Y	Y	Y	Y	Y	Y
28 Cuellar	Y	Y	Y	N	Y	Y	Y
29 Green, G.	+	+	+	+	+	Y	Y
30 Johnson, E.	N	Y	Y	Y	Y	Y	Y
31 **Carter**	Y	N	Y	N	Y	Y	Y
32 **Sessions**	Y	N	Y	N	Y	Y	Y
UTAH							
1 **Bishop**	Y	Y	Y	N	Y	Y	Y
2 Matheson	Y	Y	?	Y	Y	Y	Y
3 **Chaffetz**	Y	Y	Y	Y	Y	Y	Y
VERMONT							
AL Welch	Y	Y	Y	Y	Y	Y	Y
VIRGINIA							
1 **Wittman**	Y	Y	Y	N	Y	Y	Y
2 Nye	Y	Y	Y	Y	Y	Y	Y
3 Scott	N	Y	Y	Y	Y	Y	Y
4 **Forbes**	Y	N	Y	N	Y	Y	Y
5 Perriello	Y	Y	Y	Y	Y	Y	Y
6 **Goodlatte**	Y	N	Y	Y	Y	Y	Y
7 **Cantor**	Y	Y	Y	?	Y	Y	Y
8 Moran	Y	Y	Y	Y	Y	Y	Y
9 Boucher	Y	Y	Y	Y	Y	Y	Y
10 **Wolf**	Y	Y	Y	N	Y	Y	Y
11 Connolly	Y	Y	Y	N	Y	Y	Y
WASHINGTON							
1 Inslee	Y	Y	Y	Y	Y	Y	Y
2 Larsen	Y	Y	Y	Y	Y	Y	Y
3 Baird	Y	Y	Y	Y	Y	Y	Y
4 **Hastings**	Y	Y	Y	N	Y	Y	Y
5 **McMorris Rodgers**	Y	N	Y	N	Y	Y	Y
6 Dicks	Y	Y	Y	Y	Y	Y	Y
7 McDermott	Y	Y	Y	Y	Y	Y	Y
8 **Reichert**	Y	Y	Y	N	Y	Y	Y
9 Smith	Y	Y	Y	Y	Y	Y	Y
WEST VIRGINIA							
1 Mollohan	Y	Y	?	Y	Y	Y	Y
2 **Capito**	Y	Y	Y	N	Y	Y	Y
3 Rahall	Y	Y	Y	Y	Y	Y	Y
WISCONSIN							
1 **Ryan**	Y	N	Y	N	Y	Y	Y
2 Baldwin	Y	Y	Y	Y	Y	Y	Y
3 Kind	Y	Y	Y	Y	Y	Y	Y
4 Moore	N	Y	Y	Y	Y	Y	Y
5 **Sensenbrenner**	Y	N	Y	N	Y	Y	Y
6 **Petri**	Y	N	Y	N	Y	Y	Y
7 Obey	Y	Y	Y	Y	Y	Y	Y
8 Kagen	Y	Y	Y	Y	Y	Y	Y
WYOMING							
AL **Lummis**	Y	Y	Y	N	Y	Y	Y
DELEGATES							
Faleomavaega (A.S.)							
Norton (D.C.)							
Bordallo (Guam)							
Sablan (N. Marianas)							
Pierluisi (P.R.)							
Christensen (V.I.)							

IN THE HOUSE | By Vote Number

157. **Procedural Motion/Journal.** Approval of the House Journal of Saturday, March 20, 2010. Approved 229-189: D 215-27; R 14-162. March 21, 2010.

158. **H Res 1075. National Guard Agri-Business Development Teams/Adoption.** Skelton, D-Mo., motion to suspend the rules and adopt the resolution that would commend the members of the Agri-Business Development Teams of the National Guard for their efforts, together with personnel of the Agriculture Department and the U.S. Agency for International Development, to modernize agriculture practices and increase food production in war-torn countries. Motion agreed to 418-3: D 245-0; R 173-3. A two-thirds majority of those present and voting (281 in this case) is required for adoption under suspension of the rules. March 21, 2010.

159. **HR 3590, HR 4872. Health Care Overhaul/Question of Consideration.** Question of whether the House should consider the rule (H Res 1203) to provide for House floor consideration of Senate amendments to a health care overhaul bill (HR 3590) and of a reconciliation bill (HR 4872) that would modify the health care overhaul legislation. Agreed to consider 228-195: D 228-19; R 0-176. (Ryan, R-Wis., had raised a point of order that the rule would waive points of order against unfunded mandates in violation of the Budget Act.) March 21, 2010.

160. **HR 3590, HR 4872. Health Care Overhaul/Question of Consideration.** Question of whether the House should consider the rule (H Res 1203) to provide for House floor consideration of Senate amendments to a health care overhaul bill (HR 3590) and of a reconciliation bill (HR 4872) that would modify the health care overhaul legislation. Agreed to consider 230-200: D 230-22; R 0-178. (Issa, R-Calif., had raised a point of order that the rule would waive points of order against Clause 9 of Rule 21, which refers to the earmark rules of the House.) March 21, 2010.

161. **H Res 900. Cold War Veterans Recognition Day/Adoption.** Bordallo, D-Guam, motion to suspend the rules and adopt the resolution that would honor the sacrifices and contributions made by members of the military during the Cold War. Motion agreed to 429-0: D 252-0; R 177-0. A two-thirds majority of those present and voting (286 in this case) is required for adoption under suspension of the rules. March 21, 2010.

162. **HR 3590, HR 4872. Health Care Overhaul/Previous Question.** Slaughter, D-N.Y., motion to order the previous question (thus ending debate and possibility of amendment) on adoption of the rule (H Res 1203) to provide for House floor consideration of Senate amendments to a health care overhaul bill (HR 3590) and of a reconciliation bill (HR 4872) that would modify the health care overhaul legislation. The rule would provide for the automatic adoption of a substitute amendment to HR 4872, as modified by a manager's amendment, upon adoption of the rule. The substitute would increase federal subsidies to help low- and moderate-income families purchase coverage through new health insurance exchanges, phase out the coverage gap for Medicare prescription drug enrollees, adjust the federal matching funds for Medicaid, make the federal government the sole originator of federal student loans, and eliminate special Medicaid funding for Nebraska. Motion agreed to 228-202: D 228-24; R 0-178. March 21, 2010.

	157	158	159	160	161	162
ALABAMA						
1 **Bonner**	N	Y	N	N	Y	N
2 **Bright**	N	Y	N	N	Y	N
3 **Rogers**	N	Y	?	N	Y	N
4 **Aderholt**	N	Y	N	N	Y	N
5 **Griffith**	N	Y	N	N	Y	N
6 **Bachus**	N	Y	N	N	Y	N
7 Davis	?	?	?	N	Y	N
ALASKA						
AL **Young**	N	N	N	N	Y	N
ARIZONA						
1 Kirkpatrick	?	?	Y	Y	Y	Y
2 **Franks**	N	Y	N	N	Y	N
3 **Shadegg**	N	Y	N	N	Y	N
4 Pastor	Y	Y	Y	Y	Y	Y
5 Mitchell	N	Y	Y	Y	Y	Y
6 **Flake**	N	Y	N	N	Y	N
7 Grijalva	Y	Y	Y	Y	Y	Y
8 Giffords	Y	Y	Y	Y	Y	Y
ARKANSAS						
1 Berry	Y	Y	Y	Y	Y	Y
2 Snyder	Y	Y	Y	Y	Y	Y
3 **Boozman**	N	Y	N	N	Y	N
4 Ross	Y	Y	N	N	Y	N
CALIFORNIA						
1 Thompson	N	Y	Y	Y	Y	Y
2 **Herger**	N	Y	N	N	Y	N
3 **Lungren**	N	Y	N	N	Y	N
4 **McClintock**	Y	Y	N	N	Y	N
5 Matsui	Y	Y	Y	Y	Y	Y
6 Woolsey	Y	Y	Y	Y	Y	Y
7 Miller, George	Y	Y	Y	Y	Y	Y
8 Pelosi						
9 Lee	Y	Y	Y	Y	Y	Y
10 Garamendi	Y	Y	Y	Y	Y	Y
11 McNerney	Y	Y	Y	Y	Y	Y
12 Speier	Y	?	Y	Y	Y	Y
13 Stark	Y	Y	Y	Y	Y	Y
14 Eshoo	Y	Y	Y	Y	Y	Y
15 Honda	Y	Y	Y	Y	Y	Y
16 Lofgren	Y	Y	Y	Y	Y	Y
17 Farr	Y	Y	Y	Y	Y	Y
18 Cardoza	Y	Y	Y	Y	Y	Y
19 **Radanovich**	N	Y	N	N	Y	N
20 Costa	N	Y	Y	Y	Y	Y
21 **Nunes**	N	Y	N	N	Y	N
22 **McCarthy**	N	Y	N	N	Y	N
23 Capps	Y	Y	Y	Y	Y	Y
24 **Gallegly**	N	Y	N	N	Y	N
25 **McKeon**	N	Y	N	N	Y	N
26 **Dreier**	N	Y	N	N	Y	N
27 Sherman	Y	Y	Y	Y	Y	Y
28 Berman	Y	Y	Y	Y	Y	Y
29 Schiff	Y	Y	Y	Y	Y	Y
30 Waxman	Y	Y	Y	Y	Y	Y
31 Becerra	Y	Y	Y	Y	Y	Y
32 Chu	Y	Y	Y	Y	Y	Y
33 Watson	N	Y	Y	Y	Y	Y
34 Roybal-Allard	Y	Y	Y	Y	Y	Y
35 Waters	Y	Y	Y	Y	Y	Y
36 Harman	Y	Y	Y	Y	Y	Y
37 Richardson	Y	Y	Y	Y	Y	Y
38 Napolitano	Y	Y	Y	Y	Y	Y
39 Sánchez, Linda	Y	Y	Y	Y	Y	Y
40 **Royce**	N	Y	N	N	Y	N
41 **Lewis**	N	Y	N	N	Y	N
42 **Miller, Gary**	N	Y	N	N	Y	N
43 Baca	Y	Y	Y	Y	Y	Y
44 **Calvert**	N	Y	N	N	Y	N
45 **Bono Mack**	N	Y	N	N	Y	N
46 **Rohrabacher**	N	Y	N	N	Y	N
47 Sanchez, Loretta	Y	Y	Y	Y	Y	Y
48 **Campbell**	N	Y	N	N	Y	N
49 **Issa**	N	Y	N	N	Y	N
50 **Bilbray**	Y	Y	Y	Y	Y	Y
51 Filner	Y	Y	Y	Y	Y	Y
52 **Hunter**	Y	Y	N	N	Y	N
53 Davis	Y	Y	Y	Y	Y	Y

	157	158	159	160	161	162
COLORADO						
1 DeGette	Y	Y	Y	Y	Y	Y
2 Polis	Y	Y	Y	Y	Y	Y
3 Salazar	Y	Y	Y	Y	Y	Y
4 Markey	N	Y	Y	Y	Y	Y
5 **Lamborn**	N	Y	N	N	Y	N
6 **Coffman**	N	Y	N	N	Y	N
7 Perlmutter	Y	Y	Y	Y	Y	Y
CONNECTICUT						
1 Larson	Y	Y	Y	Y	Y	Y
2 Courtney	Y	Y	Y	Y	Y	Y
3 DeLauro	Y	Y	Y	Y	Y	Y
4 Himes	N	Y	Y	Y	Y	Y
5 Murphy	Y	Y	Y	Y	Y	Y
DELAWARE						
AL **Castle**	Y	Y	N	N	Y	N
FLORIDA						
1 **Miller**	N	Y	N	N	Y	N
2 Boyd	Y	Y	Y	Y	Y	Y
3 Brown	Y	Y	Y	Y	Y	Y
4 **Crenshaw**	N	Y	N	N	Y	N
5 **Brown-Waite**	N	Y	N	N	Y	N
6 **Stearns**	N	Y	N	N	Y	N
7 **Mica**	N	Y	N	N	Y	N
8 Grayson	Y	Y	Y	Y	Y	Y
9 **Bilirakis**	N	Y	N	N	Y	N
10 **Young**	N	Y	N	N	Y	N
11 Castor	Y	Y	Y	Y	Y	Y
12 **Putnam**	N	Y	N	N	Y	N
13 **Buchanan**	N	Y	N	N	Y	N
14 **Mack**	N	Y	N	N	Y	N
15 **Posey**	N	Y	N	N	Y	N
16 **Rooney**	N	Y	N	N	Y	N
17 Meek	Y	Y	Y	Y	Y	Y
18 **Ros-Lehtinen**	N	Y	N	N	Y	N
19 Vacant						
20 Wasserman Schultz	Y	Y	Y	Y	Y	Y
21 **Diaz-Balart, L.**	N	Y	N	N	Y	N
22 Klein	Y	Y	+	Y	Y	Y
23 Hastings	Y	Y	Y	Y	Y	Y
24 Kosmas	Y	Y	Y	Y	Y	Y
25 **Diaz-Balart, M.**	N	Y	N	N	Y	N
GEORGIA						
1 **Kingston**	N	Y	N	N	Y	N
2 Bishop	Y	Y	Y	Y	Y	Y
3 **Westmoreland**	N	Y	N	N	Y	N
4 Johnson	Y	Y	Y	Y	Y	Y
5 Lewis	Y	Y	Y	Y	Y	Y
6 **Price**	N	Y	N	N	Y	N
7 **Linder**	N	Y	N	N	Y	N
8 Marshall	Y	Y	N	N	Y	N
9 **Deal**	N	Y	N	N	Y	N
10 **Broun**	N	N	N	N	Y	N
11 **Gingrey**	N	Y	N	N	Y	N
12 Barrow	Y	Y	N	N	Y	N
13 Scott	Y	Y	Y	Y	Y	Y
HAWAII						
1 Vacant						
2 Hirono	Y	Y	Y	Y	Y	Y
IDAHO						
1 Minnick	N	Y	N	N	Y	N
2 **Simpson**	N	Y	N	N	Y	N
ILLINOIS						
1 Rush	Y	Y	Y	Y	Y	Y
2 Jackson	Y	Y	Y	Y	Y	Y
3 Lipinski	Y	Y	Y	N	Y	Y
4 Gutierrez	+	+	+	Y	Y	Y
5 Quigley	Y	Y	Y	Y	Y	Y
6 **Roskam**	N	Y	N	N	Y	N
7 Davis	Y	Y	Y	Y	Y	Y
8 Bean	Y	Y	Y	Y	Y	Y
9 Schakowsky	Y	Y	?	Y	Y	Y
10 **Kirk**	N	Y	N	N	Y	N
11 Halvorson	Y	Y	Y	Y	Y	Y
12 Costello	Y	Y	Y	Y	Y	Y
13 **Biggert**	N	Y	N	N	Y	N
14 Foster	Y	Y	Y	Y	Y	Y
15 **Johnson**	Y	Y	N	N	Y	N

KEY   **Republicans**   Democrats

Y Voted for (yea)	X Paired against	C Voted "present" to avoid possible conflict of interest
# Paired for	– Announced against	
+ Announced for	P Voted "present"	? Did not vote or otherwise make a position known
N Voted against (nay)		

	157	158	159	160	161	162
16 **Manzullo**	N	Y	N	N	Y	N
17 Hare	Y	Y	Y	Y	Y	Y
18 **Schock**	N	Y	N	N	Y	N
19 **Shimkus**	N	Y	N	N	Y	N
INDIANA						
1 Visclosky	Y	Y	Y	Y	Y	Y
2 Donnelly	Y	Y	Y	Y	Y	Y
3 **Souder**	N	Y	N	N	Y	N
4 **Buyer**	?	Y	N	N	Y	N
5 **Burton**	N	Y	N	N	Y	N
6 **Pence**	N	Y	N	N	Y	N
7 Carson	Y	Y	Y	Y	Y	Y
8 Ellsworth	N	Y	Y	Y	Y	Y
9 Hill	Y	Y	Y	Y	Y	Y
IOWA						
1 Braley	Y	Y	Y	Y	Y	Y
2 Loebsack	Y	Y	Y	Y	Y	Y
3 Boswell	Y	Y	Y	Y	Y	Y
4 **Latham**	N	Y	N	N	Y	N
5 **King**	N	Y	N	N	Y	N
KANSAS						
1 **Moran**	N	Y	N	N	Y	N
2 **Jenkins**	N	Y	N	N	Y	N
3 Moore	Y	Y	Y	Y	Y	Y
4 **Tiahrt**	N	Y	N	N	Y	N
KENTUCKY						
1 **Whitfield**	N	Y	N	N	Y	N
2 **Guthrie**	N	Y	N	N	Y	N
3 Yarmuth	Y	Y	Y	Y	Y	Y
4 **Davis**	N	Y	N	N	Y	N
5 **Rogers**	N	Y	N	N	Y	N
6 Chandler	Y	Y	Y	Y	Y	N
LOUISIANA						
1 **Scalise**	N	Y	N	N	Y	N
2 **Cao**	N	Y	N	N	?	N
3 Melancon	N	Y	N	N	Y	N
4 **Fleming**	N	Y	N	N	Y	N
5 **Alexander**	N	Y	N	N	Y	N
6 **Cassidy**	N	Y	N	N	Y	N
7 **Boustany**	N	?	N	N	Y	N
MAINE						
1 Pingree	Y	Y	Y	Y	Y	Y
2 Michaud	Y	Y	Y	Y	Y	Y
MARYLAND						
1 Kratovil	Y	Y	N	N	Y	N
2 Ruppersberger	Y	Y	Y	Y	Y	Y
3 Sarbanes	Y	Y	Y	Y	Y	Y
4 Edwards	Y	Y	Y	Y	Y	Y
5 Hoyer	Y	Y	Y	Y	Y	Y
6 **Bartlett**	N	Y	N	N	Y	N
7 Cummings	Y	Y	Y	Y	Y	Y
8 Van Hollen	Y	Y	Y	Y	Y	Y
MASSACHUSETTS						
1 Olver	Y	Y	Y	Y	Y	Y
2 Neal	Y	Y	Y	Y	Y	Y
3 McGovern	Y	Y	Y	Y	Y	Y
4 Frank	Y	Y	Y	Y	Y	Y
5 Tsongas	Y	Y	Y	Y	Y	Y
6 Tierney	Y	Y	Y	Y	Y	Y
7 Markey	Y	Y	Y	Y	Y	Y
8 Capuano	Y	Y	Y	Y	Y	Y
9 Lynch	Y	Y	Y	Y	Y	Y
10 Delahunt	Y	Y	Y	Y	Y	Y
MICHIGAN						
1 Stupak	N	Y	Y	Y	Y	Y
2 **Hoekstra**	N	Y	N	N	Y	N
3 **Ehlers**	N	Y	N	N	Y	N
4 **Camp**	N	Y	N	N	Y	N
5 Kildee	Y	Y	Y	Y	Y	Y
6 **Upton**	N	Y	N	N	Y	N
7 Schauer	Y	Y	Y	Y	Y	Y
8 **Rogers**	N	Y	N	N	Y	N
9 Peters	N	Y	Y	Y	Y	Y
10 **Miller**	N	Y	N	N	Y	N
11 **McCotter**	N	Y	N	N	Y	N
12 Levin	Y	Y	Y	Y	Y	Y
13 Kilpatrick	Y	Y	Y	Y	Y	Y
14 Conyers	Y	Y	Y	Y	Y	Y
15 Dingell	Y	Y	Y	Y	Y	Y
MINNESOTA						
1 Walz	Y	Y	Y	Y	Y	Y
2 **Kline**	N	Y	N	N	Y	N
3 **Paulsen**	Y	Y	N	N	Y	N
4 McCollum	Y	Y	Y	Y	Y	Y

	157	158	159	160	161	162
5 Ellison	Y	Y	Y	Y	Y	Y
6 **Bachmann**	N	Y	N	N	Y	N
7 Peterson	N	Y	Y	Y	Y	Y
8 Oberstar	Y	Y	Y	Y	Y	Y
MISSISSIPPI						
1 Childers	N	Y	N	N	Y	N
2 Thompson	Y	Y	Y	Y	Y	Y
3 **Harper**	N	Y	N	N	Y	N
4 Taylor	N	Y	N	N	Y	N
MISSOURI						
1 Clay	Y	Y	Y	Y	Y	Y
2 **Akin**	N	Y	N	N	Y	N
3 Carnahan	Y	Y	Y	Y	Y	Y
4 Skelton	Y	Y	Y	Y	Y	Y
5 Cleaver	Y	Y	Y	Y	Y	Y
6 **Graves**	N	Y	N	N	Y	N
7 **Blunt**	Y	Y	N	N	Y	N
8 **Emerson**	Y	Y	N	N	Y	N
9 **Luetkemeyer**	N	Y	N	N	Y	N
MONTANA						
AL **Rehberg**	N	Y	N	N	Y	N
NEBRASKA						
1 **Fortenberry**	N	Y	N	N	Y	N
2 **Terry**	N	Y	N	N	Y	N
3 **Smith**	N	Y	N	N	Y	N
NEVADA						
1 Berkley	Y	Y	Y	Y	Y	Y
2 **Heller**	Y	Y	N	N	Y	N
3 Titus	Y	Y	Y	Y	Y	Y
NEW HAMPSHIRE						
1 Shea-Porter	Y	Y	Y	Y	Y	Y
2 Hodes	Y	Y	Y	Y	Y	Y
NEW JERSEY						
1 Andrews	Y	Y	Y	Y	Y	Y
2 **LoBiondo**	N	Y	N	N	Y	N
3 Adler	N	Y	N	N	Y	N
4 **Smith**	N	Y	N	N	Y	N
5 **Garrett**	N	Y	N	N	Y	N
6 Pallone	Y	Y	Y	Y	Y	Y
7 **Lance**	N	Y	N	N	Y	N
8 Pascrell	Y	Y	Y	Y	Y	Y
9 Rothman	Y	Y	Y	Y	Y	Y
10 Payne	Y	Y	Y	Y	Y	Y
11 **Frelinghuysen**	N	Y	N	N	Y	N
12 Holt	Y	Y	Y	Y	Y	Y
13 Sires	?	?	Y	Y	Y	Y
NEW MEXICO						
1 Heinrich	Y	Y	Y	Y	Y	Y
2 Teague	Y	Y	Y	Y	Y	Y
3 Luján	Y	Y	Y	Y	Y	Y
NEW YORK						
1 Bishop	Y	Y	Y	Y	Y	Y
2 Israel	Y	Y	Y	Y	Y	Y
3 **King**	N	Y	N	N	Y	N
4 McCarthy	Y	Y	Y	Y	Y	Y
5 Ackerman	Y	Y	Y	Y	Y	Y
6 Meeks	Y	Y	Y	Y	Y	Y
7 Crowley	Y	Y	Y	Y	Y	Y
8 Nadler	Y	Y	Y	Y	Y	Y
9 Weiner	Y	Y	Y	Y	Y	Y
10 Towns	?	?	Y	Y	Y	Y
11 Clarke	Y	Y	Y	Y	Y	Y
12 Velázquez	Y	Y	Y	Y	Y	Y
13 McMahon	N	Y	N	N	Y	N
14 Maloney	Y	Y	Y	Y	Y	Y
15 Rangel	Y	Y	Y	Y	Y	Y
16 Serrano	Y	Y	Y	Y	Y	Y
17 Engel	Y	Y	Y	Y	Y	Y
18 Lowey	Y	Y	Y	Y	Y	Y
19 Hall	Y	Y	Y	Y	Y	Y
20 Murphy	N	Y	Y	Y	Y	Y
21 Tonko	Y	Y	Y	Y	Y	Y
22 Hinchey	?	?	Y	Y	Y	Y
23 Owens	?	Y	Y	Y	Y	Y
24 Arcuri	Y	Y	N	N	Y	N
25 Maffei	Y	Y	Y	Y	Y	Y
26 **Lee**	N	Y	N	N	Y	N
27 Higgins	Y	Y	Y	Y	Y	Y
28 Slaughter	Y	Y	Y	Y	Y	Y
29 Vacant						
NORTH CAROLINA						
1 Butterfield	Y	Y	Y	Y	Y	Y
2 Etheridge	N	Y	Y	Y	Y	Y
3 **Jones**	N	Y	N	N	Y	N
4 Price	Y	Y	Y	Y	Y	Y

	157	158	159	160	161	162
5 **Foxx**	N	Y	N	N	Y	N
6 **Coble**	N	Y	N	N	Y	N
7 McIntyre	Y	Y	N	N	Y	N
8 Kissell	Y	Y	Y	Y	Y	Y
9 **Myrick**	N	Y	N	N	Y	N
10 **McHenry**	N	Y	N	N	Y	N
11 Shuler	N	Y	N	N	Y	N
12 Watt	Y	Y	Y	Y	Y	Y
13 Miller	Y	Y	Y	Y	Y	Y
NORTH DAKOTA						
AL Pomeroy	Y	Y	Y	Y	Y	Y
OHIO						
1 Driehaus	Y	Y	Y	Y	Y	Y
2 **Schmidt**	N	?	N	N	Y	N
3 **Turner**	N	Y	N	N	Y	N
4 **Jordan**	N	Y	N	N	Y	N
5 **Latta**	N	Y	N	N	Y	N
6 Wilson	Y	Y	Y	Y	Y	Y
7 **Austria**	N	Y	N	N	Y	N
8 **Boehner**	N	Y	N	N	Y	N
9 Kaptur	Y	Y	Y	Y	Y	Y
10 Kucinich	Y	Y	Y	Y	Y	Y
11 Fudge	Y	Y	Y	Y	Y	Y
12 **Tiberi**	N	Y	N	N	Y	N
13 Sutton	Y	Y	Y	Y	Y	Y
14 **LaTourette**	N	Y	N	N	Y	N
15 Kilroy	Y	Y	Y	Y	Y	Y
16 Boccieri	N	Y	Y	Y	Y	Y
17 Ryan	Y	Y	Y	Y	Y	Y
18 Space	Y	Y	Y	Y	Y	N
OKLAHOMA						
1 **Sullivan**	N	Y	N	N	Y	N
2 Boren	N	Y	N	N	Y	N
3 **Lucas**	N	Y	N	N	Y	N
4 **Cole**	N	Y	N	N	Y	N
5 **Fallin**	N	Y	N	N	Y	N
OREGON						
1 Wu	Y	Y	Y	Y	Y	Y
2 **Walden**	N	Y	N	N	Y	N
3 Blumenauer	Y	Y	Y	Y	Y	Y
4 DeFazio	Y	Y	Y	Y	Y	Y
5 Schrader	?	Y	Y	Y	Y	Y
PENNSYLVANIA						
1 Brady	Y	Y	Y	Y	Y	Y
2 Fattah	?	Y	Y	Y	Y	Y
3 Dahlkemper	Y	Y	Y	Y	Y	Y
4 Altmire	N	Y	Y	Y	Y	Y
5 **Thompson**	N	Y	N	N	Y	N
6 **Gerlach**	N	Y	N	N	Y	N
7 Sestak	Y	Y	Y	Y	Y	Y
8 Murphy, P.	Y	Y	Y	Y	Y	Y
9 **Shuster**	N	Y	N	N	Y	N
10 Carney	N	Y	Y	Y	Y	Y
11 Kanjorski	Y	Y	Y	Y	Y	Y
12 Vacant						
13 Schwartz	Y	Y	Y	Y	Y	Y
14 Doyle	Y	Y	Y	Y	Y	Y
15 **Dent**	Y	Y	N	N	Y	N
16 **Pitts**	N	Y	N	N	Y	N
17 Holden	Y	Y	N	N	Y	N
18 **Murphy, T.**	N	Y	N	N	Y	N
19 **Platts**	N	Y	N	N	Y	N
RHODE ISLAND						
1 Kennedy	Y	Y	Y	Y	Y	Y
2 Langevin	Y	Y	Y	Y	Y	Y
SOUTH CAROLINA						
1 **Brown**	N	Y	N	N	Y	N
2 **Wilson**	N	Y	N	N	Y	N
3 **Barrett**	N	Y	N	N	Y	N
4 **Inglis**	N	Y	N	N	Y	N
5 Spratt	Y	Y	Y	Y	Y	Y
6 Clyburn	Y	Y	Y	Y	Y	Y
SOUTH DAKOTA						
AL Herseth Sandlin	N	Y	N	N	Y	N
TENNESSEE						
1 **Roe**	N	Y	N	N	Y	N
2 **Duncan**	N	Y	N	N	Y	N
3 **Wamp**	N	Y	N	N	Y	N
4 Davis	?	Y	?	Y	Y	Y
5 Cooper	Y	Y	Y	Y	Y	Y
6 Gordon	Y	Y	Y	Y	Y	Y
7 **Blackburn**	N	Y	N	N	Y	N
8 Tanner	Y	Y	Y	Y	Y	Y
9 Cohen	Y	Y	Y	Y	Y	Y

	157	158	159	160	161	162
TEXAS						
1 **Gohmert**	?	Y	N	N	Y	N
2 **Poe**	N	Y	N	N	Y	N
3 **Johnson, S.**	N	Y	N	N	Y	N
4 **Hall**	Y	Y	N	N	Y	N
5 **Hensarling**	N	Y	N	N	Y	N
6 **Barton**	N	Y	N	N	Y	N
7 **Culberson**	N	Y	N	N	Y	N
8 **Brady**	N	Y	N	N	Y	N
9 Green, A.	Y	Y	Y	Y	Y	Y
10 **McCaul**	N	Y	N	N	Y	N
11 **Conaway**	N	Y	N	N	Y	N
12 **Granger**	N	Y	N	N	Y	N
13 **Thornberry**	N	Y	N	N	Y	N
14 **Paul**	N	N	N	N	Y	N
15 Hinojosa	Y	Y	Y	Y	Y	Y
16 Reyes	Y	Y	Y	Y	Y	Y
17 Edwards	Y	Y	N	N	Y	N
18 Jackson Lee	Y	Y	Y	Y	Y	Y
19 **Neugebauer**	N	Y	N	N	Y	N
20 Gonzalez	Y	Y	Y	Y	Y	Y
21 **Smith**	N	Y	N	N	Y	N
22 **Olson**	N	Y	N	N	Y	N
23 Rodriguez	Y	Y	Y	Y	Y	Y
24 **Marchant**	N	Y	?	N	Y	N
25 Doggett	Y	Y	Y	Y	Y	Y
26 **Burgess**	N	Y	N	N	Y	N
27 Ortiz	Y	Y	Y	Y	Y	Y
28 Cuellar	N	Y	Y	Y	Y	Y
29 Green, G.	Y	Y	Y	Y	Y	Y
30 Johnson, E.	Y	Y	Y	Y	Y	Y
31 **Carter**	N	Y	N	N	Y	N
32 **Sessions**	Y	Y	N	N	Y	N
UTAH						
1 **Bishop**	N	Y	N	N	Y	N
2 Matheson	Y	Y	Y	Y	Y	N
3 **Chaffetz**	N	Y	N	N	Y	N
VERMONT						
AL Welch	Y	Y	Y	Y	Y	Y
VIRGINIA						
1 **Wittman**	N	Y	N	N	Y	N
2 Nye	Y	Y	N	N	Y	N
3 Scott	Y	Y	Y	Y	Y	Y
4 **Forbes**	N	Y	N	N	Y	N
5 Perriello	N	Y	Y	Y	Y	Y
6 **Goodlatte**	Y	Y	N	N	Y	N
7 **Cantor**	N	Y	N	N	Y	N
8 Moran	Y	Y	Y	Y	Y	Y
9 Boucher	Y	Y	Y	Y	Y	N
10 **Wolf**	N	Y	N	N	Y	N
11 Connolly	N	Y	Y	Y	Y	Y
WASHINGTON						
1 Inslee	Y	Y	Y	Y	Y	Y
2 Larsen	Y	Y	Y	Y	Y	Y
3 Baird	Y	Y	Y	Y	Y	Y
4 **Hastings**	N	Y	N	N	Y	N
5 **McMorris Rodgers**	N	Y	N	N	Y	N
6 Dicks	Y	Y	Y	Y	Y	Y
7 McDermott	Y	Y	Y	Y	Y	Y
8 **Reichert**	N	Y	N	N	Y	N
9 Smith	Y	Y	Y	Y	Y	Y
WEST VIRGINIA						
1 Mollohan	Y	Y	Y	Y	Y	Y
2 **Capito**	N	Y	N	N	Y	N
3 Rahall	Y	Y	Y	Y	Y	Y
WISCONSIN						
1 **Ryan**	N	Y	N	N	Y	N
2 Baldwin	Y	Y	Y	Y	Y	Y
3 Kind	Y	Y	Y	Y	Y	Y
4 Moore	Y	Y	Y	Y	Y	Y
5 **Sensenbrenner**	N	Y	N	N	Y	N
6 **Petri**	N	Y	N	N	Y	N
7 Obey	Y	Y	Y	Y	Y	Y
8 Kagen	Y	Y	Y	Y	Y	Y
WYOMING						
AL **Lummis**	N	Y	N	N	Y	N
DELEGATES						
Faleomavaega (A.S.)						
Norton (D.C.)						
Bordallo (Guam)						
Sablan (N. Marianas)						
Pierluisi (P.R.)						
Christensen (V.I.)						

IN THE HOUSE | By Vote Number

163. **HR 3590, HR 4872. Health Care Overhaul/Rule.** Adoption of the rule (H Res 1203) to provide for House floor consideration of the Senate amendments to a bill (HR 3590) that would remake the nation's health care system and would require nearly all individuals to purchase health insurance by 2014, and a reconciliation bill (HR 4872) that would modify the health care overhaul legislation. Adopted 224-206: D 224-28; R 0-178. March 21, 2010.

164. **H Res 925. Recognition for Military Aviators/Adoption.** Bordallo, D-Guam, motion to suspend the rules and adopt the resolution that would urge recognition of the extraordinary service of military aviators who were shot down over, or otherwise forced to land in, hostile territory yet evaded enemy capture or who were captured but subsequently escaped and resumed their service. It would urge secretaries of military departments to consider the aviators for appropriate recognition. Motion agreed to 426-0: D 251-0; R 175-0. A two-thirds majority of those present and voting (284 in this case) is required for adoption under suspension of the rules. March 21, 2010.

165. **HR 3590. Health Care Overhaul/Motion to Concur.** Spratt, D-S.C., motion to concur in the Senate amendment to the bill that would overhaul the nation's health insurance system and would require most individuals to buy health insurance by 2014. It would create a system of private insurance plans supervised by the Office of Personnel Management and create state-run marketplaces for purchasing health insurance. Those who do not obtain coverage would be subject to an excise tax, with exceptions. Employers with more than 50 workers would have to provide coverage or pay a fine if any employee gets a subsidized plan on the exchange. Certain small businesses would get tax credits for providing coverage, and individuals with low incomes, excluding illegal immigrants, could get subsidies. It would bar the use of federal funds to pay for abortions in the new programs, except in the cases of rape or incest or if the woman's life is in danger. Insurance companies could not deny coverage based on pre-existing medical conditions beginning in 2014 and could not drop coverage of people who become ill. It would expand eligibility for Medicaid and would shrink Medicare's so-called doughnut hole. Motion agreed to, thus clearing the bill for the president, 219-212: D 219-34; R 0-178. A "yea" was a vote in support of the president's position. March 21, 2010.

166. **HR 4872. Health Care Reconciliation/Recommit.** Camp, R-Mich., motion to recommit the bill to the House Budget Committee with instructions that it be immediately reported back with amendments that would bar the use of federal funds authorized in the bill to pay for an abortion or for a health plan that includes abortion coverage, unless the pregnancy is the result of rape or incest or if the woman suffers from a physical disorder, injury or illness that would, as certified by a physician, endanger her life. Individuals with subsidized policies could purchase abortion coverage separately with their own money. Motion rejected 199-232: D 21-232; R 178-0. March 21, 2010.

	163	164	165	166
ALABAMA				
1 **Bonner**	N	Y	N	Y
2 Bright	N	Y	N	Y
3 **Rogers**	N	Y	N	Y
4 **Aderholt**	N	Y	N	Y
5 **Griffith**	N	Y	N	Y
6 **Bachus**	N	Y	N	Y
7 Davis	N	Y	N	N
ALASKA				
AL **Young**	N	Y	N	Y
ARIZONA				
1 Kirkpatrick	Y	Y	Y	N
2 **Franks**	N	Y	N	Y
3 **Shadegg**	N	Y	N	Y
4 Pastor	Y	Y	Y	N
5 Mitchell	N	Y	Y	N
6 **Flake**	N	Y	N	Y
7 Grijalva	Y	Y	Y	N
8 Giffords	Y	Y	Y	N
ARKANSAS				
1 Berry	Y	Y	N	Y
2 Snyder	Y	Y	Y	N
3 **Boozman**	N	Y	N	Y
4 Ross	N	Y	N	Y
CALIFORNIA				
1 Thompson	Y	Y	Y	N
2 **Herger**	N	Y	N	Y
3 **Lungren**	N	Y	N	Y
4 **McClintock**	N	Y	N	Y
5 Matsui	Y	Y	Y	N
6 Woolsey	Y	Y	Y	N
7 Miller, George	Y	Y	Y	N
8 Pelosi		Y	Y	N
9 Lee	Y	Y	Y	N
10 Garamendi	Y	Y	Y	N
11 McNerney	Y	Y	Y	N
12 Speier	Y	Y	Y	N
13 Stark	Y	Y	Y	N
14 Eshoo	Y	Y	Y	N
15 Honda	Y	Y	Y	N
16 Lofgren	Y	Y	Y	N
17 Farr	Y	Y	Y	N
18 Cardoza	Y	Y	Y	N
19 **Radanovich**	N	Y	N	Y
20 Costa	Y	Y	Y	N
21 **Nunes**	N	Y	N	Y
22 **McCarthy**	N	Y	N	Y
23 Capps	Y	Y	Y	N
24 **Gallegly**	N	Y	N	Y
25 **McKeon**	N	Y	N	Y
26 **Dreier**	N	Y	N	Y
27 Sherman	Y	Y	Y	N
28 Berman	Y	Y	Y	N
29 Schiff	Y	Y	Y	N
30 Waxman	Y	Y	Y	N
31 Becerra	Y	Y	Y	N
32 Chu	Y	Y	Y	N
33 Watson	Y	Y	Y	N
34 Roybal-Allard	Y	Y	Y	N
35 Waters	Y	Y	Y	N
36 Harman	Y	Y	Y	N
37 Richardson	Y	Y	Y	N
38 Napolitano	Y	Y	Y	N
39 Sánchez, Linda	Y	Y	Y	N
40 **Royce**	N	Y	N	Y
41 **Lewis**	N	Y	N	Y
42 **Miller, Gary**	N	Y	N	Y
43 Baca	Y	Y	Y	N
44 **Calvert**	N	Y	N	Y
45 **Bono Mack**	N	Y	N	Y
46 **Rohrabacher**	N	Y	N	Y
47 Sanchez, Loretta	Y	Y	Y	N
48 **Campbell**	N	Y	N	Y
49 **Issa**	N	Y	N	Y
50 **Bilbray**	N	Y	N	Y
51 Filner	Y	Y	Y	N
52 **Hunter**	N	Y	N	Y
53 Davis	Y	Y	Y	N

	163	164	165	166
COLORADO				
1 DeGette	Y	Y	Y	N
2 Polis	Y	Y	Y	N
3 Salazar	Y	Y	Y	N
4 Markey	Y	Y	Y	N
5 **Lamborn**	N	Y	N	Y
6 **Coffman**	N	Y	N	Y
7 Perlmutter	Y	Y	Y	N
CONNECTICUT				
1 Larson	Y	Y	Y	N
2 Courtney	Y	Y	Y	N
3 DeLauro	Y	Y	Y	N
4 Himes	Y	Y	Y	N
5 Murphy	Y	Y	Y	N
DELAWARE				
AL **Castle**	N	Y	N	Y
FLORIDA				
1 **Miller**	N	Y	N	Y
2 Boyd	Y	Y	Y	N
3 Brown	Y	Y	Y	N
4 **Crenshaw**	N	Y	N	Y
5 **Brown-Waite**	N	Y	N	Y
6 **Stearns**	N	Y	N	Y
7 **Mica**	N	Y	N	Y
8 Grayson	Y	Y	Y	N
9 **Bilirakis**	N	Y	N	Y
10 **Young**	N	Y	N	Y
11 Castor	Y	Y	Y	N
12 **Putnam**	N	Y	N	Y
13 **Buchanan**	N	Y	N	Y
14 **Mack**	N	Y	N	Y
15 **Posey**	N	Y	N	Y
16 **Rooney**	N	Y	N	Y
17 Meek	Y	Y	Y	N
18 **Ros-Lehtinen**	N	Y	N	Y
19 Vacant				
20 Wasserman Schultz	Y	Y	Y	N
21 **Diaz-Balart, L.**	N	Y	N	Y
22 Klein	Y	Y	Y	N
23 Hastings	Y	Y	Y	N
24 Kosmas	Y	Y	Y	N
25 **Diaz-Balart, M.**	N	Y	N	Y
GEORGIA				
1 **Kingston**	N	Y	N	Y
2 Bishop	Y	Y	Y	N
3 **Westmoreland**	N	Y	N	Y
4 Johnson	Y	Y	Y	N
5 Lewis	Y	Y	Y	N
6 **Price**	N	Y	N	Y
7 **Linder**	N	Y	N	Y
8 Marshall	N	Y	N	Y
9 **Deal**	N	Y	N	Y
10 **Broun**	N	Y	N	Y
11 **Gingrey**	N	Y	N	Y
12 Barrow	N	Y	N	Y
13 Scott	Y	Y	Y	N
HAWAII				
1 Vacant				
2 Hirono	Y	Y	Y	N
IDAHO				
1 **Minnick**	N	Y	N	N
2 **Simpson**	N	Y	N	Y
ILLINOIS				
1 Rush	Y	Y	Y	N
2 Jackson	Y	Y	Y	N
3 Lipinski	N	Y	N	Y
4 Gutierrez	Y	Y	Y	N
5 Quigley	Y	Y	Y	N
6 **Roskam**	N	Y	N	Y
7 Davis	Y	Y	Y	N
8 Bean	Y	Y	Y	N
9 Schakowsky	Y	Y	Y	N
10 **Kirk**	N	Y	N	Y
11 Halvorson	Y	Y	Y	N
12 Costello	Y	Y	Y	Y
13 **Biggert**	N	Y	N	Y
14 Foster	Y	Y	Y	N
15 Johnson	N	Y	N	Y

KEY

	Republicans	Democrats					
Y	Voted for (yea)		X	Paired against		C	Voted "present" to avoid possible conflict of interest
#	Paired for		–	Announced against			
+	Announced for		P	Voted "present"		?	Did not vote or otherwise make a position known
N	Voted against (nay)						

	163	164	165	166
16 Manzullo	N	Y	N	Y
17 Hare	Y	Y	Y	N
18 Schock	N	Y	N	Y
19 Shimkus	N	Y	N	Y
INDIANA				
1 Visclosky	Y	Y	Y	N
2 Donnelly	Y	Y	Y	Y
3 Souder	N	Y	N	Y
4 Buyer	N	Y	N	Y
5 Burton	N	Y	N	Y
6 Pence	N	Y	N	Y
7 Carson	Y	Y	Y	N
8 Ellsworth	Y	Y	Y	N
9 Hill	Y	Y	Y	N
IOWA				
1 Braley	Y	Y	Y	N
2 Loebsack	Y	Y	Y	N
3 Boswell	Y	Y	Y	N
4 Latham	N	Y	N	Y
5 King	N	Y	N	Y
KANSAS				
1 Moran	N	Y	N	Y
2 Jenkins	N	Y	N	Y
3 Moore	Y	Y	Y	N
4 Tiahrt	N	Y	N	Y
KENTUCKY				
1 Whitfield	N	Y	N	Y
2 Guthrie	N	Y	N	Y
3 Yarmuth	Y	Y	Y	N
4 Davis	N	Y	N	Y
5 Rogers	N	Y	N	Y
6 Chandler	N	Y	N	Y
LOUISIANA				
1 Scalise	N	Y	N	Y
2 Cao	N	Y	N	Y
3 Melancon	N	Y	N	Y
4 Fleming	N	Y	N	Y
5 Alexander	N	Y	N	Y
6 Cassidy	N	Y	N	Y
7 Boustany	N	Y	N	Y
MAINE				
1 Pingree	Y	Y	Y	N
2 Michaud	Y	Y	Y	N
MARYLAND				
1 Kratovil	N	Y	N	N
2 Ruppersberger	Y	Y	Y	N
3 Sarbanes	Y	Y	Y	N
4 Edwards	Y	Y	Y	N
5 Hoyer	Y	Y	Y	N
6 Bartlett	N	Y	N	Y
7 Cummings	Y	Y	Y	N
8 Van Hollen	Y	Y	Y	N
MASSACHUSETTS				
1 Olver	Y	Y	Y	N
2 Neal	Y	Y	Y	N
3 McGovern	Y	Y	Y	N
4 Frank	Y	Y	Y	N
5 Tsongas	Y	Y	Y	N
6 Tierney	Y	Y	Y	N
7 Markey	Y	Y	Y	N
8 Capuano	Y	Y	Y	N
9 Lynch	N	Y	N	N
10 Delahunt	Y	Y	Y	N
MICHIGAN				
1 Stupak	Y	Y	Y	N
2 Hoekstra	N	Y	N	Y
3 Ehlers	N	Y	N	Y
4 Camp	N	Y	N	Y
5 Kildee	Y	Y	Y	N
6 Upton	N	Y	N	Y
7 Schauer	Y	Y	Y	N
8 Rogers	N	Y	N	Y
9 Peters	Y	Y	Y	N
10 Miller	N	Y	N	Y
11 McCotter	N	Y	N	Y
12 Levin	Y	Y	Y	N
13 Kilpatrick	Y	?	Y	N
14 Conyers	Y	Y	Y	N
15 Dingell	Y	Y	Y	N
MINNESOTA				
1 Walz	Y	Y	Y	N
2 Kline	N	Y	N	Y
3 Paulsen	N	Y	N	Y
4 McCollum	Y	Y	Y	N

	163	164	165	166
5 Ellison	Y	Y	Y	N
6 Bachmann	N	Y	N	Y
7 Peterson	Y	Y	Y	N
8 Oberstar	Y	Y	Y	N
MISSISSIPPI				
1 Childers	N	Y	N	Y
2 Thompson	Y	Y	Y	N
3 Harper	N	Y	N	Y
4 Taylor	N	Y	N	Y
MISSOURI				
1 Clay	Y	Y	Y	N
2 Akin	N	Y	N	Y
3 Carnahan	Y	Y	Y	N
4 Skelton	N	Y	N	Y
5 Cleaver	Y	Y	Y	N
6 Graves	N	Y	N	Y
7 Blunt	N	Y	N	Y
8 Emerson	N	Y	N	Y
9 Luetkemeyer	N	Y	N	Y
MONTANA				
AL Rehberg	N	Y	N	Y
NEBRASKA				
1 Fortenberry	N	Y	N	Y
2 Terry	N	Y	N	Y
3 Smith	N	Y	N	Y
NEVADA				
1 Berkley	Y	Y	Y	N
2 Heller	N	Y	N	Y
3 Titus	Y	Y	Y	N
NEW HAMPSHIRE				
1 Shea-Porter	Y	Y	Y	N
2 Hodes	Y	Y	Y	N
NEW JERSEY				
1 Andrews	Y	Y	Y	N
2 LoBiondo	N	Y	N	Y
3 Adler	N	Y	N	Y
4 Smith	N	Y	N	Y
5 Garrett	N	Y	N	Y
6 Pallone	Y	Y	Y	N
7 Lance	N	Y	N	Y
8 Pascrell	Y	Y	Y	N
9 Rothman	Y	Y	Y	N
10 Payne	Y	Y	Y	N
11 Frelinghuysen	N	Y	N	Y
12 Holt	Y	Y	Y	N
13 Sires	Y	Y	Y	N
NEW MEXICO				
1 Heinrich	Y	Y	Y	N
2 Teague	Y	Y	N	N
3 Luján	Y	Y	Y	N
NEW YORK				
1 Bishop	Y	Y	Y	N
2 Israel	Y	Y	Y	N
3 King	N	Y	N	Y
4 McCarthy	Y	Y	Y	N
5 Ackerman	Y	Y	Y	N
6 Meeks	Y	Y	Y	N
7 Crowley	Y	Y	Y	N
8 Nadler	Y	Y	Y	N
9 Weiner	Y	Y	Y	N
10 Towns	Y	Y	Y	N
11 Clarke	Y	Y	Y	N
12 Velázquez	Y	Y	Y	N
13 McMahon	Y	Y	N	N
14 Maloney	Y	Y	Y	N
15 Rangel	Y	Y	Y	N
16 Serrano	Y	Y	Y	N
17 Engel	Y	Y	Y	N
18 Lowey	Y	Y	Y	N
19 Hall	Y	Y	Y	N
20 Murphy	Y	Y	Y	N
21 Tonko	Y	Y	Y	N
22 Hinchey	Y	Y	Y	N
23 Owens	Y	Y	Y	N
24 Arcuri	N	Y	N	N
25 Maffei	Y	Y	Y	N
26 Lee	N	Y	N	Y
27 Higgins	Y	Y	Y	N
28 Slaughter	Y	Y	Y	N
29 Vacant				
NORTH CAROLINA				
1 Butterfield	Y	Y	Y	N
2 Etheridge	Y	Y	Y	N
3 Jones	N	Y	N	Y
4 Price	Y	Y	Y	N

	163	164	165	166
5 Foxx	N	?	N	Y
6 Coble	N	Y	N	Y
7 McIntyre	N	Y	N	Y
8 Kissell	N	Y	N	N
9 Myrick	N	Y	N	Y
10 McHenry	N	Y	N	Y
11 Shuler	N	Y	N	Y
12 Watt	Y	Y	Y	N
13 Miller	Y	Y	Y	N
NORTH DAKOTA				
AL Pomeroy	Y	Y	Y	N
OHIO				
1 Driehaus	Y	Y	Y	N
2 Schmidt	N	Y	N	Y
3 Turner	N	Y	N	Y
4 Jordan	N	Y	N	Y
5 Latta	N	Y	N	Y
6 Wilson	Y	Y	Y	N
7 Austria	N	Y	N	Y
8 Boehner	N	?	N	Y
9 Kaptur	Y	Y	Y	N
10 Kucinich	Y	Y	Y	N
11 Fudge	Y	Y	Y	N
12 Tiberi	N	Y	N	Y
13 Sutton	Y	Y	Y	N
14 LaTourette	N	Y	N	Y
15 Kilroy	Y	Y	Y	N
16 Boccieri	Y	Y	Y	N
17 Ryan	Y	Y	Y	N
18 Space	N	Y	N	N
OKLAHOMA				
1 Sullivan	N	Y	N	Y
2 Boren	N	Y	N	Y
3 Lucas	N	Y	N	Y
4 Cole	N	Y	N	Y
5 Fallin	N	Y	N	Y
OREGON				
1 Wu	Y	Y	Y	N
2 Walden	N	Y	N	Y
3 Blumenauer	Y	Y	Y	N
4 DeFazio	Y	Y	Y	N
5 Schrader	Y	Y	Y	N
PENNSYLVANIA				
1 Brady	Y	Y	Y	N
2 Fattah	Y	Y	Y	N
3 Dahlkemper	Y	Y	Y	N
4 Altmire	Y	Y	N	Y
5 Thompson	N	Y	N	Y
6 Gerlach	N	Y	N	Y
7 Sestak	Y	Y	Y	N
8 Murphy, P.	Y	Y	Y	N
9 Shuster	N	Y	N	Y
10 Carney	Y	Y	Y	N
11 Kanjorski	Y	Y	Y	N
12 Vacant				
13 Schwartz	Y	Y	Y	N
14 Doyle	Y	Y	Y	N
15 Dent	N	Y	N	Y
16 Pitts	N	Y	N	Y
17 Holden	N	Y	N	Y
18 Murphy, T.	N	Y	N	Y
19 Platts	N	Y	N	Y
RHODE ISLAND				
1 Kennedy	Y	Y	Y	N
2 Langevin	Y	Y	Y	N
SOUTH CAROLINA				
1 Brown	N	Y	N	Y
2 Wilson	N	Y	N	Y
3 Barrett	N	Y	N	Y
4 Inglis	N	Y	N	Y
5 Spratt	Y	Y	Y	N
6 Clyburn	Y	Y	Y	N
SOUTH DAKOTA				
AL Herseth Sandlin	N	Y	N	N
TENNESSEE				
1 Roe	N	Y	N	Y
2 Duncan	N	Y	N	Y
3 Wamp	N	Y	N	Y
4 Davis	N	Y	N	Y
5 Cooper	N	Y	N	Y
6 Gordon	Y	Y	Y	N
7 Blackburn	N	Y	N	Y
8 Tanner	Y	Y	N	N
9 Cohen	Y	Y	Y	N

	163	164	165	166
TEXAS				
1 Gohmert	N	Y	N	Y
2 Poe	N	Y	N	Y
3 Johnson, S.	N	Y	N	Y
4 Hall	N	Y	N	Y
5 Hensarling	N	Y	N	Y
6 Barton	N	Y	N	Y
7 Culberson	N	Y	N	Y
8 Brady	N	Y	N	Y
9 Green, A.	Y	Y	Y	N
10 McCaul	N	Y	N	Y
11 Conaway	N	Y	N	Y
12 Granger	N	Y	N	Y
13 Thornberry	N	Y	N	Y
14 Paul	N	Y	N	Y
15 Hinojosa	Y	Y	Y	N
16 Reyes	Y	Y	Y	N
17 Edwards	Y	Y	Y	N
18 Jackson Lee	Y	Y	Y	N
19 Neugebauer	N	Y	N	Y
20 Gonzalez	Y	Y	Y	N
21 Smith	N	?	N	Y
22 Olson	N	Y	N	Y
23 Rodriguez	Y	Y	Y	N
24 Marchant	N	Y	N	Y
25 Doggett	Y	Y	Y	N
26 Burgess	N	Y	N	Y
27 Ortiz	Y	Y	Y	N
28 Cuellar	Y	Y	Y	N
29 Green, G.	Y	Y	Y	N
30 Johnson, E.	Y	Y	Y	N
31 Carter	N	Y	N	Y
32 Sessions	N	Y	N	Y
UTAH				
1 Bishop	N	Y	N	Y
2 Matheson	N	Y	N	Y
3 Chaffetz	N	Y	N	Y
VERMONT				
AL Welch	Y	Y	Y	N
VIRGINIA				
1 Wittman	N	Y	N	Y
2 Nye	N	Y	N	N
3 Scott	Y	Y	Y	N
4 Forbes	N	Y	N	Y
5 Perriello	Y	Y	Y	N
6 Goodlatte	N	Y	N	Y
7 Cantor	N	Y	N	Y
8 Moran	Y	Y	Y	N
9 Boucher	N	Y	N	Y
10 Wolf	N	Y	N	Y
11 Connolly	Y	Y	Y	N
WASHINGTON				
1 Inslee	Y	Y	Y	N
2 Larsen	Y	Y	Y	N
3 Baird	Y	Y	Y	N
4 Hastings	N	Y	N	Y
5 McMorris Rodgers	N	Y	N	Y
6 Dicks	Y	Y	Y	N
7 McDermott	Y	Y	Y	N
8 Reichert	N	Y	N	Y
9 Smith	Y	Y	Y	N
WEST VIRGINIA				
1 Mollohan	Y	Y	Y	N
2 Capito	N	Y	N	Y
3 Rahall	Y	Y	Y	N
WISCONSIN				
1 Ryan	N	Y	N	Y
2 Baldwin	Y	Y	Y	N
3 Kind	Y	Y	Y	N
4 Moore	Y	Y	Y	N
5 Sensenbrenner	N	Y	N	Y
6 Petri	N	Y	N	Y
7 Obey	Y	Y	Y	N
8 Kagen	Y	Y	Y	N
WYOMING				
AL Lummis	N	Y	N	Y
DELEGATES				
Faleomavaega (A.S.)				
Norton (D.C.)				
Bordallo (Guam)				
Sablan (N. Marianas)				
Pierluisi (P.R.)				
Christensen (V.I.)				

IN THE HOUSE | By Vote Number

167. **HR 4872. Health Care Reconciliation/Passage.** Passage of the bill that would make changes to the health care overhaul measure (HR 3590), revise student loan programs and include revenue-raising provisions. It would increase federal subsidies to help low- and moderate-income families purchase coverage in health insurance exchanges, phase out the coverage gap for Medicare prescription drug enrollees and adjust federal matching funds for Medicaid. It would change penalties on employers that do not offer health benefits. It would freeze Medicare Advantage payments in 2011 and then reformulate them. The federal government would cover 100 percent of the cost of coverage to newly eligible Medicaid recipients in 2014-16. It would delay until 2018 the effective date of a tax on high-cost health plans and adjust the dollar amounts used to determine who would be affected by the tax. It would repeal a tax credit for a paper-processing byproduct called "black liquor." It also would make the federal government the sole originator of federal student loans and direct the savings to education programs. Passed 220-211: D 220-33; R 0-178. A "yea" was a vote in support of the president's position. March 21, 2010.

168. **H Res 1099. Anniversary of Battle of Iwo Jima/Adoption.** Owens, D-N.Y., motion to suspend the rules and adopt the resolution that would recognize the 65th anniversary of the Battle of Iwo Jima. It would commend all members of the U.S. armed forces who participated in the battle for their service and sacrifice. Motion agreed to 421-0: D 248-0; R 173-0. A two-thirds majority of those present and voting (281 in this case) is required for adoption under suspension of the rules. March 21, 2010.

169. **H Res 1119. Moment of Silence for Military Personnel/Adoption.** Bordallo, D-Guam, motion to suspend the rules and adopt the resolution that would express the sense of the House that all Americans should participate in a moment of silence to reflect on the service and sacrifice of members of the U.S. armed forces at home and abroad. Motion agreed to 400-0: D 231-0; R 169-0. A two-thirds majority of those present and voting (267 in this case) is required for adoption under suspension of the rules. March 21, 2010.

170. **HR 4810. Programs for Homeless Veterans/Passage.** Filner, D-Calif., motion to suspend the rules and pass the bill that would increase to $200 million the annual authorization for Veterans Affairs Department programs for homeless veterans, starting in fiscal 2010, and authorize funds to support very low-income veterans in permanent housing. Motion agreed to 413-0: D 242-0; R 171-0. A two-thirds majority of those present and voting (276 in this case) is required for passage under suspension of the rules. March 22, 2010.

171. **HR 4667. Veterans' Cost-of-Living Adjustment/Passage.** Filner, D-Calif., motion to suspend the rules and pass the bill that would increase veterans' disability compensation and their survivors' dependency and indemnity compensation by the same cost-of-living adjustment payable to Social Security recipients. The increase would take effect Dec. 1, 2010. Motion agreed to 407-0: D 240-0; R 167-0. A two-thirds majority of those present and voting (272 in this case) is required for passage under suspension of the rules. March 22, 2010.

	167	168	169	170	171
ALABAMA					
1 Bonner	N	Y	Y	Y	Y
2 Bright	N	Y	Y	Y	Y
3 Rogers	N	Y	Y	Y	Y
4 Aderholt	N	Y	Y	Y	Y
5 Griffith	N	Y	Y	Y	Y
6 Bachus	N	Y	Y	Y	Y
7 Davis	N	?	?	?	?
ALASKA					
AL Young	N	Y	Y	Y	Y
ARIZONA					
1 Kirkpatrick	Y	Y	Y	Y	Y
2 Franks	N	Y	Y	Y	Y
3 Shadegg	N	Y	Y	?	?
4 Pastor	Y	Y	Y	Y	Y
5 Mitchell	Y	Y	Y	Y	Y
6 Flake	N	Y	Y	Y	Y
7 Grijalva	Y	Y	Y	Y	Y
8 Giffords	Y	Y	Y	Y	Y
ARKANSAS					
1 Berry	N	Y	Y	Y	Y
2 Snyder	Y	Y	Y	Y	Y
3 Boozman	N	Y	Y	Y	Y
4 Ross	N	Y	Y	Y	Y
CALIFORNIA					
1 Thompson	Y	Y	Y	Y	Y
2 Herger	N	Y	Y	Y	Y
3 Lungren	N	Y	Y	Y	Y
4 McClintock	N	Y	Y	Y	Y
5 Matsui	Y	Y	Y	Y	Y
6 Woolsey	Y	Y	Y	Y	Y
7 Miller, George	Y	Y	Y	Y	Y
8 Pelosi	Y				
9 Lee	Y	Y	?	Y	Y
10 Garamendi	Y	Y	Y	Y	Y
11 McNerney	Y	Y	Y	Y	Y
12 Speier	Y	Y	Y	Y	Y
13 Stark	Y	Y	Y	Y	Y
14 Eshoo	Y	Y	Y	Y	Y
15 Honda	Y	Y	?	Y	Y
16 Lofgren	Y	Y	Y	Y	Y
17 Farr	Y	Y	Y	Y	Y
18 Cardoza	Y	Y	Y	Y	Y
19 Radanovich	N	Y	Y	Y	Y
20 Costa	Y	Y	Y	Y	Y
21 Nunes	N	Y	Y	Y	Y
22 McCarthy	N	Y	Y	Y	Y
23 Capps	Y	Y	Y	Y	Y
24 Gallegly	N	Y	Y	Y	Y
25 McKeon	N	Y	Y	Y	Y
26 Dreier	N	Y	Y	Y	Y
27 Sherman	Y	Y	Y	Y	Y
28 Berman	Y	Y	Y	Y	Y
29 Schiff	Y	Y	Y	Y	Y
30 Waxman	Y	Y	Y	Y	Y
31 Becerra	Y	Y	Y	Y	Y
32 Chu	Y	Y	Y	Y	Y
33 Watson	Y	Y	Y	Y	Y
34 Roybal-Allard	Y	Y	Y	Y	Y
35 Waters	Y	Y	?	Y	Y
36 Harman	Y	Y	Y	Y	Y
37 Richardson	Y	Y	Y	Y	Y
38 Napolitano	Y	Y	Y	Y	Y
39 Sánchez, Linda	Y	Y	Y	Y	Y
40 Royce	N	Y	?	Y	Y
41 Lewis	N	Y	Y	Y	Y
42 Miller, Gary	N	Y	Y	Y	Y
43 Baca	Y	Y	Y	Y	Y
44 Calvert	N	Y	Y	Y	Y
45 Bono Mack	N	Y	Y	Y	Y
46 Rohrabacher	N	Y	Y	Y	Y
47 Sanchez, Loretta	Y	Y	Y	Y	Y
48 Campbell	N	Y	Y	Y	Y
49 Issa	N	Y	?	Y	Y
50 Bilbray	N	Y	Y	Y	Y
51 Filner	Y	Y	Y	Y	Y
52 Hunter	N	Y	Y	Y	Y
53 Davis	Y	Y	Y	Y	Y
COLORADO					
1 DeGette	Y	Y	Y	Y	Y
2 Polis	Y	Y	Y	Y	Y
3 Salazar	Y	Y	Y	Y	Y
4 Markey	Y	Y	Y	Y	Y
5 Lamborn	N	Y	Y	Y	Y
6 Coffman	N	Y	Y	Y	Y
7 Perlmutter	Y	Y	Y	Y	Y
CONNECTICUT					
1 Larson	Y	Y	?	Y	Y
2 Courtney	Y	Y	Y	?	Y
3 DeLauro	Y	Y	Y	Y	Y
4 Himes	Y	Y	Y	Y	Y
5 Murphy	Y	Y	Y	Y	Y
DELAWARE					
AL Castle	N	Y	Y	Y	Y
FLORIDA					
1 Miller	N	Y	Y	Y	Y
2 Boyd	Y	Y	Y	Y	Y
3 Brown	Y	Y	Y	Y	Y
4 Crenshaw	N	Y	Y	Y	Y
5 Brown-Waite	N	Y	Y	Y	Y
6 Stearns	N	Y	Y	Y	Y
7 Mica	N	Y	Y	Y	Y
8 Grayson	Y	Y	Y	Y	Y
9 Bilirakis	N	Y	Y	Y	Y
10 Young	N	Y	Y	Y	Y
11 Castor	Y	Y	?	Y	Y
12 Putnam	N	Y	Y	Y	Y
13 Buchanan	N	Y	Y	Y	Y
14 Mack	N	Y	Y	Y	Y
15 Posey	N	Y	Y	Y	Y
16 Rooney	N	Y	Y	Y	Y
17 Meek	Y	Y	Y	Y	Y
18 Ros-Lehtinen	N	Y	Y	Y	Y
19 Vacant					
20 Wasserman Schultz	Y	Y	Y	Y	Y
21 Diaz-Balart, L.	N	Y	Y	Y	Y
22 Klein	Y	+	Y	Y	Y
23 Hastings	Y	Y	Y	Y	Y
24 Kosmas	Y	Y	Y	Y	Y
25 Diaz-Balart, M.	N	Y	Y	Y	Y
GEORGIA					
1 Kingston	N	Y	Y	Y	Y
2 Bishop	Y	Y	Y	Y	?
3 Westmoreland	N	Y	Y	Y	Y
4 Johnson	Y	Y	Y	Y	Y
5 Lewis	Y	Y	Y	Y	Y
6 Price	N	Y	Y	Y	Y
7 Linder	N	?	?	Y	Y
8 Marshall	N	Y	Y	Y	Y
9 Deal*	N	?			
10 Broun	N	Y	Y	Y	Y
11 Gingrey	N	Y	Y	Y	Y
12 Barrow	N	Y	Y	Y	Y
13 Scott	Y	Y	Y	Y	Y
HAWAII					
1 Vacant					
2 Hirono	Y	Y	Y	Y	Y
IDAHO					
1 Minnick	N	Y	Y	Y	Y
2 Simpson	N	Y	Y	Y	Y
ILLINOIS					
1 Rush	Y	Y	Y	Y	Y
2 Jackson	Y	Y	Y	Y	Y
3 Lipinski	Y	Y	Y	Y	Y
4 Gutierrez	Y	Y	Y	Y	Y
5 Quigley	Y	Y	?	Y	Y
6 Roskam	N	Y	Y	Y	Y
7 Davis	Y	Y	Y	Y	Y
8 Bean	Y	Y	Y	Y	Y
9 Schakowsky	Y	Y	?	Y	Y
10 Kirk	N	Y	Y	Y	Y
11 Halvorson	Y	Y	Y	Y	Y
12 Costello	Y	Y	Y	Y	Y
13 Biggert	N	Y	Y	Y	Y
14 Foster	Y	Y	Y	Y	Y
15 Johnson	N	Y	Y	Y	Y

KEY   Republicans   Democrats

Y Voted for (yea)	X Paired against
# Paired for	− Announced against
+ Announced for	P Voted "present"
N Voted against (nay)	C Voted "present" to avoid possible conflict of interest
	? Did not vote or otherwise make a position known

* Rep. Nathan Deal, R-Ga., resigned March 21, 2010. The last vote for which he was eligible was vote 168.

H-62   2010 CQ ALMANAC | www.cq.com

	167	168	169	170	171
16 Manzullo	N	Y	Y	Y	Y
17 Hare	Y	Y	Y	Y	Y
18 Schock	N	Y	Y	Y	Y
19 Shimkus	N	Y	Y	Y	Y
INDIANA					
1 Visclosky	Y	Y	Y	Y	Y
2 Donnelly	Y	Y	Y	Y	Y
3 Souder	N	Y	Y	Y	Y
4 Buyer	N	Y	Y	?	?
5 Burton	N	Y	Y	Y	Y
6 Pence	N	Y	Y	Y	Y
7 Carson	Y	Y	Y	Y	Y
8 Ellsworth	Y	Y	Y	Y	Y
9 Hill	Y	Y	Y	Y	Y
IOWA					
1 Braley	Y	Y	Y	Y	Y
2 Loebsack	Y	Y	Y	Y	Y
3 Boswell	Y	Y	Y	Y	Y
4 Latham	N	Y	Y	Y	Y
5 King	N	Y	Y	Y	Y
KANSAS					
1 Moran	N	Y	Y	Y	Y
2 Jenkins	N	Y	Y	Y	Y
3 Moore	Y	?	?	Y	Y
4 Tiahrt	N	Y	Y	Y	Y
KENTUCKY					
1 Whitfield	N	Y	Y	Y	Y
2 Guthrie	N	Y	Y	Y	Y
3 Yarmuth	Y	Y	Y	Y	Y
4 Davis	N	Y	Y	Y	Y
5 Rogers	N	Y	Y	Y	Y
6 Chandler	N	Y	Y	Y	?
LOUISIANA					
1 Scalise	N	Y	Y	Y	Y
2 Cao	N	Y	Y	Y	Y
3 Melancon	N	Y	Y	Y	Y
4 Fleming	N	Y	Y	Y	Y
5 Alexander	N	Y	Y	Y	Y
6 Cassidy	N	Y	Y	Y	Y
7 Boustany	N	Y	Y	Y	Y
MAINE					
1 Pingree	Y	Y	Y	Y	Y
2 Michaud	Y	Y	Y	Y	Y
MARYLAND					
1 Kratovil	N	Y	Y	Y	Y
2 Ruppersberger	Y	Y	Y	Y	Y
3 Sarbanes	Y	Y	Y	Y	Y
4 Edwards	Y	Y	Y	Y	Y
5 Hoyer	Y	Y	Y	Y	Y
6 Bartlett	N	Y	Y	Y	Y
7 Cummings	Y	Y	Y	Y	Y
8 Van Hollen	Y	Y	Y	Y	Y
MASSACHUSETTS					
1 Olver	Y	Y	Y	Y	Y
2 Neal	Y	Y	Y	?	?
3 McGovern	Y	Y	Y	Y	Y
4 Frank	Y	Y	Y	Y	Y
5 Tsongas	Y	Y	Y	Y	Y
6 Tierney	Y	Y	Y	Y	Y
7 Markey	Y	Y	?	Y	Y
8 Capuano	Y	Y	Y	Y	Y
9 Lynch	Y	Y	Y	?	?
10 Delahunt	Y	Y	Y	Y	Y
MICHIGAN					
1 Stupak	Y	Y	Y	Y	Y
2 Hoekstra	N	Y	Y	?	?
3 Ehlers	N	Y	Y	Y	Y
4 Camp	N	Y	Y	Y	Y
5 Kildee	Y	Y	Y	Y	Y
6 Upton	N	Y	Y	Y	Y
7 Schauer	Y	Y	Y	Y	Y
8 Rogers	N	Y	Y	Y	Y
9 Peters	Y	Y	Y	Y	Y
10 Miller	N	Y	Y	Y	Y
11 McCotter	N	Y	Y	Y	Y
12 Levin	Y	Y	Y	Y	Y
13 Kilpatrick	Y	Y	Y	?	+
14 Conyers	Y	?	Y	Y	Y
15 Dingell	Y	Y	?	Y	Y
MINNESOTA					
1 Walz	Y	Y	Y	Y	Y
2 Kline	N	Y	?	Y	Y
3 Paulsen	N	Y	Y	Y	Y
4 McCollum	Y	Y	Y	Y	Y

	167	168	169	170	171
5 Ellison	Y	Y	Y	Y	Y
6 Bachmann	N	Y	Y	Y	?
7 Peterson	N	Y	Y	Y	Y
8 Oberstar	Y	Y	Y	Y	Y
MISSISSIPPI					
1 Childers	N	Y	Y	Y	Y
2 Thompson	Y	Y	Y	Y	Y
3 Harper	N	Y	Y	Y	Y
4 Taylor	N	Y	?	Y	Y
MISSOURI					
1 Clay	Y	?	?	Y	Y
2 Akin	N	Y	Y	Y	Y
3 Carnahan	Y	Y	Y	Y	Y
4 Skelton	N	Y	Y	Y	Y
5 Cleaver	Y	Y	Y	Y	Y
6 Graves	N	Y	Y	Y	Y
7 Blunt	N	Y	Y	?	?
8 Emerson	N	Y	Y	Y	Y
9 Luetkemeyer	N	Y	Y	Y	Y
MONTANA					
AL Rehberg	N	Y	Y	Y	Y
NEBRASKA					
1 Fortenberry	N	Y	Y	Y	Y
2 Terry	N	Y	Y	Y	Y
3 Smith	N	Y	Y	Y	Y
NEVADA					
1 Berkley	Y	Y	Y	Y	Y
2 Heller	N	Y	Y	Y	Y
3 Titus	Y	Y	Y	Y	Y
NEW HAMPSHIRE					
1 Shea-Porter	Y	Y	?	Y	Y
2 Hodes	Y	Y	Y	Y	Y
NEW JERSEY					
1 Andrews	Y	Y	Y	Y	Y
2 LoBiondo	N	Y	Y	Y	Y
3 Adler	Y	Y	Y	Y	Y
4 Smith	N	Y	Y	Y	Y
5 Garrett	N	Y	Y	Y	Y
6 Pallone	Y	Y	Y	Y	Y
7 Lance	N	Y	Y	Y	Y
8 Pascrell	Y	Y	Y	Y	Y
9 Rothman	Y	Y	Y	Y	Y
10 Payne	Y	Y	Y	?	?
11 Frelinghuysen	N	?	?	Y	Y
12 Holt	Y	Y	Y	Y	Y
13 Sires	Y	Y	Y	Y	Y
NEW MEXICO					
1 Heinrich	Y	Y	Y	Y	Y
2 Teague	N	Y	Y	Y	Y
3 Luján	Y	Y	Y	Y	Y
NEW YORK					
1 Bishop	Y	Y	Y	Y	?
2 Israel	Y	Y	Y	Y	Y
3 King	N	Y	Y	Y	Y
4 McCarthy	Y	Y	Y	?	?
5 Ackerman	Y	Y	Y	Y	Y
6 Meeks	Y	Y	Y	Y	Y
7 Crowley	Y	Y	Y	Y	Y
8 Nadler	Y	Y	Y	Y	Y
9 Weiner	Y	Y	Y	Y	Y
10 Towns	Y	Y	Y	Y	Y
11 Clarke	Y	Y	Y	Y	Y
12 Velázquez	Y	Y	Y	Y	Y
13 McMahon	N	Y	Y	Y	Y
14 Maloney	Y	Y	Y	Y	Y
15 Rangel	Y	Y	Y	Y	Y
16 Serrano	Y	Y	Y	Y	Y
17 Engel	Y	Y	Y	Y	Y
18 Lowey	Y	Y	?	Y	Y
19 Hall	Y	Y	Y	Y	Y
20 Murphy	Y	Y	Y	Y	Y
21 Tonko	Y	Y	Y	Y	Y
22 Hinchey	Y	Y	Y	Y	Y
23 Owens	Y	Y	Y	Y	Y
24 Arcuri	N	Y	Y	Y	Y
25 Maffei	Y	Y	Y	Y	Y
26 Lee	N	Y	Y	Y	Y
27 Higgins	Y	Y	Y	Y	Y
28 Slaughter	Y	Y	Y	Y	Y
29 Vacant					
NORTH CAROLINA					
1 Butterfield	Y	Y	Y	Y	Y
2 Etheridge	Y	Y	Y	Y	Y
3 Jones	N	Y	Y	Y	Y
4 Price	Y	Y	Y	Y	Y

	167	168	169	170	171
5 Foxx	N	Y	Y	Y	Y
6 Coble	N	Y	Y	Y	Y
7 McIntyre	N	Y	?	Y	Y
8 Kissell	N	Y	Y	Y	Y
9 Myrick	N	Y	Y	Y	Y
10 McHenry	N	Y	Y	Y	Y
11 Shuler	N	Y	Y	Y	Y
12 Watt	Y	Y	Y	Y	Y
13 Miller	Y	Y	Y	Y	Y
NORTH DAKOTA					
AL Pomeroy	Y	Y	Y	Y	Y
OHIO					
1 Driehaus	Y	Y	Y	Y	Y
2 Schmidt	N	Y	Y	Y	Y
3 Turner	N	Y	Y	Y	Y
4 Jordan	N	Y	Y	Y	Y
5 Latta	N	Y	Y	Y	Y
6 Wilson	Y	Y	Y	Y	Y
7 Austria	N	Y	Y	Y	Y
8 Boehner	N	?	?	Y	Y
9 Kaptur	Y	Y	Y	Y	Y
10 Kucinich	Y	Y	Y	Y	Y
11 Fudge	Y	Y	Y	Y	Y
12 Tiberi	N	Y	Y	Y	Y
13 Sutton	Y	Y	Y	Y	Y
14 LaTourette	N	?	?	Y	Y
15 Kilroy	Y	Y	Y	Y	Y
16 Boccieri	Y	Y	Y	Y	Y
17 Ryan	Y	Y	Y	Y	Y
18 Space	N	Y	Y	Y	Y
OKLAHOMA					
1 Sullivan	N	Y	Y	Y	Y
2 Boren	N	Y	Y	Y	Y
3 Lucas	N	Y	Y	Y	Y
4 Cole	N	Y	Y	Y	Y
5 Fallin	N	Y	Y	Y	+
OREGON					
1 Wu	Y	Y	Y	Y	Y
2 Walden	N	Y	Y	Y	Y
3 Blumenauer	Y	Y	Y	Y	Y
4 DeFazio	Y	Y	?	Y	Y
5 Schrader	Y	Y	Y	Y	Y
PENNSYLVANIA					
1 Brady	Y	Y	Y	Y	Y
2 Fattah	Y	Y	Y	Y	Y
3 Dahlkemper	Y	Y	Y	Y	Y
4 Altmire	N	Y	Y	Y	Y
5 Thompson	N	Y	Y	Y	Y
6 Gerlach	N	Y	Y	Y	Y
7 Sestak	Y	Y	Y	Y	Y
8 Murphy, P.	Y	Y	Y	Y	Y
9 Shuster	N	Y	Y	Y	Y
10 Carney	Y	Y	Y	Y	Y
11 Kanjorski	Y	Y	Y	Y	Y
12 Vacant					
13 Schwartz	Y	Y	Y	Y	Y
14 Doyle	Y	Y	Y	Y	Y
15 Dent	N	Y	Y	Y	Y
16 Pitts	N	Y	Y	Y	Y
17 Holden	N	Y	Y	Y	Y
18 Murphy, T.	N	Y	Y	Y	Y
19 Platts	N	Y	Y	Y	Y
RHODE ISLAND					
1 Kennedy	Y	Y	?	Y	Y
2 Langevin	Y	Y	Y	Y	Y
SOUTH CAROLINA					
1 Brown	N	Y	Y	Y	Y
2 Wilson	N	Y	Y	Y	Y
3 Barrett	N	Y	?	?	?
4 Inglis	N	Y	Y	Y	Y
5 Spratt	Y	Y	Y	Y	Y
6 Clyburn	Y	Y	Y	Y	Y
SOUTH DAKOTA					
AL Herseth Sandlin	N	Y	Y	Y	Y
TENNESSEE					
1 Roe	N	Y	Y	Y	Y
2 Duncan	N	Y	Y	Y	Y
3 Wamp	N	Y	?	?	?
4 Davis	N	Y	Y	?	?
5 Cooper	N	Y	Y	Y	Y
6 Gordon	Y	Y	Y	Y	Y
7 Blackburn	N	Y	Y	Y	Y
8 Tanner	N	Y	Y	Y	Y
9 Cohen	Y	Y	Y	Y	Y

	167	168	169	170	171
TEXAS					
1 Gohmert	N	Y	Y	Y	Y
2 Poe	N	Y	Y	Y	Y
3 Johnson, S.	N	Y	Y	Y	?
4 Hall	N	Y	Y	Y	Y
5 Hensarling	N	Y	Y	Y	Y
6 Barton	N	Y	Y	Y	Y
7 Culberson	N	Y	Y	Y	Y
8 Brady	N	Y	Y	Y	Y
9 Green, A.	Y	Y	Y	Y	Y
10 McCaul	N	Y	Y	Y	Y
11 Conaway	N	Y	Y	Y	Y
12 Granger	N	Y	Y	Y	Y
13 Thornberry	N	Y	Y	Y	Y
14 Paul	N	Y	Y	Y	Y
15 Hinojosa	Y	Y	Y	Y	Y
16 Reyes	Y	Y	Y	Y	Y
17 Edwards	N	Y	Y	Y	Y
18 Jackson Lee	Y	Y	Y	Y	Y
19 Neugebauer	N	Y	Y	Y	Y
20 Gonzalez	Y	Y	Y	Y	Y
21 Smith	N	Y	Y	Y	Y
22 Olson	N	Y	Y	Y	?
23 Rodriguez	Y	Y	Y	Y	Y
24 Marchant	N	Y	Y	Y	Y
25 Doggett	Y	Y	Y	Y	Y
26 Burgess	N	Y	Y	Y	Y
27 Ortiz	Y	Y	Y	Y	Y
28 Cuellar	Y	Y	Y	Y	Y
29 Green, G.	Y	Y	Y	Y	Y
30 Johnson, E.	Y	Y	Y	Y	Y
31 Carter	N	Y	Y	Y	Y
32 Sessions	N	Y	Y	Y	Y
UTAH					
1 Bishop	N	Y	Y	Y	Y
2 Matheson	N	Y	Y	Y	Y
3 Chaffetz	N	Y	Y	Y	Y
VERMONT					
AL Welch	Y	Y	Y	Y	Y
VIRGINIA					
1 Wittman	N	Y	Y	Y	Y
2 Nye	N	Y	Y	Y	Y
3 Scott	Y	Y	Y	Y	Y
4 Forbes	N	Y	Y	Y	Y
5 Perriello	N	Y	Y	Y	Y
6 Goodlatte	N	Y	Y	Y	Y
7 Cantor	N	Y	Y	Y	Y
8 Moran	Y	Y	?	?	?
9 Boucher	Y	Y	Y	Y	Y
10 Wolf	N	Y	Y	Y	Y
11 Connolly	Y	Y	Y	Y	Y
WASHINGTON					
1 Inslee	Y	Y	Y	Y	Y
2 Larsen	Y	Y	Y	Y	Y
3 Baird	Y	Y	Y	Y	Y
4 Hastings	N	Y	Y	Y	Y
5 McMorris Rodgers	N	Y	Y	Y	Y
6 Dicks	Y	Y	Y	?	?
7 McDermott	Y	Y	Y	Y	Y
8 Reichert	N	Y	Y	Y	Y
9 Smith	Y	Y	?	Y	Y
WEST VIRGINIA					
1 Mollohan	Y	Y	Y	Y	Y
2 Capito	N	Y	Y	Y	Y
3 Rahall	Y	Y	Y	Y	Y
WISCONSIN					
1 Ryan	N	Y	Y	Y	Y
2 Baldwin	Y	Y	Y	Y	Y
3 Kind	Y	Y	Y	Y	Y
4 Moore	Y	Y	Y	Y	Y
5 Sensenbrenner	N	Y	Y	Y	Y
6 Petri	Y	Y	Y	Y	Y
7 Obey	Y	Y	Y	Y	Y
8 Kagen	Y	Y	?	Y	Y
WYOMING					
AL Lummis	N	Y	Y	Y	Y
DELEGATES					
Faleomavaega (A.S.)					
Norton (D.C.)					
Bordallo (Guam)					
Sablan (N. Marianas)					
Pierluisi (P.R.)					
Christensen (V.I.)					

IN THE HOUSE | By Vote Number

172. **HR 4849. Small-Business Tax Credits/Previous Question.** Cardoza, D-Calif., motion to order the previous question (thus ending debate and possibility of amendment) on adoption of the rule (H Res 1205) to provide for House floor consideration of the bill that would extend the Build America Bonds program and temporarily eliminate capital gains taxes on certain small-business stock. Motion agreed to 240-179: D 240-5; R 0-174. March 23, 2010.

173. **HR 4849. Small-Business Tax Credits/Rule.** Adoption of the rule (H Res 1205) that would provide for House floor consideration of the bill that would extend the Build America Bonds program and temporarily eliminate capital gains taxes on certain small-business stock. Adopted 233-187: D 233-14; R 0-173. March 23, 2010.

174. **H J Res 80. Blinded Veterans Association/Passage.** Filner, D-Calif., motion to suspend the rules and pass the joint resolution that would recognize the Blinded Veterans Association's efforts and support Blinded Veterans Day. Motion agreed to 416-0: D 244-0; R 172-0. A two-thirds majority of those present and voting (278 in this case) is required for passage under suspension of the rules. March 23, 2010.

175. **H Res 1186. Distracted Driving Awareness Month/Adoption.** Markey, D-Colo., motion to suspend the rules and adopt the resolution that would support the designation of Distracted Driving Awareness Month. Motion agreed to 410-2: D 243-0; R 167-2. A two-thirds majority of those present and voting (275 in this case) is required for adoption under suspension of the rules. March 23, 2010.

176. **HR 3976. Servicemember Mortgage Protections/Passage.** Filner, D-Calif., motion to suspend the rules and pass the bill that would extend through Dec. 31, 2015, a provision that bars lenders from initiating mortgage foreclosures for nine months after a servicemember returns from military service. Motion agreed to 416-4: D 248-0; R 168-4. A two-thirds majority of those present and voting (280 in this case) is required for passage under suspension of the rules. March 23, 2010.

177. **HR 4592. Energy Jobs for Veterans/Passage.** Filner, D-Calif., motion to suspend the rules and pass the bill that would authorize $10 million annually through fiscal 2015 for a Labor Department pilot program to encourage the employment of veterans in energy-related jobs. Motion agreed to 397-19: D 245-0; R 152-19. A two-thirds majority of those present and voting (278 in this case) is required for passage under suspension of the rules. March 23, 2010.

178. **H Con Res 257. Adjournment/Adoption.** Adoption of the concurrent resolution that would provide for the adjournment of the House until 2 p.m. on Tuesday, April 13, 2010, and the Senate until noon Monday, April 12, 2010. Adopted 236-175: D 225-17; R 11-158. March 24, 2010.

	172	173	174	175	176	177	178
ALABAMA							
1 Bonner	N	N	Y	Y	Y	Y	N
2 Bright	Y	N	Y	Y	Y	Y	Y
3 Rogers	N	N	Y	Y	Y	Y	N
4 Aderholt	N	N	Y	Y	Y	Y	N
5 Griffith	N	N	Y	Y	Y	Y	N
6 Bachus	N	N	Y	Y	Y	Y	N
7 Davis	?	?	?	?	?	?	?
ALASKA							
AL Young	N	N	Y	Y	Y	Y	N
ARIZONA							
1 Kirkpatrick	Y	N	Y	Y	Y	Y	Y
2 Franks	N	N	Y	Y	Y	N	N
3 Shadegg	N	N	Y	Y	Y	N	N
4 Pastor	Y	Y	Y	Y	Y	Y	Y
5 Mitchell	N	N	Y	Y	Y	Y	Y
6 Flake	N	N	Y	Y	N	N	Y
7 Grijalva	Y	Y	Y	Y	Y	Y	Y
8 Giffords	Y	Y	Y	+	Y	Y	Y
ARKANSAS							
1 Berry	Y	Y	Y	Y	Y	Y	Y
2 Snyder	Y	Y	Y	Y	Y	Y	Y
3 Boozman	N	N	Y	Y	Y	Y	N
4 Ross	Y	Y	Y	Y	Y	Y	Y
CALIFORNIA							
1 Thompson	Y	Y	Y	Y	Y	Y	Y
2 Herger	N	N	Y	Y	Y	N	N
3 Lungren	N	N	Y	Y	Y	Y	N
4 McClintock	N	N	Y	Y	N	N	N
5 Matsui	Y	Y	Y	Y	Y	Y	Y
6 Woolsey	Y	Y	Y	Y	Y	Y	Y
7 Miller, George	Y	Y	Y	Y	Y	Y	Y
8 Pelosi							
9 Lee	Y	Y	Y	Y	Y	Y	Y
10 Garamendi	Y	Y	Y	?	Y	Y	Y
11 McNerney	Y	Y	Y	Y	Y	Y	Y
12 Speier	Y	Y	Y	Y	Y	Y	Y
13 Stark	Y	Y	Y	Y	Y	Y	Y
14 Eshoo	Y	Y	Y	Y	Y	Y	?
15 Honda	Y	Y	Y	Y	Y	Y	Y
16 Lofgren	Y	Y	Y	Y	Y	Y	Y
17 Farr	Y	Y	Y	Y	Y	Y	Y
18 Cardoza	Y	Y	Y	Y	Y	Y	?
19 Radanovich	N	N	Y	Y	Y	Y	N
20 Costa	Y	Y	Y	?	Y	Y	Y
21 Nunes	N	N	Y	Y	Y	Y	N
22 McCarthy	N	N	Y	Y	Y	Y	N
23 Capps	Y	Y	Y	Y	Y	Y	Y
24 Gallegly	N	N	Y	Y	Y	Y	N
25 McKeon	N	N	Y	Y	Y	Y	N
26 Dreier	N	N	Y	Y	Y	Y	N
27 Sherman	Y	Y	Y	Y	Y	Y	Y
28 Berman	Y	Y	Y	Y	Y	Y	Y
29 Schiff	Y	Y	Y	Y	Y	Y	Y
30 Waxman	Y	Y	Y	Y	Y	Y	Y
31 Becerra	Y	Y	Y	Y	Y	Y	Y
32 Chu	Y	Y	Y	Y	Y	Y	Y
33 Watson	Y	Y	Y	Y	Y	Y	Y
34 Roybal-Allard	Y	Y	Y	Y	Y	Y	Y
35 Waters	Y	Y	Y	Y	Y	Y	?
36 Harman	Y	Y	Y	Y	Y	Y	Y
37 Richardson	Y	Y	Y	Y	Y	Y	Y
38 Napolitano	Y	Y	Y	Y	Y	Y	Y
39 Sánchez, Linda	Y	Y	Y	Y	Y	Y	Y
40 Royce	N	N	Y	Y	Y	Y	N
41 Lewis	N	N	Y	Y	Y	Y	N
42 Miller, Gary	N	N	Y	Y	Y	Y	N
43 Baca	Y	Y	Y	Y	Y	Y	Y
44 Calvert	N	N	Y	Y	Y	Y	N
45 Bono Mack	N	N	Y	Y	Y	Y	?
46 Rohrabacher	N	N	Y	Y	Y	Y	N
47 Sanchez, Loretta	Y	Y	Y	Y	Y	Y	Y
48 Campbell	N	N	Y	Y	Y	N	N
49 Issa	N	N	Y	Y	Y	Y	N
50 Bilbray	N	N	Y	Y	Y	Y	Y
51 Filner	Y	Y	Y	Y	Y	Y	Y
52 Hunter	N	N	Y	Y	Y	Y	N
53 Davis	Y	Y	Y	Y	Y	Y	Y

	172	173	174	175	176	177	178
COLORADO							
1 DeGette	Y	Y	Y	Y	Y	Y	Y
2 Polis	Y	Y	Y	Y	Y	Y	Y
3 Salazar	Y	Y	Y	Y	Y	Y	Y
4 Markey	Y	Y	Y	Y	Y	Y	Y
5 Lamborn	N	N	Y	Y	Y	N	N
6 Coffman	N	N	Y	Y	Y	Y	N
7 Perlmutter	Y	Y	Y	Y	Y	Y	Y
CONNECTICUT							
1 Larson	Y	Y	Y	Y	Y	Y	Y
2 Courtney	Y	Y	Y	Y	Y	Y	Y
3 DeLauro	Y	Y	Y	Y	Y	Y	Y
4 Himes	Y	Y	Y	Y	Y	Y	N
5 Murphy	Y	Y	Y	Y	Y	Y	Y
DELAWARE							
AL Castle	N	N	Y	Y	Y	Y	N
FLORIDA							
1 Miller	N	N	?	Y	Y	Y	N
2 Boyd	Y	Y	Y	Y	Y	Y	Y
3 Brown	Y	Y	Y	Y	Y	Y	Y
4 Crenshaw	N	N	Y	Y	Y	Y	N
5 Brown-Waite	N	N	Y	Y	Y	Y	?
6 Stearns	N	N	Y	Y	Y	Y	N
7 Mica	N	N	Y	Y	Y	Y	N
8 Grayson	Y	Y	Y	Y	Y	Y	Y
9 Bilirakis	N	?	Y	Y	Y	?	N
10 Young	N	N	Y	Y	Y	Y	N
11 Castor	Y	Y	Y	Y	Y	Y	Y
12 Putnam	N	N	Y	Y	Y	Y	N
13 Buchanan	N	N	Y	Y	Y	Y	N
14 Mack	N	N	Y	Y	Y	Y	?
15 Posey	N	N	Y	Y	Y	Y	N
16 Rooney	N	N	Y	Y	Y	Y	N
17 Meek	Y	Y	Y	Y	Y	Y	Y
18 Ros-Lehtinen	N	N	Y	Y	Y	Y	N
19 Vacant							
20 Wasserman Schultz	Y	Y	Y	Y	Y	Y	Y
21 Diaz-Balart, L.	N	N	Y	Y	Y	Y	?
22 Klein	Y	Y	Y	Y	Y	Y	Y
23 Hastings	Y	Y	Y	Y	Y	Y	Y
24 Kosmas	Y	Y	Y	Y	Y	Y	N
25 Diaz-Balart, M.	N	N	Y	Y	Y	Y	N
GEORGIA							
1 Kingston	N	N	Y	Y	N	N	N
2 Bishop	Y	Y	Y	Y	Y	Y	Y
3 Westmoreland	N	N	Y	Y	N	N	N
4 Johnson	Y	Y	Y	Y	Y	Y	Y
5 Lewis	Y	Y	Y	Y	Y	Y	Y
6 Price	N	N	Y	Y	+	N	N
7 Linder	N	N	Y	Y	Y	Y	N
8 Marshall	Y	Y	Y	Y	Y	Y	Y
9 Vacant							
10 Broun	N	N	Y	Y	N	N	N
11 Gingrey	N	N	Y	Y	Y	N	N
12 Barrow	Y	Y	Y	Y	Y	Y	Y
13 Scott	Y	Y	Y	Y	Y	Y	Y
HAWAII							
1 Vacant							
2 Hirono	Y	Y	Y	Y	Y	Y	Y
IDAHO							
1 Minnick	N	N	Y	Y	Y	Y	N
2 Simpson	N	N	Y	Y	Y	Y	N
ILLINOIS							
1 Rush	Y	Y	Y	Y	Y	Y	Y
2 Jackson	Y	Y	Y	Y	Y	Y	Y
3 Lipinski	Y	Y	Y	Y	Y	Y	Y
4 Gutierrez	Y	Y	Y	Y	Y	?	Y
5 Quigley	Y	N	Y	Y	Y	Y	Y
6 Roskam	N	N	Y	Y	Y	Y	N
7 Davis	Y	Y	Y	Y	Y	Y	Y
8 Bean	Y	Y	Y	Y	Y	Y	Y
9 Schakowsky	Y	Y	Y	Y	Y	Y	Y
10 Kirk	N	N	Y	Y	Y	Y	N
11 Halvorson	Y	Y	Y	Y	Y	Y	Y
12 Costello	Y	Y	Y	Y	Y	Y	Y
13 Biggert	N	N	Y	Y	Y	Y	N
14 Foster	Y	Y	Y	Y	Y	Y	Y
15 Johnson	N	N	Y	N	Y	Y	?

KEY   Republicans   Democrats

Y	Voted for (yea)	X	Paired against	C	Voted "present" to avoid possible conflict of interest
#	Paired for	–	Announced against		
+	Announced for	P	Voted "present"	?	Did not vote or otherwise make a position known
N	Voted against (nay)				

	172	173	174	175	176	177	178
16 **Manzullo**	N	N	Y	Y	Y	Y	N
17 Hare	Y	Y	Y	Y	Y	Y	Y
18 **Schock**	N	N	Y	Y	Y	Y	?
19 **Shimkus**	N	N	Y	Y	Y	Y	N
INDIANA							
1 Visclosky	Y	Y	Y	Y	Y	Y	Y
2 Donnelly	Y	Y	Y	Y	Y	Y	N
3 **Souder**	N	N	Y	Y	Y	Y	N
4 **Buyer**	N	N	Y	Y	Y	Y	N
5 **Burton**	N	N	Y	Y	Y	Y	N
6 **Pence**	N	N	Y	Y	Y	Y	N
7 Carson	Y	Y	Y	Y	Y	Y	Y
8 Ellsworth	Y	N	Y	Y	Y	Y	N
9 Hill	N	N	Y	Y	Y	Y	?
IOWA							
1 Braley	Y	Y	Y	Y	Y	Y	Y
2 Loebsack	Y	Y	Y	Y	Y	Y	Y
3 Boswell	Y	Y	Y	Y	Y	Y	Y
4 **Latham**	N	N	Y	Y	Y	Y	N
5 **King**	N	N	Y	Y	Y	Y	N
KANSAS							
1 **Moran**	N	N	Y	Y	Y	Y	N
2 **Jenkins**	N	N	Y	Y	Y	Y	N
3 Moore	?	Y	Y	Y	Y	Y	Y
4 **Tiahrt**	–	–	+	+	+	+	N
KENTUCKY							
1 **Whitfield**	N	N	Y	Y	Y	Y	N
2 **Guthrie**	N	N	Y	Y	Y	Y	N
3 Yarmuth	Y	Y	Y	Y	Y	Y	Y
4 **Davis**	N	N	Y	Y	Y	Y	N
5 **Rogers**	N	N	Y	Y	Y	Y	N
6 Chandler	Y	Y	Y	Y	Y	Y	Y
LOUISIANA							
1 **Scalise**	N	N	Y	Y	Y	Y	N
2 **Cao**	N	N	Y	Y	Y	Y	N
3 Melancon	Y	Y	Y	Y	Y	Y	Y
4 **Fleming**	N	N	Y	Y	Y	Y	N
5 **Alexander**	N	N	Y	Y	Y	Y	?
6 **Cassidy**	N	N	Y	Y	Y	Y	N
7 **Boustany**	N	N	Y	Y	Y	Y	N
MAINE							
1 Pingree	Y	Y	Y	Y	Y	Y	Y
2 Michaud	Y	Y	Y	Y	Y	Y	Y
MARYLAND							
1 Kratovil	Y	Y	Y	Y	Y	Y	N
2 Ruppersberger	Y	Y	Y	Y	Y	Y	Y
3 Sarbanes	Y	Y	Y	Y	Y	Y	Y
4 Edwards	Y	Y	Y	Y	Y	Y	Y
5 Hoyer	Y	Y	Y	Y	Y	Y	Y
6 **Bartlett**	N	N	Y	Y	Y	Y	Y
7 Cummings	Y	Y	Y	Y	Y	Y	?
8 Van Hollen	Y	Y	Y	Y	Y	Y	Y
MASSACHUSETTS							
1 Olver	Y	Y	Y	Y	Y	Y	Y
2 Neal	Y	Y	Y	Y	Y	Y	Y
3 McGovern	Y	Y	Y	Y	Y	Y	Y
4 Frank	Y	Y	?	Y	Y	Y	Y
5 Tsongas	Y	Y	Y	Y	Y	Y	Y
6 Tierney	Y	Y	Y	Y	Y	Y	Y
7 Markey	Y	Y	Y	Y	Y	Y	Y
8 Capuano	Y	Y	Y	Y	Y	Y	Y
9 Lynch	Y	Y	Y	Y	Y	Y	Y
10 Delahunt	Y	Y	Y	Y	Y	Y	Y
MICHIGAN							
1 Stupak	Y	Y	Y	Y	Y	Y	Y
2 **Hoekstra**	?	?	?	?	?	?	?
3 **Ehlers**	N	N	Y	Y	Y	Y	Y
4 **Camp**	N	N	Y	Y	Y	Y	N
5 Kildee	Y	Y	Y	Y	Y	Y	Y
6 **Upton**	N	N	Y	Y	Y	Y	N
7 Schauer	Y	Y	Y	Y	Y	Y	N
8 **Rogers**	N	N	Y	Y	Y	Y	N
9 Peters	Y	Y	Y	Y	Y	Y	Y
10 **Miller**	N	N	Y	Y	Y	Y	N
11 **McCotter**	N	N	Y	Y	Y	Y	N
12 Levin	Y	Y	Y	Y	Y	Y	Y
13 Kilpatrick	?	?	?	+	+	+	+
14 Conyers	Y	Y	Y	Y	Y	Y	Y
15 Dingell	Y	Y	Y	Y	Y	Y	Y
MINNESOTA							
1 Walz	Y	Y	Y	Y	Y	Y	Y
2 **Kline**	N	N	Y	Y	Y	Y	N
3 **Paulsen**	N	N	Y	Y	Y	Y	N
4 McCollum	Y	Y	Y	?	Y	Y	Y
5 Ellison	Y	Y	?	Y	Y	Y	Y
6 **Bachmann**	N	N	Y	Y	Y	Y	N
7 Peterson	Y	Y	Y	Y	Y	Y	Y
8 Oberstar	Y	Y	Y	Y	Y	Y	Y
MISSISSIPPI							
1 Childers	Y	Y	Y	Y	Y	Y	Y
2 Thompson	Y	Y	Y	Y	Y	?	Y
3 **Harper**	N	N	Y	Y	Y	Y	N
4 Taylor	N	N	Y	Y	Y	Y	Y
MISSOURI							
1 Clay	Y	Y	Y	Y	Y	Y	Y
2 **Akin**	N	N	Y	Y	Y	?	N
3 Carnahan	Y	Y	Y	Y	Y	Y	Y
4 Skelton	Y	Y	Y	Y	Y	Y	Y
5 Cleaver	Y	Y	Y	Y	Y	Y	Y
6 **Graves**	N	N	Y	Y	Y	Y	N
7 **Blunt**	N	N	Y	Y	Y	Y	N
8 **Emerson**	N	N	Y	Y	Y	Y	N
9 **Luetkemeyer**	N	N	Y	Y	Y	Y	N
MONTANA							
AL **Rehberg**	N	N	Y	Y	Y	Y	N
NEBRASKA							
1 **Fortenberry**	N	N	?	Y	Y	Y	N
2 **Terry**	N	N	Y	Y	Y	Y	N
3 **Smith**	N	N	Y	Y	Y	Y	N
NEVADA							
1 Berkley	Y	Y	Y	Y	Y	Y	Y
2 **Heller**	N	N	Y	Y	Y	Y	N
3 Titus	Y	Y	Y	Y	Y	Y	Y
NEW HAMPSHIRE							
1 Shea-Porter	Y	Y	Y	Y	Y	Y	Y
2 Hodes	Y	Y	Y	Y	Y	Y	Y
NEW JERSEY							
1 Andrews	Y	Y	Y	Y	Y	Y	Y
2 **LoBiondo**	N	N	Y	Y	Y	Y	N
3 Adler	Y	N	Y	Y	Y	Y	N
4 **Smith**	N	N	Y	Y	Y	Y	N
5 **Garrett**	N	N	Y	Y	Y	N	N
6 Pallone	Y	Y	Y	Y	Y	Y	Y
7 **Lance**	N	N	Y	Y	Y	Y	N
8 Pascrell	Y	Y	Y	Y	Y	Y	Y
9 Rothman	Y	Y	Y	Y	Y	Y	Y
10 Payne	Y	Y	Y	?	Y	Y	Y
11 **Frelinghuysen**	N	N	Y	Y	Y	Y	N
12 Holt	Y	Y	Y	Y	Y	Y	Y
13 Sires	Y	Y	Y	Y	Y	Y	Y
NEW MEXICO							
1 Heinrich	Y	Y	Y	Y	Y	Y	Y
2 Teague	Y	Y	Y	Y	Y	Y	Y
3 Luján	Y	Y	Y	Y	Y	Y	Y
NEW YORK							
1 Bishop	Y	Y	Y	Y	Y	Y	Y
2 Israel	Y	Y	Y	Y	Y	Y	Y
3 **King**	N	N	Y	Y	Y	Y	N
4 McCarthy	Y	Y	Y	Y	Y	Y	Y
5 Ackerman	Y	Y	Y	Y	Y	Y	Y
6 Meeks	Y	Y	Y	Y	Y	Y	Y
7 Crowley	Y	Y	Y	Y	Y	Y	Y
8 Nadler	Y	Y	Y	Y	Y	Y	Y
9 Weiner	Y	Y	Y	Y	Y	Y	Y
10 Towns	Y	Y	Y	Y	Y	Y	Y
11 Clarke	Y	Y	Y	Y	Y	Y	Y
12 Velázquez	Y	Y	Y	Y	Y	Y	Y
13 McMahon	Y	Y	Y	Y	Y	Y	N
14 Maloney	Y	Y	Y	Y	Y	Y	Y
15 Rangel	Y	Y	Y	Y	Y	Y	Y
16 Serrano	Y	Y	Y	Y	Y	Y	Y
17 Engel	Y	Y	Y	Y	Y	Y	Y
18 Lowey	Y	+	Y	Y	Y	Y	Y
19 Hall	Y	Y	Y	Y	Y	Y	Y
20 Murphy	Y	N	Y	Y	Y	Y	N
21 Tonko	Y	Y	Y	Y	Y	Y	Y
22 Hinchey	Y	Y	Y	Y	Y	Y	Y
23 Owens	Y	Y	Y	Y	Y	Y	Y
24 Arcuri	Y	Y	Y	Y	Y	Y	N
25 Maffei	Y	Y	Y	Y	Y	Y	Y
26 **Lee**	N	N	Y	Y	Y	Y	N
27 Higgins	Y	Y	Y	Y	Y	Y	Y
28 Slaughter	Y	Y	?	Y	Y	Y	Y
29 Vacant							
NORTH CAROLINA							
1 Butterfield	Y	Y	Y	Y	Y	Y	Y
2 Etheridge	Y	Y	Y	Y	Y	Y	Y
3 **Jones**	N	N	Y	Y	Y	Y	Y
4 Price	Y	Y	Y	Y	Y	Y	Y
5 **Foxx**	N	N	Y	Y	Y	Y	N
6 **Coble**	N	N	Y	Y	Y	Y	N
7 McIntyre	Y	Y	Y	Y	Y	Y	Y
8 Kissell	Y	Y	Y	Y	Y	Y	Y
9 **Myrick**	N	N	Y	Y	Y	Y	N
10 **McHenry**	N	N	Y	Y	Y	Y	Y
11 Shuler	Y	N	Y	Y	Y	Y	?
12 Watt	Y	Y	Y	Y	Y	Y	Y
13 Miller	Y	Y	Y	Y	Y	Y	Y
NORTH DAKOTA							
AL Pomeroy	Y	Y	Y	Y	Y	Y	Y
OHIO							
1 Driehaus	Y	Y	Y	Y	Y	Y	Y
2 **Schmidt**	N	N	Y	Y	Y	Y	N
3 **Turner**	N	N	Y	Y	Y	Y	N
4 **Jordan**	N	N	Y	Y	Y	N	N
5 **Latta**	N	N	Y	Y	Y	Y	N
6 Wilson	Y	Y	Y	Y	Y	Y	Y
7 **Austria**	N	N	Y	Y	Y	Y	N
8 **Boehner**	N	N	Y	Y	Y	Y	N
9 Kaptur	Y	Y	Y	Y	Y	Y	Y
10 Kucinich	Y	Y	Y	Y	Y	Y	Y
11 Fudge	Y	Y	Y	Y	Y	Y	Y
12 **Tiberi**	N	N	Y	Y	Y	Y	N
13 Sutton	Y	Y	Y	Y	Y	Y	Y
14 **LaTourette**	N	N	Y	Y	Y	Y	N
15 Kilroy	Y	Y	Y	Y	Y	Y	Y
16 Boccieri	+	Y	Y	Y	Y	Y	Y
17 Ryan	Y	Y	Y	Y	Y	Y	Y
18 Space	Y	Y	Y	Y	Y	Y	Y
OKLAHOMA							
1 **Sullivan**	N	N	Y	Y	Y	Y	N
2 Boren	Y	Y	Y	Y	Y	Y	Y
3 **Lucas**	N	N	Y	Y	Y	Y	N
4 **Cole**	N	N	Y	Y	Y	Y	N
5 **Fallin**	N	N	Y	Y	Y	Y	N
OREGON							
1 Wu	Y	Y	Y	Y	Y	Y	Y
2 **Walden**	N	N	Y	Y	Y	Y	N
3 Blumenauer	Y	Y	Y	Y	Y	Y	Y
4 DeFazio	Y	Y	Y	Y	Y	Y	Y
5 Schrader	Y	Y	Y	Y	Y	?	Y
PENNSYLVANIA							
1 Brady	Y	Y	Y	Y	Y	Y	Y
2 Fattah	Y	Y	?	Y	Y	Y	Y
3 Dahlkemper	Y	Y	Y	Y	Y	Y	Y
4 Altmire	Y	Y	Y	Y	Y	Y	N
5 **Thompson**	N	N	Y	Y	Y	Y	N
6 **Gerlach**	N	N	Y	Y	Y	Y	?
7 Sestak	Y	Y	Y	Y	Y	Y	N
8 Murphy, P.	Y	Y	Y	Y	Y	Y	?
9 **Shuster**	N	N	Y	Y	Y	Y	N
10 Carney	Y	Y	Y	Y	Y	Y	N
11 Kanjorski	Y	Y	Y	Y	Y	Y	Y
12 Vacant							
13 Schwartz	Y	Y	Y	Y	Y	Y	Y
14 Doyle	Y	Y	Y	Y	Y	Y	Y
15 **Dent**	N	N	Y	Y	Y	Y	N
16 **Pitts**	N	N	Y	Y	Y	Y	N
17 Holden	Y	Y	Y	Y	Y	Y	Y
18 **Murphy, T.**	N	N	Y	Y	Y	Y	N
19 **Platts**	N	N	Y	Y	Y	Y	N
RHODE ISLAND							
1 Kennedy	?	?	?	?	?	?	Y
2 Langevin	Y	Y	Y	Y	Y	Y	Y
SOUTH CAROLINA							
1 **Brown**	N	N	Y	Y	Y	Y	N
2 **Wilson**	N	N	Y	Y	Y	Y	N
3 **Barrett**	N	N	Y	Y	Y	N	N
4 **Inglis**	N	N	Y	Y	Y	Y	N
5 Spratt	Y	Y	Y	Y	Y	Y	Y
6 Clyburn	Y	Y	Y	Y	Y	Y	Y
SOUTH DAKOTA							
AL Herseth Sandlin	Y	N	Y	Y	Y	Y	Y
TENNESSEE							
1 **Roe**	N	N	Y	Y	Y	Y	N
2 **Duncan**	N	N	Y	Y	Y	Y	N
3 **Wamp**	?	?	?	?	?	?	N
4 Davis	?	?	?	?	?	?	Y
5 Cooper	Y	Y	Y	Y	Y	Y	Y
6 Gordon	Y	Y	Y	Y	Y	Y	Y
7 **Blackburn**	N	N	Y	Y	Y	Y	N
8 Tanner	Y	Y	Y	Y	Y	Y	Y
9 Cohen	Y	Y	Y	Y	Y	Y	Y
TEXAS							
1 **Gohmert**	N	N	Y	?	Y	Y	Y
2 **Poe**	N	N	?	?	Y	Y	N
3 **Johnson, S.**	N	N	Y	Y	Y	Y	N
4 **Hall**	N	N	Y	Y	Y	Y	N
5 **Hensarling**	N	N	Y	Y	Y	N	N
6 **Barton**	N	N	Y	Y	Y	Y	N
7 **Culberson**	N	N	Y	Y	Y	Y	N
8 **Brady**	N	N	Y	Y	Y	Y	N
9 Green, A.	Y	Y	Y	Y	Y	Y	Y
10 **McCaul**	N	N	Y	Y	Y	Y	N
11 **Conaway**	N	N	Y	Y	Y	N	N
12 **Granger**	N	N	Y	Y	Y	Y	N
13 **Thornberry**	N	N	Y	Y	Y	Y	N
14 **Paul**	N	N	Y	N	N	N	Y
15 Hinojosa	Y	Y	Y	Y	Y	Y	Y
16 Reyes	Y	Y	Y	Y	Y	Y	?
17 Edwards	Y	Y	Y	Y	Y	Y	Y
18 Jackson Lee	Y	Y	Y	Y	Y	Y	Y
19 **Neugebauer**	N	N	Y	Y	Y	Y	N
20 Gonzalez	Y	Y	Y	Y	Y	Y	Y
21 **Smith**	N	N	Y	Y	Y	Y	N
22 **Olson**	N	N	Y	?	Y	Y	Y
23 Rodriguez	Y	Y	Y	Y	Y	Y	Y
24 **Marchant**	N	N	Y	Y	Y	Y	N
25 Doggett	Y	Y	Y	Y	Y	Y	Y
26 **Burgess**	N	N	Y	Y	Y	Y	N
27 Ortiz	Y	Y	Y	Y	Y	Y	Y
28 Cuellar	Y	Y	Y	Y	Y	Y	Y
29 Green, G.	Y	Y	Y	Y	Y	Y	Y
30 Johnson, E.	Y	Y	Y	Y	Y	Y	Y
31 **Carter**	N	N	Y	Y	Y	Y	N
32 **Sessions**	N	N	Y	?	?	?	N
UTAH							
1 **Bishop**	N	N	Y	?	Y	N	N
2 Matheson	Y	Y	Y	Y	Y	Y	Y
3 **Chaffetz**	N	N	Y	Y	Y	N	Y
VERMONT							
AL Welch	Y	Y	Y	Y	Y	Y	Y
VIRGINIA							
1 **Wittman**	N	N	Y	Y	Y	Y	N
2 Nye	N	N	Y	Y	Y	Y	Y
3 Scott	Y	Y	Y	Y	Y	Y	Y
4 **Forbes**	N	N	Y	Y	Y	Y	N
5 Perriello	Y	Y	Y	Y	Y	Y	N
6 **Goodlatte**	N	N	Y	Y	Y	Y	N
7 **Cantor**	N	N	Y	Y	Y	Y	N
8 Moran	Y	Y	Y	Y	Y	Y	Y
9 Boucher	Y	Y	Y	Y	Y	Y	Y
10 **Wolf**	N	N	Y	Y	Y	Y	N
11 Connolly	Y	Y	Y	Y	Y	Y	Y
WASHINGTON							
1 Inslee	Y	Y	Y	Y	Y	Y	Y
2 Larsen	Y	Y	Y	Y	Y	Y	Y
3 Baird	Y	Y	Y	Y	Y	Y	Y
4 **Hastings**	N	N	Y	Y	Y	Y	N
5 **McMorris Rodgers**	N	N	Y	Y	Y	Y	N
6 Dicks	?	Y	Y	Y	Y	Y	Y
7 McDermott	Y	Y	Y	Y	Y	Y	Y
8 **Reichert**	N	N	Y	Y	Y	Y	N
9 Smith	Y	Y	Y	Y	Y	Y	Y
WEST VIRGINIA							
1 Mollohan	Y	Y	Y	Y	Y	Y	Y
2 **Capito**	N	N	Y	Y	Y	Y	N
3 Rahall	Y	Y	Y	Y	Y	Y	Y
WISCONSIN							
1 **Ryan**	N	N	Y	Y	Y	Y	N
2 Baldwin	Y	Y	Y	Y	Y	Y	Y
3 Kind	Y	Y	Y	Y	Y	Y	Y
4 Moore	Y	Y	Y	Y	Y	Y	Y
5 **Sensenbrenner**	N	N	Y	Y	Y	N	N
6 **Petri**	N	N	Y	Y	Y	Y	N
7 Obey	Y	Y	Y	Y	Y	Y	Y
8 Kagen	Y	Y	Y	Y	Y	Y	Y
WYOMING							
AL **Lummis**	N	N	Y	Y	Y	N	N
DELEGATES							
Faleomavaega (A.S.)							
Norton (D.C.)							
Bordallo (Guam)							
Sablan (N. Marianas)							
Pierluisi (P.R.)							
Christensen (V.I.)							

IN THE HOUSE | By Vote Number

179. **HR 4899. Disaster Relief and Summer Jobs Funding/Rule.** Adoption of the rule (H Res 1204) that would provide for House floor consideration of the bill that would provide $5.1 billion in emergency supplemental funding for the Federal Emergency Management Agency and $600 million for Labor Department grants for youth summer jobs programs. Adopted 233-191: D 232-17; R 1-174. March 24, 2010.

180. **H Res 917. Florida Keys Scenic Highway/Adoption.** Perriello, D-Va., motion to suspend the rules and adopt the resolution that would recognize the Florida Keys Scenic Highway on its designation as an All-American Road by the Transportation Department. Motion agreed to 420-2: D 247-0; R 173-2. A two-thirds majority of those present and voting (282 in this case) is required for adoption under suspension of the rules. March 24, 2010.

181. **HR 4849. Small-Business Tax Credits/Recommit.** Camp, R-Mich., motion to recommit the bill to the Ways and Means Committee with instructions that it be immediately reported back with an amendment that would provide tax incentives for small businesses and repeal certain provisions of the health care overhaul law that cap the amount that can be deposited in flexible spending accounts and bar the use of such funds for over-the-counter medicine. It would offset the cost of the legislation by excluding certain low-quality fuels from a biofuel producer credit. Motion rejected 184-239: D 10-239; R 174-0. March 24, 2010.

182. **HR 4849. Small-Business Tax Credits/Passage.** Passage of the bill that would provide $16.8 billion over 10 years in tax incentives for state and local governments and small businesses. It includes $13.2 billion for bond programs for state and local governments, used largely for infrastructure and to extend the Build America Bonds program. It would provide $3.6 billion in small-business tax incentives, including an exemption from capital gains taxes on the sale of small-business stock. It would be offset by various tax provisions, including new limits on foreign-owned companies' abilities to use protections under U.S. tax treaties to move money to other countries. Passed 246-178: D 242-7; R 4-171. March 24, 2010.

183. **HR 4098. Federal File-Sharing Guidelines/Passage.** Towns, D-N.Y., motion to suspend the rules and pass the bill that would require the Office of Management and Budget to issue guidelines for federal employees and contractors on the use of peer-to-peer file-sharing programs. Motion agreed to 408-13: D 248-0; R 160-13. A two-thirds majority of those present and voting (281 in this case) is required for passage under suspension of the rules. March 24, 2010.

184. **HR 1879. National Guard Employment Protection/Passage.** Filner, D-Calif., motion to suspend the rules and pass the bill that would exempt full-time National Guard service from the five-year cumulative limit that employees are allowed to be absent from work on military service and still be guaranteed their jobs with their civilian employers. Motion agreed to 416-1: D 245-0; R 171-1. A two-thirds majority of those present and voting (278 in this case) is required for passage under suspension of the rules. March 24, 2010.

	179	180	181	182	183	184
ALABAMA						
1 **Bonner**	N	Y	Y	N	Y	Y
2 Bright	Y	Y	Y	N	Y	Y
3 **Rogers**	N	Y	Y	N	Y	Y
4 **Aderholt**	N	Y	Y	N	Y	Y
5 **Griffith**	N	Y	Y	N	Y	Y
6 **Bachus**	N	Y	Y	N	Y	Y
7 Davis	?	?	?	?	?	?
ALASKA						
AL **Young**	N	N	Y	N	N	Y
ARIZONA						
1 Kirkpatrick	N	Y	N	Y	Y	Y
2 **Franks**	N	Y	Y	N	Y	Y
3 **Shadegg**	N	Y	Y	N	Y	Y
4 Pastor	Y	Y	N	Y	Y	Y
5 Mitchell	N	Y	N	Y	Y	Y
6 **Flake**	N	Y	Y	N	Y	Y
7 Grijalva	Y	Y	N	Y	Y	Y
8 Giffords	Y	Y	N	Y	Y	Y
ARKANSAS						
1 Berry	Y	Y	N	Y	Y	Y
2 Snyder	Y	Y	N	Y	Y	Y
3 **Boozman**	N	Y	Y	N	Y	Y
4 Ross	Y	Y	Y	Y	Y	Y
CALIFORNIA						
1 Thompson	Y	Y	N	Y	Y	Y
2 **Herger**	N	Y	Y	N	Y	Y
3 **Lungren**	N	Y	Y	N	Y	Y
4 **McClintock**	N	Y	Y	N	Y	Y
5 Matsui	Y	Y	N	Y	Y	Y
6 Woolsey	Y	Y	N	Y	Y	Y
7 Miller, George	Y	Y	N	Y	Y	Y
8 Pelosi						
9 Lee	Y	Y	N	Y	Y	Y
10 Garamendi	Y	Y	N	Y	Y	Y
11 McNerney	Y	Y	N	Y	Y	Y
12 Speier	Y	Y	N	Y	Y	Y
13 Stark	Y	Y	N	Y	Y	Y
14 Eshoo	Y	Y	N	Y	Y	Y
15 Honda	Y	?	N	Y	Y	Y
16 Lofgren	Y	Y	N	Y	P	Y
17 Farr	Y	Y	N	Y	Y	Y
18 Cardoza	?	?	N	Y	Y	Y
19 **Radanovich**	N	Y	Y	N	Y	Y
20 Costa	Y	Y	N	Y	Y	Y
21 **Nunes**	N	Y	Y	N	Y	Y
22 **McCarthy**	N	Y	Y	N	Y	Y
23 Capps	Y	Y	N	Y	Y	Y
24 **Gallegly**	N	Y	Y	N	Y	Y
25 **McKeon**	N	Y	Y	N	Y	Y
26 **Dreier**	N	Y	Y	N	Y	Y
27 Sherman	Y	Y	N	Y	Y	Y
28 Berman	Y	Y	N	Y	Y	Y
29 Schiff	Y	Y	N	Y	Y	Y
30 Waxman	Y	Y	N	Y	Y	Y
31 Becerra	Y	Y	N	Y	Y	?
32 Chu	Y	Y	N	Y	Y	Y
33 Watson	Y	Y	N	Y	Y	Y
34 Roybal-Allard	Y	Y	N	Y	Y	Y
35 Waters	Y	Y	N	Y	Y	Y
36 Harman	Y	Y	N	Y	Y	Y
37 Richardson	Y	Y	N	Y	Y	Y
38 Napolitano	Y	Y	N	Y	Y	Y
39 Sánchez, Linda	Y	Y	N	Y	Y	Y
40 **Royce**	N	Y	Y	N	N	Y
41 **Lewis**	N	Y	Y	N	Y	Y
42 **Miller, Gary**	N	Y	Y	N	Y	Y
43 Baca	Y	Y	N	Y	Y	Y
44 **Calvert**	N	Y	Y	N	Y	Y
45 **Bono Mack**	N	Y	Y	N	Y	Y
46 **Rohrabacher**	N	Y	Y	N	Y	Y
47 Sanchez, Loretta	Y	Y	N	Y	Y	Y
48 **Campbell**	N	Y	Y	N	Y	Y
49 **Issa**	N	Y	Y	N	Y	Y
50 **Bilbray**	N	Y	Y	N	Y	Y
51 Filner	Y	Y	N	Y	Y	Y
52 **Hunter**	N	Y	Y	N	Y	Y
53 Davis	Y	Y	N	Y	Y	Y

	179	180	181	182	183	184
COLORADO						
1 DeGette	Y	Y	N	Y	Y	Y
2 Polis	Y	Y	N	Y	Y	Y
3 Salazar	Y	Y	N	Y	Y	Y
4 Markey	Y	Y	N	Y	Y	Y
5 **Lamborn**	N	Y	Y	N	Y	Y
6 **Coffman**	N	Y	Y	N	Y	Y
7 Perlmutter	Y	Y	N	Y	Y	Y
CONNECTICUT						
1 Larson	Y	Y	N	Y	Y	Y
2 Courtney	Y	Y	N	Y	Y	Y
3 DeLauro	Y	Y	N	Y	Y	Y
4 Himes	Y	Y	N	Y	Y	Y
5 Murphy	Y	Y	N	Y	Y	Y
DELAWARE						
AL **Castle**	N	Y	Y	Y	Y	Y
FLORIDA						
1 **Miller**	N	Y	Y	N	Y	Y
2 Boyd	N	Y	N	Y	Y	Y
3 Brown	Y	Y	N	Y	Y	Y
4 **Crenshaw**	N	Y	Y	N	Y	Y
5 **Brown-Waite**	?	?	?	N	Y	Y
6 **Stearns**	N	Y	Y	N	Y	Y
7 **Mica**	N	Y	Y	N	Y	Y
8 Grayson	Y	Y	N	Y	Y	Y
9 **Bilirakis**	N	Y	Y	N	Y	Y
10 **Young**	N	Y	Y	N	Y	Y
11 Castor	Y	Y	N	Y	Y	Y
12 **Putnam**	N	Y	Y	N	Y	Y
13 **Buchanan**	N	Y	Y	N	Y	Y
14 **Mack**	N	Y	Y	N	Y	Y
15 **Posey**	N	Y	Y	N	Y	Y
16 **Rooney**	N	Y	Y	N	Y	Y
17 Meek	Y	Y	N	Y	Y	Y
18 **Ros-Lehtinen**	N	Y	Y	N	Y	Y
19 Vacant						
20 Wasserman Schultz	Y	Y	N	Y	Y	Y
21 **Diaz-Balart, L.**	N	Y	Y	N	Y	Y
22 Klein	Y	Y	N	Y	Y	Y
23 Hastings	Y	Y	N	Y	Y	Y
24 Kosmas	Y	Y	N	Y	Y	Y
25 **Diaz-Balart, M.**	N	Y	Y	N	Y	Y
GEORGIA						
1 **Kingston**	N	Y	Y	N	N	Y
2 Bishop	Y	Y	N	Y	Y	Y
3 **Westmoreland**	N	Y	Y	N	N	Y
4 Johnson	Y	Y	N	Y	Y	Y
5 Lewis	Y	Y	N	Y	Y	Y
6 **Price**	N	Y	Y	N	N	Y
7 **Linder**	N	N	Y	N	Y	Y
8 Marshall	Y	Y	N	Y	Y	Y
9 Vacant						
10 **Broun**	N	Y	Y	N	N	Y
11 **Gingrey**	N	Y	Y	N	N	Y
12 Barrow	Y	Y	N	Y	Y	Y
13 Scott	Y	Y	N	Y	Y	Y
HAWAII						
1 Vacant						
2 Hirono	Y	Y	N	Y	Y	Y
IDAHO						
1 Minnick	N	Y	Y	N	Y	?
2 **Simpson**	N	Y	Y	N	Y	Y
ILLINOIS						
1 Rush	Y	Y	N	Y	Y	Y
2 Jackson	Y	Y	N	Y	Y	Y
3 Lipinski	Y	Y	N	Y	Y	Y
4 Gutierrez	Y	Y	?	Y	Y	Y
5 Quigley	Y	Y	N	Y	Y	Y
6 **Roskam**	N	Y	Y	N	Y	Y
7 Davis	Y	Y	N	Y	Y	Y
8 Bean	Y	Y	N	Y	Y	Y
9 Schakowsky	Y	Y	N	Y	Y	Y
10 **Kirk**	N	Y	Y	N	Y	Y
11 Halvorson	N	Y	N	Y	Y	Y
12 Costello	Y	Y	N	Y	Y	Y
13 **Biggert**	N	Y	Y	N	Y	Y
14 Foster	Y	Y	N	Y	Y	Y
15 **Johnson**	N	Y	Y	N	Y	Y

KEY	**Republicans**	Democrats			
Y Voted for (yea)		X Paired against		C Voted "present" to avoid possible conflict of interest
# Paired for		− Announced against		
+ Announced for		P Voted "present"		? Did not vote or otherwise make a position known
N Voted against (nay)				

	179	180	181	182	183	184
16 **Manzullo**	N	Y	Y	N	Y	Y
17 Hare	Y	Y	N	Y	Y	Y
18 **Schock**	N	Y	Y	N	Y	Y
19 **Shimkus**	N	Y	Y	N	Y	Y
INDIANA						
1 Visclosky	Y	Y	N	Y	Y	Y
2 Donnelly	N	Y	N	Y	Y	Y
3 **Souder**	N	Y	Y	N	Y	Y
4 **Buyer**	N	Y	Y	N	Y	Y
5 **Burton**	N	Y	Y	N	Y	Y
6 **Pence**	N	Y	Y	N	Y	Y
7 Carson	Y	Y	N	Y	Y	Y
8 Ellsworth	N	Y	N	Y	Y	Y
9 Hill	N	Y	N	Y	Y	Y
IOWA						
1 Braley	Y	Y	N	Y	Y	Y
2 Loebsack	Y	Y	N	Y	Y	Y
3 Boswell	Y	Y	N	Y	Y	Y
4 **Latham**	N	Y	Y	N	Y	Y
5 **King**	N	Y	Y	N	Y	?
KANSAS						
1 **Moran**	N	Y	Y	N	Y	Y
2 **Jenkins**	N	Y	Y	N	Y	Y
3 Moore	Y	Y	N	Y	Y	Y
4 **Tiahrt**	N	Y	Y	N	Y	Y
KENTUCKY						
1 **Whitfield**	N	Y	Y	N	Y	Y
2 **Guthrie**	N	Y	Y	N	Y	Y
3 Yarmuth	Y	Y	N	Y	Y	Y
4 **Davis**	N	Y	Y	N	Y	Y
5 **Rogers**	N	Y	Y	N	Y	Y
6 Chandler	Y	Y	N	Y	Y	Y
LOUISIANA						
1 **Scalise**	N	Y	Y	N	Y	Y
2 **Cao**	Y	Y	Y	Y	Y	Y
3 Melancon	Y	Y	N	Y	Y	Y
4 **Fleming**	N	Y	Y	N	Y	Y
5 **Alexander**	N	Y	Y	N	Y	Y
6 **Cassidy**	N	Y	Y	N	?	?
7 **Boustany**	N	Y	Y	N	Y	Y
MAINE						
1 Pingree	Y	Y	N	Y	Y	Y
2 Michaud	Y	Y	N	Y	Y	Y
MARYLAND						
1 Kratovil	N	Y	N	Y	Y	Y
2 Ruppersberger	Y	Y	N	Y	Y	Y
3 Sarbanes	Y	Y	N	Y	Y	Y
4 Edwards	Y	Y	N	Y	Y	Y
5 Hoyer	Y	Y	N	Y	Y	Y
6 **Bartlett**	N	Y	Y	N	Y	Y
7 Cummings	Y	Y	N	Y	Y	Y
8 Van Hollen	Y	Y	N	Y	Y	Y
MASSACHUSETTS						
1 Olver	Y	Y	N	Y	Y	Y
2 Neal	Y	Y	N	Y	Y	Y
3 McGovern	Y	Y	N	Y	Y	Y
4 Frank	Y	Y	N	Y	Y	Y
5 Tsongas	Y	Y	N	Y	Y	Y
6 Tierney	Y	Y	N	Y	Y	Y
7 Markey	Y	Y	N	Y	Y	Y
8 Capuano	Y	Y	N	Y	Y	Y
9 Lynch	Y	Y	N	Y	Y	Y
10 Delahunt	Y	Y	N	Y	Y	Y
MICHIGAN						
1 Stupak	Y	Y	N	Y	Y	Y
2 **Hoekstra**	?	?	?	?	?	?
3 **Ehlers**	N	Y	Y	N	Y	Y
4 **Camp**	N	Y	Y	N	Y	Y
5 Kildee	Y	Y	N	Y	Y	Y
6 **Upton**	N	Y	Y	N	Y	Y
7 Schauer	Y	Y	N	Y	Y	Y
8 **Rogers**	N	Y	Y	N	Y	Y
9 Peters	Y	Y	N	Y	Y	Y
10 **Miller**	N	Y	Y	N	Y	Y
11 **McCotter**	N	Y	Y	N	Y	Y
12 Levin	Y	Y	N	Y	Y	Y
13 Kilpatrick	+	+	–	+	+	+
14 Conyers	Y	Y	N	Y	Y	Y
15 Dingell	Y	Y	N	Y	Y	Y
MINNESOTA						
1 Walz	Y	Y	N	Y	Y	Y
2 **Kline**	N	Y	Y	N	Y	Y
3 **Paulsen**	N	Y	Y	N	Y	Y
4 McCollum	Y	Y	N	Y	Y	Y

	179	180	181	182	183	184
5 Ellison	Y	Y	N	Y	Y	Y
6 **Bachmann**	N	Y	Y	N	Y	Y
7 Peterson	Y	Y	N	Y	Y	Y
8 Oberstar	Y	Y	N	Y	Y	Y
MISSISSIPPI						
1 Childers	N	Y	N	Y	Y	Y
2 Thompson	Y	Y	N	Y	Y	Y
3 **Harper**	N	Y	Y	N	Y	Y
4 Taylor	N	Y	Y	N	Y	Y
MISSOURI						
1 Clay	Y	Y	N	Y	Y	Y
2 **Akin**	N	Y	Y	N	N	Y
3 Carnahan	Y	Y	N	Y	Y	Y
4 Skelton	Y	Y	N	Y	Y	Y
5 Cleaver	Y	Y	N	?	Y	Y
6 **Graves**	N	Y	Y	N	Y	Y
7 **Blunt**	N	Y	Y	N	Y	Y
8 **Emerson**	N	Y	Y	N	Y	Y
9 **Luetkemeyer**	N	Y	Y	N	Y	Y
MONTANA						
AL **Rehberg**	N	Y	Y	N	Y	Y
NEBRASKA						
1 **Fortenberry**	N	Y	Y	N	Y	Y
2 **Terry**	N	Y	Y	N	Y	Y
3 **Smith**	N	Y	Y	N	Y	Y
NEVADA						
1 Berkley	Y	Y	N	Y	Y	Y
2 **Heller**	N	Y	Y	N	Y	Y
3 Titus	Y	Y	N	Y	Y	Y
NEW HAMPSHIRE						
1 Shea-Porter	Y	Y	N	Y	Y	Y
2 Hodes	Y	Y	N	Y	Y	Y
NEW JERSEY						
1 Andrews	Y	Y	N	Y	Y	Y
2 **LoBiondo**	N	Y	Y	N	Y	Y
3 Adler	N	Y	N	Y	Y	Y
4 **Smith**	N	Y	Y	N	Y	Y
5 **Garrett**	N	Y	Y	N	Y	Y
6 Pallone	Y	Y	N	Y	Y	Y
7 **Lance**	N	Y	Y	N	Y	Y
8 Pascrell	Y	Y	N	Y	Y	Y
9 Rothman	Y	Y	N	Y	Y	Y
10 Payne	Y	Y	N	Y	Y	Y
11 **Frelinghuysen**	N	Y	Y	N	Y	Y
12 Holt	Y	Y	N	Y	Y	Y
13 Sires	Y	Y	N	Y	Y	Y
NEW MEXICO						
1 Heinrich	Y	Y	N	Y	Y	Y
2 Teague	Y	Y	N	Y	Y	?
3 Luján	Y	Y	N	Y	Y	Y
NEW YORK						
1 Bishop	Y	Y	N	Y	Y	Y
2 Israel	Y	Y	N	Y	Y	Y
3 **King**	N	Y	Y	N	Y	Y
4 McCarthy	Y	Y	N	Y	Y	Y
5 Ackerman	Y	Y	N	Y	Y	Y
6 Meeks	Y	Y	N	Y	Y	Y
7 Crowley	Y	Y	N	Y	Y	?
8 Nadler	Y	Y	N	Y	Y	Y
9 Weiner	Y	Y	N	Y	Y	Y
10 Towns	Y	Y	N	Y	Y	Y
11 Clarke	Y	Y	N	Y	Y	Y
12 Velázquez	Y	Y	N	Y	Y	Y
13 McMahon	Y	Y	N	Y	Y	Y
14 Maloney	Y	Y	N	Y	Y	Y
15 Rangel	Y	Y	N	Y	Y	Y
16 Serrano	Y	Y	N	Y	Y	Y
17 Engel	Y	Y	N	Y	Y	Y
18 Lowey	Y	Y	N	Y	Y	Y
19 Hall	Y	Y	N	Y	Y	Y
20 Murphy	N	Y	N	Y	Y	?
21 Tonko	Y	Y	N	Y	Y	Y
22 Hinchey	Y	Y	N	Y	Y	Y
23 Owens	Y	Y	Y	N	Y	Y
24 Arcuri	Y	Y	N	Y	Y	Y
25 Maffei	Y	Y	N	Y	Y	Y
26 **Lee**	N	Y	Y	N	Y	Y
27 Higgins	Y	Y	N	Y	Y	Y
28 Slaughter	Y	?	N	Y	Y	Y
29 Vacant						
NORTH CAROLINA						
1 Butterfield	Y	Y	N	Y	?	Y
2 Etheridge	Y	Y	N	Y	Y	Y
3 **Jones**	N	Y	Y	N	Y	Y
4 Price	Y	Y	N	Y	Y	Y

	179	180	181	182	183	184
5 **Foxx**	N	Y	Y	N	Y	Y
6 **Coble**	N	Y	Y	N	Y	Y
7 McIntyre	Y	Y	Y	Y	Y	Y
8 Kissell	Y	Y	N	Y	Y	Y
9 **Myrick**	N	Y	Y	N	Y	Y
10 **McHenry**	N	Y	Y	N	Y	Y
11 Shuler	N	Y	N	Y	Y	Y
12 Watt	Y	Y	N	Y	Y	Y
13 Miller	Y	Y	N	Y	Y	Y
NORTH DAKOTA						
AL Pomeroy	Y	Y	N	Y	Y	Y
OHIO						
1 Driehaus	Y	Y	N	Y	Y	Y
2 **Schmidt**	N	Y	Y	N	Y	Y
3 **Turner**	N	Y	Y	N	Y	Y
4 **Jordan**	N	Y	Y	N	Y	Y
5 **Latta**	N	Y	Y	N	Y	Y
6 Wilson	Y	Y	N	Y	Y	Y
7 **Austria**	N	Y	Y	N	Y	Y
8 **Boehner**	N	Y	Y	N	Y	Y
9 Kaptur	Y	Y	N	Y	Y	Y
10 Kucinich	Y	Y	N	Y	Y	Y
11 Fudge	Y	Y	N	Y	Y	Y
12 **Tiberi**	N	Y	Y	N	Y	Y
13 Sutton	Y	Y	N	Y	Y	Y
14 **LaTourette**	N	Y	Y	N	Y	Y
15 Kilroy	Y	Y	N	Y	Y	Y
16 Boccieri	Y	Y	N	Y	Y	Y
17 Ryan	Y	Y	N	Y	Y	Y
18 Space	Y	Y	N	Y	Y	Y
OKLAHOMA						
1 **Sullivan**	N	Y	Y	N	Y	Y
2 Boren	Y	Y	N	Y	Y	Y
3 **Lucas**	N	Y	Y	N	Y	Y
4 **Cole**	N	Y	Y	N	Y	Y
5 **Fallin**	N	Y	Y	N	Y	Y
OREGON						
1 Wu	Y	Y	N	Y	Y	Y
2 **Walden**	N	Y	Y	N	Y	Y
3 Blumenauer	Y	Y	N	Y	Y	Y
4 DeFazio	Y	Y	N	Y	Y	Y
5 Schrader	Y	Y	N	Y	Y	Y
PENNSYLVANIA						
1 Brady	Y	Y	N	Y	Y	Y
2 Fattah	Y	Y	N	Y	Y	Y
3 Dahlkemper	N	Y	N	Y	Y	Y
4 Altmire	Y	Y	Y	Y	Y	Y
5 **Thompson**	N	Y	Y	N	Y	Y
6 **Gerlach**	N	Y	Y	N	Y	Y
7 Sestak	Y	Y	N	Y	Y	Y
8 Murphy, P.	Y	Y	N	Y	Y	Y
9 **Shuster**	N	Y	Y	N	Y	Y
10 Carney	Y	Y	N	Y	Y	Y
11 Kanjorski	Y	Y	N	Y	Y	Y
12 Vacant						
13 Schwartz	Y	Y	N	Y	Y	Y
14 Doyle	Y	Y	N	Y	Y	Y
15 **Dent**	N	Y	Y	N	Y	Y
16 **Pitts**	N	Y	Y	N	Y	Y
17 Holden	Y	Y	N	Y	Y	Y
18 **Murphy, T.**	N	Y	Y	Y	Y	Y
19 **Platts**	N	Y	Y	N	Y	Y
RHODE ISLAND						
1 Kennedy	Y	Y	N	Y	Y	Y
2 Langevin	Y	Y	N	Y	Y	Y
SOUTH CAROLINA						
1 **Brown**	N	Y	?	?	?	?
2 **Wilson**	N	Y	Y	N	Y	Y
3 **Barrett**	N	Y	Y	N	?	?
4 **Inglis**	N	Y	Y	N	Y	Y
5 Spratt	Y	Y	N	Y	Y	Y
6 Clyburn	Y	Y	N	Y	Y	Y
SOUTH DAKOTA						
AL Herseth Sandlin	N	Y	N	Y	Y	Y
TENNESSEE						
1 **Roe**	N	Y	Y	N	Y	Y
2 **Duncan**	N	Y	Y	N	N	Y
3 **Wamp**	N	Y	Y	N	Y	Y
4 Davis	Y	Y	N	Y	Y	Y
5 Cooper	Y	Y	N	Y	Y	Y
6 Gordon	Y	Y	N	Y	Y	Y
7 **Blackburn**	N	Y	Y	N	Y	Y
8 Tanner	Y	Y	N	Y	Y	Y
9 Cohen	Y	Y	N	Y	Y	Y

	179	180	181	182	183	184
TEXAS						
1 **Gohmert**	N	Y	Y	N	Y	Y
2 **Poe**	N	Y	Y	N	N	Y
3 **Johnson, S.**	N	Y	Y	N	Y	Y
4 **Hall**	N	Y	Y	N	Y	Y
5 **Hensarling**	N	Y	Y	N	Y	Y
6 **Barton**	N	Y	Y	N	Y	Y
7 **Culberson**	N	Y	Y	N	Y	Y
8 **Brady**	N	Y	Y	N	Y	Y
9 Green, A.	Y	Y	N	Y	Y	Y
10 **McCaul**	N	Y	Y	N	Y	Y
11 **Conaway**	N	Y	Y	N	Y	Y
12 **Granger**	N	Y	Y	N	Y	Y
13 **Thornberry**	N	Y	Y	N	Y	Y
14 **Paul**	N	Y	Y	N	N	N
15 Hinojosa	Y	Y	N	Y	Y	Y
16 Reyes	Y	Y	N	Y	Y	Y
17 Edwards	Y	Y	Y	Y	Y	Y
18 Jackson Lee	Y	Y	N	Y	Y	Y
19 **Neugebauer**	N	Y	Y	N	Y	Y
20 Gonzalez	Y	Y	N	Y	Y	Y
21 **Smith**	N	Y	Y	N	Y	Y
22 **Olson**	N	Y	Y	N	Y	Y
23 Rodriguez	Y	Y	N	Y	Y	Y
24 **Marchant**	N	Y	Y	N	N	Y
25 Doggett	Y	Y	N	Y	Y	Y
26 **Burgess**	N	Y	Y	N	Y	Y
27 Ortiz	Y	Y	N	Y	Y	Y
28 Cuellar	Y	Y	N	Y	Y	Y
29 Green, G.	Y	Y	N	Y	Y	Y
30 Johnson, E.	Y	Y	N	Y	Y	Y
31 **Carter**	N	Y	Y	N	Y	Y
32 **Sessions**	N	Y	Y	N	Y	Y
UTAH						
1 **Bishop**	N	Y	Y	N	Y	Y
2 Matheson	Y	Y	N	Y	Y	Y
3 **Chaffetz**	N	Y	Y	N	Y	Y
VERMONT						
AL Welch	Y	Y	N	Y	Y	Y
VIRGINIA						
1 **Wittman**	N	Y	Y	N	Y	Y
2 Nye	Y	Y	Y	N	Y	Y
3 Scott	Y	Y	N	Y	Y	Y
4 **Forbes**	N	Y	Y	N	Y	Y
5 Perriello	Y	Y	N	Y	Y	Y
6 **Goodlatte**	N	Y	Y	N	Y	Y
7 **Cantor**	N	Y	Y	N	Y	Y
8 Moran	Y	Y	N	Y	Y	Y
9 Boucher	Y	Y	Y	Y	Y	Y
10 **Wolf**	N	Y	Y	N	Y	Y
11 Connolly	Y	Y	N	Y	Y	Y
WASHINGTON						
1 Inslee	Y	Y	N	Y	Y	Y
2 Larsen	Y	Y	N	Y	Y	Y
3 Baird	N	Y	N	Y	Y	Y
4 **Hastings**	N	Y	Y	N	Y	Y
5 **McMorris Rodgers**	N	Y	Y	N	Y	Y
6 Dicks	Y	Y	N	Y	Y	Y
7 McDermott	Y	Y	N	Y	Y	Y
8 **Reichert**	N	Y	Y	N	Y	Y
9 Smith	Y	Y	N	N	Y	Y
WEST VIRGINIA						
1 Mollohan	Y	Y	N	Y	Y	Y
2 **Capito**	N	Y	Y	N	Y	Y
3 Rahall	Y	Y	N	Y	Y	Y
WISCONSIN						
1 **Ryan**	N	Y	Y	N	Y	Y
2 Baldwin	Y	Y	N	Y	Y	Y
3 Kind	Y	Y	N	Y	Y	Y
4 Moore	Y	Y	N	Y	Y	Y
5 **Sensenbrenner**	N	Y	Y	N	N	Y
6 **Petri**	N	Y	Y	N	Y	Y
7 Obey	Y	Y	N	Y	Y	Y
8 Kagen	Y	Y	N	Y	Y	Y
WYOMING						
AL **Lummis**	N	Y	Y	N	Y	Y
DELEGATES						
Faleomavaega (A.S.)						
Norton (D.C.)						
Bordallo (Guam)						
Sablan (N. Marianas)						
Pierluisi (P.R.)						
Christensen (V.I.)						

IN THE HOUSE | By Vote Number

185. **HR 4899. Disaster Relief and Summer Jobs Funding/Motion to Table.** Obey, D-Wis., motion to table (kill) the Lewis, R-Calif., appeal of the ruling of the chair with respect to the Obey point of order that the Lewis motion to recommit the bill constituted legislating on an appropriations bill. The motion would recommit the bill to the Appropriations Committee with instructions that it be immediately reported back with an amendment that would strike the $600 million that the bill would appropriate for summer jobs programs and also rescind $5.1 billion in funds appropriated in the 2009 economic stimulus law. Motion agreed to 239-176: D 239-3; R 0-173. March 24, 2010.

186. **HR 4899. Disaster Relief and Summer Jobs Funding/Passage.** Passage of the bill that would appropriate $5.1 billion in emergency supplemental funding for the Federal Emergency Management Agency Disaster Relief Fund and $600 million for Labor Department grants for youth summer jobs programs. The cost of the bill would be partially off-set by rescinding $620 million in funds that were appropriated for several existing programs at various agencies. Passed 239-175: D 234-8; R 5-167. A "yea" was a vote in support of the president's position. March 24, 2010.

187. **H Res 1220. PMA Group Investigation/Motion to Refer.** McGovern, D-Mass., motion to refer the Flake, R-Ariz., privileged resolution to the Committee on Standards of Official Conduct. The resolution would require the committee to issue a report detailing the number of interviews conducted, subpoenas issued and documents reviewed in the panel's investigation of members' dealings with the PMA Group. Motion agreed to 406-1: D 243-1; R 163-0. March 25, 2010.

188. **HR 1586. FAA Reauthorization/Rule.** Adoption of the rule (H Res 1212) that would provide for House floor consideration of the Senate amendment to the bill that would reauthorize the Federal Aviation Administration. It also would permit the Speaker to entertain motions to suspend the rules through the calendar day of March 28, 2010, and waive the two-thirds majority vote requirement for same-day consideration of resolutions reported from the Rules Committee through the calendar day of March 29, 2010. Adopted 231-190: D 231-17; R 0-173. March 25, 2010.

189. **Procedural Motion/Journal.** Approval of the House Journal of Wednesday, March 24, 2010. Approved 241-178: D 221-27; R 20-151. March 25, 2010.

190. **HR 1586. FAA Reauthorization/Motion to Concur.** Oberstar, D-Minn., motion to concur in the Senate amendment with a House amendment to the bill that would authorize $53.5 billion through fiscal 2012 for the Federal Aviation Administration. It would require airlines and airports to develop contingency plans for stranded passengers and increase the number of daily long-distance flights permitted from Ronald Reagan Washington National Airport. It would increase the maximum passenger facility charge to $7 from $4.50 and establish a new labor dispute system for FAA personnel. It also would require commercial pilots to obtain a license requiring 1,500 flight hours. Motion agreed to 276-145: D 242-6; R 34-139. March 25, 2010.

	185	186	187	188	189	190
ALABAMA						
1 Bonner	N	N	P	N	N	N
2 Bright	Y	Y	Y	N	N	N
3 Rogers	N	N	Y	N	N	N
4 Aderholt	N	N	Y	N	N	N
5 Griffith	N	N	Y	N	N	Y
6 Bachus	N	N	Y	N	N	N
7 Davis	?	?	?	?	?	?
ALASKA						
AL Young	N	N	Y	N	N	Y
ARIZONA						
1 Kirkpatrick	Y	N	Y	N	N	Y
2 Franks	N	N	Y	N	N	N
3 Shadegg	N	N	Y	N	N	N
4 Pastor	Y	Y	Y	Y	Y	Y
5 Mitchell	Y	Y	Y	N	N	Y
6 Flake	N	N	Y	N	N	N
7 Grijalva	Y	Y	Y	Y	Y	Y
8 Giffords	Y	Y	Y	Y	N	Y
ARKANSAS						
1 Berry	Y	Y	Y	Y	Y	Y
2 Snyder	Y	Y	Y	Y	Y	Y
3 Boozman	N	N	Y	N	N	N
4 Ross	Y	Y	Y	Y	Y	Y
CALIFORNIA						
1 Thompson	Y	Y	Y	Y	Y	Y
2 Herger	N	N	Y	N	N	N
3 Lungren	N	N	Y	N	N	N
4 McClintock	N	N	Y	N	N	N
5 Matsui	Y	Y	Y	Y	?	Y
6 Woolsey	Y	Y	Y	Y	Y	Y
7 Miller, George	Y	Y	Y	Y	Y	Y
8 Pelosi						
9 Lee	Y	Y	Y	Y	Y	Y
10 Garamendi	Y	Y	Y	Y	Y	Y
11 McNerney	Y	Y	Y	Y	Y	Y
12 Speier	Y	Y	Y	Y	Y	Y
13 Stark	Y	Y	Y	Y	Y	Y
14 Eshoo	Y	Y	Y	Y	Y	Y
15 Honda	Y	Y	?	Y	Y	Y
16 Lofgren	Y	Y	P	Y	Y	Y
17 Farr	Y	Y	Y	Y	Y	Y
18 Cardoza	Y	Y	Y	N	N	Y
19 Radanovich	N	N	Y	N	N	?
20 Costa	Y	Y	Y	N	N	Y
21 Nunes	N	N	Y	N	N	N
22 McCarthy	N	N	Y	N	N	N
23 Capps	Y	Y	Y	Y	Y	Y
24 Gallegly	N	N	Y	N	N	N
25 McKeon	N	N	Y	N	N	N
26 Dreier	N	N	Y	N	N	N
27 Sherman	Y	Y	Y	Y	Y	Y
28 Berman	Y	Y	Y	Y	Y	Y
29 Schiff	Y	Y	Y	Y	Y	Y
30 Waxman	Y	Y	Y	Y	Y	Y
31 Becerra	Y	Y	Y	Y	Y	Y
32 Chu	Y	Y	Y	Y	Y	Y
33 Watson	Y	Y	Y	Y	Y	Y
34 Roybal-Allard	Y	Y	Y	Y	Y	Y
35 Waters	Y	Y	Y	Y	Y	Y
36 Harman	Y	Y	Y	Y	Y	Y
37 Richardson	?	Y	Y	Y	Y	Y
38 Napolitano	Y	Y	Y	Y	Y	Y
39 Sánchez, Linda	Y	Y	Y	Y	Y	Y
40 Royce	N	N	Y	N	N	N
41 Lewis	N	N	Y	N	N	N
42 Miller, Gary	N	N	Y	N	N	Y
43 Baca	Y	Y	Y	Y	Y	Y
44 Calvert	N	N	Y	N	N	N
45 Bono Mack	N	N	Y	N	N	Y
46 Rohrabacher	N	N	Y	N	N	N
47 Sanchez, Loretta	Y	Y	Y	Y	Y	Y
48 Campbell	N	N	Y	N	N	N
49 Issa	N	?	Y	N	Y	N
50 Bilbray	N	N	Y	N	Y	Y
51 Filner	Y	Y	Y	Y	Y	Y
52 Hunter	N	N	Y	N	Y	N
53 Davis	Y	Y	Y	Y	Y	Y

	185	186	187	188	189	190
COLORADO						
1 DeGette	Y	Y	Y	Y	Y	Y
2 Polis	Y	N	Y	Y	Y	Y
3 Salazar	Y	Y	Y	Y	Y	Y
4 Markey	Y	Y	Y	Y	Y	Y
5 Lamborn	N	N	Y	N	N	N
6 Coffman	N	N	Y	N	N	N
7 Perlmutter	Y	Y	Y	Y	?	Y
CONNECTICUT						
1 Larson	Y	Y	Y	Y	Y	Y
2 Courtney	Y	Y	Y	Y	Y	Y
3 DeLauro	Y	Y	Y	Y	Y	Y
4 Himes	Y	Y	Y	N	Y	Y
5 Murphy	Y	N	Y	Y	Y	Y
DELAWARE						
AL Castle	N	N	Y	N	Y	Y
FLORIDA						
1 Miller	N	N	Y	N	N	N
2 Boyd	Y	Y	Y	Y	Y	Y
3 Brown	Y	Y	Y	Y	Y	Y
4 Crenshaw	N	N	Y	N	N	N
5 Brown-Waite	N	N	Y	N	N	N
6 Stearns	N	N	Y	N	N	N
7 Mica	N	N	Y	N	N	N
8 Grayson	Y	Y	Y	Y	Y	Y
9 Bilirakis	N	N	Y	N	N	N
10 Young	N	N	Y	N	N	N
11 Castor	Y	Y	P	Y	Y	Y
12 Putnam	N	N	Y	N	N	N
13 Buchanan	?	N	Y	N	N	N
14 Mack	N	N	Y	N	N	N
15 Posey	N	N	Y	N	N	N
16 Rooney	N	N	Y	N	N	N
17 Meek	Y	Y	Y	Y	Y	Y
18 Ros-Lehtinen	N	N	Y	N	N	N
19 Vacant						
20 Wasserman Schultz	Y	+	Y	Y	Y	Y
21 Diaz-Balart, L.	N	N	P	N	N	Y
22 Klein	Y	Y	Y	Y	Y	Y
23 Hastings	Y	Y	Y	Y	Y	Y
24 Kosmas	Y	Y	Y	Y	Y	Y
25 Diaz-Balart, M.	N	N	Y	N	N	Y
GEORGIA						
1 Kingston	N	N	Y	N	N	N
2 Bishop	Y	Y	Y	Y	Y	Y
3 Westmoreland	N	N	Y	N	N	N
4 Johnson	?	Y	?	Y	Y	Y
5 Lewis	Y	Y	Y	Y	Y	Y
6 Price	N	N	Y	N	N	N
7 Linder	N	N	Y	N	N	N
8 Marshall	Y	Y	Y	Y	Y	Y
9 Vacant						
10 Broun	N	N	Y	N	N	N
11 Gingrey	N	N	Y	N	N	N
12 Barrow	Y	Y	Y	Y	Y	Y
13 Scott	Y	Y	Y	Y	Y	Y
HAWAII						
1 Vacant						
2 Hirono	Y	Y	Y	Y	Y	Y
IDAHO						
1 Minnick	N	Y	Y	N	N	N
2 Simpson	N	N	P	N	N	N
ILLINOIS						
1 Rush	Y	?	Y	Y	Y	Y
2 Jackson	Y	Y	Y	Y	Y	Y
3 Lipinski	Y	Y	Y	Y	Y	Y
4 Gutierrez	Y	?	Y	Y	Y	Y
5 Quigley	Y	Y	Y	Y	Y	Y
6 Roskam	N	N	Y	N	N	N
7 Davis	Y	Y	Y	Y	Y	Y
8 Bean	Y	Y	Y	Y	Y	Y
9 Schakowsky	Y	Y	Y	Y	Y	Y
10 Kirk	N	N	Y	N	N	N
11 Halvorson	Y	Y	Y	Y	Y	Y
12 Costello	Y	Y	Y	Y	Y	Y
13 Biggert	N	N	Y	N	N	Y
14 Foster	Y	Y	Y	Y	Y	Y
15 Johnson	N	N	Y	N	Y	Y

KEY   **Republicans**   Democrats

Y Voted for (yea)	X Paired against	C Voted "present" to avoid possible conflict of interest
# Paired for	– Announced against	
+ Announced for	P Voted "present"	? Did not vote or otherwise make a position known
N Voted against (nay)		

	185	186	187	188	189	190
16 **Manzullo**	N	N	Y	N	N	–
17 Hare	Y	Y	Y	Y	Y	Y
18 **Schock**	N	N	Y	N	N	N
19 **Shimkus**	N	N	Y	N	N	Y
INDIANA						
1 Visclosky	Y	Y	Y	Y	Y	Y
2 Donnelly	+	Y	Y	Y	N	Y
3 **Souder**	N	N	?	?	?	N
4 **Buyer**	N	N	?	?	?	?
5 **Burton**	N	N	Y	N	N	N
6 **Pence**	N	N	Y	N	N	N
7 Carson	Y	Y	Y	Y	Y	Y
8 Ellsworth	?	Y	Y	Y	N	Y
9 Hill	Y	Y	Y	N	N	Y
IOWA						
1 Braley	Y	Y	Y	Y	Y	Y
2 Loebsack	Y	Y	Y	Y	Y	Y
3 Boswell	Y	Y	Y	Y	Y	Y
4 **Latham**	N	N	P	N	Y	N
5 **King**	N	N	Y	N	N	N
KANSAS						
1 **Moran**	N	N	Y	N	N	N
2 **Jenkins**	N	N	Y	N	N	Y
3 Moore	Y	Y	Y	Y	Y	Y
4 **Tiahrt**	N	N	Y	N	N	Y
KENTUCKY						
1 **Whitfield**	N	N	Y	N	N	N
2 **Guthrie**	N	N	Y	N	N	N
3 Yarmuth	Y	Y	Y	Y	Y	Y
4 **Davis**	N	N	Y	N	N	N
5 **Rogers**	N	N	Y	N	N	N
6 Chandler	Y	Y	P	Y	Y	Y
LOUISIANA						
1 **Scalise**	N	Y	Y	N	N	N
2 **Cao**	N	Y	Y	N	N	Y
3 Melancon	Y	Y	Y	Y	Y	Y
4 **Fleming**	N	N	Y	N	N	N
5 **Alexander**	N	N	Y	N	N	N
6 **Cassidy**	N	P	Y	N	N	N
7 **Boustany**	N	N	Y	N	N	N
MAINE						
1 Pingree	Y	Y	Y	Y	Y	Y
2 Michaud	Y	Y	Y	Y	Y	Y
MARYLAND						
1 Kratovil	Y	Y	Y	N	N	Y
2 Ruppersberger	Y	Y	Y	Y	Y	Y
3 Sarbanes	Y	Y	Y	Y	Y	Y
4 Edwards	Y	Y	Y	Y	Y	Y
5 Hoyer	Y	Y	Y	Y	Y	Y
6 **Bartlett**	N	N	Y	N	N	N
7 Cummings	Y	Y	Y	Y	Y	Y
8 Van Hollen	Y	Y	Y	Y	Y	Y
MASSACHUSETTS						
1 Olver	Y	Y	Y	Y	Y	Y
2 Neal	Y	Y	Y	Y	Y	?
3 McGovern	Y	Y	Y	Y	Y	Y
4 Frank	Y	Y	Y	Y	Y	Y
5 Tsongas	Y	Y	Y	Y	Y	Y
6 Tierney	Y	Y	Y	Y	Y	?
7 Markey	Y	Y	Y	Y	Y	Y
8 Capuano	Y	Y	Y	Y	Y	Y
9 Lynch	Y	Y	Y	Y	Y	Y
10 Delahunt	Y	Y	Y	Y	Y	Y
MICHIGAN						
1 Stupak	Y	Y	Y	Y	N	Y
2 **Hoekstra**	?	?	Y	N	N	N
3 **Ehlers**	N	Y	Y	N	N	Y
4 **Camp**	N	N	Y	N	N	N
5 Kildee	Y	Y	Y	Y	Y	Y
6 **Upton**	N	N	Y	N	N	N
7 Schauer	Y	Y	Y	Y	Y	Y
8 **Rogers**	N	N	Y	N	N	N
9 Peters	Y	N	Y	Y	Y	Y
10 **Miller**	N	N	Y	N	N	Y
11 **McCotter**	N	N	Y	N	N	Y
12 Levin	Y	Y	Y	Y	Y	Y
13 Kilpatrick	+	+	Y	Y	Y	Y
14 Conyers	Y	Y	Y	Y	Y	Y
15 Dingell	Y	Y	Y	Y	Y	Y
MINNESOTA						
1 Walz	Y	Y	Y	Y	Y	Y
2 **Kline**	N	N	Y	N	N	N
3 **Paulsen**	N	N	Y	N	Y	N
4 McCollum	Y	Y	Y	Y	Y	Y

	185	186	187	188	189	190
5 Ellison	Y	Y	Y	?	Y	Y
6 **Bachmann**	N	N	Y	N	N	N
7 Peterson	Y	Y	Y	Y	Y	Y
8 Oberstar	Y	Y	Y	Y	Y	Y
MISSISSIPPI						
1 Childers	Y	Y	Y	N	N	Y
2 Thompson	Y	Y	Y	Y	Y	Y
3 **Harper**	N	N	P	N	N	N
4 Taylor	N	Y	Y	N	N	Y
MISSOURI						
1 Clay	Y	Y	Y	Y	Y	Y
2 **Akin**	N	N	Y	N	N	N
3 Carnahan	Y	Y	Y	Y	Y	Y
4 Skelton	Y	Y	Y	Y	Y	Y
5 Cleaver	Y	Y	Y	Y	Y	Y
6 **Graves**	N	N	Y	N	Y	N
7 **Blunt**	N	N	Y	N	N	N
8 **Emerson**	N	N	Y	N	N	N
9 **Luetkemeyer**	N	N	Y	N	Y	N
MONTANA						
AL **Rehberg**	N	N	Y	N	N	N
NEBRASKA						
1 **Fortenberry**	N	N	Y	N	N	N
2 **Terry**	N	N	Y	N	N	N
3 **Smith**	N	N	Y	N	N	N
NEVADA						
1 Berkley	Y	Y	Y	Y	Y	Y
2 **Heller**	N	N	Y	N	Y	N
3 Titus	Y	Y	Y	Y	Y	Y
NEW HAMPSHIRE						
1 Shea-Porter	Y	Y	Y	Y	Y	Y
2 Hodes	Y	Y	Y	Y	Y	Y
NEW JERSEY						
1 Andrews	Y	Y	Y	Y	Y	Y
2 **LoBiondo**	N	N	Y	N	N	Y
3 Adler	Y	Y	Y	Y	N	Y
4 **Smith**	N	N	Y	N	N	Y
5 **Garrett**	N	N	Y	N	N	N
6 Pallone	Y	Y	Y	Y	Y	Y
7 **Lance**	N	N	Y	N	N	Y
8 Pascrell	Y	Y	Y	Y	Y	Y
9 Rothman	Y	Y	Y	Y	Y	Y
10 Payne	Y	Y	Y	Y	Y	Y
11 **Frelinghuysen**	N	N	Y	N	N	N
12 Holt	Y	Y	Y	Y	Y	Y
13 Sires	Y	Y	Y	Y	Y	Y
NEW MEXICO						
1 Heinrich	Y	Y	Y	Y	Y	Y
2 Teague	Y	Y	Y	Y	Y	Y
3 Luján	Y	Y	Y	Y	Y	Y
NEW YORK						
1 Bishop	Y	Y	Y	Y	Y	Y
2 Israel	Y	Y	Y	Y	Y	Y
3 **King**	N	N	Y	N	N	Y
4 McCarthy	Y	Y	Y	Y	Y	Y
5 Ackerman	Y	Y	Y	Y	Y	Y
6 Meeks	Y	Y	Y	Y	Y	Y
7 Crowley	Y	Y	Y	Y	Y	Y
8 Nadler	Y	Y	Y	Y	Y	Y
9 Weiner	Y	Y	Y	Y	Y	Y
10 Towns	Y	Y	Y	Y	Y	Y
11 Clarke	Y	Y	Y	Y	Y	Y
12 Velázquez	Y	Y	Y	Y	Y	Y
13 McMahon	Y	Y	Y	Y	Y	Y
14 Maloney	?	?	Y	Y	Y	Y
15 Rangel	Y	Y	Y	Y	Y	Y
16 Serrano	Y	Y	Y	Y	Y	Y
17 Engel	Y	Y	Y	Y	Y	N
18 Lowey	Y	Y	Y	Y	Y	Y
19 Hall	Y	Y	Y	Y	Y	Y
20 Murphy	Y	Y	Y	Y	N	Y
21 Tonko	Y	Y	Y	Y	Y	Y
22 Hinchey	Y	Y	Y	Y	Y	Y
23 Owens	Y	Y	Y	Y	N	Y
24 Arcuri	Y	Y	Y	N	N	Y
25 Maffei	Y	Y	Y	Y	Y	Y
26 **Lee**	N	N	Y	N	N	Y
27 Higgins	Y	Y	Y	Y	Y	Y
28 Slaughter	Y	Y	Y	Y	Y	Y
29 Vacant						
NORTH CAROLINA						
1 Butterfield	Y	Y	P	Y	Y	Y
2 Etheridge	Y	Y	Y	Y	N	Y
3 **Jones**	N	Y	Y	N	N	N
4 Price	Y	Y	Y	Y	Y	Y

	185	186	187	188	189	190
5 **Foxx**	N	N	Y	N	N	N
6 **Coble**	N	N	Y	N	Y	N
7 McIntyre	Y	Y	Y	Y	Y	Y
8 Kissell	Y	Y	Y	Y	Y	Y
9 **Myrick**	N	N	Y	N	N	N
10 **McHenry**	N	N	Y	N	N	N
11 Shuler	Y	Y	Y	N	N	Y
12 Watt	Y	Y	Y	Y	Y	Y
13 Miller	Y	Y	Y	Y	Y	Y
NORTH DAKOTA						
AL Pomeroy	Y	Y	Y	Y	Y	Y
OHIO						
1 Driehaus	Y	Y	Y	Y	Y	Y
2 **Schmidt**	N	N	Y	N	N	N
3 **Turner**	N	N	Y	N	N	N
4 **Jordan**	N	N	Y	N	N	N
5 **Latta**	N	N	Y	N	N	N
6 Wilson	Y	Y	Y	Y	?	Y
7 **Austria**	N	N	Y	N	N	N
8 **Boehner**	N	N	Y	N	N	N
9 Kaptur	Y	Y	Y	Y	Y	?
10 Kucinich	Y	Y	Y	Y	Y	Y
11 Fudge	Y	Y	Y	Y	Y	Y
12 **Tiberi**	N	N	Y	N	N	N
13 Sutton	Y	Y	Y	Y	Y	Y
14 **LaTourette**	N	N	Y	N	N	Y
15 Kilroy	Y	Y	Y	Y	Y	Y
16 Boccieri	Y	Y	Y	Y	N	Y
17 Ryan	Y	Y	Y	Y	Y	Y
18 Space	Y	Y	Y	Y	Y	Y
OKLAHOMA						
1 **Sullivan**	N	N	Y	N	N	N
2 Boren	Y	Y	Y	N	N	Y
3 **Lucas**	N	N	Y	N	N	N
4 **Cole**	N	N	Y	N	N	Y
5 **Fallin**	N	N	Y	N	N	N
OREGON						
1 Wu	Y	Y	Y	Y	Y	Y
2 **Walden**	N	N	P	N	N	N
3 Blumenauer	Y	Y	Y	Y	Y	Y
4 DeFazio	Y	Y	Y	Y	Y	Y
5 Schrader	Y	?	Y	Y	Y	Y
PENNSYLVANIA						
1 Brady	Y	Y	Y	Y	Y	Y
2 Fattah	Y	Y	Y	Y	Y	Y
3 Dahlkemper	Y	Y	Y	Y	Y	Y
4 Altmire	Y	Y	Y	Y	Y	Y
5 **Thompson**	N	N	Y	N	N	Y
6 **Gerlach**	N	N	Y	N	Y	Y
7 Sestak	Y	Y	Y	Y	Y	Y
8 Murphy, P.	Y	Y	Y	Y	Y	Y
9 **Shuster**	N	N	Y	N	N	N
10 Carney	Y	Y	Y	Y	N	Y
11 Kanjorski	Y	Y	Y	Y	Y	Y
12 Vacant						
13 Schwartz	Y	Y	Y	Y	Y	Y
14 Doyle	Y	Y	Y	Y	Y	Y
15 **Dent**	N	N	P	N	Y	Y
16 **Pitts**	N	N	Y	N	N	N
17 Holden	Y	Y	Y	Y	Y	Y
18 **Murphy, T.**	N	Y	Y	N	N	Y
19 **Platts**	N	N	Y	N	Y	Y
RHODE ISLAND						
1 Kennedy	Y	Y	Y	Y	Y	Y
2 Langevin	Y	Y	Y	Y	Y	Y
SOUTH CAROLINA						
1 **Brown**	N	N	Y	N	N	N
2 **Wilson**	N	N	Y	N	N	N
3 **Barrett**	?	?	?	?	?	N
4 **Inglis**	N	N	Y	N	N	N
5 Spratt	Y	Y	Y	Y	Y	Y
6 Clyburn	Y	Y	Y	Y	Y	Y
SOUTH DAKOTA						
AL Herseth Sandlin	Y	N	Y	N	N	Y
TENNESSEE						
1 **Roe**	N	N	Y	N	N	N
2 **Duncan**	N	N	Y	N	N	Y
3 **Wamp**	N	N	Y	N	N	N
4 Davis	Y	Y	Y	Y	Y	Y
5 Cooper	Y	?	Y	Y	Y	N
6 Gordon	Y	Y	Y	Y	Y	Y
7 **Blackburn**	N	N	Y	N	N	N
8 Tanner	Y	Y	Y	N	N	N
9 Cohen	Y	Y	Y	N	Y	N

	185	186	187	188	189	190
TEXAS						
1 **Gohmert**	N	N	Y	N	?	N
2 **Poe**	N	N	Y	N	N	N
3 **Johnson, S.**	N	N	Y	N	N	N
4 **Hall**	N	N	Y	N	?	N
5 **Hensarling**	N	N	Y	N	N	N
6 **Barton**	N	N	Y	N	N	N
7 **Culberson**	N	N	Y	N	N	N
8 **Brady**	N	N	Y	N	N	N
9 Green, A.	Y	Y	Y	Y	Y	Y
10 **McCaul**	N	N	P	N	N	N
11 **Conaway**	N	N	P	N	N	N
12 **Granger**	N	N	Y	N	N	N
13 **Thornberry**	N	N	Y	N	N	N
14 **Paul**	N	N	Y	N	N	N
15 Hinojosa	Y	Y	Y	Y	Y	Y
16 Reyes	Y	Y	Y	Y	Y	Y
17 Edwards	?	Y	Y	Y	Y	Y
18 Jackson Lee	?	?	Y	Y	Y	Y
19 **Neugebauer**	N	N	Y	N	N	N
20 Gonzalez	Y	Y	Y	Y	Y	Y
21 **Smith**	N	N	Y	N	N	N
22 **Olson**	N	N	Y	N	N	N
23 Rodriguez	Y	Y	Y	Y	Y	Y
24 **Marchant**	N	N	Y	N	N	N
25 Doggett	Y	Y	Y	Y	Y	Y
26 **Burgess**	N	N	Y	N	N	N
27 Ortiz	Y	Y	Y	Y	Y	Y
28 Cuellar	Y	Y	Y	Y	Y	Y
29 Green, G.	Y	Y	Y	Y	Y	Y
30 Johnson, E.	Y	Y	Y	Y	Y	Y
31 **Carter**	N	N	Y	N	N	N
32 **Sessions**	N	N	Y	N	N	N
UTAH						
1 **Bishop**	N	N	Y	N	N	N
2 Matheson	Y	N	Y	Y	Y	Y
3 **Chaffetz**	N	N	Y	N	Y	N
VERMONT						
AL Welch	Y	Y	P	Y	Y	Y
VIRGINIA						
1 **Wittman**	N	N	Y	N	N	Y
2 Nye	N	Y	Y	N	Y	Y
3 Scott	Y	Y	Y	Y	Y	Y
4 **Forbes**	N	N	Y	N	N	N
5 Perriello	Y	Y	Y	Y	Y	Y
6 **Goodlatte**	N	N	Y	N	Y	N
7 **Cantor**	N	N	Y	N	N	N
8 Moran	Y	Y	Y	Y	Y	Y
9 Boucher	?	?	Y	Y	Y	Y
10 **Wolf**	N	N	Y	N	N	Y
11 Connolly	Y	Y	Y	Y	N	Y
WASHINGTON						
1 Inslee	Y	Y	Y	Y	Y	Y
2 Larsen	Y	Y	Y	Y	Y	Y
3 Baird	Y	N	Y	Y	Y	Y
4 **Hastings**	N	N	P	N	N	N
5 **McMorris Rodgers**	N	N	Y	N	N	N
6 Dicks	Y	Y	Y	Y	Y	Y
7 McDermott	Y	Y	Y	Y	Y	Y
8 **Reichert**	?	?	?	?	?	?
9 Smith	Y	N	Y	?	Y	Y
WEST VIRGINIA						
1 Mollohan	Y	Y	Y	Y	Y	Y
2 **Capito**	N	N	Y	N	Y	Y
3 Rahall	Y	Y	N	Y	Y	Y
WISCONSIN						
1 **Ryan**	N	N	Y	N	N	N
2 Baldwin	Y	Y	Y	Y	Y	Y
3 Kind	Y	Y	Y	Y	Y	Y
4 Moore	Y	Y	Y	?	Y	Y
5 **Sensenbrenner**	N	N	Y	N	N	N
6 **Petri**	N	N	Y	N	N	N
7 Obey	Y	Y	Y	Y	Y	Y
8 Kagen	Y	Y	Y	Y	Y	Y
WYOMING						
AL **Lummis**	N	N	Y	N	N	N
DELEGATES						
Faleomavaega (A.S.)						
Norton (D.C.)						
Bordallo (Guam)						
Sablan (N. Marianas)						
Pierluisi (P.R.)						
Christensen (V.I.)						

IN THE HOUSE | By Vote Number

191. **H Res 1125. National Public Works Week/Adoption.** Perriello, D-Va., motion to suspend the rules and adopt the resolution that would support National Public Works Week and recognize the 50th anniversary of the week. Motion rejected 249-172: D 249-1; R 0-171. A two-thirds majority of those present and voting (281 in this case) is required for adoption under suspension of the rules. March 25, 2010.

192. **HR 4360. Soltes VA Department Building/Passage.** Filner, D-Calif., motion to suspend the rules and pass the bill that would designate a Veterans Affairs Department building in Long Beach, Calif., as the "Maj. Charles Robert Soltes Jr., O.D. Department of Veterans Affairs Blind Rehabilitation Center." Motion agreed to 417-0: D 246-0; R 171-0. A two-thirds majority of those present and voting (278 in this case) is required for passage under suspension of the rules. March 25, 2010.

193. **HR 4872. Health Care Reconciliation/Rule.** Adoption of the rule (H Res 1225) to provide for House floor consideration of the motion to concur in the Senate amendment to the reconciliation bill that would modify the 2010 health care overhaul law, revise student loan procedures and provide new revenue-raising provisions. Adopted 225-199: D 225-25; R 0-174. March 25, 2010.

194. **HR 4872. Health Care Reconciliation/Motion to Concur.** Miller, D-Calif., motion to concur in the Senate amendments to the bill that would make changes to the 2010 health care overhaul law, revise student loan procedures and include revenue-raising provisions. It would increase federal subsidies to help low- and moderate-income families purchase coverage through new health insurance exchanges, phase out the coverage gap for Medicare prescription drug enrollees and adjust the federal matching funds for Medicaid. It would delay a tax on high-cost health plans and reduce the reach of the tax, and it would modify a Medicare payroll tax for high-income taxpayers. The federal government would cover 100 percent of the cost of coverage for newly eligible Medicaid recipients in all states from 2014 to 2016. The bill also would make the federal government the sole originator of federal student loans and direct the savings generated to education programs, including Pell grants. Motion agreed to, thus clearing the bill for the president, 220-207: D 220-32; R 0-175. A "yea" was a vote in support of the president's position. March 25, 2010.

195. **H Res 1215. Support for Bangladesh Democracy/Adoption.** Crowley, D-N.Y., motion to suspend the rules and adopt the resolution that would express support for the people of Bangladesh and encourage the strengthening of democracy in the country. Motion agreed to 380-7: D 230-0; R 150-7. A two-thirds majority of those present and voting (258 in this case) is required for adoption under suspension of the rules. March 25, 2010.

	191	192	193	194	195
ALABAMA					
1 **Bonner**	N	Y	N	N	Y
2 Bright	Y	Y	N	N	Y
3 **Rogers**	N	Y	N	N	Y
4 **Aderholt**	N	Y	N	N	Y
5 **Griffith**	N	Y	N	N	Y
6 **Bachus**	N	Y	N	N	Y
7 Davis	?	?	?	?	?
ALASKA					
AL **Young**	N	Y	N	N	Y
ARIZONA					
1 Kirkpatrick	Y	Y	Y	Y	Y
2 **Franks**	N	Y	N	N	Y
3 **Shadegg**	?	Y	N	N	Y
4 Pastor	Y	Y	Y	Y	Y
5 Mitchell	Y	Y	Y	Y	Y
6 **Flake**	N	Y	N	N	Y
7 Grijalva	Y	Y	Y	Y	Y
8 Giffords	Y	Y	Y	Y	Y
ARKANSAS					
1 Berry	Y	Y	N	N	Y
2 Snyder	Y	Y	Y	Y	Y
3 **Boozman**	N	Y	N	N	Y
4 Ross	Y	Y	N	N	Y
CALIFORNIA					
1 Thompson	Y	Y	Y	Y	Y
2 **Herger**	N	Y	N	N	Y
3 **Lungren**	N	Y	N	N	Y
4 **McClintock**	N	Y	N	N	Y
5 Matsui	Y	Y	Y	Y	Y
6 Woolsey	?	Y	Y	Y	Y
7 Miller, George	Y	Y	Y	Y	Y
8 Pelosi				Y	
9 Lee	Y	Y	Y	Y	Y
10 Garamendi	Y	Y	Y	Y	Y
11 McNerney	Y	Y	Y	Y	Y
12 Speier	Y	Y	Y	Y	Y
13 Stark	Y	Y	Y	Y	Y
14 Eshoo	Y	Y	Y	Y	Y
15 Honda	Y	Y	Y	Y	Y
16 Lofgren	Y	Y	Y	Y	Y
17 Farr	Y	Y	Y	Y	Y
18 Cardoza	Y	Y	Y	Y	Y
19 **Radanovich**	?	?	N	N	?
20 Costa	Y	Y	Y	Y	Y
21 **Nunes**	N	Y	N	N	Y
22 **McCarthy**	N	Y	N	N	Y
23 Capps	Y	Y	Y	Y	Y
24 **Gallegly**	N	Y	N	N	?
25 **McKeon**	N	Y	N	N	Y
26 **Dreier**	N	Y	N	N	Y
27 Sherman	Y	Y	Y	Y	Y
28 Berman	Y	Y	Y	Y	?
29 Schiff	Y	Y	Y	Y	Y
30 Waxman	Y	Y	Y	Y	Y
31 Becerra	Y	Y	Y	Y	Y
32 Chu	Y	Y	Y	Y	Y
33 Watson	Y	Y	Y	Y	Y
34 Roybal-Allard	Y	Y	Y	Y	Y
35 Waters	Y	Y	Y	Y	Y
36 Harman	Y	Y	Y	Y	Y
37 Richardson	Y	Y	Y	Y	Y
38 Napolitano	Y	Y	Y	Y	?
39 Sánchez, Linda	Y	Y	Y	Y	Y
40 **Royce**	N	Y	N	N	Y
41 **Lewis**	N	Y	N	N	Y
42 **Miller, Gary**	N	Y	N	N	?
43 Baca	Y	Y	Y	Y	Y
44 **Calvert**	N	Y	N	N	?
45 **Bono Mack**	N	Y	N	N	?
46 **Rohrabacher**	N	Y	N	N	?
47 Sanchez, Loretta	Y	Y	Y	Y	?
48 **Campbell**	N	Y	N	N	Y
49 **Issa**	N	Y	N	N	Y
50 **Bilbray**	N	?	N	N	Y
51 Filner	Y	Y	Y	Y	Y
52 **Hunter**	N	Y	N	N	Y
53 Davis	Y	Y	Y	Y	Y

	191	192	193	194	195
COLORADO					
1 DeGette	Y	Y	Y	Y	Y
2 Polis	Y	Y	Y	Y	Y
3 Salazar	Y	Y	Y	Y	Y
4 Markey	Y	Y	Y	Y	Y
5 **Lamborn**	N	Y	N	N	Y
6 **Coffman**	N	Y	N	N	?
7 Perlmutter	Y	Y	Y	Y	Y
CONNECTICUT					
1 Larson	Y	Y	Y	Y	Y
2 Courtney	Y	Y	Y	Y	?
3 DeLauro	Y	Y	Y	Y	?
4 Himes	Y	Y	Y	Y	Y
5 Murphy	Y	Y	Y	Y	Y
DELAWARE					
AL **Castle**	N	Y	N	N	Y
FLORIDA					
1 **Miller**	N	Y	N	N	Y
2 Boyd	Y	Y	Y	Y	Y
3 Brown	Y	Y	Y	Y	Y
4 **Crenshaw**	N	Y	N	N	Y
5 **Brown-Waite**	N	Y	N	N	Y
6 **Stearns**	N	Y	N	N	Y
7 **Mica**	N	Y	N	N	Y
8 Grayson	Y	Y	Y	Y	Y
9 **Bilirakis**	N	Y	N	N	Y
10 **Young**	N	Y	N	N	Y
11 Castor	Y	Y	Y	Y	?
12 **Putnam**	N	Y	N	N	?
13 **Buchanan**	N	Y	N	N	Y
14 **Mack**	N	Y	N	N	Y
15 **Posey**	N	Y	N	N	Y
16 **Rooney**	N	Y	N	N	Y
17 Meek	Y	Y	Y	Y	Y
18 **Ros-Lehtinen**	N	Y	N	N	Y
19 Vacant					
20 Wasserman Schultz	Y	Y	Y	Y	Y
21 **Diaz-Balart, L.**	N	Y	N	N	?
22 Klein	Y	Y	Y	Y	Y
23 Hastings	Y	Y	Y	Y	Y
24 Kosmas	Y	Y	Y	Y	?
25 **Diaz-Balart, M.**	N	Y	N	N	Y
GEORGIA					
1 **Kingston**	N	Y	N	N	Y
2 Bishop	Y	Y	Y	Y	Y
3 **Westmoreland**	N	Y	N	N	Y
4 Johnson	Y	Y	Y	Y	Y
5 Lewis	Y	Y	Y	Y	Y
6 **Price**	N	Y	N	N	Y
7 **Linder**	N	Y	N	N	?
8 Marshall	Y	Y	N	N	Y
9 Vacant					
10 **Broun**	N	Y	N	N	N
11 **Gingrey**	N	Y	N	N	?
12 Barrow	Y	Y	N	N	Y
13 Scott	Y	Y	Y	Y	Y
HAWAII					
1 Vacant					
2 Hirono	Y	Y	Y	Y	Y
IDAHO					
1 **Minnick**	Y	Y	N	N	Y
2 **Simpson**	N	Y	N	N	Y
ILLINOIS					
1 Rush	Y	Y	Y	Y	Y
2 Jackson	Y	Y	Y	Y	Y
3 Lipinski	Y	Y	Y	Y	Y
4 Gutierrez	Y	Y	Y	Y	?
5 Quigley	Y	Y	Y	Y	Y
6 **Roskam**	N	Y	N	N	?
7 Davis	Y	Y	Y	Y	Y
8 Bean	Y	Y	Y	Y	Y
9 Schakowsky	Y	Y	Y	Y	Y
10 **Kirk**	N	Y	N	N	Y
11 Halvorson	Y	Y	Y	Y	Y
12 Costello	Y	Y	Y	Y	Y
13 **Biggert**	N	Y	N	N	Y
14 Foster	Y	Y	Y	Y	Y
15 **Johnson**	N	Y	N	N	Y

KEY **Republicans** Democrats

Y Voted for (yea)	X Paired against	C Voted "present" to avoid possible conflict of interes
# Paired for	– Announced against	
+ Announced for	P Voted "present"	? Did not vote or otherwise make a position known
N Voted against (nay)		

	191	192	193	194	195
16 Manzullo	–	+	N	N	Y
17 Hare	Y	Y	Y	Y	Y
18 Schock	N	Y	N	N	Y
19 Shimkus	N	Y	N	N	?
INDIANA					
1 Visclosky	Y	Y	Y	Y	Y
2 Donnelly	Y	Y	Y	Y	Y
3 Souder	N	Y	N	N	Y
4 Buyer	?	?	?	?	?
5 Burton	N	Y	N	N	Y
6 Pence	N	Y	N	N	Y
7 Carson	Y	Y	Y	Y	Y
8 Ellsworth	Y	Y	Y	Y	Y
9 Hill	Y	Y	Y	Y	Y
IOWA					
1 Braley	Y	Y	Y	Y	Y
2 Loebsack	Y	Y	Y	Y	Y
3 Boswell	Y	Y	Y	Y	Y
4 Latham	N	Y	N	N	Y
5 King	N	Y	N	N	Y
KANSAS					
1 Moran	N	Y	N	N	Y
2 Jenkins	N	Y	N	N	Y
3 Moore	Y	Y	Y	Y	Y
4 Tiahrt	N	Y	N	N	Y
KENTUCKY					
1 Whitfield	N	Y	N	N	Y
2 Guthrie	N	Y	N	N	Y
3 Yarmuth	Y	Y	Y	Y	Y
4 Davis	N	Y	N	N	Y
5 Rogers	N	Y	N	N	Y
6 Chandler	Y	?	N	N	Y
LOUISIANA					
1 Scalise	N	Y	N	N	Y
2 Cao	N	Y	N	N	?
3 Melancon	Y	Y	N	N	Y
4 Fleming	N	Y	N	N	Y
5 Alexander	N	Y	N	N	Y
6 Cassidy	N	Y	N	N	Y
7 Boustany	N	Y	N	N	Y
MAINE					
1 Pingree	Y	Y	Y	Y	Y
2 Michaud	Y	Y	Y	Y	Y
MARYLAND					
1 Kratovil	Y	Y	N	N	Y
2 Ruppersberger	Y	Y	Y	Y	Y
3 Sarbanes	Y	Y	Y	Y	Y
4 Edwards	Y	Y	Y	Y	Y
5 Hoyer	Y	Y	Y	Y	Y
6 Bartlett	N	Y	N	N	Y
7 Cummings	Y	Y	Y	Y	Y
8 Van Hollen	Y	Y	Y	Y	Y
MASSACHUSETTS					
1 Olver	Y	Y	Y	Y	Y
2 Neal	Y	?	Y	Y	Y
3 McGovern	Y	Y	Y	Y	Y
4 Frank	Y	Y	Y	Y	Y
5 Tsongas	Y	Y	Y	Y	Y
6 Tierney	Y	Y	Y	Y	Y
7 Markey	Y	Y	Y	Y	Y
8 Capuano	Y	Y	Y	Y	Y
9 Lynch	Y	?	Y	Y	Y
10 Delahunt	Y	Y	Y	Y	?
MICHIGAN					
1 Stupak	Y	Y	Y	Y	Y
2 Hoekstra	N	Y	N	N	Y
3 Ehlers	N	Y	N	N	Y
4 Camp	N	Y	N	N	Y
5 Kildee	Y	Y	Y	Y	Y
6 Upton	N	Y	N	N	Y
7 Schauer	Y	Y	Y	Y	Y
8 Rogers	N	Y	N	N	Y
9 Peters	Y	Y	Y	Y	Y
10 Miller	N	Y	N	N	Y
11 McCotter	N	Y	N	N	Y
12 Levin	Y	Y	Y	Y	Y
13 Kilpatrick	Y	Y	Y	Y	?
14 Conyers	Y	Y	Y	Y	Y
15 Dingell	Y	Y	Y	Y	Y
MINNESOTA					
1 Walz	Y	Y	Y	Y	Y
2 Kline	N	Y	N	N	Y
3 Paulsen	N	Y	N	N	Y
4 McCollum	Y	Y	Y	Y	Y

	191	192	193	194	195
5 Ellison	Y	Y	Y	Y	Y
6 Bachmann	N	Y	N	N	Y
7 Peterson	Y	Y	Y	N	?
8 Oberstar	Y	Y	Y	Y	Y
MISSISSIPPI					
1 Childers	Y	Y	N	N	Y
2 Thompson	Y	Y	Y	Y	Y
3 Harper	N	Y	N	N	Y
4 Taylor	N	Y	N	N	Y
MISSOURI					
1 Clay	Y	Y	Y	Y	Y
2 Akin	N	Y	N	N	Y
3 Carnahan	Y	Y	Y	Y	Y
4 Skelton	Y	Y	N	N	Y
5 Cleaver	Y	Y	Y	Y	Y
6 Graves	N	Y	N	N	Y
7 Blunt	N	Y	N	N	Y
8 Emerson	N	Y	N	N	Y
9 Luetkemeyer	N	Y	N	N	Y
MONTANA					
AL Rehberg	N	Y	N	N	Y
NEBRASKA					
1 Fortenberry	N	Y	N	N	Y
2 Terry	N	Y	N	N	Y
3 Smith	N	Y	N	N	Y
NEVADA					
1 Berkley	Y	Y	Y	Y	Y
2 Heller	N	Y	N	N	Y
3 Titus	Y	Y	Y	Y	Y
NEW HAMPSHIRE					
1 Shea-Porter	Y	Y	Y	Y	Y
2 Hodes	Y	Y	Y	Y	Y
NEW JERSEY					
1 Andrews	Y	Y	Y	Y	Y
2 LoBiondo	N	Y	N	N	Y
3 Adler	Y	Y	N	N	Y
4 Smith	N	Y	N	N	Y
5 Garrett	N	Y	N	N	Y
6 Pallone	Y	Y	Y	Y	Y
7 Lance	N	Y	N	N	Y
8 Pascrell	Y	Y	Y	Y	Y
9 Rothman	Y	Y	Y	Y	Y
10 Payne	Y	Y	Y	Y	Y
11 Frelinghuysen	N	Y	N	N	Y
12 Holt	Y	Y	Y	Y	Y
13 Sires	Y	Y	Y	Y	Y
NEW MEXICO					
1 Heinrich	Y	Y	Y	Y	Y
2 Teague	Y	Y	Y	N	Y
3 Luján	Y	Y	Y	Y	Y
NEW YORK					
1 Bishop	Y	Y	Y	Y	Y
2 Israel	Y	Y	Y	Y	Y
3 King	N	Y	N	N	Y
4 McCarthy	Y	Y	Y	Y	Y
5 Ackerman	Y	Y	Y	Y	Y
6 Meeks	Y	?	Y	Y	Y
7 Crowley	Y	Y	Y	Y	Y
8 Nadler	Y	Y	Y	Y	Y
9 Weiner	Y	Y	Y	Y	Y
10 Towns	Y	Y	Y	Y	Y
11 Clarke	Y	Y	Y	Y	Y
12 Velázquez	Y	Y	Y	Y	?
13 McMahon	Y	Y	Y	N	Y
14 Maloney	Y	Y	Y	Y	Y
15 Rangel	Y	Y	Y	Y	Y
16 Serrano	Y	Y	Y	Y	Y
17 Engel	Y	Y	Y	Y	Y
18 Lowey	Y	Y	Y	Y	Y
19 Hall	Y	Y	Y	Y	Y
20 Murphy	Y	Y	Y	Y	?
21 Tonko	Y	Y	Y	Y	Y
22 Hinchey	Y	Y	Y	Y	Y
23 Owens	Y	?	Y	Y	Y
24 Arcuri	Y	Y	N	N	Y
25 Maffei	Y	Y	Y	Y	Y
26 Lee	N	Y	N	N	Y
27 Higgins	Y	Y	Y	Y	Y
28 Slaughter	Y	Y	Y	Y	Y
29 Vacant					
NORTH CAROLINA					
1 Butterfield	Y	Y	Y	Y	Y
2 Etheridge	Y	Y	Y	Y	Y
3 Jones	N	Y	N	N	Y
4 Price	Y	Y	Y	Y	Y

	191	192	193	194	195
5 Foxx	N	Y	N	N	Y
6 Coble	N	Y	N	N	Y
7 McIntyre	Y	Y	Y	N	?
8 Kissell	Y	Y	Y	N	Y
9 Myrick	N	Y	N	N	Y
10 McHenry	N	Y	N	N	Y
11 Shuler	Y	Y	N	N	?
12 Watt	Y	Y	Y	Y	Y
13 Miller	Y	Y	Y	Y	Y
NORTH DAKOTA					
AL Pomeroy	Y	Y	Y	Y	Y
OHIO					
1 Driehaus	Y	Y	Y	Y	Y
2 Schmidt	N	Y	N	N	Y
3 Turner	N	Y	N	N	Y
4 Jordan	N	Y	N	N	?
5 Latta	N	Y	N	N	Y
6 Wilson	Y	Y	Y	Y	Y
7 Austria	N	Y	N	N	?
8 Boehner	?	?	N	N	?
9 Kaptur	Y	Y	Y	Y	Y
10 Kucinich	Y	Y	Y	Y	Y
11 Fudge	Y	Y	Y	Y	?
12 Tiberi	N	Y	N	N	Y
13 Sutton	Y	Y	Y	Y	?
14 LaTourette	N	Y	N	N	Y
15 Kilroy	Y	Y	Y	Y	Y
16 Boccieri	Y	Y	Y	Y	Y
17 Ryan	Y	Y	Y	Y	Y
18 Space	Y	Y	?	N	Y
OKLAHOMA					
1 Sullivan	N	Y	N	N	Y
2 Boren	Y	Y	N	N	Y
3 Lucas	N	Y	N	N	Y
4 Cole	N	Y	N	N	Y
5 Fallin	N	Y	N	N	Y
OREGON					
1 Wu	Y	Y	Y	Y	Y
2 Walden	N	Y	N	N	Y
3 Blumenauer	Y	Y	Y	Y	Y
4 DeFazio	Y	Y	Y	Y	Y
5 Schrader	Y	Y	Y	Y	Y
PENNSYLVANIA					
1 Brady	Y	Y	Y	Y	Y
2 Fattah	Y	Y	Y	Y	Y
3 Dahlkemper	Y	Y	Y	Y	Y
4 Altmire	Y	Y	N	N	Y
5 Thompson	N	Y	N	N	Y
6 Gerlach	N	Y	N	N	Y
7 Sestak	Y	Y	Y	Y	Y
8 Murphy, P.	Y	Y	Y	Y	Y
9 Shuster	N	Y	N	N	Y
10 Carney	Y	Y	Y	Y	Y
11 Kanjorski	Y	Y	Y	Y	Y
12 Vacant					
13 Schwartz	Y	Y	Y	Y	Y
14 Doyle	Y	Y	Y	Y	Y
15 Dent	N	Y	N	N	Y
16 Pitts	N	Y	N	N	Y
17 Holden	Y	Y	N	N	Y
18 Murphy, T.	N	Y	N	N	Y
19 Platts	N	Y	N	N	Y
RHODE ISLAND					
1 Kennedy	Y	Y	Y	Y	Y
2 Langevin	Y	Y	Y	Y	Y
SOUTH CAROLINA					
1 Brown	N	Y	N	N	Y
2 Wilson	N	Y	N	N	Y
3 Barrett	N	Y	N	N	Y
4 Inglis	N	Y	N	N	Y
5 Spratt	Y	Y	Y	Y	Y
6 Clyburn	Y	Y	Y	Y	Y
SOUTH DAKOTA					
AL Herseth Sandlin	Y	Y	N	N	Y
TENNESSEE					
1 Roe	N	Y	N	N	Y
2 Duncan	N	Y	N	N	Y
3 Wamp	N	Y	N	N	Y
4 Davis	Y	Y	N	N	Y
5 Cooper	Y	Y	N	N	Y
6 Gordon	Y	Y	Y	N	?
7 Blackburn	N	Y	N	N	Y
8 Tanner	Y	Y	Y	Y	Y
9 Cohen	Y	Y	Y	Y	Y

	191	192	193	194	195
TEXAS					
1 Gohmert	N	Y	N	N	N
2 Poe	N	Y	N	N	N
3 Johnson, S.	N	Y	N	N	Y
4 Hall	N	Y	N	N	Y
5 Hensarling	N	Y	N	N	Y
6 Barton	N	Y	N	N	Y
7 Culberson	N	Y	N	N	Y
8 Brady	N	Y	?	N	Y
9 Green, A.	Y	Y	Y	Y	Y
10 McCaul	N	Y	N	N	Y
11 Conaway	N	Y	N	N	N
12 Granger	N	Y	N	N	Y
13 Thornberry	N	Y	N	N	Y
14 Paul	N	Y	N	N	N
15 Hinojosa	Y	Y	Y	Y	Y
16 Reyes	Y	Y	Y	Y	Y
17 Edwards	Y	Y	Y	Y	Y
18 Jackson Lee	Y	Y	Y	Y	Y
19 Neugebauer	N	Y	N	N	Y
20 Gonzalez	Y	Y	Y	Y	Y
21 Smith	N	Y	N	N	Y
22 Olson	N	Y	N	N	Y
23 Rodriguez	Y	Y	Y	Y	Y
24 Marchant	N	Y	N	N	Y
25 Doggett	Y	Y	Y	Y	Y
26 Burgess	N	Y	N	N	Y
27 Ortiz	Y	Y	Y	Y	Y
28 Cuellar	Y	Y	Y	Y	Y
29 Green, G.	Y	Y	Y	Y	Y
30 Johnson, E.	Y	Y	Y	Y	Y
31 Carter	N	Y	N	N	N
32 Sessions	N	Y	N	N	Y
UTAH					
1 Bishop	N	Y	N	N	Y
2 Matheson	Y	Y	Y	Y	Y
3 Chaffetz	N	Y	N	N	Y
VERMONT					
AL Welch	Y	Y	Y	Y	Y
VIRGINIA					
1 Wittman	N	Y	N	N	Y
2 Nye	Y	Y	N	N	Y
3 Scott	Y	Y	Y	Y	Y
4 Forbes	N	Y	N	N	Y
5 Perriello	Y	Y	Y	Y	Y
6 Goodlatte	N	Y	N	N	Y
7 Cantor	N	Y	N	N	Y
8 Moran	Y	Y	Y	Y	Y
9 Boucher	Y	Y	Y	Y	Y
10 Wolf	N	Y	N	N	Y
11 Connolly	Y	Y	Y	Y	Y
WASHINGTON					
1 Inslee	Y	Y	Y	Y	Y
2 Larsen	Y	Y	Y	Y	Y
3 Baird	Y	Y	Y	Y	Y
4 Hastings	N	Y	N	N	Y
5 McMorris Rodgers	N	Y	N	N	Y
6 Dicks	Y	Y	Y	Y	Y
7 McDermott	Y	Y	Y	Y	Y
8 Reichert	?	?	?	?	?
9 Smith	Y	Y	Y	Y	Y
WEST VIRGINIA					
1 Mollohan	Y	Y	Y	Y	Y
2 Capito	N	Y	N	N	Y
3 Rahall	Y	Y	Y	Y	Y
WISCONSIN					
1 Ryan	N	Y	N	N	Y
2 Baldwin	Y	Y	Y	Y	Y
3 Kind	Y	Y	Y	Y	Y
4 Moore	Y	Y	Y	Y	Y
5 Sensenbrenner	N	Y	N	N	Y
6 Petri	N	Y	N	N	Y
7 Obey	Y	Y	Y	Y	?
8 Kagen	Y	Y	Y	Y	Y
WYOMING					
AL Lummis	N	Y	N	N	N
DELEGATES					
Faleomavaega (A.S.)					
Norton (D.C.)					
Bordallo (Guam)					
Sablan (N. Marianas)					
Pierluisi (P.R.)					
Christensen (V.I.)					

IN THE HOUSE | By Vote Number

196. **H Res 1222. National Library Week/Adoption.** Chu, D-Calif., motion to suspend the rules and adopt the resolution that would support the goals and ideals of National Library Week, encourage residents to visit libraries and support efforts to ensure that all Americans have access to libraries. Motion agreed to 397-0: D 240-0; R 157-0. A two-thirds majority of those present and voting (265 in this case) is required for adoption under suspension of the rules. April 13, 2010.

197. **H Res 1041. University of Idaho Football/Adoption.** Chu, D-Calif., motion to suspend the rules and adopt the resolution that would commend the University of Idaho's football team for winning the 2009 Humanitarian Bowl. Motion agreed to 394-1: D 238-1; R 156-0. A two-thirds majority of those present and voting (265 in this case) is required for adoption under suspension of the rules. April 13, 2010.

198. **H Res 1042. Boise State Football/Adoption.** Chu, D-Calif., motion to suspend the rules and adopt the resolution that would commend the Boise State University Broncos football team for winning the 2010 Fiesta Bowl and congratulate the team on an undefeated season. Motion agreed to 385-1: D 233-1; R 152-0. A two-thirds majority of those present and voting (258 in this case) is required for adoption under suspension of the rules. April 13, 2010.

199. **H Res 1236. Tribute to West Virginia Miners/Adoption.** Miller, D-Calif., motion to suspend the rules and adopt the resolution that would recognize the 29 coal miners lost at the Upper Big Branch Mine-South in West Virginia and extend condolences to the miners' families. Motion agreed to 409-0: D 241-0; R 168-0. A two-thirds majority of those present and voting (273 in this case) is required for adoption under suspension of the rules. April 14, 2010.

200. **HR 4994. Cell Phone Deductions and Tax Relief/Passage.** Lewis, D-Ga., motion to suspend the rules and pass the bill that would remove filing requirements for claiming a business cell phone deduction. It also would require the IRS to notify taxpayers who were eligible but did not receive a refund in any preceding tax year and authorize $20 million per year in grants for tax assistance programs for low- and moderate-income taxpayers. Motion agreed to 399-9: D 243-0; R 156-9. A two-thirds majority of those present and voting (272 in this case) is required for passage under suspension of the rules. April 14, 2010.

	196	197	198	199	200
ALABAMA					
1 Bonner	Y	Y	Y	Y	Y
2 Bright	Y	Y	Y	Y	Y
3 Rogers	Y	Y	Y	Y	Y
4 Aderholt	Y	Y	Y	Y	Y
5 Griffith	Y	Y	Y	Y	+
6 Bachus	Y	Y	Y	Y	Y
7 Davis	?	?	?	?	?
ALASKA					
AL Young	?	?	?	?	?
ARIZONA					
1 Kirkpatrick	Y	Y	Y	Y	Y
2 Franks	Y	Y	Y	Y	Y
3 Shadegg	Y	Y	Y	Y	Y
4 Pastor	Y	Y	Y	Y	Y
5 Mitchell	Y	Y	Y	Y	Y
6 Flake	Y	Y	Y	Y	N
7 Grijalva	?	?	?	Y	Y
8 Giffords	Y	Y	Y	Y	Y
ARKANSAS					
1 Berry	Y	Y	Y	Y	Y
2 Snyder	Y	Y	Y	Y	Y
3 Boozman	Y	Y	Y	Y	Y
4 Ross	Y	Y	Y	Y	Y
CALIFORNIA					
1 Thompson	Y	Y	Y	Y	Y
2 Herger	Y	Y	Y	Y	Y
3 Lungren	Y	Y	Y	Y	Y
4 McClintock	Y	Y	Y	Y	N
5 Matsui	Y	Y	Y	Y	Y
6 Woolsey	Y	Y	Y	Y	Y
7 Miller, George	Y	Y	Y	Y	Y
8 Pelosi					
9 Lee	Y	Y	Y	Y	Y
10 Garamendi	Y	Y	Y	Y	Y
11 McNerney	Y	Y	Y	Y	Y
12 Speier	Y	Y	Y	Y	Y
13 Stark	Y	Y	Y	Y	Y
14 Eshoo	Y	Y	Y	Y	Y
15 Honda	Y	Y	Y	Y	Y
16 Lofgren	Y	Y	Y	Y	Y
17 Farr	Y	Y	Y	Y	Y
18 Cardoza	Y	Y	Y	Y	Y
19 Radanovich	Y	Y	Y	Y	Y
20 Costa	Y	Y	Y	Y	+
21 Nunes	Y	Y	Y	Y	Y
22 McCarthy	Y	Y	Y	Y	Y
23 Capps	Y	Y	Y	Y	Y
24 Gallegly	?	?	?	?	?
25 McKeon	?	?	?	Y	Y
26 Dreier	Y	Y	Y	Y	Y
27 Sherman	+	+	+	+	+
28 Berman	Y	Y	Y	Y	Y
29 Schiff	Y	Y	Y	Y	Y
30 Waxman	Y	Y	Y	Y	Y
31 Becerra	Y	Y	Y	Y	Y
32 Chu	Y	Y	Y	Y	Y
33 Watson	Y	Y	Y	Y	Y
34 Roybal-Allard	Y	Y	Y	Y	Y
35 Waters	Y	Y	Y	Y	Y
36 Harman	Y	Y	Y	Y	Y
37 Richardson	Y	Y	Y	Y	Y
38 Napolitano	Y	Y	Y	Y	Y
39 Sánchez, Linda	Y	Y	Y	?	?
40 Royce	Y	Y	Y	Y	N
41 Lewis	Y	Y	Y	Y	Y
42 Miller, Gary	Y	Y	Y	Y	Y
43 Baca	Y	Y	Y	Y	Y
44 Calvert	Y	Y	Y	Y	Y
45 Bono Mack	Y	Y	Y	Y	Y
46 Rohrabacher	Y	Y	Y	Y	Y
47 Sanchez, Loretta	Y	Y	Y	Y	Y
48 Campbell	?	?	?	?	?
49 Issa	Y	Y	Y	Y	Y
50 Bilbray	?	?	?	?	?
51 Filner	Y	Y	Y	Y	Y
52 Hunter	Y	Y	Y	Y	Y
53 Davis	Y	Y	Y	Y	Y

	196	197	198	199	200
COLORADO					
1 DeGette	Y	Y	Y	Y	Y
2 Polis	Y	Y	Y	Y	Y
3 Salazar	Y	Y	Y	Y	Y
4 Markey	Y	Y	Y	Y	Y
5 Lamborn	Y	Y	Y	Y	Y
6 Coffman	Y	Y	Y	Y	Y
7 Perlmutter	Y	Y	Y	Y	Y
CONNECTICUT					
1 Larson	Y	Y	Y	Y	Y
2 Courtney	Y	Y	Y	Y	Y
3 DeLauro	Y	Y	Y	Y	Y
4 Himes	Y	Y	Y	Y	Y
5 Murphy	Y	Y	Y	Y	Y
DELAWARE					
AL Castle	Y	Y	Y	Y	Y
FLORIDA					
1 Miller	Y	Y	Y	Y	Y
2 Boyd	Y	Y	Y	Y	Y
3 Brown	?	?	?	Y	Y
4 Crenshaw	Y	Y	Y	Y	Y
5 Brown-Waite	?	?	?	Y	Y
6 Stearns	Y	Y	Y	Y	Y
7 Mica	Y	Y	Y	Y	Y
8 Grayson	Y	Y	Y	Y	Y
9 Bilirakis	Y	Y	Y	Y	Y
10 Young	Y	Y	Y	Y	Y
11 Castor	Y	Y	Y	Y	Y
12 Putnam	Y	Y	Y	Y	Y
13 Buchanan	Y	Y	Y	Y	Y
14 Mack	Y	Y	Y	Y	Y
15 Posey	Y	Y	Y	Y	Y
16 Rooney	Y	Y	Y	Y	Y
17 Meek	Y	Y	Y	Y	Y
18 Ros-Lehtinen	Y	Y	Y	Y	Y
19 Vacant					
20 Wasserman Schultz	Y	Y	Y	?	?
21 Diaz-Balart, L.	Y	Y	Y	Y	Y
22 Klein	Y	Y	Y	Y	Y
23 Hastings	Y	Y	Y	Y	Y
24 Kosmas	Y	Y	Y	Y	Y
25 Diaz-Balart, M.	Y	Y	Y	Y	Y
GEORGIA					
1 Kingston	?	?	?	Y	Y
2 Bishop	Y	Y	Y	?	Y
3 Westmoreland	Y	Y	Y	Y	Y
4 Johnson	Y	Y	Y	Y	Y
5 Lewis	Y	Y	Y	Y	Y
6 Price	Y	Y	Y	?	?
7 Linder	Y	Y	?	Y	Y
8 Marshall	Y	Y	Y	Y	Y
9 Vacant					
10 Broun	Y	Y	Y	Y	Y
11 Gingrey	Y	Y	Y	Y	Y
12 Barrow	Y	Y	Y	Y	Y
13 Scott	?	?	?	?	?
HAWAII					
1 Vacant					
2 Hirono	Y	Y	Y	Y	Y
IDAHO					
1 Minnick	Y	Y	Y	Y	Y
2 Simpson	Y	Y	Y	Y	Y
ILLINOIS					
1 Rush	Y	Y	Y	Y	Y
2 Jackson	Y	Y	Y	Y	Y
3 Lipinski	Y	Y	Y	Y	Y
4 Gutierrez	?	?	?	Y	Y
5 Quigley	Y	Y	Y	Y	Y
6 Roskam	Y	Y	Y	Y	Y
7 Davis	Y	Y	Y	Y	Y
8 Bean	Y	Y	Y	Y	Y
9 Schakowsky	Y	Y	Y	Y	Y
10 Kirk	Y	Y	Y	Y	?
11 Halvorson	Y	Y	Y	Y	Y
12 Costello	Y	Y	Y	Y	Y
13 Biggert	Y	Y	Y	Y	Y
14 Foster	Y	Y	Y	Y	Y
15 Johnson	Y	Y	Y	Y	N

KEY	Republicans	Democrats

Y	Voted for (yea)		X	Paired against		C	Voted "present" to avoid possible conflict of interest
#	Paired for		–	Announced against			
+	Announced for		P	Voted "present"		?	Did not vote or otherwise make a position known
N	Voted against (nay)						

	196	197	198	199	200
16 Manzullo	Y	Y	Y	Y	Y
17 Hare	Y	Y	Y	Y	Y
18 Schock	Y	Y	Y	Y	Y
19 Shimkus	Y	Y	Y	Y	Y
INDIANA					
1 Visclosky	Y	Y	Y	Y	Y
2 Donnelly	Y	Y	Y	Y	Y
3 Souder	?	?	?	Y	Y
4 Buyer	Y	Y	Y	Y	Y
5 Burton	Y	Y	Y	Y	Y
6 Pence	Y	Y	Y	Y	Y
7 Carson	Y	Y	Y	Y	Y
8 Ellsworth	Y	Y	Y	Y	Y
9 Hill	Y	Y	Y	Y	Y
IOWA					
1 Braley	Y	Y	Y	Y	Y
2 Loebsack	Y	Y	Y	Y	Y
3 Boswell	Y	Y	Y	Y	Y
4 Latham	Y	Y	Y	Y	Y
5 King	Y	Y	Y	Y	Y
KANSAS					
1 Moran	Y	Y	Y	Y	Y
2 Jenkins	Y	Y	Y	Y	Y
3 Moore	Y	Y	Y	?	Y
4 Tiahrt	Y	Y	Y	Y	Y
KENTUCKY					
1 Whitfield	Y	Y	Y	Y	Y
2 Guthrie	Y	Y	Y	Y	Y
3 Yarmuth	Y	Y	Y	Y	Y
4 Davis	Y	Y	Y	Y	Y
5 Rogers	Y	Y	Y	Y	Y
6 Chandler	Y	Y	Y	Y	Y
LOUISIANA					
1 Scalise	Y	Y	Y	Y	Y
2 Cao	Y	Y	Y	Y	Y
3 Melancon	Y	Y	Y	Y	Y
4 Fleming	Y	Y	Y	Y	Y
5 Alexander	Y	Y	Y	Y	Y
6 Cassidy	Y	Y	Y	Y	Y
7 Boustany	Y	Y	Y	Y	Y
MAINE					
1 Pingree	Y	Y	Y	Y	Y
2 Michaud	Y	Y	Y	Y	Y
MARYLAND					
1 Kratovil	Y	Y	Y	Y	Y
2 Ruppersberger	?	?	?	?	?
3 Sarbanes	Y	Y	Y	Y	Y
4 Edwards	Y	Y	Y	Y	Y
5 Hoyer	Y	Y	Y	Y	Y
6 Bartlett	Y	Y	Y	Y	Y
7 Cummings	Y	Y	Y	Y	Y
8 Van Hollen	Y	Y	Y	Y	Y
MASSACHUSETTS					
1 Olver	Y	Y	Y	Y	Y
2 Neal	Y	Y	Y	Y	Y
3 McGovern	Y	Y	Y	Y	Y
4 Frank	Y	Y	Y	Y	Y
5 Tsongas	Y	Y	Y	Y	Y
6 Tierney	Y	Y	Y	Y	Y
7 Markey	Y	Y	Y	Y	Y
8 Capuano	Y	Y	Y	Y	Y
9 Lynch	Y	Y	Y	Y	Y
10 Delahunt	?	Y	Y	Y	Y
MICHIGAN					
1 Stupak	?	Y	Y	Y	Y
2 Hoekstra	?	?	?	?	?
3 Ehlers	Y	Y	Y	Y	Y
4 Camp	Y	Y	Y	Y	Y
5 Kildee	Y	Y	Y	Y	Y
6 Upton	Y	Y	Y	Y	Y
7 Schauer	Y	Y	Y	Y	Y
8 Rogers	Y	Y	Y	Y	Y
9 Peters	Y	Y	Y	Y	Y
10 Miller	Y	Y	Y	Y	Y
11 McCotter	Y	Y	Y	Y	Y
12 Levin	Y	Y	Y	Y	Y
13 Kilpatrick	Y	Y	Y	Y	Y
14 Conyers	Y	Y	Y	Y	Y
15 Dingell	Y	Y	Y	Y	Y
MINNESOTA					
1 Walz	Y	Y	Y	Y	Y
2 Kline	Y	Y	Y	Y	Y
3 Paulsen	Y	Y	Y	Y	Y
4 McCollum	Y	Y	Y	Y	Y

	196	197	198	199	200
5 Ellison	Y	Y	Y	Y	Y
6 Bachmann	Y	Y	Y	Y	Y
7 Peterson	Y	Y	Y	Y	Y
8 Oberstar	Y	P	P	Y	Y
MISSISSIPPI					
1 Childers	Y	Y	Y	Y	Y
2 Thompson	Y	Y	Y	Y	Y
3 Harper	Y	Y	Y	Y	Y
4 Taylor	Y	Y	Y	Y	Y
MISSOURI					
1 Clay	Y	Y	Y	Y	Y
2 Akin	Y	Y	Y	Y	Y
3 Carnahan	Y	Y	Y	Y	Y
4 Skelton	Y	Y	Y	Y	Y
5 Cleaver	Y	Y	Y	Y	Y
6 Graves	Y	Y	Y	Y	Y
7 Blunt	?	?	?	Y	Y
8 Emerson	Y	Y	Y	Y	Y
9 Luetkemeyer	Y	Y	Y	Y	Y
MONTANA					
AL Rehberg	Y	Y	Y	Y	Y
NEBRASKA					
1 Fortenberry	Y	Y	Y	Y	Y
2 Terry	?	?	?	?	?
3 Smith	Y	Y	Y	Y	Y
NEVADA					
1 Berkley	Y	Y	Y	Y	Y
2 Heller	Y	Y	Y	Y	Y
3 Titus	Y	Y	Y	Y	Y
NEW HAMPSHIRE					
1 Shea-Porter	Y	Y	Y	Y	Y
2 Hodes	Y	Y	?	Y	Y
NEW JERSEY					
1 Andrews	Y	Y	Y	Y	Y
2 LoBiondo	Y	Y	Y	Y	Y
3 Adler	Y	Y	Y	Y	Y
4 Smith	Y	Y	Y	Y	Y
5 Garrett	Y	Y	Y	Y	Y
6 Pallone	Y	Y	Y	Y	Y
7 Lance	Y	Y	Y	Y	Y
8 Pascrell	Y	Y	?	Y	Y
9 Rothman	Y	Y	Y	Y	Y
10 Payne	Y	Y	Y	Y	Y
11 Frelinghuysen	Y	Y	Y	Y	Y
12 Holt	Y	Y	Y	Y	Y
13 Sires	Y	Y	Y	Y	Y
NEW MEXICO					
1 Heinrich	Y	Y	Y	Y	Y
2 Teague	Y	Y	Y	Y	Y
3 Luján	Y	Y	Y	Y	Y
NEW YORK					
1 Bishop	Y	Y	Y	Y	Y
2 Israel	Y	Y	Y	Y	Y
3 King	Y	Y	Y	Y	Y
4 McCarthy	Y	Y	Y	Y	Y
5 Ackerman	Y	Y	Y	Y	Y
6 Meeks	Y	Y	Y	Y	Y
7 Crowley	Y	Y	Y	Y	Y
8 Nadler	Y	Y	Y	Y	Y
9 Weiner	Y	Y	Y	Y	Y
10 Towns	Y	Y	Y	Y	Y
11 Clarke	Y	Y	Y	Y	Y
12 Velázquez	Y	Y	Y	?	Y
13 McMahon	Y	Y	Y	Y	Y
14 Maloney	Y	Y	Y	Y	Y
15 Rangel	Y	Y	Y	Y	Y
16 Serrano	Y	Y	Y	Y	Y
17 Engel	Y	Y	Y	Y	Y
18 Lowey	Y	Y	Y	Y	Y
19 Hall	Y	Y	Y	Y	Y
20 Murphy	Y	Y	Y	Y	Y
21 Tonko	Y	Y	Y	Y	Y
22 Hinchey	Y	Y	Y	Y	Y
23 Owens	Y	Y	Y	Y	Y
24 Arcuri	Y	Y	Y	Y	Y
25 Maffei	Y	Y	Y	Y	Y
26 Lee	?	?	?	Y	Y
27 Higgins	Y	Y	Y	Y	Y
28 Slaughter	Y	Y	Y	Y	Y
29 Vacant					
NORTH CAROLINA					
1 Butterfield	Y	Y	Y	Y	Y
2 Etheridge	Y	Y	Y	Y	Y
3 Jones	Y	Y	Y	Y	?
4 Price	Y	Y	Y	Y	Y

	196	197	198	199	200
5 Foxx	Y	Y	Y	Y	Y
6 Coble	Y	Y	Y	Y	Y
7 McIntyre	Y	Y	Y	Y	Y
8 Kissell	Y	Y	Y	Y	Y
9 Myrick	Y	Y	Y	Y	Y
10 McHenry	Y	Y	Y	Y	Y
11 Shuler	Y	Y	Y	Y	Y
12 Watt	Y	Y	Y	Y	Y
13 Miller	Y	Y	Y	Y	Y
NORTH DAKOTA					
AL Pomeroy	Y	Y	Y	Y	Y
OHIO					
1 Driehaus	Y	Y	Y	Y	Y
2 Schmidt	Y	Y	Y	Y	Y
3 Turner	Y	Y	Y	Y	Y
4 Jordan	+	+	+	Y	Y
5 Latta	Y	Y	Y	Y	Y
6 Wilson	Y	Y	Y	Y	Y
7 Austria	Y	Y	Y	Y	Y
8 Boehner	Y	Y	?	Y	Y
9 Kaptur	Y	Y	Y	Y	Y
10 Kucinich	Y	Y	Y	Y	Y
11 Fudge	Y	Y	Y	Y	Y
12 Tiberi	Y	Y	Y	Y	Y
13 Sutton	Y	Y	Y	Y	Y
14 LaTourette	Y	Y	?	Y	Y
15 Kilroy	Y	Y	Y	Y	Y
16 Boccieri	Y	Y	Y	Y	Y
17 Ryan	Y	Y	Y	Y	Y
18 Space	Y	Y	Y	Y	Y
OKLAHOMA					
1 Sullivan	Y	Y	Y	Y	Y
2 Boren	Y	Y	Y	Y	Y
3 Lucas	Y	Y	Y	Y	Y
4 Cole	Y	Y	Y	Y	Y
5 Fallin	?	?	?	Y	Y
OREGON					
1 Wu	Y	Y	Y	Y	Y
2 Walden	Y	Y	Y	Y	Y
3 Blumenauer	Y	Y	Y	Y	Y
4 DeFazio	Y	P	P	Y	Y
5 Schrader	Y	Y	Y	Y	Y
PENNSYLVANIA					
1 Brady	Y	Y	Y	Y	Y
2 Fattah	Y	Y	Y	Y	Y
3 Dahlkemper	Y	Y	Y	Y	Y
4 Altmire	Y	N	N	Y	Y
5 Thompson	Y	Y	Y	Y	Y
6 Gerlach	Y	Y	Y	Y	Y
7 Sestak	Y	Y	Y	Y	Y
8 Murphy, P.	Y	Y	Y	Y	Y
9 Shuster	Y	Y	Y	Y	Y
10 Carney	+	+	+	Y	Y
11 Kanjorski	Y	Y	Y	Y	Y
12 Vacant					
13 Schwartz	Y	Y	Y	Y	Y
14 Doyle	Y	Y	Y	Y	Y
15 Dent	Y	Y	Y	Y	Y
16 Pitts	Y	Y	Y	Y	Y
17 Holden	Y	Y	Y	Y	Y
18 Murphy, T.	Y	Y	Y	Y	Y
19 Platts	Y	Y	Y	Y	Y
RHODE ISLAND					
1 Kennedy	Y	Y	Y	Y	Y
2 Langevin	Y	Y	Y	Y	Y
SOUTH CAROLINA					
1 Brown	Y	Y	Y	Y	Y
2 Wilson	Y	Y	Y	Y	Y
3 Barrett	?	?	?	?	?
4 Inglis	?	?	?	Y	Y
5 Spratt	Y	Y	Y	Y	Y
6 Clyburn	Y	Y	Y	Y	Y
SOUTH DAKOTA					
AL Herseth Sandlin	Y	Y	Y	Y	Y
TENNESSEE					
1 Roe	Y	Y	Y	Y	Y
2 Duncan	Y	Y	Y	Y	N
3 Wamp	Y	Y	Y	?	Y
4 Davis	Y	Y	Y	Y	?
5 Cooper	Y	Y	Y	Y	Y
6 Gordon	Y	Y	?	Y	Y
7 Blackburn	Y	Y	Y	Y	Y
8 Tanner	Y	Y	Y	Y	Y
9 Cohen	Y	Y	Y	Y	Y

	196	197	198	199	200
TEXAS					
1 Gohmert	?	?	?	Y	Y
2 Poe	Y	Y	Y	Y	Y
3 Johnson, S.	Y	Y	Y	Y	Y
4 Hall	Y	Y	Y	Y	Y
5 Hensarling	Y	Y	Y	Y	Y
6 Barton	Y	Y	Y	Y	Y
7 Culberson	Y	Y	Y	Y	Y
8 Brady	Y	Y	Y	Y	Y
9 Green, A.	Y	Y	Y	Y	Y
10 McCaul	Y	Y	Y	Y	Y
11 Conaway	Y	Y	Y	Y	Y
12 Granger	Y	Y	P	Y	Y
13 Thornberry	Y	Y	Y	Y	Y
14 Paul	Y	Y	Y	Y	N
15 Hinojosa	Y	Y	Y	Y	Y
16 Reyes	Y	Y	Y	Y	Y
17 Edwards	Y	?	?	Y	Y
18 Jackson Lee	Y	Y	Y	Y	Y
19 Neugebauer	Y	Y	Y	Y	Y
20 Gonzalez	?	?	?	?	?
21 Smith	Y	Y	Y	Y	Y
22 Olson	Y	Y	Y	Y	Y
23 Rodriguez	Y	Y	Y	Y	Y
24 Marchant	Y	Y	Y	Y	Y
25 Doggett	Y	Y	Y	Y	Y
26 Burgess	Y	Y	Y	Y	Y
27 Ortiz	Y	Y	Y	Y	Y
28 Cuellar	Y	Y	Y	Y	Y
29 Green, G.	Y	Y	Y	Y	Y
30 Johnson, E.	Y	Y	Y	Y	Y
31 Carter	?	?	?	Y	Y
32 Sessions	Y	Y	Y	Y	Y
UTAH					
1 Bishop	?	?	?	Y	Y
2 Matheson	Y	Y	Y	Y	Y
3 Chaffetz	?	?	?	Y	N
VERMONT					
AL Welch	Y	Y	Y	Y	?
VIRGINIA					
1 Wittman	Y	Y	Y	Y	Y
2 Nye	Y	Y	Y	Y	Y
3 Scott	Y	Y	Y	Y	Y
4 Forbes	Y	Y	Y	Y	Y
5 Perriello	Y	Y	Y	Y	Y
6 Goodlatte	Y	Y	Y	Y	Y
7 Cantor	Y	?	?	Y	Y
8 Moran	Y	Y	Y	Y	Y
9 Boucher	Y	Y	Y	Y	Y
10 Wolf	Y	Y	Y	Y	Y
11 Connolly	Y	Y	Y	Y	Y
WASHINGTON					
1 Inslee	+	+	+	Y	Y
2 Larsen	Y	Y	?	Y	Y
3 Baird	Y	Y	Y	Y	Y
4 Hastings	Y	Y	Y	Y	Y
5 McMorris Rodgers	Y	Y	Y	Y	Y
6 Dicks	Y	Y	Y	Y	Y
7 McDermott	Y	Y	Y	Y	Y
8 Reichert	Y	Y	Y	Y	Y
9 Smith	Y	Y	?	Y	Y
WEST VIRGINIA					
1 Mollohan	Y	Y	Y	Y	Y
2 Capito	Y	Y	Y	Y	Y
3 Rahall	Y	Y	Y	Y	Y
WISCONSIN					
1 Ryan	Y	Y	Y	Y	Y
2 Baldwin	Y	Y	Y	Y	Y
3 Kind	Y	Y	Y	Y	Y
4 Moore	Y	Y	Y	+	Y
5 Sensenbrenner	Y	Y	Y	Y	N
6 Petri	Y	Y	Y	Y	Y
7 Obey	Y	Y	Y	Y	Y
8 Kagen	Y	Y	Y	Y	Y
WYOMING					
AL Lummis	Y	Y	Y	Y	N
DELEGATES					
Faleomavaega (A.S.)					
Norton (D.C.)					
Bordallo (Guam)					
Sablan (N. Marianas)					
Pierluisi (P.R.)					
Christensen (V.I.)					

IN THE HOUSE | By Vote Number

201. **HR 3125. Radio Spectrum Inventory/Passage.** Boucher, D-Va., motion to suspend the rules and pass the bill that would require the National Telecommunications and Information Administration and the Federal Communications Commission to conduct an inventory of radio spectrum and determine where reallocating or sharing portions would be feasible. It would require a report on which spectrum blocks should be reallocated or made available for shared access. Motion agreed to 394-18: D 244-0; R 150-18. A two-thirds majority of those present and voting (275 in this case) is required for passage under suspension of the rules. April 14, 2010.

202. **H Res 1249. Reporting of Massa Allegations/Motion to Refer.** McGovern, D-Mass., motion to refer the Boehner, R-Ohio, privileged resolution to the Committee on Standards of Official Conduct. The resolution would require the committee to investigate whether House Democratic leaders and their staff knew of allegations of misconduct by former Rep. Eric Massa, D-N.Y., before March 3, 2010. Motion agreed to 235-157: D 235-3; R 0-154. April 14, 2010.

203. **H Res 1246. Tribute to Polish Plane Crash Victims/Adoption.** Delahunt, D-Mass., motion to suspend the rules and adopt the resolution that would express sympathy for the people of Poland as they mourn the death of Polish President Lech Kaczynski and 95 others who died in a plane crash April 10, 2010, in Russia. Motion agreed to 404-0: D 240-0; R 164-0. A two-thirds majority of those present and voting (270 in this case) is required for adoption under suspension of the rules. April 14, 2010.

204. **HR 4715. Estuary Protection Program/Rule.** Adoption of the rule (H Res 1248) that would provide for House floor consideration of the bill that would authorize $50 million annually through fiscal 2016 for the EPA's National Estuary Program. It also would permit the Speaker to entertain motions to suspend the rules on legislation related to the extension of unemployment benefits and waive the two-thirds majority vote requirement for same-day consideration of resolutions reported from the Rules Committee providing for consideration of legislation dealing with unemployment insurance through the legislative day of April 16, 2010. Adopted 235-171: D 235-3; R 0-168. April 15, 2010.

205. **H Res 1062. Tribute to Coast Guard Group Astoria/Adoption.** Cummings, D-Md., motion to suspend the rules and adopt the resolution that would recognize the Coast Guard Group Astoria's more than 60 years of service to the Pacific Northwest and honor the men and women of the organization. Motion agreed to 401-0: D 236-0; R 165-0. A two-thirds majority of those present and voting (268 in this case) is required for adoption under suspension of the rules. April 15, 2010.

*Rep. Ted Deutch, D-Fla., was sworn in April 15 to fill the seat vacated by the Jan. 3 resignation of Democrat Robert Wexler. The first vote for which Deutch was eligible was vote 205.

	201	202	203	204	205
ALABAMA					
1 **Bonner**	Y	P	Y	N	Y
2 Bright	Y	Y	Y	Y	Y
3 **Rogers**	Y	N	Y	N	Y
4 **Aderholt**	Y	N	Y	N	Y
5 **Griffith**	Y	N	?	N	Y
6 **Bachus**	Y	N	Y	N	Y
7 Davis	?	?	?	Y	Y
ALASKA					
AL **Young**	?	?	?	?	?
ARIZONA					
1 Kirkpatrick	Y	N	Y	N	Y
2 **Franks**	Y	N	Y	N	Y
3 **Shadegg**	Y	N	Y	N	Y
4 Pastor	Y	Y	Y	Y	Y
5 Mitchell	Y	Y	Y	Y	Y
6 **Flake**	N	N	Y	N	Y
7 Grijalva	Y	Y	Y	Y	Y
8 Giffords	Y	Y	Y	Y	Y
ARKANSAS					
1 Berry	Y	Y	Y	Y	Y
2 Snyder	Y	Y	Y	Y	Y
3 **Boozman**	Y	N	Y	N	Y
4 Ross	Y	Y	Y	Y	Y
CALIFORNIA					
1 Thompson	Y	Y	Y	Y	Y
2 **Herger**	Y	N	Y	N	Y
3 **Lungren**	Y	N	Y	N	?
4 **McClintock**	Y	N	Y	N	Y
5 Matsui	Y	Y	Y	Y	Y
6 Woolsey	Y	Y	Y	Y	Y
7 Miller, George	Y	Y	Y	Y	Y
8 Pelosi		Y			
9 Lee	Y	Y	Y	Y	Y
10 Garamendi	Y	Y	Y	Y	Y
11 McNerney	Y	Y	Y	Y	Y
12 Speier	Y	Y	Y	Y	Y
13 Stark	Y	Y	Y	Y	Y
14 Eshoo	Y	Y	Y	Y	Y
15 Honda	Y	Y	Y	Y	Y
16 Lofgren	Y	P	Y	Y	Y
17 Farr	Y	Y	Y	Y	Y
18 Cardoza	Y	Y	Y	?	?
19 **Radanovich**	Y	?	?	N	Y
20 Costa	Y	Y	Y	Y	Y
21 **Nunes**	Y	N	Y	N	Y
22 **McCarthy**	Y	N	Y	N	Y
23 Capps	Y	Y	Y	Y	Y
24 **Gallegly**	?	?	?	?	?
25 **McKeon**	Y	N	Y	N	Y
26 **Dreier**	Y	N	Y	N	Y
27 Sherman	+	+	+	Y	Y
28 Berman	Y	Y	Y	Y	Y
29 Schiff	Y	Y	Y	Y	Y
30 Waxman	Y	Y	Y	Y	?
31 Becerra	Y	Y	Y	Y	Y
32 Chu	Y	Y	Y	Y	Y
33 Watson	Y	Y	Y	Y	Y
34 Roybal-Allard	Y	Y	Y	Y	Y
35 Waters	Y	Y	Y	Y	Y
36 Harman	Y	Y	Y	Y	Y
37 Richardson	Y	Y	?	Y	Y
38 Napolitano	Y	Y	Y	Y	Y
39 Sánchez, Linda	?	?	?	?	?
40 **Royce**	N	N	Y	N	Y
41 **Lewis**	Y	N	Y	N	Y
42 **Miller, Gary**	Y	N	Y	N	Y
43 Baca	Y	Y	Y	Y	Y
44 **Calvert**	Y	N	Y	N	Y
45 **Bono Mack**	Y	N	Y	N	Y
46 **Rohrabacher**	Y	N	Y	N	Y
47 Sanchez, Loretta	Y	Y	Y	Y	Y
48 **Campbell**	?	?	?	N	Y
49 **Issa**	Y	N	Y	N	Y
50 **Bilbray**	?	?	?	?	?
51 Filner	Y	Y	Y	Y	Y
52 **Hunter**	Y	N	Y	N	Y
53 Davis	Y	Y	Y	Y	Y

	201	202	203	204	205
COLORADO					
1 DeGette	Y	Y	Y	Y	Y
2 Polis	Y	Y	Y	Y	Y
3 Salazar	Y	Y	Y	Y	Y
4 Markey	Y	Y	Y	Y	Y
5 **Lamborn**	Y	N	Y	N	Y
6 **Coffman**	Y	N	Y	N	Y
7 Perlmutter	Y	Y	Y	Y	Y
CONNECTICUT					
1 Larson	Y	Y	Y	Y	Y
2 Courtney	Y	Y	Y	Y	Y
3 DeLauro	Y	Y	Y	Y	Y
4 Himes	Y	Y	Y	Y	Y
5 Murphy	Y	Y	Y	Y	Y
DELAWARE					
AL **Castle**	Y	N	Y	N	Y
FLORIDA					
1 **Miller**	N	N	Y	?	?
2 Boyd	Y	Y	?	?	?
3 Brown	Y	Y	Y	Y	?
4 **Crenshaw**	Y	N	Y	N	Y
5 **Brown-Waite**	Y	N	Y	N	Y
6 **Stearns**	Y	N	Y	N	Y
7 **Mica**	Y	N	Y	N	Y
8 Grayson	Y	Y	Y	Y	Y
9 **Bilirakis**	Y	N	Y	N	?
10 **Young**	Y	N	Y	N	Y
11 Castor	Y	P	Y	Y	Y
12 **Putnam**	Y	N	Y	N	Y
13 **Buchanan**	Y	N	Y	N	Y
14 **Mack**	N	N	Y	N	Y
15 **Posey**	Y	N	Y	N	Y
16 **Rooney**	N	N	Y	N	Y
17 **Meek**	Y	Y	?	?	?
18 **Ros-Lehtinen**	Y	N	Y	N	Y
19 Deutch*					Y
20 Wasserman Schultz	?	?	?	?	?
21 **Diaz-Balart, L.**	Y	P	Y	N	Y
22 Klein	Y	Y	Y	Y	Y
23 Hastings	Y	Y	Y	Y	Y
24 Kosmas	Y	Y	Y	?	?
25 **Diaz-Balart, M.**	Y	N	Y	N	Y
GEORGIA					
1 **Kingston**	Y	N	Y	N	Y
2 Bishop	Y	Y	Y	Y	Y
3 **Westmoreland**	Y	N	Y	N	Y
4 Johnson	Y	Y	?	Y	Y
5 Lewis	Y	Y	Y	Y	Y
6 **Price**	?	?	?	N	Y
7 **Linder**	Y	N	Y	N	Y
8 Marshall	Y	Y	Y	Y	Y
9 Vacant					
10 **Broun**	Y	N	Y	N	Y
11 **Gingrey**	Y	N	Y	N	Y
12 Barrow	Y	Y	Y	Y	Y
13 Scott	?	?	?	Y	Y
HAWAII					
1 Vacant					
2 Hirono	Y	Y	Y	Y	Y
IDAHO					
1 Minnick	Y	Y	Y	N	Y
2 **Simpson**	Y	P	Y	N	Y
ILLINOIS					
1 Rush	Y	Y	Y	Y	Y
2 Jackson	Y	Y	Y	Y	Y
3 Lipinski	Y	Y	Y	Y	Y
4 Gutierrez	Y	Y	Y	Y	Y
5 Quigley	Y	N	Y	Y	Y
6 **Roskam**	Y	N	Y	N	Y
7 Davis	Y	Y	Y	Y	Y
8 Bean	Y	Y	Y	Y	Y
9 Schakowsky	Y	Y	Y	?	Y
10 **Kirk**	Y	N	Y	N	Y
11 Halvorson	Y	Y	Y	Y	Y
12 Costello	Y	Y	Y	Y	Y
13 **Biggert**	Y	N	Y	N	Y
14 Foster	Y	Y	Y	Y	Y
15 **Johnson**	Y	N	Y	N	Y

KEY   **Republicans**   Democrats

Y Voted for (yea)	**X** Paired against	**C** Voted "present" to avoid possible conflict of interest
# Paired for	**–** Announced against	
+ Announced for	**P** Voted "present"	**?** Did not vote or otherwise make a position known
N Voted against (nay)		

	201	202	203	204	205
16 Manzullo	Y	N	Y	N	Y
17 Hare	Y	Y	Y	Y	Y
18 Schock	Y	N	Y	N	Y
19 Shimkus	Y	N	Y	N	Y
INDIANA					
1 Visclosky	Y	Y	Y	Y	Y
2 Donnelly	Y	Y	Y	Y	Y
3 Souder	Y	N	Y	N	Y
4 Buyer	Y	N	Y	N	Y
5 Burton	Y	N	Y	N	Y
6 Pence	Y	N	Y	N	Y
7 Carson	Y	Y	Y	Y	Y
8 Ellsworth	Y	Y	Y	Y	Y
9 Hill	Y	Y	Y	Y	Y
IOWA					
1 Braley	Y	Y	Y	Y	Y
2 Loebsack	Y	Y	Y	Y	Y
3 Boswell	Y	Y	Y	Y	Y
4 Latham	Y	P	Y	N	Y
5 King	Y	N	Y	N	Y
KANSAS					
1 Moran	Y	N	Y	N	Y
2 Jenkins	Y	N	Y	N	Y
3 Moore	Y	Y	Y	Y	Y
4 Tiahrt	Y	N	Y	?	?
KENTUCKY					
1 Whitfield	Y	N	Y	N	Y
2 Guthrie	Y	N	Y	N	Y
3 Yarmuth	Y	Y	Y	Y	Y
4 Davis	Y	N	Y	N	Y
5 Rogers	Y	N	Y	N	Y
6 Chandler	Y	P	Y	Y	Y
LOUISIANA					
1 Scalise	Y	N	Y	N	Y
2 Cao	Y	N	Y	N	Y
3 Melancon	Y	Y	Y	Y	Y
4 Fleming	Y	N	Y	N	Y
5 Alexander	Y	N	Y	N	Y
6 Cassidy	Y	N	Y	N	Y
7 Boustany	Y	N	Y	N	Y
MAINE					
1 Pingree	Y	Y	Y	Y	Y
2 Michaud	Y	Y	Y	Y	Y
MARYLAND					
1 Kratovil	Y	Y	Y	Y	Y
2 Ruppersberger	?	?	?	?	?
3 Sarbanes	Y	Y	Y	Y	Y
4 Edwards	Y	Y	Y	Y	Y
5 Hoyer	Y	Y	Y	Y	Y
6 Bartlett	Y	N	Y	N	Y
7 Cummings	Y	Y	Y	Y	Y
8 Van Hollen	Y	Y	Y	Y	Y
MASSACHUSETTS					
1 Olver	Y	Y	Y	Y	?
2 Neal	Y	Y	Y	Y	Y
3 McGovern	Y	Y	Y	Y	Y
4 Frank	Y	Y	Y	Y	Y
5 Tsongas	Y	Y	Y	?	Y
6 Tierney	Y	Y	Y	Y	Y
7 Markey	Y	Y	Y	Y	Y
8 Capuano	Y	Y	Y	Y	Y
9 Lynch	Y	?	?	Y	Y
10 Delahunt	Y	Y	Y	Y	Y
MICHIGAN					
1 Stupak	Y	Y	Y	Y	Y
2 Hoekstra	?	?	?	?	?
3 Ehlers	Y	N	Y	N	+
4 Camp	Y	N	Y	N	Y
5 Kildee	Y	Y	Y	Y	Y
6 Upton	Y	N	Y	N	Y
7 Schauer	Y	Y	Y	Y	Y
8 Rogers	Y	N	Y	N	Y
9 Peters	Y	Y	Y	Y	Y
10 Miller	Y	N	Y	N	Y
11 McCotter	Y	N	Y	?	?
12 Levin	Y	Y	Y	Y	Y
13 Kilpatrick	Y	Y	Y	Y	Y
14 Conyers	Y	Y	Y	Y	Y
15 Dingell	Y	Y	Y	Y	Y
MINNESOTA					
1 Walz	Y	N	Y	Y	Y
2 Kline	Y	N	Y	N	Y
3 Paulsen	Y	N	Y	N	Y
4 McCollum	Y	Y	Y	Y	Y

	201	202	203	204	205
5 Ellison	Y	Y	Y	Y	Y
6 Bachmann	Y	N	Y	N	Y
7 Peterson	Y	Y	Y	Y	Y
8 Oberstar	Y	Y	Y	Y	Y
MISSISSIPPI					
1 Childers	Y	Y	Y	Y	Y
2 Thompson	Y	Y	Y	Y	Y
3 Harper	Y	P	Y	N	Y
4 Taylor	Y	Y	Y	Y	Y
MISSOURI					
1 Clay	Y	Y	Y	?	Y
2 Akin	N	N	Y	N	Y
3 Carnahan	Y	Y	Y	Y	Y
4 Skelton	Y	Y	Y	Y	Y
5 Cleaver	Y	Y	Y	Y	Y
6 Graves	Y	N	Y	N	Y
7 Blunt	Y	N	Y	N	Y
8 Emerson	Y	N	Y	N	Y
9 Luetkemeyer	Y	N	Y	N	Y
MONTANA					
AL Rehberg	Y	N	Y	N	Y
NEBRASKA					
1 Fortenberry	Y	N	Y	N	Y
2 Terry	?	?	?	N	Y
3 Smith	Y	N	Y	N	Y
NEVADA					
1 Berkley	Y	Y	Y	Y	Y
2 Heller	Y	N	Y	N	Y
3 Titus	Y	Y	Y	Y	Y
NEW HAMPSHIRE					
1 Shea-Porter	Y	Y	Y	Y	Y
2 Hodes	Y	Y	Y	Y	Y
NEW JERSEY					
1 Andrews	Y	Y	Y	Y	Y
2 LoBiondo	Y	N	Y	N	Y
3 Adler	Y	Y	Y	Y	Y
4 Smith	Y	N	Y	N	Y
5 Garrett	Y	N	Y	N	Y
6 Pallone	Y	Y	Y	Y	Y
7 Lance	Y	N	Y	N	Y
8 Pascrell	Y	Y	Y	Y	Y
9 Rothman	Y	Y	Y	Y	?
10 Payne	Y	Y	Y	Y	Y
11 Frelinghuysen	Y	N	Y	N	Y
12 Holt	Y	Y	Y	Y	Y
13 Sires	Y	Y	Y	Y	Y
NEW MEXICO					
1 Heinrich	Y	Y	Y	Y	Y
2 Teague	Y	Y	Y	Y	Y
3 Luján	Y	Y	Y	Y	Y
NEW YORK					
1 Bishop	Y	Y	Y	Y	Y
2 Israel	Y	Y	Y	Y	Y
3 King	Y	N	Y	N	Y
4 McCarthy	Y	Y	Y	Y	Y
5 Ackerman	Y	Y	Y	Y	?
6 Meeks	Y	Y	Y	Y	Y
7 Crowley	Y	Y	Y	Y	Y
8 Nadler	Y	Y	Y	Y	Y
9 Weiner	Y	Y	Y	Y	Y
10 Towns	Y	Y	Y	?	?
11 Clarke	Y	Y	Y	Y	Y
12 Velázquez	Y	Y	Y	Y	Y
13 McMahon	Y	Y	Y	Y	Y
14 Maloney	Y	Y	Y	Y	Y
15 Rangel	Y	Y	Y	Y	Y
16 Serrano	Y	Y	Y	Y	Y
17 Engel	Y	Y	Y	Y	?
18 Lowey	Y	Y	Y	Y	Y
19 Hall	Y	Y	Y	Y	Y
20 Murphy	Y	Y	Y	Y	Y
21 Tonko	Y	Y	Y	Y	Y
22 Hinchey	Y	Y	Y	Y	Y
23 Owens	Y	Y	Y	Y	Y
24 Arcuri	Y	Y	Y	Y	Y
25 Maffei	Y	Y	Y	Y	Y
26 Lee	Y	N	Y	N	Y
27 Higgins	Y	Y	Y	Y	Y
28 Slaughter	Y	Y	Y	?	?
29 Vacant					
NORTH CAROLINA					
1 Butterfield	Y	P	Y	Y	Y
2 Etheridge	Y	Y	Y	Y	Y
3 Jones	Y	N	Y	N	Y
4 Price	Y	Y	Y	Y	Y

	201	202	203	204	205
5 Foxx	N	N	Y	N	Y
6 Coble	Y	N	Y	N	Y
7 McIntyre	Y	Y	Y	Y	Y
8 Kissell	Y	Y	Y	Y	Y
9 Myrick	Y	P	+	N	Y
10 McHenry	Y	N	Y	N	Y
11 Shuler	Y	Y	Y	Y	Y
12 Watt	Y	Y	Y	Y	Y
13 Miller	Y	Y	Y	Y	Y
NORTH DAKOTA					
AL Pomeroy	Y	Y	Y	Y	Y
OHIO					
1 Driehaus	Y	Y	Y	Y	Y
2 Schmidt	Y	N	Y	N	Y
3 Turner	Y	N	Y	N	Y
4 Jordan	Y	N	Y	N	Y
5 Latta	Y	N	Y	N	Y
6 Wilson	Y	Y	Y	Y	Y
7 Austria	Y	N	Y	N	Y
8 Boehner	Y	N	?	N	Y
9 Kaptur	Y	Y	Y	Y	Y
10 Kucinich	Y	Y	Y	Y	Y
11 Fudge	Y	Y	Y	Y	Y
12 Tiberi	Y	N	Y	N	Y
13 Sutton	Y	Y	Y	Y	Y
14 LaTourette	Y	N	Y	N	Y
15 Kilroy	Y	Y	Y	Y	Y
16 Boccieri	Y	Y	Y	Y	Y
17 Ryan	Y	Y	Y	Y	Y
18 Space	Y	Y	Y	Y	Y
OKLAHOMA					
1 Sullivan	Y	N	Y	N	Y
2 Boren	Y	Y	Y	Y	Y
3 Lucas	Y	?	Y	N	Y
4 Cole	Y	N	Y	N	Y
5 Fallin	Y	N	Y	N	Y
OREGON					
1 Wu	Y	Y	Y	Y	Y
2 Walden	Y	P	Y	N	Y
3 Blumenauer	Y	Y	Y	Y	Y
4 DeFazio	Y	Y	Y	Y	Y
5 Schrader	Y	Y	?	Y	Y
PENNSYLVANIA					
1 Brady	Y	Y	Y	Y	Y
2 Fattah	Y	Y	Y	Y	Y
3 Dahlkemper	Y	Y	Y	Y	Y
4 Altmire	Y	Y	Y	Y	Y
5 Thompson	Y	N	Y	N	Y
6 Gerlach	Y	N	Y	N	Y
7 Sestak	Y	Y	Y	Y	Y
8 Murphy, P.	Y	Y	Y	Y	Y
9 Shuster	Y	N	Y	N	Y
10 Carney	Y	Y	Y	Y	Y
11 Kanjorski	Y	Y	Y	Y	Y
12 Vacant					
13 Schwartz	Y	Y	Y	Y	Y
14 Doyle	Y	Y	Y	Y	Y
15 Dent	Y	P	Y	N	Y
16 Pitts	Y	N	Y	N	Y
17 Holden	Y	Y	Y	Y	Y
18 Murphy, T.	Y	N	Y	N	Y
19 Platts	Y	N	Y	N	Y
RHODE ISLAND					
1 Kennedy	Y	Y	Y	Y	Y
2 Langevin	Y	Y	Y	Y	Y
SOUTH CAROLINA					
1 Brown	Y	N	Y	N	Y
2 Wilson	Y	N	Y	N	Y
3 Barrett	?	?	?	?	?
4 Inglis	Y	N	Y	N	Y
5 Spratt	Y	Y	Y	Y	Y
6 Clyburn	Y	Y	Y	Y	Y
SOUTH DAKOTA					
AL Herseth Sandlin	Y	Y	Y	Y	Y
TENNESSEE					
1 Roe	Y	N	Y	N	Y
2 Duncan	Y	N	Y	N	Y
3 Wamp	?	?	?	?	?
4 Davis	Y	Y	Y	Y	Y
5 Cooper	Y	Y	Y	Y	Y
6 Gordon	Y	?	Y	Y	Y
7 Blackburn	Y	N	Y	N	Y
8 Tanner	Y	Y	Y	Y	Y
9 Cohen	Y	Y	Y	Y	Y

	201	202	203	204	205
TEXAS					
1 Gohmert	Y	N	Y	N	Y
2 Poe	N	P	Y	N	Y
3 Johnson, S.	N	N	Y	N	Y
4 Hall	Y	N	Y	N	Y
5 Hensarling	N	N	Y	N	Y
6 Barton	Y	N	Y	N	Y
7 Culberson	N	N	Y	N	Y
8 Brady	N	N	Y	N	Y
9 Green, A.	Y	Y	Y	Y	Y
10 McCaul	Y	P	Y	N	Y
11 Conaway	N	P	Y	N	Y
12 Granger	N	N	Y	N	Y
13 Thornberry	Y	N	Y	N	Y
14 Paul	N	N	Y	N	Y
15 Hinojosa	Y	Y	Y	Y	Y
16 Reyes	Y	Y	Y	Y	Y
17 Edwards	Y	Y	Y	Y	Y
18 Jackson Lee	Y	Y	Y	?	?
19 Neugebauer	N	N	Y	N	Y
20 Gonzalez	?	?	?	?	?
21 Smith	Y	N	Y	N	Y
22 Olson	Y	N	Y	N	Y
23 Rodriguez	Y	Y	Y	Y	Y
24 Marchant	N	N	Y	N	Y
25 Doggett	Y	Y	Y	Y	Y
26 Burgess	Y	Y	Y	Y	Y
27 Ortiz	Y	Y	Y	Y	Y
28 Cuellar	Y	Y	Y	Y	Y
29 Green, G.	Y	Y	Y	Y	Y
30 Johnson, E.	Y	Y	Y	Y	Y
31 Carter	Y	N	Y	N	Y
32 Sessions	Y	N	Y	N	Y
UTAH					
1 Bishop	Y	N	Y	N	Y
2 Matheson	Y	Y	Y	Y	Y
3 Chaffetz	Y	N	Y	N	Y
VERMONT					
AL Welch	Y	P	Y	Y	Y
VIRGINIA					
1 Wittman	Y	N	Y	N	Y
2 Nye	Y	Y	Y	Y	Y
3 Scott	Y	Y	Y	Y	Y
4 Forbes	Y	N	Y	N	Y
5 Perriello	Y	Y	Y	Y	Y
6 Goodlatte	Y	N	Y	N	Y
7 Cantor	Y	N	Y	N	Y
8 Moran	Y	Y	Y	Y	Y
9 Boucher	Y	Y	Y	Y	Y
10 Wolf	Y	N	Y	N	Y
11 Connolly	Y	Y	Y	Y	Y
WASHINGTON					
1 Inslee	Y	Y	Y	Y	Y
2 Larsen	Y	Y	Y	Y	Y
3 Baird	Y	Y	Y	Y	Y
4 Hastings	Y	P	Y	N	Y
5 McMorris Rodgers	Y	N	Y	N	Y
6 Dicks	Y	Y	Y	Y	Y
7 McDermott	Y	Y	Y	Y	Y
8 Reichert	Y	N	Y	N	Y
9 Smith	Y	Y	Y	Y	Y
WEST VIRGINIA					
1 Mollohan	Y	Y	Y	Y	Y
2 Capito	Y	N	Y	N	Y
3 Rahall	Y	Y	Y	Y	Y
WISCONSIN					
1 Ryan	Y	N	Y	N	Y
2 Baldwin	Y	Y	Y	Y	Y
3 Kind	Y	Y	Y	Y	Y
4 Moore	Y	Y	Y	Y	Y
5 Sensenbrenner	N	N	Y	N	Y
6 Petri	Y	N	Y	N	Y
7 Obey	?	Y	Y	Y	Y
8 Kagen	Y	Y	Y	Y	Y
WYOMING					
AL Lummis	Y	N	Y	N	Y
DELEGATES					
Faleomavaega (A.S.)					
Norton (D.C.)					
Bordallo (Guam)					
Sablan (N. Marianas)					
Pierluisi (P.R.)					
Christensen (V.I.)					

IN THE HOUSE | By Vote Number

206. **H Res 1255. PMA Group Investigation/Motion to Refer.** Oberstar, D-Minn., motion to refer the Flake, R-Ariz., privileged resolution to the Committee on Standards of Official Conduct. The resolution would require the committee to issue a report detailing the number of interviews conducted, subpoenas issued and documents reviewed in the panel's investigation of members' dealings with the PMA Group. Motion agreed to 385-0: D 234-0; R 151-0. April 15, 2010.

207. **HR 4715. Estuary Protection Program/Sea Level Changes.** Shea-Porter, D-N.H., amendment that would require EPA estuary conservation and management plans to monitor the effect of sea level changes on estuaries. Adopted in Committee of the Whole 294-109: D 238-2; R 56-107. April 15, 2010.

208. **HR 4715. Estuary Protection Program/Recommit.** Jordan, R-Ohio, motion to recommit the bill to the Transportation and Infrastructure Committee with instructions that it be immediately reported back with an amendment that would cap authorization for the EPA's National Estuary Program at $35 million per fiscal year if the nation had a deficit in the previous fiscal year. Motion rejected 192-214: D 28-214; R 164-0. April 15, 2010.

209. **HR 4715. Estuary Protection Program/Passage.** Passage of the bill that would authorize $50 million annually through fiscal 2016 for the EPA's National Estuary Program. It would require the EPA to evaluate estuary management plans every four years. As amended, it would require EPA plans to evaluate the impact of climate change on estuaries and require the agency to evaluate the effectiveness of the estuary program and identify best practices. Passed 278-128: D 240-2; R 38-126. April 15, 2010.

210. **H Res 1242. Tribute to Duke University Men's Basketball Team/Adoption.** Fudge, D-Ohio, motion to suspend the rules and adopt the resolution that would congratulate the Duke University Blue Devils for winning the 2010 NCAA Division I men's basketball tournament. Motion agreed to 390-0: D 229-0; R 161-0. A two-thirds majority of those present and voting (260 in this case) is required for adoption under suspension of the rules. April 15, 2010.

211. **HR 4851. Short-Term Extensions/Motion to Concur.** Levin, D-Mich., motion to concur in the Senate amendment to the bill that would extend for two months federal unemployment benefits, flood insurance programs, increased payment rates to Medicare providers and COBRA health care premium assistance. It would provide for payment to certain previously furloughed transportation workers. It also would extend for one month certain satellite TV laws and small-business lending programs. Motion agreed to, thus clearing the bill for the president, 289-112: D 240-1; R 49-111. A "yea" was a vote in support of the president's position. April 15, 2010.

	206	207	208	209	210	211
ALABAMA						
1 Bonner	P	N	Y	N	Y	Y
2 Bright	Y	Y	Y	N	Y	Y
3 Rogers	Y	Y	Y	Y	Y	Y
4 Aderholt	Y	N	Y	N	Y	Y
5 Griffith	Y	N	Y	N	Y	Y
6 Bachus	Y	N	Y	N	Y	N
7 Davis	Y	Y	N	Y	Y	Y
ALASKA						
AL Young	?	?	?	?	?	?
ARIZONA						
1 Kirkpatrick	Y	Y	Y	Y	Y	Y
2 Franks	Y	N	Y	N	Y	N
3 Shadegg	Y	N	Y	N	Y	N
4 Pastor	Y	Y	N	Y	Y	Y
5 Mitchell	Y	?	Y	Y	Y	Y
6 Flake	Y	N	Y	N	Y	N
7 Grijalva	Y	Y	N	Y	?	Y
8 Giffords	Y	Y	Y	Y	Y	Y
ARKANSAS						
1 Berry	?	?	?	?	?	?
2 Snyder	Y	Y	N	Y	Y	Y
3 Boozman	Y	Y	Y	N	Y	N
4 Ross	Y	Y	Y	Y	Y	Y
CALIFORNIA						
1 Thompson	Y	Y	N	Y	Y	Y
2 Herger	Y	N	Y	N	Y	N
3 Lungren	Y	N	Y	N	Y	N
4 McClintock	Y	N	Y	N	Y	N
5 Matsui	Y	Y	N	Y	Y	Y
6 Woolsey	Y	Y	N	Y	Y	Y
7 Miller, George	Y	Y	N	Y	Y	Y
8 Pelosi						
9 Lee	Y	Y	N	Y	Y	Y
10 Garamendi	Y	Y	N	Y	Y	Y
11 McNerney	Y	Y	Y	Y	Y	Y
12 Speier	Y	Y	N	Y	Y	?
13 Stark	Y	Y	N	Y	Y	Y
14 Eshoo	Y	Y	N	Y	Y	Y
15 Honda	Y	Y	N	Y	Y	Y
16 Lofgren	P	Y	N	Y	Y	Y
17 Farr	Y	Y	N	Y	Y	Y
18 Cardoza	Y	Y	N	Y	P	Y
19 Radanovich	?	?	?	?	?	?
20 Costa	Y	Y	N	Y	Y	Y
21 Nunes	Y	N	Y	N	Y	N
22 McCarthy	Y	N	Y	N	Y	N
23 Capps	Y	Y	N	Y	Y	Y
24 Gallegly	?	?	?	?	?	?
25 McKeon	Y	N	Y	N	Y	N
26 Dreier	Y	Y	Y	Y	Y	Y
27 Sherman	Y	Y	N	Y	Y	Y
28 Berman	Y	Y	N	Y	Y	Y
29 Schiff	Y	Y	N	Y	Y	Y
30 Waxman	Y	Y	N	Y	Y	Y
31 Becerra	Y	Y	N	Y	Y	Y
32 Chu	Y	Y	N	Y	Y	Y
33 Watson	Y	Y	N	Y	Y	Y
34 Roybal-Allard	Y	Y	N	Y	Y	Y
35 Waters	Y	Y	N	Y	Y	Y
36 Harman	Y	Y	N	Y	Y	Y
37 Richardson	Y	Y	N	Y	Y	Y
38 Napolitano	Y	Y	N	Y	Y	Y
39 Sánchez, Linda	?	?	?	?	?	?
40 Royce	Y	N	Y	N	Y	N
41 Lewis	Y	N	Y	N	Y	N
42 Miller, Gary	Y	N	Y	N	Y	N
43 Baca	Y	Y	N	Y	Y	Y
44 Calvert	Y	N	Y	N	Y	N
45 Bono Mack	Y	N	Y	N	Y	N
46 Rohrabacher	Y	N	Y	N	Y	N
47 Sanchez, Loretta	Y	Y	N	Y	Y	Y
48 Campbell	Y	N	Y	N	Y	N
49 Issa	Y	N	Y	N	Y	N
50 Bilbray	?	?	?	?	?	?
51 Filner	Y	Y	N	Y	Y	Y
52 Hunter	Y	N	Y	N	Y	N
53 Davis	Y	Y	N	Y	Y	Y

	206	207	208	209	210	211
COLORADO						
1 DeGette	Y	Y	N	Y	Y	Y
2 Polis	Y	Y	N	Y	Y	Y
3 Salazar	Y	Y	N	Y	Y	Y
4 Markey	Y	Y	N	Y	Y	Y
5 Lamborn	Y	N	Y	N	Y	N
6 Coffman	Y	N	Y	N	Y	N
7 Perlmutter	Y	Y	N	Y	Y	Y
CONNECTICUT						
1 Larson	Y	Y	N	Y	Y	Y
2 Courtney	Y	Y	N	Y	P	Y
3 DeLauro	Y	Y	N	Y	Y	Y
4 Himes	Y	Y	Y	Y	Y	Y
5 Murphy	Y	Y	N	Y	Y	Y
DELAWARE						
AL Castle	Y	Y	Y	Y	Y	Y
FLORIDA						
1 Miller	?	?	?	?	?	?
2 Boyd	?	?	?	+	?	?
3 Brown	Y	Y	N	Y	Y	Y
4 Crenshaw	Y	Y	Y	Y	Y	Y
5 Brown-Waite	Y	N	Y	N	?	Y
6 Stearns	Y	N	Y	N	Y	Y
7 Mica	Y	Y	Y	Y	Y	N
8 Grayson	Y	Y	N	Y	Y	Y
9 Bilirakis	Y	Y	Y	Y	Y	Y
10 Young	Y	Y	Y	Y	Y	Y
11 Castor	P	Y	N	Y	Y	Y
12 Putnam	Y	Y	Y	Y	Y	Y
13 Buchanan	Y	Y	Y	Y	Y	Y
14 Mack	Y	N	Y	N	Y	N
15 Posey	Y	N	Y	Y	Y	N
16 Rooney	Y	N	Y	Y	Y	N
17 Meek	?	?	?	?	?	?
18 Ros-Lehtinen	Y	Y	Y	Y	Y	Y
19 Deutch	Y	Y	N	Y	Y	Y
20 Wasserman Schultz	?	?	?	?	?	?
21 Diaz-Balart, L.	P	Y	Y	Y	Y	Y
22 Klein	Y	Y	N	Y	Y	Y
23 Hastings	Y	Y	N	Y	Y	Y
24 Kosmas	?	?	?	?	?	?
25 Diaz-Balart, M.	Y	Y	Y	Y	Y	Y
GEORGIA						
1 Kingston	Y	N	Y	N	Y	N
2 Bishop	Y	Y	N	Y	Y	Y
3 Westmoreland	Y	N	Y	N	Y	N
4 Johnson	Y	Y	N	Y	Y	Y
5 Lewis	Y	Y	N	Y	Y	Y
6 Price	Y	N	Y	N	Y	N
7 Linder	Y	N	Y	N	Y	N
8 Marshall	?	?	Y	Y	Y	Y
9 Vacant						
10 Broun	Y	N	Y	N	Y	N
11 Gingrey	Y	N	Y	N	Y	N
12 Barrow	Y	Y	N	Y	Y	Y
13 Scott	Y	Y	N	Y	Y	Y
HAWAII						
1 Vacant						
2 Hirono	Y	Y	N	Y	Y	Y
IDAHO						
1 Minnick	Y	Y	Y	Y	Y	Y
2 Simpson	P	N	Y	N	Y	N
ILLINOIS						
1 Rush	Y	?	N	Y	Y	Y
2 Jackson	Y	Y	N	Y	Y	Y
3 Lipinski	Y	Y	N	Y	Y	Y
4 Gutierrez	Y	Y	N	Y	Y	Y
5 Quigley	Y	Y	N	Y	Y	Y
6 Roskam	Y	Y	Y	N	Y	N
7 Davis	Y	Y	N	Y	Y	Y
8 Bean	?	Y	Y	Y	Y	Y
9 Schakowsky	Y	Y	N	Y	Y	Y
10 Kirk	Y	Y	Y	Y	Y	Y
11 Halvorson	Y	Y	N	Y	Y	Y
12 Costello	Y	Y	N	Y	Y	Y
13 Biggert	Y	Y	Y	Y	Y	Y
14 Foster	Y	Y	N	Y	Y	Y
15 Johnson	Y	Y	Y	Y	Y	Y

KEY   **Republicans**   Democrats

Y Voted for (yea)	X Paired against	C Voted "present" to avoid possible conflict of interest
# Paired for	− Announced against	
+ Announced for	P Voted "present"	? Did not vote or otherwise make a position known
N Voted against (nay)		

	206	207	208	209	210	211
16 **Manzullo**	Y	Y	Y	N	Y	Y
17 Hare	Y	Y	N	Y	Y	Y
18 **Schock**	Y	N	Y	N	Y	Y
19 **Shimkus**	Y	N	Y	N	Y	Y
INDIANA						
1 Visclosky	Y	Y	N	Y	Y	Y
2 Donnelly	Y	Y	Y	Y	Y	Y
3 **Souder**	Y	N	Y	N	Y	N
4 **Buyer**	P	N	Y	N	Y	N
5 **Burton**	Y	N	Y	N	Y	N
6 **Pence**	?	?	?	?	?	?
7 Carson	Y	Y	N	Y	Y	Y
8 Ellsworth	Y	Y	Y	Y	Y	Y
9 Hill	Y	Y	N	Y	Y	Y
IOWA						
1 Braley	Y	Y	N	Y	P	Y
2 Loebsack	Y	Y	N	Y	Y	Y
3 Boswell	Y	Y	N	Y	Y	Y
4 **Latham**	P	N	Y	N	Y	N
5 **King**	Y	N	Y	N	Y	N
KANSAS						
1 **Moran**	Y	Y	Y	N	Y	N
2 **Jenkins**	Y	Y	Y	N	Y	N
3 Moore	Y	Y	N	Y	Y	Y
4 **Tiahrt**	?	?	?	?	?	?
KENTUCKY						
1 **Whitfield**	Y	N	Y	N	Y	Y
2 **Guthrie**	Y	N	Y	N	Y	N
3 Yarmuth	Y	Y	N	Y	Y	Y
4 **Davis**	Y	Y	Y	N	Y	Y
5 **Rogers**	Y	N	Y	N	Y	N
6 Chandler	P	Y	N	Y	Y	Y
LOUISIANA						
1 **Scalise**	Y	Y	Y	N	Y	N
2 **Cao**	Y	Y	Y	Y	Y	Y
3 Melancon	Y	Y	N	Y	Y	Y
4 **Fleming**	Y	N	Y	N	Y	N
5 **Alexander**	Y	N	Y	N	Y	N
6 **Cassidy**	Y	N	Y	N	Y	Y
7 **Boustany**	Y	Y	Y	N	Y	N
MAINE						
1 Pingree	Y	Y	N	Y	Y	Y
2 Michaud	Y	Y	N	Y	Y	Y
MARYLAND						
1 Kratovil	Y	Y	N	Y	P	Y
2 Ruppersberger	?	?	?	?	?	?
3 Sarbanes	Y	Y	N	Y	Y	Y
4 Edwards	Y	Y	N	Y	P	?
5 Hoyer	Y	Y	N	Y	Y	Y
6 **Bartlett**	Y	N	Y	Y	Y	N
7 Cummings	Y	Y	N	Y	Y	Y
8 Van Hollen	Y	Y	N	Y	Y	Y
MASSACHUSETTS						
1 Olver	Y	Y	N	Y	Y	Y
2 Neal	Y	Y	N	Y	Y	Y
3 McGovern	Y	Y	N	Y	Y	Y
4 Frank	Y	Y	N	Y	Y	Y
5 Tsongas	Y	Y	N	Y	Y	Y
6 Tierney	Y	Y	N	Y	Y	Y
7 Markey	Y	Y	N	Y	Y	Y
8 Capuano	Y	Y	N	Y	Y	Y
9 Lynch	Y	Y	N	Y	Y	Y
10 Delahunt	Y	Y	N	Y	Y	Y
MICHIGAN						
1 Stupak	Y	Y	N	Y	Y	Y
2 **Hoekstra**	?	?	?	?	?	?
3 **Ehlers**	Y	Y	Y	Y	Y	Y
4 **Camp**	Y	Y	Y	N	Y	Y
5 Kildee	Y	Y	N	Y	Y	Y
6 **Upton**	Y	Y	Y	N	Y	Y
7 Schauer	Y	Y	N	Y	Y	Y
8 **Rogers**	Y	Y	Y	Y	?	Y
9 Peters	Y	Y	Y	Y	Y	Y
10 **Miller**	Y	Y	Y	N	Y	Y
11 **McCotter**	?	?	?	?	?	?
12 Levin	Y	Y	N	Y	Y	Y
13 Kilpatrick	Y	Y	N	Y	Y	Y
14 Conyers	Y	Y	N	Y	Y	Y
15 Dingell	Y	Y	N	Y	Y	Y
MINNESOTA						
1 Walz	Y	Y	N	Y	Y	Y
2 **Kline**	?	N	Y	N	Y	?
3 **Paulsen**	Y	Y	Y	Y	Y	Y
4 McCollum	Y	Y	N	Y	Y	Y

	206	207	208	209	210	211
5 Ellison	Y	Y	N	Y	Y	Y
6 **Bachmann**	Y	N	Y	N	Y	N
7 Peterson	Y	Y	N	Y	Y	Y
8 Oberstar	Y	Y	N	Y	P	Y
MISSISSIPPI						
1 Childers	Y	Y	Y	Y	Y	Y
2 Thompson	Y	Y	N	Y	Y	Y
3 **Harper**	P	N	Y	N	Y	N
4 Taylor	Y	?	Y	Y	Y	Y
MISSOURI						
1 Clay	Y	Y	N	Y	Y	Y
2 **Akin**	Y	N	Y	N	Y	N
3 Carnahan	Y	Y	N	Y	Y	Y
4 Skelton	Y	Y	Y	Y	Y	Y
5 Cleaver	Y	Y	N	Y	Y	Y
6 **Graves**	Y	N	Y	N	Y	N
7 **Blunt**	Y	N	Y	N	?	N
8 **Emerson**	Y	N	Y	N	Y	N
9 **Luetkemeyer**	Y	N	Y	N	Y	?
MONTANA						
AL **Rehberg**	Y	N	Y	N	Y	N
NEBRASKA						
1 **Fortenberry**	Y	Y	Y	Y	Y	N
2 **Terry**	Y	N	Y	N	Y	N
3 **Smith**	Y	N	Y	N	Y	N
NEVADA						
1 Berkley	Y	Y	N	Y	Y	Y
2 **Heller**	Y	Y	Y	N	Y	Y
3 Titus	Y	Y	N	Y	Y	Y
NEW HAMPSHIRE						
1 Shea-Porter	Y	Y	N	Y	Y	Y
2 Hodes	Y	Y	Y	Y	Y	Y
NEW JERSEY						
1 Andrews	Y	Y	N	Y	Y	Y
2 **LoBiondo**	Y	Y	Y	Y	Y	Y
3 Adler	Y	Y	N	Y	Y	Y
4 **Smith**	Y	Y	Y	Y	Y	Y
5 **Garrett**	Y	N	Y	N	Y	N
6 Pallone	Y	Y	N	Y	Y	Y
7 **Lance**	Y	Y	Y	Y	Y	N
8 Pascrell	Y	Y	N	Y	Y	Y
9 Rothman	Y	Y	N	Y	Y	Y
10 Payne	Y	Y	N	Y	Y	Y
11 **Frelinghuysen**	Y	Y	Y	Y	Y	N
12 Holt	Y	Y	N	Y	Y	Y
13 Sires	Y	Y	N	Y	Y	Y
NEW MEXICO						
1 Heinrich	Y	Y	N	Y	Y	Y
2 Teague	Y	Y	N	Y	Y	Y
3 Luján	Y	Y	N	Y	Y	Y
NEW YORK						
1 Bishop	Y	Y	N	Y	Y	Y
2 Israel	Y	Y	N	Y	Y	Y
3 **King**	Y	N	Y	N	Y	N
4 McCarthy	Y	Y	N	Y	Y	Y
5 Ackerman	Y	Y	N	Y	Y	Y
6 Meeks	Y	Y	N	Y	Y	Y
7 Crowley	Y	Y	N	Y	Y	Y
8 Nadler	Y	?	N	Y	Y	Y
9 Weiner	Y	Y	N	Y	Y	Y
10 Towns	?	?	?	?	?	?
11 Clarke	Y	Y	N	Y	Y	Y
12 Velázquez	Y	Y	N	Y	Y	Y
13 McMahon	Y	Y	N	Y	Y	Y
14 Maloney	Y	Y	N	Y	Y	Y
15 Rangel	Y	Y	N	Y	Y	Y
16 Serrano	Y	Y	N	Y	Y	Y
17 Engel	Y	Y	N	Y	Y	Y
18 Lowey	Y	Y	N	Y	Y	Y
19 Hall	Y	Y	N	Y	Y	Y
20 Murphy	Y	Y	Y	Y	Y	Y
21 Tonko	Y	Y	N	Y	Y	Y
22 Hinchey	Y	Y	N	Y	Y	Y
23 Owens	Y	N	N	N	Y	Y
24 Arcuri	Y	Y	Y	Y	Y	Y
25 Maffei	Y	Y	Y	Y	P	Y
26 **Lee**	Y	Y	Y	N	Y	N
27 Higgins	Y	Y	N	Y	Y	Y
28 Slaughter	Y	Y	?	Y	Y	Y
29 Vacant						
NORTH CAROLINA						
1 Butterfield	P	Y	N	Y	Y	Y
2 Etheridge	Y	Y	N	Y	Y	Y
3 **Jones**	Y	Y	Y	Y	Y	Y
4 Price	Y	?	N	Y	Y	Y

	206	207	208	209	210	211
5 **Foxx**	Y	N	Y	N	Y	N
6 **Coble**	Y	N	Y	N	Y	N
7 McIntyre	Y	Y	Y	Y	Y	Y
8 Kissell	Y	Y	N	Y	Y	Y
9 **Myrick**	P	Y	Y	N	Y	N
10 **McHenry**	Y	N	Y	N	Y	Y
11 Shuler	Y	Y	Y	Y	Y	Y
12 Watt	Y	Y	N	Y	Y	Y
13 Miller	Y	Y	N	Y	Y	Y
NORTH DAKOTA						
AL Pomeroy	Y	Y	N	Y	Y	Y
OHIO						
1 Driehaus	Y	Y	N	Y	Y	Y
2 **Schmidt**	Y	N	Y	N	Y	N
3 **Turner**	Y	Y	Y	N	Y	Y
4 **Jordan**	Y	N	Y	N	Y	N
5 **Latta**	Y	N	Y	N	Y	N
6 Wilson	Y	Y	N	Y	Y	Y
7 **Austria**	Y	Y	Y	N	Y	N
8 **Boehner**	Y	N	Y	N	Y	?
9 Kaptur	Y	Y	N	Y	Y	Y
10 Kucinich	Y	Y	N	Y	Y	Y
11 Fudge	Y	Y	N	Y	Y	Y
12 **Tiberi**	Y	Y	Y	Y	Y	Y
13 Sutton	Y	Y	N	Y	Y	Y
14 **LaTourette**	Y	Y	Y	Y	Y	Y
15 Kilroy	Y	Y	N	Y	Y	Y
16 Boccieri	Y	Y	N	Y	Y	Y
17 Ryan	Y	Y	N	Y	Y	Y
18 Space	Y	Y	N	Y	Y	Y
OKLAHOMA						
1 **Sullivan**	Y	N	Y	N	Y	N
2 Boren	Y	Y	Y	Y	Y	Y
3 **Lucas**	Y	N	Y	N	Y	N
4 **Cole**	Y	N	Y	N	Y	N
5 **Fallin**	Y	N	Y	N	Y	N
OREGON						
1 Wu	Y	Y	N	Y	Y	Y
2 **Walden**	P	Y	Y	Y	Y	Y
3 Blumenauer	Y	Y	N	Y	Y	Y
4 DeFazio	Y	Y	N	Y	P	Y
5 Schrader	Y	Y	N	Y	Y	Y
PENNSYLVANIA						
1 Brady	Y	Y	N	Y	Y	Y
2 Fattah	Y	Y	N	Y	Y	Y
3 Dahlkemper	Y	Y	Y	Y	Y	Y
4 Altmire	Y	N	Y	Y	Y	Y
5 **Thompson**	Y	N	Y	Y	Y	N
6 **Gerlach**	Y	Y	Y	Y	Y	Y
7 Sestak	Y	Y	N	Y	Y	Y
8 Murphy, P.	Y	Y	N	?	Y	Y
9 **Shuster**	Y	?	Y	N	Y	N
10 Carney	Y	Y	Y	Y	P	Y
11 Kanjorski	Y	Y	N	Y	Y	Y
12 Vacant						
13 Schwartz	Y	Y	N	Y	Y	Y
14 Doyle	Y	Y	N	Y	Y	Y
15 **Dent**	P	Y	Y	Y	Y	Y
16 **Pitts**	Y	N	Y	N	Y	N
17 Holden	Y	Y	N	Y	Y	Y
18 **Murphy, T.**	Y	Y	Y	N	Y	Y
19 **Platts**	Y	Y	Y	Y	Y	Y
RHODE ISLAND						
1 Kennedy	Y	Y	N	Y	Y	Y
2 Langevin	Y	Y	N	Y	Y	Y
SOUTH CAROLINA						
1 **Brown**	Y	?	?	?	?	?
2 **Wilson**	Y	Y	Y	Y	Y	N
3 **Barrett**	?	?	?	?	?	?
4 **Inglis**	Y	Y	Y	N	Y	N
5 Spratt	Y	Y	N	Y	Y	Y
6 Clyburn	Y	Y	N	Y	Y	Y
SOUTH DAKOTA						
AL Herseth Sandlin	Y	Y	N	Y	Y	Y
TENNESSEE						
1 **Roe**	Y	N	Y	N	Y	Y
2 **Duncan**	Y	N	Y	N	Y	N
3 **Wamp**	?	?	?	?	?	?
4 Davis	Y	Y	N	Y	Y	Y
5 Cooper	Y	Y	N	Y	P	N
6 Gordon	Y	Y	N	Y	Y	Y
7 **Blackburn**	P	N	Y	N	Y	N
8 Tanner	Y	Y	N	Y	Y	Y
9 Cohen	Y	Y	N	Y	Y	Y

	206	207	208	209	210	211
TEXAS						
1 **Gohmert**	Y	N	Y	N	Y	N
2 **Poe**	Y	N	Y	N	Y	N
3 **Johnson, S.**	Y	N	Y	N	Y	N
4 **Hall**	Y	Y	Y	N	Y	N
5 **Hensarling**	Y	N	Y	N	Y	N
6 **Barton**	Y	N	Y	N	Y	N
7 **Culberson**	Y	N	Y	N	Y	N
8 **Brady**	Y	N	Y	N	Y	N
9 Green, A.	Y	Y	N	Y	Y	Y
10 **McCaul**	P	N	Y	N	Y	N
11 **Conaway**	P	N	Y	N	Y	N
12 **Granger**	Y	Y	Y	N	Y	N
13 **Thornberry**	Y	N	Y	N	Y	N
14 **Paul**	Y	N	Y	N	Y	N
15 Hinojosa	Y	Y	N	Y	Y	Y
16 Reyes	Y	Y	N	Y	Y	Y
17 Edwards	Y	Y	N	Y	Y	Y
18 Jackson Lee	?	?	?	?	?	?
19 **Neugebauer**	?	?	?	?	?	?
20 Gonzalez	?	?	?	?	?	?
21 **Smith**	Y	N	Y	N	Y	N
22 **Olson**	Y	N	Y	N	Y	N
23 Rodriguez	Y	Y	N	Y	Y	Y
24 **Marchant**	Y	N	Y	N	Y	N
25 Doggett	Y	Y	N	Y	Y	Y
26 **Burgess**	Y	N	Y	N	Y	Y
27 Ortiz	Y	Y	N	Y	Y	Y
28 Cuellar	Y	Y	Y	Y	Y	Y
29 Green, G.	Y	Y	N	Y	Y	Y
30 Johnson, E.	Y	Y	N	Y	Y	Y
31 **Carter**	Y	N	Y	N	Y	N
32 **Sessions**	Y	N	Y	N	Y	N
UTAH						
1 **Bishop**	Y	N	Y	N	Y	N
2 Matheson	Y	Y	N	Y	Y	Y
3 **Chaffetz**	Y	N	Y	N	Y	N
VERMONT						
AL Welch	P	Y	N	Y	?	Y
VIRGINIA						
1 **Wittman**	Y	Y	Y	N	Y	N
2 Nye	Y	Y	Y	Y	P	Y
3 Scott	Y	Y	N	Y	Y	Y
4 **Forbes**	Y	N	Y	N	Y	N
5 Perriello	Y	Y	N	Y	Y	Y
6 **Goodlatte**	Y	N	Y	N	Y	N
7 **Cantor**	Y	N	Y	N	Y	N
8 Moran	Y	Y	N	Y	Y	Y
9 Boucher	Y	Y	N	Y	Y	Y
10 **Wolf**	Y	Y	Y	N	Y	N
11 Connolly	Y	Y	N	Y	Y	Y
WASHINGTON						
1 Inslee	Y	Y	N	Y	Y	Y
2 Larsen	Y	Y	N	Y	Y	Y
3 Baird	Y	Y	N	Y	Y	Y
4 **Hastings**	P	N	Y	N	Y	N
5 **McMorris Rodgers**	Y	N	Y	N	Y	N
6 Dicks	Y	Y	N	Y	Y	Y
7 McDermott	Y	Y	N	Y	Y	Y
8 **Reichert**	Y	Y	Y	Y	Y	Y
9 Smith	Y	Y	N	Y	Y	Y
WEST VIRGINIA						
1 Mollohan	?	Y	N	Y	Y	Y
2 **Capito**	?	Y	Y	Y	Y	?
3 Rahall	?	Y	N	Y	Y	Y
WISCONSIN						
1 **Ryan**	Y	N	Y	N	Y	N
2 Baldwin	Y	Y	N	Y	Y	Y
3 Kind	Y	Y	N	Y	Y	Y
4 Moore	Y	Y	N	Y	Y	Y
5 **Sensenbrenner**	Y	N	Y	N	Y	N
6 **Petri**	Y	N	Y	N	Y	Y
7 Obey	Y	Y	N	Y	Y	Y
8 Kagen	Y	Y	N	Y	P	Y
WYOMING						
AL **Lummis**	Y	N	Y	N	Y	N
DELEGATES						
Faleomavaega (A.S.)		?				
Norton (D.C.)		?				
Bordallo (Guam)		+				
Sablan (N. Marianas)		Y				
Pierluisi (P.R.)		Y				
Christensen (V.I.)		Y				

IN THE HOUSE | By Vote Number

212. **H Res 1257. Financial Literacy Month/Adoption.** Hinojosa, D-Texas, motion to suspend the rules and adopt the resolution that would support the goals and ideals of Financial Literacy Month. Motion agreed to 397-4: D 236-0; R 161-4. A two-thirds majority of those present and voting (268 in this case) is required for adoption under suspension of the rules. April 20, 2010.

213. **H Res 1271. Tribute to Benjamin Lawson Hooks/Adoption.** Cohen, D-Tenn., motion to suspend the rules and adopt the resolution that would honor the life and achievements of civil rights leader Benjamin Lawson Hooks. Motion agreed to 407-0: D 242-0; R 165-0. A two-thirds majority of those present and voting (272 in this case) is required for adoption under suspension of the rules. April 20, 2010.

214. **S 1963. Veterans' Health Programs/Passage.** Filner, D-Calif., motion to suspend the rules and pass the bill that would authorize $2.9 billion for veterans' health programs, assistance to their caregivers and veterans' medical facility construction projects. Motion agreed to 419-0: D 245-0; R 174-0. A two-thirds majority of those present and voting (280 in this case) is required for passage under suspension of the rules. April 21, 2010.

215. **H Res 1104. National Crime Victims' Rights Week/Adoption.** Cohen, D-Tenn., motion to suspend the rules and adopt the resolution that would support the goals of 2010 National Crime Victims' Rights Week to increase public awareness of the impact of crime on victims and survivors. Motion agreed to 417-0: D 243-0; R 174-0. A two-thirds majority of those present and voting (278 in this case) is required for adoption under suspension of the rules. April 21, 2010.

216. **H Res 1216. Tribute to Daniel Coughlin/Adoption.** Capuano, D-Mass., motion to suspend the rules and adopt the resolution that would congratulate the Rev. Daniel P. Coughlin on his 10th year of service as chaplain of the House of Representatives. Motion agreed to 412-0: D 239-0; R 173-0. A two-thirds majority of those present and voting (275 in this case) is required for adoption under suspension of the rules. April 21, 2010.

	212	213	214	215	216
ALABAMA					
1 **Bonner**	Y	Y	Y	Y	Y
2 Bright	Y	Y	Y	Y	Y
3 **Rogers**	Y	Y	Y	Y	Y
4 **Aderholt**	Y	Y	Y	Y	Y
5 **Griffith**	Y	Y	Y	Y	Y
6 **Bachus**	Y	Y	Y	Y	Y
7 Davis	?	?	?	?	?
ALASKA					
AL **Young**	Y	Y	Y	Y	Y
ARIZONA					
1 Kirkpatrick	Y	Y	Y	Y	Y
2 **Franks**	Y	Y	Y	Y	Y
3 **Shadegg**	Y	Y	Y	Y	Y
4 Pastor	Y	Y	Y	Y	Y
5 Mitchell	Y	Y	Y	Y	Y
6 **Flake**	N	Y	Y	Y	Y
7 Grijalva	Y	Y	Y	Y	Y
8 Giffords	Y	Y	Y	Y	Y
ARKANSAS					
1 Berry	?	Y	Y	Y	Y
2 Snyder	Y	Y	Y	Y	Y
3 **Boozman**	Y	Y	Y	Y	Y
4 Ross	Y	Y	Y	Y	Y
CALIFORNIA					
1 Thompson	Y	Y	Y	Y	Y
2 **Herger**	Y	Y	Y	Y	?
3 **Lungren**	Y	Y	Y	Y	Y
4 **McClintock**	Y	Y	Y	Y	Y
5 Matsui	Y	Y	Y	Y	Y
6 Woolsey	Y	Y	Y	Y	Y
7 Miller, George	Y	Y	Y	Y	Y
8 Pelosi					Y
9 Lee	Y	Y	Y	Y	Y
10 Garamendi	Y	Y	Y	Y	Y
11 McNerney	Y	Y	Y	Y	Y
12 Speier	Y	Y	Y	Y	Y
13 Stark	Y	Y	Y	Y	Y
14 Eshoo	Y	Y	Y	Y	Y
15 Honda	?	?	Y	Y	Y
16 Lofgren	Y	Y	Y	Y	Y
17 Farr	Y	Y	Y	Y	Y
18 Cardoza	Y	Y	Y	Y	Y
19 **Radanovich**	Y	Y	Y	Y	Y
20 Costa	Y	Y	Y	Y	Y
21 **Nunes**	Y	Y	Y	Y	Y
22 **McCarthy**	Y	Y	Y	Y	Y
23 Capps	+	Y	Y	Y	Y
24 **Gallegly**	Y	Y	Y	Y	Y
25 **McKeon**	Y	Y	Y	Y	Y
26 **Dreier**	Y	Y	Y	Y	Y
27 Sherman	Y	Y	Y	Y	Y
28 Berman	Y	Y	Y	Y	Y
29 Schiff	Y	Y	Y	Y	Y
30 Waxman	Y	Y	Y	Y	Y
31 Becerra	Y	Y	Y	Y	Y
32 Chu	Y	Y	Y	Y	Y
33 Watson	Y	Y	Y	Y	Y
34 Roybal-Allard	Y	Y	Y	Y	Y
35 Waters	Y	Y	Y	Y	?
36 Harman	Y	Y	Y	Y	Y
37 Richardson	Y	Y	Y	Y	Y
38 Napolitano	Y	Y	Y	Y	Y
39 Sánchez, Linda	Y	Y	Y	Y	Y
40 **Royce**	Y	Y	Y	Y	Y
41 **Lewis**	Y	Y	Y	Y	Y
42 **Miller, Gary**	Y	Y	Y	Y	Y
43 Baca	Y	Y	Y	Y	Y
44 **Calvert**	Y	Y	Y	Y	Y
45 **Bono Mack**	Y	Y	Y	Y	Y
46 **Rohrabacher**	Y	Y	Y	Y	Y
47 Sanchez, Loretta	Y	Y	Y	Y	Y
48 **Campbell**	Y	Y	Y	Y	Y
49 **Issa**	Y	Y	Y	Y	Y
50 **Bilbray**	Y	Y	Y	Y	Y
51 Filner	Y	Y	Y	Y	Y
52 **Hunter**	Y	Y	Y	Y	Y
53 Davis	Y	Y	Y	Y	Y

	212	213	214	215	216
COLORADO					
1 DeGette	Y	Y	Y	Y	Y
2 Polis	Y	Y	Y	Y	?
3 Salazar	Y	Y	Y	Y	Y
4 Markey	Y	Y	Y	Y	Y
5 **Lamborn**	Y	Y	Y	Y	Y
6 **Coffman**	Y	Y	Y	Y	Y
7 Perlmutter	Y	Y	Y	Y	Y
CONNECTICUT					
1 Larson	Y	Y	Y	Y	Y
2 Courtney	Y	Y	Y	Y	Y
3 DeLauro	Y	Y	Y	Y	Y
4 Himes	Y	Y	Y	Y	Y
5 Murphy	Y	Y	Y	Y	Y
DELAWARE					
AL **Castle**	Y	Y	Y	Y	Y
FLORIDA					
1 **Miller**	Y	Y	Y	Y	Y
2 Boyd	Y	Y	Y	Y	Y
3 Brown	Y	Y	?	?	?
4 **Crenshaw**	Y	Y	Y	Y	Y
5 **Brown-Waite**	Y	Y	Y	Y	Y
6 **Stearns**	Y	Y	Y	Y	Y
7 **Mica**	Y	Y	Y	Y	Y
8 Grayson	Y	Y	Y	Y	Y
9 **Bilirakis**	+	Y	Y	Y	Y
10 **Young**	Y	Y	Y	Y	Y
11 Castor	Y	Y	Y	Y	Y
12 **Putnam**	Y	Y	Y	Y	Y
13 **Buchanan**	Y	Y	Y	Y	Y
14 **Mack**	Y	Y	Y	Y	Y
15 **Posey**	Y	Y	Y	Y	Y
16 **Rooney**	Y	Y	Y	Y	Y
17 Meek	Y	Y	Y	Y	Y
18 **Ros-Lehtinen**	Y	Y	Y	Y	Y
19 Deutch	Y	Y	Y	Y	Y
20 Wasserman Schultz	Y	Y	Y	Y	?
21 **Diaz-Balart, L.**	?	?	Y	Y	Y
22 Klein	Y	Y	Y	Y	Y
23 Hastings	Y	Y	Y	Y	Y
24 Kosmas	Y	Y	Y	Y	Y
25 **Diaz-Balart, M.**	Y	Y	Y	Y	Y
GEORGIA					
1 **Kingston**	Y	Y	Y	Y	Y
2 Bishop	?	?	Y	Y	Y
3 **Westmoreland**	Y	Y	Y	Y	Y
4 Johnson	Y	Y	Y	Y	Y
5 Lewis	Y	Y	?	?	?
6 **Price**	Y	Y	Y	Y	Y
7 **Linder**	Y	Y	Y	Y	Y
8 Marshall	Y	Y	Y	Y	Y
9 Vacant					
10 **Broun**	N	?	Y	Y	Y
11 **Gingrey**	Y	Y	Y	Y	Y
12 Barrow	Y	Y	Y	Y	Y
13 Scott	Y	Y	Y	Y	Y
HAWAII					
1 Vacant					
2 Hirono	Y	Y	Y	Y	Y
IDAHO					
1 Minnick	Y	Y	Y	Y	Y
2 **Simpson**	Y	Y	Y	Y	Y
ILLINOIS					
1 Rush	Y	Y	Y	Y	Y
2 Jackson	Y	Y	Y	Y	Y
3 Lipinski	Y	Y	Y	Y	Y
4 Gutierrez	Y	Y	Y	Y	Y
5 Quigley	Y	Y	Y	Y	Y
6 **Roskam**	Y	Y	Y	Y	Y
7 Davis	Y	Y	Y	Y	Y
8 Bean	Y	Y	Y	Y	Y
9 Schakowsky	Y	Y	Y	Y	Y
10 **Kirk**	?	?	Y	Y	Y
11 Halvorson	Y	Y	Y	Y	Y
12 Costello	Y	Y	Y	Y	Y
13 **Biggert**	Y	Y	Y	Y	Y
14 Foster	Y	Y	Y	Y	Y
15 **Johnson**	Y	Y	Y	Y	Y

KEY	Republicans	Democrats			
Y Voted for (yea)		X Paired against		C Voted "present" to avoid possible conflict of interest	
# Paired for		– Announced against			
+ Announced for		P Voted "present"		? Did not vote or otherwise make a position known	
N Voted against (nay)					

	212	213	214	215	216
16 **Manzullo**	Y	Y	Y	Y	Y
17 Hare	Y	?	Y	Y	Y
18 **Schock**	Y	Y	Y	Y	Y
19 **Shimkus**	Y	Y	Y	Y	Y
INDIANA					
1 Visclosky	Y	Y	Y	Y	Y
2 Donnelly	Y	Y	Y	Y	Y
3 **Souder**	?	?	Y	Y	Y
4 **Buyer**	Y	Y	Y	Y	Y
5 **Burton**	Y	Y	Y	Y	Y
6 **Pence**	Y	Y	Y	Y	Y
7 Carson	Y	Y	Y	Y	Y
8 Ellsworth	Y	Y	Y	Y	Y
9 Hill	Y	Y	Y	Y	Y
IOWA					
1 Braley	Y	Y	Y	Y	Y
2 Loebsack	Y	Y	Y	Y	Y
3 Boswell	Y	Y	Y	Y	Y
4 **Latham**	Y	Y	Y	Y	Y
5 **King**	Y	Y	Y	Y	Y
KANSAS					
1 **Moran**	Y	Y	Y	Y	Y
2 **Jenkins**	Y	Y	Y	Y	Y
3 Moore	Y	Y	Y	Y	Y
4 **Tiahrt**	Y	Y	Y	Y	Y
KENTUCKY					
1 **Whitfield**	Y	Y	Y	Y	Y
2 **Guthrie**	Y	Y	Y	Y	Y
3 Yarmuth	Y	Y	Y	Y	Y
4 **Davis**	Y	Y	Y	Y	Y
5 **Rogers**	Y	Y	Y	Y	Y
6 Chandler	Y	Y	Y	Y	Y
LOUISIANA					
1 **Scalise**	Y	Y	Y	Y	Y
2 **Cao**	Y	Y	Y	Y	Y
3 Melancon	Y	Y	Y	Y	Y
4 **Fleming**	Y	Y	Y	Y	Y
5 **Alexander**	?	?	Y	Y	Y
6 **Cassidy**	Y	Y	Y	Y	Y
7 **Boustany**	?	?	Y	Y	Y
MAINE					
1 Pingree	Y	Y	Y	Y	Y
2 Michaud	Y	Y	Y	Y	Y
MARYLAND					
1 Kratovil	Y	Y	Y	Y	Y
2 Ruppersberger	?	?	?	?	?
3 Sarbanes	Y	Y	Y	Y	Y
4 Edwards	Y	Y	Y	Y	Y
5 Hoyer	Y	Y	Y	Y	Y
6 **Bartlett**	Y	Y	Y	Y	Y
7 Cummings	Y	Y	Y	Y	Y
8 Van Hollen	Y	Y	Y	Y	Y
MASSACHUSETTS					
1 Olver	Y	Y	Y	Y	Y
2 Neal	Y	Y	?	?	?
3 McGovern	?	Y	Y	Y	Y
4 Frank	Y	Y	Y	Y	Y
5 Tsongas	Y	Y	Y	Y	Y
6 Tierney	Y	Y	Y	Y	Y
7 Markey	Y	Y	Y	Y	Y
8 Capuano	Y	Y	Y	Y	Y
9 Lynch	Y	Y	Y	Y	Y
10 Delahunt	Y	Y	Y	Y	Y
MICHIGAN					
1 Stupak	Y	Y	Y	Y	Y
2 **Hoekstra**	?	?	?	?	?
3 **Ehlers**	Y	Y	Y	Y	Y
4 **Camp**	Y	Y	Y	Y	Y
5 Kildee	Y	Y	Y	Y	Y
6 **Upton**	Y	Y	Y	Y	Y
7 Schauer	Y	Y	Y	Y	Y
8 **Rogers**	Y	Y	Y	Y	Y
9 Peters	Y	Y	Y	Y	Y
10 **Miller**	Y	Y	Y	Y	Y
11 **McCotter**	Y	Y	Y	Y	Y
12 Levin	Y	Y	Y	Y	Y
13 Kilpatrick	+	+	Y	Y	Y
14 Conyers	?	Y	+	+	+
15 Dingell	Y	Y	Y	Y	Y
MINNESOTA					
1 Walz	Y	Y	Y	Y	Y
2 **Kline**	Y	Y	Y	Y	Y
3 **Paulsen**	Y	Y	Y	Y	Y
4 McCollum	Y	Y	Y	Y	Y

	212	213	214	215	216
5 Ellison	Y	Y	Y	Y	Y
6 **Bachmann**	Y	Y	Y	Y	Y
7 Peterson	Y	Y	Y	Y	Y
8 Oberstar	Y	Y	Y	Y	Y
MISSISSIPPI					
1 Childers	Y	Y	Y	Y	Y
2 Thompson	Y	Y	Y	Y	Y
3 **Harper**	Y	Y	Y	Y	Y
4 Taylor	Y	Y	Y	Y	Y
MISSOURI					
1 Clay	Y	Y	Y	Y	Y
2 **Akin**	Y	Y	Y	Y	Y
3 Carnahan	Y	Y	Y	Y	Y
4 Skelton	Y	Y	Y	Y	Y
5 Cleaver	Y	Y	Y	?	Y
6 **Graves**	Y	Y	Y	Y	Y
7 **Blunt**	?	?	Y	Y	Y
8 **Emerson**	Y	Y	Y	Y	Y
9 **Luetkemeyer**	Y	Y	Y	Y	Y
MONTANA					
AL **Rehberg**	Y	Y	Y	Y	Y
NEBRASKA					
1 **Fortenberry**	Y	Y	Y	Y	Y
2 **Terry**	Y	Y	Y	Y	Y
3 **Smith**	Y	Y	Y	Y	Y
NEVADA					
1 Berkley	Y	Y	Y	Y	Y
2 **Heller**	Y	Y	Y	Y	Y
3 Titus	Y	Y	Y	Y	Y
NEW HAMPSHIRE					
1 Shea-Porter	Y	Y	Y	Y	Y
2 Hodes	Y	Y	Y	Y	Y
NEW JERSEY					
1 Andrews	Y	Y	Y	Y	Y
2 **LoBiondo**	Y	Y	Y	Y	Y
3 Adler	Y	Y	Y	Y	Y
4 **Smith**	Y	Y	Y	Y	Y
5 **Garrett**	Y	Y	Y	Y	Y
6 Pallone	Y	Y	Y	Y	Y
7 **Lance**	Y	Y	Y	Y	Y
8 Pascrell	Y	Y	Y	Y	Y
9 Rothman	Y	Y	Y	Y	Y
10 Payne	Y	Y	Y	Y	Y
11 **Frelinghuysen**	Y	Y	Y	Y	Y
12 Holt	Y	Y	Y	Y	Y
13 Sires	Y	Y	Y	Y	Y
NEW MEXICO					
1 Heinrich	Y	Y	Y	Y	Y
2 Teague	Y	Y	Y	Y	Y
3 Luján	Y	Y	Y	Y	Y
NEW YORK					
1 Bishop	Y	Y	Y	Y	Y
2 Israel	Y	Y	Y	Y	Y
3 **King**	Y	Y	Y	Y	Y
4 McCarthy	Y	Y	Y	Y	Y
5 Ackerman	Y	Y	Y	Y	Y
6 Meeks	Y	Y	Y	Y	Y
7 Crowley	Y	Y	Y	Y	Y
8 Nadler	Y	Y	Y	Y	Y
9 Weiner	Y	Y	Y	Y	Y
10 Towns	Y	Y	Y	Y	Y
11 Clarke	?	Y	Y	Y	Y
12 Velázquez	Y	Y	Y	Y	Y
13 McMahon	Y	Y	Y	?	?
14 Maloney	Y	Y	Y	Y	Y
15 Rangel	Y	Y	Y	Y	Y
16 Serrano	Y	Y	Y	Y	Y
17 Engel	Y	Y	Y	Y	Y
18 Lowey	Y	Y	Y	Y	Y
19 Hall	Y	Y	Y	Y	Y
20 Murphy	+	Y	Y	Y	Y
21 Tonko	Y	Y	Y	Y	Y
22 Hinchey	Y	Y	Y	Y	Y
23 Owens	Y	Y	Y	Y	Y
24 Arcuri	Y	Y	Y	Y	Y
25 Maffei	Y	Y	Y	Y	Y
26 Lee	Y	Y	Y	Y	Y
27 Higgins	Y	Y	Y	Y	Y
28 Slaughter	Y	Y	Y	Y	Y
29 Vacant					
NORTH CAROLINA					
1 Butterfield	Y	Y	Y	Y	Y
2 Etheridge	Y	Y	Y	Y	Y
3 **Jones**	Y	Y	Y	Y	Y
4 Price	Y	Y	Y	Y	Y

	212	213	214	215	216
5 **Foxx**	Y	Y	Y	Y	Y
6 **Coble**	Y	Y	Y	Y	Y
7 McIntyre	Y	Y	Y	Y	Y
8 Kissell	Y	Y	Y	Y	Y
9 **Myrick**	Y	Y	Y	Y	Y
10 **McHenry**	Y	Y	Y	Y	Y
11 Shuler	Y	Y	Y	Y	Y
12 Watt	Y	Y	Y	Y	Y
13 Miller	Y	?	Y	Y	Y
NORTH DAKOTA					
AL Pomeroy	Y	Y	Y	Y	Y
OHIO					
1 Driehaus	Y	Y	Y	Y	Y
2 **Schmidt**	Y	Y	Y	Y	Y
3 Turner	Y	Y	Y	Y	Y
4 **Jordan**	Y	Y	Y	Y	Y
5 **Latta**	Y	Y	Y	Y	Y
6 Wilson	Y	Y	Y	Y	Y
7 **Austria**	Y	Y	Y	Y	Y
8 **Boehner**	?	?	Y	Y	Y
9 Kaptur	Y	Y	Y	Y	Y
10 Kucinich	Y	Y	Y	Y	Y
11 Fudge	Y	Y	Y	Y	Y
12 **Tiberi**	Y	Y	Y	Y	Y
13 Sutton	?	?	Y	Y	Y
14 **LaTourette**	Y	Y	Y	Y	Y
15 Kilroy	Y	Y	Y	Y	Y
16 Boccieri	?	?	Y	Y	Y
17 Ryan	Y	Y	Y	Y	Y
18 Space	Y	Y	Y	Y	Y
OKLAHOMA					
1 **Sullivan**		Y	Y	Y	Y
2 Boren	Y	Y	Y	Y	?
3 **Lucas**	Y	Y	Y	Y	Y
4 **Cole**	Y	Y	Y	Y	Y
5 **Fallin**	Y	Y	Y	Y	Y
OREGON					
1 Wu	Y	Y	Y	Y	Y
2 **Walden**	Y	Y	Y	Y	Y
3 Blumenauer	?	?	Y	Y	Y
4 DeFazio	Y	?	Y	Y	Y
5 Schrader	Y	Y	Y	Y	?
PENNSYLVANIA					
1 Brady	Y	Y	Y	Y	Y
2 Fattah	?	Y	Y	Y	Y
3 Dahlkemper	Y	Y	Y	Y	Y
4 Altmire	Y	Y	Y	Y	Y
5 **Thompson**	Y	Y	Y	Y	Y
6 **Gerlach**	Y	Y	Y	Y	Y
7 Sestak	Y	Y	Y	Y	Y
8 Murphy, P.	Y	Y	Y	Y	Y
9 **Shuster**	Y	Y	Y	Y	Y
10 Carney	Y	Y	Y	Y	Y
11 Kanjorski	Y	Y	Y	Y	Y
12 Vacant					
13 Schwartz	Y	Y	Y	Y	Y
14 Doyle	Y	Y	Y	Y	Y
15 **Dent**	Y	Y	Y	Y	Y
16 **Pitts**	Y	Y	Y	Y	Y
17 Holden	Y	Y	Y	Y	Y
18 **Murphy, T.**	Y	Y	Y	Y	Y
19 **Platts**	Y	Y	Y	Y	Y
RHODE ISLAND					
1 Kennedy	Y	Y	Y	Y	Y
2 Langevin	?	Y	Y	Y	Y
SOUTH CAROLINA					
1 **Brown**	Y	Y	Y	Y	Y
2 **Wilson**	Y	Y	Y	Y	Y
3 **Barrett**	?	?	?	?	?
4 **Inglis**	Y	Y	Y	Y	Y
5 Spratt	Y	Y	Y	Y	Y
6 Clyburn	Y	Y	Y	Y	Y
SOUTH DAKOTA					
AL Herseth Sandlin	Y	Y	Y	Y	Y
TENNESSEE					
1 **Roe**	Y	Y	Y	Y	Y
2 **Duncan**	Y	Y	Y	Y	Y
3 **Wamp**	?	?	Y	Y	Y
4 Davis	Y	Y	Y	Y	Y
5 Cooper	Y	Y	Y	Y	Y
6 Gordon	Y	Y	Y	Y	Y
7 **Blackburn**	Y	Y	Y	Y	Y
8 Tanner	Y	Y	Y	Y	Y
9 Cohen	Y	Y	+	+	+

	212	213	214	215	216
TEXAS					
1 **Gohmert**	?	?	Y	Y	Y
2 **Poe**	Y	Y	Y	Y	Y
3 **Johnson, S.**	Y	Y	Y	Y	Y
4 **Hall**	Y	Y	Y	Y	Y
5 **Hensarling**	Y	Y	Y	Y	Y
6 **Barton**	Y	Y	Y	Y	Y
7 **Culberson**	Y	Y	Y	Y	Y
8 **Brady**	Y	Y	Y	Y	Y
9 Green, A.	Y	Y	Y	Y	Y
10 **McCaul**	Y	Y	Y	Y	Y
11 **Conaway**	Y	Y	Y	Y	Y
12 **Granger**	Y	Y	Y	Y	Y
13 **Thornberry**	Y	Y	Y	Y	Y
14 **Paul**	N	Y	Y	Y	Y
15 Hinojosa	Y	Y	Y	Y	Y
16 Reyes	Y	Y	Y	Y	Y
17 Edwards	Y	Y	Y	Y	Y
18 Jackson Lee	Y	Y	Y	Y	Y
19 **Neugebauer**	Y	Y	Y	Y	Y
20 Gonzalez	Y	Y	Y	Y	Y
21 **Smith**	Y	Y	?	?	?
22 **Olson**	Y	Y	Y	Y	Y
23 Rodriguez	Y	Y	Y	Y	Y
24 **Marchant**	Y	Y	Y	Y	Y
25 Doggett	Y	Y	Y	Y	Y
26 **Burgess**	N	Y	Y	Y	Y
27 Ortiz	Y	Y	Y	Y	Y
28 Cuellar	Y	Y	Y	Y	Y
29 Green, G.	Y	Y	Y	Y	Y
30 Johnson, E.	+	+	+	+	+
31 **Carter**	Y	Y	Y	Y	Y
32 **Sessions**	Y	Y	Y	Y	Y
UTAH					
1 **Bishop**	Y	Y	Y	Y	Y
2 Matheson	Y	Y	Y	Y	Y
3 **Chaffetz**	Y	Y	Y	Y	Y
VERMONT					
AL Welch	Y	Y	Y	Y	?
VIRGINIA					
1 **Wittman**	Y	Y	Y	Y	Y
2 Nye	Y	Y	Y	Y	Y
3 Scott	Y	Y	Y	Y	Y
4 **Forbes**	Y	Y	Y	Y	Y
5 Perriello	Y	Y	Y	Y	Y
6 **Goodlatte**	Y	Y	Y	Y	Y
7 **Cantor**	Y	Y	Y	Y	Y
8 Moran	Y	Y	Y	Y	Y
9 Boucher	Y	Y	Y	Y	Y
10 **Wolf**	Y	Y	Y	Y	Y
11 Connolly	Y	Y	Y	Y	Y
WASHINGTON					
1 Inslee	Y	Y	Y	Y	Y
2 Larsen	Y	Y	Y	Y	Y
3 Baird	Y	Y	Y	Y	?
4 **Hastings**	Y	Y	Y	Y	Y
5 **McMorris Rodgers**	Y	Y	Y	Y	Y
6 Dicks	Y	Y	Y	Y	Y
7 McDermott	Y	Y	Y	Y	Y
8 **Reichert**	Y	Y	Y	Y	Y
9 Smith	Y	Y	Y	Y	+
WEST VIRGINIA					
1 Mollohan	Y	Y	Y	Y	Y
2 **Capito**	Y	Y	Y	Y	Y
3 Rahall	Y	Y	Y	Y	Y
WISCONSIN					
1 **Ryan**	Y	Y	Y	Y	Y
2 Baldwin	Y	Y	Y	Y	Y
3 Kind	Y	Y	Y	Y	Y
4 Moore	Y	Y	Y	Y	Y
5 **Sensenbrenner**	Y	Y	Y	Y	Y
6 **Petri**	Y	Y	Y	Y	Y
7 Obey	Y	Y	Y	Y	Y
8 Kagen	Y	Y	Y	Y	Y
WYOMING					
AL **Lummis**	Y	Y	Y	Y	Y
DELEGATES					
Faleomavaega (A.S.)					
Norton (D.C.)					
Bordallo (Guam)					
Sablan (N. Marianas)					
Pierluisi (P.R.)					
Christensen (V.I.)					

IN THE HOUSE | By Vote Number

217. **H Res 1287. PMA Group Investigation/Previous Question.**
Flake, R-Ariz., motion to order the previous question on the Flake privileged resolution. The resolution would require the Committee on Standards of Official Conduct to issue a report detailing the number of interviews conducted, subpoenas issued and documents reviewed in the panel's investigation of members' dealings with the PMA Group. Motion rejected 187-218: D 24-218; R 163-0. April 22, 2010.

218. **H Res 1287. PMA Group Investigation/Motion to Refer.**
Hastings, D-Fla., motion to refer the Flake, R-Ariz., privileged resolution to the Committee on Standards of Official Conduct. Motion agreed to 402-0: D 241-0; R 161-0. April 22, 2010.

219. **HR 2194. Iran Sanctions/Motion to Instruct.** Ros-Lehtinen, R-Fla., motion to instruct conferees to insist on House provisions of the bill that would impose sanctions against companies that supply Iran with, or support its domestic production of, gasoline and other refined-petroleum products, and present a conference report by May 28. Motion agreed to 403-11: D 232-7; R 171-4. April 22, 2010.

220. **H Res 1270. Mathematics Awareness Month/Adoption.** Sablan, D-N. Marianas, motion to suspend the rules and adopt the resolution that would support the goals and ideals of Mathematics Awareness Month. Motion agreed to 407-2: D 239-0; R 168-2. A two-thirds majority of those present and voting (273 in this case) is required for adoption under suspension of the rules. April 22, 2010.

		217	218	219	220
ALABAMA					
1	**Bonner**	P	P	Y	Y
2	Bright	Y	Y	Y	Y
3	**Rogers**	Y	Y	Y	Y
4	**Aderholt**	Y	Y	Y	?
5	**Griffith**	Y	Y	Y	Y
6	**Bachus**	Y	Y	Y	Y
7	Davis	?	?	?	?
ALASKA					
AL	**Young**	Y	Y	Y	N
ARIZONA					
1	Kirkpatrick	Y	Y	Y	Y
2	**Franks**	Y	Y	Y	Y
3	**Shadegg**	Y	Y	Y	Y
4	Pastor	N	Y	Y	Y
5	Mitchell	Y	Y	Y	Y
6	**Flake**	Y	Y	N	Y
7	Grijalva	N	Y	Y	?
8	Giffords	Y	Y	Y	Y
ARKANSAS					
1	Berry	N	Y	Y	Y
2	Snyder	N	Y	Y	Y
3	**Boozman**	Y	Y	Y	Y
4	Ross	N	Y	Y	Y
CALIFORNIA					
1	Thompson	N	Y	Y	Y
2	**Herger**	Y	Y	Y	Y
3	**Lungren**	Y	Y	Y	Y
4	**McClintock**	Y	Y	Y	Y
5	Matsui	N	Y	Y	Y
6	Woolsey	N	Y	Y	Y
7	Miller, George	N	Y	Y	Y
8	Pelosi				
9	Lee	N	Y	P	Y
10	Garamendi	N	Y	Y	Y
11	McNerney	Y	Y	Y	Y
12	Speier	N	Y	Y	Y
13	Stark	N	Y	P	Y
14	Eshoo	N	Y	Y	Y
15	Honda	N	Y	Y	Y
16	Lofgren	P	P	Y	Y
17	Farr	N	Y	Y	Y
18	Cardoza	N	Y	Y	Y
19	**Radanovich**	Y	Y	Y	Y
20	Costa	N	Y	Y	Y
21	**Nunes**	Y	Y	Y	Y
22	**McCarthy**	Y	Y	Y	Y
23	Capps	N	Y	Y	Y
24	**Gallegly**	Y	Y	Y	Y
25	**McKeon**	Y	Y	Y	Y
26	**Dreier**	Y	Y	Y	Y
27	Sherman	N	Y	Y	Y
28	Berman	N	?	Y	Y
29	Schiff	N	Y	Y	Y
30	Waxman	N	Y	Y	Y
31	Becerra	N	Y	Y	Y
32	Chu	N	Y	Y	Y
33	Watson	N	Y	Y	Y
34	Roybal-Allard	N	Y	Y	Y
35	Waters	N	Y	N	Y
36	Harman	N	Y	Y	Y
37	Richardson	N	Y	Y	Y
38	Napolitano	N	Y	Y	Y
39	Sánchez, Linda	N	Y	Y	Y
40	**Royce**	Y	Y	Y	Y
41	**Lewis**	Y	Y	Y	Y
42	**Miller, Gary**	Y	Y	Y	Y
43	Baca	N	Y	Y	Y
44	**Calvert**	Y	Y	Y	Y
45	**Bono Mack**	Y	Y	Y	Y
46	**Rohrabacher**	Y	Y	Y	Y
47	Sanchez, Loretta	N	Y	Y	Y
48	**Campbell**	Y	Y	Y	Y
49	**Issa**	Y	Y	Y	Y
50	**Bilbray**	Y	Y	Y	Y
51	Filner	N	Y	Y	Y
52	**Hunter**	Y	Y	Y	Y
53	Davis	N	Y	Y	Y

		217	218	219	220
COLORADO					
1	DeGette	N	Y	Y	Y
2	Polis	?	?	?	?
3	Salazar	N	Y	Y	Y
4	Markey	Y	Y	Y	Y
5	**Lamborn**	Y	Y	Y	Y
6	**Coffman**	Y	Y	Y	Y
7	Perlmutter	N	Y	Y	Y
CONNECTICUT					
1	Larson	N	Y	Y	Y
2	Courtney	N	Y	Y	Y
3	DeLauro	N	Y	Y	Y
4	Himes	Y	Y	Y	Y
5	Murphy	N	Y	Y	Y
DELAWARE					
AL	**Castle**	Y	Y	Y	Y
FLORIDA					
1	**Miller**	Y	Y	Y	Y
2	Boyd	N	Y	Y	Y
3	Brown	N	Y	Y	Y
4	**Crenshaw**	Y	Y	Y	Y
5	**Brown-Waite**	Y	Y	Y	Y
6	**Stearns**	Y	Y	Y	Y
7	**Mica**	Y	Y	Y	Y
8	Grayson	N	Y	Y	Y
9	**Bilirakis**	Y	Y	Y	Y
10	**Young**	Y	Y	Y	Y
11	Castor	P	P	Y	Y
12	**Putnam**	Y	Y	Y	Y
13	**Buchanan**	Y	Y	Y	Y
14	**Mack**	Y	Y	Y	Y
15	**Posey**	Y	Y	Y	Y
16	**Rooney**	Y	Y	Y	Y
17	Meek	N	Y	Y	Y
18	**Ros-Lehtinen**	Y	Y	Y	Y
19	Deutch	N	Y	Y	Y
20	Wasserman Schultz	N	Y	Y	Y
21	**Diaz-Balart, L.**	P	P	Y	Y
22	Klein	N	Y	Y	Y
23	Hastings	N	Y	Y	Y
24	Kosmas	N	Y	Y	Y
25	**Diaz-Balart, M.**	Y	Y	Y	Y
GEORGIA					
1	**Kingston**	Y	Y	Y	Y
2	Bishop	N	Y	Y	Y
3	**Westmoreland**	Y	Y	Y	Y
4	Johnson	N	Y	Y	Y
5	Lewis	N	Y	Y	Y
6	**Price**	Y	Y	Y	Y
7	**Linder**	Y	Y	Y	Y
8	Marshall	N	Y	Y	Y
9	Vacant				
10	**Broun**	Y	Y	Y	Y
11	**Gingrey**	Y	?	Y	Y
12	Barrow	N	Y	Y	Y
13	Scott	N	Y	Y	Y
HAWAII					
1	Vacant				
2	Hirono	N	Y	Y	Y
IDAHO					
1	Minnick	Y	Y	Y	Y
2	**Simpson**	Y	P	Y	Y
ILLINOIS					
1	Rush	?	?	?	?
2	Jackson	N	Y	Y	Y
3	Lipinski	N	Y	Y	Y
4	Gutierrez	N	Y	Y	Y
5	Quigley	Y	Y	Y	?
6	**Roskam**	Y	Y	Y	Y
7	Davis	N	Y	Y	Y
8	Bean	N	Y	Y	Y
9	Schakowsky	N	Y	Y	Y
10	**Kirk**	Y	Y	Y	Y
11	Halvorson	Y	Y	Y	Y
12	Costello	N	Y	Y	Y
13	**Biggert**	Y	Y	Y	Y
14	Foster	Y	Y	Y	Y
15	**Johnson**	Y	Y	Y	Y

KEY	**Republicans**	Democrats		
Y	Voted for (yea)	X	Paired against	C	Voted "present" to avoid possible conflict of interest
#	Paired for	−	Announced against	
+	Announced for	P	Voted "present"	?	Did not vote or otherwise make a position known
N	Voted against (nay)			

	217	218	219	220
16 Manzullo	Y	Y	Y	Y
17 Hare	N	Y	Y	Y
18 Schock	Y	Y	Y	Y
19 Shimkus	Y	Y	Y	Y
INDIANA				
1 Visclosky	N	Y	Y	Y
2 Donnelly	Y	Y	Y	Y
3 Souder	Y	Y	Y	Y
4 Buyer	P	Y	Y	Y
5 Burton	Y	Y	Y	Y
6 Pence	Y	Y	Y	Y
7 Carson	N	Y	Y	Y
8 Ellsworth	N	Y	Y	Y
9 Hill	N	Y	Y	Y
IOWA				
1 Braley	N	Y	Y	Y
2 Loebsack	Y	Y	Y	Y
3 Boswell	N	Y	Y	Y
4 Latham	P	P	Y	Y
5 King	Y	Y	Y	Y
KANSAS				
1 Moran	Y	Y	Y	Y
2 Jenkins	Y	Y	Y	Y
3 Moore	N	Y	Y	Y
4 Tiahrt	Y	Y	Y	Y
KENTUCKY				
1 Whitfield	Y	Y	Y	?
2 Guthrie	Y	Y	Y	Y
3 Yarmuth	N	Y	Y	Y
4 Davis	Y	Y	Y	Y
5 Rogers	Y	Y	Y	Y
6 Chandler	P	P	Y	Y
LOUISIANA				
1 Scalise	Y	Y	Y	Y
2 Cao	Y	Y	Y	Y
3 Melancon	N	Y	Y	Y
4 Fleming	Y	Y	Y	Y
5 Alexander	Y	Y	Y	Y
6 Cassidy	Y	Y	Y	Y
7 Boustany	Y	Y	Y	Y
MAINE				
1 Pingree	N	Y	Y	Y
2 Michaud	N	Y	Y	Y
MARYLAND				
1 Kratovil	N	Y	Y	Y
2 Ruppersberger	?	?	?	?
3 Sarbanes	N	Y	Y	Y
4 Edwards	N	Y	Y	Y
5 Hoyer	N	Y	Y	Y
6 Bartlett	Y	Y	Y	Y
7 Cummings	N	Y	Y	Y
8 Van Hollen	N	Y	Y	Y
MASSACHUSETTS				
1 Olver	N	Y	Y	Y
2 Neal	N	Y	Y	Y
3 McGovern	N	Y	Y	Y
4 Frank	N	Y	Y	Y
5 Tsongas	N	Y	Y	Y
6 Tierney	N	Y	?	Y
7 Markey	N	Y	+	Y
8 Capuano	N	Y	Y	Y
9 Lynch	N	Y	Y	Y
10 Delahunt	N	Y	Y	Y
MICHIGAN				
1 Stupak	N	Y	Y	Y
2 Hoekstra	Y	Y	Y	Y
3 Ehlers	Y	Y	Y	Y
4 Camp	Y	Y	Y	Y
5 Kildee	N	Y	Y	Y
6 Upton	Y	Y	Y	Y
7 Schauer	N	Y	Y	Y
8 Rogers	Y	Y	Y	Y
9 Peters	N	Y	Y	Y
10 Miller	Y	Y	Y	Y
11 McCotter	Y	Y	Y	Y
12 Levin	N	Y	Y	Y
13 Kilpatrick	N	Y	Y	Y
14 Conyers	–	+	?	?
15 Dingell	N	Y	Y	Y
MINNESOTA				
1 Walz	Y	Y	Y	Y
2 Kline	Y	Y	Y	Y
3 Paulsen	Y	Y	Y	Y
4 McCollum	N	Y	Y	Y
5 Ellison	N	Y	P	Y
6 Bachmann	Y	Y	Y	Y
7 Peterson	N	Y	Y	Y
8 Oberstar	N	Y	Y	Y
MISSISSIPPI				
1 Childers	Y	Y	Y	Y
2 Thompson	N	Y	Y	Y
3 Harper	P	P	Y	Y
4 Taylor	Y	Y	Y	Y
MISSOURI				
1 Clay	N	Y	Y	Y
2 Akin	Y	Y	Y	Y
3 Carnahan	N	Y	Y	Y
4 Skelton	N	Y	Y	Y
5 Cleaver	N	Y	Y	?
6 Graves	Y	Y	Y	Y
7 Blunt	Y	Y	Y	Y
8 Emerson	Y	Y	Y	Y
9 Luetkemeyer	Y	Y	Y	Y
MONTANA				
AL Rehberg	Y	Y	Y	Y
NEBRASKA				
1 Fortenberry	Y	Y	Y	Y
2 Terry	Y	Y	Y	Y
3 Smith	Y	Y	Y	Y
NEVADA				
1 Berkley	N	Y	Y	Y
2 Heller	Y	Y	Y	Y
3 Titus	N	Y	Y	Y
NEW HAMPSHIRE				
1 Shea-Porter	N	Y	Y	Y
2 Hodes	Y	Y	Y	Y
NEW JERSEY				
1 Andrews	N	Y	P	Y
2 LoBiondo	Y	Y	Y	Y
3 Adler	Y	Y	Y	Y
4 Smith	Y	Y	Y	Y
5 Garrett	Y	Y	Y	Y
6 Pallone	N	Y	Y	Y
7 Lance	Y	Y	Y	Y
8 Pascrell	N	Y	Y	Y
9 Rothman	N	Y	Y	Y
10 Payne	N	Y	Y	Y
11 Frelinghuysen	Y	Y	Y	Y
12 Holt	N	Y	Y	Y
13 Sires	N	Y	Y	Y
NEW MEXICO				
1 Heinrich	N	Y	Y	Y
2 Teague	N	Y	Y	Y
3 Luján	N	Y	Y	Y
NEW YORK				
1 Bishop	N	Y	Y	Y
2 Israel	N	Y	Y	Y
3 King	Y	Y	Y	Y
4 McCarthy	N	Y	Y	Y
5 Ackerman	N	Y	Y	?
6 Meeks	N	Y	Y	Y
7 Crowley	N	Y	Y	Y
8 Nadler	N	Y	Y	Y
9 Weiner	N	Y	Y	Y
10 Towns	N	Y	Y	Y
11 Clarke	N	Y	Y	Y
12 Velázquez	N	Y	Y	Y
13 McMahon	Y	Y	Y	Y
14 Maloney	?	?	?	?
15 Rangel	N	Y	Y	Y
16 Serrano	N	Y	Y	Y
17 Engel	N	Y	Y	Y
18 Lowey	N	Y	Y	Y
19 Hall	N	Y	Y	Y
20 Murphy	Y	Y	Y	Y
21 Tonko	N	Y	Y	Y
22 Hinchey	N	Y	Y	Y
23 Owens	Y	Y	Y	Y
24 Arcuri	N	Y	Y	Y
25 Maffei	N	Y	Y	Y
26 Lee	Y	Y	Y	Y
27 Higgins	N	Y	?	Y
28 Slaughter	N	Y	Y	Y
29 Vacant				
NORTH CAROLINA				
1 Butterfield	P	P	Y	Y
2 Etheridge	N	Y	Y	Y
3 Jones	Y	Y	N	Y
4 Price	N	Y	Y	Y
5 Foxx	Y	Y	Y	Y
6 Coble	Y	Y	Y	Y
7 McIntyre	N	Y	Y	?
8 Kissell	N	Y	Y	Y
9 Myrick	P	P	Y	Y
10 McHenry	Y	Y	Y	Y
11 Shuler	N	Y	Y	Y
12 Watt	N	Y	Y	Y
13 Miller	N	Y	Y	Y
NORTH DAKOTA				
AL Pomeroy	N	Y	Y	Y
OHIO				
1 Driehaus	N	Y	Y	Y
2 Schmidt	Y	Y	Y	Y
3 Turner	Y	Y	Y	Y
4 Jordan	Y	Y	Y	?
5 Latta	Y	Y	Y	Y
6 Wilson	N	Y	Y	Y
7 Austria	Y	Y	Y	Y
8 Boehner	Y	Y	Y	Y
9 Kaptur	N	Y	Y	?
10 Kucinich	N	Y	N	Y
11 Fudge	N	Y	Y	Y
12 Tiberi	Y	Y	Y	Y
13 Sutton	N	Y	?	Y
14 LaTourette	Y	Y	Y	?
15 Kilroy	N	Y	Y	Y
16 Boccieri	N	Y	Y	Y
17 Ryan	N	Y	Y	Y
18 Space	N	Y	Y	Y
OKLAHOMA				
1 Sullivan	Y	Y	Y	Y
2 Boren	N	Y	Y	Y
3 Lucas	Y	Y	Y	Y
4 Cole	Y	Y	Y	Y
5 Fallin	Y	Y	Y	Y
OREGON				
1 Wu	N	Y	Y	Y
2 Walden	P	P	Y	Y
3 Blumenauer	N	Y	N	Y
4 DeFazio	N	Y	Y	Y
5 Schrader	N	Y	Y	Y
PENNSYLVANIA				
1 Brady	N	Y	Y	Y
2 Fattah	N	Y	Y	Y
3 Dahlkemper	N	Y	Y	Y
4 Altmire	N	Y	Y	Y
5 Thompson	Y	Y	Y	Y
6 Gerlach	Y	Y	Y	Y
7 Sestak	N	Y	Y	Y
8 Murphy, P.	N	Y	Y	Y
9 Shuster	Y	Y	Y	Y
10 Carney	N	Y	Y	Y
11 Kanjorski	N	Y	Y	Y
12 Vacant				
13 Schwartz	N	Y	Y	Y
14 Doyle	N	Y	Y	Y
15 Dent	P	P	Y	+
16 Pitts	Y	Y	Y	Y
17 Holden	N	Y	Y	Y
18 Murphy, T.	Y	Y	Y	Y
19 Platts	Y	Y	Y	Y
RHODE ISLAND				
1 Kennedy	N	Y	Y	Y
2 Langevin	N	Y	Y	Y
SOUTH CAROLINA				
1 Brown	Y	Y	Y	Y
2 Wilson	Y	Y	Y	Y
3 Barrett	?	?	?	?
4 Inglis	?	Y	Y	Y
5 Spratt	N	Y	Y	Y
6 Clyburn	N	Y	Y	Y
SOUTH DAKOTA				
AL Herseth Sandlin	N	Y	Y	Y
TENNESSEE				
1 Roe	Y	Y	Y	Y
2 Duncan	Y	Y	N	Y
3 Wamp	Y	Y	Y	Y
4 Davis	N	Y	Y	Y
5 Cooper	Y	Y	Y	Y
6 Gordon	N	Y	?	Y
7 Blackburn	Y	P	Y	Y
8 Tanner	N	Y	Y	Y
9 Cohen	N	Y	Y	Y
TEXAS				
1 Gohmert	?	?	?	?
2 Poe	Y	Y	Y	Y
3 Johnson, S.	Y	Y	Y	Y
4 Hall	Y	Y	Y	Y
5 Hensarling	Y	Y	Y	Y
6 Barton	Y	Y	Y	Y
7 Culberson	Y	Y	Y	Y
8 Brady	Y	Y	Y	Y
9 Green, A.	N	Y	Y	Y
10 McCaul	P	P	Y	Y
11 Conaway	P	P	Y	Y
12 Granger	Y	Y	Y	Y
13 Thornberry	Y	Y	Y	Y
14 Paul	Y	Y	N	N
15 Hinojosa	N	Y	Y	Y
16 Reyes	N	Y	Y	Y
17 Edwards	N	Y	Y	Y
18 Jackson Lee	N	Y	Y	Y
19 Neugebauer	Y	Y	Y	Y
20 Gonzalez	N	Y	Y	Y
21 Smith	Y	Y	Y	Y
22 Olson	Y	Y	Y	Y
23 Rodriguez	N	Y	Y	Y
24 Marchant	Y	Y	Y	Y
25 Doggett	N	Y	Y	Y
26 Burgess	Y	?	Y	Y
27 Ortiz	N	Y	Y	Y
28 Cuellar	N	Y	Y	Y
29 Green, G.	N	Y	Y	Y
30 Johnson, E.	N	Y	Y	Y
31 Carter	Y	Y	Y	Y
32 Sessions	Y	Y	Y	Y
UTAH				
1 Bishop	Y	Y	Y	Y
2 Matheson	N	Y	Y	Y
3 Chaffetz	Y	Y	Y	Y
VERMONT				
AL Welch	P	P	Y	?
VIRGINIA				
1 Wittman	Y	Y	Y	Y
2 Nye	N	Y	Y	Y
3 Scott	N	Y	Y	Y
4 Forbes	Y	Y	Y	Y
5 Perriello	Y	Y	Y	Y
6 Goodlatte	Y	Y	Y	Y
7 Cantor	Y	Y	Y	Y
8 Moran	N	Y	Y	Y
9 Boucher	N	Y	Y	Y
10 Wolf	Y	Y	Y	Y
11 Connolly	N	Y	Y	Y
WASHINGTON				
1 Inslee	N	Y	Y	Y
2 Larsen	N	Y	Y	Y
3 Baird	N	Y	N	Y
4 Hastings	P	P	Y	Y
5 McMorris Rodgers	Y	Y	Y	Y
6 Dicks	N	Y	Y	?
7 McDermott	N	Y	N	Y
8 Reichert	Y	Y	Y	Y
9 Smith	N	Y	Y	Y
WEST VIRGINIA				
1 Mollohan	N	Y	Y	Y
2 Capito	Y	Y	Y	Y
3 Rahall	N	Y	Y	Y
WISCONSIN				
1 Ryan	Y	Y	Y	Y
2 Baldwin	N	Y	N	Y
3 Kind	N	Y	Y	Y
4 Moore	N	Y	N	Y
5 Sensenbrenner	Y	Y	Y	Y
6 Petri	Y	Y	Y	Y
7 Obey	N	Y	Y	Y
8 Kagen	N	Y	Y	Y
WYOMING				
AL Lummis	Y	Y	Y	Y
DELEGATES				
Faleomavaega (A.S.)				
Norton (D.C.)				
Bordallo (Guam)				
Sablan (N. Marianas)				
Pierluisi (P.R.)				
Christensen (V.I.)				

IN THE HOUSE | By Vote Number

221. **HR 4543. Anthony J. Cortese Post Office/Passage.** Lynch, D-Mass., motion to suspend the rules and pass the bill that would designate a post office in San Jose, Calif., as the "Anthony J. Cortese Post Office Building." Motion agreed to 370-0. D 214-0; R 156-0. A two-thirds majority of those present and voting (247 in this case) is required for passage under suspension of the rules. April 26, 2010.

222. **H Res 1103. Tribute to Sam Houston/Adoption.** Lynch, D-Mass., motion to suspend the rules and adopt the resolution that would recognize the contributions of American statesman and politician Sam Houston to Texas and to the expansion of the United States. Motion agreed to 375-0: D 219-0; R 156-0. A two-thirds majority of those present and voting (250 in this case) is required for adoption under suspension of the rules. April 26, 2010.

223. **HR 4861. Steve Goodman Post Office/Passage.** Lynch, D-Mass., motion to suspend the rules and pass the bill that would designate a post office in Chicago as the "Steve Goodman Post Office Building." Motion agreed to 371-0: D 218-0; R 153-0. A two-thirds majority of those present and voting (248 in this case) is required for passage under suspension of the rules. April 26, 2010.

224. **H Res 1131. National Assistant Principals Week/Adoption.** Woolsey, D-Calif., motion to suspend the rules and adopt the resolution that would support the designation of National Assistant Principals Week. Motion agreed to 411-0: D 242-0; R 169-0. A two-thirds majority of those present and voting (274 in this case) is required for adoption under suspension of the rules. April 27, 2010.

225. **HR 5017. Rural Housing Loan Program Modifications/Passage.** Kanjorski, D-Pa., motion to suspend the rules and pass the bill that would authorize the Agriculture Department to guarantee up to $30 billion in mortgages in fiscal 2010 under a rural housing program and increase fees for mortgage lenders participating in the program to up to 4 percent of the loan principal. Motion agreed to 352-62: D 244-0; R 108-62. A two-thirds majority of those present and voting (276 in this case) is required for passage under suspension of the rules. April 27, 2010.

226. **HR 5146. Block of Member Pay Increase/Passage.** Davis, D-Calif., motion to suspend the rules and pass the bill that would block a scheduled 2011 cost-of-living pay increase for members of Congress. Motion agreed to 402-15: D 232-15; R 170-0. A two-thirds majority of those present and voting (278 in this case) is required for passage under suspension of the rules. April 27, 2010.

	221	222	223	224	225	226
ALABAMA						
1 Bonner	Y	Y	Y	Y	Y	Y
2 Bright	Y	Y	Y	Y	Y	Y
3 Rogers	Y	Y	Y	Y	Y	Y
4 Aderholt	Y	Y	Y	Y	Y	Y
5 Griffith	Y	Y	Y	Y	Y	Y
6 Bachus	Y	Y	Y	Y	Y	Y
7 Davis	?	?	?	?	?	?
ALASKA						
AL Young	Y	Y	Y	Y	Y	Y
ARIZONA						
1 Kirkpatrick	Y	Y	Y	Y	Y	Y
2 Franks	Y	Y	?	Y	N	Y
3 Shadegg	?	?	?	Y	N	Y
4 Pastor	Y	Y	Y	Y	Y	Y
5 Mitchell	Y	Y	Y	Y	Y	Y
6 Flake	Y	Y	Y	Y	N	Y
7 Grijalva	?	?	?	Y	Y	Y
8 Giffords	Y	Y	Y	Y	Y	Y
ARKANSAS						
1 Berry	?	?	?	?	?	?
2 Snyder	Y	Y	Y	Y	Y	Y
3 Boozman	Y	Y	Y	Y	Y	Y
4 Ross	Y	Y	Y	Y	Y	Y
CALIFORNIA						
1 Thompson	Y	Y	Y	Y	Y	Y
2 Herger	Y	Y	Y	Y	N	Y
3 Lungren	Y	Y	Y	Y	Y	Y
4 McClintock	Y	Y	Y	Y	N	Y
5 Matsui	Y	Y	Y	Y	Y	Y
6 Woolsey	+	+	+	Y	Y	N
7 Miller, George	Y	Y	Y	Y	Y	Y
8 Pelosi						
9 Lee	Y	Y	Y	Y	Y	N
10 Garamendi	Y	Y	Y	Y	Y	Y
11 McNerney	Y	Y	Y	Y	Y	Y
12 Speier	?	Y	Y	Y	Y	Y
13 Stark	Y	Y	Y	Y	Y	Y
14 Eshoo	Y	Y	Y	Y	Y	Y
15 Honda	Y	Y	Y	Y	Y	Y
16 Lofgren	Y	Y	Y	Y	Y	Y
17 Farr	Y	Y	Y	Y	Y	Y
18 Cardoza	Y	Y	Y	Y	Y	Y
19 Radanovich	Y	Y	Y	Y	Y	Y
20 Costa	?	Y	Y	Y	Y	Y
21 Nunes	Y	Y	Y	Y	N	Y
22 McCarthy	Y	Y	Y	Y	Y	Y
23 Capps	Y	Y	Y	Y	Y	Y
24 Gallegly	Y	Y	Y	Y	Y	Y
25 McKeon	Y	Y	Y	Y	Y	Y
26 Dreier	Y	Y	Y	Y	Y	Y
27 Sherman	Y	Y	Y	Y	Y	Y
28 Berman	Y	Y	Y	Y	Y	Y
29 Schiff	Y	Y	Y	Y	Y	Y
30 Waxman	Y	Y	Y	Y	Y	Y
31 Becerra	+	+	+	+	+	Y
32 Chu	Y	Y	Y	Y	Y	Y
33 Watson	Y	Y	Y	Y	Y	Y
34 Roybal-Allard	Y	Y	Y	Y	Y	Y
35 Waters	Y	Y	?	Y	Y	?
36 Harman	?	?	?	?	?	?
37 Richardson	Y	Y	Y	?	Y	Y
38 Napolitano	Y	Y	Y	Y	Y	Y
39 Sánchez, Linda	Y	Y	Y	Y	Y	Y
40 Royce	Y	Y	Y	Y	N	Y
41 Lewis	Y	Y	Y	Y	N	Y
42 Miller, Gary	Y	Y	Y	Y	N	Y
43 Baca	Y	Y	Y	Y	Y	Y
44 Calvert	Y	Y	Y	Y	N	Y
45 Bono Mack	Y	Y	Y	Y	Y	Y
46 Rohrabacher	?	?	?	Y	N	Y
47 Sanchez, Loretta	?	?	?	Y	Y	Y
48 Campbell	Y	Y	Y	Y	N	Y
49 Issa	Y	Y	Y	Y	Y	Y
50 Bilbray	Y	Y	Y	Y	Y	Y
51 Filner	Y	Y	Y	Y	Y	Y
52 Hunter	Y	Y	Y	Y	N	Y
53 Davis	Y	Y	Y	Y	Y	Y

	221	222	223	224	225	226
COLORADO						
1 DeGette	Y	Y	Y	Y	Y	Y
2 Polis	Y	Y	Y	Y	Y	Y
3 Salazar	Y	Y	Y	Y	Y	Y
4 Markey	Y	Y	Y	Y	Y	Y
5 Lamborn	Y	Y	Y	Y	N	Y
6 Coffman	Y	Y	Y	Y	N	Y
7 Perlmutter	Y	Y	Y	Y	Y	Y
CONNECTICUT						
1 Larson	Y	Y	Y	Y	Y	Y
2 Courtney	Y	Y	Y	Y	Y	Y
3 DeLauro	Y	Y	Y	Y	Y	Y
4 Himes	Y	Y	Y	Y	Y	Y
5 Murphy	Y	Y	Y	Y	Y	Y
DELAWARE						
AL Castle	Y	Y	Y	Y	Y	Y
FLORIDA						
1 Miller	Y	Y	Y	Y	N	Y
2 Boyd	Y	Y	Y	Y	Y	Y
3 Brown	?	?	?	Y	Y	Y
4 Crenshaw	Y	Y	Y	Y	Y	Y
5 Brown-Waite	Y	Y	Y	Y	Y	Y
6 Stearns	Y	Y	Y	Y	N	Y
7 Mica	Y	Y	Y	Y	N	Y
8 Grayson	Y	Y	Y	Y	Y	Y
9 Bilirakis	Y	Y	Y	Y	Y	Y
10 Young	?	?	?	Y	Y	Y
11 Castor	?	?	?	Y	Y	Y
12 Putnam	Y	Y	Y	Y	Y	Y
13 Buchanan	Y	Y	Y	Y	Y	Y
14 Mack	?	?	?	Y	N	Y
15 Posey	Y	Y	Y	Y	Y	Y
16 Rooney	Y	Y	Y	Y	N	Y
17 Meek	Y	Y	Y	Y	Y	Y
18 Ros-Lehtinen	Y	Y	Y	Y	Y	Y
19 Deutch	Y	Y	Y	Y	Y	Y
20 Wasserman Schultz	Y	Y	Y	Y	Y	Y
21 Diaz-Balart, L.	Y	Y	Y	Y	Y	Y
22 Klein	Y	Y	Y	Y	Y	Y
23 Hastings	Y	Y	Y	Y	Y	Y
24 Kosmas	?	Y	Y	Y	Y	Y
25 Diaz-Balart, M.	Y	Y	Y	Y	Y	Y
GEORGIA						
1 Kingston	Y	Y	Y	Y	N	Y
2 Bishop	?	Y	Y	Y	Y	Y
3 Westmoreland	Y	Y	Y	Y	N	Y
4 Johnson	Y	Y	Y	Y	Y	Y
5 Lewis	Y	Y	Y	Y	Y	Y
6 Price	?	?	?	?	?	?
7 Linder	Y	Y	Y	Y	N	Y
8 Marshall	Y	Y	Y	Y	Y	?
9 Vacant						
10 Broun	Y	Y	Y	Y	N	Y
11 Gingrey	?	?	?	Y	N	Y
12 Barrow	Y	Y	Y	Y	Y	Y
13 Scott	Y	Y	Y	Y	Y	Y
HAWAII						
1 Vacant						
2 Hirono	Y	Y	Y	Y	Y	Y
IDAHO						
1 Minnick	Y	Y	Y	Y	Y	Y
2 Simpson	?	?	?	Y	Y	Y
ILLINOIS						
1 Rush	?	?	?	Y	Y	Y
2 Jackson	Y	Y	Y	Y	Y	Y
3 Lipinski	?	?	?	Y	Y	Y
4 Gutierrez	+	+	+	Y	Y	Y
5 Quigley	Y	Y	Y	Y	Y	Y
6 Roskam	Y	Y	Y	Y	N	Y
7 Davis	?	?	?	Y	Y	Y
8 Bean	Y	Y	Y	Y	Y	Y
9 Schakowsky	Y	Y	Y	Y	Y	Y
10 Kirk	?	?	?	Y	Y	Y
11 Halvorson	Y	Y	Y	Y	Y	Y
12 Costello	Y	Y	Y	Y	Y	Y
13 Biggert	Y	Y	Y	Y	Y	Y
14 Foster	Y	Y	Y	Y	Y	Y
15 Johnson	?	?	?	Y	Y	Y

	221	222	223	224	225	226
16 **Manzullo**	Y	Y	Y	Y	Y	Y
17 Hare	Y	Y	Y	Y	Y	Y
18 **Schock**	Y	Y	Y	Y	Y	Y
19 **Shimkus**	Y	Y	Y	Y	N	Y
INDIANA						
1 Visclosky	Y	Y	Y	Y	Y	Y
2 Donnelly	Y	Y	Y	Y	Y	Y
3 **Souder**	?	?	?	?	?	+
4 **Buyer**	Y	Y	?	Y	Y	Y
5 **Burton**	Y	Y	Y	Y	N	Y
6 **Pence**	Y	Y	Y	Y	N	Y
7 Carson	Y	Y	Y	Y	Y	Y
8 Ellsworth	Y	Y	Y	Y	Y	Y
9 Hill	Y	Y	Y	Y	Y	Y
IOWA						
1 Braley	Y	Y	Y	Y	Y	Y
2 Loebsack	Y	Y	Y	Y	Y	Y
3 Boswell	Y	Y	Y	Y	Y	Y
4 **Latham**	Y	Y	Y	Y	Y	Y
5 **King**	Y	Y	Y	Y	N	Y
KANSAS						
1 **Moran**	Y	Y	Y	Y	Y	Y
2 **Jenkins**	Y	Y	Y	Y	Y	Y
3 Moore	Y	Y	Y	Y	Y	Y
4 **Tiahrt**	?	?	?	Y	Y	Y
KENTUCKY						
1 **Whitfield**	Y	Y	Y	Y	Y	Y
2 **Guthrie**	Y	Y	Y	Y	Y	Y
3 Yarmuth	Y	Y	Y	Y	Y	Y
4 **Davis**	Y	Y	Y	Y	Y	Y
5 **Rogers**	Y	Y	Y	Y	Y	Y
6 Chandler	Y	Y	Y	Y	Y	Y
LOUISIANA						
1 **Scalise**	Y	Y	Y	Y	N	Y
2 **Cao**	?	?	?	Y	Y	Y
3 Melancon	Y	Y	Y	Y	Y	Y
4 **Fleming**	?	?	?	Y	N	Y
5 **Alexander**	Y	Y	Y	Y	Y	Y
6 **Cassidy**	Y	Y	Y	Y	Y	Y
7 **Boustany**	Y	Y	Y	Y	Y	Y
MAINE						
1 Pingree	Y	Y	Y	Y	Y	Y
2 Michaud	Y	Y	Y	Y	Y	Y
MARYLAND						
1 Kratovil	Y	Y	Y	Y	Y	Y
2 Ruppersberger	?	?	?	Y	?	Y
3 Sarbanes	Y	Y	Y	Y	Y	Y
4 Edwards	Y	Y	Y	Y	Y	N
5 Hoyer	Y	Y	Y	Y	Y	Y
6 **Bartlett**	Y	Y	Y	Y	Y	Y
7 Cummings	?	?	?	Y	Y	Y
8 Van Hollen	Y	Y	Y	Y	Y	Y
MASSACHUSETTS						
1 Olver	Y	Y	Y	Y	Y	Y
2 Neal	?	?	?	Y	Y	Y
3 McGovern	Y	Y	Y	Y	Y	Y
4 Frank	Y	Y	Y	Y	Y	Y
5 Tsongas	Y	Y	Y	Y	Y	Y
6 Tierney	Y	Y	Y	Y	Y	Y
7 Markey	Y	Y	Y	Y	Y	Y
8 Capuano	?	?	?	Y	Y	Y
9 Lynch	Y	Y	Y	Y	Y	Y
10 Delahunt	Y	Y	Y	Y	Y	Y
MICHIGAN						
1 Stupak	+	+	+	Y	Y	Y
2 **Hoekstra**	?	?	?	?	?	?
3 **Ehlers**	Y	Y	Y	Y	Y	Y
4 **Camp**	Y	Y	Y	Y	Y	Y
5 Kildee	Y	Y	Y	Y	Y	Y
6 **Upton**	Y	Y	Y	Y	Y	Y
7 Schauer	Y	Y	Y	Y	Y	Y
8 **Rogers**	Y	Y	Y	Y	Y	Y
9 Peters	Y	Y	Y	Y	Y	Y
10 **Miller**	Y	Y	Y	Y	Y	Y
11 **McCotter**	Y	Y	Y	Y	Y	Y
12 Levin	Y	Y	Y	Y	Y	Y
13 Kilpatrick	+	+	+	Y	Y	N
14 Conyers	Y	Y	Y	Y	Y	N
15 Dingell	?	?	?	Y	Y	Y
MINNESOTA						
1 Walz	Y	Y	Y	Y	Y	Y
2 **Kline**	Y	Y	Y	Y	Y	Y
3 **Paulsen**	Y	Y	Y	Y	Y	Y
4 McCollum	Y	Y	Y	Y	Y	Y

	221	222	223	224	225	226
5 Ellison	Y	Y	Y	Y	Y	N
6 **Bachmann**	Y	Y	Y	Y	Y	Y
7 Peterson	Y	Y	Y	Y	Y	Y
8 Oberstar	Y	Y	Y	Y	Y	Y
MISSISSIPPI						
1 Childers	Y	Y	Y	Y	Y	Y
2 Thompson	Y	Y	Y	Y	Y	N
3 **Harper**	Y	Y	Y	Y	Y	Y
4 Taylor	Y	Y	Y	Y	Y	Y
MISSOURI						
1 Clay	Y	Y	Y	Y	Y	Y
2 **Akin**	Y	Y	Y	Y	N	Y
3 Carnahan	Y	Y	Y	Y	Y	Y
4 Skelton	Y	Y	Y	Y	Y	Y
5 Cleaver	Y	Y	Y	Y	Y	Y
6 **Graves**	Y	Y	Y	Y	Y	Y
7 **Blunt**	Y	Y	Y	Y	Y	Y
8 **Emerson**	Y	Y	Y	Y	Y	Y
9 **Luetkemeyer**	Y	Y	Y	Y	Y	Y
MONTANA						
AL **Rehberg**	Y	Y	Y	Y	Y	Y
NEBRASKA						
1 **Fortenberry**	Y	Y	Y	Y	Y	Y
2 **Terry**	Y	Y	Y	Y	Y	Y
3 **Smith**	Y	Y	Y	Y	Y	Y
NEVADA						
1 Berkley	Y	Y	Y	Y	Y	Y
2 **Heller**	Y	Y	Y	Y	Y	Y
3 Titus	Y	Y	Y	Y	Y	Y
NEW HAMPSHIRE						
1 Shea-Porter	Y	Y	Y	Y	Y	Y
2 Hodes	Y	Y	Y	Y	Y	Y
NEW JERSEY						
1 Andrews	Y	Y	Y	Y	Y	Y
2 **LoBiondo**	Y	Y	Y	Y	Y	Y
3 Adler	Y	Y	Y	Y	Y	Y
4 **Smith**	Y	Y	Y	Y	Y	Y
5 **Garrett**	Y	Y	Y	Y	N	Y
6 Pallone	Y	Y	Y	Y	Y	Y
7 **Lance**	Y	Y	Y	Y	Y	Y
8 Pascrell	?	?	?	Y	Y	Y
9 Rothman	Y	Y	Y	Y	Y	Y
10 Payne	Y	Y	Y	Y	Y	N
11 **Frelinghuysen**	Y	Y	Y	Y	Y	Y
12 Holt	Y	Y	Y	Y	Y	Y
13 Sires	Y	Y	Y	Y	Y	Y
NEW MEXICO						
1 Heinrich	Y	Y	Y	Y	Y	Y
2 Teague	Y	Y	Y	Y	Y	Y
3 Luján	Y	Y	Y	Y	Y	Y
NEW YORK						
1 Bishop	Y	Y	Y	Y	Y	Y
2 Israel	?	?	?	Y	Y	Y
3 **King**	Y	Y	Y	Y	Y	Y
4 McCarthy	Y	Y	Y	Y	Y	Y
5 Ackerman	Y	Y	Y	Y	Y	Y
6 Meeks	Y	Y	Y	Y	Y	N
7 Crowley	Y	Y	Y	Y	Y	Y
8 Nadler	Y	Y	Y	Y	Y	Y
9 Weiner	?	?	?	Y	Y	Y
10 Towns	?	?	?	Y	Y	N
11 Clarke	Y	Y	Y	Y	Y	Y
12 Volázquoz	Y	Y	Y	?	Y	Y
13 McMahon	Y	Y	Y	Y	Y	Y
14 Maloney	Y	Y	Y	Y	Y	Y
15 Rangel	Y	Y	Y	Y	Y	Y
16 Serrano	Y	Y	Y	Y	Y	Y
17 Engel	Y	Y	Y	Y	Y	Y
18 Lowey	Y	Y	Y	Y	Y	Y
19 Hall	Y	Y	Y	Y	Y	Y
20 Murphy	Y	Y	Y	Y	Y	Y
21 Tonko	Y	Y	Y	Y	Y	Y
22 Hinchey	?	?	?	Y	Y	Y
23 Owens	Y	Y	Y	Y	Y	Y
24 Arcuri	Y	Y	Y	Y	Y	Y
25 Maffei	?	?	?	Y	Y	Y
26 **Lee**	Y	Y	Y	Y	Y	Y
27 Higgins	?	?	?	Y	Y	Y
28 Slaughter	Y	Y	Y	Y	Y	Y
29 Vacant						
NORTH CAROLINA						
1 Butterfield	Y	Y	Y	Y	Y	Y
2 Etheridge	Y	Y	Y	Y	Y	Y
3 **Jones**	Y	Y	Y	Y	Y	Y
4 Price	Y	Y	Y	Y	Y	Y

	221	222	223	224	225	226
5 **Foxx**	Y	Y	Y	Y	N	Y
6 **Coble**	?	?	?	Y	Y	Y
7 McIntyre	Y	Y	Y	Y	Y	Y
8 Kissell	?	?	?	Y	Y	Y
9 **Myrick**	Y	Y	Y	Y	N	Y
10 **McHenry**	Y	Y	Y	Y	Y	Y
11 Shuler	Y	Y	Y	Y	Y	Y
12 Watt	Y	Y	Y	Y	Y	N
13 Miller	Y	Y	Y	Y	Y	Y
NORTH DAKOTA						
AL Pomeroy	Y	Y	Y	Y	Y	Y
OHIO						
1 Driehaus	Y	Y	Y	Y	Y	Y
2 **Schmidt**	Y	Y	Y	Y	N	Y
3 **Turner**	Y	Y	Y	Y	Y	Y
4 **Jordan**	Y	Y	Y	Y	N	Y
5 **Latta**	Y	Y	Y	Y	Y	Y
6 Wilson	Y	Y	Y	Y	Y	Y
7 **Austria**	Y	Y	Y	Y	Y	Y
8 **Boehner**	Y	Y	Y	Y	Y	Y
9 Kaptur	?	?	?	Y	Y	Y
10 Kucinich	Y	Y	Y	Y	Y	Y
11 Fudge	?	?	?	Y	Y	Y
12 **Tiberi**	Y	Y	Y	Y	Y	Y
13 Sutton	Y	Y	Y	Y	Y	Y
14 **LaTourette**	Y	Y	Y	Y	Y	Y
15 Kilroy	Y	Y	Y	Y	Y	Y
16 Boccieri	Y	Y	Y	Y	Y	Y
17 Ryan	?	Y	Y	Y	Y	Y
18 Space	Y	Y	Y	Y	Y	Y
OKLAHOMA						
1 **Sullivan**	Y	Y	Y	Y	Y	Y
2 Boren	Y	Y	Y	Y	Y	Y
3 **Lucas**	Y	Y	Y	Y	Y	Y
4 **Cole**	Y	Y	Y	Y	Y	Y
5 **Fallin**	?	?	?	?	?	?
OREGON						
1 Wu	Y	Y	Y	Y	Y	Y
2 **Walden**	Y	Y	Y	Y	Y	Y
3 Blumenauer	Y	Y	Y	Y	Y	Y
4 DeFazio	Y	Y	Y	Y	Y	Y
5 Schrader	Y	Y	Y	Y	Y	Y
PENNSYLVANIA						
1 Brady	?	?	?	Y	Y	Y
2 Fattah	Y	Y	Y	Y	Y	Y
3 Dahlkemper	Y	Y	Y	Y	Y	Y
4 Altmire	Y	Y	Y	Y	Y	Y
5 **Thompson**	Y	Y	Y	Y	Y	Y
6 **Gerlach**	Y	Y	Y	Y	Y	Y
7 Sestak	Y	Y	Y	Y	Y	Y
8 Murphy, P.	Y	Y	Y	Y	Y	Y
9 **Shuster**	Y	Y	Y	Y	Y	Y
10 Carney	Y	Y	Y	Y	Y	Y
11 Kanjorski	Y	Y	Y	Y	Y	Y
12 Vacant						
13 Schwartz	Y	Y	Y	+	Y	Y
14 Doyle	Y	Y	Y	Y	Y	Y
15 **Dent**	Y	Y	Y	Y	Y	Y
16 **Pitts**	Y	Y	Y	Y	Y	Y
17 Holden	Y	Y	Y	Y	Y	Y
18 **Murphy, T.**	Y	Y	Y	Y	Y	Y
19 **Platts**	Y	Y	Y	Y	Y	Y
RIIODE ISLAND						
1 Kennedy	Y	Y	Y	Y	Y	Y
2 Langevin	Y	Y	Y	Y	Y	Y
SOUTH CAROLINA						
1 **Brown**	Y	Y	Y	Y	N	Y
2 **Wilson**	Y	Y	Y	Y	Y	Y
3 **Barrett**	?	?	?	?	?	?
4 **Inglis**	?	?	?	Y	N	Y
5 Spratt	Y	Y	Y	Y	Y	Y
6 Clyburn	Y	Y	Y	Y	Y	N
SOUTH DAKOTA						
AL Herseth Sandlin	Y	Y	Y	Y	Y	Y
TENNESSEE						
1 **Roe**	Y	Y	Y	Y	Y	Y
2 **Duncan**	Y	Y	Y	Y	N	Y
3 **Wamp**	?	?	?	?	?	?
4 Davis	Y	Y	Y	Y	Y	Y
5 Cooper	Y	Y	Y	Y	Y	Y
6 Gordon	Y	Y	Y	Y	Y	Y
7 **Blackburn**	Y	Y	Y	Y	N	Y
8 Tanner	Y	Y	Y	Y	Y	Y
9 Cohen	Y	Y	Y	Y	Y	Y

	221	222	223	224	225	226
TEXAS						
1 **Gohmert**	?	?	?	?	?	?
2 **Poe**	Y	Y	Y	Y	N	Y
3 **Johnson, S.**	Y	Y	Y	Y	N	Y
4 **Hall**	Y	Y	Y	Y	Y	Y
5 **Hensarling**	Y	Y	Y	Y	N	Y
6 **Barton**	Y	Y	Y	Y	Y	Y
7 **Culberson**	Y	Y	Y	Y	N	Y
8 **Brady**	?	?	?	?	N	Y
9 Green, A.	Y	Y	Y	Y	Y	Y
10 **McCaul**	Y	Y	Y	Y	Y	Y
11 **Conaway**	Y	Y	Y	Y	Y	Y
12 **Granger**	Y	Y	Y	Y	N	Y
13 **Thornberry**	Y	Y	Y	Y	Y	Y
14 **Paul**	Y	Y	Y	Y	N	Y
15 Hinojosa	Y	Y	Y	Y	Y	Y
16 Reyes	Y	Y	Y	?	?	Y
17 Edwards	Y	Y	Y	Y	Y	Y
18 Jackson Lee	Y	Y	Y	Y	Y	N
19 **Neugebauer**	Y	Y	Y	Y	Y	Y
20 Gonzalez	Y	Y	Y	?	?	Y
21 **Smith**	Y	Y	Y	Y	Y	Y
22 **Olson**	Y	Y	?	Y	Y	Y
23 Rodriguez	Y	Y	Y	Y	Y	Y
24 **Marchant**	Y	Y	Y	Y	N	Y
25 Doggett	Y	Y	Y	Y	Y	Y
26 **Burgess**	Y	Y	Y	Y	N	Y
27 Ortiz	Y	Y	Y	Y	Y	Y
28 Cuellar	Y	Y	Y	Y	Y	Y
29 Green, G.	Y	Y	Y	Y	Y	Y
30 Johnson, E.	Y	Y	Y	Y	Y	N
31 **Carter**	Y	Y	Y	Y	N	Y
32 **Sessions**	Y	Y	Y	Y	N	Y
UTAH						
1 **Bishop**	Y	Y	Y	Y	N	Y
2 Matheson	Y	Y	Y	Y	Y	Y
3 **Chaffetz**	Y	Y	Y	Y	N	Y
VERMONT						
AL Welch	Y	Y	Y	Y	Y	Y
VIRGINIA						
1 **Wittman**	Y	Y	Y	Y	Y	Y
2 Nye	Y	Y	Y	Y	Y	Y
3 Scott	Y	Y	Y	Y	Y	Y
4 **Forbes**	Y	Y	Y	Y	Y	Y
5 Perriello	Y	Y	Y	Y	Y	Y
6 **Goodlatte**	Y	Y	Y	Y	N	Y
7 **Cantor**	Y	Y	Y	Y	N	Y
8 Moran	?	?	?	Y	Y	N
9 Boucher	Y	Y	Y	Y	Y	Y
10 **Wolf**	Y	Y	Y	Y	Y	Y
11 Connolly	Y	Y	Y	Y	Y	Y
WASHINGTON						
1 Inslee	Y	Y	Y	Y	Y	Y
2 Larsen	Y	Y	Y	Y	Y	Y
3 Baird	Y	Y	Y	Y	Y	Y
4 **Hastings**	Y	Y	Y	Y	N	Y
5 **McMorris Rodgers**	Y	Y	Y	Y	Y	Y
6 Dicks	Y	Y	Y	Y	Y	Y
7 McDermott	Y	Y	Y	Y	Y	Y
8 **Reichert**	Y	Y	Y	Y	Y	Y
9 Smith	Y	Y	Y	Y	Y	Y
WEST VIRGINIA						
1 Mollohan	?	?	?	?	?	Y
2 **Capito**	Y	Y	Y	Y	Y	Y
3 Rahall	Y	Y	Y	Y	Y	Y
WISCONSIN						
1 **Ryan**	Y	Y	Y	Y	N	Y
2 Baldwin	Y	Y	Y	Y	Y	Y
3 Kind	Y	Y	Y	Y	Y	Y
4 Moore	?	?	?	?	?	?
5 **Sensenbrenner**	Y	Y	Y	Y	N	Y
6 **Petri**	Y	Y	Y	Y	N	Y
7 Obey	Y	Y	Y	Y	Y	Y
8 Kagen	Y	Y	Y	Y	Y	Y
WYOMING						
AL **Lummis**	Y	Y	Y	Y	N	Y
DELEGATES						
Faleomavaega (A.S.)						
Norton (D.C.)						
Bordallo (Guam)						
Sablan (N. Marianas)						
Pierluisi (P.R.)						
Christensen (V.I.)						

IN THE HOUSE | By Vote Number

227. HR 5013. Defense Department Acquisition Overhaul/ **Significant Findings Report.** Hall, D-N.Y., amendment that would require the director of the Office of Performance Assessment and Root Cause Analysis to include performance assessments with significant findings in its annual report. Adopted in Committee of the Whole 416-0: D 247-0; R 169-0. April 28, 2010.

228. HR 5013. Defense Department Acquisition Overhaul/ **Industrial Base Council.** Connolly, D-Va., amendment that would establish an Industrial Base Council within the Defense Department to provide input on budget and policy matters, including matters pertaining to the national defense technology and industrial base. It also would require an annual report to Congress on the council's activities. Adopted in Committee of the Whole 417-2: D 249-0; R 168-2. April 28, 2010.

229. HR 5013. Defense Department Acquisition Overhaul/ **Recommit.** Buyer, R-Ind., motion to recommit the bill to the Armed Services Committee with instructions that it be immediately reported back with an amendment that would require Defense Department health care contract bids to include the cost of compliance with health care overhaul laws. It also would require the Defense secretary to submit a report to Congress that includes the cost of agency compliance with such laws. Motion agreed to 419-1: D 247-1; R 172-0. April 28, 2010.

230. HR 5013. Defense Department Acquisition Overhaul/Passage. Passage of the bill that would require the Defense Department to improve its acquisition practices. It would require the department to create a performance management system, establish financial incentives and penalties to ensure that goals are being met, and reward and provide career development for its acquisition workforce. It would require potential federal contractors to provide certification that they do not have seriously delinquent tax debts. Passed 417-3: D 247-0; R 170-3. A "yea" was a vote in support of the president's position. April 28, 2010.

231. HR 2499. Puerto Rico Political Status/Previous Question. Polis, D-Colo., motion to order the previous question (thus ending debate and possibility of amendment) on adoption of the rule (H Res 1305) to provide for House floor consideration of the bill that would establish a two-stage process to determine Puerto Rico's political status. Motion agreed to 218-188: D 218-17; R 0-171. April 29, 2010.

232. HR 2499. Puerto Rico Political Status/Rule. Adoption of the rule (H Res 1305) that would provide for House floor consideration of the bill that would establish a two-stage process to determine Puerto Rico's political status. Adopted 222-190: D 221-20; R 1-170. April 29, 2010.

	227	228	229	230	231	232
ALABAMA						
1 Bonner	Y	Y	Y	Y	N	N
2 Bright	Y	Y	Y	Y	Y	Y
3 Rogers	Y	Y	Y	Y	N	N
4 Aderholt	Y	Y	Y	Y	N	N
5 Griffith	Y	Y	Y	Y	N	N
6 Bachus	Y	Y	Y	Y	N	N
7 Davis	?	?	?	?	?	?
ALASKA						
AL Young	Y	Y	Y	Y	N	N
ARIZONA						
1 Kirkpatrick	Y	Y	Y	Y	N	N
2 Franks	Y	Y	Y	Y	N	N
3 Shadegg	Y	Y	Y	Y	N	N
4 Pastor	Y	Y	Y	Y	Y	Y
5 Mitchell	Y	Y	Y	Y	N	N
6 Flake	Y	N	Y	N	N	N
7 Grijalva	Y	Y	Y	Y	Y	Y
8 Giffords	Y	Y	Y	Y	N	N
ARKANSAS						
1 Berry	Y	Y	Y	Y	Y	Y
2 Snyder	Y	Y	Y	Y	Y	Y
3 Boozman	Y	Y	Y	Y	N	N
4 Ross	Y	Y	Y	Y	Y	Y
CALIFORNIA						
1 Thompson	Y	Y	Y	Y	Y	Y
2 Herger	Y	Y	Y	Y	N	N
3 Lungren	Y	Y	Y	Y	N	N
4 McClintock	Y	Y	Y	Y	N	N
5 Matsui	Y	Y	Y	Y	Y	Y
6 Woolsey	Y	Y	Y	Y	Y	Y
7 Miller, George	Y	Y	Y	Y	Y	Y
8 Pelosi						
9 Lee	Y	Y	Y	Y	Y	Y
10 Garamendi	Y	Y	Y	Y	Y	Y
11 McNerney	Y	Y	Y	Y	Y	Y
12 Speier	Y	Y	Y	Y	Y	Y
13 Stark	Y	Y	Y	Y	Y	?
14 Eshoo	Y	Y	Y	Y	Y	Y
15 Honda	Y	Y	Y	Y	N	N
16 Lofgren	Y	Y	Y	Y	Y	Y
17 Farr	Y	Y	Y	Y	Y	Y
18 Cardoza	Y	Y	Y	Y	Y	Y
19 Radanovich	Y	Y	Y	Y	N	N
20 Costa	Y	Y	Y	Y	Y	Y
21 Nunes	Y	Y	Y	Y	N	N
22 McCarthy	Y	Y	Y	Y	N	N
23 Capps	Y	Y	Y	Y	Y	Y
24 Gallegly	Y	Y	Y	Y	N	N
25 McKeon	Y	Y	Y	Y	N	N
26 Dreier	Y	Y	Y	Y	N	N
27 Sherman	Y	Y	Y	Y	Y	Y
28 Berman	Y	Y	Y	Y	Y	Y
29 Schiff	Y	Y	Y	Y	Y	Y
30 Waxman	Y	Y	Y	Y	Y	Y
31 Becerra	Y	Y	Y	Y	Y	Y
32 Chu	Y	Y	Y	Y	Y	Y
33 Watson	Y	Y	Y	Y	Y	Y
34 Roybal-Allard	Y	Y	Y	Y	?	Y
35 Waters	?	Y	Y	Y	?	Y
36 Harman	?	?	?	?	Y	Y
37 Richardson	Y	Y	Y	Y	Y	Y
38 Napolitano	Y	Y	Y	Y	Y	Y
39 Sánchez, Linda	Y	Y	Y	Y	Y	Y
40 Royce	Y	Y	Y	Y	N	N
41 Lewis	Y	Y	Y	Y	N	N
42 Miller, Gary	Y	Y	Y	Y	N	N
43 Baca	Y	Y	Y	Y	Y	Y
44 Calvert	Y	Y	Y	Y	N	N
45 Bono Mack	Y	Y	Y	Y	N	N
46 Rohrabacher	Y	Y	Y	Y	N	N
47 Sanchez, Loretta	Y	Y	Y	Y	Y	Y
48 Campbell	Y	N	Y	Y	N	N
49 Issa	Y	Y	Y	Y	N	N
50 Bilbray	Y	Y	Y	Y	N	N
51 Filner	Y	Y	Y	Y	Y	Y
52 Hunter	Y	Y	Y	Y	N	N
53 Davis	Y	Y	Y	Y	Y	Y
COLORADO						
1 DeGette	?	?	?	?	?	?
2 Polis	Y	Y	Y	Y	Y	Y
3 Salazar	Y	Y	Y	Y	Y	Y
4 Markey	Y	Y	Y	Y	Y	Y
5 Lamborn	Y	Y	Y	Y	N	N
6 Coffman	Y	Y	Y	Y	N	N
7 Perlmutter	Y	Y	Y	Y	Y	Y
CONNECTICUT						
1 Larson	Y	Y	Y	Y	Y	Y
2 Courtney	Y	Y	Y	Y	Y	Y
3 DeLauro	Y	Y	Y	Y	Y	Y
4 Himes	Y	Y	Y	Y	Y	Y
5 Murphy	Y	Y	Y	Y	Y	Y
DELAWARE						
AL Castle	Y	Y	Y	Y	N	N
FLORIDA						
1 Miller	Y	Y	Y	Y	N	N
2 Boyd	Y	Y	Y	Y	Y	Y
3 Brown	Y	Y	Y	Y	Y	Y
4 Crenshaw	Y	Y	Y	Y	N	N
5 Brown-Waite	Y	Y	Y	Y	N	N
6 Stearns	Y	Y	Y	Y	N	N
7 Mica	Y	Y	Y	Y	N	N
8 Grayson	Y	Y	Y	Y	Y	Y
9 Bilirakis	Y	Y	Y	Y	N	N
10 Young	Y	Y	Y	Y	N	N
11 Castor	Y	Y	Y	Y	Y	Y
12 Putnam	Y	Y	Y	Y	N	N
13 Buchanan	Y	Y	Y	Y	?	N
14 Mack	Y	Y	Y	Y	N	N
15 Posey	Y	Y	Y	Y	N	N
16 Rooney	Y	Y	Y	Y	N	N
17 Meek	Y	Y	Y	Y	Y	Y
18 Ros-Lehtinen	Y	Y	Y	Y	N	N
19 Deutch	Y	Y	Y	Y	Y	Y
20 Wasserman Schultz	Y	Y	Y	Y	Y	Y
21 Diaz-Balart, L.	Y	Y	Y	Y	N	N
22 Klein	Y	Y	Y	Y	Y	Y
23 Hastings	Y	Y	Y	Y	Y	Y
24 Kosmas	Y	Y	Y	Y	Y	Y
25 Diaz-Balart, M.	Y	Y	Y	Y	N	N
GEORGIA						
1 Kingston	Y	Y	Y	Y	N	N
2 Bishop	Y	Y	Y	Y	Y	Y
3 Westmoreland	Y	Y	Y	Y	N	N
4 Johnson	Y	?	Y	Y	?	Y
5 Lewis	Y	Y	Y	Y	Y	Y
6 Price	Y	Y	Y	Y	N	N
7 Linder	Y	Y	Y	Y	N	N
8 Marshall	Y	Y	Y	Y	Y	Y
9 Vacant						
10 Broun	Y	Y	Y	N	N	N
11 Gingrey	Y	Y	Y	N	N	N
12 Barrow	Y	Y	Y	Y	Y	Y
13 Scott	Y	Y	Y	Y	Y	Y
HAWAII						
1 Vacant						
2 Hirono	Y	Y	Y	Y	Y	Y
IDAHO						
1 Minnick	Y	Y	Y	Y	N	N
2 Simpson	Y	Y	Y	Y	N	N
ILLINOIS						
1 Rush	Y	Y	Y	Y	Y	Y
2 Jackson	Y	Y	Y	Y	Y	Y
3 Lipinski	Y	Y	Y	Y	Y	Y
4 Gutierrez	Y	Y	Y	Y	N	Y
5 Quigley	Y	Y	Y	Y	Y	Y
6 Roskam	Y	Y	Y	Y	N	N
7 Davis	Y	Y	Y	Y	Y	N
8 Bean	Y	Y	Y	Y	Y	Y
9 Schakowsky	Y	Y	Y	Y	Y	Y
10 Kirk	Y	Y	Y	Y	N	N
11 Halvorson	Y	Y	Y	Y	Y	Y
12 Costello	Y	Y	Y	Y	Y	Y
13 Biggert	Y	Y	Y	Y	N	N
14 Foster	Y	Y	Y	Y	Y	Y
15 Johnson	Y	Y	Y	Y	N	N

KEY Republicans Democrats

Y Voted for (yea)	X Paired against
# Paired for	– Announced against
+ Announced for	P Voted "present"
N Voted against (nay)	

C Voted "present" to avoid possible conflict of interest
? Did not vote or otherwise make a position known

	227	228	229	230	231	232
16 **Manzullo**	Y	Y	Y	Y	N	N
17 Hare	Y	Y	Y	Y	Y	Y
18 **Schock**	Y	Y	Y	Y	N	N
19 **Shimkus**	Y	Y	Y	Y	N	N
INDIANA						
1 Visclosky	Y	Y	Y	Y	Y	Y
2 Donnelly	Y	Y	Y	Y	N	Y
3 **Souder**	Y	Y	Y	Y	N	N
4 **Buyer**	Y	Y	Y	Y	N	N
5 **Burton**	Y	Y	Y	Y	N	N
6 **Pence**	Y	Y	Y	Y	N	N
7 Carson	Y	Y	Y	Y	Y	Y
8 Ellsworth	Y	Y	Y	Y	Y	Y
9 Hill	Y	Y	Y	Y	N	N
IOWA						
1 Braley	Y	Y	Y	Y	Y	Y
2 Loebsack	Y	Y	Y	Y	Y	Y
3 Boswell	Y	Y	Y	Y	Y	Y
4 **Latham**	Y	Y	Y	Y	N	N
5 **King**	Y	Y	Y	Y	N	N
KANSAS						
1 **Moran**	Y	Y	Y	Y	N	N
2 **Jenkins**	Y	Y	Y	Y	N	N
3 Moore	Y	Y	Y	Y	Y	Y
4 **Tiahrt**	Y	Y	Y	Y	N	N
KENTUCKY						
1 **Whitfield**	Y	Y	Y	Y	N	N
2 **Guthrie**	Y	Y	Y	Y	N	N
3 Yarmuth	Y	Y	Y	Y	Y	Y
4 **Davis**	Y	Y	Y	Y	N	N
5 **Rogers**	Y	Y	Y	Y	N	N
6 Chandler	Y	Y	Y	Y	Y	Y
LOUISIANA						
1 **Scalise**	Y	Y	Y	Y	N	N
2 **Cao**	Y	Y	Y	Y	N	Y
3 Melancon	Y	Y	Y	Y	?	?
4 **Fleming**	Y	Y	Y	Y	N	N
5 **Alexander**	Y	Y	Y	Y	N	N
6 **Cassidy**	Y	Y	Y	Y	N	N
7 **Boustany**	Y	Y	Y	Y	N	N
MAINE						
1 Pingree	Y	Y	Y	Y	?	?
2 Michaud	Y	Y	Y	Y	Y	Y
MARYLAND						
1 Kratovil	Y	Y	Y	Y	N	N
2 Ruppersberger	Y	Y	Y	Y	Y	Y
3 Sarbanes	Y	Y	Y	Y	Y	Y
4 Edwards	Y	Y	Y	Y	Y	Y
5 Hoyer	Y	Y	Y	Y	Y	Y
6 **Bartlett**	Y	Y	Y	Y	N	N
7 Cummings	Y	Y	Y	Y	Y	Y
8 Van Hollen	Y	Y	Y	Y	Y	Y
MASSACHUSETTS						
1 Olver	Y	Y	Y	Y	Y	Y
2 Neal	Y	Y	Y	Y	Y	Y
3 McGovern	Y	Y	Y	Y	Y	Y
4 Frank	Y	Y	Y	Y	Y	Y
5 Tsongas	Y	Y	Y	Y	Y	Y
6 Tierney	Y	Y	Y	Y	Y	Y
7 Markey	Y	Y	Y	Y	Y	Y
8 Capuano	Y	Y	Y	Y	Y	Y
9 Lynch	Y	Y	Y	Y	Y	Y
10 Delahunt	Y	Y	Y	Y	Y	Y
MICHIGAN						
1 Stupak	Y	Y	Y	Y	Y	Y
2 **Hoekstra**	?	?	?	?	?	?
3 **Ehlers**	Y	Y	+	Y	N	N
4 **Camp**	Y	Y	Y	Y	N	N
5 Kildee	Y	Y	Y	Y	Y	Y
6 **Upton**	Y	Y	Y	Y	N	N
7 Schauer	Y	Y	Y	Y	Y	Y
8 **Rogers**	Y	Y	Y	Y	N	N
9 Peters	Y	Y	Y	Y	Y	Y
10 **Miller**	Y	Y	Y	Y	N	N
11 **McCotter**	Y	Y	Y	Y	N	N
12 Levin	Y	Y	Y	Y	Y	Y
13 Kilpatrick	Y	Y	Y	Y	Y	Y
14 Conyers	Y	Y	Y	Y	?	Y
15 Dingell	Y	Y	Y	Y	Y	Y
MINNESOTA						
1 Walz	Y	Y	Y	Y	Y	Y
2 **Kline**	Y	?	Y	Y	N	N
3 **Paulsen**	Y	Y	Y	Y	N	N
4 McCollum	Y	Y	Y	Y	Y	Y

	227	228	229	230	231	232
5 Ellison	Y	Y	Y	Y	N	N
6 **Bachmann**	Y	Y	Y	Y	N	N
7 Peterson	Y	Y	Y	Y	Y	Y
8 Oberstar	Y	Y	Y	Y	Y	Y
MISSISSIPPI						
1 Childers	Y	Y	Y	Y	N	N
2 Thompson	Y	Y	Y	Y	Y	Y
3 **Harper**	Y	Y	Y	Y	N	N
4 Taylor	Y	Y	Y	Y	N	N
MISSOURI						
1 Clay	Y	Y	Y	Y	Y	Y
2 **Akin**	Y	Y	Y	Y	N	N
3 Carnahan	Y	Y	Y	Y	Y	Y
4 Skelton	Y	Y	Y	Y	Y	Y
5 Cleaver	Y	Y	Y	Y	Y	Y
6 **Graves**	Y	Y	Y	Y	N	N
7 **Blunt**	Y	Y	Y	Y	N	N
8 **Emerson**	Y	Y	Y	Y	N	N
9 **Luetkemeyer**	Y	Y	Y	Y	N	N
MONTANA						
AL **Rehberg**	Y	Y	Y	Y	N	N
NEBRASKA						
1 **Fortenberry**	Y	Y	Y	Y	N	N
2 **Terry**	Y	Y	Y	Y	N	N
3 **Smith**	Y	Y	Y	Y	N	N
NEVADA						
1 Berkley	Y	Y	Y	Y	Y	Y
2 **Heller**	Y	Y	Y	Y	N	N
3 Titus	Y	Y	Y	Y	Y	Y
NEW HAMPSHIRE						
1 Shea-Porter	Y	Y	Y	Y	Y	Y
2 Hodes	Y	Y	Y	Y	Y	Y
NEW JERSEY						
1 Andrews	Y	Y	Y	Y	Y	Y
2 **LoBiondo**	Y	Y	Y	Y	N	N
3 Adler	Y	Y	Y	Y	Y	Y
4 **Smith**	Y	Y	Y	Y	N	N
5 **Garrett**	Y	Y	Y	Y	N	N
6 Pallone	Y	Y	Y	Y	Y	Y
7 **Lance**	Y	Y	Y	Y	N	N
8 Pascrell	Y	Y	N	Y	Y	Y
9 Rothman	Y	Y	Y	Y	Y	Y
10 Payne	Y	Y	Y	Y	Y	Y
11 **Frelinghuysen**	Y	Y	Y	Y	N	N
12 Holt	Y	Y	Y	Y	Y	Y
13 Sires	Y	Y	Y	Y	Y	Y
NEW MEXICO						
1 Heinrich	Y	Y	Y	Y	Y	Y
2 Teague	?	?	?	?	?	?
3 Luján	Y	Y	Y	Y	Y	Y
NEW YORK						
1 Bishop	Y	Y	Y	Y	Y	Y
2 Israel	Y	Y	Y	Y	Y	Y
3 **King**	Y	Y	Y	Y	N	N
4 McCarthy	Y	Y	Y	Y	Y	Y
5 Ackerman	Y	Y	Y	Y	Y	Y
6 Meeks	?	Y	Y	Y	?	?
7 Crowley	Y	Y	Y	Y	Y	Y
8 Nadler	Y	Y	Y	Y	Y	Y
9 Weiner	Y	Y	Y	Y	N	Y
10 Towns	Y	Y	Y	Y	N	N
11 Clarke	Y	Y	Y	Y	Y	Y
12 Velázquez	Y	Y	Y	Y	N	N
13 McMahon	Y	Y	Y	Y	Y	Y
14 Maloney	Y	Y	Y	Y	Y	Y
15 Rangel	?	?	Y	Y	Y	Y
16 Serrano	?	Y	Y	Y	Y	Y
17 Engel	Y	Y	Y	Y	Y	Y
18 Lowey	Y	Y	Y	Y	Y	Y
19 Hall	Y	Y	Y	Y	Y	Y
20 Murphy	Y	Y	Y	Y	Y	Y
21 Tonko	Y	Y	Y	Y	Y	Y
22 Hinchey	Y	Y	Y	Y	Y	Y
23 Owens	Y	Y	Y	Y	Y	Y
24 Arcuri	Y	Y	Y	Y	Y	Y
25 Maffei	Y	Y	Y	Y	Y	Y
26 **Lee**	Y	Y	Y	Y	N	N
27 Higgins	Y	Y	Y	Y	Y	Y
28 Slaughter	Y	Y	Y	Y	Y	Y
29 Vacant						
NORTH CAROLINA						
1 Butterfield	Y	Y	Y	Y	Y	Y
2 Etheridge	Y	Y	Y	Y	Y	Y
3 **Jones**	Y	Y	Y	Y	N	N
4 Price	Y	Y	Y	Y	Y	Y

	227	228	229	230	231	232
5 **Foxx**	Y	Y	Y	Y	N	N
6 **Coble**	Y	Y	Y	Y	N	N
7 McIntyre	Y	Y	Y	Y	Y	Y
8 Kissell	Y	Y	Y	Y	Y	Y
9 **Myrick**	Y	Y	Y	Y	N	N
10 **McHenry**	Y	Y	Y	Y	N	N
11 Shuler	Y	Y	Y	Y	?	?
12 Watt	Y	Y	Y	Y	Y	Y
13 Miller	Y	?	Y	Y	Y	Y
NORTH DAKOTA						
AL Pomeroy	Y	Y	Y	Y	Y	Y
OHIO						
1 Driehaus	Y	Y	Y	Y	Y	Y
2 **Schmidt**	Y	Y	Y	Y	N	N
3 **Turner**	Y	Y	Y	Y	N	N
4 **Jordan**	Y	Y	Y	Y	N	N
5 **Latta**	Y	Y	Y	Y	N	N
6 Wilson	Y	Y	Y	Y	?	?
7 **Austria**	Y	Y	Y	Y	N	N
8 **Boehner**	Y	Y	Y	Y	N	N
9 Kaptur	Y	Y	Y	Y	Y	Y
10 Kucinich	Y	Y	Y	Y	Y	N
11 Fudge	?	?	?	?	Y	Y
12 **Tiberi**	Y	Y	Y	Y	N	N
13 Sutton	Y	Y	Y	Y	?	Y
14 **LaTourette**	Y	Y	Y	Y	N	N
15 Kilroy	Y	Y	Y	Y	?	N
16 Boccieri	Y	Y	Y	Y	Y	Y
17 Ryan	Y	Y	Y	Y	Y	Y
18 Space	Y	Y	Y	Y	Y	N
OKLAHOMA						
1 **Sullivan**	Y	Y	Y	Y	N	N
2 Boren	Y	Y	Y	Y	N	Y
3 **Lucas**	Y	Y	Y	Y	N	N
4 **Cole**	Y	Y	Y	Y	N	N
5 **Fallin**	?	?	?	?	?	?
OREGON						
1 Wu	Y	Y	Y	Y	Y	Y
2 **Walden**	Y	Y	Y	Y	N	N
3 Blumenauer	Y	Y	Y	Y	Y	Y
4 DeFazio	Y	Y	Y	Y	Y	Y
5 Schrader	Y	Y	Y	Y	Y	Y
PENNSYLVANIA						
1 Brady	Y	Y	Y	Y	Y	Y
2 Fattah	Y	Y	Y	?	Y	Y
3 Dahlkemper	Y	Y	Y	Y	Y	Y
4 Altmire	Y	Y	Y	Y	Y	N
5 **Thompson**	Y	Y	Y	Y	N	N
6 **Gerlach**	Y	Y	Y	Y	N	N
7 Sestak	Y	Y	Y	Y	Y	Y
8 Murphy, P.	Y	Y	Y	Y	Y	Y
9 **Shuster**	Y	Y	Y	Y	N	N
10 Carney	Y	Y	Y	Y	Y	Y
11 Kanjorski	Y	Y	Y	Y	Y	Y
12 Vacant						
13 Schwartz	Y	Y	Y	Y	Y	Y
14 Doyle	Y	Y	Y	Y	Y	Y
15 **Dent**	Y	Y	Y	Y	N	N
16 **Pitts**	Y	Y	Y	Y	N	N
17 Holden	Y	Y	Y	Y	Y	Y
18 **Murphy, T.**	Y	Y	Y	Y	N	N
19 **Platts**	Y	Y	Y	Y	–	N
RHODE ISLAND						
1 Kennedy	Y	Y	Y	Y	Y	Y
2 Langevin	Y	Y	Y	Y	?	Y
SOUTH CAROLINA						
1 **Brown**	Y	Y	Y	Y	N	N
2 **Wilson**	Y	Y	Y	Y	N	N
3 **Barrett**	?	?	?	?	?	?
4 **Inglis**	Y	Y	Y	Y	N	N
5 Spratt	Y	Y	Y	Y	Y	Y
6 Clyburn	Y	Y	Y	Y	Y	Y
SOUTH DAKOTA						
AL Herseth Sandlin	Y	Y	Y	Y	Y	N
TENNESSEE						
1 **Roe**	Y	Y	Y	Y	N	N
2 **Duncan**	Y	Y	Y	Y	N	N
3 **Wamp**	?	?	?	?	?	?
4 Davis	Y	Y	Y	Y	Y	Y
5 Cooper	Y	Y	Y	Y	Y	Y
6 Gordon	?	Y	Y	Y	?	?
7 **Blackburn**	Y	Y	Y	Y	N	N
8 Tanner	?	?	Y	Y	Y	Y
9 Cohen	Y	Y	Y	Y	Y	Y

	227	228	229	230	231	232
TEXAS						
1 **Gohmert**	?	Y	Y	Y	N	N
2 **Poe**	Y	Y	Y	Y	N	?
3 **Johnson, S.**	Y	Y	Y	Y	N	N
4 **Hall**	Y	Y	Y	Y	N	N
5 **Hensarling**	Y	Y	Y	Y	N	N
6 **Barton**	Y	Y	Y	Y	N	N
7 **Culberson**	?	?	Y	Y	N	N
8 **Brady**	Y	Y	Y	Y	N	N
9 Green, A.	Y	Y	Y	Y	Y	Y
10 **McCaul**	Y	Y	Y	Y	N	?
11 **Conaway**	Y	Y	Y	Y	N	N
12 **Granger**	Y	Y	Y	Y	N	N
13 **Thornberry**	?	?	Y	Y	N	N
14 **Paul**	Y	Y	Y	N	N	N
15 Hinojosa	Y	Y	Y	Y	Y	Y
16 Reyes	Y	Y	Y	Y	Y	Y
17 Edwards	Y	Y	Y	Y	Y	Y
18 Jackson Lee	Y	Y	Y	Y	Y	Y
19 **Neugebauer**	Y	Y	Y	Y	N	N
20 Gonzalez	Y	Y	Y	Y	Y	Y
21 **Smith**	Y	Y	Y	Y	N	N
22 **Olson**	Y	Y	Y	Y	N	N
23 Rodriguez	Y	Y	Y	Y	Y	Y
24 **Marchant**	Y	Y	Y	Y	N	N
25 Doggett	Y	Y	Y	Y	Y	Y
26 **Burgess**	Y	Y	Y	Y	N	N
27 Ortiz	Y	Y	Y	Y	Y	Y
28 Cuellar	Y	Y	Y	Y	Y	Y
29 Green, G.	Y	Y	Y	Y	Y	Y
30 Johnson, E.	Y	Y	Y	Y	Y	Y
31 **Carter**	Y	Y	Y	Y	N	N
32 **Sessions**	Y	Y	Y	Y	N	N
UTAH						
1 **Bishop**	Y	Y	Y	Y	N	N
2 Matheson	Y	Y	Y	Y	Y	Y
3 **Chaffetz**	Y	Y	Y	Y	N	N
VERMONT						
AL Welch	Y	Y	Y	Y	Y	Y
VIRGINIA						
1 **Wittman**	Y	Y	Y	Y	N	N
2 Nye	Y	Y	Y	Y	N	N
3 Scott	Y	Y	Y	Y	Y	Y
4 **Forbes**	Y	Y	Y	Y	N	N
5 Perriello	Y	Y	Y	Y	Y	Y
6 **Goodlatte**	Y	Y	Y	Y	N	N
7 **Cantor**	Y	Y	Y	Y	N	N
8 Moran	Y	Y	Y	Y	Y	Y
9 Boucher	Y	Y	Y	Y	Y	Y
10 **Wolf**	?	Y	Y	Y	N	N
11 Connolly	Y	Y	Y	Y	Y	Y
WASHINGTON						
1 Inslee	Y	Y	Y	Y	Y	Y
2 Larsen	Y	Y	Y	Y	Y	Y
3 Baird	Y	Y	Y	Y	Y	Y
4 **Hastings**	Y	Y	Y	Y	N	N
5 **McMorris Rodgers**	Y	Y	Y	Y	N	N
6 Dicks	Y	Y	Y	Y	Y	Y
7 McDermott	Y	Y	Y	Y	Y	Y
8 **Reichert**	Y	Y	Y	Y	N	N
9 Smith	Y	Y	Y	Y	Y	Y
WEST VIRGINIA						
1 Mollohan	Y	Y	Y	Y	?	?
2 **Capito**	Y	Y	Y	Y	N	N
3 Rahall	Y	Y	Y	Y	Y	Y
WISCONSIN						
1 **Ryan**	Y	Y	Y	Y	N	N
2 Baldwin	Y	Y	Y	Y	Y	Y
3 Kind	Y	Y	Y	Y	Y	Y
4 Moore	Y	Y	Y	Y	?	?
5 **Sensenbrenner**	Y	Y	Y	Y	N	N
6 **Petri**	Y	Y	Y	Y	N	N
7 Obey	Y	Y	Y	Y	Y	Y
8 Kagen	Y	Y	Y	Y	Y	Y
WYOMING						
AL **Lummis**	Y	Y	Y	Y	N	N
DELEGATES						
Faleomavaega (A.S.)	?	?				
Norton (D.C.)	Y	Y				
Bordallo (Guam)	Y	Y				
Sablan (N. Marianas)	Y	Y				
Pierluisi (P.R.)	Y	Y				
Christensen (V.I.)	Y	Y				

IN THE HOUSE | By Vote Number

233. HR 2499. Puerto Rico Political Status/Motion to Table.
Slaughter, D-N.Y., motion to table (kill) the Gutierrez, D-Ill., motion to reconsider the vote on adoption of the rule (H Res 1305) that would provide for House floor consideration of the bill that would establish a two-stage process to determine Puerto Rico's political status. Motion agreed to 199-186: D 196-21; R 3-165. April 29, 2010.

234. HR 2499. Puerto Rico Political Status/Commonwealth Option.
Foxx, R-N.C., amendment that would give voters an option to support the current commonwealth status during the second stage of the plebiscite. Adopted in Committee of the Whole 223-179: D 74-160; R 149-19. April 29, 2010.

235. HR 2499. Puerto Rico Political Status/'None of the Above'
Option. Gutierrez, D-Ill., amendment that would give voters an option to choose "none of the above" during the second stage of the plebiscite. Rejected in Committee of the Whole 164-236: D 46-187; R 118-49. April 29, 2010.

236. HR 2499. Puerto Rico Political Status/Spanish Language
Ballots. Gutierrez, D-Ill., amendment that would require plebiscite ballots to be printed in Spanish. Ballots in English would be available upon request. Rejected in Committee of the Whole 13-386: D 12-221; R 1-165. April 29, 2010.

237. HR 2499. Puerto Rico Political Status/Language
Requirements. Burton, R-Ind., amendment that would require plebiscite ballots to be printed in English. It also would require the Puerto Rico election commission to inform voters that if Puerto Rico retains its current political status or is admitted for statehood, the official language requirements of the federal government would apply. Adopted in Committee of the Whole 301-100: D 187-47; R 114-53. April 29, 2010.

	233	234	235	236	237
ALABAMA					
1 **Bonner**	N	Y	Y	N	N
2 Bright	Y	Y	N	N	Y
3 **Rogers**	N	Y	Y	N	N
4 **Aderholt**	N	Y	Y	N	Y
5 **Griffith**	N	Y	Y	N	Y
6 **Bachus**	N	Y	Y	N	N
7 Davis	?	?	?	?	?
ALASKA					
AL **Young**	Y	N	N	N	Y
ARIZONA					
1 Kirkpatrick	N	N	N	N	Y
2 **Franks**	N	Y	Y	N	N
3 **Shadegg**	N	Y	Y	N	N
4 Pastor	Y	N	N	N	Y
5 Mitchell	N	Y	Y	N	Y
6 **Flake**	N	Y	Y	N	Y
7 Grijalva	Y	N	Y	Y	N
8 Giffords	N	Y	Y	N	Y
ARKANSAS					
1 Berry	Y	N	N	N	Y
2 Snyder	Y	N	N	N	Y
3 **Boozman**	N	Y	Y	N	N
4 Ross	Y	Y	N	N	Y
CALIFORNIA					
1 Thompson	Y	N	N	N	Y
2 **Herger**	N	Y	Y	N	Y
3 **Lungren**	N	N	N	N	Y
4 **McClintock**	N	Y	Y	N	Y
5 Matsui	Y	N	N	N	Y
6 Woolsey	Y	Y	Y	N	N
7 Miller, George	Y	N	N	N	Y
8 Pelosi					
9 Lee	Y	N	Y	Y	N
10 Garamendi	Y	N	N	N	Y
11 McNerney	Y	N	N	N	Y
12 Speier	Y	?	?	?	?
13 Stark	?	N	N	N	Y
14 Eshoo	Y	N	N	N	Y
15 Honda	N	Y	Y	Y	N
16 Lofgren	Y	N	N	N	Y
17 Farr	N	N	N	N	Y
18 Cardoza	Y	N	N	N	Y
19 **Radanovich**	N	Y	Y	N	Y
20 Costa	Y	N	N	N	Y
21 **Nunes**	N	?	?	?	?
22 **McCarthy**	N	Y	N	N	Y
23 Capps	Y	N	N	N	Y
24 **Gallegly**	N	Y	Y	N	Y
25 **McKeon**	N	Y	Y	N	N
26 **Dreier**	N	Y	Y	N	Y
27 Sherman	Y	Y	N	N	Y
28 Berman	Y	N	N	N	Y
29 Schiff	Y	N	N	N	Y
30 Waxman	?	?	?	?	?
31 Becerra	Y	Y	Y	N	Y
32 Chu	Y	N	N	N	N
33 Watson	Y	N	N	N	Y
34 Roybal-Allard	Y	Y	Y	N	Y
35 Waters	Y	?	?	?	?
36 Harman	Y	Y	N	N	Y
37 Richardson	Y	Y	N	N	Y
38 Napolitano	Y	N	N	Y	N
39 Sánchez, Linda	?	N	N	N	Y
40 **Royce**	N	Y	Y	N	N
41 **Lewis**	?	Y	Y	N	Y
42 **Miller, Gary**	N	Y	Y	N	N
43 Baca	Y	N	N	N	Y
44 **Calvert**	N	Y	Y	N	Y
45 **Bono Mack**	N	Y	Y	N	Y
46 **Rohrabacher**	N	Y	Y	N	Y
47 Sanchez, Loretta	Y	N	N	N	Y
48 **Campbell**	N	N	N	N	Y
49 **Issa**	N	Y	Y	N	Y
50 **Bilbray**	N	Y	Y	N	N
51 Filner	Y	N	–	–	+
52 **Hunter**	N	Y	Y	N	N
53 Davis	Y	N	N	N	Y

	233	234	235	236	237
COLORADO					
1 DeGette	?	?	?	?	?
2 Polis	Y	N	N	N	Y
3 Salazar	Y	N	N	N	N
4 Markey	Y	N	N	N	Y
5 **Lamborn**	N	Y	Y	N	N
6 **Coffman**	N	Y	Y	N	N
7 Perlmutter	Y	N	N	N	Y
CONNECTICUT					
1 Larson	Y	N	N	N	N
2 Courtney	Y	N	N	N	N
3 DeLauro	Y	Y	N	N	N
4 Himes	Y	Y	N	N	Y
5 Murphy	Y	N	N	N	Y
DELAWARE					
AL Castle	N	N	N	N	Y
FLORIDA					
1 **Miller**	N	Y	Y	N	N
2 Boyd	Y	N	N	N	Y
3 Brown	Y	N	N	N	N
4 **Crenshaw**	N	N	N	N	Y
5 **Brown-Waite**	N	N	N	N	Y
6 **Stearns**	N	Y	Y	N	Y
7 **Mica**	N	Y	N	N	Y
8 Grayson	Y	N	N	N	N
9 **Bilirakis**	N	Y	Y	N	N
10 **Young**	N	Y	Y	N	N
11 Castor	?	?	?	?	?
12 **Putnam**	N	N	N	N	Y
13 **Buchanan**	N	Y	Y	N	N
14 **Mack**	N	Y	N	N	Y
15 **Posey**	N	Y	Y	N	Y
16 **Rooney**	N	Y	Y	?	Y
17 Meek	?	N	N	N	Y
18 **Ros-Lehtinen**	N	N	N	N	Y
19 Deutch	Y	N	N	N	N
20 Wasserman Schultz	Y	N	N	N	Y
21 **Diaz-Balart, L.**	N	N	N	N	Y
22 **Klein**	Y	N	N	N	Y
23 Hastings	?	N	N	N	Y
24 Kosmas	Y	N	N	N	Y
25 **Diaz-Balart, M.**	N	N	N	N	Y
GEORGIA					
1 **Kingston**	N	Y	Y	N	N
2 Bishop	Y	Y	N	N	Y
3 **Westmoreland**	N	Y	Y	N	N
4 Johnson	?	N	N	N	Y
5 Lewis	Y	N	N	?	Y
6 **Price**	N	Y	Y	N	N
7 **Linder**	?	?	?	?	?
8 Marshall	Y	Y	Y	N	Y
9 Vacant					
10 **Broun**	N	Y	Y	N	N
11 **Gingrey**	?	Y	Y	N	N
12 Barrow	Y	N	N	N	Y
13 Scott	Y	N	Y	N	Y
HAWAII					
1 Vacant					
2 Hirono	Y	N	N	N	N
IDAHO					
1 Minnick	N	Y	Y	N	Y
2 **Simpson**	N	Y	Y	N	Y
ILLINOIS					
1 Rush	Y	Y	N	N	N
2 Jackson	Y	Y	N	N	N
3 Lipinski	Y	Y	N	N	Y
4 Gutierrez	N	Y	Y	Y	N
5 Quigley	Y	Y	Y	N	Y
6 **Roskam**	N	Y	Y	N	Y
7 Davis	N	Y	Y	N	N
8 Bean	?	Y	N	N	Y
9 Schakowsky	Y	Y	Y	N	Y
10 **Kirk**	N	Y	Y	N	N
11 Halvorson	Y	Y	N	N	Y
12 Costello	Y	Y	Y	N	Y
13 **Biggert**	N	Y	N	N	Y
14 Foster	Y	Y	N	N	Y
15 **Johnson**	N	N	Y	N	Y

KEY

Member	233	234	235	236	237
16 Manzullo	N	Y	Y	N	Y
17 Hare	Y	N	N	N	Y
18 Schock	N	N	N	N	Y
19 Shimkus	N	Y	Y	N	Y
INDIANA					
1 Visclosky	Y	N	N	N	Y
2 Donnelly	Y	N	N	N	Y
3 Souder	N	Y	Y	N	N
4 Buyer	N	Y	N	N	Y
5 Burton	N	N	N	N	Y
6 Pence	N	Y	N	N	Y
7 Carson	Y	N	N	N	N
8 Ellsworth	?	Y	Y	N	Y
9 Hill	Y	N	N	N	Y
IOWA					
1 Braley	Y	N	N	N	Y
2 Loebsack	Y	N	N	N	Y
3 Boswell	?	N	N	N	Y
4 Latham	N	Y	Y	N	Y
5 King	N	Y	Y	N	N
KANSAS					
1 Moran	N	Y	Y	N	N
2 Jenkins	N	Y	Y	N	N
3 Moore	Y	N	N	N	Y
4 Tiahrt	N	Y	N	N	N
KENTUCKY					
1 Whitfield	N	Y	Y	N	Y
2 Guthrie	N	Y	Y	N	Y
3 Yarmuth	?	N	N	N	Y
4 Davis	N	Y	Y	N	Y
5 Rogers	N	Y	Y	N	Y
6 Chandler	Y	N	N	N	Y
LOUISIANA					
1 Scalise	N	Y	Y	N	Y
2 Cao	Y	N	N	N	Y
3 Melancon	?	?	?	?	?
4 Fleming	N	Y	Y	N	N
5 Alexander	N	Y	Y	N	Y
6 Cassidy	N	Y	Y	N	Y
7 Boustany	N	Y	Y	N	Y
MAINE					
1 Pingree	?	?	?	?	?
2 Michaud	Y	Y	N	N	N
MARYLAND					
1 Kratovil	Y	N	N	N	Y
2 Ruppersberger	Y	N	N	N	Y
3 Sarbanes	?	Y	N	N	Y
4 Edwards	Y	N	Y	Y	N
5 Hoyer	Y	N	N	N	Y
6 Bartlett	N	Y	N	N	Y
7 Cummings	Y	Y	N	N	N
8 Van Hollen	Y	N	N	N	Y
MASSACHUSETTS					
1 Olver	Y	N	N	N	Y
2 Neal	Y	N	Y	N	Y
3 McGovern	Y	N	N	N	Y
4 Frank	Y	Y	Y	N	N
5 Tsongas	?	N	N	N	Y
6 Tierney	Y	?	N	N	Y
7 Markey	Y	N	N	N	Y
8 Capuano	Y	N	N	N	Y
9 Lynch	Y	N	Y	N	Y
10 Delahunt	Y	?	?	?	?
MICHIGAN					
1 Stupak	Y	N	N	N	Y
2 Hoekstra	?	?	?	?	?
3 Ehlers	N	N	N	N	Y
4 Camp	N	Y	N	N	Y
5 Kildee	Y	N	N	N	Y
6 Upton	N	Y	N	N	Y
7 Schauer	Y	N	N	N	Y
8 Rogers	N	Y	N	N	Y
9 Peters	Y	Y	N	N	Y
10 Miller	N	Y	N	N	Y
11 McCotter	N	Y	N	N	Y
12 Levin	Y	N	N	N	Y
13 Kilpatrick	?	Y	N	N	Y
14 Conyers	Y	N	N	N	N
15 Dingell	?	N	N	N	Y
MINNESOTA					
1 Walz	Y	N	N	N	Y
2 Kline	N	N	N	N	Y
3 Paulsen	N	Y	N	N	Y
4 McCollum	Y	Y	N	N	Y
5 Ellison	?	Y	Y	N	N
6 Bachmann	N	Y	Y	N	N
7 Peterson	Y	N	N	N	Y
8 Oberstar	Y	Y	N	N	N
MISSISSIPPI					
1 Childers	N	N	N	N	Y
2 Thompson	Y	N	N	N	Y
3 Harper	N	Y	N	N	Y
4 Taylor	N	N	N	N	Y
MISSOURI					
1 Clay	N	?	?	?	?
2 Akin	N	Y	N	N	Y
3 Carnahan	Y	N	N	N	Y
4 Skelton	N	N	N	N	N
5 Cleaver	?	Y	?	N	Y
6 Graves	N	Y	N	N	Y
7 Blunt	?	Y	N	N	Y
8 Emerson	?	Y	N	N	Y
9 Luetkemeyer	N	Y	Y	N	N
MONTANA					
AL Rehberg	N	Y	Y	N	Y
NEBRASKA					
1 Fortenberry	N	Y	Y	N	N
2 Terry	N	Y	Y	N	N
3 Smith	N	Y	Y	N	Y
NEVADA					
1 Berkley	Y	N	N	N	Y
2 Heller	N	Y	Y	N	N
3 Titus	Y	N	N	N	Y
NEW HAMPSHIRE					
1 Shea-Porter	Y	N	N	N	Y
2 Hodes	Y	?	?	?	?
NEW JERSEY					
1 Andrews	Y	N	N	N	N
2 LoBiondo	N	Y	Y	N	Y
3 Adler	Y	Y	N	N	Y
4 Smith	N	Y	Y	N	Y
5 Garrett	N	Y	Y	N	Y
6 Pallone	Y	N	N	N	Y
7 Lance	N	Y	Y	N	Y
8 Pascrell	?	N	N	N	Y
9 Rothman	Y	N	N	N	Y
10 Payne	Y	N	N	N	Y
11 Frelinghuysen	N	Y	Y	N	Y
12 Holt	Y	N	N	N	Y
13 Sires	Y	N	N	N	Y
NEW MEXICO					
1 Heinrich	Y	N	N	N	Y
2 Teague	?	?	?	?	?
3 Luján	Y	N	N	N	Y
NEW YORK					
1 Bishop	Y	N	N	N	Y
2 Israel	Y	N	N	N	Y
3 King	N	N	N	N	Y
4 McCarthy	Y	N	N	N	Y
5 Ackerman	Y	N	N	N	Y
6 Meeks	?	?	?	?	?
7 Crowley	Y	N	N	N	Y
8 Nadler	Y	N	N	N	Y
9 Weiner	Y	Y	Y	N	N
10 Towns	Y	Y	Y	N	N
11 Clarke	Y	N	N	N	Y
12 Velázquez	Y	Y	Y	N	Y
13 McMahon	Y	Y	N	N	Y
14 Maloney	N	N	N	N	Y
15 Rangel	Y	Y	N	N	Y
16 Serrano	Y	N	N	N	Y
17 Engel	Y	N	N	N	Y
18 Lowey	Y	N	N	N	Y
19 Hall	Y	Y	Y	N	Y
20 Murphy	Y	Y	N	N	Y
21 Tonko	Y	Y	N	N	Y
22 Hinchey	Y	?	?	?	?
23 Owens	Y	N	N	N	Y
24 Arcuri	Y	N	N	N	Y
25 Maffei	Y	N	N	N	Y
26 Lee	N	Y	Y	N	N
27 Higgins	?	N	N	N	Y
28 Slaughter	Y	N	N	N	N
29 Vacant					
NORTH CAROLINA					
1 Butterfield	?	?	?	?	?
2 Etheridge	Y	N	N	N	Y
3 Jones	Y	Y	Y	N	Y
4 Price	Y	N	N	N	Y
5 Foxx	N	Y	Y	N	N
6 Coble	N	Y	Y	N	Y
7 McIntyre	Y	N	N	N	Y
8 Kissell	Y	N	N	N	Y
9 Myrick	N	Y	N	N	N
10 McHenry	N	Y	N	N	N
11 Shuler	?	?	?	?	?
12 Watt	Y	Y	Y	N	N
13 Miller	Y	N	N	N	Y
NORTH DAKOTA					
AL Pomeroy	Y	N	N	N	Y
OHIO					
1 Driehaus	Y	N	N	N	Y
2 Schmidt	N	Y	Y	N	N
3 Turner	N	Y	N	N	Y
4 Jordan	N	Y	Y	N	N
5 Latta	N	Y	Y	N	N
6 Wilson	?	?	?	?	?
7 Austria	N	Y	Y	N	Y
8 Boehner	N	Y	Y	N	Y
9 Kaptur	Y	Y	Y	N	Y
10 Kucinich	N	Y	Y	N	N
11 Fudge	Y	N	N	N	Y
12 Tiberi	N	Y	N	N	Y
13 Sutton	Y	N	N	N	Y
14 LaTourette	N	Y	N	N	Y
15 Kilroy	Y	N	N	N	Y
16 Boccieri	Y	N	N	N	Y
17 Ryan	Y	N	N	N	Y
18 Space	N	Y	Y	N	Y
OKLAHOMA					
1 Sullivan	N	Y	Y	N	N
2 Boren	Y	Y	N	N	Y
3 Lucas	N	Y	Y	N	N
4 Cole	N	Y	N	N	Y
5 Fallin	?	?	?	?	?
OREGON					
1 Wu	N	Y	N	N	Y
2 Walden	N	Y	N	N	Y
3 Blumenauer	N	N	N	N	Y
4 DeFazio	Y	N	N	N	Y
5 Schrader	?	N	N	N	Y
PENNSYLVANIA					
1 Brady	Y	N	N	N	Y
2 Fattah	Y	Y	N	N	N
3 Dahlkemper	Y	N	N	N	Y
4 Altmire	N	Y	N	N	Y
5 Thompson	N	Y	Y	N	Y
6 Gerlach	N	Y	Y	N	Y
7 Sestak	Y	N	N	N	Y
8 Murphy, P.	Y	N	N	N	Y
9 Shuster	N	Y	Y	N	Y
10 Carney	Y	N	N	N	Y
11 Kanjorski	Y	Y	Y	N	Y
12 Vacant					
13 Schwartz	?	N	N	N	Y
14 Doyle	Y	N	N	N	Y
15 Dent	N	Y	N	N	Y
16 Pitts	N	Y	Y	N	N
17 Holden	Y	Y	Y	N	Y
18 Murphy, T.	N	Y	N	N	Y
19 Platts	N	Y	Y	N	Y
RHODE ISLAND					
1 Kennedy	Y	N	N	N	Y
2 Langevin	Y	N	N	N	Y
SOUTH CAROLINA					
1 Brown	N	?	?	?	?
2 Wilson	N	Y	Y	N	Y
3 Barrett	?	?	?	?	?
4 Inglis	N	Y	Y	N	N
5 Spratt	Y	Y	N	N	Y
6 Clyburn	Y	N	N	N	Y
SOUTH DAKOTA					
AL Herseth Sandlin	Y	Y	Y	N	Y
TENNESSEE					
1 Roe	N	Y	Y	N	Y
2 Duncan	N	Y	Y	N	Y
3 Wamp	?	?	?	?	?
4 Davis	Y	N	N	N	Y
5 Cooper	N	Y	N	N	Y
6 Gordon	?	N	N	N	N
7 Blackburn	N	Y	Y	N	Y
8 Tanner	?	N	N	N	Y
9 Cohen	?	?	?	?	?
TEXAS					
1 Gohmert	N	Y	Y	?	?
2 Poe	N	Y	Y	N	N
3 Johnson, S.	N	Y	N	N	Y
4 Hall	N	Y	N	N	Y
5 Hensarling	N	Y	Y	N	Y
6 Barton	N	Y	N	N	Y
7 Culberson	N	Y	Y	N	Y
8 Brady	?	Y	N	N	Y
9 Green, A.	Y	N	N	N	N
10 McCaul	N	Y	N	N	Y
11 Conaway	N	Y	N	N	Y
12 Granger	N	?	?	?	?
13 Thornberry	N	Y	Y	N	Y
14 Paul	N	?	?	?	?
15 Hinojosa	Y	?	?	?	?
16 Reyes	Y	?	?	?	?
17 Edwards	Y	N	N	N	Y
18 Jackson Lee	N	N	N	Y	N
19 Neugebauer	N	Y	Y	N	Y
20 Gonzalez	Y	N	N	N	Y
21 Smith	N	Y	Y	N	Y
22 Olson	N	Y	Y	N	Y
23 Rodriguez	Y	N	N	N	Y
24 Marchant	N	Y	Y	N	Y
25 Doggett	Y	N	N	N	Y
26 Burgess	N	Y	Y	N	Y
27 Ortiz	Y	N	N	N	Y
28 Cuellar	Y	N	N	N	Y
29 Green, G.	Y	?	?	?	?
30 Johnson, E.	Y	N	N	N	Y
31 Carter	N	Y	Y	N	Y
32 Sessions	N	Y	Y	N	Y
UTAH					
1 Bishop	N	Y	N	N	Y
2 Matheson	Y	N	N	N	Y
3 Chaffetz	N	Y	Y	Y	Y
VERMONT					
AL Welch	Y	N	N	N	Y
VIRGINIA					
1 Wittman	N	Y	N	N	N
2 Nye	Y	N	N	N	Y
3 Scott	Y	N	N	N	Y
4 Forbes	N	Y	N	N	N
5 Perriello	Y	Y	Y	N	Y
6 Goodlatte	N	Y	N	N	Y
7 Cantor	N	N	?	N	Y
8 Moran	Y	N	N	N	Y
9 Boucher	N	?	?	?	?
10 Wolf	N	Y	N	N	Y
11 Connolly	Y	N	N	N	Y
WASHINGTON					
1 Inslee	Y	N	N	N	Y
2 Larsen	Y	N	N	N	Y
3 Baird	Y	N	N	N	Y
4 Hastings	N	Y	Y	N	Y
5 McMorris Rodgers	N	Y	Y	N	Y
6 Dicks	N	N	N	N	Y
7 McDermott	Y	N	N	N	Y
8 Reichert	N	N	N	N	Y
9 Smith	Y	N	N	N	Y
WEST VIRGINIA					
1 Mollohan	?	?	?	?	?
2 Capito	N	Y	Y	N	Y
3 Rahall	Y	N	N	N	Y
WISCONSIN					
1 Ryan	N	Y	Y	N	Y
2 Baldwin	Y	N	N	N	Y
3 Kind	N	N	N	N	Y
4 Moore	?	Y	Y	N	Y
5 Sensenbrenner	N	Y	Y	N	Y
6 Petri	N	Y	N	N	Y
7 Obey	Y	N	N	N	Y
8 Kagen	?	N	N	N	Y
WYOMING					
AL Lummis	N	Y	N	N	N
DELEGATES					
Faleomavaega (A.S.)		?	?	?	?
Norton (D.C.)		N	N	N	Y
Bordallo (Guam)		N	N	N	Y
Sablan (N. Marianas)		N	N	N	Y
Pierluisi (P.R.)		N	N	N	Y
Christensen (V.I.)		Y	Y	N	N

IN THE HOUSE | By Vote Number

238. **HR 2499. Puerto Rico Political Status/Puerto Rican Descent Eligibility.** Velázquez, D-N.Y., amendment that would make U.S. citizens of Puerto Rican descent eligible to vote in the plebiscites authorized by the bill. Rejected in Committee of the Whole 11-387: D 11-221; R 0-166. April 29, 2010.

239. **HR 2499. Puerto Rico Political Status/Single Plebiscite.** Velázquez, D-N.Y., amendment that would authorize Puerto Rico to hold one plebiscite to choose between four options: statehood, full independence, independence with a special political association with the United States, or the current commonwealth status. It also would authorize a runoff process, between the two options that receive the highest number of votes, if no option receives more than 50 percent of the vote. Rejected in Committee of the Whole 112-285: D 50-181; R 62-104. April 29, 2010.

240. **HR 2499. Puerto Rico Political Status/Substitute.** Velázquez, D-N.Y., substitute amendment that would strike the text of the bill and insert language to express the sense of Congress that the government of Puerto Rico can hold a vote on whether to conduct a plebiscite to change its political status. Rejected in Committee of the Whole 171-223: D 55-175; R 116-48. April 29, 2010.

241. **HR 2499. Puerto Rico Political Status/Recommit.** Hastings, R-Wash., motion to recommit the bill to the Natural Resources Committee with instructions that it be immediately reported back with an amendment that would redefine the Puerto Rican statehood option to specify that English would be the official language and state laws would have to permit residents to own and carry firearms. Motion rejected 194-198: D 32-192; R 162-6. April 29, 2010.

242. **HR 2499. Puerto Rico Political Status/Passage.** Passage of a bill that would establish a two-stage process to determine Puerto Rico's political status. It would allow the Puerto Rican government to conduct a plebiscite on the question of whether to maintain or change Puerto Rico's current status as a commonwealth. If a majority voted for a new status, then a second vote could be held to ask participants whether they favor statehood, full independence, independence with a special political association with the United States, or the current commonwealth status. It also would require plebiscite ballots to be printed in English. Passed 223-169: D 184-40; R 39-129. April 29, 2010.

	238	239	240	241	242
ALABAMA					
1 **Bonner**	N	Y	Y	Y	N
2 **Bright**	N	Y	Y	Y	N
3 **Rogers**	N	N	Y	Y	N
4 **Aderholt**	N	N	Y	Y	N
5 **Griffith**	N	N	Y	Y	N
6 **Bachus**	N	N	Y	Y	N
7 Davis	?	?	?	?	?
ALASKA					
AL **Young**	N	N	N	N	Y
ARIZONA					
1 Kirkpatrick	N	N	N	N	Y
2 **Franks**	N	Y	Y	Y	N
3 **Shadegg**	N	Y	Y	Y	N
4 Pastor	N	N	N	N	Y
5 Mitchell	N	Y	Y	Y	N
6 **Flake**	N	Y	Y	Y	Y
7 Grijalva	N	Y	Y	N	Y
8 Giffords	N	Y	Y	Y	N
ARKANSAS					
1 Berry	N	N	N	N	N
2 Snyder	N	N	N	N	Y
3 **Boozman**	N	Y	Y	Y	N
4 Ross	N	N	N	?	N
CALIFORNIA					
1 Thompson	N	N	N	N	Y
2 **Herger**	N	Y	Y	Y	N
3 **Lungren**	N	N	N	Y	Y
4 **McClintock**	N	N	Y	Y	N
5 Matsui	N	N	N	N	Y
6 Woolsey	N	N	N	N	Y
7 Miller, George	N	N	N	N	Y
8 Pelosi					
9 Lee	Y	Y	N	N	Y
10 Garamendi	N	N	N	N	Y
11 McNerney	N	N	N	Y	Y
12 Speier	?	?	?	?	?
13 Stark	N	N	N	N	Y
14 Eshoo	N	N	N	N	Y
15 Honda	Y	Y	Y	N	N
16 Lofgren	N	N	N	N	Y
17 Farr	N	N	N	N	Y
18 Cardoza	N	N	N	N	Y
19 **Radanovich**	N	N	N	Y	N
20 Costa	N	N	N	N	Y
21 **Nunes**	?	?	?	?	?
22 **McCarthy**	N	N	N	Y	Y
23 Capps	N	N	N	N	Y
24 **Gallegly**	N	N	Y	Y	N
25 **McKeon**	N	N	Y	Y	N
26 **Dreier**	N	Y	Y	Y	N
27 Sherman	N	Y	N	N	Y
28 Berman	N	N	N	N	Y
29 Schiff	N	N	N	N	Y
30 Waxman	?	?	?	?	?
31 Becerra	N	N	Y	N	Y
32 Chu	N	N	N	N	Y
33 Watson	N	N	N	N	Y
34 Roybal-Allard	N	Y	Y	N	Y
35 Waters	?	?	?	?	?
36 Harman	N	N	N	N	Y
37 Richardson	N	Y	N	N	Y
38 Napolitano	N	N	N	N	Y
39 Sánchez, Linda	N	N	N	N	Y
40 **Royce**	N	Y	Y	Y	N
41 **Lewis**	N	N	Y	Y	N
42 **Miller, Gary**	N	Y	Y	Y	N
43 Baca	N	N	N	N	Y
44 **Calvert**	N	N	Y	Y	N
45 **Bono Mack**	N	N	Y	Y	N
46 **Rohrabacher**	N	Y	Y	Y	N
47 Sanchez, Loretta	N	N	N	N	Y
48 **Campbell**	N	N	N	Y	N
49 **Issa**	N	N	Y	Y	N
50 **Bilbray**	N	Y	Y	Y	N
51 Filner	–	–	?	–	–
52 **Hunter**	N	N	Y	Y	N
53 Davis	N	N	N	N	Y
COLORADO					
1 DeGette	?	?	?	?	?
2 Polis	N	N	N	N	Y
3 Salazar	N	N	N	N	Y
4 Markey	N	N	N	N	Y
5 **Lamborn**	N	Y	Y	Y	N
6 **Coffman**	N	Y	Y	Y	Y
7 Perlmutter	N	N	N	N	Y
CONNECTICUT					
1 Larson	N	Y	Y	N	Y
2 Courtney	N	Y	Y	N	N
3 DeLauro	N	Y	Y	N	Y
4 Himes	N	Y	N	N	Y
5 Murphy	N	Y	N	N	N
DELAWARE					
AL **Castle**	N	N	N	Y	Y
FLORIDA					
1 **Miller**	N	N	N	Y	N
2 Boyd	N	N	–	+	+
3 Brown	N	N	N	N	Y
4 **Crenshaw**	N	N	N	Y	Y
5 **Brown-Waite**	N	N	N	Y	Y
6 **Stearns**	N	Y	Y	Y	N
7 **Mica**	N	N	N	Y	Y
8 Grayson	N	N	N	N	Y
9 **Bilirakis**	N	N	Y	Y	N
10 **Young**	N	N	N	Y	N
11 Castor	?	?	?	?	?
12 **Putnam**	N	N	N	Y	N
13 **Buchanan**	N	N	Y	Y	N
14 **Mack**	N	N	?	Y	Y
15 **Posey**	N	N	N	Y	N
16 **Rooney**	N	Y	Y	Y	N
17 Meek	N	N	N	N	Y
18 **Ros-Lehtinen**	N	N	N	Y	N
19 Deutch	N	N	N	N	Y
20 Wasserman Schultz	N	N	N	N	Y
21 **Diaz-Balart, L.**	N	N	N	N	Y
22 Klein	N	N	N	N	?
23 Hastings	N	N	N	N	Y
24 Kosmas	N	N	N	N	Y
25 **Diaz-Balart, M.**	N	N	N	N	Y
GEORGIA					
1 **Kingston**	N	Y	N	Y	N
2 Bishop	N	Y	Y	N	Y
3 **Westmoreland**	N	Y	Y	Y	N
4 Johnson	N	N	N	N	Y
5 Lewis	N	N	N	N	Y
6 **Price**	N	Y	Y	Y	N
7 **Linder**	?	?	?	?	?
8 Marshall	N	Y	Y	Y	N
9 Vacant					
10 **Broun**	N	Y	Y	Y	N
11 **Gingrey**	N	Y	Y	Y	N
12 Barrow	N	N	N	Y	Y
13 Scott	N	N	N	Y	N
HAWAII					
1 Vacant					
2 Hirono	N	N	N	N	Y
IDAHO					
1 Minnick	N	Y	Y	Y	N
2 **Simpson**	N	N	Y	Y	N
ILLINOIS					
1 Rush	N	N	Y	N	N
2 Jackson	N	N	N	N	Y
3 Lipinski	N	N	Y	N	N
4 Gutierrez	Y	Y	N	N	N
5 Quigley	N	N	N	N	N
6 **Roskam**	N	Y	Y	N	N
7 Davis	N	N	N	N	N
8 Bean	N	N	N	N	N
9 Schakowsky	N	Y	N	N	Y
10 **Kirk**	N	N	N	Y	Y
11 Halvorson	N	N	N	N	Y
12 Costello	N	Y	Y	Y	N
13 **Biggert**	N	N	N	Y	Y
14 Foster	N	Y	N	Y	Y
15 **Johnson**	N	Y	Y	Y	N

KEY	**Republicans**	Democrats		
Y	Voted for (yea)	X	Paired against	
#	Paired for	–	Announced against	
+	Announced for	P	Voted "present"	
N	Voted against (nay)			
		C	Voted "present" to avoid possible conflict of interest	
		?	Did not vote or otherwise make a position known	

	238	239	240	241	242
16 Manzullo	N	N	Y	Y	N
17 Hare	N	N	N	N	Y
18 Schock	?	N	N	N	Y
19 Shimkus	N	N	Y	Y	N
INDIANA					
1 Visclosky	N	N	N	N	Y
2 Donnelly	N	N	N	Y	N
3 Souder	N	Y	Y	Y	N
4 Buyer	N	Y	Y	Y	Y
5 Burton	N	N	N	Y	Y
6 Pence	N	Y	N	Y	Y
7 Carson	N	N	N	N	Y
8 Ellsworth	N	Y	Y	Y	Y
9 Hill	N	N	N	N	Y
IOWA					
1 Braley	N	N	N	N	Y
2 Loebsack	N	N	N	N	Y
3 Boswell	N	N	N	N	Y
4 Latham	N	Y	Y	Y	N
5 King	N	Y	Y	Y	N
KANSAS					
1 Moran	N	N	Y	Y	N
2 Jenkins	N	N	Y	Y	N
3 Moore	N	N	N	N	Y
4 Tiahrt	N	N	N	Y	N
KENTUCKY					
1 Whitfield	N	N	Y	Y	N
2 Guthrie	N	Y	Y	Y	N
3 Yarmuth	N	?	?	?	?
4 Davis	N	Y	Y	Y	N
5 Rogers	N	Y	Y	Y	N
6 Chandler	N	N	Y	?	N
LOUISIANA					
1 Scalise	N	Y	Y	Y	N
2 Cao	N	N	N	N	Y
3 Melancon	?	?	?	?	?
4 Fleming	N	N	N	Y	N
5 Alexander	N	N	N	Y	N
6 Cassidy	N	N	Y	Y	N
7 Boustany	N	N	Y	Y	N
MAINE					
1 Pingree	?	?	?	?	?
2 Michaud	N	Y	Y	N	Y
MARYLAND					
1 Kratovil	N	N	N	N	Y
2 Ruppersberger	N	N	N	N	Y
3 Sarbanes	N	N	N	N	Y
4 Edwards	N	N	N	N	Y
5 Hoyer	N	N	N	N	Y
6 Bartlett	N	Y	Y	Y	Y
7 Cummings	N	N	N	N	Y
8 Van Hollen	N	N	N	N	Y
MASSACHUSETTS					
1 Olver	N	N	N	N	Y
2 Neal	N	Y	Y	N	Y
3 McGovern	N	N	N	N	Y
4 Frank	N	Y	Y	N	N
5 Tsongas	N	N	N	N	Y
6 Tierney	N	N	N	N	Y
7 Markey	N	N	N	N	Y
8 Capuano	N	N	N	N	Y
9 Lynch	N	N	Y	N	Y
10 Delahunt	?	?	?	?	?
MICHIGAN					
1 Stupak	N	N	N	N	Y
2 Hoekstra	?	?	?	?	?
3 Ehlers	N	N	N	Y	Y
4 Camp	N	N	Y	Y	N
5 Kildee	N	N	N	N	Y
6 Upton	N	N	Y	N	N
7 Schauer	N	N	N	N	Y
8 Rogers	N	N	Y	Y	N
9 Peters	N	N	N	N	Y
10 Miller	N	Y	Y	Y	N
11 McCotter	N	N	Y	N	N
12 Levin	N	N	N	N	Y
13 Kilpatrick	Y	Y	Y	–	–
14 Conyers	N	N	N	N	Y
15 Dingell	N	N	N	N	Y
MINNESOTA					
1 Walz	N	N	N	N	Y
2 Kline	N	Y	Y	Y	Y
3 Paulsen	N	N	Y	Y	N
4 McCollum	N	N	Y	N	Y

	238	239	240	241	242
5 Ellison	N	Y	Y	N	N
6 Bachmann	N	N	Y	Y	N
7 Peterson	N	N	N	Y	Y
8 Oberstar	N	N	N	N	Y
MISSISSIPPI					
1 Childers	N	N	N	Y	N
2 Thompson	N	N	N	N	Y
3 Harper	N	N	N	Y	N
4 Taylor	N	N	N	N	Y
MISSOURI					
1 Clay	?	?	?	?	?
2 Akin	?	N	Y	Y	N
3 Carnahan	?	N	N	N	Y
4 Skelton	N	Y	Y	Y	Y
5 Cleaver	N	N	N	N	Y
6 Graves	N	Y	Y	Y	N
7 Blunt	N	Y	Y	Y	N
8 Emerson	N	N	Y	Y	N
9 Luetkemeyer	N	N	Y	Y	N
MONTANA					
AL Rehberg	N	N	N	Y	N
NEBRASKA					
1 Fortenberry	N	Y	Y	Y	N
2 Terry	N	N	N	Y	N
3 Smith	N	Y	N	Y	N
NEVADA					
1 Berkley	N	N	N	N	Y
2 Heller	N	N	Y	Y	N
3 Titus	N	N	N	N	Y
NEW HAMPSHIRE					
1 Shea-Porter	N	N	N	N	Y
2 Hodes	?	?	?	?	?
NEW JERSEY					
1 Andrews	N	N	N	N	Y
2 LoBiondo	N	N	Y	Y	N
3 Adler	N	N	Y	Y	Y
4 Smith	N	N	N	N	Y
5 Garrett	N	N	N	Y	N
6 Pallone	N	N	N	N	Y
7 Lance	N	Y	Y	Y	N
8 Pascrell	N	N	N	N	Y
9 Rothman	N	N	N	N	Y
10 Payne	N	N	N	N	Y
11 Frelinghuysen	N	Y	N	Y	N
12 Holt	N	N	N	N	Y
13 Sires	N	N	N	N	Y
NEW MEXICO					
1 Heinrich	N	N	N	N	Y
2 Teague	?	?	?	?	?
3 Luján	N	N	N	N	Y
NEW YORK					
1 Bishop	N	N	N	N	Y
2 Israel	N	N	N	N	Y
3 King	N	N	N	Y	Y
4 McCarthy	N	N	Y	N	Y
5 Ackerman	N	N	N	N	Y
6 Meeks	?	?	?	?	?
7 Crowley	N	N	N	N	Y
8 Nadler	N	Y	Y	N	Y
9 Weiner	Y	Y	Y	N	N
10 Towns	Y	Y	Y	N	Y
11 Clarke	N	Y	Y	N	Y
12 Velázquez	Y	Y	Y	N	N
13 McMahon	N	Y	Y	Y	N
14 Maloney	N	N	N	N	Y
15 Rangel	N	N	N	N	Y
16 Serrano	N	N	N	N	Y
17 Engel	N	N	N	N	Y
18 Lowey	N	Y	Y	N	Y
19 Hall	N	N	N	N	Y
20 Murphy	N	N	N	N	Y
21 Tonko	N	Y	Y	N	Y
22 Hinchey	?	?	?	?	?
23 Owens	N	N	N	Y	Y
24 Arcuri	N	N	Y	Y	Y
25 Maffei	N	N	N	N	Y
26 Lee	N	Y	Y	Y	N
27 Higgins	N	N	N	N	Y
28 Slaughter	N	?	N	N	P
29 Vacant					
NORTH CAROLINA					
1 Butterfield	?	?	?	?	?
2 Etheridge	N	N	N	N	Y
3 Jones	N	N	Y	Y	N
4 Price	N	N	N	N	Y

	238	239	240	241	242
5 Foxx	N	Y	Y	Y	N
6 Coble	N	Y	Y	Y	N
7 McIntyre	N	N	N	Y	N
8 Kissell	N	N	N	N	Y
9 Myrick	N	N	Y	Y	N
10 McHenry	N	N	Y	Y	N
11 Shuler	?	?	?	?	?
12 Watt	N	Y	N	Y	N
13 Miller	N	N	N	N	Y
NORTH DAKOTA					
AL Pomeroy	N	N	N	N	Y
OHIO					
1 Driehaus	N	N	N	Y	Y
2 Schmidt	N	N	Y	Y	N
3 Turner	N	N	Y	Y	N
4 Jordan	N	Y	Y	Y	N
5 Latta	N	N	Y	Y	N
6 Wilson	?	?	?	?	?
7 Austria	N	N	Y	Y	N
8 Boehner	N	N	Y	Y	N
9 Kaptur	Y	Y	Y	Y	Y
10 Kucinich	Y	Y	N	N	Y
11 Fudge	N	N	N	N	Y
12 Tiberi	N	N	Y	Y	N
13 Sutton	N	N	N	N	Y
14 LaTourette	N	N	Y	Y	N
15 Kilroy	N	N	N	N	Y
16 Boccieri	N	N	N	Y	Y
17 Ryan	N	N	N	N	Y
18 Space	N	Y	Y	Y	N
OKLAHOMA					
1 Sullivan	N	Y	Y	Y	N
2 Boren	N	Y	Y	Y	N
3 Lucas	N	N	Y	Y	N
4 Cole	N	Y	N	Y	Y
5 Fallin	?	?	?	?	?
OREGON					
1 Wu	N	N	N	N	Y
2 Walden	N	N	N	Y	Y
3 Blumenauer	N	N	?	N	Y
4 DeFazio	N	N	N	N	Y
5 Schrader	N	Y	N	N	Y
PENNSYLVANIA					
1 Brady	N	N	N	N	Y
2 Fattah	N	N	N	N	Y
3 Dahlkemper	N	N	N	N	Y
4 Altmire	N	Y	Y	Y	N
5 Thompson	N	N	Y	Y	Y
6 Gerlach	N	Y	Y	Y	N
7 Sestak	N	N	N	N	Y
8 Murphy, P.	N	N	N	N	Y
9 Shuster	N	N	Y	Y	N
10 Carney	N	N	Y	N	N
11 Kanjorski	N	N	Y	N	Y
12 Vacant					
13 Schwartz	N	N	N	N	Y
14 Doyle	N	N	N	N	Y
15 Dent	N	N	Y	Y	N
16 Pitts	N	Y	Y	Y	N
17 Holden	N	N	Y	N	N
18 Murphy, T.	N	N	N	Y	N
19 Platts	N	Y	Y	Y	N
RHODE ISLAND					
1 Kennedy	N	N	N	N	Y
2 Langevin	N	N	N	N	Y
SOUTH CAROLINA					
1 Brown	?	?	?	?	?
2 Wilson	N	Y	Y	Y	N
3 Barrett	?	?	?	?	?
4 Inglis	N	Y	Y	Y	N
5 Spratt	N	N	N	N	Y
6 Clyburn	N	N	N	N	Y
SOUTH DAKOTA					
AL Herseth Sandlin	N	Y	N	N	Y
TENNESSEE					
1 Roe	N	N	Y	Y	N
2 Duncan	N	Y	Y	Y	N
3 Wamp	?	?	?	?	?
4 Davis	N	N	N	N	Y
5 Cooper	N	Y	Y	N	N
6 Gordon	N	N	N	N	Y
7 Blackburn	N	N	?	Y	Y
8 Tanner	N	Y	N	Y	Y
9 Cohen	?	?	?	?	?

	238	239	240	241	242
TEXAS					
1 Gohmert	N	?	?	Y	N
2 Poe	N	Y	Y	Y	N
3 Johnson, S.	N	N	Y	Y	N
4 Hall	N	Y	Y	Y	N
5 Hensarling	N	Y	Y	Y	Y
6 Barton	N	N	Y	Y	N
7 Culberson	N	Y	?	Y	N
8 Brady	N	Y	Y	Y	N
9 Green, A.	?	N	N	N	Y
10 McCaul	N	?	Y	Y	N
11 Conaway	N	Y	Y	Y	N
12 Granger	?	?	?	?	?
13 Thornberry	N	Y	Y	Y	N
14 Paul	?	?	?	?	?
15 Hinojosa	?	?	?	?	?
16 Reyes	?	?	?	?	?
17 Edwards	N	N	N	N	Y
18 Jackson Lee	Y	N	N	N	Y
19 Neugebauer	N	Y	Y	Y	N
20 Gonzalez	N	N	N	N	Y
21 Smith	N	Y	Y	Y	N
22 Olson	N	Y	Y	Y	N
23 Rodriguez	N	N	N	N	Y
24 Marchant	N	Y	Y	Y	N
25 Doggett	N	N	N	N	Y
26 Burgess	N	N	Y	Y	N
27 Ortiz	N	N	N	N	Y
28 Cuellar	N	N	N	N	Y
29 Green, G.	?	?	?	?	+
30 Johnson, E.	N	N	N	N	Y
31 Carter	N	Y	Y	Y	N
32 Sessions	N	Y	Y	Y	N
UTAH					
1 Bishop	N	N	N	Y	N
2 Matheson	N	Y	Y	N	N
3 Chaffetz	N	N	Y	Y	N
VERMONT					
AL Welch	N	N	N	N	Y
VIRGINIA					
1 Wittman	N	N	Y	Y	N
2 Nye	N	Y	Y	Y	N
3 Scott	N	N	N	N	Y
4 Forbes	N	N	Y	Y	N
5 Perriello	N	N	Y	Y	N
6 Goodlatte	N	Y	Y	Y	N
7 Cantor	N	N	Y	Y	Y
8 Moran	N	N	N	N	Y
9 Boucher	?	?	?	?	?
10 Wolf	N	Y	Y	Y	N
11 Connolly	N	N	N	N	Y
WASHINGTON					
1 Inslee	N	N	N	N	Y
2 Larsen	N	N	N	N	Y
3 Baird	N	N	N	N	Y
4 Hastings	N	Y	Y	Y	N
5 McMorris Rodgers	N	Y	Y	Y	N
6 Dicks	N	N	N	N	Y
7 McDermott	N	N	N	N	Y
8 Reichert	N	N	N	Y	Y
9 Smith	N	N	N	N	Y
WEST VIRGINIA					
1 Mollohan	?	?	?	?	?
2 Capito	N	Y	Y	Y	N
3 Rahall	N	N	N	N	Y
WISCONSIN					
1 Ryan	N	N	Y	Y	N
2 Baldwin	N	N	N	N	Y
3 Kind	N	N	N	N	Y
4 Moore	Y	Y	Y	N	Y
5 Sensenbrenner	N	N	Y	Y	N
6 Petri	N	Y	Y	Y	N
7 Obey	N	?	N	N	Y
8 Kagen	N	N	N	N	Y
WYOMING					
AL Lummis	N	N	N	Y	N
DELEGATES					
Faleomavaega (A.S.)	?	?	?		
Norton (D.C.)	N	N	N		
Bordallo (Guam)	N	N	N		
Sablan (N. Marianas)	N	N	N		
Pierluisi (P.R.)	N	N	N		
Christensen (V.I.)	N	Y	?		

IN THE HOUSE | By Vote Number

243. **H Res 1307. Tribute to National Science Foundation/Adoption.** Fudge, D-Ohio, motion to suspend the rules and adopt the resolution that would recognize the 60th anniversary of the National Science Foundation; acknowledge its advancement of scientific discovery, innovation and learning; and reaffirm Congress' commitment to support basic research, education and technological advancement through the foundation. Motion agreed to 370-2: D 220-0; R 150-2. A two-thirds majority of those present and voting (248 in this case) is required for adoption under suspension of the rules. May 4, 2010.

244. **H Res 1213. National Lab Day/Adoption.** Fudge, D-Ohio, motion to suspend the rules and adopt the resolution that would support National Lab Day and encourage scientists, educators and volunteers to participate. Motion agreed to 378-2: D 227-0; R 151-2. A two-thirds majority of those present and voting (254 in this case) is required for adoption under suspension of the rules. May 4, 2010.

245. **H Res 1132. Tribute to *USS New Mexico*/Adoption.** Heinrich, D-N.M., motion to suspend the rules and adopt the resolution that would honor the *USS New Mexico*, commend individuals involved in building the submarine and honor the Navy submarine's crew. Motion agreed to 378-1: D 226-1; R 152-0. A two-thirds majority of those present and voting (253 in this case) is required for adoption under suspension of the rules. May 4, 2010.

246. **H Res 1320. New York Car Bomb Case/Adoption.** Pascrell, D-N.J., motion to suspend the rules and adopt the resolution that would commend Lance Orton and Duane Jackson for promptly alerting authorities about a suspicious vehicle in New York City's Times Square on May 1 and recognize the New York City Police Department and others for their professionalism and preparedness. It also would urge Americans to be vigilant and report potential terrorist or suspicious activity in their communities. Motion agreed to 418-0: D 246-0; R 172-0. A two-thirds majority of those present and voting (279 in this case) is required for adoption under suspension of the rules. May 5, 2010.

247. **H Res 1272. Kent State University Shootings Anniversary/Adoption.** Chu, D-Calif., motion to suspend the rules and adopt the resolution that would recognize the 40th anniversary of the Kent State University shootings on May 4, 1970, and the implications of the incident on the school and the nation. Motion agreed to 415-0: D 247-0; R 168-0. A two-thirds majority of those present and voting (277 in this case) is required for adoption under suspension of the rules. May 5, 2010.

248. **H Res 1301. National Train Day/Adoption.** Brown, D-Fla., motion to suspend the rules and adopt the resolution that would support the goals and ideals of National Train Day on May 8 and recognize the contributions of trains and Amtrak to the national transportation system. Motion agreed to 296-119: D 246-0; R 50-119. A two-thirds majority of those present and voting (277 in this case) is required for adoption under suspension of the rules. May 5, 2010.

249. **HR 5019. Home Star Energy Retrofit Programs/Rule.** Adoption of the rule (H Res 1329) that would provide for House floor consideration of the bill to authorize $6.6 billion for rebate and assistance programs for energy-efficient home renovations. Adopted 229-182: D 229-11; R 0-171. May 6, 2010.

	243	244	245	246	247	248	249
ALABAMA							
1 **Bonner**	Y	Y	Y	Y	Y	N	?
2 Bright	Y	Y	Y	Y	Y	Y	Y
3 **Rogers**	Y	Y	Y	Y	Y	N	N
4 **Aderholt**	Y	?	?	Y	Y	N	N
5 **Griffith**	+	Y	Y	Y	Y	N	N
6 **Bachus**	Y	Y	?	Y	Y	N	N
7 Davis	?	?	?	?	?	?	?
ALASKA							
AL **Young**	Y	Y	Y	Y	Y	N	N
ARIZONA							
1 Kirkpatrick	Y	Y	Y	Y	Y	Y	Y
2 **Franks**	Y	Y	Y	Y	Y	N	N
3 **Shadegg**	Y	Y	Y	Y	Y	N	N
4 Pastor	Y	Y	Y	Y	Y	Y	Y
5 Mitchell	Y	Y	Y	Y	Y	Y	N
6 **Flake**	?	?	Y	Y	Y	N	N
7 Grijalva	?	?	?	Y	Y	Y	Y
8 Giffords	Y	Y	Y	Y	Y	Y	Y
ARKANSAS							
1 Berry	Y	Y	Y	Y	Y	Y	Y
2 Snyder	Y	Y	Y	Y	Y	Y	Y
3 **Boozman**	Y	Y	Y	Y	Y	N	N
4 Ross	Y	Y	Y	Y	Y	Y	Y
CALIFORNIA							
1 Thompson	Y	Y	Y	Y	Y	Y	Y
2 **Herger**	Y	Y	Y	Y	Y	N	N
3 **Lungren**	Y	Y	Y	Y	Y	N	N
4 **McClintock**	Y	Y	Y	Y	Y	N	N
5 Matsui	Y	Y	Y	Y	Y	Y	Y
6 Woolsey	Y	Y	Y	Y	Y	Y	Y
7 Miller, George	Y	Y	Y	Y	Y	Y	Y
8 Pelosi							
9 **Lee**	+	+	+	Y	Y	Y	Y
10 Garamendi	Y	Y	Y	Y	Y	Y	?
11 McNerney	Y	Y	Y	Y	Y	Y	Y
12 Speier	Y	Y	Y	Y	Y	Y	Y
13 Stark	Y	Y	Y	Y	Y	Y	Y
14 Eshoo	Y	Y	Y	Y	Y	Y	Y
15 Honda	Y	Y	Y	Y	Y	Y	Y
16 Lofgren	Y	Y	Y	Y	Y	Y	Y
17 Farr	Y	Y	Y	Y	Y	Y	Y
18 Cardoza	?	?	?	Y	Y	Y	Y
19 **Radanovich**	?	?	?	Y	Y	Y	N
20 Costa	?	Y	Y	Y	Y	Y	?
21 **Nunes**	Y	Y	Y	Y	Y	N	N
22 **McCarthy**	Y	Y	Y	Y	Y	N	N
23 Capps	Y	Y	Y	Y	Y	Y	Y
24 **Gallegly**	Y	Y	Y	Y	Y	N	N
25 **McKeon**	Y	?	Y	Y	Y	N	N
26 **Dreier**	Y	Y	Y	Y	Y	N	N
27 Sherman	Y	Y	Y	Y	Y	Y	Y
28 Berman	Y	Y	Y	Y	Y	Y	Y
29 Schiff	Y	Y	Y	Y	Y	Y	Y
30 Waxman	Y	Y	Y	Y	Y	Y	Y
31 Becerra	Y	Y	Y	Y	Y	Y	Y
32 Chu	Y	Y	Y	Y	Y	Y	Y
33 Watson	?	Y	Y	Y	Y	Y	Y
34 Roybal-Allard	?	?	?	Y	Y	Y	Y
35 Waters	Y	Y	Y	Y	Y	Y	Y
36 Harman	Y	Y	Y	Y	Y	Y	Y
37 Richardson	Y	Y	Y	Y	Y	Y	Y
38 Napolitano	Y	Y	Y	Y	Y	+	Y
39 Sánchez, Linda	Y	Y	Y	Y	Y	Y	Y
40 **Royce**	Y	Y	Y	Y	Y	N	N
41 **Lewis**	Y	Y	Y	Y	Y	N	N
42 **Miller, Gary**	Y	Y	Y	Y	Y	N	N
43 Baca	Y	Y	Y	Y	Y	Y	Y
44 **Calvert**	Y	Y	Y	Y	Y	N	N
45 **Bono Mack**	Y	Y	Y	Y	Y	N	N
46 **Rohrabacher**	?	?	?	Y	Y	N	N
47 Sanchez, Loretta	Y	Y	Y	Y	Y	Y	Y
48 **Campbell**	?	?	?	?	?	?	?
49 **Issa**	Y	Y	Y	Y	Y	N	N
50 **Bilbray**	Y	Y	Y	Y	Y	Y	N
51 Filner	Y	Y	Y	Y	Y	Y	Y
52 **Hunter**	Y	Y	Y	Y	Y	N	N
53 Davis	Y	Y	Y	Y	Y	Y	Y

	243	244	245	246	247	248	249
COLORADO							
1 DeGette	?	?	?	?	?	?	?
2 Polis	Y	Y	Y	Y	Y	Y	Y
3 Salazar	Y	Y	Y	Y	Y	Y	Y
4 Markey	?	?	?	Y	Y	Y	Y
5 **Lamborn**	?	?	?	Y	Y	N	N
6 **Coffman**	Y	Y	Y	Y	Y	N	N
7 Perlmutter	+	Y	Y	Y	Y	Y	Y
CONNECTICUT							
1 Larson	+	+	+	Y	Y	Y	Y
2 Courtney	Y	Y	Y	Y	Y	Y	N
3 DeLauro	Y	Y	Y	Y	Y	Y	Y
4 Himes	Y	Y	Y	Y	Y	Y	Y
5 Murphy	Y	Y	Y	Y	Y	Y	Y
DELAWARE							
AL **Castle**	Y	Y	Y	Y	Y	N	N
FLORIDA							
1 **Miller**	Y	Y	Y	Y	Y	?	N
2 Boyd	Y	Y	Y	Y	Y	Y	Y
3 Brown	Y	Y	Y	Y	Y	Y	Y
4 **Crenshaw**	Y	Y	Y	Y	Y	N	N
5 **Brown-Waite**	Y	Y	Y	Y	Y	N	N
6 **Stearns**	Y	Y	Y	Y	Y	N	N
7 **Mica**	Y	Y	Y	Y	Y	N	N
8 Grayson	Y	Y	Y	Y	Y	Y	Y
9 **Bilirakis**	Y	Y	Y	Y	Y	N	N
10 **Young**	Y	Y	Y	Y	Y	N	N
11 Castor	Y	Y	Y	Y	Y	Y	Y
12 **Putnam**	Y	Y	Y	Y	Y	N	N
13 **Buchanan**	Y	Y	Y	Y	Y	N	N
14 **Mack**	Y	Y	Y	Y	Y	N	N
15 **Posey**	Y	Y	Y	Y	Y	N	N
16 **Rooney**	Y	Y	Y	Y	Y	N	N
17 Meek	Y	Y	?	?	?	Y	Y
18 **Ros-Lehtinen**	Y	Y	Y	Y	Y	Y	N
19 Deutch	Y	Y	Y	Y	Y	Y	Y
20 Wasserman Schultz	Y	Y	Y	Y	Y	Y	Y
21 **Diaz-Balart, L.**	Y	Y	Y	Y	Y	N	Y
22 Klein	Y	Y	Y	Y	Y	Y	Y
23 Hastings	Y	Y	Y	Y	Y	Y	Y
24 Kosmas	Y	Y	Y	Y	Y	Y	Y
25 **Diaz-Balart, M.**	Y	Y	Y	Y	Y	N	N
GEORGIA							
1 **Kingston**	Y	Y	Y	Y	Y	N	N
2 Bishop	Y	Y	Y	Y	Y	Y	Y
3 **Westmoreland**	Y	Y	Y	Y	Y	N	N
4 Johnson	Y	Y	Y	Y	Y	Y	?
5 Lewis	Y	Y	Y	Y	Y	Y	Y
6 **Price**	Y	Y	Y	Y	Y	N	N
7 **Linder**	Y	Y	Y	Y	Y	N	N
8 Marshall	Y	Y	Y	Y	Y	Y	Y
9 Vacant							
10 **Broun**	N	N	Y	Y	Y	N	N
11 **Gingrey**	Y	Y	Y	Y	Y	N	N
12 Barrow	Y	Y	Y	Y	Y	Y	Y
13 Scott	Y	Y	Y	Y	Y	Y	Y
HAWAII							
1 Vacant							
2 Hirono	Y	Y	Y	Y	Y	Y	Y
IDAHO							
1 Minnick	Y	Y	Y	Y	Y	Y	Y
2 **Simpson**	Y	Y	Y	Y	Y	N	N
ILLINOIS							
1 Rush	?	?	?	Y	Y	Y	Y
2 Jackson	Y	Y	Y	Y	Y	Y	Y
3 Lipinski	Y	Y	Y	Y	Y	Y	Y
4 Gutierrez	Y	Y	Y	Y	Y	Y	Y
5 Quigley	Y	Y	Y	Y	Y	Y	Y
6 **Roskam**	Y	Y	?	Y	Y	N	N
7 Davis	Y	Y	Y	Y	Y	Y	Y
8 Bean	?	?	?	Y	Y	Y	Y
9 Schakowsky	Y	Y	Y	Y	Y	Y	Y
10 **Kirk**	?	?	?	Y	Y	N	N
11 Halvorson	Y	Y	Y	Y	Y	Y	Y
12 Costello	?	?	?	Y	Y	Y	Y
13 **Biggert**	Y	Y	Y	Y	Y	Y	N
14 Foster	Y	Y	Y	Y	Y	Y	Y
15 **Johnson**	Y	Y	Y	Y	Y	N	N

KEY   **Republicans**   Democrats

Y Voted for (yea)	X Paired against	C Voted "present" to avoid possible conflict of interest
# Paired for	– Announced against	
+ Announced for	P Voted "present"	? Did not vote or otherwise make a position known
N Voted against (nay)		

	243	244	245	246	247	248	249
16 **Manzullo**	Y	Y	Y	Y	Y	Y	N
17 Hare	Y	Y	Y	Y	Y	Y	Y
18 **Schock**	Y	Y	Y	Y	Y	?	?
19 **Shimkus**	Y	Y	Y	Y	Y	Y	N
INDIANA							
1 Visclosky	Y	Y	Y	Y	Y	Y	Y
2 Donnelly	Y	Y	Y	Y	Y	Y	N
3 **Souder**	Y	Y	Y	Y	Y	N	N
4 **Buyer**	?	?	?	Y	Y	N	N
5 **Burton**	?	?	?	Y	Y	N	N
6 **Pence**	Y	?	?	Y	Y	N	N
7 Carson	?	?	?	Y	Y	Y	Y
8 Ellsworth	Y	Y	Y	Y	Y	Y	Y
9 Hill	Y	Y	Y	Y	Y	Y	N
IOWA							
1 Braley	Y	Y	Y	Y	Y	Y	Y
2 Loebsack	Y	Y	Y	Y	Y	Y	Y
3 Boswell	Y	Y	Y	Y	Y	Y	N
4 **Latham**	Y	Y	Y	Y	Y	Y	N
5 **King**	Y	Y	Y	Y	Y	N	N
KANSAS							
1 **Moran**	Y	Y	Y	Y	Y	N	N
2 **Jenkins**	Y	Y	Y	Y	Y	N	N
3 Moore	Y	Y	Y	Y	Y	Y	Y
4 **Tiahrt**	Y	Y	Y	Y	Y	N	N
KENTUCKY							
1 **Whitfield**	Y	Y	Y	Y	Y	Y	N
2 **Guthrie**	?	?	?	Y	Y	N	N
3 Yarmuth	Y	Y	Y	Y	Y	Y	Y
4 **Davis**	Y	Y	Y	Y	Y	N	N
5 **Rogers**	Y	Y	Y	Y	Y	Y	N
6 Chandler	Y	Y	Y	Y	Y	Y	Y
LOUISIANA							
1 **Scalise**	Y	Y	Y	Y	Y	N	N
2 **Cao**	Y	Y	Y	Y	Y	Y	N
3 Melancon	?	?	?	?	?	?	?
4 **Fleming**	Y	Y	Y	Y	Y	N	N
5 **Alexander**	Y	Y	Y	Y	Y	N	N
6 **Cassidy**	Y	Y	Y	Y	Y	N	N
7 **Boustany**	Y	Y	Y	Y	Y	N	N
MAINE							
1 Pingree	Y	Y	Y	Y	Y	Y	Y
2 Michaud	Y	Y	Y	Y	Y	Y	Y
MARYLAND							
1 Kratovil	Y	Y	Y	Y	Y	Y	?
2 Ruppersberger	Y	Y	Y	Y	Y	Y	Y
3 Sarbanes	Y	Y	Y	Y	Y	Y	Y
4 Edwards	Y	Y	Y	Y	Y	Y	Y
5 Hoyer	Y	Y	Y	Y	Y	Y	Y
6 **Bartlett**	Y	Y	Y	Y	Y	N	N
7 Cummings	Y	Y	Y	Y	Y	Y	Y
8 Van Hollen	Y	Y	Y	Y	Y	Y	Y
MASSACHUSETTS							
1 Olver	Y	Y	Y	Y	Y	Y	Y
2 Neal	Y	Y	Y	Y	Y	Y	Y
3 McGovern	Y	Y	Y	Y	Y	Y	Y
4 Frank	Y	Y	Y	Y	Y	Y	Y
5 Tsongas	Y	Y	Y	Y	Y	Y	Y
6 Tierney	Y	Y	Y	Y	Y	Y	Y
7 Markey	Y	Y	N	Y	Y	Y	Y
8 Capuano	Y	Y	Y	Y	Y	Y	Y
9 Lynch	Y	Y	Y	Y	Y	Y	Y
10 Delahunt	Y	Y	Y	Y	Y	Y	Y
MICHIGAN							
1 Stupak	Y	Y	Y	Y	Y	Y	Y
2 **Hoekstra**	?	?	?	?	?	?	?
3 **Ehlers**	Y	Y	Y	Y	Y	Y	N
4 **Camp**	Y	Y	Y	Y	Y	N	N
5 Kildee	Y	Y	Y	Y	Y	Y	Y
6 **Upton**	Y	Y	Y	Y	Y	N	N
7 Schauer	Y	Y	Y	Y	Y	Y	N
8 **Rogers**	Y	Y	Y	Y	Y	Y	N
9 Peters	Y	Y	Y	Y	Y	Y	Y
10 **Miller**	Y	Y	Y	Y	Y	N	N
11 **McCotter**	Y	Y	Y	Y	Y	Y	N
12 Levin	Y	Y	Y	Y	Y	Y	Y
13 Kilpatrick	Y	Y	Y	Y	Y	Y	Y
14 Conyers	?	?	?	Y	Y	Y	Y
15 Dingell	Y	Y	Y	Y	Y	Y	Y
MINNESOTA							
1 Walz	Y	Y	Y	Y	Y	Y	Y
2 **Kline**	Y	Y	Y	Y	Y	N	N
3 **Paulsen**	Y	Y	Y	Y	Y	Y	N
4 McCollum	Y	Y	Y	Y	Y	Y	?

	243	244	245	246	247	248	249
5 Ellison	Y	Y	Y	Y	Y	Y	Y
6 **Bachmann**	Y	Y	Y	Y	Y	N	N
7 Peterson	?	?	?	Y	Y	Y	Y
8 Oberstar	?	Y	Y	Y	Y	Y	Y
MISSISSIPPI							
1 Childers	Y	Y	Y	Y	Y	Y	N
2 Thompson	?	?	?	Y	Y	Y	Y
3 **Harper**	Y	Y	Y	Y	Y	N	N
4 Taylor	?	?	?	Y	Y	Y	N
MISSOURI							
1 Clay	Y	Y	Y	Y	Y	Y	Y
2 **Akin**	Y	Y	Y	Y	Y	N	N
3 Carnahan	Y	Y	Y	Y	Y	Y	Y
4 Skelton	Y	Y	Y	Y	Y	Y	Y
5 Cleaver	Y	Y	Y	Y	Y	Y	Y
6 **Graves**	Y	Y	Y	Y	Y	N	N
7 **Blunt**	?	?	?	Y	Y	N	N
8 **Emerson**	Y	Y	Y	Y	Y	N	N
9 **Luetkemeyer**	Y	Y	Y	Y	Y	N	N
MONTANA							
AL **Rehberg**	Y	Y	Y	Y	Y	Y	N
NEBRASKA							
1 **Fortenberry**	+	+	+	Y	Y	Y	N
2 **Terry**	Y	Y	Y	Y	Y	Y	N
3 **Smith**	+	+	+	Y	Y	N	N
NEVADA							
1 Berkley	Y	Y	Y	Y	Y	Y	Y
2 **Heller**	Y	Y	Y	Y	Y	N	N
3 Titus	Y	Y	Y	Y	Y	Y	Y
NEW HAMPSHIRE							
1 Shea-Porter	Y	Y	Y	Y	Y	Y	Y
2 Hodes	?	?	?	Y	Y	Y	Y
NEW JERSEY							
1 Andrews	Y	Y	Y	Y	Y	Y	Y
2 **LoBiondo**	Y	Y	Y	Y	Y	Y	N
3 Adler	Y	Y	Y	Y	Y	Y	Y
4 **Smith**	Y	Y	Y	Y	Y	Y	N
5 **Garrett**	Y	Y	Y	Y	Y	N	N
6 Pallone	Y	Y	Y	Y	Y	Y	Y
7 **Lance**	Y	Y	Y	Y	Y	Y	N
8 Pascrell	Y	Y	Y	Y	Y	Y	Y
9 Rothman	Y	Y	Y	Y	Y	Y	Y
10 Payne	?	?	?	Y	Y	Y	Y
11 **Frelinghuysen**	Y	Y	Y	Y	Y	Y	N
12 Holt	Y	Y	Y	Y	Y	Y	Y
13 Sires	Y	Y	Y	Y	Y	Y	Y
NEW MEXICO							
1 Heinrich	Y	Y	Y	Y	Y	Y	Y
2 Teague	Y	Y	Y	Y	Y	Y	Y
3 Luján	Y	Y	Y	Y	Y	Y	Y
NEW YORK							
1 Bishop	Y	Y	Y	Y	Y	Y	N
2 Israel	Y	Y	Y	Y	Y	Y	Y
3 **King**	Y	Y	Y	Y	Y	Y	N
4 McCarthy	Y	Y	Y	Y	Y	Y	Y
5 Ackerman	Y	Y	Y	Y	Y	Y	Y
6 Meeks	Y	Y	Y	Y	Y	Y	Y
7 Crowley	Y	Y	Y	Y	Y	Y	Y
8 Nadler	Y	Y	Y	Y	Y	Y	Y
9 Weiner	Y	Y	Y	Y	Y	Y	Y
10 Towns	?	?	?	Y	Y	Y	Y
11 Clarke	Y	Y	Y	Y	Y	Y	Y
12 Velázquez	Y	Y	Y	Y	Y	Y	Y
13 McMahon	Y	Y	Y	Y	Y	Y	Y
14 Maloney	Y	Y	Y	Y	Y	Y	Y
15 Rangel	Y	Y	Y	Y	Y	Y	Y
16 Serrano	Y	Y	Y	Y	Y	Y	Y
17 Engel	Y	Y	Y	Y	Y	Y	Y
18 Lowey	Y	Y	Y	Y	Y	Y	Y
19 Hall	Y	Y	Y	Y	Y	Y	Y
20 Murphy	Y	Y	Y	Y	Y	Y	Y
21 Tonko	+	Y	Y	Y	Y	Y	Y
22 Hinchey	Y	Y	Y	Y	Y	Y	Y
23 Owens	Y	Y	Y	Y	Y	Y	Y
24 Arcuri	Y	Y	Y	Y	Y	Y	Y
25 Maffei	Y	Y	Y	Y	Y	Y	Y
26 **Lee**	Y	Y	Y	Y	Y	Y	N
27 Higgins	Y	Y	Y	Y	Y	Y	Y
28 Slaughter	Y	Y	Y	Y	Y	Y	Y
29 Vacant							
NORTH CAROLINA							
1 Butterfield	?	?	?	Y	Y	Y	Y
2 Etheridge	Y	Y	Y	Y	Y	Y	Y
3 **Jones**	Y	Y	Y	Y	Y	N	N
4 Price	Y	Y	Y	Y	Y	Y	Y

	243	244	245	246	247	248	249
5 **Foxx**	Y	Y	Y	Y	P	N	N
6 **Coble**	?	?	?	?	?	?	N
7 McIntyre	Y	Y	Y	Y	Y	Y	Y
8 Kissell	Y	Y	Y	Y	Y	Y	Y
9 **Myrick**	Y	Y	Y	Y	Y	N	N
10 **McHenry**	?	?	?	Y	Y	N	N
11 Shuler	Y	Y	Y	Y	Y	Y	N
12 Watt	Y	Y	Y	Y	Y	Y	Y
13 Miller	Y	Y	Y	Y	Y	Y	Y
NORTH DAKOTA							
AL Pomeroy	Y	Y	Y	Y	Y	Y	Y
OHIO							
1 Driehaus	Y	Y	Y	Y	Y	Y	Y
2 **Schmidt**	Y	Y	Y	Y	Y	N	N
3 **Turner**	Y	Y	Y	Y	Y	Y	N
4 **Jordan**	Y	Y	Y	Y	Y	N	N
5 **Latta**	Y	Y	Y	Y	Y	N	N
6 Wilson	?	?	?	Y	Y	Y	Y
7 **Austria**	?	?	?	Y	Y	N	N
8 **Boehner**	Y	Y	Y	Y	?	N	N
9 Kaptur	Y	Y	Y	Y	Y	Y	Y
10 Kucinich	Y	Y	Y	Y	Y	Y	Y
11 Fudge	Y	Y	Y	Y	Y	Y	Y
12 **Tiberi**	Y	Y	Y	Y	Y	Y	N
13 Sutton	Y	Y	Y	Y	Y	Y	Y
14 **LaTourette**	Y	Y	Y	Y	Y	Y	N
15 Kilroy	Y	Y	Y	Y	Y	Y	Y
16 Boccieri	Y	Y	Y	Y	Y	Y	Y
17 Ryan	Y	Y	Y	Y	Y	Y	Y
18 Space	Y	Y	Y	Y	Y	Y	Y
OKLAHOMA							
1 **Sullivan**	Y	Y	Y	Y	Y	Y	N
2 Boren	Y	Y	Y	Y	Y	Y	Y
3 **Lucas**	?	?	?	Y	Y	Y	N
4 **Cole**	Y	Y	Y	Y	Y	Y	N
5 **Fallin**	?	?	?	Y	Y	Y	N
OREGON							
1 Wu	Y	Y	Y	Y	Y	Y	Y
2 **Walden**	Y	Y	Y	Y	Y	N	N
3 Blumenauer	Y	Y	Y	Y	Y	Y	Y
4 DeFazio	Y	Y	Y	Y	Y	Y	Y
5 Schrader	Y	Y	Y	Y	Y	Y	Y
PENNSYLVANIA							
1 Brady	Y	Y	Y	Y	Y	Y	Y
2 Fattah	Y	Y	Y	Y	Y	Y	Y
3 Dahlkemper	Y	Y	Y	Y	Y	Y	+
4 Altmire	Y	Y	Y	Y	Y	Y	Y
5 **Thompson**	Y	Y	Y	Y	Y	N	N
6 **Gerlach**	Y	Y	Y	Y	Y	Y	N
7 Sestak	Y	Y	Y	Y	Y	Y	Y
8 Murphy, P.	Y	Y	Y	Y	Y	Y	Y
9 **Shuster**	Y	Y	Y	Y	Y	Y	N
10 Carney	Y	Y	Y	Y	Y	Y	Y
11 Kanjorski	Y	Y	Y	Y	Y	Y	Y
12 Vacant							
13 Schwartz	Y	Y	Y	Y	Y	Y	Y
14 Doyle	Y	Y	Y	Y	Y	Y	Y
15 **Dent**	Y	Y	Y	Y	Y	Y	N
16 **Pitts**	Y	Y	Y	Y	Y	Y	N
17 Holden	Y	Y	Y	Y	Y	Y	Y
18 **Murphy, T.**	Y	Y	Y	Y	Y	Y	N
19 **Platts**	?	Y	Y	Y	Y	N	N
RHODE ISLAND							
1 Kennedy	Y	Y	Y	Y	Y	Y	?
2 Langevin	Y	Y	Y	Y	Y	Y	Y
SOUTH CAROLINA							
1 **Brown**	Y	Y	Y	Y	Y	Y	N
2 **Wilson**	Y	Y	Y	Y	Y	N	N
3 **Barrett**	Y	Y	Y	?	?	?	?
4 **Inglis**	Y	Y	Y	Y	Y	N	N
5 Spratt	Y	Y	Y	Y	Y	Y	Y
6 Clyburn	Y	Y	Y	Y	Y	Y	Y
SOUTH DAKOTA							
AL Herseth Sandlin	Y	Y	Y	Y	Y	Y	Y
TENNESSEE							
1 **Roe**	Y	Y	Y	Y	Y	N	N
2 **Duncan**	Y	Y	Y	Y	Y	Y	N
3 **Wamp**	Y	Y	Y	Y	Y	Y	N
4 Davis	Y	Y	Y	Y	Y	Y	Y
5 Cooper	Y	Y	Y	Y	Y	Y	Y
6 Gordon	Y	Y	Y	Y	Y	Y	Y
7 **Blackburn**	?	?	?	?	?	?	?
8 Tanner	Y	Y	Y	Y	Y	Y	Y
9 Cohen	+	+	+	Y	Y	Y	Y

	243	244	245	246	247	248	249
TEXAS							
1 **Gohmert**	Y	Y	Y	Y	Y	?	N
2 **Poe**	Y	Y	Y	Y	Y	N	N
3 **Johnson, S.**	Y	Y	Y	Y	Y	N	N
4 **Hall**	Y	Y	Y	Y	Y	Y	N
5 **Hensarling**	Y	Y	Y	Y	Y	N	N
6 **Barton**	Y	Y	Y	Y	Y	N	N
7 **Culberson**	Y	Y	Y	Y	Y	N	N
8 **Brady**	?	Y	Y	Y	Y	N	N
9 Green, A.	Y	Y	Y	Y	Y	Y	Y
10 **McCaul**	?	Y	Y	Y	Y	Y	N
11 **Conaway**	+	+	+	Y	Y	N	N
12 **Granger**	Y	Y	Y	Y	Y	N	N
13 **Thornberry**	Y	Y	Y	Y	Y	N	N
14 **Paul**	N	N	Y	Y	Y	N	N
15 Hinojosa	?	?	?	?	?	?	Y
16 Reyes	Y	Y	Y	Y	Y	Y	?
17 Edwards	?	Y	Y	Y	Y	Y	Y
18 Jackson Lee	Y	Y	Y	?	?	?	Y
19 **Neugebauer**	Y	Y	Y	Y	Y	N	N
20 Gonzalez	Y	Y	Y	Y	Y	Y	Y
21 **Smith**	Y	Y	Y	Y	Y	N	N
22 **Olson**	Y	Y	Y	Y	Y	N	N
23 Rodriguez	Y	Y	Y	Y	Y	Y	Y
24 **Marchant**	Y	Y	Y	Y	Y	N	N
25 Doggett	Y	Y	Y	Y	Y	Y	Y
26 **Burgess**	Y	Y	Y	Y	P	N	N
27 Ortiz	Y	Y	Y	Y	Y	Y	Y
28 Cuellar	Y	Y	Y	Y	Y	Y	Y
29 Green, G.	Y	Y	Y	Y	Y	Y	Y
30 Johnson, E.	Y	Y	Y	Y	Y	Y	Y
31 **Carter**	Y	Y	Y	Y	Y	N	N
32 **Sessions**	Y	Y	Y	Y	Y	N	N
UTAH							
1 **Bishop**	Y	Y	Y	Y	Y	N	N
2 Matheson	Y	Y	Y	Y	Y	Y	Y
3 **Chaffetz**	Y	Y	Y	Y	Y	N	N
VERMONT							
AL Welch	?	Y	Y	Y	Y	Y	Y
VIRGINIA							
1 **Wittman**	Y	Y	Y	Y	Y	N	N
2 Nye	Y	Y	Y	Y	Y	Y	Y
3 Scott	?	?	?	Y	Y	Y	Y
4 **Forbes**	Y	Y	Y	Y	Y	Y	N
5 Perriello	Y	Y	Y	Y	Y	Y	Y
6 **Goodlatte**	Y	Y	Y	Y	Y	N	N
7 **Cantor**	Y	Y	Y	Y	?	Y	N
8 Moran	Y	Y	Y	Y	Y	Y	Y
9 Boucher	Y	Y	Y	Y	Y	Y	Y
10 **Wolf**	Y	Y	Y	Y	Y	N	N
11 Connolly	Y	Y	Y	Y	Y	Y	Y
WASHINGTON							
1 Inslee	Y	Y	Y	Y	Y	Y	Y
2 Larsen	Y	Y	Y	Y	Y	Y	Y
3 Baird	Y	Y	Y	?	Y	Y	Y
4 **Hastings**	Y	Y	Y	Y	Y	N	N
5 **McMorris Rodgers**	Y	Y	Y	Y	Y	N	N
6 Dicks	?	?	?	Y	Y	Y	Y
7 McDermott	Y	Y	Y	Y	Y	Y	Y
8 **Reichert**	Y	Y	Y	Y	Y	N	N
9 Smith	Y	Y	Y	Y	Y	Y	Y
WEST VIRGINIA							
1 Mollohan	Y	Y	Y	Y	Y	Y	?
2 **Capito**	Y	Y	Y	Y	Y	Y	N
3 Rahall	Y	Y	Y	Y	Y	Y	Y
WISCONSIN							
1 **Ryan**	Y	Y	Y	Y	Y	N	N
2 Baldwin	Y	Y	Y	Y	Y	Y	Y
3 Kind	Y	Y	Y	Y	Y	Y	Y
4 Moore	Y	Y	Y	Y	Y	Y	?
5 **Sensenbrenner**	Y	Y	Y	Y	Y	N	N
6 **Petri**	Y	Y	Y	Y	Y	N	N
7 Obey	Y	Y	Y	Y	Y	Y	Y
8 Kagen	Y	Y	Y	Y	Y	Y	Y
WYOMING							
AL **Lummis**	?	?	?	Y	Y	Y	N
DELEGATES							
Faleomavaega (A.S.)							
Norton (D.C.)							
Bordallo (Guam)							
Sablan (N. Marianas)							
Pierluisi (P.R.)							
Christensen (V.I.)							

IN THE HOUSE | By Vote Number

250. **H Res 1295. Tribute to Mother's Day/Adoption.** Lynch, D-Mass., motion to suspend the rules and adopt the resolution that would celebrate the role of mothers and support the goals and ideals of Mother's Day. Motion agreed to 417-0: D 247-0; R 170-0. A two-thirds majority of those present and voting (278 in this case) is required for adoption under suspension of the rules. May 6, 2010.

251. **HR 1722. Telework for Federal Employees/Passage.** Lynch, D-Mass., motion to suspend the rules and pass the bill that would require the heads of each executive agency to establish and implement a policy that would authorize employees to telework as much as possible without diminishing agency operations or performance. It also would require the agency heads to provide training for telework employees and designate a telework managing officer. Motion rejected 268-147: D 244-0; R 24-147. A two-thirds majority of those present and voting (277 in this case) is required for passage under suspension of the rules. May 6, 2010.

252. **HR 5019. Home Star Energy Retrofit Program/Repaid Loan Funds.** Barton, R-Texas, amendment that would strike a provision in the bill that would allow financing entities to use repaid Home Star Energy Efficiency Loan Program funds to provide financial assistance to additional participants. Rejected in Committee of the Whole 180-237: D 14-236; R 166-1. May 6, 2010.

253. **HR 5019. Home Star Energy Retrofit Program/Public Information Campaign.** Burgess, R-Texas, amendment that would strike a provision in the bill that would require the development of a public information campaign about the new Home Star program. Rejected in Committee of the Whole 190-228: D 23-227; R 167-1. May 6, 2010.

254. **HR 5019. Home Star Energy Retrofit Program/Recommit.** Barton, R-Texas, motion to recommit the bill to the Energy and Commerce Committee with instructions that it be immediately reported back with amendments that would eliminate the Home Star Energy Efficiency Loan Program, sunset the bill if it would increase the federal deficit, and make homeowners with annual household incomes of more than $250,000 ineligible for the rebate program. It also would eliminate a provision that would require the development of a public information campaign, prohibit authorized funds from being used under official business to travel to gambling establishments, and require qualified contractors to certify that employees have not been convicted of or have not pleaded guilty to child molestation, rape or other sexual assault. Motion agreed to 346-68: D 178-67; R 168-1. May 6, 2010.

255. **HR 5019. Home Star Energy Retrofit Program/Passage.** Passage of the bill that would authorize $6.6 billion for a rebate program for energy-efficient home renovations, as well as a program to assist low-income households living in certain manufactured homes to buy new Energy Star-qualified manufactured homes. The bill would require that contractors be certified to perform efficiency installations. As amended, the bill would sunset if it would increase the federal deficit. Households with annual incomes of more than $250,000 would be ineligible for the rebate program. It also would require qualified contractors to certify that employees have not been convicted of or have not pleaded guilty to child molestation, rape or other sexual assault, and it would prohibit authorized funds from being used under official business to travel to gambling establishments. Passed 246-161: D 234-7; R 12-154. A "yea" was a vote in support of the president's position. May 6, 2010.

	250	251	252	253	254	255
ALABAMA						
1 Bonner	?	?	?	?	?	?
2 Bright	Y	Y	Y	N	Y	Y
3 Rogers	Y	N	Y	Y	Y	N
4 Aderholt	Y	N	Y	Y	Y	N
5 Griffith	Y	N	Y	Y	Y	N
6 Bachus	Y	N	Y	Y	Y	N
7 Davis	?	?	?	?	?	?
ALASKA						
AL Young	Y	N	Y	Y	Y	N
ARIZONA						
1 Kirkpatrick	Y	Y	Y	Y	Y	N
2 Franks	Y	N	Y	Y	Y	N
3 Shadegg	Y	N	Y	Y	Y	N
4 Pastor	Y	Y	N	N	Y	Y
5 Mitchell	Y	Y	Y	N	Y	Y
6 Flake	Y	N	Y	Y	Y	N
7 Grijalva	Y	Y	N	N	N	Y
8 Giffords	Y	Y	N	N	Y	Y
ARKANSAS						
1 Berry	Y	Y	N	N	Y	Y
2 Snyder	Y	Y	N	N	Y	Y
3 Boozman	Y	N	Y	Y	Y	N
4 Ross	Y	Y	N	N	Y	Y
CALIFORNIA						
1 Thompson	Y	Y	N	N	Y	Y
2 Herger	Y	N	Y	Y	Y	N
3 Lungren	Y	N	Y	N	Y	N
4 McClintock	Y	N	Y	Y	Y	N
5 Matsui	Y	Y	N	N	Y	Y
6 Woolsey	Y	Y	N	N	N	Y
7 Miller, George	Y	Y	N	N	Y	Y
8 Pelosi						
9 Lee	Y	Y	N	N	N	Y
10 Garamendi	Y	Y	N	N	Y	Y
11 McNerney	Y	Y	N	N	Y	Y
12 Speier	Y	Y	N	N	Y	Y
13 Stark	Y	Y	N	N	N	Y
14 Eshoo	Y	Y	N	N	Y	Y
15 Honda	Y	Y	N	N	N	Y
16 Lofgren	Y	Y	N	N	Y	Y
17 Farr	Y	Y	N	N	N	Y
18 Cardoza	Y	Y	N	Y	Y	Y
19 Radanovich	Y	N	Y	Y	Y	N
20 Costa	Y	Y	N	Y	Y	Y
21 Nunes	Y	N	Y	Y	Y	N
22 McCarthy	Y	N	Y	Y	Y	?
23 Capps	Y	Y	N	N	N	Y
24 Gallegly	Y	N	Y	Y	Y	N
25 McKeon	Y	N	Y	Y	Y	N
26 Dreier	Y	N	Y	Y	Y	N
27 Sherman	Y	Y	N	N	Y	Y
28 Berman	Y	Y	N	N	N	Y
29 Schiff	Y	Y	N	N	Y	Y
30 Waxman	Y	Y	N	N	N	Y
31 Becerra	Y	Y	N	N	N	Y
32 Chu	Y	Y	N	N	N	Y
33 Watson	Y	Y	N	N	N	Y
34 Roybal-Allard	Y	Y	N	N	N	Y
35 Waters	Y	Y	N	N	N	Y
36 Harman	Y	Y	N	N	Y	Y
37 Richardson	Y	Y	N	Y	Y	Y
38 Napolitano	Y	?	N	N	N	Y
39 Sánchez, Linda	Y	Y	N	N	N	Y
40 Royce	Y	N	Y	Y	Y	N
41 Lewis	Y	N	Y	Y	Y	N
42 Miller, Gary	Y	N	Y	Y	Y	N
43 Baca	Y	Y	N	N	Y	Y
44 Calvert	Y	N	Y	Y	Y	N
45 Bono Mack	Y	N	Y	Y	Y	N
46 Rohrabacher	Y	N	Y	Y	Y	Y
47 Sanchez, Loretta	Y	Y	N	N	N	Y
48 Campbell	?	?	?	?	?	?
49 Issa	Y	N	Y	Y	Y	N
50 Bilbray	Y	Y	Y	Y	Y	Y
51 Filner	Y	Y	N	N	N	+
52 Hunter	Y	N	Y	Y	Y	N
53 Davis	Y	Y	N	N	Y	Y

	250	251	252	253	254	255
COLORADO						
1 DeGette	?	?	?	?	?	?
2 Polis	Y	Y	N	N	Y	Y
3 Salazar	Y	Y	N	N	Y	Y
4 Markey	Y	Y	Y	N	Y	Y
5 Lamborn	Y	N	Y	Y	Y	N
6 Coffman	Y	N	Y	Y	Y	N
7 Perlmutter	Y	Y	N	N	Y	Y
CONNECTICUT						
1 Larson	Y	Y	N	N	Y	Y
2 Courtney	Y	Y	N	N	Y	Y
3 DeLauro	Y	Y	N	N	Y	Y
4 Himes	Y	Y	N	N	Y	Y
5 Murphy	Y	Y	N	N	Y	Y
DELAWARE						
AL Castle	Y	N	?	Y	Y	Y
FLORIDA						
1 Miller	Y	N	Y	Y	Y	N
2 Boyd	Y	Y	N	N	Y	?
3 Brown	Y	Y	N	?	?	?
4 Crenshaw	Y	N	Y	Y	Y	N
5 Brown-Waite	Y	N	Y	Y	Y	N
6 Stearns	Y	N	Y	Y	Y	N
7 Mica	Y	N	Y	Y	Y	N
8 Grayson	Y	Y	N	N	Y	Y
9 Bilirakis	Y	Y	Y	Y	Y	N
10 Young	Y	N	Y	Y	Y	N
11 Castor	Y	Y	N	N	N	Y
12 Putnam	Y	N	Y	Y	Y	N
13 Buchanan	Y	N	Y	Y	Y	N
14 Mack	Y	N	Y	Y	Y	N
15 Posey	Y	N	Y	Y	Y	N
16 Rooney	Y	N	Y	Y	Y	N
17 Meek	Y	Y	N	N	Y	Y
18 Ros-Lehtinen	Y	N	Y	Y	Y	N
19 Deutch	Y	Y	N	N	Y	Y
20 Wasserman Schultz	Y	Y	N	N	Y	Y
21 Diaz-Balart, L.	Y	N	Y	Y	Y	N
22 Klein	Y	Y	N	N	Y	Y
23 Hastings	Y	Y	N	N	N	Y
24 Kosmas	Y	Y	N	N	Y	Y
25 Diaz-Balart, M.	Y	N	Y	Y	Y	N
GEORGIA						
1 Kingston	Y	N	Y	Y	Y	N
2 Bishop	Y	Y	N	N	Y	Y
3 Westmoreland	Y	N	Y	Y	Y	N
4 Johnson	Y	Y	N	N	Y	Y
5 Lewis	Y	Y	N	N	Y	Y
6 Price	Y	N	Y	Y	Y	N
7 Linder	Y	Y	Y	Y	Y	N
8 Marshall	Y	Y	Y	Y	Y	N
9 Vacant						
10 Broun	Y	N	Y	Y	Y	N
11 Gingrey	Y	N	Y	Y	Y	N
12 Barrow	Y	Y	N	N	Y	Y
13 Scott	Y	Y	N	N	Y	Y
HAWAII						
1 Vacant						
2 Hirono	Y	Y	N	N	N	Y
IDAHO						
1 Minnick	Y	Y	N	N	Y	Y
2 Simpson	Y	N	Y	Y	Y	N
ILLINOIS						
1 Rush	Y	Y	N	N	N	Y
2 Jackson	Y	Y	N	N	Y	Y
3 Lipinski	Y	Y	N	N	Y	Y
4 Gutierrez	Y	Y	N	N	Y	Y
5 Quigley	Y	Y	N	N	Y	Y
6 Roskam	Y	N	Y	Y	Y	N
7 Davis	Y	Y	N	N	N	Y
8 Bean	Y	Y	N	N	Y	Y
9 Schakowsky	Y	Y	N	N	N	Y
10 Kirk	Y	Y	Y	Y	Y	N
11 Halvorson	Y	Y	N	N	Y	Y
12 Costello	Y	Y	N	N	N	Y
13 Biggert	Y	N	Y	Y	Y	Y
14 Foster	Y	Y	N	N	Y	Y
15 Johnson	Y	N	Y	Y	Y	N

KEY   **Republicans**   Democrats

Y Voted for (yea)	X Paired against	C Voted "present" to avoid possible conflict of interest
# Paired for	– Announced against	
+ Announced for	P Voted "present"	? Did not vote or otherwise make a position known
N Voted against (nay)		

	250	251	252	253	254	255
16 **Manzullo**	Y	N	Y	Y	Y	N
17 Hare	Y	Y	N	N	Y	Y
18 **Schock**	Y	N	Y	Y	Y	N
19 **Shimkus**	Y	N	Y	Y	Y	N
INDIANA						
1 Visclosky	Y	Y	N	N	Y	Y
2 Donnelly	Y	Y	N	Y	Y	Y
3 **Souder**	Y	N	Y	Y	Y	N
4 **Buyer**	Y	N	Y	Y	Y	N
5 **Burton**	Y	N	Y	Y	Y	N
6 **Pence**	Y	N	Y	Y	Y	N
7 Carson	Y	Y	N	N	Y	Y
8 Ellsworth	Y	Y	N	Y	Y	Y
9 Hill	Y	Y	N	N	Y	Y
IOWA						
1 Braley	Y	Y	N	N	Y	Y
2 Loebsack	Y	Y	N	N	Y	Y
3 Boswell	Y	Y	N	N	Y	Y
4 **Latham**	Y	Y	Y	Y	Y	N
5 **King**	Y	N	Y	Y	Y	N
KANSAS						
1 **Moran**	Y	N	Y	Y	Y	N
2 **Jenkins**	Y	N	Y	Y	Y	N
3 Moore	Y	Y	N	N	Y	Y
4 **Tiahrt**	Y	N	Y	Y	Y	N
KENTUCKY						
1 **Whitfield**	Y	N	Y	Y	Y	?
2 **Guthrie**	Y	N	?	?	?	?
3 Yarmuth	Y	Y	N	N	Y	Y
4 **Davis**	Y	N	Y	Y	Y	N
5 **Rogers**	Y	N	Y	Y	Y	N
6 Chandler	Y	Y	Y	N	Y	Y
LOUISIANA						
1 **Scalise**	Y	N	Y	Y	Y	N
2 **Cao**	Y	Y	Y	Y	Y	Y
3 Melancon	?	?	?	?	?	?
4 **Fleming**	Y	N	Y	Y	Y	N
5 **Alexander**	Y	N	Y	Y	Y	N
6 **Cassidy**	Y	N	Y	Y	Y	N
7 **Boustany**	Y	N	Y	Y	Y	N
MAINE						
1 Pingree	Y	Y	N	N	N	Y
2 Michaud	Y	Y	N	N	N	Y
MARYLAND						
1 Kratovil	Y	Y	N	N	Y	Y
2 Ruppersberger	Y	Y	N	N	Y	Y
3 Sarbanes	Y	Y	N	N	Y	Y
4 Edwards	Y	Y	N	N	Y	Y
5 Hoyer	Y	Y	N	N	N	Y
6 **Bartlett**	Y	Y	Y	Y	Y	Y
7 Cummings	Y	Y	N	N	Y	Y
8 Van Hollen	Y	Y	N	N	Y	Y
MASSACHUSETTS						
1 Olver	Y	Y	N	N	N	Y
2 Neal	Y	Y	N	N	Y	Y
3 McGovern	Y	Y	N	N	Y	Y
4 Frank	Y	Y	N	N	N	Y
5 Tsongas	Y	Y	N	N	Y	Y
6 Tierney	Y	Y	N	N	Y	Y
7 Markey	Y	Y	N	N	N	Y
8 Capuano	Y	Y	N	N	Y	Y
9 Lynch	Y	Y	N	N	Y	Y
10 Delahunt	Y	Y	N	N	N	?
MICHIGAN						
1 Stupak	Y	Y	N	N	N	Y
2 **Hoekstra**	?	?	?	?	?	?
3 **Ehlers**	Y	Y	N	Y	Y	Y
4 **Camp**	Y	N	Y	Y	Y	Y
5 Kildee	Y	Y	N	N	Y	Y
6 **Upton**	Y	N	Y	Y	Y	N
7 Schauer	Y	Y	Y	Y	Y	N
8 **Rogers**	Y	N	Y	Y	Y	N
9 Peters	Y	Y	N	Y	Y	Y
10 **Miller**	Y	N	Y	Y	Y	N
11 **McCotter**	Y	Y	Y	Y	Y	N
12 Levin	Y	Y	N	N	Y	Y
13 Kilpatrick	Y	Y	N	N	N	Y
14 Conyers	Y	Y	N	N	N	Y
15 Dingell	Y	Y	N	N	N	Y
MINNESOTA						
1 Walz	Y	Y	N	N	Y	Y
2 **Kline**	Y	N	Y	Y	Y	N
3 **Paulsen**	Y	N	Y	Y	Y	N
4 McCollum	?	?	?	?	?	?

	250	251	252	253	254	255
5 Ellison	Y	Y	N	N	Y	Y
6 **Bachmann**	Y	N	Y	Y	Y	N
7 Peterson	Y	Y	N	N	Y	Y
8 Oberstar	Y	Y	N	N	N	Y
MISSISSIPPI						
1 Childers	Y	Y	N	Y	Y	Y
2 Thompson	Y	Y	N	N	N	Y
3 **Harper**	Y	N	Y	Y	Y	N
4 Taylor	Y	Y	Y	Y	Y	Y
MISSOURI						
1 Clay	Y	Y	N	N	N	Y
2 **Akin**	Y	N	Y	?	Y	N
3 Carnahan	Y	Y	N	N	Y	Y
4 Skelton	Y	Y	N	N	Y	Y
5 Cleaver	Y	Y	N	N	N	Y
6 **Graves**	Y	Y	Y	Y	Y	N
7 **Blunt**	Y	N	Y	Y	Y	N
8 **Emerson**	Y	N	Y	Y	Y	N
9 **Luetkemeyer**	Y	N	Y	Y	Y	N
MONTANA						
AL **Rehberg**	Y	N	Y	Y	Y	N
NEBRASKA						
1 **Fortenberry**	Y	Y	Y	Y	Y	N
2 **Terry**	Y	N	Y	Y	Y	N
3 **Smith**	Y	N	Y	Y	Y	N
NEVADA						
1 Berkley	Y	Y	N	N	N	Y
2 **Heller**	Y	N	Y	Y	N	N
3 Titus	Y	Y	N	N	N	Y
NEW HAMPSHIRE						
1 Shea-Porter	Y	Y	N	N	Y	Y
2 Hodes	Y	Y	N	N	Y	Y
NEW JERSEY						
1 Andrews	Y	Y	N	N	N	Y
2 **LoBiondo**	Y	N	Y	Y	Y	N
3 Adler	Y	Y	N	N	Y	Y
4 **Smith**	Y	N	Y	Y	Y	N
5 **Garrett**	Y	N	Y	Y	Y	N
6 Pallone	Y	Y	N	N	N	Y
7 **Lance**	Y	N	Y	Y	Y	N
8 Pascrell	Y	Y	N	N	N	N
9 Rothman	Y	Y	N	N	N	Y
10 Payne	Y	Y	N	N	N	Y
11 **Frelinghuysen**	Y	N	Y	Y	Y	N
12 Holt	Y	Y	N	N	N	Y
13 Sires	Y	Y	N	N	N	Y
NEW MEXICO						
1 Heinrich	Y	Y	N	N	Y	Y
2 Teague	Y	Y	N	Y	Y	Y
3 Luján	Y	Y	N	N	Y	Y
NEW YORK						
1 Bishop	Y	Y	N	N	Y	Y
2 Israel	Y	Y	N	N	Y	Y
3 **King**	Y	N	Y	Y	Y	N
4 McCarthy	Y	Y	N	N	Y	Y
5 Ackerman	Y	Y	N	N	Y	Y
6 Meeks	Y	Y	N	N	Y	Y
7 Crowley	Y	Y	N	N	Y	Y
8 Nadler	Y	Y	N	N	N	Y
9 Weiner	Y	Y	N	N	Y	Y
10 Towns	Y	Y	N	N	N	Y
11 Clarke	Y	Y	N	N	N	Y
12 Velázquez	Y	?	N	N	N	Y
13 McMahon	Y	Y	N	N	Y	Y
14 Maloney	Y	Y	N	N	Y	Y
15 Rangel	Y	Y	N	N	Y	Y
16 Serrano	Y	Y	N	N	Y	Y
17 Engel	Y	Y	N	N	N	Y
18 Lowey	Y	Y	N	N	Y	Y
19 Hall	Y	Y	N	N	Y	Y
20 Murphy	Y	Y	N	Y	Y	Y
21 Tonko	Y	Y	N	N	Y	Y
22 Hinchey	Y	Y	N	N	N	Y
23 Owens	Y	Y	N	N	Y	Y
24 Arcuri	Y	Y	N	Y	Y	Y
25 Maffei	Y	Y	N	N	Y	Y
26 **Lee**	Y	N	Y	Y	Y	N
27 Higgins	Y	Y	N	N	Y	Y
28 Slaughter	Y	Y	N	N	Y	Y
29 Vacant						
NORTH CAROLINA						
1 Butterfield	Y	Y	N	N	Y	Y
2 Etheridge	Y	Y	N	N	Y	Y
3 **Jones**	Y	N	Y	Y	Y	N
4 Price	Y	Y	N	N	Y	Y

	250	251	252	253	254	255
5 **Foxx**	Y	N	Y	Y	Y	N
6 **Coble**	Y	N	Y	Y	Y	N
7 McIntyre	Y	Y	N	N	Y	Y
8 Kissell	Y	Y	N	N	Y	Y
9 **Myrick**	Y	N	Y	Y	Y	N
10 **McHenry**	Y	N	Y	Y	Y	N
11 Shuler	Y	Y	N	N	Y	Y
12 Watt	Y	Y	N	N	N	Y
13 Miller	Y	Y	N	N	Y	Y
NORTH DAKOTA						
AL Pomeroy	Y	Y	N	N	Y	Y
OHIO						
1 Driehaus	Y	Y	N	N	Y	Y
2 **Schmidt**	Y	N	Y	Y	Y	N
3 **Turner**	Y	N	Y	Y	Y	N
4 **Jordan**	Y	N	Y	Y	Y	N
5 **Latta**	Y	N	Y	Y	Y	N
6 Wilson	Y	Y	N	N	Y	Y
7 **Austria**	Y	N	Y	Y	Y	N
8 **Boehner**	?	N	Y	Y	Y	N
9 Kaptur	Y	Y	N	N	Y	Y
10 Kucinich	Y	Y	N	N	Y	Y
11 Fudge	Y	Y	N	N	N	Y
12 **Tiberi**	Y	N	Y	Y	Y	N
13 Sutton	Y	Y	N	N	Y	Y
14 **LaTourette**	Y	Y	Y	Y	Y	N
15 Kilroy	Y	Y	N	Y	Y	Y
16 Boccieri	Y	Y	Y	N	Y	Y
17 Ryan	Y	Y	N	N	N	Y
18 Space	Y	Y	N	N	Y	Y
OKLAHOMA						
1 **Sullivan**	Y	N	Y	Y	Y	N
2 Boren	Y	Y	Y	Y	Y	N
3 **Lucas**	Y	N	Y	Y	Y	N
4 **Cole**	Y	N	Y	Y	Y	N
5 **Fallin**	Y	N	Y	Y	Y	N
OREGON						
1 Wu	Y	Y	N	N	Y	Y
2 **Walden**	Y	N	Y	Y	Y	N
3 Blumenauer	Y	Y	N	N	N	?
4 DeFazio	Y	Y	N	N	Y	Y
5 Schrader	Y	Y	N	Y	Y	Y
PENNSYLVANIA						
1 Brady	Y	Y	N	N	Y	Y
2 Fattah	Y	?	N	N	Y	Y
3 Dahlkemper	Y	Y	N	N	Y	Y
4 Altmire	Y	Y	N	N	Y	Y
5 **Thompson**	Y	N	Y	Y	Y	N
6 **Gerlach**	Y	N	Y	Y	Y	N
7 Sestak	Y	Y	N	N	Y	Y
8 Murphy, P.	Y	Y	N	N	Y	Y
9 **Shuster**	Y	N	Y	Y	Y	N
10 Carney	Y	Y	Y	Y	Y	Y
11 Kanjorski	Y	Y	N	N	N	N
12 Vacant						
13 Schwartz	Y	Y	N	N	Y	Y
14 Doyle	Y	Y	N	N	Y	Y
15 **Dent**	Y	Y	Y	Y	Y	N
16 **Pitts**	Y	N	?	?	?	?
17 Holden	Y	Y	N	N	Y	Y
18 **Murphy, T.**	Y	N	Y	Y	Y	Y
19 **Platts**	Y	N	?	Y	Y	N
RHODE ISLAND						
1 Kennedy	?	?	?	?	?	?
2 Langevin	Y	Y	N	N	Y	Y
SOUTH CAROLINA						
1 **Brown**	Y	N	Y	Y	Y	N
2 **Wilson**	Y	N	Y	Y	Y	N
3 **Barrett**	?	?	?	?	?	?
4 **Inglis**	Y	N	Y	Y	Y	N
5 Spratt	Y	Y	N	N	Y	Y
6 Clyburn	Y	Y	N	N	N	Y
SOUTH DAKOTA						
AL Herseth Sandlin	Y	Y	Y	N	Y	Y
TENNESSEE						
1 **Roe**	Y	N	Y	Y	Y	N
2 **Duncan**	Y	N	Y	Y	Y	N
3 **Wamp**	Y	N	?	?	?	?
4 Davis	Y	Y	N	N	Y	Y
5 Cooper	Y	Y	N	N	Y	Y
6 Gordon	Y	Y	N	Y	Y	Y
7 **Blackburn**	?	?	?	?	?	?
8 Tanner	Y	Y	N	N	Y	Y
9 Cohen	Y	Y	N	N	Y	Y

	250	251	252	253	254	255
TEXAS						
1 **Gohmert**	?	N	Y	Y	Y	Y
2 **Poe**	Y	N	Y	Y	Y	N
3 **Johnson, S.**	Y	N	Y	Y	Y	N
4 **Hall**	Y	Y	Y	Y	Y	Y
5 **Hensarling**	Y	N	Y	Y	Y	N
6 **Barton**	Y	N	Y	Y	Y	Y
7 **Culberson**	Y	N	Y	Y	Y	N
8 **Brady**	Y	?	Y	Y	Y	N
9 Green, A.	Y	Y	N	N	Y	Y
10 **McCaul**	Y	N	Y	Y	Y	N
11 **Conaway**	Y	N	Y	Y	Y	N
12 **Granger**	Y	N	Y	Y	Y	N
13 **Thornberry**	Y	N	Y	Y	Y	N
14 **Paul**	Y	N	Y	Y	Y	N
15 Hinojosa	Y	Y	N	N	N	Y
16 Reyes	Y	Y	N	N	N	Y
17 Edwards	Y	Y	Y	Y	Y	Y
18 Jackson Lee	Y	Y	N	N	Y	Y
19 **Neugebauer**	Y	N	Y	Y	Y	N
20 Gonzalez	Y	Y	N	N	Y	Y
21 **Smith**	Y	Y	Y	Y	Y	N
22 **Olson**	Y	N	Y	Y	Y	N
23 Rodriguez	Y	Y	N	N	Y	Y
24 **Marchant**	Y	N	Y	Y	Y	N
25 Doggett	Y	Y	N	Y	Y	Y
26 **Burgess**	Y	N	Y	Y	Y	N
27 Ortiz	Y	Y	N	N	Y	Y
28 Cuellar	Y	Y	N	N	Y	Y
29 Green, G.	Y	Y	N	N	Y	Y
30 Johnson, E.	Y	Y	N	N	Y	Y
31 **Carter**	Y	N	Y	Y	Y	N
32 **Sessions**	Y	N	Y	Y	Y	N
UTAH						
1 **Bishop**	Y	N	Y	Y	Y	N
2 Matheson	Y	Y	N	N	Y	Y
3 **Chaffetz**	Y	Y	Y	Y	Y	N
VERMONT						
AL Welch	Y	Y	N	N	N	Y
VIRGINIA						
1 **Wittman**	Y	Y	Y	Y	Y	N
2 Nye	Y	Y	Y	Y	Y	Y
3 Scott	Y	Y	N	N	N	Y
4 **Forbes**	Y	N	Y	Y	Y	N
5 Perriello	Y	Y	N	Y	Y	Y
6 **Goodlatte**	Y	Y	Y	Y	Y	N
7 **Cantor**	Y	N	Y	Y	Y	N
8 Moran	Y	Y	?	N	N	Y
9 Boucher	Y	Y	N	N	Y	Y
10 **Wolf**	Y	Y	Y	Y	Y	N
11 Connolly	Y	Y	N	N	Y	Y
WASHINGTON						
1 Inslee	Y	Y	N	N	Y	Y
2 Larsen	Y	Y	N	N	Y	Y
3 Baird	Y	Y	N	N	N	Y
4 **Hastings**	Y	Y	Y	Y	Y	?
5 **McMorris Rodgers**	Y	N	Y	Y	Y	N
6 Dicks	Y	Y	N	N	Y	Y
7 McDermott	Y	Y	N	N	N	Y
8 **Reichert**	Y	Y	Y	Y	Y	N
9 Smith	Y	Y	N	N	Y	Y
WEST VIRGINIA						
1 Mollohan	?	?	?	?	?	?
2 **Capito**	Y	Y	Y	Y	Y	N
3 Rahall	Y	Y	N	N	Y	Y
WISCONSIN						
1 **Ryan**	Y	N	Y	Y	Y	N
2 Baldwin	Y	Y	N	N	N	Y
3 Kind	Y	Y	N	N	Y	Y
4 Moore	Y	Y	N	N	N	Y
5 **Sensenbrenner**	Y	N	Y	Y	Y	N
6 **Petri**	Y	Y	Y	Y	Y	N
7 Obey	Y	Y	?	?	?	?
8 Kagen	Y	Y	N	N	Y	Y
WYOMING						
AL **Lummis**	Y	N	Y	Y	Y	N
DELEGATES						
Faleomavaega (A.S.)			?	?		
Norton (D.C.)			N	N		
Bordallo (Guam)			N	N		
Sablan (N. Marianas)			N	N		
Pierluisi (P.R.)			N	N		
Christensen (V.I.)			N	N		

IN THE HOUSE | By Vote Number

256. H Res 1294. National Explosive Ordnance Disposal Day/ **Adoption.** Towns, D-N.Y., motion to suspend the rules and adopt the resolution that would express support for the designation of National Explosive Ordnance Disposal Day and honor those who are serving and have served in the profession in the U.S. armed forces. Motion agreed to 388-0: D 228-0; R 160-0. A two-thirds majority of those present and voting (259 in this case) is required for adoption under suspension of the rules. May 11, 2010.

257. H Res 1328. Tribute to Ernie Harwell/Adoption. Towns, D-N.Y., motion to suspend the rules and adopt the resolution that would honor broadcaster William Earnest "Ernie" Harwell for his contributions to Major League Baseball, express sorrow at his death on May 4, 2010, and offer condolences to his family, friends, colleagues and admirers. Motion agreed to 394-0: D 231-0; R 163-0. A two-thirds majority of those present and voting (263 in this case) is required for adoption under suspension of the rules. May 11, 2010.

258. H Res 1299. Peace Officers Memorial Day/Adoption. Deutch, D-Fla., motion to suspend the rules and adopt the resolution that would support Peace Officers Memorial Day and honor federal, state and local law enforcement officers killed or disabled in the line of duty. Motion agreed to 395-0: D 234-0; R 161-0. A two-thirds majority of those present and voting (264 in this case) is required for adoption under suspension of the rules. May 11, 2010.

259. HR 5116. Science and Technology Programs Reauthorization/ **Rule.** Adoption of the rule (H Res 1344) that would provide for House floor consideration of the bill that would reauthorize science and technology programs for five years at the National Science Foundation, the National Institute of Standards and Technology, the Energy Department's Office of Science and the Advanced Research Projects Agency-Energy. Adopted 243-177: D 243-5; R 0-172. May 12, 2010.

260. HR 5014. VA Spina Bifida Program/Passage. Levin, D-Mich., motion to suspend the rules and pass the bill that would clarify that the Veterans Affairs Department Spina Bifida Health Care Program and Children of Women Vietnam Veterans Health Care Program qualify as minimum essential coverage under the health care overhaul law. Motion agreed to 417-0: D 246-0; R 171-0. A majority of two-thirds of those present and voting (278 in this case) is required for passage under suspension of the rules. May 12, 2010.

261. H Con Res 268. National Women's Health Week/Adoption. Towns, D-N.Y., motion to suspend the rules and adopt the concurrent resolution that would support the goals and ideals of National Women's Health Week. Motion agreed to 418-0: D 247-0; R 171-0. A two-thirds majority of those present and voting (279 in this case) is required for adoption under suspension of the rules. May 12, 2010.

	256	257	258	259	260	261
ALABAMA						
1 Bonner	Y	Y	Y	N	Y	Y
2 Bright	Y	Y	Y	N	Y	Y
3 Rogers	Y	Y	Y	N	Y	Y
4 Aderholt	Y	Y	Y	N	Y	Y
5 Griffith	Y	Y	Y	N	Y	Y
6 Bachus	Y	Y	Y	N	Y	Y
7 Davis	?	?	?	?	?	?
ALASKA						
AL Young	Y	Y	Y	N	Y	Y
ARIZONA						
1 Kirkpatrick	Y	Y	Y	Y	Y	Y
2 Franks	Y	Y	Y	N	Y	Y
3 Shadegg	Y	Y	Y	N	Y	Y
4 Pastor	Y	Y	Y	Y	Y	Y
5 Mitchell	Y	Y	Y	N	Y	Y
6 Flake	Y	Y	Y	N	Y	Y
7 Grijalva	Y	?	Y	Y	Y	Y
8 Giffords	Y	Y	Y	Y	Y	Y
ARKANSAS						
1 Berry	?	?	?	Y	Y	Y
2 Snyder	Y	Y	Y	Y	Y	Y
3 Boozman	Y	Y	Y	N	Y	Y
4 Ross	Y	Y	Y	Y	Y	Y
CALIFORNIA						
1 Thompson	Y	Y	Y	Y	Y	Y
2 Herger	Y	Y	Y	N	Y	Y
3 Lungren	Y	Y	Y	N	Y	Y
4 McClintock	Y	Y	Y	N	Y	Y
5 Matsui	Y	Y	Y	Y	Y	Y
6 Woolsey	Y	Y	Y	Y	Y	?
7 Miller, George	Y	Y	Y	Y	Y	Y
8 Pelosi						
9 Lee	+	+	+	Y	Y	Y
10 Garamendi	Y	Y	Y	Y	Y	Y
11 McNerney	Y	Y	Y	Y	Y	Y
12 Speier	?	?	?	Y	Y	Y
13 Stark	Y	Y	Y	Y	Y	Y
14 Eshoo	Y	Y	Y	Y	Y	Y
15 Honda	Y	Y	Y	Y	Y	Y
16 Lofgren	Y	Y	Y	Y	Y	Y
17 Farr	Y	Y	Y	Y	Y	Y
18 Cardoza	Y	Y	Y	Y	Y	Y
19 Radanovich	?	?	?	N	Y	Y
20 Costa	Y	Y	Y	Y	Y	Y
21 Nunes	Y	Y	Y	N	Y	Y
22 McCarthy	Y	Y	Y	N	Y	Y
23 Capps	Y	Y	Y	Y	Y	Y
24 Gallegly	Y	Y	Y	N	Y	Y
25 McKeon	?	Y	?	N	Y	Y
26 Dreier	Y	Y	Y	N	Y	Y
27 Sherman	Y	Y	Y	Y	Y	Y
28 Berman	Y	Y	Y	Y	Y	Y
29 Schiff	Y	Y	Y	Y	Y	Y
30 Waxman	Y	Y	Y	Y	Y	Y
31 Becerra	Y	Y	Y	Y	Y	Y
32 Chu	Y	Y	Y	Y	Y	Y
33 Watson	Y	Y	?	Y	Y	Y
34 Roybal-Allard	Y	Y	Y	Y	Y	Y
35 Waters	?	?	?	Y	Y	Y
36 Harman	Y	Y	Y	Y	Y	Y
37 Richardson	Y	Y	Y	Y	Y	Y
38 Napolitano	Y	Y	Y	Y	Y	Y
39 Sánchez, Linda	Y	Y	Y	Y	Y	Y
40 Royce	Y	Y	Y	N	Y	Y
41 Lewis	Y	Y	Y	N	Y	Y
42 Miller, Gary	Y	Y	Y	N	Y	Y
43 Baca	Y	?	Y	Y	Y	Y
44 Calvert	Y	Y	Y	N	Y	Y
45 Bono Mack	Y	Y	Y	N	Y	Y
46 Rohrabacher	Y	Y	Y	N	Y	Y
47 Sanchez, Loretta	Y	Y	Y	Y	Y	Y
48 Campbell	Y	Y	Y	N	Y	Y
49 Issa	Y	Y	Y	N	Y	Y
50 Bilbray	Y	Y	Y	N	Y	Y
51 Filner	Y	Y	Y	Y	Y	Y
52 Hunter	Y	Y	Y	N	Y	Y
53 Davis	Y	Y	Y	Y	Y	Y

	256	257	258	259	260	261
COLORADO						
1 DeGette	Y	Y	Y	Y	Y	Y
2 Polis	Y	Y	Y	Y	Y	Y
3 Salazar	Y	Y	Y	Y	Y	Y
4 Markey	?	Y	Y	Y	Y	Y
5 Lamborn	Y	Y	Y	N	Y	Y
6 Coffman	Y	Y	Y	N	Y	Y
7 Perlmutter	Y	Y	Y	Y	Y	Y
CONNECTICUT						
1 Larson	Y	Y	Y	Y	Y	Y
2 Courtney	Y	Y	Y	Y	Y	Y
3 DeLauro	Y	Y	Y	Y	Y	Y
4 Himes	Y	Y	Y	Y	Y	Y
5 Murphy	Y	?	Y	Y	Y	Y
DELAWARE						
AL Castle	Y	Y	Y	N	Y	Y
FLORIDA						
1 Miller	Y	Y	Y	N	Y	Y
2 Boyd	Y	Y	Y	Y	Y	Y
3 Brown	Y	Y	Y	Y	Y	Y
4 Crenshaw	Y	Y	Y	N	Y	Y
5 Brown-Waite	Y	Y	Y	N	Y	Y
6 Stearns	Y	Y	Y	N	Y	Y
7 Mica	Y	Y	Y	N	Y	Y
8 Grayson	Y	Y	Y	Y	Y	Y
9 Bilirakis	Y	Y	Y	N	Y	Y
10 Young	Y	Y	Y	N	Y	Y
11 Castor	Y	Y	Y	Y	Y	Y
12 Putnam	Y	Y	Y	N	+	Y
13 Buchanan	Y	Y	Y	N	Y	Y
14 Mack	Y	Y	Y	N	Y	Y
15 Posey	Y	Y	Y	N	Y	Y
16 Rooney	Y	Y	Y	N	Y	Y
17 Meek	?	?	?	Y	Y	Y
18 Ros-Lehtinen	Y	Y	Y	N	Y	Y
19 Deutch	Y	Y	Y	Y	Y	Y
20 Wasserman Schultz	?	?	?	Y	Y	Y
21 Diaz-Balart, L.	Y	Y	Y	N	Y	Y
22 Klein	Y	?	Y	Y	Y	Y
23 Hastings	Y	Y	Y	Y	Y	Y
24 Kosmas	Y	Y	Y	Y	Y	Y
25 Diaz-Balart, M.	Y	Y	Y	N	Y	Y
GEORGIA						
1 Kingston	Y	Y	Y	N	Y	Y
2 Bishop	Y	Y	Y	Y	Y	Y
3 Westmoreland	Y	Y	Y	N	Y	Y
4 Johnson	Y	Y	Y	Y	Y	Y
5 Lewis	Y	?	Y	Y	Y	Y
6 Price	Y	Y	Y	N	Y	Y
7 Linder	Y	Y	Y	N	Y	Y
8 Marshall	Y	Y	Y	Y	Y	Y
9 Vacant						
10 Broun	Y	Y	Y	N	Y	Y
11 Gingrey	Y	Y	Y	N	Y	Y
12 Barrow	Y	Y	Y	Y	Y	Y
13 Scott	Y	?	Y	Y	Y	Y
HAWAII						
1 Vacant						
2 Hirono	Y	Y	Y	Y	Y	Y
IDAHO						
1 Minnick	Y	Y	Y	Y	Y	Y
2 Simpson	Y	Y	Y	N	Y	Y
ILLINOIS						
1 Rush	?	?	?	Y	Y	Y
2 Jackson	Y	Y	Y	Y	Y	Y
3 Lipinski	Y	Y	Y	Y	Y	Y
4 Gutierrez	+	+	+	Y	Y	Y
5 Quigley	Y	Y	Y	Y	Y	Y
6 Roskam	Y	Y	Y	N	Y	Y
7 Davis	Y	Y	Y	Y	Y	Y
8 Bean	Y	Y	Y	Y	Y	Y
9 Schakowsky	Y	Y	Y	Y	Y	Y
10 Kirk	?	?	?	N	Y	Y
11 Halvorson	Y	Y	Y	Y	Y	Y
12 Costello	Y	Y	Y	Y	Y	Y
13 Biggert	Y	Y	Y	N	Y	Y
14 Foster	Y	Y	Y	Y	Y	Y
15 Johnson	Y	Y	Y	N	Y	Y

KEY   **Republicans**   Democrats

Y Voted for (yea)	X Paired against	C Voted "present" to avoid possible conflict of interest
# Paired for	– Announced against	
+ Announced for	P Voted "present"	? Did not vote or otherwise make a position known
N Voted against (nay)		

	256	257	258	259	260	261
16 **Manzullo**	Y	Y	Y	N	Y	Y
17 Hare	Y	Y	Y	Y	Y	Y
18 **Schock**	Y	Y	Y	N	Y	Y
19 **Shimkus**	Y	Y	Y	N	Y	Y
INDIANA						
1 Visclosky	Y	Y	Y	Y	Y	Y
2 Donnelly	Y	Y	Y	N	Y	?
3 **Souder**	?	?	?	?	?	?
4 **Buyer**	Y	Y	Y	N	Y	Y
5 **Burton**	Y	Y	Y	N	Y	Y
6 **Pence**	Y	Y	Y	N	Y	Y
7 Carson	Y	Y	Y	Y	Y	Y
8 Ellsworth	Y	Y	Y	Y	Y	Y
9 Hill	Y	Y	Y	N	Y	Y
IOWA						
1 Braley	Y	Y	Y	Y	Y	Y
2 Loebsack	Y	Y	Y	Y	Y	Y
3 Boswell	Y	Y	Y	Y	Y	Y
4 **Latham**	?	Y	Y	N	Y	Y
5 **King**	?	Y	Y	N	Y	?
KANSAS						
1 **Moran**	Y	Y	Y	N	Y	Y
2 **Jenkins**	Y	Y	Y	N	Y	Y
3 Moore	Y	Y	Y	Y	Y	Y
4 **Tiahrt**	Y	Y	Y	N	Y	Y
KENTUCKY						
1 **Whitfield**	Y	Y	Y	N	Y	Y
2 **Guthrie**	Y	Y	Y	N	Y	Y
3 Yarmuth	Y	Y	Y	Y	Y	Y
4 **Davis**	Y	Y	Y	N	Y	Y
5 **Rogers**	Y	Y	Y	N	Y	Y
6 Chandler	Y	Y	Y	Y	Y	Y
LOUISIANA						
1 **Scalise**	Y	Y	Y	N	Y	Y
2 **Cao**	?	?	?	N	Y	Y
3 Melancon	Y	Y	?	Y	?	Y
4 **Fleming**	Y	Y	Y	N	Y	Y
5 **Alexander**	Y	Y	Y	N	Y	Y
6 **Cassidy**	Y	Y	Y	N	Y	Y
7 **Boustany**	Y	Y	Y	N	Y	Y
MAINE						
1 Pingree	Y	Y	Y	Y	Y	Y
2 Michaud	Y	Y	Y	Y	Y	Y
MARYLAND						
1 Kratovil	Y	Y	Y	Y	Y	Y
2 Ruppersberger	Y	Y	Y	Y	Y	Y
3 Sarbanes	Y	Y	Y	Y	Y	Y
4 Edwards	Y	Y	Y	Y	Y	Y
5 Hoyer	Y	Y	Y	Y	Y	Y
6 **Bartlett**	Y	Y	Y	N	Y	Y
7 Cummings	Y	Y	Y	Y	Y	Y
8 Van Hollen	Y	Y	Y	Y	Y	Y
MASSACHUSETTS						
1 Olver	Y	Y	Y	Y	Y	Y
2 Neal	Y	Y	Y	Y	Y	Y
3 McGovern	Y	Y	Y	Y	Y	Y
4 Frank	Y	Y	Y	Y	Y	Y
5 Tsongas	Y	Y	Y	Y	+	Y
6 Tierney	Y	Y	Y	Y	Y	Y
7 Markey	Y	Y	Y	Y	Y	Y
8 Capuano	Y	Y	Y	Y	Y	Y
9 Lynch	?	?	?	Y	Y	Y
10 Delahunt	?	Y	Y	Y	Y	Y
MICHIGAN						
1 Stupak	Y	Y	Y	Y	Y	Y
2 **Hoekstra**	?	?	?	?	?	?
3 **Ehlers**	Y	Y	Y	N	Y	Y
4 **Camp**	Y	Y	Y	N	Y	Y
5 Kildee	Y	Y	Y	Y	Y	Y
6 **Upton**	Y	Y	Y	N	Y	Y
7 Schauer	Y	Y	Y	Y	Y	Y
8 **Rogers**	Y	Y	Y	N	Y	Y
9 Peters	?	Y	Y	Y	Y	Y
10 **Miller**	Y	Y	Y	N	Y	Y
11 **McCotter**	Y	Y	Y	N	Y	Y
12 Levin	Y	Y	Y	Y	Y	Y
13 Kilpatrick	Y	Y	Y	Y	Y	Y
14 Conyers	Y	Y	?	Y	Y	Y
15 Dingell	Y	Y	Y	Y	Y	Y
MINNESOTA						
1 Walz	Y	Y	Y	Y	Y	Y
2 **Kline**	Y	Y	Y	N	Y	Y
3 **Paulsen**	Y	Y	Y	N	Y	Y
4 McCollum	Y	Y	Y	Y	Y	Y

	256	257	258	259	260	261
5 Ellison	Y	Y	Y	Y	Y	Y
6 **Bachmann**	Y	Y	Y	N	Y	Y
7 Peterson	Y	Y	Y	Y	Y	Y
8 Oberstar	Y	Y	Y	Y	Y	Y
MISSISSIPPI						
1 Childers	Y	Y	Y	Y	Y	Y
2 Thompson	Y	Y	Y	Y	Y	Y
3 **Harper**	Y	Y	Y	N	Y	Y
4 Taylor	Y	Y	Y	Y	Y	Y
MISSOURI						
1 Clay	Y	Y	Y	Y	Y	Y
2 **Akin**	Y	Y	Y	N	Y	Y
3 Carnahan	Y	Y	Y	Y	+	Y
4 Skelton	Y	Y	Y	Y	Y	Y
5 Cleaver	Y	Y	Y	Y	Y	Y
6 **Graves**	Y	Y	Y	N	Y	Y
7 **Blunt**	?	?	?	N	Y	Y
8 **Emerson**	Y	Y	Y	N	Y	Y
9 **Luetkemeyer**	Y	Y	Y	N	Y	Y
MONTANA						
AL **Rehberg**	Y	Y	Y	N	Y	Y
NEBRASKA						
1 **Fortenberry**	Y	Y	Y	N	Y	Y
2 **Terry**	Y	Y	Y	N	Y	Y
3 **Smith**	Y	Y	Y	N	Y	Y
NEVADA						
1 Berkley	Y	Y	Y	Y	Y	Y
2 **Heller**	+	+	+	N	Y	Y
3 Titus	Y	Y	Y	Y	Y	Y
NEW HAMPSHIRE						
1 Shea-Porter	Y	Y	Y	Y	Y	Y
2 Hodes	?	Y	Y	Y	Y	Y
NEW JERSEY						
1 Andrews	Y	Y	Y	Y	Y	Y
2 **LoBiondo**	Y	Y	Y	N	Y	Y
3 Adler	Y	Y	Y	Y	Y	Y
4 **Smith**	Y	Y	Y	N	Y	Y
5 **Garrett**	Y	Y	Y	N	Y	Y
6 Pallone	Y	Y	Y	Y	Y	Y
7 **Lance**	Y	Y	Y	N	Y	Y
8 Pascrell	Y	Y	Y	Y	Y	Y
9 Rothman	Y	Y	Y	Y	Y	Y
10 Payne	?	?	?	Y	Y	Y
11 **Frelinghuysen**	Y	Y	Y	N	Y	Y
12 Holt	Y	Y	Y	Y	Y	Y
13 Sires	Y	Y	Y	Y	Y	Y
NEW MEXICO						
1 Heinrich	Y	Y	Y	Y	Y	Y
2 Teague	Y	Y	Y	Y	Y	Y
3 Luján	Y	Y	Y	Y	Y	Y
NEW YORK						
1 Bishop	Y	Y	Y	Y	Y	Y
2 Israel	Y	Y	Y	Y	Y	Y
3 **King**	Y	Y	Y	N	Y	Y
4 McCarthy	Y	Y	Y	Y	Y	Y
5 Ackerman	Y	Y	Y	Y	Y	Y
6 Meeks	?	?	?	?	?	?
7 Crowley	Y	Y	Y	Y	Y	Y
8 Nadler	Y	Y	Y	Y	Y	Y
9 Weiner	Y	Y	Y	Y	Y	Y
10 Towns	Y	Y	Y	Y	Y	Y
11 Clarke	?	Y	Y	Y	Y	Y
12 Velázquez	Y	Y	Y	Y	Y	Y
13 McMahon	?	Y	Y	Y	Y	Y
14 Maloney	Y	Y	Y	Y	Y	Y
15 Rangel	Y	Y	Y	?	Y	Y
16 Serrano	Y	Y	Y	Y	Y	Y
17 Engel	?	?	Y	Y	Y	Y
18 Lowey	Y	Y	?	Y	Y	Y
19 Hall	Y	Y	Y	Y	Y	Y
20 Murphy	Y	Y	Y	Y	Y	Y
21 Tonko	Y	Y	Y	Y	Y	Y
22 Hinchey	Y	Y	Y	Y	Y	Y
23 Owens	Y	Y	Y	Y	Y	Y
24 Arcuri	Y	Y	Y	Y	Y	Y
25 Maffei	Y	Y	Y	Y	Y	Y
26 **Lee**	Y	Y	Y	N	Y	Y
27 Higgins	Y	Y	Y	Y	Y	Y
28 Slaughter	Y	Y	Y	Y	Y	Y
29 Vacant						
NORTH CAROLINA						
1 Butterfield	Y	Y	Y	Y	Y	Y
2 Etheridge	Y	Y	Y	Y	Y	Y
3 **Jones**	Y	Y	Y	N	Y	Y
4 Price	Y	Y	Y	Y	Y	Y

	256	257	258	259	260	261
5 **Foxx**	Y	Y	Y	N	Y	Y
6 **Coble**	Y	Y	Y	N	Y	Y
7 McIntyre	Y	Y	Y	Y	Y	Y
8 Kissell	Y	Y	Y	Y	Y	Y
9 **Myrick**	Y	Y	Y	N	Y	Y
10 **McHenry**	Y	Y	Y	N	Y	Y
11 Shuler	Y	Y	Y	N	Y	Y
12 Watt	Y	Y	Y	Y	Y	Y
13 Miller	Y	Y	Y	Y	Y	Y
NORTH DAKOTA						
AL Pomeroy	Y	Y	Y	Y	Y	Y
OHIO						
1 Driehaus	Y	Y	Y	Y	Y	Y
2 **Schmidt**	Y	Y	Y	N	Y	Y
3 **Turner**	Y	Y	Y	N	Y	Y
4 **Jordan**	Y	Y	Y	N	Y	Y
5 **Latta**	Y	Y	Y	N	Y	Y
6 Wilson	Y	Y	Y	Y	Y	Y
7 **Austria**	Y	Y	Y	N	Y	Y
8 **Boehner**	Y	Y	Y	N	Y	Y
9 Kaptur	Y	Y	Y	Y	Y	Y
10 Kucinich	Y	Y	Y	Y	Y	Y
11 Fudge	Y	Y	Y	Y	Y	Y
12 **Tiberi**	Y	Y	Y	N	Y	Y
13 Sutton	Y	Y	Y	Y	Y	Y
14 **LaTourette**	Y	Y	?	N	Y	Y
15 Kilroy	Y	Y	Y	Y	Y	Y
16 Boccieri	Y	Y	Y	Y	Y	Y
17 Ryan	Y	Y	Y	Y	Y	Y
18 Space	Y	Y	Y	Y	Y	Y
OKLAHOMA						
1 **Sullivan**	Y	Y	Y	N	Y	Y
2 Boren	Y	Y	Y	Y	Y	Y
3 **Lucas**	Y	Y	Y	N	Y	Y
4 **Cole**	?	?	?	?	?	?
5 **Fallin**	?	?	?	N	Y	Y
OREGON						
1 Wu	Y	Y	Y	Y	Y	Y
2 **Walden**	Y	Y	Y	N	Y	Y
3 Blumenauer	Y	Y	Y	Y	Y	Y
4 DeFazio	?	Y	Y	Y	Y	Y
5 Schrader	Y	Y	Y	Y	Y	Y
PENNSYLVANIA						
1 Brady	Y	Y	Y	Y	Y	Y
2 Fattah	Y	Y	Y	Y	Y	Y
3 Dahlkemper	Y	Y	Y	Y	Y	Y
4 Altmire	Y	Y	Y	Y	Y	Y
5 **Thompson**	Y	Y	Y	N	Y	Y
6 **Gerlach**	Y	Y	Y	N	Y	Y
7 Sestak	Y	Y	Y	Y	Y	Y
8 Murphy, P.	Y	Y	Y	Y	Y	Y
9 **Shuster**	Y	Y	Y	N	Y	Y
10 Carney	Y	Y	Y	?	?	?
11 Kanjorski	Y	Y	Y	Y	Y	Y
12 Vacant						
13 Schwartz	Y	Y	Y	Y	Y	Y
14 Doyle	Y	Y	Y	Y	Y	Y
15 **Dent**	Y	Y	Y	N	Y	Y
16 **Pitts**	Y	Y	Y	N	Y	Y
17 Holden	Y	Y	Y	Y	Y	Y
18 **Murphy, T.**	Y	Y	Y	N	Y	Y
19 **Platts**	Y	Y	Y	N	Y	Y
RHODE ISLAND						
1 Kennedy	Y	Y	Y	Y	Y	Y
2 Langevin	Y	Y	Y	Y	Y	Y
SOUTH CAROLINA						
1 **Brown**	Y	Y	Y	N	Y	Y
2 **Wilson**	Y	Y	Y	N	Y	Y
3 **Barrett**	?	?	?	?	?	?
4 **Inglis**	?	?	?	N	Y	Y
5 Spratt	Y	Y	Y	Y	Y	Y
6 Clyburn	Y	Y	Y	Y	Y	Y
SOUTH DAKOTA						
AL Herseth Sandlin	Y	Y	Y	Y	Y	Y
TENNESSEE						
1 **Roe**	Y	Y	Y	N	Y	Y
2 **Duncan**	Y	Y	Y	N	Y	Y
3 **Wamp**	?	?	?	?	?	?
4 Davis	?	?	?	Y	Y	Y
5 Cooper	Y	Y	Y	Y	Y	Y
6 Gordon	Y	Y	Y	Y	Y	Y
7 **Blackburn**	Y	Y	Y	N	Y	Y
8 Tanner	Y	Y	Y	Y	Y	Y
9 Cohen	Y	Y	Y	Y	Y	Y

	256	257	258	259	260	261
TEXAS						
1 **Gohmert**	?	?	?	N	Y	Y
2 **Poe**	Y	Y	Y	N	Y	Y
3 **Johnson, S.**	Y	Y	Y	N	Y	Y
4 **Hall**	Y	Y	Y	N	Y	Y
5 **Hensarling**	Y	Y	Y	N	Y	Y
6 **Barton**	Y	Y	Y	N	Y	Y
7 **Culberson**	Y	Y	Y	N	Y	Y
8 **Brady**	Y	Y	Y	N	Y	Y
9 Green, A.	Y	Y	Y	Y	Y	Y
10 **McCaul**	Y	Y	Y	N	Y	Y
11 **Conaway**	Y	Y	Y	N	Y	Y
12 **Granger**	Y	Y	Y	N	Y	Y
13 **Thornberry**	Y	Y	Y	N	Y	Y
14 **Paul**	Y	Y	Y	N	Y	Y
15 Hinojosa	Y	Y	Y	Y	Y	Y
16 Reyes	?	Y	Y	Y	Y	Y
17 Edwards	Y	Y	Y	Y	Y	Y
18 Jackson Lee	Y	Y	Y	?	?	?
19 **Neugebauer**	Y	Y	Y	N	Y	Y
20 Gonzalez	Y	Y	Y	Y	Y	Y
21 **Smith**	Y	Y	Y	N	Y	Y
22 **Olson**	Y	Y	Y	N	Y	Y
23 Rodriguez	?	?	?	Y	Y	Y
24 **Marchant**	Y	Y	Y	N	Y	Y
25 Doggett	Y	Y	Y	Y	Y	Y
26 **Burgess**	Y	Y	Y	N	Y	Y
27 Ortiz	Y	Y	Y	Y	Y	Y
28 Cuellar	Y	Y	Y	Y	Y	Y
29 Green, G.	Y	Y	Y	Y	Y	Y
30 Johnson, E.	Y	Y	Y	Y	Y	Y
31 **Carter**	Y	Y	Y	N	Y	Y
32 **Sessions**	Y	Y	Y	N	Y	Y
UTAH						
1 **Bishop**	?	?	?	N	Y	Y
2 Matheson	Y	Y	Y	Y	Y	Y
3 **Chaffetz**	Y	Y	Y	N	Y	Y
VERMONT						
AL Welch	Y	Y	Y	Y	Y	Y
VIRGINIA						
1 **Wittman**	Y	Y	Y	N	Y	Y
2 Nye	Y	Y	Y	Y	Y	Y
3 Scott	Y	Y	Y	Y	Y	Y
4 **Forbes**	Y	Y	Y	N	Y	Y
5 Perriello	Y	Y	Y	Y	Y	Y
6 **Goodlatte**	Y	Y	Y	N	Y	Y
7 **Cantor**	Y	Y	Y	N	Y	Y
8 Moran	Y	Y	Y	Y	Y	Y
9 Boucher	Y	Y	Y	Y	Y	Y
10 **Wolf**	Y	Y	Y	N	Y	Y
11 Connolly	+	Y	Y	Y	Y	Y
WASHINGTON						
1 Inslee	Y	Y	Y	Y	Y	Y
2 Larsen	Y	Y	Y	Y	Y	Y
3 Baird	Y	Y	Y	Y	Y	Y
4 **Hastings**	Y	Y	Y	N	Y	Y
5 **McMorris Rodgers**	Y	Y	Y	N	Y	Y
6 Dicks	Y	Y	Y	Y	Y	Y
7 McDermott	Y	Y	Y	Y	Y	Y
8 **Reichert**	Y	Y	Y	N	Y	Y
9 Smith	Y	Y	Y	Y	Y	Y
WEST VIRGINIA						
1 Mollohan	?	?	?	Y	Y	Y
2 **Capito**	Y	Y	Y	N	Y	Y
3 Rahall	Y	Y	Y	Y	Y	Y
WISCONSIN						
1 **Ryan**	Y	Y	Y	N	Y	Y
2 Baldwin	Y	Y	Y	Y	Y	Y
3 Kind	Y	Y	Y	Y	Y	Y
4 Moore	Y	Y	Y	Y	Y	Y
5 **Sensenbrenner**	Y	Y	Y	N	Y	Y
6 **Petri**	Y	Y	Y	N	Y	Y
7 Obey	Y	Y	Y	Y	Y	Y
8 Kagen	Y	Y	Y	Y	Y	Y
WYOMING						
AL **Lummis**	Y	Y	Y	N	Y	Y
DELEGATES						
Faleomavaega (A.S.)						
Norton (D.C.)						
Bordallo (Guam)						
Sablan (N. Marianas)						
Pierluisi (P.R.)						
Christensen (V.I.)						

IN THE HOUSE | By Vote Number

262. HR 5116. Science and Technology Programs Reauthorization/ Use of Funds. Gordon, D-Tenn., amendment that would clarify matching requirements for the teacher training scholarship program and require the National Institute of Standards and Technology to report on the use of computer modeling by manufacturers. It also would stipulate that educational institutions serving a high number of individuals with disabilities receive special consideration when applying for funding and disallow the use of funds to employ individuals who have been convicted of or pleaded guilty to sexual assault or child molestation. Adopted in Committee of the Whole 417-6: D 252-1; R 165-5. May 12, 2010.

263. HR 5116. Science and Technology Programs Reauthorization/ Office of Innovation and Entrepreneurship. Hall, R-Texas, amendment that would strike language creating an Office of Innovation and Entrepreneurship, authorize loan guarantees to small- and medium-sized manufacturers and create a new grant program for regional innovation strategies. Rejected in Committee of the Whole 163-258: D 2-250; R 161-8. May 12, 2010.

264. HR 5116. Science and Technology Programs Reauthorization/ Clean Energy Consortium. Markey, D-Mass., amendment that would create a new Energy Department Clean Energy Consortium to promote the commercial application of clean-energy technologies. The consortium, which would be regionally based, could include research universities, national laboratories, industry or other state and non-governmental organizations. Adopted in Committee of the Whole 254-173: D 253-3; R 1-170. May 12, 2010.

265. HR 5116. Science and Technology Programs Reauthorization/ Union Access to Information. Miller, D-Calif., amendment that would require that institutions of higher education that employ members of a labor union must respond within 15 days to union requests for information to which they are legally entitled, or lose funding for programs authorized under the bill. Adopted in Committee of the Whole 250-174: D 241-13; R 9-161. May 12, 2010.

266. HR 5116. Science and Technology Programs Reauthorization/ Minority Outreach. Reyes, D-Texas, amendment that would require the science, technology, engineering and math coordinating committee created by the bill to include outreach to Latinos, African-Americans and other underrepresented groups in its five-year plan. Adopted in Committee of the Whole 413-10: D 254-0; R 159-10. May 12, 2010.

267. HR 5116. Science and Technology Programs Reauthorization/ Loan Guarantee Program. Boccieri, D-Ohio, amendment that would increase the annual authorization to $100 million for fiscal 2011 to 2015 for loan guarantees to small- and medium-sized manufacturers for innovative technology projects. Adopted in Committee of the Whole 248-171: D 246-3; R 2-168. May 13, 2010.

	262	263	264	265	266	267
ALABAMA						
1 **Bonner**	Y	Y	N	N	Y	N
2 Bright	Y	N	Y	N	Y	Y
3 **Rogers**	Y	Y	N	N	Y	N
4 **Aderholt**	Y	Y	N	N	Y	N
5 **Griffith**	Y	Y	N	N	Y	N
6 **Bachus**	Y	Y	N	N	Y	N
7 Davis	?	?	?	?	?	?
ALASKA						
AL **Young**	Y	Y	N	N	N	N
ARIZONA						
1 Kirkpatrick	Y	N	Y	Y	Y	N
2 **Franks**	Y	Y	N	?	Y	N
3 **Shadegg**	Y	Y	N	N	Y	N
4 Pastor	Y	N	Y	Y	Y	Y
5 Mitchell	Y	N	Y	N	Y	Y
6 **Flake**	N	Y	N	N	N	N
7 Grijalva	Y	N	Y	Y	Y	Y
8 Giffords	Y	N	Y	Y	Y	Y
ARKANSAS						
1 Berry	Y	N	Y	Y	Y	Y
2 Snyder	Y	N	Y	N	Y	Y
3 **Boozman**	Y	Y	N	N	Y	N
4 Ross	Y	N	Y	Y	Y	Y
CALIFORNIA						
1 Thompson	Y	N	Y	Y	Y	Y
2 **Herger**	Y	Y	N	N	Y	N
3 **Lungren**	Y	Y	N	N	Y	N
4 **McClintock**	N	Y	N	N	N	N
5 Matsui	Y	N	Y	Y	Y	Y
6 Woolsey	Y	N	Y	Y	Y	Y
7 Miller, George	Y	N	Y	Y	Y	Y
8 Pelosi						
9 Lee	Y	N	Y	Y	Y	Y
10 Garamendi	Y	N	Y	Y	Y	Y
11 McNerney	Y	N	Y	Y	Y	Y
12 Speier	Y	N	Y	Y	Y	Y
13 Stark	Y	N	Y	Y	Y	Y
14 Eshoo	Y	N	Y	Y	Y	Y
15 Honda	Y	N	Y	Y	Y	?
16 Lofgren	Y	N	Y	Y	Y	Y
17 Farr	Y	N	Y	Y	Y	Y
18 Cardoza	Y	N	N	Y	Y	Y
19 **Radanovich**	Y	Y	N	?	?	N
20 Costa	Y	N	N	Y	Y	Y
21 **Nunes**	Y	Y	N	N	Y	N
22 **McCarthy**	Y	Y	N	N	Y	N
23 Capps	Y	N	Y	Y	Y	Y
24 **Gallegly**	Y	Y	N	N	Y	N
25 **McKeon**	Y	Y	N	N	Y	N
26 **Dreier**	Y	Y	N	N	N	N
27 Sherman	?	?	Y	Y	Y	Y
28 Berman	Y	N	Y	Y	Y	Y
29 Schiff	Y	N	Y	Y	Y	Y
30 Waxman	?	N	Y	Y	Y	Y
31 Becerra	Y	N	Y	Y	Y	Y
32 Chu	Y	N	Y	Y	Y	Y
33 Watson	Y	N	Y	Y	Y	Y
34 Roybal-Allard	Y	N	Y	Y	Y	Y
35 Waters	Y	N	Y	?	?	Y
36 Harman	Y	N	Y	Y	Y	Y
37 Richardson	Y	Y	Y	Y	Y	Y
38 Napolitano	Y	N	Y	Y	Y	Y
39 Sánchez, Linda	Y	N	Y	Y	Y	Y
40 **Royce**	Y	Y	N	N	N	N
41 **Lewis**	Y	Y	N	N	Y	N
42 **Miller, Gary**	Y	Y	N	N	N	N
43 Baca	Y	N	Y	Y	Y	Y
44 **Calvert**	Y	Y	N	N	Y	N
45 **Bono Mack**	Y	Y	N	N	Y	N
46 **Rohrabacher**	Y	Y	N	N	N	N
47 Sanchez, Loretta	Y	N	Y	?	Y	Y
48 **Campbell**	Y	Y	N	N	Y	N
49 **Issa**	Y	Y	N	N	Y	N
50 **Bilbray**	Y	Y	N	N	Y	N
51 Filner	Y	N	Y	Y	Y	Y
52 **Hunter**	Y	Y	N	N	Y	N
53 Davis	Y	N	Y	Y	Y	Y

	262	263	264	265	266	267
COLORADO						
1 DeGette	Y	N	Y	Y	Y	Y
2 Polis	Y	N	Y	Y	Y	Y
3 Salazar	Y	N	Y	Y	Y	Y
4 Markey	Y	N	Y	Y	Y	Y
5 **Lamborn**	Y	Y	N	N	Y	N
6 **Coffman**	Y	Y	N	N	N	N
7 Perlmutter	Y	N	Y	Y	Y	Y
CONNECTICUT						
1 Larson	Y	N	Y	Y	Y	Y
2 Courtney	Y	N	Y	Y	Y	Y
3 DeLauro	Y	N	Y	Y	Y	Y
4 Himes	Y	N	Y	Y	Y	Y
5 Murphy	Y	N	Y	Y	Y	Y
DELAWARE						
AL **Castle**	Y	N	N	N	Y	N
FLORIDA						
1 **Miller**	Y	Y	N	N	Y	N
2 Boyd	Y	N	Y	Y	Y	Y
3 Brown	Y	N	Y	Y	Y	Y
4 **Crenshaw**	Y	Y	N	N	Y	N
5 **Brown-Waite**	Y	Y	N	N	Y	N
6 **Stearns**	+	Y	N	N	Y	N
7 **Mica**	Y	Y	N	N	Y	N
8 Grayson	Y	N	Y	Y	Y	Y
9 **Bilirakis**	Y	Y	N	N	Y	N
10 **Young**	Y	Y	N	N	N	N
11 Castor	Y	N	Y	Y	Y	Y
12 **Putnam**	Y	Y	N	N	Y	N
13 **Buchanan**	Y	Y	N	N	Y	N
14 **Mack**	Y	Y	N	N	N	N
15 **Posey**	Y	Y	N	N	Y	N
16 **Rooney**	Y	Y	N	N	Y	N
17 Meek	Y	N	Y	Y	Y	Y
18 **Ros-Lehtinen**	Y	Y	N	N	Y	N
19 Deutch	Y	N	Y	Y	Y	Y
20 Wasserman Schultz	Y	N	Y	Y	Y	Y
21 **Diaz-Balart, L.**	Y	Y	N	Y	Y	?
22 Klein	Y	N	Y	Y	Y	Y
23 Hastings	Y	N	Y	Y	Y	Y
24 Kosmas	Y	N	Y	Y	Y	Y
25 **Diaz-Balart, M.**	Y	Y	N	Y	Y	N
GEORGIA						
1 **Kingston**	Y	Y	N	N	Y	N
2 Bishop	Y	N	Y	Y	Y	Y
3 **Westmoreland**	Y	Y	N	N	Y	N
4 Johnson	Y	N	Y	Y	Y	Y
5 Lewis	Y	?	Y	Y	Y	Y
6 **Price**	Y	Y	N	N	Y	N
7 **Linder**	Y	Y	N	N	N	N
8 Marshall	Y	N	Y	Y	Y	Y
9 Vacant						
10 **Broun**	Y	Y	N	N	N	N
11 **Gingrey**	Y	Y	N	N	?	N
12 Barrow	Y	N	Y	Y	Y	Y
13 Scott	Y	N	Y	Y	Y	Y
HAWAII						
1 Vacant						
2 Hirono	Y	N	Y	Y	Y	Y
IDAHO						
1 Minnick	Y	N	Y	Y	Y	Y
2 **Simpson**	Y	Y	N	N	Y	N
ILLINOIS						
1 Rush	Y	N	Y	Y	Y	?
2 Jackson	Y	N	Y	Y	Y	Y
3 Lipinski	Y	N	Y	Y	Y	Y
4 Gutierrez	Y	N	Y	Y	Y	Y
5 Quigley	Y	N	Y	Y	Y	Y
6 **Roskam**	Y	Y	N	N	Y	N
7 Davis	Y	N	Y	Y	Y	Y
8 Bean	Y	N	Y	Y	Y	Y
9 Schakowsky	Y	N	Y	Y	Y	Y
10 **Kirk**	Y	Y	N	N	Y	N
11 Halvorson	Y	N	Y	Y	Y	Y
12 Costello	Y	N	Y	Y	Y	Y
13 **Biggert**	Y	Y	N	N	Y	N
14 Foster	Y	N	Y	Y	Y	Y
15 **Johnson**	Y	Y	Y	N	Y	N

	262	263	264	265	266	267
16 **Manzullo**	Y	Y	N	N	Y	N
17 Hare	Y	N	Y	Y	Y	Y
18 **Schock**	Y	Y	N	N	Y	N
19 **Shimkus**	Y	Y	N	N	Y	N
INDIANA						
1 Visclosky	Y	N	Y	Y	Y	Y
2 Donnelly	Y	N	Y	Y	Y	Y
3 **Souder**	?	?	?	?	?	N
4 **Buyer**	Y	Y	N	N	Y	N
5 **Burton**	Y	Y	N	N	Y	N
6 **Pence**	Y	Y	N	N	Y	N
7 Carson	Y	N	Y	Y	Y	Y
8 Ellsworth	Y	N	Y	Y	Y	Y
9 Hill	Y	N	Y	Y	Y	Y
IOWA						
1 Braley	Y	N	Y	Y	Y	Y
2 Loebsack	Y	N	Y	Y	Y	Y
3 Boswell	Y	N	Y	Y	Y	Y
4 **Latham**	Y	Y	N	N	Y	N
5 **King**	Y	Y	N	N	Y	N
KANSAS						
1 **Moran**	Y	Y	N	N	Y	N
2 **Jenkins**	Y	Y	N	N	Y	N
3 Moore	Y	N	Y	Y	Y	Y
4 **Tiahrt**	Y	Y	N	N	Y	N
KENTUCKY						
1 **Whitfield**	Y	Y	N	N	Y	N
2 **Guthrie**	Y	Y	N	N	Y	N
3 Yarmuth	Y	N	Y	Y	Y	Y
4 **Davis**	Y	Y	N	N	Y	N
5 **Rogers**	Y	Y	N	N	Y	N
6 Chandler	Y	N	Y	Y	Y	Y
LOUISIANA						
1 **Scalise**	Y	Y	N	N	Y	N
2 **Cao**	Y	N	N	N	Y	N
3 Melancon	Y	N	Y	Y	Y	Y
4 **Fleming**	Y	Y	N	N	Y	N
5 **Alexander**	Y	Y	N	N	Y	N
6 **Cassidy**	Y	Y	N	N	Y	N
7 **Boustany**	Y	Y	N	N	Y	N
MAINE						
1 Pingree	Y	N	Y	Y	Y	Y
2 Michaud	Y	N	Y	Y	Y	Y
MARYLAND						
1 Kratovil	Y	N	Y	Y	Y	Y
2 Ruppersberger	Y	N	Y	Y	Y	Y
3 Sarbanes	Y	N	Y	Y	Y	Y
4 Edwards	Y	N	Y	Y	Y	Y
5 Hoyer	Y	N	Y	Y	Y	Y
6 **Bartlett**	Y	N	N	N	Y	N
7 Cummings	Y	N	Y	Y	Y	Y
8 Van Hollen	Y	N	Y	Y	Y	Y
MASSACHUSETTS						
1 Olver	Y	N	Y	Y	?	Y
2 Neal	Y	N	Y	Y	Y	Y
3 McGovern	Y	N	Y	Y	Y	Y
4 Frank	Y	N	Y	Y	Y	Y
5 Tsongas	Y	N	Y	Y	Y	Y
6 Tierney	Y	N	Y	Y	Y	Y
7 Markey	Y	N	Y	Y	Y	Y
8 Capuano	Y	N	Y	Y	Y	Y
9 Lynch	Y	N	Y	Y	Y	Y
10 Delahunt	Y	N	Y	Y	Y	Y
MICHIGAN						
1 Stupak	Y	N	Y	Y	Y	Y
2 **Hoekstra**	?	?	?	?	?	?
3 **Ehlers**	Y	N	N	N	Y	Y
4 **Camp**	Y	Y	N	N	Y	N
5 Kildee	Y	N	Y	Y	Y	Y
6 **Upton**	Y	Y	N	N	Y	N
7 Schauer	Y	N	Y	Y	Y	Y
8 **Rogers**	Y	Y	N	N	Y	N
9 Peters	Y	N	N	Y	Y	Y
10 **Miller**	Y	Y	N	Y	Y	N
11 **McCotter**	Y	Y	N	Y	Y	N
12 Levin	Y	N	Y	Y	Y	Y
13 Kilpatrick	Y	N	Y	Y	Y	Y
14 Conyers	Y	N	Y	Y	Y	Y
15 Dingell	Y	N	Y	Y	Y	Y
MINNESOTA						
1 Walz	Y	N	Y	Y	Y	Y
2 **Kline**	Y	Y	N	N	Y	N
3 **Paulsen**	Y	Y	N	N	Y	N
4 McCollum	Y	N	Y	Y	Y	Y

	262	263	264	265	266	267
5 Ellison	Y	N	Y	Y	Y	Y
6 **Bachmann**	Y	Y	N	N	Y	N
7 Peterson	Y	N	Y	Y	Y	Y
8 Oberstar	Y	N	Y	Y	Y	Y
MISSISSIPPI						
1 Childers	Y	N	Y	N	Y	Y
2 Thompson	Y	N	Y	Y	Y	Y
3 **Harper**	Y	Y	N	N	Y	N
4 Taylor	Y	Y	Y	N	Y	Y
MISSOURI						
1 Clay	Y	N	Y	Y	Y	Y
2 **Akin**	Y	Y	N	N	Y	N
3 Carnahan	Y	N	Y	Y	Y	Y
4 Skelton	Y	N	Y	Y	Y	Y
5 Cleaver	Y	N	Y	Y	Y	Y
6 **Graves**	Y	Y	N	N	Y	N
7 **Blunt**	Y	Y	N	N	Y	N
8 **Emerson**	Y	Y	N	N	Y	N
9 **Luetkemeyer**	Y	Y	N	N	Y	N
MONTANA						
AL **Rehberg**	Y	Y	N	N	Y	N
NEBRASKA						
1 **Fortenberry**	Y	N	N	N	Y	N
2 **Terry**	Y	Y	N	N	Y	N
3 **Smith**	Y	Y	N	N	Y	N
NEVADA						
1 Berkley	Y	N	Y	Y	Y	Y
2 **Heller**	Y	Y	N	N	Y	N
3 Titus	Y	N	Y	Y	Y	Y
NEW HAMPSHIRE						
1 Shea-Porter	Y	N	Y	Y	Y	Y
2 Hodes	Y	N	Y	Y	Y	Y
NEW JERSEY						
1 Andrews	Y	N	Y	Y	Y	Y
2 **LoBiondo**	Y	Y	N	N	Y	N
3 Adler	Y	N	Y	Y	Y	N
4 **Smith**	Y	Y	N	N	?	N
5 **Garrett**	?	?	?	N	Y	N
6 Pallone	Y	N	Y	Y	Y	Y
7 **Lance**	Y	Y	N	N	Y	N
8 Pascrell	Y	N	Y	Y	Y	Y
9 Rothman	Y	N	Y	Y	Y	Y
10 Payne	Y	N	Y	Y	Y	Y
11 **Frelinghuysen**	Y	Y	N	N	Y	N
12 Holt	Y	N	Y	Y	Y	Y
13 Sires	Y	N	Y	Y	Y	Y
NEW MEXICO						
1 Heinrich	Y	N	Y	Y	Y	Y
2 Teague	Y	N	Y	Y	Y	?
3 Luján	Y	N	Y	Y	Y	Y
NEW YORK						
1 Bishop	Y	N	Y	Y	Y	Y
2 Israel	Y	N	Y	Y	Y	Y
3 **King**	Y	Y	N	N	Y	N
4 McCarthy	Y	N	Y	Y	Y	Y
5 Ackerman	Y	N	Y	Y	Y	Y
6 Meeks	Y	N	Y	Y	Y	Y
7 Crowley	Y	N	Y	Y	Y	Y
8 Nadler	N	N	Y	Y	Y	Y
9 Weiner	Y	N	Y	Y	Y	Y
10 Towns	Y	N	Y	Y	Y	Y
11 Clarke	Y	N	Y	Y	Y	Y
12 Velázquez	Y	N	Y	Y	Y	Y
13 McMahon	Y	N	Y	Y	Y	Y
14 Maloney	Y	N	Y	Y	Y	Y
15 Rangel	Y	N	Y	Y	Y	Y
16 Serrano	Y	N	Y	Y	Y	?
17 Engel	Y	N	Y	Y	Y	Y
18 Lowey	Y	N	Y	Y	Y	Y
19 Hall	Y	N	Y	Y	Y	Y
20 Murphy	Y	N	Y	Y	Y	Y
21 Tonko	Y	N	Y	Y	Y	Y
22 Hinchey	Y	N	Y	Y	Y	Y
23 Owens	Y	N	Y	Y	Y	N
24 Arcuri	Y	N	Y	Y	Y	Y
25 Maffei	Y	N	Y	Y	Y	Y
26 **Lee**	Y	N	N	N	Y	?
27 Higgins	Y	N	Y	Y	Y	?
28 Slaughter	Y	N	Y	Y	Y	+
29 Vacant						
NORTH CAROLINA						
1 Butterfield	Y	N	Y	Y	Y	Y
2 Etheridge	Y	N	Y	N	Y	Y
3 **Jones**	Y	Y	N	N	Y	N
4 Price	Y	N	Y	Y	Y	Y

	262	263	264	265	266	267
5 **Foxx**	Y	Y	N	N	Y	N
6 **Coble**	Y	Y	N	N	Y	N
7 McIntyre	Y	N	Y	N	Y	Y
8 Kissell	Y	N	Y	Y	Y	Y
9 **Myrick**	Y	Y	N	N	Y	N
10 **McHenry**	Y	Y	N	N	Y	N
11 Shuler	Y	N	Y	N	Y	Y
12 Watt	Y	?	Y	Y	Y	Y
13 Miller	Y	N	Y	Y	Y	Y
NORTH DAKOTA						
AL Pomeroy	Y	N	Y	Y	Y	Y
OHIO						
1 Driehaus	Y	N	Y	Y	Y	Y
2 **Schmidt**	Y	Y	N	N	Y	Y
3 **Turner**	Y	Y	N	Y	Y	N
4 **Jordan**	Y	Y	N	N	Y	N
5 **Latta**	Y	Y	N	N	Y	N
6 Wilson	Y	N	Y	Y	Y	Y
7 **Austria**	Y	Y	N	N	Y	N
8 **Boehner**	Y	Y	N	N	Y	N
9 Kaptur	Y	N	Y	Y	Y	Y
10 Kucinich	Y	N	Y	Y	Y	Y
11 Fudge	Y	N	Y	Y	Y	Y
12 **Tiberi**	Y	Y	N	Y	Y	N
13 Sutton	Y	N	Y	Y	Y	Y
14 **LaTourette**	Y	Y	N	Y	Y	N
15 Kilroy	Y	N	Y	Y	Y	Y
16 Boccieri	Y	N	Y	Y	Y	Y
17 Ryan	Y	N	Y	Y	Y	Y
18 Space	Y	N	Y	Y	Y	Y
OKLAHOMA						
1 **Sullivan**	Y	Y	N	N	Y	N
2 Boren	Y	N	Y	Y	Y	Y
3 **Lucas**	Y	Y	N	N	Y	N
4 **Cole**	?	?	?	?	?	?
5 **Fallin**	Y	Y	N	N	Y	N
OREGON						
1 Wu	Y	N	Y	Y	Y	Y
2 **Walden**	Y	Y	N	N	Y	N
3 Blumenauer	Y	N	Y	Y	Y	Y
4 DeFazio	Y	N	Y	Y	Y	Y
5 Schrader	Y	N	Y	Y	Y	Y
PENNSYLVANIA						
1 Brady	Y	N	Y	Y	Y	Y
2 Fattah	Y	N	Y	Y	Y	Y
3 Dahlkemper	Y	N	Y	Y	Y	Y
4 Altmire	Y	N	Y	Y	Y	Y
5 **Thompson**	Y	Y	N	N	Y	N
6 **Gerlach**	Y	Y	N	N	Y	N
7 Sestak	Y	N	Y	Y	Y	Y
8 Murphy, P.	Y	N	Y	Y	Y	Y
9 **Shuster**	Y	Y	N	N	Y	N
10 Carney	?	?	?	?	?	?
11 Kanjorski	Y	N	Y	Y	Y	Y
12 Vacant						
13 Schwartz	Y	N	Y	Y	Y	Y
14 Doyle	Y	N	Y	Y	Y	?
15 **Dent**	Y	Y	N	N	Y	N
16 **Pitts**	Y	Y	N	N	Y	N
17 Holden	Y	N	Y	Y	Y	Y
18 **Murphy, T.**	Y	Y	N	Y	Y	N
19 **Platts**	Y	Y	N	Y	Y	N
RHODE ISLAND						
1 Kennedy	Y	N	Y	Y	Y	Y
2 Langevin	Y	N	Y	Y	Y	Y
SOUTH CAROLINA						
1 **Brown**	Y	Y	N	N	Y	N
2 **Wilson**	Y	Y	N	N	Y	N
3 **Barrett**	?	?	?	?	?	?
4 **Inglis**	Y	Y	N	N	Y	N
5 Spratt	Y	N	Y	Y	Y	Y
6 Clyburn	Y	N	Y	Y	Y	Y
SOUTH DAKOTA						
AL Herseth Sandlin	Y	N	Y	Y	Y	Y
TENNESSEE						
1 **Roe**	Y	Y	N	N	Y	N
2 **Duncan**	Y	Y	N	N	Y	N
3 **Wamp**	?	?	?	?	?	?
4 Davis	Y	N	Y	Y	Y	Y
5 Cooper	Y	N	Y	N	Y	Y
6 Gordon	Y	N	Y	Y	Y	Y
7 **Blackburn**	Y	Y	N	N	Y	N
8 Tanner	Y	N	Y	Y	Y	Y
9 Cohen	Y	N	Y	Y	Y	Y

	262	263	264	265	266	267
TEXAS						
1 **Gohmert**	Y	Y	N	N	Y	N
2 **Poe**	Y	Y	N	N	Y	N
3 **Johnson, S.**	Y	Y	N	N	N	N
4 **Hall**	Y	Y	N	N	Y	N
5 **Hensarling**	Y	Y	N	N	Y	N
6 **Barton**	Y	Y	N	N	Y	N
7 **Culberson**	Y	Y	N	N	Y	N
8 **Brady**	Y	Y	N	N	Y	N
9 Green, A.	Y	N	Y	Y	Y	Y
10 **McCaul**	Y	Y	N	N	Y	N
11 **Conaway**	Y	Y	N	N	Y	N
12 **Granger**	Y	Y	N	N	Y	N
13 **Thornberry**	Y	Y	N	N	Y	N
14 **Paul**	N	Y	N	N	Y	N
15 Hinojosa	Y	N	Y	Y	Y	Y
16 Reyes	Y	N	Y	Y	Y	Y
17 Edwards	Y	N	Y	N	Y	Y
18 Jackson Lee	?	?	?	?	?	Y
19 **Neugebauer**	Y	Y	N	N	Y	N
20 Gonzalez	Y	N	Y	Y	Y	Y
21 **Smith**	Y	Y	N	N	Y	N
22 **Olson**	Y	Y	N	N	Y	N
23 Rodriguez	Y	N	Y	Y	Y	Y
24 **Marchant**	Y	Y	N	N	Y	N
25 Doggett	Y	N	Y	Y	Y	Y
26 **Burgess**	N	Y	N	N	N	N
27 Ortiz	Y	N	Y	Y	Y	Y
28 Cuellar	Y	N	Y	Y	Y	Y
29 Green, G.	Y	N	Y	Y	Y	Y
30 Johnson, E.	Y	N	Y	Y	Y	Y
31 **Carter**	Y	Y	N	N	Y	N
32 **Sessions**	Y	?	N	N	N	N
UTAH						
1 **Bishop**	Y	Y	N	N	Y	?
2 Matheson	Y	N	Y	Y	Y	Y
3 **Chaffetz**	Y	Y	N	N	Y	N
VERMONT						
AL Welch	Y	N	Y	Y	Y	Y
VIRGINIA						
1 **Wittman**	Y	Y	N	N	Y	N
2 Nye	Y	N	Y	Y	Y	Y
3 Scott	Y	N	Y	Y	Y	Y
4 **Forbes**	Y	Y	N	N	Y	N
5 Perriello	Y	N	Y	Y	Y	Y
6 **Goodlatte**	Y	Y	N	N	Y	N
7 **Cantor**	Y	Y	N	N	Y	N
8 Moran	Y	N	Y	Y	Y	Y
9 Boucher	Y	N	Y	Y	Y	Y
10 **Wolf**	Y	N	N	N	Y	N
11 Connolly	Y	N	Y	Y	Y	Y
WASHINGTON						
1 Inslee	Y	N	Y	Y	Y	Y
2 Larsen	Y	N	Y	Y	Y	Y
3 Baird	Y	N	Y	N	Y	Y
4 **Hastings**	Y	Y	N	N	Y	N
5 **McMorris Rodgers**	Y	Y	N	N	Y	N
6 Dicks	Y	N	Y	Y	Y	Y
7 McDermott	Y	N	Y	Y	Y	Y
8 **Reichert**	Y	N	N	N	Y	N
9 Smith	Y	N	Y	Y	Y	Y
WEST VIRGINIA						
1 Mollohan	Y	N	Y	Y	Y	Y
2 **Capito**	Y	Y	N	N	Y	N
3 Rahall	Y	N	Y	Y	Y	Y
WISCONSIN						
1 **Ryan**	Y	Y	N	N	Y	N
2 Baldwin	Y	N	Y	Y	Y	Y
3 Kind	Y	N	Y	N	Y	Y
4 Moore	?	?	Y	Y	Y	Y
5 **Sensenbrenner**	Y	Y	N	N	Y	N
6 **Petri**	Y	Y	N	N	Y	N
7 Obey	Y	N	Y	Y	Y	Y
8 Kagen	Y	N	Y	Y	Y	Y
WYOMING						
AL **Lummis**	N	?	N	N	Y	N
DELEGATES						
Faleomavaega (A.S.)	Y	N	Y	Y	Y	Y
Norton (D.C.)	Y	N	Y	Y	Y	Y
Bordallo (Guam)	Y	N	Y	Y	Y	Y
Sablan (N. Marianas)	Y	N	Y	Y	Y	Y
Pierluisi (P.R.)	Y	N	Y	Y	Y	Y
Christensen (V.I.)	Y	N	Y	Y	Y	?

IN THE HOUSE | By Vote Number

268. HR 5116. Science and Technology Programs Reauthorization/ **Consideration of Veterans.** Halvorson, D-Ill., amendment that would require the National Science Foundation to give consideration to the goal of promoting the participation of veterans in a postdoctoral research fellowship program. Adopted in Committee of the Whole 419-0: D 249-0; R 170-0. May 13, 2010.

269. HR 5116. Science and Technology Programs Reauthorization/ **Talent Retention.** Flake, R-Ariz., amendment that would express the sense of Congress that retaining graduate-level talent trained at U.S. universities in science, technology, engineering and math fields is critical to enhancing American business competitiveness. Adopted in Committee of the Whole 419-0: D 251-0; R 168-0. May 13, 2010.

270. HR 5116. Science and Technology Programs Reauthorization/ **Recommit.** Hall, R-Texas, motion to recommit the bill to the House Science and Technology Committee with instructions that it be immediately reported back with amendments that would freeze the authorization levels for the National Science Foundation, National Institute of Standards and Technology, and Energy Department Office of Science at fiscal 2010 levels and eliminate fiscal 2014 and 2015 authorizations. It would also bar the use of funds to pay the salaries of individuals who have been disciplined for viewing, downloading or exchanging pornography on a federal government computer or while performing their duties. Motion agreed to 292-126: D 121-125; R 171-1. May 13, 2010.

271. H Res 1338. Tribute to AmeriCorps/ **Adoption.** Titus, D-Nev., motion to suspend the rules and adopt the resolution that would acknowledge the accomplishments of AmeriCorps members, alumni and community partners. It would encourage citizens to raise awareness about the importance of national and community service. Motion agreed to 280-128: D 236-0; R 44-128. A two-thirds majority of those present and voting (272 in this case) is required for adoption under suspension of the rules. May 13, 2010.

272. H Res 1337. Condolences to Families of Flood Victims/ **Adoption.** Cohen, D-Tenn., motion to suspend the rules and adopt the resolution that would offer condolences to families of those who died as a result of the floods in Tennessee, Kentucky and Mississippi on May 2, 2010. It also would express condolences to families who lost their homes, honor emergency responders and express appreciation to people who continue to help in recovery efforts. Motion agreed to 402-0: D 231-0; R 171-0. A two-thirds majority of those present and voting (268 in this case) is required for adoption under suspension of the rules. May 13, 2010.

	268	269	270	271	272
ALABAMA					
1 **Bonner**	Y	Y	Y	N	Y
2 Bright	Y	Y	Y	Y	Y
3 **Rogers**	Y	Y	Y	Y	Y
4 **Aderholt**	Y	Y	Y	Y	Y
5 **Griffith**	Y	Y	Y	Y	Y
6 **Bachus**	Y	Y	Y	N	Y
7 Davis	?	?	?	?	?
ALASKA					
AL **Young**	Y	Y	Y	Y	Y
ARIZONA					
1 Kirkpatrick	Y	Y	Y	Y	Y
2 **Franks**	Y	Y	Y	N	Y
3 **Shadegg**	Y	Y	Y	N	Y
4 Pastor	Y	Y	Y	Y	Y
5 Mitchell	Y	Y	Y	Y	Y
6 **Flake**	Y	Y	Y	N	Y
7 Grijalva	Y	Y	N	Y	Y
8 Giffords	Y	Y	Y	Y	?
ARKANSAS					
1 Berry	Y	Y	N	Y	Y
2 Snyder	Y	Y	N	Y	Y
3 **Boozman**	Y	Y	Y	N	Y
4 Ross	Y	Y	Y	Y	Y
CALIFORNIA					
1 Thompson	Y	Y	N	Y	Y
2 **Herger**	Y	Y	Y	N	Y
3 **Lungren**	Y	Y	Y	N	Y
4 **McClintock**	Y	Y	Y	N	Y
5 Matsui	Y	Y	N	Y	Y
6 Woolsey	Y	Y	N	Y	Y
7 Miller, George	Y	Y	N	Y	Y
8 Pelosi					
9 Lee	Y	Y	N	Y	Y
10 Garamendi	Y	Y	Y	Y	Y
11 McNerney	Y	Y	Y	Y	Y
12 Speier	Y	Y	N	Y	Y
13 Stark	Y	Y	N	Y	Y
14 Eshoo	Y	Y	N	Y	?
15 Honda	Y	Y	N	Y	Y
16 Lofgren	Y	Y	N	Y	Y
17 Farr	Y	Y	N	Y	Y
18 Cardoza	Y	Y	N	Y	Y
19 **Radanovich**	Y	?	Y	N	Y
20 Costa	Y	Y	Y	Y	Y
21 **Nunes**	Y	Y	Y	N	Y
22 **McCarthy**	Y	Y	Y	N	Y
23 Capps	Y	Y	N	Y	Y
24 **Gallegly**	Y	Y	Y	N	Y
25 **McKeon**	Y	Y	Y	N	Y
26 **Dreier**	Y	Y	Y	N	Y
27 Sherman	Y	Y	N	Y	Y
28 Berman	Y	Y	N	Y	?
29 Schiff	Y	Y	Y	Y	Y
30 Waxman	Y	Y	N	Y	Y
31 Becerra	Y	Y	N	Y	Y
32 Chu	Y	Y	N	Y	Y
33 Watson	Y	Y	N	Y	Y
34 Roybal-Allard	Y	Y	N	Y	Y
35 Waters	Y	Y	N	?	Y
36 Harman	Y	Y	N	Y	Y
37 Richardson	Y	Y	Y	Y	Y
38 Napolitano	Y	Y	N	Y	Y
39 Sánchez, Linda	Y	Y	N	Y	Y
40 **Royce**	Y	Y	Y	N	Y
41 **Lewis**	Y	Y	Y	N	Y
42 **Miller, Gary**	Y	Y	Y	N	Y
43 Baca	Y	Y	Y	Y	Y
44 **Calvert**	Y	Y	Y	N	Y
45 **Bono Mack**	Y	Y	Y	N	Y
46 **Rohrabacher**	Y	Y	Y	N	Y
47 Sanchez, Loretta	Y	Y	Y	Y	Y
48 **Campbell**	Y	Y	Y	N	Y
49 **Issa**	Y	Y	Y	N	Y
50 **Bilbray**	Y	Y	Y	Y	Y
51 Filner	Y	Y	N	Y	Y
52 **Hunter**	Y	Y	Y	N	Y
53 Davis	Y	Y	Y	Y	Y

	268	269	270	271	272
COLORADO					
1 DeGette	Y	Y	N	Y	Y
2 Polis	Y	Y	N	Y	Y
3 Salazar	Y	Y	Y	?	?
4 Markey	Y	Y	Y	Y	Y
5 **Lamborn**	Y	Y	Y	N	Y
6 **Coffman**	Y	Y	Y	N	Y
7 Perlmutter	Y	Y	N	Y	Y
CONNECTICUT					
1 Larson	Y	Y	N	Y	Y
2 Courtney	Y	Y	Y	Y	Y
3 DeLauro	Y	Y	N	Y	Y
4 Himes	Y	Y	N	Y	Y
5 Murphy	Y	Y	N	Y	Y
DELAWARE					
AL **Castle**	Y	Y	Y	Y	Y
FLORIDA					
1 **Miller**	Y	Y	Y	N	Y
2 Boyd	Y	Y	Y	Y	Y
3 Brown	Y	Y	N	Y	Y
4 **Crenshaw**	Y	Y	Y	N	Y
5 **Brown-Waite**	Y	Y	Y	N	Y
6 **Stearns**	Y	Y	Y	N	Y
7 **Mica**	Y	Y	N	Y	Y
8 Grayson	Y	Y	N	Y	Y
9 **Bilirakis**	Y	Y	Y	N	Y
10 **Young**	Y	Y	Y	N	Y
11 Castor	Y	Y	N	Y	Y
12 **Putnam**	Y	Y	Y	Y	Y
13 **Buchanan**	Y	Y	Y	N	Y
14 **Mack**	Y	Y	Y	N	?
15 **Posey**	Y	Y	Y	N	Y
16 **Rooney**	Y	Y	Y	N	Y
17 Meek	Y	Y	Y	Y	Y
18 **Ros-Lehtinen**	Y	Y	Y	Y	Y
19 Deutch	Y	Y	Y	Y	Y
20 Wasserman Schultz	Y	Y	N	Y	Y
21 **Diaz-Balart, L.**	Y	Y	Y	Y	Y
22 Klein	Y	Y	Y	Y	Y
23 Hastings	Y	Y	N	Y	Y
24 **Kosmas**	Y	Y	Y	Y	Y
25 **Diaz-Balart, M.**	Y	Y	Y	Y	Y
GEORGIA					
1 **Kingston**	Y	Y	Y	N	Y
2 Bishop	Y	Y	Y	Y	Y
3 **Westmoreland**	Y	Y	Y	N	Y
4 Johnson	Y	Y	N	Y	Y
5 Lewis	Y	Y	N	Y	Y
6 **Price**	Y	Y	Y	N	Y
7 **Linder**	Y	Y	Y	N	Y
8 Marshall	Y	Y	Y	Y	Y
9 Vacant					
10 **Broun**	Y	Y	Y	N	Y
11 **Gingrey**	Y	Y	Y	N	Y
12 Barrow	Y	Y	Y	Y	Y
13 Scott	Y	Y	N	Y	Y
HAWAII					
1 Vacant					
2 Hirono	Y	Y	N	Y	Y
IDAHO					
1 Minnick	Y	Y	Y	Y	Y
2 **Simpson**	Y	Y	Y	N	Y
ILLINOIS					
1 Rush	?	?	?	?	?
2 Jackson	Y	Y	N	Y	Y
3 Lipinski	Y	Y	Y	Y	Y
4 Gutierrez	Y	Y	Y	Y	Y
5 Quigley	Y	Y	N	Y	Y
6 **Roskam**	Y	Y	Y	N	Y
7 Davis	Y	Y	N	Y	Y
8 Bean	Y	Y	Y	Y	Y
9 Schakowsky	Y	Y	N	?	?
10 **Kirk**	Y	Y	Y	Y	Y
11 Halvorson	Y	Y	Y	Y	Y
12 Costello	Y	Y	Y	Y	Y
13 **Biggert**	Y	Y	Y	Y	Y
14 Foster	Y	Y	Y	Y	Y
15 **Johnson**	Y	Y	Y	N	Y

KEY   Republicans   Democrats

Y   Voted for (yea)
\#   Paired for
\+   Announced for
N   Voted against (nay)

X   Paired against
\-   Announced against
P   Voted "present"

C   Voted "present" to avoid possible conflict of interest
?   Did not vote or otherwise make a position known

	268	269	270	271	272
16 Manzullo	Y	Y	Y	N	Y
17 Hare	Y	Y	Y	Y	Y
18 Schock	Y	Y	Y	Y	Y
19 Shimkus	Y	Y	Y	N	Y
INDIANA					
1 Visclosky	Y	Y	Y	Y	Y
2 Donnelly	Y	Y	Y	Y	Y
3 Souder	Y	Y	Y	Y	Y
4 Buyer	Y	Y	Y	N	Y
5 Burton	Y	Y	Y	N	Y
6 Pence	?	Y	Y	N	Y
7 Carson	Y	Y	N	Y	Y
8 Ellsworth	Y	Y	Y	Y	Y
9 Hill	Y	Y	Y	Y	Y
IOWA					
1 Braley	Y	Y	Y	+	+
2 Loebsack	Y	Y	Y	Y	Y
3 Boswell	Y	Y	Y	Y	Y
4 Latham	Y	Y	Y	Y	Y
5 King	Y	Y	Y	N	Y
KANSAS					
1 Moran	Y	Y	Y	N	Y
2 Jenkins	Y	Y	Y	N	Y
3 Moore	Y	Y	Y	?	?
4 Tiahrt	Y	Y	Y	N	Y
KENTUCKY					
1 Whitfield	Y	Y	Y	Y	Y
2 Guthrie	Y	Y	Y	N	Y
3 Yarmuth	Y	Y	N	Y	Y
4 Davis	Y	Y	Y	N	Y
5 Rogers	Y	Y	Y	Y	Y
6 Chandler	Y	Y	Y	Y	Y
LOUISIANA					
1 Scalise	Y	Y	Y	N	Y
2 Cao	Y	Y	Y	Y	Y
3 Melancon	Y	Y	?	Y	Y
4 Fleming	Y	Y	Y	N	Y
5 Alexander	Y	Y	Y	N	Y
6 Cassidy	Y	Y	Y	Y	Y
7 Boustany	Y	Y	Y	Y	Y
MAINE					
1 Pingree	Y	Y	N	Y	Y
2 Michaud	Y	Y	N	Y	Y
MARYLAND					
1 Kratovil	Y	Y	Y	Y	Y
2 Ruppersberger	Y	Y	Y	Y	Y
3 Sarbanes	Y	Y	N	Y	Y
4 Edwards	Y	Y	N	Y	Y
5 Hoyer	Y	Y	N	Y	Y
6 Bartlett	Y	Y	Y	N	Y
7 Cummings	Y	Y	N	Y	Y
8 Van Hollen	Y	Y	N	Y	Y
MASSACHUSETTS					
1 Olver	Y	Y	N	Y	Y
2 Neal	Y	Y	Y	N	Y
3 McGovern	Y	Y	N	Y	Y
4 Frank	Y	Y	N	Y	Y
5 Tsongas	Y	Y	N	Y	Y
6 Tierney	Y	Y	N	Y	?
7 Markey	Y	Y	N	Y	Y
8 Capuano	Y	Y	N	Y	Y
9 Lynch	Y	Y	N	Y	Y
10 Delahunt	Y	Y	N	Y	Y
MICHIGAN					
1 Stupak	Y	Y	N	Y	Y
2 Hoekstra	?	?	?	?	?
3 Ehlers	Y	Y	N	Y	Y
4 Camp	Y	?	Y	N	Y
5 Kildee	Y	Y	Y	Y	Y
6 Upton	Y	Y	Y	Y	Y
7 Schauer	Y	Y	Y	Y	Y
8 Rogers	Y	Y	Y	N	Y
9 Peters	Y	Y	Y	Y	Y
10 Miller	Y	Y	Y	N	Y
11 McCotter	Y	Y	Y	N	Y
12 Levin	Y	Y	N	Y	Y
13 Kilpatrick	Y	Y	N	Y	Y
14 Conyers	Y	Y	N	Y	Y
15 Dingell	Y	Y	N	Y	Y
MINNESOTA					
1 Walz	Y	Y	Y	Y	Y
2 Kline	Y	Y	Y	N	Y
3 Paulsen	Y	Y	Y	N	Y
4 McCollum	Y	Y	N	Y	Y

	268	269	270	271	272
5 Ellison	Y	Y	Y	N	Y
6 Bachmann	Y	Y	Y	N	Y
7 Peterson	Y	Y	Y	Y	Y
8 Oberstar	Y	Y	N	Y	Y
MISSISSIPPI					
1 Childers	Y	Y	Y	Y	Y
2 Thompson	Y	Y	N	Y	Y
3 Harper	Y	Y	Y	N	Y
4 Taylor	Y	Y	Y	Y	Y
MISSOURI					
1 Clay	Y	Y	N	Y	Y
2 Akin	Y	Y	Y	N	Y
3 Carnahan	Y	Y	Y	N	Y
4 Skelton	Y	Y	Y	Y	?
5 Cleaver	Y	?	N	Y	?
6 Graves	Y	Y	Y	N	Y
7 Blunt	Y	Y	Y	N	Y
8 Emerson	Y	Y	Y	N	Y
9 Luetkemeyer	Y	Y	Y	N	Y
MONTANA					
AL Rehberg	Y	Y	Y	N	Y
NEBRASKA					
1 Fortenberry	Y	Y	Y	Y	Y
2 Terry	Y	Y	Y	Y	Y
3 Smith	Y	Y	Y	Y	Y
NEVADA					
1 Berkley	Y	Y	N	Y	Y
2 Heller	Y	Y	Y	N	Y
3 Titus	Y	Y	Y	Y	Y
NEW HAMPSHIRE					
1 Shea-Porter	Y	Y	Y	Y	Y
2 Hodes	Y	Y	Y	?	?
NEW JERSEY					
1 Andrews	Y	Y	N	Y	Y
2 LoBiondo	Y	Y	Y	N	Y
3 Adler	Y	Y	Y	Y	Y
4 Smith	Y	?	Y	N	Y
5 Garrett	Y	Y	Y	N	Y
6 Pallone	Y	Y	N	Y	Y
7 Lance	Y	Y	Y	Y	Y
8 Pascrell	Y	Y	N	Y	Y
9 Rothman	Y	Y	N	Y	Y
10 Payne	Y	Y	N	Y	Y
11 Frelinghuysen	Y	Y	Y	Y	Y
12 Holt	Y	Y	N	Y	Y
13 Sires	Y	Y	N	Y	Y
NEW MEXICO					
1 Heinrich	Y	Y	Y	Y	Y
2 Teague	?	?	?	?	?
3 Luján	Y	Y	N	Y	Y
NEW YORK					
1 Bishop	Y	Y	Y	Y	Y
2 Israel	Y	Y	Y	Y	Y
3 King	Y	Y	Y	N	Y
4 McCarthy	Y	Y	Y	Y	Y
5 Ackerman	Y	Y	N	Y	Y
6 Meeks	Y	Y	N	Y	Y
7 Crowley	Y	Y	N	Y	Y
8 Nadler	Y	Y	N	?	?
9 Weiner	Y	Y	Y	Y	Y
10 Towns	Y	Y	N	Y	Y
11 Clarke	Y	Y	N	Y	Y
12 Velázquez	Y	Y	N	Y	Y
13 McMahon	Y	Y	Y	Y	Y
14 Maloney	Y	Y	N	Y	Y
15 Rangel	?	Y	N	?	?
16 Serrano	?	Y	Y	Y	Y
17 Engel	Y	Y	N	Y	Y
18 Lowey	Y	Y	N	Y	Y
19 Hall	Y	Y	N	Y	Y
20 Murphy	Y	Y	Y	Y	Y
21 Tonko	Y	Y	N	Y	Y
22 Hinchey	Y	Y	N	Y	Y
23 Owens	Y	Y	N	Y	Y
24 Arcuri	Y	Y	Y	Y	Y
25 Maffei	Y	Y	Y	Y	Y
26 Lee	?	?	?	?	?
27 Higgins	?	?	?	?	?
28 Slaughter	+	+	−	+	+
29 Vacant					
NORTH CAROLINA					
1 Butterfield	Y	Y	N	Y	Y
2 Etheridge	Y	Y	Y	Y	Y
3 Jones	Y	Y	Y	N	Y
4 Price	Y	Y	N	Y	Y

	268	269	270	271	272
5 Foxx	Y	Y	Y	N	Y
6 Coble	Y	Y	Y	N	Y
7 McIntyre	Y	Y	Y	Y	Y
8 Kissell	Y	Y	Y	Y	Y
9 Myrick	Y	Y	Y	N	Y
10 McHenry	Y	Y	Y	N	Y
11 Shuler	Y	Y	Y	Y	Y
12 Watt	Y	Y	N	Y	Y
13 Miller	Y	Y	N	Y	Y
NORTH DAKOTA					
AL Pomeroy	Y	Y	Y	Y	Y
OHIO					
1 Driehaus	Y	Y	Y	Y	Y
2 Schmidt	Y	Y	Y	N	Y
3 Turner	Y	Y	Y	Y	Y
4 Jordan	Y	Y	Y	N	Y
5 Latta	Y	Y	Y	N	Y
6 Wilson	Y	Y	N	Y	Y
7 Austria	Y	Y	Y	N	Y
8 Boehner	Y	Y	Y	N	Y
9 Kaptur	Y	Y	Y	Y	Y
10 Kucinich	Y	Y	N	Y	Y
11 Fudge	Y	Y	N	Y	Y
12 Tiberi	Y	Y	Y	N	Y
13 Sutton	Y	Y	N	Y	Y
14 LaTourette	Y	Y	Y	Y	Y
15 Kilroy	Y	Y	Y	Y	Y
16 Boccieri	Y	Y	Y	Y	Y
17 Ryan	Y	Y	N	Y	Y
18 Space	Y	Y	Y	Y	Y
OKLAHOMA					
1 Sullivan	Y	Y	Y	N	Y
2 Boren	Y	Y	Y	Y	Y
3 Lucas	Y	Y	Y	Y	Y
4 Cole	?	?	?	?	?
5 Fallin	Y	Y	Y	N	Y
OREGON					
1 Wu	Y	Y	Y	Y	Y
2 Walden	Y	Y	Y	Y	Y
3 Blumenauer	Y	Y	N	Y	Y
4 DeFazio	Y	Y	Y	Y	Y
5 Schrader	Y	Y	Y	?	Y
PENNSYLVANIA					
1 Brady	Y	Y	Y	Y	Y
2 Fattah	Y	Y	Y	Y	Y
3 Dahlkemper	Y	Y	Y	Y	Y
4 Altmire	Y	Y	Y	Y	Y
5 Thompson	Y	Y	Y	N	Y
6 Gerlach	Y	Y	Y	Y	Y
7 Sestak	Y	Y	Y	Y	Y
8 Murphy, P.	Y	Y	Y	Y	Y
9 Shuster	Y	Y	Y	N	Y
10 Carney	?	Y	Y	Y	Y
11 Kanjorski	Y	Y	Y	Y	Y
12 Vacant					
13 Schwartz	Y	Y	Y	Y	Y
14 Doyle	?	?	?	?	?
15 Dent	Y	Y	Y	N	Y
16 Pitts	Y	?	Y	N	Y
17 Holden	Y	Y	Y	Y	Y
18 Murphy, T.	Y	Y	Y	Y	Y
19 Platts	Y	Y	Y	Y	Y
RHODE ISLAND					
1 Kennedy	Y	Y	N	Y	Y
2 Langevin	Y	Y	Y	Y	Y
SOUTH CAROLINA					
1 Brown	Y	Y	Y	N	Y
2 Wilson	Y	Y	Y	N	Y
3 Barrett	?	?	?	?	?
4 Inglis	Y	Y	Y	N	Y
5 Spratt	Y	Y	Y	Y	Y
6 Clyburn	Y	Y	N	Y	Y
SOUTH DAKOTA					
AL Herseth Sandlin	Y	Y	Y	Y	Y
TENNESSEE					
1 Roe	Y	Y	Y	N	Y
2 Duncan	Y	Y	Y	N	Y
3 Wamp	?	?	?	?	?
4 Davis	Y	Y	Y	Y	Y
5 Cooper	Y	Y	N	Y	Y
6 Gordon	Y	Y	N	?	Y
7 Blackburn	Y	Y	Y	N	Y
8 Tanner	Y	Y	Y	Y	Y
9 Cohen	Y	Y	N	Y	Y

	268	269	270	271	272
TEXAS					
1 Gohmert	Y	Y	Y	N	Y
2 Poe	Y	Y	Y	N	Y
3 Johnson, S.	Y	Y	Y	N	Y
4 Hall	Y	Y	Y	Y	Y
5 Hensarling	Y	Y	Y	N	Y
6 Barton	Y	Y	Y	Y	Y
7 Culberson	Y	Y	Y	N	Y
8 Brady	Y	Y	Y	N	Y
9 Green, A.	Y	Y	N	Y	Y
10 McCaul	Y	Y	Y	Y	Y
11 Conaway	Y	Y	Y	N	Y
12 Granger	Y	Y	Y	N	Y
13 Thornberry	Y	Y	Y	N	Y
14 Paul	Y	Y	Y	N	Y
15 Hinojosa	Y	Y	Y	Y	Y
16 Reyes	Y	Y	N	Y	Y
17 Edwards	Y	Y	Y	Y	Y
18 Jackson Lee	Y	Y	N	Y	Y
19 Neugebauer	Y	Y	Y	N	Y
20 Gonzalez	Y	Y	N	Y	Y
21 Smith	Y	Y	Y	N	Y
22 Olson	Y	Y	Y	N	Y
23 Rodriguez	Y	Y	Y	Y	Y
24 Marchant	Y	Y	Y	N	Y
25 Doggett	Y	Y	N	Y	Y
26 Burgess	Y	Y	Y	N	Y
27 Ortiz	Y	Y	Y	N	Y
28 Cuellar	Y	Y	Y	?	?
29 Green, G.	Y	Y	N	Y	Y
30 Johnson, E.	Y	Y	N	Y	Y
31 Carter	Y	Y	Y	N	Y
32 Sessions	Y	Y	Y	N	Y
UTAH					
1 Bishop	?	Y	Y	N	Y
2 Matheson	Y	Y	Y	Y	Y
3 Chaffetz	Y	Y	Y	N	Y
VERMONT					
AL Welch	Y	Y	N	Y	Y
VIRGINIA					
1 Wittman	Y	Y	Y	N	Y
2 Nye	Y	Y	Y	Y	Y
3 Scott	Y	Y	N	Y	Y
4 Forbes	Y	Y	Y	N	Y
5 Perriello	Y	Y	Y	Y	Y
6 Goodlatte	Y	Y	Y	N	Y
7 Cantor	Y	Y	Y	N	Y
8 Moran	Y	Y	N	Y	Y
9 Boucher	Y	Y	Y	Y	Y
10 Wolf	Y	Y	Y	N	Y
11 Connolly	Y	Y	Y	Y	Y
WASHINGTON					
1 Inslee	Y	Y	N	Y	Y
2 Larsen	Y	Y	Y	Y	Y
3 Baird	Y	Y	N	Y	Y
4 Hastings	Y	Y	Y	N	Y
5 McMorris Rodgers	Y	Y	Y	N	Y
6 Dicks	Y	Y	N	Y	Y
7 McDermott	Y	Y	N	Y	Y
8 Reichert	Y	Y	Y	N	Y
9 Smith	Y	Y	Y	Y	Y
WEST VIRGINIA					
1 Mollohan	Y	Y	Y	Y	Y
2 Capito	Y	Y	Y	N	Y
3 Rahall	Y	Y	Y	Y	Y
WISCONSIN					
1 Ryan	Y	Y	Y	N	Y
2 Baldwin	Y	Y	N	Y	Y
3 Kind	Y	Y	Y	Y	Y
4 Moore	Y	Y	N	Y	Y
5 Sensenbrenner	Y	Y	Y	N	Y
6 Petri	Y	Y	Y	N	Y
7 Obey	Y	Y	N	Y	Y
8 Kagen	Y	Y	Y	Y	Y
WYOMING					
AL Lummis	Y	Y	Y	N	Y
DELEGATES					
Faleomavaega (A.S.)	Y	Y			
Norton (D.C.)	Y	Y			
Bordallo (Guam)	Y	Y			
Sablan (N. Marianas)	Y	Y			
Pierluisi (P.R.)	Y	Y			
Christensen (V.I.)	?	?			

IN THE HOUSE | By Vote Number

273. **HR 2288. Endangered Fish Recovery Programs/Passage.** Napolitano, D-Calif., motion to suspend the rules and pass the bill that would authorize funding, as necessary, through fiscal 2023 for the Bureau of Reclamation to provide base funding for the Upper Colorado River Basin and San Juan River endangered fish recovery implementation programs. Motion agreed to 264-122: D 228-3; R 36-119. A two-thirds majority of those present and voting (258 in this case) is required for passage under suspension of the rules. May 18, 2010.

274. **HR 4614. DNA Collection Incentives Program/Passage.** Johnson, D-Ga., motion to suspend the rules and pass the bill that would authorize bonus payments of 5 percent or 10 percent of Byrne grants to states that have implemented a collection system for DNA evidence from arrested individuals. The bill would authorize funding, as necessary, for the payments in fiscal 2011 through 2015. Motion agreed to 357-32: D 233-0; R 124-32. A two-thirds majority of those present and voting (260 in this case) is required for passage under suspension of the rules. May 18, 2010.

275. **H Res 1327. Tribute to Floyd Dominy/Adoption.** Napolitano, D-Calif., motion to suspend the rules and adopt the resolution that would honor former Bureau of Reclamation commissioner Floyd Dominy for his contributions to the nation's water and food supply, recreation and environment. Motion agreed to 390-0: D 235-0; R 155-0. A two-thirds majority of those present and voting (260 in this case) is required for adoption under suspension of the rules. May 18, 2010.

276. **HR 1514. Juvenile Accountability Block Grants/Passage.** Scott, D-Va., motion to suspend the rules and pass the bill that would reauthorize the Juvenile Accountability Block Grants program through fiscal 2014 at $350 million per year. Motion agreed to 364-45: D 245-1; R 119-44. A two-thirds majority of those present and voting (273 in this case) is required for passage under suspension of the rules. May 19, 2010.

277. **HR 5325. Science and Technology Programs Reauthorization/Passage.** Gordon, D-Tenn., motion to suspend the rules and pass the bill that would authorize approximately $48 billion in fiscal 2011 through 2013 for science and technology research initiatives and programs. It also would authorize new and existing federal programs for continuing education in the fields of science, technology, engineering and math. It would disallow the use of funds to pay the salaries of federal employees who are disciplined for viewing pornography on the job. Motion rejected 261-148: D 246-0; R 15-148. A two-thirds majority of those present and voting (273 in this case) is required for passage under suspension of the rules. May 19, 2010.

278. **H Res 1325. National Missing Children's Day/Adoption.** Scott, D-Va., motion to suspend the rules and adopt the resolution that would recognize National Missing Children's Day and encourage people to plan events to raise public awareness of the problem. Motion agreed to 410-0: D 246-0; R 164-0. A two-thirds majority of those present and voting (274 in this case) is required for adoption under suspension of the rules. May 19, 2010.

ALABAMA	273	274	275	276	277	278
1 Bonner	N	Y	Y	Y	N	Y
2 Bright	N	Y	Y	Y	Y	Y
3 Rogers	N	Y	Y	Y	N	Y
4 Aderholt	N	Y	Y	N	N	Y
5 Griffith	N	Y	Y	N	N	Y
6 Bachus	Y	Y	Y	?	?	?
7 Davis	?	?	?	?	?	?
ALASKA						
AL Young	?	?	?	Y	N	Y
ARIZONA						
1 Kirkpatrick	Y	Y	Y	Y	Y	Y
2 Franks	N	N	Y	N	N	Y
3 Shadegg	N	N	Y	N	N	Y
4 Pastor	Y	Y	Y	Y	Y	Y
5 Mitchell	Y	Y	Y	Y	Y	Y
6 Flake	?	?	?	N	N	Y
7 Grijalva	?	?	?	Y	Y	Y
8 Giffords	Y	Y	Y	Y	Y	Y
ARKANSAS						
1 Berry	Y	Y	Y	Y	Y	Y
2 Snyder	Y	Y	Y	Y	Y	Y
3 Boozman	?	?	?	?	?	?
4 Ross	Y	Y	Y	Y	Y	Y
CALIFORNIA						
1 Thompson	+	+	+	Y	Y	Y
2 Herger	N	Y	Y	N	N	Y
3 Lungren	N	Y	Y	N	N	Y
4 McClintock	N	Y	Y	N	N	Y
5 Matsui	Y	Y	Y	Y	Y	Y
6 Woolsey	+	Y	Y	Y	Y	Y
7 Miller, George	Y	Y	Y	Y	Y	Y
8 Pelosi					Y	
9 Lee	Y	Y	Y	Y	Y	Y
10 Garamendi	Y	Y	Y	?	+	?
11 McNerney	Y	Y	Y	Y	Y	Y
12 Speier	Y	Y	Y	Y	Y	Y
13 Stark	Y	Y	?	Y	Y	Y
14 Eshoo	Y	Y	Y	Y	Y	Y
15 Honda	Y	Y	Y	Y	Y	Y
16 Lofgren	Y	Y	Y	Y	Y	Y
17 Farr	Y	Y	Y	+	?	+
18 Cardoza	Y	Y	Y	Y	Y	Y
19 Radanovich	N	Y	Y	N	N	Y
20 Costa	?	?	?	?	?	?
21 Nunes	N	Y	Y	N	N	Y
22 McCarthy	N	Y	Y	Y	N	Y
23 Capps	Y	Y	Y	Y	Y	Y
24 Gallegly	N	Y	Y	Y	N	Y
25 McKeon	N	Y	Y	N	N	Y
26 Dreier	N	Y	Y	N	N	Y
27 Sherman	Y	Y	Y	Y	Y	Y
28 Berman	Y	Y	Y	Y	Y	Y
29 Schiff	Y	Y	Y	Y	Y	Y
30 Waxman	Y	Y	Y	Y	Y	Y
31 Becerra	+	+	?	Y	Y	Y
32 Chu	Y	Y	Y	Y	Y	Y
33 Watson	Y	Y	Y	Y	Y	Y
34 Roybal-Allard	Y	Y	Y	Y	Y	Y
35 Waters	Y	Y	Y	Y	Y	Y
36 Harman	Y	Y	Y	Y	Y	Y
37 Richardson	Y	Y	Y	Y	Y	Y
38 Napolitano	Y	Y	Y	Y	Y	Y
39 Sánchez, Linda	Y	Y	Y	Y	Y	Y
40 Royce	N	Y	Y	N	N	Y
41 Lewis	N	Y	Y	N	N	Y
42 Miller, Gary	N	Y	Y	N	N	Y
43 Baca	Y	Y	Y	Y	Y	Y
44 Calvert	N	Y	Y	N	N	Y
45 Bono Mack	N	Y	Y	Y · N		Y
46 Rohrabacher	N	Y	Y	N	N	Y
47 Sanchez, Loretta	Y	Y	Y	Y	Y	Y
48 Campbell	N	N	Y	N	N	Y
49 Issa	N	Y	Y	N	N	Y
50 Bilbray	?	?	?	?	?	?
51 Filner	Y	Y	Y	Y	Y	Y
52 Hunter	N	Y	Y	N	N	Y
53 Davis	Y	Y	Y	Y	Y	Y

COLORADO	273	274	275	276	277	278
1 DeGette	Y	Y	Y	Y	Y	Y
2 Polis	Y	Y	Y	Y	Y	Y
3 Salazar	Y	Y	Y	Y	Y	Y
4 Markey	Y	Y	Y	Y	Y	Y
5 Lamborn	N	N	Y	N	N	Y
6 Coffman	Y	N	Y	N	N	Y
7 Perlmutter	Y	Y	Y	Y	Y	Y
CONNECTICUT						
1 Larson	Y	Y	Y	Y	Y	Y
2 Courtney	Y	Y	Y	Y	Y	Y
3 DeLauro	Y	Y	Y	Y	Y	Y
4 Himes	Y	Y	Y	Y	Y	Y
5 Murphy	Y	Y	Y	Y	Y	Y
DELAWARE						
AL Castle	Y	Y	Y	Y	Y	Y
FLORIDA						
1 Miller	N	N	Y	N	N	Y
2 Boyd	Y	Y	Y	Y	Y	Y
3 Brown	Y	Y	Y	Y	Y	Y
4 Crenshaw	N	Y	Y	Y	N	Y
5 Brown-Waite	N	Y	Y	Y	N	Y
6 Stearns	N	Y	Y	Y	N	Y
7 Mica	N	Y	Y	N	N	Y
8 Grayson	+	+	+	Y	Y	Y
9 Bilirakis	N	Y	?	Y	N	Y
10 Young	N	Y	Y	Y	N	Y
11 Castor	Y	Y	Y	Y	Y	Y
12 Putnam	?	?	?	?	?	?
13 Buchanan	Y	Y	Y	Y	N	Y
14 Mack	N	N	Y	?	?	?
15 Posey	Y	Y	Y	Y	N	Y
16 Rooney	N	Y	Y	Y	N	Y
17 Meek	Y	Y	Y	Y	Y	Y
18 Ros-Lehtinen	Y	Y	Y	Y	Y	Y
19 Deutch	Y	Y	Y	Y	Y	Y
20 Wasserman Schultz	Y	Y	Y	Y	Y	Y
21 Diaz-Balart, L.	Y	Y	Y	Y	N	Y
22 Klein	Y	Y	Y	Y	Y	Y
23 Hastings	Y	Y	Y	Y	Y	Y
24 Kosmas	Y	Y	Y	Y	Y	Y
25 Diaz-Balart, M.	?	?	?	?	?	?
GEORGIA						
1 Kingston	N	N	Y	N	N	Y
2 Bishop	Y	Y	Y	Y	Y	Y
3 Westmoreland	N	N	Y	N	N	Y
4 Johnson	Y	?	Y	Y	Y	Y
5 Lewis	Y	Y	Y	Y	Y	Y
6 Price	?	?	?	N	N	Y
7 Linder	N	Y	Y	N	N	Y
8 Marshall	Y	Y	Y	Y	Y	Y
9 Vacant						
10 Broun	N	N	Y	N	N	Y
11 Gingrey	N	Y	Y	N	N	Y
12 Barrow	Y	Y	Y	Y	Y	Y
13 Scott	Y	Y	Y	Y	Y	Y
HAWAII						
1 Vacant						
2 Hirono	Y	Y	Y	Y	Y	Y
IDAHO						
1 Minnick	Y	Y	Y	Y	Y	Y
2 Simpson	Y	Y	Y	Y	N	Y
ILLINOIS						
1 Rush	?	?	?	Y	Y	Y
2 Jackson	Y	Y	Y	Y	Y	Y
3 Lipinski	Y	Y	Y	Y	Y	Y
4 Gutierrez	+	Y	Y	Y	Y	Y
5 Quigley	Y	Y	Y	Y	Y	Y
6 Roskam	N	Y	Y	Y	N	Y
7 Davis	Y	Y	Y	Y	Y	Y
8 Bean	Y	Y	Y	Y	Y	Y
9 Schakowsky	Y	Y	Y	Y	Y	Y
10 Kirk	?	?	?	?	?	?
11 Halvorson	Y	Y	Y	Y	N	Y
12 Costello	Y	Y	Y	Y	Y	Y
13 Biggert	N	Y	Y	Y	Y	Y
14 Foster	Y	Y	Y	Y	Y	Y
15 Johnson	Y	Y	Y	Y	Y	Y

	273	274	275	276	277	278
16 **Manzullo**	–	+	+	N	N	Y
17 Hare	Y	Y	Y	Y	Y	Y
18 **Schock**	N	Y	Y	Y	N	Y
19 **Shimkus**	N	Y	Y	Y	N	Y
INDIANA						
1 Visclosky	Y	Y	Y	Y	Y	Y
2 Donnelly	Y	Y	Y	Y	Y	Y
3 **Souder**	?	?	?	?	?	?
4 **Buyer**	N	Y	Y	Y	N	Y
5 **Burton**	N	Y	Y	Y	N	Y
6 **Pence**	N	N	Y	Y	?	Y
7 Carson	Y	Y	Y	Y	Y	Y
8 Ellsworth	Y	Y	Y	Y	Y	Y
9 Hill	Y	Y	Y	Y	Y	Y
IOWA						
1 Braley	Y	Y	Y	Y	Y	Y
2 Loebsack	Y	Y	Y	Y	Y	Y
3 Boswell	Y	Y	Y	Y	Y	Y
4 **Latham**	Y	Y	Y	Y	N	Y
5 **King**	N	Y	Y	Y	N	Y
KANSAS						
1 **Moran**	N	Y	Y	Y	N	Y
2 **Jenkins**	N	Y	Y	Y	N	Y
3 Moore	Y	Y	Y	Y	Y	Y
4 **Tiahrt**	N	Y	Y	Y	N	Y
KENTUCKY						
1 **Whitfield**	N	Y	Y	Y	N	Y
2 **Guthrie**	N	Y	Y	Y	N	Y
3 Yarmuth	Y	Y	Y	Y	Y	Y
4 **Davis**	N	Y	Y	Y	N	Y
5 **Rogers**	N	Y	Y	Y	N	Y
6 Chandler	Y	Y	Y	Y	Y	Y
LOUISIANA						
1 **Scalise**	N	Y	Y	Y	N	Y
2 **Cao**	N	Y	Y	Y	Y	Y
3 Melancon	?	Y	Y	Y	Y	Y
4 **Fleming**	N	Y	Y	N	N	Y
5 **Alexander**	N	Y	Y	Y	N	Y
6 **Cassidy**	N	Y	Y	Y	N	Y
7 **Boustany**	N	Y	Y	Y	N	Y
MAINE						
1 Pingree	Y	Y	Y	Y	Y	Y
2 Michaud	Y	Y	Y	Y	Y	Y
MARYLAND						
1 Kratovil	Y	Y	Y	Y	Y	Y
2 Ruppersberger	Y	Y	Y	Y	Y	Y
3 Sarbanes	Y	Y	Y	Y	Y	Y
4 Edwards	Y	Y	Y	Y	Y	Y
5 Hoyer	Y	Y	Y	Y	Y	Y
6 **Bartlett**	N	Y	Y	N	Y	Y
7 Cummings	Y	Y	Y	Y	Y	Y
8 Van Hollen	?	Y	Y	Y	Y	Y
MASSACHUSETTS						
1 Olver	Y	Y	Y	Y	Y	Y
2 Neal	Y	Y	Y	Y	Y	Y
3 McGovern	Y	Y	Y	Y	Y	Y
4 Frank	Y	Y	Y	Y	Y	Y
5 Tsongas	Y	Y	Y	Y	Y	Y
6 Tierney	Y	Y	Y	Y	Y	Y
7 Markey	Y	Y	Y	Y	Y	Y
8 Capuano	Y	Y	Y	Y	Y	Y
9 Lynch	Y	Y	Y	Y	?	Y
10 Delahunt	Y	Y	Y	Y	Y	Y
MICHIGAN						
1 Stupak	Y	Y	Y	Y	Y	Y
2 **Hoekstra**	?	N	Y	Y	N	Y
3 **Ehlers**	Y	Y	Y	Y	Y	Y
4 **Camp**	N	Y	Y	Y	N	Y
5 Kildee	Y	Y	Y	Y	Y	Y
6 **Upton**	N	Y	Y	Y	N	Y
7 Schauer	Y	Y	Y	Y	Y	Y
8 **Rogers**	Y	Y	Y	?	N	Y
9 Peters	Y	Y	Y	Y	Y	Y
10 **Miller**	N	Y	Y	Y	N	Y
11 **McCotter**	Y	Y	Y	Y	N	Y
12 Levin	Y	Y	Y	Y	Y	Y
13 Kilpatrick	Y	Y	Y	Y	Y	Y
14 Conyers	Y	Y	Y	Y	Y	Y
15 Dingell	Y	Y	Y	Y	Y	Y
MINNESOTA						
1 Walz	Y	Y	Y	Y	Y	Y
2 **Kline**	N	Y	Y	Y	N	Y
3 **Paulsen**	N	Y	Y	Y	N	Y
4 McCollum	Y	Y	Y	Y	Y	Y

	273	274	275	276	277	278
5 Ellison	Y	Y	Y	+	Y	Y
6 **Bachmann**	?	?	?	Y	N	Y
7 Peterson	Y	Y	Y	Y	Y	Y
8 Oberstar	Y	Y	Y	Y	Y	Y
MISSISSIPPI						
1 Childers	Y	Y	Y	Y	Y	Y
2 Thompson	Y	Y	Y	Y	Y	Y
3 **Harper**	N	N	Y	Y	N	Y
4 Taylor	Y	Y	Y	Y	Y	Y
MISSOURI						
1 Clay	Y	Y	Y	Y	Y	Y
2 **Akin**	N	N	Y	N	N	Y
3 Carnahan	Y	Y	Y	Y	Y	Y
4 Skelton	Y	Y	Y	Y	Y	Y
5 Cleaver	Y	Y	Y	Y	Y	Y
6 **Graves**	N	Y	Y	?	?	?
7 **Blunt**	?	?	?	Y	N	Y
8 **Emerson**	N	Y	Y	Y	Y	Y
9 **Luetkemeyer**	N	Y	Y	Y	N	Y
MONTANA						
AL **Rehberg**	N	Y	Y	Y	N	Y
NEBRASKA						
1 **Fortenberry**	Y	Y	Y	Y	N	Y
2 **Terry**	Y	Y	Y	Y	N	Y
3 **Smith**	Y	Y	Y	Y	N	Y
NEVADA						
1 Berkley	Y	Y	Y	Y	Y	Y
2 **Heller**	Y	Y	Y	Y	N	Y
3 Titus	Y	Y	Y	Y	Y	Y
NEW HAMPSHIRE						
1 Shea-Porter	Y	Y	Y	Y	Y	Y
2 Hodes	Y	Y	Y	Y	Y	Y
NEW JERSEY						
1 Andrews	Y	Y	Y	Y	Y	Y
2 **LoBiondo**	Y	Y	Y	Y	N	Y
3 Adler	Y	Y	Y	Y	Y	Y
4 **Smith**	Y	Y	Y	Y	N	Y
5 **Garrett**	N	N	Y	N	N	Y
6 Pallone	Y	Y	Y	Y	Y	Y
7 **Lance**	Y	Y	Y	Y	N	Y
8 Pascrell	Y	Y	Y	Y	Y	Y
9 Rothman	?	?	?	Y	Y	Y
10 Payne	Y	Y	Y	Y	Y	Y
11 **Frelinghuysen**	Y	Y	Y	Y	N	Y
12 Holt	Y	Y	Y	Y	Y	Y
13 Sires	?	?	?	Y	Y	Y
NEW MEXICO						
1 Heinrich	Y	Y	Y	Y	Y	Y
2 Teague	Y	Y	Y	Y	Y	Y
3 Luján	Y	Y	Y	Y	Y	Y
NEW YORK						
1 Bishop	Y	Y	Y	Y	Y	Y
2 Israel	Y	Y	Y	Y	Y	Y
3 **King**	N	Y	Y	Y	N	Y
4 McCarthy	Y	Y	Y	Y	Y	Y
5 Ackerman	Y	Y	Y	Y	Y	Y
6 Meeks	Y	Y	Y	Y	Y	Y
7 Crowley	Y	Y	Y	Y	Y	Y
8 Nadler	Y	Y	Y	Y	Y	Y
9 Weiner	Y	Y	Y	Y	Y	Y
10 Towns	?	?	?	Y	Y	Y
11 Clarke	Y	Y	Y	Y	Y	Y
12 Velázquez	Y	Y	Y	Y	Y	?
13 McMahon	Y	Y	Y	Y	Y	Y
14 Maloney	Y	Y	Y	Y	Y	Y
15 Rangel	Y	Y	Y	Y	Y	Y
16 Serrano	Y	Y	Y	Y	Y	Y
17 Engel	Y	Y	Y	Y	Y	Y
18 Lowey	Y	Y	Y	Y	Y	Y
19 Hall	Y	Y	Y	Y	+	Y
20 Murphy	N	Y	Y	Y	Y	Y
21 Tonko	Y	Y	Y	Y	Y	Y
22 Hinchey	?	?	?	?	?	?
23 Owens	N	Y	Y	N	Y	Y
24 Arcuri	Y	Y	Y	Y	Y	Y
25 Maffei	Y	Y	Y	Y	Y	Y
26 **Lee**	Y	Y	Y	Y	Y	Y
27 Higgins	Y	Y	Y	Y	Y	Y
28 Slaughter	Y	Y	Y	Y	Y	Y
29 Vacant						
NORTH CAROLINA						
1 Butterfield	Y	Y	Y	Y	Y	Y
2 Etheridge	Y	Y	Y	Y	Y	Y
3 **Jones**	Y	Y	Y	Y	Y	Y
4 Price	Y	Y	Y	Y	Y	Y

	273	274	275	276	277	278
5 **Foxx**	N	N	Y	N	N	Y
6 **Coble**	N	Y	Y	Y	N	Y
7 McIntyre	Y	Y	Y	Y	Y	Y
8 Kissell	Y	Y	Y	Y	Y	Y
9 **Myrick**	N	Y	Y	Y	N	Y
10 **McHenry**	N	Y	Y	Y	N	Y
11 Shuler	Y	Y	Y	Y	Y	Y
12 Watt	Y	Y	Y	Y	Y	Y
13 Miller	Y	Y	Y	Y	Y	Y
NORTH DAKOTA						
AL Pomeroy	Y	Y	Y	Y	Y	Y
OHIO						
1 Driehaus	Y	Y	Y	Y	Y	Y
2 **Schmidt**	N	Y	Y	Y	N	Y
3 **Turner**	Y	Y	Y	Y	N	Y
4 **Jordan**	N	N	Y	N	N	Y
5 **Latta**	N	Y	Y	Y	N	Y
6 Wilson	Y	Y	Y	Y	Y	Y
7 **Austria**	N	Y	Y	Y	N	Y
8 **Boehner**	N	Y	Y	Y	N	Y
9 Kaptur	Y	Y	Y	Y	Y	Y
10 Kucinich	Y	Y	Y	Y	Y	Y
11 Fudge	Y	Y	Y	Y	Y	Y
12 **Tiberi**	Y	Y	Y	Y	N	Y
13 Sutton	Y	Y	Y	Y	Y	Y
14 **LaTourette**	Y	Y	Y	Y	N	Y
15 Kilroy	Y	Y	Y	Y	Y	Y
16 Boccieri	Y	Y	Y	Y	Y	Y
17 Ryan	Y	Y	Y	Y	Y	Y
18 Space	Y	Y	Y	Y	Y	Y
OKLAHOMA						
1 **Sullivan**	N	Y	Y	Y	N	Y
2 Boren	Y	Y	Y	Y	Y	Y
3 **Lucas**	N	Y	Y	Y	N	Y
4 **Cole**	N	Y	Y	Y	N	Y
5 **Fallin**	N	Y	Y	Y	N	Y
OREGON						
1 Wu	Y	Y	Y	Y	Y	Y
2 **Walden**	Y	Y	Y	Y	N	Y
3 Blumenauer	Y	Y	Y	Y	Y	Y
4 DeFazio	Y	Y	Y	Y	Y	Y
5 Schrader	Y	Y	Y	Y	Y	Y
PENNSYLVANIA						
1 Brady	?	?	?	Y	Y	Y
2 Fattah	Y	Y	Y	Y	Y	Y
3 Dahlkemper	Y	Y	Y	Y	Y	Y
4 Altmire	Y	Y	Y	Y	Y	Y
5 **Thompson**	N	Y	Y	Y	N	Y
6 **Gerlach**	+	+	+	Y	Y	Y
7 Sestak	?	?	?	Y	Y	Y
8 Murphy, P.	Y	Y	Y	Y	Y	Y
9 **Shuster**	?	?	?	Y	N	Y
10 Carney	Y	Y	Y	Y	Y	Y
11 Kanjorski	Y	Y	Y	Y	Y	Y
12 Vacant						
13 Schwartz	Y	Y	Y	Y	Y	Y
14 Doyle	Y	Y	Y	Y	Y	Y
15 **Dent**	Y	Y	Y	Y	Y	Y
16 **Pitts**	N	Y	Y	Y	N	Y
17 Holden	?	?	?	?	?	?
18 **Murphy, T.**	N	Y	Y	Y	N	Y
19 **Platts**	?	?	?	Y	Y	Y
RHODE ISLAND						
1 Kennedy	Y	Y	Y	Y	Y	Y
2 Langevin	Y	Y	Y	Y	Y	Y
SOUTH CAROLINA						
1 **Brown**	N	Y	Y	Y	N	Y
2 **Wilson**	N	N	Y	Y	N	Y
3 **Barrett**	?	?	?	?	?	?
4 **Inglis**	?	?	?	N	N	Y
5 Spratt	Y	Y	Y	Y	Y	Y
6 Clyburn	Y	Y	Y	Y	Y	Y
SOUTH DAKOTA						
AL Herseth Sandlin	Y	Y	Y	Y	Y	Y
TENNESSEE						
1 **Roe**	N	Y	Y	Y	N	Y
2 **Duncan**	N	N	Y	Y	N	Y
3 **Wamp**	?	?	?	?	?	?
4 Davis	Y	Y	Y	Y	Y	Y
5 Cooper	Y	Y	Y	Y	Y	Y
6 Gordon	Y	?	Y	Y	Y	Y
7 **Blackburn**	N	N	Y	Y	N	Y
8 Tanner	Y	Y	Y	Y	Y	Y
9 Cohen	Y	Y	Y	Y	Y	Y

	273	274	275	276	277	278
TEXAS						
1 **Gohmert**	N	N	Y	Y	N	Y
2 **Poe**	N	N	Y	N	N	Y
3 **Johnson, S.**	N	N	Y	Y	N	Y
4 **Hall**	N	Y	Y	Y	N	Y
5 **Hensarling**	N	N	Y	N	N	Y
6 **Barton**	N	N	Y	Y	N	Y
7 **Culberson**	?	?	?	N	N	Y
8 **Brady**	N	N	Y	N	N	Y
9 Green, A.	Y	Y	Y	Y	Y	Y
10 **McCaul**	?	?	?	Y	Y	Y
11 **Conaway**	N	N	Y	N	N	Y
12 **Granger**	N	Y	Y	?	?	?
13 **Thornberry**	N	N	Y	N	N	Y
14 **Paul**	?	?	?	?	?	?
15 Hinojosa	Y	Y	Y	Y	Y	Y
16 Reyes	Y	Y	Y	Y	Y	Y
17 Edwards	Y	Y	Y	Y	Y	Y
18 Jackson Lee	?	?	?	Y	Y	Y
19 **Neugebauer**	N	N	Y	N	N	Y
20 Gonzalez	Y	Y	Y	Y	Y	Y
21 **Smith**	Y	Y	Y	Y	N	Y
22 **Olson**	N	Y	Y	Y	N	Y
23 Rodriguez	Y	Y	Y	Y	Y	Y
24 **Marchant**	N	N	Y	N	N	Y
25 Doggett	Y	Y	Y	Y	Y	Y
26 **Burgess**	N	Y	Y	N	N	Y
27 Ortiz	Y	Y	Y	Y	Y	Y
28 Cuellar	Y	Y	Y	Y	Y	Y
29 Green, G.	?	Y	Y	Y	Y	Y
30 Johnson, E.	Y	Y	Y	Y	Y	Y
31 **Carter**	N	Y	Y	N	N	Y
32 **Sessions**	N	Y	Y	Y	N	Y
UTAH						
1 **Bishop**	Y	Y	Y	Y	N	Y
2 Matheson	Y	Y	Y	Y	Y	Y
3 **Chaffetz**	Y	Y	Y	N	N	Y
VERMONT						
AL Welch	Y	Y	Y	Y	Y	Y
VIRGINIA						
1 **Wittman**	N	Y	Y	Y	N	Y
2 Nye	Y	Y	Y	Y	Y	Y
3 Scott	Y	Y	Y	Y	Y	Y
4 **Forbes**	N	Y	Y	Y	N	Y
5 Perriello	Y	Y	Y	Y	Y	Y
6 **Goodlatte**	N	Y	Y	Y	N	Y
7 **Cantor**	N	Y	Y	Y	N	Y
8 Moran	Y	Y	Y	Y	Y	Y
9 Boucher	Y	?	Y	Y	Y	Y
10 **Wolf**	N	Y	Y	Y	Y	Y
11 Connolly	Y	Y	Y	Y	Y	Y
WASHINGTON						
1 Inslee	Y	Y	Y	Y	Y	Y
2 Larsen	Y	Y	Y	Y	Y	Y
3 Baird	Y	Y	Y	Y	Y	Y
4 **Hastings**	Y	Y	Y	Y	N	Y
5 **McMorris Rodgers**	Y	Y	Y	Y	N	Y
6 Dicks	?	?	?	Y	Y	Y
7 McDermott	Y	Y	Y	Y	Y	Y
8 **Reichert**	Y	Y	Y	Y	Y	Y
9 Smith	Y	Y	Y	Y	Y	Y
WEST VIRGINIA						
1 Mollohan	Y	Y	Y	Y	Y	Y
2 **Capito**	Y	Y	Y	Y	N	Y
3 Rahall	+	+	+	Y	Y	Y
WISCONSIN						
1 **Ryan**	N	Y	Y	Y	N	Y
2 Baldwin	Y	Y	Y	Y	Y	Y
3 Kind	Y	Y	Y	Y	Y	Y
4 Moore	Y	Y	Y	Y	Y	Y
5 **Sensenbrenner**	N	N	Y	Y	N	Y
6 **Petri**	N	Y	Y	Y	N	Y
7 Obey	Y	Y	Y	Y	Y	Y
8 Kagen	Y	Y	Y	Y	Y	Y
WYOMING						
AL **Lummis**	Y	N	Y	N	N	Y
DELEGATES						
Faleomavaega (A.S.)						
Norton (D.C.)						
Bordallo (Guam)						
Sablan (N. Marianas)						
Pierluisi (P.R.)						
Christensen (V.I.)						

IN THE HOUSE | By Vote Number

279. **H Res 1362. Tribute to Lena Horne/Adoption.** Conyers, D-Mich., motion to suspend the rules and adopt the resolution that would celebrate the life and achievements of entertainer Lena Horne and honor her triumphs against racial discrimination and commitment to civil rights. Motion agreed to 405-1: D 243-0; R 162-1. A two-thirds majority of those present and voting (271 in this case) is required for adoption under suspension of the rules. May 19, 2010.

280. **HR 5099. Michael C. Rothberg Post Office/Passage.** Davis, D-Ill., motion to suspend the rules and pass the bill that would designate a post office in Sharon, Mass., as the "Michael C. Rothberg Post Office." Motion agreed to 410-1: D 247-0; R 163-1. A two-thirds majority of those present and voting (274 in this case) is required for passage under suspension of the rules. May 19, 2010.

281. **H Res 403. National Teacher Day/Adoption.** Davis, D-Ill., motion to suspend the rules and adopt the resolution that would support the establishment of National Teacher Day to honor teachers. Motion agreed to 405-2: D 246-0; R 159-2. A two-thirds majority of those present and voting (272 in this case) is required for adoption under suspension of the rules. May 19, 2010.

282. **H Res 1292. Tribute to Emporia State University Women's Basketball Team/Adoption.** Fudge, D-Ohio, motion to suspend the rules and adopt the resolution that would congratulate the Emporia State University Lady Hornets basketball team for winning the 2010 NCAA Division II national championship. Motion agreed to 407-1: D 245-0; R 162-1. A two-thirds majority of those present and voting (272 in this case) is required for adoption under suspension of the rules. May 19, 2010.

283. **H Res 1364. Tribute to the Chatham County Courthouse/Adoption.** Johnson, D-Ga., motion to suspend the rules and adopt the resolution that would express condolences to the North Carolina court system, Chatham County and the town of Pittsboro for the loss of the Chatham County Courthouse in a fire. It would commend the firefighters and first-responders who fought the fire and recognize the significance of the courthouse and its impact on the community. Motion agreed to 406-1: D 242-0; R 164-1. A two-thirds majority of those present and voting (272 in this case) is required for adoption under suspension of the rules. May 19, 2010.

284. **HR 5327. U.S.-Israel Missile Defense Cooperation/Passage.** McMahon, D-N.Y., motion to suspend the rules and pass the bill that would authorize the president, acting through the secretaries of Defense and State, to provide assistance to the government of Israel for the procurement, maintenance and sustainment of the "Iron Dome" anti-missile defense system for purposes of intercepting short-range missiles launched against Israel. Motion agreed to 410-4: D 244-0; R 166-1. A two-thirds majority of those present and voting (276 in this case) is required for passage under suspension of the rules. May 20, 2010.

285. **H Res 1256. Tribute to Phil Mickelson/Adoption.** Davis, D-Ill., motion to suspend the rules and adopt the resolution that would congratulate Phil Mickelson for winning the 2010 Masters golf tournament. Motion agreed to 401-0: D 239-0; R 162-0. A two-thirds majority of those present and voting (268 in this case) is required for adoption under suspension of the rules. May 20, 2010.

	279	280	281	282	283	284	285
ALABAMA							
1 **Bonner**	Y	Y	Y	Y	Y	?	?
2 Bright	Y	Y	Y	Y	Y	Y	Y
3 **Rogers**	Y	Y	Y	Y	Y	Y	Y
4 **Aderholt**	Y	Y	Y	Y	Y	Y	Y
5 **Griffith**	Y	Y	Y	Y	Y	Y	Y
6 **Bachus**	?	?	?	?	?	?	?
7 Davis	?	?	?	?	?	Y	Y
ALASKA							
AL **Young**	Y	N	N	N	N	Y	?
ARIZONA							
1 Kirkpatrick	Y	Y	Y	Y	Y	Y	Y
2 **Franks**	Y	Y	Y	Y	Y	Y	Y
3 **Shadegg**	Y	Y	Y	Y	Y	Y	Y
4 Pastor	Y	Y	Y	Y	Y	Y	Y
5 Mitchell	Y	Y	Y	Y	Y	Y	Y
6 **Flake**	Y	Y	N	Y	Y	Y	Y
7 Grijalva	Y	Y	Y	?	Y	Y	Y
8 Giffords	Y	Y	Y	Y	Y	Y	Y
ARKANSAS							
1 Berry	Y	Y	Y	Y	Y	Y	P
2 Snyder	Y	Y	Y	Y	Y	Y	Y
3 **Boozman**	?	?	?	?	?	Y	Y
4 Ross	Y	Y	Y	Y	Y	Y	Y
CALIFORNIA							
1 Thompson	Y	Y	Y	Y	Y	Y	Y
2 **Herger**	Y	Y	Y	?	Y	Y	Y
3 **Lungren**	Y	Y	Y	Y	Y	Y	Y
4 **McClintock**	Y	Y	Y	Y	Y	Y	Y
5 Matsui	Y	Y	Y	Y	Y	Y	Y
6 Woolsey	Y	Y	Y	Y	Y	Y	Y
7 Miller, George	Y	Y	Y	Y	Y	Y	Y
8 Pelosi							
9 Lee	Y	Y	Y	Y	Y	Y	Y
10 Garamendi	?	?	?	?	?	?	?
11 McNerney	Y	Y	Y	Y	Y	Y	Y
12 Speier	Y	Y	Y	Y	Y	Y	Y
13 Stark	Y	Y	Y	Y	Y	N	Y
14 Eshoo	Y	Y	Y	Y	Y	Y	Y
15 Honda	Y	Y	Y	Y	Y	Y	Y
16 Lofgren	Y	Y	Y	Y	Y	Y	Y
17 Farr	+	Y	Y	Y	Y	Y	Y
18 Cardoza	Y	Y	Y	Y	Y	Y	Y
19 **Radanovich**	Y	Y	Y	Y	Y	Y	Y
20 Costa	?	?	?	?	?	Y	Y
21 **Nunes**	Y	Y	Y	Y	Y	Y	Y
22 **McCarthy**	Y	?	Y	Y	Y	Y	Y
23 Capps	Y	Y	Y	Y	Y	Y	Y
24 **Gallegly**	Y	Y	Y	Y	Y	Y	Y
25 **McKeon**	Y	Y	Y	Y	Y	Y	Y
26 **Dreier**	Y	Y	Y	Y	Y	Y	Y
27 Sherman	Y	Y	Y	Y	Y	Y	Y
28 Berman	Y	Y	Y	Y	Y	Y	Y
29 Schiff	Y	Y	Y	Y	Y	Y	Y
30 Waxman	Y	Y	Y	Y	Y	Y	?
31 Becerra	Y	Y	Y	Y	Y	Y	Y
32 Chu	Y	Y	Y	Y	Y	Y	Y
33 Watson	Y	Y	Y	Y	Y	Y	Y
34 Roybal-Allard	Y	Y	Y	Y	Y	Y	Y
35 Waters	Y	Y	Y	Y	Y	Y	Y
36 Harman	Y	Y	Y	Y	Y	Y	Y
37 Richardson	Y	Y	Y	Y	Y	Y	Y
38 Napolitano	Y	Y	Y	Y	Y	Y	Y
39 Sánchez, Linda	Y	Y	Y	Y	Y	?	?
40 **Royce**	Y	Y	Y	Y	Y	Y	Y
41 **Lewis**	Y	Y	?	Y	Y	Y	Y
42 **Miller, Gary**	Y	Y	Y	Y	Y	Y	Y
43 Baca	Y	Y	Y	Y	Y	Y	Y
44 **Calvert**	Y	Y	Y	Y	Y	Y	Y
45 **Bono Mack**	Y	Y	Y	Y	Y	Y	Y
46 **Rohrabacher**	N	Y	Y	Y	Y	Y	Y
47 Sanchez, Loretta	Y	Y	Y	Y	Y	Y	Y
48 **Campbell**	Y	Y	Y	Y	Y	Y	Y
49 **Issa**	Y	Y	Y	Y	Y	Y	Y
50 **Bilbray**	?	?	?	?	?	?	?
51 Filner	Y	Y	Y	Y	Y	Y	Y
52 **Hunter**	Y	Y	Y	Y	Y	Y	Y
53 Davis	Y	Y	Y	Y	Y	Y	Y

	279	280	281	282	283	284	285
COLORADO							
1 DeGette	Y	Y	Y	Y	Y	Y	Y
2 Polis	Y	Y	Y	Y	Y	Y	Y
3 Salazar	Y	Y	Y	Y	Y	Y	Y
4 Markey	Y	Y	Y	Y	Y	Y	Y
5 **Lamborn**	Y	Y	Y	Y	Y	Y	Y
6 **Coffman**	Y	Y	Y	Y	Y	Y	Y
7 Perlmutter	Y	Y	Y	Y	Y	Y	Y
CONNECTICUT							
1 Larson	Y	Y	Y	Y	Y	Y	Y
2 Courtney	Y	Y	Y	Y	Y	Y	Y
3 DeLauro	Y	Y	Y	Y	Y	Y	Y
4 Himes	Y	Y	Y	Y	Y	Y	Y
5 Murphy	Y	Y	Y	Y	Y	Y	Y
DELAWARE							
AL **Castle**	Y	Y	Y	Y	Y	Y	Y
FLORIDA							
1 **Miller**	Y	Y	Y	Y	Y	Y	Y
2 Boyd	Y	Y	Y	Y	Y	Y	Y
3 Brown	Y	Y	Y	Y	Y	Y	Y
4 **Crenshaw**	Y	Y	Y	Y	Y	Y	Y
5 **Brown-Waite**	Y	Y	Y	Y	Y	Y	Y
6 **Stearns**	Y	Y	Y	Y	Y	Y	Y
7 **Mica**	Y	Y	Y	Y	Y	Y	Y
8 Grayson	Y	Y	Y	Y	Y	Y	Y
9 **Bilirakis**	Y	Y	Y	Y	Y	Y	Y
10 **Young**	Y	Y	Y	Y	Y	Y	Y
11 Castor	Y	Y	Y	Y	Y	Y	Y
12 **Putnam**	?	?	?	?	?	Y	Y
13 **Buchanan**	Y	Y	Y	Y	Y	Y	Y
14 **Mack**	?	Y	Y	Y	Y	Y	Y
15 **Posey**	Y	Y	Y	Y	Y	Y	Y
16 **Rooney**	Y	Y	Y	Y	Y	Y	P
17 Meek	Y	Y	Y	Y	Y	Y	Y
18 **Ros-Lehtinen**	Y	Y	Y	Y	Y	Y	Y
19 Deutch	Y	Y	Y	Y	Y	Y	Y
20 Wasserman Schultz	Y	Y	Y	Y	Y	Y	Y
21 **Diaz-Balart, L.**	Y	Y	Y	Y	Y	Y	Y
22 Klein	Y	Y	Y	Y	Y	Y	Y
23 Hastings	Y	Y	Y	Y	Y	Y	Y
24 Kosmas	Y	Y	Y	Y	Y	Y	Y
25 **Diaz-Balart, M.**	?	?	?	?	?	?	?
GEORGIA							
1 **Kingston**	Y	Y	Y	Y	Y	Y	Y
2 Bishop	Y	Y	Y	Y	Y	Y	Y
3 **Westmoreland**	Y	Y	Y	Y	Y	Y	Y
4 Johnson	Y	Y	Y	Y	Y	?	Y
5 Lewis	Y	Y	Y	Y	Y	Y	Y
6 **Price**	Y	Y	Y	Y	Y	Y	Y
7 **Linder**	Y	Y	Y	Y	Y	Y	Y
8 **Marshall**	?	Y	Y	Y	Y	Y	P
9 Vacant							
10 **Broun**	Y	Y	Y	Y	Y	Y	Y
11 **Gingrey**	Y	Y	Y	Y	Y	Y	Y
12 Barrow	Y	Y	Y	Y	Y	Y	Y
13 Scott	Y	Y	Y	Y	Y	Y	Y
HAWAII							
1 Vacant							
2 Hirono	Y	Y	Y	Y	Y	Y	Y
IDAHO							
1 Minnick	Y	Y	Y	Y	Y	Y	Y
2 **Simpson**	Y	Y	Y	Y	Y	Y	Y
ILLINOIS							
1 Rush	Y	Y	Y	Y	Y	Y	Y
2 Jackson	Y	Y	Y	Y	Y	Y	Y
3 Lipinski	Y	Y	Y	Y	Y	Y	Y
4 Gutierrez	Y	Y	Y	Y	Y	?	Y
5 Quigley	Y	Y	Y	Y	Y	Y	Y
6 **Roskam**	Y	Y	Y	Y	Y	Y	Y
7 Davis	Y	Y	Y	Y	Y	Y	Y
8 Bean	Y	Y	Y	Y	Y	Y	Y
9 Schakowsky	Y	Y	Y	Y	Y	Y	Y
10 **Kirk**	?	?	?	?	?	?	?
11 Halvorson	Y	Y	Y	Y	Y	Y	Y
12 Costello	Y	Y	Y	Y	Y	Y	Y
13 **Biggert**	Y	Y	Y	Y	Y	Y	Y
14 Foster	Y	Y	Y	Y	Y	Y	Y
15 **Johnson**	Y	Y	Y	Y	Y	Y	Y

KEY   **Republicans**   Democrats

Y	Voted for (yea)
#	Paired for
+	Announced for
N	Voted against (nay)
X	Paired against
−	Announced against
P	Voted "present"
C	Voted "present" to avoid possible conflict of interest
?	Did not vote or otherwise make a position known

	279	280	281	282	283	284	285
16 **Manzullo**	Y	Y	Y	Y	Y	Y	Y
17 Hare	Y	Y	Y	Y	Y	Y	Y
18 **Schock**	Y	Y	Y	Y	Y	?	Y
19 **Shimkus**	Y	Y	Y	Y	Y	Y	Y
INDIANA							
1 Visclosky	Y	Y	Y	Y	Y	Y	Y
2 Donnelly	Y	Y	Y	Y	Y	Y	Y
3 **Souder**	?	?	?	?	?	?	?
4 **Buyer**	Y	Y	Y	Y	Y	Y	Y
5 **Burton**	Y	Y	Y	Y	Y	Y	Y
6 **Pence**	Y	Y	Y	Y	Y	Y	Y
7 Carson	Y	Y	Y	Y	Y	Y	Y
8 Ellsworth	Y	Y	Y	Y	Y	Y	Y
9 Hill	Y	Y	Y	Y	Y	Y	Y
IOWA							
1 Braley	Y	Y	Y	Y	Y	Y	Y
2 Loebsack	Y	Y	Y	Y	Y	Y	Y
3 Boswell	Y	Y	Y	Y	?	Y	Y
4 **Latham**	Y	Y	Y	Y	Y	Y	Y
5 **King**	Y	Y	Y	Y	Y	Y	Y
KANSAS							
1 **Moran**	Y	Y	Y	Y	Y	Y	Y
2 **Jenkins**	Y	Y	Y	Y	Y	Y	Y
3 Moore	Y	Y	Y	Y	Y	Y	Y
4 **Tiahrt**	Y	Y	Y	Y	Y	Y	Y
KENTUCKY							
1 **Whitfield**	Y	Y	Y	Y	Y	Y	Y
2 **Guthrie**	Y	Y	Y	Y	Y	Y	Y
3 Yarmuth	Y	Y	Y	Y	Y	Y	Y
4 **Davis**	Y	Y	Y	Y	Y	Y	Y
5 **Rogers**	Y	Y	Y	Y	Y	Y	Y
6 Chandler	Y	Y	Y	Y	Y	Y	Y
LOUISIANA							
1 **Scalise**	Y	Y	Y	Y	Y	Y	Y
2 **Cao**	Y	Y	Y	Y	Y	Y	Y
3 Melancon	Y	Y	Y	Y	Y	Y	Y
4 **Fleming**	Y	Y	Y	Y	Y	Y	Y
5 **Alexander**	Y	Y	Y	Y	Y	Y	Y
6 **Cassidy**	Y	Y	Y	Y	Y	Y	P
7 **Boustany**	Y	Y	Y	Y	Y	Y	Y
MAINE							
1 Pingree	Y	Y	Y	Y	Y	Y	Y
2 Michaud	Y	Y	Y	Y	Y	Y	Y
MARYLAND							
1 Kratovil	Y	Y	Y	Y	Y	Y	Y
2 Ruppersberger	Y	Y	Y	Y	Y	Y	Y
3 Sarbanes	Y	Y	Y	Y	?	Y	Y
4 Edwards	Y	Y	Y	Y	Y	Y	Y
5 Hoyer	Y	Y	Y	Y	Y	Y	Y
6 **Bartlett**	Y	Y	Y	Y	Y	Y	Y
7 Cummings	Y	Y	Y	Y	Y	Y	Y
8 Van Hollen	Y	Y	Y	Y	Y	Y	Y
MASSACHUSETTS							
1 Olver	Y	Y	Y	Y	Y	Y	Y
2 Neal	Y	Y	Y	Y	Y	Y	Y
3 McGovern	Y	Y	Y	Y	Y	Y	Y
4 Frank	Y	Y	Y	Y	Y	Y	Y
5 Tsongas	Y	Y	Y	Y	Y	Y	Y
6 Tierney	Y	Y	Y	Y	Y	Y	Y
7 Markey	Y	Y	Y	Y	Y	Y	?
8 Capuano	Y	Y	Y	Y	Y	Y	Y
9 Lynch	Y	?	Y	Y	Y	Y	Y
10 Delahunt	Y	Y	Y	Y	Y	Y	Y
MICHIGAN							
1 Stupak	Y	Y	Y	Y	Y	Y	Y
2 **Hoekstra**	Y	Y	Y	Y	Y	?	?
3 **Ehlers**	Y	Y	Y	Y	Y	Y	+
4 **Camp**	Y	Y	Y	?	Y	Y	Y
5 Kildee	Y	Y	Y	Y	Y	Y	Y
6 **Upton**	Y	Y	Y	Y	Y	Y	Y
7 Schauer	Y	Y	Y	Y	Y	Y	Y
8 **Rogers**	Y	Y	Y	Y	?	Y	Y
9 Peters	Y	Y	Y	Y	Y	Y	Y
10 **Miller**	Y	Y	Y	Y	Y	Y	Y
11 **McCotter**	Y	Y	Y	Y	Y	Y	Y
12 Levin	Y	Y	Y	Y	Y	Y	Y
13 Kilpatrick	Y	Y	Y	Y	Y	Y	Y
14 Conyers	Y	Y	Y	Y	Y	N	Y
15 Dingell	Y	Y	Y	Y	Y	Y	Y
MINNESOTA							
1 Walz	Y	Y	Y	Y	Y	Y	Y
2 **Kline**	Y	Y	Y	Y	Y	Y	Y
3 **Paulsen**	Y	Y	Y	Y	Y	Y	Y
4 McCollum	Y	Y	Y	Y	Y	Y	Y

	279	280	281	282	283	284	285
5 Ellison	Y	Y	Y	Y	?	Y	Y
6 **Bachmann**	Y	Y	Y	Y	Y	Y	Y
7 Peterson	Y	Y	Y	Y	Y	Y	Y
8 Oberstar	Y	Y	Y	Y	Y	Y	P
MISSISSIPPI							
1 Childers	Y	Y	Y	Y	Y	Y	Y
2 Thompson	Y	Y	Y	Y	Y	Y	Y
3 **Harper**	Y	Y	Y	Y	Y	Y	Y
4 Taylor	Y	Y	Y	Y	Y	Y	Y
MISSOURI							
1 Clay	Y	Y	Y	Y	Y	Y	Y
2 **Akin**	Y	Y	Y	Y	Y	Y	Y
3 Carnahan	Y	Y	Y	Y	Y	Y	Y
4 Skelton	Y	Y	Y	Y	Y	Y	Y
5 Cleaver	Y	Y	Y	Y	Y	Y	Y
6 **Graves**	?	?	?	?	?	Y	Y
7 **Blunt**	Y	Y	Y	Y	Y	Y	Y
8 **Emerson**	Y	Y	Y	Y	Y	Y	Y
9 **Luetkemeyer**	Y	Y	Y	Y	Y	Y	Y
MONTANA							
AL **Rehberg**	Y	Y	Y	Y	Y	Y	Y
NEBRASKA							
1 **Fortenberry**	Y	Y	Y	Y	Y	Y	Y
2 **Terry**	Y	Y	Y	Y	Y	Y	Y
3 **Smith**	Y	Y	Y	Y	Y	Y	Y
NEVADA							
1 Berkley	Y	Y	Y	Y	Y	Y	Y
2 **Heller**	Y	Y	Y	Y	Y	Y	Y
3 Titus	Y	Y	Y	Y	Y	Y	Y
NEW HAMPSHIRE							
1 Shea-Porter	Y	Y	Y	Y	Y	Y	Y
2 Hodes	Y	Y	Y	Y	Y	Y	Y
NEW JERSEY							
1 Andrews	Y	Y	Y	Y	Y	Y	Y
2 **LoBiondo**	Y	Y	Y	Y	Y	Y	Y
3 Adler	Y	Y	Y	Y	Y	Y	Y
4 **Smith**	Y	Y	Y	Y	Y	Y	Y
5 **Garrett**	Y	Y	Y	Y	Y	Y	Y
6 Pallone	Y	Y	Y	Y	Y	Y	Y
7 **Lance**	Y	Y	Y	Y	Y	Y	Y
8 Pascrell	Y	Y	Y	Y	Y	Y	Y
9 Rothman	Y	Y	Y	Y	Y	Y	Y
10 Payne	Y	Y	Y	Y	Y	Y	Y
11 **Frelinghuysen**	Y	Y	Y	Y	Y	Y	Y
12 Holt	Y	Y	Y	Y	Y	Y	Y
13 Sires	Y	Y	Y	Y	Y	Y	Y
NEW MEXICO							
1 Heinrich	Y	Y	Y	Y	Y	Y	Y
2 Teague	Y	Y	Y	Y	Y	Y	Y
3 Luján	Y	Y	Y	Y	Y	Y	Y
NEW YORK							
1 Bishop	Y	Y	Y	Y	Y	Y	Y
2 Israel	Y	Y	Y	Y	Y	Y	Y
3 **King**	Y	Y	Y	Y	Y	Y	Y
4 McCarthy	Y	Y	Y	Y	Y	Y	Y
5 Ackerman	Y	Y	Y	Y	Y	Y	Y
6 Meeks	Y	Y	?	Y	Y	Y	Y
7 Crowley	Y	Y	Y	Y	Y	Y	Y
8 Nadler	Y	Y	Y	Y	Y	Y	Y
9 Weiner	Y	Y	Y	Y	Y	Y	Y
10 Towns	Y	Y	Y	Y	Y	Y	Y
11 Clarke	Y	Y	Y	Y	Y	Y	Y
12 Velázquez	?	Y	Y	?	?	Y	Y
13 McMahon	Y	Y	Y	Y	Y	Y	Y
14 Maloney	Y	Y	Y	Y	Y	Y	Y
15 Rangel	Y	Y	Y	Y	Y	Y	Y
16 Serrano	Y	Y	Y	Y	Y	Y	Y
17 Engel	Y	Y	Y	Y	Y	+	?
18 Lowey	Y	Y	Y	Y	Y	Y	Y
19 Hall	Y	Y	Y	Y	Y	Y	Y
20 Murphy	Y	Y	Y	Y	Y	Y	Y
21 Tonko	Y	Y	Y	Y	Y	Y	Y
22 Hinchey	?	?	?	?	?	Y	Y
23 Owens	Y	Y	?	Y	Y	Y	Y
24 Arcuri	Y	Y	Y	Y	Y	Y	Y
25 Maffei	Y	Y	Y	Y	Y	Y	Y
26 **Lee**	Y	Y	Y	Y	Y	Y	Y
27 Higgins	Y	Y	Y	Y	Y	Y	Y
28 Slaughter	Y	Y	Y	Y	Y	Y	Y
29 Vacant							
NORTH CAROLINA							
1 Butterfield	Y	Y	Y	Y	Y	Y	Y
2 Etheridge	Y	Y	Y	Y	Y	Y	Y
3 **Jones**	Y	Y	Y	Y	Y	Y	Y
4 Price	Y	Y	Y	Y	Y	Y	Y

	279	280	281	282	283	284	285
5 **Foxx**	Y	Y	Y	Y	Y	Y	Y
6 **Coble**	Y	Y	Y	Y	Y	Y	Y
7 McIntyre	Y	Y	Y	Y	Y	Y	Y
8 Kissell	Y	Y	Y	Y	Y	Y	Y
9 **Myrick**	Y	Y	Y	Y	Y	Y	Y
10 **McHenry**	Y	Y	Y	Y	Y	Y	Y
11 Shuler	Y	Y	Y	Y	Y	Y	Y
12 Watt	Y	Y	Y	Y	Y	Y	Y
13 Miller	Y	Y	Y	Y	Y	Y	Y
NORTH DAKOTA							
AL Pomeroy	Y	Y	Y	Y	Y	Y	Y
OHIO							
1 Driehaus	Y	Y	Y	Y	Y	Y	Y
2 **Schmidt**	Y	Y	Y	Y	Y	Y	Y
3 **Turner**	Y	Y	Y	Y	Y	Y	Y
4 **Jordan**	Y	Y	Y	Y	Y	Y	Y
5 **Latta**	Y	Y	Y	Y	Y	Y	Y
6 Wilson	Y	Y	Y	Y	Y	Y	Y
7 **Austria**	Y	Y	Y	Y	Y	Y	Y
8 **Boehner**	Y	Y	Y	Y	Y	Y	Y
9 Kaptur	Y	Y	Y	Y	Y	Y	Y
10 Kucinich	Y	Y	Y	Y	Y	N	Y
11 Fudge	Y	Y	Y	Y	Y	Y	Y
12 **Tiberi**	Y	Y	Y	Y	Y	Y	Y
13 Sutton	Y	Y	Y	Y	Y	Y	Y
14 **LaTourette**	Y	Y	Y	Y	Y	Y	Y
15 Kilroy	Y	Y	Y	Y	Y	Y	Y
16 Boccieri	Y	Y	Y	Y	Y	Y	Y
17 Ryan	Y	Y	Y	Y	Y	Y	Y
18 Space	Y	Y	Y	Y	Y	Y	Y
OKLAHOMA							
1 **Sullivan**	Y	Y	Y	Y	Y	Y	Y
2 Boren	Y	Y	Y	Y	Y	Y	Y
3 **Lucas**	Y	Y	Y	Y	Y	Y	Y
4 **Cole**	Y	Y	Y	Y	Y	Y	Y
5 **Fallin**	Y	Y	Y	Y	Y	Y	Y
OREGON							
1 Wu	Y	Y	Y	Y	Y	Y	Y
2 **Walden**	Y	Y	Y	Y	Y	Y	Y
3 Blumenauer	Y	Y	Y	Y	Y	Y	Y
4 DeFazio	Y	Y	Y	P	Y	Y	P
5 Schrader	Y	Y	Y	Y	Y	Y	Y
PENNSYLVANIA							
1 Brady	Y	Y	Y	Y	Y	Y	Y
2 Fattah	Y	Y	Y	Y	Y	Y	Y
3 Dahlkemper	Y	Y	Y	Y	Y	Y	Y
4 Altmire	Y	Y	Y	Y	Y	Y	Y
5 **Thompson**	Y	Y	Y	Y	Y	Y	Y
6 **Gerlach**	Y	Y	Y	Y	Y	Y	Y
7 Sestak	Y	Y	Y	Y	Y	Y	Y
8 Murphy, P.	Y	Y	Y	Y	Y	Y	Y
9 **Shuster**	Y	Y	Y	Y	Y	Y	Y
10 Carney	Y	Y	Y	Y	Y	Y	Y
11 Kanjorski	Y	Y	Y	Y	Y	Y	Y
12 Vacant							
13 Schwartz	Y	Y	Y	Y	Y	Y	?
14 Doyle	Y	Y	Y	Y	Y	Y	Y
15 **Dent**	Y	Y	Y	Y	Y	Y	Y
16 **Pitts**	Y	Y	Y	Y	Y	Y	Y
17 Holden	?	?	?	?	?	Y	Y
18 **Murphy, T.**	Y	Y	Y	Y	Y	Y	Y
19 **Platts**	Y	Y	Y	Y	Y	Y	Y
RHODE ISLAND							
1 Kennedy	Y	Y	Y	Y	Y	Y	Y
2 Langevin	Y	Y	Y	Y	Y	Y	Y
SOUTH CAROLINA							
1 **Brown**	Y	Y	Y	Y	Y	Y	Y
2 **Wilson**	Y	Y	Y	Y	Y	Y	Y
3 **Barrett**	?	?	?	?	?	?	?
4 **Inglis**	Y	Y	Y	Y	Y	Y	Y
5 Spratt	Y	Y	Y	Y	Y	Y	Y
6 Clyburn	Y	Y	Y	Y	Y	Y	Y
SOUTH DAKOTA							
AL Herseth Sandlin	Y	Y	Y	Y	Y	Y	Y
TENNESSEE							
1 **Roe**	Y	Y	Y	?	Y	Y	Y
2 **Duncan**	Y	Y	Y	Y	Y	Y	Y
3 **Wamp**	?	?	?	?	?	?	?
4 Davis	Y	Y	Y	Y	Y	Y	Y
5 Cooper	Y	Y	Y	Y	Y	Y	Y
6 Gordon	?	Y	Y	Y	?	?	?
7 **Blackburn**	Y	Y	Y	Y	Y	Y	Y
8 Tanner	Y	Y	Y	Y	Y	Y	Y
9 Cohen	Y	Y	Y	Y	Y	Y	Y

	279	280	281	282	283	284	285
TEXAS							
1 **Gohmert**	Y	Y	Y	Y	Y	Y	Y
2 **Poe**	?	Y	Y	Y	Y	Y	Y
3 **Johnson, S.**	Y	Y	Y	Y	Y	Y	Y
4 **Hall**	Y	Y	Y	Y	Y	Y	Y
5 **Hensarling**	Y	Y	Y	Y	Y	Y	Y
6 **Barton**	Y	Y	Y	Y	Y	Y	Y
7 **Culberson**	Y	Y	Y	Y	Y	Y	Y
8 **Brady**	Y	Y	Y	Y	Y	Y	Y
9 Green, A.	Y	Y	Y	Y	Y	Y	?
10 **McCaul**	Y	Y	?	Y	Y	Y	Y
11 **Conaway**	Y	Y	Y	Y	Y	Y	Y
12 **Granger**	?	Y	?	Y	Y	Y	Y
13 **Thornberry**	Y	Y	Y	Y	Y	Y	Y
14 **Paul**	?	?	?	?	?	N	Y
15 Hinojosa	Y	Y	Y	Y	Y	Y	Y
16 Reyes	?	Y	Y	Y	Y	Y	Y
17 Edwards	Y	Y	Y	Y	Y	Y	?
18 Jackson Lee	Y	Y	Y	Y	Y	?	?
19 **Neugebauer**	Y	Y	Y	Y	Y	Y	Y
20 Gonzalez	Y	Y	Y	Y	Y	Y	Y
21 **Smith**	Y	Y	Y	Y	Y	Y	Y
22 **Olson**	Y	Y	Y	Y	Y	Y	Y
23 Rodriguez	Y	Y	Y	Y	Y	Y	Y
24 **Marchant**	Y	Y	Y	Y	Y	Y	Y
25 Doggett	Y	Y	Y	Y	Y	Y	Y
26 **Burgess**	Y	Y	Y	Y	Y	Y	Y
27 Ortiz	Y	Y	Y	Y	Y	Y	Y
28 Cuellar	Y	Y	Y	Y	Y	Y	Y
29 Green, G.	Y	Y	Y	Y	Y	Y	Y
30 Johnson, E.	Y	Y	Y	Y	Y	Y	Y
31 **Carter**	Y	Y	Y	Y	Y	Y	Y
32 **Sessions**	Y	Y	Y	Y	Y	Y	Y
UTAH							
1 **Bishop**	Y	Y	P	Y	Y	Y	Y
2 Matheson	Y	Y	Y	Y	Y	Y	Y
3 **Chaffetz**	Y	Y	Y	Y	Y	Y	P
VERMONT							
AL Welch	Y	Y	Y	Y	Y	Y	Y
VIRGINIA							
1 **Wittman**	Y	Y	Y	Y	Y	Y	Y
2 Nye	Y	Y	Y	Y	Y	Y	Y
3 Scott	Y	Y	Y	Y	Y	Y	Y
4 **Forbes**	Y	Y	Y	Y	Y	Y	Y
5 Perriello	Y	Y	Y	Y	Y	Y	Y
6 **Goodlatte**	Y	Y	Y	Y	Y	Y	Y
7 **Cantor**	Y	?	?	Y	Y	Y	Y
8 Moran	Y	Y	Y	Y	Y	Y	Y
9 Boucher	Y	Y	Y	Y	Y	Y	Y
10 **Wolf**	Y	Y	Y	Y	Y	Y	Y
11 Connolly	Y	Y	Y	Y	Y	Y	Y
WASHINGTON							
1 Inslee	Y	Y	Y	Y	Y	Y	Y
2 Larsen	Y	Y	Y	Y	Y	Y	Y
3 Baird	Y	Y	Y	Y	Y	Y	Y
4 **Hastings**	Y	Y	Y	Y	Y	Y	Y
5 **McMorris Rodgers**	Y	Y	Y	Y	Y	Y	Y
6 Dicks	Y	Y	Y	Y	Y	Y	Y
7 McDermott	Y	Y	Y	Y	Y	Y	Y
8 **Reichert**	Y	Y	Y	Y	Y	Y	Y
9 Smith	Y	Y	Y	Y	Y	Y	Y
WEST VIRGINIA							
1 Mollohan	Y	Y	Y	Y	Y	Y	Y
2 **Capito**	Y	Y	Y	Y	Y	Y	Y
3 Rahall	Y	Y	Y	Y	Y	Y	Y
WISCONSIN							
1 **Ryan**	Y	Y	Y	Y	Y	Y	Y
2 Baldwin	Y	Y	Y	Y	Y	Y	Y
3 Kind	Y	Y	Y	Y	Y	Y	Y
4 Moore	Y	Y	Y	Y	Y	Y	Y
5 **Sensenbrenner**	Y	Y	Y	Y	Y	Y	Y
6 **Petri**	Y	Y	Y	Y	Y	Y	Y
7 Obey	Y	Y	Y	Y	Y	Y	Y
8 Kagen	Y	Y	Y	Y	Y	Y	Y
WYOMING							
AL **Lummis**	Y	Y	Y	Y	Y	Y	P
DELEGATES							
Faleomavaega (A.S.)							
Norton (D.C.)							
Bordallo (Guam)							
Sablan (N. Marianas)							
Pierluisi (P.R.)							
Christensen (V.I.)							

IN THE HOUSE | By Vote Number

286. H Res 1336. Tribute to the University of Texas Men's Swimming and Diving Team/Adoption. Fudge, D-Ohio, motion to suspend the rules and adopt the resolution that would congratulate the University of Texas men's swimming and diving team for winning the 2010 NCAA Division I national championship. Motion agreed to 405-0: D 241-0; R 164-0. A two-thirds majority of those present and voting (270 in this case) is required for adoption under suspension of the rules. May 20, 2010.

287. H Res 1361. Tribute to North Carolina Central University/Adoption. Fudge, D-Ohio, motion to suspend the rules and adopt the resolution that would celebrate the 100th anniversary of North Carolina Central University. Motion agreed to 408-1: D 242-0; R 166-1. A two-thirds majority of those present and voting (273 in this case) is required for adoption under suspension of the rules. May 20, 2010.

288. H Res 1363. Deposition Authority on Mine Blast/Previous Question. Slaughter, D-N.Y., motion to order the previous question (thus ending debate and the possibility of amendment) on the Miller, D-Calif., resolution that would provide deposition authority to the Education and Labor Committee to aid in the panel's investigation into the April 5, 2010, explosion at the Upper Big Branch mine in West Virginia. Motion agreed to 240-177: D 240-9; R 0-168. May 20, 2010.

289. H Res 1363. Deposition Authority on Mine Blast/Adoption. Adoption of the resolution that would provide deposition authority to the Education and Labor Committee to aid in the panel's investigation into the April 5, 2010, explosion at the Upper Big Branch mine in West Virginia. Adopted 413-1: D 247-0; R 166-1. May 20, 2010.

290. HR 5128. Stewart Lee Udall Department of the Interior Building/Passage. Teague, D-N.M., motion to suspend the rules and pass the bill that would designate the Interior Department building located at 1849 C St. NW in Washington, D.C., as the "Stewart Lee Udall Department of the Interior Building." Motion agreed to 409-1: D 245-0; R 164-1. A two-thirds majority of those present and voting (274 in this case) is required for passage under suspension of the rules. May 20, 2010.

	286	287	288	289	290
ALABAMA					
1 **Bonner**	?	?	?	?	?
2 Bright	Y	Y	N	Y	Y
3 **Rogers**	Y	Y	N	Y	Y
4 **Aderholt**	Y	Y	N	Y	Y
5 **Griffith**	Y	Y	N	Y	Y
6 **Bachus**	?	?	?	?	?
7 Davis	Y	Y	Y	Y	Y
ALASKA					
AL **Young**	Y	N	N	Y	N
ARIZONA					
1 Kirkpatrick	Y	Y	N	Y	Y
2 **Franks**	Y	Y	N	Y	Y
3 **Shadegg**	Y	Y	N	Y	Y
4 Pastor	Y	Y	Y	Y	Y
5 Mitchell	Y	Y	N	Y	Y
6 **Flake**	Y	Y	N	Y	Y
7 Grijalva	Y	Y	Y	Y	Y
8 Giffords	Y	Y	N	Y	Y
ARKANSAS					
1 Berry	P	?	Y	Y	Y
2 Snyder	Y	Y	Y	Y	Y
3 **Boozman**	Y	Y	N	Y	Y
4 Ross	Y	Y	Y	Y	Y
CALIFORNIA					
1 Thompson	Y	Y	Y	Y	Y
2 **Herger**	Y	Y	N	Y	Y
3 **Lungren**	Y	Y	N	Y	Y
4 **McClintock**	Y	Y	N	Y	Y
5 Matsui	Y	Y	Y	Y	Y
6 Woolsey	Y	Y	Y	Y	Y
7 Miller, George	Y	Y	Y	Y	Y
8 Pelosi					
9 Lee	Y	Y	Y	Y	Y
10 Garamendi	?	?	?	?	+
11 McNerney	Y	Y	Y	Y	Y
12 Speier	Y	Y	Y	Y	Y
13 Stark	Y	Y	Y	Y	Y
14 Eshoo	Y	Y	Y	Y	Y
15 Honda	Y	Y	Y	Y	Y
16 Lofgren	Y	Y	Y	Y	Y
17 Farr	Y	Y	Y	Y	Y
18 Cardoza	Y	Y	Y	Y	Y
19 **Radanovich**	Y	Y	N	Y	Y
20 Costa	Y	Y	Y	Y	Y
21 **Nunes**	Y	Y	N	Y	Y
22 **McCarthy**	Y	Y	N	Y	Y
23 Capps	Y	Y	Y	Y	Y
24 **Gallegly**	Y	Y	N	Y	Y
25 **McKeon**	Y	Y	N	Y	Y
26 **Dreier**	Y	Y	N	Y	Y
27 Sherman	Y	Y	Y	Y	Y
28 Berman	Y	Y	Y	Y	Y
29 Schiff	Y	Y	Y	Y	Y
30 Waxman	Y	Y	Y	Y	Y
31 Becerra	Y	Y	Y	Y	Y
32 Chu	Y	Y	Y	Y	Y
33 Watson	Y	Y	Y	Y	Y
34 Roybal-Allard	Y	Y	Y	Y	Y
35 Waters	Y	Y	Y	Y	Y
36 Harman	Y	Y	Y	Y	Y
37 Richardson	Y	Y	Y	Y	Y
38 Napolitano	Y	Y	Y	Y	Y
39 Sánchez, Linda	?	?	?	?	?
40 **Royce**	Y	Y	N	Y	Y
41 **Lewis**	Y	Y	N	Y	Y
42 **Miller, Gary**	Y	Y	N	Y	Y
43 Baca	Y	Y	Y	Y	Y
44 **Calvert**	Y	Y	N	Y	Y
45 **Bono Mack**	Y	Y	N	Y	Y
46 **Rohrabacher**	Y	Y	N	Y	Y
47 Sanchez, Loretta	Y	Y	Y	Y	Y
48 **Campbell**	Y	Y	N	Y	Y
49 **Issa**	Y	Y	N	Y	Y
50 **Bilbray**	?	?	?	?	?
51 Filner	Y	Y	Y	Y	Y
52 **Hunter**	Y	Y	N	Y	Y
53 Davis	Y	Y	Y	Y	Y

	286	287	288	289	290
COLORADO					
1 DeGette	Y	Y	Y	Y	Y
2 Polis	Y	Y	Y	Y	Y
3 Salazar	Y	Y	Y	Y	Y
4 Markey	Y	Y	Y	Y	Y
5 **Lamborn**	Y	Y	N	Y	Y
6 **Coffman**	Y	Y	N	Y	Y
7 Perlmutter	Y	Y	Y	Y	Y
CONNECTICUT					
1 Larson	Y	Y	Y	Y	Y
2 Courtney	Y	Y	Y	Y	Y
3 DeLauro	Y	Y	Y	Y	Y
4 Himes	Y	Y	Y	Y	Y
5 Murphy	Y	Y	Y	Y	Y
DELAWARE					
AL Castle	Y	Y	N	Y	Y
FLORIDA					
1 **Miller**	Y	Y	N	Y	Y
2 Boyd	Y	Y	Y	Y	Y
3 Brown	Y	Y	Y	Y	Y
4 **Crenshaw**	Y	Y	N	Y	Y
5 **Brown-Waite**	Y	Y	N	Y	Y
6 **Stearns**	Y	Y	N	Y	Y
7 **Mica**	Y	Y	N	Y	Y
8 Grayson	Y	Y	Y	Y	Y
9 **Bilirakis**	Y	+	N	Y	Y
10 **Young**	Y	Y	N	Y	Y
11 Castor	Y	Y	Y	Y	Y
12 **Putnam**	Y	Y	N	Y	Y
13 **Buchanan**	Y	Y	N	Y	Y
14 **Mack**	Y	Y	N	Y	Y
15 **Posey**	Y	Y	N	Y	Y
16 **Rooney**	P	Y	N	Y	Y
17 Meek	Y	Y	Y	Y	Y
18 **Ros-Lehtinen**	Y	Y	N	Y	Y
19 Deutch	Y	Y	Y	Y	Y
20 Wasserman Schultz	Y	Y	Y	Y	Y
21 **Diaz-Balart, L.**	Y	Y	N	Y	Y
22 Klein	Y	Y	Y	Y	Y
23 Hastings	Y	Y	Y	Y	Y
24 Kosmas	Y	Y	Y	Y	Y
25 **Diaz-Balart, M.**	?	?	?	?	?
GEORGIA					
1 **Kingston**	Y	Y	N	Y	Y
2 Bishop	Y	Y	Y	Y	Y
3 **Westmoreland**	P	Y	N	Y	Y
4 Johnson	Y	Y	Y	Y	Y
5 Lewis	Y	Y	Y	Y	Y
6 **Price**	Y	Y	N	Y	Y
7 **Linder**	Y	Y	N	Y	Y
8 Marshall	Y	Y	Y	Y	Y
9 Vacant					
10 **Broun**	Y	Y	N	Y	Y
11 **Gingrey**	Y	Y	N	Y	Y
12 Barrow	Y	Y	Y	Y	Y
13 Scott	Y	Y	Y	Y	Y
HAWAII					
1 Vacant					
2 Hirono	Y	Y	Y	Y	Y
IDAHO					
1 Minnick	Y	?	N	Y	Y
2 **Simpson**	Y	Y	N	Y	Y
ILLINOIS					
1 Rush	?	Y	Y	?	Y
2 Jackson	Y	Y	Y	Y	Y
3 Lipinski	Y	Y	Y	Y	Y
4 Gutierrez	Y	Y	Y	Y	Y
5 Quigley	Y	Y	Y	Y	Y
6 **Roskam**	Y	Y	N	Y	Y
7 Davis	Y	Y	Y	Y	Y
8 Bean	Y	Y	Y	Y	Y
9 Schakowsky	Y	Y	Y	Y	Y
10 **Kirk**	?	?	?	?	?
11 Halvorson	Y	Y	Y	Y	Y
12 Costello	Y	Y	Y	Y	Y
13 **Biggert**	Y	Y	N	Y	Y
14 Foster	Y	Y	Y	Y	Y
15 **Johnson**	Y	Y	N	Y	Y

* Rep. Mark Critz, D-Pa., was sworn in May 20, 2010, to fill the seat vacated by the Feb. 8 death of Democrat John P. Murtha. The first vote for which Critz was eligible was vote 286.

	286	287	288	289	290
16 Manzullo	Y	Y	N	Y	Y
17 Hare	Y	Y	Y	Y	Y
18 Schock	Y	Y	N	Y	Y
19 Shimkus	Y	Y	N	Y	Y
INDIANA					
1 Visclosky	Y	Y	Y	Y	Y
2 Donnelly	Y	Y	N	Y	Y
3 Souder	?	?	?	?	?
4 Buyer	Y	Y	N	Y	Y
5 Burton	Y	Y	N	Y	Y
6 Pence	Y	Y	N	Y	Y
7 Carson	Y	Y	Y	Y	Y
8 Ellsworth	Y	Y	Y	Y	Y
9 Hill	Y	Y	Y	Y	Y
IOWA					
1 Braley	Y	Y	Y	Y	?
2 Loebsack	Y	Y	Y	Y	Y
3 Boswell	Y	Y	Y	Y	Y
4 Latham	Y	Y	N	Y	Y
5 King	Y	Y	N	Y	Y
KANSAS					
1 Moran	Y	Y	N	Y	?
2 Jenkins	Y	Y	N	Y	Y
3 Moore	Y	Y	Y	Y	?
4 Tiahrt	Y	Y	N	Y	Y
KENTUCKY					
1 Whitfield	Y	Y	N	Y	Y
2 Guthrie	Y	Y	N	Y	Y
3 Yarmuth	Y	Y	Y	Y	Y
4 Davis	Y	Y	N	?	?
5 Rogers	Y	Y	N	Y	Y
6 Chandler	Y	Y	Y	Y	Y
LOUISIANA					
1 Scalise	Y	Y	N	Y	Y
2 Cao	Y	Y	N	Y	Y
3 Melancon	Y	Y	Y	Y	Y
4 Fleming	Y	Y	N	Y	Y
5 Alexander	Y	Y	N	Y	Y
6 Cassidy	Y	Y	N	Y	Y
7 Boustany	Y	Y	N	Y	Y
MAINE					
1 Pingree	Y	Y	Y	Y	Y
2 Michaud	Y	Y	Y	Y	Y
MARYLAND					
1 Kratovil	Y	Y	Y	Y	Y
2 Ruppersberger	Y	Y	Y	Y	Y
3 Sarbanes	Y	Y	Y	Y	Y
4 Edwards	Y	Y	Y	Y	Y
5 Hoyer	Y	Y	Y	Y	Y
6 Bartlett	Y	Y	N	Y	Y
7 Cummings	Y	Y	Y	Y	Y
8 Van Hollen	Y	Y	Y	Y	Y
MASSACHUSETTS					
1 Olver	Y	Y	Y	Y	Y
2 Neal	Y	Y	Y	Y	Y
3 McGovern	Y	Y	Y	Y	Y
4 Frank	Y	Y	Y	Y	Y
5 Tsongas	Y	Y	Y	Y	Y
6 Tierney	Y	Y	Y	Y	Y
7 Markey	Y	Y	Y	Y	Y
8 Capuano	Y	Y	Y	Y	Y
9 Lynch	Y	Y	Y	?	Y
10 Delahunt	Y	?	Y	Y	Y
MICHIGAN					
1 Stupak	Y	Y	Y	Y	Y
2 Hoekstra	?	?	?	?	?
3 Ehlers	Y	Y	N	Y	Y
4 Camp	Y	Y	N	Y	Y
5 Kildee	Y	Y	Y	Y	Y
6 Upton	Y	Y	N	Y	Y
7 Schauer	Y	Y	Y	Y	Y
8 Rogers	Y	Y	N	Y	Y
9 Peters	Y	Y	Y	Y	Y
10 Miller	Y	Y	N	Y	Y
11 McCotter	Y	Y	Y	Y	Y
12 Levin	Y	Y	Y	Y	Y
13 Kilpatrick	Y	Y	Y	Y	Y
14 Conyers	Y	Y	Y	Y	Y
15 Dingell	Y	Y	Y	Y	Y
MINNESOTA					
1 Walz	Y	Y	Y	Y	Y
2 Kline	Y	Y	N	Y	Y
3 Paulsen	Y	Y	N	Y	Y
4 McCollum	Y	Y	Y	Y	Y

	286	287	288	289	290
5 Ellison	Y	Y	Y	Y	Y
6 Bachmann	Y	Y	N	Y	Y
7 Peterson	Y	Y	Y	Y	Y
8 Oberstar	P	Y	Y	Y	Y
MISSISSIPPI					
1 Childers	Y	Y	Y	Y	Y
2 Thompson	Y	Y	Y	Y	Y
3 Harper	Y	Y	N	Y	Y
4 Taylor	Y	Y	N	Y	Y
MISSOURI					
1 Clay	Y	Y	Y	Y	Y
2 Akin	Y	Y	N	Y	Y
3 Carnahan	Y	Y	Y	Y	Y
4 Skelton	Y	Y	Y	Y	Y
5 Cleaver	Y	Y	Y	Y	Y
6 Graves	Y	Y	N	Y	Y
7 Blunt	Y	Y	N	Y	Y
8 Emerson	Y	Y	N	Y	Y
9 Luetkemeyer	Y	Y	N	Y	Y
MONTANA					
AL Rehberg	Y	Y	N	Y	Y
NEBRASKA					
1 Fortenberry	Y	Y	N	Y	Y
2 Terry	Y	Y	N	Y	Y
3 Smith	Y	Y	N	Y	Y
NEVADA					
1 Berkley	Y	Y	Y	Y	Y
2 Heller	Y	Y	N	Y	Y
3 Titus	Y	Y	Y	Y	Y
NEW HAMPSHIRE					
1 Shea-Porter	Y	Y	Y	Y	Y
2 Hodes	Y	Y	Y	Y	Y
NEW JERSEY					
1 Andrews	Y	Y	Y	Y	Y
2 LoBiondo	Y	Y	N	Y	Y
3 Adler	Y	Y	Y	Y	Y
4 Smith	Y	Y	N	Y	Y
5 Garrett	Y	Y	N	Y	Y
6 Pallone	Y	Y	Y	Y	Y
7 Lance	Y	Y	N	Y	Y
8 Pascrell	Y	Y	Y	Y	Y
9 Rothman	Y	Y	Y	Y	Y
10 Payne	Y	Y	Y	Y	Y
11 Frelinghuysen	Y	Y	N	Y	Y
12 Holt	Y	Y	Y	Y	Y
13 Sires	Y	Y	Y	Y	Y
NEW MEXICO					
1 Heinrich	Y	Y	Y	Y	Y
2 Teague	Y	Y	Y	Y	Y
3 Luján	Y	Y	Y	Y	Y
NEW YORK					
1 Bishop	Y	Y	Y	Y	Y
2 Israel	Y	Y	Y	Y	Y
3 King	Y	Y	N	Y	Y
4 McCarthy	Y	Y	Y	Y	Y
5 Ackerman	Y	Y	Y	Y	Y
6 Meeks	Y	Y	Y	Y	Y
7 Crowley	Y	Y	Y	Y	Y
8 Nadler	Y	Y	Y	Y	Y
9 Weiner	Y	Y	Y	Y	Y
10 Towns	Y	Y	Y	Y	Y
11 Clarke	Y	Y	Y	Y	Y
12 Velázquez	Y	Y	Y	Y	Y
13 McMahon	Y	Y	Y	Y	Y
14 Maloney	Y	Y	Y	Y	Y
15 Rangel	Y	Y	Y	Y	Y
16 Serrano	Y	Y	Y	Y	Y
17 Engel	?	Y	Y	Y	Y
18 Lowey	Y	Y	Y	Y	Y
19 Hall	Y	Y	Y	Y	Y
20 Murphy	Y	Y	Y	Y	Y
21 Tonko	Y	Y	Y	Y	Y
22 Hinchey	Y	Y	Y	Y	Y
23 Owens	Y	Y	Y	Y	Y
24 Arcuri	Y	Y	Y	Y	Y
25 Maffei	Y	Y	Y	Y	Y
26 Lee	Y	Y	N	Y	Y
27 Higgins	Y	Y	Y	Y	Y
28 Slaughter	Y	Y	Y	Y	Y
29 Vacant					
NORTH CAROLINA					
1 Butterfield	Y	Y	Y	Y	Y
2 Etheridge	Y	Y	Y	Y	Y
3 Jones	Y	Y	N	Y	Y
4 Price	Y	Y	Y	Y	Y

	286	287	288	289	290
5 Foxx	Y	Y	N	Y	Y
6 Coble	Y	Y	N	Y	Y
7 McIntyre	Y	Y	N	Y	Y
8 Kissell	Y	Y	Y	Y	Y
9 Myrick	Y	Y	N	Y	Y
10 McHenry	Y	Y	N	Y	Y
11 Shuler	Y	Y	Y	Y	Y
12 Watt	Y	Y	Y	Y	Y
13 Miller	Y	Y	Y	Y	?
NORTH DAKOTA					
AL Pomeroy	Y	Y	Y	Y	Y
OHIO					
1 Driehaus	Y	Y	N	Y	Y
2 Schmidt	Y	Y	N	Y	Y
3 Turner	Y	Y	N	Y	Y
4 Jordan	Y	Y	N	Y	Y
5 Latta	Y	Y	N	Y	Y
6 Wilson	Y	Y	Y	Y	Y
7 Austria	Y	Y	N	Y	Y
8 Boehner	Y	Y	N	Y	Y
9 Kaptur	Y	Y	Y	Y	Y
10 Kucinich	Y	Y	Y	Y	Y
11 Fudge	Y	Y	Y	Y	Y
12 Tiberi	Y	Y	N	Y	Y
13 Sutton	Y	Y	Y	Y	Y
14 LaTourette	Y	Y	N	Y	Y
15 Kilroy	Y	Y	Y	Y	Y
16 Boccieri	Y	Y	Y	Y	Y
17 Ryan	Y	Y	Y	Y	Y
18 Space	Y	Y	Y	Y	Y
OKLAHOMA					
1 Sullivan	Y	Y	N	Y	Y
2 Boren	Y	Y	Y	Y	Y
3 Lucas	Y	Y	N	Y	Y
4 Cole	Y	Y	N	Y	Y
5 Fallin	Y	Y	N	Y	Y
OREGON					
1 Wu	Y	Y	Y	Y	Y
2 Walden	Y	Y	N	Y	Y
3 Blumenauer	Y	Y	Y	Y	Y
4 DeFazio	P	Y	Y	Y	Y
5 Schrader	Y	Y	Y	Y	Y
PENNSYLVANIA					
1 Brady	Y	Y	Y	Y	Y
2 Fattah	Y	Y	Y	Y	Y
3 Dahlkemper	Y	Y	Y	Y	Y
4 Altmire	Y	Y	Y	Y	Y
5 Thompson	Y	Y	N	Y	Y
6 Gerlach	Y	Y	N	Y	Y
7 Sestak	Y	Y	Y	Y	Y
8 Murphy, P.	Y	Y	Y	Y	Y
9 Shuster	Y	Y	N	Y	Y
10 Carney	Y	Y	Y	Y	Y
11 Kanjorski	Y	Y	Y	Y	Y
12 Critz*	Y	Y	Y	Y	Y
13 Schwartz	?	?	?	?	?
14 Doyle	Y	Y	Y	Y	Y
15 Dent	Y	Y	N	Y	Y
16 Pitts	Y	Y	N	Y	Y
17 Holden	Y	Y	Y	Y	Y
18 Murphy, T.	Y	Y	N	Y	Y
19 Platts	Y	Y	N	Y	Y
RHODE ISLAND					
1 Kennedy	Y	Y	Y	Y	Y
2 Langevin	Y	Y	Y	Y	Y
SOUTH CAROLINA					
1 Brown	Y	Y	N	Y	Y
2 Wilson	Y	Y	N	Y	Y
3 Barrett	?	?	?	?	?
4 Inglis	Y	Y	N	Y	Y
5 Spratt	Y	Y	Y	Y	Y
6 Clyburn	Y	Y	Y	Y	Y
SOUTH DAKOTA					
AL Herseth Sandlin	Y	Y	Y	Y	Y
TENNESSEE					
1 Roe	Y	Y	N	Y	Y
2 Duncan	Y	Y	N	Y	Y
3 Wamp	?	?	?	?	?
4 Davis	Y	Y	Y	Y	Y
5 Cooper	Y	Y	Y	Y	Y
6 Gordon	?	?	?	?	?
7 Blackburn	Y	Y	N	Y	Y
8 Tanner	Y	Y	Y	Y	Y
9 Cohen	Y	Y	Y	Y	Y

	286	287	288	289	290
TEXAS					
1 Gohmert	Y	Y	N	Y	Y
2 Poe	Y	Y	N	Y	Y
3 Johnson, S.	Y	Y	N	Y	Y
4 Hall	Y	Y	N	Y	Y
5 Hensarling	Y	Y	N	Y	Y
6 Barton	Y	Y	N	Y	Y
7 Culberson	Y	Y	N	Y	Y
8 Brady	Y	Y	N	Y	Y
9 Green, A.	Y	Y	Y	Y	Y
10 McCaul	Y	Y	N	Y	Y
11 Conaway	Y	Y	N	Y	Y
12 Granger	Y	Y	N	Y	Y
13 Thornberry	Y	Y	N	Y	Y
14 Paul	Y	Y	N	N	Y
15 Hinojosa	+	+	Y	Y	?
16 Reyes	?	?	Y	Y	Y
17 Edwards	Y	Y	Y	Y	Y
18 Jackson Lee	?	?	?	?	?
19 Neugebauer	Y	Y	N	Y	Y
20 Gonzalez	Y	Y	Y	Y	Y
21 Smith	Y	Y	N	Y	Y
22 Olson	Y	Y	N	Y	Y
23 Rodriguez	Y	Y	Y	Y	Y
24 Marchant	Y	Y	N	Y	Y
25 Doggett	Y	Y	Y	Y	Y
26 Burgess	Y	Y	N	Y	?
27 Ortiz	+	+	Y	Y	Y
28 Cuellar	Y	Y	Y	Y	Y
29 Green, G.	Y	Y	Y	Y	Y
30 Johnson, E.	Y	Y	Y	Y	Y
31 Carter	Y	Y	N	Y	Y
32 Sessions	Y	Y	N	Y	Y
UTAH					
1 Bishop	Y	Y	N	Y	Y
2 Matheson	Y	Y	Y	Y	Y
3 Chaffetz	P	Y	N	Y	Y
VERMONT					
AL Welch	Y	Y	Y	Y	Y
VIRGINIA					
1 Wittman	Y	Y	N	Y	Y
2 Nye	Y	?	N	Y	Y
3 Scott	Y	Y	Y	Y	Y
4 Forbes	Y	Y	N	Y	Y
5 Perriello	Y	Y	Y	Y	Y
6 Goodlatte	Y	Y	N	Y	Y
7 Cantor	Y	Y	N	Y	Y
8 Moran	Y	Y	Y	Y	Y
9 Boucher	Y	Y	Y	Y	Y
10 Wolf	Y	Y	N	Y	Y
11 Connolly	Y	Y	Y	Y	Y
WASHINGTON					
1 Inslee	Y	Y	Y	Y	Y
2 Larsen	Y	Y	Y	Y	Y
3 Baird	Y	Y	Y	Y	Y
4 Hastings	Y	Y	N	Y	Y
5 McMorris Rodgers	Y	Y	N	Y	Y
6 Dicks	Y	Y	Y	Y	Y
7 McDermott	Y	Y	Y	Y	Y
8 Reichert	Y	Y	N	Y	Y
9 Smith	Y	Y	Y	Y	Y
WEST VIRGINIA					
1 Mollohan	Y	Y	Y	Y	Y
2 Capito	Y	Y	N	Y	Y
3 Rahall	Y	Y	Y	Y	Y
WISCONSIN					
1 Ryan	Y	Y	N	Y	Y
2 Baldwin	Y	Y	Y	Y	Y
3 Kind	Y	Y	Y	Y	Y
4 Moore	Y	Y	Y	Y	Y
5 Sensenbrenner	Y	Y	N	Y	Y
6 Petri	Y	Y	N	Y	Y
7 Obey	Y	Y	Y	Y	Y
8 Kagen	Y	Y	Y	Y	Y
WYOMING					
AL Lummis	P	Y	N	Y	Y
DELEGATES					
Faleomavaega (A.S.)					
Norton (D.C.)					
Bordallo (Guam)					
Sablan (N. Marianas)					
Pierluisi (P.R.)					
Christensen (V.I.)					

IN THE HOUSE | By Vote Number

291. **H Con Res 278. Tribute to Sons and Daughters in Touch/ Adoption.** Filner, D-Calif., motion to suspend the rules and adopt the concurrent resolution that would express the sense of Congress in support of the Sons and Daughters in Touch on its 20th anniversary. The group is dedicated to bringing together children and families of U.S. servicemembers killed in Southeast Asia. Motion agreed to 371-0: D 218-0; R 153-0. A two-thirds majority of those present and voting (248 in this case) is required for adoption under suspension of the rules. May 24, 2010.

292. **HR 1017. Chiropractic Care for Veterans/Passage.** Filner, D-Calif., motion to suspend the rules and pass the bill that would require the Department of Veterans Affairs (VA) to provide chiropractic care and services to veterans at no fewer than 75 VA medical centers by Dec. 31, 2011, and at all VA medical centers by Dec. 31, 2013. Motion agreed to 365-6: D 219-0; R 146-6. A two-thirds majority of those present and voting (248 in this case) is required for passage under suspension of the rules. May 24, 2010.

293. **HR 5330. Antitrust Violation Penalties/Passage.** Nadler, D-N.Y., motion to suspend the rules and pass the bill that would extend until June 22, 2020, provisions in current law that set a maximum prison sentence of 10 years for antitrust violations, with a maximum fine of $1 million for individuals and $100 million for corporations. It also would extend a Justice Department program to provide leniency to whistleblowers in certain antitrust cases. Motion agreed to 366-4: D 216-0; R 150-4. A two-thirds majority of those present and voting (247 in this case) is required for passage under suspension of the rules. May 24, 2010.

294. **HR 5145. VA Staff Education/Passage.** Filner, D-Calif., motion to suspend the rules and pass the bill that would increase to $1,600 per year, from $1,000 per year, the amount that the VA could reimburse employees of the Veterans Health Administration for continuing professional education. It also would expand reimbursement eligibility to all full-time VA health professionals. Motion agreed to 413-2: D 248-0; R 165-2. A two-thirds majority of those present and voting (277 in this case) is required for passage under suspension of the rules. May 25, 2010.

295. **H Res 1258. Mental Health Month/Adoption.** Matsui, D-Calif., motion to suspend the rules and adopt the resolution that would support the designation of Mental Health Month in order to educate the public regarding mental health and to remove the stigma associated with mental illness. Motion agreed to 414-1: D 248-0; R 166-1. A two-thirds majority of those present and voting (277 in this case) is required for adoption under suspension of the rules. May 25, 2010.

296. **H Res 1382. Attack on South Korean Warship/Adoption.** Faleo-mavaega, D-A.S., motion to suspend the rules and adopt the resolution that would condemn North Korea for its alleged attack on the South Korean warship, the *Cheonan*, and call for an apology. It would express sympathy and condolences to the families and loved ones of the sailors who were killed. Motion agreed to 411-3: D 245-0; R 166-2. A two-thirds majority of those present and voting (276 in this case) is required for adoption under suspension of the rules. May 25, 2010.

[1] Rep. Charles K. Djou, R-Hawaii, was sworn in May 25, 2010, to fill the seat vacated by Democrat Neil Abercrombie, who resigned Feb. 28 to run for governor. The first vote for which Djou was eligible was vote 296.

[2] Rep. Mark Souder, R-Ind., resigned May 21, 2010. The last vote for which he was eligible was vote 290.

	291	292	293	294	295	296
ALABAMA						
1 Bonner	Y	Y	Y	Y	Y	Y
2 Bright	Y	Y	Y	Y	Y	Y
3 Rogers	Y	Y	Y	Y	Y	Y
4 Aderholt	Y	Y	Y	Y	Y	
5 Griffith	?	?	?	?	?	?
6 Bachus	Y	Y	Y	Y	Y	
7 Davis	?	?	?	?	?	?
ALASKA						
AL Young	Y	Y	Y	Y	Y	Y
ARIZONA						
1 Kirkpatrick	Y	Y	Y	Y	Y	Y
2 Franks	Y	Y	Y	Y	Y	
3 Shadegg	Y	Y	Y	Y	Y	
4 Pastor	Y	Y	Y	Y	Y	
5 Mitchell	Y	Y	Y	Y	Y	
6 Flake	Y	N	Y	N	Y	Y
7 Grijalva	Y	Y	Y	Y	Y	
8 Giffords	Y	Y	Y	Y	Y	Y
ARKANSAS						
1 Berry	?	?	?	Y	Y	Y
2 Snyder	Y	Y	Y	Y	Y	
3 Boozman	Y	Y	Y	Y	Y	
4 Ross	+	+	+	Y	Y	Y
CALIFORNIA						
1 Thompson	Y	Y	Y	Y	Y	
2 Herger	Y	Y	Y	Y	Y	
3 Lungren	Y	Y	Y	Y	Y	
4 McClintock	Y	N	N	Y	Y	
5 Matsui	Y	Y	Y	Y	Y	
6 Woolsey	Y	Y	Y	Y	Y	
7 Miller, George	Y	Y	?	Y	Y	Y
8 Pelosi						
9 Lee	Y	Y	Y	Y	Y	
10 Garamendi	Y	Y	Y	Y	Y	
11 McNerney	?	?	?	Y	Y	Y
12 Speier	Y	Y	Y	Y	Y	
13 Stark	Y	Y	Y	Y	Y	
14 Eshoo	Y	Y	Y	Y	Y	
15 Honda	Y	Y	Y	Y	?	
16 Lofgren	Y	Y	Y	Y	Y	
17 Farr	Y	Y	Y	Y	Y	
18 Cardoza	Y	Y	Y	Y	Y	
19 Radanovich	Y	Y	Y	Y	Y	
20 Costa	Y	Y	Y	Y	Y	
21 Nunes	Y	Y	Y	Y	Y	
22 McCarthy	Y	Y	Y	Y	Y	
23 Capps	Y	Y	Y	Y	Y	
24 Gallegly	Y	Y	Y	Y	Y	
25 McKeon	Y	Y	Y	Y	Y	
26 Dreier	Y	Y	Y	Y	Y	
27 Sherman	Y	Y	Y	Y	Y	
28 Berman	Y	Y	Y	Y	Y	Y
29 Schiff	+	+	+	Y	Y	Y
30 Waxman	Y	Y	Y	Y	Y	
31 Becerra	Y	Y	Y	Y	Y	
32 Chu	Y	Y	Y	Y	Y	
33 Watson	Y	Y	Y	Y	?	
34 Roybal-Allard	Y	Y	Y	Y	Y	
35 Waters	Y	Y	Y	Y	Y	
36 Harman	Y	Y	Y	Y	Y	
37 Richardson	Y	Y	Y	Y	Y	
38 Napolitano	Y	Y	Y	Y	Y	
39 Sánchez, Linda	?	?	?	Y	Y	Y
40 Royce	Y	Y	Y	Y	Y	
41 Lewis	Y	Y	Y	Y	Y	
42 Miller, Gary	Y	Y	Y	Y	Y	
43 Baca	Y	Y	Y	Y	Y	
44 Calvert	Y	Y	Y	Y	Y	
45 Bono Mack	?	?	?	Y	Y	Y
46 Rohrabacher	?	?	?	Y	Y	Y
47 Sanchez, Loretta	Y	Y	Y	Y	Y	
48 Campbell	Y	N	Y	N	Y	
49 Issa	Y	N	Y	Y	Y	
50 Bilbray	Y	Y	Y	Y	Y	
51 Filner	Y	Y	Y	Y	Y	
52 Hunter	Y	Y	Y	Y	Y	
53 Davis	Y	Y	Y	Y	Y	

	291	292	293	294	295	296
COLORADO						
1 DeGette	Y	Y	Y	Y	Y	Y
2 Polis	Y	Y	Y	Y	Y	Y
3 Salazar	Y	Y	Y	Y	Y	Y
4 Markey	Y	Y	Y	Y	Y	Y
5 Lamborn	?	?	?	Y	Y	Y
6 Coffman	Y	Y	Y	Y	Y	Y
7 Perlmutter	Y	Y	Y	Y	Y	Y
CONNECTICUT						
1 Larson	Y	Y	Y	Y	Y	Y
2 Courtney	Y	Y	Y	Y	Y	Y
3 DeLauro	Y	Y	Y	Y	Y	Y
4 Himes	Y	Y	Y	Y	Y	Y
5 Murphy	Y	Y	Y	Y	Y	Y
DELAWARE						
AL Castle	Y	Y	Y	Y	Y	Y
FLORIDA						
1 Miller	Y	Y	Y	Y	Y	Y
2 Boyd	Y	Y	Y	Y	Y	Y
3 Brown	Y	Y	Y	Y	Y	Y
4 Crenshaw	Y	Y	Y	Y	Y	Y
5 Brown-Waite	?	?	?	Y	Y	Y
6 Stearns	Y	Y	Y	Y	Y	Y
7 Mica	Y	Y	Y	Y	Y	Y
8 Grayson	Y	Y	Y	Y	Y	Y
9 Bilirakis	Y	Y	Y	Y	Y	Y
10 Young	Y	Y	Y	Y	Y	Y
11 Castor	Y	Y	Y	Y	Y	Y
12 Putnam	Y	Y	Y	Y	Y	Y
13 Buchanan	Y	Y	Y	Y	Y	Y
14 Mack	Y	Y	Y	Y	Y	Y
15 Posey	Y	Y	Y	Y	Y	Y
16 Rooney	Y	Y	Y	Y	Y	Y
17 Meek	Y	Y	Y	Y	Y	Y
18 Ros-Lehtinen	?	?	?	Y	Y	Y
19 Deutch	Y	Y	Y	Y	Y	Y
20 Wasserman Schultz	Y	Y	Y	Y	Y	Y
21 Diaz-Balart, L.	?	?	?	Y	Y	Y
22 Klein	Y	Y	Y	Y	Y	Y
23 Hastings	Y	Y	Y	Y	Y	Y
24 Kosmas	Y	Y	Y	Y	Y	Y
25 Diaz-Balart, M.	Y	Y	Y	Y	Y	Y
GEORGIA						
1 Kingston	Y	Y	Y	Y	Y	Y
2 Bishop	Y	Y	Y	Y	Y	Y
3 Westmoreland	Y	Y	Y	Y	Y	Y
4 Johnson	Y	Y	Y	Y	Y	Y
5 Lewis	Y	Y	Y	Y	Y	Y
6 Price	Y	Y	Y	Y	Y	Y
7 Linder	Y	Y	Y	Y	Y	Y
8 Marshall	Y	Y	Y	Y	Y	Y
9 Vacant						
10 Broun	Y	Y	N	Y	Y	Y
11 Gingrey	Y	Y	Y	Y	Y	Y
12 Barrow	Y	Y	Y	Y	Y	Y
13 Scott	Y	Y	Y	?	Y	Y
HAWAII						
1 Djou[1]						Y
2 Hirono	Y	Y	Y	Y	Y	Y
IDAHO						
1 Minnick	Y	Y	Y	Y	Y	Y
2 Simpson	?	?	?	Y	Y	Y
ILLINOIS						
1 Rush	?	?	?	Y	Y	Y
2 Jackson	Y	Y	Y	Y	Y	Y
3 Lipinski	?	?	?	Y	Y	Y
4 Gutierrez	+	+	+	Y	Y	Y
5 Quigley	Y	Y	Y	Y	Y	Y
6 Roskam	Y	Y	Y	Y	Y	Y
7 Davis	Y	Y	Y	Y	Y	Y
8 Bean	Y	Y	Y	Y	Y	Y
9 Schakowsky	Y	Y	Y	Y	Y	Y
10 Kirk	?	?	?	Y	Y	Y
11 Halvorson	Y	Y	Y	Y	Y	Y
12 Costello	Y	Y	Y	Y	Y	Y
13 Biggert	Y	Y	Y	Y	Y	Y
14 Foster	Y	Y	Y	Y	Y	Y
15 Johnson	+	+	+	Y	Y	Y

	291	292	293	294	295	296
16 Manzullo	+	+	+	+	+	+
17 Hare	Y	Y	Y	Y	Y	Y
18 Schock	Y	Y	Y	Y	Y	Y
19 Shimkus	Y	Y	Y	Y	Y	Y
INDIANA						
1 Visclosky	Y	Y	Y	Y	Y	Y
2 Donnelly	Y	Y	Y	Y	Y	Y
3 Vacant[2]						
4 Buyer	Y	Y	Y	Y	Y	Y
5 Burton	Y	Y	Y	Y	Y	Y
6 Pence	Y	Y	Y	Y	Y	Y
7 Carson	Y	Y	Y	Y	Y	Y
8 Ellsworth	Y	Y	Y	Y	Y	Y
9 Hill	Y	Y	Y	Y	Y	Y
IOWA						
1 Braley	Y	Y	Y	Y	Y	Y
2 Loebsack	Y	Y	Y	Y	Y	Y
3 Boswell	Y	+	+	Y	Y	Y
4 Latham	Y	Y	Y	Y	Y	Y
5 King	Y	Y	Y	Y	Y	Y
KANSAS						
1 Moran	Y	Y	Y	Y	Y	Y
2 Jenkins	Y	Y	Y	Y	Y	Y
3 Moore	Y	?	Y	Y	Y	Y
4 Tiahrt	?	?	?	Y	Y	Y
KENTUCKY						
1 Whitfield	Y	Y	Y	Y	Y	Y
2 Guthrie	Y	Y	Y	Y	Y	Y
3 Yarmuth	Y	Y	Y	Y	Y	Y
4 Davis	Y	Y	Y	Y	Y	Y
5 Rogers	Y	Y	Y	Y	Y	Y
6 Chandler	Y	Y	Y	Y	Y	Y
LOUISIANA						
1 Scalise	Y	Y	Y	Y	Y	Y
2 Cao	?	?	?	Y	Y	Y
3 Melancon	?	?	?	Y	Y	Y
4 Fleming	?	?	?	Y	Y	Y
5 Alexander	?	?	?	Y	Y	Y
6 Cassidy	+	+	Y	Y	Y	Y
7 Boustany	Y	Y	Y	Y	Y	Y
MAINE						
1 Pingree	?	?	?	Y	Y	Y
2 Michaud	Y	Y	Y	Y	Y	Y
MARYLAND						
1 Kratovil	Y	Y	Y	Y	Y	Y
2 Ruppersberger	Y	Y	Y	Y	Y	Y
3 Sarbanes	Y	Y	Y	Y	Y	Y
4 Edwards	Y	Y	Y	Y	Y	Y
5 Hoyer	Y	Y	Y	Y	Y	Y
6 Bartlett	Y	Y	Y	Y	Y	Y
7 Cummings	Y	Y	Y	Y	Y	Y
8 Van Hollen	Y	Y	Y	Y	Y	Y
MASSACHUSETTS						
1 Olver	Y	Y	Y	Y	Y	Y
2 Neal	Y	Y	Y	Y	Y	Y
3 McGovern	Y	Y	Y	Y	Y	Y
4 Frank	Y	Y	Y	Y	Y	Y
5 Tsongas	Y	Y	Y	Y	Y	Y
6 Tierney	Y	Y	Y	Y	Y	Y
7 Markey	Y	Y	Y	Y	Y	Y
8 Capuano	Y	Y	Y	Y	Y	Y
9 Lynch	Y	Y	Y	Y	Y	Y
10 Delahunt	?	?	?	Y	Y	Y
MICHIGAN						
1 Stupak	?	?	?	Y	Y	Y
2 Hoekstra	?	?	?	?	?	?
3 Ehlers	Y	Y	Y	Y	Y	Y
4 Camp	Y	Y	Y	Y	Y	Y
5 Kildee	Y	Y	Y	Y	Y	Y
6 Upton	Y	Y	Y	Y	Y	Y
7 Schauer	Y	Y	Y	Y	Y	Y
8 Rogers	Y	Y	Y	Y	Y	Y
9 Peters	Y	Y	Y	Y	Y	Y
10 Miller	Y	Y	Y	Y	Y	Y
11 McCotter	Y	Y	Y	Y	Y	Y
12 Levin	Y	Y	Y	Y	Y	Y
13 Kilpatrick	Y	Y	Y	+	+	+
14 Conyers	?	?	?	?	?	?
15 Dingell	Y	Y	Y	Y	Y	Y
MINNESOTA						
1 Walz	Y	Y	Y	Y	Y	Y
2 Kline	Y	Y	Y	Y	Y	Y
3 Paulsen	Y	Y	Y	Y	Y	Y
4 McCollum	Y	Y	Y	Y	Y	Y

	291	292	293	294	295	296
5 Ellison	Y	Y	Y	Y	Y	Y
6 Bachmann	Y	Y	Y	Y	Y	Y
7 Peterson	Y	Y	Y	Y	Y	Y
8 Oberstar	Y	Y	Y	Y	Y	
MISSISSIPPI						
1 Childers	?	?	?	Y	Y	Y
2 Thompson	Y	Y	Y	Y	Y	Y
3 Harper	Y	Y	Y	Y	Y	Y
4 Taylor	?	?	?	Y	Y	Y
MISSOURI						
1 Clay	Y	Y	Y	Y	Y	Y
2 Akin	Y	Y	Y	Y	Y	Y
3 Carnahan	Y	Y	Y	Y	Y	Y
4 Skelton	Y	Y	Y	Y	Y	Y
5 Cleaver	Y	Y	Y	Y	Y	Y
6 Graves	?	?	?	?	?	?
7 Blunt	?	?	?	?	?	?
8 Emerson	Y	Y	Y	Y	Y	Y
9 Luetkemeyer	Y	Y	Y	Y	Y	Y
MONTANA						
AL Rehberg	Y	Y	Y	Y	Y	Y
NEBRASKA						
1 Fortenberry	Y	Y	Y	Y	Y	Y
2 Terry	Y	Y	Y	Y	Y	Y
3 Smith	Y	Y	Y	Y	Y	Y
NEVADA						
1 Berkley	Y	Y	Y	Y	Y	Y
2 Heller	Y	Y	Y	Y	Y	Y
3 Titus	Y	Y	Y	Y	Y	Y
NEW HAMPSHIRE						
1 Shea-Porter	Y	Y	Y	Y	Y	Y
2 Hodes	?	?	?	Y	Y	Y
NEW JERSEY						
1 Andrews	Y	Y	Y	Y	Y	Y
2 LoBiondo	Y	Y	Y	Y	Y	Y
3 Adler	Y	Y	Y	Y	Y	Y
4 Smith	Y	Y	Y	Y	Y	Y
5 Garrett	Y	Y	Y	Y	Y	Y
6 Pallone	Y	Y	Y	Y	Y	Y
7 Lance	Y	Y	Y	Y	Y	Y
8 Pascrell	Y	Y	Y	Y	Y	Y
9 Rothman	Y	Y	Y	Y	Y	Y
10 Payne	?	?	?	Y	Y	Y
11 Frelinghuysen	Y	Y	Y	Y	Y	Y
12 Holt	Y	Y	Y	Y	Y	Y
13 Sires	Y	Y	Y	Y	Y	Y
NEW MEXICO						
1 Heinrich	Y	Y	Y	Y	Y	Y
2 Teague	Y	Y	Y	Y	Y	Y
3 Luján	Y	Y	Y	Y	Y	
NEW YORK						
1 Bishop	?	?	?	Y	Y	Y
2 Israel	Y	Y	Y	Y	Y	Y
3 King	Y	Y	Y	Y	Y	Y
4 McCarthy	Y	Y	Y	Y	Y	Y
5 Ackerman	Y	Y	Y	Y	Y	Y
6 Meeks	Y	Y	Y	Y	Y	Y
7 Crowley	Y	Y	Y	Y	Y	+
8 Nadler	Y	Y	Y	Y	Y	Y
9 Weiner	Y	Y	Y	Y	Y	Y
10 Towns	?	?	?	Y	Y	Y
11 Clarke	Y	Y	Y	Y	Y	Y
12 Velázquez	Y	Y	Y	Y	Y	Y
13 McMahon	Y	?	Y	Y	Y	Y
14 Maloney	Y	Y	Y	Y	Y	Y
15 Rangel	Y	Y	Y	Y	Y	Y
16 Serrano	Y	Y	Y	Y	Y	Y
17 Engel	Y	Y	Y	Y	Y	Y
18 Lowey	Y	Y	Y	Y	Y	Y
19 Hall	?	?	?	Y	Y	Y
20 Murphy	Y	Y	Y	Y	Y	Y
21 Tonko	Y	Y	?	Y	Y	Y
22 Hinchey	Y	Y	Y	Y	Y	Y
23 Owens	Y	Y	Y	Y	Y	Y
24 Arcuri	?	Y	Y	Y	Y	Y
25 Maffei	?	Y	Y	Y	Y	Y
26 Lee	Y	Y	Y	Y	Y	Y
27 Higgins	?	?	?	Y	Y	Y
28 Slaughter	Y	Y	Y	Y	Y	Y
29 Vacant						
NORTH CAROLINA						
1 Butterfield	Y	Y	Y	Y	Y	Y
2 Etheridge	Y	Y	Y	Y	Y	Y
3 Jones	Y	Y	Y	Y	Y	N
4 Price	Y	Y	Y	Y	Y	

	291	292	293	294	295	296
5 Foxx	Y	Y	Y	Y	Y	
6 Coble	Y	Y	Y	Y	Y	
7 McIntyre	Y	Y	Y	Y	Y	
8 Kissell	Y	Y	Y	Y	Y	
9 Myrick	Y	Y	Y	Y	Y	
10 McHenry	Y	Y	Y	Y	Y	
11 Shuler	Y	Y	Y	Y	Y	
12 Watt	Y	Y	Y	Y	Y	
13 Miller	Y	Y	Y	Y	Y	
NORTH DAKOTA						
AL Pomeroy	Y	Y	Y	Y	Y	
OHIO						
1 Driehaus	Y	Y	Y	Y	Y	Y
2 Schmidt	Y	Y	Y	Y	Y	Y
3 Turner	Y	Y	Y	Y	Y	Y
4 Jordan	Y	Y	Y	Y	Y	Y
5 Latta	Y	Y	Y	Y	Y	Y
6 Wilson	Y	Y	Y	Y	Y	Y
7 Austria	Y	Y	Y	Y	Y	Y
8 Boehner	Y	Y	Y	Y	Y	Y
9 Kaptur	Y	Y	Y	Y	Y	Y
10 Kucinich	Y	Y	Y	Y	Y	N
11 Fudge	Y	Y	Y	Y	Y	Y
12 Tiberi	Y	Y	Y	Y	Y	Y
13 Sutton	Y	Y	Y	Y	Y	Y
14 LaTourette	Y	Y	Y	Y	Y	Y
15 Kilroy	Y	Y	Y	Y	Y	Y
16 Boccieri	?	?	?	Y	Y	Y
17 Ryan	?	?	?	Y	Y	Y
18 Space	?	?	?	Y	Y	Y
OKLAHOMA						
1 Sullivan	Y	Y	Y	Y	Y	Y
2 Boren	Y	Y	Y	Y	Y	Y
3 Lucas	Y	Y	Y	Y	Y	Y
4 Cole	Y	Y	Y	Y	Y	Y
5 Fallin	?	?	?	?	?	?
OREGON						
1 Wu	Y	Y	Y	Y	Y	Y
2 Walden	Y	Y	Y	Y	Y	Y
3 Blumenauer	?	?	?	Y	Y	Y
4 DeFazio	Y	Y	Y	Y	Y	Y
5 Schrader	Y	Y	Y	Y	Y	Y
PENNSYLVANIA						
1 Brady	Y	Y	Y	Y	Y	Y
2 Fattah	Y	Y	Y	Y	Y	Y
3 Dahlkemper	Y	Y	Y	Y	Y	Y
4 Altmire	Y	Y	Y	Y	Y	Y
5 Thompson	Y	Y	Y	Y	Y	Y
6 Gerlach	Y	Y	Y	Y	Y	Y
7 Sestak	Y	Y	Y	Y	Y	Y
8 Murphy, P.	?	?	?	Y	Y	Y
9 Shuster	Y	Y	Y	Y	Y	Y
10 Carney	Y	Y	Y	Y	Y	Y
11 Kanjorski	Y	Y	Y	Y	Y	Y
12 Critz	Y	Y	Y	Y	Y	Y
13 Schwartz	Y	Y	Y	Y	Y	Y
14 Doyle	Y	Y	Y	Y	Y	Y
15 Dent	Y	Y	Y	Y	Y	Y
16 Pitts	Y	Y	Y	Y	Y	Y
17 Holden	Y	Y	Y	Y	Y	Y
18 Murphy, T.	Y	Y	Y	Y	Y	Y
19 Platts	Y	Y	Y	Y	Y	Y
RHODE ISLAND						
1 Kennedy	Y	Y	Y	Y	Y	Y
2 Langevin	Y	Y	Y	Y	Y	Y
SOUTH CAROLINA						
1 Brown	Y	Y	Y	Y	Y	Y
2 Wilson	Y	Y	Y	Y	Y	Y
3 Barrett	?	?	?	?	?	?
4 Inglis	?	?	?	Y	Y	Y
5 Spratt	?	?	?	Y	Y	Y
6 Clyburn	Y	Y	Y	Y	Y	Y
SOUTH DAKOTA						
AL Herseth Sandlin	Y	Y	Y	Y	Y	Y
TENNESSEE						
1 Roe	Y	Y	Y	Y	Y	Y
2 Duncan	Y	Y	Y	Y	Y	Y
3 Wamp	?	?	?	?	?	?
4 Davis	Y	Y	?	Y	Y	Y
5 Cooper	Y	Y	Y	Y	Y	Y
6 Gordon	Y	Y	Y	Y	Y	Y
7 Blackburn	Y	Y	Y	Y	Y	Y
8 Tanner	Y	Y	Y	Y	Y	Y
9 Cohen	Y	Y	Y	Y	Y	Y

	291	292	293	294	295	296
TEXAS						
1 Gohmert	Y	Y	Y	Y	Y	
2 Poe	Y	Y	Y	Y	Y	
3 Johnson, S.	Y	N	Y	Y	Y	
4 Hall	Y	Y	Y	Y	Y	
5 Hensarling	Y	Y	Y	Y	Y	
6 Barton	Y	Y	Y	Y	Y	
7 Culberson	Y	Y	Y	Y	Y	
8 Brady	Y	Y	Y	Y	Y	
9 Green, A.	Y	Y	Y	Y	Y	
10 McCaul	Y	Y	Y	Y	Y	
11 Conaway	Y	Y	Y	Y	Y	
12 Granger	Y	Y	Y	Y	Y	
13 Thornberry	Y	N	N	N	N	
14 Paul	Y	N	N	N	N	N
15 Hinojosa	?	?	?	?	?	?
16 Reyes	Y	Y	Y	Y	Y	
17 Edwards	Y	Y	Y	Y	Y	
18 Jackson Lee	?	?	?	?	?	?
19 Neugebauer	Y	Y	Y	Y	Y	
20 Gonzalez	Y	Y	Y	Y	Y	
21 Smith	Y	Y	Y	Y	Y	
22 Olson	Y	Y	Y	Y	Y	
23 Rodriguez	Y	Y	Y	Y	Y	
24 Marchant	Y	Y	Y	Y	Y	
25 Doggett	Y	Y	Y	Y	Y	
26 Burgess	Y	?	N	Y	Y	
27 Ortiz	?	?	?	Y	Y	Y
28 Cuellar	Y	Y	Y	Y	Y	
29 Green, G.	Y	Y	Y	Y	Y	
30 Johnson, E.	Y	Y	Y	Y	Y	
31 Carter	Y	Y	Y	Y	Y	
32 Sessions	Y	Y	Y	Y	Y	
UTAH						
1 Bishop	Y	Y	Y	Y	Y	
2 Matheson	?	?	?	Y	Y	Y
3 Chaffetz	Y	N	Y	Y	Y	
VERMONT						
AL Welch	Y	Y	Y	Y	Y	Y
VIRGINIA						
1 Wittman	Y	Y	Y	Y	Y	Y
2 Nye	Y	Y	Y	Y	Y	Y
3 Scott	Y	Y	Y	Y	Y	Y
4 Forbes	Y	Y	Y	Y	Y	Y
5 Perriello	Y	Y	Y	Y	Y	Y
6 Goodlatte	Y	Y	Y	Y	Y	Y
7 Cantor	Y	Y	Y	Y	Y	Y
8 Moran	Y	Y	Y	Y	Y	Y
9 Boucher	?	Y	Y	Y	?	Y
10 Wolf	Y	Y	Y	Y	Y	Y
11 Connolly	Y	Y	Y	Y	Y	Y
WASHINGTON						
1 Inslee	Y	Y	Y	Y	Y	Y
2 Larsen	Y	Y	Y	Y	Y	Y
3 Baird	Y	Y	Y	Y	Y	Y
4 Hastings	Y	Y	Y	Y	Y	Y
5 McMorris Rodgers	Y	Y	Y	Y	Y	Y
6 Dicks	Y	Y	Y	Y	Y	Y
7 McDermott	Y	Y	Y	Y	Y	Y
8 Reichert	Y	Y	Y	Y	Y	Y
9 Smith	Y	Y	Y	Y	Y	Y
WEST VIRGINIA						
1 Mollohan	?	?	?	Y	Y	Y
2 Capito	Y	Y	Y	Y	Y	Y
3 Rahall	Y	Y	Y	Y	Y	Y
WISCONSIN						
1 Ryan	?	?	?	?	?	?
2 Baldwin	Y	Y	Y	Y	Y	Y
3 Kind	Y	Y	Y	Y	Y	Y
4 Moore	Y	Y	Y	Y	Y	Y
5 Sensenbrenner	Y	Y	Y	Y	Y	Y
6 Petri	Y	Y	Y	Y	Y	Y
7 Obey	Y	Y	Y	Y	Y	Y
8 Kagen	Y	Y	Y	Y	Y	Y
WYOMING						
AL Lummis	Y	N	Y	Y	Y	Y
DELEGATES						
Faleomavaega (A.S.)						
Norton (D.C.)						
Bordallo (Guam)						
Sablan (N. Marianas)						
Pierluisi (P.R.)						
Christensen (V.I.)						

IN THE HOUSE | By Vote Number

297. **H Res 584. Tribute to Manufactured and Modular Housing/Adoption.** Donnelly, D-Ind., motion to suspend the rules and adopt the resolution that would recognize the importance of manufactured and modular housing to homeownership in the United States. It also would support the goals and ideals of Manufactured and Modular Housing Week and National Homeownership Month. Motion agreed to 408-4: D 246-0; R 162-4. A two-thirds majority of those present and voting (275 in this case) is required for adoption under suspension of the rules. May 25, 2010.

298. **HR 3885. Veterans' Dog Therapy Pilot Program/Passage.** Filner, D-Calif., motion to suspend the rules and pass the bill that would create a five-year pilot program in which veterans diagnosed with post-traumatic stress disorder or other mental health conditions would train service dogs for use by disabled veterans. It also would require the Veterans Affairs Department to collect data to evaluate the effectiveness of the program and to report annually to Congress. Motion agreed to 403-4: D 244-0; R 159-4. A two-thirds majority of those present and voting (272 in this case) is required for passage under suspension of the rules. May 25, 2010.

299. **HR 2711. Expenses for Families of Fallen Federal Agents/Passage.** Lynch, D-Mass., motion to suspend the rules and concur in the Senate amendments to the bill that would authorize departments to pay transportation and moving expenses for families of federal law enforcement officers, including customs and border protection officers, who are killed in the line of duty. Motion agreed to, thus clearing the bill for the president, 416-0: D 249-0; R 167-0. A two-thirds majority of those present and voting (278 in this case) is required for passage under suspension of the rules. May 25, 2010.

300. **H Res 1189. Tribute to Lance Mackey/Adoption.** Lynch, D-Mass., motion to suspend the rules and adopt the resolution that would commend Lance Mackey on his record-breaking fourth consecutive Iditarod Trail Sled Dog Race win, and applaud participants in the 2010 race, including volunteers and staff. Motion agreed to 411-0: D 246-0; R 165-0. A two-thirds majority of those present and voting (274 in this case) is required for adoption under suspension of the rules. May 25, 2010.

301. **H Res 1172. Tribute to Will Keith 'W.K.' Kellogg/Adoption.** Lynch, D-Mass., motion to suspend the rules and adopt the resolution that would recognize the 150th anniversary of the birth of breakfast cereal manufacturer Will Keith "W.K." Kellogg, founder of the Kellogg Co. Motion agreed to 410-0: D 244-0; R 166-0. A two-thirds majority of those present and voting (274 in this case) is required for adoption under suspension of the rules. May 25, 2010.

302. **H Res 1347. Deepwater Horizon Explosion Victims/Adoption.** Speier, D-Calif., motion to suspend the rules and adopt the resolution that would honor the 11 workers who died in the explosion on the Deepwater Horizon oil platform in the Gulf of Mexico off the coast of Louisiana, and would extend condolences to their families. Motion agreed to 403-0: D 239-0; R 164-0. A two-thirds majority of those present and voting (269 in this case) is required for adoption under suspension of the rules. May 26, 2010.

	297	298	299	300	301	302
ALABAMA						
1 Bonner	Y	Y	Y	Y	Y	Y
2 Bright	Y	Y	Y	Y	Y	Y
3 Rogers	Y	Y	Y	Y	Y	Y
4 Aderholt	Y	Y	Y	Y	Y	Y
5 Griffith	?	Y	Y	Y	Y	Y
6 Bachus	Y	Y	Y	Y	Y	Y
7 Davis	?	?	?	?	?	?
ALASKA						
AL Young	N	Y	Y	Y	Y	Y
ARIZONA						
1 Kirkpatrick	Y	Y	Y	Y	Y	Y
2 Franks	Y	Y	Y	Y	Y	Y
3 Shadegg	Y	N	Y	Y	Y	Y
4 Pastor	Y	Y	Y	Y	Y	Y
5 Mitchell	Y	Y	Y	Y	Y	Y
6 Flake	Y	N	Y	Y	Y	Y
7 Grijalva	Y	Y	Y	Y	Y	?
8 Giffords	Y	Y	Y	Y	Y	Y
ARKANSAS						
1 Berry	Y	Y	Y	Y	Y	Y
2 Snyder	Y	Y	Y	Y	Y	Y
3 Boozman	Y	Y	Y	Y	Y	Y
4 Ross	Y	Y	Y	Y	Y	Y
CALIFORNIA						
1 Thompson	Y	Y	Y	Y	Y	Y
2 Herger	Y	Y	Y	Y	Y	Y
3 Lungren	Y	Y	Y	Y	Y	Y
4 McClintock	Y	Y	Y	Y	Y	?
5 Matsui	Y	Y	Y	Y	Y	Y
6 Woolsey	Y	Y	Y	Y	Y	?
7 Miller, George	Y	Y	Y	Y	Y	Y
8 Pelosi						
9 Lee	Y	Y	Y	Y	Y	Y
10 Garamendi	Y	Y	Y	Y	Y	Y
11 McNerney	Y	Y	Y	Y	Y	Y
12 Speier	Y	Y	Y	Y	Y	Y
13 Stark	Y	Y	Y	Y	Y	Y
14 Eshoo	Y	Y	Y	Y	Y	Y
15 Honda	Y	Y	Y	Y	Y	?
16 Lofgren	Y	Y	Y	Y	Y	Y
17 Farr	Y	Y	Y	Y	Y	Y
18 Cardoza	Y	?	Y	Y	Y	Y
19 Radanovich	Y	?	?	?	?	?
20 Costa	Y	Y	Y	Y	Y	Y
21 Nunes	Y	Y	Y	Y	Y	Y
22 McCarthy	Y	?	Y	Y	Y	Y
23 Capps	Y	Y	Y	Y	Y	Y
24 Gallegly	Y	Y	Y	Y	Y	Y
25 McKeon	Y	Y	Y	Y	Y	Y
26 Dreier	Y	Y	Y	Y	Y	Y
27 Sherman	Y	Y	Y	Y	Y	Y
28 Berman	Y	Y	Y	Y	Y	Y
29 Schiff	Y	Y	Y	Y	Y	Y
30 Waxman	Y	Y	Y	Y	Y	Y
31 Becerra	Y	Y	Y	Y	Y	?
32 Chu	Y	Y	Y	?	Y	Y
33 Watson	Y	Y	Y	Y	Y	Y
34 Roybal-Allard	Y	Y	Y	Y	Y	Y
35 Waters	Y	Y	Y	Y	Y	Y
36 Harman	Y	Y	Y	Y	Y	Y
37 Richardson	Y	Y	Y	Y	Y	Y
38 Napolitano	Y	Y	Y	Y	Y	Y
39 Sánchez, Linda	Y	Y	Y	Y	Y	Y
40 Royce	Y	Y	Y	Y	Y	Y
41 Lewis	Y	?	Y	Y	Y	Y
42 Miller, Gary	Y	Y	Y	Y	Y	Y
43 Baca	Y	Y	Y	Y	Y	Y
44 Calvert	Y	Y	Y	Y	Y	Y
45 Bono Mack	Y	Y	Y	Y	Y	Y
46 Rohrabacher	Y	Y	Y	Y	Y	Y
47 Sanchez, Loretta	Y	Y	Y	Y	Y	Y
48 Campbell	Y	N	Y	Y	Y	Y
49 Issa	Y	N	Y	Y	Y	Y
50 Bilbray	Y	Y	Y	Y	Y	Y
51 Filner	Y	Y	Y	Y	Y	Y
52 Hunter	Y	Y	Y	Y	Y	Y
53 Davis	Y	Y	Y	Y	Y	Y
COLORADO						
1 DeGette	Y	Y	Y	Y	Y	Y
2 Polis	Y	?	Y	Y	Y	Y
3 Salazar	Y	Y	Y	Y	Y	Y
4 Markey	Y	Y	Y	Y	Y	Y
5 Lamborn	Y	Y	Y	Y	Y	Y
6 Coffman	Y	Y	Y	Y	Y	Y
7 Perlmutter	Y	Y	Y	Y	Y	Y
CONNECTICUT						
1 Larson	Y	Y	Y	Y	Y	+
2 Courtney	Y	Y	Y	Y	Y	Y
3 DeLauro	Y	Y	Y	Y	Y	Y
4 Himes	Y	?	Y	Y	Y	Y
5 Murphy	Y	Y	Y	Y	Y	Y
DELAWARE						
AL Castle	Y	Y	Y	Y	Y	Y
FLORIDA						
1 Miller	Y	Y	Y	Y	Y	Y
2 Boyd	?	Y	Y	Y	Y	Y
3 Brown	Y	Y	Y	Y	Y	?
4 Crenshaw	Y	Y	Y	Y	Y	Y
5 Brown-Waite	Y	Y	Y	Y	Y	Y
6 Stearns	Y	Y	Y	Y	Y	Y
7 Mica	Y	Y	Y	Y	Y	Y
8 Grayson	Y	Y	Y	Y	Y	Y
9 Bilirakis	Y	Y	Y	Y	Y	Y
10 Young	Y	Y	Y	Y	Y	Y
11 Castor	Y	Y	Y	Y	Y	Y
12 Putnam	Y	Y	Y	Y	Y	Y
13 Buchanan	Y	Y	Y	Y	Y	Y
14 Mack	Y	Y	Y	Y	Y	Y
15 Posey	Y	Y	Y	Y	Y	Y
16 Rooney	Y	Y	Y	Y	Y	Y
17 Meek	Y	Y	Y	Y	Y	Y
18 Ros-Lehtinen	Y	Y	Y	Y	Y	Y
19 Deutch	Y	Y	Y	Y	Y	Y
20 Wasserman Schultz	Y	Y	Y	Y	Y	Y
21 Diaz-Balart, L.	Y	Y	Y	Y	Y	Y
22 Klein	Y	Y	Y	Y	Y	Y
23 Hastings	Y	Y	Y	Y	Y	Y
24 Kosmas	Y	Y	Y	Y	Y	Y
25 Diaz-Balart, M.	Y	Y	Y	Y	Y	Y
GEORGIA						
1 Kingston	Y	Y	Y	Y	Y	Y
2 Bishop	Y	Y	Y	Y	Y	Y
3 Westmoreland	Y	Y	Y	Y	Y	Y
4 Johnson	Y	Y	Y	Y	Y	Y
5 Lewis	Y	Y	Y	Y	Y	Y
6 Price	Y	Y	Y	Y	Y	Y
7 Linder	Y	Y	Y	Y	Y	?
8 Marshall	Y	Y	Y	Y	Y	Y
9 Vacant						
10 Broun	N	Y	Y	Y	Y	Y
11 Gingrey	Y	Y	Y	Y	Y	Y
12 Barrow	Y	Y	Y	Y	Y	Y
13 Scott	Y	Y	Y	Y	Y	Y
HAWAII						
1 Djou	Y	Y	Y	Y	Y	Y
2 Hirono	Y	Y	Y	Y	Y	+
IDAHO						
1 Minnick	Y	Y	Y	Y	Y	Y
2 Simpson	Y	Y	Y	Y	Y	Y
ILLINOIS						
1 Rush	Y	Y	Y	Y	Y	Y
2 Jackson	Y	Y	Y	Y	Y	Y
3 Lipinski	Y	Y	Y	Y	Y	Y
4 Gutierrez	?	Y	Y	Y	?	Y
5 Quigley	Y	Y	Y	Y	Y	Y
6 Roskam	Y	Y	Y	Y	Y	Y
7 Davis	Y	Y	Y	Y	Y	Y
8 Bean	Y	Y	Y	Y	Y	Y
9 Schakowsky	Y	Y	Y	Y	Y	Y
10 Kirk	Y	Y	Y	Y	?	Y
11 Halvorson	Y	Y	Y	Y	Y	Y
12 Costello	Y	Y	Y	Y	Y	Y
13 Biggert	Y	Y	Y	Y	Y	Y
14 Foster	Y	Y	Y	Y	Y	Y
15 Johnson	Y	Y	Y	Y	Y	Y

KEY   Republicans   Democrats

Y Voted for (yea)	**X** Paired against	**C** Voted "present" to avoid possible conflict of interest
# Paired for	**–** Announced against	
+ Announced for	**P** Voted "present"	**?** Did not vote or otherwise make a position known
N Voted against (nay)		

	297	298	299	300	301	302
16 **Manzullo**	+	+	?	+	+	Y
17 Hare	Y	Y	Y	Y	Y	Y
18 **Schock**	Y	Y	Y	Y	Y	Y
19 **Shimkus**	Y	Y	Y	Y	Y	Y
INDIANA						
1 Visclosky	Y	Y	Y	Y	Y	Y
2 Donnelly	Y	Y	Y	Y	Y	Y
3 Vacant						
4 **Buyer**	Y	Y	Y	Y	Y	Y
5 **Burton**	Y	Y	Y	Y	Y	Y
6 **Pence**	Y	Y	Y	Y	Y	Y
7 Carson	Y	Y	Y	Y	Y	Y
8 Ellsworth	Y	Y	Y	Y	Y	Y
9 Hill	Y	Y	Y	Y	Y	Y
IOWA						
1 Braley	Y	Y	Y	Y	Y	Y
2 Loebsack	Y	Y	Y	Y	Y	Y
3 Boswell	Y	Y	Y	Y	Y	Y
4 **Latham**	Y	Y	Y	Y	Y	Y
5 **King**	Y	Y	Y	Y	Y	Y
KANSAS						
1 **Moran**	Y	Y	Y	Y	Y	Y
2 **Jenkins**	Y	Y	Y	Y	Y	Y
3 Moore	Y	Y	Y	Y	Y	Y
4 **Tiahrt**	Y	Y	Y	Y	Y	+
KENTUCKY						
1 **Whitfield**	Y	Y	Y	Y	Y	Y
2 **Guthrie**	Y	Y	Y	Y	Y	Y
3 Yarmuth	Y	Y	Y	Y	Y	Y
4 **Davis**	Y	Y	Y	Y	Y	Y
5 **Rogers**	Y	Y	Y	Y	Y	Y
6 Chandler	Y	Y	Y	Y	?	Y
LOUISIANA						
1 **Scalise**	Y	Y	Y	Y	Y	Y
2 **Cao**	N	Y	Y	Y	Y	Y
3 Melancon	Y	Y	Y	Y	Y	Y
4 **Fleming**	Y	Y	Y	Y	Y	Y
5 **Alexander**	Y	Y	Y	Y	Y	Y
6 **Cassidy**	Y	Y	Y	Y	Y	+
7 **Boustany**	Y	Y	Y	Y	Y	Y
MAINE						
1 Pingree	Y	Y	Y	Y	Y	Y
2 Michaud	Y	Y	Y	Y	Y	Y
MARYLAND						
1 Kratovil	Y	Y	Y	Y	Y	Y
2 Ruppersberger	Y	?	Y	Y	Y	Y
3 Sarbanes	Y	Y	Y	Y	Y	Y
4 Edwards	Y	Y	Y	Y	Y	Y
5 Hoyer	Y	Y	Y	Y	Y	Y
6 **Bartlett**	Y	Y	Y	Y	Y	Y
7 Cummings	Y	Y	Y	Y	Y	Y
8 Van Hollen	Y	Y	Y	Y	Y	Y
MASSACHUSETTS						
1 Olver	Y	Y	Y	Y	Y	Y
2 Neal	Y	Y	Y	Y	Y	Y
3 McGovern	Y	?	Y	Y	Y	Y
4 Frank	Y	Y	Y	Y	Y	Y
5 Tsongas	Y	Y	Y	Y	Y	Y
6 Tierney	Y	Y	Y	Y	Y	?
7 Markey	Y	Y	Y	Y	Y	Y
8 Capuano	Y	Y	Y	Y	Y	Y
9 Lynch	Y	Y	Y	Y	Y	Y
10 Delahunt	Y	Y	Y	Y	Y	Y
MICHIGAN						
1 Stupak	Y	Y	Y	Y	Y	Y
2 **Hoekstra**	?	?	?	?	?	?
3 **Ehlers**	Y	Y	Y	Y	Y	Y
4 **Camp**	Y	Y	Y	Y	Y	Y
5 Kildee	Y	Y	Y	Y	Y	Y
6 **Upton**	Y	Y	Y	Y	Y	Y
7 Schauer	Y	Y	Y	Y	Y	Y
8 **Rogers**	P	Y	Y	Y	Y	Y
9 Peters	Y	Y	Y	Y	Y	Y
10 **Miller**	Y	Y	Y	Y	Y	Y
11 **McCotter**	Y	Y	Y	Y	Y	Y
12 Levin	Y	Y	Y	Y	Y	Y
13 Kilpatrick	?	+	+	+	?	+
14 Conyers	?	?	?	?	?	?
15 Dingell	Y	Y	Y	Y	Y	Y
MINNESOTA						
1 Walz	Y	Y	Y	Y	Y	Y
2 **Kline**	Y	Y	Y	Y	Y	Y
3 **Paulsen**	Y	Y	Y	Y	Y	Y
4 McCollum	Y	Y	Y	Y	Y	Y

	297	298	299	300	301	302
5 Ellison	Y	Y	Y	Y	Y	Y
6 **Bachmann**	Y	Y	Y	Y	Y	Y
7 Peterson	Y	Y	Y	Y	Y	Y
8 Oberstar	Y	Y	Y	Y	Y	Y
MISSISSIPPI						
1 Childers	Y	Y	Y	Y	Y	Y
2 Thompson	Y	Y	Y	Y	Y	Y
3 **Harper**	Y	Y	Y	Y	Y	Y
4 Taylor	Y	Y	Y	Y	Y	Y
MISSOURI						
1 Clay	Y	Y	Y	Y	?	Y
2 **Akin**	Y	Y	Y	Y	Y	Y
3 Carnahan	Y	Y	Y	Y	Y	Y
4 Skelton	Y	Y	Y	Y	Y	Y
5 Cleaver	Y	Y	Y	?	Y	Y
6 **Graves**	?	?	?	?	?	?
7 **Blunt**	?	?	?	?	?	Y
8 **Emerson**	Y	Y	Y	Y	Y	Y
9 **Luetkemeyer**	Y	Y	Y	Y	Y	Y
MONTANA						
AL **Rehberg**	Y	Y	Y	Y	Y	Y
NEBRASKA						
1 **Fortenberry**	Y	Y	Y	Y	Y	Y
2 **Terry**	Y	Y	Y	Y	Y	Y
3 **Smith**	Y	Y	Y	Y	Y	Y
NEVADA						
1 Berkley	Y	Y	Y	Y	Y	Y
2 **Heller**	Y	Y	Y	Y	Y	Y
3 Titus	Y	Y	Y	Y	Y	Y
NEW HAMPSHIRE						
1 Shea-Porter	Y	Y	Y	Y	Y	Y
2 Hodes	?	Y	Y	Y	Y	Y
NEW JERSEY						
1 Andrews	Y	Y	Y	Y	Y	?
2 **LoBiondo**	Y	Y	Y	Y	Y	Y
3 Adler	Y	Y	Y	Y	Y	Y
4 **Smith**	Y	Y	Y	Y	Y	Y
5 **Garrett**	Y	Y	Y	Y	Y	Y
6 Pallone	Y	Y	Y	Y	Y	Y
7 **Lance**	Y	Y	Y	Y	Y	Y
8 Pascrell	Y	Y	Y	Y	Y	Y
9 Rothman	Y	Y	Y	Y	Y	Y
10 Payne	Y	Y	Y	Y	Y	Y
11 **Frelinghuysen**	Y	Y	Y	Y	Y	Y
12 Holt	Y	Y	Y	Y	Y	Y
13 Sires	Y	Y	Y	Y	Y	Y
NEW MEXICO						
1 Heinrich	Y	Y	Y	Y	Y	Y
2 Teague	Y	Y	Y	Y	Y	Y
3 Luján	Y	Y	Y	Y	Y	Y
NEW YORK						
1 Bishop	Y	Y	Y	Y	Y	Y
2 Israel	Y	Y	Y	Y	Y	Y
3 **King**	Y	Y	Y	Y	Y	Y
4 McCarthy	Y	Y	Y	Y	Y	Y
5 Ackerman	Y	Y	Y	Y	Y	Y
6 Meeks	Y	Y	Y	Y	Y	Y
7 Crowley	Y	Y	Y	Y	Y	Y
8 Nadler	Y	Y	Y	Y	Y	Y
9 Weiner	Y	Y	Y	Y	Y	Y
10 Towns	Y	Y	Y	Y	Y	Y
11 Clarke	Y	Y	Y	Y	Y	Y
12 Velázquez	Y	Y	Y	Y	Y	Y
13 McMahon	Y	Y	Y	Y	Y	Y
14 Maloney	Y	Y	Y	Y	Y	?
15 Rangel	Y	Y	Y	Y	Y	Y
16 Serrano	Y	Y	Y	Y	Y	Y
17 Engel	Y	Y	Y	Y	Y	Y
18 Lowey	Y	Y	Y	Y	Y	Y
19 Hall	Y	Y	Y	Y	Y	Y
20 Murphy	Y	Y	Y	Y	Y	Y
21 Tonko	Y	Y	Y	Y	Y	Y
22 Hinchey	Y	Y	Y	Y	Y	Y
23 Owens	Y	Y	Y	Y	Y	Y
24 Arcuri	Y	Y	Y	Y	Y	Y
25 Maffei	Y	Y	Y	Y	Y	Y
26 **Lee**	Y	Y	Y	Y	Y	Y
27 Higgins	Y	Y	Y	Y	Y	Y
28 Slaughter	Y	Y	Y	?	Y	Y
29 Vacant						
NORTH CAROLINA						
1 Butterfield	Y	Y	Y	Y	Y	Y
2 Etheridge	Y	Y	Y	Y	Y	Y
3 **Jones**	Y	Y	Y	Y	Y	Y
4 Price	Y	Y	Y	Y	Y	Y

	297	298	299	300	301	302
5 **Foxx**	Y	Y	Y	Y	Y	Y
6 **Coble**	Y	Y	Y	Y	Y	Y
7 McIntyre	Y	Y	Y	Y	Y	Y
8 Kissell	Y	Y	Y	Y	Y	Y
9 **Myrick**	Y	Y	Y	Y	Y	Y
10 **McHenry**	Y	Y	Y	Y	Y	Y
11 Shuler	Y	Y	Y	Y	Y	Y
12 Watt	Y	Y	Y	Y	Y	Y
13 Miller	Y	Y	Y	Y	Y	Y
NORTH DAKOTA						
AL Pomeroy	Y	Y	Y	Y	Y	Y
OHIO						
1 Driehaus	Y	Y	Y	Y	Y	Y
2 **Schmidt**	Y	Y	Y	Y	Y	Y
3 **Turner**	Y	Y	Y	Y	Y	Y
4 **Jordan**	Y	Y	Y	Y	Y	Y
5 **Latta**	Y	Y	Y	Y	Y	Y
6 Wilson	Y	Y	Y	Y	Y	Y
7 **Austria**	Y	Y	Y	Y	Y	Y
8 **Boehner**	Y	Y	Y	Y	Y	Y
9 Kaptur	Y	Y	Y	Y	Y	Y
10 Kucinich	Y	Y	Y	Y	Y	Y
11 Fudge	Y	Y	Y	Y	Y	Y
12 **Tiberi**	Y	Y	Y	Y	Y	Y
13 Sutton	Y	Y	Y	Y	Y	Y
14 **LaTourette**	Y	Y	Y	Y	Y	Y
15 Kilroy	Y	Y	Y	Y	Y	Y
16 Boccieri	Y	Y	Y	Y	Y	Y
17 Ryan	Y	Y	Y	Y	Y	Y
18 Space	Y	Y	Y	Y	Y	Y
OKLAHOMA						
1 **Sullivan**	Y	Y	Y	Y	Y	Y
2 Boren	Y	Y	Y	Y	Y	?
3 **Lucas**	Y	Y	Y	Y	Y	Y
4 **Cole**	Y	Y	Y	Y	Y	?
5 **Fallin**	?	?	?	?	?	Y
OREGON						
1 Wu	Y	Y	Y	Y	Y	Y
2 **Walden**	Y	Y	Y	Y	Y	Y
3 Blumenauer	Y	Y	Y	Y	Y	Y
4 DeFazio	Y	Y	Y	P	Y	Y
5 Schrader	Y	Y	Y	Y	Y	Y
PENNSYLVANIA						
1 Brady	Y	Y	Y	Y	Y	Y
2 Fattah	Y	Y	Y	Y	Y	Y
3 Dahlkemper	Y	Y	Y	Y	Y	Y
4 Altmire	Y	Y	Y	Y	Y	Y
5 **Thompson**	Y	Y	Y	Y	Y	Y
6 **Gerlach**	Y	Y	Y	Y	Y	Y
7 Sestak	Y	Y	Y	Y	Y	Y
8 Murphy, P.	Y	Y	Y	Y	Y	Y
9 **Shuster**	Y	Y	Y	Y	Y	Y
10 Carney	Y	Y	Y	Y	Y	Y
11 Kanjorski	Y	Y	Y	Y	Y	Y
12 Critz	Y	Y	Y	Y	Y	Y
13 Schwartz	Y	Y	Y	Y	Y	Y
14 Doyle	Y	Y	Y	Y	Y	Y
15 **Dent**	Y	Y	Y	Y	Y	Y
16 **Pitts**	Y	Y	Y	Y	Y	Y
17 Holden	Y	Y	Y	Y	Y	Y
18 **Murphy, T.**	Y	Y	Y	Y	Y	Y
19 **Platts**	Y	Y	Y	Y	Y	Y
RHODE ISLAND						
1 Kennedy	Y	Y	?	Y	Y	Y
2 Langevin	Y	+	Y	Y	Y	Y
SOUTH CAROLINA						
1 **Brown**	Y	Y	Y	Y	Y	Y
2 **Wilson**	Y	Y	Y	Y	Y	Y
3 **Barrett**	?	?	?	?	?	?
4 **Inglis**	Y	Y	Y	Y	Y	Y
5 Spratt	Y	Y	Y	Y	Y	Y
6 Clyburn	Y	Y	Y	Y	Y	Y
SOUTH DAKOTA						
AL Herseth Sandlin	Y	Y	Y	Y	Y	Y
TENNESSEE						
1 **Roe**	Y	Y	Y	Y	Y	Y
2 **Duncan**	Y	Y	Y	Y	Y	Y
3 **Wamp**	?	?	?	?	?	Y
4 Davis	Y	Y	Y	Y	Y	Y
5 Cooper	Y	Y	Y	Y	Y	Y
6 Gordon	Y	Y	Y	Y	Y	Y
7 **Blackburn**	Y	Y	Y	Y	Y	Y
8 Tanner	Y	Y	Y	Y	Y	Y
9 Cohen	Y	Y	Y	Y	Y	Y

	297	298	299	300	301	302
TEXAS						
1 **Gohmert**	Y	Y	Y	Y	Y	?
2 **Poe**	Y	Y	Y	Y	Y	Y
3 **Johnson, S.**	Y	Y	Y	Y	Y	Y
4 **Hall**	Y	Y	Y	Y	Y	Y
5 **Hensarling**	Y	Y	Y	Y	Y	Y
6 **Barton**	Y	Y	Y	Y	Y	Y
7 **Culberson**	Y	Y	Y	Y	Y	?
8 **Brady**	Y	?	Y	Y	Y	Y
9 Green, A.	Y	Y	Y	Y	?	Y
10 **McCaul**	Y	Y	Y	Y	Y	Y
11 **Conaway**	Y	Y	Y	Y	Y	Y
12 **Granger**	Y	Y	Y	Y	Y	Y
13 **Thornberry**	Y	Y	Y	Y	Y	Y
14 **Paul**	N	Y	Y	Y	Y	Y
15 Hinojosa	?	Y	Y	Y	Y	Y
16 Reyes	Y	Y	Y	Y	Y	Y
17 Edwards	Y	Y	Y	Y	Y	Y
18 Jackson Lee	?	?	?	?	?	?
19 **Neugebauer**	Y	Y	Y	Y	Y	Y
20 Gonzalez	Y	Y	Y	Y	Y	Y
21 **Smith**	Y	Y	Y	Y	Y	Y
22 **Olson**	Y	Y	Y	Y	Y	Y
23 Rodriguez	Y	Y	Y	Y	Y	Y
24 **Marchant**	Y	Y	Y	Y	Y	Y
25 Doggett	Y	Y	Y	Y	Y	Y
26 **Burgess**	Y	Y	Y	Y	Y	Y
27 Ortiz	Y	Y	Y	Y	Y	Y
28 Cuellar	Y	Y	Y	Y	Y	Y
29 Green, G.	Y	Y	Y	Y	Y	Y
30 Johnson, E.	Y	Y	Y	Y	Y	Y
31 **Carter**	Y	Y	Y	Y	Y	Y
32 **Sessions**	Y	Y	Y	Y	Y	Y
UTAH						
1 **Bishop**	Y	?	Y	Y	Y	Y
2 Matheson	Y	Y	Y	Y	Y	Y
3 **Chaffetz**	Y	Y	Y	P	Y	Y
VERMONT						
AL Welch	Y	Y	Y	Y	Y	Y
VIRGINIA						
1 **Wittman**	Y	Y	Y	Y	Y	Y
2 Nye	Y	Y	Y	Y	Y	Y
3 Scott	Y	Y	Y	Y	Y	Y
4 **Forbes**	Y	Y	Y	Y	Y	Y
5 Perriello	Y	Y	Y	Y	Y	Y
6 **Goodlatte**	Y	Y	Y	Y	Y	Y
7 **Cantor**	Y	Y	Y	Y	Y	Y
8 Moran	Y	Y	Y	Y	Y	Y
9 Boucher	Y	Y	Y	Y	Y	Y
10 **Wolf**	?	?	?	?	?	Y
11 Connolly	Y	Y	Y	Y	Y	Y
WASHINGTON						
1 Inslee	Y	Y	Y	Y	Y	Y
2 Larsen	Y	Y	Y	Y	Y	Y
3 Baird	Y	Y	Y	Y	?	Y
4 **Hastings**	Y	Y	Y	Y	Y	Y
5 **McMorris Rodgers**	Y	Y	Y	Y	Y	Y
6 Dicks	Y	Y	Y	Y	Y	Y
7 McDermott	Y	Y	Y	Y	Y	Y
8 **Reichert**	Y	Y	Y	Y	Y	Y
9 Smith	Y	Y	Y	Y	Y	Y
WEST VIRGINIA						
1 Mollohan	Y	Y	Y	Y	?	Y
2 **Capito**	Y	Y	Y	Y	Y	Y
3 Rahall	Y	Y	Y	Y	Y	Y
WISCONSIN						
1 **Ryan**	?	?	?	?	?	?
2 Baldwin	Y	Y	Y	Y	Y	Y
3 Kind	Y	Y	Y	Y	Y	Y
4 Moore	Y	Y	Y	Y	Y	Y
5 **Sensenbrenner**	Y	Y	Y	Y	Y	Y
6 **Petri**	Y	?	?	?	?	?
7 Obey	Y	Y	Y	Y	Y	Y
8 Kagen	Y	Y	Y	Y	Y	Y
WYOMING						
AL **Lummis**	?	Y	Y	P	Y	Y
DELEGATES						
Faleomavaega (A.S.)						
Norton (D.C.)						
Bordallo (Guam)						
Sablan (N. Marianas)						
Pierluisi (P.R.)						
Christensen (V.I.)						

IN THE HOUSE | By Vote Number

303. **H Res 1385. Tribute to Military Members/Adoption.** Skelton, D-Mo., motion to suspend the rules and adopt the resolution that would recognize and honor current and former members of the armed forces and urge Americans to thank them for their service. Motion agreed to 414-0: D 245-0; R 169-0. A two-thirds majority of those present and voting (276 in this case) is required for adoption under suspension of the rules. May 26, 2010.

304. **H Res 1316. Tribute to Asian-Americans and Pacific Islanders/ Adoption.** Lynch, D-Mass., motion to suspend the rules and adopt the resolution that would recognize the Asian-American and Pacific Islander communities for their contributions to the United States. Motion agreed to 408-0: D 241-0; R 167-0. A two-thirds majority of those present and voting (272 in this case) is required for adoption under suspension of the rules. May 26, 2010.

305. **H Res 1169. Tribute to Rollins College/Adoption.** Bishop, D-N.Y., motion to suspend the rules and adopt the resolution that would recognize Rollins College on its 125th anniversary. Motion agreed to 371-36: D 239-0; R 132-36. A two-thirds majority of those present and voting (272 in this case) is required for adoption under suspension of the rules. May 26, 2010.

306. **H Con Res 282. Adjournment/Adoption.** Adoption of the concurrent resolution that would provide for the adjournment of the House until 2 p.m. Tuesday, June 8, 2010, and the Senate until noon Monday, June 7, 2010. Adopted 230-187: D 220-27; R 10-160. May 27, 2010.

307. **H Res 1404, HR 5136. Fiscal 2011 Defense Authorization/ Rule.** Adoption of the rule (H Res 1404) that would provide for House floor consideration of the bill that would authorize roughly $760 billion for defense programs, including $725.9 billion for fiscal 2011 and $33.7 billion for fiscal 2010. It also would waive, through the legislative day of June 1, 2010, the two-thirds majority requirement to consider a rule on the same day it is reported from the Rules Committee, and it would allow for consideration of measures under suspension of the rules at any time through Sunday, May 30, 2010. Adopted 241-178: D 240-11; R 1-167. May 27, 2010.

308. **H Res 1161. Women at Marquette University/Adoption.** Bishop, D-N.Y., motion to suspend the rules and adopt the resolution that would honor the Centennial Celebration of Women at Marquette University, the first Catholic university to offer education for men and women. Motion agreed to 380-0: D 212-0; R 168-0. A two-thirds majority of those present and voting (254 in this case) is required for adoption under suspension of the rules. May 27, 2010.

309. **H Res 1372. Tribute to University of Georgia Graduate School/ Adoption.** Bishop, D-N.Y., motion to suspend the rules and adopt the resolution that would recognize the 100th anniversary of the founding of the University of Georgia Graduate School. Motion agreed to 412-0: D 245-0; R 167-0. A two-thirds majority of those present and voting (275 in this case) is required for adoption under suspension of the rules. May 27, 2010.

	303	304	305	306	307	308	309
ALABAMA							
1 **Bonner**	Y	Y	Y	N	N	Y	Y
2 Bright	Y	Y	Y	N	N	Y	Y
3 **Rogers**	Y	Y	?	N	N	Y	Y
4 **Aderholt**	Y	Y	Y	N	N	Y	Y
5 **Griffith**	Y	Y	Y	N	N	Y	Y
6 **Bachus**	Y	Y	Y	N	N	Y	Y
7 Davis	?	?	?	?	?	?	?
ALASKA							
AL **Young**	Y	Y	N	N	N	Y	Y
ARIZONA							
1 Kirkpatrick	Y	Y	Y	Y	N	P	Y
2 **Franks**	Y	Y	Y	N	N	Y	Y
3 **Shadegg**	Y	Y	N	N	Y	Y	Y
4 Pastor	Y	Y	Y	Y	Y	Y	Y
5 Mitchell	Y	Y	Y	N	N	Y	Y
6 **Flake**	Y	?	Y	N	N	Y	Y
7 Grijalva	Y	Y	Y	Y	Y	Y	Y
8 Giffords	Y	Y	Y	Y	Y	P	Y
ARKANSAS							
1 Berry	Y	Y	Y	Y	Y	Y	Y
2 Snyder	Y	Y	Y	Y	Y	Y	Y
3 **Boozman**	Y	Y	Y	N	N	Y	Y
4 Ross	Y	Y	Y	Y	Y	Y	Y
CALIFORNIA							
1 Thompson	Y	Y	Y	Y	Y	Y	Y
2 **Herger**	Y	Y	N	N	N	Y	Y
3 **Lungren**	Y	Y	Y	N	N	Y	Y
4 **McClintock**	?	?	?	N	N	Y	Y
5 Matsui	Y	Y	Y	Y	Y	Y	Y
6 Woolsey	Y	Y	Y	Y	P	P	Y
7 Miller, George	Y	Y	Y	Y	P	P	Y
8 Pelosi							
9 Lee	Y	Y	Y	Y	P	P	Y
10 Garamendi	Y	Y	Y	Y	Y	Y	Y
11 McNerney	Y	Y	Y	Y	Y	Y	Y
12 Speier	Y	?	Y	Y	Y	Y	Y
13 Stark	Y	Y	Y	Y	N	P	Y
14 Eshoo	Y	Y	Y	Y	P	P	Y
15 Honda	Y	Y	Y	Y	P	P	Y
16 Lofgren	Y	Y	Y	Y	P	P	Y
17 Farr	Y	Y	Y	Y	P	P	Y
18 Cardoza	Y	Y	Y	Y	Y	Y	Y
19 **Radanovich**	Y	Y	Y	N	N	Y	Y
20 Costa	Y	Y	Y	Y	Y	Y	Y
21 **Nunes**	Y	Y	Y	N	N	Y	Y
22 **McCarthy**	Y	Y	Y	N	N	Y	Y
23 Capps	Y	Y	Y	Y	Y	Y	Y
24 **Gallegly**	Y	Y	Y	N	N	Y	Y
25 **McKeon**	Y	Y	Y	N	N	Y	Y
26 **Dreier**	Y	Y	Y	N	N	Y	Y
27 Sherman	Y	Y	Y	Y	Y	Y	Y
28 Berman	Y	Y	Y	Y	Y	Y	?
29 Schiff	Y	Y	Y	Y	Y	Y	Y
30 Waxman	Y	Y	Y	Y	Y	Y	Y
31 Becerra	?	?	?	Y	Y	Y	Y
32 Chu	Y	Y	Y	Y	Y	Y	Y
33 Watson	Y	Y	Y	Y	Y	Y	Y
34 Roybal-Allard	Y	Y	Y	Y	Y	Y	Y
35 Waters	Y	Y	Y	Y	Y	Y	Y
36 Harman	Y	Y	Y	Y	Y	Y	Y
37 Richardson	Y	?	Y	Y	Y	Y	Y
38 Napolitano	Y	Y	Y	Y	Y	Y	Y
39 Sánchez, Linda	Y	Y	Y	Y	P	Y	Y
40 **Royce**	Y	Y	Y	N	N	Y	Y
41 **Lewis**	Y	Y	Y	N	N	Y	Y
42 **Miller, Gary**	Y	Y	Y	N	N	Y	Y
43 Baca	Y	Y	Y	Y	Y	Y	Y
44 **Calvert**	Y	Y	Y	N	N	Y	Y
45 **Bono Mack**	Y	Y	Y	N	N	Y	Y
46 **Rohrabacher**	Y	Y	N	N	N	Y	Y
47 Sanchez, Loretta	Y	Y	Y	Y	Y	Y	Y
48 **Campbell**	Y	Y	Y	N	N	Y	Y
49 **Issa**	Y	Y	N	N	N	Y	Y
50 **Bilbray**	Y	?	Y	N	N	Y	Y
51 Filner	Y	Y	Y	Y	Y	Y	Y
52 **Hunter**	Y	Y	N	N	N	Y	Y
53 Davis	Y	Y	Y	Y	Y	Y	Y

	303	304	305	306	307	308	309
COLORADO							
1 DeGette	Y	Y	Y	Y	Y	Y	Y
2 Polis	Y	Y	Y	Y	Y	Y	Y
3 Salazar	Y	Y	Y	Y	N	Y	Y
4 Markey	Y	Y	Y	N	Y	Y	Y
5 **Lamborn**	Y	Y	N	N	N	Y	Y
6 **Coffman**	Y	Y	N	N	N	Y	Y
7 Perlmutter	Y	Y	Y	Y	Y	Y	Y
CONNECTICUT							
1 Larson	Y	Y	Y	Y	Y	Y	Y
2 Courtney	Y	Y	Y	Y	Y	Y	Y
3 DeLauro	Y	Y	Y	Y	Y	Y	Y
4 Himes	Y	Y	Y	Y	Y	Y	Y
5 Murphy	Y	Y	Y	Y	Y	Y	Y
DELAWARE							
AL **Castle**	Y	Y	Y	Y	N	Y	Y
FLORIDA							
1 **Miller**	Y	Y	Y	N	N	Y	Y
2 Boyd	Y	Y	Y	N	N	Y	Y
3 Brown	?	?	?	Y	Y	Y	Y
4 **Crenshaw**	Y	Y	Y	N	N	Y	Y
5 **Brown-Waite**	Y	?	?	?	?	?	?
6 **Stearns**	Y	Y	Y	N	N	Y	Y
7 **Mica**	Y	Y	Y	N	N	Y	Y
8 Grayson	Y	Y	N	N	N	Y	Y
9 **Bilirakis**	Y	Y	Y	N	N	Y	Y
10 **Young**	Y	Y	Y	?	?	?	?
11 Castor	Y	Y	Y	Y	Y	Y	Y
12 **Putnam**	Y	Y	Y	N	N	Y	Y
13 **Buchanan**	Y	Y	Y	N	N	Y	Y
14 **Mack**	Y	Y	N	N	N	Y	Y
15 **Posey**	Y	Y	Y	N	N	Y	Y
16 **Rooney**	Y	Y	Y	N	N	Y	Y
17 Meek	Y	Y	Y	Y	Y	Y	Y
18 **Ros-Lehtinen**	Y	Y	Y	N	N	Y	Y
19 Deutch	Y	Y	Y	Y	Y	Y	Y
20 Wasserman Schultz	Y	Y	Y	Y	P	Y	Y
21 **Diaz-Balart, L.**	Y	Y	Y	N	N	?	?
22 Klein	Y	Y	Y	Y	Y	Y	Y
23 Hastings	Y	Y	Y	Y	Y	Y	Y
24 Kosmas	Y	Y	Y	N	Y	Y	Y
25 **Diaz-Balart, M.**	Y	Y	Y	N	N	Y	Y
GEORGIA							
1 **Kingston**	Y	Y	N	N	N	Y	Y
2 Bishop	Y	Y	Y	Y	Y	Y	Y
3 **Westmoreland**	Y	Y	N	N	N	Y	Y
4 Johnson	Y	Y	Y	Y	Y	Y	?
5 Lewis	Y	Y	Y	?	Y	Y	Y
6 **Price**	Y	?	Y	N	N	Y	Y
7 **Linder**	Y	Y	Y	N	N	Y	Y
8 Marshall	Y	Y	Y	Y	Y	Y	Y
9 Vacant							
10 **Broun**	Y	Y	N	N	N	Y	Y
11 **Gingrey**	Y	Y	N	N	N	Y	Y
12 Barrow	Y	Y	Y	Y	Y	Y	Y
13 Scott	Y	Y	Y	Y	Y	Y	Y
HAWAII							
1 **Djou**	Y	Y	Y	N	N	Y	Y
2 Hirono	Y	Y	Y	Y	Y	Y	Y
IDAHO							
1 Minnick	Y	Y	N	Y	N	Y	Y
2 **Simpson**	Y	Y	N	N	N	Y	Y
ILLINOIS							
1 Rush	Y	Y	Y	?	Y	Y	Y
2 Jackson	Y	Y	Y	Y	Y	Y	Y
3 Lipinski	Y	Y	Y	Y	Y	Y	Y
4 Gutierrez	Y	?	?	Y	Y	Y	Y
5 Quigley	Y	Y	Y	Y	Y	Y	Y
6 **Roskam**	Y	Y	Y	N	N	Y	Y
7 Davis	Y	Y	Y	Y	Y	Y	Y
8 Bean	Y	Y	Y	Y	Y	Y	Y
9 Schakowsky	Y	Y	Y	Y	Y	Y	Y
10 **Kirk**	Y	Y	Y	N	N	Y	Y
11 Halvorson	Y	Y	Y	Y	Y	Y	Y
12 Costello	Y	Y	Y	Y	Y	Y	Y
13 **Biggert**	Y	Y	Y	N	N	Y	Y
14 Foster	Y	Y	Y	Y	Y	Y	Y
15 **Johnson**	Y	Y	N	Y	N	Y	Y

KEY   **Republicans**   Democrats

Y Voted for (yea)	X Paired against	C Voted "present" to avoid possible conflict of interest
# Paired for	– Announced against	
+ Announced for	P Voted "present"	? Did not vote or otherwise make a position known
N Voted against (nay)		

	303	304	305	306	307	308	309
16 **Manzullo**	Y	Y	Y	N	N	Y	Y
17 Hare	Y	Y	Y	Y	Y	P	Y
18 **Schock**	Y	Y	N	N	N	Y	Y
19 **Shimkus**	Y	Y	Y	N	N	Y	Y
INDIANA							
1 Visclosky	Y	Y	Y	Y	Y	Y	Y
2 Donnelly	Y	Y	Y	N	Y	Y	Y
3 Vacant							
4 **Buyer**	Y	Y	Y	N	N	?	Y
5 **Burton**	Y	Y	N	N	N	Y	Y
6 **Pence**	Y	Y	Y	N	N	Y	Y
7 Carson	Y	Y	Y	Y	Y	Y	Y
8 Ellsworth	Y	Y	Y	N	Y	Y	Y
9 Hill	Y	Y	Y	Y	N	Y	Y
IOWA							
1 Braley	Y	Y	Y	Y	Y	Y	Y
2 Loebsack	Y	Y	Y	Y	Y	Y	Y
3 Boswell	Y	Y	Y	Y	Y	Y	Y
4 **Latham**	Y	Y	Y	N	N	Y	Y
5 **King**	Y	Y	N	N	N	Y	Y
KANSAS							
1 **Moran**	Y	Y	Y	N	N	Y	Y
2 **Jenkins**	Y	Y	Y	N	N	Y	Y
3 Moore	Y	Y	Y	?	Y	Y	Y
4 **Tiahrt**	+	Y	Y	N	N	Y	Y
KENTUCKY							
1 **Whitfield**	Y	Y	Y	N	N	Y	Y
2 **Guthrie**	Y	Y	Y	N	N	Y	Y
3 Yarmuth	Y	Y	Y	Y	Y	Y	Y
4 **Davis**	Y	Y	Y	?	?	?	?
5 **Rogers**	Y	Y	N	N	N	Y	Y
6 Chandler	Y	Y	Y	Y	Y	Y	Y
LOUISIANA							
1 **Scalise**	Y	Y	N	N	N	Y	Y
2 **Cao**	Y	Y	N	N	N	Y	Y
3 Melancon	Y	Y	Y	Y	Y	?	?
4 **Fleming**	Y	Y	N	N	N	Y	Y
5 **Alexander**	Y	Y	Y	N	N	Y	Y
6 **Cassidy**	Y	Y	N	N	N	Y	Y
7 **Boustany**	Y	Y	N	N	N	Y	Y
MAINE							
1 Pingree	Y	Y	Y	Y	Y	P	Y
2 Michaud	Y	Y	Y	N	Y	Y	Y
MARYLAND							
1 Kratovil	Y	Y	Y	N	Y	Y	Y
2 Ruppersberger	Y	Y	Y	Y	Y	Y	Y
3 Sarbanes	Y	Y	Y	Y	Y	P	Y
4 Edwards	Y	Y	Y	Y	Y	Y	Y
5 Hoyer	Y	Y	Y	Y	Y	Y	Y
6 **Bartlett**	Y	Y	Y	N	N	Y	Y
7 Cummings	Y	Y	Y	Y	Y	Y	Y
8 Van Hollen	Y	Y	Y	Y	Y	Y	Y
MASSACHUSETTS							
1 Olver	Y	Y	Y	Y	Y	P	Y
2 Neal	Y	Y	Y	Y	Y	Y	Y
3 McGovern	Y	Y	Y	Y	Y	P	Y
4 Frank	Y	Y	?	Y	Y	Y	Y
5 Tsongas	Y	Y	Y	Y	Y	P	Y
6 Tierney	Y	Y	Y	Y	Y	P	?
7 Markey	Y	Y	Y	Y	Y	Y	Y
8 Capuano	Y	Y	Y	Y	Y	P	Y
9 Lynch	Y	Y	Y	?	Y	Y	Y
10 Delahunt	Y	Y	Y	Y	Y	P	Y
MICHIGAN							
1 Stupak	Y	Y	Y	Y	Y	Y	Y
2 **Hoekstra**	?	?	?	?	?	?	?
3 **Ehlers**	Y	Y	?	Y	N	Y	Y
4 **Camp**	Y	Y	Y	N	N	Y	Y
5 Kildee	Y	Y	Y	Y	Y	Y	Y
6 **Upton**	Y	Y	Y	N	N	Y	Y
7 Schauer	Y	Y	Y	N	Y	Y	Y
8 **Rogers**	Y	Y	Y	N	N	Y	Y
9 Peters	Y	Y	Y	N	Y	P	Y
10 **Miller**	Y	Y	Y	N	N	Y	Y
11 **McCotter**	Y	Y	Y	N	N	Y	Y
12 Levin	Y	Y	Y	Y	Y	Y	Y
13 Kilpatrick	+	+	+	Y	Y	Y	Y
14 Conyers	?	?	+	Y	Y	Y	Y
15 Dingell	Y	Y	Y	Y	Y	Y	Y
MINNESOTA							
1 Walz	Y	Y	Y	Y	Y	P	Y
2 **Kline**	Y	Y	Y	N	N	Y	Y
3 **Paulsen**	Y	Y	Y	N	N	Y	Y
4 McCollum	Y	Y	Y	Y	Y	P	Y
5 Ellison	Y	Y	Y	Y	Y	Y	Y
6 **Bachmann**	Y	Y	Y	N	N	Y	Y
7 Peterson	Y	Y	Y	Y	Y	Y	Y
8 Oberstar	Y	Y	Y	Y	Y	Y	Y
MISSISSIPPI							
1 Childers	Y	Y	Y	N	Y	?	Y
2 Thompson	Y	Y	Y	Y	Y	Y	Y
3 **Harper**	Y	Y	Y	N	N	Y	Y
4 Taylor	Y	Y	Y	N	N	Y	Y
MISSOURI							
1 Clay	Y	Y	Y	Y	Y	Y	Y
2 **Akin**	Y	Y	N	N	N	Y	?
3 Carnahan	Y	Y	Y	Y	Y	Y	Y
4 Skelton	Y	Y	Y	Y	Y	Y	Y
5 Cleaver	Y	Y	Y	Y	Y	Y	Y
6 **Graves**	?	?	?	?	?	?	?
7 **Blunt**	Y	Y	Y	N	N	Y	Y
8 **Emerson**	Y	Y	N	N	N	Y	Y
9 **Luetkemeyer**	Y	Y	N	N	N	Y	Y
MONTANA							
AL **Rehberg**	Y	Y	Y	N	N	Y	Y
NEBRASKA							
1 **Fortenberry**	Y	Y	Y	N	?	Y	Y
2 **Terry**	Y	Y	Y	N	N	Y	Y
3 **Smith**	Y	Y	Y	N	N	Y	Y
NEVADA							
1 Berkley	Y	Y	Y	Y	Y	Y	Y
2 **Heller**	Y	Y	Y	Y	N	Y	Y
3 Titus	Y	Y	Y	Y	Y	Y	Y
NEW HAMPSHIRE							
1 Shea-Porter	Y	Y	Y	Y	Y	Y	Y
2 Hodes	Y	Y	Y	Y	Y	P	Y
NEW JERSEY							
1 Andrews	?	?	?	Y	Y	Y	Y
2 **LoBiondo**	Y	Y	Y	N	N	Y	Y
3 Adler	Y	Y	Y	N	Y	Y	Y
4 **Smith**	Y	Y	Y	N	N	Y	Y
5 **Garrett**	Y	Y	Y	N	N	Y	Y
6 Pallone	Y	Y	Y	Y	Y	Y	Y
7 **Lance**	Y	Y	Y	N	N	Y	Y
8 Pascrell	Y	Y	Y	?	?	?	?
9 Rothman	Y	Y	Y	Y	Y	Y	Y
10 Payne	Y	Y	Y	Y	Y	Y	Y
11 **Frelinghuysen**	Y	Y	Y	N	N	Y	Y
12 Holt	Y	Y	Y	Y	Y	Y	Y
13 Sires	Y	Y	Y	Y	Y	Y	Y
NEW MEXICO							
1 Heinrich	Y	Y	Y	Y	Y	Y	Y
2 Teague	Y	Y	Y	Y	Y	Y	?
3 Luján	Y	Y	Y	Y	Y	Y	Y
NEW YORK							
1 Bishop	Y	Y	Y	N	Y	Y	Y
2 Israel	Y	Y	Y	Y	Y	Y	Y
3 **King**	Y	Y	Y	N	N	Y	Y
4 McCarthy	Y	Y	Y	Y	Y	Y	Y
5 Ackerman	Y	Y	Y	Y	Y	Y	Y
6 Meeks	Y	Y	Y	Y	Y	Y	Y
7 Crowley	Y	Y	Y	Y	Y	Y	Y
8 Nadler	Y	Y	Y	Y	Y	P	Y
9 Weiner	Y	Y	Y	Y	Y	P	Y
10 Towns	Y	Y	?	Y	Y	Y	Y
11 Clarke	Y	Y	Y	Y	Y	Y	Y
12 Velázquez	Y	Y	Y	Y	Y	Y	Y
13 McMahon	Y	Y	Y	N	Y	Y	Y
14 Maloney	?	?	?	Y	Y	Y	Y
15 Rangel	Y	Y	Y	Y	Y	Y	Y
16 Serrano	Y	Y	Y	Y	Y	Y	Y
17 Engel	Y	Y	Y	Y	Y	Y	Y
18 Lowey	Y	Y	Y	Y	Y	Y	Y
19 Hall	Y	Y	Y	Y	Y	P	Y
20 Murphy	Y	Y	Y	Y	Y	Y	Y
21 Tonko	Y	Y	Y	Y	Y	Y	Y
22 Hinchey	Y	Y	Y	Y	Y	Y	Y
23 Owens	Y	Y	Y	Y	Y	Y	Y
24 Arcuri	Y	Y	Y	Y	Y	?	Y
25 Maffei	Y	Y	Y	Y	Y	Y	Y
26 **Lee**	Y	Y	N	N	N	Y	Y
27 Higgins	Y	Y	Y	Y	Y	Y	Y
28 Slaughter	Y	Y	Y	Y	Y	Y	Y
29 Vacant							
NORTH CAROLINA							
1 Butterfield	Y	Y	Y	Y	Y	Y	Y
2 Etheridge	Y	Y	Y	Y	Y	Y	Y
3 **Jones**	Y	Y	Y	Y	N	Y	Y
4 Price	Y	Y	Y	Y	Y	Y	
5 **Foxx**	Y	Y	Y	N	N	Y	Y
6 **Coble**	Y	Y	Y	N	N	Y	Y
7 McIntyre	Y	Y	Y	Y	Y	Y	Y
8 Kissell	Y	Y	Y	Y	Y	Y	Y
9 **Myrick**	Y	Y	N	N	N	Y	Y
10 **McHenry**	Y	Y	N	N	N	Y	Y
11 Shuler	Y	Y	Y	Y	N	Y	Y
12 Watt	Y	Y	Y	Y	Y	Y	Y
13 Miller	Y	Y	Y	Y	Y	Y	Y
NORTH DAKOTA							
AL Pomeroy	Y	Y	Y	Y	Y	Y	Y
OHIO							
1 Driehaus	Y	Y	Y	N	N	Y	Y
2 **Schmidt**	Y	Y	N	N	N	Y	Y
3 **Turner**	Y	Y	Y	N	N	Y	Y
4 **Jordan**	Y	Y	Y	N	N	Y	Y
5 **Latta**	Y	Y	Y	N	N	Y	Y
6 Wilson	Y	Y	Y	Y	Y	Y	Y
7 **Austria**	Y	Y	Y	N	N	Y	Y
8 **Boehner**	Y	Y	Y	N	N	Y	Y
9 Kaptur	Y	Y	Y	Y	Y	Y	Y
10 Kucinich	Y	Y	Y	Y	N	P	Y
11 Fudge	Y	Y	Y	Y	Y	Y	Y
12 **Tiberi**	Y	Y	Y	N	N	Y	Y
13 Sutton	Y	Y	Y	Y	Y	P	Y
14 **LaTourette**	Y	Y	Y	N	N	Y	Y
15 Kilroy	Y	Y	Y	N	Y	P	Y
16 Boccieri	Y	Y	Y	Y	Y	Y	Y
17 Ryan	Y	Y	Y	Y	Y	Y	Y
18 Space	Y	Y	Y	N	Y	Y	Y
OKLAHOMA							
1 **Sullivan**	Y	Y	Y	N	N	Y	Y
2 Boren	?	?	?	?	?	?	?
3 **Lucas**	Y	Y	Y	N	N	Y	Y
4 **Cole**	Y	Y	Y	N	N	Y	Y
5 **Fallin**	Y	Y	Y	N	N	Y	Y
OREGON							
1 Wu	Y	Y	Y	Y	Y	Y	Y
2 **Walden**	Y	Y	Y	N	N	Y	Y
3 Blumenauer	Y	Y	Y	Y	Y	P	Y
4 DeFazio	Y	Y	Y	Y	Y	Y	Y
5 Schrader	Y	Y	Y	Y	Y	Y	Y
PENNSYLVANIA							
1 Brady	Y	Y	Y	Y	Y	Y	Y
2 Fattah	Y	Y	Y	Y	Y	Y	Y
3 Dahlkemper	Y	Y	Y	N	Y	Y	Y
4 Altmire	Y	Y	Y	N	Y	Y	Y
5 **Thompson**	Y	Y	Y	N	N	Y	Y
6 **Gerlach**	Y	Y	Y	N	N	Y	Y
7 Sestak	Y	Y	Y	N	Y	Y	Y
8 Murphy, P.	Y	Y	Y	Y	Y	Y	Y
9 **Shuster**	Y	Y	Y	N	N	Y	Y
10 Carney	Y	Y	Y	N	Y	Y	Y
11 Kanjorski	Y	Y	Y	Y	Y	Y	Y
12 Critz	Y	Y	Y	Y	Y	Y	Y
13 Schwartz	Y	Y	Y	Y	Y	Y	Y
14 Doyle	Y	Y	Y	Y	Y	Y	Y
15 **Dent**	Y	Y	Y	N	N	Y	Y
16 **Pitts**	Y	Y	Y	N	N	Y	Y
17 Holden	Y	Y	Y	Y	Y	Y	Y
18 **Murphy, T.**	Y	Y	Y	N	N	Y	Y
19 **Platts**	Y	Y	Y	N	N	Y	Y
RHODE ISLAND							
1 Kennedy	Y	Y	Y	Y	Y	P	Y
2 Langevin	Y	Y	Y	Y	Y	Y	Y
SOUTH CAROLINA							
1 **Brown**	Y	Y	Y	N	N	Y	Y
2 **Wilson**	Y	Y	N	N	N	Y	Y
3 **Barrett**	?	?	?	?	?	?	?
4 **Inglis**	Y	Y	Y	N	N	Y	Y
5 Spratt	Y	Y	Y	Y	Y	Y	Y
6 Clyburn	Y	Y	Y	Y	Y	Y	Y
SOUTH DAKOTA							
AL Herseth Sandlin	Y	Y	Y	Y	Y	Y	Y
TENNESSEE							
1 **Roe**	Y	Y	Y	N	N	Y	Y
2 **Duncan**	Y	Y	Y	N	N	Y	Y
3 **Wamp**	Y	Y	Y	N	N	Y	Y
4 Davis	Y	Y	Y	Y	Y	Y	Y
5 Cooper	Y	Y	Y	Y	Y	Y	Y
6 Gordon	Y	Y	Y	Y	Y	Y	Y
7 **Blackburn**	Y	Y	Y	N	?	Y	Y
8 Tanner	Y	Y	Y	Y	Y	Y	Y
9 Cohen	Y	Y	Y	Y	Y	Y	Y
TEXAS							
1 **Gohmert**	Y	Y	Y	Y	N	Y	Y
2 **Poe**	Y	Y	Y	N	N	Y	Y
3 **Johnson, S.**	Y	Y	N	N	N	Y	Y
4 **Hall**	Y	Y	N	N	N	Y	Y
5 **Hensarling**	Y	Y	N	N	N	Y	Y
6 **Barton**	Y	Y	Y	N	N	Y	Y
7 **Culberson**	?	Y	Y	N	N	Y	Y
8 **Brady**	Y	Y	Y	N	N	Y	Y
9 Green, A.	Y	Y	Y	Y	Y	Y	Y
10 **McCaul**	Y	Y	Y	N	N	Y	?
11 **Conaway**	Y	Y	Y	N	N	Y	Y
12 **Granger**	Y	Y	N	N	N	Y	Y
13 **Thornberry**	Y	Y	Y	N	N	Y	Y
14 **Paul**	Y	Y	Y	Y	N	Y	Y
15 Hinojosa	Y	Y	Y	Y	Y	Y	Y
16 Reyes	Y	Y	Y	Y	Y	Y	Y
17 Edwards	Y	Y	?	Y	Y	Y	Y
18 Jackson Lee	?	?	?	Y	Y	Y	Y
19 **Neugebauer**	Y	Y	N	N	N	Y	Y
20 Gonzalez	Y	Y	Y	Y	Y	Y	Y
21 **Smith**	Y	Y	Y	N	N	Y	Y
22 **Olson**	Y	Y	Y	Y	N	Y	Y
23 Rodriguez	Y	Y	Y	Y	Y	Y	Y
24 **Marchant**	Y	Y	Y	N	N	Y	Y
25 Doggett	Y	Y	Y	Y	Y	Y	Y
26 **Burgess**	Y	Y	Y	N	N	Y	Y
27 Ortiz	Y	Y	Y	Y	Y	Y	Y
28 Cuellar	Y	?	Y	Y	Y	Y	Y
29 Green, G.	Y	Y	Y	Y	Y	Y	Y
30 Johnson, E.	Y	Y	Y	Y	Y	Y	Y
31 **Carter**	Y	Y	N	N	N	Y	Y
32 **Sessions**	Y	Y	Y	N	N	Y	Y
UTAH							
1 **Bishop**	Y	Y	Y	N	N	Y	Y
2 Matheson	Y	Y	Y	Y	Y	Y	Y
3 **Chaffetz**	Y	Y	Y	Y	N	Y	Y
VERMONT							
AL Welch	Y	Y	Y	Y	Y	Y	Y
VIRGINIA							
1 **Wittman**	Y	Y	Y	N	N	Y	Y
2 Nye	Y	Y	Y	N	Y	Y	Y
3 Scott	Y	Y	?	Y	Y	Y	Y
4 **Forbes**	Y	Y	Y	N	N	Y	Y
5 Perriello	Y	Y	Y	N	Y	Y	Y
6 **Goodlatte**	Y	Y	Y	N	N	Y	Y
7 **Cantor**	Y	Y	Y	N	N	Y	Y
8 Moran	Y	Y	Y	Y	Y	Y	Y
9 Boucher	Y	Y	Y	Y	Y	Y	Y
10 **Wolf**	Y	Y	Y	N	N	Y	Y
11 Connolly	Y	Y	Y	Y	Y	Y	Y
WASHINGTON							
1 Inslee	Y	Y	Y	Y	Y	Y	Y
2 Larsen	Y	Y	Y	Y	Y	Y	Y
3 Baird	Y	?	?	Y	Y	Y	Y
4 **Hastings**	Y	Y	Y	N	N	Y	Y
5 **McMorris Rodgers**	Y	Y	Y	N	N	Y	Y
6 Dicks	Y	Y	Y	Y	Y	Y	Y
7 McDermott	Y	Y	Y	Y	Y	P	Y
8 **Reichert**	Y	Y	Y	N	N	Y	Y
9 Smith	Y	Y	Y	Y	Y	Y	Y
WEST VIRGINIA							
1 Mollohan	Y	Y	Y	Y	Y	Y	Y
2 **Capito**	Y	Y	Y	N	N	Y	Y
3 Rahall	Y	Y	Y	Y	Y	Y	Y
WISCONSIN							
1 **Ryan**	?	?	?	?	?	?	?
2 Baldwin	Y	Y	Y	Y	Y	P	Y
3 Kind	Y	Y	Y	Y	Y	Y	Y
4 Moore	Y	Y	Y	Y	Y	Y	Y
5 **Sensenbrenner**	Y	Y	Y	N	N	Y	Y
6 **Petri**	?	?	?	N	N	Y	Y
7 Obey	Y	Y	Y	N	Y	P	P
8 Kagen	Y	Y	Y	Y	Y	Y	Y
WYOMING							
AL **Lummis**	Y	Y	Y	Y	N	Y	Y
DELEGATES							
Faleomavaega (A.S.)							
Norton (D.C.)							
Bordallo (Guam)							
Sablan (N. Marianas)							
Pierluisi (P.R.)							
Christensen (V.I.)							

IN THE HOUSE | By Vote Number

310. **HR 5136. Fiscal 2011 Defense Authorization/Manager's Amendment.** Skelton, D-Mo., amendment that would make a number of technical changes. Adopted in Committee of the Whole 421-0: D 249-0; R 172-0. May 27, 2010.

311. **HR 5136. Fiscal 2011 Defense Authorization/Fire-Resistant Equipment for National Guard.** Marshall, D-Ga., amendment that would express the sense of Congress that the chief of the National Guard Bureau should issue fire-resistant utility ensembles to National Guard personnel who are engaged, or likely to become engaged, in defense support to civil authority missions, such as wildfire recovery efforts, that routinely involve serious fire hazards. Adopted in Committee of the Whole 423-0: D 252-0; R 171-0. May 27, 2010.

312. **HR 5136. Fiscal 2011 Defense Authorization/Effect of Hunger on Recruitment.** McGovern, D-Mass., amendment that would express the sense of Congress that hunger and obesity are impairing military recruitment and must be appropriately addressed. Adopted in Committee of the Whole 341-85: D 254-0; R 87-85. May 27, 2010.

313. **HR 5136. Fiscal 2011 Defense Authorization/Aerial Tanker Program.** Inslee, D-Wash., amendment that would require the Department of Defense to take into consideration during any aerial tanker replacement program any unfair competitive advantage a bidder may possess, and to report any such issues to congressional defense committees within 60 days of bid submissions. Adopted in Committee of the Whole 410-8: D 246-0; R 164-8. May 27, 2010.

314. **HR 5136. Fiscal 2011 Defense Authorization/Debarment of BP.** Gutierrez, D-Ill., amendment that would stipulate that, if the Defense secretary determines that BP or its subsidiaries performing any contracts with the department are no longer a "responsible source," the secretary would consider debarring BP or its subsidiaries from contracting with the department within 90 days. Adopted in Committee of the Whole 372-52: D 246-5; R 126-47. May 27, 2010.

	310	311	312	313	314
ALABAMA					
1 **Bonner**	Y	Y	Y	Y	Y
2 Bright	Y	Y	Y	Y	Y
3 **Rogers**	Y	Y	Y	Y	Y
4 **Aderholt**	Y	Y	Y	Y	Y
5 **Griffith**	Y	Y	N	Y	N
6 **Bachus**	Y	Y	N	Y	Y
7 Davis	?	?	?	?	?
ALASKA					
AL **Young**	Y	Y	N	Y	N
ARIZONA					
1 Kirkpatrick	Y	Y	Y	Y	Y
2 **Franks**	Y	Y	N	Y	N
3 **Shadegg**	Y	Y	N	N	N
4 Pastor	Y	Y	Y	Y	Y
5 Mitchell	Y	Y	Y	Y	Y
6 **Flake**	Y	Y	N	N	N
7 Grijalva	Y	Y	Y	Y	Y
8 Giffords	Y	Y	Y	Y	Y
ARKANSAS					
1 Berry	Y	Y	Y	Y	Y
2 Snyder	Y	Y	Y	Y	Y
3 **Boozman**	Y	Y	N	Y	Y
4 Ross	Y	Y	Y	Y	Y
CALIFORNIA					
1 Thompson	Y	Y	Y	Y	Y
2 **Herger**	?	?	N	N	N
3 **Lungren**	Y	Y	N	Y	Y
4 **McClintock**	Y	Y	N	N	Y
5 Matsui	Y	Y	Y	Y	Y
6 Woolsey	Y	Y	Y	Y	Y
7 Miller, George	Y	Y	Y	Y	Y
8 Pelosi					
9 Lee	Y	Y	Y	Y	Y
10 Garamendi	Y	Y	Y	Y	Y
11 McNerney	Y	Y	Y	Y	Y
12 Speier	Y	Y	Y	Y	Y
13 Stark	Y	Y	Y	Y	Y
14 Eshoo	Y	Y	Y	Y	Y
15 Honda	Y	Y	Y	Y	Y
16 Lofgren	Y	Y	Y	Y	Y
17 Farr	Y	Y	Y	Y	Y
18 Cardoza	Y	?	Y	Y	Y
19 **Radanovich**	Y	Y	Y	Y	Y
20 Costa	Y	Y	Y	?	Y
21 **Nunes**	Y	Y	N	Y	Y
22 **McCarthy**	Y	Y	N	Y	Y
23 Capps	Y	Y	Y	Y	Y
24 **Gallegly**	Y	Y	N	Y	Y
25 **McKeon**	Y	Y	Y	Y	Y
26 **Dreier**	Y	Y	Y	Y	Y
27 Sherman	Y	Y	Y	Y	Y
28 Berman	Y	Y	Y	Y	Y
29 Schiff	+	Y	Y	Y	Y
30 Waxman	Y	Y	Y	Y	Y
31 Becerra	Y	Y	Y	Y	Y
32 Chu	Y	Y	Y	Y	Y
33 Watson	Y	Y	Y	Y	Y
34 Roybal-Allard	Y	Y	Y	Y	Y
35 Waters	Y	Y	Y	Y	Y
36 Harman	Y	Y	Y	Y	Y
37 Richardson	Y	Y	?	Y	Y
38 Napolitano	Y	Y	Y	Y	Y
39 Sánchez, Linda	Y	Y	Y	Y	Y
40 **Royce**	Y	Y	N	Y	Y
41 **Lewis**	Y	Y	N	Y	Y
42 **Miller, Gary**	Y	Y	N	Y	Y
43 Baca	Y	Y	Y	Y	Y
44 **Calvert**	Y	Y	N	Y	Y
45 **Bono Mack**	Y	Y	Y	Y	Y
46 **Rohrabacher**	Y	Y	N	Y	Y
47 Sanchez, Loretta	Y	Y	Y	Y	Y
48 **Campbell**	Y	Y	N	N	N
49 **Issa**	Y	Y	N	Y	N
50 **Bilbray**	Y	Y	Y	Y	Y
51 Filner	Y	Y	Y	Y	Y
52 **Hunter**	Y	Y	N	Y	Y
53 Davis	Y	Y	Y	Y	Y

	310	311	312	313	314
COLORADO					
1 DeGette	Y	Y	Y	Y	Y
2 Polis	Y	Y	Y	Y	Y
3 Salazar	Y	Y	Y	Y	Y
4 Markey	Y	Y	Y	Y	Y
5 **Lamborn**	Y	Y	N	Y	N
6 **Coffman**	Y	Y	Y	Y	Y
7 Perlmutter	Y	Y	Y	Y	Y
CONNECTICUT					
1 Larson	Y	Y	Y	Y	Y
2 Courtney	Y	Y	Y	Y	Y
3 DeLauro	Y	Y	Y	Y	Y
4 Himes	Y	Y	Y	Y	Y
5 Murphy	Y	Y	Y	Y	Y
DELAWARE					
AL **Castle**	Y	Y	Y	Y	Y
FLORIDA					
1 **Miller**	Y	Y	N	Y	Y
2 Boyd	Y	Y	Y	Y	Y
3 Brown	Y	Y	Y	Y	Y
4 **Crenshaw**	Y	Y	Y	Y	Y
5 **Brown-Waite**	?	?	?	?	?
6 **Stearns**	Y	Y	N	Y	Y
7 **Mica**	Y	Y	N	Y	Y
8 Grayson	Y	Y	Y	Y	Y
9 **Bilirakis**	Y	Y	Y	Y	Y
10 **Young**	Y	Y	Y	Y	Y
11 Castor	Y	Y	Y	Y	Y
12 **Putnam**	Y	Y	Y	Y	Y
13 **Buchanan**	Y	Y	Y	Y	Y
14 **Mack**	Y	Y	N	Y	Y
15 **Posey**	Y	Y	N	Y	Y
16 **Rooney**	Y	Y	N	Y	N
17 Meek	Y	Y	Y	Y	Y
18 **Ros-Lehtinen**	Y	Y	Y	Y	Y
19 Deutch	?	?	Y	Y	Y
20 Wasserman Schultz	Y	Y	Y	Y	Y
21 **Diaz-Balart, L.**	Y	Y	Y	Y	Y
22 Klein	Y	Y	?	Y	Y
23 Hastings	Y	Y	Y	?	?
24 Kosmas	Y	Y	Y	Y	Y
25 **Diaz-Balart, M.**	Y	Y	Y	Y	Y
GEORGIA					
1 **Kingston**	Y	Y	N	Y	Y
2 Bishop	Y	Y	Y	Y	Y
3 **Westmoreland**	Y	Y	N	Y	N
4 Johnson	Y	Y	Y	Y	Y
5 Lewis	Y	Y	Y	Y	Y
6 **Price**	Y	Y	N	Y	N
7 **Linder**	Y	Y	N	Y	N
8 Marshall	Y	Y	Y	?	Y
9 Vacant					
10 **Broun**	Y	Y	N	Y	N
11 **Gingrey**	Y	Y	N	Y	N
12 Barrow	Y	Y	Y	Y	Y
13 Scott	Y	Y	Y	Y	Y
HAWAII					
1 **Djou**	Y	Y	Y	Y	Y
2 Hirono	Y	Y	Y	Y	Y
IDAHO					
1 Minnick	Y	Y	Y	Y	N
2 **Simpson**	Y	Y	Y	Y	Y
ILLINOIS					
1 Rush	Y	Y	Y	Y	?
2 Jackson	Y	Y	Y	Y	Y
3 Lipinski	Y	Y	Y	Y	Y
4 Gutierrez	?	Y	Y	Y	Y
5 Quigley	Y	Y	Y	Y	Y
6 **Roskam**	Y	Y	Y	Y	Y
7 Davis	Y	Y	Y	Y	Y
8 Bean	Y	Y	Y	Y	Y
9 Schakowsky	Y	Y	Y	Y	Y
10 **Kirk**	Y	Y	Y	Y	Y
11 Halvorson	Y	Y	Y	Y	Y
12 Costello	Y	Y	Y	Y	Y
13 **Biggert**	Y	Y	Y	Y	Y
14 Foster	Y	Y	Y	Y	Y
15 **Johnson**	Y	Y	Y	Y	Y

	310	311	312	313	314
16 Manzullo	Y	Y	N	Y	Y
17 Hare	Y	Y	Y	Y	Y
18 Schock	Y	Y	Y	Y	Y
19 Shimkus	Y	Y	N	Y	N
INDIANA					
1 Visclosky	Y	Y	Y	Y	N
2 Donnelly	Y	Y	Y	Y	Y
3 Vacant					
4 Buyer	Y	Y	Y	Y	N
5 Burton	Y	Y	N	Y	N
6 Pence	Y	Y	N	Y	N
7 Carson	Y	Y	Y	Y	Y
8 Ellsworth	Y	Y	Y	Y	Y
9 Hill	Y	Y	Y	Y	Y
IOWA					
1 Braley	Y	Y	Y	?	Y
2 Loebsack	Y	Y	Y	Y	Y
3 Boswell	Y	Y	Y	Y	Y
4 Latham	Y	Y	Y	Y	Y
5 King	Y	Y	N	Y	N
KANSAS					
1 Moran	Y	Y	N	Y	Y
2 Jenkins	Y	Y	Y	Y	Y
3 Moore	Y	Y	Y	?	Y
4 Tiahrt	Y	Y	N	Y	Y
KENTUCKY					
1 Whitfield	Y	Y	Y	Y	Y
2 Guthrie	Y	Y	Y	Y	Y
3 Yarmuth	Y	Y	Y	Y	Y
4 Davis	?	?	?	?	?
5 Rogers	Y	Y	Y	Y	Y
6 Chandler	Y	Y	Y	Y	Y
LOUISIANA					
1 Scalise	Y	Y	N	Y	N
2 Cao	Y	Y	Y	Y	Y
3 Melancon	?	?	?	?	?
4 Fleming	Y	Y	N	Y	N
5 Alexander	Y	Y	N	Y	N
6 Cassidy	Y	Y	N	Y	N
7 Boustany	Y	Y	Y	Y	N
MAINE					
1 Pingree	Y	Y	Y	Y	?
2 Michaud	Y	Y	Y	Y	Y
MARYLAND					
1 Kratovil	Y	Y	Y	Y	Y
2 Ruppersberger	Y	Y	Y	Y	Y
3 Sarbanes	Y	Y	Y	Y	?
4 Edwards	Y	Y	Y	Y	Y
5 Hoyer	Y	Y	Y	Y	Y
6 Bartlett	Y	Y	N	Y	N
7 Cummings	Y	Y	Y	Y	Y
8 Van Hollen	Y	Y	Y	Y	Y
MASSACHUSETTS					
1 Olver	Y	?	Y	Y	Y
2 Neal	Y	Y	Y	Y	Y
3 McGovern	Y	Y	Y	Y	Y
4 Frank	Y	Y	Y	Y	Y
5 Tsongas	Y	Y	Y	Y	Y
6 Tierney	Y	Y	Y	Y	Y
7 Markey	Y	Y	Y	Y	Y
8 Capuano	Y	Y	Y	Y	Y
9 Lynch	Y	Y	Y	Y	Y
10 Delahunt	Y	Y	Y	Y	Y
MICHIGAN					
1 Stupak	Y	Y	Y	Y	Y
2 Hoekstra	Y	Y	N	Y	Y
3 Ehlers	Y	Y	Y	Y	Y
4 Camp	Y	Y	Y	Y	Y
5 Kildee	Y	Y	Y	Y	Y
6 Upton	Y	Y	Y	Y	Y
7 Schauer	Y	Y	Y	Y	Y
8 Rogers	Y	Y	Y	Y	Y
9 Peters	Y	Y	Y	Y	Y
10 Miller	Y	Y	N	Y	Y
11 McCotter	Y	Y	N	Y	Y
12 Levin	Y	Y	Y	Y	Y
13 Kilpatrick	Y	Y	Y	?	Y
14 Conyers	Y	Y	Y	?	Y
15 Dingell	Y	Y	Y	Y	Y
MINNESOTA					
1 Walz	Y	Y	Y	Y	Y
2 Kline	Y	Y	N	Y	Y
3 Paulsen	Y	Y	Y	Y	Y
4 McCollum	Y	Y	Y	Y	Y

	310	311	312	313	314
5 Ellison	Y	Y	Y	Y	Y
6 Bachmann	Y	Y	N	Y	Y
7 Peterson	Y	Y	Y	Y	Y
8 Oberstar	Y	Y	Y	Y	Y
MISSISSIPPI					
1 Childers	Y	Y	Y	Y	Y
2 Thompson	Y	Y	Y	Y	Y
3 Harper	Y	Y	Y	Y	Y
4 Taylor	Y	Y	Y	Y	Y
MISSOURI					
1 Clay	Y	Y	Y	Y	Y
2 Akin	Y	Y	Y	Y	N
3 Carnahan	Y	Y	Y	Y	Y
4 Skelton	Y	Y	Y	Y	Y
5 Cleaver	Y	Y	Y	Y	Y
6 Graves	?	?	?	?	?
7 Blunt	Y	Y	Y	Y	Y
8 Emerson	Y	Y	Y	Y	Y
9 Luetkemeyer	Y	Y	Y	Y	Y
MONTANA					
AL Rehberg	Y	Y	Y	Y	Y
NEBRASKA					
1 Fortenberry	Y	Y	Y	Y	Y
2 Terry	Y	Y	N	Y	Y
3 Smith	Y	Y	Y	Y	Y
NEVADA					
1 Berkley	?	Y	Y	Y	Y
2 Heller	Y	Y	Y	Y	Y
3 Titus	Y	Y	Y	Y	Y
NEW HAMPSHIRE					
1 Shea-Porter	Y	Y	Y	Y	Y
2 Hodes	Y	Y	Y	Y	Y
NEW JERSEY					
1 Andrews	Y	Y	Y	Y	Y
2 LoBiondo	Y	Y	Y	Y	Y
3 Adler	Y	Y	Y	Y	Y
4 Smith	Y	Y	Y	Y	Y
5 Garrett	Y	Y	N	Y	N
6 Pallone	Y	Y	Y	Y	Y
7 Lance	Y	Y	Y	Y	Y
8 Pascrell	Y	Y	Y	Y	Y
9 Rothman	Y	Y	Y	Y	Y
10 Payne	Y	Y	Y	Y	Y
11 Frelinghuysen	Y	Y	Y	Y	Y
12 Holt	Y	Y	Y	Y	Y
13 Sires	Y	Y	Y	Y	Y
NEW MEXICO					
1 Heinrich	Y	Y	Y	Y	Y
2 Teague	Y	Y	Y	Y	Y
3 Luján	Y	Y	Y	Y	Y
NEW YORK					
1 Bishop	Y	Y	Y	Y	Y
2 Israel	Y	Y	Y	Y	Y
3 King	Y	Y	Y	Y	Y
4 McCarthy	Y	Y	Y	Y	Y
5 Ackerman	Y	Y	Y	Y	Y
6 Meeks	Y	Y	Y	Y	Y
7 Crowley	Y	Y	Y	Y	Y
8 Nadler	?	Y	Y	Y	Y
9 Weiner	Y	Y	Y	Y	Y
10 Towns	Y	Y	Y	Y	Y
11 Clarke	Y	Y	Y	Y	Y
12 Velázquez	Y	Y	Y	Y	Y
13 McMahon	Y	Y	Y	Y	Y
14 Maloney	Y	Y	Y	Y	Y
15 Rangel	Y	Y	Y	Y	Y
16 Serrano	Y	Y	Y	Y	Y
17 Engel	Y	Y	Y	Y	Y
18 Lowey	?	Y	Y	Y	Y
19 Hall	Y	Y	Y	Y	Y
20 Murphy	Y	Y	Y	Y	Y
21 Tonko	Y	Y	Y	Y	Y
22 Hinchey	Y	Y	Y	Y	Y
23 Owens	Y	Y	Y	Y	N
24 Arcuri	Y	Y	Y	Y	Y
25 Maffei	Y	Y	Y	Y	Y
26 Lee	Y	Y	Y	Y	Y
27 Higgins	Y	Y	Y	Y	Y
28 Slaughter	Y	Y	Y	Y	Y
29 Vacant					
NORTH CAROLINA					
1 Butterfield	Y	Y	Y	Y	Y
2 Etheridge	Y	Y	Y	Y	Y
3 Jones	Y	Y	Y	Y	Y
4 Price	Y	Y	Y	Y	Y

	310	311	312	313	314
5 Foxx	Y	Y	N	Y	Y
6 Coble	Y	Y	N	Y	Y
7 McIntyre	Y	Y	Y	Y	Y
8 Kissell	Y	Y	Y	Y	Y
9 Myrick	Y	Y	N	Y	Y
10 McHenry	Y	Y	Y	Y	Y
11 Shuler	Y	Y	Y	Y	Y
12 Watt	Y	Y	Y	Y	Y
13 Miller	Y	Y	Y	Y	Y
NORTH DAKOTA					
AL Pomeroy	Y	Y	Y	Y	Y
OHIO					
1 Driehaus	Y	Y	Y	Y	Y
2 Schmidt	Y	Y	?	Y	Y
3 Turner	Y	Y	Y	Y	Y
4 Jordan	Y	Y	N	Y	Y
5 Latta	Y	Y	N	Y	Y
6 Wilson	Y	Y	Y	Y	Y
7 Austria	Y	Y	Y	Y	Y
8 Boehner	Y	Y	N	Y	Y
9 Kaptur	Y	Y	Y	Y	Y
10 Kucinich	Y	Y	Y	Y	Y
11 Fudge	Y	Y	Y	Y	Y
12 Tiberi	Y	Y	Y	Y	Y
13 Sutton	Y	Y	Y	Y	Y
14 LaTourette	Y	Y	Y	Y	Y
15 Kilroy	Y	Y	Y	Y	Y
16 Boccieri	Y	Y	Y	Y	Y
17 Ryan	Y	Y	Y	?	Y
18 Space	Y	Y	Y	Y	Y
OKLAHOMA					
1 Sullivan	Y	Y	Y	Y	N
2 Boren	?	?	?	?	?
3 Lucas	Y	Y	Y	Y	Y
4 Cole	Y	Y	Y	Y	Y
5 Fallin	Y	Y	N	Y	Y
OREGON					
1 Wu	Y	Y	Y	?	Y
2 Walden	Y	Y	Y	Y	Y
3 Blumenauer	Y	Y	Y	Y	Y
4 DeFazio	Y	Y	Y	?	Y
5 Schrader	Y	Y	Y	Y	Y
PENNSYLVANIA					
1 Brady	Y	Y	Y	Y	Y
2 Fattah	Y	Y	Y	Y	Y
3 Dahlkemper	Y	Y	Y	Y	Y
4 Altmire	Y	Y	Y	Y	Y
5 Thompson	Y	Y	Y	Y	Y
6 Gerlach	Y	Y	Y	Y	Y
7 Sestak	Y	Y	Y	Y	Y
8 Murphy, P.	Y	Y	Y	Y	Y
9 Shuster	Y	?	Y	Y	Y
10 Carney	Y	Y	Y	Y	Y
11 Kanjorski	Y	Y	Y	Y	Y
12 Critz	Y	Y	Y	Y	Y
13 Schwartz	Y	Y	Y	Y	Y
14 Doyle	Y	Y	Y	Y	Y
15 Dent	Y	Y	Y	Y	Y
16 Pitts	Y	Y	N	Y	Y
17 Holden	Y	Y	Y	Y	Y
18 Murphy, T.	Y	Y	Y	Y	Y
19 Platts	Y	Y	Y	Y	Y
RHODE ISLAND					
1 Kennedy	Y	Y	Y	Y	Y
2 Langevin	Y	Y	Y	Y	Y
SOUTH CAROLINA					
1 Brown	Y	Y	Y	Y	Y
2 Wilson	Y	Y	Y	Y	Y
3 Barrett	Y	Y	N	Y	N
4 Inglis	Y	Y	N	Y	Y
5 Spratt	Y	Y	Y	Y	Y
6 Clyburn	Y	Y	Y	Y	Y
SOUTH DAKOTA					
AL Herseth Sandlin	Y	Y	Y	Y	Y
TENNESSEE					
1 Roe	Y	Y	Y	Y	Y
2 Duncan	Y	Y	N	Y	Y
3 Wamp	Y	Y	Y	Y	Y
4 Davis	Y	Y	Y	Y	Y
5 Cooper	Y	Y	Y	Y	Y
6 Gordon	Y	Y	Y	Y	Y
7 Blackburn	Y	Y	N	Y	Y
8 Tanner	Y	Y	Y	Y	Y
9 Cohen	Y	Y	Y	Y	Y

	310	311	312	313	314
TEXAS					
1 Gohmert	Y	Y	N	Y	Y
2 Poe	Y	Y	N	Y	N
3 Johnson, S.	Y	Y	N	Y	N
4 Hall	Y	Y	N	Y	N
5 Hensarling	Y	Y	N	N	N
6 Barton	Y	Y	Y	Y	N
7 Culberson	Y	Y	N	Y	N
8 Brady	Y	Y	N	N	N
9 Green, A.	Y	Y	Y	Y	Y
10 McCaul	Y	Y	Y	Y	Y
11 Conaway	Y	Y	N	Y	Y
12 Granger	Y	Y	N	Y	Y
13 Thornberry	Y	Y	N	Y	Y
14 Paul	Y	Y	N	N	N
15 Hinojosa	Y	Y	Y	Y	Y
16 Reyes	Y	Y	Y	Y	Y
17 Edwards	Y	Y	Y	Y	Y
18 Jackson Lee	Y	Y	Y	Y	Y
19 Neugebauer	Y	Y	N	Y	Y
20 Gonzalez	Y	Y	Y	Y	Y
21 Smith	Y	Y	Y	Y	Y
22 Olson	Y	Y	Y	Y	Y
23 Rodriguez	Y	Y	Y	Y	Y
24 Marchant	Y	Y	N	Y	N
25 Doggett	Y	Y	Y	Y	Y
26 Burgess	Y	Y	Y	Y	Y
27 Ortiz	Y	Y	Y	Y	Y
28 Cuellar	Y	Y	Y	Y	Y
29 Green, G.	Y	Y	Y	Y	Y
30 Johnson, E.	Y	Y	Y	Y	Y
31 Carter	Y	Y	N	Y	N
32 Sessions	Y	Y	N	Y	N
UTAH					
1 Bishop	Y	Y	N	?	N
2 Matheson	Y	Y	Y	Y	Y
3 Chaffetz	Y	Y	N	Y	Y
VERMONT					
AL Welch	Y	Y	Y	Y	Y
VIRGINIA					
1 Wittman	Y	Y	Y	Y	Y
2 Nye	Y	Y	Y	Y	Y
3 Scott	Y	Y	Y	Y	Y
4 Forbes	Y	Y	N	Y	Y
5 Perriello	Y	Y	Y	Y	Y
6 Goodlatte	Y	Y	N	Y	Y
7 Cantor	Y	Y	Y	Y	Y
8 Moran	Y	Y	Y	Y	Y
9 Boucher	Y	Y	Y	Y	Y
10 Wolf	Y	Y	Y	Y	Y
11 Connolly	Y	Y	Y	Y	Y
WASHINGTON					
1 Inslee	Y	Y	Y	Y	Y
2 Larsen	Y	Y	Y	Y	Y
3 Baird	Y	Y	Y	Y	N
4 Hastings	Y	Y	Y	Y	Y
5 McMorris Rodgers	Y	Y	Y	Y	Y
6 Dicks	Y	Y	Y	Y	Y
7 McDermott	Y	Y	Y	Y	Y
8 Reichert	Y	Y	Y	Y	Y
9 Smith	Y	Y	Y	Y	Y
WEST VIRGINIA					
1 Mollohan	Y	Y	Y	Y	Y
2 Capito	Y	Y	Y	Y	Y
3 Rahall	Y	Y	Y	Y	Y
WISCONSIN					
1 Ryan	?	?	?	?	?
2 Baldwin	Y	Y	Y	Y	Y
3 Kind	Y	Y	Y	Y	Y
4 Moore	Y	Y	Y	Y	Y
5 Sensenbrenner	Y	Y	Y	Y	N
6 Petri	Y	Y	Y	Y	N
7 Obey	Y	Y	Y	Y	Y
8 Kagen	Y	Y	Y	Y	Y
WYOMING					
AL Lummis	Y	Y	N	Y	Y
DELEGATES					
Faleomavaega (A.S.)	Y	Y	Y	Y	Y
Norton (D.C.)	Y	Y	Y	Y	Y
Bordallo (Guam)	Y	Y	Y	Y	Y
Sablan (N. Marianas)	?	?	?	?	?
Pierluisi (P.R.)	?	?	?	?	?
Christensen (V.I.)	Y	Y	Y	Y	Y

IN THE HOUSE | By Vote Number

315. **HR 5136. Fiscal 2011 Defense Authorization/GAO Intelligence Audits.** Eshoo, D-Calif., amendment that would require the director of national intelligence (DNI) to cooperate with Government Accountability Office (GAO) inquiries initiated by congressional committees. It also would allow committees to request GAO audits of the intelligence community and allow the DNI to designate certain reports or portions of reports as sensitive or reportable only to the intelligence committees. Adopted in Committee of the Whole 218-210: D 206-49; R 12-161. May 27, 2010.

316. **HR 5136. Fiscal 2011 Defense Authorization/F-35 Alternative Engine.** Pingree, D-Maine, amendment that would strike funds authorized for the F-35 alternative-engine program. Rejected in Committee of the Whole 193-231: D 136-115; R 57-116. A "yea" was a vote in support of the president's position. May 27, 2010.

317. **HR 5136. Fiscal 2011 Defense Authorization/'Don't Ask, Don't Tell' Policy Repeal.** Murphy, D-Pa., amendment that would repeal the "don't ask, don't tell" policy on military service by openly gay men and women after receipt of Pentagon recommendations on how to implement a repeal. It would take effect 60 days after certification by the Defense secretary, the chairman of the Joint Chiefs and the president that the repeal is consistent with the standards of military readiness, military effectiveness, unit cohesion and recruiting. Adopted in Committee of the Whole 234-194: D 229-26; R 5-168. A "yea" was a vote in support of the president's position. May 27, 2010.

318. **HR 5136. Fiscal 2011 Defense Authorization/Contractor Insourcing Policies.** Sarbanes, D-Md., amendment that would require non-defense agencies to establish contractor inventories and insourcing programs to mirror current law for the Defense Department. It also would bar agencies from establishing any numerical goal, target or quota for converting jobs from contractors to federal employees and would require the Office of Management and Budget to report to Congress on agency insourcing policies. Adopted in Committee of the Whole 253-172: D 243-11; R 10-161. May 27, 2010.

	315	316	317	318
ALABAMA				
1 **Bonner**	N	N	N	N
2 Bright	Y	N	N	N
3 **Rogers**	N	N	N	N
4 **Aderholt**	Y	N	N	N
5 **Griffith**	N	Y	N	N
6 **Bachus**	N	N	N	N
7 Davis	?	?	?	?
ALASKA				
AL **Young**	N	N	N	N
ARIZONA				
1 Kirkpatrick	Y	Y	Y	Y
2 **Franks**	N	N	N	N
3 **Shadegg**	N	Y	N	N
4 Pastor	N	Y	Y	Y
5 Mitchell	Y	Y	Y	Y
6 **Flake**	N	Y	N	N
7 Grijalva	N	Y	Y	Y
8 Giffords	Y	Y	Y	Y
ARKANSAS				
1 Berry	Y	Y	N	Y
2 Snyder	N	N	Y	Y
3 **Boozman**	N	N	N	N
4 Ross	N	Y	N	Y
CALIFORNIA				
1 Thompson	Y	Y	Y	Y
2 **Herger**	N	Y	N	N
3 **Lungren**	N	N	N	N
4 **McClintock**	Y	Y	N	N
5 Matsui	Y	Y	Y	Y
6 Woolsey	Y	P	Y	Y
7 Miller, George	Y	Y	Y	Y
8 Pelosi	Y		Y	
9 Lee	Y	Y	Y	Y
10 Garamendi	Y	N	Y	Y
11 McNerney	Y	N	Y	Y
12 Speier	Y	Y	Y	Y
13 Stark	Y	Y	Y	Y
14 Eshoo	Y	Y	Y	Y
15 Honda	Y	Y	Y	Y
16 Lofgren	Y	Y	Y	N
17 Farr	Y	Y	Y	Y
18 Cardoza	Y	Y	Y	Y
19 **Radanovich**	N	N	N	?
20 Costa	Y	Y	Y	N
21 **Nunes**	N	N	N	N
22 **McCarthy**	N	N	N	N
23 Capps	Y	Y	Y	Y
24 **Gallegly**	N	N	N	N
25 **McKeon**	N	N	N	N
26 **Dreier**	N	N	N	N
27 Sherman	Y	Y	Y	Y
28 Berman	Y	Y	Y	Y
29 Schiff	Y	Y	Y	Y
30 Waxman	Y	Y	Y	Y
31 Becerra	Y	Y	Y	Y
32 Chu	Y	N	Y	Y
33 Watson	Y	N	Y	Y
34 Roybal-Allard	N	N	Y	Y
35 Waters	Y	P	Y	Y
36 Harman	Y	Y	Y	Y
37 Richardson	Y	N	Y	Y
38 Napolitano	Y	Y	Y	Y
39 Sánchez, Linda	Y	Y	Y	Y
40 **Royce**	N	N	N	N
41 **Lewis**	N	N	N	N
42 **Miller, Gary**	N	N	N	N
43 Baca	N	N	Y	Y
44 **Calvert**	N	N	N	N
45 **Bono Mack**	N	N	N	N
46 **Rohrabacher**	Y	Y	N	N
47 Sanchez, Loretta	Y	N	Y	Y
48 **Campbell**	N	Y	N	N
49 **Issa**	N	N	N	N
50 **Bilbray**	N	N	N	N
51 Filner	N	Y	Y	Y
52 **Hunter**	N	N	N	N
53 Davis	Y	N	Y	Y
COLORADO				
1 DeGette	Y	Y	Y	Y
2 Polis	Y	Y	Y	Y
3 Salazar	N	Y	Y	Y
4 Markey	Y	Y	Y	Y
5 **Lamborn**	N	N	N	N
6 **Coffman**	N	Y	N	N
7 Perlmutter	Y	Y	Y	Y
CONNECTICUT				
1 Larson	Y	Y	Y	Y
2 Courtney	Y	Y	Y	Y
3 DeLauro	Y	Y	Y	Y
4 Himes	N	Y	Y	Y
5 Murphy	Y	Y	Y	Y
DELAWARE				
AL **Castle**	N	N	N	N
FLORIDA				
1 **Miller**	N	Y	N	N
2 Boyd	Y	Y	Y	Y
3 Brown	Y	Y	Y	Y
4 **Crenshaw**	N	N	N	N
5 **Brown-Waite**	?	?	?	?
6 **Stearns**	N	Y	N	N
7 **Mica**	N	N	N	N
8 Grayson	Y	Y	Y	Y
9 **Bilirakis**	N	N	N	N
10 **Young**	N	Y	N	N
11 Castor	Y	Y	Y	Y
12 **Putnam**	N	N	N	N
13 **Buchanan**	N	Y	N	N
14 **Mack**	N	Y	N	N
15 **Posey**	N	Y	N	N
16 **Rooney**	N	Y	N	N
17 Meek	Y	Y	Y	Y
18 **Ros-Lehtinen**	N	N	Y	N
19 Deutch	Y	Y	Y	Y
20 Wasserman Schultz	Y	N	Y	Y
21 **Diaz-Balart, L.**	N	N	N	N
22 Klein	Y	Y	Y	Y
23 Hastings	?	?	?	?
24 Kosmas	Y	Y	Y	N
25 **Diaz-Balart, M.**	N	N	N	N
GEORGIA				
1 **Kingston**	Y	N	N	N
2 Bishop	Y	Y	N	Y
3 **Westmoreland**	N	Y	N	N
4 Johnson	Y	Y	Y	Y
5 Lewis	Y	Y	Y	Y
6 **Price**	N	N	N	N
7 **Linder**	N	Y	N	?
8 Marshall	N	N	N	Y
9 Vacant				
10 **Broun**	N	Y	N	N
11 **Gingrey**	N	Y	N	N
12 Barrow	Y	Y	Y	Y
13 Scott	Y	N	Y	Y
HAWAII				
1 **Djou**	N	N	Y	Y
2 Hirono	Y	Y	Y	Y
IDAHO				
1 Minnick	N	Y	N	N
2 **Simpson**	N	N	N	N
ILLINOIS				
1 Rush	Y	Y	Y	Y
2 Jackson	Y	Y	Y	Y
3 Lipinski	N	N	N	Y
4 Gutierrez	N	N	Y	Y
5 Quigley	Y	Y	Y	Y
6 **Roskam**	N	N	N	N
7 Davis	Y	Y	Y	Y
8 Bean	N	Y	Y	Y
9 Schakowsky	Y	N	Y	Y
10 **Kirk**	N	Y	N	N
11 Halvorson	N	N	Y	Y
12 Costello	N	N	N	Y
13 **Biggert**	N	N	Y	N
14 Foster	Y	N	Y	Y
15 **Johnson**	N	Y	N	N

KEY **Republicans** Democrats

Y Voted for (yea)	X Paired against	C Voted "present" to avoid possible conflict of interest
# Paired for	– Announced against	
+ Announced for	P Voted "present"	? Did not vote or otherwise make a position known
N Voted against (nay)		

Member	315	316	317	318
16 Manzullo	N	N	N	N
17 Hare	Y	Y	Y	Y
18 Schock	N	N	N	N
19 Shimkus	N	N	N	N
INDIANA				
1 Visclosky	N	N	Y	Y
2 Donnelly	N	N	N	Y
3 Vacant				
4 Buyer	N	N	N	N
5 Burton	N	N	N	N
6 Pence	N	N	N	N
7 Carson	Y	N	Y	Y
8 Ellsworth	N	N	Y	Y
9 Hill	N	N	Y	Y
IOWA				
1 Braley	Y	Y	Y	Y
2 Loebsack	Y	N	Y	Y
3 Boswell	Y	N	Y	Y
4 Latham	N	N	N	N
5 King	N	N	N	N
KANSAS				
1 Moran	N	Y	N	N
2 Jenkins	N	Y	N	N
3 Moore	Y	N	Y	Y
4 Tiahrt	N	Y	N	N
KENTUCKY				
1 Whitfield	N	N	N	N
2 Guthrie	N	N	N	N
3 Yarmuth	Y	N	Y	Y
4 Davis	?	?	?	?
5 Rogers	N	N	N	N
6 Chandler	Y	N	Y	Y
LOUISIANA				
1 Scalise	N	N	N	N
2 Cao	N	N	Y	Y
3 Melancon	?	?	?	?
4 Fleming	N	N	N	N
5 Alexander	N	N	N	N
6 Cassidy	N	Y	N	Y
7 Boustany	N	Y	N	N
MAINE				
1 Pingree	Y	Y	Y	Y
2 Michaud	Y	Y	Y	Y
MARYLAND				
1 Kratovil	Y	Y	Y	Y
2 Ruppersberger	Y	N	Y	Y
3 Sarbanes	Y	N	Y	Y
4 Edwards	Y	Y	Y	Y
5 Hoyer	Y	Y	Y	Y
6 Bartlett	Y	N	N	N
7 Cummings	Y	Y	Y	Y
8 Van Hollen	Y	Y	Y	Y
MASSACHUSETTS				
1 Olver	Y	Y	Y	Y
2 Neal	Y	Y	Y	Y
3 McGovern	Y	N	Y	Y
4 Frank	Y	N	Y	Y
5 Tsongas	Y	N	Y	Y
6 Tierney	Y	N	Y	Y
7 Markey	Y	N	Y	Y
8 Capuano	Y	N	Y	Y
9 Lynch	Y	N	Y	Y
10 Delahunt	Y	N	Y	Y
MICHIGAN				
1 Stupak	Y	Y	Y	Y
2 Hoekstra	N	Y	N	N
3 Ehlers	Y	N	N	N
4 Camp	N	Y	N	N
5 Kildee	Y	N	Y	Y
6 Upton	N	Y	N	N
7 Schauer	Y	N	Y	Y
8 Rogers	N	N	N	N
9 Peters	Y	N	Y	Y
10 Miller	N	N	N	N
11 McCotter	N	N	N	N
12 Levin	Y	N	Y	Y
13 Kilpatrick	Y	N	Y	Y
14 Conyers	Y	Y	Y	Y
15 Dingell	Y	N	Y	Y
MINNESOTA				
1 Walz	Y	Y	Y	Y
2 Kline	N	N	N	N
3 Paulsen	N	Y	N	N
4 McCollum	Y	Y	Y	Y
5 Ellison	Y	Y	Y	Y
6 Bachmann	N	N	N	N
7 Peterson	N	Y	N	Y
8 Oberstar	Y	Y	Y	Y
MISSISSIPPI				
1 Childers	N	N	N	Y
2 Thompson	Y	N	Y	Y
3 Harper	N	N	N	N
4 Taylor	N	N	N	Y
MISSOURI				
1 Clay	N	N	Y	Y
2 Akin	N	N	N	N
3 Carnahan	Y	Y	Y	Y
4 Skelton	N	N	N	Y
5 Cleaver	N	N	N	Y
6 Graves	?	?	?	?
7 Blunt	N	N	N	N
8 Emerson	N	N	N	Y
9 Luetkemeyer	N	N	N	N
MONTANA				
AL Rehberg	N	Y	N	N
NEBRASKA				
1 Fortenberry	N	N	N	N
2 Terry	N	N	N	N
3 Smith	N	N	N	N
NEVADA				
1 Berkley	Y	Y	Y	Y
2 Heller	N	N	N	N
3 Titus	Y	Y	Y	Y
NEW HAMPSHIRE				
1 Shea-Porter	Y	N	Y	Y
2 Hodes	Y	Y	Y	Y
NEW JERSEY				
1 Andrews	Y	N	Y	Y
2 LoBiondo	N	N	N	Y
3 Adler	Y	N	N	Y
4 Smith	N	N	N	Y
5 Garrett	N	Y	N	N
6 Pallone	Y	Y	Y	Y
7 Lance	N	Y	N	N
8 Pascrell	Y	Y	Y	Y
9 Rothman	Y	N	Y	Y
10 Payne	Y	N	Y	Y
11 Frelinghuysen	N	N	N	N
12 Holt	Y	Y	Y	Y
13 Sires	N	N	Y	Y
NEW MEXICO				
1 Heinrich	Y	Y	Y	Y
2 Teague	N	Y	Y	Y
3 Luján	N	Y	Y	Y
NEW YORK				
1 Bishop	Y	Y	Y	Y
2 Israel	Y	N	Y	Y
3 King	N	Y	N	N
4 McCarthy	Y	N	Y	Y
5 Ackerman	Y	N	Y	Y
6 Meeks	Y	Y	Y	Y
7 Crowley	Y	N	Y	Y
8 Nadler	Y	Y	Y	Y
9 Weiner	Y	N	Y	Y
10 Towns	Y	Y	Y	Y
11 Clarke	Y	N	Y	Y
12 Velázquez	Y	N	Y	Y
13 McMahon	N	N	Y	Y
14 Maloney	Y	Y	Y	Y
15 Rangel	Y	N	Y	Y
16 Serrano	Y	N	Y	Y
17 Engel	Y	N	Y	Y
18 Lowey	Y	Y	Y	Y
19 Hall	Y	N	Y	Y
20 Murphy	Y	N	Y	Y
21 Tonko	Y	N	Y	Y
22 Hinchey	Y	Y	Y	Y
23 Owens	N	Y	Y	Y
24 Arcuri	Y	N	Y	Y
25 Maffei	Y	N	Y	Y
26 Lee	N	Y	N	N
27 Higgins	Y	N	Y	Y
28 Slaughter	Y	P	Y	Y
29 Vacant				
NORTH CAROLINA				
1 Butterfield	Y	N	Y	Y
2 Etheridge	N	N	N	Y
3 Jones	Y	Y	N	Y
4 Price	Y	N	Y	Y
5 Foxx	N	N	N	N
6 Coble	N	N	N	N
7 McIntyre	N	N	N	Y
8 Kissell	Y	N	N	Y
9 Myrick	N	N	N	N
10 McHenry	N	N	N	N
11 Shuler	Y	N	N	Y
12 Watt	N	Y	Y	Y
13 Miller	Y	N	Y	Y
NORTH DAKOTA				
AL Pomeroy	Y	N	N	Y
OHIO				
1 Driehaus	Y	N	N	Y
2 Schmidt	N	N	N	N
3 Turner	N	N	N	N
4 Jordan	N	N	N	N
5 Latta	N	N	N	N
6 Wilson	N	Y	N	Y
7 Austria	N	N	N	N
8 Boehner	N	N	N	N
9 Kaptur	Y	N	Y	Y
10 Kucinich	Y	N	Y	Y
11 Fudge	Y	N	Y	Y
12 Tiberi	N	N	N	N
13 Sutton	Y	N	Y	Y
14 LaTourette	N	N	N	Y
15 Kilroy	Y	N	Y	Y
16 Boccieri	N	N	Y	Y
17 Ryan	Y	N	Y	Y
18 Space	Y	N	Y	Y
OKLAHOMA				
1 Sullivan	N	Y	N	N
2 Boren	?	?	?	?
3 Lucas	N	N	N	N
4 Cole	N	Y	N	N
5 Fallin	N	N	N	N
OREGON				
1 Wu	Y	Y	Y	Y
2 Walden	N	Y	N	N
3 Blumenauer	Y	Y	Y	Y
4 DeFazio	Y	Y	Y	Y
5 Schrader	Y	Y	Y	Y
PENNSYLVANIA				
1 Brady	Y	N	Y	Y
2 Fattah	Y	Y	Y	Y
3 Dahlkemper	N	N	Y	Y
4 Altmire	N	Y	Y	Y
5 Thompson	N	Y	N	N
6 Gerlach	N	N	N	N
7 Sestak	Y	N	Y	Y
8 Murphy, P.	N	Y	Y	Y
9 Shuster	N	N	N	N
10 Carney	N	N	Y	Y
11 Kanjorski	Y	N	Y	Y
12 Critz	Y	N	N	Y
13 Schwartz	Y	Y	Y	Y
14 Doyle	Y	Y	Y	Y
15 Dent	N	Y	N	N
16 Pitts	N	N	N	N
17 Holden	Y	Y	Y	Y
18 Murphy, T.	N	N	N	N
19 Platts	Y	N	N	N
RHODE ISLAND				
1 Kennedy	Y	N	Y	Y
2 Langevin	Y	N	Y	Y
SOUTH CAROLINA				
1 Brown	N	N	N	N
2 Wilson	N	N	N	N
3 Barrett	N	N	N	N
4 Inglis	N	N	N	N
5 Spratt	Y	N	N	Y
6 Clyburn	Y	N	Y	Y
SOUTH DAKOTA				
AL Herseth Sandlin	Y	Y	Y	Y
TENNESSEE				
1 Roe	N	Y	N	N
2 Duncan	Y	Y	N	N
3 Wamp	N	Y	N	N
4 Davis	Y	N	N	Y
5 Cooper	N	Y	N	Y
6 Gordon	Y	Y	Y	Y
7 Blackburn	N	Y	N	N
8 Tanner	Y	N	N	Y
9 Cohen	Y	Y	Y	Y
TEXAS				
1 Gohmert	N	Y	N	N
2 Poe	N	N	N	N
3 Johnson, S.	N	Y	N	N
4 Hall	N	N	N	N
5 Hensarling	N	Y	N	N
6 Barton	Y	Y	N	N
7 Culberson	N	N	N	N
8 Brady	N	Y	N	N
9 Green, A.	Y	Y	Y	Y
10 McCaul	N	N	N	N
11 Conaway	N	N	N	N
12 Granger	N	Y	N	N
13 Thornberry	N	N	N	N
14 Paul	Y	Y	Y	N
15 Hinojosa	N	N	Y	Y
16 Reyes	N	Y	Y	Y
17 Edwards	N	Y	N	Y
18 Jackson Lee	Y	Y	Y	Y
19 Neugebauer	N	Y	N	N
20 Gonzalez	N	Y	Y	Y
21 Smith	N	N	N	N
22 Olson	N	N	N	N
23 Rodriguez	Y	Y	Y	Y
24 Marchant	N	N	N	N
25 Doggett	Y	Y	Y	Y
26 Burgess	N	Y	N	N
27 Ortiz	N	Y	N	Y
28 Cuellar	Y	Y	Y	Y
29 Green, G.	N	Y	N	Y
30 Johnson, E.	Y	Y	Y	Y
31 Carter	N	N	N	N
32 Sessions	N	N	N	N
UTAH				
1 Bishop	N	N	N	N
2 Matheson	Y	N	Y	Y
3 Chaffetz	N	Y	N	N
VERMONT				
AL Welch	Y	N	Y	Y
VIRGINIA				
1 Wittman	N	N	N	N
2 Nye	Y	N	Y	Y
3 Scott	Y	N	Y	Y
4 Forbes	N	N	N	N
5 Perriello	N	N	Y	Y
6 Goodlatte	N	N	N	N
7 Cantor	N	N	N	N
8 Moran	Y	N	Y	N
9 Boucher	Y	N	N	Y
10 Wolf	N	N	N	N
11 Connolly	Y	N	Y	Y
WASHINGTON				
1 Inslee	Y	Y	Y	Y
2 Larsen	Y	N	Y	Y
3 Baird	Y	Y	Y	Y
4 Hastings	N	N	N	N
5 McMorris Rodgers	N	N	N	N
6 Dicks	N	Y	Y	Y
7 McDermott	Y	Y	Y	Y
8 Reichert	N	N	N	N
9 Smith	Y	N	Y	Y
WEST VIRGINIA				
1 Mollohan	Y	N	Y	Y
2 Capito	N	Y	N	N
3 Rahall	N	Y	N	Y
WISCONSIN				
1 Ryan	?	?	?	?
2 Baldwin	Y	Y	Y	Y
3 Kind	Y	Y	Y	Y
4 Moore	Y	Y	Y	Y
5 Sensenbrenner	N	Y	N	N
6 Petri	Y	Y	N	N
7 Obey	Y	Y	Y	Y
8 Kagen	Y	Y	Y	Y
WYOMING				
AL Lummis	N	N	N	N
DELEGATES				
Faleomavaega (A.S.)	Y	Y	Y	Y
Norton (D.C.)	Y	N	Y	Y
Bordallo (Guam)	Y	Y	Y	Y
Sablan (N. Marianas)	?	?	?	?
Pierluisi (P.R.)	?	?	?	?
Christensen (V.I.)	Y	Y	Y	Y

IN THE HOUSE | By Vote Number

319. **Procedural Motion/Journal.** Approval of the House Journal of Thursday, May 28, 2010. Approved 230-182: D 214-31; R 16-151. May 28, 2010.

320. **H Res 1391. Israel Membership in OECD/Adoption.** Berkley, D-Nev., motion to suspend the rules and adopt the resolution that would congratulate Israel for its accession to membership in the Organization for Economic Co-operation and Development, commend the 31 OECD nations for recognizing Israel's economic success and recognize the strong U.S. role in Israel's successful bid for membership. Motion agreed to 418-0: D 246-0; R 172-0. A two-thirds majority of those present and voting (279 in this case) is required for adoption under suspension of the rules. May 28, 2010.

321. **HR 4213. Tax Extensions/Previous Question.** Slaughter, D-N.Y., motion to order the previous question (thus ending debate and possibility of amendment) on adoption of the rule (H Res 1403) and a Slaughter amendment to the rule. The rule would provide for House floor consideration of the motion to concur in the Senate amendment with a House amendment to the bill that would extend several expired or expiring tax provisions and block a scheduled cut to Medicare payments to physicians. Motion agreed to 235-182: D 235-13; R 0-169. May 28, 2010.

322. **HR 4213. Tax Extensions/Amendment to Rule.** Slaughter, D-N.Y., amendment to the rule (H Res 1403). The Slaughter amendment would provide for a separate vote on a provision that would block a scheduled cut to Medicare payments to physicians. It would strike an extension of COBRA health insurance premium subsidies for jobless workers, as well as an extension of extra federal Medicaid assistance to the states. It would delay the effective date of a provision on carried interest. Adopted 215-206: D 215-34; R 0-172. May 28, 2010.

323. **HR 4213. Tax Extensions/Rule.** Adoption of the rule (H Res 1403) to provide for House floor consideration of the motion to concur in the Senate amendment with a House amendment to the bill that would extend several expired or expiring tax provisions and block a scheduled cut to Medicare payments to physicians. Adopted 221-199: D 221-29; R 0-170. May 28, 2010.

324. **HR 4213. Tax Extensions/Motion to Concur.** Adoption of the Levin, D-Mich., motion to concur in the Senate amendment to the bill with all except Section 523 of a House amendment. The House amendment would extend tax provisions such as the research and development credit and the tuition deduction. It would provide $1 billion for a summer jobs program as well as funding for states that would lose money due to changes in the transportation funding formula. It would increase the Oil Spill Liability Trust Fund financing rate to 34 cents per barrel and tax a portion of the carried interest received by investment managers as ordinary income. Motion agreed to 215-204: D 214-34; R 1-170. May 28, 2010.

	319	320	321	322	323	324
ALABAMA						
1 **Bonner**	N	Y	N	N	N	N
2 Bright	Y	Y	N	N	N	N
3 **Rogers**	N	Y	N	N	N	N
4 **Aderholt**	?	Y	N	N	N	N
5 **Griffith**	N	Y	N	N	N	N
6 **Bachus**	N	Y	N	N	N	N
7 Davis	?	?	?	?	?	?
ALASKA						
AL **Young**	N	Y	N	N	N	N
ARIZONA						
1 Kirkpatrick	N	Y	Y	N	N	Y
2 **Franks**	N	Y	N	N	N	N
3 **Shadegg**	N	Y	N	N	N	N
4 Pastor	Y	Y	Y	Y	Y	Y
5 Mitchell	N	Y	N	N	N	N
6 **Flake**	N	Y	N	N	N	N
7 Grijalva	Y	Y	Y	Y	Y	Y
8 Giffords	N	Y	N	N	N	N
ARKANSAS						
1 Berry	Y	Y	N	Y	Y	Y
2 Snyder	Y	Y	Y	Y	Y	Y
3 **Boozman**	N	Y	N	N	N	N
4 Ross	Y	Y	Y	Y	Y	Y
CALIFORNIA						
1 Thompson	N	Y	Y	Y	Y	Y
2 **Herger**	N	Y	N	N	N	N
3 **Lungren**	N	Y	N	N	N	N
4 **McClintock**	N	Y	N	N	N	N
5 Matsui	Y	Y	Y	Y	Y	Y
6 Woolsey	Y	Y	Y	Y	Y	Y
7 Miller, George	Y	Y	Y	Y	Y	Y
8 Pelosi				Y	Y	Y
9 Lee	Y	Y	Y	Y	Y	Y
10 Garamendi	Y	Y	Y	Y	Y	Y
11 McNerney	Y	Y	Y	Y	Y	N
12 Speier	Y	Y	Y	Y	Y	Y
13 Stark	Y	Y	Y	Y	Y	N
14 Eshoo	Y	Y	Y	Y	Y	Y
15 Honda	Y	Y	Y	Y	Y	Y
16 Lofgren	Y	Y	Y	Y	Y	Y
17 Farr	Y	Y	Y	Y	Y	Y
18 Cardoza	N	Y	Y	Y	Y	Y
19 **Radanovich**	N	Y	N	N	?	N
20 Costa	N	Y	Y	Y	Y	Y
21 **Nunes**	N	Y	N	N	N	N
22 **McCarthy**	N	Y	N	N	N	N
23 Capps	Y	Y	Y	Y	Y	Y
24 **Gallegly**	N	Y	N	N	N	N
25 **McKeon**	N	Y	N	N	N	N
26 **Dreier**	N	Y	N	N	N	N
27 Sherman	Y	Y	Y	Y	Y	Y
28 Berman	Y	Y	Y	Y	Y	Y
29 Schiff	Y	Y	Y	Y	Y	Y
30 Waxman	Y	Y	Y	Y	Y	Y
31 Becerra	Y	Y	Y	Y	Y	Y
32 Chu	Y	Y	Y	Y	Y	Y
33 Watson	Y	Y	Y	Y	Y	Y
34 Roybal-Allard	Y	Y	Y	Y	Y	Y
35 Waters	Y	Y	?	Y	Y	Y
36 Harman	?	Y	Y	Y	Y	Y
37 Richardson	Y	Y	Y	Y	Y	Y
38 Napolitano	Y	Y	Y	Y	N	Y
39 Sánchez, Linda	Y	Y	Y	Y	Y	Y
40 **Royce**	N	Y	N	N	N	N
41 **Lewis**	Y	Y	N	N	N	N
42 **Miller, Gary**	N	Y	N	N	N	N
43 Baca	Y	Y	Y	Y	Y	Y
44 **Calvert**	N	Y	N	N	N	N
45 **Bono Mack**	N	Y	N	N	N	N
46 **Rohrabacher**	N	Y	N	N	N	N
47 Sanchez, Loretta	Y	Y	Y	Y	Y	Y
48 **Campbell**	N	Y	N	N	N	N
49 **Issa**	N	Y	N	N	N	N
50 **Bilbray**	Y	Y	N	N	N	N
51 Filner	Y	Y	Y	Y	Y	Y
52 **Hunter**	N	Y	N	N	N	N
53 Davis	Y	Y	Y	Y	Y	Y

	319	320	321	322	323	324
COLORADO						
1 DeGette	Y	Y	Y	Y	Y	Y
2 Polis	Y	Y	Y	Y	Y	N
3 Salazar	N	Y	Y	N	N	N
4 Markey	N	Y	Y	Y	N	N
5 **Lamborn**	N	Y	N	N	N	N
6 **Coffman**	N	Y	N	N	N	N
7 Perlmutter	Y	Y	Y	Y	Y	Y
CONNECTICUT						
1 Larson	Y	Y	Y	Y	Y	Y
2 Courtney	Y	Y	Y	Y	Y	Y
3 DeLauro	Y	Y	Y	Y	Y	Y
4 Himes	N	Y	Y	Y	N	N
5 Murphy	Y	Y	Y	Y	Y	Y
DELAWARE						
AL **Castle**	Y	Y	N	N	N	N
FLORIDA						
1 **Miller**	N	Y	N	N	N	N
2 Boyd	Y	Y	Y	Y	N	N
3 Brown	Y	Y	Y	Y	Y	Y
4 **Crenshaw**	N	Y	N	N	N	N
5 **Brown-Waite**	?	?	?	?	?	?
6 **Stearns**	N	Y	N	N	N	N
7 **Mica**	N	Y	N	N	N	N
8 Grayson	Y	Y	Y	Y	Y	Y
9 **Bilirakis**	N	Y	N	N	N	N
10 **Young**	N	Y	N	N	N	N
11 Castor	Y	Y	Y	Y	Y	Y
12 **Putnam**	N	Y	N	N	N	N
13 **Buchanan**	N	Y	N	N	N	N
14 **Mack**	N	Y	N	N	N	N
15 **Posey**	Y	Y	N	N	N	N
16 **Rooney**	N	Y	N	N	N	N
17 Meek	Y	Y	Y	Y	Y	Y
18 **Ros-Lehtinen**	N	Y	N	N	N	N
19 Deutch	Y	Y	Y	Y	Y	Y
20 Wasserman Schultz	?	Y	Y	Y	Y	Y
21 **Diaz-Balart, L.**	N	Y	N	N	N	N
22 Klein	Y	Y	Y	N	Y	N
23 Hastings	?	?	?	?	?	?
24 Kosmas	N	Y	Y	N	N	N
25 **Diaz-Balart, M.**	N	Y	N	N	N	N
GEORGIA						
1 **Kingston**	N	Y	N	N	N	N
2 Bishop	Y	Y	Y	Y	Y	Y
3 **Westmoreland**	N	Y	N	N	N	N
4 Johnson	?	?	Y	Y	Y	Y
5 Lewis	Y	Y	Y	Y	Y	Y
6 **Price**	N	Y	N	N	N	N
7 **Linder**	N	Y	N	N	N	N
8 Marshall	Y	Y	Y	Y	Y	Y
9 Vacant						
10 **Broun**	N	Y	N	N	N	N
11 **Gingrey**	N	Y	N	N	N	N
12 Barrow	Y	Y	Y	Y	Y	Y
13 Scott	Y	Y	Y	Y	Y	Y
HAWAII						
1 **Djou**	N	Y	N	N	N	N
2 Hirono	Y	Y	Y	Y	Y	Y
IDAHO						
1 Minnick	N	Y	N	N	N	N
2 **Simpson**	N	Y	N	N	N	N
ILLINOIS						
1 Rush	?	Y	Y	Y	Y	Y
2 Jackson	Y	Y	Y	Y	Y	Y
3 Lipinski	Y	Y	Y	Y	Y	Y
4 Gutierrez	Y	Y	Y	Y	Y	Y
5 Quigley	Y	Y	Y	Y	Y	Y
6 **Roskam**	N	Y	N	N	N	N
7 Davis	Y	Y	Y	Y	Y	Y
8 Bean	Y	Y	Y	Y	Y	Y
9 Schakowsky	Y	Y	Y	Y	Y	Y
10 **Kirk**	Y	Y	N	N	N	N
11 Halvorson	Y	Y	Y	Y	Y	Y
12 Costello	Y	Y	Y	Y	Y	Y
13 **Biggert**	N	Y	N	N	N	N
14 Foster	Y	Y	Y	Y	N	Y
15 **Johnson**	Y	Y	N	N	N	N

	319	320	321	322	323	324
16 **Manzullo**	N	Y	N	N	N	N
17 Hare	Y	Y	Y	Y	Y	Y
18 **Schock**	?	Y	N	N	N	N
19 **Shimkus**	N	Y	N	N	N	N
INDIANA						
1 Visclosky	Y	Y	Y	Y	Y	Y
2 Donnelly	N	Y	Y	Y	Y	N
3 Vacant						
4 **Buyer**	N	Y	?	N	N	N
5 **Burton**	N	Y	N	N	N	N
6 **Pence**	N	Y	N	N	N	N
7 Carson	Y	Y	Y	Y	Y	Y
8 Ellsworth	N	Y	Y	Y	Y	Y
9 Hill	Y	Y	N	N	N	N
IOWA						
1 Braley	Y	Y	Y	N	Y	Y
2 Loebsack	Y	Y	Y	N	Y	Y
3 Boswell	Y	Y	Y	N	N	Y
4 **Latham**	Y	Y	N	N	N	N
5 **King**	N	Y	N	N	N	N
KANSAS						
1 **Moran**	N	Y	N	N	N	N
2 **Jenkins**	N	Y	N	N	N	N
3 Moore	Y	Y	Y	Y	Y	Y
4 **Tiahrt**	N	Y	N	N	N	N
KENTUCKY						
1 **Whitfield**	N	Y	N	N	N	N
2 **Guthrie**	N	Y	N	N	N	N
3 Yarmuth	Y	Y	Y	Y	Y	Y
4 **Davis**	–	+	–	–	–	–
5 **Rogers**	N	Y	N	N	N	N
6 Chandler	Y	Y	Y	Y	Y	Y
LOUISIANA						
1 **Scalise**	N	Y	N	N	N	N
2 **Cao**	N	Y	N	N	N	Y
3 Melancon	?	?	?	?	?	?
4 **Fleming**	N	Y	N	N	N	N
5 **Alexander**	N	Y	N	N	N	N
6 **Cassidy**	N	Y	N	N	N	N
7 **Boustany**	N	Y	N	N	N	N
MAINE						
1 Pingree	Y	Y	Y	Y	Y	Y
2 Michaud	Y	Y	Y	N	N	N
MARYLAND						
1 Kratovil	N	Y	N	N	N	N
2 Ruppersberger	Y	Y	Y	Y	Y	Y
3 Sarbanes	Y	Y	Y	N	Y	Y
4 Edwards	Y	Y	Y	Y	Y	Y
5 Hoyer	Y	Y	Y	Y	Y	Y
6 **Bartlett**	N	Y	N	N	N	N
7 Cummings	Y	Y	Y	Y	Y	Y
8 Van Hollen	Y	Y	Y	Y	Y	Y
MASSACHUSETTS						
1 Olver	Y	Y	Y	Y	Y	Y
2 Neal	Y	Y	Y	Y	Y	Y
3 McGovern	Y	Y	Y	Y	Y	Y
4 Frank	Y	Y	Y	Y	Y	Y
5 Tsongas	Y	Y	Y	Y	Y	Y
6 Tierney	Y	Y	Y	Y	Y	Y
7 Markey	Y	Y	Y	Y	Y	Y
8 Capuano	Y	Y	Y	Y	Y	N
9 Lynch	Y	Y	Y	Y	Y	Y
10 Delahunt	Y	Y	Y	Y	Y	Y
MICHIGAN						
1 Stupak	N	Y	Y	Y	Y	+
2 **Hoekstra**	N	Y	N	N	N	N
3 **Ehlers**	N	Y	N	N	N	N
4 **Camp**	N	Y	N	N	N	N
5 Kildee	Y	Y	Y	Y	Y	Y
6 **Upton**	N	Y	N	N	N	N
7 Schauer	Y	Y	Y	Y	Y	Y
8 **Rogers**	N	Y	N	N	N	N
9 Peters	N	Y	Y	Y	Y	Y
10 **Miller**	N	Y	N	N	N	N
11 **McCotter**	N	Y	N	N	N	N
12 Levin	Y	Y	Y	Y	Y	Y
13 Kilpatrick	Y	Y	Y	Y	Y	Y
14 Conyers	Y	Y	Y	Y	Y	Y
15 Dingell	Y	Y	Y	Y	Y	Y
MINNESOTA						
1 Walz	Y	Y	Y	Y	Y	Y
2 **Kline**	N	Y	N	N	N	N
3 **Paulsen**	N	Y	N	N	N	N
4 McCollum	Y	Y	Y	Y	Y	Y
5 Ellison	Y	Y	Y	Y	Y	Y
6 **Bachmann**	N	Y	N	N	N	N
7 Peterson	N	Y	Y	Y	Y	Y
8 Oberstar	Y	Y	Y	Y	Y	Y
MISSISSIPPI						
1 Childers	N	Y	N	N	N	Y
2 Thompson	Y	Y	Y	Y	Y	Y
3 **Harper**	N	Y	N	N	N	N
4 Taylor	N	Y	N	N	N	N
MISSOURI						
1 Clay	Y	Y	Y	Y	Y	Y
2 **Akin**	N	Y	N	N	N	N
3 Carnahan	Y	Y	Y	Y	Y	Y
4 Skelton	Y	Y	Y	Y	Y	Y
5 Cleaver	Y	Y	Y	Y	Y	Y
6 **Graves**	–	+	?	–	+	–
7 **Blunt**	N	Y	N	N	N	N
8 **Emerson**	N	Y	N	N	N	N
9 **Luetkemeyer**	N	Y	N	N	N	N
MONTANA						
AL **Rehberg**	N	Y	N	N	N	N
NEBRASKA						
1 **Fortenberry**	Y	Y	N	N	N	N
2 **Terry**	N	Y	N	N	N	N
3 **Smith**	N	Y	N	N	N	N
NEVADA						
1 Berkley	Y	Y	Y	Y	Y	Y
2 **Heller**	Y	Y	–	N	N	N
3 Titus	Y	Y	Y	Y	Y	Y
NEW HAMPSHIRE						
1 Shea-Porter	Y	Y	Y	Y	Y	Y
2 Hodes	Y	Y	Y	Y	Y	Y
NEW JERSEY						
1 Andrews	Y	Y	Y	Y	Y	Y
2 **LoBiondo**	N	Y	N	N	N	N
3 Adler	N	Y	Y	Y	N	Y
4 **Smith**	N	Y	N	N	N	N
5 **Garrett**	N	Y	N	N	N	N
6 Pallone	Y	Y	Y	Y	Y	Y
7 **Lance**	N	Y	N	N	N	N
8 Pascrell	Y	Y	Y	Y	Y	Y
9 Rothman	Y	Y	Y	Y	Y	Y
10 Payne	Y	Y	Y	Y	Y	Y
11 **Frelinghuysen**	N	Y	N	N	N	N
12 Holt	Y	Y	Y	Y	Y	Y
13 Sires	Y	Y	Y	Y	Y	Y
NEW MEXICO						
1 Heinrich	Y	Y	Y	Y	Y	Y
2 Teague	Y	Y	Y	Y	Y	Y
3 Luján	Y	Y	Y	Y	Y	Y
NEW YORK						
1 Bishop	Y	Y	Y	Y	Y	Y
2 Israel	Y	Y	Y	Y	Y	Y
3 **King**	N	Y	N	N	N	N
4 McCarthy	Y	Y	Y	Y	Y	Y
5 Ackerman	Y	Y	Y	Y	Y	Y
6 Meeks	Y	Y	Y	Y	Y	Y
7 Crowley	Y	Y	Y	Y	Y	Y
8 Nadler	Y	Y	Y	Y	Y	Y
9 Weiner	Y	Y	Y	N	Y	Y
10 Towns	Y	Y	Y	Y	Y	Y
11 Clarke	Y	Y	Y	Y	Y	Y
12 Velázquez	Y	Y	Y	Y	Y	Y
13 McMahon	Y	Y	Y	N	N	N
14 Maloney	N	Y	Y	Y	Y	Y
15 Rangel	Y	?	Y	Y	Y	Y
16 Serrano	Y	Y	Y	Y	Y	Y
17 Engel	Y	Y	Y	Y	Y	Y
18 Lowey	Y	Y	Y	Y	Y	Y
19 Hall	Y	Y	Y	Y	Y	Y
20 Murphy	N	Y	Y	N	N	N
21 Tonko	Y	Y	Y	Y	Y	Y
22 Hinchey	Y	Y	Y	Y	Y	Y
23 Owens	N	Y	Y	N	Y	Y
24 Arcuri	N	Y	Y	Y	Y	Y
25 Maffei	Y	Y	Y	Y	Y	Y
26 **Lee**	N	Y	N	N	N	N
27 Higgins	Y	Y	Y	Y	Y	Y
28 Slaughter	Y	Y	Y	Y	Y	Y
29 Vacant						
NORTH CAROLINA						
1 Butterfield	Y	Y	Y	Y	Y	Y
2 Etheridge	Y	Y	Y	N	Y	Y
3 **Jones**	?	?	?	?	?	?
4 Price	Y	Y	Y	Y	Y	Y
5 **Foxx**	N	Y	N	N	N	N
6 **Coble**	N	Y	N	N	N	N
7 McIntyre	Y	Y	Y	?	N	N
8 Kissell	Y	Y	Y	Y	Y	Y
9 **Myrick**	N	Y	N	N	N	N
10 **McHenry**	N	Y	N	N	N	N
11 Shuler	?	?	?	?	?	?
12 Watt	Y	Y	Y	Y	Y	Y
13 Miller	Y	Y	Y	Y	Y	Y
NORTH DAKOTA						
AL Pomeroy	Y	Y	Y	Y	Y	Y
OHIO						
1 Driehaus	N	Y	N	N	N	N
2 **Schmidt**	N	Y	N	N	N	N
3 **Turner**	N	Y	N	N	N	N
4 **Jordan**	N	Y	N	N	N	N
5 **Latta**	N	Y	N	N	N	–
6 Wilson	Y	Y	Y	Y	Y	Y
7 **Austria**	N	Y	N	N	N	N
8 **Boehner**	N	Y	N	N	N	N
9 Kaptur	Y	Y	Y	Y	Y	Y
10 Kucinich	Y	Y	Y	Y	Y	Y
11 Fudge	Y	Y	Y	Y	Y	Y
12 **Tiberi**	N	Y	N	N	N	N
13 Sutton	Y	Y	Y	Y	Y	Y
14 **LaTourette**	N	Y	N	N	N	N
15 Kilroy	N	Y	Y	Y	Y	Y
16 Boccieri	N	Y	Y	N	Y	Y
17 Ryan	Y	Y	Y	Y	Y	Y
18 Space	Y	Y	Y	N	Y	Y
OKLAHOMA						
1 **Sullivan**	N	Y	?	N	N	N
2 Boren	?	?	?	?	?	–
3 **Lucas**	N	Y	N	N	N	N
4 **Cole**	Y	Y	N	N	N	N
5 **Fallin**	N	Y	N	N	N	N
OREGON						
1 Wu	Y	Y	Y	N	Y	Y
2 **Walden**	N	Y	N	N	N	N
3 Blumenauer	Y	Y	Y	Y	Y	Y
4 DeFazio	Y	Y	Y	N	Y	N
5 Schrader	Y	Y	Y	Y	Y	Y
PENNSYLVANIA						
1 Brady	Y	Y	Y	Y	Y	Y
2 Fattah	Y	Y	Y	Y	Y	Y
3 Dahlkemper	Y	Y	N	N	N	Y
4 Altmire	N	Y	Y	Y	Y	Y
5 **Thompson**	N	Y	N	N	N	N
6 **Gerlach**	N	Y	N	N	N	N
7 Sestak	Y	Y	Y	Y	Y	Y
8 Murphy, P.	Y	Y	Y	Y	Y	Y
9 **Shuster**	N	Y	N	N	N	N
10 Carney	N	Y	Y	N	Y	Y
11 Kanjorski	Y	Y	Y	Y	Y	Y
12 Critz	Y	Y	Y	Y	Y	Y
13 Schwartz	Y	Y	Y	Y	Y	Y
14 Doyle	Y	Y	Y	Y	Y	Y
15 **Dent**	Y	Y	N	N	N	N
16 **Pitts**	N	Y	N	N	N	N
17 Holden	Y	Y	Y	Y	Y	Y
18 **Murphy, T.**	N	Y	N	N	N	N
19 **Platts**	N	Y	N	N	N	N
RHODE ISLAND						
1 Kennedy	Y	Y	Y	Y	Y	Y
2 Langevin	Y	Y	Y	Y	Y	Y
SOUTH CAROLINA						
1 **Brown**	N	Y	N	N	N	N
2 **Wilson**	N	Y	N	N	N	N
3 **Barrett**	N	Y	N	N	N	N
4 **Inglis**	N	Y	N	N	N	N
5 Spratt	Y	Y	Y	Y	Y	Y
6 Clyburn	Y	Y	Y	Y	Y	Y
SOUTH DAKOTA						
AL Herseth Sandlin	Y	Y	Y	N	N	N
TENNESSEE						
1 **Roe**	Y	Y	N	N	N	N
2 **Duncan**	N	Y	N	N	N	N
3 **Wamp**	N	Y	N	N	N	N
4 Davis	Y	Y	Y	Y	Y	Y
5 Cooper	Y	Y	Y	Y	N	N
6 Gordon	Y	Y	Y	Y	Y	Y
7 **Blackburn**	N	Y	N	N	N	N
8 Tanner	Y	Y	Y	Y	Y	Y
9 Cohen	Y	Y	Y	Y	Y	Y
TEXAS						
1 **Gohmert**	P	Y	N	N	N	N
2 **Poe**	N	Y	N	N	N	N
3 **Johnson, S.**	N	Y	N	N	N	N
4 **Hall**	N	Y	N	N	N	N
5 **Hensarling**	N	Y	N	N	N	N
6 **Barton**	N	Y	N	N	N	N
7 **Culberson**	N	Y	N	N	N	N
8 **Brady**	N	Y	N	N	N	N
9 Green, A.	Y	Y	Y	Y	Y	Y
10 **McCaul**	N	Y	N	N	N	N
11 **Conaway**	N	Y	N	N	N	N
12 **Granger**	N	Y	N	N	N	N
13 **Thornberry**	N	Y	N	N	N	N
14 **Paul**	N	Y	N	N	N	N
15 Hinojosa	Y	Y	Y	Y	Y	Y
16 Reyes	Y	Y	Y	Y	Y	Y
17 Edwards	Y	Y	Y	Y	Y	N
18 Jackson Lee	Y	Y	Y	Y	Y	Y
19 **Neugebauer**	N	Y	N	N	N	N
20 Gonzalez	Y	Y	Y	Y	Y	Y
21 **Smith**	N	Y	N	N	N	N
22 **Olson**	N	Y	N	N	N	N
23 Rodriguez	Y	Y	Y	Y	Y	Y
24 **Marchant**	N	Y	N	N	N	N
25 Doggett	Y	Y	Y	Y	Y	N
26 **Burgess**	N	Y	N	N	N	N
27 Ortiz	Y	Y	Y	Y	Y	Y
28 Cuellar	Y	Y	Y	Y	Y	Y
29 Green, G.	Y	Y	Y	Y	Y	Y
30 Johnson, E.	Y	Y	Y	Y	Y	Y
31 **Carter**	N	Y	N	N	N	N
32 **Sessions**	N	Y	N	N	?	N
UTAH						
1 **Bishop**	?	Y	N	N	N	N
2 Matheson	Y	Y	Y	Y	Y	Y
3 **Chaffetz**	Y	Y	N	N	N	N
VERMONT						
AL Welch	Y	Y	Y	Y	Y	Y
VIRGINIA						
1 **Wittman**	N	Y	N	N	N	N
2 Nye	N	Y	N	N	N	N
3 Scott	Y	Y	Y	Y	Y	Y
4 **Forbes**	N	Y	N	N	N	N
5 Perriello	Y	Y	N	N	N	Y
6 **Goodlatte**	Y	Y	N	N	N	N
7 **Cantor**	N	Y	N	N	N	N
8 Moran	Y	Y	Y	Y	Y	Y
9 Boucher	Y	Y	Y	Y	Y	Y
10 **Wolf**	N	Y	N	N	N	N
11 Connolly	N	Y	Y	Y	Y	N
WASHINGTON						
1 Inslee	Y	Y	Y	Y	Y	N
2 Larsen	Y	Y	Y	Y	Y	Y
3 Baird	Y	?	Y	Y	Y	Y
4 **Hastings**	N	Y	N	N	N	N
5 **McMorris Rodgers**	?	Y	N	N	N	N
6 Dicks	Y	Y	Y	Y	Y	Y
7 McDermott	Y	Y	Y	Y	Y	Y
8 **Reichert**	N	Y	N	N	N	N
9 Smith	Y	Y	Y	Y	Y	N
WEST VIRGINIA						
1 Mollohan	Y	Y	Y	Y	Y	Y
2 **Capito**	N	Y	N	N	N	N
3 Rahall	Y	Y	Y	Y	Y	Y
WISCONSIN						
1 **Ryan**	–	+	?	–	–	–
2 Baldwin	Y	Y	Y	Y	Y	Y
3 Kind	Y	Y	Y	Y	Y	Y
4 Moore	Y	Y	Y	Y	Y	Y
5 **Sensenbrenner**	N	Y	N	N	N	N
6 **Petri**	N	Y	N	N	N	N
7 Obey	Y	Y	Y	Y	Y	Y
8 Kagen	Y	Y	Y	Y	Y	Y
WYOMING						
AL **Lummis**	N	Y	N	N	N	N
DELEGATES						
Faleomavaega (A.S.)						
Norton (D.C.)						
Bordallo (Guam)						
Sablan (N. Marianas)						
Pierluisi (P.R.)						
Christensen (V.I.)						

IN THE HOUSE | By Vote Number

325. **HR 4213. Tax Extensions/Motion to Concur.** Adoption of the Levin, D-Mich., motion to concur in the Senate amendment to the bill with Section 523 of the House amendment. Section 523 would increase Medicare reimbursements to doctors by 2.2 percent for the rest of 2010 and by 1 percent in 2011. Motion agreed to 245-171: D 230-15; R 15-156. May 28, 2010.

326. **HR 5116. Science and Technology Programs Reauthorization/ Innovation Prize Program.** Division I of the Gordon, D-Tenn., amendment reported pursuant to the Hall, R-Texas, motion to recommit with instructions. Division I would strike provisions that would authorize $12 million for fiscal 2011 through 2013 for a pilot program of cash prizes for innovation in any area of research supported by the National Science Foundation. Rejected 175-243: D 5-242; R 170-1. The House adopted the motion to recommit with instructions on May 13; Gordon reported the amendment and moved to divide it into nine parts. May 28, 2010.

327. **HR 5116. Science and Technology Programs Reauthorization/ Innovation Services Program.** Division II of the Gordon, D-Tenn., amendment reported pursuant to the Hall, R-Texas, motion to recommit with instructions. Division II would strike provisions that would create an innovative services program within the National Institute of Standards and Technology. Rejected 163-244: D 0-239; R 163-5. The House adopted the motion to recommit with instructions on May 13; Gordon reported the amendment and moved to divide it into nine parts. May 28, 2010.

328. **HR 5116. Science and Technology Programs Reauthorization/ Special Consideration.** Division VI of the Gordon, D-Tenn., amendment reported pursuant to the Hall, R-Texas, motion to recommit with instructions. Division VI would require educational institutions that serve a large number of students with disabilities and disabled veterans to receive special consideration when applying for funds authorized by the bill. Rejected 197-215: D 26-215; R 171-0. The House adopted the motion to recommit with instructions on May 13; Gordon reported the amendment and moved to divide it into nine parts. May 28, 2010.

329. **HR 5116. Science and Technology Programs Reauthorization/ Pornography Violation Exclusion.** Division VII of the Gordon, D-Tenn., amendment reported pursuant to the Hall, R-Texas, motion to recommit with instructions. Division VII would prohibit the use of funds authorized in the bill to pay the salary of any individual who has been disciplined for viewing, downloading or exchanging pornographic materials on a government computer or while performing official duties. Adopted 409-0: D 244-0; R 165-0. The House adopted the motion to recommit with instructions on May 13; Gordon reported the amendment and moved to divide it into nine parts. May 28, 2010.

330. **HR 5116. Science and Technology Programs Reauthorization/ Military Recruiter Restriction.** Division VIII of the Gordon, D-Tenn., amendment reported pursuant to the Hall, R-Texas, motion to recommit with instructions. Division VIII would disallow the use of funds authorized by the bill from going to educational institutions that restrict or deny military recruiting on campus. Adopted 348-68: D 179-68; R 169-0. The House adopted the motion to recommit with instructions on May 13; Gordon reported the amendment and moved to divide it into nine parts. May 28, 2010.

	325	326	327	328	329	330
ALABAMA						
1 **Bonner**	N	Y	Y	Y	Y	Y
2 Bright	N	Y	N	Y	Y	Y
3 **Rogers**	N	Y	Y	Y	Y	?
4 **Aderholt**	N	Y	?	Y	Y	Y
5 **Griffith**	N	Y	Y	Y	Y	Y
6 **Bachus**	N	Y	Y	Y	?	Y
7 Davis	?	?	?	?	?	?
ALASKA						
AL **Young**	Y	Y	?	Y	Y	Y
ARIZONA						
1 Kirkpatrick	Y	N	N	Y	Y	Y
2 **Franks**	N	Y	Y	Y	Y	Y
3 **Shadegg**	N	Y	Y	Y	Y	Y
4 Pastor	Y	N	N	N	Y	Y
5 Mitchell	Y	N	N	Y	Y	Y
6 **Flake**	N	Y	Y	Y	Y	Y
7 Grijalva	Y	N	N	N	Y	N
8 Giffords	Y	N	N	Y	Y	Y
ARKANSAS						
1 Berry	Y	N	N	N	Y	Y
2 Snyder	Y	N	N	Y	Y	Y
3 **Boozman**	N	Y	Y	Y	Y	Y
4 Ross	Y	N	N	Y	Y	Y
CALIFORNIA						
1 Thompson	Y	N	N	N	Y	N
2 **Herger**	N	Y	Y	Y	Y	Y
3 **Lungren**	N	Y	Y	Y	Y	Y
4 **McClintock**	N	Y	Y	Y	Y	Y
5 Matsui	Y	N	N	N	Y	Y
6 Woolsey	Y	N	N	N	Y	N
7 Miller, George	Y	N	N	N	Y	N
8 Pelosi	Y					
9 Lee	Y	N	N	N	Y	N
10 Garamendi	Y	N	N	N	Y	N
11 McNerney	Y	N	N	Y	Y	Y
12 Speier	Y	N	N	N	Y	Y
13 Stark	Y	N	N	N	Y	N
14 Eshoo	Y	N	N	N	Y	N
15 Honda	Y	N	N	N	Y	N
16 Lofgren	Y	N	N	N	Y	N
17 Farr	Y	N	N	N	Y	N
18 Cardoza	Y	N	N	N	Y	Y
19 **Radanovich**	N	Y	Y	Y	Y	Y
20 Costa	Y	N	N	Y	Y	Y
21 **Nunes**	N	Y	Y	Y	Y	Y
22 **McCarthy**	N	Y	Y	Y	Y	Y
23 Capps	Y	N	N	N	Y	N
24 **Gallegly**	N	Y	Y	Y	Y	Y
25 **McKeon**	N	Y	Y	Y	Y	Y
26 **Dreier**	N	Y	Y	Y	Y	Y
27 Sherman	Y	N	N	N	Y	N
28 Berman	Y	N	N	N	Y	Y
29 Schiff	Y	N	N	N	Y	Y
30 Waxman	Y	N	?	N	?	N
31 Becerra	Y	N	N	N	Y	N
32 Chu	Y	N	N	N	Y	N
33 Watson	Y	N	N	N	Y	N
34 Roybal-Allard	Y	N	N	N	Y	N
35 Waters	Y	N	N	N	Y	N
36 Harman	N	N	N	N	Y	Y
37 Richardson	?	N	N	N	Y	N
38 Napolitano	Y	N	?	N	Y	N
39 Sánchez, Linda	Y	N	N	N	Y	N
40 **Royce**	N	Y	Y	Y	Y	Y
41 **Lewis**	N	Y	Y	Y	Y	Y
42 **Miller, Gary**	N	Y	Y	Y	Y	Y
43 Baca	Y	N	N	N	Y	Y
44 **Calvert**	N	Y	Y	Y	Y	Y
45 **Bono Mack**	N	Y	Y	Y	Y	Y
46 **Rohrabacher**	N	Y	Y	Y	Y	Y
47 Sanchez, Loretta	?	N	N	N	Y	N
48 **Campbell**	N	Y	Y	Y	Y	Y
49 **Issa**	N	Y	Y	Y	Y	Y
50 **Bilbray**	Y	Y	Y	Y	Y	Y
51 Filner	Y	N	N	N	Y	N
52 **Hunter**	N	Y	Y	Y	Y	Y
53 Davis	Y	N	N	N	Y	N

	325	326	327	328	329	330
COLORADO						
1 DeGette	Y	N	N	N	Y	N
2 Polis	Y	N	N	N	Y	N
3 Salazar	N	N	N	N	Y	Y
4 Markey	Y	N	N	N	Y	Y
5 **Lamborn**	N	Y	Y	Y	Y	Y
6 **Coffman**	N	Y	Y	Y	Y	Y
7 Perlmutter	Y	N	N	N	Y	Y
CONNECTICUT						
1 Larson	Y	N	N	N	Y	N
2 Courtney	Y	N	—	Y	Y	Y
3 DeLauro	Y	N	N	N	Y	N
4 Himes	Y	N	N	N	Y	N
5 Murphy	Y	N	N	N	Y	Y
DELAWARE						
AL **Castle**	N	Y	N	Y	Y	Y
FLORIDA						
1 **Miller**	N	Y	Y	Y	Y	Y
2 Boyd	Y	N	N	N	Y	Y
3 Brown	Y	N	N	N	Y	Y
4 **Crenshaw**	N	Y	Y	Y	Y	Y
5 **Brown-Waite**	?	?	?	?	?	?
6 **Stearns**	N	Y	Y	Y	Y	Y
7 **Mica**	N	Y	Y	?	Y	Y
8 Grayson	Y	N	N	N	Y	N
9 **Bilirakis**	Y	Y	Y	Y	Y	Y
10 **Young**	Y	Y	Y	Y	Y	Y
11 Castor	Y	N	N	N	Y	N
12 **Putnam**	N	Y	Y	Y	Y	Y
13 **Buchanan**	N	Y	Y	Y	Y	Y
14 **Mack**	N	Y	Y	Y	Y	Y
15 **Posey**	N	Y	Y	Y	Y	Y
16 **Rooney**	N	Y	Y	Y	Y	Y
17 Meek	Y	N	N	N	Y	Y
18 **Ros-Lehtinen**	N	Y	Y	Y	Y	Y
19 Deutch	Y	N	N	N	Y	Y
20 Wasserman Schultz	Y	N	N	N	Y	N
21 **Diaz-Balart, L.**	N	Y	Y	Y	Y	Y
22 Klein	Y	N	N	N	Y	Y
23 Hastings	?	?	?	?	?	?
24 Kosmas	Y	N	N	N	Y	Y
25 **Diaz-Balart, M.**	N	Y	Y	Y	Y	Y
GEORGIA						
1 **Kingston**	N	Y	Y	Y	Y	Y
2 Bishop	Y	N	N	N	Y	Y
3 **Westmoreland**	N	Y	Y	Y	Y	Y
4 Johnson	Y	N	N	N	Y	N
5 Lewis	Y	N	N	N	Y	N
6 **Price**	N	Y	Y	Y	Y	Y
7 **Linder**	N	Y	Y	Y	Y	Y
8 Marshall	Y	N	N	N	Y	Y
9 Vacant						
10 **Broun**	N	Y	Y	Y	Y	Y
11 **Gingrey**	N	Y	Y	Y	Y	Y
12 Barrow	Y	N	N	N	Y	Y
13 Scott	Y	N	N	N	Y	Y
HAWAII						
1 **Djou**	N	Y	Y	Y	Y	Y
2 Hirono	Y	N	N	N	Y	Y
IDAHO						
1 Minnick	N	N	N	N	Y	Y
2 **Simpson**	N	Y	Y	Y	Y	Y
ILLINOIS						
1 Rush	Y	N	?	N	Y	N
2 Jackson	Y	N	N	N	Y	Y
3 Lipinski	N	N	N	N	Y	Y
4 Gutierrez	?	N	N	N	Y	N
5 Quigley	Y	N	N	N	Y	N
6 **Roskam**	N	Y	Y	Y	Y	Y
7 Davis	Y	N	N	N	Y	N
8 Bean	Y	N	N	?	Y	Y
9 Schakowsky	Y	N	N	N	Y	N
10 **Kirk**	Y	Y	Y	Y	Y	Y
11 Halvorson	Y	N	N	Y	Y	Y
12 Costello	Y	N	?	N	Y	Y
13 **Biggert**	N	Y	Y	Y	Y	Y
14 Foster	Y	N	N	N	Y	Y
15 **Johnson**	N	Y	Y	Y	Y	Y

	325	326	327	328	329	330
16 **Manzullo**	N	Y	Y	Y	Y	Y
17 Hare	Y	N	N	N	Y	Y
18 **Schock**	N	Y	Y	Y	Y	Y
19 **Shimkus**	N	Y	Y	Y	Y	Y
INDIANA						
1 Visclosky	Y	N	N	N	Y	Y
2 Donnelly	Y	N	N	Y	Y	Y
3 Vacant						
4 **Buyer**	Y	Y	Y	Y	Y	Y
5 **Burton**	N	Y	Y	Y	Y	Y
6 **Pence**	N	Y	Y	Y	Y	Y
7 Carson	Y	N	N	N	Y	Y
8 Ellsworth	Y	N	N	N	Y	Y
9 Hill	Y	N	N	N	Y	Y
IOWA						
1 Braley	Y	N	N	N	Y	Y
2 Loebsack	Y	N	N	N	Y	Y
3 Boswell	Y	N	N	N	Y	Y
4 **Latham**	N	Y	Y	Y	Y	Y
5 **King**	N	Y	Y	Y	?	Y
KANSAS						
1 **Moran**	N	Y	Y	Y	Y	Y
2 **Jenkins**	N	Y	Y	Y	Y	Y
3 Moore	Y	N	N	N	Y	Y
4 **Tiahrt**	N	Y	Y	Y	Y	Y
KENTUCKY						
1 **Whitfield**	Y	Y	Y	Y	Y	Y
2 **Guthrie**	N	Y	Y	Y	Y	Y
3 Yarmuth	Y	N	N	N	Y	Y
4 **Davis**	–	?	+	+	+	+
5 **Rogers**	Y	Y	Y	Y	Y	Y
6 Chandler	Y	N	N	N	Y	Y
LOUISIANA						
1 **Scalise**	N	Y	Y	Y	Y	Y
2 **Cao**	N	Y	Y	Y	Y	Y
3 Melancon	?	?	?	?	?	?
4 **Fleming**	N	Y	Y	Y	Y	Y
5 **Alexander**	N	Y	Y	Y	?	Y
6 **Cassidy**	Y	Y	Y	Y	Y	Y
7 **Boustany**	N	Y	Y	Y	Y	Y
MAINE						
1 Pingree	Y	N	N	N	Y	N
2 Michaud	Y	N	N	N	Y	Y
MARYLAND						
1 Kratovil	Y	N	N	N	Y	Y
2 Ruppersberger	Y	N	N	?	Y	Y
3 Sarbanes	Y	N	N	N	Y	Y
4 Edwards	Y	N	N	N	Y	N
5 Hoyer	Y	N	N	N	Y	Y
6 **Bartlett**	N	Y	Y	Y	Y	Y
7 Cummings	Y	N	N	N	Y	Y
8 Van Hollen	Y	N	N	N	Y	Y
MASSACHUSETTS						
1 Olver	Y	N	N	N	Y	N
2 Neal	Y	N	N	N	Y	N
3 McGovern	Y	N	N	N	Y	N
4 Frank	Y	N	N	N	Y	N
5 Tsongas	Y	N	N	N	Y	N
6 Tierney	Y	N	N	N	Y	N
7 Markey	Y	N	N	N	Y	N
8 Capuano	Y	N	N	N	Y	N
9 Lynch	N	N	N	N	Y	Y
10 Delahunt	?	?	?	?	?	?
MICHIGAN						
1 Stupak	–	–	–	–	+	+
2 **Hoekstra**	N	Y	Y	Y	Y	Y
3 **Ehlers**	Y	N	N	Y	Y	Y
4 **Camp**	N	Y	Y	Y	Y	Y
5 Kildee	Y	N	N	N	Y	Y
6 **Upton**	N	Y	Y	Y	Y	Y
7 Schauer	Y	N	N	N	Y	Y
8 **Rogers**	N	Y	Y	Y	Y	Y
9 Peters	Y	N	N	N	Y	Y
10 **Miller**	N	Y	Y	Y	Y	Y
11 **McCotter**	N	Y	Y	Y	Y	Y
12 Levin	Y	N	N	N	Y	Y
13 Kilpatrick	Y	N	N	N	Y	Y
14 Conyers	Y	N	N	N	Y	N
15 Dingell	Y	N	N	N	Y	Y
MINNESOTA						
1 Walz	Y	N	N	N	Y	Y
2 **Kline**	N	Y	Y	Y	Y	Y
3 **Paulsen**	N	Y	N	Y	Y	Y
4 McCollum	Y	N	N	N	Y	Y

	325	326	327	328	329	330
5 Ellison	Y	N	N	N	Y	N
6 **Bachmann**	N	Y	Y	Y	Y	Y
7 Peterson	Y	N	N	N	Y	Y
8 Oberstar	Y	N	N	N	Y	N
MISSISSIPPI						
1 Childers	Y	N	N	N	Y	Y
2 Thompson	Y	N	N	N	Y	Y
3 **Harper**	N	Y	Y	Y	Y	Y
4 Taylor	N	Y	N	Y	Y	Y
MISSOURI						
1 Clay	Y	N	N	N	Y	Y
2 **Akin**	N	Y	Y	Y	Y	Y
3 Carnahan	Y	N	N	N	Y	Y
4 Skelton	Y	N	N	N	Y	Y
5 Cleaver	Y	N	N	N	Y	Y
6 **Graves**	–	+	+	+	+	+
7 **Blunt**	N	Y	N	Y	Y	Y
8 **Emerson**	N	Y	Y	Y	Y	Y
9 **Luetkemeyer**	N	Y	Y	Y	Y	Y
MONTANA						
AL **Rehberg**	N	Y	Y	Y	Y	Y
NEBRASKA						
1 **Fortenberry**	N	Y	Y	Y	Y	Y
2 **Terry**	N	Y	Y	Y	Y	Y
3 **Smith**	N	Y	Y	Y	Y	Y
NEVADA						
1 Berkley	Y	N	N	N	Y	Y
2 **Heller**	N	Y	Y	Y	Y	Y
3 Titus	Y	N	N	Y	Y	Y
NEW HAMPSHIRE						
1 Shea-Porter	Y	N	N	N	Y	Y
2 Hodes	Y	Y	N	Y	Y	Y
NEW JERSEY						
1 Andrews	Y	N	N	N	Y	N
2 **LoBiondo**	N	Y	Y	Y	Y	Y
3 Adler	Y	N	N	Y	Y	Y
4 **Smith**	N	Y	Y	Y	Y	Y
5 **Garrett**	N	Y	Y	Y	Y	Y
6 Pallone	Y	N	N	N	Y	Y
7 **Lance**	N	Y	Y	Y	Y	Y
8 Pascrell	Y	N	N	N	Y	Y
9 Rothman	Y	N	N	N	Y	Y
10 Payne	Y	N	N	N	Y	N
11 **Frelinghuysen**	N	Y	Y	Y	Y	?
12 Holt	Y	N	N	N	Y	N
13 Sires	Y	N	N	N	Y	Y
NEW MEXICO						
1 Heinrich	Y	N	N	Y	Y	Y
2 Teague	N	N	N	Y	Y	Y
3 Luján	Y	N	N	N	Y	Y
NEW YORK						
1 Bishop	Y	N	N	N	Y	Y
2 Israel	Y	N	N	N	Y	Y
3 **King**	N	Y	Y	Y	Y	Y
4 McCarthy	Y	N	N	N	Y	Y
5 Ackerman	Y	N	N	N	Y	Y
6 Meeks	Y	N	?	N	Y	N
7 Crowley	Y	N	N	N	Y	N
8 Nadler	Y	N	N	N	Y	N
9 Weiner	Y	N	N	N	Y	N
10 Towns	Y	N	N	N	Y	N
11 Clarke	Y	N	N	?	Y	Y
12 Velázquez	Y	N	N	N	Y	N
13 McMahon	N	N	N	N	Y	Y
14 Maloney	Y	N	N	N	Y	Y
15 Rangel	Y	N	N	N	Y	N
16 Serrano	?	N	N	N	Y	N
17 Engel	Y	N	N	N	Y	Y
18 Lowey	Y	N	N	N	Y	Y
19 Hall	Y	N	N	N	Y	Y
20 Murphy	Y	N	N	?	Y	Y
21 Tonko	Y	N	N	N	Y	Y
22 Hinchey	Y	N	N	N	Y	N
23 Owens	Y	N	N	Y	Y	Y
24 Arcuri	Y	N	N	N	Y	Y
25 Maffei	Y	Y	N	Y	Y	Y
26 **Lee**	N	Y	N	Y	Y	Y
27 Higgins	Y	N	N	N	Y	Y
28 Slaughter	Y	N	N	N	Y	N
29 Vacant						
NORTH CAROLINA						
1 Butterfield	Y	N	N	N	Y	Y
2 Etheridge	Y	N	N	N	Y	Y
3 **Jones**	?	?	?	?	?	?
4 Price	Y	N	N	N	Y	N

	325	326	327	328	329	330
5 **Foxx**	N	Y	Y	Y	Y	Y
6 **Coble**	N	Y	Y	Y	Y	Y
7 McIntyre	N	N	N	N	Y	Y
8 Kissell	Y	N	N	N	Y	Y
9 **Myrick**	N	Y	Y	Y	Y	Y
10 **McHenry**	N	Y	Y	Y	Y	Y
11 Shuler	?	?	?	?	?	?
12 Watt	Y	N	N	N	Y	N
13 Miller	Y	N	N	N	Y	Y
NORTH DAKOTA						
AL Pomeroy	Y	N	N	N	Y	Y
OHIO						
1 Driehaus	Y	N	N	N	Y	Y
2 **Schmidt**	N	Y	Y	Y	Y	Y
3 **Turner**	N	Y	Y	Y	Y	Y
4 **Jordan**	N	Y	Y	Y	Y	Y
5 **Latta**	–	+	+	+	?	+
6 Wilson	Y	N	N	N	Y	Y
7 **Austria**	N	Y	Y	Y	Y	Y
8 **Boehner**	N	Y	Y	Y	Y	Y
9 Kaptur	Y	N	N	N	?	Y
10 Kucinich	Y	N	N	N	Y	N
11 Fudge	Y	N	N	N	Y	Y
12 **Tiberi**	N	Y	Y	Y	Y	Y
13 Sutton	Y	N	N	N	Y	Y
14 **LaTourette**	Y	Y	?	Y	Y	Y
15 Kilroy	Y	N	N	?	Y	Y
16 Boccieri	Y	N	N	Y	Y	Y
17 Ryan	Y	N	?	N	Y	Y
18 Space	Y	N	N	Y	Y	Y
OKLAHOMA						
1 **Sullivan**	N	Y	Y	Y	Y	Y
2 Boren	–	–	–	–	+	+
3 **Lucas**	N	Y	Y	Y	Y	Y
4 **Cole**	N	Y	Y	Y	Y	Y
5 **Fallin**	N	Y	Y	Y	Y	Y
OREGON						
1 Wu	Y	N	N	N	Y	N
2 **Walden**	N	Y	Y	Y	Y	Y
3 Blumenauer	Y	N	N	N	Y	N
4 DeFazio	Y	N	N	Y	Y	Y
5 Schrader	Y	N	N	Y	Y	Y
PENNSYLVANIA						
1 Brady	Y	N	N	N	Y	Y
2 Fattah	Y	N	N	N	Y	Y
3 Dahlkemper	N	N	N	N	Y	Y
4 Altmire	Y	N	N	Y	Y	Y
5 **Thompson**	N	Y	Y	Y	Y	Y
6 **Gerlach**	N	Y	Y	Y	Y	Y
7 Sestak	Y	N	N	N	Y	Y
8 Murphy, P.	Y	N	N	N	Y	Y
9 **Shuster**	N	Y	Y	Y	Y	Y
10 Carney	Y	N	N	Y	Y	Y
11 Kanjorski	Y	N	N	N	Y	Y
12 Critz	Y	N	N	N	Y	Y
13 Schwartz	Y	N	N	N	Y	Y
14 Doyle	Y	N	N	N	Y	N
15 **Dent**	Y	Y	Y	Y	Y	Y
16 **Pitts**	N	Y	Y	Y	Y	Y
17 Holden	Y	N	N	Y	Y	Y
18 **Murphy, T.**	N	Y	Y	Y	Y	Y
19 **Platts**	N	Y	Y	Y	Y	Y
RHODE ISLAND						
1 Kennedy	Y	N	N	N	Y	Y
2 Langevin	Y	N	N	N	Y	Y
SOUTH CAROLINA						
1 **Brown**	N	Y	Y	Y	Y	Y
2 **Wilson**	N	Y	Y	Y	Y	Y
3 **Barrett**	N	Y	Y	Y	Y	Y
4 **Inglis**	N	Y	Y	Y	Y	Y
5 Spratt	Y	N	?	N	Y	Y
6 Clyburn	Y	N	N	N	Y	Y
SOUTH DAKOTA						
AL Herseth Sandlin	N	N	N	N	Y	Y
TENNESSEE						
1 **Roe**	N	Y	Y	Y	Y	Y
2 **Duncan**	N	Y	Y	Y	Y	Y
3 **Wamp**	N	Y	Y	Y	Y	Y
4 Davis	Y	N	N	N	Y	Y
5 Cooper	N	N	N	N	Y	Y
6 Gordon	Y	N	N	N	Y	Y
7 **Blackburn**	N	Y	Y	Y	Y	Y
8 Tanner	Y	N	N	N	Y	Y
9 Cohen	Y	N	N	N	Y	N

	325	326	327	328	329	330
TEXAS						
1 **Gohmert**	N	Y	Y	Y	Y	Y
2 **Poe**	N	Y	Y	Y	Y	Y
3 **Johnson, S.**	N	Y	Y	Y	Y	Y
4 **Hall**	N	Y	Y	Y	?	Y
5 **Hensarling**	N	Y	Y	Y	Y	Y
6 **Barton**	N	Y	Y	Y	Y	Y
7 **Culberson**	N	Y	Y	Y	Y	Y
8 **Brady**	N	Y	Y	Y	Y	Y
9 Green, A.	Y	N	N	N	Y	Y
10 **McCaul**	Y	Y	Y	Y	Y	Y
11 **Conaway**	N	Y	Y	Y	Y	Y
12 **Granger**	N	Y	Y	Y	Y	Y
13 **Thornberry**	N	Y	Y	Y	Y	Y
14 **Paul**	N	Y	Y	Y	Y	Y
15 Hinojosa	Y	N	N	N	Y	Y
16 Reyes	Y	N	N	N	Y	Y
17 Edwards	Y	N	N	N	Y	Y
18 Jackson Lee	Y	N	N	N	Y	Y
19 **Neugebauer**	N	Y	Y	Y	Y	Y
20 Gonzalez	Y	N	N	N	Y	Y
21 **Smith**	N	Y	Y	Y	Y	Y
22 **Olson**	N	Y	Y	Y	Y	Y
23 Rodriguez	Y	N	N	N	Y	Y
24 **Marchant**	N	Y	Y	Y	Y	Y
25 Doggett	Y	N	N	N	Y	Y
26 **Burgess**	Y	Y	Y	Y	Y	Y
27 Ortiz	Y	N	N	N	Y	Y
28 Cuellar	Y	N	N	N	Y	Y
29 Green, G.	Y	N	N	N	Y	Y
30 Johnson, E.	Y	N	N	N	Y	N
31 **Carter**	N	Y	Y	Y	Y	Y
32 **Sessions**	N	Y	Y	Y	?	Y
UTAH						
1 **Bishop**	N	Y	Y	Y	Y	Y
2 Matheson	Y	N	N	N	Y	Y
3 **Chaffetz**	N	Y	Y	Y	Y	Y
VERMONT						
AL Welch	Y	N	N	N	Y	N
VIRGINIA						
1 **Wittman**	N	Y	Y	Y	Y	Y
2 Nye	Y	Y	N	Y	Y	Y
3 Scott	Y	N	N	N	Y	N
4 **Forbes**	N	Y	Y	Y	Y	Y
5 Perriello	Y	N	N	N	Y	Y
6 **Goodlatte**	N	Y	Y	Y	Y	Y
7 **Cantor**	N	Y	Y	Y	Y	Y
8 Moran	Y	N	N	N	Y	Y
9 Boucher	Y	N	N	Y	Y	Y
10 **Wolf**	N	Y	Y	Y	Y	Y
11 Connolly	Y	N	N	N	Y	Y
WASHINGTON						
1 Inslee	Y	N	N	N	Y	Y
2 Larsen	Y	N	N	N	Y	Y
3 Baird	N	N	N	N	Y	Y
4 **Hastings**	N	Y	Y	Y	Y	Y
5 **McMorris Rodgers**	N	Y	Y	Y	Y	Y
6 Dicks	Y	N	N	Y	Y	Y
7 McDermott	N	N	N	N	Y	N
8 **Reichert**	N	Y	Y	Y	Y	Y
9 Smith	Y	N	N	N	Y	Y
WEST VIRGINIA						
1 Mollohan	Y	N	N	N	Y	N
2 **Capito**	Y	Y	Y	Y	Y	Y
3 Rahall	Y	N	N	N	Y	Y
WISCONSIN						
1 **Ryan**	–	+	+	+	+	+
2 Baldwin	Y	N	N	N	Y	N
3 Kind	Y	N	N	N	Y	Y
4 Moore	Y	N	N	N	Y	N
5 **Sensenbrenner**	N	Y	Y	Y	Y	Y
6 **Petri**	N	Y	Y	Y	Y	Y
7 Obey	Y	N	?	N	?	N
8 Kagen	Y	N	N	N	Y	Y
WYOMING						
AL **Lummis**	N	Y	Y	Y	Y	Y
DELEGATES						
Faleomavaega (A.S.)						
Norton (D.C.)						
Bordallo (Guam)						
Sablan (N. Marianas)						
Pierluisi (P.R.)						
Christensen (V.I.)						

IN THE HOUSE | By Vote Number

331. **HR 5116. Science and Technology Programs Reauthorization/ Authorization Level Decrease.** Division IX of the Gordon, D-Tenn., amendment reported pursuant to the Hall, R-Texas, motion to recommit with instructions. Division IX would reauthorize programs in the bill though fiscal 2013, instead of through fiscal 2015, and would freeze authorization levels for most programs under the bill at the fiscal 2010 level in any year with a budget deficit. It also would eliminate funding for the Advanced Research Projects Agency-Energy. Rejected 181-234: D 12-233; R 169-1. The House adopted the motion to recommit with instructions on May 13; Gordon reported the amendment and moved to divide it into nine parts. May 28, 2010.

332. **HR 5116. Science and Technology Programs Reauthorization/ Passage.** Passage of the bill that would authorize $85.6 billion in fiscal 2011 through 2015 for science and research programs at the National Science Foundation, the National Institute of Standards and Technology and the Energy Department. As amended, it would disallow authorized funds from going to educational institutions that restrict or deny military recruiting on campus or to pay the salary of any individual who has been disciplined regarding pornographic materials. Passed 262-150: D 245-0; R 17-150. May 28, 2010.

333. **HR 5136. Fiscal 2011 Defense Authorization/En Bloc Amendments.** Skelton, D-Mo., en bloc amendments that would require the Defense Department to ensure that certain individuals who have served at least one tour in Iraq or Afghanistan receive at least quarterly counseling, create a scholarship program for veterans pursuing degrees in behavioral health sciences and add numerous other provisions. Adopted in Committee of the Whole 416-1: D 248-0; R 168-1. May 28, 2010.

334. **HR 5136. Fiscal 2011 Defense Authorization/Motion to Table.** Skelton, D-Mo., motion to table (kill) the Bachmann, R-Minn., appeal of the ruling of the chair with respect to the Skelton point of order that the Bachmann motion to recommit the bill was not germane to the bill. The motion would recommit the bill to the Armed Services Committee with instructions that it be reported back immediately with an amendment that would freeze the pay of members of Congress and non-uniformed federal employees. Motion agreed to 227-183: D 224-18; R 3-165. May 28, 2010.

335. **HR 5136. Fiscal 2011 Defense Authorization/Recommit.** Forbes, R-Va., motion to recommit the bill to the Armed Services Committee with instructions that it be reported back immediately with an amendment that would prohibit the use of funds authorized in the bill to transfer or release individuals detained at the U.S. facility at Guantánamo Bay, Cuba, into the United States or its territories. Motion agreed to 282-131: D 114-130; R 168-1. A "nay" was a vote in support of the president's position. May 28, 2010.

336. **HR 5136. Fiscal 2011 Defense Authorization/Passage.** Passage of the bill that would authorize $725.9 billion in discretionary funding for defense programs in fiscal 2011, including $159.3 billion for the wars in Iraq and Afghanistan and other overseas contingency operations. It would authorize $167.6 billion for operations and maintenance accounts, $111 billion for procurement and $138.5 billion for military personnel. The bill would authorize $20 billion for military construction and family housing, $32.4 billion for the Defense Health Program, and a 1.9 percent pay raise for military personnel. The measure would repeal the military's policy on the service of openly gay personnel, contingent upon certification and the results of a Dec. 1 review. It would prohibit the use of funds authorized in the bill to transfer or release detainees at Guantánamo Bay, Cuba, into the United States or its territories. Passed 229-186: D 220-26; R 9-160. A "nay" was a vote in support of the president's position. May 28, 2010.

	331	332	333	334	335	336
ALABAMA						
1 Bonner	Y	N	Y	N	Y	N
2 Bright	Y	Y	Y	N	Y	N
3 Rogers	Y	N	Y	N	Y	N
4 Aderholt	Y	N	Y	N	Y	N
5 Griffith	Y	N	Y	N	Y	N
6 Bachus	Y	N	Y	N	Y	N
7 Davis	?	?	?	?	?	?
ALASKA						
AL Young	Y	N	Y	Y	Y	N
ARIZONA						
1 Kirkpatrick	N	Y	Y	N	Y	N
2 Franks	Y	N	Y	N	Y	N
3 Shadegg	Y	N	Y	Y	Y	N
4 Pastor	N	Y	Y	Y	N	Y
5 Mitchell	N	Y	Y	Y	N	Y
6 Flake	Y	N	Y	N	Y	N
7 Grijalva	N	Y	Y	Y	N	Y
8 Giffords	N	Y	Y	N	Y	Y
ARKANSAS						
1 Berry	N	Y	Y	Y	N	Y
2 Snyder	N	Y	Y	Y	N	Y
3 Boozman	Y	N	Y	N	Y	N
4 Ross	N	Y	Y	Y	N	Y
CALIFORNIA						
1 Thompson	N	Y	Y	Y	N	Y
2 Herger	Y	N	Y	N	Y	N
3 Lungren	Y	N	Y	N	Y	N
4 McClintock	Y	N	Y	N	Y	N
5 Matsui	N	Y	Y	Y	N	Y
6 Woolsey	N	Y	Y	N	N	Y
7 Miller, George	N	Y	Y	Y	N	N
8 Pelosi		Y				Y
9 Lee	N	Y	Y	N	N	Y
10 Garamendi	N	Y	Y	Y	Y	Y
11 McNerney	N	+	Y	Y	Y	Y
12 Speier	N	Y	Y	Y	N	Y
13 Stark	N	Y	Y	N	N	N
14 Eshoo	N	Y	Y	Y	N	Y
15 Honda	N	Y	Y	Y	N	Y
16 Lofgren	N	Y	Y	N	N	Y
17 Farr	?	Y	Y	Y	N	Y
18 Cardoza	N	Y	Y	Y	Y	Y
19 Radanovich	Y	?	Y	N	Y	N
20 Costa	N	Y	Y	Y	Y	Y
21 Nunes	Y	N	Y	N	Y	N
22 McCarthy	Y	N	Y	N	Y	N
23 Capps	N	Y	Y	Y	N	Y
24 Gallegly	Y	N	Y	N	Y	N
25 McKeon	?	N	Y	N	Y	N
26 Dreier	Y	N	Y	N	Y	N
27 Sherman	N	Y	Y	Y	N	Y
28 Berman	N	Y	Y	Y	?	Y
29 Schiff	N	Y	Y	Y	N	Y
30 Waxman	N	Y	Y	N	N	Y
31 Becerra	N	Y	Y	Y	N	Y
32 Chu	N	Y	Y	?	N	N
33 Watson	N	Y	Y	Y	N	N
34 Roybal-Allard	N	Y	Y	Y	N	Y
35 Waters	N	Y	Y	Y	N	Y
36 Harman	N	Y	Y	Y	N	Y
37 Richardson	N	Y	Y	Y	Y	Y
38 Napolitano	N	Y	Y	Y	N	Y
39 Sánchez, Linda	N	Y	Y	Y	N	Y
40 Royce	Y	N	Y	N	Y	N
41 Lewis	Y	N	Y	N	Y	N
42 Miller, Gary	Y	N	Y	N	Y	N
43 Baca	N	Y	Y	Y	Y	Y
44 Calvert	Y	N	Y	N	Y	N
45 Bono Mack	Y	N	Y	N	Y	Y
46 Rohrabacher	Y	N	Y	N	Y	N
47 Sanchez, Loretta	N	Y	Y	Y	N	Y
48 Campbell	Y	N	Y	N	Y	N
49 Issa	Y	N	Y	N	Y	N
50 Bilbray	Y	N	Y	N	Y	N
51 Filner	N	Y	Y	N	N	Y
52 Hunter	Y	N	Y	N	Y	N
53 Davis	N	Y	Y	N	Y	N

	331	332	333	334	335	336
COLORADO						
1 DeGette	N	Y	Y	?	N	Y
2 Polis	N	Y	Y	Y	N	Y
3 Salazar	N	Y	Y	Y	Y	Y
4 Markey	N	Y	Y	Y	Y	Y
5 Lamborn	Y	N	Y	N	Y	N
6 Coffman	Y	N	Y	N	Y	N
7 Perlmutter	N	Y	Y	Y	N	Y
CONNECTICUT						
1 Larson	N	Y	Y	Y	N	Y
2 Courtney	N	Y	Y	Y	Y	Y
3 DeLauro	N	Y	Y	Y	N	Y
4 Himes	N	Y	Y	Y	N	Y
5 Murphy	N	Y	Y	Y	N	Y
DELAWARE						
AL Castle	Y	Y	Y	N	Y	Y
FLORIDA						
1 Miller	Y	N	Y	N	Y	N
2 Boyd	N	Y	Y	Y	Y	Y
3 Brown	N	Y	Y	Y	N	Y
4 Crenshaw	Y	Y	Y	N	Y	N
5 Brown-Waite	?	?	?	?	?	?
6 Stearns	Y	N	Y	N	Y	N
7 Mica	Y	N	Y	?	Y	N
8 Grayson	N	Y	Y	Y	N	Y
9 Bilirakis	Y	N	Y	N	Y	N
10 Young	Y	N	Y	N	Y	N
11 Castor	N	Y	Y	Y	N	Y
12 Putnam	Y	N	Y	N	Y	N
13 Buchanan	Y	N	Y	N	Y	N
14 Mack	Y	N	Y	N	Y	N
15 Posey	Y	N	Y	N	Y	N
16 Rooney	Y	N	Y	N	Y	N
17 Meek	N	Y	Y	Y	N	Y
18 Ros-Lehtinen	Y	N	Y	N	Y	N
19 Deutch	N	Y	Y	Y	N	Y
20 Wasserman Schultz	N	Y	Y	Y	N	Y
21 Diaz-Balart, L.	Y	N	Y	N	Y	N
22 Klein	N	Y	Y	Y	Y	Y
23 Hastings	?	?	?	?	?	?
24 Kosmas	N	Y	Y	N	Y	N
25 Diaz-Balart, M.	Y	N	Y	N	Y	N
GEORGIA						
1 Kingston	Y	N	Y	N	Y	N
2 Bishop	N	Y	Y	Y	Y	Y
3 Westmoreland	Y	N	Y	N	Y	N
4 Johnson	N	Y	Y	Y	N	Y
5 Lewis	N	Y	Y	Y	N	Y
6 Price	Y	N	Y	N	Y	N
7 Linder	Y	N	Y	N	?	N
8 Marshall	N	Y	Y	Y	N	N
9 Vacant						
10 Broun	Y	N	Y	N	Y	N
11 Gingrey	Y	N	Y	N	Y	N
12 Barrow	N	Y	Y	Y	Y	Y
13 Scott	N	Y	Y	Y	N	Y
HAWAII						
1 Djou	Y	?	Y	N	Y	Y
2 Hirono	N	Y	Y	Y	N	N
IDAHO						
1 Minnick	N	Y	Y	N	Y	Y
2 Simpson	Y	N	Y	N	Y	N
ILLINOIS						
1 Rush	N	Y	Y	Y	N	Y
2 Jackson	N	Y	Y	Y	Y	Y
3 Lipinski	N	Y	Y	Y	N	Y
4 Gutierrez	N	Y	Y	?	N	Y
5 Quigley	N	Y	Y	Y	N	Y
6 Roskam	Y	N	Y	N	Y	N
7 Davis	N	Y	Y	N	Y	N
8 Bean	N	Y	Y	Y	Y	Y
9 Schakowsky	N	Y	Y	Y	N	Y
10 Kirk	Y	Y	Y	N	Y	Y
11 Halvorson	N	Y	Y	N	Y	Y
12 Costello	N	Y	Y	Y	N	Y
13 Biggert	Y	Y	Y	N	Y	Y
14 Foster	N	Y	Y	N	Y	Y
15 Johnson	Y	Y	Y	N	Y	N

KEY | **Republicans** | Democrats

Y Voted for (yea)	X Paired against	C Voted "present" to avoid possible conflict of interest
# Paired for	– Announced against	
+ Announced for	P Voted "present"	? Did not vote or otherwise make a position known
N Voted against (nay)		

	331	332	333	334	335	336
16 **Manzullo**	Y	N	Y	N	Y	N
17 Hare	N	Y	Y	Y	N	Y
18 **Schock**	Y	N	Y	N	Y	N
19 **Shimkus**	Y	N	Y	N	Y	N
INDIANA						
1 Visclosky	N	Y	Y	Y	Y	Y
2 Donnelly	Y	Y	Y	Y	Y	Y
3 Vacant						
4 **Buyer**	Y	N	Y	N	Y	N
5 **Burton**	Y	N	Y	N	Y	N
6 **Pence**	Y	N	Y	N	Y	N
7 Carson	N	Y	Y	Y	Y	Y
8 Ellsworth	Y	Y	Y	Y	Y	Y
9 Hill	N	Y	Y	Y	Y	Y
IOWA						
1 Braley	N	Y	Y	Y	N	Y
2 Loebsack	N	Y	Y	Y	N	Y
3 Boswell	N	Y	Y	Y	Y	Y
4 **Latham**	Y	N	Y	N	Y	N
5 **King**	Y	N	Y	N	Y	N
KANSAS						
1 **Moran**	Y	N	Y	N	Y	N
2 **Jenkins**	Y	N	Y	N	Y	N
3 Moore	N	Y	Y	Y	Y	Y
4 **Tiahrt**	Y	N	Y	N	Y	N
KENTUCKY						
1 **Whitfield**	Y	?	Y	N	Y	N
2 **Guthrie**	Y	N	Y	N	Y	N
3 Yarmuth	N	Y	Y	Y	N	Y
4 **Davis**	?	?	?	–	+	–
5 **Rogers**	Y	N	Y	N	Y	N
6 Chandler	N	Y	Y	Y	Y	Y
LOUISIANA						
1 **Scalise**	Y	N	Y	N	Y	N
2 **Cao**	Y	Y	Y	N	Y	Y
3 Melancon	?	?	?	?	?	?
4 **Fleming**	Y	N	Y	N	Y	N
5 **Alexander**	Y	N	Y	N	Y	N
6 **Cassidy**	Y	N	Y	N	Y	N
7 **Boustany**	Y	N	Y	N	Y	N
MAINE						
1 Pingree	N	Y	Y	Y	N	Y
2 Michaud	N	Y	Y	Y	N	N
MARYLAND						
1 Kratovil	N	Y	Y	Y	Y	Y
2 Ruppersberger	N	Y	Y	Y	Y	Y
3 Sarbanes	N	Y	Y	Y	N	Y
4 Edwards	N	Y	Y	Y	N	Y
5 Hoyer	N	Y	Y	Y	N	Y
6 **Bartlett**	Y	Y	Y	N	Y	N
7 Cummings	N	Y	Y	Y	N	Y
8 Van Hollen	N	Y	Y	Y	N	Y
MASSACHUSETTS						
1 Olver	N	Y	Y	Y	N	N
2 Neal	N	Y	Y	Y	N	Y
3 McGovern	N	Y	Y	Y	N	Y
4 Frank	N	Y	Y	Y	N	Y
5 Tsongas	N	Y	Y	Y	N	Y
6 Tierney	N	Y	Y	Y	N	Y
7 Markey	N	Y	Y	Y	N	Y
8 Capuano	N	Y	Y	Y	N	Y
9 Lynch	N	Y	Y	Y	Y	Y
10 Delahunt	?	?	?	?	?	?
MICHIGAN						
1 Stupak	+	+	+	+	–	+
2 **Hoekstra**	Y	N	Y	N	Y	N
3 **Ehlers**	N	Y	Y	N	Y	N
4 **Camp**	Y	N	Y	N	Y	N
5 Kildee	N	Y	Y	Y	N	Y
6 **Upton**	Y	N	Y	N	Y	N
7 Schauer	N	Y	Y	Y	Y	Y
8 **Rogers**	Y	N	Y	?	Y	N
9 Peters	N	Y	Y	Y	Y	Y
10 **Miller**	Y	N	Y	N	Y	N
11 **McCotter**	Y	N	Y	N	Y	N
12 Levin	N	Y	Y	Y	N	?
13 Kilpatrick	N	Y	Y	Y	N	Y
14 Conyers	N	Y	Y	Y	N	?
15 Dingell	N	Y	Y	Y	N	Y
MINNESOTA						
1 Walz	N	Y	Y	Y	Y	Y
2 **Kline**	Y	N	Y	N	Y	N
3 **Paulsen**	Y	N	Y	N	Y	N
4 McCollum	N	Y	Y	Y	N	Y

	331	332	333	334	335	336
5 Ellison	N	Y	Y	Y	N	N
6 **Bachmann**	Y	N	Y	N	Y	N
7 Peterson	N	Y	Y	Y	Y	N
8 Oberstar	N	Y	Y	Y	N	Y
MISSISSIPPI						
1 Childers	Y	Y	Y	N	Y	N
2 Thompson	N	Y	Y	Y	N	Y
3 **Harper**	Y	N	Y	N	Y	N
4 Taylor	Y	Y	Y	N	Y	N
MISSOURI						
1 Clay	N	Y	Y	Y	N	Y
2 **Akin**	Y	N	Y	N	Y	N
3 Carnahan	N	Y	Y	Y	Y	Y
4 Skelton	N	Y	Y	Y	Y	Y
5 Cleaver	N	Y	Y	Y	N	Y
6 **Graves**	+	–	+	–	+	–
7 **Blunt**	Y	N	Y	N	Y	N
8 **Emerson**	Y	N	Y	N	Y	N
9 **Luetkemeyer**	Y	N	Y	N	Y	N
MONTANA						
AL **Rehberg**	Y	N	Y	N	Y	N
NEBRASKA						
1 **Fortenberry**	Y	N	Y	N	Y	N
2 **Terry**	Y	Y	Y	N	Y	N
3 **Smith**	Y	N	Y	N	Y	N
NEVADA						
1 Berkley	?	Y	Y	Y	Y	Y
2 **Heller**	Y	N	Y	N	Y	N
3 Titus	N	Y	Y	N	Y	Y
NEW HAMPSHIRE						
1 Shea-Porter	N	Y	Y	Y	Y	Y
2 Hodes	Y	Y	Y	N	Y	Y
NEW JERSEY						
1 Andrews	N	Y	Y	Y	Y	Y
2 **LoBiondo**	Y	N	Y	N	Y	N
3 Adler	N	Y	Y	Y	Y	Y
4 **Smith**	Y	N	Y	N	Y	N
5 **Garrett**	Y	N	Y	N	Y	N
6 Pallone	N	Y	Y	Y	N	Y
7 **Lance**	Y	N	Y	N	Y	N
8 Pascrell	N	Y	Y	Y	N	Y
9 Rothman	N	Y	Y	Y	N	Y
10 Payne	N	Y	Y	Y	N	N
11 **Frelinghuysen**	Y	N	Y	N	Y	N
12 Holt	N	Y	Y	Y	N	Y
13 Sires	N	Y	Y	Y	Y	Y
NEW MEXICO						
1 Heinrich	N	Y	Y	Y	N	Y
2 Teague	N	Y	Y	N	Y	Y
3 Luján	N	Y	Y	Y	N	Y
NEW YORK						
1 Bishop	N	Y	Y	Y	Y	Y
2 Israel	N	Y	Y	Y	Y	Y
3 **King**	Y	N	Y	N	?	?
4 McCarthy	N	Y	Y	Y	N	Y
5 Ackerman	N	Y	Y	Y	?	Y
6 Meeks	N	Y	Y	Y	N	Y
7 Crowley	N	Y	Y	Y	N	Y
8 Nadler	N	Y	Y	Y	N	Y
9 Weiner	N	Y	Y	Y	N	Y
10 Towns	N	Y	Y	Y	N	Y
11 Clarke	N	Y	Y	Y	N	Y
12 Velázquez	N	Y	Y	Y	N	Y
13 McMahon	Y	Y	Y	Y	Y	Y
14 Maloney	N	Y	Y	Y	Y	Y
15 Rangel	N	Y	Y	Y	N	Y
16 Serrano	N	?	Y	Y	N	Y
17 Engel	N	Y	Y	?	Y	Y
18 Lowey	N	Y	Y	Y	N	Y
19 Hall	N	Y	Y	Y	Y	Y
20 Murphy	N	Y	Y	Y	Y	Y
21 Tonko	N	Y	Y	Y	Y	Y
22 Hinchey	N	Y	Y	Y	N	Y
23 Owens	N	Y	Y	Y	Y	Y
24 Arcuri	N	Y	Y	Y	Y	Y
25 Maffei	N	Y	Y	Y	Y	Y
26 **Lee**	Y	Y	Y	N	Y	N
27 Higgins	N	Y	Y	Y	Y	Y
28 Slaughter	N	Y	Y	Y	?	Y
29 Vacant						
NORTH CAROLINA						
1 Butterfield	N	Y	Y	Y	N	Y
2 Etheridge	N	Y	Y	Y	Y	Y
3 **Jones**	?	?	?	?	?	?
4 Price	N	Y	Y	Y	N	Y

	331	332	333	334	335	336
5 **Foxx**	Y	N	Y	N	Y	N
6 **Coble**	Y	N	Y	N	Y	N
7 McIntyre	Y	Y	Y	N	Y	N
8 Kissell	N	Y	Y	Y	Y	Y
9 **Myrick**	Y	N	?	N	Y	N
10 **McHenry**	Y	N	Y	N	Y	N
11 Shuler	?	?	?	?	?	?
12 Watt	N	Y	Y	Y	N	N
13 Miller	N	Y	Y	Y	Y	Y
NORTH DAKOTA						
AL Pomeroy	N	Y	Y	Y	Y	Y
OHIO						
1 Driehaus	N	Y	Y	Y	Y	Y
2 **Schmidt**	Y	N	Y	N	Y	N
3 **Turner**	Y	N	Y	N	Y	N
4 **Jordan**	Y	N	Y	N	Y	N
5 **Latta**	+	–	+	–	+	–
6 Wilson	N	Y	Y	Y	Y	Y
7 **Austria**	Y	N	Y	N	Y	N
8 **Boehner**	Y	N	Y	N	Y	N
9 Kaptur	N	Y	Y	Y	N	Y
10 Kucinich	N	Y	Y	Y	N	N
11 Fudge	N	Y	Y	Y	N	Y
12 **Tiberi**	Y	N	Y	N	Y	N
13 Sutton	N	Y	Y	Y	Y	Y
14 **LaTourette**	Y	N	Y	N	Y	N
15 Kilroy	N	Y	Y	Y	N	Y
16 Boccieri	N	Y	Y	Y	Y	Y
17 Ryan	N	Y	Y	Y	Y	Y
18 Space	N	Y	Y	Y	Y	Y
OKLAHOMA						
1 **Sullivan**	Y	N	Y	N	Y	N
2 Boren	–	+	+	–	+	–
3 **Lucas**	Y	N	Y	N	Y	N
4 **Cole**	Y	N	Y	N	Y	N
5 **Fallin**	Y	N	Y	N	Y	N
OREGON						
1 Wu	N	Y	Y	Y	N	Y
2 **Walden**	Y	N	Y	N	Y	N
3 Blumenauer	N	Y	Y	Y	N	Y
4 DeFazio	N	Y	Y	?	N	Y
5 Schrader	N	Y	Y	Y	Y	Y
PENNSYLVANIA						
1 Brady	N	Y	Y	Y	N	Y
2 Fattah	N	Y	Y	Y	N	Y
3 Dahlkemper	N	Y	Y	N	Y	Y
4 Altmire	N	Y	Y	Y	Y	Y
5 **Thompson**	Y	N	Y	N	Y	N
6 **Gerlach**	Y	Y	Y	N	Y	N
7 Sestak	N	Y	Y	Y	N	Y
8 Murphy, P.	N	Y	Y	Y	Y	Y
9 **Shuster**	Y	N	Y	N	Y	N
10 Carney	N	Y	Y	Y	Y	Y
11 Kanjorski	N	Y	Y	Y	Y	Y
12 Critz	N	Y	Y	Y	Y	Y
13 Schwartz	N	Y	Y	Y	Y	Y
14 Doyle	N	Y	Y	Y	N	Y
15 **Dent**	Y	Y	Y	N	Y	Y
16 **Pitts**	Y	N	Y	N	Y	N
17 Holden	N	Y	Y	N	Y	Y
18 **Murphy, T.**	Y	N	Y	N	Y	N
19 **Platts**	Y	N	Y	N	Y	N
RHODE ISLAND						
1 Kennedy	N	Y	Y	Y	N	Y
2 Langevin	N	Y	Y	Y	Y	Y
SOUTH CAROLINA						
1 **Brown**	Y	N	Y	N	Y	?
2 **Wilson**	Y	N	Y	N	Y	N
3 **Barrett**	Y	N	Y	N	Y	N
4 **Inglis**	Y	N	Y	N	Y	N
5 Spratt	N	Y	Y	Y	Y	Y
6 Clyburn	N	Y	Y	Y	N	Y
SOUTH DAKOTA						
AL Herseth Sandlin	N	Y	Y	Y	Y	Y
TENNESSEE						
1 **Roe**	Y	N	Y	N	Y	N
2 **Duncan**	Y	N	Y	N	Y	N
3 **Wamp**	Y	Y	Y	N	Y	N
4 Davis	N	Y	Y	Y	Y	N
5 Cooper	N	Y	Y	Y	Y	Y
6 Gordon	N	Y	Y	Y	Y	Y
7 **Blackburn**	Y	N	Y	N	Y	N
8 Tanner	N	Y	Y	Y	Y	Y
9 Cohen	N	Y	+	Y	N	Y

	331	332	333	334	335	336
TEXAS						
1 **Gohmert**	Y	N	Y	N	Y	N
2 **Poe**	Y	N	Y	N	Y	N
3 **Johnson, S.**	Y	N	Y	N	Y	N
4 **Hall**	Y	N	Y	N	Y	N
5 **Hensarling**	Y	N	Y	N	Y	N
6 **Barton**	Y	N	?	N	Y	N
7 **Culberson**	Y	N	Y	N	Y	N
8 **Brady**	Y	N	Y	N	Y	N
9 Green, A.	N	Y	Y	Y	N	Y
10 **McCaul**	Y	Y	Y	N	Y	N
11 **Conaway**	Y	N	Y	N	Y	N
12 **Granger**	Y	N	Y	N	Y	N
13 **Thornberry**	Y	N	Y	N	Y	N
14 **Paul**	Y	N	N	N	N	N
15 Hinojosa	N	Y	Y	Y	Y	Y
16 Reyes	N	Y	Y	Y	Y	Y
17 Edwards	N	Y	Y	Y	Y	Y
18 Jackson Lee	N	Y	Y	Y	N	Y
19 **Neugebauer**	Y	N	Y	N	Y	N
20 Gonzalez	N	Y	Y	Y	Y	Y
21 **Smith**	Y	?	Y	N	Y	N
22 **Olson**	Y	N	Y	N	Y	N
23 Rodriguez	N	Y	Y	Y	Y	Y
24 **Marchant**	Y	N	Y	N	Y	N
25 Doggett	N	Y	Y	Y	N	Y
26 **Burgess**	Y	N	Y	N	Y	N
27 Ortiz	N	Y	Y	Y	Y	Y
28 Cuellar	Y	Y	Y	Y	Y	Y
29 Green, G.	N	Y	Y	Y	Y	Y
30 Johnson, E.	N	Y	Y	Y	N	Y
31 **Carter**	Y	N	Y	N	Y	N
32 **Sessions**	Y	N	Y	N	Y	N
UTAH						
1 **Bishop**	Y	N	Y	?	Y	N
2 Matheson	N	Y	Y	Y	Y	Y
3 **Chaffetz**	Y	N	Y	N	Y	N
VERMONT						
AL Welch	N	Y	Y	Y	N	N
VIRGINIA						
1 **Wittman**	Y	N	Y	N	Y	N
2 Nye	Y	Y	Y	N	Y	Y
3 Scott	N	Y	Y	Y	N	Y
4 **Forbes**	Y	N	Y	N	Y	N
5 Perriello	N	Y	Y	Y	Y	Y
6 **Goodlatte**	Y	N	Y	N	Y	N
7 **Cantor**	Y	N	Y	N	Y	N
8 Moran	N	Y	Y	Y	N	Y
9 Boucher	N	Y	Y	Y	Y	Y
10 **Wolf**	Y	Y	Y	Y	Y	N
11 Connolly	N	Y	Y	Y	Y	Y
WASHINGTON						
1 Inslee	N	Y	Y	Y	N	Y
2 Larsen	N	Y	Y	Y	N	Y
3 Baird	N	Y	Y	Y	N	Y
4 **Hastings**	Y	N	Y	N	Y	N
5 **McMorris Rodgers**	Y	N	Y	N	Y	N
6 Dicks	N	Y	Y	Y	N	Y
7 McDermott	N	?	Y	Y	N	N
8 **Reichert**	Y	Y	Y	N	Y	N
9 Smith	N	Y	Y	Y	N	Y
WEST VIRGINIA						
1 Mollohan	N	Y	Y	Y	N	Y
2 **Capito**	Y	Y	Y	N	Y	N
3 Rahall	Y	Y	Y	Y	Y	Y
WISCONSIN						
1 **Ryan**	+	–	+	–	+	–
2 Baldwin	N	Y	Y	Y	N	Y
3 Kind	N	Y	Y	Y	Y	Y
4 Moore	N	Y	Y	Y	N	N
5 **Sensenbrenner**	Y	N	Y	N	Y	N
6 **Petri**	Y	N	Y	N	Y	N
7 Obey	N	Y	Y	Y	N	N
8 Kagen	N	Y	Y	Y	N	Y
WYOMING						
AL **Lummis**	Y	N	Y	N	Y	N
DELEGATES						
Faleomavaega (A.S.)			?			
Norton (D.C.)			Y			
Bordallo (Guam)			+			
Sablan (N. Marianas)			?			
Pierluisi (P.R.)			Y			
Christensen (V.I.)			?			

IN THE HOUSE | By Vote Number

337. **HR 1061. Hoh Indian Tribe Land/Passage.** Bordallo, D-Guam, motion to suspend the rules and pass the bill that would entrust to the Hoh Indian Tribe certain non-federal land owned by the tribe and certain federal land administered by the National Park Service located south of the Hoh River in Washington state. The bill would prohibit gaming activities on land taken into trust, and ban logging, hunting and the building of structures on the federal lands. Motion agreed to 347-0: D 201-0; R 146-0. A two-thirds majority of those present and voting (232 in this case) is required for passage under suspension of the rules. June 8, 2010.

338. **H Res 518. Tribute to Jacques-Yves Cousteau/Adoption.** Bordallo, D-Guam, motion to suspend the rules and adopt the resolution that would honor the life, achievements and career of explorer and marine conservationist Jacques-Yves Cousteau. Motion agreed to 354-0: D 208-0; R 146-0. A two-thirds majority of those present and voting (236 in this case) is required for adoption under suspension of the rules. June 8, 2010.

339. **HR 5072. FHA Mortgage Rates Revisions/Previous Question.** Perlmutter, D-Colo., motion to order the previous question (thus ending debate and possibility of amendment) on adoption of the rule (HR 5072) to provide for House floor consideration of the bill that would provide the Federal Housing Administration with the authority to adjust the premium structure for mortgage insurance. Motion agreed to 230-180: D 230-10; R 0-170. June 9, 2010.

340. **H Res 1424, HR 5072. FHA Mortgage Rates Revisions/Rule.** Adoption of the rule (H Res 1424) to provide for House floor consideration of the bill that would provide the Federal Housing Administration with the authority to adjust the premium structure for mortgage insurance. Adopted 239-172: D 239-4; R 0-168. June 9, 2010.

341. **H Res 989. Ocean Acidification Prevention/Adoption.** Inslee, D-Wash., motion to suspend the rules and adopt the resolution that would express the sense of the House that the United States should adopt national policies and pursue international agreements to prevent ocean acidification and address its effect on marine ecosystems and coastal economies. Motion rejected 241-170: D 222-20; R 19-150. A two-thirds majority of those present and voting (274 in this case) is required for adoption under suspension of the rules. June 9, 2010.

342. **H Res 1178. CBO Cost Estimates/Adoption.** Brady, D-Pa., motion to suspend the rules and adopt the resolution that would direct the clerk of the House of Representatives to ensure that Congressional Budget Office (CBO) cost estimates are available to the public by including a link to the CBO website on the clerk's public website. Motion agreed to 390-22: D 243-0; R 147-22. A two-thirds majority of those present and voting (275 in this case) is required for adoption under suspension of the rules. June 9, 2010.

	337	338	339	340	341	342
ALABAMA						
1 Bonner	?	?	N	N	N	Y
2 Bright	Y	Y	N	Y	N	Y
3 Rogers	Y	?	N	N	N	Y
4 Aderholt	Y	Y	N	N	N	Y
5 Griffith	?	?	N	N	N	Y
6 Bachus	Y	Y	N	?	N	?
7 Davis	Y	Y	Y	Y	Y	Y
ALASKA						
AL Young	Y	Y	N	N	N	N
ARIZONA						
1 Kirkpatrick	Y	Y	N	Y	Y	Y
2 Franks	Y	Y	N	N	N	Y
3 Shadegg	Y	Y	N	N	N	Y
4 Pastor	Y	Y	Y	Y	Y	Y
5 Mitchell	Y	Y	N	Y	Y	Y
6 Flake	?	?	N	N	N	N
7 Grijalva	?	?	Y	N	N	Y
8 Giffords	+	+	N	?	Y	Y
ARKANSAS						
1 Berry	?	?	Y	Y	Y	Y
2 Snyder	Y	Y	Y	Y	Y	Y
3 Boozman	Y	Y	N	N	N	Y
4 Ross	Y	Y	Y	Y	Y	Y
CALIFORNIA						
1 Thompson	+	+	Y	Y	Y	Y
2 Herger	?	Y	N	N	N	Y
3 Lungren	Y	Y	N	N	N	N
4 McClintock	Y	Y	N	N	N	Y
5 Matsui	Y	Y	Y	Y	Y	Y
6 Woolsey	Y	Y	Y	Y	Y	Y
7 Miller, George	?	?	?	Y	Y	Y
8 Pelosi						
9 Lee	Y	Y	Y	Y	Y	Y
10 Garamendi	Y	Y	Y	Y	Y	Y
11 McNerney	Y	Y	Y	Y	Y	Y
12 Speier	?	?	Y	Y	Y	Y
13 Stark	?	?	Y	Y	Y	Y
14 Eshoo	Y	Y	Y	Y	Y	Y
15 Honda	Y	Y	Y	Y	Y	Y
16 Lofgren	?	?	Y	Y	Y	Y
17 Farr	Y	Y	Y	Y	Y	Y
18 Cardoza	?	Y	Y	Y	Y	Y
19 Radanovich	?	?	N	N	N	Y
20 Costa	?	Y	Y	Y	Y	Y
21 Nunes	Y	Y	N	N	N	N
22 McCarthy	Y	Y	N	N	N	Y
23 Capps	Y	Y	Y	Y	Y	Y
24 Gallegly	Y	Y	N	N	N	Y
25 McKeon	Y	Y	N	N	N	Y
26 Dreier	Y	Y	N	N	N	N
27 Sherman	Y	Y	Y	Y	Y	Y
28 Berman	Y	Y	Y	Y	Y	Y
29 Schiff	Y	Y	Y	Y	Y	Y
30 Waxman	?	?	Y	Y	?	Y
31 Becerra	Y	Y	Y	Y	Y	Y
32 Chu	Y	Y	Y	Y	Y	Y
33 Watson	?	?	?	?	?	?
34 Roybal-Allard	Y	Y	Y	Y	Y	Y
35 Waters	?	?	Y	Y	?	Y
36 Harman	?	?	?	?	?	?
37 Richardson	+	+	+	?	Y	Y
38 Napolitano	Y	Y	Y	Y	Y	Y
39 Sánchez, Linda	Y	Y	Y	Y	Y	Y
40 Royce	Y	Y	N	N	N	Y
41 Lewis	?	?	N	N	N	N
42 Miller, Gary	?	?	?	?	?	?
43 Baca	Y	Y	Y	N	Y	Y
44 Calvert	+	+	-	-	-	+
45 Bono Mack	?	?	N	N	Y	Y
46 Rohrabacher	?	?	N	N	N	Y
47 Sanchez, Loretta	Y	Y	Y	Y	Y	Y
48 Campbell	?	?	?	?	?	?
49 Issa	?	?	N	N	N	Y
50 Bilbray	Y	Y	N	N	Y	Y
51 Filner	Y	Y	Y	Y	Y	Y
52 Hunter	Y	Y	N	N	N	Y
53 Davis	Y	Y	Y	Y	Y	Y

	337	338	339	340	341	342
COLORADO						
1 DeGette	Y	?	Y	Y	Y	Y
2 Polis	Y	Y	Y	Y	Y	Y
3 Salazar	Y	Y	Y	Y	N	Y
4 Markey	Y	Y	Y	Y	Y	Y
5 Lamborn	Y	Y	N	N	N	Y
6 Coffman	Y	Y	N	N	N	Y
7 Perlmutter	Y	Y	Y	Y	Y	Y
CONNECTICUT						
1 Larson	?	?	Y	Y	Y	Y
2 Courtney	Y	Y	Y	Y	Y	Y
3 DeLauro	Y	Y	Y	Y	Y	Y
4 Himes	Y	Y	Y	Y	Y	Y
5 Murphy	Y	Y	Y	Y	Y	Y
DELAWARE						
AL Castle	Y	Y	N	N	Y	Y
FLORIDA						
1 Miller	Y	Y	N	N	N	Y
2 Boyd	Y	Y	?	?	?	?
3 Brown	Y	Y	Y	Y	Y	Y
4 Crenshaw	Y	Y	Y	Y	Y	Y
5 Brown-Waite	Y	Y	N	N	N	Y
6 Stearns	Y	Y	N	N	N	Y
7 Mica	Y	Y	N	N	N	Y
8 Grayson	Y	Y	Y	Y	Y	Y
9 Bilirakis	Y	Y	N	-	N	Y
10 Young	Y	Y	N	N	N	Y
11 Castor	Y	Y	Y	Y	Y	Y
12 Putnam	Y	Y	N	N	N	Y
13 Buchanan	Y	Y	N	N	N	Y
14 Mack	?	?	N	N	N	Y
15 Posey	Y	Y	N	N	N	Y
16 Rooney	Y	Y	N	N	N	Y
17 Meek	Y	Y	Y	Y	Y	Y
18 Ros-Lehtinen	Y	Y	N	N	N	Y
19 Deutch	Y	Y	Y	Y	Y	Y
20 Wasserman Schultz	Y	Y	Y	Y	Y	Y
21 Diaz-Balart, L.	Y	Y	N	N	Y	Y
22 Klein	Y	Y	Y	Y	Y	Y
23 Hastings	Y	Y	Y	Y	Y	Y
24 Kosmas	Y	Y	Y	Y	Y	Y
25 Diaz-Balart, M.	Y	Y	N	N	N	Y
GEORGIA						
1 Kingston	Y	Y	N	N	N	Y
2 Bishop	Y	Y	Y	Y	Y	Y
3 Westmoreland	Y	?	N	N	N	N
4 Johnson	Y	Y	?	Y	Y	Y
5 Lewis	Y	Y	Y	?	Y	Y
6 Price	?	Y	N	N	N	Y
7 Linder	Y	Y	N	N	N	Y
8 Marshall	Y	Y	Y	Y	Y	Y
9 Vacant						
10 Broun	Y	Y	N	N	N	N
11 Gingrey	Y	Y	N	N	N	Y
12 Barrow	Y	Y	Y	Y	Y	Y
13 Scott	Y	Y	?	Y	Y	Y
HAWAII						
1 Djou	Y	Y	N	N	Y	Y
2 Hirono	Y	Y	Y	Y	Y	Y
IDAHO						
1 Minnick	Y	Y	N	Y	Y	Y
2 Simpson	Y	Y	N	N	N	N
ILLINOIS						
1 Rush	Y	Y	Y	Y	Y	Y
2 Jackson	Y	Y	Y	Y	Y	Y
3 Lipinski	Y	Y	Y	Y	Y	Y
4 Gutierrez	+	+	Y	Y	Y	?
5 Quigley	Y	Y	Y	Y	Y	Y
6 Roskam	Y	Y	N	N	N	Y
7 Davis	Y	Y	Y	Y	Y	Y
8 Bean	Y	Y	Y	Y	Y	Y
9 Schakowsky	?	?	Y	Y	Y	Y
10 Kirk	Y	Y	N	N	N	Y
11 Halvorson	Y	Y	Y	Y	Y	Y
12 Costello	Y	Y	Y	Y	Y	Y
13 Biggert	Y	Y	N	N	Y	Y
14 Foster	Y	Y	Y	Y	Y	Y
15 Johnson	Y	Y	N	N	Y	Y

	337	338	339	340	341	342
16 **Manzullo**	Y	?	N	N	N	Y
17 Hare	Y	Y	Y	Y	Y	Y
18 **Schock**	Y	Y	N	N	N	Y
19 **Shimkus**	Y	Y	N	N	N	Y
INDIANA						
1 Visclosky	Y	Y	Y	Y	Y	Y
2 Donnelly	Y	Y	Y	Y	Y	Y
3 Vacant						
4 **Buyer**	Y	Y	N	N	N	Y
5 **Burton**	Y	Y	N	N	N	Y
6 **Pence**	Y	Y	N	N	N	Y
7 Carson	Y	Y	Y	Y	Y	Y
8 Ellsworth	Y	Y	?	?	?	?
9 Hill	Y	Y	N	N	Y	Y
IOWA						
1 Braley	Y	Y	Y	Y	Y	Y
2 Loebsack	Y	Y	Y	Y	Y	Y
3 Boswell	Y	Y	Y	Y	Y	Y
4 **Latham**	Y	Y	N	N	N	Y
5 **King**	Y	Y	N	N	N	N
KANSAS						
1 **Moran**	Y	Y	N	N	N	Y
2 **Jenkins**	Y	Y	N	N	N	Y
3 Moore	Y	Y	Y	Y	Y	Y
4 **Tiahrt**	Y	Y	N	N	N	Y
KENTUCKY						
1 **Whitfield**	Y	Y	N	N	N	Y
2 **Guthrie**	Y	Y	N	N	N	Y
3 Yarmuth	Y	Y	?	?	?	?
4 **Davis**	Y	Y	N	N	N	Y
5 **Rogers**	Y	Y	N	N	N	Y
6 Chandler	Y	Y	Y	Y	Y	Y
LOUISIANA						
1 **Scalise**	Y	Y	N	N	N	Y
2 **Cao**	Y	Y	N	N	N	Y
3 Melancon	Y	Y	Y	Y	Y	Y
4 **Fleming**	Y	Y	N	N	N	Y
5 **Alexander**	Y	Y	N	N	Y	Y
6 **Cassidy**	Y	Y	N	N	Y	Y
7 **Boustany**	Y	Y	N	N	N	Y
MAINE						
1 Pingree	Y	Y	Y	Y	Y	Y
2 Michaud	Y	Y	Y	Y	Y	Y
MARYLAND						
1 Kratovil	Y	Y	N	Y	Y	Y
2 Ruppersberger	Y	Y	Y	Y	Y	Y
3 Sarbanes	Y	Y	Y	Y	Y	Y
4 Edwards	Y	Y	Y	Y	Y	Y
5 Hoyer	?	?	?	Y	Y	Y
6 **Bartlett**	Y	Y	N	N	N	Y
7 Cummings	Y	Y	Y	Y	Y	Y
8 Van Hollen	Y	?	Y	Y	Y	Y
MASSACHUSETTS						
1 Olver	Y	Y	Y	Y	Y	Y
2 Neal	Y	Y	Y	Y	Y	Y
3 McGovern	Y	Y	Y	Y	Y	Y
4 Frank	Y	Y	Y	Y	Y	Y
5 Tsongas	?	?	Y	Y	Y	Y
6 Tierney	?	?	Y	Y	Y	Y
7 Markey	Y	Y	Y	Y	Y	Y
8 Capuano	Y	Y	Y	Y	Y	Y
9 Lynch	Y	Y	Y	Y	Y	Y
10 Delahunt	Y	Y	Y	Y	Y	Y
MICHIGAN						
1 Stupak	?	?	Y	Y	Y	Y
2 **Hoekstra**	?	?	?	?	?	?
3 **Ehlers**	Y	Y	N	N	N	Y
4 **Camp**	Y	Y	N	N	N	Y
5 Kildee	Y	Y	Y	Y	Y	Y
6 **Upton**	Y	Y	N	N	N	Y
7 Schauer	Y	Y	Y	Y	Y	Y
8 **Rogers**	Y	Y	N	N	N	Y
9 Peters	Y	Y	Y	Y	Y	Y
10 **Miller**	Y	Y	N	N	N	Y
11 **McCotter**	Y	Y	N	N	N	Y
12 Levin	Y	Y	Y	Y	Y	Y
13 Kilpatrick	+	+	?	?	?	?
14 Conyers	+	+	Y	Y	Y	Y
15 Dingell	Y	Y	Y	Y	?	Y
MINNESOTA						
1 Walz	Y	Y	Y	Y	Y	Y
2 **Kline**	Y	Y	N	N	N	N
3 **Paulsen**	Y	Y	N	N	N	Y
4 McCollum	Y	Y	Y	Y	Y	?

	337	338	339	340	341	342
5 Ellison	Y	Y	Y	Y	Y	Y
6 **Bachmann**	Y	Y	N	N	N	Y
7 Peterson	Y	Y	Y	Y	Y	Y
8 Oberstar	Y	Y	Y	Y	Y	Y
MISSISSIPPI						
1 Childers	Y	Y	Y	Y	Y	Y
2 Thompson	Y	Y	Y	Y	Y	Y
3 **Harper**	Y	Y	N	N	N	N
4 Taylor	Y	Y	N	N	N	Y
MISSOURI						
1 Clay	Y	Y	Y	Y	Y	Y
2 **Akin**	Y	Y	N	N	N	Y
3 Carnahan	Y	Y	Y	Y	Y	Y
4 Skelton	Y	Y	Y	Y	N	Y
5 Cleaver	Y	Y	Y	Y	Y	Y
6 **Graves**	Y	Y	N	N	N	Y
7 **Blunt**	?	?	N	N	N	Y
8 **Emerson**	Y	Y	N	N	N	Y
9 **Luetkemeyer**	Y	Y	N	N	N	Y
MONTANA						
AL **Rehberg**	Y	Y	N	N	N	Y
NEBRASKA						
1 **Fortenberry**	Y	Y	N	N	Y	Y
2 **Terry**	Y	Y	N	N	N	Y
3 **Smith**	Y	Y	N	N	N	Y
NEVADA						
1 Berkley	?	?	?	?	?	?
2 **Heller**	Y	Y	N	N	N	Y
3 Titus	?	?	Y	Y	Y	Y
NEW HAMPSHIRE						
1 Shea-Porter	Y	Y	Y	Y	Y	Y
2 Hodes	?	?	Y	Y	Y	Y
NEW JERSEY						
1 Andrews	?	?	Y	Y	Y	Y
2 **LoBiondo**	Y	Y	N	N	N	Y
3 Adler	Y	Y	Y	Y	Y	Y
4 **Smith**	Y	Y	N	N	N	Y
5 **Garrett**	Y	Y	N	N	N	Y
6 Pallone	Y	Y	Y	Y	Y	Y
7 **Lance**	Y	Y	N	N	N	Y
8 Pascrell	Y	Y	Y	Y	Y	Y
9 Rothman	Y	Y	Y	Y	Y	Y
10 Payne	?	?	Y	Y	Y	Y
11 **Frelinghuysen**	Y	Y	N	N	N	Y
12 Holt	?	Y	Y	Y	Y	Y
13 Sires	?	?	Y	Y	Y	Y
NEW MEXICO						
1 Heinrich	Y	Y	Y	Y	Y	Y
2 Teague	Y	Y	Y	Y	Y	Y
3 Luján	Y	Y	Y	Y	Y	Y
NEW YORK						
1 Bishop	Y	Y	Y	Y	Y	Y
2 Israel	Y	Y	Y	Y	Y	Y
3 **King**	Y	Y	N	N	Y	Y
4 McCarthy	Y	Y	Y	Y	Y	Y
5 Ackerman	?	?	Y	Y	Y	Y
6 Meeks	Y	Y	Y	Y	Y	Y
7 Crowley	Y	Y	Y	Y	Y	Y
8 Nadler	?	Y	Y	Y	Y	Y
9 Weiner	Y	Y	Y	Y	Y	Y
10 Towns	?	?	Y	Y	Y	Y
11 Clarke	?	Y	Y	Y	Y	Y
12 Velázquez	?	Y	Y	Y	Y	Y
13 McMahon	Y	Y	Y	Y	Y	Y
14 Maloney	Y	Y	Y	Y	Y	Y
15 Rangel	Y	Y	Y	Y	Y	Y
16 Serrano	Y	Y	Y	Y	Y	Y
17 Engel	Y	Y	Y	Y	Y	Y
18 Lowey	+	Y	Y	Y	Y	Y
19 Hall	Y	Y	Y	Y	Y	Y
20 Murphy	Y	Y	Y	Y	Y	Y
21 Tonko	Y	Y	Y	Y	Y	Y
22 Hinchey	Y	Y	Y	Y	Y	Y
23 Owens	Y	Y	Y	Y	Y	Y
24 Arcuri	Y	Y	Y	Y	Y	Y
25 Maffei	Y	Y	Y	Y	Y	Y
26 **Lee**	Y	Y	N	N	Y	Y
27 Higgins	Y	Y	Y	Y	Y	Y
28 Slaughter	?	Y	Y	Y	Y	Y
29 Vacant						
NORTH CAROLINA						
1 Butterfield	Y	Y	Y	Y	Y	Y
2 Etheridge	Y	Y	Y	Y	Y	Y
3 **Jones**	Y	Y	N	N	Y	Y
4 Price	?	?	Y	Y	Y	Y

	337	338	339	340	341	342
5 **Foxx**	Y	Y	N	N	N	Y
6 **Coble**	Y	Y	N	N	N	N
7 McIntyre	Y	Y	N	Y	Y	Y
8 Kissell	Y	Y	Y	Y	Y	Y
9 **Myrick**	Y	Y	N	N	N	Y
10 **McHenry**	?	?	?	?	?	?
11 Shuler	Y	Y	Y	N	Y	Y
12 Watt	Y	Y	Y	Y	Y	Y
13 Miller	Y	Y	Y	Y	Y	Y
NORTH DAKOTA						
AL Pomeroy	Y	Y	?	Y	Y	Y
OHIO						
1 Driehaus	Y	Y	Y	Y	Y	Y
2 **Schmidt**	Y	Y	N	N	N	Y
3 **Turner**	Y	Y	N	N	N	Y
4 **Jordan**	Y	Y	N	N	N	N
5 **Latta**	Y	Y	N	N	N	Y
6 Wilson	Y	Y	Y	Y	N	Y
7 **Austria**	Y	Y	N	N	N	Y
8 **Boehner**	?	?	N	N	N	N
9 Kaptur	Y	Y	Y	Y	?	Y
10 Kucinich	Y	Y	Y	Y	Y	Y
11 Fudge	Y	Y	Y	Y	Y	Y
12 **Tiberi**	Y	Y	N	N	N	Y
13 Sutton	Y	Y	Y	Y	Y	Y
14 **LaTourette**	?	?	N	N	N	Y
15 Kilroy	?	Y	Y	Y	Y	Y
16 Boccieri	Y	Y	Y	Y	Y	Y
17 Ryan	?	Y	Y	Y	Y	Y
18 Space	Y	Y	Y	Y	N	Y
OKLAHOMA						
1 **Sullivan**	Y	Y	N	N	N	Y
2 Boren	Y	Y	Y	Y	Y	Y
3 **Lucas**	Y	Y	N	N	N	Y
4 **Cole**	Y	Y	N	N	N	Y
5 **Fallin**	?	?	N	N	N	Y
OREGON						
1 Wu	Y	Y	Y	Y	Y	Y
2 **Walden**	Y	Y	N	N	N	Y
3 Blumenauer	?	?	Y	Y	Y	Y
4 DeFazio	Y	Y	Y	Y	Y	Y
5 Schrader	Y	Y	Y	Y	Y	Y
PENNSYLVANIA						
1 Brady	Y	Y	Y	Y	Y	Y
2 Fattah	Y	Y	Y	Y	Y	?
3 Dahlkemper	Y	Y	Y	Y	Y	Y
4 Altmire	Y	Y	Y	Y	N	Y
5 **Thompson**	Y	Y	N	N	N	Y
6 **Gerlach**	+	+	N	N	N	Y
7 Sestak	Y	Y	Y	Y	Y	Y
8 Murphy, P.	Y	Y	Y	Y	N	Y
9 **Shuster**	Y	Y	N	N	N	Y
10 Carney	Y	Y	Y	Y	Y	Y
11 Kanjorski	Y	Y	Y	Y	N	Y
12 Critz	Y	Y	Y	Y	N	Y
13 Schwartz	?	Y	Y	Y	Y	Y
14 Doyle	?	?	Y	Y	Y	Y
15 **Dent**	Y	Y	N	N	N	Y
16 **Pitts**	Y	?	N	N	N	Y
17 Holden	Y	Y	Y	Y	N	Y
18 **Murphy, T.**	Y	Y	N	N	N	Y
19 **Platts**	Y	Y	N	N	N	Y
RHODE ISLAND						
1 Kennedy	+	+	+	+	+	+
2 Langevin	?	Y	Y	Y	Y	Y
SOUTH CAROLINA						
1 **Brown**	?	?	N	N	N	Y
2 **Wilson**	?	+	N	N	N	Y
3 **Barrett**	?	?	?	?	?	?
4 **Inglis**	?	?	?	?	?	?
5 Spratt	?	?	Y	Y	Y	Y
6 Clyburn	?	?	Y	Y	Y	Y
SOUTH DAKOTA						
AL Herseth Sandlin	Y	Y	Y	Y	N	Y
TENNESSEE						
1 **Roe**	Y	Y	N	N	N	Y
2 **Duncan**	Y	Y	N	N	N	Y
3 **Wamp**	?	?	N	N	N	Y
4 Davis	Y	Y	Y	Y	Y	Y
5 Cooper	Y	Y	Y	Y	Y	Y
6 Gordon	?	?	Y	Y	Y	Y
7 **Blackburn**	Y	Y	N	N	N	Y
8 Tanner	Y	Y	Y	Y	N	Y
9 Cohen	Y	Y	Y	Y	Y	Y

	337	338	339	340	341	342
TEXAS						
1 **Gohmert**	Y	Y	N	N	N	Y
2 **Poe**	Y	Y	N	N	N	Y
3 **Johnson, S.**	Y	Y	N	N	N	N
4 **Hall**	Y	Y	N	N	N	Y
5 **Hensarling**	Y	Y	N	N	N	Y
6 **Barton**	Y	?	N	N	?	Y
7 **Culberson**	Y	Y	N	N	N	Y
8 **Brady**	?	?	N	N	N	N
9 Green, A.	Y	Y	Y	Y	Y	Y
10 **McCaul**	Y	Y	N	N	N	Y
11 **Conaway**	Y	Y	N	N	N	Y
12 **Granger**	?	Y	N	N	N	Y
13 **Thornberry**	Y	Y	N	N	N	Y
14 **Paul**	Y	Y	N	N	N	Y
15 Hinojosa	Y	Y	Y	Y	Y	Y
16 Reyes	Y	Y	Y	Y	N	Y
17 Edwards	?	?	Y	Y	Y	Y
18 Jackson Lee	Y	Y	Y	Y	Y	Y
19 **Neugebauer**	Y	Y	N	N	N	Y
20 Gonzalez	Y	Y	Y	Y	Y	Y
21 **Smith**	Y	Y	N	N	N	Y
22 **Olson**	Y	Y	N	N	N	Y
23 Rodriguez	?	?	Y	Y	Y	Y
24 **Marchant**	Y	Y	N	N	N	Y
25 Doggett	Y	Y	Y	Y	Y	Y
26 **Burgess**	?	Y	N	N	N	Y
27 Ortiz	Y	Y	Y	Y	N	Y
28 Cuellar	Y	Y	Y	Y	Y	Y
29 Green, G.	Y	Y	Y	Y	N	Y
30 Johnson, E.	Y	Y	Y	Y	Y	Y
31 **Carter**	?	?	N	N	N	N
32 **Sessions**	Y	Y	N	N	N	Y
UTAH						
1 **Bishop**	Y	Y	N	N	N	N
2 Matheson	Y	Y	Y	Y	Y	Y
3 **Chaffetz**	Y	Y	N	N	N	N
VERMONT						
AL Welch	Y	Y	Y	Y	Y	Y
VIRGINIA						
1 **Wittman**	Y	Y	N	N	Y	Y
2 Nye	Y	Y	N	Y	Y	Y
3 Scott	Y	Y	Y	Y	Y	Y
4 **Forbes**	Y	Y	N	N	N	Y
5 Perriello	Y	Y	Y	Y	Y	Y
6 **Goodlatte**	Y	Y	N	N	N	Y
7 **Cantor**	Y	Y	N	N	N	Y
8 Moran	Y	Y	Y	Y	Y	Y
9 Boucher	Y	Y	Y	Y	Y	Y
10 **Wolf**	Y	Y	N	N	N	Y
11 Connolly	Y	Y	Y	Y	Y	Y
WASHINGTON						
1 Inslee	Y	Y	Y	Y	Y	Y
2 Larsen	Y	Y	Y	Y	Y	Y
3 Baird	Y	?	Y	Y	Y	Y
4 **Hastings**	Y	Y	N	N	N	Y
5 **McMorris Rodgers**	?	Y	N	N	N	Y
6 Dicks	Y	?	Y	Y	Y	Y
7 McDermott	?	Y	Y	Y	Y	Y
8 **Reichert**	Y	Y	N	N	Y	Y
9 Smith	+	+	Y	Y	Y	Y
WEST VIRGINIA						
1 Mollohan	?	?	Y	Y	N	Y
2 **Capito**	Y	Y	N	N	N	Y
3 Rahall	Y	Y	Y	Y	N	Y
WISCONSIN						
1 **Ryan**	Y	Y	N	N	N	Y
2 Baldwin	Y	Y	Y	Y	Y	Y
3 Kind	Y	Y	Y	Y	Y	Y
4 Moore	Y	Y	Y	Y	Y	Y
5 **Sensenbrenner**	Y	Y	N	N	N	N
6 **Petri**	Y	Y	N	N	N	N
7 Obey	Y	Y	Y	Y	Y	Y
8 Kagen	Y	Y	Y	Y	Y	Y
WYOMING						
AL **Lummis**	Y	Y	N	N	N	Y
DELEGATES						
Faleomavaega (A.S.)						
Norton (D.C.)						
Bordallo (Guam)						
Sablan (N. Marianas)						
Pierluisi (P.R.)						
Christensen (V.I.)						

IN THE HOUSE | By Vote Number

343. HR 4173. **Financial Regulatory Overhaul/Motion to Instruct.**
Bachus, R-Ala., motion to instruct the conferees to disagree to provisions
in the House bill regarding the dissolution of large financial institutions.
It would instruct conferees to disagree to Senate provisions related to the
commencement of orderly liquidation and the appointment of the Federal Deposit Insurance Corporation (FDIC) as receiver for failing financial companies, as well as provisions related to FDIC powers and duties
as receiver. It would instruct conferees to withhold approval of the final
conference agreement unless it has been available to the managers for at
least 72 hours. Motion rejected 198-217: D 28-217; R 170-0. June 9, 2010.

344. H Res 1330. **World Ocean Day/Adoption.** Chu, D-Calif., motion to suspend the rules and adopt the resolution that would recognize
World Ocean Day. Motion agreed to 369-44: D 244-0; R 125-44. A two-
thirds majority of those present and voting (276 in this case) is required
for adoption under suspension of the rules. June 9, 2010.

345. HR 5278. **Ronald Reagan Post Office/Passage.** Chu, D-Calif.,
motion to suspend the rules and pass the bill that would designate a
post office in Dixon, Ill., as the "President Ronald W. Reagan Post Office
Building." Motion agreed to 416-0: D 247-0; R 169-0. A two-thirds majority of those present and voting (278 in this case) is required for passage
under suspension of the rules. June 9, 2010.

346. HR 5133. **Carvill and Schwarz Post Office/Passage.** Chu,
D-Calif., motion to suspend the rules and pass the bill that would designate a post office in Carlstadt, N.J., as the "Staff Sgt. Frank T. Carvill
and Lance Cpl. Michael A. Schwarz Post Office Building." Motion agreed
to 409-0: D 244-0; R 165-0. A two-thirds majority of those present and
voting (273 in this case) is required for passage under suspension of the
rules. June 9, 2010.

347. HR 5072. **FHA Mortgage Rates Revisions/Manager's
Amendment.** Waters, D-Calif., amendment that would make various
technical corrections, make modifications to the Government Accountability Office report called for in the bill, allow the Department of Housing and Urban Development to increase loan limits for micropolitan
counties surrounded by higher-cost areas and experiencing significant
growth, and address documentation standards for Federal Housing Administration (FHA)-insured loans. Adopted in Committee of the Whole
417-3: D 250-0; R 167-3. June 10, 2010.

348. HR 5072. **FHA Mortgage Rates Revisions/Down Payment
Requirement.** Garrett, R-N.J., amendment that would increase the FHA
loan minimum down payment requirement from 3.5 percent to 5 percent
and prohibit closing costs from being financed through FHA-insured
loans. Rejected in Committee of the Whole 131-289: D 7-243; R 124-46.
June 10, 2010.

	343	344	345	346	347	348
ALABAMA						
1 **Bonner**	Y	Y	Y	Y	Y	Y
2 Bright	Y	Y	Y	Y	Y	N
3 **Rogers**	Y	Y	Y	Y	Y	Y
4 **Aderholt**	Y	Y	Y	Y	Y	Y
5 **Griffith**	Y	Y	Y	Y	Y	Y
6 **Bachus**	Y	Y	Y	Y	Y	Y
7 Davis	N	Y	Y	?	Y	N
ALASKA						
AL **Young**	Y	N	Y	Y	Y	N
ARIZONA						
1 **Kirkpatrick**	Y	Y	Y	Y	Y	N
2 **Franks**	Y	N	Y	Y	Y	Y
3 **Shadegg**	Y	N	Y	Y	Y	Y
4 Pastor	N	Y	Y	Y	Y	N
5 Mitchell	Y	Y	Y	Y	Y	N
6 **Flake**	Y	Y	Y	Y	N	Y
7 Grijalva	N	Y	Y	Y	Y	N
8 **Giffords**	Y	Y	Y	Y	Y	N
ARKANSAS						
1 Berry	N	Y	Y	Y	Y	N
2 Snyder	N	Y	Y	Y	Y	N
3 **Boozman**	Y	Y	Y	Y	Y	Y
4 Ross	N	Y	Y	Y	Y	N
CALIFORNIA						
1 Thompson	N	Y	Y	Y	Y	N
2 **Herger**	Y	N	Y	Y	Y	Y
3 **Lungren**	Y	Y	Y	Y	Y	N
4 **McClintock**	Y	Y	Y	Y	Y	Y
5 Matsui	N	Y	Y	Y	Y	N
6 Woolsey	N	Y	Y	Y	Y	N
7 Miller, George	N	Y	Y	Y	Y	N
8 Pelosi						
9 Lee	N	Y	Y	Y	Y	N
10 Garamendi	N	Y	Y	Y	Y	N
11 McNerney	Y	Y	Y	Y	Y	N
12 Speier	N	Y	Y	Y	Y	N
13 Stark	N	Y	Y	Y	Y	N
14 Eshoo	N	Y	Y	Y	?	?
15 Honda	N	Y	Y	Y	Y	N
16 Lofgren	N	Y	Y	Y	Y	N
17 Farr	N	Y	Y	Y	Y	N
18 Cardoza	N	Y	Y	Y	Y	N
19 **Radanovich**	Y	Y	Y	Y	Y	?
20 Costa	N	Y	Y	Y	Y	N
21 **Nunes**	Y	N	Y	Y	Y	Y
22 **McCarthy**	Y	Y	Y	Y	Y	N
23 Capps	N	Y	Y	Y	Y	N
24 **Gallegly**	Y	Y	Y	Y	Y	N
25 **McKeon**	Y	Y	Y	Y	Y	N
26 **Dreier**	Y	Y	Y	Y	Y	Y
27 Sherman	N	Y	Y	Y	Y	N
28 Berman	N	Y	Y	Y	Y	N
29 Schiff	N	Y	Y	Y	Y	N
30 Waxman	N	Y	Y	Y	Y	N
31 Becerra	N	Y	Y	Y	Y	N
32 Chu	N	Y	Y	Y	Y	N
33 Watson	?	?	?	?	Y	N
34 Roybal-Allard	N	Y	Y	Y	Y	N
35 Waters	N	Y	Y	Y	Y	N
36 Harman	?	?	?	?	?	N
37 Richardson	N	Y	Y	Y	Y	N
38 Napolitano	N	Y	Y	Y	Y	N
39 Sánchez, Linda	N	Y	Y	Y	Y	N
40 **Royce**	Y	Y	Y	Y	Y	Y
41 **Lewis**	Y	Y	Y	Y	Y	N
42 **Miller, Gary**	?	?	?	?	Y	N
43 Baca	N	Y	Y	Y	Y	N
44 **Calvert**	+	+	+	+	Y	N
45 **Bono Mack**	Y	Y	Y	Y	Y	Y
46 **Rohrabacher**	Y	Y	Y	Y	Y	Y
47 Sanchez, Loretta	N	Y	Y	Y	Y	N
48 **Campbell**	?	?	?	?	Y	Y
49 **Issa**	Y	Y	Y	Y	Y	Y
50 **Bilbray**	Y	Y	Y	Y	Y	N
51 Filner	N	Y	Y	Y	Y	N
52 **Hunter**	Y	Y	Y	Y	Y	Y
53 Davis	N	Y	Y	Y	+	—

	343	344	345	346	347	348
COLORADO						
1 DeGette	N	Y	Y	Y	Y	N
2 Polis	N	Y	Y	Y	Y	N
3 Salazar	N	Y	Y	Y	Y	N
4 Markey	Y	Y	Y	Y	Y	N
5 **Lamborn**	Y	N	Y	Y	Y	Y
6 **Coffman**	Y	N	Y	Y	Y	Y
7 Perlmutter	N	Y	Y	Y	Y	N
CONNECTICUT						
1 Larson	N	Y	Y	Y	Y	N
2 Courtney	Y	Y	Y	Y	Y	N
3 DeLauro	N	Y	Y	Y	Y	N
4 Himes	N	Y	Y	Y	Y	N
5 Murphy	N	Y	Y	Y	Y	N
DELAWARE						
AL **Castle**	Y	Y	Y	Y	Y	N
FLORIDA						
1 **Miller**	Y	Y	Y	Y	Y	Y
2 Boyd	N	Y	Y	Y	Y	N
3 Brown	N	Y	Y	Y	Y	N
4 **Crenshaw**	Y	Y	Y	Y	Y	Y
5 **Brown-Waite**	Y	Y	Y	Y	Y	Y
6 **Stearns**	Y	Y	Y	Y	Y	Y
7 **Mica**	Y	Y	Y	Y	Y	Y
8 Grayson	N	Y	Y	Y	Y	N
9 **Bilirakis**	Y	Y	Y	Y	Y	Y
10 **Young**	Y	Y	Y	Y	Y	Y
11 Castor	N	Y	Y	Y	Y	N
12 **Putnam**	Y	Y	Y	Y	?	?
13 **Buchanan**	Y	Y	Y	Y	Y	Y
14 **Mack**	Y	Y	Y	Y	Y	Y
15 **Posey**	Y	Y	Y	Y	Y	Y
16 **Rooney**	Y	Y	Y	Y	Y	Y
17 Meek	N	?	Y	Y	Y	N
18 **Ros-Lehtinen**	Y	Y	Y	Y	Y	Y
19 Deutch	N	Y	Y	Y	Y	N
20 Wasserman Schultz	N	Y	Y	Y	Y	N
21 **Diaz-Balart, L.**	Y	Y	Y	Y	Y	Y
22 Klein	N	Y	Y	Y	Y	N
23 Hastings	N	Y	Y	Y	Y	N
24 Kosmas	?	Y	Y	Y	Y	N
25 **Diaz-Balart, M.**	Y	Y	Y	Y	Y	Y
GEORGIA						
1 **Kingston**	Y	Y	Y	Y	Y	Y
2 Bishop	N	Y	Y	Y	Y	N
3 **Westmoreland**	Y	N	Y	Y	Y	Y
4 Johnson	N	?	Y	Y	?	N
5 Lewis	N	Y	Y	Y	?	N
6 **Price**	Y	N	Y	Y	Y	Y
7 **Linder**	Y	N	Y	Y	Y	Y
8 Marshall	N	Y	Y	Y	Y	N
9 Vacant						
10 **Broun**	Y	N	Y	Y	N	Y
11 **Gingrey**	Y	Y	Y	Y	Y	Y
12 Barrow	N	Y	Y	Y	Y	N
13 Scott	N	Y	Y	Y	Y	N
HAWAII						
1 **Djou**	Y	Y	Y	Y	Y	Y
2 Hirono	N	Y	Y	Y	Y	N
IDAHO						
1 **Minnick**	Y	Y	Y	Y	Y	Y
2 **Simpson**	Y	Y	Y	Y	Y	N
ILLINOIS						
1 Rush	N	Y	Y	Y	Y	N
2 Jackson	N	Y	Y	Y	Y	N
3 Lipinski	N	Y	Y	Y	Y	N
4 Gutierrez	N	Y	Y	Y	Y	N
5 Quigley	?	?	?	?	Y	N
6 **Roskam**	Y	Y	Y	Y	Y	Y
7 Davis	N	Y	Y	Y	?	?
8 Bean	N	Y	Y	Y	Y	N
9 Schakowsky	N	Y	Y	Y	Y	N
10 **Kirk**	Y	Y	Y	?	Y	Y
11 Halvorson	Y	Y	Y	Y	Y	N
12 Costello	N	Y	Y	Y	Y	N
13 **Biggert**	Y	Y	Y	Y	Y	N
14 Foster	N	Y	Y	Y	Y	N
15 **Johnson**	Y	Y	Y	Y	Y	Y

	343	344	345	346	347	348
16 **Manzullo**	Y	Y	Y	Y	Y	Y
17 Hare	N	Y	Y	Y	Y	N
18 **Schock**	Y	Y	Y	Y	Y	Y
19 **Shimkus**	Y	N	Y	Y	Y	Y
INDIANA						
1 Visclosky	N	Y	Y	Y	Y	N
2 Donnelly	N	Y	Y	Y	Y	N
3 Vacant						
4 **Buyer**	Y	Y	Y	Y	Y	Y
5 **Burton**	Y	N	Y	Y	Y	Y
6 **Pence**	Y	Y	Y	Y	Y	Y
7 Carson	N	Y	Y	Y	Y	N
8 Ellsworth	N	Y	Y	?	Y	N
9 Hill	N	Y	Y	Y	Y	N
IOWA						
1 Braley	N	Y	Y	Y	Y	N
2 Loebsack	N	Y	Y	Y	Y	N
3 Boswell	N	Y	Y	?	Y	N
4 **Latham**	Y	Y	Y	Y	Y	N
5 **King**	Y	N	Y	Y	Y	N
KANSAS						
1 **Moran**	Y	N	Y	Y	Y	Y
2 **Jenkins**	Y	N	Y	Y	Y	Y
3 Moore	N	Y	Y	Y	Y	N
4 **Tiahrt**	Y	N	Y	Y	Y	Y
KENTUCKY						
1 **Whitfield**	Y	Y	Y	Y	Y	Y
2 **Guthrie**	Y	Y	Y	Y	Y	N
3 Yarmuth	N	Y	Y	Y	Y	N
4 **Davis**	Y	N	Y	Y	Y	Y
5 **Rogers**	Y	Y	Y	Y	Y	N
6 Chandler	N	Y	Y	Y	Y	N
LOUISIANA						
1 **Scalise**	Y	N	Y	Y	Y	Y
2 **Cao**	Y	Y	Y	Y	Y	N
3 Melancon	N	Y	Y	Y	Y	N
4 **Fleming**	Y	N	Y	Y	Y	N
5 **Alexander**	Y	N	Y	Y	Y	Y
6 **Cassidy**	Y	N	Y	Y	Y	Y
7 **Boustany**	Y	N	Y	Y	Y	Y
MAINE						
1 Pingree	N	Y	Y	Y	Y	N
2 Michaud	N	Y	Y	Y	Y	N
MARYLAND						
1 Kratovil	N	Y	Y	Y	Y	N
2 Ruppersberger	N	Y	Y	Y	Y	N
3 Sarbanes	N	Y	Y	Y	Y	N
4 Edwards	N	Y	Y	Y	Y	N
5 Hoyer	N	Y	Y	?	Y	N
6 **Bartlett**	Y	Y	Y	Y	Y	Y
7 Cummings	N	Y	Y	Y	Y	N
8 Van Hollen	N	Y	Y	Y	Y	N
MASSACHUSETTS						
1 Olver	N	Y	Y	Y	Y	N
2 Neal	N	Y	Y	Y	Y	N
3 McGovern	N	Y	Y	Y	Y	?
4 Frank	N	Y	Y	Y	Y	N
5 Tsongas	N	Y	Y	Y	Y	N
6 Tierney	N	Y	Y	Y	Y	N
7 Markey	N	Y	Y	Y	Y	N
8 Capuano	N	Y	Y	Y	Y	N
9 Lynch	N	Y	Y	Y	Y	N
10 Delahunt	N	Y	Y	Y	Y	N
MICHIGAN						
1 Stupak	N	Y	Y	Y	Y	N
2 **Hoekstra**	?	?	?	?	?	?
3 **Ehlers**	Y	Y	Y	Y	Y	N
4 **Camp**	Y	Y	Y	Y	Y	Y
5 Kildee	N	Y	Y	Y	Y	N
6 **Upton**	Y	Y	Y	Y	Y	Y
7 Schauer	Y	Y	Y	Y	Y	N
8 **Rogers**	Y	Y	Y	Y	Y	Y
9 Peters	N	Y	Y	Y	Y	N
10 **Miller**	Y	Y	Y	Y	Y	N
11 **McCotter**	Y	Y	Y	Y	Y	N
12 Levin	N	Y	Y	Y	Y	N
13 Kilpatrick	–	+	+	+	+	–
14 Conyers	N	Y	Y	Y	Y	N
15 Dingell	N	Y	Y	Y	Y	N
MINNESOTA						
1 Walz	N	Y	Y	Y	Y	N
2 **Kline**	Y	Y	Y	Y	Y	N
3 **Paulsen**	Y	Y	Y	Y	Y	N
4 McCollum	N	Y	Y	Y	Y	N

	343	344	345	346	347	348
5 Ellison	N	Y	Y	Y	Y	N
6 **Bachmann**	Y	Y	Y	Y	Y	Y
7 Peterson	Y	Y	Y	Y	Y	N
8 Oberstar	N	Y	Y	Y	Y	N
MISSISSIPPI						
1 Childers	Y	Y	Y	Y	Y	N
2 Thompson	N	Y	Y	Y	Y	N
3 **Harper**	Y	Y	Y	Y	Y	Y
4 Taylor	Y	Y	Y	Y	Y	N
MISSOURI						
1 Clay	N	Y	Y	Y	Y	N
2 **Akin**	Y	N	Y	Y	Y	Y
3 Carnahan	N	Y	Y	Y	Y	N
4 Skelton	Y	Y	Y	Y	Y	N
5 Cleaver	N	Y	Y	Y	Y	N
6 **Graves**	Y	Y	Y	Y	Y	Y
7 **Blunt**	Y	Y	Y	Y	Y	Y
8 **Emerson**	Y	N	Y	Y	Y	Y
9 **Luetkemeyer**	Y	N	Y	Y	Y	Y
MONTANA						
AL **Rehberg**	Y	N	Y	Y	Y	N
NEBRASKA						
1 **Fortenberry**	Y	Y	Y	Y	Y	Y
2 **Terry**	Y	Y	Y	Y	Y	N
3 **Smith**	Y	Y	Y	Y	Y	Y
NEVADA						
1 Berkley	?	?	?	Y	Y	N
2 **Heller**	Y	Y	Y	Y	Y	N
3 Titus	N	Y	Y	Y	Y	N
NEW HAMPSHIRE						
1 Shea-Porter	N	Y	Y	Y	Y	N
2 Hodes	Y	Y	Y	Y	Y	N
NEW JERSEY						
1 Andrews	N	Y	Y	Y	Y	N
2 **LoBiondo**	Y	Y	Y	Y	Y	N
3 Adler	N	Y	Y	Y	Y	N
4 **Smith**	Y	Y	Y	Y	Y	N
5 **Garrett**	Y	N	Y	Y	Y	Y
6 Pallone	N	Y	Y	Y	Y	N
7 **Lance**	Y	Y	Y	Y	Y	N
8 Pascrell	N	Y	Y	Y	Y	N
9 Rothman	N	Y	Y	Y	Y	N
10 Payne	N	Y	Y	Y	Y	N
11 **Frelinghuysen**	Y	Y	Y	Y	Y	N
12 Holt	N	Y	Y	Y	Y	N
13 Sires	N	Y	Y	Y	Y	N
NEW MEXICO						
1 Heinrich	Y	Y	Y	Y	Y	N
2 Teague	Y	Y	Y	Y	Y	N
3 Luján	N	Y	Y	Y	Y	N
NEW YORK						
1 Bishop	N	Y	Y	Y	Y	N
2 Israel	N	Y	Y	Y	Y	N
3 **King**	Y	Y	Y	Y	Y	Y
4 McCarthy	N	Y	Y	Y	Y	N
5 Ackerman	N	Y	Y	Y	Y	N
6 Meeks	N	Y	Y	Y	Y	N
7 Crowley	N	Y	Y	Y	Y	N
8 Nadler	N	Y	Y	Y	Y	N
9 Weiner	N	Y	Y	Y	Y	N
10 Towns	N	Y	Y	Y	Y	N
11 Clarke	N	Y	Y	Y	Y	N
12 Velázquez	N	Y	Y	Y	Y	N
13 McMahon	N	Y	Y	Y	Y	N
14 Maloney	N	Y	Y	Y	Y	N
15 Rangel	N	Y	Y	Y	Y	N
16 Serrano	N	Y	Y	Y	Y	N
17 Engel	N	Y	Y	Y	Y	N
18 Lowey	N	Y	Y	Y	Y	N
19 Hall	N	Y	Y	Y	Y	N
20 Murphy	N	Y	Y	Y	Y	N
21 Tonko	N	Y	Y	Y	Y	N
22 Hinchey	N	Y	Y	Y	Y	N
23 Owens	Y	Y	Y	Y	Y	N
24 Arcuri	N	Y	Y	Y	Y	N
25 Maffei	N	Y	Y	Y	Y	N
26 **Lee**	Y	Y	Y	Y	Y	N
27 Higgins	?	?	?	?	Y	N
28 Slaughter	N	Y	Y	Y	Y	N
29 Vacant						
NORTH CAROLINA						
1 Butterfield	N	Y	Y	Y	Y	?
2 Etheridge	N	Y	Y	Y	Y	N
3 **Jones**	Y	Y	Y	Y	Y	Y
4 Price	N	Y	Y	Y	Y	N

	343	344	345	346	347	348
5 **Foxx**	Y	Y	Y	Y	Y	Y
6 **Coble**	Y	Y	Y	Y	Y	N
7 McIntyre	Y	Y	Y	Y	Y	N
8 Kissell	N	Y	Y	Y	Y	N
9 **Myrick**	Y	Y	Y	Y	Y	Y
10 **McHenry**	?	?	?	?	?	?
11 Shuler	N	Y	Y	Y	Y	N
12 Watt	N	Y	Y	Y	Y	N
13 Miller	N	Y	Y	Y	Y	N
NORTH DAKOTA						
AL Pomeroy	N	Y	Y	Y	Y	N
OHIO						
1 Driehaus	N	Y	Y	Y	Y	N
2 **Schmidt**	Y	Y	Y	Y	Y	Y
3 **Turner**	Y	Y	Y	Y	Y	N
4 **Jordan**	Y	Y	Y	Y	Y	Y
5 **Latta**	Y	Y	Y	Y	Y	Y
6 Wilson	N	Y	Y	Y	Y	N
7 **Austria**	Y	Y	Y	Y	Y	Y
8 **Boehner**	Y	Y	?	?	Y	Y
9 Kaptur	N	Y	Y	Y	Y	N
10 Kucinich	N	Y	Y	Y	Y	N
11 Fudge	N	Y	Y	Y	Y	N
12 **Tiberi**	Y	Y	Y	Y	Y	Y
13 Sutton	N	Y	Y	Y	Y	N
14 **LaTourette**	Y	Y	Y	Y	Y	N
15 Kilroy	N	Y	Y	Y	Y	N
16 Boccieri	N	Y	Y	Y	Y	N
17 Ryan	Y	Y	Y	Y	Y	N
18 Space	Y	Y	Y	Y	Y	N
OKLAHOMA						
1 **Sullivan**	Y	Y	Y	?	Y	Y
2 Boren	N	Y	Y	Y	Y	N
3 **Lucas**	Y	Y	Y	Y	Y	Y
4 **Cole**	Y	Y	Y	Y	Y	Y
5 **Fallin**	Y	Y	Y	Y	Y	Y
OREGON						
1 Wu	N	Y	Y	Y	Y	N
2 **Walden**	Y	Y	Y	Y	Y	Y
3 Blumenauer	N	Y	Y	Y	Y	?
4 DeFazio	N	Y	Y	Y	Y	N
5 Schrader	Y	Y	Y	Y	Y	Y
PENNSYLVANIA						
1 Brady	N	Y	Y	Y	Y	N
2 Fattah	N	Y	Y	Y	Y	N
3 Dahlkemper	N	Y	Y	Y	Y	N
4 Altmire	N	Y	Y	Y	Y	N
5 **Thompson**	Y	Y	Y	Y	Y	Y
6 **Gerlach**	Y	Y	Y	Y	Y	N
7 Sestak	N	Y	Y	Y	Y	N
8 Murphy, P.	N	Y	Y	Y	Y	N
9 **Shuster**	Y	Y	Y	Y	?	?
10 Carney	N	Y	Y	Y	Y	N
11 Kanjorski	N	Y	Y	Y	Y	N
12 Critz	N	Y	Y	Y	Y	N
13 Schwartz	N	Y	Y	Y	Y	N
14 Doyle	N	Y	Y	Y	Y	N
15 **Dent**	Y	Y	Y	Y	Y	Y
16 **Pitts**	Y	Y	Y	?	Y	Y
17 Holden	N	Y	Y	Y	Y	N
18 **Murphy, T.**	Y	Y	Y	Y	Y	N
19 **Platts**	Y	Y	Y	Y	Y	N
RHODE ISLAND						
1 Kennedy	–	+	+	+	?	N
2 Langevin	N	Y	Y	Y	Y	N
SOUTH CAROLINA						
1 **Brown**	Y	Y	Y	Y	Y	Y
2 **Wilson**	Y	Y	Y	Y	Y	Y
3 **Barrett**	?	?	?	?	?	?
4 **Inglis**	?	?	?	?	?	?
5 Spratt	Y	Y	Y	Y	Y	?
6 Clyburn	N	Y	Y	Y	Y	N
SOUTH DAKOTA						
AL Herseth Sandlin	N	Y	Y	Y	Y	N
TENNESSEE						
1 **Roe**	Y	N	Y	Y	Y	Y
2 **Duncan**	Y	N	Y	Y	Y	Y
3 **Wamp**	Y	Y	Y	Y	Y	Y
4 Davis	?	?	Y	Y	Y	N
5 Cooper	N	Y	Y	Y	Y	N
6 Gordon	N	Y	Y	Y	Y	N
7 **Blackburn**	Y	N	Y	Y	Y	Y
8 Tanner	N	Y	Y	Y	Y	N
9 Cohen	N	Y	Y	Y	Y	N

	343	344	345	346	347	348
TEXAS						
1 **Gohmert**	Y	?	Y	Y	Y	Y
2 **Poe**	Y	N	Y	Y	Y	Y
3 **Johnson, S.**	Y	N	Y	Y	Y	Y
4 **Hall**	Y	Y	Y	Y	Y	Y
5 **Hensarling**	Y	Y	Y	Y	Y	Y
6 **Barton**	Y	N	Y	Y	Y	Y
7 **Culberson**	Y	Y	Y	Y	Y	Y
8 **Brady**	Y	N	Y	Y	Y	Y
9 Green, A.	N	Y	Y	Y	Y	N
10 **McCaul**	Y	Y	Y	Y	Y	Y
11 **Conaway**	Y	N	Y	Y	Y	Y
12 **Granger**	Y	Y	Y	Y	Y	Y
13 **Thornberry**	Y	Y	Y	Y	Y	Y
14 **Paul**	Y	N	Y	Y	N	Y
15 Hinojosa	N	Y	Y	Y	?	?
16 Reyes	N	Y	Y	Y	Y	N
17 Edwards	Y	Y	Y	Y	Y	N
18 Jackson Lee	N	Y	Y	Y	Y	N
19 **Neugebauer**	Y	N	Y	Y	Y	Y
20 Gonzalez	N	Y	Y	Y	Y	N
21 **Smith**	Y	Y	Y	?	Y	Y
22 **Olson**	Y	Y	Y	Y	?	Y
23 Rodriguez	Y	Y	Y	Y	Y	N
24 **Marchant**	Y	Y	Y	Y	Y	N
25 Doggett	N	Y	Y	Y	Y	Y
26 **Burgess**	Y	N	Y	Y	Y	Y
27 Ortiz	N	Y	Y	Y	Y	N
28 Cuellar	N	Y	Y	Y	Y	N
29 Green, G.	N	Y	Y	Y	Y	N
30 Johnson, E.	N	Y	Y	Y	Y	N
31 **Carter**	Y	Y	Y	Y	Y	Y
32 **Sessions**	Y	Y	Y	Y	Y	Y
UTAH						
1 **Bishop**	Y	N	Y	Y	Y	Y
2 Matheson	N	Y	Y	Y	Y	N
3 **Chaffetz**	Y	N	Y	Y	Y	Y
VERMONT						
AL Welch	N	Y	Y	Y	Y	N
VIRGINIA						
1 **Wittman**	Y	Y	Y	Y	Y	N
2 Nye	N	Y	Y	Y	Y	N
3 Scott	N	Y	Y	Y	Y	N
4 **Forbes**	Y	Y	Y	Y	Y	Y
5 Perriello	Y	Y	Y	Y	Y	N
6 **Goodlatte**	Y	Y	Y	Y	Y	Y
7 **Cantor**	Y	N	Y	Y	Y	Y
8 Moran	N	Y	Y	Y	Y	N
9 Boucher	Y	Y	Y	Y	Y	N
10 **Wolf**	Y	Y	Y	Y	Y	Y
11 Connolly	Y	Y	Y	Y	Y	N
WASHINGTON						
1 Inslee	N	Y	Y	Y	Y	N
2 Larsen	N	Y	Y	Y	Y	N
3 Baird	N	Y	Y	Y	Y	N
4 **Hastings**	Y	N	Y	Y	Y	Y
5 **McMorris Rodgers**	Y	Y	Y	Y	Y	Y
6 Dicks	N	Y	Y	Y	Y	N
7 McDermott	N	Y	Y	Y	Y	N
8 **Reichert**	Y	Y	Y	Y	Y	N
9 Smith	N	Y	Y	Y	Y	Y
WEST VIRGINIA						
1 Mollohan	N	Y	Y	Y	Y	N
2 **Capito**	Y	Y	Y	Y	Y	N
3 Rahall	N	Y	Y	Y	Y	N
WISCONSIN						
1 **Ryan**	Y	Y	Y	Y	Y	Y
2 Baldwin	N	Y	Y	Y	Y	N
3 Kind	N	Y	Y	Y	Y	N
4 Moore	N	Y	Y	Y	Y	N
5 **Sensenbrenner**	Y	Y	Y	Y	Y	Y
6 **Petri**	Y	Y	Y	Y	Y	Y
7 Obey	N	Y	Y	Y	Y	N
8 Kagen	N	Y	Y	Y	Y	Y
WYOMING						
AL **Lummis**	Y	N	Y	Y	Y	Y
DELEGATES						
Faleomavaega (A.S.)					?	?
Norton (D.C.)					Y	N
Bordallo (Guam)					Y	N
Sablan (N. Marianas)					Y	N
Pierluisi (P.R.)					Y	N
Christensen (V.I.)					Y	N

IN THE HOUSE | By Vote Number

349. **HR 5072. FHA Mortgage Rates Revisions/Cap on Insured Loans.** Price, R-Ga., amendment that would cap the number of mortgages the Federal Housing Administration (FHA) can insure at 10 percent of total loans originated in each year, starting in fiscal 2012. Within 90 days of enactment, FHA would have to submit a plan to Congress to decrease FHA market share to 10 percent of loans originated each year. Rejected in Committee of the Whole 106-316: D 1-251; R 105-65. June 10, 2010.

350. **HR 5072. FHA Mortgage Rates Revisions/Maximum Loan Limits.** Turner, R-Ohio, amendment that would repeal the emergency authority that allows the Federal Housing Administration (FHA) to insure loans up to $720,000 in certain high-cost areas. The amendment would create a maximum FHA-insured loan limit of $500,000 for a single-family unit and a percentage of the same ratio for two-, three- or four-family residences. Rejected in Committee of the Whole 121-301: D 12-240; R 109-61. June 10, 2010.

351. **HR 5072. FHA Mortgage Rates Revisions/Sex Offenders.** Edwards, D-Texas, amendment that would require individuals to certify that they have not been convicted of a sex offense against a minor in order to obtain a Federal Housing Administration-insured mortgage. Adopted in Committee of the Whole 420-4: D 250-3; R 170-1. June 10, 2010.

352. **HR 5072. FHA Mortgage Rates Revisions/Pornography Violation.** Maffei, D-N.Y., amendment that would prohibit the use of funds authorized in the bill to pay the salary of any Federal Housing Administration (FHA) employee who has been disciplined for viewing, downloading or exchanging pornography on a federal computer or while performing official job duties. Adopted in Committee of the Whole 416-0: D 247-0; R 169-0. June 10, 2010.

353. **HR 5072. FHA Mortgage Rates Revisions/Passage.** Passage of the bill that would allow the Federal Housing Administration (FHA) to adjust the premium structure for mortgage insurance. It would authorize the FHA to increase the maximum annual mortgage insurance premium on the mortgages it approves by 1 percentage point. It would permit the FHA to reimburse loan-servicing companies for the costs of conducting counseling with households that are more than 60 days past due on loan payments. Passed 406-4: D 241-1; R 165-3. June 10, 2010.

354. **S 3473. Oil Spill Trust Fund Advances/Passage.** Oberstar, D-Minn., motion to suspend the rules and pass the bill that would remove the limitation on the amount the president can withdraw from the Oil Spill Liability Trust Fund in response to the discharge of oil in connection with the explosion of the Deepwater Horizon mobile offshore drilling unit. It would allow advances of $100 million at a time, not to exceed the amounts available, and would require the administration to notify Congress within seven days of each advance. Motion agreed to, thus clearing the bill for the president, 410-0: D 245-0; R 165-0. A two-thirds majority of those present and voting (274 in this case) is required for passage under suspension of the rules. June 10, 2010.

	349	350	351	352	353	354
ALABAMA						
1 **Bonner**	Y	Y	Y	Y	Y	Y
2 Bright	N	N	Y	Y	Y	Y
3 **Rogers**	Y	Y	Y	Y	Y	Y
4 **Aderholt**	N	N	Y	Y	Y	Y
5 **Griffith**	Y	Y	Y	Y	Y	Y
6 **Bachus**	Y	Y	Y	Y	Y	Y
7 Davis	N	N	Y	Y	Y	Y
ALASKA						
AL **Young**	Y	Y	Y	Y	Y	Y
ARIZONA						
1 Kirkpatrick	N	Y	Y	Y	Y	Y
2 **Franks**	Y	Y	Y	Y	Y	Y
3 **Shadegg**	Y	Y	Y	Y	Y	Y
4 Pastor	N	N	Y	Y	Y	Y
5 Mitchell	N	N	Y	Y	Y	Y
6 **Flake**	Y	Y	Y	Y	N	Y
7 Grijalva	N	N	Y	Y	Y	Y
8 Giffords	N	N	Y	?	Y	Y
ARKANSAS						
1 Berry	N	N	Y	Y	Y	Y
2 Snyder	N	N	Y	Y	Y	Y
3 **Boozman**	N	N	Y	Y	Y	Y
4 Ross	N	N	Y	Y	Y	Y
CALIFORNIA						
1 Thompson	N	N	Y	Y	Y	Y
2 **Herger**	Y	Y	Y	Y	Y	Y
3 Lungren	N	N	Y	Y	Y	Y
4 **McClintock**	Y	Y	Y	Y	Y	Y
5 Matsui	N	N	Y	Y	Y	Y
6 Woolsey	N	N	Y	Y	Y	Y
7 Miller, George	N	N	Y	Y	Y	Y
8 Pelosi						
9 Lee	N	N	Y	Y	Y	Y
10 Garamendi	?	?	Y	Y	Y	Y
11 McNerney	N	N	Y	Y	Y	Y
12 Speier	N	N	Y	Y	Y	Y
13 Stark	N	N	Y	?	Y	Y
14 Eshoo	–	–	+	+	+	+
15 Honda	N	N	Y	N	Y	Y
16 Lofgren	N	N	?	?	Y	Y
17 Farr	N	N	Y	Y	Y	Y
18 Cardoza	N	N	Y	Y	Y	Y
19 **Radanovich**	N	N	Y	Y	Y	Y
20 Costa	N	N	Y	Y	+	Y
21 **Nunes**	Y	N	Y	Y	Y	Y
22 **McCarthy**	N	N	Y	Y	Y	Y
23 Capps	N	N	Y	Y	Y	Y
24 **Gallegly**	N	N	Y	Y	Y	Y
25 **McKeon**	N	N	Y	Y	Y	Y
26 **Dreier**	N	N	Y	Y	Y	Y
27 Sherman	N	N	Y	Y	Y	Y
28 Berman	N	N	Y	Y	+	Y
29 Schiff	N	N	Y	Y	Y	Y
30 Waxman	N	N	Y	Y	Y	?
31 Becerra	N	N	Y	Y	Y	Y
32 Chu	N	N	Y	Y	Y	Y
33 Watson	N	N	Y	Y	Y	Y
34 Roybal-Allard	N	N	Y	Y	Y	Y
35 Waters	N	N	Y	Y	Y	Y
36 Harman	N	N	Y	Y	Y	Y
37 Richardson	N	N	Y	Y	Y	Y
38 Napolitano	N	N	Y	Y	Y	Y
39 Sánchez, Linda	N	N	Y	Y	Y	Y
40 **Royce**	Y	Y	Y	Y	Y	Y
41 **Lewis**	N	N	Y	Y	Y	Y
42 **Miller, Gary**	N	N	Y	Y	Y	?
43 Baca	N	N	Y	Y	Y	Y
44 **Calvert**	N	N	Y	Y	Y	Y
45 **Bono Mack**	N	N	Y	Y	Y	Y
46 **Rohrabacher**	N	N	Y	Y	Y	Y
47 Sanchez, Loretta	N	N	Y	Y	Y	Y
48 **Campbell**	N	N	Y	Y	Y	Y
49 **Issa**	Y	N	Y	Y	Y	Y
50 **Bilbray**	N	N	Y	Y	Y	Y
51 Filner	N	N	N	Y	Y	Y
52 **Hunter**	N	N	Y	Y	Y	Y
53 Davis	–	–	+	+	+	+

	349	350	351	352	353	354
COLORADO						
1 DeGette	N	N	Y	Y	Y	Y
2 Polis	N	N	Y	Y	Y	Y
3 Salazar	N	N	Y	Y	Y	Y
4 Markey	N	N	Y	Y	Y	Y
5 **Lamborn**	Y	Y	Y	Y	Y	Y
6 **Coffman**	Y	Y	Y	Y	Y	Y
7 Perlmutter	N	N	Y	Y	Y	Y
CONNECTICUT						
1 Larson	N	N	Y	Y	Y	Y
2 Courtney	N	N	Y	Y	Y	Y
3 DeLauro	N	N	Y	Y	Y	Y
4 Himes	N	N	Y	Y	Y	Y
5 Murphy	N	N	Y	Y	Y	Y
DELAWARE						
AL **Castle**	Y	Y	Y	Y	Y	Y
FLORIDA						
1 **Miller**	Y	Y	Y	Y	Y	Y
2 Boyd	N	N	Y	Y	Y	Y
3 Brown	N	N	Y	Y	Y	Y
4 **Crenshaw**	Y	Y	Y	Y	Y	Y
5 **Brown-Waite**	N	N	Y	Y	Y	Y
6 **Stearns**	Y	Y	Y	Y	Y	Y
7 **Mica**	N	N	Y	Y	Y	Y
8 Grayson	N	N	Y	Y	Y	Y
9 **Bilirakis**	Y	Y	Y	Y	Y	Y
10 **Young**	N	N	Y	Y	Y	Y
11 Castor	N	N	Y	Y	Y	Y
12 **Putnam**	–	+	+	+	+	+
13 **Buchanan**	N	Y	Y	Y	Y	?
14 **Mack**	Y	Y	Y	Y	Y	Y
15 **Posey**	N	Y	Y	Y	Y	+
16 **Rooney**	Y	Y	Y	Y	Y	Y
17 Meek	N	N	Y	Y	Y	Y
18 **Ros-Lehtinen**	Y	N	Y	Y	Y	Y
19 Deutch	N	N	Y	Y	Y	Y
20 Wasserman Schultz	N	N	Y	Y	Y	Y
21 **Diaz-Balart, L.**	Y	Y	Y	Y	Y	Y
22 Klein	N	N	Y	Y	Y	Y
23 Hastings	N	N	Y	Y	Y	Y
24 Kosmas	N	N	Y	Y	Y	Y
25 **Diaz-Balart, M.**	Y	Y	Y	Y	Y	Y
GEORGIA						
1 **Kingston**	Y	Y	Y	Y	Y	Y
2 Bishop	N	N	Y	Y	Y	Y
3 **Westmoreland**	Y	N	Y	Y	Y	Y
4 Johnson	N	N	Y	Y	Y	Y
5 Lewis	N	N	Y	Y	Y	Y
6 **Price**	Y	Y	Y	Y	Y	Y
7 **Linder**	Y	Y	Y	Y	Y	?
8 Marshall	N	Y	Y	Y	+	Y
9 Vacant						
10 **Broun**	Y	Y	Y	Y	N	Y
11 **Gingrey**	Y	Y	Y	Y	Y	Y
12 Barrow	N	N	Y	Y	Y	Y
13 Scott	N	N	Y	Y	Y	Y
HAWAII						
1 **Djou**	N	N	Y	Y	Y	Y
2 Hirono	N	N	Y	Y	Y	Y
IDAHO						
1 Minnick	N	Y	Y	Y	Y	Y
2 **Simpson**	N	N	Y	Y	Y	Y
ILLINOIS						
1 Rush	N	N	Y	Y	Y	Y
2 Jackson	N	N	Y	Y	Y	Y
3 Lipinski	N	N	Y	Y	Y	Y
4 Gutierrez	N	N	Y	?	Y	Y
5 Quigley	N	N	Y	Y	Y	Y
6 **Roskam**	N	Y	Y	Y	Y	Y
7 Davis	–	–	–	+	+	+
8 Bean	N	N	Y	Y	Y	Y
9 Schakowsky	N	N	Y	Y	Y	Y
10 **Kirk**	N	N	Y	Y	Y	Y
11 Halvorson	N	N	Y	Y	Y	Y
12 Costello	N	N	Y	Y	Y	Y
13 **Biggert**	N	N	Y	Y	Y	Y
14 Foster	N	N	Y	Y	Y	Y
15 Johnson	Y	Y	Y	Y	Y	Y

	349	350	351	352	353	354
16 **Manzullo**	–	N	Y	Y	Y	Y
17 Hare	N	N	Y	Y	Y	Y
18 **Schock**	Y	Y	Y	Y	Y	Y
19 **Shimkus**	Y	Y	Y	Y	Y	Y
INDIANA						
1 Visclosky	N	N	Y	Y	Y	Y
2 Donnelly	N	N	Y	Y	Y	Y
3 Vacant						
4 **Buyer**	Y	Y	Y	Y	Y	?
5 **Burton**	Y	Y	Y	Y	Y	Y
6 **Pence**	Y	Y	Y	Y	Y	Y
7 Carson	N	N	Y	Y	Y	Y
8 Ellsworth	N	N	Y	Y	Y	Y
9 Hill	N	N	Y	Y	Y	Y
IOWA						
1 Braley	N	N	Y	Y	Y	Y
2 Loebsack	N	Y	Y	Y	Y	Y
3 Boswell	N	N	Y	Y	Y	Y
4 **Latham**	N	N	Y	Y	Y	Y
5 **King**	Y	Y	Y	Y	Y	Y
KANSAS						
1 **Moran**	Y	Y	Y	Y	Y	Y
2 **Jenkins**	Y	Y	Y	Y	Y	Y
3 Moore	N	N	Y	Y	Y	Y
4 **Tiahrt**	Y	Y	Y	Y	Y	Y
KENTUCKY						
1 **Whitfield**	Y	N	Y	Y	Y	Y
2 **Guthrie**	N	N	Y	Y	Y	Y
3 Yarmuth	N	N	Y	Y	Y	Y
4 **Davis**	Y	Y	Y	Y	Y	Y
5 **Rogers**	N	Y	Y	Y	Y	Y
6 Chandler	N	N	Y	Y	Y	Y
LOUISIANA						
1 **Scalise**	Y	Y	Y	Y	Y	Y
2 **Cao**	N	N	Y	Y	Y	Y
3 Melancon	N	Y	Y	Y	Y	Y
4 **Fleming**	Y	Y	Y	Y	Y	Y
5 **Alexander**	Y	Y	Y	Y	Y	Y
6 **Cassidy**	Y	Y	Y	Y	Y	Y
7 **Boustany**	Y	Y	Y	Y	Y	Y
MAINE						
1 Pingree	N	N	Y	Y	Y	Y
2 Michaud	N	N	Y	Y	Y	Y
MARYLAND						
1 Kratovil	N	N	Y	Y	Y	Y
2 Ruppersberger	N	N	Y	Y	Y	Y
3 Sarbanes	N	N	Y	Y	Y	Y
4 Edwards	N	N	Y	P	Y	Y
5 Hoyer	N	N	Y	Y	Y	Y
6 **Bartlett**	Y	Y	Y	Y	Y	Y
7 Cummings	N	N	Y	Y	Y	Y
8 Van Hollen	N	N	Y	Y	Y	Y
MASSACHUSETTS						
1 Olver	N	N	Y	Y	Y	Y
2 Neal	N	N	Y	Y	Y	Y
3 McGovern	N	N	Y	Y	Y	Y
4 Frank	N	N	Y	Y	Y	Y
5 Tsongas	N	N	Y	Y	Y	Y
6 Tierney	N	N	Y	Y	Y	Y
7 Markey	N	N	Y	Y	Y	Y
8 Capuano	N	N	Y	Y	Y	Y
9 Lynch	N	N	Y	Y	Y	Y
10 Delahunt	N	N	Y	?	?	?
MICHIGAN						
1 Stupak	N	N	Y	Y	Y	Y
2 **Hoekstra**	?	?	?	?	?	?
3 **Ehlers**	N	N	Y	Y	Y	Y
4 **Camp**	Y	Y	Y	Y	Y	Y
5 Kildee	N	N	Y	Y	Y	Y
6 **Upton**	Y	Y	Y	Y	Y	Y
7 Schauer	N	N	Y	Y	Y	Y
8 **Rogers**	Y	Y	Y	Y	Y	Y
9 Peters	N	N	Y	Y	Y	Y
10 **Miller**	N	N	Y	Y	Y	Y
11 **McCotter**	N	Y	Y	Y	Y	Y
12 Levin	N	N	Y	Y	Y	Y
13 Kilpatrick	–	–	+	+	+	+
14 Conyers	N	N	Y	Y	Y	Y
15 Dingell	N	N	Y	Y	Y	Y
MINNESOTA						
1 Walz	N	N	Y	Y	Y	Y
2 **Kline**	N	Y	Y	Y	Y	Y
3 **Paulsen**	N	Y	Y	Y	Y	Y
4 McCollum	N	N	Y	Y	Y	Y

	349	350	351	352	353	354
5 Ellison	N	N	Y	Y	Y	Y
6 **Bachmann**	Y	Y	Y	Y	Y	?
7 Peterson	N	N	Y	Y	?	Y
8 Oberstar	N	N	Y	Y	Y	Y
MISSISSIPPI						
1 Childers	N	N	Y	Y	Y	Y
2 Thompson	N	N	Y	Y	Y	Y
3 **Harper**	Y	Y	Y	Y	Y	Y
4 Taylor	N	N	Y	Y	Y	Y
MISSOURI						
1 Clay	N	N	Y	Y	Y	Y
2 **Akin**	Y	N	Y	Y	Y	Y
3 Carnahan	N	?	Y	Y	Y	Y
4 Skelton	N	N	Y	Y	Y	Y
5 Cleaver	N	N	Y	Y	Y	Y
6 **Graves**	Y	Y	Y	Y	Y	Y
7 **Blunt**	N	N	Y	Y	Y	Y
8 **Emerson**	Y	Y	Y	Y	Y	Y
9 **Luetkemeyer**	Y	Y	Y	Y	Y	Y
MONTANA						
AL **Rehberg**	N	Y	Y	Y	Y	Y
NEBRASKA						
1 **Fortenberry**	Y	Y	Y	Y	Y	Y
2 **Terry**	N	Y	Y	Y	Y	Y
3 **Smith**	Y	Y	Y	Y	Y	Y
NEVADA						
1 Berkley	N	N	Y	Y	Y	Y
2 **Heller**	N	N	Y	Y	Y	Y
3 Titus	N	N	Y	Y	Y	Y
NEW HAMPSHIRE						
1 Shea-Porter	N	N	Y	Y	Y	P
2 Hodes	N	N	Y	Y	Y	Y
NEW JERSEY						
1 Andrews	N	N	Y	Y	Y	Y
2 **LoBiondo**	N	N	Y	Y	Y	Y
3 Adler	N	N	Y	Y	Y	Y
4 **Smith**	N	N	Y	Y	Y	Y
5 **Garrett**	Y	Y	Y	Y	Y	Y
6 Pallone	N	N	Y	Y	Y	Y
7 **Lance**	N	N	Y	Y	Y	Y
8 Pascrell	N	N	Y	Y	Y	Y
9 Rothman	N	N	Y	Y	Y	Y
10 Payne	N	N	Y	Y	Y	Y
11 **Frelinghuysen**	N	N	Y	Y	Y	Y
12 Holt	N	N	Y	Y	Y	Y
13 Sires	N	N	Y	Y	Y	Y
NEW MEXICO						
1 Heinrich	N	N	Y	Y	Y	Y
2 Teague	N	Y	Y	Y	Y	Y
3 Luján	N	N	Y	Y	Y	Y
NEW YORK						
1 Bishop	N	N	Y	Y	Y	Y
2 Israel	N	N	Y	Y	Y	Y
3 **King**	N	N	Y	Y	Y	Y
4 McCarthy	N	N	?	Y	Y	Y
5 Ackerman	N	N	Y	Y	Y	Y
6 Meeks	N	N	Y	Y	Y	Y
7 Crowley	N	N	Y	Y	Y	Y
8 Nadler	N	N	N	Y	Y	Y
9 Weiner	N	N	Y	Y	Y	Y
10 Towns	N	N	Y	Y	Y	Y
11 Clarke	N	N	Y	Y	Y	Y
12 Velázquez	N	N	Y	Y	Y	Y
13 McMahon	N	N	Y	Y	Y	Y
14 Maloney	N	N	Y	Y	Y	Y
15 Rangel	Y	N	Y	Y	Y	Y
16 Serrano	N	N	Y	Y	Y	Y
17 Engel	N	N	Y	Y	Y	Y
18 Lowey	N	N	Y	Y	Y	Y
19 Hall	N	N	Y	Y	Y	Y
20 Murphy	N	N	Y	Y	Y	Y
21 Tonko	N	N	Y	Y	Y	Y
22 Hinchey	N	N	Y	Y	Y	Y
23 Owens	N	N	Y	Y	Y	Y
24 Arcuri	N	N	Y	Y	Y	Y
25 Maffei	N	N	Y	Y	Y	Y
26 **Lee**	N	N	Y	Y	Y	Y
27 Higgins	N	N	Y	Y	Y	Y
28 Slaughter	N	N	Y	Y	Y	Y
29 Vacant						
NORTH CAROLINA						
1 Butterfield	N	N	Y	Y	Y	Y
2 Etheridge	N	N	Y	Y	Y	Y
3 **Jones**	Y	Y	Y	Y	Y	Y
4 Price	N	N	Y	Y	Y	Y

	349	350	351	352	353	354
5 **Foxx**	Y	Y	Y	Y	Y	Y
6 **Coble**	N	Y	Y	Y	Y	Y
7 McIntyre	N	N	Y	Y	Y	Y
8 Kissell	N	Y	Y	Y	Y	Y
9 **Myrick**	Y	Y	Y	Y	Y	Y
10 **McHenry**	?	?	?	?	?	?
11 Shuler	N	N	Y	Y	Y	Y
12 Watt	N	N	Y	Y	Y	Y
13 Miller	N	N	Y	Y	Y	Y
NORTH DAKOTA						
AL Pomeroy	N	N	Y	Y	Y	Y
OHIO						
1 Driehaus	N	N	Y	Y	Y	Y
2 **Schmidt**	N	N	Y	Y	Y	Y
3 **Turner**	N	Y	Y	Y	Y	Y
4 **Jordan**	Y	Y	Y	Y	Y	Y
5 **Latta**	Y	Y	Y	Y	Y	Y
6 Wilson	N	N	Y	Y	Y	Y
7 **Austria**	Y	Y	Y	Y	Y	Y
8 **Boehner**	Y	Y	Y	Y	Y	Y
9 Kaptur	N	N	Y	Y	Y	Y
10 Kucinich	N	N	Y	Y	Y	Y
11 Fudge	N	N	Y	Y	Y	Y
12 **Tiberi**	N	Y	Y	Y	Y	Y
13 Sutton	N	Y	Y	Y	Y	Y
14 **LaTourette**	N	Y	Y	Y	Y	Y
15 Kilroy	N	N	Y	Y	Y	Y
16 Boccieri	N	N	Y	Y	Y	Y
17 Ryan	N	N	Y	Y	Y	Y
18 Space	N	N	Y	Y	Y	Y
OKLAHOMA						
1 **Sullivan**	N	Y	Y	Y	Y	Y
2 Boren	N	N	Y	Y	Y	Y
3 **Lucas**	N	N	Y	Y	Y	Y
4 **Cole**	N	N	Y	Y	Y	Y
5 **Fallin**	N	N	Y	Y	Y	Y
OREGON						
1 Wu	N	N	Y	?	Y	Y
2 **Walden**	N	N	Y	Y	Y	Y
3 Blumenauer	N	N	Y	Y	Y	Y
4 DeFazio	N	N	Y	Y	Y	Y
5 Schrader	N	?	Y	Y	Y	Y
PENNSYLVANIA						
1 Brady	N	N	Y	Y	Y	Y
2 Fattah	N	N	Y	Y	Y	Y
3 Dahlkemper	N	N	Y	Y	Y	Y
4 Altmire	N	N	Y	Y	Y	Y
5 **Thompson**	Y	N	Y	Y	Y	Y
6 **Gerlach**	N	N	Y	Y	Y	Y
7 Sestak	N	N	Y	Y	Y	Y
8 Murphy, P.	N	N	Y	Y	Y	Y
9 **Shuster**	?	?	?	?	+	+
10 Carney	N	N	Y	Y	Y	Y
11 Kanjorski	N	N	Y	Y	Y	Y
12 Critz	N	N	Y	Y	Y	Y
13 Schwartz	N	N	Y	Y	Y	Y
14 Doyle	N	N	Y	Y	Y	Y
15 **Dent**	N	N	Y	Y	Y	Y
16 **Pitts**	Y	Y	Y	Y	Y	Y
17 Holden	N	N	Y	Y	Y	Y
18 **Murphy, T.**	Y	Y	Y	Y	Y	Y
19 **Platts**	N	N	Y	Y	Y	Y
RHODE ISLAND						
1 Kennedy	N	N	Y	Y	Y	Y
2 Langevin	N	N	Y	Y	Y	Y
SOUTH CAROLINA						
1 **Brown**	N	Y	Y	Y	Y	Y
2 **Wilson**	Y	Y	Y	Y	Y	Y
3 **Barrett**	?	?	?	?	?	?
4 **Inglis**	?	?	?	?	?	?
5 Spratt	N	N	Y	Y	Y	Y
6 Clyburn	N	N	Y	Y	Y	Y
SOUTH DAKOTA						
AL Herseth Sandlin	N	Y	Y	Y	Y	Y
TENNESSEE						
1 **Roe**	Y	N	Y	Y	+	Y
2 **Duncan**	N	Y	Y	Y	Y	Y
3 **Wamp**	N	Y	Y	Y	Y	Y
4 Davis	N	Y	Y	Y	Y	Y
5 Cooper	N	N	Y	Y	Y	Y
6 Gordon	?	N	Y	?	Y	Y
7 **Blackburn**	Y	Y	Y	Y	Y	Y
8 Tanner	N	N	Y	Y	Y	Y
9 Cohen	N	N	Y	Y	Y	Y

	349	350	351	352	353	354
TEXAS						
1 **Gohmert**	Y	?	Y	Y	Y	Y
2 **Poe**	Y	Y	Y	Y	Y	Y
3 **Johnson, S.**	Y	Y	Y	Y	Y	Y
4 **Hall**	Y	N	Y	Y	Y	Y
5 **Hensarling**	Y	Y	Y	Y	?	Y
6 **Barton**	Y	Y	Y	Y	Y	Y
7 **Culberson**	Y	N	Y	Y	Y	Y
8 **Brady**	Y	N	Y	Y	Y	Y
9 Green, A.	N	N	Y	Y	Y	Y
10 **McCaul**	Y	Y	Y	Y	Y	Y
11 **Conaway**	Y	Y	Y	Y	Y	Y
12 **Granger**	Y	Y	Y	Y	Y	Y
13 **Thornberry**	Y	Y	Y	Y	Y	Y
14 **Paul**	Y	Y	N	Y	N	Y
15 Hinojosa	?	?	?	?	?	?
16 Reyes	N	N	Y	Y	Y	Y
17 Edwards	N	N	Y	Y	Y	Y
18 Jackson Lee	N	N	Y	Y	Y	Y
19 **Neugebauer**	Y	Y	Y	Y	Y	Y
20 Gonzalez	N	N	Y	Y	Y	Y
21 **Smith**	Y	Y	Y	?	Y	Y
22 **Olson**	Y	Y	Y	Y	Y	Y
23 Rodriguez	N	N	Y	Y	Y	Y
24 **Marchant**	Y	Y	Y	Y	Y	Y
25 Doggett	N	Y	Y	Y	Y	Y
26 **Burgess**	Y	Y	Y	Y	Y	Y
27 Ortiz	N	N	Y	Y	Y	Y
28 Cuellar	N	N	Y	Y	Y	Y
29 Green, G.	N	N	Y	Y	Y	Y
30 Johnson, E.	N	N	Y	Y	Y	Y
31 **Carter**	Y	Y	Y	Y	Y	Y
32 **Sessions**	Y	Y	Y	?	Y	Y
UTAH						
1 **Bishop**	Y	Y	Y	Y	Y	Y
2 Matheson	N	N	Y	Y	Y	Y
3 **Chaffetz**	Y	Y	Y	Y	Y	Y
VERMONT						
AL Welch	N	N	Y	Y	?	Y
VIRGINIA						
1 **Wittman**	N	N	Y	Y	Y	Y
2 Nye	N	N	Y	Y	Y	Y
3 Scott	N	N	N	Y	Y	Y
4 **Forbes**	N	N	Y	Y	Y	Y
5 Perriello	N	N	Y	Y	Y	Y
6 **Goodlatte**	N	Y	Y	Y	Y	Y
7 **Cantor**	Y	Y	Y	Y	Y	Y
8 Moran	N	N	Y	Y	Y	Y
9 Boucher	N	N	Y	Y	Y	Y
10 **Wolf**	N	N	Y	Y	Y	Y
11 Connolly	N	N	Y	Y	Y	Y
WASHINGTON						
1 Inslee	N	N	Y	Y	Y	Y
2 Larsen	N	N	Y	Y	Y	Y
3 Baird	N	N	Y	Y	Y	Y
4 **Hastings**	Y	Y	Y	Y	Y	Y
5 **McMorris Rodgers**	Y	Y	Y	Y	Y	Y
6 Dicks	N	N	Y	Y	Y	Y
7 McDermott	N	N	Y	Y	Y	Y
8 **Reichert**	N	N	Y	Y	Y	Y
9 Smith	N	N	Y	Y	Y	Y
WEST VIRGINIA						
1 Mollohan	N	N	Y	Y	Y	Y
2 **Capito**	Y	Y	Y	Y	Y	Y
3 Rahall	N	N	Y	Y	Y	Y
WISCONSIN						
1 **Ryan**	Y	Y	Y	Y	Y	Y
2 Baldwin	N	N	Y	Y	Y	Y
3 Kind	N	N	Y	Y	Y	Y
4 Moore	N	N	Y	Y	Y	Y
5 **Sensenbrenner**	Y	Y	Y	Y	Y	Y
6 **Petri**	Y	Y	Y	Y	Y	Y
7 Obey	N	N	Y	Y	?	?
8 Kagen	N	N	Y	Y	Y	Y
WYOMING						
AL **Lummis**	Y	N	Y	Y	?	Y
DELEGATES						
Faleomavaega (A.S.)	?	N	Y	Y		
Norton (D.C.)	N	N	Y	Y		
Bordallo (Guam)	N	N	Y	Y		
Sablan (N. Marianas)	N	N	Y	Y		
Pierluisi (P.R.)	N	N	Y	Y		
Christensen (V.I.)	N	N	Y	Y		

IN THE HOUSE | By Vote Number

355. H Res 1368. National Dairy Month/Adoption. Bright, D-Ala., motion to suspend the rules and adopt the resolution that would express support for the goals of National Dairy Month. Motion agreed to 359-0: D 214-0; R 145-0. A two-thirds majority of those present and voting (240 in this case) is required for adoption under suspension of the rules. June 14, 2010.

356. H Res 1409. American Eagle Day/Adoption. Hinojosa, D-Texas, motion to suspend the rules and adopt the resolution that would support the designation of American Eagle Day. Motion agreed to 360-0: D 212-0; R 148-0. A two-thirds majority of those present and voting (240 in this case) is required for adoption under suspension of the rules. June 14, 2010.

357. HR 5502. Gift Card Disclosure Extension/Passage. Hinojosa, D-Texas, motion to suspend the rules and pass the bill that would extend the effective date of disclosure requirements from Aug. 22, 2010, to Jan. 31, 2011, for gift cards produced prior to April 1, 2010. To qualify for the extension, issuers of gift cards would be required to eliminate the expiration date on those cards, if applicable, or issue consumers free replacement cards. Motion agreed to 357-0: D 210-0; R 147-0. A two-thirds majority of those present and voting (238 in this case) is required for passage under suspension of the rules. June 14, 2010.

358. H Res 1383. Tribute to Larry Case/Adoption. Bright, D-Ala., motion to suspend the rules and adopt the resolution that would pay tribute to Dr. Larry Case on his retirement as National Future Farmers of America Organization adviser. Motion agreed to 409-0: D 245-0; R 164-0. A two-thirds majority of those present and voting (273 in this case) is required for adoption under suspension of the rules. June 15, 2010.

359. HR 5297, HR 5486. Small-Business Lending and Tax Relief/Rule. Adoption of the rule (H Res 1436) to provide for House floor consideration of two small business-related bills: one (HR 5297) that would authorize $30 billion for the creation of a lending fund, and another (HR 5486) that would provide $3.6 billion in tax incentives for small businesses. Adopted 228-186: D 228-20; R 0-166. June 15, 2010.

360. HR 4855. Work-Life Balance Award/Passage. Woolsey, D-Calif., motion to suspend the rules and pass the bill that would establish an annual award under the Labor Department to recognize employers with policies that promote work-life balance. Motion rejected 249-163: D 230-16; R 19-147. A two-thirds majority of those present and voting (275 in this case) is required for passage under suspension of the rules. June 15, 2010.

361. H Res 1389. Father's Day/Adoption. Woolsey, D-Calif., motion to suspend the rules and adopt the resolution that would call on fathers to spend Father's Day with their children and encourage their active involvement in the rearing and development of their children. Motion agreed to 416-0: D 249-0; R 167-0. A two-thirds majority of those present and voting (278 in this case) is required for adoption under suspension of the rules. June 15, 2010.

	355	356	357	358	359	360	361
ALABAMA							
1 Bonner	?	?	?	Y	N	N	Y
2 Bright	Y	Y	Y	Y	N	Y	Y
3 Rogers	Y	Y	Y	Y	N	N	Y
4 Aderholt	Y	Y	Y	Y	N	N	Y
5 Griffith	Y	Y	Y	Y	N	N	Y
6 Bachus	Y	Y	Y	Y	N	N	Y
7 Davis	?	?	?	Y	Y	Y	Y
ALASKA							
AL Young	Y	Y	Y	Y	N	Y	Y
ARIZONA							
1 Kirkpatrick	Y	Y	Y	Y	N	N	Y
2 Franks	Y	Y	Y	Y	N	N	N
3 Shadegg	Y	Y	Y	Y	N	N	Y
4 Pastor	Y	Y	Y	Y	Y	Y	Y
5 Mitchell	Y	Y	Y	Y	N	Y	Y
6 Flake	Y	Y	Y	Y	N	N	Y
7 Grijalva	?	?	?	Y	Y	Y	Y
8 Giffords	?	Y	Y	Y	N	Y	Y
ARKANSAS							
1 Berry	Y	Y	Y	Y	Y	Y	Y
2 Snyder	Y	Y	Y	Y	Y	Y	Y
3 Boozman	?	?	?	Y	N	N	Y
4 Ross	Y	Y	Y	Y	Y	Y	Y
CALIFORNIA							
1 Thompson	Y	Y	Y	Y	Y	Y	Y
2 Herger	Y	Y	Y	Y	N	N	Y
3 Lungren	Y	Y	Y	Y	N	N	Y
4 McClintock	Y	Y	Y	Y	N	N	Y
5 Matsui	Y	Y	Y	Y	Y	Y	Y
6 Woolsey	Y	Y	Y	Y	Y	Y	Y
7 Miller, George	Y	Y	Y	Y	Y	Y	Y
8 Pelosi							
9 Lee	Y	Y	Y	Y	Y	Y	Y
10 Garamendi	Y	Y	Y	Y	Y	Y	Y
11 McNerney	Y	Y	Y	Y	Y	Y	Y
12 Speier	Y	?	Y	Y	Y	Y	Y
13 Stark	?	?	?	Y	Y	Y	Y
14 Eshoo	Y	Y	Y	Y	Y	Y	Y
15 Honda	?	?	?	?	?	?	Y
16 Lofgren	Y	Y	Y	Y	Y	Y	Y
17 Farr	Y	Y	Y	Y	Y	Y	Y
18 Cardoza	Y	Y	Y	Y	N	N	Y
19 Radanovich	?	?	?	Y	N	N	Y
20 Costa	+	Y	Y	Y	N	N	Y
21 Nunes	+	+	+	Y	N	N	Y
22 McCarthy	Y	Y	Y	Y	N	N	Y
23 Capps	Y	Y	Y	Y	Y	Y	Y
24 Gallegly	Y	Y	Y	Y	N	Y	Y
25 McKeon	Y	Y	Y	Y	N	N	Y
26 Dreier	Y	Y	Y	Y	N	N	Y
27 Sherman	Y	Y	Y	Y	Y	Y	Y
28 Berman	Y	?	?	Y	Y	Y	Y
29 Schiff	Y	Y	Y	Y	Y	Y	Y
30 Waxman	Y	Y	Y	Y	Y	Y	Y
31 Becerra	Y	Y	Y	Y	Y	Y	Y
32 Chu	Y	Y	Y	Y	Y	Y	Y
33 Watson	Y	Y	Y	Y	Y	Y	Y
34 Roybal-Allard	Y	Y	Y	Y	Y	Y	Y
35 Waters	?	?	?	Y	Y	Y	Y
36 Harman	Y	Y	Y	Y	Y	Y	Y
37 Richardson	Y	Y	Y	Y	Y	Y	Y
38 Napolitano	+	+	+	Y	Y	Y	Y
39 Sánchez, Linda	Y	Y	Y	Y	Y	Y	Y
40 Royce	Y	Y	Y	Y	N	N	Y
41 Lewis	Y	Y	Y	Y	N	N	Y
42 Miller, Gary	Y	Y	Y	Y	N	N	Y
43 Baca	Y	Y	Y	Y	Y	Y	Y
44 Calvert	Y	Y	Y	Y	N	N	Y
45 Bono Mack	Y	Y	Y	Y	N	N	Y
46 Rohrabacher	?	?	?	Y	N	N	Y
47 Sanchez, Loretta	?	?	?	Y	Y	Y	Y
48 Campbell	?	?	?	Y	N	N	Y
49 Issa	?	?	?	Y	N	N	Y
50 Bilbray	Y	Y	Y	Y	N	N	Y
51 Filner	Y	Y	Y	Y	Y	Y	Y
52 Hunter	Y	Y	Y	?	N	N	Y
53 Davis	Y	Y	Y	Y	Y	Y	Y

	355	356	357	358	359	360	361
COLORADO							
1 DeGette	Y	Y	Y	Y	Y	Y	Y
2 Polis	Y	Y	Y	Y	Y	Y	Y
3 Salazar	?	?	?	Y	Y	Y	Y
4 Markey	Y	?	?	Y	Y	Y	Y
5 Lamborn	Y	Y	Y	Y	N	N	Y
6 Coffman	Y	Y	Y	Y	N	N	Y
7 Perlmutter	Y	Y	Y	Y	Y	Y	Y
CONNECTICUT							
1 Larson	Y	Y	Y	Y	Y	Y	Y
2 Courtney	Y	Y	Y	Y	Y	Y	Y
3 DeLauro	Y	Y	Y	Y	Y	Y	Y
4 Himes	Y	Y	Y	Y	N	Y	Y
5 Murphy	Y	Y	Y	Y	Y	Y	Y
DELAWARE							
AL Castle	Y	Y	Y	Y	N	Y	Y
FLORIDA							
1 Miller	+	+	+	+	−	−	+
2 Boyd	?	?	?	Y	N	Y	Y
3 Brown	?	?	?	?	?	?	?
4 Crenshaw	Y	Y	Y	Y	N	N	Y
5 Brown-Waite	Y	Y	Y	?	?	?	Y
6 Stearns	Y	Y	Y	Y	N	N	Y
7 Mica	Y	Y	Y	Y	N	N	Y
8 Grayson	Y	Y	Y	Y	Y	Y	Y
9 Bilirakis	Y	Y	Y	+	N	N	Y
10 Young	?	?	?	Y	N	N	Y
11 Castor	Y	Y	Y	Y	Y	Y	Y
12 Putnam	Y	Y	Y	Y	N	N	Y
13 Buchanan	Y	Y	Y	Y	N	N	Y
14 Mack	Y	Y	Y	N	N	N	Y
15 Posey	Y	Y	Y	Y	N	N	Y
16 Rooney	Y	Y	Y	Y	N	N	Y
17 Meek	Y	Y	Y	Y	Y	Y	Y
18 Ros-Lehtinen	Y	Y	Y	Y	N	N	Y
19 Deutch	Y	Y	Y	?	?	?	Y
20 Wasserman Schultz	Y	Y	Y	Y	Y	Y	Y
21 Diaz-Balart, L.	?	?	?	Y	N	N	Y
22 Klein	Y	Y	Y	Y	Y	Y	Y
23 Hastings	Y	Y	Y	Y	Y	Y	Y
24 Kosmas	Y	Y	Y	Y	Y	Y	Y
25 Diaz-Balart, M.	Y	Y	Y	Y	N	N	Y
GEORGIA							
1 Kingston	Y	Y	Y	Y	N	N	Y
2 Bishop	Y	Y	Y	Y	Y	Y	Y
3 Westmoreland	Y	Y	Y	Y	N	N	Y
4 Johnson	Y	Y	Y	Y	Y	Y	Y
5 Lewis	Y	Y	Y	Y	Y	Y	Y
6 Price	Y	Y	Y	Y	N	N	Y
7 Linder	Y	Y	?	Y	N	N	?
8 Marshall	Y	Y	Y	Y	Y	Y	Y
9 Graves*		Y	Y	Y	N	N	Y
10 Broun	Y	Y	Y	Y	N	N	Y
11 Gingrey	Y	Y	Y	Y	N	N	Y
12 Barrow	Y	Y	Y	Y	Y	Y	Y
13 Scott	Y	Y	Y	Y	Y	Y	Y
HAWAII							
1 Djou	Y	Y	Y	Y	N	N	Y
2 Hirono	Y	Y	Y	Y	Y	Y	Y
IDAHO							
1 Minnick	Y	Y	Y	Y	Y	Y	Y
2 Simpson	?	?	?	Y	N	N	Y
ILLINOIS							
1 Rush	Y	Y	Y	Y	Y	Y	Y
2 Jackson	Y	Y	Y	Y	Y	Y	Y
3 Lipinski	?	?	?	Y	Y	Y	Y
4 Gutierrez	+	+	+	Y	Y	Y	Y
5 Quigley	?	?	?	Y	Y	Y	Y
6 Roskam	Y	Y	Y	Y	N	N	Y
7 Davis	+	+	+	+	+	+	Y
8 Bean	Y	Y	Y	Y	N	Y	Y
9 Schakowsky	Y	Y	Y	Y	Y	Y	Y
10 Kirk	?	?	?	Y	N	N	Y
11 Halvorson	Y	Y	Y	Y	N	Y	Y
12 Costello	?	?	?	Y	Y	Y	Y
13 Biggert	Y	Y	Y	Y	N	N	Y
14 Foster	Y	Y	Y	Y	Y	Y	Y
15 Johnson	Y	Y	Y	Y	N	Y	Y

KEY   Republicans   Democrats

Y Voted for (yea)	X Paired against	C Voted "present" to avoid possible conflict of interest
# Paired for	− Announced against	
+ Announced for	P Voted "present"	? Did not vote or otherwise make a position known
N Voted against (nay)		

* Rep. Tom Graves, R-Ga., was sworn in June 14 to fill the seat vacated by Nathan Deal, who resigned March 21 to run for governor. The first vote for which Graves was eligible was vote 356.

	355	356	357	358	359	360	361
16 **Manzullo**	Y	Y	Y	Y	N	N	Y
17 Hare	Y	Y	Y	Y	Y	Y	Y
18 **Schock**	Y	Y	Y	Y	N	N	Y
19 **Shimkus**	Y	Y	Y	Y	N	N	Y
INDIANA							
1 Visclosky	Y	Y	Y	Y	Y	Y	Y
2 Donnelly	Y	Y	Y	Y	Y	Y	Y
3 Vacant							
4 **Buyer**	Y	Y	Y	?	?	?	Y
5 **Burton**	Y	Y	Y	Y	N	N	Y
6 **Pence**	Y	Y	Y	Y	N	N	Y
7 Carson	Y	Y	Y	Y	Y	Y	Y
8 Ellsworth	Y	Y	Y	Y	Y	Y	Y
9 Hill	?	?	?	Y	N	N	Y
IOWA							
1 Braley	Y	Y	Y	Y	Y	Y	Y
2 Loebsack	Y	Y	Y	Y	Y	Y	Y
3 Boswell	Y	Y	Y	Y	Y	Y	Y
4 **Latham**	Y	Y	Y	Y	N	N	Y
5 **King**	Y	Y	Y	Y	N	N	Y
KANSAS							
1 **Moran**	?	?	?	Y	N	N	Y
2 **Jenkins**	Y	Y	Y	Y	N	N	Y
3 Moore	Y	Y	Y	Y	Y	Y	Y
4 **Tiahrt**	Y	Y	Y	Y	N	N	Y
KENTUCKY							
1 **Whitfield**	Y	Y	Y	Y	N	N	Y
2 **Guthrie**	Y	Y	Y	Y	N	N	Y
3 Yarmuth	?	?	?	Y	Y	Y	Y
4 **Davis**	Y	Y	Y	Y	N	N	Y
5 **Rogers**	?	?	?	Y	N	N	Y
6 Chandler	Y	Y	Y	Y	Y	Y	Y
LOUISIANA							
1 **Scalise**	Y	Y	Y	Y	N	N	Y
2 **Cao**	?	?	?	Y	N	Y	Y
3 Melancon	?	?	?	Y	N	N	Y
4 **Fleming**	Y	Y	Y	Y	N	N	Y
5 **Alexander**	Y	Y	Y	Y	N	N	Y
6 **Cassidy**	Y	Y	Y	Y	N	Y	Y
7 **Boustany**	Y	Y	Y	Y	N	N	Y
MAINE							
1 Pingree	Y	Y	Y	Y	Y	Y	Y
2 Michaud	Y	Y	Y	Y	Y	Y	Y
MARYLAND							
1 Kratovil	Y	Y	Y	Y	N	Y	Y
2 Ruppersberger	Y	Y	Y	Y	Y	Y	Y
3 Sarbanes	Y	Y	?	Y	Y	Y	Y
4 Edwards	Y	Y	Y	Y	Y	Y	Y
5 Hoyer	Y	Y	Y	Y	Y	Y	Y
6 **Bartlett**	Y	Y	Y	Y	N	N	Y
7 Cummings	Y	Y	Y	Y	Y	Y	Y
8 Van Hollen	Y	Y	Y	Y	Y	Y	Y
MASSACHUSETTS							
1 Olver	Y	Y	Y	Y	Y	Y	Y
2 Neal	Y	Y	Y	Y	Y	Y	Y
3 McGovern	Y	Y	Y	Y	Y	Y	Y
4 Frank	Y	Y	Y	Y	Y	Y	Y
5 Tsongas	Y	Y	Y	Y	Y	Y	Y
6 Tierney	Y	Y	Y	Y	Y	Y	Y
7 Markey	Y	Y	Y	Y	Y	Y	Y
8 Capuano	Y	Y	?	Y	Y	Y	Y
9 Lynch	?	?	?	?	Y	Y	?
10 Delahunt	?	?	?	Y	Y	Y	Y
MICHIGAN							
1 Stupak	Y	Y	Y	Y	Y	Y	Y
2 **Hoekstra**	?	?	?	?	?	?	?
3 **Ehlers**	Y	Y	Y	Y	N	N	Y
4 **Camp**	Y	Y	Y	Y	N	N	Y
5 Kildee	Y	Y	Y	Y	Y	Y	Y
6 **Upton**	Y	Y	Y	Y	N	N	Y
7 Schauer	Y	Y	Y	Y	Y	Y	Y
8 **Rogers**	?	Y	Y	Y	N	N	Y
9 Peters	Y	Y	Y	Y	Y	Y	Y
10 **Miller**	Y	Y	Y	Y	N	N	Y
11 **McCotter**	Y	Y	Y	Y	N	N	Y
12 Levin	Y	Y	Y	Y	Y	Y	Y
13 Kilpatrick	+	+	+	Y	Y	Y	Y
14 Conyers	Y	Y	Y	Y	Y	Y	Y
15 Dingell	Y	Y	Y	Y	Y	Y	Y
MINNESOTA							
1 Walz	Y	Y	Y	Y	Y	Y	Y
2 **Kline**	Y	Y	Y	Y	N	N	Y
3 **Paulsen**	Y	Y	Y	Y	N	N	Y
4 McCollum	Y	Y	Y	Y	Y	Y	Y

	355	356	357	358	359	360	361
5 Ellison	Y	Y	Y	?	Y	Y	Y
6 **Bachmann**	Y	Y	Y	Y	N	N	Y
7 Peterson	Y	Y	Y	Y	Y	N	Y
8 Oberstar	Y	Y	Y	Y	Y	Y	Y
MISSISSIPPI							
1 Childers	Y	Y	Y	Y	N	N	Y
2 Thompson	Y	Y	Y	Y	Y	Y	Y
3 **Harper**	Y	Y	Y	Y	N	N	Y
4 Taylor	?	?	?	Y	N	N	Y
MISSOURI							
1 Clay	Y	Y	Y	Y	Y	Y	Y
2 **Akin**	?	Y	Y	Y	N	N	Y
3 Carnahan	?	Y	Y	Y	Y	Y	Y
4 Skelton	?	?	?	Y	Y	Y	Y
5 Cleaver	Y	Y	Y	Y	Y	Y	Y
6 **Graves**	Y	Y	Y	Y	N	N	Y
7 **Blunt**	Y	Y	Y	Y	N	N	Y
8 **Emerson**	Y	Y	Y	Y	N	N	Y
9 **Luetkemeyer**	?	Y	Y	Y	N	N	Y
MONTANA							
AL **Rehberg**	Y	Y	Y	Y	N	N	Y
NEBRASKA							
1 **Fortenberry**	+	+	+	Y	N	N	Y
2 **Terry**	Y	Y	Y	Y	N	N	Y
3 **Smith**	Y	Y	Y	Y	N	N	Y
NEVADA							
1 Berkley	Y	Y	Y	Y	Y	Y	Y
2 **Heller**	Y	Y	Y	Y	N	N	Y
3 Titus	Y	Y	Y	Y	Y	Y	Y
NEW HAMPSHIRE							
1 Shea-Porter	Y	Y	Y	Y	Y	Y	Y
2 Hodes	?	?	?	?	?	?	?
NEW JERSEY							
1 Andrews	Y	Y	Y	Y	Y	Y	Y
2 **LoBiondo**	Y	Y	Y	Y	N	N	Y
3 Adler	Y	Y	Y	Y	Y	N	Y
4 **Smith**	Y	Y	Y	Y	N	N	Y
5 **Garrett**	?	Y	Y	Y	N	N	Y
6 Pallone	Y	Y	Y	?	?	?	?
7 **Lance**	Y	Y	Y	Y	N	N	Y
8 Pascrell	Y	Y	Y	Y	Y	Y	Y
9 Rothman	Y	Y	Y	Y	Y	Y	Y
10 Payne	Y	Y	Y	Y	Y	Y	Y
11 **Frelinghuysen**	Y	Y	Y	Y	N	Y	Y
12 Holt	Y	Y	Y	Y	Y	Y	Y
13 Sires	?	?	?	Y	Y	Y	Y
NEW MEXICO							
1 Heinrich	Y	Y	Y	Y	Y	Y	Y
2 Teague	Y	Y	Y	Y	Y	Y	Y
3 Luján	Y	Y	Y	Y	Y	Y	Y
NEW YORK							
1 Bishop	Y	Y	Y	Y	Y	Y	Y
2 Israel	Y	Y	Y	Y	Y	Y	Y
3 **King**	Y	Y	Y	Y	N	N	Y
4 McCarthy	Y	Y	Y	Y	Y	Y	Y
5 Ackerman	Y	Y	Y	Y	Y	Y	Y
6 Meeks	Y	Y	Y	Y	Y	Y	Y
7 Crowley	Y	Y	Y	Y	Y	Y	Y
8 Nadler	Y	Y	Y	Y	Y	Y	Y
9 Weiner	?	?	?	Y	Y	Y	Y
10 Towns	?	?	?	Y	Y	Y	Y
11 Clarke	Y	Y	Y	Y	Y	Y	Y
12 Velázquez	Y	Y	Y	Y	Y	Y	Y
13 McMahon	Y	Y	Y	Y	Y	Y	Y
14 Maloney	?	?	?	Y	Y	Y	Y
15 Rangel	Y	Y	Y	Y	Y	Y	Y
16 Serrano	Y	Y	Y	Y	Y	Y	Y
17 Engel	Y	Y	Y	Y	Y	Y	Y
18 Lowey	Y	Y	Y	Y	Y	Y	Y
19 Hall	Y	Y	Y	Y	Y	Y	Y
20 Murphy	Y	Y	Y	Y	N	Y	Y
21 Tonko	Y	Y	Y	Y	Y	Y	Y
22 Hinchey	Y	Y	Y	Y	Y	Y	Y
23 Owens	Y	Y	Y	Y	Y	N	Y
24 Arcuri	Y	Y	Y	Y	Y	Y	Y
25 Maffei	Y	Y	Y	Y	Y	N	Y
26 **Lee**	Y	Y	Y	Y	N	N	Y
27 Higgins	Y	Y	Y	Y	Y	Y	Y
28 Slaughter	?	?	?	Y	Y	Y	Y
29 Vacant							
NORTH CAROLINA							
1 Butterfield	?	?	?	Y	Y	Y	Y
2 Etheridge	Y	Y	Y	Y	Y	Y	Y
3 **Jones**	Y	Y	Y	Y	N	Y	Y
4 Price	Y	Y	Y	Y	Y	Y	Y

	355	356	357	358	359	360	361
5 **Foxx**	Y	Y	Y	Y	N	N	Y
6 **Coble**	Y	Y	Y	Y	N	N	Y
7 McIntyre	Y	Y	Y	Y	N	N	Y
8 Kissell	Y	Y	Y	Y	Y	Y	Y
9 **Myrick**	+	+	+	+	–	–	+
10 **McHenry**	Y	Y	Y	Y	N	Y	Y
11 Shuler	?	?	?	Y	N	N	Y
12 Watt	Y	Y	Y	Y	Y	Y	Y
13 Miller	Y	Y	Y	Y	Y	Y	Y
NORTH DAKOTA							
AL Pomeroy	Y	Y	Y	Y	Y	Y	Y
OHIO							
1 Driehaus	Y	Y	Y	Y	Y	Y	Y
2 **Schmidt**	Y	Y	Y	Y	N	N	Y
3 **Turner**	Y	Y	Y	Y	N	N	Y
4 **Jordan**	Y	Y	Y	Y	N	N	Y
5 **Latta**	Y	Y	Y	Y	N	N	Y
6 Wilson	Y	Y	Y	Y	N	Y	Y
7 **Austria**	Y	Y	Y	Y	N	N	Y
8 **Boehner**	Y	Y	Y	Y	N	N	Y
9 Kaptur	Y	Y	Y	Y	Y	Y	Y
10 Kucinich	Y	Y	Y	Y	Y	Y	Y
11 Fudge	Y	Y	Y	Y	Y	Y	Y
12 **Tiberi**	Y	Y	Y	Y	N	N	Y
13 Sutton	Y	Y	?	Y	Y	Y	Y
14 **LaTourette**	Y	Y	Y	Y	N	N	Y
15 Kilroy	Y	Y	Y	Y	Y	Y	Y
16 Boccieri	Y	Y	Y	Y	Y	Y	Y
17 Ryan	Y	Y	Y	Y	Y	Y	Y
18 Space	Y	Y	Y	Y	N	Y	Y
OKLAHOMA							
1 **Sullivan**	Y	Y	Y	Y	N	N	Y
2 Boren	Y	Y	Y	Y	Y	N	Y
3 **Lucas**	Y	Y	Y	Y	N	N	Y
4 **Cole**	Y	Y	Y	Y	N	N	Y
5 **Fallin**	?	?	?	?	?	?	+
OREGON							
1 Wu	Y	Y	Y	Y	Y	Y	Y
2 **Walden**	Y	?	?	Y	N	N	Y
3 Blumenauer	Y	Y	Y	Y	Y	Y	Y
4 DeFazio	Y	Y	Y	Y	Y	Y	Y
5 Schrader	Y	Y	Y	Y	Y	Y	Y
PENNSYLVANIA							
1 Brady	?	?	?	Y	Y	Y	Y
2 Fattah	?	?	?	Y	Y	Y	Y
3 Dahlkemper	Y	Y	Y	Y	N	Y	Y
4 Altmire	Y	Y	Y	Y	Y	Y	Y
5 **Thompson**	Y	Y	Y	Y	N	N	Y
6 **Gerlach**	+	+	+	Y	N	N	Y
7 Sestak	Y	Y	Y	Y	Y	Y	Y
8 Murphy, P.	Y	Y	Y	Y	Y	Y	Y
9 **Shuster**	Y	Y	Y	Y	N	N	Y
10 Carney	Y	Y	Y	Y	Y	Y	Y
11 Kanjorski	Y	Y	Y	Y	Y	Y	Y
12 Critz	Y	Y	Y	Y	Y	Y	Y
13 Schwartz	Y	Y	Y	Y	Y	Y	Y
14 Doyle	Y	Y	Y	Y	Y	Y	Y
15 **Dent**	Y	Y	Y	Y	N	Y	Y
16 **Pitts**	Y	Y	Y	Y	N	N	Y
17 Holden	?	?	?	Y	Y	Y	Y
18 **Murphy, T.**	Y	Y	Y	Y	N	N	Y
19 **Platts**	Y	Y	Y	Y	N	N	Y
RHODE ISLAND							
1 Kennedy	Y	Y	Y	Y	Y	Y	Y
2 Langevin	Y	Y	Y	Y	Y	Y	Y
SOUTH CAROLINA							
1 **Brown**	?	?	?	?	?	?	?
2 **Wilson**	?	+	+	Y	N	N	Y
3 **Barrett**	?	?	?	?	?	?	?
4 **Inglis**	?	?	?	?	?	?	?
5 Spratt	Y	Y	Y	Y	Y	Y	Y
6 Clyburn	Y	Y	Y	Y	Y	Y	Y
SOUTH DAKOTA							
AL Herseth Sandlin	Y	Y	Y	Y	N	Y	Y
TENNESSEE							
1 **Roe**	Y	Y	Y	Y	N	N	Y
2 **Duncan**	Y	Y	Y	Y	N	N	Y
3 **Wamp**	?	?	?	?	?	?	?
4 Davis	Y	Y	Y	Y	Y	Y	Y
5 Cooper	Y	Y	Y	Y	Y	Y	Y
6 Gordon	?	?	?	Y	Y	Y	Y
7 **Blackburn**	Y	Y	Y	Y	N	N	Y
8 Tanner	?	?	?	Y	Y	N	Y
9 Cohen	Y	Y	Y	Y	Y	Y	Y

	355	356	357	358	359	360	361
TEXAS							
1 **Gohmert**	Y	?	?	?	?	?	?
2 **Poe**	Y	Y	Y	Y	N	N	Y
3 **Johnson, S.**	Y	Y	Y	Y	N	N	Y
4 **Hall**	Y	Y	Y	Y	N	N	Y
5 **Hensarling**	Y	Y	Y	Y	N	N	Y
6 **Barton**	Y	Y	Y	Y	N	N	Y
7 **Culberson**	Y	Y	Y	Y	N	N	Y
8 **Brady**	?	?	?	Y	N	N	Y
9 Green, A.	Y	Y	Y	Y	Y	Y	Y
10 **McCaul**	Y	Y	Y	Y	N	N	Y
11 **Conaway**	Y	Y	Y	Y	N	N	Y
12 **Granger**	Y	Y	Y	Y	N	N	Y
13 **Thornberry**	Y	Y	Y	Y	N	N	Y
14 **Paul**	Y	Y	Y	Y	N	N	Y
15 Hinojosa	Y	Y	Y	Y	Y	Y	Y
16 Reyes	Y	?	Y	Y	Y	Y	Y
17 Edwards	Y	Y	Y	Y	Y	Y	Y
18 Jackson Lee	Y	Y	Y	Y	Y	Y	Y
19 **Neugebauer**	Y	Y	Y	Y	N	N	Y
20 Gonzalez	Y	Y	Y	Y	Y	Y	Y
21 **Smith**	Y	Y	Y	Y	N	N	Y
22 **Olson**	Y	Y	Y	Y	N	N	Y
23 Rodriguez	Y	Y	Y	Y	Y	Y	Y
24 **Marchant**	Y	Y	Y	Y	N	N	Y
25 Doggett	Y	Y	Y	Y	Y	Y	Y
26 **Burgess**	Y	Y	Y	Y	N	N	Y
27 Ortiz	Y	Y	Y	Y	Y	Y	Y
28 Cuellar	Y	Y	Y	Y	Y	Y	Y
29 Green, G.	Y	Y	Y	Y	Y	Y	Y
30 Johnson, E.	Y	Y	Y	Y	Y	Y	Y
31 **Carter**	?	?	?	Y	N	N	Y
32 **Sessions**	Y	Y	Y	Y	N	N	Y
UTAH							
1 **Bishop**	Y	Y	Y	Y	N	N	Y
2 Matheson	?	?	?	Y	Y	Y	Y
3 **Chaffetz**	Y	Y	Y	Y	N	N	Y
VERMONT							
AL Welch	Y	Y	Y	Y	Y	Y	Y
VIRGINIA							
1 **Wittman**	Y	Y	Y	Y	N	N	Y
2 Nye	Y	Y	Y	Y	Y	Y	Y
3 Scott	Y	Y	Y	Y	Y	Y	Y
4 **Forbes**	?	?	?	Y	N	N	Y
5 Perriello	Y	Y	Y	Y	Y	Y	Y
6 **Goodlatte**	Y	Y	Y	Y	N	N	Y
7 **Cantor**	Y	Y	Y	?	?	?	?
8 Moran	Y	Y	?	Y	Y	Y	Y
9 Boucher	Y	Y	Y	Y	Y	Y	Y
10 **Wolf**	Y	Y	Y	Y	N	N	Y
11 Connolly	Y	Y	Y	Y	Y	Y	Y
WASHINGTON							
1 Inslee	+	+	+	Y	Y	Y	Y
2 Larsen	Y	Y	Y	Y	Y	Y	Y
3 Baird	Y	?	?	Y	Y	Y	Y
4 **Hastings**	Y	Y	Y	Y	N	N	Y
5 **McMorris Rodgers**	Y	Y	Y	Y	N	Y	Y
6 Dicks	Y	Y	Y	Y	Y	Y	Y
7 McDermott	Y	Y	Y	Y	Y	Y	Y
8 **Reichert**	Y	Y	Y	Y	N	Y	Y
9 Smith	Y	Y	Y	Y	Y	Y	Y
WEST VIRGINIA							
1 Mollohan	Y	Y	Y	Y	Y	Y	Y
2 **Capito**	Y	Y	Y	Y	N	Y	Y
3 Rahall	Y	Y	Y	Y	Y	?	Y
WISCONSIN							
1 **Ryan**	Y	Y	Y	Y	N	N	Y
2 Baldwin	Y	Y	Y	Y	Y	Y	Y
3 Kind	Y	Y	Y	Y	Y	Y	Y
4 Moore	Y	Y	Y	Y	Y	Y	Y
5 **Sensenbrenner**	Y	Y	Y	Y	N	N	Y
6 **Petri**	Y	Y	Y	Y	N	N	Y
7 Obey	Y	Y	Y	Y	Y	Y	Y
8 Kagen	Y	Y	Y	Y	Y	Y	Y
WYOMING							
AL **Lummis**	Y	Y	Y	Y	N	Y	Y
DELEGATES							
Faleomavaega (A.S.)							
Norton (D.C.)							
Bordallo (Guam)							
Sablan (N. Marianas)							
Pierluisi (P.R.)							
Christensen (V.I.)							

IN THE HOUSE | By Vote Number

362. HR 5486. Small-Business Tax Relief/Recommit. Camp, R-Mich., motion to recommit the bill to the Ways and Means Committee with instructions that it be immediately reported back with language that would repeal the individual mandate to purchase health insurance in the 2010 health care overhaul law. Motion rejected 187-230: D 21-229; R 166-1. June 15, 2010.

363. HR 5486. Small-Business Tax Relief/Passage. Passage of the bill that would provide $3.6 billion in tax incentives for small businesses by increasing deductions for startup expenses and eliminating taxation on certain small-business stocks. Passed 247-170: D 242-8; R 5-162. June 15, 2010.

364. H Res 1322. Tribute to Albert Einstein Fellows/Adoption. Woolsey, D-Calif., motion to suspend the rules and adopt the resolution that would mark the 20th anniversary of the Albert Einstein Distinguished Educator Fellowship Program. Motion agreed to 405-5: D 246-0; R 159-5. A two-thirds majority of those present and voting (274 in this case) is required for adoption under suspension of the rules. June 15, 2010.

365. H Con Res 242. NAACP Anniversary/Adoption. Cohen, D-Tenn., motion to suspend the rules and adopt the concurrent resolution that would mark the 101st anniversary of the founding the National Association for the Advancement of Colored People (NAACP) and recognize its accomplishments. Motion agreed to 421-0: D 249-0; R 172-0. A two-thirds majority of those present and voting (281 in this case) is required for adoption under suspension of the rules. June 16, 2010.

366. H Res 1422. Justice Department Anniversary/Adoption. Cohen, D-Tenn., motion to suspend the rules and adopt the resolution that would recognize the Justice Department on its 140th anniversary. Motion agreed to 416-3: D 248-0; R 168-3. A two-thirds majority of those present and voting (280 in this case) is required for adoption under suspension of the rules. June 16, 2010.

367. H Res 1414. Commend College Acceptances/Adoption. Woolsey, D-Calif., motion to suspend the rules and adopt the resolution that would congratulate the 2010 graduates of Urban Prep Charter Academy for Young Men-Englewood Campus for achieving a 100 percent college acceptance rate. Motion agreed to 420-0: D 249-0; R 171-0. A two-thirds majority of those present and voting (280 in this case) is required for adoption under suspension of the rules. June 16, 2010.

368. HR 5297. Small-Business Lending/Previous Question. Perlmutter, D-Colo., motion to order the previous question (thus ending debate and the possibility of amendment) on adoption of the rule (H Res 1448) that would provide for further House floor consideration of the bill that would create a lending fund through which the Treasury Department could make up to $30 billion in investments to encourage certain financial institutions to make credit available for small businesses. Motion agreed to 241-179: D 241-7; R 0-172. June 17, 2010.

	362	363	364	365	366	367	368
ALABAMA							
1 Bonner	Y	N	Y	Y	Y	Y	N
2 Bright	Y	Y	Y	Y	Y	Y	N
3 Rogers	Y	N	Y	Y	Y	Y	N
4 Aderholt	Y	N	Y	Y	Y	Y	N
5 Griffith	Y	N	Y	Y	Y	Y	N
6 Bachus	Y	N	Y	Y	Y	Y	N
7 Davis	N	Y	Y	Y	Y	Y	Y
ALASKA							
AL Young	Y	N	Y	Y	N	Y	N
ARIZONA							
1 Kirkpatrick	N	Y	Y	Y	Y	Y	?
2 Franks	Y	N	Y	Y	Y	Y	N
3 Shadegg	Y	N	Y	Y	Y	Y	N
4 Pastor	N	Y	Y	Y	Y	Y	Y
5 Mitchell	N	N	Y	Y	Y	Y	N
6 Flake	Y	N	N	Y	Y	Y	N
7 Grijalva	N	Y	Y	Y	Y	Y	Y
8 Giffords	N	Y	Y	Y	Y	Y	N
ARKANSAS							
1 Berry	N	N	Y	Y	Y	Y	Y
2 Snyder	N	Y	Y	Y	Y	Y	Y
3 Boozman	Y	N	Y	Y	Y	Y	N
4 Ross	Y	Y	Y	Y	Y	Y	Y
CALIFORNIA							
1 Thompson	N	Y	Y	Y	Y	Y	Y
2 Herger	Y	N	Y	Y	Y	Y	N
3 Lungren	Y	N	Y	Y	Y	Y	N
4 McClintock	Y	N	Y	Y	Y	Y	N
5 Matsui	N	Y	Y	Y	Y	Y	Y
6 Woolsey	N	Y	Y	Y	Y	Y	Y
7 Miller, George	N	Y	Y	Y	Y	Y	Y
8 Pelosi							
9 Lee	N	Y	Y	Y	Y	Y	Y
10 Garamendi	N	Y	Y	Y	Y	Y	Y
11 McNerney	N	Y	Y	Y	Y	Y	Y
12 Speier	N	Y	Y	Y	Y	Y	Y
13 Stark	N	Y	Y	Y	Y	Y	Y
14 Eshoo	N	Y	Y	Y	Y	Y	Y
15 Honda	N	Y	Y	Y	Y	Y	Y
16 Lofgren	N	Y	Y	Y	Y	Y	Y
17 Farr	N	Y	Y	Y	Y	Y	Y
18 Cardoza	N	Y	Y	Y	Y	Y	Y
19 Radanovich	Y	N	Y	Y	Y	Y	N
20 Costa	N	N	Y	Y	Y	Y	Y
21 Nunes	Y	N	Y	Y	Y	Y	N
22 McCarthy	Y	N	Y	Y	Y	Y	N
23 Capps	N	Y	+	Y	Y	Y	Y
24 Gallegly	Y	N	Y	Y	Y	Y	N
25 McKeon	Y	N	Y	Y	Y	Y	N
26 Dreier	Y	N	Y	Y	Y	Y	N
27 Sherman	N	Y	Y	Y	Y	Y	Y
28 Berman	N	Y	Y	Y	Y	Y	Y
29 Schiff	N	Y	Y	Y	Y	Y	Y
30 Waxman	N	Y	Y	Y	Y	Y	Y
31 Becerra	N	Y	Y	Y	Y	Y	Y
32 Chu	N	Y	Y	Y	Y	Y	Y
33 Watson	N	Y	Y	Y	Y	Y	Y
34 Roybal-Allard	N	Y	Y	Y	Y	Y	Y
35 Waters	N	Y	?	Y	Y	Y	Y
36 Harman	N	Y	Y	Y	Y	Y	Y
37 Richardson	N	Y	Y	Y	Y	Y	Y
38 Napolitano	N	Y	Y	Y	Y	Y	Y
39 Sánchez, Linda	N	Y	Y	Y	Y	Y	Y
40 Royce	Y	N	Y	Y	Y	Y	N
41 Lewis	Y	N	Y	Y	Y	Y	N
42 Miller, Gary	Y	N	Y	Y	Y	Y	N
43 Baca	N	Y	Y	Y	Y	Y	Y
44 Calvert	Y	N	Y	Y	Y	Y	N
45 Bono Mack	Y	N	Y	Y	Y	Y	N
46 Rohrabacher	Y	N	Y	Y	Y	Y	N
47 Sanchez, Loretta	N	Y	Y	Y	Y	Y	Y
48 Campbell	Y	N	N	Y	Y	Y	N
49 Issa	Y	N	Y	Y	Y	Y	N
50 Bilbray	Y	N	?	Y	Y	Y	N
51 Filner	N	Y	Y	Y	Y	Y	Y
52 Hunter	Y	N	Y	Y	Y	Y	N
53 Davis	N	Y	Y	Y	Y	Y	Y

	362	363	364	365	366	367	368
COLORADO							
1 DeGette	N	Y	Y	Y	Y	Y	Y
2 Polis	N	Y	Y	Y	Y	Y	Y
3 Salazar	N	Y	Y	Y	Y	Y	Y
4 Markey	N	Y	Y	Y	Y	Y	Y
5 Lamborn	Y	N	Y	Y	Y	Y	N
6 Coffman	Y	N	Y	Y	Y	Y	N
7 Perlmutter	N	Y	Y	Y	Y	Y	Y
CONNECTICUT							
1 Larson	N	Y	Y	Y	Y	Y	Y
2 Courtney	N	Y	Y	Y	Y	Y	Y
3 DeLauro	N	Y	Y	Y	Y	Y	Y
4 Himes	N	Y	Y	?	Y	Y	Y
5 Murphy	N	Y	Y	Y	Y	Y	Y
DELAWARE							
AL Castle	Y	Y	Y	Y	Y	Y	N
FLORIDA							
1 Miller	+	–	+	Y	Y	Y	N
2 Boyd	N	N	Y	Y	Y	Y	Y
3 Brown	?	?	?	Y	Y	Y	Y
4 Crenshaw	Y	N	Y	Y	Y	Y	N
5 Brown-Waite	Y	N	Y	Y	Y	Y	N
6 Stearns	Y	N	Y	Y	Y	Y	N
7 Mica	Y	N	Y	Y	Y	Y	N
8 Grayson	N	Y	Y	Y	Y	Y	Y
9 Bilirakis	Y	N	Y	Y	Y	Y	N
10 Young	Y	N	Y	Y	Y	Y	?
11 Castor	N	Y	Y	Y	Y	Y	Y
12 Putnam	Y	–	+	Y	Y	Y	N
13 Buchanan	Y	N	Y	Y	Y	Y	N
14 Mack	Y	N	Y	Y	Y	Y	N
15 Posey	Y	N	Y	Y	Y	Y	N
16 Rooney	Y	N	Y	Y	Y	Y	N
17 Meek	N	Y	Y	Y	Y	?	Y
18 Ros-Lehtinen	Y	N	Y	Y	Y	Y	N
19 Deutch	?	?	?	Y	Y	Y	Y
20 Wasserman Schultz	N	Y	Y	Y	Y	Y	Y
21 Diaz-Balart, L.	Y	N	Y	Y	Y	Y	N
22 Klein	N	Y	Y	Y	Y	Y	Y
23 Hastings	N	Y	Y	Y	Y	Y	Y
24 Kosmas	N	Y	Y	Y	Y	Y	Y
25 Diaz-Balart, M.	Y	N	Y	Y	Y	Y	N
GEORGIA							
1 Kingston	Y	N	?	Y	Y	Y	N
2 Bishop	N	Y	?	Y	Y	Y	Y
3 Westmoreland	Y	N	Y	Y	Y	Y	N
4 Johnson	N	Y	Y	?	Y	Y	Y
5 Lewis	N	Y	Y	Y	Y	Y	Y
6 Price	Y	N	Y	Y	Y	Y	N
7 Linder	?	N	Y	Y	Y	Y	N
8 Marshall	Y	Y	Y	Y	Y	Y	Y
9 Graves	Y	N	Y	Y	Y	Y	N
10 Broun	Y	N	Y	Y	Y	Y	N
11 Gingrey	Y	N	Y	Y	Y	Y	N
12 Barrow	N	Y	Y	Y	Y	Y	Y
13 Scott	N	Y	Y	Y	Y	Y	Y
HAWAII							
1 Djou	Y	N	Y	Y	Y	Y	N
2 Hirono	N	Y	Y	Y	Y	?	Y
IDAHO							
1 Minnick	Y	Y	Y	Y	Y	Y	N
2 Simpson	Y	N	Y	Y	?	Y	N
ILLINOIS							
1 Rush	N	Y	Y	Y	Y	Y	Y
2 Jackson	N	Y	Y	Y	Y	Y	Y
3 Lipinski	N	Y	Y	Y	Y	Y	Y
4 Gutierrez	N	Y	Y	Y	Y	Y	?
5 Quigley	N	Y	Y	Y	Y	Y	Y
6 Roskam	Y	N	Y	Y	Y	Y	N
7 Davis	N	Y	Y	+	+	+	Y
8 Bean	N	Y	Y	Y	Y	Y	Y
9 Schakowsky	N	Y	Y	Y	Y	Y	Y
10 Kirk	Y	Y	Y	Y	Y	Y	N
11 Halvorson	N	Y	Y	Y	Y	Y	Y
12 Costello	N	Y	Y	Y	Y	Y	Y
13 Biggert	Y	N	Y	Y	Y	Y	N
14 Foster	N	Y	Y	Y	Y	Y	Y
15 Johnson	Y	N	Y	N	Y	N	N

KEY | **Republicans** | Democrats

Y Voted for (yea)	X Paired against	C Voted "present" to avoid possible conflict of interest
# Paired for	– Announced against	
+ Announced for	P Voted "present"	? Did not vote or otherwise make a position known
N Voted against (nay)		

	362	363	364	365	366	367	368
16 **Manzullo**	Y	N	Y	Y	Y	Y	N
17 Hare	N	Y	Y	Y	Y	Y	Y
18 **Schock**	Y	N	Y	Y	Y	Y	N
19 **Shimkus**	Y	N	Y	Y	Y	Y	N
INDIANA							
1 Visclosky	N	Y	Y	Y	Y	Y	Y
2 Donnelly	N	Y	Y	Y	Y	Y	Y
3 Vacant							
4 **Buyer**	Y	N	Y	Y	Y	Y	N
5 **Burton**	Y	N	Y	Y	Y	Y	N
6 **Pence**	Y	N	Y	Y	Y	Y	N
7 Carson	N	Y	Y	Y	Y	Y	Y
8 Ellsworth	N	Y	Y	Y	?	?	Y
9 Hill	N	Y	Y	Y	Y	Y	Y
IOWA							
1 Braley	N	Y	Y	Y	Y	Y	Y
2 Loebsack	N	Y	Y	Y	Y	Y	Y
3 Boswell	N	Y	Y	Y	Y	Y	Y
4 **Latham**	Y	N	Y	Y	Y	Y	N
5 **King**	Y	N	Y	Y	Y	Y	N
KANSAS							
1 **Moran**	Y	N	Y	Y	Y	Y	N
2 **Jenkins**	Y	N	Y	Y	Y	Y	N
3 Moore	N	Y	Y	Y	?	Y	Y
4 **Tiahrt**	Y	N	Y	Y	Y	Y	N
KENTUCKY							
1 **Whitfield**	Y	N	Y	Y	Y	Y	N
2 **Guthrie**	Y	N	Y	Y	Y	Y	N
3 Yarmuth	N	Y	Y	Y	Y	Y	Y
4 **Davis**	Y	N	Y	Y	Y	Y	N
5 **Rogers**	Y	N	Y	Y	Y	Y	N
6 Chandler	Y	Y	Y	Y	Y	Y	Y
LOUISIANA							
1 **Scalise**	Y	N	Y	Y	Y	Y	N
2 **Cao**	N	Y	Y	Y	Y	Y	N
3 Melancon	N	Y	Y	?	?	?	Y
4 **Fleming**	Y	N	Y	Y	Y	Y	N
5 **Alexander**	Y	N	Y	Y	Y	Y	N
6 **Cassidy**	Y	N	Y	Y	Y	?	N
7 **Boustany**	Y	N	Y	Y	Y	Y	N
MAINE							
1 Pingree	N	Y	Y	Y	Y	Y	Y
2 Michaud	N	Y	Y	Y	Y	Y	Y
MARYLAND							
1 Kratovil	N	Y	Y	Y	Y	Y	N
2 Ruppersberger	N	Y	Y	Y	Y	Y	Y
3 Sarbanes	N	Y	Y	Y	Y	Y	Y
4 Edwards	N	Y	Y	Y	Y	Y	Y
5 Hoyer	N	Y	Y	Y	Y	Y	Y
6 **Bartlett**	Y	N	Y	Y	Y	Y	N
7 Cummings	N	Y	Y	Y	Y	Y	Y
8 Van Hollen	N	Y	Y	Y	Y	Y	Y
MASSACHUSETTS							
1 Olver	N	Y	Y	Y	Y	?	Y
2 Neal	N	Y	Y	Y	Y	Y	Y
3 McGovern	N	Y	Y	Y	Y	Y	Y
4 Frank	N	Y	Y	Y	Y	Y	Y
5 Tsongas	N	Y	Y	Y	Y	Y	Y
6 Tierney	N	Y	Y	Y	Y	Y	Y
7 Markey	N	Y	Y	Y	Y	Y	Y
8 Capuano	N	Y	Y	Y	Y	Y	Y
9 Lynch	N	Y	Y	Y	Y	Y	Y
10 Delahunt	N	Y	Y	Y	Y	Y	Y
MICHIGAN							
1 Stupak	N	Y	Y	Y	Y	Y	Y
2 **Hoekstra**	?	?	?	?	?	?	?
3 **Ehlers**	Y	N	Y	Y	Y	Y	N
4 **Camp**	Y	N	Y	Y	Y	Y	N
5 Kildee	N	Y	Y	Y	Y	Y	Y
6 **Upton**	Y	N	Y	Y	Y	Y	N
7 Schauer	N	Y	Y	Y	Y	Y	Y
8 **Rogers**	Y	N	Y	Y	Y	Y	N
9 Peters	N	Y	Y	Y	Y	Y	Y
10 **Miller**	Y	N	Y	Y	Y	Y	N
11 **McCotter**	Y	N	Y	Y	Y	Y	N
12 Levin	N	Y	Y	Y	Y	Y	Y
13 Kilpatrick	N	Y	Y	Y	Y	Y	Y
14 Conyers	N	Y	Y	Y	Y	Y	Y
15 Dingell	N	Y	Y	Y	Y	Y	Y
MINNESOTA							
1 Walz	N	Y	Y	Y	Y	Y	Y
2 **Kline**	Y	N	Y	Y	Y	Y	N
3 **Paulsen**	Y	N	Y	Y	Y	Y	N
4 McCollum	N	Y	Y	Y	Y	Y	Y

	362	363	364	365	366	367	368
5 Ellison	N	Y	Y	Y	Y	Y	Y
6 **Bachmann**	Y	N	Y	Y	Y	Y	N
7 Peterson	Y	N	Y	Y	Y	Y	Y
8 Oberstar	N	Y	Y	Y	Y	Y	Y
MISSISSIPPI							
1 Childers	Y	Y	Y	Y	Y	Y	?
2 Thompson	N	Y	Y	Y	Y	Y	Y
3 **Harper**	Y	N	Y	Y	Y	Y	N
4 Taylor	Y	Y	Y	Y	Y	Y	?
MISSOURI							
1 Clay	N	Y	Y	Y	Y	Y	Y
2 **Akin**	Y	N	Y	Y	Y	Y	N
3 Carnahan	N	Y	Y	Y	Y	Y	Y
4 Skelton	Y	Y	Y	Y	Y	Y	Y
5 Cleaver	N	Y	Y	Y	?	Y	Y
6 **Graves**	Y	N	Y	Y	Y	Y	N
7 **Blunt**	Y	N	Y	Y	Y	Y	N
8 **Emerson**	Y	N	Y	Y	Y	Y	N
9 **Luetkemeyer**	Y	N	Y	Y	Y	Y	N
MONTANA							
AL **Rehberg**	Y	N	Y	Y	Y	Y	N
NEBRASKA							
1 **Fortenberry**	Y	N	Y	Y	Y	Y	N
2 **Terry**	Y	N	Y	Y	Y	Y	N
3 **Smith**	Y	N	Y	Y	Y	Y	N
NEVADA							
1 Berkley	N	Y	Y	Y	Y	Y	Y
2 **Heller**	Y	N	Y	Y	Y	Y	N
3 Titus	N	Y	Y	Y	Y	Y	Y
NEW HAMPSHIRE							
1 Shea-Porter	N	Y	Y	Y	Y	Y	Y
2 Hodes	?	?	?	Y	Y	Y	Y
NEW JERSEY							
1 Andrews	N	Y	Y	Y	Y	Y	Y
2 **LoBiondo**	Y	N	Y	Y	Y	Y	N
3 Adler	N	Y	Y	Y	Y	Y	Y
4 **Smith**	Y	N	Y	Y	Y	Y	N
5 **Garrett**	Y	N	Y	Y	Y	Y	N
6 Pallone	?	?	?	Y	Y	Y	Y
7 **Lance**	Y	N	Y	Y	Y	Y	N
8 Pascrell	N	Y	Y	Y	Y	Y	Y
9 Rothman	N	Y	Y	Y	Y	Y	Y
10 Payne	N	Y	Y	Y	Y	Y	Y
11 **Frelinghuysen**	Y	N	Y	Y	Y	Y	N
12 Holt	N	Y	Y	Y	Y	Y	Y
13 Sires	N	Y	Y	Y	Y	Y	Y
NEW MEXICO							
1 Heinrich	N	Y	Y	Y	Y	Y	Y
2 Teague	Y	Y	Y	Y	Y	Y	Y
3 Luján	N	Y	Y	Y	Y	Y	Y
NEW YORK							
1 Bishop	N	Y	Y	Y	Y	Y	Y
2 Israel	N	Y	Y	Y	Y	Y	Y
3 **King**	Y	N	Y	Y	Y	Y	N
4 McCarthy	N	Y	Y	Y	Y	Y	Y
5 Ackerman	N	Y	Y	Y	Y	Y	Y
6 Meeks	N	Y	Y	Y	Y	Y	Y
7 Crowley	N	Y	Y	Y	Y	Y	Y
8 Nadler	N	Y	Y	Y	Y	Y	Y
9 Weiner	N	Y	Y	Y	Y	Y	Y
10 Towns	N	Y	Y	Y	Y	Y	Y
11 Clarke	N	Y	Y	Y	Y	Y	Y
12 Velázquez	N	Y	Y	Y	?	Y	Y
13 McMahon	N	Y	Y	Y	Y	Y	Y
14 Maloney	N	Y	Y	Y	Y	Y	Y
15 Rangel	N	Y	Y	Y	Y	Y	Y
16 Serrano	N	Y	Y	Y	Y	Y	Y
17 Engel	N	Y	Y	Y	Y	Y	Y
18 Lowey	N	Y	Y	Y	Y	Y	Y
19 Hall	N	Y	Y	Y	Y	Y	Y
20 Murphy	N	Y	Y	Y	Y	Y	Y
21 Tonko	N	Y	Y	Y	Y	Y	Y
22 Hinchey	N	Y	Y	Y	Y	Y	Y
23 Owens	N	Y	Y	Y	Y	Y	Y
24 Arcuri	N	Y	Y	Y	Y	Y	Y
25 Maffei	N	Y	Y	Y	Y	Y	Y
26 **Lee**	Y	N	Y	Y	Y	Y	N
27 Higgins	N	Y	Y	Y	Y	Y	Y
28 Slaughter	N	Y	Y	Y	Y	Y	Y
29 Vacant							
NORTH CAROLINA							
1 Butterfield	N	Y	Y	Y	Y	Y	Y
2 Etheridge	N	Y	Y	Y	Y	Y	Y
3 **Jones**	Y	N	Y	Y	Y	Y	N
4 Price	N	Y	Y	Y	Y	Y	Y

	362	363	364	365	366	367	368
5 **Foxx**	Y	N	Y	Y	Y	Y	N
6 **Coble**	Y	N	Y	Y	Y	Y	N
7 McIntyre	Y	Y	Y	Y	Y	Y	Y
8 Kissell	N	Y	Y	Y	Y	Y	Y
9 **Myrick**	+	–	+	Y	Y	Y	N
10 **McHenry**	Y	N	Y	Y	Y	Y	N
11 Shuler	Y	Y	Y	Y	Y	Y	Y
12 Watt	N	Y	Y	Y	Y	Y	Y
13 Miller	N	Y	Y	Y	Y	Y	Y
NORTH DAKOTA							
AL Pomeroy	N	Y	Y	Y	Y	Y	Y
OHIO							
1 Driehaus	N	Y	Y	Y	Y	Y	Y
2 **Schmidt**	Y	N	Y	Y	Y	Y	N
3 **Turner**	Y	N	Y	Y	Y	Y	N
4 **Jordan**	Y	N	Y	Y	Y	Y	N
5 **Latta**	Y	N	Y	Y	Y	Y	N
6 Wilson	N	Y	Y	Y	Y	Y	Y
7 **Austria**	Y	N	Y	Y	Y	Y	N
8 **Boehner**	Y	N	?	Y	Y	Y	N
9 Kaptur	N	Y	Y	Y	Y	Y	Y
10 Kucinich	N	Y	Y	Y	Y	Y	Y
11 Fudge	N	Y	Y	Y	Y	Y	Y
12 **Tiberi**	Y	N	Y	Y	Y	Y	N
13 Sutton	N	Y	Y	Y	Y	Y	Y
14 **LaTourette**	Y	N	Y	Y	Y	Y	N
15 Kilroy	N	Y	Y	Y	Y	Y	Y
16 Boccieri	N	Y	Y	Y	Y	Y	Y
17 Ryan	N	Y	Y	Y	Y	Y	Y
18 Space	N	Y	Y	Y	Y	Y	Y
OKLAHOMA							
1 **Sullivan**	Y	N	Y	Y	Y	Y	N
2 Boren	Y	Y	Y	Y	Y	Y	Y
3 **Lucas**	Y	N	Y	Y	Y	Y	N
4 **Cole**	Y	N	Y	Y	Y	Y	N
5 **Fallin**	+	–	+	Y	Y	Y	N
OREGON							
1 Wu	N	Y	Y	Y	Y	Y	Y
2 **Walden**	Y	N	Y	Y	Y	Y	N
3 Blumenauer	N	Y	Y	Y	Y	Y	Y
4 DeFazio	N	Y	Y	Y	Y	Y	Y
5 Schrader	N	Y	Y	Y	Y	Y	Y
PENNSYLVANIA							
1 Brady	N	Y	Y	Y	Y	Y	Y
2 Fattah	N	Y	Y	Y	Y	Y	Y
3 Dahlkemper	N	Y	Y	Y	Y	Y	N
4 Altmire	Y	Y	Y	Y	Y	Y	Y
5 **Thompson**	Y	N	Y	Y	Y	Y	N
6 **Gerlach**	Y	N	Y	Y	Y	Y	N
7 Sestak	N	Y	Y	Y	Y	Y	Y
8 Murphy, P.	N	Y	Y	Y	Y	Y	Y
9 **Shuster**	Y	N	Y	Y	Y	Y	N
10 Carney	N	Y	Y	Y	Y	Y	Y
11 Kanjorski	N	Y	Y	Y	Y	Y	Y
12 Critz	Y	Y	Y	Y	Y	Y	Y
13 Schwartz	N	Y	Y	Y	Y	Y	Y
14 Doyle	N	Y	Y	Y	Y	Y	Y
15 **Dent**	Y	Y	Y	Y	Y	Y	N
16 **Pitts**	Y	N	Y	Y	Y	Y	N
17 Holden	Y	Y	Y	Y	Y	Y	Y
18 **Murphy, T.**	Y	N	Y	Y	Y	Y	N
19 **Platts**	Y	N	Y	Y	Y	Y	N
RHODE ISLAND							
1 Kennedy	N	Y	Y	Y	Y	Y	Y
2 Langevin	N	Y	Y	Y	Y	Y	Y
SOUTH CAROLINA							
1 **Brown**	?	?	?	?	?	?	?
2 **Wilson**	Y	N	Y	Y	Y	Y	N
3 **Barrett**	?	?	?	?	?	?	?
4 **Inglis**	?	?	?	?	?	?	?
5 Spratt	N	Y	Y	Y	Y	Y	Y
6 Clyburn	N	Y	Y	Y	Y	Y	Y
SOUTH DAKOTA							
AL Herseth Sandlin	N	N	Y	Y	Y	Y	Y
TENNESSEE							
1 **Roe**	Y	N	Y	Y	Y	Y	N
2 **Duncan**	Y	N	Y	Y	Y	Y	N
3 **Wamp**	?	?	?	?	?	?	?
4 Davis	Y	Y	Y	Y	Y	Y	Y
5 Cooper	N	N	Y	Y	Y	Y	Y
6 Gordon	N	Y	Y	Y	Y	Y	Y
7 **Blackburn**	Y	N	Y	Y	Y	Y	N
8 Tanner	Y	Y	Y	Y	Y	Y	Y
9 Cohen	N	Y	Y	Y	Y	Y	Y

	362	363	364	365	366	367	368
TEXAS							
1 **Gohmert**	?	?	?	Y	Y	Y	N
2 **Poe**	Y	N	Y	Y	Y	Y	N
3 **Johnson, S.**	Y	N	Y	Y	Y	Y	N
4 **Hall**	Y	N	Y	Y	Y	Y	N
5 **Hensarling**	Y	N	Y	Y	Y	Y	N
6 **Barton**	Y	N	Y	Y	Y	Y	N
7 **Culberson**	Y	N	Y	Y	Y	Y	N
8 **Brady**	Y	N	Y	Y	Y	Y	N
9 Green, A.	N	Y	Y	Y	Y	Y	Y
10 **McCaul**	Y	N	Y	Y	Y	Y	N
11 **Conaway**	Y	N	N	Y	Y	Y	N
12 **Granger**	Y	N	Y	Y	Y	Y	N
13 **Thornberry**	Y	N	Y	Y	Y	Y	N
14 **Paul**	Y	Y	Y	Y	N	Y	N
15 Hinojosa	N	Y	Y	Y	Y	Y	Y
16 Reyes	N	Y	Y	Y	Y	Y	Y
17 Edwards	Y	N	Y	Y	Y	Y	Y
18 Jackson Lee	N	Y	Y	+	Y	Y	Y
19 **Neugebauer**	Y	N	N	Y	Y	Y	N
20 Gonzalez	N	Y	Y	Y	Y	Y	Y
21 **Smith**	Y	N	Y	Y	Y	Y	N
22 **Olson**	Y	N	Y	Y	Y	Y	N
23 Rodriguez	N	Y	Y	Y	Y	Y	Y
24 **Marchant**	Y	N	Y	Y	Y	Y	N
25 Doggett	N	Y	Y	Y	Y	Y	Y
26 **Burgess**	Y	N	Y	Y	Y	Y	N
27 Ortiz	N	Y	Y	Y	Y	Y	Y
28 Cuellar	N	Y	Y	Y	Y	Y	Y
29 Green, G.	N	Y	Y	Y	Y	Y	Y
30 Johnson, E.	N	Y	Y	Y	Y	Y	Y
31 **Carter**	Y	N	Y	Y	Y	Y	N
32 **Sessions**	Y	N	Y	Y	Y	Y	N
UTAH							
1 **Bishop**	Y	N	Y	?	?	?	N
2 Matheson	N	Y	Y	Y	Y	Y	Y
3 **Chaffetz**	Y	N	Y	Y	Y	Y	N
VERMONT							
AL Welch	N	Y	Y	Y	Y	Y	Y
VIRGINIA							
1 **Wittman**	Y	N	Y	Y	Y	Y	N
2 Nye	Y	Y	Y	Y	Y	Y	N
3 Scott	N	Y	Y	Y	Y	Y	Y
4 **Forbes**	Y	N	Y	Y	Y	Y	N
5 Perriello	N	Y	Y	Y	Y	Y	Y
6 **Goodlatte**	Y	N	Y	Y	Y	Y	N
7 **Cantor**	?	?	?	Y	Y	Y	N
8 Moran	N	Y	Y	Y	Y	Y	Y
9 Boucher	Y	Y	Y	Y	Y	Y	Y
10 **Wolf**	Y	N	Y	Y	Y	Y	N
11 Connolly	N	Y	Y	Y	Y	Y	Y
WASHINGTON							
1 Inslee	N	Y	Y	Y	Y	Y	Y
2 Larsen	N	Y	Y	Y	Y	Y	Y
3 Baird	N	Y	Y	Y	Y	Y	Y
4 **Hastings**	Y	N	Y	Y	Y	Y	N
5 **McMorris Rodgers**	Y	N	Y	Y	Y	Y	N
6 Dicks	N	Y	?	Y	Y	Y	Y
7 McDermott	N	Y	Y	Y	Y	Y	Y
8 **Reichert**	Y	N	Y	Y	Y	Y	N
9 Smith	N	Y	Y	Y	Y	Y	Y
WEST VIRGINIA							
1 Mollohan	N	Y	Y	Y	Y	Y	Y
2 **Capito**	Y	N	Y	Y	Y	Y	N
3 Rahall	N	Y	Y	Y	Y	Y	Y
WISCONSIN							
1 **Ryan**	Y	N	Y	Y	Y	Y	N
2 Baldwin	N	Y	Y	Y	Y	Y	Y
3 Kind	N	Y	Y	Y	Y	Y	Y
4 Moore	N	Y	Y	Y	Y	Y	?
5 **Sensenbrenner**	Y	N	Y	Y	Y	Y	N
6 **Petri**	Y	N	Y	Y	Y	Y	N
7 Obey	N	Y	Y	Y	Y	Y	Y
8 Kagen	N	Y	Y	Y	Y	Y	Y
WYOMING							
AL **Lummis**	Y	N	N	Y	Y	Y	N
DELEGATES							
Faleomavaega (A.S.)							
Norton (D.C.)							
Bordallo (Guam)							
Sablan (N. Marianas)							
Pierluisi (P.R.)							
Christensen (V.I.)							

IN THE HOUSE | By Vote Number

369. **HR 5297. Small-Business Lending/Rule.** Adoption of the rule (H Res 1448) that would provide for further House floor consideration of the bill that would create a lending fund through which the Treasury Department could make up to $30 billion in investments to encourage certain financial institutions to make credit available for small businesses. Adopted 237-179: D 237-10; R 0-169. June 17, 2010.

370. **H Res 1429. Flag Day/Adoption.** Watson, D-Calif, motion to suspend the rules and adopt the resolution that would celebrate the U.S. flag and support Flag Day. Motion agreed to 418-0: D 248-0; R 170-0. A two-thirds majority of those present and voting (279 in this case) is required for adoption under suspension of the rules. June 17, 2010.

371. **HR 5297. Small-Business Lending/Veteran- and Women-Owned Businesses.** Israel, D-N.Y., amendment that would add veteran- and women-owned businesses to the groups that would receive outreach under the new fund established by the bill and require that they be included in the study on lending assistance called for in the bill. Adopted in Committee of the Whole 420-0: D 255-0; R 165-0. June 17, 2010.

372. **HR 5297. Small-Business Lending/Oil Spill Impact.** Cao, R-La., amendment that would provide funding to eligible institutions that serve small businesses affected by the Deepwater Horizon oil spill. Adopted in Committee of the Whole 414-0: D 249-0; R 165-0. June 17, 2010.

373. **HR 5297. Small-Business Lending/Loans to Construction Businesses.** Miller, D-N.C., amendment that would expand the definition of "small-business lending" to include loans to small businesses acquiring or constructing industrial, commercial, residential and farm buildings. Adopted in Committee of the Whole 418-3: D 252-0; R 166-3. June 17, 2010.

374. **HR 5297. Small-Business Lending/Recommit.** Neugebauer, R-Texas, motion to recommit the bill to the House Financial Services Committee with instructions that it be immediately reported back with language that would place the inspector general for the Troubled Asset Relief Program in charge of oversight of the lending fund established by the bill. It also would add language certifying that each decision to provide loans to banks is based on merit. Motion rejected 180-237: D 9-237; R 171-0. June 17, 2010.

375. **HR 5297. Small-Business Lending/Passage.** Passage of the bill that would create a lending fund through which the Treasury Department could make up to $30 billion in investments to encourage certain financial institutions to make credit available for small businesses. It also would create a $2 billion state small-business credit initiative fund to assist state and municipal programs that provide small businesses access to capital and a $1 billion Small Business Administration program to provide financing to "early stage" small businesses. As amended, it would provide funding to eligible institutions that serve small businesses affected by the Deepwater Horizon oil spill. Passed 241-182: D 238-13; R 3-169. A "yea" was a vote in support of the president's position. June 17, 2010.

	369	370	371	372	373	374	375
ALABAMA							
1 **Bonner**	N	Y	Y	Y	Y	Y	N
2 **Bright**	N	Y	Y	Y	Y	N	N
3 **Rogers**	N	Y	Y	Y	Y	Y	N
4 **Aderholt**	N	Y	Y	Y	Y	Y	N
5 **Griffith**	N	Y	?	?	?	Y	N
6 **Bachus**	N	Y	Y	Y	Y	Y	N
7 Davis	Y	Y	Y	Y	Y	N	Y
ALASKA							
AL **Young**	N	Y	Y	Y	Y	Y	N
ARIZONA							
1 Kirkpatrick	Y	Y	Y	Y	Y	N	Y
2 **Franks**	N	Y	Y	Y	Y	Y	N
3 **Shadegg**	N	Y	Y	Y	Y	Y	N
4 Pastor	Y	Y	Y	Y	Y	N	Y
5 Mitchell	N	Y	Y	Y	Y	Y	N
6 **Flake**	N	Y	Y	Y	N	Y	N
7 Grijalva	Y	Y	Y	Y	Y	N	Y
8 Giffords	N	Y	Y	Y	Y	N	Y
ARKANSAS							
1 Berry	Y	Y	Y	Y	Y	N	N
2 Snyder	Y	Y	Y	Y	Y	N	Y
3 **Boozman**	N	Y	Y	Y	Y	Y	N
4 Ross	Y	Y	Y	Y	Y	N	Y
CALIFORNIA							
1 Thompson	Y	Y	Y	Y	Y	N	N
2 **Herger**	N	Y	Y	Y	Y	Y	N
3 **Lungren**	N	Y	Y	Y	Y	Y	N
4 **McClintock**	N	Y	Y	Y	N	Y	N
5 Matsui	Y	Y	Y	Y	Y	N	Y
6 Woolsey	Y	Y	Y	?	Y	N	Y
7 Miller, George	Y	Y	Y	Y	Y	N	Y
8 Pelosi							
9 Lee	Y	Y	Y	Y	Y	N	Y
10 Garamendi	Y	Y	Y	Y	Y	N	Y
11 McNerney	Y	Y	Y	Y	Y	N	Y
12 Speer	Y	Y	Y	Y	Y	N	Y
13 Stark	Y	Y	Y	?	Y	N	Y
14 Eshoo	Y	Y	Y	Y	Y	N	Y
15 Honda	Y	Y	Y	Y	Y	N	Y
16 Lofgren	Y	Y	Y	Y	Y	N	Y
17 Farr	Y	Y	Y	Y	Y	N	Y
18 Cardoza	Y	Y	Y	Y	Y	N	Y
19 **Radanovich**	N	Y	Y	Y	Y	Y	N
20 Costa	Y	Y	Y	Y	Y	N	Y
21 **Nunes**	N	Y	Y	Y	Y	Y	N
22 **McCarthy**	N	Y	Y	Y	Y	Y	N
23 Capps	+	Y	Y	Y	Y	N	Y
24 **Gallegly**	N	Y	Y	Y	Y	Y	N
25 **McKeon**	N	Y	Y	Y	Y	Y	N
26 **Dreier**	N	Y	Y	Y	Y	Y	N
27 Sherman	Y	Y	Y	Y	Y	N	Y
28 Berman	Y	Y	Y	Y	Y	N	Y
29 Schiff	Y	Y	Y	Y	Y	N	Y
30 Waxman	Y	Y	Y	Y	Y	N	Y
31 Becerra	Y	Y	Y	Y	Y	N	Y
32 Chu	Y	Y	Y	Y	Y	N	Y
33 Watson	Y	Y	Y	Y	Y	N	Y
34 Roybal-Allard	Y	Y	Y	Y	Y	N	Y
35 Waters	Y	Y	Y	Y	?	N	Y
36 Harman	Y	Y	Y	Y	Y	N	Y
37 Richardson	Y	Y	Y	Y	Y	–	Y
38 Napolitano	Y	Y	Y	Y	Y	N	Y
39 Sánchez, Linda	Y	Y	Y	Y	Y	N	Y
40 **Royce**	N	Y	Y	Y	Y	Y	N
41 **Lewis**	N	Y	Y	Y	Y	Y	N
42 **Miller, Gary**	N	Y	Y	P	Y	Y	N
43 Baca	Y	Y	Y	Y	Y	N	Y
44 **Calvert**	N	Y	Y	Y	Y	Y	N
45 **Bono Mack**	N	Y	Y	Y	Y	Y	N
46 **Rohrabacher**	N	Y	Y	Y	Y	Y	N
47 Sanchez, Loretta	Y	Y	Y	Y	Y	N	Y
48 **Campbell**	N	Y	Y	Y	N	Y	N
49 **Issa**	N	Y	Y	Y	Y	Y	N
50 **Bilbray**	N	Y	Y	Y	Y	Y	N
51 Filner	Y	Y	Y	Y	Y	N	Y
52 **Hunter**	N	Y	Y	Y	Y	Y	N
53 Davis	Y	Y	Y	Y	Y	N	Y

	369	370	371	372	373	374	375
COLORADO							
1 DeGette	Y	Y	Y	Y	Y	N	Y
2 Polis	Y	Y	Y	Y	Y	N	Y
3 Salazar	Y	Y	Y	Y	Y	N	Y
4 Markey	Y	Y	Y	Y	Y	N	Y
5 **Lamborn**	N	Y	Y	Y	Y	Y	N
6 **Coffman**	N	Y	Y	Y	Y	Y	N
7 Perlmutter	Y	Y	Y	Y	Y	N	Y
CONNECTICUT							
1 Larson	Y	Y	Y	Y	Y	N	Y
2 Courtney	Y	Y	Y	Y	Y	N	Y
3 DeLauro	Y	Y	Y	Y	Y	N	Y
4 Himes	Y	Y	Y	Y	Y	?	Y
5 Murphy	Y	Y	Y	Y	Y	N	Y
DELAWARE							
AL **Castle**	N	Y	Y	Y	Y	Y	Y
FLORIDA							
1 **Miller**	N	Y	Y	Y	Y	Y	N
2 Boyd	N	Y	Y	Y	Y	N	N
3 Brown	Y	Y	Y	Y	Y	N	Y
4 **Crenshaw**	N	Y	Y	Y	Y	Y	N
5 **Brown-Waite**	N	Y	Y	?	Y	Y	N
6 **Stearns**	N	Y	Y	Y	Y	Y	N
7 **Mica**	N	Y	Y	Y	Y	Y	N
8 Grayson	Y	Y	Y	Y	Y	N	Y
9 **Bilirakis**	N	Y	Y	Y	Y	Y	N
10 **Young**	?	?	Y	Y	Y	Y	N
11 Castor	Y	Y	Y	Y	?	N	Y
12 **Putnam**	N	Y	Y	Y	Y	Y	N
13 **Buchanan**	N	Y	Y	Y	Y	Y	N
14 **Mack**	N	Y	Y	Y	Y	Y	N
15 **Posey**	N	Y	Y	Y	Y	Y	N
16 **Rooney**	N	Y	Y	Y	Y	Y	N
17 Meek	?	?	?	?	?	?	?
18 **Ros-Lehtinen**	N	Y	?	+	Y	Y	N
19 Deutch	N	Y	Y	Y	Y	N	Y
20 Wasserman Schultz	Y	Y	Y	Y	Y	N	Y
21 **Diaz-Balart, L.**	N	Y	Y	Y	Y	Y	N
22 Klein	Y	Y	Y	Y	Y	N	Y
23 Hastings	Y	Y	Y	Y	Y	N	Y
24 Kosmas	Y	Y	Y	Y	Y	N	Y
25 **Diaz-Balart, M.**	N	Y	Y	Y	Y	Y	N
GEORGIA							
1 **Kingston**	N	Y	Y	Y	Y	Y	N
2 Bishop	Y	Y	Y	?	Y	N	Y
3 **Westmoreland**	N	Y	Y	Y	Y	Y	N
4 Johnson	?	Y	Y	Y	Y	N	Y
5 Lewis	Y	Y	Y	Y	Y	N	Y
6 **Price**	N	Y	Y	Y	Y	Y	N
7 **Linder**	N	Y	Y	Y	?	Y	N
8 Marshall	Y	Y	Y	?	Y	N	Y
9 **Graves**	N	Y	Y	Y	Y	Y	N
10 **Broun**	N	Y	Y	Y	N	Y	N
11 **Gingrey**	N	Y	Y	Y	Y	Y	N
12 Barrow	Y	Y	Y	Y	Y	N	Y
13 Scott	Y	Y	Y	Y	Y	N	Y
HAWAII							
1 **Djou**	N	Y	Y	Y	Y	Y	N
2 Hirono	Y	Y	Y	Y	Y	N	Y
IDAHO							
1 Minnick	Y	Y	Y	Y	Y	N	N
2 **Simpson**	N	Y	Y	Y	Y	Y	N
ILLINOIS							
1 Rush	Y	Y	Y	Y	Y	N	Y
2 Jackson	Y	Y	Y	Y	Y	N	Y
3 Lipinski	Y	Y	Y	Y	Y	N	Y
4 Gutierrez	Y	Y	Y	Y	?	N	Y
5 Quigley	Y	Y	Y	Y	Y	N	Y
6 **Roskam**	N	Y	Y	Y	Y	Y	N
7 Davis	Y	Y	Y	Y	Y	N	Y
8 Bean	Y	Y	Y	Y	Y	N	Y
9 Schakowsky	Y	Y	Y	Y	Y	N	Y
10 **Kirk**	N	Y	Y	Y	Y	Y	N
11 Halvorson	Y	Y	Y	Y	Y	N	N
12 Costello	Y	Y	Y	Y	Y	N	Y
13 **Biggert**	N	Y	Y	Y	Y	Y	N
14 Foster	Y	Y	Y	Y	Y	N	N
15 **Johnson**	N	Y	Y	Y	Y	Y	N

	369	370	371	372	373	374	375
16 **Manzullo**	N	Y	Y	Y	Y	Y	N
17 Hare	Y	Y	Y	Y	Y	N	Y
18 **Schock**	N	Y	Y	Y	Y	Y	N
19 **Shimkus**	N	Y	Y	Y	Y	Y	N
INDIANA							
1 Visclosky	Y	Y	Y	Y	Y	N	Y
2 Donnelly	Y	Y	Y	Y	Y	N	Y
3 Vacant							
4 **Buyer**	N	Y	?	Y	Y	Y	N
5 **Burton**	N	Y	Y	Y	Y	Y	N
6 **Pence**	N	Y	Y	Y	Y	Y	N
7 Carson	Y	Y	Y	Y	Y	N	Y
8 Ellsworth	Y	Y	Y	Y	Y	N	Y
9 Hill	N	Y	Y	Y	Y	N	Y
IOWA							
1 Braley	Y	Y	Y	Y	Y	N	Y
2 Loebsack	Y	Y	Y	Y	Y	N	Y
3 Boswell	Y	Y	Y	Y	Y	N	Y
4 **Latham**	N	Y	Y	?	Y	Y	N
5 **King**	?	Y	Y	Y	Y	Y	N
KANSAS							
1 **Moran**	N	Y	Y	Y	Y	Y	N
2 **Jenkins**	N	Y	Y	Y	Y	Y	N
3 Moore	Y	Y	Y	Y	Y	N	Y
4 **Tiahrt**	N	Y	Y	Y	Y	Y	N
KENTUCKY							
1 **Whitfield**	N	Y	Y	Y	Y	Y	N
2 **Guthrie**	N	Y	Y	Y	Y	Y	N
3 Yarmuth	Y	Y	Y	Y	Y	N	Y
4 **Davis**	N	Y	Y	Y	Y	Y	N
5 **Rogers**	N	Y	Y	Y	Y	Y	N
6 Chandler	Y	Y	Y	Y	Y	N	Y
LOUISIANA							
1 **Scalise**	N	Y	Y	Y	Y	Y	N
2 **Cao**	N	Y	Y	Y	Y	Y	Y
3 Melancon	Y	Y	Y	Y	Y	N	Y
4 **Fleming**	N	Y	Y	Y	Y	Y	N
5 **Alexander**	N	?	Y	Y	Y	Y	N
6 **Cassidy**	N	Y	Y	Y	Y	Y	N
7 **Boustany**	N	Y	Y	Y	Y	Y	N
MAINE							
1 Pingree	Y	Y	Y	Y	Y	N	Y
2 Michaud	Y	Y	Y	Y	Y	N	Y
MARYLAND							
1 Kratovil	N	Y	Y	Y	Y	N	Y
2 Ruppersberger	Y	Y	Y	Y	Y	N	Y
3 Sarbanes	Y	Y	Y	Y	Y	N	Y
4 Edwards	Y	Y	Y	Y	Y	N	Y
5 Hoyer	Y	Y	Y	Y	Y	N	Y
6 **Bartlett**	N	Y	Y	Y	Y	Y	N
7 Cummings	Y	Y	Y	?	Y	N	Y
8 Van Hollen	Y	Y	Y	Y	Y	N	Y
MASSACHUSETTS							
1 Olver	Y	Y	Y	Y	Y	N	Y
2 Neal	Y	Y	Y	Y	Y	N	Y
3 McGovern	Y	Y	Y	Y	Y	N	Y
4 Frank	Y	Y	Y	Y	Y	N	Y
5 Tsongas	Y	Y	Y	Y	Y	N	Y
6 Tierney	Y	Y	Y	Y	Y	N	Y
7 Markey	Y	Y	Y	Y	Y	N	Y
8 Capuano	Y	Y	Y	Y	Y	N	Y
9 Lynch	Y	Y	Y	Y	Y	N	Y
10 Delahunt	Y	Y	Y	Y	Y	N	Y
MICHIGAN							
1 Stupak	Y	Y	Y	Y	Y	N	Y
2 **Hoekstra**	?	?	?	?	?	?	?
3 **Ehlers**	N	Y	Y	Y	Y	Y	N
4 **Camp**	N	Y	Y	Y	Y	Y	N
5 Kildee	Y	Y	Y	Y	Y	N	Y
6 **Upton**	N	Y	Y	Y	Y	Y	N
7 Schauer	Y	Y	Y	Y	Y	N	Y
8 **Rogers**	N	Y	Y	Y	Y	Y	N
9 Peters	Y	Y	Y	Y	Y	N	Y
10 **Miller**	N	Y	Y	Y	Y	Y	N
11 **McCotter**	N	Y	Y	Y	Y	Y	N
12 Levin	Y	Y	Y	Y	Y	N	Y
13 Kilpatrick	Y	Y	Y	Y	Y	N	Y
14 Conyers	Y	Y	Y	Y	Y	N	Y
15 Dingell	Y	Y	Y	Y	Y	N	Y
MINNESOTA							
1 Walz	Y	Y	Y	Y	Y	N	Y
2 **Kline**	N	Y	Y	Y	Y	Y	N
3 **Paulsen**	N	Y	Y	Y	Y	Y	N
4 McCollum	Y	Y	Y	Y	Y	N	Y
5 Ellison	Y	Y	Y	Y	Y	N	Y
6 **Bachmann**	N	Y	Y	Y	Y	Y	N
7 Peterson	Y	Y	Y	Y	Y	N	Y
8 Oberstar	Y	Y	Y	Y	Y	N	Y
MISSISSIPPI							
1 Childers	?	?	?	?	?	?	?
2 Thompson	Y	Y	Y	Y	Y	N	Y
3 **Harper**	N	Y	Y	Y	Y	Y	N
4 Taylor	N	Y	Y	Y	Y	Y	N
MISSOURI							
1 Clay	Y	Y	Y	Y	Y	N	Y
2 **Akin**	N	Y	Y	Y	Y	Y	N
3 Carnahan	Y	Y	Y	Y	Y	N	Y
4 Skelton	Y	Y	Y	Y	Y	N	Y
5 Cleaver	Y	Y	Y	Y	?	N	Y
6 **Graves**	N	Y	Y	Y	Y	Y	N
7 **Blunt**	N	Y	Y	Y	Y	Y	N
8 **Emerson**	N	Y	Y	Y	Y	Y	N
9 **Luetkemeyer**	N	Y	Y	Y	Y	Y	N
MONTANA							
AL **Rehberg**	N	Y	Y	Y	Y	Y	N
NEBRASKA							
1 **Fortenberry**	N	Y	Y	?	Y	Y	N
2 **Terry**	N	Y	Y	Y	Y	Y	N
3 **Smith**	N	Y	Y	Y	Y	Y	N
NEVADA							
1 Berkley	Y	Y	Y	Y	Y	N	Y
2 **Heller**	N	Y	Y	Y	Y	Y	N
3 Titus	Y	Y	Y	Y	Y	N	N
NEW HAMPSHIRE							
1 Shea-Porter	Y	Y	Y	Y	Y	N	Y
2 Hodes	Y	Y	Y	Y	Y	N	Y
NEW JERSEY							
1 Andrews	Y	Y	Y	Y	Y	N	Y
2 **LoBiondo**	N	Y	Y	Y	Y	Y	N
3 Adler	Y	Y	Y	Y	Y	N	Y
4 **Smith**	N	Y	Y	Y	Y	Y	N
5 **Garrett**	N	Y	Y	Y	Y	Y	N
6 Pallone	Y	Y	Y	Y	Y	N	Y
7 **Lance**	N	Y	Y	Y	Y	Y	N
8 Pascrell	Y	Y	Y	?	Y	N	Y
9 Rothman	Y	Y	Y	Y	Y	N	Y
10 Payne	Y	Y	?	Y	Y	N	Y
11 **Frelinghuysen**	N	Y	Y	Y	Y	Y	N
12 Holt	Y	Y	Y	Y	Y	N	Y
13 Sires	Y	Y	Y	Y	Y	N	Y
NEW MEXICO							
1 Heinrich	Y	Y	Y	Y	Y	N	Y
2 Teague	Y	Y	Y	Y	Y	N	Y
3 Luján	Y	Y	Y	Y	Y	N	Y
NEW YORK							
1 Bishop	Y	Y	Y	Y	Y	N	Y
2 Israel	Y	Y	Y	Y	Y	N	Y
3 **King**	N	Y	Y	Y	Y	Y	N
4 McCarthy	Y	Y	Y	Y	Y	N	Y
5 Ackerman	Y	Y	Y	Y	Y	N	Y
6 Meeks	Y	Y	Y	Y	Y	N	Y
7 Crowley	Y	Y	Y	Y	Y	N	Y
8 Nadler	Y	Y	Y	Y	Y	N	Y
9 Weiner	Y	Y	Y	Y	Y	N	Y
10 Towns	Y	Y	Y	Y	Y	N	Y
11 Clarke	Y	Y	Y	Y	Y	N	Y
12 Velázquez	?	Y	Y	Y	Y	N	Y
13 McMahon	Y	Y	Y	Y	Y	Y	Y
14 Maloney	Y	Y	Y	Y	Y	N	Y
15 Rangel	Y	Y	Y	Y	Y	N	Y
16 Serrano	Y	Y	Y	Y	Y	N	Y
17 Engel	Y	Y	Y	Y	Y	N	Y
18 Lowey	Y	Y	Y	Y	Y	N	Y
19 Hall	Y	Y	Y	Y	Y	N	Y
20 Murphy	Y	Y	Y	Y	Y	N	Y
21 Tonko	Y	Y	Y	Y	Y	N	Y
22 Hinchey	Y	Y	Y	Y	Y	N	Y
23 Owens	Y	Y	Y	Y	Y	N	Y
24 Arcuri	Y	Y	Y	Y	Y	N	Y
25 Maffei	Y	Y	Y	Y	Y	N	Y
26 **Lee**	N	Y	Y	Y	Y	Y	N
27 Higgins	Y	Y	Y	Y	Y	N	Y
28 Slaughter	Y	Y	Y	Y	Y	N	Y
29 Vacant							
NORTH CAROLINA							
1 Butterfield	Y	Y	Y	Y	Y	N	Y
2 Etheridge	Y	Y	Y	Y	Y	N	Y
3 **Jones**	N	Y	Y	Y	Y	Y	Y
4 Price	Y	Y	Y	Y	Y	N	Y
5 **Foxx**	N	Y	Y	Y	Y	Y	N
6 **Coble**	N	Y	Y	Y	Y	Y	N
7 McIntyre	Y	Y	Y	Y	Y	Y	Y
8 Kissell	Y	Y	Y	Y	Y	N	Y
9 **Myrick**	N	Y	Y	Y	Y	Y	N
10 **McHenry**	N	Y	Y	Y	Y	Y	N
11 Shuler	N	Y	Y	Y	Y	N	Y
12 Watt	Y	Y	Y	Y	Y	N	Y
13 Miller	Y	Y	Y	Y	Y	N	Y
NORTH DAKOTA							
AL Pomeroy	?	Y	Y	Y	Y	N	Y
OHIO							
1 Driehaus	Y	Y	Y	Y	Y	N	Y
2 **Schmidt**	N	Y	Y	Y	Y	Y	N
3 **Turner**	N	Y	Y	Y	Y	Y	N
4 **Jordan**	N	Y	Y	Y	Y	Y	N
5 **Latta**	N	Y	Y	Y	Y	Y	N
6 Wilson	Y	Y	Y	Y	Y	N	Y
7 **Austria**	N	Y	Y	Y	Y	Y	N
8 **Boehner**	N	Y	?	?	?	Y	N
9 Kaptur	Y	Y	Y	Y	Y	N	Y
10 Kucinich	Y	Y	Y	Y	Y	N	Y
11 Fudge	Y	Y	Y	Y	Y	N	Y
12 **Tiberi**	N	Y	Y	Y	Y	Y	N
13 Sutton	Y	Y	Y	Y	Y	N	Y
14 **LaTourette**	N	Y	Y	?	Y	Y	N
15 Kilroy	Y	Y	Y	Y	Y	N	Y
16 Boccieri	Y	Y	Y	+	Y	N	Y
17 Ryan	Y	Y	Y	Y	Y	N	Y
18 Space	Y	Y	Y	Y	Y	N	Y
OKLAHOMA							
1 **Sullivan**	?	?	?	Y	Y	Y	N
2 Boren	Y	Y	Y	Y	Y	N	Y
3 **Lucas**	N	Y	Y	Y	Y	Y	N
4 **Cole**	N	Y	Y	Y	Y	Y	N
5 **Fallin**	N	Y	Y	Y	Y	?	N
OREGON							
1 Wu	Y	?	Y	?	Y	N	Y
2 **Walden**	N	Y	Y	Y	Y	Y	N
3 Blumenauer	Y	Y	Y	Y	Y	Y	Y
4 DeFazio	Y	Y	Y	Y	Y	N	Y
5 Schrader	Y	?	Y	Y	Y	N	Y
PENNSYLVANIA							
1 Brady	Y	Y	Y	Y	Y	N	Y
2 Fattah	Y	Y	Y	Y	Y	N	Y
3 Dahlkemper	N	Y	Y	Y	Y	N	N
4 Altmire	Y	Y	Y	Y	Y	N	Y
5 **Thompson**	N	Y	Y	Y	Y	Y	N
6 **Gerlach**	N	Y	Y	Y	Y	Y	N
7 Sestak	Y	Y	Y	Y	Y	N	Y
8 Murphy, P.	Y	Y	Y	Y	Y	N	Y
9 **Shuster**	N	Y	Y	Y	Y	Y	N
10 Carney	Y	Y	Y	Y	Y	N	Y
11 Kanjorski	Y	Y	Y	Y	Y	N	Y
12 Critz	Y	Y	Y	Y	Y	N	Y
13 Schwartz	Y	Y	Y	Y	Y	N	Y
14 Doyle	Y	Y	Y	Y	Y	N	Y
15 **Dent**	N	Y	Y	Y	Y	Y	N
16 **Pitts**	N	Y	Y	Y	Y	Y	N
17 Holden	Y	Y	Y	Y	Y	N	Y
18 **Murphy, T.**	N	Y	Y	Y	Y	Y	N
19 **Platts**	N	Y	Y	Y	Y	Y	N
RHODE ISLAND							
1 Kennedy	Y	Y	Y	Y	Y	N	Y
2 Langevin	Y	Y	Y	Y	Y	N	Y
SOUTH CAROLINA							
1 **Brown**	?	?	?	?	?	?	?
2 **Wilson**	N	Y	Y	Y	Y	Y	N
3 **Barrett**	?	?	?	?	?	?	?
4 **Inglis**	?	?	?	?	?	?	?
5 Spratt	Y	Y	Y	Y	Y	N	Y
6 Clyburn	Y	Y	Y	Y	Y	N	Y
SOUTH DAKOTA							
AL Herseth Sandlin	N	Y	Y	Y	Y	Y	N
TENNESSEE							
1 **Roe**	?	Y	Y	Y	Y	Y	N
2 **Duncan**	N	Y	Y	Y	Y	Y	N
3 **Wamp**	?	?	?	?	?	?	?
4 Davis	Y	Y	Y	Y	Y	N	Y
5 Cooper	Y	Y	Y	Y	Y	N	N
6 Gordon	Y	Y	Y	Y	Y	?	Y
7 **Blackburn**	N	Y	Y	Y	Y	Y	N
8 Tanner	Y	Y	Y	Y	Y	N	Y
9 Cohen	Y	Y	Y	Y	Y	N	Y
TEXAS							
1 **Gohmert**	N	Y	Y	?	Y	Y	N
2 **Poe**	N	Y	Y	Y	Y	Y	N
3 **Johnson, S.**	N	Y	Y	Y	Y	Y	N
4 **Hall**	N	Y	Y	Y	Y	Y	N
5 **Hensarling**	N	Y	Y	Y	Y	Y	N
6 **Barton**	N	Y	?	Y	Y	Y	?
7 **Culberson**	N	Y	Y	Y	Y	Y	N
8 **Brady**	N	Y	Y	Y	Y	Y	N
9 Green, A.	Y	Y	Y	Y	Y	N	Y
10 **McCaul**	N	Y	Y	Y	Y	Y	N
11 **Conaway**	N	Y	Y	Y	Y	Y	N
12 **Granger**	N	Y	Y	Y	Y	Y	N
13 **Thornberry**	N	Y	Y	Y	Y	Y	N
14 **Paul**	N	Y	Y	Y	Y	Y	N
15 Hinojosa	Y	Y	Y	Y	Y	N	Y
16 Reyes	Y	Y	Y	Y	Y	N	Y
17 Edwards	Y	Y	Y	Y	Y	Y	N
18 Jackson Lee	Y	Y	Y	Y	Y	N	Y
19 **Neugebauer**	N	Y	Y	Y	Y	Y	N
20 Gonzalez	Y	Y	Y	Y	Y	N	Y
21 **Smith**	N	Y	Y	Y	Y	?	N
22 **Olson**	N	Y	?	Y	Y	Y	N
23 Rodriguez	Y	Y	Y	Y	Y	N	Y
24 **Marchant**	N	Y	Y	Y	Y	Y	N
25 Doggett	Y	Y	Y	Y	Y	Y	N
26 **Burgess**	N	Y	?	Y	Y	Y	N
27 Ortiz	Y	Y	Y	Y	Y	N	Y
28 Cuellar	Y	Y	Y	Y	Y	N	Y
29 Green, G.	Y	Y	Y	Y	Y	N	Y
30 Johnson, E.	Y	Y	Y	Y	Y	N	Y
31 **Carter**	N	Y	Y	Y	Y	Y	N
32 **Sessions**	N	Y	Y	Y	Y	Y	N
UTAH							
1 **Bishop**	N	Y	Y	Y	Y	Y	N
2 Matheson	Y	Y	Y	Y	Y	N	Y
3 **Chaffetz**	N	Y	Y	Y	Y	Y	N
VERMONT							
AL Welch	Y	Y	Y	Y	Y	N	Y
VIRGINIA							
1 **Wittman**	N	Y	Y	Y	Y	Y	N
2 Nye	Y	Y	Y	Y	Y	Y	Y
3 Scott	Y	Y	Y	Y	Y	N	Y
4 **Forbes**	N	Y	Y	Y	Y	Y	N
5 Perriello	Y	Y	Y	Y	Y	N	Y
6 **Goodlatte**	N	Y	Y	Y	Y	Y	N
7 **Cantor**	N	Y	Y	Y	Y	Y	N
8 Moran	Y	Y	Y	Y	Y	?	Y
9 Boucher	Y	?	Y	Y	Y	?	Y
10 **Wolf**	N	Y	Y	Y	Y	Y	N
11 Connolly	Y	Y	Y	Y	Y	N	Y
WASHINGTON							
1 Inslee	Y	Y	Y	Y	Y	N	Y
2 Larsen	Y	Y	Y	Y	Y	N	Y
3 Baird	Y	Y	Y	Y	Y	N	Y
4 **Hastings**	N	Y	Y	Y	Y	Y	N
5 **McMorris Rodgers**	N	Y	Y	Y	Y	Y	N
6 Dicks	Y	Y	Y	Y	Y	N	Y
7 McDermott	Y	Y	Y	Y	Y	N	Y
8 **Reichert**	N	Y	Y	Y	Y	Y	N
9 Smith	Y	Y	Y	Y	Y	N	Y
WEST VIRGINIA							
1 Mollohan	Y	Y	Y	Y	Y	N	Y
2 **Capito**	N	Y	Y	Y	Y	Y	N
3 Rahall	Y	Y	Y	Y	Y	N	Y
WISCONSIN							
1 **Ryan**	N	Y	Y	Y	Y	Y	N
2 Baldwin	Y	Y	Y	Y	Y	N	Y
3 Kind	Y	Y	Y	Y	Y	N	Y
4 Moore	?	?	?	?	?	?	?
5 **Sensenbrenner**	N	Y	Y	Y	Y	Y	N
6 **Petri**	N	Y	Y	Y	Y	Y	N
7 Obey	Y	Y	?	Y	Y	N	Y
8 Kagen	Y	Y	Y	Y	Y	N	Y
WYOMING							
AL **Lummis**	N	Y	Y	Y	Y	Y	N
DELEGATES							
Faleomavaega (A.S.)			Y	Y	Y		
Norton (D.C.)			Y	Y	Y		
Bordallo (Guam)			Y	Y	Y		
Sablan (N. Marianas)			Y	Y	?		
Pierluisi (P.R.)			Y	Y	Y		
Christensen (V.I.)			Y	Y	Y		

IN THE HOUSE | By Vote Number

376. H Con Res 288. National Men's Health Week/Adoption. Davis, D-Ill., motion to suspend the rules and adopt the concurrent resolution that would support the annual National Men's Health Week. Motion agreed to 388-0: D 234-0; R 154-0. A two-thirds majority of those present and voting (259 in this case) is required for adoption under suspension of the rules. June 22, 2010.

377. H Res 546. Juneteenth Independence Day/Adoption. Davis, D-Ill., motion to suspend the rules and adopt the resolution that would recognize the historical significance of and support the celebration of Juneteenth Independence Day. Motion agreed to 390-0: D 234-0; R 156-0. A two-thirds majority of those present and voting (260 in this case) is required for adoption under suspension of the rules. June 22, 2010.

378. H Res 1407. High-Performance Building Week/Adoption. Carnahan, D-Mo., motion to suspend the rules and adopt the resolution that would support the goals and ideals of High-Performance Building Week and encourage further research and development on high-performance building standards. Motion agreed to 371-20: D 235-0; R 136-20. A two-thirds majority of those present and voting (261 in this case) is required for adoption under suspension of the rules. June 22, 2010.

379. HR 5551. Small Business Lending Fund Certification/Passage. Kosmas, D-Fla., motion to suspend the rules and pass the bill that would require the Treasury Department to certify under oath before making a purchase under the Small Business Lending Fund Program that the purchase and decision process has been designed so that purchases are based solely on economic fundamentals and not political considerations. Motion agreed to 411-0: D 247-0; R 164-0. A two-thirds majority of those present and voting (274 in this case) is required for passage under suspension of the rules. June 23, 2010.

380. H Res 1434. National Homeownership Month/Adoption. Kosmas, D-Fla., motion to suspend the rules and adopt the resolution that would support the goals and ideals of National Homeownership Month. Motion agreed to 405-6: D 246-0; R 159-6. A two-thirds majority of those present and voting (274 in this case) is required for adoption under suspension of the rules. June 23, 2010.

381. H Res 1369. Caribbean-American Heritage Month/Adoption. Davis, D-Ill., motion to suspend the rules and adopt the resolution that would support the goals and ideals of Caribbean-American Heritage Month. Motion agreed to 410-0: D 247-0; R 163-0. A two-thirds majority of those present and voting (274 in this case) is required for adoption under suspension of the rules. June 23, 2010.

382. HR 5481. Oil Spill Investigation Commission Subpoena Authority/Passage. Rahall, D-W.Va., motion to suspend the rules and pass the bill that would authorize the National Commission on the BP Deepwater Horizon Oil Spill and Offshore Drilling to issue subpoenas. The commission could not issue a subpoena if the Justice Department objects on the basis of interference with any criminal or civil investigations. Motion agreed to 420-1: D 251-0; R 169-1. A two-thirds majority of those present and voting (281 in this case) is required for passage under suspension of the rules. June 23, 2010.

	376	377	378	379	380	381	382
ALABAMA							
1 Bonner	Y	Y	Y	Y	Y	Y	Y
2 Bright	Y	Y	Y	Y	Y	Y	Y
3 Rogers	Y	Y	Y	Y	Y	Y	Y
4 Aderholt	Y	Y	Y	Y	Y	Y	Y
5 Griffith	?	?	?	?	?	?	Y
6 Bachus	Y	Y	Y	Y	Y	Y	Y
7 Davis	?	?	?	?	?	?	Y
ALASKA							
AL Young	Y	Y	N	Y	Y	Y	Y
ARIZONA							
1 Kirkpatrick	Y	Y	Y	Y	Y	Y	Y
2 Franks	Y	Y	N	Y	Y	Y	Y
3 Shadegg	Y	Y	N	Y	Y	Y	Y
4 Pastor	Y	Y	Y	Y	Y	Y	Y
5 Mitchell	Y	Y	Y	Y	Y	Y	Y
6 Flake	Y	Y	N	Y	N	Y	Y
7 Grijalva	?	?	?	Y	Y	Y	Y
8 Giffords	Y	Y	Y	Y	Y	Y	Y
ARKANSAS							
1 Berry	Y	Y	Y	Y	Y	Y	Y
2 Snyder	Y	Y	Y	Y	Y	Y	Y
3 Boozman	Y	Y	Y	Y	Y	Y	Y
4 Ross	Y	Y	Y	Y	Y	Y	Y
CALIFORNIA							
1 Thompson	Y	Y	Y	Y	Y	Y	Y
2 Herger	Y	Y	Y	Y	Y	Y	Y
3 Lungren	Y	Y	Y	Y	Y	Y	Y
4 McClintock	Y	Y	N	Y	N	Y	Y
5 Matsui	Y	Y	Y	Y	Y	Y	Y
6 Woolsey	?	?	?	Y	Y	Y	Y
7 Miller, George	Y	Y	Y	Y	Y	Y	Y
8 Pelosi							
9 Lee	+	+	+	Y	Y	Y	Y
10 Garamendi	Y	Y	Y	?	?	Y	Y
11 McNerney	?	?	?	Y	Y	Y	Y
12 Speier	Y	Y	Y	Y	Y	Y	Y
13 Stark	?	?	?	Y	Y	Y	Y
14 Eshoo	Y	Y	Y	Y	Y	Y	Y
15 Honda	?	?	?	Y	Y	Y	Y
16 Lofgren	?	?	?	Y	Y	Y	Y
17 Farr	?	?	?	Y	Y	Y	Y
18 Cardoza	Y	Y	Y	Y	Y	Y	Y
19 Radanovich	Y	Y	Y	Y	Y	Y	Y
20 Costa	Y	Y	Y	Y	Y	Y	Y
21 Nunes	Y	Y	Y	Y	Y	Y	P
22 McCarthy	Y	Y	Y	Y	?	?	Y
23 Capps	Y	Y	Y	Y	Y	Y	Y
24 Gallegly	Y	Y	Y	Y	Y	Y	Y
25 McKeon	Y	Y	Y	Y	Y	Y	Y
26 Dreier	Y	Y	Y	Y	Y	Y	Y
27 Sherman	Y	Y	Y	Y	Y	Y	Y
28 Berman	Y	Y	Y	Y	Y	Y	Y
29 Schiff	Y	Y	Y	Y	+	+	Y
30 Waxman	Y	Y	?	Y	Y	Y	Y
31 Becerra	Y	Y	Y	Y	Y	Y	Y
32 Chu	Y	Y	Y	Y	Y	Y	Y
33 Watson	Y	Y	Y	Y	Y	Y	Y
34 Roybal-Allard	Y	Y	Y	Y	Y	Y	Y
35 Waters	Y	Y	Y	Y	Y	Y	Y
36 Harman	Y	Y	Y	Y	Y	Y	Y
37 Richardson	Y	Y	Y	Y	Y	Y	Y
38 Napolitano	Y	Y	Y	Y	Y	Y	Y
39 Sánchez, Linda	Y	Y	Y	Y	Y	Y	Y
40 Royce	Y	Y	Y	Y	Y	Y	Y
41 Lewis	Y	Y	Y	Y	Y	Y	Y
42 Miller, Gary	Y	Y	Y	Y	Y	Y	P
43 Baca	Y	Y	Y	Y	Y	Y	Y
44 Calvert	Y	Y	Y	Y	Y	Y	Y
45 Bono Mack	Y	Y	Y	Y	Y	Y	Y
46 Rohrabacher	Y	Y	Y	Y	Y	Y	Y
47 Sanchez, Loretta	Y	Y	Y	Y	Y	Y	Y
48 Campbell	Y	Y	Y	Y	Y	Y	Y
49 Issa	Y	Y	Y	Y	Y	Y	Y
50 Bilbray	Y	Y	Y	Y	Y	Y	Y
51 Filner	Y	Y	Y	Y	Y	Y	Y
52 Hunter	Y	Y	Y	Y	Y	Y	Y
53 Davis	Y	Y	Y	Y	Y	Y	Y

	376	377	378	379	380	381	382
COLORADO							
1 DeGette	Y	Y	Y	Y	Y	Y	Y
2 Polis	Y	Y	Y	Y	Y	Y	Y
3 Salazar	Y	Y	Y	Y	Y	Y	Y
4 Markey	Y	Y	Y	Y	Y	Y	Y
5 Lamborn	Y	Y	N	Y	Y	Y	Y
6 Coffman	Y	Y	Y	Y	Y	Y	Y
7 Perlmutter	Y	Y	Y	Y	Y	Y	Y
CONNECTICUT							
1 Larson	Y	Y	Y	Y	Y	Y	Y
2 Courtney	Y	Y	Y	Y	Y	Y	Y
3 DeLauro	Y	Y	Y	Y	Y	Y	Y
4 Himes	?	?	?	Y	Y	Y	Y
5 Murphy	Y	Y	Y	Y	Y	Y	Y
DELAWARE							
AL Castle	Y	Y	Y	Y	Y	Y	Y
FLORIDA							
1 Miller	Y	Y	N	Y	Y	Y	Y
2 Boyd	Y	Y	Y	Y	Y	Y	Y
3 Brown	Y	Y	Y	Y	Y	Y	Y
4 Crenshaw	Y	Y	Y	Y	Y	Y	Y
5 Brown-Waite	Y	Y	Y	N	Y	Y	Y
6 Stearns	Y	Y	Y	Y	Y	Y	Y
7 Mica	Y	Y	Y	Y	Y	Y	Y
8 Grayson	Y	Y	Y	Y	Y	Y	Y
9 Bilirakis	Y	Y	Y	Y	Y	Y	Y
10 Young	?	?	?	?	?	?	Y
11 Castor	Y	Y	Y	Y	Y	Y	Y
12 Putnam	+	+	+	+	+	+	Y
13 Buchanan	Y	Y	Y	Y	Y	Y	Y
14 Mack	Y	Y	N	Y	Y	Y	Y
15 Posey	Y	Y	Y	Y	Y	Y	Y
16 Rooney	Y	Y	Y	Y	Y	Y	Y
17 Meek	Y	Y	Y	Y	Y	Y	Y
18 Ros-Lehtinen	Y	Y	Y	Y	Y	Y	Y
19 Deutch	Y	Y	Y	Y	Y	Y	Y
20 Wasserman Schultz	Y	Y	Y	Y	Y	Y	Y
21 Diaz-Balart, L.	Y	Y	Y	Y	Y	Y	Y
22 Klein	Y	Y	Y	Y	Y	Y	Y
23 Hastings	Y	Y	Y	Y	Y	Y	Y
24 Kosmas	Y	Y	Y	Y	Y	Y	Y
25 Diaz-Balart, M.	Y	Y	Y	Y	Y	Y	Y
GEORGIA							
1 Kingston	Y	Y	N	Y	Y	Y	Y
2 Bishop	Y	Y	Y	Y	Y	Y	Y
3 Westmoreland	Y	Y	N	Y	Y	Y	Y
4 Johnson	Y	Y	Y	Y	?	Y	Y
5 Lewis	Y	Y	Y	Y	Y	Y	Y
6 Price	Y	Y	N	?	Y	Y	Y
7 Linder	Y	Y	Y	Y	Y	Y	Y
8 Marshall	Y	Y	Y	Y	Y	Y	Y
9 Graves	Y	Y	N	Y	N	Y	Y
10 Broun	Y	Y	N	Y	N	Y	Y
11 Gingrey	Y	Y	N	Y	Y	Y	Y
12 Barrow	Y	Y	Y	Y	Y	Y	Y
13 Scott	Y	Y	Y	Y	Y	Y	Y
HAWAII							
1 Djou	Y	Y	Y	Y	Y	Y	Y
2 Hirono	Y	Y	Y	Y	Y	Y	Y
IDAHO							
1 Minnick	Y	Y	Y	Y	Y	Y	Y
2 Simpson	Y	Y	Y	Y	Y	Y	Y
ILLINOIS							
1 Rush	Y	Y	Y	?	Y	Y	Y
2 Jackson	Y	Y	Y	Y	Y	Y	Y
3 Lipinski	Y	Y	Y	Y	Y	Y	Y
4 Gutierrez	Y	Y	Y	Y	Y	Y	Y
5 Quigley	Y	Y	Y	Y	Y	Y	Y
6 Roskam	Y	Y	Y	?	Y	Y	Y
7 Davis	Y	Y	Y	Y	Y	Y	Y
8 Bean	Y	Y	Y	Y	Y	Y	Y
9 Schakowsky	Y	Y	Y	Y	Y	Y	Y
10 Kirk	?	?	?	?	?	?	?
11 Halvorson	Y	Y	Y	Y	Y	Y	Y
12 Costello	Y	Y	Y	Y	Y	Y	Y
13 Biggert	Y	Y	Y	Y	Y	Y	Y
14 Foster	Y	Y	Y	Y	Y	Y	Y
15 Johnson	Y	Y	Y	Y	Y	Y	Y

KEY **Republicans** Democrats

Y Voted for (yea)	X Paired against	C Voted "present" to avoid possible conflict of interest
# Paired for	– Announced against	
+ Announced for	P Voted "present"	? Did not vote or otherwise make a position known
N Voted against (nay)		

	376	377	378	379	380	381	382
16 **Manzullo**	Y	Y	Y	Y	Y	Y	Y
17 Hare	Y	Y	Y	Y	Y	Y	Y
18 **Schock**	Y	Y	Y	Y	Y	Y	Y
19 **Shimkus**	Y	Y	Y	Y	Y	Y	Y
INDIANA							
1 Visclosky	Y	Y	Y	Y	Y	Y	?
2 Donnelly	Y	Y	Y	Y	Y	Y	Y
3 Vacant							
4 **Buyer**	?	?	?	?	?	?	Y
5 **Burton**	Y	Y	Y	Y	Y	Y	Y
6 **Pence**	Y	Y	Y	Y	Y	Y	Y
7 Carson	Y	Y	Y	Y	Y	Y	Y
8 Ellsworth	Y	Y	Y	Y	Y	Y	Y
9 Hill	Y	Y	Y	?	?	Y	Y
IOWA							
1 Braley	Y	Y	Y	Y	Y	Y	Y
2 Loebsack	?	?	?	Y	Y	Y	Y
3 Boswell	Y	Y	Y	Y	Y	Y	Y
4 **Latham**	Y	Y	Y	Y	Y	Y	Y
5 **King**	Y	Y	N	Y	Y	Y	Y
KANSAS							
1 **Moran**	Y	Y	Y	Y	Y	Y	Y
2 **Jenkins**	Y	Y	Y	Y	Y	Y	Y
3 Moore	Y	Y	Y	Y	Y	Y	Y
4 **Tiahrt**	Y	Y	Y	Y	Y	?	Y
KENTUCKY							
1 **Whitfield**	Y	Y	Y	Y	Y	Y	Y
2 **Guthrie**	Y	Y	Y	Y	Y	Y	Y
3 Yarmuth	Y	Y	Y	Y	Y	Y	Y
4 **Davis**	Y	Y	Y	Y	Y	Y	Y
5 **Rogers**	Y	Y	Y	Y	Y	Y	Y
6 Chandler	Y	Y	Y	Y	Y	Y	Y
LOUISIANA							
1 **Scalise**	Y	Y	Y	Y	Y	Y	Y
2 **Cao**	Y	Y	Y	Y	Y	Y	Y
3 Melancon	Y	Y	Y	Y	Y	Y	Y
4 **Fleming**	Y	Y	Y	Y	Y	Y	Y
5 **Alexander**	?	?	?	Y	Y	Y	Y
6 **Cassidy**	Y	Y	Y	Y	Y	Y	Y
7 **Boustany**	Y	Y	Y	Y	Y	Y	Y
MAINE							
1 Pingree	Y	Y	Y	Y	Y	Y	Y
2 Michaud	Y	Y	Y	Y	Y	Y	Y
MARYLAND							
1 Kratovil	Y	Y	Y	Y	Y	Y	Y
2 Ruppersberger	Y	Y	Y	Y	Y	Y	Y
3 Sarbanes	Y	Y	Y	Y	Y	Y	Y
4 Edwards	Y	Y	Y	Y	Y	Y	Y
5 Hoyer	Y	Y	Y	Y	Y	Y	Y
6 **Bartlett**	Y	Y	Y	Y	Y	Y	Y
7 Cummings	Y	Y	Y	Y	Y	Y	Y
8 Van Hollen	Y	Y	Y	Y	Y	Y	Y
MASSACHUSETTS							
1 Olver	Y	Y	Y	Y	Y	?	Y
2 Neal	Y	Y	Y	Y	Y	Y	Y
3 McGovern	Y	Y	Y	Y	Y	Y	Y
4 Frank	Y	Y	Y	Y	Y	Y	Y
5 Tsongas	Y	Y	Y	Y	Y	Y	Y
6 Tierney	Y	Y	Y	Y	Y	Y	Y
7 Markey	Y	Y	Y	Y	Y	Y	Y
8 Capuano	Y	Y	Y	Y	Y	Y	Y
9 Lynch	Y	Y	Y	Y	Y	Y	Y
10 Delahunt	Y	?	Y	Y	Y	Y	?
MICHIGAN							
1 Stupak	Y	Y	Y	Y	Y	Y	Y
2 **Hoekstra**	?	?	?	?	?	?	Y
3 **Ehlers**	Y	Y	Y	Y	Y	Y	Y
4 **Camp**	Y	Y	Y	Y	Y	Y	Y
5 Kildee	Y	Y	Y	Y	Y	Y	Y
6 **Upton**	Y	Y	Y	Y	Y	Y	Y
7 Schauer	Y	Y	Y	Y	Y	Y	Y
8 **Rogers**	Y	Y	Y	Y	Y	Y	Y
9 Peters	Y	Y	Y	Y	Y	Y	Y
10 **Miller**	Y	Y	Y	Y	Y	Y	Y
11 **McCotter**	Y	Y	Y	Y	Y	Y	Y
12 Levin	Y	Y	Y	Y	Y	Y	Y
13 Kilpatrick	Y	Y	Y	Y	Y	Y	Y
14 Conyers	Y	?	?	Y	Y	Y	Y
15 Dingell	Y	Y	Y	Y	Y	Y	Y
MINNESOTA							
1 Walz	Y	Y	Y	Y	Y	Y	Y
2 **Kline**	Y	Y	Y	Y	Y	Y	Y
3 **Paulsen**	Y	Y	Y	Y	Y	Y	Y
4 McCollum	Y	Y	Y	Y	Y	Y	Y
5 Ellison	Y	Y	Y	Y	Y	Y	Y
6 **Bachmann**	Y	Y	Y	Y	Y	Y	Y
7 Peterson	Y	Y	Y	Y	Y	Y	Y
8 Oberstar	Y	Y	Y	Y	Y	Y	Y
MISSISSIPPI							
1 Childers	Y	Y	Y	Y	Y	Y	Y
2 Thompson	Y	Y	Y	Y	Y	Y	Y
3 **Harper**	Y	Y	Y	Y	Y	Y	Y
4 Taylor	Y	Y	Y	Y	Y	Y	Y
MISSOURI							
1 Clay	Y	Y	Y	Y	Y	Y	Y
2 **Akin**	Y	Y	Y	Y	Y	Y	Y
3 Carnahan	Y	Y	Y	Y	Y	Y	Y
4 Skelton	Y	Y	Y	Y	Y	Y	Y
5 Cleaver	Y	Y	Y	Y	Y	Y	Y
6 **Graves**	?	Y	Y	Y	Y	Y	Y
7 **Blunt**	?	?	?	Y	Y	Y	Y
8 **Emerson**	Y	Y	Y	Y	Y	Y	Y
9 **Luetkemeyer**	Y	Y	Y	Y	Y	Y	Y
MONTANA							
AL **Rehberg**	Y	Y	Y	Y	Y	Y	Y
NEBRASKA							
1 **Fortenberry**	+	+	+	Y	Y	Y	Y
2 **Terry**	Y	Y	Y	Y	Y	Y	Y
3 **Smith**	Y	Y	Y	Y	Y	Y	Y
NEVADA							
1 Berkley	Y	Y	Y	Y	Y	Y	Y
2 **Heller**	Y	Y	Y	Y	Y	Y	Y
3 Titus	Y	Y	Y	Y	Y	Y	Y
NEW HAMPSHIRE							
1 Shea-Porter	Y	Y	Y	Y	Y	Y	Y
2 Hodes	?	?	?	?	?	?	Y
NEW JERSEY							
1 Andrews	Y	Y	Y	Y	Y	Y	Y
2 **LoBiondo**	Y	Y	Y	Y	Y	Y	Y
3 Adler	Y	Y	Y	Y	Y	Y	Y
4 **Smith**	Y	Y	Y	Y	Y	Y	?
5 **Garrett**	Y	Y	Y	Y	Y	Y	Y
6 Pallone	Y	Y	Y	Y	Y	Y	Y
7 **Lance**	Y	Y	Y	Y	Y	Y	Y
8 Pascrell	Y	Y	Y	Y	Y	Y	Y
9 Rothman	Y	Y	Y	Y	Y	Y	Y
10 Payne	Y	Y	Y	Y	Y	Y	Y
11 **Frelinghuysen**	Y	Y	Y	Y	Y	Y	Y
12 Holt	Y	Y	Y	Y	Y	Y	Y
13 Sires	Y	Y	Y	Y	Y	Y	Y
NEW MEXICO							
1 Heinrich	Y	Y	Y	Y	Y	Y	Y
2 Teague	Y	Y	Y	Y	Y	Y	Y
3 Luján	Y	Y	Y	Y	Y	Y	Y
NEW YORK							
1 Bishop	Y	Y	Y	Y	Y	Y	Y
2 Israel	Y	Y	Y	Y	Y	Y	Y
3 **King**	Y	Y	Y	Y	Y	Y	Y
4 McCarthy	+	+	+	Y	Y	Y	Y
5 Ackerman	Y	Y	Y	Y	Y	Y	Y
6 Meeks	Y	Y	Y	?	Y	Y	Y
7 Crowley	Y	Y	Y	Y	Y	Y	Y
8 Nadler	Y	Y	Y	Y	Y	Y	Y
9 Weiner	Y	Y	Y	Y	Y	Y	Y
10 Towns	Y	Y	Y	Y	Y	Y	Y
11 Clarke	Y	Y	Y	Y	Y	Y	Y
12 Velázquez	Y	Y	Y	Y	Y	Y	Y
13 McMahon	Y	Y	Y	Y	Y	Y	Y
14 Maloney	Y	Y	Y	Y	Y	Y	Y
15 Rangel	?	Y	Y	Y	Y	Y	Y
16 Serrano	Y	Y	Y	Y	Y	Y	Y
17 Engel	Y	Y	Y	Y	Y	Y	Y
18 Lowey	Y	Y	Y	Y	Y	Y	Y
19 Hall	Y	Y	Y	Y	Y	Y	Y
20 Murphy	Y	Y	Y	Y	Y	Y	Y
21 Tonko	Y	Y	Y	Y	Y	Y	Y
22 Hinchey	?	?	Y	Y	Y	Y	Y
23 Owens	Y	Y	Y	Y	Y	Y	Y
24 Arcuri	Y	Y	Y	Y	Y	Y	Y
25 Maffei	Y	Y	Y	Y	Y	Y	Y
26 **Lee**	Y	Y	Y	Y	Y	Y	Y
27 Higgins	Y	Y	Y	Y	Y	Y	Y
28 Slaughter	Y	Y	Y	Y	Y	Y	Y
29 Vacant							
NORTH CAROLINA							
1 Butterfield	?	?	?	Y	Y	Y	Y
2 Etheridge	Y	Y	Y	Y	Y	Y	Y
3 **Jones**	Y	Y	Y	Y	Y	Y	Y
4 Price	Y	Y	Y	Y	Y	Y	Y
5 **Foxx**	Y	Y	N	Y	Y	Y	Y
6 **Coble**	Y	Y	Y	Y	Y	Y	Y
7 McIntyre	Y	Y	Y	Y	Y	Y	Y
8 Kissell	Y	Y	Y	Y	Y	Y	Y
9 **Myrick**	Y	Y	Y	Y	Y	Y	Y
10 **McHenry**	Y	Y	Y	Y	Y	Y	Y
11 Shuler	Y	Y	Y	Y	Y	Y	Y
12 Watt	Y	Y	Y	Y	Y	Y	Y
13 Miller	Y	Y	Y	Y	Y	Y	Y
NORTH DAKOTA							
AL Pomeroy	Y	Y	Y	Y	Y	Y	Y
OHIO							
1 Driehaus	Y	Y	Y	Y	Y	Y	Y
2 **Schmidt**	Y	Y	Y	Y	Y	Y	Y
3 **Turner**	Y	Y	Y	Y	Y	Y	Y
4 **Jordan**	+	+	+	Y	Y	Y	Y
5 **Latta**	Y	Y	Y	Y	Y	Y	Y
6 Wilson	Y	Y	Y	Y	Y	Y	Y
7 **Austria**	Y	Y	Y	Y	Y	Y	Y
8 **Boehner**	Y	Y	Y	Y	Y	Y	Y
9 Kaptur	Y	Y	Y	Y	Y	Y	Y
10 Kucinich	Y	Y	Y	Y	Y	Y	Y
11 Fudge	Y	Y	Y	Y	Y	Y	Y
12 **Tiberi**	Y	Y	Y	Y	Y	Y	Y
13 Sutton	Y	Y	Y	Y	Y	Y	Y
14 **LaTourette**	Y	Y	Y	Y	Y	Y	Y
15 Kilroy	Y	Y	Y	Y	Y	Y	Y
16 Boccieri	Y	Y	Y	Y	Y	Y	Y
17 Ryan	Y	Y	Y	Y	Y	Y	Y
18 Space	Y	Y	Y	Y	Y	Y	Y
OKLAHOMA							
1 **Sullivan**	Y	Y	Y	Y	Y	Y	Y
2 Boren	Y	Y	Y	Y	Y	Y	Y
3 **Lucas**	Y	Y	Y	Y	Y	Y	Y
4 **Cole**	Y	Y	Y	Y	Y	Y	Y
5 **Fallin**	?	?	?	?	?	?	Y
OREGON							
1 Wu	Y	Y	Y	Y	Y	Y	Y
2 **Walden**	Y	Y	Y	Y	Y	Y	Y
3 Blumenauer	Y	Y	Y	Y	Y	Y	Y
4 DeFazio	Y	Y	Y	Y	Y	Y	Y
5 Schrader	?	?	?	Y	Y	Y	Y
PENNSYLVANIA							
1 Brady	Y	Y	Y	Y	Y	Y	Y
2 Fattah	Y	Y	Y	Y	Y	Y	Y
3 Dahlkemper	Y	Y	Y	Y	Y	Y	Y
4 Altmire	Y	Y	Y	Y	Y	Y	Y
5 **Thompson**	Y	Y	Y	Y	Y	Y	Y
6 **Gerlach**	Y	Y	Y	Y	Y	Y	Y
7 Sestak	Y	Y	Y	Y	Y	Y	?
8 Murphy, P.	?	Y	Y	Y	Y	Y	Y
9 **Shuster**	Y	Y	Y	Y	Y	Y	Y
10 Carney	Y	Y	Y	Y	Y	Y	Y
11 Kanjorski	Y	Y	Y	Y	Y	Y	Y
12 Critz	Y	Y	Y	Y	Y	Y	Y
13 Schwartz	Y	Y	Y	Y	Y	Y	Y
14 Doyle	Y	Y	Y	Y	Y	Y	Y
15 **Dent**	Y	Y	Y	Y	Y	Y	Y
16 **Pitts**	Y	Y	Y	Y	Y	Y	Y
17 Holden	Y	Y	Y	Y	Y	Y	Y
18 **Murphy, T.**	Y	Y	Y	Y	Y	Y	Y
19 **Platts**	?	?	?	?	?	?	?
RHODE ISLAND							
1 Kennedy	Y	Y	Y	Y	Y	Y	Y
2 Langevin	Y	Y	Y	Y	Y	Y	Y
SOUTH CAROLINA							
1 **Brown**	?	?	?	?	?	?	?
2 **Wilson**	+	+	+	Y	Y	Y	Y
3 **Barrett**	?	?	?	?	?	?	?
4 **Inglis**	?	?	?	?	?	?	Y
5 Spratt	Y	Y	Y	Y	Y	Y	Y
6 Clyburn	Y	Y	Y	Y	Y	Y	Y
SOUTH DAKOTA							
AL Herseth Sandlin	Y	Y	Y	Y	Y	Y	Y
TENNESSEE							
1 **Roe**	Y	Y	Y	Y	Y	Y	Y
2 **Duncan**	Y	Y	Y	Y	Y	Y	Y
3 **Wamp**	?	?	?	?	?	?	?
4 Davis	Y	Y	Y	Y	Y	Y	Y
5 Cooper	Y	Y	Y	Y	Y	Y	Y
6 Gordon	Y	?	?	Y	Y	Y	Y
7 **Blackburn**	Y	Y	Y	Y	Y	Y	Y
8 Tanner	Y	Y	Y	Y	Y	Y	Y
9 Cohen	Y	Y	Y	Y	Y	Y	Y
TEXAS							
1 **Gohmert**	Y	Y	Y	Y	Y	Y	Y
2 **Poe**	Y	Y	N	Y	Y	Y	Y
3 **Johnson, S.**	?	?	?	Y	Y	Y	Y
4 **Hall**	Y	Y	N	Y	Y	Y	Y
5 **Hensarling**	Y	Y	Y	Y	Y	Y	Y
6 **Barton**	Y	Y	Y	Y	Y	Y	Y
7 **Culberson**	?	?	?	Y	Y	Y	Y
8 **Brady**	Y	Y	Y	Y	Y	Y	Y
9 Green, A.	Y	Y	Y	Y	Y	Y	Y
10 **McCaul**	Y	Y	Y	Y	Y	Y	Y
11 **Conaway**	Y	Y	Y	Y	Y	Y	Y
12 **Granger**	Y	Y	Y	Y	Y	Y	Y
13 **Thornberry**	Y	Y	Y	Y	Y	Y	Y
14 **Paul**	Y	Y	N	Y	N	Y	N
15 Hinojosa	Y	Y	Y	Y	Y	Y	Y
16 Reyes	Y	Y	Y	Y	Y	Y	Y
17 Edwards	Y	Y	Y	Y	Y	Y	Y
18 Jackson Lee	Y	Y	Y	Y	Y	Y	Y
19 **Neugebauer**	Y	Y	Y	Y	Y	Y	Y
20 Gonzalez	Y	Y	Y	Y	Y	Y	Y
21 **Smith**	Y	Y	Y	Y	Y	Y	Y
22 **Olson**	?	?	?	Y	Y	?	Y
23 Rodriguez	Y	Y	Y	Y	Y	Y	Y
24 **Marchant**	Y	Y	Y	Y	Y	Y	Y
25 Doggett	Y	Y	Y	Y	Y	Y	Y
26 **Burgess**	Y	Y	N	Y	Y	Y	Y
27 Ortiz	Y	Y	Y	Y	Y	Y	Y
28 Cuellar	Y	Y	Y	Y	Y	Y	Y
29 Green, G.	Y	Y	Y	Y	Y	Y	Y
30 Johnson, E.	Y	Y	Y	Y	Y	Y	Y
31 **Carter**	?	?	?	Y	Y	Y	Y
32 **Sessions**	?	Y	Y	Y	Y	Y	Y
UTAH							
1 **Bishop**	Y	Y	Y	Y	Y	Y	Y
2 Matheson	?	?	?	?	?	?	Y
3 **Chaffetz**	Y	Y	Y	Y	Y	Y	Y
VERMONT							
AL Welch	Y	Y	Y	Y	Y	Y	Y
VIRGINIA							
1 **Wittman**	Y	Y	Y	Y	Y	Y	Y
2 Nye	Y	Y	Y	Y	Y	Y	Y
3 Scott	Y	Y	Y	Y	Y	Y	Y
4 **Forbes**	Y	Y	Y	Y	Y	Y	Y
5 Perriello	Y	Y	Y	Y	Y	Y	Y
6 **Goodlatte**	+	+	+	Y	Y	Y	Y
7 **Cantor**	Y	Y	Y	Y	Y	Y	Y
8 Moran	?	Y	Y	Y	Y	Y	Y
9 Boucher	Y	Y	Y	Y	Y	Y	Y
10 **Wolf**	Y	Y	Y	Y	Y	Y	Y
11 Connolly	Y	Y	Y	Y	Y	Y	Y
WASHINGTON							
1 Inslee	Y	Y	Y	Y	Y	Y	Y
2 Larsen	Y	Y	Y	Y	Y	Y	Y
3 Baird	Y	Y	Y	Y	?	?	Y
4 **Hastings**	Y	Y	Y	Y	Y	Y	Y
5 **McMorris Rodgers**	Y	Y	Y	Y	Y	Y	Y
6 Dicks	Y	Y	Y	Y	Y	?	Y
7 McDermott	Y	Y	Y	Y	Y	Y	Y
8 **Reichert**	Y	Y	Y	Y	Y	Y	Y
9 Smith	Y	Y	Y	Y	Y	Y	Y
WEST VIRGINIA							
1 Mollohan	Y	Y	Y	Y	Y	Y	Y
2 **Capito**	Y	Y	Y	Y	Y	Y	Y
3 Rahall	Y	Y	Y	Y	Y	Y	Y
WISCONSIN							
1 **Ryan**	Y	Y	Y	Y	Y	Y	Y
2 Baldwin	Y	Y	Y	Y	Y	Y	Y
3 Kind	Y	Y	Y	Y	Y	Y	Y
4 Moore	Y	Y	Y	Y	Y	Y	Y
5 **Sensenbrenner**	Y	Y	Y	Y	Y	Y	Y
6 **Petri**	Y	Y	Y	Y	Y	Y	Y
7 Obey	Y	Y	Y	Y	Y	Y	Y
8 Kagen	Y	Y	Y	Y	Y	Y	Y
WYOMING							
AL **Lummis**	Y	Y	Y	Y	Y	Y	Y
DELEGATES							
Faleomavaega (A.S.)							
Norton (D.C.)							
Bordallo (Guam)							
Sablan (N. Marianas)							
Pierluisi (P.R.)							
Christensen (V.I.)							

IN THE HOUSE | By Vote Number

383. **HR 3993. Calling-Card Disclosure/Passage.** Matsui, D-Calif., motion to suspend the rules and pass the bill that would require prepaid calling-card providers and distributors to disclose additional information to consumers, including fees, refund policies, and the number of domestic and international preferred minutes available. The Federal Trade Commission would be authorized to enforce the new rules. Motion agreed to 381-41: D 248-0; R 133-41. A two-thirds majority of those present and voting (282 in this case) is required for passage under suspension of the rules. June 23, 2010.

384. **H Res 1388. National Hurricane Preparedness Week/Adoption.** Carnahan, D-Mo., motion to suspend the rules and adopt the resolution that would support the goals and ideals of National Hurricane Preparedness Week and encourage federal agencies to continue educating the public about hurricane preparedness. Motion agreed to 419-0: D 247-0; R 172-0. A two-thirds majority of those present and voting (280 in this case) is required for adoption under suspension of the rules. June 23, 2010.

385. **HR 5175. Campaign Finance Disclosure/Previous Question.** McGovern, D-Mass., motion to order the previous question (thus ending debate and possibility of amendment) on adoption of the rule (H Res 1468) to provide for House floor consideration of the bill that would establish new reporting requirements for corporations, unions and other interest groups for campaign-related activities. Motion agreed to 243-181: D 243-8; R 0-173. June 24, 2010.

386. **HR 5175. Campaign Finance Disclosure/Rule.** Adoption of the rule (H Res 1468) to provide for House floor consideration of the bill that would establish new reporting requirements for corporations, unions and other interest groups for campaign-related activities. It also would waive through the legislative day of June 25 the two-thirds majority requirement to consider a rule on the same day it is reported by the Rules Committee for a bill to revive and extend certain tax credits and benefits, and it would allow for consideration of measures under suspension of the rules at any time through the legislative day of June 25. Adopted 220-205: D 220-34; R 0-171. June 24, 2010.

387. **H Con Res 285. 'Year of the Father'/Adoption.** Payne, D-N.J., motion to suspend the rules and adopt the concurrent resolution that would support the goals and ideals of designating 2010 as the "Year of the Father." It would recognize the important role fathers play in their families' lives. Motion agreed to 423-0: D 250-0; R 173-0. A two-thirds majority of those present and voting (282 in this case) is required for adoption under suspension of the rules. June 24, 2010.

388. **HR 5175. Campaign Finance Disclosure/Removal of Limitations.** King, R-Iowa, amendment that would exempt contributions made beginning in 2009 from limits in current law on federal campaign contributions. Rejected in Committee of the Whole 57-369: D 0-255; R 57-114. June 24, 2010.

389. **HR 5175. Campaign Finance Disclosure/Location of Advertisement Sponsors.** Murphy, D-Pa., amendment that would require sponsors of political advertisements to disclose their locations. Adopted in Committee of the Whole 274-152: D 243-12; R 31-140. June 24, 2010.

	383	384	385	386	387	388	389
ALABAMA							
1 **Bonner**	Y	Y	N	Y	N	N	Y
2 **Bright**	Y	Y	N	N	Y	N	N
3 **Rogers**	Y	Y	N	N	Y	N	N
4 **Aderholt**	Y	Y	N	Y	N	N	N
5 **Griffith**	Y	Y	N	N	Y	N	N
6 **Bachus**	Y	Y	N	N	Y	N	Y
7 Davis	Y	Y	Y	Y	Y	N	Y
ALASKA							
AL **Young**	N	Y	N	N	Y	Y	Y
ARIZONA							
1 Kirkpatrick	Y	Y	Y	Y	Y	N	Y
2 **Franks**	N	?	N	N	Y	Y	N
3 **Shadegg**	N	Y	N	N	Y	Y	N
4 Pastor	Y	Y	Y	Y	Y	N	Y
5 Mitchell	Y	Y	N	N	Y	N	Y
6 **Flake**	N	Y	N	N	Y	Y	N
7 Grijalva	Y	Y	Y	Y	Y	N	Y
8 Giffords	Y	Y	N	N	Y	N	Y
ARKANSAS							
1 Berry	Y	Y	Y	Y	Y	N	Y
2 Snyder	Y	Y	Y	Y	Y	N	N
3 **Boozman**	Y	Y	N	N	Y	N	N
4 Ross	Y	Y	Y	Y	Y	N	Y
CALIFORNIA							
1 Thompson	Y	Y	Y	Y	Y	N	Y
2 **Herger**	N	Y	N	N	Y	Y	N
3 **Lungren**	Y	Y	N	N	Y	Y	N
4 **McClintock**	N	Y	N	N	Y	Y	N
5 Matsui	Y	Y	Y	Y	Y	N	Y
6 Woolsey	Y	?	Y	Y	Y	N	Y
7 Miller, George	Y	Y	Y	Y	Y	N	Y
8 Pelosi				Y			
9 Lee	Y	Y	Y	Y	Y	N	Y
10 Garamendi	Y	Y	Y	Y	Y	N	Y
11 McNerney	Y	Y	Y	Y	Y	N	Y
12 Speier	Y	Y	Y	Y	Y	N	Y
13 Stark	Y	Y	Y	Y	Y	N	Y
14 Eshoo	Y	Y	Y	Y	Y	N	Y
15 Honda	Y	Y	Y	Y	Y	N	Y
16 Lofgren	Y	Y	Y	Y	?	N	Y
17 Farr	Y	Y	Y	Y	Y	N	Y
18 Cardoza	Y	Y	Y	Y	Y	N	Y
19 **Radanovich**	Y	Y	N	N	Y	N	N
20 Costa	Y	Y	Y	Y	Y	N	Y
21 **Nunes**	N	Y	N	N	Y	Y	N
22 **McCarthy**	Y	Y	N	N	Y	N	N
23 Capps	Y	Y	Y	Y	Y	N	Y
24 **Gallegly**	Y	Y	N	N	Y	N	N
25 **McKeon**	Y	Y	N	N	Y	N	N
26 **Dreier**	Y	Y	N	N	Y	N	N
27 Sherman	Y	Y	Y	Y	Y	N	Y
28 Berman	Y	Y	Y	Y	Y	N	Y
29 Schiff	Y	Y	Y	Y	Y	N	Y
30 Waxman	Y	Y	Y	Y	Y	N	Y
31 Becerra	Y	Y	Y	Y	Y	N	Y
32 Chu	Y	Y	Y	Y	Y	N	Y
33 Watson	Y	Y	Y	Y	Y	N	Y
34 Roybal-Allard	Y	Y	Y	Y	Y	N	Y
35 Waters	Y	Y	Y	Y	Y	N	Y
36 Harman	Y	Y	Y	Y	Y	N	Y
37 Richardson	Y	Y	Y	Y	Y	N	Y
38 Napolitano	Y	Y	Y	Y	?	N	Y
39 Sánchez, Linda	Y	Y	Y	Y	Y	N	Y
40 **Royce**	N	Y	N	N	Y	Y	N
41 **Lewis**	Y	Y	N	N	Y	N	N
42 **Miller, Gary**	Y	Y	N	N	Y	N	N
43 Baca	Y	Y	Y	Y	Y	N	Y
44 **Calvert**	Y	Y	N	N	Y	N	N
45 **Bono Mack**	Y	Y	N	N	Y	N	N
46 **Rohrabacher**	N	Y	N	N	Y	N	N
47 Sanchez, Loretta	Y	Y	Y	Y	Y	N	Y
48 **Campbell**	N	Y	N	N	Y	N	N
49 **Issa**	N	Y	N	N	Y	Y	Y
50 **Bilbray**	Y	Y	N	N	Y	N	N
51 Filner	Y	Y	Y	Y	Y	N	Y
52 **Hunter**	Y	Y	N	N	Y	N	N
53 Davis	Y	Y	Y	Y	Y	N	Y
COLORADO							
1 DeGette	Y	Y	Y	Y	Y	N	Y
2 Polis	Y	Y	Y	Y	Y	N	Y
3 Salazar	Y	Y	Y	Y	Y	N	Y
4 Markey	Y	Y	Y	Y	Y	N	Y
5 **Lamborn**	N	Y	N	N	Y	Y	N
6 **Coffman**	Y	Y	N	N	Y	N	N
7 Perlmutter	Y	Y	Y	Y	Y	N	Y
CONNECTICUT							
1 Larson	Y	Y	Y	Y	Y	N	Y
2 Courtney	Y	Y	Y	Y	Y	N	Y
3 DeLauro	Y	Y	Y	Y	Y	N	Y
4 Himes	Y	Y	Y	Y	Y	N	Y
5 Murphy	Y	Y	Y	Y	Y	N	Y
DELAWARE							
AL **Castle**	Y	Y	N	N	Y	N	N
FLORIDA							
1 **Miller**	N	Y	N	N	Y	N	N
2 Boyd	Y	?	Y	N	Y	N	N
3 Brown	Y	Y	Y	Y	Y	N	Y
4 **Crenshaw**	Y	Y	N	?	Y	N	N
5 **Brown-Waite**	Y	Y	N	?	Y	N	N
6 **Stearns**	Y	Y	N	N	Y	N	N
7 **Mica**	Y	Y	N	N	Y	N	N
8 Grayson	Y	Y	Y	Y	Y	N	Y
9 **Bilirakis**	Y	Y	N	N	Y	N	N
10 **Young**	Y	Y	N	N	Y	N	N
11 Castor	?	Y	Y	Y	Y	N	Y
12 **Putnam**	Y	Y	N	N	Y	N	N
13 **Buchanan**	Y	Y	N	N	Y	N	N
14 **Mack**	N	Y	N	N	Y	Y	N
15 **Posey**	Y	Y	N	N	Y	N	N
16 **Rooney**	N	Y	N	N	Y	N	N
17 Meek	Y	Y	Y	Y	Y	N	Y
18 **Ros-Lehtinen**	Y	Y	N	N	Y	N	N
19 Deutch	Y	Y	Y	Y	Y	N	Y
20 Wasserman Schultz	Y	Y	Y	Y	Y	N	Y
21 **Diaz-Balart, L.**	Y	Y	N	N	Y	N	N
22 Klein	Y	Y	Y	Y	Y	N	Y
23 Hastings	Y	Y	Y	Y	Y	N	Y
24 Kosmas	Y	Y	Y	Y	Y	N	Y
25 **Diaz-Balart, M.**	Y	Y	N	N	Y	N	N
GEORGIA							
1 **Kingston**	N	Y	N	N	Y	Y	Y
2 Bishop	Y	Y	Y	N	Y	N	Y
3 **Westmoreland**	N	Y	N	N	Y	Y	N
4 Johnson	Y	Y	Y	Y	Y	N	Y
5 Lewis	Y	Y	Y	Y	Y	N	Y
6 **Price**	N	Y	N	N	Y	Y	N
7 **Linder**	Y	Y	N	N	Y	N	N
8 Marshall	Y	Y	Y	Y	Y	N	N
9 **Graves**	N	Y	N	N	Y	Y	N
10 **Broun**	N	Y	N	N	Y	Y	N
11 **Gingrey**	Y	Y	N	N	Y	Y	N
12 Barrow	Y	Y	Y	N	Y	N	N
13 Scott	Y	Y	Y	Y	Y	N	Y
HAWAII							
1 **Djou**	Y	Y	N	N	Y	N	N
2 Hirono	Y	Y	Y	Y	Y	N	Y
IDAHO							
1 **Minnick**	Y	Y	Y	N	Y	N	N
2 **Simpson**	Y	Y	N	N	Y	N	N
ILLINOIS							
1 Rush	Y	Y	Y	N	Y	N	Y
2 Jackson	Y	Y	Y	N	Y	N	Y
3 Lipinski	Y	Y	Y	Y	Y	N	Y
4 Gutierrez	Y	Y	Y	N	Y	N	Y
5 Quigley	Y	Y	Y	Y	Y	N	Y
6 **Roskam**	Y	Y	N	N	Y	N	N
7 Davis	Y	Y	Y	Y	Y	N	Y
8 Bean	Y	Y	Y	Y	Y	N	Y
9 Schakowsky	Y	Y	Y	Y	Y	N	Y
10 **Kirk**	Y	Y	N	N	Y	N	N
11 Halvorson	Y	Y	Y	Y	Y	N	Y
12 Costello	Y	Y	Y	Y	Y	N	Y
13 **Biggert**	Y	Y	N	N	Y	N	N
14 Foster	Y	Y	Y	Y	Y	N	Y
15 **Johnson**	N	Y	N	N	Y	N	N

	383	384	385	386	387	388	389
16 **Manzullo**	Y	Y	N	N	Y	N	N
17 Hare	Y	Y	Y	Y	Y	N	Y
18 **Schock**	N	Y	N	N	Y	N	N
19 **Shimkus**	Y	Y	N	N	Y	Y	Y
INDIANA							
1 Visclosky	?	?	?	?	?	?	?
2 Donnelly	Y	Y	Y	N	Y	N	Y
3 Vacant							
4 **Buyer**	Y	Y	N	N	Y	N	N
5 **Burton**	Y	Y	N	N	Y	Y	N
6 **Pence**	Y	Y	N	N	Y	+	–
7 Carson	Y	Y	Y	Y	Y	N	Y
8 Ellsworth	Y	Y	Y	Y	Y	N	Y
9 Hill	Y	Y	N	N	Y	N	Y
IOWA							
1 Braley	Y	Y	Y	Y	Y	N	Y
2 Loebsack	Y	Y	Y	Y	Y	N	Y
3 Boswell	Y	Y	Y	Y	Y	N	Y
4 **Latham**	Y	Y	N	N	Y	N	N
5 **King**	Y	Y	N	N	Y	Y	N
KANSAS							
1 **Moran**	Y	Y	N	N	Y	N	N
2 **Jenkins**	Y	Y	N	N	Y	N	N
3 Moore	Y	Y	Y	Y	Y	N	Y
4 **Tiahrt**	Y	Y	N	N	Y	Y	N
KENTUCKY							
1 **Whitfield**	Y	Y	N	N	Y	N	Y
2 **Guthrie**	Y	Y	N	N	Y	N	N
3 Yarmuth	Y	Y	Y	Y	Y	N	Y
4 **Davis**	Y	Y	N	N	Y	N	N
5 **Rogers**	Y	Y	N	N	Y	N	N
6 Chandler	Y	Y	Y	Y	Y	N	Y
LOUISIANA							
1 **Scalise**	Y	Y	N	N	Y	N	N
2 **Cao**	Y	Y	N	N	Y	N	Y
3 Melancon	Y	Y	N	Y	Y	N	Y
4 **Fleming**	Y	Y	N	N	Y	N	N
5 **Alexander**	Y	Y	N	N	Y	N	N
6 **Cassidy**	Y	Y	N	N	Y	N	N
7 **Boustany**	Y	Y	N	N	Y	N	N
MAINE							
1 Pingree	Y	Y	Y	Y	Y	N	Y
2 Michaud	Y	Y	Y	Y	Y	N	Y
MARYLAND							
1 Kratovil	Y	Y	Y	N	Y	N	N
2 Ruppersberger	Y	Y	Y	Y	Y	N	Y
3 Sarbanes	Y	Y	Y	Y	Y	N	Y
4 Edwards	Y	Y	Y	Y	Y	N	Y
5 Hoyer	Y	Y	Y	Y	Y	N	Y
6 **Bartlett**	Y	Y	N	N	Y	Y	N
7 Cummings	Y	Y	Y	Y	Y	N	Y
8 Van Hollen	Y	Y	Y	Y	Y	N	Y
MASSACHUSETTS							
1 Olver	Y	Y	Y	Y	Y	N	Y
2 Neal	Y	Y	Y	Y	Y	N	Y
3 McGovern	Y	Y	Y	Y	Y	N	Y
4 Frank	Y	Y	Y	Y	Y	N	Y
5 Tsongas	Y	Y	Y	Y	Y	N	Y
6 Tierney	Y	Y	Y	Y	Y	N	Y
7 Markey	Y	Y	Y	Y	Y	N	Y
8 Capuano	Y	Y	Y	Y	Y	N	Y
9 Lynch	Y	Y	Y	Y	Y	N	Y
10 Delahunt	?	?	Y	Y	Y	N	Y
MICHIGAN							
1 Stupak	Y	Y	Y	N	Y	N	Y
2 **Hoekstra**	Y	Y	?	?	?	?	?
3 **Ehlers**	Y	?	N	N	Y	Y	N
4 **Camp**	Y	Y	N	N	Y	N	N
5 Kildee	Y	Y	Y	Y	Y	N	Y
6 **Upton**	Y	Y	N	N	Y	N	N
7 Schauer	Y	Y	Y	Y	Y	N	Y
8 **Rogers**	Y	Y	N	N	Y	N	N
9 Peters	Y	Y	Y	Y	Y	N	Y
10 **Miller**	Y	Y	N	N	Y	N	N
11 **McCotter**	Y	Y	N	N	Y	N	N
12 Levin	Y	Y	Y	Y	Y	N	Y
13 Kilpatrick	Y	Y	Y	Y	Y	N	Y
14 Conyers	Y	Y	Y	Y	Y	N	Y
15 Dingell	Y	Y	Y	Y	?	N	Y
MINNESOTA							
1 Walz	Y	Y	Y	Y	Y	N	Y
2 **Kline**	Y	Y	N	N	Y	N	N
3 **Paulsen**	Y	Y	N	N	Y	N	Y
4 McCollum	Y	Y	Y	Y	Y	N	Y
5 Ellison	Y	Y	?	Y	Y	N	Y
6 **Bachmann**	Y	Y	N	N	Y	N	N
7 Peterson	Y	Y	Y	Y	Y	N	Y
8 Oberstar	Y	Y	Y	Y	Y	N	Y
MISSISSIPPI							
1 Childers	Y	Y	N	N	Y	N	Y
2 Thompson	Y	Y	Y	Y	Y	N	Y
3 **Harper**	Y	Y	N	N	Y	N	N
4 Taylor	Y	Y	N	N	Y	N	Y
MISSOURI							
1 Clay	Y	Y	Y	Y	Y	N	Y
2 **Akin**	N	Y	N	N	Y	N	N
3 Carnahan	Y	Y	Y	Y	Y	N	Y
4 Skelton	Y	Y	Y	Y	Y	N	Y
5 Cleaver	Y	Y	Y	Y	Y	N	Y
6 **Graves**	Y	Y	N	N	Y	N	N
7 **Blunt**	Y	Y	?	?	?	?	?
8 **Emerson**	Y	Y	N	N	Y	N	Y
9 **Luetkemeyer**	Y	Y	N	N	Y	N	N
MONTANA							
AL **Rehberg**	Y	Y	N	N	Y	Y	N
NEBRASKA							
1 **Fortenberry**	Y	Y	N	N	Y	N	Y
2 **Terry**	Y	Y	N	N	Y	N	N
3 **Smith**	Y	Y	N	N	Y	Y	N
NEVADA							
1 Berkley	Y	Y	Y	Y	Y	N	Y
2 **Heller**	Y	Y	N	N	Y	N	N
3 Titus	Y	Y	Y	Y	Y	N	Y
NEW HAMPSHIRE							
1 Shea-Porter	Y	Y	Y	Y	Y	N	Y
2 Hodes	Y	Y	Y	N	Y	N	Y
NEW JERSEY							
1 Andrews	Y	Y	Y	Y	Y	N	Y
2 **LoBiondo**	Y	Y	N	N	Y	N	Y
3 Adler	Y	Y	Y	N	Y	N	Y
4 **Smith**	Y	Y	N	N	Y	N	Y
5 **Garrett**	N	Y	N	N	Y	Y	N
6 Pallone	Y	Y	Y	Y	Y	N	Y
7 **Lance**	Y	Y	N	N	Y	N	N
8 Pascrell	Y	Y	Y	Y	Y	N	Y
9 Rothman	Y	Y	Y	Y	Y	?	?
10 Payne	Y	Y	Y	Y	Y	N	Y
11 **Frelinghuysen**	Y	Y	N	N	Y	N	N
12 Holt	Y	Y	Y	Y	Y	N	Y
13 Sires	Y	Y	Y	Y	Y	N	Y
NEW MEXICO							
1 Heinrich	Y	Y	Y	Y	Y	N	Y
2 Teague	Y	Y	Y	Y	Y	N	Y
3 Luján	Y	Y	Y	Y	Y	N	Y
NEW YORK							
1 Bishop	Y	Y	Y	Y	Y	N	Y
2 Israel	Y	Y	Y	Y	Y	N	Y
3 **King**	Y	Y	N	N	Y	N	N
4 McCarthy	Y	Y	Y	N	Y	N	Y
5 Ackerman	Y	Y	Y	Y	Y	N	Y
6 Meeks	Y	Y	Y	Y	Y	N	Y
7 Crowley	Y	?	Y	Y	Y	N	Y
8 Nadler	Y	Y	Y	Y	Y	N	Y
9 Weiner	Y	Y	Y	Y	Y	N	Y
10 Towns	Y	Y	Y	Y	Y	N	Y
11 Clarke	Y	Y	Y	Y	Y	N	Y
12 Velázquez	Y	Y	Y	Y	Y	N	Y
13 McMahon	Y	Y	Y	Y	Y	N	Y
14 Maloney	Y	Y	Y	Y	Y	N	Y
15 Rangel	Y	Y	Y	Y	Y	N	Y
16 Serrano	Y	Y	Y	Y	Y	N	Y
17 Engel	Y	Y	Y	Y	Y	N	Y
18 Lowey	Y	Y	Y	Y	Y	N	Y
19 Hall	Y	Y	Y	Y	Y	N	Y
20 Murphy	Y	Y	Y	Y	Y	N	Y
21 Tonko	Y	Y	Y	Y	Y	N	Y
22 Hinchey	Y	Y	Y	Y	Y	N	Y
23 Owens	Y	Y	Y	Y	Y	N	N
24 Arcuri	Y	Y	Y	Y	Y	N	Y
25 Maffei	Y	Y	Y	Y	Y	N	Y
26 **Lee**	Y	Y	N	N	Y	N	N
27 Higgins	Y	Y	Y	Y	Y	N	Y
28 Slaughter	Y	Y	Y	Y	Y	N	Y
29 Vacant							
NORTH CAROLINA							
1 Butterfield	Y	Y	Y	Y	Y	N	Y
2 Etheridge	Y	Y	Y	Y	Y	N	Y
3 **Jones**	Y	Y	N	N	Y	N	Y
4 Price	Y	Y	Y	Y	Y	N	Y
5 **Foxx**	N	Y	N	N	Y	N	N
6 **Coble**	N	Y	N	N	Y	N	N
7 McIntyre	Y	Y	N	N	Y	N	Y
8 Kissell	Y	Y	Y	Y	Y	N	Y
9 **Myrick**	Y	Y	N	N	Y	N	N
10 **McHenry**	Y	Y	N	N	Y	Y	N
11 Shuler	Y	Y	Y	N	Y	N	Y
12 Watt	Y	Y	Y	N	Y	N	Y
13 Miller	Y	Y	Y	Y	Y	N	Y
NORTH DAKOTA							
AL Pomeroy	Y	Y	Y	Y	Y	N	Y
OHIO							
1 Driehaus	Y	Y	Y	Y	Y	N	Y
2 **Schmidt**	Y	Y	N	N	Y	N	N
3 **Turner**	Y	Y	N	N	Y	N	Y
4 **Jordan**	N	Y	N	N	Y	Y	N
5 **Latta**	Y	Y	N	N	Y	N	N
6 Wilson	Y	Y	Y	Y	Y	N	Y
7 **Austria**	Y	Y	N	N	Y	N	N
8 **Boehner**	Y	Y	N	N	Y	N	?
9 Kaptur	Y	Y	Y	Y	Y	N	Y
10 Kucinich	Y	Y	Y	Y	Y	N	Y
11 Fudge	Y	Y	Y	Y	Y	N	Y
12 **Tiberi**	Y	Y	N	N	Y	N	Y
13 Sutton	Y	Y	Y	Y	Y	N	Y
14 **LaTourette**	Y	Y	N	N	Y	N	Y
15 Kilroy	Y	Y	Y	Y	Y	N	Y
16 Boccieri	Y	Y	Y	Y	Y	N	Y
17 Ryan	Y	Y	Y	Y	Y	N	Y
18 Space	Y	Y	Y	Y	Y	N	Y
OKLAHOMA							
1 **Sullivan**	Y	Y	N	N	Y	N	N
2 Boren	Y	Y	Y	N	Y	N	Y
3 **Lucas**	Y	Y	N	N	Y	N	N
4 **Cole**	Y	Y	N	N	Y	N	N
5 **Fallin**	Y	Y	N	N	Y	N	N
OREGON							
1 Wu	Y	Y	Y	N	Y	N	N
2 **Walden**	Y	Y	N	N	Y	N	N
3 Blumenauer	Y	Y	Y	Y	Y	N	Y
4 DeFazio	Y	Y	Y	Y	Y	N	Y
5 Schrader	Y	Y	Y	Y	Y	N	Y
PENNSYLVANIA							
1 Brady	Y	Y	Y	Y	Y	N	Y
2 Fattah	Y	Y	Y	Y	Y	N	Y
3 Dahlkemper	Y	Y	Y	N	Y	N	Y
4 Altmire	Y	Y	Y	Y	Y	N	Y
5 **Thompson**	Y	Y	N	N	Y	Y	N
6 **Gerlach**	Y	Y	N	N	Y	N	Y
7 Sestak	?	?	Y	N	Y	N	Y
8 Murphy, P.	Y	Y	Y	Y	Y	N	Y
9 **Shuster**	Y	Y	N	N	Y	N	N
10 Carney	Y	Y	Y	Y	Y	N	Y
11 Kanjorski	Y	Y	Y	Y	Y	N	Y
12 Critz	Y	Y	Y	Y	Y	N	N
13 Schwartz	Y	Y	Y	Y	Y	N	Y
14 Doyle	Y	Y	Y	Y	Y	N	Y
15 **Dent**	Y	Y	N	N	Y	N	Y
16 **Pitts**	Y	Y	N	N	Y	N	N
17 Holden	Y	Y	Y	Y	Y	N	N
18 **Murphy, T.**	Y	Y	N	N	Y	N	Y
19 **Platts**	?	?	N	N	Y	N	Y
RHODE ISLAND							
1 Kennedy	?	?	Y	Y	Y	N	Y
2 Langevin	?	Y	Y	Y	Y	N	Y
SOUTH CAROLINA							
1 **Brown**	?	?	?	?	?	?	?
2 **Wilson**	Y	Y	N	N	Y	N	N
3 **Barrett**	?	?	?	?	?	?	?
4 **Inglis**	Y	Y	N	N	Y	N	Y
5 Spratt	Y	Y	Y	Y	Y	N	Y
6 Clyburn	Y	Y	Y	Y	Y	N	Y
SOUTH DAKOTA							
AL Herseth Sandlin	Y	Y	Y	N	Y	N	Y
TENNESSEE							
1 **Roe**	Y	Y	N	N	Y	N	N
2 **Duncan**	Y	Y	N	N	Y	N	N
3 **Wamp**	?	?	?	?	?	?	?
4 Davis	Y	Y	Y	N	Y	N	Y
5 Cooper	Y	Y	Y	N	Y	N	Y
6 Gordon	Y	Y	Y	Y	Y	N	?
7 **Blackburn**	Y	Y	N	N	Y	Y	N
8 Tanner	Y	Y	Y	Y	Y	N	Y
9 Cohen	Y	Y	Y	Y	Y	N	Y
TEXAS							
1 **Gohmert**	Y	Y	N	N	Y	?	N
2 **Poe**	N	Y	N	N	Y	Y	N
3 **Johnson, S.**	N	Y	N	N	Y	Y	N
4 **Hall**	Y	Y	N	N	Y	Y	N
5 **Hensarling**	N	Y	N	N	Y	Y	N
6 **Barton**	Y	Y	N	N	Y	N	N
7 **Culberson**	Y	Y	N	N	Y	Y	N
8 **Brady**	Y	Y	N	N	Y	Y	N
9 Green, A.	Y	Y	Y	Y	Y	N	Y
10 **McCaul**	Y	Y	N	N	Y	Y	N
11 **Conaway**	N	Y	N	N	Y	Y	N
12 **Granger**	Y	Y	N	N	Y	Y	N
13 **Thornberry**	Y	Y	N	N	Y	Y	N
14 **Paul**	N	Y	N	N	Y	Y	N
15 Hinojosa	Y	Y	Y	Y	Y	N	Y
16 Reyes	Y	Y	Y	Y	Y	N	Y
17 Edwards	Y	Y	Y	Y	Y	N	Y
18 Jackson Lee	Y	Y	Y	Y	Y	N	Y
19 **Neugebauer**	N	Y	N	N	Y	Y	N
20 Gonzalez	Y	Y	Y	Y	Y	N	Y
21 **Smith**	Y	Y	N	N	Y	N	N
22 **Olson**	Y	Y	N	N	Y	Y	N
23 Rodriguez	Y	Y	Y	Y	Y	N	Y
24 **Marchant**	N	Y	N	N	Y	N	N
25 Doggett	Y	Y	Y	Y	Y	N	Y
26 **Burgess**	N	Y	N	N	Y	N	N
27 Ortiz	Y	Y	Y	Y	Y	N	Y
28 Cuellar	Y	Y	Y	Y	Y	N	Y
29 Green, G.	Y	Y	Y	Y	Y	N	Y
30 Johnson, E.	Y	Y	Y	Y	Y	N	Y
31 **Carter**	Y	Y	N	N	Y	N	N
32 **Sessions**	Y	Y	N	N	Y	Y	N
UTAH							
1 **Bishop**	N	Y	N	N	Y	Y	N
2 Matheson	Y	Y	Y	Y	Y	N	Y
3 **Chaffetz**	N	Y	N	N	Y	Y	N
VERMONT							
AL Welch	Y	Y	Y	Y	Y	N	Y
VIRGINIA							
1 **Wittman**	Y	Y	N	N	Y	N	N
2 Nye	Y	Y	Y	N	Y	N	N
3 Scott	Y	Y	Y	Y	Y	N	Y
4 **Forbes**	Y	Y	N	N	Y	N	N
5 Perriello	Y	Y	Y	Y	Y	N	Y
6 **Goodlatte**	N	Y	N	N	Y	Y	N
7 **Cantor**	N	Y	N	N	Y	Y	N
8 Moran	Y	Y	Y	Y	Y	N	Y
9 Boucher	Y	Y	Y	Y	Y	N	N
10 **Wolf**	Y	Y	N	N	Y	N	N
11 Connolly	Y	Y	Y	Y	Y	N	Y
WASHINGTON							
1 Inslee	Y	Y	Y	Y	Y	N	Y
2 Larsen	Y	Y	Y	Y	Y	N	Y
3 Baird	Y	Y	Y	Y	Y	N	Y
4 **Hastings**	Y	Y	N	N	Y	Y	N
5 **McMorris Rodgers**	Y	Y	N	N	Y	N	N
6 Dicks	Y	Y	Y	Y	Y	N	Y
7 McDermott	Y	Y	Y	Y	Y	N	Y
8 **Reichert**	Y	Y	N	N	Y	N	N
9 Smith	Y	Y	Y	Y	Y	N	Y
WEST VIRGINIA							
1 Mollohan	Y	Y	Y	Y	Y	N	Y
2 **Capito**	Y	Y	N	N	Y	N	Y
3 Rahall	Y	Y	Y	Y	Y	N	Y
WISCONSIN							
1 **Ryan**	Y	Y	N	N	Y	N	N
2 Baldwin	Y	Y	Y	N	Y	N	Y
3 Kind	Y	Y	Y	Y	Y	N	Y
4 Moore	Y	Y	?	N	Y	?	Y
5 **Sensenbrenner**	N	Y	N	N	Y	N	N
6 **Petri**	N	Y	N	N	Y	N	N
7 Obey	Y	Y	Y	Y	Y	N	Y
8 Kagen	Y	Y	Y	Y	Y	N	Y
WYOMING							
AL **Lummis**	Y	Y	N	N	Y	Y	N
DELEGATES							
Faleomavaega (A.S.)						?	?
Norton (D.C.)						–	+
Bordallo (Guam)						N	Y
Sablan (N. Marianas)						N	Y
Pierluisi (P.R.)						N	Y
Christensen (V.I.)						N	Y

IN THE HOUSE | By Vote Number

390. **HR 5175. Campaign Finance Disclosure/Recommit.** Lungren, R-Calif., motion to recommit the bill to the House Administration Committee with instructions that it be immediately reported back with an amendment that would require that legal actions challenging the bill's constitutionality be considered as expeditiously as possible by the U.S. District Court for the District of Columbia. It also would ban campaign contributions by registered lobbyists who have as clients certain foreign governments or individuals, such as those who have repeatedly supported acts of international terrorism. It also would prohibit the use of campaign funds for political robocalls to individuals listed on the national "do not call" registry. Motion rejected 208-217: D 37-216; R 171-1. June 24, 2010.

391. **HR 5175. Campaign Finance Disclosure/Passage.** Passage of the bill that would establish new reporting requirements for corporations, unions and other interest groups for campaign-related activities. It would prohibit corporations that are foreign-controlled or have received a specified amount of government assistance from making expenditures in political campaigns. As amended, it would exempt from some identification disclosure rules certain charitable organizations as well as organizations that are at least 10 years old, have at least 500,000 dues-paying members, have members in each state and receive no more than 15 percent of their funding from corporations and unions. Passed 219-206: D 217-36; R 2-170. A "yea" was a vote in support of the president's position. June 24, 2010.

392. **H Res 1464. Tribute to Japan as Security Partner/Adoption.** Watson, D-Calif., motion to suspend the rules and adopt the resolution that would state that the House recognizes Japan as a security partner of the United States for peace, prosperity and stability in the Asia-Pacific region and expresses appreciation to the Japanese people for hosting U.S. forces. Motion agreed to 412-2: D 247-1; R 165-1. A two-thirds majority of those present and voting (276 in this case) is required for adoption under suspension of the rules. June 24, 2010.

393. **HR 3962. Medicare Physician Payments/Passage.** Levin, D-Mich., motion to suspend the rules and concur in the Senate amendments to the bill that would reverse until after Nov. 30 a scheduled 21 percent payment cut to doctors under Medicare and make the cut prevention retroactive to June 1. The cost would be offset, including by changes to pension law. The bill also would authorize data matching by the IRS and the Centers for Medicare and Medicaid Services to identify fraud. Motion agreed to, thus clearing the bill for the president, 417-1: D 247-1; R 170-0. A two-thirds majority of those present and voting (279 in this case) is required for passage under suspension of the rules. June 24, 2010.

394. **HR 2194. Iran Sanctions/Conference Report.** Berman, D-Calif., motion to suspend the rules and adopt the conference report on the bill that would impose new sanctions on companies doing business with Iran. It would expand the list of available sanctions for the president to impose on companies that engage in certain trade with Iran relating to petroleum and gasoline production and refinement. It would cut off international financial institutions from the U.S. banking system if they do business with the Islamic Revolutionary Guard Corps or facilitate Tehran's efforts to acquire weapons of mass destruction. The measure would require the administration to investigate and issue findings on possible violations but would also give the president the ability to waive many of the provisions if doing so is necessary to the national interest. Motion agreed to, thus clearing the bill for the president, 408-8: D 241-6; R 167-2. A two-thirds majority of those present and voting (278 in this case) is required for adoption under suspension of the rules. June 24, 2010.

	390	391	392	393	394
ALABAMA					
1 Bonner	Y	N	Y	Y	Y
2 Bright	Y	N	Y	Y	Y
3 Rogers	Y	N	Y	Y	Y
4 Aderholt	Y	N	Y	Y	Y
5 Griffith	Y	N	Y	Y	Y
6 Bachus	Y	N	Y	Y	Y
7 Davis	N	Y	Y	Y	Y
ALASKA					
AL Young	Y	N	?	?	?
ARIZONA					
1 Kirkpatrick	Y	Y	Y	Y	Y
2 Franks	Y	N	Y	Y	Y
3 Shadegg	Y	N	Y	Y	Y
4 Pastor	N	Y	Y	Y	Y
5 Mitchell	Y	N	Y	Y	Y
6 Flake	Y	N	Y	Y	N
7 Grijalva	N	Y	Y	Y	Y
8 Giffords	Y	Y	Y	Y	Y
ARKANSAS					
1 Berry	N	Y	Y	Y	Y
2 Snyder	N	Y	Y	Y	Y
3 Boozman	Y	N	Y	Y	Y
4 Ross	N	Y	Y	Y	Y
CALIFORNIA					
1 Thompson	N	Y	Y	Y	Y
2 Herger	Y	N	?	Y	Y
3 Lungren	Y	N	Y	Y	Y
4 McClintock	Y	N	Y	Y	Y
5 Matsui	N	Y	Y	Y	Y
6 Woolsey	N	Y	Y	Y	?
7 Miller, George	N	Y	Y	N	Y
8 Pelosi	N	Y			Y
9 Lee	N	Y	Y	Y	Y
10 Garamendi	N	Y	Y	Y	Y
11 McNerney	Y	Y	Y	Y	Y
12 Speier	N	Y	Y	Y	Y
13 Stark	N	Y	Y	Y	N
14 Eshoo	N	Y	Y	Y	Y
15 Honda	N	Y	Y	Y	Y
16 Lofgren	N	Y	Y	Y	Y
17 Farr	N	Y	Y	Y	Y
18 Cardoza	N	Y	Y	Y	Y
19 Radanovich	Y	N	Y	Y	Y
20 Costa	N	Y	Y	Y	Y
21 Nunes	Y	N	Y	Y	Y
22 McCarthy	Y	N	Y	Y	Y
23 Capps	N	Y	Y	Y	Y
24 Gallegly	Y	N	Y	Y	Y
25 McKeon	Y	N	Y	Y	Y
26 Dreier	Y	N	Y	Y	Y
27 Sherman	N	Y	Y	Y	Y
28 Berman	N	Y	Y	Y	Y
29 Schiff	N	Y	Y	Y	Y
30 Waxman	N	Y	Y	Y	Y
31 Becerra	N	Y	Y	Y	Y
32 Chu	N	Y	Y	Y	Y
33 Watson	N	Y	Y	Y	Y
34 Roybal-Allard	N	Y	Y	Y	Y
35 Waters	N	N	?	Y	P
36 Harman	N	Y	Y	Y	Y
37 Richardson	N	Y	Y	?	Y
38 Napolitano	N	Y	Y	Y	Y
39 Sánchez, Linda	N	Y	Y	Y	Y
40 Royce	Y	N	Y	Y	Y
41 Lewis	Y	N	Y	Y	Y
42 Miller, Gary	Y	N	Y	Y	Y
43 Baca	N	Y	Y	Y	Y
44 Calvert	Y	N	Y	Y	Y
45 Bono Mack	Y	N	Y	Y	Y
46 Rohrabacher	Y	N	Y	Y	Y
47 Sanchez, Loretta	N	Y	Y	Y	Y
48 Campbell	Y	N	?	?	?
49 Issa	Y	N	Y	Y	Y
50 Bilbray	Y	N	Y	Y	Y
51 Filner	N	Y	Y	Y	Y
52 Hunter	Y	N	Y	Y	Y
53 Davis	N	Y	Y	Y	Y

	390	391	392	393	394
COLORADO					
1 DeGette	N	Y	Y	Y	Y
2 Polis	N	Y	Y	Y	Y
3 Salazar	N	Y	Y	Y	Y
4 Markey	N	Y	Y	Y	Y
5 Lamborn	Y	N	Y	Y	Y
6 Coffman	Y	N	Y	Y	Y
7 Perlmutter	N	Y	Y	Y	Y
CONNECTICUT					
1 Larson	N	Y	Y	Y	Y
2 Courtney	N	Y	Y	Y	Y
3 DeLauro	N	Y	Y	Y	Y
4 Himes	N	Y	Y	Y	Y
5 Murphy	N	Y	Y	Y	Y
DELAWARE					
AL Castle	Y	Y	Y	Y	Y
FLORIDA					
1 Miller	Y	N	Y	Y	Y
2 Boyd	N	N	Y	Y	Y
3 Brown	N	Y	Y	Y	Y
4 Crenshaw	Y	N	Y	Y	Y
5 Brown-Waite	Y	N	Y	Y	Y
6 Stearns	Y	N	Y	Y	Y
7 Mica	Y	N	Y	Y	Y
8 Grayson	N	Y	?	Y	Y
9 Bilirakis	Y	N	Y	Y	Y
10 Young	Y	N	Y	Y	Y
11 Castor	N	Y	Y	Y	Y
12 Putnam	Y	N	Y	Y	Y
13 Buchanan	Y	N	Y	Y	Y
14 Mack	Y	N	Y	Y	Y
15 Posey	Y	N	Y	Y	Y
16 Rooney	Y	N	Y	Y	Y
17 Meek	N	Y	Y	Y	Y
18 Ros-Lehtinen	Y	N	Y	Y	Y
19 Deutch	N	Y	Y	Y	Y
20 Wasserman Schultz	N	Y	Y	Y	Y
21 Diaz-Balart, L.	Y	N	Y	Y	Y
22 Klein	Y	Y	Y	Y	Y
23 Hastings	N	N	Y	Y	Y
24 Kosmas	N	Y	Y	Y	Y
25 Diaz-Balart, M.	Y	N	Y	Y	Y
GEORGIA					
1 Kingston	Y	N	Y	Y	Y
2 Bishop	N	N	Y	Y	Y
3 Westmoreland	Y	N	Y	Y	Y
4 Johnson	N	Y	Y	Y	Y
5 Lewis	N	Y	Y	Y	Y
6 Price	Y	N	Y	Y	Y
7 Linder	Y	N	Y	Y	Y
8 Marshall	Y	N	Y	Y	Y
9 Graves	Y	N	Y	Y	Y
10 Broun	Y	N	Y	Y	Y
11 Gingrey	Y	N	Y	Y	Y
12 Barrow	Y	N	Y	Y	Y
13 Scott	N	Y	Y	Y	Y
HAWAII					
1 Djou	Y	N	Y	Y	Y
2 Hirono	N	Y	Y	Y	Y
IDAHO					
1 Minnick	Y	N	Y	Y	Y
2 Simpson	Y	N	Y	Y	Y
ILLINOIS					
1 Rush	N	N	Y	Y	Y
2 Jackson	N	Y	Y	Y	Y
3 Lipinski	N	Y	Y	Y	Y
4 Gutierrez	N	Y	Y	Y	Y
5 Quigley	N	Y	Y	Y	Y
6 Roskam	Y	N	?	Y	Y
7 Davis	N	Y	Y	Y	Y
8 Bean	N	Y	Y	Y	Y
9 Schakowsky	N	Y	Y	Y	Y
10 Kirk	Y	N	Y	Y	Y
11 Halvorson	N	Y	Y	Y	Y
12 Costello	N	Y	Y	Y	Y
13 Biggert	Y	N	Y	Y	Y
14 Foster	Y	Y	Y	Y	Y
15 Johnson	Y	N	Y	Y	Y

KEY — **Republicans** — Democrats

Y	Voted for (yea)	X Paired against
#	Paired for	– Announced against
+	Announced for	P Voted "present"
N	Voted against (nay)	

C Voted "present" to avoid possible conflict of interest

? Did not vote or otherwise make a position known

	390	391	392	393	394
16 Manzullo	Y	N	Y	Y	Y
17 Hare	N	Y	Y	Y	Y
18 Schock	Y	N	Y	Y	?
19 Shimkus	Y	N	Y	Y	Y
INDIANA					
1 Visclosky	?	?	?	?	?
2 Donnelly	Y	N	Y	Y	Y
3 Vacant					
4 Buyer	Y	N	Y	Y	Y
5 Burton	Y	N	Y	Y	Y
6 Pence	+	–	+	Y	Y
7 Carson	N	Y	Y	Y	Y
8 Ellsworth	Y	Y	Y	Y	Y
9 Hill	Y	N	Y	Y	Y
IOWA					
1 Braley	N	Y	Y	Y	Y
2 Loebsack	N	Y	Y	Y	Y
3 Boswell	N	Y	Y	Y	Y
4 Latham	Y	N	Y	Y	Y
5 King	Y	N	Y	Y	Y
KANSAS					
1 Moran	Y	N	Y	Y	Y
2 Jenkins	Y	N	Y	Y	Y
3 Moore	N	Y	Y	Y	Y
4 Tiahrt	Y	N	Y	Y	Y
KENTUCKY					
1 Whitfield	Y	N	Y	Y	Y
2 Guthrie	Y	N	Y	Y	Y
3 Yarmuth	N	Y	Y	Y	Y
4 Davis	Y	N	Y	Y	Y
5 Rogers	Y	N	Y	Y	Y
6 Chandler	Y	Y	Y	Y	Y
LOUISIANA					
1 Scalise	Y	N	Y	Y	Y
2 Cao	Y	Y	Y	Y	Y
3 Melancon	N	Y	Y	Y	Y
4 Fleming	Y	N	Y	Y	Y
5 Alexander	Y	N	Y	Y	Y
6 Cassidy	Y	N	Y	Y	Y
7 Boustany	Y	N	Y	Y	Y
MAINE					
1 Pingree	N	Y	Y	Y	Y
2 Michaud	N	Y	Y	Y	Y
MARYLAND					
1 Kratovil	Y	N	Y	Y	Y
2 Ruppersberger	N	Y	Y	Y	Y
3 Sarbanes	N	Y	Y	Y	Y
4 Edwards	N	N	Y	Y	Y
5 Hoyer	N	Y	Y	Y	Y
6 Bartlett	Y	N	Y	Y	Y
7 Cummings	N	Y	Y	Y	Y
8 Van Hollen	N	Y	Y	Y	Y
MASSACHUSETTS					
1 Olver	N	Y	Y	Y	Y
2 Neal	N	Y	Y	Y	Y
3 McGovern	N	Y	Y	Y	Y
4 Frank	N	Y	Y	Y	Y
5 Tsongas	N	Y	Y	Y	Y
6 Tierney	N	Y	Y	Y	Y
7 Markey	N	Y	Y	Y	Y
8 Capuano	N	Y	Y	Y	Y
9 Lynch	N	Y	Y	Y	Y
10 Delahunt	N	Y	Y	Y	Y
MICHIGAN					
1 Stupak	N	Y	Y	Y	Y
2 Hoekstra	?	?	?	?	?
3 Ehlers	Y	N	Y	Y	Y
4 Camp	Y	N	Y	Y	Y
5 Kildee	N	Y	Y	Y	Y
6 Upton	Y	N	Y	Y	Y
7 Schauer	N	Y	Y	Y	Y
8 Rogers	Y	N	Y	Y	Y
9 Peters	N	Y	Y	Y	Y
10 Miller	Y	N	Y	Y	Y
11 McCotter	Y	N	Y	Y	Y
12 Levin	N	Y	Y	Y	Y
13 Kilpatrick	N	N	Y	Y	Y
14 Conyers	N	Y	Y	Y	N
15 Dingell	N	Y	Y	Y	Y
MINNESOTA					
1 Walz	N	Y	Y	Y	Y
2 Kline	Y	N	Y	Y	Y
3 Paulsen	Y	N	Y	Y	Y
4 McCollum	N	Y	Y	Y	Y

	390	391	392	393	394
5 Ellison	N	Y	Y	Y	Y
6 Bachmann	Y	N	Y	Y	Y
7 Peterson	Y	N	Y	Y	Y
8 Oberstar	N	Y	Y	?	?
MISSISSIPPI					
1 Childers	Y	N	Y	Y	Y
2 Thompson	N	N	Y	Y	Y
3 Harper	Y	N	Y	Y	Y
4 Taylor	Y	N	Y	Y	Y
MISSOURI					
1 Clay	N	Y	Y	Y	Y
2 Akin	Y	N	Y	Y	Y
3 Carnahan	N	Y	Y	Y	Y
4 Skelton	N	Y	Y	Y	Y
5 Cleaver	N	Y	Y	Y	Y
6 Graves	Y	N	Y	Y	Y
7 Blunt	?	?	?	?	?
8 Emerson	Y	N	Y	Y	Y
9 Luetkemeyer	Y	N	Y	Y	Y
MONTANA					
AL Rehberg	Y	N	Y	Y	Y
NEBRASKA					
1 Fortenberry	Y	N	Y	Y	Y
2 Terry	Y	N	Y	Y	Y
3 Smith	Y	N	Y	Y	Y
NEVADA					
1 Berkley	N	Y	Y	Y	Y
2 Heller	Y	N	Y	Y	Y
3 Titus	Y	Y	Y	Y	Y
NEW HAMPSHIRE					
1 Shea-Porter	N	Y	Y	Y	Y
2 Hodes	Y	Y	Y	Y	Y
NEW JERSEY					
1 Andrews	N	Y	Y	Y	Y
2 LoBiondo	Y	N	Y	Y	Y
3 Adler	N	Y	Y	Y	Y
4 Smith	Y	N	Y	Y	Y
5 Garrett	Y	N	Y	Y	Y
6 Pallone	N	Y	Y	Y	Y
7 Lance	Y	N	Y	Y	Y
8 Pascrell	N	Y	Y	Y	Y
9 Rothman	+	?	?	?	+
10 Payne	N	Y	Y	Y	Y
11 Frelinghuysen	Y	N	Y	Y	Y
12 Holt	N	Y	Y	Y	Y
13 Sires	N	Y	Y	Y	Y
NEW MEXICO					
1 Heinrich	N	Y	Y	Y	Y
2 Teague	Y	Y	Y	+	+
3 Luján	N	Y	Y	Y	Y
NEW YORK					
1 Bishop	N	Y	Y	Y	Y
2 Israel	N	Y	Y	Y	Y
3 King	Y	N	Y	Y	Y
4 McCarthy	N	N	Y	Y	Y
5 Ackerman	N	Y	Y	Y	Y
6 Meeks	N	Y	Y	Y	Y
7 Crowley	N	Y	Y	Y	Y
8 Nadler	N	Y	Y	Y	Y
9 Weiner	N	Y	Y	Y	Y
10 Towns	N	Y	Y	Y	Y
11 Clarke	N	N	Y	Y	Y
12 Velázquez	N	Y	Y	Y	Y
13 McMahon	N	Y	Y	Y	Y
14 Maloney	N	Y	Y	Y	Y
15 Rangel	N	Y	?	Y	Y
16 Serrano	N	Y	Y	Y	Y
17 Engel	N	Y	Y	Y	Y
18 Lowey	N	Y	Y	Y	Y
19 Hall	N	Y	Y	Y	Y
20 Murphy	N	Y	Y	Y	Y
21 Tonko	N	Y	Y	Y	Y
22 Hinchey	N	Y	Y	Y	Y
23 Owens	N	N	Y	Y	Y
24 Arcuri	Y	Y	Y	Y	Y
25 Maffei	Y	Y	Y	Y	Y
26 Lee	Y	N	Y	Y	Y
27 Higgins	N	Y	Y	Y	Y
28 Slaughter	N	Y	Y	Y	Y
29 Vacant					
NORTH CAROLINA					
1 Butterfield	N	N	Y	Y	Y
2 Etheridge	N	Y	Y	Y	Y
3 Jones	Y	N	Y	Y	Y
4 Price	N	Y	Y	Y	Y

	390	391	392	393	394
5 Foxx	Y	N	Y	Y	Y
6 Coble	Y	N	Y	Y	Y
7 McIntyre	Y	N	Y	Y	Y
8 Kissell	N	Y	Y	Y	Y
9 Myrick	Y	N	Y	Y	Y
10 McHenry	Y	N	Y	Y	Y
11 Shuler	Y	Y	Y	Y	Y
12 Watt	N	N	Y	Y	Y
13 Miller	N	Y	Y	Y	Y
NORTH DAKOTA					
AL Pomeroy	N	Y	Y	Y	Y
OHIO					
1 Driehaus	N	Y	Y	Y	Y
2 Schmidt	Y	N	Y	Y	Y
3 Turner	Y	N	Y	Y	Y
4 Jordan	Y	N	Y	Y	Y
5 Latta	Y	N	Y	Y	Y
6 Wilson	N	Y	Y	Y	Y
7 Austria	Y	N	Y	?	Y
8 Boehner	Y	N	Y	?	Y
9 Kaptur	N	Y	Y	Y	Y
10 Kucinich	N	Y	N	Y	N
11 Fudge	N	N	Y	Y	Y
12 Tiberi	Y	N	Y	Y	Y
13 Sutton	N	Y	Y	Y	Y
14 LaTourette	Y	N	Y	Y	Y
15 Kilroy	N	Y	Y	Y	Y
16 Boccieri	Y	Y	Y	Y	Y
17 Ryan	N	Y	Y	Y	Y
18 Space	Y	Y	Y	Y	Y
OKLAHOMA					
1 Sullivan	Y	N	Y	Y	Y
2 Boren	Y	N	Y	Y	Y
3 Lucas	Y	N	Y	Y	Y
4 Cole	Y	N	Y	Y	Y
5 Fallin	Y	N	Y	Y	Y
OREGON					
1 Wu	N	Y	Y	Y	Y
2 Walden	Y	N	Y	Y	Y
3 Blumenauer	N	Y	Y	Y	N
4 DeFazio	N	Y	Y	Y	Y
5 Schrader	N	Y	Y	Y	Y
PENNSYLVANIA					
1 Brady	N	Y	Y	Y	Y
2 Fattah	N	Y	Y	Y	Y
3 Dahlkemper	N	N	Y	Y	Y
4 Altmire	Y	Y	Y	Y	Y
5 Thompson	Y	N	Y	Y	Y
6 Gerlach	Y	N	Y	Y	Y
7 Sestak	N	Y	Y	Y	Y
8 Murphy, P.	N	Y	Y	Y	Y
9 Shuster	Y	N	Y	Y	Y
10 Carney	N	Y	Y	Y	Y
11 Kanjorski	N	Y	Y	Y	Y
12 Critz	N	Y	Y	Y	Y
13 Schwartz	N	Y	Y	Y	Y
14 Doyle	N	Y	Y	Y	Y
15 Dent	Y	N	Y	Y	Y
16 Pitts	Y	N	Y	Y	Y
17 Holden	N	N	Y	Y	Y
18 Murphy, T.	Y	N	Y	Y	Y
19 Platts	Y	N	Y	Y	Y
RHODE ISLAND					
1 Kennedy	N	Y	Y	Y	Y
2 Langevin	N	Y	Y	Y	Y
SOUTH CAROLINA					
1 Brown	?	?	?	?	?
2 Wilson	Y	N	Y	Y	Y
3 Barrett	?	?	?	?	?
4 Inglis	Y	N	Y	Y	Y
5 Spratt	N	Y	Y	Y	Y
6 Clyburn	N	Y	Y	Y	Y
SOUTH DAKOTA					
AL Herseth Sandlin	Y	N	Y	Y	Y
TENNESSEE					
1 Roe	Y	N	Y	Y	Y
2 Duncan	Y	N	Y	Y	?
3 Wamp	?	?	?	?	?
4 Davis	N	Y	Y	Y	Y
5 Cooper	N	Y	Y	Y	Y
6 Gordon	N	Y	Y	Y	Y
7 Blackburn	Y	N	Y	Y	Y
8 Tanner	N	Y	Y	Y	Y
9 Cohen	N	Y	Y	Y	Y

	390	391	392	393	394
TEXAS					
1 Gohmert	Y	N	Y	Y	Y
2 Poe	Y	N	Y	Y	Y
3 Johnson, S.	Y	N	?	Y	Y
4 Hall	Y	N	Y	Y	Y
5 Hensarling	Y	N	Y	Y	Y
6 Barton	Y	N	Y	Y	Y
7 Culberson	Y	N	Y	Y	Y
8 Brady	Y	N	Y	Y	Y
9 Green, A.	N	Y	Y	Y	Y
10 McCaul	Y	N	Y	Y	Y
11 Conaway	Y	N	Y	Y	Y
12 Granger	Y	N	Y	Y	Y
13 Thornberry	Y	N	Y	Y	Y
14 Paul	N	N	N	Y	N
15 Hinojosa	N	Y	Y	?	?
16 Reyes	N	Y	Y	Y	Y
17 Edwards	Y	Y	Y	Y	Y
18 Jackson Lee	N	Y	Y	Y	Y
19 Neugebauer	Y	N	Y	Y	Y
20 Gonzalez	N	Y	Y	Y	Y
21 Smith	Y	N	Y	Y	Y
22 Olson	Y	N	Y	Y	Y
23 Rodriguez	N	Y	Y	Y	Y
24 Marchant	Y	N	Y	Y	Y
25 Doggett	N	Y	Y	Y	Y
26 Burgess	Y	N	Y	Y	Y
27 Ortiz	N	Y	Y	Y	Y
28 Cuellar	Y	Y	Y	Y	Y
29 Green, G.	N	Y	Y	Y	Y
30 Johnson, E.	N	Y	Y	Y	Y
31 Carter	Y	N	Y	Y	Y
32 Sessions	Y	N	?	Y	Y
UTAH					
1 Bishop	Y	N	Y	Y	Y
2 Matheson	N	Y	Y	Y	Y
3 Chaffetz	Y	N	Y	Y	Y
VERMONT					
AL Welch	N	Y	Y	Y	Y
VIRGINIA					
1 Wittman	Y	N	Y	Y	Y
2 Nye	Y	N	Y	Y	Y
3 Scott	N	Y	Y	Y	Y
4 Forbes	Y	N	Y	Y	Y
5 Perriello	Y	N	Y	Y	Y
6 Goodlatte	Y	N	Y	Y	Y
7 Cantor	Y	N	Y	Y	Y
8 Moran	N	Y	Y	Y	Y
9 Boucher	Y	Y	Y	Y	Y
10 Wolf	Y	N	Y	Y	Y
11 Connolly	N	Y	Y	Y	Y
WASHINGTON					
1 Inslee	N	Y	Y	Y	Y
2 Larsen	N	Y	Y	Y	Y
3 Baird	N	Y	Y	Y	N
4 Hastings	Y	N	Y	Y	Y
5 McMorris Rodgers	Y	N	Y	Y	Y
6 Dicks	N	Y	?	Y	Y
7 McDermott	N	Y	Y	Y	+
8 Reichert	Y	N	Y	Y	Y
9 Smith	N	Y	Y	Y	Y
WEST VIRGINIA					
1 Mollohan	N	Y	Y	Y	Y
2 Capito	Y	N	Y	Y	Y
3 Rahall	N	Y	Y	Y	Y
WISCONSIN					
1 Ryan	Y	N	Y	Y	Y
2 Baldwin	N	Y	Y	Y	N
3 Kind	N	Y	Y	Y	Y
4 Moore	N	Y	Y	Y	Y
5 Sensenbrenner	Y	N	Y	Y	Y
6 Petri	Y	N	Y	Y	Y
7 Obey	N	Y	Y	Y	Y
8 Kagen	N	Y	Y	Y	Y
WYOMING					
AL Lummis	Y	N	Y	Y	Y
DELEGATES					
Faleomavaega (A.S.)					
Norton (D.C.)					
Bordallo (Guam)					
Sablan (N. Marianas)					
Pierluisi (P.R.)					
Christensen (V.I.)					

IN THE HOUSE | By Vote Number

395. **Procedural Motion/Journal.** Approval of the House Journal of June 28, 2010. Approved 219-175: D 206-26; R 13-149. June 29, 2010.

396. **H Res 1439. Tribute to Chicago Blackhawks/Adoption.** Norton, D-D.C., motion to suspend the rules and adopt the resolution that would congratulate the Chicago Blackhawks on winning the National Hockey League 2010 Stanley Cup Championship. Motion agreed to 395-5: D 232-4; R 163-1. A two-thirds majority of those present and voting (267 in this case) is required for adoption under suspension of the rules. June 29, 2010.

397. **Procedural Motion/Motion to Adjourn.** Broun, R-Ga., motion to adjourn. Motion rejected 23-379: D 3-232; R 20-147. June 29, 2010.

398. **HR 5618. Unemployment Benefits Extension/Passage.** Levin, D-Mich., motion to suspend the rules and pass the bill that would extend through Nov. 30 and make retroactive to June 2 eligibility for unemployment insurance for laid-off workers and 100 percent federal funding for extended jobless benefits. States could not reduce their regular unemployment compensation programs below June 2 levels and be eligible for the funding. Motion rejected 261-155: D 231-16; R 30-139. A two-thirds majority of those present and voting (278 in this case) is required for passage under suspension of the rules. June 29, 2010.

399. **H Res 1244. Tribute to National Collegiate Cyber Defense Competition/Adoption.** Hirono, D-Hawaii, motion to suspend the rules and adopt the resolution that would recognize the five-year effort of the National Collegiate Cyber Defense Competition in promoting cybersecurity curricula in higher education institutions. Motion agreed to 412-2: D 243-0; R 169-2. A two-thirds majority of those present and voting (276 in this case) is required for adoption under suspension of the rules. June 29, 2010.

400. **HR 5552. Firearms Excise Tax Alterations/Passage.** Kind, D-Wis., motion to suspend the rules and pass the bill that would alter the manufacturer's excise tax on recreational firearms and ammunition equipment to be paid quarterly, rather than every two weeks. Motion agreed to 412-6: D 242-5; R 170-1. A two-thirds majority of those present and voting (279 in this case) is required for passage under suspension of the rules. June 29, 2010.

401. **HR 5623. Extension of Homebuyer Tax Credit/Passage.** Levin, D-Mich., motion to suspend the rules and pass the bill that would extend the required closing date for a first-time-homebuyer tax credit. Individuals who entered into a written binding contract before May 1 would have to close on the purchase of a principal residence before Oct. 1, 2010. The cost would be offset by extending fees for travel promotion and by applying a bad-check penalty to electronic payments. Motion agreed to 409-5: D 244-0; R 165-5. A two-thirds majority of those present and voting (276 in this case) is required for passage under suspension of the rules. June 29, 2010.

	395	396	397	398	399	400	401
ALABAMA							
1 Bonner	N	Y	N	N	Y	Y	Y
2 Bright	N	Y	N	N	Y	Y	Y
3 Rogers	N	Y	N	N	Y	Y	Y
4 Aderholt	N	Y	N	N	Y	Y	Y
5 Griffith	?	?	?	?	?	?	?
6 Bachus	N	Y	N	N	Y	Y	Y
7 Davis	Y	Y	N	Y	Y	Y	Y
ALASKA							
AL Young	?	?	?	?	?	?	?
ARIZONA							
1 Kirkpatrick	N	Y	N	Y	Y	Y	Y
2 Franks	N	Y	N	N	Y	Y	Y
3 Shadegg	N	Y	N	N	Y	Y	Y
4 Pastor	Y	Y	N	Y	Y	Y	Y
5 Mitchell	N	Y	N	Y	Y	Y	Y
6 Flake	N	Y	Y	N	N	Y	N
7 Grijalva	Y	Y	N	Y	Y	Y	Y
8 Giffords	+	+	−	Y	Y	Y	Y
ARKANSAS							
1 Berry	Y	N	N	N	Y	Y	Y
2 Snyder	Y	Y	N	Y	Y	Y	Y
3 Boozman	N	Y	N	N	Y	Y	Y
4 Ross	Y	Y	N	Y	Y	Y	Y
CALIFORNIA							
1 Thompson	N	Y	N	Y	Y	Y	Y
2 Herger	N	Y	N	N	Y	Y	Y
3 Lungren	N	Y	N	N	Y	Y	Y
4 McClintock	Y	Y	N	N	Y	Y	N
5 Matsui	Y	Y	N	Y	Y	Y	Y
6 Woolsey	?	?	?	?	?	?	?
7 Miller, George	Y	Y	Y	Y	?	Y	Y
8 Pelosi				Y			
9 Lee	Y	Y	N	Y	Y	Y	Y
10 Garamendi	Y	Y	N	Y	Y	Y	Y
11 McNerney	Y	Y	N	Y	Y	Y	Y
12 Speier	Y	Y	N	Y	Y	Y	Y
13 Stark	Y	Y	N	Y	Y	Y	Y
14 Eshoo	Y	Y	N	Y	Y	Y	Y
15 Honda	Y	Y	N	Y	Y	Y	Y
16 Lofgren	Y	Y	N	Y	Y	Y	Y
17 Farr	Y	Y	N	Y	Y	N	Y
18 Cardoza	Y	Y	N	Y	Y	Y	Y
19 Radanovich	N	Y	N	N	Y	Y	Y
20 Costa	?	Y	N	Y	Y	Y	Y
21 Nunes	N	Y	N	N	Y	Y	Y
22 McCarthy	N	Y	N	N	Y	Y	Y
23 Capps	Y	Y	N	Y	Y	Y	Y
24 Gallegly	N	Y	N	N	Y	Y	Y
25 McKeon	N	Y	N	N	Y	Y	Y
26 Dreier	N	Y	N	N	Y	Y	Y
27 Sherman	Y	Y	N	Y	Y	Y	Y
28 Berman	Y	Y	N	Y	Y	Y	Y
29 Schiff	Y	Y	N	Y	Y	Y	Y
30 Waxman	Y	Y	N	Y	Y	Y	Y
31 Becerra	Y	Y	N	Y	Y	Y	Y
32 Chu	Y	Y	N	Y	Y	Y	Y
33 Watson	Y	Y	N	Y	Y	Y	Y
34 Roybal-Allard	Y	Y	N	Y	Y	Y	Y
35 Waters	Y	Y	N	Y	Y	N	Y
36 Harman	Y	Y	N	Y	Y	Y	Y
37 Richardson	Y	Y	N	Y	Y	Y	Y
38 Napolitano	Y	Y	N	Y	Y	Y	Y
39 Sánchez, Linda	Y	Y	N	Y	Y	Y	Y
40 Royce	N	Y	N	N	Y	Y	Y
41 Lewis	N	Y	N	N	Y	Y	Y
42 Miller, Gary	N	Y	N	N	Y	Y	Y
43 Baca	Y	Y	N	Y	Y	Y	Y
44 Calvert	Y	Y	N	N	Y	Y	Y
45 Bono Mack	N	Y	N	N	Y	Y	Y
46 Rohrabacher	N	Y	N	N	Y	Y	Y
47 Sanchez, Loretta	Y	Y	Y	Y	Y	Y	Y
48 Campbell	N	Y	N	N	Y	Y	N
49 Issa	N	Y	N	N	Y	Y	Y
50 Bilbray	N	Y	N	Y	Y	Y	Y
51 Filner	Y	Y	N	Y	Y	Y	Y
52 Hunter	N	Y	Y	N	Y	Y	Y
53 Davis	Y	Y	N	Y	Y	Y	Y

	395	396	397	398	399	400	401
COLORADO							
1 DeGette	Y	Y	N	Y	Y	Y	Y
2 Polis	Y	Y	N	Y	Y	Y	Y
3 Salazar	Y	Y	N	Y	Y	Y	Y
4 Markey	N	Y	N	Y	Y	Y	Y
5 Lamborn	N	Y	N	Y	Y	Y	Y
6 Coffman	N	Y	N	N	Y	Y	Y
7 Perlmutter	Y	Y	N	Y	Y	Y	Y
CONNECTICUT							
1 Larson	Y	Y	N	Y	Y	Y	Y
2 Courtney	Y	Y	N	Y	Y	Y	Y
3 DeLauro	Y	Y	N	Y	Y	Y	Y
4 Himes	N	Y	N	Y	Y	Y	Y
5 Murphy	Y	Y	N	Y	Y	Y	Y
DELAWARE							
AL Castle	Y	Y	N	Y	Y	Y	Y
FLORIDA							
1 Miller	N	Y	N	N	Y	Y	Y
2 Boyd	Y	Y	N	Y	Y	Y	Y
3 Brown	?	?	?	Y	Y	Y	Y
4 Crenshaw	N	Y	N	Y	Y	Y	Y
5 Brown-Waite	N	Y	N	N	Y	Y	Y
6 Stearns	N	Y	N	N	Y	Y	Y
7 Mica	N	Y	N	N	Y	Y	Y
8 Grayson	Y	Y	N	Y	Y	Y	Y
9 Bilirakis	N	Y	N	Y	Y	Y	Y
10 Young	N	Y	N	Y	Y	Y	Y
11 Castor	Y	Y	N	Y	Y	Y	Y
12 Putnam	−	+	−	−	+	+	+
13 Buchanan	N	Y	N	N	Y	Y	Y
14 Mack	N	Y	N	N	Y	Y	Y
15 Posey	Y	Y	N	N	Y	Y	Y
16 Rooney	N	Y	N	N	Y	Y	Y
17 Meek	Y	Y	N	Y	Y	Y	Y
18 Ros-Lehtinen	N	Y	N	Y	Y	Y	Y
19 Deutch	Y	Y	N	Y	Y	Y	Y
20 Wasserman Schultz	Y	Y	N	Y	Y	Y	Y
21 Diaz-Balart, L.	N	Y	N	N	Y	Y	Y
22 Klein	Y	Y	N	Y	Y	Y	Y
23 Hastings	Y	Y	N	Y	Y	Y	Y
24 Kosmas	Y	Y	N	Y	Y	Y	Y
25 Diaz-Balart, M.	N	Y	N	Y	Y	Y	Y
GEORGIA							
1 Kingston	N	Y	N	N	Y	Y	Y
2 Bishop	Y	Y	N	Y	Y	Y	Y
3 Westmoreland	N	Y	N	N	Y	Y	Y
4 Johnson	Y	Y	N	Y	Y	Y	Y
5 Lewis	Y	Y	N	Y	Y	Y	Y
6 Price	N	Y	N	Y	Y	Y	Y
7 Linder	N	Y	N	N	Y	Y	N
8 Marshall	Y	Y	N	Y	Y	Y	Y
9 Graves	N	Y	N	Y	Y	Y	Y
10 Broun	N	Y	N	Y	Y	Y	Y
11 Gingrey	N	?	Y	N	Y	Y	Y
12 Barrow	Y	Y	N	Y	Y	Y	Y
13 Scott	Y	Y	N	Y	Y	Y	Y
HAWAII							
1 Djou	N	Y	N	N	Y	Y	Y
2 Hirono	Y	Y	N	Y	Y	Y	Y
IDAHO							
1 Minnick	N	Y	N	N	Y	Y	Y
2 Simpson	N	Y	N	N	Y	Y	Y
ILLINOIS							
1 Rush	?	?	?	?	Y	Y	Y
2 Jackson	Y	Y	N	Y	Y	Y	Y
3 Lipinski	?	?	?	Y	Y	Y	Y
4 Gutierrez	Y	Y	N	Y	Y	Y	Y
5 Quigley	Y	Y	N	Y	Y	Y	Y
6 Roskam	N	Y	N	N	Y	Y	Y
7 Davis	Y	Y	N	Y	Y	Y	Y
8 Bean	Y	Y	N	Y	Y	Y	Y
9 Schakowsky	Y	Y	N	Y	?	Y	Y
10 Kirk	?	?	?	−	?	?	+
11 Halvorson	Y	Y	N	Y	Y	Y	Y
12 Costello	Y	Y	N	Y	Y	Y	Y
13 Biggert	N	Y	N	N	Y	Y	Y
14 Foster	Y	Y	N	Y	Y	Y	Y
15 Johnson	+	+	+	Y	Y	Y	Y

KEY   **Republicans**   Democrats

Y Voted for (yea)	X Paired against	C Voted "present" to avoid possible conflict of interest
# Paired for	− Announced against	
+ Announced for	P Voted "present"	? Did not vote or otherwise make a position known
N Voted against (nay)		

	395	396	397	398	399	400	401
16 **Manzullo**	N	Y	N	Y	Y	Y	Y
17 Hare	Y	Y	N	Y	Y	Y	Y
18 **Schock**	N	Y	N	?	Y	Y	Y
19 **Shimkus**	N	Y	N	N	Y	Y	Y
INDIANA							
1 Visclosky	Y	Y	N	Y	Y	Y	+
2 Donnelly	N	Y	N	N	Y	Y	Y
3 Vacant							
4 **Buyer**	N	Y	N	N	Y	Y	Y
5 **Burton**	?	?	?	N	Y	Y	Y
6 **Pence**	N	Y	N	N	Y	Y	Y
7 Carson	Y	Y	N	Y	Y	Y	Y
8 Ellsworth	?	?	?	Y	Y	Y	Y
9 Hill	Y	Y	N	N	Y	Y	Y
IOWA							
1 Braley	Y	Y	N	Y	Y	Y	Y
2 Loebsack	Y	Y	N	Y	?	Y	Y
3 Boswell	+	+	–	Y	Y	Y	Y
4 **Latham**	N	Y	N	N	Y	Y	Y
5 **King**	N	Y	Y	N	Y	Y	Y
KANSAS							
1 **Moran**	N	Y	N	N	Y	Y	Y
2 **Jenkins**	N	Y	N	N	Y	Y	Y
3 Moore	Y	Y	N	Y	Y	Y	Y
4 **Tiahrt**	?	Y	Y	N	Y	Y	Y
KENTUCKY							
1 **Whitfield**	N	Y	N	Y	Y	Y	Y
2 **Guthrie**	N	Y	N	N	Y	Y	Y
3 Yarmuth	Y	Y	N	Y	Y	Y	Y
4 **Davis**	N	Y	N	N	Y	Y	Y
5 **Rogers**	N	Y	N	N	Y	Y	Y
6 Chandler	Y	Y	N	Y	Y	Y	Y
LOUISIANA							
1 **Scalise**	N	Y	N	N	Y	Y	Y
2 **Cao**	?	?	?	?	?	?	?
3 Melancon	Y	Y	N	Y	Y	Y	Y
4 **Fleming**	N	Y	N	N	Y	Y	Y
5 **Alexander**	N	Y	N	N	Y	Y	Y
6 **Cassidy**	N	Y	N	N	Y	Y	Y
7 **Boustany**	N	Y	N	N	Y	Y	Y
MAINE							
1 Pingree	Y	Y	N	Y	Y	Y	Y
2 Michaud	Y	Y	N	Y	Y	Y	Y
MARYLAND							
1 Kratovil	Y	Y	N	N	Y	Y	Y
2 Ruppersberger	Y	Y	N	Y	Y	Y	Y
3 Sarbanes	Y	Y	N	Y	Y	Y	Y
4 Edwards	Y	Y	N	Y	Y	Y	Y
5 Hoyer	Y	Y	N	Y	Y	Y	Y
6 **Bartlett**	N	Y	Y	N	Y	Y	Y
7 Cummings	Y	Y	N	?	?	?	?
8 Van Hollen	Y	Y	N	Y	Y	Y	Y
MASSACHUSETTS							
1 Olver	Y	?	N	Y	Y	Y	Y
2 Neal	Y	Y	N	Y	Y	Y	Y
3 McGovern	Y	Y	N	Y	Y	Y	Y
4 Frank	Y	Y	N	Y	Y	Y	Y
5 Tsongas	Y	Y	N	Y	Y	Y	Y
6 Tierney	Y	Y	N	Y	Y	Y	Y
7 Markey	Y	Y	N	Y	Y	Y	Y
8 Capuano	Y	Y	N	Y	Y	Y	Y
9 Lynch	Y	Y	N	Y	Y	Y	Y
10 Delahunt	?	?	?	Y	Y	Y	Y
MICHIGAN							
1 Stupak	N	Y	N	Y	Y	Y	Y
2 **Hoekstra**	?	?	?	?	?	?	?
3 **Ehlers**	N	Y	N	Y	Y	Y	Y
4 **Camp**	N	Y	N	N	Y	Y	Y
5 Kildee	Y	Y	N	Y	Y	Y	Y
6 **Upton**	N	Y	N	Y	Y	Y	Y
7 Schauer	Y	Y	N	Y	Y	Y	Y
8 **Rogers**	N	Y	N	Y	Y	Y	Y
9 Peters	N	Y	N	Y	Y	Y	Y
10 **Miller**	N	Y	N	N	Y	Y	Y
11 **McCotter**	N	Y	N	Y	Y	Y	Y
12 Levin	Y	Y	N	Y	Y	Y	Y
13 Kilpatrick	Y	Y	N	Y	Y	Y	Y
14 Conyers	Y	Y	N	Y	Y	N	Y
15 Dingell	Y	Y	N	Y	Y	Y	Y
MINNESOTA							
1 Walz	Y	Y	N	Y	Y	Y	Y
2 **Kline**	N	Y	N	N	Y	Y	Y
3 **Paulsen**	Y	Y	N	N	Y	Y	Y
4 McCollum	Y	Y	N	Y	Y	Y	Y

	395	396	397	398	399	400	401
5 Ellison	Y	Y	N	Y	Y	Y	Y
6 **Bachmann**	Y	Y	N	N	Y	Y	Y
7 Peterson	N	Y	N	Y	?	Y	?
8 Oberstar	+	?	–	+	+	+	+
MISSISSIPPI							
1 Childers	N	Y	N	N	Y	Y	Y
2 Thompson	Y	Y	N	Y	Y	Y	Y
3 **Harper**	Y	Y	N	N	Y	Y	Y
4 Taylor	?	?	?	?	?	?	?
MISSOURI							
1 Clay	Y	Y	N	Y	Y	Y	Y
2 **Akin**	N	Y	N	N	Y	Y	Y
3 Carnahan	Y	Y	N	Y	Y	Y	Y
4 Skelton	Y	Y	N	Y	Y	Y	Y
5 Cleaver	Y	Y	?	Y	Y	Y	Y
6 **Graves**	Y	Y	N	N	Y	Y	Y
7 **Blunt**	N	Y	N	N	Y	Y	Y
8 **Emerson**	N	Y	N	N	Y	Y	Y
9 **Luetkemeyer**	N	Y	N	N	Y	Y	Y
MONTANA							
AL **Rehberg**	N	Y	N	N	Y	Y	Y
NEBRASKA							
1 **Fortenberry**	Y	Y	N	N	Y	Y	Y
2 **Terry**	N	Y	N	N	Y	Y	Y
3 **Smith**	N	Y	N	N	Y	Y	Y
NEVADA							
1 Berkley	?	?	?	Y	Y	Y	Y
2 **Heller**	N	Y	Y	Y	Y	Y	Y
3 Titus	Y	Y	N	Y	Y	Y	Y
NEW HAMPSHIRE							
1 Shea-Porter	Y	Y	N	Y	Y	Y	Y
2 Hodes	?	?	?	Y	Y	Y	Y
NEW JERSEY							
1 Andrews	Y	N	N	Y	Y	Y	Y
2 **LoBiondo**	N	Y	N	Y	Y	Y	Y
3 Adler	N	N	N	N	Y	Y	Y
4 **Smith**	N	Y	N	Y	Y	Y	Y
5 **Garrett**	N	Y	Y	N	Y	Y	Y
6 Pallone	Y	Y	N	Y	Y	Y	Y
7 **Lance**	N	Y	N	N	Y	Y	Y
8 Pascrell	Y	Y	N	Y	Y	Y	Y
9 Rothman	Y	Y	N	Y	Y	Y	Y
10 Payne	?	?	?	Y	Y	Y	Y
11 **Frelinghuysen**	N	Y	N	N	Y	Y	Y
12 Holt	Y	Y	N	Y	Y	Y	Y
13 Sires	Y	Y	N	Y	Y	Y	Y
NEW MEXICO							
1 Heinrich	Y	Y	N	Y	Y	Y	Y
2 Teague	Y	Y	N	Y	Y	Y	Y
3 Luján	Y	Y	N	Y	Y	Y	Y
NEW YORK							
1 Bishop	Y	Y	N	Y	Y	Y	Y
2 Israel	Y	Y	N	Y	Y	Y	Y
3 **King**	N	Y	N	N	Y	Y	Y
4 McCarthy	Y	Y	N	Y	Y	Y	Y
5 Ackerman	Y	Y	N	Y	Y	Y	Y
6 Meeks	Y	Y	N	Y	Y	Y	Y
7 Crowley	Y	Y	N	Y	Y	Y	Y
8 Nadler	Y	Y	N	Y	Y	N	Y
9 Weiner	Y	Y	N	Y	Y	Y	Y
10 Towns	Y	Y	N	Y	Y	Y	Y
11 Clarke	Y	Y	N	Y	Y	Y	Y
12 Velázquez	Y	Y	N	Y	Y	Y	Y
13 McMahon	Y	Y	N	Y	Y	Y	Y
14 Maloney	Y	Y	N	Y	Y	Y	Y
15 Rangel	Y	Y	?	Y	Y	Y	Y
16 Serrano	Y	Y	N	Y	Y	Y	Y
17 Engel	?	?	?	+	?	?	?
18 Lowey	Y	Y	N	Y	Y	Y	Y
19 Hall	Y	Y	N	Y	Y	Y	Y
20 Murphy	N	Y	N	Y	Y	Y	Y
21 Tonko	Y	Y	N	Y	Y	Y	Y
22 Hinchey	Y	Y	N	Y	Y	Y	Y
23 Owens	N	Y	N	Y	Y	Y	Y
24 Arcuri	N	Y	N	Y	Y	Y	Y
25 Maffei	?	Y	Y	Y	Y	Y	Y
26 **Lee**	N	Y	N	Y	Y	Y	Y
27 Higgins	Y	Y	N	Y	Y	Y	Y
28 Slaughter	Y	Y	N	Y	Y	?	Y
29 Vacant							
NORTH CAROLINA							
1 Butterfield	Y	Y	N	Y	Y	Y	Y
2 Etheridge	Y	Y	N	Y	Y	Y	Y
3 **Jones**	N	Y	N	Y	Y	Y	Y
4 Price	Y	Y	N	Y	Y	Y	Y

	395	396	397	398	399	400	401
5 **Foxx**	N	Y	Y	N	Y	Y	Y
6 **Coble**	N	Y	N	N	Y	Y	Y
7 McIntyre	Y	Y	N	+	Y	Y	Y
8 Kissell	Y	Y	N	Y	Y	Y	Y
9 **Myrick**	N	Y	N	N	Y	Y	Y
10 **McHenry**	N	Y	N	N	Y	Y	Y
11 Shuler	N	Y	N	N	Y	Y	Y
12 Watt	Y	Y	N	Y	Y	Y	Y
13 Miller	Y	Y	N	Y	Y	Y	Y
NORTH DAKOTA							
AL Pomeroy	Y	Y	N	Y	Y	Y	Y
OHIO							
1 Driehaus	Y	Y	N	Y	Y	Y	Y
2 **Schmidt**	N	Y	N	N	Y	Y	Y
3 **Turner**	N	Y	N	Y	Y	Y	Y
4 **Jordan**	N	Y	N	N	Y	Y	Y
5 **Latta**	N	Y	N	N	Y	Y	Y
6 Wilson	Y	Y	N	Y	Y	Y	Y
7 **Austria**	N	Y	N	N	Y	Y	Y
8 **Boehner**	?	?	N	N	Y	Y	Y
9 Kaptur	Y	Y	N	Y	Y	Y	Y
10 Kucinich	Y	Y	N	Y	Y	N	Y
11 Fudge	Y	Y	N	Y	Y	Y	Y
12 **Tiberi**	N	Y	N	N	Y	Y	Y
13 Sutton	?	Y	N	Y	Y	Y	Y
14 **LaTourette**	Y	Y	N	Y	Y	Y	Y
15 Kilroy	N	Y	N	Y	Y	Y	Y
16 Boccieri	N	Y	N	Y	Y	Y	Y
17 Ryan	Y	Y	N	Y	Y	Y	Y
18 Space	Y	Y	N	Y	Y	Y	Y
OKLAHOMA							
1 **Sullivan**	N	Y	N	N	Y	Y	Y
2 Boren	Y	Y	N	Y	Y	Y	Y
3 **Lucas**	N	Y	N	N	Y	Y	Y
4 **Cole**	N	Y	N	N	Y	Y	Y
5 **Fallin**	?	?	?	N	Y	Y	Y
OREGON							
1 Wu	N	Y	N	Y	Y	Y	Y
2 **Walden**	N	Y	N	N	Y	Y	Y
3 Blumenauer	Y	Y	N	Y	Y	Y	Y
4 DeFazio	Y	Y	N	Y	Y	Y	Y
5 Schrader	Y	Y	N	Y	?	Y	Y
PENNSYLVANIA							
1 Brady	Y	Y	N	Y	Y	Y	Y
2 Fattah	Y	Y	N	Y	Y	Y	Y
3 Dahlkemper	Y	Y	N	Y	Y	Y	Y
4 Altmire	N	Y	N	Y	Y	Y	Y
5 **Thompson**	N	Y	N	N	Y	Y	Y
6 **Gerlach**	N	Y	N	Y	Y	Y	Y
7 Sestak	Y	Y	N	Y	Y	Y	Y
8 Murphy, P.	Y	Y	N	Y	Y	Y	Y
9 **Shuster**	N	Y	N	N	Y	Y	Y
10 Carney	N	Y	N	Y	Y	Y	Y
11 Kanjorski	Y	Y	N	Y	Y	Y	Y
12 Critz	N	Y	N	Y	Y	Y	Y
13 Schwartz	Y	Y	N	Y	Y	Y	?
14 Doyle	Y	Y	N	Y	Y	Y	Y
15 **Dent**	Y	Y	N	Y	Y	Y	Y
16 **Pitts**	N	Y	N	N	Y	Y	Y
17 Holden	Y	Y	N	Y	Y	Y	Y
18 **Murphy, T.**	N	Y	N	Y	Y	Y	Y
19 **Platts**	N	Y	N	Y	Y	Y	Y
RHODE ISLAND							
1 Kennedy	Y	Y	N	Y	Y	Y	Y
2 Langevin	?	Y	N	Y	Y	Y	Y
SOUTH CAROLINA							
1 **Brown**	N	Y	N	N	Y	Y	Y
2 **Wilson**	N	Y	N	N	Y	Y	Y
3 **Barrett**	N	Y	N	N	Y	Y	Y
4 **Inglis**	N	Y	N	N	Y	Y	Y
5 Spratt	Y	Y	N	Y	Y	Y	Y
6 Clyburn	Y	Y	N	Y	Y	Y	Y
SOUTH DAKOTA							
AL Herseth Sandlin	Y	Y	N	N	Y	Y	Y
TENNESSEE							
1 **Roe**	N	Y	N	N	Y	Y	Y
2 **Duncan**	N	Y	N	N	Y	Y	Y
3 **Wamp**	?	?	?	?	?	?	?
4 Davis	Y	Y	N	Y	Y	Y	Y
5 Cooper	Y	Y	N	N	Y	Y	Y
6 Gordon	Y	Y	N	Y	Y	Y	Y
7 **Blackburn**	N	Y	N	N	Y	Y	Y
8 Tanner	Y	Y	N	Y	Y	Y	Y
9 Cohen	?	?	?	Y	Y	Y	Y

	395	396	397	398	399	400	401
TEXAS							
1 **Gohmert**	P	Y	Y	N	Y	Y	Y
2 **Poe**	?	Y	N	N	Y	Y	Y
3 **Johnson, S.**	N	Y	Y	N	Y	Y	Y
4 **Hall**	N	Y	N	N	Y	Y	Y
5 **Hensarling**	N	Y	N	N	Y	Y	N
6 **Barton**	?	Y	N	N	Y	Y	Y
7 **Culberson**	?	?	N	N	Y	Y	Y
8 **Brady**	N	Y	N	N	Y	Y	Y
9 Green, A.	Y	Y	N	Y	Y	Y	Y
10 **McCaul**	N	Y	N	N	Y	Y	Y
11 **Conaway**	N	Y	N	N	Y	Y	Y
12 **Granger**	N	Y	N	N	Y	Y	Y
13 **Thornberry**	N	Y	N	N	Y	Y	Y
14 **Paul**	N	Y	Y	N	N	N	Y
15 Hinojosa	Y	Y	N	Y	Y	Y	Y
16 Reyes	Y	Y	N	Y	Y	Y	Y
17 Edwards	Y	Y	N	Y	Y	Y	Y
18 Jackson Lee	Y	Y	N	Y	Y	Y	Y
19 **Neugebauer**	N	Y	N	N	Y	Y	Y
20 Gonzalez	Y	Y	N	Y	Y	Y	Y
21 **Smith**	N	Y	?	N	Y	Y	Y
22 **Olson**	N	Y	Y	N	Y	Y	Y
23 Rodriguez	Y	Y	N	Y	Y	Y	Y
24 **Marchant**	N	Y	N	N	Y	Y	Y
25 Doggett	Y	Y	N	Y	Y	Y	Y
26 **Burgess**	N	Y	N	N	Y	Y	Y
27 Ortiz	Y	Y	N	Y	Y	Y	Y
28 Cuellar	Y	Y	N	Y	Y	Y	Y
29 Green, G.	Y	Y	N	Y	Y	Y	Y
30 Johnson, E.	Y	Y	N	Y	Y	Y	Y
31 **Carter**	N	Y	N	N	Y	Y	Y
32 **Sessions**	N	Y	N	N	Y	Y	+
UTAH							
1 **Bishop**	N	Y	Y	?	Y	Y	Y
2 Matheson	Y	Y	N	Y	Y	Y	Y
3 **Chaffetz**	Y	P	Y	N	Y	Y	Y
VERMONT							
AL Welch	Y	Y	N	Y	Y	Y	Y
VIRGINIA							
1 **Wittman**	N	Y	N	N	Y	Y	Y
2 Nye	N	N	N	Y	Y	Y	Y
3 Scott	Y	Y	N	Y	Y	Y	Y
4 **Forbes**	N	Y	N	N	Y	Y	Y
5 Perriello	N	Y	N	Y	Y	Y	Y
6 **Goodlatte**	Y	Y	N	N	Y	Y	Y
7 **Cantor**	N	Y	N	N	Y	Y	Y
8 Moran	?	?	?	Y	Y	Y	Y
9 Boucher	Y	Y	N	Y	Y	Y	Y
10 **Wolf**	N	Y	N	N	Y	Y	Y
11 Connolly	N	Y	N	Y	Y	Y	Y
WASHINGTON							
1 Inslee	Y	Y	N	Y	Y	Y	Y
2 Larsen	Y	Y	N	Y	Y	Y	Y
3 Baird	Y	Y	N	N	Y	Y	Y
4 **Hastings**	N	Y	N	N	Y	Y	Y
5 **McMorris Rodgers**	N	Y	N	N	Y	Y	Y
6 Dicks	Y	Y	N	Y	Y	Y	Y
7 McDermott	Y	Y	N	Y	Y	Y	Y
8 **Reichert**	N	Y	N	Y	Y	Y	Y
9 Smith	Y	Y	N	Y	Y	Y	Y
WEST VIRGINIA							
1 Mollohan	Y	Y	N	Y	Y	Y	Y
2 **Capito**	N	Y	N	Y	Y	Y	Y
3 Rahall	Y	Y	N	Y	Y	Y	Y
WISCONSIN							
1 **Ryan**	N	Y	N	N	Y	Y	Y
2 Baldwin	Y	Y	N	Y	Y	Y	Y
3 Kind	Y	Y	N	Y	Y	Y	Y
4 Moore	?	?	?	+	+	+	+
5 **Sensenbrenner**	N	Y	N	N	Y	Y	Y
6 **Petri**	N	Y	N	Y	Y	Y	Y
7 Obey	Y	Y	N	Y	Y	Y	Y
8 Kagen	?	Y	N	Y	Y	Y	Y
WYOMING							
AL **Lummis**	N	Y	Y	N	Y	Y	Y
DELEGATES							
Faleomavaega (A.S.)							
Norton (D.C.)							
Bordallo (Guam)							
Sablan (N. Marianas)							
Pierluisi (P.R.)							
Christensen (V.I.)							

IN THE HOUSE | By Vote Number

402. H Con Res 284. Tribute to Special Education Teachers/ **Adoption.** Hirono, D-Hawaii, motion to suspend the rules and adopt the concurrent resolution that would recognize the work required of special education teachers and commend their sacrifice and dedication as well as the quality-of-life skills they provide to individuals with special needs. Motion agreed to 415-0: D 244-0; R 171-0. A two-thirds majority of those present and voting (277 in this case) is required for adoption under suspension of the rules. June 29, 2010.

403. HR 5395. Paula Hawkins Post Office/Passage. Norton, D-D.C., motion to suspend the rules and pass the bill that would designate a postal building in Maitland, Fla., as the "Paula Hawkins Post Office Building." Motion agreed to 409-0: D 239-0; R 170-0. A two-thirds majority of those present and voting (273 in this case) is required for passage under suspension of the rules. June 30, 2010.

404. H Res 1446. Tribute to Residents of Tracy, Calif./Adoption. Filner, D-Calif., motion to suspend the rules and adopt the resolution that would express gratitude to the veterans and residents of Tracy, Calif., for serving the country. Motion agreed to 419-0: D 248-0; R 171-0. A two-thirds majority of those present and voting (280 in this case) is required for adoption under suspension of the rules. June 30, 2010.

405. HR 4307. Alejandro Renteria Ruiz Clinic/Passage. Filner, D-Calif., motion to suspend the rules and pass the bill that would name the Veterans Affairs Department outpatient clinic in Artesia, N.M., the "Alejandro Renteria Ruiz Department of Veterans Affairs Clinic." Motion agreed to 417-0: D 246-0; R 171-0. A two-thirds majority of those present and voting (278 in this case) is required for passage under suspension of the rules. June 30, 2010.

406. HR 4173, HR 4213. Same-Day Consideration/Previous **Question.** McGovern, D-Mass., motion to order the previous question (thus ending debate and possibility of amendment) on adoption of the rule (H Res 1487) that would waive the two-thirds majority vote requirement for same-day consideration of rules reported from the Rules Committee through the legislative day of July 3 for the conference report on the financial regulatory overhaul bill (HR 4173) and any measure relating to an extension package (HR 4213). Motion agreed to 243-182: D 242-9; R 1-173. June 30, 2010.

	402	403	404	405	406
ALABAMA					
1 Bonner	Y	Y	Y	Y	N
2 Bright	Y	Y	Y	Y	N
3 Rogers	Y	Y	Y	Y	N
4 Aderholt	Y	Y	Y	Y	N
5 Griffith	Y	Y	Y	Y	N
6 Bachus	Y	Y	Y	Y	N
7 Davis	Y	Y	Y	Y	?
ALASKA					
AL Young	?	?	?	?	?
ARIZONA					
1 Kirkpatrick	Y	Y	Y	Y	Y
2 Franks	Y	Y	Y	Y	N
3 Shadegg	Y	Y	Y	Y	N
4 Pastor	Y	Y	Y	Y	Y
5 Mitchell	Y	Y	Y	Y	N
6 Flake	Y	Y	Y	Y	N
7 Grijalva	Y	Y	Y	Y	Y
8 Giffords	Y	Y	Y	Y	Y
ARKANSAS					
1 Berry	Y	Y	Y	Y	Y
2 Snyder	Y	Y	Y	Y	Y
3 Boozman	Y	Y	Y	Y	N
4 Ross	Y	Y	Y	Y	Y
CALIFORNIA					
1 Thompson	Y	Y	Y	Y	Y
2 Herger	Y	Y	Y	Y	N
3 Lungren	Y	Y	Y	Y	N
4 McClintock	Y	Y	Y	Y	N
5 Matsui	Y	Y	Y	Y	Y
6 Woolsey	?	?	?	?	?
7 Miller, George	Y	Y	Y	Y	Y
8 Pelosi					
9 Lee	Y	Y	Y	Y	Y
10 Garamendi	Y	Y	Y	Y	Y
11 McNerney	Y	Y	Y	Y	Y
12 Speier	Y	Y	Y	Y	Y
13 Stark	?	?	Y	Y	Y
14 Eshoo	Y	Y	Y	Y	Y
15 Honda	Y	Y	Y	Y	Y
16 Lofgren	Y	Y	Y	Y	Y
17 Farr	Y	Y	Y	Y	Y
18 Cardoza	Y	Y	Y	Y	Y
19 Radanovich	Y	Y	Y	Y	N
20 Costa	Y	Y	Y	Y	Y
21 Nunes	Y	Y	Y	Y	N
22 McCarthy	Y	Y	Y	Y	N
23 Capps	Y	Y	Y	Y	Y
24 Gallegly	Y	Y	Y	Y	N
25 McKeon	Y	Y	Y	Y	N
26 Dreier	Y	Y	Y	Y	N
27 Sherman	Y	Y	Y	Y	Y
28 Berman	Y	Y	Y	Y	Y
29 Schiff	Y	Y	Y	Y	Y
30 Waxman	Y	Y	Y	Y	Y
31 Becerra	+	Y	Y	Y	Y
32 Chu	Y	Y	Y	Y	Y
33 Watson	Y	Y	Y	Y	Y
34 Roybal-Allard	Y	Y	Y	Y	Y
35 Waters	Y	Y	Y	Y	Y
36 Harman	Y	Y	Y	Y	Y
37 Richardson	Y	Y	Y	Y	Y
38 Napolitano	Y	Y	Y	Y	Y
39 Sánchez, Linda	Y	Y	Y	Y	Y
40 Royce	Y	Y	Y	Y	N
41 Lewis	Y	Y	Y	Y	N
42 Miller, Gary	Y	Y	Y	Y	N
43 Baca	Y	Y	Y	Y	Y
44 Calvert	Y	Y	Y	Y	N
45 Bono Mack	Y	Y	Y	Y	N
46 Rohrabacher	Y	Y	Y	Y	N
47 Sanchez, Loretta	Y	Y	Y	Y	Y
48 Campbell	Y	Y	Y	Y	N
49 Issa	Y	Y	Y	Y	N
50 Bilbray	Y	Y	Y	Y	N
51 Filner	Y	Y	Y	Y	Y
52 Hunter	Y	Y	Y	Y	N
53 Davis	Y	Y	Y	Y	Y

	402	403	404	405	406
COLORADO					
1 DeGette	Y	Y	Y	Y	Y
2 Polis	Y	Y	Y	Y	Y
3 Salazar	Y	Y	Y	Y	Y
4 Markey	Y	Y	Y	Y	Y
5 Lamborn	Y	Y	Y	Y	N
6 Coffman	Y	Y	Y	Y	N
7 Perlmutter	Y	Y	Y	Y	Y
CONNECTICUT					
1 Larson	Y	Y	Y	Y	Y
2 Courtney	Y	Y	Y	Y	Y
3 DeLauro	Y	Y	Y	Y	Y
4 Himes	Y	Y	Y	Y	Y
5 Murphy	Y	Y	Y	Y	Y
DELAWARE					
AL Castle	Y	Y	Y	Y	N
FLORIDA					
1 Miller	Y	Y	Y	Y	N
2 Boyd	Y	Y	Y	Y	Y
3 Brown	Y	Y	Y	Y	Y
4 Crenshaw	Y	Y	Y	Y	N
5 Brown-Waite	Y	Y	Y	Y	N
6 Stearns	Y	Y	Y	Y	N
7 Mica	Y	Y	Y	Y	N
8 Grayson	Y	Y	Y	Y	Y
9 Bilirakis	Y	Y	Y	Y	N
10 Young	Y	Y	Y	Y	N
11 Castor	Y	Y	Y	Y	Y
12 Putnam	Y	Y	Y	Y	N
13 Buchanan	Y	Y	Y	Y	N
14 Mack	Y	Y	Y	Y	N
15 Posey	Y	Y	Y	Y	N
16 Rooney	Y	Y	Y	+	N
17 Meek	Y	Y	Y	Y	Y
18 Ros-Lehtinen	Y	Y	Y	Y	N
19 Deutch	Y	Y	Y	Y	Y
20 Wasserman Schultz	Y	?	Y	Y	Y
21 Diaz-Balart, L.	Y	Y	Y	Y	N
22 Klein	Y	Y	Y	Y	Y
23 Hastings	Y	?	Y	Y	Y
24 Kosmas	Y	Y	Y	Y	Y
25 Diaz-Balart, M.	Y	Y	Y	Y	N
GEORGIA					
1 Kingston	Y	Y	Y	Y	N
2 Bishop	Y	Y	Y	Y	Y
3 Westmoreland	Y	Y	Y	Y	N
4 Johnson	Y	Y	Y	Y	Y
5 Lewis	Y	Y	Y	Y	Y
6 Price	Y	Y	Y	Y	N
7 Linder	Y	Y	Y	Y	N
8 Marshall	Y	Y	Y	Y	Y
9 Graves	Y	Y	Y	Y	N
10 Broun	Y	Y	Y	Y	N
11 Gingrey	Y	Y	Y	Y	N
12 Barrow	Y	Y	Y	Y	Y
13 Scott	Y	Y	Y	Y	Y
HAWAII					
1 Djou	Y	Y	Y	Y	N
2 Hirono	Y	Y	Y	Y	Y
IDAHO					
1 Minnick	Y	Y	Y	Y	N
2 Simpson	Y	Y	Y	Y	N
ILLINOIS					
1 Rush	Y	Y	Y	Y	Y
2 Jackson	Y	Y	Y	Y	Y
3 Lipinski	Y	Y	Y	Y	Y
4 Gutierrez	Y	?	Y	Y	Y
5 Quigley	Y	Y	Y	Y	Y
6 Roskam	Y	Y	Y	Y	N
7 Davis	Y	Y	Y	Y	Y
8 Bean	Y	Y	Y	Y	Y
9 Schakowsky	Y	Y	Y	Y	Y
10 Kirk	Y	Y	Y	Y	N
11 Halvorson	Y	Y	Y	Y	Y
12 Costello	Y	Y	Y	Y	Y
13 Biggert	Y	Y	Y	Y	N
14 Foster	Y	Y	Y	Y	Y
15 Johnson	Y	Y	Y	Y	N

KEY Republicans Democrats

Y Voted for (yea)
\# Paired for
\+ Announced for
N Voted against (nay)

X Paired against
– Announced against
P Voted "present"

C Voted "present" to avoid possible conflict of interest
? Did not vote or otherwise make a position known

	402	403	404	405	406
16 Manzullo	Y	Y	Y	Y	N
17 Hare	Y	Y	Y	Y	Y
18 Schock	Y	Y	Y	Y	N
19 Shimkus	Y	Y	Y	Y	N
INDIANA					
1 Visclosky	Y	Y	Y	Y	Y
2 Donnelly	Y	Y	Y	Y	Y
3 Vacant					
4 **Buyer**	Y	Y	Y	Y	N
5 **Burton**	Y	Y	?	Y	N
6 **Pence**	Y	Y	Y	Y	N
7 Carson	Y	Y	Y	Y	Y
8 Ellsworth	?	?	?	?	Y
9 Hill	Y	Y	Y	Y	Y
IOWA					
1 Braley	Y	?	Y	Y	Y
2 Loebsack	Y	Y	Y	?	Y
3 Boswell	Y	Y	Y	Y	Y
4 **Latham**	Y	Y	Y	Y	N
5 **King**	Y	Y	Y	Y	N
KANSAS					
1 **Moran**	Y	?	?	?	N
2 **Jenkins**	Y	Y	Y	Y	N
3 Moore	Y	Y	Y	Y	Y
4 **Tiahrt**	Y	Y	Y	Y	N
KENTUCKY					
1 **Whitfield**	Y	Y	Y	Y	N
2 **Guthrie**	Y	Y	Y	Y	N
3 Yarmuth	Y	Y	Y	Y	Y
4 **Davis**	Y	Y	Y	Y	N
5 **Rogers**	Y	Y	Y	Y	N
6 Chandler	Y	Y	Y	Y	Y
LOUISIANA					
1 **Scalise**	Y	Y	Y	Y	N
2 **Cao**	Y	Y	Y	Y	N
3 Melancon	Y	Y	Y	Y	N
4 **Fleming**	Y	Y	Y	Y	N
5 **Alexander**	Y	Y	Y	Y	N
6 **Cassidy**	Y	Y	Y	Y	N
7 **Boustany**	Y	Y	Y	Y	N
MAINE					
1 Pingree	Y	Y	Y	Y	Y
2 Michaud	Y	Y	Y	Y	Y
MARYLAND					
1 Kratovil	Y	Y	Y	Y	Y
2 Ruppersberger	Y	Y	Y	Y	Y
3 Sarbanes	Y	Y	Y	Y	Y
4 Edwards	Y	Y	Y	Y	Y
5 Hoyer	Y	Y	Y	Y	Y
6 **Bartlett**	Y	Y	Y	Y	N
7 Cummings	Y	Y	Y	Y	Y
8 Van Hollen	Y	Y	Y	Y	Y
MASSACHUSETTS					
1 Olver	Y	Y	Y	Y	Y
2 Neal	Y	Y	Y	Y	Y
3 McGovern	Y	Y	Y	Y	Y
4 Frank	Y	Y	Y	Y	Y
5 Tsongas	Y	Y	Y	Y	Y
6 Tierney	Y	Y	Y	Y	Y
7 Markey	Y	Y	Y	Y	Y
8 Capuano	Y	Y	Y	Y	Y
9 Lynch	Y	Y	Y	Y	Y
10 Delahunt	Y	Y	Y	Y	Y
MICHIGAN					
1 Stupak	Y	Y	Y	Y	Y
2 **Hoekstra**	?	?	?	?	N
3 **Ehlers**	Y	Y	Y	Y	N
4 **Camp**	Y	Y	Y	Y	N
5 Kildee	Y	Y	Y	Y	Y
6 **Upton**	Y	Y	Y	Y	N
7 Schauer	Y	Y	Y	Y	Y
8 **Rogers**	Y	Y	Y	Y	N
9 Peters	Y	Y	Y	Y	Y
10 **Miller**	Y	Y	Y	Y	N
11 **McCotter**	Y	Y	Y	Y	N
12 Levin	Y	Y	Y	Y	Y
13 Kilpatrick	Y	Y	Y	Y	Y
14 Conyers	Y	Y	Y	Y	Y
15 Dingell	Y	Y	Y	Y	Y
MINNESOTA					
1 Walz	Y	Y	Y	Y	Y
2 **Kline**	Y	Y	Y	Y	N
3 **Paulsen**	Y	Y	Y	Y	N
4 McCollum	Y	Y	Y	Y	Y

	402	403	404	405	406
5 Ellison	Y	Y	Y	Y	Y
6 **Bachmann**	Y	Y	Y	Y	N
7 Peterson	Y	Y	Y	Y	Y
8 Oberstar	Y	Y	Y	?	Y
MISSISSIPPI					
1 Childers	Y	Y	Y	Y	N
2 Thompson	Y	Y	Y	Y	Y
3 **Harper**	Y	Y	Y	Y	N
4 Taylor	?	?	?	?	?
MISSOURI					
1 Clay	?	?	?	?	Y
2 **Akin**	Y	Y	Y	Y	N
3 Carnahan	Y	Y	Y	Y	Y
4 Skelton	Y	Y	Y	Y	Y
5 Cleaver	Y	Y	Y	Y	Y
6 **Graves**	Y	Y	Y	Y	N
7 **Blunt**	Y	Y	Y	Y	N
8 **Emerson**	Y	Y	Y	Y	N
9 **Luetkemeyer**	?	Y	Y	Y	N
MONTANA					
AL **Rehberg**	Y	Y	Y	Y	N
NEBRASKA					
1 **Fortenberry**	Y	Y	Y	Y	N
2 **Terry**	Y	Y	Y	Y	N
3 **Smith**	Y	Y	Y	Y	N
NEVADA					
1 Berkley	Y	Y	Y	Y	Y
2 **Heller**	Y	Y	Y	Y	N
3 Titus	Y	Y	Y	Y	Y
NEW HAMPSHIRE					
1 Shea-Porter	Y	Y	Y	Y	Y
2 Hodes	Y	Y	Y	Y	Y
NEW JERSEY					
1 Andrews	Y	Y	Y	Y	Y
2 **LoBiondo**	Y	Y	Y	Y	N
3 Adler	Y	Y	Y	Y	Y
4 **Smith**	Y	Y	Y	Y	N
5 **Garrett**	Y	Y	Y	Y	N
6 Pallone	Y	Y	Y	Y	Y
7 **Lance**	Y	Y	Y	Y	N
8 Pascrell	Y	Y	Y	Y	Y
9 Rothman	Y	Y	Y	Y	Y
10 Payne	Y	Y	Y	Y	Y
11 **Frelinghuysen**	Y	Y	Y	Y	N
12 Holt	Y	Y	Y	Y	Y
13 Sires	Y	Y	Y	Y	Y
NEW MEXICO					
1 Heinrich	Y	Y	Y	Y	Y
2 Teague	Y	Y	Y	Y	Y
3 Luján	Y	Y	Y	Y	Y
NEW YORK					
1 Bishop	Y	Y	Y	Y	Y
2 Israel	Y	Y	Y	Y	Y
3 **King**	Y	Y	Y	Y	N
4 McCarthy	Y	Y	Y	Y	Y
5 Ackerman	?	?	Y	Y	Y
6 Meeks	Y	Y	Y	Y	Y
7 Crowley	Y	Y	Y	Y	Y
8 Nadler	Y	Y	Y	Y	Y
9 Weiner	Y	Y	Y	Y	Y
10 Towns	Y	Y	Y	Y	Y
11 Clarke	Y	Y	Y	Y	Y
12 Velázquez	Y	Y	Y	Y	Y
13 McMahon	Y	Y	Y	Y	Y
14 Maloney	Y	Y	Y	Y	Y
15 Rangel	Y	?	Y	Y	Y
16 Serrano	Y	Y	Y	Y	Y
17 Engel	Y	Y	Y	Y	Y
18 Lowey	Y	Y	Y	Y	Y
19 Hall	Y	Y	Y	Y	Y
20 Murphy	Y	Y	Y	Y	Y
21 Tonko	Y	Y	Y	Y	Y
22 Hinchey	Y	Y	Y	Y	Y
23 Owens	Y	Y	Y	Y	Y
24 Arcuri	Y	Y	Y	Y	Y
25 Maffei	Y	Y	Y	Y	Y
26 **Lee**	Y	Y	Y	Y	N
27 Higgins	Y	Y	Y	Y	Y
28 Slaughter	Y	Y	Y	Y	Y
29 Vacant					
NORTH CAROLINA					
1 Butterfield	Y	Y	Y	Y	Y
2 Etheridge	Y	Y	Y	Y	Y
3 **Jones**	Y	Y	Y	Y	N
4 Price	Y	Y	Y	Y	Y

	402	403	404	405	406
5 **Foxx**	Y	Y	Y	Y	N
6 **Coble**	Y	Y	Y	Y	N
7 McIntyre	Y	Y	Y	Y	Y
8 Kissell	Y	Y	Y	Y	Y
9 **Myrick**	Y	Y	Y	Y	N
10 **McHenry**	Y	Y	Y	Y	N
11 Shuler	Y	Y	Y	Y	Y
12 Watt	Y	Y	Y	Y	Y
13 Miller	Y	Y	Y	Y	Y
NORTH DAKOTA					
AL Pomeroy	Y	Y	Y	Y	Y
OHIO					
1 Driehaus	Y	Y	Y	Y	Y
2 **Schmidt**	Y	Y	Y	Y	N
3 **Turner**	Y	Y	Y	Y	N
4 **Jordan**	Y	Y	Y	Y	N
5 **Latta**	Y	Y	Y	Y	N
6 **Wilson**	Y	Y	Y	Y	Y
7 **Austria**	Y	Y	Y	Y	N
8 **Boehner**	Y	Y	Y	Y	N
9 Kaptur	Y	Y	Y	Y	Y
10 Kucinich	Y	Y	Y	Y	Y
11 Fudge	Y	?	?	?	Y
12 **Tiberi**	Y	Y	Y	Y	N
13 Sutton	?	Y	Y	Y	Y
14 **LaTourette**	Y	?	Y	Y	N
15 Kilroy	Y	Y	Y	Y	Y
16 Boccieri	Y	Y	Y	Y	Y
17 Ryan	Y	Y	Y	Y	Y
18 Space	Y	Y	Y	Y	Y
OKLAHOMA					
1 **Sullivan**	Y	Y	Y	Y	N
2 Boren	Y	Y	Y	Y	N
3 **Lucas**	Y	Y	Y	Y	N
4 **Cole**	Y	Y	Y	Y	N
5 **Fallin**	Y	Y	Y	Y	N
OREGON					
1 Wu	Y	Y	Y	Y	Y
2 **Walden**	Y	Y	Y	Y	N
3 Blumenauer	Y	Y	Y	Y	Y
4 DeFazio	Y	Y	Y	Y	Y
5 Schrader	Y	Y	Y	Y	Y
PENNSYLVANIA					
1 Brady	Y	Y	Y	Y	Y
2 Fattah	Y	Y	Y	Y	Y
3 Dahlkemper	Y	Y	Y	Y	Y
4 Altmire	Y	Y	Y	Y	Y
5 **Thompson**	Y	Y	Y	Y	N
6 **Gerlach**	Y	Y	Y	Y	Y
7 Sestak	Y	Y	Y	Y	Y
8 Murphy, P.	Y	Y	Y	Y	Y
9 **Shuster**	Y	?	Y	Y	N
10 Carney	Y	Y	Y	Y	Y
11 Kanjorski	Y	Y	Y	Y	Y
12 Critz	Y	Y	Y	Y	Y
13 Schwartz	Y	Y	Y	Y	Y
14 Doyle	Y	Y	Y	Y	Y
15 **Dent**	Y	Y	Y	Y	N
16 **Pitts**	Y	Y	Y	Y	N
17 Holden	Y	Y	Y	Y	Y
18 **Murphy, T.**	Y	Y	Y	Y	N
19 **Platts**	?	?	?	?	N
RHODE ISLAND					
1 Kennedy	Y	Y	Y	Y	Y
2 Langevin	Y	Y	Y	Y	Y
SOUTH CAROLINA					
1 **Brown**	Y	Y	Y	Y	N
2 **Wilson**	Y	Y	Y	Y	N
3 **Barrett**	Y	Y	Y	Y	N
4 **Inglis**	Y	Y	Y	Y	N
5 Spratt	Y	Y	Y	Y	Y
6 Clyburn	Y	Y	Y	Y	Y
SOUTH DAKOTA					
AL Herseth Sandlin	Y	Y	Y	Y	Y
TENNESSEE					
1 **Roe**	Y	Y	Y	Y	N
2 **Duncan**	Y	Y	Y	Y	N
3 **Wamp**	?	?	?	?	?
4 Davis	Y	Y	Y	Y	Y
5 Cooper	Y	Y	Y	Y	Y
6 Gordon	Y	Y	Y	Y	Y
7 **Blackburn**	Y	Y	Y	Y	N
8 Tanner	Y	Y	Y	Y	Y
9 Cohen	Y	Y	Y	Y	Y

	402	403	404	405	406
TEXAS					
1 **Gohmert**	Y	Y	Y	Y	?
2 **Poe**	Y	Y	Y	Y	N
3 **Johnson, S.**	Y	Y	Y	Y	N
4 **Hall**	Y	Y	Y	Y	N
5 **Hensarling**	Y	Y	Y	Y	N
6 **Barton**	Y	Y	Y	Y	N
7 **Culberson**	?	Y	Y	Y	N
8 **Brady**	?	?	?	?	N
9 Green, A.	Y	Y	Y	Y	Y
10 **McCaul**	Y	Y	Y	Y	N
11 **Conaway**	Y	Y	Y	Y	N
12 **Granger**	Y	Y	Y	Y	N
13 **Thornberry**	Y	Y	Y	Y	N
14 **Paul**	Y	Y	Y	Y	N
15 Hinojosa	Y	Y	Y	Y	Y
16 Reyes	Y	Y	Y	Y	Y
17 Edwards	Y	?	Y	Y	Y
18 Jackson Lee	Y	Y	Y	Y	Y
19 **Neugebauer**	Y	Y	Y	Y	N
20 Gonzalez	Y	Y	Y	Y	Y
21 **Smith**	Y	Y	Y	Y	N
22 **Olson**	Y	Y	Y	Y	N
23 Rodriguez	Y	Y	Y	Y	Y
24 **Marchant**	Y	Y	Y	Y	?
25 Doggett	Y	Y	Y	Y	Y
26 **Burgess**	Y	Y	Y	Y	N
27 Ortiz	Y	?	Y	Y	Y
28 Cuellar	Y	Y	Y	Y	N
29 Green, G.	Y	Y	Y	Y	Y
30 Johnson, E.	+	+	+	+	Y
31 **Carter**	Y	Y	Y	Y	N
32 **Sessions**	Y	Y	Y	Y	N
UTAH					
1 **Bishop**	Y	Y	Y	Y	N
2 Matheson	Y	Y	Y	Y	Y
3 **Chaffetz**	Y	Y	Y	Y	N
VERMONT					
AL Welch	Y	Y	Y	Y	Y
VIRGINIA					
1 **Wittman**	Y	Y	Y	Y	N
2 Nye	Y	Y	Y	Y	N
3 Scott	Y	Y	Y	Y	Y
4 **Forbes**	Y	Y	Y	Y	N
5 Perriello	Y	Y	Y	Y	Y
6 **Goodlatte**	Y	Y	Y	Y	N
7 **Cantor**	Y	Y	Y	Y	N
8 Moran	Y	Y	Y	Y	Y
9 Boucher	Y	Y	Y	Y	Y
10 **Wolf**	Y	Y	Y	Y	N
11 Connolly	Y	Y	Y	Y	Y
WASHINGTON					
1 Inslee	Y	Y	Y	Y	Y
2 Larsen	Y	Y	Y	Y	Y
3 Baird	Y	Y	Y	Y	Y
4 **Hastings**	Y	Y	Y	Y	?
5 **McMorris Rodgers**	Y	Y	Y	Y	N
6 Dicks	Y	Y	Y	Y	Y
7 McDermott	Y	Y	Y	Y	Y
8 **Reichert**	Y	Y	Y	Y	Y
9 Smith	Y	Y	Y	Y	Y
WEST VIRGINIA					
1 Mollohan	Y	Y	Y	Y	Y
2 **Capito**	Y	Y	Y	Y	N
3 Rahall	Y	Y	Y	Y	Y
WISCONSIN					
1 **Ryan**	Y	Y	Y	Y	N
2 Baldwin	Y	Y	Y	Y	Y
3 Kind	Y	Y	Y	Y	Y
4 Moore	?	Y	Y	Y	Y
5 **Sensenbrenner**	Y	Y	Y	Y	N
6 **Petri**	Y	Y	Y	Y	N
7 Obey	Y	Y	Y	Y	Y
8 Kagen	Y	Y	Y	Y	Y
WYOMING					
AL **Lummis**	Y	Y	Y	Y	N
DELEGATES					
Faleomavaega (A.S.)					
Norton (D.C.)					
Bordallo (Guam)					
Sablan (N. Marianas)					
Pierluisi (P.R.)					
Christensen (V.I.)					

IN THE HOUSE | By Vote Number

407. **HR 4173, HR 4213. Same-Day Consideration/Rule.** Adoption of the rule (H Res 1487) that would waive the two-thirds majority vote requirement for same-day consideration of rules reported from the Rules Committee through the legislative day of July 3 for the conference report on the financial regulatory overhaul bill (HR 4173) and any measure relating to an extension package (HR 4213). The rule also would allow consideration of measures under suspension of the rules at any time through the legislative day of July 3. Adopted 237-189: D 237-14; R 0-175. June 30, 2010.

408. **HR 4505. 'Gold Star' Parents/Passage.** Filner, D-Calif., motion to suspend the rules and pass the bill that would allow admission to veterans' homes for any "Gold Star" parent — a parent whose son or daughter died while serving in the military. Motion agreed to 420-0: D 249-0; R 171-0. A two-thirds majority of those present and voting (280 in this case) is required for passage under suspension of the rules. June 30, 2010.

409. **H Con Res 293. Adjournment/Adoption.** Adoption of the concurrent resolution that would provide for the adjournment of the House until 2 p.m. Tuesday, July 13, 2010, and the Senate until noon Monday, July 12, 2010. Adopted 222-186: D 213-27; R 9-159. June 30, 2010.

410. **HR 4173. Financial Regulatory Overhaul/Rule.** Adoption of the rule (H Res 1490) to provide for House floor consideration of the conference report on the bill that would overhaul federal regulations for the financial services industry. Adopted 234-189: D 234-14; R 0-175. June 30, 2010.

411. **HR 1554. Oklahoma Land Transfer/Passage.** Boren, D-Okla., motion to suspend the rules and pass the bill that would transfer approximately 18 acres of federal land in McIntosh County, Okla., into trust for the benefit of the Muscogee (Creek) Nation. The measure also would prohibit gambling operations on the land. Motion agreed to 421-1: D 246-1; R 175-0. A two-thirds majority of those present and voting (282 in this case) is required for passage under suspension of the rules. June 30, 2010.

412. **HR 4173. Financial Regulatory Overhaul/Motion to Recommit.** Bachus, R-Ala., motion to recommit the bill and instruct conferees to disagree to language in the conference report that would give the Government Accountability Office (GAO) authority to conduct a one-time audit of the Federal Reserve's emergency lending activities during the financial crisis. It would direct conferees to insist on House language to give the GAO other expanded audit authority over the Federal Reserve, including the ability to monitor some of its most sensitive monetary policy deliberations. It also would instruct conferees to insist on Senate language to expand the exemption for commercial businesses using financial derivatives to hedge their business risks from the margin requirements in the bill. Motion rejected 198-229: D 23-229; R 175-0. June 30, 2010.

	407	408	409	410	411	412
ALABAMA						
1 Bonner	N	Y	N	N	Y	Y
2 Bright	N	Y	N	Y	N	N
3 Rogers	N	Y	N	N	Y	Y
4 Aderholt	N	Y	N	N	Y	Y
5 Griffith	N	Y	N	N	Y	Y
6 Bachus	N	Y	N	N	Y	Y
7 Davis	?	?	Y	Y	Y	N
ALASKA						
AL Young	?	?	?	?	?	?
ARIZONA						
1 Kirkpatrick	N	Y	Y	N	Y	Y
2 Franks	N	Y	N	N	Y	Y
3 Shadegg	N	Y	N	N	Y	Y
4 Pastor	Y	Y	N	Y	Y	N
5 Mitchell	N	Y	N	N	Y	Y
6 Flake	N	Y	N	N	Y	Y
7 Grijalva	Y	Y	Y	Y	Y	N
8 Giffords	N	Y	N	N	Y	Y
ARKANSAS						
1 Berry	Y	Y	Y	Y	Y	N
2 Snyder	Y	Y	Y	Y	Y	N
3 Boozman	N	Y	N	N	Y	Y
4 Ross	Y	Y	Y	N	Y	N
CALIFORNIA						
1 Thompson	Y	Y	Y	Y	Y	N
2 Herger	N	Y	N	N	Y	Y
3 Lungren	N	Y	N	N	Y	Y
4 McClintock	N	Y	N	N	Y	Y
5 Matsui	Y	Y	Y	Y	Y	N
6 Woolsey	?	?	?	?	?	?
7 Miller, George	Y	Y	Y	Y	Y	N
8 Pelosi						
9 Lee	Y	Y	Y	Y	Y	N
10 Garamendi	Y	Y	Y	Y	Y	N
11 McNerney	Y	Y	Y	Y	Y	N
12 Speier	Y	Y	Y	Y	Y	N
13 Stark	Y	Y	Y	Y	Y	N
14 Eshoo	Y	Y	Y	Y	Y	N
15 Honda	Y	Y	Y	Y	Y	N
16 Lofgren	Y	Y	Y	Y	Y	N
17 Farr	Y	Y	?	Y	Y	N
18 Cardoza	Y	Y	Y	Y	Y	N
19 Radanovich	N	?	N	N	Y	Y
20 Costa	Y	Y	Y	Y	Y	N
21 Nunes	N	Y	N	N	Y	Y
22 McCarthy	N	Y	N	N	Y	Y
23 Capps	Y	Y	Y	Y	Y	N
24 Gallegly	N	Y	N	N	Y	Y
25 McKeon	N	Y	N	N	Y	Y
26 Dreier	N	Y	N	N	Y	Y
27 Sherman	Y	Y	Y	Y	Y	N
28 Berman	Y	Y	Y	Y	Y	N
29 Schiff	Y	Y	Y	Y	Y	N
30 Waxman	Y	Y	Y	Y	Y	N
31 Becerra	Y	+	Y	Y	Y	N
32 Chu	Y	Y	Y	Y	Y	N
33 Watson	Y	Y	Y	Y	Y	N
34 Roybal-Allard	Y	Y	Y	Y	Y	N
35 Waters	Y	Y	Y	Y	Y	N
36 Harman	Y	Y	Y	Y	Y	N
37 Richardson	Y	Y	Y	Y	Y	N
38 Napolitano	Y	Y	Y	Y	Y	N
39 Sánchez, Linda	Y	Y	Y	Y	Y	N
40 Royce	N	Y	N	N	Y	Y
41 Lewis	N	Y	?	N	Y	Y
42 Miller, Gary	N	Y	N	N	Y	Y
43 Baca	Y	Y	Y	Y	Y	N
44 Calvert	N	Y	N	N	Y	Y
45 Bono Mack	N	Y	N	N	Y	Y
46 Rohrabacher	N	Y	N	N	Y	Y
47 Sanchez, Loretta	Y	Y	Y	Y	Y	N
48 Campbell	N	Y	N	N	Y	Y
49 Issa	N	Y	N	N	Y	Y
50 Bilbray	N	Y	N	N	Y	Y
51 Filner	Y	Y	Y	Y	Y	N
52 Hunter	N	Y	N	N	Y	Y
53 Davis	Y	Y	Y	Y	Y	N

	407	408	409	410	411	412
COLORADO						
1 DeGette	Y	Y	Y	Y	Y	N
2 Polis	Y	Y	Y	Y	Y	N
3 Salazar	Y	Y	Y	Y	Y	N
4 Markey	Y	Y	N	Y	Y	Y
5 Lamborn	N	Y	N	N	Y	Y
6 Coffman	N	Y	N	N	Y	Y
7 Perlmutter	Y	Y	Y	Y	Y	N
CONNECTICUT						
1 Larson	Y	Y	Y	Y	Y	N
2 Courtney	Y	Y	Y	Y	Y	N
3 DeLauro	Y	Y	?	Y	Y	N
4 Himes	Y	Y	Y	Y	Y	N
5 Murphy	Y	Y	Y	Y	Y	N
DELAWARE						
AL Castle	N	Y	Y	N	Y	Y
FLORIDA						
1 Miller	N	Y	N	N	Y	Y
2 Boyd	Y	Y	?	Y	Y	N
3 Brown	Y	Y	?	Y	Y	N
4 Crenshaw	N	Y	N	N	Y	Y
5 Brown-Waite	N	Y	N	N	Y	Y
6 Stearns	N	Y	N	N	Y	Y
7 Mica	N	Y	N	N	Y	Y
8 Grayson	Y	Y	Y	Y	Y	Y
9 Bilirakis	N	Y	N	N	Y	Y
10 Young	N	Y	N	N	Y	Y
11 Castor	Y	Y	Y	Y	Y	N
12 Putnam	N	Y	N	N	Y	Y
13 Buchanan	N	Y	N	N	Y	Y
14 Mack	N	Y	N	N	Y	Y
15 Posey	N	Y	Y	N	Y	Y
16 Rooney	N	Y	N	N	Y	Y
17 Meek	Y	Y	Y	Y	Y	N
18 Ros-Lehtinen	N	Y	N	N	Y	Y
19 Deutch	Y	Y	Y	Y	Y	N
20 Wasserman Schultz	Y	Y	Y	Y	Y	N
21 Diaz-Balart, L.	N	Y	N	N	Y	Y
22 Klein	Y	Y	Y	Y	Y	N
23 Hastings	Y	Y	Y	Y	Y	N
24 Kosmas	Y	Y	Y	Y	Y	N
25 Diaz-Balart, M.	N	Y	N	N	Y	Y
GEORGIA						
1 Kingston	N	Y	?	N	Y	Y
2 Bishop	Y	Y	?	Y	Y	N
3 Westmoreland	N	Y	N	N	Y	Y
4 Johnson	Y	Y	Y	Y	Y	N
5 Lewis	Y	Y	Y	Y	Y	N
6 Price	N	Y	N	N	Y	Y
7 Linder	N	?	N	N	Y	Y
8 Marshall	Y	Y	Y	Y	Y	N
9 Graves	N	Y	N	N	Y	Y
10 Broun	N	Y	N	N	Y	Y
11 Gingrey	N	Y	N	N	Y	Y
12 Barrow	Y	Y	Y	Y	Y	N
13 Scott	Y	Y	Y	Y	Y	N
HAWAII						
1 Djou	N	Y	N	N	Y	Y
2 Hirono	Y	Y	Y	Y	Y	N
IDAHO						
1 Minnick	N	Y	N	N	Y	Y
2 Simpson	N	Y	N	N	Y	Y
ILLINOIS						
1 Rush	Y	Y	Y	Y	?	N
2 Jackson	Y	Y	Y	Y	Y	N
3 Lipinski	N	Y	Y	Y	Y	Y
4 Gutierrez	Y	Y	Y	Y	Y	N
5 Quigley	Y	Y	Y	Y	Y	N
6 Roskam	N	Y	N	N	Y	Y
7 Davis	Y	Y	Y	Y	Y	N
8 Bean	Y	Y	Y	Y	Y	N
9 Schakowsky	Y	Y	Y	Y	Y	N
10 Kirk	N	Y	N	N	Y	Y
11 Halvorson	Y	Y	Y	Y	Y	N
12 Costello	Y	Y	Y	Y	Y	N
13 Biggert	N	Y	N	N	Y	Y
14 Foster	Y	Y	Y	Y	Y	N
15 Johnson	N	Y	Y	N	Y	Y

	407	408	409	410	411	412
16 **Manzullo**	N	Y	N	N	Y	Y
17 Hare	Y	Y	Y	Y	Y	N
18 **Schock**	N	Y	N	N	Y	Y
19 **Shimkus**	N	Y	N	N	Y	Y
INDIANA						
1 Visclosky	Y	Y	Y	Y	Y	N
2 Donnelly	Y	Y	N	Y	Y	N
3 Vacant						
4 **Buyer**	N	Y	N	N	Y	Y
5 **Burton**	N	Y	?	N	Y	Y
6 **Pence**	N	Y	N	N	Y	Y
7 Carson	Y	Y	Y	Y	Y	N
8 Ellsworth	N	Y	N	Y	Y	N
9 Hill	Y	Y	Y	N	Y	N
IOWA						
1 Braley	Y	Y	Y	Y	Y	N
2 Loebsack	Y	Y	Y	Y	Y	N
3 Boswell	Y	Y	Y	Y	Y	N
4 **Latham**	N	Y	?	N	Y	Y
5 **King**	N	Y	N	N	Y	Y
KANSAS						
1 **Moran**	N	Y	N	N	Y	Y
2 **Jenkins**	N	Y	N	N	Y	Y
3 Moore	Y	Y	Y	Y	Y	N
4 **Tiahrt**	N	Y	N	N	Y	Y
KENTUCKY						
1 **Whitfield**	N	Y	N	N	Y	Y
2 **Guthrie**	N	Y	N	N	Y	Y
3 Yarmuth	Y	Y	Y	Y	Y	N
4 **Davis**	N	Y	N	N	Y	Y
5 **Rogers**	N	Y	N	N	Y	Y
6 Chandler	Y	Y	Y	N	Y	N
LOUISIANA						
1 **Scalise**	N	Y	N	N	Y	Y
2 **Cao**	N	Y	N	N	Y	Y
3 Melancon	Y	Y	Y	Y	Y	N
4 **Fleming**	N	Y	N	N	Y	Y
5 **Alexander**	N	Y	?	N	Y	Y
6 **Cassidy**	N	Y	N	N	Y	Y
7 **Boustany**	N	Y	N	N	Y	Y
MAINE						
1 Pingree	Y	Y	Y	Y	?	N
2 Michaud	Y	Y	N	Y	Y	N
MARYLAND						
1 Kratovil	N	Y	N	N	Y	Y
2 Ruppersberger	Y	Y	Y	Y	Y	N
3 Sarbanes	Y	Y	Y	Y	Y	N
4 Edwards	Y	Y	Y	Y	Y	N
5 Hoyer	Y	Y	Y	Y	Y	N
6 **Bartlett**	N	Y	N	N	Y	Y
7 Cummings	Y	Y	Y	Y	Y	N
8 Van Hollen	Y	Y	Y	Y	Y	N
MASSACHUSETTS						
1 Olver	Y	Y	Y	Y	Y	N
2 Neal	Y	Y	Y	Y	Y	N
3 McGovern	Y	Y	Y	Y	Y	N
4 Frank	Y	Y	Y	Y	Y	N
5 Tsongas	Y	Y	Y	Y	Y	N
6 Tierney	Y	Y	Y	Y	Y	N
7 Markey	Y	Y	Y	Y	Y	N
8 Capuano	Y	Y	Y	Y	Y	N
9 Lynch	Y	Y	Y	Y	Y	N
10 Delahunt	Y	Y	Y	?	Y	N
MICHIGAN						
1 Stupak	Y	Y	Y	Y	Y	N
2 **Hoekstra**	N	Y	N	N	Y	Y
3 **Ehlers**	N	Y	N	N	Y	Y
4 **Camp**	N	Y	N	N	Y	Y
5 Kildee	Y	Y	Y	Y	Y	N
6 **Upton**	N	Y	N	N	Y	Y
7 Schauer	Y	Y	Y	Y	Y	N
8 **Rogers**	N	Y	N	N	Y	Y
9 Peters	Y	Y	N	Y	Y	N
10 **Miller**	N	Y	N	N	Y	Y
11 **McCotter**	N	Y	N	N	Y	Y
12 Levin	Y	Y	Y	Y	Y	N
13 Kilpatrick	Y	Y	Y	Y	Y	N
14 Conyers	Y	Y	Y	Y	Y	N
15 Dingell	Y	Y	Y	Y	Y	N
MINNESOTA						
1 Walz	Y	Y	Y	Y	Y	N
2 **Kline**	N	Y	N	N	Y	Y
3 **Paulsen**	N	Y	N	N	Y	Y
4 McCollum	Y	Y	Y	Y	Y	N

	407	408	409	410	411	412
5 Ellison	Y	Y	Y	Y	Y	N
6 **Bachmann**	N	Y	N	N	Y	Y
7 Peterson	Y	Y	Y	Y	Y	N
8 Oberstar	Y	Y	Y	Y	Y	N
MISSISSIPPI						
1 Childers	Y	Y	Y	N	Y	Y
2 Thompson	Y	Y	Y	Y	Y	N
3 **Harper**	N	Y	N	N	Y	Y
4 Taylor	?	?	?	?	?	?
MISSOURI						
1 Clay	Y	Y	Y	Y	Y	N
2 **Akin**	N	Y	N	N	Y	Y
3 Carnahan	Y	Y	Y	Y	Y	N
4 Skelton	Y	Y	Y	Y	Y	Y
5 Cleaver	Y	Y	Y	Y	Y	N
6 **Graves**	N	Y	N	N	Y	Y
7 **Blunt**	N	Y	N	N	Y	Y
8 **Emerson**	N	Y	?	N	Y	Y
9 **Luetkemeyer**	N	Y	N	N	Y	Y
MONTANA						
AL **Rehberg**	N	Y	N	N	Y	Y
NEBRASKA						
1 **Fortenberry**	N	Y	N	N	Y	Y
2 **Terry**	N	Y	N	N	Y	Y
3 **Smith**	N	Y	N	N	Y	Y
NEVADA						
1 Berkley	Y	Y	Y	Y	Y	N
2 **Heller**	N	Y	N	N	Y	Y
3 Titus	N	Y	Y	Y	Y	Y
NEW HAMPSHIRE						
1 Shea-Porter	Y	Y	Y	Y	Y	N
2 Hodes	Y	Y	Y	Y	Y	Y
NEW JERSEY						
1 Andrews	Y	Y	Y	Y	Y	N
2 **LoBiondo**	N	Y	N	N	Y	Y
3 Adler	Y	Y	N	Y	Y	N
4 **Smith**	N	Y	N	N	Y	Y
5 **Garrett**	N	Y	N	N	Y	Y
6 Pallone	Y	Y	Y	Y	Y	N
7 **Lance**	N	Y	N	N	Y	Y
8 Pascrell	Y	Y	Y	Y	Y	N
9 Rothman	Y	Y	?	?	?	N
10 Payne	Y	Y	Y	Y	Y	N
11 **Frelinghuysen**	N	Y	N	N	Y	Y
12 Holt	Y	Y	Y	Y	Y	N
13 Sires	Y	Y	N	Y	Y	N
NEW MEXICO						
1 Heinrich	Y	Y	Y	Y	Y	N
2 Teague	Y	Y	N	Y	Y	Y
3 Luján	Y	Y	Y	Y	Y	N
NEW YORK						
1 Bishop	Y	Y	N	Y	Y	N
2 Israel	Y	Y	Y	Y	Y	N
3 **King**	N	Y	N	N	Y	Y
4 McCarthy	Y	Y	Y	Y	Y	N
5 Ackerman	Y	Y	Y	Y	Y	N
6 Meeks	Y	Y	Y	Y	Y	N
7 Crowley	Y	Y	Y	Y	Y	N
8 Nadler	Y	Y	Y	Y	Y	N
9 Weiner	Y	Y	Y	Y	Y	N
10 Towns	Y	Y	Y	Y	Y	N
11 Clarke	Y	Y	Y	Y	Y	N
12 Velázquez	Y	Y	Y	Y	Y	N
13 McMahon	Y	Y	N	Y	Y	N
14 Maloney	Y	Y	Y	Y	Y	N
15 Rangel	Y	Y	Y	Y	Y	N
16 Serrano	Y	Y	Y	Y	Y	N
17 Engel	Y	Y	Y	Y	Y	N
18 Lowey	Y	Y	Y	Y	Y	N
19 Hall	Y	Y	Y	Y	Y	N
20 Murphy	Y	?	N	Y	Y	N
21 Tonko	Y	Y	Y	Y	Y	N
22 Hinchey	Y	Y	?	Y	Y	N
23 Owens	Y	Y	Y	Y	Y	N
24 Arcuri	Y	Y	N	Y	Y	N
25 Maffei	Y	Y	N	Y	Y	N
26 **Lee**	N	Y	N	N	Y	Y
27 Higgins	Y	Y	?	?	?	N
28 Slaughter	Y	Y	Y	Y	Y	N
29 Vacant						
NORTH CAROLINA						
1 Butterfield	Y	Y	Y	Y	Y	N
2 Etheridge	Y	Y	Y	Y	Y	N
3 **Jones**	N	Y	Y	N	Y	Y
4 Price	Y	Y	Y	Y	Y	N

	407	408	409	410	411	412
5 **Foxx**	N	Y	N	N	Y	Y
6 **Coble**	N	Y	N	N	Y	Y
7 McIntyre	Y	Y	Y	Y	Y	Y
8 Kissell	Y	Y	Y	Y	Y	N
9 **Myrick**	N	Y	N	N	Y	Y
10 **McHenry**	N	Y	N	N	Y	Y
11 Shuler	N	Y	N	N	Y	N
12 Watt	Y	Y	Y	Y	Y	N
13 Miller	Y	Y	Y	Y	Y	N
NORTH DAKOTA						
AL Pomeroy	Y	Y	Y	Y	Y	N
OHIO						
1 Driehaus	Y	Y	Y	Y	Y	N
2 **Schmidt**	N	Y	N	N	Y	Y
3 **Turner**	N	Y	N	N	Y	Y
4 **Jordan**	N	Y	N	N	Y	Y
5 **Latta**	N	Y	N	N	Y	Y
6 Wilson	Y	Y	Y	Y	Y	N
7 **Austria**	N	Y	N	N	Y	Y
8 **Boehner**	N	Y	N	N	Y	Y
9 Kaptur	N	Y	?	N	Y	N
10 Kucinich	Y	Y	Y	Y	Y	N
11 Fudge	Y	Y	Y	Y	Y	N
12 **Tiberi**	N	Y	N	N	Y	Y
13 Sutton	Y	Y	Y	Y	Y	N
14 **LaTourette**	N	Y	N	N	Y	Y
15 Kilroy	Y	Y	Y	Y	Y	N
16 Boccieri	Y	Y	N	Y	Y	N
17 Ryan	Y	Y	Y	Y	Y	N
18 Space	Y	Y	Y	Y	Y	Y
OKLAHOMA						
1 **Sullivan**	N	Y	N	N	Y	Y
2 Boren	N	Y	Y	N	Y	N
3 **Lucas**	N	Y	N	N	Y	Y
4 **Cole**	N	Y	N	N	Y	Y
5 **Fallin**	N	Y	N	N	Y	Y
OREGON						
1 Wu	Y	Y	Y	Y	Y	N
2 **Walden**	N	Y	N	N	Y	Y
3 Blumenauer	Y	Y	Y	Y	Y	N
4 DeFazio	Y	Y	Y	Y	Y	N
5 Schrader	Y	Y	Y	Y	Y	N
PENNSYLVANIA						
1 Brady	Y	Y	Y	Y	Y	N
2 Fattah	Y	Y	Y	Y	Y	N
3 Dahlkemper	Y	Y	Y	Y	Y	N
4 Altmire	Y	Y	Y	Y	Y	N
5 **Thompson**	N	Y	N	N	Y	Y
6 **Gerlach**	N	Y	Y	N	Y	Y
7 Sestak	Y	Y	N	Y	Y	N
8 Murphy, P.	Y	Y	Y	Y	Y	N
9 **Shuster**	N	Y	N	N	Y	Y
10 Carney	Y	Y	N	Y	Y	Y
11 Kanjorski	Y	Y	Y	Y	Y	N
12 Critz	Y	Y	Y	N	Y	Y
13 Schwartz	Y	Y	Y	Y	Y	N
14 Doyle	Y	Y	Y	Y	Y	N
15 **Dent**	N	Y	N	N	Y	Y
16 **Pitts**	N	Y	N	N	Y	Y
17 Holden	Y	Y	Y	Y	Y	N
18 **Murphy, T.**	N	Y	N	N	Y	Y
19 **Platts**	N	Y	N	N	Y	Y
RHODE ISLAND						
1 Kennedy	Y	Y	Y	Y	Y	N
2 Langevin	Y	Y	Y	Y	Y	N
SOUTH CAROLINA						
1 **Brown**	N	Y	N	N	Y	Y
2 **Wilson**	N	Y	N	N	Y	Y
3 **Barrett**	N	?	N	N	Y	Y
4 **Inglis**	N	Y	N	N	Y	Y
5 Spratt	Y	Y	Y	Y	Y	N
6 Clyburn	Y	Y	Y	Y	Y	N
SOUTH DAKOTA						
AL Herseth Sandlin	N	Y	N	Y	Y	N
TENNESSEE						
1 **Roe**	N	Y	N	N	Y	Y
2 **Duncan**	N	Y	N	N	Y	Y
3 **Wamp**	?	?	?	?	?	?
4 Davis	Y	Y	?	Y	Y	N
5 Cooper	Y	Y	Y	Y	Y	N
6 Gordon	Y	Y	Y	Y	Y	N
7 **Blackburn**	N	Y	N	N	Y	Y
8 Tanner	Y	Y	Y	Y	Y	N
9 Cohen	Y	Y	Y	Y	Y	N

	407	408	409	410	411	412
TEXAS						
1 **Gohmert**	?	?	?	?	?	Y
2 **Poe**	N	Y	N	N	Y	Y
3 **Johnson, S.**	N	Y	N	N	Y	Y
4 **Hall**	N	Y	N	N	Y	Y
5 **Hensarling**	N	Y	N	N	Y	Y
6 **Barton**	N	Y	N	N	Y	Y
7 **Culberson**	N	Y	N	N	Y	Y
8 **Brady**	N	Y	N	N	Y	Y
9 Green, A.	Y	Y	Y	Y	Y	N
10 **McCaul**	N	Y	N	N	Y	Y
11 **Conaway**	N	Y	N	N	Y	Y
12 **Granger**	N	Y	N	N	Y	Y
13 **Thornberry**	N	Y	N	N	Y	Y
14 **Paul**	N	Y	N	N	Y	Y
15 Hinojosa	Y	Y	Y	Y	Y	N
16 Reyes	Y	Y	Y	Y	Y	N
17 Edwards	Y	Y	?	Y	Y	Y
18 Jackson Lee	Y	Y	Y	Y	Y	N
19 **Neugebauer**	N	Y	N	N	Y	Y
20 Gonzalez	Y	Y	Y	Y	Y	N
21 **Smith**	N	Y	N	N	Y	Y
22 **Olson**	N	Y	Y	N	Y	Y
23 Rodriguez	Y	Y	Y	Y	Y	N
24 **Marchant**	N	Y	N	N	Y	Y
25 Doggett	Y	Y	Y	Y	Y	N
26 **Burgess**	N	Y	N	N	Y	Y
27 Ortiz	Y	Y	Y	Y	Y	N
28 Cuellar	Y	Y	Y	Y	Y	N
29 Green, G.	Y	Y	Y	Y	+	N
30 Johnson, E.	Y	Y	Y	Y	Y	N
31 **Carter**	N	Y	N	N	Y	Y
32 **Sessions**	N	Y	N	N	Y	Y
UTAH						
1 **Bishop**	N	Y	?	N	Y	+
2 Matheson	Y	Y	Y	Y	Y	N
3 **Chaffetz**	N	Y	Y	N	Y	Y
VERMONT						
AL Welch	Y	Y	Y	Y	Y	N
VIRGINIA						
1 **Wittman**	N	Y	N	N	Y	Y
2 Nye	Y	Y	N	N	Y	Y
3 Scott	Y	Y	Y	Y	Y	N
4 **Forbes**	N	Y	N	N	Y	Y
5 Perriello	Y	Y	N	Y	Y	Y
6 **Goodlatte**	N	Y	N	N	Y	Y
7 **Cantor**	N	?	N	N	Y	Y
8 Moran	Y	Y	Y	Y	Y	N
9 Boucher	Y	Y	Y	Y	Y	Y
10 **Wolf**	N	Y	N	N	Y	Y
11 Connolly	Y	Y	N	Y	Y	N
WASHINGTON						
1 Inslee	Y	Y	Y	?	Y	N
2 Larsen	Y	Y	Y	Y	Y	N
3 Baird	Y	Y	Y	Y	Y	N
4 **Hastings**	N	Y	N	N	Y	Y
5 **McMorris Rodgers**	N	Y	N	N	Y	Y
6 Dicks	Y	Y	Y	Y	Y	N
7 McDermott	Y	Y	Y	Y	Y	N
8 **Reichert**	N	Y	N	N	Y	Y
9 Smith	Y	Y	Y	Y	Y	N
WEST VIRGINIA						
1 Mollohan	Y	Y	Y	Y	Y	N
2 **Capito**	N	Y	N	N	Y	Y
3 Rahall	Y	Y	Y	Y	Y	N
WISCONSIN						
1 **Ryan**	N	Y	N	N	Y	Y
2 Baldwin	Y	Y	Y	Y	Y	N
3 Kind	Y	Y	Y	Y	Y	N
4 Moore	Y	Y	Y	Y	Y	N
5 **Sensenbrenner**	N	Y	N	N	Y	Y
6 **Petri**	N	Y	N	N	Y	Y
7 Obey	Y	Y	?	Y	Y	N
8 Kagen	Y	Y	Y	Y	Y	N
WYOMING						
AL **Lummis**	N	Y	Y	N	Y	Y
DELEGATES						
Faleomavaega (A.S.)						
Norton (D.C.)						
Bordallo (Guam)						
Sablan (N. Marianas)						
Pierluisi (P.R.)						
Christensen (V.I.)						

IN THE HOUSE | By Vote Number

413. **HR 4173. Financial Regulatory Overhaul/Conference Report.**
Adoption of the conference report on the bill that would overhaul the regulation of the financial services industry. The measure would create a new regulatory mechanism to assess risks posed by very large financial institutions and facilitate the orderly dissolution of failing businesses that pose a threat to the economy. It would create a new federal agency to oversee consumer financial products, bring the derivatives market under significant federal regulation for the first time and give company shareholders and regulators greater say on executive pay packages. The costs would be offset by terminating the Troubled Asset Relief Program and increasing deposit insurance premiums paid by some banks. Adopted (thus sent to the Senate) 237-192: D 234-19; R 3-173. A "yea" was a vote in support of the president's position. June 30, 2010.

414. **HR 4445. Indian Pueblo Land Trust/Passage.** Heinrich, D-N.M., motion to suspend the rules and pass the bill that would provide the same legal status for the Indian Pueblo Cultural Center in New Mexico as for other land taken into trust for the American Indian pueblos in New Mexico. The measure would prohibit gambling operations on the Pueblo Cultural Center land. Motion agreed to 411-0: D 242-0; R 169-0. A two-thirds majority of those present and voting (274 in this case) is required for passage under suspension of the rules. June 30, 2010.

415. **H Res 1228. Helicopter Attack Light Squadron Three/ Adoption.** Filner, D-Calif., motion to suspend the rules and adopt the resolution that would honor the veterans of Helicopter Attack Light Squadron Three, express condolences to the families and comrades of those killed in action, and recognize the squadron as unique in naval aviation history. Motion agreed to 410-0: D 238-0; R 172-0. A two-thirds majority of those present and voting (274 in this case) is required for adoption under suspension of the rules. July 1, 2010.

416. **HR 2340. Salmon Lake Land Transfer/Passage.** Heinrich, D-N.M., motion to suspend the rules and pass the bill that would ratify a land transfer agreement among the Bering Straits Native Corporation, the state of Alaska and the Bureau of Land Management. Motion agreed to 410-0: D 237-0; R 173-0. A two-thirds majority of those present and voting (274 in this case) is required for passage under suspension of the rules. July 1, 2010.

417. **H Res 1460. National Pollinator Week/Adoption.** Cardoza, D-Calif., motion to suspend the rules and adopt the resolution that would support the goals and ideals of National Pollinator Week and recognize the role of pollinators in agriculture and in maintaining a diverse ecosystem. Motion agreed to 412-0: D 241-0; R 171-0. A two-thirds majority of those present and voting (275 in this case) is required for adoption under suspension of the rules. July 1, 2010.

418. **HR 5618. Unemployment Benefits Extension/Rule.** Adoption of the rule (H Res 1495) to provide for House floor consideration of the bill that would extend expired unemployment benefits through Nov. 30, 2010. The rule would also waive through the legislative day of July 3, 2010, the two-thirds majority requirement to consider a rule on the same day the Rules Committee reports it. Adopted 231-189: D 231-14; R 0-175. July 1, 2010.

	413	414	415	416	417	418
ALABAMA						
1 **Bonner**	N	Y	Y	Y	Y	N
2 **Bright**	N	Y	Y	Y	Y	N
3 **Rogers**	N	Y	Y	Y	Y	N
4 **Aderholt**	N	Y	Y	Y	Y	N
5 **Griffith**	N	Y	Y	Y	Y	N
6 **Bachus**	N	Y	Y	Y	Y	N
7 Davis	Y	Y	Y	Y	Y	Y
ALASKA						
AL **Young**	?	?	?	?	?	?
ARIZONA						
1 Kirkpatrick	N	Y	Y	Y	Y	N
2 **Franks**	N	Y	Y	Y	Y	N
3 **Shadegg**	N	Y	Y	Y	Y	N
4 Pastor	Y	Y	Y	Y	Y	Y
5 Mitchell	N	Y	Y	Y	Y	N
6 **Flake**	N	Y	?	?	?	N
7 Grijalva	Y	Y	Y	Y	Y	Y
8 Giffords	Y	Y	Y	Y	Y	N
ARKANSAS						
1 Berry	N	Y	Y	Y	Y	Y
2 Snyder	Y	Y	Y	Y	Y	Y
3 **Boozman**	N	Y	Y	Y	Y	N
4 Ross	N	Y	Y	Y	Y	
CALIFORNIA						
1 Thompson	Y	Y	Y	+	Y	Y
2 **Herger**	N	Y	Y	Y	?	N
3 **Lungren**	N	Y	Y	Y	Y	N
4 **McClintock**	N	Y	Y	Y	Y	N
5 Matsui	Y	Y	Y	Y	Y	Y
6 Woolsey	?	?	?	?	?	?
7 Miller, George	Y	Y	Y	Y	Y	Y
8 Pelosi	Y					
9 Lee	Y	Y	Y	Y	Y	Y
10 Garamendi	Y	?	Y	Y	Y	Y
11 McNerney	Y	Y	Y	Y	Y	Y
12 Speier	Y	Y	?	Y	Y	Y
13 Stark	Y	Y	Y	Y	Y	Y
14 Eshoo	Y	Y	Y	Y	Y	Y
15 Honda	Y	Y	Y	Y	Y	Y
16 Lofgren	Y	Y	Y	Y	Y	Y
17 Farr	Y	Y	Y	Y	Y	Y
18 Cardoza	Y	Y	Y	Y	Y	Y
19 **Radanovich**	N	Y	Y	Y	?	N
20 Costa	Y	Y	Y	Y	Y	Y
21 **Nunes**	N	Y	Y	Y	Y	N
22 **McCarthy**	N	?	Y	Y	Y	N
23 Capps	Y	Y	Y	Y	Y	Y
24 **Gallegly**	N	Y	Y	Y	Y	N
25 **McKeon**	N	Y	Y	Y	Y	N
26 **Dreier**	N	Y	Y	Y	Y	N
27 Sherman	Y	Y	Y	Y	Y	Y
28 Berman	Y	Y	Y	Y	Y	Y
29 Schiff	Y	Y	Y	Y	Y	Y
30 Waxman	Y	Y	Y	Y	Y	Y
31 Becerra	Y	Y	Y	Y	Y	Y
32 Chu	Y	Y	Y	Y	Y	Y
33 Watson	Y	Y	Y	Y	Y	Y
34 Roybal-Allard	Y	Y	Y	Y	Y	Y
35 Waters	Y	?	Y	Y	Y	Y
36 Harman	Y	Y	Y	Y	Y	Y
37 Richardson	Y	Y	Y	Y	?	Y
38 Napolitano	Y	Y	Y	?	Y	Y
39 Sánchez, Linda	Y	Y	Y	Y	Y	Y
40 **Royce**	N	?	Y	Y	Y	N
41 **Lewis**	N	Y	Y	Y	Y	N
42 **Miller, Gary**	N	Y	Y	Y	Y	N
43 Baca	Y	Y	Y	Y	Y	Y
44 **Calvert**	N	Y	Y	Y	Y	N
45 **Bono Mack**	N	Y	Y	Y	Y	N
46 **Rohrabacher**	N	Y	Y	Y	Y	N
47 Sanchez, Loretta	Y	Y	?	?	?	Y
48 **Campbell**	N	Y	Y	Y	Y	N
49 **Issa**	N	Y	Y	Y	Y	N
50 **Bilbray**	N	Y	Y	Y	Y	N
51 Filner	Y	Y	Y	Y	Y	Y
52 **Hunter**	N	Y	Y	Y	Y	N
53 Davis	Y	Y	Y	Y	Y	Y

	413	414	415	416	417	418
COLORADO						
1 DeGette	Y	Y	Y	Y	Y	Y
2 Polis	Y	Y	Y	Y	Y	Y
3 Salazar	Y	Y	Y	Y	Y	Y
4 Markey	Y	Y	Y	Y	Y	N
5 **Lamborn**	N	Y	Y	Y	Y	N
6 **Coffman**	N	Y	Y	Y	Y	N
7 Perlmutter	Y	Y	Y	Y	Y	Y
CONNECTICUT						
1 Larson	Y	Y	Y	Y	Y	Y
2 Courtney	Y	Y	Y	Y	Y	Y
3 DeLauro	Y	Y	Y	Y	Y	Y
4 Himes	Y	Y	Y	Y	Y	Y
5 Murphy	Y	Y	Y	Y	Y	Y
DELAWARE						
AL **Castle**	Y	Y	Y	Y	Y	N
FLORIDA						
1 **Miller**	N	Y	Y	Y	Y	N
2 Boyd	Y	Y	Y	Y	Y	Y
3 Brown	Y	Y	Y	Y	Y	Y
4 **Crenshaw**	N	Y	Y	Y	Y	N
5 **Brown-Waite**	N	Y	Y	Y	Y	N
6 **Stearns**	N	Y	Y	Y	Y	N
7 **Mica**	N	Y	Y	Y	Y	N
8 Grayson	Y	Y	Y	Y	Y	Y
9 **Bilirakis**	N	Y	Y	Y	Y	N
10 **Young**	N	Y	Y	Y	Y	N
11 Castor	Y	Y	Y	Y	Y	Y
12 **Putnam**	N	Y	Y	Y	Y	N
13 **Buchanan**	N	Y	Y	Y	Y	N
14 **Mack**	N	Y	Y	Y	Y	N
15 **Posey**	N	Y	Y	Y	Y	N
16 **Rooney**	N	Y	Y	Y	Y	N
17 Meek	Y	Y	Y	Y	Y	Y
18 **Ros-Lehtinen**	N	Y	Y	Y	Y	N
19 Deutch	Y	Y	Y	Y	Y	Y
20 Wasserman Schultz	Y	Y	Y	Y	Y	Y
21 **Diaz-Balart, L.**	N	?	Y	Y	Y	N
22 Klein	Y	Y	Y	?	Y	Y
23 Hastings	Y	Y	Y	Y	Y	Y
24 Kosmas	Y	Y	Y	Y	Y	Y
25 **Diaz-Balart, M.**	N	?	Y	Y	Y	N
GEORGIA						
1 **Kingston**	N	Y	Y	Y	Y	N
2 Bishop	Y	Y	Y	Y	Y	Y
3 **Westmoreland**	N	Y	Y	Y	Y	N
4 Johnson	Y	Y	Y	Y	Y	Y
5 Lewis	Y	Y	?	?	Y	Y
6 **Price**	N	Y	Y	Y	Y	N
7 **Linder**	N	Y	Y	Y	Y	N
8 Marshall	Y	Y	Y	Y	Y	Y
9 **Graves**	N	Y	Y	Y	Y	N
10 **Broun**	N	Y	Y	Y	Y	N
11 **Gingrey**	N	Y	Y	Y	Y	N
12 Barrow	Y	Y	Y	Y	Y	Y
13 Scott	Y	Y	Y	Y	Y	Y
HAWAII						
1 **Djou**	N	Y	Y	Y	Y	N
2 Hirono	Y	Y	Y	Y	Y	N
IDAHO						
1 Minnick	Y	Y	Y	Y	Y	N
2 **Simpson**	N	Y	Y	Y	Y	N
ILLINOIS						
1 Rush	Y	?	?	Y	Y	Y
2 Jackson	Y	Y	?	Y	Y	Y
3 Lipinski	Y	Y	Y	Y	Y	Y
4 Gutierrez	Y	Y	+	+	+	Y
5 Quigley	Y	?	Y	Y	Y	Y
6 **Roskam**	N	Y	Y	Y	Y	N
7 Davis	Y	Y	Y	Y	Y	Y
8 Bean	Y	Y	Y	Y	Y	Y
9 Schakowsky	Y	Y	Y	Y	Y	Y
10 **Kirk**	N	?	Y	Y	Y	N
11 Halvorson	Y	Y	Y	Y	Y	Y
12 Costello	Y	Y	Y	Y	Y	Y
13 **Biggert**	N	Y	Y	Y	Y	N
14 Foster	Y	Y	Y	Y	Y	Y
15 **Johnson**	N	Y	Y	Y	Y	N

KEY **Republicans** Democrats

Y Voted for (yea) X Paired against C Voted "present" to avoid possible conflict of interest
\# Paired for − Announced against
\+ Announced for P Voted "present" ? Did not vote or otherwise make a position known
N Voted against (nay)

	413	414	415	416	417	418
16 **Manzullo**	N	Y	Y	Y	Y	N
17 Hare	Y	Y	Y	Y	Y	Y
18 **Schock**	N	Y	Y	Y	Y	N
19 **Shimkus**	N	Y	Y	Y	Y	N
INDIANA						
1 Visclosky	Y	Y	Y	Y	Y	Y
2 Donnelly	Y	Y	Y	Y	Y	Y
3 Vacant						
4 **Buyer**	N	Y	Y	Y	Y	N
5 **Burton**	N	Y	Y	Y	Y	N
6 **Pence**	N	Y	Y	Y	Y	N
7 Carson	Y	Y	Y	Y	Y	Y
8 Ellsworth	Y	Y	Y	Y	Y	N
9 Hill	Y	Y	Y	Y	Y	N
IOWA						
1 Braley	Y	Y	Y	Y	Y	Y
2 Loebsack	Y	Y	Y	Y	Y	Y
3 Boswell	Y	Y	Y	Y	Y	Y
4 **Latham**	N	Y	Y	Y	Y	N
5 **King**	N	Y	Y	Y	Y	N
KANSAS						
1 **Moran**	N	Y	Y	Y	Y	N
2 **Jenkins**	N	Y	Y	Y	Y	N
3 Moore	Y	Y	Y	Y	Y	Y
4 **Tiahrt**	N	Y	Y	Y	Y	N
KENTUCKY						
1 **Whitfield**	N	Y	Y	Y	Y	N
2 **Guthrie**	N	Y	Y	Y	Y	N
3 Yarmuth	Y	Y	Y	Y	Y	Y
4 **Davis**	N	Y	Y	Y	Y	N
5 **Rogers**	N	Y	Y	Y	Y	N
6 Chandler	N	Y	Y	Y	Y	Y
LOUISIANA						
1 **Scalise**	N	Y	Y	Y	Y	N
2 **Cao**	Y	Y	Y	Y	Y	N
3 Melancon	Y	Y	Y	Y	Y	Y
4 **Fleming**	N	Y	Y	Y	Y	N
5 **Alexander**	N	Y	Y	Y	Y	N
6 **Cassidy**	N	Y	Y	Y	Y	N
7 **Boustany**	N	Y	?	?	Y	N
MAINE						
1 Pingree	Y	Y	Y	Y	Y	Y
2 Michaud	Y	Y	Y	Y	Y	Y
MARYLAND						
1 Kratovil	Y	Y	Y	Y	Y	N
2 Ruppersberger	Y	Y	Y	Y	Y	Y
3 Sarbanes	Y	Y	Y	Y	?	Y
4 Edwards	Y	Y	Y	Y	Y	?
5 Hoyer	Y	Y	Y	Y	Y	Y
6 **Bartlett**	N	Y	Y	Y	Y	N
7 Cummings	Y	Y	?	?	Y	Y
8 Van Hollen	Y	Y	Y	Y	Y	Y
MASSACHUSETTS						
1 Olver	Y	Y	Y	Y	Y	Y
2 Neal	Y	Y	Y	Y	Y	Y
3 McGovern	Y	Y	Y	Y	Y	Y
4 Frank	Y	?	Y	Y	Y	Y
5 Tsongas	Y	Y	Y	Y	Y	Y
6 Tierney	Y	Y	Y	Y	Y	Y
7 Markey	Y	Y	Y	Y	Y	Y
8 Capuano	Y	Y	Y	Y	Y	Y
9 Lynch	Y	Y	Y	Y	?	?
10 Delahunt	Y	?	?	?	?	Y
MICHIGAN						
1 Stupak	Y	Y	Y	Y	Y	Y
2 **Hoekstra**	N	Y	?	?	?	?
3 **Ehlers**	N	?	Y	Y	Y	N
4 **Camp**	N	Y	Y	Y	Y	N
5 Kildee	Y	Y	Y	Y	Y	Y
6 **Upton**	N	Y	Y	Y	Y	N
7 Schauer	Y	Y	Y	Y	Y	Y
8 **Rogers**	N	Y	Y	Y	Y	N
9 Peters	Y	Y	Y	Y	Y	Y
10 **Miller**	N	Y	Y	Y	Y	N
11 **McCotter**	N	Y	Y	Y	Y	N
12 Levin	Y	Y	Y	Y	Y	Y
13 Kilpatrick	Y	Y	Y	Y	Y	Y
14 Conyers	Y	Y	Y	Y	Y	Y
15 Dingell	Y	Y	Y	Y	Y	Y
MINNESOTA						
1 Walz	Y	Y	Y	Y	Y	Y
2 **Kline**	N	Y	Y	Y	Y	N
3 **Paulsen**	N	Y	Y	Y	Y	N
4 McCollum	Y	Y	Y	Y	Y	Y

	413	414	415	416	417	418
5 Ellison	Y	Y	Y	Y	Y	+
6 **Bachmann**	N	Y	Y	Y	Y	N
7 Peterson	Y	Y	Y	Y	Y	Y
8 Oberstar	Y	Y	Y	Y	Y	Y
MISSISSIPPI						
1 Childers	N	Y	Y	Y	Y	N
2 Thompson	Y	Y	Y	Y	Y	Y
3 **Harper**	N	Y	Y	Y	Y	N
4 Taylor	?	?	Y	Y	Y	N
MISSOURI						
1 Clay	Y	Y	?	Y	Y	Y
2 **Akin**	N	?	Y	Y	Y	N
3 Carnahan	Y	Y	Y	Y	?	Y
4 Skelton	N	Y	?	?	?	Y
5 Cleaver	Y	Y	Y	Y	Y	Y
6 **Graves**	N	Y	Y	Y	Y	N
7 **Blunt**	N	Y	Y	Y	Y	N
8 **Emerson**	N	Y	Y	Y	Y	N
9 **Luetkemeyer**	N	Y	Y	Y	Y	N
MONTANA						
AL **Rehberg**	N	Y	Y	Y	Y	N
NEBRASKA						
1 **Fortenberry**	N	Y	Y	Y	Y	N
2 **Terry**	N	Y	Y	Y	Y	N
3 **Smith**	N	Y	Y	Y	Y	N
NEVADA						
1 Berkley	Y	Y	Y	Y	Y	Y
2 **Heller**	N	Y	Y	Y	Y	N
3 Titus	Y	Y	Y	Y	Y	Y
NEW HAMPSHIRE						
1 Shea-Porter	Y	Y	Y	Y	Y	Y
2 Hodes	Y	Y	Y	Y	Y	Y
NEW JERSEY						
1 Andrews	Y	Y	Y	Y	Y	Y
2 **LoBiondo**	N	Y	Y	Y	Y	N
3 Adler	Y	Y	Y	Y	Y	N
4 **Smith**	N	Y	Y	Y	Y	N
5 **Garrett**	N	Y	Y	Y	Y	N
6 Pallone	Y	Y	Y	Y	Y	Y
7 **Lance**	N	Y	Y	Y	Y	N
8 Pascrell	Y	Y	Y	Y	Y	Y
9 Rothman	Y	Y	Y	Y	Y	Y
10 Payne	Y	Y	?	?	?	?
11 **Frelinghuysen**	N	Y	?	Y	Y	N
12 Holt	Y	Y	Y	Y	Y	Y
13 Sires	Y	Y	Y	Y	Y	Y
NEW MEXICO						
1 Heinrich	Y	Y	Y	Y	Y	Y
2 Teague	Y	Y	Y	Y	Y	Y
3 Luján	Y	Y	Y	Y	Y	Y
NEW YORK						
1 Bishop	Y	Y	Y	Y	Y	Y
2 Israel	Y	Y	Y	Y	Y	Y
3 **King**	N	Y	Y	Y	Y	N
4 McCarthy	Y	Y	Y	Y	Y	Y
5 Ackerman	Y	Y	Y	Y	Y	Y
6 Meeks	Y	Y	Y	Y	Y	Y
7 Crowley	Y	Y	Y	Y	Y	Y
8 Nadler	Y	Y	Y	Y	Y	Y
9 Weiner	Y	Y	Y	Y	Y	Y
10 Towns	Y	Y	Y	Y	Y	Y
11 Clarke	Y	Y	Y	Y	Y	Y
12 Velázquez	Y	Y	?	?	?	Y
13 McMahon	Y	Y	Y	Y	Y	Y
14 Maloney	Y	Y	Y	Y	Y	Y
15 Rangel	Y	?	Y	Y	Y	Y
16 Serrano	Y	Y	?	Y	Y	Y
17 Engel	Y	Y	?	?	Y	Y
18 Lowey	Y	Y	Y	Y	Y	Y
19 Hall	Y	?	Y	Y	Y	Y
20 Murphy	Y	Y	Y	Y	Y	Y
21 Tonko	Y	Y	Y	Y	Y	Y
22 Hinchey	Y	Y	Y	Y	Y	Y
23 Owens	N	Y	Y	Y	Y	Y
24 Arcuri	Y	Y	Y	Y	Y	Y
25 Maffei	Y	Y	Y	Y	Y	Y
26 **Lee**	N	Y	Y	Y	Y	N
27 Higgins	Y	Y	Y	Y	Y	Y
28 Slaughter	Y	Y	Y	Y	Y	Y
29 Vacant						
NORTH CAROLINA						
1 Butterfield	Y	Y	Y	Y	Y	Y
2 Etheridge	Y	Y	Y	Y	Y	Y
3 **Jones**	Y	Y	Y	Y	Y	N
4 Price	Y	Y	Y	Y	Y	Y

	413	414	415	416	417	418
5 **Foxx**	N	Y	Y	Y	Y	N
6 **Coble**	N	Y	Y	Y	Y	N
7 McIntyre	N	Y	Y	Y	Y	Y
8 Kissell	Y	Y	Y	Y	Y	Y
9 **Myrick**	N	Y	Y	Y	Y	N
10 **McHenry**	N	Y	Y	Y	Y	N
11 Shuler	Y	Y	Y	Y	Y	N
12 Watt	Y	Y	Y	Y	Y	Y
13 Miller	Y	Y	Y	Y	Y	Y
NORTH DAKOTA						
AL Pomeroy	Y	Y	Y	Y	Y	Y
OHIO						
1 Driehaus	Y	Y	Y	Y	Y	Y
2 **Schmidt**	N	Y	Y	Y	Y	N
3 **Turner**	N	Y	Y	Y	Y	N
4 **Jordan**	N	Y	Y	Y	Y	N
5 **Latta**	N	Y	Y	Y	Y	N
6 Wilson	Y	Y	Y	Y	Y	Y
7 **Austria**	N	Y	Y	Y	Y	N
8 **Boehner**	N	Y	Y	Y	Y	N
9 Kaptur	N	Y	Y	Y	Y	Y
10 Kucinich	Y	Y	Y	Y	Y	Y
11 Fudge	Y	Y	Y	Y	Y	Y
12 **Tiberi**	N	Y	Y	Y	Y	N
13 Sutton	Y	Y	Y	Y	Y	Y
14 **LaTourette**	N	Y	Y	Y	Y	N
15 Kilroy	Y	Y	Y	Y	Y	Y
16 Boccieri	Y	Y	Y	Y	Y	Y
17 Ryan	Y	Y	Y	Y	Y	Y
18 Space	Y	Y	Y	Y	Y	Y
OKLAHOMA						
1 **Sullivan**	N	Y	Y	Y	Y	N
2 Boren	N	Y	Y	Y	Y	Y
3 **Lucas**	N	Y	Y	Y	Y	N
4 **Cole**	N	Y	Y	Y	Y	N
5 **Fallin**	N	Y	Y	Y	Y	N
OREGON						
1 Wu	Y	Y	Y	Y	Y	Y
2 **Walden**	N	Y	Y	Y	Y	N
3 Blumenauer	Y	Y	Y	Y	Y	Y
4 DeFazio	Y	?	Y	Y	Y	Y
5 Schrader	Y	Y	Y	?	Y	Y
PENNSYLVANIA						
1 Brady	Y	Y	Y	Y	Y	Y
2 Fattah	Y	Y	Y	Y	Y	Y
3 Dahlkemper	Y	Y	Y	Y	Y	Y
4 Altmire	Y	Y	Y	Y	Y	Y
5 **Thompson**	N	Y	Y	Y	Y	N
6 **Gerlach**	N	Y	Y	Y	Y	N
7 Sestak	Y	Y	Y	Y	Y	Y
8 Murphy, P.	Y	Y	Y	Y	Y	Y
9 **Shuster**	N	Y	Y	Y	Y	N
10 Carney	Y	Y	Y	Y	Y	Y
11 Kanjorski	Y	Y	Y	Y	Y	Y
12 Critz	N	Y	Y	Y	Y	Y
13 Schwartz	Y	Y	Y	Y	Y	Y
14 Doyle	Y	Y	Y	Y	Y	Y
15 **Dent**	N	Y	Y	Y	Y	N
16 **Pitts**	N	Y	Y	Y	Y	N
17 Holden	Y	Y	Y	Y	Y	Y
18 **Murphy, T.**	N	Y	Y	Y	Y	N
19 **Platts**	N	Y	Y	Y	Y	N
RHODE ISLAND						
1 Kennedy	Y	Y	Y	Y	?	Y
2 Langevin	Y	Y	Y	Y	Y	Y
SOUTH CAROLINA						
1 **Brown**	N	Y	Y	Y	Y	N
2 **Wilson**	N	Y	Y	Y	Y	N
3 **Barrett**	N	Y	Y	Y	Y	N
4 **Inglis**	N	Y	Y	Y	Y	N
5 Spratt	Y	Y	Y	Y	Y	Y
6 Clyburn	Y	Y	Y	Y	Y	Y
SOUTH DAKOTA						
AL Herseth Sandlin	Y	Y	Y	Y	Y	Y
TENNESSEE						
1 **Roe**	N	Y	Y	Y	Y	N
2 **Duncan**	N	Y	Y	Y	Y	N
3 **Wamp**	?	?	?	?	?	?
4 Davis	N	Y	Y	Y	Y	Y
5 Cooper	N	Y	Y	Y	Y	Y
6 Gordon	Y	Y	Y	Y	Y	Y
7 **Blackburn**	N	Y	Y	Y	Y	N
8 Tanner	Y	Y	Y	Y	Y	Y
9 Cohen	Y	Y	Y	Y	Y	Y

	413	414	415	416	417	418
TEXAS						
1 **Gohmert**	N	Y	Y	Y	Y	N
2 **Poe**	N	Y	Y	Y	Y	N
3 **Johnson, S.**	N	Y	Y	Y	Y	N
4 **Hall**	N	Y	Y	Y	Y	N
5 **Hensarling**	N	Y	Y	Y	Y	N
6 **Barton**	N	Y	Y	Y	Y	N
7 **Culberson**	N	Y	Y	Y	P	N
8 **Brady**	N	Y	Y	Y	Y	N
9 Green, A.	Y	Y	Y	Y	Y	Y
10 **McCaul**	N	Y	Y	Y	Y	N
11 **Conaway**	N	Y	Y	Y	Y	N
12 **Granger**	N	Y	Y	Y	Y	N
13 **Thornberry**	N	Y	Y	Y	Y	N
14 **Paul**	N	Y	Y	Y	Y	N
15 Hinojosa	Y	Y	Y	+	Y	Y
16 Reyes	Y	Y	Y	Y	Y	Y
17 Edwards	N	Y	Y	Y	Y	Y
18 Jackson Lee	Y	Y	Y	Y	Y	Y
19 **Neugebauer**	N	Y	Y	Y	Y	N
20 Gonzalez	Y	Y	Y	Y	Y	Y
21 **Smith**	N	Y	Y	Y	Y	N
22 **Olson**	N	Y	Y	Y	Y	N
23 Rodriguez	Y	?	?	?	?	?
24 **Marchant**	N	Y	Y	Y	Y	N
25 Doggett	Y	Y	Y	Y	Y	Y
26 **Burgess**	N	Y	Y	Y	Y	N
27 Ortiz	Y	Y	Y	Y	Y	Y
28 Cuellar	N	Y	Y	Y	Y	Y
29 Green, G.	Y	Y	Y	Y	Y	Y
30 Johnson, E.	Y	Y	Y	Y	Y	Y
31 **Carter**	N	Y	Y	Y	Y	N
32 **Sessions**	N	Y	Y	Y	Y	N
UTAH						
1 **Bishop**	N	Y	Y	Y	Y	N
2 Matheson	N	Y	Y	Y	Y	Y
3 **Chaffetz**	N	Y	Y	Y	Y	N
VERMONT						
AL Welch	Y	Y	Y	Y	Y	?
VIRGINIA						
1 **Wittman**	N	Y	Y	Y	Y	N
2 Nye	Y	Y	Y	Y	Y	N
3 Scott	Y	Y	Y	Y	Y	Y
4 **Forbes**	N	Y	Y	Y	Y	N
5 Perriello	N	Y	Y	Y	Y	Y
6 **Goodlatte**	N	Y	Y	Y	Y	N
7 **Cantor**	N	Y	Y	Y	Y	N
8 Moran	Y	Y	?	?	Y	?
9 Boucher	N	Y	Y	Y	Y	Y
10 **Wolf**	N	Y	Y	Y	Y	N
11 Connolly	Y	Y	Y	Y	Y	Y
WASHINGTON						
1 Inslee	Y	Y	Y	Y	Y	Y
2 Larsen	Y	Y	Y	Y	Y	Y
3 Baird	Y	Y	Y	Y	Y	?
4 **Hastings**	N	Y	Y	Y	Y	N
5 **McMorris Rodgers**	N	Y	Y	Y	Y	N
6 Dicks	Y	Y	Y	Y	Y	Y
7 McDermott	Y	Y	Y	Y	Y	Y
8 **Reichert**	N	Y	Y	Y	Y	N
9 Smith	Y	Y	Y	Y	Y	Y
WEST VIRGINIA						
1 Mollohan	Y	Y	Y	Y	Y	Y
2 **Capito**	N	Y	Y	Y	Y	N
3 Rahall	Y	Y	Y	Y	Y	Y
WISCONSIN						
1 **Ryan**	N	Y	Y	Y	Y	N
2 Baldwin	Y	Y	Y	Y	Y	Y
3 Kind	Y	Y	Y	Y	Y	Y
4 Moore	Y	Y	Y	Y	Y	Y
5 **Sensenbrenner**	N	Y	Y	Y	Y	N
6 **Petri**	N	Y	Y	Y	Y	N
7 Obey	Y	Y	Y	Y	Y	Y
8 Kagen	Y	Y	Y	Y	Y	Y
WYOMING						
AL **Lummis**	N	Y	Y	Y	Y	N
DELEGATES						
Faleomavaega (A.S.)						
Norton (D.C.)						
Bordallo (Guam)						
Sablan (N. Marianas)						
Pierluisi (P.R.)						
Christensen (V.I.)						

IN THE HOUSE | By Vote Number

419. **H Res 1321. Political Crisis in Thailand/Adoption.** Watson, D-Calif., motion to suspend the rules and adopt the resolution that would express the sense of the House in support of the strong U.S. alliance with Thailand and call on all parties involved in that country's political crisis to renounce the use of violence and pledge to resolve the country's political problems through dialogue. Motion agreed to 411-4: D 239-1; R 172-3. A two-thirds majority of those present and voting (277 in this case) is required for adoption under suspension of the rules. July 1, 2010.

420. **H Res 1405. 50th Independence Anniversary of 17 African Countries/Adoption.** Watson, D-Calif., motion to suspend the rules and adopt the resolution that would congratulate the people of the 17 African countries that in 2010 are marking the 50th anniversary of their national independence. It also would renew the U.S. commitment to helping foster democracy, civic participation, market-based economic growth and the alleviation of poverty and disease in sub-Saharan Africa. Motion agreed to 410-0: D 236-0; R 174-0. A two-thirds majority of those present and voting (274 in this case) is required for adoption under suspension of the rules. July 1, 2010.

421. **H Res 1412. South African Trafficking Convictions/Adoption.** Watson, D-Calif., motion to suspend the rules and adopt the resolution that would congratulate the South African government on its first two successful convictions for human trafficking. It also would urge the government to expeditiously adopt additional legislation to facilitate future anti-trafficking prosecutions. Motion agreed to 414-1: D 246-0; R 168-1. A two-thirds majority of those present and voting (277 in this case) is required for adoption under suspension of the rules. July 1, 2010.

422. **HR 5618. Unemployment Benefits Extension/Motion to Table.** Levin, D-Mich., motion to table (kill) the Camp, R-Mich., appeal of the ruling of the chair with respect to the Levin point of order that the Camp motion to recommit the bill was not germane to the bill. The motion would recommit the bill to the Ways and Means Committee with instructions that it be immediately reported back with an amendment that would require the rescission of $34 billion in unobligated stimulus funds to offset the net increase in spending resulting from the bill. Motion agreed to 220-196: D 220-27; R 0-169. July 1, 2010.

423. **HR 5618. Unemployment Benefits Extension/Passage.** Passage of the bill that would extend through Nov. 30, 2010, and make retroactive to June 2, eligibility for extended federal unemployment insurance for laid-off workers and 100 percent federal funding for the extended benefits. States could not reduce their regular unemployment compensation programs below June 2 levels to be eligible for the funding. As amended, it would prevent payment of emergency unemployment compensation benefits to known or suspected terrorists, individuals convicted of sex offenses against minors, and illegal immigrants. Passed 270-153: D 241-11; R 29-142. July 1, 2010.

	419	420	421	422	423
ALABAMA					
1 **Bonner**	Y	Y	Y	N	N
2 **Bright**	Y	Y	Y	N	N
3 **Rogers**	Y	Y	Y	N	N
4 **Aderholt**	Y	Y	Y	N	N
5 **Griffith**	Y	Y	Y	N	N
6 **Bachus**	Y	Y	Y	N	N
7 Davis	Y	Y	Y	Y	Y
ALASKA					
AL **Young**	?	?	?	?	?
ARIZONA					
1 Kirkpatrick	Y	Y	Y	N	Y
2 **Franks**	Y	Y	Y	N	N
3 **Shadegg**	Y	Y	Y	N	N
4 Pastor	Y	Y	Y	Y	Y
5 Mitchell	Y	?	Y	N	Y
6 **Flake**	Y	Y	Y	N	N
7 Grijalva	Y	Y	Y	Y	Y
8 Giffords	Y	Y	Y	N	Y
ARKANSAS					
1 Berry	Y	Y	Y	Y	N
2 Snyder	Y	Y	Y	Y	Y
3 **Boozman**	Y	Y	Y	N	N
4 Ross	Y	Y	Y	Y	Y
CALIFORNIA					
1 Thompson	Y	Y	Y	Y	Y
2 **Herger**	N	Y	?	?	N
3 **Lungren**	Y	Y	Y	N	N
4 **McClintock**	Y	Y	Y	N	N
5 Matsui	Y	Y	Y	Y	Y
6 Woolsey	?	?	?	?	?
7 Miller, George	Y	Y	Y	?	Y
8 Pelosi					Y
9 Lee	Y	Y	Y	Y	Y
10 Garamendi	Y	Y	Y	Y	Y
11 McNerney	Y	Y	Y	Y	Y
12 Speier	Y	Y	Y	Y	Y
13 Stark	Y	Y	Y	Y	Y
14 Eshoo	Y	Y	Y	Y	Y
15 Honda	Y	Y	Y	Y	Y
16 Lofgren	Y	Y	Y	Y	Y
17 Farr	Y	Y	Y	Y	Y
18 Cardoza	Y	Y	Y	Y	Y
19 **Radanovich**	Y	Y	?	?	?
20 Costa	Y	Y	Y	Y	Y
21 **Nunes**	Y	Y	Y	N	N
22 **McCarthy**	Y	Y	Y	N	N
23 Capps	Y	?	Y	Y	Y
24 **Gallegly**	Y	Y	Y	N	N
25 **McKeon**	Y	Y	Y	N	N
26 **Dreier**	Y	Y	Y	N	N
27 Sherman	Y	Y	Y	Y	Y
28 Berman	Y	Y	Y	Y	Y
29 Schiff	Y	Y	Y	Y	Y
30 Waxman	Y	Y	Y	Y	Y
31 Becerra	Y	Y	Y	Y	Y
32 Chu	Y	Y	Y	Y	Y
33 Watson	Y	Y	Y	Y	Y
34 Roybal-Allard	Y	Y	Y	Y	Y
35 Waters	Y	Y	Y	Y	Y
36 Harman	Y	Y	Y	Y	Y
37 Richardson	Y	Y	Y	Y	Y
38 Napolitano	Y	Y	Y	Y	Y
39 Sánchez, Linda	Y	Y	Y	Y	Y
40 **Royce**	Y	Y	Y	N	N
41 **Lewis**	Y	Y	Y	N	N
42 **Miller, Gary**	Y	Y	Y	N	N
43 Baca	Y	Y	Y	Y	Y
44 **Calvert**	Y	Y	Y	N	N
45 **Bono Mack**	Y	Y	Y	N	Y
46 **Rohrabacher**	Y	Y	Y	N	N
47 Sanchez, Loretta	Y	Y	Y	Y	Y
48 **Campbell**	Y	Y	Y	N	N
49 **Issa**	Y	Y	Y	N	N
50 **Bilbray**	Y	Y	Y	N	Y
51 Filner	Y	Y	Y	Y	Y
52 **Hunter**	Y	Y	Y	N	N
53 Davis	Y	Y	Y	Y	Y
COLORADO					
1 DeGette	Y	Y	Y	Y	Y
2 Polis	Y	?	Y	Y	Y
3 Salazar	Y	Y	Y	Y	Y
4 Markey	Y	Y	Y	N	N
5 **Lamborn**	Y	Y	Y	N	N
6 **Coffman**	Y	Y	Y	N	N
7 Perlmutter	Y	Y	Y	Y	Y
CONNECTICUT					
1 Larson	Y	Y	Y	Y	Y
2 Courtney	Y	Y	Y	Y	Y
3 DeLauro	Y	Y	Y	Y	Y
4 Himes	Y	Y	Y	N	Y
5 Murphy	Y	Y	Y	Y	Y
DELAWARE					
AL **Castle**	Y	Y	Y	N	Y
FLORIDA					
1 **Miller**	Y	Y	Y	N	N
2 Boyd	Y	Y	Y	Y	Y
3 Brown	Y	Y	Y	Y	Y
4 **Crenshaw**	Y	Y	Y	N	N
5 **Brown-Waite**	Y	Y	Y	N	N
6 **Stearns**	Y	Y	Y	N	N
7 **Mica**	Y	Y	Y	N	N
8 Grayson	Y	Y	Y	Y	Y
9 **Bilirakis**	Y	Y	Y	N	Y
10 **Young**	Y	Y	Y	N	N
11 Castor	Y	Y	Y	Y	Y
12 **Putnam**	Y	Y	Y	N	N
13 **Buchanan**	Y	Y	Y	N	N
14 **Mack**	Y	Y	Y	N	N
15 **Posey**	Y	Y	Y	N	N
16 **Rooney**	Y	Y	Y	N	N
17 Meek	Y	Y	Y	Y	Y
18 **Ros-Lehtinen**	Y	Y	Y	N	Y
19 Deutch	Y	Y	Y	Y	Y
20 Wasserman Schultz	Y	Y	Y	Y	Y
21 **Diaz-Balart, L.**	Y	Y	Y	Y	Y
22 Klein	Y	Y	Y	Y	Y
23 Hastings	Y	Y	Y	Y	Y
24 Kosmas	Y	Y	Y	N	Y
25 **Diaz-Balart, M.**	Y	Y	Y	N	Y
GEORGIA					
1 **Kingston**	Y	Y	Y	N	N
2 Bishop	Y	Y	Y	Y	Y
3 **Westmoreland**	Y	Y	Y	N	N
4 Johnson	Y	Y	Y	Y	Y
5 Lewis	Y	Y	Y	?	Y
6 **Price**	Y	Y	Y	N	N
7 **Linder**	Y	Y	?	N	N
8 Marshall	Y	Y	Y	N	N
9 **Graves**	Y	Y	Y	N	N
10 **Broun**	Y	Y	Y	N	N
11 **Gingrey**	Y	Y	Y	N	N
12 Barrow	Y	Y	Y	Y	Y
13 Scott	Y	Y	Y	Y	Y
HAWAII					
1 **Djou**	Y	Y	Y	N	N
2 Hirono	Y	Y	Y	Y	Y
IDAHO					
1 Minnick	N	Y	Y	N	N
2 **Simpson**	Y	Y	Y	N	N
ILLINOIS					
1 Rush	Y	Y	Y	Y	Y
2 Jackson	Y	Y	Y	Y	Y
3 Lipinski	Y	Y	Y	Y	Y
4 Gutierrez	Y	?	Y	?	Y
5 Quigley	Y	Y	Y	Y	Y
6 **Roskam**	Y	Y	Y	N	N
7 Davis	Y	Y	Y	Y	Y
8 Bean	Y	Y	Y	Y	Y
9 Schakowsky	Y	Y	Y	Y	Y
10 **Kirk**	Y	Y	Y	N	N
11 Halvorson	Y	Y	Y	Y	Y
12 Costello	Y	Y	Y	Y	Y
13 **Biggert**	Y	Y	Y	N	N
14 Foster	Y	?	Y	N	Y
15 **Johnson**	N	Y	Y	N	Y

	419	420	421	422	423
16 Manzullo	Y	Y	Y	N	Y
17 Hare	Y	Y	Y	Y	Y
18 **Schock**	Y	Y	Y	N	N
19 **Shimkus**	Y	?	Y	N	N
INDIANA					
1 Visclosky	Y	Y	Y	Y	Y
2 Donnelly	Y	Y	Y	N	Y
3 Vacant					
4 **Buyer**	Y	Y	Y	N	N
5 **Burton**	Y	Y	Y	N	N
6 **Pence**	Y	Y	Y	N	N
7 Carson	Y	Y	Y	Y	Y
8 Ellsworth	Y	Y	Y	Y	Y
9 Hill	Y	Y	Y	N	N
IOWA					
1 Braley	Y	Y	Y	Y	Y
2 Loebsack	Y	Y	Y	Y	Y
3 Boswell	Y	Y	Y	Y	Y
4 **Latham**	Y	Y	Y	N	N
5 **King**	Y	Y	Y	N	N
KANSAS					
1 **Moran**	Y	Y	Y	N	N
2 **Jenkins**	Y	Y	Y	N	N
3 Moore	Y	Y	Y	Y	Y
4 **Tiahrt**	Y	Y	Y	N	N
KENTUCKY					
1 **Whitfield**	Y	Y	Y	N	Y
2 **Guthrie**	Y	Y	Y	N	N
3 Yarmuth	Y	Y	Y	Y	Y
4 **Davis**	Y	Y	Y	N	N
5 **Rogers**	Y	Y	Y	N	N
6 Chandler	Y	Y	Y	Y	Y
LOUISIANA					
1 **Scalise**	Y	Y	Y	N	N
2 **Cao**	Y	Y	Y	N	Y
3 Melancon	?	Y	Y	N	Y
4 **Fleming**	Y	Y	Y	N	N
5 **Alexander**	Y	Y	?	?	?
6 **Cassidy**	Y	Y	Y	N	N
7 **Boustany**	Y	Y	Y	N	N
MAINE					
1 Pingree	Y	Y	Y	Y	Y
2 Michaud	Y	Y	Y	Y	Y
MARYLAND					
1 Kratovil	Y	Y	Y	N	Y
2 Ruppersberger	Y	Y	Y	Y	Y
3 Sarbanes	Y	Y	Y	Y	Y
4 Edwards	?	?	Y	Y	Y
5 Hoyer	Y	Y	Y	Y	Y
6 **Bartlett**	Y	Y	Y	?	N
7 Cummings	Y	Y	Y	Y	Y
8 Van Hollen	Y	Y	Y	Y	Y
MASSACHUSETTS					
1 Olver	Y	Y	Y	Y	Y
2 Neal	Y	Y	Y	Y	Y
3 McGovern	Y	Y	Y	Y	Y
4 Frank	Y	Y	Y	Y	Y
5 Tsongas	Y	Y	Y	Y	Y
6 Tierney	Y	Y	Y	Y	Y
7 Markey	Y	Y	Y	Y	Y
8 Capuano	Y	Y	Y	Y	Y
9 Lynch	?	?	Y	Y	Y
10 Delahunt	Y	Y	Y	Y	Y
MICHIGAN					
1 Stupak	Y	Y	Y	Y	Y
2 **Hoekstra**	?	?	?	?	?
3 **Ehlers**	Y	Y	Y	N	Y
4 **Camp**	Y	Y	Y	N	N
5 Kildee	Y	Y	Y	Y	Y
6 **Upton**	Y	Y	Y	N	Y
7 Schauer	Y	Y	Y	Y	Y
8 **Rogers**	Y	Y	Y	N	Y
9 Peters	Y	Y	Y	Y	Y
10 **Miller**	Y	Y	Y	N	N
11 **McCotter**	Y	Y	Y	N	Y
12 Levin	Y	Y	Y	Y	Y
13 Kilpatrick	Y	Y	Y	Y	Y
14 Conyers	Y	Y	Y	Y	Y
15 Dingell	Y	Y	Y	Y	Y
MINNESOTA					
1 Walz	Y	Y	Y	Y	Y
2 **Kline**	Y	Y	Y	N	N
3 **Paulsen**	Y	Y	Y	N	N
4 McCollum	?	?	Y	Y	Y

	419	420	421	422	423
5 Ellison	+	+	Y	Y	Y
6 **Bachmann**	Y	Y	Y	N	N
7 Peterson	Y	Y	Y	Y	Y
8 Oberstar	Y	Y	Y	Y	Y
MISSISSIPPI					
1 Childers	Y	Y	Y	N	Y
2 Thompson	Y	Y	Y	Y	Y
3 **Harper**	Y	Y	Y	N	N
4 Taylor	Y	Y	Y	N	Y
MISSOURI					
1 Clay	Y	Y	Y	Y	Y
2 **Akin**	Y	Y	Y	N	N
3 Carnahan	Y	Y	Y	Y	Y
4 Skelton	Y	Y	Y	Y	Y
5 Cleaver	Y	Y	Y	Y	Y
6 **Graves**	Y	Y	Y	N	N
7 **Blunt**	Y	Y	Y	N	N
8 **Emerson**	Y	Y	Y	N	N
9 **Luetkemeyer**	Y	Y	Y	N	N
MONTANA					
AL **Rehberg**	Y	Y	Y	N	N
NEBRASKA					
1 **Fortenberry**	Y	Y	Y	N	N
2 **Terry**	Y	Y	Y	N	N
3 **Smith**	Y	Y	Y	N	N
NEVADA					
1 Berkley	Y	Y	Y	Y	Y
2 **Heller**	Y	Y	Y	N	Y
3 Titus	Y	Y	Y	Y	Y
NEW HAMPSHIRE					
1 Shea-Porter	Y	Y	?	Y	Y
2 Hodes	?	?	Y	Y	Y
NEW JERSEY					
1 Andrews	Y	Y	Y	Y	Y
2 **LoBiondo**	Y	Y	Y	N	Y
3 Adler	Y	Y	Y	N	Y
4 **Smith**	Y	Y	Y	N	Y
5 **Garrett**	Y	Y	Y	N	N
6 Pallone	Y	Y	Y	Y	Y
7 **Lance**	Y	Y	Y	N	N
8 Pascrell	Y	Y	Y	Y	Y
9 Rothman	Y	Y	Y	Y	Y
10 Payne	?	?	?	?	?
11 **Frelinghuysen**	Y	Y	Y	N	N
12 Holt	Y	Y	Y	Y	Y
13 Sires	Y	Y	?	Y	Y
NEW MEXICO					
1 Heinrich	Y	Y	Y	Y	Y
2 Teague	Y	Y	Y	Y	Y
3 Luján	Y	Y	Y	Y	Y
NEW YORK					
1 Bishop	Y	Y	Y	Y	Y
2 Israel	Y	Y	Y	Y	Y
3 **King**	Y	Y	Y	N	N
4 McCarthy	Y	Y	Y	Y	Y
5 Ackerman	Y	Y	Y	Y	Y
6 Meeks	Y	Y	Y	Y	Y
7 Crowley	Y	+	Y	Y	Y
8 Nadler	Y	Y	Y	Y	Y
9 Weiner	Y	Y	Y	Y	Y
10 Towns	Y	Y	Y	Y	Y
11 Clarke	Y	Y	?	Y	Y
12 Velázquez	Y	Y	Y	Y	Y
13 McMahon	Y	Y	Y	N	Y
14 Maloney	Y	Y	Y	Y	Y
15 Rangel	Y	Y	Y	Y	Y
16 Serrano	Y	Y	Y	Y	Y
17 Engel	Y	Y	Y	Y	Y
18 Lowey	Y	Y	Y	Y	Y
19 Hall	Y	Y	Y	Y	Y
20 Murphy	Y	Y	Y	Y	Y
21 Tonko	Y	Y	Y	Y	Y
22 Hinchey	Y	Y	Y	Y	Y
23 Owens	Y	Y	Y	Y	Y
24 Arcuri	Y	Y	Y	N	Y
25 Maffei	Y	Y	Y	Y	Y
26 **Lee**	Y	Y	Y	N	N
27 Higgins	Y	Y	Y	Y	Y
28 Slaughter	Y	Y	Y	Y	Y
29 Vacant					
NORTH CAROLINA					
1 Butterfield	Y	Y	Y	Y	Y
2 Etheridge	Y	Y	Y	Y	Y
3 **Jones**	Y	Y	Y	N	Y
4 Price	Y	Y	Y	Y	Y

	419	420	421	422	423
5 **Foxx**	Y	Y	Y	N	N
6 **Coble**	Y	Y	Y	N	N
7 McIntyre	Y	Y	Y	N	Y
8 Kissell	Y	Y	Y	Y	Y
9 **Myrick**	Y	Y	N	N	N
10 **McHenry**	Y	Y	Y	N	N
11 Shuler	Y	Y	Y	N	N
12 Watt	Y	Y	Y	Y	Y
13 Miller	Y	Y	Y	N	Y
NORTH DAKOTA					
AL Pomeroy	Y	Y	Y	Y	Y
OHIO					
1 Driehaus	Y	Y	Y	Y	Y
2 **Schmidt**	Y	Y	Y	N	N
3 **Turner**	Y	Y	Y	N	Y
4 **Jordan**	Y	Y	Y	N	N
5 **Latta**	Y	Y	Y	N	N
6 Wilson	Y	Y	Y	Y	Y
7 **Austria**	Y	Y	Y	N	N
8 **Boehner**	Y	Y	Y	N	N
9 Kaptur	Y	Y	Y	Y	Y
10 Kucinich	Y	Y	Y	Y	Y
11 Fudge	Y	Y	Y	Y	Y
12 **Tiberi**	Y	Y	Y	N	N
13 Sutton	Y	Y	Y	Y	Y
14 **LaTourette**	Y	Y	Y	N	Y
15 Kilroy	Y	Y	Y	Y	Y
16 Boccieri	Y	Y	Y	Y	Y
17 Ryan	Y	Y	Y	Y	Y
18 Space	Y	Y	Y	Y	Y
OKLAHOMA					
1 **Sullivan**	Y	Y	Y	N	N
2 Boren	Y	Y	Y	Y	Y
3 **Lucas**	Y	Y	Y	N	N
4 **Cole**	Y	Y	Y	N	N
5 **Fallin**	Y	Y	Y	N	N
OREGON					
1 Wu	Y	Y	Y	Y	Y
2 **Walden**	Y	Y	Y	N	N
3 Blumenauer	Y	Y	Y	Y	Y
4 DeFazio	Y	Y	Y	Y	Y
5 Schrader	Y	Y	Y	Y	Y
PENNSYLVANIA					
1 Brady	Y	Y	Y	Y	Y
2 Fattah	Y	Y	Y	Y	Y
3 Dahlkemper	Y	Y	Y	N	Y
4 Altmire	Y	Y	Y	N	Y
5 **Thompson**	Y	Y	Y	N	N
6 **Gerlach**	Y	Y	Y	N	Y
7 Sestak	Y	Y	Y	Y	Y
8 Murphy, P.	Y	Y	Y	Y	Y
9 **Shuster**	Y	Y	Y	N	N
10 Carney	Y	Y	Y	N	Y
11 Kanjorski	Y	Y	Y	Y	Y
12 Critz	Y	Y	Y	Y	Y
13 Schwartz	Y	Y	Y	Y	Y
14 Doyle	Y	Y	Y	Y	Y
15 **Dent**	Y	Y	Y	N	Y
16 **Pitts**	Y	Y	Y	N	N
17 Holden	Y	Y	Y	Y	Y
18 **Murphy, T.**	Y	Y	Y	N	Y
19 **Platts**	Y	Y	Y	N	Y
RHODE ISLAND					
1 Kennedy	Y	Y	Y	Y	Y
2 Langevin	Y	Y	Y	Y	Y
SOUTH CAROLINA					
1 **Brown**	Y	Y	Y	N	N
2 **Wilson**	Y	Y	Y	N	N
3 **Barrett**	Y	Y	Y	N	N
4 **Inglis**	Y	Y	Y	N	N
5 Spratt	Y	Y	?	Y	Y
6 Clyburn	Y	Y	Y	Y	Y
SOUTH DAKOTA					
AL Herseth Sandlin	Y	Y	Y	N	Y
TENNESSEE					
1 **Roe**	Y	Y	Y	N	N
2 **Duncan**	Y	Y	Y	N	N
3 **Wamp**	?	?	?	?	?
4 Davis	Y	Y	Y	Y	Y
5 Cooper	Y	Y	Y	Y	Y
6 Gordon	Y	Y	Y	?	Y
7 **Blackburn**	Y	Y	Y	N	N
8 Tanner	Y	Y	Y	N	Y
9 Cohen	Y	Y	Y	Y	Y

	419	420	421	422	423
TEXAS					
1 **Gohmert**	Y	Y	Y	N	N
2 **Poe**	Y	Y	Y	N	N
3 **Johnson, S.**	Y	Y	Y	N	N
4 **Hall**	Y	Y	Y	N	N
5 **Hensarling**	Y	Y	Y	N	N
6 **Barton**	Y	Y	Y	N	N
7 **Culberson**	Y	Y	Y	N	N
8 **Brady**	Y	Y	Y	N	N
9 Green, A.	Y	Y	Y	Y	Y
10 **McCaul**	Y	Y	Y	N	N
11 **Conaway**	Y	Y	Y	N	N
12 **Granger**	Y	Y	Y	N	N
13 **Thornberry**	Y	Y	Y	N	N
14 **Paul**	N	Y	N	N	N
15 Hinojosa	Y	Y	Y	Y	Y
16 Reyes	Y	Y	Y	Y	Y
17 Edwards	Y	Y	Y	Y	Y
18 Jackson Lee	Y	Y	Y	Y	Y
19 **Neugebauer**	Y	Y	Y	N	N
20 Gonzalez	Y	Y	Y	Y	Y
21 **Smith**	Y	Y	Y	N	N
22 **Olson**	Y	Y	Y	N	N
23 Rodriguez	?	?	?	?	?
24 **Marchant**	Y	Y	Y	N	N
25 Doggett	Y	Y	Y	Y	Y
26 **Burgess**	Y	Y	Y	N	N
27 Ortiz	Y	Y	Y	Y	Y
28 Cuellar	Y	Y	Y	Y	Y
29 Green, G.	Y	Y	Y	Y	Y
30 Johnson, E.	Y	Y	Y	Y	Y
31 **Carter**	Y	Y	Y	N	N
32 **Sessions**	Y	Y	Y	N	N
UTAH					
1 **Bishop**	Y	Y	?	–	?
2 Matheson	Y	Y	Y	Y	Y
3 **Chaffetz**	Y	Y	Y	N	N
VERMONT					
AL Welch	?	?	Y	Y	Y
VIRGINIA					
1 **Wittman**	Y	Y	Y	N	N
2 Nye	Y	Y	Y	N	N
3 Scott	Y	Y	?	Y	Y
4 **Forbes**	Y	Y	Y	N	N
5 Perriello	Y	Y	Y	Y	Y
6 **Goodlatte**	Y	Y	Y	N	N
7 **Cantor**	Y	Y	Y	N	N
8 Moran	?	?	Y	Y	Y
9 Boucher	Y	Y	Y	Y	Y
10 **Wolf**	Y	Y	Y	N	N
11 Connolly	Y	Y	Y	N	Y
WASHINGTON					
1 Inslee	Y	Y	Y	Y	Y
2 Larsen	Y	Y	Y	Y	Y
3 Baird	?	?	Y	Y	Y
4 **Hastings**	Y	Y	Y	N	N
5 **McMorris Rodgers**	Y	Y	Y	N	N
6 Dicks	Y	?	Y	Y	Y
7 McDermott	+	Y	Y	Y	Y
8 **Reichert**	Y	Y	Y	N	Y
9 Smith	Y	Y	Y	Y	Y
WEST VIRGINIA					
1 Mollohan	Y	Y	Y	Y	Y
2 **Capito**	Y	Y	?	?	?
3 Rahall	Y	Y	Y	Y	Y
WISCONSIN					
1 **Ryan**	Y	Y	Y	N	N
2 Baldwin	Y	Y	Y	Y	Y
3 Kind	Y	Y	Y	Y	Y
4 Moore	?	Y	Y	Y	Y
5 **Sensenbrenner**	Y	Y	Y	N	N
6 **Petri**	Y	Y	Y	N	Y
7 Obey	Y	Y	Y	Y	Y
8 Kagen	Y	Y	Y	Y	Y
WYOMING					
AL **Lummis**	Y	Y	Y	N	N
DELEGATES					
Faleomavaega (A.S.)					
Norton (D.C.)					
Bordallo (Guam)					
Sablan (N. Marianas)					
Pierluisi (P.R.)					
Christensen (V.I.)					

IN THE HOUSE | By Vote Number

424. **Procedural Matter/Quorum Call.*** Call of the House. A quorum was present with 416 members responding (17 members did not respond). July 1, 2010.

425. **HR 5609. Lobbying Ban for Terrorism Sponsors/Passage.** Conyers, D-Mich., motion to suspend the rules and pass the bill that would prohibit lobbying on behalf of countries designated by the State Department as repeated supporters of international terrorism. Motion agreed to 408-4: D 241-3; R 167-1. A two-thirds majority of those present and voting (275 in this case) is required for passage under suspension of the rules. July 1, 2010.

426. **H Con Res 290. National ESIGN Day/Adoption.** McDermott, D-Wash., motion to suspend the rules and adopt the concurrent resolution that would support the designation of June 30 as "National ESIGN Day" and reaffirm Congress' commitment to facilitating interstate and foreign commerce in an increasingly digital world. Motion agreed to 397-15: D 242-0; R 155-15. A two-thirds majority of those present and voting (275 in this case) is required for adoption under suspension of the rules. July 1, 2010.

427. **Procedural Matter/Quorum Call.*** Call of the House. A quorum was present with 419 members responding (14 members did not respond). July 1, 2010.

428. **HR 4899. Supplemental Appropriations/Rule.** Adoption of the rule (H Res 1500) that would provide for House floor consideration of the Senate amendment to the bill that would provide $58.8 billion in supplemental funds for fiscal 2010. The rule would also provide for the automatic adoption by the House of a resolution (H Res 1493) that would set a discretionary spending limit of $1.12 trillion for fiscal 2011. The rule would also amend the House pay-as-you-go rule to align it with the statutory pay-as-you-go law. Adopted 215-210: D 215-38; R 0-172. July 1, 2010.

	425	426	428
ALABAMA			
1 **Bonner**	Y	Y	N
2 Bright	Y	Y	N
3 **Rogers**	Y	Y	N
4 **Aderholt**	Y	Y	N
5 **Griffith**	?	?	?
6 **Bachus**	Y	Y	N
7 Davis	Y	Y	Y
ALASKA			
AL **Young**	?	?	?
ARIZONA			
1 Kirkpatrick	Y	Y	Y
2 **Franks**	Y	Y	N
3 **Shadegg**	Y	N	N
4 Pastor	Y	Y	Y
5 Mitchell	Y	Y	N
6 **Flake**	Y	N	N
7 Grijalva	Y	Y	N
8 Giffords	Y	Y	N
ARKANSAS			
1 Berry	Y	Y	N
2 Snyder	Y	Y	Y
3 **Boozman**	Y	Y	N
4 Ross	Y	Y	Y
CALIFORNIA			
1 Thompson	Y	Y	Y
2 **Herger**	Y	Y	N
3 **Lungren**	Y	Y	N
4 **McClintock**	Y	Y	N
5 Matsui	Y	Y	Y
6 Woolsey	?	?	?
7 Miller, George	?	Y	Y
8 Pelosi			Y
9 Lee	Y	Y	Y
10 Garamendi	Y	Y	Y
11 McNerney	Y	Y	Y
12 Speier	Y	Y	Y
13 Stark	Y	Y	Y
14 Eshoo	Y	Y	Y
15 Honda	Y	Y	Y
16 Lofgren	Y	Y	Y
17 Farr	?	Y	Y
18 Cardoza	Y	Y	Y
19 **Radanovich**	Y	Y	N
20 Costa	Y	Y	Y
21 **Nunes**	Y	Y	N
22 **McCarthy**	Y	Y	N
23 Capps	Y	Y	Y
24 **Gallegly**	Y	Y	N
25 **McKeon**	Y	Y	N
26 **Dreier**	Y	Y	N
27 Sherman	Y	Y	Y
28 Berman	Y	?	Y
29 Schiff	Y	Y	Y
30 Waxman	Y	Y	Y
31 Becerra	Y	Y	Y
32 Chu	Y	Y	Y
33 Watson	Y	Y	Y
34 Roybal-Allard	Y	Y	Y
35 Waters	?	Y	Y
36 Harman	Y	Y	Y
37 Richardson	Y	Y	Y
38 Napolitano	Y	Y	N
39 Sánchez, Linda	Y	Y	Y
40 **Royce**	Y	Y	N
41 **Lewis**	Y	Y	N
42 **Miller, Gary**	Y	Y	N
43 Baca	Y	Y	Y
44 **Calvert**	Y	Y	N
45 **Bono Mack**	Y	Y	N
46 **Rohrabacher**	Y	Y	N
47 Sanchez, Loretta	Y	Y	Y
48 **Campbell**	Y	N	N
49 **Issa**	Y	Y	N
50 **Bilbray**	Y	Y	N
51 Filner	Y	Y	N
52 **Hunter**	Y	Y	N
53 Davis	Y	Y	Y

	425	426	428
COLORADO			
1 DeGette	Y	Y	Y
2 Polis	Y	Y	Y
3 Salazar	Y	Y	Y
4 Markey	Y	Y	Y
5 **Lamborn**	Y	Y	N
6 **Coffman**	Y	Y	N
7 Perlmutter	Y	Y	Y
CONNECTICUT			
1 Larson	Y	Y	Y
2 Courtney	Y	Y	Y
3 DeLauro	Y	Y	Y
4 Himes	Y	Y	N
5 Murphy	Y	Y	N
DELAWARE			
AL **Castle**	Y	Y	N
FLORIDA			
1 **Miller**	Y	Y	N
2 Boyd	Y	Y	Y
3 Brown	Y	Y	Y
4 **Crenshaw**	Y	Y	N
5 **Brown-Waite**	Y	Y	N
6 **Stearns**	Y	Y	N
7 **Mica**	Y	Y	N
8 Grayson	Y	Y	N
9 **Bilirakis**	Y	Y	N
10 **Young**	Y	Y	N
11 Castor	Y	?	Y
12 **Putnam**	Y	Y	N
13 **Buchanan**	Y	Y	N
14 **Mack**	Y	Y	N
15 **Posey**	Y	Y	N
16 **Rooney**	Y	Y	N
17 Meek	Y	Y	Y
18 **Ros-Lehtinen**	Y	Y	N
19 Deutch	Y	Y	Y
20 Wasserman Schultz	Y	Y	Y
21 **Diaz-Balart, L.**	Y	Y	N
22 Klein	Y	?	Y
23 Hastings	Y	Y	Y
24 Kosmas	?	Y	Y
25 **Diaz-Balart, M.**	Y	Y	N
GEORGIA			
1 **Kingston**	Y	Y	N
2 Bishop	Y	Y	Y
3 **Westmoreland**	Y	Y	N
4 Johnson	Y	Y	Y
5 Lewis	Y	Y	Y
6 **Price**	Y	Y	N
7 **Linder**	Y	Y	N
8 Marshall	Y	Y	N
9 **Graves**	Y	Y	N
10 **Broun**	Y	Y	N
11 **Gingrey**	Y	Y	N
12 Barrow	Y	Y	Y
13 Scott	Y	Y	Y
HAWAII			
1 **Djou**	Y	Y	N
2 Hirono	Y	Y	Y
IDAHO			
1 Minnick	Y	Y	N
2 **Simpson**	Y	Y	N
ILLINOIS			
1 Rush	Y	Y	Y
2 Jackson	Y	Y	Y
3 Lipinski	Y	Y	N
4 Gutierrez	Y	Y	Y
5 Quigley	Y	Y	Y
6 **Roskam**	Y	Y	N
7 Davis	Y	Y	Y
8 Bean	Y	Y	Y
9 Schakowsky	Y	Y	Y
10 **Kirk**	Y	Y	N
11 Halvorson	Y	Y	N
12 Costello	Y	Y	Y
13 **Biggert**	Y	Y	N
14 Foster	Y	Y	N
15 **Johnson**	Y	Y	N

KEY	**Republicans**	Democrats

Y	Voted for (yea)	X	Paired against	C	Voted "present" to avoid possible conflict of interest
#	Paired for	–	Announced against		
+	Announced for	P	Voted "present"	?	Did not vote or otherwise make a position known
N	Voted against (nay)				

* CQ does not include quorum calls in its vote charts.

		425	426	428
16	**Manzullo**	Y	Y	N
17	Hare	Y	Y	Y
18	**Schock**	Y	Y	N
19	**Shimkus**	Y	Y	N
INDIANA				
1	Visclosky	Y	Y	Y
2	Donnelly	Y	Y	Y
3	Vacant			
4	**Buyer**	Y	Y	N
5	**Burton**	Y	Y	N
6	**Pence**	Y	?	N
7	Carson	Y	Y	Y
8	Ellsworth	Y	Y	Y
9	Hill	Y	Y	Y
IOWA				
1	Braley	Y	Y	Y
2	Loebsack	Y	Y	Y
3	Boswell	Y	Y	Y
4	Latham	Y	Y	N
5	**King**	Y	N	N
KANSAS				
1	**Moran**	Y	Y	N
2	**Jenkins**	Y	Y	N
3	Moore	Y	Y	Y
4	**Tiahrt**	Y	Y	N
KENTUCKY				
1	**Whitfield**	Y	Y	N
2	**Guthrie**	Y	Y	N
3	Yarmuth	Y	Y	Y
4	**Davis**	Y	Y	N
5	**Rogers**	Y	Y	N
6	Chandler	Y	Y	Y
LOUISIANA				
1	**Scalise**	Y	Y	N
2	**Cao**	Y	Y	N
3	Melancon	Y	Y	Y
4	**Fleming**	Y	Y	N
5	**Alexander**	Y	Y	N
6	**Cassidy**	Y	Y	N
7	**Boustany**	Y	Y	N
MAINE				
1	Pingree	Y	Y	N
2	Michaud	Y	Y	N
MARYLAND				
1	Kratovil	Y	Y	N
2	Ruppersberger	Y	Y	Y
3	Sarbanes	Y	Y	Y
4	Edwards	Y	Y	Y
5	Hoyer	Y	Y	Y
6	**Bartlett**	Y	Y	N
7	Cummings	Y	Y	Y
8	Van Hollen	Y	Y	Y
MASSACHUSETTS				
1	Olver	?	Y	Y
2	Neal	Y	Y	Y
3	McGovern	Y	Y	Y
4	Frank	Y	Y	Y
5	Tsongas	Y	Y	Y
6	Tierney	Y	Y	Y
7	Markey	Y	Y	Y
8	Capuano	Y	Y	Y
9	Lynch	Y	Y	Y
10	Delahunt	Y	Y	Y
MICHIGAN				
1	Stupak	Y	Y	Y
2	**Hoekstra**	?	?	?
3	**Ehlers**	?	Y	N
4	**Camp**	Y	Y	N
5	Kildee	Y	Y	Y
6	**Upton**	Y	Y	N
7	Schauer	Y	Y	Y
8	**Rogers**	Y	Y	N
9	Peters	Y	Y	N
10	**Miller**	Y	Y	N
11	**McCotter**	Y	Y	N
12	Levin	Y	?	Y
13	Kilpatrick	?	Y	Y
14	Conyers	?	?	N
15	Dingell	Y	Y	Y
MINNESOTA				
1	Walz	Y	Y	Y
2	**Kline**	Y	Y	N
3	**Paulsen**	Y	Y	N
4	McCollum	Y	Y	Y

		425	426	428
5	Ellison	Y	Y	Y
6	**Bachmann**	Y	Y	N
7	Peterson	Y	Y	N
8	Oberstar	Y	Y	Y
MISSISSIPPI				
1	Childers	Y	Y	N
2	Thompson	Y	Y	Y
3	**Harper**	Y	Y	N
4	Taylor	Y	Y	N
MISSOURI				
1	Clay	Y	Y	Y
2	**Akin**	Y	N	N
3	Carnahan	Y	Y	Y
4	Skelton	Y	Y	N
5	Cleaver	Y	?	Y
6	**Graves**	Y	Y	N
7	**Blunt**	?	Y	N
8	**Emerson**	Y	Y	N
9	**Luetkemeyer**	Y	Y	N
MONTANA				
AL	**Rehberg**	Y	Y	N
NEBRASKA				
1	**Fortenberry**	Y	Y	N
2	**Terry**	Y	Y	N
3	**Smith**	Y	Y	N
NEVADA				
1	Berkley	Y	Y	Y
2	**Heller**	Y	Y	N
3	Titus	Y	Y	N
NEW HAMPSHIRE				
1	Shea-Porter	Y	Y	N
2	Hodes	Y	Y	Y
NEW JERSEY				
1	Andrews	Y	?	Y
2	**LoBiondo**	Y	Y	N
3	Adler	Y	Y	N
4	**Smith**	Y	Y	N
5	**Garrett**	?	Y	N
6	Pallone	Y	Y	Y
7	**Lance**	Y	Y	N
8	Pascrell	Y	Y	Y
9	Rothman	Y	Y	Y
10	Payne	Y	Y	Y
11	**Frelinghuysen**	Y	Y	N
12	Holt	Y	Y	Y
13	Sires	Y	Y	Y
NEW MEXICO				
1	Heinrich	Y	Y	Y
2	Teague	Y	Y	Y
3	Luján	Y	Y	Y
NEW YORK				
1	Bishop	Y	Y	Y
2	Israel	Y	Y	Y
3	**King**	Y	Y	N
4	McCarthy	Y	Y	Y
5	Ackerman	Y	?	Y
6	Meeks	Y	Y	Y
7	Crowley	Y	Y	Y
8	Nadler	Y	Y	Y
9	Weiner	Y	Y	Y
10	Towns	Y	Y	Y
11	Clarke	Y	Y	Y
12	Velázquez	Y	Y	Y
13	McMahon	Y	?	Y
14	Maloney	Y	Y	Y
15	Rangel	Y	Y	Y
16	Serrano	Y	Y	Y
17	Engel	Y	Y	Y
18	Lowey	?	Y	Y
19	Hall	Y	Y	Y
20	Murphy	Y	Y	N
21	Tonko	Y	Y	Y
22	Hinchey	Y	Y	Y
23	Owens	Y	Y	Y
24	Arcuri	Y	Y	Y
25	Maffei	Y	Y	N
26	**Lee**	Y	Y	N
27	Higgins	Y	Y	Y
28	Slaughter	Y	?	Y
29	Vacant			
NORTH CAROLINA				
1	Butterfield	Y	Y	Y
2	Etheridge	Y	Y	Y
3	**Jones**	Y	Y	N
4	Price	Y	Y	Y

		425	426	428
5	**Foxx**	Y	Y	N
6	**Coble**	Y	Y	N
7	McIntyre	Y	Y	Y
8	Kissell	Y	Y	Y
9	**Myrick**	Y	Y	N
10	**McHenry**	Y	Y	N
11	Shuler	Y	Y	N
12	Watt	Y	Y	Y
13	Miller	Y	Y	Y
NORTH DAKOTA				
AL	Pomeroy	Y	Y	N
OHIO				
1	Driehaus	Y	Y	N
2	**Schmidt**	Y	Y	N
3	**Turner**	Y	Y	N
4	**Jordan**	Y	Y	N
5	**Latta**	Y	Y	N
6	Wilson	Y	Y	Y
7	**Austria**	Y	Y	N
8	**Boehner**	Y	Y	N
9	Kaptur	Y	Y	Y
10	Kucinich	N	Y	N
11	Fudge	Y	Y	Y
12	**Tiberi**	Y	Y	N
13	Sutton	Y	Y	Y
14	**LaTourette**	Y	Y	N
15	Kilroy	Y	Y	Y
16	Boccieri	Y	Y	N
17	Ryan	Y	Y	Y
18	Space	Y	Y	N
OKLAHOMA				
1	**Sullivan**	Y	Y	N
2	Boren	Y	Y	Y
3	**Lucas**	Y	Y	N
4	**Cole**	Y	Y	N
5	**Fallin**	Y	Y	N
OREGON				
1	Wu	Y	Y	Y
2	**Walden**	Y	Y	N
3	Blumenauer	Y	Y	Y
4	DeFazio	Y	Y	Y
5	Schrader	Y	Y	N
PENNSYLVANIA				
1	Brady	Y	Y	Y
2	Fattah	Y	Y	Y
3	Dahlkemper	Y	Y	N
4	Altmire	Y	Y	N
5	**Thompson**	Y	Y	N
6	**Gerlach**	Y	Y	N
7	Sestak	Y	Y	Y
8	Murphy, P.	Y	Y	Y
9	**Shuster**	Y	Y	N
10	Carney	Y	Y	Y
11	Kanjorski	Y	Y	Y
12	Critz	Y	Y	N
13	Schwartz	Y	Y	Y
14	Doyle	Y	Y	Y
15	**Dent**	Y	Y	N
16	**Pitts**	Y	Y	N
17	Holden	Y	Y	N
18	**Murphy, T.**	Y	Y	N
19	**Platts**	Y	Y	N
RHODE ISLAND				
1	Kennedy	Y	Y	Y
2	Langevin	Y	Y	Y
SOUTH CAROLINA				
1	**Brown**	Y	?	N
2	**Wilson**	Y	Y	N
3	**Barrett**	Y	Y	N
4	**Inglis**	Y	Y	N
5	Spratt	Y	Y	N
6	Clyburn	Y	Y	Y
SOUTH DAKOTA				
AL	Herseth Sandlin	Y	Y	N
TENNESSEE				
1	**Roe**	Y	Y	N
2	**Duncan**	Y	N	N
3	**Wamp**	?	?	?
4	Davis	Y	Y	Y
5	Cooper	Y	Y	Y
6	Gordon	Y	Y	Y
7	**Blackburn**	Y	Y	N
8	Tanner	Y	Y	N
9	Cohen	N	Y	Y

		425	426	428
TEXAS				
1	**Gohmert**	Y	Y	N
2	**Poe**	Y	Y	N
3	**Johnson, S.**	?	?	?
4	**Hall**	Y	Y	N
5	**Hensarling**	Y	Y	N
6	**Barton**	Y	Y	N
7	**Culberson**	Y	Y	N
8	**Brady**	Y	Y	N
9	Green, A.	Y	Y	Y
10	**McCaul**	Y	Y	N
11	**Conaway**	Y	N	N
12	**Granger**	Y	Y	N
13	**Thornberry**	Y	Y	N
14	**Paul**	N	N	N
15	Hinojosa	Y	Y	Y
16	Reyes	Y	Y	Y
17	Edwards	Y	Y	Y
18	Jackson Lee	Y	Y	Y
19	**Neugebauer**	Y	N	N
20	Gonzalez	Y	Y	Y
21	**Smith**	Y	Y	N
22	**Olson**	Y	Y	N
23	Rodriguez	?	?	?
24	**Marchant**	Y	N	N
25	Doggett	Y	Y	Y
26	**Burgess**	Y	N	N
27	Ortiz	Y	Y	Y
28	Cuellar	Y	Y	Y
29	Green, G.	Y	Y	Y
30	Johnson, E.	Y	Y	Y
31	**Carter**	Y	N	N
32	**Sessions**	Y	Y	N
UTAH				
1	**Bishop**	Y	N	N
2	Matheson	Y	Y	Y
3	**Chaffetz**	Y	N	N
VERMONT				
AL	Welch	Y	Y	Y
VIRGINIA				
1	**Wittman**	Y	Y	N
2	Nye	Y	Y	N
3	Scott	Y	Y	Y
4	**Forbes**	Y	Y	N
5	Perriello	Y	Y	N
6	**Goodlatte**	Y	Y	N
7	**Cantor**	Y	Y	N
8	Moran	Y	Y	Y
9	Boucher	Y	Y	Y
10	**Wolf**	Y	Y	N
11	Connolly	Y	Y	Y
WASHINGTON				
1	Inslee	Y	Y	Y
2	Larsen	Y	Y	Y
3	Baird	N	Y	Y
4	**Hastings**	Y	Y	N
5	**McMorris Rodgers**	Y	Y	N
6	Dicks	Y	Y	Y
7	McDermott	Y	Y	Y
8	**Reichert**	Y	Y	N
9	Smith	Y	Y	Y
WEST VIRGINIA				
1	Mollohan	Y	Y	Y
2	**Capito**	?	?	?
3	Rahall	Y	Y	Y
WISCONSIN				
1	**Ryan**	Y	Y	N
2	Baldwin	Y	Y	Y
3	Kind	Y	Y	Y
4	Moore	?	Y	Y
5	**Sensenbrenner**	?	Y	N
6	**Petri**	Y	Y	N
7	Obey	Y	Y	Y
8	Kagen	Y	Y	Y
WYOMING				
AL	**Lummis**	Y	Y	N
DELEGATES				
Faleomavaega (A.S.)				
Norton (D.C.)				
Bordallo (Guam)				
Sablan (N. Marianas)				
Pierluisi (P.R.)				
Christensen (V.I.)				

IN THE HOUSE | By Vote Number

429. **H Res 1462. Tribute to Victims of Tropical Storm Agatha/Adoption.** Watson, D-Calif., motion to suspend the rules and adopt the resolution that would mourn the loss of life related to Tropical Storm Agatha; commend the people of Guatemala, Honduras and El Salvador as they recover from the storm; and recognize the international community's assistance in recovery efforts. Motion agreed to 403-1: D 238-0; R 165-1. A two-thirds majority of those present and voting (270 in this case) is required for adoption under suspension of the rules. July 1, 2010.

430. **HR 4899. Supplemental Appropriations/Motion to Concur.** Second portion of the divided question on the Obey, D-Wis., motion to concur in the Senate amendments to the bill with House amendments. The second portion consists of an Obey amendment that would appropriate $10 billion to assist in the hiring and retention of teachers, $4.95 billion for Pell grants, $701 million for border security and $142 million in additional funding related to the Gulf Coast oil spill response. It also would include $11.7 billion in rescissions of previously appropriated funds and $4.7 billion in expected savings from changes to mandatory programs. Motion agreed to, thus returning the bill to the Senate, 239-182: D 236-15; R 3-167. July 1, 2010.

431. **HR 4899. Supplemental Appropriations/Motion to Concur.** Third portion of the divided question on the Obey, D-Wis., motion to concur in the Senate amendments to the bill with House amendments. The third portion consists of an amendment that would strike military funding for Afghanistan from the bill. Motion rejected 25-376: D 22-208; R 3-168. A "nay" was a vote in support of the president's position. July 1, 2010.

432. **HR 4899. Supplemental Appropriations/Motion to Concur.** Fourth portion of the divided question on the Obey, D-Wis., motion to concur in the Senate amendments to the bill with House amendments. The fourth portion consists of a Lee, D-Calif., amendment that would limit the use of military funding for Afghanistan to activities relating to the safe withdrawal of U.S. troops and protection of civilian and military personnel in the country. Motion rejected 100-321: D 93-157; R 7-164. A "nay" was a vote in support of the president's position. July 1, 2010.

433. **HR 4899. Supplemental Appropriations/Motion to Concur.** Fifth portion of the divided question on the Obey, D-Wis., motion to concur in the Senate amendments to the bill with House amendments. The fifth portion consists of a McGovern, D-Mass., amendment that would require the president to send Congress a new National Intelligence Estimate on Afghanistan by Jan. 31, 2011. The president would be required to send Congress a plan by April 4, 2011, for redeployment of U.S. troops from Afghanistan. The amendment also would require Congress to vote by July 2011 in order to allow the use of funds for Afghanistan in a way not consistent with the president's policy to begin drawing down troops by July 2011. Motion rejected 162-260: D 153-98; R 9-162. July 1, 2010.

	429	430	431	432	433
ALABAMA					
1 **Bonner**	Y	N	N	N	N
2 Bright	?	N	N	N	N
3 **Rogers**	Y	N	N	N	N
4 **Aderholt**	Y	N	N	N	N
5 **Griffith**	?	?	?	?	?
6 **Bachus**	Y	N	N	N	N
7 Davis	?	Y	N	N	N
ALASKA					
AL **Young**	?	?	?	?	?
ARIZONA					
1 Kirkpatrick	Y	Y	N	N	N
2 **Franks**	Y	N	N	N	N
3 **Shadegg**	Y	N	N	N	N
4 Pastor	Y	Y	N	Y	Y
5 Mitchell	Y	Y	N	N	N
6 **Flake**	Y	N	N	N	N
7 Grijalva	Y	Y	Y	Y	Y
8 Giffords	Y	Y	N	N	N
ARKANSAS					
1 Berry	Y	Y	N	N	Y
2 Snyder	Y	N	N	N	N
3 **Boozman**	Y	N	N	N	N
4 Ross	Y	Y	N	N	N
CALIFORNIA					
1 Thompson	Y	Y	P	N	Y
2 **Herger**	Y	N	N	N	N
3 **Lungren**	Y	N	N	N	N
4 **McClintock**	Y	N	N	N	N
5 Matsui	Y	Y	N	Y	Y
6 Woolsey	?	?	?	?	?
7 Miller, George	Y	Y	P	Y	Y
8 Pelosi		Y	N		Y
9 Lee	Y	Y	P	Y	Y
10 Garamendi	Y	Y	Y	Y	Y
11 McNerney	Y	Y	N	N	N
12 Speier	?	Y	N	Y	Y
13 Stark	Y	Y	Y	Y	Y
14 Eshoo	Y	Y	N	Y	Y
15 Honda	Y	Y	N	Y	Y
16 Lofgren	Y	Y	P	Y	Y
17 Farr	Y	Y	N	Y	Y
18 Cardoza	Y	Y	N	N	Y
19 **Radanovich**	?	?	?	?	?
20 Costa	Y	Y	N	N	N
21 **Nunes**	Y	N	N	N	N
22 **McCarthy**	Y	N	N	N	N
23 Capps	Y	Y	N	N	Y
24 **Gallegly**	Y	N	N	N	N
25 **McKeon**	Y	N	N	N	N
26 **Dreier**	Y	N	N	N	N
27 Sherman	Y	Y	N	N	N
28 Berman	Y	Y	N	N	N
29 Schiff	Y	Y	N	N	N
30 Waxman	Y	Y	N	Y	Y
31 Becerra	Y	Y	N	Y	Y
32 Chu	Y	Y	P	Y	Y
33 Watson	Y	Y	P	?	Y
34 Roybal-Allard	Y	Y	N	Y	Y
35 Waters	?	Y	P	Y	Y
36 Harman	?	Y	N	Y	Y
37 Richardson	Y	Y	N	Y	Y
38 Napolitano	Y	Y	Y	Y	Y
39 Sánchez, Linda	Y	Y	P	Y	Y
40 **Royce**	Y	N	N	N	N
41 **Lewis**	Y	N	N	N	N
42 **Miller, Gary**	Y	P	N	N	N
43 Baca	Y	Y	N	N	Y
44 **Calvert**	Y	N	N	N	N
45 **Bono Mack**	Y	N	N	N	N
46 **Rohrabacher**	Y	N	N	Y	Y
47 Sanchez, Loretta	Y	Y	N	Y	Y
48 **Campbell**	Y	N	N	Y	N
49 **Issa**	Y	N	N	N	N
50 **Bilbray**	Y	N	N	N	N
51 Filner	Y	Y	Y	Y	Y
52 **Hunter**	Y	N	N	N	N
53 Davis	Y	Y	N	N	N
COLORADO					
1 DeGette	Y	Y	N	Y	Y
2 Polis	?	N	N	Y	Y
3 Salazar	Y	Y	N	N	N
4 Markey	Y	N	N	N	N
5 **Lamborn**	Y	N	N	N	N
6 **Coffman**	Y	N	N	N	N
7 Perlmutter	Y	Y	N	N	Y
CONNECTICUT					
1 Larson	Y	Y	N	Y	Y
2 Courtney	Y	Y	N	N	Y
3 DeLauro	Y	Y	N	Y	Y
4 Himes	Y	Y	N	N	Y
5 Murphy	Y	Y	N	N	Y
DELAWARE					
AL **Castle**	Y	Y	N	N	N
FLORIDA					
1 **Miller**	Y	N	N	N	N
2 Boyd	Y	Y	N	N	N
3 Brown	Y	Y	N	N	Y
4 **Crenshaw**	Y	N	N	N	N
5 **Brown-Waite**	?	N	N	N	Y
6 **Stearns**	Y	N	N	N	N
7 **Mica**	Y	N	N	N	N
8 Grayson	Y	Y	Y	Y	Y
9 **Bilirakis**	Y	N	N	N	N
10 **Young**	Y	N	N	N	N
11 Castor	Y	Y	P	N	Y
12 **Putnam**	Y	N	N	N	N
13 **Buchanan**	Y	N	N	N	N
14 **Mack**	Y	N	N	N	N
15 **Posey**	Y	N	N	N	N
16 **Rooney**	Y	N	N	N	N
17 Meek	Y	Y	N	N	N
18 **Ros-Lehtinen**	Y	Y	N	N	N
19 Deutch	Y	Y	N	N	Y
20 Wasserman Schultz	Y	Y	N	N	Y
21 **Diaz-Balart, L.**	Y	N	N	N	N
22 Klein	Y	Y	N	N	N
23 Hastings	Y	Y	N	N	Y
24 Kosmas	Y	Y	N	N	N
25 **Diaz-Balart, M.**	Y	N	N	N	N
GEORGIA					
1 **Kingston**	Y	N	N	N	N
2 Bishop	Y	Y	N	N	N
3 **Westmoreland**	Y	N	N	N	N
4 Johnson	Y	Y	N	N	Y
5 Lewis	Y	Y	Y	Y	Y
6 **Price**	Y	N	N	N	N
7 **Linder**	Y	N	N	N	N
8 Marshall	Y	N	N	N	N
9 **Graves**	Y	N	N	N	N
10 **Broun**	Y	N	N	N	N
11 **Gingrey**	Y	N	N	N	N
12 Barrow	Y	Y	N	N	N
13 Scott	Y	Y	N	N	N
HAWAII					
1 **Djou**	Y	N	N	N	N
2 Hirono	Y	Y	P	Y	Y
IDAHO					
1 Minnick	Y	Y	N	N	N
2 **Simpson**	Y	N	N	N	N
ILLINOIS					
1 Rush	Y	Y	N	Y	Y
2 Jackson	Y	Y	Y	Y	Y
3 Lipinski	Y	N	N	N	N
4 Gutierrez	?	Y	Y	Y	?
5 Quigley	Y	Y	N	Y	Y
6 **Roskam**	Y	N	N	N	N
7 Davis	Y	Y	N	Y	Y
8 Bean	Y	+	N	N	N
9 Schakowsky	Y	Y	P	Y	Y
10 **Kirk**	Y	Y	N	N	N
11 Halvorson	Y	Y	N	N	N
12 Costello	Y	Y	N	Y	Y
13 **Biggert**	Y	N	N	N	N
14 Foster	Y	Y	N	N	N
15 **Johnson**	Y	Y	Y	Y	Y

KEY   **Republicans**   Democrats

Y	Voted for (yea)
#	Paired for
+	Announced for
N	Voted against (nay)
X	Paired against
–	Announced against
P	Voted "present"
C	Voted "present" to avoid possible conflict of interest
?	Did not vote or otherwise make a position known

	429	430	431	432	433
16 Manzullo	Y	N	N	N	N
17 Hare	Y	Y	N	N	Y
18 Schock	Y	N	N	N	N
19 Shimkus	Y	N	N	N	N
INDIANA					
1 Visclosky	Y	N	N	N	Y
2 Donnelly	Y	Y	N	N	N
3 Vacant					
4 Buyer	Y	N	N	N	N
5 Burton	Y	N	N	N	N
6 Pence	Y	N	N	N	N
7 Carson	Y	Y	N	N	N
8 Ellsworth	Y	Y	N	N	N
9 Hill	Y	Y	N	N	N
IOWA					
1 Braley	Y	Y	N	N	Y
2 Loebsack	Y	Y	N	N	Y
3 Boswell	Y	Y	N	N	Y
4 Latham	Y	N	N	N	N
5 King	Y	N	N	N	N
KANSAS					
1 Moran	Y	N	N	N	N
2 Jenkins	Y	N	N	N	N
3 Moore	Y	Y	N	N	N
4 Tiahrt	Y	N	N	N	N
KENTUCKY					
1 Whitfield	Y	N	N	N	N
2 Guthrie	Y	N	N	N	N
3 Yarmuth	Y	Y	P	Y	Y
4 Davis	Y	N	N	N	N
5 Rogers	Y	N	N	N	N
6 Chandler	Y	Y	N	N	N
LOUISIANA					
1 Scalise	Y	N	N	N	N
2 Cao	Y	N	N	N	N
3 Melancon	Y	N	N	N	N
4 Fleming	Y	N	N	N	N
5 Alexander	Y	N	N	N	N
6 Cassidy	Y	N	N	N	N
7 Boustany	Y	N	N	N	N
MAINE					
1 Pingree	?	Y	Y	Y	Y
2 Michaud	Y	Y	Y	Y	Y
MARYLAND					
1 Kratovil	Y	Y	N	N	N
2 Ruppersberger	Y	Y	N	N	N
3 Sarbanes	Y	Y	N	N	Y
4 Edwards	Y	Y	Y	Y	Y
5 Hoyer	Y	Y	N	N	N
6 Bartlett	Y	N	N	N	N
7 Cummings	Y	Y	N	Y	Y
8 Van Hollen	Y	Y	N	N	Y
MASSACHUSETTS					
1 Olver	Y	Y	N	Y	Y
2 Neal	Y	Y	N	Y	Y
3 McGovern	Y	Y	P	Y	Y
4 Frank	Y	Y	N	Y	Y
5 Tsongas	Y	Y	N	Y	Y
6 Tierney	Y	Y	N	Y	Y
7 Markey	Y	Y	N	Y	Y
8 Capuano	Y	Y	N	Y	Y
9 Lynch	Y	Y	N	Y	Y
10 Delahunt	Y	Y	N	Y	Y
MICHIGAN					
1 Stupak	Y	Y	N	Y	Y
2 Hoekstra	?	?	?	?	?
3 Ehlers	Y	N	N	N	N
4 Camp	Y	N	N	N	N
5 Kildee	Y	Y	N	N	Y
6 Upton	Y	N	N	N	N
7 Schauer	Y	Y	N	N	Y
8 Rogers	Y	N	N	N	N
9 Peters	Y	Y	N	N	Y
10 Miller	Y	N	N	N	N
11 McCotter	Y	N	N	N	N
12 Levin	Y	Y	N	N	Y
13 Kilpatrick	Y	Y	N	Y	Y
14 Conyers	Y	?	?	?	?
15 Dingell	Y	Y	N	N	Y
MINNESOTA					
1 Walz	Y	Y	N	N	Y
2 Kline	Y	N	N	N	N
3 Paulsen	Y	N	N	N	N
4 McCollum	Y	Y	N	Y	Y

	429	430	431	432	433
5 Ellison	Y	Y	Y	Y	Y
6 Bachmann	Y	N	N	N	N
7 Peterson	Y	N	N	N	N
8 Oberstar	Y	Y	N	Y	Y
MISSISSIPPI					
1 Childers	Y	Y	N	N	N
2 Thompson	Y	Y	N	Y	Y
3 Harper	Y	N	N	N	N
4 Taylor	Y	N	N	N	N
MISSOURI					
1 Clay	Y	Y	Y	Y	Y
2 Akin	Y	N	N	N	N
3 Carnahan	Y	Y	N	N	Y
4 Skelton	Y	N	N	N	N
5 Cleaver	Y	Y	N	Y	Y
6 Graves	Y	N	N	N	N
7 Blunt	?	N	N	N	N
8 Emerson	?	N	N	N	N
9 Luetkemeyer	Y	N	N	N	N
MONTANA					
AL Rehberg	Y	N	N	N	N
NEBRASKA					
1 Fortenberry	Y	N	N	N	N
2 Terry	Y	N	N	N	N
3 Smith	Y	N	N	N	N
NEVADA					
1 Berkley	Y	Y	N	N	Y
2 Heller	Y	N	N	N	N
3 Titus	Y	Y	N	N	N
NEW HAMPSHIRE					
1 Shea-Porter	Y	Y	N	N	Y
2 Hodes	Y	Y	N	N	Y
NEW JERSEY					
1 Andrews	Y	Y	N	N	N
2 LoBiondo	Y	N	N	N	N
3 Adler	Y	Y	N	N	N
4 Smith	Y	N	N	N	N
5 Garrett	Y	N	N	N	N
6 Pallone	Y	Y	N	Y	Y
7 Lance	Y	N	N	N	N
8 Pascrell	Y	Y	N	N	Y
9 Rothman	Y	Y	N	N	Y
10 Payne	Y	Y	N	Y	Y
11 Frelinghuysen	Y	N	N	N	N
12 Holt	Y	Y	N	Y	Y
13 Sires	Y	Y	Y	Y	Y
NEW MEXICO					
1 Heinrich	Y	Y	N	N	Y
2 Teague	Y	Y	N	N	N
3 Luján	Y	Y	N	N	Y
NEW YORK					
1 Bishop	Y	Y	N	N	Y
2 Israel	Y	Y	N	N	N
3 King	Y	N	N	N	N
4 McCarthy	?	Y	N	N	Y
5 Ackerman	Y	Y	N	N	N
6 Meeks	Y	Y	N	N	N
7 Crowley	Y	Y	N	Y	Y
8 Nadler	Y	Y	Y	Y	Y
9 Weiner	Y	Y	N	Y	Y
10 Towns	Y	Y	N	Y	Y
11 Clarke	Y	Y	Y	Y	Y
12 Velázquez	Y	Y	Y	Y	Y
13 McMahon	Y	Y	N	N	N
14 Maloney	Y	Y	P	Y	Y
15 Rangel	Y	Y	P	Y	Y
16 Serrano	Y	Y	N	Y	Y
17 Engel	Y	Y	N	N	Y
18 Lowey	Y	Y	N	N	Y
19 Hall	Y	Y	N	N	N
20 Murphy	Y	Y	N	N	N
21 Tonko	Y	Y	N	Y	Y
22 Hinchey	Y	Y	P	Y	Y
23 Owens	Y	Y	N	N	N
24 Arcuri	Y	Y	N	N	N
25 Maffei	Y	Y	N	Y	Y
26 Lee	Y	N	N	N	N
27 Higgins	Y	Y	N	N	Y
28 Slaughter	?	Y	P	Y	Y
29 Vacant					
NORTH CAROLINA					
1 Butterfield	Y	Y	N	N	N
2 Etheridge	Y	Y	N	N	N
3 Jones	Y	N	N	Y	Y
4 Price	Y	Y	N	Y	Y

	429	430	431	432	433
5 Foxx	Y	N	N	N	N
6 Coble	?	N	N	N	Y
7 McIntyre	Y	Y	N	N	N
8 Kissell	Y	Y	N	N	N
9 Myrick	Y	N	N	N	N
10 McHenry	Y	N	N	N	N
11 Shuler	Y	N	N	N	Y
12 Watt	Y	Y	N	Y	Y
13 Miller	Y	Y	N	N	Y
NORTH DAKOTA					
AL Pomeroy	Y	Y	N	N	N
OHIO					
1 Driehaus	Y	Y	N	N	N
2 Schmidt	Y	N	N	N	N
3 Turner	Y	N	N	N	N
4 Jordan	Y	N	N	N	N
5 Latta	Y	N	N	N	N
6 Wilson	Y	Y	N	N	Y
7 Austria	Y	N	N	N	N
8 Boehner	Y	N	N	N	N
9 Kaptur	Y	Y	N	N	Y
10 Kucinich	Y	Y	Y	Y	Y
11 Fudge	Y	Y	N	Y	Y
12 Tiberi	Y	N	N	N	N
13 Sutton	Y	Y	N	N	Y
14 LaTourette	Y	N	N	N	N
15 Kilroy	Y	Y	N	N	Y
16 Boccieri	Y	Y	N	N	N
17 Ryan	Y	Y	N	N	Y
18 Space	Y	Y	N	N	N
OKLAHOMA					
1 Sullivan	Y	N	N	N	N
2 Boren	Y	N	N	N	N
3 Lucas	Y	N	N	N	N
4 Cole	Y	N	N	N	N
5 Fallin	Y	N	N	N	N
OREGON					
1 Wu	Y	Y	N	N	N
2 Walden	Y	N	N	N	N
3 Blumenauer	Y	Y	N	Y	Y
4 DeFazio	Y	Y	N	Y	Y
5 Schrader	Y	Y	Y	Y	Y
PENNSYLVANIA					
1 Brady	Y	Y	N	N	Y
2 Fattah	Y	Y	N	N	Y
3 Dahlkemper	?	N	N	N	Y
4 Altmire	Y	Y	N	N	N
5 Thompson	Y	N	N	N	N
6 Gerlach	Y	N	N	N	N
7 Sestak	Y	Y	N	N	N
8 Murphy, P.	Y	Y	N	N	N
9 Shuster	Y	N	N	N	N
10 Carney	Y	Y	N	N	N
11 Kanjorski	Y	Y	N	N	Y
12 Critz	Y	Y	N	N	N
13 Schwartz	Y	Y	N	N	Y
14 Doyle	Y	Y	N	Y	Y
15 Dent	Y	N	N	N	N
16 Pitts	Y	N	N	N	N
17 Holden	Y	Y	N	N	N
18 Murphy, T.	Y	N	N	N	N
19 Platts	Y	N	N	N	N
RHODE ISLAND					
1 Kennedy	Y	Y	N	Y	Y
2 Langevin	Y	Y	N	N	Y
SOUTH CAROLINA					
1 Brown	Y	N	N	N	N
2 Wilson	Y	N	N	N	N
3 Barrett	Y	N	N	N	N
4 Inglis	Y	N	N	N	N
5 Spratt	Y	Y	N	N	N
6 Clyburn	Y	Y	N	N	N
SOUTH DAKOTA					
AL Herseth Sandlin	Y	N	N	N	N
TENNESSEE					
1 Roe	Y	N	N	N	N
2 Duncan	Y	N	Y	Y	Y
3 Wamp	?	?	?	?	?
4 Davis	Y	N	N	N	N
5 Cooper	Y	N	N	N	N
6 Gordon	?	Y	N	N	N
7 Blackburn	Y	N	N	N	N
8 Tanner	Y	Y	N	N	N
9 Cohen	Y	Y	P	Y	Y

	429	430	431	432	433
TEXAS					
1 Gohmert	Y	N	N	N	N
2 Poe	Y	N	N	N	N
3 Johnson, S.	?	?	?	?	?
4 Hall	Y	N	N	N	N
5 Hensarling	Y	N	N	N	N
6 Barton	Y	N	N	N	N
7 Culberson	Y	N	N	N	N
8 Brady	Y	N	N	N	N
9 Green, A.	Y	Y	N	N	N
10 McCaul	?	N	N	N	N
11 Conaway	Y	N	N	N	N
12 Granger	Y	N	N	N	N
13 Thornberry	Y	N	N	N	N
14 Paul	N	N	Y	Y	Y
15 Hinojosa	Y	Y	N	Y	Y
16 Reyes	Y	Y	N	N	N
17 Edwards	Y	Y	N	N	N
18 Jackson Lee	Y	Y	P	Y	Y
19 Neugebauer	Y	N	N	N	N
20 Gonzalez	Y	Y	N	N	Y
21 Smith	Y	N	N	N	N
22 Olson	Y	N	N	N	N
23 Rodriguez	?	?	?	?	?
24 Marchant	Y	N	N	N	N
25 Doggett	Y	Y	N	Y	Y
26 Burgess	Y	N	N	N	N
27 Ortiz	Y	Y	N	N	N
28 Cuellar	Y	Y	N	N	N
29 Green, G.	?	Y	N	N	N
30 Johnson, E.	Y	Y	N	N	N
31 Carter	Y	N	N	N	N
32 Sessions	Y	N	N	N	N
UTAH					
1 Bishop	Y	N	N	N	N
2 Matheson	Y	Y	N	N	N
3 Chaffetz	Y	N	N	Y	Y
VERMONT					
AL Welch	Y	N	Y	Y	N
VIRGINIA					
1 Wittman	Y	N	N	N	N
2 Nye	Y	Y	N	N	N
3 Scott	Y	Y	N	Y	Y
4 Forbes	Y	N	N	N	N
5 Perriello	Y	Y	N	N	N
6 Goodlatte	Y	N	N	N	N
7 Cantor	Y	N	N	N	N
8 Moran	Y	Y	N	N	Y
9 Boucher	Y	Y	N	N	N
10 Wolf	Y	N	N	N	N
11 Connolly	Y	Y	N	N	Y
WASHINGTON					
1 Inslee	Y	N	N	Y	Y
2 Larsen	Y	N	N	N	N
3 Baird	Y	N	N	N	N
4 Hastings	Y	N	N	N	N
5 McMorris Rodgers	Y	N	N	N	N
6 Dicks	?	Y	N	N	N
7 McDermott	Y	Y	P	Y	Y
8 Reichert	Y	N	N	N	N
9 Smith	Y	Y	N	N	Y
WEST VIRGINIA					
1 Mollohan	Y	Y	N	N	N
2 Capito	?	?	?	?	?
3 Rahall	Y	Y	N	N	N
WISCONSIN					
1 Ryan	Y	N	N	N	N
2 Baldwin	Y	Y	P	Y	Y
3 Kind	Y	N	N	Y	Y
4 Moore	Y	Y	N	Y	Y
5 Sensenbrenner	Y	N	N	N	N
6 Petri	Y	N	N	N	N
7 Obey	Y	N	N	Y	Y
8 Kagen	Y	Y	P	Y	Y
WYOMING					
AL Lummis	Y	N	N	N	N
DELEGATES					
Faleomavaega (A.S.)					
Norton (D.C.)					
Bordallo (Guam)					
Sablan (N. Marianas)					
Pierluisi (P.R.)					
Christensen (V.I.)					

IN THE HOUSE | By Vote Number

434. **HR 4514. Col. Charles Young Home Study/Passage.** Bordallo, D-Guam, motion to suspend the rules and pass the bill that would authorize the Interior Department to conduct a study to determine the suitability and feasibility of designating the Col. Charles Young Home, a national historic landmark in Xenia, Ohio, as a unit of the National Park System. Motion agreed to 350-26: D 225-0; R 125-26. A two-thirds majority of those present and voting (251 in this case) is required for passage under suspension of the rules. July 13, 2010.

435. **HR 4438. San Antonio Missions Park Expansion/Passage.** Bordallo, D-Guam, motion to suspend the rules and pass the bill that would authorize the Interior Department to expand the boundary of the San Antonio Missions National Historical Park by approximately 151 acres. Motion agreed to 264-114: D 225-1; R 39-113. A two-thirds majority of those present and voting (252 in this case) is required for passage under suspension of the rules. July 13, 2010.

436. **HR 4773. Fort Pulaski Lease Authorization/Passage.** Bordallo, D-Guam, motion to suspend the rules and pass the bill that would permit the National Park Service to lease a site at the Fort Pulaski National Monument on Cockspur Island, Ga., to the Savannah Bar Pilots Association. Motion agreed to 379-0: D 228-0; R 151-0. A two-thirds majority of those present and voting (253 in this case) is required for passage under suspension of the rules. July 13, 2010.

437. **HR 1722. Telework for Federal Employees/Previous Question.** McGovern, D-Mass., motion to order the previous question (thus ending debate and possibility of amendment) on adoption of the rule (H Res 1509) to provide for House floor consideration of the bill that would require the head of each executive agency to establish and implement a policy that would allow employees to telework as much as possible without diminishing agency operations or performance. Motion agreed to 232-184: D 232-11; R 0-173. July 14, 2010.

438. **HR 1722. Telework for Federal Employees/Rule.** Adoption of the rule (H Res 1509) to provide for House floor consideration of the bill. The rule would provide for automatic adoption of an amendment to exclude employees who have been disciplined for certain activities from teleworking and require the Office of Management and Budget to issue guidelines to prevent inappropriate use of official time and resources. Adopted 238-180: D 237-9; R 1-171. July 14, 2010.

439. **HR 2864. NOAA Arctic Study/Passage.** Bordallo, D-Guam, motion to suspend the rules and pass the bill that would permit the National Oceanic and Atmospheric Administration (NOAA) to use $7 million annually from amounts previously authorized for fiscal 2011-12 to collect and analyze hydrographic and coastal-change data in order to ensure safe navigation, improve the management of coastal change and delineate the U.S. extended continental shelf in the Arctic. Motion agreed to 420-0: D 247-0; R 173-0. A two-thirds majority of those present and voting (280 in this case) is required for passage under suspension of the rules. July 14, 2010.

440. **HR 1722. Telework for Federal Employees/Recommit.** Issa, R-Calif., motion to recommit the bill to the House Oversight and Government Reform Committee with instructions that it be immediately reported back with an amendment that would require agency heads to certify to the Office of Personnel Management that a telework program will result in agency savings. It would prohibit certain employees from participating in telework programs, including those who have taken more than five unexcused absences or are seriously delinquent in taxes. Motion agreed to 303-119: D 129-119; R 174-0. July 14, 2010.

	434	435	436	437	438	439	440
ALABAMA							
1 Bonner	Y	Y	Y	N	N	Y	Y
2 Bright	Y	Y	Y	N	Y	Y	Y
3 Rogers	Y	Y	?	N	N	Y	Y
4 Aderholt	Y	N	Y	N	N	Y	Y
5 Griffith	?	?	Y	N	Y	Y	Y
6 Bachus	Y	Y	Y	–	–	+	Y
7 Davis	?	?	?	Y	Y	Y	Y
ALASKA							
AL Young	Y	N	Y	N	N	Y	Y
ARIZONA							
1 Kirkpatrick	Y	Y	Y	N	Y	Y	Y
2 Franks	Y	N	Y	N	N	Y	Y
3 Shadegg	N	N	Y	N	N	Y	Y
4 Pastor	Y	Y	Y	Y	N	Y	Y
5 Mitchell	Y	Y	Y	N	N	Y	Y
6 Flake	N	N	Y	N	N	Y	Y
7 Grijalva	Y	Y	Y	?	Y	Y	N
8 Giffords	?	?	?	N	N	Y	Y
ARKANSAS							
1 Berry	?	?	?	Y	Y	Y	N
2 Snyder	Y	Y	Y	Y	Y	Y	N
3 Boozman	Y	N	Y	N	N	Y	Y
4 Ross	Y	Y	Y	Y	Y	Y	Y
CALIFORNIA							
1 Thompson	Y	Y	Y	Y	Y	Y	N
2 Herger	N	N	Y	N	N	Y	Y
3 Lungren	Y	N	Y	N	N	Y	Y
4 McClintock	Y	N	Y	N	N	Y	Y
5 Matsui	Y	Y	Y	Y	Y	Y	N
6 Woolsey	Y	Y	Y	Y	Y	Y	N
7 Miller, George	Y	Y	Y	Y	Y	Y	N
8 Pelosi							
9 Lee	+	+	+	Y	Y	Y	N
10 Garamendi	Y	Y	Y	?	Y	Y	N
11 McNerney	Y	Y	Y	Y	Y	Y	Y
12 Speier	Y	Y	Y	Y	Y	Y	N
13 Stark	Y	Y	Y	Y	Y	Y	N
14 Eshoo	Y	Y	Y	Y	Y	Y	N
15 Honda	Y	Y	Y	Y	Y	Y	N
16 Lofgren	Y	Y	Y	Y	Y	Y	N
17 Farr	Y	Y	Y	Y	Y	Y	N
18 Cardoza	Y	Y	Y	Y	Y	Y	N
19 Radanovich	Y	Y	Y	N	Y	Y	Y
20 Costa	Y	Y	Y	Y	Y	Y	Y
21 Nunes	N	N	Y	N	N	Y	Y
22 McCarthy	Y	N	Y	N	N	Y	Y
23 Capps	Y	Y	Y	Y	Y	Y	N
24 Gallegly	Y	N	Y	N	N	Y	Y
25 McKeon	Y	N	Y	N	?	Y	Y
26 Dreier	Y	N	Y	N	N	Y	Y
27 Sherman	Y	Y	Y	Y	Y	Y	N
28 Berman	Y	Y	Y	Y	Y	Y	N
29 Schiff	Y	Y	Y	Y	Y	Y	N
30 Waxman	Y	Y	Y	Y	Y	Y	N
31 Becerra	Y	Y	Y	Y	Y	Y	N
32 Chu	Y	Y	Y	Y	Y	Y	N
33 Watson	Y	Y	Y	Y	Y	Y	N
34 Roybal-Allard	Y	Y	Y	Y	Y	Y	N
35 Waters	Y	Y	Y	Y	Y	Y	N
36 Harman	Y	Y	Y	Y	Y	Y	Y
37 Richardson	Y	?	Y	Y	Y	Y	N
38 Napolitano	Y	Y	Y	Y	Y	Y	N
39 Sánchez, Linda	?	?	?	?	?	?	?
40 Royce	N	N	Y	N	N	Y	Y
41 Lewis	Y	N	Y	N	N	Y	Y
42 Miller, Gary	Y	N	Y	N	N	Y	Y
43 Baca	Y	Y	Y	Y	N	Y	Y
44 Calvert	Y	N	Y	N	N	Y	Y
45 Bono Mack	Y	Y	Y	N	N	Y	Y
46 Rohrabacher	?	?	?	N	N	Y	Y
47 Sanchez, Loretta	Y	Y	Y	Y	Y	Y	N
48 Campbell	N	N	Y	N	N	Y	Y
49 Issa	N	N	Y	N	N	Y	Y
50 Bilbray	Y	N	Y	N	N	Y	Y
51 Filner	+	+	+	Y	Y	Y	N
52 Hunter	N	N	Y	N	N	Y	Y
53 Davis	Y	Y	Y	Y	Y	Y	N
COLORADO							
1 DeGette	Y	Y	Y	Y	Y	Y	N
2 Polis	Y	Y	Y	Y	Y	Y	N
3 Salazar	Y	Y	Y	Y	Y	Y	Y
4 Markey	Y	Y	Y	Y	Y	Y	Y
5 Lamborn	N	N	Y	N	N	Y	Y
6 Coffman	Y	–	Y	N	N	Y	Y
7 Perlmutter	?	?	?	Y	Y	Y	Y
CONNECTICUT							
1 Larson	Y	Y	Y	Y	Y	Y	N
2 Courtney	Y	Y	Y	Y	Y	Y	N
3 DeLauro	Y	Y	Y	Y	Y	Y	N
4 Himes	Y	Y	Y	Y	Y	Y	N
5 Murphy	Y	Y	Y	Y	Y	Y	N
DELAWARE							
AL Castle	Y	N	Y	N	N	Y	Y
FLORIDA							
1 Miller	+	–	+	N	N	Y	Y
2 Boyd	Y	Y	Y	Y	Y	Y	N
3 Brown	Y	Y	Y	Y	Y	Y	N
4 Crenshaw	Y	Y	Y	N	N	Y	Y
5 Brown-Waite	Y	N	Y	N	N	Y	Y
6 Stearns	N	N	Y	N	N	Y	Y
7 Mica	Y	Y	Y	N	N	Y	Y
8 Grayson	Y	Y	Y	Y	Y	Y	N
9 Bilirakis	Y	N	Y	N	N	Y	Y
10 Young	?	?	?	N	N	Y	Y
11 Castor	Y	Y	Y	Y	Y	Y	N
12 Putnam	+	+	+	N	N	Y	Y
13 Buchanan	Y	Y	Y	N	N	Y	Y
14 Mack	N	N	Y	N	N	Y	Y
15 Posey	Y	N	Y	N	N	Y	Y
16 Rooney	Y	N	Y	N	N	Y	Y
17 Meek	Y	Y	Y	Y	Y	Y	N
18 Ros-Lehtinen	Y	Y	Y	N	N	Y	Y
19 Deutch	?	?	?	?	?	?	?
20 Wasserman Schultz	Y	Y	Y	Y	Y	Y	N
21 Diaz-Balart, L.	Y	Y	Y	N	N	Y	Y
22 Klein	Y	Y	Y	Y	Y	Y	Y
23 Hastings	?	?	?	?	?	?	?
24 Kosmas	Y	Y	Y	Y	Y	Y	Y
25 Diaz-Balart, M.	Y	Y	Y	N	N	Y	Y
GEORGIA							
1 Kingston	N	N	Y	N	N	Y	Y
2 Bishop	Y	Y	Y	Y	Y	Y	N
3 Westmoreland	Y	N	Y	N	N	Y	Y
4 Johnson	Y	Y	Y	Y	Y	Y	N
5 Lewis	Y	Y	Y	Y	Y	Y	N
6 Price	Y	N	Y	N	N	Y	Y
7 Linder	?	?	?	N	N	Y	Y
8 Marshall	Y	Y	Y	?	?	Y	Y
9 Graves	N	N	Y	N	N	Y	Y
10 Broun	N	N	Y	N	N	Y	Y
11 Gingrey	Y	N	Y	N	N	Y	Y
12 Barrow	Y	Y	Y	Y	Y	Y	N
13 Scott	Y	Y	Y	Y	Y	Y	N
HAWAII							
1 Djou	Y	Y	Y	N	N	Y	Y
2 Hirono	Y	Y	Y	Y	Y	Y	N
IDAHO							
1 Minnick	Y	Y	?	N	N	Y	Y
2 Simpson	Y	Y	Y	N	N	Y	Y
ILLINOIS							
1 Rush	?	?	?	Y	Y	Y	Y
2 Jackson	Y	Y	Y	Y	Y	Y	Y
3 Lipinski	Y	Y	Y	Y	Y	Y	Y
4 Gutierrez	Y	?	Y	Y	Y	Y	N
5 Quigley	Y	Y	Y	Y	Y	Y	N
6 Roskam	Y	N	Y	N	N	Y	Y
7 Davis	?	?	Y	Y	Y	Y	N
8 Bean	?	N	Y	Y	Y	Y	Y
9 Schakowsky	Y	Y	Y	Y	Y	Y	N
10 Kirk	Y	Y	Y	N	N	Y	Y
11 Halvorson	Y	Y	Y	Y	Y	Y	N
12 Costello	?	?	?	Y	Y	Y	N
13 Biggert	Y	N	Y	N	N	Y	Y
14 Foster	Y	Y	Y	Y	Y	Y	N
15 Johnson	Y	Y	Y	N	N	Y	Y

KEY   **Republicans**   Democrats

Y Voted for (yea)	X Paired against	C Voted "present" to avoid possible conflict of interest
# Paired for	– Announced against	
+ Announced for	P Voted "present"	? Did not vote or otherwise make a position known
N Voted against (nay)		

	434	435	436	437	438	439	440
16 **Manzullo**	Y	N	Y	N	N	Y	Y
17 Hare	+	+	+	Y	Y	Y	Y
18 **Schock**	Y	N	Y	N	N	Y	Y
19 **Shimkus**	?	?	?	N	N	Y	Y
INDIANA							
1 Visclosky	Y	Y	Y	Y	Y	Y	Y
2 Donnelly	Y	Y	Y	Y	Y	Y	Y
3 Vacant							
4 **Buyer**	?	?	?	N	N	Y	Y
5 **Burton**	Y	N	Y	N	N	Y	Y
6 **Pence**	?	N	Y	N	N	Y	Y
7 Carson	Y	Y	Y	Y	Y	Y	Y
8 Ellsworth	?	Y	Y	Y	Y	Y	Y
9 Hill	Y	Y	Y	N	N	Y	Y
IOWA							
1 Braley	Y	Y	Y	Y	Y	Y	N
2 Loebsack	Y	Y	Y	Y	Y	Y	Y
3 Boswell	Y	Y	Y	Y	Y	Y	Y
4 **Latham**	Y	Y	Y	N	N	Y	Y
5 **King**	N	N	Y	N	N	Y	Y
KANSAS							
1 **Moran**	?	?	?	N	N	Y	Y
2 **Jenkins**	Y	N	Y	N	N	Y	Y
3 Moore	Y	Y	Y	Y	Y	Y	Y
4 **Tiahrt**	–	–	+	–	–	+	+
KENTUCKY							
1 **Whitfield**	Y	Y	Y	?	?	Y	Y
2 **Guthrie**	Y	N	Y	N	N	Y	Y
3 Yarmuth	Y	Y	Y	Y	Y	Y	Y
4 **Davis**	Y	N	Y	N	N	Y	Y
5 **Rogers**	Y	N	Y	N	N	Y	Y
6 Chandler	Y	Y	Y	Y	Y	Y	Y
LOUISIANA							
1 **Scalise**	Y	N	Y	N	N	Y	Y
2 **Cao**	Y	Y	Y	N	N	Y	Y
3 Melancon	Y	Y	Y	Y	Y	Y	Y
4 **Fleming**	?	?	?	N	N	Y	Y
5 **Alexander**	?	?	?	N	N	Y	Y
6 **Cassidy**	Y	N	Y	N	N	Y	Y
7 **Boustany**	Y	N	Y	N	N	Y	Y
MAINE							
1 Pingree	Y	Y	Y	Y	Y	Y	N
2 Michaud	Y	Y	Y	Y	Y	Y	N
MARYLAND							
1 Kratovil	Y	Y	Y	N	N	Y	Y
2 Ruppersberger	Y	Y	Y	Y	Y	Y	N
3 Sarbanes	Y	Y	Y	Y	Y	Y	N
4 Edwards	Y	Y	Y	Y	Y	Y	N
5 Hoyer	Y	Y	Y	Y	Y	Y	N
6 **Bartlett**	Y	N	Y	N	N	Y	Y
7 Cummings	Y	Y	Y	?	Y	Y	N
8 Van Hollen	Y	Y	Y	Y	Y	Y	N
MASSACHUSETTS							
1 Olver	Y	Y	Y	Y	Y	Y	N
2 Neal	Y	Y	Y	Y	Y	Y	N
3 McGovern	Y	Y	Y	Y	Y	Y	N
4 Frank	?	?	Y	Y	Y	Y	N
5 Tsongas	Y	Y	Y	Y	Y	Y	N
6 Tierney	Y	Y	Y	Y	Y	Y	N
7 Markey	Y	Y	Y	Y	Y	Y	N
8 Capuano	Y	Y	Y	?	Y	Y	N
9 Lynch	Y	Y	Y	Y	Y	Y	N
10 Delahunt	Y	Y	Y	?	Y	Y	N
MICHIGAN							
1 Stupak	Y	Y	Y	Y	Y	Y	Y
2 **Hoekstra**	?	?	?	?	?	?	?
3 **Ehlers**	+	+	+	N	N	Y	Y
4 **Camp**	?	?	?	N	N	Y	Y
5 Kildee	Y	Y	Y	Y	Y	Y	Y
6 **Upton**	Y	N	Y	N	N	Y	Y
7 Schauer	Y	Y	Y	Y	Y	Y	Y
8 **Rogers**	Y	N	Y	N	N	Y	Y
9 Peters	Y	Y	Y	Y	Y	Y	Y
10 **Miller**	Y	N	Y	N	N	Y	Y
11 **McCotter**	Y	N	Y	N	N	Y	Y
12 Levin	Y	Y	Y	Y	Y	Y	N
13 Kilpatrick	Y	Y	Y	Y	Y	Y	N
14 Conyers	Y	Y	Y	Y	Y	?	Y
15 Dingell	Y	Y	Y	Y	Y	Y	N
MINNESOTA							
1 Walz	Y	Y	Y	Y	Y	Y	Y
2 **Kline**	Y	N	Y	N	N	Y	Y
3 **Paulsen**	Y	Y	Y	N	N	Y	Y
4 McCollum	Y	Y	Y	Y	Y	Y	N

	434	435	436	437	438	439	440
5 Ellison	Y	Y	Y	Y	Y	Y	N
6 **Bachmann**	Y	N	Y	N	N	Y	Y
7 Peterson	Y	Y	Y	Y	Y	Y	Y
8 Oberstar	Y	Y	Y	Y	Y	Y	N
MISSISSIPPI							
1 Childers	Y	Y	Y	N	N	Y	Y
2 Thompson	Y	Y	Y	Y	Y	Y	N
3 **Harper**	Y	N	Y	N	N	Y	Y
4 Taylor	?	?	?	N	N	Y	Y
MISSOURI							
1 Clay	Y	Y	Y	Y	Y	Y	N
2 **Akin**	+	+	+	N	N	Y	Y
3 Carnahan	?	?	?	Y	Y	Y	Y
4 Skelton	Y	Y	Y	Y	Y	Y	Y
5 Cleaver	Y	Y	Y	Y	Y	Y	N
6 **Graves**	Y	N	Y	N	N	Y	Y
7 **Blunt**	?	?	?	N	N	Y	Y
8 **Emerson**	Y	N	Y	N	N	Y	Y
9 **Luetkemeyer**	?	?	?	N	N	Y	Y
MONTANA							
AL **Rehberg**	+	–	+	N	N	Y	Y
NEBRASKA							
1 **Fortenberry**	?	?	?	N	N	Y	Y
2 **Terry**	Y	Y	Y	N	N	Y	Y
3 **Smith**	Y	N	Y	N	N	Y	Y
NEVADA							
1 Berkley	Y	Y	Y	Y	Y	Y	Y
2 **Heller**	Y	N	Y	N	N	Y	Y
3 Titus	Y	Y	Y	Y	Y	Y	Y
NEW HAMPSHIRE							
1 Shea-Porter	Y	Y	Y	Y	Y	Y	Y
2 Hodes	Y	Y	Y	Y	Y	Y	Y
NEW JERSEY							
1 Andrews	Y	Y	Y	Y	Y	?	N
2 **LoBiondo**	Y	N	Y	N	N	Y	Y
3 Adler	Y	Y	Y	Y	Y	Y	Y
4 **Smith**	Y	Y	Y	N	N	Y	Y
5 **Garrett**	Y	N	Y	N	N	Y	Y
6 Pallone	Y	Y	Y	Y	Y	Y	N
7 **Lance**	Y	Y	Y	N	N	Y	Y
8 Pascrell	Y	Y	Y	Y	Y	Y	N
9 Rothman	Y	Y	Y	Y	Y	Y	Y
10 Payne	Y	Y	Y	Y	Y	Y	N
11 **Frelinghuysen**	Y	N	Y	N	N	Y	Y
12 Holt	Y	Y	Y	Y	Y	Y	N
13 Sires	Y	Y	Y	Y	?	Y	N
NEW MEXICO							
1 Heinrich	Y	Y	Y	Y	Y	Y	Y
2 Teague	Y	Y	Y	Y	Y	Y	Y
3 Luján	Y	Y	Y	Y	Y	Y	Y
NEW YORK							
1 Bishop	Y	Y	Y	Y	Y	Y	Y
2 Israel	?	Y	Y	Y	Y	Y	Y
3 **King**	Y	N	Y	N	N	Y	Y
4 McCarthy	Y	Y	Y	Y	Y	Y	N
5 Ackerman	Y	Y	Y	Y	Y	Y	Y
6 Meeks	Y	Y	Y	Y	Y	Y	N
7 Crowley	Y	Y	Y	Y	Y	Y	N
8 Nadler	Y	Y	Y	Y	Y	Y	N
9 Weiner	Y	Y	Y	Y	Y	Y	N
10 Towns	Y	Y	Y	Y	Y	Y	N
11 Clarke	Y	Y	Y	Y	Y	Y	N
12 Velázquez	Y	Y	Y	Y	Y	Y	N
13 McMahon	Y	Y	Y	Y	+	Y	Y
14 Maloney	Y	Y	Y	Y	Y	Y	N
15 Rangel	Y	Y	Y	Y	Y	Y	N
16 Serrano	Y	Y	Y	Y	Y	Y	N
17 Engel	Y	Y	Y	Y	Y	Y	N
18 Lowey	Y	Y	Y	Y	Y	Y	N
19 Hall	Y	Y	Y	Y	Y	Y	Y
20 Murphy	Y	Y	Y	Y	Y	Y	Y
21 Tonko	Y	Y	Y	Y	Y	Y	N
22 Hinchey	Y	Y	Y	Y	Y	Y	N
23 Owens	Y	Y	Y	Y	Y	Y	N
24 Arcuri	Y	Y	Y	Y	Y	Y	Y
25 Maffei	?	?	?	Y	Y	Y	Y
26 **Lee**	Y	N	Y	N	N	Y	Y
27 Higgins	Y	Y	Y	Y	Y	Y	?
28 Slaughter	Y	Y	Y	Y	Y	Y	N
29 Vacant							
NORTH CAROLINA							
1 Butterfield	Y	Y	Y	Y	Y	Y	N
2 Etheridge	Y	Y	Y	Y	Y	Y	Y
3 **Jones**	Y	Y	Y	N	N	Y	Y
4 Price	Y	Y	Y	Y	Y	Y	N

	434	435	436	437	438	439	440
5 **Foxx**	N	N	Y	N	N	Y	Y
6 **Coble**	N	N	Y	N	N	Y	Y
7 McIntyre	Y	Y	Y	Y	Y	Y	Y
8 Kissell	Y	Y	Y	Y	Y	Y	Y
9 **Myrick**	Y	N	Y	N	N	Y	Y
10 **McHenry**	Y	N	Y	N	N	Y	Y
11 Shuler	?	?	?	Y	N	Y	Y
12 Watt	Y	Y	Y	Y	Y	Y	N
13 Miller	Y	Y	Y	Y	Y	Y	N
NORTH DAKOTA							
AL Pomeroy	Y	Y	Y	Y	Y	Y	Y
OHIO							
1 Driehaus	Y	Y	Y	Y	Y	Y	Y
2 **Schmidt**	?	?	?	N	N	Y	Y
3 **Turner**	Y	N	Y	N	N	Y	Y
4 **Jordan**	Y	N	Y	N	N	Y	Y
5 **Latta**	Y	N	Y	N	N	Y	Y
6 Wilson	Y	Y	Y	Y	Y	Y	Y
7 **Austria**	Y	Y	Y	N	N	Y	Y
8 **Boehner**	Y	N	Y	N	N	Y	Y
9 Kaptur	?	?	?	Y	Y	Y	Y
10 Kucinich	Y	Y	Y	Y	Y	Y	N
11 Fudge	Y	Y	Y	Y	Y	Y	N
12 **Tiberi**	Y	N	Y	N	N	Y	Y
13 Sutton	Y	Y	Y	Y	Y	Y	Y
14 **LaTourette**	Y	Y	Y	N	N	Y	Y
15 Kilroy	Y	Y	Y	Y	Y	Y	N
16 Boccieri	Y	Y	Y	Y	Y	Y	Y
17 Ryan	Y	Y	Y	Y	Y	Y	Y
18 Space	Y	Y	Y	N	Y	Y	Y
OKLAHOMA							
1 **Sullivan**	Y	N	Y	N	N	Y	Y
2 Boren	Y	Y	Y	Y	Y	Y	Y
3 **Lucas**	Y	Y	Y	N	N	Y	Y
4 **Cole**	Y	Y	Y	N	N	Y	Y
5 **Fallin**	?	?	?	N	N	Y	Y
OREGON							
1 Wu	Y	Y	Y	Y	Y	Y	Y
2 **Walden**	?	N	Y	N	N	Y	Y
3 Blumenauer	Y	Y	Y	Y	Y	Y	N
4 DeFazio	Y	Y	Y	Y	Y	Y	Y
5 Schrader	Y	Y	Y	Y	Y	Y	Y
PENNSYLVANIA							
1 Brady	Y	Y	Y	Y	Y	Y	N
2 Fattah	Y	Y	?	Y	Y	Y	N
3 Dahlkemper	Y	Y	Y	Y	Y	Y	Y
4 Altmire	Y	Y	Y	Y	Y	Y	Y
5 **Thompson**	Y	N	Y	N	N	Y	Y
6 **Gerlach**	Y	N	Y	N	N	Y	Y
7 Sestak	Y	Y	Y	Y	Y	Y	Y
8 Murphy, P.	Y	Y	Y	Y	Y	Y	Y
9 **Shuster**	Y	N	Y	N	N	Y	Y
10 Carney	?	?	?	Y	Y	Y	Y
11 Kanjorski	Y	Y	Y	Y	Y	Y	N
12 Critz	Y	Y	Y	Y	Y	Y	Y
13 Schwartz	Y	Y	Y	Y	Y	Y	Y
14 Doyle	?	?	?	Y	Y	Y	N
15 **Dent**	Y	Y	Y	N	N	Y	Y
16 **Pitts**	Y	N	Y	N	N	Y	Y
17 Holden	Y	Y	Y	Y	Y	Y	Y
18 **Murphy, T.**	Y	N	Y	N	N	Y	Y
19 **Platts**	Y	N	Y	N	N	Y	Y
RHODE ISLAND							
1 Kennedy	Y	Y	Y	Y	Y	Y	N
2 Langevin	Y	Y	Y	Y	Y	Y	N
SOUTH CAROLINA							
1 **Brown**	Y	N	Y	N	N	Y	Y
2 **Wilson**	Y	N	Y	N	N	Y	Y
3 **Barrett**	+	–	+	N	N	Y	Y
4 **Inglis**	Y	N	Y	N	N	Y	Y
5 Spratt	Y	Y	Y	Y	Y	Y	Y
6 Clyburn	Y	Y	Y	Y	Y	Y	N
SOUTH DAKOTA							
AL Herseth Sandlin	Y	Y	Y	Y	Y	Y	Y
TENNESSEE							
1 **Roe**	Y	N	Y	N	N	Y	Y
2 **Duncan**	N	N	Y	N	N	Y	Y
3 **Wamp**	?	?	?	N	N	Y	Y
4 Davis	Y	Y	Y	Y	Y	Y	Y
5 Cooper	Y	Y	Y	Y	Y	Y	Y
6 Gordon	Y	Y	Y	Y	Y	Y	Y
7 **Blackburn**	Y	N	Y	N	N	Y	Y
8 Tanner	Y	Y	Y	Y	Y	Y	Y
9 Cohen	+	+	+	Y	Y	Y	N

	434	435	436	437	438	439	440
TEXAS							
1 **Gohmert**	N	N	Y	N	N	Y	Y
2 **Poe**	N	Y	Y	N	N	Y	Y
3 **Johnson, S.**	Y	N	Y	N	N	Y	Y
4 **Hall**	Y	Y	Y	N	N	Y	Y
5 **Hensarling**	Y	N	Y	N	N	Y	Y
6 **Barton**	Y	Y	Y	N	N	Y	Y
7 **Culberson**	N	N	Y	N	N	Y	Y
8 **Brady**	N	Y	Y	N	N	?	Y
9 Green, A.	Y	Y	Y	Y	Y	Y	Y
10 **McCaul**	Y	Y	Y	N	N	Y	Y
11 **Conaway**	Y	N	Y	N	N	Y	Y
12 **Granger**	Y	Y	Y	N	N	Y	Y
13 **Thornberry**	N	N	Y	N	N	Y	Y
14 **Paul**	N	N	Y	N	N	Y	Y
15 Hinojosa	?	?	?	?	?	?	?
16 Reyes	Y	Y	Y	Y	Y	Y	N
17 Edwards	Y	Y	Y	Y	Y	Y	Y
18 Jackson Lee	Y	Y	Y	Y	Y	Y	Y
19 **Neugebauer**	N	N	Y	N	N	Y	Y
20 Gonzalez	Y	Y	Y	Y	Y	Y	Y
21 **Smith**	Y	Y	Y	N	N	Y	Y
22 **Olson**	?	?	?	?	?	?	?
23 Rodriguez	Y	Y	Y	Y	Y	Y	Y
24 **Marchant**	Y	N	Y	N	N	Y	Y
25 Doggett	Y	Y	Y	Y	Y	Y	Y
26 **Burgess**	N	N	Y	N	N	Y	Y
27 Ortiz	Y	Y	Y	Y	Y	Y	Y
28 Cuellar	Y	Y	Y	Y	Y	Y	Y
29 Green, G.	Y	Y	Y	Y	Y	Y	Y
30 Johnson, E.	?	?	?	Y	Y	Y	N
31 **Carter**	Y	Y	?	N	N	Y	Y
32 **Sessions**	Y	Y	Y	N	N	Y	Y
UTAH							
1 **Bishop**	Y	N	Y	N	N	Y	Y
2 Matheson	Y	Y	Y	Y	Y	Y	Y
3 **Chaffetz**	Y	N	Y	N	N	Y	Y
VERMONT							
AL Welch	Y	Y	Y	Y	Y	Y	Y
VIRGINIA							
1 **Wittman**	Y	Y	Y	N	N	Y	Y
2 Nye	Y	Y	Y	N	Y	Y	Y
3 Scott	Y	Y	Y	Y	Y	Y	N
4 **Forbes**	Y	N	Y	N	N	Y	Y
5 Perriello	Y	Y	Y	Y	Y	Y	Y
6 **Goodlatte**	Y	N	Y	N	N	Y	Y
7 **Cantor**	Y	N	Y	N	N	Y	Y
8 Moran	Y	Y	Y	Y	Y	Y	Y
9 Boucher	?	?	?	Y	Y	Y	Y
10 **Wolf**	Y	N	Y	N	Y	Y	Y
11 Connolly	Y	Y	Y	Y	Y	Y	Y
WASHINGTON							
1 Inslee	Y	Y	Y	Y	Y	Y	N
2 Larsen	Y	Y	Y	Y	Y	Y	N
3 Baird	Y	Y	Y	Y	Y	Y	N
4 **Hastings**	Y	N	Y	N	N	Y	?
5 **McMorris Rodgers**	Y	N	Y	N	N	Y	Y
6 Dicks	Y	Y	Y	Y	Y	Y	N
7 McDermott	Y	Y	Y	Y	Y	Y	N
8 **Reichert**	Y	Y	Y	N	N	Y	Y
9 Smith	Y	Y	Y	Y	Y	Y	N
WEST VIRGINIA							
1 Mollohan	Y	Y	Y	Y	Y	Y	Y
2 **Capito**	Y	Y	Y	N	N	Y	Y
3 Rahall	Y	Y	Y	Y	Y	Y	Y
WISCONSIN							
1 **Ryan**	N	N	Y	N	N	Y	Y
2 Baldwin	Y	Y	Y	Y	Y	Y	N
3 Kind	Y	Y	Y	Y	Y	Y	Y
4 Moore	Y	Y	Y	Y	Y	Y	N
5 **Sensenbrenner**	N	N	Y	N	N	Y	Y
6 **Petri**	Y	N	Y	N	N	Y	Y
7 Obey	Y	Y	Y	Y	Y	Y	N
8 Kagen	?	?	?	?	?	?	?
WYOMING							
AL **Lummis**	Y	N	Y	N	N	Y	Y
DELEGATES							
Faleomavaega (A.S.)							
Norton (D.C.)							
Bordallo (Guam)							
Sablan (N. Marianas)							
Pierluisi (P.R.)							
Christensen (V.I.)							

IN THE HOUSE | By Vote Number

441. **HR 1722. Telework for Federal Employees/Passage.**
Passage of the bill that would require the head of each executive agency to establish and implement a policy that would allow employees to work remotely as much as possible without diminishing agency operations or performance. It also would require agency heads to provide training for teleworking employees and designate a telework managing officer. The bill would exclude certain employees from teleworking, including those disciplined for viewing, downloading or exchanging pornography on the job, as well as those who are seriously delinquent in taxes. Passed 290-131: D 245-2; R 45-129. July 14, 2010.

442. **S 1508. Improper Payments Reporting/Passage.** Davis, D-Ill., motion to suspend the rules and pass the bill that would lower the reporting threshold above which federal agencies are required to report improper payments. It also would require federal agencies to report their plans to prevent improper payments and seek to recover overpayments if a program's outlays exceed $1 million. Motion agreed to 414-0: D 244-0; R 170-0. A two-thirds majority of those present and voting (276 in this case) is required for passage under suspension of the rules. July 14, 2010.

443. **HR 5114. National Flood Insurance Program Reauthorization/ Rule.** Adoption of the rule (H Res 1517) to provide for House floor consideration of the bill that would reauthorize the National Flood Insurance Program through September 2015. Adopted 239-182: D 238-8; R 1-174. July 15, 2010.

444. **HR 5114. National Flood Insurance Program Reauthorization/ Earmark Ban.** Flake, R-Ariz., amendment that would bar the use of funds in the bill for earmarks. Adopted in Committee of the Whole 423-3: D 252-1; R 171-2. July 15, 2010.

445. **HR 5114. National Flood Insurance Program Reauthorization/ Ethical Expenditures.** Murphy, D-N.Y., amendment that would require all funds authorized under the bill to be expended in a manner consistent with the manual on Standards of Ethical Conduct for Employees of the Executive Branch. Adopted in Committee of the Whole 421-0: D 249-0; R 172-0. July 15, 2010.

446. **HR 5114. National Flood Insurance Program Reauthorization/ Recommit.** Hensarling, R-Texas, motion to recommit the bill to the House Financial Services Committee with instructions that it be immediately reported back with an amendment that would strike the section of the bill that would authorize $250 million over five years for a new flood insurance education and outreach grant program administered by the Federal Emergency Management Agency. Motion rejected 191-229: D 19-227; R 172-2. July 15, 2010.

447. **HR 5114. National Flood Insurance Program Reauthorization/ Passage.** Passage of the bill that would reauthorize the National Flood Insurance Program through September 2015. It would delay for five years the effective date of a requirement for homeowners in newly designated flood hazard areas to purchase insurance and would phase in risk rates in those areas over the following five years. It would increase coverage limits and raise the maximum annual increases allowed for flood insurance premiums to 20 percent. As amended, it would phase out subsidized premiums for severe repetitive-loss properties, substantially damaged or improved properties and policyholders who voluntarily allow flood coverage to lapse. Passed 329-90: D 244-1; R 85-89. July 15, 2010.

	441	442	443	444	445	446	447
ALABAMA							
1 **Bonner**	N	Y	N	Y	Y	Y	Y
2 Bright	Y	Y	?	?	?	?	?
3 **Rogers**	N	Y	N	Y	Y	Y	N
4 **Aderholt**	N	Y	N	Y	Y	Y	N
5 **Griffith**	N	Y	N	Y	Y	Y	N
6 **Bachus**	N	Y	N	+	Y	Y	N
7 Davis	Y	Y	Y	Y	Y	N	Y
ALASKA							
AL **Young**	N	Y	N	N	Y	Y	Y
ARIZONA							
1 Kirkpatrick	Y	Y	Y	Y	Y	N	Y
2 **Franks**	N	Y	N	Y	Y	Y	N
3 **Shadegg**	N	?	N	Y	Y	Y	N
4 Pastor	Y	Y	Y	Y	Y	N	Y
5 Mitchell	Y	Y	N	Y	Y	Y	Y
6 **Flake**	Y	Y	N	Y	Y	Y	N
7 Grijalva	Y	Y	Y	Y	Y	N	Y
8 Giffords	Y	Y	Y	Y	Y	N	Y
ARKANSAS							
1 Berry	N	Y	Y	N	Y	N	Y
2 Snyder	Y	Y	Y	Y	Y	N	Y
3 **Boozman**	N	Y	N	Y	Y	Y	Y
4 Ross	Y	Y	Y	Y	Y	N	Y
CALIFORNIA							
1 Thompson	Y	Y	Y	Y	Y	N	Y
2 **Herger**	N	?	N	Y	Y	Y	N
3 **Lungren**	Y	Y	N	Y	Y	Y	Y
4 **McClintock**	N	Y	N	Y	Y	Y	N
5 Matsui	Y	Y	Y	Y	Y	N	Y
6 Woolsey	Y	Y	Y	Y	Y	N	Y
7 Miller, George	Y	Y	Y	Y	Y	N	Y
8 Pelosi							
9 Lee	Y	Y	Y	Y	Y	N	Y
10 Garamendi	Y	Y	Y	Y	Y	N	Y
11 McNerney	Y	Y	Y	Y	Y	N	Y
12 Speier	Y	Y	Y	Y	Y	N	Y
13 Stark	Y	Y	Y	Y	Y	N	Y
14 Eshoo	Y	Y	Y	Y	Y	N	Y
15 Honda	Y	Y	Y	Y	Y	N	Y
16 Lofgren	Y	Y	Y	Y	Y	N	Y
17 Farr	Y	Y	Y	Y	Y	N	Y
18 Cardoza	Y	Y	Y	Y	Y	N	?
19 **Radanovich**	N	Y	N	Y	Y	Y	N
20 Costa	Y	Y	Y	Y	Y	Y	Y
21 **Nunes**	N	Y	N	Y	Y	Y	N
22 **McCarthy**	N	Y	N	Y	Y	Y	N
23 Capps	Y	Y	Y	Y	Y	N	Y
24 **Gallegly**	N	Y	N	Y	Y	Y	N
25 **McKeon**	N	Y	N	Y	Y	Y	N
26 **Dreier**	Y	Y	N	Y	Y	Y	Y
27 Sherman	Y	Y	Y	Y	Y	N	Y
28 Berman	Y	Y	Y	Y	Y	N	Y
29 Schiff	Y	Y	Y	Y	Y	N	Y
30 Waxman	Y	Y	Y	?	N	Y	Y
31 Becerra	Y	Y	Y	Y	Y	N	Y
32 Chu	Y	Y	Y	Y	Y	N	Y
33 Watson	Y	Y	Y	Y	Y	N	Y
34 Roybal-Allard	Y	Y	Y	Y	Y	N	Y
35 Waters	Y	Y	Y	Y	Y	N	Y
36 Harman	Y	Y	Y	Y	Y	N	Y
37 Richardson	Y	Y	Y	Y	Y	N	Y
38 Napolitano	Y	Y	Y	Y	Y	N	Y
39 Sánchez, Linda	?	?	Y	Y	Y	N	Y
40 **Royce**	N	Y	N	Y	Y	Y	N
41 **Lewis**	N	Y	N	Y	Y	Y	N
42 **Miller, Gary**	N	Y	N	Y	Y	Y	N
43 Baca	Y	Y	Y	Y	Y	N	Y
44 **Calvert**	N	Y	N	Y	Y	Y	N
45 **Bono Mack**	Y	Y	N	Y	Y	Y	N
46 **Rohrabacher**	N	Y	N	Y	Y	Y	N
47 Sanchez, Loretta	Y	Y	Y	Y	Y	N	Y
48 **Campbell**	N	Y	N	Y	Y	Y	N
49 **Issa**	Y	Y	N	Y	Y	Y	N
50 **Bilbray**	Y	Y	N	Y	Y	Y	N
51 Filner	Y	Y	Y	Y	Y	N	Y
52 **Hunter**	N	Y	N	Y	Y	Y	N
53 Davis	Y	Y	Y	Y	Y	N	Y

	441	442	443	444	445	446	447
COLORADO							
1 DeGette	Y	Y	Y	Y	Y	N	Y
2 Polis	Y	Y	Y	Y	Y	N	Y
3 Salazar	Y	Y	Y	Y	Y	N	Y
4 Markey	Y	Y	Y	Y	Y	N	Y
5 **Lamborn**	N	Y	N	Y	Y	Y	N
6 **Coffman**	N	Y	N	Y	Y	Y	N
7 Perlmutter	Y	Y	Y	Y	Y	N	Y
CONNECTICUT							
1 Larson	Y	Y	Y	Y	Y	N	Y
2 Courtney	Y	Y	Y	Y	Y	N	Y
3 DeLauro	Y	Y	Y	Y	Y	N	Y
4 Himes	Y	Y	Y	Y	Y	N	Y
5 Murphy	Y	Y	Y	Y	Y	N	Y
DELAWARE							
AL **Castle**	Y	Y	N	Y	Y	Y	N
FLORIDA							
1 **Miller**	N	Y	N	Y	Y	Y	Y
2 Boyd	Y	Y	Y	Y	Y	N	Y
3 Brown	Y	Y	Y	Y	Y	N	Y
4 **Crenshaw**	N	Y	N	Y	Y	Y	Y
5 **Brown-Waite**	N	Y	N	Y	Y	Y	Y
6 **Stearns**	N	Y	N	Y	Y	Y	N
7 **Mica**	N	Y	N	Y	Y	Y	N
8 Grayson	Y	Y	Y	Y	Y	N	Y
9 **Bilirakis**	Y	Y	N	Y	Y	Y	Y
10 **Young**	N	Y	N	Y	Y	Y	Y
11 Castor	Y	Y	Y	Y	Y	N	Y
12 **Putnam**	Y	Y	N	Y	Y	Y	N
13 **Buchanan**	N	Y	N	Y	Y	Y	Y
14 **Mack**	N	Y	N	Y	Y	Y	Y
15 **Posey**	N	Y	N	Y	Y	Y	N
16 **Rooney**	N	Y	N	Y	Y	Y	Y
17 Meek	Y	Y	Y	Y	Y	N	Y
18 **Ros-Lehtinen**	Y	Y	N	Y	Y	Y	N
19 Deutch	?	?	Y	Y	Y	N	Y
20 Wasserman Schultz	Y	Y	Y	Y	Y	N	Y
21 **Diaz-Balart, L.**	N	Y	N	Y	Y	N	Y
22 Klein	Y	Y	Y	Y	Y	N	Y
23 Hastings	?	?	?	?	?	?	?
24 Kosmas	Y	Y	Y	Y	Y	N	Y
25 **Diaz-Balart, M.**	N	Y	N	Y	Y	Y	Y
GEORGIA							
1 **Kingston**	N	Y	N	Y	Y	Y	Y
2 Bishop	Y	Y	Y	Y	Y	N	Y
3 **Westmoreland**	N	Y	N	Y	Y	Y	Y
4 Johnson	Y	Y	Y	Y	Y	N	Y
5 Lewis	Y	Y	Y	Y	Y	N	Y
6 **Price**	N	Y	N	Y	Y	Y	N
7 **Linder**	N	Y	N	Y	Y	Y	Y
8 Marshall	Y	Y	Y	Y	Y	N	Y
9 **Graves**	N	Y	N	Y	Y	Y	N
10 **Broun**	N	Y	N	Y	Y	Y	N
11 **Gingrey**	N	Y	N	Y	Y	Y	N
12 Barrow	Y	Y	Y	Y	Y	N	Y
13 Scott	Y	Y	Y	Y	Y	N	Y
HAWAII							
1 **Djou**	Y	Y	N	Y	Y	Y	Y
2 Hirono	Y	Y	Y	Y	Y	N	Y
IDAHO							
1 Minnick	Y	Y	N	Y	Y	Y	Y
2 **Simpson**	N	Y	N	Y	Y	Y	Y
ILLINOIS							
1 Rush	Y	Y	Y	Y	?	N	+
2 Jackson	Y	Y	Y	Y	Y	N	Y
3 Lipinski	Y	Y	Y	Y	Y	N	Y
4 Gutierrez	Y	Y	Y	Y	Y	N	Y
5 Quigley	Y	Y	Y	Y	Y	N	Y
6 **Roskam**	N	Y	N	Y	Y	Y	N
7 Davis	Y	Y	Y	Y	Y	N	Y
8 Bean	Y	Y	Y	Y	Y	N	Y
9 Schakowsky	Y	Y	Y	Y	Y	N	Y
10 **Kirk**	Y	Y	N	?	?	?	?
11 Halvorson	Y	Y	Y	Y	Y	N	Y
12 Costello	Y	Y	Y	Y	Y	N	Y
13 **Biggert**	Y	Y	N	Y	Y	N	Y
14 Foster	Y	Y	Y	Y	Y	N	Y
15 **Johnson**	N	Y	N	Y	Y	Y	Y

	441	442	443	444	445	446	447
16 **Manzullo**	N	Y	N	Y	Y	Y	N
17 Hare	Y	Y	Y	Y	Y	N	Y
18 **Schock**	N	Y	N	Y	Y	Y	Y
19 **Shimkus**	N	Y	N	Y	Y	Y	Y
INDIANA							
1 Visclosky	Y	Y	Y	Y	Y	N	Y
2 Donnelly	Y	Y	Y	Y	Y	Y	Y
3 Vacant							
4 **Buyer**	N	Y	N	Y	Y	Y	N
5 **Burton**	N	Y	N	Y	Y	Y	N
6 **Pence**	N	Y	N	Y	Y	Y	N
7 Carson	Y	Y	Y	Y	Y	N	Y
8 Ellsworth	Y	Y	Y	Y	Y	Y	Y
9 Hill	Y	Y	Y	Y	Y	N	Y
IOWA							
1 Braley	Y	Y	Y	Y	Y	N	Y
2 Loebsack	Y	Y	Y	Y	Y	N	Y
3 Boswell	Y	Y	Y	Y	Y	N	Y
4 **Latham**	Y	Y	N	Y	Y	Y	Y
5 **King**	N	Y	N	Y	Y	Y	N
KANSAS							
1 **Moran**	N	Y	N	Y	Y	Y	N
2 **Jenkins**	N	Y	N	Y	Y	Y	N
3 Moore	Y	Y	Y	Y	Y	N	Y
4 **Tiahrt**	–	?	N	Y	Y	Y	N
KENTUCKY							
1 **Whitfield**	N	Y	Y	Y	Y	Y	Y
2 **Guthrie**	N	Y	N	Y	Y	Y	Y
3 Yarmuth	Y	Y	Y	Y	Y	N	Y
4 **Davis**	N	Y	N	Y	Y	Y	Y
5 **Rogers**	N	Y	N	Y	Y	Y	Y
6 Chandler	Y	Y	Y	Y	Y	N	Y
LOUISIANA							
1 **Scalise**	N	Y	N	Y	Y	Y	Y
2 **Cao**	Y	Y	N	Y	Y	N	Y
3 Melancon	Y	Y	Y	Y	Y	N	Y
4 **Fleming**	N	Y	N	Y	Y	Y	N
5 **Alexander**	N	Y	N	Y	Y	Y	N
6 **Cassidy**	Y	Y	N	Y	Y	Y	Y
7 **Boustany**	N	Y	N	Y	Y	Y	Y
MAINE							
1 Pingree	Y	Y	Y	Y	Y	N	Y
2 Michaud	Y	Y	Y	Y	Y	N	Y
MARYLAND							
1 Kratovil	Y	Y	N	Y	Y	Y	Y
2 Ruppersberger	Y	Y	Y	Y	Y	N	Y
3 Sarbanes	Y	Y	Y	Y	Y	N	Y
4 Edwards	Y	Y	Y	Y	Y	N	Y
5 Hoyer	Y	Y	Y	Y	Y	N	Y
6 **Bartlett**	Y	Y	N	Y	Y	Y	N
7 Cummings	Y	Y	Y	Y	Y	N	Y
8 Van Hollen	Y	Y	Y	Y	Y	N	Y
MASSACHUSETTS							
1 Olver	Y	Y	Y	Y	Y	N	Y
2 Neal	Y	Y	Y	Y	Y	N	Y
3 McGovern	Y	?	Y	Y	Y	N	Y
4 Frank	Y	Y	Y	Y	Y	N	Y
5 Tsongas	Y	Y	Y	Y	+	N	Y
6 Tierney	Y	Y	Y	Y	Y	N	Y
7 Markey	Y	Y	Y	Y	Y	N	Y
8 Capuano	Y	Y	Y	Y	Y	N	Y
9 Lynch	Y	Y	Y	Y	Y	N	Y
10 Delahunt	Y	Y	Y	Y	Y	N	Y
MICHIGAN							
1 Stupak	Y	Y	N	Y	Y	N	N
2 **Hoekstra**	?	?	?	?	?	?	?
3 **Ehlers**	Y	Y	N	Y	Y	Y	Y
4 **Camp**	N	Y	N	Y	Y	Y	N
5 Kildee	Y	Y	Y	Y	Y	N	Y
6 **Upton**	Y	Y	N	Y	Y	Y	N
7 Schauer	Y	Y	Y	Y	Y	N	Y
8 **Rogers**	N	Y	N	Y	Y	Y	N
9 Peters	Y	Y	Y	Y	Y	Y	Y
10 **Miller**	Y	Y	N	Y	Y	Y	N
11 **McCotter**	Y	Y	N	Y	Y	Y	N
12 Levin	Y	Y	Y	Y	Y	N	Y
13 Kilpatrick	Y	Y	Y	Y	Y	N	Y
14 Conyers	Y	Y	Y	Y	Y	N	Y
15 Dingell	Y	Y	Y	Y	Y	N	Y
MINNESOTA							
1 Walz	Y	Y	Y	Y	Y	N	Y
2 **Kline**	Y	Y	N	Y	Y	Y	N
3 **Paulsen**	Y	Y	N	Y	Y	Y	N
4 McCollum	Y	Y	Y	Y	Y	N	Y

	441	442	443	444	445	446	447
5 Ellison	Y	Y	Y	Y	Y	N	Y
6 **Bachmann**	N	Y	N	Y	Y	Y	N
7 Peterson	Y	Y	Y	Y	Y	Y	Y
8 Oberstar	Y	Y	Y	Y	Y	N	Y
MISSISSIPPI							
1 Childers	Y	Y	N	Y	Y	Y	Y
2 Thompson	Y	Y	Y	Y	Y	N	Y
3 **Harper**	N	Y	N	Y	Y	Y	Y
4 Taylor	Y	Y	N	Y	Y	Y	Y
MISSOURI							
1 Clay	Y	Y	Y	Y	Y	N	Y
2 **Akin**	N	Y	N	Y	Y	Y	N
3 Carnahan	Y	Y	Y	Y	Y	N	Y
4 Skelton	Y	Y	Y	Y	Y	N	Y
5 Cleaver	?	Y	Y	Y	Y	N	Y
6 **Graves**	Y	Y	N	Y	Y	Y	Y
7 **Blunt**	N	Y	N	?	Y	Y	Y
8 **Emerson**	N	Y	N	Y	Y	Y	Y
9 **Luetkemeyer**	N	Y	N	Y	Y	Y	Y
MONTANA							
AL **Rehberg**	N	Y	N	Y	Y	Y	Y
NEBRASKA							
1 **Fortenberry**	Y	Y	N	Y	Y	Y	Y
2 **Terry**	Y	Y	N	Y	Y	Y	Y
3 **Smith**	N	Y	N	Y	Y	Y	N
NEVADA							
1 Berkley	Y	Y	Y	Y	Y	N	Y
2 **Heller**	N	Y	N	Y	Y	Y	Y
3 Titus	Y	Y	Y	Y	Y	Y	Y
NEW HAMPSHIRE							
1 Shea-Porter	Y	Y	Y	Y	Y	N	Y
2 Hodes	Y	Y	Y	Y	Y	N	Y
NEW JERSEY							
1 Andrews	Y	Y	Y	Y	Y	N	Y
2 **LoBiondo**	Y	Y	N	Y	Y	Y	Y
3 Adler	Y	Y	Y	Y	Y	N	Y
4 **Smith**	Y	Y	N	Y	Y	Y	Y
5 **Garrett**	N	Y	N	Y	Y	Y	N
6 Pallone	Y	Y	Y	Y	Y	N	Y
7 **Lance**	N	Y	N	Y	Y	Y	Y
8 Pascrell	Y	Y	Y	Y	Y	N	Y
9 Rothman	Y	Y	Y	Y	Y	N	Y
10 Payne	Y	Y	Y	Y	Y	N	Y
11 **Frelinghuysen**	N	Y	N	Y	Y	Y	N
12 Holt	Y	Y	Y	Y	Y	N	Y
13 Sires	Y	Y	Y	Y	Y	N	Y
NEW MEXICO							
1 Heinrich	Y	Y	Y	Y	Y	N	Y
2 Teague	Y	?	Y	Y	Y	Y	Y
3 Luján	Y	Y	Y	Y	Y	N	Y
NEW YORK							
1 Bishop	Y	Y	Y	Y	Y	N	Y
2 Israel	Y	Y	Y	Y	Y	N	Y
3 **King**	N	Y	N	Y	Y	Y	Y
4 McCarthy	Y	Y	Y	Y	Y	N	Y
5 Ackerman	Y	Y	Y	Y	Y	N	Y
6 Meeks	Y	Y	Y	Y	Y	N	Y
7 Crowley	Y	Y	Y	Y	Y	N	Y
8 Nadler	Y	Y	Y	Y	Y	N	Y
9 Weiner	Y	Y	Y	Y	Y	N	Y
10 Towns	Y	Y	Y	Y	Y	N	Y
11 Clarke	Y	Y	Y	Y	Y	N	Y
12 Velázquez	Y	Y	Y	Y	Y	N	Y
13 McMahon	Y	Y	Y	Y	Y	N	Y
14 Maloney	Y	Y	Y	Y	Y	N	Y
15 Rangel	Y	Y	Y	Y	Y	N	Y
16 Serrano	Y	Y	Y	Y	?	N	Y
17 Engel	Y	Y	Y	Y	Y	N	Y
18 Lowey	Y	Y	Y	Y	Y	N	Y
19 Hall	Y	Y	Y	Y	Y	N	Y
20 Murphy	Y	Y	Y	Y	Y	Y	Y
21 Tonko	Y	Y	Y	Y	Y	N	Y
22 Hinchey	Y	Y	Y	Y	Y	N	Y
23 Owens	Y	?	Y	Y	Y	N	Y
24 Arcuri	Y	Y	Y	Y	Y	N	Y
25 Maffei	Y	Y	Y	Y	Y	N	Y
26 **Lee**	N	Y	N	Y	Y	Y	Y
27 Higgins	?	?	?	?	?	?	?
28 Slaughter	Y	Y	Y	Y	Y	N	Y
29 Vacant							
NORTH CAROLINA							
1 Butterfield	Y	Y	Y	Y	Y	N	Y
2 Etheridge	Y	Y	Y	Y	Y	N	Y
3 **Jones**	Y	Y	N	Y	Y	Y	Y
4 Price	Y	Y	Y	Y	Y	N	Y

	441	442	443	444	445	446	447
5 **Foxx**	N	Y	N	Y	Y	Y	N
6 **Coble**	N	Y	N	Y	Y	Y	N
7 McIntyre	Y	Y	Y	Y	Y	N	Y
8 Kissell	Y	Y	Y	Y	Y	N	Y
9 **Myrick**	N	Y	N	Y	Y	Y	N
10 **McHenry**	N	Y	N	Y	Y	Y	N
11 Shuler	Y	Y	N	Y	Y	N	Y
12 Watt	Y	Y	Y	Y	Y	N	Y
13 Miller	Y	Y	Y	Y	Y	N	Y
NORTH DAKOTA							
AL Pomeroy	Y	Y	Y	Y	Y	?	Y
OHIO							
1 Driehaus	Y	Y	Y	Y	Y	N	Y
2 **Schmidt**	N	Y	N	Y	Y	Y	N
3 **Turner**	N	Y	N	Y	Y	Y	Y
4 **Jordan**	N	Y	N	Y	Y	Y	N
5 **Latta**	N	Y	N	Y	Y	Y	N
6 Wilson	Y	Y	Y	Y	Y	N	Y
7 **Austria**	N	Y	N	Y	Y	Y	Y
8 **Boehner**	N	Y	N	Y	Y	Y	N
9 Kaptur	Y	Y	Y	Y	Y	N	Y
10 Kucinich	Y	Y	Y	Y	Y	N	Y
11 Fudge	Y	Y	Y	Y	Y	N	Y
12 **Tiberi**	N	Y	N	Y	Y	Y	Y
13 Sutton	Y	Y	Y	Y	Y	N	Y
14 **LaTourette**	Y	Y	N	Y	Y	Y	Y
15 Kilroy	Y	Y	Y	Y	Y	N	Y
16 Boccieri	Y	Y	Y	Y	Y	N	Y
17 Ryan	Y	Y	Y	Y	Y	N	Y
18 Space	Y	Y	Y	Y	Y	N	Y
OKLAHOMA							
1 **Sullivan**	N	Y	N	Y	Y	Y	N
2 Boren	Y	Y	Y	Y	Y	N	Y
3 **Lucas**	N	Y	N	Y	Y	Y	N
4 **Cole**	N	Y	N	Y	Y	Y	N
5 **Fallin**	N	Y	N	Y	Y	Y	Y
OREGON							
1 Wu	N	Y	Y	Y	Y	N	Y
2 **Walden**	Y	Y	N	Y	Y	Y	Y
3 Blumenauer	Y	Y	Y	Y	Y	N	Y
4 DeFazio	Y	Y	Y	Y	Y	N	Y
5 Schrader	Y	Y	?	?	?	?	?
PENNSYLVANIA							
1 Brady	Y	Y	Y	Y	Y	N	Y
2 Fattah	Y	Y	Y	Y	Y	N	Y
3 Dahlkemper	Y	Y	Y	Y	Y	N	Y
4 Altmire	Y	Y	Y	Y	Y	N	Y
5 **Thompson**	N	Y	N	Y	Y	Y	Y
6 **Gerlach**	Y	Y	N	Y	Y	Y	Y
7 Sestak	Y	Y	Y	Y	Y	Y	Y
8 Murphy, P.	Y	Y	Y	Y	Y	Y	Y
9 **Shuster**	N	Y	N	Y	Y	Y	Y
10 Carney	Y	Y	Y	Y	Y	N	Y
11 Kanjorski	Y	Y	Y	Y	Y	N	Y
12 Critz	Y	Y	Y	Y	Y	N	Y
13 Schwartz	Y	Y	Y	Y	Y	N	Y
14 Doyle	Y	Y	Y	Y	Y	N	Y
15 **Dent**	Y	Y	N	Y	Y	Y	Y
16 **Pitts**	N	Y	N	Y	Y	Y	N
17 Holden	Y	Y	Y	Y	Y	N	Y
18 **Murphy, T.**	N	Y	N	Y	Y	Y	Y
19 **Platts**	Y	Y	N	Y	Y	Y	Y
RHODE ISLAND							
1 Kennedy	Y	Y	Y	Y	Y	N	Y
2 Langevin	Y	Y	Y	Y	Y	N	Y
SOUTH CAROLINA							
1 **Brown**	N	Y	N	Y	Y	Y	Y
2 **Wilson**	N	Y	N	Y	Y	Y	Y
3 **Barrett**	N	Y	N	Y	Y	Y	N
4 **Inglis**	N	Y	N	Y	Y	Y	N
5 Spratt	Y	Y	Y	Y	Y	N	Y
6 Clyburn	Y	Y	Y	Y	Y	N	Y
SOUTH DAKOTA							
AL Herseth Sandlin	Y	Y	Y	Y	Y	–	Y
TENNESSEE							
1 **Roe**	N	Y	N	Y	Y	Y	Y
2 **Duncan**	N	Y	N	Y	Y	Y	N
3 **Wamp**	N	Y	N	?	?	?	?
4 Davis	Y	Y	Y	Y	Y	N	Y
5 Cooper	Y	Y	Y	Y	Y	Y	Y
6 Gordon	Y	Y	Y	Y	Y	N	Y
7 **Blackburn**	N	Y	N	Y	Y	Y	N
8 Tanner	Y	Y	N	Y	Y	N	Y
9 Cohen	Y	Y	Y	Y	Y	N	Y

	441	442	443	444	445	446	447
TEXAS							
1 **Gohmert**	N	Y	N	Y	Y	Y	Y
2 **Poe**	N	Y	N	Y	Y	Y	Y
3 **Johnson, S.**	N	Y	N	Y	Y	Y	N
4 **Hall**	Y	Y	N	Y	Y	Y	Y
5 **Hensarling**	N	Y	N	Y	Y	Y	N
6 **Barton**	N	Y	N	Y	Y	Y	N
7 **Culberson**	N	Y	?	Y	Y	Y	N
8 **Brady**	N	Y	N	Y	Y	Y	Y
9 Green, A.	Y	Y	Y	Y	Y	N	Y
10 **McCaul**	N	Y	N	Y	Y	Y	Y
11 **Conaway**	N	Y	N	Y	Y	Y	Y
12 **Granger**	Y	Y	N	Y	Y	Y	Y
13 **Thornberry**	N	Y	N	Y	Y	Y	Y
14 **Paul**	N	Y	N	N	Y	Y	N
15 Hinojosa	?	?	?	?	?	?	?
16 Reyes	Y	Y	Y	Y	Y	N	?
17 Edwards	Y	Y	Y	Y	Y	N	Y
18 Jackson Lee	Y	Y	Y	Y	Y	N	Y
19 **Neugebauer**	N	Y	N	Y	Y	Y	N
20 Gonzalez	Y	Y	Y	Y	Y	N	Y
21 **Smith**	N	Y	N	Y	Y	Y	N
22 **Olson**	?	?	?	?	?	?	?
23 Rodriguez	Y	Y	Y	Y	Y	N	Y
24 **Marchant**	N	Y	N	Y	Y	Y	N
25 Doggett	Y	Y	Y	Y	Y	N	Y
26 **Burgess**	N	Y	N	Y	Y	Y	Y
27 Ortiz	Y	Y	Y	Y	Y	N	Y
28 Cuellar	Y	Y	Y	Y	Y	N	Y
29 Green, G.	Y	Y	Y	Y	Y	N	Y
30 Johnson, E.	Y	Y	Y	Y	Y	N	Y
31 **Carter**	N	?	N	Y	Y	Y	Y
32 **Sessions**	N	Y	N	Y	Y	Y	N
UTAH							
1 **Bishop**	N	Y	N	Y	Y	Y	Y
2 Matheson	Y	Y	Y	Y	Y	Y	Y
3 **Chaffetz**	Y	Y	N	Y	Y	Y	N
VERMONT							
AL Welch	Y	Y	?	Y	Y	N	Y
VIRGINIA							
1 **Wittman**	Y	Y	N	Y	+	Y	Y
2 Nye	Y	Y	Y	Y	Y	Y	Y
3 Scott	Y	Y	Y	Y	Y	N	Y
4 **Forbes**	Y	Y	N	Y	Y	Y	Y
5 Perriello	Y	Y	Y	Y	Y	N	Y
6 **Goodlatte**	Y	Y	N	Y	Y	Y	N
7 **Cantor**	N	Y	N	Y	Y	Y	N
8 Moran	Y	Y	Y	?	?	N	Y
9 Boucher	Y	Y	Y	Y	Y	N	Y
10 **Wolf**	Y	Y	N	Y	Y	Y	Y
11 Connolly	Y	Y	Y	Y	Y	N	Y
WASHINGTON							
1 Inslee	Y	Y	Y	Y	Y	N	Y
2 Larsen	Y	Y	Y	Y	Y	N	Y
3 Baird	Y	Y	Y	Y	Y	N	Y
4 **Hastings**	?	?	N	Y	Y	Y	N
5 **McMorris Rodgers**	N	?	N	Y	Y	Y	N
6 Dicks	Y	Y	Y	Y	Y	N	Y
7 McDermott	Y	Y	Y	Y	Y	N	Y
8 **Reichert**	Y	Y	N	Y	Y	N	Y
9 Smith	Y	Y	Y	Y	Y	N	Y
WEST VIRGINIA							
1 Mollohan	Y	?	Y	Y	Y	N	Y
2 **Capito**	Y	Y	N	Y	Y	Y	Y
3 Rahall	Y	Y	Y	Y	Y	N	Y
WISCONSIN							
1 **Ryan**	N	Y	N	Y	Y	Y	N
2 Baldwin	Y	Y	Y	Y	Y	N	Y
3 Kind	Y	Y	?	Y	Y	N	Y
4 Moore	Y	Y	Y	Y	Y	N	Y
5 **Sensenbrenner**	N	Y	N	Y	Y	Y	N
6 **Petri**	Y	Y	N	Y	Y	Y	Y
7 Obey	Y	Y	Y	Y	Y	N	Y
8 Kagen	?	?	?	?	?	?	?
WYOMING							
AL **Lummis**	N	Y	N	Y	Y	Y	Y
DELEGATES							
Faleomavaega (A.S.)				Y	Y		
Norton (D.C.)				Y	Y		
Bordallo (Guam)				Y	Y		
Sablan (N. Marianas)				Y	Y		
Pierluisi (P.R.)				Y	Y		
Christensen (V.I.)				Y	Y		

IN THE HOUSE | By Vote Number

448. **H Res 1472. National Adult Education and Family Literacy Week/Adoption.** Loebsack, D-Iowa, motion to suspend the rules and adopt the resolution that would support the designation of National Adult Education and Family Literacy Week and request a presidential proclamation recognizing adult education and family literacy programs. Motion agreed to 369-0: D 225-0; R 144-0. A two-thirds majority of those present and voting (246 in this case) is required for adoption under suspension of the rules. July 19, 2010.

449. **H Con Res 126. Support for International Education Programs/ Adoption.** Loebsack, D-Iowa, motion to suspend the rules and adopt the concurrent resolution that would express support for the goals and ideals of Title VI international education programs. Motion agreed to 355-16: D 224-0; R 131-16. A two-thirds majority of those present and voting (248 in this case) is required for adoption under suspension of the rules. July 19, 2010.

450. **H Res 1219. National Child Awareness Month/Adoption.** Loebsack, D-Iowa, motion to suspend the rules and adopt the resolution that would support the designation of a National Child Awareness Month and recognize the efforts of children's charities and youth-serving organizations. Motion agreed to 373-0: D 222-0; R 151-0. A two-thirds majority of those present and voting (249 in this case) is required for adoption under suspension of the rules. July 19, 2010.

451. **H Res 1491. Tribute to University of South Carolina Baseball Team/Adoption.** Loebsack, D-Iowa, motion to suspend the rules and adopt the resolution that would congratulate the University of South Carolina Gamecocks for winning the 2010 NCAA Division I College World Series. Motion agreed to 400-6: D 236-2; R 164-4. A two-thirds majority of those present and voting (271 in this case) is required for adoption under suspension of the rules. July 20, 2010.

452. **HR 5604. Surface Transportation Rescissions/Passage.** Perriello, D-Va., motion to suspend the rules and pass the bill that would rescind $106.8 million of contract authority from the National Highway Traffic Safety Administration and the Federal Transit Administration. Motion agreed to 402-0: D 239-0; R 163-0. A two-thirds majority of those present and voting (268 in this case) is required for passage under suspension of the rules. July 20, 2010.

453. **H Res 1516. World War II Anniversary/Adoption.** Skelton, D-Mo., motion to suspend the rules and adopt the resolution that would recognize the 65th anniversary of the end of World War II, honor the service and sacrifice of those who fought and contributed to the war effort, and honor servicemembers currently serving in combat operations. Motion agreed to 408-0: D 241-0; R 167-0. A two-thirds majority of those present and voting (272 in this case) is required for adoption under suspension of the rules. July 20, 2010.

454. **H Con Res 292. National Aerospace Week/Adoption.** Gordon, D-Tenn., motion to suspend the rules and adopt the concurrent resolution that would support the goals and ideals of National Aerospace Week and recognize the contributions of the aerospace industry. Motion agreed to 413-0: D 242-0; R 171-0. A two-thirds majority of those present and voting (276 in this case) is required for adoption under suspension of the rules. July 21, 2010.

	448	449	450	451	452	453	454
ALABAMA							
1 **Bonner**	Y	Y	Y	Y	Y	Y	Y
2 **Bright**	Y	Y	Y	Y	Y	Y	Y
3 **Rogers**	Y	Y	Y	Y	Y	Y	Y
4 **Aderholt**	Y	Y	Y	Y	Y	Y	Y
5 **Griffith**	Y	Y	Y	Y	Y	Y	Y
6 **Bachus**	Y	Y	?	Y	Y	Y	Y
7 Davis	?	?	?	?	?	?	Y
ALASKA							
AL **Young**	Y	Y	Y	Y	Y	Y	Y
ARIZONA							
1 Kirkpatrick	?	?	?	Y	Y	Y	Y
2 **Franks**	Y	N	?	Y	Y	Y	Y
3 **Shadegg**	Y	N	Y	Y	Y	Y	Y
4 Pastor	Y	Y	Y	Y	Y	Y	Y
5 Mitchell	Y	Y	Y	Y	Y	Y	Y
6 **Flake**	?	?	?	Y	Y	Y	Y
7 Grijalva	?	?	?	Y	Y	Y	Y
8 Giffords	Y	Y	Y	Y	Y	Y	Y
ARKANSAS							
1 Berry	?	?	?	N	Y	Y	Y
2 Snyder	Y	Y	Y	Y	Y	Y	Y
3 **Boozman**	Y	Y	Y	Y	Y	Y	Y
4 Ross	Y	Y	Y	Y	Y	Y	Y
CALIFORNIA							
1 Thompson	Y	Y	Y	Y	Y	Y	Y
2 **Herger**	Y	Y	Y	Y	Y	Y	Y
3 **Lungren**	Y	Y	Y	Y	Y	Y	Y
4 **McClintock**	Y	Y	Y	Y	Y	Y	Y
5 Matsui	Y	Y	Y	Y	Y	Y	Y
6 Woolsey	Y	Y	Y	Y	Y	Y	Y
7 Miller, George	Y	Y	Y	Y	Y	Y	Y
8 Pelosi							
9 Lee	+	+	+	Y	Y	Y	Y
10 Garamendi	Y	Y	Y	Y	?	Y	Y
11 McNerney	Y	Y	Y	Y	Y	Y	Y
12 Speier	Y	Y	Y	Y	Y	Y	Y
13 Stark	Y	Y	Y	Y	Y	Y	Y
14 Eshoo	Y	Y	Y	Y	Y	Y	Y
15 Honda	Y	Y	Y	Y	Y	Y	Y
16 Lofgren	Y	Y	Y	Y	Y	Y	Y
17 Farr	Y	Y	Y	Y	Y	Y	Y
18 Cardoza	Y	Y	Y	Y	Y	Y	Y
19 **Radanovich**	Y	N	Y	Y	Y	Y	Y
20 Costa	Y	?	Y	Y	Y	Y	Y
21 **Nunes**	Y	Y	Y	Y	Y	Y	Y
22 **McCarthy**	Y	Y	Y	Y	Y	Y	Y
23 Capps	Y	Y	Y	Y	Y	Y	Y
24 **Gallegly**	Y	Y	Y	Y	Y	Y	Y
25 **McKeon**	?	?	?	Y	Y	Y	Y
26 **Dreier**	Y	Y	Y	Y	Y	Y	Y
27 Sherman	Y	Y	Y	Y	Y	Y	Y
28 Berman	Y	Y	Y	Y	Y	Y	Y
29 Schiff	Y	Y	Y	Y	Y	Y	Y
30 Waxman	Y	Y	Y	Y	Y	Y	Y
31 Becerra	Y	Y	Y	Y	Y	Y	Y
32 Chu	Y	Y	Y	Y	Y	Y	Y
33 Watson	Y	Y	Y	Y	Y	Y	Y
34 Roybal-Allard	Y	Y	Y	Y	Y	Y	Y
35 Waters	Y	Y	Y	Y	+	Y	Y
36 Harman	Y	Y	Y	Y	Y	Y	Y
37 Richardson	Y	Y	Y	Y	Y	Y	Y
38 Napolitano	Y	Y	Y	Y	Y	Y	Y
39 Sánchez, Linda	Y	Y	Y	Y	Y	Y	Y
40 **Royce**	Y	Y	Y	Y	Y	Y	Y
41 **Lewis**	Y	Y	Y	Y	Y	Y	Y
42 **Miller, Gary**	Y	Y	Y	Y	Y	Y	Y
43 Baca	Y	Y	Y	Y	Y	Y	Y
44 **Calvert**	Y	Y	Y	Y	Y	Y	Y
45 **Bono Mack**	Y	Y	Y	Y	Y	Y	Y
46 **Rohrabacher**	?	?	?	Y	Y	Y	Y
47 Sanchez, Loretta	?	?	?	?	?	?	Y
48 **Campbell**	?	N	Y	Y	Y	Y	Y
49 **Issa**	Y	Y	Y	Y	Y	Y	Y
50 Bilbray	Y	N	Y	N	Y	Y	Y
51 Filner	Y	Y	Y	Y	Y	Y	Y
52 **Hunter**	Y	Y	Y	Y	Y	Y	Y
53 Davis	Y	Y	Y	Y	Y	Y	Y

	448	449	450	451	452	453	454
COLORADO							
1 DeGette	Y	Y	?	Y	Y	Y	Y
2 Polis	Y	Y	Y	Y	Y	Y	Y
3 Salazar	Y	Y	Y	Y	Y	Y	Y
4 Markey	Y	Y	Y	Y	Y	?	
5 **Lamborn**	Y	N	Y	Y	Y	Y	Y
6 **Coffman**	Y	Y	Y	Y	Y	Y	Y
7 Perlmutter	Y	Y	Y	Y	Y	Y	Y
CONNECTICUT							
1 Larson	Y	Y	Y	Y	Y	Y	Y
2 Courtney	?	Y	Y	Y	Y	Y	Y
3 DeLauro	Y	Y	Y	Y	Y	Y	Y
4 Himes	Y	Y	Y	Y	Y	Y	Y
5 Murphy	Y	Y	Y	Y	Y	Y	Y
DELAWARE							
AL **Castle**	Y	Y	Y	Y	Y	Y	Y
FLORIDA							
1 **Miller**	+	Y	Y	Y	Y	Y	Y
2 Boyd	Y	Y	Y	Y	Y	Y	Y
3 Brown	Y	Y	Y	Y	Y	Y	Y
4 **Crenshaw**	Y	Y	Y	Y	Y	Y	Y
5 **Brown-Waite**	?	?	?	Y	Y	Y	Y
6 **Stearns**	Y	Y	Y	Y	Y	Y	Y
7 **Mica**	Y	Y	Y	Y	Y	Y	Y
8 Grayson	Y	Y	Y	Y	Y	Y	Y
9 **Bilirakis**	Y	Y	Y	Y	Y	Y	Y
10 **Young**	?	?	?	Y	Y	Y	Y
11 Castor	Y	Y	Y	Y	Y	Y	Y
12 **Putnam**	+	+	+	Y	Y	Y	Y
13 **Buchanan**	?	?	?	Y	Y	Y	Y
14 **Mack**	Y	Y	Y	?	?	?	Y
15 **Posey**	Y	Y	Y	Y	Y	Y	Y
16 **Rooney**	Y	Y	Y	Y	Y	Y	Y
17 Meek	?	?	?	?	?	?	Y
18 **Ros-Lehtinen**	Y	Y	Y	Y	Y	Y	Y
19 Deutch	Y	Y	Y	Y	Y	Y	Y
20 Wasserman Schultz	Y	Y	Y	Y	Y	Y	Y
21 **Diaz-Balart, L.**	Y	Y	Y	Y	Y	Y	Y
22 Klein	Y	Y	Y	Y	Y	Y	Y
23 Hastings	Y	Y	Y	Y	Y	Y	Y
24 Kosmas	Y	Y	Y	Y	Y	Y	Y
25 **Diaz-Balart, M.**	Y	Y	Y	Y	Y	Y	Y
GEORGIA							
1 **Kingston**	?	?	?	Y	Y	Y	Y
2 Bishop	Y	Y	Y	Y	Y	Y	Y
3 **Westmoreland**	Y	Y	Y	Y	Y	Y	Y
4 Johnson	+	+	+	+	+	+	?
5 Lewis	Y	Y	Y	Y	Y	Y	Y
6 **Price**	Y	Y	Y	Y	Y	Y	Y
7 **Linder**	Y	Y	Y	Y	Y	Y	Y
8 Marshall	Y	Y	Y	Y	Y	Y	Y
9 **Graves**	Y	N	Y	N	Y	Y	Y
10 **Broun**	Y	N	Y	Y	Y	Y	Y
11 **Gingrey**	?	?	?	Y	Y	Y	Y
12 Barrow	?	?	?	?	?	Y	Y
13 Scott	Y	Y	Y	Y	Y	Y	Y
HAWAII							
1 **Djou**	Y	Y	Y	Y	?	Y	Y
2 Hirono	Y	Y	Y	Y	Y	Y	Y
IDAHO							
1 Minnick	Y	Y	Y	Y	Y	Y	Y
2 **Simpson**	?	?	?	Y	Y	Y	Y
ILLINOIS							
1 Rush	?	?	?	Y	Y	Y	Y
2 Jackson	Y	Y	Y	Y	Y	Y	Y
3 Lipinski	Y	Y	Y	Y	Y	Y	Y
4 Gutierrez	+	+	+	Y	Y	Y	Y
5 Quigley	Y	Y	Y	Y	Y	Y	Y
6 **Roskam**	Y	Y	Y	Y	Y	Y	Y
7 Davis	Y	Y	Y	Y	Y	Y	Y
8 Bean	Y	Y	Y	Y	Y	Y	Y
9 Schakowsky	Y	Y	Y	Y	Y	Y	Y
10 **Kirk**	?	?	?	Y	Y	Y	Y
11 Halvorson	Y	Y	Y	Y	Y	Y	Y
12 Costello	Y	Y	Y	Y	Y	Y	Y
13 **Biggert**	Y	Y	Y	Y	Y	Y	Y
14 Foster	Y	Y	Y	Y	Y	Y	Y
15 **Johnson**	?	?	?	Y	Y	Y	Y

	448	449	450	451	452	453	454
16 **Manzullo**	Y	Y	Y	Y	Y	Y	Y
17 Hare	Y	Y	Y	Y	Y	Y	Y
18 **Schock**	Y	Y	Y	Y	Y	Y	Y
19 **Shimkus**	Y	Y	Y	Y	Y	Y	Y
INDIANA							
1 Visclosky	Y	Y	Y	+	+	+	Y
2 Donnelly	Y	Y	Y	Y	Y	Y	Y
3 Vacant							
4 **Buyer**	?	?	?	Y	Y	Y	Y
5 **Burton**	Y	N	Y	Y	Y	Y	Y
6 **Pence**	Y	Y	Y	Y	Y	Y	Y
7 Carson	Y	Y	Y	Y	Y	Y	Y
8 Ellsworth	?	?	?	?	?	?	Y
9 Hill	Y	Y	Y	Y	Y	Y	Y
IOWA							
1 Braley	Y	Y	Y	Y	Y	Y	Y
2 Loebsack	Y	Y	Y	Y	Y	Y	Y
3 Boswell	Y	Y	Y	Y	Y	Y	Y
4 **Latham**	Y	Y	Y	Y	Y	Y	Y
5 **King**	Y	Y	Y	Y	Y	Y	Y
KANSAS							
1 **Moran**	?	?	?	?	?	?	?
2 **Jenkins**	Y	Y	Y	Y	Y	Y	Y
3 Moore	Y	Y	Y	Y	Y	Y	Y
4 **Tiahrt**	?	?	?	?	?	?	?
KENTUCKY							
1 **Whitfield**	Y	Y	Y	Y	Y	Y	Y
2 **Guthrie**	Y	Y	Y	Y	Y	Y	Y
3 Yarmuth	Y	Y	Y	Y	Y	Y	Y
4 **Davis**	Y	Y	Y	Y	Y	Y	Y
5 **Rogers**	Y	Y	Y	?	?	?	Y
6 Chandler	Y	Y	Y	Y	Y	Y	Y
LOUISIANA							
1 **Scalise**	Y	Y	Y	Y	Y	Y	Y
2 **Cao**	Y	?	Y	Y	Y	Y	Y
3 Melancon	Y	Y	Y	Y	Y	Y	Y
4 **Fleming**	Y	Y	Y	Y	Y	Y	Y
5 **Alexander**	Y	Y	Y	Y	Y	Y	Y
6 **Cassidy**	Y	Y	Y	Y	Y	Y	Y
7 **Boustany**	Y	Y	Y	Y	Y	Y	Y
MAINE							
1 Pingree	Y	Y	Y	Y	Y	Y	Y
2 Michaud	Y	Y	Y	Y	Y	Y	Y
MARYLAND							
1 Kratovil	Y	Y	Y	Y	Y	Y	Y
2 Ruppersberger	Y	Y	Y	Y	Y	Y	Y
3 Sarbanes	Y	Y	Y	Y	Y	Y	Y
4 Edwards	Y	Y	Y	Y	Y	Y	Y
5 Hoyer	Y	Y	Y	Y	Y	Y	Y
6 **Bartlett**	Y	N	Y	Y	Y	Y	Y
7 Cummings	Y	Y	Y	Y	Y	Y	Y
8 Van Hollen	Y	Y	Y	Y	Y	Y	Y
MASSACHUSETTS							
1 Olver	Y	Y	Y	Y	Y	Y	Y
2 Neal	?	Y	Y	Y	Y	Y	Y
3 McGovern	Y	Y	Y	Y	Y	Y	Y
4 Frank	Y	Y	Y	?	Y	Y	Y
5 Tsongas	Y	Y	Y	Y	Y	Y	Y
6 Tierney	Y	Y	Y	Y	Y	Y	Y
7 Markey	Y	Y	Y	Y	Y	Y	Y
8 Capuano	?	?	?	?	?	?	?
9 Lynch	Y	?	Y	Y	Y	Y	Y
10 Delahunt	?	?	?	Y	Y	Y	Y
MICHIGAN							
1 Stupak	Y	Y	Y	Y	Y	Y	Y
2 **Hoekstra**	?	?	?	?	?	?	?
3 **Ehlers**	Y	Y	Y	N	+	+	Y
4 **Camp**	Y	Y	Y	Y	Y	Y	Y
5 Kildee	Y	Y	Y	Y	Y	Y	Y
6 **Upton**	Y	Y	Y	Y	Y	Y	Y
7 Schauer	Y	Y	Y	Y	Y	Y	Y
8 **Rogers**	Y	Y	Y	Y	Y	Y	Y
9 Peters	Y	Y	Y	Y	Y	Y	Y
10 **Miller**	Y	Y	Y	Y	Y	Y	Y
11 **McCotter**	Y	Y	Y	Y	Y	Y	Y
12 Levin	Y	Y	Y	Y	Y	Y	Y
13 Kilpatrick	+	+	+	Y	Y	Y	Y
14 Conyers	+	+	+	+	+	+	Y
15 Dingell	Y	Y	Y	Y	Y	Y	Y
MINNESOTA							
1 Walz	Y	Y	Y	Y	Y	Y	Y
2 **Kline**	Y	Y	Y	Y	Y	Y	Y
3 **Paulsen**	Y	Y	Y	Y	Y	Y	Y
4 McCollum	Y	Y	Y	Y	Y	Y	Y
5 Ellison	Y	Y	Y	Y	Y	Y	Y
6 **Bachmann**	Y	N	Y	Y	Y	Y	Y
7 Peterson	Y	Y	Y	Y	Y	Y	Y
8 Oberstar	Y	Y	?	P	Y	Y	Y
MISSISSIPPI							
1 Childers	Y	Y	Y	Y	Y	Y	Y
2 Thompson	Y	Y	Y	Y	Y	Y	Y
3 **Harper**	Y	Y	Y	Y	Y	Y	Y
4 Taylor	Y	Y	Y	Y	Y	Y	Y
MISSOURI							
1 Clay	Y	Y	Y	Y	Y	Y	Y
2 **Akin**	+	–	+	Y	Y	Y	Y
3 Carnahan	Y	Y	Y	Y	?	Y	Y
4 Skelton	Y	Y	Y	Y	Y	Y	Y
5 Cleaver	Y	Y	Y	Y	Y	Y	Y
6 **Graves**	Y	Y	Y	Y	Y	Y	Y
7 **Blunt**	Y	Y	Y	?	?	?	Y
8 **Emerson**	?	?	?	Y	Y	Y	Y
9 **Luetkemeyer**	Y	Y	Y	Y	Y	Y	Y
MONTANA							
AL **Rehberg**	Y	Y	Y	Y	Y	Y	Y
NEBRASKA							
1 **Fortenberry**	Y	Y	Y	Y	Y	Y	Y
2 **Terry**	Y	Y	Y	Y	Y	Y	Y
3 **Smith**	Y	Y	Y	Y	Y	Y	Y
NEVADA							
1 Berkley	Y	Y	Y	Y	Y	Y	Y
2 **Heller**	Y	Y	Y	Y	+	Y	Y
3 Titus	Y	Y	Y	Y	Y	Y	Y
NEW HAMPSHIRE							
1 Shea-Porter	Y	Y	Y	Y	Y	Y	?
2 Hodes	?	?	?	Y	Y	Y	Y
NEW JERSEY							
1 Andrews	Y	Y	Y	?	?	?	Y
2 **LoBiondo**	Y	Y	Y	Y	Y	Y	Y
3 Adler	Y	Y	Y	Y	Y	Y	Y
4 **Smith**	Y	Y	Y	Y	Y	Y	Y
5 **Garrett**	Y	Y	Y	Y	Y	Y	Y
6 Pallone	Y	Y	Y	Y	Y	Y	Y
7 **Lance**	Y	Y	Y	Y	Y	Y	Y
8 Pascrell	Y	Y	Y	Y	Y	Y	Y
9 Rothman	Y	Y	Y	Y	Y	Y	Y
10 Payne	Y	Y	Y	Y	Y	Y	Y
11 **Frelinghuysen**	Y	Y	Y	Y	Y	Y	Y
12 Holt	Y	Y	Y	Y	Y	Y	Y
13 Sires	Y	Y	Y	Y	Y	Y	Y
NEW MEXICO							
1 Heinrich	Y	Y	Y	Y	Y	Y	Y
2 Teague	?	?	?	Y	Y	Y	Y
3 Luján	Y	Y	Y	Y	Y	Y	Y
NEW YORK							
1 Bishop	Y	Y	Y	Y	Y	Y	Y
2 Israel	Y	Y	Y	Y	Y	Y	Y
3 **King**	?	?	?	?	?	?	?
4 McCarthy	Y	Y	Y	Y	Y	Y	Y
5 Ackerman	Y	Y	Y	Y	Y	Y	Y
6 Meeks	?	?	?	Y	Y	Y	Y
7 Crowley	Y	Y	Y	Y	Y	?	Y
8 Nadler	Y	Y	Y	Y	Y	Y	Y
9 Weiner	Y	Y	Y	Y	Y	Y	Y
10 Towns	?	?	?	Y	Y	Y	Y
11 Clarke	Y	Y	Y	Y	Y	Y	+
12 Velázquez	Y	Y	Y	Y	Y	Y	Y
13 McMahon	Y	Y	Y	Y	Y	Y	Y
14 Maloney	?	?	?	Y	Y	Y	Y
15 Rangel	Y	Y	Y	Y	Y	Y	Y
16 Serrano	Y	Y	Y	Y	Y	Y	Y
17 Engel	?	?	?	Y	Y	Y	Y
18 Lowey	Y	Y	Y	Y	Y	Y	Y
19 Hall	Y	Y	Y	Y	Y	Y	Y
20 Murphy	Y	Y	Y	Y	Y	Y	Y
21 Tonko	Y	Y	Y	Y	Y	Y	Y
22 Hinchey	Y	Y	Y	Y	Y	Y	Y
23 Owens	Y	Y	Y	Y	Y	Y	Y
24 Arcuri	Y	Y	Y	Y	Y	Y	Y
25 Maffei	Y	Y	Y	Y	Y	Y	?
26 **Lee**	Y	Y	Y	Y	Y	Y	Y
27 Higgins	Y	Y	Y	Y	Y	Y	Y
28 Slaughter	Y	Y	?	Y	Y	Y	Y
29 Vacant							
NORTH CAROLINA							
1 Butterfield	Y	Y	Y	Y	Y	Y	Y
2 Etheridge	Y	Y	Y	Y	Y	Y	Y
3 **Jones**	Y	Y	Y	Y	Y	Y	Y
4 Price	Y	Y	Y	Y	Y	Y	Y
5 **Foxx**	Y	N	Y	Y	Y	Y	Y
6 **Coble**	Y	Y	Y	Y	Y	Y	Y
7 McIntyre	Y	Y	Y	Y	Y	Y	Y
8 Kissell	Y	Y	?	Y	Y	Y	Y
9 **Myrick**	Y	Y	Y	Y	Y	Y	Y
10 **McHenry**	Y	Y	Y	Y	Y	Y	Y
11 Shuler	Y	Y	Y	Y	Y	Y	Y
12 Watt	Y	Y	Y	Y	Y	Y	Y
13 Miller	Y	Y	Y	Y	Y	Y	Y
NORTH DAKOTA							
AL Pomeroy	Y	Y	Y	Y	Y	Y	Y
OHIO							
1 Driehaus	Y	Y	Y	Y	Y	Y	+
2 **Schmidt**	Y	Y	Y	Y	Y	Y	Y
3 **Turner**	Y	Y	Y	Y	Y	Y	Y
4 **Jordan**	+	+	+	Y	Y	Y	Y
5 **Latta**	Y	Y	Y	Y	Y	Y	Y
6 Wilson	Y	Y	Y	Y	Y	Y	Y
7 **Austria**	Y	Y	Y	Y	Y	Y	Y
8 **Boehner**	?	?	?	Y	?	?	Y
9 Kaptur	Y	Y	Y	Y	Y	Y	Y
10 Kucinich	Y	Y	Y	Y	Y	Y	Y
11 Fudge	Y	Y	Y	Y	Y	Y	Y
12 **Tiberi**	Y	Y	Y	Y	Y	Y	Y
13 Sutton	Y	Y	Y	Y	Y	Y	Y
14 **LaTourette**	Y	Y	Y	Y	Y	Y	Y
15 Kilroy	Y	Y	Y	Y	Y	Y	Y
16 Boccieri	?	?	?	Y	Y	Y	?
17 Ryan	Y	Y	Y	Y	Y	Y	Y
18 Space	Y	Y	Y	Y	Y	Y	Y
OKLAHOMA							
1 **Sullivan**	Y	Y	Y	Y	Y	Y	Y
2 Boren	Y	Y	Y	Y	Y	Y	Y
3 **Lucas**	Y	Y	Y	Y	Y	Y	Y
4 **Cole**	Y	Y	Y	Y	Y	Y	Y
5 **Fallin**	?	?	?	?	?	?	?
OREGON							
1 Wu	Y	Y	Y	Y	Y	Y	Y
2 **Walden**	Y	Y	Y	Y	Y	Y	Y
3 Blumenauer	Y	Y	Y	Y	Y	Y	Y
4 DeFazio	Y	Y	Y	P	Y	Y	Y
5 Schrader	?	?	?	?	Y	Y	Y
PENNSYLVANIA							
1 Brady	?	?	?	Y	Y	Y	Y
2 Fattah	Y	Y	Y	Y	Y	Y	Y
3 Dahlkemper	Y	Y	Y	Y	Y	Y	Y
4 Altmire	Y	Y	Y	Y	Y	Y	Y
5 **Thompson**	+	Y	Y	Y	Y	Y	Y
6 **Gerlach**	Y	Y	Y	Y	?	Y	Y
7 Sestak	Y	Y	Y	Y	Y	Y	Y
8 Murphy, P.	Y	Y	Y	Y	Y	Y	Y
9 **Shuster**	+	+	Y	Y	Y	Y	Y
10 Carney	Y	Y	Y	Y	Y	Y	Y
11 Kanjorski	Y	?	Y	Y	Y	Y	Y
12 Critz	Y	Y	Y	Y	Y	Y	Y
13 Schwartz	Y	Y	Y	Y	Y	Y	Y
14 Doyle	Y	Y	Y	Y	Y	Y	Y
15 **Dent**	Y	Y	Y	Y	Y	Y	Y
16 **Pitts**	Y	Y	Y	Y	Y	Y	Y
17 Holden	Y	Y	Y	Y	Y	Y	Y
18 **Murphy, T.**	+	+	Y	Y	Y	Y	Y
19 **Platts**	?	Y	Y	Y	Y	Y	Y
RHODE ISLAND							
1 Kennedy	Y	Y	Y	Y	Y	Y	Y
2 Langevin	Y	Y	Y	Y	Y	Y	Y
SOUTH CAROLINA							
1 **Brown**	Y	Y	Y	Y	Y	Y	Y
2 **Wilson**	Y	Y	Y	Y	Y	Y	Y
3 **Barrett**	+	+	+	Y	Y	Y	Y
4 **Inglis**	Y	Y	Y	Y	Y	Y	Y
5 Spratt	Y	Y	Y	Y	Y	Y	Y
6 Clyburn	Y	Y	Y	Y	Y	Y	Y
SOUTH DAKOTA							
AL Herseth Sandlin	Y	Y	Y	Y	Y	Y	Y
TENNESSEE							
1 **Roe**	Y	Y	Y	Y	Y	Y	Y
2 **Duncan**	Y	N	Y	Y	Y	Y	Y
3 **Wamp**	?	?	?	?	?	?	?
4 Davis	Y	Y	Y	Y	Y	Y	Y
5 Cooper	Y	Y	Y	Y	Y	Y	Y
6 Gordon	Y	Y	Y	Y	Y	Y	Y
7 **Blackburn**	Y	Y	Y	Y	Y	Y	Y
8 Tanner	Y	Y	Y	Y	Y	Y	Y
9 Cohen	Y	Y	Y	Y	Y	Y	Y
TEXAS							
1 **Gohmert**	Y	?	Y	Y	Y	Y	Y
2 **Poe**	Y	N	Y	Y	Y	Y	Y
3 **Johnson, S.**	Y	Y	Y	Y	Y	Y	Y
4 **Hall**	Y	Y	Y	Y	Y	Y	Y
5 **Hensarling**	Y	Y	Y	Y	Y	Y	Y
6 **Barton**	Y	Y	Y	Y	Y	Y	Y
7 **Culberson**	Y	Y	Y	Y	Y	Y	Y
8 **Brady**	Y	Y	Y	Y	Y	Y	Y
9 Green, A.	Y	Y	Y	Y	Y	Y	Y
10 **McCaul**	Y	Y	Y	Y	Y	Y	Y
11 **Conaway**	Y	Y	Y	Y	Y	Y	Y
12 **Granger**	Y	Y	Y	Y	Y	Y	Y
13 **Thornberry**	Y	Y	Y	Y	Y	Y	Y
14 **Paul**	Y	N	Y	Y	Y	Y	Y
15 Hinojosa	?	?	?	?	?	?	Y
16 Reyes	?	?	?	?	?	?	Y
17 Edwards	Y	Y	Y	Y	Y	Y	Y
18 Jackson Lee	Y	Y	Y	Y	Y	Y	Y
19 **Neugebauer**	Y	Y	Y	Y	Y	Y	Y
20 Gonzalez	Y	Y	Y	Y	Y	Y	Y
21 **Smith**	Y	Y	Y	Y	Y	Y	Y
22 **Olson**	Y	Y	Y	Y	Y	Y	Y
23 Rodriguez	Y	Y	Y	Y	Y	Y	Y
24 **Marchant**	Y	Y	Y	Y	Y	Y	Y
25 Doggett	Y	Y	Y	Y	Y	Y	Y
26 **Burgess**	Y	Y	Y	Y	Y	Y	Y
27 Ortiz	Y	Y	Y	Y	Y	Y	?
28 Cuellar	Y	Y	Y	Y	Y	Y	Y
29 Green, G.	Y	Y	Y	Y	Y	Y	Y
30 Johnson, E.	Y	Y	Y	Y	Y	Y	Y
31 **Carter**	Y	Y	Y	Y	?	Y	Y
32 **Sessions**	?	Y	Y	Y	Y	Y	Y
UTAH							
1 **Bishop**	?	?	?	Y	Y	Y	Y
2 Matheson	Y	Y	Y	Y	Y	Y	Y
3 **Chaffetz**	Y	N	Y	N	Y	Y	Y
VERMONT							
AL Welch	Y	Y	Y	Y	Y	Y	?
VIRGINIA							
1 **Wittman**	Y	Y	Y	Y	Y	Y	Y
2 Nye	Y	Y	Y	N	Y	Y	Y
3 Scott	Y	Y	Y	Y	Y	Y	Y
4 **Forbes**	Y	Y	Y	Y	Y	Y	Y
5 Perriello	Y	Y	Y	Y	Y	Y	?
6 **Goodlatte**	Y	Y	Y	Y	Y	Y	Y
7 **Cantor**	Y	Y	Y	Y	Y	Y	Y
8 Moran	Y	Y	Y	Y	Y	Y	Y
9 Boucher	Y	Y	Y	Y	Y	Y	Y
10 **Wolf**	Y	Y	Y	Y	Y	Y	Y
11 Connolly	Y	Y	Y	Y	Y	Y	Y
WASHINGTON							
1 Inslee	Y	Y	Y	Y	Y	Y	Y
2 Larsen	Y	Y	Y	Y	Y	Y	Y
3 Baird	Y	Y	Y	Y	Y	Y	Y
4 **Hastings**	?	?	?	Y	Y	Y	Y
5 **McMorris Rodgers**	Y	?	Y	Y	Y	Y	Y
6 Dicks	Y	Y	Y	Y	Y	Y	Y
7 McDermott	Y	Y	Y	Y	Y	Y	Y
8 **Reichert**	Y	Y	Y	Y	Y	Y	Y
9 Smith	Y	Y	+	Y	Y	Y	Y
WEST VIRGINIA							
1 Mollohan	Y	Y	Y	Y	Y	Y	Y
2 **Capito**	?	Y	Y	Y	Y	Y	Y
3 Rahall	Y	Y	Y	Y	Y	Y	Y
WISCONSIN							
1 **Ryan**	Y	Y	Y	Y	Y	Y	Y
2 Baldwin	Y	Y	Y	Y	Y	Y	Y
3 Kind	Y	Y	Y	Y	Y	Y	Y
4 Moore	Y	Y	Y	Y	Y	Y	Y
5 **Sensenbrenner**	Y	Y	Y	Y	Y	Y	Y
6 **Petri**	Y	Y	Y	Y	Y	Y	Y
7 Obey	Y	Y	Y	Y	Y	Y	Y
8 Kagen	Y	Y	Y	Y	Y	Y	Y
WYOMING							
AL **Lummis**	Y	Y	Y	Y	Y	Y	Y
DELEGATES							
Faleomavaega (A.S.)							
Norton (D.C.)							
Bordallo (Guam)							
Sablan (N. Marianas)							
Pierluisi (P.R.)							
Christensen (V.I.)							

IN THE HOUSE | By Vote Number

455. **HR 725. Tribal Law Enforcement/Passage.** Rahall, D-W.Va., motion to suspend the rules and concur in the Senate amendment to the bill that would permit federal law enforcement officials to investigate the production and sale of counterfeit American Indian arts and crafts. The Senate amendment would establish or reauthorize various programs and offices within the Bureau of Indian Affairs and Justice Department to support the criminal justice system on Indian lands. Motion agreed to, thus clearing the bill for the president, 326-92: D 248-0; R 78-92. A two-thirds majority of those present and voting (279 in this case) is required for passage under suspension of the rules. July 21, 2010.

456. **HR 4380. Tariff and Trade Provisions/Passage.** Levin, D-Mich., motion to suspend the rules and pass the bill that would temporarily suspend or reduce duties on hundreds of specific imported goods, make several technical corrections to trade laws and streamline current customs laws. Motion agreed to 378-43: D 249-1; R 129-42. A two-thirds majority of those present and voting (281 in this case) is required for passage under suspension of the rules. July 21, 2010.

457. **H Res 1513. Tribute to Saratoga Race Course/Adoption.** Norton, D-D.C., motion to suspend the rules and adopt the resolution that would congratulate the Saratoga Race Course on its 142nd season and recognize its place in horse racing history. Motion agreed to 396-14: D 240-3; R 156-11. A two-thirds majority of those present and voting (274 in this case) is required for adoption under suspension of the rules. July 21, 2010.

458. **HR 4213. Unemployment Benefits/Same-Day Consideration.** Adoption of the rule (H Res 1537) that would waive, through the legislative day of July 23, the two-thirds majority vote requirement to consider a rule related to the unemployment compensation measure (HR 4213) on the same day it is reported from the Rules Committee. The rule also would allow for consideration of measures under suspension of the rules at any time through the legislative day of July 23, 2010. Adopted 233-185: D 233-15; R 0-170. July 21, 2010.

459. **HR 5566. Animal 'Crush' Videos/Passage.** Scott, D-Va., motion to suspend the rules and pass the bill that would make it a federal crime to sell or distribute animal "crush" videos, which depict live animals being intentionally tortured or killed. Motion agreed to 416-3: D 249-0; R 167-3. A two-thirds majority of those present and voting (280 in this case) is required for passage under suspension of the rules. July 21, 2010.

460. **H Res 1411. Tribute to the 111th Fighter Wing/Adoption.** Critz, D-Pa., motion to suspend the rules and adopt the resolution that would honor the service of past and present members of the 111th Fighter Wing of the Pennsylvania Air National Guard. Motion agreed to 417-0: D 249-0; R 168-0. A two-thirds majority of those present and voting (278 in this case) is required for adoption under suspension of the rules. July 21, 2010.

	455	456	457	458	459	460
ALABAMA						
1 **Bonner**	Y	N	Y	N	Y	Y
2 Bright	Y	Y	Y	N	Y	Y
3 **Rogers**	N	Y	Y	N	Y	Y
4 **Aderholt**	Y	Y	Y	N	Y	Y
5 Griffith	Y	N	Y	N	Y	Y
6 **Bachus**	Y	Y	?	N	Y	Y
7 Davis	Y	Y	?	Y	Y	Y
ALASKA						
AL **Young**	Y	Y	Y	N	Y	Y
ARIZONA						
1 Kirkpatrick	Y	Y	Y	N	Y	Y
2 **Franks**	N	N	Y	N	Y	Y
3 **Shadegg**	N	Y	N	N	Y	Y
4 Pastor	Y	Y	Y	Y	Y	Y
5 Mitchell	Y	Y	Y	N	Y	Y
6 **Flake**	N	N	N	N	Y	Y
7 Grijalva	Y	Y	Y	Y	Y	Y
8 Giffords	Y	Y	Y	N	Y	Y
ARKANSAS						
1 Berry	Y	Y	N	Y	Y	Y
2 Snyder	Y	Y	Y	Y	Y	Y
3 **Boozman**	Y	Y	Y	N	Y	Y
4 Ross	Y	Y	Y	Y	Y	Y
CALIFORNIA						
1 Thompson	Y	Y	Y	Y	Y	Y
2 **Herger**	N	N	Y	N	Y	Y
3 **Lungren**	Y	Y	Y	N	Y	Y
4 **McClintock**	Y	Y	Y	N	Y	Y
5 Matsui	Y	Y	Y	Y	Y	Y
6 Woolsey	Y	Y	Y	Y	Y	Y
7 Miller, George	Y	Y	Y	Y	Y	Y
8 Pelosi						
9 Lee	Y	Y	Y	?	Y	Y
10 Garamendi	Y	Y	Y	Y	Y	Y
11 McNerney	Y	Y	Y	Y	Y	Y
12 Speier	Y	Y	Y	Y	Y	Y
13 Stark	Y	Y	Y	Y	Y	Y
14 Eshoo	Y	Y	Y	Y	Y	Y
15 Honda	Y	Y	Y	Y	Y	Y
16 Lofgren	Y	Y	Y	Y	Y	Y
17 Farr	Y	Y	Y	Y	Y	Y
18 Cardoza	Y	Y	Y	Y	Y	Y
19 **Radanovich**	N	N	Y	?	?	?
20 Costa	Y	Y	Y	Y	Y	Y
21 **Nunes**	Y	Y	Y	N	Y	Y
22 **McCarthy**	Y	N	Y	N	Y	Y
23 Capps	Y	Y	Y	Y	Y	Y
24 **Gallegly**	Y	Y	Y	N	Y	Y
25 **McKeon**	Y	Y	Y	N	Y	Y
26 **Dreier**	N	Y	Y	N	Y	Y
27 Sherman	Y	Y	Y	Y	Y	Y
28 Berman	Y	Y	Y	Y	Y	Y
29 Schiff	Y	Y	Y	Y	Y	Y
30 Waxman	Y	Y	Y	Y	Y	Y
31 Becerra	Y	Y	Y	Y	Y	Y
32 Chu	Y	Y	Y	Y	Y	Y
33 Watson	Y	Y	Y	Y	Y	?
34 Roybal-Allard	Y	Y	Y	Y	Y	Y
35 Waters	Y	Y	Y	Y	Y	Y
36 Harman	Y	Y	Y	Y	Y	Y
37 Richardson	Y	Y	Y	Y	Y	Y
38 Napolitano	Y	Y	Y	Y	Y	Y
39 Sánchez, Linda	Y	Y	Y	Y	Y	Y
40 **Royce**	N	Y	Y	N	Y	Y
41 **Lewis**	Y	N	Y	N	Y	Y
42 **Miller, Gary**	N	Y	Y	N	Y	Y
43 Baca	Y	Y	Y	Y	Y	Y
44 **Calvert**	Y	Y	Y	N	Y	Y
45 **Bono Mack**	Y	Y	Y	N	Y	Y
46 **Rohrabacher**	N	Y	Y	N	Y	Y
47 Sanchez, Loretta	Y	Y	Y	Y	Y	Y
48 **Campbell**	N	Y	N	N	Y	Y
49 **Issa**	Y	Y	Y	N	Y	Y
50 **Bilbray**	Y	N	Y	N	Y	Y
51 Filner	Y	Y	Y	Y	Y	Y
52 **Hunter**	N	Y	Y	N	Y	Y
53 Davis	Y	Y	Y	Y	Y	Y

	455	456	457	458	459	460
COLORADO						
1 DeGette	Y	Y	Y	Y	Y	Y
2 Polis	Y	Y	Y	Y	Y	Y
3 Salazar	Y	Y	Y	Y	Y	Y
4 Markey	?	Y	Y	N	Y	Y
5 **Lamborn**	N	N	Y	N	Y	Y
6 **Coffman**	N	N	Y	N	Y	Y
7 Perlmutter	Y	Y	Y	Y	Y	Y
CONNECTICUT						
1 Larson	Y	Y	Y	Y	Y	Y
2 Courtney	Y	Y	Y	Y	Y	Y
3 DeLauro	Y	Y	Y	Y	Y	Y
4 Himes	Y	Y	Y	Y	Y	Y
5 Murphy	Y	Y	Y	Y	Y	Y
DELAWARE						
AL **Castle**	Y	Y	Y	N	Y	Y
FLORIDA						
1 **Miller**	Y	Y	Y	N	Y	Y
2 Boyd	Y	Y	Y	Y	Y	Y
3 Brown	Y	Y	Y	Y	Y	Y
4 **Crenshaw**	Y	Y	Y	Y	Y	Y
5 **Brown-Waite**	N	Y	Y	N	Y	Y
6 **Stearns**	N	Y	Y	N	Y	Y
7 **Mica**	N	N	Y	N	Y	Y
8 Grayson	Y	Y	Y	Y	Y	Y
9 **Bilirakis**	N	Y	Y	N	Y	Y
10 **Young**	Y	Y	Y	N	Y	Y
11 Castor	Y	Y	Y	Y	Y	Y
12 **Putnam**	Y	Y	Y	N	Y	Y
13 **Buchanan**	Y	Y	Y	N	Y	Y
14 **Mack**	?	?	?	?	?	?
15 **Posey**	Y	Y	Y	N	Y	Y
16 **Rooney**	N	Y	Y	N	Y	Y
17 Meek	?	?	?	?	?	?
18 **Ros-Lehtinen**	?	Y	Y	N	Y	Y
19 Deutch	Y	Y	Y	Y	Y	Y
20 Wasserman Schultz	Y	Y	Y	Y	Y	Y
21 **Diaz-Balart, L.**	Y	Y	Y	Y	Y	Y
22 Klein	Y	Y	Y	Y	Y	Y
23 Hastings	Y	Y	Y	Y	Y	Y
24 Kosmas	Y	Y	Y	Y	Y	Y
25 **Diaz-Balart, M.**	Y	Y	Y	N	Y	Y
GEORGIA						
1 **Kingston**	N	N	Y	N	Y	Y
2 Bishop	Y	Y	?	Y	Y	Y
3 **Westmoreland**	N	Y	?	N	Y	Y
4 Johnson	?	?	?	Y	Y	Y
5 Lewis	Y	Y	Y	Y	Y	Y
6 **Price**	N	N	Y	N	Y	Y
7 **Linder**	N	N	N	N	Y	Y
8 Marshall	Y	Y	Y	Y	Y	Y
9 **Graves**	N	N	N	N	Y	Y
10 **Broun**	N	N	Y	N	Y	Y
11 **Gingrey**	N	Y	Y	N	Y	Y
12 Barrow	Y	Y	Y	Y	Y	Y
13 Scott	Y	Y	Y	Y	Y	Y
HAWAII						
1 **Djou**	Y	Y	Y	N	Y	Y
2 Hirono	Y	Y	Y	Y	Y	Y
IDAHO						
1 Minnick	Y	Y	Y	N	Y	Y
2 **Simpson**	Y	Y	Y	N	Y	?
ILLINOIS						
1 Rush	Y	Y	?	Y	Y	Y
2 Jackson	Y	Y	Y	Y	Y	Y
3 Lipinski	Y	Y	Y	Y	Y	Y
4 Gutierrez	Y	Y	Y	Y	Y	Y
5 Quigley	Y	Y	Y	Y	Y	Y
6 **Roskam**	Y	N	Y	N	Y	Y
7 Davis	Y	Y	Y	Y	Y	Y
8 Bean	Y	Y	Y	Y	Y	Y
9 Schakowsky	Y	Y	Y	Y	Y	Y
10 **Kirk**	Y	Y	Y	N	Y	Y
11 Halvorson	Y	Y	Y	Y	Y	Y
12 Costello	Y	Y	Y	Y	Y	Y
13 **Biggert**	N	Y	Y	N	Y	Y
14 Foster	Y	Y	Y	Y	Y	Y
15 **Johnson**	Y	N	Y	N	Y	Y

KEY   **Republicans**   Democrats

Y Voted for (yea)	**X** Paired against
# Paired for	**−** Announced against
+ Announced for	**P** Voted "present"
N Voted against (nay)	

C Voted "present" to avoid possible conflict of interest

? Did not vote or otherwise make a position known

	455	456	457	458	459	460
16 **Manzullo**	N	Y	Y	N	Y	Y
17 Hare	Y	Y	Y	Y	Y	Y
18 **Schock**	N	Y	Y	N	Y	Y
19 **Shimkus**	Y	Y	Y	N	Y	Y
INDIANA						
1 Visclosky	Y	Y	Y	Y	Y	Y
2 Donnelly	Y	Y	Y	Y	Y	Y
3 Vacant						
4 **Buyer**	N	Y	Y	N	Y	?
5 **Burton**	Y	Y	Y	N	Y	Y
6 **Pence**	N	N	Y	N	Y	Y
7 Carson	Y	Y	Y	Y	Y	Y
8 Ellsworth	Y	Y	Y	N	Y	Y
9 Hill	Y	Y	Y	N	Y	Y
IOWA						
1 Braley	Y	Y	Y	Y	Y	Y
2 Loebsack	Y	Y	Y	Y	Y	Y
3 Boswell	Y	Y	Y	Y	Y	Y
4 **Latham**	Y	Y	Y	N	Y	Y
5 **King**	N	Y	Y	N	Y	Y
KANSAS						
1 **Moran**	?	?	?	?	?	?
2 **Jenkins**	Y	Y	Y	N	Y	Y
3 Moore	Y	Y	Y	Y	Y	Y
4 **Tiahrt**	?	?	?	?	?	?
KENTUCKY						
1 **Whitfield**	Y	Y	Y	N	Y	Y
2 **Guthrie**	Y	Y	Y	N	Y	Y
3 Yarmuth	Y	Y	Y	Y	Y	Y
4 **Davis**	N	Y	Y	N	Y	Y
5 **Rogers**	N	Y	Y	N	Y	Y
6 Chandler	Y	Y	Y	Y	Y	Y
LOUISIANA						
1 **Scalise**	N	N	Y	N	Y	Y
2 **Cao**	Y	Y	Y	N	Y	Y
3 Melancon	Y	Y	Y	?	Y	Y
4 **Fleming**	N	Y	Y	N	Y	Y
5 **Alexander**	Y	Y	Y	N	Y	Y
6 **Cassidy**	Y	Y	Y	N	Y	Y
7 **Boustany**	N	N	Y	N	Y	Y
MAINE						
1 Pingree	Y	Y	Y	Y	Y	Y
2 Michaud	Y	Y	Y	Y	Y	Y
MARYLAND						
1 Kratovil	Y	Y	Y	Y	Y	Y
2 Ruppersberger	Y	Y	Y	Y	Y	Y
3 Sarbanes	Y	Y	Y	Y	Y	Y
4 Edwards	Y	Y	Y	Y	Y	Y
5 Hoyer	Y	Y	Y	Y	Y	Y
6 **Bartlett**	N	N	Y	N	Y	Y
7 Cummings	Y	Y	Y	Y	Y	Y
8 Van Hollen	Y	Y	Y	Y	Y	Y
MASSACHUSETTS						
1 Olver	Y	Y	Y	Y	Y	Y
2 Neal	Y	Y	Y	Y	Y	Y
3 McGovern	Y	Y	Y	Y	Y	Y
4 Frank	Y	Y	Y	Y	Y	Y
5 Tsongas	Y	Y	Y	Y	Y	Y
6 Tierney	Y	Y	Y	Y	Y	Y
7 Markey	Y	Y	Y	Y	Y	?
8 Capuano	?	?	?	?	?	?
9 Lynch	Y	Y	Y	Y	Y	Y
10 Delahunt	Y	Y	Y	Y	Y	Y
MICHIGAN						
1 Stupak	Y	Y	Y	Y	Y	Y
2 **Hoekstra**	?	?	?	?	?	?
3 **Ehlers**	Y	Y	N	N	Y	Y
4 **Camp**	Y	N	Y	N	Y	Y
5 Kildee	Y	Y	Y	Y	Y	Y
6 **Upton**	Y	Y	Y	N	Y	Y
7 Schauer	Y	Y	Y	Y	Y	Y
8 **Rogers**	N	Y	Y	N	Y	Y
9 Peters	Y	Y	Y	Y	Y	Y
10 **Miller**	Y	Y	Y	N	Y	Y
11 **McCotter**	N	Y	Y	N	Y	Y
12 Levin	Y	Y	Y	Y	Y	Y
13 Kilpatrick	Y	Y	Y	Y	Y	Y
14 Conyers	Y	Y	Y	Y	Y	Y
15 Dingell	Y	Y	Y	Y	Y	Y
MINNESOTA						
1 Walz	Y	Y	Y	Y	Y	Y
2 **Kline**	Y	Y	Y	N	Y	Y
3 **Paulsen**	Y	Y	Y	N	Y	Y
4 McCollum	Y	Y	Y	Y	Y	Y
5 Ellison	Y	Y	Y	Y	Y	Y
6 **Bachmann**	N	N	Y	N	Y	Y
7 Peterson	Y	Y	Y	Y	Y	Y
8 Oberstar	Y	Y	Y	Y	Y	Y
MISSISSIPPI						
1 Childers	Y	Y	Y	N	Y	Y
2 Thompson	Y	Y	Y	Y	Y	Y
3 **Harper**	N	N	Y	N	Y	Y
4 Taylor	Y	Y	Y	Y	Y	Y
MISSOURI						
1 Clay	Y	Y	Y	Y	Y	Y
2 **Akin**	N	Y	Y	N	Y	Y
3 Carnahan	Y	Y	Y	Y	Y	Y
4 Skelton	Y	Y	Y	Y	Y	Y
5 Cleaver	Y	Y	?	Y	?	Y
6 **Graves**	N	Y	Y	N	Y	Y
7 **Blunt**	N	Y	Y	N	Y	Y
8 **Emerson**	Y	Y	Y	N	Y	Y
9 **Luetkemeyer**	N	Y	Y	N	Y	Y
MONTANA						
AL **Rehberg**	Y	Y	Y	N	Y	Y
NEBRASKA						
1 **Fortenberry**	Y	Y	Y	N	Y	Y
2 **Terry**	Y	Y	Y	N	Y	Y
3 **Smith**	N	N	Y	N	Y	Y
NEVADA						
1 Berkley	Y	Y	Y	Y	Y	Y
2 **Heller**	N	Y	Y	N	Y	Y
3 Titus	Y	Y	Y	Y	Y	Y
NEW HAMPSHIRE						
1 Shea-Porter	Y	Y	Y	Y	Y	Y
2 Hodes	Y	N	Y	Y	Y	Y
NEW JERSEY						
1 Andrews	Y	Y	Y	Y	Y	Y
2 **LoBiondo**	N	Y	Y	N	Y	Y
3 Adler	Y	Y	Y	N	Y	Y
4 **Smith**	Y	Y	Y	N	Y	Y
5 **Garrett**	N	N	Y	N	Y	Y
6 Pallone	Y	Y	Y	Y	Y	Y
7 **Lance**	N	Y	Y	N	Y	Y
8 Pascrell	Y	Y	Y	Y	Y	Y
9 Rothman	Y	Y	Y	Y	Y	Y
10 Payne	Y	Y	Y	Y	Y	Y
11 **Frelinghuysen**	Y	Y	Y	N	Y	Y
12 Holt	Y	Y	Y	Y	Y	Y
13 Sires	Y	Y	Y	Y	Y	Y
NEW MEXICO						
1 Heinrich	Y	Y	Y	Y	Y	Y
2 Teague	Y	Y	Y	N	Y	Y
3 Luján	Y	Y	Y	Y	Y	Y
NEW YORK						
1 Bishop	Y	Y	Y	Y	Y	Y
2 Israel	Y	Y	Y	Y	Y	Y
3 **King**	?	?	?	?	?	?
4 McCarthy	Y	Y	Y	Y	Y	Y
5 Ackerman	Y	Y	Y	Y	Y	Y
6 Meeks	Y	Y	Y	Y	Y	Y
7 Crowley	Y	Y	Y	Y	Y	Y
8 Nadler	Y	Y	Y	Y	Y	Y
9 Weiner	Y	Y	Y	Y	Y	Y
10 Towns	Y	Y	Y	Y	Y	Y
11 Clarke	+	Y	Y	+	+	Y
12 Velázquez	Y	Y	Y	Y	Y	Y
13 McMahon	Y	Y	Y	Y	Y	Y
14 Maloney	Y	Y	Y	Y	Y	Y
15 Rangel	Y	Y	Y	Y	Y	Y
16 Serrano	Y	Y	Y	Y	Y	Y
17 Engel	Y	Y	Y	Y	Y	Y
18 Lowey	Y	Y	Y	Y	Y	Y
19 Hall	Y	Y	Y	Y	Y	Y
20 Murphy	Y	Y	Y	Y	Y	Y
21 Tonko	Y	Y	Y	Y	Y	Y
22 Hinchey	Y	Y	Y	Y	Y	Y
23 Owens	Y	Y	Y	Y	Y	Y
24 Arcuri	Y	Y	Y	Y	Y	Y
25 Maffei	Y	Y	Y	Y	Y	Y
26 **Lee**	N	Y	Y	N	Y	Y
27 Higgins	Y	Y	Y	Y	Y	Y
28 Slaughter	Y	Y	Y	Y	Y	Y
29 Vacant						
NORTH CAROLINA						
1 Butterfield	Y	Y	?	Y	Y	Y
2 Etheridge	Y	Y	Y	Y	Y	Y
3 **Jones**	Y	Y	Y	N	Y	Y
4 Price	Y	Y	Y	Y	Y	Y
5 **Foxx**	N	N	Y	N	Y	Y
6 **Coble**	N	Y	Y	N	Y	Y
7 McIntyre	Y	Y	Y	Y	Y	Y
8 Kissell	Y	Y	Y	Y	Y	Y
9 **Myrick**	Y	Y	Y	N	Y	Y
10 **McHenry**	Y	Y	Y	N	Y	Y
11 Shuler	Y	Y	Y	N	Y	Y
12 Watt	Y	Y	Y	Y	Y	Y
13 Miller	Y	Y	Y	Y	Y	Y
NORTH DAKOTA						
AL Pomeroy	Y	Y	Y	Y	Y	Y
OHIO						
1 Driehaus	Y	Y	Y	Y	Y	Y
2 **Schmidt**	N	Y	Y	N	Y	Y
3 **Turner**	Y	Y	Y	N	Y	Y
4 **Jordan**	N	N	Y	N	Y	Y
5 **Latta**	N	N	Y	N	Y	Y
6 Wilson	Y	Y	Y	Y	Y	Y
7 **Austria**	N	Y	Y	N	Y	Y
8 **Boehner**	N	N	?	N	Y	Y
9 Kaptur	Y	Y	Y	Y	Y	Y
10 Kucinich	Y	Y	Y	Y	Y	Y
11 Fudge	Y	Y	Y	Y	Y	Y
12 **Tiberi**	N	Y	Y	N	Y	Y
13 Sutton	Y	Y	Y	Y	Y	Y
14 **LaTourette**	Y	Y	Y	N	Y	Y
15 Kilroy	Y	Y	Y	Y	Y	Y
16 Boccieri	Y	Y	Y	Y	Y	Y
17 Ryan	Y	Y	Y	Y	Y	Y
18 Space	Y	Y	Y	Y	Y	Y
OKLAHOMA						
1 **Sullivan**	Y	Y	Y	N	Y	Y
2 Boren	Y	Y	Y	Y	Y	Y
3 **Lucas**	Y	Y	Y	N	Y	Y
4 **Cole**	Y	Y	Y	N	Y	Y
5 **Fallin**	?	?	?	?	?	?
OREGON						
1 Wu	Y	Y	Y	Y	Y	Y
2 **Walden**	Y	Y	Y	N	Y	Y
3 Blumenauer	Y	Y	Y	Y	Y	Y
4 DeFazio	Y	Y	P	Y	Y	Y
5 Schrader	Y	Y	Y	Y	Y	Y
PENNSYLVANIA						
1 Brady	Y	Y	Y	Y	Y	Y
2 Fattah	Y	Y	Y	Y	Y	Y
3 Dahlkemper	Y	Y	Y	Y	Y	Y
4 Altmire	Y	Y	N	Y	Y	Y
5 **Thompson**	N	Y	Y	N	Y	Y
6 **Gerlach**	Y	Y	Y	N	Y	Y
7 Sestak	Y	Y	Y	Y	Y	Y
8 Murphy, P.	Y	Y	Y	Y	Y	Y
9 **Shuster**	N	Y	Y	N	Y	Y
10 Carney	Y	Y	Y	N	Y	Y
11 Kanjorski	Y	Y	Y	Y	Y	Y
12 Critz	Y	Y	Y	Y	Y	Y
13 Schwartz	Y	Y	Y	Y	Y	Y
14 Doyle	Y	Y	Y	Y	Y	Y
15 **Dent**	Y	Y	Y	N	Y	Y
16 **Pitts**	N	N	Y	N	Y	Y
17 Holden	Y	Y	Y	Y	Y	Y
18 **Murphy, T.**	Y	Y	Y	N	Y	Y
19 **Platts**	Y	Y	Y	N	Y	Y
RHODE ISLAND						
1 Kennedy	Y	Y	Y	Y	Y	Y
2 Langevin	Y	Y	Y	Y	Y	Y
SOUTH CAROLINA						
1 **Brown**	N	Y	Y	N	Y	Y
2 **Wilson**	Y	Y	Y	N	Y	Y
3 **Barrett**	N	Y	Y	N	Y	Y
4 **Inglis**	N	Y	Y	N	Y	Y
5 Spratt	Y	Y	Y	Y	Y	Y
6 Clyburn	Y	Y	Y	Y	Y	Y
SOUTH DAKOTA						
AL Herseth Sandlin	Y	Y	Y	Y	Y	Y
TENNESSEE						
1 **Roe**	N	Y	Y	N	Y	Y
2 **Duncan**	N	Y	Y	N	Y	Y
3 **Wamp**	?	?	?	?	?	?
4 Davis	Y	Y	Y	Y	Y	Y
5 Cooper	Y	Y	Y	Y	Y	Y
6 Gordon	Y	Y	Y	Y	Y	Y
7 **Blackburn**	Y	Y	Y	N	Y	Y
8 Tanner	Y	Y	Y	Y	Y	Y
9 Cohen	Y	Y	Y	Y	Y	Y
TEXAS						
1 **Gohmert**	N	Y	N	N	Y	Y
2 **Poe**	N	Y	N	N	Y	Y
3 **Johnson, S.**	N	Y	Y	N	Y	Y
4 **Hall**	N	N	Y	N	Y	Y
5 **Hensarling**	N	Y	Y	N	Y	Y
6 **Barton**	N	N	Y	N	Y	Y
7 **Culberson**	N	N	Y	N	Y	Y
8 **Brady**	Y	N	Y	N	Y	Y
9 Green, A.	Y	Y	Y	Y	Y	Y
10 **McCaul**	Y	N	Y	N	Y	Y
11 **Conaway**	N	Y	Y	N	Y	Y
12 **Granger**	Y	Y	Y	N	Y	Y
13 **Thornberry**	Y	Y	Y	N	Y	Y
14 **Paul**	N	Y	Y	N	N	Y
15 Hinojosa	Y	Y	Y	Y	Y	Y
16 Reyes	Y	Y	Y	Y	Y	Y
17 Edwards	Y	Y	Y	Y	Y	Y
18 Jackson Lee	Y	Y	Y	Y	Y	Y
19 **Neugebauer**	N	Y	Y	N	Y	Y
20 Gonzalez	Y	Y	Y	Y	Y	Y
21 **Smith**	N	Y	Y	N	Y	Y
22 **Olson**	N	Y	Y	N	Y	Y
23 Rodriguez	Y	Y	Y	Y	Y	Y
24 **Marchant**	N	N	Y	N	Y	Y
25 Doggett	Y	Y	Y	Y	Y	Y
26 **Burgess**	N	Y	N	N	Y	Y
27 Ortiz	?	?	?	?	?	?
28 Cuellar	Y	Y	Y	Y	Y	Y
29 Green, G.	Y	Y	Y	Y	Y	Y
30 Johnson, E.	Y	Y	Y	Y	Y	Y
31 **Carter**	Y	Y	N	N	Y	Y
32 **Sessions**	N	N	Y	N	Y	Y
UTAH						
1 **Bishop**	N	Y	Y	N	Y	Y
2 Matheson	Y	Y	Y	Y	Y	Y
3 **Chaffetz**	N	Y	N	N	Y	Y
VERMONT						
AL Welch	Y	Y	P	Y	Y	Y
VIRGINIA						
1 **Wittman**	Y	Y	Y	N	Y	Y
2 Nye	Y	Y	N	N	Y	Y
3 Scott	Y	Y	Y	Y	Y	Y
4 **Forbes**	Y	Y	?	N	Y	Y
5 Perriello	Y	Y	Y	Y	Y	Y
6 **Goodlatte**	N	Y	Y	N	Y	Y
7 **Cantor**	N	N	Y	N	Y	Y
8 Moran	Y	Y	Y	Y	Y	Y
9 Boucher	Y	Y	Y	Y	Y	Y
10 **Wolf**	Y	Y	Y	N	Y	Y
11 Connolly	Y	Y	Y	Y	Y	Y
WASHINGTON						
1 Inslee	Y	Y	Y	Y	Y	Y
2 Larsen	Y	Y	Y	Y	Y	Y
3 Baird	Y	Y	Y	N	Y	Y
4 **Hastings**	N	Y	Y	N	Y	Y
5 **McMorris Rodgers**	N	Y	Y	N	Y	Y
6 Dicks	Y	Y	Y	Y	Y	Y
7 McDermott	Y	Y	Y	Y	Y	Y
8 **Reichert**	Y	Y	Y	N	Y	Y
9 Smith	Y	Y	Y	Y	Y	Y
WEST VIRGINIA						
1 Mollohan	Y	Y	Y	Y	Y	Y
2 **Capito**	Y	Y	Y	N	Y	Y
3 Rahall	Y	Y	Y	Y	Y	Y
WISCONSIN						
1 **Ryan**	N	Y	Y	N	Y	Y
2 Baldwin	Y	Y	Y	Y	Y	Y
3 Kind	Y	Y	Y	Y	Y	Y
4 Moore	Y	Y	Y	Y	Y	Y
5 **Sensenbrenner**	N	N	Y	N	Y	Y
6 **Petri**	N	Y	Y	N	Y	Y
7 Obey	Y	Y	Y	Y	Y	Y
8 Kagen	Y	Y	Y	Y	Y	Y
WYOMING						
AL **Lummis**	N	Y	Y	N	Y	Y
DELEGATES						
Faleomavaega (A.S.)						
Norton (D.C.)						
Bordallo (Guam)						
Sablan (N. Marianas)						
Pierluisi (P.R.)						
Christensen (V.I.)						

IN THE HOUSE | By Vote Number

461. **HR 4213. Unemployment Benefits Extension/Rule.** Adoption of the rule (H Res 1550) to provide for House floor consideration of the motion to concur in the Senate amendment to the House amendment to the Senate amendment to the bill that would extend eligibility for extended federal unemployment insurance through Nov. 30, 2010, applied retroactively to June 2. Adopted 237-180: D 236-10; R 1-170. July 22, 2010.

462. **HR 1469. Background Check Availability/Passage.** Scott, D-Va., motion to suspend the rules and pass the bill that would direct the Justice Department to create a program to streamline the process of national criminal history background checks for those who work with children. Motion agreed to 413-4: D 246-0; R 167-4. A two-thirds majority of those present and voting (278 in this case) is required for passage under suspension of the rules. July 22, 2010.

463. **HR 4213. Unemployment Benefits Extension/Motion to Concur.** Levin, D-Mich., motion to concur in the Senate amendment to the House amendment to the Senate amendment to the bill that would extend eligibility for extended federal unemployment insurance until Nov. 30, 2010, applied retroactively to June 2. Motion agreed to, thus clearing the bill for the president, 272-152: D 241-10; R 31-142. A "yea" was a vote in support of the president's position. July 22, 2010.

464. **HR 5341. Joyce Rogers Post Office/Passage.** Norton, D-D.C., motion to suspend the rules and pass the bill that would designate a postal building in Brighton, Mich., as the "Joyce Rogers Post Office Building." Motion agreed to 411-0: D 246-0; R 165-0. A two-thirds majority of those present and voting (274 in this case) is required for passage under suspension of the rules. July 22, 2010.

465. **HR 1264. Wind Insurance/Previous Question.** Slaughter, D-N.Y., motion to order the previous question (thus ending debate and possibility of amendment) on adoption of the rule (H Res 1549) to provide for House floor consideration of the bill that would make multiperil coverage for damage resulting from windstorms or floods available through the National Flood Insurance Program. Motion agreed to 234-179: D 234-11; R 0-168. July 22, 2010.

466. **HR 1264. Wind Insurance/Rule.** Adoption of the rule (H Res 1549) that would provide for House floor consideration of the bill that would make multiperil coverage for damage resulting from windstorms or floods available through the National Flood Insurance Program. Adopted 228-183: D 227-17; R 1-166. July 22, 2010.

	461	462	463	464	465	466
ALABAMA						
1 **Bonner**	N	Y	N	Y	N	N
2 Bright	N	Y	N	Y	Y	N
3 **Rogers**	N	Y	N	Y	N	N
4 **Aderholt**	N	Y	N	Y	N	N
5 **Griffith**	N	Y	N	Y	N	N
6 **Bachus**	N	Y	N	Y	N	N
7 Davis	Y	Y	Y	?	?	?
ALASKA						
AL **Young**	N	Y	Y	Y	N	N
ARIZONA						
1 Kirkpatrick	Y	Y	Y	Y	N	Y
2 **Franks**	N	Y	N	Y	N	N
3 **Shadegg**	N	Y	N	N	N	N
4 Pastor	Y	Y	Y	Y	Y	Y
5 Mitchell	N	Y	Y	Y	N	N
6 **Flake**	N	N	N	Y	N	N
7 Grijalva	Y	Y	Y	Y	Y	Y
8 Giffords	N	Y	Y	Y	N	N
ARKANSAS						
1 Berry	Y	Y	N	Y	Y	Y
2 Snyder	Y	?	Y	Y	Y	Y
3 **Boozman**	N	Y	N	Y	N	N
4 Ross	Y	Y	Y	Y	Y	Y
CALIFORNIA						
1 Thompson	Y	Y	Y	Y	Y	Y
2 **Herger**	N	Y	N	Y	N	N
3 **Lungren**	N	Y	N	N	N	N
4 **McClintock**	N	Y	N	Y	N	N
5 Matsui	Y	Y	Y	Y	Y	Y
6 Woolsey	Y	Y	Y	Y	Y	Y
7 Miller, George	Y	Y	Y	Y	Y	Y
8 Pelosi		Y				
9 Lee	Y	Y	Y	Y	Y	Y
10 Garamendi	Y	Y	Y	Y	Y	Y
11 McNerney	Y	Y	Y	Y	?	Y
12 Speier	Y	Y	Y	Y	Y	Y
13 Stark	Y	Y	Y	Y	Y	N
14 Eshoo	Y	Y	Y	Y	Y	Y
15 Honda	Y	Y	Y	Y	Y	Y
16 Lofgren	Y	Y	Y	?	?	?
17 Farr	Y	Y	Y	Y	Y	Y
18 Cardoza	Y	Y	Y	Y	Y	Y
19 **Radanovich**	N	Y	N	?	N	N
20 Costa	Y	Y	Y	Y	Y	Y
21 **Nunes**	N	Y	N	N	N	N
22 **McCarthy**	N	Y	N	Y	N	N
23 Capps	Y	Y	Y	Y	Y	Y
24 **Gallegly**	N	Y	N	Y	N	N
25 **McKeon**	N	Y	N	N	N	N
26 **Dreier**	N	Y	N	N	N	N
27 Sherman	Y	Y	Y	Y	Y	Y
28 Berman	Y	Y	Y	Y	Y	?
29 Schiff	Y	Y	Y	Y	Y	Y
30 Waxman	Y	Y	Y	Y	Y	Y
31 Becerra	Y	Y	Y	Y	Y	Y
32 Chu	Y	Y	Y	Y	Y	Y
33 Watson	Y	Y	Y	Y	Y	Y
34 Roybal-Allard	Y	Y	Y	Y	Y	Y
35 Waters	Y	Y	Y	Y	Y	Y
36 Harman	Y	Y	Y	Y	Y	Y
37 Richardson	Y	Y	Y	Y	Y	Y
38 Napolitano	Y	Y	Y	Y	Y	Y
39 Sánchez, Linda	Y	Y	Y	Y	Y	Y
40 **Royce**	N	Y	N	Y	N	N
41 **Lewis**	N	Y	N	Y	N	N
42 **Miller, Gary**	N	Y	N	Y	N	N
43 Baca	Y	Y	Y	Y	Y	Y
44 **Calvert**	N	Y	N	Y	N	N
45 **Bono Mack**	N	Y	Y	Y	N	N
46 **Rohrabacher**	N	Y	N	Y	N	N
47 Sanchez, Loretta	Y	Y	Y	Y	Y	?
48 **Campbell**	N	Y	N	Y	N	N
49 **Issa**	N	Y	N	Y	N	N
50 **Bilbray**	N	Y	Y	Y	N	N
51 Filner	Y	Y	Y	Y	Y	Y
52 **Hunter**	N	Y	N	Y	N	N
53 Davis	Y	Y	Y	Y	Y	Y

	461	462	463	464	465	466
COLORADO						
1 DeGette	Y	Y	Y	Y	Y	Y
2 Polis	Y	Y	Y	Y	Y	Y
3 Salazar	Y	Y	Y	Y	Y	Y
4 Markey	N	Y	N	Y	N	N
5 **Lamborn**	N	Y	N	N	N	N
6 **Coffman**	N	Y	N	Y	N	N
7 Perlmutter	Y	Y	Y	Y	Y	Y
CONNECTICUT						
1 Larson	Y	Y	Y	Y	Y	Y
2 Courtney	Y	Y	Y	Y	Y	Y
3 DeLauro	Y	Y	Y	Y	Y	Y
4 Himes	Y	Y	Y	Y	Y	Y
5 Murphy	Y	Y	Y	Y	Y	Y
DELAWARE						
AL **Castle**	N	Y	Y	Y	N	N
FLORIDA						
1 **Miller**	N	Y	N	Y	N	N
2 Boyd	Y	Y	Y	Y	Y	Y
3 Brown	Y	Y	Y	Y	Y	Y
4 **Crenshaw**	N	Y	N	Y	N	N
5 **Brown-Waite**	N	Y	N	N	N	N
6 **Stearns**	N	Y	N	Y	N	N
7 **Mica**	N	Y	N	Y	N	N
8 Grayson	Y	Y	Y	Y	Y	Y
9 **Bilirakis**	N	Y	Y	Y	N	N
10 **Young**	?	?	Y	Y	N	N
11 Castor	Y	Y	Y	Y	Y	Y
12 **Putnam**	N	Y	N	N	N	N
13 **Buchanan**	N	Y	N	N	N	N
14 **Mack**	N	Y	N	Y	N	N
15 **Posey**	N	Y	Y	N	N	N
16 **Rooney**	N	Y	N	Y	N	N
17 Meek	Y	Y	Y	Y	Y	Y
18 **Ros-Lehtinen**	N	Y	Y	Y	N	N
19 Deutch	Y	Y	Y	Y	Y	Y
20 Wasserman Schultz	Y	Y	Y	Y	Y	Y
21 **Diaz-Balart, L.**	N	Y	?	?	?	?
22 Klein	Y	Y	Y	Y	Y	Y
23 Hastings	Y	Y	Y	Y	Y	Y
24 Kosmas	Y	Y	Y	Y	Y	Y
25 **Diaz-Balart, M.**	N	Y	Y	Y	?	N
GEORGIA						
1 **Kingston**	N	Y	N	Y	N	N
2 Bishop	Y	Y	Y	Y	Y	Y
3 **Westmoreland**	N	Y	N	Y	N	N
4 Johnson	Y	Y	Y	Y	Y	Y
5 Lewis	Y	Y	Y	Y	Y	Y
6 **Price**	N	Y	N	Y	N	N
7 **Linder**	N	Y	N	N	N	N
8 Marshall	Y	Y	Y	Y	Y	Y
9 **Graves**	N	N	N	Y	N	N
10 **Broun**	N	N	N	N	N	N
11 **Gingrey**	N	Y	N	Y	N	N
12 Barrow	Y	Y	Y	Y	Y	Y
13 Scott	Y	Y	Y	Y	Y	Y
HAWAII						
1 **Djou**	N	Y	N	Y	N	N
2 Hirono	Y	Y	Y	Y	Y	Y
IDAHO						
1 Minnick	N	Y	N	Y	N	N
2 **Simpson**	N	Y	N	Y	N	?
ILLINOIS						
1 Rush	Y	?	Y	?	Y	Y
2 Jackson	Y	Y	Y	Y	Y	Y
3 Lipinski	Y	Y	Y	Y	Y	Y
4 Gutierrez	Y	Y	Y	?	Y	Y
5 Quigley	?	?	Y	Y	Y	Y
6 **Roskam**	N	Y	N	Y	N	N
7 Davis	Y	Y	Y	Y	Y	Y
8 Bean	Y	Y	Y	Y	Y	Y
9 Schakowsky	Y	Y	Y	Y	Y	Y
10 **Kirk**	N	Y	N	Y	N	N
11 Halvorson	Y	Y	Y	Y	Y	N
12 Costello	Y	Y	Y	Y	Y	?
13 **Biggert**	N	Y	N	Y	N	N
14 Foster	Y	Y	Y	Y	Y	Y
15 **Johnson**	N	Y	Y	Y	N	N

KEY   **Republicans**   Democrats

Y Voted for (yea)	X Paired against	C Voted "present" to avoid possible conflict of interest
# Paired for	– Announced against	
+ Announced for	P Voted "present"	? Did not vote or otherwise make a position known
N Voted against (nay)		

	461	462	463	464	465	466
16 **Manzullo**	N	Y	Y	Y	N	N
17 Hare	Y	Y	Y	Y	Y	Y
18 **Schock**	N	Y	N	Y	N	N
19 **Shimkus**	N	Y	N	Y	N	N
INDIANA						
1 Visclosky	Y	Y	Y	Y	Y	Y
2 Donnelly	Y	Y	Y	Y	Y	N
3 Vacant						
4 **Buyer**	N	Y	N	Y	?	?
5 **Burton**	N	Y	N	Y	N	N
6 **Pence**	N	Y	N	Y	?	?
7 Carson	Y	Y	Y	Y	Y	Y
8 Ellsworth	Y	Y	Y	Y	N	N
9 Hill	N	Y	N	Y	N	N
IOWA						
1 Braley	Y	Y	Y	Y	Y	Y
2 Loebsack	Y	Y	Y	Y	Y	Y
3 Boswell	Y	Y	Y	Y	Y	Y
4 **Latham**	N	Y	N	Y	N	N
5 **King**	N	Y	N	Y	N	N
KANSAS						
1 **Moran**	N	Y	N	Y	N	N
2 **Jenkins**	N	Y	N	Y	N	N
3 Moore	Y	Y	Y	?	Y	Y
4 **Tiahrt**	?	?	?	?	?	?
KENTUCKY						
1 **Whitfield**	N	Y	Y	Y	N	N
2 **Guthrie**	N	Y	N	Y	N	N
3 Yarmuth	Y	Y	Y	Y	Y	Y
4 **Davis**	N	Y	N	Y	N	N
5 **Rogers**	N	Y	N	Y	N	N
6 Chandler	Y	Y	Y	Y	Y	Y
LOUISIANA						
1 **Scalise**	N	Y	N	Y	N	N
2 **Cao**	N	Y	Y	Y	N	Y
3 Melancon	Y	Y	Y	Y	Y	Y
4 **Fleming**	N	Y	N	Y	N	N
5 **Alexander**	N	Y	N	Y	N	N
6 **Cassidy**	N	Y	N	Y	N	N
7 **Boustany**	N	Y	N	Y	N	N
MAINE						
1 Pingree	Y	Y	Y	Y	Y	Y
2 Michaud	Y	Y	Y	Y	Y	Y
MARYLAND						
1 Kratovil	Y	Y	Y	Y	N	N
2 Ruppersberger	Y	Y	Y	Y	Y	Y
3 Sarbanes	Y	Y	Y	Y	Y	Y
4 Edwards	Y	Y	Y	Y	Y	Y
5 Hoyer	Y	Y	Y	Y	Y	Y
6 **Bartlett**	N	Y	N	Y	N	N
7 Cummings	Y	Y	Y	Y	Y	Y
8 Van Hollen	Y	Y	Y	Y	Y	Y
MASSACHUSETTS						
1 Olver	Y	Y	Y	Y	Y	Y
2 Neal	Y	Y	Y	Y	Y	Y
3 McGovern	Y	Y	Y	Y	Y	Y
4 Frank	Y	Y	Y	Y	Y	Y
5 Tsongas	Y	Y	Y	Y	Y	Y
6 Tierney	Y	Y	Y	Y	?	?
7 Markey	Y	Y	Y	Y	Y	Y
8 Capuano	?	?	?	?	?	?
9 Lynch	Y	Y	Y	Y	Y	Y
0 Delahunt	Y	Y	Y	Y	Y	?
MICHIGAN						
1 Stupak	Y	Y	Y	Y	Y	Y
2 **Hoekstra**	?	?	?	?	?	?
3 **Ehlers**	Y	Y	Y	Y	N	N
4 **Camp**	N	Y	N	Y	N	N
5 Kildee	Y	Y	Y	Y	Y	Y
6 **Upton**	N	Y	Y	Y	N	N
7 Schauer	Y	Y	Y	Y	Y	Y
8 **Rogers**	N	Y	Y	Y	N	N
9 Peters	Y	Y	Y	Y	Y	N
0 **Miller**	N	Y	N	Y	N	N
1 **McCotter**	N	Y	Y	Y	N	N
2 Levin	Y	Y	Y	Y	Y	Y
3 Kilpatrick	Y	Y	Y	Y	Y	Y
4 Conyers	Y	Y	Y	Y	Y	Y
5 Dingell	Y	Y	Y	Y	Y	Y
MINNESOTA						
1 Walz	Y	Y	Y	Y	Y	Y
2 **Kline**	N	Y	N	Y	N	N
3 **Paulsen**	N	Y	N	Y	N	N
4 McCollum	Y	Y	Y	Y	Y	Y

	461	462	463	464	465	466
5 Ellison	Y	Y	Y	Y	Y	Y
6 **Bachmann**	N	Y	N	Y	N	N
7 Peterson	Y	Y	Y	Y	Y	Y
8 Oberstar	Y	Y	Y	Y	Y	Y
MISSISSIPPI						
1 Childers	Y	Y	Y	Y	Y	Y
2 Thompson	Y	Y	Y	Y	Y	Y
3 **Harper**	N	Y	N	Y	N	N
4 Taylor	Y	Y	Y	Y	Y	Y
MISSOURI						
1 Clay	Y	Y	Y	Y	Y	Y
2 **Akin**	N	Y	N	?	N	N
3 Carnahan	Y	Y	Y	Y	Y	Y
4 Skelton	Y	Y	Y	Y	Y	Y
5 Cleaver	Y	Y	Y	Y	Y	Y
6 **Graves**	N	Y	N	Y	N	N
7 **Blunt**	N	Y	N	Y	N	N
8 **Emerson**	N	Y	N	Y	N	N
9 **Luetkemeyer**	N	Y	N	Y	N	N
MONTANA						
AL **Rehberg**	N	Y	N	Y	N	N
NEBRASKA						
1 **Fortenberry**	N	Y	N	Y	N	N
2 **Terry**	N	Y	N	Y	N	N
3 **Smith**	N	Y	N	Y	N	N
NEVADA						
1 Berkley	Y	Y	Y	Y	Y	Y
2 **Heller**	N	Y	Y	Y	N	N
3 Titus	?	Y	Y	Y	Y	Y
NEW HAMPSHIRE						
1 Shea-Porter	Y	Y	Y	Y	Y	Y
2 Hodes	?	?	?	?	?	?
NEW JERSEY						
1 Andrews	Y	Y	Y	Y	Y	Y
2 **LoBiondo**	N	Y	Y	Y	N	N
3 Adler	Y	Y	Y	Y	Y	N
4 **Smith**	N	Y	Y	?	N	N
5 **Garrett**	N	Y	N	Y	N	N
6 Pallone	Y	Y	Y	Y	Y	Y
7 **Lance**	N	Y	N	Y	N	N
8 Pascrell	Y	Y	Y	Y	Y	Y
9 Rothman	Y	Y	Y	Y	Y	Y
10 Payne	Y	Y	Y	Y	Y	Y
11 **Frelinghuysen**	N	Y	N	Y	N	N
12 Holt	Y	Y	Y	Y	Y	Y
13 Sires	Y	Y	Y	Y	Y	Y
NEW MEXICO						
1 Heinrich	Y	Y	Y	Y	Y	Y
2 Teague	Y	Y	Y	Y	Y	Y
3 Luján	Y	Y	Y	Y	Y	Y
NEW YORK						
1 Bishop	Y	Y	Y	Y	Y	Y
2 Israel	Y	Y	Y	Y	Y	Y
3 **King**	?	?	?	?	?	?
4 McCarthy	Y	Y	Y	?	Y	Y
5 Ackerman	Y	Y	Y	Y	Y	Y
6 Meeks	Y	Y	Y	Y	Y	Y
7 Crowley	Y	Y	Y	Y	Y	Y
8 Nadler	Y	Y	Y	Y	Y	Y
9 Weiner	Y	Y	Y	Y	Y	Y
10 Towns	Y	Y	Y	Y	Y	Y
11 Clarke	Y	Y	Y	Y	Y	Y
12 Velázquez	Y	Y	Y	Y	Y	Y
13 McMahon	Y	Y	Y	Y	Y	Y
14 Maloney	?	Y	Y	Y	Y	Y
15 Rangel	Y	Y	Y	Y	Y	Y
16 Serrano	Y	Y	Y	Y	Y	Y
17 Engel	Y	Y	Y	Y	Y	Y
18 Lowey	Y	Y	Y	Y	Y	Y
19 Hall	Y	Y	Y	Y	Y	Y
20 Murphy	Y	Y	Y	Y	Y	N
21 Tonko	Y	Y	Y	Y	Y	Y
22 Hinchey	Y	Y	Y	Y	Y	Y
23 Owens	Y	Y	Y	Y	Y	Y
24 Arcuri	Y	Y	Y	Y	Y	Y
25 Maffei	Y	Y	Y	Y	Y	Y
26 **Lee**	N	Y	N	Y	N	N
27 Higgins	Y	Y	Y	Y	Y	Y
28 Slaughter	Y	Y	Y	Y	Y	Y
29 Vacant						
NORTH CAROLINA						
1 Butterfield	Y	Y	Y	Y	Y	Y
2 Etheridge	Y	Y	Y	Y	Y	Y
3 **Jones**	N	Y	Y	?	N	N
4 Price	Y	Y	Y	Y	Y	Y

	461	462	463	464	465	466
5 **Foxx**	N	Y	N	Y	N	N
6 **Coble**	N	Y	N	Y	N	N
7 McIntyre	Y	Y	N	Y	N	Y
8 Kissell	Y	Y	Y	Y	Y	Y
9 **Myrick**	N	Y	N	Y	N	N
10 **McHenry**	N	Y	N	Y	N	N
11 Shuler	N	Y	N	Y	Y	N
12 Watt	Y	Y	Y	Y	Y	Y
13 Miller	Y	Y	Y	Y	Y	Y
NORTH DAKOTA						
AL Pomeroy	Y	Y	Y	Y	Y	Y
OHIO						
1 Driehaus	Y	Y	Y	Y	Y	Y
2 **Schmidt**	N	Y	N	Y	N	N
3 **Turner**	N	Y	Y	Y	N	N
4 **Jordan**	N	Y	N	Y	N	N
5 **Latta**	N	Y	N	Y	N	N
6 Wilson	Y	Y	Y	Y	Y	Y
7 **Austria**	N	Y	N	Y	N	N
8 **Boehner**	N	Y	N	Y	N	N
9 Kaptur	Y	Y	Y	Y	Y	Y
10 Kucinich	Y	Y	Y	Y	Y	Y
11 Fudge	Y	Y	Y	Y	Y	Y
12 **Tiberi**	N	Y	N	Y	N	N
13 Sutton	Y	Y	Y	Y	Y	Y
14 **LaTourette**	N	Y	Y	Y	N	N
15 Kilroy	Y	Y	Y	Y	Y	Y
16 Boccieri	Y	Y	Y	Y	N	N
17 Ryan	Y	Y	Y	Y	Y	Y
18 Space	Y	Y	Y	Y	Y	Y
OKLAHOMA						
1 **Sullivan**	N	Y	N	Y	N	N
2 Boren	Y	Y	Y	Y	Y	Y
3 **Lucas**	N	Y	N	Y	N	N
4 **Cole**	N	Y	N	Y	N	N
5 **Fallin**	?	?	?	?	?	?
OREGON						
1 Wu	Y	Y	Y	Y	Y	Y
2 **Walden**	N	Y	N	Y	N	N
3 Blumenauer	Y	Y	Y	Y	Y	Y
4 DeFazio	Y	Y	Y	Y	Y	Y
5 Schrader	Y	Y	Y	Y	Y	Y
PENNSYLVANIA						
1 Brady	Y	Y	Y	Y	Y	Y
2 Fattah	Y	Y	Y	Y	Y	Y
3 Dahlkemper	Y	Y	Y	Y	Y	Y
4 Altmire	Y	Y	Y	Y	Y	Y
5 **Thompson**	N	Y	N	Y	N	N
6 **Gerlach**	N	Y	Y	Y	N	N
7 Sestak	Y	Y	Y	Y	Y	Y
8 Murphy, P.	?	?	Y	Y	Y	Y
9 **Shuster**	N	Y	N	?	N	N
10 Carney	Y	Y	Y	Y	Y	Y
11 Kanjorski	Y	Y	Y	Y	Y	Y
12 Critz	Y	Y	Y	Y	Y	Y
13 Schwartz	Y	Y	Y	Y	Y	Y
14 Doyle	?	?	+	Y	Y	Y
15 **Dent**	N	Y	Y	Y	N	N
16 **Pitts**	N	Y	N	Y	N	N
17 Holden	Y	Y	Y	Y	Y	Y
18 **Murphy, T.**	N	Y	Y	Y	N	N
19 **Platts**	N	Y	Y	Y	N	N
RHODE ISLAND						
1 Kennedy	Y	Y	Y	Y	Y	Y
2 Langevin	Y	Y	Y	Y	Y	Y
SOUTH CAROLINA						
1 **Brown**	N	Y	N	Y	N	N
2 **Wilson**	N	Y	N	Y	N	N
3 **Barrett**	N	Y	N	Y	N	N
4 **Inglis**	N	Y	N	Y	N	N
5 Spratt	Y	Y	Y	Y	Y	Y
6 Clyburn	Y	Y	Y	Y	Y	Y
SOUTH DAKOTA						
AL Herseth Sandlin	Y	Y	Y	Y	Y	Y
TENNESSEE						
1 **Roe**	N	Y	N	Y	N	N
2 **Duncan**	N	Y	N	Y	N	?
3 **Wamp**	?	?	?	?	?	?
4 Davis	Y	Y	Y	Y	Y	Y
5 Cooper	Y	Y	N	Y	Y	Y
6 Gordon	Y	Y	Y	Y	Y	Y
7 **Blackburn**	N	Y	N	Y	N	N
8 Tanner	Y	Y	Y	Y	Y	Y
9 Cohen	Y	Y	Y	Y	Y	Y

	461	462	463	464	465	466
TEXAS						
1 **Gohmert**	N	Y	N	Y	N	N
2 **Poe**	N	Y	N	Y	N	N
3 **Johnson, S.**	N	Y	N	?	N	N
4 **Hall**	N	Y	N	Y	N	N
5 **Hensarling**	N	Y	N	Y	N	N
6 **Barton**	N	Y	N	Y	N	N
7 **Culberson**	N	Y	N	?	?	?
8 **Brady**	N	?	N	Y	N	N
9 Green, A.	Y	Y	Y	Y	Y	Y
10 **McCaul**	N	Y	N	Y	N	N
11 **Conaway**	N	Y	N	Y	N	N
12 **Granger**	N	Y	N	Y	N	N
13 **Thornberry**	N	Y	N	Y	N	N
14 **Paul**	N	N	N	Y	N	N
15 Hinojosa	Y	Y	Y	Y	Y	Y
16 Reyes	Y	Y	Y	Y	Y	Y
17 Edwards	Y	Y	Y	Y	Y	Y
18 Jackson Lee	Y	Y	Y	Y	Y	Y
19 **Neugebauer**	N	Y	N	Y	N	N
20 Gonzalez	Y	Y	Y	Y	Y	Y
21 **Smith**	N	Y	N	Y	N	N
22 **Olson**	N	Y	N	Y	N	N
23 Rodriguez	Y	Y	Y	Y	Y	Y
24 **Marchant**	N	Y	N	Y	N	N
25 Doggett	Y	Y	Y	Y	Y	Y
26 **Burgess**	N	Y	N	Y	N	N
27 Ortiz	?	?	?	?	?	?
28 Cuellar	Y	Y	Y	Y	Y	Y
29 Green, G.	Y	Y	Y	Y	Y	Y
30 Johnson, E.	Y	Y	Y	Y	Y	Y
31 **Carter**	N	Y	N	Y	N	N
32 **Sessions**	N	Y	N	Y	N	N
UTAH						
1 **Bishop**	N	Y	N	Y	N	N
2 Matheson	Y	Y	Y	Y	Y	Y
3 **Chaffetz**	N	Y	N	Y	N	N
VERMONT						
AL Welch	Y	Y	Y	Y	Y	Y
VIRGINIA						
1 **Wittman**	N	Y	N	Y	N	N
2 Nye	N	Y	N	Y	N	Y
3 Scott	Y	Y	Y	Y	Y	Y
4 **Forbes**	N	Y	N	Y	N	N
5 Perriello	Y	Y	Y	Y	Y	N
6 **Goodlatte**	N	Y	N	Y	N	N
7 **Cantor**	?	Y	N	Y	N	N
8 Moran	Y	Y	Y	Y	Y	Y
9 Boucher	Y	Y	Y	Y	Y	Y
10 **Wolf**	N	Y	N	Y	N	N
11 Connolly	Y	Y	Y	Y	Y	Y
WASHINGTON						
1 Inslee	Y	Y	Y	Y	Y	Y
2 Larsen	Y	Y	Y	Y	Y	Y
3 Baird	N	Y	N	Y	Y	Y
4 **Hastings**	N	Y	N	Y	N	N
5 **McMorris Rodgers**	N	Y	N	Y	N	N
6 Dicks	Y	Y	Y	Y	Y	Y
7 McDermott	Y	Y	Y	Y	Y	Y
8 **Reichert**	N	Y	Y	Y	N	N
9 Smith	Y	Y	Y	Y	Y	Y
WEST VIRGINIA						
1 Mollohan	Y	Y	Y	Y	?	Y
2 **Capito**	N	Y	Y	Y	N	N
3 Rahall	Y	Y	Y	Y	Y	Y
WISCONSIN						
1 **Ryan**	N	Y	N	Y	N	N
2 Baldwin	Y	Y	Y	Y	Y	Y
3 Kind	Y	Y	Y	Y	Y	Y
4 Moore	Y	Y	Y	Y	Y	Y
5 **Sensenbrenner**	N	Y	N	Y	N	N
6 **Petri**	N	Y	Y	Y	N	N
7 Obey	Y	Y	Y	Y	Y	Y
8 Kagen	Y	Y	Y	Y	Y	Y
WYOMING						
AL **Lummis**	N	Y	N	Y	N	N
DELEGATES						
Faleomavaega (A.S.)						
Norton (D.C.)						
Bordallo (Guam)						
Sablan (N. Marianas)						
Pierluisi (P.R.)						
Christensen (V.I.)						

IN THE HOUSE | By Vote Number

467. **HR 1320. Federal Advisory Committee Disclosure/Passage.**
Norton, D-D.C., motion to suspend the rules and pass the bill that would direct federal agency heads to disclose information on advisory committees reporting to them, including information on the appointment process, membership and decision-making process. It would require that appointments to advisory committees be made without regard to political affiliation or activity, unless required by federal law. Motion agreed to 250-124: D 223-0; R 27-124. A two-thirds majority of those present and voting (250 in this case) is required for passage under suspension of the rules. July 26, 2010.

468. **H Res 1504. Americans with Disabilities Act Anniversary/ Adoption.** Polis, D-Colo., motion to suspend the rules and adopt the resolution that would recognize and honor the 20th anniversary of the enactment of the Americans with Disabilities Act of 1990. Motion agreed to 377-0: D 224-0; R 153-0. A two-thirds majority of those present and voting (252 in this case) is required for adoption under suspension of the rules. July 26, 2010.

469. **HR 3101. Communications Technology Accessibility/Passage.**
Markey, D-Mass., motion to suspend the rules and pass the bill that would require that equipment used for advanced communications, such as phone calls over the Internet and video conferencing, be accessible to people with disabilities. Motion agreed to 348-23: D 220-0; R 128-23. A two-thirds majority of those present and voting (248 in this case) is required for passage under suspension of the rules. July 26, 2010.

470. **H Con Res 301. Pakistan Troop Withdrawal/Rule.** Adoption of the rule (H Res 1556) that would provide for House floor consideration of the concurrent resolution that would direct the president to remove U.S. troops from Pakistan. Adopted 222-196: D 217-31; R 5-165. July 27, 2010.

471. **HR 5730. Surface Transportation Earmark Rescission/ Passage.** Markey, D-Colo., motion to suspend the rules and pass the bill that would rescind about $713 million in contract authority for unspent earmark funds for 309 surface transportation projects. Motion agreed to 394-23: D 231-17; R 163-6. A two-thirds majority of those present and voting (278 in this case) is required for passage under suspension of the rules. July 27, 2010.

472. **H Res 1366. Tribute to the Freight Rail Industry/Adoption.**
Costello, D-Ill., motion to suspend the rules and adopt the resolution that would recognize the contributions of the freight rail industry and its employees to the national transportation system and support their efforts to continue improving safety. Motion agreed to 411-0: D 242-0; R 169-0. A two-thirds majority of those present and voting (274 in this case) is required for adoption under suspension of the rules. July 27, 2010.

473. **H Con Res 301. Pakistan Troop Withdrawal/Adoption.** Adoption of the concurrent resolution that would direct the president to remove U.S. armed forces from Pakistan within 30 days of adoption or by Dec. 31 if the president determined that a withdrawal could not be accomplished safely within 30 days. Rejected 38-372: D 32-209; R 6-163. A "nay" was a vote in support of the president's position. July 27, 2010.

	467	468	469	470	471	472	473
ALABAMA							
1 **Bonner**	Y	Y	Y	N	Y	Y	N
2 **Bright**	?	?	?	N	Y	Y	N
3 **Rogers**	N	Y	Y	N	N	Y	N
4 **Aderholt**	N	Y	Y	N	N	Y	N
5 **Griffith**	?	?	?	N	Y	Y	N
6 **Bachus**	N	Y	Y	N	Y	Y	N
7 Davis	?	?	?	Y	Y	Y	N
ALASKA							
AL **Young**	Y	Y	N	N	N	Y	N
ARIZONA							
1 Kirkpatrick	Y	Y	Y	N	Y	Y	N
2 **Franks**	N	Y	N	N	Y	Y	N
3 **Shadegg**	?	?	?	N	Y	Y	N
4 Pastor	Y	Y	Y	Y	Y	Y	–
5 Mitchell	Y	Y	Y	N	Y	Y	N
6 **Flake**	N	Y	N	N	Y	Y	N
7 Grijalva	Y	Y	Y	Y	Y	Y	Y
8 Giffords	Y	Y	Y	N	Y	Y	N
ARKANSAS							
1 Berry	Y	Y	Y	Y	N	Y	N
2 Snyder	Y	Y	Y	Y	Y	Y	N
3 **Boozman**	N	Y	Y	N	Y	Y	N
4 Ross	Y	Y	Y	Y	Y	Y	N
CALIFORNIA							
1 Thompson	Y	Y	Y	Y	Y	Y	N
2 **Herger**	N	Y	Y	N	Y	Y	N
3 **Lungren**	N	Y	Y	N	Y	Y	N
4 **McClintock**	N	N	N	N	Y	Y	N
5 Matsui	Y	Y	Y	?	?	?	N
6 Woolsey	Y	Y	Y	Y	Y	Y	Y
7 Miller, George	Y	Y	Y	Y	Y	Y	Y
8 Pelosi							
9 Lee	Y	Y	Y	Y	Y	Y	Y
10 Garamendi	Y	Y	Y	Y	Y	Y	N
11 McNerney	Y	Y	Y	Y	Y	Y	N
12 Speier	?	?	?	Y	Y	Y	N
13 Stark	Y	Y	?	Y	Y	Y	Y
14 Eshoo	Y	Y	Y	Y	Y	Y	N
15 Honda	Y	Y	Y	Y	Y	Y	P
16 Lofgren	Y	Y	?	Y	Y	Y	Y
17 Farr	Y	Y	Y	Y	Y	Y	Y
18 Cardoza	Y	Y	Y	Y	Y	Y	N
19 **Radanovich**	?	?	?	?	?	?	?
20 Costa	Y	Y	Y	Y	Y	Y	N
21 **Nunes**	N	Y	Y	N	Y	Y	N
22 **McCarthy**	N	Y	Y	N	Y	Y	N
23 Capps	Y	Y	Y	Y	Y	Y	N
24 **Gallegly**	N	Y	Y	N	Y	Y	N
25 **McKeon**	N	Y	Y	N	Y	Y	N
26 **Dreier**	N	Y	Y	N	Y	Y	N
27 Sherman	Y	Y	Y	Y	Y	Y	N
28 Berman	Y	Y	Y	Y	Y	Y	N
29 Schiff	Y	Y	Y	Y	Y	Y	N
30 Waxman	Y	Y	Y	?	Y	Y	N
31 Becerra	Y	Y	Y	Y	Y	Y	N
32 Chu	+	+	+	Y	Y	Y	N
33 Watson	?	?	?	?	?	?	?
34 Roybal-Allard	Y	Y	Y	Y	Y	Y	N
35 Waters	?	?	?	Y	Y	Y	?
36 Harman	Y	Y	Y	Y	Y	Y	N
37 Richardson	Y	Y	Y	Y	Y	Y	N
38 Napolitano	Y	Y	Y	Y	Y	Y	Y
39 Sánchez, Linda	Y	Y	Y	Y	Y	?	Y
40 **Royce**	N	Y	N	N	Y	Y	N
41 **Lewis**	N	Y	N	N	Y	Y	N
42 **Miller, Gary**	N	Y	N	N	Y	Y	N
43 Baca	Y	Y	Y	Y	Y	Y	N
44 **Calvert**	N	Y	N	N	Y	Y	N
45 **Bono Mack**	N	Y	N	N	Y	Y	N
46 **Rohrabacher**	?	?	?	N	Y	Y	Y
47 Sanchez, Loretta	Y	Y	Y	Y	Y	Y	N
48 **Campbell**	N	Y	N	N	Y	Y	Y
49 **Issa**	Y	Y	Y	N	Y	Y	N
50 **Bilbray**	Y	Y	Y	N	Y	Y	N
51 Filner	Y	Y	Y	Y	Y	Y	Y
52 **Hunter**	N	Y	Y	N	Y	Y	N
53 Davis	Y	Y	Y	Y	Y	Y	N

	467	468	469	470	471	472	473
COLORADO							
1 DeGette	Y	Y	Y	Y	Y	Y	N
2 Polis	Y	Y	Y	Y	Y	Y	N
3 Salazar	Y	Y	Y	Y	Y	Y	N
4 Markey	Y	Y	Y	Y	Y	Y	N
5 **Lamborn**	N	Y	N	N	Y	Y	N
6 **Coffman**	Y	Y	N	N	Y	Y	N
7 Perlmutter	Y	Y	Y	Y	+	Y	N
CONNECTICUT							
1 Larson	Y	Y	Y	Y	Y	Y	N
2 Courtney	Y	Y	Y	Y	Y	Y	N
3 DeLauro	Y	Y	Y	Y	Y	Y	N
4 Himes	Y	Y	Y	Y	Y	Y	N
5 Murphy	Y	Y	Y	Y	Y	Y	N
DELAWARE							
AL **Castle**	N	Y	Y	N	Y	Y	N
FLORIDA							
1 **Miller**	–	Y	Y	N	N	Y	N
2 Boyd	Y	Y	Y	Y	Y	Y	N
3 Brown	Y	Y	Y	Y	Y	Y	N
4 **Crenshaw**	N	Y	Y	N	Y	Y	N
5 **Brown-Waite**	N	Y	Y	N	Y	Y	N
6 **Stearns**	N	Y	Y	N	Y	Y	N
7 **Mica**	N	Y	Y	N	Y	Y	N
8 Grayson	?	?	?	Y	Y	Y	+
9 **Bilirakis**	N	Y	Y	N	Y	Y	N
10 **Young**	?	?	?	?	?	?	?
11 Castor	Y	Y	Y	Y	Y	Y	N
12 **Putnam**	+	+	+	N	Y	Y	N
13 **Buchanan**	N	Y	Y	N	Y	Y	N
14 **Mack**	N	Y	N	N	Y	Y	N
15 **Posey**	N	Y	N	N	Y	Y	N
16 **Rooney**	N	Y	Y	N	Y	Y	N
17 Meek	?	?	?	?	?	?	?
18 **Ros-Lehtinen**	N	Y	Y	N	Y	Y	N
19 Deutch	Y	Y	Y	Y	Y	Y	N
20 Wasserman Schultz	Y	Y	Y	Y	Y	Y	N
21 **Diaz-Balart, L.**	N	Y	Y	N	Y	Y	N
22 Klein	Y	Y	Y	Y	Y	Y	N
23 Hastings	Y	Y	Y	Y	Y	Y	N
24 Kosmas	?	?	?	N	Y	Y	N
25 **Diaz-Balart, M.**	N	Y	N	N	Y	Y	N
GEORGIA							
1 **Kingston**	N	Y	N	N	Y	Y	N
2 Bishop	+	+	+	Y	Y	Y	N
3 **Westmoreland**	N	Y	N	N	Y	Y	N
4 Johnson	?	Y	Y	Y	Y	Y	N
5 Lewis	Y	Y	Y	Y	Y	Y	N
6 **Price**	N	Y	N	N	Y	Y	N
7 **Linder**	?	Y	Y	N	Y	Y	N
8 Marshall	Y	Y	Y	Y	Y	Y	N
9 **Graves**	N	Y	N	N	Y	Y	N
10 **Broun**	N	?	?	N	Y	Y	N
11 **Gingrey**	N	Y	N	N	Y	Y	N
12 Barrow	Y	Y	Y	Y	Y	Y	N
13 Scott	Y	Y	Y	Y	Y	Y	N
HAWAII							
1 **Djou**	Y	Y	Y	N	N	Y	N
2 Hirono	Y	Y	Y	Y	Y	Y	N
IDAHO							
1 Minnick	Y	Y	Y	N	Y	Y	N
2 **Simpson**	N	Y	Y	N	Y	Y	N
ILLINOIS							
1 Rush	?	?	?	Y	Y	Y	Y
2 Jackson	Y	Y	Y	Y	Y	Y	Y
3 Lipinski	?	?	?	Y	Y	Y	Y
4 Gutierrez	+	+	+	Y	Y	?	Y
5 Quigley	Y	Y	Y	Y	Y	Y	N
6 **Roskam**	N	Y	Y	N	Y	Y	N
7 Davis	+	+	+	Y	Y	Y	Y
8 Bean	Y	Y	Y	Y	Y	P	N
9 Schakowsky	Y	Y	Y	Y	Y	Y	N
10 **Kirk**	Y	Y	Y	N	Y	Y	N
11 Halvorson	Y	Y	Y	Y	Y	Y	N
12 Costello	Y	Y	Y	Y	Y	Y	N
13 **Biggert**	N	Y	Y	N	Y	Y	N
14 Foster	Y	Y	Y	Y	Y	Y	N
15 **Johnson**	–	+	+	Y	Y	Y	N

KEY   **Republicans**   Democrats

Y Voted for (yea)	**X** Paired against
# Paired for	**–** Announced against
+ Announced for	**P** Voted "present"
N Voted against (nay)	

C Voted "present" to avoid possible conflict of interes[t]

? Did not vote or otherwise make a position known

	467	468	469	470	471	472	473
16 **Manzullo**	N	Y	Y	N	Y	Y	N
17 Hare	Y	Y	Y	Y	Y	Y	N
18 **Schock**	Y	Y	Y	N	Y	Y	N
19 **Shimkus**	?	Y	Y	N	Y	Y	N
INDIANA							
1 Visclosky	Y	Y	Y	Y	Y	Y	N
2 Donnelly	Y	Y	Y	N	Y	Y	N
3 Vacant							
4 **Buyer**	?	?	?	N	Y	Y	N
5 **Burton**	N	Y	Y	N	Y	Y	N
6 **Pence**	N	Y	Y	N	Y	Y	N
7 Carson	Y	Y	Y	Y	Y	Y	?
8 Ellsworth	?	?	?	N	Y	Y	N
9 Hill	Y	Y	Y	N	Y	Y	N
IOWA							
1 Braley	+	+	+	Y	Y	Y	N
2 Loebsack	Y	Y	Y	Y	Y	Y	N
3 Boswell	Y	Y	Y	Y	Y	Y	N
4 **Latham**	N	Y	Y	N	Y	Y	N
5 **King**	N	Y	N	N	Y	Y	–
KANSAS							
1 **Moran**	?	?	?	?	?	?	?
2 **Jenkins**	N	Y	Y	N	Y	Y	N
3 Moore	Y	Y	Y	Y	Y	Y	N
4 **Tiahrt**	?	?	?	?	?	?	?
KENTUCKY							
1 **Whitfield**	N	Y	Y	N	Y	?	N
2 **Guthrie**	Y	Y	Y	N	N	Y	N
3 Yarmuth	Y	Y	Y	Y	Y	Y	N
4 **Davis**	N	Y	Y	N	Y	Y	N
5 **Rogers**	N	Y	Y	N	Y	Y	N
6 Chandler	Y	Y	Y	Y	Y	Y	N
LOUISIANA							
1 **Scalise**	N	Y	Y	N	Y	Y	N
2 **Cao**	?	?	?	N	Y	Y	N
3 Melancon	Y	Y	Y	Y	Y	Y	N
4 **Fleming**	N	Y	Y	N	Y	Y	N
5 **Alexander**	?	Y	Y	N	Y	Y	N
6 **Cassidy**	N	Y	Y	N	Y	Y	N
7 **Boustany**	N	Y	Y	N	Y	Y	N
MAINE							
1 Pingree	Y	Y	?	Y	Y	Y	Y
2 Michaud	Y	Y	Y	Y	Y	Y	N
MARYLAND							
1 Kratovil	Y	Y	Y	N	Y	Y	N
2 Ruppersberger	Y	Y	Y	Y	Y	Y	N
3 Sarbanes	Y	Y	Y	Y	Y	Y	N
4 Edwards	Y	Y	Y	Y	Y	Y	Y
5 Hoyer	Y	Y	Y	Y	Y	Y	N
6 **Bartlett**	N	Y	N	N	Y	Y	P
7 Cummings	Y	Y	Y	Y	Y	Y	N
8 Van Hollen	Y	Y	Y	Y	Y	Y	N
MASSACHUSETTS							
1 Olver	Y	Y	Y	Y	Y	Y	N
2 Neal	Y	Y	Y	Y	N	Y	N
3 McGovern	Y	Y	Y	Y	Y	Y	N
4 Frank	Y	Y	Y	Y	N	Y	N
5 Tsongas	Y	Y	Y	Y	Y	Y	N
6 Tierney	Y	Y	Y	Y	N	Y	N
7 Markey	Y	Y	Y	Y	N	Y	N
8 Capuano	Y	Y	Y	Y	N	Y	N
9 Lynch	Y	Y	Y	Y	N	Y	N
10 Delahunt	?	?	?	Y	N	Y	Y
MICHIGAN							
1 Stupak	?	?	?	Y	Y	Y	N
2 **Hoekstra**	?	?	?	N	Y	Y	N
3 **Ehlers**	N	?	Y	N	Y	Y	N
4 **Camp**	N	Y	Y	N	Y	Y	N
5 Kildee	Y	Y	Y	Y	Y	Y	N
6 **Upton**	N	Y	Y	N	Y	Y	N
7 Schauer	Y	Y	Y	Y	Y	Y	N
8 **Rogers**	N	Y	Y	N	Y	Y	N
9 Peters	Y	Y	Y	N	Y	Y	N
10 **Miller**	N	Y	Y	N	Y	Y	N
11 **McCotter**	N	Y	Y	N	Y	Y	N
12 Levin	Y	Y	Y	Y	Y	Y	N
13 Kilpatrick	+	+	+	Y	Y	Y	N
14 Conyers	+	+	+	Y	N	Y	?
15 Dingell	Y	Y	Y	Y	Y	Y	N
MINNESOTA							
1 Walz	Y	Y	Y	Y	Y	Y	N
2 **Kline**	N	Y	Y	N	Y	Y	N
3 **Paulsen**	Y	Y	Y	N	Y	Y	N
4 McCollum	Y	Y	Y	Y	Y	Y	N

	467	468	469	470	471	472	473
5 Ellison	Y	Y	Y	Y	Y	Y	Y
6 **Bachmann**	N	Y	?	N	Y	Y	N
7 Peterson	Y	Y	Y	N	Y	Y	N
8 Oberstar	Y	Y	Y	Y	Y	Y	N
MISSISSIPPI							
1 Childers	Y	Y	Y	N	Y	Y	N
2 Thompson	?	?	?	Y	Y	Y	N
3 **Harper**	N	Y	Y	N	Y	Y	N
4 Taylor	Y	Y	Y	N	Y	Y	N
MISSOURI							
1 Clay	Y	Y	Y	Y	Y	Y	Y
2 **Akin**	–	+	+	–	+	+	–
3 Carnahan	Y	Y	Y	Y	Y	Y	N
4 Skelton	Y	Y	Y	Y	Y	Y	N
5 Cleaver	Y	Y	Y	Y	Y	Y	Y
6 **Graves**	?	?	?	?	?	?	?
7 **Blunt**	N	Y	Y	N	Y	Y	N
8 **Emerson**	Y	Y	Y	N	Y	Y	N
9 **Luetkemeyer**	N	Y	Y	N	Y	Y	N
MONTANA							
AL **Rehberg**	N	Y	Y	N	Y	Y	N
NEBRASKA							
1 **Fortenberry**	Y	Y	Y	N	Y	Y	N
2 **Terry**	N	Y	Y	N	Y	Y	N
3 **Smith**	N	Y	Y	N	Y	Y	N
NEVADA							
1 Berkley	Y	Y	Y	Y	Y	Y	N
2 **Heller**	?	?	?	–	+	+	?
3 Titus	Y	Y	Y	Y	Y	Y	N
NEW HAMPSHIRE							
1 Shea-Porter	Y	Y	Y	Y	Y	Y	P
2 Hodes	?	?	?	Y	Y	Y	N
NEW JERSEY							
1 Andrews	Y	Y	Y	Y	Y	Y	N
2 **LoBiondo**	N	Y	Y	N	Y	Y	N
3 Adler	Y	Y	Y	N	Y	Y	N
4 **Smith**	N	Y	Y	N	Y	Y	N
5 **Garrett**	N	Y	N	N	Y	Y	N
6 Pallone	Y	Y	Y	Y	Y	Y	N
7 **Lance**	N	Y	Y	N	Y	Y	N
8 Pascrell	Y	Y	Y	Y	Y	Y	N
9 Rothman	Y	Y	Y	Y	Y	Y	N
10 Payne	Y	Y	P	Y	Y	Y	+
11 **Frelinghuysen**	N	Y	Y	N	Y	Y	N
12 Holt	Y	Y	Y	Y	Y	Y	N
13 Sires	Y	Y	Y	Y	Y	Y	Y
NEW MEXICO							
1 Heinrich	Y	Y	Y	Y	Y	Y	N
2 Teague	Y	Y	Y	N	Y	Y	N
3 Luján	Y	Y	Y	Y	Y	Y	N
NEW YORK							
1 Bishop	Y	Y	Y	Y	Y	Y	N
2 Israel	Y	Y	Y	Y	Y	Y	N
3 **King**	N	Y	Y	N	Y	Y	N
4 McCarthy	Y	Y	Y	Y	Y	Y	N
5 Ackerman	Y	Y	Y	Y	Y	Y	N
6 Meeks	Y	Y	Y	Y	Y	Y	N
7 Crowley	Y	Y	Y	Y	Y	Y	N
8 Nadler	Y	Y	Y	Y	Y	Y	N
9 Weiner	?	?	?	Y	N	Y	N
10 Towns	?	?	?	Y	Y	Y	Y
11 Clarke	Y	Y	Y	Y	Y	Y	Y
12 Velázquez	Y	Y	Y	Y	Y	Y	Y
13 McMahon	Y	Y	Y	Y	Y	Y	N
14 Maloney	Y	Y	Y	Y	Y	Y	N
15 Rangel	Y	Y	Y	Y	Y	Y	N
16 Serrano	Y	Y	Y	Y	Y	Y	Y
17 Engel	Y	Y	Y	?	?	?	N
18 Lowey	Y	Y	Y	Y	Y	Y	N
19 Hall	Y	Y	Y	Y	Y	Y	N
20 Murphy	Y	Y	Y	Y	Y	Y	N
21 Tonko	Y	Y	Y	Y	Y	Y	N
22 Hinchey	Y	Y	Y	Y	N	Y	N
23 Owens	Y	Y	Y	Y	Y	Y	N
24 Arcuri	Y	Y	Y	Y	Y	Y	N
25 Maffei	Y	Y	Y	Y	Y	Y	Y
26 **Lee**	N	Y	Y	N	Y	Y	N
27 Higgins	Y	Y	Y	Y	Y	Y	N
28 Slaughter	Y	Y	Y	Y	Y	P	P
29 Vacant							
NORTH CAROLINA							
1 Butterfield	Y	Y	Y	Y	Y	Y	N
2 Etheridge	Y	Y	Y	Y	Y	Y	N
3 **Jones**	Y	Y	Y	Y	Y	Y	Y
4 Price	Y	Y	Y	Y	Y	Y	N

	467	468	469	470	471	472	473
5 **Foxx**	N	Y	N	N	Y	Y	N
6 **Coble**	N	Y	Y	N	Y	Y	N
7 McIntyre	Y	Y	Y	N	Y	Y	N
8 Kissell	Y	Y	Y	N	Y	Y	N
9 **Myrick**	N	Y	Y	N	Y	Y	N
10 **McHenry**	Y	Y	Y	N	Y	Y	N
11 Shuler	?	?	?	N	Y	Y	N
12 Watt	Y	Y	Y	Y	Y	Y	N
13 Miller	Y	Y	Y	Y	Y	Y	N
NORTH DAKOTA							
AL Pomeroy	Y	Y	Y	Y	Y	Y	N
OHIO							
1 Driehaus	Y	Y	Y	Y	Y	Y	N
2 **Schmidt**	N	Y	Y	N	Y	Y	N
3 **Turner**	N	Y	Y	N	Y	Y	N
4 **Jordan**	N	Y	N	N	Y	Y	N
5 **Latta**	N	Y	Y	N	Y	Y	N
6 Wilson	Y	Y	Y	Y	N	Y	N
7 **Austria**	N	Y	Y	N	Y	Y	N
8 **Boehner**	N	Y	Y	N	?	Y	N
9 Kaptur	Y	Y	Y	Y	Y	Y	N
10 Kucinich	Y	Y	Y	Y	Y	Y	Y
11 Fudge	Y	Y	Y	Y	Y	Y	N
12 **Tiberi**	N	Y	Y	N	Y	Y	N
13 Sutton	Y	Y	Y	Y	Y	Y	N
14 **LaTourette**	Y	Y	Y	N	N	Y	N
15 Kilroy	Y	Y	Y	Y	Y	Y	N
16 Boccieri	Y	Y	Y	Y	Y	Y	N
17 Ryan	Y	Y	Y	Y	Y	Y	N
18 Space	?	?	?	Y	N	Y	N
OKLAHOMA							
1 **Sullivan**	?	?	?	N	Y	Y	N
2 Boren	?	?	?	?	?	?	N
3 **Lucas**	N	Y	Y	N	Y	Y	N
4 **Cole**	+	+	+	N	Y	Y	N
5 **Fallin**	?	?	?	N	Y	Y	N
OREGON							
1 Wu	Y	Y	Y	N	Y	Y	N
2 **Walden**	N	Y	?	N	Y	Y	N
3 Blumenauer	Y	Y	Y	Y	Y	Y	N
4 DeFazio	Y	Y	Y	Y	Y	Y	N
5 Schrader	Y	Y	Y	Y	Y	Y	N
PENNSYLVANIA							
1 Brady	Y	Y	Y	Y	Y	Y	N
2 Fattah	Y	Y	Y	Y	Y	Y	N
3 Dahlkemper	Y	Y	Y	N	Y	Y	N
4 Altmire	Y	Y	Y	N	Y	Y	N
5 **Thompson**	N	Y	Y	N	N	Y	N
6 **Gerlach**	Y	Y	Y	N	Y	Y	N
7 Sestak	Y	Y	Y	Y	Y	Y	N
8 Murphy, P.	Y	Y	Y	N	Y	Y	N
9 **Shuster**	N	Y	Y	N	Y	Y	N
10 Carney	Y	Y	Y	Y	Y	Y	N
11 Kanjorski	Y	Y	Y	N	N	Y	N
12 Critz	Y	Y	Y	N	Y	Y	N
13 Schwartz	Y	Y	Y	Y	Y	Y	N
14 Doyle	Y	Y	Y	Y	Y	Y	N
15 **Dent**	Y	Y	Y	N	Y	Y	N
16 **Pitts**	N	Y	Y	N	Y	Y	N
17 Holden	Y	Y	Y	N	N	Y	N
18 **Murphy, T.**	Y	Y	Y	N	Y	Y	N
19 **Platts**	Y	Y	Y	N	Y	Y	N
RHODE ISLAND							
1 Kennedy	?	?	?	Y	Y	?	N
2 Langevin	Y	Y	Y	Y	Y	Y	N
SOUTH CAROLINA							
1 **Brown**	N	Y	Y	N	Y	Y	N
2 **Wilson**	N	Y	Y	N	Y	Y	N
3 **Barrett**	?	?	?	N	Y	Y	N
4 **Inglis**	N	Y	Y	N	Y	Y	N
5 Spratt	Y	Y	Y	Y	Y	Y	N
6 Clyburn	Y	Y	Y	Y	Y	Y	?
SOUTH DAKOTA							
AL Herseth Sandlin	Y	Y	Y	Y	Y	Y	N
TENNESSEE							
1 **Roe**	N	Y	Y	N	Y	Y	N
2 **Duncan**	N	Y	Y	Y	Y	Y	Y
3 **Wamp**	?	?	?	N	Y	Y	N
4 Davis	?	?	?	Y	Y	Y	N
5 Cooper	Y	Y	Y	Y	Y	Y	N
6 Gordon	Y	Y	Y	Y	Y	Y	N
7 **Blackburn**	N	Y	Y	N	Y	Y	N
8 Tanner	Y	Y	Y	N	Y	Y	N
9 Cohen	Y	Y	Y	Y	Y	Y	N

	467	468	469	470	471	472	473
TEXAS							
1 **Gohmert**	Y	Y	?	N	Y	Y	N
2 **Poe**	?	?	?	–	+	+	N
3 **Johnson, S.**	N	Y	N	N	Y	Y	N
4 **Hall**	Y	Y	Y	N	Y	Y	N
5 **Hensarling**	N	Y	N	N	Y	Y	N
6 **Barton**	N	Y	Y	N	Y	Y	N
7 **Culberson**	Y	Y	Y	N	Y	Y	N
8 **Brady**	N	Y	Y	N	Y	Y	N
9 Green, A.	Y	Y	?	Y	Y	Y	N
10 **McCaul**	N	Y	Y	N	Y	Y	N
11 **Conaway**	N	Y	N	N	Y	Y	N
12 **Granger**	N	Y	Y	N	Y	Y	N
13 **Thornberry**	N	Y	Y	N	Y	Y	N
14 **Paul**	N	?	N	Y	Y	Y	Y
15 Hinojosa	Y	Y	Y	Y	Y	Y	N
16 Reyes	Y	Y	Y	Y	Y	Y	N
17 Edwards	Y	Y	Y	N	Y	Y	N
18 Jackson Lee	Y	Y	Y	Y	Y	Y	–
19 **Neugebauer**	N	Y	Y	N	Y	Y	N
20 Gonzalez	Y	Y	Y	Y	Y	Y	N
21 **Smith**	N	Y	Y	N	Y	Y	N
22 **Olson**	N	Y	Y	N	Y	Y	N
23 Rodriguez	Y	Y	Y	Y	Y	Y	N
24 **Marchant**	N	Y	Y	N	Y	Y	N
25 Doggett	Y	Y	Y	Y	Y	Y	N
26 **Burgess**	N	Y	Y	N	Y	Y	N
27 Ortiz	Y	Y	Y	Y	Y	Y	Y
28 Cuellar	Y	Y	Y	Y	Y	Y	N
29 Green, G.	Y	Y	Y	Y	Y	Y	N
30 Johnson, E.	Y	Y	Y	Y	Y	Y	N
31 **Carter**	N	Y	Y	N	Y	Y	N
32 **Sessions**	N	Y	Y	N	Y	Y	N
UTAH							
1 **Bishop**	?	Y	Y	N	Y	Y	N
2 Matheson	Y	Y	Y	Y	Y	Y	N
3 **Chaffetz**	Y	Y	N	N	Y	Y	N
VERMONT							
AL Welch	Y	Y	Y	Y	Y	Y	N
VIRGINIA							
1 **Wittman**	Y	Y	Y	N	Y	Y	N
2 Nye	Y	Y	Y	N	N	Y	N
3 Scott	Y	Y	Y	Y	N	Y	N
4 **Forbes**	?	?	?	N	Y	Y	N
5 Perriello	Y	Y	Y	Y	Y	Y	N
6 **Goodlatte**	N	Y	Y	N	Y	Y	N
7 **Cantor**	N	Y	Y	N	Y	Y	N
8 Moran	Y	Y	Y	Y	Y	Y	N
9 Boucher	Y	Y	Y	N	Y	Y	N
10 **Wolf**	Y	Y	Y	N	Y	Y	N
11 Connolly	Y	Y	Y	Y	Y	Y	N
WASHINGTON							
1 Inslee	Y	Y	Y	Y	Y	Y	N
2 Larsen	Y	Y	Y	Y	Y	Y	N
3 Baird	Y	Y	Y	Y	Y	Y	N
4 **Hastings**	N	Y	Y	N	Y	Y	N
5 **McMorris Rodgers**	N	Y	Y	N	Y	Y	N
6 Dicks	Y	Y	Y	Y	Y	Y	N
7 McDermott	Y	Y	Y	Y	Y	Y	Y
8 **Reichert**	Y	Y	Y	N	Y	Y	N
9 Smith	+	+	+	Y	Y	Y	N
WEST VIRGINIA							
1 Mollohan	Y	Y	Y	Y	Y	Y	N
2 **Capito**	N	Y	Y	N	Y	Y	N
3 Rahall	Y	Y	Y	Y	Y	Y	N
WISCONSIN							
1 **Ryan**	N	Y	Y	N	Y	Y	N
2 Baldwin	Y	Y	Y	Y	Y	Y	Y
3 Kind	Y	Y	Y	Y	Y	Y	N
4 Moore	Y	Y	Y	Y	Y	Y	N
5 **Sensenbrenner**	N	Y	Y	N	Y	Y	N
6 **Petri**	N	Y	Y	N	Y	Y	N
7 Obey	Y	Y	Y	Y	Y	Y	N
8 Kagen	Y	Y	Y	Y	Y	Y	N
WYOMING							
AL **Lummis**	N	Y	Y	N	Y	Y	N
DELEGATES							
Faleomavaega (A.S.)							
Norton (D.C.)							
Bordallo (Guam)							
Sablan (N. Marianas)							
Pierluisi (P.R.)							
Christensen (V.I.)							

IN THE HOUSE | By Vote Number

474. **HR 4899. Supplemental Appropriations/Passage.** Obey, D-Wis., motion to suspend the rules, recede from the House amendment to the Senate amendment and concur in the Senate amendment to the bill that would provide $58.8 billion in supplemental funds for fiscal 2010. That total includes $33.5 billion for the Defense Department for the addition of 30,000 troops in Afghanistan, $3.6 billion for Afghan and Iraqi security forces, and $4.9 billion for Defense Department procurement. It would provide $162 million in funds related to the oil spill in the Gulf of Mexico. It would also provide $5.1 billion for the Federal Emergency Management Agency to pay for costs of past disasters and $13.4 billion in mandatory funds to compensate Vietnam War veterans exposed to Agent Orange. Motion agreed to, thus clearing the bill for the president, 308-114: D 148-102; R 160-12. A two-thirds majority of those present and voting (282 in this case) is required for passage under suspension of the rules. A "yea" was a vote in support of the president's position. July 27, 2010.

475. **HR 4748. Border Drug Control Policy/Passage.** Scott, D-Va., motion to suspend the rules and pass the bill that would require the Office of National Drug Control Policy to develop a strategy to address illegal drug trafficking along the U.S.-Canada border. Motion agreed to 413-0: D 248-0; R 165-0. A two-thirds majority of those present and voting (276 in this case) is required for passage under suspension of the rules. July 27, 2010.

476. **HR 5822. Fiscal 2011 Military Construction-VA Appropriations/Rule.** Adoption of the rule (H Res 1559) that would provide for House floor consideration of the bill that would appropriate $141.1 billion in fiscal 2011 for the Department of Veterans Affairs and for Defense Department military construction and military housing projects. Adopted 243-178: D 243-7; R 0-171. July 28, 2010.

477. **HR 4692. National Manufacturing Strategy/Passage.** Rush, D-Ill., motion to suspend the rules and pass the bill that would require the president to prepare a national manufacturing strategy policy plan every four years, with the first plan to be submitted one year after enactment. It would also require the president to establish a Manufacturing Strategy Board within the Commerce Department, including members from the public and private sectors. Motion agreed to 379-38: D 247-0; R 132-38. A two-thirds majority of those present and voting (278 in this case) is required for passage under suspension of the rules. July 28, 2010.

478. **H Res 1543. Tribute to Jane Goodall/Adoption.** Polis, D-Colo., motion to suspend the rules and adopt the resolution that would recognize the environmental education advancements by the Jane Goodall Institute's Roots and Shoots initiative on the 50th anniversary of the beginning of Dr. Jane Goodall's research. Motion agreed to 416-0: D 246-0; R 170-0. A two-thirds majority of those present and voting (278 in this case) is required for adoption under suspension of the rules. July 28, 2010.

479. **HR 5827. Bankruptcy Firearms Exemption/Passage.** Scott, D-Va., motion to suspend the rules and pass the bill that would add firearms valued at up to $3,000 to the list of items exempted from repossession during the bankruptcy process. Motion agreed to 307-113: D 139-112; R 168-1. A two-thirds majority of those present and voting (280 in this case) is required for passage under suspension of the rules. July 28, 2010.

	474	475	476	477	478	479
ALABAMA						
1 Bonner	Y	Y	N	Y	Y	Y
2 Bright	Y	Y	N	Y	Y	Y
3 Rogers	Y	Y	N	Y	Y	Y
4 Aderholt	Y	Y	N	Y	Y	Y
5 Griffith	Y	Y	N	Y	Y	Y
6 Bachus	Y	Y	N	Y	Y	Y
7 Davis	Y	Y	Y	Y	Y	Y
ALASKA						
AL Young	Y	Y	N	N	Y	Y
ARIZONA						
1 Kirkpatrick	Y	Y	Y	Y	Y	Y
2 Franks	Y	Y	N	N	Y	Y
3 Shadegg	Y	Y	N	N	Y	Y
4 Pastor	Y	Y	Y	Y	Y	Y
5 Mitchell	Y	Y	N	Y	Y	Y
6 Flake	N	Y	N	N	Y	Y
7 Grijalva	N	Y	Y	Y	Y	N
8 Giffords	Y	Y	Y	Y	Y	Y
ARKANSAS						
1 Berry	Y	Y	Y	Y	Y	N
2 Snyder	Y	Y	Y	Y	Y	Y
3 Boozman	Y	Y	N	Y	Y	Y
4 Ross	Y	Y	Y	Y	Y	Y
CALIFORNIA						
1 Thompson	N	Y	Y	Y	Y	Y
2 Herger	Y	?	N	N	Y	Y
3 Lungren	Y	Y	N	N	Y	Y
4 McClintock	Y	Y	N	N	Y	Y
5 Matsui	N	Y	Y	Y	Y	N
6 Woolsey	N	Y	+	Y	Y	N
7 Miller, George	N	Y	Y	Y	Y	N
8 Pelosi						
9 Lee	N	Y	Y	Y	Y	N
10 Garamendi	N	Y	Y	Y	Y	Y
11 McNerney	Y	Y	Y	Y	Y	Y
12 Speier	N	Y	Y	Y	Y	N
13 Stark	N	Y	Y	Y	Y	N
14 Eshoo	N	Y	Y	Y	Y	N
15 Honda	N	Y	Y	Y	Y	N
16 Lofgren	N	Y	Y	Y	?	N
17 Farr	N	Y	Y	Y	Y	N
18 Cardoza	Y	Y	Y	Y	Y	Y
19 Radanovich	Y	?	N	Y	Y	Y
20 Costa	Y	Y	Y	Y	Y	Y
21 Nunes	Y	Y	N	N	Y	Y
22 McCarthy	Y	Y	Y	Y	Y	Y
23 Capps	Y	Y	Y	Y	Y	N
24 Gallegly	Y	Y	N	Y	Y	Y
25 McKeon	Y	Y	Y	Y	Y	Y
26 Dreier	Y	Y	Y	Y	Y	Y
27 Sherman	Y	Y	Y	Y	Y	N
28 Berman	Y	Y	Y	Y	Y	N
29 Schiff	Y	Y	Y	Y	Y	N
30 Waxman	N	Y	Y	Y	Y	N
31 Becerra	N	Y	Y	Y	Y	N
32 Chu	N	Y	Y	Y	Y	N
33 Watson	?	?	?	?	?	?
34 Roybal-Allard	Y	Y	Y	Y	Y	N
35 Waters	N	Y	Y	Y	Y	N
36 Harman	Y	Y	Y	Y	Y	N
37 Richardson	N	Y	Y	Y	Y	N
38 Napolitano	N	Y	Y	Y	Y	N
39 Sánchez, Linda	N	Y	Y	Y	Y	N
40 Royce	Y	Y	N	N	Y	Y
41 Lewis	Y	Y	Y	Y	Y	Y
42 Miller, Gary	Y	Y	N	Y	Y	Y
43 Baca	Y	Y	Y	Y	Y	Y
44 Calvert	Y	Y	N	Y	Y	Y
45 Bono Mack	Y	Y	Y	Y	Y	Y
46 Rohrabacher	N	Y	N	N	Y	Y
47 Sanchez, Loretta	N	Y	Y	Y	?	N
48 Campbell	N	Y	N	N	Y	Y
49 Issa	Y	Y	N	Y	Y	Y
50 Bilbray	Y	Y	N	Y	Y	Y
51 Filner	N	Y	Y	Y	Y	N
52 Hunter	Y	Y	N	Y	Y	Y
53 Davis	Y	Y	Y	Y	Y	N

	474	475	476	477	478	479
COLORADO						
1 DeGette	Y	Y	Y	Y	Y	Y
2 Polis	N	Y	Y	Y	Y	Y
3 Salazar	Y	Y	Y	Y	Y	Y
4 Markey	Y	Y	Y	Y	Y	Y
5 Lamborn	Y	Y	N	Y	Y	Y
6 Coffman	Y	Y	N	Y	Y	Y
7 Perlmutter	Y	Y	Y	Y	Y	Y
CONNECTICUT						
1 Larson	N	Y	Y	Y	Y	Y
2 Courtney	Y	Y	Y	Y	Y	Y
3 DeLauro	N	Y	Y	Y	Y	N
4 Himes	Y	Y	Y	Y	Y	N
5 Murphy	N	Y	Y	Y	Y	N
DELAWARE						
AL Castle	Y	Y	N	Y	Y	Y
FLORIDA						
1 Miller	Y	Y	N	N	Y	Y
2 Boyd	Y	Y	Y	Y	Y	Y
3 Brown	N	Y	Y	Y	Y	N
4 Crenshaw	Y	Y	N	Y	Y	Y
5 Brown-Waite	Y	Y	N	Y	Y	Y
6 Stearns	Y	Y	N	Y	Y	Y
7 Mica	Y	Y	N	Y	Y	Y
8 Grayson	–	Y	Y	Y	Y	Y
9 Bilirakis	Y	Y	N	Y	Y	Y
10 Young	?	?	?	?	?	?
11 Castor	N	?	Y	Y	Y	N
12 Putnam	Y	Y	N	Y	Y	Y
13 Buchanan	Y	Y	N	Y	Y	Y
14 Mack	Y	Y	N	N	Y	Y
15 Posey	Y	Y	Y	Y	Y	Y
16 Rooney	Y	Y	N	N	Y	Y
17 Meek	?	?	Y	Y	Y	Y
18 Ros-Lehtinen	Y	Y	N	Y	Y	Y
19 Deutch	Y	Y	Y	Y	Y	Y
20 Wasserman Schultz	Y	Y	Y	Y	Y	Y
21 Diaz-Balart, L.	Y	Y	N	Y	Y	Y
22 Klein	Y	Y	Y	Y	Y	N
23 Hastings	N	Y	Y	Y	Y	N
24 Kosmas	Y	Y	Y	Y	Y	Y
25 Diaz-Balart, M.	Y	Y	N	Y	Y	Y
GEORGIA						
1 Kingston	Y	Y	N	N	Y	Y
2 Bishop	Y	Y	Y	Y	Y	Y
3 Westmoreland	Y	Y	N	N	Y	Y
4 Johnson	N	Y	Y	Y	Y	Y
5 Lewis	N	Y	?	?	?	?
6 Price	Y	Y	N	N	Y	Y
7 Linder	N	Y	N	N	Y	Y
8 Marshall	Y	Y	Y	Y	Y	Y
9 Graves	Y	Y	N	N	Y	Y
10 Broun	N	Y	N	N	Y	Y
11 Gingrey	N	Y	N	Y	Y	?
12 Barrow	Y	Y	Y	Y	Y	Y
13 Scott	Y	Y	Y	Y	?	Y
HAWAII						
1 Djou	Y	Y	N	N	Y	N
2 Hirono	N	Y	Y	Y	Y	N
IDAHO						
1 Minnick	Y	Y	Y	Y	Y	Y
2 Simpson	Y	Y	N	Y	Y	Y
ILLINOIS						
1 Rush	N	Y	Y	Y	Y	Y
2 Jackson	N	Y	Y	Y	Y	N
3 Lipinski	Y	Y	Y	Y	Y	Y
4 Gutierrez	N	Y	Y	Y	Y	Y
5 Quigley	N	Y	Y	Y	Y	Y
6 Roskam	Y	Y	N	Y	Y	Y
7 Davis	N	Y	Y	Y	Y	Y
8 Bean	Y	Y	Y	Y	Y	Y
9 Schakowsky	N	Y	Y	Y	Y	N
10 Kirk	Y	Y	N	Y	Y	Y
11 Halvorson	Y	Y	Y	Y	Y	Y
12 Costello	N	Y	Y	?	Y	Y
13 Biggert	Y	Y	N	Y	Y	Y
14 Foster	Y	Y	Y	Y	Y	Y
15 Johnson	N	Y	N	Y	Y	Y

KEY   **Republicans**   Democrats

Y Voted for (yea)	**X** Paired against	**C** Voted "present" to avoid possible conflict of interest
# Paired for	**–** Announced against	
+ Announced for	**P** Voted "present"	**?** Did not vote or otherwise make a position known
N Voted against (nay)		

	474	475	476	477	478	479
16 **Manzullo**	Y	Y	N	Y	Y	Y
17 Hare	Y	Y	Y	Y	Y	Y
18 **Schock**	Y	Y	N	Y	Y	Y
19 **Shimkus**	Y	Y	N	Y	Y	Y
INDIANA						
1 Visclosky	Y	Y	Y	Y	Y	N
2 Donnelly	Y	Y	Y	Y	Y	Y
3 Vacant						
4 **Buyer**	Y	?	N	Y	?	Y
5 **Burton**	Y	Y	N	N	Y	Y
6 **Pence**	Y	Y	N	N	Y	Y
7 Carson	?	Y	Y	Y	Y	Y
8 Ellsworth	Y	Y	N	Y	Y	Y
9 Hill	Y	Y	Y	Y	Y	Y
IOWA						
1 Braley	Y	Y	Y	Y	Y	Y
2 Loebsack	Y	?	Y	Y	Y	Y
3 Boswell	Y	Y	Y	Y	Y	Y
4 **Latham**	Y	?	N	Y	Y	Y
5 **King**	Y	Y	N	N	Y	Y
KANSAS						
1 **Moran**	?	?	N	Y	Y	Y
2 **Jenkins**	Y	Y	N	Y	Y	Y
3 Moore	Y	Y	Y	Y	Y	Y
4 **Tiahrt**	?	?	?	?	?	?
KENTUCKY						
1 **Whitfield**	Y	Y	N	Y	Y	Y
2 **Guthrie**	Y	Y	N	Y	Y	Y
3 Yarmuth	Y	Y	Y	Y	Y	N
4 **Davis**	Y	Y	N	Y	Y	Y
5 **Rogers**	Y	Y	N	Y	Y	Y
6 Chandler	Y	Y	Y	Y	Y	Y
LOUISIANA						
1 **Scalise**	Y	Y	N	Y	Y	Y
2 **Cao**	Y	Y	N	Y	Y	Y
3 Melancon	Y	Y	Y	Y	Y	Y
4 **Fleming**	Y	Y	N	Y	Y	Y
5 **Alexander**	Y	Y	N	Y	Y	Y
6 **Cassidy**	Y	Y	N	Y	Y	Y
7 **Boustany**	Y	Y	N	Y	Y	Y
MAINE						
1 Pingree	N	Y	Y	Y	Y	Y
2 Michaud	N	Y	Y	Y	Y	Y
MARYLAND						
1 Kratovil	Y	Y	N	Y	Y	Y
2 Ruppersberger	Y	Y	Y	Y	Y	Y
3 Sarbanes	Y	Y	Y	Y	Y	N
4 Edwards	N	Y	Y	Y	Y	N
5 Hoyer	Y	Y	Y	Y	Y	Y
6 **Bartlett**	Y	Y	N	N	Y	Y
7 Cummings	N	Y	Y	Y	Y	N
8 Van Hollen	Y	Y	Y	Y	Y	N
MASSACHUSETTS						
1 Olver	N	Y	Y	Y	Y	N
2 Neal	N	Y	Y	Y	Y	N
3 McGovern	N	Y	Y	Y	Y	N
4 Frank	N	Y	Y	Y	Y	N
5 Tsongas	N	Y	Y	Y	Y	N
6 Tierney	N	Y	Y	Y	Y	N
7 Markey	N	Y	Y	Y	Y	N
8 Capuano	N	Y	Y	Y	Y	N
9 Lynch	Y	Y	Y	Y	Y	N
10 Delahunt	N	Y	Y	Y	Y	N
MICHIGAN						
1 Stupak	N	Y	Y	Y	Y	Y
2 **Hoekstra**	Y	?	?	?	?	?
3 **Ehlers**	N	Y	N	Y	Y	Y
4 **Camp**	Y	Y	N	Y	Y	Y
5 Kildee	Y	Y	Y	Y	Y	Y
6 **Upton**	Y	Y	N	Y	Y	Y
7 Schauer	Y	Y	Y	Y	Y	Y
8 **Rogers**	Y	Y	N	Y	Y	Y
9 Peters	Y	Y	Y	Y	Y	Y
10 **Miller**	Y	Y	N	Y	Y	Y
11 **McCotter**	Y	Y	N	Y	Y	Y
12 Levin	Y	Y	Y	Y	Y	N
13 Kilpatrick	N	Y	Y	Y	Y	N
14 Conyers	N	Y	Y	Y	Y	N
15 Dingell	Y	Y	Y	Y	Y	Y
MINNESOTA						
1 Walz	Y	Y	Y	Y	Y	Y
2 **Kline**	Y	Y	N	Y	Y	Y
3 **Paulsen**	Y	Y	N	Y	Y	Y
4 McCollum	N	Y	Y	Y	Y	N

	474	475	476	477	478	479
5 Ellison	N	Y	Y	Y	Y	N
6 **Bachmann**	Y	Y	N	N	Y	Y
7 Peterson	Y	Y	Y	Y	Y	Y
8 Oberstar	N	Y	Y	Y	Y	Y
MISSISSIPPI						
1 Childers	Y	Y	Y	Y	Y	Y
2 Thompson	N	Y	Y	Y	Y	N
3 **Harper**	Y	Y	N	Y	Y	Y
4 Taylor	Y	Y	Y	Y	Y	Y
MISSOURI						
1 Clay	N	Y	Y	Y	Y	N
2 **Akin**	+	+	−	+	+	+
3 Carnahan	Y	Y	Y	Y	Y	Y
4 Skelton	Y	Y	Y	Y	Y	Y
5 Cleaver	N	Y	Y	Y	Y	N
6 **Graves**	?	?	N	Y	Y	Y
7 **Blunt**	Y	Y	N	Y	Y	Y
8 **Emerson**	Y	Y	N	Y	Y	Y
9 **Luetkemeyer**	Y	Y	N	Y	Y	Y
MONTANA						
AL **Rehberg**	Y	Y	N	Y	Y	Y
NEBRASKA						
1 **Fortenberry**	Y	Y	N	Y	Y	Y
2 **Terry**	Y	Y	N	Y	Y	Y
3 **Smith**	Y	Y	N	N	Y	Y
NEVADA						
1 Berkley	Y	Y	Y	Y	Y	Y
2 **Heller**	+	?	N	Y	Y	Y
3 Titus	Y	Y	Y	Y	Y	Y
NEW HAMPSHIRE						
1 Shea-Porter	N	Y	Y	Y	Y	Y
2 Hodes	Y	Y	Y	Y	Y	Y
NEW JERSEY						
1 Andrews	Y	Y	?	?	?	?
2 **LoBiondo**	Y	Y	N	Y	Y	Y
3 Adler	Y	Y	Y	Y	Y	Y
4 **Smith**	Y	Y	N	Y	Y	Y
5 **Garrett**	Y	Y	N	Y	Y	Y
6 Pallone	N	Y	Y	Y	Y	N
7 **Lance**	Y	Y	N	Y	Y	Y
8 Pascrell	Y	Y	Y	Y	Y	Y
9 Rothman	Y	Y	Y	Y	Y	N
10 Payne	N	Y	Y	Y	Y	N
11 **Frelinghuysen**	Y	Y	N	Y	Y	Y
12 Holt	N	Y	Y	Y	Y	N
13 Sires	Y	Y	Y	Y	Y	N
NEW MEXICO						
1 Heinrich	Y	Y	Y	Y	Y	Y
2 Teague	Y	Y	Y	Y	Y	Y
3 Luján	Y	Y	Y	Y	Y	Y
NEW YORK						
1 Bishop	Y	Y	Y	?	Y	N
2 Israel	Y	Y	Y	Y	Y	N
3 **King**	Y	Y	N	Y	Y	Y
4 McCarthy	Y	Y	Y	Y	Y	N
5 Ackerman	Y	Y	Y	Y	Y	N
6 Meeks	N	Y	Y	Y	Y	N
7 Crowley	N	Y	Y	Y	Y	N
8 Nadler	N	Y	Y	Y	Y	N
9 Weiner	N	Y	Y	Y	Y	N
10 Towns	N	Y	Y	Y	?	N
11 Clarke	N	Y	Y	Y	Y	N
12 Velázquez	N	Y	Y	Y	Y	N
13 McMahon	Y	Y	Y	Y	Y	N
14 Maloney	N	Y	Y	Y	Y	N
15 Rangel	N	Y	Y	Y	Y	N
16 Serrano	N	Y	Y	Y	Y	N
17 Engel	Y	Y	Y	Y	Y	N
18 Lowey	Y	Y	Y	Y	Y	N
19 Hall	Y	Y	Y	Y	Y	N
20 Murphy	Y	Y	Y	Y	Y	Y
21 Tonko	N	Y	Y	Y	Y	N
22 Hinchey	N	?	Y	Y	Y	Y
23 Owens	Y	Y	Y	Y	Y	Y
24 Arcuri	Y	Y	Y	Y	Y	Y
25 Maffei	N	Y	Y	Y	Y	Y
26 **Lee**	Y	Y	N	Y	Y	Y
27 Higgins	Y	Y	Y	Y	Y	Y
28 Slaughter	N	Y	Y	Y	Y	N
29 Vacant						
NORTH CAROLINA						
1 Butterfield	Y	Y	Y	Y	Y	N
2 Etheridge	Y	Y	Y	Y	Y	Y
3 **Jones**	N	Y	N	Y	Y	Y
4 Price	Y	Y	Y	Y	Y	N

	474	475	476	477	478	479
5 **Foxx**	Y	Y	N	Y	Y	Y
6 **Coble**	Y	Y	N	Y	Y	Y
7 McIntyre	Y	Y	Y	Y	Y	Y
8 Kissell	Y	Y	Y	Y	Y	Y
9 **Myrick**	Y	Y	N	N	Y	Y
10 **McHenry**	Y	Y	N	Y	Y	Y
11 Shuler	Y	Y	N	Y	Y	Y
12 Watt	N	Y	Y	Y	Y	N
13 Miller	Y	Y	Y	Y	Y	Y
NORTH DAKOTA						
AL Pomeroy	Y	Y	Y	Y	Y	Y
OHIO						
1 Driehaus	Y	Y	Y	Y	Y	Y
2 **Schmidt**	Y	Y	N	Y	Y	Y
3 **Turner**	Y	Y	N	Y	Y	Y
4 **Jordan**	Y	Y	N	Y	Y	Y
5 **Latta**	Y	Y	N	Y	Y	Y
6 Wilson	Y	?	Y	Y	Y	Y
7 **Austria**	Y	Y	N	Y	Y	Y
8 **Boehner**	Y	Y	N	Y	Y	Y
9 Kaptur	N	Y	Y	Y	Y	Y
10 Kucinich	N	Y	Y	Y	Y	N
11 Fudge	N	Y	Y	Y	Y	N
12 **Tiberi**	Y	Y	N	Y	Y	Y
13 Sutton	Y	Y	Y	Y	Y	Y
14 **LaTourette**	Y	Y	N	Y	Y	Y
15 Kilroy	Y	Y	Y	Y	Y	N
16 Boccieri	Y	Y	Y	Y	Y	Y
17 Ryan	Y	Y	Y	Y	Y	Y
18 Space	Y	Y	Y	Y	Y	Y
OKLAHOMA						
1 **Sullivan**	Y	Y	N	Y	Y	Y
2 Boren	Y	Y	Y	Y	Y	Y
3 **Lucas**	Y	Y	N	Y	Y	Y
4 **Cole**	Y	?	N	Y	Y	Y
5 **Fallin**	Y	?	?	?	?	?
OREGON						
1 Wu	N	Y	Y	Y	Y	Y
2 **Walden**	Y	Y	N	Y	Y	Y
3 Blumenauer	N	Y	Y	Y	Y	N
4 DeFazio	N	Y	Y	Y	Y	Y
5 Schrader	N	Y	Y	Y	Y	Y
PENNSYLVANIA						
1 Brady	Y	Y	Y	Y	Y	N
2 Fattah	N	Y	Y	Y	Y	N
3 Dahlkemper	Y	Y	Y	Y	Y	Y
4 Altmire	Y	Y	Y	Y	Y	Y
5 **Thompson**	Y	Y	N	Y	Y	Y
6 **Gerlach**	Y	Y	N	Y	Y	Y
7 Sestak	Y	Y	Y	Y	Y	Y
8 Murphy, P.	Y	Y	Y	Y	Y	Y
9 **Shuster**	Y	Y	N	Y	Y	Y
10 Carney	Y	Y	Y	Y	Y	Y
11 Kanjorski	Y	Y	Y	Y	Y	Y
12 Critz	Y	Y	Y	Y	Y	Y
13 Schwartz	Y	Y	Y	Y	Y	Y
14 Doyle	N	Y	Y	Y	Y	N
15 **Dent**	Y	Y	N	Y	Y	Y
16 **Pitts**	Y	Y	N	Y	Y	Y
17 Holden	Y	Y	Y	Y	Y	Y
18 **Murphy, T.**	Y	Y	N	Y	Y	Y
19 **Platts**	Y	Y	N	Y	Y	Y
RHODE ISLAND						
1 Kennedy	Y	Y	Y	Y	Y	N
2 Langevin	Y	Y	Y	Y	Y	N
SOUTH CAROLINA						
1 **Brown**	Y	Y	N	Y	Y	Y
2 **Wilson**	Y	Y	N	Y	Y	Y
3 **Barrett**	Y	Y	N	N	Y	Y
4 **Inglis**	Y	Y	N	N	Y	Y
5 Spratt	Y	Y	Y	Y	Y	Y
6 Clyburn	Y	Y	Y	Y	Y	Y
SOUTH DAKOTA						
AL Herseth Sandlin	Y	Y	N	Y	Y	Y
TENNESSEE						
1 **Roe**	Y	Y	N	Y	Y	Y
2 **Duncan**	N	Y	N	Y	Y	Y
3 **Wamp**	Y	Y	?	?	?	?
4 Davis	Y	Y	Y	Y	Y	Y
5 Cooper	Y	Y	Y	Y	Y	Y
6 Gordon	Y	Y	Y	?	Y	Y
7 **Blackburn**	Y	Y	N	Y	Y	Y
8 Tanner	Y	Y	Y	Y	Y	Y
9 Cohen	N	Y	Y	Y	Y	N

	474	475	476	477	478	479
TEXAS						
1 **Gohmert**	Y	Y	N	N	Y	Y
2 **Poe**	Y	Y	N	N	Y	Y
3 **Johnson, S.**	Y	Y	N	Y	Y	Y
4 **Hall**	Y	Y	N	Y	Y	?
5 **Hensarling**	Y	Y	N	N	Y	Y
6 **Barton**	Y	Y	N	Y	Y	Y
7 **Culberson**	Y	Y	N	?	Y	Y
8 **Brady**	Y	Y	N	Y	Y	Y
9 Green, A.	Y	Y	Y	Y	Y	Y
10 **McCaul**	Y	Y	N	Y	Y	Y
11 **Conaway**	Y	Y	N	N	Y	Y
12 **Granger**	Y	Y	N	Y	Y	Y
13 **Thornberry**	Y	Y	N	N	Y	Y
14 **Paul**	N	Y	N	N	Y	Y
15 Hinojosa	Y	Y	Y	Y	Y	Y
16 Reyes	Y	Y	Y	Y	Y	Y
17 Edwards	Y	Y	Y	Y	Y	Y
18 Jackson Lee	N	Y	Y	Y	Y	N
19 **Neugebauer**	Y	Y	N	?	?	?
20 Gonzalez	Y	Y	Y	Y	Y	N
21 **Smith**	Y	Y	?	Y	Y	Y
22 **Olson**	Y	Y	N	Y	Y	Y
23 Rodriguez	Y	Y	Y	Y	Y	Y
24 **Marchant**	Y	Y	N	Y	Y	Y
25 Doggett	N	Y	Y	Y	Y	Y
26 **Burgess**	Y	Y	N	Y	Y	Y
27 Ortiz	Y	Y	Y	Y	Y	Y
28 Cuellar	Y	Y	Y	Y	Y	Y
29 Green, G.	Y	Y	Y	Y	Y	Y
30 Johnson, E.	N	Y	Y	Y	Y	N
31 **Carter**	Y	Y	N	N	Y	Y
32 **Sessions**	Y	Y	N	Y	Y	Y
UTAH						
1 **Bishop**	Y	Y	N	Y	Y	Y
2 Matheson	Y	Y	Y	Y	Y	Y
3 **Chaffetz**	N	Y	N	N	Y	Y
VERMONT						
AL Welch	N	Y	Y	Y	Y	Y
VIRGINIA						
1 **Wittman**	Y	Y	N	Y	Y	Y
2 Nye	Y	Y	Y	Y	Y	Y
3 Scott	N	Y	Y	Y	Y	Y
4 **Forbes**	Y	Y	N	Y	Y	Y
5 Perriello	Y	Y	Y	Y	Y	Y
6 **Goodlatte**	Y	Y	N	Y	Y	Y
7 **Cantor**	Y	Y	N	Y	Y	Y
8 Moran	N	Y	Y	Y	Y	N
9 Boucher	Y	Y	Y	Y	Y	Y
10 **Wolf**	Y	Y	N	Y	Y	Y
11 Connolly	Y	Y	Y	Y	Y	Y
WASHINGTON						
1 Inslee	N	Y	Y	Y	Y	Y
2 Larsen	Y	Y	Y	Y	Y	Y
3 Baird	Y	Y	Y	Y	Y	N
4 **Hastings**	Y	Y	N	Y	Y	Y
5 **McMorris Rodgers**	Y	Y	N	Y	Y	Y
6 Dicks	Y	Y	Y	Y	Y	Y
7 McDermott	N	Y	Y	Y	Y	N
8 **Reichert**	Y	Y	N	Y	Y	Y
9 Smith	Y	Y	Y	Y	Y	Y
WEST VIRGINIA						
1 Mollohan	Y	Y	Y	Y	Y	Y
2 **Capito**	Y	Y	N	Y	Y	Y
3 Rahall	Y	Y	Y	Y	Y	Y
WISCONSIN						
1 **Ryan**	Y	Y	N	Y	Y	Y
2 Baldwin	N	Y	Y	Y	Y	N
3 Kind	Y	Y	Y	Y	Y	Y
4 Moore	N	Y	Y	?	Y	Y
5 **Sensenbrenner**	Y	Y	N	Y	Y	Y
6 **Petri**	Y	Y	N	Y	Y	Y
7 Obey	N	Y	Y	Y	?	Y
8 Kagen	N	Y	Y	Y	Y	Y
WYOMING						
AL **Lummis**	Y	Y	N	Y	Y	Y
DELEGATES						
Faleomavaega (A.S.)						
Norton (D.C.)						
Bordallo (Guam)						
Sablan (N. Marianas)						
Pierluisi (P.R.)						
Christensen (V.I.)						

IN THE HOUSE | By Vote Number

480. HR 5822. Fiscal 2011 Military Construction-VA Appropriations/ **Guantánamo Bay Detainees.** Gingrey, R-Ga., amendment that would bar the use of funds in the bill to renovate or construct any facility within the continental United States for the purpose of housing any individual who has been detained, at any time after Sept. 11, 2001, at U.S. Naval Station, Guantánamo Bay. Adopted in Committee of the Whole 353-69: D 182-69; R 171-0. July 28, 2010.

481. HR 5822. Fiscal 2011 Military Construction-VA Appropriations/ **State Veterans' Cemetery Funding.** Garrett, R-N.J., amendment that would increase grant funding for construction of state veterans' cemeteries by $7 million and decrease grant funding for minor construction projects by the same amount. Rejected in Committee of the Whole 128-296: D 20-234; R 108-62. July 28, 2010.

482. HR 5822. Fiscal 2011 Military Construction-VA Appropriations/ **Passage.** Passage of the bill that would provide $141.1 billion in fiscal 2011 for the Department of Veterans Affairs, military construction and military housing, including $77.3 billion in discretionary funding. It would provide $120.8 billion for the department, including $48.8 billion for veterans' health programs. The bill would provide $53.5 billion in mandatory spending for veterans' service-connected compensation benefits and pensions. The total also includes $13.7 billion for military construction, $1.8 billion for military family housing and $2.8 billion for the latest round of base realignment and closure. The bill would provide $50.6 billion in advance appropriations for three veterans' medical care accounts for fiscal 2012. Passed 411-6: D 247-0; R 164-6. A "yea" was a vote in support of the president's position. July 28, 2010.

483. H Con Res 308. **Adjournment/Adoption.** Adoption of the concurrent resolution that would provide for the adjournment of the House until Tuesday, Sept. 14, 2010. Adopted 231-189: D 218-32; R 13-157. July 29, 2010.

484. HR 5850. Fiscal 2011 Transportation-HUD Appropriations/ **Previous Question.** Arcuri, D-N.Y., motion to order the previous question (thus ending debate and possibility of amendment) on adoption of the rule (H Res 1569) to provide for House floor consideration of the bill that would appropriate $126.4 billion in fiscal 2011 for the departments of Transportation and Housing and Urban Development and related agencies. Motion agreed to 236-179: D 236-12; R 0-167. July 29, 2010.

485. HR 5850. Fiscal 2011 Transportation-HUD Appropriations/ **Rule.** Adoption of the rule (H Res 1569) that would provide for House floor consideration of the bill that would appropriate $126.4 billion in fiscal 2011 for the departments of Transportation and Housing and Urban Development and related agencies. Adopted 231-185: D 231-17; R 0-168. July 29, 2010.

486. HR 5893. **Tax Incentives and Emergency Spending/Rule.** Adoption of the rule (H Res 1568) that would provide for House floor consideration of the bill that would provide $7.9 billion in infrastructure tax incentives and extend the Temporary Assistance to Needy Families emergency fund. The rule also would waive, through Aug. 1, 2010, the two-thirds majority requirement to consider a rule on the same day it is reported by the Rules Committee. Adopted 233-182: D 233-13; R 0-169. July 29, 2010.

	480	481	482	483	484	485	486
ALABAMA							
1 **Bonner**	Y	Y	Y	N	N	N	N
2 Bright	Y	N	Y	N	N	N	N
3 **Rogers**	Y	Y	Y	N	N	N	N
4 **Aderholt**	Y	Y	Y	N	N	N	N
5 **Griffith**	Y	N	N	N	N	N	N
6 **Bachus**	Y	Y	Y	N	N	N	N
7 Davis	?	N	Y	Y	Y	Y	Y
ALASKA							
AL **Young**	Y	N	Y	N	?	N	N
ARIZONA							
1 Kirkpatrick	Y	N	Y	Y	N	Y	Y
2 **Franks**	Y	Y	Y	N	N	?	N
3 **Shadegg**	Y	Y	Y	?	?	?	?
4 Pastor	N	N	Y	Y	Y	Y	Y
5 Mitchell	Y	Y	Y	N	N	N	N
6 **Flake**	Y	Y	N	Y	N	N	N
7 Grijalva	N	N	Y	Y	Y	Y	Y
8 Giffords	Y	Y	Y	N	N	N	N
ARKANSAS							
1 Berry	Y	N	Y	Y	Y	Y	Y
2 Snyder	N	N	Y	Y	Y	Y	Y
3 **Boozman**	Y	N	N	N	N	N	N
4 Ross	Y	N	Y	Y	Y	Y	Y
CALIFORNIA							
1 Thompson	Y	N	Y	Y	Y	Y	Y
2 **Herger**	Y	Y	Y	N	N	N	N
3 **Lungren**	Y	Y	Y	N	N	N	N
4 **McClintock**	Y	Y	Y	N	N	N	N
5 Matsui	Y	N	Y	Y	Y	Y	Y
6 Woolsey	N	N	Y	Y	Y	Y	Y
7 Miller, George	Y	N	Y	Y	Y	Y	Y
8 Pelosi							
9 Lee	N	N	Y	Y	Y	Y	Y
10 Garamendi	N	N	Y	?	Y	Y	Y
11 McNerney	Y	N	Y	N	Y	Y	Y
12 Speier	Y	N	Y	Y	Y	Y	Y
13 Stark	?	N	Y	Y	Y	Y	Y
14 Eshoo	Y	N	Y	Y	Y	Y	Y
15 Honda	N	N	Y	Y	Y	Y	Y
16 Lofgren	N	N	Y	Y	Y	Y	Y
17 Farr	N	N	Y	?	?	Y	Y
18 Cardoza	Y	N	Y	Y	Y	Y	Y
19 **Radanovich**	Y	Y	Y	N	N	N	?
20 Costa	Y	N	Y	Y	Y	Y	Y
21 **Nunes**	Y	Y	Y	N	N	?	N
22 **McCarthy**	Y	Y	Y	N	N	N	N
23 Capps	N	N	Y	Y	Y	Y	Y
24 **Gallegly**	Y	Y	Y	N	N	N	N
25 **McKeon**	Y	Y	Y	N	N	N	N
26 **Dreier**	Y	Y	Y	N	N	N	N
27 Sherman	Y	N	Y	Y	Y	Y	Y
28 Berman	N	N	Y	Y	Y	Y	Y
29 Schiff	Y	N	Y	Y	Y	Y	Y
30 Waxman	N	N	Y	Y	Y	?	?
31 Becerra	N	N	Y	Y	Y	Y	Y
32 Chu	N	N	Y	Y	Y	Y	Y
33 Watson	?	?	?	?	?	?	?
34 Roybal-Allard	N	N	Y	Y	Y	Y	Y
35 Waters	N	N	?	Y	Y	Y	?
36 Harman	N	N	Y	Y	Y	Y	Y
37 Richardson	Y	N	Y	Y	Y	Y	Y
38 Napolitano	Y	N	Y	Y	Y	Y	Y
39 Sánchez, Linda	N	N	Y	Y	Y	Y	Y
40 **Royce**	Y	N	Y	N	N	N	N
41 **Lewis**	Y	Y	Y	N	N	N	N
42 **Miller, Gary**	Y	Y	Y	N	N	N	N
43 Baca	Y	N	Y	Y	Y	Y	Y
44 **Calvert**	Y	Y	Y	N	N	N	N
45 **Bono Mack**	Y	Y	Y	N	N	N	N
46 **Rohrabacher**	Y	Y	Y	N	N	N	N
47 Sanchez, Loretta	Y	N	Y	Y	Y	Y	Y
48 **Campbell**	Y	Y	N	N	N	N	N
49 **Issa**	Y	Y	Y	N	N	N	N
50 **Bilbray**	Y	Y	Y	N	?	N	N
51 Filner	N	N	Y	Y	Y	Y	Y
52 **Hunter**	Y	Y	Y	N	N	N	N
53 Davis	Y	N	Y	Y	Y	Y	Y

	480	481	482	483	484	485	486
COLORADO							
1 DeGette	N	N	Y	Y	Y	Y	Y
2 Polis	Y	N	Y	Y	Y	Y	Y
3 Salazar	Y	N	Y	Y	Y	Y	Y
4 Markey	Y	N	Y	N	Y	Y	Y
5 **Lamborn**	Y	Y	Y	N	N	N	N
6 **Coffman**	Y	N	Y	N	N	N	N
7 Perlmutter	Y	N	Y	Y	Y	Y	Y
CONNECTICUT							
1 Larson	Y	N	Y	Y	Y	Y	Y
2 Courtney	Y	N	Y	Y	Y	Y	Y
3 DeLauro	Y	N	Y	Y	Y	Y	Y
4 Himes	Y	N	Y	Y	Y	Y	Y
5 Murphy	Y	N	Y	Y	Y	Y	Y
DELAWARE							
AL **Castle**	Y	N	Y	N	N	N	N
FLORIDA							
1 **Miller**	Y	N	Y	N	N	N	N
2 Boyd	Y	N	Y	Y	Y	Y	Y
3 Brown	Y	N	Y	Y	Y	Y	Y
4 **Crenshaw**	Y	Y	Y	N	N	N	N
5 **Brown-Waite**	Y	N	N	N	N	N	N
6 **Stearns**	Y	Y	Y	N	N	N	N
7 **Mica**	Y	Y	Y	N	N	N	N
8 Grayson	Y	N	Y	Y	Y	Y	Y
9 **Bilirakis**	Y	Y	Y	N	N	N	N
10 **Young**	?	?	?	?	?	?	?
11 Castor	N	N	Y	Y	Y	Y	Y
12 **Putnam**	Y	N	Y	N	N	N	N
13 **Buchanan**	Y	Y	Y	N	N	N	N
14 **Mack**	Y	Y	Y	N	N	N	N
15 **Posey**	Y	N	Y	N	N	N	N
16 **Rooney**	Y	N	Y	N	N	N	N
17 Meek	Y	N	Y	Y	Y	Y	Y
18 **Ros-Lehtinen**	Y	Y	Y	N	N	N	N
19 Deutch	Y	Y	Y	Y	Y	Y	Y
20 Wasserman Schultz	N	N	Y	Y	Y	Y	Y
21 **Diaz-Balart, L.**	Y	Y	Y	N	N	N	N
22 Klein	Y	N	Y	?	Y	Y	Y
23 Hastings	Y	N	Y	Y	Y	Y	Y
24 Kosmas	Y	N	Y	N	Y	Y	Y
25 **Diaz-Balart, M.**	Y	Y	Y	N	N	N	N
GEORGIA							
1 **Kingston**	Y	N	Y	N	N	N	N
2 Bishop	Y	N	Y	Y	Y	Y	Y
3 **Westmoreland**	Y	Y	Y	N	N	N	N
4 Johnson	N	N	Y	Y	Y	Y	Y
5 Lewis	?	?	?	Y	Y	Y	Y
6 **Price**	Y	Y	Y	N	N	N	N
7 **Linder**	Y	Y	Y	N	N	N	N
8 Marshall	Y	Y	Y	N	N	N	N
9 **Graves**	Y	Y	Y	N	N	N	N
10 **Broun**	Y	N	N	N	N	N	N
11 **Gingrey**	Y	Y	Y	N	N	N	N
12 Barrow	Y	Y	Y	Y	Y	Y	Y
13 Scott	Y	N	Y	Y	Y	Y	Y
HAWAII							
1 Djou	Y	N	Y	N	N	N	N
2 Hirono	Y	N	Y	Y	Y	Y	Y
IDAHO							
1 Minnick	Y	N	Y	N	N	N	N
2 **Simpson**	Y	Y	Y	N	N	N	N
ILLINOIS							
1 Rush	Y	N	Y	Y	Y	Y	Y
2 Jackson	Y	N	Y	Y	Y	Y	Y
3 Lipinski	Y	N	Y	Y	Y	Y	Y
4 Gutierrez	N	N	Y	Y	Y	Y	Y
5 Quigley	N	N	Y	Y	Y	Y	Y
6 **Roskam**	Y	Y	Y	N	N	N	N
7 Davis	N	N	Y	Y	Y	Y	Y
8 Bean	Y	N	Y	N	Y	Y	Y
9 Schakowsky	N	N	Y	Y	Y	Y	Y
10 **Kirk**	Y	N	Y	N	N	N	N
11 Halvorson	Y	N	Y	Y	Y	Y	Y
12 Costello	Y	N	Y	Y	Y	Y	Y
13 **Biggert**	Y	N	Y	N	N	N	N
14 Foster	Y	N	Y	N	Y	Y	Y
15 **Johnson**	Y	Y	Y	N	N	N	N

	480	481	482	483	484	485	486
16 **Manzullo**	Y	N	Y	N	N	N	N
17 Hare	Y	N	Y	Y	Y	Y	Y
18 **Schock**	Y	N	Y	N	N	N	N
19 **Shimkus**	Y	N	Y	N	N	N	N
INDIANA							
1 Visclosky	Y	N	Y	Y	Y	Y	Y
2 Donnelly	Y	N	Y	N	Y	N	Y
3 Vacant							
4 **Buyer**	Y	Y	Y	?	?	N	N
5 **Burton**	Y	Y	Y	N	N	N	N
6 **Pence**	Y	Y	Y	N	N	N	N
7 Carson	Y	N	Y	Y	Y	Y	Y
8 Ellsworth	Y	N	Y	N	N	N	N
9 Hill	Y	N	Y	Y	N	N	N
IOWA							
1 Braley	N	N	?	Y	Y	Y	Y
2 Loebsack	Y	N	Y	Y	Y	Y	Y
3 Boswell	Y	N	Y	Y	Y	Y	Y
4 **Latham**	Y	Y	Y	N	N	N	N
5 **King**	Y	N	Y	N	N	N	N
KANSAS							
1 **Moran**	Y	?	?	?	?	?	?
2 **Jenkins**	Y	N	Y	N	N	N	N
3 Moore	Y	N	Y	Y	Y	Y	Y
4 **Tiahrt**	?	?	?	?	?	?	?
KENTUCKY							
1 **Whitfield**	Y	N	Y	N	N	N	N
2 **Guthrie**	Y	Y	Y	N	N	N	N
3 Yarmuth	Y	N	Y	Y	Y	Y	Y
4 **Davis**	Y	Y	Y	N	N	N	N
5 **Rogers**	Y	Y	Y	N	N	N	N
6 Chandler	Y	N	Y	Y	Y	Y	Y
LOUISIANA							
1 **Scalise**	Y	Y	Y	N	N	N	N
2 **Cao**	Y	N	Y	N	N	N	N
3 Melancon	Y	N	Y	Y	Y	Y	Y
4 **Fleming**	Y	Y	Y	N	N	N	N
5 **Alexander**	Y	Y	Y	N	N	N	N
6 **Cassidy**	Y	Y	Y	N	N	N	N
7 **Boustany**	Y	Y	Y	N	N	N	N
MAINE							
1 Pingree	N	Y	Y	Y	Y	Y	Y
2 Michaud	Y	Y	Y	N	Y	Y	Y
MARYLAND							
1 Kratovil	Y	N	Y	N	Y	N	N
2 Ruppersberger	Y	Y	Y	Y	Y	Y	Y
3 Sarbanes	Y	N	Y	Y	Y	Y	Y
4 Edwards	N	N	Y	Y	Y	Y	Y
5 Hoyer	Y	N	Y	Y	Y	Y	Y
6 **Bartlett**	Y	Y	Y	Y	N	N	N
7 Cummings	Y	N	Y	Y	Y	Y	Y
8 Van Hollen	Y	N	Y	Y	Y	Y	Y
MASSACHUSETTS							
1 Olver	N	N	Y	Y	Y	Y	Y
2 Neal	Y	N	Y	Y	Y	Y	Y
3 McGovern	Y	N	Y	Y	Y	Y	Y
4 Frank	N	N	Y	Y	Y	Y	Y
5 Tsongas	N	N	Y	Y	Y	Y	Y
6 Tierney	Y	N	Y	Y	Y	Y	Y
7 Markey	Y	N	Y	Y	Y	Y	Y
8 Capuano	Y	N	Y	Y	Y	Y	Y
9 Lynch	Y	N	Y	?	?	?	?
10 Delahunt	Y	N	Y	Y	Y	Y	Y
MICHIGAN							
1 Stupak	Y	N	Y	Y	Y	Y	Y
2 **Hoekstra**	?	?	?	?	?	?	?
3 **Ehlers**	?	?	?	Y	N	N	N
4 **Camp**	Y	N	Y	N	N	N	N
5 Kildee	Y	N	Y	Y	Y	Y	Y
6 **Upton**	Y	N	Y	N	N	N	N
7 Schauer	Y	N	Y	N	Y	Y	Y
8 **Rogers**	Y	Y	Y	N	N	N	N
9 Peters	Y	N	Y	N	Y	Y	Y
10 **Miller**	Y	Y	Y	N	N	N	N
11 **McCotter**	Y	Y	Y	N	N	N	N
12 Levin	Y	N	Y	Y	Y	Y	Y
13 Kilpatrick	Y	N	Y	Y	Y	Y	Y
14 Conyers	Y	N	Y	Y	Y	Y	Y
15 Dingell	N	N	Y	Y	Y	Y	Y
MINNESOTA							
1 Walz	Y	N	Y	Y	Y	Y	Y
2 **Kline**	Y	Y	Y	N	N	N	N
3 **Paulsen**	Y	N	Y	N	N	N	N
4 McCollum	Y	N	Y	Y	Y	Y	Y

	480	481	482	483	484	485	486
5 Ellison	N	N	Y	Y	Y	Y	Y
6 **Bachmann**	Y	Y	Y	N	N	N	N
7 Peterson	Y	N	Y	Y	Y	Y	Y
8 Oberstar	Y	N	Y	Y	Y	Y	Y
MISSISSIPPI							
1 Childers	Y	N	Y	Y	N	N	N
2 Thompson	Y	N	Y	Y	Y	Y	Y
3 **Harper**	Y	Y	Y	N	N	N	N
4 Taylor	Y	N	Y	Y	N	N	Y
MISSOURI							
1 Clay	N	N	Y	Y	Y	Y	Y
2 **Akin**	+	+	+	–	–	–	–
3 Carnahan	Y	N	Y	Y	Y	Y	Y
4 Skelton	Y	N	Y	Y	Y	Y	Y
5 Cleaver	?	N	Y	Y	Y	Y	Y
6 **Graves**	Y	Y	Y	N	N	N	N
7 **Blunt**	Y	N	Y	N	N	N	N
8 **Emerson**	Y	Y	Y	N	N	N	N
9 **Luetkemeyer**	Y	N	Y	Y	N	N	N
MONTANA							
AL **Rehberg**	Y	Y	Y	N	N	N	N
NEBRASKA							
1 **Fortenberry**	Y	N	Y	N	N	N	N
2 **Terry**	Y	N	Y	N	N	N	N
3 **Smith**	Y	Y	Y	N	N	N	N
NEVADA							
1 Berkley	Y	N	Y	Y	Y	Y	Y
2 **Heller**	Y	Y	Y	N	N	N	N
3 Titus	Y	N	Y	Y	Y	Y	Y
NEW HAMPSHIRE							
1 Shea-Porter	Y	N	Y	Y	Y	Y	Y
2 Hodes	Y	Y	Y	Y	Y	Y	Y
NEW JERSEY							
1 Andrews	?	?	?	?	?	?	?
2 **LoBiondo**	Y	Y	Y	N	N	N	N
3 Adler	Y	Y	Y	N	N	Y	Y
4 **Smith**	Y	Y	Y	N	N	N	N
5 **Garrett**	Y	Y	Y	N	N	N	N
6 Pallone	Y	Y	Y	Y	Y	Y	Y
7 **Lance**	Y	Y	Y	N	N	N	N
8 Pascrell	Y	Y	Y	Y	Y	Y	Y
9 Rothman	Y	Y	Y	Y	Y	Y	Y
10 Payne	Y	N	Y	Y	Y	Y	Y
11 **Frelinghuysen**	Y	Y	Y	N	N	N	N
12 Holt	Y	Y	Y	Y	Y	Y	Y
13 Sires	Y	Y	Y	Y	Y	Y	Y
NEW MEXICO							
1 Heinrich	Y	N	Y	Y	Y	Y	Y
2 Teague	Y	N	Y	N	Y	Y	Y
3 Luján	Y	N	Y	Y	Y	Y	Y
NEW YORK							
1 Bishop	Y	N	Y	N	Y	Y	Y
2 Israel	N	N	Y	Y	Y	Y	?
3 **King**	Y	Y	Y	N	N	N	N
4 McCarthy	Y	N	Y	Y	Y	Y	Y
5 Ackerman	Y	N	Y	Y	Y	Y	Y
6 Meeks	Y	N	Y	Y	Y	Y	?
7 Crowley	–	–	+	Y	Y	?	Y
8 Nadler	N	N	Y	Y	Y	Y	Y
9 Weiner	Y	N	Y	Y	Y	Y	Y
10 Towns	N	N	Y	Y	Y	Y	Y
11 Clarke	Y	N	Y	Y	Y	Y	Y
12 Velázquez	N	N	Y	Y	Y	Y	Y
13 McMahon	Y	Y	Y	Y	Y	Y	Y
14 Maloney	Y	N	Y	Y	Y	Y	Y
15 Rangel	Y	Y	Y	N	Y	Y	Y
16 Serrano	Y	N	Y	Y	Y	Y	Y
17 Engel	N	N	Y	Y	Y	Y	Y
18 Lowey	Y	N	Y	Y	Y	Y	Y
19 Hall	Y	N	Y	Y	Y	Y	Y
20 Murphy	N	N	Y	N	Y	N	N
21 Tonko	Y	N	Y	Y	Y	Y	Y
22 Hinchey	N	N	Y	Y	Y	Y	Y
23 Owens	Y	N	Y	Y	Y	Y	Y
24 Arcuri	Y	N	Y	N	Y	Y	Y
25 Maffei	Y	N	Y	N	Y	Y	Y
26 **Lee**	Y	Y	Y	N	N	N	N
27 Higgins	Y	N	Y	Y	Y	Y	?
28 Slaughter	?	?	?	Y	Y	Y	Y
29 Vacant							
NORTH CAROLINA							
1 Butterfield	Y	N	Y	Y	Y	Y	Y
2 Etheridge	Y	N	Y	Y	Y	Y	Y
3 **Jones**	Y	N	Y	Y	N	N	N
4 Price	N	N	Y	Y	Y	Y	Y

	480	481	482	483	484	485	486
5 **Foxx**	Y	Y	Y	N	N	N	N
6 **Coble**	Y	N	Y	N	N	N	N
7 McIntyre	Y	N	Y	Y	N	Y	Y
8 Kissell	Y	N	Y	Y	Y	Y	Y
9 **Myrick**	Y	Y	Y	N	N	N	N
10 **McHenry**	Y	Y	Y	N	N	N	N
11 Shuler	Y	N	Y	Y	Y	N	N
12 Watt	N	N	Y	Y	Y	Y	Y
13 Miller	Y	N	Y	Y	Y	Y	Y
NORTH DAKOTA							
AL Pomeroy	Y	N	Y	Y	Y	Y	Y
OHIO							
1 Driehaus	Y	N	Y	Y	Y	Y	Y
2 **Schmidt**	Y	Y	Y	N	N	N	N
3 **Turner**	Y	N	Y	N	N	N	N
4 **Jordan**	Y	N	Y	N	N	N	N
5 **Latta**	Y	N	Y	N	N	N	N
6 Wilson	Y	N	Y	Y	Y	Y	Y
7 **Austria**	Y	N	Y	N	N	N	N
8 **Boehner**	Y	Y	Y	N	N	N	N
9 Kaptur	Y	N	Y	Y	Y	Y	Y
10 Kucinich	N	N	Y	Y	Y	Y	Y
11 Fudge	N	N	Y	Y	Y	Y	Y
12 **Tiberi**	Y	N	Y	N	N	N	N
13 Sutton	Y	N	Y	Y	Y	Y	Y
14 **LaTourette**	Y	Y	Y	N	N	N	N
15 Kilroy	Y	N	Y	N	Y	Y	Y
16 Boccieri	Y	N	Y	N	Y	Y	Y
17 Ryan	N	N	Y	Y	Y	Y	Y
18 Space	Y	N	Y	Y	Y	Y	Y
OKLAHOMA							
1 **Sullivan**	Y	Y	Y	N	N	N	N
2 Boren	Y	N	Y	Y	Y	Y	Y
3 **Lucas**	Y	Y	Y	N	N	N	N
4 **Cole**	Y	Y	Y	N	N	N	N
5 **Fallin**	?	?	?	N	N	N	N
OREGON							
1 Wu	N	Y	Y	Y	Y	Y	Y
2 **Walden**	Y	Y	Y	N	N	N	N
3 Blumenauer	N	N	Y	Y	Y	Y	Y
4 DeFazio	Y	Y	Y	Y	Y	Y	Y
5 Schrader	Y	N	Y	Y	Y	Y	Y
PENNSYLVANIA							
1 Brady	Y	N	Y	Y	Y	Y	Y
2 Fattah	N	N	Y	Y	Y	Y	Y
3 Dahlkemper	Y	N	Y	Y	Y	Y	Y
4 Altmire	Y	N	Y	N	Y	Y	Y
5 **Thompson**	Y	N	Y	N	N	N	N
6 **Gerlach**	Y	N	Y	N	N	N	N
7 Sestak	N	N	Y	N	Y	Y	Y
8 Murphy, P.	Y	N	Y	N	Y	Y	Y
9 **Shuster**	Y	N	Y	N	N	N	N
10 Carney	Y	N	Y	N	Y	Y	Y
11 Kanjorski	Y	N	Y	Y	Y	Y	Y
12 Critz	Y	N	Y	Y	Y	Y	Y
13 Schwartz	Y	N	Y	Y	Y	Y	Y
14 Doyle	Y	N	Y	Y	Y	Y	Y
15 **Dent**	Y	N	Y	N	N	N	N
16 **Pitts**	Y	Y	Y	N	N	N	N
17 Holden	Y	N	Y	Y	Y	Y	Y
18 **Murphy, T.**	Y	N	Y	N	N	N	N
19 **Platts**	Y	N	Y	N	N	N	N
RHODE ISLAND							
1 Kennedy	Y	N	Y	Y	Y	Y	Y
2 Langevin	Y	N	Y	Y	Y	Y	Y
SOUTH CAROLINA							
1 **Brown**	Y	N	Y	N	N	N	N
2 **Wilson**	Y	Y	Y	N	N	N	N
3 **Barrett**	Y	Y	Y	N	N	N	N
4 **Inglis**	Y	N	Y	N	N	N	N
5 Spratt	Y	N	Y	Y	Y	Y	Y
6 Clyburn	Y	N	Y	Y	Y	Y	Y
SOUTH DAKOTA							
AL Herseth Sandlin	Y	Y	Y	N	Y	N	N
TENNESSEE							
1 **Roe**	Y	Y	Y	N	N	N	N
2 **Duncan**	Y	Y	N	N	N	N	N
3 **Wamp**	?	?	?	?	?	?	?
4 Davis	Y	N	Y	Y	Y	Y	Y
5 Cooper	Y	N	Y	Y	Y	Y	Y
6 Gordon	Y	N	Y	Y	Y	Y	Y
7 **Blackburn**	Y	Y	Y	N	N	N	N
8 Tanner	Y	N	Y	Y	Y	Y	Y
9 Cohen	N	N	Y	Y	Y	Y	Y

	480	481	482	483	484	485	486
TEXAS							
1 **Gohmert**	Y	Y	Y	Y	N	N	N
2 **Poe**	Y	Y	Y	N	?	?	?
3 **Johnson, S.**	Y	Y	Y	N	N	N	N
4 **Hall**	Y	Y	Y	N	N	N	N
5 **Hensarling**	Y	Y	Y	N	N	N	N
6 **Barton**	Y	N	Y	N	N	N	N
7 **Culberson**	Y	N	Y	N	N	N	N
8 **Brady**	Y	Y	Y	N	N	N	N
9 Green, A.	Y	N	Y	Y	Y	Y	Y
10 **McCaul**	Y	Y	Y	N	N	N	N
11 **Conaway**	Y	Y	Y	N	N	N	N
12 **Granger**	Y	N	Y	N	N	N	N
13 **Thornberry**	Y	N	Y	N	N	N	N
14 **Paul**	Y	Y	N	Y	N	N	N
15 Hinojosa	Y	N	Y	Y	Y	Y	Y
16 Reyes	Y	N	Y	Y	Y	Y	Y
17 Edwards	Y	N	Y	Y	Y	Y	Y
18 Jackson Lee	N	N	Y	Y	Y	Y	Y
19 **Neugebauer**	Y	Y	Y	N	N	N	N
20 Gonzalez	Y	N	Y	Y	Y	Y	Y
21 **Smith**	Y	Y	Y	N	N	N	N
22 **Olson**	Y	Y	Y	Y	N	N	N
23 Rodriguez	Y	N	Y	Y	Y	Y	Y
24 **Marchant**	Y	N	Y	N	N	N	N
25 Doggett	N	N	Y	Y	Y	Y	Y
26 **Burgess**	Y	N	Y	N	N	N	N
27 Ortiz	Y	N	Y	Y	Y	Y	Y
28 Cuellar	Y	N	Y	Y	Y	Y	Y
29 Green, G.	Y	N	Y	Y	?	Y	Y
30 Johnson, E.	N	N	Y	Y	Y	Y	Y
31 **Carter**	Y	N	Y	N	N	N	N
32 **Sessions**	Y	N	Y	N	N	N	N
UTAH							
1 **Bishop**	Y	Y	Y	N	N	N	N
2 Matheson	Y	N	Y	Y	N	N	N
3 **Chaffetz**	Y	Y	Y	Y	N	N	N
VERMONT							
AL Welch	Y	N	Y	Y	Y	Y	Y
VIRGINIA							
1 **Wittman**	Y	N	Y	N	N	N	N
2 Nye	Y	N	Y	N	N	N	N
3 Scott	N	N	Y	Y	Y	Y	Y
4 **Forbes**	Y	N	Y	N	N	N	N
5 Perriello	Y	N	Y	N	Y	Y	Y
6 **Goodlatte**	Y	N	Y	N	N	N	N
7 **Cantor**	Y	Y	Y	N	N	N	N
8 Moran	N	N	Y	Y	Y	Y	Y
9 Boucher	Y	N	Y	Y	Y	Y	Y
10 **Wolf**	Y	N	Y	N	N	N	N
11 Connolly	Y	N	Y	N	Y	Y	Y
WASHINGTON							
1 Inslee	N	N	Y	Y	Y	Y	Y
2 Larsen	Y	N	Y	Y	Y	Y	Y
3 Baird	N	N	Y	Y	Y	Y	Y
4 **Hastings**	Y	Y	Y	N	N	N	N
5 **McMorris Rodgers**	Y	N	Y	N	N	N	N
6 Dicks	Y	N	Y	Y	Y	Y	Y
7 McDermott	N	N	Y	Y	Y	Y	Y
8 **Reichert**	Y	N	Y	N	N	N	N
9 Smith	N	N	Y	Y	Y	Y	Y
WEST VIRGINIA							
1 Mollohan	Y	N	Y	Y	Y	Y	Y
2 **Capito**	Y	Y	Y	N	N	N	N
3 Rahall	Y	Y	Y	Y	Y	Y	Y
WISCONSIN							
1 **Ryan**	Y	Y	Y	N	N	N	N
2 Baldwin	N	N	Y	Y	Y	Y	Y
3 Kind	Y	N	Y	Y	Y	Y	Y
4 Moore	N	N	Y	Y	Y	Y	Y
5 **Sensenbrenner**	Y	Y	N	N	N	N	N
6 **Petri**	Y	Y	Y	N	N	N	N
7 Obey	Y	N	Y	Y	Y	Y	Y
8 Kagen	Y	N	Y	Y	Y	Y	Y
WYOMING							
AL **Lummis**	Y	Y	Y	Y	N	N	N
DELEGATES							
Faleomavaega (A.S.)	?	?					
Norton (D.C.)	N	N					
Bordallo (Guam)	N	N					
Sablan (N. Marianas)	N	N					
Pierluisi (P.R.)	N	N					
Christensen (V.I.)	N	N					

www.cq.com | 2010 CQ ALMANAC H-169

IN THE HOUSE | By Vote Number

487. **HR 3040. Senior Fraud Education/Passage.** Scott, D-Va., motion to suspend the rules and pass the bill that would authorize $150 million over five years for the Federal Trade Commission and Justice Department to conduct consumer education and outreach programs regarding fraud targeting senior citizens. Motion agreed to 335-81: D 246-2; R 89-79. A two-thirds majority of those present and voting (278 in this case) is required for passage under suspension of the rules. July 29, 2010.

488. **HR 5850. Fiscal 2011 Transportation-HUD Appropriations/ Transformation Initiative Funds.** Boehner, R-Ohio, amendment that would reduce funding for the Department of Housing and Urban Development's Transformation Initiative by $40 million. Rejected in Committee of the Whole 206-217: D 41-214; R 165-3. July 29, 2010.

489. **HR 5850. Fiscal 2011 Transportation-HUD Appropriations/ Funding Decrease.** Latham, R-Iowa, amendment that would cut $1.8 billion from funds provided for specific accounts in the bill, including $400 million for national infrastructure investment, $400 million for capital assistance for high-speed rail corridors and intercity passenger rail service, and $456 million for the public housing capital fund. Rejected in Committee of the Whole 197-225: D 30-224; R 167-1. July 29, 2010.

490. **HR 5850. Fiscal 2011 Transportation-HUD Appropriations/ Spending Reduction.** Culberson, R-Texas, amendment that would reduce spending in the bill by $12.4 billion. Rejected in Committee of the Whole 169-252: D 13-240; R 156-12. July 29, 2010.

491. **HR 847. Sept. 11 Health and Compensation Fund/Passage.** Pallone, D-N.J., motion to suspend the rules and pass the bill that would create a program to provide medical services and health monitoring for first-responders and others with conditions related to the Sept. 11 attacks. It also would reopen the Sept. 11 Victim Compensation Fund to provide compensation for economic losses and amend tax-withholding rules for certain payments made by U.S. subsidiaries of foreign corporations. Motion rejected 255-159: D 243-4; R 12-155. A two-thirds majority of those present and voting (276 in this case) is required for passage under suspension of the rules. July 29, 2010.

492. **HR 5850. Fiscal 2011 Transportation-HUD Appropriations/ Spending Reduction.** Neugebauer, R-Texas, amendment that would reduce spending in the bill by $10.5 billion. Rejected in Committee of the Whole 177-247: D 12-244; R 165-3. A "nay" was a vote in support of the president's position. July 29, 2010.

493. **HR 5850. Fiscal 2011 Transportation-HUD Appropriations/ Spending Reduction.** Jordan, R-Ohio, amendment that would reduce spending in the bill by $18.6 billion. Rejected in Committee of the Whole 159-265: D 7-250; R 152-15. July 29, 2010.

	487	488	489	490	491	492	493
ALABAMA							
1 **Bonner**	Y	Y	Y	Y	N	Y	Y
2 **Bright**	Y	Y	Y	N	Y	Y	Y
3 **Rogers**	Y	Y	Y	Y	N	Y	Y
4 **Aderholt**	Y	Y	Y	Y	N	Y	Y
5 **Griffith**	Y	?	?	?	?	?	?
6 **Bachus**	Y	Y	Y	Y	N	Y	Y
7 Davis	Y	Y	N	N	Y	N	N
ALASKA							
AL **Young**	N	Y	Y	N	Y	Y	N
ARIZONA							
1 Kirkpatrick	Y	Y	Y	Y	Y	Y	Y
2 **Franks**	N	Y	Y	Y	N	Y	Y
3 **Shadegg**	?	?	?	?	?	?	?
4 Pastor	Y	N	N	N	Y	N	N
5 Mitchell	Y	Y	Y	Y	N	N	N
6 **Flake**	N	Y	Y	N	Y	Y	Y
7 Grijalva	Y	N	N	N	?	N	N
8 Giffords	Y	Y	Y	Y	Y	Y	Y
ARKANSAS							
1 Berry	Y	N	N	N	N	N	N
2 Snyder	Y	N	N	N	Y	N	N
3 **Boozman**	Y	Y	Y	N	N	Y	Y
4 Ross	Y	N	N	N	Y	N	N
CALIFORNIA							
1 Thompson	Y	N	N	N	Y	N	N
2 **Herger**	N	Y	Y	Y	N	Y	Y
3 **Lungren**	Y	Y	Y	Y	N	Y	Y
4 **McClintock**	N	Y	Y	Y	N	Y	Y
5 Matsui	Y	N	N	N	Y	N	N
6 Woolsey	Y	N	N	N	Y	N	N
7 Miller, George	Y	N	N	N	Y	N	N
8 Pelosi							
9 Lee	Y	N	N	N	Y	N	N
10 Garamendi	Y	N	N	N	Y	N	N
11 McNerney	Y	Y	N	N	Y	N	N
12 Speier	Y	N	N	N	Y	N	N
13 Stark	Y	N	N	N	Y	N	N
14 Eshoo	Y	N	N	N	Y	N	N
15 Honda	Y	N	N	N	Y	N	N
16 Lofgren	Y	N	N	N	Y	N	N
17 Farr	Y	N	N	N	Y	N	N
18 Cardoza	Y	N	N	N	Y	N	N
19 **Radanovich**	N	?	?	?	?	?	?
20 Costa	Y	N	N	N	Y	N	N
21 **Nunes**	N	Y	Y	Y	N	Y	Y
22 **McCarthy**	N	?	?	?	?	?	?
23 Capps	Y	N	N	N	Y	N	N
24 **Gallegly**	Y	Y	Y	Y	N	Y	Y
25 **McKeon**	N	Y	Y	Y	N	Y	Y
26 **Dreier**	Y	Y	Y	Y	N	Y	Y
27 Sherman	Y	N	N	N	Y	N	N
28 Berman	Y	N	N	N	Y	N	N
29 Schiff	Y	N	N	N	Y	N	N
30 Waxman	?	N	N	Y	N	N	N
31 Becerra	Y	N	N	N	Y	N	N
32 Chu	Y	N	N	N	Y	N	N
33 Watson	?	?	?	?	?	?	?
34 Roybal-Allard	Y	N	N	N	Y	N	N
35 Waters	Y	N	N	N	Y	N	N
36 Harman	Y	N	N	N	Y	N	N
37 Richardson	Y	N	N	N	Y	N	N
38 Napolitano	Y	N	N	N	Y	N	N
39 Sánchez, Linda	Y	N	N	N	Y	N	N
40 **Royce**	N	Y	Y	Y	N	Y	Y
41 **Lewis**	Y	Y	Y	Y	N	Y	Y
42 **Miller, Gary**	N	Y	Y	Y	N	Y	Y
43 Baca	Y	N	N	N	Y	N	N
44 **Calvert**	Y	Y	Y	Y	N	Y	Y
45 **Bono Mack**	N	Y	Y	Y	N	Y	Y
46 **Rohrabacher**	N	Y	Y	Y	N	Y	Y
47 Sanchez, Loretta	Y	N	N	N	Y	N	N
48 **Campbell**	N	Y	Y	Y	N	Y	Y
49 **Issa**	N	Y	Y	Y	N	Y	Y
50 **Bilbray**	Y	Y	Y	Y	N	Y	Y
51 Filner	Y	N	N	N	Y	N	N
52 **Hunter**	N	Y	Y	Y	N	Y	Y
53 Davis	Y	N	N	N	Y	N	N

	487	488	489	490	491	492	493
COLORADO							
1 DeGette	Y	N	N	N	Y	N	N
2 Polis	Y	N	N	N	Y	N	N
3 Salazar	Y	N	N	N	Y	N	N
4 Markey	Y	N	N	Y	Y	N	N
5 **Lamborn**	N	Y	Y	Y	N	Y	Y
6 **Coffman**	N	Y	Y	N	Y	Y	Y
7 Perlmutter	Y	N	N	N	Y	N	N
CONNECTICUT							
1 Larson	Y	N	N	N	Y	N	N
2 Courtney	Y	N	N	N	Y	N	N
3 DeLauro	Y	N	N	N	Y	N	N
4 Himes	Y	Y	Y	N	Y	N	N
5 Murphy	Y	N	N	N	Y	N	N
DELAWARE							
AL Castle	Y	Y	Y	N	N	N	N
FLORIDA							
1 **Miller**	N	Y	Y	Y	N	Y	Y
2 Boyd	Y	N	N	N	Y	N	N
3 Brown	Y	N	N	N	Y	N	N
4 **Crenshaw**	Y	Y	Y	Y	N	Y	Y
5 **Brown-Waite**	Y	Y	Y	N	N	Y	Y
6 **Stearns**	N	Y	Y	Y	N	Y	Y
7 **Mica**	Y	Y	Y	Y	N	Y	Y
8 Grayson	Y	N	N	Y	N	Y	N
9 **Bilirakis**	Y	Y	Y	Y	N	Y	Y
10 Young	?	?	?	?	?	?	?
11 Castor	Y	N	N	N	Y	N	N
12 **Putnam**	Y	Y	Y	Y	N	Y	Y
13 **Buchanan**	Y	Y	Y	Y	N	Y	Y
14 **Mack**	N	Y	Y	Y	N	Y	Y
15 **Posey**	Y	Y	Y	Y	N	Y	Y
16 **Rooney**	Y	Y	Y	Y	N	Y	Y
17 Meek	Y	N	N	N	Y	N	N
18 **Ros-Lehtinen**	Y	Y	Y	Y	N	Y	Y
19 Deutch	Y	N	N	N	Y	N	N
20 Wasserman Schultz	Y	N	N	N	Y	N	N
21 **Diaz-Balart, L.**	Y	Y	Y	Y	N	Y	Y
22 Klein	Y	N	N	N	Y	N	N
23 Hastings	Y	N	N	N	Y	N	N
24 Kosmas	Y	N	N	N	Y	N	N
25 **Diaz-Balart, M.**	Y	Y	Y	Y	N	Y	Y
GEORGIA							
1 **Kingston**	N	Y	Y	Y	N	Y	Y
2 Bishop	Y	N	N	N	Y	N	N
3 **Westmoreland**	N	Y	Y	Y	N	Y	Y
4 Johnson	Y	N	N	N	Y	N	N
5 Lewis	Y	N	N	N	Y	N	N
6 **Price**	N	Y	Y	Y	N	Y	Y
7 **Linder**	?	Y	Y	Y	N	Y	Y
8 Marshall	Y	N	N	N	Y	N	N
9 **Graves**	N	Y	Y	Y	N	Y	Y
10 **Broun**	N	Y	Y	Y	N	Y	Y
11 **Gingrey**	N	Y	Y	Y	N	Y	Y
12 Barrow	Y	N	N	N	Y	N	N
13 Scott	Y	N	N	N	Y	N	N
HAWAII							
1 **Djou**	Y	Y	Y	N	Y	Y	N
2 Hirono	Y	N	N	N	Y	N	N
IDAHO							
1 Minnick	Y	Y	Y	Y	Y	Y	Y
2 **Simpson**	N	Y	Y	Y	N	Y	Y
ILLINOIS							
1 Rush	Y	N	N	N	Y	N	N
2 Jackson	Y	N	N	N	Y	N	N
3 Lipinski	Y	N	N	N	Y	N	N
4 Gutierrez	Y	N	?	?	Y	N	N
5 Quigley	Y	N	N	N	Y	N	N
6 **Roskam**	N	Y	Y	Y	N	Y	Y
7 Davis	Y	N	N	N	Y	N	N
8 Bean	N	Y	Y	N	N	Y	N
9 Schakowsky	Y	N	N	N	Y	N	N
10 **Kirk**	Y	Y	Y	N	Y	N	N
11 Halvorson	Y	N	N	N	Y	N	N
12 Costello	Y	N	N	N	Y	N	N
13 **Biggert**	Y	Y	Y	Y	N	Y	Y
14 Foster	Y	Y	Y	N	Y	N	N
15 **Johnson**	N	Y	Y	Y	N	Y	Y

KEY   **Republicans**   Democrats

Y Voted for (yea)	**X** Paired against
# Paired for	**–** Announced against
+ Announced for	**P** Voted "present"
N Voted against (nay)	

C Voted "present" to avoid possible conflict of interest

? Did not vote or otherwise make a position known

	487	488	489	490	491	492	493
16 **Manzullo**	N	Y	Y	Y	N	Y	Y
17 Hare	Y	N	N	N	Y	N	N
18 **Schock**	?	Y	Y	Y	N	Y	Y
19 **Shimkus**	Y	Y	Y	Y	N	Y	Y
INDIANA							
1 Visclosky	Y	N	N	N	Y	N	N
2 Donnelly	Y	Y	Y	N	Y	Y	N
3 Vacant							
4 **Buyer**	N	N	Y	Y	N	Y	Y
5 **Burton**	N	Y	Y	Y	N	Y	Y
6 **Pence**	N	Y	Y	Y	N	Y	Y
7 Carson	Y	?	N	N	Y	N	N
8 Ellsworth	Y	Y	N	N	Y	N	N
9 Hill	Y	N	Y	N	Y	N	N
IOWA							
1 Braley	Y	N	N	N	Y	N	N
2 Loebsack	?	N	N	N	Y	N	N
3 Boswell	Y	N	N	N	Y	N	N
4 **Latham**	Y	Y	Y	Y	N	Y	Y
5 **King**	N	Y	Y	Y	N	Y	Y
KANSAS							
1 **Moran**	?	?	?	?	?	?	?
2 **Jenkins**	Y	Y	Y	Y	N	Y	Y
3 Moore	Y	N	Y	N	Y	N	N
4 **Tiahrt**	?	?	?	?	?	?	?
KENTUCKY							
1 **Whitfield**	Y	Y	Y	Y	N	Y	Y
2 **Guthrie**	Y	Y	Y	Y	?	Y	Y
3 Yarmuth	Y	?	?	?	Y	N	N
4 **Davis**	Y	Y	Y	Y	N	Y	Y
5 **Rogers**	Y	Y	Y	Y	N	Y	Y
6 Chandler	Y	Y	N	N	Y	N	N
LOUISIANA							
1 **Scalise**	Y	Y	Y	Y	N	Y	Y
2 **Cao**	Y	N	Y	N	Y	N	N
3 Melancon	Y	N	Y	N	Y	N	N
4 **Fleming**	N	Y	Y	Y	N	Y	Y
5 **Alexander**	Y	Y	Y	Y	N	Y	Y
6 **Cassidy**	Y	Y	Y	Y	N	Y	Y
7 **Boustany**	Y	Y	Y	Y	N	Y	Y
MAINE							
1 Pingree	Y	N	N	N	Y	N	N
2 Michaud	Y	N	Y	N	Y	N	N
MARYLAND							
1 Kratovil	Y	Y	Y	N	Y	N	N
2 Ruppersberger	Y	N	N	N	Y	N	N
3 Sarbanes	Y	N	N	N	Y	N	N
4 Edwards	Y	N	N	N	Y	N	N
5 Hoyer	Y	N	N	N	Y	N	N
6 **Bartlett**	N	Y	Y	Y	N	Y	Y
7 Cummings	Y	N	N	N	Y	N	N
8 Van Hollen	Y	N	N	N	Y	N	N
MASSACHUSETTS							
1 Olver	Y	N	N	N	Y	N	N
2 Neal	Y	N	N	N	Y	N	N
3 McGovern	Y	N	N	N	Y	N	N
4 Frank	?	N	N	N	Y	N	N
5 Tsongas	Y	N	N	N	Y	N	N
6 Tierney	Y	N	N	N	Y	Y	N
7 Markey	Y	N	N	N	Y	N	N
8 Capuano	Y	N	N	N	Y	N	N
9 Lynch	?	?	?	?	Y	N	N
10 Delahunt	Y	N	N	N	Y	N	N
MICHIGAN							
1 Stupak	Y	N	N	N	Y	N	N
2 **Hoekstra**	?	?	?	?	?	?	?
3 **Ehlers**	Y	Y	Y	Y	N	Y	Y
4 **Camp**	N	Y	Y	Y	N	Y	Y
5 Kildee	Y	N	N	N	Y	N	N
6 **Upton**	N	Y	Y	Y	N	Y	Y
7 Schauer	Y	Y	N	N	Y	N	N
8 **Rogers**	N	Y	Y	Y	N	Y	Y
9 Peters	Y	Y	Y	Y	Y	N	N
10 **Miller**	N	Y	Y	Y	Y	Y	Y
11 **McCotter**	Y	Y	Y	Y	N	Y	Y
12 Levin	Y	N	N	N	Y	N	N
13 Kilpatrick	Y	N	?	?	?	?	?
14 Conyers	Y	N	N	N	?	N	N
15 Dingell	Y	N	N	N	Y	N	N
MINNESOTA							
1 Walz	Y	N	N	N	Y	N	N
2 **Kline**	Y	Y	Y	Y	N	Y	Y
3 **Paulsen**	Y	Y	Y	Y	N	Y	Y
4 McCollum	Y	N	N	N	Y	N	N

	487	488	489	490	491	492	493
5 Ellison	Y	N	N	N	Y	N	N
6 **Bachmann**	Y	Y	Y	Y	N	Y	Y
7 Peterson	Y	Y	Y	N	Y	N	N
8 Oberstar	Y	N	N	N	Y	N	N
MISSISSIPPI							
1 Childers	Y	Y	Y	N	Y	Y	N
2 Thompson	Y	N	N	N	Y	N	N
3 **Harper**	Y	Y	Y	Y	N	Y	Y
4 Taylor	Y	Y	Y	Y	Y	Y	N
MISSOURI							
1 Clay	Y	N	N	N	?	N	N
2 **Akin**	+	+	+	+	?	?	?
3 Carnahan	Y	N	N	N	Y	N	N
4 Skelton	Y	N	N	N	Y	N	N
5 Cleaver	Y	N	N	N	Y	N	N
6 **Graves**	Y	Y	Y	Y	N	Y	Y
7 **Blunt**	Y	Y	Y	Y	N	Y	Y
8 **Emerson**	Y	Y	Y	Y	N	Y	Y
9 **Luetkemeyer**	Y	Y	Y	Y	N	Y	Y
MONTANA							
AL **Rehberg**	Y	Y	Y	Y	N	Y	Y
NEBRASKA							
1 **Fortenberry**	Y	Y	Y	Y	N	Y	Y
2 **Terry**	Y	Y	Y	Y	N	Y	Y
3 **Smith**	Y	Y	Y	Y	N	Y	Y
NEVADA							
1 Berkley	Y	N	N	N	Y	N	N
2 **Heller**	Y	Y	Y	Y	N	Y	Y
3 Titus	Y	N	N	N	Y	N	N
NEW HAMPSHIRE							
1 Shea-Porter	Y	N	N	N	Y	N	N
2 Hodes	Y	Y	N	Y	Y	N	Y
NEW JERSEY							
1 Andrews	?	?	?	?	Y	N	N
2 **LoBiondo**	Y	Y	Y	N	Y	Y	N
3 Adler	Y	Y	Y	N	Y	N	N
4 **Smith**	Y	Y	Y	N	Y	Y	N
5 **Garrett**	N	Y	Y	Y	N	Y	Y
6 Pallone	Y	N	N	N	Y	N	N
7 **Lance**	Y	Y	Y	Y	Y	Y	Y
8 Pascrell	Y	N	N	N	Y	N	N
9 Rothman	Y	N	N	N	Y	N	N
10 Payne	Y	N	N	N	Y	N	N
11 **Frelinghuysen**	Y	Y	Y	Y	Y	Y	Y
12 Holt	Y	N	N	N	Y	N	N
13 Sires	Y	N	N	N	Y	N	N
NEW MEXICO							
1 Heinrich	Y	Y	Y	N	Y	N	N
2 Teague	Y	Y	N	N	Y	N	N
3 Luján	Y	N	N	N	Y	N	N
NEW YORK							
1 Bishop	Y	N	N	N	Y	N	N
2 Israel	Y	N	N	N	Y	N	N
3 **King**	Y	Y	Y	N	Y	Y	Y
4 McCarthy	Y	N	N	N	Y	N	N
5 Ackerman	Y	N	N	N	Y	N	N
6 Meeks	Y	N	N	N	Y	N	N
7 Crowley	Y	N	N	N	Y	N	N
8 Nadler	Y	N	N	N	Y	N	N
9 Weiner	Y	N	N	N	Y	N	N
10 Towns	Y	N	N	N	Y	N	N
11 Clarke	Y	N	N	N	Y	N	N
12 Velázquez	Y	N	N	N	Y	N	N
13 McMahon	Y	Y	Y	N	Y	N	N
14 Maloney	Y	N	N	N	Y	N	N
15 Rangel	Y	N	N	N	Y	N	N
16 Serrano	Y	N	N	N	Y	N	N
17 Engel	Y	N	N	N	Y	N	N
18 Lowey	Y	N	N	N	Y	N	N
19 Hall	Y	N	N	N	Y	N	N
20 Murphy	Y	Y	Y	Y	Y	N	N
21 Tonko	Y	N	N	N	Y	N	N
22 Hinchey	Y	N	N	N	Y	N	N
23 Owens	Y	Y	Y	N	Y	N	N
24 Arcuri	Y	Y	N	N	Y	N	N
25 Maffei	Y	Y	N	N	Y	N	N
26 **Lee**	Y	Y	Y	Y	N	Y	Y
27 Higgins	Y	N	N	N	Y	N	N
28 Slaughter	Y	N	N	N	Y	N	N
29 Vacant							
NORTH CAROLINA							
1 Butterfield	Y	N	N	N	Y	N	N
2 Etheridge	Y	N	N	N	Y	N	N
3 **Jones**	Y	Y	Y	Y	Y	Y	Y
4 Price	Y	N	N	N	Y	N	N

	487	488	489	490	491	492	493
5 **Foxx**	N	Y	Y	Y	N	Y	Y
6 **Coble**	N	Y	Y	Y	N	Y	Y
7 McIntyre	Y	N	N	N	Y	N	N
8 Kissell	Y	N	N	N	Y	N	N
9 **Myrick**	N	Y	Y	Y	N	Y	Y
10 **McHenry**	Y	Y	Y	Y	N	Y	Y
11 Shuler	Y	N	Y	N	Y	N	N
12 Watt	Y	N	N	N	?	N	N
13 Miller	Y	N	N	N	Y	N	N
NORTH DAKOTA							
AL Pomeroy	Y	N	N	N	Y	N	N
OHIO							
1 Driehaus	Y	N	Y	N	Y	N	N
2 **Schmidt**	N	Y	Y	Y	N	Y	Y
3 **Turner**	Y	Y	Y	Y	N	Y	N
4 **Jordan**	N	Y	Y	Y	N	Y	Y
5 **Latta**	N	Y	Y	Y	N	Y	Y
6 Wilson	Y	N	N	N	Y	N	N
7 **Austria**	Y	Y	Y	Y	N	Y	Y
8 **Boehner**	N	Y	Y	Y	N	Y	Y
9 Kaptur	Y	N	N	N	Y	N	N
10 Kucinich	Y	N	N	N	Y	N	N
11 Fudge	Y	N	N	N	Y	N	N
12 **Tiberi**	N	Y	Y	Y	N	Y	Y
13 Sutton	Y	N	N	N	Y	N	N
14 **LaTourette**	Y	Y	Y	N	N	N	N
15 Kilroy	Y	N	N	N	Y	N	N
16 Boccieri	Y	N	N	N	Y	N	N
17 Ryan	Y	N	N	N	Y	N	N
18 Space	Y	N	N	N	Y	N	N
OKLAHOMA							
1 **Sullivan**	Y	Y	Y	Y	N	Y	Y
2 Boren	Y	Y	N	N	Y	N	N
3 **Lucas**	Y	Y	Y	Y	N	Y	Y
4 **Cole**	Y	Y	Y	Y	N	Y	Y
5 **Fallin**	Y	Y	Y	Y	N	Y	Y
OREGON							
1 Wu	Y	N	N	N	Y	N	N
2 **Walden**	N	Y	Y	Y	N	Y	Y
3 Blumenauer	Y	N	N	N	Y	N	N
4 DeFazio	Y	Y	N	N	Y	N	N
5 Schrader	Y	N	N	N	Y	N	N
PENNSYLVANIA							
1 Brady	Y	N	N	N	Y	N	N
2 Fattah	Y	N	N	N	Y	N	N
3 Dahlkemper	Y	Y	N	N	Y	N	N
4 Altmire	Y	Y	N	Y	Y	N	N
5 **Thompson**	N	Y	Y	Y	N	Y	Y
6 **Gerlach**	Y	Y	Y	N	N	Y	N
7 Sestak	Y	N	N	N	Y	N	N
8 Murphy, P.	Y	Y	N	N	Y	N	N
9 **Shuster**	?	Y	Y	Y	N	Y	Y
10 Carney	Y	N	Y	N	?	?	?
11 Kanjorski	Y	N	N	N	Y	N	N
12 Critz	Y	N	N	N	Y	N	N
13 Schwartz	Y	N	N	N	Y	N	N
14 Doyle	Y	N	N	N	Y	N	N
15 **Dent**	Y	Y	Y	Y	N	Y	N
16 **Pitts**	Y	Y	Y	Y	N	Y	Y
17 Holden	Y	N	N	N	Y	N	N
18 **Murphy, T.**	Y	Y	Y	N	Y	Y	N
19 **Platts**	Y	Y	Y	Y	N	Y	N
RHODE ISLAND							
1 Kennedy	Y	N	N	N	Y	N	N
2 Langevin	Y	N	N	N	Y	N	N
SOUTH CAROLINA							
1 **Brown**	N	Y	Y	Y	N	Y	Y
2 **Wilson**	N	Y	Y	Y	N	Y	Y
3 **Barrett**	N	Y	Y	Y	N	Y	Y
4 **Inglis**	N	Y	Y	Y	N	Y	Y
5 Spratt	Y	N	N	N	Y	N	N
6 Clyburn	Y	N	N	N	Y	N	N
SOUTH DAKOTA							
AL Herseth Sandlin	Y	Y	N	Y	Y	Y	N
TENNESSEE							
1 **Roe**	N	Y	Y	Y	N	Y	Y
2 **Duncan**	N	Y	Y	Y	N	Y	Y
3 **Wamp**	?	?	?	?	?	?	?
4 Davis	Y	N	N	N	Y	?	N
5 Cooper	Y	Y	Y	N	N	Y	N
6 Gordon	Y	N	N	N	Y	N	N
7 **Blackburn**	N	Y	Y	Y	N	Y	Y
8 Tanner	Y	N	Y	N	Y	N	N
9 Cohen	Y	N	N	N	Y	N	N

	487	488	489	490	491	492	493
TEXAS							
1 **Gohmert**	Y	Y	Y	Y	N	Y	Y
2 **Poe**	Y	Y	Y	Y	N	Y	Y
3 **Johnson, S.**	N	Y	Y	Y	N	Y	Y
4 **Hall**	Y	Y	Y	Y	N	Y	Y
5 **Hensarling**	N	Y	Y	Y	N	Y	Y
6 **Barton**	N	Y	Y	Y	N	Y	Y
7 **Culberson**	Y	Y	Y	Y	N	Y	Y
8 **Brady**	N	Y	Y	Y	N	Y	Y
9 Green, A.	Y	N	N	N	Y	N	N
10 **McCaul**	Y	Y	Y	Y	N	Y	Y
11 **Conaway**	N	Y	Y	Y	N	Y	Y
12 **Granger**	Y	Y	Y	Y	N	Y	?
13 **Thornberry**	N	Y	Y	Y	N	Y	Y
14 **Paul**	N	Y	Y	Y	N	Y	Y
15 Hinojosa	Y	N	N	N	Y	N	N
16 Reyes	Y	N	N	N	Y	N	N
17 Edwards	Y	N	N	N	Y	N	N
18 Jackson Lee	Y	N	N	N	Y	N	N
19 **Neugebauer**	Y	Y	Y	Y	N	Y	Y
20 Gonzalez	Y	N	N	N	Y	N	N
21 **Smith**	Y	Y	Y	Y	N	Y	Y
22 **Olson**	N	Y	Y	Y	N	Y	Y
23 Rodriguez	Y	N	N	N	Y	N	N
24 **Marchant**	N	Y	Y	Y	N	Y	Y
25 Doggett	Y	N	N	N	Y	N	N
26 **Burgess**	N	Y	Y	Y	N	Y	Y
27 Ortiz	Y	N	N	N	Y	N	N
28 Cuellar	Y	N	N	N	Y	N	N
29 Green, G.	Y	N	N	N	Y	N	N
30 Johnson, E.	Y	N	N	N	Y	N	N
31 **Carter**	N	Y	Y	Y	N	Y	Y
32 **Sessions**	Y	Y	Y	Y	N	Y	Y
UTAH							
1 **Bishop**	N	Y	Y	Y	N	Y	Y
2 Matheson	Y	Y	Y	N	Y	Y	N
3 **Chaffetz**	N	Y	Y	Y	N	Y	Y
VERMONT							
AL Welch	Y	N	N	N	Y	N	N
VIRGINIA							
1 **Wittman**	Y	Y	Y	Y	N	Y	N
2 Nye	Y	Y	N	Y	Y	N	Y
3 Scott	Y	N	N	N	Y	N	N
4 **Forbes**	Y	Y	Y	Y	N	Y	Y
5 Perriello	Y	N	N	N	Y	N	N
6 **Goodlatte**	N	Y	Y	Y	N	Y	Y
7 **Cantor**	N	Y	Y	Y	N	Y	Y
8 Moran	Y	N	N	N	Y	N	N
9 Boucher	Y	Y	N	N	Y	N	N
10 **Wolf**	Y	Y	Y	Y	N	Y	N
11 Connolly	Y	Y	N	?	Y	N	N
WASHINGTON							
1 Inslee	Y	N	N	N	Y	N	N
2 Larsen	Y	N	N	N	Y	N	N
3 Baird	N	N	N	N	Y	N	N
4 **Hastings**	N	Y	Y	Y	N	Y	Y
5 **McMorris Rodgers**	Y	Y	Y	Y	N	Y	Y
6 Dicks	Y	N	N	N	Y	N	N
7 McDermott	Y	N	N	N	Y	N	N
8 **Reichert**	Y	Y	Y	Y	N	Y	Y
9 Smith	Y	N	Y	N	Y	N	N
WEST VIRGINIA							
1 Mollohan	Y	N	N	N	Y	N	N
2 **Capito**	Y	Y	Y	Y	N	Y	Y
3 Rahall	Y	N	N	N	Y	N	N
WISCONSIN							
1 **Ryan**	N	Y	Y	Y	N	Y	Y
2 Baldwin	Y	N	N	N	Y	N	N
3 Kind	Y	N	N	N	Y	N	N
4 Moore	Y	N	N	N	Y	N	N
5 **Sensenbrenner**	N	Y	Y	Y	N	Y	Y
6 **Petri**	N	Y	Y	Y	N	Y	Y
7 Obey	Y	N	N	N	Y	N	N
8 Kagen	Y	N	N	N	Y	N	N
WYOMING							
AL **Lummis**	N	Y	Y	Y	N	Y	Y
DELEGATES							
Faleomavaega (A.S.)		N	N	N		N	N
Norton (D.C.)		N	N	N		N	N
Bordallo (Guam)		N	N	N		N	N
Sablan (N. Marianas)		N	N	N		N	N
Pierluisi (P.R.)		N	N	N		N	N
Christensen (V.I.)		N	N	N		N	N

IN THE HOUSE | By Vote Number

494. HR 5850. Fiscal 2011 Transportation-HUD Appropriations/ **Amtrak.** Flake, R-Ariz., amendment that would strike $1.2 billion in funding provided for capital investments and debt service grants to Amtrak. Rejected in Committee of the Whole 129-293: D 6-250; R 123-43. July 29, 2010.

495. HR 5850. Fiscal 2011 Transportation-HUD Appropriations/ **Blackstone River Bikeway.** Flake, R-Ariz., amendment that would strike $1 million in funding provided for the Blackstone River Bikeway in Rhode Island. Rejected in Committee of the Whole 163-260: D 12-243; R 151-17. July 29, 2010.

496. HR 5850. Fiscal 2011 Transportation-HUD Appropriations/ **Tacoma Downtown Streetscapes.** Flake, R-Ariz., amendment that would strike $1 million in funding provided for a downtown streetscapes improvement project in Tacoma, Wash. Rejected in Committee of the Whole 157-267: D 9-247; R 148-20. July 29, 2010.

497. HR 5850. Fiscal 2011 Transportation-HUD Appropriations/ **Darwin Martin House Home.** Flake, R-Ariz., amendment that would strike $1 million in funding provided for the restoration and improvements to the historical Darwin Martin House Home and complex in New York. Rejected in Committee of the Whole 165-258: D 14-242; R 151-16. July 29, 2010.

498. HR 5850. Fiscal 2011 Transportation-HUD Appropriations/ **Yauco Playground.** Flake, R-Ariz., amendment that would strike $150,000 in funding provided for the construction of a children's playground in the municipality of Yauco, Puerto Rico. Rejected in Committee of the Whole 159-264: D 13-243; R 146-21. July 29, 2010.

499. HR 5850. Fiscal 2011 Transportation-HUD Appropriations/ **Passage.** Passage of the bill that would appropriate $126.3 billion in fiscal 2011, including $67.4 billion in discretionary spending, for the departments of Transportation and Housing and Urban Development and related agencies. It would provide $79.4 billion for the Transportation Department, including $16.5 billion for the Federal Aviation Administration, $45.2 billion for highway programs and $11.3 billion for transit programs. It also would provide $46.6 billion for the Housing and Urban Development Department, including $19.4 billion for the tenant-based Section 8 rental assistance program. Passed 251-167: D 237-13; R 14-154. A "yea" was a vote in support of the president's position. July 29, 2010.

	494	495	496	497	498	499
ALABAMA						
1 Bonner	Y	N	N	N	N	N
2 Bright	Y	Y	Y	Y	Y	Y
3 Rogers	Y	N	N	N	N	N
4 Aderholt	N	N	N	?	N	N
5 Griffith	?	?	?	?	?	?
6 Bachus	N	N	N	N	N	N
7 Davis	N	N	N	N	N	Y
ALASKA						
AL Young	N	N	N	N	N	Y
ARIZONA						
1 Kirkpatrick	Y	N	N	N	Y	Y
2 Franks	Y	Y	Y	Y	Y	N
3 Shadegg	?	?	?	?	?	?
4 Pastor	N	N	N	N	N	Y
5 Mitchell	N	Y	Y	Y	Y	Y
6 Flake	Y	Y	Y	Y	Y	N
7 Grijalva	N	N	N	N	N	Y
8 Giffords	N	Y	N	Y	Y	Y
ARKANSAS						
1 Berry	N	N	N	N	N	Y
2 Snyder	N	N	N	N	N	Y
3 Boozman	Y	Y	Y	Y	N	Y
4 Ross	N	N	N	N	N	Y
CALIFORNIA						
1 Thompson	N	N	N	N	N	Y
2 Herger	Y	Y	Y	Y	Y	N
3 Lungren	Y	Y	Y	Y	Y	N
4 McClintock	Y	Y	Y	Y	Y	N
5 Matsui	N	N	N	N	N	Y
6 Woolsey	N	N	N	N	N	Y
7 Miller, George	N	N	N	N	N	Y
8 Pelosi						
9 Lee	N	N	N	N	N	Y
10 Garamendi	N	N	N	N	N	Y
11 McNerney	N	N	N	N	N	Y
12 Speier	N	N	N	N	N	Y
13 Stark	N	N	N	N	N	Y
14 Eshoo	N	N	N	N	N	Y
15 Honda	N	N	N	N	N	Y
16 Lofgren	N	N	N	N	N	Y
17 Farr	N	N	N	N	N	Y
18 Cardoza	?	N	N	N	N	Y
19 Radanovich	?	?	?	?	?	?
20 Costa	N	N	N	N	N	Y
21 Nunes	Y	Y	Y	Y	Y	N
22 McCarthy	?	?	?	?	?	?
23 Capps	N	N	N	N	N	Y
24 Gallegly	Y	Y	Y	Y	N	N
25 McKeon	Y	Y	Y	Y	Y	N
26 Dreier	Y	Y	Y	Y	Y	N
27 Sherman	N	N	N	N	N	Y
28 Berman	N	N	N	N	N	Y
29 Schiff	N	N	N	N	N	Y
30 Waxman	N	N	N	N	N	Y
31 Becerra	N	N	N	N	N	Y
32 Chu	N	N	N	N	N	Y
33 Watson	?	?	?	?	?	?
34 Roybal-Allard	N	N	N	N	N	Y
35 Waters	N	N	N	?	N	Y
36 Harman	N	N	N	N	N	Y
37 Richardson	N	?	N	N	N	Y
38 Napolitano	N	N	N	N	N	Y
39 Sánchez, Linda	N	N	N	N	N	Y
40 Royce	Y	Y	Y	Y	Y	N
41 Lewis	Y	N	N	N	N	N
42 Miller, Gary	Y	Y	Y	Y	Y	N
43 Baca	N	N	N	N	N	Y
44 Calvert	Y	Y	N	Y	N	N
45 Bono Mack	Y	Y	Y	Y	N	N
46 Rohrabacher	Y	Y	Y	Y	Y	N
47 Sanchez, Loretta	N	N	N	N	N	Y
48 Campbell	Y	Y	Y	Y	Y	N
49 Issa	Y	Y	Y	Y	Y	N
50 Bilbray	Y	Y	Y	Y	Y	N
51 Filner	N	N	N	N	N	Y
52 Hunter	Y	Y	N	Y	N	N
53 Davis	N	N	N	N	N	Y

	494	495	496	497	498	499
COLORADO						
1 DeGette	N	N	N	N	N	Y
2 Polis	N	N	N	N	N	Y
3 Salazar	N	N	N	N	N	Y
4 Markey	N	N	N	N	N	Y
5 Lamborn	Y	Y	Y	Y	Y	N
6 Coffman	Y	Y	Y	Y	Y	N
7 Perlmutter	N	N	N	N	N	Y
CONNECTICUT						
1 Larson	N	N	N	N	N	Y
2 Courtney	N	N	N	N	N	Y
3 DeLauro	N	N	N	N	N	Y
4 Himes	N	N	N	N	N	Y
5 Murphy	N	N	N	N	N	Y
DELAWARE						
AL Castle	N	Y	Y	Y	Y	N
FLORIDA						
1 Miller	Y	Y	Y	Y	Y	N
2 Boyd	N	N	N	N	N	Y
3 Brown	N	N	N	N	N	Y
4 Crenshaw	N	Y	Y	Y	Y	N
5 Brown-Waite	Y	Y	Y	Y	Y	N
6 Stearns	Y	Y	Y	Y	Y	N
7 Mica	Y	Y	Y	Y	Y	N
8 Grayson	N	N	N	N	N	Y
9 Bilirakis	N	Y	Y	Y	Y	N
10 Young	?	?	?	?	?	?
11 Castor	N	N	N	N	N	Y
12 Putnam	N	Y	Y	Y	Y	N
13 Buchanan	Y	Y	Y	Y	Y	N
14 Mack	Y	Y	Y	Y	Y	N
15 Posey	Y	Y	Y	Y	Y	N
16 Rooney	Y	Y	Y	Y	Y	N
17 Meek	N	N	N	N	N	Y
18 Ros-Lehtinen	Y	Y	Y	Y	Y	N
19 Deutch	N	N	N	N	N	Y
20 Wasserman Schultz	N	N	N	N	N	Y
21 Diaz-Balart, L.	N	N	N	N	N	Y
22 Klein	N	N	N	N	N	Y
23 Hastings	N	N	N	N	N	Y
24 Kosmas	N	N	N	N	N	Y
25 Diaz-Balart, M.	N	Y	Y	Y	Y	N
GEORGIA						
1 Kingston	Y	Y	N	Y	Y	Y
2 Bishop	N	N	N	N	N	Y
3 Westmoreland	Y	Y	Y	Y	Y	N
4 Johnson	N	N	N	N	N	Y
5 Lewis	N	N	N	N	N	Y
6 Price	Y	Y	Y	Y	Y	N
7 Linder	Y	Y	Y	Y	Y	N
8 Marshall	N	N	N	Y	N	N
9 Graves	Y	Y	Y	Y	Y	N
10 Broun	Y	Y	Y	Y	Y	N
11 Gingrey	?	Y	Y	Y	Y	N
12 Barrow	N	N	N	N	N	Y
13 Scott	Y	N	N	N	N	Y
HAWAII						
1 Djou	Y	Y	Y	Y	Y	Y
2 Hirono	N	N	N	N	N	Y
IDAHO						
1 Minnick	Y	Y	Y	Y	Y	Y
2 Simpson	N	N	N	N	N	N
ILLINOIS						
1 Rush	N	N	N	N	N	Y
2 Jackson	N	N	N	N	N	Y
3 Lipinski	N	N	N	N	N	Y
4 Gutierrez	N	?	?	N	N	Y
5 Quigley	N	N	N	N	N	Y
6 Roskam	Y	Y	Y	Y	Y	N
7 Davis	N	N	N	N	N	Y
8 Bean	N	Y	Y	Y	N	Y
9 Schakowsky	N	N	N	N	N	Y
10 Kirk	N	Y	Y	Y	N	Y
11 Halvorson	N	Y	N	N	N	Y
12 Costello	N	N	N	N	N	Y
13 Biggert	Y	Y	Y	Y	Y	N
14 Foster	N	N	N	Y	N	Y
15 Johnson	N	Y	Y	Y	Y	N

	494	495	496	497	498	499
16 **Manzullo**	N	Y	Y	Y	Y	N
17 Hare	N	N	N	N	N	Y
18 **Schock**	N	Y	Y	Y	Y	N
19 **Shimkus**	Y	Y	Y	Y	Y	N
INDIANA						
1 Visclosky	N	N	N	N	N	Y
2 Donnelly	N	N	N	N	N	Y
3 Vacant						
4 **Buyer**	Y	Y	Y	Y	Y	N
5 **Burton**	Y	Y	Y	Y	Y	N
6 **Pence**	Y	Y	Y	Y	Y	N
7 Carson	N	N	N	N	N	Y
8 Ellsworth	N	N	N	N	N	Y
9 Hill	N	N	N	N	N	Y
IOWA						
1 Braley	N	N	N	N	N	Y
2 Loebsack	N	N	N	N	N	Y
3 Boswell	N	N	N	N	N	Y
4 **Latham**	N	N	N	N	N	N
5 **King**	Y	Y	Y	Y	Y	N
KANSAS						
1 **Moran**	?	?	?	?	?	?
2 **Jenkins**	Y	Y	Y	Y	Y	N
3 Moore	N	N	N	N	N	Y
4 **Tiahrt**	?	?	?	?	?	?
KENTUCKY						
1 **Whitfield**	Y	Y	Y	Y	Y	Y
2 **Guthrie**	Y	Y	Y	Y	Y	N
3 Yarmuth	N	N	N	N	N	Y
4 **Davis**	Y	Y	Y	Y	Y	N
5 **Rogers**	Y	Y	Y	Y	Y	N
6 Chandler	N	N	N	N	N	Y
LOUISIANA						
1 **Scalise**	Y	Y	Y	Y	Y	N
2 **Cao**	N	Y	N	N	N	Y
3 Melancon	N	N	N	N	N	Y
4 **Fleming**	Y	Y	Y	Y	Y	N
5 **Alexander**	Y	Y	Y	Y	Y	N
6 **Cassidy**	Y	Y	Y	Y	Y	N
7 **Boustany**	Y	Y	Y	Y	Y	N
MAINE						
1 Pingree	N	N	N	N	N	Y
2 Michaud	N	N	N	N	N	Y
MARYLAND						
1 Kratovil	N	N	N	N	N	Y
2 Ruppersberger	N	N	N	N	N	Y
3 Sarbanes	N	N	N	N	N	Y
4 Edwards	N	N	N	N	N	Y
5 Hoyer	N	N	N	N	N	Y
6 **Bartlett**	Y	Y	Y	Y	Y	N
7 Cummings	N	N	N	N	N	Y
8 Van Hollen	N	N	N	N	N	Y
MASSACHUSETTS						
1 Olver	N	N	N	N	N	Y
2 Neal	N	N	N	N	N	Y
3 McGovern	N	N	N	N	N	Y
4 Frank	N	N	N	N	N	Y
5 Tsongas	N	N	N	N	N	Y
6 Tierney	N	N	N	N	N	Y
7 Markey	N	N	N	N	N	Y
8 Capuano	N	N	N	N	N	Y
9 Lynch	N	N	N	N	N	Y
10 Delahunt	N	N	N	N	N	Y
MICHIGAN						
1 Stupak	N	N	N	N	N	Y
2 **Hoekstra**	?	?	?	?	?	?
3 **Ehlers**	N	N	Y	Y	N	N
4 **Camp**	Y	Y	Y	Y	Y	N
5 Kildee	N	N	N	N	N	Y
6 **Upton**	N	Y	Y	Y	Y	N
7 Schauer	N	Y	Y	Y	Y	Y
8 **Rogers**	Y	Y	Y	Y	Y	N
9 Peters	N	Y	Y	Y	Y	N
10 **Miller**	N	Y	Y	Y	Y	N
11 **McCotter**	N	Y	Y	Y	Y	N
12 Levin	N	N	N	N	N	Y
13 Kilpatrick	?	?	?	?	?	?
14 Conyers	N	N	N	N	N	Y
15 Dingell	N	N	N	N	N	Y
MINNESOTA						
1 Walz	N	N	N	N	N	Y
2 **Kline**	Y	Y	Y	Y	Y	N
3 **Paulsen**	Y	Y	Y	Y	Y	N
4 McCollum	N	N	N	N	N	Y

	494	495	496	497	498	499
5 Ellison	N	N	N	N	N	Y
6 **Bachmann**	Y	Y	Y	Y	Y	N
7 Peterson	N	N	N	N	N	Y
8 Oberstar	N	N	N	N	N	Y
MISSISSIPPI						
1 Childers	N	N	N	N	N	Y
2 Thompson	N	N	N	N	N	Y
3 **Harper**	Y	Y	Y	Y	Y	N
4 Taylor	N	N	N	N	N	N
MISSOURI						
1 Clay	N	N	N	N	N	Y
2 **Akin**	?	?	?	?	?	?
3 Carnahan	N	N	N	N	N	Y
4 Skelton	N	N	N	N	N	Y
5 Cleaver	N	N	N	N	N	Y
6 **Graves**	Y	Y	Y	Y	Y	N
7 **Blunt**	Y	Y	Y	Y	Y	N
8 **Emerson**	Y	Y	Y	Y	Y	N
9 **Luetkemeyer**	Y	Y	Y	Y	Y	N
MONTANA						
AL **Rehberg**	N	Y	Y	Y	Y	N
NEBRASKA						
1 **Fortenberry**	N	Y	Y	Y	Y	N
2 **Terry**	Y	Y	Y	Y	Y	N
3 **Smith**	Y	Y	Y	Y	Y	N
NEVADA						
1 Berkley	N	N	N	N	N	Y
2 **Heller**	Y	Y	Y	Y	Y	N
3 Titus	N	N	N	N	Y	Y
NEW HAMPSHIRE						
1 Shea-Porter	N	N	N	N	N	Y
2 Hodes	Y	Y	Y	Y	Y	N
NEW JERSEY						
1 Andrews	N	N	N	N	N	Y
2 **LoBiondo**	N	Y	Y	Y	Y	Y
3 Adler	N	N	N	N	N	N
4 **Smith**	N	Y	Y	Y	Y	Y
5 **Garrett**	N	Y	Y	Y	Y	N
6 Pallone	N	N	N	N	N	Y
7 **Lance**	N	Y	Y	Y	Y	N
8 Pascrell	N	N	N	N	N	Y
9 Rothman	N	N	N	N	N	Y
10 Payne	N	N	N	N	N	Y
11 **Frelinghuysen**	N	N	N	N	N	N
12 Holt	N	N	N	N	N	Y
13 Sires	N	N	N	N	N	Y
NEW MEXICO						
1 Heinrich	N	N	N	N	N	Y
2 Teague	N	N	N	N	N	Y
3 Luján	N	N	N	N	N	Y
NEW YORK						
1 Bishop	N	N	N	N	N	Y
2 Israel	N	N	N	N	N	Y
3 **King**	N	Y	Y	Y	Y	Y
4 McCarthy	N	N	N	N	N	Y
5 Ackerman	N	N	N	N	N	Y
6 Meeks	N	N	N	N	N	Y
7 Crowley	N	N	N	N	N	Y
8 Nadler	N	N	N	N	N	Y
9 Weiner	N	N	N	N	N	Y
10 Towns	N	N	N	N	N	Y
11 Clarke	N	N	N	N	N	Y
12 Velázquez	N	N	N	?	N	Y
13 McMahon	N	N	N	N	N	Y
14 Maloney	N	N	N	N	N	Y
15 Rangel	N	N	N	N	N	Y
16 Serrano	N	N	N	N	N	Y
17 Engel	N	N	N	N	N	Y
18 Lowey	N	N	N	N	N	Y
19 Hall	N	N	N	N	N	Y
20 Murphy	N	N	N	N	N	N
21 Tonko	N	N	N	N	N	Y
22 Hinchey	N	N	N	N	N	Y
23 Owens	N	N	N	N	N	Y
24 Arcuri	N	N	N	N	N	Y
25 Maffei	N	N	N	N	N	Y
26 **Lee**	N	Y	Y	N	Y	N
27 Higgins	N	N	N	N	N	Y
28 Slaughter	N	N	N	N	N	Y
29 Vacant						
NORTH CAROLINA						
1 Butterfield	N	N	N	N	N	Y
2 Etheridge	N	N	N	N	N	Y
3 **Jones**	Y	N	N	N	N	N
4 Price	N	N	N	N	N	Y

	494	495	496	497	498	499
5 **Foxx**	Y	Y	Y	Y	Y	N
6 **Coble**	Y	Y	Y	Y	Y	N
7 McIntyre	N	N	N	N	N	Y
8 Kissell	N	N	N	N	N	Y
9 **Myrick**	Y	Y	Y	Y	Y	N
10 **McHenry**	Y	Y	Y	Y	Y	N
11 Shuler	N	N	N	N	N	Y
12 Watt	N	N	N	N	N	Y
13 Miller	N	N	N	N	N	Y
NORTH DAKOTA						
AL Pomeroy	N	N	N	N	N	Y
OHIO						
1 Driehaus	N	N	N	N	N	Y
2 **Schmidt**	Y	Y	Y	Y	Y	N
3 **Turner**	N	Y	Y	Y	Y	N
4 **Jordan**	Y	Y	Y	Y	Y	N
5 **Latta**	Y	Y	Y	Y	Y	N
6 Wilson	N	N	N	N	N	Y
7 **Austria**	Y	Y	Y	Y	Y	N
8 **Boehner**	Y	Y	Y	Y	Y	N
9 Kaptur	N	N	N	N	N	Y
10 Kucinich	N	N	N	N	N	Y
11 Fudge	N	N	N	N	N	Y
12 **Tiberi**	N	Y	Y	Y	Y	N
13 Sutton	N	N	N	N	N	Y
14 **LaTourette**	N	N	N	N	N	Y
15 Kilroy	N	N	N	N	N	Y
16 Boccieri	N	N	N	N	N	Y
17 Ryan	N	N	N	N	N	Y
18 Space	N	N	N	N	N	Y
OKLAHOMA						
1 **Sullivan**	Y	Y	Y	Y	Y	N
2 Boren	N	N	N	N	N	Y
3 **Lucas**	Y	Y	Y	Y	Y	N
4 **Cole**	Y	Y	N	Y	Y	N
5 **Fallin**	Y	Y	Y	Y	Y	N
OREGON						
1 Wu	N	N	N	N	N	Y
2 **Walden**	N	Y	Y	Y	Y	N
3 Blumenauer	N	N	N	N	N	Y
4 DeFazio	N	N	N	N	N	Y
5 Schrader	N	N	N	N	N	Y
PENNSYLVANIA						
1 Brady	N	N	N	N	N	Y
2 Fattah	N	N	N	N	N	Y
3 Dahlkemper	N	N	N	N	N	Y
4 Altmire	N	N	N	N	N	Y
5 **Thompson**	Y	N	N	N	N	N
6 **Gerlach**	N	Y	Y	Y	Y	Y
7 Sestak	N	N	N	N	N	Y
8 Murphy, P.	N	N	N	N	N	Y
9 **Shuster**	N	Y	Y	Y	Y	N
10 Carney	?	?	?	?	?	?
11 Kanjorski	N	N	N	N	N	Y
12 Critz	N	N	N	N	N	Y
13 Schwartz	N	N	N	N	N	Y
14 Doyle	N	N	N	N	N	Y
15 **Dent**	N	Y	Y	Y	Y	N
16 **Pitts**	Y	Y	Y	Y	Y	N
17 Holden	N	N	N	N	N	Y
18 **Murphy, T.**	N	N	N	N	N	Y
19 **Platts**	N	Y	Y	Y	Y	N
RHODE ISLAND						
1 Kennedy	N	N	N	N	N	Y
2 Langevin	N	N	N	N	N	Y
SOUTH CAROLINA						
1 **Brown**	Y	Y	Y	Y	Y	N
2 **Wilson**	Y	Y	Y	Y	Y	N
3 **Barrett**	Y	Y	Y	Y	Y	N
4 **Inglis**	Y	Y	Y	Y	Y	N
5 Spratt	N	N	N	N	N	Y
6 Clyburn	N	N	N	N	N	Y
SOUTH DAKOTA						
AL Herseth Sandlin	N	N	N	N	N	N
TENNESSEE						
1 **Roe**	Y	Y	Y	Y	Y	N
2 **Duncan**	Y	Y	Y	Y	Y	N
3 **Wamp**	?	?	?	?	?	?
4 Davis	N	N	N	N	N	Y
5 Cooper	N	Y	Y	Y	Y	N
6 Gordon	N	N	N	N	N	Y
7 **Blackburn**	Y	Y	Y	Y	Y	N
8 Tanner	N	N	N	N	N	Y
9 Cohen	N	N	N	N	N	Y

	494	495	496	497	498	499
TEXAS						
1 **Gohmert**	Y	Y	Y	Y	?	N
2 **Poe**	Y	Y	Y	Y	Y	N
3 **Johnson, S.**	Y	Y	Y	Y	Y	N
4 **Hall**	?	Y	Y	Y	Y	N
5 **Hensarling**	Y	Y	Y	Y	Y	N
6 **Barton**	Y	Y	Y	Y	Y	N
7 **Culberson**	Y	Y	N	N	Y	N
8 **Brady**	Y	Y	Y	Y	Y	N
9 Green, A.	N	N	N	N	N	Y
10 **McCaul**	Y	Y	Y	Y	Y	N
11 **Conaway**	Y	Y	Y	Y	Y	N
12 **Granger**	Y	N	Y	Y	Y	N
13 **Thornberry**	Y	Y	Y	Y	Y	N
14 **Paul**	Y	Y	Y	Y	Y	N
15 Hinojosa	N	N	N	N	N	Y
16 Reyes	N	N	N	N	N	Y
17 Edwards	N	N	N	N	N	Y
18 Jackson Lee	N	N	N	N	N	Y
19 **Neugebauer**	Y	Y	Y	Y	Y	N
20 Gonzalez	N	N	N	N	N	Y
21 **Smith**	Y	Y	Y	Y	N	N
22 **Olson**	Y	Y	Y	Y	Y	N
23 Rodriguez	N	N	N	N	N	Y
24 **Marchant**	Y	Y	Y	Y	Y	N
25 Doggett	N	N	N	N	N	Y
26 **Burgess**	Y	Y	Y	Y	Y	N
27 Ortiz	N	N	N	N	N	Y
28 Cuellar	N	N	N	N	N	Y
29 Green, G.	N	N	N	N	N	Y
30 Johnson, E.	N	N	N	N	N	Y
31 **Carter**	Y	N	Y	Y	Y	N
32 **Sessions**	Y	Y	Y	Y	Y	N
UTAH						
1 **Bishop**	Y	Y	Y	Y	Y	N
2 Matheson	N	N	N	Y	N	N
3 **Chaffetz**	Y	Y	Y	Y	Y	N
VERMONT						
AL Welch	N	N	N	N	N	Y
VIRGINIA						
1 **Wittman**	N	Y	Y	Y	Y	Y
2 Nye	Y	Y	N	Y	Y	N
3 Scott	N	N	N	N	N	Y
4 **Forbes**	N	Y	Y	Y	Y	N
5 Perriello	N	N	N	N	N	Y
6 **Goodlatte**	N	Y	Y	Y	Y	N
7 **Cantor**	N	Y	Y	Y	Y	N
8 Moran	N	N	N	N	N	Y
9 Boucher	N	N	N	N	N	Y
10 **Wolf**	N	Y	Y	Y	Y	Y
11 Connolly	N	N	N	N	N	Y
WASHINGTON						
1 Inslee	N	N	N	N	N	Y
2 Larsen	N	N	N	N	N	Y
3 Baird	N	N	N	N	N	Y
4 **Hastings**	Y	Y	Y	Y	Y	N
5 **McMorris Rodgers**	Y	Y	Y	Y	Y	N
6 Dicks	N	N	N	N	N	Y
7 McDermott	N	N	N	N	N	Y
8 **Reichert**	Y	Y	Y	Y	Y	N
9 Smith	N	N	N	N	N	Y
WEST VIRGINIA						
1 Mollohan	N	N	N	N	N	Y
2 **Capito**	Y	Y	Y	Y	Y	N
3 Rahall	N	N	N	N	N	Y
WISCONSIN						
1 **Ryan**	Y	Y	Y	Y	Y	N
2 Baldwin	N	N	N	N	N	Y
3 Kind	N	Y	Y	Y	Y	N
4 Moore	N	N	N	N	N	Y
5 **Sensenbrenner**	Y	Y	Y	Y	Y	N
6 **Petri**	Y	Y	Y	Y	Y	N
7 Obey	N	N	N	N	N	Y
8 Kagen	N	N	N	N	N	?
WYOMING						
AL **Lummis**	Y	Y	Y	Y	Y	N
DELEGATES						
Faleomavaega (A.S.)	N	N	N	N	N	
Norton (D.C.)	N	N	N	N	N	
Bordallo (Guam)	N	N	N	N	N	
Sablan (N. Marianas)	N	N	N	N	N	
Pierluisi (P.R.)	N	N	N	N	N	
Christensen (V.I.)	N	N	N	N	N	

IN THE HOUSE | By Vote Number

500. **HR 3534; HR 5851. Offshore Drilling Regulation Overhaul, Whistleblower Protections/Rule.** Adoption of the rule (H Res 1574) that would provide for House floor consideration of the bill (HR 3534) that would increase safety regulatory standards for offshore oil drilling and a bill (HR 5851) that would extend whistleblower protections to workers on the outer continental shelf. The rule would also provide for the automatic adoption of a Miller, D-Calif., manager's amendment to HR 5851 that would make technical changes. The rule stipulates that the text of HR 5851 would be added to HR 3534 upon engrossment of that legislation. Adopted 220-194: D 220-29; R 0-165. July 30, 2010.

501. **H Res 1558. U.S.-Grown Produce/Adoption.** Cardoza, D-Calif., motion to suspend the rules and adopt the resolution that would express the sense of the House that fruit, vegetable and commodity producers are encouraged to display the American flag on labels of products grown in the United States. Motion agreed to 403-1: D 241-0; R 162-1. A two-thirds majority of those present and voting (270 in this case) is required for adoption under suspension of the rules. July 30, 2010.

502. **HR 5901. Real Estate Jobs and Investment/Passage.** Crowley, D-N.Y., motion to suspend the rules and pass the bill that would raise to 10 percent, from 5 percent, the stake that a foreign investor could have in a publicly traded Real Estate Investment Trust before higher tax rates would apply. Motion agreed to 402-11: D 247-1; R 155-10. A two-thirds majority of those present and voting (276 in this case) is required for passage under suspension of the rules. July 30, 2010.

503. **H Res 1566. SNCC 50th Anniversary/Adoption.** Cohen, D-Tenn., motion to suspend the rules and adopt the resolution that would recognize the 50th anniversary of the founding of the Student Nonviolent Coordinating Committee (SNCC) and its role in the organization of the national sit-in movement and in desegregation. Motion agreed to 410-0: D 249-0; R 161-0. A two-thirds majority of those present and voting (274 in this case) is required for adoption under suspension of the rules. July 30, 2010.

504. **HR 5414. Francis Marion National Forest Land Conveyance/Passage.** Scott, D-Ga., motion to suspend the rules and pass the bill that would authorize the Agriculture Department to convey a parcel of National Forest System land in the Francis Marion National Forest in South Carolina to the First Baptist Church of Bonneau, S.C. Motion agreed to 408-0: D 246-0; R 162-0. A two-thirds majority of those present and voting (272 in this case) is required for passage under suspension of the rules. July 30, 2010.

	500	501	502	503	504
ALABAMA					
1 **Bonner**	N	Y	Y	Y	Y
2 Bright	N	Y	Y	Y	Y
3 **Rogers**	N	Y	Y	Y	Y
4 **Aderholt**	N	Y	Y	Y	Y
5 **Griffith**	?	?	?	?	?
6 **Bachus**	N	Y	Y	Y	Y
7 Davis	Y	Y	Y	Y	
ALASKA					
AL **Young**	N	Y	Y	Y	Y
ARIZONA					
1 Kirkpatrick	N	Y	Y	Y	Y
2 **Franks**	N	Y	Y	Y	Y
3 **Shadegg**	?	?	?	?	?
4 Pastor	Y	Y	Y	Y	Y
5 Mitchell	N	Y	Y	Y	Y
6 **Flake**	N	Y	N	Y	Y
7 Grijalva	Y	Y	Y	Y	Y
8 Giffords	N	Y	Y	Y	Y
ARKANSAS					
1 Berry	N	Y	Y	Y	Y
2 Snyder	Y	Y	Y	Y	Y
3 **Boozman**	N	Y	Y	Y	Y
4 Ross	N	Y	Y	Y	Y
CALIFORNIA					
1 Thompson	Y	Y	Y	Y	Y
2 **Herger**	N	Y	Y	Y	Y
3 **Lungren**	N	Y	Y	Y	Y
4 **McClintock**	N	Y	N	Y	Y
5 Matsui	Y	Y	Y	Y	Y
6 Woolsey	Y	Y	Y	Y	Y
7 Miller, George	Y	Y	Y	Y	Y
8 Pelosi					
9 Lee	Y	Y	Y	Y	Y
10 Garamendi	Y	Y	Y	Y	Y
11 McNerney	Y	Y	Y	Y	Y
12 Speier	Y	Y	Y	Y	Y
13 Stark	Y	Y	Y	Y	Y
14 Eshoo	Y	Y	Y	Y	Y
15 Honda	Y	Y	Y	Y	Y
16 Lofgren	Y	Y	Y	Y	Y
17 Farr	Y	Y	Y	Y	Y
18 Cardoza	Y	Y	Y	Y	Y
19 **Radanovich**	?	?	?	?	?
20 Costa	N	Y	Y	Y	Y
21 **Nunes**	Y	Y	Y	Y	Y
22 **McCarthy**	?	?	?	?	?
23 Capps	Y	Y	Y	Y	Y
24 **Gallegly**	N	Y	Y	Y	Y
25 **McKeon**	N	Y	Y	Y	Y
26 **Dreier**	N	Y	Y	Y	Y
27 Sherman	Y	Y	Y	Y	Y
28 Berman	Y	Y	Y	Y	Y
29 Schiff	Y	Y	Y	Y	Y
30 Waxman	Y	Y	Y	Y	Y
31 Becerra	Y	?	Y	Y	Y
32 Chu	Y	Y	Y	Y	Y
33 Watson	?	?	?	?	?
34 Roybal-Allard	Y	Y	Y	Y	Y
35 Waters	Y	Y	Y	Y	Y
36 Harman	Y	Y	Y	Y	Y
37 Richardson	Y	Y	Y	Y	Y
38 Napolitano	Y	Y	Y	Y	Y
39 Sánchez, Linda	Y	Y	Y	Y	Y
40 **Royce**	N	Y	N	Y	Y
41 **Lewis**	N	Y	Y	Y	Y
42 **Miller, Gary**	N	Y	Y	Y	Y
43 Baca	Y	Y	Y	Y	Y
44 **Calvert**	N	Y	Y	Y	Y
45 **Bono Mack**	N	Y	Y	Y	Y
46 **Rohrabacher**	N	Y	N	Y	Y
47 Sanchez, Loretta	Y	Y	Y	Y	Y
48 **Campbell**	N	Y	N	Y	Y
49 **Issa**	N	Y	Y	Y	Y
50 **Bilbray**	N	Y	Y	Y	Y
51 Filner	Y	Y	Y	Y	Y
52 **Hunter**	N	Y	Y	Y	Y
53 Davis	Y	Y	Y	Y	Y

	500	501	502	503	504
COLORADO					
1 DeGette	Y	Y	Y	Y	Y
2 Polis	Y	Y	Y	Y	Y
3 Salazar	N	Y	Y	Y	Y
4 Markey	Y	Y	Y	Y	Y
5 **Lamborn**	N	Y	Y	Y	Y
6 **Coffman**	N	Y	Y	Y	Y
7 Perlmutter	Y	Y	Y	Y	Y
CONNECTICUT					
1 Larson	Y	Y	Y	Y	Y
2 Courtney	Y	Y	Y	Y	Y
3 DeLauro	Y	Y	Y	Y	Y
4 Himes	+	+	+	+	?
5 Murphy	Y	Y	Y	Y	Y
DELAWARE					
AL **Castle**	N	Y	Y	Y	Y
FLORIDA					
1 **Miller**	N	Y	Y	Y	Y
2 Boyd	N	Y	Y	Y	Y
3 Brown	Y	Y	Y	Y	Y
4 **Crenshaw**	N	Y	Y	Y	Y
5 **Brown-Waite**	N	Y	Y	Y	Y
6 **Stearns**	N	Y	Y	Y	Y
7 **Mica**	N	Y	Y	Y	Y
8 Grayson	Y	Y	Y	Y	Y
9 **Bilirakis**	N	Y	Y	Y	Y
10 **Young**	?	?	?	?	?
11 Castor	Y	Y	Y	Y	Y
12 **Putnam**	N	Y	Y	Y	Y
13 **Buchanan**	N	Y	Y	Y	Y
14 **Mack**	N	Y	Y	Y	?
15 **Posey**	N	Y	Y	Y	Y
16 **Rooney**	N	Y	Y	Y	Y
17 Meek	Y	Y	Y	Y	Y
18 **Ros-Lehtinen**	N	Y	Y	Y	Y
19 Deutch	Y	Y	Y	Y	Y
20 Wasserman Schultz	Y	Y	Y	Y	Y
21 **Diaz-Balart, L.**	N	Y	Y	Y	Y
22 Klein	Y	Y	Y	Y	Y
23 Hastings	Y	Y	Y	Y	Y
24 Kosmas	Y	Y	Y	Y	Y
25 **Diaz-Balart, M.**	N	Y	Y	Y	Y
GEORGIA					
1 **Kingston**	N	Y	Y	Y	Y
2 Bishop	N	Y	Y	Y	Y
3 **Westmoreland**	N	Y	Y	Y	Y
4 Johnson	Y	Y	Y	Y	Y
5 Lewis	Y	Y	Y	Y	Y
6 **Price**	N	Y	Y	Y	Y
7 **Linder**	?	?	?	?	?
8 Marshall	N	Y	Y	Y	Y
9 **Graves**	N	Y	Y	Y	Y
10 **Broun**	N	Y	N	Y	Y
11 **Gingrey**	N	Y	Y	Y	Y
12 Barrow	Y	Y	Y	Y	Y
13 Scott	Y	Y	Y	Y	Y
HAWAII					
1 **Djou**	N	Y	Y	Y	Y
2 Hirono	Y	Y	Y	Y	Y
IDAHO					
1 Minnick	N	Y	Y	Y	Y
2 **Simpson**	N	Y	Y	Y	Y
ILLINOIS					
1 Rush	Y	Y	Y	Y	Y
2 Jackson	Y	Y	Y	Y	Y
3 Lipinski	Y	Y	Y	Y	Y
4 Gutierrez	Y	Y	Y	Y	?
5 Quigley	Y	Y	Y	Y	Y
6 **Roskam**	N	Y	Y	Y	Y
7 Davis	Y	Y	Y	Y	Y
8 Bean	Y	Y	Y	Y	Y
9 Schakowsky	Y	Y	Y	Y	Y
10 **Kirk**	N	Y	Y	Y	Y
11 Halvorson	Y	Y	Y	Y	Y
12 Costello	Y	Y	Y	Y	Y
13 **Biggert**	N	Y	Y	Y	Y
14 Foster	Y	Y	Y	Y	Y
15 Johnson	N	Y	Y	Y	Y

KEY **Republicans** Democrats

- Y Voted for (yea)
- # Paired for
- + Announced for
- N Voted against (nay)
- X Paired against
- − Announced against
- P Voted "present"
- C Voted "present" to avoid possible conflict of interest
- ? Did not vote or otherwise make a position known

	500	501	502	503	504
16 Manzullo	N	Y	Y	Y	Y
17 Hare	Y	Y	Y	Y	Y
18 Schock	N	Y	Y	Y	Y
19 Shimkus	N	Y	Y	Y	Y
INDIANA					
1 Visclosky	Y	Y	Y	Y	Y
2 Donnelly	N	Y	Y	Y	Y
3 Vacant					
4 Buyer	?	?	?	?	?
5 Burton	N	Y	Y	Y	Y
6 Pence	N	Y	Y	Y	Y
7 Carson	Y	Y	Y	Y	Y
8 Ellsworth	N	Y	Y	Y	Y
9 Hill	N	Y	Y	Y	Y
IOWA					
1 Braley	Y	Y	Y	Y	Y
2 Loebsack	Y	Y	Y	Y	Y
3 Boswell	Y	Y	Y	Y	Y
4 Latham	N	Y	Y	Y	Y
5 King	N	Y	Y	Y	Y
KANSAS					
1 Moran	?	?	?	?	?
2 Jenkins	N	Y	Y	Y	Y
3 Moore	Y	Y	Y	Y	Y
4 Tiahrt	?	?	?	?	?
KENTUCKY					
1 Whitfield	N	Y	Y	Y	Y
2 Guthrie	N	Y	Y	Y	Y
3 Yarmuth	Y	Y	Y	Y	Y
4 Davis	N	Y	Y	Y	Y
5 Rogers	N	Y	Y	Y	Y
6 Chandler	Y	Y	Y	Y	Y
LOUISIANA					
1 Scalise	N	Y	Y	Y	Y
2 Cao	N	Y	Y	Y	Y
3 Melancon	Y	Y	+	Y	Y
4 Fleming	N	Y	Y	Y	Y
5 Alexander	N	Y	Y	Y	Y
6 Cassidy	N	Y	Y	Y	Y
7 Boustany	N	Y	Y	Y	Y
MAINE					
1 Pingree	Y	Y	Y	Y	Y
2 Michaud	Y	Y	Y	Y	Y
MARYLAND					
1 Kratovil	Y	Y	Y	Y	Y
2 Ruppersberger	Y	Y	Y	Y	Y
3 Sarbanes	Y	Y	Y	Y	Y
4 Edwards	Y	Y	Y	Y	Y
5 Hoyer	Y	Y	Y	Y	Y
6 Bartlett	N	Y	Y	Y	Y
7 Cummings	Y	Y	Y	Y	Y
8 Van Hollen	Y	Y	Y	Y	Y
MASSACHUSETTS					
1 Olver	Y	Y	Y	Y	Y
2 Neal	Y	Y	Y	Y	Y
3 McGovern	Y	Y	Y	Y	Y
4 Frank	Y	Y	Y	Y	Y
5 Tsongas	Y	Y	Y	Y	Y
6 Tierney	Y	Y	Y	Y	Y
7 Markey	Y	Y	Y	Y	Y
8 Capuano	Y	Y	Y	Y	Y
9 Lynch	Y	Y	Y	Y	Y
10 Delahunt	Y	?	?	?	?
MICHIGAN					
1 Stupak	Y	Y	Y	Y	Y
2 Hoekstra	?	?	?	?	?
3 Ehlers	N	Y	Y	Y	Y
4 Camp	N	Y	Y	Y	Y
5 Kildee	Y	Y	Y	Y	Y
6 Upton	N	Y	Y	Y	Y
7 Schauer	Y	Y	Y	Y	Y
8 Rogers	?	?	?	?	?
9 Peters	Y	Y	Y	Y	Y
10 Miller	N	Y	Y	Y	Y
11 McCotter	N	Y	Y	Y	Y
12 Levin	Y	Y	Y	Y	Y
13 Kilpatrick	+	+	+	+	+
14 Conyers	Y	?	Y	Y	Y
15 Dingell	Y	Y	Y	Y	Y
MINNESOTA					
1 Walz	Y	Y	Y	Y	Y
2 Kline	N	Y	Y	Y	Y
3 Paulsen	N	Y	Y	Y	Y
4 McCollum	Y	Y	Y	Y	Y

	500	501	502	503	504
5 Ellison	Y	Y	Y	Y	?
6 Bachmann	N	?	Y	Y	Y
7 Peterson	N	?	Y	Y	Y
8 Oberstar	Y	Y	Y	Y	Y
MISSISSIPPI					
1 Childers	Y	Y	Y	Y	Y
2 Thompson	Y	Y	Y	Y	Y
3 Harper	N	Y	Y	Y	Y
4 Taylor	Y	Y	N	Y	Y
MISSOURI					
1 Clay	Y	Y	Y	Y	Y
2 Akin	−	+	+	+	+
3 Carnahan	Y	Y	Y	Y	Y
4 Skelton	Y	Y	Y	Y	Y
5 Cleaver	Y	Y	Y	Y	Y
6 Graves	N	Y	Y	Y	Y
7 Blunt	N	Y	Y	Y	Y
8 Emerson	N	Y	Y	Y	Y
9 Luetkemeyer	N	Y	Y	Y	Y
MONTANA					
AL Rehberg	N	Y	Y	Y	Y
NEBRASKA					
1 Fortenberry	N	Y	Y	Y	Y
2 Terry	N	Y	Y	Y	Y
3 Smith	N	Y	Y	Y	Y
NEVADA					
1 Berkley	Y	Y	Y	Y	Y
2 Heller	N	Y	Y	Y	Y
3 Titus	Y	Y	Y	Y	Y
NEW HAMPSHIRE					
1 Shea-Porter	Y	Y	Y	Y	Y
2 Hodes	Y	Y	Y	Y	Y
NEW JERSEY					
1 Andrews	Y	Y	Y	Y	Y
2 LoBiondo	N	Y	Y	Y	Y
3 Adler	N	Y	Y	Y	Y
4 Smith	N	Y	Y	Y	Y
5 Garrett	N	Y	N	Y	Y
6 Pallone	Y	Y	Y	Y	Y
7 Lance	N	Y	Y	Y	Y
8 Pascrell	Y	Y	Y	Y	Y
9 Rothman	Y	Y	Y	Y	Y
10 Payne	Y	Y	Y	Y	Y
11 Frelinghuysen	N	Y	Y	Y	Y
12 Holt	Y	Y	Y	Y	Y
13 Sires	Y	Y	Y	Y	Y
NEW MEXICO					
1 Heinrich	Y	Y	Y	Y	Y
2 Teague	N	Y	Y	Y	Y
3 Luján	Y	?	Y	Y	Y
NEW YORK					
1 Bishop	Y	Y	Y	Y	Y
2 Israel	Y	Y	Y	Y	Y
3 King	N	Y	Y	Y	Y
4 McCarthy	Y	Y	Y	Y	Y
5 Ackerman	Y	Y	Y	Y	?
6 Meeks	Y	Y	Y	Y	Y
7 Crowley	Y	Y	Y	Y	Y
8 Nadler	Y	Y	Y	Y	Y
9 Weiner	Y	Y	Y	Y	Y
10 Towns	Y	Y	Y	Y	Y
11 Clarke	Y	Y	Y	Y	Y
12 Velázquez	Y	Y	Y	Y	Y
13 McMahon	Y	Y	Y	Y	Y
14 Maloney	Y	Y	Y	Y	Y
15 Rangel	Y	Y	Y	Y	Y
16 Serrano	Y	Y	Y	Y	Y
17 Engel	Y	Y	Y	Y	Y
18 Lowey	Y	Y	Y	Y	Y
19 Hall	Y	Y	Y	Y	Y
20 Murphy	Y	Y	Y	Y	Y
21 Tonko	Y	Y	Y	Y	Y
22 Hinchey	Y	Y	Y	Y	Y
23 Owens	Y	Y	Y	Y	Y
24 Arcuri	Y	Y	Y	Y	Y
25 Maffei	Y	Y	Y	Y	Y
26 Lee	N	Y	Y	Y	Y
27 Higgins	Y	Y	Y	Y	Y
28 Slaughter	Y	Y	Y	Y	Y
29 Vacant					
NORTH CAROLINA					
1 Butterfield	Y	?	Y	Y	Y
2 Etheridge	Y	Y	Y	Y	Y
3 Jones	N	Y	Y	Y	Y
4 Price	Y	Y	Y	Y	Y

	500	501	502	503	504
5 Foxx	N	Y	Y	Y	Y
6 Coble	N	Y	Y	Y	Y
7 McIntyre	Y	Y	Y	Y	Y
8 Kissell	Y	Y	Y	Y	Y
9 Myrick	N	Y	Y	Y	Y
10 McHenry	N	Y	Y	Y	Y
11 Shuler	N	Y	Y	Y	Y
12 Watt	Y	Y	Y	Y	Y
13 Miller	Y	Y	Y	Y	?
NORTH DAKOTA					
AL Pomeroy	N	Y	Y	Y	Y
OHIO					
1 Driehaus	Y	Y	Y	Y	Y
2 Schmidt	N	Y	Y	Y	Y
3 Turner	N	Y	Y	Y	Y
4 Jordan	N	Y	Y	Y	Y
5 Latta	N	Y	Y	Y	Y
6 Wilson	Y	Y	Y	Y	Y
7 Austria	N	Y	Y	Y	Y
8 Boehner	N	Y	Y	Y	Y
9 Kaptur	Y	Y	Y	Y	Y
10 Kucinich	Y	Y	Y	Y	Y
11 Fudge	Y	Y	Y	Y	Y
12 Tiberi	N	Y	Y	Y	Y
13 Sutton	Y	Y	Y	Y	Y
14 LaTourette	N	Y	Y	Y	?
15 Kilroy	Y	Y	Y	Y	Y
16 Boccieri	Y	Y	Y	Y	Y
17 Ryan	Y	Y	Y	Y	Y
18 Space	N	Y	Y	Y	Y
OKLAHOMA					
1 Sullivan	N	Y	Y	Y	Y
2 Boren	N	Y	Y	Y	Y
3 Lucas	N	Y	Y	Y	Y
4 Cole	N	Y	Y	Y	Y
5 Fallin	N	Y	Y	Y	Y
OREGON					
1 Wu	Y	Y	Y	Y	Y
2 Walden	N	Y	Y	Y	Y
3 Blumenauer	Y	Y	Y	Y	Y
4 DeFazio	Y	Y	Y	Y	Y
5 Schrader	Y	Y	Y	Y	Y
PENNSYLVANIA					
1 Brady	Y	Y	Y	Y	Y
2 Fattah	Y	Y	Y	Y	Y
3 Dahlkemper	Y	Y	Y	Y	Y
4 Altmire	N	Y	Y	Y	Y
5 Thompson	N	Y	Y	Y	Y
6 Gerlach	N	Y	Y	Y	Y
7 Sestak	Y	Y	Y	Y	Y
8 Murphy, P.	Y	Y	Y	Y	Y
9 Shuster	N	Y	Y	Y	Y
10 Carney	?	?	?	?	?
11 Kanjorski	Y	Y	Y	Y	Y
12 Critz	Y	Y	Y	Y	Y
13 Schwartz	Y	Y	Y	Y	Y
14 Doyle	Y	Y	Y	Y	Y
15 Dent	N	Y	Y	Y	Y
16 Pitts	N	Y	Y	Y	Y
17 Holden	Y	Y	Y	Y	Y
18 Murphy, T.	N	Y	Y	Y	Y
19 Platts	N	Y	Y	Y	Y
RHODE ISLAND					
1 Kennedy	Y	?	Y	Y	Y
2 Langevin	Y	Y	Y	Y	Y
SOUTH CAROLINA					
1 Brown	N	Y	Y	Y	Y
2 Wilson	N	Y	Y	Y	Y
3 Barrett	N	Y	Y	Y	Y
4 Inglis	N	Y	Y	?	Y
5 Spratt	Y	Y	Y	Y	Y
6 Clyburn	Y	Y	Y	Y	Y
SOUTH DAKOTA					
AL Herseth Sandlin	N	Y	Y	Y	Y
TENNESSEE					
1 Roe	N	Y	Y	Y	Y
2 Duncan	N	Y	N	Y	Y
3 Wamp	?	?	?	?	?
4 Davis	N	Y	Y	Y	Y
5 Cooper	Y	Y	Y	Y	Y
6 Gordon	Y	Y	Y	Y	Y
7 Blackburn	N	Y	Y	Y	Y
8 Tanner	Y	Y	Y	Y	Y
9 Cohen	Y	Y	Y	Y	Y

	500	501	502	503	504
TEXAS					
1 Gohmert	N	Y	Y	?	?
2 Poe	N	Y	Y	Y	Y
3 Johnson, S.	N	Y	Y	Y	Y
4 Hall	N	Y	Y	Y	Y
5 Hensarling	N	Y	Y	Y	Y
6 Barton	N	Y	Y	Y	Y
7 Culberson	N	Y	Y	Y	Y
8 Brady	N	Y	Y	Y	Y
9 Green, A.	Y	Y	Y	Y	Y
10 McCaul	N	Y	Y	Y	Y
11 Conaway	N	?	Y	Y	Y
12 Granger	N	Y	Y	Y	Y
13 Thornberry	N	Y	Y	Y	Y
14 Paul	N	N	N	Y	Y
15 Hinojosa	+	Y	Y	Y	Y
16 Reyes	Y	Y	Y	Y	Y
17 Edwards	N	?	Y	Y	Y
18 Jackson Lee	Y	Y	Y	Y	Y
19 Neugebauer	N	Y	Y	Y	Y
20 Gonzalez	Y	Y	Y	Y	Y
21 Smith	N	Y	Y	Y	Y
22 Olson	N	Y	Y	Y	Y
23 Rodriguez	Y	?	Y	Y	Y
24 Marchant	N	Y	Y	Y	Y
25 Doggett	Y	Y	Y	Y	Y
26 Burgess	N	Y	Y	Y	Y
27 Ortiz	Y	Y	Y	Y	Y
28 Cuellar	Y	Y	Y	Y	Y
29 Green, G.	N	Y	Y	Y	Y
30 Johnson, E.	Y	Y	Y	Y	Y
31 Carter	N	Y	Y	Y	Y
32 Sessions	N	Y	Y	Y	Y
UTAH					
1 Bishop	N	Y	Y	Y	Y
2 Matheson	N	Y	Y	Y	Y
3 Chaffetz	N	Y	Y	Y	Y
VERMONT					
AL Welch	Y	Y	Y	Y	Y
VIRGINIA					
1 Wittman	N	Y	Y	Y	Y
2 Nye	N	Y	Y	Y	Y
3 Scott	Y	Y	Y	Y	Y
4 Forbes	N	Y	Y	Y	Y
5 Perriello	Y	Y	Y	Y	Y
6 Goodlatte	N	Y	Y	Y	Y
7 Cantor	N	Y	Y	Y	Y
8 Moran	Y	Y	Y	Y	Y
9 Boucher	Y	Y	Y	Y	Y
10 Wolf	N	Y	Y	Y	Y
11 Connolly	Y	Y	Y	Y	Y
WASHINGTON					
1 Inslee	Y	Y	Y	Y	Y
2 Larsen	Y	Y	Y	Y	Y
3 Baird	Y	Y	Y	Y	Y
4 Hastings	N	Y	Y	Y	Y
5 McMorris Rodgers	N	Y	Y	?	Y
6 Dicks	Y	Y	Y	Y	Y
7 McDermott	Y	Y	Y	Y	Y
8 Reichert	N	Y	Y	Y	Y
9 Smith	Y	Y	Y	Y	Y
WEST VIRGINIA					
1 Mollohan	Y	Y	Y	Y	Y
2 Capito	N	Y	Y	Y	Y
3 Rahall	Y	Y	Y	Y	Y
WISCONSIN					
1 Ryan	N	Y	Y	Y	Y
2 Baldwin	Y	Y	Y	Y	Y
3 Kind	Y	Y	Y	Y	Y
4 Moore	Y	Y	Y	Y	Y
5 Sensenbrenner	N	Y	Y	Y	Y
6 Petri	N	Y	N	Y	Y
7 Obey	Y	Y	Y	Y	Y
8 Kagen	Y	Y	Y	Y	Y
WYOMING					
AL Lummis	N	Y	Y	Y	Y
DELEGATES					
Faleomavaega (A.S.)					
Norton (D.C.)					
Bordallo (Guam)					
Sablan (N. Marianas)					
Pierluisi (P.R.)					
Christensen (V.I.)					

IN THE HOUSE | By Vote Number

505. HR 5851. Offshore Drilling, Whistleblower Protections/
Recommit. Kline, R-Minn., motion to recommit the bill to the House
Education and Labor Committee with instructions that it be immediately reported back with an amendment that would strike all language after
the enacting clause and insert language that would grant whistleblower
protections to an employee engaged in activities on or in waters above
the outer continental shelf relating to oil production and who has filed
a complaint or prompted a proceeding related to workplace safety and
health regulation. It would require the employee to file a complaint with
the Labor secretary within 30 days after such a violation occurs. Motion
rejected 171-234: D 10-234; R 161-0. July 30, 2010.

506. HR 5851. Offshore Drilling, Whistleblower Protections/
Passage. Passage of the bill that would prohibit employers from discriminating against workers in the offshore energy development industry
who report suspected safety violations to federal or state authorities. The
measure would apply to any employer, including contractors and subcon-
tractors, who hires workers engaged in activities related to oil and natural
gas exploration and development on waters on the outer continental
shelf. Passed 315-93: D 247-1; R 68-92. A "yea" was a vote in support of
the president's position. July 30, 2010.

507. HR 3534. Offshore Drilling Regulation Overhaul/Manager's
Amendment. Rahall, D-W.Va., manager's amendment that would make a
number of changes to the bill, including adding provisions that would allow discharges resulting from salvage activities in the oil spill cleanup to
be exempt from liability under the Clean Water Act; require redundancy
in accident and spill response plans as part of the permitting process for
drilling; require oil and gas companies to pay royalties on all oil that is
discharged from a well, including spilled oil; and strike "biomass" from
the renewable-energy resource definition. Adopted in Committee of the
Whole 250-161: D 238-13; R 12-148. July 30, 2010.

508. HR 3534. Offshore Drilling Regulation Overhaul/Funds for
Public Recreation. Kind, D-Wis., amendment that would require that at
least 1.5 percent of funds appropriated for the Land and Water Conservation Fund each year go to projects to make federal lands available for
public recreational use, including hunting, fishing and other outdoor
recreational activities. Adopted in Committee of the Whole 404-1:
D 249-0; R 155-1. July 30, 2010.

509. HR 3534. Offshore Drilling Regulation Overhaul/Financial
Responsibility Pooling. Teague, D-N.M., amendment that would allow
oil companies to participate in cooperative arrangements such as resource pooling or joint insurance to meet financial responsibility requirements under the bill. Adopted in Committee of the Whole 399-8:
D 247-3; R 152-5. July 30, 2010.

	505	506	507	508	509
ALABAMA					
1 **Bonner**	Y	N	N	Y	Y
2 Bright	N	Y	Y	Y	Y
3 **Rogers**	Y	N	N	Y	Y
4 **Aderholt**	Y	N	N	Y	Y
5 **Griffith**	?	?	?	?	?
6 **Bachus**	Y	N	N	Y	Y
7 Davis	N	Y	Y	Y	Y
ALASKA					
AL **Young**	Y	N	N	Y	Y
ARIZONA					
1 Kirkpatrick	Y	Y	Y	Y	Y
2 **Franks**	Y	N	N	Y	N
3 **Shadegg**	?	?	?	?	?
4 Pastor	N	Y	Y	Y	Y
5 Mitchell	N	Y	Y	Y	Y
6 **Flake**	Y	N	N	Y	Y
7 Grijalva	N	Y	Y	Y	Y
8 Giffords	N	Y	Y	Y	Y
ARKANSAS					
1 Berry	?	?	?	?	?
2 Snyder	N	Y	Y	Y	Y
3 **Boozman**	Y	Y	N	Y	Y
4 Ross	N	Y	Y	Y	Y
CALIFORNIA					
1 Thompson	N	Y	Y	Y	Y
2 **Herger**	Y	N	N	Y	Y
3 **Lungren**	Y	N	Y	Y	Y
4 **McClintock**	Y	N	N	Y	Y
5 Matsui	N	Y	Y	Y	Y
6 Woolsey	N	Y	Y	Y	Y
7 Miller, George	N	Y	Y	Y	Y
8 Pelosi		Y			
9 Lee	N	Y	Y	Y	Y
10 Garamendi	N	Y	Y	Y	N
11 McNerney	N	Y	Y	Y	Y
12 Speier	N	Y	Y	Y	Y
13 Stark	N	Y	Y	Y	Y
14 Eshoo	N	Y	Y	Y	Y
15 Honda	N	Y	Y	Y	Y
16 Lofgren	N	Y	Y	Y	Y
17 Farr	N	Y	Y	Y	Y
18 Cardoza	N	Y	Y	Y	?
19 **Radanovich**	?	?	?	?	?
20 Costa	N	Y	N	Y	Y
21 **Nunes**	?	?	?	?	?
22 **McCarthy**	?	?	?	?	?
23 Capps	N	Y	Y	Y	Y
24 **Gallegly**	Y	N	N	Y	Y
25 **McKeon**	Y	N	N	Y	Y
26 **Dreier**	Y	Y	N	Y	Y
27 Sherman	N	Y	Y	Y	Y
28 Berman	N	Y	Y	Y	Y
29 Schiff	N	Y	Y	Y	Y
30 Waxman	N	Y	Y	Y	Y
31 Becerra	N	Y	Y	Y	Y
32 Chu	N	Y	Y	Y	Y
33 Watson	?	?	?	?	?
34 Roybal-Allard	N	Y	Y	Y	Y
35 Waters	N	Y	Y	Y	Y
36 Harman	N	Y	Y	Y	Y
37 Richardson	N	Y	Y	Y	Y
38 Napolitano	N	Y	Y	Y	Y
39 Sánchez, Linda	N	Y	Y	Y	Y
40 **Royce**	Y	N	N	Y	Y
41 **Lewis**	Y	N	N	Y	Y
42 **Miller, Gary**	Y	N	P	Y	Y
43 Baca	N	Y	Y	Y	Y
44 **Calvert**	Y	N	N	Y	Y
45 **Bono Mack**	Y	Y	N	Y	Y
46 **Rohrabacher**	Y	N	N	Y	Y
47 Sanchez, Loretta	N	Y	Y	Y	Y
48 **Campbell**	Y	N	N	?	?
49 **Issa**	Y	Y	N	?	Y
50 **Bilbray**	Y	Y	N	Y	Y
51 Filner	N	Y	Y	Y	Y
52 **Hunter**	Y	N	N	Y	Y
53 Davis	N	Y	Y	Y	Y

	505	506	507	508	509
COLORADO					
1 DeGette	N	Y	Y	Y	Y
2 Polis	N	Y	Y	Y	Y
3 Salazar	N	Y	Y	Y	Y
4 Markey	N	Y	Y	Y	Y
5 **Lamborn**	Y	N	N	Y	?
6 **Coffman**	Y	N	N	Y	Y
7 Perlmutter	N	Y	?	?	?
CONNECTICUT					
1 Larson	N	Y	Y	Y	Y
2 Courtney	N	Y	Y	Y	Y
3 DeLauro	N	Y	Y	Y	Y
4 Himes	+	+	+	+	+
5 Murphy	N	Y	Y	Y	Y
DELAWARE					
AL **Castle**	Y	Y	Y	Y	Y
FLORIDA					
1 **Miller**	Y	N	N	Y	Y
2 Boyd	N	Y	Y	Y	Y
3 Brown	N	Y	Y	Y	Y
4 **Crenshaw**	Y	N	N	Y	Y
5 **Brown-Waite**	Y	Y	N	Y	Y
6 **Stearns**	Y	Y	N	Y	Y
7 **Mica**	Y	N	N	Y	Y
8 Grayson	N	Y	Y	Y	Y
9 **Bilirakis**	Y	Y	N	Y	Y
10 **Young**	?	?	?	?	?
11 Castor	N	Y	Y	Y	N
12 **Putnam**	Y	Y	N	Y	Y
13 **Buchanan**	Y	Y	N	Y	Y
14 **Mack**	Y	N	N	Y	Y
15 **Posey**	Y	Y	N	Y	Y
16 **Rooney**	Y	Y	N	Y	Y
17 Meek	N	Y	Y	Y	Y
18 **Ros-Lehtinen**	Y	Y	Y	Y	Y
19 Deutch	N	Y	Y	Y	Y
20 Wasserman Schultz	N	Y	Y	Y	Y
21 **Diaz-Balart, L.**	Y	Y	N	Y	Y
22 Klein	N	Y	Y	Y	Y
23 Hastings	N	Y	Y	Y	Y
24 Kosmas	N	Y	Y	Y	Y
25 **Diaz-Balart, M.**	Y	Y	N	Y	Y
GEORGIA					
1 **Kingston**	Y	N	N	Y	Y
2 Bishop	N	Y	Y	Y	Y
3 **Westmoreland**	Y	N	N	Y	Y
4 Johnson	?	Y	Y	Y	Y
5 Lewis	N	Y	Y	Y	Y
6 **Price**	Y	N	N	Y	Y
7 **Linder**	?	?	?	?	?
8 Marshall	Y	Y	Y	Y	Y
9 **Graves**	Y	N	N	Y	Y
10 **Broun**	Y	N	N	Y	Y
11 **Gingrey**	Y	N	N	Y	Y
12 Barrow	N	Y	Y	Y	Y
13 Scott	N	Y	Y	Y	Y
HAWAII					
1 **Djou**	Y	Y	Y	Y	Y
2 Hirono	N	Y	Y	Y	Y
IDAHO					
1 Minnick	Y	Y	Y	Y	Y
2 **Simpson**	Y	Y	N	Y	Y
ILLINOIS					
1 Rush	N	Y	Y	Y	Y
2 Jackson	N	Y	Y	Y	Y
3 Lipinski	N	Y	Y	Y	Y
4 Gutierrez	N	Y	Y	Y	Y
5 Quigley	N	Y	Y	Y	Y
6 **Roskam**	Y	Y	N	Y	Y
7 Davis	N	Y	Y	Y	Y
8 Bean	N	Y	Y	Y	Y
9 Schakowsky	N	Y	Y	Y	Y
10 **Kirk**	Y	Y	Y	Y	Y
11 Halvorson	N	Y	Y	Y	Y
12 Costello	N	Y	Y	Y	Y
13 **Biggert**	Y	N	N	Y	Y
14 Foster	N	Y	Y	Y	Y
15 Johnson	Y	Y	Y	Y	Y

KEY **Republicans** Democrats

Y	Voted for (yea)		X	Paired against		C	Voted "present" to avoid possible conflict of interest
#	Paired for		–	Announced against			
+	Announced for		P	Voted "present"		?	Did not vote or otherwise make a position known
N	Voted against (nay)						

	505	506	507	508	509
16 Manzullo	Y	N	N	Y	Y
17 Hare	N	Y	Y	Y	Y
18 Schock	Y	Y	N	Y	Y
19 Shimkus	Y	Y	N	Y	Y
INDIANA					
1 Visclosky	N	Y	Y	Y	Y
2 Donnelly	N	Y	Y	Y	Y
3 Vacant					
4 **Buyer**	?	?	?	?	?
5 **Burton**	Y	N	N	Y	Y
6 **Pence**	Y	N	N	Y	Y
7 Carson	N	Y	Y	Y	Y
8 Ellsworth	N	Y	Y	Y	Y
9 Hill	N	Y	Y	Y	Y
IOWA					
1 Braley	N	Y	Y	Y	Y
2 Loebsack	N	Y	Y	Y	Y
3 Boswell	N	Y	Y	Y	Y
4 **Latham**	Y	N	N	?	Y
5 **King**	Y	N	N	Y	Y
KANSAS					
1 **Moran**	?	?	?	?	?
2 **Jenkins**	Y	N	N	Y	Y
3 Moore	N	Y	Y	Y	Y
4 **Tiahrt**	?	?	?	?	?
KENTUCKY					
1 **Whitfield**	Y	Y	N	Y	Y
2 **Guthrie**	Y	Y	N	Y	Y
3 Yarmuth	N	Y	Y	Y	Y
4 **Davis**	Y	–	–	+	+
5 **Rogers**	Y	N	N	Y	Y
6 Chandler	N	Y	Y	Y	Y
LOUISIANA					
1 **Scalise**	Y	Y	N	Y	Y
2 **Cao**	Y	Y	N	Y	Y
3 Melancon	N	Y	Y	Y	Y
4 **Fleming**	Y	N	N	Y	Y
5 **Alexander**	Y	Y	N	Y	Y
6 **Cassidy**	Y	Y	N	Y	Y
7 **Boustany**	Y	Y	N	Y	Y
MAINE					
1 Pingree	N	Y	Y	Y	Y
2 Michaud	N	Y	Y	Y	Y
MARYLAND					
1 Kratovil	N	Y	Y	Y	Y
2 Ruppersberger	N	Y	Y	?	Y
3 Sarbanes	N	Y	Y	Y	Y
4 Edwards	N	Y	Y	Y	Y
5 Hoyer	N	Y	Y	Y	Y
6 **Bartlett**	Y	N	N	Y	Y
7 Cummings	N	Y	Y	Y	Y
8 Van Hollen	N	Y	Y	Y	Y
MASSACHUSETTS					
1 Olver	N	Y	Y	Y	Y
2 Neal	N	Y	Y	Y	Y
3 McGovern	N	Y	Y	Y	Y
4 Frank	N	Y	Y	Y	Y
5 Tsongas	N	Y	Y	Y	Y
6 Tierney	N	Y	Y	Y	Y
7 Markey	N	Y	Y	Y	Y
8 Capuano	N	Y	Y	Y	Y
9 Lynch	N	Y	Y	Y	Y
10 Delahunt	?	?	?	?	?
MICHIGAN					
1 Stupak	N	Y	Y	Y	Y
2 **Hoekstra**	?	?	?	?	?
3 **Ehlers**	Y	Y	Y	Y	Y
4 **Camp**	Y	Y	N	Y	Y
5 Kildee	N	Y	Y	Y	Y
6 **Upton**	Y	Y	N	Y	Y
7 Schauer	N	Y	Y	Y	Y
8 **Rogers**	?	?	?	?	?
9 Peters	N	Y	Y	Y	Y
10 **Miller**	Y	Y	N	Y	Y
11 **McCotter**	Y	Y	N	Y	Y
12 Levin	N	Y	Y	Y	Y
13 Kilpatrick	–	+	+	+	+
14 Conyers	N	Y	Y	Y	Y
15 Dingell	N	Y	Y	Y	Y
MINNESOTA					
1 Walz	N	Y	Y	Y	Y
2 **Kline**	Y	N	N	Y	Y
3 **Paulsen**	Y	Y	N	Y	Y
4 McCollum	N	Y	Y	Y	Y

	505	506	507	508	509
5 Ellison	N	Y	Y	Y	Y
6 **Bachmann**	?	?	?	?	?
7 Peterson	N	Y	Y	Y	Y
8 Oberstar	N	Y	Y	Y	Y
MISSISSIPPI					
1 Childers	Y	Y	N	Y	Y
2 Thompson	N	Y	Y	Y	Y
3 **Harper**	Y	N	N	Y	Y
4 Taylor	Y	Y	Y	Y	Y
MISSOURI					
1 Clay	N	Y	Y	Y	Y
2 **Akin**	+	–	–	+	+
3 Carnahan	N	Y	Y	Y	Y
4 Skelton	N	Y	N	Y	Y
5 Cleaver	N	Y	Y	Y	Y
6 **Graves**	Y	Y	N	Y	Y
7 **Blunt**	Y	Y	N	Y	Y
8 **Emerson**	Y	Y	N	Y	Y
9 **Luetkemeyer**	Y	Y	N	Y	Y
MONTANA					
AL **Rehberg**	Y	N	N	Y	Y
NEBRASKA					
1 **Fortenberry**	Y	Y	N	Y	Y
2 **Terry**	Y	Y	N	Y	Y
3 **Smith**	Y	N	N	Y	Y
NEVADA					
1 Berkley	N	Y	Y	Y	Y
2 **Heller**	Y	N	N	Y	Y
3 Titus	N	Y	Y	Y	Y
NEW HAMPSHIRE					
1 Shea-Porter	N	Y	Y	Y	Y
2 Hodes	N	Y	Y	Y	Y
NEW JERSEY					
1 Andrews	N	Y	Y	Y	Y
2 **LoBiondo**	Y	Y	Y	Y	Y
3 Adler	N	Y	Y	Y	Y
4 **Smith**	Y	Y	N	Y	Y
5 **Garrett**	Y	N	N	Y	Y
6 Pallone	N	Y	Y	Y	Y
7 **Lance**	Y	Y	N	Y	Y
8 Pascrell	N	Y	Y	Y	Y
9 Rothman	N	Y	Y	Y	Y
10 Payne	N	Y	Y	Y	Y
11 **Frelinghuysen**	Y	Y	N	Y	Y
12 Holt	N	Y	Y	Y	Y
13 Sires	N	Y	Y	Y	Y
NEW MEXICO					
1 Heinrich	N	Y	Y	Y	Y
2 Teague	N	Y	Y	Y	Y
3 Luján	N	Y	Y	Y	Y
NEW YORK					
1 Bishop	N	Y	Y	Y	Y
2 Israel	N	Y	Y	Y	Y
3 **King**	Y	Y	N	Y	Y
4 McCarthy	N	Y	Y	Y	Y
5 Ackerman	N	Y	Y	Y	Y
6 Meeks	N	Y	Y	Y	Y
7 Crowley	N	Y	Y	Y	Y
8 Nadler	N	Y	Y	Y	Y
9 Weiner	N	Y	Y	Y	Y
10 Towns	N	Y	Y	Y	Y
11 Clarke	N	Y	Y	Y	Y
12 Velázquez	N	Y	Y	Y	Y
13 McMahon	N	Y	Y	Y	Y
14 Maloney	N	Y	Y	Y	Y
15 Rangel	N	Y	Y	Y	Y
16 Serrano	N	Y	Y	Y	Y
17 Engel	N	Y	Y	Y	Y
18 Lowey	N	Y	Y	Y	Y
19 Hall	N	Y	Y	Y	Y
20 Murphy	N	Y	Y	Y	Y
21 Tonko	N	Y	Y	Y	Y
22 Hinchey	N	Y	Y	Y	Y
23 Owens	N	Y	Y	Y	Y
24 Arcuri	N	Y	Y	Y	Y
25 Maffei	N	Y	Y	Y	Y
26 **Lee**	Y	Y	N	Y	Y
27 Higgins	N	Y	Y	Y	Y
28 Slaughter	–	Y	Y	Y	Y
29 Vacant					
NORTH CAROLINA					
1 Butterfield	N	Y	Y	Y	Y
2 Etheridge	N	Y	Y	Y	Y
3 **Jones**	Y	Y	N	Y	Y
4 Price	N	Y	Y	Y	Y

	505	506	507	508	509
5 **Foxx**	?	N	N	Y	Y
6 **Coble**	Y	N	N	Y	Y
7 McIntyre	Y	Y	Y	Y	Y
8 Kissell	N	Y	Y	Y	Y
9 **Myrick**	Y	N	N	Y	Y
10 **McHenry**	Y	N	N	Y	Y
11 Shuler	N	Y	Y	Y	Y
12 Watt	N	?	Y	Y	Y
13 Miller	N	Y	Y	Y	Y
NORTH DAKOTA					
AL Pomeroy	N	Y	Y	Y	Y
OHIO					
1 Driehaus	N	Y	Y	Y	Y
2 **Schmidt**	Y	N	N	Y	Y
3 **Turner**	Y	Y	N	Y	Y
4 **Jordan**	Y	N	N	Y	Y
5 **Latta**	Y	N	N	Y	Y
6 Wilson	N	Y	Y	Y	Y
7 **Austria**	Y	Y	N	Y	Y
8 **Boehner**	Y	N	N	?	?
9 Kaptur	N	Y	Y	Y	Y
10 Kucinich	N	Y	Y	Y	Y
11 Fudge	N	Y	Y	Y	Y
12 **Tiberi**	Y	Y	N	Y	Y
13 Sutton	N	Y	Y	?	Y
14 **LaTourette**	Y	Y	N	Y	Y
15 Kilroy	N	Y	Y	Y	Y
16 Boccieri	N	Y	Y	Y	Y
17 Ryan	N	Y	Y	Y	Y
18 Space	N	Y	Y	Y	Y
OKLAHOMA					
1 **Sullivan**	Y	N	N	Y	Y
2 Boren	Y	Y	N	Y	Y
3 **Lucas**	Y	N	N	Y	Y
4 **Cole**	Y	N	N	Y	Y
5 **Fallin**	Y	N	N	Y	Y
OREGON					
1 Wu	?	Y	N	Y	Y
2 **Walden**	Y	Y	Y	Y	Y
3 Blumenauer	N	Y	Y	Y	Y
4 DeFazio	N	Y	Y	Y	Y
5 Schrader	N	Y	Y	Y	Y
PENNSYLVANIA					
1 Brady	N	Y	Y	Y	Y
2 Fattah	N	Y	Y	Y	Y
3 Dahlkemper	N	Y	Y	Y	Y
4 Altmire	N	Y	Y	Y	Y
5 **Thompson**	Y	N	N	Y	Y
6 **Gerlach**	Y	Y	Y	Y	Y
7 Sestak	N	Y	Y	Y	Y
8 Murphy, P.	N	Y	Y	Y	Y
9 **Shuster**	Y	N	N	Y	Y
10 Carney	?	?	?	?	?
11 Kanjorski	N	Y	Y	Y	Y
12 Critz	N	Y	N	Y	Y
13 Schwartz	N	Y	Y	Y	Y
14 Doyle	N	Y	Y	Y	Y
15 **Dent**	Y	Y	N	Y	Y
16 **Pitts**	Y	N	N	Y	Y
17 Holden	N	Y	Y	Y	Y
18 **Murphy, T.**	Y	Y	N	Y	Y
19 **Platts**	Y	Y	N	Y	Y
RHODE ISLAND					
1 Kennedy	N	Y	Y	Y	Y
2 Langevin	N	Y	Y	Y	Y
SOUTH CAROLINA					
1 **Brown**	?	?	?	?	?
2 **Wilson**	Y	N	N	Y	Y
3 **Barrett**	Y	N	N	Y	Y
4 **Inglis**	Y	N	N	Y	Y
5 Spratt	N	Y	Y	Y	Y
6 Clyburn	N	Y	Y	Y	Y
SOUTH DAKOTA					
AL Herseth Sandlin	N	Y	Y	Y	Y
TENNESSEE					
1 **Roe**	Y	N	N	Y	Y
2 **Duncan**	Y	N	N	Y	Y
3 **Wamp**	?	?	?	?	?
4 Davis	N	Y	Y	Y	Y
5 Cooper	N	Y	Y	Y	Y
6 Gordon	N	Y	Y	Y	Y
7 **Blackburn**	Y	N	N	Y	Y
8 Tanner	N	Y	Y	Y	Y
9 Cohen	N	Y	Y	Y	Y

	505	506	507	508	509
TEXAS					
1 **Gohmert**	Y	N	N	Y	Y
2 **Poe**	Y	N	N	Y	Y
3 **Johnson, S.**	Y	N	N	Y	N
4 **Hall**	Y	N	N	Y	N
5 **Hensarling**	Y	N	N	Y	Y
6 **Barton**	Y	N	N	Y	Y
7 **Culberson**	Y	N	N	Y	Y
8 **Brady**	Y	N	N	Y	Y
9 Green, A.	N	Y	Y	Y	Y
10 **McCaul**	Y	N	N	Y	Y
11 **Conaway**	Y	N	N	Y	Y
12 **Granger**	Y	N	N	Y	Y
13 **Thornberry**	Y	N	N	Y	Y
14 **Paul**	Y	N	N	Y	Y
15 Hinojosa	N	Y	Y	Y	Y
16 Reyes	N	Y	Y	Y	Y
17 Edwards	N	Y	Y	Y	Y
18 Jackson Lee	N	Y	Y	Y	Y
19 **Neugebauer**	Y	N	N	Y	Y
20 Gonzalez	N	Y	Y	Y	Y
21 **Smith**	Y	N	N	Y	Y
22 **Olson**	Y	N	N	Y	Y
23 Rodriguez	N	Y	Y	Y	Y
24 **Marchant**	Y	?	N	Y	Y
25 Doggett	N	Y	Y	Y	Y
26 **Burgess**	Y	N	N	Y	Y
27 Ortiz	N	Y	Y	Y	Y
28 Cuellar	N	Y	Y	Y	Y
29 Green, G.	N	Y	Y	Y	Y
30 Johnson, E.	N	Y	Y	Y	Y
31 **Carter**	Y	N	N	Y	Y
32 **Sessions**	Y	N	N	Y	?
UTAH					
1 **Bishop**	Y	N	N	Y	Y
2 Matheson	N	Y	N	Y	Y
3 **Chaffetz**	Y	N	N	Y	Y
VERMONT					
AL Welch	N	Y	Y	Y	Y
VIRGINIA					
1 **Wittman**	Y	N	N	Y	Y
2 Nye	Y	N	N	Y	N
3 Scott	N	Y	Y	Y	Y
4 **Forbes**	Y	N	N	Y	Y
5 Perriello	N	Y	Y	Y	Y
6 **Goodlatte**	Y	N	N	Y	Y
7 **Cantor**	Y	N	N	Y	Y
8 Moran	N	Y	Y	Y	Y
9 Boucher	N	Y	Y	Y	Y
10 **Wolf**	Y	N	N	Y	Y
11 Connolly	N	Y	Y	Y	Y
WASHINGTON					
1 Inslee	N	Y	Y	Y	Y
2 Larsen	N	Y	Y	Y	Y
3 Baird	?	Y	Y	Y	Y
4 **Hastings**	Y	N	N	Y	Y
5 **McMorris Rodgers**	Y	N	N	Y	Y
6 Dicks	N	Y	Y	Y	Y
7 McDermott	N	Y	Y	Y	Y
8 **Reichert**	Y	N	N	Y	Y
9 Smith	N	Y	Y	Y	Y
WEST VIRGINIA					
1 Mollohan	N	Y	Y	Y	Y
2 **Capito**	Y	Y	N	Y	Y
3 Rahall	N	Y	Y	Y	Y
WISCONSIN					
1 **Ryan**	Y	N	N	?	N
2 Baldwin	N	Y	Y	Y	Y
3 Kind	N	Y	Y	Y	Y
4 Moore	N	Y	Y	Y	Y
5 **Sensenbrenner**	Y	N	N	Y	N
6 **Petri**	Y	Y	Y	Y	Y
7 Obey	N	Y	Y	Y	Y
8 Kagen	N	Y	Y	Y	Y
WYOMING					
AL **Lummis**	Y	N	N	N	Y
DELEGATES					
Faleomavaega (A.S.)			?	?	?
Norton (D.C.)			Y	Y	Y
Bordallo (Guam)			Y	Y	Y
Sablan (N. Marianas)			Y	Y	Y
Pierluisi (P.R.)			Y	Y	Y
Christensen (V.I.)			?	?	?

IN THE HOUSE | By Vote Number

510. HR 3534. **Offshore Drilling Regulation Overhaul/Land Acquisition Consideration.** Oberstar, D-Minn., amendment that would require trustees developing plans to restore, rehabilitate or replace natural resources damaged after an oil spill to give equal and full consideration to acquisition of non-affected land. Adopted in Committee of the Whole 258-149: D 243-5; R 15-144. July 30, 2010.

511. HR 3534. **Offshore Drilling Regulation Overhaul/Drilling Permits.** Melancon, D-La., amendment that would seek to end the federal moratorium on deep-water drilling by allowing the Interior secretary to provide permits to applicants that have complied with increased safety measures outlined by the Minerals Management Service on June 8, 2010, and June 18, 2010. Applicants would also have to comply with any additional safety measures recommended by the Interior Department and complete all required safety inspections before they could be granted a permit. Adopted in Committee of the Whole 216-195: D 213-39; R 3-156. July 30, 2010.

512. HR 3534. **Offshore Drilling Regulation Overhaul/Recommit.** Cassidy, R-La., motion to recommit the bill to the House Natural Resources Committee with instructions that it be reported back immediately with an amendment that would provide for the termination of the moratoriums set forth in the Minerals Management Service Notice dated May 30, 2010; the decision memorandum from the Interior secretary dated July 12, 2010; and any suspension of operations issued in connection with either moratorium. A "nay" was a vote in support of the president's position. Motion rejected 166-239: D 17-228; R 149-11. July 30, 2010.

513. HR 3534. **Offshore Drilling Regulation Overhaul/Passage.** Passage of the bill that would repeal the current $75 million cap on liability for offshore oil spills. It also would abolish the agency formerly known as the Minerals Management Service in the Interior Department and assign its responsibilities to three new agencies in the department. It would create numerous new safety regulations for leases for offshore oil and gas development, including features designed to prevent well blowouts, and it would require some holders of leases to renegotiate royalty payments disputed by industry. As amended, it would prevent oil companies from shifting oil spill cleanup costs to taxpayers in the event one of its subsidiaries goes bankrupt. Passed 209-193: D 207-39; R 2-154. A "yea" was a vote in support of the president's position. July 30, 2010.

514. HR 5982. **IRS Filing Requirement Repeal/Passage.** Levin, D-Mich., motion to suspend the rules and pass the bill that would repeal tax compliance language in the health care overhaul law that would require businesses to file information reports to the IRS for payments of $600 or more made to any vendor in a single year. The repeal of the reporting requirement would be offset by placing new limits on the ability of U.S.-based companies to use certain foreign tax-credit transactions to lower their tax liability. Motion rejected 241-154: D 239-1; R 2-153. A two-thirds majority of those present and voting (264 in this case) is required for passage under suspension of the rules. July 30, 2010.

	510	511	512	513	514
ALABAMA					
1 **Bonner**	N	N	Y	N	N
2 Bright	Y	Y	N	N	Y
3 **Rogers**	N	N	Y	N	N
4 **Aderholt**	N	N	Y	N	N
5 **Griffith**	?	?	?	?	?
6 **Bachus**	N	N	Y	N	N
7 Davis	Y	Y	N	N	Y
ALASKA					
AL **Young**	N	N	Y	N	N
ARIZONA					
1 Kirkpatrick	Y	Y	N	N	Y
2 **Franks**	N	N	Y	N	N
3 **Shadegg**	?	?	?	?	?
4 Pastor	Y	N	N	Y	Y
5 Mitchell	Y	Y	Y	N	Y
6 **Flake**	N	N	Y	N	N
7 Grijalva	Y	N	N	Y	Y
8 Giffords	Y	Y	N	Y	Y
ARKANSAS					
1 Berry	?	?	?	?	?
2 Snyder	Y	Y	N	Y	Y
3 **Boozman**	N	N	Y	N	N
4 Ross	Y	Y	Y	N	Y
CALIFORNIA					
1 Thompson	Y	Y	N	Y	Y
2 **Herger**	N	N	Y	N	N
3 **Lungren**	N	N	Y	N	N
4 **McClintock**	N	N	Y	N	N
5 Matsui	Y	Y	N	Y	Y
6 Woolsey	Y	Y	N	Y	Y
7 Miller, George	Y	Y	N	Y	Y
8 Pelosi		Y		Y	
9 Lee	Y	Y	N	Y	Y
10 Garamendi	Y	Y	N	Y	Y
11 McNerney	Y	Y	N	Y	Y
12 Speier	Y	N	N	Y	Y
13 Stark	Y	Y	N	Y	Y
14 Eshoo	Y	Y	N	Y	Y
15 Honda	Y	Y	N	Y	Y
16 Lofgren	Y	Y	N	Y	Y
17 Farr	Y	Y	N	Y	?
18 Cardoza	Y	Y	N	Y	Y
19 **Radanovich**	?	?	?	?	?
20 Costa	N	Y	N	Y	Y
21 **Nunes**	?	?	?	?	?
22 **McCarthy**	?	?	?	?	?
23 Capps	Y	Y	N	Y	Y
24 **Gallegly**	N	N	Y	N	N
25 **McKeon**	N	N	Y	?	?
26 **Dreier**	N	N	Y	N	N
27 Sherman	Y	N	N	Y	Y
28 Berman	Y	Y	N	Y	Y
29 Schiff	Y	Y	N	Y	Y
30 Waxman	Y	Y	N	Y	Y
31 Becerra	Y	Y	N	Y	Y
32 Chu	Y	N	N	Y	Y
33 Watson	?	?	?	?	?
34 Roybal-Allard	Y	N	N	Y	Y
35 Waters	Y	N	N	Y	Y
36 Harman	Y	Y	N	Y	?
37 Richardson	Y	Y	N	Y	Y
38 Napolitano	Y	N	N	Y	Y
39 Sánchez, Linda	Y	Y	N	Y	Y
40 **Royce**	N	N	Y	N	N
41 **Lewis**	N	N	Y	N	N
42 **Miller, Gary**	N	P	Y	P	N
43 Baca	Y	Y	N	Y	Y
44 **Calvert**	N	N	Y	N	N
45 **Bono Mack**	N	N	Y	N	N
46 **Rohrabacher**	N	N	Y	N	N
47 Sanchez, Loretta	Y	Y	N	Y	Y
48 **Campbell**	?	?	?	?	?
49 **Issa**	N	N	Y	N	N
50 **Bilbray**	N	N	Y	N	N
51 Filner	Y	Y	N	Y	Y
52 **Hunter**	N	N	Y	N	N
53 Davis	Y	Y	N	Y	Y

	510	511	512	513	514
COLORADO					
1 DeGette	Y	Y	N	Y	Y
2 Polis	Y	Y	N	Y	Y
3 Salazar	Y	N	Y	N	Y
4 Markey	Y	Y	N	Y	Y
5 **Lamborn**	N	N	Y	N	N
6 **Coffman**	N	N	Y	N	N
7 Perlmutter	?	?	?	?	?
CONNECTICUT					
1 Larson	Y	Y	N	Y	Y
2 Courtney	Y	Y	N	Y	Y
3 DeLauro	Y	Y	N	Y	Y
4 Himes	+	–	–	+	+
5 Murphy	Y	Y	N	Y	Y
DELAWARE					
AL **Castle**	Y	N	N	N	N
FLORIDA					
1 **Miller**	N	N	N	N	N
2 Boyd	Y	Y	N	Y	Y
3 Brown	Y	Y	N	Y	Y
4 **Crenshaw**	N	N	N	N	N
5 **Brown-Waite**	N	N	Y	N	N
6 **Stearns**	N	N	N	N	N
7 **Mica**	N	N	Y	N	N
8 Grayson	Y	N	N	Y	Y
9 **Bilirakis**	N	N	N	N	N
10 **Young**	?	?	?	?	?
11 Castor	Y	N	N	Y	Y
12 **Putnam**	N	Y	N	N	N
13 **Buchanan**	N	N	N	N	N
14 **Mack**	N	N	N	N	N
15 **Posey**	N	N	N	N	N
16 **Rooney**	N	N	Y	N	N
17 Meek	Y	N	N	Y	Y
18 **Ros-Lehtinen**	N	N	N	N	N
19 Deutch	Y	Y	N	Y	Y
20 Wasserman Schultz	Y	N	N	Y	Y
21 **Diaz-Balart, L.**	N	N	Y	N	N
22 Klein	Y	N	N	Y	Y
23 Hastings	?	Y	N	Y	Y
24 Kosmas	Y	Y	N	Y	Y
25 **Diaz-Balart, M.**	N	N	Y	N	N
GEORGIA					
1 **Kingston**	N	N	Y	N	N
2 Bishop	Y	Y	N	Y	Y
3 **Westmoreland**	N	N	Y	N	N
4 Johnson	Y	Y	N	Y	Y
5 Lewis	Y	Y	N	Y	Y
6 **Price**	N	N	Y	N	N
7 **Linder**	?	?	?	?	?
8 Marshall	Y	Y	Y	N	Y
9 **Graves**	N	N	Y	N	N
10 **Broun**	N	N	Y	N	N
11 **Gingrey**	N	N	Y	N	N
12 Barrow	Y	Y	Y	Y	Y
13 Scott	Y	Y	N	Y	Y
HAWAII					
1 **Djou**	Y	N	N	N	N
2 Hirono	Y	Y	N	Y	Y
IDAHO					
1 Minnick	Y	N	Y	N	N
2 **Simpson**	N	N	Y	N	N
ILLINOIS					
1 Rush	Y	Y	N	Y	Y
2 Jackson	Y	Y	N	Y	Y
3 Lipinski	Y	N	N	Y	Y
4 Gutierrez	Y	N	N	Y	Y
5 Quigley	Y	N	N	Y	Y
6 **Roskam**	N	N	Y	N	N
7 Davis	Y	N	N	Y	Y
8 Bean	Y	N	N	Y	Y
9 Schakowsky	Y	N	N	Y	Y
10 **Kirk**	Y	Y	N	N	N
11 Halvorson	N	Y	N	Y	Y
12 Costello	Y	Y	N	Y	Y
13 **Biggert**	N	N	Y	N	N
14 Foster	Y	Y	?	Y	Y
15 **Johnson**	Y	N	N	Y	N

KEY	**Republicans**	Democrats		
Y	Voted for (yea)	X	Paired against	C Voted "present" to avoid possible conflict of interest
#	Paired for	–	Announced against	
+	Announced for	P	Voted "present"	? Did not vote or otherwise make a position known
N	Voted against (nay)			

	510	511	512	513	514
16 Manzullo	N	N	Y	N	N
17 Hare	Y	N	Y	N	Y
18 Schock	N	N	Y	N	N
19 Shimkus	N	N	Y	N	N
INDIANA					
1 Visclosky	Y	Y	N	Y	Y
2 Donnelly	Y	Y	Y	N	Y
3 Vacant					
4 Buyer	?	?	?	?	?
5 Burton	N	N	Y	N	N
6 Pence	N	N	Y	N	N
7 Carson	Y	Y	N	Y	Y
8 Ellsworth	Y	Y	Y	N	Y
9 Hill	Y	Y	N	Y	Y
IOWA					
1 Braley	Y	Y	N	Y	Y
2 Loebsack	Y	Y	N	Y	Y
3 Boswell	Y	Y	N	Y	Y
4 Latham	N	N	Y	N	N
5 King	N	N	Y	N	N
KANSAS					
1 Moran	?	?	?	?	?
2 Jenkins	N	N	Y	N	N
3 Moore	Y	Y	N	Y	Y
4 Tiahrt	?	?	?	?	?
KENTUCKY					
1 Whitfield	N	N	Y	N	N
2 Guthrie	N	N	Y	N	N
3 Yarmuth	Y	Y	N	Y	Y
4 Davis	–	–	+	–	–
5 Rogers	N	N	Y	N	N
6 Chandler	Y	Y	N	Y	?
LOUISIANA					
1 Scalise	N	N	Y	N	N
2 Cao	Y	N	Y	N	Y
3 Melancon	Y	Y	N	Y	Y
4 Fleming	N	N	Y	N	N
5 Alexander	N	N	Y	N	N
6 Cassidy	N	N	Y	N	N
7 Boustany	N	N	Y	N	N
MAINE					
1 Pingree	Y	Y	N	Y	Y
2 Michaud	Y	Y	N	Y	Y
MARYLAND					
1 Kratovil	Y	Y	N	Y	Y
2 Ruppersberger	Y	N	N	Y	Y
3 Sarbanes	Y	Y	N	Y	Y
4 Edwards	Y	Y	P	Y	Y
5 Hoyer	Y	Y	N	Y	Y
6 Bartlett	N	N	Y	N	N
7 Cummings	Y	Y	N	Y	Y
8 Van Hollen	Y	Y	N	Y	Y
MASSACHUSETTS					
1 Olver	Y	Y	N	Y	Y
2 Neal	Y	Y	N	Y	Y
3 McGovern	Y	Y	N	Y	Y
4 Frank	Y	Y	N	Y	Y
5 Tsongas	Y	Y	N	Y	Y
6 Tierney	Y	Y	N	Y	Y
7 Markey	Y	Y	N	Y	Y
8 Capuano	Y	Y	N	Y	Y
9 Lynch	Y	N	N	Y	Y
10 Delahunt	?	?	?	?	?
MICHIGAN					
1 Stupak	Y	Y	N	Y	Y
2 Hoekstra	?	?	?	?	?
3 Ehlers	Y	N	Y	Y	N
4 Camp	N	N	Y	N	N
5 Kildee	Y	Y	N	Y	Y
6 Upton	Y	N	Y	N	N
7 Schauer	Y	Y	N	Y	Y
8 Rogers	?	?	?	?	?
9 Peters	Y	Y	N	Y	Y
10 Miller	N	N	Y	N	N
11 McCotter	N	N	Y	N	N
12 Levin	Y	Y	N	Y	Y
13 Kilpatrick	+	+	–	+	+
14 Conyers	Y	Y	N	Y	Y
15 Dingell	Y	Y	N	Y	Y
MINNESOTA					
1 Walz	Y	Y	N	Y	Y
2 Kline	N	N	Y	N	N
3 Paulsen	N	N	Y	N	N
4 McCollum	Y	Y	N	Y	Y

	510	511	512	513	514
5 Ellison	Y	Y	N	Y	Y
6 Bachmann	?	?	?	N	N
7 Peterson	Y	Y	N	N	Y
8 Oberstar	Y	Y	N	Y	Y
MISSISSIPPI					
1 Childers	Y	Y	N	N	?
2 Thompson	Y	Y	N	Y	Y
3 Harper	N	N	Y	N	N
4 Taylor	Y	Y	N	Y	Y
MISSOURI					
1 Clay	Y	N	N	Y	Y
2 Akin	–	–	+	–	–
3 Carnahan	Y	Y	N	Y	Y
4 Skelton	Y	Y	N	N	Y
5 Cleaver	Y	Y	N	Y	Y
6 Graves	N	N	Y	N	N
7 Blunt	N	N	Y	?	?
8 Emerson	N	N	Y	N	N
9 Luetkemeyer	N	N	Y	N	?
MONTANA					
AL Rehberg	N	N	Y	N	N
NEBRASKA					
1 Fortenberry	Y	N	Y	N	N
2 Terry	N	N	Y	N	N
3 Smith	N	N	Y	N	N
NEVADA					
1 Berkley	Y	Y	N	Y	Y
2 Heller	N	N	Y	N	N
3 Titus	Y	Y	N	N	Y
NEW HAMPSHIRE					
1 Shea-Porter	Y	N	N	Y	Y
2 Hodes	Y	N	N	Y	Y
NEW JERSEY					
1 Andrews	Y	Y	N	Y	Y
2 LoBiondo	Y	N	Y	N	N
3 Adler	Y	Y	N	Y	Y
4 Smith	Y	Y	N	Y	N
5 Garrett	N	N	Y	N	N
6 Pallone	Y	N	N	Y	Y
7 Lance	N	N	Y	N	N
8 Pascrell	Y	Y	N	Y	Y
9 Rothman	Y	Y	N	Y	Y
10 Payne	Y	Y	N	Y	Y
11 Frelinghuysen	N	N	Y	N	N
12 Holt	Y	N	N	Y	Y
13 Sires	Y	Y	N	Y	Y
NEW MEXICO					
1 Heinrich	Y	Y	N	Y	Y
2 Teague	Y	Y	N	N	Y
3 Luján	Y	N	N	Y	Y
NEW YORK					
1 Bishop	Y	Y	N	Y	Y
2 Israel	Y	Y	N	Y	Y
3 King	N	N	Y	N	N
4 McCarthy	Y	Y	N	Y	Y
5 Ackerman	Y	Y	N	Y	Y
6 Meeks	Y	Y	N	Y	Y
7 Crowley	Y	Y	N	Y	Y
8 Nadler	Y	Y	N	Y	Y
9 Weiner	Y	Y	N	Y	Y
10 Towns	Y	Y	N	Y	Y
11 Clarke	Y	Y	N	Y	Y
12 Velázquez	Y	Y	N	Y	Y
13 McMahon	Y	N	N	N	Y
14 Maloney	Y	Y	N	Y	Y
15 Rangel	Y	Y	N	Y	Y
16 Serrano	Y	Y	N	Y	Y
17 Engel	Y	Y	N	Y	Y
18 Lowey	Y	Y	N	Y	Y
19 Hall	Y	N	N	Y	Y
20 Murphy	Y	Y	N	Y	Y
21 Tonko	Y	Y	N	Y	Y
22 Hinchey	Y	Y	N	Y	Y
23 Owens	Y	Y	N	Y	Y
24 Arcuri	Y	N	N	Y	Y
25 Maffei	Y	N	N	Y	Y
26 Lee	N	N	Y	N	N
27 Higgins	Y	Y	N	Y	Y
28 Slaughter	Y	Y	N	Y	Y
29 Vacant					
NORTH CAROLINA					
1 Butterfield	Y	Y	N	Y	Y
2 Etheridge	Y	Y	N	Y	Y
3 Jones	N	Y	N	N	Y
4 Price	Y	Y	N	Y	Y

	510	511	512	513	514
5 Foxx	N	N	Y	N	N
6 Coble	N	N	Y	N	N
7 McIntyre	Y	Y	N	Y	Y
8 Kissell	Y	Y	N	Y	Y
9 Myrick	N	N	Y	N	N
10 McHenry	N	N	Y	N	N
11 Shuler	Y	Y	N	Y	Y
12 Watt	Y	Y	N	Y	Y
13 Miller	Y	Y	N	Y	Y
NORTH DAKOTA					
AL Pomeroy	Y	Y	Y	N	Y
OHIO					
1 Driehaus	Y	Y	N	Y	Y
2 Schmidt	N	N	Y	N	N
3 Turner	N	N	Y	N	N
4 Jordan	N	N	Y	N	N
5 Latta	N	N	Y	N	N
6 Wilson	Y	Y	N	Y	Y
7 Austria	N	N	Y	N	N
8 Boehner	N	N	Y	N	N
9 Kaptur	Y	Y	N	Y	Y
10 Kucinich	Y	N	Y	Y	Y
11 Fudge	Y	Y	N	Y	Y
12 Tiberi	N	N	Y	N	N
13 Sutton	Y	Y	N	Y	Y
14 LaTourette	N	N	Y	Y	N
15 Kilroy	Y	Y	N	Y	Y
16 Boccieri	Y	Y	N	Y	Y
17 Ryan	Y	Y	N	Y	Y
18 Space	Y	Y	Y	N	Y
OKLAHOMA					
1 Sullivan	N	N	Y	N	N
2 Boren	N	Y	N	Y	Y
3 Lucas	N	N	Y	N	N
4 Cole	N	N	Y	N	N
5 Fallin	N	N	Y	N	N
OREGON					
1 Wu	?	Y	N	Y	Y
2 Walden	N	N	Y	N	N
3 Blumenauer	Y	Y	N	Y	Y
4 DeFazio	Y	Y	N	Y	Y
5 Schrader	Y	Y	N	Y	Y
PENNSYLVANIA					
1 Brady	Y	Y	N	Y	Y
2 Fattah	Y	Y	N	Y	Y
3 Dahlkemper	Y	Y	N	Y	Y
4 Altmire	Y	Y	N	Y	Y
5 Thompson	N	N	Y	N	N
6 Gerlach	N	N	Y	N	N
7 Sestak	?	Y	N	Y	Y
8 Murphy, P.	Y	Y	N	Y	Y
9 Shuster	N	N	Y	N	N
10 Carney	?	?	?	?	?
11 Kanjorski	Y	Y	N	Y	Y
12 Critz	Y	Y	N	Y	Y
13 Schwartz	Y	Y	N	Y	Y
14 Doyle	Y	Y	N	Y	Y
15 Dent	Y	N	Y	N	N
16 Pitts	N	N	Y	N	N
17 Holden	Y	N	N	Y	Y
18 Murphy, T.	N	N	Y	N	N
19 Platts	Y	N	Y	N	N
RHODE ISLAND					
1 Kennedy	Y	Y	N	Y	Y
2 Langevin	Y	N	N	Y	Y
SOUTH CAROLINA					
1 Brown	?	?	?	?	?
2 Wilson	N	N	Y	N	N
3 Barrett	N	N	Y	?	?
4 Inglis	N	N	Y	N	N
5 Spratt	Y	Y	N	Y	?
6 Clyburn	Y	Y	N	Y	Y
SOUTH DAKOTA					
AL Herseth Sandlin	Y	Y	N	N	Y
TENNESSEE					
1 Roe	N	N	Y	N	N
2 Duncan	N	N	Y	N	N
3 Wamp	?	?	?	?	?
4 Davis	Y	Y	N	N	Y
5 Cooper	Y	Y	N	Y	Y
6 Gordon	Y	Y	N	Y	Y
7 Blackburn	N	N	Y	N	N
8 Tanner	Y	Y	N	N	?
9 Cohen	Y	N	N	Y	Y

	510	511	512	513	514
TEXAS					
1 Gohmert	N	N	Y	N	N
2 Poe	N	N	Y	N	N
3 Johnson, S.	N	N	Y	?	?
4 Hall	N	N	Y	N	N
5 Hensarling	N	N	Y	N	N
6 Barton	N	N	Y	N	N
7 Culberson	N	N	Y	N	N
8 Brady	N	N	Y	N	N
9 Green, A.	Y	Y	N	Y	Y
10 McCaul	N	N	Y	N	N
11 Conaway	N	N	Y	N	N
12 Granger	N	N	Y	N	N
13 Thornberry	N	N	Y	N	N
14 Paul	N	N	Y	N	N
15 Hinojosa	Y	Y	N	Y	Y
16 Reyes	Y	Y	N	?	Y
17 Edwards	Y	Y	N	Y	Y
18 Jackson Lee	Y	Y	N	Y	Y
19 Neugebauer	N	N	Y	N	N
20 Gonzalez	Y	Y	N	Y	Y
21 Smith	N	N	Y	N	N
22 Olson	N	N	Y	N	N
23 Rodriguez	Y	Y	N	Y	Y
24 Marchant	N	N	Y	N	N
25 Doggett	Y	Y	N	Y	Y
26 Burgess	N	N	Y	N	N
27 Ortiz	Y	Y	N	Y	Y
28 Cuellar	Y	Y	N	Y	Y
29 Green, G.	Y	Y	N	Y	Y
30 Johnson, E.	Y	Y	N	Y	Y
31 Carter	N	N	Y	N	N
32 Sessions	?	N	N	N	N
UTAH					
1 Bishop	N	N	Y	N	N
2 Matheson	N	Y	N	N	Y
3 Chaffetz	N	N	Y	N	?
VERMONT					
AL Welch	Y	N	N	Y	Y
VIRGINIA					
1 Wittman	N	N	Y	N	N
2 Nye	N	Y	N	N	Y
3 Scott	Y	N	N	Y	Y
4 Forbes	N	N	Y	N	N
5 Perriello	Y	Y	N	Y	Y
6 Goodlatte	N	N	Y	N	N
7 Cantor	N	N	Y	N	N
8 Moran	Y	Y	N	Y	Y
9 Boucher	Y	Y	N	Y	Y
10 Wolf	N	N	Y	N	N
11 Connolly	Y	Y	N	Y	Y
WASHINGTON					
1 Inslee	Y	Y	N	Y	Y
2 Larsen	Y	Y	N	Y	Y
3 Baird	Y	Y	N	Y	Y
4 Hastings	N	N	Y	N	N
5 McMorris Rodgers	N	N	Y	N	N
6 Dicks	Y	Y	N	Y	Y
7 McDermott	Y	Y	N	Y	Y
8 Reichert	Y	Y	N	Y	Y
9 Smith	Y	Y	N	Y	Y
WEST VIRGINIA					
1 Mollohan	Y	Y	N	Y	Y
2 Capito	N	N	Y	N	N
3 Rahall	Y	Y	N	Y	Y
WISCONSIN					
1 Ryan	N	N	Y	N	N
2 Baldwin	Y	Y	N	Y	Y
3 Kind	Y	Y	N	Y	Y
4 Moore	Y	Y	N	Y	Y
5 Sensenbrenner	N	N	Y	N	N
6 Petri	N	N	Y	N	N
7 Obey	Y	Y	N	?	?
8 Kagen	Y	Y	N	Y	Y
WYOMING					
AL Lummis	N	N	Y	N	N
DELEGATES					
Faleomavaega (A.S.)	?	?			
Norton (D.C.)	Y	Y			
Bordallo (Guam)	Y	Y			
Sablan (N. Marianas)	Y	Y			
Pierluisi (P.R.)	Y	Y			
Christensen (V.I.)	?	?			

IN THE HOUSE | By Vote Number

515. **Opposition to Lame-Duck Session/Motion to Table.** Polis, D-Colo., motion to table (kill) the Price, R-Ga., appeal of the ruling of the chair that the Price draft resolution does not constitute a question of the privileges of the House under Rule 9 of the House. The draft resolution would pledge that the House would not assemble on or between the dates of Nov. 2, 2010, and Jan. 3, 2011, except in the case of an unforeseen, sudden emergency requiring immediate action from Congress. Motion agreed to 236-163: D 235-6; R 1-157. Aug. 10, 2010.

516. **HR 1586. Medicaid and Education Assistance/Previous Question.** Polis, D-Colo., motion to order the previous question (thus ending debate and possibility of amendment) on adoption of the rule (H Res 1606) to provide for House floor consideration of the Senate amendment to the House amendment to the Senate amendment to the bill that would provide $16.1 billion to extend increased Medicaid assistance to states and $10 billion in education funding for states. Motion agreed to 244-164: D 244-4; R 0-160. Aug. 10, 2010.

517. **HR 1586. Medicaid and Education Assistance/Rule.** Adoption of the rule (H Res 1606) that would provide for House floor consideration of the Senate amendment to the House amendment to the Senate amendment to the bill that would provide $16.1 billion to extend increased Medicaid assistance to states and $10 billion in education funding for states. Adopted 229-173: D 229-16; R 0-157. Aug. 10, 2010.

518. **HR 1586. Medicaid and Education Assistance/Motion to Concur.** Obey, D-Wis., motion to concur in the Senate amendment to the House amendment to the Senate amendment to the bill that would provide $16.1 billion to extend increased Medicaid assistance to states and $10 billion in funding for states to create or retain teachers' jobs. The costs would be offset by changing foreign tax provisions, ending increased food stamp benefits beginning in April 2014 and rescinding previously enacted spending. Motion agreed to, thus clearing the bill for the president, 247-161: D 245-3; R 2-158. A "yea" was a vote in support of the president's position. Aug. 10, 2010.

	515	516	517	518
ALABAMA				
1 **Bonner**	N	N	N	N
2 Bright	N	Y	N	N
3 **Rogers**	N	N	N	N
4 **Aderholt**	N	N	N	N
5 **Griffith**	N	N	N	N
6 **Bachus**	N	N	N	N
7 Davis	Y	Y	Y	Y
ALASKA				
AL **Young**	?	?	?	?
ARIZONA				
1 Kirkpatrick	Y	Y	Y	Y
2 **Franks**	N	N	N	N
3 **Shadegg**	N	N	N	N
4 Pastor	Y	Y	Y	Y
5 Mitchell	Y	N	Y	Y
6 **Flake**	N	N	N	N
7 Grijalva	Y	Y	Y	Y
8 Giffords	Y	N	N	Y
ARKANSAS				
1 Berry	?	?	?	?
2 Snyder	?	?	?	?
3 **Boozman**	N	N	N	N
4 Ross	Y	Y	Y	Y
CALIFORNIA				
1 Thompson	Y	Y	Y	Y
2 **Herger**	N	N	N	N
3 **Lungren**	?	?	?	?
4 **McClintock**	N	N	N	N
5 Matsui	Y	Y	Y	Y
6 Woolsey	Y	Y	Y	Y
7 Miller, George	Y	Y	Y	Y
8 Pelosi				Y
9 Lee	Y	Y	Y	Y
10 Garamendi	Y	Y	Y	Y
11 McNerney	Y	Y	Y	Y
12 Speier	?	?	?	?
13 Stark	Y	Y	Y	Y
14 Eshoo	Y	Y	Y	Y
15 Honda	Y	Y	Y	Y
16 Lofgren	Y	Y	Y	Y
17 Farr	Y	Y	Y	Y
18 Cardoza	Y	Y	Y	Y
19 **Radanovich**	?	?	?	?
20 Costa	Y	Y	N	Y
21 **Nunes**	N	N	N	N
22 **McCarthy**	N	N	N	N
23 Capps	Y	Y	Y	Y
24 **Gallegly**	N	N	N	N
25 **McKeon**	N	N	N	N
26 **Dreier**	N	N	N	N
27 Sherman	Y	Y	Y	Y
28 Berman	Y	Y	Y	Y
29 Schiff	Y	Y	Y	Y
30 Waxman	Y	Y	Y	Y
31 Becerra	Y	Y	Y	Y
32 Chu	Y	Y	Y	Y
33 Watson	Y	Y	Y	Y
34 Roybal-Allard	Y	Y	Y	Y
35 Waters	Y	Y	Y	Y
36 Harman	Y	Y	Y	Y
37 Richardson	Y	Y	Y	Y
38 Napolitano	Y	Y	Y	Y
39 Sánchez, Linda	Y	Y	Y	Y
40 **Royce**	N	N	N	N
41 **Lewis**	N	N	N	N
42 **Miller, Gary**	?	?	?	?
43 Baca	Y	Y	Y	Y
44 **Calvert**	N	N	N	N
45 **Bono Mack**	N	N	N	N
46 **Rohrabacher**	N	N	N	N
47 Sanchez, Loretta	Y	Y	Y	Y
48 **Campbell**	N	N	N	N
49 **Issa**	N	N	N	N
50 **Bilbray**	N	N	N	N
51 Filner	Y	Y	Y	Y
52 **Hunter**	N	N	N	N
53 Davis	Y	Y	Y	Y

	515	516	517	518
COLORADO				
1 DeGette	?	?	?	?
2 Polis	Y	Y	Y	Y
3 Salazar	?	Y	Y	Y
4 Markey	Y	Y	Y	Y
5 **Lamborn**	N	N	N	N
6 **Coffman**	N	N	N	N
7 Perlmutter	Y	Y	Y	Y
CONNECTICUT				
1 Larson	Y	Y	Y	Y
2 Courtney	Y	Y	Y	Y
3 DeLauro	Y	Y	Y	Y
4 Himes	Y	Y	Y	Y
5 Murphy	Y	Y	Y	Y
DELAWARE				
AL **Castle**	N	N	N	Y
FLORIDA				
1 **Miller**	N	N	N	N
2 Boyd	Y	Y	Y	Y
3 Brown	Y	Y	Y	Y
4 **Crenshaw**	N	N	N	N
5 **Brown-Waite**	N	N	N	N
6 **Stearns**	N	N	N	N
7 **Mica**	N	N	N	N
8 Grayson	Y	Y	Y	Y
9 **Bilirakis**	N	N	N	N
10 **Young**	?	?	?	?
11 Castor	Y	Y	Y	Y
12 **Putnam**	N	N	N	N
13 **Buchanan**	?	?	?	?
14 **Mack**	N	N	N	N
15 **Posey**	N	N	N	N
16 **Rooney**	?	?	?	?
17 **Meek**	?	?	?	?
18 **Ros-Lehtinen**	N	N	N	N
19 Deutch	Y	Y	Y	Y
20 Wasserman Schultz	Y	Y	Y	Y
21 **Diaz-Balart, L.**	?	?	?	?
22 Klein	Y	Y	Y	Y
23 Hastings	Y	Y	Y	Y
24 Kosmas	Y	Y	Y	Y
25 **Diaz-Balart, M.**	N	N	N	N
GEORGIA				
1 **Kingston**	N	N	N	N
2 Bishop	N	N	+	Y
3 **Westmoreland**	N	N	N	N
4 Johnson	Y	Y	Y	Y
5 Lewis	Y	Y	Y	Y
6 **Price**	N	N	N	N
7 **Linder**	?	?	?	?
8 Marshall	Y	Y	N	Y
9 **Graves**	N	N	N	N
10 **Broun**	?	?	?	?
11 **Gingrey**	?	?	?	?
12 Barrow	Y	Y	Y	Y
13 Scott	Y	Y	Y	Y
HAWAII				
1 **Djou**	?	N	N	N
2 Hirono	Y	Y	Y	Y
IDAHO				
1 Minnick	N	N	N	Y
2 **Simpson**	Y	N	N	N
ILLINOIS				
1 Rush	Y	Y	Y	Y
2 Jackson	Y	Y	Y	Y
3 Lipinski	Y	Y	Y	Y
4 Gutierrez	?	Y	?	Y
5 Quigley	Y	Y	Y	Y
6 **Roskam**	?	?	?	?
7 Davis	Y	Y	Y	Y
8 Bean	Y	Y	Y	Y
9 Schakowsky	Y	Y	Y	Y
10 **Kirk**	N	N	N	N
11 Halvorson	Y	Y	Y	Y
12 Costello	Y	Y	Y	Y
13 **Biggert**	N	N	N	N
14 Foster	Y	Y	Y	Y
15 **Johnson**	N	N	N	N

KEY	**Republicans**	Democrats	
Y Voted for (yea)		X Paired against	C Voted "present" to avoid possible conflict of interest
# Paired for		– Announced against	
+ Announced for		P Voted "present"	? Did not vote or otherwise make a position known
N Voted against (nay)			

	515	516	517	518
16 Manzullo	N	N	N	N
17 Hare	Y	Y	Y	Y
18 **Schock**	?	N	N	N
19 **Shimkus**	N	N	N	N
INDIANA				
1 Visclosky	Y	Y	Y	Y
2 Donnelly	Y	Y	N	Y
3 Vacant				
4 **Buyer**	N	N	?	N
5 **Burton**	N	N	N	N
6 **Pence**	N	N	N	N
7 Carson	Y	Y	Y	Y
8 Ellsworth	Y	Y	Y	Y
9 Hill	Y	Y	N	Y
IOWA				
1 Braley	Y	Y	Y	Y
2 Loebsack	Y	Y	Y	Y
3 Boswell	Y	Y	Y	Y
4 **Latham**	N	N	N	N
5 **King**	N	N	N	N
KANSAS				
1 Moran	N	N	N	N
2 Jenkins	N	N	N	N
3 Moore	Y	Y	Y	Y
4 Tiahrt	N	N	N	N
KENTUCKY				
1 **Whitfield**	N	N	N	N
2 **Guthrie**	N	N	N	N
3 Yarmuth	Y	Y	Y	Y
4 **Davis**	N	N	N	N
5 Rogers	N	N	N	N
6 Chandler	Y	Y	Y	Y
LOUISIANA				
1 **Scalise**	N	N	N	N
2 **Cao**	N	N	N	Y
3 Melancon	N	Y	Y	Y
4 **Fleming**	N	N	N	N
5 **Alexander**	N	N	N	N
6 **Cassidy**	N	N	N	N
7 **Boustany**	?	?	?	?
MAINE				
1 Pingree	Y	Y	Y	Y
2 Michaud	Y	Y	Y	Y
MARYLAND				
1 Kratovil	Y	Y	Y	Y
2 Ruppersberger	Y	Y	Y	Y
3 Sarbanes	Y	Y	Y	Y
4 Edwards	Y	Y	Y	Y
5 Hoyer	Y	Y	Y	Y
6 **Bartlett**	N	N	N	N
7 Cummings	Y	Y	Y	Y
8 Van Hollen	Y	Y	Y	Y
MASSACHUSETTS				
1 Olver	Y	Y	Y	Y
2 Neal	Y	Y	Y	Y
3 McGovern	Y	Y	Y	Y
4 Frank	Y	Y	Y	Y
5 Tsongas	Y	Y	Y	Y
6 Tierney	Y	Y	Y	Y
7 Markey	Y	Y	Y	Y
8 Capuano	Y	Y	Y	Y
9 Lynch	Y	Y	Y	Y
10 Delahunt	?	Y	Y	Y
MICHIGAN				
1 Stupak	Y	Y	Y	Y
2 **Hoekstra**	N	N	N	N
3 **Ehlers**	N	N	N	N
4 **Camp**	N	N	N	N
5 Kildee	Y	Y	Y	Y
6 **Upton**	N	N	N	N
7 Schauer	Y	Y	Y	Y
8 **Rogers**	N	N	N	N
9 Peters	Y	Y	Y	Y
10 **Miller**	N	N	N	N
11 **McCotter**	N	N	N	N
12 Levin	Y	Y	Y	Y
13 Kilpatrick	Y	Y	Y	Y
14 Conyers	Y	Y	Y	Y
15 Dingell	Y	Y	Y	Y
MINNESOTA				
1 Walz	Y	Y	Y	Y
2 **Kline**	N	N	N	N
3 **Paulsen**	N	N	N	N
4 McCollum	Y	Y	Y	Y

	515	516	517	518
5 Ellison	Y	Y	Y	Y
6 **Bachmann**	N	N	N	N
7 Peterson	Y	Y	N	Y
8 Oberstar	Y	Y	Y	Y
MISSISSIPPI				
1 Childers	Y	Y	Y	Y
2 Thompson	Y	Y	Y	Y
3 **Harper**	N	N	N	N
4 Taylor	Y	N	N	N
MISSOURI				
1 Clay	Y	Y	Y	Y
2 **Akin**	N	N	N	N
3 Carnahan	Y	Y	Y	Y
4 Skelton	Y	Y	Y	Y
5 Cleaver	Y	Y	Y	Y
6 **Graves**	N	N	N	N
7 **Blunt**	?	?	?	?
8 **Emerson**	N	N	N	N
9 **Luetkemeyer**	N	N	N	N
MONTANA				
AL **Rehberg**	N	N	N	N
NEBRASKA				
1 **Fortenberry**	N	N	N	N
2 **Terry**	N	N	N	N
3 **Smith**	N	N	N	N
NEVADA				
1 Berkley	Y	Y	Y	Y
2 **Heller**	N	N	N	N
3 Titus	?	Y	Y	Y
NEW HAMPSHIRE				
1 Shea-Porter	Y	Y	Y	Y
2 Hodes	Y	Y	Y	Y
NEW JERSEY				
1 Andrews	Y	Y	Y	Y
2 **LoBiondo**	N	N	N	N
3 Adler	Y	Y	Y	Y
4 **Smith**	N	N	N	N
5 **Garrett**	N	N	N	N
6 Pallone	Y	Y	Y	Y
7 **Lance**	N	N	N	N
8 Pascrell	Y	Y	Y	Y
9 Rothman	Y	Y	Y	Y
10 Payne	Y	Y	Y	Y
11 **Frelinghuysen**	N	N	N	N
12 Holt	Y	Y	Y	Y
13 Sires	Y	Y	Y	Y
NEW MEXICO				
1 Heinrich	Y	Y	Y	Y
2 Teague	Y	Y	Y	Y
3 Luján	Y	Y	Y	Y
NEW YORK				
1 Bishop	Y	Y	Y	Y
2 Israel	Y	Y	Y	Y
3 **King**	N	N	N	N
4 McCarthy	Y	Y	Y	Y
5 Ackerman	Y	Y	Y	Y
6 Meeks	Y	Y	Y	Y
7 Crowley	Y	Y	Y	Y
8 Nadler	Y	Y	Y	Y
9 Weiner	Y	Y	Y	Y
10 Towns	Y	Y	Y	Y
11 Clarke	Y	Y	Y	Y
12 Velázquez	Y	Y	Y	Y
13 McMahon	N	Y	Y	Y
14 Maloney	Y	Y	Y	Y
15 Rangel	Y	Y	Y	Y
16 Serrano	Y	Y	Y	Y
17 Engel	Y	Y	Y	Y
18 Lowey	?	Y	Y	Y
19 Hall	Y	Y	Y	Y
20 Murphy	Y	Y	Y	Y
21 Tonko	Y	Y	Y	Y
22 Hinchey	Y	Y	Y	Y
23 Owens	Y	Y	Y	Y
24 Arcuri	Y	Y	Y	Y
25 Maffei	Y	Y	Y	Y
26 **Lee**	N	N	N	N
27 Higgins	Y	Y	Y	Y
28 Slaughter	Y	Y	Y	Y
29 Vacant				
NORTH CAROLINA				
1 Butterfield	Y	Y	Y	Y
2 Etheridge	Y	Y	Y	Y
3 **Jones**	?	?	?	?
4 Price	Y	Y	Y	Y

	515	516	517	518
5 **Foxx**	N	N	N	N
6 **Coble**	N	N	N	N
7 McIntyre	N	Y	N	Y
8 Kissell	Y	Y	Y	Y
9 **Myrick**	N	N	N	N
10 **McHenry**	N	N	N	N
11 Shuler	Y	Y	N	Y
12 Watt	Y	Y	Y	Y
13 Miller	Y	Y	Y	Y
NORTH DAKOTA				
AL Pomeroy	Y	Y	Y	Y
OHIO				
1 Driehaus	Y	Y	Y	Y
2 **Schmidt**	N	N	N	N
3 **Turner**	N	N	N	N
4 **Jordan**	N	N	N	N
5 **Latta**	N	N	N	N
6 Wilson	Y	Y	Y	Y
7 **Austria**	N	N	N	N
8 **Boehner**	N	N	N	N
9 Kaptur	Y	Y	Y	Y
10 Kucinich	Y	Y	Y	Y
11 Fudge	Y	Y	Y	Y
12 **Tiberi**	N	N	N	N
13 Sutton	Y	Y	Y	Y
14 **LaTourette**	?	?	?	?
15 Kilroy	Y	Y	Y	Y
16 Boccieri	Y	Y	Y	Y
17 Ryan	Y	Y	Y	Y
18 Space	Y	Y	Y	Y
OKLAHOMA				
1 **Sullivan**	N	N	N	N
2 Boren	Y	Y	Y	Y
3 **Lucas**	N	N	N	N
4 **Cole**	N	N	N	N
5 **Fallin**	N	N	N	N
OREGON				
1 Wu	Y	Y	Y	Y
2 **Walden**	N	N	N	N
3 Blumenauer	Y	Y	Y	Y
4 DeFazio	Y	Y	Y	Y
5 Schrader	Y	Y	Y	Y
PENNSYLVANIA				
1 Brady	Y	Y	Y	Y
2 Fattah	Y	Y	Y	Y
3 Dahlkemper	Y	Y	N	Y
4 Altmire	Y	Y	Y	Y
5 **Thompson**	N	N	N	N
6 **Gerlach**	N	N	N	N
7 Sestak	Y	Y	Y	Y
8 Murphy, P.	Y	Y	Y	Y
9 **Shuster**	N	N	N	N
10 Carney	Y	Y	Y	Y
11 Kanjorski	Y	Y	Y	Y
12 Critz	Y	Y	Y	Y
13 Schwartz	Y	Y	Y	Y
14 Doyle	Y	Y	Y	Y
15 **Dent**	N	N	N	N
16 **Pitts**	N	N	N	N
17 Holden	Y	Y	Y	Y
18 **Murphy, T.**	N	N	N	N
19 **Platts**	N	N	N	N
RHODE ISLAND				
1 Kennedy	Y	Y	Y	Y
2 Langevin	Y	Y	Y	Y
SOUTH CAROLINA				
1 **Brown**	N	N	N	N
2 **Wilson**	N	N	N	N
3 **Barrett**	N	N	N	N
4 **Inglis**	N	N	N	N
5 Spratt	Y	Y	Y	Y
6 Clyburn	Y	Y	Y	Y
SOUTH DAKOTA				
AL Herseth Sandlin	Y	Y	N	Y
TENNESSEE				
1 **Roe**	N	N	N	N
2 **Duncan**	N	N	N	N
3 **Wamp**	?	?	?	?
4 Davis	?	Y	Y	Y
5 Cooper	Y	Y	N	N
6 Gordon	Y	Y	Y	Y
7 **Blackburn**	N	N	N	N
8 Tanner	?	?	?	?
9 Cohen	Y	Y	Y	Y

	515	516	517	518
TEXAS				
1 **Gohmert**	N	N	?	N
2 **Poe**	N	N	N	N
3 **Johnson, S.**	N	N	N	N
4 **Hall**	N	N	?	N
5 **Hensarling**	N	N	N	N
6 **Barton**	N	N	N	N
7 **Culberson**	N	N	N	N
8 **Brady**	N	N	N	N
9 Green, A.	Y	Y	Y	Y
10 **McCaul**	N	N	N	N
11 **Conaway**	N	N	N	N
12 **Granger**	N	N	N	N
13 **Thornberry**	N	N	N	N
14 **Paul**	N	N	N	N
15 Hinojosa	Y	Y	?	?
16 Reyes	Y	Y	Y	Y
17 Edwards	Y	Y	Y	Y
18 Jackson Lee	Y	Y	Y	Y
19 **Neugebauer**	?	?	?	?
20 Gonzalez	Y	Y	Y	Y
21 **Smith**	N	N	N	N
22 Olson	N	N	N	N
23 Rodriguez	Y	Y	Y	Y
24 **Marchant**	N	N	N	N
25 Doggett	Y	Y	Y	Y
26 **Burgess**	N	N	N	N
27 Ortiz	Y	Y	Y	Y
28 Cuellar	Y	Y	Y	Y
29 Green, G.	Y	Y	Y	Y
30 Johnson, E.	Y	Y	Y	Y
31 **Carter**	N	N	N	N
32 **Sessions**	N	N	N	N
UTAH				
1 **Bishop**	N	N	N	N
2 Matheson	Y	Y	Y	Y
3 **Chaffetz**	N	N	N	N
VERMONT				
AL Welch	?	Y	Y	Y
VIRGINIA				
1 **Wittman**	N	N	N	N
2 Nye	N	Y	N	Y
3 Scott	Y	Y	Y	Y
4 **Forbes**	N	N	N	N
5 Perriello	Y	Y	Y	Y
6 **Goodlatte**	N	N	N	N
7 **Cantor**	N	N	N	N
8 Moran	Y	Y	Y	Y
9 Boucher	Y	Y	Y	Y
10 **Wolf**	N	N	N	N
11 Connolly	Y	Y	Y	Y
WASHINGTON				
1 Inslee	Y	Y	Y	Y
2 Larsen	Y	Y	Y	Y
3 Baird	Y	Y	Y	Y
4 **Hastings**	N	N	N	N
5 **McMorris Rodgers**	N	N	N	N
6 Dicks	Y	Y	Y	Y
7 McDermott	Y	Y	Y	Y
8 **Reichert**	N	N	N	N
9 Smith	Y	Y	Y	Y
WEST VIRGINIA				
1 Mollohan	Y	Y	Y	Y
2 **Capito**	N	N	N	N
3 Rahall	Y	Y	Y	Y
WISCONSIN				
1 **Ryan**	N	N	N	N
2 Baldwin	Y	Y	Y	Y
3 Kind	Y	Y	Y	Y
4 Moore	Y	Y	Y	Y
5 **Sensenbrenner**	N	N	N	N
6 **Petri**	N	N	N	N
7 Obey	Y	Y	Y	Y
8 Kagen	Y	Y	Y	Y
WYOMING				
AL **Lummis**	N	N	N	N
DELEGATES				
Faleomavaega (A.S.)				
Norton (D.C.)				
Bordallo (Guam)				
Sablan (N. Marianas)				
Pierluisi (P.R.)				
Christensen (V.I.)				

IN THE HOUSE | By Vote Number

519. **H Res 1052. Tribute to Oklahoma National Guard/Adoption.** Boren, D-Okla., motion to suspend the rules and adopt the resolution that would express the gratitude of the House to the members of the Oklahoma National Guard for their service since Sept. 11, 2001. Motion agreed to 378-0: D 220-0; R 158-0. A two-thirds majority of those present and voting (252 in this case) is required for adoption under suspension of the rules. Sept. 14, 2010.

520. **H Res 1571. Miami Dade College 50th Anniversary/Adoption.** Watson, D-Calif., motion to suspend the rules and adopt the resolution that would congratulate Miami Dade College on its 50th anniversary of academic excellence and service to the residents of Florida. Motion agreed to 378-0: D 220-0; R 158-0. A two-thirds majority of those present and voting (252 in this case) is required for adoption under suspension of the rules. Sept. 14, 2010.

521. **HR 2039. Legislative Branch 'Buy American' Requirements/ Passage.** Brady, D-Pa., motion to suspend the rules and pass the bill that would clarify that the Buy American Act applies to products purchased for use by the legislative branch. It also would establish additional restrictions for products bearing a congressional seal. Motion agreed to 371-36: D 232-1; R 139-35. A two-thirds majority of those present and voting (272 in this case) is required for passage under suspension of the rules. Sept. 15, 2010.

522. **HR 5873. Capt. Rhett W. Schiller Post Office/Passage.** Clay, D-Mo., motion to suspend the rules and pass the bill that would designate a postal building in Waterford, Wis., as the "Capt. Rhett W. Schiller Post Office." Motion agreed to 411-0: D 237-0; R 174-0. A two-thirds majority of those present and voting (274 in this case) is required for passage under suspension of the rules. Sept. 15, 2010.

523. **H Res 1522. Hereditary Breast and Ovarian Cancer Week/ Adoption.** Clay, D-Mo., motion to suspend the rules and adopt the resolution that would support the designation of National Hereditary Breast and Ovarian Cancer Week and National Previvor Day. Motion agreed to 408-0: D 235-0; R 173-0. A two-thirds majority of those present and voting (272 in this case) is required for adoption under suspension of the rules. Sept. 15, 2010.

524. **HR 5366. Overseas Contractor Violations/Passage.** Clay, D-Mo., motion to suspend the rules and pass the bill that would remove individuals or companies convicted of violating the Foreign Corrupt Practices Act from any federal contracts or grants and state that it is U.S. policy to bar such individuals or companies from receiving such contracts. Motion agreed to 409-0: D 236-0; R 173-0. A two-thirds majority of those present and voting (273 in this case) is required for passage under suspension of the rules. Sept. 15, 2010.

525. **H Res 1610. Sept. 11 Remembrance/Adoption.** Connolly, D-Va., motion to suspend the rules and adopt the resolution that would extend the sympathies of the House to the friends, families and loved ones of the victims of the Sept. 11 attacks and express gratitude to the leaders and citizens of nations that have assisted the United States in its fight against terrorism. Motion agreed to 410-0: D 237-0; R 173-0. A two-thirds majority of those present and voting (274 in this case) is required for adoption under suspension of the rules. Sept. 15, 2010.

	519	520	521	522	523	524	525
ALABAMA							
1 Bonner	?	?	Y	Y	Y	Y	Y
2 Bright	Y	Y	Y	Y	Y	Y	Y
3 Rogers	Y	Y	Y	Y	Y	Y	Y
4 Aderholt	Y	Y	Y	Y	Y	Y	Y
5 Griffith	Y	Y	Y	Y	Y	Y	Y
6 Bachus	Y	Y	Y	Y	Y	Y	Y
7 Davis	Y	Y	Y	Y	Y	Y	Y
ALASKA							
AL Young	Y	Y	Y	Y	Y	Y	Y
ARIZONA							
1 Kirkpatrick	Y	Y	Y	Y	Y	Y	Y
2 Franks	Y	Y	N	Y	Y	Y	Y
3 Shadegg	Y	Y	N	Y	Y	Y	Y
4 Pastor	Y	Y	Y	Y	Y	Y	Y
5 Mitchell	Y	Y	Y	Y	Y	Y	Y
6 Flake	Y	Y	N	Y	Y	Y	Y
7 Grijalva	?	?	?	Y	Y	Y	Y
8 Giffords	Y	Y	Y	Y	Y	Y	Y
ARKANSAS							
1 Berry	Y	Y	Y	Y	Y	Y	Y
2 Snyder	Y	Y	Y	Y	Y	Y	Y
3 Boozman	?	?	Y	Y	Y	Y	Y
4 Ross	Y	Y	Y	Y	Y	Y	Y
CALIFORNIA							
1 Thompson	Y	Y	Y	Y	Y	Y	Y
2 Herger	Y	Y	N	Y	Y	Y	Y
3 Lungren	Y	Y	Y	Y	Y	Y	Y
4 McClintock	Y	Y	N	Y	Y	Y	Y
5 Matsui	Y	Y	Y	Y	Y	Y	Y
6 Woolsey	Y	Y	Y	Y	Y	Y	Y
7 Miller, George	Y	?	Y	Y	Y	Y	Y
8 Pelosi							
9 Lee	+	+	?	?	?	?	?
10 Garamendi	Y	Y	Y	Y	Y	Y	Y
11 McNerney	Y	Y	Y	Y	Y	Y	Y
12 Speier	?	?	Y	Y	Y	Y	Y
13 Stark	Y	Y	Y	Y	Y	Y	Y
14 Eshoo	Y	Y	?	?	?	?	?
15 Honda	Y	Y	Y	Y	Y	Y	Y
16 Lofgren	Y	Y	Y	Y	Y	Y	Y
17 Farr	Y	Y	Y	Y	Y	Y	Y
18 Cardoza	Y	Y	Y	Y	Y	Y	Y
19 Radanovich	?	?	Y	Y	Y	Y	Y
20 Costa	Y	Y	Y	Y	Y	Y	Y
21 Nunes	Y	Y	Y	Y	Y	Y	Y
22 McCarthy	?	?	Y	Y	Y	Y	Y
23 Capps	Y	Y	Y	Y	Y	Y	Y
24 Gallegly	Y	Y	Y	Y	Y	Y	Y
25 McKeon	Y	Y	Y	Y	Y	Y	Y
26 Dreier	Y	Y	N	Y	Y	Y	Y
27 Sherman	Y	Y	Y	Y	Y	Y	Y
28 Berman	Y	Y	Y	Y	Y	Y	Y
29 Schiff	Y	Y	Y	Y	Y	Y	Y
30 Waxman	Y	Y	Y	Y	Y	Y	Y
31 Becerra	Y	Y	Y	Y	Y	Y	Y
32 Chu	Y	Y	Y	Y	Y	Y	Y
33 Watson	Y	Y	Y	Y	Y	Y	Y
34 Roybal-Allard	Y	Y	Y	Y	Y	Y	Y
35 Waters	Y	Y	Y	Y	Y	Y	Y
36 Harman	Y	Y	Y	Y	Y	Y	Y
37 Richardson	+	Y	Y	Y	Y	Y	Y
38 Napolitano	Y	Y	Y	Y	Y	Y	Y
39 Sánchez, Linda	Y	Y	Y	Y	Y	Y	Y
40 Royce	Y	Y	Y	Y	Y	Y	Y
41 Lewis	Y	Y	Y	Y	Y	Y	Y
42 Miller, Gary	Y	Y	Y	Y	Y	Y	Y
43 Baca	Y	Y	Y	Y	Y	Y	Y
44 Calvert	Y	Y	Y	Y	Y	Y	Y
45 Bono Mack	Y	Y	Y	Y	Y	Y	Y
46 Rohrabacher	Y	Y	Y	Y	Y	Y	Y
47 Sanchez, Loretta	Y	Y	Y	Y	Y	Y	Y
48 Campbell	Y	Y	N	Y	Y	Y	Y
49 Issa	Y	Y	Y	Y	Y	Y	Y
50 Bilbray	Y	Y	Y	Y	Y	Y	Y
51 Filner	+	+	Y	Y	Y	Y	Y
52 Hunter	Y	Y	Y	Y	Y	Y	Y
53 Davis	Y	Y	Y	Y	Y	Y	Y

	519	520	521	522	523	524	525
COLORADO							
1 DeGette	Y	Y	Y	Y	Y	Y	Y
2 Polis	Y	Y	N	Y	Y	Y	Y
3 Salazar	Y	Y	Y	Y	Y	Y	Y
4 Markey	Y	Y	Y	Y	Y	Y	Y
5 Lamborn	Y	Y	N	Y	Y	Y	Y
6 Coffman	Y	Y	Y	Y	Y	Y	Y
7 Perlmutter	Y	Y	Y	Y	Y	Y	Y
CONNECTICUT							
1 Larson	Y	Y	Y	Y	Y	Y	Y
2 Courtney	Y	Y	Y	Y	Y	Y	Y
3 DeLauro	Y	Y	Y	Y	Y	Y	Y
4 Himes	Y	Y	Y	Y	Y	Y	Y
5 Murphy	Y	Y	Y	Y	Y	Y	Y
DELAWARE							
AL Castle	?	?	Y	Y	Y	Y	Y
FLORIDA							
1 Miller	Y	Y	N	Y	Y	Y	Y
2 Boyd	Y	Y	Y	Y	Y	Y	Y
3 Brown	Y	Y	Y	Y	Y	Y	Y
4 Crenshaw	Y	Y	Y	Y	Y	Y	Y
5 Brown-Waite	?	?	Y	Y	Y	Y	Y
6 Stearns	Y	Y	Y	Y	Y	Y	Y
7 Mica	Y	Y	Y	Y	Y	Y	Y
8 Grayson	Y	Y	Y	Y	Y	Y	Y
9 Bilirakis	Y	Y	Y	Y	Y	Y	Y
10 Young	?	?	?	?	?	?	?
11 Castor	Y	Y	Y	Y	Y	Y	Y
12 Putnam	?	?	?	?	?	?	?
13 Buchanan	Y	Y	Y	Y	Y	Y	Y
14 Mack	Y	Y	Y	Y	Y	Y	Y
15 Posey	Y	Y	Y	Y	Y	Y	Y
16 Rooney	Y	Y	Y	Y	Y	Y	Y
17 Meek	?	?	?	?	?	?	?
18 Ros-Lehtinen	Y	Y	Y	Y	Y	Y	Y
19 Deutch	Y	Y	Y	Y	Y	Y	Y
20 Wasserman Schultz	Y	Y	Y	Y	Y	Y	Y
21 Diaz-Balart, L.	Y	Y	Y	Y	Y	Y	Y
22 Klein	Y	Y	Y	Y	Y	Y	Y
23 Hastings	Y	Y	?	?	?	?	?
24 Kosmas	Y	Y	Y	Y	Y	Y	Y
25 Diaz-Balart, M.	Y	Y	Y	Y	Y	Y	Y
GEORGIA							
1 Kingston	Y	Y	N	Y	Y	Y	Y
2 Bishop	Y	Y	Y	Y	Y	Y	Y
3 Westmoreland	Y	Y	N	Y	Y	Y	Y
4 Johnson	Y	Y	Y	Y	Y	Y	Y
5 Lewis	Y	Y	Y	Y	Y	Y	Y
6 Price	?	?	N	Y	Y	Y	Y
7 Linder	Y	Y	N	Y	Y	Y	Y
8 Marshall	Y	Y	Y	Y	Y	Y	Y
9 Graves	Y	Y	N	Y	Y	Y	Y
10 Broun	Y	Y	N	Y	Y	Y	Y
11 Gingrey	Y	Y	N	Y	Y	Y	Y
12 Barrow	Y	Y	Y	Y	Y	Y	Y
13 Scott	Y	Y	Y	Y	Y	Y	Y
HAWAII							
1 Djou	Y	Y	Y	Y	Y	Y	Y
2 Hirono	Y	Y	Y	Y	Y	Y	Y
IDAHO							
1 Minnick	Y	Y	Y	Y	Y	Y	Y
2 Simpson	Y	Y	Y	Y	Y	Y	Y
ILLINOIS							
1 Rush	?	?	Y	Y	Y	Y	Y
2 Jackson	Y	Y	Y	Y	Y	Y	Y
3 Lipinski	Y	Y	Y	Y	Y	Y	Y
4 Gutierrez	Y	Y	Y	Y	Y	Y	Y
5 Quigley	Y	Y	Y	Y	Y	Y	Y
6 Roskam	Y	Y	Y	Y	Y	Y	Y
7 Davis	Y	Y	Y	Y	Y	Y	Y
8 Bean	Y	Y	Y	Y	Y	Y	Y
9 Schakowsky	Y	Y	Y	Y	Y	Y	Y
10 Kirk	?	?	Y	Y	Y	Y	Y
11 Halvorson	Y	Y	Y	Y	Y	Y	Y
12 Costello	Y	Y	Y	Y	Y	Y	Y
13 Biggert	+	Y	Y	Y	Y	Y	Y
14 Foster	Y	Y	Y	Y	Y	Y	Y
15 Johnson	Y	Y	Y	Y	Y	Y	Y

KEY **Republicans** Democrats

Y Voted for (yea)	X Paired against	C Voted "present" to avoid possible conflict of interest
# Paired for	– Announced against	
+ Announced for	P Voted "present"	? Did not vote or otherwise make a position known
N Voted against (nay)		

	519	520	521	522	523	524	525
16 **Manzullo**	Y	Y	Y	Y	Y	Y	Y
17 Hare	Y	Y	Y	Y	Y	Y	Y
18 **Schock**	Y	Y	Y	Y	Y	Y	Y
19 **Shimkus**	Y	Y	Y	Y	Y	Y	Y
INDIANA							
1 Visclosky	Y	Y	Y	Y	Y	Y	Y
2 Donnelly	Y	Y	Y	Y	Y	Y	Y
3 Vacant							
4 **Buyer**	Y	?	Y	Y	Y	Y	Y
5 **Burton**	Y	Y	Y	Y	Y	Y	Y
6 **Pence**	Y	Y	N	Y	Y	Y	Y
7 Carson	Y	Y	Y	Y	Y	Y	Y
8 Ellsworth	?	?	?	?	?	?	?
9 Hill	Y	Y	Y	Y	Y	Y	Y
IOWA							
1 Braley	Y	Y	Y	Y	Y	Y	Y
2 Loebsack	Y	Y	Y	Y	Y	Y	Y
3 Boswell	Y	Y	Y	Y	Y	Y	Y
4 **Latham**	Y	Y	Y	Y	Y	Y	Y
5 **King**	Y	Y	N	Y	Y	Y	Y
KANSAS							
1 **Moran**	?	?	Y	Y	Y	Y	Y
2 **Jenkins**	Y	Y	Y	Y	Y	Y	Y
3 Moore	Y	Y	Y	Y	Y	Y	Y
4 **Tiahrt**	Y	Y	Y	Y	Y	Y	Y
KENTUCKY							
1 **Whitfield**	Y	Y	Y	Y	Y	Y	Y
2 **Guthrie**	Y	Y	Y	Y	Y	Y	Y
3 Yarmuth	Y	Y	Y	Y	Y	Y	Y
4 **Davis**	Y	Y	Y	Y	Y	Y	Y
5 **Rogers**	Y	Y	Y	Y	Y	Y	Y
6 Chandler	Y	Y	Y	Y	Y	Y	Y
LOUISIANA							
1 **Scalise**	Y	Y	Y	Y	Y	Y	Y
2 **Cao**	Y	Y	Y	Y	Y	Y	Y
3 Melancon	?	?	Y	Y	Y	Y	Y
4 **Fleming**	Y	?	N	Y	Y	Y	Y
5 **Alexander**	Y	Y	Y	Y	Y	Y	Y
6 **Cassidy**	Y	Y	Y	Y	Y	Y	Y
7 **Boustany**	Y	Y	Y	Y	Y	Y	Y
MAINE							
1 Pingree	Y	Y	Y	Y	Y	Y	Y
2 Michaud	Y	Y	Y	Y	Y	Y	Y
MARYLAND							
1 Kratovil	Y	Y	Y	Y	Y	Y	Y
2 Ruppersberger	Y	Y	Y	Y	Y	Y	?
3 Sarbanes	Y	Y	Y	Y	Y	Y	Y
4 Edwards	Y	Y	Y	Y	Y	Y	Y
5 Hoyer	Y	Y	Y	Y	Y	Y	Y
6 **Bartlett**	Y	Y	N	Y	Y	Y	Y
7 Cummings	Y	Y	?	?	?	?	?
8 Van Hollen	Y	Y	Y	Y	Y	Y	Y
MASSACHUSETTS							
1 Olver	Y	Y	Y	Y	Y	Y	Y
2 Neal	Y	Y	Y	Y	Y	Y	Y
3 McGovern	Y	Y	Y	Y	Y	Y	Y
4 Frank	Y	Y	Y	Y	?	Y	Y
5 Tsongas	?	?	Y	Y	Y	Y	Y
6 Tierney	?	?	?	?	?	?	?
7 Markey	Y	Y	Y	Y	Y	Y	Y
8 Capuano	Y	Y	Y	Y	Y	Y	Y
9 Lynch	?	?	Y	Y	Y	Y	Y
10 Delahunt	?	?	?	?	?	?	?
MICHIGAN							
1 Stupak	Y	Y	+	+	+	+	+
2 **Hoekstra**	?	?	N	Y	Y	Y	Y
3 **Ehlers**	Y	Y	Y	Y	Y	Y	Y
4 **Camp**	Y	Y	Y	Y	Y	Y	Y
5 Kildee	Y	Y	Y	Y	Y	Y	Y
6 **Upton**	Y	Y	Y	Y	Y	Y	Y
7 Schauer	Y	Y	Y	Y	Y	Y	Y
8 **Rogers**	Y	Y	Y	Y	Y	Y	Y
9 Peters	Y	Y	Y	Y	Y	Y	Y
10 **Miller**	Y	Y	Y	Y	Y	Y	Y
11 **McCotter**	Y	Y	Y	Y	Y	Y	Y
12 Levin	Y	Y	Y	Y	Y	Y	Y
13 Kilpatrick	Y	Y	Y	Y	Y	Y	Y
14 Conyers	Y	Y	Y	Y	Y	Y	Y
15 Dingell	Y	Y	Y	Y	Y	Y	Y
MINNESOTA							
1 Walz	Y	Y	Y	Y	Y	Y	Y
2 **Kline**	Y	Y	Y	Y	Y	Y	Y
3 **Paulsen**	Y	Y	Y	Y	Y	Y	Y
4 McCollum	Y	Y	Y	Y	Y	Y	Y
5 Ellison	Y	Y	Y	Y	Y	Y	Y
6 **Bachmann**	Y	Y	Y	Y	Y	Y	Y
7 Peterson	Y	Y	Y	Y	Y	Y	Y
8 Oberstar	Y	Y	Y	Y	Y	Y	Y
MISSISSIPPI							
1 Childers	Y	Y	Y	Y	Y	Y	Y
2 Thompson	Y	Y	Y	Y	Y	Y	Y
3 **Harper**	Y	Y	N	Y	Y	Y	Y
4 Taylor	Y	Y	Y	Y	Y	Y	Y
MISSOURI							
1 Clay	Y	Y	Y	Y	Y	Y	Y
2 **Akin**	Y	Y	Y	Y	Y	Y	Y
3 Carnahan	Y	Y	Y	Y	Y	Y	Y
4 Skelton	Y	Y	Y	Y	Y	Y	Y
5 Cleaver	Y	Y	Y	Y	Y	Y	Y
6 **Graves**	Y	Y	Y	Y	Y	Y	Y
7 **Blunt**	Y	Y	?	?	?	?	?
8 **Emerson**	Y	Y	Y	Y	Y	Y	Y
9 **Luetkemeyer**	Y	Y	Y	Y	Y	Y	Y
MONTANA							
AL **Rehberg**	+	+	Y	Y	Y	Y	Y
NEBRASKA							
1 **Fortenberry**	Y	Y	Y	Y	Y	Y	Y
2 **Terry**	Y	Y	Y	Y	Y	Y	Y
3 **Smith**	Y	Y	Y	Y	Y	Y	Y
NEVADA							
1 Berkley	Y	Y	Y	Y	Y	Y	Y
2 **Heller**	Y	Y	Y	Y	Y	Y	Y
3 Titus	Y	Y	Y	Y	Y	Y	Y
NEW HAMPSHIRE							
1 Shea-Porter	?	?	Y	Y	Y	Y	Y
2 Hodes	?	?	?	?	?	?	?
NEW JERSEY							
1 Andrews	Y	Y	Y	Y	Y	Y	Y
2 **LoBiondo**	Y	Y	Y	Y	Y	Y	Y
3 Adler	Y	Y	Y	Y	Y	Y	Y
4 **Smith**	Y	Y	Y	Y	?	?	?
5 **Garrett**	Y	Y	Y	Y	Y	Y	Y
6 Pallone	Y	Y	Y	Y	Y	Y	Y
7 **Lance**	Y	Y	Y	Y	Y	Y	Y
8 Pascrell	Y	Y	Y	Y	Y	Y	Y
9 Rothman	Y	Y	Y	Y	Y	Y	Y
10 Payne	Y	Y	?	?	?	?	?
11 **Frelinghuysen**	Y	Y	Y	Y	Y	Y	Y
12 Holt	Y	Y	Y	Y	Y	Y	Y
13 Sires	Y	Y	Y	Y	Y	Y	Y
NEW MEXICO							
1 Heinrich	Y	Y	Y	Y	Y	Y	Y
2 Teague	Y	Y	Y	Y	Y	Y	Y
3 Luján	Y	Y	Y	Y	Y	Y	Y
NEW YORK							
1 Bishop	Y	Y	Y	Y	Y	Y	Y
2 Israel	Y	Y	Y	Y	Y	Y	Y
3 **King**	Y	Y	Y	Y	Y	Y	Y
4 McCarthy	Y	Y	Y	Y	Y	Y	Y
5 Ackerman	?	?	?	?	?	?	?
6 Meeks	?	?	Y	Y	Y	Y	Y
7 Crowley	+	+	Y	Y	Y	Y	Y
8 Nadler	?	?	Y	Y	Y	Y	Y
9 Weiner	Y	Y	Y	Y	Y	Y	Y
10 Towns	?	?	Y	Y	Y	Y	Y
11 Clarke	?	?	Y	Y	Y	Y	Y
12 Velázquez	Y	Y	?	?	?	?	?
13 McMahon	Y	Y	Y	Y	Y	Y	Y
14 Maloney	?	?	Y	Y	Y	Y	Y
15 Rangel	?	?	Y	Y	Y	Y	Y
16 Serrano	?	?	Y	Y	Y	Y	Y
17 Engel	?	?	Y	Y	Y	Y	Y
18 Lowey	Y	Y	Y	Y	Y	Y	Y
19 Hall	?	?	Y	Y	Y	Y	Y
20 Murphy	Y	Y	Y	Y	Y	Y	Y
21 Tonko	Y	Y	Y	Y	Y	Y	Y
22 Hinchey	Y	Y	Y	Y	Y	Y	Y
23 Owens	Y	Y	Y	Y	Y	Y	Y
24 Arcuri	Y	Y	Y	Y	Y	Y	Y
25 Maffei	Y	Y	Y	Y	Y	Y	Y
26 **Lee**	Y	Y	Y	Y	Y	Y	Y
27 Higgins	?	?	Y	Y	Y	Y	Y
28 Slaughter	Y	Y	Y	Y	Y	Y	Y
29 Vacant							
NORTH CAROLINA							
1 Butterfield	Y	Y	Y	Y	Y	Y	Y
2 Etheridge	Y	Y	Y	Y	Y	Y	Y
3 **Jones**	Y	Y	Y	Y	Y	Y	Y
4 Price	Y	Y	Y	Y	Y	Y	Y
5 **Foxx**	Y	Y	Y	Y	Y	Y	Y
6 **Coble**	Y	Y	Y	Y	Y	Y	Y
7 McIntyre	Y	Y	Y	Y	Y	Y	Y
8 Kissell	Y	Y	Y	Y	Y	Y	Y
9 **Myrick**	Y	Y	Y	Y	Y	Y	Y
10 **McHenry**	Y	Y	Y	Y	Y	Y	Y
11 Shuler	Y	Y	Y	Y	Y	Y	Y
12 Watt	Y	Y	Y	Y	Y	Y	Y
13 Miller	Y	Y	Y	Y	Y	Y	Y
NORTH DAKOTA							
AL Pomeroy	Y	Y	Y	Y	Y	Y	Y
OHIO							
1 Driehaus	Y	Y	Y	Y	Y	Y	Y
2 **Schmidt**	Y	Y	Y	Y	Y	Y	Y
3 **Turner**	Y	Y	Y	Y	Y	Y	Y
4 **Jordan**	Y	Y	Y	Y	Y	Y	Y
5 **Latta**	Y	Y	Y	Y	Y	Y	Y
6 Wilson	Y	Y	Y	Y	Y	Y	Y
7 **Austria**	Y	Y	Y	Y	Y	Y	Y
8 **Boehner**	?	?	Y	Y	Y	Y	Y
9 Kaptur	Y	Y	Y	Y	Y	Y	Y
10 Kucinich	Y	Y	Y	Y	Y	Y	Y
11 Fudge	Y	Y	Y	Y	Y	Y	Y
12 **Tiberi**	Y	Y	Y	Y	Y	Y	Y
13 Sutton	Y	Y	Y	Y	Y	Y	Y
14 **LaTourette**	Y	Y	Y	Y	Y	Y	Y
15 Kilroy	+	+	Y	Y	Y	Y	Y
16 Boccieri	Y	Y	Y	Y	Y	Y	Y
17 Ryan	Y	Y	Y	Y	Y	Y	Y
18 Space	Y	Y	Y	Y	?	Y	Y
OKLAHOMA							
1 **Sullivan**	Y	Y	Y	Y	Y	Y	Y
2 Boren	Y	Y	Y	Y	Y	Y	Y
3 **Lucas**	Y	Y	Y	Y	Y	Y	Y
4 **Cole**	Y	Y	Y	Y	Y	Y	Y
5 **Fallin**	?	?	?	?	?	?	?
OREGON							
1 Wu	Y	Y	Y	Y	Y	Y	?
2 **Walden**	Y	Y	Y	Y	Y	Y	Y
3 Blumenauer	Y	Y	Y	Y	Y	Y	Y
4 DeFazio	?	?	Y	Y	Y	Y	Y
5 Schrader	Y	Y	Y	Y	Y	Y	Y
PENNSYLVANIA							
1 Brady	Y	Y	Y	Y	Y	Y	Y
2 Fattah	Y	Y	Y	Y	Y	Y	Y
3 Dahlkemper	Y	Y	Y	Y	Y	Y	Y
4 Altmire	Y	Y	Y	Y	Y	Y	Y
5 **Thompson**	Y	Y	Y	Y	Y	Y	Y
6 **Gerlach**	Y	Y	Y	Y	Y	Y	Y
7 Sestak	Y	Y	Y	Y	Y	Y	Y
8 Murphy, P.	Y	Y	Y	Y	Y	Y	Y
9 **Shuster**	Y	Y	Y	Y	Y	Y	Y
10 Carney	?	?	Y	Y	Y	Y	Y
11 Kanjorski	Y	Y	Y	Y	Y	Y	Y
12 Critz	Y	Y	Y	Y	Y	Y	Y
13 Schwartz	Y	Y	Y	Y	Y	Y	Y
14 Doyle	Y	Y	Y	Y	Y	Y	Y
15 **Dent**	Y	Y	Y	Y	Y	Y	Y
16 **Pitts**	Y	Y	Y	Y	Y	Y	Y
17 Holden	Y	Y	Y	Y	Y	Y	Y
18 **Murphy, T.**	Y	Y	Y	Y	Y	Y	Y
19 **Platts**	?	Y	Y	Y	Y	Y	Y
RHODE ISLAND							
1 Kennedy	Y	Y	?	?	?	?	Y
2 Langevin	?	?	?	?	?	?	?
SOUTH CAROLINA							
1 **Brown**	Y	Y	Y	Y	Y	Y	Y
2 **Wilson**	Y	Y	Y	Y	Y	Y	Y
3 **Barrett**	Y	Y	N	Y	Y	Y	Y
4 **Inglis**	?	Y	Y	Y	Y	Y	Y
5 Spratt	Y	Y	Y	Y	Y	Y	Y
6 Clyburn	Y	Y	Y	Y	Y	Y	Y
SOUTH DAKOTA							
AL Herseth Sandlin	Y	Y	Y	Y	Y	Y	Y
TENNESSEE							
1 **Roe**	Y	Y	Y	Y	Y	Y	Y
2 **Duncan**	Y	Y	Y	Y	Y	Y	Y
3 **Wamp**	Y	Y	Y	Y	Y	Y	Y
4 Davis	Y	Y	Y	Y	Y	Y	Y
5 Cooper	?	Y	Y	Y	Y	Y	Y
6 Gordon	?	?	Y	Y	Y	Y	Y
7 **Blackburn**	Y	?	N	Y	Y	Y	Y
8 Tanner	Y	Y	Y	Y	Y	Y	Y
9 Cohen	Y	Y	Y	Y	Y	Y	Y
TEXAS							
1 **Gohmert**	Y	Y	N	Y	Y	Y	Y
2 **Poe**	Y	Y	Y	Y	Y	Y	Y
3 **Johnson, S.**	Y	Y	N	Y	Y	Y	Y
4 **Hall**	Y	Y	Y	Y	Y	Y	Y
5 **Hensarling**	Y	Y	N	Y	Y	Y	Y
6 **Barton**	Y	Y	Y	Y	Y	Y	Y
7 **Culberson**	?	?	Y	Y	Y	Y	Y
8 **Brady**	Y	Y	N	Y	Y	Y	Y
9 Green, A.	Y	Y	Y	Y	Y	Y	Y
10 **McCaul**	Y	Y	Y	Y	Y	Y	Y
11 **Conaway**	Y	Y	N	Y	Y	Y	Y
12 **Granger**	Y	Y	Y	Y	Y	Y	Y
13 **Thornberry**	Y	Y	N	Y	Y	Y	Y
14 **Paul**	Y	Y	N	Y	Y	Y	Y
15 Hinojosa	Y	Y	?	Y	Y	?	Y
16 Reyes	Y	Y	Y	Y	Y	Y	Y
17 Edwards	Y	?	Y	Y	Y	Y	Y
18 Jackson Lee	Y	Y	Y	Y	Y	Y	Y
19 **Neugebauer**	Y	Y	N	Y	Y	Y	Y
20 Gonzalez	Y	Y	Y	Y	Y	Y	Y
21 **Smith**	Y	Y	Y	Y	Y	Y	Y
22 **Olson**	Y	Y	Y	Y	Y	Y	Y
23 Rodriguez	Y	Y	Y	Y	Y	Y	Y
24 **Marchant**	Y	Y	N	Y	Y	Y	Y
25 Doggett	Y	Y	Y	Y	Y	Y	Y
26 **Burgess**	Y	Y	Y	Y	Y	Y	Y
27 Ortiz	Y	Y	Y	Y	Y	Y	Y
28 Cuellar	Y	Y	Y	Y	Y	Y	Y
29 Green, G.	Y	Y	Y	Y	Y	Y	Y
30 Johnson, E.	Y	Y	Y	Y	Y	Y	Y
31 **Carter**	Y	Y	N	Y	Y	Y	Y
32 **Sessions**	Y	Y	N	Y	Y	Y	Y
UTAH							
1 **Bishop**	Y	Y	Y	Y	Y	Y	Y
2 Matheson	Y	Y	Y	Y	Y	Y	Y
3 **Chaffetz**	Y	Y	Y	Y	Y	Y	Y
VERMONT							
AL Welch	Y	Y	Y	Y	Y	Y	Y
VIRGINIA							
1 **Wittman**	Y	Y	Y	Y	Y	Y	Y
2 Nye	Y	Y	Y	Y	Y	Y	Y
3 Scott	Y	Y	Y	Y	Y	Y	Y
4 **Forbes**	Y	Y	Y	Y	Y	Y	Y
5 Perriello	Y	Y	Y	Y	Y	Y	Y
6 **Goodlatte**	Y	Y	Y	Y	Y	Y	Y
7 **Cantor**	?	?	Y	Y	Y	Y	Y
8 Moran	Y	Y	Y	Y	Y	Y	Y
9 Boucher	Y	Y	?	Y	Y	Y	Y
10 **Wolf**	Y	Y	Y	Y	Y	Y	Y
11 Connolly	Y	Y	Y	Y	Y	Y	Y
WASHINGTON							
1 Inslee	Y	Y	Y	Y	Y	Y	Y
2 Larsen	Y	Y	Y	Y	Y	Y	Y
3 Baird	Y	Y	Y	Y	Y	Y	Y
4 **Hastings**	Y	Y	Y	Y	Y	Y	Y
5 **McMorris Rodgers**	Y	Y	Y	Y	Y	Y	Y
6 Dicks	Y	Y	Y	Y	Y	Y	Y
7 McDermott	Y	Y	Y	Y	Y	Y	Y
8 **Reichert**	Y	Y	Y	Y	Y	Y	Y
9 Smith	Y	Y	Y	Y	Y	Y	Y
WEST VIRGINIA							
1 Mollohan	Y	Y	?	?	?	?	?
2 **Capito**	Y	Y	Y	Y	Y	Y	Y
3 Rahall	Y	Y	Y	Y	Y	Y	Y
WISCONSIN							
1 **Ryan**	Y	Y	Y	Y	Y	Y	Y
2 Baldwin	Y	Y	Y	Y	Y	Y	Y
3 Kind	Y	Y	Y	Y	Y	Y	Y
4 Moore	?	?	?	?	?	?	?
5 **Sensenbrenner**	Y	Y	Y	Y	Y	Y	Y
6 **Petri**	Y	Y	Y	Y	Y	Y	Y
7 Obey	Y	Y	Y	Y	Y	Y	Y
8 Kagen	Y	Y	Y	Y	Y	Y	Y
WYOMING							
AL **Lummis**	Y	Y	N	Y	Y	Y	Y
DELEGATES							
Faleomavaega (A.S.)							
Norton (D.C.)							
Bordallo (Guam)							
Sablan (N. Marianas)							
Pierluisi (P.R.)							
Christensen (V.I.)							

IN THE HOUSE | By Vote Number

526. HR 4785. Energy Efficiency Loan Programs/Previous Question. McGovern, D-Mass., motion to order the previous question (thus ending debate and possibility of amendment) on adoption of the rule (H Res 1620) to provide for House floor consideration of the bill that would authorize $5 billion over five years to create two energy efficiency loan programs. Motion agreed to 226-186: D 226-15; R 0-171. Sept. 16, 2010.

527. HR 4785. Energy Efficiency Loan Programs/Rule. Adoption of the rule (H Res 1620) that would provide for House floor consideration of the bill that would authorize $5 billion over five years to create two energy efficiency loan programs: the Home Star Energy Efficiency Loan Program, to be administered by the Energy Department, and the Rural Star Savings Energy Program, to be administered by the Agriculture Department. Adopted 225-188: D 223-17; R 2-171. Sept. 16, 2010.

528. HR 3562. Mississippi Civil Rights Heroes Federal Building/Passage. Johnson, D-Texas, motion to suspend the rules and concur in the Senate amendment to the bill that would designate the federally occupied building located at 1220 Echelon Parkway in Jackson, Miss., as the "James Chaney, Andrew Goodman, Michael Schwerner, and Roy K. Moore Federal Building." Motion agreed to 409-0: D 239-0; R 170-0. A two-thirds majority of those present and voting (273 in this case) is required for passage under suspension of the rules. Sept. 16, 2010.

529. HR 4785. Energy Efficiency Loan Programs/Manager's Amendment. Holden, D-Pa., amendment that would make several changes to the bill, including specifying that loan funds may not be used to purchase manufactured homes. It also would prohibit certain federal employees from receiving loans under the bill, including those who are seriously delinquent in tax debt or have been officially disciplined for viewing, downloading or exchanging pornography. Adopted in Committee of the Whole 402-0: D 238-0; R 164-0. Sept. 16, 2010.

530. HR 4785. Energy Efficiency Loan Programs/Passage. Passage of the bill that would authorize $5 billion over five years to create two energy efficiency loan programs: the Home Star Energy Efficiency Loan Program, to support loans to finance energy-efficient home renovations, and the Rural Star Savings Energy Program, to make loans to eligible entities to provide loans for energy efficiency measures in rural areas. Passed 240-172: D 234-5; R 6-167. Sept. 16, 2010.

531. H Res 1613. Pakistan Flood Condolences/Adoption. Barrow, D-Ga., motion to suspend the rules and adopt the resolution that would express condolences and sympathy for the loss of life and the damage in Pakistan caused by the floods that began on July 22, 2010, and commend relief and humanitarian efforts in the region. Motion agreed to 396-2: D 231-0; R 165-2. A two-thirds majority of those present and voting (266 in this case) is required for adoption under suspension of the rules. Sept. 16, 2010.

	526	527	528	529	530	531
ALABAMA						
1 Bonner	?	N	Y	Y	N	Y
2 Bright	N	N	Y	Y	Y	Y
3 Rogers	N	N	Y	Y	N	Y
4 Aderholt	N	N	Y	Y	N	Y
5 Griffith	N	N	Y	Y	N	Y
6 Bachus	N	N	Y	N	Y	Y
7 Davis	?	?	?	Y	Y	?
ALASKA						
AL Young	N	N	Y	Y	N	?
ARIZONA						
1 Kirkpatrick	N	N	Y	Y	N	Y
2 Franks	N	N	Y	Y	N	Y
3 Shadegg	N	N	Y	Y	N	Y
4 Pastor	Y	Y	Y	Y	Y	Y
5 Mitchell	N	N	Y	Y	Y	Y
6 Flake	N	N	Y	N	Y	Y
7 Grijalva	Y	Y	Y	Y	Y	Y
8 Giffords	N	N	Y	Y	Y	?
ARKANSAS						
1 Berry	Y	Y	Y	Y	Y	Y
2 Snyder	Y	Y	Y	Y	Y	Y
3 Boozman	N	N	Y	Y	N	Y
4 Ross	Y	N	Y	Y	Y	Y
CALIFORNIA						
1 Thompson	Y	Y	Y	Y	Y	Y
2 Herger	N	N	Y	Y	N	Y
3 Lungren	N	N	Y	Y	N	Y
4 McClintock	N	N	?	Y	N	Y
5 Matsui	Y	Y	Y	Y	Y	Y
6 Woolsey	Y	Y	Y	Y	Y	Y
7 Miller, George	Y	Y	Y	Y	Y	Y
8 Pelosi						
9 Lee	Y	Y	Y	Y	Y	Y
10 Garamendi	Y	Y	Y	Y	Y	Y
11 McNerney	N	Y	Y	Y	Y	Y
12 Speier	Y	Y	Y	Y	Y	Y
13 Stark	Y	Y	Y	Y	Y	Y
14 Eshoo	?	?	?	?	?	?
15 Honda	Y	Y	Y	Y	Y	Y
16 Lofgren	Y	Y	Y	Y	Y	Y
17 Farr	Y	Y	Y	Y	Y	Y
18 Cardoza	Y	Y	Y	Y	Y	Y
19 Radanovich	N	N	Y	?	N	?
20 Costa	Y	Y	Y	Y	Y	Y
21 Nunes	N	N	Y	Y	N	Y
22 McCarthy	N	N	Y	Y	N	Y
23 Capps	Y	Y	Y	Y	Y	Y
24 Gallegly	N	N	Y	Y	N	Y
25 McKeon	N	N	Y	Y	N	Y
26 Dreier	N	N	Y	Y	N	Y
27 Sherman	Y	Y	Y	Y	Y	Y
28 Berman	Y	Y	Y	Y	Y	Y
29 Schiff	Y	Y	Y	Y	Y	Y
30 Waxman	Y	Y	Y	Y	Y	?
31 Becerra	Y	Y	Y	Y	Y	Y
32 Chu	Y	Y	Y	Y	Y	Y
33 Watson	Y	Y	Y	Y	Y	Y
34 Roybal-Allard	Y	Y	Y	Y	Y	Y
35 Waters	Y	Y	Y	Y	Y	Y
36 Harman	Y	Y	Y	?	Y	Y
37 Richardson	Y	Y	Y	+	Y	Y
38 Napolitano	Y	Y	Y	Y	Y	Y
39 Sánchez, Linda	Y	Y	Y	Y	Y	Y
40 Royce	N	N	Y	Y	N	Y
41 Lewis	N	N	Y	Y	N	Y
42 Miller, Gary	N	N	Y	Y	N	Y
43 Baca	Y	Y	Y	Y	Y	Y
44 Calvert	N	N	Y	Y	N	Y
45 Bono Mack	N	N	Y	Y	N	Y
46 Rohrabacher	N	N	Y	Y	N	Y
47 Sanchez, Loretta	Y	Y	Y	Y	Y	
48 Campbell	N	N	Y	Y	N	Y
49 Issa	N	N	Y	Y	N	Y
50 Bilbray	N	N	Y	?	N	Y
51 Filner	Y	Y	Y	Y	Y	Y
52 Hunter	N	N	Y	Y	N	Y
53 Davis	Y	Y	Y	Y	Y	Y

	526	527	528	529	530	531
COLORADO						
1 DeGette	Y	Y	Y	Y	Y	Y
2 Polis	Y	Y	Y	Y	Y	Y
3 Salazar	Y	Y	Y	Y	Y	Y
4 Markey	Y	Y	Y	Y	Y	Y
5 Lamborn	N	N	Y	Y	N	Y
6 Coffman	N	N	Y	Y	N	Y
7 Perlmutter	Y	Y	Y	Y	Y	Y
CONNECTICUT						
1 Larson	Y	Y	Y	Y	Y	Y
2 Courtney	Y	Y	Y	Y	Y	Y
3 DeLauro	Y	Y	Y	Y	Y	Y
4 Himes	Y	Y	Y	Y	Y	Y
5 Murphy	Y	Y	Y	Y	Y	Y
DELAWARE						
AL Castle	N	N	Y	Y	Y	Y
FLORIDA						
1 Miller	N	N	Y	Y	N	Y
2 Boyd	Y	Y	Y	Y	Y	Y
3 Brown	Y	Y	Y	Y	Y	Y
4 Crenshaw	N	N	Y	Y	N	Y
5 Brown-Waite	N	N	Y	Y	N	?
6 Stearns	N	N	Y	Y	N	Y
7 Mica	N	N	Y	Y	N	Y
8 Grayson	Y	Y	Y	Y	Y	Y
9 Bilirakis	N	N	Y	Y	N	Y
10 Young	?	?	?	?	?	?
11 Castor	Y	Y	Y	Y	Y	Y
12 Putnam	?	?	?	?	?	?
13 Buchanan	N	N	Y	Y	N	Y
14 Mack	N	N	Y	Y	N	Y
15 Posey	N	N	Y	Y	N	Y
16 Rooney	N	N	Y	Y	N	Y
17 Meek	?	?	?	?	?	?
18 Ros-Lehtinen	N	N	Y	Y	N	Y
19 Deutch	Y	Y	Y	Y	Y	Y
20 Wasserman Schultz	Y	Y	Y	Y	Y	Y
21 Diaz-Balart, L.	N	N	Y	?	N	Y
22 Klein	Y	Y	Y	Y	Y	Y
23 Hastings	Y	Y	Y	Y	Y	Y
24 Kosmas	Y	Y	Y	Y	Y	Y
25 Diaz-Balart, M.	N	N	Y	?	N	Y
GEORGIA						
1 Kingston	N	N	Y	Y	N	Y
2 Bishop	Y	Y	?	Y	Y	?
3 Westmoreland	N	N	Y	Y	N	Y
4 Johnson	Y	Y	Y	?	Y	Y
5 Lewis	Y	Y	Y	Y	Y	Y
6 Price	N	N	Y	Y	N	Y
7 Linder	N	N	Y	Y	N	Y
8 Marshall	Y	Y	Y	Y	Y	Y
9 Graves	N	N	Y	Y	N	Y
10 Broun	N	N	Y	Y	N	N
11 Gingrey	N	N	Y	Y	N	Y
12 Barrow	Y	Y	Y	Y	Y	Y
13 Scott	Y	Y	Y	Y	Y	Y
HAWAII						
1 Djou	N	N	Y	Y	Y	Y
2 Hirono	Y	Y	Y	Y	Y	Y
IDAHO						
1 Minnick	N	N	Y	Y	Y	Y
2 Simpson	N	N	Y	Y	N	?
ILLINOIS						
1 Rush	?	?	?	Y	Y	Y
2 Jackson	Y	Y	Y	Y	Y	Y
3 Lipinski	Y	Y	Y	Y	Y	Y
4 Gutierrez	Y	Y	Y	Y	Y	+
5 Quigley	Y	Y	Y	Y	Y	Y
6 Roskam	N	N	Y	Y	N	Y
7 Davis	Y	Y	Y	Y	Y	Y
8 Bean	Y	Y	Y	Y	Y	Y
9 Schakowsky	Y	Y	Y	Y	Y	Y
10 Kirk	N	N	Y	Y	N	Y
11 Halvorson	Y	Y	Y	Y	Y	Y
12 Costello	Y	Y	Y	Y	Y	Y
13 Biggert	N	N	Y	Y	N	Y
14 Foster	Y	Y	Y	Y	Y	Y
15 Johnson	N	N	Y	Y	N	Y

	526	527	528	529	530	531
16 **Manzullo**	N	N	Y	Y	N	Y
17 Hare	Y	Y	Y	Y	Y	Y
18 **Schock**	N	N	Y	Y	N	Y
19 **Shimkus**	N	N	Y	Y	N	Y
INDIANA						
1 Visclosky	Y	+	+	Y	Y	Y
2 Donnelly	Y	N	Y	Y	Y	Y
3 Vacant						
4 **Buyer**	N	N	Y	Y	N	Y
5 **Burton**	N	N	Y	Y	N	Y
6 **Pence**	N	N	Y	Y	N	Y
7 Carson	Y	Y	Y	Y	Y	Y
8 Ellsworth	?	?	?	?	?	?
9 Hill	N	N	Y	Y	Y	Y
IOWA						
1 Braley	+	+	+	Y	Y	Y
2 Loebsack	Y	Y	Y	Y	Y	Y
3 Boswell	Y	Y	Y	Y	Y	Y
4 **Latham**	N	N	Y	Y	N	Y
5 **King**	N	N	Y	Y	N	Y
KANSAS						
1 **Moran**	N	N	Y	Y	N	Y
2 **Jenkins**	N	N	Y	Y	N	Y
3 Moore	Y	Y	Y	Y	Y	Y
4 **Tiahrt**	N	N	Y	Y	N	Y
KENTUCKY						
1 **Whitfield**	N	N	Y	Y	Y	Y
2 **Guthrie**	N	N	Y	Y	N	Y
3 Yarmuth	Y	Y	Y	Y	Y	Y
4 **Davis**	N	N	Y	Y	N	Y
5 **Rogers**	N	N	Y	Y	N	Y
6 Chandler	Y	Y	Y	Y	Y	Y
LOUISIANA						
1 **Scalise**	N	N	Y	Y	N	Y
2 **Cao**	N	N	Y	Y	N	Y
3 Melancon	Y	N	Y	Y	Y	Y
4 **Fleming**	N	N	?	?	?	?
5 **Alexander**	N	N	Y	Y	N	Y
6 **Cassidy**	N	N	Y	Y	N	Y
7 **Boustany**	N	N	Y	Y	N	Y
MAINE						
1 Pingree	Y	Y	Y	Y	Y	Y
2 Michaud	Y	Y	Y	Y	Y	Y
MARYLAND						
1 Kratovil	N	N	Y	Y	Y	Y
2 Ruppersberger	Y	Y	Y	Y	?	Y
3 Sarbanes	Y	Y	Y	Y	Y	Y
4 Edwards	Y	Y	Y	Y	Y	Y
5 Hoyer	Y	Y	Y	Y	Y	Y
6 **Bartlett**	N	N	Y	Y	N	Y
7 Cummings	Y	Y	Y	Y	Y	Y
8 Van Hollen	Y	Y	Y	Y	Y	Y
MASSACHUSETTS						
1 Olver	Y	Y	Y	Y	Y	Y
2 Neal	Y	Y	Y	Y	Y	Y
3 McGovern	Y	Y	Y	Y	Y	Y
4 Frank	Y	Y	Y	Y	Y	Y
5 Tsongas	Y	Y	Y	Y	Y	Y
6 Tierney	?	?	?	?	?	?
7 Markey	Y	Y	Y	Y	Y	Y
8 Capuano	Y	Y	Y	Y	Y	Y
9 Lynch	Y	Y	Y	Y	Y	Y
10 Delahunt	Y	Y	Y	?	?	?
MICHIGAN						
1 Stupak	Y	Y	Y	Y	Y	Y
2 **Hoekstra**	N	N	Y	Y	N	Y
3 **Ehlers**	N	Y	Y	Y	Y	Y
4 **Camp**	N	N	?	Y	N	Y
5 Kildee	Y	Y	Y	Y	Y	Y
6 **Upton**	N	N	Y	Y	N	Y
7 Schauer	Y	Y	Y	Y	N	Y
8 **Rogers**	N	N	Y	?	N	Y
9 Peters	Y	Y	Y	Y	Y	Y
10 **Miller**	N	N	Y	Y	N	Y
11 **McCotter**	N	N	Y	Y	N	Y
12 Levin	Y	Y	Y	Y	Y	Y
13 Kilpatrick	Y	Y	Y	Y	Y	Y
14 Conyers	Y	Y	Y	Y	Y	Y
15 Dingell	Y	Y	Y	Y	Y	Y
MINNESOTA						
1 Walz	Y	Y	Y	Y	Y	Y
2 **Kline**	N	N	Y	Y	N	Y
3 **Paulsen**	N	N	Y	Y	N	Y
4 McCollum	Y	Y	Y	Y	Y	Y

	526	527	528	529	530	531
5 Ellison	Y	Y	Y	?	?	Y
6 **Bachmann**	N	N	Y	Y	N	Y
7 Peterson	Y	Y	Y	Y	Y	Y
8 Oberstar	Y	Y	Y	?	Y	Y
MISSISSIPPI						
1 Childers	N	N	Y	Y	Y	Y
2 Thompson	Y	Y	Y	Y	Y	Y
3 **Harper**	N	N	Y	Y	N	Y
4 Taylor	N	N	Y	Y	Y	Y
MISSOURI						
1 Clay	Y	Y	Y	Y	Y	Y
2 **Akin**	N	N	Y	Y	N	Y
3 Carnahan	Y	Y	Y	Y	Y	Y
4 Skelton	Y	Y	Y	Y	N	Y
5 Cleaver	Y	Y	Y	Y	Y	Y
6 **Graves**	N	N	Y	Y	N	Y
7 **Blunt**	?	?	?	?	?	?
8 **Emerson**	N	N	Y	Y	N	Y
9 **Luetkemeyer**	N	N	Y	Y	N	Y
MONTANA						
AL **Rehberg**	N	N	Y	Y	N	Y
NEBRASKA						
1 **Fortenberry**	N	N	Y	Y	N	Y
2 **Terry**	N	N	Y	Y	N	?
3 **Smith**	N	N	Y	Y	N	Y
NEVADA						
1 Berkley	Y	Y	Y	Y	Y	Y
2 **Heller**	N	N	Y	?	N	Y
3 Titus	Y	Y	Y	Y	Y	Y
NEW HAMPSHIRE						
1 Shea-Porter	?	?	?	?	?	?
2 Hodes	?	?	?	?	?	?
NEW JERSEY						
1 Andrews	Y	Y	Y	Y	Y	Y
2 **LoBiondo**	N	N	Y	Y	N	Y
3 Adler	Y	N	Y	Y	N	Y
4 **Smith**	N	N	Y	Y	N	Y
5 **Garrett**	N	N	Y	?	N	Y
6 Pallone	Y	Y	Y	Y	Y	Y
7 **Lance**	N	N	Y	Y	N	Y
8 Pascrell	Y	Y	Y	Y	Y	Y
9 Rothman	Y	Y	Y	Y	Y	Y
10 Payne	Y	Y	Y	Y	Y	Y
11 **Frelinghuysen**	N	N	Y	Y	N	Y
12 Holt	Y	Y	Y	Y	Y	Y
13 Sires	Y	Y	Y	Y	Y	Y
NEW MEXICO						
1 Heinrich	Y	Y	Y	Y	Y	Y
2 Teague	Y	Y	Y	Y	Y	Y
3 Luján	Y	Y	Y	Y	Y	Y
NEW YORK						
1 Bishop	Y	Y	Y	Y	Y	Y
2 Israel	Y	Y	Y	Y	Y	Y
3 **King**	N	N	Y	Y	N	Y
4 McCarthy	Y	Y	Y	Y	Y	Y
5 Ackerman	?	?	?	?	?	?
6 Meeks	Y	Y	Y	Y	Y	Y
7 Crowley	Y	Y	Y	Y	Y	Y
8 Nadler	Y	Y	Y	Y	Y	Y
9 Weiner	Y	Y	Y	Y	Y	Y
10 Towns	Y	Y	Y	Y	Y	Y
11 Clarke	Y	Y	Y	Y	Y	Y
12 Velázquez	Y	Y	Y	Y	Y	?
13 McMahon	Y	Y	Y	Y	Y	Y
14 Maloney	Y	Y	Y	Y	Y	Y
15 Rangel	Y	Y	Y	Y	Y	Y
16 Serrano	Y	Y	Y	Y	Y	Y
17 Engel	Y	Y	Y	?	Y	Y
18 Lowey	Y	Y	Y	Y	Y	Y
19 Hall	Y	Y	Y	Y	Y	Y
20 Murphy	Y	Y	Y	Y	Y	Y
21 Tonko	Y	Y	Y	Y	Y	Y
22 Hinchey	Y	Y	Y	Y	Y	Y
23 Owens	Y	Y	Y	Y	Y	Y
24 Arcuri	Y	Y	Y	Y	Y	Y
25 Maffei	Y	Y	Y	Y	Y	Y
26 **Lee**	N	N	Y	Y	N	Y
27 Higgins	Y	Y	Y	Y	Y	Y
28 Slaughter	Y	Y	Y	Y	Y	?
29 Vacant						
NORTH CAROLINA						
1 Butterfield	Y	Y	Y	Y	Y	Y
2 Etheridge	Y	Y	Y	Y	Y	Y
3 **Jones**	N	N	Y	Y	N	Y
4 Price	Y	Y	Y	Y	Y	Y

	526	527	528	529	530	531
5 **Foxx**	N	N	Y	Y	N	Y
6 **Coble**	N	N	Y	Y	N	Y
7 McIntyre	N	Y	Y	Y	Y	Y
8 Kissell	Y	Y	Y	Y	Y	Y
9 **Myrick**	N	N	Y	Y	N	Y
10 **McHenry**	N	N	Y	Y	N	Y
11 Shuler	Y	N	Y	Y	Y	Y
12 Watt	Y	Y	?	Y	Y	Y
13 Miller	Y	Y	Y	Y	Y	Y
NORTH DAKOTA						
AL Pomeroy	Y	Y	Y	Y	Y	Y
OHIO						
1 Driehaus	Y	Y	Y	Y	Y	Y
2 **Schmidt**	N	N	Y	Y	N	Y
3 **Turner**	N	N	Y	Y	N	Y
4 **Jordan**	N	N	Y	Y	N	Y
5 **Latta**	N	N	Y	Y	N	Y
6 Wilson	Y	Y	Y	Y	Y	Y
7 **Austria**	N	N	Y	Y	N	Y
8 **Boehner**	N	N	Y	?	N	Y
9 Kaptur	Y	Y	Y	Y	Y	Y
10 Kucinich	Y	Y	Y	Y	Y	Y
11 Fudge	Y	Y	Y	Y	Y	Y
12 **Tiberi**	N	N	Y	Y	N	Y
13 Sutton	Y	?	Y	Y	Y	Y
14 **LaTourette**	N	N	Y	Y	N	Y
15 Kilroy	Y	Y	Y	Y	Y	Y
16 Boccieri	Y	Y	Y	Y	Y	Y
17 Ryan	Y	Y	Y	Y	Y	Y
18 Space	N	Y	Y	Y	Y	Y
OKLAHOMA						
1 **Sullivan**	N	N	Y	Y	N	Y
2 Boren	Y	N	Y	Y	Y	?
3 **Lucas**	N	N	Y	Y	N	Y
4 **Cole**	N	N	Y	Y	N	Y
5 **Fallin**	?	?	?	?	?	?
OREGON						
1 Wu	Y	Y	Y	Y	Y	Y
2 **Walden**	N	N	Y	Y	N	Y
3 Blumenauer	Y	Y	Y	Y	Y	Y
4 DeFazio	Y	Y	Y	Y	Y	Y
5 Schrader	Y	Y	Y	Y	Y	Y
PENNSYLVANIA						
1 Brady	Y	Y	Y	Y	Y	Y
2 Fattah	Y	Y	Y	Y	Y	Y
3 Dahlkemper	Y	Y	Y	Y	Y	Y
4 Altmire	Y	Y	Y	Y	Y	Y
5 **Thompson**	N	N	Y	Y	N	Y
6 **Gerlach**	N	N	Y	Y	N	Y
7 Sestak	Y	Y	Y	Y	Y	Y
8 Murphy, P.	Y	Y	Y	Y	Y	?
9 **Shuster**	N	N	Y	Y	N	Y
10 Carney	Y	Y	Y	Y	Y	Y
11 Kanjorski	Y	Y	Y	Y	Y	Y
12 Critz	Y	Y	Y	Y	Y	Y
13 Schwartz	?	?	?	Y	Y	Y
14 Doyle	Y	Y	Y	Y	Y	Y
15 **Dent**	N	N	Y	Y	N	Y
16 **Pitts**	N	N	Y	Y	N	Y
17 Holden	Y	Y	Y	Y	Y	Y
18 **Murphy, T.**	N	N	Y	Y	N	Y
19 **Platts**	N	N	Y	Y	N	Y
RHODE ISLAND						
1 Kennedy	Y	Y	Y	+	+	+
2 Langevin	Y	Y	Y	Y	Y	Y
SOUTH CAROLINA						
1 **Brown**	N	N	Y	Y	N	Y
2 **Wilson**	N	N	Y	Y	N	Y
3 **Barrett**	N	N	Y	Y	Y	Y
4 **Inglis**	?	N	Y	Y	Y	Y
5 Spratt	Y	Y	Y	Y	Y	Y
6 Clyburn	Y	Y	Y	Y	Y	Y
SOUTH DAKOTA						
AL Herseth Sandlin	Y	Y	Y	Y	Y	Y
TENNESSEE						
1 **Roe**	N	N	Y	Y	N	Y
2 **Duncan**	N	N	Y	Y	N	Y
3 **Wamp**	N	N	Y	Y	N	Y
4 Davis	Y	Y	Y	Y	Y	Y
5 Cooper	Y	Y	Y	Y	Y	Y
6 Gordon	?	Y	Y	Y	Y	Y
7 **Blackburn**	N	N	Y	Y	N	Y
8 Tanner	Y	Y	Y	?	?	?
9 Cohen	Y	Y	Y	Y	Y	Y

	526	527	528	529	530	531
TEXAS						
1 **Gohmert**	N	N	Y	Y	N	Y
2 **Poe**	N	N	Y	Y	N	Y
3 **Johnson, S.**	N	N	Y	Y	N	Y
4 **Hall**	N	N	Y	Y	N	Y
5 **Hensarling**	N	N	Y	Y	N	Y
6 **Barton**	N	N	Y	Y	N	Y
7 **Culberson**	N	N	Y	Y	N	Y
8 **Brady**	N	N	Y	Y	N	Y
9 Green, A.	Y	Y	Y	Y	Y	Y
10 **McCaul**	N	N	Y	Y	N	Y
11 **Conaway**	N	N	Y	Y	N	Y
12 **Granger**	N	N	Y	Y	N	Y
13 **Thornberry**	N	N	Y	Y	N	Y
14 **Paul**	N	N	Y	Y	N	N
15 Hinojosa	Y	Y	Y	Y	Y	Y
16 Reyes	Y	Y	Y	Y	Y	Y
17 Edwards	Y	Y	Y	Y	Y	Y
18 Jackson Lee	Y	Y	Y	Y	Y	Y
19 **Neugebauer**	N	N	Y	Y	N	Y
20 Gonzalez	Y	Y	Y	Y	Y	Y
21 **Smith**	N	N	Y	Y	N	Y
22 **Olson**	N	N	Y	?	N	Y
23 Rodriguez	Y	Y	Y	Y	Y	Y
24 **Marchant**	?	?	?	Y	N	?
25 Doggett	Y	Y	Y	Y	Y	Y
26 **Burgess**	N	N	Y	Y	N	Y
27 Ortiz	Y	Y	Y	Y	Y	Y
28 Cuellar	Y	Y	Y	Y	Y	Y
29 Green, G.	Y	Y	Y	Y	Y	Y
30 Johnson, E.	Y	Y	Y	Y	Y	Y
31 **Carter**	N	N	Y	Y	N	Y
32 **Sessions**	N	N	Y	Y	N	Y
UTAH						
1 **Bishop**	N	N	Y	Y	N	Y
2 Matheson	N	N	Y	Y	Y	Y
3 **Chaffetz**	N	N	Y	Y	N	Y
VERMONT						
AL Welch	Y	Y	Y	Y	Y	?
VIRGINIA						
1 **Wittman**	N	N	Y	Y	N	Y
2 Nye	N	Y	Y	Y	Y	Y
3 Scott	Y	Y	Y	Y	Y	Y
4 **Forbes**	N	N	Y	Y	N	Y
5 Perriello	Y	Y	Y	Y	Y	Y
6 **Goodlatte**	N	N	Y	Y	N	Y
7 **Cantor**	N	N	Y	Y	N	Y
8 Moran	Y	Y	Y	Y	Y	Y
9 Boucher	Y	Y	Y	Y	Y	Y
10 **Wolf**	N	N	Y	Y	N	Y
11 Connolly	Y	Y	Y	Y	Y	Y
WASHINGTON						
1 Inslee	Y	Y	Y	Y	Y	Y
2 Larsen	Y	Y	Y	Y	Y	Y
3 Baird	Y	Y	Y	Y	Y	?
4 **Hastings**	N	N	Y	Y	N	Y
5 **McMorris Rodgers**	N	N	Y	Y	N	Y
6 Dicks	Y	Y	Y	Y	Y	Y
7 McDermott	Y	Y	Y	Y	Y	Y
8 **Reichert**	N	N	Y	Y	N	Y
9 Smith	Y	Y	Y	Y	Y	Y
WEST VIRGINIA						
1 Mollohan	?	?	?	?	?	?
2 **Capito**	N	N	Y	Y	N	Y
3 Rahall	Y	Y	Y	Y	Y	Y
WISCONSIN						
1 **Ryan**	N	N	Y	Y	N	Y
2 Baldwin	Y	Y	Y	Y	+	Y
3 Kind	Y	Y	Y	Y	Y	Y
4 Moore	Y	Y	Y	?	Y	Y
5 **Sensenbrenner**	N	N	Y	Y	N	Y
6 **Petri**	N	N	Y	Y	N	Y
7 Obey	Y	Y	Y	?	?	?
8 Kagen	Y	Y	Y	Y	Y	Y
WYOMING						
AL **Lummis**	N	N	Y	Y	N	Y
DELEGATES						
Faleomavaega (A.S.)				Y		
Norton (D.C.)				?		
Bordallo (Guam)				Y		
Sablan (N. Marianas)				Y		
Pierluisi (P.R.)				Y		
Christensen (V.I.)				?		

IN THE HOUSE | By Vote Number

532. HR 5131. Coltsville National Historical Park/Passage.
Christensen, D-V.I., motion to suspend the rules and pass the bill that would authorize $10 million to establish the Coltsville National Historical Park in Hartford, Conn., as part of the National Park System, subject to certain conditions. Motion rejected 215-174: D 214-6; R 1-168. A two-thirds majority of those present and voting (260 in this case) is required for passage under suspension of the rules. Sept. 22, 2010.

533. HR 3470. Infant Mortality Pilot Programs/Passage.
Pallone, D-N.J., motion to suspend the rules and pass the bill that would authorize $10 million annually in fiscal 2011 through 2015 for grants to state, tribal and local health departments that create pilot programs to reduce infant mortality. Preference would be given to health departments that serve any of the 15 counties or groups of counties with the highest infant mortality rates in the United States in the past three years. Motion agreed to 324-64: D 218-0; R 106-64. A two-thirds majority of those present and voting (259 in this case) is required for passage under suspension of the rules. Sept. 22, 2010.

534. Opposition to Lame-Duck Session/Motion to Table.
Hastings, D-Fla., motion to table (kill) the Price, R-Ga., appeal of the ruling of the chair that the Price draft resolution does not constitute a question of the privileges of the House under Rule 9 of the House. The draft resolution would pledge that the House would not assemble on or between the dates of Nov. 2, 2010, and Jan. 3, 2011, except in the case of a sudden unforeseen emergency requiring immediate action from Congress. It would specify that certain items of legislation, including any measure "increasing any tax on any American," could not be considered as an emergency. Motion agreed to 236-172: D 235-6; R 1-166. Sept. 23, 2010.

535. HR 5297. Small-Business Tax and Lending/Previous Question.
Pingree, D-Maine, motion to order the previous question (thus ending debate and possibility of amendment) on adoption of the rule (H Res 1640) to provide for House floor consideration of the Senate amendment to the bill that would provide a variety of small-business tax benefits and establish a $30 billion small-business lending fund to be administered by the Treasury Department, with funds directed to community banks. Motion agreed to 230-181: D 230-11; R 0-170. Sept. 23, 2010.

536. HR 5297. Small-Business Tax and Lending/Rule.
Adoption of the rule (H Res 1640) to provide for House floor consideration of the Senate amendment to the bill that would provide a variety of small-business tax benefits and establish a $30 billion small-business lending fund to be administered by the Treasury Department, with funds directed to community banks. The rule also would waive, through the legislative day of Oct. 1, 2010, the two-thirds majority requirement to consider a resolution on the same day it is reported by the Rules Committee, and would allow for consideration of measures under suspension of the rules at any time through the legislative day of Oct. 1, 2010. Adopted 226-186: D 226-16; R 0-170. Sept. 23, 2010.

	532	533	534	535	536
ALABAMA					
1 **Bonner**	N	Y	N	N	N
2 Bright	N	Y	?	?	?
3 **Rogers**	N	N	N	N	N
4 **Aderholt**	N	Y	N	N	N
5 **Griffith**	N	Y	N	N	N
6 **Bachus**	N	Y	N	N	N
7 Davis	?	?	Y	Y	Y
ALASKA					
AL **Young**	N	Y	N	N	N
ARIZONA					
1 Kirkpatrick	Y	Y	Y	N	N
2 **Franks**	N	Y	N	N	N
3 **Shadegg**	N	N	N	N	N
4 Pastor	Y	Y	Y	Y	Y
5 Mitchell	N	Y	Y	N	N
6 **Flake**	?	?	N	N	N
7 Grijalva	Y	Y	Y	Y	Y
8 Giffords	Y	Y	Y	N	N
ARKANSAS					
1 Berry	?	?	Y	Y	Y
2 Snyder	Y	Y	Y	Y	Y
3 **Boozman**	N	Y	N	N	N
4 Ross	Y	Y	Y	N	N
CALIFORNIA					
1 Thompson	Y	Y	Y	Y	Y
2 **Herger**	N	N	N	N	N
3 **Lungren**	N	Y	N	N	N
4 **McClintock**	N	N	N	N	N
5 Matsui	Y	Y	Y	Y	Y
6 Woolsey	Y	Y	Y	Y	Y
7 Miller, George	?	Y	Y	Y	Y
8 Pelosi					
9 Lee	Y	Y	Y	Y	Y
10 Garamendi	Y	Y	Y	Y	Y
11 McNerney	Y	Y	Y	Y	Y
12 Speier	Y	Y	Y	Y	Y
13 Stark	Y	Y	Y	?	Y
14 Eshoo	Y	Y	Y	Y	Y
15 Honda	Y	Y	?	?	?
16 Lofgren	Y	Y	Y	Y	Y
17 Farr	Y	Y	Y	Y	Y
18 Cardoza	Y	Y	Y	Y	Y
19 **Radanovich**	?	?	N	N	N
20 Costa	N	Y	?	Y	Y
21 **Nunes**	N	N	N	N	N
22 **McCarthy**	N	N	?	N	N
23 Capps	Y	Y	Y	Y	Y
24 **Gallegly**	N	Y	N	N	N
25 **McKeon**	N	Y	N	N	N
26 **Dreier**	N	Y	N	N	N
27 Sherman	Y	Y	Y	Y	Y
28 Berman	Y	Y	Y	Y	Y
29 Schiff	Y	Y	Y	Y	Y
30 Waxman	Y	Y	Y	Y	Y
31 Becerra	Y	Y	?	?	?
32 Chu	Y	Y	Y	Y	Y
33 Watson	Y	Y	Y	Y	Y
34 Roybal-Allard	Y	Y	Y	Y	Y
35 Waters	Y	Y	Y	Y	?
36 Harman	Y	?	Y	Y	Y
37 Richardson	Y	Y	Y	Y	Y
38 Napolitano	Y	Y	Y	Y	Y
39 Sánchez, Linda	?	?	Y	Y	Y
40 **Royce**	N	N	N	N	N
41 **Lewis**	N	Y	N	N	N
42 **Miller, Gary**	N	Y	N	N	N
43 Baca	Y	Y	Y	Y	Y
44 **Calvert**	N	Y	N	N	N
45 **Bono Mack**	N	Y	N	N	N
46 **Rohrabacher**	N	N	N	N	N
47 Sanchez, Loretta	Y	Y	Y	Y	Y
48 **Campbell**	N	N	N	N	N
49 **Issa**	N	N	N	N	N
50 **Bilbray**	N	Y	N	–	–
51 Filner	Y	Y	Y	Y	Y
52 **Hunter**	N	N	N	N	N
53 Davis	Y	Y	Y	Y	Y

	532	533	534	535	536
COLORADO					
1 DeGette	Y	Y	Y	Y	Y
2 Polis	Y	Y	Y	Y	Y
3 Salazar	Y	Y	Y	Y	Y
4 Markey	Y	Y	Y	Y	Y
5 **Lamborn**	N	N	N	N	N
6 **Coffman**	N	Y	N	N	N
7 Perlmutter	Y	Y	Y	Y	Y
CONNECTICUT					
1 Larson	Y	Y	Y	Y	Y
2 Courtney	Y	Y	Y	Y	Y
3 DeLauro	Y	Y	Y	Y	Y
4 Himes	Y	Y	Y	Y	Y
5 Murphy	Y	Y	Y	Y	Y
DELAWARE					
AL **Castle**	N	Y	N	N	N
FLORIDA					
1 **Miller**	N	N	N	N	N
2 Boyd	Y	Y	Y	Y	Y
3 Brown	Y	Y	Y	Y	Y
4 **Crenshaw**	N	Y	N	N	N
5 **Brown-Waite**	N	Y	N	N	N
6 **Stearns**	N	Y	N	N	N
7 **Mica**	N	N	N	N	N
8 Grayson	Y	Y	Y	Y	Y
9 **Bilirakis**	N	Y	–	N	N
10 **Young**	?	?	?	?	?
11 Castor	Y	Y	Y	Y	?
12 **Putnam**	N	Y	N	N	N
13 **Buchanan**	N	Y	N	N	N
14 **Mack**	N	N	N	N	N
15 **Posey**	N	N	N	N	N
16 **Rooney**	N	Y	N	N	N
17 Meek	Y	Y	?	?	Y
18 **Ros-Lehtinen**	N	Y	N	N	N
19 Deutch	Y	Y	Y	Y	Y
20 Wasserman Schultz	Y	Y	Y	Y	Y
21 **Diaz-Balart, L.**	N	Y	?	N	N
22 Klein	Y	Y	Y	Y	Y
23 Hastings	Y	Y	Y	Y	Y
24 Kosmas	Y	Y	Y	Y	Y
25 **Diaz-Balart, M.**	N	Y	N	N	N
GEORGIA					
1 **Kingston**	N	N	N	N	N
2 Bishop	Y	Y	Y	Y	Y
3 **Westmoreland**	N	N	N	N	N
4 Johnson	Y	Y	Y	Y	Y
5 Lewis	Y	Y	Y	Y	Y
6 **Price**	N	N	N	N	N
7 **Linder**	N	N	N	N	N
8 Marshall	Y	Y	Y	Y	Y
9 **Graves**	N	N	N	N	N
10 **Broun**	N	N	N	N	N
11 **Gingrey**	N	N	N	N	N
12 Barrow	?	?	Y	Y	Y
13 Scott	Y	Y	Y	Y	Y
HAWAII					
1 **Djou**	N	Y	N	N	N
2 Hirono	Y	Y	Y	Y	Y
IDAHO					
1 Minnick	Y	Y	N	N	N
2 **Simpson**	N	Y	N	N	N
ILLINOIS					
1 Rush	Y	Y	Y	Y	Y
2 Jackson	?	?	Y	Y	Y
3 Lipinski	Y	Y	Y	Y	Y
4 Gutierrez	+	+	Y	Y	Y
5 Quigley	Y	Y	Y	Y	Y
6 **Roskam**	N	Y	?	N	N
7 Davis	Y	Y	?	Y	Y
8 Bean	N	Y	Y	Y	Y
9 Schakowsky	Y	Y	Y	Y	Y
10 **Kirk**	?	?	N	N	?
11 Halvorson	Y	Y	Y	Y	Y
12 Costello	Y	Y	Y	Y	Y
13 **Biggert**	N	Y	N	N	N
14 Foster	Y	Y	Y	Y	Y
15 Johnson	N	Y	N	N	N

KEY   Republicans   Democrats

Y Voted for (yea)	X Paired against	C Voted "present" to avoid possible conflict of interest
# Paired for	– Announced against	
+ Announced for	P Voted "present"	? Did not vote or otherwise make a position known
N Voted against (nay)		

	532	533	534	535	536
16 Manzullo	N	N	N	N	N
17 Hare	Y	Y	Y	Y	Y
18 Schock	N	Y	N	N	N
19 Shimkus	N	Y	N	N	N
INDIANA					
1 Visclosky	Y	Y	Y	Y	Y
2 Donnelly	Y	Y	Y	Y	N
3 Vacant					
4 Buyer	N	Y	N	?	N
5 Burton	N	N	N	N	N
6 Pence	N	Y	?	N	N
7 Carson	Y	Y	Y	Y	Y
8 Ellsworth	Y	Y	Y	Y	Y
9 Hill	Y	Y	Y	N	N
IOWA					
1 Braley	Y	Y	?	?	Y
2 Loebsack	Y	Y	Y	Y	Y
3 Boswell	Y	Y	Y	Y	Y
4 Latham	N	Y	N	N	N
5 King	N	N	N	N	N
KANSAS					
1 Moran	N	Y	N	N	N
2 Jenkins	N	N	N	N	N
3 Moore	Y	Y	Y	?	?
4 Tiahrt	N	N	N	N	N
KENTUCKY					
1 Whitfield	N	Y	N	N	N
2 Guthrie	N	Y	N	N	N
3 Yarmuth	Y	Y	?	Y	Y
4 Davis	N	Y	N	N	N
5 Rogers	N	Y	N	N	N
6 Chandler	Y	Y	Y	Y	Y
LOUISIANA					
1 Scalise	N	Y	N	N	N
2 Cao	N	Y	N	N	N
3 Melancon	Y	Y	N	Y	Y
4 Fleming	N	N	N	N	N
5 Alexander	N	Y	N	N	N
6 Cassidy	N	Y	N	N	N
7 Boustany	N	Y	N	N	N
MAINE					
1 Pingree	Y	Y	Y	Y	Y
2 Michaud	Y	Y	Y	Y	Y
MARYLAND					
1 Kratovil	Y	Y	Y	N	N
2 Ruppersberger	Y	Y	Y	Y	Y
3 Sarbanes	Y	Y	Y	Y	Y
4 Edwards	Y	Y	Y	Y	Y
5 Hoyer	Y	Y	Y	Y	Y
6 Bartlett	N	Y	N	N	N
7 Cummings	Y	Y	Y	Y	Y
8 Van Hollen	?	?	Y	Y	Y
MASSACHUSETTS					
1 Olver	Y	Y	Y	Y	Y
2 Neal	Y	Y	Y	Y	Y
3 McGovern	Y	Y	Y	Y	Y
4 Frank	Y	Y	Y	Y	Y
5 Tsongas	Y	Y	Y	Y	Y
6 Tierney	Y	Y	Y	Y	Y
7 Markey	Y	Y	Y	Y	Y
8 Capuano	Y	Y	?	?	?
9 Lynch	Y	Y	Y	Y	Y
10 Delahunt	Y	Y	Y	Y	Y
MICHIGAN					
1 Stupak	Y	Y	Y	Y	Y
2 Hoekstra	N	N	N	N	N
3 Ehlers	N	Y	N	N	N
4 Camp	N	Y	N	N	N
5 Kildee	Y	Y	Y	Y	Y
6 Upton	N	Y	N	N	N
7 Schauer	Y	Y	Y	Y	Y
8 Rogers	N	Y	N	N	N
9 Peters	Y	Y	Y	Y	Y
10 Miller	N	Y	N	N	N
11 McCotter	N	Y	N	N	N
12 Levin	Y	Y	Y	Y	Y
13 Kilpatrick	+	+	Y	Y	Y
14 Conyers	Y	Y	Y	Y	Y
15 Dingell	Y	Y	Y	Y	Y
MINNESOTA					
1 Walz	Y	Y	Y	Y	Y
2 Kline	N	N	N	N	N
3 Paulsen	N	Y	N	N	N
4 McCollum	Y	Y	Y	Y	Y
5 Ellison	Y	Y	+	Y	Y
6 Bachmann	N	N	N	N	N
7 Peterson	Y	Y	Y	Y	N
8 Oberstar	Y	?	Y	Y	Y
MISSISSIPPI					
1 Childers	Y	Y	N	N	N
2 Thompson	Y	Y	Y	Y	Y
3 Harper	N	Y	N	N	N
4 Taylor	Y	Y	Y	N	N
MISSOURI					
1 Clay	Y	Y	Y	Y	Y
2 Akin	N	N	N	N	N
3 Carnahan	Y	Y	Y	Y	Y
4 Skelton	Y	Y	Y	Y	Y
5 Cleaver	Y	Y	Y	Y	?
6 Graves	N	Y	N	N	N
7 Blunt	N	?	?	?	?
8 Emerson	N	Y	N	N	N
9 Luetkemeyer	N	Y	N	N	N
MONTANA					
AL Rehberg	N	Y	N	N	N
NEBRASKA					
1 Fortenberry	N	Y	N	N	N
2 Terry	N	Y	N	N	N
3 Smith	N	N	N	N	N
NEVADA					
1 Berkley	Y	Y	Y	Y	Y
2 Heller	N	Y	?	N	N
3 Titus	Y	Y	Y	Y	Y
NEW HAMPSHIRE					
1 Shea-Porter	?	?	Y	Y	Y
2 Hodes	?	?	Y	Y	Y
NEW JERSEY					
1 Andrews	Y	Y	Y	Y	Y
2 LoBiondo	N	Y	N	N	N
3 Adler	Y	Y	Y	Y	Y
4 Smith	N	Y	N	N	N
5 Garrett	N	N	N	N	N
6 Pallone	Y	Y	Y	Y	Y
7 Lance	N	Y	N	N	N
8 Pascrell	Y	Y	Y	Y	Y
9 Rothman	Y	Y	Y	Y	Y
10 Payne	Y	Y	Y	Y	Y
11 Frelinghuysen	N	Y	N	N	N
12 Holt	Y	Y	Y	Y	Y
13 Sires	Y	Y	Y	Y	Y
NEW MEXICO					
1 Heinrich	Y	Y	Y	Y	Y
2 Teague	Y	Y	?	Y	Y
3 Luján	Y	Y	Y	Y	Y
NEW YORK					
1 Bishop	Y	Y	Y	Y	Y
2 Israel	?	?	Y	Y	Y
3 King	N	Y	N	N	N
4 McCarthy	Y	Y	Y	Y	Y
5 Ackerman	Y	Y	Y	Y	Y
6 Meeks	?	?	Y	Y	Y
7 Crowley	Y	Y	Y	Y	Y
8 Nadler	?	?	Y	Y	?
9 Weiner	Y	Y	Y	Y	Y
10 Towns	?	?	Y	?	Y
11 Clarke	Y	Y	Y	Y	Y
12 Velázquez	?	?	Y	?	Y
13 McMahon	Y	Y	N	Y	Y
14 Maloney	+	+	Y	Y	Y
15 Rangel	?	?	Y	Y	Y
16 Serrano	Y	Y	Y	Y	Y
17 Engel	?	?	Y	Y	Y
18 Lowey	+	+	Y	Y	Y
19 Hall	?	?	?	?	?
20 Murphy	?	?	Y	Y	Y
21 Tonko	Y	Y	Y	Y	Y
22 Hinchey	Y	Y	Y	Y	Y
23 Owens	N	Y	Y	Y	Y
24 Arcuri	Y	Y	Y	Y	Y
25 Maffei	Y	Y	Y	Y	Y
26 Lee	N	Y	N	N	N
27 Higgins	Y	Y	Y	Y	Y
28 Slaughter	Y	Y	Y	Y	Y
29 Vacant					
NORTH CAROLINA					
1 Butterfield	?	?	Y	Y	Y
2 Etheridge	Y	Y	Y	Y	Y
3 Jones	Y	Y	N	N	N
4 Price	Y	Y	Y	Y	Y
5 Foxx	N	N	N	N	N
6 Coble	N	Y	N	N	N
7 McIntyre	Y	Y	Y	Y	Y
8 Kissell	Y	Y	Y	Y	Y
9 Myrick	N	Y	N	N	N
10 McHenry	N	Y	N	N	N
11 Shuler	Y	Y	Y	Y	N
12 Watt	Y	Y	Y	Y	Y
13 Miller	Y	Y	Y	Y	Y
NORTH DAKOTA					
AL Pomeroy	Y	Y	Y	Y	Y
OHIO					
1 Driehaus	Y	Y	Y	Y	Y
2 Schmidt	N	Y	N	N	N
3 Turner	N	Y	N	N	N
4 Jordan	N	N	N	N	N
5 Latta	N	Y	N	N	N
6 Wilson	?	?	Y	Y	Y
7 Austria	N	Y	N	N	N
8 Boehner	?	Y	N	N	N
9 Kaptur	Y	Y	Y	Y	Y
10 Kucinich	Y	Y	Y	Y	Y
11 Fudge	Y	Y	Y	Y	Y
12 Tiberi	N	Y	N	N	N
13 Sutton	Y	Y	Y	Y	Y
14 LaTourette	N	Y	N	N	N
15 Kilroy	Y	Y	Y	Y	Y
16 Boccieri	Y	Y	Y	Y	Y
17 Ryan	Y	Y	Y	Y	Y
18 Space	?	?	Y	Y	Y
OKLAHOMA					
1 Sullivan	N	N	?	N	N
2 Boren	?	?	?	?	?
3 Lucas	N	N	N	N	N
4 Cole	N	Y	N	N	N
5 Fallin	?	?	?	?	?
OREGON					
1 Wu	Y	Y	Y	Y	Y
2 Walden	N	Y	N	N	N
3 Blumenauer	?	?	Y	Y	Y
4 DeFazio	Y	Y	Y	Y	Y
5 Schrader	?	Y	Y	Y	Y
PENNSYLVANIA					
1 Brady	?	?	Y	Y	Y
2 Fattah	Y	Y	Y	Y	Y
3 Dahlkemper	Y	Y	Y	Y	N
4 Altmire	Y	Y	Y	Y	Y
5 Thompson	N	Y	N	N	N
6 Gerlach	N	Y	N	N	N
7 Sestak	Y	Y	Y	Y	Y
8 Murphy, P.	Y	Y	Y	Y	Y
9 Shuster	N	N	N	N	N
10 Carney	?	?	Y	Y	Y
11 Kanjorski	Y	Y	Y	Y	Y
12 Critz	Y	Y	Y	Y	Y
13 Schwartz	Y	Y	Y	Y	Y
14 Doyle	Y	Y	Y	Y	Y
15 Dent	N	Y	N	N	N
16 Pitts	N	Y	N	N	N
17 Holden	Y	Y	Y	Y	Y
18 Murphy, T.	N	Y	N	N	N
19 Platts	N	Y	N	N	N
RHODE ISLAND					
1 Kennedy	Y	Y	Y	Y	Y
2 Langevin	Y	Y	Y	Y	Y
SOUTH CAROLINA					
1 Brown	N	Y	N	N	N
2 Wilson	N	Y	N	N	N
3 Barrett	?	?	N	N	N
4 Inglis	N	Y	N	N	N
5 Spratt	Y	Y	Y	Y	Y
6 Clyburn	Y	Y	Y	Y	Y
SOUTH DAKOTA					
AL Herseth Sandlin	Y	Y	Y	Y	N
TENNESSEE					
1 Roe	N	Y	N	N	N
2 Duncan	N	N	N	N	N
3 Wamp	N	Y	N	N	N
4 Davis	Y	Y	Y	Y	Y
5 Cooper	N	Y	Y	N	Y
6 Gordon	Y	Y	Y	Y	Y
7 Blackburn	N	Y	N	N	N
8 Tanner	Y	Y	Y	Y	Y
9 Cohen	Y	Y	Y	?	Y
TEXAS					
1 Gohmert	N	N	N	N	N
2 Poe	N	?	N	N	N
3 Johnson, S.	N	?	N	N	N
4 Hall	N	N	N	N	N
5 Hensarling	N	N	N	N	N
6 Barton	N	Y	N	N	N
7 Culberson	N	N	N	N	N
8 Brady	N	N	N	N	N
9 Green, A.	Y	Y	Y	Y	Y
10 McCaul	N	Y	N	N	N
11 Conaway	N	N	—	—	—
12 Granger	N	N	N	N	N
13 Thornberry	N	N	N	?	?
14 Paul	N	N	N	N	N
15 Hinojosa	Y	Y	Y	Y	Y
16 Reyes	Y	Y	Y	Y	Y
17 Edwards	Y	Y	Y	Y	Y
18 Jackson Lee	Y	Y	Y	Y	Y
19 Neugebauer	N	N	N	N	N
20 Gonzalez	Y	?	Y	Y	Y
21 Smith	N	Y	N	N	N
22 Olson	N	N	N	N	N
23 Rodriguez	Y	Y	Y	Y	Y
24 Marchant	N	N	N	N	?
25 Doggett	Y	Y	Y	Y	Y
26 Burgess	N	Y	N	N	N
27 Ortiz	Y	Y	Y	Y	Y
28 Cuellar	Y	Y	Y	Y	Y
29 Green, G.	Y	Y	Y	Y	Y
30 Johnson, E.	Y	Y	Y	Y	Y
31 Carter	?	N	N	N	N
32 Sessions	N	N	N	N	N
UTAH					
1 Bishop	?	N	N	N	N
2 Matheson	Y	Y	Y	N	N
3 Chaffetz	N	N	N	N	N
VERMONT					
AL Welch	Y	Y	Y	Y	Y
VIRGINIA					
1 Wittman	N	Y	N	N	N
2 Nye	Y	Y	N	N	Y
3 Scott	Y	Y	Y	Y	Y
4 Forbes	N	Y	N	N	N
5 Perriello	Y	Y	Y	Y	Y
6 Goodlatte	N	N	N	N	N
7 Cantor	N	Y	N	N	N
8 Moran	Y	Y	Y	Y	Y
9 Boucher	?	?	Y	Y	Y
10 Wolf	N	Y	N	N	N
11 Connolly	Y	Y	Y	Y	Y
WASHINGTON					
1 Inslee	Y	Y	Y	Y	Y
2 Larsen	Y	Y	Y	Y	Y
3 Baird	Y	Y	Y	Y	Y
4 Hastings	N	N	N	N	N
5 McMorris Rodgers	N	Y	N	?	N
6 Dicks	?	?	Y	Y	Y
7 McDermott	Y	Y	Y	Y	Y
8 Reichert	N	Y	N	N	N
9 Smith	Y	Y	Y	Y	Y
WEST VIRGINIA					
1 Mollohan	?	?	Y	Y	Y
2 Capito	N	Y	N	N	N
3 Rahall	Y	Y	Y	Y	Y
WISCONSIN					
1 Ryan	N	Y	N	N	N
2 Baldwin	Y	Y	Y	Y	Y
3 Kind	Y	Y	Y	Y	Y
4 Moore	?	?	Y	Y	Y
5 Sensenbrenner	N	N	N	N	N
6 Petri	N	N	N	N	N
7 Obey	?	?	Y	Y	Y
8 Kagen	Y	Y	Y	Y	Y
WYOMING					
AL Lummis	N	N	N	N	N
DELEGATES					
Faleomavaega (A.S.)					
Norton (D.C.)					
Bordallo (Guam)					
Sablan (N. Marianas)					
Pierluisi (P.R.)					
Christensen (V.I.)					

IN THE HOUSE | By Vote Number

537. **HR 5110. Casa Grande Ruins National Monument Boundary/ Passage.** Christensen, D-V.I., motion to suspend the rules and pass the bill that would authorize the Interior Department to expand the boundary of the Casa Grande Ruins National Monument in Arizona by approximately 415 acres. Motion rejected 244-174: D 242-2; R 2-172. A two-thirds majority of those present and voting (279 in this case) is required for passage under suspension of the rules. Sept. 23, 2010.

538. **HR 4823. Sedona-Red Rock National Scenic Area/Passage.** Christensen, D-V.I., motion to suspend the rules and pass the bill that would designate approximately 160,000 acres of National Forest System land in the Coconino National Forest near Sedona, Ariz., as a National Scenic Area. Motion rejected 258-160: D 246-0; R 12-160. A two-thirds majority of those present and voting (279 in this case) is required for passage under suspension of the rules. Sept. 23, 2010.

539. **HR 5297. Small-Business Tax and Lending/Motion to Concur.** Bean, D-Ill., motion to concur in the Senate amendment to the bill that would provide for a variety of small-business tax benefits, including a revival of an expired bonus depreciation provision to allow companies to write off assets more quickly. It also would establish a $30 billion small-business lending fund administered by the Treasury Department, with funds directed to community banks. The cost would be offset with increased penalties for failing to file information returns, new limits on papermakers' ability to claim a biofuel tax credit and new rules on tax-delinquent federal contractors. Motion agreed to, thus clearing the bill for the president, 237-187: D 236-13; R 1-174. A "yea" was a vote in support of the president's position. Sept. 23, 2010.

540. **HR 5307. Smuggling on Ultralight Aircraft/Passage.** Tanner, D-Tenn., motion to suspend the rules and pass the bill that would amend the Tariff Act of 1930 to include small aircraft known as ultralights under its aviation smuggling provisions, thus permitting the prosecution of individuals for smuggling drugs using such aircraft. Motion agreed to 412-3: D 246-0; R 166-3. A two-thirds majority of those present and voting (277 in this case) is required for passage under suspension of the rules. Sept. 23, 2010.

	537	538	539	540
ALABAMA				
1 **Bonner**	N	N	N	Y
2 Bright	?	?	?	?
3 **Rogers**	N	N	N	Y
4 **Aderholt**	N	N	N	Y
5 **Griffith**	N	N	N	Y
6 **Bachus**	N	N	N	Y
7 Davis	Y	?	Y	Y
ALASKA				
AL **Young**	N	N	N	N
ARIZONA				
1 Kirkpatrick	Y	Y	Y	Y
2 **Franks**	N	N	N	Y
3 **Shadegg**	N	N	N	Y
4 Pastor	Y	Y	Y	Y
5 Mitchell	Y	Y	Y	Y
6 **Flake**	N	N	N	Y
7 Grijalva	Y	Y	Y	Y
8 Giffords	Y	Y	Y	Y
ARKANSAS				
1 Berry	?	Y	N	Y
2 Snyder	Y	Y	Y	Y
3 **Boozman**	N	N	N	Y
4 Ross	Y	Y	Y	Y
CALIFORNIA				
1 Thompson	Y	Y	Y	Y
2 **Herger**	N	N	N	Y
3 **Lungren**	N	N	N	Y
4 **McClintock**	N	N	N	Y
5 Matsui	Y	Y	Y	Y
6 Woolsey	+	Y	Y	Y
7 Miller, George	Y	Y	Y	?
8 Pelosi			Y	
9 Lee	Y	Y	Y	Y
10 Garamendi	Y	Y	Y	?
11 McNerney	Y	Y	Y	Y
12 Speier	Y	Y	Y	Y
13 Stark	Y	Y	Y	Y
14 Eshoo	Y	Y	Y	Y
15 Honda	?	?	Y	Y
16 Lofgren	Y	Y	Y	Y
17 Farr	Y	Y	Y	Y
18 Cardoza	Y	Y	Y	Y
19 **Radanovich**	N	N	N	Y
20 Costa	Y	Y	Y	Y
21 **Nunes**	N	N	N	?
22 **McCarthy**	N	N	N	Y
23 Capps	Y	Y	Y	Y
24 **Gallegly**	N	N	N	Y
25 **McKeon**	N	N	N	Y
26 **Dreier**	N	N	N	Y
27 Sherman	Y	Y	Y	Y
28 Berman	Y	Y	Y	Y
29 Schiff	Y	Y	Y	Y
30 Waxman	Y	Y	Y	Y
31 Becerra	Y	Y	Y	Y
32 Chu	Y	Y	Y	Y
33 Watson	Y	Y	Y	Y
34 Roybal-Allard	Y	Y	Y	Y
35 Waters	Y	Y	Y	Y
36 Harman	Y	Y	Y	Y
37 Richardson	Y	Y	Y	Y
38 Napolitano	Y	Y	Y	Y
39 Sánchez, Linda	Y	Y	Y	Y
40 **Royce**	N	N	N	Y
41 **Lewis**	N	N	N	Y
42 **Miller, Gary**	N	N	N	Y
43 Baca	Y	Y	Y	Y
44 **Calvert**	N	N	N	Y
45 **Bono Mack**	N	Y	N	Y
46 **Rohrabacher**	N	N	N	Y
47 Sanchez, Loretta	Y	Y	Y	Y
48 **Campbell**	N	N	N	Y
49 **Issa**	N	N	N	Y
50 **Bilbray**	N	N	N	Y
51 Filner	Y	Y	Y	Y
52 **Hunter**	N	N	N	Y
53 Davis	Y	Y	Y	Y

	537	538	539	540
COLORADO				
1 DeGette	Y	Y	Y	Y
2 Polis	Y	Y	N	Y
3 Salazar	Y	Y	Y	Y
4 Markey	Y	Y	Y	Y
5 **Lamborn**	N	N	N	Y
6 **Coffman**	N	N	N	Y
7 Perlmutter	Y	Y	Y	Y
CONNECTICUT				
1 Larson	Y	Y	Y	Y
2 Courtney	Y	Y	Y	Y
3 DeLauro	Y	Y	Y	Y
4 Himes	Y	Y	Y	Y
5 Murphy	Y	Y	Y	Y
DELAWARE				
AL **Castle**	N	Y	N	Y
FLORIDA				
1 **Miller**	N	N	N	Y
2 Boyd	Y	Y	Y	Y
3 Brown	Y	Y	Y	Y
4 **Crenshaw**	N	N	N	Y
5 **Brown-Waite**	N	N	N	Y
6 **Stearns**	N	N	N	Y
7 **Mica**	N	N	N	Y
8 Grayson	Y	Y	Y	Y
9 **Bilirakis**	N	N	N	Y
10 **Young**	?	?	?	?
11 Castor	Y	Y	+	Y
12 **Putnam**	N	N	N	Y
13 **Buchanan**	N	N	N	Y
14 **Mack**	N	N	N	Y
15 **Posey**	N	N	N	Y
16 **Rooney**	N	N	N	Y
17 Meek	?	?	?	?
18 **Ros-Lehtinen**	N	N	N	Y
19 Deutch	Y	Y	Y	Y
20 Wasserman Schultz	Y	Y	Y	Y
21 **Diaz-Balart, L.**	N	N	N	Y
22 Klein	Y	Y	Y	Y
23 Hastings	Y	Y	Y	Y
24 Kosmas	Y	Y	Y	Y
25 **Diaz-Balart, M.**	N	N	N	Y
GEORGIA				
1 **Kingston**	N	N	N	Y
2 Bishop	Y	Y	Y	Y
3 **Westmoreland**	N	N	N	Y
4 Johnson	Y	Y	Y	Y
5 Lewis	Y	Y	Y	Y
6 **Price**	N	N	N	Y
7 **Linder**	N	N	N	Y
8 Marshall	Y	Y	Y	Y
9 **Graves**	N	N	N	Y
10 **Broun**	N	N	N	Y
11 **Gingrey**	N	N	N	Y
12 Barrow	Y	Y	Y	Y
13 Scott	Y	Y	Y	Y
HAWAII				
1 **Djou**	N	Y	N	Y
2 Hirono	Y	Y	Y	Y
IDAHO				
1 Minnick	Y	Y	Y	Y
2 **Simpson**	N	N	N	Y
ILLINOIS				
1 Rush	Y	Y	Y	Y
2 Jackson	Y	Y	Y	Y
3 Lipinski	Y	Y	Y	Y
4 Gutierrez	Y	Y	Y	Y
5 Quigley	Y	Y	Y	Y
6 **Roskam**	N	N	N	Y
7 Davis	Y	Y	Y	Y
8 Bean	N	Y	Y	Y
9 Schakowsky	Y	Y	Y	Y
10 **Kirk**	N	N	N	Y
11 Halvorson	Y	Y	Y	Y
12 Costello	Y	Y	Y	Y
13 **Biggert**	N	N	N	Y
14 Foster	Y	Y	Y	Y
15 Johnson	N	N	N	N

KEY   **Republicans**   Democrats

Y Voted for (yea)	X Paired against	C Voted "present" to avoid possible conflict of interest
# Paired for	– Announced against	
+ Announced for	P Voted "present"	? Did not vote or otherwise make a position known
N Voted against (nay)		

Member	537	538	539	540
16 Manzullo	N	N	N	Y
17 Hare	Y	Y	Y	Y
18 Schock	N	N	N	Y
19 Shimkus	N	N	N	Y
INDIANA				
1 Visclosky	Y	Y	Y	Y
2 Donnelly	Y	Y	Y	Y
3 Vacant				
4 Buyer	N	N	N	Y
5 Burton	N	N	N	Y
6 Pence	N	N	N	Y
7 Carson	Y	Y	Y	Y
8 Ellsworth	Y	Y	Y	Y
9 Hill	Y	Y	Y	Y
IOWA				
1 Braley	Y	Y	Y	Y
2 Loebsack	Y	Y	Y	Y
3 Boswell	Y	Y	Y	Y
4 Latham	N	Y	N	Y
5 King	N	N	N	?
KANSAS				
1 Moran	N	N	N	Y
2 Jenkins	N	N	N	Y
3 Moore	Y	Y	Y	Y
4 Tiahrt	N	N	N	Y
KENTUCKY				
1 Whitfield	N	N	N	Y
2 Guthrie	N	N	N	Y
3 Yarmuth	Y	Y	Y	Y
4 Davis	N	N	N	Y
5 Rogers	N	N	N	Y
6 Chandler	Y	Y	Y	Y
LOUISIANA				
1 Scalise	N	N	N	Y
2 Cao	N	N	N	Y
3 Melancon	Y	Y	Y	Y
4 Fleming	N	N	N	Y
5 Alexander	N	N	N	Y
6 Cassidy	N	N	N	+
7 Boustany	N	N	N	Y
MAINE				
1 Pingree	Y	Y	Y	Y
2 Michaud	Y	Y	Y	Y
MARYLAND				
1 Kratovil	Y	Y	Y	Y
2 Ruppersberger	Y	Y	Y	Y
3 Sarbanes	Y	Y	Y	Y
4 Edwards	Y	Y	Y	Y
5 Hoyer	Y	Y	Y	Y
6 Bartlett	N	N	N	Y
7 Cummings	Y	Y	Y	Y
8 Van Hollen	Y	Y	Y	Y
MASSACHUSETTS				
1 Olver	Y	Y	Y	Y
2 Neal	Y	Y	Y	Y
3 McGovern	Y	Y	Y	Y
4 Frank	Y	Y	Y	+
5 Tsongas	Y	Y	Y	Y
6 Tierney	Y	Y	Y	Y
7 Markey	Y	Y	Y	Y
8 Capuano	?	Y	Y	Y
9 Lynch	Y	Y	Y	Y
10 Delahunt	Y	Y	Y	Y
MICHIGAN				
1 Stupak	Y	Y	Y	Y
2 Hoekstra	N	N	N	Y
3 Ehlers	Y	Y	N	Y
4 Camp	N	N	N	Y
5 Kildee	Y	Y	Y	Y
6 Upton	N	N	N	Y
7 Schauer	Y	Y	Y	Y
8 Rogers	N	N	N	Y
9 Peters	Y	Y	Y	Y
10 Miller	N	N	N	Y
11 McCotter	N	N	N	Y
12 Levin	Y	Y	Y	Y
13 Kilpatrick	Y	Y	Y	Y
14 Conyers	Y	Y	Y	Y
15 Dingell	Y	Y	Y	Y
MINNESOTA				
1 Walz	Y	Y	Y	Y
2 Kline	N	N	N	Y
3 Paulsen	N	N	N	Y
4 McCollum	Y	Y	Y	Y
5 Ellison	Y	Y	Y	Y
6 Bachmann	N	?	N	Y
7 Peterson	Y	Y	N	Y
8 Oberstar	Y	Y	Y	Y
MISSISSIPPI				
1 Childers	Y	Y	N	Y
2 Thompson	Y	Y	Y	Y
3 Harper	N	N	N	Y
4 Taylor	Y	Y	N	Y
MISSOURI				
1 Clay	Y	Y	Y	Y
2 Akin	N	N	N	Y
3 Carnahan	Y	Y	Y	Y
4 Skelton	Y	Y	Y	Y
5 Cleaver	Y	Y	Y	Y
6 Graves	N	N	N	Y
7 Blunt	?	?	?	?
8 Emerson	N	N	N	Y
9 Luetkemeyer	N	N	N	Y
MONTANA				
AL Rehberg	N	N	N	Y
NEBRASKA				
1 Fortenberry	N	Y	N	Y
2 Terry	N	N	N	Y
3 Smith	N	N	N	Y
NEVADA				
1 Berkley	Y	Y	Y	Y
2 Heller	N	N	N	Y
3 Titus	Y	Y	N	Y
NEW HAMPSHIRE				
1 Shea-Porter	Y	Y	Y	Y
2 Hodes	Y	Y	Y	Y
NEW JERSEY				
1 Andrews	Y	Y	Y	Y
2 LoBiondo	N	N	N	Y
3 Adler	Y	Y	Y	Y
4 Smith	N	Y	N	Y
5 Garrett	N	?	N	Y
6 Pallone	Y	Y	Y	Y
7 Lance	N	N	N	Y
8 Pascrell	Y	Y	Y	?
9 Rothman	Y	Y	Y	Y
10 Payne	Y	Y	Y	Y
11 Frelinghuysen	N	N	N	Y
12 Holt	Y	Y	Y	Y
13 Sires	Y	Y	Y	Y
NEW MEXICO				
1 Heinrich	Y	Y	Y	Y
2 Teague	Y	Y	Y	Y
3 Luján	Y	Y	Y	Y
NEW YORK				
1 Bishop	Y	Y	Y	Y
2 Israel	Y	Y	Y	Y
3 King	N	N	N	Y
4 McCarthy	Y	Y	Y	Y
5 Ackerman	Y	Y	Y	Y
6 Meeks	Y	Y	Y	Y
7 Crowley	Y	Y	Y	Y
8 Nadler	Y	Y	Y	Y
9 Weiner	Y	Y	Y	Y
10 Towns	Y	Y	Y	Y
11 Clarke	Y	Y	Y	Y
12 Velázquez	Y	Y	N	Y
13 McMahon	Y	Y	Y	Y
14 Maloney	Y	Y	Y	Y
15 Rangel	Y	Y	Y	Y
16 Serrano	Y	Y	Y	Y
17 Engel	Y	Y	Y	Y
18 Lowey	Y	Y	Y	Y
19 Hall	?	?	?	?
20 Murphy	Y	Y	Y	Y
21 Tonko	Y	Y	Y	Y
22 Hinchey	Y	Y	Y	Y
23 Owens	N	Y	Y	Y
24 Arcuri	Y	Y	Y	Y
25 Maffei	Y	Y	Y	Y
26 Lee	N	N	N	Y
27 Higgins	Y	Y	Y	Y
28 Slaughter	Y	Y	Y	Y
29 Vacant				
NORTH CAROLINA				
1 Butterfield	Y	Y	Y	Y
2 Etheridge	Y	Y	Y	Y
3 Jones	N	Y	Y	Y
4 Price	Y	Y	Y	Y
5 Foxx	N	N	N	Y
6 Coble	N	N	N	Y
7 McIntyre	Y	Y	Y	Y
8 Kissell	Y	Y	Y	Y
9 Myrick	N	N	N	Y
10 McHenry	N	N	N	Y
11 Shuler	Y	Y	N	Y
12 Watt	Y	Y	Y	Y
13 Miller	Y	Y	Y	Y
NORTH DAKOTA				
AL Pomeroy	Y	Y	Y	Y
OHIO				
1 Driehaus	Y	Y	Y	Y
2 Schmidt	N	N	N	Y
3 Turner	N	Y	N	Y
4 Jordan	N	N	N	Y
5 Latta	N	N	N	Y
6 Wilson	Y	Y	Y	Y
7 Austria	N	N	N	Y
8 Boehner	N	N	N	?
9 Kaptur	Y	Y	Y	Y
10 Kucinich	Y	Y	Y	Y
11 Fudge	Y	Y	Y	Y
12 Tiberi	N	Y	N	Y
13 Sutton	Y	Y	Y	Y
14 LaTourette	N	Y	N	Y
15 Kilroy	Y	Y	Y	Y
16 Boccieri	Y	Y	Y	Y
17 Ryan	Y	Y	Y	Y
18 Space	Y	Y	Y	Y
OKLAHOMA				
1 Sullivan	N	N	N	Y
2 Boren	?	?	?	?
3 Lucas	N	N	N	Y
4 Cole	N	N	N	Y
5 Fallin	?	?	?	?
OREGON				
1 Wu	Y	Y	Y	Y
2 Walden	N	N	N	Y
3 Blumenauer	Y	Y	Y	Y
4 DeFazio	?	?	N	Y
5 Schrader	?	?	Y	Y
PENNSYLVANIA				
1 Brady	Y	Y	Y	Y
2 Fattah	Y	Y	Y	Y
3 Dahlkemper	Y	Y	Y	Y
4 Altmire	Y	Y	Y	Y
5 Thompson	N	N	N	Y
6 Gerlach	N	N	N	?
7 Sestak	Y	Y	Y	Y
8 Murphy, P.	Y	Y	Y	Y
9 Shuster	N	N	N	Y
10 Carney	Y	Y	Y	Y
11 Kanjorski	Y	Y	Y	Y
12 Critz	Y	Y	Y	Y
13 Schwartz	Y	Y	Y	Y
14 Doyle	Y	Y	Y	Y
15 Dent	N	N	N	Y
16 Pitts	N	N	N	Y
17 Holden	Y	Y	Y	Y
18 Murphy, T.	N	N	N	Y
19 Platts	N	N	N	Y
RHODE ISLAND				
1 Kennedy	Y	Y	?	Y
2 Langevin	Y	Y	Y	Y
SOUTH CAROLINA				
1 Brown	N	N	N	Y
2 Wilson	N	N	N	Y
3 Barrett	N	N	N	Y
4 Inglis	N	N	N	Y
5 Spratt	Y	Y	Y	Y
6 Clyburn	Y	Y	Y	Y
SOUTH DAKOTA				
AL Herseth Sandlin	Y	Y	N	Y
TENNESSEE				
1 Roe	N	N	N	Y
2 Duncan	N	N	N	Y
3 Wamp	N	N	N	Y
4 Davis	Y	Y	Y	Y
5 Cooper	Y	Y	Y	Y
6 Gordon	Y	Y	Y	Y
7 Blackburn	N	N	N	Y
8 Tanner	Y	Y	Y	Y
9 Cohen	Y	Y	Y	Y
TEXAS				
1 Gohmert	N	N	N	Y
2 Poe	N	N	N	Y
3 Johnson, S.	N	N	N	Y
4 Hall	N	N	N	Y
5 Hensarling	N	N	N	Y
6 Barton	N	N	N	Y
7 Culberson	Y	N	N	Y
8 Brady	N	N	N	Y
9 Green, A.	Y	Y	Y	Y
10 McCaul	N	N	N	Y
11 Conaway	–	–	N	Y
12 Granger	N	N	N	Y
13 Thornberry	N	N	N	Y
14 Paul	N	N	N	N
15 Hinojosa	Y	Y	Y	Y
16 Reyes	Y	Y	Y	Y
17 Edwards	Y	Y	Y	Y
18 Jackson Lee	Y	Y	Y	Y
19 Neugebauer	Y	Y	Y	Y
20 Gonzalez	Y	Y	Y	Y
21 Smith	N	N	N	Y
22 Olson	N	N	N	Y
23 Rodriguez	Y	Y	Y	Y
24 Marchant	N	N	N	Y
25 Doggett	Y	Y	Y	Y
26 Burgess	N	N	N	Y
27 Ortiz	Y	Y	Y	Y
28 Cuellar	Y	Y	Y	Y
29 Green, G.	Y	Y	Y	Y
30 Johnson, E.	Y	Y	Y	Y
31 Carter	N	N	N	Y
32 Sessions	N	N	N	?
UTAH				
1 Bishop	N	N	N	Y
2 Matheson	Y	Y	Y	Y
3 Chaffetz	N	N	N	Y
VERMONT				
AL Welch	Y	Y	Y	Y
VIRGINIA				
1 Wittman	N	N	N	Y
2 Nye	Y	Y	Y	Y
3 Scott	Y	Y	Y	Y
4 Forbes	N	N	N	Y
5 Perriello	Y	Y	Y	Y
6 Goodlatte	N	N	N	Y
7 Cantor	N	N	N	Y
8 Moran	Y	Y	Y	Y
9 Boucher	Y	Y	Y	Y
10 Wolf	N	N	N	Y
11 Connolly	Y	Y	Y	Y
WASHINGTON				
1 Inslee	Y	Y	Y	Y
2 Larsen	Y	Y	Y	Y
3 Baird	Y	Y	Y	Y
4 Hastings	N	N	N	Y
5 McMorris Rodgers	N	N	N	Y
6 Dicks	Y	Y	Y	Y
7 McDermott	Y	Y	Y	Y
8 Reichert	N	Y	N	Y
9 Smith	Y	Y	Y	Y
WEST VIRGINIA				
1 Mollohan	Y	Y	Y	Y
2 Capito	N	N	N	Y
3 Rahall	Y	Y	Y	Y
WISCONSIN				
1 Ryan	N	N	N	Y
2 Baldwin	Y	Y	Y	Y
3 Kind	Y	Y	Y	Y
4 Moore	Y	Y	Y	Y
5 Sensenbrenner	N	N	N	Y
6 Petri	N	N	N	Y
7 Obey	Y	Y	Y	Y
8 Kagen	Y	Y	Y	Y
WYOMING				
AL Lummis	N	N	N	Y
DELEGATES				
Faleomavaega (A.S.)				
Norton (D.C.)				
Bordallo (Guam)				
Sablan (N. Marianas)				
Pierluisi (P.R.)				
Christensen (V.I.)				

IN THE HOUSE | By Vote Number

541. **HR 5756. Autism Training and Research/Passage.** Pallone, D-N.J., motion to suspend the rules and pass the bill that would authorize $18 million annually in fiscal 2012 through 2016 for grants for autism research and services, including interdisciplinary training, continuing education and technical assistance, for children and adults with autism, their families, and health and education professionals. Motion agreed to 393-24: D 246-0; R 147-24. A two-thirds majority of those present and voting (278 in this case) is required for passage under suspension of the rules. Sept. 23, 2010.

542. **HR 3199. Military Emergency Medical Technicians/Passage.** Pallone, D-N.J., motion to suspend the rules and pass the bill that would require the Department of Health and Human Services to create a program to award grants to states to aid veterans who completed military emergency medical training while serving in the armed forces to become state-licensed or certified emergency medical technicians. It would authorize $5 million per year from fiscal 2011 through 2015. Motion agreed to 412-5: D 247-0; R 165-5. A two-thirds majority of those present and voting (278 in this case) is required for passage under suspension of the rules. Sept. 23, 2010.

543. **HR 1745. Health Center Volunteer Liability Protection/ Passage.** Pallone, D-N.J., motion to suspend the rules and pass the bill that would provide liability protection to health care professionals who volunteer at certain health facilities. Any health care volunteer who provides services eligible for funding under the community health center grant program would be considered an employee of the Public Health Service for purposes of any civil actions that may arise. Motion agreed to 417-1: D 247-0; R 170-1. A two-thirds majority of those present and voting (279 in this case) is required for passage under suspension of the rules. Sept. 23, 2010.

544. **HR 5710. Prescription Electronic Reporting/Passage.** Pallone, D-N.J., motion to suspend the rules and pass the bill that would authorize $15 million in fiscal 2011 and $10 million per year in fiscal 2012 and 2013 to reauthorize the National All Schedules Prescription Electronic Reporting Act, which provides grants to states to track drug prescriptions. Motion agreed to 384-32: D 244-1; R 140-31. A two-thirds majority of those present and voting (278 in this case) is required for passage under suspension of the rules. Sept. 23, 2010.

	541	542	543	544
ALABAMA				
1 Bonner	Y	Y	Y	Y
2 Bright	?	?	?	?
3 Rogers	Y	Y	Y	Y
4 Aderholt	Y	Y	Y	Y
5 Griffith	Y	Y	Y	Y
6 Bachus	Y	Y	Y	Y
7 Davis	Y	Y	Y	Y
ALASKA				
AL Young	Y	Y	Y	Y
ARIZONA				
1 Kirkpatrick	Y	Y	Y	Y
2 Franks	N	Y	Y	N
3 Shadegg	N	Y	Y	Y
4 Pastor	Y	Y	Y	Y
5 Mitchell	Y	Y	Y	Y
6 Flake	N	N	Y	N
7 Grijalva	Y	Y	Y	Y
8 Giffords	Y	Y	Y	Y
ARKANSAS				
1 Berry	Y	Y	Y	Y
2 Snyder	Y	Y	Y	Y
3 Boozman	Y	Y	Y	Y
4 Ross	Y	Y	Y	Y
CALIFORNIA				
1 Thompson	Y	Y	Y	Y
2 Herger	N	Y	Y	N
3 Lungren	Y	Y	Y	Y
4 McClintock	N	Y	Y	N
5 Matsui	Y	Y	Y	Y
6 Woolsey	Y	Y	Y	Y
7 Miller, George	Y	Y	Y	Y
8 Pelosi				
9 Lee	Y	Y	Y	Y
10 Garamendi	Y	Y	Y	Y
11 McNerney	Y	Y	Y	Y
12 Speier	Y	Y	Y	Y
13 Stark	Y	Y	Y	Y
14 Eshoo	Y	Y	Y	Y
15 Honda	Y	Y	Y	Y
16 Lofgren	Y	Y	Y	Y
17 Farr	Y	Y	Y	Y
18 Cardoza	Y	Y	Y	Y
19 Radanovich	Y	?	?	?
20 Costa	Y	Y	Y	Y
21 Nunes	Y	Y	Y	N
22 McCarthy	Y	Y	Y	Y
23 Capps	Y	Y	Y	Y
24 Gallegly	Y	Y	Y	Y
25 McKeon	Y	Y	Y	Y
26 Dreier	Y	Y	Y	Y
27 Sherman	Y	Y	Y	Y
28 Berman	Y	Y	Y	Y
29 Schiff	Y	Y	Y	Y
30 Waxman	Y	Y	Y	Y
31 Becerra	Y	Y	Y	Y
32 Chu	Y	Y	Y	Y
33 Watson	Y	Y	Y	Y
34 Roybal-Allard	Y	Y	Y	Y
35 Waters	Y	Y	Y	Y
36 Harman	Y	Y	Y	Y
37 Richardson	Y	Y	Y	Y
38 Napolitano	Y	Y	Y	Y
39 Sánchez, Linda	Y	Y	Y	Y
40 Royce	Y	Y	Y	Y
41 Lewis	Y	Y	Y	Y
42 Miller, Gary	Y	Y	Y	Y
43 Baca	Y	Y	Y	Y
44 Calvert	Y	Y	Y	Y
45 Bono Mack	Y	Y	Y	Y
46 Rohrabacher	Y	Y	Y	N
47 Sanchez, Loretta	Y	Y	Y	Y
48 Campbell	N	Y	N	N
49 Issa	N	Y	Y	Y
50 Bilbray	Y	Y	Y	Y
51 Filner	Y	Y	Y	Y
52 Hunter	Y	Y	Y	Y
53 Davis	Y	Y	Y	Y

	541	542	543	544
COLORADO				
1 DeGette	Y	Y	Y	Y
2 Polis	Y	Y	Y	Y
3 Salazar	Y	Y	Y	Y
4 Markey	Y	Y	Y	Y
5 Lamborn	Y	Y	Y	Y
6 Coffman	Y	Y	Y	Y
7 Perlmutter	Y	Y	Y	Y
CONNECTICUT				
1 Larson	Y	Y	Y	Y
2 Courtney	Y	Y	Y	Y
3 DeLauro	Y	Y	Y	Y
4 Himes	Y	Y	Y	Y
5 Murphy	Y	Y	Y	Y
DELAWARE				
AL Castle	Y	Y	Y	Y
FLORIDA				
1 Miller	Y	Y	Y	Y
2 Boyd	Y	Y	Y	Y
3 Brown	Y	Y	Y	Y
4 Crenshaw	Y	Y	Y	Y
5 Brown-Waite	Y	Y	Y	Y
7 Stearns	Y	Y	Y	Y
7 Mica	Y	Y	Y	Y
8 Grayson	Y	Y	Y	Y
9 Bilirakis	Y	Y	Y	Y
10 Young	?	?	?	?
11 Castor	Y	Y	Y	Y
12 Putnam	Y	Y	Y	Y
13 Buchanan	Y	Y	Y	Y
14 Mack	N	Y	N	N
15 Posey	Y	Y	Y	Y
16 Rooney	Y	Y	Y	N
17 Meek	?	?	?	?
18 Ros-Lehtinen	?	Y	Y	Y
19 Deutch	Y	Y	Y	Y
20 Wasserman Schultz	Y	Y	Y	Y
21 Diaz-Balart, L.	Y	Y	Y	Y
22 Klein	Y	Y	Y	Y
23 Hastings	Y	Y	Y	Y
24 Kosmas	Y	Y	Y	Y
25 Diaz-Balart, M.	Y	Y	Y	Y
GEORGIA				
1 Kingston	Y	Y	Y	N
2 Bishop	Y	Y	Y	Y
3 Westmoreland	Y	Y	Y	N
4 Johnson	Y	Y	Y	Y
5 Lewis	Y	Y	Y	Y
6 Price	Y	Y	Y	N
7 Linder	Y	Y	Y	Y
8 Marshall	Y	Y	Y	Y
9 Graves	N	Y	Y	N
10 Broun	N	N	Y	N
11 Gingrey	N	Y	Y	Y
12 Barrow	Y	Y	Y	Y
13 Scott	?	Y	Y	Y
HAWAII				
1 Djou	Y	Y	Y	Y
2 Hirono	Y	Y	Y	Y
IDAHO				
1 Minnick	Y	Y	Y	Y
2 Simpson	Y	Y	Y	Y
ILLINOIS				
1 Rush	Y	Y	Y	Y
2 Jackson	Y	Y	Y	Y
3 Lipinski	Y	Y	Y	Y
4 Gutierrez	Y	Y	Y	Y
5 Quigley	Y	Y	Y	Y
6 Roskam	Y	Y	Y	?
7 Davis	Y	Y	Y	Y
8 Bean	Y	Y	Y	Y
9 Schakowsky	Y	Y	Y	Y
10 Kirk	Y	Y	?	Y
11 Halvorson	Y	Y	Y	Y
12 Costello	Y	Y	Y	Y
13 Biggert	Y	Y	Y	Y
14 Foster	Y	Y	Y	Y
15 Johnson	Y	Y	Y	Y

KEY	**Republicans**	Democrats		
Y Voted for (yea)		X Paired against		C Voted "present" to avoid possible conflict of interest
# Paired for		– Announced against		
+ Announced for		P Voted "present"		? Did not vote or otherwise make a position known
N Voted against (nay)				

	541	542	543	544
16 **Manzullo**	Y	Y	Y	N
17 Hare	Y	Y	Y	Y
18 **Schock**	Y	?	Y	Y
19 **Shimkus**	Y	Y	Y	Y
INDIANA				
1 Visclosky	Y	Y	Y	Y
2 Donnelly	Y	Y	Y	Y
3 Vacant				
4 **Buyer**	Y	Y	Y	Y
5 **Burton**	Y	Y	Y	Y
6 **Pence**	Y	Y	Y	Y
7 Carson	Y	Y	Y	Y
8 Ellsworth	Y	Y	Y	Y
9 Hill	Y	Y	Y	Y
IOWA				
1 Braley	Y	Y	Y	Y
2 Loebsack	Y	Y	Y	Y
3 Boswell	Y	Y	Y	Y
4 **Latham**	Y	Y	Y	Y
5 **King**	N	N	Y	Y
KANSAS				
1 **Moran**	Y	Y	Y	Y
2 **Jenkins**	Y	Y	Y	Y
3 Moore	Y	Y	Y	Y
4 **Tiahrt**	Y	Y	Y	Y
KENTUCKY				
1 **Whitfield**	Y	Y	Y	Y
2 **Guthrie**	Y	Y	Y	Y
3 Yarmuth	Y	Y	Y	Y
4 **Davis**	Y	Y	Y	Y
5 **Rogers**	Y	Y	Y	Y
6 Chandler	Y	Y	Y	Y
LOUISIANA				
1 **Scalise**	Y	Y	Y	Y
2 **Cao**	Y	Y	Y	Y
3 Melancon	Y	Y	Y	Y
4 **Fleming**	Y	Y	Y	Y
5 **Alexander**	Y	Y	Y	Y
6 **Cassidy**	Y	Y	Y	Y
7 **Boustany**	Y	Y	Y	Y
MAINE				
1 Pingree	Y	Y	Y	Y
2 Michaud	Y	Y	Y	Y
MARYLAND				
1 Kratovil	Y	Y	Y	Y
2 Ruppersberger	Y	Y	Y	Y
3 Sarbanes	Y	Y	Y	Y
4 Edwards	Y	Y	Y	Y
5 Hoyer	Y	Y	Y	Y
6 **Bartlett**	Y	Y	Y	Y
7 Cummings	Y	Y	Y	Y
8 Van Hollen	Y	Y	Y	Y
MASSACHUSETTS				
1 Olver	Y	Y	Y	Y
2 Neal	Y	Y	Y	Y
3 McGovern	Y	Y	Y	Y
4 Frank	+	+	+	+
5 Tsongas	Y	Y	Y	Y
6 Tierney	Y	?	?	?
7 Markey	Y	Y	Y	Y
8 Capuano	Y	Y	Y	Y
9 Lynch	Y	Y	Y	Y
10 Delahunt	Y	Y	Y	Y
MICHIGAN				
1 Stupak	Y	Y	Y	Y
2 **Hoekstra**	Y	Y	Y	Y
3 **Ehlers**	Y	Y	+	Y
4 **Camp**	Y	Y	Y	Y
5 Kildee	Y	Y	Y	Y
6 **Upton**	Y	Y	Y	Y
7 Schauer	Y	Y	Y	Y
8 **Rogers**	Y	Y	Y	Y
9 Peters	Y	Y	Y	Y
10 **Miller**	Y	Y	Y	Y
11 **McCotter**	Y	Y	Y	Y
12 Levin	Y	Y	Y	Y
13 Kilpatrick	Y	Y	Y	Y
14 Conyers	Y	Y	Y	?
15 Dingell	Y	Y	Y	Y
MINNESOTA				
1 Walz	Y	Y	Y	Y
2 **Kline**	Y	Y	Y	Y
3 **Paulsen**	Y	Y	Y	Y
4 McCollum	Y	Y	Y	Y

	541	542	543	544
5 Ellison	Y	Y	Y	Y
6 **Bachmann**	Y	Y	Y	Y
7 Peterson	Y	Y	Y	Y
8 Oberstar	Y	Y	Y	Y
MISSISSIPPI				
1 **Childers**	Y	Y	Y	Y
2 Thompson	Y	Y	Y	Y
3 **Harper**	Y	Y	Y	Y
4 Taylor	Y	Y	Y	Y
MISSOURI				
1 Clay	Y	Y	Y	Y
2 **Akin**	N	Y	Y	N
3 Carnahan	Y	Y	Y	Y
4 Skelton	Y	Y	Y	Y
5 Cleaver	Y	Y	Y	Y
6 **Graves**	Y	Y	Y	Y
7 **Blunt**	?	?	?	?
8 **Emerson**	Y	Y	Y	Y
9 **Luetkemeyer**	Y	Y	Y	Y
MONTANA				
AL **Rehberg**	Y	Y	Y	Y
NEBRASKA				
1 **Fortenberry**	Y	Y	Y	Y
2 **Terry**	Y	Y	Y	Y
3 **Smith**	Y	Y	Y	Y
NEVADA				
1 Berkley	Y	Y	Y	Y
2 **Heller**	Y	Y	Y	Y
3 Titus	Y	Y	Y	Y
NEW HAMPSHIRE				
1 Shea-Porter	Y	Y	Y	Y
2 Hodes	Y	Y	Y	Y
NEW JERSEY				
1 Andrews	Y	Y	Y	Y
2 **LoBiondo**	Y	Y	Y	Y
3 Adler	Y	Y	Y	Y
4 **Smith**	Y	Y	Y	Y
5 **Garrett**	Y	Y	Y	Y
6 Pallone	Y	Y	Y	Y
7 **Lance**	Y	Y	Y	Y
8 Pascrell	Y	Y	Y	Y
9 Rothman	Y	Y	Y	Y
10 Payne	Y	Y	Y	Y
11 **Frelinghuysen**	Y	Y	Y	Y
12 Holt	Y	Y	Y	Y
13 Sires	Y	Y	Y	Y
NEW MEXICO				
1 Heinrich	Y	Y	Y	Y
2 Teague	Y	Y	Y	Y
3 Luján	Y	Y	Y	Y
NEW YORK				
1 Bishop	Y	?	?	?
2 Israel	Y	Y	Y	Y
3 **King**	Y	Y	Y	Y
4 McCarthy	Y	Y	Y	Y
5 Ackerman	Y	Y	Y	Y
6 Meeks	Y	Y	Y	Y
7 Crowley	Y	Y	Y	Y
8 Nadler	Y	Y	Y	Y
9 Weiner	Y	Y	Y	Y
10 Towns	Y	Y	Y	Y
11 Clarke	Y	Y	Y	Y
12 Velázquez	Y	Y	Y	Y
13 McMahon	Y	Y	Y	Y
14 Maloney	Y	Y	Y	Y
15 Rangel	Y	Y	Y	Y
16 Serrano	Y	Y	Y	Y
17 Engel	Y	Y	Y	Y
18 Lowey	Y	Y	Y	Y
19 Hall	?	?	?	?
20 Murphy	Y	Y	Y	Y
21 Tonko	Y	Y	Y	Y
22 Hinchey	Y	Y	Y	Y
23 Owens	Y	Y	Y	N
24 Arcuri	Y	Y	Y	Y
25 Maffei	Y	Y	Y	Y
26 **Lee**	Y	Y	Y	Y
27 Higgins	Y	Y	Y	Y
28 Slaughter	Y	Y	Y	Y
29 Vacant				
NORTH CAROLINA				
1 Butterfield	Y	Y	Y	Y
2 Etheridge	Y	Y	Y	Y
3 **Jones**	Y	Y	Y	Y
4 Price	Y	Y	Y	Y

	541	542	543	544
5 **Foxx**	N	Y	Y	N
6 **Coble**	N	Y	Y	N
7 McIntyre	Y	Y	Y	Y
8 Kissell	Y	Y	Y	Y
9 **Myrick**	Y	Y	Y	Y
10 **McHenry**	Y	Y	Y	Y
11 Shuler	Y	Y	Y	?
12 Watt	Y	Y	Y	Y
13 Miller	Y	Y	Y	Y
NORTH DAKOTA				
AL Pomeroy	Y	Y	Y	Y
OHIO				
1 Driehaus	Y	Y	Y	Y
2 **Schmidt**	Y	Y	Y	Y
3 **Turner**	Y	Y	Y	Y
4 **Jordan**	N	Y	Y	N
5 **Latta**	Y	Y	Y	Y
6 Wilson	Y	Y	Y	Y
7 **Austria**	Y	Y	Y	Y
8 **Boehner**	?	?	Y	Y
9 Kaptur	Y	Y	Y	Y
10 Kucinich	Y	Y	Y	Y
11 Fudge	Y	Y	Y	Y
12 **Tiberi**	Y	Y	Y	Y
13 Sutton	Y	Y	Y	Y
14 **LaTourette**	Y	Y	Y	Y
15 Kilroy	Y	Y	Y	Y
16 Boccieri	Y	Y	Y	Y
17 Ryan	Y	Y	Y	Y
18 Space	Y	Y	Y	Y
OKLAHOMA				
1 **Sullivan**	Y	?	Y	Y
2 Boren	?	?	?	?
3 **Lucas**	Y	Y	Y	Y
4 **Cole**	Y	Y	Y	Y
5 **Fallin**	?	?	?	?
OREGON				
1 Wu	Y	Y	Y	Y
2 **Walden**	Y	Y	Y	Y
3 Blumenauer	Y	Y	Y	Y
4 DeFazio	Y	Y	Y	Y
5 Schrader	?	Y	Y	Y
PENNSYLVANIA				
1 Brady	Y	Y	Y	Y
2 Fattah	Y	Y	Y	Y
3 Dahlkemper	Y	Y	Y	Y
4 Altmire	Y	Y	Y	Y
5 **Thompson**	Y	Y	Y	Y
6 **Gerlach**	?	?	?	?
7 Sestak	Y	Y	Y	Y
8 Murphy, P.	Y	Y	Y	Y
9 **Shuster**	Y	Y	Y	Y
10 Carney	Y	Y	Y	Y
11 Kanjorski	Y	Y	Y	Y
12 Critz	Y	Y	Y	N
13 Schwartz	Y	Y	Y	Y
14 Doyle	Y	Y	Y	Y
15 **Dent**	Y	Y	Y	Y
16 **Pitts**	Y	Y	Y	Y
17 Holden	Y	Y	Y	Y
18 **Murphy, T.**	Y	Y	Y	Y
19 **Platts**	Y	Y	Y	Y
RHODE ISLAND				
1 Kennedy	Y	Y	Y	Y
2 Langevin	Y	Y	Y	Y
SOUTH CAROLINA				
1 **Brown**	Y	Y	Y	Y
2 **Wilson**	Y	Y	Y	Y
3 **Barrett**	Y	Y	Y	Y
4 **Inglis**	Y	Y	Y	Y
5 Spratt	Y	Y	Y	Y
6 Clyburn	Y	Y	Y	Y
SOUTH DAKOTA				
AL Herseth Sandlin	Y	Y	Y	Y
TENNESSEE				
1 **Roe**	Y	Y	Y	Y
2 **Duncan**	Y	Y	Y	Y
3 **Wamp**	Y	Y	Y	Y
4 Davis	Y	Y	Y	Y
5 Cooper	Y	Y	Y	Y
6 Gordon	Y	Y	Y	Y
7 **Blackburn**	Y	Y	Y	Y
8 Tanner	Y	Y	Y	Y
9 Cohen	Y	Y	Y	Y

	541	542	543	544
TEXAS				
1 **Gohmert**	N	Y	Y	?
2 **Poe**	?	Y	Y	N
3 **Johnson, S.**	Y	Y	Y	Y
4 **Hall**	Y	Y	Y	Y
5 **Hensarling**	N	Y	Y	N
6 **Barton**	Y	Y	Y	N
7 **Culberson**	Y	Y	Y	N
8 **Brady**	Y	Y	Y	Y
9 Green, A.	Y	Y	Y	Y
10 **McCaul**	Y	Y	Y	Y
11 **Conaway**	N	Y	Y	Y
12 **Granger**	Y	Y	Y	Y
13 **Thornberry**	N	Y	Y	N
14 **Paul**	N	N	N	N
15 Hinojosa	?	Y	Y	Y
16 Reyes	Y	Y	Y	Y
17 Edwards	Y	Y	Y	Y
18 Jackson Lee	Y	Y	Y	Y
19 **Neugebauer**	Y	Y	Y	N
20 Gonzalez	Y	Y	Y	Y
21 **Smith**	Y	Y	Y	Y
22 **Olson**	Y	Y	Y	Y
23 Rodriguez	Y	Y	Y	Y
24 **Marchant**	N	Y	Y	N
25 Doggett	Y	Y	Y	Y
26 **Burgess**	Y	Y	Y	Y
27 Ortiz	Y	Y	Y	Y
28 Cuellar	Y	Y	Y	Y
29 Green, G.	Y	Y	Y	Y
30 Johnson, E.	Y	Y	Y	Y
31 **Carter**	Y	Y	Y	N
32 **Sessions**	Y	Y	Y	Y
UTAH				
1 **Bishop**	Y	Y	Y	Y
2 Matheson	Y	Y	Y	Y
3 **Chaffetz**	N	Y	Y	Y
VERMONT				
AL Welch	Y	Y	Y	Y
VIRGINIA				
1 **Wittman**	Y	Y	Y	Y
2 Nye	Y	Y	Y	Y
3 Scott	Y	Y	Y	Y
4 **Forbes**	Y	Y	Y	Y
5 Perriello	Y	Y	Y	Y
6 **Goodlatte**	Y	Y	Y	N
7 **Cantor**	Y	Y	Y	Y
8 Moran	Y	Y	Y	Y
9 Boucher	Y	Y	Y	Y
10 **Wolf**	Y	Y	Y	Y
11 Connolly	Y	Y	Y	Y
WASHINGTON				
1 Inslee	Y	Y	Y	Y
2 Larsen	Y	Y	Y	Y
3 Baird	Y	Y	Y	Y
4 **Hastings**	Y	Y	Y	Y
5 **McMorris Rodgers**	Y	Y	Y	Y
6 Dicks	Y	Y	Y	Y
7 McDermott	Y	Y	Y	Y
8 **Reichert**	Y	Y	Y	Y
9 Smith	Y	Y	Y	Y
WEST VIRGINIA				
1 Mollohan	Y	Y	Y	Y
2 **Capito**	Y	Y	Y	Y
3 Rahall	Y	Y	Y	Y
WISCONSIN				
1 **Ryan**	Y	Y	Y	Y
2 Baldwin	Y	Y	Y	Y
3 Kind	Y	Y	Y	Y
4 Moore	Y	Y	Y	Y
5 **Sensenbrenner**	Y	Y	Y	N
6 **Petri**	Y	Y	Y	Y
7 Obey	Y	Y	Y	Y
8 Kagen	Y	Y	Y	Y
WYOMING				
AL **Lummis**	N	N	Y	N
DELEGATES				
Faleomavaega (A.S.)				
Norton (D.C.)				
Bordallo (Guam)				
Sablan (N. Marianas)				
Pierluisi (P.R.)				
Christensen (V.I.)				

IN THE HOUSE | By Vote Number

545. **Procedural Motion/Motion to Adjourn.** Diaz-Balart, R-Fla., motion to adjourn. Motion rejected 2-409: D 1-241; R 1-168. Sept. 29, 2010.

546. **H Con Res 321. Adjournment/Adoption.** Adoption of the concurrent resolution that would provide for the adjournment of the House until 2 p.m. Monday, Nov. 15, 2010, and the conditional adjournment of the Senate until noon Monday, Nov. 15, 2010. Adopted 210-209: D 210-39; R 0-170. Sept. 29, 2010.

547. **HR 847, HR 2378, HR 2701. Health, Currency and Intelligence Authorization Bills/Previous Question.** Arcuri, D-N.Y., motion to order the previous question (thus ending debate and possibility of amendment) on adoption of the rule (H Res 1674) to provide for House floor consideration of the bill (HR 847) that would create a program to provide medical services for individuals with conditions related to the Sept. 11 attacks, a bill (HR 2378) that would allow the Commerce Department to impose countervailing duties on imports from a country that undervalues its currency, and the Senate amendment to a bill (HR 2701) that would authorize intelligence programs for fiscal 2010. Motion agreed to 235-183: D 235-12; R 0-171. Sept. 29, 2010.

548. **HR 847, HR 2378, HR 2701. Health, Currency and Intelligence Authorization Bills/Rule.** Adoption of the rule (H Res 1674) that would provide for House floor consideration of a bill (HR 847) that would create a program to provide medical services for individuals with conditions related to the Sept. 11 attacks, a bill (HR 2378) that would allow the Commerce Department to impose countervailing duties on imports from a country that undervalues its currency, and the Senate amendment to a bill (HR 2701) that would authorize intelligence programs for fiscal 2010. Adopted 234-183: D 233-14; R 1-169. Sept. 29, 2010.

549. **HR 847. Sept. 11 Health and Compensation Fund/Recommit.** Lee, R-N.Y., motion to recommit the bill to the House Energy and Commerce Committee with instructions that it be immediately reported back with an amendment that would replace the payment rates for health treatment and services in the bill with rates equal to Medicare rates. It also would repeal certain provisions of the health care overhaul law. It would add a section to the law that would establish a statute of limitations on commencing a health care lawsuit and cap the awards that plaintiffs and their attorneys could receive in medical malpractice cases. Motion rejected 185-244: D 14-240; R 171-4. Sept. 29, 2010.

550. **HR 847. Sept. 11 Health and Compensation Fund/Passage.** Passage of the bill that would create a program to provide medical services and health monitoring for first-responders and others with conditions related to the Sept. 11 attacks. It also would reopen the Sept. 11 Victim Compensation Fund to provide compensation for economic losses suffered by those affected by the attacks and amend tax-withholding rules for certain payments made by U.S. subsidiaries of foreign corporations. Passed 268-160: D 251-3; R 17-157. Sept. 29, 2010.

551. **HR 3685. VetSuccess Website Promotion/Passage.** Filner, D-Calif., motion to suspend the rules and pass the bill that would require the secretary of Veterans Affairs to include a hyperlink to the VetSuccess website and other appropriate employment websites on the main page of the VA website. It also would direct the secretary to promote the site through advertising and outreach to veterans. Motion agreed to 425-0: D 251-0; R 174-0. A two-thirds majority of those present and voting (284 in this case) is required for passage under suspension of the rules. Sept. 29, 2010.

	545	546	547	548	549	550	551
ALABAMA							
1 **Bonner**	N	N	N	N	Y	N	Y
2 Bright	N	N	N	N	Y	N	Y
3 **Rogers**	N	N	N	Y	N	N	Y
4 **Aderholt**	N	?	?	N	Y	N	Y
5 Griffith	?	?	?	?	Y	N	Y
6 **Bachus**	N	N	N	N	Y	N	Y
7 Davis	N	Y	Y	Y	N	Y	Y
ALASKA							
AL **Young**	Y	N	N	N	Y	N	Y
ARIZONA							
1 Kirkpatrick	N	N	N	N	Y	Y	Y
2 **Franks**	N	N	N	Y	N	N	Y
3 **Shadegg**	N	N	N	N	Y	N	Y
4 Pastor	N	Y	Y	Y	N	Y	Y
5 Mitchell	N	N	N	N	Y	Y	Y
6 **Flake**	N	N	N	Y	N	N	Y
7 Grijalva	?	Y	Y	Y	N	Y	Y
8 Giffords	N	N	N	N	Y	Y	Y
ARKANSAS							
1 Berry	N	Y	Y	Y	N	N	Y
2 Snyder	N	Y	Y	Y	N	Y	Y
3 **Boozman**	N	N	N	Y	N	N	Y
4 Ross	N	Y	Y	Y	N	Y	Y
CALIFORNIA							
1 Thompson	N	Y	Y	Y	N	Y	Y
2 **Herger**	N	N	N	N	Y	N	Y
3 **Lungren**	N	N	N	Y	N	Y	Y
4 **McClintock**	N	N	N	Y	N	N	Y
5 Matsui	N	Y	Y	N	Y	Y	Y
6 Woolsey	N	Y	Y	Y	N	Y	Y
7 Miller, George	N	Y	Y	Y	N	Y	Y
8 Pelosi		Y			N	Y	
9 Lee	N	Y	Y	Y	N	Y	Y
10 Garamendi	N	Y	Y	Y	N	Y	Y
11 McNerney	N	N	?	Y	N	Y	Y
12 Speier	N	Y	Y	Y	N	Y	Y
13 Stark	N	Y	Y	Y	N	Y	Y
14 Eshoo	N	Y	Y	Y	N	Y	Y
15 Honda	N	Y	Y	?	N	Y	Y
16 Lofgren	N	Y	Y	Y	N	Y	Y
17 Farr	N	Y	Y	Y	N	Y	Y
18 Cardoza	N	Y	Y	Y	N	Y	Y
19 **Radanovich**	N	N	N	N	Y	N	Y
20 Costa	N	Y	Y	Y	N	Y	Y
21 **Nunes**	N	N	N	N	Y	N	Y
22 **McCarthy**	N	N	N	N	Y	N	Y
23 Capps	N	Y	Y	Y	N	Y	Y
24 **Gallegly**	N	N	N	Y	N	N	Y
25 **McKeon**	N	N	N	N	Y	N	Y
26 **Dreier**	N	N	N	N	Y	N	Y
27 Sherman	N	Y	Y	Y	N	Y	Y
28 Berman	N	Y	Y	Y	N	Y	Y
29 Schiff	N	Y	Y	Y	N	Y	Y
30 Waxman	N	Y	Y	Y	N	Y	Y
31 Becerra	N	Y	Y	Y	N	Y	Y
32 Chu	N	Y	Y	Y	N	Y	Y
33 Watson	N	Y	Y	Y	N	Y	Y
34 Roybal-Allard	N	Y	Y	Y	N	Y	Y
35 Waters	N	Y	Y	Y	N	Y	Y
36 Harman	N	Y	Y	Y	N	Y	Y
37 Richardson	N	Y	Y	Y	N	Y	Y
38 Napolitano	N	Y	Y	Y	N	Y	Y
39 Sánchez, Linda	?	Y	Y	Y	N	Y	Y
40 **Royce**	N	N	N	N	Y	N	Y
41 **Lewis**	N	N	N	N	Y	N	Y
42 **Miller, Gary**	N	N	N	N	Y	N	Y
43 Baca	N	Y	Y	Y	N	Y	Y
44 **Calvert**	N	N	N	N	Y	N	Y
45 **Bono Mack**	N	N	N	N	Y	N	Y
46 **Rohrabacher**	N	N	N	N	Y	N	Y
47 Sanchez, Loretta	N	Y	Y	Y	N	Y	Y
48 **Campbell**	N	N	N	N	Y	N	Y
49 **Issa**	N	N	N	N	Y	N	Y
50 **Bilbray**	N	N	N	N	Y	N	Y
51 Filner	N	Y	Y	Y	N	Y	Y
52 **Hunter**	N	N	N	N	Y	N	Y
53 Davis	N	Y	Y	Y	N	Y	Y
COLORADO							
1 DeGette	N	Y	Y	Y	N	Y	Y
2 Polis	N	Y	Y	Y	N	Y	Y
3 Salazar	N	Y	Y	N	Y	N	Y
4 Markey	N	Y	Y	Y	N	Y	Y
5 **Lamborn**	N	N	N	N	Y	N	Y
6 **Coffman**	N	N	N	Y	N	N	Y
7 Perlmutter	N	Y	Y	Y	N	Y	Y
CONNECTICUT							
1 Larson	N	Y	Y	Y	N	Y	Y
2 Courtney	N	Y	Y	Y	N	Y	Y
3 DeLauro	N	Y	Y	Y	N	Y	Y
4 Himes	N	Y	Y	Y	N	Y	Y
5 Murphy	N	Y	Y	Y	N	Y	Y
DELAWARE							
AL **Castle**	N	N	N	N	Y	Y	Y
FLORIDA							
1 **Miller**	N	N	N	N	Y	N	Y
2 Boyd	N	?	?	?	?	?	?
3 Brown	N	Y	Y	Y	N	Y	Y
4 **Crenshaw**	N	N	N	N	Y	N	Y
5 **Brown-Waite**	N	N	N	N	Y	N	Y
6 **Stearns**	N	N	N	N	Y	N	Y
7 **Mica**	N	N	N	Y	N	N	Y
8 Grayson	N	Y	Y	Y	N	Y	Y
9 **Bilirakis**	N	N	N	N	Y	N	Y
10 **Young**	?	?	?	?	?	?	?
11 Castor	N	Y	Y	Y	N	Y	Y
12 **Putnam**	N	N	N	N	Y	N	Y
13 **Buchanan**	N	N	N	N	Y	N	Y
14 **Mack**	N	N	N	N	Y	N	Y
15 **Posey**	N	N	N	N	Y	N	Y
16 **Rooney**	N	N	N	N	Y	N	Y
17 Meek	N	Y	Y	Y	N	Y	Y
18 **Ros-Lehtinen**	N	N	N	Y	N	Y	Y
19 Deutch	N	Y	Y	Y	N	Y	Y
20 Wasserman Schultz	N	Y	Y	Y	N	Y	Y
21 **Diaz-Balart, L.**	N	?	?	?	Y	?	Y
22 Klein	N	Y	Y	Y	N	Y	Y
23 Hastings	N	Y	Y	Y	N	Y	Y
24 Kosmas	N	Y	Y	Y	N	Y	Y
25 **Diaz-Balart, M.**	N	N	N	N	Y	N	Y
GEORGIA							
1 **Kingston**	N	N	N	N	Y	N	Y
2 Bishop	N	Y	Y	Y	N	Y	Y
3 **Westmoreland**	N	N	N	N	Y	N	Y
4 Johnson	N	Y	Y	Y	N	Y	Y
5 Lewis	N	Y	Y	Y	N	Y	Y
6 **Price**	N	N	N	N	Y	N	Y
7 **Linder**	N	N	N	N	Y	N	Y
8 Marshall	N	Y	Y	Y	N	Y	Y
9 **Graves**	N	N	N	N	Y	N	Y
10 **Broun**	N	N	N	N	Y	N	Y
11 **Gingrey**	N	N	N	N	Y	N	Y
12 Barrow	N	Y	Y	Y	N	Y	Y
13 Scott	N	Y	Y	Y	N	Y	Y
HAWAII							
1 **Djou**	N	N	N	Y	N	N	Y
2 Hirono	N	Y	Y	Y	N	Y	Y
IDAHO							
1 Minnick	N	N	N	N	Y	Y	Y
2 **Simpson**	N	N	N	N	Y	N	Y
ILLINOIS							
1 Rush	N	Y	Y	Y	N	Y	Y
2 Jackson	N	Y	Y	Y	N	Y	Y
3 Lipinski	N	Y	Y	Y	N	Y	Y
4 Gutierrez	N	Y	Y	Y	N	Y	Y
5 Quigley	N	Y	Y	Y	N	Y	Y
6 **Roskam**	N	N	N	N	Y	N	Y
7 Davis	N	Y	Y	Y	N	Y	Y
8 Bean	N	Y	Y	Y	N	Y	Y
9 Schakowsky	N	Y	Y	Y	N	Y	Y
10 **Kirk**	N	N	N	?	Y	Y	Y
11 Halvorson	N	Y	Y	Y	N	Y	Y
12 Costello	N	Y	Y	Y	N	Y	Y
13 **Biggert**	N	N	N	Y	N	N	Y
14 Foster	N	Y	Y	Y	N	Y	Y
15 **Johnson**	N	N	N	N	N	N	Y

	545	546	547	548	549	550	551
16 **Manzullo**	N	N	N	N	Y	N	Y
17 Hare	N	Y	Y	Y	N	Y	Y
18 **Schock**	N	?	N	N	Y	N	Y
19 **Shimkus**	N	N	N	N	Y	N	Y
INDIANA							
1 Visclosky	N	Y	Y	Y	N	Y	Y
2 Donnelly	N	N	Y	N	N	Y	Y
3 Vacant							
4 **Buyer**	N	?	?	?	Y	N	Y
5 **Burton**	N	N	N	N	Y	N	Y
6 **Pence**	N	N	N	N	Y	N	Y
7 Carson	N	Y	Y	Y	N	Y	Y
8 Ellsworth	N	N	Y	N	N	Y	Y
9 Hill	N	Y	N	N	N	Y	Y
IOWA							
1 Braley	N	Y	Y	Y	N	Y	Y
2 Loebsack	N	Y	Y	Y	N	Y	Y
3 Boswell	N	Y	Y	Y	N	Y	Y
4 **Latham**	N	N	N	N	Y	N	Y
5 **King**	N	N	N	N	Y	N	Y
KANSAS							
1 **Moran**	N	N	N	N	Y	N	Y
2 **Jenkins**	N	N	N	N	Y	N	Y
3 Moore	N	Y	Y	Y	N	Y	Y
4 **Tiahrt**	N	N	N	N	Y	N	Y
KENTUCKY							
1 **Whitfield**	N	N	N	N	Y	N	Y
2 **Guthrie**	N	N	N	N	Y	N	Y
3 Yarmuth	N	Y	Y	Y	N	Y	Y
4 **Davis**	N	N	N	N	Y	N	Y
5 **Rogers**	N	N	N	N	Y	N	Y
6 Chandler	N	Y	Y	Y	N	Y	?
LOUISIANA							
1 **Scalise**	N	N	N	N	Y	N	Y
2 **Cao**	N	N	N	N	N	Y	Y
3 Melancon	N	N	Y	Y	Y	Y	Y
4 **Fleming**	N	N	N	N	Y	N	Y
5 **Alexander**	?	N	N	N	Y	N	Y
6 **Cassidy**	N	N	N	N	Y	N	Y
7 **Boustany**	N	N	N	N	Y	N	Y
MAINE							
1 Pingree	N	Y	Y	Y	N	Y	Y
2 Michaud	N	N	Y	Y	N	Y	Y
MARYLAND							
1 Kratovil	N	N	N	N	N	Y	Y
2 Ruppersberger	N	Y	Y	Y	N	Y	Y
3 Sarbanes	N	Y	Y	Y	N	Y	Y
4 Edwards	N	Y	Y	Y	N	Y	Y
5 Hoyer	N	Y	Y	Y	N	Y	Y
6 **Bartlett**	N	N	N	N	Y	N	Y
7 Cummings	N	Y	Y	Y	N	Y	Y
8 Van Hollen	N	Y	Y	Y	N	Y	Y
MASSACHUSETTS							
1 Olver	N	Y	Y	Y	N	Y	Y
2 Neal	N	Y	Y	Y	N	Y	Y
3 McGovern	N	Y	Y	Y	N	Y	Y
4 Frank	N	Y	Y	Y	N	Y	Y
5 Tsongas	N	Y	Y	Y	N	Y	Y
6 Tierney	N	Y	Y	Y	N	Y	Y
7 Markey	?	Y	Y	Y	N	Y	Y
8 Capuano	N	Y	Y	Y	N	Y	Y
9 Lynch	N	Y	Y	Y	N	Y	Y
10 Delahunt	N	Y	Y	Y	N	Y	Y
MICHIGAN							
1 Stupak	N	Y	Y	Y	N	Y	Y
2 **Hoekstra**	N	N	N	N	Y	N	Y
3 **Ehlers**	N	N	N	N	Y	N	Y
4 **Camp**	N	N	N	N	Y	N	Y
5 Kildee	N	Y	Y	Y	N	Y	Y
6 **Upton**	N	N	N	N	Y	N	Y
7 Schauer	N	N	Y	Y	N	Y	Y
8 **Rogers**	N	N	N	N	Y	N	Y
9 Peters	N	N	Y	Y	N	Y	Y
10 **Miller**	N	N	N	N	Y	Y	Y
11 **McCotter**	N	N	N	N	Y	N	Y
12 Levin	N	Y	Y	Y	N	Y	Y
13 Kilpatrick	N	Y	Y	Y	N	Y	Y
14 Conyers	N	Y	Y	Y	N	Y	Y
15 Dingell	N	?	Y	Y	N	Y	Y
MINNESOTA							
1 Walz	N	Y	Y	Y	N	Y	Y
2 **Kline**	N	N	N	N	Y	N	Y
3 **Paulsen**	N	N	N	N	Y	N	Y
4 McCollum	N	Y	?	Y	N	Y	Y

	545	546	547	548	549	550	551
5 Ellison	N	Y	Y	Y	N	Y	Y
6 **Bachmann**	N	N	N	N	Y	N	Y
7 Peterson	N	Y	Y	Y	Y	Y	Y
8 Oberstar	N	Y	Y	Y	N	Y	Y
MISSISSIPPI							
1 Childers	N	N	N	N	N	Y	Y
2 Thompson	N	Y	Y	Y	N	Y	Y
3 **Harper**	N	N	N	N	Y	N	Y
4 Taylor	?	N	N	Y	Y	Y	Y
MISSOURI							
1 Clay	N	Y	Y	Y	N	Y	Y
2 **Akin**	N	N	N	N	Y	N	Y
3 Carnahan	N	Y	Y	Y	N	Y	Y
4 Skelton	N	Y	Y	Y	N	Y	Y
5 Cleaver	P	Y	Y	Y	N	Y	Y
6 **Graves**	N	N	N	N	Y	N	Y
7 **Blunt**	?	?	?	?	?	?	?
8 **Emerson**	N	N	N	N	Y	N	Y
9 **Luetkemeyer**	N	N	N	N	Y	N	Y
MONTANA							
AL **Rehberg**	N	N	N	N	Y	N	Y
NEBRASKA							
1 **Fortenberry**	N	N	N	N	Y	N	Y
2 **Terry**	N	N	N	N	Y	N	Y
3 **Smith**	N	N	N	N	Y	N	Y
NEVADA							
1 Berkley	N	Y	Y	Y	N	Y	Y
2 **Heller**	N	N	N	N	Y	N	Y
3 Titus	N	N	Y	Y	N	Y	Y
NEW HAMPSHIRE							
1 Shea-Porter	N	Y	Y	Y	N	Y	Y
2 Hodes	N	Y	Y	Y	N	Y	Y
NEW JERSEY							
1 Andrews	N	Y	Y	Y	N	Y	Y
2 **LoBiondo**	N	N	N	N	Y	Y	Y
3 Adler	N	N	N	Y	Y	Y	Y
4 **Smith**	N	N	N	N	Y	Y	Y
5 **Garrett**	N	N	N	N	Y	N	Y
6 Pallone	N	Y	Y	Y	N	Y	Y
7 **Lance**	N	N	N	N	Y	Y	Y
8 Pascrell	N	Y	Y	Y	N	Y	Y
9 Rothman	N	Y	Y	Y	N	Y	Y
10 Payne	N	Y	Y	Y	N	Y	Y
11 **Frelinghuysen**	N	N	N	N	Y	Y	Y
12 Holt	N	Y	Y	Y	N	Y	Y
13 Sires	N	Y	Y	Y	N	Y	Y
NEW MEXICO							
1 Heinrich	N	N	Y	Y	N	Y	Y
2 Teague	N	Y	Y	Y	Y	Y	Y
3 Luján	N	Y	Y	Y	N	Y	Y
NEW YORK							
1 Bishop	N	N	Y	Y	N	Y	Y
2 Israel	N	Y	Y	Y	N	Y	Y
3 **King**	N	N	N	N	Y	N	Y
4 McCarthy	N	Y	Y	Y	N	Y	Y
5 Ackerman	N	Y	Y	Y	N	Y	Y
6 Meeks	N	Y	Y	Y	N	Y	Y
7 Crowley	N	Y	Y	Y	N	Y	Y
8 Nadler	N	Y	Y	Y	N	Y	Y
9 Weiner	N	Y	Y	Y	N	Y	Y
10 Towns	N	Y	Y	Y	N	Y	Y
11 Clarke	N	Y	Y	Y	N	Y	Y
12 Velázquez	N	Y	Y	Y	N	Y	Y
13 McMahon	N	N	Y	Y	N	Y	Y
14 Maloney	N	Y	Y	Y	N	Y	Y
15 Rangel	Y	Y	Y	Y	N	Y	Y
16 Serrano	N	Y	Y	Y	N	Y	Y
17 Engel	?	Y	Y	Y	N	Y	Y
18 Lowey	N	Y	Y	Y	N	Y	?
19 Hall	N	Y	Y	Y	N	Y	Y
20 Murphy	N	Y	Y	Y	N	Y	Y
21 Tonko	N	Y	Y	Y	N	Y	Y
22 Hinchey	N	Y	Y	Y	N	Y	Y
23 Owens	N	Y	Y	?	N	Y	Y
24 Arcuri	N	N	Y	Y	N	Y	Y
25 Maffei	N	?	Y	Y	N	Y	Y
26 **Lee**	N	N	N	N	Y	N	Y
27 Higgins	N	Y	Y	Y	N	Y	Y
28 Slaughter	N	Y	Y	Y	N	Y	Y
29 Vacant							
NORTH CAROLINA							
1 Butterfield	?	?	?	Y	N	Y	Y
2 Etheridge	N	Y	Y	Y	N	Y	Y
3 **Jones**	N	N	N	N	N	Y	Y
4 Price	N	Y	Y	Y	N	Y	Y

	545	546	547	548	549	550	551
5 **Foxx**	N	N	N	N	Y	N	Y
6 **Coble**	N	N	N	N	Y	N	Y
7 McIntyre	N	N	Y	Y	N	Y	Y
8 Kissell	N	Y	Y	Y	N	Y	Y
9 **Myrick**	N	N	N	N	Y	N	Y
10 **McHenry**	N	N	N	N	Y	N	Y
11 Shuler	N	N	?	N	Y	Y	Y
12 Watt	N	Y	Y	Y	N	Y	Y
13 Miller	N	Y	Y	Y	N	Y	Y
NORTH DAKOTA							
AL Pomeroy	N	Y	Y	Y	N	Y	Y
OHIO							
1 Driehaus	N	N	Y	Y	N	Y	Y
2 **Schmidt**	N	N	N	N	Y	N	Y
3 **Turner**	N	N	N	N	Y	N	Y
4 **Jordan**	N	N	N	N	Y	N	Y
5 **Latta**	N	N	N	N	Y	N	Y
6 Wilson	N	Y	Y	Y	N	Y	Y
7 **Austria**	N	N	N	N	Y	N	Y
8 **Boehner**	N	N	N	N	Y	N	Y
9 Kaptur	N	Y	Y	Y	N	Y	Y
10 Kucinich	N	Y	Y	Y	N	Y	Y
11 Fudge	N	Y	Y	Y	N	Y	Y
12 **Tiberi**	N	N	N	N	Y	N	Y
13 Sutton	N	Y	Y	?	N	Y	Y
14 **LaTourette**	N	N	N	N	Y	N	Y
15 Kilroy	N	N	Y	Y	N	Y	Y
16 Boccieri	N	Y	Y	Y	N	Y	Y
17 Ryan	N	Y	Y	Y	N	Y	Y
18 Space	N	N	Y	Y	Y	Y	Y
OKLAHOMA							
1 **Sullivan**	N	N	N	N	Y	N	Y
2 Boren	N	Y	Y	Y	N	Y	Y
3 **Lucas**	N	N	N	N	Y	N	Y
4 **Cole**	N	N	N	N	Y	Y	Y
5 **Fallin**	?	?	?	?	?	?	?
OREGON							
1 Wu	N	Y	Y	Y	N	Y	Y
2 **Walden**	N	N	N	N	Y	N	Y
3 Blumenauer	N	Y	Y	Y	N	Y	Y
4 DeFazio	N	Y	Y	Y	N	Y	Y
5 Schrader	N	Y	Y	Y	N	Y	Y
PENNSYLVANIA							
1 Brady	N	Y	Y	Y	N	Y	Y
2 Fattah	N	Y	Y	Y	N	Y	Y
3 Dahlkemper	N	Y	Y	Y	N	Y	Y
4 Altmire	N	N	Y	Y	N	Y	Y
5 **Thompson**	N	N	N	N	Y	N	Y
6 **Gerlach**	N	N	N	N	Y	Y	Y
7 Sestak	N	N	Y	Y	N	Y	Y
8 Murphy, P.	N	N	Y	Y	N	Y	Y
9 **Shuster**	N	N	N	N	Y	N	Y
10 Carney	N	N	Y	Y	N	Y	Y
11 Kanjorski	N	Y	Y	Y	N	Y	Y
12 Critz	N	Y	Y	Y	N	Y	Y
13 Schwartz	N	Y	Y	Y	N	Y	Y
14 Doyle	N	Y	Y	Y	N	Y	Y
15 **Dent**	N	N	N	N	Y	Y	Y
16 **Pitts**	N	N	N	N	Y	N	Y
17 Holden	?	Y	Y	Y	N	Y	Y
18 **Murphy, T.**	N	N	N	N	Y	Y	Y
19 **Platts**	N	N	N	N	Y	Y	Y
RHODE ISLAND							
1 Kennedy	N	?	Y	Y	N	Y	Y
2 Langevin	N	Y	Y	Y	N	Y	Y
SOUTH CAROLINA							
1 **Brown**	N	N	N	N	Y	N	Y
2 **Wilson**	N	N	N	N	Y	N	Y
3 **Barrett**	N	N	N	N	Y	N	Y
4 **Inglis**	N	N	N	N	Y	N	Y
5 Spratt	N	Y	Y	Y	N	Y	Y
6 Clyburn	N	Y	Y	Y	N	Y	Y
SOUTH DAKOTA							
AL Herseth Sandlin	N	N	Y	N	N	Y	Y
TENNESSEE							
1 **Roe**	N	N	N	N	Y	Y	Y
2 **Duncan**	N	N	N	N	Y	N	Y
3 **Wamp**	N	N	N	N	Y	N	Y
4 Davis	N	Y	Y	Y	Y	Y	Y
5 Cooper	N	Y	Y	N	N	N	Y
6 Gordon	N	Y	?	Y	N	Y	Y
7 **Blackburn**	N	N	N	N	Y	N	Y
8 Tanner	N	Y	Y	Y	N	Y	Y
9 Cohen	N	Y	Y	Y	N	Y	Y

	545	546	547	548	549	550	551
TEXAS							
1 **Gohmert**	N	N	N	N	Y	N	Y
2 **Poe**	N	N	N	N	Y	N	?
3 **Johnson, S.**	N	N	N	N	Y	N	Y
4 **Hall**	N	N	N	N	Y	N	Y
5 **Hensarling**	N	N	N	N	Y	N	Y
6 **Barton**	N	N	N	N	Y	N	Y
7 **Culberson**	?	N	N	N	Y	N	Y
8 **Brady**	N	N	N	N	Y	N	Y
9 Green, A.	N	Y	Y	Y	N	Y	Y
10 **McCaul**	N	N	N	N	Y	N	Y
11 **Conaway**	N	N	N	N	Y	N	Y
12 **Granger**	N	N	N	?	Y	N	Y
13 **Thornberry**	N	N	N	N	Y	N	Y
14 **Paul**	N	N	N	N	Y	N	Y
15 Hinojosa	N	Y	Y	Y	N	Y	Y
16 Reyes	N	Y	Y	Y	N	Y	Y
17 Edwards	N	N	Y	Y	N	Y	Y
18 Jackson Lee	N	Y	Y	Y	N	Y	Y
19 **Neugebauer**	N	N	N	N	Y	N	Y
20 Gonzalez	N	Y	Y	Y	N	Y	Y
21 **Smith**	N	N	N	N	Y	N	Y
22 **Olson**	N	N	N	N	Y	N	Y
23 Rodriguez	N	Y	Y	Y	N	Y	Y
24 **Marchant**	N	N	N	N	Y	N	Y
25 Doggett	N	Y	Y	Y	N	Y	Y
26 **Burgess**	N	N	N	N	Y	N	Y
27 Ortiz	N	Y	Y	Y	N	Y	Y
28 Cuellar	N	Y	Y	Y	N	Y	Y
29 Green, G.	N	Y	Y	Y	N	Y	Y
30 Johnson, E.	N	Y	Y	Y	N	Y	Y
31 **Carter**	N	N	N	N	Y	N	Y
32 **Sessions**	N	N	N	N	Y	N	Y
UTAH							
1 **Bishop**	?	N	N	N	Y	N	Y
2 Matheson	N	Y	Y	Y	Y	Y	Y
3 **Chaffetz**	N	N	N	N	Y	N	Y
VERMONT							
AL Welch	N	Y	Y	Y	N	Y	Y
VIRGINIA							
1 **Wittman**	?	N	N	N	Y	N	Y
2 Nye	?	N	N	Y	Y	Y	Y
3 Scott	?	Y	Y	Y	N	Y	Y
4 **Forbes**	?	N	N	N	Y	N	Y
5 Perriello	N	N	N	Y	N	Y	Y
6 **Goodlatte**	N	N	N	N	Y	N	Y
7 **Cantor**	N	N	N	N	Y	N	Y
8 Moran	N	Y	Y	?	N	Y	Y
9 Boucher	N	Y	Y	Y	Y	Y	Y
10 **Wolf**	N	N	N	N	Y	N	Y
11 Connolly	N	N	Y	Y	N	Y	Y
WASHINGTON							
1 Inslee	N	Y	Y	Y	N	Y	Y
2 Larsen	N	Y	Y	Y	N	Y	Y
3 Baird	N	Y	Y	Y	N	Y	Y
4 **Hastings**	N	N	N	N	Y	N	Y
5 **McMorris Rodgers**	N	N	N	N	Y	N	Y
6 Dicks	N	Y	Y	Y	N	Y	Y
7 McDermott	N	Y	Y	Y	N	Y	Y
8 **Reichert**	N	N	N	N	Y	N	Y
9 Smith	N	Y	Y	Y	N	Y	Y
WEST VIRGINIA							
1 Mollohan	N	Y	Y	Y	N	Y	Y
2 **Capito**	N	N	N	N	Y	N	Y
3 Rahall	–	+	+	+	N	Y	Y
WISCONSIN							
1 **Ryan**	N	N	N	N	Y	N	Y
2 Baldwin	N	Y	Y	Y	N	Y	Y
3 Kind	N	Y	Y	?	N	Y	Y
4 Moore	N	Y	Y	Y	N	Y	Y
5 **Sensenbrenner**	N	N	N	N	Y	N	Y
6 **Petri**	N	N	N	N	Y	N	Y
7 Obey	?	Y	Y	Y	N	Y	Y
8 Kagen	N	Y	Y	Y	N	Y	Y
WYOMING							
AL **Lummis**	N	N	N	N	Y	N	Y
DELEGATES							
Faleomavaega (A.S.)							
Norton (D.C.)							
Bordallo (Guam)							
Sablan (N. Marianas)							
Pierluisi (P.R.)							
Christensen (V.I.)							

IN THE HOUSE | By Vote Number

552. **HR 5993. Veterans' Life Insurance Disclosure/Passage.**
Filner, D-Calif., motion to suspend the rules and pass the bill that would direct the Veterans Affairs Department to ensure that beneficiaries of Servicemembers' Group Life Insurance receive financial counseling and disclosure information regarding life insurance payments. Motion agreed to 358-66: D 249-2; R 109-64. A two-thirds majority of those present and voting (283 in this case) is required for passage under suspension of the rules. Sept. 29, 2010.

553. **H Res 1326. U.S.-Japan Custody Disputes/Adoption.** Berman, D-Calif., motion to suspend the rules and adopt the resolution that would condemn the abduction of minors who are being held in Japan away from a U.S. parent and call on the government of Japan to facilitate the resolution of all abduction cases, recognize U.S. court orders and allow communication between the children and their parents. Motion agreed to 416-1: D 247-0; R 169-1. A two-thirds majority of those present and voting (278 in this case) is required for adoption under suspension of the rules. Sept. 29, 2010.

554. **HR 2378. U.S. Trade Currency Policy/Passage.** Passage of the bill that would permit the Commerce Department to impose countervailing duties on imported goods if it finds that a foreign government has undervalued its currency. Passed 348-79: D 249-5; R 99-74. Sept. 29, 2010.

555. **HR 6160. 'Rare Earth' Materials Development/Passage.**
Gordon, D-Tenn., motion to suspend the rules and pass the bill that would create a program in the Energy Department to support research and development to ensure a long-term supply of "rare earth" materials for the nation's security and production needs. It also would expand a loan guarantee program for commercial applications of new or improved technologies to include using rare-earth materials. Motion agreed to 325-98: D 251-1; R 74-97. A two-thirds majority of those present and voting (282 in this case) is required for passage under suspension of the rules. Sept. 29, 2010.

556. **HR 4072. Workforce Training Programs/Passage.** Hirono, D-Hawaii, motion to suspend the rules and pass the bill that would direct neighborhood training centers to give priority to programs that lead to credentials that are in high demand and recognized by private industry nationwide. Motion agreed to 412-10: D 251-0; R 161-10. A two-thirds majority of those present and voting (282 in this case) is required for passage under suspension of the rules. Sept. 29, 2010.

557. **HR 3421. Medical Debt Credit Reporting/Passage.** Kilroy, D-Ohio, motion to suspend the rules and pass the bill that would amend the Fair Credit Reporting Act to prohibit credit-reporting agencies from listing in consumer credit reports medical debts that have been paid or settled more than 45 days before the report is issued. Motion agreed to 336-82: D 249-1; R 87-81. A two-thirds majority of those present and voting (279 in this case) is required for passage under suspension of the rules. Sept. 29, 2010.

558. **HR 2701. Fiscal 2010 Intelligence Authorization/Motion to Concur.** Reyes, D-Texas, motion to concur in the Senate amendment to the bill that would authorize intelligence programs for fiscal 2010. The bill would expand disclosure requirements and congressional oversight of intelligence agencies, and it would require the director of national intelligence to allow access for GAO personnel to audit certain intelligence agencies. Motion agreed to, thus clearing the bill for the president, 244-181: D 243-9; R 1-172. Sept. 29, 2010.

	552	553	554	555	556	557	558
ALABAMA							
1 Bonner	N	Y	Y	Y	Y	N	N
2 Bright	Y	Y	Y	Y	Y	Y	Y
3 Rogers	N	Y	Y	N	Y	N	Y
4 Aderholt	N	Y	Y	Y	Y	Y	N
5 Griffith	N	Y	Y	Y	Y	Y	Y
6 Bachus	N	Y	Y	Y	Y	N	N
7 Davis	Y	Y	Y	Y	Y	Y	Y
ALASKA							
AL Young	N	Y	Y	N	Y	N	N
ARIZONA							
1 Kirkpatrick	Y	Y	Y	Y	Y	Y	Y
2 Franks	N	Y	N	N	N	N	N
3 Shadegg	N	Y	N	N	Y	N	N
4 Pastor	Y	Y	Y	Y	Y	Y	Y
5 Mitchell	Y	Y	N	Y	Y	Y	Y
6 Flake	N	Y	N	N	N	N	N
7 Grijalva	Y	Y	Y	Y	Y	Y	Y
8 Giffords	Y	Y	Y	Y	Y	Y	Y
ARKANSAS							
1 Berry	Y	Y	Y	Y	Y	Y	Y
2 Snyder	Y	Y	N	N	Y	Y	Y
3 Boozman	Y	Y	Y	Y	Y	Y	N
4 Ross	Y	Y	Y	Y	Y	Y	Y
CALIFORNIA							
1 Thompson	Y	Y	Y	Y	Y	Y	Y
2 Herger	Y	Y	N	N	Y	Y	N
3 Lungren	Y	Y	N	N	Y	Y	N
4 McClintock	Y	Y	N	N	Y	N	N
5 Matsui	Y	Y	Y	Y	Y	Y	Y
6 Woolsey	Y	Y	Y	Y	Y	Y	Y
7 Miller, George	Y	Y	Y	Y	Y	Y	Y
8 Pelosi		Y					
9 Lee	Y	Y	Y	Y	Y	Y	N
10 Garamendi	Y	Y	Y	Y	Y	Y	Y
11 McNerney	Y	Y	Y	Y	Y	Y	Y
12 Speier	Y	Y	Y	Y	Y	Y	Y
13 Stark	Y	Y	Y	Y	Y	Y	N
14 Eshoo	Y	Y	Y	Y	Y	Y	Y
15 Honda	Y	Y	Y	Y	Y	Y	Y
16 Lofgren	Y	Y	Y	Y	Y	Y	Y
17 Farr	Y	Y	Y	Y	Y	Y	Y
18 Cardoza	Y	Y	Y	Y	Y	Y	Y
19 Radanovich	N	?	?	?	?	?	?
20 Costa	Y	Y	Y	Y	Y	Y	Y
21 Nunes	N	Y	N	N	Y	N	N
22 McCarthy	Y	Y	N	N	Y	N	N
23 Capps	Y	Y	Y	Y	Y	Y	Y
24 Gallegly	Y	Y	N	N	Y	Y	N
25 McKeon	N	Y	Y	Y	Y	Y	N
26 Dreier	Y	Y	N	N	Y	Y	N
27 Sherman	Y	Y	Y	Y	Y	Y	Y
28 Berman	Y	Y	Y	Y	Y	Y	Y
29 Schiff	Y	Y	Y	Y	Y	Y	Y
30 Waxman	Y	Y	Y	Y	Y	Y	N
31 Becerra	Y	Y	Y	Y	Y	Y	Y
32 Chu	Y	Y	Y	Y	Y	Y	Y
33 Watson	Y	Y	Y	Y	Y	N	Y
34 Roybal-Allard	Y	Y	Y	Y	Y	Y	Y
35 Waters	Y	Y	Y	Y	Y	Y	Y
36 Harman	Y	Y	Y	Y	Y	Y	Y
37 Richardson	Y	Y	Y	Y	Y	Y	?
38 Napolitano	Y	Y	Y	Y	Y	Y	Y
39 Sánchez, Linda	Y	Y	Y	Y	Y	Y	Y
40 Royce	Y	Y	Y	N	Y	Y	N
41 Lewis	Y	Y	N	N	Y	N	N
42 Miller, Gary	N	Y	N	N	Y	N	N
43 Baca	Y	Y	Y	Y	Y	Y	Y
44 Calvert	Y	Y	N	N	Y	Y	N
45 Bono Mack	Y	Y	N	N	Y	Y	N
46 Rohrabacher	N	Y	Y	N	Y	N	N
47 Sanchez, Loretta	Y	Y	Y	Y	Y	N	Y
48 Campbell	N	Y	N	N	N	Y	N
49 Issa	N	Y	N	N	Y	N	N
50 Bilbray	Y	Y	Y	Y	Y	Y	N
51 Filner	Y	Y	Y	Y	Y	Y	Y
52 Hunter	Y	Y	Y	N	Y	Y	N
53 Davis	Y	Y	Y	Y	Y	Y	Y

	552	553	554	555	556	557	558
COLORADO							
1 DeGette	Y	Y	Y	Y	Y	Y	Y
2 Polis	?	Y	N	Y	Y	Y	Y
3 Salazar	Y	Y	Y	Y	Y	?	Y
4 Markey	Y	Y	Y	Y	Y	Y	Y
5 Lamborn	N	Y	N	N	Y	N	N
6 Coffman	N	Y	Y	Y	Y	N	N
7 Perlmutter	Y	Y	Y	Y	Y	Y	Y
CONNECTICUT							
1 Larson	Y	Y	Y	Y	Y	Y	Y
2 Courtney	Y	Y	Y	Y	Y	Y	Y
3 DeLauro	Y	Y	Y	Y	Y	Y	Y
4 Himes	Y	Y	Y	Y	Y	Y	Y
5 Murphy	Y	Y	Y	Y	Y	Y	Y
DELAWARE							
AL Castle	Y	Y	Y	Y	Y	Y	N
FLORIDA							
1 Miller	Y	Y	Y	N	Y	N	N
2 Boyd	?	?	Y	Y	Y	Y	Y
3 Brown	Y	Y	Y	Y	Y	Y	Y
4 Crenshaw	Y	Y	Y	N	Y	N	N
5 Brown-Waite	Y	Y	Y	N	Y	N	N
6 Stearns	Y	Y	Y	N	Y	N	N
7 Mica	Y	Y	Y	N	Y	N	N
8 Grayson	Y	Y	Y	Y	Y	Y	Y
9 Bilirakis	Y	Y	Y	Y	Y	N	N
10 Young	?	?	?	?	?	?	?
11 Castor	Y	Y	Y	Y	Y	Y	Y
12 Putnam	Y	Y	N	Y	Y	Y	N
13 Buchanan	Y	Y	N	Y	Y	Y	N
14 Mack	Y	Y	N	N	Y	N	N
15 Posey	Y	Y	N	Y	Y	N	N
16 Rooney	Y	Y	N	Y	Y	Y	N
17 Meek	Y	Y	Y	Y	Y	Y	Y
18 Ros-Lehtinen	Y	Y	Y	Y	Y	Y	N
19 Deutch	Y	Y	Y	Y	Y	Y	Y
20 Wasserman Schultz	Y	Y	Y	Y	Y	Y	Y
21 Diaz-Balart, L.	Y	?	Y	N	Y	?	N
22 Klein	Y	Y	Y	Y	Y	Y	Y
23 Hastings	Y	Y	Y	Y	Y	Y	Y
24 Kosmas	Y	Y	Y	Y	Y	Y	Y
25 Diaz-Balart, M.	Y	?	Y	N	Y	Y	N
GEORGIA							
1 Kingston	N	Y	N	N	Y	N	N
2 Bishop	Y	Y	Y	Y	Y	Y	Y
3 Westmoreland	Y	Y	Y	N	Y	N	N
4 Johnson	Y	Y	Y	Y	Y	Y	Y
5 Lewis	Y	Y	Y	Y	Y	Y	Y
6 Price	N	Y	N	N	Y	N	N
7 Linder	N	Y	N	N	Y	N	N
8 Marshall	Y	Y	Y	Y	Y	Y	N
9 Graves	N	Y	N	N	N	N	N
10 Broun	N	Y	N	N	N	N	N
11 Gingrey	N	Y	N	N	Y	N	N
12 Barrow	Y	Y	Y	Y	Y	Y	Y
13 Scott	N	Y	Y	Y	Y	Y	Y
HAWAII							
1 Djou	Y	Y	N	Y	Y	Y	N
2 Hirono	Y	Y	Y	Y	Y	Y	Y
IDAHO							
1 Minnick	Y	Y	Y	Y	Y	Y	Y
2 Simpson	N	Y	Y	Y	Y	Y	N
ILLINOIS							
1 Rush	Y	Y	Y	Y	Y	Y	Y
2 Jackson	Y	Y	Y	Y	Y	Y	Y
3 Lipinski	Y	Y	Y	Y	Y	Y	Y
4 Gutierrez	Y	Y	Y	Y	Y	Y	Y
5 Quigley	Y	Y	Y	Y	Y	Y	Y
6 Roskam	Y	Y	Y	Y	Y	N	N
7 Davis	Y	Y	Y	Y	Y	Y	Y
8 Bean	Y	Y	Y	Y	Y	Y	Y
9 Schakowsky	Y	Y	Y	Y	Y	Y	Y
10 Kirk	?	?	Y	?	?	?	N
11 Halvorson	Y	Y	Y	Y	Y	Y	Y
12 Costello	Y	Y	Y	Y	Y	Y	Y
13 Biggert	Y	Y	Y	Y	Y	Y	N
14 Foster	Y	Y	Y	Y	Y	Y	Y
15 Johnson	Y	Y	Y	Y	Y	Y	N

	552	553	554	555	556	557	558
16 **Manzullo**	Y	Y	Y	Y	Y	Y	N
17 Hare	Y	Y	Y	Y	Y	Y	Y
18 **Schock**	Y	Y	Y	Y	Y	Y	N
19 **Shimkus**	Y	Y	Y	Y	Y	Y	N
INDIANA							
1 Visclosky	Y	Y	Y	Y	Y	Y	Y
2 Donnelly	Y	Y	Y	Y	Y	Y	Y
3 Vacant							
4 **Buyer**	N	Y	?	?	?	?	N
5 **Burton**	Y	Y	Y	N	Y	N	N
6 **Pence**	N	Y	N	N	Y	N	N
7 Carson	Y	Y	Y	Y	Y	Y	Y
8 Ellsworth	Y	Y	Y	Y	Y	Y	Y
9 Hill	Y	Y	Y	Y	Y	Y	Y
IOWA							
1 Braley	Y	Y	Y	Y	Y	Y	Y
2 Loebsack	Y	Y	Y	Y	Y	Y	Y
3 Boswell	Y	Y	Y	Y	Y	Y	Y
4 **Latham**	Y	Y	N	Y	Y	N	N
5 **King**	N	Y	N	N	N	N	N
KANSAS							
1 **Moran**	Y	Y	Y	Y	Y	Y	N
2 **Jenkins**	Y	Y	N	N	Y	Y	N
3 Moore	Y	Y	Y	Y	Y	Y	Y
4 **Tiahrt**	N	Y	N	N	Y	N	N
KENTUCKY							
1 **Whitfield**	Y	Y	Y	Y	Y	N	N
2 **Guthrie**	Y	Y	Y	Y	Y	N	N
3 Yarmuth	Y	Y	Y	Y	Y	Y	Y
4 **Davis**	Y	Y	Y	N	Y	Y	N
5 **Rogers**	Y	Y	Y	Y	Y	Y	N
6 Chandler	Y	Y	Y	Y	Y	Y	Y
LOUISIANA							
1 **Scalise**	Y	Y	N	N	Y	N	N
2 **Cao**	Y	Y	Y	Y	Y	Y	N
3 Melancon	Y	Y	Y	Y	Y	Y	Y
4 **Fleming**	N	Y	N	N	Y	N	N
5 **Alexander**	Y	Y	N	N	Y	Y	N
6 **Cassidy**	Y	Y	Y	N	Y	Y	N
7 **Boustany**	Y	Y	N	N	Y	Y	N
MAINE							
1 Pingree	Y	Y	Y	Y	Y	Y	Y
2 Michaud	Y	Y	Y	Y	Y	Y	Y
MARYLAND							
1 Kratovil	Y	Y	Y	Y	Y	Y	Y
2 Ruppersberger	Y	Y	Y	Y	Y	Y	Y
3 Sarbanes	Y	Y	Y	Y	Y	Y	Y
4 Edwards	Y	Y	Y	Y	Y	Y	Y
5 Hoyer	Y	Y	Y	Y	Y	Y	Y
6 **Bartlett**	N	Y	N	Y	Y	N	N
7 Cummings	Y	Y	Y	Y	Y	Y	Y
8 Van Hollen	Y	Y	Y	Y	Y	Y	Y
MASSACHUSETTS							
1 Olver	Y	Y	Y	Y	Y	Y	Y
2 Neal	Y	Y	Y	Y	Y	Y	Y
3 McGovern	Y	Y	Y	Y	Y	Y	Y
4 Frank	Y	Y	Y	Y	Y	Y	Y
5 Tsongas	Y	Y	Y	Y	Y	Y	Y
6 Tierney	Y	Y	Y	Y	Y	Y	Y
7 Markey	Y	Y	Y	Y	Y	Y	Y
8 Capuano	Y	?	Y	Y	Y	Y	N
9 Lynch	Y	Y	Y	Y	Y	Y	Y
10 Delahunt	Y	Y	?	?	?	?	?
MICHIGAN							
1 Stupak	Y	Y	Y	Y	Y	Y	Y
2 **Hoekstra**	N	Y	Y	N	N	N	N
3 **Ehlers**	Y	Y	Y	Y	Y	Y	N
4 **Camp**	Y	Y	Y	Y	Y	Y	N
5 Kildee	Y	Y	Y	Y	Y	Y	Y
6 **Upton**	Y	Y	Y	Y	Y	Y	N
7 Schauer	Y	Y	Y	Y	Y	Y	Y
8 **Rogers**	Y	Y	Y	Y	Y	Y	N
9 Peters	Y	Y	Y	Y	Y	Y	Y
10 **Miller**	Y	Y	Y	Y	Y	Y	N
11 **McCotter**	Y	Y	Y	Y	Y	Y	N
12 Levin	Y	Y	Y	Y	Y	Y	Y
13 Kilpatrick	Y	Y	Y	Y	Y	Y	Y
14 Conyers	Y	Y	Y	Y	?	Y	Y
15 Dingell	Y	Y	Y	Y	Y	Y	Y
MINNESOTA							
1 Walz	N	Y	Y	Y	Y	Y	Y
2 **Kline**	Y	Y	N	N	Y	N	N
3 **Paulsen**	Y	Y	N	N	Y	N	N
4 McCollum	Y	Y	Y	Y	Y	Y	Y

	552	553	554	555	556	557	558
5 Ellison	Y	Y	Y	Y	Y	Y	Y
6 **Bachmann**	Y	Y	N	N	Y	N	N
7 Peterson	Y	Y	Y	Y	Y	Y	Y
8 Oberstar	Y	Y	Y	Y	Y	Y	Y
MISSISSIPPI							
1 Childers	Y	Y	Y	Y	Y	Y	Y
2 Thompson	Y	Y	Y	Y	Y	Y	Y
3 **Harper**	N	Y	Y	N	Y	N	N
4 Taylor	Y	Y	Y	Y	Y	Y	Y
MISSOURI							
1 Clay	Y	Y	Y	Y	Y	Y	Y
2 **Akin**	Y	Y	Y	Y	Y	N	N
3 Carnahan	Y	Y	Y	Y	Y	Y	Y
4 Skelton	Y	Y	Y	Y	Y	Y	Y
5 Cleaver	Y	Y	Y	Y	Y	Y	Y
6 **Graves**	Y	Y	Y	N	Y	N	?
7 **Blunt**	?	?	?	?	?	?	?
8 **Emerson**	Y	Y	Y	Y	Y	Y	N
9 **Luetkemeyer**	Y	Y	Y	Y	Y	N	N
MONTANA							
AL **Rehberg**	Y	Y	Y	Y	Y	Y	N
NEBRASKA							
1 **Fortenberry**	Y	Y	Y	Y	Y	Y	N
2 **Terry**	Y	Y	Y	Y	Y	N	N
3 **Smith**	N	Y	N	N	Y	N	N
NEVADA							
1 Berkley	Y	Y	Y	Y	Y	Y	Y
2 **Heller**	Y	Y	N	Y	Y	N	N
3 Titus	Y	Y	Y	Y	Y	Y	Y
NEW HAMPSHIRE							
1 Shea-Porter	Y	Y	Y	Y	Y	Y	Y
2 Hodes	Y	Y	Y	?	?	?	Y
NEW JERSEY							
1 Andrews	Y	Y	Y	Y	Y	Y	Y
2 **LoBiondo**	Y	Y	Y	Y	Y	Y	N
3 Adler	Y	Y	Y	Y	Y	Y	Y
4 **Smith**	Y	Y	Y	Y	Y	Y	N
5 **Garrett**	Y	Y	N	N	Y	N	N
6 Pallone	Y	Y	Y	Y	Y	Y	Y
7 **Lance**	Y	Y	N	Y	Y	Y	N
8 Pascrell	Y	Y	Y	Y	Y	Y	Y
9 Rothman	Y	Y	Y	Y	Y	Y	Y
10 Payne	Y	Y	Y	Y	Y	Y	Y
11 **Frelinghuysen**	Y	Y	N	N	Y	Y	N
12 Holt	Y	Y	Y	Y	Y	Y	Y
13 Sires	Y	Y	Y	Y	Y	Y	Y
NEW MEXICO							
1 Heinrich	Y	Y	Y	Y	Y	Y	Y
2 Teague	Y	Y	Y	Y	Y	Y	Y
3 Luján	Y	Y	Y	Y	Y	Y	Y
NEW YORK							
1 Bishop	Y	Y	Y	Y	Y	Y	Y
2 Israel	Y	Y	Y	Y	Y	Y	Y
3 **King**	Y	Y	N	N	Y	Y	N
4 McCarthy	Y	Y	Y	Y	Y	Y	Y
5 Ackerman	Y	Y	Y	Y	Y	Y	Y
6 Meeks	Y	Y	Y	Y	Y	Y	Y
7 Crowley	Y	Y	Y	Y	Y	Y	Y
8 Nadler	Y	Y	Y	Y	Y	Y	Y
9 Weiner	Y	Y	Y	Y	Y	Y	Y
10 Towns	Y	Y	Y	Y	Y	Y	Y
11 Clarke	Y	Y	Y	Y	Y	Y	Y
12 Velázquez	Y	Y	Y	Y	Y	Y	Y
13 McMahon	Y	Y	Y	Y	Y	Y	Y
14 Maloney	Y	?	Y	Y	Y	Y	Y
15 Rangel	Y	?	Y	Y	Y	Y	Y
16 Serrano	Y	Y	Y	Y	Y	Y	Y
17 Engel	Y	Y	Y	Y	Y	Y	Y
18 Lowey	Y	Y	Y	Y	Y	Y	Y
19 Hall	Y	Y	Y	Y	Y	Y	Y
20 Murphy	Y	Y	Y	Y	Y	Y	Y
21 Tonko	Y	Y	Y	Y	Y	Y	Y
22 Hinchey	Y	Y	Y	Y	Y	Y	Y
23 Owens	Y	Y	Y	Y	Y	Y	Y
24 Arcuri	Y	Y	Y	Y	Y	Y	Y
25 Maffei	Y	Y	Y	Y	Y	Y	Y
26 **Lee**	Y	Y	Y	Y	Y	N	N
27 Higgins	Y	Y	Y	Y	Y	Y	Y
28 Slaughter	Y	Y	Y	Y	Y	Y	Y
29 Vacant							
NORTH CAROLINA							
1 Butterfield	Y	Y	Y	Y	Y	Y	Y
2 Etheridge	Y	Y	Y	Y	Y	Y	Y
3 **Jones**	Y	Y	Y	Y	Y	Y	N
4 Price	Y	Y	Y	Y	Y	Y	Y

	552	553	554	555	556	557	558
5 **Foxx**	N	Y	Y	N	Y	N	N
6 **Coble**	N	Y	Y	Y	Y	N	N
7 McIntyre	Y	Y	Y	Y	Y	Y	Y
8 Kissell	Y	Y	Y	Y	Y	Y	Y
9 **Myrick**	N	Y	Y	Y	Y	N	N
10 **McHenry**	N	Y	Y	N	Y	?	N
11 Shuler	Y	Y	Y	Y	Y	Y	Y
12 Watt	Y	Y	Y	Y	Y	Y	Y
13 Miller	Y	Y	Y	Y	Y	Y	Y
NORTH DAKOTA							
AL Pomeroy	Y	?	Y	Y	Y	Y	Y
OHIO							
1 Driehaus	Y	Y	Y	Y	Y	Y	Y
2 **Schmidt**	Y	Y	N	N	Y	N	N
3 **Turner**	Y	Y	Y	Y	Y	Y	N
4 **Jordan**	N	Y	N	N	N	N	N
5 **Latta**	N	Y	N	N	Y	N	N
6 Wilson	Y	Y	Y	Y	Y	Y	Y
7 **Austria**	Y	Y	Y	Y	Y	N	N
8 **Boehner**	?	?	N	N	?	?	N
9 Kaptur	Y	Y	Y	Y	Y	Y	Y
10 Kucinich	Y	Y	Y	Y	Y	Y	N
11 Fudge	Y	Y	Y	Y	Y	Y	Y
12 **Tiberi**	Y	Y	Y	Y	Y	N	N
13 Sutton	Y	Y	Y	Y	Y	Y	Y
14 **LaTourette**	Y	Y	Y	Y	Y	N	N
15 Kilroy	Y	Y	Y	Y	Y	Y	Y
16 Boccieri	Y	Y	Y	Y	Y	Y	Y
17 Ryan	Y	Y	Y	Y	Y	Y	Y
18 Space	Y	Y	Y	Y	Y	Y	Y
OKLAHOMA							
1 **Sullivan**	Y	Y	N	N	Y	Y	N
2 Boren	Y	Y	Y	Y	Y	Y	Y
3 **Lucas**	Y	Y	Y	Y	Y	Y	N
4 **Cole**	Y	Y	Y	Y	Y	Y	N
5 **Fallin**	?	?	?	?	?	?	?
OREGON							
1 Wu	Y	Y	Y	Y	Y	Y	N
2 **Walden**	Y	Y	N	Y	Y	Y	N
3 Blumenauer	Y	Y	Y	Y	Y	Y	Y
4 DeFazio	Y	?	Y	Y	Y	Y	Y
5 Schrader	Y	Y	Y	Y	Y	Y	Y
PENNSYLVANIA							
1 Brady	Y	Y	Y	Y	Y	Y	Y
2 Fattah	Y	Y	Y	Y	Y	Y	Y
3 Dahlkemper	Y	Y	Y	Y	Y	Y	Y
4 Altmire	Y	Y	Y	Y	Y	Y	Y
5 **Thompson**	Y	Y	Y	Y	Y	Y	N
6 **Gerlach**	Y	Y	Y	Y	Y	Y	N
7 Sestak	Y	Y	Y	Y	Y	Y	Y
8 Murphy, P.	Y	Y	Y	Y	Y	Y	Y
9 **Shuster**	Y	Y	Y	N	Y	Y	N
10 Carney	Y	Y	Y	Y	Y	Y	Y
11 Kanjorski	Y	Y	Y	Y	Y	Y	Y
12 Critz	Y	Y	Y	Y	Y	Y	Y
13 Schwartz	Y	Y	Y	Y	Y	Y	Y
14 Doyle	Y	Y	Y	Y	Y	Y	Y
15 **Dent**	Y	Y	Y	Y	Y	Y	N
16 **Pitts**	N	Y	Y	Y	Y	Y	N
17 Holden	Y	Y	Y	Y	Y	Y	Y
18 **Murphy, T.**	Y	Y	Y	Y	Y	Y	N
19 **Platts**	Y	Y	Y	Y	Y	Y	N
RHODE ISLAND							
1 Kennedy	Y	Y	Y	Y	Y	Y	Y
2 Langevin	Y	Y	Y	Y	Y	Y	Y
SOUTH CAROLINA							
1 **Brown**	Y	Y	Y	N	Y	N	N
2 **Wilson**	Y	Y	Y	N	Y	N	N
3 **Barrett**	Y	Y	Y	N	Y	N	N
4 **Inglis**	N	Y	Y	Y	Y	N	N
5 Spratt	Y	Y	Y	Y	Y	Y	Y
6 Clyburn	Y	Y	Y	Y	Y	?	Y
SOUTH DAKOTA							
AL Herseth Sandlin	Y	Y	Y	Y	Y	Y	Y
TENNESSEE							
1 **Roe**	N	Y	Y	N	Y	Y	N
2 **Duncan**	Y	Y	Y	N	Y	Y	N
3 **Wamp**	N	Y	Y	Y	Y	Y	N
4 Davis	Y	Y	Y	Y	Y	Y	Y
5 Cooper	Y	Y	Y	Y	Y	Y	Y
6 Gordon	Y	?	Y	Y	Y	Y	Y
7 **Blackburn**	N	Y	N	N	Y	Y	N
8 Tanner	Y	Y	Y	Y	Y	Y	Y
9 Cohen	Y	Y	Y	Y	Y	Y	Y

	552	553	554	555	556	557	558
TEXAS							
1 **Gohmert**	Y	Y	N	N	Y	Y	N
2 **Poe**	N	Y	N	N	Y	N	N
3 **Johnson, S.**	N	Y	N	N	Y	N	N
4 **Hall**	N	Y	N	Y	Y	Y	N
5 **Hensarling**	N	Y	N	N	N	N	N
6 **Barton**	N	Y	N	N	Y	Y	N
7 **Culberson**	Y	Y	N	Y	Y	N	N
8 **Brady**	N	Y	N	N	Y	N	N
9 Green, A.	Y	Y	Y	Y	Y	Y	Y
10 **McCaul**	N	Y	N	Y	Y	Y	N
11 **Conaway**	N	Y	N	N	Y	N	N
12 **Granger**	N	Y	N	N	Y	N	N
13 **Thornberry**	N	Y	N	N	Y	N	N
14 **Paul**	N	N	N	N	N	N	N
15 Hinojosa	Y	Y	Y	Y	Y	Y	Y
16 Reyes	Y	Y	Y	Y	Y	Y	Y
17 Edwards	Y	Y	Y	Y	Y	Y	Y
18 Jackson Lee	Y	Y	Y	Y	Y	Y	Y
19 **Neugebauer**	N	Y	N	N	Y	N	N
20 Gonzalez	Y	Y	Y	Y	Y	Y	Y
21 **Smith**	Y	Y	N	Y	Y	N	N
22 **Olson**	Y	Y	N	?	Y	N	N
23 Rodriguez	Y	Y	Y	Y	Y	Y	Y
24 **Marchant**	N	Y	N	N	Y	N	N
25 Doggett	Y	Y	Y	Y	Y	Y	Y
26 **Burgess**	Y	Y	Y	N	Y	Y	N
27 Ortiz	Y	Y	Y	Y	Y	Y	Y
28 Cuellar	Y	Y	N	Y	Y	Y	Y
29 Green, G.	Y	Y	Y	Y	Y	Y	Y
30 Johnson, E.	Y	Y	Y	Y	Y	Y	Y
31 **Carter**	N	Y	N	N	Y	N	N
32 **Sessions**	N	Y	N	N	Y	Y	N
UTAH							
1 **Bishop**	Y	Y	Y	Y	Y	N	N
2 Matheson	Y	Y	Y	Y	Y	Y	Y
3 **Chaffetz**	Y	Y	N	N	Y	N	N
VERMONT							
AL Welch	Y	Y	Y	Y	Y	Y	N
VIRGINIA							
1 **Wittman**	Y	Y	Y	Y	Y	Y	N
2 Nye	Y	Y	Y	Y	Y	Y	Y
3 Scott	?	Y	Y	Y	Y	Y	Y
4 **Forbes**	Y	Y	Y	Y	Y	Y	N
5 Perriello	Y	Y	Y	Y	Y	Y	Y
6 **Goodlatte**	Y	Y	Y	N	Y	N	N
7 **Cantor**	N	Y	N	N	Y	N	N
8 Moran	Y	Y	Y	Y	Y	Y	Y
9 Boucher	Y	Y	Y	Y	Y	Y	Y
10 **Wolf**	Y	Y	Y	Y	Y	Y	N
11 Connolly	Y	Y	Y	Y	Y	Y	Y
WASHINGTON							
1 Inslee	Y	Y	Y	Y	Y	Y	Y
2 Larsen	Y	Y	N	Y	Y	Y	Y
3 Baird	Y	Y	Y	Y	Y	Y	Y
4 **Hastings**	N	Y	N	N	Y	N	N
5 **McMorris Rodgers**	Y	Y	N	N	Y	N	N
6 Dicks	Y	Y	Y	Y	Y	Y	Y
7 McDermott	Y	Y	Y	Y	Y	Y	Y
8 **Reichert**	Y	Y	N	Y	Y	Y	N
9 Smith	Y	Y	Y	Y	Y	N	Y
WEST VIRGINIA							
1 Mollohan	Y	Y	Y	Y	Y	Y	Y
2 **Capito**	Y	Y	Y	Y	Y	Y	Y
3 Rahall	Y	Y	Y	Y	Y	Y	Y
WISCONSIN							
1 **Ryan**	N	Y	N	N	Y	N	N
2 Baldwin	Y	Y	Y	Y	Y	Y	Y
3 Kind	Y	Y	Y	Y	Y	Y	Y
4 Moore	Y	Y	Y	Y	Y	Y	Y
5 **Sensenbrenner**	N	Y	N	N	Y	N	N
6 **Petri**	Y	Y	Y	N	Y	N	N
7 Obey	Y	Y	Y	Y	Y	Y	Y
8 Kagen	Y	Y	Y	Y	Y	Y	Y
WYOMING							
AL **Lummis**	N	Y	N	N	Y	N	N
DELEGATES							
Faleomavaega (A.S.)							
Norton (D.C.)							
Bordallo (Guam)							
Sablan (N. Marianas)							
Pierluisi (P.R.)							
Christensen (V.I.)							

IN THE HOUSE | By Vote Number

559. **HR 3081. Continuing Appropriations/Previous Question.** Slaughter, D-N.Y., motion to order the previous question (thus ending debate and possibility of amendment) on adoption of the rule (H Res 1682) to provide for House floor consideration of the Senate amendments to the bill that would provide continuing appropriations through Dec. 3, 2010. Motion agreed to 240-186: D 240-13; R 0-173. Sept. 29, 2010.

560. **HR 3081. Continuing Appropriations/Rule.** Adoption of the rule (H Res 1682) that would provide for House floor consideration of the Senate amendments to the bill that would provide continuing appropriations through Dec. 3, 2010. Adopted 233-191: D 233-19; R 0-172. Sept. 29, 2010.

561. **S 3729. NASA Reauthorization/Passage.** Gordon, D-Tenn., motion to suspend the rules and pass the bill that would authorize $58.4 billion for NASA in fiscal 2011 through 2013, including $1.6 billion for commercial crew and cargo systems development, $6.9 billion for a NASA space launch system, $3.9 billion for a crew vehicle and $1.6 billion for space shuttle flight operations. It would allow for one additional shuttle flight, support using the International Space Station through at least 2020 and authorize $8.9 billion for the station. Motion agreed to, thus clearing the bill for the president, 304-118: D 185-64; R 119-54. A two-thirds majority of those present and voting (282 in this case) is required for passage under suspension of the rules. Sept. 29, 2010.

562. **HR 946. Plain Language in Government Communications/ Passage.** Clay, D-Mo., motion to suspend the rules and concur in the Senate amendments to the bill that would require executive branch agencies to use plain language in documents issued to the public, excluding regulations. Motion agreed to 341-82: D 249-2; R 92-80. A two-thirds majority of those present and voting (282 in this case) is required for passage under suspension of the rules. Sept. 29, 2010.

563. **HR 512. State Election Official Political Activity/Passage.** Davis, D-Calif., motion to suspend the rules and pass the bill that would prohibit a chief state election administration official from taking an active part in a federal election campaign that the official supervises, except for their own or that of a family member. Motion agreed to 296-129: D 251-1; R 45-128. A two-thirds majority of those present and voting (284 in this case) is required for passage under suspension of the rules. Sept. 29, 2010.

564. **HR 3081. Continuing Appropriations/Motion to Concur.** Obey, D-Wis., motion to concur in the Senate amendments to the bill that would provide continuing appropriations through Dec. 3, 2010, for all federal departments and agencies, none of whose fiscal 2011 appropriations bills have been enacted. It includes several spending adjustments including an increase of $624 million for the National Nuclear Security Administration. It also would extend year-round child nutrition programs and the Federal Emergency Management Agency's pre-disaster mitigation operations. It would allow the District of Columbia to implement its local budget beginning on Oct. 1, 2010. Motion agreed to, thus clearing the bill for the president, 228-194: D 227-22; R 1-172. Sept. 30, 2010 (in the session that began and the Congressional Record dated Sept. 29, 2010).

565. **HR 3940. Minimum-Wage Increase Delay/Motion to Concur.** Miller, D-Calif., motion to suspend the rules and concur in the Senate amendments to the bill that would delay a scheduled minimum-wage increase in American Samoa in 2010 and 2011, and in the Commonwealth of the Northern Mariana Islands in 2011. Motion agreed to 386-5: D 227-2; R 159-3. A two-thirds majority of those present and voting (261 in this case) is required for passage under suspension of the rules. Sept. 30, 2010 (in the session that began and the Congressional Record dated Sept. 29, 2010).

	559	560	561	562	563	564	565
ALABAMA							
1 **Bonner**	N	N	Y	Y	N	N	Y
2 **Bright**	N	N	Y	N	Y	N	Y
3 **Rogers**	N	N	Y	Y	N	N	Y
4 **Aderholt**	N	N	Y	N	N	N	Y
5 **Griffith**	N	N	Y	Y	N	N	Y
6 **Bachus**	N	N	Y	Y	N	N	Y
7 Davis	Y	Y	Y	Y	Y	Y	?
ALASKA							
AL **Young**	N	N	N	N	N	N	Y
ARIZONA							
1 **Kirkpatrick**	N	N	Y	Y	Y	N	?
2 **Franks**	N	N	Y	N	N	N	Y
3 **Shadegg**	N	N	N	N	N	N	Y
4 **Pastor**	Y	Y	Y	Y	Y	Y	Y
5 **Mitchell**	N	Y	Y	Y	Y	N	Y
6 **Flake**	N	N	N	N	N	N	Y
7 **Grijalva**	Y	Y	N	Y	Y	Y	Y
8 **Giffords**	N	N	N	Y	N	N	Y
ARKANSAS							
1 **Berry**	Y	Y	N	Y	Y	Y	?
2 **Snyder**	Y	Y	N	Y	Y	Y	Y
3 **Boozman**	N	N	Y	N	Y	N	Y
4 **Ross**	Y	Y	Y	Y	Y	Y	Y
CALIFORNIA							
1 **Thompson**	Y	Y	Y	Y	Y	Y	?
2 **Herger**	N	N	N	N	N	N	Y
3 **Lungren**	N	N	Y	N	N	N	Y
4 **McClintock**	N	N	Y	N	N	N	Y
5 **Matsui**	Y	Y	Y	Y	Y	Y	Y
6 **Woolsey**	Y	Y	N	Y	Y	Y	Y
7 **Miller, George**	Y	Y	Y	Y	Y	Y	Y
8 Pelosi							
9 Lee	Y	Y	N	Y	Y	Y	Y
10 Garamendi	Y	Y	Y	Y	Y	Y	Y
11 McNerney	Y	Y	Y	Y	Y	Y	Y
12 Speier	Y	Y	Y	Y	Y	Y	Y
13 Stark	Y	N	N	Y	Y	N	?
14 Eshoo	Y	Y	Y	Y	Y	Y	Y
15 Honda	Y	Y	Y	Y	Y	Y	Y
16 Lofgren	Y	Y	Y	Y	Y	Y	Y
17 Farr	Y	Y	Y	Y	Y	Y	Y
18 Cardoza	Y	Y	Y	Y	Y	Y	Y
19 **Radanovich**	?	?	?	?	?	?	?
20 Costa	Y	Y	Y	Y	Y	Y	Y
21 **Nunes**	N	N	Y	N	N	N	N
22 **McCarthy**	N	N	Y	N	N	N	Y
23 Capps	Y	Y	Y	Y	Y	Y	Y
24 **Gallegly**	N	N	Y	Y	N	?	Y
25 **McKeon**	N	N	Y	Y	N	N	Y
26 **Dreier**	N	N	Y	N	N	N	Y
27 Sherman	Y	Y	N	Y	?	Y	Y
28 Berman	Y	Y	N	Y	Y	Y	Y
29 Schiff	Y	Y	Y	Y	Y	Y	Y
30 Waxman	Y	Y	Y	Y	Y	Y	?
31 Becerra	Y	Y	Y	Y	Y	Y	Y
32 Chu	Y	Y	Y	Y	Y	Y	Y
33 Watson	Y	Y	Y	Y	Y	Y	Y
34 Roybal-Allard	Y	Y	Y	Y	Y	Y	Y
35 Waters	Y	Y	Y	Y	Y	Y	Y
36 Harman	Y	Y	Y	Y	Y	Y	Y
37 Richardson	Y	Y	?	Y	Y	Y	Y
38 Napolitano	Y	Y	Y	Y	Y	Y	Y
39 Sánchez, Linda	Y	Y	Y	Y	Y	Y	Y
40 **Royce**	N	N	Y	N	N	N	Y
41 **Lewis**	N	N	Y	N	N	N	Y
42 **Miller, Gary**	N	N	Y	N	N	N	?
43 Baca	Y	Y	Y	Y	Y	Y	Y
44 **Calvert**	N	N	Y	N	N	N	Y
45 **Bono Mack**	N	N	Y	Y	Y	N	Y
46 **Rohrabacher**	N	N	Y	N	N	N	Y
47 Sanchez, Loretta	Y	Y	Y	Y	Y	Y	?
48 **Campbell**	N	N	Y	N	N	N	Y
49 **Issa**	N	N	Y	Y	N	N	Y
50 **Bilbray**	N	N	N	Y	N	N	Y
51 Filner	Y	Y	Y	Y	Y	Y	Y
52 **Hunter**	N	N	Y	N	N	N	Y
53 Davis	Y	Y	Y	Y	Y	Y	Y

	559	560	561	562	563	564	565
COLORADO							
1 DeGette	Y	Y	Y	Y	Y	Y	?
2 Polis	Y	Y	Y	Y	Y	Y	Y
3 Salazar	Y	Y	Y	Y	Y	Y	Y
4 Markey	Y	Y	Y	Y	Y	Y	Y
5 **Lamborn**	N	N	Y	N	N	N	Y
6 **Coffman**	N	N	Y	Y	N	N	Y
7 Perlmutter	Y	Y	Y	Y	Y	Y	Y
CONNECTICUT							
1 Larson	Y	Y	Y	Y	Y	Y	Y
2 Courtney	Y	Y	N	Y	Y	Y	Y
3 DeLauro	Y	Y	Y	Y	Y	Y	Y
4 Himes	Y	Y	Y	Y	Y	?	Y
5 Murphy	Y	Y	Y	Y	Y	Y	Y
DELAWARE							
AL **Castle**	N	N	Y	Y	Y	N	Y
FLORIDA							
1 **Miller**	N	N	Y	N	N	N	Y
2 Boyd	Y	Y	Y	Y	Y	Y	Y
3 Brown	Y	Y	Y	Y	Y	Y	Y
4 **Crenshaw**	N	N	Y	N	N	N	Y
5 **Brown-Waite**	N	N	Y	Y	Y	N	?
6 **Stearns**	N	N	Y	N	N	N	Y
7 **Mica**	N	N	Y	N	N	N	Y
8 Grayson	Y	Y	Y	Y	Y	Y	Y
9 **Bilirakis**	N	N	Y	N	N	N	Y
10 **Young**	?	?	?	?	?	?	?
11 Castor	Y	Y	Y	Y	Y	Y	Y
12 **Putnam**	N	N	Y	N	N	N	Y
13 **Buchanan**	N	N	Y	Y	N	N	Y
14 **Mack**	N	N	Y	N	N	N	Y
15 **Posey**	N	N	Y	N	N	N	Y
16 **Rooney**	N	N	Y	Y	N	N	Y
17 Meek	Y	Y	Y	Y	Y	Y	Y
18 **Ros-Lehtinen**	N	N	Y	N	N	N	Y
19 Deutch	Y	Y	Y	Y	Y	Y	Y
20 Wasserman Schultz	Y	Y	Y	Y	Y	Y	Y
21 **Diaz-Balart, L.**	N	N	Y	Y	Y	N	Y
22 Klein	Y	Y	Y	Y	Y	Y	Y
23 Hastings	Y	Y	Y	Y	Y	Y	Y
24 Kosmas	Y	Y	Y	Y	Y	Y	Y
25 **Diaz-Balart, M.**	N	N	Y	Y	Y	N	Y
GEORGIA							
1 **Kingston**	N	N	N	N	N	N	Y
2 Bishop	Y	Y	Y	Y	Y	Y	Y
3 **Westmoreland**	N	N	N	N	N	N	Y
4 Johnson	Y	Y	Y	Y	Y	Y	Y
5 Lewis	Y	Y	Y	Y	Y	Y	Y
6 **Price**	N	N	N	N	N	N	Y
7 **Linder**	N	N	Y	N	N	N	?
8 Marshall	Y	Y	Y	Y	Y	N	Y
9 **Graves**	N	N	N	N	N	N	Y
10 **Broun**	N	N	N	N	N	N	Y
11 **Gingrey**	N	N	Y	N	N	N	Y
12 Barrow	Y	Y	N	Y	Y	Y	Y
13 Scott	Y	Y	Y	Y	Y	Y	Y
HAWAII							
1 **Djou**	N	N	Y	Y	Y	N	Y
2 Hirono	Y	Y	N	Y	Y	Y	Y
IDAHO							
1 Minnick	N	N	Y	Y	N	N	Y
2 **Simpson**	N	N	N	N	Y	N	Y
ILLINOIS							
1 Rush	Y	Y	Y	Y	Y	Y	Y
2 Jackson	Y	Y	N	Y	Y	Y	Y
3 Lipinski	Y	Y	Y	Y	Y	Y	Y
4 Gutierrez	Y	Y	Y	Y	Y	Y	Y
5 Quigley	Y	Y	Y	Y	Y	Y	Y
6 **Roskam**	N	N	N	N	N	N	Y
7 Davis	Y	Y	Y	Y	Y	Y	Y
8 Bean	Y	Y	Y	Y	Y	N	Y
9 Schakowsky	Y	Y	Y	Y	Y	Y	Y
10 **Kirk**	N	N	Y	Y	N	N	Y
11 Halvorson	Y	Y	Y	Y	Y	Y	?
12 Costello	Y	Y	Y	Y	Y	Y	Y
13 **Biggert**	N	N	Y	N	N	N	Y
14 Foster	Y	Y	Y	Y	Y	Y	Y
15 **Johnson**	N	N	N	Y	Y	N	Y

	559	560	561	562	563	564	565
16 **Manzullo**	N	N	Y	N	N	N	Y
17 Hare	Y	Y	Y	Y	Y	Y	Y
18 **Schock**	N	N	Y	Y	N	N	Y
19 **Shimkus**	N	N	N	Y	N	N	Y
INDIANA							
1 Visclosky	Y	Y	N	Y	Y	N	Y
2 Donnelly	Y	N	Y	Y	Y	Y	Y
3 Vacant							
4 **Buyer**	N	N	Y	?	Y	N	Y
5 **Burton**	N	N	Y	Y	N	N	Y
6 **Pence**	N	N	Y	N	N	N	Y
7 Carson	Y	Y	Y	Y	Y	Y	Y
8 Ellsworth	Y	Y	Y	Y	Y	Y	Y
9 Hill	N	N	N	Y	Y	Y	?
IOWA							
1 Braley	Y	Y	Y	Y	Y	Y	Y
2 Loebsack	Y	Y	Y	Y	Y	Y	Y
3 Boswell	Y	Y	N	Y	Y	Y	Y
4 **Latham**	N	N	Y	Y	N	N	Y
5 **King**	N	N	Y	N	N	N	Y
KANSAS							
1 **Moran**	N	N	Y	Y	N	N	Y
2 **Jenkins**	N	N	Y	Y	N	N	Y
3 Moore	Y	Y	Y	Y	Y	Y	Y
4 **Tiahrt**	N	N	Y	N	N	N	Y
KENTUCKY							
1 **Whitfield**	N	N	Y	N	Y	N	Y
2 **Guthrie**	N	N	Y	Y	Y	N	Y
3 Yarmuth	Y	Y	N	Y	Y	Y	?
4 **Davis**	N	N	Y	Y	N	N	Y
5 **Rogers**	N	N	Y	Y	Y	N	Y
6 Chandler	Y	Y	N	Y	Y	Y	Y
LOUISIANA							
1 **Scalise**	N	N	Y	N	N	N	Y
2 **Cao**	N	N	Y	Y	Y	Y	Y
3 Melancon	Y	Y	Y	Y	Y	Y	Y
4 **Fleming**	N	N	Y	Y	N	N	Y
5 **Alexander**	N	N	Y	Y	N	N	Y
6 **Cassidy**	N	N	Y	N	N	N	Y
7 **Boustany**	N	N	Y	Y	N	N	Y
MAINE							
1 Pingree	Y	Y	N	Y	Y	Y	Y
2 Michaud	Y	Y	N	Y	Y	Y	Y
MARYLAND							
1 Kratovil	N	N	Y	Y	Y	N	Y
2 Ruppersberger	Y	Y	Y	Y	Y	Y	Y
3 Sarbanes	Y	Y	Y	Y	Y	Y	Y
4 Edwards	Y	Y	N	Y	Y	Y	Y
5 Hoyer	Y	Y	Y	Y	Y	Y	Y
6 **Bartlett**	N	N	Y	N	N	N	Y
7 Cummings	Y	Y	Y	Y	Y	Y	Y
8 Van Hollen	Y	Y	Y	Y	Y	Y	Y
MASSACHUSETTS							
1 Olver	Y	Y	Y	Y	Y	Y	Y
2 Neal	Y	Y	Y	Y	Y	Y	?
3 McGovern	Y	Y	N	Y	Y	Y	Y
4 Frank	Y	Y	N	Y	Y	Y	Y
5 Tsongas	Y	Y	Y	Y	Y	Y	?
6 Tierney	Y	Y	N	Y	Y	Y	Y
7 Markey	Y	Y	Y	Y	Y	Y	Y
8 Capuano	Y	Y	N	Y	Y	Y	Y
9 Lynch	Y	Y	N	Y	Y	Y	Y
10 Delahunt	?	?	?	?	?	?	?
MICHIGAN							
1 Stupak	Y	Y	Y	Y	Y	Y	Y
2 **Hoekstra**	N	N	N	N	N	N	Y
3 **Ehlers**	N	N	N	Y	Y	N	Y
4 **Camp**	N	N	N	Y	N	N	Y
5 Kildee	Y	Y	Y	Y	Y	Y	N
6 **Upton**	N	N	N	Y	N	N	Y
7 Schauer	Y	Y	Y	Y	Y	Y	Y
8 **Rogers**	N	N	N	Y	Y	N	Y
9 Peters	Y	N	Y	Y	Y	Y	Y
10 **Miller**	N	N	N	Y	N	N	Y
11 **McCotter**	N	N	N	Y	Y	N	Y
12 Levin	Y	Y	Y	Y	Y	Y	Y
13 Kilpatrick	Y	Y	Y	Y	Y	Y	?
14 Conyers	Y	Y	N	Y	Y	Y	Y
15 Dingell	Y	Y	Y	Y	Y	Y	Y
MINNESOTA							
1 Walz	Y	Y	N	Y	Y	Y	Y
2 **Kline**	N	N	Y	Y	N	N	Y
3 **Paulsen**	N	N	N	Y	N	N	Y
4 McCollum	Y	Y	Y	Y	Y	Y	Y

	559	560	561	562	563	564	565
5 Ellison	Y	Y	Y	Y	Y	Y	Y
6 **Bachmann**	N	N	Y	Y	N	N	Y
7 Peterson	Y	Y	Y	Y	Y	Y	Y
8 Oberstar	Y	Y	N	Y	Y	Y	Y
MISSISSIPPI							
1 Childers	N	N	N	Y	Y	?	Y
2 Thompson	Y	Y	N	Y	Y	Y	Y
3 **Harper**	N	N	Y	Y	N	N	Y
4 Taylor	N	N	Y	Y	Y	N	Y
MISSOURI							
1 Clay	Y	Y	N	Y	Y	?	Y
2 **Akin**	N	N	Y	N	N	N	Y
3 Carnahan	Y	Y	Y	Y	Y	Y	Y
4 Skelton	Y	Y	Y	Y	Y	Y	Y
5 Cleaver	Y	Y	Y	Y	Y	Y	Y
6 **Graves**	?	?	?	?	?	?	?
7 **Blunt**	?	?	?	?	?	?	?
8 **Emerson**	N	N	N	Y	N	N	Y
9 **Luetkemeyer**	N	N	Y	Y	Y	N	Y
MONTANA							
AL **Rehberg**	N	N	Y	Y	N	N	Y
NEBRASKA							
1 **Fortenberry**	N	N	Y	Y	Y	N	Y
2 **Terry**	N	N	N	Y	N	N	Y
3 **Smith**	N	N	Y	N	N	N	Y
NEVADA							
1 Berkley	Y	Y	Y	Y	Y	Y	?
2 **Heller**	N	N	N	Y	N	N	Y
3 Titus	Y	Y	Y	Y	Y	Y	Y
NEW HAMPSHIRE							
1 Shea-Porter	Y	Y	N	Y	Y	Y	Y
2 Hodes	Y	Y	N	Y	Y	N	?
NEW JERSEY							
1 Andrews	Y	Y	N	Y	Y	Y	Y
2 **LoBiondo**	N	N	Y	Y	Y	N	Y
3 Adler	N	N	N	Y	Y	N	Y
4 **Smith**	N	N	Y	Y	Y	N	Y
5 **Garrett**	N	N	N	N	N	N	Y
6 Pallone	Y	Y	Y	Y	Y	Y	Y
7 **Lance**	N	N	N	Y	N	N	Y
8 Pascrell	Y	Y	Y	Y	Y	Y	Y
9 Rothman	Y	Y	Y	Y	Y	Y	Y
10 Payne	Y	Y	N	Y	Y	Y	Y
11 **Frelinghuysen**	N	N	N	N	N	N	Y
12 Holt	Y	Y	N	Y	Y	Y	Y
13 Sires	Y	Y	Y	Y	Y	Y	Y
NEW MEXICO							
1 Heinrich	Y	Y	Y	Y	Y	Y	Y
2 Teague	Y	Y	Y	Y	Y	Y	Y
3 Luján	Y	Y	Y	Y	Y	Y	Y
NEW YORK							
1 Bishop	Y	Y	Y	Y	Y	Y	Y
2 Israel	Y	Y	N	Y	Y	Y	Y
3 **King**	N	N	Y	Y	Y	N	?
4 McCarthy	Y	Y	Y	Y	Y	Y	Y
5 Ackerman	Y	Y	Y	Y	Y	Y	Y
6 Meeks	Y	Y	Y	Y	Y	Y	Y
7 Crowley	Y	Y	N	Y	Y	Y	?
8 Nadler	Y	Y	Y	Y	Y	Y	Y
9 Weiner	Y	Y	Y	Y	Y	Y	Y
10 Towns	Y	Y	Y	Y	Y	Y	Y
11 Clarke	Y	Y	N	Y	Y	Y	Y
12 Velázquez	Y	Y	Y	Y	Y	Y	Y
13 McMahon	Y	Y	+	Y	Y	Y	Y
14 Maloney	Y	Y	Y	Y	Y	Y	Y
15 Rangel	Y	Y	Y	Y	Y	Y	?
16 Serrano	Y	Y	Y	Y	Y	Y	Y
17 Engel	Y	Y	N	Y	Y	Y	Y
18 Lowey	Y	Y	Y	Y	Y	Y	Y
19 Hall	Y	Y	Y	Y	Y	Y	Y
20 Murphy	Y	N	N	Y	Y	N	Y
21 Tonko	Y	Y	Y	Y	Y	Y	Y
22 Hinchey	Y	Y	N	Y	Y	Y	Y
23 Owens	Y	Y	N	Y	Y	Y	N
24 Arcuri	Y	Y	Y	Y	Y	Y	Y
25 Maffei	Y	Y	N	Y	Y	Y	Y
26 **Lee**	N	N	Y	Y	N	N	?
27 Higgins	Y	Y	Y	Y	Y	Y	Y
28 Slaughter	Y	Y	Y	Y	Y	Y	?
29 Vacant							
NORTH CAROLINA							
1 Butterfield	Y	Y	N	Y	Y	Y	Y
2 Etheridge	Y	Y	?	Y	Y	Y	Y
3 **Jones**	N	N	N	N	Y	N	Y
4 Price	Y	Y	Y	Y	Y	Y	Y

	559	560	561	562	563	564	565
5 **Foxx**	N	N	Y	Y	N	N	Y
6 **Coble**	N	N	N	N	N	N	Y
7 McIntyre	Y	Y	Y	Y	Y	N	Y
8 Kissell	Y	Y	Y	Y	Y	Y	Y
9 **Myrick**	N	N	N	N	N	N	Y
10 **McHenry**	N	N	N	N	N	N	N
11 Shuler	Y	N	Y	Y	Y	N	Y
12 Watt	Y	Y	N	Y	Y	?	Y
13 Miller	Y	Y	N	Y	Y	Y	Y
NORTH DAKOTA							
AL Pomeroy	Y	Y	Y	Y	Y	Y	Y
OHIO							
1 Driehaus	Y	N	Y	Y	Y	N	Y
2 **Schmidt**	N	N	N	Y	N	N	Y
3 **Turner**	N	N	N	Y	Y	N	Y
4 **Jordan**	N	N	N	N	N	N	Y
5 **Latta**	N	N	N	N	N	N	Y
6 Wilson	Y	Y	Y	Y	Y	Y	Y
7 **Austria**	N	N	N	Y	Y	N	Y
8 **Boehner**	N	N	N	N	N	N	Y
9 Kaptur	Y	?	Y	Y	Y	Y	Y
10 Kucinich	Y	Y	N	N	Y	N	Y
11 Fudge	Y	Y	Y	Y	Y	Y	?
12 **Tiberi**	N	N	N	Y	Y	N	Y
13 Sutton	Y	Y	Y	Y	Y	Y	Y
14 **LaTourette**	N	N	N	N	Y	N	?
15 Kilroy	Y	Y	N	Y	Y	Y	Y
16 Boccieri	Y	Y	Y	Y	Y	Y	Y
17 Ryan	Y	Y	Y	Y	Y	Y	Y
18 Space	N	Y	Y	Y	Y	N	Y
OKLAHOMA							
1 **Sullivan**	N	N	N	N	N	N	Y
2 Boren	Y	Y	Y	Y	Y	Y	Y
3 **Lucas**	N	N	Y	Y	N	N	Y
4 **Cole**	N	N	Y	Y	N	N	Y
5 **Fallin**	?	?	?	?	?	?	?
OREGON							
1 Wu	Y	Y	N	Y	Y	Y	Y
2 **Walden**	N	N	N	Y	N	N	Y
3 Blumenauer	Y	Y	Y	Y	Y	Y	Y
4 DeFazio	Y	Y	N	Y	Y	N	Y
5 Schrader	Y	Y	Y	Y	Y	Y	Y
PENNSYLVANIA							
1 Brady	Y	Y	Y	Y	Y	Y	Y
2 Fattah	Y	Y	Y	Y	Y	Y	Y
3 Dahlkemper	Y	Y	N	Y	Y	Y	Y
4 Altmire	Y	N	Y	Y	Y	Y	Y
5 **Thompson**	N	N	Y	Y	Y	N	Y
6 **Gerlach**	N	N	Y	Y	Y	N	Y
7 Sestak	Y	Y	Y	Y	Y	Y	?
8 Murphy, P.	Y	Y	Y	Y	Y	Y	Y
9 **Shuster**	N	N	N	N	N	N	Y
10 Carney	Y	Y	Y	Y	Y	Y	Y
11 Kanjorski	Y	Y	Y	Y	Y	Y	Y
12 Critz	Y	Y	Y	Y	Y	Y	Y
13 Schwartz	Y	Y	Y	Y	Y	Y	Y
14 Doyle	Y	Y	Y	Y	Y	Y	Y
15 **Dent**	N	N	Y	Y	Y	N	Y
16 **Pitts**	N	N	Y	N	N	N	Y
17 Holden	Y	Y	Y	Y	Y	Y	Y
18 **Murphy, T.**	N	N	Y	Y	Y	N	Y
19 **Platts**	N	N	Y	Y	Y	N	Y
RHODE ISLAND							
1 Kennedy	Y	Y	Y	Y	Y	Y	?
2 Langevin	Y	Y	Y	Y	Y	Y	Y
SOUTH CAROLINA							
1 **Brown**	N	N	Y	Y	Y	N	Y
2 **Wilson**	N	N	N	Y	N	N	Y
3 **Barrett**	N	N	N	Y	N	N	Y
4 **Inglis**	N	N	N	N	N	N	Y
5 Spratt	Y	Y	Y	Y	Y	Y	Y
6 Clyburn	Y	Y	Y	Y	Y	Y	Y
SOUTH DAKOTA							
AL Herseth Sandlin	Y	N	Y	Y	Y	N	Y
TENNESSEE							
1 **Roe**	N	N	Y	Y	N	N	Y
2 **Duncan**	N	N	N	N	N	N	Y
3 **Wamp**	N	N	Y	Y	N	N	Y
4 Davis	Y	Y	Y	?	Y	Y	Y
5 Cooper	Y	Y	Y	Y	Y	Y	Y
6 Gordon	Y	Y	Y	Y	Y	Y	Y
7 **Blackburn**	N	N	N	Y	N	N	Y
8 Tanner	Y	Y	N	Y	Y	Y	Y
9 Cohen	Y	Y	N	Y	Y	Y	Y

	559	560	561	562	563	564	565
TEXAS							
1 **Gohmert**	N	N	Y	N	N	N	Y
2 **Poe**	N	N	Y	N	N	N	Y
3 **Johnson, S.**	N	N	Y	N	N	N	Y
4 **Hall**	N	N	Y	Y	N	N	N
5 **Hensarling**	N	N	N	N	N	N	Y
6 **Barton**	N	N	Y	Y	N	N	?
7 **Culberson**	N	N	Y	N	N	N	Y
8 **Brady**	N	N	Y	N	N	N	Y
9 Green, A.	Y	Y	Y	Y	Y	Y	Y
10 **McCaul**	N	N	Y	Y	Y	N	Y
11 **Conaway**	N	N	Y	N	N	N	Y
12 **Granger**	N	N	Y	N	N	N	Y
13 **Thornberry**	N	N	Y	N	N	N	Y
14 **Paul**	N	N	N	N	N	N	Y
15 Hinojosa	Y	Y	?	Y	Y	Y	Y
16 Reyes	Y	Y	Y	Y	Y	Y	Y
17 Edwards	Y	Y	Y	Y	Y	Y	Y
18 Jackson Lee	Y	Y	Y	Y	Y	Y	Y
19 **Neugebauer**	N	N	Y	N	N	N	Y
20 Gonzalez	Y	Y	Y	Y	Y	Y	Y
21 **Smith**	N	N	Y	Y	Y	N	Y
22 **Olson**	N	N	Y	N	N	N	Y
23 Rodriguez	Y	Y	Y	Y	Y	Y	Y
24 **Marchant**	N	N	Y	N	N	N	?
25 Doggett	Y	Y	Y	Y	Y	Y	Y
26 **Burgess**	N	N	Y	N	N	N	Y
27 Ortiz	Y	Y	Y	Y	Y	Y	Y
28 Cuellar	Y	Y	Y	Y	Y	Y	Y
29 Green, G.	Y	Y	Y	Y	Y	Y	Y
30 Johnson, E.	Y	Y	Y	Y	Y	Y	Y
31 **Carter**	N	N	Y	N	N	N	Y
32 **Sessions**	N	N	Y	Y	N	N	Y
UTAH							
1 **Bishop**	N	N	Y	N	N	N	Y
2 Matheson	Y	Y	Y	Y	Y	Y	Y
3 **Chaffetz**	N	N	Y	N	N	N	Y
VERMONT							
AL Welch	Y	Y	Y	Y	Y	Y	Y
VIRGINIA							
1 **Wittman**	N	N	Y	Y	Y	N	Y
2 Nye	N	N	Y	Y	Y	N	Y
3 Scott	Y	Y	Y	Y	Y	Y	Y
4 **Forbes**	N	N	Y	Y	N	N	Y
5 Perriello	N	Y	Y	Y	Y	N	Y
6 **Goodlatte**	N	N	N	Y	N	N	Y
7 **Cantor**	N	?	Y	N	N	N	Y
8 Moran	Y	Y	Y	Y	Y	Y	Y
9 Boucher	Y	Y	Y	Y	Y	Y	Y
10 **Wolf**	N	N	Y	Y	N	N	Y
11 Connolly	Y	Y	Y	Y	Y	Y	Y
WASHINGTON							
1 Inslee	Y	Y	Y	Y	Y	Y	Y
2 Larsen	Y	Y	Y	Y	Y	Y	Y
3 Baird	Y	Y	N	Y	N	Y	Y
4 **Hastings**	N	N	Y	N	N	N	Y
5 **McMorris Rodgers**	N	N	Y	Y	N	N	Y
6 Dicks	Y	Y	Y	Y	Y	Y	?
7 McDermott	Y	Y	N	Y	Y	Y	Y
8 **Reichert**	N	N	Y	Y	Y	N	Y
9 Smith	Y	Y	N	Y	Y	Y	Y
WEST VIRGINIA							
1 Mollohan	Y	Y	Y	Y	Y	Y	Y
2 **Capito**	N	N	Y	Y	Y	N	Y
3 Rahall	Y	Y	Y	Y	Y	Y	Y
WISCONSIN							
1 **Ryan**	N	N	N	Y	N	N	Y
2 Baldwin	Y	Y	N	Y	Y	Y	Y
3 Kind	Y	Y	Y	Y	Y	Y	Y
4 Moore	Y	Y	N	Y	?	Y	Y
5 **Sensenbrenner**	N	N	N	N	N	N	Y
6 **Petri**	N	N	N	N	N	N	Y
7 Obey	Y	Y	Y	Y	Y	Y	Y
8 Kagen	Y	Y	N	Y	Y	Y	Y
WYOMING							
AL **Lummis**	N	N	N	N	N	N	Y
DELEGATES							
Faleomavaega (A.S.)							
Norton (D.C.)							
Bordallo (Guam)							
Sablan (N. Marianas)							
Pierluisi (P.R.)							
Christensen (V.I.)							

IN THE HOUSE | By Vote Number

566. **S 3689. Copyright Law Changes/Passage.** Conyers, D-Mich., motion to suspend the rules and pass the bill that would make corrections and clarifications to copyright laws, including permitting the Register of Copyrights to establish regulations for electronic certification of copyrights. Motion agreed to 385-0: D 221-0; R 164-0. A two-thirds majority of those present and voting (257 in this case) is required for passage under suspension of the rules. Nov. 15, 2010.

567. **H Res 1713. Tribute to Ruby Bridges/Adoption.** Conyers, D-Mich., motion to suspend the rules and adopt the resolution that would recognize the 50th anniversary of Ruby Bridges desegregating a previously all-white public elementary school in New Orleans. Motion agreed to 376-0: D 214-0; R 162-0. A two-thirds majority of those present and voting (251 in this case) is required for adoption under suspension of the rules. Nov. 15, 2010.

568. **H Con Res 328. Bayh-Dole Act Anniversary/Adoption.** Conyers, D-Mich., motion to suspend the rules and adopt the concurrent resolution that would recognize the 30th anniversary of the enactment of the Bayh-Dole Act, which granted patent rights to inventions resulting from government-sponsored research. Motion agreed to 385-1: D 224-0; R 161-1. A two-thirds majority of those present and voting (258 in this case) is required for adoption under suspension of the rules. Nov. 15, 2010.

569. **H Res 716. Gail Abarbanel Tribute/Adoption.** Conyers, D-Mich., motion to suspend the rules and adopt the resolution that would honor Gail Abarbanel, the founder and director of the Rape Treatment Center at the Santa Monica-UCLA Medical Center, and commend the center for its work. Motion agreed to 415-0: D 242-0; R 173-0. A two-thirds majority of those present and voting (277 in this case) is required for adoption under suspension of the rules. Nov. 16, 2010.

570. **H Res 1475. Town of Tarboro Anniversary/Adoption.** Norton, D-D.C., motion to suspend the rules and adopt the resolution that would congratulate the town of Tarboro, N.C., on its 250th anniversary. Motion agreed to 406-0: D 235-0; R 171-0. A two-thirds majority of those present and voting (271 in this case) is required for adoption under suspension of the rules. Nov. 16, 2010.

	566	567	568	569	570
ALABAMA					
1 **Bonner**	Y	Y	Y	Y	Y
2 Bright	Y	Y	Y	Y	Y
3 **Rogers**	Y	Y	Y	Y	Y
4 **Aderholt**	Y	Y	Y	Y	Y
5 **Griffith**	Y	Y	Y	Y	Y
6 **Bachus**	Y	Y	Y	Y	Y
7 Davis	?	?	?	?	?
ALASKA					
AL **Young**	Y	Y	Y	Y	Y
ARIZONA					
1 Kirkpatrick	Y	Y	Y	Y	Y
2 **Franks**	Y	Y	Y	Y	Y
3 **Shadegg**	Y	Y	Y	Y	Y
4 Pastor	?	?	?	Y	Y
5 Mitchell	Y	Y	Y	Y	Y
6 **Flake**	Y	Y	Y	Y	Y
7 Grijalva	Y	Y	Y	Y	Y
8 Giffords	Y	Y	Y	Y	Y
ARKANSAS					
1 Berry	?	?	?	Y	Y
2 Snyder	Y	Y	Y	Y	Y
3 **Boozman**	Y	Y	Y	?	?
4 Ross	Y	Y	Y	Y	Y
CALIFORNIA					
1 Thompson	Y	Y	Y	Y	Y
2 **Herger**	Y	Y	Y	Y	Y
3 **Lungren**	Y	Y	Y	Y	Y
4 **McClintock**	Y	Y	Y	Y	Y
5 Matsui	Y	Y	Y	Y	Y
6 Woolsey	Y	Y	Y	Y	Y
7 Miller, George	Y	Y	Y	Y	Y
8 Pelosi					
9 Lee	Y	Y	Y	Y	Y
10 Garamendi	Y	Y	Y	Y	Y
11 McNerney	Y	Y	Y	Y	Y
12 Speier	?	?	?	Y	Y
13 Stark	?	?	?	?	?
14 Eshoo	Y	Y	Y	Y	Y
15 Honda	Y	Y	Y	Y	Y
16 Lofgren	Y	Y	Y	Y	Y
17 Farr	Y	Y	Y	Y	Y
18 Cardoza	Y	Y	Y	Y	Y
19 **Radanovich**	Y	Y	Y	Y	Y
20 Costa	Y	Y	Y	Y	Y
21 **Nunes**	Y	Y	Y	Y	Y
22 **McCarthy**	Y	Y	Y	Y	Y
23 Capps	+	+	+	Y	Y
24 **Gallegly**	Y	Y	Y	Y	Y
25 **McKeon**	Y	Y	Y	Y	Y
26 **Dreier**	Y	Y	Y	Y	Y
27 Sherman	Y	Y	Y	Y	Y
28 Berman	Y	?	Y	Y	Y
29 Schiff	Y	Y	Y	Y	Y
30 Waxman	Y	Y	Y	Y	Y
31 Becerra	Y	Y	Y	Y	Y
32 Chu	Y	Y	Y	Y	Y
33 Watson	Y	?	Y	Y	Y
34 Roybal-Allard	Y	Y	Y	Y	Y
35 Waters	Y	?	Y	Y	Y
36 Harman	Y	Y	Y	Y	Y
37 Richardson	Y	Y	Y	Y	Y
38 Napolitano	Y	Y	Y	Y	?
39 Sánchez, Linda	?	?	?	Y	Y
40 **Royce**	Y	Y	Y	Y	Y
41 **Lewis**	Y	Y	Y	Y	Y
42 **Miller, Gary**	Y	Y	Y	Y	Y
43 Baca	Y	Y	Y	Y	Y
44 **Calvert**	Y	Y	Y	Y	Y
45 **Bono Mack**	Y	Y	Y	Y	Y
46 **Rohrabacher**	Y	Y	Y	Y	Y
47 Sanchez, Loretta	Y	Y	Y	Y	Y
48 **Campbell**	Y	Y	Y	Y	Y
49 **Issa**	Y	Y	Y	Y	Y
50 **Bilbray**	Y	Y	Y	Y	Y
51 Filner	Y	Y	Y	Y	Y
52 **Hunter**	Y	Y	Y	Y	Y
53 Davis	Y	Y	Y	Y	Y

	566	567	568	569	570
COLORADO					
1 DeGette	Y	Y	Y	Y	Y
2 Polis	Y	Y	Y	Y	Y
3 Salazar	Y	Y	Y	Y	Y
4 Markey	Y	Y	Y	Y	Y
5 **Lamborn**	?	?	?	Y	Y
6 **Coffman**	Y	Y	Y	Y	Y
7 Perlmutter	Y	?	Y	Y	Y
CONNECTICUT					
1 Larson	?	Y	Y	Y	?
2 Courtney	Y	Y	Y	Y	Y
3 DeLauro	Y	Y	Y	Y	Y
4 Himes	Y	Y	Y	Y	Y
5 Murphy	Y	Y	Y	Y	Y
DELAWARE					
AL Castle	Y	Y	Y	Y	Y
FLORIDA					
1 **Miller**	Y	Y	Y	Y	Y
2 Boyd	Y	Y	Y	Y	Y
3 Brown	Y	Y	Y	Y	Y
4 **Crenshaw**	Y	Y	Y	Y	Y
5 **Brown-Waite**	?	?	?	Y	Y
6 **Stearns**	Y	Y	Y	Y	Y
7 **Mica**	Y	Y	Y	Y	Y
8 Grayson	Y	Y	Y	Y	Y
9 **Bilirakis**	Y	Y	Y	Y	Y
10 **Young**	Y	Y	Y	Y	Y
11 Castor	Y	Y	Y	Y	Y
12 **Putnam**	+	+	+	+	+
13 **Buchanan**	Y	Y	Y	Y	Y
14 **Mack**	Y	Y	Y	Y	Y
15 **Posey**	Y	Y	Y	Y	Y
16 **Rooney**	Y	Y	Y	Y	Y
17 Meek	Y	Y	Y	?	?
18 **Ros-Lehtinen**	Y	Y	Y	Y	Y
19 Deutch	Y	Y	Y	Y	Y
20 Wasserman Schultz	Y	Y	Y	Y	Y
21 **Diaz-Balart, L.**	Y	Y	Y	Y	Y
22 Klein	Y	Y	Y	Y	Y
23 Hastings	Y	?	Y	Y	Y
24 Kosmas	Y	Y	Y	Y	Y
25 **Diaz-Balart, M.**	Y	Y	Y	Y	Y
GEORGIA					
1 **Kingston**	Y	Y	Y	Y	Y
2 Bishop	Y	Y	Y	Y	Y
3 **Westmoreland**	Y	Y	Y	Y	Y
4 Johnson	Y	Y	Y	Y	Y
5 Lewis	Y	Y	Y	Y	Y
6 **Price**	Y	Y	Y	Y	Y
7 **Linder**	Y	Y	Y	Y	Y
8 Marshall	Y	Y	Y	Y	Y
9 **Graves**	Y	Y	Y	Y	Y
10 **Broun**	Y	Y	N	Y	Y
11 **Gingrey**	?	?	?	Y	Y
12 Barrow	Y	Y	Y	Y	Y
13 Scott	Y	Y	Y	Y	Y
HAWAII					
1 **Djou**	Y	Y	Y	Y	Y
2 Hirono	+	?	Y	Y	Y
IDAHO					
1 Minnick	Y	Y	Y	Y	Y
2 **Simpson**	Y	Y	Y	Y	Y
ILLINOIS					
1 Rush	?	?	?	Y	Y
2 Jackson	Y	Y	Y	Y	Y
3 Lipinski	Y	Y	Y	Y	Y
4 Gutierrez	+	+	+	Y	?
5 Quigley	Y	Y	Y	Y	Y
6 **Roskam**	Y	Y	Y	Y	Y
7 Davis	+	+	+	Y	Y
8 Bean	Y	Y	Y	?	?
9 Schakowsky	Y	Y	Y	Y	Y
10 **Kirk**	?	?	?	Y	?
11 Halvorson	Y	Y	Y	Y	Y
12 Costello	Y	Y	Y	Y	Y
13 **Biggert**	Y	Y	Y	Y	Y
14 Foster	Y	Y	Y	Y	Y
15 **Johnson**	+	+	+	Y	Y

	566	567	568	569	570
16 Manzullo	Y	Y	Y	Y	Y
17 Hare	Y	Y	Y	Y	Y
18 Schock	Y	Y	Y	Y	Y
19 Shimkus	Y	Y	Y	Y	Y
INDIANA					
1 Visclosky	Y	Y	Y	Y	Y
2 Donnelly	Y	Y	Y	Y	Y
3 Vacant					
4 Buyer	Y	Y	Y	Y	?
5 Burton	Y	Y	Y	Y	Y
6 Pence	Y	Y	Y	Y	Y
7 Carson	Y	Y	Y	Y	Y
8 Ellsworth	Y	Y	Y	Y	Y
9 Hill	Y	Y	Y	Y	Y
IOWA					
1 Braley	Y	?	?	Y	Y
2 Loebsack	Y	Y	Y	Y	Y
3 Boswell	Y	Y	Y	Y	Y
4 Latham	Y	Y	Y	Y	Y
5 King	Y	Y	Y	Y	Y
KANSAS					
1 Moran	Y	Y	Y	Y	Y
2 Jenkins	Y	Y	Y	Y	Y
3 Moore	Y	Y	Y	Y	Y
4 Tiahrt	Y	Y	Y	Y	Y
KENTUCKY					
1 Whitfield	Y	?	Y	Y	Y
2 Guthrie	Y	Y	Y	Y	Y
3 Yarmuth	Y	Y	Y	Y	Y
4 Davis	Y	Y	Y	Y	Y
5 Rogers	Y	Y	Y	Y	Y
6 Chandler	Y	Y	Y	Y	Y
LOUISIANA					
1 Scalise	Y	Y	Y	Y	Y
2 Cao	Y	Y	Y	Y	Y
3 Melancon	Y	Y	Y	?	?
4 Fleming	Y	Y	Y	Y	Y
5 Alexander	Y	?	Y	Y	Y
6 Cassidy	Y	Y	Y	Y	Y
7 Boustany	Y	Y	Y	Y	Y
MAINE					
1 Pingree	Y	Y	Y	Y	Y
2 Michaud	Y	Y	Y	Y	Y
MARYLAND					
1 Kratovil	Y	?	Y	Y	Y
2 Ruppersberger	Y	Y	Y	Y	Y
3 Sarbanes	Y	Y	Y	Y	Y
4 Edwards	Y	Y	Y	Y	Y
5 Hoyer	Y	Y	Y	Y	Y
6 Bartlett	Y	Y	Y	Y	Y
7 Cummings	Y	Y	Y	Y	Y
8 Van Hollen	Y	?	Y	Y	Y
MASSACHUSETTS					
1 Olver	Y	Y	Y	Y	Y
2 Neal	Y	Y	Y	Y	Y
3 McGovern	Y	Y	Y	Y	Y
4 Frank	Y	Y	Y	Y	Y
5 Tsongas	Y	Y	Y	Y	Y
6 Tierney	Y	Y	Y	Y	Y
7 Markey	Y	Y	Y	Y	Y
8 Capuano	Y	Y	Y	Y	Y
9 Lynch	Y	Y	Y	Y	Y
10 Delahunt	?	?	?	Y	Y
MICHIGAN					
1 Stupak	?	?	?	Y	Y
2 Hoekstra	Y	Y	Y	Y	Y
3 Ehlers	Y	Y	Y	Y	Y
4 Camp	Y	Y	Y	Y	Y
5 Kildee	Y	Y	Y	Y	Y
6 Upton	Y	Y	Y	Y	Y
7 Schauer	Y	Y	Y	Y	Y
8 Rogers	Y	Y	Y	Y	Y
9 Peters	Y	Y	Y	Y	Y
10 Miller	Y	Y	Y	Y	Y
11 McCotter	Y	Y	Y	Y	Y
12 Levin	Y	Y	Y	Y	Y
13 Kilpatrick	Y	Y	Y	Y	Y
14 Conyers	Y	Y	Y	Y	Y
15 Dingell	?	?	?	Y	Y
MINNESOTA					
1 Walz	Y	Y	Y	Y	Y
2 Kline	Y	Y	Y	Y	Y
3 Paulsen	Y	Y	Y	Y	Y
4 McCollum	Y	Y	Y	Y	Y

	566	567	568	569	570
5 Ellison	Y	Y	Y	Y	Y
6 Bachmann	Y	Y	Y	Y	Y
7 Peterson	Y	Y	Y	Y	Y
8 Oberstar	Y	Y	Y	?	?
MISSISSIPPI					
1 Childers	Y	Y	Y	Y	Y
2 Thompson	Y	Y	Y	Y	Y
3 Harper	Y	Y	Y	Y	Y
4 Taylor	?	?	?	Y	?
MISSOURI					
1 Clay	Y	Y	Y	Y	Y
2 Akin	Y	Y	Y	Y	Y
3 Carnahan	Y	Y	Y	Y	Y
4 Skelton	Y	Y	Y	Y	Y
5 Cleaver	Y	Y	Y	Y	Y
6 Graves	Y	Y	Y	Y	Y
7 Blunt	Y	Y	Y	Y	Y
8 Emerson	Y	Y	Y	Y	Y
9 Luetkemeyer	Y	Y	Y	Y	Y
MONTANA					
AL Rehberg	Y	Y	Y	Y	Y
NEBRASKA					
1 Fortenberry	Y	Y	Y	Y	Y
2 Terry	Y	Y	Y	Y	Y
3 Smith	Y	Y	Y	Y	Y
NEVADA					
1 Berkley	Y	Y	Y	Y	Y
2 Heller	Y	Y	Y	Y	Y
3 Titus	Y	Y	Y	Y	Y
NEW HAMPSHIRE					
1 Shea-Porter	Y	Y	Y	Y	?
2 Hodes	Y	Y	Y	Y	Y
NEW JERSEY					
1 Andrews	Y	Y	Y	Y	Y
2 LoBiondo	Y	Y	Y	Y	Y
3 Adler	Y	Y	Y	Y	Y
4 Smith	Y	Y	Y	Y	Y
5 Garrett	Y	Y	Y	Y	Y
6 Pallone	Y	Y	Y	Y	Y
7 Lance	Y	Y	Y	Y	Y
8 Pascrell	Y	Y	Y	Y	Y
9 Rothman	?	?	?	Y	Y
10 Payne	?	?	?	Y	Y
11 Frelinghuysen	?	?	?	Y	Y
12 Holt	Y	Y	Y	Y	Y
13 Sires	Y	Y	Y	Y	Y
NEW MEXICO					
1 Heinrich	?	?	?	Y	Y
2 Teague	Y	Y	Y	Y	Y
3 Luján	Y	Y	Y	Y	Y
NEW YORK					
1 Bishop	Y	Y	Y	Y	Y
2 Israel	Y	Y	Y	Y	Y
3 King	Y	Y	Y	Y	Y
4 McCarthy	Y	Y	Y	Y	Y
5 Ackerman	Y	Y	Y	Y	Y
6 Meeks	Y	Y	Y	Y	Y
7 Crowley	Y	Y	Y	Y	Y
8 Nadler	Y	Y	Y	Y	Y
9 Weiner	Y	Y	Y	Y	Y
10 Towns	Y	Y	Y	Y	Y
11 Clarke	Y	Y	Y	Y	Y
12 Velázquez	Y	Y	Y	Y	Y
13 McMahon	Y	Y	Y	Y	Y
14 Maloney	+	+	+	Y	Y
15 Rangel	Y	Y	Y	Y	Y
16 Serrano	Y	Y	Y	Y	Y
17 Engel	Y	Y	Y	Y	Y
18 Lowey	Y	Y	Y	Y	Y
19 Hall	P	Y	Y	Y	Y
20 Murphy	Y	Y	Y	Y	Y
21 Tonko	Y	Y	Y	Y	Y
22 Hinchey	Y	Y	Y	Y	Y
23 Owens	+	+	+	Y	Y
24 Arcuri	?	?	?	Y	Y
25 Maffei	Y	Y	Y	Y	Y
26 Lee	?	?	?	Y	Y
27 Higgins	Y	Y	Y	Y	Y
28 Slaughter	Y	Y	Y	Y	Y
29 Vacant					
NORTH CAROLINA					
1 Butterfield	Y	Y	Y	Y	Y
2 Etheridge	Y	Y	Y	Y	Y
3 Jones	Y	Y	Y	Y	Y
4 Price	Y	Y	Y	Y	Y

	566	567	568	569	570
5 Foxx	Y	Y	Y	Y	Y
6 Coble	Y	Y	Y	Y	Y
7 McIntyre	Y	Y	Y	Y	Y
8 Kissell	Y	Y	Y	Y	Y
9 Myrick	Y	Y	Y	Y	Y
10 McHenry	Y	Y	Y	Y	Y
11 Shuler	Y	Y	Y	Y	Y
12 Watt	Y	Y	Y	Y	Y
13 Miller	Y	Y	Y	Y	Y
NORTH DAKOTA					
AL Pomeroy	?	?	?	Y	Y
OHIO					
1 Driehaus	Y	Y	Y	Y	Y
2 Schmidt	Y	Y	Y	Y	Y
3 Turner	Y	Y	Y	Y	Y
4 Jordan	Y	Y	Y	Y	Y
5 Latta	Y	Y	Y	Y	Y
6 Wilson	Y	Y	Y	Y	Y
7 Austria	Y	Y	Y	Y	Y
8 Boehner	Y	Y	?	Y	Y
9 Kaptur	Y	Y	Y	Y	Y
10 Kucinich	Y	Y	Y	Y	Y
11 Fudge	Y	Y	Y	Y	Y
12 Tiberi	?	?	?	Y	Y
13 Sutton	Y	Y	Y	Y	Y
14 LaTourette	Y	Y	Y	Y	Y
15 Kilroy	Y	Y	Y	Y	Y
16 Boccieri	Y	Y	Y	Y	Y
17 Ryan	Y	Y	Y	Y	?
18 Space	?	?	?	?	?
OKLAHOMA					
1 Sullivan	?	?	?	Y	Y
2 Boren	Y	Y	Y	Y	Y
3 Lucas	Y	Y	Y	Y	Y
4 Cole	Y	Y	Y	Y	Y
5 Fallin	?	?	?	?	?
OREGON					
1 Wu	Y	Y	Y	Y	Y
2 Walden	Y	Y	Y	Y	Y
3 Blumenauer	Y	Y	Y	Y	?
4 DeFazio	Y	Y	Y	Y	Y
5 Schrader	Y	?	Y	Y	Y
PENNSYLVANIA					
1 Brady	Y	Y	Y	Y	Y
2 Fattah	Y	Y	Y	Y	Y
3 Dahlkemper	Y	Y	Y	Y	Y
4 Altmire	Y	Y	Y	Y	Y
5 Thompson	Y	Y	Y	Y	Y
6 Gerlach	Y	Y	Y	Y	Y
7 Sestak	Y	Y	Y	Y	Y
8 Murphy, P.	?	Y	Y	Y	Y
9 Shuster	Y	Y	Y	Y	Y
10 Carney	?	?	?	Y	Y
11 Kanjorski	Y	Y	Y	Y	Y
12 Critz	Y	Y	Y	Y	Y
13 Schwartz	Y	Y	Y	Y	Y
14 Doyle	Y	Y	Y	Y	Y
15 Dent	Y	Y	Y	Y	Y
16 Pitts	Y	Y	Y	Y	Y
17 Holden	Y	Y	Y	Y	Y
18 Murphy, T.	Y	Y	Y	Y	Y
19 Platts	?	?	?	?	?
RHODE ISLAND					
1 Kennedy	+	+	+	+	+
2 Langevin	Y	Y	Y	Y	Y
SOUTH CAROLINA					
1 Brown	Y	Y	Y	Y	Y
2 Wilson	Y	Y	Y	Y	Y
3 Barrett	Y	Y	Y	Y	Y
4 Inglis	Y	Y	Y	Y	Y
5 Spratt	Y	Y	Y	Y	Y
6 Clyburn	?	?	?	Y	Y
SOUTH DAKOTA					
AL Herseth Sandlin	Y	Y	Y	Y	Y
TENNESSEE					
1 Roe	Y	Y	Y	Y	Y
2 Duncan	Y	Y	Y	Y	Y
3 Wamp	Y	Y	Y	Y	Y
4 Davis	Y	Y	Y	Y	Y
5 Cooper	Y	Y	Y	Y	Y
6 Gordon	Y	Y	Y	Y	Y
7 Blackburn	Y	Y	Y	Y	Y
8 Tanner	?	?	?	?	?
9 Cohen	Y	Y	Y	Y	Y

	566	567	568	569	570
TEXAS					
1 Gohmert	Y	Y	?	?	Y
2 Poe	Y	Y	Y	Y	Y
3 Johnson, S.	Y	Y	Y	Y	Y
4 Hall	Y	Y	Y	Y	Y
5 Hensarling	Y	Y	Y	Y	Y
6 Barton	Y	Y	Y	Y	Y
7 Culberson	Y	Y	Y	Y	Y
8 Brady	Y	Y	Y	Y	Y
9 Green, A.	Y	Y	Y	Y	Y
10 McCaul	Y	Y	Y	Y	?
11 Conaway	Y	Y	Y	Y	Y
12 Granger	Y	Y	Y	Y	Y
13 Thornberry	Y	Y	Y	Y	Y
14 Paul	Y	Y	Y	Y	Y
15 Hinojosa	Y	Y	Y	Y	Y
16 Reyes	Y	Y	Y	Y	Y
17 Edwards	Y	Y	Y	Y	Y
18 Jackson Lee	Y	Y	Y	Y	Y
19 Neugebauer	Y	Y	Y	Y	Y
20 Gonzalez	Y	Y	Y	Y	Y
21 Smith	Y	Y	Y	Y	Y
22 Olson	Y	Y	Y	Y	Y
23 Rodriguez	Y	Y	Y	Y	Y
24 Marchant	?	?	?	Y	Y
25 Doggett	Y	Y	Y	Y	Y
26 Burgess	Y	Y	Y	Y	Y
27 Ortiz	Y	Y	Y	Y	Y
28 Cuellar	Y	Y	Y	Y	Y
29 Green, G.	Y	Y	Y	Y	Y
30 Johnson, E.	Y	Y	Y	Y	Y
31 Carter	Y	Y	Y	Y	Y
32 Sessions	Y	Y	Y	Y	Y
UTAH					
1 Bishop	Y	Y	Y	Y	Y
2 Matheson	Y	Y	Y	?	?
3 Chaffetz	Y	Y	Y	Y	Y
VERMONT					
AL Welch	Y	Y	Y	Y	Y
VIRGINIA					
1 Wittman	Y	Y	Y	Y	Y
2 Nye	Y	Y	Y	Y	Y
3 Scott	Y	Y	Y	Y	Y
4 Forbes	Y	Y	Y	Y	Y
5 Perriello	?	?	?	Y	Y
6 Goodlatte	Y	Y	Y	Y	Y
7 Cantor	Y	Y	Y	Y	Y
8 Moran	?	?	?	Y	Y
9 Boucher	Y	Y	Y	Y	Y
10 Wolf	?	?	?	Y	Y
11 Connolly	Y	Y	Y	Y	Y
WASHINGTON					
1 Inslee	Y	Y	Y	Y	Y
2 Larsen	Y	Y	Y	Y	Y
3 Baird	Y	Y	Y	Y	Y
4 Hastings	Y	Y	Y	Y	Y
5 McMorris Rodgers	Y	Y	Y	Y	Y
6 Dicks	Y	Y	Y	Y	Y
7 McDermott	?	?	?	?	?
8 Reichert	Y	Y	Y	Y	Y
9 Smith	Y	Y	Y	Y	Y
WEST VIRGINIA					
1 Mollohan	Y	Y	Y	?	?
2 Capito	Y	Y	Y	Y	Y
3 Rahall	Y	?	Y	Y	Y
WISCONSIN					
1 Ryan	Y	Y	Y	Y	Y
2 Baldwin	Y	Y	Y	Y	Y
3 Kind	Y	Y	Y	Y	Y
4 Moore	Y	Y	Y	Y	Y
5 Sensenbrenner	Y	Y	Y	Y	Y
6 Petri	Y	Y	Y	Y	Y
7 Obey	Y	Y	Y	Y	Y
8 Kagen	Y	Y	Y	Y	Y
WYOMING					
AL Lummis	Y	Y	Y	Y	Y
DELEGATES					
Faleomavaega (A.S.)					
Norton (D.C.)					
Bordallo (Guam)					
Sablan (N. Marianas)					
Pierluisi (P.R.)					
Christensen (V.I.)					

IN THE HOUSE | By Vote Number

571. **H Res 1428. Brooklyn Botanic Garden Anniversary/Adoption.** Norton, D-D.C., motion to suspend the rules and adopt the resolution that would recognize the Brooklyn Botanic Garden on its 100th anniversary. Motion agreed to 401-0: D 236-0; R 165-0. A two-thirds majority of those present and voting (268 in this case) is required for adoption under suspension of the rules. Nov. 16, 2010.

572. **H Con Res 332. Adjournment/Adoption.** Adoption of the concurrent resolution that would provide for the adjournment of the House until 2 p.m., Monday, Nov. 29, 2010, and the conditional adjournment of the Senate until noon, Monday, Nov. 29, 2010. Adopted 234-184: D 223-21; R 11-163. Nov. 17, 2010.

573. **HR 3808. Interstate Recognition of Notarizations/Veto Override.** Passage, over President Obama's Oct. 8, 2010, veto, of the bill that would require federal and state courts to recognize legal documents that have been notarized in another state. Rejected 185-235: D 16-230; R 169-5. A two-thirds majority of those present and voting of both chambers (280 in this case for the House) is required to override a veto. A "nay" was a vote in support of the president's position. Nov. 17, 2010.

574. **HR 5758. Sgt. Robert Barrett Post Office/Passage.** Norton, D-D.C., motion to suspend the rules and pass the bill that would designate a post office in Fall River, Mass., as the "Sgt. Robert Barrett Post Office Building." Motion agreed to 417-0: D 245-0; R 172-0. A two-thirds majority of those present and voting (278 in this case) is required for passage under suspension of the rules. Nov. 17, 2010.

575. **H Res 1715. Joe Paterno Tribute/Adoption.** Hirono, D-Hawaii, motion to suspend the rules and adopt the resolution that would congratulate Joe Paterno on his success with the Penn State football program, including 400 wins as head coach. Motion agreed to 417-3: D 245-2; R 172-1. A two-thirds majority of those present and voting (280 in this case) is required for adoption under suspension of the rules. Nov. 17, 2010.

	571	572	573	574	575
ALABAMA					
1 **Bonner**	Y	N	Y	Y	Y
2 Bright	Y	N	Y	Y	Y
3 **Rogers**	Y	N	Y	Y	Y
4 **Aderholt**	Y	N	Y	Y	Y
5 **Griffith**	Y	N	Y	Y	Y
6 **Bachus**	Y	N	Y	Y	Y
7 Davis	?	Y	N	?	?
ALASKA					
AL **Young**	Y	Y	Y	Y	Y
ARIZONA					
1 Kirkpatrick	Y	Y	N	Y	Y
2 **Franks**	Y	N	Y	Y	Y
3 **Shadegg**	Y	N	Y	Y	Y
4 Pastor	Y	Y	N	Y	Y
5 Mitchell	Y	Y	N	Y	Y
6 **Flake**	Y	N	Y	Y	Y
7 Grijalva	Y	Y	N	Y	Y
8 Giffords	Y	N	Y	Y	Y
ARKANSAS					
1 Berry	Y	Y	N	Y	Y
2 Snyder	Y	Y	N	Y	Y
3 **Boozman**	?	?	?	?	?
4 Ross	Y	N	N	Y	Y
CALIFORNIA					
1 Thompson	Y	Y	N	Y	Y
2 **Herger**	Y	N	Y	Y	Y
3 **Lungren**	Y	N	Y	Y	Y
4 **McClintock**	Y	N	Y	Y	Y
5 Matsui	Y	Y	N	Y	Y
6 Woolsey	Y	Y	N	Y	Y
7 Miller, George	Y	Y	N	Y	Y
8 Pelosi					
9 Lee	Y	Y	N	Y	Y
10 Garamendi	Y	Y	N	Y	Y
11 McNerney	Y	Y	N	Y	Y
12 Speier	Y	Y	N	Y	Y
13 Stark	?	Y	N	Y	Y
14 Eshoo	?	Y	N	Y	Y
15 Honda	Y	Y	N	Y	Y
16 Lofgren	Y	Y	N	Y	Y
17 Farr	Y	Y	N	Y	Y
18 Cardoza	?	Y	N	Y	Y
19 **Radanovich**	Y	?	?	?	?
20 Costa	Y	Y	N	Y	Y
21 **Nunes**	Y	N	Y	Y	Y
22 **McCarthy**	?	N	Y	Y	Y
23 Capps	Y	Y	N	Y	Y
24 **Gallegly**	Y	?	?	?	?
25 **McKeon**	?	N	Y	Y	Y
26 **Dreier**	Y	N	Y	Y	Y
27 Sherman	Y	Y	N	Y	Y
28 Berman	Y	Y	N	Y	Y
29 Schiff	Y	Y	N	Y	Y
30 Waxman	Y	?	?	Y	Y
31 Becerra	Y	Y	N	Y	Y
32 Chu	Y	Y	N	Y	Y
33 Watson	Y	Y	N	Y	Y
34 Roybal-Allard	Y	Y	N	Y	Y
35 Waters	Y	Y	N	Y	Y
36 Harman	Y	Y	N	Y	Y
37 Richardson	Y	Y	N	Y	Y
38 Napolitano	Y	Y	N	Y	Y
39 Sánchez, Linda	Y	Y	N	Y	Y
40 **Royce**	Y	N	Y	Y	Y
41 **Lewis**	Y	N	Y	Y	Y
42 **Miller, Gary**	Y	N	Y	Y	Y
43 Baca	Y	Y	N	Y	Y
44 **Calvert**	Y	N	Y	Y	Y
45 **Bono Mack**	Y	N	Y	Y	Y
46 **Rohrabacher**	Y	N	Y	Y	Y
47 Sanchez, Loretta	Y	Y	N	Y	Y
48 **Campbell**	Y	N	Y	Y	Y
49 **Issa**	Y	N	Y	Y	Y
50 **Bilbray**	Y	N	Y	Y	Y
51 Filner	Y	Y	N	Y	Y
52 **Hunter**	Y	N	Y	Y	Y
53 Davis	Y	Y	N	Y	Y

	571	572	573	574	575
COLORADO					
1 DeGette	Y	Y	N	Y	Y
2 Polis	Y	Y	N	Y	Y
3 Salazar	Y	Y	N	Y	Y
4 Markey	Y	Y	N	Y	Y
5 **Lamborn**	Y	N	Y	Y	Y
6 **Coffman**	Y	N	Y	Y	Y
7 Perlmutter	Y	Y	N	Y	Y
CONNECTICUT					
1 Larson	Y	+	N	Y	Y
2 Courtney	Y	Y	N	Y	Y
3 DeLauro	Y	Y	N	Y	Y
4 Himes	Y	Y	N	Y	Y
5 Murphy	Y	Y	N	Y	Y
DELAWARE					
AL **Castle**	Y	N	Y	Y	Y
FLORIDA					
1 **Miller**	Y	N	Y	Y	Y
2 Boyd	Y	Y	N	Y	Y
3 Brown	Y	Y	N	Y	Y
4 **Crenshaw**	Y	N	Y	Y	Y
5 **Brown-Waite**	Y	N	Y	Y	Y
6 **Stearns**	?	N	Y	Y	Y
7 **Mica**	Y	N	Y	Y	Y
8 Grayson	Y	Y	N	Y	Y
9 **Bilirakis**	Y	N	Y	Y	Y
10 **Young**	Y	N	Y	Y	Y
11 Castor	Y	Y	N	Y	Y
12 **Putnam**	+	N	Y	Y	Y
13 **Buchanan**	Y	N	Y	Y	Y
14 **Mack**	Y	N	Y	Y	Y
15 **Posey**	Y	N	Y	Y	Y
16 **Rooney**	Y	N	Y	Y	Y
17 **Meek**	?	?	?	Y	Y
18 **Ros-Lehtinen**	Y	N	Y	Y	Y
19 Deutch	Y	Y	N	Y	Y
20 Wasserman Schultz	Y	Y	N	Y	Y
21 **Diaz-Balart, L.**	Y	N	Y	Y	Y
22 Klein	Y	?	?	?	?
23 Hastings	Y	Y	N	Y	Y
24 Kosmas	Y	Y	N	Y	Y
25 **Diaz-Balart, M.**	Y	N	Y	Y	Y
GEORGIA					
1 **Kingston**	Y	N	Y	Y	Y
2 Bishop	Y	Y	N	Y	Y
3 **Westmoreland**	Y	N	Y	Y	Y
4 Johnson	Y	Y	N	Y	Y
5 Lewis	Y	Y	N	Y	Y
6 **Price**	Y	N	Y	Y	Y
7 **Linder**	?	N	Y	Y	Y
8 Marshall	Y	Y	?	Y	Y
9 **Graves**	Y	N	Y	Y	Y
10 **Broun**	Y	N	Y	Y	Y
11 **Gingrey**	Y	N	Y	Y	Y
12 Barrow	Y	Y	N	Y	Y
13 Scott	Y	Y	N	Y	Y
HAWAII					
1 **Djou**	Y	Y	N	Y	Y
2 Hirono	Y	Y	N	Y	Y
IDAHO					
1 Minnick	Y	Y	Y	?	?
2 **Simpson**	Y	N	Y	?	Y
ILLINOIS					
1 Rush	Y	Y	N	Y	Y
2 Jackson	Y	Y	N	Y	Y
3 Lipinski	Y	Y	N	Y	Y
4 Gutierrez	Y	Y	N	Y	Y
5 Quigley	Y	Y	N	Y	Y
6 **Roskam**	Y	N	Y	Y	Y
7 Davis	Y	Y	N	Y	Y
8 Bean	?	Y	Y	Y	Y
9 Schakowsky	Y	Y	N	Y	Y
10 **Kirk**	?	?	?	?	?
11 Halvorson	Y	?	?	?	?
12 Costello	Y	Y	N	Y	Y
13 **Biggert**	Y	N	Y	Y	Y
14 Foster	Y	Y	N	Y	Y
15 **Johnson**	Y	N	Y	Y	Y

KEY **Republicans** Democrats

Y Voted for (yea)	X Paired against	C Voted "present" to avoid possible conflict of interest
# Paired for	− Announced against	
+ Announced for	P Voted "present"	? Did not vote or otherwise make a position known
N Voted against (nay)		

* Rep. Marlin Stutzman, R-Ind., was sworn in Nov. 16 to fill the vacancy created by the May 21 resignation of Republican Mark Souder. The first vote for which Stutzman was eligible was vote 571.

	571	572	573	574	575
16 Manzullo	Y	Y	Y	Y	Y
17 Hare	?	Y	N	Y	Y
18 Schock	?	N	Y	Y	Y
19 Shimkus	Y	N	Y	Y	Y
INDIANA					
1 Visclosky	Y	Y	N	Y	Y
2 Donnelly	Y	N	Y	Y	Y
3 Stutzman*	Y	N	Y	Y	Y
4 Buyer	Y	N	Y	Y	Y
5 Burton	Y	N	Y	Y	Y
6 Pence	Y	N	Y	Y	Y
7 Carson	Y	Y	N	Y	Y
8 Ellsworth	Y	N	N	Y	Y
9 Hill	Y	Y	N	Y	Y
IOWA					
1 Braley	Y	+	Y	Y	Y
2 Loebsack	Y	Y	N	Y	Y
3 Boswell	Y	Y	N	Y	Y
4 Latham	Y	N	Y	Y	Y
5 King	Y	N	Y	Y	Y
KANSAS					
1 Moran	Y	N	Y	Y	Y
2 Jenkins	Y	N	Y	Y	Y
3 Moore	?	Y	N	Y	Y
4 Tiahrt	Y	N	Y	Y	Y
KENTUCKY					
1 Whitfield	Y	N	Y	Y	Y
2 Guthrie	Y	N	Y	Y	Y
3 Yarmuth	Y	Y	N	Y	Y
4 Davis	Y	N	Y	Y	Y
5 Rogers	Y	N	Y	Y	Y
6 Chandler	Y	Y	N	Y	Y
LOUISIANA					
1 Scalise	Y	N	Y	Y	Y
2 Cao	Y	Y	N	Y	Y
3 Melancon	?	Y	N	Y	Y
4 Fleming	Y	N	Y	Y	Y
5 Alexander	Y	N	Y	Y	Y
6 Cassidy	Y	N	Y	Y	Y
7 Boustany	Y	N	Y	Y	Y
MAINE					
1 Pingree	Y	?	?	?	?
2 Michaud	Y	N	N	Y	Y
MARYLAND					
1 Kratovil	Y	N	N	Y	Y
2 Ruppersberger	Y	Y	N	Y	Y
3 Sarbanes	Y	Y	N	Y	Y
4 Edwards	Y	Y	N	Y	Y
5 Hoyer	Y	Y	N	Y	Y
6 Bartlett	Y	N	Y	Y	Y
7 Cummings	Y	Y	N	Y	Y
8 Van Hollen	Y	Y	N	Y	Y
MASSACHUSETTS					
1 Olver	Y	Y	N	Y	Y
2 Neal	Y	Y	N	Y	Y
3 McGovern	Y	Y	N	Y	Y
4 Frank	Y	Y	N	Y	Y
5 Tsongas	Y	Y	N	Y	Y
6 Tierney	Y	Y	N	Y	Y
7 Markey	Y	Y	N	Y	Y
8 Capuano	Y	Y	N	Y	Y
9 Lynch	Y	Y	N	Y	Y
10 Delahunt	Y	Y	N	Y	Y
MICHIGAN					
1 Stupak	Y	Y	N	Y	Y
2 Hoekstra	Y	N	Y	Y	Y
3 Ehlers	Y	Y	Y	Y	Y
4 Camp	Y	N	Y	Y	Y
5 Kildee	Y	Y	N	Y	Y
6 Upton	Y	N	Y	Y	Y
7 Schauer	Y	Y	N	Y	Y
8 Rogers	Y	N	Y	Y	Y
9 Peters	Y	N	N	Y	Y
10 Miller	Y	N	Y	Y	Y
11 McCotter	Y	Y	N	Y	Y
12 Levin	Y	Y	N	Y	Y
13 Kilpatrick	Y	Y	N	Y	Y
14 Conyers	Y	Y	N	Y	Y
15 Dingell	Y	Y	N	Y	Y
MINNESOTA					
1 Walz	Y	Y	N	Y	Y
2 Kline	Y	N	Y	Y	Y
3 Paulsen	Y	N	Y	Y	Y
4 McCollum	Y	Y	N	Y	Y

	571	572	573	574	575
5 Ellison	Y	Y	Y	Y	Y
6 Bachmann	Y	N	Y	Y	Y
7 Peterson	Y	Y	Y	Y	Y
8 Oberstar	?	Y	N	Y	Y
MISSISSIPPI					
1 Childers	Y	N	N	Y	Y
2 Thompson	Y	Y	N	Y	Y
3 Harper	Y	N	Y	Y	Y
4 Taylor	Y	N	Y	Y	Y
MISSOURI					
1 Clay	Y	Y	N	Y	Y
2 Akin	Y	N	Y	Y	Y
3 Carnahan	Y	Y	N	Y	Y
4 Skelton	Y	Y	N	Y	Y
5 Cleaver	Y	Y	N	Y	Y
6 Graves	Y	N	Y	Y	Y
7 Blunt	?	N	Y	?	?
8 Emerson	Y	N	Y	Y	Y
9 Luetkemeyer	Y	N	Y	Y	Y
MONTANA					
AL Rehberg	Y	N	Y	Y	Y
NEBRASKA					
1 Fortenberry	Y	N	Y	Y	Y
2 Terry	Y	Y	Y	Y	Y
3 Smith	Y	N	Y	Y	Y
NEVADA					
1 Berkley	Y	Y	N	Y	Y
2 Heller	Y	N	N	Y	Y
3 Titus	Y	Y	N	Y	Y
NEW HAMPSHIRE					
1 Shea-Porter	Y	Y	N	Y	Y
2 Hodes	Y	Y	N	Y	Y
NEW JERSEY					
1 Andrews	Y	Y	N	Y	Y
2 LoBiondo	Y	N	Y	Y	Y
3 Adler	Y	N	N	Y	Y
4 Smith	Y	N	Y	Y	Y
5 Garrett	Y	N	Y	Y	Y
6 Pallone	Y	Y	N	Y	Y
7 Lance	Y	N	Y	Y	Y
8 Pascrell	Y	Y	N	Y	Y
9 Rothman	Y	Y	N	Y	Y
10 Payne	Y	Y	N	Y	Y
11 Frelinghuysen	Y	N	Y	Y	Y
12 Holt	Y	Y	N	Y	Y
13 Sires	Y	Y	N	Y	Y
NEW MEXICO					
1 Heinrich	Y	Y	N	Y	Y
2 Teague	Y	Y	N	Y	Y
3 Luján	Y	Y	N	Y	Y
NEW YORK					
1 Bishop	Y	N	N	Y	Y
2 Israel	Y	Y	N	Y	Y
3 King	Y	N	Y	Y	Y
4 McCarthy	Y	Y	N	Y	Y
5 Ackerman	Y	Y	N	Y	Y
6 Meeks	Y	Y	N	Y	Y
7 Crowley	Y	Y	N	Y	Y
8 Nadler	Y	Y	N	Y	Y
9 Weiner	Y	Y	N	Y	Y
10 Towns	Y	Y	N	Y	Y
11 Clarke	Y	Y	N	Y	Y
12 Velázquez	Y	Y	N	?	Y
13 McMahon	Y	Y	Y	Y	Y
14 Maloney	Y	Y	N	Y	Y
15 Rangel	Y	Y	N	Y	Y
16 Serrano	Y	Y	N	Y	Y
17 Engel	Y	Y	N	Y	Y
18 Lowey	Y	Y	N	Y	Y
19 Hall	Y	Y	N	Y	Y
20 Murphy	Y	N	Y	Y	Y
21 Tonko	Y	Y	N	Y	Y
22 Hinchey	Y	Y	N	Y	Y
23 Owens	Y	N	Y	Y	Y
24 Arcuri	Y	Y	N	Y	Y
25 Maffei	Y	Y	N	Y	Y
26 Lee	Y	N	Y	Y	Y
27 Higgins	Y	Y	N	Y	Y
28 Slaughter	Y	Y	N	Y	N
29 Vacant					
NORTH CAROLINA					
1 Butterfield	Y	Y	N	Y	Y
2 Etheridge	Y	Y	N	Y	Y
3 Jones	Y	Y	N	Y	Y
4 Price	Y	Y	N	Y	Y

	571	572	573	574	575
5 Foxx	Y	N	Y	Y	Y
6 Coble	Y	N	Y	Y	Y
7 McIntyre	Y	Y	N	Y	Y
8 Kissell	Y	Y	N	Y	Y
9 Myrick	Y	N	Y	Y	Y
10 McHenry	Y	N	Y	Y	Y
11 Shuler	Y	Y	Y	Y	Y
12 Watt	Y	Y	N	Y	Y
13 Miller	Y	Y	N	Y	Y
NORTH DAKOTA					
AL Pomeroy	Y	Y	N	Y	Y
OHIO					
1 Driehaus	Y	Y	N	Y	Y
2 Schmidt	Y	N	Y	Y	Y
3 Turner	Y	N	Y	Y	Y
4 Jordan	Y	N	Y	Y	Y
5 Latta	Y	N	Y	Y	Y
6 Wilson	Y	Y	N	Y	Y
7 Austria	Y	N	Y	Y	Y
8 Boehner	Y	N	Y	Y	Y
9 Kaptur	Y	Y	N	Y	Y
10 Kucinich	Y	Y	N	Y	Y
11 Fudge	Y	Y	N	Y	Y
12 Tiberi	Y	N	Y	Y	Y
13 Sutton	Y	Y	N	Y	Y
14 LaTourette	Y	N	Y	Y	Y
15 Kilroy	Y	Y	N	Y	Y
16 Boccieri	Y	Y	N	Y	Y
17 Ryan	Y	Y	N	Y	Y
18 Space	?	Y	Y	Y	Y
OKLAHOMA					
1 Sullivan	Y	N	Y	Y	Y
2 Boren	Y	N	Y	Y	Y
3 Lucas	Y	N	Y	Y	Y
4 Cole	Y	N	Y	Y	Y
5 Fallin	?	?	?	?	?
OREGON					
1 Wu	Y	Y	Y	Y	Y
2 Walden	Y	N	Y	Y	Y
3 Blumenauer	Y	Y	N	Y	Y
4 DeFazio	Y	Y	N	Y	N
5 Schrader	?	Y	N	Y	Y
PENNSYLVANIA					
1 Brady	Y	Y	N	Y	Y
2 Fattah	Y	Y	N	Y	Y
3 Dahlkemper	Y	Y	N	Y	Y
4 Altmire	Y	N	Y	Y	Y
5 Thompson	Y	N	Y	Y	Y
6 Gerlach	Y	N	Y	Y	Y
7 Sestak	Y	N	N	Y	Y
8 Murphy, P.	Y	Y	N	Y	Y
9 Shuster	Y	N	Y	Y	Y
10 Carney	Y	Y	N	Y	Y
11 Kanjorski	Y	Y	N	Y	Y
12 Critz	Y	Y	N	Y	Y
13 Schwartz	Y	Y	N	Y	Y
14 Doyle	Y	Y	N	Y	Y
15 Dent	Y	N	Y	Y	Y
16 Pitts	Y	N	Y	Y	Y
17 Holden	Y	Y	N	Y	Y
18 Murphy, T.	Y	N	Y	Y	Y
19 Platts	?	N	Y	Y	Y
RHODE ISLAND					
1 Kennedy	+	Y	N	?	?
2 Langevin	Y	Y	N	Y	Y
SOUTH CAROLINA					
1 Brown	Y	N	Y	Y	Y
2 Wilson	Y	N	Y	Y	Y
3 Barrett	Y	N	Y	Y	Y
4 Inglis	Y	N	Y	Y	Y
5 Spratt	Y	Y	N	Y	Y
6 Clyburn	Y	Y	N	Y	Y
SOUTH DAKOTA					
AL Herseth Sandlin	Y	Y	N	Y	Y
TENNESSEE					
1 Roe	Y	N	Y	Y	Y
2 Duncan	Y	N	Y	Y	Y
3 Wamp	Y	N	Y	Y	Y
4 Davis	Y	Y	N	Y	Y
5 Cooper	Y	Y	N	Y	Y
6 Gordon	Y	?	?	?	?
7 Blackburn	Y	N	Y	Y	Y
8 Tanner	?	?	?	?	?
9 Cohen	Y	Y	N	Y	Y

	571	572	573	574	575
TEXAS					
1 Gohmert	Y	Y	Y	Y	Y
2 Poe	Y	N	Y	Y	Y
3 Johnson, S.	Y	N	Y	Y	Y
4 Hall	Y	N	Y	Y	Y
5 Hensarling	Y	N	Y	Y	Y
6 Barton	Y	N	Y	Y	Y
7 Culberson	Y	N	Y	Y	Y
8 Brady	Y	N	Y	Y	Y
9 Green, A.	Y	Y	N	Y	Y
10 McCaul	Y	N	Y	Y	Y
11 Conaway	Y	N	Y	Y	Y
12 Granger	Y	N	Y	Y	Y
13 Thornberry	Y	N	Y	Y	Y
14 Paul	Y	Y	N	Y	Y
15 Hinojosa	Y	Y	N	Y	Y
16 Reyes	Y	?	N	Y	Y
17 Edwards	?	Y	N	Y	Y
18 Jackson Lee	Y	Y	N	Y	Y
19 Neugebauer	Y	N	Y	Y	Y
20 Gonzalez	Y	Y	N	Y	Y
21 Smith	Y	N	Y	Y	Y
22 Olson	Y	Y	Y	Y	Y
23 Rodriguez	Y	Y	N	Y	Y
24 Marchant	Y	N	Y	Y	Y
25 Doggett	Y	Y	N	Y	Y
26 Burgess	Y	N	Y	Y	Y
27 Ortiz	Y	Y	N	Y	Y
28 Cuellar	Y	Y	N	Y	Y
29 Green, G.	Y	Y	N	Y	Y
30 Johnson, E.	Y	Y	N	Y	Y
31 Carter	Y	N	Y	Y	Y
32 Sessions	Y	N	Y	Y	Y
UTAH					
1 Bishop	Y	N	Y	Y	Y
2 Matheson	?	N	N	Y	Y
3 Chaffetz	P	N	Y	Y	N
VERMONT					
AL Welch	Y	Y	N	Y	Y
VIRGINIA					
1 Wittman	Y	N	Y	Y	Y
2 Nye	Y	N	N	Y	Y
3 Scott	Y	Y	N	Y	Y
4 Forbes	Y	N	Y	Y	Y
5 Perriello	Y	Y	N	Y	Y
6 Goodlatte	Y	Y	Y	Y	Y
7 Cantor	Y	N	Y	Y	Y
8 Moran	Y	Y	N	Y	Y
9 Boucher	Y	Y	N	Y	Y
10 Wolf	Y	N	Y	Y	Y
11 Connolly	Y	N	N	Y	Y
WASHINGTON					
1 Inslee	Y	Y	N	Y	Y
2 Larsen	Y	Y	N	Y	Y
3 Baird	Y	Y	N	Y	Y
4 Hastings	Y	N	Y	Y	Y
5 McMorris Rodgers	?	N	Y	Y	Y
6 Dicks	Y	Y	N	Y	Y
7 McDermott	?	Y	N	Y	Y
8 Reichert	Y	N	Y	Y	Y
9 Smith	Y	Y	N	Y	Y
WEST VIRGINIA					
1 Mollohan	?	Y	N	Y	Y
2 Capito	Y	N	Y	Y	Y
3 Rahall	Y	Y	N	Y	Y
WISCONSIN					
1 Ryan	Y	N	Y	Y	Y
2 Baldwin	Y	Y	N	Y	Y
3 Kind	Y	Y	N	Y	Y
4 Moore	Y	Y	N	Y	Y
5 Sensenbrenner	Y	N	Y	Y	Y
6 Petri	Y	N	Y	Y	Y
7 Obey	Y	Y	N	Y	Y
8 Kagen	Y	Y	N	Y	Y
WYOMING					
AL Lummis	?	N	Y	Y	Y
DELEGATES					
Faleomavaega (A.S.)					
Norton (D.C.)					
Bordallo (Guam)					
Sablan (N. Marianas)					
Pierluisi (P.R.)					
Christensen (V.I.)					

IN THE HOUSE | By Vote Number

576. HR 1722. Telework for Federal Employees/Previous Question. Arcuri, D-N.Y., motion to order the previous question (thus ending debate and possibility of amendment) on adoption of the rule (H Res 1721) to provide for House floor consideration of the Senate amendment to the bill that would require executive agencies to allow employees to work remotely as much as possible without diminishing agency operations or performance. Motion agreed to 239-171: D 239-3; R 0-168. Nov. 18, 2010.

577. HR 1722. Telework for Federal Employees/Rule. Adoption of the rule (H Res 1721) that would provide for House floor consideration of the Senate amendment to the bill that would require executive agencies to allow employees to work remotely as much as possible without diminishing agency operations or performance. The rule also would allow for consideration of measures under suspension of the rules at any time through the legislative day of Nov. 19, 2010. Adopted 235-171: D 234-4; R 1-167. Nov. 18, 2010.

578. HR 1722. Telework for Federal Employees/Motion to Concur. Lynch, D-Mass., motion to concur in the Senate amendment to the bill that would require the head of each executive agency to establish and implement a policy that would allow employees to work remotely as much as possible without diminishing agency operation or performance and would require each agency to designate a telework managing officer. Motion agreed to, thus clearing the bill for the president, 254-152: D 240-3; R 14-149. Nov. 18, 2010.

579. HR 6419. Unemployment Benefits Extension/Passage. Levin, D-Mich., motion to suspend the rules and pass the bill that would extend eligibility for expanded unemployment benefits through Feb. 28, 2011. It also would extend federal funding to states for the costs of additional unemployment benefits through March 1, 2011. Motion rejected 258-154: D 237-11; R 21-143. A two-thirds majority of those present and voting (275 in this case) is required for passage under suspension of the rules. A "yea" was a vote in support of the president's position. Nov. 18, 2010.

580. S 3774. Disaster Relief/Passage. McDermott, D-Wash., motion to suspend the rules and pass the bill that would extend through Sept. 30, 2011, the deadline for states to spend supplemental disaster relief funds provided through the Social Services Block Grant program under the 2008 supplemental appropriations law. Motion agreed to 366-40: D 239-8; R 127-32. A two-thirds majority of those present and voting (271 in this case) is required for passage under suspension of the rules. Nov. 18, 2010.

	576	577	578	579	580
ALABAMA					
1 **Bonner**	N	N	N	N	Y
2 Bright	?	?	N	Y	N
3 **Rogers**	N	N	N	N	?
4 **Aderholt**	N	N	N	N	Y
5 **Griffith**	N	N	N	N	?
6 **Bachus**	N	N	N	N	Y
7 Davis	Y	Y	Y	Y	Y
ALASKA					
AL **Young**	N	N	N	N	Y
ARIZONA					
1 Kirkpatrick	Y	Y	Y	Y	Y
2 **Franks**	N	N	N	N	N
3 **Shadegg**	N	N	N	N	N
4 Pastor	Y	Y	Y	Y	Y
5 Mitchell	Y	Y	Y	Y	Y
6 **Flake**	N	N	N	N	N
7 Grijalva	Y	Y	Y	Y	Y
8 Giffords	N	N	Y	Y	Y
ARKANSAS					
1 Berry	Y	Y	N	N	Y
2 Snyder	Y	Y	Y	Y	Y
3 **Boozman**	?	?	?	?	?
4 Ross	Y	Y	Y	Y	Y
CALIFORNIA					
1 Thompson	Y	Y	Y	Y	Y
2 **Herger**	N	N	N	N	N
3 **Lungren**	N	N	N	N	N
4 **McClintock**	N	N	N	N	N
5 Matsui	Y	Y	Y	Y	Y
6 Woolsey	Y	Y	Y	Y	Y
7 Miller, George	Y	Y	Y	Y	Y
8 Pelosi			Y		
9 Lee	Y	Y	Y	Y	Y
10 Garamendi	Y	Y	?	Y	Y
11 McNerney	Y	?	Y	Y	Y
12 Speier	Y	Y	Y	Y	Y
13 Stark	Y	Y	Y	Y	Y
14 Eshoo	Y	Y	Y	Y	Y
15 Honda	Y	Y	Y	Y	Y
16 Lofgren	Y	Y	Y	Y	Y
17 Farr	Y	Y	Y	Y	Y
18 Cardoza	Y	Y	Y	Y	Y
19 **Radanovich**	?	?	?	?	?
20 Costa	Y	Y	Y	Y	Y
21 **Nunes**	N	N	N	N	Y
22 **McCarthy**	N	N	N	N	Y
23 Capps	Y	Y	Y	Y	Y
24 **Gallegly**	?	?	?	?	?
25 **McKeon**	N	N	N	N	Y
26 **Dreier**	N	N	N	N	Y
27 Sherman	Y	Y	Y	Y	Y
28 Berman	Y	Y	Y	Y	Y
29 Schiff	Y	Y	Y	Y	Y
30 Waxman	Y	Y	Y	Y	Y
31 Becerra	Y	Y	Y	Y	Y
32 Chu	Y	Y	Y	Y	Y
33 Watson	Y	Y	?	Y	Y
34 Roybal-Allard	Y	Y	Y	Y	Y
35 Waters	?	?	Y	Y	Y
36 Harman	Y	Y	Y	Y	Y
37 Richardson	Y	Y	Y	Y	Y
38 Napolitano	Y	Y	Y	Y	Y
39 Sánchez, Linda	Y	Y	Y	Y	+
40 **Royce**	N	N	N	N	N
41 **Lewis**	N	N	N	N	Y
42 **Miller, Gary**	N	N	N	N	?
43 Baca	Y	Y	Y	Y	Y
44 **Calvert**	N	N	N	N	Y
45 **Bono Mack**	N	N	N	N	Y
46 **Rohrabacher**	N	N	N	N	Y
47 Sanchez, Loretta	Y	Y	Y	Y	Y
48 **Campbell**	N	N	N	N	N
49 **Issa**	N	N	N	N	N
50 **Bilbray**	N	N	Y	Y	Y
51 Filner	Y	Y	Y	Y	Y
52 **Hunter**	N	N	N	N	N
53 Davis	Y	Y	Y	Y	Y

	576	577	578	579	580
COLORADO					
1 DeGette	Y	Y	Y	Y	Y
2 Polis	Y	Y	Y	Y	Y
3 Salazar	Y	Y	Y	Y	Y
4 Markey	Y	Y	Y	Y	Y
5 **Lamborn**	N	N	N	N	N
6 **Coffman**	N	N	N	N	N
7 Perlmutter	Y	?	Y	Y	Y
CONNECTICUT					
1 Larson	Y	Y	Y	Y	Y
2 Courtney	Y	Y	Y	Y	Y
3 DeLauro	Y	Y	Y	Y	Y
4 Himes	Y	Y	Y	Y	Y
5 Murphy	Y	Y	Y	Y	Y
DELAWARE					
AL **Castle**	N	N	N	Y	Y
FLORIDA					
1 **Miller**	N	N	N	N	N
2 Boyd	Y	Y	Y	N	Y
3 Brown	Y	Y	+	+	+
4 **Crenshaw**	N	N	N	N	Y
5 **Brown-Waite**	?	?	?	?	?
6 **Stearns**	N	N	N	N	N
7 **Mica**	N	N	N	N	N
8 Grayson	Y	Y	Y	Y	Y
9 **Bilirakis**	N	N	–	N	Y
10 **Young**	N	N	N	N	Y
11 Castor	Y	Y	Y	Y	Y
12 **Putnam**	N	N	N	N	?
13 **Buchanan**	N	N	Y	N	Y
14 **Mack**	N	N	N	N	N
15 **Posey**	N	N	N	Y	Y
16 **Rooney**	N	N	N	N	Y
17 Meek	Y	Y	Y	Y	Y
18 **Ros-Lehtinen**	N	N	N	Y	?
19 Deutch	Y	Y	Y	Y	Y
20 Wasserman Schultz	Y	Y	Y	Y	Y
21 **Diaz-Balart, L.**	N	N	N	Y	Y
22 Klein	Y	Y	Y	Y	Y
23 Hastings	Y	Y	Y	Y	Y
24 Kosmas	Y	Y	Y	Y	Y
25 **Diaz-Balart, M.**	N	N	N	Y	Y
GEORGIA					
1 **Kingston**	N	N	N	N	N
2 Bishop	Y	Y	Y	Y	Y
3 **Westmoreland**	N	N	?	?	N
4 Johnson	Y	Y	Y	Y	Y
5 Lewis	Y	Y	Y	Y	Y
6 **Price**	N	N	N	N	N
7 **Linder**	N	N	?	?	?
8 Marshall	Y	Y	Y	Y	Y
9 **Graves**	N	N	N	N	N
10 **Broun**	N	N	?	N	N
11 **Gingrey**	N	N	N	N	N
12 Barrow	Y	Y	Y	Y	Y
13 Scott	Y	Y	Y	Y	Y
HAWAII					
1 **Djou**	N	Y	Y	N	Y
2 Hirono	Y	Y	Y	Y	Y
IDAHO					
1 Minnick	Y	Y	Y	N	Y
2 **Simpson**	N	N	N	N	N
ILLINOIS					
1 Rush	Y	Y	Y	Y	Y
2 Jackson	Y	Y	Y	Y	Y
3 Lipinski	Y	Y	Y	Y	Y
4 Gutierrez	Y	Y	Y	Y	Y
5 Quigley	Y	Y	Y	Y	Y
6 **Roskam**	N	N	N	N	Y
7 Davis	Y	Y	Y	Y	Y
8 Bean	Y	Y	Y	Y	N
9 Schakowsky	Y	Y	Y	Y	Y
10 **Kirk**	?	?	?	?	?
11 Halvorson	Y	Y	Y	Y	Y
12 Costello	Y	Y	Y	Y	Y
13 **Biggert**	N	N	N	N	Y
14 Foster	Y	Y	Y	Y	Y
15 **Johnson**	N	N	N	Y	Y

KEY **Republicans**   Democrats

Y Voted for (yea)	X Paired against	C Voted "present" to avoid possible conflict of interest
# Paired for	– Announced against	
+ Announced for	P Voted "present"	? Did not vote or otherwise make a position known
N Voted against (nay)		

* Rep. Tom Reed, R-N.Y., was sworn in Nov. 18 to fill the vacancy created by the March 8 resignation of Democrat Eric Massa. The first vote for which Reed was eligible was vote 580.

	576	577	578	579	580
16 Manzullo	N	N	N	Y	Y
17 Hare	Y	Y	Y	Y	Y
18 **Schock**	N	N	N	N	Y
19 **Shimkus**	N	N	N	N	Y
INDIANA					
1 Visclosky	Y	Y	Y	Y	Y
2 Donnelly	Y	Y	Y	Y	Y
3 **Stutzman**	N	N	N	N	N
4 **Buyer**	N	N	N	N	?
5 **Burton**	N	N	N	N	Y
6 **Pence**	N	N	N	N	Y
7 Carson	Y	Y	Y	Y	Y
8 Ellsworth	Y	Y	Y	Y	Y
9 Hill	?	?	Y	N	Y
IOWA					
1 Braley	Y	Y	Y	Y	Y
2 Loebsack	Y	Y	Y	Y	Y
3 Boswell	Y	Y	Y	Y	Y
4 Latham	N	N	N	N	Y
5 **King**	N	N	N	N	Y
KANSAS					
1 **Moran**	N	N	?	?	?
2 **Jenkins**	N	N	N	N	N
3 Moore	Y	Y	Y	Y	Y
4 **Tiahrt**	?	?	N	N	N
KENTUCKY					
1 **Whitfield**	N	N	N	N	Y
2 **Guthrie**	N	N	N	N	Y
3 Yarmuth	Y	Y	Y	Y	Y
4 **Davis**	–	–	–	–	+
5 **Rogers**	N	N	N	N	Y
6 Chandler	Y	Y	Y	Y	Y
LOUISIANA					
1 **Scalise**	N	N	N	N	Y
2 **Cao**	N	N	Y	N	Y
3 Melancon	Y	Y	Y	Y	Y
4 **Fleming**	N	N	N	N	Y
5 **Alexander**	N	N	N	N	Y
6 **Cassidy**	N	N	N	N	Y
7 **Boustany**	N	N	N	N	Y
MAINE					
1 Pingree	Y	Y	Y	Y	?
2 Michaud	Y	Y	Y	Y	Y
MARYLAND					
1 Kratovil	Y	Y	Y	Y	Y
2 Ruppersberger	Y	Y	Y	Y	Y
3 Sarbanes	Y	Y	Y	Y	Y
4 Edwards	Y	Y	Y	Y	Y
5 Hoyer	?	?	Y	Y	Y
6 **Bartlett**	N	N	N	N	Y
7 Cummings	Y	Y	Y	Y	Y
8 Van Hollen	?	?	Y	Y	Y
MASSACHUSETTS					
1 Olver	Y	Y	Y	Y	Y
2 Neal	Y	Y	Y	Y	Y
3 McGovern	Y	Y	Y	Y	Y
4 Frank	Y	Y	Y	Y	Y
5 Tsongas	Y	Y	Y	Y	Y
6 Tierney	Y	Y	Y	Y	Y
7 Markey	Y	?	Y	Y	Y
8 Capuano	Y	Y	Y	Y	Y
9 Lynch	Y	Y	Y	?	Y
10 Dolahunt	?	?	?	?	?
MICHIGAN					
1 Stupak	Y	Y	Y	Y	Y
2 **Hoekstra**	N	N	N	Y	Y
3 **Ehlers**	N	N	N	Y	Y
4 **Camp**	N	N	N	N	Y
5 Kildee	Y	Y	Y	Y	Y
6 **Upton**	N	N	N	N	Y
7 Schauer	Y	Y	Y	Y	Y
8 **Rogers**	N	N	N	N	Y
9 Peters	Y	Y	Y	Y	Y
10 **Miller**	N	N	N	N	Y
11 **McCotter**	N	N	Y	N	Y
12 Levin	Y	Y	Y	Y	Y
13 Kilpatrick	Y	Y	Y	Y	Y
14 Conyers	Y	Y	Y	Y	Y
15 Dingell	Y	Y	Y	Y	Y
MINNESOTA					
1 Walz	Y	Y	Y	Y	Y
2 **Kline**	N	N	N	N	Y
3 **Paulsen**	N	N	N	N	Y
4 McCollum	Y	Y	Y	Y	Y

	576	577	578	579	580
5 Ellison	Y	Y	Y	Y	Y
6 **Bachmann**	N	N	N	N	Y
7 Peterson	Y	Y	Y	N	N
8 Oberstar	Y	Y	?	Y	Y
MISSISSIPPI					
1 Childers	Y	Y	Y	Y	Y
2 Thompson	Y	Y	Y	Y	Y
3 **Harper**	N	N	N	N	N
4 Taylor	N	N	Y	N	Y
MISSOURI					
1 Clay	?	?	Y	Y	Y
2 Akin	N	N	N	N	Y
3 Carnahan	Y	Y	Y	Y	Y
4 Skelton	Y	Y	Y	Y	Y
5 Cleaver	Y	Y	Y	Y	Y
6 **Graves**	N	N	N	N	Y
7 **Blunt**	N	N	N	N	Y
8 **Emerson**	N	N	N	N	Y
9 **Luetkemeyer**	N	N	N	N	Y
MONTANA					
AL **Rehberg**	N	N	N	N	Y
NEBRASKA					
1 **Fortenberry**	N	N	N	N	Y
2 **Terry**	N	N	N	?	?
3 **Smith**	N	N	N	N	Y
NEVADA					
1 Berkley	Y	Y	Y	Y	Y
2 **Heller**	N	N	N	N	Y
3 Titus	Y	Y	Y	Y	Y
NEW HAMPSHIRE					
1 Shea-Porter	Y	Y	Y	Y	Y
2 Hodes	Y	Y	Y	Y	Y
NEW JERSEY					
1 Andrews	Y	Y	Y	Y	Y
2 **LoBiondo**	N	N	N	Y	Y
3 Adler	N	Y	Y	Y	Y
4 **Smith**	N	N	N	Y	Y
5 **Garrett**	N	N	N	N	N
6 Pallone	Y	Y	Y	Y	Y
7 **Lance**	N	N	N	N	Y
8 Pascrell	Y	Y	Y	Y	Y
9 Rothman	Y	Y	Y	Y	Y
10 Payne	Y	Y	Y	Y	Y
11 **Frelinghuysen**	N	N	N	N	Y
12 Holt	Y	Y	Y	Y	Y
13 Sires	Y	Y	Y	Y	Y
NEW MEXICO					
1 Heinrich	Y	Y	Y	Y	Y
2 Teague	Y	Y	Y	Y	Y
3 Luján	Y	Y	Y	Y	Y
NEW YORK					
1 Bishop	Y	Y	Y	Y	Y
2 Israel	Y	Y	Y	Y	Y
3 **King**	N	N	N	N	Y
4 McCarthy	Y	Y	Y	Y	Y
5 Ackerman	Y	Y	Y	Y	Y
6 Meeks	Y	Y	Y	Y	Y
7 Crowley	Y	Y	Y	Y	Y
8 Nadler	Y	?	Y	Y	Y
9 Weiner	Y	Y	Y	Y	Y
10 Towns	Y	Y	Y	Y	Y
11 Clarke	Y	Y	Y	Y	Y
12 Velázquez	Y	Y	Y	Y	Y
13 McMahon	Y	Y	?	?	?
14 Maloney	Y	Y	Y	Y	Y
15 Rangel	Y	Y	Y	Y	Y
16 Serrano	Y	Y	Y	Y	Y
17 Engel	Y	Y	Y	Y	Y
18 Lowey	Y	Y	Y	Y	Y
19 Hall	Y	Y	Y	Y	Y
20 Murphy	Y	Y	Y	Y	N
21 Tonko	Y	Y	Y	Y	Y
22 Hinchey	Y	Y	Y	Y	Y
23 Owens	Y	Y	Y	Y	Y
24 Arcuri	Y	Y	Y	Y	N
25 Maffei	Y	Y	Y	Y	Y
26 Lee	N	N	N	N	Y
27 Higgins	Y	Y	Y	Y	Y
28 Slaughter	Y	Y	Y	Y	?
29 Reed*					Y
NORTH CAROLINA					
1 Butterfield	Y	Y	Y	Y	Y
2 Etheridge	Y	Y	Y	Y	Y
3 **Jones**	N	N	Y	Y	Y
4 Price	Y	Y	?	Y	Y

	576	577	578	579	580
5 **Foxx**	N	N	N	N	N
6 **Coble**	N	?	?	?	?
7 McIntyre	Y	Y	Y	Y	Y
8 Kissell	Y	Y	Y	Y	Y
9 **Myrick**	N	N	N	N	Y
10 **McHenry**	N	N	N	N	N
11 Shuler	Y	N	N	N	Y
12 Watt	Y	Y	Y	Y	Y
13 Miller	Y	Y	Y	Y	Y
NORTH DAKOTA					
AL Pomeroy	Y	Y	Y	Y	Y
OHIO					
1 Driehaus	Y	Y	Y	Y	Y
2 **Schmidt**	N	N	N	N	Y
3 **Turner**	N	N	N	N	Y
4 **Jordan**	N	N	N	N	N
5 **Latta**	N	N	N	N	Y
6 Wilson	Y	Y	Y	Y	Y
7 **Austria**	N	N	N	N	Y
8 **Boehner**	N	N	N	N	Y
9 Kaptur	Y	Y	Y	Y	Y
10 Kucinich	Y	Y	Y	Y	Y
11 Fudge	Y	Y	Y	Y	Y
12 **Tiberi**	N	N	N	N	Y
13 Sutton	Y	Y	Y	Y	?
14 **LaTourette**	N	Y	Y	Y	Y
15 Kilroy	Y	Y	Y	Y	Y
16 Boccieri	Y	Y	Y	Y	Y
17 Ryan	Y	Y	Y	Y	Y
18 Space	Y	Y	?	?	Y
OKLAHOMA					
1 **Sullivan**	N	N	N	Y	Y
2 Boren	Y	Y	Y	Y	Y
3 **Lucas**	N	N	N	N	Y
4 **Cole**	N	N	N	Y	Y
5 **Fallin**	?	?	?	?	?
OREGON					
1 Wu	Y	N	N	Y	Y
2 **Walden**	N	N	N	N	Y
3 Blumenauer	Y	Y	Y	Y	Y
4 DeFazio	Y	Y	Y	Y	Y
5 Schrader	Y	Y	Y	Y	Y
PENNSYLVANIA					
1 Brady	Y	Y	Y	Y	Y
2 Fattah	?	?	Y	Y	Y
3 Dahlkemper	Y	Y	Y	Y	Y
4 Altmire	Y	Y	Y	Y	Y
5 **Thompson**	N	N	N	N	Y
6 **Gerlach**	N	N	N	Y	Y
7 Sestak	Y	Y	Y	Y	Y
8 Murphy, P.	Y	?	?	Y	Y
9 **Shuster**	N	N	N	N	Y
10 Carney	Y	Y	Y	Y	Y
11 Kanjorski	Y	Y	Y	Y	Y
12 Critz	Y	Y	Y	Y	Y
13 Schwartz	Y	Y	Y	Y	Y
14 Doyle	Y	Y	Y	Y	Y
15 **Dent**	N	N	Y	Y	Y
16 **Pitts**	N	N	N	N	Y
17 Holden	Y	Y	N	Y	Y
18 **Murphy, T.**	N	N	N	Y	Y
19 **Platts**	N	N	N	Y	Y
RHODE ISLAND					
1 Kennedy	Y	Y	+	+	Y
2 Langevin	Y	Y	Y	Y	Y
SOUTH CAROLINA					
1 **Brown**	N	N	?	?	?
2 **Wilson**	N	N	N	N	Y
3 **Barrett**	?	?	?	?	?
4 **Inglis**	?	?	N	N	Y
5 Spratt	Y	Y	Y	Y	Y
6 Clyburn	?	?	Y	Y	Y
SOUTH DAKOTA					
AL Herseth Sandlin	Y	Y	Y	Y	Y
TENNESSEE					
1 **Roe**	N	N	N	N	Y
2 **Duncan**	N	N	?	?	?
3 **Wamp**	N	N	N	N	Y
4 Davis	?	?	Y	N	N
5 Cooper	Y	Y	Y	N	N
6 Gordon	Y	Y	Y	Y	Y
7 **Blackburn**	?	N	N	N	Y
8 Tanner	Y	Y	Y	Y	Y
9 Cohen	Y	Y	Y	Y	Y

	576	577	578	579	580
TEXAS					
1 **Gohmert**	N	N	N	N	Y
2 **Poe**	N	N	N	N	Y
3 **Johnson, S.**	N	N	N	N	Y
4 **Hall**	N	N	N	N	Y
5 **Hensarling**	N	N	N	N	Y
6 **Barton**	N	N	N	N	Y
7 **Culberson**	N	N	N	N	Y
8 **Brady**	N	N	N	N	Y
9 Green, A.	Y	Y	Y	Y	Y
10 **McCaul**	N	N	N	N	Y
11 **Conaway**	N	N	N	N	Y
12 **Granger**	N	N	N	N	Y
13 **Thornberry**	N	N	N	N	Y
14 **Paul**	N	N	N	N	N
15 Hinojosa	Y	Y	Y	Y	Y
16 Reyes	Y	Y	Y	Y	Y
17 Edwards	?	Y	Y	Y	Y
18 Jackson Lee	Y	Y	Y	Y	Y
19 **Neugebauer**	N	N	N	N	Y
20 Gonzalez	Y	Y	Y	Y	Y
21 **Smith**	N	N	N	N	Y
22 **Olson**	N	N	N	N	Y
23 Rodriguez	Y	Y	Y	Y	Y
24 **Marchant**	N	N	N	N	Y
25 Doggett	Y	Y	Y	Y	Y
26 **Burgess**	N	N	N	N	?
27 Ortiz	Y	Y	Y	Y	Y
28 Cuellar	Y	Y	Y	Y	Y
29 Green, G.	Y	Y	Y	Y	Y
30 Johnson, E.	Y	Y	Y	Y	Y
31 **Carter**	N	N	N	N	Y
32 **Sessions**	N	N	N	N	Y
UTAH					
1 **Bishop**	N	N	N	N	Y
2 Matheson	Y	Y	Y	Y	Y
3 **Chaffetz**	N	N	N	N	N
VERMONT					
AL Welch	Y	Y	Y	Y	Y
VIRGINIA					
1 **Wittman**	N	N	Y	N	Y
2 Nye	Y	Y	Y	N	Y
3 Scott	Y	Y	Y	Y	Y
4 **Forbes**	N	N	Y	N	Y
5 Perriello	Y	Y	Y	Y	Y
6 **Goodlatte**	N	N	N	N	Y
7 **Cantor**	N	N	N	N	Y
8 Moran	Y	Y	?	+	N
9 Boucher	?	?	Y	Y	Y
10 **Wolf**	N	N	Y	N	Y
11 Connolly	Y	Y	Y	Y	Y
WASHINGTON					
1 Inslee	Y	Y	Y	Y	Y
2 Larsen	Y	Y	Y	Y	Y
3 Baird	Y	Y	Y	Y	N
4 **Hastings**	N	N	N	N	Y
5 **McMorris Rodgers**	N	N	N	N	Y
6 Dicks	Y	Y	Y	Y	Y
7 McDermott	Y	Y	Y	Y	Y
8 **Reichert**	N	N	Y	N	Y
9 Smith	Y	Y	Y	Y	Y
WEST VIRGINIA					
1 Mollohan	Y	Y	Y	Y	Y
2 **Capito**	N	N	Y	N	Y
3 Rahall	Y	Y	Y	Y	Y
WISCONSIN					
1 **Ryan**	N	N	N	N	Y
2 Baldwin	Y	Y	Y	Y	Y
3 Kind	Y	Y	Y	Y	Y
4 Moore	Y	Y	Y	Y	Y
5 **Sensenbrenner**	N	N	N	N	N
6 **Petri**	N	N	N	N	N
7 Obey	Y	Y	Y	Y	Y
8 Kagen	Y	Y	Y	Y	Y
WYOMING					
AL **Lummis**	N	N	N	N	Y
DELEGATES					
Faleomavaega (A.S.)					
Norton (D.C.)					
Bordallo (Guam)					
Sablan (N. Marianas)					
Pierluisi (P.R.)					
Christensen (V.I.)					

IN THE HOUSE | By Vote Number

581. **HR 5877. Lance Cpl. Alexander Scott Arredondo Post Office/ Passage.** Clay, D-Mo., motion to suspend the rules and pass the bill that would designate a post office in Jamaica Plain, Mass., as the "Lance Cpl. Alexander Scott Arredondo, United States Marine Corps Post Office Building." Motion agreed to 366-0: D 212-0; R 154-0. A two-thirds majority of those present and voting (244 in this case) is required for passage under suspension of the rules. Nov. 29, 2010.

582. **H Res 771. National Mesothelioma Awareness Day/Adoption.** Clay, D-Mo., motion to suspend the rules and adopt the resolution that would support the goals and ideals of a National Mesothelioma Awareness Day. Motion agreed to 363-0: D 211-0; R 152-0. A two-thirds majority of those present and voting (242 in this case) is required for adoption under suspension of the rules. Nov. 29, 2010.

583. **HR 4783. Claims Settlement/Rule.** Adoption of the rule (H Res 1736) that would provide for House floor consideration of the Senate amendments to the bill that would approve the settlement of claims in the cases of *Cobell v. Salazar* and Pigford II. Adopted 223-168: D 221-9; R 2-159. Nov. 30, 2010.

584. **HR 4783. Claims Settlement/Motion to Concur.** Rahall, D-W.Va., motion to concur in the Senate amendments to the bill that would approve the settlement of claims in the cases of *Cobell v. Salazar*, involving allegations that the Interior Department mismanaged royalties owed to American Indians, and Pigford II, concerning alleged discrimination by Agriculture Department officials against African-American farmers. It also would approve water rights settlements with American Indian tribes and extend the Temporary Assistance for Needy Families program through fiscal 2011. The bill also includes a variety of offsets. Motion agreed to, thus clearing the bill for the president, 256-152: D 240-3; R 16-149. Nov. 30, 2010.

585. **H Res 1585. Tribute to Travis Air Force Base/Adoption.** Garamendi, D-Calif., motion to suspend the rules and adopt the resolution that would recognize the service of the 60th Air Mobility Wing, the 349th Air Mobility Wing, the 15th Expeditionary Mobility Task Force and the 615th Contingency Response Wing civilians and families serving at Travis Air Force Base, Calif. Motion agreed to 408-0: D 240-0; R 168-0. A two-thirds majority of those present and voting (272 in this case) is required for adoption under suspension of the rules. Nov. 30, 2010.

586. **H Res 1740. National Guard Anniversary/Adoption.** Garamendi, D-Calif., motion to suspend the rules and adopt the resolution that would recognize the National Guard's 374th anniversary and thank the members of the National Guard for their service in response to the Sept. 11 attacks and their continuing role in homeland security and military operations. Motion agreed to 404-0: D 238-0; R 166-0. A two-thirds majority of those present and voting (270 in this case) is required for adoption under suspension of the rules. Nov. 30, 2010.

587. **S 3307. Child Nutrition Programs/Previous Question.** McGovern, D-Mass., motion to order the previous question (thus ending debate and possibility of amendment) on adoption of the rule (H Res 1742) that would provide for House floor consideration of the bill that would reauthorize child nutrition programs though fiscal 2015 and make changes to the programs, including increasing spending by $4.5 billion over 10 years. Motion agreed to 232-180: D 232-11; R 0-169. Dec. 1, 2010.

	581	582	583	584	585	586	587
ALABAMA							
1 **Bonner**	Y	Y	N	N	Y	Y	N
2 **Bright**	Y	Y	N	N	Y	Y	N
3 **Rogers**	Y	Y	N	N	Y	Y	N
4 **Aderholt**	Y	Y	N	N	Y	Y	N
5 **Griffith**	Y	Y	N	N	Y	Y	N
6 **Bachus**	Y	Y	N	N	Y	Y	N
7 Davis	?	?	?	Y	Y	Y	Y
ALASKA							
AL **Young**	?	?	N	Y	Y	Y	N
ARIZONA							
1 Kirkpatrick	Y	Y	Y	Y	Y	Y	Y
2 **Franks**	Y	Y	N	N	Y	Y	N
3 **Shadegg**	?	?	?	Y	Y	Y	N
4 Pastor	?	?	Y	Y	Y	Y	Y
5 Mitchell	Y	Y	Y	Y	Y	Y	Y
6 **Flake**	Y	Y	N	N	Y	Y	N
7 Grijalva	?	?	Y	Y	Y	?	Y
8 Giffords	Y	Y	+	Y	Y	Y	Y
ARKANSAS							
1 Berry	?	?	N	Y	Y	Y	N
2 Snyder	Y	Y	Y	Y	Y	Y	Y
3 **Boozman**	?	?	N	N	Y	Y	N
4 Ross	Y	Y	Y	Y	Y	Y	N
CALIFORNIA							
1 Thompson	Y	Y	Y	Y	Y	Y	Y
2 **Herger**	Y	Y	N	N	Y	Y	N
3 **Lungren**	Y	Y	N	N	Y	Y	N
4 **McClintock**	Y	Y	N	N	Y	Y	N
5 Matsui	Y	Y	Y	Y	Y	Y	Y
6 Woolsey	Y	Y	+	Y	Y	Y	Y
7 Miller, George	Y	Y	Y	Y	+	Y	Y
8 Pelosi							
9 Lee	Y	Y	?	Y	Y	Y	Y
10 Garamendi	Y	Y	Y	Y	Y	Y	Y
11 McNerney	Y	?	Y	Y	Y	Y	Y
12 Speier	?	?	Y	Y	Y	Y	?
13 Stark	?	?	Y	Y	Y	Y	Y
14 Eshoo	Y	Y	Y	Y	?	?	Y
15 Honda	Y	Y	?	Y	Y	Y	Y
16 Lofgren	Y	Y	Y	Y	Y	Y	Y
17 Farr	Y	Y	Y	Y	Y	Y	Y
18 Cardoza	Y	Y	Y	Y	Y	Y	Y
19 **Radanovich**	?	?	?	?	?	?	?
20 Costa	Y	Y	Y	Y	Y	Y	Y
21 **Nunes**	Y	Y	N	N	Y	Y	N
22 **McCarthy**	Y	Y	N	N	Y	Y	N
23 Capps	Y	Y	Y	Y	Y	Y	Y
24 **Gallegly**	Y	Y	N	Y	Y	Y	N
25 **McKeon**	Y	Y	N	N	Y	Y	N
26 **Dreier**	Y	Y	N	N	Y	Y	N
27 Sherman	Y	Y	Y	Y	Y	Y	Y
28 Berman	?	?	Y	Y	Y	Y	Y
29 Schiff	Y	Y	Y	Y	Y	Y	Y
30 Waxman	Y	Y	?	Y	Y	Y	Y
31 Becerra	Y	Y	Y	Y	Y	Y	Y
32 Chu	Y	Y	Y	Y	Y	Y	Y
33 Watson	Y	Y	Y	Y	Y	Y	Y
34 Roybal-Allard	Y	Y	Y	Y	Y	Y	Y
35 Waters	Y	Y	Y	Y	?	Y	Y
36 Harman	Y	Y	Y	Y	Y	Y	Y
37 Richardson	Y	Y	Y	Y	Y	Y	Y
38 Napolitano	Y	Y	Y	Y	Y	Y	Y
39 Sánchez, Linda	+	+	Y	Y	Y	Y	Y
40 **Royce**	Y	Y	N	N	Y	Y	N
41 **Lewis**	Y	Y	N	N	Y	Y	N
42 **Miller, Gary**	Y	Y	N	N	Y	Y	N
43 Baca	Y	Y	Y	Y	Y	Y	Y
44 **Calvert**	Y	Y	N	N	Y	?	N
45 **Bono Mack**	?	?	N	N	Y	Y	N
46 **Rohrabacher**	Y	Y	N	N	Y	Y	N
47 Sanchez, Loretta	?	?	Y	Y	Y	Y	Y
48 **Campbell**	Y	Y	N	N	Y	Y	N
49 **Issa**	Y	N	N	?	Y	Y	N
50 **Bilbray**	Y	Y	N	N	Y	Y	N
51 Filner	Y	Y	Y	Y	Y	Y	Y
52 **Hunter**	Y	Y	N	N	Y	Y	N
53 Davis	Y	Y	Y	Y	Y	Y	Y

	581	582	583	584	585	586	587
COLORADO							
1 DeGette	Y	Y	Y	Y	Y	Y	Y
2 Polis	Y	Y	Y	Y	Y	Y	Y
3 Salazar	Y	Y	Y	Y	Y	Y	Y
4 Markey	?	?	Y	Y	Y	Y	Y
5 **Lamborn**	Y	Y	N	N	Y	Y	N
6 **Coffman**	Y	Y	N	N	Y	Y	N
7 Perlmutter	Y	Y	Y	Y	Y	Y	Y
CONNECTICUT							
1 Larson	Y	Y	Y	Y	Y	Y	Y
2 Courtney	Y	Y	Y	Y	?	?	Y
3 DeLauro	Y	Y	Y	Y	Y	Y	Y
4 Himes	Y	Y	?	Y	Y	Y	Y
5 Murphy	Y	Y	Y	Y	Y	Y	Y
DELAWARE							
AL **Castle**	Y	Y	N	N	Y	Y	N
FLORIDA							
1 **Miller**	Y	Y	N	N	Y	Y	N
2 Boyd	Y	Y	Y	Y	Y	Y	Y
3 Brown	Y	Y	Y	Y	Y	Y	Y
4 **Crenshaw**	Y	Y	N	N	Y	Y	N
5 **Brown-Waite**	?	?	?	?	?	?	?
6 **Stearns**	Y	Y	N	N	Y	Y	N
7 **Mica**	Y	Y	N	N	Y	Y	N
8 Grayson	Y	Y	Y	Y	Y	Y	Y
9 **Bilirakis**	Y	Y	N	N	Y	Y	N
10 **Young**	Y	Y	N	N	Y	Y	N
11 Castor	Y	Y	Y	Y	Y	Y	Y
12 **Putnam**	+	+	–	–	+	+	N
13 **Buchanan**	Y	Y	N	N	Y	Y	N
14 **Mack**	?	?	N	N	Y	Y	N
15 **Posey**	Y	Y	N	N	Y	Y	N
16 **Rooney**	Y	Y	N	N	Y	Y	N
17 Meek	Y	Y	Y	Y	Y	Y	Y
18 **Ros-Lehtinen**	Y	Y	?	?	Y	Y	N
19 Deutch	Y	Y	?	?	?	?	Y
20 Wasserman Schultz	Y	Y	Y	Y	Y	Y	Y
21 **Diaz-Balart, L.**	Y	Y	N	Y	Y	Y	N
22 Klein	Y	Y	Y	Y	Y	Y	Y
23 Hastings	?	?	?	?	?	?	?
24 Kosmas	Y	Y	Y	Y	Y	Y	Y
25 **Diaz-Balart, M.**	Y	Y	?	Y	Y	Y	N
GEORGIA							
1 **Kingston**	Y	Y	N	N	Y	Y	N
2 Bishop	?	?	Y	Y	Y	Y	Y
3 **Westmoreland**	Y	Y	N	N	Y	Y	N
4 Johnson	Y	Y	Y	Y	Y	Y	Y
5 Lewis	Y	Y	Y	Y	Y	Y	Y
6 **Price**	Y	Y	N	N	Y	Y	N
7 **Linder**	?	?	N	N	Y	Y	N
8 Marshall	Y	Y	Y	Y	Y	Y	N
9 **Graves**	Y	Y	N	N	Y	Y	N
10 **Broun**	Y	Y	N	N	Y	Y	N
11 **Gingrey**	Y	Y	N	N	Y	Y	N
12 Barrow	Y	Y	Y	Y	Y	Y	Y
13 Scott	Y	Y	Y	Y	Y	Y	Y
HAWAII							
1 **Djou**	Y	Y	Y	Y	Y	Y	Y
2 Hirono	Y	Y	Y	Y	Y	Y	Y
IDAHO							
1 Minnick	Y	Y	Y	Y	Y	Y	?
2 **Simpson**	Y	Y	N	Y	Y	Y	N
ILLINOIS							
1 Rush	?	?	Y	Y	?	?	Y
2 Jackson	Y	Y	Y	Y	Y	Y	Y
3 Lipinski	?	?	Y	Y	Y	Y	Y
4 Gutierrez	+	+	Y	Y	Y	Y	Y
5 Quigley	Y	Y	Y	Y	Y	Y	Y
6 **Roskam**	Y	?	N	N	Y	Y	N
7 Davis	Y	Y	Y	Y	Y	Y	?
8 Bean	Y	Y	Y	Y	Y	Y	Y
9 Schakowsky	Y	Y	Y	+	Y	Y	Y
10 Vacant*							
11 Halvorson	Y	Y	Y	Y	Y	Y	Y
12 Costello	Y	Y	Y	Y	Y	Y	?
13 **Biggert**	Y	Y	N	N	Y	Y	N
14 Foster	Y	Y	Y	Y	Y	Y	Y
15 **Johnson**	–	+	N	N	Y	Y	N

KEY   Republicans   Democrats

Y Voted for (yea)	**X** Paired against	**C** Voted "present" to avoid possible conflict of interest
# Paired for	**–** Announced against	
+ Announced for	**P** Voted "present"	**?** Did not vote or otherwise make a position known
N Voted against (nay)		

* Rep. Mark Steven Kirk, R-Ill., resigned Nov. 29, 2010, to assume the Senate seat he won in a Nov. 2 special election. The last vote for which he was eligible was vote 580.

	581	582	583	584	585	586	587
16 **Manzullo**	Y	Y	N	N	Y	Y	N
17 Hare	Y	Y	Y	Y	Y	Y	Y
18 **Schock**	Y	Y	N	N	Y	Y	N
19 **Shimkus**	Y	Y	N	N	Y	Y	N
INDIANA							
1 Visclosky	Y	Y	Y	Y	Y	Y	Y
2 Donnelly	Y	Y	N	Y	Y	Y	Y
3 **Stutzman**	Y	Y	N	N	Y	Y	N
4 **Buyer**	Y	Y	?	?	?	?	?
5 **Burton**	+	+	–	–	+	+	–
6 **Pence**	+	+	N	N	Y	Y	N
7 Carson	Y	Y	Y	Y	Y	Y	Y
8 Ellsworth	Y	Y	Y	Y	Y	Y	Y
9 Hill	Y	Y	?	Y	Y	Y	Y
IOWA							
1 Braley	Y	Y	Y	Y	Y	Y	Y
2 Loebsack	Y	Y	Y	Y	Y	Y	Y
3 Boswell	Y	Y	Y	Y	Y	Y	Y
4 **Latham**	Y	Y	N	N	Y	Y	N
5 **King**	Y	Y	N	N	Y	Y	N
KANSAS							
1 **Moran**	?	?	?	?	?	?	N
2 **Jenkins**	Y	Y	N	N	Y	Y	N
3 Moore	Y	Y	Y	Y	Y	Y	Y
4 **Tiahrt**	Y	Y	?	N	Y	Y	N
KENTUCKY							
1 **Whitfield**	Y	Y	N	N	Y	Y	N
2 **Guthrie**	Y	Y	N	N	Y	Y	N
3 Yarmuth	Y	Y	Y	Y	Y	Y	Y
4 **Davis**	Y	Y	N	N	Y	Y	N
5 **Rogers**	Y	Y	N	N	Y	Y	N
6 Chandler	Y	Y	?	Y	Y	Y	Y
LOUISIANA							
1 **Scalise**	Y	Y	N	N	Y	Y	N
2 **Cao**	Y	Y	N	N	Y	Y	N
3 Melancon	Y	Y	Y	Y	Y	Y	?
4 **Fleming**	?	?	N	N	Y	Y	N
5 **Alexander**	Y	Y	N	N	Y	Y	?
6 **Cassidy**	Y	Y	N	Y	Y	Y	N
7 **Boustany**	Y	Y	N	N	Y	Y	N
MAINE							
1 Pingree	Y	Y	Y	Y	Y	Y	Y
2 Michaud	Y	Y	Y	Y	Y	Y	Y
MARYLAND							
1 Kratovil	Y	Y	Y	Y	Y	Y	Y
2 Ruppersberger	Y	Y	Y	Y	Y	Y	Y
3 Sarbanes	Y	Y	Y	Y	Y	Y	Y
4 Edwards	Y	Y	Y	Y	Y	Y	Y
5 Hoyer	Y	Y	Y	Y	Y	Y	Y
6 **Bartlett**	Y	Y	N	N	Y	Y	N
7 Cummings	Y	Y	Y	Y	Y	Y	Y
8 Van Hollen	Y	Y	Y	Y	Y	Y	Y
MASSACHUSETTS							
1 Olver	Y	Y	Y	Y	Y	Y	Y
2 Neal	?	Y	Y	Y	Y	Y	Y
3 McGovern	Y	Y	Y	Y	Y	Y	Y
4 Frank	Y	Y	Y	Y	Y	Y	Y
5 Tsongas	?	?	?	?	?	?	Y
6 Tierney	Y	Y	Y	Y	Y	Y	Y
7 Markey	?	?	Y	Y	Y	Y	?
8 Capuano	Y	Y	Y	Y	Y	Y	Y
9 Lynch	Y	Y	Y	Y	Y	Y	Y
10 Delahunt	?	?	Y	Y	Y	Y	Y
MICHIGAN							
1 Stupak	Y	Y	Y	Y	Y	Y	Y
2 **Hoekstra**	Y	Y	N	N	Y	Y	N
3 **Ehlers**	Y	Y	N	N	Y	Y	N
4 **Camp**	Y	Y	N	N	Y	Y	N
5 Kildee	Y	Y	Y	Y	Y	Y	Y
6 **Upton**	Y	Y	N	N	Y	Y	N
7 Schauer	Y	Y	Y	Y	Y	Y	Y
8 **Rogers**	Y	Y	N	N	Y	Y	N
9 Peters	Y	Y	Y	Y	Y	Y	Y
10 **Miller**	Y	Y	N	N	Y	Y	N
11 **McCotter**	Y	Y	N	N	Y	Y	N
12 Levin	Y	Y	Y	Y	Y	Y	Y
13 Kilpatrick	?	?	Y	Y	Y	Y	Y
14 Conyers	+	+	?	Y	Y	Y	Y
15 Dingell	Y	Y	Y	Y	Y	Y	Y
MINNESOTA							
1 Walz	Y	Y	Y	Y	Y	Y	Y
2 **Kline**	Y	Y	N	N	Y	Y	N
3 **Paulsen**	Y	Y	N	N	Y	Y	N
4 McCollum	Y	Y	Y	Y	Y	Y	Y

	581	582	583	584	585	586	587
5 Ellison	Y	Y	Y	Y	Y	Y	Y
6 **Bachmann**	Y	Y	N	N	Y	Y	N
7 Peterson	Y	Y	Y	Y	Y	Y	Y
8 Oberstar	Y	Y	?	Y	Y	Y	Y
MISSISSIPPI							
1 Childers	?	?	Y	Y	Y	Y	N
2 Thompson	Y	Y	Y	Y	Y	Y	Y
3 **Harper**	Y	Y	N	Y	Y	Y	N
4 Taylor	?	?	?	N	Y	Y	N
MISSOURI							
1 Clay	Y	Y	Y	Y	Y	Y	Y
2 **Akin**	Y	Y	N	N	Y	Y	N
3 Carnahan	Y	Y	Y	Y	Y	Y	Y
4 Skelton	Y	Y	Y	Y	Y	Y	Y
5 Cleaver	Y	Y	?	Y	Y	Y	Y
6 **Graves**	Y	Y	N	N	Y	Y	N
7 **Blunt**	Y	Y	N	N	Y	Y	N
8 **Emerson**	Y	Y	N	Y	Y	Y	N
9 **Luetkemeyer**	Y	Y	N	N	Y	Y	N
MONTANA							
AL **Rehberg**	Y	Y	N	N	Y	Y	N
NEBRASKA							
1 **Fortenberry**	Y	Y	N	N	Y	Y	N
2 **Terry**	Y	Y	N	N	Y	Y	N
3 **Smith**	Y	Y	N	N	Y	Y	N
NEVADA							
1 Berkley	Y	Y	Y	Y	Y	Y	Y
2 **Heller**	Y	Y	N	N	Y	Y	N
3 Titus	Y	Y	Y	Y	Y	Y	Y
NEW HAMPSHIRE							
1 Shea-Porter	Y	Y	Y	Y	Y	Y	Y
2 Hodes	Y	Y	Y	Y	Y	Y	?
NEW JERSEY							
1 Andrews	Y	Y	Y	Y	Y	Y	Y
2 **LoBiondo**	Y	Y	N	N	Y	Y	N
3 Adler	Y	Y	N	Y	Y	Y	N
4 **Smith**	Y	Y	N	N	Y	Y	N
5 **Garrett**	Y	Y	N	N	Y	Y	N
6 Pallone	Y	Y	Y	Y	Y	Y	Y
7 **Lance**	Y	Y	N	N	Y	Y	N
8 Pascrell	Y	Y	Y	Y	Y	Y	Y
9 Rothman	Y	Y	Y	Y	Y	Y	Y
10 Payne	Y	Y	Y	Y	Y	Y	Y
11 **Frelinghuysen**	Y	Y	N	N	Y	Y	N
12 Holt	Y	Y	Y	Y	Y	Y	Y
13 Sires	Y	Y	Y	Y	Y	Y	Y
NEW MEXICO							
1 Heinrich	Y	Y	Y	Y	Y	Y	Y
2 Teague	Y	Y	Y	Y	Y	Y	Y
3 Luján	Y	Y	Y	Y	Y	Y	Y
NEW YORK							
1 Bishop	Y	Y	Y	Y	Y	Y	Y
2 Israel	Y	Y	Y	Y	Y	Y	Y
3 **King**	Y	Y	N	N	Y	Y	N
4 McCarthy	Y	Y	Y	Y	Y	Y	Y
5 Ackerman	Y	Y	Y	Y	Y	Y	Y
6 Meeks	Y	Y	Y	Y	Y	Y	Y
7 Crowley	Y	Y	Y	Y	Y	Y	Y
8 Nadler	Y	Y	Y	Y	Y	Y	Y
9 Weiner	Y	Y	Y	Y	Y	Y	Y
10 Towns	Y	Y	Y	Y	Y	Y	Y
11 Clarke	Y	Y	Y	Y	Y	Y	Y
12 Velázquez	Y	Y	Y	Y	Y	Y	Y
13 McMahon	?	?	Y	Y	Y	Y	Y
14 Maloney	Y	Y	Y	Y	Y	Y	Y
15 Rangel	Y	Y	Y	Y	Y	Y	Y
16 Serrano	Y	?	Y	Y	Y	Y	Y
17 Engel	Y	Y	Y	Y	Y	Y	Y
18 Lowey	Y	Y	Y	Y	Y	Y	Y
19 Hall	?	?	Y	Y	Y	Y	Y
20 Murphy	Y	Y	N	Y	Y	Y	Y
21 Tonko	+	+	Y	Y	Y	Y	Y
22 Hinchey	Y	Y	Y	Y	Y	Y	Y
23 Owens	Y	Y	Y	Y	Y	Y	Y
24 Arcuri	?	?	Y	Y	Y	Y	Y
25 Maffei	Y	Y	Y	Y	Y	Y	Y
26 **Lee**	Y	Y	N	N	Y	Y	N
27 Higgins	Y	Y	Y	Y	Y	Y	Y
28 Slaughter	Y	Y	Y	Y	Y	Y	Y
29 **Reed**	Y	Y	N	N	Y	Y	N
NORTH CAROLINA							
1 Butterfield	Y	Y	Y	Y	Y	Y	Y
2 Etheridge	Y	Y	Y	Y	Y	Y	Y
3 **Jones**	Y	Y	N	N	Y	Y	N
4 Price	Y	Y	Y	Y	Y	Y	Y

	581	582	583	584	585	586	587
5 **Foxx**	Y	Y	N	N	Y	Y	N
6 **Coble**	Y	Y	N	N	Y	Y	N
7 McIntyre	Y	Y	Y	Y	Y	Y	N
8 Kissell	Y	Y	Y	Y	Y	Y	Y
9 **Myrick**	+	+	–	–	+	+	–
10 **McHenry**	Y	Y	N	N	Y	Y	N
11 Shuler	Y	Y	N	Y	Y	Y	Y
12 Watt	Y	Y	Y	Y	Y	Y	Y
13 Miller	Y	Y	Y	Y	Y	Y	Y
NORTH DAKOTA							
AL Pomeroy	Y	Y	Y	Y	Y	Y	Y
OHIO							
1 Driehaus	Y	Y	Y	Y	Y	Y	Y
2 **Schmidt**	Y	Y	N	N	Y	Y	N
3 **Turner**	Y	Y	N	N	Y	Y	N
4 **Jordan**	Y	Y	N	N	Y	Y	N
5 **Latta**	Y	Y	N	N	Y	Y	N
6 Wilson	Y	Y	Y	Y	Y	Y	Y
7 **Austria**	?	?	N	N	Y	Y	N
8 **Boehner**	?	?	N	N	Y	?	N
9 Kaptur	Y	Y	Y	Y	Y	Y	Y
10 Kucinich	Y	Y	Y	Y	Y	Y	Y
11 Fudge	Y	Y	?	Y	Y	Y	Y
12 **Tiberi**	?	?	N	N	Y	Y	N
13 Sutton	Y	Y	Y	Y	Y	Y	Y
14 **LaTourette**	Y	Y	N	Y	Y	Y	N
15 Kilroy	Y	Y	Y	Y	Y	Y	Y
16 Boccieri	Y	Y	Y	Y	Y	Y	Y
17 Ryan	+	+	Y	Y	Y	Y	Y
18 Space	Y	Y	Y	?	?	?	Y
OKLAHOMA							
1 **Sullivan**	Y	Y	N	Y	Y	Y	N
2 Boren	Y	Y	N	Y	Y	Y	Y
3 **Lucas**	Y	Y	N	N	Y	Y	N
4 **Cole**	Y	Y	N	Y	Y	Y	N
5 **Fallin**	?	?	?	?	?	?	?
OREGON							
1 Wu	?	?	?	?	?	?	?
2 **Walden**	Y	Y	N	N	Y	Y	N
3 Blumenauer	Y	Y	Y	Y	Y	Y	Y
4 DeFazio	?	?	?	?	?	?	?
5 Schrader	Y	Y	Y	Y	Y	?	Y
PENNSYLVANIA							
1 Brady	?	?	Y	Y	Y	Y	Y
2 Fattah	?	?	Y	Y	Y	Y	Y
3 Dahlkemper	?	?	Y	Y	Y	Y	Y
4 Altmire	Y	Y	Y	Y	Y	Y	Y
5 **Thompson**	Y	Y	N	N	Y	Y	N
6 **Gerlach**	+	+	N	N	Y	Y	N
7 Sestak	Y	Y	Y	Y	Y	Y	Y
8 Murphy, P.	?	?	Y	Y	Y	Y	Y
9 **Shuster**	?	?	N	N	Y	Y	N
10 Carney	?	?	?	?	?	?	Y
11 Kanjorski	Y	Y	Y	Y	Y	Y	Y
12 Critz	Y	Y	Y	Y	Y	Y	Y
13 Schwartz	Y	Y	Y	Y	Y	Y	Y
14 Doyle	Y	Y	Y	Y	Y	Y	Y
15 **Dent**	Y	Y	N	N	Y	Y	N
16 **Pitts**	Y	Y	N	N	Y	Y	N
17 Holden	Y	Y	Y	Y	Y	Y	Y
18 **Murphy, T.**	Y	Y	N	Y	Y	Y	N
19 **Platts**	Y	Y	N	N	Y	Y	N
RHODE ISLAND							
1 Kennedy	Y	Y	Y	Y	Y	Y	Y
2 Langevin	Y	Y	?	Y	Y	Y	Y
SOUTH CAROLINA							
1 **Brown**	Y	Y	N	N	Y	Y	N
2 **Wilson**	Y	Y	N	N	Y	Y	N
3 **Barrett**	?	?	?	?	?	?	?
4 **Inglis**	Y	Y	?	N	Y	Y	N
5 Spratt	Y	Y	Y	Y	Y	Y	Y
6 Clyburn	Y	Y	Y	Y	Y	Y	Y
SOUTH DAKOTA							
AL Herseth Sandlin	Y	Y	N	Y	Y	Y	Y
TENNESSEE							
1 **Roe**	Y	Y	N	N	Y	Y	N
2 **Duncan**	Y	Y	N	N	Y	Y	N
3 **Wamp**	?	?	?	?	?	?	N
4 Davis	Y	Y	Y	Y	Y	Y	Y
5 Cooper	Y	Y	Y	N	Y	Y	Y
6 Gordon	Y	Y	Y	Y	Y	?	Y
7 **Blackburn**	Y	Y	N	N	Y	Y	N
8 Tanner	?	?	Y	Y	Y	Y	Y
9 Cohen	Y	Y	Y	Y	Y	Y	Y

	581	582	583	584	585	586	587
TEXAS							
1 **Gohmert**	Y	Y	N	N	Y	Y	N
2 **Poe**	Y	Y	N	N	Y	Y	N
3 **Johnson, S.**	Y	Y	N	N	Y	Y	N
4 **Hall**	Y	Y	N	N	Y	Y	N
5 **Hensarling**	Y	Y	N	N	Y	Y	N
6 **Barton**	Y	Y	N	N	Y	Y	N
7 **Culberson**	Y	Y	N	N	Y	Y	N
8 **Brady**	Y	Y	N	N	Y	Y	N
9 Green, A.	Y	Y	Y	Y	Y	Y	Y
10 **McCaul**	Y	Y	N	N	Y	Y	N
11 **Conaway**	Y	Y	N	N	Y	Y	N
12 **Granger**	Y	Y	N	N	Y	Y	N
13 **Thornberry**	Y	Y	N	N	Y	Y	N
14 **Paul**	Y	Y	N	N	Y	Y	N
15 Hinojosa	Y	Y	Y	Y	Y	Y	Y
16 Reyes	?	?	Y	Y	Y	?	Y
17 Edwards	?	?	?	Y	Y	Y	Y
18 Jackson Lee	Y	Y	Y	Y	Y	Y	Y
19 **Neugebauer**	Y	Y	N	–	Y	Y	N
20 Gonzalez	Y	Y	Y	?	Y	Y	Y
21 **Smith**	Y	Y	N	N	Y	Y	N
22 **Olson**	Y	Y	N	N	Y	Y	N
23 Rodriguez	?	?	Y	Y	Y	Y	Y
24 **Marchant**	?	?	?	?	?	?	?
25 Doggett	Y	Y	Y	Y	Y	Y	Y
26 **Burgess**	Y	Y	N	N	Y	Y	N
27 Ortiz	?	?	?	?	?	?	Y
28 Cuellar	Y	Y	Y	Y	Y	Y	Y
29 Green, G.	Y	Y	Y	Y	Y	Y	Y
30 Johnson, E.	Y	Y	Y	Y	Y	?	Y
31 **Carter**	Y	Y	N	N	Y	Y	N
32 **Sessions**	Y	Y	N	N	Y	Y	N
UTAH							
1 **Bishop**	Y	Y	?	N	Y	Y	N
2 Matheson	Y	Y	N	Y	Y	Y	Y
3 **Chaffetz**	Y	Y	N	N	Y	Y	N
VERMONT							
AL Welch	Y	Y	Y	Y	Y	Y	?
VIRGINIA							
1 **Wittman**	?	?	?	N	Y	Y	N
2 Nye	Y	Y	Y	Y	Y	Y	N
3 Scott	?	?	Y	Y	Y	Y	Y
4 **Forbes**	Y	Y	N	N	Y	Y	N
5 Perriello	Y	Y	Y	Y	Y	Y	Y
6 **Goodlatte**	Y	Y	N	N	Y	Y	N
7 **Cantor**	Y	?	N	N	Y	Y	N
8 Moran	?	?	Y	Y	Y	Y	Y
9 Boucher	Y	Y	Y	?	Y	Y	Y
10 **Wolf**	Y	Y	N	N	Y	Y	N
11 Connolly	Y	Y	Y	Y	Y	Y	Y
WASHINGTON							
1 Inslee	Y	Y	Y	Y	Y	Y	Y
2 Larsen	Y	Y	Y	Y	Y	Y	Y
3 Baird	Y	Y	?	Y	Y	Y	Y
4 **Hastings**	Y	Y	N	N	Y	Y	N
5 **McMorris Rodgers**	Y	Y	N	N	Y	Y	–
6 Dicks	Y	Y	Y	Y	Y	Y	Y
7 McDermott	Y	Y	Y	Y	Y	Y	Y
8 **Reichert**	Y	Y	N	N	Y	Y	N
9 Smith	Y	Y	Y	Y	Y	Y	Y
WEST VIRGINIA							
1 Mollohan	?	?	Y	Y	Y	Y	Y
2 **Capito**	Y	Y	N	N	Y	Y	N
3 Rahall	Y	Y	Y	Y	Y	Y	Y
WISCONSIN							
1 **Ryan**	Y	Y	N	N	Y	Y	N
2 Baldwin	Y	Y	Y	Y	Y	Y	Y
3 Kind	Y	Y	Y	Y	Y	Y	Y
4 Moore	Y	Y	Y	Y	?	Y	Y
5 **Sensenbrenner**	Y	Y	N	N	Y	Y	N
6 **Petri**	Y	Y	N	N	Y	Y	N
7 Obey	Y	Y	Y	Y	Y	Y	Y
8 Kagen	Y	Y	Y	Y	Y	Y	Y
WYOMING							
AL **Lummis**	Y	Y	N	Y	Y	Y	N
DELEGATES							
Faleomavaega (A.S.)							
Norton (D.C.)							
Bordallo (Guam)							
Sablan (N. Marianas)							
Pierluisi (P.R.)							
Christensen (V.I.)							

IN THE HOUSE | By Vote Number

588. **S 3307. Child Nutrition Programs/Rule.** Adoption of the rule (H Res 1742) that would provide for House floor consideration of the bill that would reauthorize child nutrition programs though fiscal 2015 and make changes to the programs, including increasing spending by $4.5 billion over 10 years. Adopted 230-174: D 229-12; R 1-162. Dec. 1, 2010.

589. **H J Res 101. Continuing Appropriations/Rule.** Adoption of the rule (H Res 1741) that would provide for House floor consideration of the joint resolution that would provide continuing appropriations through Dec. 18, 2010. Adopted 236-172: D 236-6; R 0-166. Dec. 1, 2010.

590. **H Con Res 323. Holocaust Survivors Support/Adoption.** McCarthy, D-N.Y., motion to suspend the rules and adopt the concurrent resolution that would honor the nonprofit organizations and agencies that work to assist Holocaust survivors and support the goal of ensuring that all survivors are able to live with dignity, comfort and security in their remaining years. Motion agreed to 406-0: D 238-0; R 168-0. A two-thirds majority of those present and voting (271 in this case) is required for adoption under suspension of the rules. Dec. 1, 2010.

591. **H Res 1735. Attack on South Korean Island/Adoption.** Berman, D-Calif., motion to suspend the rules and adopt the resolution that would condemn North Korea in the strongest terms for its Nov. 23 military attack against Yeonpyeong Island in South Korea in violation of the Korean War Armistice Agreement. Motion agreed to 403-2: D 238-1; R 165-1. A two-thirds majority of those present and voting (270 in this case) is required for adoption under suspension of the rules. Dec. 1, 2010.

592. **H Res 1430. Juan Antonio 'Chi Chi' Rodriguez Tribute/ Adoption.** Woolsey, D-Calif., motion to suspend the rules and adopt the resolution that would honor Juan Antonio "Chi Chi" Rodriguez for his contributions to the youth programs at the Congressional Hispanic Caucus Institute and his work with at-risk youth through the Chi Chi Rodriguez Youth Foundation. Motion agreed to 405-2: D 240-0; R 165-2. A two-thirds majority of those present and voting (272 in this case) is required for adoption under suspension of the rules. Dec. 1, 2010.

593. **H J Res 101. Continuing Appropriations/Passage.** Passage of the joint resolution that would provide continuing appropriations through Dec. 18, 2010, for all federal departments and agencies, none of whose fiscal 2011 appropriations bills have been enacted. Funding would be set mostly at fiscal 2010 levels. Passed 239-178: D 237-8; R 2-170. Dec. 1, 2010.

594. **H Res 1217. Tribute to the 10th Mountain Division/Adoption.** Owens, D-N.Y., motion to suspend the rules and adopt the resolution that would recognize the achievements of soldiers serving in the 10th Mountain Division, as well as Army Reserve and National Guard members who have fought with the division. Motion agreed to 415-0: D 243-0; R 172-0. A two-thirds majority of those present and voting (277 in this case) is required for adoption under suspension of the rules. Dec. 1, 2010.

	588	589	590	591	592	593	594
ALABAMA							
1 Bonner	N	N	Y	Y	Y	N	Y
2 Bright	?	N	Y	Y	Y	N	Y
3 Rogers	N	N	Y	Y	Y	N	Y
4 Aderholt	N	N	Y	Y	Y	N	Y
5 Griffith	N	N	Y	Y	Y	N	Y
6 Bachus	N	N	Y	Y	Y	N	Y
7 Davis	Y	Y	Y	Y	?	Y	Y
ALASKA							
AL Young	N	N	Y	Y	Y	Y	Y
ARIZONA							
1 Kirkpatrick	Y	Y	Y	Y	Y	Y	Y
2 Franks	N	N	Y	Y	Y	N	Y
3 Shadegg	?	N	Y	Y	Y	N	Y
4 Pastor	Y	Y	Y	Y	Y	Y	Y
5 Mitchell	Y	Y	Y	Y	Y	Y	Y
6 Flake	N	N	Y	Y	Y	N	Y
7 Grijalva	Y	Y	Y	Y	Y	Y	Y
8 Giffords	Y	Y	Y	Y	Y	N	Y
ARKANSAS							
1 Berry	Y	Y	Y	Y	Y	Y	Y
2 Snyder	Y	Y	Y	Y	Y	Y	Y
3 Boozman	N	N	Y	Y	Y	N	Y
4 Ross	Y	Y	Y	Y	Y	Y	Y
CALIFORNIA							
1 Thompson	Y	Y	Y	Y	Y	Y	Y
2 Herger	N	N	Y	Y	Y	N	Y
3 Lungren	N	N	Y	Y	Y	N	Y
4 McClintock	N	N	Y	Y	Y	N	Y
5 Matsui	Y	Y	Y	Y	Y	Y	Y
6 Woolsey	Y	Y	Y	Y	Y	Y	Y
7 Miller, George	Y	Y	Y	Y	Y	Y	Y
8 Pelosi							
9 Lee	Y	Y	Y	Y	Y	Y	Y
10 Garamendi	Y	Y	Y	Y	Y	Y	Y
11 McNerney	Y	Y	Y	Y	Y	Y	Y
12 Speier	?	?	?	?	?	?	?
13 Stark	Y	Y	Y	Y	Y	Y	Y
14 Eshoo	Y	Y	Y	Y	Y	Y	Y
15 Honda	Y	Y	Y	Y	Y	Y	Y
16 Lofgren	Y	Y	Y	Y	Y	Y	Y
17 Farr	Y	Y	Y	Y	Y	Y	Y
18 Cardoza	Y	Y	Y	Y	Y	Y	Y
19 Radanovich	?	?	?	?	?	?	?
20 Costa	Y	Y	Y	Y	Y	Y	Y
21 Nunes	N	N	Y	Y	Y	N	Y
22 McCarthy	N	N	Y	Y	Y	N	Y
23 Capps	Y	Y	Y	Y	Y	Y	Y
24 Gallegly	N	N	Y	Y	Y	N	Y
25 McKeon	?	N	Y	Y	Y	N	Y
26 Dreier	N	N	Y	Y	Y	N	Y
27 Sherman	Y	Y	Y	Y	Y	Y	Y
28 Berman	Y	Y	Y	Y	Y	Y	Y
29 Schiff	Y	Y	Y	Y	Y	Y	Y
30 Waxman	Y	Y	Y	Y	Y	Y	Y
31 Becerra	Y	Y	Y	Y	Y	Y	Y
32 Chu	Y	Y	Y	Y	Y	Y	Y
33 Watson	Y	Y	Y	Y	Y	Y	Y
34 Roybal-Allard	Y	Y	Y	Y	Y	Y	Y
35 Waters	Y	?	?	Y	Y	Y	Y
36 Harman	Y	Y	?	?	?	Y	Y
37 Richardson	Y	Y	Y	Y	Y	Y	Y
38 Napolitano	Y	Y	Y	Y	Y	Y	Y
39 Sánchez, Linda	Y	Y	Y	Y	Y	Y	Y
40 Royce	N	N	Y	Y	Y	N	Y
41 Lewis	N	N	Y	Y	Y	N	Y
42 Miller, Gary	N	N	Y	Y	Y	N	Y
43 Baca	Y	Y	Y	Y	Y	Y	Y
44 Calvert	N	N	Y	Y	Y	N	Y
45 Bono Mack	N	N	Y	Y	Y	N	Y
46 Rohrabacher	N	N	Y	Y	Y	N	Y
47 Sanchez, Loretta	Y	Y	Y	Y	Y	Y	Y
48 Campbell	N	N	Y	Y	Y	N	Y
49 Issa	N	N	Y	Y	N	N	Y
50 Bilbray	N	N	Y	Y	Y	N	Y
51 Filner	Y	Y	Y	Y	Y	Y	Y
52 Hunter	N	N	Y	Y	Y	N	Y
53 Davis	Y	Y	Y	Y	Y	Y	Y

	588	589	590	591	592	593	594
COLORADO							
1 DeGette	Y	Y	Y	Y	Y	Y	Y
2 Polis	Y	Y	Y	Y	Y	Y	Y
3 Salazar	Y	Y	Y	Y	Y	Y	Y
4 Markey	Y	Y	Y	Y	Y	Y	Y
5 Lamborn	N	N	Y	Y	Y	N	Y
6 Coffman	?	N	Y	Y	Y	N	Y
7 Perlmutter	Y	Y	Y	Y	Y	Y	Y
CONNECTICUT							
1 Larson	Y	Y	Y	Y	Y	Y	Y
2 Courtney	Y	Y	Y	Y	Y	Y	Y
3 DeLauro	Y	Y	Y	Y	Y	Y	Y
4 Himes	Y	Y	Y	Y	Y	Y	Y
5 Murphy	Y	Y	?	Y	Y	Y	Y
DELAWARE							
AL Castle	N	N	Y	Y	Y	N	Y
FLORIDA							
1 Miller	N	N	Y	Y	Y	N	Y
2 Boyd	N	Y	Y	Y	Y	Y	Y
3 Brown	Y	Y	Y	Y	Y	Y	Y
4 Crenshaw	N	N	Y	Y	Y	N	Y
5 Brown-Waite	?	?	?	?	?	?	?
6 Stearns	N	N	Y	Y	Y	N	Y
7 Mica	N	N	Y	Y	Y	N	Y
8 Grayson	Y	Y	Y	Y	Y	Y	Y
9 Bilirakis	N	N	Y	Y	Y	N	Y
10 Young	N	N	Y	Y	Y	N	Y
11 Castor	Y	Y	Y	Y	Y	Y	Y
12 Putnam	N	N	Y	Y	Y	N	Y
13 Buchanan	N	N	Y	Y	Y	N	Y
14 Mack	N	N	Y	Y	Y	N	Y
15 Posey	N	N	Y	Y	Y	N	Y
16 Rooney	N	N	Y	Y	Y	N	Y
17 Meek	Y	Y	Y	Y	Y	Y	Y
18 Ros-Lehtinen	N	N	Y	Y	Y	N	Y
19 Deutch	Y	Y	Y	Y	Y	Y	Y
20 Wasserman Schultz	Y	Y	Y	Y	Y	Y	Y
21 Diaz-Balart, L.	N	N	Y	?	Y	N	Y
22 Klein	Y	Y	Y	?	Y	Y	Y
23 Hastings	?	?	?	?	?	?	?
24 Kosmas	Y	Y	Y	Y	Y	Y	Y
25 Diaz-Balart, M.	N	N	Y	Y	Y	N	Y
GEORGIA							
1 Kingston	N	N	Y	Y	Y	N	Y
2 Bishop	Y	Y	Y	Y	Y	Y	Y
3 Westmoreland	N	N	Y	Y	Y	N	Y
4 Johnson	Y	Y	Y	Y	Y	Y	Y
5 Lewis	Y	Y	Y	Y	Y	Y	Y
6 Price	N	N	Y	Y	Y	N	Y
7 Linder	N	N	Y	Y	Y	N	Y
8 Marshall	N	Y	Y	Y	Y	N	Y
9 Graves	N	N	Y	Y	Y	N	Y
10 Broun	N	N	Y	Y	Y	N	Y
11 Gingrey	N	N	Y	Y	Y	N	Y
12 Barrow	Y	Y	Y	Y	Y	Y	Y
13 Scott	Y	Y	Y	Y	Y	Y	Y
HAWAII							
1 Djou	Y	N	Y	Y	Y	N	Y
2 Hirono	Y	+	Y	Y	Y	Y	Y
IDAHO							
1 Minnick	?	?	?	?	?	?	?
2 Simpson	N	N	Y	Y	Y	N	Y
ILLINOIS							
1 Rush	Y	Y	Y	Y	Y	Y	Y
2 Jackson	Y	Y	Y	Y	Y	Y	Y
3 Lipinski	Y	Y	Y	Y	Y	Y	Y
4 Gutierrez	Y	Y	Y	Y	Y	Y	Y
5 Quigley	N	Y	Y	Y	Y	Y	Y
6 Roskam	N	N	Y	Y	Y	N	Y
7 Davis	?	?	?	?	?	?	?
8 Bean	Y	Y	Y	Y	Y	Y	Y
9 Schakowsky	Y	Y	Y	Y	Y	Y	Y
10 Vacant							
11 Halvorson	Y	Y	Y	Y	Y	Y	Y
12 Costello	Y	Y	Y	Y	Y	Y	Y
13 Biggert	N	N	Y	Y	Y	N	Y
14 Foster	Y	Y	Y	Y	Y	Y	Y
15 Johnson	N	N	Y	Y	Y	N	Y

KEY	**Republicans**	Democrats			
Y	Voted for (yea)		X	Paired against	C	Voted "present" to avoid possible conflict of interest
#	Paired for		–	Announced against	
+	Announced for		P	Voted "present"	?	Did not vote or otherwise make a position known
N	Voted against (nay)				

	588	589	590	591	592	593	594
16 **Manzullo**	N	N	Y	Y	Y	N	Y
17 Hare	Y	Y	Y	Y	Y	Y	Y
18 **Schock**	N	N	Y	Y	Y	N	Y
19 **Shimkus**	N	N	Y	Y	Y	N	Y
INDIANA							
1 Visclosky	Y	Y	Y	Y	Y	Y	Y
2 Donnelly	N	Y	Y	Y	Y	Y	Y
3 **Stutzman**	N	N	Y	Y	Y	N	Y
4 **Buyer**	?	?	?	?	?	?	?
5 **Burton**	–	–	+	+	+	N	Y
6 **Pence**	N	N	Y	Y	Y	N	Y
7 Carson	Y	Y	Y	Y	Y	Y	Y
8 Ellsworth	Y	Y	Y	Y	Y	Y	Y
9 Hill	Y	Y	Y	Y	Y	Y	Y
IOWA							
1 Braley	Y	Y	?	Y	Y	Y	Y
2 Loebsack	Y	Y	Y	Y	Y	Y	Y
3 Boswell	Y	Y	Y	Y	Y	Y	Y
4 **Latham**	N	N	Y	Y	Y	N	Y
5 **King**	N	N	Y	Y	Y	N	Y
KANSAS							
1 **Moran**	N	N	Y	Y	Y	N	Y
2 **Jenkins**	N	N	Y	Y	Y	N	Y
3 Moore	Y	Y	Y	Y	Y	Y	Y
4 **Tiahrt**	N	?	Y	Y	Y	N	Y
KENTUCKY							
1 **Whitfield**	?	?	Y	?	Y	N	Y
2 **Guthrie**	N	N	Y	Y	Y	N	Y
3 Yarmuth	Y	Y	Y	Y	Y	Y	Y
4 **Davis**	N	N	Y	Y	Y	N	Y
5 **Rogers**	N	N	?	Y	Y	N	Y
6 Chandler	N	Y	Y	Y	Y	Y	Y
LOUISIANA							
1 **Scalise**	N	N	Y	Y	Y	N	Y
2 **Cao**	N	?	Y	Y	Y	Y	Y
3 Melancon	?	?	?	?	?	Y	Y
4 **Fleming**	N	N	Y	Y	Y	N	Y
5 **Alexander**	?	?	?	?	?	N	Y
6 **Cassidy**	N	N	Y	Y	Y	N	Y
7 **Boustany**	N	N	Y	Y	Y	N	Y
MAINE							
1 Pingree	Y	Y	Y	Y	Y	Y	Y
2 Michaud	Y	Y	Y	Y	Y	Y	Y
MARYLAND							
1 Kratovil	Y	N	Y	Y	Y	N	Y
2 Ruppersberger	?	Y	Y	Y	Y	Y	Y
3 Sarbanes	Y	Y	Y	Y	Y	Y	Y
4 Edwards	Y	Y	Y	Y	Y	Y	Y
5 Hoyer	Y	Y	Y	Y	Y	Y	Y
6 **Bartlett**	N	N	Y	Y	Y	N	Y
7 Cummings	Y	Y	Y	Y	Y	Y	Y
8 Van Hollen	Y	Y	Y	Y	Y	Y	Y
MASSACHUSETTS							
1 Olver	Y	Y	Y	Y	Y	Y	Y
2 Neal	Y	Y	Y	?	Y	Y	Y
3 McGovern	Y	Y	Y	Y	Y	Y	Y
4 Frank	Y	Y	Y	Y	Y	Y	Y
5 Tsongas	Y	Y	Y	Y	Y	Y	Y
6 Tierney	Y	?	?	Y	Y	Y	Y
7 Markey	Y	Y	Y	Y	Y	Y	Y
8 Capuano	Y	Y	Y	Y	Y	Y	Y
9 Lynch	?	Y	Y	Y	Y	Y	Y
10 Delahunt	Y	Y	Y	Y	Y	?	?
MICHIGAN							
1 Stupak	Y	Y	Y	Y	Y	Y	Y
2 **Hoekstra**	N	N	Y	Y	?	N	Y
3 **Ehlers**	N	N	Y	Y	Y	N	Y
4 **Camp**	N	N	Y	Y	Y	N	Y
5 Kildee	Y	Y	Y	Y	Y	Y	Y
6 **Upton**	N	N	Y	Y	Y	N	Y
7 Schauer	Y	Y	Y	Y	Y	Y	Y
8 **Rogers**	N	N	Y	Y	Y	N	Y
9 Peters	Y	N	Y	Y	Y	N	Y
10 **Miller**	N	N	Y	Y	Y	N	Y
11 **McCotter**	N	N	Y	Y	Y	N	Y
12 Levin	Y	Y	Y	Y	Y	Y	Y
13 Kilpatrick	Y	Y	Y	Y	Y	Y	Y
14 Conyers	Y	Y	Y	Y	Y	Y	Y
15 Dingell	Y	Y	Y	Y	Y	Y	?
MINNESOTA							
1 Walz	Y	Y	Y	Y	Y	Y	Y
2 **Kline**	N	N	Y	Y	Y	N	Y
3 **Paulsen**	N	N	Y	Y	Y	N	Y
4 McCollum	Y	Y	Y	Y	Y	Y	Y
5 Ellison	Y	Y	Y	Y	Y	Y	Y
6 **Bachmann**	N	N	Y	Y	Y	N	Y
7 Peterson	Y	Y	Y	Y	Y	Y	Y
8 Oberstar	Y	Y	Y	Y	Y	Y	Y
MISSISSIPPI							
1 Childers	N	Y	Y	Y	Y	Y	Y
2 Thompson	Y	Y	Y	Y	Y	Y	Y
3 **Harper**	N	N	Y	Y	Y	N	Y
4 Taylor	Y	Y	Y	Y	Y	N	Y
MISSOURI							
1 Clay	Y	Y	Y	Y	Y	Y	Y
2 **Akin**	N	N	Y	Y	Y	N	Y
3 Carnahan	Y	Y	Y	Y	Y	Y	Y
4 Skelton	Y	Y	Y	Y	Y	Y	Y
5 Cleaver	Y	Y	Y	Y	Y	Y	Y
6 **Graves**	N	N	Y	Y	Y	N	Y
7 **Blunt**	N	N	Y	Y	Y	N	Y
8 **Emerson**	N	N	Y	Y	Y	N	Y
9 **Luetkemeyer**	N	N	Y	Y	Y	N	Y
MONTANA							
AL **Rehberg**	N	N	Y	Y	Y	N	Y
NEBRASKA							
1 **Fortenberry**	N	N	Y	Y	Y	N	Y
2 **Terry**	N	N	Y	Y	Y	N	Y
3 **Smith**	N	N	Y	Y	Y	N	Y
NEVADA							
1 Berkley	?	Y	Y	Y	Y	Y	Y
2 **Heller**	N	N	Y	Y	Y	N	Y
3 Titus	Y	Y	Y	Y	Y	Y	Y
NEW HAMPSHIRE							
1 Shea-Porter	Y	Y	Y	Y	Y	Y	Y
2 Hodes	?	?	?	?	?	?	?
NEW JERSEY							
1 Andrews	Y	Y	Y	Y	Y	Y	Y
2 **LoBiondo**	N	N	Y	Y	Y	N	Y
3 Adler	N	N	Y	Y	Y	N	Y
4 **Smith**	N	N	Y	Y	Y	N	Y
5 **Garrett**	N	N	Y	Y	Y	N	Y
6 Pallone	Y	Y	Y	Y	Y	Y	Y
7 **Lance**	N	N	Y	Y	Y	N	Y
8 Pascrell	Y	Y	Y	Y	Y	Y	Y
9 Rothman	Y	Y	Y	Y	Y	Y	Y
10 Payne	Y	Y	Y	Y	Y	Y	Y
11 **Frelinghuysen**	N	N	Y	Y	Y	N	Y
12 Holt	Y	Y	+	Y	Y	Y	Y
13 Sires	Y	Y	Y	Y	Y	Y	Y
NEW MEXICO							
1 Heinrich	Y	Y	Y	Y	Y	Y	Y
2 Teague	Y	Y	Y	Y	Y	Y	Y
3 Luján	Y	Y	Y	Y	Y	Y	Y
NEW YORK							
1 Bishop	Y	Y	Y	Y	Y	Y	Y
2 Israel	Y	Y	Y	Y	Y	Y	Y
3 **King**	N	N	Y	Y	Y	N	Y
4 McCarthy	Y	Y	Y	Y	Y	Y	Y
5 Ackerman	Y	Y	Y	Y	Y	Y	Y
6 Meeks	Y	Y	Y	Y	Y	Y	Y
7 Crowley	Y	Y	Y	Y	Y	Y	Y
8 Nadler	Y	Y	Y	Y	Y	Y	Y
9 Weiner	Y	Y	Y	Y	Y	Y	Y
10 Towns	Y	Y	Y	Y	Y	Y	Y
11 Clarke	Y	Y	Y	Y	Y	Y	Y
12 Velázquez	Y	Y	Y	Y	Y	Y	Y
13 McMahon	Y	Y	Y	Y	Y	Y	Y
14 Maloney	Y	Y	Y	Y	Y	Y	Y
15 Rangel	Y	Y	Y	?	?	Y	Y
16 Serrano	Y	Y	Y	Y	Y	Y	Y
17 Engel	Y	Y	Y	Y	Y	Y	Y
18 Lowey	Y	Y	Y	Y	Y	Y	Y
19 Hall	Y	Y	?	?	?	Y	Y
20 Murphy	N	Y	Y	Y	Y	Y	Y
21 Tonko	Y	Y	Y	Y	Y	Y	Y
22 Hinchey	Y	Y	Y	Y	Y	Y	Y
23 Owens	Y	Y	Y	Y	Y	Y	Y
24 Arcuri	Y	Y	Y	Y	Y	Y	Y
25 Maffei	Y	Y	Y	Y	Y	Y	Y
26 **Lee**	N	N	Y	Y	Y	N	Y
27 Higgins	Y	Y	Y	Y	Y	Y	Y
28 Slaughter	Y	Y	Y	Y	Y	Y	Y
29 **Reed**	N	N	Y	Y	Y	N	Y
NORTH CAROLINA							
1 Butterfield	Y	Y	Y	Y	Y	Y	Y
2 Etheridge	Y	Y	Y	Y	Y	Y	+
3 **Jones**	N	N	Y	Y	Y	N	Y
4 Price	Y	Y	Y	Y	Y	Y	Y
5 **Foxx**	N	N	Y	Y	Y	N	Y
6 **Coble**	N	N	Y	Y	Y	N	Y
7 McIntyre	Y	Y	Y	Y	Y	Y	Y
8 Kissell	Y	Y	Y	Y	Y	Y	Y
9 **Myrick**	–	–	+	+	+	N	Y
10 **McHenry**	N	N	Y	Y	Y	N	Y
11 Shuler	N	N	Y	Y	Y	Y	Y
12 Watt	Y	Y	Y	Y	Y	Y	Y
13 Miller	Y	Y	Y	Y	Y	Y	Y
NORTH DAKOTA							
AL Pomeroy	Y	Y	Y	Y	Y	Y	Y
OHIO							
1 Driehaus	Y	Y	Y	Y	Y	Y	Y
2 **Schmidt**	N	N	Y	Y	Y	N	Y
3 **Turner**	N	N	Y	Y	Y	N	Y
4 **Jordan**	N	N	Y	Y	Y	N	Y
5 **Latta**	N	N	Y	Y	Y	N	Y
6 Wilson	Y	Y	Y	Y	Y	Y	Y
7 **Austria**	N	N	Y	Y	Y	N	Y
8 **Boehner**	N	N	Y	Y	Y	N	Y
9 Kaptur	Y	Y	Y	Y	Y	Y	Y
10 Kucinich	Y	Y	Y	Y	Y	Y	Y
11 Fudge	Y	Y	Y	Y	Y	Y	Y
12 **Tiberi**	N	N	Y	Y	Y	N	Y
13 Sutton	Y	Y	Y	Y	Y	Y	Y
14 **LaTourette**	N	N	Y	Y	Y	N	Y
15 Kilroy	Y	Y	Y	Y	Y	Y	Y
16 Boccieri	Y	Y	Y	Y	Y	Y	Y
17 Ryan	Y	Y	Y	Y	Y	Y	Y
18 Space	Y	Y	Y	Y	Y	Y	Y
OKLAHOMA							
1 **Sullivan**	N	N	Y	Y	Y	N	Y
2 Boren	N	Y	Y	Y	Y	Y	Y
3 **Lucas**	N	N	Y	Y	Y	N	Y
4 **Cole**	N	N	Y	Y	Y	N	Y
5 **Fallin**	?	?	?	?	?	N	Y
OREGON							
1 Wu	?	?	?	?	?	?	?
2 **Walden**	N	N	Y	Y	Y	N	Y
3 Blumenauer	Y	Y	Y	Y	Y	Y	Y
4 DeFazio	?	?	?	?	?	?	?
5 Schrader	Y	Y	Y	Y	Y	Y	Y
PENNSYLVANIA							
1 Brady	Y	Y	Y	Y	Y	Y	Y
2 Fattah	Y	Y	Y	Y	Y	Y	Y
3 Dahlkemper	Y	Y	Y	Y	Y	Y	Y
4 Altmire	Y	Y	Y	Y	Y	Y	Y
5 **Thompson**	N	N	Y	Y	Y	N	Y
6 **Gerlach**	N	N	Y	Y	Y	N	Y
7 Sestak	Y	Y	Y	Y	Y	Y	Y
8 Murphy, P.	Y	Y	Y	Y	Y	Y	Y
9 **Shuster**	N	N	Y	Y	Y	N	Y
10 Carney	Y	Y	Y	Y	Y	Y	Y
11 Kanjorski	Y	Y	Y	Y	Y	Y	Y
12 Critz	Y	Y	Y	Y	Y	Y	Y
13 Schwartz	Y	?	Y	Y	Y	Y	Y
14 Doyle	Y	Y	Y	Y	Y	Y	Y
15 **Dent**	N	N	Y	Y	Y	N	Y
16 **Pitts**	N	N	Y	Y	Y	N	Y
17 Holden	Y	Y	Y	Y	Y	Y	Y
18 **Murphy, T.**	N	N	Y	Y	Y	N	Y
19 **Platts**	N	N	Y	Y	Y	N	Y
RHODE ISLAND							
1 Kennedy	Y	Y	Y	Y	Y	Y	?
2 Langevin	Y	Y	Y	Y	Y	Y	Y
SOUTH CAROLINA							
1 **Brown**	N	N	Y	Y	Y	N	Y
2 **Wilson**	N	N	Y	Y	Y	N	Y
3 **Barrett**	?	?	?	?	?	?	?
4 **Inglis**	N	N	Y	Y	Y	N	Y
5 Spratt	Y	Y	Y	Y	Y	?	Y
6 Clyburn	Y	Y	Y	Y	Y	Y	Y
SOUTH DAKOTA							
AL Herseth Sandlin	N	Y	Y	Y	Y	Y	Y
TENNESSEE							
1 **Roe**	N	N	Y	Y	Y	N	Y
2 **Duncan**	N	N	Y	Y	Y	N	Y
3 **Wamp**	N	N	Y	Y	Y	N	Y
4 Davis	?	Y	Y	Y	Y	Y	Y
5 Cooper	Y	Y	Y	Y	Y	Y	Y
6 Gordon	Y	Y	?	?	?	Y	Y
7 **Blackburn**	N	N	Y	Y	Y	N	Y
8 Tanner	N	Y	Y	Y	Y	Y	Y
9 Cohen	Y	Y	Y	Y	Y	Y	Y
TEXAS							
1 **Gohmert**	?	N	Y	Y	?	N	Y
2 **Poe**	N	N	Y	Y	Y	N	Y
3 **Johnson, S.**	?	N	Y	Y	Y	N	Y
4 **Hall**	N	N	Y	Y	Y	N	Y
5 **Hensarling**	N	N	Y	Y	Y	N	Y
6 **Barton**	N	N	Y	Y	Y	N	Y
7 **Culberson**	N	N	Y	Y	Y	N	Y
8 **Brady**	N	N	Y	Y	Y	N	Y
9 Green, A.	Y	Y	Y	Y	Y	Y	Y
10 **McCaul**	N	N	Y	Y	Y	N	Y
11 **Conaway**	N	N	Y	Y	Y	N	Y
12 **Granger**	N	N	Y	?	Y	N	Y
13 **Thornberry**	N	N	Y	Y	Y	N	Y
14 **Paul**	N	N	Y	N	Y	N	Y
15 Hinojosa	Y	Y	Y	Y	Y	Y	Y
16 Reyes	Y	Y	Y	?	Y	Y	Y
17 Edwards	Y	Y	Y	Y	Y	Y	Y
18 Jackson Lee	Y	Y	Y	Y	Y	Y	Y
19 **Neugebauer**	N	N	Y	Y	Y	N	Y
20 Gonzalez	Y	Y	Y	Y	Y	Y	Y
21 **Smith**	N	N	Y	Y	Y	N	Y
22 **Olson**	N	N	Y	Y	Y	N	Y
23 Rodriguez	Y	Y	Y	Y	Y	Y	Y
24 **Marchant**	?	?	?	?	?	?	?
25 Doggett	Y	Y	Y	Y	Y	Y	Y
26 **Burgess**	N	N	Y	Y	Y	N	Y
27 Ortiz	Y	Y	Y	Y	Y	Y	Y
28 Cuellar	Y	Y	Y	Y	Y	Y	Y
29 Green, G.	Y	Y	Y	Y	Y	Y	Y
30 Johnson, E.	Y	Y	Y	Y	Y	Y	Y
31 **Carter**	N	N	Y	Y	Y	N	Y
32 **Sessions**	N	N	Y	Y	Y	N	?
UTAH							
1 **Bishop**	N	N	Y	Y	Y	N	Y
2 Matheson	Y	Y	Y	Y	Y	Y	Y
3 **Chaffetz**	N	N	Y	Y	N	N	Y
VERMONT							
AL Welch	Y	Y	Y	Y	Y	Y	Y
VIRGINIA							
1 **Wittman**	N	N	Y	Y	Y	N	Y
2 Nye	Y	N	Y	Y	Y	N	Y
3 Scott	Y	Y	Y	Y	Y	Y	Y
4 **Forbes**	N	N	Y	Y	Y	N	Y
5 Perriello	Y	Y	Y	Y	Y	Y	Y
6 **Goodlatte**	N	N	Y	Y	Y	N	Y
7 **Cantor**	N	N	Y	Y	Y	N	Y
8 Moran	Y	Y	Y	Y	Y	Y	Y
9 Boucher	Y	Y	Y	Y	Y	Y	Y
10 **Wolf**	N	N	Y	Y	Y	N	Y
11 Connolly	Y	Y	Y	Y	Y	N	Y
WASHINGTON							
1 Inslee	Y	Y	Y	Y	Y	Y	Y
2 Larsen	Y	Y	Y	Y	Y	Y	Y
3 Baird	Y	Y	Y	Y	Y	Y	Y
4 **Hastings**	N	N	Y	Y	Y	?	Y
5 **McMorris Rodgers**	–	–	+	+	+	–	+
6 Dicks	Y	Y	Y	Y	Y	Y	Y
7 McDermott	Y	Y	Y	Y	Y	Y	Y
8 **Reichert**	N	N	Y	Y	Y	N	Y
9 Smith	Y	Y	Y	Y	Y	Y	Y
WEST VIRGINIA							
1 Mollohan	Y	Y	Y	Y	Y	Y	Y
2 **Capito**	N	N	Y	Y	Y	N	Y
3 Rahall	Y	Y	Y	Y	Y	Y	Y
WISCONSIN							
1 **Ryan**	N	N	Y	Y	Y	N	Y
2 Baldwin	Y	Y	Y	Y	Y	Y	Y
3 Kind	Y	Y	Y	Y	Y	Y	Y
4 Moore	Y	Y	Y	Y	Y	Y	Y
5 **Sensenbrenner**	N	N	Y	Y	Y	N	Y
6 **Petri**	N	N	Y	Y	Y	N	Y
7 Obey	Y	Y	Y	Y	Y	Y	Y
8 Kagen	Y	Y	Y	N	Y	Y	Y
WYOMING							
AL **Lummis**	N	N	Y	Y	Y	N	Y
DELEGATES							
Faleomavaega (A.S.)							
Norton (D.C.)							
Bordallo (Guam)							
Sablan (N. Marianas)							
Pierluisi (P.R.)							
Christensen (V.I.)							

IN THE HOUSE | By Vote Number

595. **H Res 1724. Tribute to City of Jacksonville/Adoption.** Snyder, D-Ark., motion to suspend the rules and adopt the resolution that would commend the city of Jacksonville, Ark., for its support of and partnership with the Little Rock Air Force Base. Motion agreed to 411-0: D 241-0; R 170-0. A two-thirds majority of those present and voting (274 in this case) is required for adoption under suspension of the rules. Dec. 1, 2010.

596. **HR 4853. Tax Rates Extensions/Previous Question.** Pingree, D-Maine, motion to order the previous question (thus ending debate and possibility of amendment) on adoption of the rule (H Res 1745) that would allow for a motion to concur in the Senate amendment to the bill with a House amendment that would extend certain tax provisions, including making permanent the rates and benefits enacted under 2001 and 2003 tax-cut laws for taxable incomes of up to $200,000 for individuals and $250,000 for couples. Motion agreed to 224-186: D 224-17; R 0-169. Dec. 2, 2010.

597. **HR 4853. Tax Rates Extensions/Rule.** Adoption of the rule (H Res 1745) that would provide for House floor consideration of the Senate amendment to the bill by allowing for a motion to concur with a House amendment that would extend certain tax provisions, including making permanent the rates and benefits under 2001 and 2003 tax cut laws for taxable incomes of up to $200,000 for individuals and $250,000 for couples. The rule also would allow for House floor consideration of measures under suspension of the rules through Dec. 3, 2010. Adopted 213-203: D 213-33; R 0-170. Dec. 2, 2010.

598. **H Res 1638. National GEAR UP Day/Adoption.** Woolsey, D-Calif., motion to suspend the rules and adopt the resolution that would support the goals and ideals of National GEAR UP Day. Motion agreed to 405-0: D 239-0; R 166-0. A two-thirds majority of those present and voting (270 in this case) is required for adoption under suspension of the rules. Dec. 2, 2010.

599. **H Res 1598. National Work and Family Month/Adoption.** Woolsey, D-Calif., motion to suspend the rules and adopt the resolution that would support the designation of National Work and Family Month. Motion agreed to 412-0: D 244-0; R 168-0. A two-thirds majority of those present and voting (275 in this case) is required for adoption under suspension of the rules. Dec. 2, 2010.

600. **H Res 1576. Recognition for Parents of Special Needs Children/Adoption.** Woolsey, D-Calif., motion to suspend the rules and adopt the resolution that would support the establishment of a National Day of Recognition for Parents of Children with Special Needs. Motion agreed to 413-0: D 243-0; R 170-0. A two-thirds majority of those present and voting (276 in this case) is required for adoption under suspension of the rules. Dec. 2, 2010.

601. **HR 6469. Child Care Worker Background Checks/Passage.** Miller, D-Calif., motion to suspend the rules and pass the bill that would make an institution ineligible for funds under the Child and Adult Care Food Program if it employs a child care staff member who refuses to consent to or makes a false statement on a background check, is registered or required to be registered as a sex offender, or has been convicted of a certain type of felony. Motion agreed to 416-3: D 250-0; R 166-3. A two-thirds majority of those present and voting (280 in this case) is required for passage under suspension of the rules. Dec. 2, 2010.

	595	596	597	598	599	600	601
ALABAMA							
1 Bonner	Y	N	N	Y	Y	Y	Y
2 Bright	Y	N	N	Y	Y	Y	Y
3 Rogers	Y	N	N	Y	Y	Y	Y
4 Aderholt	Y	N	N	Y	Y	Y	Y
5 Griffith	Y	N	N	Y	Y	Y	Y
6 Bachus	Y	N	N	Y	Y	Y	Y
7 Davis	Y	N	N	Y	Y	Y	Y
ALASKA							
AL Young	Y	N	N	Y	Y	Y	Y
ARIZONA							
1 Kirkpatrick	Y	Y	N	Y	Y	Y	Y
2 Franks	Y	N	N	Y	Y	Y	Y
3 Shadegg	Y	?	?	Y	Y	Y	Y
4 Pastor	Y	Y	Y	Y	Y	Y	Y
5 Mitchell	Y	N	N	Y	Y	Y	Y
6 Flake	Y	N	N	Y	Y	Y	Y
7 Grijalva	Y	Y	Y	Y	Y	Y	Y
8 Giffords	Y	Y	Y	Y	Y	Y	Y
ARKANSAS							
1 Berry	Y	N	N	Y	Y	Y	?
2 Snyder	Y	Y	Y	Y	Y	Y	Y
3 Boozman	Y	N	N	Y	Y	Y	Y
4 Ross	Y	N	N	Y	Y	Y	Y
CALIFORNIA							
1 Thompson	Y	Y	Y	Y	Y	Y	Y
2 Herger	Y	N	N	Y	Y	Y	Y
3 Lungren	Y	N	N	Y	Y	Y	Y
4 McClintock	Y	N	N	Y	Y	Y	Y
5 Matsui	Y	Y	Y	Y	Y	Y	Y
6 Woolsey	+	Y	Y	Y	Y	Y	Y
7 Miller, George	Y	Y	Y	Y	Y	Y	Y
8 Pelosi			Y				Y
9 Lee	Y	Y	Y	Y	Y	Y	Y
10 Garamendi	Y	Y	Y	?	?	?	Y
11 McNerney	Y	Y	Y	Y	Y	Y	Y
12 Speier	?	Y	Y	Y	Y	Y	Y
13 Stark	Y	Y	Y	Y	Y	Y	Y
14 Eshoo	Y	Y	Y	Y	Y	Y	Y
15 Honda	Y	Y	Y	Y	Y	Y	Y
16 Lofgren	Y	Y	Y	Y	Y	Y	Y
17 Farr	Y	Y	Y	Y	Y	Y	Y
18 Cardoza	?	?	?	?	Y	Y	Y
19 Radanovich	?	N	N	Y	Y	Y	Y
20 Costa	Y	N	N	Y	Y	Y	Y
21 Nunes	Y	N	N	Y	Y	Y	Y
22 McCarthy	Y	N	N	Y	Y	Y	Y
23 Capps	Y	Y	Y	Y	Y	Y	Y
24 Gallegly	Y	N	N	Y	Y	Y	Y
25 McKeon	Y	N	N	Y	Y	Y	Y
26 Dreier	Y	N	N	Y	Y	Y	Y
27 Sherman	Y	Y	Y	Y	Y	Y	Y
28 Berman	Y	?	Y	Y	Y	Y	Y
29 Schiff	Y	Y	Y	Y	Y	Y	Y
30 Waxman	Y	?	Y	Y	Y	Y	Y
31 Becerra	Y	Y	Y	Y	Y	Y	Y
32 Chu	Y	Y	Y	Y	Y	Y	Y
33 Watson	Y	Y	Y	Y	Y	Y	Y
34 Roybal-Allard	Y	Y	Y	Y	Y	Y	Y
35 Waters	Y	Y	Y	Y	Y	?	Y
36 Harman	Y	Y	Y	Y	Y	Y	Y
37 Richardson	Y	Y	Y	Y	Y	Y	Y
38 Napolitano	Y	Y	Y	Y	Y	Y	Y
39 Sánchez, Linda	Y	Y	Y	Y	Y	Y	Y
40 Royce	Y	N	N	Y	Y	Y	Y
41 Lewis	Y	N	N	Y	Y	Y	Y
42 Miller, Gary	Y	N	N	Y	Y	Y	Y
43 Baca	Y	Y	Y	Y	Y	Y	Y
44 Calvert	Y	N	N	Y	Y	Y	Y
45 Bono Mack	Y	N	N	Y	Y	Y	Y
46 Rohrabacher	Y	N	N	Y	Y	Y	Y
47 Sanchez, Loretta	Y	Y	Y	Y	Y	Y	Y
48 Campbell	Y	N	N	Y	Y	Y	Y
49 Issa	Y	N	N	Y	Y	Y	Y
50 Bilbray	Y	N	N	Y	Y	Y	Y
51 Filner	Y	Y	Y	Y	Y	Y	Y
52 Hunter	Y	N	N	Y	Y	Y	Y
53 Davis	Y	Y	Y	Y	Y	Y	Y

	595	596	597	598	599	600	601
COLORADO							
1 DeGette	Y	Y	Y	Y	Y	Y	Y
2 Polis	Y	Y	Y	Y	Y	Y	Y
3 Salazar	Y	Y	Y	Y	Y	Y	Y
4 Markey	Y	Y	Y	Y	Y	Y	Y
5 Lamborn	Y	N	N	Y	Y	Y	Y
6 Coffman	Y	N	N	Y	Y	Y	Y
7 Perlmutter	Y	Y	Y	Y	Y	Y	?
CONNECTICUT							
1 Larson	Y	Y	Y	Y	Y	Y	Y
2 Courtney	Y	Y	Y	Y	Y	Y	Y
3 DeLauro	Y	Y	Y	Y	Y	Y	Y
4 Himes	Y	Y	N	Y	Y	Y	Y
5 Murphy	Y	Y	Y	Y	Y	Y	Y
DELAWARE							
AL Castle	Y	N	N	Y	Y	Y	Y
FLORIDA							
1 Miller	?	N	N	Y	Y	Y	Y
2 Boyd	Y	Y	N	Y	Y	Y	Y
3 Brown	Y	Y	Y	Y	Y	Y	Y
4 Crenshaw	Y	N	N	Y	Y	Y	Y
5 Brown-Waite	?	?	?	?	?	?	?
6 Stearns	Y	N	N	Y	Y	Y	Y
7 Mica	Y	N	N	Y	Y	Y	Y
8 Grayson	Y	+	Y	Y	Y	Y	Y
9 Bilirakis	Y	N	N	Y	Y	Y	Y
10 Young	Y	N	N	Y	Y	Y	Y
11 Castor	Y	Y	Y	Y	Y	Y	Y
12 Putnam	Y	?	?	?	?	?	?
13 Buchanan	Y	N	N	Y	Y	Y	Y
14 Mack	Y	N	N	Y	Y	Y	Y
15 Posey	Y	N	N	Y	Y	Y	Y
16 Rooney	Y	N	N	Y	Y	Y	Y
17 Meek	Y	?	Y	Y	Y	Y	Y
18 Ros-Lehtinen	Y	N	N	Y	Y	Y	Y
19 Deutch	Y	Y	Y	Y	Y	Y	Y
20 Wasserman Schultz	Y	Y	Y	Y	Y	Y	Y
21 Diaz-Balart, L.	Y	N	N	Y	Y	Y	Y
22 Klein	Y	Y	Y	Y	Y	Y	Y
23 Hastings	?	?	?	?	?	?	?
24 Kosmas	Y	Y	Y	Y	Y	Y	Y
25 Diaz-Balart, M.	Y	N	N	Y	Y	Y	Y
GEORGIA							
1 Kingston	Y	N	N	Y	Y	Y	Y
2 Bishop	Y	Y	Y	Y	Y	Y	Y
3 Westmoreland	Y	N	N	Y	Y	Y	Y
4 Johnson	Y	Y	Y	Y	Y	Y	Y
5 Lewis	Y	?	?	?	?	?	Y
6 Price	Y	N	N	?	Y	Y	Y
7 Linder	Y	N	N	Y	Y	Y	Y
8 Marshall	Y	N	N	Y	Y	Y	Y
9 Graves	Y	N	N	Y	Y	Y	Y
10 Broun	Y	N	N	Y	Y	Y	N
11 Gingrey	Y	N	N	Y	Y	Y	Y
12 Barrow	Y	Y	Y	Y	Y	?	Y
13 Scott	Y	Y	Y	Y	Y	Y	Y
HAWAII							
1 Djou	Y	N	N	Y	Y	Y	Y
2 Hirono	Y	Y	Y	Y	Y	Y	Y
IDAHO							
1 Minnick	?	N	N	Y	Y	Y	Y
2 Simpson	Y	N	N	Y	Y	Y	Y
ILLINOIS							
1 Rush	Y	Y	Y	Y	Y	Y	Y
2 Jackson	Y	Y	Y	Y	Y	Y	Y
3 Lipinski	Y	N	N	Y	Y	Y	Y
4 Gutierrez	Y	Y	Y	Y	Y	Y	Y
5 Quigley	Y	Y	Y	Y	Y	Y	Y
6 Roskam	Y	N	N	Y	Y	Y	Y
7 Davis	?	Y	Y	Y	Y	Y	Y
8 Bean	Y	N	N	Y	Y	Y	Y
9 Schakowsky	Y	Y	Y	Y	Y	Y	Y
10 Vacant							
11 Halvorson	Y	N	N	Y	Y	Y	Y
12 Costello	Y	Y	N	Y	Y	Y	Y
13 Biggert	Y	N	N	Y	Y	Y	Y
14 Foster	Y	Y	Y	Y	Y	Y	Y
15 Johnson	Y	N	N	Y	Y	Y	Y

KEY

Republicans Democrats

Y Voted for (yea)	X Paired against	C Voted "present" to avoid possible conflict of interest
# Paired for	− Announced against	
+ Announced for	P Voted "present"	? Did not vote or otherwise make a position known
N Voted against (nay)		

	595	596	597	598	599	600	601
16 **Manzullo**	Y	N	N	Y	Y	Y	Y
17 Hare	Y	Y	Y	Y	Y	Y	Y
18 **Schock**	Y	N	N	Y	Y	Y	Y
19 **Shimkus**	Y	N	N	Y	Y	Y	Y
INDIANA							
1 Visclosky	Y	Y	Y	Y	Y	Y	Y
2 Donnelly	Y	Y	Y	Y	Y	Y	Y
3 **Stutzman**	Y	N	N	Y	Y	Y	Y
4 **Buyer**	?	?	?	?	?	?	?
5 **Burton**	Y	N	N	Y	Y	Y	Y
6 **Pence**	Y	N	N	Y	Y	Y	Y
7 Carson	Y	Y	Y	Y	Y	Y	Y
8 Ellsworth	Y	Y	N	Y	Y	Y	Y
9 Hill	Y	Y	Y	Y	Y	Y	Y
IOWA							
1 Braley	Y	Y	Y	Y	Y	Y	Y
2 Loebsack	Y	Y	Y	Y	Y	Y	Y
3 Boswell	Y	Y	Y	Y	Y	Y	Y
4 **Latham**	Y	N	N	Y	Y	Y	Y
5 **King**	Y	N	N	Y	Y	Y	N
KANSAS							
1 **Moran**	Y	N	N	Y	Y	Y	Y
2 **Jenkins**	Y	N	N	Y	Y	Y	Y
3 Moore	Y	Y	Y	Y	Y	Y	Y
4 **Tiahrt**	Y	N	N	Y	Y	Y	Y
KENTUCKY							
1 **Whitfield**	Y	N	N	Y	Y	Y	Y
2 **Guthrie**	Y	N	N	Y	Y	Y	Y
3 Yarmuth	Y	Y	Y	Y	Y	Y	Y
4 **Davis**	Y	N	N	Y	Y	Y	Y
5 **Rogers**	Y	N	N	Y	Y	Y	Y
6 Chandler	Y	Y	N	Y	Y	Y	Y
LOUISIANA							
1 **Scalise**	Y	N	N	Y	Y	Y	Y
2 **Cao**	Y	N	N	Y	Y	Y	Y
3 Melancon	Y	Y	Y	Y	Y	?	Y
4 **Fleming**	Y	N	N	Y	Y	Y	Y
5 **Alexander**	Y	?	N	Y	Y	Y	Y
6 **Cassidy**	Y	N	N	Y	Y	?	Y
7 **Boustany**	Y	N	N	Y	Y	Y	Y
MAINE							
1 Pingree	?	Y	Y	Y	Y	Y	Y
2 Michaud	Y	Y	Y	Y	Y	Y	Y
MARYLAND							
1 Kratovil	Y	N	Y	Y	Y	Y	Y
2 Ruppersberger	Y	Y	Y	Y	Y	Y	Y
3 Sarbanes	Y	Y	Y	Y	Y	Y	Y
4 Edwards	Y	Y	Y	Y	Y	Y	Y
5 Hoyer	Y	Y	Y	Y	Y	Y	Y
6 **Bartlett**	Y	N	N	Y	Y	Y	Y
7 Cummings	Y	Y	Y	Y	Y	Y	Y
8 Van Hollen	Y	Y	Y	Y	Y	Y	Y
MASSACHUSETTS							
1 Olver	Y	Y	Y	Y	Y	Y	Y
2 Neal	Y	Y	Y	Y	Y	Y	Y
3 McGovern	Y	Y	Y	Y	Y	Y	Y
4 Frank	Y	Y	Y	Y	Y	Y	Y
5 Tsongas	Y	Y	Y	Y	Y	Y	Y
6 Tierney	Y	Y	Y	Y	Y	Y	Y
7 Markey	Y	Y	Y	Y	Y	Y	Y
8 Capuano	Y	Y	Y	Y	Y	Y	Y
9 Lynch	Y	Y	Y	Y	Y	Y	Y
10 Delahunt	?	?	?	?	?	?	?
MICHIGAN							
1 Stupak	Y	Y	Y	Y	Y	Y	Y
2 **Hoekstra**	Y	N	N	Y	Y	Y	Y
3 **Ehlers**	Y	N	N	Y	Y	Y	Y
4 **Camp**	Y	N	N	Y	Y	Y	Y
5 Kildee	Y	Y	Y	Y	Y	Y	Y
6 **Upton**	Y	N	N	Y	Y	Y	Y
7 Schauer	Y	Y	Y	Y	Y	Y	Y
8 **Rogers**	Y	N	N	Y	Y	Y	Y
9 Peters	Y	Y	N	Y	Y	Y	Y
10 **Miller**	Y	N	N	Y	Y	Y	Y
11 **McCotter**	Y	N	N	Y	Y	Y	Y
12 Levin	Y	Y	Y	Y	Y	Y	Y
13 Kilpatrick	Y	Y	Y	Y	Y	Y	Y
14 Conyers	Y	Y	Y	?	Y	Y	Y
15 Dingell	Y	Y	Y	Y	Y	Y	Y
MINNESOTA							
1 Walz	Y	Y	Y	Y	Y	Y	Y
2 **Kline**	Y	N	N	Y	Y	Y	Y
3 **Paulsen**	Y	N	N	Y	Y	Y	Y
4 McCollum	Y	Y	Y	Y	Y	Y	Y

	595	596	597	598	599	600	601
5 Ellison	Y	Y	Y	Y	Y	Y	Y
6 **Bachmann**	Y	?	?	?	?	?	?
7 Peterson	Y	N	N	Y	Y	Y	Y
8 Oberstar	Y	?	Y	Y	Y	Y	Y
MISSISSIPPI							
1 Childers	Y	N	Y	Y	Y	Y	Y
2 Thompson	Y	Y	Y	Y	Y	Y	Y
3 **Harper**	Y	N	N	Y	Y	Y	Y
4 Taylor	Y	?	?	Y	Y	Y	Y
MISSOURI							
1 Clay	Y	Y	Y	Y	Y	Y	Y
2 **Akin**	Y	N	N	Y	Y	Y	Y
3 Carnahan	Y	Y	Y	Y	Y	Y	Y
4 Skelton	Y	Y	Y	Y	Y	Y	Y
5 Cleaver	Y	Y	Y	Y	Y	Y	Y
6 **Graves**	Y	N	N	Y	Y	Y	Y
7 **Blunt**	Y	N	N	Y	Y	Y	Y
8 **Emerson**	Y	N	N	Y	Y	Y	Y
9 **Luetkemeyer**	Y	N	N	Y	Y	Y	Y
MONTANA							
AL **Rehberg**	Y	N	N	Y	Y	Y	Y
NEBRASKA							
1 **Fortenberry**	Y	N	N	Y	Y	Y	Y
2 **Terry**	Y	N	N	Y	Y	Y	Y
3 **Smith**	Y	N	N	Y	Y	Y	Y
NEVADA							
1 Berkley	Y	Y	Y	Y	Y	Y	Y
2 **Heller**	Y	N	N	Y	Y	Y	Y
3 Titus	Y	Y	Y	Y	Y	Y	Y
NEW HAMPSHIRE							
1 Shea-Porter	Y	Y	Y	Y	Y	Y	Y
2 Hodes	?	Y	Y	Y	Y	Y	Y
NEW JERSEY							
1 Andrews	Y	Y	Y	Y	Y	Y	Y
2 **LoBiondo**	Y	N	N	Y	Y	Y	Y
3 Adler	Y	N	N	Y	Y	Y	Y
4 **Smith**	Y	N	N	Y	Y	Y	Y
5 **Garrett**	Y	N	N	Y	Y	Y	Y
6 Pallone	Y	Y	Y	Y	Y	Y	Y
7 **Lance**	Y	N	N	Y	Y	Y	Y
8 Pascrell	Y	Y	Y	Y	Y	Y	Y
9 Rothman	Y	Y	Y	Y	Y	Y	Y
10 Payne	Y	Y	Y	Y	Y	Y	Y
11 **Frelinghuysen**	Y	N	N	Y	Y	Y	Y
12 Holt	Y	Y	Y	Y	Y	Y	Y
13 Sires	Y	Y	Y	Y	Y	Y	Y
NEW MEXICO							
1 Heinrich	Y	Y	Y	Y	Y	Y	Y
2 Teague	Y	Y	Y	Y	Y	Y	Y
3 Luján	Y	Y	Y	Y	Y	Y	Y
NEW YORK							
1 Bishop	Y	Y	Y	Y	Y	Y	Y
2 Israel	Y	Y	Y	Y	Y	Y	Y
3 **King**	Y	N	N	Y	Y	Y	Y
4 McCarthy	Y	Y	Y	Y	Y	Y	Y
5 Ackerman	Y	Y	Y	Y	Y	Y	Y
6 Meeks	Y	Y	Y	Y	Y	Y	Y
7 Crowley	Y	Y	Y	Y	Y	Y	Y
8 Nadler	Y	Y	Y	Y	Y	Y	Y
9 Weiner	Y	Y	Y	Y	Y	Y	Y
10 Towns	Y	Y	Y	Y	Y	Y	Y
11 Clarke	Y	Y	Y	?	Y	Y	Y
12 Velázquez	Y	Y	Y	Y	Y	Y	Y
13 McMahon	Y	Y	Y	Y	Y	Y	Y
14 Maloney	Y	Y	Y	Y	Y	Y	Y
15 Rangel	Y	Y	Y	Y	Y	Y	Y
16 Serrano	Y	Y	Y	Y	Y	Y	Y
17 Engel	Y	Y	Y	Y	Y	Y	Y
18 Lowey	Y	Y	Y	Y	Y	Y	Y
19 Hall	Y	Y	Y	Y	Y	Y	Y
20 Murphy	Y	Y	Y	Y	Y	Y	Y
21 Tonko	Y	Y	Y	Y	Y	Y	Y
22 Hinchey	Y	Y	Y	Y	Y	Y	Y
23 Owens	Y	Y	?	Y	Y	Y	Y
24 Arcuri	Y	Y	Y	Y	Y	Y	Y
25 Maffei	Y	Y	Y	Y	Y	Y	Y
26 **Lee**	Y	N	N	Y	Y	Y	Y
27 Higgins	Y	Y	Y	Y	Y	Y	Y
28 Slaughter	Y	Y	Y	Y	Y	Y	Y
29 **Reed**	Y	N	N	Y	Y	Y	Y
NORTH CAROLINA							
1 Butterfield	Y	Y	Y	?	Y	Y	Y
2 Etheridge	Y	Y	Y	Y	Y	Y	Y
3 **Jones**	Y	N	N	Y	Y	Y	Y
4 Price	Y	Y	Y	Y	Y	Y	Y

	595	596	597	598	599	600	601
5 **Foxx**	Y	N	N	Y	Y	Y	Y
6 **Coble**	Y	N	N	Y	Y	Y	Y
7 McIntyre	Y	N	N	Y	Y	Y	Y
8 Kissell	Y	Y	Y	Y	Y	Y	Y
9 **Myrick**	Y	N	N	Y	Y	Y	Y
10 **McHenry**	Y	N	N	Y	Y	Y	Y
11 Shuler	Y	Y	N	Y	Y	Y	Y
12 Watt	Y	Y	Y	Y	Y	Y	Y
13 Miller	Y	Y	Y	Y	Y	Y	Y
NORTH DAKOTA							
AL Pomeroy	Y	Y	N	?	?	?	Y
OHIO							
1 Driehaus	Y	Y	Y	Y	Y	Y	Y
2 **Schmidt**	Y	N	N	Y	Y	Y	Y
3 **Turner**	Y	N	N	Y	Y	Y	Y
4 **Jordan**	Y	N	N	Y	Y	Y	Y
5 **Latta**	Y	N	N	Y	Y	Y	Y
6 Wilson	Y	Y	Y	Y	Y	Y	Y
7 **Austria**	Y	N	N	Y	Y	Y	Y
8 **Boehner**	?	N	N	?	?	Y	Y
9 Kaptur	Y	Y	Y	?	Y	Y	Y
10 Kucinich	Y	Y	Y	Y	Y	Y	Y
11 Fudge	Y	Y	Y	Y	Y	Y	Y
12 **Tiberi**	Y	N	N	Y	Y	Y	Y
13 Sutton	Y	Y	Y	Y	Y	Y	Y
14 **LaTourette**	Y	N	N	Y	Y	Y	Y
15 Kilroy	Y	Y	Y	Y	Y	Y	Y
16 Boccieri	Y	Y	Y	Y	Y	Y	Y
17 Ryan	Y	Y	Y	Y	Y	Y	Y
18 Space	Y	Y	N	Y	Y	Y	Y
OKLAHOMA							
1 **Sullivan**	Y	N	N	Y	Y	Y	Y
2 Boren	Y	N	N	Y	Y	Y	Y
3 **Lucas**	Y	N	N	Y	Y	Y	Y
4 **Cole**	Y	N	N	Y	Y	Y	Y
5 **Fallin**	Y	?	?	?	?	?	?
OREGON							
1 Wu	?	Y	Y	Y	Y	Y	Y
2 **Walden**	Y	N	N	?	?	Y	Y
3 Blumenauer	Y	Y	Y	Y	Y	Y	Y
4 DeFazio	?	?	?	?	?	?	?
5 Schrader	Y	?	?	?	?	?	Y
PENNSYLVANIA							
1 Brady	Y	Y	Y	Y	Y	Y	Y
2 Fattah	Y	Y	Y	Y	Y	Y	Y
3 Dahlkemper	Y	Y	N	Y	Y	Y	Y
4 Altmire	Y	N	N	Y	Y	Y	Y
5 **Thompson**	Y	N	N	Y	Y	Y	Y
6 **Gerlach**	Y	N	N	Y	Y	Y	Y
7 Sestak	Y	Y	Y	Y	Y	Y	Y
8 Murphy, P.	Y	Y	Y	Y	Y	Y	Y
9 **Shuster**	Y	N	N	Y	Y	Y	Y
10 Carney	Y	Y	Y	Y	Y	Y	Y
11 Kanjorski	Y	Y	Y	Y	Y	Y	Y
12 Critz	Y	Y	Y	Y	Y	Y	Y
13 Schwartz	Y	Y	Y	Y	Y	Y	Y
14 Doyle	Y	Y	Y	Y	Y	Y	Y
15 **Dent**	Y	N	N	Y	Y	Y	Y
16 **Pitts**	Y	N	N	Y	Y	Y	Y
17 Holden	Y	Y	Y	Y	Y	Y	Y
18 **Murphy, T.**	Y	N	N	Y	Y	Y	Y
19 **Platts**	Y	N	N	Y	Y	Y	Y
RHODE ISLAND							
1 Kennedy	?	Y	Y	Y	Y	Y	Y
2 Langevin	Y	Y	Y	Y	Y	Y	Y
SOUTH CAROLINA							
1 **Brown**	Y	N	N	Y	Y	Y	Y
2 **Wilson**	Y	N	N	Y	Y	Y	Y
3 **Barrett**	?	?	?	?	?	?	?
4 **Inglis**	Y	N	N	Y	Y	Y	Y
5 Spratt	Y	Y	Y	Y	Y	Y	Y
6 Clyburn	Y	Y	Y	?	Y	Y	Y
SOUTH DAKOTA							
AL Herseth Sandlin	Y	Y	N	Y	Y	Y	Y
TENNESSEE							
1 **Roe**	Y	N	N	Y	Y	Y	Y
2 **Duncan**	Y	N	N	Y	Y	Y	Y
3 **Wamp**	Y	N	N	Y	Y	Y	Y
4 Davis	Y	Y	Y	Y	Y	Y	Y
5 Cooper	Y	N	N	Y	Y	Y	Y
6 Gordon	?	Y	Y	Y	?	Y	Y
7 **Blackburn**	?	N	N	Y	Y	Y	Y
8 Tanner	Y	Y	Y	Y	Y	Y	Y
9 Cohen	Y	Y	Y	Y	Y	Y	Y

	595	596	597	598	599	600	601
TEXAS							
1 **Gohmert**	Y	N	N	?	Y	Y	Y
2 **Poe**	Y	N	N	Y	Y	Y	Y
3 **Johnson, S.**	Y	N	N	Y	Y	Y	Y
4 **Hall**	Y	N	N	Y	Y	Y	Y
5 **Hensarling**	Y	N	N	Y	Y	Y	Y
6 **Barton**	Y	N	N	Y	Y	Y	Y
7 **Culberson**	Y	N	N	Y	Y	Y	Y
8 **Brady**	Y	N	N	Y	Y	Y	Y
9 Green, A.	Y	Y	Y	Y	Y	Y	Y
10 **McCaul**	Y	N	N	Y	Y	Y	Y
11 **Conaway**	Y	N	N	Y	Y	Y	Y
12 **Granger**	Y	N	N	Y	Y	Y	?
13 **Thornberry**	Y	N	N	Y	Y	Y	Y
14 **Paul**	Y	N	N	Y	Y	Y	N
15 Hinojosa	Y	Y	Y	?	Y	Y	Y
16 Reyes	Y	Y	Y	Y	Y	Y	Y
17 Edwards	Y	Y	Y	Y	Y	Y	Y
18 Jackson Lee	Y	Y	Y	Y	Y	Y	Y
19 **Neugebauer**	Y	N	N	Y	Y	Y	Y
20 Gonzalez	Y	Y	Y	Y	Y	Y	Y
21 **Smith**	Y	N	N	Y	Y	Y	Y
22 **Olson**	Y	N	N	Y	Y	Y	Y
23 Rodriguez	Y	Y	Y	Y	Y	Y	Y
24 **Marchant**	?	?	?	?	?	?	?
25 Doggett	Y	Y	Y	Y	Y	Y	Y
26 **Burgess**	Y	N	N	Y	Y	Y	Y
27 Ortiz	Y	Y	Y	Y	?	Y	Y
28 Cuellar	Y	Y	Y	Y	Y	Y	Y
29 Green, G.	Y	Y	Y	Y	Y	Y	Y
30 Johnson, E.	Y	Y	Y	Y	Y	Y	Y
31 **Carter**	Y	N	N	Y	Y	Y	?
32 **Sessions**	Y	N	N	Y	Y	Y	Y
UTAH							
1 **Bishop**	Y	N	N	?	?	Y	Y
2 Matheson	Y	N	N	Y	Y	Y	Y
3 **Chaffetz**	Y	N	N	Y	Y	Y	Y
VERMONT							
AL Welch	Y	Y	Y	Y	Y	Y	Y
VIRGINIA							
1 **Wittman**	Y	N	N	Y	Y	Y	Y
2 Nye	Y	Y	Y	Y	Y	Y	Y
3 Scott	Y	Y	Y	Y	Y	Y	Y
4 **Forbes**	Y	N	N	Y	Y	Y	Y
5 Perriello	Y	Y	N	Y	Y	Y	Y
6 **Goodlatte**	Y	N	N	Y	Y	Y	Y
7 **Cantor**	Y	N	N	Y	Y	Y	Y
8 Moran	Y	Y	N	Y	Y	Y	Y
9 Boucher	Y	?	?	?	?	?	Y
10 **Wolf**	Y	N	N	Y	Y	Y	Y
11 Connolly	Y	Y	N	Y	Y	Y	Y
WASHINGTON							
1 Inslee	Y	Y	Y	Y	Y	Y	Y
2 Larsen	Y	Y	Y	Y	Y	Y	Y
3 Baird	Y	Y	N	Y	Y	Y	Y
4 **Hastings**	Y	N	N	Y	Y	Y	Y
5 **McMorris Rodgers**	+	?	?	?	?	?	?
6 Dicks	Y	Y	Y	Y	Y	Y	Y
7 McDermott	Y	Y	Y	Y	Y	Y	Y
8 **Reichert**	Y	N	N	Y	Y	Y	Y
9 Smith	Y	Y	Y	Y	Y	Y	Y
WEST VIRGINIA							
1 Mollohan	Y	Y	Y	Y	Y	Y	Y
2 **Capito**	Y	N	N	Y	Y	Y	Y
3 Rahall	Y	Y	Y	Y	Y	Y	Y
WISCONSIN							
1 **Ryan**	Y	N	N	Y	Y	Y	Y
2 Baldwin	Y	Y	Y	Y	Y	Y	Y
3 Kind	Y	Y	Y	Y	Y	Y	Y
4 Moore	Y	Y	Y	Y	Y	Y	Y
5 **Sensenbrenner**	Y	N	N	Y	Y	Y	Y
6 **Petri**	Y	N	N	Y	Y	Y	Y
7 Obey	Y	Y	Y	Y	Y	Y	Y
8 Kagen	Y	Y	Y	Y	Y	Y	Y
WYOMING							
AL **Lummis**	Y	N	N	Y	Y	Y	Y
DELEGATES							
Faleomavaega (A.S.)							
Norton (D.C.)							
Bordallo (Guam)							
Sablan (N. Marianas)							
Pierluisi (P.R.)							
Christensen (V.I.)							

IN THE HOUSE | By Vote Number

602. S 3307. Child Nutrition Programs/Recommit. Kline, R-Minn., motion to recommit the bill to the House Education and Labor Committee with instructions that it be immediately reported back with an amendment that would strike the provision of the bill that would set price requirements for paid school lunches and insert provisions that would make an institution ineligible for funds under the Child and Adult Care Food Program if it employs a child care staff member who refuses to consent to specified background checks or is registered or required to be registered as a sex offender. Motion rejected 200-221: D 30-220; R 170-1. Dec. 2, 2010.

603. S 3307. Child Nutrition Programs/Passage. Passage of the bill that would reauthorize child nutrition programs through fiscal 2015 and make changes to the programs, including a $4.5 billion increase in new spending over 10 years. The bill would expand eligibility for school meal programs, direct the Agriculture Department to set nutrition rules for food sold in schools and increase reimbursement rates for schools that comply with the standards. The costs of the bill would be partially offset by moving up the end date of a temporary boost in food stamp benefits. Passed, thus clearing the bill for the president, 264-157: D 247-4; R 17-153. A "yea" was a vote in support of the president's position. Dec. 2, 2010.

604. HR 4853. Tax Rates Extensions/Motion to Concur. Levin, D-Mich., motion to concur in the Senate amendment to the bill with a House amendment that would make permanent the 2001 and 2003 tax cuts on income less than $200,000 for individuals and $250,000 for married couples. It also would provide through 2011 a "patch" that would shield millions of taxpayers from the alternative minimum tax. Motion agreed to, thus sent to the Senate, 234-188: D 231-20; R 3-168. A "yea" was a vote in support of the president's position. Dec. 2, 2010.

605. H Res 1313. Child Advocacy Center Month/Adoption. Woolsey, D-Calif., motion to suspend the rules and adopt the resolution that would support the designation of Child Advocacy Center Month and commend the National Child Advocacy Center in Huntsville, Ala., on its 25th anniversary. Motion agreed to 413-0: D 248-0; R 165-0. A two-thirds majority of those present and voting (276 in this case) is required for adoption under suspension of the rules. Dec. 2, 2010.

606. H Res 1737. Censure of Rep. Charles B. Rangel/Reduction of Sentence to Reprimand. Butterfield, D-N.C., amendment that would strike all instances of "censure" in the resolution and replace them with "reprimand." It would strike the paragraphs of the resolution that would provide for the censure of Rep. Charles B. Rangel, D-N.Y., by the Speaker in the well of the House. Rejected 146-267: D 143-105; R 3-162. Dec. 2, 2010.

607. H Res 1737. Censure of Rep. Charles B. Rangel/Adoption. Adoption of the resolution that would provide for the censure of Democratic Rep. Charles B. Rangel of New York. It would require Rangel to present himself in the well of the House for the pronouncement of censure, including a public reading of the resolution by the Speaker, to pay restitution for any unpaid estimated taxes on income from his property in the Dominican Republic and to provide proof of payment to the Committee on Standards of Official Conduct. Adopted 333-79: D 170-77; R 163-2. Dec. 2, 2010.

	602	603	604	605	606	607
ALABAMA						
1 **Bonner**	Y	N	N	Y	N	Y
2 Bright	Y	Y	Y	Y	N	Y
3 **Rogers**	Y	N	N	Y	N	Y
4 **Aderholt**	Y	N	N	Y	N	Y
5 **Griffith**	Y	N	N	Y	N	Y
6 **Bachus**	Y	Y	N	Y	N	Y
7 Davis	N	Y	N	Y	N	Y
ALASKA						
AL **Young**	Y	Y	N	Y	Y	N
ARIZONA						
1 Kirkpatrick	Y	Y	Y	Y	N	Y
2 **Franks**	Y	N	N	Y	N	Y
3 **Shadegg**	Y	N	N	Y	N	Y
4 Pastor	N	Y	Y	Y	Y	N
5 Mitchell	Y	Y	Y	Y	N	Y
6 **Flake**	Y	N	N	Y	N	Y
7 Grijalva	N	Y	Y	Y	Y	N
8 Giffords	Y	Y	Y	Y	N	Y
ARKANSAS						
1 Berry	?	?	?	?	?	?
2 Snyder	N	Y	Y	Y	N	Y
3 **Boozman**	Y	N	N	Y	N	Y
4 Ross	Y	Y	Y	Y	N	Y
CALIFORNIA						
1 Thompson	N	Y	N	Y	N	Y
2 **Herger**	Y	N	N	?	N	Y
3 **Lungren**	Y	N	N	Y	N	Y
4 **McClintock**	Y	N	N	Y	N	Y
5 Matsui	N	Y	Y	Y	Y	Y
6 Woolsey	N	Y	Y	Y	Y	N
7 Miller, George	N	Y	Y	Y	Y	Y
8 Pelosi		Y	Y			
9 Lee	N	Y	Y	Y	Y	N
10 Garamendi	N	Y	Y	Y	Y	Y
11 McNerney	Y	Y	N	Y	N	Y
12 Speier	N	Y	Y	Y	?	Y
13 Stark	N	Y	Y	Y	Y	N
14 Eshoo	N	Y	Y	Y	N	Y
15 Honda	N	Y	Y	Y	Y	N
16 Lofgren	N	Y	Y	Y	N	Y
17 Farr	N	Y	Y	Y	Y	Y
18 Cardoza	N	Y	Y	Y	N	Y
19 **Radanovich**	Y	N	N	Y	N	Y
20 Costa	N	Y	Y	Y	N	Y
21 **Nunes**	Y	N	N	Y	N	Y
22 **McCarthy**	Y	N	N	Y	N	Y
23 Capps	N	Y	Y	Y	Y	Y
24 **Gallegly**	Y	N	N	Y	N	Y
25 **McKeon**	Y	N	N	Y	N	Y
26 **Dreier**	Y	N	N	Y	N	Y
27 Sherman	N	Y	Y	Y	N	Y
28 Berman	N	Y	Y	Y	N	Y
29 Schiff	N	Y	Y	Y	N	Y
30 Waxman	N	Y	Y	Y	Y	Y
31 Becerra	N	Y	Y	Y	Y	N
32 Chu	N	Y	Y	Y	Y	N
33 Watson	N	Y	Y	Y	Y	N
34 Roybal-Allard	N	Y	Y	Y	Y	N
35 Waters	N	Y	Y	Y	Y	N
36 Harman	N	Y	Y	Y	N	Y
37 Richardson	N	Y	Y	Y	Y	N
38 Napolitano	N	Y	Y	Y	Y	N
39 Sánchez, Linda	N	Y	Y	Y	N	Y
40 **Royce**	Y	N	N	Y	N	Y
41 **Lewis**	Y	N	N	Y	N	Y
42 **Miller, Gary**	Y	N	N	Y	?	?
43 Baca	N	Y	Y	Y	Y	N
44 **Calvert**	Y	N	N	Y	N	Y
45 **Bono Mack**	Y	N	N	Y	N	Y
46 **Rohrabacher**	Y	N	N	Y	N	Y
47 Sanchez, Loretta	N	Y	Y	Y	Y	Y
48 **Campbell**	Y	N	N	Y	N	Y
49 **Issa**	Y	N	N	Y	N	?
50 **Bilbray**	Y	N	N	Y	N	Y
51 Filner	N	Y	Y	Y	Y	N
52 **Hunter**	Y	N	N	Y	N	Y
53 Davis	N	Y	Y	Y	Y	Y

	602	603	604	605	606	607
COLORADO						
1 DeGette	N	Y	Y	Y	N	Y
2 Polis	N	Y	Y	Y	N	Y
3 Salazar	N	Y	Y	Y	Y	N
4 Markey	N	Y	Y	Y	N	Y
5 **Lamborn**	Y	N	N	Y	N	Y
6 **Coffman**	Y	N	N	Y	N	Y
7 Perlmutter	N	Y	Y	Y	N	Y
CONNECTICUT						
1 Larson	N	Y	Y	Y	Y	Y
2 Courtney	N	Y	Y	Y	N	Y
3 DeLauro	N	Y	Y	Y	Y	Y
4 Himes	N	Y	Y	Y	N	Y
5 Murphy	N	Y	Y	Y	N	Y
DELAWARE						
AL **Castle**	Y	Y	N	Y	N	Y
FLORIDA						
1 **Miller**	Y	N	N	Y	N	Y
2 Boyd	N	N	Y	Y	Y	?
3 Brown	N	Y	Y	Y	Y	N
4 **Crenshaw**	Y	N	N	Y	N	Y
5 **Brown-Waite**	?	?	?	?	?	?
6 **Stearns**	Y	N	N	Y	N	Y
7 **Mica**	Y	N	N	Y	N	Y
8 Grayson	N	Y	Y	Y	Y	Y
9 **Bilirakis**	Y	N	N	Y	N	Y
10 **Young**	Y	N	N	Y	N	Y
11 Castor	N	Y	Y	Y	N	Y
12 **Putnam**	?	?	?	?	?	?
13 **Buchanan**	Y	N	N	Y	?	Y
14 **Mack**	Y	N	N	Y	N	Y
15 **Posey**	Y	N	N	Y	N	Y
16 **Rooney**	Y	N	N	Y	N	Y
17 Meek	N	Y	Y	Y	?	Y
18 **Ros-Lehtinen**	Y	N	N	Y	N	Y
19 Deutch	N	Y	Y	Y	N	Y
20 Wasserman Schultz	N	Y	Y	Y	Y	Y
21 **Diaz-Balart, L.**	Y	?	N	Y	N	Y
22 Klein	N	Y	N	Y	N	Y
23 Hastings	?	?	?	?	?	?
24 Kosmas	N	Y	Y	Y	Y	Y
25 **Diaz-Balart, M.**	Y	N	N	Y	N	Y
GEORGIA						
1 **Kingston**	Y	N	N	Y	N	Y
2 Bishop	N	Y	Y	Y	Y	N
3 **Westmoreland**	Y	N	N	Y	N	Y
4 Johnson	N	Y	Y	Y	Y	N
5 Lewis	N	Y	Y	Y	Y	N
6 **Price**	Y	N	N	Y	N	Y
7 **Linder**	Y	N	N	?	N	Y
8 Marshall	Y	Y	Y	Y	N	Y
9 **Graves**	Y	N	N	Y	N	Y
10 **Broun**	Y	N	N	Y	N	Y
11 **Gingrey**	Y	N	N	?	N	Y
12 Barrow	N	Y	Y	Y	Y	Y
13 Scott	N	Y	Y	Y	Y	N
HAWAII						
1 **Djou**	Y	Y	N	Y	N	Y
2 Hirono	N	Y	Y	Y	Y	N
IDAHO						
1 Minnick	N	Y	N	Y	N	Y
2 **Simpson**	Y	N	Y	N	Y	N
ILLINOIS						
1 Rush	N	Y	Y	Y	Y	N
2 Jackson	N	Y	Y	Y	Y	N
3 Lipinski	N	Y	Y	Y	N	Y
4 Gutierrez	N	Y	Y	Y	Y	N
5 Quigley	N	Y	Y	Y	N	Y
6 **Roskam**	Y	N	N	Y	N	Y
7 Davis	N	Y	Y	Y	Y	N
8 Bean	N	Y	Y	Y	N	Y
9 Schakowsky	N	Y	Y	Y	Y	Y
10 Vacant						
11 Halvorson	N	Y	Y	Y	N	Y
12 Costello	N	Y	Y	Y	N	Y
13 **Biggert**	Y	N	N	Y	N	Y
14 Foster	N	Y	Y	Y	N	Y
15 **Johnson**	Y	N	N	Y	N	Y

	602	603	604	605	606	607
16 **Manzullo**	Y	N	N	?	N	Y
17 Hare	N	Y	Y	Y	N	Y
18 **Schock**	Y	N	N	Y	N	Y
19 **Shimkus**	Y	N	N	Y	N	Y
INDIANA						
1 Visclosky	N	Y	N	Y	N	Y
2 Donnelly	Y	Y	Y	Y	N	Y
3 **Stutzman**	Y	N	N	Y	N	Y
4 **Buyer**	?	?	?	?	?	?
5 **Burton**	Y	N	N	Y	N	Y
6 **Pence**	Y	N	N	Y	N	Y
7 Carson	N	Y	Y	Y	Y	N
8 Ellsworth	N	Y	Y	Y	N	Y
9 Hill	N	Y	Y	Y	N	Y
IOWA						
1 Braley	N	Y	Y	Y	N	Y
2 Loebsack	N	Y	Y	Y	N	Y
3 Boswell	N	Y	Y	Y	Y	Y
4 **Latham**	Y	Y	N	Y	N	Y
5 **King**	Y	N	N	Y	N	Y
KANSAS						
1 **Moran**	Y	N	N	Y	N	Y
2 **Jenkins**	Y	N	N	Y	N	Y
3 Moore	N	Y	Y	Y	Y	N
4 **Tiahrt**	Y	N	N	Y	N	Y
KENTUCKY						
1 **Whitfield**	Y	N	N	Y	N	Y
2 **Guthrie**	Y	N	N	Y	N	Y
3 Yarmuth	N	Y	Y	Y	N	Y
4 **Davis**	Y	N	N	Y	N	Y
5 **Rogers**	Y	N	N	Y	N	Y
6 Chandler	Y	Y	Y	Y	N	Y
LOUISIANA						
1 **Scalise**	Y	N	N	Y	N	Y
2 **Cao**	Y	Y	N	Y	N	Y
3 Melancon	Y	Y	Y	Y	Y	N
4 **Fleming**	Y	N	N	Y	N	Y
5 **Alexander**	Y	N	N	Y	N	Y
6 **Cassidy**	Y	N	N	Y	N	Y
7 **Boustany**	Y	N	N	Y	N	Y
MAINE						
1 Pingree	Y	Y	Y	Y	Y	Y
2 Michaud	N	Y	Y	Y	N	Y
MARYLAND						
1 Kratovil	Y	Y	Y	Y	N	Y
2 Ruppersberger	N	Y	Y	Y	Y	Y
3 Sarbanes	N	Y	Y	Y	Y	Y
4 Edwards	N	Y	Y	Y	Y	N
5 Hoyer	N	Y	Y	Y	Y	Y
6 **Bartlett**	Y	N	N	Y	N	Y
7 Cummings	N	Y	Y	Y	Y	N
8 Van Hollen	N	Y	Y	Y	Y	Y
MASSACHUSETTS						
1 Olver	N	Y	Y	Y	Y	Y
2 Neal	N	Y	Y	Y	Y	Y
3 McGovern	N	Y	Y	Y	Y	Y
4 Frank	N	Y	Y	Y	Y	N
5 Tsongas	N	Y	Y	Y	N	Y
6 Tierney	N	Y	Y	Y	N	Y
7 Markey	N	Y	Y	Y	N	Y
8 Capuano	N	Y	Y	Y	Y	Y
9 Lynch	N	Y	Y	Y	N	Y
10 Delahunt	?	?	?	?	?	?
MICHIGAN						
1 Stupak	N	N	Y	Y	Y	N
2 **Hoekstra**	Y	N	N	Y	N	Y
3 **Ehlers**	Y	Y	N	Y	N	Y
4 **Camp**	Y	N	N	Y	N	Y
5 Kildee	N	Y	Y	Y	Y	Y
6 **Upton**	Y	N	N	Y	N	Y
7 Schauer	N	Y	Y	Y	N	Y
8 **Rogers**	Y	N	N	Y	?	Y
9 Peters	Y	Y	Y	Y	N	Y
10 **Miller**	Y	N	N	Y	N	Y
11 **McCotter**	Y	N	N	Y	N	Y
12 Levin	N	Y	Y	Y	Y	N
13 Kilpatrick	N	Y	Y	Y	Y	N
14 Conyers	N	Y	Y	Y	Y	N
15 Dingell	N	Y	Y	Y	Y	Y
MINNESOTA						
1 Walz	N	Y	Y	Y	N	Y
2 **Kline**	Y	N	N	Y	N	Y
3 **Paulsen**	Y	N	N	Y	N	Y
4 McCollum	N	Y	Y	Y	Y	Y

	602	603	604	605	606	607
5 Ellison	N	Y	Y	Y	Y	N
6 **Bachmann**	?	?	?	?	?	?
7 Peterson	N	Y	N	Y	N	Y
8 Oberstar	N	Y	Y	Y	Y	Y
MISSISSIPPI						
1 Childers	Y	Y	Y	Y	N	Y
2 Thompson	N	Y	Y	Y	Y	N
3 **Harper**	Y	N	N	?	N	Y
4 Taylor	Y	Y	N	Y	N	Y
MISSOURI						
1 Clay	N	Y	Y	Y	Y	N
2 **Akin**	Y	N	N	Y	N	Y
3 Carnahan	N	Y	Y	Y	N	Y
4 Skelton	N	Y	Y	Y	N	Y
5 Cleaver	N	Y	Y	?	Y	N
6 **Graves**	Y	N	N	Y	N	Y
7 **Blunt**	Y	N	N	Y	N	Y
8 **Emerson**	Y	Y	N	Y	N	Y
9 **Luetkemeyer**	Y	N	N	Y	N	Y
MONTANA						
AL **Rehberg**	Y	N	N	Y	N	Y
NEBRASKA						
1 **Fortenberry**	Y	Y	N	Y	N	Y
2 **Terry**	Y	N	N	Y	N	Y
3 **Smith**	Y	N	N	Y	N	Y
NEVADA						
1 Berkley	N	Y	Y	Y	Y	Y
2 **Heller**	Y	N	N	Y	N	Y
3 Titus	Y	Y	Y	Y	N	Y
NEW HAMPSHIRE						
1 Shea-Porter	N	Y	Y	Y	N	Y
2 Hodes	N	Y	Y	Y	Y	Y
NEW JERSEY						
1 Andrews	N	Y	Y	Y	Y	Y
2 **LoBiondo**	Y	N	N	Y	N	Y
3 Adler	N	Y	Y	Y	N	Y
4 **Smith**	Y	N	N	Y	N	Y
5 **Garrett**	Y	N	N	Y	N	Y
6 Pallone	N	Y	Y	Y	N	Y
7 **Lance**	Y	N	N	Y	N	Y
8 Pascrell	N	Y	Y	Y	Y	Y
9 Rothman	N	Y	Y	Y	Y	Y
10 Payne	N	Y	Y	Y	Y	N
11 **Frelinghuysen**	Y	N	N	Y	N	Y
12 Holt	N	Y	Y	Y	Y	Y
13 Sires	N	Y	Y	Y	Y	Y
NEW MEXICO						
1 Heinrich	N	Y	Y	Y	N	Y
2 Teague	N	Y	Y	Y	Y	Y
3 Luján	N	Y	Y	Y	Y	Y
NEW YORK						
1 Bishop	N	Y	Y	Y	N	Y
2 Israel	N	Y	Y	Y	N	Y
3 **King**	Y	N	N	Y	Y	N
4 McCarthy	N	Y	Y	Y	N	Y
5 Ackerman	N	Y	Y	Y	Y	N
6 Meeks	N	Y	Y	Y	Y	N
7 Crowley	N	Y	Y	Y	Y	N
8 Nadler	N	Y	Y	Y	Y	N
9 Weiner	N	Y	Y	Y	Y	N
10 Towns	N	Y	Y	Y	Y	N
11 Clarke	N	Y	Y	Y	Y	N
12 Velázquez	N	Y	Y	?	Y	N
13 McMahon	Y	Y	N	Y	N	Y
14 Maloney	N	Y	Y	Y	Y	N
15 Rangel	N	Y	Y	Y	Y	N
16 Serrano	N	Y	Y	Y	Y	N
17 Engel	N	Y	Y	Y	Y	N
18 Lowey	N	Y	Y	Y	Y	N
19 Hall	N	Y	Y	Y	Y	N
20 Murphy	N	Y	Y	Y	N	Y
21 Tonko	N	Y	Y	Y	Y	N
22 Hinchey	N	Y	Y	Y	Y	N
23 Owens	N	Y	Y	Y	N	Y
24 Arcuri	N	Y	Y	Y	Y	Y
25 Maffei	N	Y	Y	Y	Y	Y
26 **Lee**	Y	N	N	Y	N	Y
27 Higgins	N	Y	Y	Y	N	Y
28 Slaughter	N	Y	Y	Y	Y	N
29 **Reed**	Y	N	N	Y	N	Y
NORTH CAROLINA						
1 Butterfield	N	Y	Y	Y	Y	N
2 Etheridge	N	Y	Y	Y	Y	Y
3 **Jones**	Y	Y	Y	Y	N	Y
4 Price	N	Y	Y	Y	Y	Y

	602	603	604	605	606	607
5 **Foxx**	Y	N	N	Y	N	Y
6 **Coble**	Y	N	N	Y	N	Y
7 McIntyre	Y	Y	N	Y	N	Y
8 Kissell	Y	Y	Y	Y	Y	Y
9 **Myrick**	Y	N	N	Y	N	Y
10 **McHenry**	Y	N	N	Y	N	Y
11 Shuler	Y	Y	Y	Y	N	?
12 Watt	N	Y	Y	Y	Y	N
13 Miller	N	Y	Y	Y	Y	Y
NORTH DAKOTA						
AL Pomeroy	N	Y	N	Y	Y	Y
OHIO						
1 Driehaus	N	Y	Y	Y	Y	Y
2 **Schmidt**	Y	N	N	Y	N	Y
3 **Turner**	Y	N	N	Y	N	Y
4 **Jordan**	Y	N	N	Y	N	Y
5 **Latta**	Y	N	N	Y	N	Y
6 Wilson	N	Y	Y	Y	N	Y
7 **Austria**	Y	N	N	Y	N	Y
8 **Boehner**	Y	N	N	Y	N	Y
9 Kaptur	N	Y	Y	Y	Y	Y
10 Kucinich	N	Y	Y	Y	Y	Y
11 Fudge	N	Y	Y	Y	Y	N
12 **Tiberi**	Y	N	N	Y	N	Y
13 Sutton	N	Y	Y	Y	N	Y
14 **LaTourette**	Y	Y	N	Y	N	Y
15 Kilroy	N	Y	Y	Y	N	Y
16 Boccieri	Y	Y	Y	Y	N	Y
17 Ryan	N	Y	Y	Y	N	Y
18 Space	Y	Y	Y	Y	N	Y
OKLAHOMA						
1 **Sullivan**	Y	N	N	Y	N	Y
2 Boren	Y	Y	N	Y	N	Y
3 **Lucas**	Y	N	N	Y	N	Y
4 **Cole**	Y	N	N	Y	N	Y
5 **Fallin**	?	?	?	?	?	?
OREGON						
1 Wu	N	Y	Y	Y	Y	Y
2 **Walden**	Y	N	N	Y	N	Y
3 Blumenauer	N	Y	Y	Y	Y	Y
4 DeFazio	?	?	?	?	?	?
5 Schrader	N	Y	Y	Y	N	Y
PENNSYLVANIA						
1 Brady	N	Y	Y	Y	Y	N
2 Fattah	N	Y	Y	Y	Y	N
3 Dahlkemper	N	Y	N	Y	Y	Y
4 Altmire	Y	Y	Y	Y	N	Y
5 **Thompson**	Y	N	N	Y	N	Y
6 **Gerlach**	Y	Y	N	Y	N	Y
7 Sestak	N	Y	Y	Y	N	Y
8 Murphy, P.	Y	Y	Y	Y	N	Y
9 **Shuster**	Y	N	N	Y	N	Y
10 Carney	N	Y	Y	Y	N	Y
11 Kanjorski	N	Y	Y	Y	Y	N
12 Critz	N	Y	Y	Y	Y	Y
13 Schwartz	N	Y	Y	Y	N	Y
14 Doyle	N	Y	Y	Y	Y	Y
15 **Dent**	Y	Y	N	Y	N	Y
16 **Pitts**	Y	N	N	Y	N	Y
17 Holden	Y	Y	Y	Y	N	Y
18 **Murphy, T.**	Y	Y	N	Y	N	Y
19 **Platts**	Y	Y	N	Y	N	Y
RHODE ISLAND						
1 Kennedy	N	Y	Y	Y	Y	N
2 Langevin	N	Y	Y	Y	N	Y
SOUTH CAROLINA						
1 **Brown**	Y	N	N	Y	?	?
2 **Wilson**	Y	N	N	Y	N	Y
3 **Barrett**	?	?	?	?	?	?
4 **Inglis**	Y	N	N	?	?	?
5 Spratt	N	Y	Y	Y	Y	Y
6 Clyburn	N	Y	Y	Y	Y	N
SOUTH DAKOTA						
AL Herseth Sandlin	N	Y	N	Y	N	Y
TENNESSEE						
1 **Roe**	Y	N	N	Y	N	Y
2 **Duncan**	Y	N	N	Y	N	Y
3 **Wamp**	Y	N	N	Y	N	Y
4 Davis	N	Y	Y	Y	N	Y
5 Cooper	N	Y	Y	Y	N	Y
6 Gordon	N	Y	Y	Y	Y	Y
7 **Blackburn**	Y	N	N	Y	N	Y
8 Tanner	N	N	Y	Y	Y	N
9 Cohen	N	Y	Y	Y	Y	Y

	602	603	604	605	606	607
TEXAS						
1 **Gohmert**	Y	N	N	Y	N	Y
2 **Poe**	Y	N	N	Y	N	Y
3 **Johnson, S.**	Y	N	N	Y	N	Y
4 **Hall**	Y	N	N	Y	N	Y
5 **Hensarling**	Y	N	N	Y	N	Y
6 **Barton**	Y	N	N	Y	N	Y
7 **Culberson**	Y	N	N	Y	N	Y
8 **Brady**	Y	N	N	Y	N	Y
9 Green, A.	N	Y	Y	Y	Y	N
10 **McCaul**	Y	N	N	Y	N	Y
11 **Conaway**	Y	N	N	Y	N	Y
12 **Granger**	Y	N	N	Y	?	?
13 **Thornberry**	Y	N	N	Y	N	Y
14 **Paul**	N	N	Y	Y	Y	Y
15 Hinojosa	N	Y	Y	Y	Y	N
16 Reyes	N	Y	Y	Y	Y	N
17 Edwards	N	Y	Y	Y	Y	Y
18 Jackson Lee	N	Y	Y	Y	Y	N
19 **Neugebauer**	Y	N	N	Y	N	Y
20 Gonzalez	N	Y	Y	Y	Y	N
21 **Smith**	Y	N	N	Y	N	Y
22 **Olson**	Y	N	N	Y	N	Y
23 Rodriguez	N	Y	Y	Y	Y	Y
24 **Marchant**	?	?	?	?	?	?
25 Doggett	N	Y	N	Y	N	Y
26 **Burgess**	Y	N	N	Y	N	Y
27 Ortiz	N	Y	Y	Y	Y	N
28 Cuellar	N	Y	Y	Y	N	Y
29 Green, G.	N	Y	Y	Y	Y	Y
30 Johnson, E.	N	Y	Y	Y	Y	N
31 **Carter**	Y	N	N	Y	N	Y
32 **Sessions**	Y	N	N	Y	N	Y
UTAH						
1 **Bishop**	Y	N	N	Y	N	Y
2 Matheson	Y	Y	N	Y	N	Y
3 **Chaffetz**	Y	N	N	Y	N	Y
VERMONT						
AL Welch	N	N	Y	Y	N	Y
VIRGINIA						
1 **Wittman**	Y	N	N	Y	N	Y
2 Nye	Y	Y	Y	Y	N	Y
3 Scott	N	Y	N	Y	Y	N
4 **Forbes**	Y	N	N	Y	N	Y
5 Perriello	Y	Y	Y	Y	N	Y
6 **Goodlatte**	Y	N	N	Y	N	Y
7 **Cantor**	Y	N	N	Y	N	Y
8 Moran	N	Y	N	Y	Y	Y
9 Boucher	N	Y	Y	Y	Y	Y
10 **Wolf**	Y	N	N	Y	N	Y
11 Connolly	N	Y	Y	Y	N	Y
WASHINGTON						
1 Inslee	N	Y	Y	Y	N	Y
2 Larsen	N	Y	Y	Y	N	Y
3 Baird	N	Y	N	Y	Y	Y
4 **Hastings**	Y	N	N	Y	N	Y
5 **McMorris Rodgers**	?	?	?	?	?	?
6 Dicks	N	Y	Y	Y	Y	Y
7 McDermott	N	Y	Y	Y	Y	N
8 **Reichert**	Y	Y	N	Y	N	Y
9 Smith	N	Y	Y	Y	Y	N
WEST VIRGINIA						
1 Mollohan	Y	Y	Y	Y	N	Y
2 **Capito**	Y	N	N	Y	N	Y
3 Rahall	N	Y	Y	Y	N	Y
WISCONSIN						
1 **Ryan**	Y	N	N	Y	N	Y
2 Baldwin	N	Y	Y	Y	Y	Y
3 Kind	N	Y	Y	Y	N	Y
4 Moore	N	Y	Y	Y	Y	N
5 **Sensenbrenner**	Y	N	N	Y	N	Y
6 **Petri**	Y	N	N	Y	N	Y
7 Obey	N	Y	Y	Y	Y	Y
8 Kagen	N	Y	Y	Y	Y	Y
WYOMING						
AL **Lummis**	Y	N	N	Y	N	Y
DELEGATES						
Faleomavaega (A.S.)						
Norton (D.C.)						
Bordallo (Guam)						
Sablan (N. Marianas)						
Pierluisi (P.R.)						
Christensen (V.I.)						

IN THE HOUSE | By Vote Number

608. **HR 6400. Earl Wilson Jr. Post Office/Passage.** Clay, D-Mo., motion to suspend the rules and pass the bill that would designate a post office in St. Louis, Mo., as the "Earl Wilson Jr. Post Office." Motion agreed to 382-0: D 225-0; R 157-0. A two-thirds majority of those present and voting (255 in this case) is required for passage under suspension of the rules. Dec. 7, 2010.

609. **H Res 1642. City of Lilburn, Ga., Anniversary/Adoption.** Clay, D-Mo., motion to suspend the rules and adopt the resolution that would recognize the centennial anniversary of the city of Lilburn, Ga. Motion agreed to 379-0: D 225-0; R 154-0. A two-thirds majority of those present and voting (253 in this case) is required for adoption under suspension of the rules. Dec. 7, 2010.

610. **H Res 1264. National Essential Tremor Awareness Month/ Adoption.** Clay, D-Mo., motion to suspend the rules and adopt the resolution that would support the designation of National Essential Tremor Awareness Month and encourage participation in the International Essential Tremor Foundation's educational activities. Motion agreed to 387-1: D 230-0; R 157-1. A two-thirds majority of those present and voting (259 in this case) is required for adoption under suspension of the rules. Dec. 7, 2010.

611. **HR 5987. One-Time Supplemental Payment/Passage.** Pomeroy, D-N.D., motion to suspend the rules and pass the bill that would provide a one-time payment of $250 to recipients of Social Security, railroad retirement benefits and veterans' disability compensation or pension benefits if there is no cost-of-living adjustment payable in 2011. Motion rejected 254-153: D 228-12; R 26-141. A two-thirds majority of those present and voting (272 in this case) is required for passage under suspension of the rules. A "yea" was a vote in support of the president's position. Dec. 8, 2010.

612. **H Res 1717. Tribute to Liu Xiaobo/Adoption.** Klein, D-Fla., motion to suspend the rules and adopt the resolution that would congratulate Liu Xiaobo on the award of the 2010 Nobel Peace Prize, honor his work promoting democracy in China and call on Chinese officials to release him from prison. Motion agreed to 402-1: D 238-0; R 164-1. A two-thirds majority of those present and voting (269 in this case) is required for adoption under suspension of the rules. Dec. 8, 2010.

613. **H Res 1540. Marijuana Cultivation on Federal Lands/ Adoption.** Scott, D-Va., motion to suspend the rules and adopt the resolution that would declare that drug trafficking organizations cultivating illicit marijuana on federal lands pose an unacceptable threat to the safety of law enforcement and the public. Motion agreed to 400-4: D 235-3; R 165-1. A two-thirds majority of those present and voting (270 in this case) is required for adoption under suspension of the rules. Dec. 8, 2010.

	608	609	610	611	612	613
ALABAMA						
1 **Bonner**	Y	Y	Y	N	Y	Y
2 **Bright**	?	?	?	Y	Y	Y
3 **Rogers**	Y	Y	Y	N	Y	Y
4 **Aderholt**	Y	Y	Y	N	Y	Y
5 **Griffith**	?	?	?	?	?	?
6 **Bachus**	Y	Y	Y	?	Y	Y
7 Davis	?	?	?	?	?	?
ALASKA						
AL **Young**	Y	?	N	N	Y	Y
ARIZONA						
1 Kirkpatrick	Y	Y	Y	?	?	?
2 **Franks**	Y	Y	Y	N	Y	Y
3 **Shadegg**	Y	Y	Y	N	Y	Y
4 Pastor	Y	Y	Y	Y	Y	Y
5 Mitchell	Y	Y	Y	Y	Y	Y
6 **Flake**	Y	Y	Y	N	Y	Y
7 Grijalva	Y	Y	Y	Y	Y	Y
8 Giffords	Y	Y	Y	Y	Y	Y
ARKANSAS						
1 Berry	?	?	?	?	?	?
2 Snyder	Y	Y	Y	Y	Y	Y
3 **Boozman**	Y	Y	Y	N	Y	Y
4 Ross	Y	Y	Y	Y	Y	Y
CALIFORNIA						
1 Thompson	Y	Y	Y	Y	Y	Y
2 **Herger**	Y	Y	Y	N	Y	Y
3 **Lungren**	Y	Y	Y	N	Y	Y
4 **McClintock**	Y	Y	Y	N	Y	Y
5 Matsui	Y	Y	Y	Y	Y	Y
6 Woolsey	Y	Y	Y	Y	Y	Y
7 Miller, George	Y	?	Y	Y	Y	Y
8 Pelosi				Y	Y	
9 Lee	Y	Y	Y	Y	Y	Y
10 Garamendi	?	Y	Y	Y	Y	Y
11 McNerney	Y	Y	Y	Y	Y	Y
12 Speier	?	?	?	Y	Y	Y
13 Stark	?	?	?	Y	Y	Y
14 Eshoo	Y	Y	Y	Y	Y	Y
15 Honda	Y	Y	Y	Y	Y	Y
16 Lofgren	Y	Y	Y	Y	Y	Y
17 Farr	Y	Y	Y	Y	Y	Y
18 Cardoza	Y	Y	Y	Y	Y	Y
19 **Radanovich**	?	?	?	?	?	?
20 Costa	?	?	?	Y	Y	Y
21 **Nunes**	Y	Y	Y	N	Y	Y
22 **McCarthy**	Y	Y	Y	N	Y	Y
23 Capps	Y	Y	Y	Y	Y	Y
24 **Gallegly**	Y	Y	Y	N	Y	Y
25 **McKeon**	Y	Y	Y	N	Y	Y
26 **Dreier**	Y	Y	Y	N	Y	Y
27 Sherman	Y	Y	Y	Y	Y	Y
28 Berman	Y	Y	Y	Y	Y	Y
29 Schiff	Y	Y	Y	Y	Y	Y
30 Waxman	Y	Y	Y	Y	Y	Y
31 Becerra	Y	Y	Y	Y	Y	Y
32 Chu	Y	+	Y	Y	Y	Y
33 Watson	Y	Y	Y	Y	Y	Y
34 Roybal-Allard	Y	Y	Y	Y	Y	Y
35 Waters	Y	Y	Y	Y	Y	Y
36 Harman	?	?	?	Y	Y	Y
37 Richardson	Y	Y	Y	Y	Y	Y
38 Napolitano	Y	Y	Y	Y	Y	Y
39 Sánchez, Linda	Y	Y	Y	Y	Y	Y
40 **Royce**	Y	Y	Y	N	Y	Y
41 **Lewis**	?	?	?	N	Y	Y
42 **Miller, Gary**	Y	Y	Y	N	Y	Y
43 Baca	?	?	?	Y	Y	Y
44 **Calvert**	Y	Y	Y	N	Y	Y
45 **Bono Mack**	Y	Y	Y	N	Y	Y
46 **Rohrabacher**	Y	Y	Y	N	Y	Y
47 Sanchez, Loretta	Y	Y	Y	Y	Y	Y
48 **Campbell**	Y	Y	Y	N	Y	Y
49 **Issa**	Y	Y	Y	N	Y	Y
50 **Bilbray**	Y	Y	Y	?	?	?
51 Filner	Y	Y	Y	+	Y	Y
52 **Hunter**	Y	Y	Y	N	Y	Y
53 Davis	Y	Y	Y	Y	Y	Y

	608	609	610	611	612	613
COLORADO						
1 DeGette	Y	Y	Y	Y	Y	Y
2 Polis	Y	Y	Y	Y	Y	N
3 Salazar	?	?	?	Y	Y	Y
4 Markey	Y	Y	Y	N	?	?
5 **Lamborn**	Y	Y	Y	N	Y	Y
6 **Coffman**	Y	Y	Y	N	Y	Y
7 Perlmutter	Y	Y	Y	Y	Y	Y
CONNECTICUT						
1 Larson	Y	Y	Y	Y	Y	Y
2 Courtney	Y	Y	Y	Y	Y	Y
3 DeLauro	Y	Y	Y	Y	Y	Y
4 Himes	Y	Y	Y	Y	Y	Y
5 Murphy	Y	Y	Y	Y	Y	Y
DELAWARE						
AL **Castle**	Y	Y	Y	Y	?	Y
FLORIDA						
1 **Miller**	Y	Y	Y	N	Y	Y
2 Boyd	Y	Y	Y	?	?	?
3 Brown	Y	Y	Y	Y	Y	Y
4 **Crenshaw**	Y	Y	Y	N	Y	Y
5 **Brown-Waite**	Y	Y	Y	Y	Y	Y
6 **Stearns**	Y	Y	Y	N	Y	Y
7 **Mica**	Y	Y	Y	N	Y	Y
8 Grayson	Y	Y	Y	Y	Y	Y
9 **Bilirakis**	Y	Y	Y	N	Y	Y
10 **Young**	Y	Y	Y	?	?	?
11 Castor	Y	Y	Y	Y	Y	Y
12 **Putnam**	+	+	+	Y	Y	Y
13 **Buchanan**	Y	Y	Y	Y	Y	Y
14 **Mack**	Y	Y	Y	N	Y	Y
15 **Posey**	Y	Y	Y	N	Y	Y
16 **Rooney**	Y	Y	Y	N	Y	Y
17 Meek	Y	Y	Y	?	?	?
18 **Ros-Lehtinen**	Y	Y	Y	Y	Y	Y
19 Deutch	Y	Y	Y	Y	Y	Y
20 Wasserman Schultz	Y	Y	Y	Y	Y	Y
21 **Diaz-Balart, L.**	Y	Y	Y	Y	Y	Y
22 Klein	Y	Y	Y	Y	Y	Y
23 Hastings	Y	Y	Y	Y	Y	Y
24 Kosmas	Y	Y	Y	Y	Y	Y
25 **Diaz-Balart, M.**	?	?	?	Y	Y	Y
GEORGIA						
1 **Kingston**	Y	Y	Y	N	Y	Y
2 Bishop	Y	Y	Y	Y	Y	Y
3 **Westmoreland**	Y	Y	Y	N	Y	Y
4 Johnson	Y	Y	Y	?	Y	Y
5 Lewis	Y	Y	Y	Y	Y	Y
6 **Price**	Y	Y	Y	N	Y	+
7 **Linder**	?	?	?	N	Y	Y
8 Marshall	Y	Y	Y	Y	Y	Y
9 **Graves**	Y	Y	Y	N	Y	Y
10 **Broun**	Y	Y	Y	N	Y	Y
11 **Gingrey**	Y	Y	Y	N	Y	Y
12 Barrow	Y	Y	Y	Y	Y	Y
13 Scott	Y	Y	Y	Y	Y	Y
HAWAII						
1 **Djou**	Y	Y	Y	N	Y	Y
2 Hirono	Y	Y	Y	Y	Y	Y
IDAHO						
1 Minnick	Y	Y	Y	N	Y	Y
2 **Simpson**	Y	?	Y	N	Y	Y
ILLINOIS						
1 Rush	Y	Y	?	Y	Y	Y
2 Jackson	Y	Y	Y	Y	Y	Y
3 Lipinski	Y	Y	Y	Y	Y	Y
4 Gutierrez	?	?	?	Y	Y	Y
5 Quigley	Y	Y	Y	Y	Y	Y
6 **Roskam**	Y	Y	Y	N	Y	Y
7 Davis	?	?	?	Y	Y	Y
8 Bean	?	?	?	Y	Y	Y
9 Schakowsky	Y	Y	Y	Y	Y	Y
10 Vacant						
11 Halvorson	Y	Y	Y	Y	Y	Y
12 Costello	Y	Y	Y	Y	Y	Y
13 **Biggert**	Y	Y	Y	Y	Y	Y
14 Foster	Y	Y	Y	Y	Y	Y
15 Johnson	Y	Y	Y	N	Y	Y

KEY   Republicans   Democrats

Y Voted for (yea)	X Paired against
# Paired for	– Announced against
+ Announced for	P Voted "present"
N Voted against (nay)	

C Voted "present" to avoid possible conflict of interest

? Did not vote or otherwise make a position known

	608	609	610	611	612	613
16 **Manzullo**	Y	Y	Y	N	Y	Y
17 Hare	Y	Y	Y	Y	Y	Y
18 **Schock**	Y	Y	Y	Y	Y	Y
19 **Shimkus**	Y	Y	Y	N	Y	Y
INDIANA						
1 Visclosky	Y	Y	Y	Y	Y	Y
2 Donnelly	Y	Y	Y	Y	Y	Y
3 **Stutzman**	Y	Y	Y	N	Y	Y
4 **Buyer**	Y	Y	Y	N	Y	Y
5 **Burton**	Y	Y	Y	N	Y	Y
6 **Pence**	Y	Y	Y	N	Y	Y
7 Carson	Y	Y	Y	Y	Y	Y
8 Ellsworth	?	?	?	Y	Y	Y
9 Hill	Y	Y	Y	Y	Y	Y
IOWA						
1 Braley	Y	Y	Y	Y	Y	Y
2 Loebsack	Y	Y	Y	Y	Y	Y
3 Boswell	Y	Y	Y	Y	Y	Y
4 **Latham**	Y	Y	Y	N	Y	Y
5 **King**	Y	Y	Y	N	Y	Y
KANSAS						
1 **Moran**	?	?	?	N	Y	Y
2 **Jenkins**	Y	Y	Y	N	Y	Y
3 Moore	Y	Y	Y	Y	Y	Y
4 **Tiahrt**	?	?	?	?	?	?
KENTUCKY						
1 **Whitfield**	Y	Y	Y	Y	Y	Y
2 **Guthrie**	Y	Y	Y	N	Y	Y
3 Yarmuth	+	+	+	Y	Y	Y
4 **Davis**	Y	Y	Y	N	Y	Y
5 **Rogers**	Y	Y	Y	N	Y	Y
6 Chandler	Y	Y	Y	Y	Y	Y
LOUISIANA						
1 **Scalise**	Y	Y	Y	N	Y	Y
2 **Cao**	Y	Y	Y	Y	Y	Y
3 Melancon	Y	Y	Y	Y	Y	Y
4 **Fleming**	Y	Y	Y	N	Y	Y
5 **Alexander**	Y	Y	Y	N	Y	Y
6 **Cassidy**	Y	Y	Y	N	Y	Y
7 **Boustany**	Y	Y	Y	N	Y	Y
MAINE						
1 Pingree	Y	Y	Y	Y	Y	Y
2 Michaud	Y	Y	Y	Y	Y	Y
MARYLAND						
1 Kratovil	Y	Y	Y	Y	Y	Y
2 Ruppersberger	Y	Y	Y	Y	Y	Y
3 Sarbanes	Y	Y	Y	Y	Y	Y
4 Edwards	Y	Y	Y	Y	Y	Y
5 Hoyer	Y	Y	Y	Y	Y	Y
6 **Bartlett**	Y	Y	Y	N	Y	Y
7 Cummings	Y	Y	Y	Y	Y	Y
8 Van Hollen	Y	Y	Y	Y	Y	Y
MASSACHUSETTS						
1 Olver	Y	Y	Y	Y	Y	Y
2 Neal	Y	Y	Y	Y	Y	Y
3 McGovern	Y	Y	Y	Y	Y	Y
4 Frank	Y	Y	Y	Y	Y	N
5 Tsongas	Y	Y	Y	Y	Y	Y
6 Tierney	Y	Y	Y	Y	Y	Y
7 Markey	Y	Y	Y	Y	Y	Y
8 Capuano	Y	Y	Y	Y	Y	Y
9 Lynch	Y	Y	Y	Y	Y	Y
10 Delahunt	?	?	?	?	?	?
MICHIGAN						
1 Stupak	Y	Y	Y	Y	Y	Y
2 **Hoekstra**	?	?	?	?	?	?
3 **Ehlers**	Y	Y	Y	N	Y	Y
4 **Camp**	Y	Y	Y	N	Y	Y
5 Kildee	Y	Y	Y	Y	Y	Y
6 **Upton**	Y	Y	Y	N	Y	Y
7 Schauer	Y	Y	Y	Y	Y	Y
8 **Rogers**	Y	Y	Y	N	Y	Y
9 Peters	Y	Y	Y	Y	Y	Y
10 **Miller**	Y	Y	Y	N	Y	Y
11 **McCotter**	Y	Y	Y	Y	Y	Y
12 Levin	Y	Y	Y	Y	Y	Y
13 Kilpatrick	Y	Y	Y	+	+	+
14 Conyers	Y	Y	Y	Y	Y	Y
15 Dingell	Y	Y	Y	Y	Y	Y
MINNESOTA						
1 Walz	Y	Y	Y	Y	Y	Y
2 **Kline**	Y	Y	Y	N	Y	Y
3 **Paulsen**	Y	Y	Y	N	Y	Y
4 McCollum	Y	Y	Y	Y	Y	Y

	608	609	610	611	612	613
5 Ellison	Y	Y	Y	Y	Y	Y
6 **Bachmann**	Y	Y	Y	N	Y	Y
7 Peterson	Y	Y	Y	Y	Y	Y
8 Oberstar	?	?	?	Y	Y	Y
MISSISSIPPI						
1 Childers	Y	Y	Y	?	?	?
2 Thompson	Y	Y	Y	Y	Y	Y
3 **Harper**	Y	Y	Y	N	Y	Y
4 Taylor	Y	Y	Y	N	Y	Y
MISSOURI						
1 Clay	Y	Y	Y	Y	Y	Y
2 **Akin**	Y	Y	Y	N	Y	Y
3 Carnahan	Y	Y	Y	Y	Y	Y
4 Skelton	Y	Y	Y	Y	Y	Y
5 Cleaver	Y	Y	Y	Y	Y	Y
6 **Graves**	+	+	+	N	Y	Y
7 **Blunt**	?	?	?	?	?	?
8 **Emerson**	Y	Y	Y	Y	Y	Y
9 **Luetkemeyer**	Y	Y	Y	N	Y	Y
MONTANA						
AL **Rehberg**	Y	Y	Y	N	Y	Y
NEBRASKA						
1 **Fortenberry**	Y	Y	Y	N	Y	Y
2 **Terry**	?	?	?	N	Y	Y
3 **Smith**	Y	Y	Y	N	Y	Y
NEVADA						
1 Berkley	Y	Y	Y	Y	Y	Y
2 **Heller**	Y	Y	Y	N	Y	Y
3 Titus	Y	Y	Y	Y	Y	Y
NEW HAMPSHIRE						
1 Shea-Porter	?	Y	Y	Y	?	Y
2 Hodes	Y	Y	Y	Y	Y	Y
NEW JERSEY						
1 Andrews	Y	Y	Y	Y	Y	Y
2 **LoBiondo**	Y	Y	Y	Y	Y	Y
3 Adler	Y	Y	Y	Y	Y	Y
4 **Smith**	Y	Y	Y	Y	Y	Y
5 **Garrett**	Y	Y	Y	N	Y	Y
6 Pallone	Y	Y	Y	Y	Y	Y
7 **Lance**	Y	Y	Y	N	Y	Y
8 Pascrell	Y	Y	Y	Y	Y	Y
9 Rothman	Y	Y	Y	Y	Y	Y
10 Payne	Y	Y	Y	Y	Y	Y
11 **Frelinghuysen**	Y	Y	Y	N	Y	Y
12 Holt	Y	Y	Y	Y	Y	Y
13 Sires	?	?	?	Y	Y	Y
NEW MEXICO						
1 Heinrich	Y	Y	Y	Y	Y	Y
2 Teague	Y	Y	Y	Y	Y	Y
3 Luján	Y	Y	Y	Y	Y	Y
NEW YORK						
1 Bishop	Y	Y	Y	Y	Y	Y
2 Israel	Y	Y	Y	Y	Y	Y
3 **King**	Y	Y	Y	N	Y	Y
4 McCarthy	Y	Y	Y	Y	Y	Y
5 Ackerman	Y	Y	Y	Y	Y	Y
6 Meeks	Y	Y	Y	Y	Y	Y
7 Crowley	Y	Y	Y	Y	Y	Y
8 Nadler	Y	Y	Y	Y	Y	Y
9 Weiner	Y	Y	Y	Y	Y	Y
10 Towns	Y	Y	Y	Y	Y	Y
11 Clarke	Y	Y	Y	Y	Y	Y
12 Velázquez	Y	?	Y	Y	Y	Y
13 McMahon	?	?	?	Y	Y	Y
14 Maloney	Y	Y	Y	Y	Y	Y
15 Rangel	Y	Y	Y	Y	Y	Y
16 Serrano	Y	Y	Y	Y	Y	Y
17 Engel	Y	Y	Y	Y	Y	Y
18 Lowey	Y	Y	Y	Y	Y	Y
19 Hall	Y	Y	Y	Y	Y	?
20 Murphy	?	Y	Y	N	Y	Y
21 Tonko	Y	Y	Y	Y	Y	Y
22 Hinchey	Y	Y	Y	Y	Y	Y
23 Owens	Y	Y	Y	Y	Y	Y
24 Arcuri	?	?	?	?	?	?
25 Maffei	Y	Y	Y	Y	Y	Y
26 **Lee**	Y	Y	Y	N	Y	Y
27 Higgins	Y	Y	Y	Y	Y	Y
28 Slaughter	Y	Y	Y	Y	Y	Y
29 **Reed**	Y	Y	Y	N	Y	Y
NORTH CAROLINA						
1 Butterfield	Y	Y	Y	Y	Y	Y
2 Etheridge	Y	Y	Y	Y	Y	Y
3 **Jones**	Y	Y	Y	Y	Y	?
4 Price	Y	Y	Y	Y	Y	Y

	608	609	610	611	612	613
5 **Foxx**	Y	Y	Y	N	Y	Y
6 **Coble**	Y	Y	Y	N	Y	Y
7 McIntyre	Y	Y	Y	Y	Y	+
8 Kissell	Y	Y	Y	Y	Y	Y
9 **Myrick**	Y	Y	Y	N	Y	Y
10 **McHenry**	Y	Y	Y	N	Y	Y
11 Shuler	Y	Y	Y	Y	Y	Y
12 Watt	Y	Y	Y	Y	Y	Y
13 Miller	Y	Y	Y	Y	Y	Y
NORTH DAKOTA						
AL Pomeroy	Y	Y	Y	Y	Y	Y
OHIO						
1 Driehaus	Y	Y	Y	Y	Y	Y
2 **Schmidt**	Y	Y	Y	N	Y	Y
3 **Turner**	Y	Y	Y	N	Y	Y
4 **Jordan**	Y	Y	Y	N	Y	Y
5 **Latta**	Y	Y	Y	N	Y	Y
6 Wilson	Y	Y	Y	Y	Y	Y
7 **Austria**	Y	Y	Y	N	Y	Y
8 **Boehner**	?	?	?	N	Y	Y
9 Kaptur	Y	Y	Y	Y	Y	Y
10 Kucinich	Y	Y	Y	Y	Y	N
11 Fudge	Y	Y	Y	Y	Y	Y
12 **Tiberi**	?	?	?	N	Y	Y
13 Sutton	?	Y	Y	Y	Y	Y
14 **LaTourette**	Y	Y	Y	N	Y	Y
15 Kilroy	Y	Y	Y	Y	Y	Y
16 Boccieri	Y	Y	Y	Y	Y	Y
17 Ryan	Y	Y	Y	Y	Y	Y
18 Space	Y	Y	Y	Y	Y	Y
OKLAHOMA						
1 **Sullivan**	Y	Y	Y	N	Y	Y
2 Boren	Y	Y	Y	Y	Y	Y
3 **Lucas**	Y	Y	Y	N	Y	Y
4 **Cole**	Y	Y	Y	N	Y	Y
5 **Fallin**	?	?	?	?	?	?
OREGON						
1 Wu	Y	Y	Y	Y	Y	Y
2 **Walden**	Y	?	Y	N	Y	Y
3 Blumenauer	Y	Y	Y	N	Y	Y
4 DeFazio	Y	Y	Y	Y	Y	Y
5 Schrader	Y	Y	Y	N	Y	Y
PENNSYLVANIA						
1 Brady	?	?	?	Y	Y	Y
2 Fattah	Y	Y	Y	Y	Y	Y
3 Dahlkemper	Y	Y	Y	Y	Y	Y
4 Altmire	Y	Y	Y	Y	Y	Y
5 **Thompson**	Y	Y	Y	N	Y	Y
6 **Gerlach**	Y	Y	Y	Y	Y	Y
7 Sestak	Y	Y	Y	Y	Y	Y
8 Murphy, P.	?	?	?	?	?	?
9 **Shuster**	Y	Y	Y	N	Y	Y
10 Carney	?	?	?	Y	Y	Y
11 Kanjorski	Y	Y	Y	Y	Y	Y
12 Critz	Y	Y	Y	Y	Y	Y
13 Schwartz	Y	Y	Y	Y	Y	Y
14 Doyle	Y	Y	Y	Y	Y	Y
15 **Dent**	Y	Y	Y	Y	Y	Y
16 **Pitts**	Y	Y	Y	N	Y	Y
17 Holden	Y	Y	Y	Y	Y	Y
18 **Murphy, T.**	Y	Y	Y	Y	Y	Y
19 **Platts**	Y	Y	Y	Y	Y	Y
RHODE ISLAND						
1 Kennedy	Y	Y	Y	?	?	?
2 Langevin	?	Y	Y	Y	Y	Y
SOUTH CAROLINA						
1 **Brown**	Y	Y	Y	Y	Y	Y
2 **Wilson**	Y	Y	Y	N	Y	Y
3 **Barrett**	Y	Y	Y	N	Y	Y
4 **Inglis**	Y	Y	Y	N	Y	Y
5 Spratt	Y	Y	Y	Y	Y	Y
6 Clyburn	Y	Y	Y	Y	Y	Y
SOUTH DAKOTA						
AL Herseth Sandlin	Y	Y	Y	Y	Y	Y
TENNESSEE						
1 **Roe**	Y	Y	Y	N	Y	Y
2 **Duncan**	Y	Y	Y	N	Y	Y
3 **Wamp**	Y	Y	Y	Y	?	Y
4 Davis	Y	?	Y	Y	Y	Y
5 Cooper	Y	Y	Y	N	Y	Y
6 Gordon	Y	Y	Y	?	?	?
7 **Blackburn**	Y	Y	Y	N	Y	Y
8 Tanner	Y	Y	Y	N	Y	Y
9 Cohen	+	+	+	+	+	+

	608	609	610	611	612	613
TEXAS						
1 **Gohmert**	Y	Y	Y	N	Y	Y
2 **Poe**	?	?	?	N	Y	Y
3 **Johnson, S.**	Y	Y	Y	N	Y	Y
4 **Hall**	Y	Y	Y	N	Y	Y
5 **Hensarling**	Y	Y	Y	N	Y	Y
6 **Barton**	Y	Y	Y	N	Y	Y
7 **Culberson**	?	?	?	N	Y	Y
8 **Brady**	Y	Y	Y	N	Y	Y
9 Green, A.	Y	Y	Y	Y	Y	Y
10 **McCaul**	Y	Y	Y	N	Y	Y
11 **Conaway**	Y	Y	Y	N	Y	Y
12 **Granger**	?	?	?	?	?	?
13 **Thornberry**	Y	Y	Y	N	Y	Y
14 **Paul**	?	?	?	N	N	N
15 Hinojosa	Y	Y	Y	Y	Y	Y
16 Reyes	Y	?	Y	Y	Y	Y
17 Edwards	?	?	?	Y	?	Y
18 Jackson Lee	Y	Y	Y	N	Y	Y
19 **Neugebauer**	Y	Y	Y	N	Y	Y
20 Gonzalez	Y	Y	Y	Y	Y	Y
21 **Smith**	Y	Y	Y	N	Y	Y
22 **Olson**	Y	Y	Y	N	Y	Y
23 Rodriguez	Y	Y	Y	Y	Y	Y
24 **Marchant**	?	?	?	?	?	?
25 Doggett	Y	Y	Y	Y	Y	Y
26 **Burgess**	Y	Y	Y	N	Y	Y
27 Ortiz	Y	Y	Y	Y	Y	Y
28 Cuellar	Y	Y	Y	Y	Y	Y
29 Green, G.	Y	Y	Y	Y	Y	Y
30 Johnson, E.	Y	Y	Y	Y	Y	Y
31 **Carter**	?	Y	Y	N	Y	Y
32 **Sessions**	Y	Y	Y	N	Y	Y
UTAH						
1 **Bishop**	Y	Y	Y	N	Y	Y
2 Matheson	Y	Y	Y	Y	Y	Y
3 **Chaffetz**	Y	Y	Y	N	Y	Y
VERMONT						
AL Welch	Y	Y	Y	Y	?	Y
VIRGINIA						
1 **Wittman**	Y	Y	Y	N	Y	Y
2 Nye	Y	Y	Y	Y	Y	Y
3 Scott	Y	Y	Y	Y	Y	Y
4 **Forbes**	Y	Y	Y	N	Y	Y
5 Perriello	Y	Y	Y	Y	Y	Y
6 **Goodlatte**	Y	Y	Y	N	Y	Y
7 **Cantor**	Y	?	Y	N	Y	Y
8 Moran	Y	Y	Y	N	Y	Y
9 Boucher	Y	Y	Y	Y	Y	Y
10 **Wolf**	Y	Y	Y	N	Y	Y
11 Connolly	Y	Y	Y	Y	Y	Y
WASHINGTON						
1 Inslee	Y	Y	Y	N	Y	Y
2 Larsen	Y	Y	Y	Y	Y	Y
3 Baird	Y	Y	Y	N	Y	Y
4 **Hastings**	Y	Y	Y	N	Y	Y
5 **McMorris Rodgers**	?	+	+	?	?	?
6 Dicks	Y	Y	Y	Y	Y	Y
7 McDermott	Y	Y	Y	Y	Y	Y
8 **Reichert**	Y	Y	Y	N	Y	Y
9 Smith	Y	Y	Y	Y	Y	Y
WEST VIRGINIA						
1 Mollohan	Y	Y	Y	Y	Y	Y
2 **Capito**	Y	Y	Y	Y	Y	Y
3 Rahall	Y	Y	Y	Y	Y	Y
WISCONSIN						
1 **Ryan**	Y	Y	Y	N	Y	Y
2 Baldwin	Y	Y	Y	Y	Y	Y
3 Kind	Y	Y	Y	N	Y	Y
4 Moore	Y	Y	Y	Y	Y	Y
5 **Sensenbrenner**	Y	Y	Y	N	Y	Y
6 **Petri**	Y	Y	Y	Y	Y	Y
7 Obey	Y	Y	Y	Y	Y	Y
8 Kagen	Y	Y	Y	Y	Y	Y
WYOMING						
AL **Lummis**	Y	Y	Y	N	Y	Y
DELEGATES						
Faleomavaega (A.S.)						
Norton (D.C.)						
Bordallo (Guam)						
Sablan (N. Marianas)						
Pierluisi (P.R.)						
Christensen (V.I.)						

IN THE HOUSE | By Vote Number

614. **H Res 1531. World Veterinary Year/Adoption.** Clay, D-Mo., motion to suspend the rules and adopt the resolution that would support the designation of 2011 as World Veterinary Year and commend veterinarians' contributions to animal health and welfare, public health, and food safety. Motion agreed to 406-0: D 239-0; R 167-0. A two-thirds majority of those present and voting (271 in this case) is required for adoption under suspension of the rules. Dec. 8, 2010.

615. **H Res 1752. Same-Day Consideration/Rule.** Adoption of the rule (H Res 1752) that would waive, through the legislative day of Dec. 18, 2010, the two-thirds majority vote requirement to consider a rule on the same day it is reported from the Rules Committee. The rule also would allow for consideration of measures under suspension of the rules at any time through the legislative day of Dec. 18. Adopted 215-194: D 215-27; R 0-167. Dec. 8, 2010.

616. **HR 6495. Mine Safety and Regulation/Passage.** Miller, D-Calif., motion to suspend the rules and pass the bill that would provide additional authorities to the Mine Safety and Health Administration, including the power to subpoena documents and testimony in carrying out investigations and inspections. It would increase civil and criminal penalties for mines that violate safety and health regulations and create a system by which mines could be identified as having a history of citations for substantial violations. The bill would provide for independent investigations for certain mine accidents and increase whistleblower protections for mine workers. Motion rejected 214-193: D 213-27; R 1-166. A two-thirds majority of those present and voting (272 in this case) is required for passage under suspension of the rules. Dec. 8, 2010.

617. **H Res 1402. Tribute to Citizen Diplomats/Adoption.** Klein, D-Fla., motion to suspend the rules and adopt the resolution that would recognize the 50th anniversary of the National Council for International Visitors and support the designation of Feb. 16, 2011, as Citizen Diplomacy Day. Motion agreed to 394-13: D 240-0; R 154-13. A two-thirds majority of those present and voting (272 in this case) is required for adoption under suspension of the rules. Dec. 8, 2010.

618. **H Res 1704. Battle of Marathon Anniversary/Adoption.** Klein, D-Fla., motion to suspend the rules and adopt the resolution that would honor the 2,500th anniversary of the Battle of Marathon, Greece. Motion agreed to 359-44: D 235-2; R 124-42. A two-thirds majority of those present and voting (269 in this case) is required for adoption under suspension of the rules. Dec. 8, 2010.

619. **HR 3082. Continuing Appropriations and Food Safety/Rule.** Adoption of the rule (H Res 1755) that would provide for House floor consideration of the Senate amendment to the bill by allowing for a motion to concur with a House amendment that would provide continuing appropriations through Sept. 30, 2011, for all federal departments and agencies, none of whose fiscal 2011 appropriations bills have been enacted. The amendment also would include provisions of a Senate-passed bill that would overhaul food safety laws and expand Food and Drug Administration enforcement powers. Adopted 207-206: D 207-37; R 0-169. Dec. 8, 2010.

	614	615	616	617	618	619
ALABAMA						
1 **Bonner**	Y	N	N	Y	Y	N
2 **Bright**	Y	N	N	Y	Y	N
3 **Rogers**	Y	N	N	?	Y	N
4 **Aderholt**	Y	N	N	Y	Y	N
5 **Griffith**	?	?	?	?	?	?
6 **Bachus**	Y	N	N	Y	Y	N
7 Davis	?	Y	N	Y	Y	?
ALASKA						
AL **Young**	Y	N	N	N	N	N
ARIZONA						
1 Kirkpatrick	?	?	?	?	?	?
2 **Franks**	Y	N	N	Y	Y	N
3 **Shadegg**	Y	N	N	Y	N	N
4 Pastor	Y	Y	Y	Y	Y	Y
5 Mitchell	Y	N	Y	Y	Y	Y
6 **Flake**	Y	N	N	N	N	N
7 Grijalva	Y	Y	Y	Y	Y	Y
8 Giffords	Y	Y	N	Y	Y	N
ARKANSAS						
1 Berry	?	?	?	?	?	?
2 Snyder	Y	Y	Y	Y	Y	Y
3 **Boozman**	Y	N	N	Y	Y	N
4 Ross	Y	N	N	Y	Y	N
CALIFORNIA						
1 Thompson	Y	Y	Y	Y	Y	N
2 **Herger**	Y	N	N	Y	N	N
3 **Lungren**	Y	N	N	Y	Y	N
4 **McClintock**	Y	N	N	Y	N	N
5 Matsui	Y	Y	Y	Y	Y	Y
6 Woolsey	Y	Y	Y	Y	Y	Y
7 Miller, George	Y	Y	Y	Y	Y	Y
8 Pelosi						Y
9 Lee	Y	Y	Y	Y	Y	Y
10 Garamendi	Y	Y	Y	Y	Y	Y
11 McNerney	Y	Y	Y	Y	Y	Y
12 Speier	Y	Y	Y	Y	Y	Y
13 Stark	Y	Y	Y	Y	Y	Y
14 Eshoo	Y	Y	Y	Y	Y	Y
15 Honda	Y	Y	Y	Y	Y	Y
16 Lofgren	Y	Y	Y	Y	Y	Y
17 Farr	Y	Y	Y	Y	Y	Y
18 Cardoza	Y	N	Y	Y	Y	N
19 **Radanovich**	?	?	?	?	?	?
20 Costa	Y	N	N	Y	Y	N
21 **Nunes**	Y	N	N	N	N	N
22 **McCarthy**	Y	N	N	Y	Y	N
23 Capps	Y	Y	Y	Y	Y	Y
24 **Gallegly**	Y	N	N	Y	Y	N
25 **McKeon**	Y	N	N	Y	Y	N
26 **Dreier**	Y	N	N	Y	Y	N
27 Sherman	Y	Y	Y	Y	Y	Y
28 Berman	Y	Y	Y	Y	Y	Y
29 Schiff	Y	Y	Y	Y	Y	Y
30 Waxman	Y	Y	Y	Y	Y	Y
31 Becerra	Y	Y	Y	Y	Y	Y
32 Chu	Y	Y	Y	Y	?	Y
33 Watson	Y	Y	Y	Y	Y	Y
34 Roybal-Allard	Y	Y	Y	Y	Y	Y
35 Waters	Y	?	Y	Y	Y	Y
36 Harman	Y	Y	Y	Y	Y	N
37 Richardson	Y	Y	Y	Y	Y	Y
38 Napolitano	Y	Y	Y	Y	Y	Y
39 Sánchez, Linda	Y	Y	Y	Y	Y	Y
40 **Royce**	Y	N	N	Y	N	N
41 **Lewis**	Y	N	N	Y	N	N
42 **Miller, Gary**	Y	N	N	Y	Y	N
43 Baca	Y	Y	Y	Y	Y	Y
44 **Calvert**	Y	N	N	Y	Y	N
45 **Bono Mack**	Y	N	N	Y	Y	N
46 **Rohrabacher**	Y	N	N	Y	N	N
47 Sanchez, Loretta	Y	Y	Y	Y	Y	Y
48 **Campbell**	Y	N	N	N	N	N
49 **Issa**	Y	N	N	Y	Y	N
50 **Bilbray**	?	?	?	?	?	?
51 Filner	Y	Y	Y	Y	Y	Y
52 **Hunter**	Y	N	N	Y	Y	N
53 Davis	Y	Y	Y	Y	Y	Y

	614	615	616	617	618	619
COLORADO						
1 DeGette	Y	Y	Y	Y	Y	Y
2 Polis	Y	Y	Y	Y	Y	Y
3 Salazar	Y	Y	N	Y	Y	N
4 Markey	?	Y	Y	Y	Y	Y
5 **Lamborn**	Y	N	N	Y	N	N
6 **Coffman**	Y	N	N	Y	N	N
7 Perlmutter	Y	Y	N	Y	Y	Y
CONNECTICUT						
1 Larson	Y	Y	Y	Y	Y	Y
2 Courtney	Y	Y	Y	Y	Y	N
3 DeLauro	Y	Y	Y	Y	Y	Y
4 Himes	Y	Y	Y	Y	Y	Y
5 Murphy	Y	Y	Y	Y	Y	Y
DELAWARE						
AL Castle	Y	N	N	Y	Y	N
FLORIDA						
1 **Miller**	Y	N	N	Y	N	N
2 Boyd	Y	Y	N	Y	N	N
3 Brown	Y	Y	Y	Y	Y	Y
4 **Crenshaw**	Y	N	N	Y	Y	N
5 **Brown-Waite**	Y	N	N	Y	N	N
6 **Stearns**	Y	N	N	Y	N	N
7 **Mica**	Y	N	N	Y	Y	N
8 Grayson	Y	Y	Y	Y	Y	Y
9 **Bilirakis**	Y	N	N	N	Y	N
10 **Young**	?	N	N	Y	N	N
11 Castor	Y	Y	Y	Y	Y	Y
12 **Putnam**	Y	N	N	Y	N	N
13 **Buchanan**	Y	N	N	Y	N	N
14 **Mack**	Y	N	N	Y	N	N
15 **Posey**	Y	N	N	Y	Y	N
16 **Rooney**	Y	N	N	N	N	N
17 Meek	?	Y	Y	Y	Y	Y
18 **Ros-Lehtinen**	Y	N	N	Y	Y	N
19 Deutch	Y	Y	Y	+	Y	Y
20 Wasserman Schultz	Y	Y	Y	Y	Y	Y
21 **Diaz-Balart, L.**	Y	N	N	Y	Y	N
22 Klein	Y	Y	Y	Y	Y	Y
23 Hastings	Y	Y	Y	Y	Y	Y
24 Kosmas	Y	Y	Y	Y	Y	Y
25 **Diaz-Balart, M.**	Y	N	N	Y	Y	N
GEORGIA						
1 **Kingston**	Y	N	N	N	Y	N
2 Bishop	Y	Y	Y	Y	Y	Y
3 **Westmoreland**	Y	N	N	N	N	N
4 Johnson	Y	Y	Y	Y	Y	Y
5 Lewis	Y	Y	Y	Y	Y	Y
6 **Price**	Y	N	N	Y	N	N
7 **Linder**	Y	N	N	Y	N	N
8 Marshall	Y	N	?	Y	P	Y
9 **Graves**	Y	N	N	N	N	N
10 **Broun**	Y	N	N	N	N	N
11 **Gingrey**	Y	N	N	N	Y	N
12 Barrow	Y	N	Y	Y	Y	Y
13 Scott	?	Y	Y	Y	Y	Y
HAWAII						
1 **Djou**	Y	N	N	Y	Y	N
2 Hirono	Y	Y	Y	Y	Y	Y
IDAHO						
1 Minnick	Y	N	N	Y	Y	N
2 **Simpson**	Y	N	N	Y	N	N
ILLINOIS						
1 Rush	Y	Y	Y	Y	Y	?
2 Jackson	Y	Y	Y	Y	Y	Y
3 Lipinski	Y	Y	Y	Y	Y	Y
4 Gutierrez	Y	Y	Y	Y	Y	Y
5 Quigley	Y	?	?	?	Y	Y
6 **Roskam**	Y	N	?	Y	Y	N
7 Davis	Y	Y	Y	Y	Y	Y
8 Bean	Y	N	Y	Y	Y	Y
9 Schakowsky	Y	Y	Y	Y	Y	Y
10 Vacant						
11 Halvorson	Y	Y	Y	Y	Y	Y
12 Costello	Y	Y	Y	Y	Y	Y
13 **Biggert**	Y	N	N	Y	Y	N
14 Foster	Y	Y	Y	Y	Y	Y
15 **Johnson**	Y	N	N	Y	N	N

	614	615	616	617	618	619
16 **Manzullo**	Y	N	N	Y	Y	N
17 Hare	Y	N	Y	Y	Y	Y
18 **Schock**	Y	N	N	Y	N	N
19 **Shimkus**	Y	N	N	Y	N	N
INDIANA						
1 Visclosky	Y	Y	Y	Y	Y	Y
2 Donnelly	Y	N	N	Y	Y	N
3 **Stutzman**	Y	N	N	Y	N	N
4 **Buyer**	Y	N	N	Y	Y	?
5 **Burton**	Y	N	N	N	Y	N
6 **Pence**	Y	N	N	Y	Y	N
7 Carson	Y	Y	Y	Y	Y	Y
8 Ellsworth	?	N	N	?	?	?
9 Hill	Y	Y	?	?	?	Y
IOWA						
1 Braley	Y	Y	Y	Y	Y	Y
2 Loebsack	Y	Y	Y	Y	Y	Y
3 Boswell	Y	Y	Y	Y	Y	Y
4 **Latham**	Y	N	N	Y	Y	N
5 **King**	Y	N	N	Y	N	N
KANSAS						
1 **Moran**	Y	N	N	Y	Y	N
2 **Jenkins**	Y	N	N	Y	Y	N
3 Moore	Y	Y	Y	Y	?	Y
4 **Tiahrt**	?	?	?	?	?	?
KENTUCKY						
1 **Whitfield**	Y	N	N	Y	Y	N
2 **Guthrie**	Y	N	N	Y	Y	N
3 Yarmuth	Y	Y	Y	Y	Y	Y
4 **Davis**	Y	N	N	Y	N	N
5 **Rogers**	Y	N	N	Y	Y	N
6 Chandler	Y	Y	Y	Y	Y	Y
LOUISIANA						
1 **Scalise**	Y	N	N	Y	Y	N
2 **Cao**	Y	N	N	Y	Y	N
3 Melancon	Y	Y	Y	Y	Y	Y
4 **Fleming**	Y	N	N	Y	Y	N
5 **Alexander**	Y	N	N	Y	Y	N
6 **Cassidy**	Y	N	N	Y	N	N
7 **Boustany**	Y	N	N	Y	Y	N
MAINE						
1 Pingree	Y	Y	Y	Y	?	Y
2 Michaud	Y	N	Y	Y	Y	N
MARYLAND						
1 Kratovil	Y	N	Y	Y	Y	N
2 Ruppersberger	Y	Y	Y	Y	Y	Y
3 Sarbanes	Y	Y	Y	Y	Y	Y
4 Edwards	Y	Y	Y	Y	Y	Y
5 Hoyer	Y	Y	Y	Y	Y	Y
6 **Bartlett**	Y	N	N	N	N	N
7 Cummings	Y	Y	Y	Y	Y	Y
8 Van Hollen	Y	Y	Y	Y	Y	Y
MASSACHUSETTS						
1 Olver	Y	Y	Y	Y	Y	Y
2 Neal	Y	Y	Y	Y	Y	Y
3 McGovern	Y	Y	Y	Y	Y	Y
4 Frank	Y	Y	Y	Y	Y	Y
5 Tsongas	Y	Y	Y	Y	Y	Y
6 Tierney	Y	Y	Y	Y	Y	Y
7 Markey	Y	Y	Y	Y	Y	Y
8 Capuano	Y	Y	Y	Y	Y	Y
9 Lynch	Y	Y	Y	Y	Y	Y
10 Delahunt	?	?	?	?	?	?
MICHIGAN						
1 Stupak	Y	Y	Y	Y	Y	Y
2 **Hoekstra**	?	?	?	?	?	N
3 **Ehlers**	Y	N	N	Y	Y	N
4 **Camp**	Y	?	N	Y	Y	N
5 Kildee	Y	Y	Y	Y	Y	Y
6 **Upton**	Y	N	N	Y	Y	N
7 Schauer	Y	Y	Y	Y	Y	Y
8 **Rogers**	Y	N	N	Y	N	N
9 Peters	Y	N	Y	Y	Y	N
10 **Miller**	Y	N	N	Y	N	N
11 **McCotter**	Y	N	N	Y	Y	N
12 Levin	Y	Y	Y	Y	Y	Y
13 Kilpatrick	+	+	+	+	+	?
14 Conyers	Y	?	Y	Y	?	N
15 Dingell	Y	Y	Y	Y	Y	Y
MINNESOTA						
1 Walz	Y	Y	Y	?	Y	Y
2 **Kline**	Y	N	N	Y	Y	N
3 **Paulsen**	Y	N	N	Y	Y	N
4 McCollum	Y	Y	Y	Y	Y	Y

	614	615	616	617	618	619
5 Ellison	Y	Y	Y	?	Y	Y
6 **Bachmann**	Y	N	N	Y	Y	N
7 Peterson	Y	Y	N	Y	Y	N
8 Oberstar	Y	Y	?	Y	Y	Y
MISSISSIPPI						
1 Childers	?	N	N	Y	Y	N
2 Thompson	Y	Y	Y	Y	Y	Y
3 **Harper**	Y	N	N	Y	Y	N
4 Taylor	Y	N	Y	Y	N	N
MISSOURI						
1 Clay	Y	Y	Y	Y	Y	Y
2 **Akin**	Y	N	N	Y	Y	N
3 Carnahan	Y	Y	Y	Y	Y	Y
4 Skelton	Y	Y	Y	Y	Y	Y
5 Cleaver	Y	Y	Y	Y	Y	Y
6 **Graves**	Y	N	N	Y	N	N
7 **Blunt**	?	?	?	?	?	?
8 **Emerson**	Y	N	N	Y	N	N
9 **Luetkemeyer**	Y	N	N	Y	Y	N
MONTANA						
AL **Rehberg**	Y	N	N	Y	N	N
NEBRASKA						
1 **Fortenberry**	Y	N	N	Y	N	N
2 **Terry**	Y	N	N	Y	N	N
3 **Smith**	Y	N	N	Y	N	N
NEVADA						
1 Berkley	Y	Y	N	Y	Y	Y
2 **Heller**	Y	N	N	Y	N	N
3 Titus	Y	Y	N	Y	Y	Y
NEW HAMPSHIRE						
1 Shea-Porter	Y	Y	Y	Y	Y	Y
2 Hodes	Y	Y	Y	Y	Y	Y
NEW JERSEY						
1 Andrews	Y	Y	Y	Y	Y	Y
2 **LoBiondo**	Y	N	N	Y	Y	N
3 Adler	Y	N	Y	Y	Y	N
4 **Smith**	Y	?	N	Y	Y	N
5 **Garrett**	Y	N	?	Y	?	N
6 Pallone	Y	Y	Y	Y	Y	Y
7 **Lance**	Y	N	N	Y	Y	N
8 Pascrell	Y	Y	Y	Y	Y	Y
9 Rothman	Y	Y	Y	Y	Y	Y
10 Payne	Y	Y	Y	Y	Y	Y
11 **Frelinghuysen**	Y	N	N	Y	Y	N
12 Holt	Y	Y	Y	Y	Y	Y
13 Sires	Y	Y	Y	Y	Y	Y
NEW MEXICO						
1 Heinrich	Y	Y	Y	Y	Y	Y
2 Teague	Y	Y	Y	Y	Y	Y
3 Luján	Y	Y	Y	Y	Y	Y
NEW YORK						
1 Bishop	Y	Y	Y	Y	Y	Y
2 Israel	Y	Y	Y	Y	Y	Y
3 **King**	Y	N	N	Y	Y	N
4 McCarthy	Y	Y	Y	Y	Y	Y
5 Ackerman	Y	Y	Y	Y	Y	Y
6 Meeks	Y	Y	Y	Y	Y	Y
7 Crowley	Y	Y	Y	Y	Y	Y
8 Nadler	Y	Y	?	Y	Y	N
9 Weiner	Y	Y	Y	Y	Y	Y
10 Towns	Y	Y	Y	Y	Y	Y
11 Clarke	Y	Y	Y	Y	Y	Y
12 Velázquez	Y	Y	Y	?	Y	Y
13 McMahon	Y	?	?	Y	Y	Y
14 Maloney	Y	Y	Y	Y	Y	Y
15 Rangel	Y	Y	Y	Y	Y	Y
16 Serrano	Y	Y	Y	Y	Y	Y
17 Engel	Y	Y	Y	Y	Y	Y
18 Lowey	Y	Y	Y	Y	Y	Y
19 Hall	?	Y	Y	Y	P	N
20 Murphy	Y	N	Y	Y	P	N
21 Tonko	Y	Y	Y	Y	Y	Y
22 Hinchey	Y	Y	Y	Y	Y	Y
23 Owens	Y	Y	Y	Y	P	Y
24 Arcuri	?	Y	Y	Y	Y	Y
25 Maffei	Y	Y	Y	Y	Y	Y
26 **Lee**	Y	N	N	Y	N	N
27 Higgins	Y	Y	Y	Y	Y	Y
28 Slaughter	Y	Y	Y	Y	Y	Y
29 **Reed**	Y	N	N	Y	Y	N
NORTH CAROLINA						
1 Butterfield	Y	Y	Y	Y	Y	Y
2 Etheridge	Y	Y	Y	Y	Y	Y
3 **Jones**	?	N	Y	Y	N	N
4 Price	Y	Y	Y	Y	Y	Y

	614	615	616	617	618	619
5 **Foxx**	Y	N	N	Y	Y	N
6 **Coble**	Y	N	N	Y	Y	N
7 McIntyre	Y	Y	Y	Y	Y	N
8 Kissell	Y	Y	Y	Y	Y	Y
9 **Myrick**	Y	N	N	Y	Y	N
10 **McHenry**	Y	N	N	Y	Y	N
11 Shuler	Y	N	Y	Y	Y	N
12 Watt	Y	Y	Y	Y	Y	N
13 Miller	Y	Y	Y	Y	Y	Y
NORTH DAKOTA						
AL Pomeroy	Y	Y	N	Y	Y	Y
OHIO						
1 Driehaus	Y	Y	Y	Y	Y	N
2 **Schmidt**	Y	N	N	Y	Y	N
3 **Turner**	Y	N	N	Y	Y	N
4 **Jordan**	Y	N	N	Y	N	N
5 **Latta**	Y	N	N	Y	Y	N
6 Wilson	Y	Y	Y	Y	Y	Y
7 **Austria**	Y	N	N	Y	Y	N
8 **Boehner**	Y	N	N	Y	Y	N
9 Kaptur	Y	Y	Y	Y	Y	Y
10 Kucinich	Y	Y	Y	Y	Y	Y
11 Fudge	Y	Y	Y	Y	Y	Y
12 **Tiberi**	Y	N	N	Y	Y	N
13 Sutton	Y	Y	Y	Y	Y	Y
14 **LaTourette**	Y	N	N	Y	Y	N
15 Kilroy	Y	Y	Y	Y	Y	Y
16 Boccieri	Y	N	N	Y	Y	N
17 Ryan	Y	Y	N	Y	Y	Y
18 Space	Y	N	Y	Y	Y	Y
OKLAHOMA						
1 **Sullivan**	Y	N	N	Y	Y	N
2 Boren	Y	N	N	Y	Y	N
3 **Lucas**	Y	N	N	Y	Y	N
4 **Cole**	Y	N	N	Y	Y	N
5 **Fallin**	?	?	?	?	?	?
OREGON						
1 Wu	Y	Y	Y	Y	Y	?
2 **Walden**	Y	N	N	Y	Y	N
3 Blumenauer	Y	Y	Y	Y	Y	Y
4 DeFazio	Y	Y	Y	Y	Y	Y
5 Schrader	Y	Y	Y	Y	Y	Y
PENNSYLVANIA						
1 Brady	Y	Y	Y	Y	Y	Y
2 Fattah	Y	Y	Y	Y	Y	Y
3 Dahlkemper	Y	Y	Y	Y	Y	Y
4 Altmire	Y	N	Y	Y	Y	N
5 **Thompson**	Y	N	N	Y	Y	N
6 **Gerlach**	Y	N	N	Y	Y	N
7 Sestak	Y	Y	Y	Y	Y	Y
8 Murphy, P.	Y	Y	Y	Y	Y	Y
9 **Shuster**	Y	N	N	Y	Y	N
10 Carney	Y	Y	N	Y	Y	Y
11 Kanjorski	Y	Y	Y	Y	Y	Y
12 Critz	Y	Y	Y	Y	Y	Y
13 Schwartz	Y	Y	Y	Y	Y	Y
14 Doyle	Y	Y	Y	Y	Y	Y
15 **Dent**	Y	N	N	Y	Y	N
16 **Pitts**	Y	N	N	Y	Y	N
17 Holden	Y	Y	N	Y	Y	Y
18 **Murphy, T.**	Y	N	N	Y	Y	N
19 **Platts**	Y	N	N	Y	Y	N
RHODE ISLAND						
1 Kennedy	?	Y	Y	Y	Y	Y
2 Langevin	Y	Y	Y	Y	Y	N
SOUTH CAROLINA						
1 **Brown**	Y	N	N	Y	Y	N
2 **Wilson**	Y	N	N	Y	Y	N
3 **Barrett**	Y	N	N	Y	Y	N
4 **Inglis**	Y	N	N	Y	Y	N
5 Spratt	Y	Y	Y	Y	Y	Y
6 Clyburn	Y	Y	Y	Y	Y	Y
SOUTH DAKOTA						
AL Herseth Sandlin	Y	N	N	Y	Y	N
TENNESSEE						
1 **Roe**	Y	N	N	Y	N	N
2 **Duncan**	Y	N	N	Y	Y	N
3 **Wamp**	Y	N	N	Y	Y	N
4 Davis	Y	Y	N	Y	Y	Y
5 Cooper	Y	Y	Y	Y	Y	Y
6 Gordon	?	?	?	?	?	?
7 **Blackburn**	Y	N	N	Y	Y	N
8 Tanner	Y	Y	N	Y	Y	Y
9 Cohen	+	+	+	+	+	+

	614	615	616	617	618	619
TEXAS						
1 **Gohmert**	Y	N	N	P	P	N
2 **Poe**	Y	N	N	N	Y	N
3 **Johnson, S.**	Y	N	N	Y	Y	N
4 **Hall**	Y	N	N	Y	Y	N
5 **Hensarling**	Y	N	N	Y	Y	N
6 **Barton**	Y	N	N	N	N	N
7 **Culberson**	Y	N	N	Y	Y	N
8 **Brady**	Y	N	N	Y	Y	N
9 Green, A.	Y	Y	Y	Y	Y	Y
10 **McCaul**	Y	N	N	Y	Y	N
11 **Conaway**	Y	N	N	Y	N	N
12 **Granger**	?	?	?	?	?	?
13 **Thornberry**	Y	N	N	Y	Y	N
14 **Paul**	Y	N	N	N	N	N
15 Hinojosa	Y	Y	Y	Y	Y	Y
16 Reyes	Y	Y	Y	Y	Y	Y
17 Edwards	Y	Y	Y	Y	Y	Y
18 Jackson Lee	Y	Y	Y	Y	Y	Y
19 **Neugebauer**	Y	N	N	Y	Y	N
20 Gonzalez	Y	Y	Y	Y	Y	Y
21 **Smith**	Y	N	N	Y	Y	N
22 **Olson**	Y	N	N	Y	Y	N
23 Rodriguez	Y	Y	Y	Y	Y	Y
24 **Marchant**	?	?	?	?	?	?
25 Doggett	Y	Y	Y	Y	Y	Y
26 **Burgess**	Y	N	N	Y	Y	N
27 Ortiz	Y	Y	Y	Y	Y	Y
28 Cuellar	Y	Y	N	Y	Y	Y
29 Green, G.	Y	Y	Y	Y	Y	Y
30 Johnson, E.	Y	Y	Y	Y	Y	Y
31 **Carter**	Y	N	N	Y	Y	N
32 **Sessions**	Y	N	N	Y	Y	N
UTAH						
1 **Bishop**	Y	N	N	Y	Y	N
2 Matheson	Y	N	N	Y	Y	N
3 **Chaffetz**	Y	N	N	N	N	N
VERMONT						
AL Welch	Y	Y	Y	Y	Y	Y
VIRGINIA						
1 **Wittman**	Y	N	N	Y	Y	N
2 Nye	Y	N	Y	Y	Y	N
3 Scott	Y	Y	Y	Y	Y	Y
4 **Forbes**	Y	N	N	Y	Y	N
5 Perriello	Y	N	Y	Y	Y	N
6 **Goodlatte**	Y	N	N	Y	Y	N
7 **Cantor**	Y	N	N	Y	N	N
8 Moran	Y	Y	Y	Y	Y	Y
9 Boucher	Y	Y	?	Y	Y	Y
10 **Wolf**	Y	N	N	Y	Y	N
11 Connolly	Y	Y	Y	Y	Y	Y
WASHINGTON						
1 Inslee	Y	Y	Y	Y	Y	Y
2 Larsen	Y	Y	Y	Y	Y	Y
3 Baird	Y	N	Y	Y	Y	N
4 **Hastings**	Y	N	N	Y	Y	N
5 **McMorris Rodgers**	?	?	?	?	?	?
6 Dicks	Y	Y	Y	Y	Y	Y
7 McDermott	Y	Y	Y	Y	Y	Y
8 **Reichert**	Y	N	N	Y	Y	N
9 Smith	Y	Y	Y	Y	Y	Y
WEST VIRGINIA						
1 Mollohan	Y	?	?	?	?	?
2 **Capito**	Y	N	N	Y	?	N
3 Rahall	Y	Y	Y	Y	Y	Y
WISCONSIN						
1 **Ryan**	Y	N	N	Y	Y	N
2 Baldwin	Y	Y	Y	Y	Y	Y
3 Kind	Y	Y	Y	Y	N	Y
4 Moore	Y	Y	Y	Y	Y	Y
5 **Sensenbrenner**	Y	N	N	Y	N	N
6 **Petri**	Y	N	N	Y	Y	N
7 Obey	Y	?	Y	Y	Y	Y
8 Kagen	Y	Y	Y	Y	Y	Y
WYOMING						
AL **Lummis**	Y	N	N	Y	N	N
DELEGATES						
Faleomavaega (A.S.)						
Norton (D.C.)						
Bordallo (Guam)						
Sablan (N. Marianas)						
Pierluisi (P.R.)						
Christensen (V.I.)						

IN THE HOUSE | By Vote Number

620. **HR 4501. Return Requirements for Precious Metals/Passage.**
Weiner, D-N.Y., motion to suspend the rules and pass the bill that would require the adoption of return policies by businesses that purchase precious metals from consumers and solicit such transactions through a website. It would direct the Federal Trade Commission to issue regulations for such transactions. Motion agreed to 324-81: D 239-0; R 85-81. A two-thirds majority of those present and voting (270 in this case) is required for passage under suspension of the rules. Dec. 8, 2010.

621. **H Res 1746. PTSD Treatment and Research/Adoption.**
Donnelly, D-Ind., motion to suspend the rules and adopt the resolution that would recognize the efforts of Welcome Back Veterans in augmenting the care for veterans and members of the armed forces suffering from post-traumatic stress disorder and related psychiatric disorders and encourage the secretary of Veterans Affairs to establish partnerships for the treatment and research of PTSD. Motion agreed to 409-0: D 242-0; R 167-0. A two-thirds majority of those present and voting (273 in this case) is required for adoption under suspension of the rules. Dec. 8, 2010.

622. **HR 3082. Continuing Appropriations and Food Safety/Motion to Concur.** Obey, D-Wis., motion to concur in the Senate amendment to the bill with a House amendment that would provide continuing appropriations through Sept. 30, 2011, for all federal departments and agencies, none of whose fiscal 2011 appropriations bills have been enacted. It would keep total discretionary funding at the same level that was provided for fiscal 2010 but would shift billions of dollars among programs. The amendment would also include provisions of a Senate-passed bill that would overhaul food safety laws and expand Food and Drug Administration enforcement powers, including giving the FDA authority to force a company to recall foods believed to be contaminated. Motion agreed to, thus sent to the Senate, 212-206: D 212-35; R 0-171. Dec. 8, 2010.

623. **HR 5281. Immigration Policy Revisions/Rule.** Adoption of the rule (H Res 1756) that would provide for House floor consideration of the Senate amendments to the bill by allowing for a motion to concur in the Senate amendments with a House amendment. The bill would clarify that pre-trial proceedings would be covered under a law that allows certain civil and criminal cases against federal officials to be moved from state to federal courts. The House amendment would allow the secretary of Homeland Security to grant conditional non-immigrant status to the undocumented children of illegal immigrants if they meet certain requirements, including military enlistment or college enrollment. Adopted 211-208: D 211-37; R 0-171. Dec. 8, 2010.

	620	621	622	623
ALABAMA				
1 **Bonner**	Y	Y	N	N
2 Bright	Y	Y	N	N
3 **Rogers**	Y	Y	N	N
4 **Aderholt**	Y	Y	N	N
5 **Griffith**	?	?	?	?
6 **Bachus**	N	Y	N	N
7 Davis	?	?	Y	Y
ALASKA				
AL **Young**	N	Y	N	N
ARIZONA				
1 Kirkpatrick	?	?	?	?
2 **Franks**	N	Y	N	N
3 **Shadegg**	N	Y	N	N
4 Pastor	Y	Y	Y	Y
5 Mitchell	Y	Y	Y	Y
6 **Flake**	N	Y	N	N
7 Grijalva	Y	Y	Y	Y
8 Giffords	Y	Y	N	Y
ARKANSAS				
1 Berry	?	?	?	?
2 Snyder	Y	Y	Y	Y
3 **Boozman**	Y	Y	N	N
4 Ross	Y	Y	N	N
CALIFORNIA				
1 Thompson	Y	Y	Y	Y
2 **Herger**	Y	Y	N	N
3 **Lungren**	N	Y	N	N
4 **McClintock**	N	N	N	N
5 Matsui	Y	Y	Y	Y
6 Woolsey	Y	Y	Y	Y
7 Miller, George	Y	Y	Y	Y
8 Pelosi		Y	Y	Y
9 Lee	Y	Y	Y	Y
10 Garamendi	?	?	Y	Y
11 McNerney	Y	Y	Y	Y
12 Speier	Y	Y	Y	Y
13 Stark	Y	Y	Y	Y
14 Eshoo	Y	Y	Y	Y
15 Honda	Y	Y	Y	Y
16 Lofgren	Y	Y	Y	Y
17 Farr	Y	Y	N	Y
18 Cardoza	Y	Y	N	Y
19 **Radanovich**	?	?	?	?
20 Costa	Y	Y	N	Y
21 **Nunes**	N	Y	N	N
22 **McCarthy**	N	Y	N	N
23 Capps	+	Y	Y	Y
24 **Gallegly**	Y	Y	N	N
25 **McKeon**	Y	Y	N	N
26 **Dreier**	Y	Y	N	N
27 Sherman	Y	Y	Y	Y
28 Berman	Y	Y	Y	Y
29 Schiff	Y	Y	Y	Y
30 Waxman	Y	Y	Y	Y
31 Becerra	Y	Y	Y	Y
32 Chu	Y	Y	Y	Y
33 Watson	Y	Y	Y	Y
34 Roybal-Allard	Y	Y	Y	Y
35 Waters	Y	Y	Y	Y
36 Harman	Y	Y	Y	Y
37 Richardson	Y	Y	Y	Y
38 Napolitano	Y	Y	Y	Y
39 Sánchez, Linda	Y	Y	Y	Y
40 **Royce**	N	Y	N	N
41 **Lewis**	Y	Y	N	N
42 **Miller, Gary**	Y	Y	N	N
43 Baca	Y	Y	Y	Y
44 **Calvert**	Y	Y	N	N
45 **Bono Mack**	Y	Y	N	N
46 **Rohrabacher**	Y	Y	N	N
47 Sanchez, Loretta	Y	Y	Y	Y
48 **Campbell**	N	Y	N	N
49 **Issa**	Y	Y	N	N
50 **Bilbray**	?	?	?	?
51 Filner	Y	Y	Y	Y
52 **Hunter**	N	Y	N	N
53 Davis	Y	Y	Y	Y

	620	621	622	623
COLORADO				
1 DeGette	Y	Y	Y	Y
2 Polis	Y	Y	Y	Y
3 Salazar	Y	Y	N	Y
4 Markey	Y	Y	Y	Y
5 **Lamborn**	N	Y	N	N
6 **Coffman**	N	Y	N	N
7 Perlmutter	Y	Y	Y	Y
CONNECTICUT				
1 Larson	Y	Y	Y	Y
2 Courtney	Y	Y	N	Y
3 DeLauro	Y	Y	Y	Y
4 Himes	Y	Y	Y	Y
5 Murphy	Y	Y	Y	Y
DELAWARE				
AL **Castle**	Y	Y	N	N
FLORIDA				
1 **Miller**	Y	Y	N	N
2 Boyd	Y	Y	Y	Y
3 Brown	Y	Y	Y	Y
4 **Crenshaw**	Y	Y	N	N
5 **Brown-Waite**	Y	Y	N	N
6 **Stearns**	Y	Y	N	N
7 **Mica**	Y	Y	N	N
8 Grayson	Y	Y	Y	Y
9 **Bilirakis**	Y	Y	N	N
10 **Young**	N	Y	N	N
11 Castor	Y	Y	Y	Y
12 **Putnam**	Y	Y	N	N
13 **Buchanan**	Y	Y	N	N
14 **Mack**	Y	Y	N	N
15 **Posey**	N	Y	N	N
16 **Rooney**	N	Y	N	N
17 Meek	Y	Y	Y	Y
18 **Ros-Lehtinen**	?	Y	N	N
19 Deutch	Y	Y	Y	Y
20 Wasserman Schultz	Y	Y	Y	Y
21 **Diaz-Balart, L.**	N	Y	N	N
22 Klein	Y	Y	Y	Y
23 Hastings	Y	Y	Y	Y
24 Kosmas	Y	Y	Y	Y
25 **Diaz-Balart, M.**	N	Y	N	N
GEORGIA				
1 **Kingston**	N	Y	N	N
2 Bishop	Y	Y	Y	N
3 **Westmoreland**	N	Y	N	N
4 Johnson	Y	Y	Y	Y
5 Lewis	Y	Y	Y	Y
6 **Price**	N	Y	N	N
7 **Linder**	N	Y	N	N
8 Marshall	Y	Y	N	N
9 **Graves**	N	Y	N	N
10 **Broun**	N	Y	N	N
11 **Gingrey**	Y	Y	N	N
12 Barrow	Y	Y	Y	Y
13 Scott	Y	Y	Y	Y
HAWAII				
1 **Djou**	N	Y	N	N
2 Hirono	Y	Y	Y	Y
IDAHO				
1 Minnick	Y	Y	N	N
2 **Simpson**	N	Y	N	N
ILLINOIS				
1 Rush	?	?	Y	Y
2 Jackson	Y	Y	Y	Y
3 Lipinski	Y	Y	N	N
4 Gutierrez	Y	Y	Y	Y
5 Quigley	Y	Y	Y	Y
6 **Roskam**	Y	Y	N	N
7 Davis	Y	Y	Y	Y
8 Bean	Y	Y	N	N
9 Schakowsky	Y	Y	Y	Y
10 Vacant				
11 Halvorson	Y	Y	N	N
12 Costello	Y	Y	N	Y
13 **Biggert**	Y	Y	N	N
14 Foster	Y	Y	Y	Y
15 Johnson	Y	Y	N	N

KEY | **Republicans** | Democrats

Y Voted for (yea)	X Paired against
# Paired for	– Announced against
+ Announced for	P Voted "present"
N Voted against (nay)	
	C Voted "present" to avoid possible conflict of interest
	? Did not vote or otherwise make a position known

	620	621	622	623
16 Manzullo	Y	Y	N	N
17 Hare	Y	Y	Y	Y
18 Schock	N	Y	N	N
19 Shimkus	Y	Y	N	N
INDIANA				
1 Visclosky	Y	Y	Y	Y
2 Donnelly	Y	Y	Y	N
3 Stutzman	N	Y	N	N
4 Buyer	?	?	N	N
5 Burton	N	Y	N	N
6 Pence	N	Y	N	N
7 Carson	Y	Y	Y	Y
8 Ellsworth	?	?	Y	N
9 Hill	Y	Y	Y	Y
IOWA				
1 Braley	Y	Y	Y	Y
2 Loebsack	Y	Y	Y	Y
3 Boswell	Y	Y	Y	Y
4 Latham	Y	Y	N	N
5 King	N	Y	N	N
KANSAS				
1 Moran	Y	Y	N	N
2 Jenkins	Y	Y	N	N
3 Moore	Y	Y	Y	Y
4 Tiahrt	?	?	N	N
KENTUCKY				
1 Whitfield	Y	Y	N	N
2 Guthrie	Y	Y	N	N
3 Yarmuth	Y	Y	Y	Y
4 Davis	N	Y	N	N
5 Rogers	Y	Y	N	N
6 Chandler	Y	Y	Y	N
LOUISIANA				
1 Scalise	N	Y	N	N
2 Cao	N	Y	N	N
3 Melancon	Y	Y	N	Y
4 Fleming	N	Y	N	N
5 Alexander	N	Y	N	N
6 Cassidy	N	Y	N	N
7 Boustany	N	Y	N	N
MAINE				
1 Pingree	Y	Y	Y	Y
2 Michaud	Y	Y	N	N
MARYLAND				
1 Kratovil	Y	Y	N	N
2 Ruppersberger	Y	Y	Y	Y
3 Sarbanes	Y	Y	Y	Y
4 Edwards	Y	Y	Y	Y
5 Hoyer	Y	Y	Y	Y
6 Bartlett	N	Y	N	N
7 Cummings	Y	Y	Y	Y
8 Van Hollen	Y	Y	Y	Y
MASSACHUSETTS				
1 Olver	Y	Y	Y	Y
2 Neal	Y	Y	Y	Y
3 McGovern	Y	Y	Y	Y
4 Frank	Y	Y	Y	Y
5 Tsongas	Y	Y	Y	Y
6 Tierney	Y	Y	Y	Y
7 Markey	Y	Y	Y	Y
8 Capuano	Y	Y	Y	Y
9 Lynch	Y	Y	Y	Y
10 Delahunt	?	?	?	?
MICHIGAN				
1 Stupak	Y	Y	Y	N
2 Hoekstra	N	Y	N	N
3 Ehlers	Y	Y	N	N
4 Camp	Y	Y	N	N
5 Kildee	Y	Y	Y	Y
6 Upton	Y	Y	N	N
7 Schauer	Y	Y	N	N
8 Rogers	Y	Y	N	N
9 Peters	Y	Y	N	N
10 Miller	Y	Y	N	N
11 McCotter	N	Y	N	N
12 Levin	Y	Y	Y	Y
13 Kilpatrick	+	?	+	?
14 Conyers	Y	Y	Y	Y
15 Dingell	Y	Y	Y	Y
MINNESOTA				
1 Walz	Y	Y	Y	Y
2 Kline	N	Y	N	N
3 Paulsen	Y	Y	N	N
4 McCollum	Y	Y	Y	Y

	620	621	622	623
5 Ellison	Y	Y	Y	Y
6 Bachmann	N	Y	N	N
7 Peterson	Y	Y	N	N
8 Oberstar	Y	Y	Y	Y
MISSISSIPPI				
1 Childers	Y	Y	N	N
2 Thompson	Y	Y	Y	Y
3 Harper	Y	Y	N	N
4 Taylor	Y	Y	N	N
MISSOURI				
1 Clay	Y	Y	Y	Y
2 Akin	N	Y	N	N
3 Carnahan	Y	Y	Y	Y
4 Skelton	Y	Y	Y	Y
5 Cleaver	?	Y	Y	Y
6 Graves	Y	Y	N	N
7 Blunt	?	?	?	?
8 Emerson	N	Y	N	N
9 Luetkemeyer	Y	Y	N	N
MONTANA				
AL Rehberg	N	Y	N	N
NEBRASKA				
1 Fortenberry	Y	Y	N	N
2 Terry	N	Y	N	N
3 Smith	N	Y	N	N
NEVADA				
1 Berkley	Y	Y	Y	Y
2 Heller	N	Y	N	N
3 Titus	Y	Y	Y	Y
NEW HAMPSHIRE				
1 Shea-Porter	Y	Y	Y	Y
2 Hodes	Y	Y	Y	Y
NEW JERSEY				
1 Andrews	Y	Y	Y	Y
2 LoBiondo	N	Y	N	N
3 Adler	Y	Y	N	Y
4 Smith	Y	Y	N	N
5 Garrett	N	Y	N	N
6 Pallone	Y	Y	Y	Y
7 Lance	N	Y	N	N
8 Pascrell	Y	Y	Y	Y
9 Rothman	Y	Y	Y	Y
10 Payne	Y	Y	Y	Y
11 Frelinghuysen	Y	Y	N	N
12 Holt	Y	Y	Y	Y
13 Sires	Y	Y	Y	Y
NEW MEXICO				
1 Heinrich	Y	Y	Y	Y
2 Teague	Y	Y	Y	Y
3 Luján	Y	Y	Y	Y
NEW YORK				
1 Bishop	Y	Y	Y	N
2 Israel	Y	Y	Y	Y
3 King	Y	Y	N	N
4 McCarthy	Y	Y	Y	Y
5 Ackerman	Y	Y	Y	Y
6 Meeks	Y	Y	Y	Y
7 Crowley	Y	Y	Y	Y
8 Nadler	Y	Y	Y	Y
9 Weiner	Y	Y	Y	Y
10 Towns	Y	Y	Y	Y
11 Clarke	Y	Y	Y	Y
12 Velázquez	Y	Y	Y	Y
13 McMahon	Y	Y	N	Y
14 Maloney	Y	Y	Y	Y
15 Rangel	Y	Y	Y	Y
16 Serrano	Y	Y	Y	Y
17 Engel	Y	Y	Y	Y
18 Lowey	Y	Y	Y	Y
19 Hall	Y	Y	Y	Y
20 Murphy	Y	Y	Y	N
21 Tonko	Y	Y	Y	Y
22 Hinchey	Y	Y	Y	Y
23 Owens	Y	Y	Y	Y
24 Arcuri	Y	Y	N	Y
25 Maffei	Y	Y	N	Y
26 Lee	Y	Y	N	N
27 Higgins	Y	Y	Y	Y
28 Slaughter	Y	Y	Y	Y
29 Reed	Y	Y	N	N
NORTH CAROLINA				
1 Butterfield	Y	Y	Y	Y
2 Etheridge	Y	Y	Y	Y
3 Jones	?	?	N	N
4 Price	Y	Y	Y	Y

	620	621	622	623
5 Foxx	N	Y	N	N
6 Coble	Y	Y	N	N
7 McIntyre	Y	Y	N	N
8 Kissell	Y	Y	Y	Y
9 Myrick	N	Y	N	N
10 McHenry	Y	Y	N	N
11 Shuler	Y	Y	N	N
12 Watt	Y	Y	Y	Y
13 Miller	Y	Y	Y	Y
NORTH DAKOTA				
AL Pomeroy	Y	Y	Y	Y
OHIO				
1 Driehaus	Y	Y	N	Y
2 Schmidt	N	Y	N	N
3 Turner	Y	Y	N	N
4 Jordan	N	Y	N	N
5 Latta	N	Y	N	N
6 Wilson	Y	Y	N	N
7 Austria	Y	Y	N	N
8 Boehner	?	?	N	N
9 Kaptur	?	Y	Y	Y
10 Kucinich	Y	Y	N	Y
11 Fudge	Y	Y	Y	Y
12 Tiberi	Y	Y	N	N
13 Sutton	Y	Y	Y	Y
14 LaTourette	Y	Y	N	N
15 Kilroy	Y	Y	Y	Y
16 Boccieri	Y	Y	Y	Y
17 Ryan	Y	Y	Y	Y
18 Space	Y	Y	Y	Y
OKLAHOMA				
1 Sullivan	N	Y	N	N
2 Boren	Y	Y	N	N
3 Lucas	Y	Y	N	N
4 Cole	Y	Y	N	N
5 Fallin	?	?	?	?
OREGON				
1 Wu	?	?	?	?
2 Walden	Y	Y	N	N
3 Blumenauer	Y	Y	Y	Y
4 DeFazio	Y	Y	Y	Y
5 Schrader	Y	Y	N	Y
PENNSYLVANIA				
1 Brady	Y	Y	Y	Y
2 Fattah	Y	Y	Y	Y
3 Dahlkemper	Y	Y	Y	N
4 Altmire	Y	Y	Y	N
5 Thompson	N	Y	N	N
6 Gerlach	Y	Y	N	N
7 Sestak	Y	Y	Y	Y
8 Murphy, P.	N	Y	N	N
9 Shuster	N	Y	N	N
10 Carney	Y	Y	Y	Y
11 Kanjorski	Y	Y	Y	Y
12 Critz	Y	?	Y	Y
13 Schwartz	Y	Y	Y	Y
14 Doyle	Y	Y	Y	Y
15 Dent	Y	Y	N	N
16 Pitts	Y	Y	N	N
17 Holden	Y	Y	Y	N
18 Murphy, T.	Y	Y	N	N
19 Platts	N	Y	N	N
RHODE ISLAND				
1 Kennedy	Y	Y	Y	Y
2 Langevin	Y	Y	N	Y
SOUTH CAROLINA				
1 Brown	Y	Y	N	N
2 Wilson	Y	Y	N	N
3 Barrett	N	Y	N	N
4 Inglis	N	Y	N	N
5 Spratt	Y	Y	Y	Y
6 Clyburn	Y	Y	Y	Y
SOUTH DAKOTA				
AL Herseth Sandlin	Y	Y	Y	Y
TENNESSEE				
1 Roe	Y	Y	N	N
2 Duncan	Y	Y	N	N
3 Wamp	N	Y	N	N
4 Davis	Y	Y	?	Y
5 Cooper	Y	Y	Y	Y
6 Gordon	?	Y	Y	Y
7 Blackburn	Y	Y	N	N
8 Tanner	Y	Y	N	N
9 Cohen	+	+	+	+

	620	621	622	623
TEXAS				
1 Gohmert	Y	Y	N	N
2 Poe	N	Y	N	N
3 Johnson, S.	N	Y	N	N
4 Hall	N	Y	N	N
5 Hensarling	N	Y	N	N
6 Barton	N	Y	N	N
7 Culberson	N	Y	N	N
8 Brady	N	Y	N	N
9 Green, A.	Y	Y	Y	Y
10 McCaul	Y	Y	N	N
11 Conaway	N	Y	N	N
12 Granger	?	?	-	?
13 Thornberry	N	Y	N	N
14 Paul	N	Y	N	N
15 Hinojosa	Y	Y	Y	Y
16 Reyes	Y	Y	Y	Y
17 Edwards	Y	Y	Y	Y
18 Jackson Lee	Y	Y	Y	Y
19 Neugebauer	N	Y	N	N
20 Gonzalez	Y	Y	Y	Y
21 Smith	Y	Y	N	N
22 Olson	Y	Y	N	N
23 Rodriguez	Y	Y	N	N
24 Marchant	?	?	?	?
25 Doggett	Y	Y	Y	Y
26 Burgess	Y	Y	N	N
27 Ortiz	Y	Y	Y	Y
28 Cuellar	Y	Y	Y	Y
29 Green, G.	Y	Y	Y	Y
30 Johnson, E.	Y	Y	Y	Y
31 Carter	Y	Y	N	N
32 Sessions	N	Y	N	N
UTAH				
1 Bishop	Y	Y	N	N
2 Matheson	Y	Y	N	N
3 Chaffetz	Y	Y	N	N
VERMONT				
AL Welch	Y	Y	Y	Y
VIRGINIA				
1 Wittman	Y	Y	N	N
2 Nye	Y	Y	Y	Y
3 Scott	Y	Y	Y	Y
4 Forbes	Y	Y	N	N
5 Perriello	Y	Y	N	N
6 Goodlatte	Y	Y	N	N
7 Cantor	N	Y	N	N
8 Moran	Y	Y	Y	Y
9 Boucher	Y	Y	Y	Y
10 Wolf	Y	Y	N	N
11 Connolly	Y	Y	N	N
WASHINGTON				
1 Inslee	Y	Y	Y	Y
2 Larsen	Y	Y	Y	Y
3 Baird	Y	Y	N	N
4 Hastings	Y	Y	N	N
5 McMorris Rodgers	?	?	?	?
6 Dicks	Y	Y	Y	Y
7 McDermott	Y	Y	Y	Y
8 Reichert	Y	Y	N	N
9 Smith	Y	Y	Y	Y
WEST VIRGINIA				
1 Mollohan	?	?	?	?
2 Capito	Y	Y	N	N
3 Rahall	Y	Y	N	N
WISCONSIN				
1 Ryan	N	Y	N	N
2 Baldwin	Y	Y	Y	Y
3 Kind	Y	Y	Y	Y
4 Moore	Y	Y	Y	Y
5 Sensenbrenner	N	Y	N	N
6 Petri	N	Y	N	N
7 Obey	Y	Y	Y	Y
8 Kagen	Y	Y	Y	Y
WYOMING				
AL Lummis	Y	Y	N	N
DELEGATES				
Faleomavaega (A.S.)				
Norton (D.C.)				
Bordallo (Guam)				
Sablan (N. Marianas)				
Pierluisi (P.R.)				
Christensen (V.I.)				

IN THE HOUSE | By Vote Number

624. S 3998. Background Checks Pilot Program Extension/Passage.
Scott, D-Va., motion to suspend the rules and pass the bill that would extend, through Dec. 31, 2011, the Child Safety Pilot Program, which allows youth-serving organizations to request from the FBI fingerprint background checks for employees or volunteers. Motion agreed to 401-2: D 238-0; R 163-2. A two-thirds majority of those present and voting (269 in this case) is required for passage under suspension of the rules. Dec. 8, 2010.

625. HR 5281. Immigration Policy Revisions/Motion to Concur.
Conyers, D-Mich., motion to concur in Senate amendments to the bill with a House amendment that would add language to allow the Homeland Security Department to grant conditional non-immigrant status to the undocumented children of illegal immigrants if they meet certain requirements, including having been in the United States continuously for more than five years, been younger than 16 when they entered the country and been admitted to a U.S. college or university or enlisted in the military. The individuals would have to pay a $525 application surcharge and a subsequent fee and could be eligible to apply for legal permanent status after 10 years. Motion agreed to, thus sent to the Senate, 216-198: D 208-38; R 8-160. A "yea" was a vote in support of the president's position. Dec. 8, 2010.

626. HR 4994. Medicare Physician Payment Rates/Passage.
Stark, D-Calif., motion to suspend the rules and concur in the Senate amendments to the bill that would extend, through Dec. 31, 2011, the current Medicare reimbursement rates for physicians and extend several expiring Medicare programs. The costs would be fully offset, mainly by modifying the amount that recipients of insurance subsidy overpayments under the 2010 health care law would have to pay back to the government. Motion agreed to, thus clearing the bill for the president, 409-2: D 243-1; R 166-1. A two-thirds majority of those present and voting (274 in this case) is required for passage under suspension of the rules. A "yea" was a vote in support of the president's position. Dec. 9, 2010.

627. HR 6412. Federal-State Criminal Record Sharing/Passage.
Scott, D-Va., motion to suspend the rules and pass the bill that would require the Justice Department to share criminal records with state sentencing commissions. Motion agreed to 371-1: D 220-0; R 151-1. A two-thirds majority of those present and voting (248 in this case) is required for passage under suspension of the rules. Dec. 9, 2010.

	624	625	626	627
ALABAMA				
1 **Bonner**	Y	N	Y	Y
2 Bright	Y	N	Y	Y
3 **Rogers**	Y	N	Y	Y
4 **Aderholt**	?	N	Y	Y
5 **Griffith**	?	?	?	?
6 **Bachus**	Y	N	Y	?
7 Davis	?	Y	Y	Y
ALASKA				
AL **Young**	N	N	Y	Y
ARIZONA				
1 Kirkpatrick	?	?	Y	?
2 **Franks**	Y	N	Y	Y
3 **Shadegg**	Y	N	Y	Y
4 Pastor	Y	Y	Y	Y
5 Mitchell	Y	Y	Y	Y
6 **Flake**	Y	N	?	?
7 Grijalva	Y	Y	Y	Y
8 Giffords	Y	Y	Y	Y
ARKANSAS				
1 Berry	?	?	?	?
2 Snyder	Y	Y	Y	Y
3 **Boozman**	Y	N	Y	Y
4 Ross	Y	N	Y	Y
CALIFORNIA				
1 Thompson	Y	Y	Y	Y
2 **Herger**	Y	N	Y	Y
3 **Lungren**	Y	N	Y	Y
4 **McClintock**	Y	N	N	Y
5 Matsui	Y	Y	Y	Y
6 Woolsey	+	Y	Y	Y
7 Miller, George	Y	Y	Y	?
8 Pelosi		Y		
9 Lee	Y	Y	Y	Y
10 Garamendi	Y	Y	Y	Y
11 McNerney	Y	Y	Y	Y
12 Speier	Y	Y	Y	?
13 Stark	Y	Y	Y	?
14 Eshoo	Y	Y	Y	Y
15 Honda	Y	Y	Y	Y
16 Lofgren	Y	Y	Y	Y
17 Farr	Y	Y	Y	Y
18 Cardoza	?	Y	Y	?
19 **Radanovich**	?	?	?	?
20 Costa	Y	Y	Y	Y
21 **Nunes**	Y	N	Y	Y
22 **McCarthy**	Y	N	Y	Y
23 Capps	Y	Y	Y	Y
24 **Gallegly**	Y	N	Y	?
25 **McKeon**	Y	N	Y	?
26 **Dreier**	Y	N	Y	Y
27 Sherman	Y	Y	Y	Y
28 Berman	Y	Y	Y	Y
29 Schiff	Y	?	Y	Y
30 Waxman	Y	Y	Y	Y
31 Becerra	Y	Y	Y	Y
32 Chu	Y	Y	Y	Y
33 Watson	Y	Y	?	?
34 Roybal-Allard	Y	Y	Y	Y
35 Waters	Y	Y	Y	Y
36 Harman	Y	Y	Y	Y
37 Richardson	Y	Y	Y	Y
38 Napolitano	Y	Y	Y	?
39 Sánchez, Linda	Y	Y	Y	Y
40 **Royce**	Y	N	Y	Y
41 **Lewis**	Y	N	Y	Y
42 **Miller, Gary**	Y	N	Y	?
43 Baca	Y	Y	Y	Y
44 **Calvert**	Y	N	Y	?
45 **Bono Mack**	Y	N	Y	Y
46 **Rohrabacher**	?	N	Y	Y
47 Sanchez, Loretta	Y	Y	Y	Y
48 **Campbell**	Y	N	Y	Y
49 **Issa**	Y	N	Y	Y
50 **Bilbray**	?	?	Y	Y
51 Filner	Y	Y	Y	Y
52 **Hunter**	Y	N	Y	Y
53 Davis	Y	Y	Y	?

	624	625	626	627
COLORADO				
1 DeGette	Y	Y	Y	?
2 Polis	Y	Y	Y	Y
3 Salazar	Y	Y	Y	Y
4 Markey	Y	Y	Y	?
5 **Lamborn**	Y	N	Y	Y
6 **Coffman**	Y	N	Y	?
7 Perlmutter	Y	Y	Y	Y
CONNECTICUT				
1 Larson	Y	Y	Y	Y
2 Courtney	Y	Y	Y	Y
3 DeLauro	Y	Y	Y	Y
4 Himes	Y	Y	Y	Y
5 Murphy	Y	Y	Y	Y
DELAWARE				
AL **Castle**	Y	Y	Y	Y
FLORIDA				
1 **Miller**	Y	N	Y	Y
2 Boyd	Y	Y	?	?
3 Brown	Y	Y	Y	Y
4 **Crenshaw**	Y	N	Y	?
5 **Brown-Waite**	Y	N	Y	Y
6 **Stearns**	Y	N	Y	Y
7 **Mica**	Y	N	Y	Y
8 Grayson	Y	Y	Y	Y
9 **Bilirakis**	Y	N	Y	Y
10 **Young**	Y	N	Y	Y
11 Castor	Y	Y	Y	Y
12 **Putnam**	Y	N	?	?
13 **Buchanan**	Y	N	Y	Y
14 **Mack**	Y	N	Y	Y
15 **Posey**	Y	N	Y	Y
16 **Rooney**	Y	N	Y	Y
17 Meek	Y	Y	?	Y
18 **Ros-Lehtinen**	Y	Y	Y	Y
19 Deutch	Y	Y	Y	Y
20 Wasserman Schultz	Y	Y	Y	Y
21 **Diaz-Balart, L.**	Y	Y	Y	Y
22 Klein	Y	Y	Y	Y
23 Hastings	Y	Y	Y	Y
24 Kosmas	Y	Y	Y	Y
25 **Diaz-Balart, M.**	Y	Y	Y	Y
GEORGIA				
1 **Kingston**	Y	N	Y	Y
2 Bishop	Y	Y	Y	Y
3 **Westmoreland**	Y	N	Y	Y
4 Johnson	Y	Y	Y	Y
5 Lewis	Y	Y	Y	Y
6 **Price**	Y	N	Y	Y
7 **Linder**	Y	N	?	?
8 Marshall	Y	?	Y	Y
9 **Graves**	Y	N	Y	Y
10 **Broun**	Y	N	Y	Y
11 **Gingrey**	Y	?	Y	Y
12 Barrow	Y	N	Y	Y
13 Scott	Y	Y	Y	?
HAWAII				
1 **Djou**	Y	Y	Y	Y
2 Hirono	Y	Y	Y	Y
IDAHO				
1 Minnick	Y	Y	Y	Y
2 **Simpson**	Y	N	Y	Y
ILLINOIS				
1 Rush	Y	Y	Y	Y
2 Jackson	Y	Y	Y	Y
3 Lipinski	Y	N	Y	Y
4 Gutierrez	?	Y	Y	Y
5 Quigley	Y	Y	Y	Y
6 **Roskam**	Y	N	Y	Y
7 Davis	Y	Y	Y	Y
8 Bean	Y	Y	Y	Y
9 Schakowsky	Y	Y	Y	Y
10 Vacant				
11 Halvorson	Y	Y	Y	Y
12 Costello	Y	N	Y	Y
13 **Biggert**	Y	N	Y	Y
14 Foster	Y	Y	Y	Y
15 **Johnson**	Y	N	Y	Y

	624	625	626	627
16 Manzullo	Y	N	Y	Y
17 Hare	Y	Y	Y	Y
18 Schock	Y	N	Y	Y
19 Shimkus	Y	N	Y	Y
INDIANA				
1 Visclosky	Y	N	Y	Y
2 Donnelly	Y	N	Y	Y
3 Stutzman	Y	–	Y	Y
4 Buyer	Y	?	Y	?
5 Burton	Y	N	Y	Y
6 Pence	Y	Y	Y	Y
7 Carson	Y	Y	Y	Y
8 Ellsworth	Y	N	Y	?
9 Hill	Y	Y	Y	?
IOWA				
1 Braley	Y	Y	Y	Y
2 Loebsack	Y	Y	Y	Y
3 Boswell	Y	Y	Y	Y
4 Latham	Y	N	Y	Y
5 King	Y	N	Y	Y
KANSAS				
1 Moran	Y	N	?	?
2 Jenkins	Y	N	Y	Y
3 Moore	Y	Y	Y	Y
4 Tiahrt	Y	N	Y	?
KENTUCKY				
1 Whitfield	Y	N	Y	Y
2 Guthrie	Y	N	Y	Y
3 Yarmuth	Y	Y	Y	Y
4 Davis	Y	N	Y	Y
5 Rogers	Y	N	Y	Y
6 Chandler	Y	N	Y	Y
LOUISIANA				
1 Scalise	Y	N	Y	Y
2 Cao	Y	Y	Y	Y
3 Melancon	Y	N	Y	Y
4 Fleming	Y	N	Y	Y
5 Alexander	Y	N	Y	Y
6 Cassidy	Y	N	Y	Y
7 Boustany	Y	N	Y	Y
MAINE				
1 Pingree	Y	Y	Y	?
2 Michaud	Y	Y	Y	Y
MARYLAND				
1 Kratovil	Y	N	Y	Y
2 Ruppersberger	Y	Y	Y	Y
3 Sarbanes	Y	Y	Y	?
4 Edwards	Y	Y	Y	Y
5 Hoyer	Y	Y	Y	Y
6 Bartlett	Y	N	Y	Y
7 Cummings	Y	Y	Y	Y
8 Van Hollen	Y	Y	Y	Y
MASSACHUSETTS				
1 Olver	Y	Y	Y	?
2 Neal	Y	Y	Y	Y
3 McGovern	Y	Y	Y	Y
4 Frank	Y	Y	Y	Y
5 Tsongas	Y	Y	Y	Y
6 Tierney	Y	Y	Y	Y
7 Markey	Y	Y	Y	Y
8 Capuano	Y	Y	Y	Y
9 Lynch	Y	Y	Y	Y
10 Delahunt	?	?	?	?
MICHIGAN				
1 Stupak	Y	N	Y	Y
2 Hoekstra	Y	N	Y	Y
3 Ehlers	?	N	Y	Y
4 Camp	Y	N	Y	Y
5 Kildee	Y	Y	Y	Y
6 Upton	Y	N	Y	Y
7 Schauer	Y	Y	Y	Y
8 Rogers	Y	N	Y	Y
9 Peters	Y	Y	Y	?
10 Miller	Y	N	Y	Y
11 McCotter	Y	N	Y	Y
12 Levin	Y	Y	Y	Y
13 Kilpatrick	?	?	Y	Y
14 Conyers	Y	Y	Y	Y
15 Dingell	Y	Y	Y	Y
MINNESOTA				
1 Walz	Y	Y	Y	Y
2 Kline	Y	N	Y	Y
3 Paulsen	Y	N	Y	Y
4 McCollum	Y	Y	Y	Y

	624	625	626	627
5 Ellison	Y	Y	Y	Y
6 Bachmann	Y	N	Y	Y
7 Peterson	Y	N	Y	Y
8 Oberstar	Y	Y	Y	Y
MISSISSIPPI				
1 Childers	Y	N	Y	Y
2 Thompson	Y	Y	Y	Y
3 Harper	Y	N	Y	Y
4 Taylor	Y	N	Y	Y
MISSOURI				
1 Clay	Y	Y	Y	Y
2 Akin	Y	N	Y	Y
3 Carnahan	Y	Y	Y	?
4 Skelton	Y	N	Y	?
5 Cleaver	Y	Y	Y	Y
6 Graves	Y	N	Y	?
7 Blunt	?	?	?	?
8 Emerson	Y	N	Y	Y
9 Luetkemeyer	Y	N	Y	Y
MONTANA				
AL Rehberg	Y	N	Y	Y
NEBRASKA				
1 Fortenberry	Y	N	Y	Y
2 Terry	Y	N	Y	Y
3 Smith	Y	N	Y	Y
NEVADA				
1 Berkley	Y	Y	Y	Y
2 Heller	Y	N	Y	Y
3 Titus	Y	Y	Y	Y
NEW HAMPSHIRE				
1 Shea-Porter	Y	Y	Y	Y
2 Hodes	Y	Y	Y	Y
NEW JERSEY				
1 Andrews	Y	Y	Y	Y
2 LoBiondo	Y	N	Y	Y
3 Adler	Y	Y	Y	Y
4 Smith	Y	N	Y	Y
5 Garrett	Y	N	Y	Y
6 Pallone	Y	Y	Y	Y
7 Lance	Y	N	Y	Y
8 Pascrell	Y	Y	Y	Y
9 Rothman	Y	Y	Y	Y
10 Payne	Y	Y	Y	Y
11 Frelinghuysen	Y	N	Y	Y
12 Holt	Y	Y	Y	Y
13 Sires	Y	Y	Y	Y
NEW MEXICO				
1 Heinrich	Y	Y	Y	Y
2 Teague	Y	Y	Y	Y
3 Luján	Y	Y	Y	Y
NEW YORK				
1 Bishop	Y	Y	Y	Y
2 Israel	Y	Y	Y	Y
3 King	Y	N	Y	?
4 McCarthy	Y	Y	Y	Y
5 Ackerman	Y	Y	Y	Y
6 Meeks	Y	Y	Y	Y
7 Crowley	Y	Y	Y	Y
8 Nadler	Y	Y	Y	Y
9 Weiner	Y	Y	Y	Y
10 Towns	Y	Y	Y	Y
11 Clarke	Y	Y	Y	Y
12 Velázquez	Y	Y	Y	Y
13 McMahon	Y	Y	Y	Y
14 Maloney	Y	Y	Y	Y
15 Rangel	Y	Y	Y	Y
16 Serrano	?	Y	Y	Y
17 Engel	Y	Y	Y	Y
18 Lowey	Y	Y	Y	Y
19 Hall	Y	Y	Y	Y
20 Murphy	Y	?	Y	Y
21 Tonko	Y	Y	Y	Y
22 Hinchey	Y	Y	Y	Y
23 Owens	?	N	Y	Y
24 Arcuri	Y	N	Y	?
25 Maffei	Y	Y	Y	Y
26 Lee	Y	N	Y	Y
27 Higgins	Y	Y	Y	Y
28 Slaughter	Y	Y	Y	Y
29 Reed	Y	N	Y	Y
NORTH CAROLINA				
1 Butterfield	Y	Y	Y	Y
2 Etheridge	Y	Y	Y	Y
3 Jones	Y	N	Y	Y
4 Price	Y	Y	Y	Y

	624	625	626	627
5 Foxx	Y	N	Y	?
6 Coble	Y	N	Y	?
7 McIntyre	Y	N	Y	Y
8 Kissell	Y	N	Y	Y
9 Myrick	Y	N	Y	+
10 McHenry	Y	N	Y	Y
11 Shuler	Y	N	?	?
12 Watt	Y	Y	Y	Y
13 Miller	Y	Y	Y	Y
NORTH DAKOTA				
AL Pomeroy	?	Y	Y	Y
OHIO				
1 Driehaus	Y	Y	Y	?
2 Schmidt	Y	N	Y	?
3 Turner	Y	N	Y	Y
4 Jordan	Y	N	Y	Y
5 Latta	Y	N	Y	Y
6 Wilson	Y	N	Y	Y
7 Austria	Y	N	Y	Y
8 Boehner	Y	N	?	?
9 Kaptur	?	N	Y	Y
10 Kucinich	Y	Y	Y	Y
11 Fudge	Y	Y	Y	?
12 Tiberi	?	N	Y	?
13 Sutton	Y	Y	Y	Y
14 LaTourette	Y	N	Y	Y
15 Kilroy	Y	Y	Y	Y
16 Boccieri	Y	N	Y	Y
17 Ryan	Y	Y	Y	Y
18 Space	Y	N	Y	Y
OKLAHOMA				
1 Sullivan	Y	N	Y	Y
2 Boren	Y	N	Y	Y
3 Lucas	Y	N	Y	Y
4 Cole	?	N	Y	Y
5 Fallin	?	?	?	?
OREGON				
1 Wu	?	?	?	?
2 Walden	Y	N	Y	Y
3 Blumenauer	Y	Y	Y	Y
4 DeFazio	Y	Y	Y	Y
5 Schrader	Y	N	Y	Y
PENNSYLVANIA				
1 Brady	Y	Y	Y	Y
2 Fattah	Y	Y	Y	Y
3 Dahlkemper	Y	N	Y	Y
4 Altmire	Y	N	Y	Y
5 Thompson	Y	N	Y	Y
6 Gerlach	Y	N	Y	Y
7 Sestak	Y	Y	Y	Y
8 Murphy, P.	Y	N	Y	Y
9 Shuster	Y	N	Y	Y
10 Carney	Y	N	Y	Y
11 Kanjorski	Y	N	Y	Y
12 Critz	Y	N	Y	Y
13 Schwartz	Y	Y	Y	Y
14 Doyle	Y	Y	Y	Y
15 Dent	Y	N	Y	Y
16 Pitts	Y	N	Y	Y
17 Holden	Y	N	Y	Y
18 Murphy, T.	Y	N	Y	Y
19 Platts	Y	N	Y	Y
RHODE ISLAND				
1 Kennedy	Y	Y	Y	Y
2 Langevin	Y	Y	Y	Y
SOUTH CAROLINA				
1 Brown	Y	N	Y	Y
2 Wilson	Y	N	Y	Y
3 Barrett	Y	N	Y	Y
4 Inglis	Y	Y	Y	Y
5 Spratt	Y	Y	Y	Y
6 Clyburn	Y	Y	Y	?
SOUTH DAKOTA				
AL Herseth Sandlin	Y	Y	Y	Y
TENNESSEE				
1 Roe	Y	N	Y	Y
2 Duncan	Y	N	Y	Y
3 Wamp	Y	N	Y	?
4 Davis	Y	Y	Y	Y
5 Cooper	Y	Y	Y	Y
6 Gordon	?	Y	Y	Y
7 Blackburn	Y	N	Y	Y
8 Tanner	Y	Y	Y	Y
9 Cohen	+	+	?	?

	624	625	626	627
TEXAS				
1 Gohmert	Y	N	Y	Y
2 Poe	Y	N	Y	Y
3 Johnson, S.	Y	N	Y	Y
4 Hall	Y	N	Y	Y
5 Hensarling	Y	N	Y	Y
6 Barton	Y	N	Y	Y
7 Culberson	Y	N	Y	Y
8 Brady	Y	N	Y	Y
9 Green, A.	Y	Y	Y	Y
10 McCaul	Y	N	Y	Y
11 Conaway	Y	N	Y	Y
12 Granger	?	–	+	?
13 Thornberry	Y	N	Y	Y
14 Paul	N	N	Y	N
15 Hinojosa	Y	Y	Y	Y
16 Reyes	Y	Y	Y	Y
17 Edwards	Y	Y	Y	Y
18 Jackson Lee	Y	Y	Y	Y
19 Neugebauer	Y	N	Y	Y
20 Gonzalez	Y	Y	Y	Y
21 Smith	Y	N	Y	Y
22 Olson	Y	N	Y	Y
23 Rodriguez	Y	Y	Y	Y
24 Marchant	?	?	?	?
25 Doggett	Y	Y	Y	Y
26 Burgess	Y	Y	Y	Y
27 Ortiz	Y	Y	Y	Y
28 Cuellar	Y	Y	Y	Y
29 Green, G.	Y	Y	Y	Y
30 Johnson, E.	Y	Y	Y	Y
31 Carter	Y	Y	Y	Y
32 Sessions	Y	N	Y	Y
UTAH				
1 Bishop	?	N	Y	Y
2 Matheson	Y	N	Y	Y
3 Chaffetz	Y	N	Y	Y
VERMONT				
AL Welch	Y	Y	Y	?
VIRGINIA				
1 Wittman	Y	N	Y	Y
2 Nye	Y	N	Y	Y
3 Scott	Y	Y	Y	Y
4 Forbes	Y	N	Y	Y
5 Perriello	Y	N	Y	Y
6 Goodlatte	Y	N	Y	Y
7 Cantor	Y	N	Y	Y
8 Moran	Y	Y	Y	Y
9 Boucher	Y	N	?	Y
10 Wolf	Y	N	Y	Y
11 Connolly	Y	Y	Y	?
WASHINGTON				
1 Inslee	Y	Y	Y	Y
2 Larsen	Y	Y	Y	Y
3 Baird	Y	N	N	Y
4 Hastings	Y	N	Y	Y
5 McMorris Rodgers	?	?	?	?
6 Dicks	Y	Y	Y	Y
7 McDermott	Y	Y	Y	Y
8 Reichert	Y	N	Y	Y
9 Smith	Y	Y	Y	Y
WEST VIRGINIA				
1 Mollohan	?	?	Y	Y
2 Capito	Y	N	Y	Y
3 Rahall	Y	N	Y	Y
WISCONSIN				
1 Ryan	Y	N	Y	Y
2 Baldwin	Y	Y	Y	Y
3 Kind	Y	Y	Y	?
4 Moore	Y	Y	Y	Y
5 Sensenbrenner	Y	N	Y	Y
6 Petri	Y	N	Y	?
7 Obey	Y	Y	Y	Y
8 Kagen	Y	Y	Y	Y
WYOMING				
AL Lummis	Y	N	Y	Y
DELEGATES				
Faleomavaega (A.S.)				
Norton (D.C.)				
Bordallo (Guam)				
Sablan (N. Marianas)				
Pierluisi (P.R.)				
Christensen (V.I.)				

IN THE HOUSE | By Vote Number

628. S 1405. National Historic Site Redesignation/Passage. Rahall, D-W.Va., motion to suspend the rules and pass the bill that would redesignate the Longfellow National Historic Site in Cambridge, Mass., as the "Longfellow House-Washington's Headquarters National Historic Site." Motion agreed to 364-0: D 211-0; R 153-0. A two-thirds majority of those present and voting (243 in this case) is required for passage under suspension of the rules. Dec. 14, 2010.

629. S 3167. Census Bureau Oversight and Organization/Passage. Maloney, D-N.Y., motion to suspend the rules and pass the bill that would establish five-year fixed terms for the census director beginning Jan. 1, 2012, and identify the authority and duties of the director and deputy director. The bill would require the census director to report directly to the Commerce secretary and provide a plan to Congress on how the Census Bureau will test, develop and implement an Internet response option for the 2020 Census and the American Community Survey. Motion rejected 201-167: D 200-13; R 1-154. A two-thirds majority of those present and voting (246 in this case) is required for passage under suspension of the rules. Dec. 14, 2010.

630. HR 6510. Property Transfer to Military Museum of Texas/Passage. Norton, D-D.C., motion to suspend the rules and pass the bill that would direct the General Services Administration to convey a 3.673-acre parcel of real property in Houston, Texas, to the Military Museum of Texas. Motion agreed to 363-0: D 210-0; R 153-0. A two-thirds majority of those present and voting (242 in this case) is required for passage under suspension of the rules. Dec. 14, 2010.

631. HR 5446. Harry T. and Harriette Moore Post Office/Passage. Chu, D-Calif., motion to suspend the rules and pass the bill that would designate a postal facility in Cocoa, Fla., as the "Harry T. and Harriette Moore Post Office." Motion agreed to 405-0: D 239-0; R 166-0. A two-thirds majority of those present and voting (270 in this case) is required for passage under suspension of the rules. Dec. 15, 2010.

632. H Res 1759. Ed Roberts Day/Adoption. Grijalva, D-Ariz., motion to suspend the rules and adopt the resolution that would support the designation of Jan. 23 as Ed Roberts Day and acknowledge the accomplishments of activist Ed Roberts in improving the lives of people with disabilities. Motion agreed to 390-8: D 236-0; R 154-8. A two-thirds majority of those present and voting (266 in this case) is required for adoption under suspension of the rules. Dec. 15, 2010.

633. S Con Res 72. White House Fellows Program Anniversary/Adoption. Chu, D-Calif., motion to suspend the rules and adopt the concurrent resolution that would recognize the 45th anniversary of the White House Fellows program. Motion agreed to 401-1: D 236-0; R 165-1. A two-thirds majority of those present and voting (268 in this case) is required for adoption under suspension of the rules. Dec. 15, 2010.

634. HR 6205. Pvt. Isaac T. Cortes Post Office/Passage. Chu, D-Calif., motion to suspend the rules and pass the bill that would designate a post office in Bronx, N.Y., as the "Pvt. Isaac T. Cortes Post Office." Motion agreed to 399-0: D 234-0; R 165-0. A two-thirds majority of those present and voting (266 in this case) is required for passage under suspension of the rules. Dec. 15, 2010.

	628	629	630	631	632	633	634
ALABAMA							
1 Bonner	?	?	?	?	?	?	?
2 Bright	Y	Y	Y	Y	Y	Y	Y
3 Rogers	Y	N	Y	Y	Y	Y	Y
4 Aderholt	Y	N	Y	Y	Y	Y	Y
5 Griffith	?	?	?	?	?	?	?
6 Bachus	Y	N	Y	Y	Y	Y	Y
7 Davis	?	?	?	?	?	?	?
ALASKA							
AL Young	Y	N	Y	Y	N	N	Y
ARIZONA							
1 Kirkpatrick	?	?	?	Y	Y	Y	Y
2 Franks	Y	N	Y	Y	Y	Y	Y
3 Shadegg	?	?	?	?	?	?	?
4 Pastor	Y	Y	Y	Y	Y	Y	Y
5 Mitchell	Y	Y	Y	Y	Y	Y	Y
6 Flake	Y	N	Y	Y	Y	Y	Y
7 Grijalva	Y	Y	Y	Y	Y	Y	Y
8 Giffords	Y	Y	Y	Y	Y	Y	Y
ARKANSAS							
1 Berry	?	?	?	?	?	?	?
2 Snyder	Y	Y	Y	Y	Y	Y	Y
3 Boozman	Y	N	Y	Y	Y	Y	Y
4 Ross	Y	N	Y	Y	Y	Y	Y
CALIFORNIA							
1 Thompson	Y	Y	Y	Y	Y	Y	Y
2 Herger	Y	N	Y	Y	Y	Y	Y
3 Lungren	Y	N	Y	Y	Y	Y	Y
4 McClintock	Y	N	Y	Y	Y	Y	Y
5 Matsui	Y	Y	Y	Y	Y	Y	Y
6 Woolsey	+	+	+	+	+	+	+
7 Miller, George	Y	Y	Y	Y	Y	Y	Y
8 Pelosi							
9 Lee	Y	Y	Y	Y	Y	Y	Y
10 Garamendi	Y	Y	Y	Y	Y	Y	Y
11 McNerney	Y	Y	Y	Y	Y	Y	Y
12 Speier	?	?	?	Y	Y	Y	Y
13 Stark	Y	Y	?	Y	Y	Y	Y
14 Eshoo	Y	Y	Y	Y	Y	Y	Y
15 Honda	?	?	?	Y	Y	Y	Y
16 Lofgren	Y	Y	Y	Y	Y	Y	Y
17 Farr	Y	Y	Y	Y	Y	Y	Y
18 Cardoza	?	?	?	?	?	?	?
19 Radanovich	?	?	?	?	?	?	?
20 Costa	Y	Y	Y	Y	Y	Y	Y
21 Nunes	Y	N	Y	Y	Y	Y	Y
22 McCarthy	Y	N	Y	Y	Y	Y	Y
23 Capps	+	+	+	Y	Y	Y	Y
24 Gallegly	Y	N	Y	Y	Y	Y	Y
25 McKeon	Y	N	Y	Y	Y	Y	Y
26 Dreier	Y	N	Y	Y	Y	Y	Y
27 Sherman	Y	N	Y	Y	?	Y	Y
28 Berman	Y	Y	Y	Y	Y	Y	Y
29 Schiff	Y	Y	Y	Y	Y	Y	Y
30 Waxman	Y	Y	Y	Y	Y	Y	Y
31 Becerra	Y	Y	Y	Y	Y	Y	Y
32 Chu	Y	Y	Y	Y	Y	Y	Y
33 Watson	?	Y	Y	Y	Y	Y	Y
34 Roybal-Allard	Y	Y	Y	Y	Y	Y	Y
35 Waters	?	?	?	Y	Y	?	Y
36 Harman	Y	Y	Y	Y	Y	Y	Y
37 Richardson	Y	Y	Y	Y	Y	Y	Y
38 Napolitano	Y	Y	Y	Y	Y	Y	Y
39 Sánchez, Linda	Y	Y	Y	Y	Y	Y	Y
40 Royce	Y	N	Y	Y	Y	Y	Y
41 Lewis	Y	N	Y	Y	Y	Y	Y
42 Miller, Gary	Y	N	Y	Y	Y	Y	Y
43 Baca	Y	Y	Y	Y	Y	Y	Y
44 Calvert	Y	N	Y	Y	Y	Y	Y
45 Bono Mack	Y	N	Y	Y	Y	Y	Y
46 Rohrabacher	?	?	?	Y	Y	Y	Y
47 Sanchez, Loretta	Y	Y	Y	Y	Y	Y	Y
48 Campbell	Y	N	Y	Y	N	Y	Y
49 Issa	?	?	?	Y	Y	Y	Y
50 Bilbray	Y	N	Y	Y	Y	Y	Y
51 Filner	Y	Y	Y	Y	Y	Y	Y
52 Hunter	Y	N	Y	Y	Y	Y	Y
53 Davis	Y	Y	Y	Y	Y	Y	Y

	628	629	630	631	632	633	634
COLORADO							
1 DeGette	Y	Y	Y	Y	Y	Y	Y
2 Polis	Y	Y	Y	Y	Y	Y	Y
3 Salazar	?	?	?	?	?	?	?
4 Markey	?	?	?	?	?	?	?
5 Lamborn	Y	N	Y	Y	Y	Y	Y
6 Coffman	Y	N	Y	Y	Y	Y	Y
7 Perlmutter	?	Y	Y	Y	Y	Y	Y
CONNECTICUT							
1 Larson	Y	Y	Y	Y	Y	Y	Y
2 Courtney	Y	Y	Y	Y	Y	Y	Y
3 DeLauro	Y	Y	Y	Y	Y	Y	Y
4 Himes	Y	Y	Y	Y	Y	Y	Y
5 Murphy	Y	Y	Y	Y	Y	Y	Y
DELAWARE							
AL Castle	Y	N	Y	Y	Y	Y	Y
FLORIDA							
1 Miller	Y	N	Y	Y	Y	Y	Y
2 Boyd	Y	Y	Y	Y	Y	Y	Y
3 Brown	Y	Y	Y	Y	Y	Y	Y
4 Crenshaw	Y	N	Y	Y	Y	Y	Y
5 Brown-Waite	?	?	?	?	?	?	?
6 Stearns	Y	N	Y	Y	N	Y	Y
7 Mica	Y	N	Y	Y	Y	Y	Y
8 Grayson	Y	Y	Y	Y	Y	Y	Y
9 Bilirakis	Y	N	Y	Y	Y	Y	Y
10 Young	Y	N	Y	?	?	?	?
11 Castor	Y	Y	Y	Y	Y	Y	Y
12 Putnam	+	-	+	+	+	+	+
13 Buchanan	Y	N	?	Y	Y	Y	Y
14 Mack	Y	N	Y	Y	Y	Y	Y
15 Posey	Y	N	Y	Y	Y	Y	Y
16 Rooney	Y	N	Y	N	Y	Y	Y
17 Meek	Y	Y	Y	?	Y	Y	Y
18 Ros-Lehtinen	Y	N	Y	Y	Y	Y	Y
19 Deutch	Y	Y	Y	Y	?	Y	Y
20 Wasserman Schultz	Y	Y	Y	Y	Y	Y	Y
21 Diaz-Balart, L.	?	?	?	Y	Y	Y	Y
22 Klein	Y	Y	Y	?	?	?	Y
23 Hastings	Y	Y	Y	Y	Y	Y	Y
24 Kosmas	Y	Y	Y	Y	Y	Y	Y
25 Diaz-Balart, M.	Y	N	Y	Y	Y	Y	Y
GEORGIA							
1 Kingston	Y	N	Y	Y	Y	Y	Y
2 Bishop	Y	Y	Y	Y	Y	Y	Y
3 Westmoreland	Y	Y	Y	Y	Y	Y	Y
4 Johnson	Y	Y	Y	Y	Y	Y	Y
5 Lewis	Y	Y	Y	Y	Y	Y	?
6 Price	Y	N	Y	Y	?	Y	Y
7 Linder	Y	N	Y	Y	Y	Y	Y
8 Marshall	Y	Y	Y	Y	Y	Y	Y
9 Graves	Y	N	Y	Y	Y	Y	Y
10 Broun	Y	N	Y	Y	N	Y	Y
11 Gingrey	Y	N	Y	Y	Y	Y	Y
12 Barrow	Y	Y	Y	Y	Y	Y	Y
13 Scott	Y	Y	Y	Y	Y	Y	Y
HAWAII							
1 Djou	Y	N	Y	Y	Y	Y	Y
2 Hirono	Y	Y	Y	Y	Y	Y	Y
IDAHO							
1 Minnick	Y	N	Y	Y	Y	Y	Y
2 Simpson	?	?	?	Y	Y	Y	Y
ILLINOIS							
1 Rush	Y	Y	Y	Y	Y	Y	Y
2 Jackson	Y	Y	Y	Y	Y	Y	Y
3 Lipinski	Y	Y	Y	Y	Y	Y	Y
4 Gutierrez	+	+	+	Y	?	Y	Y
5 Quigley	Y	Y	Y	Y	Y	Y	Y
6 Roskam	Y	N	Y	Y	Y	Y	Y
7 Davis	?	?	?	?	?	?	?
8 Bean	Y	Y	Y	Y	Y	Y	Y
9 Schakowsky	Y	Y	Y	Y	Y	Y	Y
10 Vacant							
11 Halvorson	Y	Y	Y	Y	Y	Y	?
12 Costello	?	?	?	Y	Y	Y	Y
13 Biggert	Y	N	Y	Y	Y	Y	Y
14 Foster	Y	Y	Y	Y	Y	Y	Y
15 Johnson	Y	N	Y	Y	Y	Y	Y

KEY   **Republicans**   Democrats

Y Voted for (yea)	X Paired against	C Voted "present" to avoid possible conflict of interest
# Paired for	– Announced against	? Did not vote or otherwise make a position known
+ Announced for	P Voted "present"	
N Voted against (nay)		

	628	629	630	631	632	633	634
16 **Manzullo**	Y	N	?	Y	Y	Y	Y
17 Hare	Y	Y	Y	Y	Y	Y	Y
18 **Schock**	Y	N	Y	Y	Y	Y	Y
19 **Shimkus**	Y	N	Y	Y	Y	Y	Y
INDIANA							
1 Visclosky	Y	Y	Y	Y	Y	Y	Y
2 Donnelly	Y	Y	Y	Y	Y	Y	Y
3 **Stutzman**	?	?	?	Y	Y	Y	Y
4 **Buyer**	?	N	Y	Y	Y	Y	Y
5 **Burton**	+	–	+	Y	Y	Y	Y
6 **Pence**	+	–	+	Y	Y	Y	Y
7 Carson	Y	Y	Y	Y	Y	Y	Y
8 Ellsworth	Y	Y	Y	Y	Y	Y	Y
9 Hill	Y	Y	Y	Y	Y	Y	Y
IOWA							
1 Braley	Y	Y	Y	Y	Y	Y	Y
2 Loebsack	Y	Y	Y	Y	Y	Y	Y
3 Boswell	Y	Y	Y	Y	Y	Y	Y
4 **Latham**	Y	N	Y	Y	Y	Y	Y
5 **King**	Y	N	Y	Y	Y	Y	Y
KANSAS							
1 **Moran**	?	?	?	Y	Y	Y	Y
2 **Jenkins**	Y	N	Y	Y	Y	Y	Y
3 Moore	Y	Y	Y	Y	Y	Y	Y
4 **Tiahrt**	Y	N	Y	Y	Y	Y	Y
KENTUCKY							
1 **Whitfield**	Y	N	Y	Y	Y	Y	Y
2 **Guthrie**	Y	N	Y	Y	Y	Y	Y
3 Yarmuth	Y	Y	Y	Y	Y	Y	Y
4 **Davis**	Y	N	Y	Y	Y	Y	Y
5 **Rogers**	Y	N	Y	Y	Y	Y	Y
6 Chandler	?	Y	Y	Y	Y	Y	Y
LOUISIANA							
1 **Scalise**	Y	N	Y	Y	Y	Y	Y
2 **Cao**	Y	N	Y	Y	Y	Y	Y
3 Melancon	Y	N	Y	Y	?	?	?
4 **Fleming**	Y	N	Y	Y	Y	Y	Y
5 **Alexander**	Y	N	Y	Y	Y	Y	Y
6 **Cassidy**	Y	N	Y	Y	P	Y	Y
7 **Boustany**	Y	N	Y	Y	Y	Y	Y
MAINE							
1 Pingree	Y	Y	Y	Y	Y	Y	Y
2 Michaud	Y	Y	Y	Y	Y	Y	Y
MARYLAND							
1 Kratovil	Y	N	Y	Y	Y	Y	Y
2 Ruppersberger	Y	Y	Y	Y	Y	Y	Y
3 Sarbanes	Y	Y	Y	Y	Y	Y	Y
4 Edwards	Y	N	Y	Y	Y	Y	Y
5 Hoyer	Y	Y	Y	Y	Y	Y	Y
6 **Bartlett**	Y	N	Y	Y	Y	Y	Y
7 Cummings	Y	Y	Y	Y	Y	Y	Y
8 Van Hollen	Y	Y	Y	Y	Y	Y	Y
MASSACHUSETTS							
1 Olver	Y	Y	Y	Y	Y	Y	Y
2 Neal	Y	Y	Y	Y	Y	Y	Y
3 McGovern	Y	Y	Y	Y	Y	Y	Y
4 Frank	Y	Y	?	Y	Y	Y	Y
5 Tsongas	Y	Y	Y	Y	Y	Y	Y
6 Tierney	Y	Y	Y	Y	Y	Y	Y
7 Markey	Y	Y	Y	Y	Y	Y	Y
8 Capuano	Y	Y	Y	Y	Y	Y	Y
9 Lynch	?	?	?	Y	Y	Y	Y
10 Delahunt	?	?	?	Y	Y	Y	Y
MICHIGAN							
1 Stupak	Y	Y	Y	Y	Y	Y	Y
2 **Hoekstra**	Y	N	Y	Y	Y	Y	Y
3 **Ehlers**	Y	N	Y	Y	Y	Y	Y
4 **Camp**	Y	N	Y	Y	Y	Y	Y
5 Kildee	Y	Y	Y	Y	Y	Y	Y
6 **Upton**	Y	N	Y	Y	Y	Y	Y
7 Schauer	Y	Y	Y	Y	Y	Y	Y
8 **Rogers**	Y	N	Y	Y	Y	Y	Y
9 Peters	Y	Y	Y	Y	Y	Y	Y
10 **Miller**	Y	N	Y	Y	Y	Y	Y
11 **McCotter**	Y	N	Y	Y	Y	Y	Y
12 Levin	Y	Y	Y	Y	Y	Y	Y
13 Kilpatrick	Y	Y	Y	Y	Y	Y	Y
14 Conyers	Y	Y	Y	Y	Y	Y	Y
15 Dingell	Y	Y	Y	Y	Y	Y	Y
MINNESOTA							
1 Walz	Y	Y	Y	Y	Y	Y	Y
2 **Kline**	Y	N	Y	Y	Y	Y	Y
3 **Paulsen**	Y	N	Y	Y	Y	Y	Y
4 McCollum	Y	Y	Y	Y	Y	Y	Y

	628	629	630	631	632	633	634
5 Ellison	Y	Y	Y	Y	Y	?	Y
6 **Bachmann**	Y	N	Y	Y	Y	Y	Y
7 Peterson	Y	Y	Y	Y	Y	Y	Y
8 Oberstar	Y	Y	Y	Y	Y	Y	Y
MISSISSIPPI							
1 Childers	?	?	?	Y	Y	Y	Y
2 Thompson	Y	Y	Y	Y	Y	Y	Y
3 **Harper**	Y	N	Y	Y	Y	Y	Y
4 Taylor	Y	Y	Y	Y	Y	Y	Y
MISSOURI							
1 Clay	Y	N	Y	Y	Y	Y	Y
2 **Akin**	Y	N	Y	Y	Y	Y	Y
3 Carnahan	Y	Y	Y	Y	Y	Y	Y
4 Skelton	Y	Y	Y	Y	Y	Y	Y
5 Cleaver	Y	Y	Y	Y	Y	Y	Y
6 **Graves**	+	–	+	Y	Y	Y	Y
7 **Blunt**	?	?	?	Y	Y	Y	Y
8 **Emerson**	Y	N	Y	Y	Y	Y	Y
9 **Luetkemeyer**	Y	N	Y	Y	Y	Y	Y
MONTANA							
AL **Rehberg**	Y	N	Y	Y	Y	Y	Y
NEBRASKA							
1 **Fortenberry**	Y	N	Y	Y	Y	Y	Y
2 **Terry**	Y	N	Y	Y	Y	Y	Y
3 **Smith**	Y	N	Y	Y	Y	Y	Y
NEVADA							
1 Berkley	Y	Y	Y	Y	Y	Y	Y
2 **Heller**	Y	N	Y	Y	Y	Y	Y
3 Titus	Y	Y	Y	Y	Y	Y	Y
NEW HAMPSHIRE							
1 Shea-Porter	Y	Y	Y	Y	Y	Y	Y
2 Hodes	Y	Y	Y	Y	Y	Y	Y
NEW JERSEY							
1 Andrews	Y	Y	Y	Y	Y	Y	Y
2 **LoBiondo**	Y	N	Y	Y	Y	Y	Y
3 Adler	?	?	?	Y	Y	Y	Y
4 **Smith**	Y	N	Y	Y	Y	Y	Y
5 **Garrett**	Y	N	Y	Y	Y	Y	Y
6 Pallone	Y	Y	Y	Y	Y	Y	Y
7 **Lance**	Y	N	Y	Y	Y	Y	Y
8 Pascrell	Y	Y	Y	Y	Y	Y	Y
9 Rothman	Y	Y	Y	Y	Y	Y	Y
10 Payne	Y	Y	Y	Y	Y	Y	Y
11 **Frelinghuysen**	Y	N	Y	Y	Y	Y	Y
12 Holt	Y	Y	Y	Y	Y	Y	Y
13 Sires	Y	Y	Y	Y	Y	Y	Y
NEW MEXICO							
1 Heinrich	Y	Y	Y	Y	Y	Y	Y
2 Teague	Y	Y	Y	Y	Y	Y	Y
3 Luján	Y	Y	Y	Y	Y	Y	Y
NEW YORK							
1 Bishop	Y	Y	Y	Y	Y	Y	Y
2 Israel	Y	Y	Y	Y	Y	Y	Y
3 **King**	Y	N	Y	Y	Y	Y	Y
4 McCarthy	+	+	+	+	+	+	+
5 Ackerman	Y	Y	Y	Y	Y	Y	?
6 Meeks	Y	Y	Y	Y	Y	Y	Y
7 Crowley	Y	Y	Y	Y	Y	Y	Y
8 Nadler	Y	Y	Y	Y	Y	Y	Y
9 Weiner	Y	Y	Y	Y	Y	Y	Y
10 Towns	?	?	?	Y	Y	Y	Y
11 Clarke	Y	Y	Y	Y	Y	Y	Y
12 Velázquez	Y	Y	?	Y	Y	Y	Y
13 McMahon	Y	Y	?	Y	Y	Y	Y
14 Maloney	Y	Y	Y	Y	Y	Y	Y
15 Rangel	Y	?	Y	Y	Y	Y	Y
16 Serrano	Y	Y	Y	Y	Y	Y	Y
17 Engel	?	?	?	Y	Y	Y	Y
18 Lowey	+	+	+	Y	Y	Y	Y
19 Hall	?	?	?	Y	Y	Y	Y
20 Murphy	Y	N	Y	Y	Y	Y	Y
21 Tonko	Y	Y	Y	Y	Y	Y	Y
22 Hinchey	Y	Y	Y	Y	Y	Y	Y
23 Owens	+	+	+	+	+	+	+
24 Arcuri	?	?	?	Y	Y	Y	Y
25 Maffei	Y	Y	Y	Y	Y	Y	Y
26 **Lee**	Y	N	Y	Y	Y	?	?
27 Higgins	Y	Y	Y	Y	Y	Y	Y
28 Slaughter	Y	Y	Y	Y	Y	Y	Y
29 **Reed**	Y	N	Y	Y	Y	Y	Y
NORTH CAROLINA							
1 Butterfield	Y	Y	Y	Y	Y	Y	Y
2 Etheridge	+	+	+	Y	Y	Y	Y
3 **Jones**	Y	N	Y	Y	Y	Y	Y
4 Price	Y	Y	Y	Y	Y	Y	Y

	628	629	630	631	632	633	634
5 **Foxx**	Y	N	Y	Y	P	Y	Y
6 **Coble**	Y	N	Y	Y	Y	Y	Y
7 McIntyre	Y	Y	Y	Y	Y	Y	Y
8 Kissell	Y	Y	Y	Y	Y	Y	Y
9 **Myrick**	Y	N	Y	Y	Y	Y	Y
10 **McHenry**	Y	N	Y	Y	Y	Y	Y
11 Shuler	Y	N	Y	Y	Y	Y	Y
12 Watt	Y	Y	Y	Y	Y	Y	Y
13 Miller	Y	Y	Y	Y	Y	Y	Y
NORTH DAKOTA							
AL Pomeroy	Y	Y	Y	?	?	?	?
OHIO							
1 Driehaus	Y	Y	Y	Y	Y	Y	Y
2 **Schmidt**	Y	N	Y	Y	Y	Y	Y
3 **Turner**	Y	N	Y	Y	Y	Y	Y
4 **Jordan**	Y	N	Y	Y	Y	Y	Y
5 **Latta**	Y	N	Y	Y	Y	Y	Y
6 Wilson	Y	Y	Y	Y	Y	Y	Y
7 **Austria**	Y	N	Y	Y	Y	Y	Y
8 **Boehner**	Y	N	Y	Y	Y	Y	Y
9 Kaptur	Y	Y	Y	Y	Y	Y	Y
10 Kucinich	Y	Y	Y	Y	Y	Y	Y
11 Fudge	Y	Y	Y	Y	Y	Y	Y
12 **Tiberi**	?	?	?	Y	Y	Y	Y
13 Sutton	?	?	?	Y	Y	Y	Y
14 **LaTourette**	Y	N	Y	Y	Y	Y	Y
15 Kilroy	Y	Y	Y	Y	Y	Y	Y
16 Boccieri	Y	Y	Y	Y	Y	Y	Y
17 Ryan	Y	Y	Y	Y	Y	Y	Y
18 Space	Y	Y	Y	?	?	?	?
OKLAHOMA							
1 **Sullivan**	Y	N	Y	Y	Y	Y	Y
2 Boren	Y	N	Y	Y	Y	Y	Y
3 **Lucas**	Y	N	Y	Y	Y	Y	Y
4 **Cole**	Y	N	Y	Y	Y	Y	Y
5 **Fallin**	?	?	?	?	?	?	?
OREGON							
1 Wu	Y	Y	Y	Y	Y	Y	Y
2 **Walden**	Y	N	Y	Y	Y	Y	Y
3 Blumenauer	Y	Y	Y	Y	Y	Y	Y
4 DeFazio	Y	Y	Y	Y	Y	Y	Y
5 Schrader	Y	Y	Y	Y	Y	Y	Y
PENNSYLVANIA							
1 Brady	Y	Y	Y	Y	Y	Y	Y
2 Fattah	Y	Y	Y	Y	Y	Y	Y
3 Dahlkemper	?	?	?	Y	Y	Y	Y
4 Altmire	Y	N	Y	Y	Y	Y	Y
5 **Thompson**	Y	N	Y	Y	Y	Y	Y
6 **Gerlach**	Y	N	Y	Y	Y	Y	Y
7 Sestak	?	?	?	Y	Y	Y	Y
8 Murphy, P.	?	?	?	Y	Y	Y	Y
9 **Shuster**	Y	N	Y	Y	Y	Y	Y
10 Carney	?	?	?	Y	Y	Y	Y
11 Kanjorski	Y	Y	Y	Y	Y	Y	Y
12 Critz	Y	Y	Y	Y	Y	Y	Y
13 Schwartz	Y	Y	Y	Y	Y	Y	Y
14 Doyle	Y	Y	Y	Y	Y	Y	Y
15 **Dent**	Y	Y	Y	Y	Y	Y	Y
16 **Pitts**	Y	N	Y	Y	Y	Y	Y
17 Holden	Y	Y	Y	Y	Y	Y	Y
18 **Murphy, T.**	Y	N	Y	Y	Y	Y	Y
19 **Platts**	Y	N	Y	Y	Y	Y	Y
RHODE ISLAND							
1 Kennedy	?	?	?	Y	Y	Y	Y
2 Langevin	?	?	?	Y	Y	Y	Y
SOUTH CAROLINA							
1 **Brown**	Y	N	Y	Y	Y	Y	Y
2 **Wilson**	Y	N	Y	Y	Y	Y	Y
3 **Barrett**	?	?	?	Y	Y	Y	Y
4 **Inglis**	Y	N	Y	Y	Y	Y	Y
5 Spratt	Y	Y	Y	Y	Y	Y	Y
6 Clyburn	Y	Y	Y	Y	Y	Y	Y
SOUTH DAKOTA							
AL Herseth Sandlin	Y	Y	Y	+	+	+	+
TENNESSEE							
1 **Roe**	Y	N	Y	Y	P	Y	Y
2 **Duncan**	Y	N	Y	Y	Y	Y	Y
3 **Wamp**	?	?	?	?	?	?	?
4 Davis	Y	Y	Y	Y	Y	Y	Y
5 Cooper	Y	Y	Y	Y	Y	Y	Y
6 Gordon	Y	Y	Y	Y	Y	Y	Y
7 **Blackburn**	Y	N	Y	Y	Y	Y	Y
8 Tanner	?	?	?	Y	Y	Y	Y
9 Cohen	Y	Y	Y	Y	Y	Y	Y

	628	629	630	631	632	633	634
TEXAS							
1 **Gohmert**	Y	N	Y	Y	Y	Y	Y
2 **Poe**	+	N	Y	Y	P	Y	Y
3 **Johnson, S.**	Y	N	Y	Y	Y	Y	Y
4 **Hall**	Y	N	Y	Y	Y	Y	Y
5 **Hensarling**	Y	N	Y	Y	Y	Y	Y
6 **Barton**	Y	N	Y	Y	Y	Y	Y
7 **Culberson**	Y	N	Y	Y	Y	Y	Y
8 **Brady**	Y	N	Y	Y	Y	Y	Y
9 Green, A.	Y	Y	Y	Y	Y	?	Y
10 **McCaul**	Y	N	Y	Y	Y	Y	Y
11 **Conaway**	Y	N	Y	Y	Y	Y	Y
12 **Granger**	?	?	?	?	?	?	?
13 **Thornberry**	Y	N	Y	Y	Y	Y	Y
14 **Paul**	Y	N	Y	Y	N	Y	?
15 Hinojosa	?	?	?	Y	Y	Y	Y
16 Reyes	Y	Y	Y	Y	Y	Y	Y
17 Edwards	Y	Y	Y	Y	Y	Y	Y
18 Jackson Lee	Y	Y	Y	Y	Y	Y	Y
19 **Neugebauer**	Y	N	Y	Y	Y	Y	Y
20 Gonzalez	Y	Y	Y	Y	Y	Y	Y
21 **Smith**	Y	N	Y	Y	Y	Y	Y
22 **Olson**	Y	N	Y	Y	Y	Y	Y
23 Rodriguez	?	?	?	Y	Y	Y	Y
24 **Marchant**	?	?	?	?	?	?	?
25 Doggett	Y	Y	Y	Y	Y	Y	Y
26 **Burgess**	Y	N	Y	Y	Y	Y	Y
27 Ortiz	?	?	?	Y	Y	Y	Y
28 Cuellar	Y	Y	Y	Y	Y	Y	Y
29 Green, G.	+	+	+	Y	Y	Y	Y
30 Johnson, E.	Y	Y	Y	Y	Y	Y	Y
31 **Carter**	Y	N	Y	Y	Y	Y	Y
32 **Sessions**	Y	N	Y	Y	Y	Y	Y
UTAH							
1 **Bishop**	Y	N	Y	Y	Y	Y	Y
2 Matheson	Y	N	Y	Y	Y	Y	Y
3 **Chaffetz**	Y	N	Y	Y	N	Y	Y
VERMONT							
AL Welch	Y	Y	Y	Y	Y	Y	Y
VIRGINIA							
1 **Wittman**	Y	N	Y	Y	Y	Y	Y
2 Nye	Y	N	Y	Y	Y	Y	Y
3 Scott	Y	Y	Y	Y	Y	Y	?
4 **Forbes**	Y	N	Y	Y	Y	Y	Y
5 Perriello	Y	Y	Y	Y	Y	Y	Y
6 **Goodlatte**	Y	N	Y	Y	Y	Y	Y
7 **Cantor**	Y	N	Y	?	Y	Y	Y
8 Moran	Y	Y	Y	Y	Y	Y	Y
9 Boucher	?	?	?	Y	Y	Y	Y
10 **Wolf**	Y	N	Y	Y	Y	Y	Y
11 Connolly	Y	Y	Y	Y	Y	Y	Y
WASHINGTON							
1 Inslee	Y	Y	Y	Y	Y	Y	Y
2 Larsen	Y	Y	Y	Y	Y	Y	Y
3 Baird	?	?	?	Y	Y	Y	Y
4 **Hastings**	?	?	?	Y	Y	Y	Y
5 **McMorris Rodgers**	?	?	?	?	?	?	?
6 Dicks	Y	Y	Y	Y	Y	Y	Y
7 McDermott	Y	Y	Y	Y	Y	Y	Y
8 **Reichert**	Y	N	Y	Y	Y	Y	Y
9 Smith	Y	Y	Y	Y	Y	Y	Y
WEST VIRGINIA							
1 Mollohan	Y	Y	Y	Y	Y	Y	Y
2 **Capito**	Y	N	Y	Y	Y	Y	Y
3 Rahall	Y	Y	Y	Y	Y	Y	Y
WISCONSIN							
1 **Ryan**	Y	N	Y	Y	Y	Y	Y
2 Baldwin	Y	Y	Y	Y	Y	Y	Y
3 Kind	Y	Y	Y	Y	Y	Y	Y
4 Moore	Y	Y	Y	Y	Y	Y	Y
5 **Sensenbrenner**	Y	N	Y	Y	N	Y	Y
6 **Petri**	Y	N	Y	Y	Y	Y	Y
7 Obey	Y	Y	Y	Y	Y	Y	Y
8 Kagen	Y	Y	Y	Y	Y	Y	Y
WYOMING							
AL **Lummis**	Y	N	Y	Y	Y	Y	Y
DELEGATES							
Faleomavaega (A.S.)							
Norton (D.C.)							
Bordallo (Guam)							
Sablan (N. Marianas)							
Pierluisi (P.R.)							
Christensen (V.I.)							

IN THE HOUSE | By Vote Number

635. **HR 2965. 'Don't Ask, Don't Tell' Policy Repeal/Rule.** Adoption of the rule (H Res 1764) that would provide for House floor consideration of the Senate amendment to the bill by allowing for a motion to concur with a House amendment that would strike the text of the bill and insert language to allow for the repeal of the military's "don't ask, don't tell" policy, which prohibits military service by openly gay men and women, after certain requirements are met. Adopted 232-180: D 230-12; R 2-168. Dec. 15, 2010.

636. **H Res 1761. Tribute to Cameron Newton/Adoption.** Altmire, D-Pa., motion to suspend the rules and adopt the resolution that would congratulate Auburn University quarterback and College Park, Ga., native Cameron Newton on winning the 2010 Heisman Trophy. Motion agreed to 378-15: D 228-7; R 150-8. A two-thirds majority of those present and voting (262 in this case) is required for adoption under suspension of the rules. Dec. 15, 2010.

637. **H Res 1743. Tribute to Gerda Weissmann Klein/Adoption.** Chu, D-Calif., motion to suspend the rules and adopt the resolution that would congratulate Holocaust survivor Gerda Weissmann Klein on being selected to receive the Presidential Medal of Freedom. Motion agreed to 407-0: D 240-0; R 167-0. A two-thirds majority of those present and voting (272 in this case) is required for adoption under suspension of the rules. Dec. 15, 2010.

638. **HR 2965. 'Don't Ask, Don't Tell' Policy Repeal/Motion to Concur.** Davis, D-Calif., motion to concur in the Senate amendment to the bill with a House amendment that would allow for the repeal of the military's "don't ask, don't tell" policy, which prohibits military service by openly gay men and women, after certain requirements are met, including the submission of a written certification, signed by the president, the secretary of Defense and the chairman of the Joint Chiefs of Staff, that the repeal is consistent with military readiness and effectiveness. Motion agreed to, 250-175: D 235-15; R 15-160. A "yea" was a vote in support of the president's position. Dec. 15, 2010.

639. **Procedural Motion/Motion to Adjourn.** Taylor, D-Miss., motion to adjourn. Motion rejected 14-385: D 7-226; R 7-159. Dec. 16, 2010.

640. **S 841. Pedestrian Alert for Motor Vehicles/Passage.** Barrow, D-Ga., motion to suspend the rules and pass the bill that would require the Transportation Department to promulgate a motor vehicle safety standard establishing requirements for an alert sound that would allow blind and other pedestrians to detect the operation of otherwise silent vehicles. Motion agreed to 379-30: D 242-0; R 137-30. A two-thirds majority of those present and voting (273 in this case) is required for passage under suspension of the rules. Dec. 16, 2010.

641. **S 3860. Arlington National Cemetery Oversight/Passage.** Filner, D-Calif., motion to suspend the rules and pass the bill that would require the Army secretary to submit a report to Congress specifying whether grave site locations at Arlington National Cemetery are identified correctly and outlining a plan to address any deficiencies found. The bill also would require the Government Accountability Office to report on the management and oversight of contracts at the cemetery. Motion agreed to 407-3: D 243-0; R 164-3. A two-thirds majority of those present and voting (274 in this case) is required for passage under suspension of the rules. Dec. 16, 2010.

	635	636	637	638	639	640	641
ALABAMA							
1 Bonner	?	+	?	N	N	Y	Y
2 Bright	N	Y	?	N	N	Y	Y
3 Rogers	N	Y	N	N	N	Y	Y
4 Aderholt	N	Y	Y	N	N	Y	Y
5 Griffith	N	Y	Y	N	N	Y	Y
6 Bachus	N	Y	Y	N	N	Y	Y
7 Davis	N	Y	?	N	?	?	?
ALASKA							
AL Young	N	Y	Y	N	N	N	N
ARIZONA							
1 Kirkpatrick	Y	Y	Y	Y	Y	Y	Y
2 Franks	N	Y	Y	N	N	N	Y
3 Shadegg	?	?	?	N	N	N	Y
4 Pastor	Y	Y	Y	Y	N	Y	Y
5 Mitchell	Y	Y	Y	Y	N	Y	Y
6 Flake	N	Y	Y	Y	Y	N	Y
7 Grijalva	Y	Y	Y	?	Y	Y	Y
8 Giffords	Y	Y	Y	Y	N	Y	Y
ARKANSAS							
1 Berry	?	?	?	?	?	?	?
2 Snyder	Y	Y	Y	Y	N	Y	Y
3 Boozman	N	Y	N	N	N	Y	Y
4 Ross	N	Y	Y	N	N	Y	Y
CALIFORNIA							
1 Thompson	Y	Y	Y	Y	N	Y	Y
2 Herger	N	Y	Y	N	N	Y	Y
3 Lungren	N	N	Y	N	N	Y	Y
4 McClintock	N	Y	Y	N	N	N	Y
5 Matsui	Y	Y	Y	Y	N	Y	Y
6 Woolsey	+	+	+	+	N	Y	Y
7 Miller, George	Y	Y	Y	Y	N	Y	Y
8 Pelosi				Y			
9 Lee	Y	Y	Y	Y	N	Y	Y
10 Garamendi	Y	Y	Y	Y	N	Y	Y
11 McNerney	Y	Y	Y	Y	N	Y	Y
12 Speier	Y	Y	Y	Y	N	Y	Y
13 Stark	Y	Y	Y	Y	N	Y	Y
14 Eshoo	Y	Y	Y	Y	N	Y	Y
15 Honda	Y	Y	Y	Y	N	Y	Y
16 Lofgren	Y	Y	Y	Y	N	Y	Y
17 Farr	Y	Y	Y	Y	N	Y	?
18 Cardoza	?	?	?	?	?	?	?
19 Radanovich	?	?	?	N	N	?	?
20 Costa	Y	Y	Y	Y	N	Y	Y
21 Nunes	N	Y	Y	N	N	N	Y
22 McCarthy	N	Y	Y	N	N	Y	Y
23 Capps	Y	Y	Y	Y	N	Y	Y
24 Gallegly	N	Y	Y	N	N	Y	Y
25 McKeon	N	Y	Y	N	N	Y	Y
26 Dreier	N	Y	Y	N	N	Y	Y
27 Sherman	Y	Y	Y	Y	N	Y	Y
28 Berman	Y	Y	Y	Y	N	Y	Y
29 Schiff	Y	Y	Y	Y	N	Y	Y
30 Waxman	Y	Y	Y	Y	N	Y	Y
31 Becerra	Y	Y	Y	Y	N	Y	Y
32 Chu	Y	Y	Y	Y	N	Y	Y
33 Watson	Y	Y	Y	Y	N	Y	?
34 Roybal-Allard	Y	Y	Y	Y	N	Y	Y
35 Waters	Y	Y	Y	Y	N	Y	Y
36 Harman	Y	Y	Y	Y	N	Y	Y
37 Richardson	Y	Y	Y	Y	N	Y	Y
38 Napolitano	Y	Y	Y	Y	N	Y	Y
39 Sánchez, Linda	Y	Y	Y	Y	N	Y	Y
40 Royce	N	Y	Y	N	N	N	Y
41 Lewis	N	Y	Y	N	N	Y	Y
42 Miller, Gary	N	Y	Y	N	N	Y	Y
43 Baca	Y	Y	Y	Y	N	Y	Y
44 Calvert	N	Y	Y	N	N	Y	Y
45 Bono Mack	N	Y	Y	N	N	Y	Y
46 Rohrabacher	N	Y	Y	N	N	N	Y
47 Sanchez, Loretta	Y	Y	Y	Y	N	Y	Y
48 Campbell	N	N	Y	N	N	N	Y
49 Issa	N	Y	Y	N	N	Y	Y
50 Bilbray	N	P	Y	N	N	Y	Y
51 Filner	Y	Y	Y	Y	N	Y	Y
52 Hunter	N	Y	Y	N	N	N	Y
53 Davis	Y	Y	Y	Y	N	Y	Y

	635	636	637	638	639	640	641
COLORADO							
1 DeGette	Y	Y	Y	Y	N	Y	Y
2 Polis	Y	Y	Y	Y	N	Y	Y
3 Salazar	Y	Y	Y	Y	N	Y	Y
4 Markey	Y	Y	Y	Y	?	?	Y
5 Lamborn	N	Y	Y	N	N	N	Y
6 Coffman	N	Y	N	N	N	N	Y
7 Perlmutter	Y	Y	Y	N	Y	Y	Y
CONNECTICUT							
1 Larson	Y	Y	Y	Y	N	Y	Y
2 Courtney	Y	Y	Y	Y	N	Y	Y
3 DeLauro	Y	Y	Y	Y	N	Y	Y
4 Himes	Y	Y	Y	N	?	?	Y
5 Murphy	Y	Y	Y	Y	N	Y	Y
DELAWARE							
AL Castle	Y	Y	Y	N	Y	N	Y
FLORIDA							
1 Miller	N	Y	Y	N	N	N	Y
2 Boyd	Y	Y	Y	Y	N	Y	Y
3 Brown	Y	Y	Y	Y	N	Y	Y
4 Crenshaw	N	Y	Y	N	N	Y	Y
5 Brown-Waite	N	Y	Y	N	N	Y	Y
6 Stearns	N	Y	Y	N	N	Y	Y
7 Mica	N	Y	Y	N	N	Y	Y
8 Grayson	Y	Y	Y	Y	N	Y	Y
9 Bilirakis	N	Y	?	N	N	Y	Y
10 Young	N	Y	Y	N	?	?	?
11 Castor	Y	Y	Y	Y	N	Y	Y
12 Putnam	–	+	+	N	N	Y	Y
13 Buchanan	N	Y	Y	N	N	Y	Y
14 Mack	N	Y	Y	N	N	N	Y
15 Posey	N	Y	Y	N	N	N	Y
16 Rooney	N	Y	Y	N	N	Y	Y
17 Meek	Y	Y	Y	Y	?	Y	Y
18 Ros-Lehtinen	N	Y	Y	N	N	Y	Y
19 Deutch	Y	?	Y	Y	N	Y	Y
20 Wasserman Schultz	Y	Y	Y	Y	N	Y	Y
21 Diaz-Balart, L.	N	Y	Y	N	N	Y	Y
22 Klein	Y	Y	Y	Y	N	Y	Y
23 Hastings	Y	Y	Y	Y	N	Y	Y
24 Kosmas	Y	Y	Y	Y	N	Y	Y
25 Diaz-Balart, M.	N	Y	Y	N	N	Y	Y
GEORGIA							
1 Kingston	N	Y	Y	N	N	N	Y
2 Bishop	Y	Y	Y	Y	N	Y	Y
3 Westmoreland	N	Y	Y	N	N	N	Y
4 Johnson	Y	Y	Y	Y	N	Y	Y
5 Lewis	Y	Y	Y	Y	N	Y	Y
6 Price	N	Y	N	N	N	N	Y
7 Linder	N	Y	Y	N	?	N	Y
8 Marshall	N	Y	Y	N	N	Y	Y
9 Graves	N	N	Y	N	N	N	Y
10 Broun	N	N	Y	N	N	N	Y
11 Gingrey	N	P	Y	N	?	Y	Y
12 Barrow	Y	Y	Y	N	Y	Y	Y
13 Scott	Y	Y	Y	Y	N	Y	Y
HAWAII							
1 Djou	N	P	Y	N	N	Y	Y
2 Hirono	Y	Y	Y	Y	N	Y	Y
IDAHO							
1 Minnick	Y	P	Y	Y	N	Y	Y
2 Simpson	N	Y	Y	N	N	?	?
ILLINOIS							
1 Rush	?	Y	Y	Y	N	Y	Y
2 Jackson	Y	Y	Y	Y	N	Y	Y
3 Lipinski	N	N	Y	Y	N	Y	Y
4 Gutierrez	Y	Y	Y	Y	N	Y	?
5 Quigley	Y	Y	Y	Y	N	Y	Y
6 Roskam	N	Y	Y	N	N	Y	Y
7 Davis	?	?	?	Y	N	Y	Y
8 Bean	Y	Y	Y	Y	N	Y	Y
9 Schakowsky	Y	Y	Y	Y	N	Y	Y
10 Vacant							
11 Halvorson	Y	Y	Y	Y	N	Y	Y
12 Costello	Y	Y	Y	Y	N	Y	Y
13 Biggert	N	Y	Y	N	N	Y	Y
14 Foster	Y	Y	Y	Y	?	Y	Y
15 Johnson	N	Y	Y	N	N	Y	Y

KEY **Republicans** Democrats

Y Voted for (yea)	X Paired against	C Voted "present" to avoid possible conflict of interest
# Paired for	– Announced against	
+ Announced for	P Voted "present"	? Did not vote or otherwise make a position known
N Voted against (nay)		

	635	636	637	638	639	640	641
16 **Manzullo**	N	P	Y	N	N	Y	Y
17 Hare	Y	Y	Y	Y	N	Y	Y
18 **Schock**	N	Y	Y	N	N	Y	?
19 **Shimkus**	N	Y	Y	N	N	Y	Y
INDIANA							
1 Visclosky	Y	P	Y	Y	Y	Y	Y
2 Donnelly	Y	Y	Y	Y	N	Y	Y
3 **Stutzman**	N	Y	Y	N	N	N	Y
4 **Buyer**	?	?	Y	N	N	Y	Y
5 **Burton**	N	Y	Y	N	N	Y	Y
6 **Pence**	N	Y	Y	N	N	Y	?
7 Carson	Y	Y	Y	Y	N	Y	Y
8 Ellsworth	Y	Y	Y	Y	?	Y	Y
9 Hill	Y	Y	Y	Y	N	Y	Y
IOWA							
1 Braley	Y	N	Y	Y	N	Y	Y
2 Loebsack	Y	Y	Y	Y	N	Y	Y
3 Boswell	Y	Y	Y	Y	N	Y	Y
4 **Latham**	N	Y	Y	N	N	Y	Y
5 **King**	N	Y	Y	N	N	Y	Y
KANSAS							
1 **Moran**	N	Y	Y	N	N	Y	Y
2 **Jenkins**	N	Y	Y	N	N	Y	Y
3 Moore	Y	Y	Y	Y	N	Y	Y
4 **Tiahrt**	N	Y	Y	N	Y	Y	N
KENTUCKY							
1 **Whitfield**	N	Y	Y	N	?	Y	Y
2 **Guthrie**	N	Y	Y	N	N	Y	Y
3 Yarmuth	Y	Y	Y	Y	N	Y	Y
4 **Davis**	N	Y	Y	N	N	Y	Y
5 **Rogers**	N	Y	Y	N	N	Y	Y
6 Chandler	Y	Y	Y	Y	?	Y	Y
LOUISIANA							
1 **Scalise**	N	Y	Y	N	N	Y	Y
2 **Cao**	N	P	Y	Y	Y	Y	Y
3 Melancon	Y	Y	Y	Y	N	Y	Y
4 **Fleming**	N	Y	Y	N	N	Y	Y
5 **Alexander**	N	Y	Y	N	N	Y	Y
6 **Cassidy**	N	Y	Y	N	N	Y	Y
7 **Boustany**	N	N	Y	N	N	Y	Y
MAINE							
1 Pingree	Y	Y	Y	Y	N	Y	Y
2 Michaud	Y	Y	Y	Y	N	Y	Y
MARYLAND							
1 Kratovil	Y	Y	Y	Y	N	Y	Y
2 Ruppersberger	Y	Y	Y	Y	N	Y	Y
3 Sarbanes	Y	Y	Y	Y	?	Y	Y
4 Edwards	Y	Y	Y	Y	N	Y	Y
5 Hoyer	Y	Y	Y	Y	N	Y	Y
6 **Bartlett**	N	Y	Y	N	N	Y	Y
7 Cummings	Y	Y	Y	Y	N	Y	Y
8 Van Hollen	Y	Y	Y	Y	N	Y	Y
MASSACHUSETTS							
1 Olver	Y	Y	Y	Y	N	Y	Y
2 Neal	Y	Y	Y	Y	N	Y	Y
3 McGovern	Y	Y	Y	Y	N	Y	Y
4 Frank	Y	Y	Y	Y	N	Y	Y
5 Tsongas	Y	Y	Y	Y	N	Y	Y
6 Tierney	Y	Y	Y	Y	N	Y	Y
7 Markey	Y	Y	Y	Y	?	Y	Y
8 Capuano	Y	Y	Y	Y	N	Y	Y
9 Lynch	Y	Y	Y	Y	N	Y	Y
10 Delahunt	Y	Y	Y	Y	?	Y	Y
MICHIGAN							
1 Stupak	Y	Y	Y	Y	N	Y	Y
2 **Hoekstra**	N	Y	Y	N	Y	?	Y
3 **Ehlers**	N	Y	Y	Y	?	Y	Y
4 **Camp**	N	Y	Y	N	N	Y	Y
5 Kildee	Y	Y	Y	Y	N	Y	Y
6 **Upton**	N	Y	Y	N	N	Y	Y
7 Schauer	Y	Y	Y	Y	N	Y	Y
8 **Rogers**	N	Y	Y	N	N	Y	Y
9 Peters	Y	Y	Y	Y	N	?	Y
10 **Miller**	N	Y	Y	N	N	Y	Y
11 **McCotter**	N	Y	Y	N	N	Y	Y
12 Levin	Y	Y	Y	Y	N	Y	Y
13 Kilpatrick	Y	Y	Y	Y	N	?	?
14 Conyers	?	Y	Y	Y	?	Y	Y
15 Dingell	Y	Y	Y	Y	N	Y	Y
MINNESOTA							
1 Walz	Y	Y	Y	Y	N	Y	Y
2 **Kline**	N	Y	Y	N	?	Y	Y
3 **Paulsen**	N	Y	Y	N	N	Y	Y
4 McCollum	Y	Y	Y	Y	N	Y	Y
5 Ellison	Y	Y	Y	Y	N	Y	Y
6 **Bachmann**	N	Y	Y	N	N	Y	Y
7 Peterson	N	Y	Y	N	N	Y	Y
8 Oberstar	Y	Y	Y	Y	N	Y	Y
MISSISSIPPI							
1 Childers	N	Y	Y	N	N	Y	Y
2 Thompson	Y	Y	Y	Y	N	Y	Y
3 **Harper**	N	P	Y	N	N	Y	Y
4 Taylor	N	Y	Y	N	Y	Y	Y
MISSOURI							
1 Clay	Y	Y	Y	Y	N	Y	Y
2 **Akin**	N	P	Y	N	N	N	Y
3 Carnahan	Y	Y	Y	Y	N	Y	Y
4 Skelton	Y	Y	Y	N	?	Y	Y
5 Cleaver	Y	Y	Y	Y	N	Y	Y
6 **Graves**	N	Y	Y	N	N	Y	Y
7 **Blunt**	N	Y	Y	N	N	?	?
8 **Emerson**	N	Y	Y	N	N	Y	Y
9 **Luetkemeyer**	N	Y	Y	N	N	Y	Y
MONTANA							
AL **Rehberg**	N	Y	Y	N	N	Y	Y
NEBRASKA							
1 **Fortenberry**	N	Y	Y	N	N	Y	Y
2 **Terry**	N	P	Y	N	N	Y	Y
3 **Smith**	N	Y	Y	N	N	Y	Y
NEVADA							
1 Berkley	?	Y	Y	Y	N	Y	Y
2 **Heller**	N	N	Y	N	N	Y	Y
3 Titus	Y	Y	Y	Y	N	Y	Y
NEW HAMPSHIRE							
1 Shea-Porter	Y	Y	Y	Y	N	Y	Y
2 Hodes	Y	Y	Y	Y	N	Y	Y
NEW JERSEY							
1 Andrews	Y	Y	Y	Y	N	Y	Y
2 **LoBiondo**	N	Y	Y	N	N	Y	Y
3 Adler	Y	N	Y	Y	N	Y	Y
4 **Smith**	N	Y	Y	N	N	Y	Y
5 **Garrett**	N	Y	Y	N	Y	N	Y
6 Pallone	Y	Y	Y	Y	N	Y	Y
7 **Lance**	N	Y	Y	N	N	Y	Y
8 Pascrell	Y	?	Y	Y	Y	Y	Y
9 Rothman	Y	Y	Y	Y	N	Y	Y
10 Payne	Y	Y	Y	Y	N	Y	Y
11 **Frelinghuysen**	N	Y	Y	N	N	Y	Y
12 Holt	Y	Y	Y	Y	N	Y	Y
13 Sires	Y	Y	Y	Y	N	Y	Y
NEW MEXICO							
1 Heinrich	Y	Y	Y	Y	N	Y	Y
2 Teague	Y	Y	Y	Y	N	Y	Y
3 Luján	Y	Y	Y	Y	N	Y	Y
NEW YORK							
1 Bishop	Y	?	?	Y	N	Y	Y
2 Israel	Y	Y	Y	Y	N	Y	Y
3 **King**	N	Y	Y	N	N	Y	Y
4 McCarthy	+	+	+	+	?	?	?
5 Ackerman	Y	Y	Y	Y	N	Y	Y
6 Meeks	Y	Y	Y	Y	N	Y	Y
7 Crowley	Y	Y	Y	Y	N	Y	Y
8 Nadler	Y	Y	Y	Y	N	Y	Y
9 Weiner	Y	Y	Y	Y	N	Y	Y
10 Towns	Y	Y	Y	Y	N	Y	Y
11 Clarke	Y	Y	Y	Y	N	Y	Y
12 Velázquez	Y	Y	Y	Y	N	Y	Y
13 McMahon	?	?	?	Y	N	Y	Y
14 Maloney	Y	Y	Y	Y	P	Y	Y
15 Rangel	Y	Y	Y	Y	N	Y	Y
16 Serrano	Y	Y	Y	Y	N	Y	Y
17 Engel	Y	Y	Y	Y	N	Y	Y
18 Lowey	Y	Y	Y	Y	N	Y	Y
19 Hall	Y	Y	Y	Y	N	Y	Y
20 Murphy	Y	N	Y	Y	N	Y	Y
21 Tonko	Y	Y	Y	Y	N	Y	Y
22 Hinchey	Y	Y	Y	Y	N	Y	Y
23 Owens	Y	N	Y	Y	N	Y	Y
24 Arcuri	Y	P	Y	Y	N	Y	Y
25 Maffei	Y	P	Y	Y	?	Y	Y
26 **Lee**	N	Y	Y	N	N	Y	Y
27 Higgins	Y	Y	?	Y	N	Y	Y
28 Slaughter	Y	Y	Y	Y	N	Y	Y
29 **Reed**	N	Y	Y	N	N	N	Y
NORTH CAROLINA							
1 Butterfield	Y	Y	Y	Y	N	Y	Y
2 Etheridge	Y	Y	Y	Y	N	Y	Y
3 **Jones**	N	Y	Y	N	N	Y	Y
4 Price	Y	Y	Y	Y	N	Y	Y
5 **Foxx**	N	Y	Y	N	N	Y	Y
6 **Coble**	N	Y	Y	N	N	Y	Y
7 McIntyre	N	Y	Y	N	N	Y	Y
8 Kissell	Y	Y	Y	Y	N	Y	Y
9 **Myrick**	N	Y	Y	N	N	Y	Y
10 **McHenry**	N	Y	Y	N	N	Y	Y
11 Shuler	N	Y	Y	Y	N	?	Y
12 Watt	Y	Y	Y	Y	N	Y	Y
13 Miller	Y	Y	Y	Y	N	Y	Y
NORTH DAKOTA							
AL Pomeroy	Y	Y	Y	Y	?	Y	Y
OHIO							
1 Driehaus	Y	Y	Y	Y	N	Y	Y
2 **Schmidt**	N	Y	Y	N	N	Y	Y
3 **Turner**	N	Y	Y	N	?	Y	Y
4 **Jordan**	N	Y	Y	N	N	Y	Y
5 **Latta**	N	Y	Y	N	N	Y	Y
6 Wilson	Y	Y	Y	Y	N	Y	Y
7 **Austria**	N	Y	Y	N	N	Y	Y
8 **Boehner**	N	Y	?	N	N	?	Y
9 Kaptur	Y	Y	Y	Y	N	Y	Y
10 Kucinich	Y	Y	Y	Y	N	Y	Y
11 Fudge	Y	Y	Y	Y	N	Y	Y
12 **Tiberi**	N	Y	Y	N	N	Y	Y
13 Sutton	Y	Y	Y	Y	N	Y	Y
14 **LaTourette**	N	Y	Y	N	N	Y	Y
15 Kilroy	Y	Y	Y	Y	N	Y	Y
16 Boccieri	Y	Y	Y	Y	N	Y	Y
17 Ryan	Y	Y	Y	Y	N	Y	Y
18 Space	?	?	?	Y	N	Y	Y
OKLAHOMA							
1 **Sullivan**	N	Y	Y	N	N	Y	Y
2 Boren	N	Y	Y	N	N	Y	Y
3 **Lucas**	N	Y	Y	N	N	Y	Y
4 **Cole**	N	Y	Y	N	N	Y	Y
5 **Fallin**	N	Y	Y	N	N	Y	Y
OREGON							
1 Wu	Y	Y	Y	Y	N	Y	Y
2 **Walden**	N	Y	Y	N	N	Y	Y
3 Blumenauer	Y	Y	Y	Y	N	Y	Y
4 DeFazio	Y	P	Y	Y	N	Y	Y
5 Schrader	Y	Y	Y	Y	N	Y	Y
PENNSYLVANIA							
1 Brady	Y	Y	Y	Y	N	Y	Y
2 Fattah	Y	Y	Y	Y	N	Y	Y
3 Dahlkemper	Y	Y	Y	Y	Y	Y	Y
4 Altmire	Y	Y	Y	Y	N	Y	Y
5 **Thompson**	N	Y	Y	N	N	Y	Y
6 **Gerlach**	N	Y	Y	N	N	Y	Y
7 Sestak	Y	Y	Y	Y	N	Y	Y
8 Murphy, P.	Y	Y	Y	Y	N	Y	Y
9 **Shuster**	N	Y	Y	N	N	N	Y
10 Carney	Y	P	Y	Y	N	Y	Y
11 Kanjorski	Y	Y	Y	Y	N	Y	Y
12 Critz	N	Y	Y	N	N	Y	Y
13 Schwartz	Y	Y	Y	Y	N	Y	Y
14 Doyle	Y	Y	Y	Y	N	Y	Y
15 **Dent**	N	Y	Y	Y	N	Y	Y
16 **Pitts**	N	Y	Y	N	N	Y	Y
17 Holden	Y	Y	Y	Y	N	Y	Y
18 **Murphy, T.**	N	Y	Y	N	N	Y	Y
19 **Platts**	N	Y	Y	Y	?	?	?
RHODE ISLAND							
1 Kennedy	Y	Y	Y	Y	N	Y	Y
2 Langevin	Y	Y	Y	Y	N	Y	Y
SOUTH CAROLINA							
1 **Brown**	N	Y	Y	N	?	?	?
2 **Wilson**	N	Y	Y	N	N	N	Y
3 **Barrett**	N	Y	?	N	N	N	Y
4 **Inglis**	N	Y	Y	N	N	Y	Y
5 Spratt	Y	Y	Y	Y	N	Y	Y
6 Clyburn	Y	Y	Y	Y	N	Y	?
SOUTH DAKOTA							
AL Herseth Sandlin	–	+	+	Y	N	Y	Y
TENNESSEE							
1 **Roe**	N	P	Y	N	N	Y	Y
2 **Duncan**	N	Y	Y	N	N	Y	Y
3 **Wamp**	?	?	?	?	?	?	?
4 Davis	Y	Y	Y	N	?	Y	Y
5 Cooper	Y	Y	Y	Y	N	Y	Y
6 Gordon	Y	Y	Y	Y	N	Y	Y
7 **Blackburn**	N	P	Y	N	N	Y	Y
8 Tanner	Y	Y	Y	N	N	Y	Y
9 Cohen	Y	Y	Y	Y	?	Y	Y
TEXAS							
1 **Gohmert**	N	Y	Y	N	Y	Y	Y
2 **Poe**	N	P	Y	N	N	N	N
3 **Johnson, S.**	N	Y	Y	N	N	Y	Y
4 **Hall**	N	Y	Y	N	N	Y	Y
5 **Hensarling**	N	Y	Y	N	N	N	Y
6 **Barton**	N	Y	Y	N	N	Y	Y
7 **Culberson**	N	Y	Y	N	N	Y	Y
8 **Brady**	N	Y	Y	N	N	Y	Y
9 Green, A.	Y	Y	Y	Y	N	Y	Y
10 **McCaul**	N	Y	Y	N	N	Y	Y
11 **Conaway**	N	Y	Y	N	N	Y	Y
12 **Granger**	?	?	?	?	?	?	?
13 **Thornberry**	N	Y	Y	N	N	Y	Y
14 **Paul**	Y	Y	Y	Y	N	N	Y
15 Hinojosa	Y	Y	Y	Y	N	Y	Y
16 Reyes	Y	Y	Y	Y	N	?	Y
17 Edwards	Y	Y	Y	Y	N	Y	Y
18 Jackson Lee	Y	Y	Y	Y	N	Y	Y
19 **Neugebauer**	N	Y	Y	N	N	Y	Y
20 Gonzalez	Y	Y	Y	Y	N	Y	Y
21 **Smith**	N	Y	Y	N	N	Y	Y
22 **Olson**	N	Y	?	N	N	Y	Y
23 Rodriguez	Y	Y	Y	Y	N	Y	Y
24 **Marchant**	?	?	?	?	?	?	?
25 Doggett	Y	Y	Y	Y	N	Y	Y
26 **Burgess**	N	Y	Y	N	N	Y	Y
27 Ortiz	Y	Y	Y	N	N	Y	Y
28 Cuellar	Y	?	Y	Y	N	Y	Y
29 Green, G.	Y	Y	Y	Y	N	Y	Y
30 Johnson, E.	Y	Y	Y	Y	N	?	?
31 **Carter**	N	Y	Y	N	N	Y	Y
32 **Sessions**	N	Y	Y	N	N	Y	Y
UTAH							
1 **Bishop**	N	Y	Y	N	N	Y	Y
2 Matheson	Y	Y	Y	Y	N	Y	Y
3 **Chaffetz**	N	N	Y	N	N	N	Y
VERMONT							
AL Welch	Y	Y	Y	Y	N	Y	Y
VIRGINIA							
1 **Wittman**	N	Y	Y	N	N	Y	Y
2 Nye	Y	Y	Y	Y	N	Y	Y
3 Scott	Y	Y	Y	Y	N	Y	Y
4 **Forbes**	N	Y	Y	N	N	Y	Y
5 Perriello	Y	Y	Y	Y	N	Y	Y
6 **Goodlatte**	N	Y	Y	N	N	Y	Y
7 **Cantor**	N	Y	Y	N	N	Y	Y
8 Moran	Y	Y	Y	Y	N	Y	Y
9 Boucher	Y	Y	Y	Y	N	Y	Y
10 **Wolf**	N	Y	Y	N	N	Y	Y
11 Connolly	Y	Y	Y	Y	N	Y	Y
WASHINGTON							
1 Inslee	Y	Y	Y	Y	N	Y	Y
2 Larsen	Y	N	Y	Y	N	Y	Y
3 Baird	?	?	?	?	?	?	?
4 **Hastings**	N	Y	Y	N	N	Y	Y
5 **McMorris Rodgers**	?	?	?	?	?	?	?
6 Dicks	Y	Y	?	Y	N	Y	Y
7 McDermott	Y	Y	Y	Y	N	Y	Y
8 **Reichert**	N	Y	Y	Y	N	Y	Y
9 Smith	Y	Y	Y	Y	N	Y	Y
WEST VIRGINIA							
1 Mollohan	Y	Y	Y	Y	N	Y	Y
2 **Capito**	N	Y	Y	N	N	Y	Y
3 Rahall	Y	N	Y	N	N	Y	Y
WISCONSIN							
1 **Ryan**	N	Y	Y	N	N	Y	Y
2 Baldwin	Y	Y	Y	Y	N	Y	Y
3 Kind	Y	Y	Y	Y	N	Y	Y
4 Moore	Y	Y	Y	Y	N	Y	Y
5 **Sensenbrenner**	N	Y	Y	N	N	Y	Y
6 **Petri**	N	Y	Y	N	N	Y	Y
7 Obey	Y	Y	Y	Y	N	Y	Y
8 Kagen	Y	Y	Y	Y	N	Y	Y
WYOMING							
AL **Lummis**	N	P	Y	N	N	N	Y
DELEGATES							
Faleomavaega (A.S.)							
Norton (D.C.)							
Bordallo (Guam)							
Sablan (N. Marianas)							
Pierluisi (P.R.)							
Christensen (V.I.)							

IN THE HOUSE | By Vote Number

642. **S 3447. Post-Sept. 11 GI Bill Revisions/Passage.** Filner, D-Calif., motion to suspend the rules and pass the bill that would make changes to the post-Sept. 11 GI bill, which created a program that provides veterans with an educational benefit equal to the highest tuition rate of a public college or university in their state, to allow the benefits to be used at trade and vocational schools. It also would reduce the maximum allowance for tuition and fees to $17,500 from $20,000. Motion agreed to, thus clearing the bill for the president, 409-3: D 245-0; R 164-3. A two-thirds majority of those present and voting (275 in this case) is required for passage under suspension of the rules. Dec. 16, 2010.

643. **HR 4853. Tax Rates Extensions/Modification to the Rule.** Slaughter, D-N.Y., amendment to the rule (H Res 1766) that would provide for House floor consideration of the Senate amendment to the House amendment to the Senate amendment to the bill that would extend the 2001- and 2003-enacted tax cuts for two years, as well as reinstitute the estate tax at a 35 percent rate on the value of estates in excess of $5 million. The Slaughter amendment would provide for a vote on an amendment to strike the estate tax provisions and insert provisions to set the rate at 45 percent on the value of estates in excess of $3.5 million. The amendment also would provide for possible consideration of a motion to concur in the further Senate amendment with the House amendment if the House adopts the estate tax language. It also would provide for a motion to concur without amendment, which would send the measure to the president. Adopted 230-186: D 230-15; R 0-171. Dec. 16, 2010.

644. **HR 4853. Tax Rates Extensions/Rule.** Adoption of the rule (H Res 1766) that would provide for House floor consideration of the Senate amendment to the House amendment to the Senate amendment to the bill that would extend the 2001- and 2003-enacted tax cuts for all taxpayers for two years, as well as reinstitute the estate tax at a 35 percent rate on the value of estates in excess of $5 million, by making in order an amendment that would strike the estate tax provisions and insert language to set the rate at 45 percent on the value of estates in excess of $3.5 million. It would provide for possible consideration of a motion to concur in the further Senate amendment with the House amendment if the House adopts the estate tax language. It also would provide for a motion to concur without amendment, which would send the measure to the president. Adopted 214-201: D 214-31; R 0-170. Dec. 16, 2010.

645. **S 987. Prevention of Forced Child Marriage/Passage.** Berman, D-Calif., motion to suspend the rules and pass the bill that would authorize grants to establish empowerment and awareness programs aimed at eradicating forced child marriages that could be run through multilateral, non-governmental and faith-based organizations in developing countries. Motion rejected 241-166: D 229-9; R 12-157. A two-thirds majority of those present and voting (272 in this case) is required for passage under suspension of the rules. Dec. 16, 2010.

646. **HR 4853. Tax Rates Extensions/Estate Tax.** Levin, D-Mich., amendment that would strike the estate tax provisions in the bill, which would reinstitute the estate tax at a 35 percent rate on the value of estates in excess of $5 million for individuals and $10 million total for couples, and insert provisions that would set the estate tax rate for 2011 and 2012 at 45 percent rate on the value of estates in excess of $3.5 million for individuals and $7 million total for couples. Rejected in Committee of the Whole 194-233: D 194-60; R 0-173. Dec. 16, 2010.

	642	643	644	645	646
ALABAMA					
1 Bonner	Y	N	N	N	N
2 Bright	Y	N	N	Y	N
3 Rogers	Y	N	N	N	N
4 Aderholt	Y	N	N	N	N
5 Griffith	Y	N	N	N	N
6 Bachus	Y	N	N	N	N
7 Davis	?	?	Y	Y	N
ALASKA					
AL Young	N	N	N	N	N
ARIZONA					
1 Kirkpatrick	Y	Y	Y	Y	N
2 Franks	Y	N	N	N	N
3 Shadegg	Y	N	N	N	N
4 Pastor	Y	Y	Y	Y	N
5 Mitchell	Y	Y	Y	Y	N
6 Flake	N	N	N	N	N
7 Grijalva	Y	N	N	Y	Y
8 Giffords	Y	Y	Y	Y	N
ARKANSAS					
1 Berry	?	?	?	?	?
2 Snyder	Y	Y	Y	Y	N
3 Boozman	Y	N	N	N	N
4 Ross	Y	Y	Y	Y	N
CALIFORNIA					
1 Thompson	Y	Y	Y	Y	Y
2 Herger	Y	N	N	N	N
3 Lungren	Y	N	N	N	N
4 McClintock	Y	N	N	N	N
5 Matsui	Y	Y	Y	Y	Y
6 Woolsey	Y	Y	Y	Y	Y
7 Miller, George	Y	Y	Y	Y	Y
8 Pelosi	Y				
9 Lee	Y	Y	Y	Y	Y
10 Garamendi	Y	Y	Y	Y	Y
11 McNerney	Y	Y	Y	Y	Y
12 Speier	Y	?	Y	Y	Y
13 Stark	Y	Y	Y	Y	Y
14 Eshoo	Y	Y	Y	Y	Y
15 Honda	Y	Y	Y	Y	Y
16 Lofgren	Y	Y	N	Y	Y
17 Farr	Y	Y	Y	Y	Y
18 Cardoza	?	Y	Y	Y	N
19 Radanovich	?	?	?	?	N
20 Costa	Y	Y	Y	Y	N
21 Nunes	Y	N	N	N	N
22 McCarthy	Y	N	N	N	N
23 Capps	Y	Y	Y	Y	Y
24 Gallegly	Y	N	N	N	N
25 McKeon	Y	N	N	N	N
26 Dreier	Y	N	N	N	N
27 Sherman	Y	Y	Y	Y	Y
28 Berman	Y	Y	Y	Y	Y
29 Schiff	Y	Y	Y	Y	Y
30 Waxman	Y	Y	Y	Y	Y
31 Becerra	Y	Y	Y	Y	N
32 Chu	Y	Y	Y	Y	Y
33 Watson	Y	Y	Y	Y	Y
34 Roybal-Allard	Y	Y	Y	Y	Y
35 Waters	Y	Y	Y	Y	Y
36 Harman	Y	Y	Y	Y	Y
37 Richardson	Y	Y	Y	Y	Y
38 Napolitano	Y	N	N	Y	Y
39 Sánchez, Linda	Y	Y	Y	Y	Y
40 Royce	Y	N	N	N	N
41 Lewis	Y	N	N	N	N
42 Miller, Gary	Y	N	N	N	N
43 Baca	Y	Y	Y	Y	Y
44 Calvert	Y	N	N	N	N
45 Bono Mack	Y	N	N	N	N
46 Rohrabacher	Y	N	N	N	N
47 Sanchez, Loretta	Y	Y	Y	Y	Y
48 Campbell	Y	N	N	N	N
49 Issa	Y	N	N	N	N
50 Bilbray	Y	N	N	N	N
51 Filner	Y	N	N	Y	Y
52 Hunter	Y	N	N	N	N
53 Davis	Y	Y	Y	Y	Y

	642	643	644	645	646
COLORADO					
1 DeGette	Y	Y	Y	?	Y
2 Polis	Y	Y	Y	Y	Y
3 Salazar	Y	Y	Y	?	N
4 Markey	Y	Y	Y	Y	Y
5 Lamborn	Y	N	N	N	N
6 Coffman	Y	N	N	N	N
7 Perlmutter	Y	Y	Y	Y	Y
CONNECTICUT					
1 Larson	Y	Y	Y	Y	Y
2 Courtney	Y	Y	Y	Y	Y
3 DeLauro	Y	Y	Y	Y	Y
4 Himes	Y	Y	Y	Y	Y
5 Murphy	Y	Y	Y	Y	Y
DELAWARE					
AL Castle	Y	N	N	Y	N
FLORIDA					
1 Miller	Y	N	N	N	N
2 Boyd	Y	N	N	Y	Y
3 Brown	Y	Y	Y	Y	Y
4 Crenshaw	Y	N	N	N	N
5 Brown-Waite	Y	N	N	N	N
6 Stearns	Y	N	N	N	N
7 Mica	Y	N	N	N	N
8 Grayson	Y	Y	N	Y	Y
9 Bilirakis	Y	N	N	N	N
10 Young	?	?	?	?	?
11 Castor	Y	Y	Y	Y	Y
12 Putnam	Y	N	N	N	N
13 Buchanan	Y	N	N	N	N
14 Mack	Y	N	N	N	N
15 Posey	Y	N	N	N	N
16 Rooney	Y	N	N	N	N
17 Meek	Y	Y	Y	Y	Y
18 Ros-Lehtinen	Y	N	N	N	N
19 Deutch	Y	Y	Y	Y	Y
20 Wasserman Schultz	Y	Y	Y	Y	Y
21 Diaz-Balart, L.	Y	N	N	N	N
22 Klein	Y	Y	Y	Y	Y
23 Hastings	Y	Y	Y	Y	Y
24 Kosmas	Y	N	N	Y	N
25 Diaz-Balart, M.	Y	N	N	N	N
GEORGIA					
1 Kingston	Y	N	N	N	N
2 Bishop	Y	Y	Y	Y	N
3 Westmoreland	Y	N	N	N	N
4 Johnson	Y	Y	Y	Y	Y
5 Lewis	Y	Y	Y	Y	Y
6 Price	Y	N	N	N	N
7 Linder	Y	N	N	N	N
8 Marshall	Y	Y	N	Y	N
9 Graves	Y	N	N	N	N
10 Broun	Y	N	N	N	N
11 Gingrey	Y	N	N	N	N
12 Barrow	Y	Y	Y	Y	N
13 Scott	Y	Y	Y	Y	Y
HAWAII					
1 Djou	Y	N	N	N	N
2 Hirono	Y	Y	Y	Y	Y
IDAHO					
1 Minnick	Y	Y	Y	Y	N
2 Simpson	?	N	N	Y	N
ILLINOIS					
1 Rush	Y	Y	Y	?	Y
2 Jackson	Y	Y	Y	Y	Y
3 Lipinski	Y	Y	Y	N	P
4 Gutierrez	Y	Y	Y	Y	Y
5 Quigley	Y	Y	Y	Y	Y
6 Roskam	Y	N	N	N	N
7 Davis	Y	Y	Y	Y	Y
8 Bean	Y	Y	Y	Y	N
9 Schakowsky	Y	Y	Y	Y	Y
10 Vacant					
11 Halvorson	Y	Y	Y	?	N
12 Costello	Y	Y	Y	Y	N
13 Biggert	Y	N	N	N	N
14 Foster	Y	Y	Y	Y	N
15 Johnson	Y	N	N	N	N

KEY   **Republicans**   Democrats

Y	Voted for (yea)	X	Paired against
#	Paired for	–	Announced against
+	Announced for	P	Voted "present"
N	Voted against (nay)		

C   Voted "present" to avoid possible conflict of interest

?   Did not vote or otherwise make a position known

	642	643	644	645	646
16 Manzullo	Y	N	N	N	N
17 Hare	Y	Y	Y	?	N
18 Schock	Y	N	N	Y	N
19 Shimkus	Y	N	N	N	N
INDIANA					
1 Visclosky	Y	Y	Y	Y	Y
2 Donnelly	Y	Y	Y	Y	Y
3 Stutzman	Y	N	N	N	N
4 Buyer	N	?	?	?	N
5 Burton	Y	N	N	N	N
6 Pence	?	N	N	N	N
7 Carson	Y	Y	Y	Y	Y
8 Ellsworth	Y	Y	Y	Y	N
9 Hill	Y	Y	Y	Y	Y
IOWA					
1 Braley	Y	Y	N	Y	Y
2 Loebsack	Y	Y	Y	Y	Y
3 Boswell	Y	Y	Y	Y	Y
4 Latham	Y	N	N	Y	N
5 King	Y	N	N	N	N
KANSAS					
1 Moran	Y	N	N	N	N
2 Jenkins	Y	N	N	N	N
3 Moore	Y	Y	Y	Y	Y
4 Tiahrt	Y	N	N	N	N
KENTUCKY					
1 Whitfield	Y	N	N	N	N
2 Guthrie	Y	N	N	N	N
3 Yarmuth	Y	Y	Y	Y	Y
4 Davis	Y	N	N	N	N
5 Rogers	Y	N	N	N	N
6 Chandler	Y	Y	Y	Y	N
LOUISIANA					
1 Scalise	Y	N	N	N	N
2 Cao	Y	N	N	N	N
3 Melancon	Y	Y	Y	Y	Y
4 Fleming	Y	N	N	N	N
5 Alexander	Y	N	N	N	N
6 Cassidy	Y	N	N	N	N
7 Boustany	Y	N	N	N	N
MAINE					
1 Pingree	Y	Y	Y	Y	Y
2 Michaud	Y	Y	N	Y	Y
MARYLAND					
1 Kratovil	Y	Y	?	Y	N
2 Ruppersberger	Y	Y	Y	Y	N
3 Sarbanes	Y	Y	Y	Y	Y
4 Edwards	Y	Y	Y	Y	Y
5 Hoyer	Y	Y	Y	Y	Y
6 Bartlett	Y	N	N	N	N
7 Cummings	Y	Y	Y	Y	Y
8 Van Hollen	Y	?	?	?	Y
MASSACHUSETTS					
1 Olver	Y	Y	Y	?	Y
2 Neal	Y	Y	Y	Y	Y
3 McGovern	Y	Y	Y	Y	Y
4 Frank	Y	Y	Y	Y	Y
5 Tsongas	Y	Y	Y	Y	Y
6 Tierney	Y	Y	?	Y	Y
7 Markey	Y	Y	Y	Y	Y
8 Capuano	Y	Y	Y	Y	Y
9 Lynch	Y	Y	N	Y	Y
10 Delahunt	Y	Y	Y	Y	Y
MICHIGAN					
1 Stupak	Y	Y	Y	Y	Y
2 Hoekstra	?	N	N	N	N
3 Ehlers	Y	N	N	Y	N
4 Camp	Y	Y	Y	Y	Y
5 Kildee	Y	Y	Y	Y	Y
6 Upton	Y	N	N	Y	N
7 Schauer	Y	Y	Y	Y	Y
8 Rogers	Y	N	N	N	N
9 Peters	Y	Y	Y	Y	Y
10 Miller	Y	N	N	N	N
11 McCotter	Y	Y	Y	Y	N
12 Levin	Y	Y	Y	Y	Y
13 Kilpatrick	?	Y	N	Y	Y
14 Conyers	Y	Y	Y	Y	Y
15 Dingell	Y	Y	Y	Y	Y
MINNESOTA					
1 Walz	Y	Y	Y	Y	N
2 Kline	Y	N	N	N	N
3 Paulsen	Y	N	N	Y	N
4 McCollum	Y	Y	Y	Y	Y
5 Ellison	Y	Y	Y	Y	Y
6 Bachmann	Y	N	N	N	N
7 Peterson	Y	Y	Y	Y	Y
8 Oberstar	Y	Y	Y	Y	Y
MISSISSIPPI					
1 Childers	Y	Y	Y	N	Y
2 Thompson	Y	Y	Y	Y	Y
3 Harper	Y	N	N	N	N
4 Taylor	Y	N	N	N	Y
MISSOURI					
1 Clay	Y	Y	Y	Y	Y
2 Akin	Y	N	N	N	N
3 Carnahan	Y	Y	Y	Y	Y
4 Skelton	Y	N	N	Y	N
5 Cleaver	Y	Y	N	?	Y
6 Graves	Y	N	N	N	N
7 Blunt	Y	N	N	N	N
8 Emerson	Y	N	N	N	N
9 Luetkemeyer	Y	N	N	N	N
MONTANA					
AL Rehberg	Y	N	N	N	N
NEBRASKA					
1 Fortenberry	Y	N	N	N	N
2 Terry	Y	N	N	N	N
3 Smith	Y	N	N	N	N
NEVADA					
1 Berkley	Y	Y	Y	Y	Y
2 Heller	Y	N	N	N	N
3 Titus	Y	Y	Y	Y	Y
NEW HAMPSHIRE					
1 Shea-Porter	Y	Y	Y	Y	Y
2 Hodes	Y	Y	Y	Y	Y
NEW JERSEY					
1 Andrews	Y	Y	Y	Y	Y
2 LoBiondo	Y	N	N	N	N
3 Adler	Y	N	Y	N	Y
4 Smith	Y	N	N	N	N
5 Garrett	Y	N	N	N	N
6 Pallone	Y	Y	Y	Y	Y
7 Lance	Y	N	N	N	N
8 Pascrell	Y	Y	Y	Y	Y
9 Rothman	Y	Y	Y	Y	Y
10 Payne	Y	Y	Y	Y	Y
11 Frelinghuysen	Y	N	N	Y	N
12 Holt	Y	Y	Y	Y	Y
13 Sires	Y	Y	Y	Y	Y
NEW MEXICO					
1 Heinrich	Y	Y	Y	Y	Y
2 Teague	Y	Y	Y	N	N
3 Luján	Y	Y	Y	Y	Y
NEW YORK					
1 Bishop	Y	Y	Y	Y	Y
2 Israel	Y	Y	Y	Y	Y
3 King	Y	N	N	N	N
4 McCarthy	?	?	?	?	?
5 Ackerman	Y	Y	Y	Y	Y
6 Meeks	Y	Y	Y	Y	Y
7 Crowley	Y	Y	Y	Y	Y
8 Nadler	Y	Y	Y	Y	Y
9 Weiner	Y	Y	Y	Y	Y
10 Towns	Y	Y	Y	Y	Y
11 Clarke	Y	Y	Y	Y	Y
12 Velázquez	Y	Y	Y	Y	Y
13 McMahon	Y	Y	N	Y	N
14 Maloney	Y	Y	Y	Y	Y
15 Rangel	Y	Y	Y	?	Y
16 Serrano	Y	Y	Y	Y	Y
17 Engel	Y	Y	Y	Y	Y
18 Lowey	Y	Y	Y	Y	Y
19 Hall	Y	Y	Y	Y	Y
20 Murphy	Y	Y	Y	Y	Y
21 Tonko	Y	Y	Y	Y	Y
22 Hinchey	Y	Y	Y	Y	Y
23 Owens	Y	Y	Y	N	N
24 Arcuri	Y	Y	Y	Y	Y
25 Maffei	Y	Y	Y	Y	Y
26 Lee	Y	N	N	N	N
27 Higgins	Y	Y	Y	Y	Y
28 Slaughter	Y	Y	Y	Y	Y
29 Reed	Y	N	N	N	N
NORTH CAROLINA					
1 Butterfield	Y	Y	Y	Y	Y
2 Etheridge	Y	N	Y	Y	Y
3 Jones	Y	N	N	N	N
4 Price	Y	Y	Y	Y	Y
5 Foxx	Y	N	N	N	N
6 Coble	Y	N	N	N	N
7 McIntyre	Y	N	Y	Y	N
8 Kissell	Y	Y	Y	Y	Y
9 Myrick	Y	N	N	N	N
10 McHenry	Y	N	?	?	N
11 Shuler	Y	Y	Y	Y	N
12 Watt	Y	Y	N	Y	Y
13 Miller	Y	Y	Y	Y	Y
NORTH DAKOTA					
AL Pomeroy	Y	Y	Y	Y	Y
OHIO					
1 Driehaus	Y	Y	Y	Y	Y
2 Schmidt	Y	N	N	N	N
3 Turner	Y	N	N	N	N
4 Jordan	Y	N	N	N	N
5 Latta	Y	N	N	N	N
6 Wilson	Y	Y	Y	Y	Y
7 Austria	Y	N	N	N	N
8 Boehner	?	N	N	N	N
9 Kaptur	Y	Y	Y	N	Y
10 Kucinich	Y	Y	Y	Y	Y
11 Fudge	Y	Y	Y	Y	Y
12 Tiberi	Y	N	N	N	N
13 Sutton	Y	Y	Y	Y	Y
14 LaTourette	Y	N	N	Y	N
15 Kilroy	?	?	?	?	Y
16 Boccieri	Y	Y	Y	Y	Y
17 Ryan	Y	Y	Y	Y	?
18 Space	Y	Y	Y	Y	N
OKLAHOMA					
1 Sullivan	Y	N	N	N	N
2 Boren	Y	Y	Y	Y	N
3 Lucas	Y	N	N	N	N
4 Cole	Y	N	N	N	N
5 Fallin	Y	N	N	N	N
OREGON					
1 Wu	Y	N	N	Y	Y
2 Walden	Y	N	N	N	N
3 Blumenauer	Y	Y	Y	Y	Y
4 DeFazio	Y	N	N	Y	Y
5 Schrader	Y	N	Y	Y	N
PENNSYLVANIA					
1 Brady	Y	Y	Y	Y	Y
2 Fattah	Y	Y	Y	Y	Y
3 Dahlkemper	Y	Y	N	Y	Y
4 Altmire	Y	Y	Y	N	Y
5 Thompson	Y	N	N	N	N
6 Gerlach	Y	N	N	N	?
7 Sestak	Y	Y	Y	Y	Y
8 Murphy, P.	Y	Y	Y	Y	Y
9 Shuster	Y	N	N	N	N
10 Carney	Y	Y	Y	Y	Y
11 Kanjorski	Y	Y	Y	Y	Y
12 Critz	Y	Y	Y	Y	N
13 Schwartz	Y	Y	Y	Y	Y
14 Doyle	Y	Y	Y	Y	Y
15 Dent	Y	N	N	Y	N
16 Pitts	Y	N	N	N	N
17 Holden	Y	Y	N	Y	N
18 Murphy, T.	Y	N	N	N	N
19 Platts	?	N	N	N	N
RHODE ISLAND					
1 Kennedy	Y	Y	Y	Y	Y
2 Langevin	Y	Y	Y	Y	Y
SOUTH CAROLINA					
1 Brown	?	?	?	?	?
2 Wilson	Y	N	N	N	N
3 Barrett	Y	N	N	N	N
4 Inglis	Y	N	N	N	N
5 Spratt	Y	Y	Y	Y	Y
6 Clyburn	?	Y	Y	Y	Y
SOUTH DAKOTA					
AL Herseth Sandlin	Y	Y	Y	N	Y
TENNESSEE					
1 Roe	Y	N	N	N	N
2 Duncan	Y	N	N	N	N
3 Wamp	?	?	?	?	?
4 Davis	Y	Y	N	Y	Y
5 Cooper	Y	Y	N	Y	Y
6 Gordon	Y	Y	Y	Y	Y
7 Blackburn	Y	N	N	N	N
8 Tanner	Y	?	?	?	Y
9 Cohen	Y	Y	Y	Y	Y
TEXAS					
1 Gohmert	Y	N	N	?	N
2 Poe	Y	N	N	N	N
3 Johnson, S.	Y	N	N	N	N
4 Hall	Y	N	N	N	N
5 Hensarling	Y	N	N	N	N
6 Barton	Y	N	N	N	N
7 Culberson	Y	N	N	N	N
8 Brady	Y	N	N	N	N
9 Green, A.	Y	Y	Y	Y	Y
10 McCaul	Y	N	N	N	N
11 Conaway	Y	N	N	N	N
12 Granger	?	?	?	?	?
13 Thornberry	Y	N	N	N	N
14 Paul	Y	N	N	N	N
15 Hinojosa	Y	Y	Y	Y	Y
16 Reyes	Y	Y	Y	Y	Y
17 Edwards	Y	Y	Y	Y	Y
18 Jackson Lee	Y	Y	Y	Y	Y
19 Neugebauer	Y	N	N	N	N
20 Gonzalez	Y	Y	Y	Y	Y
21 Smith	Y	N	N	N	N
22 Olson	Y	N	N	N	N
23 Rodriguez	Y	Y	N	Y	Y
24 Marchant	?	?	?	?	?
25 Doggett	Y	Y	Y	Y	Y
26 Burgess	Y	N	N	Y	Y
27 Ortiz	Y	?	+	+	N
28 Cuellar	Y	Y	Y	Y	Y
29 Green, G.	Y	Y	Y	Y	Y
30 Johnson, E.	?	?	?	?	?
31 Carter	Y	N	N	N	N
32 Sessions	Y	N	N	N	N
UTAH					
1 Bishop	Y	N	N	N	N
2 Matheson	Y	Y	Y	Y	N
3 Chaffetz	Y	N	N	N	N
VERMONT					
AL Welch	Y	Y	Y	Y	Y
VIRGINIA					
1 Wittman	Y	N	N	N	N
2 Nye	Y	Y	Y	Y	N
3 Scott	Y	N	N	Y	Y
4 Forbes	Y	N	N	N	N
5 Perriello	Y	N	N	Y	N
6 Goodlatte	Y	N	N	N	N
7 Cantor	Y	N	N	N	N
8 Moran	Y	Y	Y	Y	Y
9 Boucher	Y	Y	Y	Y	Y
10 Wolf	Y	N	N	N	N
11 Connolly	Y	Y	Y	Y	N
WASHINGTON					
1 Inslee	Y	Y	Y	Y	Y
2 Larsen	Y	Y	Y	Y	Y
3 Baird	?	Y	Y	Y	Y
4 Hastings	Y	N	N	N	N
5 McMorris Rodgers	?	?	?	?	N
6 Dicks	Y	Y	Y	Y	Y
7 McDermott	Y	Y	Y	Y	Y
8 Reichert	Y	N	N	N	N
9 Smith	Y	Y	Y	Y	Y
WEST VIRGINIA					
1 Mollohan	Y	Y	Y	Y	N
2 Capito	Y	N	N	N	N
3 Rahall	Y	Y	Y	N	N
WISCONSIN					
1 Ryan	Y	N	N	N	N
2 Baldwin	Y	Y	Y	Y	Y
3 Kind	Y	Y	Y	Y	Y
4 Moore	?	Y	Y	Y	Y
5 Sensenbrenner	Y	N	N	N	N
6 Petri	Y	N	N	N	N
7 Obey	Y	N	Y	Y	N
8 Kagen	Y	Y	Y	Y	Y
WYOMING					
AL Lummis	Y	N	N	N	N
DELEGATES					
Faleomavaega (A.S.)					Y
Norton (D.C.)					Y
Bordallo (Guam)					Y
Sablan (N. Marianas)					Y
Pierluisi (P.R.)					?
Christensen (V.I.)					Y

IN THE HOUSE | By Vote Number

647. **HR 4853. Tax Rates Extensions/Motion to Concur.** Levin, D-Mich., motion to concur in the Senate amendment to the House amendment to the Senate amendment to the bill that would extend the 2001- and 2003-enacted tax cuts for all taxpayers for two years and revive the lapsed estate tax, setting the tax rate at 35 percent on the value of estates in excess of $5 million for 2011 and 2012. It would also continue expanded unemployment insurance benefits for 13 months and cut the employee portion of the Social Security tax by 2 percentage points. Motion agreed to, thus clearing the bill for the president, 277-148: D 139-112; R 138-36. A "yea" was a vote in support of the president's position. Dec. 17, 2010 (in the session that began in the Congressional Record dated Dec. 16, 2010).

648. **H Res 1377. Tribute to Norman Y. Mineta/Adoption.** Faleomavaega, D-A.S., motion to suspend the rules and adopt the resolution that would honor former Rep. (1975-95), Commerce secretary (2000-01) and Transportation secretary (2001-06) Norman Y. Mineta, D-Calif., for his contributions to the Asian-American and Pacific Islander communities. Motion agreed to 384-0: D 224-0; R 160-0. A two-thirds majority of those present and voting (256 in this case) is required for adoption under suspension of the rules. Dec. 17, 2010.

649. **HR 1107. Public Contracts/Motion to Concur.** Chu, D-Calif., motion to suspend the rules and concur in the Senate amendments to the bill that would revise, codify and enact certain laws related to public contracts as Title 41, U.S. Code, "Public Contracts." Motion agreed to, 385-0: D 226-0; R 159-0. A two-thirds majority of those present and voting (257 in this case) is required for passage under suspension of the rules. Dec. 17, 2010.

650. **HR 6523. Fiscal 2011 Defense Authorization/Passage.** Skelton, D-Mo., motion to suspend the rules and pass the bill that would authorize $725 billion for defense programs in fiscal 2011. The measure would include $158.7 billion for the wars in Afghanistan and Iraq and the general war on terrorism; $10 billion for missile defense; and $19 billion for military construction, base realignment and closure, and family housing. It would authorize a 1.4 percent pay raise for military personnel and extend Tricare coverage to dependent adult children until age 26. It also would prohibit the Defense secretary from using funds authorized by the bill in fiscal 2011 from being used to transfer, release or assist in the transfer of any detainee who is or was held on or after Jan. 20, 2009, at Guantánamo Bay, Cuba. Motion agreed to 341-48: D 187-42; R 154-6. A two-thirds majority of those present and voting (260 in this case) is required for passage under suspension of the rules. Dec. 17, 2010.

651. **HR 628. Patent Pilot Program for Judges/Motion to Concur.** Chu, D-Calif., motion to suspend the rules and concur in the Senate amendment to the bill that would establish a pilot program for judges in certain district courts to hear patent cases. Motion agreed to, 371-1: D 218-0; R 153-1. A two-thirds majority of those present and voting (248 in this case) is required for passage under suspension of the rules. Dec. 17, 2010.

652. **H Con Res 336. Adjournment/Adoption.** Adoption of the concurrent resolution that would provide for the adjournment of the House and Senate sine die or until the Speaker of the House and the majority leader of the Senate, acting in consultation with the minority leaders of each chamber, notify members to reassemble at a designated time and place. Adopted 196-153: D 185-13; R 11-140. Dec. 17, 2010.

	647	648	649	650	651	652
ALABAMA						
1 **Bonner**	Y	Y	Y	Y	Y	N
2 Bright	Y	Y	Y	Y	Y	Y
3 **Rogers**	N	Y	Y	Y	Y	N
4 **Aderholt**	Y	Y	Y	Y	N	N
5 **Griffith**	Y	?	?	?	?	?
6 **Bachus**	Y	Y	Y	Y	Y	N
7 Davis	Y	?	?	?	?	?
ALASKA						
AL **Young**	Y	Y	Y	Y	Y	Y
ARIZONA						
1 Kirkpatrick	Y	Y	Y	Y	Y	Y
2 **Franks**	N	Y	Y	Y	?	N
3 **Shadegg**	N	Y	Y	Y	N	N
4 Pastor	Y	Y	Y	Y	Y	Y
5 Mitchell	Y	Y	Y	Y	Y	?
6 **Flake**	N	Y	Y	N	N	N
7 Grijalva	N	Y	Y	Y	Y	Y
8 Giffords	Y	Y	Y	Y	Y	Y
ARKANSAS						
1 Berry	?	?	?	?	?	?
2 Snyder	Y	Y	Y	Y	Y	Y
3 **Boozman**	Y	Y	Y	Y	Y	N
4 Ross	Y	Y	Y	Y	Y	Y
CALIFORNIA						
1 Thompson	N	Y	Y	N	Y	Y
2 **Herger**	Y	Y	Y	Y	?	N
3 **Lungren**	Y	Y	Y	Y	Y	N
4 **McClintock**	Y	Y	Y	Y	Y	N
5 Matsui	N	Y	Y	N	Y	Y
6 Woolsey	N	Y	Y	N	Y	Y
7 Miller, George	N	Y	Y	N	Y	Y
8 Pelosi						
9 Lee	N	Y	Y	N	Y	Y
10 Garamendi	N	Y	Y	N	Y	Y
11 McNerney	Y	Y	Y	Y	Y	Y
12 Speier	N	?	?	?	?	?
13 Stark	N	Y	Y	N	Y	?
14 Eshoo	N	Y	Y	N	Y	Y
15 Honda	N	Y	Y	N	Y	Y
16 Lofgren	N	Y	Y	N	Y	Y
17 Farr	N	Y	Y	N	Y	Y
18 Cardoza	Y	?	?	?	?	?
19 **Radanovich**	Y	?	?	?	?	?
20 Costa	Y	Y	Y	Y	Y	Y
21 **Nunes**	Y	Y	Y	Y	Y	N
22 **McCarthy**	Y	Y	Y	Y	Y	N
23 Capps	Y	Y	Y	Y	Y	Y
24 **Gallegly**	Y	?	?	?	?	?
25 **McKeon**	Y	Y	Y	Y	Y	N
26 **Dreier**	Y	Y	Y	Y	Y	N
27 Sherman	Y	Y	Y	Y	Y	Y
28 Berman	Y	Y	Y	Y	Y	Y
29 Schiff	Y	Y	Y	Y	Y	Y
30 Waxman	Y	Y	Y	N	Y	Y
31 Becerra	N	Y	Y	Y	?	Y
32 Chu	N	Y	Y	N	Y	Y
33 Watson	N	Y	Y	N	Y	Y
34 Roybal-Allard	N	Y	Y	Y	Y	Y
35 Waters	N	?	?	?	?	?
36 Harman	Y	Y	Y	Y	Y	?
37 Richardson	Y	Y	Y	Y	Y	Y
38 Napolitano	N	?	?	?	?	?
39 Sánchez, Linda	N	Y	Y	Y	Y	Y
40 **Royce**	Y	Y	Y	Y	Y	N
41 **Lewis**	Y	Y	Y	Y	Y	N
42 **Miller, Gary**	Y	?	?	?	?	?
43 Baca	Y	Y	Y	Y	?	?
44 **Calvert**	Y	Y	Y	Y	Y	?
45 **Bono Mack**	Y	Y	Y	Y	Y	N
46 **Rohrabacher**	Y	Y	Y	Y	Y	N
47 Sanchez, Loretta	N	Y	Y	Y	Y	Y
48 **Campbell**	N	Y	Y	N	Y	Y
49 **Issa**	Y	Y	Y	Y	Y	N
50 **Bilbray**	Y	Y	Y	Y	Y	N
51 Filner	N	Y	Y	N	Y	Y
52 **Hunter**	Y	Y	Y	Y	Y	N
53 Davis	Y	Y	Y	Y	Y	+

	647	648	649	650	651	652
COLORADO						
1 DeGette	N	?	?	?	?	?
2 Polis	Y	Y	Y	Y	Y	Y
3 Salazar	Y	?	?	?	?	?
4 Markey	Y	Y	Y	Y	Y	Y
5 **Lamborn**	N	Y	Y	Y	Y	N
6 **Coffman**	Y	Y	Y	Y	Y	N
7 Perlmutter	N	Y	Y	Y	?	Y
CONNECTICUT						
1 Larson	N	Y	Y	Y	Y	Y
2 Courtney	Y	Y	Y	Y	?	Y
3 DeLauro	N	Y	Y	Y	Y	Y
4 Himes	Y	Y	Y	Y	Y	?
5 Murphy	N	Y	Y	Y	Y	Y
DELAWARE						
AL **Castle**	Y	Y	Y	Y	Y	Y
FLORIDA						
1 **Miller**	Y	Y	Y	Y	Y	N
2 Boyd	N	?	?	?	?	?
3 Brown	N	Y	Y	Y	Y	Y
4 **Crenshaw**	Y	Y	Y	Y	Y	N
5 **Brown-Waite**	Y	?	?	?	?	?
6 **Stearns**	Y	Y	Y	Y	Y	N
7 **Mica**	Y	Y	Y	Y	Y	N
8 Grayson	N	?	?	?	?	?
9 **Bilirakis**	N	Y	Y	Y	?	N
10 **Young**	?	?	?	?	?	?
11 Castor	Y	Y	Y	Y	Y	Y
12 **Putnam**	Y	Y	Y	Y	Y	N
13 **Buchanan**	Y	Y	Y	Y	Y	N
14 **Mack**	N	Y	Y	Y	Y	N
15 **Posey**	Y	Y	Y	Y	Y	N
16 **Rooney**	Y	Y	Y	Y	Y	N
17 Meek	Y	?	?	?	?	Y
18 **Ros-Lehtinen**	Y	Y	Y	Y	Y	N
19 Deutch	Y	Y	Y	Y	Y	Y
20 Wasserman Schultz	Y	Y	Y	Y	Y	?
21 **Diaz-Balart, L.**	Y	Y	Y	Y	Y	?
22 Klein	Y	Y	Y	Y	Y	Y
23 Hastings	N	Y	Y	Y	Y	Y
24 Kosmas	Y	Y	Y	Y	Y	Y
25 **Diaz-Balart, M.**	Y	Y	Y	Y	Y	Y
GEORGIA						
1 **Kingston**	N	Y	Y	Y	Y	N
2 Bishop	Y	Y	Y	Y	Y	?
3 **Westmoreland**	Y	Y	Y	Y	Y	N
4 Johnson	Y	?	Y	Y	Y	Y
5 Lewis	N	?	Y	N	Y	Y
6 **Price**	Y	Y	Y	Y	Y	N
7 **Linder**	N	Y	Y	Y	?	N
8 Marshall	Y	Y	Y	Y	Y	Y
9 **Graves**	N	Y	Y	Y	Y	N
10 **Broun**	N	Y	Y	Y	Y	N
11 **Gingrey**	N	Y	Y	Y	Y	N
12 Barrow	Y	Y	Y	Y	Y	?
13 Scott	Y	Y	Y	Y	Y	Y
HAWAII						
1 **Djou**	Y	?	?	?	?	?
2 Hirono	N	Y	Y	Y	Y	Y
IDAHO						
1 Minnick	Y	Y	Y	Y	Y	Y
2 **Simpson**	N	Y	Y	Y	Y	N
ILLINOIS						
1 Rush	N	Y	Y	Y	Y	Y
2 Jackson	N	Y	Y	N	Y	Y
3 Lipinski	Y	Y	Y	Y	Y	?
4 Gutierrez	Y	Y	Y	Y	Y	Y
5 Quigley	Y	?	?	?	?	?
6 **Roskam**	Y	Y	Y	Y	?	N
7 Davis	Y	Y	Y	Y	Y	?
8 Bean	Y	Y	Y	Y	Y	?
9 Schakowsky	Y	Y	Y	Y	Y	Y
10 Vacant						
11 Halvorson	Y	Y	Y	Y	Y	Y
12 Costello	N	Y	Y	Y	Y	Y
13 **Biggert**	Y	Y	Y	Y	Y	N
14 Foster	Y	Y	Y	Y	Y	Y
15 **Johnson**	Y	Y	N	Y	N	Y

	647	648	649	650	651	652
16 **Manzullo**	Y	Y	Y	Y	Y	N
17 Hare	Y	Y	Y	Y	Y	Y
18 **Schock**	Y	Y	Y	Y	Y	N
19 **Shimkus**	Y	Y	Y	Y	Y	N
INDIANA						
1 Visclosky	N	Y	Y	Y	Y	Y
2 Donnelly	Y	Y	Y	Y	Y	N
3 **Stutzman**	Y	Y	Y	Y	Y	N
4 **Buyer**	Y	Y	?	Y	Y	N
5 **Burton**	Y	Y	Y	Y	Y	N
6 **Pence**	N	Y	Y	Y	Y	N
7 Carson	Y	Y	Y	Y	Y	?
8 Ellsworth	Y	Y	Y	Y	Y	N
9 Hill	Y	Y	Y	Y	Y	Y
IOWA						
1 Braley	N	?	Y	Y	Y	Y
2 Loebsack	Y	Y	Y	Y	Y	Y
3 Boswell	Y	Y	Y	Y	Y	Y
4 **Latham**	Y	Y	Y	Y	Y	?
5 **King**	N	Y	Y	Y	Y	N
KANSAS						
1 **Moran**	N	?	?	?	?	?
2 **Jenkins**	Y	Y	Y	Y	Y	N
3 Moore	Y	Y	Y	Y	?	Y
4 **Tiahrt**	Y	Y	Y	Y	Y	N
KENTUCKY						
1 **Whitfield**	Y	Y	Y	Y	Y	Y
2 **Guthrie**	Y	Y	Y	Y	Y	N
3 Yarmuth	N	Y	Y	Y	Y	Y
4 **Davis**	Y	Y	Y	Y	Y	N
5 **Rogers**	Y	Y	Y	Y	Y	N
6 Chandler	Y	Y	Y	Y	Y	Y
LOUISIANA						
1 **Scalise**	Y	Y	Y	Y	Y	N
2 **Cao**	Y	Y	Y	Y	Y	N
3 Melancon	N	Y	Y	Y	?	Y
4 **Fleming**	N	Y	Y	Y	Y	N
5 **Alexander**	Y	Y	Y	Y	Y	N
6 **Cassidy**	Y	Y	Y	Y	Y	N
7 **Boustany**	Y	Y	Y	Y	Y	?
MAINE						
1 Pingree	N	Y	Y	N	Y	?
2 Michaud	N	Y	Y	N	Y	N
MARYLAND						
1 Kratovil	Y	Y	Y	Y	Y	Y
2 Ruppersberger	Y	Y	Y	Y	Y	Y
3 Sarbanes	Y	Y	Y	Y	Y	Y
4 Edwards	N	Y	Y	Y	Y	Y
5 Hoyer	Y	Y	Y	Y	Y	Y
6 **Bartlett**	Y	Y	Y	Y	Y	N
7 Cummings	N	Y	Y	Y	Y	Y
8 Van Hollen	N	Y	Y	Y	Y	Y
MASSACHUSETTS						
1 Olver	N	Y	Y	N	Y	Y
2 Neal	N	Y	Y	Y	Y	Y
3 McGovern	N	Y	Y	Y	Y	Y
4 Frank	N	Y	Y	Y	Y	Y
5 Tsongas	Y	Y	Y	Y	Y	Y
6 Tierney	N	Y	Y	N	Y	Y
7 Markey	N	Y	Y	Y	Y	Y
8 Capuano	N	Y	Y	N	Y	Y
9 Lynch	N	Y	Y	Y	Y	Y
10 Delahunt	Y	?	?	?	?	?
MICHIGAN						
1 Stupak	N	?	?	?	?	?
2 **Hoekstra**	N	Y	Y	Y	Y	N
3 **Ehlers**	Y	Y	Y	N	Y	Y
4 **Camp**	Y	Y	Y	Y	Y	?
5 Kildee	Y	Y	Y	Y	Y	Y
6 **Upton**	Y	Y	Y	Y	Y	N
7 Schauer	Y	Y	Y	Y	Y	Y
8 **Rogers**	Y	Y	Y	Y	Y	N
9 Peters	Y	Y	Y	Y	Y	?
10 **Miller**	Y	Y	Y	Y	Y	N
11 **McCotter**	N	Y	Y	Y	Y	N
12 Levin	Y	Y	Y	Y	Y	Y
13 Kilpatrick	N	?	?	?	?	?
14 Conyers	N	Y	Y	N	Y	Y
15 Dingell	Y	Y	Y	Y	Y	Y
MINNESOTA						
1 Walz	Y	Y	Y	Y	Y	Y
2 **Kline**	Y	Y	Y	Y	Y	N
3 **Paulsen**	Y	Y	Y	Y	Y	N
4 McCollum	N	Y	Y	Y	Y	Y

	647	648	649	650	651	652
5 Ellison	N	Y	Y	N	Y	Y
6 **Bachmann**	N	Y	Y	Y	Y	N
7 Peterson	Y	Y	Y	Y	Y	Y
8 Oberstar	Y	Y	Y	Y	Y	Y
MISSISSIPPI						
1 Childers	Y	Y	Y	Y	Y	?
2 Thompson	N	Y	Y	Y	Y	Y
3 **Harper**	Y	Y	Y	Y	Y	N
4 Taylor	N	Y	Y	Y	?	N
MISSOURI						
1 Clay	Y	Y	Y	Y	Y	?
2 **Akin**	Y	Y	Y	Y	Y	N
3 Carnahan	Y	Y	Y	Y	Y	Y
4 Skelton	Y	Y	Y	Y	Y	Y
5 Cleaver	N	Y	?	Y	Y	Y
6 **Graves**	Y	Y	Y	Y	Y	N
7 **Blunt**	Y	Y	Y	Y	Y	N
8 **Emerson**	Y	Y	Y	Y	Y	N
9 **Luetkemeyer**	Y	Y	Y	Y	Y	N
MONTANA						
AL **Rehberg**	N	Y	Y	Y	Y	N
NEBRASKA						
1 **Fortenberry**	N	Y	Y	Y	Y	N
2 **Terry**	Y	Y	Y	Y	Y	N
3 **Smith**	Y	Y	Y	Y	Y	N
NEVADA						
1 Berkley	Y	Y	Y	Y	Y	?
2 **Heller**	Y	Y	Y	Y	Y	N
3 Titus	Y	Y	Y	Y	Y	Y
NEW HAMPSHIRE						
1 Shea-Porter	N	?	Y	Y	Y	N
2 Hodes	Y	?	?	?	?	?
NEW JERSEY						
1 Andrews	Y	Y	Y	Y	Y	?
2 **LoBiondo**	Y	Y	Y	Y	Y	N
3 Adler	Y	Y	Y	Y	Y	Y
4 **Smith**	Y	Y	Y	?	Y	N
5 **Garrett**	N	Y	Y	Y	Y	Y
6 Pallone	Y	Y	Y	Y	Y	Y
7 **Lance**	Y	Y	Y	Y	Y	N
8 Pascrell	Y	Y	Y	Y	Y	Y
9 Rothman	Y	Y	Y	Y	Y	?
10 Payne	N	Y	Y	N	Y	Y
11 **Frelinghuysen**	Y	Y	Y	Y	Y	N
12 Holt	N	Y	Y	Y	Y	Y
13 Sires	Y	Y	Y	Y	Y	Y
NEW MEXICO						
1 Heinrich	N	Y	Y	Y	Y	Y
2 Teague	Y	Y	Y	Y	Y	Y
3 Luján	N	Y	Y	Y	Y	Y
NEW YORK						
1 Bishop	Y	Y	Y	Y	Y	N
2 Israel	Y	Y	Y	Y	Y	Y
3 **King**	Y	Y	Y	Y	Y	N
4 McCarthy	+	?	?	?	?	?
5 Ackerman	N	Y	Y	Y	Y	?
6 Meeks	Y	Y	Y	Y	Y	?
7 Crowley	Y	Y	Y	Y	Y	Y
8 Nadler	N	Y	Y	N	Y	Y
9 Weiner	N	Y	Y	Y	Y	Y
10 Towns	N	Y	Y	N	Y	Y
11 Clarke	N	Y	Y	N	Y	Y
12 Velázquez	N	Y	Y	N	Y	Y
13 McMahon	Y	Y	Y	Y	Y	Y
14 Maloney	Y	Y	Y	Y	Y	Y
15 Rangel	N	Y	Y	Y	Y	Y
16 Serrano	N	Y	Y	N	Y	Y
17 Engel	N	Y	Y	Y	Y	Y
18 Lowey	Y	Y	Y	Y	Y	Y
19 Hall	Y	Y	Y	N	Y	Y
20 Murphy	Y	Y	Y	Y	Y	?
21 Tonko	N	Y	Y	Y	Y	Y
22 Hinchey	N	Y	Y	Y	Y	Y
23 Owens	Y	Y	Y	Y	Y	N
24 Arcuri	Y	Y	Y	Y	Y	?
25 Maffei	Y	Y	Y	Y	Y	Y
26 **Lee**	Y	Y	Y	Y	Y	N
27 Higgins	Y	Y	Y	Y	Y	Y
28 Slaughter	N	Y	Y	N	Y	Y
29 **Reed**	Y	Y	Y	Y	Y	N
NORTH CAROLINA						
1 Butterfield	N	Y	?	Y	?	Y
2 Etheridge	Y	Y	Y	Y	Y	Y
3 **Jones**	Y	?	?	?	?	?
4 Price	Y	Y	Y	Y	Y	Y

	647	648	649	650	651	652
5 **Foxx**	N	Y	Y	Y	Y	N
6 **Coble**	Y	Y	Y	Y	Y	N
7 McIntyre	Y	Y	Y	Y	Y	?
8 Kissell	Y	Y	Y	Y	Y	Y
9 **Myrick**	Y	Y	Y	Y	Y	N
10 **McHenry**	Y	Y	Y	Y	Y	N
11 Shuler	Y	Y	Y	Y	Y	Y
12 Watt	Y	Y	Y	N	Y	Y
13 Miller	N	Y	Y	Y	Y	Y
NORTH DAKOTA						
AL Pomeroy	N	Y	Y	Y	?	?
OHIO						
1 Driehaus	Y	Y	Y	Y	Y	Y
2 **Schmidt**	N	Y	Y	Y	Y	N
3 **Turner**	Y	Y	Y	Y	Y	N
4 **Jordan**	N	Y	Y	Y	Y	Y
5 **Latta**	Y	Y	Y	Y	Y	N
6 Wilson	Y	Y	Y	Y	Y	Y
7 **Austria**	Y	Y	Y	Y	Y	N
8 **Boehner**	Y	Y	Y	Y	?	N
9 Kaptur	N	Y	Y	Y	Y	Y
10 Kucinich	Y	Y	Y	N	Y	Y
11 Fudge	N	Y	Y	N	Y	Y
12 **Tiberi**	Y	Y	Y	Y	Y	N
13 Sutton	Y	Y	Y	Y	Y	Y
14 **LaTourette**	Y	Y	Y	Y	Y	N
15 Kilroy	N	Y	Y	Y	Y	Y
16 Boccieri	Y	Y	Y	Y	Y	Y
17 Ryan	Y	Y	Y	Y	Y	Y
18 Space	Y	Y	Y	Y	Y	Y
OKLAHOMA						
1 **Sullivan**	N	Y	Y	Y	Y	N
2 Boren	Y	Y	Y	Y	Y	Y
3 **Lucas**	Y	Y	Y	Y	Y	N
4 **Cole**	Y	Y	?	Y	Y	N
5 **Fallin**	Y	?	?	?	?	?
OREGON						
1 Wu	N	Y	Y	Y	Y	Y
2 **Walden**	Y	Y	Y	Y	Y	N
3 Blumenauer	N	Y	Y	N	Y	Y
4 DeFazio	N	Y	Y	N	Y	Y
5 Schrader	N	Y	Y	Y	Y	Y
PENNSYLVANIA						
1 Brady	Y	?	?	?	?	?
2 Fattah	Y	Y	Y	Y	Y	Y
3 Dahlkemper	N	Y	Y	Y	Y	Y
4 Altmire	Y	Y	Y	Y	Y	Y
5 **Thompson**	Y	Y	Y	Y	Y	N
6 **Gerlach**	Y	Y	Y	Y	Y	N
7 Sestak	Y	?	?	Y	Y	N
8 Murphy, P.	Y	Y	Y	Y	Y	?
9 **Shuster**	Y	Y	Y	Y	Y	N
10 Carney	Y	?	?	?	?	N
11 Kanjorski	N	Y	Y	Y	Y	Y
12 Critz	Y	Y	Y	Y	Y	Y
13 Schwartz	Y	Y	Y	Y	Y	?
14 Doyle	Y	Y	Y	Y	?	Y
15 **Dent**	Y	Y	Y	Y	Y	N
16 **Pitts**	Y	Y	Y	Y	Y	N
17 Holden	Y	Y	Y	Y	Y	Y
18 **Murphy, T.**	Y	Y	Y	Y	Y	?
19 **Platts**	Y	Y	Y	Y	Y	N
RHODE ISLAND						
1 Kennedy	Y	Y	Y	Y	Y	Y
2 Langevin	Y	Y	Y	Y	Y	Y
SOUTH CAROLINA						
1 **Brown**	?	?	?	?	?	?
2 **Wilson**	N	Y	Y	Y	Y	N
3 **Barrett**	Y	?	?	?	?	?
4 **Inglis**	Y	Y	Y	Y	Y	N
5 Spratt	Y	Y	Y	Y	Y	Y
6 Clyburn	N	Y	Y	Y	Y	Y
SOUTH DAKOTA						
AL Herseth Sandlin	Y	Y	Y	Y	Y	Y
TENNESSEE						
1 **Roe**	Y	Y	Y	Y	Y	N
2 **Duncan**	Y	Y	Y	N	Y	N
3 **Wamp**	?	?	?	?	?	?
4 Davis	Y	?	?	?	?	?
5 Cooper	N	Y	Y	Y	Y	Y
6 Gordon	Y	Y	Y	Y	?	Y
7 **Blackburn**	Y	Y	Y	Y	Y	N
8 Tanner	N	Y	Y	Y	Y	Y
9 Cohen	N	Y	Y	N	Y	Y

	647	648	649	650	651	652
TEXAS						
1 **Gohmert**	N	Y	Y	Y	Y	N
2 **Poe**	N	Y	Y	Y	Y	N
3 **Johnson, S.**	Y	?	?	?	?	?
4 **Hall**	Y	Y	Y	Y	Y	N
5 **Hensarling**	Y	Y	Y	Y	Y	N
6 **Barton**	N	?	?	?	?	?
7 **Culberson**	Y	Y	Y	Y	Y	?
8 **Brady**	Y	Y	Y	Y	Y	N
9 Green, A.	Y	Y	Y	Y	?	+
10 **McCaul**	Y	?	Y	Y	Y	N
11 **Conaway**	Y	Y	Y	Y	Y	N
12 **Granger**	+	?	?	?	?	?
13 **Thornberry**	Y	Y	Y	Y	Y	N
14 **Paul**	Y	Y	Y	N	N	?
15 Hinojosa	Y	?	?	?	?	?
16 Reyes	N	?	?	?	?	?
17 Edwards	Y	Y	Y	Y	Y	Y
18 Jackson Lee	N	Y	Y	Y	Y	Y
19 **Neugebauer**	Y	Y	Y	Y	Y	N
20 Gonzalez	Y	Y	Y	Y	Y	Y
21 **Smith**	Y	Y	Y	Y	Y	N
22 **Olson**	Y	Y	Y	Y	Y	N
23 Rodriguez	N	Y	Y	Y	Y	?
24 **Marchant**	–	?	?	?	?	?
25 Doggett	N	Y	Y	Y	Y	Y
26 **Burgess**	N	Y	Y	Y	Y	N
27 Ortiz	N	?	?	?	?	?
28 Cuellar	Y	Y	Y	Y	Y	Y
29 Green, G.	N	Y	Y	Y	Y	Y
30 Johnson, E.	?	?	?	?	?	?
31 **Carter**	Y	Y	Y	Y	Y	N
32 **Sessions**	Y	Y	Y	Y	Y	N
UTAH						
1 **Bishop**	Y	Y	Y	Y	Y	N
2 Matheson	Y	Y	Y	Y	Y	Y
3 **Chaffetz**	N	Y	Y	Y	Y	N
VERMONT						
AL Welch	N	Y	Y	N	Y	Y
VIRGINIA						
1 **Wittman**	Y	Y	Y	Y	Y	?
2 Nye	Y	Y	Y	Y	Y	N
3 Scott	N	Y	Y	Y	Y	Y
4 **Forbes**	N	Y	Y	Y	?	N
5 Perriello	Y	Y	Y	Y	Y	N
6 **Goodlatte**	Y	Y	Y	Y	Y	N
7 **Cantor**	Y	Y	Y	Y	Y	N
8 Moran	N	Y	Y	Y	Y	N
9 Boucher	Y	Y	Y	Y	Y	Y
10 **Wolf**	N	Y	Y	Y	Y	N
11 Connolly	Y	Y	Y	Y	Y	N
WASHINGTON						
1 Inslee	N	Y	Y	Y	Y	Y
2 Larsen	Y	Y	Y	Y	Y	Y
3 Baird	N	?	?	?	?	?
4 **Hastings**	Y	Y	Y	Y	Y	N
5 **McMorris Rodgers**	Y	+	+	+	+	?
6 Dicks	Y	Y	Y	Y	Y	Y
7 McDermott	N	Y	Y	Y	Y	Y
8 **Reichert**	Y	Y	Y	Y	Y	N
9 Smith	N	Y	Y	Y	Y	Y
WEST VIRGINIA						
1 Mollohan	Y	Y	Y	Y	Y	Y
2 **Capito**	Y	Y	Y	Y	Y	N
3 Rahall	Y	Y	Y	Y	Y	Y
WISCONSIN						
1 **Ryan**	Y	Y	Y	Y	Y	N
2 Baldwin	N	Y	Y	N	Y	Y
3 Kind	N	Y	Y	Y	Y	?
4 Moore	N	Y	Y	N	Y	Y
5 **Sensenbrenner**	Y	Y	Y	Y	Y	Y
6 **Petri**	Y	Y	Y	Y	Y	N
7 Obey	N	Y	Y	Y	Y	Y
8 Kagen	N	Y	Y	N	Y	Y
WYOMING						
AL **Lummis**	Y	Y	Y	Y	Y	N
DELEGATES						
Faleomavaega (A.S.)						
Norton (D.C.)						
Bordallo (Guam)						
Sablan (N. Marianas)						
Pierluisi (P.R.)						
Christensen (V.I.)						

IN THE HOUSE | By Vote Number

653. **H J Res 105. Continuing Appropriations/Rule.** Adoption of the rule that would provide for House floor consideration of the joint resolution that would provide continuing appropriations through Dec. 21, 2010, for all federal departments and agencies, none of whose fiscal 2011 appropriations bills have been enacted. Funding would be set mostly at fiscal 2010 levels. Adopted 184-159: D 184-10; R 0-149. (Subsequently, the joint resolution was passed by voice vote.) Dec. 17, 2010.

654. **HR 2142. Federal Agency Performance Plans/Motion to Concur.** Cuellar, D-Texas, motion to suspend the rules and concur in the Senate amendment to the bill that would require federal agencies to establish performance plans for assessing performance and improving operations and to submit a strategic plan for program activities to the Office of Management and Budget. It also would establish the Performance Improvement Council within the OMB to assist in the development of performance standards and evaluation methodologies. Motion rejected 212-131: D 189-4; R 23-127. A two-thirds majority of those present and voting (229 in this case) is required for passage under suspension of the rules. Dec. 17, 2010.

655. **HR 5510. Legal Aid for Homeowners/Passage.** Capuano, D-Mass., motion to suspend the rules and pass the bill that would allow the Treasury secretary to use unobligated funds from the Troubled Asset Relief Program to provide legal assistance to homeowners who have mortgages on their principal residences that are in default or delinquency, are in danger of default or delinquency, or are subject to or at risk of foreclosure. Motion rejected 210-145: D 204-5; R 6-140. A two-thirds majority of those present and voting (237 in this case) is required for passage under suspension of the rules. Dec. 17, 2010.

656. **S 3874. Lead-Free Drinking Water/Passage.** Doyle, D-Pa., motion to suspend the rules and pass the bill that would amend current law restricting the use of lead in pipes for drinking water to modify the definition of "lead free" by reducing the allowable amount of lead on the wetted surface of pipes, pipe fittings and other fixtures. Motion agreed to 226-109: D 195-1; R 31-108. A two-thirds majority of those present and voting (224 in this case) is required for passage under suspension of the rules. Dec. 17, 2010.

657. **H Res 1771. Same-Day Consideration/Rule.** Adoption of the rule that would waive, through the legislative day of Dec. 24, 2010, the two-thirds majority vote requirement to consider a rule on the same day it is reported from the Rules Committee. The rule also would allow for consideration of measures under suspension of the rules at any time through the legislative day of Dec. 24. Adopted 199-151: D 199-5; R 0-146. Dec. 21, 2010.

658. **HR 6540. Aerial Refueling Aircraft Contracts/Passage.** Inslee, D-Wash., motion to suspend the rules and pass the bill that would require the Defense secretary to consider unfair competitive advantages in awarding contracts for the KC-X aerial refueling aircraft program or any successor to the program. Motion agreed to 325-23: D 203-2; R 122-21. A two-thirds majority of those present and voting (232 in this case) is required for passage under suspension of the rules. Dec. 21, 2010.

	653	654	655	656	657	658
ALABAMA						
1 **Bonner**	N	N	N	?	N	N
2 **Bright**	Y	Y	Y	Y	?	?
3 **Rogers**	N	Y	N	N	N	N
4 **Aderholt**	N	N	N	N	N	N
5 **Griffith**	?	?	?	?	?	?
6 **Bachus**	N	N	N	N	N	N
7 Davis	?	?	?	?	?	N
ALASKA						
AL **Young**	N	Y	Y	N	?	?
ARIZONA						
1 Kirkpatrick	Y	Y	Y	Y	Y	Y
2 **Franks**	N	N	N	N	N	Y
3 **Shadegg**	N	N	?	N	N	N
4 Pastor	?	?	?	?	?	?
5 Mitchell	?	?	?	?	?	?
6 **Flake**	N	N	N	N	N	N
7 Grijalva	Y	Y	Y	Y	Y	Y
8 Giffords	Y	Y	Y	Y	Y	Y
ARKANSAS						
1 Berry	?	?	?	?	?	?
2 Snyder	Y	Y	Y	Y	Y	Y
3 **Boozman**	N	N	N	N	N	N
4 Ross	?	?	Y	Y	Y	Y
CALIFORNIA						
1 Thompson	Y	Y	Y	Y	Y	Y
2 **Herger**	N	N	N	N	N	N
3 **Lungren**	N	Y	N	Y	N	N
4 **McClintock**	N	N	N	N	N	N
5 Matsui	Y	Y	Y	Y	Y	Y
6 Woolsey	Y	Y	Y	Y	Y	Y
7 Miller, George	Y	Y	Y	Y	Y	Y
8 Pelosi						
9 Lee	Y	Y	Y	Y	?	?
10 Garamendi	Y	Y	Y	Y	Y	Y
11 McNerney	Y	Y	Y	Y	Y	Y
12 Speier	?	?	?	?	Y	Y
13 Stark	?	?	?	?	?	?
14 Eshoo	Y	Y	Y	Y	Y	Y
15 Honda	Y	Y	Y	Y	?	?
16 Lofgren	Y	Y	Y	Y	?	?
17 Farr	Y	Y	Y	Y	Y	Y
18 Cardoza	?	?	?	?	Y	Y
19 **Radanovich**	?	?	?	?	?	?
20 Costa	Y	Y	Y	Y	Y	Y
21 **Nunes**	?	N	N	N	?	?
22 **McCarthy**	N	N	N	N	?	?
23 Capps	Y	Y	Y	?	Y	Y
24 **Gallegly**	?	?	?	?	N	Y
25 **McKeon**	N	N	N	N	N	N
26 **Dreier**	N	N	N	N	N	Y
27 Sherman	Y	Y	Y	Y	Y	Y
28 Berman	Y	Y	Y	Y	Y	?
29 Schiff	Y	Y	Y	Y	Y	Y
30 Waxman	Y	Y	Y	Y	Y	Y
31 Becerra	Y	?	Y	Y	Y	Y
32 Chu	Y	Y	Y	Y	?	?
33 Watson	Y	Y	Y	Y	Y	Y
34 Roybal-Allard	Y	Y	Y	Y	Y	Y
35 Waters	?	?	?	?	?	?
36 Harman	?	?	Y	Y	Y	Y
37 Richardson	Y	Y	Y	Y	Y	Y
38 Napolitano	?	?	?	?	Y	Y
39 Sánchez, Linda	Y	Y	Y	Y	Y	Y
40 **Royce**	N	N	N	N	N	N
41 **Lewis**	N	N	N	N	N	Y
42 **Miller, Gary**	?	?	?	?	?	?
43 Baca	?	?	Y	?	?	?
44 **Calvert**	?	?	?	?	?	?
45 **Bono Mack**	N	N	N	Y	N	Y
46 **Rohrabacher**	N	N	N	Y	N	Y
47 Sanchez, Loretta	Y	Y	Y	?	?	?
48 **Campbell**	N	N	N	N	?	Y
49 **Issa**	N	N	N	N	N	N
50 **Bilbray**	N	N	N	N	N	Y
51 Filner	Y	Y	Y	Y	Y	Y
52 **Hunter**	N	N	N	N	N	N
53 Davis	+	+	Y	Y	Y	Y

	653	654	655	656	657	658
COLORADO						
1 DeGette	?	?	?	?	Y	Y
2 Polis	Y	Y	Y	Y	Y	Y
3 Salazar	?	?	?	?	?	?
4 Markey	Y	Y	Y	Y	Y	Y
5 **Lamborn**	N	N	N	N	N	Y
6 **Coffman**	N	N	N	N	N	Y
7 Perlmutter	Y	Y	Y	Y	Y	Y
CONNECTICUT						
1 Larson	Y	Y	Y	Y	Y	Y
2 Courtney	Y	Y	Y	Y	Y	Y
3 DeLauro	Y	Y	Y	Y	Y	Y
4 Himes	?	?	Y	Y	Y	Y
5 Murphy	Y	Y	Y	Y	Y	Y
DELAWARE						
AL **Castle**	N	Y	N	Y	N	Y
FLORIDA						
1 **Miller**	N	N	N	N	N	N
2 Boyd	?	?	?	?	Y	Y
3 Brown	Y	Y	Y	?	Y	Y
4 **Crenshaw**	N	N	N	N	?	?
5 **Brown-Waite**	?	?	?	?	?	?
6 **Stearns**	N	N	N	N	N	N
7 **Mica**	N	N	N	N	N	N
8 Grayson	Y	Y	Y	Y	?	?
9 **Bilirakis**	N	N	N	N	N	N
10 **Young**	?	?	?	?	?	?
11 Castor	Y	Y	Y	?	Y	Y
12 **Putnam**	N	N	N	N	N	N
13 **Buchanan**	N	N	N	N	N	N
14 **Mack**	N	N	N	N	N	N
15 **Posey**	N	N	N	N	N	N
16 **Rooney**	N	N	N	N	N	N
17 Meek	Y	Y	Y	Y	?	?
18 **Ros-Lehtinen**	?	?	?	?	N	Y
19 Deutch	Y	Y	Y	Y	?	?
20 Wasserman Schultz	?	?	Y	Y	?	?
21 **Diaz-Balart, L.**	?	?	?	?	?	?
22 Klein	Y	Y	Y	Y	Y	Y
23 Hastings	Y	Y	Y	Y	Y	Y
24 Kosmas	Y	Y	Y	Y	Y	Y
25 **Diaz-Balart, M.**	N	Y	Y	Y	N	Y
GEORGIA						
1 **Kingston**	N	N	N	N	N	Y
2 Bishop	?	?	Y	Y	Y	Y
3 **Westmoreland**	N	N	N	N	N	Y
4 Johnson	?	?	Y	Y	Y	Y
5 Lewis	Y	Y	Y	N	N	Y
6 **Price**	N	N	N	N	N	N
7 **Linder**	N	N	?	?	?	?
8 Marshall	Y	Y	N	Y	Y	Y
9 **Graves**	N	N	N	N	N	N
10 **Broun**	N	N	N	N	N	N
11 **Gingrey**	N	N	N	N	N	N
12 Barrow	?	?	Y	Y	Y	Y
13 Scott	Y	Y	Y	Y	Y	Y
HAWAII						
1 **Djou**	?	?	?	?	N	N
2 Hirono	?	Y	Y	Y	Y	Y
IDAHO						
1 Minnick	Y	Y	Y	Y	Y	?
2 **Simpson**	N	N	N	N	N	Y
ILLINOIS						
1 Rush	Y	?	Y	Y	?	?
2 Jackson	Y	Y	Y	Y	Y	Y
3 Lipinski	?	?	?	?	?	?
4 Gutierrez	+	+	+	+	Y	Y
5 Quigley	?	?	?	?	Y	Y
6 **Roskam**	N	N	N	?	N	Y
7 Davis	?	?	Y	Y	?	?
8 Bean	?	?	Y	Y	Y	Y
9 Schakowsky	Y	Y	Y	Y	Y	Y
10 Vacant						
11 Halvorson	Y	Y	Y	Y	Y	Y
12 Costello	Y	Y	Y	Y	?	?
13 **Biggert**	N	N	N	N	N	Y
14 Foster	Y	Y	Y	Y	Y	Y
15 **Johnson**	N	Y	N	Y	N	Y

KEY   **Republicans**   Democrats

Y Voted for (yea)	X Paired against
# Paired for	– Announced against
+ Announced for	P Voted "present"
N Voted against (nay)	C Voted "present" to avoid possible conflict of interest
	? Did not vote or otherwise make a position known

	653	654	655	656	657	658
16 **Manzullo**	N	N	N	N	N	Y
17 Hare	Y	Y	Y	Y	Y	Y
18 **Schock**	N	N	N	Y	?	?
19 **Shimkus**	N	N	N	N	N	Y
INDIANA						
1 Visclosky	Y	Y	Y	Y	Y	Y
2 Donnelly	Y	Y	Y	Y	Y	Y
3 **Stutzman**	N	N	N	N	N	N
4 **Buyer**	N	N	?	?	?	?
5 **Burton**	N	N	N	N	N	Y
6 **Pence**	N	N	N	N	N	Y
7 Carson	?	?	Y	Y	Y	Y
8 Ellsworth	Y	Y	Y	Y	?	?
9 Hill	Y	Y	Y	?	Y	Y
IOWA						
1 Braley	Y	Y	Y	Y	Y	Y
2 Loebsack	Y	Y	Y	Y	Y	Y
3 Boswell	Y	Y	Y	Y	Y	Y
4 **Latham**	?	?	N	N	N	Y
5 **King**	N	N	N	N	N	Y
KANSAS						
1 **Moran**	?	?	?	?	N	Y
2 **Jenkins**	N	N	N	Y	N	Y
3 Moore	Y	Y	?	?	Y	Y
4 **Tiahrt**	N	N	N	N	N	Y
KENTUCKY						
1 **Whitfield**	?	?	?	?	N	Y
2 **Guthrie**	N	N	N	N	N	Y
3 Yarmuth	Y	Y	Y	Y	Y	Y
4 **Davis**	N	N	N	?	N	Y
5 **Rogers**	N	N	N	N	N	?
6 Chandler	Y	Y	Y	Y	Y	Y
LOUISIANA						
1 **Scalise**	N	N	N	N	N	N
2 **Cao**	N	Y	N	N	?	?
3 Melancon	N	Y	Y	Y	?	?
4 **Fleming**	N	N	N	N	N	N
5 **Alexander**	N	N	N	?	N	N
6 **Cassidy**	N	Y	N	Y	N	N
7 **Boustany**	?	?	N	Y	N	N
MAINE						
1 Pingree	?	?	?	?	Y	Y
2 Michaud	Y	Y	Y	Y	Y	Y
MARYLAND						
1 Kratovil	N	Y	Y	Y	N	Y
2 Ruppersberger	Y	Y	Y	Y	Y	Y
3 Sarbanes	Y	Y	Y	Y	Y	Y
4 Edwards	Y	Y	Y	Y	Y	Y
5 Hoyer	Y	Y	Y	Y	Y	Y
6 **Bartlett**	N	N	N	N	N	Y
7 Cummings	Y	Y	Y	Y	Y	Y
8 Van Hollen	?	Y	Y	Y	Y	Y
MASSACHUSETTS						
1 Olver	Y	Y	Y	Y	Y	Y
2 Neal	Y	Y	Y	Y	?	?
3 McGovern	Y	Y	Y	Y	Y	Y
4 Frank	Y	Y	Y	Y	Y	Y
5 Tsongas	Y	Y	Y	Y	Y	Y
6 Tierney	Y	Y	Y	Y	Y	Y
7 Markey	Y	Y	?	Y	Y	Y
8 Capuano	Y	Y	Y	Y	Y	Y
9 Lynch	Y	Y	Y	Y	Y	Y
10 Delahunt	?	?	?	?	?	?
MICHIGAN						
1 Stupak	?	?	?	?	Y	Y
2 **Hoekstra**	N	N	N	N	N	Y
3 **Ehlers**	N	N	?	?	N	Y
4 **Camp**	?	?	N	N	?	?
5 Kildee	Y	Y	Y	Y	Y	Y
6 **Upton**	N	N	N	N	N	Y
7 Schauer	Y	Y	Y	Y	Y	Y
8 **Rogers**	N	N	N	N	N	Y
9 Peters	?	?	Y	Y	Y	Y
10 **Miller**	N	Y	N	N	N	Y
11 **McCotter**	N	N	N	N	N	Y
12 Levin	Y	Y	Y	Y	Y	Y
13 Kilpatrick	?	?	?	?	?	?
14 Conyers	+	+	+	+	Y	Y
15 Dingell	Y	Y	Y	Y	Y	Y
MINNESOTA						
1 Walz	Y	Y	Y	Y	Y	Y
2 **Kline**	N	N	N	N	N	Y
3 **Paulsen**	N	N	N	Y	?	?
4 McCollum	Y	?	Y	Y	Y	Y

	653	654	655	656	657	658
5 Ellison	Y	Y	Y	Y	?	?
6 **Bachmann**	N	N	N	N	?	?
7 Peterson	Y	Y	Y	N	Y	Y
8 Oberstar	Y	Y	Y	Y	Y	Y
MISSISSIPPI						
1 Childers	N	Y	Y	?	N	Y
2 Thompson	Y	Y	Y	Y	Y	Y
3 **Harper**	N	N	N	N	N	N
4 Taylor	N	N	Y	Y	N	Y
MISSOURI						
1 Clay	?	?	Y	Y	Y	Y
2 **Akin**	N	N	N	N	N	Y
3 Carnahan	Y	Y	Y	Y	Y	Y
4 Skelton	Y	Y	Y	Y	Y	Y
5 Cleaver	Y	Y	Y	Y	Y	Y
6 **Graves**	N	N	N	Y	N	Y
7 **Blunt**	N	N	N	?	N	Y
8 **Emerson**	N	N	N	N	N	Y
9 **Luetkemeyer**	N	N	N	N	N	Y
MONTANA						
AL **Rehberg**	N	N	N	N	N	Y
NEBRASKA						
1 **Fortenberry**	N	N	N	Y	N	Y
2 **Terry**	N	Y	N	Y	N	Y
3 **Smith**	N	N	N	N	N	Y
NEVADA						
1 Berkley	?	?	Y	Y	Y	Y
2 **Heller**	N	N	N	?	?	?
3 Titus	Y	Y	Y	Y	Y	Y
NEW HAMPSHIRE						
1 Shea-Porter	Y	Y	Y	Y	?	Y
2 Hodes	?	?	?	?	?	?
NEW JERSEY						
1 Andrews	?	?	Y	Y	Y	Y
2 **LoBiondo**	N	N	N	N	N	Y
3 Adler	N	N	N	Y	?	?
4 **Smith**	N	N	N	N	N	Y
5 **Garrett**	N	N	N	N	N	N
6 Pallone	Y	Y	Y	Y	Y	Y
7 **Lance**	N	N	N	Y	N	Y
8 Pascrell	Y	Y	Y	Y	Y	Y
9 Rothman	?	?	Y	Y	Y	Y
10 Payne	Y	Y	Y	Y	Y	Y
11 **Frelinghuysen**	N	N	N	N	N	Y
12 Holt	Y	Y	Y	Y	Y	Y
13 Sires	Y	Y	Y	Y	?	?
NEW MEXICO						
1 Heinrich	Y	Y	Y	Y	Y	Y
2 Teague	Y	Y	Y	Y	Y	Y
3 Luján	Y	Y	Y	Y	Y	Y
NEW YORK						
1 Bishop	Y	Y	Y	?	Y	Y
2 Israel	Y	Y	Y	?	Y	Y
3 **King**	N	Y	?	?	?	?
4 McCarthy	?	?	?	?	?	?
5 Ackerman	?	?	?	?	Y	Y
6 Meeks	?	?	?	?	Y	Y
7 Crowley	Y	Y	Y	Y	Y	?
8 Nadler	Y	Y	Y	Y	Y	Y
9 Weiner	Y	Y	Y	Y	?	Y
10 Towns	Y	?	Y	?	Y	Y
11 Clarke	Y	Y	Y	Y	Y	Y
12 Velázquez	Y	?	?	?	Y	Y
13 McMahon	N	N	N	Y	?	?
14 Maloney	Y	Y	Y	Y	Y	Y
15 Rangel	Y	Y	Y	Y	Y	Y
16 Serrano	Y	Y	Y	Y	Y	Y
17 Engel	Y	Y	Y	Y	Y	Y
18 Lowey	Y	Y	Y	Y	Y	Y
19 Hall	Y	Y	Y	Y	Y	Y
20 Murphy	?	?	?	?	?	?
21 Tonko	Y	Y	Y	Y	Y	Y
22 Hinchey	Y	Y	Y	Y	Y	Y
23 Owens	Y	N	N	Y	Y	Y
24 Arcuri	?	?	?	?	?	?
25 Maffei	Y	Y	?	?	Y	Y
26 **Lee**	N	N	N	Y	N	Y
27 Higgins	Y	Y	Y	Y	Y	Y
28 Slaughter	Y	Y	Y	Y	Y	?
29 **Reed**	N	N	N	Y	N	Y
NORTH CAROLINA						
1 Butterfield	Y	Y	Y	Y	Y	Y
2 Etheridge	Y	Y	Y	Y	Y	Y
3 **Jones**	?	?	?	?	?	?
4 Price	Y	Y	Y	Y	Y	Y

	653	654	655	656	657	658
5 **Foxx**	N	N	N	N	N	Y
6 **Coble**	N	N	N	?	?	?
7 McIntyre	?	?	?	?	Y	Y
8 Kissell	Y	Y	Y	?	Y	Y
9 **Myrick**	N	N	N	N	N	Y
10 **McHenry**	N	N	N	N	N	Y
11 Shuler	N	Y	Y	Y	N	Y
12 Watt	Y	Y	Y	Y	Y	Y
13 Miller	Y	Y	Y	Y	Y	Y
NORTH DAKOTA						
AL Pomeroy	?	Y	Y	Y	Y	Y
OHIO						
1 Driehaus	Y	Y	Y	Y	Y	Y
2 **Schmidt**	N	N	N	N	N	Y
3 **Turner**	N	N	Y	Y	N	Y
4 **Jordan**	N	N	N	N	N	Y
5 **Latta**	N	N	N	N	N	Y
6 Wilson	Y	Y	Y	Y	Y	Y
7 **Austria**	N	N	Y	N	N	Y
8 **Boehner**	N	N	?	?	N	?
9 Kaptur	Y	Y	Y	Y	Y	Y
10 Kucinich	Y	Y	Y	Y	Y	?
11 Fudge	Y	Y	Y	Y	Y	Y
12 **Tiberi**	N	N	Y	N	N	Y
13 Sutton	Y	Y	Y	Y	Y	Y
14 **LaTourette**	N	Y	Y	N	N	Y
15 Kilroy	Y	Y	Y	Y	Y	Y
16 Boccieri	Y	Y	Y	Y	Y	Y
17 Ryan	Y	Y	Y	Y	Y	N
18 Space	Y	Y	?	?	Y	Y
OKLAHOMA						
1 **Sullivan**	N	N	N	N	N	Y
2 Boren	Y	Y	N	Y	Y	Y
3 **Lucas**	N	N	N	N	N	Y
4 **Cole**	N	Y	N	N	N	Y
5 **Fallin**	?	?	?	?	?	?
OREGON						
1 Wu	Y	Y	Y	Y	Y	Y
2 **Walden**	N	N	N	N	N	Y
3 Blumenauer	Y	Y	?	?	?	?
4 DeFazio	Y	Y	Y	Y	Y	Y
5 Schrader	Y	Y	Y	Y	Y	Y
PENNSYLVANIA						
1 Brady	?	?	?	?	Y	Y
2 Fattah	Y	Y	Y	Y	Y	Y
3 Dahlkemper	Y	Y	Y	Y	Y	Y
4 Altmire	Y	Y	Y	Y	Y	Y
5 **Thompson**	N	Y	N	Y	N	Y
6 **Gerlach**	N	Y	N	N	N	Y
7 Sestak	Y	Y	Y	Y	Y	Y
8 Murphy, P.	?	?	?	?	Y	Y
9 **Shuster**	N	Y	N	Y	N	Y
10 Carney	Y	Y	Y	Y	Y	Y
11 Kanjorski	Y	Y	Y	Y	Y	Y
12 Critz	Y	Y	Y	Y	Y	Y
13 Schwartz	?	?	Y	Y	Y	Y
14 Doyle	N	Y	Y	Y	?	?
15 **Dent**	N	Y	N	Y	N	Y
16 **Pitts**	N	N	N	N	N	Y
17 Holden	Y	Y	Y	Y	Y	Y
18 **Murphy, T.**	?	?	N	N	N	Y
19 **Platts**	N	Y	N	Y	N	Y
RHODE ISLAND						
1 Kennedy	Y	Y	Y	Y	?	?
2 Langevin	Y	Y	Y	Y	Y	Y
SOUTH CAROLINA						
1 **Brown**	?	?	?	?	N	Y
2 **Wilson**	N	N	N	N	N	Y
3 **Barrett**	?	?	?	?	?	?
4 **Inglis**	N	N	N	N	?	?
5 Spratt	Y	Y	Y	Y	Y	Y
6 Clyburn	Y	Y	Y	Y	?	?
SOUTH DAKOTA						
AL Herseth Sandlin	Y	Y	?	Y	?	?
TENNESSEE						
1 **Roe**	N	N	N	Y	N	Y
2 **Duncan**	N	N	N	N	N	Y
3 **Wamp**	?	?	?	?	N	Y
4 Davis	?	?	?	?	Y	Y
5 Cooper	Y	Y	Y	Y	Y	Y
6 Gordon	Y	Y	Y	Y	Y	Y
7 **Blackburn**	N	N	N	N	N	N
8 Tanner	Y	Y	Y	Y	?	?
9 Cohen	Y	Y	Y	?	Y	Y

	653	654	655	656	657	658
TEXAS						
1 **Gohmert**	N	Y	N	N	N	Y
2 **Poe**	N	N	N	N	N	Y
3 **Johnson, S.**	?	?	?	?	?	?
4 **Hall**	N	N	N	N	N	Y
5 **Hensarling**	N	N	N	N	N	N
6 **Barton**	?	?	?	?	?	?
7 **Culberson**	?	?	?	?	?	?
8 **Brady**	N	N	N	N	N	N
9 Green, A.	+	+	Y	Y	Y	Y
10 **McCaul**	N	Y	N	N	N	Y
11 **Conaway**	N	N	N	N	N	Y
12 **Granger**	?	?	?	?	?	?
13 **Thornberry**	N	N	N	N	N	Y
14 **Paul**	?	?	?	?	N	N
15 Hinojosa	?	?	?	?	Y	Y
16 Reyes	?	?	?	?	?	?
17 Edwards	Y	Y	Y	Y	Y	Y
18 Jackson Lee	Y	Y	Y	Y	Y	Y
19 **Neugebauer**	N	N	N	N	N	Y
20 Gonzalez	Y	Y	Y	?	Y	Y
21 **Smith**	N	Y	N	N	N	Y
22 **Olson**	N	N	N	N	N	Y
23 Rodriguez	?	?	?	?	Y	Y
24 **Marchant**	?	?	?	?	?	?
25 Doggett	Y	Y	Y	Y	Y	Y
26 **Burgess**	N	N	N	N	N	Y
27 Ortiz	?	?	?	?	?	?
28 Cuellar	Y	Y	Y	?	Y	Y
29 Green, G.	Y	Y	Y	Y	Y	Y
30 Johnson, E.	?	?	?	?	Y	Y
31 **Carter**	N	Y	?	?	N	Y
32 **Sessions**	N	N	N	N	N	Y
UTAH						
1 **Bishop**	N	N	N	N	N	?
2 Matheson	Y	Y	?	?	Y	Y
3 **Chaffetz**	N	N	?	?	N	Y
VERMONT						
AL Welch	?	Y	Y	Y	?	Y
VIRGINIA						
1 **Wittman**	?	?	?	?	N	Y
2 Nye	N	Y	Y	Y	Y	Y
3 Scott	Y	Y	Y	Y	Y	Y
4 **Forbes**	N	N	N	Y	N	Y
5 Perriello	Y	Y	Y	Y	N	Y
6 **Goodlatte**	N	N	N	N	N	Y
7 **Cantor**	N	N	N	N	N	Y
8 Moran	Y	Y	Y	Y	Y	Y
9 Boucher	Y	Y	Y	Y	Y	Y
10 **Wolf**	N	Y	N	Y	N	Y
11 Connolly	N	Y	Y	Y	?	Y
WASHINGTON						
1 Inslee	Y	Y	Y	Y	Y	Y
2 Larsen	Y	Y	Y	Y	Y	Y
3 Baird	?	?	?	?	?	?
4 **Hastings**	N	N	N	N	N	Y
5 **McMorris Rodgers**	?	?	?	?	?	?
6 Dicks	Y	Y	Y	Y	Y	Y
7 McDermott	Y	Y	Y	Y	Y	Y
8 **Reichert**	N	N	N	Y	N	Y
9 Smith	Y	Y	Y	Y	?	?
WEST VIRGINIA						
1 Mollohan	Y	Y	Y	Y	Y	Y
2 **Capito**	N	N	N	Y	N	Y
3 Rahall	Y	Y	Y	Y	Y	Y
WISCONSIN						
1 **Ryan**	N	N	N	Y	N	Y
2 Baldwin	Y	Y	Y	Y	Y	Y
3 Kind	?	?	?	?	Y	Y
4 Moore	Y	Y	Y	?	Y	Y
5 **Sensenbrenner**	N	N	N	N	N	Y
6 **Petri**	N	N	N	Y	N	Y
7 Obey	Y	Y	Y	Y	Y	Y
8 Kagen	Y	Y	Y	Y	Y	Y
WYOMING						
AL **Lummis**	N	N	N	N	N	Y
DELEGATES						
Faleomavaega (A.S.)						
Norton (D.C.)						
Bordallo (Guam)						
Sablan (N. Marianas)						
Pierluisi (P.R.)						
Christensen (V.I.)						

IN THE HOUSE | By Vote Number

659. **HR 5116. Science and Technology Programs Reauthorization/Motion to Concur.** Gordon, D-Tenn., motion to concur in the Senate amendment to the bill that would authorize roughly $45.2 billion from fiscal 2011 through 2013 for a variety of science and technology research and education programs. The bill would authorize $23.5 billion for the National Science Foundation, $2.9 billion for the National Institute of Standards and Technology, $16.9 billion for basic research at the Energy Department and $912 million for the department's Advanced Research Projects Agency. Motion agreed to, thus clearing the bill for the president, 228-130: D 212-0; R 16-130. Dec. 21, 2010.

660. **HR 2142. Federal Agency Performance Plans/Motion to Concur.** Cuellar, D-Texas, motion to concur in the Senate amendment to the bill that would require federal agencies to establish performance plans for assessing performance and improving operations and to submit a strategic plan for program activities to the Office of Management and Budget. It also would establish the Performance Improvement Council within the OMB to assist in the development of performance standards and evaluation methodologies. Motion agreed to, thus clearing the bill for the president, 216-139: D 208-1; R 8-138. Dec. 21, 2010.

661. **HR 2751. Food Safety Overhaul/Motion to Concur.** Dingell, D-Mich., motion to concur in the Senate amendments to the bill. The Senate amendments would increase the reporting and record-keeping requirements for food facilities. The measure would expand the Food and Drug Administration's oversight authority by increasing the number of required inspections, boosting access to the records of food processors and providing the authority to issue mandatory recalls. It also would increase the FDA's ability to inspect imported foods and create a foreign facility inspection program. Motion agreed to, thus clearing the bill for the president, 215-144: D 205-8; R 10-136. Dec. 21, 2010.

662. **HR 3082. Fiscal 2011 Continuing Appropriations/Motion to Concur.** Obey, D-Wis., motion to concur in the Senate amendment to the House amendment to the Senate amendment to the bill. The Senate amendment would continue most appropriations at fiscal 2010-enacted levels through March 4, 2011. The measure would provide an overall annualized spending rate that is $1.16 billion more than fiscal 2010 levels. It would provide additional funding for the Low Income Home Energy Assistance Program and Pell grants. It also would allow the awarding of a Navy contract for shipbuilding of Littoral Combat Ships to multiple suppliers. Motion agreed to, thus clearing the bill for the president, 193-165: D 192-19; R 1-146. Dec. 21, 2010.

663. **HR 6547. School Employee Background Checks/Passage.** Miller, D-Calif., motion to suspend the rules and pass the bill that would require periodic criminal background checks of current and potential elementary and secondary school employees. The requirement also would apply to private groups that contract with or provide services to the schools or to local and state educational agencies. Motion agreed to 314-20: D 201-0; R 113-20. A two-thirds majority of those present and voting (223 in this case) is required for passage under suspension of the rules. Dec. 21, 2010.

664. **HR 847. Sept. 11 Health and Compensation Fund/Motion to Concur.** Pallone, D-N.J., motion to concur in the Senate amendment to the bill that would create a program to provide medical services and health monitoring for first-responders and others with conditions related to the Sept. 11 attacks. It would reopen the Sept. 11 Victims Compensation Fund and allow claims to be filed during a five-year period. It would impose a 2 percent tax on companies in certain foreign countries that have federal procurement contracts. It also would extend for one year an increase in H1-B and L visa fees for certain companies. Motion agreed to, thus clearing the bill for the president, 206-60: D 175-1; R 31-59. Dec. 22, 2010.

	659	660	661	662	663	664
ALABAMA						
1 Bonner	N	N	?	Y	Y	?
2 Bright	?	?	?	?	?	?
3 Rogers	N	Y	N	N	Y	Y
4 Aderholt	N	N	N	N	Y	Y
5 Griffith	?	?	?	?	?	?
6 Bachus	N	N	N	N	Y	N
7 Davis	?	Y	Y	Y	?	?
ALASKA						
AL Young	?	?	?	?	?	?
ARIZONA						
1 Kirkpatrick	Y	Y	Y	Y	Y	?
2 Franks	N	N	N	N	Y	N
3 Shadegg	N	N	N	N	N	?
4 Pastor	?	?	?	?	?	?
5 Mitchell	?	?	?	?	?	?
6 Flake	N	N	N	N	N	?
7 Grijalva	Y	Y	Y	Y	Y	Y
8 Giffords	Y	Y	Y	N	Y	Y
ARKANSAS						
1 Berry	?	?	?	?	?	?
2 Snyder	Y	Y	Y	Y	Y	Y
3 Boozman	N	N	N	N	Y	N
4 Ross	Y	Y	Y	Y	Y	Y
CALIFORNIA						
1 Thompson	Y	Y	Y	Y	Y	Y
2 Herger	N	N	N	N	Y	N
3 Lungren	N	N	N	N	Y	N
4 McClintock	N	N	N	N	Y	N
5 Matsui	Y	Y	Y	Y	Y	Y
6 Woolsey	Y	Y	Y	Y	Y	Y
7 Miller, George	Y	Y	Y	Y	Y	Y
8 Pelosi						Y
9 Lee	?	?	?	?	?	?
10 Garamendi	+	Y	Y	Y	Y	?
11 McNerney	Y	Y	Y	Y	Y	Y
12 Speier	Y	Y	Y	Y	Y	Y
13 Stark	?	?	?	?	?	?
14 Eshoo	Y	Y	Y	Y	Y	Y
15 Honda	?	?	?	?	?	?
16 Lofgren	?	?	?	?	?	?
17 Farr	Y	Y	N	Y	Y	Y
18 Cardoza	Y	Y	N	Y	?	Y
19 Radanovich	?	?	?	?	?	?
20 Costa	Y	Y	N	Y	Y	Y
21 Nunes	?	?	?	?	?	?
22 McCarthy	?	?	?	?	?	?
23 Capps	Y	Y	Y	Y	Y	Y
24 Gallegly	N	N	N	N	?	?
25 McKeon	N	N	N	N	Y	?
26 Dreier	N	N	N	N	Y	Y
27 Sherman	Y	Y	Y	Y	Y	Y
28 Berman	Y	Y	Y	Y	Y	?
29 Schiff	Y	Y	Y	Y	Y	Y
30 Waxman	Y	Y	Y	Y	Y	Y
31 Becerra	Y	Y	Y	Y	Y	?
32 Chu	+	+	+	+	+	?
33 Watson	?	?	Y	Y	Y	Y
34 Roybal-Allard	Y	Y	Y	Y	Y	Y
35 Waters	Y	Y	Y	Y	Y	?
36 Harman	Y	Y	Y	Y	?	?
37 Richardson	Y	Y	Y	Y	Y	Y
38 Napolitano	Y	+	Y	Y	Y	Y
39 Sánchez, Linda	Y	Y	Y	Y	Y	?
40 Royce	N	N	N	N	Y	N
41 Lewis	N	N	N	N	Y	N
42 Miller, Gary	?	?	?	?	?	?
43 Baca	+	+	+	+	+	?
44 Calvert	?	?	?	?	?	?
45 Bono Mack	N	N	N	N	Y	?
46 Rohrabacher	N	N	N	N	Y	?
47 Sanchez, Loretta	?	?	?	?	N	?
48 Campbell	?	?	?	?	?	?
49 Issa	N	N	N	N	Y	?
50 Bilbray	N	N	N	N	Y	Y
51 Filner	Y	Y	Y	Y	Y	?
52 Hunter	N	N	N	N	Y	?
53 Davis	Y	Y	Y	Y	Y	Y

	659	660	661	662	663	664
COLORADO						
1 DeGette	Y	Y	Y	Y	Y	Y
2 Polis	Y	Y	Y	Y	Y	Y
3 Salazar	?	?	?	?	?	?
4 Markey	Y	Y	Y	Y	Y	Y
5 Lamborn	N	N	N	N	?	?
6 Coffman	N	N	N	N	N	N
7 Perlmutter	Y	Y	Y	Y	?	?
CONNECTICUT						
1 Larson	Y	?	Y	Y	Y	Y
2 Courtney	Y	Y	Y	Y	Y	Y
3 DeLauro	Y	Y	Y	Y	Y	Y
4 Himes	Y	Y	Y	Y	Y	Y
5 Murphy	Y	Y	Y	Y	Y	Y
DELAWARE						
AL Castle	Y	Y	Y	Y	Y	Y
FLORIDA						
1 Miller	N	N	N	N	N	N
2 Boyd	Y	Y	Y	?	?	?
3 Brown	Y	Y	Y	Y	Y	Y
4 Crenshaw	?	?	?	?	?	?
5 Brown-Waite	?	?	?	N	?	?
6 Stearns	N	N	N	N	Y	?
7 Mica	N	N	N	N	Y	N
8 Grayson	Y	Y	Y	Y	Y	Y
9 Bilirakis	N	?	N	N	Y	Y
10 Young	?	?	?	?	?	?
11 Castor	Y	Y	Y	Y	Y	Y
12 Putnam	N	N	N	N	Y	?
13 Buchanan	N	N	N	N	Y	?
14 Mack	N	N	N	N	Y	?
15 Posey	N	N	N	N	Y	?
16 Rooney	N	N	N	N	Y	?
17 Meek	Y	Y	Y	Y	Y	Y
18 Ros-Lehtinen	N	N	N	N	Y	?
19 Deutch	?	?	?	?	?	?
20 Wasserman Schultz	?	?	?	?	?	?
21 Diaz-Balart, L.	?	?	?	?	?	?
22 Klein	Y	Y	Y	Y	Y	Y
23 Hastings	Y	Y	Y	Y	Y	Y
24 Kosmas	Y	Y	Y	Y	Y	Y
25 Diaz-Balart, M.	N	Y	N	N	Y	N
GEORGIA						
1 Kingston	N	N	N	N	N	N
2 Bishop	Y	Y	Y	Y	Y	N
3 Westmoreland	N	N	N	N	N	?
4 Johnson	Y	Y	Y	Y	Y	Y
5 Lewis	Y	Y	Y	Y	Y	Y
6 Price	N	N	N	N	?	?
7 Linder	?	?	?	?	?	?
8 Marshall	Y	Y	Y	Y	Y	Y
9 Graves	N	N	N	N	N	?
10 Broun	N	N	N	N	N	N
11 Gingrey	N	N	N	N	Y	?
12 Barrow	Y	Y	Y	Y	Y	Y
13 Scott, D.	Y	Y	Y	Y	Y	Y
HAWAII						
1 Djou	N	N	Y	N	Y	?
2 Hirono	Y	Y	Y	Y	Y	Y
IDAHO						
1 Minnick	Y	Y	Y	Y	Y	Y
2 Simpson	N	N	N	N	Y	?
ILLINOIS						
1 Rush	?	?	?	?	?	?
2 Jackson	Y	Y	Y	Y	Y	Y
3 Lipinski	Y	Y	Y	Y	?	?
4 Gutierrez	+	+	+	?	?	?
5 Quigley	Y	Y	Y	Y	Y	Y
6 Roskam	N	N	Y	N	?	?
7 Davis	?	?	?	?	?	?
8 Bean	Y	Y	Y	Y	Y	Y
9 Schakowsky	Y	Y	Y	Y	Y	Y
10 Vacant						
11 Halvorson	Y	Y	Y	Y	Y	Y
12 Costello	?	?	?	?	?	?
13 Biggert	Y	N	Y	N	Y	?
14 Foster	Y	Y	Y	Y	Y	Y
15 Johnson	Y	N	N	Y	?	?

KEY **Republicans** Democrats

Y Voted for (yea)	X Paired against	C Voted "present" to avoid possible conflict of interest
# Paired for	– Announced against	
+ Announced for	P Voted "present"	? Did not vote or otherwise make a position known
N Voted against (nay)		

	659	660	661	662	663	664
16 **Manzullo**	N	N	N	N	Y	N
17 Hare	Y	Y	Y	Y	Y	Y
18 **Schock**	?	?	?	?	?	?
19 **Shimkus**	N	N	N	N	Y	?
INDIANA						
1 Visclosky	Y	Y	Y	N	Y	Y
2 Donnelly	Y	Y	Y	Y	Y	Y
3 **Stutzman**	N	N	N	N	N	N
4 **Buyer**	?	?	?	?	?	?
5 **Burton**	?	?	N	N	Y	?
6 **Pence**	N	N	N	N	Y	?
7 Carson	Y	Y	Y	Y	Y	Y
8 Ellsworth	Y	Y	Y	Y	Y	?
9 Hill	Y	Y	Y	?	?	?
IOWA						
1 Braley	Y	Y	Y	Y	Y	?
2 Loebsack	Y	Y	Y	Y	Y	Y
3 Boswell	Y	Y	Y	Y	Y	Y
4 **Latham**	N	N	N	N	Y	?
5 **King**	N	N	N	N	N	N
KANSAS						
1 **Moran**	N	N	N	?	?	?
2 **Jenkins**	N	N	N	N	Y	N
3 Moore	Y	Y	Y	?	Y	?
4 **Tiahrt**	N	N	N	N	Y	N
KENTUCKY						
1 **Whitfield**	N	N	N	N	Y	N
2 **Guthrie**	N	N	N	N	Y	N
3 Yarmuth	Y	Y	Y	Y	Y	Y
4 **Davis**	N	N	N	N	Y	?
5 **Rogers**	N	N	N	N	Y	N
6 Chandler	Y	Y	Y	Y	Y	Y
LOUISIANA						
1 **Scalise**	N	N	N	N	Y	N
2 **Cao**	?	?	?	?	?	?
3 Melancon	?	?	?	?	?	?
4 **Fleming**	N	N	N	N	Y	N
5 **Alexander**	N	N	N	N	Y	N
6 **Cassidy**	Y	N	N	N	Y	N
7 **Boustany**	N	N	N	N	Y	?
MAINE						
1 Pingree	Y	Y	Y	Y	Y	Y
2 Michaud	Y	Y	Y	N	Y	Y
MARYLAND						
1 Kratovil	Y	Y	Y	N	Y	Y
2 Ruppersberger	Y	Y	Y	Y	Y	Y
3 Sarbanes	Y	Y	Y	Y	Y	Y
4 Edwards	Y	Y	Y	Y	Y	Y
5 Hoyer	?	Y	Y	Y	?	Y
6 **Bartlett**	Y	N	N	N	Y	N
7 Cummings	Y	Y	Y	Y	Y	Y
8 Van Hollen	Y	Y	Y	Y	Y	Y
MASSACHUSETTS						
1 Olver	Y	Y	Y	Y	Y	Y
2 Neal	?	?	?	?	?	?
3 McGovern	Y	Y	Y	Y	?	Y
4 Frank	Y	Y	Y	Y	?	Y
5 Tsongas	Y	Y	Y	Y	Y	Y
6 Tierney	Y	Y	Y	Y	Y	Y
7 Markey	Y	Y	Y	Y	Y	Y
8 Capuano	Y	Y	Y	Y	Y	Y
9 Lynch	Y	Y	Y	Y	Y	Y
10 Delahunt	?	?	?	?	?	?
MICHIGAN						
1 Stupak	Y	Y	Y	Y	Y	?
2 **Hoekstra**	N	N	N	N	N	N
3 **Ehlers**	Y	N	Y	N	N	N
4 **Camp**	?	?	?	?	?	?
5 Kildee	Y	Y	Y	Y	Y	Y
6 **Upton**	N	N	N	N	Y	N
7 Schauer	Y	Y	Y	Y	Y	Y
8 **Rogers**	N	N	N	N	Y	?
9 Peters	Y	Y	Y	Y	Y	Y
10 **Miller**	N	N	N	N	Y	?
11 **McCotter**	N	N	N	N	Y	N
12 Levin	Y	Y	Y	Y	Y	Y
13 Kilpatrick	?	?	?	?	?	?
14 Conyers	Y	Y	Y	Y	Y	Y
15 Dingell	Y	Y	Y	Y	Y	Y
MINNESOTA						
1 Walz	Y	Y	Y	Y	Y	Y
2 **Kline**	N	N	N	N	Y	?
3 **Paulsen**	N	N	N	N	Y	N
4 McCollum	Y	Y	Y	N	Y	Y

	659	660	661	662	663	664
5 Ellison	Y	Y	Y	Y	Y	Y
6 **Bachmann**	N	N	N	N	Y	N
7 Peterson	Y	?	N	Y	Y	?
8 Oberstar	Y	Y	Y	Y	Y	?
MISSISSIPPI						
1 Childers	Y	Y	N	N	Y	?
2 Thompson	Y	Y	Y	Y	Y	Y
3 **Harper**	N	N	N	N	Y	?
4 Taylor	Y	Y	Y	N	Y	N
MISSOURI						
1 Clay	Y	Y	Y	?	?	?
2 **Akin**	N	N	N	N	Y	N
3 Carnahan	Y	Y	Y	Y	Y	Y
4 Skelton	Y	Y	Y	Y	Y	Y
5 Cleaver	Y	Y	Y	Y	Y	Y
6 **Graves**	N	N	N	N	Y	?
7 **Blunt**	N	N	N	N	Y	Y
8 **Emerson**	N	N	N	N	?	Y
9 **Luetkemeyer**	N	N	N	N	Y	?
MONTANA						
AL **Rehberg**	N	N	N	N	Y	N
NEBRASKA						
1 **Fortenberry**	N	N	Y	N	Y	Y
2 **Terry**	N	N	Y	N	Y	N
3 **Smith**	N	N	N	N	Y	N
NEVADA						
1 Berkley	Y	Y	Y	Y	Y	Y
2 **Heller**	?	?	?	?	?	?
3 Titus	Y	Y	Y	Y	Y	Y
NEW HAMPSHIRE						
1 Shea-Porter	Y	Y	Y	Y	Y	Y
2 Hodes	?	?	?	?	?	?
NEW JERSEY						
1 Andrews	Y	Y	Y	Y	Y	Y
2 **LoBiondo**	N	N	N	N	Y	Y
3 Adler	?	?	?	?	?	Y
4 **Smith**	Y	N	N	N	Y	Y
5 **Garrett**	N	N	N	N	N	Y
6 Pallone	Y	Y	Y	Y	Y	Y
7 **Lance**	N	N	N	N	Y	Y
8 Pascrell	Y	Y	Y	Y	Y	Y
9 Rothman	Y	Y	Y	Y	Y	Y
10 Payne	Y	Y	Y	Y	Y	Y
11 **Frelinghuysen**	N	N	N	N	Y	Y
12 Holt	Y	Y	Y	Y	Y	Y
13 Sires	?	?	?	?	?	Y
NEW MEXICO						
1 Heinrich	Y	Y	Y	Y	Y	Y
2 Teague	Y	Y	Y	Y	Y	Y
3 Luján	Y	Y	Y	Y	Y	Y
NEW YORK						
1 Bishop	Y	Y	Y	Y	Y	Y
2 Israel	Y	Y	Y	Y	Y	Y
3 **King**	?	?	?	?	?	Y
4 McCarthy	?	?	?	?	?	?
5 Ackerman	Y	Y	Y	Y	Y	Y
6 Meeks	Y	Y	Y	Y	Y	Y
7 Crowley	Y	Y	Y	Y	Y	Y
8 Nadler	Y	Y	Y	Y	Y	Y
9 Weiner	Y	Y	Y	Y	Y	Y
10 Towns	Y	Y	Y	Y	Y	Y
11 Clarke	Y	Y	Y	Y	Y	Y
12 Velázquez	Y	Y	Y	Y	Y	Y
13 McMahon	?	?	?	?	?	Y
14 Maloney	Y	Y	Y	Y	Y	Y
15 Rangel	Y	Y	Y	Y	Y	Y
16 Serrano	Y	Y	Y	Y	Y	Y
17 Engel	Y	Y	Y	Y	Y	Y
18 Lowey	Y	Y	Y	Y	Y	Y
19 Hall	Y	Y	Y	Y	Y	Y
20 Murphy	Y	Y	Y	Y	Y	Y
21 Tonko	+	Y	Y	Y	Y	Y
22 Hinchey	Y	Y	Y	Y	Y	Y
23 Owens	Y	N	Y	Y	Y	Y
24 Arcuri	Y	Y	Y	Y	Y	Y
25 Maffei	Y	Y	Y	N	Y	Y
26 **Lee**	Y	N	Y	N	?	Y
27 Higgins	Y	Y	Y	Y	Y	Y
28 Slaughter	Y	Y	Y	Y	Y	Y
29 **Reed**	Y	N	N	N	Y	Y
NORTH CAROLINA						
1 Butterfield	Y	Y	Y	Y	Y	Y
2 Etheridge	Y	Y	Y	Y	Y	Y
3 **Jones**	?	?	?	?	?	?
4 Price	Y	Y	Y	Y	Y	Y

	659	660	661	662	663	664
5 **Foxx**	N	N	N	N	Y	N
6 **Coble**	?	?	?	?	?	?
7 McIntyre	Y	Y	Y	N	Y	?
8 Kissell	Y	Y	Y	Y	Y	Y
9 **Myrick**	N	N	N	N	Y	N
10 **McHenry**	N	N	N	N	Y	?
11 Shuler	Y	Y	Y	Y	Y	?
12 Watt	Y	Y	Y	Y	Y	Y
13 Miller	Y	?	Y	Y	Y	Y
NORTH DAKOTA						
AL Pomeroy	Y	Y	Y	Y	Y	?
OHIO						
1 Driehaus	Y	Y	Y	Y	Y	Y
2 **Schmidt**	N	N	N	N	Y	N
3 **Turner**	N	N	N	N	Y	Y
4 **Jordan**	N	N	N	N	N	N
5 **Latta**	N	N	N	N	Y	N
6 Wilson	Y	Y	Y	Y	Y	Y
7 **Austria**	N	N	N	N	Y	Y
8 **Boehner**	?	N	N	N	?	?
9 Kaptur	Y	Y	Y	Y	Y	Y
10 Kucinich	Y	Y	Y	N	Y	Y
11 Fudge	Y	Y	Y	Y	Y	?
12 **Tiberi**	N	N	N	N	?	?
13 Sutton	?	Y	Y	Y	Y	Y
14 **LaTourette**	N	N	N	N	?	N
15 Kilroy	Y	Y	?	Y	Y	?
16 Boccieri	Y	Y	Y	N	+	?
17 Ryan	Y	Y	Y	Y	Y	Y
18 Space	Y	Y	Y	Y	Y	?
OKLAHOMA						
1 **Sullivan**	N	N	N	N	Y	?
2 Boren	Y	Y	N	Y	Y	Y
3 **Lucas**	N	N	N	N	Y	?
4 **Cole**	N	N	N	N	Y	Y
5 **Fallin**	?	?	?	?	?	?
OREGON						
1 Wu	Y	Y	Y	N	Y	?
2 **Walden**	N	N	N	N	Y	N
3 Blumenauer	+	+	+	?	?	?
4 DeFazio	Y	Y	Y	N	Y	?
5 Schrader	Y	Y	Y	Y	Y	?
PENNSYLVANIA						
1 Brady	Y	?	Y	Y	Y	?
2 Fattah	Y	Y	Y	Y	Y	Y
3 Dahlkemper	Y	Y	Y	Y	Y	Y
4 Altmire	Y	Y	Y	Y	Y	Y
5 **Thompson**	N	N	N	N	Y	Y
6 **Gerlach**	Y	N	N	N	Y	Y
7 Sestak	Y	Y	Y	Y	Y	Y
8 Murphy, P.	Y	Y	Y	Y	Y	Y
9 **Shuster**	N	N	N	N	Y	N
10 Carney	Y	Y	Y	Y	Y	Y
11 Kanjorski	Y	Y	Y	?	Y	Y
12 Critz	Y	Y	Y	Y	Y	Y
13 Schwartz	Y	Y	Y	Y	Y	Y
14 Doyle	?	?	?	?	?	Y
15 **Dent**	Y	Y	Y	N	Y	Y
16 **Pitts**	N	N	N	N	Y	?
17 Holden	Y	Y	Y	Y	Y	Y
18 **Murphy, T.**	N	N	N	N	Y	Y
19 **Platts**	N	Y	N	N	Y	Y
RHODE ISLAND						
1 Kennedy	?	?	?	?	?	?
2 Langevin	Y	Y	Y	Y	Y	Y
SOUTH CAROLINA						
1 **Brown**	N	N	N	?	?	?
2 **Wilson**	N	N	N	N	Y	N
3 **Barrett**	?	?	?	?	?	?
4 **Inglis**	?	?	?	N	N	N
5 Spratt	Y	Y	Y	Y	Y	?
6 Clyburn	Y	Y	Y	Y	Y	Y
SOUTH DAKOTA						
AL Herseth Sandlin	+	+	+	+	+	?
TENNESSEE						
1 **Roe**	N	N	N	N	Y	?
2 **Duncan**	N	N	N	N	?	?
3 **Wamp**	?	?	?	?	?	?
4 Davis	Y	Y	Y	Y	Y	?
5 Cooper	Y	Y	Y	Y	?	?
6 Gordon	Y	?	?	?	Y	?
7 **Blackburn**	N	N	N	N	?	?
8 Tanner	?	?	?	?	?	?
9 Cohen	Y	Y	Y	Y	Y	?

	659	660	661	662	663	664
TEXAS						
1 **Gohmert**	N	N	N	N	Y	?
2 **Poe**	N	N	N	N	N	?
3 **Johnson, S.**	?	?	?	?	?	?
4 **Hall**	N	N	N	N	Y	N
5 **Hensarling**	N	N	N	N	N	N
6 **Barton**	?	?	?	?	?	?
7 **Culberson**	?	?	?	?	?	?
8 **Brady**	N	N	N	N	Y	N
9 Green, A.	Y	Y	Y	Y	Y	Y
10 **McCaul**	Y	Y	N	N	Y	?
11 **Conaway**	N	N	N	N	N	N
12 **Granger**	?	?	?	?	?	?
13 **Thornberry**	N	N	N	N	N	?
14 **Paul**	N	N	N	N	N	?
15 Hinojosa	Y	?	?	?	?	?
16 Reyes	?	?	?	?	?	?
17 Edwards	Y	?	Y	Y	Y	Y
18 Jackson Lee	Y	Y	Y	Y	Y	Y
19 **Neugebauer**	N	N	N	N	N	?
20 Gonzalez	Y	Y	Y	Y	Y	Y
21 **Smith**	N	Y	?	N	Y	?
22 **Olson**	N	N	N	N	Y	N
23 Rodriguez	Y	Y	Y	N	Y	?
24 **Marchant**	?	?	?	?	?	?
25 Doggett	Y	Y	Y	N	Y	?
26 **Burgess**	N	N	N	N	Y	Y
27 Ortiz	?	?	?	?	?	?
28 Cuellar	Y	Y	Y	Y	Y	?
29 Green, G.	Y	Y	Y	+	+	?
30 Johnson, E.	Y	Y	Y	Y	Y	?
31 **Carter**	N	N	N	N	Y	?
32 **Sessions**	N	N	N	N	Y	N
UTAH						
1 **Bishop**	N	N	N	N	Y	N
2 Matheson	Y	Y	Y	N	Y	Y
3 **Chaffetz**	N	N	N	N	Y	Y
VERMONT						
AL Welch	Y	Y	Y	Y	Y	?
VIRGINIA						
1 **Wittman**	N	N	N	N	Y	N
2 Nye	Y	Y	Y	N	Y	Y
3 Scott	Y	Y	Y	Y	Y	Y
4 **Forbes**	N	N	N	N	Y	?
5 Perriello	Y	Y	N	N	Y	Y
6 **Goodlatte**	N	N	N	N	Y	N
7 **Cantor**	N	N	N	N	Y	N
8 Moran	Y	Y	Y	Y	Y	Y
9 Boucher	Y	Y	Y	Y	?	Y
10 **Wolf**	Y	N	Y	N	Y	Y
11 Connolly	Y	Y	Y	N	Y	Y
WASHINGTON						
1 Inslee	Y	Y	Y	Y	Y	Y
2 Larsen	Y	Y	Y	Y	Y	Y
3 Baird	?	?	?	?	?	?
4 **Hastings**	N	N	N	N	Y	?
5 **McMorris Rodgers**	?	?	?	?	?	?
6 Dicks	Y	Y	Y	Y	Y	Y
7 McDermott	Y	Y	Y	Y	Y	Y
8 **Reichert**	Y	N	N	N	Y	Y
9 Smith	?	?	?	?	?	?
WEST VIRGINIA						
1 Mollohan	Y	Y	Y	Y	Y	Y
2 **Capito**	Y	N	N	N	Y	Y
3 Rahall	Y	Y	Y	Y	Y	Y
WISCONSIN						
1 **Ryan**	N	N	N	N	?	?
2 Baldwin	Y	Y	Y	Y	Y	Y
3 Kind	Y	Y	Y	Y	Y	Y
4 Moore	Y	Y	Y	Y	Y	Y
5 **Sensenbrenner**	N	N	N	N	Y	?
6 **Petri**	N	N	N	N	Y	?
7 Obey	Y	Y	Y	Y	Y	Y
8 Kagen	Y	Y	+	Y	Y	?
WYOMING						
AL **Lummis**	N	N	N	N	Y	N
DELEGATES						
Faleomavaega (A.S.)						
Norton (D.C.)						
Bordallo (Guam)						
Sablan (N. Marianas)						
Pierluisi (P.R.)						
Christensen (V.I.)						

House Roll Call Index by Subject

Appendix S

Senate Votes

Senate Roll Call Index By Bill Number

IN THE SENATE | By Vote Number

1. Martin Nomination/Confirmation. Confirmation of President Obama's nomination of Beverly Baldwin Martin of Georgia to be a judge for the 11th U.S. Circuit Court of Appeals. Confirmed 97-0: D 57-0; R 38-0; I 2-0. A "yea" was a vote in support of the president's position. Jan. 20, 2010.

2. H J Res 45. Debt Limit Increase/TARP Elimination. Thune, R-S.D., amendment to the Baucus, D-Mont., substitute amendment. The Thune amendment would terminate the Troubled Asset Relief Program and require that the debt ceiling increase in the resolution be reduced by the amount of TARP funds that are repaid after the date of enactment. The substitute would increase the statutory debt limit to $14.29 trillion. Rejected 53-45: D 13-43; R 40-0; I 0-2. (By unanimous consent, the Senate agreed to raise the majority requirement for adoption of the Thune amendment to 60 votes.) A "nay" was a vote in support of the president's position. Jan. 21, 2010.

3. Peterson Nomination/Confirmation. Confirmation of President Obama's nomination of Rosanna Malouf Peterson of Washington to be a judge for the U.S. District Court for the Eastern District of Washington. Confirmed 89-0: D 54-0; R 33-0; I 2-0. A "yea" was a vote in support of the president's position. Jan. 25, 2010.

4. H J Res 45. Debt Limit Increase/Limits on Changes to Social Security. Baucus, D-Mont., amendment to the Baucus substitute amendment. The Baucus amendment would exclude fiscal task force proposals that affect programs established under Title II of the Social Security Act or related Social Security taxes from being considered under expedited procedures in the House or Senate. In the Senate, a three-fifths majority would be required to waive the exemptions or to sustain an appeal of the ruling of the chair on a point of order related to the exclusions. The substitute would increase the statutory debt limit to $14.29 trillion. Adopted 97-0: D 56-0; R 39-0; I 2-0. (By unanimous consent, the Senate agreed to raise the majority requirement for adoption of the Baucus amendment to 60 votes.) Jan. 26, 2010.

5. H J Res 45. Debt Limit Increase/Fiscal Task Force. Conrad, D-N.D., amendment to the Baucus, D-Mont., substitute amendment. The Conrad amendment would establish a bipartisan fiscal task force with the authority to propose debt and deficit reduction policies. The task force would transmit proposals in legislative language. The proposals would be considered under expedited floor procedure, could not be amended and would require a three-fifths majority vote in both chambers. Congress would have to consider any proposal supported by 14 of the panel's 18 members. Rejected 53-46: D 36-22; R 16-23; I 1-1. (By unanimous consent, the Senate agreed to raise the majority requirement for adoption of the Conrad amendment to 60 votes.) A "yea" was a vote in support of the president's position. Jan. 26, 2010.

6. H J Res 45. Debt Limit Increase/GAO Duplication Report. Division I of the Coburn, R-Okla., amendment to the Baucus, D-Mont., substitute amendment. Division I would require the Government Accountability Office to routinely investigate areas with duplicative goals and activities within the government and report annually to Congress on the findings, including the cost of the duplications and recommendations to eliminate them. Adopted 94-0: D 54-0; R 38-0; I 2-0. (By unanimous consent, the Senate agreed to divide the question on the Coburn amendment and to raise the majority requirement for adoption of each division to 60 votes.) Jan. 26, 2010.

State / Senator	1	2	3	4	5	6
ALABAMA						
Shelby	Y	Y	Y	Y	N	Y
Sessions	Y	Y	Y	Y	N	Y
ALASKA						
Murkowski	Y	Y	?	?	?	Y
Begich	Y	Y	Y	Y	Y	Y
ARIZONA						
McCain	Y	Y	Y	Y	N	Y
Kyl	Y	Y	Y	Y	N	Y
ARKANSAS						
Lincoln	Y	Y	Y	Y	Y	Y
Pryor	Y	Y	Y	Y	Y	Y
CALIFORNIA						
Feinstein	Y	Y	Y	Y	Y	Y
Boxer	Y	N	Y	Y	Y	Y
COLORADO						
Udall	+	Y	Y	Y	Y	Y
Bennet	Y	Y	Y	Y	Y	Y
CONNECTICUT						
Dodd	Y	N	Y	Y	N	Y
Lieberman	Y	N	Y	Y	N	Y
DELAWARE						
Carper	Y	N	Y	Y	Y	Y
Kaufman	Y	N	Y	Y	Y	Y
FLORIDA						
Nelson	Y	Y	Y	Y	Y	Y
LeMieux	Y	Y	Y	Y	Y	Y
GEORGIA						
Chambliss	Y	Y	Y	Y	N	Y
Isakson	Y	Y	Y	Y	Y	Y
HAWAII						
Inouye	Y	N	?	Y	N	Y
Akaka	Y	N	Y	Y	N	Y
IDAHO						
Crapo	Y	Y	Y	Y	N	Y
Risch	Y	Y	Y	Y	N	Y
ILLINOIS						
Durbin	Y	N	Y	Y	Y	Y
Burris	Y	N	Y	Y	N	Y
INDIANA						
Lugar	Y	Y	Y	Y	Y	Y
Bayh	Y	Y	Y	Y	Y	Y
IOWA						
Grassley	Y	Y	Y	Y	N	Y
Harkin	Y	N	Y	Y	N	Y
KANSAS						
Brownback	Y	Y	?	Y	N	Y
Roberts	?	Y	?	Y	N	?
KENTUCKY						
McConnell	Y	Y	Y	Y	N	Y
Bunning	Y	Y	Y	Y	N	Y
LOUISIANA						
Landrieu	Y	N	Y	Y	Y	Y
Vitter	Y	Y	Y	Y	Y	Y
MAINE						
Snowe	Y	Y	Y	Y	N	Y
Collins	Y	Y	Y	Y	Y	Y
MARYLAND						
Mikulski	Y	N	Y	Y	N	?
Cardin	Y	N	Y	Y	N	Y
MASSACHUSETTS						
Kerry	Y	N	Y	Y	Y	Y
Kirk	Y	N	Y	Y	N	Y
MICHIGAN						
Levin	Y	N	Y	Y	Y	Y
Stabenow	Y	N	Y	Y	N	Y
MINNESOTA						
Klobuchar	Y	N	?	Y	Y	Y
Franken	Y	N	Y	Y	Y	Y
MISSISSIPPI						
Cochran	Y	Y	Y	Y	N	Y
Wicker	Y	Y	Y	Y	Y	Y
MISSOURI						
Bond	?	Y	Y	Y	Y	Y
McCaskill	Y	N	Y	Y	Y	Y
MONTANA						
Baucus	Y	N	Y	Y	N	Y
Tester	Y	Y	Y	Y	Y	Y
NEBRASKA						
Nelson	Y	Y	Y	Y	Y	Y
Johanns	Y	Y	Y	Y	Y	Y
NEVADA						
Reid	Y	N	Y	Y	Y	Y
Ensign	Y	Y	Y	Y	N	Y
NEW HAMPSHIRE						
Gregg	Y	Y	Y	Y	Y	Y
Shaheen	Y	N	Y	Y	Y	Y
NEW JERSEY						
Lautenberg	Y	N	Y	Y	N	Y
Menendez	Y	N	Y	Y	Y	Y
NEW MEXICO						
Bingaman	Y	N	Y	Y	Y	Y
Udall	Y	N	Y	Y	N	Y
NEW YORK						
Schumer	Y	N	Y	Y	Y	Y
Gillibrand	Y	N	Y	Y	Y	Y
NORTH CAROLINA						
Burr	Y	Y	?	Y	N	Y
Hagan	Y	?	?	Y	Y	Y
NORTH DAKOTA						
Conrad	Y	N	Y	Y	Y	Y
Dorgan	Y	N	Y	Y	Y	Y
OHIO						
Voinovich	Y	Y	Y	Y	Y	?
Brown	Y	N	Y	Y	N	Y
OKLAHOMA						
Inhofe	Y	Y	?	Y	N	Y
Coburn	Y	Y	Y	Y	N	Y
OREGON						
Wyden	Y	Y	Y	Y	Y	Y
Merkley	Y	N	Y	Y	N	Y
PENNSYLVANIA						
Specter	Y	N	Y	Y	N	Y
Casey	Y	N	Y	Y	N	Y
RHODE ISLAND						
Reed	Y	N	Y	Y	N	Y
Whitehouse	Y	N	Y	Y	N	Y
SOUTH CAROLINA						
Graham	Y	Y	Y	Y	N	Y
DeMint	Y	Y	Y	Y	N	Y
SOUTH DAKOTA						
Johnson	Y	N	Y	Y	Y	Y
Thune	Y	Y	Y	Y	N	Y
TENNESSEE						
Alexander	Y	Y	Y	Y	Y	Y
Corker	Y	Y	Y	Y	Y	Y
TEXAS						
Hutchison	Y	Y	?	Y	N	Y
Cornyn	Y	Y	Y	Y	Y	Y
UTAH						
Hatch	Y	Y	Y	Y	N	Y
Bennett	Y	Y	?	Y	N	Y
VERMONT						
Leahy	Y	N	Y	Y	N	Y
Sanders	Y	N	Y	Y	N	Y
VIRGINIA						
Webb	Y	Y	Y	?	Y	?
Warner	Y	N	?	?	Y	?
WASHINGTON						
Murray	Y	N	Y	Y	N	Y
Cantwell	Y	N	Y	Y	N	Y
WEST VIRGINIA						
Byrd	Y	?	?	Y	N	?
Rockefeller	Y	N	Y	Y	N	Y
WISCONSIN						
Kohl	Y	N	Y	Y	Y	Y
Feingold	Y	Y	Y	Y	Y	Y
WYOMING						
Enzi	Y	Y	Y	Y	N	Y
Barrasso	Y	Y	Y	Y	N	Y

KEY — **Republicans** — Democrats — *Independents*

Y Voted for (yea)	X Paired against	C Voted "present" to avoid possible conflict of interest
# Paired for	– Announced against	
+ Announced for	P Voted "present"	? Did not vote or otherwise make a position known
N Voted against (nay)		

IN THE SENATE | By Vote Number

7. **H J Res 45. Debt Limit Increase/Legislative Branch Rescission.**
Division II of the Coburn, R-Okla., amendment to the Baucus, D-Mont.,
substitute amendment. Division II would rescind $245 million in un-
obligated funds under the fiscal 2010 Legislative Branch appropriations
law. It would bar the use of funds for Senate offices to mail postcards
to constituents announcing the location of town meetings where the
senator would be in attendance. Rejected 46-48: D 9-45; R 37-1; I 0-2.
(By unanimous consent, the Senate agreed to divide the question on the
Coburn amendment and to raise the majority requirement for adoption
of each division to 60 votes.) Jan. 26, 2010.

8. **H J Res 45. Debt Limit Increase/Department Funds Rescission.**
Division III of the Coburn, R-Okla., amendment to the Baucus, D-Mont.,
substitute amendment. Division III would rescind certain unobligated
funds made available under fiscal 2010 appropriations laws and stipulate programs to be eliminated. Rejected 33-61: D 2-52; R 31-7; I 0-2.
(By unanimous consent, the Senate agreed to divide the question on the
Coburn amendment and to raise the majority requirement for adoption
of each division to 60 votes.) Jan. 26, 2010.

9. **H J Res 45. Debt Limit Increase/Unobligated Funds Rescission.**
Division IV of the Coburn, R-Okla., amendment to the Baucus, D-Mont.,
substitute amendment. Division IV would rescind all of the discretionary
funds that were unobligated at the end of fiscal 2009, had not expired
and had been available for at least two consecutive years prior to enactment of the joint resolution. Rejected 37-57: D 2-52; R 35-3; I 0-2. (By
unanimous consent, the Senate agreed to divide the question on the
Coburn amendment and to raise the majority requirement for adoption
of each division to 60 votes.) Jan. 26, 2010.

10. **H J Res 45. Debt Limit Increase/Budgetary Accountability
Commission.** Brownback, R-Kan., amendment to the Baucus, D-Mont.,
substitute amendment. The Brownback amendment would establish a
congressional budgetary accountability commission to assess federal
agencies and programs and to make recommendations to change those
considered duplicative, inefficient and outdated. The commission would
submit legislative proposals that would be considered under expedited
procedures in the House and Senate, with no amendments in order.
Rejected 51-49: D 13-45; R 37-3; I 1-1. (By unanimous consent, the Senate
agreed to raise the majority requirement for adoption of the Brownback
amendment to 60 votes.) Jan. 28, 2010.

11. **H J Res 45. Debt Limit Increase/Spending Caps.** Sessions,
R-Ala., amendment to the Baucus, D-Mont., substitute amendment. The
Sessions amendment would establish discretionary spending limits for
five fiscal years beginning in fiscal 2010 equal to the levels for defense
and non-defense spending in the fiscal 2010 budget resolution. It also
would limit spending on overseas deployments and related operations to
$130 billion in fiscal 2010 and $50 billion in each of fiscal years 2011 to
2014. Points of order against emergency-spending designations could be
waived by a three-fifths majority vote in the Senate. Rejected 56-44:
D 16-42; R 39-1; I 1-1. (By unanimous consent, the Senate agreed to raise
the majority requirement for adoption of the Sessions amendment to
60 votes.) Jan. 28, 2010.

	7	8	9	10	11
ALABAMA					
Shelby	Y	Y	Y	Y	Y
Sessions	Y	Y	Y	Y	Y
ALASKA					
Murkowski	Y	N	Y	Y	Y
Begich	N	N	N	N	Y
ARIZONA					
McCain	Y	Y	Y	Y	Y
Kyl	Y	Y	Y	Y	Y
ARKANSAS					
Lincoln	Y	N	N	Y	Y
Pryor	N	N	N	N	Y
CALIFORNIA					
Feinstein	N	N	N	N	N
Boxer	N	N	N	N	N
COLORADO					
Udall	Y	N	N	N	Y
Bennet	Y	N	N	Y	Y
CONNECTICUT					
Dodd	N	N	N	N	N
Lieberman	N	N	N	Y	Y
DELAWARE					
Carper	N	N	N	N	Y
Kaufman	N	N	N	N	N
FLORIDA					
Nelson	N	N	N	Y	Y
LeMieux	Y	Y	Y	Y	Y
GEORGIA					
Chambliss	Y	Y	Y	Y	Y
Isakson	Y	Y	Y	Y	Y
HAWAII					
Inouye	N	N	N	N	N
Akaka	N	N	N	N	N
IDAHO					
Crapo	Y	Y	Y	Y	Y
Risch	Y	Y	Y	Y	Y
ILLINOIS					
Durbin	N	N	N	N	N
Burris	N	N	N	N	N
INDIANA					
Lugar	Y	N	Y	Y	Y
Bayh	Y	Y	Y	Y	Y
IOWA					
Grassley	Y	N	Y	Y	Y
Harkin	N	N	N	N	N
KANSAS					
Brownback	Y	Y	Y	Y	Y
Roberts	?	?	?	Y	Y
KENTUCKY					
McConnell	Y	Y	Y	Y	Y
Bunning	Y	Y	Y	Y	Y
LOUISIANA					
Landrieu	N	N	N	N	N
Vitter	Y	Y	Y	Y	Y
MAINE					
Snowe	Y	N	Y	N	Y
Collins	Y	N	N	Y	Y
MARYLAND					
Mikulski	?	?	?	N	N
Cardin	N	N	N	N	N
MASSACHUSETTS					
Kerry	N	N	N	N	N
Kirk	N	N	N	N	N
MICHIGAN					
Levin	N	N	N	N	N
Stabenow	N	N	N	N	N
MINNESOTA					
Klobuchar	Y	N	N	Y	Y
Franken	N	N	N	N	N
MISSISSIPPI					
Cochran	Y	N	N	N	N
Wicker	Y	Y	Y	Y	Y
MISSOURI					
Bond	N	N	N	Y	Y
McCaskill	Y	Y	N	Y	Y

	7	8	9	10	11
MONTANA					
Baucus	N	N	N	N	N
Tester	N	N	N	Y	Y
NEBRASKA					
Nelson	N	N	N	Y	Y
Johanns	Y	Y	Y	Y	Y
NEVADA					
Reid	N	N	N	N	N
Ensign	Y	Y	Y	Y	Y
NEW HAMPSHIRE					
Gregg	Y	Y	Y	N	Y
Shaheen	N	N	N	Y	Y
NEW JERSEY					
Lautenberg	N	N	N	N	N
Menendez	N	N	N	N	N
NEW MEXICO					
Bingaman	N	N	N	N	N
Udall	N	N	N	N	N
NEW YORK					
Schumer	N	N	N	N	N
Gillibrand	N	N	N	N	N
NORTH CAROLINA					
Burr	Y	Y	Y	Y	Y
Hagan	Y	N	N	Y	Y
NORTH DAKOTA					
Conrad	N	N	N	N	N
Dorgan	N	N	N	N	N
OHIO					
Voinovich	?	?	?	Y	Y
Brown	N	N	N	N	N
OKLAHOMA					
Inhofe	Y	Y	Y	Y	Y
Coburn	Y	Y	Y	Y	Y
OREGON					
Wyden	N	N	N	N	N
Merkley	N	N	N	Y	N
PENNSYLVANIA					
Specter	N	N	N	N	N
Casey	N	N	N	N	N
RHODE ISLAND					
Reed	N	N	N	N	N
Whitehouse	N	N	N	N	N
SOUTH CAROLINA					
Graham	Y	Y	Y	Y	Y
DeMint	Y	Y	Y	Y	Y
SOUTH DAKOTA					
Johnson	N	N	N	N	N
Thune	Y	Y	Y	Y	Y
TENNESSEE					
Alexander	Y	Y	Y	Y	Y
Corker	Y	Y	Y	Y	Y
TEXAS					
Hutchison	Y	Y	Y	Y	Y
Cornyn	Y	Y	Y	Y	Y
UTAH					
Hatch	Y	Y	Y	Y	Y
Bennett	Y	Y	Y	Y	Y
VERMONT					
Leahy	N	N	N	N	N
Sanders	N	N	N	N	N
VIRGINIA					
Webb	?	?	?	Y	Y
Warner	?	?	?	Y	Y
WASHINGTON					
Murray	N	N	N	N	N
Cantwell	N	N	N	N	N
WEST VIRGINIA					
Byrd	?	?	?	N	N
Rockefeller	N	N	N	N	N
WISCONSIN					
Kohl	Y	N	N	N	N
Feingold	Y	N	Y	N	N
WYOMING					
Enzi	Y	Y	Y	Y	Y
Barrasso	Y	Y	Y	Y	Y

KEY	**Republicans**	Democrats	*Independents*	
Y Voted for (yea)		X Paired against		C Voted "present" to avoid possible conflict of interest
# Paired for		− Announced against		? Did not vote or otherwise make a position known
+ Announced for		P Voted "present"		
N Voted against (nay)				

IN THE SENATE | By Vote Number

12. **H J Res 45. Debt Limit Increase/Statutory Pay-as-You-Go.** Reid, D-Nev., amendment to the Baucus, D-Mont., substitute amendment. The Reid amendment would establish a statutory requirement that new tax and mandatory spending legislation be budget neutral, enforced by automatic across-the-board spending cuts in non-exempt programs if the pay-as-you-go tally at the end of the year shows a deficit. It would exempt measures to extend certain tax cuts scheduled to expire in 2010 and treat the alternative minimum tax exemption as though it had been extended beyond Dec. 31, 2009. A three-fifths majority would be required to waive a point of order against emergency spending designations in the Senate. Adopted 60-40: D 58-0; R 0-40; I 2-0. (By unanimous consent, the Senate agreed to raise the majority requirement for adoption of the Reid amendment to 60 votes.) Jan. 28, 2010.

13. **H J Res 45. Debt Limit Increase/Substitute.** Baucus, D-Mont., substitute amendment that would increase the statutory debt limit by $1.9 trillion to $14.29 trillion. As amended, the substitute also would establish a statutory requirement that new tax and mandatory spending legislation be budget neutral, enforced by automatic across-the-board spending cuts in non-exempt programs if the pay-as-you-go tally at the end of the year shows a deficit. It would also require the Government Accountability Office to investigate areas with duplicative goals and activities within the government. Adopted 60-40: D 58-0; R 0-40; I 2-0. (By unanimous consent, the Senate agreed to raise the majority requirement for adoption of the Baucus substitute amendment to 60 votes.) Jan. 28, 2010.

14. **H J Res 45. Debt Limit Increase/Passage.** Passage of the joint resolution that would increase the statutory debt limit by $1.9 trillion to $14.29 trillion. It also would establish a statutory requirement that new tax and mandatory spending legislation be budget neutral, enforced by automatic across-the-board spending cuts in non-exempt programs if the pay-as-you-go tally at the end of the year shows a deficit. It would require the Government Accountability Office to investigate areas with duplicative goals and activities within the government. Passed 60-39: D 58-0; R 0-39; I 2-0. (By unanimous consent, the Senate agreed to raise the majority requirement for passage of the joint resolution to 60 votes.) A "yea" was a vote in support of the president's position. Jan. 28, 2010.

15. **Bernanke Nomination/Cloture.** Motion to invoke cloture (thus limiting debate) on the nomination of Ben S. Bernanke of New Jersey to be chairman of the Board of Governors of the Federal Reserve System. Motion agreed to 77-23: D 53-5; R 23-17; I 1-1. Three-fifths of the total Senate (60) is required to invoke cloture. Jan. 28, 2010.

16. **Bernanke Nomination/Confirmation.** Confirmation of President Obama's nomination of Ben S. Bernanke of New Jersey to be chairman of the Board of Governors of the Federal Reserve System. Confirmed 70-30: D 47-11; R 22-18; I 1-1. A "yea" was a vote in support of the president's position. Jan. 28, 2010.

	12	13	14	15	16
ALABAMA					
Shelby	N	N	N	N	N
Sessions	N	N	N	N	N
ALASKA					
Murkowski	N	N	N	Y	Y
Begich	Y	Y	Y	N	N
ARIZONA					
McCain	N	N	N	N	N
Kyl	N	N	N	Y	Y
ARKANSAS					
Lincoln	Y	Y	Y	Y	Y
Pryor	Y	Y	Y	Y	Y
CALIFORNIA					
Feinstein	Y	Y	Y	Y	Y
Boxer	Y	Y	Y	Y	N
COLORADO					
Udall	Y	Y	Y	Y	Y
Bennet	Y	Y	Y	Y	Y
CONNECTICUT					
Dodd	Y	Y	Y	Y	Y
Lieberman	Y	Y	Y	Y	Y
DELAWARE					
Carper	Y	Y	Y	Y	Y
Kaufman	Y	Y	Y	Y	N
FLORIDA					
Nelson	Y	Y	Y	Y	Y
LeMieux	N	N	N	Y	N
GEORGIA					
Chambliss	N	N	N	N	Y
Isakson	N	N	N	Y	Y
HAWAII					
Inouye	Y	Y	Y	Y	Y
Akaka	Y	Y	Y	Y	Y
IDAHO					
Crapo	N	N	N	N	N
Risch	N	N	N	N	N
ILLINOIS					
Durbin	Y	Y	Y	Y	Y
Burris	Y	Y	Y	Y	Y
INDIANA					
Lugar	N	N	N	Y	Y
Bayh	Y	Y	Y	Y	Y
IOWA					
Grassley	N	N	N	N	N
Harkin	Y	Y	Y	Y	N
KANSAS					
Brownback	N	N	N	N	N
Roberts	N	N	N	N	N
KENTUCKY					
McConnell	N	N	N	Y	Y
Bunning	N	N	N	N	N
LOUISIANA					
Landrieu	Y	Y	Y	Y	Y
Vitter	N	N	N	N	N
MAINE					
Snowe	N	N	N	Y	Y
Collins	N	N	N	Y	Y
MARYLAND					
Mikulski	Y	Y	Y	Y	Y
Cardin	Y	Y	Y	Y	Y
MASSACHUSETTS					
Kerry	Y	Y	Y	Y	Y
Kirk	Y	Y	Y	Y	Y
MICHIGAN					
Levin	Y	Y	Y	Y	Y
Stabenow	Y	Y	Y	Y	Y
MINNESOTA					
Klobuchar	Y	Y	Y	Y	Y
Franken	Y	Y	Y	Y	N
MISSISSIPPI					
Cochran	N	N	N	Y	Y
Wicker	N	N	N	N	N
MISSOURI					
Bond	N	N	N	Y	Y
McCaskill	Y	Y	Y	Y	Y
MONTANA					
Baucus	Y	Y	Y	Y	Y
Tester	Y	Y	Y	Y	Y
NEBRASKA					
Nelson	Y	Y	Y	Y	Y
Johanns	N	N	N	Y	Y
NEVADA					
Reid	Y	Y	Y	Y	Y
Ensign	N	N	N	N	N
NEW HAMPSHIRE					
Gregg	N	N	N	Y	Y
Shaheen	Y	Y	Y	Y	Y
NEW JERSEY					
Lautenberg	Y	Y	Y	Y	Y
Menendez	Y	Y	Y	Y	Y
NEW MEXICO					
Bingaman	Y	Y	Y	Y	Y
Udall	Y	Y	Y	Y	Y
NEW YORK					
Schumer	Y	Y	Y	Y	Y
Gillibrand	Y	Y	Y	Y	Y
NORTH CAROLINA					
Burr	N	N	N	Y	Y
Hagan	Y	Y	Y	Y	Y
NORTH DAKOTA					
Conrad	Y	Y	Y	Y	Y
Dorgan	Y	Y	Y	Y	N
OHIO					
Voinovich	N	N	N	Y	Y
Brown	Y	Y	Y	Y	Y
OKLAHOMA					
Inhofe	N	N	N	N	N
Coburn	N	N	N	Y	Y
OREGON					
Wyden	Y	Y	Y	Y	Y
Merkley	Y	Y	Y	N	N
PENNSYLVANIA					
Specter	Y	Y	Y	N	N
Casey	Y	Y	Y	Y	Y
RHODE ISLAND					
Reed	Y	Y	Y	Y	Y
Whitehouse	Y	Y	Y	Y	N
SOUTH CAROLINA					
Graham	N	N	N	Y	Y
DeMint	N	N	N	N	N
SOUTH DAKOTA					
Johnson	Y	Y	Y	Y	Y
Thune	N	N	N	N	N
TENNESSEE					
Alexander	N	N	N	Y	Y
Corker	N	N	N	Y	Y
TEXAS					
Hutchison	N	N	N	N	N
Cornyn	N	N	N	N	N
UTAH					
Hatch	N	N	N	Y	Y
Bennett	N	N	N	Y	Y
VERMONT					
Leahy	Y	Y	Y	Y	Y
Sanders	Y	Y	Y	N	N
VIRGINIA					
Webb	Y	Y	Y	Y	Y
Warner	Y	Y	Y	Y	Y
WASHINGTON					
Murray	Y	Y	Y	Y	Y
Cantwell	Y	Y	Y	N	N
WEST VIRGINIA					
Byrd	Y	Y	Y	Y	Y
Rockefeller	Y	Y	Y	Y	Y
WISCONSIN					
Kohl	Y	Y	Y	Y	Y
Feingold	Y	Y	Y	N	N
WYOMING					
Enzi	N	N	?	Y	Y
Barrasso	N	N	N	Y	Y

KEY   **Republicans**   Democrats   *Independents*

Y Voted for (yea)
\# Paired for
\+ Announced for
N Voted against (nay)

X Paired against
– Announced against
P Voted "present"

C Voted "present" to avoid possible conflict of interest
? Did not vote or otherwise make a position known

IN THE SENATE | By Vote Number

17. Smith Nomination/Cloture. Motion to invoke cloture (thus limiting debate) on the nomination of M. Patricia Smith of New York to be solicitor of the Labor Department. Motion agreed to 60-32: D 58-0; R 0-32; I 2-0. Three-fifths of the total Senate (60) is required to invoke cloture. Feb. 1, 2010.

18. Smith Nomination/Confirmation. Confirmation of President Obama's nomination of M. Patricia Smith of New York to be solicitor of the Labor Department. Confirmed 60-37: D 58-0; R 0-37; I 2-0. A "yea" was a vote in support of the president's position. Feb. 4, 2010.

19. Johnson Nomination/Cloture. Motion to invoke cloture (thus limiting debate) on the nomination of Martha N. Johnson of Maryland to be administrator of General Services. Motion agreed to 82-16: D 58-0; R 22-16; I 2-0. Three-fifths of the total Senate (60) is required to invoke cloture. Feb. 4, 2010.

20. Johnson Nomination/Confirmation. Confirmation of President Obama's nomination of Martha N. Johnson of Maryland to be administrator of General Services. Confirmed 96-0: D 58-0; R 36-0; I 2-0. A "yea" was a vote in support of the president's position. Feb. 4, 2010.

21. Greenaway Nomination/Confirmation. Confirmation of President Obama's nomination of Joseph A. Greenaway Jr. of New Jersey to be a judge for the 3rd U.S. Circuit Court of Appeals. Confirmed 84-0: D 52-0; R 31-0; I 1-0. A "yea" was a vote in support of the president's position. Feb. 9, 2010.

22. Becker Nomination/Cloture. Motion to invoke cloture (thus limiting debate) on the nomination of Craig Becker of Illinois to be a member of the National Labor Relations Board. Motion rejected 52-33: D 51-2; R 0-31; I 1-0. Three-fifths of the total Senate (60) is required to invoke cloture. A "yea" was a vote in support of the president's position. Feb. 9, 2010.

	17	18	19	20	21	22
ALABAMA						
Shelby	N	N	N	Y	Y	N
Sessions	N	N	N	Y	Y	N
ALASKA						
Murkowski	N	N	Y	Y	Y	N
Begich	Y	Y	Y	Y	Y	Y
ARIZONA						
McCain	?	N	Y	Y	Y	N
Kyl	N	N	N	Y	Y	N
ARKANSAS						
Lincoln	Y	Y	Y	Y	Y	N
Pryor	Y	Y	Y	Y	?	?
CALIFORNIA						
Feinstein	Y	Y	Y	Y	Y	Y
Boxer	Y	Y	Y	Y	Y	Y
COLORADO						
Udall	Y	Y	Y	Y	Y	Y
Bennet	Y	Y	Y	Y	Y	Y
CONNECTICUT						
Dodd	Y	Y	Y	Y	Y	Y
Lieberman	Y	Y	Y	Y	Y	Y
DELAWARE						
Carper	Y	Y	Y	Y	Y	Y
Kaufman	Y	Y	Y	Y	Y	Y
FLORIDA						
Nelson	Y	Y	Y	Y	Y	Y
LeMieux	N	N	Y	Y	Y	N
GEORGIA						
Chambliss	N	N	N	Y	Y	N
Isakson	N	N	N	?	Y	N
HAWAII						
Inouye	Y	Y	Y	Y	?	?
Akaka	Y	Y	Y	Y	Y	Y
IDAHO						
Crapo	N	N	N	Y	Y	N
Risch	–	N	N	Y	Y	N
ILLINOIS						
Durbin	Y	Y	Y	Y	Y	Y
Burris	Y	Y	Y	Y	Y	Y
INDIANA						
Lugar	N	N	Y	Y	Y	N
Bayh	Y	Y	Y	Y	Y	Y
IOWA						
Grassley	N	N	N	Y	Y	N
Harkin	Y	Y	Y	Y	Y	Y
KANSAS						
Brownback	N	N	Y	Y	?	?
Roberts	?	N	Y	Y	?	?
KENTUCKY						
McConnell	N	N	N	Y	Y	N
Bunning	N	N	N	Y	Y	N
LOUISIANA						
Landrieu	Y	Y	Y	Y	?	?
Vitter	?	N	Y	Y	?	?
MAINE						
Snowe	N	N	Y	Y	Y	N
Collins	N	N	Y	Y	Y	N
MARYLAND						
Mikulski	Y	Y	Y	Y	Y	Y
Cardin	Y	Y	Y	Y	Y	Y
MASSACHUSETTS						
Kerry	Y	Y	Y	Y	Y	Y
Kirk*	Y	Y	Y	Y		
Brown*					Y	N
MICHIGAN						
Levin	Y	Y	Y	Y	Y	Y
Stabenow	Y	Y	Y	Y	Y	Y
MINNESOTA						
Klobuchar	Y	Y	Y	Y	Y	Y
Franken	Y	Y	Y	Y	Y	Y
MISSISSIPPI						
Cochran	N	N	N	Y	Y	N
Wicker	N	N	N	Y	Y	N
MISSOURI						
Bond	?	N	N	Y	Y	N
McCaskill	Y	Y	Y	Y	Y	Y

	17	18	19	20	21	22
MONTANA						
Baucus	Y	Y	Y	Y	Y	Y
Tester	Y	Y	Y	Y	Y	Y
NEBRASKA						
Nelson	Y	Y	Y	Y	Y	N
Johanns	N	N	N	Y	Y	N
NEVADA						
Reid	Y	Y	Y	Y	Y	Y
Ensign	N	N	Y	Y	?	?
NEW HAMPSHIRE						
Gregg	?	N	N	Y	?	?
Shaheen	Y	Y	Y	Y	Y	Y
NEW JERSEY						
Lautenberg	Y	Y	Y	Y	Y	Y
Menendez	Y	Y	Y	Y	Y	Y
NEW MEXICO						
Bingaman	Y	Y	Y	Y	Y	Y
Udall	Y	Y	Y	Y	Y	Y
NEW YORK						
Schumer	Y	Y	Y	Y	Y	Y
Gillibrand	Y	Y	Y	Y	Y	Y
NORTH CAROLINA						
Burr	?	N	Y	Y	Y	N
Hagan	Y	Y	Y	Y	Y	Y
NORTH DAKOTA						
Conrad	Y	Y	Y	Y	Y	Y
Dorgan	Y	Y	Y	Y	Y	Y
OHIO						
Voinovich	N	?	Y	Y	Y	N
Brown	Y	Y	Y	Y	Y	Y
OKLAHOMA						
Inhofe	N	N	Y	Y	Y	N
Coburn	N	N	Y	?	Y	N
OREGON						
Wyden	Y	Y	Y	Y	Y	Y
Merkley	Y	Y	Y	Y	Y	Y
PENNSYLVANIA						
Specter	Y	Y	Y	Y	Y	Y
Casey	Y	Y	Y	Y	?	Y
RHODE ISLAND						
Reed	Y	Y	Y	Y	Y	Y
Whitehouse	Y	Y	Y	Y	Y	Y
SOUTH CAROLINA						
Graham	N	N	Y	Y	?	–
DeMint	N	N	Y	Y	+	–
SOUTH DAKOTA						
Johnson	Y	Y	Y	Y	Y	Y
Thune	N	N	Y	Y	+	–
TENNESSEE						
Alexander	N	N	N	Y	Y	N
Corker	N	N	N	Y	Y	N
TEXAS						
Hutchison	?	?	?	?	?	?
Cornyn	N	N	Y	Y	Y	N
UTAH						
Hatch	N	N	N	Y	+	–
Bennett	N	?	?	?	Y	N
VERMONT						
Leahy	Y	Y	Y	Y	Y	Y
Sanders	Y	Y	Y	Y	?	?
VIRGINIA						
Webb	Y	Y	Y	Y	Y	Y
Warner	Y	Y	Y	Y	Y	Y
WASHINGTON						
Murray	Y	Y	Y	Y	Y	Y
Cantwell	Y	Y	Y	Y	Y	Y
WEST VIRGINIA						
Byrd	Y	Y	Y	Y	?	?
Rockefeller	Y	Y	Y	Y	Y	Y
WISCONSIN						
Kohl	Y	Y	Y	Y	Y	Y
Feingold	Y	Y	Y	Y	Y	Y
WYOMING						
Enzi	N	N	Y	Y	Y	N
Barrasso	N	N	Y	Y	Y	N

KEY   **Republicans**   Democrats   *Independents*

Y Voted for (yea)	X Paired against	C Voted "present" to avoid possible conflict of interest
# Paired for	– Announced against	
+ Announced for	P Voted "present"	? Did not vote or otherwise make a position known
N Voted against (nay)		

*Sen. Scott P. Brown, R-Mass., was sworn in Feb. 4, 2010, to replace Democrat Paul G. Kirk Jr., the appointed interim successor to Democrat Edward M. Kennedy, who died Aug. 25, 2009. The first vote for which Brown was eligible was vote 21; the last vote for which Kirk was eligible was vote 20.

IN THE SENATE | By Vote Number

23. **HR 2847. Jobs Package/Cloture.** Motion to invoke cloture (thus limiting debate) on the Reid, D-Nev., motion to concur in the House amendment to the Senate amendment with a Reid substitute amendment that would exempt employers from paying Social Security payroll taxes for certain new hires made in 2010. The amendment would expand the Build America Bonds program. It also would extend the authorization for surface transportation programs and an expensing provision for small businesses, both through Dec. 31, 2010. Motion agreed to 62-30: D 55-1; R 5-29; I 2-0. Three-fifths of the total Senate (60) is required to invoke cloture. Feb. 22, 2010.

24. **HR 2847. Jobs Package/Motion to Waive.** Cardin, D-Md., motion to waive the Budget Act and budget resolutions with respect to the Gregg, R-N.H., point of order against the Reid, D-Nev., motion to concur in the House amendment to the Senate amendment to the bill with a Reid substitute amendment. Motion agreed to 62-34: D 54-1; R 6-33; I 2-0. A three-fifths majority vote (60) of the total Senate is required to waive the Budget Act. Feb. 24, 2010.

25. **HR 2847. Jobs Package/Motion to Concur.** Reid, D-Nev., motion to concur in the House amendment to the Senate amendment to the bill with a Reid substitute amendment. Motion agreed to 70-28: D 55-1; R 13-27; I 2-0. A "yea" was a vote in support of the president's position. Feb. 24, 2010.

26. **HR 1299. Travel Promotion and Capitol Police/Cloture.** Motion to invoke cloture (thus limiting debate) on the Reid, D-Nev., motion to concur in the House amendment to the Senate amendment with a Reid amendment that would set the bill's effective date for five days after enactment. Motion agreed to 76-20: D 55-0; R 19-20; I 2-0. Three-fifths of the total Senate (60) is required to invoke cloture. Feb. 25, 2010.

27. **HR 1299. Travel Promotion and Capitol Police/National Monuments.** DeMint, R-S.C., motion to suspend Senate Rule 22 to permit the consideration of a DeMint amendment that would prohibit the establishment of national monuments in certain areas by the Interior Department. Motion rejected 38-58: D 3-52; R 35-4; I 0-2. A two-thirds majority of the total Senate (67) is required to suspend Rule 22. Feb. 25, 2010.

28. **HR 1299. Travel Promotion and Capitol Police/Motion to Concur.** Reid, D-Nev., motion to concur in the House amendment to the Senate amendment to the bill that would create a nonprofit corporation to attract foreign tourists to the United States and an Office of Travel Promotion in the Commerce Department. It would require the Homeland Security Department to add $10 to existing fees on users of a visa waiver program. Money from the fee would be used to help fund the nonprofit corporation. It would also clarify that the Capitol Police is an agency of the legislative branch. Motion agreed to 78-18: D 55-0; R 21-18; I 2-0. Feb. 25, 2010.

	23	24	25	26	27	28			23	24	25	26	27	28
ALABAMA								**MONTANA**						
Shelby	N	N	N	N	Y	N		Baucus	Y	Y	Y	Y	Y	Y
Sessions	?	N	N	N	Y	N		Tester	Y	Y	Y	Y	Y	Y
ALASKA								**NEBRASKA**						
Murkowski	N	N	Y	Y	Y	Y		Nelson	N	N	N	Y	Y	Y
Begich	Y	Y	Y	Y	N	Y		Johanns	N	N	N	Y	Y	Y
ARIZONA								**NEVADA**						
McCain	N	–	N	N	Y	N		Reid	Y	Y	Y	Y	N	Y
Kyl	N	N	N	N	Y	N		Ensign	N	N	N	Y	Y	Y
ARKANSAS								**NEW HAMPSHIRE**						
Lincoln	Y	Y	Y	Y	N	Y		**Gregg**	N	N	N	N	N	N
Pryor	Y	Y	Y	Y	N	Y		Shaheen	Y	Y	Y	Y	N	Y
CALIFORNIA								**NEW JERSEY**						
Feinstein	Y	Y	Y	Y	N	Y		Lautenberg	?	?	?	?	?	?
Boxer	Y	Y	Y	Y	N	Y		Menendez	Y	Y	Y	Y	N	Y
COLORADO								**NEW MEXICO**						
Udall	Y	Y	Y	Y	N	Y		Bingaman	Y	Y	Y	Y	N	Y
Bennet	Y	Y	Y	Y	N	Y		Udall	Y	Y	Y	Y	N	Y
CONNECTICUT								**NEW YORK**						
Dodd	Y	Y	Y	Y	N	Y		Schumer	Y	Y	Y	Y	N	Y
Lieberman	Y	Y	Y	Y	N	Y		Gillibrand	Y	Y	Y	Y	N	Y
DELAWARE								**NORTH CAROLINA**						
Carper	Y	Y	Y	Y	N	Y		**Burr**	?	N	N	Y	N	N
Kaufman	Y	Y	Y	Y	N	Y		Hagan	Y	Y	Y	Y	N	Y
FLORIDA								**NORTH DAKOTA**						
Nelson	Y	Y	Y	Y	N	Y		Conrad	Y	Y	Y	Y	N	Y
LeMieux	N	N	Y	Y	Y	Y		Dorgan	Y	Y	Y	Y	N	Y
GEORGIA								**OHIO**						
Chambliss	N	N	N	Y	Y	Y		**Voinovich**	Y	Y	Y	Y	N	Y
Isakson	?	N	N	Y	Y	Y		Brown	Y	Y	Y	Y	N	Y
HAWAII								**OKLAHOMA**						
Inouye	Y	Y	Y	Y	N	Y		**Inhofe**	N	Y	Y	–	?	–
Akaka	Y	Y	Y	Y	N	Y		**Coburn**	N	N	N	N	Y	N
IDAHO								**OREGON**						
Crapo	N	N	N	N	Y	N		Wyden	Y	Y	Y	Y	N	Y
Risch	N	N	N	N	Y	N		Merkley	Y	Y	Y	Y	N	Y
ILLINOIS								**PENNSYLVANIA**						
Durbin	Y	Y	Y	Y	N	Y		Specter	Y	Y	Y	Y	N	Y
Burris	Y	Y	Y	Y	N	Y		Casey	Y	Y	Y	Y	N	Y
INDIANA								**RHODE ISLAND**						
Lugar	N	N	N	Y	Y	Y		Reed	Y	Y	Y	Y	N	Y
Bayh	Y	Y	Y	Y	N	Y		Whitehouse	Y	Y	Y	Y	N	Y
IOWA								**SOUTH CAROLINA**						
Grassley	N	N	N	Y	Y	Y		**Graham**	N	N	N	Y	Y	Y
Harkin	Y	Y	Y	Y	N	Y		**DeMint**	N	N	N	N	Y	N
KANSAS								**SOUTH DAKOTA**						
Brownback	?	N	N	N	Y	N		Johnson	Y	Y	Y	Y	N	Y
Roberts	N	N	N	N	Y	N		**Thune**	N	N	N	Y	Y	Y
KENTUCKY								**TENNESSEE**						
McConnell	N	N	N	N	Y	N		**Alexander**	N	N	Y	Y	N	Y
Bunning	N	N	N	N	Y	N		**Corker**	N	N	N	N	Y	N
LOUISIANA								**TEXAS**						
Landrieu	Y	Y	Y	Y	N	Y		**Hutchison**	N	?	?	?	?	?
Vitter	N	N	N	Y	Y	Y		**Cornyn**	N	N	N	N	Y	N
MAINE								**UTAH**						
Snowe	Y	Y	Y	Y	N	Y		**Hatch**	?	N	N	Y	Y	Y
Collins	Y	Y	Y	Y	N	Y		**Bennett**	?	N	N	Y	Y	Y
MARYLAND								**VERMONT**						
Mikulski	Y	Y	Y	Y	N	Y		Leahy	Y	Y	Y	Y	N	Y
Cardin	Y	Y	Y	Y	N	Y		*Sanders*	Y	Y	Y	Y	N	Y
MASSACHUSETTS								**VIRGINIA**						
Kerry	Y	Y	Y	Y	N	Y		Webb	Y	Y	Y	Y	N	Y
Brown	Y	Y	Y	N	Y	N		Warner	Y	Y	Y	?	?	?
MICHIGAN								**WASHINGTON**						
Levin	Y	?	Y	Y	N	Y		Murray	Y	Y	Y	Y	N	Y
Stabenow	Y	Y	Y	Y	N	Y		Cantwell	Y	Y	Y	Y	N	Y
MINNESOTA								**WEST VIRGINIA**						
Klobuchar	Y	Y	Y	Y	N	Y		Byrd	Y	Y	Y	Y	N	Y
Franken	Y	Y	Y	Y	N	Y		Rockefeller	Y	Y	Y	Y	N	Y
MISSISSIPPI								**WISCONSIN**						
Cochran	N	N	Y	Y	Y	Y		Kohl	Y	Y	Y	Y	N	Y
Wicker	N	N	Y	Y	Y	Y		Feingold	Y	Y	Y	Y	N	Y
MISSOURI								**WYOMING**						
Bond	Y	Y	Y	Y	Y	Y		**Enzi**	?	N	N	N	Y	Y
McCaskill	Y	Y	Y	Y	N	Y		**Barrasso**	N	N	N	N	Y	Y

KEY **Republicans**   Democrats   *Independents*

Y	Voted for (yea)	X	Paired against
#	Paired for	–	Announced against
+	Announced for	P	Voted "present"
N	Voted against (nay)		

C Voted "present" to avoid possible conflict of interest

? Did not vote or otherwise make a position known

IN THE SENATE | By Vote Number

29. Keenan Nomination/Cloture. Motion to invoke cloture (thus limiting debate) on the nomination of Barbara Milano Keenan of Virginia to be a judge for the 4th U.S. Circuit Court of Appeals. Motion agreed to 99-0: D 57-0; R 40-0; I 2-0. Three-fifths of the total Senate (60) is required to invoke cloture. March 2, 2010.

30. Keenan Nomination/Confirmation. Confirmation of President Obama's nomination of Barbara Milano Keenan of Virginia to be a judge for the 4th U.S. Circuit Court of Appeals. Confirmed 99-0: D 57-0; R 40-0; I 2-0. A "yea" was a vote in support of the president's position. March 2, 2010.

31. HR 4691. Short-Term Extensions/Offsets. Bunning, R-Ky., motion to waive the Budget Act and budget resolutions with respect to the Boxer, D-Calif., point of order against the Bunning substitute amendment that would retain the extensions in the underlying bill but would offset the costs by repealing a provision allowing the cellulosic biofuels producer credit to be claimed by producers of certain paper products. Motion rejected 43-53: D 3-52; R 39-0; I 1-1. A three-fifths majority vote (60) of the total Senate is required to waive the Budget Act. (Subsequently, the chair upheld the point of order, and the amendment fell.) March 2, 2010.

32. HR 4691. Short-Term Extensions/Passage. Passage of the bill that would extend COBRA health care premium assistance, the Satellite Home Viewer Act, surface transportation programs and small-business lending for one month. It would extend payment rates to Medicare providers through April 1 and extend unemployment insurance through April 5. Passed (thus cleared for the president) 78-19: D 55-0; R 21-19; I 2-0. March 2, 2010.

33. HR 4213. Tax Extenders/Small-Business Taxes. Cornyn, R-Texas., motion to waive the Budget Act with respect to the Baucus, D-Mont., point of order against the Thune, R-S.D., amendment, to the Baucus substitute. The Thune amendment would redirect unobligated funds from the 2009 economic stimulus law to offset the costs of the bill. It would also add provisions to reduce certain small-business taxes. The substitute would extend a variety of tax provisions that expired on Dec. 31, 2009. It also would extend for varying lengths of time a list of programs that expired on Feb. 28, 2010, including expanded unemployment benefits and health insurance subsidies for jobless workers, a delay to pay cuts for Medicare physicians, small-business loans, certain satellite TV broadcasting and flood insurance. Motion rejected 38-61: D 1-56; R 37-3; I 0-2. A three-fifths majority vote (60) of the total Senate is required to waive the Budget Act. (Subsequently, the chair upheld the point of order, and the amendment fell.) March 2, 2010.

	29	30	31	32	33		29	30	31	32	33
ALABAMA						**MONTANA**					
Shelby	Y	Y	Y	Y	Y	Baucus	Y	Y	N	Y	N
Sessions	Y	Y	Y	N	Y	Tester	Y	Y	N	Y	N
ALASKA						**NEBRASKA**					
Murkowski	Y	Y	Y	Y	N	Nelson	Y	Y	Y	Y	Y
Begich	Y	Y	N	Y	N	Johanns	Y	Y	Y	N	N
ARIZONA						**NEVADA**					
McCain	Y	Y	Y	Y	Y	Reid	Y	Y	N	Y	N
Kyl	Y	Y	Y	Y	Y	Ensign	Y	Y	Y	N	Y
ARKANSAS						**NEW HAMPSHIRE**					
Lincoln	Y	Y	Y	Y	N	Gregg	Y	Y	N	Y	Y
Pryor	Y	Y	N	Y	N	Shaheen	Y	Y	N	Y	N
CALIFORNIA						**NEW JERSEY**					
Feinstein	Y	Y	N	Y	N	Lautenberg	Y	Y	?	?	N
Boxer	Y	Y	N	Y	N	Menendez	Y	Y	N	Y	N
COLORADO						**NEW MEXICO**					
Udall	Y	Y	N	Y	N	Bingaman	Y	Y	N	Y	N
Bennet	Y	Y	N	Y	N	Udall	Y	Y	N	Y	N
CONNECTICUT						**NEW YORK**					
Dodd	Y	Y	N	Y	N	Schumer	Y	Y	N	Y	N
Lieberman	Y	Y	Y	Y	N	Gillibrand	Y	Y	N	Y	N
DELAWARE						**NORTH CAROLINA**					
Carper	Y	Y	N	Y	N	**Burr**	Y	Y	Y	N	Y
Kaufman	Y	Y	N	Y	N	Hagan	Y	Y	N	Y	N
FLORIDA						**NORTH DAKOTA**					
Nelson	Y	Y	N	Y	N	Conrad	Y	Y	N	Y	N
LeMieux	Y	Y	Y	Y	Y	Dorgan	Y	Y	N	Y	N
GEORGIA						**OHIO**					
Chambliss	Y	Y	Y	Y	Y	**Voinovich**	Y	Y	N	Y	N
Isakson	Y	Y	Y	Y	Y	Brown	Y	Y	N	Y	N
HAWAII						**OKLAHOMA**					
Inouye	Y	Y	N	Y	N	**Inhofe**	Y	Y	?	Y	Y
Akaka	Y	Y	N	Y	N	**Coburn**	Y	Y	Y	N	Y
IDAHO						**OREGON**					
Crapo	Y	Y	Y	N	Y	Wyden	Y	Y	N	Y	N
Risch	Y	Y	Y	N	Y	Merkley	Y	Y	N	Y	N
ILLINOIS						**PENNSYLVANIA**					
Durbin	Y	Y	N	Y	N	Specter	Y	Y	N	Y	N
Burris	Y	Y	N	Y	N	Casey	Y	Y	N	Y	N
INDIANA						**RHODE ISLAND**					
Lugar	Y	Y	Y	Y	Y	Reed	Y	Y	N	Y	N
Bayh	Y	Y	N	Y	N	Whitehouse	Y	Y	N	Y	N
IOWA						**SOUTH CAROLINA**					
Grassley	Y	Y	Y	Y	Y	**Graham**	Y	Y	Y	Y	Y
Harkin	Y	Y	N	Y	N	**DeMint**	Y	Y	Y	N	Y
KANSAS						**SOUTH DAKOTA**					
Brownback	Y	Y	Y	Y	Y	Johnson	Y	Y	N	Y	N
Roberts	Y	Y	Y	Y	Y	**Thune**	Y	Y	Y	N	Y
KENTUCKY						**TENNESSEE**					
McConnell	Y	Y	Y	N	Y	**Alexander**	Y	Y	Y	N	Y
Bunning	Y	Y	Y	N	Y	**Corker**	Y	Y	Y	N	Y
LOUISIANA						**TEXAS**					
Landrieu	Y	Y	N	Y	N	**Hutchison**	?	?	?	?	?
Vitter	Y	Y	Y	Y	Y	**Cornyn**	Y	Y	Y	N	Y
MAINE						**UTAH**					
Snowe	Y	Y	Y	Y	Y	**Hatch**	Y	Y	Y	N	Y
Collins	Y	Y	Y	Y	Y	**Bennett**	Y	Y	Y	N	Y
MARYLAND						**VERMONT**					
Mikulski	Y	Y	N	Y	N	Leahy	Y	Y	N	Y	N
Cardin	Y	Y	N	Y	N	*Sanders*	Y	Y	N	Y	N
MASSACHUSETTS						**VIRGINIA**					
Kerry	Y	Y	N	Y	N	Webb	Y	Y	N	Y	N
Brown	Y	Y	Y	Y	Y	Warner	Y	Y	N	Y	N
MICHIGAN						**WASHINGTON**					
Levin	Y	Y	N	Y	N	Murray	Y	Y	N	Y	N
Stabenow	Y	Y	N	Y	N	Cantwell	Y	Y	N	Y	N
MINNESOTA						**WEST VIRGINIA**					
Klobuchar	Y	Y	N	Y	N	Byrd	Y	Y	?	?	N
Franken	Y	Y	N	Y	N	Rockefeller	Y	Y	N	Y	N
MISSISSIPPI						**WISCONSIN**					
Cochran	Y	Y	Y	Y	Y	Kohl	Y	Y	N	Y	N
Wicker	Y	Y	Y	Y	Y	Feingold	Y	Y	Y	Y	N
MISSOURI						**WYOMING**					
Bond	Y	Y	Y	Y	Y	**Enzi**	Y	Y	Y	N	Y
McCaskill	Y	Y	N	Y	N	**Barrasso**	Y	Y	Y	N	Y

KEY   **Republicans**   Democrats   *Independents*

Y Voted for (yea)	X Paired against	C Voted "present" to avoid possible conflict of interest
# Paired for	– Announced against	
+ Announced for	P Voted "present"	? Did not vote or otherwise make a position known
N Voted against (nay)		

IN THE SENATE | By Vote Number

34. HR 4213. **Tax Extenders/Medicare Payment Rates.** Baucus, D-Mont., motion to table (kill) the Grassley, R-Iowa, amendment to the Baucus substitute amendment. The Grassley amendment would extend the increased Medicare payment rates to providers through Dec. 31, 2010, with an offset. It also would provide offsets for the substitute amendment's Medicare provisions. Motion agreed to 54-45: D 52-5; R 0-40; I 2-0. March 3, 2010.

35. HR 4213. **Tax Extenders/Social Security Payments.** Burr, R-N.C., motion to waive the Budget Act and budget resolutions with respect to the Baucus, D-Mont., point of order against the Burr amendment to the Baucus substitute. The Burr amendment would provide for a $250 payment to qualified Social Security recipients, offset with unspent funds from the 2009 stimulus law. Motion rejected 38-59: D 9-48; R 29-9; I 0-2. A three-fifths majority vote (60) of the total Senate is required to waive the Budget Act. (Subsequently, the chair upheld the point of order, and the amendment fell.) March 3, 2010.

36. HR 4213. **Tax Extenders/Social Security Payments.** Sanders, I-Vt., motion to waive the Budget Act and budget resolutions with respect to the Gregg, R-N.H., point of order against the Sanders amendment to the Baucus substitute. The Sanders amendment would provide for a $250 payment to qualified Social Security recipients. Motion rejected 47-50: D 45-12; R 1-37; I 1-1. A three-fifths majority vote (60) of the total Senate is required to waive the Budget Act. (Subsequently, the chair upheld the point of order, and the amendment fell.) March 3, 2010.

37. HR 4213. **Tax Extenders/Stimulus Funds Offset.** Baucus, D-Mont., motion to table (kill) the Bunning, R-Ky., amendment to the Baucus substitute. The Bunning amendment would offset provisions in the underlying substitute by redirecting unobligated funds from the 2009 economic stimulus law. Motion agreed to 56-41: D 54-3; R 0-38; I 2-0. March 3, 2010.

38. HR 4213. **Tax Extenders/Program Terminations.** Inouye, D-Hawaii, motion to table (kill) the Bunning, R-Ky., amendment to the Baucus substitute. The Bunning amendment would offset provisions in the underlying substitute by improving collection of federal taxes from federal workers and canceling certain government programs determined to be wasteful. Motion agreed to 61-36: D 56-1; R 3-35; I 2-0. March 3, 2010.

	34	35	36	37	38			34	35	36	37	38
ALABAMA							**MONTANA**					
Shelby	N	Y	N	N	N		Baucus	Y	N	Y	Y	Y
Sessions	N	?	N	N	N		Tester	Y	N	Y	Y	Y
ALASKA							**NEBRASKA**					
Murkowski	N	Y	N	N	N		Nelson	N	Y	N	N	Y
Begich	Y	N	Y	Y	Y		Johanns	N	N	N	N	N
ARIZONA							**NEVADA**					
McCain	N	Y	N	N	N		Reid	Y	N	Y	Y	Y
Kyl	N	N	N	N	N		Ensign	N	N	N	N	N
ARKANSAS							**NEW HAMPSHIRE**					
Lincoln	N	Y	Y	N	N		Gregg	N	N	N	N	N
Pryor	Y	Y	Y	Y	Y		Shaheen	Y	N	N	Y	Y
CALIFORNIA							**NEW JERSEY**					
Feinstein	Y	N	N	Y	Y		Lautenberg	Y	N	Y	Y	Y
Boxer	Y	N	Y	Y	Y		Menendez	Y	N	Y	Y	Y
COLORADO							**NEW MEXICO**					
Udall	Y	N	Y	Y	Y		Bingaman	N	N	Y	Y	Y
Bennet	Y	Y	N	Y	Y		Udall	Y	N	Y	Y	Y
CONNECTICUT							**NEW YORK**					
Dodd	Y	N	Y	Y	Y		Schumer	Y	N	Y	Y	Y
Lieberman	Y	N	N	Y	Y		Gillibrand	Y	N	Y	Y	Y
DELAWARE							**NORTH CAROLINA**					
Carper	Y	N	N	Y	Y		Burr	N	Y	N	N	N
Kaufman	Y	N	Y	Y	Y		Hagan	Y	N	Y	Y	Y
FLORIDA							**NORTH DAKOTA**					
Nelson	N	Y	Y	Y	Y		Conrad	Y	N	Y	Y	Y
LeMieux	N	Y	N	N	N		Dorgan	Y	N	Y	Y	Y
GEORGIA							**OHIO**					
Chambliss	N	Y	N	N	N		Voinovich	N	N	N	N	N
Isakson	N	Y	?	?	?		Brown	Y	N	Y	Y	Y
HAWAII							**OKLAHOMA**					
Inouye	Y	N	Y	Y	Y		Inhofe	N	N	N	N	N
Akaka	Y	N	Y	Y	Y		Coburn	N	N	N	N	N
IDAHO							**OREGON**					
Crapo	N	Y	N	N	N		Wyden	Y	N	Y	Y	Y
Risch	N	Y	N	N	N		Merkley	Y	N	Y	Y	Y
ILLINOIS							**PENNSYLVANIA**					
Durbin	Y	N	Y	Y	Y		Specter	Y	N	Y	Y	Y
Burris	Y	N	Y	Y	Y		Casey	Y	N	Y	Y	Y
INDIANA							**RHODE ISLAND**					
Lugar	N	Y	N	N	N		Reed	Y	N	Y	Y	Y
Bayh	Y	Y	N	N	Y		Whitehouse	Y	N	Y	Y	Y
IOWA							**SOUTH CAROLINA**					
Grassley	N	Y	N	N	N		Graham	N	Y	N	N	N
Harkin	Y	N	Y	Y	Y		DeMint	N	Y	N	N	N
KANSAS							**SOUTH DAKOTA**					
Brownback	N	Y	N	N	N		Johnson	Y	N	Y	Y	Y
Roberts	N	Y	N	N	N		Thune	N	Y	N	N	N
KENTUCKY							**TENNESSEE**					
McConnell	N	Y	N	N	N		Alexander	N	N	N	N	N
Bunning	N	Y	N	N	N		Corker	N	Y	N	N	N
LOUISIANA							**TEXAS**					
Landrieu	Y	N	N	Y	Y		Hutchison	?	?	?	?	?
Vitter	N	Y	N	N	N		Cornyn	N	Y	N	N	N
MAINE							**UTAH**					
Snowe	N	Y	Y	N	Y		Hatch	N	Y	N	N	N
Collins	N	Y	N	N	Y		Bennett	N	Y	N	N	N
MARYLAND							**VERMONT**					
Mikulski	Y	N	Y	Y	Y		Leahy	Y	N	Y	Y	Y
Cardin	Y	N	Y	Y	Y		Sanders	Y	N	Y	Y	Y
MASSACHUSETTS							**VIRGINIA**					
Kerry	Y	N	Y	Y	Y		Webb	N	Y	Y	Y	Y
Brown	N	Y	N	N	N		Warner	Y	N	Y	Y	Y
MICHIGAN							**WASHINGTON**					
Levin	Y	N	N	Y	Y		Murray	Y	N	Y	Y	Y
Stabenow	Y	N	Y	Y	Y		Cantwell	Y	N	Y	Y	Y
MINNESOTA							**WEST VIRGINIA**					
Klobuchar	Y	Y	Y	Y	Y		Byrd	Y	N	Y	Y	Y
Franken	Y	N	Y	Y	Y		Rockefeller	Y	N	Y	Y	Y
MISSISSIPPI							**WISCONSIN**					
Cochran	N	Y	N	N	N		Kohl	Y	N	Y	Y	Y
Wicker	N	N	N	N	N		Feingold	Y	N	N	Y	Y
MISSOURI							**WYOMING**					
Bond	N	?	?	?	?		Enzi	N	Y	N	N	N
McCaskill	Y	Y	N	Y	N		Barrasso	N	Y	N	N	N

KEY   **Republicans**   Democrats   *Independents*

Y Voted for (yea)	X Paired against	C Voted "present" to avoid possible conflict of interest
# Paired for	– Announced against	
+ Announced for	P Voted "present"	? Did not vote or otherwise make a position known
N Voted against (nay)		

IN THE SENATE | By Vote Number

39. **HR 4213. Tax Extenders/Motion to Waive.** Baucus, D-Mont., motion to waive the Budget Act and budget resolutions with respect to the LeMieux, R-Fla., point of order against the Baucus substitute. Motion agreed to 60-37: D 57-0; R 1-37; I 2-0. A three-fifths majority vote (60) of the total Senate is required to waive the Budget Act. March 3, 2010.

40. **HR 4213. Tax Extenders/Payroll Taxes.** Brown, R-Mass., motion to waive the Budget Act and budget resolutions with respect to the Baucus, D-Mont., point of order against the Brown amendment to the Baucus substitute amendment. The Brown amendment would provide an employee payroll tax holiday for a period of six months, offset with unobligated funds from the 2009 stimulus law. Motion rejected 44-56: D 4-53; R 40-1; I 0-2. A three-fifths majority vote (60) of the total Senate is required to waive the Budget Act. (Subsequently, the chair upheld the point of order, and the amendment fell.) March 4, 2010.

41. **HR 4213. Tax Extenders/Sales Taxes.** Burr, R-N.C., motion to waive the Budget Act and budget resolutions with respect to the Baucus, D-Mont., point of order against the Burr amendment to the Baucus substitute amendment. The Burr amendment would provide states with a 75 percent reimbursement of the amount of uncollected state and local sales taxes during a sales tax holiday. It would be offset with unobligated funds from the 2009 stimulus law. Motion rejected 22-78: D 0-57; R 22-19; I 0-2. A three-fifths majority vote (60) of the total Senate is required to waive the Budget Act. (Subsequently, the chair upheld the point of order, and the amendment fell.) March 4, 2010.

42. **HR 4213. Tax Extenders/Spending Caps.** McCaskill, D-Mo., motion to waive the Budget Act and budget resolutions with respect to the Inouye, D-Hawaii, point of order against the Sessions, R-Ala., amendment to the Baucus, D-Mont., substitute amendment. The Sessions amendment would establish discretionary spending limits for four fiscal years beginning in fiscal 2011, equal to the levels for defense and nondefense spending in the fiscal 2010 budget resolution. It also would limit spending on overseas deployments and related operations. Points of order against emergency spending designations could be waived by a three-fifths majority vote in the Senate. Motion rejected 59-41: D 17-40; R 41-0; I 1-1. A three-fifths majority vote (60) of the total Senate is required to waive the Budget Act. (Subsequently, the chair upheld the point of order, and the amendment fell.) March 4, 2010.

43. **Conley Nomination/Confirmation.** Confirmation of President Obama's nomination of William M. Conley of Wisconsin to be a judge for the U.S. District Court of the Western District of Wisconsin. Confirmed 99-0: D 56-0; R 41-0; I 2-0. A "yea" was a vote in support of the president's position. March 4, 2010.

	39	40	41	42	43			39	40	41	42	43
ALABAMA							**MONTANA**					
Shelby	N	Y	N	Y	Y		Baucus	Y	N	N	N	Y
Sessions	N	Y	N	Y	Y		Tester	Y	N	N	Y	Y
ALASKA							**NEBRASKA**					
Murkowski	N	Y	N	Y	Y		Nelson	Y	N	N	Y	Y
Begich	Y	N	N	Y	Y		**Johanns**	N	Y	Y	Y	Y
ARIZONA							**NEVADA**					
McCain	N	Y	Y	Y	Y		Reid	Y	N	N	N	Y
Kyl	N	Y	N	Y	Y		**Ensign**	N	Y	N	Y	Y
ARKANSAS							**NEW HAMPSHIRE**					
Lincoln	Y	Y	N	Y	Y		**Gregg**	N	Y	N	Y	Y
Pryor	Y	N	N	Y	Y		Shaheen	Y	N	N	Y	Y
CALIFORNIA							**NEW JERSEY**					
Feinstein	Y	N	N	N	Y		Lautenberg	Y	N	N	N	Y
Boxer	Y	N	N	N	Y		Menendez	Y	N	N	N	Y
COLORADO							**NEW MEXICO**					
Udall	Y	N	N	Y	Y		Bingaman	Y	N	N	N	Y
Bennet	Y	N	N	Y	Y		Udall	Y	N	N	N	Y
CONNECTICUT							**NEW YORK**					
Dodd	Y	Y	N	Y	Y		Schumer	Y	N	N	N	Y
Lieberman	Y	N	N	Y	Y		Gillibrand	Y	N	N	N	Y
DELAWARE							**NORTH CAROLINA**					
Carper	Y	N	N	Y	Y		**Burr**	N	Y	Y	Y	Y
Kaufman	Y	N	N	Y	Y		Hagan	Y	N	N	Y	Y
FLORIDA							**NORTH DAKOTA**					
Nelson	Y	N	N	Y	Y		Conrad	Y	N	N	N	Y
LeMieux	N	Y	Y	Y	Y		Dorgan	Y	N	N	N	?
GEORGIA							**OHIO**					
Chambliss	N	Y	Y	Y	Y		**Voinovich**	N	N	N	Y	Y
Isakson	?	Y	Y	Y	Y		Brown	Y	N	N	N	Y
HAWAII							**OKLAHOMA**					
Inouye	Y	N	N	N	Y		**Inhofe**	N	Y	Y	Y	Y
Akaka	Y	N	N	N	Y		**Coburn**	N	Y	Y	Y	Y
IDAHO							**OREGON**					
Crapo	N	Y	N	Y	Y		Wyden	Y	N	N	N	Y
Risch	N	Y	N	Y	Y		Merkley	Y	N	N	N	Y
ILLINOIS							**PENNSYLVANIA**					
Durbin	Y	N	N	N	Y		Specter	Y	N	N	N	Y
Burris	Y	N	N	N	Y		Casey	Y	N	N	N	Y
INDIANA							**RHODE ISLAND**					
Lugar	N	Y	Y	Y	Y		Reed	Y	N	N	N	Y
Bayh	Y	Y	N	Y	Y		Whitehouse	Y	N	N	N	Y
IOWA							**SOUTH CAROLINA**					
Grassley	N	Y	Y	Y	Y		**Graham**	N	Y	Y	Y	Y
Harkin	Y	N	N	N	Y		**DeMint**	N	Y	N	Y	Y
KANSAS							**SOUTH DAKOTA**					
Brownback	N	Y	N	Y	Y		Johnson	Y	N	N	N	Y
Roberts	N	Y	N	Y	Y		**Thune**	N	Y	Y	Y	Y
KENTUCKY							**TENNESSEE**					
McConnell	N	Y	Y	Y	Y		**Alexander**	N	Y	N	Y	Y
Bunning	N	Y	Y	Y	Y		**Corker**	N	Y	N	Y	Y
LOUISIANA							**TEXAS**					
Landrieu	Y	N	N	N	Y		**Hutchison**	?	Y	N	Y	Y
Vitter	N	Y	Y	Y	Y		**Cornyn**	N	Y	N	Y	Y
MAINE							**UTAH**					
Snowe	N	Y	Y	Y	Y		**Hatch**	N	Y	Y	Y	Y
Collins	Y	Y	Y	Y	Y		**Bennett**	N	Y	Y	Y	Y
MARYLAND							**VERMONT**					
Mikulski	Y	N	N	N	Y		Leahy	Y	N	N	N	Y
Cardin	Y	N	N	N	Y		*Sanders*	Y	N	N	N	Y
MASSACHUSETTS							**VIRGINIA**					
Kerry	Y	Y	N	N	Y		Webb	Y	N	N	Y	Y
Brown	N	Y	Y	Y	Y		Warner	Y	N	N	Y	Y
MICHIGAN							**WASHINGTON**					
Levin	Y	N	N	N	Y		Murray	Y	N	N	N	Y
Stabenow	Y	N	N	N	Y		Cantwell	Y	N	N	Y	Y
MINNESOTA							**WEST VIRGINIA**					
Klobuchar	Y	N	N	Y	Y		Byrd	Y	N	N	N	Y
Franken	Y	N	N	N	Y		Rockefeller	Y	N	N	N	Y
MISSISSIPPI							**WISCONSIN**					
Cochran	N	Y	N	Y	Y		Kohl	Y	N	N	N	Y
Wicker	N	Y	N	Y	Y		Feingold	Y	N	N	N	Y
MISSOURI							**WYOMING**					
Bond	?	Y	Y	Y	Y		**Enzi**	N	Y	N	Y	Y
McCaskill	Y	N	N	Y	Y		**Barrasso**	N	Y	N	Y	Y

KEY	**Republicans**	Democrats	*Independents*	
Y Voted for (yea)		**X** Paired against		**C** Voted "present" to avoid possible conflict of interest
# Paired for		**–** Announced against		
+ Announced for		**P** Voted "present"		**?** Did not vote or otherwise make a position known
N Voted against (nay)				

IN THE SENATE | By Vote Number

44. HR 4213. Tax Extenders/Spending Posting Requirement.
Coburn, R-Okla., amendment to the Baucus, D-Mont., substitute amendment. The Coburn amendment would require prominent display on the Senate's Web site of the amount of spending that has been exempted from pay-as-you-go budgetary requirements, the amount authorized in Senate-passed legislation and the number of government programs created by Senate-passed bills. The substitute would extend a variety of tax provisions that expired Dec. 31. It would also extend federal unemployment benefits and health insurance subsidies for jobless workers and a number of other expiring provisions. Adopted 100-0: D 57-0; R 41-0; I 2-0. March 9, 2010.

45. HR 4213. Tax Extenders/Motion to Waive.
Murray, D-Wash., motion to waive the Budget Act with respect to the Gregg, R-N.H., point of order against the Murray amendment to the Baucus, D-Mont., substitute amendment. The Murray amendment would appropriate $1.3 billion for a six-month extension of the Emergency Fund of the Temporary Assistance to Needy Families program and $1.3 billion for workforce development programs. It would modify the enrollment process for low-income beneficiaries of prescription drug plans and eliminate the advance earned-income tax credit in 2011. Motion rejected 55-45: D 53-4; R 0-41; I 2-0. A three-fifths majority vote (60) of the total Senate is required to waive the Budget Act. A "yea" was a vote in support of the president's position. March 9, 2010.

46. HR 4213. Tax Extenders/Cloture.
Motion to invoke cloture (thus limiting debate) on the Baucus, D-Mont., substitute amendment that would extend for one year a variety of tax provisions that expired Dec. 31. It also would extend federal unemployment benefits and health insurance subsidies for jobless workers; Medicare payment rates for physicians; and programs for small-business loans, certain satellite TV broadcasting and flood insurance. It would be partially offset. It also would extend some Medicare provisions. Motion agreed to 66-34: D 56-1; R 8-33; I 2-0. Three-fifths of the total Senate (60) is required to invoke cloture. (Subsequently, the Baucus substitute amendment was adopted by voice vote.) March 9, 2010.

47. HR 4213. Tax Extenders/Cloture.
Motion to invoke cloture (thus limiting debate) on the bill, as amended. Motion agreed to 66-33: D 55-1; R 9-32; I 2-0. Three-fifths of the total Senate (60) is required to invoke cloture. March 10, 2010.

48. HR 4213. Tax Extenders/Passage.
Passage of the bill that would extend for one year a variety of tax provisions that expired Dec. 31. It also would extend federal unemployment benefits and health insurance subsidies for jobless workers; Medicare payment rates for physicians; and programs for small-business loans, certain satellite TV broadcasting and flood insurance. It would be partially offset by repealing a provision that allows the cellulosic biofuels producer credit to be claimed by producers of certain paper products. It also would extend some Medicare provisions, including authorization for certain Medicare Advantage plans, as well as an increase in the federal medical assistance percentage for state Medicaid programs. Passed 62-36: D 54-1; R 6-35; I 2-0. A "yea" was a vote in support of the president's position. March 10, 2010.

	44	45	46	47	48
ALABAMA					
Shelby	Y	N	N	N	N
Sessions	Y	N	N	N	N
ALASKA					
Murkowski	Y	N	Y	Y	Y
Begich	Y	Y	Y	Y	Y
ARIZONA					
McCain	Y	N	N	N	N
Kyl	Y	N	N	N	N
ARKANSAS					
Lincoln	Y	Y	Y	Y	Y
Pryor	Y	Y	Y	Y	Y
CALIFORNIA					
Feinstein	Y	Y	Y	Y	Y
Boxer	Y	Y	Y	Y	Y
COLORADO					
Udall	Y	Y	Y	Y	Y
Bennet	Y	Y	Y	Y	Y
CONNECTICUT					
Dodd	Y	Y	Y	Y	Y
Lieberman	Y	Y	Y	Y	Y
DELAWARE					
Carper	Y	Y	Y	Y	Y
Kaufman	Y	Y	Y	Y	Y
FLORIDA					
Nelson	Y	Y	Y	Y	Y
LeMieux	Y	N	N	N	N
GEORGIA					
Chambliss	Y	N	N	Y	N
Isakson	Y	N	Y	N	N
HAWAII					
Inouye	Y	Y	Y	Y	Y
Akaka	Y	Y	Y	Y	Y
IDAHO					
Crapo	Y	N	N	N	N
Risch	Y	N	N	N	N
ILLINOIS					
Durbin	Y	Y	Y	Y	Y
Burris	Y	Y	Y	Y	Y
INDIANA					
Lugar	Y	N	N	N	N
Bayh	Y	Y	Y	Y	Y
IOWA					
Grassley	Y	N	N	N	N
Harkin	Y	Y	Y	Y	Y
KANSAS					
Brownback	Y	N	N	N	N
Roberts	Y	N	N	N	N
KENTUCKY					
McConnell	Y	N	N	N	N
Bunning	Y	N	N	N	N
LOUISIANA					
Landrieu	Y	Y	Y	Y	Y
Vitter	Y	N	N	N	Y
MAINE					
Snowe	Y	N	Y	Y	Y
Collins	Y	N	Y	Y	Y
MARYLAND					
Mikulski	Y	Y	Y	Y	Y
Cardin	Y	Y	Y	Y	Y
MASSACHUSETTS					
Kerry	Y	Y	Y	Y	Y
Brown	Y	N	Y	N	N
MICHIGAN					
Levin	Y	Y	Y	Y	Y
Stabenow	Y	Y	Y	Y	Y
MINNESOTA					
Klobuchar	Y	Y	Y	Y	Y
Franken	Y	Y	Y	Y	Y
MISSISSIPPI					
Cochran	Y	N	Y	N	N
Wicker	Y	N	N	N	N
MISSOURI					
Bond	Y	N	N	Y	Y
McCaskill	Y	N	Y	Y	?

	44	45	46	47	48
MONTANA					
Baucus	Y	Y	Y	Y	Y
Tester	Y	Y	Y	Y	Y
NEBRASKA					
Nelson	Y	N	N	N	N
Johanns	Y	N	N	N	N
NEVADA					
Reid	Y	Y	Y	Y	Y
Ensign	Y	N	N	N	N
NEW HAMPSHIRE					
Gregg	Y	N	N	N	N
Shaheen	Y	Y	Y	Y	Y
NEW JERSEY					
Lautenberg	Y	Y	Y	Y	Y
Menendez	Y	Y	Y	Y	Y
NEW MEXICO					
Bingaman	Y	Y	Y	Y	Y
Udall	Y	Y	Y	Y	Y
NEW YORK					
Schumer	Y	Y	Y	Y	Y
Gillibrand	Y	Y	Y	Y	Y
NORTH CAROLINA					
Burr	Y	N	N	N	N
Hagan	Y	Y	Y	Y	Y
NORTH DAKOTA					
Conrad	Y	Y	Y	Y	Y
Dorgan	Y	Y	Y	Y	Y
OHIO					
Voinovich	Y	N	Y	Y	Y
Brown	Y	Y	Y	Y	Y
OKLAHOMA					
Inhofe	Y	N	N	N	N
Coburn	Y	N	N	N	N
OREGON					
Wyden	Y	Y	Y	Y	Y
Merkley	Y	Y	Y	Y	Y
PENNSYLVANIA					
Specter	Y	Y	Y	Y	Y
Casey	Y	Y	Y	Y	Y
RHODE ISLAND					
Reed	Y	Y	Y	Y	Y
Whitehouse	Y	Y	Y	Y	Y
SOUTH CAROLINA					
Graham	Y	N	N	N	N
DeMint	Y	N	N	N	N
SOUTH DAKOTA					
Johnson	Y	Y	Y	Y	Y
Thune	Y	N	N	N	N
TENNESSEE					
Alexander	Y	N	N	N	N
Corker	Y	N	N	N	N
TEXAS					
Hutchison	Y	N	N	N	N
Cornyn	Y	N	N	N	N
UTAH					
Hatch	Y	N	N	N	N
Bennett	Y	N	N	N	N
VERMONT					
Leahy	Y	Y	Y	Y	Y
Sanders	Y	Y	Y	Y	Y
VIRGINIA					
Webb	Y	N	Y	Y	Y
Warner	Y	N	Y	Y	Y
WASHINGTON					
Murray	Y	Y	Y	Y	Y
Cantwell	Y	Y	Y	Y	Y
WEST VIRGINIA					
Byrd	Y	Y	Y	?	?
Rockefeller	Y	Y	Y	Y	Y
WISCONSIN					
Kohl	Y	Y	Y	Y	Y
Feingold	Y	Y	Y	Y	Y
WYOMING					
Enzi	Y	N	N	N	N
Barrasso	Y	N	N	N	N

KEY   **Republicans**   Democrats   *Independents*

Y Voted for (yea)	X Paired against
# Paired for	– Announced against
+ Announced for	P Voted "present"
N Voted against (nay)	

C Voted "present" to avoid possible conflict of interest

? Did not vote or otherwise make a position known

IN THE SENATE | By Vote Number

49. **HR 2847. Business Tax Exemptions and Highway Extensions/ Cloture.** Motion to invoke cloture (thus limiting debate) on the Durbin, D-Ill., motion to concur in the House amendment to the Senate amendment to the House amendment to the Senate amendment to the bill that would provide payroll tax exemptions for employers who hire new workers, extend the Highway Trust Fund and extend increased expense deductions for small businesses. Motion agreed to 61-30: D 53-1; R 6-29; I 2-0. Three-fifths of the total Senate (60) is required to invoke cloture. March 15, 2010.

50. **HR 1586. FAA Reauthorization 'Shell'/Earmark Moratorium.** Rockefeller, D-W.Va., motion to table (kill) the DeMint, R-S.C., amendment to the Rockefeller substitute. The DeMint amendment would provide for a point of order against consideration of legislation containing congressionally directed spending items in fiscal years 2010 and 2011. The substitute would authorize $34.5 billion for the Federal Aviation Administration through fiscal 2011. It would codify and accelerate completion timelines for a new satellite-based air traffic control system and would require the FAA to maintain a comprehensive database of pilot performance records. Air carriers and airports would be required to submit proposed contingency plans for long onboard tarmac delays. It would increase the general aviation jet fuel tax to a rate of 36 cents per gallon and subject fractional aircraft to the tax rate. Motion agreed to 68-29: D 51-4; R 15-25; I 2-0. March 16, 2010.

51. **HR 1586. FAA Reauthorization 'Shell'/Transportation Earmark Rescissions.** Feingold, D-Wis., amendment to the Rockefeller, D-W.Va., substitute amendment. The Feingold amendment would rescind previously appropriated unspent funds for certain transportation earmarks more than 10 years old. It also would establish general reporting requirements for unspent earmarks. Adopted 87-11: D 53-3; R 32-8; I 2-0. March 16, 2010.

52. **HR 1586. FAA Reauthorization 'Shell'/Coastal Management Assistance.** Vitter, R-La., motion to waive the Budget Act and budget resolutions with respect to the Bingaman, D-N.M., point of order against the Vitter amendment to the Rockefeller, D-W.Va., substitute amendment. The Vitter amendment would clarify that no supplemental application requirements are needed for state funding under the Coastal Impact Assistance Program once the Interior secretary has approved the project. Motion rejected 41-57: D 5-51; R 36-4; I 0-2. A three-fifths majority vote (60) of the total Senate is required to waive the Budget Act. (Subsequently, the chair upheld the point of order, and the amendment fell.) March 16, 2010.

	49	50	51	52
ALABAMA				
Shelby	N	Y	N	Y
Sessions	N	N	Y	Y
ALASKA				
Murkowski	N	Y	Y	Y
Begich	Y	Y	Y	Y
ARIZONA				
McCain	N	N	Y	Y
Kyl	N	N	Y	Y
ARKANSAS				
Lincoln	Y	Y	Y	N
Pryor	Y	Y	Y	N
CALIFORNIA				
Feinstein	Y	Y	Y	N
Boxer	Y	Y	Y	N
COLORADO				
Udall	Y	Y	Y	N
Bennet	Y	Y	Y	N
CONNECTICUT				
Dodd	Y	Y	Y	N
Lieberman	Y	Y	Y	N
DELAWARE				
Carper	Y	Y	Y	N
Kaufman	Y	N	Y	N
FLORIDA				
Nelson	Y	Y	Y	N
LeMieux	N	N	Y	Y
GEORGIA				
Chambliss	N	N	Y	Y
Isakson	N	N	Y	Y
HAWAII				
Inouye	Y	Y	Y	N
Akaka	Y	Y	Y	N
IDAHO				
Crapo	N	N	Y	Y
Risch	N	N	Y	Y
ILLINOIS				
Durbin	Y	Y	Y	N
Burris	Y	Y	Y	N
INDIANA				
Lugar	N	Y	Y	Y
Bayh	Y	N	Y	Y
IOWA				
Grassley	N	N	Y	Y
Harkin	Y	Y	Y	N
KANSAS				
Brownback	N	N	Y	Y
Roberts	N	Y	Y	Y
KENTUCKY				
McConnell	N	N	Y	Y
Bunning	–	Y	Y	Y
LOUISIANA				
Landrieu	Y	Y	N	Y
Vitter	N	N	Y	Y
MAINE				
Snowe	Y	Y	Y	N
Collins	Y	Y	Y	N
MARYLAND				
Mikulski	Y	Y	Y	N
Cardin	Y	Y	Y	N
MASSACHUSETTS				
Kerry	Y	Y	Y	N
Brown	Y	N	N	N
MICHIGAN				
Levin	Y	Y	N	N
Stabenow	Y	Y	Y	N
MINNESOTA				
Klobuchar	Y	Y	Y	N
Franken	Y	Y	Y	N
MISSISSIPPI				
Cochran	N	Y	N	Y
Wicker	N	Y	N	Y
MISSOURI				
Bond	Y	Y	N	Y
McCaskill	Y	N	Y	N

	49	50	51	52
MONTANA				
Baucus	Y	Y	Y	N
Tester	+	+	Y	N
NEBRASKA				
Nelson	N	Y	Y	Y
Johanns	N	N	Y	Y
NEVADA				
Reid	Y	Y	Y	N
Ensign	N	N	Y	Y
NEW HAMPSHIRE				
Gregg	?	Y	Y	N
Shaheen	Y	Y	Y	N
NEW JERSEY				
Lautenberg	Y	Y	Y	N
Menendez	Y	Y	Y	N
NEW MEXICO				
Bingaman	Y	Y	Y	N
Udall	Y	Y	Y	N
NEW YORK				
Schumer	Y	Y	Y	N
Gillibrand	Y	Y	Y	N
NORTH CAROLINA				
Burr	Y	N	Y	Y
Hagan	?	Y	Y	Y
NORTH DAKOTA				
Conrad	Y	Y	Y	N
Dorgan	Y	Y	Y	N
OHIO				
Voinovich	?	Y	N	Y
Brown	Y	Y	Y	N
OKLAHOMA				
Inhofe	N	Y	N	Y
Coburn	N	N	Y	N
OREGON				
Wyden	Y	Y	Y	N
Merkley	Y	Y	Y	N
PENNSYLVANIA				
Specter	Y	Y	Y	N
Casey	Y	Y	Y	N
RHODE ISLAND				
Reed	Y	Y	Y	N
Whitehouse	Y	Y	Y	N
SOUTH CAROLINA				
Graham	N	N	Y	Y
DeMint	–	N	Y	Y
SOUTH DAKOTA				
Johnson	Y	Y	Y	N
Thune	N	N	Y	Y
TENNESSEE				
Alexander	N	Y	N	Y
Corker	N	N	Y	Y
TEXAS				
Hutchison	N	Y	Y	Y
Cornyn	N	N	Y	Y
UTAH				
Hatch	?	N	Y	Y
Bennett	?	?	?	?
VERMONT				
Leahy	Y	Y	Y	N
Sanders	Y	Y	Y	N
VIRGINIA				
Webb	Y	Y	Y	N
Warner	Y	Y	Y	N
WASHINGTON				
Murray	Y	Y	Y	N
Cantwell	Y	Y	Y	N
WEST VIRGINIA				
Byrd	?	?	?	?
Rockefeller	Y	Y	N	N
WISCONSIN				
Kohl	Y	Y	Y	N
Feingold	Y	N	Y	N
WYOMING				
Enzi	N	N	Y	Y
Barrasso	N	N	Y	Y

KEY **Republicans** Democrats *Independents*

Y Voted for (yea)	X Paired against	C Voted "present" to avoid possible conflict of interest
# Paired for	– Announced against	
+ Announced for	P Voted "present"	? Did not vote or otherwise make a position known
N Voted against (nay)		

IN THE SENATE | By Vote Number

53. HR 1586. FAA Reauthorization 'Shell'/D.C. Opportunity Scholarships.
Lieberman, I-Conn., amendment to the Rockefeller, D-W.Va., substitute amendment. The Lieberman amendment would authorize $20 million in 2010 for a five-year program to provide vouchers of up to $11,000 per student per year, adjusted for inflation, to permit low-income students in the District of Columbia public school system to attend private and faith-based schools. It also would authorize $20 million each for District public and charter schools. Grant preference would be given to students in schools identified as in need of improvement in accordance with the Elementary and Secondary Education Act. Rejected 42-55: D 3-53; R 38-1; I 1-1. March 16, 2010.

54. HR 2847. Business Tax Exemptions and Highway Extensions/Motion to Waive.
Schumer, D-N.Y., motion to waive the Budget Act and budget resolutions with respect to the Gregg, R-N.H., point of order against the Durbin, D-Ill., motion to concur in the House amendments to the Senate amendment to the House amendment to the Senate amendment to the bill that would exempt employers from Social Security payroll taxes for certain new hires made in 2010. It also would allow certain tax-advantaged bonds to be converted to bonds with a direct subsidy and delay by three years the effective date of new interest allocation rules for multinational companies. It would extend the Highway Trust Fund and certain transportation safety programs through Dec. 31, 2010. It also would extend through 2010 the ability of small businesses to deduct $250,000 of qualified property purchases from income taxes in the year of purchase. Motion agreed to 63-34: D 55-1; R 6-33; I 2-0. A three-fifths majority vote (60) of the total Senate is required to waive the Budget Act. March 17, 2010.

55. HR 2847. Business Tax Exemptions and Highway Extensions/Motion to Concur.
Durbin, D-Ill., motion to concur in the House amendments to the Senate amendment to the House amendment to the Senate amendment to the bill. Motion agreed to (thus clearing the bill for the president) 68-29: D 55-1; R 11-28; I 2-0. A "yea" was a vote in support of the president's position. March 17, 2010.

56. Thompson Nomination/Confirmation.
Confirmation of President Obama's nomination of O. Rogeriee Thompson of Rhode Island to be a judge for the 1st U.S. Circuit Court of Appeals. Confirmed 98-0: D 56-0; R 40-0; I 2-0. A "yea" was a vote in support of the president's position. March 17, 2010.

	53	54	55	56			53	54	55	56
ALABAMA						**MONTANA**				
Shelby	?	N	N	Y		Baucus	N	Y	Y	Y
Sessions	Y	N	N	Y		Tester	N	Y	Y	Y
ALASKA						**NEBRASKA**				
Murkowski	Y	N	Y	Y		Nelson	N	N	N	Y
Begich	N	Y	Y	Y		Johanns	Y	N	N	Y
ARIZONA						**NEVADA**				
McCain	Y	N	N	Y		Reid	N	Y	Y	Y
Kyl	Y	N	N	Y		Ensign	Y	N	N	Y
ARKANSAS						**NEW HAMPSHIRE**				
Lincoln	N	Y	Y	Y		Gregg	Y	N	N	Y
Pryor	N	Y	Y	Y		Shaheen	N	Y	Y	Y
CALIFORNIA						**NEW JERSEY**				
Feinstein	Y	Y	Y	Y		Lautenberg	N	Y	Y	Y
Boxer	N	Y	Y	Y		Menendez	N	Y	Y	Y
COLORADO						**NEW MEXICO**				
Udall	N	Y	Y	Y		Bingaman	N	Y	Y	Y
Bennet	N	Y	Y	Y		Udall	N	Y	Y	Y
CONNECTICUT						**NEW YORK**				
Dodd	N	Y	Y	Y		Schumer	N	Y	Y	Y
Lieberman	Y	Y	Y	Y		Gillibrand	N	Y	Y	Y
DELAWARE						**NORTH CAROLINA**				
Carper	N	Y	Y	Y		Burr	Y	N	Y	Y
Kaufman	N	Y	Y	Y		Hagan	N	Y	Y	Y
FLORIDA						**NORTH DAKOTA**				
Nelson	Y	Y	Y	Y		Conrad	N	Y	Y	Y
LeMieux	Y	N	Y	Y		Dorgan	N	Y	Y	Y
GEORGIA						**OHIO**				
Chambliss	Y	N	N	Y		**Voinovich**	Y	Y	Y	Y
Isakson	Y	N	N	Y		Brown	N	Y	Y	Y
HAWAII						**OKLAHOMA**				
Inouye	N	Y	Y	Y		**Inhofe**	Y	Y	Y	Y
Akaka	N	Y	Y	Y		**Coburn**	Y	N	N	Y
IDAHO						**OREGON**				
Crapo	Y	–	–	Y		Wyden	N	Y	Y	Y
Risch	Y	N	N	Y		Merkley	N	Y	Y	Y
ILLINOIS						**PENNSYLVANIA**				
Durbin	N	Y	Y	Y		Specter	N	Y	Y	Y
Burris	N	Y	Y	Y		Casey	N	Y	Y	Y
INDIANA						**RHODE ISLAND**				
Lugar	Y	N	N	Y		Reed	N	Y	Y	Y
Bayh	N	Y	Y	Y		Whitehouse	N	Y	Y	Y
IOWA						**SOUTH CAROLINA**				
Grassley	Y	N	N	Y		**Graham**	Y	N	Y	Y
Harkin	N	Y	Y	Y		**DeMint**	Y	N	N	Y
KANSAS						**SOUTH DAKOTA**				
Brownback	Y	N	N	Y		Johnson	N	Y	Y	Y
Roberts	Y	N	N	Y		**Thune**	Y	N	N	Y
KENTUCKY						**TENNESSEE**				
McConnell	Y	N	N	Y		**Alexander**	Y	N	Y	Y
Bunning	Y	N	N	Y		**Corker**	Y	N	N	Y
LOUISIANA						**TEXAS**				
Landrieu	N	Y	Y	Y		**Hutchison**	Y	N	N	Y
Vitter	Y	N	N	Y		**Cornyn**	Y	N	N	Y
MAINE						**UTAH**				
Snowe	N	Y	Y	Y		**Hatch**	Y	N	N	Y
Collins	Y	Y	Y	Y		**Bennett**	?	?	?	?
MARYLAND						**VERMONT**				
Mikulski	N	Y	Y	Y		Leahy	N	Y	Y	Y
Cardin	N	Y	Y	Y		*Sanders*	N	Y	Y	Y
MASSACHUSETTS						**VIRGINIA**				
Kerry	N	Y	Y	Y		Webb	N	Y	Y	Y
Brown	Y	Y	Y	Y		Warner	Y	Y	Y	Y
MICHIGAN						**WASHINGTON**				
Levin	N	Y	Y	Y		Murray	N	Y	Y	Y
Stabenow	N	Y	Y	Y		Cantwell	N	Y	Y	Y
MINNESOTA						**WEST VIRGINIA**				
Klobuchar	N	Y	Y	Y		Byrd	?	?	?	?
Franken	N	Y	Y	Y		Rockefeller	N	Y	Y	Y
MISSISSIPPI						**WISCONSIN**				
Cochran	Y	N	Y	Y		Kohl	N	Y	Y	Y
Wicker	Y	N	N	Y		Feingold	N	Y	Y	Y
MISSOURI						**WYOMING**				
Bond	Y	Y	Y	Y		**Enzi**	Y	N	N	Y
McCaskill	N	Y	Y	Y		**Barrasso**	Y	N	N	Y

KEY   **Republicans**   Democrats   *Independents*

Y Voted for (yea)	X Paired against	C Voted "present" to avoid possible conflict of interest
# Paired for	– Announced against	
+ Announced for	P Voted "present"	? Did not vote or otherwise make a position known
N Voted against (nay)		

IN THE SENATE | By Vote Number

57. HR 1586. FAA Reauthorization 'Shell'/Spending Caps.

Sessions, R-Ala., motion to waive the Budget Act and budget resolutions with respect to the Inouye, D-Hawaii, point of order against the Sessions amendment to the Rockefeller, D-W.Va., substitute amendment. The Sessions amendment would establish discretionary spending limits for three years beginning in fiscal 2011. Points of order against emergency spending designations could be waived by a three-fifths majority vote in the Senate. Motion rejected 56-40: D 15-39; R 40-0; I 1-1. A three-fifths majority vote (60) of the total Senate is required to waive the Budget Act. (Subsequently, the chair upheld the point of order, and the amendment fell.) March 18, 2010.

58. HR 1586. FAA Reauthorization 'Shell'/Spending Caps.

Pryor, D-Ark., motion to waive the Budget Act and budget resolutions with respect to the Sessions, R-Ala., point of order against the Pryor amendment to the Rockefeller, D-W.Va., substitute amendment. The Pryor amendment would establish discretionary spending limits for three years beginning in fiscal 2011. The spending limits would be discontinued if Congress does not enact recommendations of a debt commission by Jan. 2, 2011. Motion rejected 27-70: D 27-28; R 0-40; I 0-2. A three-fifths majority vote (60) of the total Senate is required to waive the Budget Act. (Subsequently, the chair upheld the point of order, and the amendment fell.) March 18, 2010.

59. HR 1586. FAA Reauthorization 'Shell'/Non-Security Spending Limits.

Inhofe, R-Okla., motion to waive the Budget Act and budget resolutions with respect to the Dorgan, D-N.D., point of order against the Inhofe amendment to the McCain, R-Ariz., amendment to the Rockefeller, D-W.Va., substitute amendment. The Inhofe amendment would establish statutory non-security discretionary spending limits. It would phase spending back to fiscal 2008 levels by fiscal 2015 and keep those levels through fiscal 2020. The provisions could be waived by two-thirds of the total Senate or when Congress authorizes the use of force or declares war. The McCain amendment would establish a budget point of order against the use of earmarks in fiscal years that the Congressional Budget Office reports a federal deficit. Motion rejected 41-56: D 2-53; R 39-1; I 0-2. A three-fifths majority vote (60) of the total Senate is required to waive the Budget Act. (Subsequently, the chair upheld the point of order, and the amendment fell.) March 18, 2010.

60. HR 1586. FAA Reauthorization 'Shell'/Earmark Prohibition.

McCain, R-Ariz., amendment to the Rockefeller, D-W.Va., substitute amendment. The McCain amendment would establish a budget point of order against the use of earmarks in fiscal years that the Congressional Budget Office reports a federal deficit. The provision could be waived by a three-fifths majority vote in the Senate. Rejected 26-70: D 3-51; R 23-17; I 0-2. March 18, 2010.

	57	58	59	60			57	58	59	60
ALABAMA						**MONTANA**				
Shelby	Y	N	Y	N		Baucus	N	Y	N	N
Sessions	Y	N	Y	Y		Tester	N	Y	N	N
ALASKA						**NEBRASKA**				
Murkowski	Y	N	Y	N		Nelson	Y	N	N	N
Begich	Y	Y	N	N		**Johanns**	Y	N	Y	Y
ARIZONA						**NEVADA**				
McCain	Y	N	Y	Y		Reid	N	N	N	N
Kyl	Y	N	Y	Y		**Ensign**	Y	N	Y	Y
ARKANSAS						**NEW HAMPSHIRE**				
Lincoln	Y	Y	N	N		**Gregg**	Y	N	Y	N
Pryor	N	Y	Y	N		Shaheen	Y	N	N	N
CALIFORNIA						**NEW JERSEY**				
Feinstein	N	Y	N	N		Lautenberg	N	N	N	N
Boxer	N	Y	N	N		Menendez	N	Y	N	N
COLORADO						**NEW MEXICO**				
Udall	Y	N	N	N		Bingaman	N	N	N	N
Bennet	Y	Y	N	N		Udall	N	N	N	N
CONNECTICUT						**NEW YORK**				
Dodd	N	Y	N	N		Schumer	N	N	N	N
Lieberman	Y	N	N	N		Gillibrand	N	N	N	N
DELAWARE						**NORTH CAROLINA**				
Carper	Y	Y	N	N		**Burr**	Y	N	Y	Y
Kaufman	N	Y	N	N		Hagan	Y	Y	N	N
FLORIDA						**NORTH DAKOTA**				
Nelson	Y	N	N	N		Conrad	?	N	N	N
LeMieux	Y	N	Y	Y		Dorgan	N	Y	N	N
GEORGIA						**OHIO**				
Chambliss	Y	N	Y	Y		**Voinovich**	Y	N	N	N
Isakson	Y	N	Y	Y		Brown	N	Y	N	N
HAWAII						**OKLAHOMA**				
Inouye	N	N	N	N		**Inhofe**	Y	N	Y	N
Akaka	N	Y	N	N		**Coburn**	Y	N	Y	Y
IDAHO						**OREGON**				
Crapo	Y	N	Y	Y		Wyden	N	Y	N	N
Risch	Y	N	Y	Y		Merkley	N	Y	N	N
ILLINOIS						**PENNSYLVANIA**				
Durbin	N	Y	N	N		Specter	N	Y	N	N
Burris	N	N	N	N		Casey	N	Y	N	N
INDIANA						**RHODE ISLAND**				
Lugar	Y	N	Y	N		Reed	N	N	N	N
Bayh	Y	Y	N	Y		Whitehouse	N	N	N	N
IOWA						**SOUTH CAROLINA**				
Grassley	Y	N	Y	Y		**Graham**	Y	N	Y	Y
Harkin	N	Y	N	N		**DeMint**	Y	N	Y	Y
KANSAS						**SOUTH DAKOTA**				
Brownback	Y	N	Y	Y		Johnson	N	Y	N	N
Roberts	Y	N	Y	N		**Thune**	Y	N	Y	Y
KENTUCKY						**TENNESSEE**				
McConnell	Y	N	Y	N		**Alexander**	Y	N	Y	N
Bunning	Y	N	Y	N		**Corker**	Y	N	Y	Y
LOUISIANA						**TEXAS**				
Landrieu	N	Y	N	N		**Hutchison**	Y	N	Y	N
Vitter	Y	N	Y	Y		**Cornyn**	Y	N	Y	Y
MAINE						**UTAH**				
Snowe	Y	N	Y	N		**Hatch**	Y	N	Y	N
Collins	Y	N	Y	N		**Bennett**	?	?	?	?
MARYLAND						**VERMONT**				
Mikulski	N	N	N	N		Leahy	N	N	N	N
Cardin	N	N	N	N		*Sanders*	N	N	N	N
MASSACHUSETTS						**VIRGINIA**				
Kerry	N	Y	N	N		Webb	Y	N	N	N
Brown	Y	N	Y	N		Warner	Y	N	N	N
MICHIGAN						**WASHINGTON**				
Levin	N	N	N	N		Murray	N	N	N	?
Stabenow	N	N	N	N		Cantwell	Y	N	N	N
MINNESOTA						**WEST VIRGINIA**				
Klobuchar	Y	N	N	N		Byrd	?	?	?	?
Franken	N	N	N	N		Rockefeller	?	?	?	?
MISSISSIPPI						**WISCONSIN**				
Cochran	Y	N	Y	N		Kohl	N	Y	N	N
Wicker	Y	N	Y	N		Feingold	N	N	N	Y
MISSOURI						**WYOMING**				
Bond	Y	N	Y	N		**Enzi**	Y	N	Y	Y
McCaskill	Y	N	Y	Y		**Barrasso**	Y	N	Y	Y

KEY   **Republicans**   Democrats   *Independents*

Y Voted for (yea)	X Paired against	C Voted "present" to avoid possible conflict of interest
# Paired for	− Announced against	
+ Announced for	P Voted "present"	? Did not vote or otherwise make a position known
N Voted against (nay)		

IN THE SENATE | By Vote Number

61. **HR 1586. FAA Reauthorization/Passage.** Passage of the bill that would authorize $34.5 billion for the Federal Aviation Administration through fiscal 2011. It would authorize $9.3 billion in fiscal 2010 and $9.6 billion in fiscal 2011 for operations, as well as $3.5 billion in fiscal 2010 and $3.6 billion in fiscal 2011 for air navigation facilities and equipment. It would authorize $4 billion in fiscal 2010 and $4.1 billion in fiscal 2011 for airport planning and development and for noise compatibility planning and programs. A new Air Traffic Control System Modernization Account would receive $400 million per year through taxes imposed on jet fuel, with funding available for expenditures related to modernization and implementation of NextGen. It would increase the general aviation jet fuel tax to 36 cents per gallon and subject fractional aircraft to the tax rate. Passed 93-0: D 55-0; R 37-0; I 1-0. March 22, 2010.

62. **Procedural Motion/Motion to Adjourn.** Reid, D-Nev., motion to adjourn until 3:05 p.m. on Tuesday, March 23, 2010. Motion agreed to 57-39: D 55-0; R 0-39; I 2-0. March 23, 2010.

63. **HR 4872. Health Care Reconciliation/Motion to Proceed.** Reid, D-Nev., motion to proceed to the bill that would make changes to the 2010 health care overhaul law, revise student lending procedures and provide new revenue-raising provisions. Motion agreed to 56-40: D 54-1; R 0-39; I 2-0. March 23, 2010.

64. **HR 4872. Health Care Reconciliation/Medicare Savings.** Baucus, D-Mont., motion to table (kill) the Gregg, R-N.H., amendment that would require certification that all new spending in the 2010 health care overhaul law and the reconciliation bill be offset with savings from sources outside of Medicare. Motion agreed to 56-42: D 54-2; R 0-40; I 2-0. March 24, 2010.

65. **HR 4872. Health Care Reconciliation/Program Rescissions.** Baucus, D-Mont., motion to table (kill) the McCain, R-Ariz., amendment that would rescind certain targeted programs contained in the 2010 health care overhaul law, including federal Medicaid funding for Louisiana that exceeds levels in other states, health insurance under Medicare for residents of Libby, Mont., and hospital reimbursement rates for Connecticut and Michigan. Motion agreed to 54-43: D 52-3; R 0-40; I 2-0. March 24, 2010.

66. **HR 4872. Health Care Reconciliation/Tax Increases.** Baucus, D-Mont., motion to table (kill) the Crapo, R-Idaho, motion to commit the bill to the Finance Committee with instructions that it be reported back with changes that would provide that no provisions of existing health care law or the underlying bill could result in a federal tax increase for individuals with adjusted gross incomes of less than $200,000 and married individuals with adjusted gross incomes of less than $250,000. Motion agreed to 56-43: D 54-3; R 0-40; I 2-0. March 24, 2010.

67. **HR 4872. Health Care Reconciliation/Employer Mandates.** Baucus, D-Mont., motion to table (kill) the Enzi, R-Wyo., motion to commit the bill to the Finance Committee with instructions that it be reported back with changes that would strike provisions of the 2010 health care overhaul relating to mandates on employers to provide health insurance to their employees and add an offset. Motion agreed to 58-41: D 56-1; R 0-40; I 2-0. March 24, 2010.

	61	62	63	64	65	66	67
ALABAMA							
Shelby	Y	N	N	N	N	N	N
Sessions	Y	N	N	N	N	N	N
ALASKA							
Murkowski	Y	N	N	N	N	N	N
Begich	Y	Y	Y	Y	?	Y	Y
ARIZONA							
McCain	Y	N	N	N	N	N	N
Kyl	Y	N	N	N	N	N	N
ARKANSAS							
Lincoln	Y	Y	Y	Y	N	N	N
Pryor	Y	Y	Y	Y	Y	Y	Y
CALIFORNIA							
Feinstein	Y	Y	Y	Y	Y	Y	Y
Boxer	Y	Y	Y	Y	Y	Y	Y
COLORADO							
Udall	Y	Y	Y	Y	Y	Y	Y
Bennet	Y	Y	Y	Y	Y	Y	Y
CONNECTICUT							
Dodd	Y	Y	Y	Y	Y	Y	Y
Lieberman	Y	Y	Y	Y	Y	Y	Y
DELAWARE							
Carper	Y	Y	Y	Y	Y	Y	Y
Kaufman	Y	Y	Y	Y	Y	Y	Y
FLORIDA							
Nelson	Y	Y	Y	Y	Y	Y	Y
LeMieux	Y	N	N	N	N	N	N
GEORGIA							
Chambliss	Y	N	N	N	N	N	N
Isakson	?	?	?	?	?	?	?
HAWAII							
Inouye	Y	Y	Y	Y	Y	Y	Y
Akaka	Y	Y	Y	Y	Y	Y	Y
IDAHO							
Crapo	Y	N	N	N	N	N	N
Risch	Y	N	N	N	N	N	N
ILLINOIS							
Durbin	Y	Y	Y	Y	Y	Y	Y
Burris	Y	Y	Y	Y	Y	Y	Y
INDIANA							
Lugar	Y	N	N	N	N	N	N
Bayh	Y	Y	Y	N	N	Y	Y
IOWA							
Grassley	Y	N	N	N	N	N	N
Harkin	Y	Y	Y	Y	Y	Y	Y
KANSAS							
Brownback	Y	N	N	N	N	N	N
Roberts	Y	N	N	N	N	N	N
KENTUCKY							
McConnell	Y	N	N	N	N	N	N
Bunning	Y	N	N	N	N	N	N
LOUISIANA							
Landrieu	Y	Y	Y	Y	Y	Y	Y
Vitter	Y	N	N	N	N	N	N
MAINE							
Snowe	Y	N	N	N	N	N	N
Collins	Y	N	N	N	N	N	N
MARYLAND							
Mikulski	Y	Y	Y	Y	Y	Y	Y
Cardin	Y	Y	Y	Y	Y	Y	Y
MASSACHUSETTS							
Kerry	Y	Y	Y	Y	Y	Y	Y
Brown	Y	N	N	N	N	N	N
MICHIGAN							
Levin	Y	Y	Y	Y	Y	Y	Y
Stabenow	Y	Y	Y	Y	Y	Y	Y
MINNESOTA							
Klobuchar	Y	Y	Y	Y	Y	Y	Y
Franken	Y	Y	Y	Y	Y	Y	Y
MISSISSIPPI							
Cochran	Y	N	N	N	N	N	N
Wicker	?	N	N	N	N	N	N
MISSOURI							
Bond	Y	N	N	N	N	N	N
McCaskill	Y	Y	Y	Y	Y	Y	Y

	61	62	63	64	65	66	67
MONTANA							
Baucus	Y	Y	Y	Y	Y	Y	Y
Tester	Y	Y	Y	Y	Y	Y	Y
NEBRASKA							
Nelson	Y	Y	N	N	N	N	Y
Johanns	Y	N	N	N	N	N	N
NEVADA							
Reid	Y	Y	Y	Y	Y	Y	Y
Ensign	Y	N	N	N	N	N	N
NEW HAMPSHIRE							
Gregg	Y	N	N	N	N	N	N
Shaheen	Y	Y	Y	Y	Y	Y	Y
NEW JERSEY							
Lautenberg	Y	Y	Y	Y	Y	Y	Y
Menendez	Y	Y	Y	Y	Y	Y	Y
NEW MEXICO							
Bingaman	Y	Y	Y	Y	Y	Y	Y
Udall	+	?	?	Y	Y	Y	Y
NEW YORK							
Schumer	Y	Y	Y	Y	Y	Y	Y
Gillibrand	Y	Y	Y	Y	Y	Y	Y
NORTH CAROLINA							
Burr	Y	N	N	N	N	N	N
Hagan	Y	Y	Y	Y	Y	Y	Y
NORTH DAKOTA							
Conrad	Y	Y	Y	Y	Y	Y	Y
Dorgan	Y	Y	Y	Y	Y	Y	Y
OHIO							
Voinovich	Y	N	N	N	N	N	N
Brown	Y	Y	Y	Y	Y	Y	Y
OKLAHOMA							
Inhofe	Y	N	N	N	N	N	N
Coburn	Y	N	N	N	N	N	N
OREGON							
Wyden	Y	Y	Y	Y	Y	Y	Y
Merkley	Y	Y	Y	Y	Y	Y	Y
PENNSYLVANIA							
Specter	Y	Y	Y	Y	Y	Y	Y
Casey	Y	Y	Y	Y	Y	Y	Y
RHODE ISLAND							
Reed	Y	Y	Y	Y	Y	Y	Y
Whitehouse	Y	Y	Y	Y	Y	Y	Y
SOUTH CAROLINA							
Graham	Y	N	N	N	N	N	N
DeMint	?	N	N	N	N	N	N
SOUTH DAKOTA							
Johnson	Y	Y	Y	Y	Y	Y	Y
Thune	Y	N	N	N	N	N	N
TENNESSEE							
Alexander	Y	N	N	N	N	N	N
Corker	Y	N	N	N	N	N	N
TEXAS							
Hutchison	Y	N	N	N	N	N	N
Cornyn	Y	N	N	N	N	N	N
UTAH							
Hatch	Y	N	N	N	N	N	N
Bennett	?	?	?	N	N	N	N
VERMONT							
Leahy	Y	Y	Y	Y	Y	Y	Y
Sanders	?	Y	Y	Y	Y	Y	Y
VIRGINIA							
Webb	Y	Y	Y	N	Y	Y	Y
Warner	Y	Y	Y	Y	Y	Y	Y
WASHINGTON							
Murray	Y	Y	Y	Y	Y	Y	Y
Cantwell	Y	Y	Y	Y	N	Y	Y
WEST VIRGINIA							
Byrd	?	?	?	?	?	Y	Y
Rockefeller	Y	Y	Y	Y	Y	Y	Y
WISCONSIN							
Kohl	Y	Y	Y	Y	Y	Y	Y
Feingold	Y	Y	Y	Y	Y	Y	Y
WYOMING							
Enzi	Y	N	N	N	N	N	N
Barrasso	Y	N	N	N	N	N	N

KEY   **Republicans**   Democrats   *Independents*

Y Voted for (yea)	X Paired against	C Voted "present" to avoid possible conflict of interest
# Paired for	– Announced against	
+ Announced for	P Voted "present"	? Did not vote or otherwise make a position known
N Voted against (nay)		

IN THE SENATE | By Vote Number

68. HR 4872. Health Care Reconciliation/Premium Increases. Baucus, D-Mont., motion to table (kill) the Barrasso, R-Wyo., amendment that would require the Health and Human Services secretary to certify that programs in the 2010 health care overhaul law and health care provisions in the reconciliation measure would not increase insurance premiums more than the increases projected before enactment. Motion agreed to 57-41: D 55-1; R 0-40; I 2-0. March 24, 2010.

69. HR 4872. Health Care Reconciliation/Executive Branch Requirement. Grassley, R-Iowa, motion to waive the Budget Act and budget resolutions with respect to the Baucus, D-Mont., point of order against the Grassley amendment. The Grassley amendment would require that health insurance benefits for the president, vice president, members of Congress, certain congressional staff and certain political appointees within the executive branch may be provided only through the health insurance exchanges established by the 2010 health care overhaul law. Motion rejected 43-56: D 3-54; R 40-0; I 0-2. A three-fifths majority vote (60) of the total Senate is required to waive the Budget Act. (Subsequently, the chair upheld the point of order, and the amendment fell.) March 24, 2010.

70. HR 4872. Health Care Reconciliation/Student Loan Interest Rate. Alexander, R-Tenn., motion to waive the Budget Act and budget resolutions with respect to the Harkin, D-Iowa, motion to table (kill) the Alexander motion to commit the bill to the Health, Education, Labor and Pensions Committee with instructions that it be reported back with changes that would reduce the student loan interest rate for the direct-loan program to 5.3 percent. Motion rejected 58-41: D 56-1; R 0-40; I 2-0. A three-fifths majority vote (60) of the total Senate is required to waive the Budget Act. (Subsequently, the chair upheld the point of order, and the amendment fell.) March 24, 2010.

71. HR 4872. Health Care Reconciliation/Members of Congress on Medicaid. LeMieux, R-Fla., motion to waive the Budget Act and budget resolutions with respect to the Baucus, D-Mont., point of order against the LeMieux amendment. The LeMieux amendment would require members of Congress to receive health insurance coverage through Medicaid programs instead of through the Federal Employees Health Benefits Program. Motion rejected 40-59: D 0-57; R 40-0; I 0-2. A three-fifths majority vote (60) of the total Senate is required to waive the Budget Act. (Subsequently, the chair upheld the point of order, and the amendment fell.) March 24, 2010.

72. HR 4872. Health Care Reconciliation/Medicare Advantage Reduction Ban. Baucus, D-Mont., motion to table (kill) the Hatch, R-Utah, motion to commit the bill to the Finance Committee with instructions that it be reported back with changes that would prohibit cuts to the Medicare Advantage program and provide for an offset if the Health and Human Services Department certified that at least 1 million Medicare Advantage program participants would lose benefits under the changes in the reconciliation measure or the 2010 health care overhaul law. Motion agreed to 56-42: D 54-2; R 0-40; I 2-0. March 24, 2010.

73. HR 4872. Health Care Reconciliation/Medication for Sex Offenders. Baucus, D-Mont., motion to table (kill) the Coburn, R-Okla., amendment that would prohibit the health insurance exchanges established under the 2010 health care overhaul law from subsidizing the purchase of erectile dysfunction medication by registered sex offenders. It also would establish oversight to prevent the filing of fraudulent health care claims. Motion agreed to 57-42: D 55-2; R 0-40; I 2-0. March 24, 2010.

State / Senator	68	69	70	71	72	73
ALABAMA						
Shelby	N	Y	N	Y	N	N
Sessions	N	Y	N	Y	N	N
ALASKA						
Murkowski	N	Y	N	Y	N	N
Begich	Y	N	Y	N	Y	Y
ARIZONA						
McCain	N	Y	N	Y	N	N
Kyl	N	Y	N	Y	N	N
ARKANSAS						
Lincoln	Y	Y	Y	N	Y	Y
Pryor	Y	N	Y	N	Y	Y
CALIFORNIA						
Feinstein	Y	N	Y	N	Y	Y
Boxer	Y	N	Y	N	Y	Y
COLORADO						
Udall	Y	N	Y	N	Y	Y
Bennet	Y	N	Y	N	Y	Y
CONNECTICUT						
Dodd	Y	N	Y	N	Y	Y
Lieberman	Y	N	Y	N	Y	Y
DELAWARE						
Carper	Y	N	Y	N	Y	Y
Kaufman	?	N	Y	N	Y	Y
FLORIDA						
Nelson	Y	N	Y	N	Y	Y
LeMieux	N	Y	N	Y	N	N
GEORGIA						
Chambliss	N	Y	N	Y	N	N
Isakson	?	?	?	?	?	?
HAWAII						
Inouye	Y	N	Y	N	Y	Y
Akaka	Y	N	Y	N	Y	Y
IDAHO						
Crapo	N	Y	N	Y	N	N
Risch	N	Y	N	Y	N	N
ILLINOIS						
Durbin	Y	N	Y	N	Y	Y
Burris	Y	N	Y	N	Y	Y
INDIANA						
Lugar	N	Y	N	Y	N	N
Bayh	N	Y	Y	N	Y	N
IOWA						
Grassley	N	Y	N	Y	N	N
Harkin	Y	N	Y	N	Y	Y
KANSAS						
Brownback	N	Y	N	Y	N	N
Roberts	N	Y	N	Y	N	N
KENTUCKY						
McConnell	N	Y	N	Y	N	N
Bunning	N	Y	N	Y	N	N
LOUISIANA						
Landrieu	Y	N	Y	N	Y	Y
Vitter	N	Y	N	Y	N	N
MAINE						
Snowe	N	Y	N	Y	N	N
Collins	N	Y	N	Y	N	N
MARYLAND						
Mikulski	Y	N	Y	N	Y	Y
Cardin	Y	N	Y	N	Y	Y
MASSACHUSETTS						
Kerry	Y	N	Y	N	Y	Y
Brown	N	Y	N	Y	N	N
MICHIGAN						
Levin	Y	N	Y	N	Y	Y
Stabenow	Y	N	Y	N	Y	Y
MINNESOTA						
Klobuchar	Y	N	Y	N	Y	Y
Franken	Y	N	Y	N	Y	Y
MISSISSIPPI						
Cochran	N	Y	N	Y	N	N
Wicker	N	Y	N	Y	N	N
MISSOURI						
Bond	N	Y	N	Y	N	N
McCaskill	Y	N	Y	N	Y	Y

State / Senator	68	69	70	71	72	73
MONTANA						
Baucus	Y	N	Y	N	Y	Y
Tester	Y	N	Y	N	Y	Y
NEBRASKA						
Nelson	Y	Y	N	N	N	N
Johanns	N	Y	N	Y	N	N
NEVADA						
Reid	Y	N	Y	N	Y	Y
Ensign	N	Y	N	Y	N	N
NEW HAMPSHIRE						
Gregg	N	Y	N	Y	N	N
Shaheen	Y	N	Y	N	Y	Y
NEW JERSEY						
Lautenberg	Y	N	Y	N	Y	Y
Menendez	Y	N	Y	N	Y	Y
NEW MEXICO						
Bingaman	Y	N	Y	N	Y	Y
Udall	Y	N	Y	N	Y	Y
NEW YORK						
Schumer	Y	N	Y	N	Y	Y
Gillibrand	Y	N	Y	N	Y	Y
NORTH CAROLINA						
Burr	N	Y	N	Y	N	N
Hagan	Y	N	Y	N	Y	Y
NORTH DAKOTA						
Conrad	Y	N	Y	N	Y	Y
Dorgan	Y	N	Y	N	Y	Y
OHIO						
Voinovich	N	Y	N	Y	N	N
Brown	Y	N	Y	N	Y	Y
OKLAHOMA						
Inhofe	N	Y	N	Y	N	N
Coburn	N	Y	N	Y	N	N
OREGON						
Wyden	Y	N	Y	N	Y	Y
Merkley	Y	N	Y	N	Y	Y
PENNSYLVANIA						
Specter	Y	N	Y	N	Y	Y
Casey	Y	N	Y	N	Y	Y
RHODE ISLAND						
Reed	Y	N	Y	N	Y	Y
Whitehouse	Y	N	Y	N	Y	Y
SOUTH CAROLINA						
Graham	N	Y	N	Y	N	N
DeMint	N	Y	N	Y	N	N
SOUTH DAKOTA						
Johnson	Y	N	Y	N	Y	Y
Thune	N	Y	N	Y	N	N
TENNESSEE						
Alexander	N	Y	N	Y	N	N
Corker	N	Y	N	Y	N	N
TEXAS						
Hutchison	N	Y	N	Y	N	N
Cornyn	N	Y	N	Y	N	N
UTAH						
Hatch	N	Y	N	Y	N	N
Bennett	N	Y	N	Y	N	N
VERMONT						
Leahy	Y	N	Y	N	Y	Y
Sanders	Y	N	Y	N	Y	Y
VIRGINIA						
Webb	Y	N	Y	N	Y	Y
Warner	Y	N	Y	N	Y	Y
WASHINGTON						
Murray	Y	N	Y	N	Y	Y
Cantwell	Y	N	Y	N	Y	Y
WEST VIRGINIA						
Byrd	Y	N	Y	N	?	Y
Rockefeller	Y	N	Y	N	Y	Y
WISCONSIN						
Kohl	Y	N	Y	N	Y	Y
Feingold	Y	N	Y	N	Y	Y
WYOMING						
Enzi	N	Y	N	Y	N	N
Barrasso	N	Y	N	Y	N	N

KEY — Republicans — Democrats — *Independents*

Y Voted for (yea)	X Paired against	C Voted "present" to avoid possible conflict of interest
# Paired for	− Announced against	
+ Announced for	P Voted "present"	? Did not vote or otherwise make a position known
N Voted against (nay)		

IN THE SENATE | By Vote Number

74. **HR 4872. Health Care Reconciliation/State Opt-Out.** Baucus, D-Mont., motion to table (kill) the Hutchison, R-Texas, amendment that would allow state governments to opt out of certain Medicare and Medicaid mandates and tax provisions, including those on prescription drugs and medical devices, contained in the reconciliation measure and the 2010 health care overhaul law. Motion agreed to 58-41: D 56-1; R 0-40; I 2-0. March 24, 2010.

75. **HR 4872. Health Care Reconciliation/Previously Unemployed Workers.** Baucus, D-Mont., motion to table (kill) the Collins, R-Maine, amendment that would exempt newly hired workers who were previously unemployed from the total number of employees used to calculate employer mandate compliance with providing health insurance coverage. Motion agreed to 58-41: D 56-1; R 0-40; I 2-0. March 24, 2010.

76. **HR 4872. Health Care Reconciliation/Direct Student Loans.** Harkin, D-Iowa, motion to table (kill) the Thune, R-S.D., amendment that would prevent enactment of provisions in the bill to place student loans under the direct-lending program if any state experiences a job loss as a result of the provisions. Motion agreed to 55-43: D 53-3; R 0-40; I 2-0. March 24, 2010.

77. **HR 4872. Health Care Reconciliation/Strike CLASS Act.** Thune, R-S.D., motion to waive the Budget Act and budget resolutions with respect to the Harkin, D-Iowa, point of order against the Thune amendment. The Thune amendment would terminate the Community Living Assistance Services and Supports (CLASS) program, a new voluntary insurance program to help individuals with functional limitations purchase community living assistance services. Motion rejected 43-55: D 2-54; R 40-0; I 1-1. A three-fifths majority vote (60) of the total Senate is required to waive the Budget Act. (Subsequently, the chair upheld the point of order, and the amendment fell.) March 24, 2010.

78. **HR 4872. Health Care Reconciliation/Medicare Tax.** Baucus, D-Mont., motion to table (kill) the Cornyn, R-Texas, motion to commit the bill to the Finance Committee with instructions that it be reported back with changes that would strike a provision in the 2010 health care overhaul law that applies a 3.8 percent Medicare tax to income for certain taxpayers with adjusted gross incomes in excess of $200,000 for individuals and $250,000 for married couples filing jointly. Motion agreed to 52-46: D 50-6; R 0-40; I 2-0. March 24, 2010.

79. **HR 4872. Health Care Reconciliation/Medical-Device Tax.** Baucus, D-Mont., motion to table (kill) the Roberts, R-Kan., amendment that would strike a provision in the bill that would establish a 2.3 percent tax on certain medical devices. It would be offset by lowering, from 8 percent to 5 percent, the 2010 health care overhaul law's affordability tax exemption for individuals under the individual mandate. Motion agreed to 56-42: D 54-2; R 0-40; I 2-0. March 24, 2010.

80. **HR 4872. Health Care Reconciliation/Pediatric Assistance Devices.** Baucus, D-Mont., motion to table (kill) the Inhofe, R-Okla., amendment that would exempt certain pediatric assistive devices from a provision in the bill that would establish a 2.3 percent tax on medical devices. It would be offset by lowering, from 8 percent to 5 percent, the 2010 health care overhaul law's affordability tax exemption for individuals under the individual mandate. Motion agreed to 57-41: D 55-1; R 0-40; I 2-0. March 24, 2010.

State / Senator	74	75	76	77	78	79	80
ALABAMA							
Shelby	N	N	N	Y	N	N	N
Sessions	N	N	N	Y	N	N	N
ALASKA							
Murkowski	N	N	N	Y	N	N	N
Begich	Y	Y	Y	N	Y	Y	Y
ARIZONA							
McCain	N	N	N	Y	N	N	N
Kyl	N	N	N	Y	N	N	N
ARKANSAS							
Lincoln	Y	Y	Y	N	N	Y	Y
Pryor	Y	Y	Y	N	N	Y	Y
CALIFORNIA							
Feinstein	Y	Y	Y	N	Y	Y	Y
Boxer	Y	Y	Y	N	Y	Y	Y
COLORADO							
Udall	Y	Y	Y	N	Y	Y	Y
Bennet	Y	Y	Y	N	Y	Y	Y
CONNECTICUT							
Dodd	Y	Y	Y	N	Y	Y	Y
Lieberman	Y	Y	Y	N	Y	Y	Y
DELAWARE							
Carper	Y	Y	Y	N	Y	Y	Y
Kaufman	Y	Y	Y	N	Y	Y	Y
FLORIDA							
Nelson	Y	Y	N	N	N	Y	Y
LeMieux	N	N	N	Y	N	N	N
GEORGIA							
Chambliss	N	N	N	Y	N	N	N
Isakson	?	?	?	?	?	?	?
HAWAII							
Inouye	Y	Y	Y	N	Y	Y	Y
Akaka	Y	Y	Y	N	Y	Y	Y
IDAHO							
Crapo	N	N	N	Y	N	N	N
Risch	N	N	N	Y	N	N	N
ILLINOIS							
Durbin	Y	Y	Y	N	Y	Y	Y
Burris	Y	Y	Y	N	Y	Y	Y
INDIANA							
Lugar	N	N	N	Y	N	N	N
Bayh	Y	Y	N	Y	N	N	Y
IOWA							
Grassley	N	N	N	Y	N	N	N
Harkin	Y	Y	Y	N	Y	Y	Y
KANSAS							
Brownback	N	N	N	Y	N	N	N
Roberts	N	N	N	Y	N	N	N
KENTUCKY							
McConnell	N	N	N	Y	N	N	N
Bunning	N	N	N	Y	N	N	N
LOUISIANA							
Landrieu	Y	Y	Y	N	Y	Y	Y
Vitter	N	N	N	Y	N	N	N
MAINE							
Snowe	N	N	N	Y	N	N	N
Collins	N	N	N	Y	N	N	N
MARYLAND							
Mikulski	Y	Y	Y	N	Y	Y	Y
Cardin	Y	Y	Y	N	Y	Y	Y
MASSACHUSETTS							
Kerry	Y	Y	Y	N	Y	Y	Y
Brown	N	N	N	Y	N	N	N
MICHIGAN							
Levin	Y	Y	Y	N	Y	Y	Y
Stabenow	Y	Y	Y	N	Y	Y	Y
MINNESOTA							
Klobuchar	Y	Y	Y	N	Y	Y	Y
Franken	Y	Y	Y	N	Y	Y	Y
MISSISSIPPI							
Cochran	N	N	N	Y	N	N	N
Wicker	N	N	N	Y	N	N	N
MISSOURI							
Bond	N	N	N	Y	N	N	N
McCaskill	Y	Y	Y	N	Y	Y	Y
MONTANA							
Baucus	Y	Y	Y	N	Y	Y	Y
Tester	Y	Y	Y	N	Y	Y	Y
NEBRASKA							
Nelson	N	N	N	Y	N	N	N
Johanns	N	N	N	Y	N	N	N
NEVADA							
Reid	Y	Y	Y	N	Y	Y	Y
Ensign	N	N	N	Y	N	N	N
NEW HAMPSHIRE							
Gregg	N	N	N	Y	N	N	N
Shaheen	Y	Y	Y	N	Y	Y	Y
NEW JERSEY							
Lautenberg	Y	Y	Y	N	Y	Y	Y
Menendez	Y	Y	Y	N	Y	Y	Y
NEW MEXICO							
Bingaman	Y	Y	Y	N	Y	Y	Y
Udall	Y	Y	Y	N	Y	Y	Y
NEW YORK							
Schumer	Y	Y	Y	N	Y	Y	Y
Gillibrand	Y	Y	Y	N	Y	Y	Y
NORTH CAROLINA							
Burr	N	N	N	Y	N	N	N
Hagan	Y	Y	Y	N	Y	Y	Y
NORTH DAKOTA							
Conrad	Y	Y	Y	N	Y	Y	Y
Dorgan	Y	Y	Y	N	Y	Y	Y
OHIO							
Voinovich	N	N	N	Y	N	N	N
Brown	Y	Y	Y	N	Y	Y	Y
OKLAHOMA							
Inhofe	N	N	N	Y	N	N	N
Coburn	N	N	N	Y	N	N	N
OREGON							
Wyden	Y	Y	Y	N	Y	Y	Y
Merkley	Y	Y	Y	N	Y	Y	Y
PENNSYLVANIA							
Specter	Y	Y	Y	N	Y	Y	Y
Casey	Y	Y	Y	N	Y	Y	Y
RHODE ISLAND							
Reed	Y	Y	Y	N	Y	Y	Y
Whitehouse	Y	Y	Y	N	Y	Y	Y
SOUTH CAROLINA							
Graham	N	N	N	Y	N	N	N
DeMint	N	N	N	Y	N	N	N
SOUTH DAKOTA							
Johnson	Y	Y	Y	N	Y	Y	Y
Thune	N	N	N	Y	N	N	N
TENNESSEE							
Alexander	N	N	N	Y	N	N	N
Corker	N	N	N	Y	N	N	N
TEXAS							
Hutchison	N	N	N	Y	N	N	N
Cornyn	N	N	N	Y	N	N	N
UTAH							
Hatch	N	N	N	Y	N	N	N
Bennett	N	N	N	Y	N	N	N
VERMONT							
Leahy	Y	Y	Y	N	Y	Y	Y
Sanders	Y	Y	Y	N	Y	Y	Y
VIRGINIA							
Webb	Y	Y	Y	N	Y	Y	Y
Warner	Y	Y	Y	N	Y	Y	Y
WASHINGTON							
Murray	Y	Y	Y	N	Y	Y	Y
Cantwell	Y	Y	Y	N	Y	Y	Y
WEST VIRGINIA							
Byrd	Y	Y	?	?	?	?	?
Rockefeller	Y	Y	Y	N	Y	Y	Y
WISCONSIN							
Kohl	Y	Y	Y	N	Y	Y	Y
Feingold	Y	Y	Y	N	Y	Y	Y
WYOMING							
Enzi	N	N	N	Y	N	N	N
Barrasso	N	N	N	Y	N	N	N

KEY   **Republicans**   Democrats   *Independents*

Y Voted for (yea)	X Paired against	C Voted "present" to avoid possible conflict of interest
# Paired for	– Announced against	
+ Announced for	P Voted "present"	? Did not vote or otherwise make a position known
N Voted against (nay)		

IN THE SENATE | By Vote Number

81. HR 4872. Health Care Reconciliation/Medical-Device Tax Exemption for Veterans. Baucus, D-Mont., motion to table (kill) the Hatch, R-Utah, amendment that would exempt certain devices used by patients covered by Tricare and Veterans Affairs health programs from a provision in the bill that would establish a 2.3 percent tax on medical devices. It would be offset by lowering the affordability tax exemption for individuals under the individual mandate from 8 percent to 5 percent. Motion agreed to 54-44: D 52-4; R 0-40; I 2-0. March 24, 2010.

82. HR 4872. Health Care Reconciliation/Medicare Payment Growth Rate. Gregg, R-N.H., motion to waive the Budget Act and budget resolutions with respect to the Baucus, D-Mont., point of order against the Gregg amendment that would provide for a 0 percent rate of growth in Medicare payments to physicians through calendar year 2013. It would also provide for the adjustments through the end of 2013 to be excluded from the calculation of the Medicare sustainable growth rate in future years. Motion rejected 42-56: D 2-54; R 40-0; I 0-2. A three-fifths majority vote (60) of the total Senate is required to waive the Budget Act. (Subsequently, the chair upheld the point of order, and the amendment fell.) March 24, 2010.

83. HR 4872. Health Care Reconciliation/Veterans' Health Programs. Akaka, D-Hawaii, motion to table (kill) the Burr, R-N.C., amendment that would clarify that certain military and veterans' health programs qualify as minimum coverage under the individual insurance mandate contained in the 2010 health care overhaul law. Motion agreed to 54-44: D 52-4; R 0-40; I 2-0. March 24, 2010.

84. HR 4872. Health Care Reconciliation/Overhaul Repeal. Baucus, D-Mont., motion to table (kill) the Vitter, R-La., amendment that would repeal the 2010 health care overhaul law. Motion agreed to 58-39: D 56-0; R 0-39; I 2-0. March 24, 2010.

85. HR 4872. Health Care Reconciliation/Rural Hospitals Exemption. Roberts, R-Kan., motion to waive the Budget Act and budget resolutions with respect to the Baucus, D-Mont., point of order against the Roberts amendment that would exempt critical-access hospitals in rural areas from payment rate reductions recommended by the Medicare Independent Payment Advisory Board under the 2010 health care overhaul law. The amendment would be offset by lowering the affordability tax exemption for individuals under the individual insurance mandate in the law from 8 percent to 5 percent. Motion rejected 42-54: D 3-52; R 39-0; I 0-2. A three-fifths majority vote (60) of the total Senate is required to waive the Budget Act. (Subsequently, the chair upheld the point of order, and the amendment fell.) March 24, 2010.

86. HR 4872. Health Care Reconciliation/Program Repeal. Baucus, D-Mont., motion to table (kill) the Roberts, R-Kan., motion to commit the bill to the Finance Committee with instructions that it be reported back with changes that would repeal the Patient-Centered Outcomes Research Institute, the Center for Medicare and Medicaid Innovation, any new functions of the U.S. Preventive Services Task Force and the Independent Payment Advisory Board. Motion agreed to 59-37: D 55-0; R 2-37; I 2-0. March 25, 2010 (in the session that began and the Congressional Record dated March 24, 2010).

	81	82	83	84	85	86			81	82	83	84	85	86
ALABAMA								**MONTANA**						
Shelby	N	Y	N	N	Y	N		Baucus	Y	N	Y	Y	N	Y
Sessions	N	Y	N	N	Y	N		Tester	N	N	Y	Y	N	Y
ALASKA								**NEBRASKA**						
Murkowski	N	Y	N	N	Y	N		Nelson	N	Y	N	Y	Y	Y
Begich	Y	N	Y	Y	N	Y		Johanns	N	Y	N	N	Y	N
ARIZONA								**NEVADA**						
McCain	N	Y	N	N	Y	N		Reid	Y	N	Y	Y	N	Y
Kyl	N	Y	N	N	Y	N		Ensign	N	Y	N	N	Y	N
ARKANSAS								**NEW HAMPSHIRE**						
Lincoln	Y	Y	N	Y	Y	Y		Gregg	N	Y	N	N	Y	N
Pryor	Y	N	N	Y	N	Y		Shaheen	Y	N	Y	Y	N	Y
CALIFORNIA								**NEW JERSEY**						
Feinstein	Y	N	Y	Y	N	Y		Lautenberg	Y	N	Y	Y	N	Y
Boxer	Y	N	Y	Y	N	Y		Menendez	Y	N	Y	Y	N	Y
COLORADO								**NEW MEXICO**						
Udall	Y	N	Y	Y	N	Y		Bingaman	Y	N	Y	Y	N	Y
Bennet	Y	N	Y	Y	N	Y		Udall	Y	N	Y	Y	N	Y
CONNECTICUT								**NEW YORK**						
Dodd	Y	N	Y	Y	N	Y		Schumer	Y	N	Y	Y	N	Y
Lieberman	Y	N	Y	Y	N	Y		Gillibrand	Y	N	Y	Y	N	Y
DELAWARE								**NORTH CAROLINA**						
Carper	Y	N	Y	Y	N	Y		Burr	N	Y	N	N	Y	N
Kaufman	Y	N	Y	Y	N	Y		Hagan	N	N	N	Y	N	Y
FLORIDA								**NORTH DAKOTA**						
Nelson	Y	N	Y	Y	N	Y		Conrad	Y	N	Y	Y	N	Y
LeMieux	N	Y	N	N	Y	N		Dorgan	Y	N	Y	Y	N	Y
GEORGIA								**OHIO**						
Chambliss	N	Y	N	N	Y	N		**Voinovich**	N	Y	N	N	Y	N
Isakson	?	?	?	?	?	?		Brown	Y	N	Y	Y	N	Y
HAWAII								**OKLAHOMA**						
Inouye	Y	N	Y	Y	N	Y		**Inhofe**	N	Y	N	N	Y	N
Akaka	Y	N	Y	Y	N	Y		**Coburn**	N	Y	N	N	Y	N
IDAHO								**OREGON**						
Crapo	N	Y	N	N	Y	N		Wyden	Y	N	Y	Y	N	Y
Risch	N	Y	N	N	Y	N		Merkley	Y	N	Y	Y	N	Y
ILLINOIS								**PENNSYLVANIA**						
Durbin	Y	N	Y	Y	N	Y		Specter	Y	N	Y	Y	N	Y
Burris	Y	N	Y	Y	N	Y		Casey	Y	N	Y	Y	N	Y
INDIANA								**RHODE ISLAND**						
Lugar	N	Y	N	N	Y	N		Reed	Y	N	Y	Y	N	Y
Bayh	Y	N	Y	Y	N	Y		Whitehouse	Y	N	Y	Y	N	Y
IOWA								**SOUTH CAROLINA**						
Grassley	N	Y	N	N	Y	N		**Graham**	N	Y	N	N	Y	N
Harkin	Y	N	Y	Y	N	Y		**DeMint**	N	Y	N	N	Y	N
KANSAS								**SOUTH DAKOTA**						
Brownback	N	Y	N	N	Y	N		Johnson	Y	N	Y	Y	N	Y
Roberts	N	Y	N	N	Y	N		**Thune**	N	Y	N	N	Y	N
KENTUCKY								**TENNESSEE**						
McConnell	N	Y	N	N	Y	N		**Alexander**	N	Y	N	N	Y	N
Bunning	N	Y	N	N	Y	N		**Corker**	N	Y	N	N	Y	N
LOUISIANA								**TEXAS**						
Landrieu	Y	N	Y	Y	N	Y		**Hutchison**	N	Y	N	N	Y	N
Vitter	N	Y	N	N	Y	N		**Cornyn**	N	Y	N	N	Y	N
MAINE								**UTAH**						
Snowe	N	Y	N	N	Y	Y		**Hatch**	N	Y	N	N	Y	N
Collins	N	Y	N	N	Y	Y		**Bennett**	N	Y	N	N	Y	N
MARYLAND								**VERMONT**						
Mikulski	Y	N	Y	Y	?	?		Leahy	Y	N	Y	Y	N	Y
Cardin	Y	N	Y	Y	N	Y		*Sanders*	Y	N	Y	Y	N	Y
MASSACHUSETTS								**VIRGINIA**						
Kerry	Y	N	Y	Y	N	Y		Webb	N	N	Y	Y	Y	Y
Brown	N	Y	N	N	Y	N		Warner	Y	N	Y	Y	N	Y
MICHIGAN								**WASHINGTON**						
Levin	Y	N	Y	Y	N	Y		Murray	Y	N	Y	Y	N	Y
Stabenow	Y	N	Y	Y	N	Y		Cantwell	Y	N	Y	Y	N	Y
MINNESOTA								**WEST VIRGINIA**						
Klobuchar	Y	N	Y	Y	N	Y		Byrd	?	?	?	?	?	?
Franken	Y	N	Y	Y	N	Y		Rockefeller	Y	N	Y	Y	N	Y
MISSISSIPPI								**WISCONSIN**						
Cochran	N	Y	N	N	Y	N		Kohl	Y	N	Y	Y	N	Y
Wicker	N	Y	N	N	Y	N		Feingold	Y	N	Y	Y	N	Y
MISSOURI								**WYOMING**						
Bond	N	Y	N	?	?	?		**Enzi**	N	Y	N	N	Y	N
McCaskill	Y	N	Y	Y	N	Y		**Barrasso**	N	Y	N	N	Y	N

KEY   **Republicans**   Democrats   *Independents*

Y Voted for (yea)	X Paired against	C Voted "present" to avoid possible conflict of interest
# Paired for	– Announced against	
+ Announced for	P Voted "present"	? Did not vote or otherwise make a position known
N Voted against (nay)		

IN THE SENATE | By Vote Number

87. **HR 4872. Health Care Reconciliation/Medicare Part A Opt-Out.**
Baucus, D-Mont., motion to table (kill) the Bunning, R-Ky., amendment that would allow individuals to opt out of receiving Medicare Part A benefits. Motion agreed to 61-36: D 56-0; R 3-36; I 2-0. March 25, 2010 (in the session that began and the Congressional Record dated March 24, 2010).

88. **HR 4872. Health Care Reconciliation/Tax Extenders.** Grassley, R-Iowa, motion to waive the Budget Act with respect to the Baucus, D-Mont., point of order against the Grassley amendment that would extend, until May 5, 2010, unemployment insurance, payment rates to Medicare providers and COBRA health care premium assistance. The funding would be offset with unobligated stimulus funds and elimination of advance refunds of the earned-income tax credit. Motion rejected 40-56: D 1-54; R 39-0; I 0-2. A three-fifths majority vote (60) of the total Senate is required to waive the Budget Act. (Subsequently, the chair upheld the point of order, and the amendment fell.) March 25, 2010 (in the session that began and the Congressional Record dated March 24, 2010).

89. **HR 4872. Health Care Reconciliation/D.C. Gay Marriage Law.**
Bennett, R-Utah, motion to waive the Budget Act and budget resolutions with respect to the Baucus, D-Mont., point of order against the Bennett amendment for not being germane. The Bennett amendment would require the District of Columbia to immediately suspend the issuance of marriage licenses to any couple of the same sex until the District holds a referendum on the issue. Motion rejected 36-59: D 0-55; R 36-2; I 0-2. A three-fifths majority vote (60) of the total Senate is required to waive the Budget Act. (Subsequently, the chair upheld the point of order, and the amendment fell.) March 25, 2010 (in the session that began and the Congressional Record dated March 24, 2010).

90. **HR 4872. Health Care Reconciliation/Itemized Medical Deduction Repeal.** Baucus, D-Mont., motion to table (kill) the Risch, R-Idaho, amendment that would repeal the limitation on itemized medical expense deductions and change the affordability exception from 8 percent of a family's household income to 5 percent. Motion agreed to 55-40: D 53-2; R 0-38; I 2-0. March 25, 2010 (in the session that began and the Congressional Record dated March 24, 2010).

91. **HR 4872. Health Care Reconciliation/Tax Deductions.** Hutchison, R-Texas, motion to waive the Budget Act and budget resolutions with respect to the Baucus, D-Mont., point of order against the Hutchison amendment that would repeal the sunset of the so-called marriage penalty tax, make the sales tax deduction permanent and rescind all unobligated funds from the 2009 economic stimulus law. Motion rejected 40-55: D 3-52; R 37-1; I 0-2. A three-fifths majority vote (60) of the total Senate is required to waive the Budget Act. (Subsequently, the chair upheld the point of order, and the amendment fell.) March 25, 2010 (in the session that began and the Congressional Record dated March 24, 2010).

92. **HR 4872. Health Care Reconciliation/Mobile Mammography Exemption.** Baucus, D-Mont., motion to table (kill) the Vitter, R-La., amendment that would exempt mobile mammography units from federal excise taxes on fuel. Motion agreed to 56-39: D 54-1; R 0-38; I 2-0. March 25, 2010 (in the session that began and the Congressional Record dated March 24, 2010).

	87	88	89	90	91	92			87	88	89	90	91	92
ALABAMA								**MONTANA**						
Shelby	N	Y	Y	N	Y	N		Baucus	Y	N	N	Y	N	Y
Sessions	N	Y	Y	N	Y	N		Tester	Y	N	N	Y	N	Y
ALASKA								**NEBRASKA**						
Murkowski	N	Y	Y	N	Y	N		Nelson	Y	Y	N	Y	Y	N
Begich	Y	N	N	Y	N	Y		**Johanns**	N	Y	Y	N	Y	N
ARIZONA								**NEVADA**						
McCain	N	Y	Y	N	Y	N		Reid	Y	N	N	Y	N	Y
Kyl	N	Y	Y	N	Y	N		**Ensign**	N	Y	Y	N	Y	N
ARKANSAS								**NEW HAMPSHIRE**						
Lincoln	Y	N	N	N	N	Y		**Gregg**	Y	N	N	N	N	N
Pryor	Y	N	N	Y	N	Y		Shaheen	Y	N	N	Y	N	Y
CALIFORNIA								**NEW JERSEY**						
Feinstein	Y	N	N	Y	N	Y		Lautenberg	Y	?	?	?	?	?
Boxer	Y	N	N	Y	N	Y		Menendez	Y	N	N	Y	N	Y
COLORADO								**NEW MEXICO**						
Udall	Y	N	N	Y	N	Y		Bingaman	Y	N	N	Y	N	Y
Bennet	Y	N	N	Y	N	Y		Udall	Y	N	N	Y	N	Y
CONNECTICUT								**NEW YORK**						
Dodd	Y	N	N	Y	N	Y		Schumer	Y	N	N	Y	N	Y
Lieberman	Y	N	N	Y	N	Y		Gillibrand	Y	N	N	Y	N	Y
DELAWARE								**NORTH CAROLINA**						
Carper	Y	N	N	Y	N	Y		**Burr**	N	Y	Y	N	Y	N
Kaufman	Y	N	N	Y	N	Y		Hagan	Y	N	N	Y	N	Y
FLORIDA								**NORTH DAKOTA**						
Nelson	Y	N	N	Y	N	Y		Conrad	Y	N	N	Y	N	Y
LeMieux	N	Y	Y	N	Y	N		Dorgan	Y	N	N	Y	N	Y
GEORGIA								**OHIO**						
Chambliss	N	Y	Y	N	Y	N		**Voinovich**	Y	Y	?	?	?	?
Isakson	?	?	?	?	?	?		Brown	Y	N	N	Y	N	Y
HAWAII								**OKLAHOMA**						
Inouye	Y	N	N	Y	N	Y		**Inhofe**	N	Y	Y	N	Y	N
Akaka	Y	N	N	Y	N	Y		**Coburn**	N	Y	Y	N	Y	N
IDAHO								**OREGON**						
Crapo	N	Y	Y	N	Y	N		Wyden	Y	N	N	Y	N	Y
Risch	N	Y	Y	N	Y	N		Merkley	Y	N	N	Y	N	Y
ILLINOIS								**PENNSYLVANIA**						
Durbin	Y	N	N	Y	N	Y		Specter	Y	N	N	Y	N	Y
Burris	Y	N	N	Y	N	Y		Casey	Y	N	N	Y	N	Y
INDIANA								**RHODE ISLAND**						
Lugar	N	Y	Y	N	Y	N		Reed	Y	N	N	Y	N	Y
Bayh	Y	N	N	N	Y	Y		Whitehouse	Y	N	N	Y	N	Y
IOWA								**SOUTH CAROLINA**						
Grassley	N	Y	Y	N	Y	N		**Graham**	N	Y	Y	N	Y	N
Harkin	Y	N	N	Y	N	Y		**DeMint**	N	Y	Y	N	Y	N
KANSAS								**SOUTH DAKOTA**						
Brownback	N	Y	Y	N	Y	N		Johnson	Y	N	N	Y	N	Y
Roberts	N	Y	Y	N	Y	N		**Thune**	N	Y	Y	N	Y	N
KENTUCKY								**TENNESSEE**						
McConnell	N	Y	Y	N	Y	N		**Alexander**	N	Y	Y	N	Y	N
Bunning	N	Y	Y	N	Y	N		**Corker**	N	Y	Y	N	Y	N
LOUISIANA								**TEXAS**						
Landrieu	Y	N	N	Y	N	Y		**Hutchison**	N	Y	Y	N	Y	N
Vitter	N	Y	Y	N	Y	N		**Cornyn**	N	Y	Y	N	Y	N
MAINE								**UTAH**						
Snowe	Y	Y	N	N	Y	N		**Hatch**	N	Y	Y	N	Y	N
Collins	Y	Y	N	N	Y	N		**Bennett**	N	Y	Y	N	Y	N
MARYLAND								**VERMONT**						
Mikulski	Y	N	N	Y	N	Y		Leahy	Y	N	N	Y	N	Y
Cardin	Y	N	N	Y	N	Y		*Sanders*	Y	N	N	Y	N	Y
MASSACHUSETTS								**VIRGINIA**						
Kerry	Y	N	N	Y	N	Y		Webb	Y	N	N	Y	N	Y
Brown	N	Y	Y	N	Y	N		Warner	Y	N	N	Y	N	Y
MICHIGAN								**WASHINGTON**						
Levin	Y	N	N	Y	N	Y		Murray	Y	N	N	Y	N	Y
Stabenow	Y	N	N	Y	N	Y		Cantwell	Y	N	N	Y	Y	Y
MINNESOTA								**WEST VIRGINIA**						
Klobuchar	Y	N	N	Y	N	Y		Byrd	?	?	?	?	?	?
Franken	Y	N	N	Y	N	Y		Rockefeller	Y	N	N	Y	N	Y
MISSISSIPPI								**WISCONSIN**						
Cochran	N	Y	Y	N	Y	N		Kohl	Y	N	N	Y	N	Y
Wicker	N	Y	Y	N	Y	N		Feingold	Y	N	N	Y	N	Y
MISSOURI								**WYOMING**						
Bond	?	?	?	?	?	?		**Enzi**	N	Y	Y	N	Y	N
McCaskill	Y	N	N	Y	N	Y		**Barrasso**	N	Y	Y	N	Y	N

KEY   **Republicans**   Democrats   *Independents*

Y Voted for (yea)	X Paired against	C Voted "present" to avoid possible conflict of interest
# Paired for	– Announced against	
+ Announced for	P Voted "present"	? Did not vote or otherwise make a position known
N Voted against (nay)		

IN THE SENATE | By Vote Number

93. HR 4872. Health Care Reconciliation/Medical Malpractice.
Ensign, R-Nev., motion to waive the Budget Act and budget resolutions with respect to the Baucus, D-Mont., point of order against the Ensign amendment that would provide protection against medical-malpractice lawsuits for certain providers of pro bono care. Motion rejected 40-55: D 0-53; R 40-0; I 0-2. A three-fifths majority vote (60) of the total Senate is required to waive the Budget Act. (Subsequently, the chair upheld the point of order, and the amendment fell.) March 25, 2010.

94. HR 4872. Health Care Reconciliation/Firearms and Veterans.
Coburn, R-Okla., motion to waive the Budget Act and budget resolutions with respect to the Baucus, D-Mont., point of order against the Coburn amendment that would require that Veterans Affairs beneficiaries who are determined by the department to be mentally incapacitated, deemed mentally incompetent or experiencing an extended loss of consciousness not be prohibited from buying or transporting firearms or ammunition without a judicial order or finding that the person is a danger to himself or herself or others. Motion rejected 45-53: D 5-51; R 40-0; I 0-2. A three-fifths majority vote (60) of the total Senate is required to waive the Budget Act. (Subsequently, the chair upheld the point of order, and the amendment fell.) March 25, 2010.

95. HR 4872. Health Care Reconciliation/Immigration Status Verification.
Durbin, D-Ill., motion to table (kill) the Sessions, R-Ala., amendment that would require individuals in certain health insurance programs to sign a sworn statement indicating that they are a U.S. national or have an eligible immigration status to participate. It also would require certain documentation with respect to eligibility. Motion agreed to 55-43: D 53-3; R 0-40; I 2-0. March 25, 2010.

96. HR 4872. Health Care Reconciliation/Limitation of Application.
Baucus, D-Mont., motion to table (kill) the Cornyn, R-Texas, amendment that would prevent implementation of the 2010 health care overhaul law or the reconciliation bill until the actuary of the Centers for Medicare and Medicaid Services certifies that health expenditures will see reductions from implementation. Motion agreed to 58-40: D 56-0; R 0-40; I 2-0. March 25, 2010.

97. HR 4872. Health Care Reconciliation/Medicare Reimbursement Rates.
Baucus, D-Mont., motion to table (kill) the Grassley, R-Iowa, amendment that would repeal the higher Medicare reimbursement rates to frontier states established in the 2010 health care overhaul law. It also would redirect savings from eliminating those higher reimbursements to geographic adjustments to fees paid to certain physicians by Medicare. Motion agreed to 53-45: D 51-5; R 0-40; I 2-0. March 25, 2010.

98. HR 4872. Health Care Reconciliation/Tax Increase Inflation Indexing.
Baucus, D-Mont., motion to table (kill) the Brownback, R-Kan., amendment that would index for inflation, beginning in 2013, the 3.8 percent Medicare tax on income for certain taxpayers with adjusted gross incomes in excess of $200,000 for individuals and $250,000 for married couples filing jointly. Motion agreed to 56-42: D 54-2; R 40-0; I 2-0. March 25, 2010.

	93	94	95	96	97	98
ALABAMA						
Shelby	Y	Y	N	N	N	N
Sessions	Y	Y	N	N	N	N
ALASKA						
Murkowski	Y	Y	N	N	N	N
Begich	N	N	Y	Y	Y	Y
ARIZONA						
McCain	Y	Y	N	N	N	N
Kyl	Y	Y	N	N	N	N
ARKANSAS						
Lincoln	N	Y	N	Y	N	Y
Pryor	N	Y	N	Y	N	Y
CALIFORNIA						
Feinstein	N	N	Y	Y	Y	Y
Boxer	?	N	Y	Y	Y	Y
COLORADO						
Udall	N	N	Y	Y	Y	Y
Bennet	N	N	Y	Y	Y	Y
CONNECTICUT						
Dodd	N	N	Y	Y	Y	Y
Lieberman	N	N	Y	Y	Y	Y
DELAWARE						
Carper	N	N	Y	Y	Y	Y
Kaufman	N	N	Y	Y	Y	Y
FLORIDA						
Nelson	N	N	Y	Y	Y	Y
LeMieux	Y	Y	N	N	N	N
GEORGIA						
Chambliss	Y	Y	N	N	N	N
Isakson	?	?	?	?	?	?
HAWAII						
Inouye	N	N	Y	Y	Y	Y
Akaka	N	N	Y	Y	Y	Y
IDAHO						
Crapo	Y	Y	N	N	N	N
Risch	Y	Y	N	N	N	N
ILLINOIS						
Durbin	N	N	Y	Y	Y	Y
Burris	N	N	Y	Y	Y	Y
INDIANA						
Lugar	Y	Y	N	N	N	N
Bayh	N	Y	N	Y	N	N
IOWA						
Grassley	Y	Y	N	N	N	N
Harkin	N	N	Y	Y	Y	Y
KANSAS						
Brownback	Y	Y	N	N	N	N
Roberts	Y	Y	N	N	N	N
KENTUCKY						
McConnell	Y	Y	N	N	N	N
Bunning	Y	Y	N	N	N	N
LOUISIANA						
Landrieu	N	N	Y	Y	Y	Y
Vitter	Y	Y	N	N	N	N
MAINE						
Snowe	Y	Y	N	N	N	N
Collins	Y	Y	N	N	N	N
MARYLAND						
Mikulski	N	N	Y	Y	Y	Y
Cardin	N	N	Y	Y	Y	Y
MASSACHUSETTS						
Kerry	N	N	Y	Y	Y	Y
Brown	Y	Y	N	N	N	N
MICHIGAN						
Levin	N	N	Y	Y	Y	Y
Stabenow	N	N	Y	Y	Y	Y
MINNESOTA						
Klobuchar	N	N	Y	Y	Y	Y
Franken	N	N	Y	Y	Y	Y
MISSISSIPPI						
Cochran	Y	Y	N	N	N	N
Wicker	Y	Y	N	N	N	N
MISSOURI						
Bond	Y	Y	N	N	N	N
McCaskill	N	N	Y	Y	Y	Y
MONTANA						
Baucus	N	N	Y	Y	Y	Y
Tester	N	N	Y	Y	Y	Y
NEBRASKA						
Nelson	N	Y	N	Y	N	Y
Johanns	Y	Y	N	N	N	N
NEVADA						
Reid	N	N	Y	Y	Y	Y
Ensign	Y	Y	N	N	N	N
NEW HAMPSHIRE						
Gregg	Y	Y	N	N	N	N
Shaheen	N	N	Y	Y	Y	Y
NEW JERSEY						
Lautenberg	?	N	Y	Y	Y	Y
Menendez	N	N	Y	Y	Y	Y
NEW MEXICO						
Bingaman	N	N	Y	Y	Y	Y
Udall	N	N	Y	Y	Y	Y
NEW YORK						
Schumer	N	N	Y	Y	Y	Y
Gillibrand	N	N	Y	Y	Y	Y
NORTH CAROLINA						
Burr	Y	Y	N	N	N	N
Hagan	N	N	Y	Y	Y	Y
NORTH DAKOTA						
Conrad	N	N	Y	Y	Y	Y
Dorgan	N	N	Y	Y	Y	Y
OHIO						
Voinovich	Y	Y	N	N	N	N
Brown	N	N	Y	Y	Y	Y
OKLAHOMA						
Inhofe	Y	Y	N	N	N	N
Coburn	Y	Y	N	N	N	N
OREGON						
Wyden	N	N	Y	Y	Y	Y
Merkley	N	N	Y	Y	Y	Y
PENNSYLVANIA						
Specter	N	N	Y	Y	Y	Y
Casey	N	N	Y	Y	Y	Y
RHODE ISLAND						
Reed	N	N	Y	Y	Y	Y
Whitehouse	N	N	Y	Y	Y	Y
SOUTH CAROLINA						
Graham	Y	Y	N	N	N	N
DeMint	Y	Y	N	N	N	N
SOUTH DAKOTA						
Johnson	N	N	Y	Y	Y	Y
Thune	Y	Y	N	N	N	N
TENNESSEE						
Alexander	Y	Y	N	N	N	N
Corker	Y	Y	N	N	N	N
TEXAS						
Hutchison	Y	Y	N	N	N	N
Cornyn	Y	Y	N	N	N	N
UTAH						
Hatch	Y	Y	N	N	N	N
Bennett	Y	Y	N	N	N	N
VERMONT						
Leahy	N	N	Y	Y	Y	Y
Sanders	N	N	Y	Y	Y	Y
VIRGINIA						
Webb	N	Y	N	Y	N	N
Warner	N	N	Y	Y	Y	Y
WASHINGTON						
Murray	N	N	Y	Y	Y	Y
Cantwell	?	N	Y	Y	Y	Y
WEST VIRGINIA						
Byrd	?	?	?	?	?	?
Rockefeller	N	N	Y	Y	Y	Y
WISCONSIN						
Kohl	N	N	Y	Y	Y	Y
Feingold	N	N	Y	Y	Y	Y
WYOMING						
Enzi	Y	Y	N	N	N	N
Barrasso	Y	Y	N	N	N	N

KEY   **Republicans**   Democrats   *Independents*

Y Voted for (yea)	X Paired against	C Voted "present" to avoid possible conflict of interest
# Paired for	− Announced against	
+ Announced for	P Voted "present"	? Did not vote or otherwise make a position known
N Voted against (nay)		

IN THE SENATE | By Vote Number

99. HR 4872. Health Care Reconciliation/Deficit Targets.
Vitter, R-La., motion to waive the Budget Act and budget resolutions with respect to the Baucus, D-Mont., point of order against the Vitter amendment that would provide for the suspension of provisions of the 2010 health care overhaul law and the reconciliation bill in any fiscal year that the Office of Management and Budget determines that annual deficit targets would not be met. Motion rejected 39-56: D 0-54; R 39-0; I 0-2. A three-fifths majority vote (60) of the total Senate is required to waive the Budget Act. (Subsequently, the chair upheld the point of order, and the amendment fell.) March 25, 2010.

100. HR 4872. Health Care Reconciliation/Interstate Competition.
Baucus, D-Mont., motion to table (kill) the DeMint, R-S.C., motion to commit the bill to the Finance Committee with instructions that it be reported back with changes that would ensure no provisions of the 2010 health care overhaul law prevent the sale of health insurance policies across state lines. Motion agreed to 56-43: D 54-3; R 0-40; I 2-0. March 25, 2010.

101. HR 4872. Health Care Reconciliation/Individual Mandate Penalties.
Baucus, D-Mont., motion to table (kill) the Ensign, R-Nev., amendment that would repeal provisions of the 2010 health care overhaul law that provide for IRS penalties for certain taxpayers who do not obtain basic health insurance coverage. Motion agreed to 58-40: D 56-0; R 0-40; I 2-0. March 25, 2010.

102. HR 4872. Health Care Reconciliation/Tax Increase Inflation Index.
Murkowski, R-Alaska, motion to waive the Budget Act and budget resolutions with respect to the Baucus, D-Mont., point of order against the Murkowski amendment that would index for inflation the 3.8 percent Medicare tax on income for certain taxpayers with adjusted gross incomes in excess of $200,000 for individuals and $250,000 for married couples filing jointly. It also would rescind $1.6 billion in unobligated funds appropriated under the 2009 economic stimulus law. Motion rejected 42-57: D 2-55; R 40-0; I 0-2. A three-fifths majority vote (60) of the total Senate is required to waive the Budget Act. (Subsequently, the chair upheld the point of order, and the amendment fell.) March 25, 2010.

103. HR 4872. Health Care Reconciliation/Tax Credit Sunset Repeal.
Baucus, D-Mont., motion to table (kill) the Hutchison, R-Texas, amendment that would strike the sunset for certain small-business tax credits that are due to expire two years after implementation of the health insurance exchanges contained in the 2010 health care overhaul law. Motion agreed to 55-43: D 53-3; R 0-40; I 2-0. March 25, 2010.

104. HR 4872. Health Care Reconciliation/Improper Medicaid Payments.
Baucus, D-Mont., motion to table (kill) the Cornyn, R-Texas, amendment that would provide for a 1 percent penalty in reduced Medicaid matching funds for states that have Medicaid payment error rates in excess of 10 percent, beginning in 2014. Motion agreed to 57-41: D 55-1; R 0-40; I 2-0. March 25, 2010.

	99	100	101	102	103	104
ALABAMA						
Shelby	Y	N	N	Y	N	N
Sessions	Y	N	N	Y	N	N
ALASKA						
Murkowski	Y	N	N	Y	N	N
Begich	N	Y	Y	N	Y	Y
ARIZONA						
McCain	Y	N	N	Y	N	N
Kyl	Y	N	N	Y	N	N
ARKANSAS						
Lincoln	N	N	N	Y	N	Y
Pryor	N	Y	Y	N	Y	Y
CALIFORNIA						
Feinstein	N	Y	Y	N	Y	Y
Boxer	N	Y	Y	N	Y	Y
COLORADO						
Udall	?	Y	Y	N	Y	Y
Bennet	N	Y	Y	N	Y	Y
CONNECTICUT						
Dodd	N	Y	Y	N	Y	Y
Lieberman	N	Y	Y	N	Y	Y
DELAWARE						
Carper	N	Y	Y	N	Y	Y
Kaufman	N	Y	?	N	Y	Y
FLORIDA						
Nelson	N	Y	Y	N	Y	Y
LeMieux	Y	N	N	Y	N	N
GEORGIA						
Chambliss	Y	N	N	Y	N	N
Isakson	?	?	?	?	?	?
HAWAII						
Inouye	N	Y	Y	N	Y	Y
Akaka	N	Y	Y	N	Y	Y
IDAHO						
Crapo	Y	N	N	Y	N	N
Risch	Y	N	N	Y	N	N
ILLINOIS						
Durbin	N	Y	Y	N	Y	Y
Burris	N	Y	Y	N	Y	Y
INDIANA						
Lugar	Y	N	N	Y	N	N
Bayh	N	N	Y	Y	?	Y
IOWA						
Grassley	Y	N	N	Y	N	N
Harkin	N	Y	Y	N	Y	Y
KANSAS						
Brownback	Y	N	N	Y	N	N
Roberts	Y	N	N	Y	N	N
KENTUCKY						
McConnell	Y	N	N	Y	N	N
Bunning	Y	N	N	Y	N	N
LOUISIANA						
Landrieu	?	Y	Y	N	Y	Y
Vitter	Y	N	N	Y	N	N
MAINE						
Snowe	Y	N	N	Y	N	N
Collins	Y	N	N	Y	N	N
MARYLAND						
Mikulski	N	Y	Y	N	Y	Y
Cardin	N	Y	Y	N	Y	Y
MASSACHUSETTS						
Kerry	N	Y	Y	N	Y	Y
Brown	Y	N	N	Y	N	N
MICHIGAN						
Levin	N	Y	Y	N	Y	Y
Stabenow	N	Y	Y	N	Y	Y
MINNESOTA						
Klobuchar	N	Y	Y	N	Y	Y
Franken	N	Y	Y	N	Y	Y
MISSISSIPPI						
Cochran	Y	N	N	Y	N	N
Wicker	Y	N	N	Y	N	N
MISSOURI						
Bond	Y	N	N	Y	N	N
McCaskill	N	Y	Y	N	Y	Y
MONTANA						
Baucus	N	Y	Y	N	Y	Y
Tester	N	Y	Y	N	N	Y
NEBRASKA						
Nelson	N	N	Y	N	Y	Y
Johanns	Y	N	N	Y	N	N
NEVADA						
Reid	N	Y	Y	N	Y	Y
Ensign	Y	N	N	Y	N	N
NEW HAMPSHIRE						
Gregg	Y	N	N	Y	N	N
Shaheen	N	Y	Y	N	Y	Y
NEW JERSEY						
Lautenberg	N	Y	Y	N	Y	Y
Menendez	N	Y	Y	N	Y	Y
NEW MEXICO						
Bingaman	N	Y	Y	N	Y	Y
Udall	N	Y	Y	N	Y	Y
NEW YORK						
Schumer	N	Y	Y	N	Y	Y
Gillibrand	N	Y	Y	N	Y	Y
NORTH CAROLINA						
Burr	Y	N	N	Y	N	N
Hagan	N	Y	Y	N	Y	Y
NORTH DAKOTA						
Conrad	N	Y	Y	N	Y	Y
Dorgan	N	Y	Y	N	Y	Y
OHIO						
Voinovich	Y	N	N	Y	N	N
Brown	N	Y	Y	N	Y	Y
OKLAHOMA						
Inhofe	Y	N	N	Y	N	N
Coburn	Y	N	N	Y	N	N
OREGON						
Wyden	N	Y	Y	N	Y	Y
Merkley	N	Y	Y	N	Y	Y
PENNSYLVANIA						
Specter	N	Y	Y	N	Y	Y
Casey	N	Y	Y	N	Y	Y
RHODE ISLAND						
Reed	N	Y	Y	N	Y	Y
Whitehouse	N	Y	Y	N	Y	Y
SOUTH CAROLINA						
Graham	Y	N	N	Y	N	N
DeMint	Y	N	N	Y	N	N
SOUTH DAKOTA						
Johnson	N	Y	Y	N	Y	Y
Thune	Y	N	N	Y	N	N
TENNESSEE						
Alexander	Y	N	N	Y	N	N
Corker	Y	N	N	Y	N	N
TEXAS						
Hutchison	Y	N	N	Y	N	N
Cornyn	Y	N	N	Y	N	N
UTAH						
Hatch	Y	N	N	Y	N	N
Bennett	?	N	N	Y	N	N
VERMONT						
Leahy	N	Y	Y	N	Y	Y
Sanders	N	Y	Y	N	Y	Y
VIRGINIA						
Webb	N	Y	Y	N	Y	Y
Warner	N	Y	Y	N	Y	Y
WASHINGTON						
Murray	N	Y	Y	N	Y	Y
Cantwell	N	Y	Y	N	Y	Y
WEST VIRGINIA						
Byrd	?	Y	Y	N	N	?
Rockefeller	N	Y	Y	N	Y	Y
WISCONSIN						
Kohl	N	Y	Y	N	Y	Y
Feingold	N	Y	Y	N	Y	Y
WYOMING						
Enzi	Y	N	N	Y	N	N
Barrasso	Y	N	N	Y	N	N

KEY   Republicans   Democrats   *Independents*

Y Voted for (yea)	X Paired against	C Voted "present" to avoid possible conflict of interest
# Paired for	– Announced against	
+ Announced for	P Voted "present"	? Did not vote or otherwise make a position known
N Voted against (nay)		

IN THE SENATE | By Vote Number

105. **HR 4872. Health Care Reconciliation/Passage.** Passage of the bill that would make changes to the 2010 health care overhaul law, revise student loan programs and include revenue-raising provisions. It would increase federal subsidies to help low- and moderate-income families purchase coverage through new health insurance exchanges, phase out the coverage gap for Medicare prescription drug enrollees and adjust the federal matching funds for Medicaid. It would delay a tax on high-cost health plans and reduce the reach of the tax, and it would modify a Medicare payroll tax for high-income taxpayers. The federal government would cover 100 percent of the cost of coverage for newly eligible Medicaid recipients in all states from 2014 to 2016. The bill also would make the federal government the sole originator of federal student loans and direct the savings generated to education programs, including Pell grants. Passed 56-43: D 54-3; R 0-40; I 2-0. A "yea" was a vote in support of the president's position. March 25, 2010.

106. **S 3153. Short-Term Extensions/Motion to Table.** Reid, D-Nev., motion to table (kill) the McConnell, R-Ky., motion to proceed to the bill that would extend COBRA health care premium assistance, the Satellite Home Viewer Act and federal unemployment insurance, and extend current payment rates for Medicare providers for one month. It would repeal a provision of the 2010 health care overhaul law that would increase Medicare payment rates in "frontier states" and redirect $9.2 billion in unobligated stimulus funding to offset the extensions. Motion agreed to 59-40: D 57-0; R 0-40; I 2-0. March 25, 2010.

107. **Procedural Motion/Require Attendance.** Reid, D-Nev., motion to instruct the sergeant at arms to request the attendance of absent senators. Motion agreed to 58-35: D 54-0; R 2-35; I 2-0. March 25, 2010.

108. **H Con Res 257. Adjournment/Adoption.** Adoption of the concurrent resolution that would provide for the adjournment of the House until 2 p.m. on Tuesday, April 13, 2010, and the Senate until noon on Monday, April 12, 2010. Adopted 49-39: D 47-4; R 0-35; I 2-0. March 25, 2010.

	105	106	107	108
ALABAMA				
Shelby	N	N	N	N
Sessions	N	N	N	N
ALASKA				
Murkowski	N	N	N	?
Begich	Y	Y	Y	Y
ARIZONA				
McCain	N	N	N	N
Kyl	N	N	N	N
ARKANSAS				
Lincoln	N	Y	Y	Y
Pryor	N	Y	Y	Y
CALIFORNIA				
Feinstein	Y	Y	Y	Y
Boxer	Y	Y	Y	?
COLORADO				
Udall	Y	Y	Y	Y
Bennet	Y	Y	Y	N
CONNECTICUT				
Dodd	Y	Y	Y	Y
Lieberman	Y	Y	Y	Y
DELAWARE				
Carper	Y	Y	Y	Y
Kaufman	Y	Y	Y	Y
FLORIDA				
Nelson	Y	Y	Y	Y
LeMieux	N	N	N	N
GEORGIA				
Chambliss	N	N	N	N
Isakson	?	?	?	?
HAWAII				
Inouye	Y	Y	Y	Y
Akaka	Y	Y	Y	Y
IDAHO				
Crapo	N	N	N	?
Risch	N	N	N	N
ILLINOIS				
Durbin	Y	Y	Y	Y
Burris	Y	Y	Y	Y
INDIANA				
Lugar	N	N	N	N
Bayh	Y	Y	Y	Y
IOWA				
Grassley	N	N	N	N
Harkin	Y	Y	Y	Y
KANSAS				
Brownback	N	N	N	N
Roberts	N	N	N	N
KENTUCKY				
McConnell	N	N	N	N
Bunning	N	N	?	N
LOUISIANA				
Landrieu	Y	Y	Y	Y
Vitter	N	N	N	N
MAINE				
Snowe	N	N	N	N
Collins	N	N	N	N
MARYLAND				
Mikulski	Y	Y	Y	Y
Cardin	Y	Y	Y	Y
MASSACHUSETTS				
Kerry	Y	Y	Y	?
Brown	N	N	Y	N
MICHIGAN				
Levin	Y	Y	Y	Y
Stabenow	Y	Y	Y	Y
MINNESOTA				
Klobuchar	Y	Y	Y	Y
Franken	Y	Y	Y	Y
MISSISSIPPI				
Cochran	N	N	N	N
Wicker	N	N	?	?
MISSOURI				
Bond	N	N	N	N
McCaskill	Y	Y	Y	Y

	105	106	107	108
MONTANA				
Baucus	Y	Y	Y	Y
Tester	Y	Y	Y	Y
NEBRASKA				
Nelson	N	Y	Y	Y
Johanns	.	N	N	N
NEVADA				
Reid	Y	Y	Y	Y
Ensign	N	N	N	N
NEW HAMPSHIRE				
Gregg	N	N	N	N
Shaheen	Y	Y	Y	Y
NEW JERSEY				
Lautenberg	Y	Y	Y	Y
Menendez	Y	Y	Y	N
NEW MEXICO				
Bingaman	Y	Y	Y	Y
Udall	Y	Y	Y	Y
NEW YORK				
Schumer	Y	Y	Y	Y
Gillibrand	Y	Y	Y	Y
NORTH CAROLINA				
Burr	N	N	N	N
Hagan	Y	Y	Y	Y
NORTH DAKOTA				
Conrad	Y	Y	Y	Y
Dorgan	Y	Y	Y	?
OHIO				
Voinovich	N	N	N	N
Brown	Y	Y	Y	Y
OKLAHOMA				
Inhofe	N	N	N	N
Coburn	N	N	N	N
OREGON				
Wyden	Y	Y	Y	N
Merkley	Y	Y	Y	N
PENNSYLVANIA				
Specter	Y	Y	Y	Y
Casey	Y	Y	Y	Y
RHODE ISLAND				
Reed	Y	Y	Y	Y
Whitehouse	Y	Y	Y	Y
SOUTH CAROLINA				
Graham	N	N	N	N
DeMint	N	N	N	N
SOUTH DAKOTA				
Johnson	Y	Y	Y	Y
Thune	N	N	N	N
TENNESSEE				
Alexander	N	N	N	?
Corker	N	N	N	N
TEXAS				
Hutchison	N	N	?	?
Cornyn	N	N	N	N
UTAH				
Hatch	N	N	N	N
Bennett	N	N	N	N
VERMONT				
Leahy	Y	Y	Y	Y
Sanders	Y	Y	Y	Y
VIRGINIA				
Webb	Y	Y	Y	Y
Warner	Y	Y	Y	Y
WASHINGTON				
Murray	Y	Y	?	?
Cantwell	Y	Y	Y	Y
WEST VIRGINIA				
Byrd	Y	Y	?	?
Rockefeller	Y	Y	?	?
WISCONSIN				
Kohl	Y	Y	Y	Y
Feingold	Y	Y	Y	Y
WYOMING				
Enzi	N	N	N	N
Barrasso	N	N	N	N

KEY	**Republicans**	Democrats	*Independents*	
Y Voted for (yea)		X Paired against		C Voted "present" to avoid possible conflict of interest
# Paired for		– Announced against		
+ Announced for		P Voted "present"		? Did not vote or otherwise make a position known
N Voted against (nay)				

IN THE SENATE | By Vote Number

109. **HR 4851. Short-Term Extensions/Cloture.** Motion to invoke cloture (thus limiting debate) on the Reid, D-Nev., motion to proceed to the bill that would provide short-term extensions for certain government programs, including unemployment insurance benefits. Motion agreed to 60-34: D 54-0; R 4-34; I 2-0. Three-fifths of the total Senate (60) is required to invoke cloture. April 12, 2010.

110. **HR 4851. Short-Term Extensions/Motion to Waive.** Baucus, D-Mont., motion to waive the Budget Act and budget resolutions with respect to the LeMieux, R-Fla., point of order against the Baucus substitute amendment that would extend for two months federal unemployment benefits, flood insurance programs, increased payment rates to Medicare providers, and COBRA health care premium assistance. It would provide for payment to certain previously furloughed transportation workers. It also would extend for one month certain satellite TV laws and small-business lending programs. Motion rejected 58-40: D 55-1; R 1-39; I 2-0. A three-fifths majority vote (60) of the total Senate is required to waive the Budget Act. (At the conclusion of the vote, Reid, D-Nev., entered a motion to reconsider the vote.) April 14, 2010.

111. **HR 4851. Short-Term Extensions/Funding Rescissions.** Baucus, D-Mont., motion to table (kill) the Coburn, R-Okla., amendment to the Baucus substitute amendment. The Coburn amendment would rescind at least $20 billion in unobligated federal funds. Motion agreed to 51-46: D 49-5; R 0-41; I 2-0. April 14, 2010.

112. **HR 4851. Short-Term Extensions/Motion to Waive.** Baucus, D-Mont., motion to waive the Budget Act and budget resolutions with respect to the LeMieux, R-Fla., point of order against the Baucus substitute amendment. Motion agreed to 60-40: D 57-0; R 1-40; I 2-0. A three-fifths majority vote (60) of the total Senate is required to waive the Budget Act. (Previously, a Reid, D-Nev., motion to reconsider was adopted by unanimous consent.) April 14, 2010.

113. **HR 4851. Short-Term Extensions/Funding Rescissions and Revenue Provisions.** Baucus, D-Mont., motion to table (kill) the Coburn, R-Okla., amendment to the Baucus substitute amendment. The Coburn amendment would rescind at least $20 billion in unobligated federal funds. It also would add revenue-raising provisions and would provide pension funding relief for certain defined-benefit plans. Motion agreed to 50-48: D 48-7; R 0-41; I 2-0. April 15, 2010.

	109	110	111	112	113
ALABAMA					
Shelby	N	N	N	N	N
Sessions	N	N	N	N	N
ALASKA					
Murkowski	N	N	N	N	N
Begich	Y	Y	Y	Y	Y
ARIZONA					
McCain	N	N	N	N	N
Kyl	N	N	N	N	N
ARKANSAS					
Lincoln	Y	Y	N	Y	N
Pryor	Y	Y	Y	Y	N
CALIFORNIA					
Feinstein	Y	Y	Y	Y	Y
Boxer	Y	Y	Y	Y	Y
COLORADO					
Udall	Y	Y	Y	Y	N
Bennet	Y	Y	Y	Y	N
CONNECTICUT					
Dodd	Y	Y	Y	Y	Y
Lieberman	Y	Y	Y	Y	Y
DELAWARE					
Carper	Y	Y	Y	Y	Y
Kaufman	Y	Y	Y	Y	Y
FLORIDA					
Nelson	Y	Y	Y	Y	?
LeMieux	N	N	N	N	N
GEORGIA					
Chambliss	N	N	N	N	N
Isakson	N	N	N	N	N
HAWAII					
Inouye	Y	Y	Y	Y	Y
Akaka	Y	Y	Y	Y	Y
IDAHO					
Crapo	N	N	N	N	N
Risch	N	N	N	N	N
ILLINOIS					
Durbin	Y	Y	Y	Y	Y
Burris	Y	Y	Y	Y	Y
INDIANA					
Lugar	N	N	N	N	N
Bayh	Y	Y	N	Y	N
IOWA					
Grassley	N	N	N	N	N
Harkin	?	Y	Y	Y	Y
KANSAS					
Brownback	N	N	N	N	N
Roberts	N	N	N	N	N
KENTUCKY					
McConnell	N	N	N	N	N
Bunning	N	N	N	N	N
LOUISIANA					
Landrieu	Y	Y	Y	Y	Y
Vitter	N	N	N	N	N
MAINE					
Snowe	Y	N	N	N	N
Collins	Y	N	N	N	N
MARYLAND					
Mikulski	Y	Y	Y	Y	Y
Cardin	Y	Y	Y	Y	Y
MASSACHUSETTS					
Kerry	Y	Y	Y	Y	Y
Brown	Y	N	N	N	N
MICHIGAN					
Levin	Y	Y	Y	Y	Y
Stabenow	Y	Y	Y	Y	Y
MINNESOTA					
Klobuchar	Y	Y	N	Y	Y
Franken	Y	Y	Y	Y	Y
MISSISSIPPI					
Cochran	N	N	N	N	N
Wicker	N	N	N	N	N
MISSOURI					
Bond	?	N	N	N	N
McCaskill	Y	Y	Y	Y	Y

	109	110	111	112	113
MONTANA					
Baucus	Y	Y	Y	Y	Y
Tester	Y	Y	Y	Y	Y
NEBRASKA					
Nelson	Y	Y	N	Y	N
Johanns	N	N	N	N	N
NEVADA					
Reid	Y	N	Y	Y	Y
Ensign	N	N	N	N	N
NEW HAMPSHIRE					
Gregg	?	N	N	N	N
Shaheen	Y	Y	Y	Y	Y
NEW JERSEY					
Lautenberg	Y	Y	Y	Y	Y
Menendez	+	Y	Y	Y	Y
NEW MEXICO					
Bingaman	Y	Y	Y	Y	Y
Udall	Y	Y	Y	Y	Y
NEW YORK					
Schumer	Y	Y	Y	Y	Y
Gillibrand	Y	Y	Y	Y	Y
NORTH CAROLINA					
Burr	N	N	N	N	N
Hagan	Y	Y	Y	Y	Y
NORTH DAKOTA					
Conrad	Y	Y	Y	Y	Y
Dorgan	Y	Y	Y	Y	Y
OHIO					
Voinovich	Y	Y	N	Y	N
Brown	Y	Y	Y	Y	Y
OKLAHOMA					
Inhofe	N	N	N	N	N
Coburn	N	N	N	N	N
OREGON					
Wyden	Y	Y	Y	Y	Y
Merkley	Y	Y	Y	Y	Y
PENNSYLVANIA					
Specter	Y	Y	Y	Y	Y
Casey	Y	Y	Y	Y	Y
RHODE ISLAND					
Reed	Y	Y	Y	Y	Y
Whitehouse	Y	Y	?	Y	Y
SOUTH CAROLINA					
Graham	N	N	N	N	N
DeMint	N	N	N	N	N
SOUTH DAKOTA					
Johnson	Y	Y	Y	Y	Y
Thune	N	N	N	N	N
TENNESSEE					
Alexander	N	N	N	N	N
Corker	N	N	N	N	N
TEXAS					
Hutchison	N	N	N	N	N
Cornyn	N	N	N	N	N
UTAH					
Hatch	N	N	N	N	N
Bennett	?	?	N	N	N
VERMONT					
Leahy	Y	?	?	Y	Y
Sanders	Y	Y	Y	Y	Y
VIRGINIA					
Webb	Y	Y	Y	Y	Y
Warner	Y	Y	Y	Y	?
WASHINGTON					
Murray	Y	Y	Y	Y	Y
Cantwell	Y	Y	Y	Y	Y
WEST VIRGINIA					
Byrd	Y	Y	?	Y	Y
Rockefeller	?	Y	Y	Y	Y
WISCONSIN					
Kohl	Y	Y	Y	Y	Y
Feingold	Y	Y	N	Y	N
WYOMING					
Enzi	N	N	N	N	N
Barrasso	N	N	N	N	N

KEY **Republicans** Democrats *Independents*

Y	Voted for (yea)	X	Paired against	C	Voted "present" to avoid possible conflict of interest
#	Paired for	–	Announced against		
+	Announced for	P	Voted "present"	?	Did not vote or otherwise make a position known
N	Voted against (nay)				

IN THE SENATE | By Vote Number

114.
HR 4851. Short-Term Extensions/Modified Funding Rescissions and Revenue Provisions. Baucus, D-Mont., motion to table (kill) the Coburn, R-Okla., amendment to the Baucus substitute amendment. The Coburn amendment would rescind unobligated federal funds, including those for rebates for the purchase of new fuel-efficient cars and coupons for the purchase of digital television converter boxes. It also would add revenue-raising provisions, including increased information return penalties, and would provide pension funding relief for certain defined benefit plans. Motion agreed to 53-45: D 51-4; R 0-41; I 2-0. April 15, 2010.

115.
HR 4851. Short-Term Extensions/Value-Added Tax. McCain, R-Ariz., amendment to the Baucus, D-Mont., substitute amendment. The McCain amendment would express the sense of the Senate in opposition to implementation of a value-added tax. Adopted 85-13: D 43-12; R 40-1; I 2-0. April 15, 2010.

116.
HR 4851. Short-Term Extensions/Cloture. Motion to invoke cloture (thus limiting debate) on the Baucus, D-Mont., substitute amendment that would extend for two months federal unemployment benefits, flood insurance programs, increased payment rates to Medicare providers, and COBRA health care premium assistance. It would provide for payment to certain previously furloughed transportation workers. It also would extend for one month certain satellite TV laws and small-business lending programs. Motion agreed to 60-38: D 55-0; R 3-38; I 2-0. Three-fifths of the total Senate (60) is required to invoke cloture. April 15, 2010.

117.
HR 4851. Short-Term Extensions/Passage. Passage of the bill that would extend for two months federal unemployment benefits, flood insurance programs, increased payment rates to Medicare providers and COBRA health care premium assistance. It would provide for payment to certain previously furloughed transportation workers. It also would extend for one month certain satellite TV laws and small-business lending programs. Passed 59-38: D 54-0; R 3-38; I 2-0. A "yea" was a vote in support of the president's position. April 15, 2010.

	114	115	116	117			114	115	116	117
ALABAMA						**MONTANA**				
Shelby	N	Y	N	N		Baucus	Y	Y	Y	Y
Sessions	N	Y	N	N		Tester	Y	Y	Y	Y
ALASKA						**NEBRASKA**				
Murkowski	N	Y	N	N		Nelson	Y	Y	Y	Y
Begich	Y	Y	Y	Y		**Johanns**	N	Y	N	N
ARIZONA						**NEVADA**				
McCain	N	Y	N	N		Reid	Y	Y	Y	Y
Kyl	N	Y	N	N		**Ensign**	N	Y	N	N
ARKANSAS						**NEW HAMPSHIRE**				
Lincoln	Y	Y	Y	Y		**Gregg**	N	Y	N	N
Pryor	Y	Y	Y	Y		Shaheen	Y	Y	Y	Y
CALIFORNIA						**NEW JERSEY**				
Feinstein	Y	Y	Y	Y		Lautenberg	Y	Y	Y	Y
Boxer	Y	Y	Y	Y		Menendez	Y	Y	Y	Y
COLORADO						**NEW MEXICO**				
Udall	N	Y	Y	Y		Bingaman	Y	N	Y	Y
Bennet	N	Y	Y	Y		Udall	Y	N	Y	Y
CONNECTICUT						**NEW YORK**				
Dodd	Y	Y	Y	Y		Schumer	Y	Y	Y	Y
Lieberman	Y	Y	Y	Y		Gillibrand	Y	Y	Y	Y
DELAWARE						**NORTH CAROLINA**				
Carper	Y	Y	Y	Y		**Burr**	N	Y	N	N
Kaufman	Y	N	Y	Y		Hagan	Y	Y	Y	Y
FLORIDA						**NORTH DAKOTA**				
Nelson	?	+	+	+		Conrad	Y	Y	Y	Y
LeMieux	N	Y	N	N		Dorgan	Y	N	Y	Y
GEORGIA						**OHIO**				
Chambliss	N	Y	N	N		**Voinovich**	N	N	Y	Y
Isakson	N	Y	N	N		Brown	Y	N	Y	Y
HAWAII						**OKLAHOMA**				
Inouye	Y	Y	Y	Y		**Inhofe**	N	Y	N	N
Akaka	Y	N	Y	Y		**Coburn**	N	Y	N	N
IDAHO						**OREGON**				
Crapo	N	Y	N	N		Wyden	Y	Y	Y	Y
Risch	N	Y	N	N		Merkley	Y	Y	Y	Y
ILLINOIS						**PENNSYLVANIA**				
Durbin	Y	Y	Y	Y		Specter	Y	Y	Y	Y
Burris	Y	Y	Y	Y		Casey	Y	Y	Y	Y
INDIANA						**RHODE ISLAND**				
Lugar	N	Y	N	N		Reed	Y	N	Y	Y
Bayh	N	Y	Y	?		Whitehouse	Y	N	Y	Y
IOWA						**SOUTH CAROLINA**				
Grassley	N	Y	N	N		**Graham**	N	Y	N	N
Harkin	Y	Y	Y	Y		**DeMint**	N	Y	N	N
KANSAS						**SOUTH DAKOTA**				
Brownback	N	Y	N	N		Johnson	Y	Y	Y	Y
Roberts	N	Y	N	N		**Thune**	N	Y	N	N
KENTUCKY						**TENNESSEE**				
McConnell	N	Y	N	N		**Alexander**	N	Y	N	N
Bunning	N	Y	N	N		**Corker**	N	Y	N	N
LOUISIANA						**TEXAS**				
Landrieu	Y	Y	Y	Y		**Hutchison**	N	Y	N	N
Vitter	N	Y	N	N		**Cornyn**	N	Y	N	N
MAINE						**UTAH**				
Snowe	N	Y	Y	Y		**Hatch**	N	Y	N	N
Collins	N	Y	Y	Y		**Bennett**	N	Y	N	N
MARYLAND						**VERMONT**				
Mikulski	Y	Y	Y	Y		Leahy	Y	Y	Y	Y
Cardin	Y	N	Y	Y		*Sanders*	Y	Y	Y	Y
MASSACHUSETTS						**VIRGINIA**				
Kerry	Y	Y	Y	Y		Webb	Y	N	Y	Y
Brown	N	Y	N	N		Warner	?	?	?	?
MICHIGAN						**WASHINGTON**				
Levin	Y	N	Y	Y		Murray	Y	Y	Y	Y
Stabenow	Y	Y	Y	Y		Cantwell	Y	Y	Y	Y
MINNESOTA						**WEST VIRGINIA**				
Klobuchar	Y	Y	Y	Y		Byrd	Y	N	Y	Y
Franken	Y	Y	Y	Y		Rockefeller	Y	Y	Y	Y
MISSISSIPPI						**WISCONSIN**				
Cochran	N	Y	N	N		Kohl	Y	Y	Y	Y
Wicker	N	Y	N	N		Feingold	N	Y	Y	Y
MISSOURI						**WYOMING**				
Bond	N	Y	N	N		**Enzi**	N	Y	N	N
McCaskill	Y	Y	Y	Y		**Barrasso**	N	Y	N	N

KEY	**Republicans**	Democrats	*Independents*	
Y Voted for (yea)		X Paired against		C Voted "present" to avoid possible conflict of interest
# Paired for		− Announced against		
+ Announced for		P Voted "present"		? Did not vote or otherwise make a position known
N Voted against (nay)				

IN THE SENATE | By Vote Number

118. Brainard Nomination/Cloture. Motion to invoke cloture (thus limiting debate) on the nomination of Lael Brainard of the District of Columbia to be undersecretary of the Treasury for international affairs. Motion agreed to 84-10: D 55-0; R 27-10; I 2-0. Three-fifths of the total Senate (60) is required to invoke cloture. April 19, 2010.

119. Brainard Nomination/Confirmation. Confirmation of President Obama's nomination of Lael Brainard of the District of Columbia to be undersecretary of the Treasury for international affairs. Confirmed 78-19: D 56-0; R 20-19; I 2-0. A "yea" was a vote in support of the president's position. April 20, 2010.

120. Demeo Nomination/Confirmation. Confirmation of President Obama's nomination of Marisa J. Demeo of the District of Columbia to be an associate judge for the Superior Court of the District of Columbia. Confirmed 66-32: D 56-0; R 8-32; I 2-0. A "yea" was a vote in support of the president's position. April 20, 2010.

121. Schroeder Nomination/Confirmation. Confirmation of President Obama's nomination of Christopher H. Schroeder of North Carolina to be assistant attorney general for the Justice Department's Office of Legal Policy. Confirmed 72-24: D 56-0; R 14-24; I 2-0. A "yea" was a vote in support of the president's position. April 21, 2010.

122. Vanaskie Nomination/Confirmation. Confirmation of President Obama's nomination of Thomas I. Vanaskie of Pennsylvania to be a judge for the 3rd U.S. Circuit Court of Appeals. Confirmed 77-20: D 56-0; R 19-20; I 2-0. A "yea" was a vote in support of the president's position. April 21, 2010.

123. Chin Nomination/Confirmation. Confirmation of President Obama's nomination of Denny Chin of New York to be a judge for the 2nd U.S. Circuit Court of Appeals. Confirmed 98-0: D 56-0; R 40-0; I 2-0. A "yea" was a vote in support of the president's position. April 22, 2010.

	118	119	120	121	122	123
ALABAMA						
Shelby	Y	Y	N	Y	Y	Y
Sessions	Y	Y	N	Y	Y	Y
ALASKA						
Murkowski	Y	Y	Y	Y	Y	Y
Begich	Y	Y	Y	Y	Y	Y
ARIZONA						
McCain	Y	N	N	N	Y	Y
Kyl	Y	N	N	Y	Y	Y
ARKANSAS						
Lincoln	Y	Y	Y	Y	Y	Y
Pryor	Y	Y	Y	Y	Y	Y
CALIFORNIA						
Feinstein	Y	Y	Y	Y	Y	Y
Boxer	?	Y	Y	Y	Y	Y
COLORADO						
Udall	Y	Y	Y	Y	Y	Y
Bennet	Y	Y	Y	Y	Y	Y
CONNECTICUT						
Dodd	Y	Y	Y	Y	Y	Y
Lieberman	Y	Y	Y	Y	Y	Y
DELAWARE						
Carper	Y	Y	Y	Y	Y	Y
Kaufman	Y	Y	Y	Y	Y	?
FLORIDA						
Nelson	Y	Y	Y	Y	Y	Y
LeMieux	Y	Y	N	Y	Y	Y
GEORGIA						
Chambliss	?	Y	N	N	N	Y
Isakson	Y	Y	N	N	N	Y
HAWAII						
Inouye	Y	Y	Y	Y	Y	Y
Akaka	Y	Y	Y	Y	Y	Y
IDAHO						
Crapo	Y	Y	N	N	N	Y
Risch	Y	Y	N	N	N	Y
ILLINOIS						
Durbin	Y	Y	Y	Y	Y	Y
Burris	Y	Y	Y	Y	Y	Y
INDIANA						
Lugar	Y	Y	Y	Y	Y	Y
Bayh	Y	Y	Y	Y	Y	Y
IOWA						
Grassley	Y	N	N	Y	N	Y
Harkin	?	Y	Y	Y	Y	Y
KANSAS						
Brownback	N	N	N	N	N	Y
Roberts	N	N	N	N	N	Y
KENTUCKY						
McConnell	Y	N	N	N	Y	Y
Bunning	N	N	N	N	N	Y
LOUISIANA						
Landrieu	Y	Y	Y	Y	Y	Y
Vitter	N	N	N	N	Y	Y
MAINE						
Snowe	Y	N	Y	Y	Y	Y
Collins	Y	Y	Y	Y	Y	Y
MARYLAND						
Mikulski	Y	Y	Y	Y	Y	Y
Cardin	Y	Y	Y	Y	Y	Y
MASSACHUSETTS						
Kerry	Y	Y	Y	Y	Y	Y
Brown	Y	Y	Y	Y	Y	Y
MICHIGAN						
Levin	Y	Y	Y	Y	Y	Y
Stabenow	Y	Y	Y	Y	Y	Y
MINNESOTA						
Klobuchar	Y	Y	Y	Y	Y	Y
Franken	Y	Y	Y	Y	Y	Y
MISSISSIPPI						
Cochran	Y	Y	N	N	N	Y
Wicker	Y	Y	N	N	N	Y
MISSOURI						
Bond	Y	N	Y	N	Y	Y
McCaskill	Y	Y	Y	Y	Y	Y

	118	119	120	121	122	123
MONTANA						
Baucus	Y	Y	Y	Y	Y	Y
Tester	Y	Y	Y	Y	Y	Y
NEBRASKA						
Nelson	Y	Y	Y	Y	Y	Y
Johanns	Y	N	N	?	?	Y
NEVADA						
Reid	Y	Y	Y	Y	Y	Y
Ensign	N	N	N	N	N	Y
NEW HAMPSHIRE						
Gregg	Y	Y	Y	N	Y	Y
Shaheen	Y	Y	Y	Y	Y	Y
NEW JERSEY						
Lautenberg	Y	Y	Y	Y	Y	Y
Menendez	Y	Y	Y	Y	Y	Y
NEW MEXICO						
Bingaman	Y	Y	Y	Y	Y	Y
Udall	Y	Y	Y	Y	Y	Y
NEW YORK						
Schumer	Y	Y	Y	Y	Y	Y
Gillibrand	Y	Y	Y	Y	Y	Y
NORTH CAROLINA						
Burr	Y	N	N	N	N	Y
Hagan	Y	Y	Y	Y	Y	Y
NORTH DAKOTA						
Conrad	Y	Y	Y	Y	Y	Y
Dorgan	Y	Y	Y	Y	Y	Y
OHIO						
Voinovich	Y	Y	Y	Y	Y	Y
Brown	Y	Y	Y	Y	Y	Y
OKLAHOMA						
Inhofe	N	?	N	N	N	Y
Coburn	?	N	N	N	N	Y
OREGON						
Wyden	Y	Y	Y	Y	Y	Y
Merkley	Y	Y	Y	Y	Y	Y
PENNSYLVANIA						
Specter	Y	Y	Y	Y	Y	Y
Casey	Y	Y	Y	Y	Y	Y
RHODE ISLAND						
Reed	Y	Y	Y	Y	Y	Y
Whitehouse	Y	Y	Y	Y	Y	Y
SOUTH CAROLINA						
Graham	Y	Y	N	Y	Y	Y
DeMint	N	N	N	N	N	+
SOUTH DAKOTA						
Johnson	Y	Y	Y	Y	Y	Y
Thune	Y	N	N	N	N	Y
TENNESSEE						
Alexander	Y	Y	N	+	Y	Y
Corker	Y	Y	N	Y	Y	Y
TEXAS						
Hutchison	?	N	N	N	N	Y
Cornyn	N	N	N	N	N	Y
UTAH						
Hatch	Y	Y	N	Y	Y	Y
Bennett	?	?	?	?	?	Y
VERMONT						
Leahy	Y	Y	Y	Y	Y	Y
Sanders	Y	Y	Y	Y	Y	Y
VIRGINIA						
Webb	Y	Y	Y	Y	Y	Y
Warner	Y	Y	Y	Y	Y	Y
WASHINGTON						
Murray	Y	Y	Y	Y	Y	Y
Cantwell	Y	Y	Y	Y	Y	Y
WEST VIRGINIA						
Byrd	Y	?	?	?	?	Y
Rockefeller	Y	Y	Y	Y	Y	Y
WISCONSIN						
Kohl	Y	Y	Y	Y	Y	Y
Feingold	Y	Y	Y	Y	Y	Y
WYOMING						
Enzi	N	N	N	N	N	Y
Barrasso	N	N	N	N	N	Y

KEY   **Republicans**   Democrats   *Independents*

Y Voted for (yea)	X Paired against	C Voted "present" to avoid possible conflict of interest
# Paired for	- Announced against	
+ Announced for	P Voted "present"	? Did not vote or otherwise make a position known
N Voted against (nay)		

IN THE SENATE | By Vote Number

124. **S 3217. Financial Regulatory Overhaul/Cloture.** Motion to invoke cloture (thus limiting debate) on the Reid, D-Nev., motion to proceed to the bill that would overhaul the federal financial regulatory system. Motion rejected 57-41: D 55-2; R 0-39; I 2-0. Three-fifths of the total Senate (60) is required to invoke cloture. April 26, 2010.

125. **Procedural Motion/Require Attendance.** Reid, D-Nev., motion to instruct the sergeant at arms to request the attendance of absent senators. Motion agreed to 50-31: D 48-0; R 1-31; I 1-0. April 26, 2010.

126. **S 3217. Financial Regulatory Overhaul/Cloture.** Motion to invoke cloture (thus limiting debate) on the Reid, D-Nev., motion to proceed to the bill that would overhaul the federal financial regulatory system. Motion rejected 57-41: D 55-1; R 0-40; I 2-0. Three-fifths of the total Senate (60) is required to invoke cloture. (Previously, a Reid motion to reconsider was agreed to by unanimous consent.) April 27, 2010.

127. **S 3217. Financial Regulatory Overhaul/Cloture.** Motion to invoke cloture (thus limiting debate) on the Reid, D-Nev., motion to proceed to the bill that would overhaul the federal financial regulatory system. Motion rejected 56-42: D 54-2; R 0-40; I 2-0. Three-fifths of the total Senate (60) is required to invoke cloture. (Subsequently, the motion to proceed was agreed to by unanimous consent.) April 28, 2010.

	124	125	126	127			124	125	126	127
ALABAMA						**MONTANA**				
Shelby	N	N	N	N		Baucus	Y	Y	Y	Y
Sessions	N	N	N	N		Tester	Y	Y	Y	Y
ALASKA						**NEBRASKA**				
Murkowski	N	?	N	N		Nelson	N	Y	N	N
Begich	Y	Y	Y	Y		**Johanns**	N	?	N	N
ARIZONA						**NEVADA**				
McCain	N	N	N	N		Reid	N	Y	N	N
Kyl	N	?	N	N		**Ensign**	N	?	N	N
ARKANSAS						**NEW HAMPSHIRE**				
Lincoln	Y	Y	Y	Y		**Gregg**	N	N	N	N
Pryor	Y	Y	Y	Y		Shaheen	Y	Y	Y	Y
CALIFORNIA						**NEW JERSEY**				
Feinstein	Y	Y	Y	Y		Lautenberg	Y	Y	Y	Y
Boxer	Y	Y	Y	Y		Menendez	Y	Y	Y	Y
COLORADO						**NEW MEXICO**				
Udall	Y	Y	Y	Y		Bingaman	Y	Y	Y	Y
Bennet	Y	Y	Y	Y		Udall	Y	Y	Y	Y
CONNECTICUT						**NEW YORK**				
Dodd	Y	Y	Y	Y		Schumer	Y	Y	Y	Y
Lieberman	Y	?	Y	Y		Gillibrand	Y	Y	Y	Y
DELAWARE						**NORTH CAROLINA**				
Carper	Y	?	Y	Y		**Burr**	N	N	N	N
Kaufman	Y	Y	Y	Y		Hagan	Y	Y	Y	Y
FLORIDA						**NORTH DAKOTA**				
Nelson	Y	Y	Y	Y		Conrad	Y	Y	Y	Y
LeMieux	N	N	N	N		Dorgan	Y	Y	Y	Y
GEORGIA						**OHIO**				
Chambliss	N	N	N	N		**Voinovich**	N	?	N	N
Isakson	N	N	N	N		Brown	Y	Y	Y	Y
HAWAII						**OKLAHOMA**				
Inouye	Y	Y	Y	Y		**Inhofe**	N	N	N	N
Akaka	Y	Y	Y	Y		**Coburn**	N	N	N	N
IDAHO						**OREGON**				
Crapo	N	N	N	N		Wyden	Y	Y	Y	Y
Risch	N	N	N	N		Merkley	Y	Y	Y	Y
ILLINOIS						**PENNSYLVANIA**				
Durbin	Y	Y	Y	Y		Specter	Y	Y	Y	Y
Burris	Y	Y	Y	Y		Casey	Y	Y	Y	Y
INDIANA						**RHODE ISLAND**				
Lugar	N	N	N	N		Reed	Y	Y	Y	Y
Bayh	Y	?	?	Y		Whitehouse	Y	Y	Y	Y
IOWA						**SOUTH CAROLINA**				
Grassley	N	N	N	N		**Graham**	N	N	N	N
Harkin	Y	Y	Y	Y		**DeMint**	N	N	N	N
KANSAS						**SOUTH DAKOTA**				
Brownback	N	N	N	N		Johnson	Y	?	Y	Y
Roberts	N	?	N	N		**Thune**	N	N	N	N
KENTUCKY						**TENNESSEE**				
McConnell	N	N	N	N		**Alexander**	N	N	N	N
Bunning	N	N	N	N		**Corker**	N	N	N	N
LOUISIANA						**TEXAS**				
Landrieu	Y	?	Y	Y		**Hutchison**	N	N	N	N
Vitter	N	N	N	N		**Cornyn**	N	N	N	N
MAINE						**UTAH**				
Snowe	N	N	N	N		**Hatch**	N	N	N	N
Collins	N	N	N	N		**Bennett**	?	?	?	?
MARYLAND						**VERMONT**				
Mikulski	Y	?	Y	Y		Leahy	Y	Y	Y	Y
Cardin	Y	Y	Y	Y		*Sanders*	Y	Y	Y	Y
MASSACHUSETTS						**VIRGINIA**				
Kerry	Y	Y	Y	Y		Webb	Y	?	Y	Y
Brown	N	Y	N	N		Warner	Y	Y	Y	Y
MICHIGAN						**WASHINGTON**				
Levin	Y	Y	Y	Y		Murray	Y	Y	Y	Y
Stabenow	Y	Y	Y	Y		Cantwell	Y	Y	Y	Y
MINNESOTA						**WEST VIRGINIA**				
Klobuchar	Y	Y	Y	Y		Byrd	Y	?	Y	?
Franken	Y	Y	Y	Y		Rockefeller	Y	?	Y	Y
MISSISSIPPI						**WISCONSIN**				
Cochran	N	N	N	N		Kohl	Y	?	Y	Y
Wicker	N	?	N	N		Feingold	Y	Y	Y	Y
MISSOURI						**WYOMING**				
Bond	?	?	N	N		**Enzi**	N	N	N	N
McCaskill	Y	Y	Y	Y		**Barrasso**	N	N	N	N

KEY   **Republicans**   Democrats   *Independents*

Y Voted for (yea)	**X** Paired against	**C** Voted "present" to avoid possible conflict of interest
# Paired for	**–** Announced against	
+ Announced for	**P** Voted "present"	
N Voted against (nay)		**?** Did not vote or otherwise make a position known

IN THE SENATE | By Vote Number

128. **Navarro Nomination/Confirmation.** Confirmation of President Obama's nomination of Gloria M. Navarro of Nevada to be a judge for the U.S. District Court for the District of Nevada. Confirmed 98-0: D 56-0; R 40-0; I 2-0. A "yea" was a vote in support of the president's position. May 5, 2010.

129. **Freudenthal Nomination/Confirmation.** Confirmation of President Obama's nomination of Nancy D. Freudenthal of Wyoming to be a judge for the U.S. District Court for the District of Wyoming. Confirmed 96-1: D 55-0; R 39-1; I 2-0. A "yea" was a vote in support of the president's position. May 5, 2010.

130. **S 3217. Financial Regulatory Overhaul/Receivership.** Boxer, D-Calif., amendment to the Reid, D-Nev. (for Dodd, D-Conn., and Lincoln, D-Ark.), substitute amendment. The Boxer amendment would require that all financial companies put into receivership under the bill be liquidated. It would prohibit taxpayer funds from being used to prevent such actions and would require that liquidation costs be paid for with the proceeds of asset sales or through assessments on financial institutions. The substitute would create a new consumer protection regulator that would have the authority to write new rules for banks and non-banks offering consumer financial services. It also would create a systemic-risk council to monitor companies whose failure could threaten the economy. It would require that some over-the-counter derivatives transactions be processed through a regulated central clearinghouse, with an exemption for clearing requirements for some end users. Adopted 96-1: D 55-0; R 39-1; I 2-0. May 5, 2010.

131. **S 3217. Financial Regulatory Overhaul/Liquidation of Failed Companies.** Shelby, R-Ala., and Dodd, D-Conn., amendment to the Dodd and Lincoln, D-Ark., substitute amendment. The Shelby amendment would strike language that would create a $50 billion fund for the Federal Deposit Insurance Corporation (FDIC) to cover the cost of liquidating failing financial companies. Creditors of the failing company would have to pay back any funds received in excess of what they would have received in liquidation. If this did not raise sufficient funds, an assessment would be levied on the company. It also would require Congress to approve FDIC debt guarantees and would allow the Federal Reserve to use its emergency lending authority solely for solvent companies. Adopted 93-5: D 55-1; R 36-4; I 2-0. May 5, 2010.

	128	129	130	131			128	129	130	131
ALABAMA						**MONTANA**				
Shelby	Y	Y	Y	Y		Baucus	Y	Y	Y	Y
Sessions	Y	Y	Y	Y		Tester	Y	Y	Y	Y
ALASKA						**NEBRASKA**				
Murkowski	Y	Y	Y	Y		Nelson	Y	Y	Y	Y
Begich	Y	Y	Y	Y		Johanns	Y	Y	Y	Y
ARIZONA						**NEVADA**				
McCain	Y	Y	Y	Y		Reid	Y	Y	Y	Y
Kyl	Y	Y	N	Y		Ensign	Y	Y	Y	Y
ARKANSAS						**NEW HAMPSHIRE**				
Lincoln	Y	Y	Y	Y		Gregg	Y	Y	Y	Y
Pryor	Y	Y	Y	Y		Shaheen	Y	Y	Y	Y
CALIFORNIA						**NEW JERSEY**				
Feinstein	Y	Y	Y	Y		Lautenberg	Y	Y	Y	Y
Boxer	Y	Y	Y	Y		Menendez	Y	Y	Y	Y
COLORADO						**NEW MEXICO**				
Udall	Y	Y	Y	Y		Bingaman	Y	Y	Y	Y
Bennet	Y	Y	Y	Y		Udall	Y	Y	Y	Y
CONNECTICUT						**NEW YORK**				
Dodd	Y	Y	Y	Y		Schumer	Y	Y	Y	Y
Lieberman	Y	Y	Y	Y		Gillibrand	Y	Y	Y	Y
DELAWARE						**NORTH CAROLINA**				
Carper	Y	Y	Y	Y		Burr	Y	Y	Y	Y
Kaufman	Y	Y	Y	Y		Hagan	Y	Y	Y	Y
FLORIDA						**NORTH DAKOTA**				
Nelson	Y	Y	Y	Y		Conrad	Y	Y	Y	Y
LeMieux	Y	Y	Y	Y		Dorgan	Y	Y	Y	N
GEORGIA						**OHIO**				
Chambliss	Y	Y	Y	Y		Voinovich	Y	Y	Y	Y
Isakson	Y	Y	Y	Y		Brown	Y	Y	Y	Y
HAWAII						**OKLAHOMA**				
Inouye	Y	Y	Y	Y		Inhofe	Y	Y	Y	Y
Akaka	Y	Y	Y	Y		Coburn	Y	N	Y	N
IDAHO						**OREGON**				
Crapo	Y	Y	Y	Y		Wyden	Y	Y	Y	Y
Risch	Y	Y	Y	Y		Merkley	Y	Y	Y	Y
ILLINOIS						**PENNSYLVANIA**				
Durbin	Y	Y	Y	Y		Specter	Y	Y	Y	Y
Burris	Y	Y	Y	Y		Casey	Y	Y	Y	Y
INDIANA						**RHODE ISLAND**				
Lugar	Y	Y	Y	Y		Reed	Y	Y	Y	Y
Bayh	Y	Y	Y	Y		Whitehouse	Y	Y	Y	Y
IOWA						**SOUTH CAROLINA**				
Grassley	Y	Y	Y	Y		Graham	Y	Y	Y	Y
Harkin	Y	Y	Y	Y		DeMint	Y	Y	Y	N
KANSAS						**SOUTH DAKOTA**				
Brownback	Y	Y	Y	Y		Johnson	Y	Y	Y	Y
Roberts	Y	Y	Y	Y		Thune	Y	Y	Y	Y
KENTUCKY						**TENNESSEE**				
McConnell	Y	Y	Y	Y		Alexander	Y	Y	Y	Y
Bunning	Y	Y	Y	Y		Corker	Y	Y	Y	Y
LOUISIANA						**TEXAS**				
Landrieu	Y	Y	Y	Y		Hutchison	Y	Y	Y	Y
Vitter	Y	Y	Y	Y		Cornyn	Y	Y	Y	N
MAINE						**UTAH**				
Snowe	Y	Y	Y	Y		Hatch	Y	Y	Y	N
Collins	Y	Y	Y	Y		Bennett	?	?	?	?
MARYLAND						**VERMONT**				
Mikulski	Y	Y	Y	Y		Leahy	Y	Y	Y	Y
Cardin	Y	Y	Y	Y		*Sanders*	Y	Y	Y	Y
MASSACHUSETTS						**VIRGINIA**				
Kerry	Y	?	+	Y		Webb	Y	Y	Y	Y
Brown	Y	Y	Y	Y		Warner	Y	Y	Y	Y
MICHIGAN						**WASHINGTON**				
Levin	Y	Y	Y	Y		Murray	Y	Y	Y	Y
Stabenow	Y	Y	Y	Y		Cantwell	Y	Y	Y	Y
MINNESOTA						**WEST VIRGINIA**				
Klobuchar	Y	Y	Y	Y		Byrd	?	?	?	?
Franken	Y	Y	Y	Y		Rockefeller	Y	Y	Y	Y
MISSISSIPPI						**WISCONSIN**				
Cochran	Y	Y	Y	Y		Kohl	Y	Y	Y	Y
Wicker	Y	Y	Y	Y		Feingold	Y	Y	Y	Y
MISSOURI						**WYOMING**				
Bond	Y	Y	Y	Y		Enzi	Y	Y	Y	Y
McCaskill	Y	Y	Y	Y		Barrasso	Y	Y	Y	Y

KEY	**Republicans**	Democrats	*Independents*		
Y	Voted for (yea)	X	Paired against	C	Voted "present" to avoid possible conflict of interest
#	Paired for	–	Announced against		
+	Announced for	P	Voted "present"	?	Did not vote or otherwise make a position known
N	Voted against (nay)				

IN THE SENATE | By Vote Number

132. **S 3217. Financial Regulatory Overhaul/FDIC Deposit Insurance Fund Premiums.** Tester, D-Mont., amendment to the Dodd, D-Conn., and Lincoln, D-Ark., substitute amendment. The Tester amendment would direct the Federal Deposit Insurance Corporation to calculate the premiums that banks pay into its Deposit Insurance Fund using total assets rather than deposits. Adopted 98-0: D 56-0; R 40-0; I 2-0. May 6, 2010.

133. **S 3217. Financial Regulatory Overhaul/Consumer Protection.** Shelby, R-Ala., amendment to the Dodd, D-Conn., and Lincoln, D-Ark., substitute amendment. The Shelby amendment would replace the substitute's consumer protection language with language that would create a consumer regulator within the Federal Deposit Insurance Corporation (FDIC) with authority to write new rules for banks and non-banks offering consumer financial services, but not to enforce them. It would grant the FDIC primary supervision and enforcement authority over large non-bank mortgage originators and other financial services providers that have violated consumer protection statutes. The president would appoint the director of the consumer protection division for a four-year term to be confirmed by the Senate. Rejected 38-61: D 0-57; R 38-2; I 0-2. A "nay" was a vote in support of the president's position. May 6, 2010.

134. **Procedural Motion/Require Attendance.** Reid, D-Nev., motion to instruct the sergeant at arms to request the attendance of absent senators. Motion agreed to 61-33: D 56-0; R 3-33; I 2-0. May 6, 2010.

135. **S 3217. Financial Regulatory Overhaul/Government-Sponsored Enterprises.** Ensign, R-Nev., amendment to the Brown, D-Ohio, amendment to the Dodd, D-Conn., and Lincoln, D-Ark., substitute amendment. The Ensign amendment would apply restrictions regarding the size of financial institutions to government-sponsored enterprises. The Brown amendment would place a cap of 2 percent of gross domestic product on non-deposit liabilities. It also would establish a cap of 10 percent of the total market of depositors on the deposit base of any single financial institution. Rejected 35-59: D 7-49; R 28-8; I 0-2. May 6, 2010.

136. **S 3217. Financial Regulatory Overhaul/Limitation on Financial Institution Size.** Brown, D-Ohio, amendment to the Dodd, D-Conn., and Lincoln, D-Ark., substitute amendment. The Brown amendment would place a cap of 2 percent of gross domestic product on non-deposit liabilities. It also would establish a cap of 10 percent of the total market of depositors on the deposit base of any single financial institution. Rejected 33-61: D 29-27; R 3-33; I 1-1. May 6, 2010.

	132	133	134	135	136
ALABAMA					
Shelby	Y	Y	N	Y	Y
Sessions	Y	Y	N	Y	N
ALASKA					
Murkowski	Y	Y	N	Y	N
Begich	Y	N	Y	N	Y
ARIZONA					
McCain	Y	Y	N	Y	N
Kyl	Y	Y	?	Y	N
ARKANSAS					
Lincoln	Y	N	Y	Y	Y
Pryor	Y	N	Y	N	Y
CALIFORNIA					
Feinstein	Y	N	Y	N	N
Boxer	Y	N	Y	N	N
COLORADO					
Udall	Y	N	Y	N	N
Bennet	Y	N	Y	N	N
CONNECTICUT					
Dodd	Y	N	Y	N	N
Lieberman	Y	N	Y	N	N
DELAWARE					
Carper	Y	N	Y	N	N
Kaufman	Y	N	Y	N	Y
FLORIDA					
Nelson	Y	N	Y	N	N
LeMieux	Y	Y	N	N	N
GEORGIA					
Chambliss	Y	Y	N	Y	N
Isakson	Y	Y	N	N	N
HAWAII					
Inouye	Y	N	Y	N	N
Akaka	Y	N	Y	N	N
IDAHO					
Crapo	Y	Y	N	Y	N
Risch	Y	Y	N	Y	N
ILLINOIS					
Durbin	Y	N	Y	N	Y
Burris	Y	N	Y	N	Y
INDIANA					
Lugar	Y	Y	?	?	?
Bayh	Y	N	Y	N	N
IOWA					
Grassley	Y	N	N	Y	N
Harkin	Y	N	Y	N	Y
KANSAS					
Brownback	Y	Y	N	Y	N
Roberts	Y	Y	N	Y	N
KENTUCKY					
McConnell	Y	Y	N	Y	N
Bunning	Y	Y	N	+	+
LOUISIANA					
Landrieu	Y	N	Y	N	N
Vitter	Y	Y	N	?	?
MAINE					
Snowe	Y	N	N	Y	N
Collins	Y	Y	N	Y	N
MARYLAND					
Mikulski	Y	N	Y	N	Y
Cardin	Y	N	Y	N	Y
MASSACHUSETTS					
Kerry	Y	N	Y	N	N
Brown	Y	Y	Y	N	N
MICHIGAN					
Levin	Y	N	Y	N	Y
Stabenow	Y	N	Y	N	Y
MINNESOTA					
Klobuchar	Y	N	Y	N	N
Franken	Y	N	Y	N	Y
MISSISSIPPI					
Cochran	Y	Y	N	Y	N
Wicker	Y	Y	N	Y	N
MISSOURI					
Bond	Y	Y	N	Y	N
McCaskill	Y	N	Y	N	N

	132	133	134	135	136
MONTANA					
Baucus	Y	N	Y	N	N
Tester	Y	N	Y	N	N
NEBRASKA					
Nelson	Y	N	Y	N	N
Johanns	Y	Y	N	N	N
NEVADA					
Reid	Y	N	Y	N	Y
Ensign	Y	Y	N	Y	Y
NEW HAMPSHIRE					
Gregg	Y	Y	N	N	N
Shaheen	Y	N	Y	N	N
NEW JERSEY					
Lautenberg	Y	N	Y	N	N
Menendez	Y	N	Y	N	N
NEW MEXICO					
Bingaman	Y	N	Y	Y	Y
Udall	Y	N	Y	N	Y
NEW YORK					
Schumer	Y	N	Y	N	N
Gillibrand	Y	N	Y	N	N
NORTH CAROLINA					
Burr	Y	Y	N	Y	N
Hagan	Y	N	Y	N	N
NORTH DAKOTA					
Conrad	Y	N	Y	N	N
Dorgan	Y	N	Y	N	Y
OHIO					
Voinovich	Y	Y	?	N	N
Brown	Y	N	Y	N	Y
OKLAHOMA					
Inhofe	Y	Y	N	Y	N
Coburn	Y	Y	N	Y	Y
OREGON					
Wyden	Y	N	Y	N	Y
Merkley	Y	N	Y	Y	Y
PENNSYLVANIA					
Specter	Y	N	Y	N	Y
Casey	Y	N	Y	N	Y
RHODE ISLAND					
Reed	Y	N	Y	N	N
Whitehouse	Y	N	Y	N	Y
SOUTH CAROLINA					
Graham	Y	Y	Y	N	N
DeMint	Y	Y	?	?	?
SOUTH DAKOTA					
Johnson	Y	N	Y	N	N
Thune	Y	Y	N	Y	N
TENNESSEE					
Alexander	Y	N	Y	N	N
Corker	Y	Y	N	Y	N
TEXAS					
Hutchison	Y	Y	N	Y	N
Cornyn	Y	Y	N	Y	N
UTAH					
Hatch	Y	Y	Y	Y	N
Bennett	?	?	?	?	?
VERMONT					
Leahy	Y	N	Y	N	Y
Sanders	Y	N	Y	N	Y
VIRGINIA					
Webb	Y	N	Y	N	Y
Warner	Y	N	Y	N	N
WASHINGTON					
Murray	Y	N	Y	N	Y
Cantwell	Y	N	Y	Y	Y
WEST VIRGINIA					
Byrd	?	N	?	?	?
Rockefeller	Y	N	Y	N	Y
WISCONSIN					
Kohl	Y	N	Y	N	N
Feingold	Y	N	Y	Y	Y
WYOMING					
Enzi	Y	Y	N	Y	N
Barrasso	Y	Y	N	Y	N

KEY	**Republicans**	Democrats	*Independents*	
Y	Voted for (yea)	X Paired against	C Voted "present" to avoid possible conflict of interest
#	Paired for	– Announced against	
+	Announced for	P Voted "present"	? Did not vote or otherwise make a position known
N	Voted against (nay)		

IN THE SENATE | By Vote Number

137. S 3217. Financial Regulatory Overhaul/Federal Reserve Audit.

Sanders, I-Vt., amendment to the Reid, D-Nev., (for Dodd, D-Conn., and Lincoln, D-Ark.,) substitute amendment. The Sanders amendment would require the Government Accountability Office (GAO) to complete an audit of the Federal Reserve within one year and would require the central bank to disclose the names of the financial institutions to which it provided emergency financial assistance since December 2007. The GAO audit would cover the emergency financial assistance programs created by the Fed but would not be directed at the Fed's monetary policy deliberations, including transactions with foreign central banks. The substitute would create a new consumer protection regulator with the authority to write new rules for banks and non-banks offering consumer financial services. It would create a systemic-risk council to monitor companies whose failure could threaten the economy. It would require that some over-the-counter derivatives transactions be processed through a regulated central clearinghouse, with an exemption for some end users. Adopted 96-0: D 55-0; R 39-0; I 2-0. May 11, 2010.

138. S 3217. Financial Regulatory Overhaul/Federal Reserve Audits.

Vitter, R-La., amendment to the Dodd, D-Conn., and Lincoln, D-Ark., substitute amendment. The Vitter amendment would remove several restrictions on GAO's current authority to examine the Federal Reserve. The amendment would exempt unreleased transcripts and minutes of Federal Reserve and Federal Open Market Committee discussions from the audit and would impose a 180-day delay on the publication of information about Federal Reserve decisions to intervene in markets. Rejected 37-62: D 6-50; R 30-11; I 1-1. May 11, 2010.

139. S 3217. Financial Regulatory Overhaul/Study on Government-Sponsored Enterprises.

Dodd, D-Conn., amendment to the Dodd and Lincoln, D-Ark., substitute amendment. The Dodd amendment would require the Treasury Department to conduct a study on ending the conservatorship of Fannie Mae and Freddie Mac and report to Congress by Jan. 31, 2011. Adopted 63-36: D 55-1; R 6-35; I 2-0. May 11, 2010.

140. S 3217. Financial Regulatory Overhaul/Government-Sponsored Enterprises Conservatorship.

McCain, R-Ariz., amendment to the Dodd, D-Conn., and Lincoln, D-Ark., substitute amendment. The McCain amendment would require the Federal Housing Finance Agency to end the conservatorship of Fannie Mae and Freddie Mac within 30 months of the bill's enactment. If the government-sponsored enterprises (GSEs) were not financially viable at that point, they would be placed into receivership. The amendment also would place new limits on the GSEs' ongoing operations when the conservatorship ends, including restrictions on mortgage holdings and increased capital requirements. Rejected 43-56: D 2-54; R 41-0; I 0-2. May 12, 2010.

	137	138	139	140
ALABAMA				
Shelby	Y	Y	N	Y
Sessions	Y	Y	N	Y
ALASKA				
Murkowski	?	Y	Y	Y
Begich	Y	N	Y	N
ARIZONA				
McCain	Y	Y	N	Y
Kyl	Y	N	N	Y
ARKANSAS				
Lincoln	Y	Y	Y	N
Pryor	Y	N	Y	N
CALIFORNIA				
Feinstein	Y	N	Y	N
Boxer	Y	N	Y	N
COLORADO				
Udall	Y	N	Y	N
Bennet	Y	N	Y	N
CONNECTICUT				
Dodd	Y	N	Y	N
Lieberman	Y	N	Y	N
DELAWARE				
Carper	Y	N	Y	N
Kaufman	Y	N	Y	N
FLORIDA				
Nelson	Y	N	Y	N
LeMieux	Y	Y	N	Y
GEORGIA				
Chambliss	Y	Y	N	Y
Isakson	Y	Y	N	Y
HAWAII				
Inouye	Y	N	Y	N
Akaka	Y	N	Y	N
IDAHO				
Crapo	Y	Y	N	Y
Risch	Y	Y	N	Y
ILLINOIS				
Durbin	Y	N	Y	N
Burris	Y	N	Y	N
INDIANA				
Lugar	Y	N	N	Y
Bayh	Y	N	Y	N
IOWA				
Grassley	Y	Y	N	Y
Harkin	Y	N	Y	N
KANSAS				
Brownback	Y	Y	N	Y
Roberts	Y	Y	N	Y
KENTUCKY				
McConnell	Y	N	N	Y
Bunning	Y	Y	N	Y
LOUISIANA				
Landrieu	Y	N	Y	N
Vitter	Y	Y	N	Y
MAINE				
Snowe	Y	Y	Y	Y
Collins	Y	Y	Y	Y
MARYLAND				
Mikulski	Y	N	Y	N
Cardin	Y	N	Y	N
MASSACHUSETTS				
Kerry	Y	N	Y	N
Brown	Y	N	Y	Y
MICHIGAN				
Levin	Y	N	Y	N
Stabenow	Y	N	Y	N
MINNESOTA				
Klobuchar	Y	N	Y	N
Franken	Y	N	Y	N
MISSISSIPPI				
Cochran	Y	Y	N	Y
Wicker	Y	Y	N	Y
MISSOURI				
Bond	Y	N	N	Y
McCaskill	Y	N	Y	N

	137	138	139	140
MONTANA				
Baucus	Y	N	Y	N
Tester	Y	N	Y	N
NEBRASKA				
Nelson	Y	N	Y	N
Johanns	Y	N	Y	Y
NEVADA				
Reid	Y	N	Y	N
Ensign	Y	Y	N	Y
NEW HAMPSHIRE				
Gregg	Y	N	N	Y
Shaheen	Y	N	Y	N
NEW JERSEY				
Lautenberg	Y	N	Y	N
Menendez	Y	N	Y	N
NEW MEXICO				
Bingaman	+	N	Y	N
Udall	Y	N	Y	N
NEW YORK				
Schumer	Y	N	Y	N
Gillibrand	Y	N	Y	N
NORTH CAROLINA				
Burr	Y	Y	N	Y
Hagan	Y	N	Y	N
NORTH DAKOTA				
Conrad	Y	N	Y	N
Dorgan	Y	Y	Y	N
OHIO				
Voinovich	Y	N	Y	Y
Brown	Y	N	Y	N
OKLAHOMA				
Inhofe	?	Y	N	Y
Coburn	Y	Y	N	Y
OREGON				
Wyden	Y	Y	Y	N
Merkley	Y	N	Y	N
PENNSYLVANIA				
Specter	Y	N	Y	N
Casey	Y	N	Y	N
RHODE ISLAND				
Reed	Y	N	Y	N
Whitehouse	Y	N	Y	N
SOUTH CAROLINA				
Graham	Y	Y	N	Y
DeMint	Y	Y	N	Y
SOUTH DAKOTA				
Johnson	Y	N	Y	N
Thune	Y	Y	N	Y
TENNESSEE				
Alexander	Y	N	N	Y
Corker	Y	N	N	Y
TEXAS				
Hutchison	Y	Y	N	Y
Cornyn	Y	Y	N	Y
UTAH				
Hatch	Y	Y	N	Y
Bennett	Y	N	N	Y
VERMONT				
Leahy	Y	N	Y	N
Sanders	Y	Y	Y	N
VIRGINIA				
Webb	Y	Y	Y	N
Warner	Y	N	Y	N
WASHINGTON				
Murray	Y	N	Y	N
Cantwell	Y	Y	Y	N
WEST VIRGINIA				
Byrd	?	?	?	?
Rockefeller	Y	N	Y	N
WISCONSIN				
Kohl	Y	N	Y	N
Feingold	Y	Y	Y	N
WYOMING				
Enzi	Y	Y	N	Y
Barrasso	Y	Y	N	Y

KEY	**Republicans**	Democrats	*Independents*	
Y Voted for (yea)		X Paired against		C Voted "present" to avoid possible conflict of interest
# Paired for		– Announced against		
+ Announced for		P Voted "present"		? Did not vote or otherwise make a position known
N Voted against (nay)				

IN THE SENATE | By Vote Number

141. S 3217. Financial Regulatory Overhaul/Mortgage Broker Pay Restrictions. Merkley, D-Ore., amendment to the Dodd, D-Conn., and Lincoln, D-Ark., substitute amendment. The Merkley amendment would disallow mortgage brokers and loan originators from receiving payments based on the terms of the loans they sell. It would prohibit lenders from making a loan without verifying the borrower's ability to repay the loan from income and assets other than the home's value. It also would require that lenders assess the borrower's repayment ability based on the maximum interest rate allowed in the first five years of the loan. Adopted 63-36: D 56-0; R 5-36; I 2-0. May 12, 2010.

142. S 3217. Financial Regulatory Overhaul/Mortgage Underwriting Standards. Corker, R-Tenn., amendment to the Dodd, D-Conn., and Lincoln, D-Ark., substitute amendment. The Corker amendment would direct federal banking regulators to establish minimum loan underwriting standards, including documented income and methods for determining the borrower's ability to repay. It would require regulators to write rules mandating a minimum 5 percent down payment for home purchases and require private mortgage insurance for borrowers with less than 20 percent equity in their home. It would strike provisions from the substitute that would require securitizers to retain 5 percent of the credit risk on any loan that is transferred, sold or conveyed. Rejected 42-57: D 3-53; R 39-2; I 0-2. May 12, 2010.

143. S 3217. Financial Regulatory Overhaul/Community Bank Supervision. Hutchison, R-Texas, amendment to the Dodd, D-Conn., and Lincoln, D-Ark., substitute amendment. The Hutchison amendment would allow community banks and small bank holding companies to choose the Federal Reserve as their regulator. Adopted 91-8: D 49-7; R 41-0; I 1-1. May 12, 2010.

144. S 3217. Financial Regulatory Overhaul/Derivatives. Chambliss, R-Ga., amendment to Dodd, D-Conn., and Lincoln, D-Ark., substitute amendment. The Chambliss amendment would strike provisions related to derivatives and replace them with language that would allow the Commodity Futures Trading Commission (CFTC) to require reporting of swaps transactions. It would require the Securities and Exchange Commission (SEC), CFTC and Federal Reserve to develop requirements for clearing transactions. The SEC and CFTC also could apply new margin requirements to transactions that are entered into by major swaps participants and do not involve end users. It would also establish broader end-user exemptions from the mandatory clearing requirements. Rejected 39-59: D 0-55; R 39-2; I 0-2. May 12, 2010.

	141	142	143	144
ALABAMA				
Shelby	N	Y	Y	Y
Sessions	N	Y	Y	Y
ALASKA				
Murkowski	N	Y	Y	Y
Begich	Y	N	Y	N
ARIZONA				
McCain	N	Y	Y	Y
Kyl	N	Y	Y	Y
ARKANSAS				
Lincoln	Y	N	Y	N
Pryor	Y	N	Y	N
CALIFORNIA				
Feinstein	Y	N	Y	N
Boxer	Y	N	Y	N
COLORADO				
Udall	Y	N	Y	N
Bennet	Y	N	Y	N
CONNECTICUT				
Dodd	Y	N	N	N
Lieberman	Y	N	Y	N
DELAWARE				
Carper	Y	N	Y	N
Kaufman	Y	N	Y	N
FLORIDA				
Nelson	Y	N	Y	N
LeMieux	N	Y	Y	Y
GEORGIA				
Chambliss	N	Y	Y	Y
Isakson	N	Y	Y	Y
HAWAII				
Inouye	Y	N	N	N
Akaka	Y	N	N	N
IDAHO				
Crapo	N	Y	Y	Y
Risch	N	Y	Y	Y
ILLINOIS				
Durbin	Y	N	Y	N
Burris	Y	N	Y	N
INDIANA				
Lugar	Y	Y	Y	Y
Bayh	Y	Y	Y	N
IOWA				
Grassley	Y	N	Y	N
Harkin	Y	N	N	N
KANSAS				
Brownback	N	Y	Y	Y
Roberts	N	Y	Y	Y
KENTUCKY				
McConnell	N	Y	Y	Y
Bunning	N	Y	Y	Y
LOUISIANA				
Landrieu	Y	N	Y	N
Vitter	N	Y	Y	Y
MAINE				
Snowe	Y	Y	Y	Y
Collins	Y	Y	Y	Y
MARYLAND				
Mikulski	Y	N	Y	N
Cardin	Y	N	Y	N
MASSACHUSETTS				
Kerry	Y	N	Y	N
Brown	Y	Y	Y	Y
MICHIGAN				
Levin	Y	N	N	N
Stabenow	Y	N	Y	N
MINNESOTA				
Klobuchar	Y	N	Y	N
Franken	Y	N	Y	N
MISSISSIPPI				
Cochran	N	Y	Y	Y
Wicker	N	Y	Y	Y
MISSOURI				
Bond	N	Y	Y	Y
McCaskill	Y	N	Y	N
MONTANA				
Baucus	Y	N	Y	N
Tester	Y	N	Y	N
NEBRASKA				
Nelson	Y	N	Y	N
Johanns	N	Y	Y	Y
NEVADA				
Reid	Y	N	Y	N
Ensign	N	Y	Y	Y
NEW HAMPSHIRE				
Gregg	N	Y	Y	Y
Shaheen	Y	N	Y	N
NEW JERSEY				
Lautenberg	Y	N	Y	N
Menendez	Y	N	Y	N
NEW MEXICO				
Bingaman	Y	N	Y	N
Udall	Y	N	Y	N
NEW YORK				
Schumer	Y	N	Y	N
Gillibrand	Y	N	Y	N
NORTH CAROLINA				
Burr	N	Y	Y	Y
Hagan	Y	N	Y	N
NORTH DAKOTA				
Conrad	Y	Y	Y	N
Dorgan	Y	N	Y	N
OHIO				
Voinovich	N	Y	Y	Y
Brown	Y	N	Y	N
OKLAHOMA				
Inhofe	N	Y	Y	Y
Coburn	N	Y	Y	Y
OREGON				
Wyden	Y	N	Y	N
Merkley	Y	N	Y	N
PENNSYLVANIA				
Specter	Y	N	Y	N
Casey	Y	N	Y	N
RHODE ISLAND				
Reed	Y	N	N	N
Whitehouse	Y	N	N	N
SOUTH CAROLINA				
Graham	N	Y	Y	Y
DeMint	N	Y	Y	Y
SOUTH DAKOTA				
Johnson	Y	N	Y	N
Thune	N	Y	Y	Y
TENNESSEE				
Alexander	N	Y	Y	Y
Corker	N	Y	Y	Y
TEXAS				
Hutchison	N	Y	Y	Y
Cornyn	N	Y	Y	Y
UTAH				
Hatch	N	Y	Y	Y
Bennett	N	Y	Y	Y
VERMONT				
Leahy	Y	N	Y	N
Sanders	Y	N	N	N
VIRGINIA				
Webb	Y	N	Y	N
Warner	Y	Y	Y	N
WASHINGTON				
Murray	Y	N	Y	N
Cantwell	Y	N	Y	N
WEST VIRGINIA				
Byrd	?	?	?	?
Rockefeller	Y	N	Y	?
WISCONSIN				
Kohl	Y	N	Y	N
Feingold	Y	N	Y	N
WYOMING				
Enzi	N	Y	Y	Y
Barrasso	N	Y	Y	Y

KEY Republicans   Democrats   *Independents*

Y Voted for (yea)
\# Paired for
\+ Announced for
N Voted against (nay)
X Paired against
− Announced against
P Voted "present"
C Voted "present" to avoid possible conflict of interest
? Did not vote or otherwise make a position known

IN THE SENATE | By Vote Number

145. **S 3217. Financial Regulatory Overhaul/Office of Service Member Affairs.** Reed, D-R.I., amendment to the Dodd, D-Conn., and Lincoln, D-Ark., substitute amendment. The Reed amendment would establish an Office of Service Member Affairs within the new Bureau of Consumer Financial Protection. It would coordinate the response to complaints about financial products from servicemembers and their families and would provide educational resources to them. Adopted 98-1: D 56-0; R 40-1; I 2-0. May 12, 2010.

146. **S 3217. Financial Regulatory Overhaul/Initial Credit Ratings.** Franken, D-Minn., amendment to the Dodd, D-Conn., and Lincoln, D-Ark., substitute amendment. The Franken amendment would require that initial credit ratings for new issues of certain complex financial instruments be assigned by a newly established board. Adopted 64-35: D 52-4; R 11-30; I 1-1 May 13, 2010.

147. **S 3217. Financial Regulatory Overhaul/Credit-Rating Agencies.** LeMieux, R-Fla., amendment to the Dodd, D-Conn., and Lincoln, D-Ark., substitute amendment. The LeMieux amendment would strike certain references in current law to credit-rating agencies and operations, including related terminology. Adopted 61-38: D 19-37; R 41-0; I 1-1. May 13, 2010.

148. **S 3217. Financial Regulatory Overhaul/Bankruptcy.** Sessions, R-Ala., amendment to the Dodd, D-Conn., and Lincoln, D-Ark., substitute amendment. The Sessions amendment would prevent the Federal Reserve from using its emergency authority to provide funding to certain insolvent companies, and it would block resolution authority for non-bank financial institutions. It also would modify bankruptcy law to allow for an automatic stay of debts related to derivatives contracts. Rejected 42-58: D 1-56; R 41-0; I 0-2. May 13, 2010.

149. **S 3217. Financial Regulatory Overhaul/Interchange Fees.** Durbin, D-Ill., amendment to the Dodd, D-Conn., and Lincoln, D-Ark., substitute amendment. The Durbin amendment would require the Federal Reserve to promulgate rules for "reasonable and proportional" interchange fees relative to the costs of debit card transactions. It also would prevent the major network operators from establishing rules that bar merchants from giving preference to a particular brand of card or from offering a discount for paying in cash. Adopted 64-33: D 46-9; R 17-23; I 1-1. By unanimous consent, the Senate agreed to raise the majority requirement for adoption of the Durbin amendment to 60 votes. May 13, 2010.

150. **S 3217. Financial Regulatory Overhaul/Sunset Provision.** Thune, R-S.D., amendment to the Dodd, D-Conn., and Lincoln, D-Ark., substitute amendment. The Thune amendment would sunset the new Bureau of Consumer Financial Protection established in the bill after four years. Rejected 40-55: D 1-52; R 39-1; I 0-2. May 13, 2010.

	145	146	147	148	149	150
ALABAMA						
Shelby	Y	N	Y	Y	N	Y
Sessions	Y	N	Y	Y	N	Y
ALASKA						
Murkowski	Y	Y	Y	Y	N	Y
Begich	Y	Y	Y	N	Y	N
ARIZONA						
McCain	Y	N	Y	Y	N	Y
Kyl	Y	N	Y	Y	N	Y
ARKANSAS						
Lincoln	Y	Y	Y	N	Y	Y
Pryor	Y	Y	N	N	Y	N
CALIFORNIA						
Feinstein	Y	Y	N	N	Y	N
Boxer	Y	Y	Y	N	Y	N
COLORADO						
Udall	Y	Y	Y	N	Y	N
Bennet	Y	Y	Y	N	Y	N
CONNECTICUT						
Dodd	Y	N	N	N	Y	N
Lieberman	Y	N	N	N	N	N
DELAWARE						
Carper	Y	Y	N	N	N	N
Kaufman	Y	Y	Y	N	N	N
FLORIDA						
Nelson	Y	Y	N	N	?	?
LeMieux	Y	N	Y	Y	Y	Y
GEORGIA						
Chambliss	Y	N	Y	Y	Y	Y
Isakson	Y	N	Y	Y	Y	Y
HAWAII						
Inouye	Y	Y	N	N	Y	N
Akaka	Y	Y	N	N	N	N
IDAHO						
Crapo	Y	Y	Y	Y	Y	Y
Risch	Y	Y	Y	Y	Y	Y
ILLINOIS						
Durbin	Y	Y	N	N	Y	N
Burris	Y	Y	N	N	Y	N
INDIANA						
Lugar	Y	N	Y	Y	Y	Y
Bayh	Y	N	Y	N	N	N
IOWA						
Grassley	Y	Y	Y	Y	Y	Y
Harkin	Y	Y	N	N	Y	N
KANSAS						
Brownback	Y	N	Y	Y	N	Y
Roberts	Y	N	Y	Y	N	Y
KENTUCKY						
McConnell	Y	N	Y	Y	N	Y
Bunning	Y	N	Y	Y	N	Y
LOUISIANA						
Landrieu	Y	Y	Y	N	Y	N
Vitter	Y	N	Y	Y	Y	Y
MAINE						
Snowe	Y	Y	Y	Y	Y	N
Collins	Y	Y	Y	Y	Y	N
MARYLAND						
Mikulski	Y	Y	N	N	Y	N
Cardin	Y	Y	N	N	Y	N
MASSACHUSETTS						
Kerry	Y	Y	N	N	Y	N
Brown	Y	Y	Y	Y	Y	Y
MICHIGAN						
Levin	Y	Y	Y	N	Y	N
Stabenow	Y	Y	N	N	Y	?
MINNESOTA						
Klobuchar	Y	Y	Y	N	Y	N
Franken	Y	Y	N	N	Y	N
MISSISSIPPI						
Cochran	Y	Y	Y	Y	N	Y
Wicker	Y	Y	Y	Y	Y	Y
MISSOURI						
Bond	Y	N	Y	Y	N	Y
McCaskill	Y	Y	Y	N	N	N

	145	146	147	148	149	150
MONTANA						
Baucus	Y	Y	N	N	N	N
Tester	Y	Y	N	N	N	N
NEBRASKA						
Nelson	Y	N	N	N	Y	N
Johanns	Y	N	Y	Y	N	Y
NEVADA						
Reid	Y	Y	Y	N	Y	N
Ensign	Y	Y	Y	Y	Y	Y
NEW HAMPSHIRE						
Gregg	Y	N	Y	Y	N	Y
Shaheen	Y	Y	N	N	Y	N
NEW JERSEY						
Lautenberg	Y	Y	N	N	Y	?
Menendez	Y	Y	Y	N	Y	N
NEW MEXICO						
Bingaman	Y	Y	N	N	Y	N
Udall	Y	Y	N	N	Y	N
NEW YORK						
Schumer	Y	Y	N	N	Y	N
Gillibrand	Y	Y	N	N	Y	N
NORTH CAROLINA						
Burr	Y	N	Y	Y	Y	Y
Hagan	Y	Y	N	N	Y	N
NORTH DAKOTA						
Conrad	Y	Y	N	N	Y	N
Dorgan	Y	Y	Y	N	Y	N
OHIO						
Voinovich	Y	N	Y	Y	N	Y
Brown	Y	Y	N	N	Y	N
OKLAHOMA						
Inhofe	Y	N	Y	Y	N	Y
Coburn	N	N	Y	Y	N	Y
OREGON						
Wyden	Y	Y	Y	N	Y	N
Merkley	Y	Y	N	N	Y	N
PENNSYLVANIA						
Specter	Y	Y	N	N	Y	N
Casey	Y	Y	N	N	Y	N
RHODE ISLAND						
Reed	Y	N	N	N	Y	N
Whitehouse	Y	Y	N	N	Y	N
SOUTH CAROLINA						
Graham	Y	Y	Y	Y	Y	Y
DeMint	Y	N	Y	Y	N	Y
SOUTH DAKOTA						
Johnson	Y	Y	N	N	N	N
Thune	Y	N	Y	Y	N	Y
TENNESSEE						
Alexander	Y	N	Y	Y	N	Y
Corker	Y	N	Y	Y	N	Y
TEXAS						
Hutchison	Y	N	Y	Y	?	?
Cornyn	Y	N	Y	Y	N	Y
UTAH						
Hatch	Y	N	Y	Y	N	Y
Bennett	Y	N	Y	Y	N	Y
VERMONT						
Leahy	Y	Y	N	N	Y	N
Sanders	Y	Y	Y	N	Y	N
VIRGINIA						
Webb	Y	Y	N	N	Y	N
Warner	Y	Y	N	N	N	N
WASHINGTON						
Murray	Y	Y	Y	N	Y	N
Cantwell	Y	Y	Y	N	Y	N
WEST VIRGINIA						
Byrd	?	?	?	N	?	?
Rockefeller	Y	Y	N	N	Y	N
WISCONSIN						
Kohl	Y	Y	N	N	Y	N
Feingold	Y	Y	Y	Y	Y	N
WYOMING						
Enzi	Y	N	Y	Y	Y	Y
Barrasso	Y	N	Y	Y	Y	Y

KEY   **Republicans**   Democrats   *Independents*

Y Voted for (yea)	X Paired against	C Voted "present" to avoid possible conflict of interest
# Paired for	– Announced against	
+ Announced for	P Voted "present"	? Did not vote or otherwise make a position known
N Voted against (nay)		

IN THE SENATE | By Vote Number

151. **S 3217. Financial Regulatory Overhaul/Budgetary Treatment of Fannie Mae and Freddie Mac.** Crapo, R-Idaho, motion to waive the Budget Act and budget resolutions with respect to the Dodd, D-Conn., point of order against the Crapo amendment to the Dodd and Lincoln, D-Ark., substitute amendment. The Crapo amendment would place Fannie Mae and Freddie Mac balance sheets on the federal budget until the end of any federal conservatorship or receivership. It would cap the companies' ability to receive Treasury funds at $200 billion. The substitute would create a new consumer protection regulator with the authority to write new rules for banks and non-banks offering consumer financial services. It would create a systemic-risk council to monitor companies whose failure could threaten the economy. It would require that some over-the-counter derivatives transactions be processed through a regulated central clearinghouse, with an exemption for some end users. Motion rejected 47-46: D 7-44; R 40-0; I 0-2. A three-fifths majority vote (60) of the total Senate is required to waive the Budget Act. (Subsequently, the chair upheld the point of order, and the amendment fell.) May 17, 2010.

152. **S 3217. Financial Regulatory Overhaul/International Monetary Fund.** Cornyn, R-Texas, amendment to the Dodd, D-Conn., and Lincoln, D-Ark., substitute amendment. The Cornyn amendment would require the U.S. representative to the International Monetary Fund (IMF) to determine, and to certify to Congress, whether a proposed IMF loan to a country whose debt exceeds its gross domestic product will be repaid. If it is determined that the loan will not be repaid, the U.S. representative would be required to vote against it. Adopted 94-0: D 52-0; R 40-0; I 2-0. May 17, 2010.

153. **S 3217. Financial Regulatory Overhaul/State Bailouts.** Gregg, R-N.H., amendment to the Dodd, D-Conn., and Lincoln, D-Ark., substitute amendment. The Gregg amendment would disallow the use of federal funds to purchase or guarantee obligations, issue lines of credit or provide direct or indirect grants to state or local governments that have defaulted, are at risk of defaulting, or are likely to default absent federal assistance. Rejected 47-50: D 6-48; R 41-0; I 0-2. By unanimous consent, the Senate agreed to raise the majority requirement for adoption of the Gregg amendment to 60 votes. May 18, 2010.

154. **S 3217. Financial Regulatory Overhaul/Federal Pre-emption.** Corker, R-Tenn., amendment to the Dodd, D-Conn., and Lincoln, D-Ark., substitute amendment. The Corker amendment would provide for federal pre-emption of state consumer financial protection laws pursuant to *Barnett Bank v. Nelson*. Pre-emption standards would be determined by the Office of the Comptroller of the Currency. Rejected 43-55: D 3-52; R 40-1; I 0-2. May 18, 2010.

155. **S 3217. Financial Regulatory Overhaul/Federal Pre-emption.** Carper, D-Del., amendment to the Dodd, D-Conn., and Lincoln, D-Ark., substitute amendment. The Carper amendment would allow state attorneys general to file civil lawsuits against state-chartered institutions pursuant to the bill. It would allow for federal pre-emption of state consumer financial protection laws only if the laws would have a discriminatory effect on national banks vs. state-chartered banks in accordance with *Barnett Bank v. Nelson*. Pre-emption standards would be determined by the Office of the Comptroller of the Currency. Adopted 80-18: D 38-17; R 41-0; I 1-1. May 18, 2010.

	151	152	153	154	155		151	152	153	154	155
ALABAMA						**MONTANA**					
Shelby	Y	Y	Y	Y	Y	Baucus	N	Y	Y	N	Y
Sessions	Y	Y	Y	Y	Y	Tester	N	Y	Y	N	Y
ALASKA						**NEBRASKA**					
Murkowski	+	+	Y	Y	Y	Nelson	Y	Y	N	Y	Y
Begich	?	?	N	N	Y	Johanns	Y	Y	Y	Y	Y
ARIZONA						**NEVADA**					
McCain	Y	Y	Y	Y	Y	Reid	N	Y	N	N	N
Kyl	Y	Y	Y	Y	Y	Ensign	Y	Y	Y	Y	Y
ARKANSAS						**NEW HAMPSHIRE**					
Lincoln	?	?	?	?	?	Gregg	Y	Y	Y	Y	Y
Pryor	Y	Y	N	N	Y	Shaheen	?	?	Y	N	N
CALIFORNIA						**NEW JERSEY**					
Feinstein	N	Y	N	N	Y	Lautenberg	N	Y	N	N	Y
Boxer	N	Y	N	N	N	Menendez	N	Y	N	N	Y
COLORADO						**NEW MEXICO**					
Udall	Y	Y	N	N	Y	Bingaman	N	Y	N	N	Y
Bennet	Y	Y	N	N	Y	Udall	N	Y	N	N	N
CONNECTICUT						**NEW YORK**					
Dodd	N	Y	N	N	Y	Schumer	N	Y	N	N	Y
Lieberman	N	Y	N	N	Y	Gillibrand	N	Y	N	N	Y
DELAWARE						**NORTH CAROLINA**					
Carper	N	Y	N	N	Y	Burr	Y	Y	Y	Y	Y
Kaufman	?	Y	N	N	Y	Hagan	N	Y	N	N	Y
FLORIDA						**NORTH DAKOTA**					
Nelson	N	Y	N	N	Y	Conrad	N	Y	N	N	N
LeMieux	Y	Y	Y	Y	Y	Dorgan	N	Y	N	N	N
GEORGIA						**OHIO**					
Chambliss	Y	Y	Y	Y	Y	**Voinovich**	Y	Y	Y	Y	Y
Isakson	Y	Y	Y	Y	Y	Brown	N	Y	N	N	N
HAWAII						**OKLAHOMA**					
Inouye	N	Y	N	N	Y	**Inhofe**	Y	Y	Y	Y	Y
Akaka	N	Y	N	N	Y	**Coburn**	Y	Y	Y	Y	Y
IDAHO						**OREGON**					
Crapo	Y	Y	Y	Y	Y	Wyden	N	Y	N	N	N
Risch	Y	Y	Y	Y	Y	Merkley	N	Y	N	N	N
ILLINOIS						**PENNSYLVANIA**					
Durbin	N	Y	N	N	N	Specter	?	?	?	?	?
Burris	N	Y	N	N	Y	Casey	N	Y	N	N	Y
INDIANA						**RHODE ISLAND**					
Lugar	Y	Y	Y	Y	Y	Reed	N	Y	N	N	N
Bayh	Y	Y	Y	Y	Y	Whitehouse	N	Y	N	N	N
IOWA						**SOUTH CAROLINA**					
Grassley	Y	Y	Y	Y	Y	**Graham**	Y	Y	Y	Y	Y
Harkin	?	?	N	N	N	**DeMint**	Y	Y	Y	Y	Y
KANSAS						**SOUTH DAKOTA**					
Brownback	Y	Y	Y	Y	Y	Johnson	N	Y	N	N	Y
Roberts	Y	Y	Y	Y	Y	**Thune**	Y	Y	Y	Y	Y
KENTUCKY						**TENNESSEE**					
McConnell	Y	Y	Y	Y	Y	**Alexander**	Y	Y	Y	Y	Y
Bunning	Y	Y	Y	Y	Y	**Corker**	Y	Y	Y	Y	Y
LOUISIANA						**TEXAS**					
Landrieu	N	Y	N	N	Y	**Hutchison**	Y	Y	Y	Y	Y
Vitter	Y	Y	Y	Y	Y	**Cornyn**	Y	Y	Y	Y	Y
MAINE						**UTAH**					
Snowe	Y	Y	Y	Y	Y	**Hatch**	Y	Y	Y	Y	Y
Collins	Y	Y	Y	Y	Y	**Bennett**	Y	Y	Y	Y	Y
MARYLAND						**VERMONT**					
Mikulski	N	Y	N	N	Y	Leahy	N	Y	N	N	N
Cardin	N	Y	N	N	Y	*Sanders*	N	Y	N	N	N
MASSACHUSETTS						**VIRGINIA**					
Kerry	N	Y	N	N	Y	Webb	N	Y	N	N	Y
Brown	Y	Y	Y	N	Y	Warner	N	Y	N	N	Y
MICHIGAN						**WASHINGTON**					
Levin	N	Y	N	N	Y	Murray	N	Y	N	N	Y
Stabenow	N	Y	N	N	Y	Cantwell	N	Y	N	N	Y
MINNESOTA						**WEST VIRGINIA**					
Klobuchar	N	Y	N	N	Y	Byrd	N	Y	?	Y	Y
Franken	N	Y	N	N	N	Rockefeller	N	Y	N	N	N
MISSISSIPPI						**WISCONSIN**					
Cochran	Y	Y	Y	Y	Y	Kohl	Y	Y	N	N	Y
Wicker	Y	Y	Y	Y	Y	Feingold	Y	Y	N	N	N
MISSOURI						**WYOMING**					
Bond	Y	Y	Y	Y	Y	**Enzi**	Y	Y	Y	Y	Y
McCaskill	N	Y	N	N	N	**Barrasso**	Y	Y	Y	Y	Y

KEY	**Republicans**		Democrats	*Independents*			
Y	Voted for (yea)	X	Paired against		C	Voted "present" to avoid possible conflict of interest
#	Paired for	–	Announced against			
+	Announced for	P	Voted "present"		?	Did not vote or otherwise make a position known
N	Voted against (nay)					

IN THE SENATE | By Vote Number

156. **S 3217. Financial Regulatory Overhaul/Credit Default Swaps.** Dodd, D-Conn., motion to table (kill) the Dorgan, D-N.D., amendment to the Grassley, R-Iowa, amendment to the Dodd and Lincoln, D Ark., substitute amendment. The Dorgan amendment would prohibit trading of "naked" credit default swaps. It would provide regulators with up to 18 months to implement the prohibition after it takes effect. The Grassley amendment would strike language from the substitute that would authorize the president to appoint inspectors general for the Federal Reserve, Commodity Futures Trading Commission, National Credit Union Administration, Pension Benefit Guaranty Corporation and the Securities and Exchange Commission. Motion agreed to 57-38: D 18-35; R 38-2; I 1-1. May 18, 2010.

157. **S 3217. Financial Regulatory Overhaul/Inspector General Independence.** Grassley, R-Iowa, amendment to the Dodd, D-Conn., and Lincoln, D-Ark., substitute amendment. The Grassley amendment would strike language in the substitute that would authorize the president to appoint inspectors general for the Federal Reserve, Commodity Futures Trading Commission, National Credit Union Association, Pension Benefits Guaranty Corporation and Securities and Exchange Commission. Adopted 75-21: D 35-19; R 40-0; I 0-2. May 18, 2010.

158. **S 3217. Financial Regulatory Overhaul/Cloture.** Motion to invoke cloture (thus limiting debate) on the Dodd, D-Conn., and Lincoln, D-Ark., substitute amendment that would create a new consumer protection regulator with the authority to write new rules for banks and non-banks offering consumer financial services. It would create a systemic-risk council to monitor companies whose failure could threaten the economy. It would require that some over-the-counter derivatives transactions be processed through a regulated central clearinghouse, with an exemption for some end users. Motion rejected 57-42: D 53-3; R 2-39; I 2-0. Three-fifths of the total Senate (60) is required to invoke cloture. (At the conclusion of the vote, Reid entered a motion to reconsider the vote.). May 19, 2010.

159. **S 3217. Financial Regulatory Overhaul/Consumer Credit.** Whitehouse, D-R.I., amendment to the Dodd, D-Conn., and Lincoln, D-Ark., substitute amendment. The Whitehouse amendment would specify that the interest, fees or points on a consumer credit transaction could not exceed the maximum allowed by the law in the state where the consumer resides. It also would require additional disclosure from the Office of the Comptroller of the Currency regarding pre-emption determinations with respect to state consumer financial protection laws. Rejected 35-60: D 32-21; R 2-39; I 1-0. By unanimous consent, the Senate agreed to raise the majority requirement for adoption of the Whitehouse amendment to 60 votes. May 19, 2010.

	156	157	158	159			156	157	158	159
ALABAMA						**MONTANA**				
Shelby	Y	Y	N	N		Baucus	Y	Y	Y	N
Sessions	Y	Y	N	N		Tester	N	Y	Y	N
ALASKA						**NEBRASKA**				
Murkowski	Y	Y	N	N		Nelson	Y	Y	Y	N
Begich	N	Y	Y	Y		Johanns	Y	Y	N	N
ARIZONA						**NEVADA**				
McCain	Y	Y	N	N		Reid	N	N	N	Y
Kyl	Y	Y	N	N		Ensign	N	Y	N	N
ARKANSAS						**NEW HAMPSHIRE**				
Lincoln	?	?	Y	N		Gregg	Y	Y	N	N
Pryor	N	N	Y	N		Shaheen	N	Y	Y	N
CALIFORNIA						**NEW JERSEY**				
Feinstein	N	N	Y	Y		Lautenberg	N	N	Y	Y
Boxer	N	N	Y	Y		Menendez	N	N	Y	?
COLORADO						**NEW MEXICO**				
Udall	N	Y	Y	Y		Bingaman	Y	Y	N	N
Bennet	N	Y	Y	Y		Udall	N	Y	Y	Y
CONNECTICUT						**NEW YORK**				
Dodd	Y	N	Y	N		Schumer	?	N	Y	Y
Lieberman	Y	N	Y	?		Gillibrand	Y	N	Y	Y
DELAWARE						**NORTH CAROLINA**				
Carper	Y	Y	Y	N		**Burr**	Y	Y	N	N
Kaufman	N	Y	Y	N		Hagan	Y	Y	N	N
FLORIDA						**NORTH DAKOTA**				
Nelson	N	Y	Y	Y		Conrad	N	Y	Y	N
LeMieux	Y	Y	N	Y		Dorgan	N	Y	Y	Y
GEORGIA						**OHIO**				
Chambliss	Y	Y	N	N		**Voinovich**	?	?	N	N
Isakson	Y	Y	N	N		Brown	N	Y	Y	Y
HAWAII						**OKLAHOMA**				
Inouye	Y	N	Y	N		**Inhofe**	Y	Y	N	N
Akaka	Y	N	Y	Y		**Coburn**	Y	Y	N	N
IDAHO						**OREGON**				
Crapo	Y	Y	N	N		Wyden	N	Y	Y	Y
Risch	Y	Y	N	N		Merkley	N	N	Y	Y
ILLINOIS						**PENNSYLVANIA**				
Durbin	N	Y	Y	Y		Specter	?	?	?	?
Burris	N	N	Y	Y		Casey	N	Y	Y	Y
INDIANA						**RHODE ISLAND**				
Lugar	Y	Y	N	N		Reed	Y	N	Y	Y
Bayh	Y	Y	N	N		Whitehouse	N	Y	Y	Y
IOWA						**SOUTH CAROLINA**				
Grassley	Y	Y	N	N		**Graham**	Y	Y	N	N
Harkin	N	Y	Y	Y		**DeMint**	Y	Y	N	N
KANSAS						**SOUTH DAKOTA**				
Brownback	Y	Y	N	N		Johnson	Y	Y	Y	N
Roberts	Y	Y	N	N		**Thune**	Y	Y	N	N
KENTUCKY						**TENNESSEE**				
McConnell	Y	Y	N	N		**Alexander**	Y	Y	N	N
Bunning	N	Y	N	N		**Corker**	Y	Y	N	N
LOUISIANA						**TEXAS**				
Landrieu	Y	Y	Y	N		**Hutchison**	Y	Y	N	N
Vitter	Y	Y	N	N		**Cornyn**	Y	Y	N	N
MAINE						**UTAH**				
Snowe	Y	Y	Y	N		**Hatch**	Y	Y	N	N
Collins	Y	Y	Y	N		**Bennett**	Y	Y	N	N
MARYLAND						**VERMONT**				
Mikulski	Y	Y	Y	Y		Leahy	N	Y	Y	Y
Cardin	N	N	Y	Y		*Sanders*	N	N	Y	Y
MASSACHUSETTS						**VIRGINIA**				
Kerry	Y	Y	Y	N		Webb	N	Y	Y	Y
Brown	Y	Y	N	N		Warner	Y	N	Y	?
MICHIGAN						**WASHINGTON**				
Levin	N	N	Y	Y		Murray	N	Y	Y	N
Stabenow	Y	Y	Y	Y		Cantwell	N	Y	N	N
MINNESOTA						**WEST VIRGINIA**				
Klobuchar	N	Y	Y	Y		Byrd	?	?	Y	?
Franken	N	N	Y	Y		Rockefeller	N	N	Y	Y
MISSISSIPPI						**WISCONSIN**				
Cochran	Y	Y	N	Y		Kohl	Y	Y	Y	N
Wicker	Y	Y	N	N		Feingold	N	Y	N	Y
MISSOURI						**WYOMING**				
Bond	Y	Y	N	N		**Enzi**	Y	Y	N	N
McCaskill	N	Y	Y	Y		**Barrasso**	Y	Y	N	N

KEY   **Republicans**   Democrats   *Independents*

Y Voted for (yea)	X Paired against	C Voted "present" to avoid possible conflict of interes
# Paired for	– Announced against	
+ Announced for	P Voted "present"	? Did not vote or otherwise make a position known
N Voted against (nay)		

IN THE SENATE | By Vote Number

160. **S 3217. Financial Regulatory Overhaul/Cloture.** Motion to invoke cloture (thus limiting debate) on the Dodd, D-Conn., and Lincoln, D-Ark., substitute amendment that would create a new consumer protection regulator with the authority to write new rules for banks and non-banks offering consumer financial services. It would create a systemic-risk council to monitor companies whose failure could threaten the economy. It would require that some over-the-counter derivatives transactions be processed through a regulated central clearinghouse, with an exemption for some end users. Motion agreed to 60-40: D 55-2; R 3-38; I 2-0. Three-fifths of the total Senate (60) is required to invoke cloture. (Previously, a Reid motion to reconsider was adopted by unanimous consent.) May 20, 2010.

161. **S 3217. Financial Regulatory Overhaul/Motion to Waive.** Dodd, D-Conn., motion to waive the Budget Act with respect to the Sessions, R-Ala., point of order against the Dodd and Lincoln, D-Ark., substitute amendment. Motion agreed to 60-39: D 55-1; R 3-38; I 2-0. A three-fifths majority vote (60) of the total Senate is required to waive the Budget Act. (Subsequently, the substitute amendment was adopted by unanimous consent.) May 20, 2010.

162. **HR 4173. Financial Regulatory Overhaul/Passage.** Passage of the bill that would create a new consumer protection regulator with the authority to write new rules for banks and non-banks offering consumer financial services. It would create a systemic-risk council to monitor companies whose failure could threaten the economy, and it would provide mechanisms for dealing with large, complex financial institutions that could pose a "grave threat" to financial stability. It would require that some over-the-counter derivatives transactions be processed through a regulated central clearinghouse, with an exemption for some end users. It would prohibit financial institutions from claiming the clearing exemption and require a bank that qualifies as a "swap dealer" or a "major swap participant" to divest its swap desk or forgo access to federal credit assistance. Passed 59-39: D 53-2; R 4-37; I 2-0. (Before passage, the Senate struck all after the enacting clause and inserted the text of S 3217, as amended, into the bill.) A "yea" was a vote in support of the president's position. May 20, 2010.

163. **HR 4173. Financial Regulatory Overhaul/Motion to Instruct.** Brownback, R-Kan., motion to instruct conferees to insist on House-passed provisions to exempt auto dealers from regulation by a consumer financial protection agency, and to insist on Senate-passed provisions regarding consultation with a new Office of Service Member Affairs. Motion agreed to 60-30: D 22-29; R 37-0; I 1-1. May 24, 2010.

164. **HR 4173. Financial Regulatory Overhaul/Motion to Instruct.** Hutchison, R-Texas, motion to instruct conferees to insist on provisions to exempt insurance subsidiaries of depository institutions from regulations restricting proprietary trading activities by banks. Motion agreed to 87-4: D 50-2; R 36-1; I 1-1. May 24, 2010.

165. **HR 4899. Supplemental Appropriations/National Guard Border Deployment.** Motion to waive the Budget Act and budget resolutions with respect to the Schumer, D-N.Y., point of order against the McCain, R-Ariz., amendment that would provide $250 million to fund the deployment of 6,000 National Guard troops on the U.S.-Mexico border, offset by rescinding unspent funds from the 2009 economic stimulus law. Motion rejected 51-46: D 12-43; R 39-1; I 0-2. A three-fifths majority vote (60) of the total Senate is required to waive the Budget Act. (Subsequently, the amendment was withdrawn.) May 27, 2010 (on the legislative day of May 26, 2010).

	160	161	162	163	164	165
ALABAMA						
Shelby	N	N	N	Y	Y	Y
Sessions	N	N	N	Y	Y	Y
ALASKA						
Murkowski	N	N	N	Y	Y	Y
Begich	Y	Y	Y	Y	Y	N
ARIZONA						
McCain	N	N	N	Y	Y	Y
Kyl	N	N	N	Y	Y	Y
ARKANSAS						
Lincoln	Y	Y	Y	?	?	Y
Pryor	Y	Y	Y	Y	Y	Y
CALIFORNIA						
Feinstein	Y	Y	Y	N	Y	Y
Boxer	Y	Y	Y	Y	Y	Y
COLORADO						
Udall	Y	Y	Y	N	Y	N
Bennet	Y	Y	Y	N	Y	Y
CONNECTICUT						
Dodd	Y	Y	Y	N	Y	N
Lieberman	Y	Y	Y	Y	Y	N
DELAWARE						
Carper	Y	Y	Y	N	Y	N
Kaufman	Y	Y	Y	N	Y	N
FLORIDA						
Nelson	Y	Y	Y	Y	Y	Y
LeMieux	N	N	N	Y	Y	Y
GEORGIA						
Chambliss	N	N	N	?	?	?
Isakson	N	N	N	?	?	Y
HAWAII						
Inouye	Y	Y	Y	N	Y	N
Akaka	Y	Y	Y	N	Y	N
IDAHO						
Crapo	N	N	N	Y	Y	Y
Risch	N	N	N	Y	Y	Y
ILLINOIS						
Durbin	Y	Y	Y	N	Y	N
Burris	Y	Y	Y	N	Y	N
INDIANA						
Lugar	N	N	N	Y	Y	Y
Bayh	Y	Y	Y	Y	Y	Y
IOWA						
Grassley	N	N	Y	Y	Y	Y
Harkin	Y	Y	Y	N	Y	N
KANSAS						
Brownback	N	N	N	Y	Y	Y
Roberts	N	N	N	Y	Y	Y
KENTUCKY						
McConnell	N	N	N	Y	Y	Y
Bunning	N	N	N	Y	N	Y
LOUISIANA						
Landrieu	Y	Y	Y	Y	Y	N
Vitter	N	N	N	Y	Y	Y
MAINE						
Snowe	Y	Y	Y	Y	Y	N
Collins	Y	Y	Y	Y	Y	Y
MARYLAND						
Mikulski	Y	Y	Y	Y	Y	N
Cardin	Y	Y	Y	Y	Y	N
MASSACHUSETTS						
Kerry	Y	Y	Y	Y	Y	N
Brown	Y	Y	Y	Y	Y	Y
MICHIGAN						
Levin	Y	Y	Y	N	Y	N
Stabenow	Y	Y	Y	N	Y	N
MINNESOTA						
Klobuchar	Y	Y	Y	N	Y	N
Franken	Y	Y	Y	N	Y	N
MISSISSIPPI						
Cochran	N	N	N	Y	Y	Y
Wicker	N	N	N	?	?	Y
MISSOURI						
Bond	N	N	N	Y	Y	Y
McCaskill	Y	Y	Y	?	?	Y

	160	161	162	163	164	165
MONTANA						
Baucus	Y	Y	Y	N	Y	Y
Tester	Y	Y	Y	N	Y	Y
NEBRASKA						
Nelson	Y	Y	Y	Y	Y	Y
Johanns	N	N	N	Y	Y	Y
NEVADA						
Reid	Y	Y	Y	Y	Y	N
Ensign	N	N	N	Y	Y	Y
NEW HAMPSHIRE						
Gregg	N	N	N	Y	Y	Y
Shaheen	Y	Y	Y	Y	Y	N
NEW JERSEY						
Lautenberg	Y	Y	Y	Y	Y	N
Menendez	Y	Y	Y	Y	Y	N
NEW MEXICO						
Bingaman	Y	Y	Y	N	Y	N
Udall	Y	Y	Y	N	Y	N
NEW YORK						
Schumer	Y	Y	Y	?	?	N
Gillibrand	Y	Y	Y	N	Y	N
NORTH CAROLINA						
Burr	N	N	N	Y	Y	Y
Hagan	Y	Y	Y	Y	Y	?
NORTH DAKOTA						
Conrad	Y	Y	Y	N	Y	N
Dorgan	Y	Y	Y	N	Y	N
OHIO						
Voinovich	N	N	N	Y	Y	N
Brown	Y	Y	Y	N	Y	N
OKLAHOMA						
Inhofe	N	N	N	Y	Y	Y
Coburn	N	N	N	?	?	Y
OREGON						
Wyden	Y	Y	Y	N	Y	N
Merkley	Y	Y	Y	?	Y	N
PENNSYLVANIA						
Specter	Y	?	?	Y	Y	N
Casey	Y	Y	Y	N	Y	N
RHODE ISLAND						
Reed	Y	Y	Y	N	Y	N
Whitehouse	Y	Y	Y	N	Y	N
SOUTH CAROLINA						
Graham	N	N	N	Y	Y	Y
DeMint	N	N	N	Y	Y	Y
SOUTH DAKOTA						
Johnson	Y	Y	Y	N	Y	N
Thune	N	N	N	Y	Y	Y
TENNESSEE						
Alexander	N	N	N	Y	Y	Y
Corker	N	N	N	Y	Y	Y
TEXAS						
Hutchison	N	N	N	Y	Y	Y
Cornyn	N	N	N	Y	Y	Y
UTAH						
Hatch	N	N	N	Y	Y	Y
Bennett	N	N	N	Y	Y	Y
VERMONT						
Leahy	Y	Y	Y	N	Y	N
Sanders	Y	Y	Y	N	N	N
VIRGINIA						
Webb	Y	Y	Y	N	Y	Y
Warner	Y	Y	Y	?	?	N
WASHINGTON						
Murray	Y	Y	Y	N	Y	N
Cantwell	N	Y	N	N	N	N
WEST VIRGINIA						
Byrd	Y	Y	?	?	?	?
Rockefeller	Y	Y	Y	Y	Y	N
WISCONSIN						
Kohl	Y	Y	Y	Y	Y	N
Feingold	N	N	N	N	N	N
WYOMING						
Enzi	N	N	N	Y	Y	Y
Barrasso	N	N	N	Y	Y	Y

KEY **Republicans**   Democrats   *Independents*

Y Voted for (yea)	X Paired against	C Voted "present" to avoid possible conflict of interest
# Paired for	− Announced against	
+ Announced for	P Voted "present"	? Did not vote or otherwise make a position known
N Voted against (nay)		

IN THE SENATE | By Vote Number

166. HR 4899. Supplemental Appropriations/Illegal-Immigrant **Prosecution.** Motion to waive the Budget Act and budget resolutions with respect to the Schumer, D-N.Y., point of order against the Kyl, R-Ariz., amendment to the Cornyn, R-Texas, amendment. The Kyl amendment would provide $155 million for the U.S. Marshals Service and $45 million for federal court renovations and support related to the prosecution of illegal immigrants, offset by rescinding unspent funds from the 2009 economic stimulus law. The Cornyn amendment would provide a total of $2.25 billion for border security activities. Motion rejected 54-44: D 13-43; R 40-0; I 1-1. A three-fifths majority vote (60) of the total Senate is required to waive the Budget Act. (Subsequently, the amendment was withdrawn.) May 27, 2010 (on the legislative day of May 26, 2010).

167. HR 4899. Supplemental Appropriations/Border Security **Grants.** Motion to waive the Budget Act and budget resolutions with respect to the Schumer, D-N.Y., point of order against the Cornyn, R-Texas, amendment. Motion rejected 54-43: D 13-42; R 40-0; I 1-1. A three-fifths majority vote (60) of the total Senate is required to waive the Budget Act. (Subsequently, the amendment was withdrawn.) May 27, 2010 (on the legislative day of May 26, 2010).

168. HR 4899. Supplemental Appropriations/Afghanistan **Withdrawal Plan.** Feingold, D-Wis., amendment that would require the president to develop a non-binding plan for the withdrawal of U.S. forces from Afghanistan. Rejected 18-80: D 17-39; R 0-40; I 1-1. May 27, 2010 (on the legislative day of May 26, 2010).

169. HR 4899. Supplemental Appropriations/Rescissions and **Federal Salary Freeze.** Inouye, D-Hawaii, motion to table (kill) the Coburn, R-Okla., amendment that would provide offsets, including provisions that would freeze salaries of federal civilian employees and rescind 5 percent of fiscal 2010 budget authority for programs other than those in the departments of Defense and Veterans Affairs. Motion agreed to 53-45: D 50-6; R 1-39; I 2-0. May 27, 2010 (on the legislative day of May 26, 2010).

170. HR 4899. Supplemental Appropriations/Disposal of Federal **Property.** Inouye, D-Hawaii, motion to table (kill) the Coburn, R-Okla., amendment that would provide several offsets, including expedited disposal of surplus federal property. It also would require publication on the Senate website of discretionary and direct spending that is not offset. Motion agreed to 50-47: D 47-8; R 1-39; I 2-0. May 27, 2010 (on the legislative day of May 26, 2010).

171. HR 4899. Supplemental Appropriations/Cloture. Motion to invoke cloture (thus limiting debate) on the committee-reported substitute that would provide $58.8 billion in supplemental funds for fiscal 2010, including $33.5 billion for the Defense Department for the addition of 30,000 troops in Afghanistan, $3.6 billion for Afghan and Iraqi security forces and $4.9 billion for Defense Department procurement. It would also provide $5.1 billion for costs of past disasters and $13.4 billion in mandatory funds to compensate Vietnam War veterans exposed to Agent Orange. Motion agreed to 69-29: D 55-1; R 12-28; I 2-0. Three-fifths of the total Senate (60) is required to invoke cloture. May 27, 2010 (on the legislative day of May 26, 2010).

	166	167	168	169	170	171
ALABAMA						
Shelby	Y	Y	N	N	N	N
Sessions	Y	Y	N	N	N	N
ALASKA						
Murkowski	Y	Y	N	N	N	Y
Begich	Y	N	N	Y	N	Y
ARIZONA						
McCain	Y	Y	N	N	N	N
Kyl	Y	Y	N	N	N	N
ARKANSAS						
Lincoln	Y	Y	N	Y	Y	Y
Pryor	Y	Y	N	Y	Y	Y
CALIFORNIA						
Feinstein	Y	Y	Y	Y	Y	Y
Boxer	Y	Y	Y	Y	Y	Y
COLORADO						
Udall	N	Y	N	Y	Y	Y
Bennet	N	N	N	Y	Y	Y
CONNECTICUT						
Dodd	N	N	N	Y	Y	Y
Lieberman	Y	Y	N	Y	N	Y
DELAWARE						
Carper	N	N	N	Y	Y	Y
Kaufman	N	N	N	Y	Y	Y
FLORIDA						
Nelson	N	N	N	Y	Y	Y
LeMieux	Y	Y	N	N	N	N
GEORGIA						
Chambliss	?	?	?	?	?	?
Isakson	Y	Y	N	N	N	N
HAWAII						
Inouye	N	N	N	Y	Y	Y
Akaka	N	N	N	Y	?	Y
IDAHO						
Crapo	Y	Y	N	N	N	N
Risch	Y	Y	N	N	N	N
ILLINOIS						
Durbin	N	N	N	Y	Y	Y
Burris	N	N	N	Y	Y	Y
INDIANA						
Lugar	Y	Y	N	N	N	Y
Bayh	Y	Y	N	N	N	Y
IOWA						
Grassley	Y	Y	N	N	N	N
Harkin	N	N	Y	Y	Y	Y
KANSAS						
Brownback	Y	Y	N	N	N	N
Roberts	Y	Y	N	N	N	N
KENTUCKY						
McConnell	Y	Y	N	N	N	Y
Bunning	Y	Y	N	N	N	N
LOUISIANA						
Landrieu	Y	N	N	Y	Y	Y
Vitter	Y	Y	N	N	Y	Y
MAINE						
Snowe	Y	Y	N	Y	N	Y
Collins	Y	Y	N	Y	N	Y
MARYLAND						
Mikulski	N	N	N	Y	Y	Y
Cardin	N	N	N	Y	Y	Y
MASSACHUSETTS						
Kerry	N	N	N	Y	Y	Y
Brown	Y	Y	N	N	N	Y
MICHIGAN						
Levin	N	N	N	Y	Y	Y
Stabenow	N	N	N	Y	Y	Y
MINNESOTA						
Klobuchar	Y	Y	N	Y	N	Y
Franken	N	N	N	Y	Y	Y
MISSISSIPPI						
Cochran	Y	Y	N	N	N	Y
Wicker	Y	Y	N	N	N	N
MISSOURI						
Bond	Y	Y	N	N	N	Y
McCaskill	Y	Y	N	N	N	Y

	166	167	168	169	170	171
MONTANA						
Baucus	N	Y	Y	Y	Y	Y
Tester	N	Y	Y	N	N	Y
NEBRASKA						
Nelson	Y	Y	N	N	N	Y
Johanns	Y	Y	N	N	N	Y
NEVADA						
Reid	N	N	N	Y	Y	Y
Ensign	Y	Y	N	N	N	N
NEW HAMPSHIRE						
Gregg	Y	Y	N	N	N	N
Shaheen	N	–	N	Y	Y	Y
NEW JERSEY						
Lautenberg	N	N	N	Y	Y	Y
Menendez	N	N	N	Y	Y	Y
NEW MEXICO						
Bingaman	N	N	N	Y	Y	Y
Udall	N	N	Y	Y	Y	Y
NEW YORK						
Schumer	N	N	Y	Y	Y	Y
Gillibrand	N	N	Y	Y	Y	Y
NORTH CAROLINA						
Burr	Y	Y	N	N	N	N
Hagan	N	N	N	Y	Y	Y
NORTH DAKOTA						
Conrad	N	N	N	Y	Y	Y
Dorgan	N	N	Y	Y	Y	Y
OHIO						
Voinovich	Y	Y	N	N	Y	Y
Brown	N	N	Y	Y	Y	Y
OKLAHOMA						
Inhofe	Y	Y	N	N	N	N
Coburn	Y	Y	N	N	N	N
OREGON						
Wyden	Y	N	Y	Y	Y	Y
Merkley	Y	N	Y	Y	Y	Y
PENNSYLVANIA						
Specter	N	N	N	Y	Y	Y
Casey	N	N	N	Y	Y	Y
RHODE ISLAND						
Reed	N	N	N	Y	Y	Y
Whitehouse	N	N	N	Y	Y	Y
SOUTH CAROLINA						
Graham	Y	Y	N	N	N	N
DeMint	Y	Y	N	N	N	N
SOUTH DAKOTA						
Johnson	N	N	N	Y	Y	Y
Thune	Y	Y	N	N	N	N
TENNESSEE						
Alexander	Y	Y	N	N	N	Y
Corker	Y	Y	N	N	N	N
TEXAS						
Hutchison	Y	Y	N	N	N	Y
Cornyn	Y	Y	N	N	N	N
UTAH						
Hatch	Y	Y	N	N	N	N
Bennett	Y	Y	N	N	N	Y
VERMONT						
Leahy	N	N	Y	Y	Y	Y
Sanders	N	N	Y	Y	Y	Y
VIRGINIA						
Webb	Y	Y	N	Y	Y	Y
Warner	N	N	N	Y	N	Y
WASHINGTON						
Murray	N	N	Y	Y	Y	Y
Cantwell	N	N	Y	Y	Y	Y
WEST VIRGINIA						
Byrd	?	?	?	?	?	?
Rockefeller	N	N	N	Y	Y	Y
WISCONSIN						
Kohl	N	Y	N	Y	Y	Y
Feingold	N	N	Y	Y	Y	N
WYOMING						
Enzi	Y	Y	N	N	N	N
Barrasso	Y	Y	N	N	N	N

KEY   **Republicans**   Democrats   *Independents*

Y Voted for (yea)	X Paired against
# Paired for	– Announced against
+ Announced for	P Voted "present"
N Voted against (nay)	

C   Voted "present" to avoid possible conflict of interest

?   Did not vote or otherwise make a position known

IN THE SENATE | By Vote Number

172. **HR 4899. Supplemental Appropriations/Border Fence.** De-Mint, R-S.C., motion to suspend Senate rules to permit the consideration of the DeMint amendment that would require completion of a 700-mile southern border fence to restrain all pedestrian traffic and require a report to Congress within 180 days of the enactment detailing progress. Motion rejected 45-52: D 6-49; R 39-1; I 0-2. (A two-thirds majority of those present and voting (65 in this case) is required to suspend Senate rules.) May 27, 2010 (on the legislative day of May 26, 2010).

173. **HR 4899. Supplemental Appropriations/Lead Paint Regulations.** Collins, R-Maine, amendment that would disallow the use of funds for the EPA to enforce lead paint regulations against certain contractors. Adopted 60-37: D 19-36; R 40-0; I 1-1. May 27, 2010 (on the legislative day of May 26, 2010).

174. **HR 4899. Supplemental Appropriations/Filipino Veterans.** Inouye, D-Hawaii, amendment that would make optional a $67 million transfer from a Veterans Affairs (VA) construction account to the Filipino Veterans Equity Compensation Fund, allowing the funds to be used for major medical facility projects. Adopted 60-35: D 54-1; R 4-34; I 2-0. May 27, 2010 (on the legislative day of May 26, 2010).

175. **HR 4899. Supplemental Appropriations/Filipino Veterans.** Burr, R-N.C., amendment that would strike a $67 million transfer from a VA construction account to the Filipino Veterans Equity Compensation Fund. Rejected 37-58: D 3-52; R 34-4; I 0-2. May 27, 2010 (on the legislative day of May 26, 2010).

176. **HR 4899. Supplemental Appropriations/Passage.** Passage of the bill that would provide $58.8 billion in supplemental funds for fiscal 2010, including $33.5 billion for the Defense Department for the addition of 30,000 troops in Afghanistan, $3.6 billion for Afghan and Iraqi security forces and $4.9 billion for Defense Department procurement. It would provide $94 million for recovery efforts related to the oil spill in the Gulf of Mexico. It would provide $5.1 billion for costs of past disasters and $13.4 billion in mandatory funds to compensate Vietnam War veterans exposed to Agent Orange. Passed 67-28: D 53-2; R 12-26; I 2-0. A "yea" was a vote in support of the president's position. May 27, 2010 (on the legislative day of May 26, 2010).

	172	173	174	175	176		172	173	174	175	176
ALABAMA						**MONTANA**					
Shelby	Y	Y	N	Y	N	Baucus	Y	Y	Y	N	Y
Sessions	Y	Y	N	Y	N	Tester	Y	Y	Y	N	Y
ALASKA						**NEBRASKA**					
Murkowski	Y	Y	Y	N	Y	Nelson	Y	Y	Y	Y	Y
Begich	N	Y	Y	N	Y	**Johanns**	Y	Y	N	Y	Y
ARIZONA						**NEVADA**					
McCain	Y	Y	N	Y	N	Reid	N	N	Y	N	Y
Kyl	Y	Y	N	Y	N	**Ensign**	Y	Y	N	Y	N
ARKANSAS						**NEW HAMPSHIRE**					
Lincoln	?	?	?	?	?	**Gregg**	Y	Y	Y	N	N
Pryor	N	Y	Y	N	Y	Shaheen	N	Y	Y	N	Y
CALIFORNIA						**NEW JERSEY**					
Feinstein	N	N	Y	N	Y	Lautenberg	N	N	Y	N	Y
Boxer	N	N	Y	N	Y	Menendez	N	N	Y	N	Y
COLORADO						**NEW MEXICO**					
Udall	N	Y	Y	N	Y	Bingaman	N	N	Y	N	Y
Bennet	N	Y	Y	N	Y	Udall	N	N	Y	N	Y
CONNECTICUT						**NEW YORK**					
Dodd	N	Y	Y	N	Y	Schumer	N	N	Y	N	Y
Lieberman	N	Y	Y	N	Y	Gillibrand	N	N	Y	N	Y
DELAWARE						**NORTH CAROLINA**					
Carper	N	N	Y	N	Y	**Burr**	Y	Y	N	Y	N
Kaufman	N	N	Y	N	Y	Hagan	N	Y	N	Y	Y
FLORIDA						**NORTH DAKOTA**					
Nelson	N	N	Y	N	Y	Conrad	N	Y	Y	Y	Y
LeMieux	Y	Y	N	Y	Y	Dorgan	N	Y	Y	N	Y
GEORGIA						**OHIO**					
Chambliss	?	?	?	?	?	**Voinovich**	N	Y	N	Y	N
Isakson	Y	Y	N	Y	N	Brown	N	N	Y	N	Y
HAWAII						**OKLAHOMA**					
Inouye	N	N	Y	N	Y	**Inhofe**	Y	Y	N	Y	N
Akaka	N	N	Y	N	Y	**Coburn**	Y	Y	N	Y	N
IDAHO						**OREGON**					
Crapo	Y	Y	N	Y	N	Wyden	N	N	Y	N	N
Risch	Y	Y	N	Y	N	Merkley	N	N	Y	N	Y
ILLINOIS						**PENNSYLVANIA**					
Durbin	N	N	Y	N	Y	Specter	N	N	Y	N	Y
Burris	N	N	Y	N	Y	Casey	N	N	Y	N	Y
INDIANA						**RHODE ISLAND**					
Lugar	Y	Y	N	Y	Y	Reed	N	N	Y	N	Y
Bayh	Y	N	Y	N	Y	Whitehouse	N	N	Y	N	Y
IOWA						**SOUTH CAROLINA**					
Grassley	Y	Y	N	Y	N	**Graham**	Y	Y	N	Y	Y
Harkin	N	N	Y	N	Y	**DeMint**	Y	Y	N	Y	N
KANSAS						**SOUTH DAKOTA**					
Brownback	Y	Y	N	Y	N	Johnson	N	Y	Y	N	Y
Roberts	Y	Y	N	Y	N	**Thune**	Y	Y	N	Y	N
KENTUCKY						**TENNESSEE**					
McConnell	Y	Y	N	Y	Y	**Alexander**	Y	Y	N	Y	Y
Bunning	Y	Y	N	Y	N	**Corker**	Y	Y	N	Y	N
LOUISIANA						**TEXAS**					
Landrieu	Y	Y	Y	N	Y	**Hutchison**	Y	Y	?	?	?
Vitter	Y	Y	?	?	?	**Cornyn**	Y	Y	N	Y	N
MAINE						**UTAH**					
Snowe	Y	Y	N	Y	N	**Hatch**	Y	Y	N	Y	N
Collins	Y	Y	N	Y	Y	**Bennett**	Y	Y	N	Y	Y
MARYLAND						**VERMONT**					
Mikulski	N	N	Y	N	Y	Leahy	N	N	Y	N	Y
Cardin	N	N	Y	N	Y	*Sanders*	N	N	Y	N	Y
MASSACHUSETTS						**VIRGINIA**					
Kerry	N	N	Y	N	Y	Webb	N	Y	Y	N	Y
Brown	Y	Y	N	Y	Y	Warner	N	N	Y	N	Y
MICHIGAN						**WASHINGTON**					
Levin	N	N	Y	N	Y	Murray	N	N	Y	N	Y
Stabenow	N	N	Y	N	Y	Cantwell	N	N	Y	N	Y
MINNESOTA						**WEST VIRGINIA**					
Klobuchar	N	N	Y	N	Y	Byrd	N	Y	Y	Y	Y
Franken	N	N	Y	N	Y	Rockefeller	Y	Y	Y	N	Y
MISSISSIPPI						**WISCONSIN**					
Cochran	Y	Y	N	Y	Y	Kohl	N	N	Y	N	Y
Wicker	Y	Y	N	Y	N	Feingold	N	N	Y	N	N
MISSOURI						**WYOMING**					
Bond	Y	Y	Y	N	Y	**Enzi**	Y	Y	N	Y	N
McCaskill	?	?	?	?	?	**Barrasso**	Y	Y	N	Y	N

KEY	**Republicans**	Democrats	*Independents*		
Y	Voted for (yea)	X	Paired against	C	Voted "present" to avoid possible conflict of interest
#	Paired for	−	Announced against		
+	Announced for	P	Voted "present"	?	Did not vote or otherwise make a position known
N	Voted against (nay)				

IN THE SENATE | By Vote Number

177. **Fleissig Nomination/Confirmation.** Confirmation of President Obama's nomination of Audrey Goldstein Fleissig of Missouri to be a judge for the U.S. District Court for the Eastern District of Missouri. Confirmed 90-0: D 53-0; R 35-0; I 2-0. A "yea" was a vote in support of the president's position. June 7, 2010.

178. **Koh Nomination/Confirmation.** Confirmation of President Obama's nomination of Lucy Haeran Koh of California to be a judge for the U.S. District Court for the Northern District of California. Confirmed 90-0: D 53-0; R 35-0; I 2-0. A "yea" was a vote in support of the president's position. June 7, 2010.

179. **HR 4213. Tax Extensions/Federal Employee Health Benefits.** Cardin, D-Md., motion to waive the Budget Act and budget resolutions with respect to the Hatch, R-Utah, point of order against the Cardin amendment to the Baucus, D-Mont., substitute amendment. The Cardin amendment would expedite a provision of the 2010 health care overhaul law to increase, to 26, the age for coverage of dependents under the Federal Employee Health Benefits Program. The substitute would extend several expired tax provisions, unemployment insurance benefits, federal Medicaid assistance to states, increased payments to doctors that see Medicare patients, federal flood insurance and other programs. Motion rejected 57-42: D 55-1; R 0-41; I 2-0. A three-fifths majority vote (60) of the total Senate is required to waive the Budget Act. (Subsequently, the chair upheld the point of order, and the amendment fell.) June 9, 2010.

180. **HR 4213. Tax Extensions/Pediatric Medical Devices.** Baucus, D-Mont., motion to table (kill) the Roberts, R-Kan., amendment to the Baucus substitute amendment. The Roberts amendment would exempt certain pediatric medical devices from a provision in the 2010 health care overhaul law that would establish a 2.3 percent tax on medical devices. It would be offset by lowering, from 8 percent to 5 percent, the 2010 health care overhaul law's affordability tax exemption under the individual mandate. Motion agreed to 55-44: D 53-3; R 0-41; I 2-0. June 9, 2010.

	177	178	179	180		177	178	179	180
ALABAMA					**MONTANA**				
Shelby	Y	Y	N	N	Baucus	Y	Y	Y	Y
Sessions	Y	Y	N	N	Tester	Y	Y	Y	Y
ALASKA					**NEBRASKA**				
Murkowski	Y	Y	N	N	Nelson	Y	Y	Y	N
Begich	Y	Y	Y	Y	Johanns	Y	Y	N	N
ARIZONA					**NEVADA**				
McCain	Y	Y	N	N	Reid	Y	Y	Y	Y
Kyl	Y	Y	N	N	Ensign	?	?	N	N
ARKANSAS					**NEW HAMPSHIRE**				
Lincoln	?	?	Y	Y	Gregg	?	?	N	N
Pryor	Y	Y	Y	Y	Shaheen	Y	Y	Y	Y
CALIFORNIA					**NEW JERSEY**				
Feinstein	Y	Y	Y	Y	Lautenberg	Y	Y	Y	Y
Boxer	Y	Y	Y	N	Menendez	Y	Y	Y	Y
COLORADO					**NEW MEXICO**				
Udall	Y	Y	Y	Y	Bingaman	Y	Y	Y	Y
Bennet	Y	Y	Y	Y	Udall	Y	Y	Y	Y
CONNECTICUT					**NEW YORK**				
Dodd	Y	Y	Y	Y	Schumer	Y	Y	Y	Y
Lieberman	Y	Y	Y	Y	Gillibrand	Y	Y	Y	Y
DELAWARE					**NORTH CAROLINA**				
Carper	Y	Y	Y	Y	Burr	Y	Y	N	N
Kaufman	Y	Y	Y	Y	Hagan	Y	Y	Y	Y
FLORIDA					**NORTH DAKOTA**				
Nelson	Y	Y	Y	Y	Conrad	Y	Y	Y	Y
LeMieux	Y	Y	N	N	Dorgan	Y	Y	Y	Y
GEORGIA					**OHIO**				
Chambliss	Y	Y	N	N	Voinovich	Y	Y	N	N
Isakson	Y	Y	N	N	Brown	Y	Y	Y	Y
HAWAII					**OKLAHOMA**				
Inouye	?	?	Y	Y	Inhofe	Y	Y	N	N
Akaka	Y	Y	Y	Y	Coburn	Y	Y	N	N
IDAHO					**OREGON**				
Crapo	?	?	N	N	Wyden	Y	Y	Y	Y
Risch	Y	Y	N	N	Merkley	Y	Y	Y	Y
ILLINOIS					**PENNSYLVANIA**				
Durbin	Y	Y	Y	Y	Specter	Y	Y	Y	Y
Burris	Y	Y	Y	Y	Casey	Y	Y	Y	Y
INDIANA					**RHODE ISLAND**				
Lugar	Y	Y	N	N	Reed	Y	Y	Y	Y
Bayh	?	?	Y	Y	Whitehouse	Y	Y	Y	Y
IOWA					**SOUTH CAROLINA**				
Grassley	Y	Y	N	N	Graham	Y	Y	N	N
Harkin	Y	Y	Y	Y	DeMint	?	?	N	N
KANSAS					**SOUTH DAKOTA**				
Brownback	Y	Y	N	N	Johnson	Y	Y	Y	Y
Roberts	Y	Y	N	N	Thune	Y	Y	N	N
KENTUCKY					**TENNESSEE**				
McConnell	Y	Y	N	N	Alexander	Y	Y	N	N
Bunning	Y	Y	N	N	Corker	Y	Y	N	N
LOUISIANA					**TEXAS**				
Landrieu	Y	Y	Y	Y	Hutchison	?	?	N	N
Vitter	?	?	N	N	Cornyn	Y	Y	N	N
MAINE					**UTAH**				
Snowe	Y	Y	N	N	Hatch	Y	Y	N	N
Collins	Y	Y	N	N	Bennett	Y	Y	N	N
MARYLAND					**VERMONT**				
Mikulski	Y	Y	Y	Y	Leahy	Y	Y	Y	Y
Cardin	Y	Y	Y	Y	*Sanders*	Y	Y	Y	Y
MASSACHUSETTS					**VIRGINIA**				
Kerry	Y	Y	Y	Y	Webb	Y	Y	Y	Y
Brown	Y	Y	N	N	Warner	Y	Y	Y	Y
MICHIGAN					**WASHINGTON**				
Levin	Y	Y	Y	Y	Murray	Y	Y	Y	Y
Stabenow	Y	Y	Y	Y	Cantwell	Y	Y	Y	Y
MINNESOTA					**WEST VIRGINIA**				
Klobuchar	Y	Y	Y	N	Byrd	?	?	?	?
Franken	Y	Y	Y	Y	Rockefeller	Y	Y	Y	Y
MISSISSIPPI					**WISCONSIN**				
Cochran	Y	Y	N	N	Kohl	Y	Y	Y	Y
Wicker	Y	Y	N	N	Feingold	Y	Y	N	Y
MISSOURI					**WYOMING**				
Bond	Y	Y	N	N	Enzi	Y	Y	N	N
McCaskill	Y	Y	Y	Y	Barrasso	Y	Y	N	N

KEY **Republicans** Democrats *Independents*

Y	Voted for (yea)	X	Paired against	C	Voted "present" to avoid possible conflict of interest
#	Paired for	–	Announced against	
+	Announced for	P	Voted "present"	?	Did not vote or otherwise make a position known
N	Voted against (nay)		

N THE SENATE | By Vote Number

181. **HR 4213. Tax Extensions/Spending Caps.** Sessions, R-Ala., motion to waive the Budget Act and budget resolutions with respect to the Baucus, D-Mont., point of order against the Sessions amendment to the Baucus substitute amendment. The Sessions amendment would establish discretionary spending limits for fiscal 2011, 2012 and 2013 equal to the levels for defense and non-defense spending in the fiscal 2010 budget resolution. It would also limit spending on overseas deployments and related operations. Points of order against emergency spending designations could be waived by a three-fifths majority vote in the Senate; two-thirds would be required to waive other restrictions. Motion rejected 7-41: D 16-40; R 40-0; I 1-1. A three-fifths majority vote (60) of the total Senate is required to waive the Budget Act. (Subsequently, the chair upheld the point of order, and the amendment fell.) June 9, 2010.

182. **HR 4213. Tax Extensions/Foreign Debt Holdings.** Baucus, D-Mont., amendment to the Baucus substitute amendment. The Baucus amendment would require the Treasury Department and Government Accountability Office to report annually on the risks posed by foreign holdings of U.S. debt and by the debt itself. If the president determined that the risks were unacceptable, he would be required to provide an action plan to relevant congressional committees within 30 days. Adopted 8-41: D 56-0; R 0-41; I 2-0. June 9, 2010.

183. **HR 4213. Tax Extensions/Foreign Debt Holdings.** Baucus, D-Mont., motion to table (kill) the Cornyn, R-Texas, amendment to the Baucus substitute amendment. The Cornyn amendment would require the president to report quarterly on the risk posed by foreign holdings of U.S. debt, and the Government Accountability Office to report annually on the risk posed by the U.S. debt. If the risks were determined to be unacceptable, the president would have to provide an action plan to relevant congressional committees within 30 days. Motion rejected 8-61: D 37-19; R 0-41; I 1-1. (Subsequently, the Cornyn amendment was adopted by voice vote.) June 9, 2010.

184. **S J Res 26. Greenhouse Gas Regulation/Motion to Proceed.** Murkowski, R-Alaska, motion to proceed to consideration of a joint resolution that would provide for congressional disapproval of an EPA endangerment finding that greenhouse gases qualify as dangerous pollutants under the Clean Air Act. Motion rejected 47-53: D 6-51; R 41-0; I 0-2. A "nay" was a vote in support of the president's position. June 10, 2010.

	181	182	183	184			181	182	183	184
ALABAMA						**MONTANA**				
Shelby	Y	N	N	Y		Baucus	N	Y	Y	N
Sessions	Y	N	N	Y		Tester	N	Y	Y	N
ALASKA						**NEBRASKA**				
Murkowski	Y	N	N	Y		Nelson	Y	Y	N	Y
Begich	Y	Y	N	N		**Johanns**	Y	N	N	Y
ARIZONA						**NEVADA**				
McCain	Y	N	N	Y		Reid	N	Y	N	N
Kyl	Y	N	N	Y		**Ensign**	Y	N	N	Y
ARKANSAS						**NEW HAMPSHIRE**				
Lincoln	Y	Y	N	Y		**Gregg**	Y	N	N	Y
Pryor	N	Y	Y	Y		Shaheen	Y	Y	N	N
CALIFORNIA						**NEW JERSEY**				
Feinstein	N	Y	Y	N		Lautenberg	N	Y	Y	N
Boxer	N	Y	N	N		Menendez	N	Y	Y	N
COLORADO						**NEW MEXICO**				
Udall	Y	Y	Y	N		Bingaman	N	Y	Y	N
Bennet	Y	Y	N	N		Udall	N	Y	Y	N
CONNECTICUT						**NEW YORK**				
Dodd	N	Y	Y	N		Schumer	N	Y	Y	N
Lieberman	Y	Y	N	N		Gillibrand	N	Y	Y	N
DELAWARE						**NORTH CAROLINA**				
Carper	Y	Y	Y	N		**Burr**	Y	N	N	Y
Kaufman	N	Y	Y	N		Hagan	Y	Y	Y	N
FLORIDA						**NORTH DAKOTA**				
Nelson	Y	Y	N	N		Conrad	N	Y	Y	N
LeMieux	Y	N	N	Y		Dorgan	N	Y	N	N
GEORGIA						**OHIO**				
Chambliss	Y	N	N	Y		**Voinovich**	Y	N	N	Y
Isakson	Y	N	N	Y		Brown	N	Y	N	N
HAWAII						**OKLAHOMA**				
Inouye	N	Y	Y	N		**Inhofe**	Y	N	N	Y
Akaka	N	Y	Y	N		**Coburn**	Y	N	N	Y
IDAHO						**OREGON**				
Crapo	Y	N	N	Y		Wyden	N	Y	N	N
Risch	Y	N	N	Y		Merkley	N	Y	N	N
ILLINOIS						**PENNSYLVANIA**				
Durbin	N	Y	Y	N		Specter	N	Y	Y	N
Burris	N	Y	Y	N		Casey	Y	Y	Y	N
INDIANA						**RHODE ISLAND**				
Lugar	Y	N	N	Y		Reed	N	Y	Y	N
Bayh	Y	Y	Y	Y		Whitehouse	N	Y	Y	N
IOWA						**SOUTH CAROLINA**				
Grassley	Y	N	N	Y		**Graham**	Y	N	N	Y
Harkin	N	Y	Y	N		**DeMint**	Y	N	N	Y
KANSAS						**SOUTH DAKOTA**				
Brownback	Y	N	N	Y		Johnson	N	Y	Y	N
Roberts	?	N	N	Y		**Thune**	Y	N	N	Y
KENTUCKY						**TENNESSEE**				
McConnell	Y	N	N	Y		**Alexander**	Y	N	N	Y
Bunning	Y	N	N	Y		**Corker**	Y	N	N	Y
LOUISIANA						**TEXAS**				
Landrieu	N	Y	Y	Y		**Hutchison**	Y	N	N	Y
Vitter	Y	N	N	Y		**Cornyn**	Y	N	N	Y
MAINE						**UTAH**				
Snowe	Y	N	N	Y		**Hatch**	Y	N	N	Y
Collins	Y	N	N	Y		**Bennett**	Y	N	N	Y
MARYLAND						**VERMONT**				
Mikulski	N	Y	Y	N		Leahy	N	Y	Y	N
Cardin	N	Y	Y	N		*Sanders*	N	Y	Y	N
MASSACHUSETTS						**VIRGINIA**				
Kerry	N	Y	Y	N		Webb	Y	Y	N	N
Brown	Y	N	N	Y		Warner	Y	Y	Y	N
MICHIGAN						**WASHINGTON**				
Levin	N	Y	Y	N		Murray	N	Y	Y	N
Stabenow	N	Y	Y	N		Cantwell	Y	Y	N	N
MINNESOTA						**WEST VIRGINIA**				
Klobuchar	Y	Y	Y	N		Byrd	?	?	?	?
Franken	N	Y	Y	N		Rockefeller	N	Y	Y	Y
MISSISSIPPI						**WISCONSIN**				
Cochran	Y	N	N	Y		Kohl	N	Y	Y	N
Wicker	Y	N	N	Y		Feingold	N	Y	N	N
MISSOURI						**WYOMING**				
Bond	Y	N	N	Y		**Enzi**	Y	N	N	Y
McCaskill	Y	Y	Y	N		**Barrasso**	Y	N	N	Y

KEY	**Republicans**	Democrats	*Independents*		
Y	Voted for (yea)	X Paired against		C	Voted "present" to avoid possible conflict of interest
#	Paired for	– Announced against			
+	Announced for	P Voted "present"		?	Did not vote or otherwise make a position known
N	Voted against (nay)				

IN THE SENATE | By Vote Number

185. **Pratt Nomination/Confirmation.** Confirmation of President Obama's nomination of Tanya Walton Pratt of Indiana to be a judge for the U.S. District Court for the Southern District of Indiana. Confirmed 95-0: D 54-0; R 39-0; I 2-0. A "yea" was a vote in support of the president's position. June 15, 2010.

186. **Jackson Nomination/Confirmation.** Confirmation of President Obama's nomination of Brian Anthony Jackson of Louisiana to be a judge for the U.S. District Court for the Middle District of Louisiana. Confirmed 96-0: D 55-0; R 39-0; I 2-0. A "yea" was a vote in support of the president's position. June 15, 2010.

187. **HR 4213. Tax Extensions/Oil Tax Exemptions.** Sanders, I-Vt., amendment to the Baucus, D-Mont., substitute amendment. The Sanders amendment would repeal tax benefits for oil and gas companies, including the deduction for income attributable to domestic production of oil, natural gas and primary products of these fuels. It would appropriate $2 billion annually for the Energy Efficiency and Conservation Block Grant Program in fiscal 2011 through 2015. The substitute would extend several expired tax provisions, unemployment insurance benefits, federal Medicaid assistance to states, increased payments to doctors who serve Medicare patients, federal flood insurance and other programs. Rejected 35-61: D 34-21; R 0-39; I 1-1. (By unanimous consent, the Senate agreed to raise the majority requirement for adoption of the Sanders amendment to 60 votes.) June 15, 2010.

188. **HR 4213. Tax Extensions/Oil Spill Liability.** Vitter, R-La., amendment to the Baucus, D-Mont., substitute amendment. The Vitter amendment would prevent funds generated by an increase in taxes on oil companies for the Oil Spill Liability Trust Fund from being counted as an offset for purposes of the Budget Act or the 2010 pay-as-you-go law. Rejected 48-49: D 8-48; R 39-0; I 1-1. (By unanimous consent, the Senate agreed to raise the majority requirement for adoption of the Vitter amendment to 60 votes.) June 15, 2010.

189. **HR 4213. Tax Extensions/Homeowner Advocate.** Franken, D-Minn., amendment to the Baucus, D-Mont., substitute amendment. The Franken amendment would create an Office of the Homeowner Advocate in the Treasury Department tasked with assisting homeowners, housing counselors and housing lawyers in resolving problems related to the Home Affordable Modification Program. Adopted 63-33: D 53-2; R 8-31; I 2-0. (By unanimous consent, the Senate agreed to raise the majority requirement for adoption of the Franken amendment to 60 votes.) June 15, 2010.

190. **HR 4213. Tax Extensions/Motion to Waive.** Baucus, D-Mont., motion to waive the Budget Act and budget resolutions with respect to the Gregg, R-N.H., point of order against the Baucus motion to concur in the House amendment to the Senate amendment to the bill with a Baucus substitute amendment. Motion rejected 45-52: D 44-11; R 0-40; I 1-1. A three-fifths majority vote (60) of the total Senate is required to waive the Budget Act. (Subsequently, the motion was withdrawn.) June 16, 2010.

	185	186	187	188	189	190
ALABAMA						
Shelby	Y	Y	N	Y	N	N
Sessions	Y	Y	N	Y	N	N
ALASKA						
Murkowski	Y	Y	N	Y	Y	N
Begich	Y	Y	N	Y	Y	N
ARIZONA						
McCain	Y	Y	N	Y	N	N
Kyl	Y	Y	N	Y	N	N
ARKANSAS						
Lincoln	Y	Y	N	N	Y	?
Pryor	Y	Y	N	N	Y	N
CALIFORNIA						
Feinstein	Y	Y	Y	N	Y	Y
Boxer	+	Y	Y	N	?	Y
COLORADO						
Udall	Y	Y	N	N	Y	Y
Bennet	Y	Y	N	N	Y	Y
CONNECTICUT						
Dodd	Y	Y	N	N	Y	Y
Lieberman	Y	Y	N	Y	Y	N
DELAWARE						
Carper	Y	Y	Y	N	Y	Y
Kaufman	Y	Y	Y	N	Y	Y
FLORIDA						
Nelson	Y	Y	Y	Y	Y	N
LeMieux	?	?	?	?	?	N
GEORGIA						
Chambliss	Y	Y	N	Y	N	N
Isakson	Y	Y	N	Y	N	N
HAWAII						
Inouye	Y	Y	N	N	Y	Y
Akaka	Y	Y	N	N	Y	Y
IDAHO						
Crapo	Y	Y	N	Y	N	N
Risch	Y	Y	N	Y	N	N
ILLINOIS						
Durbin	Y	Y	N	N	Y	Y
Burris	Y	Y	Y	N	Y	Y
INDIANA						
Lugar	Y	Y	N	Y	N	N
Bayh	Y	Y	N	N	Y	N
IOWA						
Grassley	Y	Y	N	Y	Y	N
Harkin	Y	Y	N	N	Y	Y
KANSAS						
Brownback	Y	Y	N	Y	N	N
Roberts	?	?	?	?	?	?
KENTUCKY						
McConnell	Y	Y	N	Y	N	N
Bunning	Y	Y	N	Y	N	N
LOUISIANA						
Landrieu	Y	Y	N	Y	Y	N
Vitter	Y	Y	N	Y	Y	N
MAINE						
Snowe	Y	Y	N	Y	Y	N
Collins	Y	Y	N	Y	Y	N
MARYLAND						
Mikulski	Y	Y	Y	N	Y	Y
Cardin	Y	Y	Y	N	Y	Y
MASSACHUSETTS						
Kerry	Y	Y	N	N	Y	Y
Brown	Y	Y	N	Y	Y	N
MICHIGAN						
Levin	Y	Y	Y	N	Y	Y
Stabenow	Y	Y	Y	N	Y	Y
MINNESOTA						
Klobuchar	Y	Y	Y	N	Y	Y
Franken	Y	Y	Y	N	Y	Y
MISSISSIPPI						
Cochran	Y	Y	N	Y	N	N
Wicker	Y	Y	N	Y	N	N
MISSOURI						
Bond	Y	Y	N	Y	N	N
McCaskill	?	?	Y	N	Y	N

	185	186	187	188	189	190
MONTANA						
Baucus	Y	Y	N	N	Y	Y
Tester	Y	Y	N	N	Y	Y
NEBRASKA						
Nelson	Y	Y	N	Y	N	N
Johanns	Y	Y	N	Y	N	N
NEVADA						
Reid	Y	Y	N	Y	Y	Y
Ensign	Y	Y	N	Y	N	N
NEW HAMPSHIRE						
Gregg	Y	Y	Y	N	Y	Y
Shaheen	Y	Y	Y	N	Y	Y
NEW JERSEY						
Lautenberg	Y	Y	Y	N	Y	Y
Menendez	Y	Y	Y	N	Y	N
NEW MEXICO						
Bingaman	Y	Y	N	N	Y	Y
Udall	Y	Y	N	N	Y	Y
NEW YORK						
Schumer	Y	Y	Y	N	Y	Y
Gillibrand	Y	Y	Y	N	Y	Y
NORTH CAROLINA						
Burr	Y	Y	N	Y	Y	N
Hagan	Y	Y	N	Y	Y	Y
NORTH DAKOTA						
Conrad	Y	Y	N	N	Y	N
Dorgan	Y	Y	N	Y	Y	Y
OHIO						
Voinovich	Y	Y	N	Y	N	N
Brown	Y	Y	Y	N	Y	Y
OKLAHOMA						
Inhofe	Y	Y	N	Y	N	N
Coburn	Y	Y	N	Y	N	N
OREGON						
Wyden	Y	Y	N	Y	Y	Y
Merkley	Y	Y	Y	Y	Y	Y
PENNSYLVANIA						
Specter	Y	Y	Y	N	Y	Y
Casey	Y	Y	Y	N	Y	Y
RHODE ISLAND						
Reed	Y	Y	Y	N	Y	Y
Whitehouse	Y	Y	Y	N	Y	Y
SOUTH CAROLINA						
Graham	Y	Y	N	Y	Y	N
DeMint	Y	Y	N	Y	N	N
SOUTH DAKOTA						
Johnson	Y	Y	?	N	Y	Y
Thune	Y	Y	N	Y	N	N
TENNESSEE						
Alexander	Y	Y	N	Y	N	N
Corker	Y	Y	N	Y	N	N
TEXAS						
Hutchison	Y	Y	N	Y	N	N
Cornyn	Y	Y	N	Y	N	N
UTAH						
Hatch	Y	Y	N	Y	N	N
Bennett	Y	Y	N	Y	N	N
VERMONT						
Leahy	Y	Y	Y	N	Y	Y
Sanders	Y	Y	N	Y	N	Y
VIRGINIA						
Webb	Y	Y	N	N	Y	N
Warner	Y	Y	N	N	Y	Y
WASHINGTON						
Murray	Y	Y	Y	N	Y	Y
Cantwell	Y	Y	Y	N	Y	Y
WEST VIRGINIA						
Byrd	?	?	?	?	?	?
Rockefeller	Y	Y	Y	N	Y	Y
WISCONSIN						
Kohl	Y	Y	Y	N	Y	Y
Feingold	Y	Y	Y	N	Y	N
WYOMING						
Enzi	Y	Y	N	Y	N	N
Barrasso	Y	Y	N	Y	N	N

KEY	**Republicans**	Democrats	*Independents*	
Y Voted for (yea)		X Paired against		C Voted "present" to avoid possible conflict of interes
# Paired for		– Announced against		
+ Announced for		P Voted "present"		? Did not vote or otherwise make a position known
N Voted against (nay)				

IN THE SENATE | By Vote Number

191. **HR 4213. Tax Extensions/Homebuyer Tax Credit.** Reid, D-Nev., amendment that would extend, through Sept. 30, 2010, the deadline for homebuyers to close on their properties to claim a first-time homebuyer tax credit if the house was under contract as of April 30, 2010. It would be offset by eliminating the possibility of a tax deduction for punitive damages judgments against businesses. Adopted 60-37: D 54-1; R 4-36; I 2-0. (By unanimous consent, the Senate agreed to raise the majority requirement for adoption of the Reid amendment to 60 votes. Subsequently, the Reid amendment was incorporated into the Baucus, D-Mont., substitute.) June 16, 2010.

192. **HR 4213. Tax Extensions/Homebuyer Tax Credit.** Isakson, R-Ga., amendment that would extend, through Sept. 30, 2010, the deadline for homebuyers to close on their properties to claim a first-time homebuyer tax credit if the house was under contract as of April 30, 2010. It would be offset by rescinding unobligated funds from the 2009 economic stimulus law. Rejected 45-52: D 8-47; R 37-3; I 0-2. (By unanimous consent, the Senate agreed to raise the majority requirement for adoption of the Isakson amendment to 60 votes.) June 16, 2010.

193. **HR 4213. Tax Extensions/Republican Substitute.** Thune, R-S.D., motion to waive the Budget Act and budget resolutions with respect to the Baucus, D-Mont., point of order against the Thune substitute amendment that would extend several expired tax provisions, unemployment insurance benefits, increased payments to doctors that see Medicare patients, federal flood insurance and other programs. It would be offset with a medical-malpractice overhaul, a freeze on federal employees' salaries and a 5 percent cut in discretionary spending outside of the Defense and Veterans Affairs departments. Motion rejected 41-57: D 1-55; R 40-0; I 0-2. A three-fifths majority vote (60) of the total Senate is required to waive the Budget Act. (Subsequently, the motion was withdrawn). June 17, 2010.

194. **HR 4213. Tax Extensions/Cloture.** Motion to invoke cloture (thus limiting debate) on the Baucus, D-Mont., motion to concur in the House amendment to the Senate amendment with a revised Baucus substitute amendment that would extend several expired tax provisions, extend unemployment benefits and prevent a 21 percent cut to payment rates for doctors under Medicare. Changes to doctors' payment rates under Medicare would be offset. It also would raise the per-barrel excise tax on oil to 49 cents. Motion rejected 56-40: D 55-1; R 0-38; I 1-1. Three-fifths of the total Senate (60) is required to invoke cloture. June 17, 2010.

	191	192	193	194			191	192	193	194
ALABAMA						**MONTANA**				
Shelby	N	Y	Y	N		Baucus	Y	N	N	Y
Sessions	N	Y	Y	N		Tester	Y	N	N	Y
ALASKA						**NEBRASKA**				
Murkowski	N	Y	Y	N		Nelson	N	Y	Y	N
Begich	Y	N	N	Y		Johanns	N	Y	Y	N
ARIZONA						**NEVADA**				
McCain	N	Y	Y	N		Reid	Y	N	N	Y
Kyl	N	N	Y	N		Ensign	Y	Y	Y	N
ARKANSAS						**NEW HAMPSHIRE**				
Lincoln	Y	Y	N	Y		Gregg	Y	Y	Y	N
Pryor	Y	N	N	Y		Shaheen	Y	N	N	Y
CALIFORNIA						**NEW JERSEY**				
Feinstein	Y	N	N	Y		Lautenberg	Y	N	N	Y
Boxer	Y	N	N	Y		Menendez	Y	N	N	Y
COLORADO						**NEW MEXICO**				
Udall	Y	N	N	Y		Bingaman	Y	N	N	Y
Bennet	Y	N	N	Y		Udall	Y	N	N	Y
CONNECTICUT						**NEW YORK**				
Dodd	Y	N	N	Y		Schumer	Y	N	N	Y
Lieberman	Y	N	N	Y		Gillibrand	Y	N	N	Y
DELAWARE						**NORTH CAROLINA**				
Carper	Y	N	N	Y		Burr	N	Y	Y	N
Kaufman	Y	N	N	Y		Hagan	Y	N	N	Y
FLORIDA						**NORTH DAKOTA**				
Nelson	Y	Y	N	Y		Conrad	Y	Y	Y	N
LeMieux	Y	Y	Y	N		Dorgan	Y	Y	N	Y
GEORGIA						**OHIO**				
Chambliss	N	Y	Y	N		Voinovich	N	Y	Y	N
Isakson	N	Y	Y	N		Brown	Y	N	N	Y
HAWAII						**OKLAHOMA**				
Inouye	Y	N	N	Y		Inhofe	N	Y	Y	N
Akaka	Y	N	N	Y		Coburn	N	Y	Y	N
IDAHO						**OREGON**				
Crapo	N	Y	Y	N		Wyden	Y	N	N	Y
Risch	N	Y	Y	N		Merkley	Y	N	N	Y
ILLINOIS						**PENNSYLVANIA**				
Durbin	Y	N	N	Y		Specter	Y	N	N	Y
Burris	Y	N	N	Y		Casey	Y	N	N	Y
INDIANA						**RHODE ISLAND**				
Lugar	N	Y	Y	N		Reed	Y	N	N	Y
Bayh	Y	Y	N	Y		Whitehouse	Y	N	N	Y
IOWA						**SOUTH CAROLINA**				
Grassley	N	Y	Y	N		Graham	N	Y	?	?
Harkin	Y	N	N	Y		DeMint	N	N	Y	N
KANSAS						**SOUTH DAKOTA**				
Brownback	N	Y	Y	N		Johnson	Y	N	N	Y
Roberts	?	?	Y	?		Thune	N	Y	Y	N
KENTUCKY						**TENNESSEE**				
McConnell	N	Y	Y	N		Alexander	N	Y	Y	N
Bunning	N	N	Y	N		Corker	N	Y	Y	N
LOUISIANA						**TEXAS**				
Landrieu	Y	N	N	Y		Hutchison	N	Y	Y	N
Vitter	N	Y	Y	N		Cornyn	N	Y	Y	N
MAINE						**UTAH**				
Snowe	N	Y	Y	N		Hatch	N	Y	Y	N
Collins	Y	Y	Y	N		Bennett	N	Y	Y	N
MARYLAND						**VERMONT**				
Mikulski	Y	N	N	Y		Leahy	Y	N	N	Y
Cardin	Y	N	N	Y		*Sanders*	Y	N	N	Y
MASSACHUSETTS						**VIRGINIA**				
Kerry	Y	N	N	Y		Webb	Y	Y	N	Y
Brown	N	Y	Y	N		Warner	?	?	N	Y
MICHIGAN						**WASHINGTON**				
Levin	Y	N	N	Y		Murray	Y	N	N	Y
Stabenow	Y	N	N	Y		Cantwell	Y	N	N	Y
MINNESOTA						**WEST VIRGINIA**				
Klobuchar	Y	Y	?	Y		Byrd	?	?	N	?
Franken	Y	N	N	Y		Rockefeller	Y	N	N	Y
MISSISSIPPI						**WISCONSIN**				
Cochran	N	Y	Y	N		Kohl	Y	N	N	Y
Wicker	N	Y	Y	N		Feingold	Y	N	N	Y
MISSOURI						**WYOMING**				
Bond	N	Y	Y	?		Enzi	N	Y	Y	N
McCaskill	Y	N	N	Y		Barrasso	N	Y	Y	N

KEY	**Republicans**	Democrats	*Independents*	
Y Voted for (yea)		X Paired against		C Voted "present" to avoid possible conflict of interest
# Paired for		– Announced against		
+ Announced for		P Voted "present"		? Did not vote or otherwise make a position known
N Voted against (nay)				

IN THE SENATE | By Vote Number

195. Goldsmith Nomination/Confirmation. Confirmation of President Obama's nomination of Mark A. Goldsmith of Michigan to be a judge for the U.S. District Court for the Eastern District of Michigan. Confirmed 89-0: D 52-0; R 35-0; I 2-0. A "yea" was a vote in support of the president's position. June 21, 2010.

196. Treadwell Nomination/Confirmation. Confirmation of President Obama's nomination of Marc T. Treadwell of Georgia to be a judge for the U.S. District Court for the Middle District of Georgia. Confirmed 89-0: D 53-0; R 34-0; I 2-0. A "yea" was a vote in support of the president's position. June 21, 2010.

197. HR 4213. Tax Extensions/Motion to Refer. Reid, D-Nev., motion to table (kill) the DeMint, R-S.C., motion to refer the bill to the Finance Committee with instructions that it be reported back with language that would permanently extend the 15 percent capital gains tax rate. It would require offsets for the provision. Motion agreed to 57-40: D 54-1; R 1-39; I 2-0. June 23, 2010.

198. HR 4213. Tax Extensions/Motion to Table. Reid, D-Nev., motion to table (kill) the Baucus, D-Mont., motion to concur in the House amendment to the Senate amendment with a further Baucus substitute amendment that would extend several expired tax provisions, extend unemployment benefits and reverse a 21 percent payment cut to doctors under Medicare. Changes to doctors' payment rate under Medicare would be offset. It also would raise the per-barrel tax on oil to 49 cents. Motion agreed to 56-40: D 54-0; R 0-40; I 2-0. June 23, 2010.

199. HR 2194. Iran Sanctions/Conference Report. Adoption of the conference report on the bill that would impose new sanctions on companies doing business with Iran. It would expand the list of available sanctions for the president to impose on companies that engage in certain trade with Iran relating to petroleum and gasoline production and refinement. It would cut off international financial institutions from the U.S. banking system if they do business with the Islamic Revolutionary Guard Corps or facilitate Tehran's efforts to acquire weapons of mass destruction. The measure would require the administration to investigate and issue findings on possible violations but also give the president the ability to waive many of the provisions if doing so is necessary to the national interest. Adopted, (thus sent to the House), 99-0: D 56-0; R 41-0; I 2-0. June 24, 2010.

200. HR 4213. Tax Extensions/Cloture. Motion to invoke cloture (thus limiting debate) on the Reid, D-Nev., motion to concur in the House amendment to the Senate amendment with a further Baucus substitute amendment that would extend several expired tax provisions, extend unemployment benefits and reverse a 21 percent payment cut to doctors under Medicare. Provisions other than the unemployment insurance extension would be offset. The offsets include provisions that would raise the per-barrel tax on oil to 49 cents. Motion rejected 57-41: D 55-1; R 0-40; I 2-0. Three-fifths of the total Senate (60) is required to invoke cloture. June 24, 2010.

	195	196	197	198	199	200
ALABAMA						
Shelby	Y	Y	N	N	Y	N
Sessions	Y	Y	N	N	Y	N
ALASKA						
Murkowski	Y	Y	N	N	Y	?
Begich	Y	Y	Y	Y	Y	Y
ARIZONA						
McCain	Y	Y	N	N	Y	N
Kyl	Y	?	N	N	Y	N
ARKANSAS						
Lincoln	Y	Y	Y	Y	Y	Y
Pryor	Y	Y	Y	Y	Y	Y
CALIFORNIA						
Feinstein	Y	Y	Y	Y	Y	Y
Boxer	Y	Y	Y	Y	Y	Y
COLORADO						
Udall	Y	Y	Y	Y	Y	Y
Bennet	Y	Y	Y	Y	Y	Y
CONNECTICUT						
Dodd	Y	Y	Y	Y	Y	Y
Lieberman	Y	Y	Y	Y	Y	Y
DELAWARE						
Carper	Y	Y	Y	Y	Y	Y
Kaufman	Y	Y	Y	Y	Y	Y
FLORIDA						
Nelson	?	?	Y	Y	Y	Y
LeMieux	Y	Y	N	N	Y	N
GEORGIA						
Chambliss	Y	Y	N	N	Y	N
Isakson	Y	Y	N	N	Y	N
HAWAII						
Inouye	Y	Y	Y	Y	Y	Y
Akaka	Y	Y	Y	Y	Y	Y
IDAHO						
Crapo	Y	Y	N	N	Y	N
Risch	Y	Y	N	N	Y	N
ILLINOIS						
Durbin	?	Y	Y	Y	Y	Y
Burris	Y	Y	Y	Y	Y	Y
INDIANA						
Lugar	Y	Y	N	N	Y	N
Bayh	?	?	Y	Y	Y	Y
IOWA						
Grassley	Y	Y	N	N	Y	N
Harkin	Y	Y	Y	Y	Y	Y
KANSAS						
Brownback	Y	Y	N	N	Y	N
Roberts	Y	Y	?	?	Y	N
KENTUCKY						
McConnell	Y	Y	N	N	Y	N
Bunning	Y	Y	N	N	Y	N
LOUISIANA						
Landrieu	Y	Y	Y	Y	Y	Y
Vitter	?	?	N	N	Y	N
MAINE						
Snowe	Y	Y	N	N	Y	N
Collins	Y	Y	N	N	Y	N
MARYLAND						
Mikulski	Y	Y	Y	Y	Y	Y
Cardin	Y	Y	Y	Y	Y	Y
MASSACHUSETTS						
Kerry	Y	Y	Y	Y	Y	Y
Brown	Y	Y	N	N	Y	N
MICHIGAN						
Levin	Y	Y	Y	Y	Y	Y
Stabenow	Y	Y	Y	Y	Y	Y
MINNESOTA						
Klobuchar	Y	Y	Y	Y	Y	Y
Franken	Y	Y	Y	Y	Y	Y
MISSISSIPPI						
Cochran	Y	Y	N	N	Y	N
Wicker	Y	Y	N	N	Y	N
MISSOURI						
Bond	?	?	N	N	Y	N
McCaskill	Y	Y	Y	Y	Y	Y

	195	196	197	198	199	200
MONTANA						
Baucus	Y	Y	Y	Y	Y	Y
Tester	Y	Y	Y	Y	Y	Y
NEBRASKA						
Nelson	Y	Y	N	Y	Y	N
Johanns	Y	Y	N	N	Y	N
NEVADA						
Reid	Y	Y	Y	Y	Y	Y
Ensign	Y	Y	N	N	Y	N
NEW HAMPSHIRE						
Gregg	?	?	N	N	Y	N
Shaheen	Y	Y	Y	Y	Y	Y
NEW JERSEY						
Lautenberg	Y	Y	Y	Y	Y	Y
Menendez	Y	Y	Y	Y	Y	Y
NEW MEXICO						
Bingaman	Y	Y	Y	Y	Y	Y
Udall	Y	Y	Y	Y	Y	Y
NEW YORK						
Schumer	Y	Y	Y	Y	Y	Y
Gillibrand	Y	Y	Y	Y	Y	Y
NORTH CAROLINA						
Burr	Y	Y	N	N	Y	N
Hagan	Y	Y	Y	Y	Y	Y
NORTH DAKOTA						
Conrad	Y	Y	Y	Y	Y	Y
Dorgan	Y	Y	Y	?	Y	Y
OHIO						
Voinovich	Y	Y	N	N	Y	N
Brown	Y	Y	Y	Y	Y	Y
OKLAHOMA						
Inhofe	Y	Y	N	N	Y	N
Coburn	Y	Y	N	N	Y	N
OREGON						
Wyden	?	?	Y	Y	Y	Y
Merkley	Y	Y	Y	Y	Y	Y
PENNSYLVANIA						
Specter	Y	Y	Y	Y	Y	Y
Casey	Y	Y	Y	Y	Y	Y
RHODE ISLAND						
Reed	Y	Y	Y	Y	Y	Y
Whitehouse	Y	Y	Y	Y	Y	Y
SOUTH CAROLINA						
Graham	Y	Y	N	N	Y	N
DeMint	Y	Y	N	N	Y	N
SOUTH DAKOTA						
Johnson	Y	Y	Y	Y	Y	Y
Thune	?	?	N	N	Y	N
TENNESSEE						
Alexander	Y	Y	N	N	Y	N
Corker	Y	Y	N	N	Y	N
TEXAS						
Hutchison	?	?	N	N	Y	N
Cornyn	Y	Y	N	N	Y	N
UTAH						
Hatch	Y	Y	N	N	Y	N
Bennett	?	?	N	N	Y	N
VERMONT						
Leahy	Y	Y	Y	Y	Y	Y
Sanders	Y	Y	Y	Y	Y	Y
VIRGINIA						
Webb	Y	Y	Y	Y	Y	Y
Warner	Y	Y	Y	Y	Y	Y
WASHINGTON						
Murray	Y	Y	Y	Y	Y	Y
Cantwell	Y	Y	Y	Y	Y	Y
WEST VIRGINIA						
Byrd	?	?	?	?	?	?
Rockefeller	Y	Y	?	?	Y	Y
WISCONSIN						
Kohl	Y	Y	Y	Y	Y	Y
Feingold	Y	Y	Y	Y	Y	Y
WYOMING						
Enzi	Y	Y	N	N	Y	N
Barrasso	Y	Y	N	N	Y	N

KEY **Republicans** Democrats *Independents*

Y Voted for (yea)	X Paired against
# Paired for	– Announced against
+ Announced for	P Voted "present"
N Voted against (nay)	

C Voted "present" to avoid possible conflict of interest

? Did not vote or otherwise make a position known

N THE SENATE | By Vote Number

201. **Feinerman Nomination/Confirmation.** Confirmation of President Obama's nomination of Gary Scott Feinerman of Illinois to be a judge for the U.S. District Court for the Northern District of Illinois. Confirmed 80-0: D 48-0; R 31-0; I 1-0. A "yea" was a vote in support of the president's position. June 28, 2010.

202. **HR 5297. Small-Business Tax and Lending/Cloture.** Motion to invoke cloture (thus limiting debate) on the Reid, D-Nev., motion to proceed to the bill that would include small-business tax initiatives and authorize a small-business lending fund. Motion agreed to 66-33: D 56-0; R 8-33; I 2-0. Three-fifths of the total Senate (60) is required to invoke cloture. (Subsequently, the Senate agreed to proceed to the measure by unanimous consent.) June 29, 2010.

203. **Petraeus Nomination/Confirmation.** Confirmation of President Obama's nomination of Army Gen. David H. Petraeus to be commander of U.S. and coalition forces in Afghanistan. Confirmed 99-0: D 56-0; R 41-0; I 2-0. A "yea" was a vote in support of the president's position. June 30, 2010.

204. **HR 4213. Unemployment and Tax Extensions/Cloture.** Motion to invoke cloture (thus limiting debate) on the Reid, D-Nev., motion to concur in the House amendment to the Senate amendment with a further Reid substitute amendment that would extend eligibility for extended federal unemployment insurance and the deadline for consumers to benefit from the homebuyer tax credit program. Motion rejected 58-38: D 54-2; R 2-36; I 2-0. Three-fifths of the total Senate (60) is required to invoke cloture. (At the conclusion of the vote, Reid entered a motion to reconsider the vote.) June 30, 2010.

	201	202	203	204			201	202	203	204
ALABAMA						**MONTANA**				
Shelby	?	N	Y	N		Baucus	Y	Y	Y	Y
Sessions	Y	N	Y	N		Tester	Y	Y	Y	Y
ALASKA						**NEBRASKA**				
Murkowski	?	N	Y	N		Nelson	Y	Y	Y	N
Begich	Y	Y	Y	Y		**Johanns**	Y	N	Y	N
ARIZONA						**NEVADA**				
McCain	Y	N	Y	N		Reid	Y	Y	Y	N
Kyl	Y	N	Y	N		**Ensign**	Y	N	Y	N
ARKANSAS						**NEW HAMPSHIRE**				
Lincoln	Y	Y	Y	Y		**Gregg**	?	N	Y	N
Pryor	Y	Y	Y	Y		Shaheen	Y	Y	Y	Y
CALIFORNIA						**NEW JERSEY**				
Feinstein	Y	Y	Y	Y		Lautenberg	Y	Y	Y	Y
Boxer	Y	Y	Y	Y		Menendez	Y	Y	Y	Y
COLORADO						**NEW MEXICO**				
Udall	Y	Y	Y	Y		Bingaman	Y	Y	Y	Y
Bennet	Y	Y	Y	Y		Udall	Y	Y	Y	Y
CONNECTICUT						**NEW YORK**				
Dodd	Y	Y	Y	Y		Schumer	Y	Y	Y	Y
Lieberman	Y	Y	Y	Y		Gillibrand	?	Y	Y	Y
DELAWARE						**NORTH CAROLINA**				
Carper	Y	Y	Y	Y		**Burr**	?	N	Y	N
Kaufman	Y	Y	Y	Y		Hagan	Y	Y	Y	Y
FLORIDA						**NORTH DAKOTA**				
Nelson	Y	Y	Y	Y		Conrad	Y	Y	Y	Y
LeMieux	?	Y	Y	N		Dorgan	Y	Y	Y	Y
GEORGIA						**OHIO**				
Chambliss	Y	N	Y	N		**Voinovich**	?	Y	Y	N
Isakson	Y	N	Y	N		Brown	Y	Y	Y	Y
HAWAII						**OKLAHOMA**				
Inouye	Y	Y	Y	Y		**Inhofe**	Y	N	Y	N
Akaka	Y	Y	Y	Y		**Coburn**	Y	N	Y	N
IDAHO						**OREGON**				
Crapo	Y	N	Y	N		Wyden	?	Y	Y	Y
Risch	Y	N	Y	N		Merkley	?	Y	Y	Y
ILLINOIS						**PENNSYLVANIA**				
Durbin	Y	Y	Y	Y		Specter	Y	Y	Y	Y
Burris	Y	Y	Y	Y		Casey	Y	Y	Y	Y
INDIANA						**RHODE ISLAND**				
Lugar	Y	Y	Y	N		Reed	Y	Y	Y	Y
Bayh	Y	Y	Y	Y		Whitehouse	Y	Y	Y	Y
IOWA						**SOUTH CAROLINA**				
Grassley	Y	Y	Y	N		**Graham**	Y	N	Y	N
Harkin	Y	Y	Y	Y		**DeMint**	Y	N	Y	–
KANSAS						**SOUTH DAKOTA**				
Brownback	+	N	Y	N		Johnson	?	Y	Y	Y
Roberts	Y	N	Y	?		**Thune**	Y	N	Y	N
KENTUCKY						**TENNESSEE**				
McConnell	Y	N	Y	N		**Alexander**	Y	N	Y	N
Bunning	Y	N	Y	N		**Corker**	Y	N	Y	N
LOUISIANA						**TEXAS**				
Landrieu	Y	Y	Y	Y		**Hutchison**	Y	N	Y	N
Vitter	?	N	Y	N		**Cornyn**	Y	N	Y	N
MAINE						**UTAH**				
Snowe	Y	Y	Y	Y		**Hatch**	Y	N	Y	N
Collins	Y	Y	Y	Y		**Bennett**	?	N	Y	N
MARYLAND						**VERMONT**				
Mikulski	?	Y	Y	Y		Leahy	Y	Y	Y	Y
Cardin	Y	Y	Y	Y		*Sanders*	?	Y	Y	Y
MASSACHUSETTS						**VIRGINIA**				
Kerry	Y	Y	Y	Y		Webb	Y	Y	Y	Y
Brown	Y	Y	Y	Y		Warner	Y	Y	Y	Y
MICHIGAN						**WASHINGTON**				
Levin	Y	Y	Y	Y		Murray	?	Y	Y	Y
Stabenow	?	Y	Y	Y		Cantwell	?	Y	Y	Y
MINNESOTA						**WEST VIRGINIA**				
Klobuchar	Y	Y	Y	Y		Rockefeller	Y	Y	Y	Y
Franken	Y	Y	Y	Y		Vacant*				
MISSISSIPPI						**WISCONSIN**				
Cochran	Y	N	Y	N		Kohl	Y	Y	Y	Y
Wicker	Y	N	Y	N		Feingold	Y	Y	Y	Y
MISSOURI						**WYOMING**				
Bond	?	Y	Y	?		**Enzi**	Y	N	Y	N
McCaskill	Y	Y	Y	Y		**Barrasso**	Y	N	Y	N

KEY   **Republicans**   Democrats   *Independents*

Y	Voted for (yea)	X	Paired against
#	Paired for	–	Announced against
+	Announced for	P	Voted "present"
N	Voted against (nay)		

C Voted "present" to avoid possible conflict of interest

? Did not vote or otherwise make a position known

Sen. Robert C. Byrd, D-W.Va., died June 28. The last vote for which he was eligible was vote 200.

IN THE SENATE | By Vote Number

205. **Coleman Nomination/Confirmation.** Confirmation of President Obama's nomination of Sharon Johnson Coleman of Illinois to be a judge for the U.S. District Court for the Northern District of Illinois. Confirmed 86-0: D 49-0; R 35-0; I 2-0. A "yea" was a vote in support of the president's position. July 12, 2010.

206. **HR 4173. Financial Regulatory Overhaul/Cloture.** Motion to invoke cloture (thus limiting debate) on the conference report on the bill that would overhaul the regulation of the financial services industry. The measure would create new regulatory mechanisms to assess risks posed by very large financial institutions and facilitate the orderly dissolution of failing businesses that pose a threat to the economy. It would create a new federal agency to oversee consumer financial products, bring the derivatives market under significant federal regulation for the first time and give company shareholders and regulators greater say on executive pay packages. The costs would be offset by terminating the Trouble Asset Relief Program and increasing deposit insurance premiums paid by some banks. Motion agreed to 60-38: D 55-1; R 3-37; I 2-0. Three-fifths of the total Senate (60) is required to invoke cloture. July 15, 2010.

207. **HR 4173. Financial Regulatory Overhaul/Motion to Waive.** Dodd, D-Conn., motion to waive the Budget Act and budget resolutions with respect to the Gregg, R-N.H., point of order against the conference report on the bill that would overhaul the regulation of the financial services industry. Motion agreed to 60-39: D 55-1; R 3-38; I 2-0. A three-fifths majority vote (60) of the total Senate is required to waive the Budget Act. July 15, 2010.

208. **HR 4173. Financial Regulatory Overhaul/Conference Report.** Adoption of the conference report on the bill that would overhaul the regulation of the financial services industry. The measure would create new regulatory mechanisms to assess risks posed by very large financial institutions and facilitate the orderly dissolution of failing companies that pose a threat to the economy. It would create a new federal agency to oversee consumer financial products, bring the derivatives market under significant federal regulation for the first time and give company shareholders and regulators greater say on executive pay packages. The costs would be offset by terminating the Troubled Asset Relief Program and increasing deposit insurance premiums paid by some banks. Adopted (thus cleared for the president) 60-39: D 55-1; R 3-38; I 2-0. A "yea" was a vote in support of the president's position. July 15, 2010.

209. **HR 4213. Unemployment Extension/Cloture.** Motion to invoke cloture (thus limiting debate) on the Reid, D-Nev., motion to concur in the House amendment to the Senate amendment with a further Reid substitute amendment that would extend eligibility for extended federal unemployment insurance until Nov. 30, applied retroactively to June 2. Motion agreed to 60-40: D 56-1; R 2-39; I 2-0. Three-fifths of the total Senate (60) is required to invoke cloture. (Previously, a Reid motion to reconsider was adopted by unanimous consent.) July 20, 2010.

	205	206	207	208	209
ALABAMA					
Shelby	Y	N	N	N	N
Sessions	?	N	N	N	N
ALASKA					
Murkowski	?	N	N	N	N
Begich	?	Y	Y	Y	Y
ARIZONA					
McCain	Y	N	N	N	N
Kyl	Y	N	N	N	N
ARKANSAS					
Lincoln	Y	Y	Y	Y	Y
Pryor	Y	Y	Y	Y	Y
CALIFORNIA					
Feinstein	Y	Y	Y	Y	Y
Boxer	Y	Y	Y	Y	Y
COLORADO					
Udall	Y	Y	Y	Y	Y
Bennet	Y	Y	Y	Y	Y
CONNECTICUT					
Dodd	Y	Y	Y	Y	Y
Lieberman	Y	Y	Y	Y	Y
DELAWARE					
Carper	Y	Y	Y	Y	Y
Kaufman	Y	Y	Y	Y	Y
FLORIDA					
Nelson	Y	Y	Y	Y	Y
LeMieux	?	N	N	N	N
GEORGIA					
Chambliss	Y	N	N	N	N
Isakson	Y	N	N	N	N
HAWAII					
Inouye	Y	Y	Y	Y	Y
Akaka	Y	Y	Y	Y	Y
IDAHO					
Crapo	Y	?	N	N	N
Risch	Y	N	N	N	N
ILLINOIS					
Durbin	Y	Y	Y	Y	Y
Burris	Y	Y	Y	Y	Y
INDIANA					
Lugar	Y	N	N	N	N
Bayh	Y	Y	Y	Y	Y
IOWA					
Grassley	Y	N	N	N	N
Harkin	Y	Y	Y	Y	Y
KANSAS					
Brownback	?	N	N	N	N
Roberts	?	N	N	N	N
KENTUCKY					
McConnell	Y	N	N	N	N
Bunning	Y	N	N	N	N
LOUISIANA					
Landrieu	?	Y	Y	Y	Y
Vitter	?	N	N	N	N
MAINE					
Snowe	Y	Y	Y	Y	Y
Collins	Y	Y	Y	Y	Y
MARYLAND					
Mikulski	?	Y	Y	Y	Y
Cardin	Y	Y	Y	Y	Y
MASSACHUSETTS					
Kerry	Y	Y	Y	Y	Y
Brown	Y	Y	Y	Y	N
MICHIGAN					
Levin	Y	Y	Y	Y	Y
Stabenow	Y	Y	Y	Y	Y
MINNESOTA					
Klobuchar	Y	Y	Y	Y	Y
Franken	Y	Y	Y	Y	Y
MISSISSIPPI					
Cochran	Y	N	N	N	N
Wicker	Y	N	N	N	N
MISSOURI					
Bond	Y	N	N	N	N
McCaskill	Y	Y	Y	Y	Y
MONTANA					
Baucus	Y	Y	Y	Y	Y
Tester	Y	Y	Y	Y	Y
NEBRASKA					
Nelson	Y	Y	Y	Y	N
Johanns	Y	N	N	N	N
NEVADA					
Reid	Y	Y	Y	Y	Y
Ensign	Y	N	N	N	N
NEW HAMPSHIRE					
Gregg	Y	N	N	N	N
Shaheen	?	Y	Y	Y	Y
NEW JERSEY					
Lautenberg	Y	Y	Y	Y	Y
Menendez	Y	Y	Y	Y	Y
NEW MEXICO					
Bingaman	Y	Y	Y	Y	Y
Udall	Y	Y	Y	Y	Y
NEW YORK					
Schumer	Y	Y	Y	Y	Y
Gillibrand	?	Y	Y	Y	Y
NORTH CAROLINA					
Burr	Y	N	N	N	N
Hagan	?	Y	Y	Y	Y
NORTH DAKOTA					
Conrad	Y	Y	Y	Y	Y
Dorgan	Y	Y	Y	Y	Y
OHIO					
Voinovich	Y	N	N	N	N
Brown	Y	Y	Y	Y	Y
OKLAHOMA					
Inhofe	Y	N	N	N	N
Coburn	Y	N	N	N	N
OREGON					
Wyden	Y	Y	Y	Y	Y
Merkley	Y	Y	Y	Y	Y
PENNSYLVANIA					
Specter	Y	Y	Y	Y	Y
Casey	Y	Y	Y	Y	Y
RHODE ISLAND					
Reed	Y	Y	Y	Y	Y
Whitehouse	Y	Y	Y	Y	Y
SOUTH CAROLINA					
Graham	Y	N	N	N	N
DeMint	Y	N	N	N	N
SOUTH DAKOTA					
Johnson	Y	Y	Y	Y	Y
Thune	Y	N	N	N	N
TENNESSEE					
Alexander	Y	N	N	N	N
Corker	Y	N	N	N	N
TEXAS					
Hutchison	Y	N	N	N	N
Cornyn	Y	N	N	N	N
UTAH					
Hatch	Y	N	N	N	N
Bennett	Y	N	N	N	N
VERMONT					
Leahy	Y	Y	Y	Y	Y
Sanders	Y	Y	Y	Y	Y
VIRGINIA					
Webb	Y	Y	Y	Y	Y
Warner	Y	Y	Y	Y	Y
WASHINGTON					
Murray	Y	Y	Y	Y	Y
Cantwell	Y	Y	Y	Y	Y
WEST VIRGINIA					
Rockefeller	Y	Y	Y	Y	Y
Goodwin *					Y
WISCONSIN					
Kohl	?	Y	Y	Y	Y
Feingold	Y	N	N	N	Y
WYOMING					
Enzi	Y	N	N	N	N
Barrasso	Y	N	N	N	N

KEY   **Republicans**   Democrats   *Independents*

Y	Voted for (yea)	X	Paired against	C Voted "present" to avoid possible conflict of interes
#	Paired for	–	Announced against	
+	Announced for	P	Voted "present"	? Did not vote or otherwise make a position known
N	Voted against (nay)			

*Sen. Carte P. Goodwin, D-W.Va., was sworn in July 20 to fill the seat vacated by the June 28 death of Democrat Robert C. Byrd. The first vote for which Goodwin was eligible was vote 209.

N THE SENATE | By Vote Number

210. **HR 4213. Unemployment Extension/Offsets.** Brown, R-Mass., motion to suspend Rule 22 to permit the consideration of a Brown substitute amendment that would extend eligibility for extended federal unemployment insurance until Nov. 30, applied retroactively to June 2. It would be offset with funds from the 2010 economic stimulus law. Motion rejected 42-56: D 2-54; R 40-0; I 0-2. A two-thirds majority of senators voting (66 in this case), a quorum being present, is required to suspend Rule 22. July 21, 2010.

211. **HR 4213. Unemployment Extension/Offsets.** Coburn, R-Okla., motion to suspend Rule 22 to permit the consideration of a Coburn motion to commit the bill to the Finance Committee with instructions that it be reported back with language that would offset the cost of the unemployment insurance provisions through government spending reductions and revenue from the sale of surplus federal property. Motion rejected 49-49: D 9-47; R 40-0; I 0-2. A two-thirds majority of senators voting (66 in this case), a quorum being present, is required to suspend Rule 22. July 21, 2010.

212. **HR 4213. Unemployment Extension/Spending Posting Requirement.** Coburn, R-Okla., motion to suspend Rule 22 to permit the consideration of a Coburn amendment that would require prominent display on the Senate's website of the amount of spending that has been exempted from pay-as-you-go budgetary requirements, the amount authorized in Senate-passed legislation and the number of government programs created by Senate-passed bills. It also would require the Senate to post the number of new government programs created by Senate-passed legislation and the net spending authorized in legislation passed after 2009, as scored by the Congressional Budget Office. Motion rejected 44-44: D 14-42; R 40-0; I 0-2. A two-thirds majority of senators voting (66 in this case), a quorum being present, is required to suspend Rule 22. July 21, 2010.

213. **HR 4213. Unemployment Extension/Estate Tax Repeal.** DeMint, R-S.C., motion to suspend Rule 22 to permit the consideration of a DeMint motion to commit the bill to the Finance Committee with instructions that it be reported back with language that would provide for a permanent repeal of the estate tax. Motion rejected 39-59: D 2-54; R 37-3; I 0-2. A two-thirds majority of senators voting (66 in this case), a quorum being present, is required to suspend Rule 22. July 21, 2010.

214. **HR 4213. Unemployment Extension/Arizona Immigration Law.** DeMint, R-S.C., motion to suspend Rule 22 to permit the consideration of a DeMint motion to commit the bill to the Judiciary Committee with instructions that it be reported back with language that would provide that no funds may be used for any federal legal action to invalidate certain Arizona state immigration laws. Motion rejected 43-55: D 5-51; R 38-2; I 0-2. A two-thirds majority of senators voting (66 in this case), a quorum being present, is required to suspend Rule 22. July 21, 2010.

215. **HR 4213. Unemployment Extension/Motion to Concur.** Reid, D-Nev., motion to concur in the House amendment to the Senate amendment with a further Reid substitute amendment that would extend eligibility for extended federal unemployment insurance until Nov. 30, 2010, applied retroactively to June 2. Motion agreed to 59-39: D 55-1; R 2-38; I 2-0. A "yea" was a vote in support of the president's position. July 21, 2010.

	210	211	212	213	214	215
ALABAMA						
Shelby	Y	Y	Y	Y	Y	N
Sessions	Y	Y	Y	Y	Y	N
ALASKA						
Murkowski	Y	Y	Y	Y	Y	N
Begich	N	N	N	N	N	Y
ARIZONA						
McCain	Y	Y	Y	Y	Y	N
Kyl	Y	Y	Y	Y	Y	N
ARKANSAS						
Lincoln	Y	Y	Y	Y	Y	Y
Pryor	N	Y	Y	N	Y	Y
CALIFORNIA						
Feinstein	N	N	N	N	N	Y
Boxer	N	N	N	N	N	Y
COLORADO						
Udall	N	N	N	N	N	Y
Bennet	N	N	N	N	N	Y
CONNECTICUT						
Dodd	N	N	N	N	N	Y
Lieberman	N	N	N	N	N	Y
DELAWARE						
Carper	N	N	N	N	N	Y
Kaufman	N	N	N	N	N	Y
FLORIDA						
Nelson	N	Y	N	N	Y	Y
LeMieux	Y	Y	Y	Y	Y	N
GEORGIA						
Chambliss	Y	Y	Y	Y	Y	N
Isakson	Y	Y	Y	Y	Y	N
HAWAII						
Inouye	N	N	N	N	N	Y
Akaka	N	N	N	N	N	Y
IDAHO						
Crapo	Y	Y	Y	Y	Y	N
Risch	Y	Y	Y	Y	Y	N
ILLINOIS						
Durbin	N	N	N	N	N	Y
Burris	N	N	N	N	N	Y
INDIANA						
Lugar	Y	Y	Y	Y	Y	N
Bayh	?	?	?	?	?	?
IOWA						
Grassley	Y	Y	Y	Y	Y	N
Harkin	N	N	N	N	N	Y
KANSAS						
Brownback	Y	Y	Y	Y	Y	N
Roberts	Y	Y	Y	Y	Y	N
KENTUCKY						
McConnell	Y	Y	Y	Y	Y	N
Bunning	Y	Y	Y	Y	Y	N
LOUISIANA						
Landrieu	N	N	N	N	N	Y
Vitter	?	?	?	?	?	?
MAINE						
Snowe	Y	Y	Y	N	Y	Y
Collins	Y	Y	Y	N	Y	Y
MARYLAND						
Mikulski	N	N	N	N	N	Y
Cardin	N	N	N	N	N	Y
MASSACHUSETTS						
Kerry	N	N	N	N	N	Y
Brown	Y	Y	Y	Y	Y	N
MICHIGAN						
Levin	N	N	N	N	N	Y
Stabenow	N	N	N	N	N	Y
MINNESOTA						
Klobuchar	N	N	N	N	N	Y
Franken	N	N	N	N	N	Y
MISSISSIPPI						
Cochran	Y	Y	Y	Y	Y	N
Wicker	Y	Y	Y	Y	Y	N
MISSOURI						
Bond	Y	Y	Y	Y	Y	N
McCaskill	N	N	N	N	N	Y
MONTANA						
Baucus	N	N	N	N	Y	Y
Tester	N	Y	Y	N	Y	Y
NEBRASKA						
Nelson	Y	Y	Y	Y	Y	N
Johanns	Y	Y	Y	Y	N	N
NEVADA						
Reid	N	N	N	N	N	Y
Ensign	Y	Y	Y	Y	Y	N
NEW HAMPSHIRE						
Gregg	Y	Y	Y	Y	Y	N
Shaheen	N	N	N	N	N	Y
NEW JERSEY						
Lautenberg	N	N	N	N	N	Y
Menendez	N	N	N	N	N	Y
NEW MEXICO						
Bingaman	N	N	N	N	N	Y
Udall	N	N	N	N	N	Y
NEW YORK						
Schumer	N	N	N	N	N	Y
Gillibrand	N	N	N	N	N	Y
NORTH CAROLINA						
Burr	Y	Y	Y	Y	Y	N
Hagan	N	Y	Y	N	N	Y
NORTH DAKOTA						
Conrad	N	N	N	N	N	Y
Dorgan	N	N	N	N	N	Y
OHIO						
Voinovich	Y	Y	Y	N	N	N
Brown	N	N	N	N	N	Y
OKLAHOMA						
Inhofe	Y	Y	Y	Y	Y	N
Coburn	Y	Y	Y	Y	Y	N
OREGON						
Wyden	N	Y	N	N	N	Y
Merkley	N	N	N	N	N	Y
PENNSYLVANIA						
Specter	N	N	N	N	N	Y
Casey	N	N	N	N	N	Y
RHODE ISLAND						
Reed	N	N	N	N	N	Y
Whitehouse	N	N	N	N	N	Y
SOUTH CAROLINA						
Graham	Y	Y	Y	Y	Y	N
DeMint	Y	Y	Y	Y	Y	N
SOUTH DAKOTA						
Johnson	N	N	N	N	N	Y
Thune	Y	Y	Y	Y	Y	N
TENNESSEE						
Alexander	Y	Y	Y	Y	Y	N
Corker	Y	Y	Y	Y	Y	N
TEXAS						
Hutchison	Y	Y	Y	Y	Y	N
Cornyn	Y	Y	Y	Y	Y	N
UTAH						
Hatch	Y	Y	Y	Y	Y	N
Bennett	Y	Y	Y	Y	Y	N
VERMONT						
Leahy	N	N	N	N	N	Y
Sanders	N	N	N	N	N	Y
VIRGINIA						
Webb	N	Y	Y	N	N	Y
Warner	N	Y	Y	N	N	Y
WASHINGTON						
Murray	N	Y	Y	N	N	Y
Cantwell	N	Y	Y	N	N	Y
WEST VIRGINIA						
Rockefeller	N	N	N	N	N	Y
Goodwin	N	N	N	N	N	Y
WISCONSIN						
Kohl	N	N	N	N	N	Y
Feingold	N	Y	Y	N	N	Y
WYOMING						
Enzi	Y	Y	Y	Y	Y	N
Barrasso	Y	Y	Y	Y	Y	N

KEY   **Republicans**   Democrats   *Independents*

Y	Voted for (yea)	X Paired against	C Voted "present" to avoid possible conflict of interest
#	Paired for	– Announced against	
+	Announced for	P Voted "present"	? Did not vote or otherwise make a position known
N	Voted against (nay)		

IN THE SENATE | By Vote Number

216. **H J Res 83. Myanmar Sanctions/Passage.** Passage of the joint resolution that would extend for one year, through July 2011, import restrictions on products from Myanmar, formerly known as Burma, until the president certifies that the Myanmar government has made significant progress toward instituting democracy and ending human rights violations. Passed (thus cleared for the president) 99-1: D 57-0; R 40-1; I 2-0. July 22, 2010.

217. **S Res 591. Americans With Disabilities Act Anniversary/Adoption.** Adoption of the resolution that would recognize and honor the 20th anniversary of enactment of the Americans with Disabilities Act of 1990. Adopted 100-0: D 57-0; R 41-0; I 2-0. July 22, 2010.

218. **HR 5297. Small-Business Lending Fund/Cloture.** Motion to invoke cloture (thus limiting debate) on the LeMieux, R-Fla., amendment to the Baucus, D-Mont., substitute amendment. The LeMieux amendment would establish a $30 billion small-business lending fund administered by the Treasury Department. The substitute would make a variety of small-business tax changes, including a revival of an expired bonus depreciation provision to allow companies to write off assets more quickly. Motion agreed to 60-37: D 56-0; R 2-37; I 2-0. Three-fifths of the total Senate (60) is required to invoke cloture. July 22, 2010.

219. **HR 4899. Supplemental Appropriations/Cloture.** Motion to invoke cloture (thus limiting debate) on the Reid, D-Nev., motion to concur in the House amendment to the Senate amendment to the bill that would provide $58.8 billion in supplemental funds for fiscal 2010, mainly to fund military operations in Iraq and Afghanistan. The House amendment also would provide $22.8 billion in additional domestic spending. Motion rejected 46-51: D 45-11; R 0-39; I 1-1. Three-fifths of the total Senate (60) is required to invoke cloture. (Subsequently, the Senate agreed to a motion to disagree to the House amendment by unanimous consent.) July 22, 2010.

220. **S 3628. Campaign Finance Disclosure/Cloture.** Motion to invoke cloture (thus limiting debate) on the motion to proceed to the bill that would require corporations and unions to disclose in their campaign advertising the chief donors who paid for the ad. Motion rejected 57-41: D 56-1; R 0-40; I 1-0. Three-fifths of the total Senate (60) is required to invoke cloture. A "yea" was a vote in support of the president's position. July 27, 2010.

221. **HR 5297. Small-Business Tax and Lending/Cloture.** Motion to invoke cloture (thus limiting debate) on Reid, D-Nev., substitute amendment that would provide small-business tax initiatives and authorize a $30 billion small-business lending fund. Motion rejected 58-42: D 56-1; R 0-41; I 2-0. Three-fifths of the total Senate (60) is required to invoke cloture. (At the conclusion of the vote, Reid entered a motion to reconsider the vote.) A "yea" was a vote in support of the president's position. July 29, 2010.

222. **Procedural Motion/Require Attendance.** Reid, D-Nev., motion to instruct the sergeant at arms to request the attendance of absent senators. Motion agreed to 70-23: D 56-0; R 12-23; I 2-0. July 29, 2010.

	216	217	218	219	220	221	222
ALABAMA							
Shelby	Y	Y	N	N	N	N	Y
Sessions	Y	Y	N	N	N	N	N
ALASKA							
Murkowski	Y	Y	N	N	N	N	N
Begich	Y	Y	Y	N	Y	Y	Y
ARIZONA							
McCain	Y	Y	N	N	N	N	N
Kyl	Y	Y	N	N	N	N	N
ARKANSAS							
Lincoln	Y	Y	Y	Y	Y	Y	Y
Pryor	Y	Y	Y	N	Y	Y	Y
CALIFORNIA							
Feinstein	Y	Y	Y	Y	Y	Y	Y
Boxer	Y	Y	Y	Y	Y	Y	Y
COLORADO							
Udall	Y	Y	Y	N	Y	Y	Y
Bennet	Y	Y	Y	N	Y	Y	Y
CONNECTICUT							
Dodd	Y	Y	Y	Y	Y	Y	Y
Lieberman	Y	Y	Y	?	Y	Y	Y
DELAWARE							
Carper	Y	Y	Y	N	Y	Y	Y
Kaufman	Y	Y	Y	Y	Y	Y	Y
FLORIDA							
Nelson	Y	Y	Y	Y	Y	Y	Y
LeMieux	Y	Y	Y	N	N	N	N
GEORGIA							
Chambliss	Y	Y	N	N	N	N	N
Isakson	Y	Y	N	N	N	N	Y
HAWAII							
Inouye	Y	Y	Y	Y	Y	Y	Y
Akaka	Y	Y	Y	Y	Y	Y	Y
IDAHO							
Crapo	Y	Y	N	N	N	N	N
Risch	Y	Y	N	N	N	N	N
ILLINOIS							
Durbin	Y	Y	Y	Y	Y	Y	Y
Burris	Y	Y	Y	Y	Y	Y	Y
INDIANA							
Lugar	Y	Y	N	N	N	N	Y
Bayh	Y	Y	Y	N	Y	Y	Y
IOWA							
Grassley	Y	Y	N	N	N	N	Y
Harkin	Y	Y	Y	Y	Y	Y	Y
KANSAS							
Brownback	Y	Y	N	N	N	N	?
Roberts	Y	Y	N	N	N	N	N
KENTUCKY							
McConnell	Y	Y	N	N	N	N	N
Bunning	Y	Y	N	N	N	N	N
LOUISIANA							
Landrieu	Y	Y	Y	N	Y	Y	Y
Vitter	Y	Y	N	N	N	N	N
MAINE							
Snowe	Y	Y	N	N	N	N	N
Collins	Y	Y	N	N	N	N	N
MARYLAND							
Mikulski	Y	Y	Y	Y	Y	Y	Y
Cardin	Y	Y	Y	Y	Y	Y	Y
MASSACHUSETTS							
Kerry	Y	Y	Y	Y	Y	Y	Y
Brown	Y	Y	N	N	N	N	Y
MICHIGAN							
Levin	Y	Y	Y	Y	Y	Y	Y
Stabenow	Y	Y	Y	Y	Y	Y	Y
MINNESOTA							
Klobuchar	Y	Y	Y	Y	Y	Y	Y
Franken	Y	Y	Y	Y	Y	Y	Y
MISSISSIPPI							
Cochran	Y	Y	N	N	N	N	N
Wicker	Y	Y	N	N	N	N	N
MISSOURI							
Bond	Y	Y	?	?	N	N	N
McCaskill	Y	Y	N	Y	N	Y	Y

	216	217	218	219	220	221
MONTANA						
Baucus	Y	Y	Y	Y	Y	Y
Tester	Y	Y	Y	Y	Y	Y
NEBRASKA						
Nelson	Y	Y	Y	Y	Y	Y
Johanns	Y	Y	N	N	N	N
NEVADA						
Reid	Y	Y	Y	Y	N	N
Ensign	Y	Y	N	N	?	N
NEW HAMPSHIRE						
Gregg	Y	Y	N	N	N	N
Shaheen	Y	Y	Y	Y	Y	Y
NEW JERSEY						
Lautenberg	Y	Y	Y	Y	Y	Y
Menendez	Y	Y	Y	Y	Y	Y
NEW MEXICO						
Bingaman	Y	Y	Y	Y	Y	Y
Udall	Y	Y	Y	Y	Y	Y
NEW YORK						
Schumer	Y	Y	Y	Y	Y	Y
Gillibrand	Y	Y	Y	Y	Y	Y
NORTH CAROLINA						
Burr	Y	Y	N	N	N	N
Hagan	Y	Y	Y	Y	Y	Y
NORTH DAKOTA						
Conrad	Y	Y	Y	Y	Y	Y
Dorgan	Y	Y	Y	Y	Y	Y
OHIO						
Voinovich	Y	Y	N	N	N	N
Brown	Y	Y	Y	Y	Y	Y
OKLAHOMA						
Inhofe	Y	Y	N	N	N	N
Coburn	Y	Y	N	N	N	N
OREGON						
Wyden	Y	Y	Y	Y	Y	Y
Merkley	Y	Y	Y	Y	Y	Y
PENNSYLVANIA						
Specter	Y	Y	Y	Y	Y	Y
Casey	Y	Y	Y	Y	Y	Y
RHODE ISLAND						
Reed	Y	Y	Y	Y	Y	Y
Whitehouse	Y	Y	Y	Y	Y	Y
SOUTH CAROLINA						
Graham	Y	Y	N	N	N	N
DeMint	Y	Y	-	-	N	N
SOUTH DAKOTA						
Johnson	Y	Y	Y	Y	Y	Y
Thune	Y	Y	N	N	N	N
TENNESSEE						
Alexander	Y	Y	N	N	N	N
Corker	Y	Y	N	N	N	N
TEXAS						
Hutchison	Y	Y	N	N	N	N
Cornyn	Y	Y	N	N	N	N
UTAH						
Hatch	Y	Y	N	N	N	N
Bennett	Y	Y	N	N	N	N
VERMONT						
Leahy	Y	Y	?	?	Y	Y
Sanders	Y	Y	Y	Y	Y	Y
VIRGINIA						
Webb	Y	Y	Y	N	Y	Y
Warner	Y	Y	Y	N	Y	Y
WASHINGTON						
Murray	Y	Y	Y	Y	Y	Y
Cantwell	Y	Y	Y	Y	Y	Y
WEST VIRGINIA						
Rockefeller	Y	Y	Y	Y	Y	Y
Goodwin	Y	Y	Y	Y	Y	Y
WISCONSIN						
Kohl	Y	Y	Y	Y	Y	Y
Feingold	Y	Y	Y	Y	Y	Y
WYOMING						
Enzi	N	Y	N	N	N	N
Barrasso	Y	Y	N	N	N	N

KEY   **Republicans**   Democrats   *Independents*

Y Voted for (yea)	X Paired against	C Voted "present" to avoid possible conflict of interes
# Paired for	– Announced against	
+ Announced for	P Voted "present"	? Did not vote or otherwise make a position known
N Voted against (nay)		

N THE SENATE | By Vote Number

223. HR 1586. Medicaid and Education Assistance/Motion to Table. Reid, D-Nev., motion to table (kill) the Reid motion to concur in the House amendment to the Senate amendment with a further Murray, D-Wash., substitute amendment that would provide $16.1 billion for an extension of expanded Medicaid assistance to states and $10 billion in funding for states to create or retain teachers' jobs. Motion agreed to 5-0: D 57-0; R 36-0; I 2-0. Aug. 2, 2010.

224. HR 1586. Medicaid and Education Assistance/Cloture. Motion to invoke cloture (thus limiting debate) on the Reid, D-Nev., motion to concur in the House amendment to the Senate amendment with a further Murray, D-Wash., substitute amendment that would provide 16.1 billion for an extension of expanded Medicaid assistance to states and $10 billion in funding for states to create or retain teachers' jobs. Motion agreed to 61-38: D 57-0; R 2-38; I 2-0. Three-fifths of the total Senate (60) is required to invoke cloture. Aug. 4, 2010.

225. HR 1586. Medicaid and Education Assistance/Motion to Waive. Murray, D-Wash., motion to waive the Budget Act and budget resolutions with respect to the Gregg, R-N.H., point of order against the Reid, D-Nev., motion to concur in the House amendment to the Senate amendment with the further Murray substitute amendment. Motion agreed to 61-38: D 57-0; R 2-38; I 2-0. A three-fifths majority vote (60) of the total Senate is required to waive the Budget Act. Aug. 4, 2010.

226. HR 1586. Medicaid and Education Assistance/Individual Income Taxes. DeMint, R-S.C., motion to suspend Rule 22 to permit the consideration of a DeMint motion to commit the bill to the Finance Committee with instructions that it be reported back with language that would provide for a permanent extension of 2010 individual income tax rates, offset with spending reductions. Motion rejected 42-58: D 2-55; R 40-1; I 0-2. A two-thirds majority of senators voting (67 in this case), a quorum being present, is required to suspend Rule 22. A "nay" was a vote in support of the president's position. Aug. 5, 2010.

227. HR 1586. Medicaid and Education Assistance/Small-Business Taxes. DeMint, R-S.C., motion to suspend Rule 22 to permit the consideration of a DeMint motion to commit the bill to the Finance Committee with instructions that it be reported back with language that would provide for a permanent extension of the small-business tax rates in effect in 2010, offset with spending reductions. Motion rejected 2-58: D 2-55; R 40-1; I 0-2. A two-thirds majority of senators voting (67 in this case), a quorum being present, is required to suspend Rule 22. Aug. 5, 2010.

228. HR 1586. Medicaid and Education Assistance/Motion to Concur. Reid, D-Nev., motion to concur in the House amendment to the Senate amendment with the further Murray, D-Wash., substitute amendment that would provide $16.1 billion to extend increased Medicaid assistance to states and $10 billion in funding for states to create or retain teachers' jobs. The costs would be offset by changing foreign tax provisions, ending increased food stamp benefits beginning in April 2014 and rescinding previously enacted spending. Motion agreed to 61-39: D 57-0; R 2-39; I 2-0. A "yea" was a vote in support of the president's position. Aug. 5, 2010.

229. Kagan Nomination/Confirmation. Confirmation of President Obama's nomination of Elena Kagan of Massachusetts to be an associate justice of the U.S. Supreme Court. Confirmed 63-37: D 56-1; R 5-36; I 2-0. A "yea" was a vote in support of the president's position. Aug. 5, 2010.

	223	224	225	226	227	228	229
ALABAMA							
Shelby	Y	N	N	Y	Y	N	N
Sessions	Y	N	N	Y	Y	N	N
ALASKA							
Murkowski	+	N	N	Y	Y	N	N
Begich	Y	Y	Y	N	N	Y	Y
ARIZONA							
McCain	Y	N	N	Y	Y	N	N
Kyl	Y	N	N	Y	Y	N	N
ARKANSAS							
Lincoln	Y	Y	Y	Y	Y	Y	Y
Pryor	Y	Y	Y	N	N	Y	Y
CALIFORNIA							
Feinstein	Y	Y	Y	N	N	Y	Y
Boxer	Y	Y	Y	N	N	Y	Y
COLORADO							
Udall	Y	Y	Y	N	N	Y	Y
Bennet	Y	Y	Y	N	N	Y	Y
CONNECTICUT							
Dodd	Y	Y	Y	N	N	Y	Y
Lieberman	Y	Y	Y	N	N	Y	Y
DELAWARE							
Carper	Y	Y	Y	N	N	Y	Y
Kaufman	Y	Y	Y	N	N	Y	Y
FLORIDA							
Nelson	Y	Y	Y	N	N	Y	Y
LeMieux	Y	N	N	Y	Y	N	N
GEORGIA							
Chambliss	?	N	N	Y	Y	N	N
Isakson	Y	N	N	Y	Y	N	N
HAWAII							
Inouye	Y	Y	Y	N	N	Y	Y
Akaka	Y	Y	Y	N	N	Y	Y
IDAHO							
Crapo	Y	N	N	Y	Y	N	N
Risch	Y	N	N	Y	Y	N	N
ILLINOIS							
Durbin	Y	Y	Y	N	N	Y	Y
Burris	Y	Y	Y	N	N	Y	Y
INDIANA							
Lugar	Y	N	N	Y	N	Y	Y
Bayh	Y	Y	Y	N	N	Y	Y
IOWA							
Grassley	Y	N	N	Y	Y	N	N
Harkin	Y	Y	Y	N	N	Y	Y
KANSAS							
Brownback	Y	N	N	Y	Y	N	N
Roberts	Y	N	N	Y	Y	N	N
KENTUCKY							
McConnell	Y	N	N	Y	Y	N	N
Bunning	Y	N	N	Y	Y	N	N
LOUISIANA							
Landrieu	Y	Y	Y	N	N	Y	Y
Vitter	?	?	?	Y	Y	N	N
MAINE							
Snowe	Y	Y	Y	Y	Y	Y	Y
Collins	Y	Y	Y	Y	Y	Y	Y
MARYLAND							
Mikulski	Y	Y	Y	N	N	Y	Y
Cardin	Y	Y	Y	N	N	Y	Y
MASSACHUSETTS							
Kerry	Y	Y	Y	N	N	Y	Y
Brown	Y	N	N	Y	Y	N	N
MICHIGAN							
Levin	Y	Y	Y	N	N	Y	Y
Stabenow	Y	Y	Y	N	N	Y	Y
MINNESOTA							
Klobuchar	Y	Y	Y	N	N	Y	Y
Franken	Y	Y	Y	N	N	Y	Y
MISSISSIPPI							
Cochran	Y	N	N	Y	Y	N	N
Wicker	Y	N	N	Y	Y	N	N
MISSOURI							
Bond	Y	N	N	Y	Y	N	N
McCaskill	Y	Y	Y	N	N	Y	Y
MONTANA							
Baucus	Y	Y	Y	N	N	Y	Y
Tester	Y	Y	Y	N	N	Y	Y
NEBRASKA							
Nelson	Y	Y	Y	Y	Y	Y	N
Johanns	Y	N	N	Y	Y	N	N
NEVADA							
Reid	Y	Y	Y	N	N	Y	Y
Ensign	Y	N	N	Y	Y	N	N
NEW HAMPSHIRE							
Gregg	?	N	N	Y	Y	N	Y
Shaheen	Y	Y	Y	N	N	Y	Y
NEW JERSEY							
Lautenberg	Y	Y	Y	N	N	Y	Y
Menendez	Y	Y	Y	N	N	Y	Y
NEW MEXICO							
Bingaman	Y	Y	Y	N	N	Y	Y
Udall	Y	Y	Y	N	N	Y	Y
NEW YORK							
Schumer	Y	Y	Y	N	N	Y	Y
Gillibrand	Y	Y	Y	N	N	Y	Y
NORTH CAROLINA							
Burr	Y	N	N	Y	Y	N	N
Hagan	Y	Y	Y	N	N	Y	Y
NORTH DAKOTA							
Conrad	Y	Y	Y	N	N	Y	Y
Dorgan	Y	Y	Y	N	N	Y	Y
OHIO							
Voinovich	Y	N	N	N	N	N	N
Brown	Y	Y	Y	N	N	Y	Y
OKLAHOMA							
Inhofe	Y	N	N	Y	Y	N	N
Coburn	?	N	N	Y	Y	N	N
OREGON							
Wyden	Y	Y	Y	N	N	Y	Y
Merkley	Y	Y	Y	N	N	Y	Y
PENNSYLVANIA							
Specter	Y	Y	Y	N	N	Y	Y
Casey	Y	Y	Y	N	N	Y	Y
RHODE ISLAND							
Reed	Y	Y	Y	N	N	Y	Y
Whitehouse	Y	Y	Y	N	N	Y	Y
SOUTH CAROLINA							
Graham	Y	N	N	Y	N	Y	Y
DeMint	Y	N	N	Y	Y	N	N
SOUTH DAKOTA							
Johnson	Y	Y	Y	N	N	Y	Y
Thune	Y	N	N	Y	Y	N	N
TENNESSEE							
Alexander	Y	N	N	Y	Y	N	N
Corker	Y	N	N	Y	Y	N	N
TEXAS							
Hutchison	Y	N	N	Y	Y	N	N
Cornyn	Y	N	N	Y	Y	N	N
UTAH							
Hatch	Y	N	N	Y	Y	N	N
Bennett	Y	N	N	Y	Y	N	N
VERMONT							
Leahy	Y	Y	Y	N	N	Y	Y
Sanders	Y	Y	Y	N	N	Y	Y
VIRGINIA							
Webb	Y	Y	Y	N	N	Y	Y
Warner	Y	Y	Y	N	N	Y	Y
WASHINGTON							
Murray	Y	Y	Y	N	N	Y	Y
Cantwell	Y	Y	Y	N	N	Y	Y
WEST VIRGINIA							
Rockefeller	Y	Y	Y	N	N	Y	Y
Goodwin	Y	Y	Y	N	N	Y	Y
WISCONSIN							
Kohl	Y	Y	Y	N	N	Y	Y
Feingold	Y	Y	Y	N	N	Y	Y
WYOMING							
Enzi	Y	N	N	Y	Y	N	N
Barrasso	Y	N	N	Y	Y	N	N

KEY	**Republicans**		Democrats	*Independents*		
Y	Voted for (yea)		X	Paired against	C	Voted "present" to avoid possible conflict of interest
#	Paired for		–	Announced against		
+	Announced for		P	Voted "present"	?	Did not vote or otherwise make a position known
N	Voted against (nay)					

IN THE SENATE | By Vote Number

230. Stranch Nomination/Confirmation. Confirmation of President Obama's nomination of Jane Branstetter Stranch of Tennessee to be a judge for the 6th U.S. Circuit Court of Appeals. Confirmed 71-21: D 53-0; R 16-21; I 2-0. A "yea" was a vote in support of the president's position. Sept. 13, 2010.

231. HR 5297. Small-Business Tax and Lending/Cloture. Motion to invoke cloture (thus limiting debate) on the Johanns, R-Neb., amendment to the Nelson, D-Fla., amendment to the Baucus, D-Mont., and Landrieu, D-La., substitute amendment. The Johanns amendment would repeal a tax information-reporting requirement from the 2010 health care overhaul law, offset by increasing the affordability exemption to the individual mandate in the health care law and cutting funding allocated for prevention programs. The Nelson amendment would exempt businesses with fewer than 25 employees from the tax compliance provision in the health care law and raise the reporting threshold for the remaining companies from $600 to $5,000. The substitute would provide a variety of small-business tax initiatives, including reviving an expired bonus depreciation provision, and would authorize a small-business lending fund. Motion rejected 46-52: D 7-50; R 39-0; I 0-2. Three-fifths of the total Senate (60) is required to invoke cloture. Sept. 14, 2010.

232. HR 5297. Small-Business Tax and Lending/Cloture. Motion to invoke cloture (thus limiting debate) on the Nelson, D-Fla., amendment to the Baucus, D-Mont., and Landrieu, D-La., substitute amendment. The Nelson amendment would exempt businesses with fewer than 25 employees from the tax compliance provision in the 2010 health care overhaul law and would raise the reporting threshold for the remaining companies from $600 to $5,000. It also would exempt credit card purchases and give the Treasury Department more flexibility in implementing the reporting requirements. It would be offset by eliminating a 6 percent tax deduction for certain oil companies. Motion rejected 56-42: D 54-3; R 0-39; I 2-0. Three-fifths of the total Senate (60) is required to invoke cloture. Sept. 14, 2010.

233. HR 5297. Small-Business Tax and Lending/Cloture. Motion to invoke cloture (thus limiting debate) on the Baucus, D-Mont., and Landrieu, D-La., substitute amendment. The substitute would provide a variety of small-business tax initiatives, including reviving an expired bonus depreciation provision, and authorize a small-business lending fund. It would be offset with increased penalties for failing to file information returns, new limits on papermakers' ability to claim a biofuel tax credit and new rules on tax-delinquent federal contractors. Motion agreed to 61-37: D 57-0; R 2-37; I 2-0. Three-fifths of the total Senate (60) is required to invoke cloture. (Subsequently, the substitute was adopted by voice vote.) Sept. 14, 2010.

	230	231	232	233
ALABAMA				
Shelby	Y	Y	N	N
Sessions	Y	Y	N	N
ALASKA				
Murkowski	?	?	?	?
Begich	Y	N	N	Y
ARIZONA				
McCain	Y	Y	N	N
Kyl	N	Y	N	N
ARKANSAS				
Lincoln	Y	Y	N	Y
Pryor	Y	Y	Y	Y
CALIFORNIA				
Feinstein	Y	N	Y	Y
Boxer	Y	N	Y	Y
COLORADO				
Udall	+	N	Y	Y
Bennet	Y	Y	Y	Y
CONNECTICUT				
Dodd	Y	N	Y	Y
Lieberman	Y	N	Y	Y
DELAWARE				
Carper	Y	N	Y	Y
Kaufman	Y	N	Y	Y
FLORIDA				
Nelson	Y	N	Y	Y
LeMieux	Y	Y	N	Y
GEORGIA				
Chambliss	N	Y	N	N
Isakson	N	Y	N	N
HAWAII				
Inouye	Y	N	Y	Y
Akaka	Y	N	Y	Y
IDAHO				
Crapo	N	Y	N	N
Risch	N	Y	N	N
ILLINOIS				
Durbin	Y	N	Y	Y
Burris	Y	N	Y	Y
INDIANA				
Lugar	Y	Y	N	N
Bayh	?	Y	Y	Y
IOWA				
Grassley	N	Y	N	N
Harkin	Y	N	Y	Y
KANSAS				
Brownback	?	Y	N	N
Roberts	N	Y	N	N
KENTUCKY				
McConnell	N	Y	N	N
Bunning	N	Y	N	N
LOUISIANA				
Landrieu	Y	N	N	Y
Vitter	N	Y	N	N
MAINE				
Snowe	Y	Y	N	N
Collins	Y	Y	N	N
MARYLAND				
Mikulski	?	N	Y	Y
Cardin	Y	N	Y	Y
MASSACHUSETTS				
Kerry	Y	N	Y	Y
Brown	Y	Y	N	N
MICHIGAN				
Levin	Y	N	Y	Y
Stabenow	Y	N	Y	Y
MINNESOTA				
Klobuchar	Y	N	Y	Y
Franken	Y	N	Y	Y
MISSISSIPPI				
Cochran	Y	Y	N	N
Wicker	N	Y	N	N
MISSOURI				
Bond	N	Y	N	N
McCaskill	Y	N	Y	Y

	230	231	232	233
MONTANA				
Baucus	+	N	Y	Y
Tester	Y	N	Y	Y
NEBRASKA				
Nelson	Y	Y	Y	Y
Johanns	Y	Y	N	N
NEVADA				
Reid	Y	N	Y	Y
Ensign	N	Y	N	N
NEW HAMPSHIRE				
Gregg	?	?	?	?
Shaheen	Y	N	Y	Y
NEW JERSEY				
Lautenberg	Y	N	Y	Y
Menendez	Y	N	Y	Y
NEW MEXICO				
Bingaman	Y	N	Y	Y
Udall	Y	N	Y	Y
NEW YORK				
Schumer	Y	N	Y	Y
Gillibrand	Y	N	Y	Y
NORTH CAROLINA				
Burr	N	Y	N	N
Hagan	Y	N	Y	Y
NORTH DAKOTA				
Conrad	Y	N	Y	Y
Dorgan	Y	N	Y	Y
OHIO				
Voinovich	Y	Y	N	Y
Brown	Y	N	Y	Y
OKLAHOMA				
Inhofe	N	Y	N	N
Coburn	N	Y	N	N
OREGON				
Wyden	Y	N	Y	Y
Merkley	Y	N	Y	Y
PENNSYLVANIA				
Specter	Y	N	Y	Y
Casey	Y	N	Y	Y
RHODE ISLAND				
Reed	Y	N	Y	Y
Whitehouse	Y	N	Y	Y
SOUTH CAROLINA				
Graham	Y	Y	N	N
DeMint	N	Y	N	N
SOUTH DAKOTA				
Johnson	Y	N	Y	Y
Thune	N	Y	N	N
TENNESSEE				
Alexander	Y	Y	N	N
Corker	Y	Y	N	N
TEXAS				
Hutchison	N	Y	N	N
Cornyn	N	Y	N	N
UTAH				
Hatch	Y	Y	N	N
Bennett	Y	Y	N	N
VERMONT				
Leahy	Y	N	Y	Y
Sanders	Y	N	Y	Y
VIRGINIA				
Webb	Y	Y	Y	Y
Warner	Y	Y	Y	Y
WASHINGTON				
Murray	Y	N	Y	Y
Cantwell	Y	N	Y	Y
WEST VIRGINIA				
Rockefeller	Y	N	Y	Y
Goodwin	Y	N	Y	Y
WISCONSIN				
Kohl	Y	N	Y	Y
Feingold	Y	N	Y	Y
WYOMING				
Enzi	?	Y	N	N
Barrasso	N	Y	N	N

KEY	**Republicans**	Democrats	*Independents*	
Y Voted for (yea)		X Paired against		C Voted "present" to avoid possible conflict of interes
# Paired for		– Announced against		
+ Announced for		P Voted "present"		? Did not vote or otherwise make a position known
N Voted against (nay)				

IN THE SENATE | By Vote Number

234. **HR 5297. Small-Business Tax and Lending/Biodiesel Tax Incentives.** Grassley, R-Iowa, motion to suspend Rule 22 to permit the consideration of a Grassley amendment that would revive, for one year, lapsed tax incentives for the production of biodiesel fuels. Motion rejected 41-58: D 16-40; R 25-16; I 0-2. A two-thirds majority of senators voting (66 in this case), a quorum being present, is required to suspend Rule 22. Sept. 16, 2010.

235. **HR 5297. Small-Business Tax and Lending/Research and Development Tax Credit.** Hatch, R-Utah, motion to suspend Rule 22 to permit the consideration of a Hatch motion to commit the bill to the Finance Committee with instructions that it be reported back with language that would make permanent an expired tax credit for research and development investment. Motion rejected 51-48: D 12-45; R 39-1; I 0-2. A two-thirds majority of senators voting (66 in this case), a quorum being present, is required to suspend Rule 22. Sept. 16, 2010.

236. **HR 5297. Small-Business Tax and Lending/Cloture.** Motion to invoke cloture (thus limiting debate) on the bill that would provide a variety of small-business tax initiatives, including reviving an expired bonus depreciation provision, and would authorize a small-business lending fund. It would be offset with increased penalties for failing to file information returns, new limits on papermakers' ability to claim a biofuel tax credit and new rules on tax-delinquent federal contractors. Motion agreed to 61-38: D 57-0; R 2-38; I 2-0. Three-fifths of the total Senate (60) is required to invoke cloture. Sept. 16, 2010.

237. **HR 5297. Small-Business Tax and Lending/Passage.** Passage of the bill that would provide a variety of small-business tax initiatives, including reviving an expired bonus depreciation provision and establishment of a $30 billion small-business lending fund administered by the Treasury Department, with funds directed to community banks. It would be offset with increased penalties for failing to file information returns, new limits on papermakers' ability to claim a biofuel tax credit and new rules on tax-delinquent federal contractors. Passed 61-38: D 57-0; R 2-38; I 2-0. A "yea" was a vote in support of the president's position. Sept. 16, 2010.

	234	235	236	237		234	235	236	237
ALABAMA					**MONTANA**				
Shelby	N	Y	N	N	Baucus	N	N	Y	Y
Sessions	N	?	N	N	Tester	N	N	Y	Y
ALASKA					**NEBRASKA**				
Murkowski	Y	Y	N	N	Nelson	Y	Y	Y	Y
Begich	N	N	Y	Y	Johanns	Y	Y	N	N
ARIZONA					**NEVADA**				
McCain	N	Y	N	N	Reid	N	N	Y	Y
Kyl	N	Y	N	N	Ensign	N	Y	N	N
ARKANSAS					**NEW HAMPSHIRE**				
Lincoln	?	Y	Y	Y	Gregg	N	Y	N	N
Pryor	Y	N	Y	Y	Shaheen	Y	N	Y	Y
CALIFORNIA					**NEW JERSEY**				
Feinstein	N	N	Y	Y	Lautenberg	N	N	Y	Y
Boxer	N	Y	Y	Y	Menendez	N	N	Y	Y
COLORADO					**NEW MEXICO**				
Udall	N	N	Y	Y	Bingaman	N	N	Y	Y
Bennet	Y	Y	Y	Y	Udall	N	N	Y	Y
CONNECTICUT					**NEW YORK**				
Dodd	N	N	Y	Y	Schumer	N	N	Y	Y
Lieberman	N	N	Y	Y	Gillibrand	N	N	Y	Y
DELAWARE					**NORTH CAROLINA**				
Carper	N	N	Y	Y	**Burr**	Y	Y	N	N
Kaufman	N	N	Y	Y	Hagan	Y	Y	Y	Y
FLORIDA					**NORTH DAKOTA**				
Nelson	N	N	Y	Y	Conrad	Y	N	Y	Y
LeMieux	N	Y	Y	Y	Dorgan	Y	N	Y	Y
GEORGIA					**OHIO**				
Chambliss	Y	Y	N	N	**Voinovich**	N	N	Y	Y
Isakson	Y	Y	N	N	Brown	N	N	Y	Y
HAWAII					**OKLAHOMA**				
Inouye	N	N	Y	Y	**Inhofe**	Y	Y	N	N
Akaka	N	N	Y	Y	**Coburn**	N	Y	N	N
IDAHO					**OREGON**				
Crapo	N	Y	N	N	Wyden	Y	N	Y	Y
Risch	N	Y	N	N	Merkley	N	N	Y	Y
ILLINOIS					**PENNSYLVANIA**				
Durbin	N	N	Y	Y	Specter	Y	Y	Y	Y
Burris	N	N	Y	Y	Casey	N	N	Y	Y
INDIANA					**RHODE ISLAND**				
Lugar	Y	Y	N	N	Reed	N	N	Y	Y
Bayh	Y	Y	Y	Y	Whitehouse	N	N	Y	Y
IOWA					**SOUTH CAROLINA**				
Grassley	Y	Y	N	N	**Graham**	Y	Y	N	N
Harkin	Y	N	Y	Y	**DeMint**	N	Y	N	N
KANSAS					**SOUTH DAKOTA**				
Brownback	Y	Y	N	N	Johnson	N	N	Y	Y
Roberts	Y	Y	N	N	**Thune**	Y	Y	N	N
KENTUCKY					**TENNESSEE**				
McConnell	Y	Y	N	N	**Alexander**	Y	Y	N	N
Bunning	N	Y	N	N	**Corker**	N	Y	N	N
LOUISIANA					**TEXAS**				
Landrieu	N	N	Y	Y	**Hutchison**	Y	Y	N	N
Vitter	Y	Y	?	?	**Cornyn**	Y	Y	N	N
MAINE					**UTAH**				
Snowe	Y	Y	N	N	**Hatch**	Y	Y	N	N
Collins	Y	Y	N	N	**Bennett**	Y	Y	N	N
MARYLAND					**VERMONT**				
Mikulski	N	N	Y	Y	Leahy	N	N	Y	Y
Cardin	N	N	Y	Y	*Sanders*	N	N	Y	Y
MASSACHUSETTS					**VIRGINIA**				
Kerry	N	N	Y	Y	Webb	N	N	Y	Y
Brown	Y	Y	N	N	Warner	N	Y	Y	Y
MICHIGAN					**WASHINGTON**				
Levin	N	N	Y	Y	Murray	Y	Y	Y	Y
Stabenow	N	N	Y	Y	Cantwell	Y	N	Y	Y
MINNESOTA					**WEST VIRGINIA**				
Klobuchar	Y	Y	Y	Y	Rockefeller	N	N	Y	Y
Franken	Y	Y	Y	Y	Goodwin	N	N	Y	Y
MISSISSIPPI					**WISCONSIN**				
Cochran	Y	Y	N	N	Kohl	N	N	Y	Y
Wicker	Y	Y	N	N	Feingold	N	N	Y	Y
MISSOURI					**WYOMING**				
Bond	Y	Y	N	N	**Enzi**	N	Y	N	N
McCaskill	Y	Y	Y	Y	**Barrasso**	N	Y	N	N

KEY   **Republicans**   Democrats   *Independents*

Y Voted for (yea)	X Paired against	C Voted "present" to avoid possible conflict of interest
# Paired for	− Announced against	
+ Announced for	P Voted "present"	? Did not vote or otherwise make a position known
N Voted against (nay)		

IN THE SENATE | By Vote Number

238. **S 3454. Fiscal 2011 Defense Authorization/Cloture.** Motion to invoke cloture (thus limiting debate) on the motion to proceed to the bill that would authorize $725.7 billion in discretionary funding for defense programs in fiscal 2011. It also would repeal a 1993 law that codifies the "don't ask, don't tell" policy on military service by openly gay men and women. Motion rejected 56-43: D 54-3; R 0-40; I 2-0. Three-fifths of the total Senate (60) is required to invoke cloture. (At the conclusion of the vote, Reid, D-Nev., entered a motion to reconsider the vote.) Sept. 21, 2010.

239. **S J Res 30. Union Elections/Motion to Proceed.** Isakson, R-Ga., motion to proceed to consideration of a joint resolution that would provide for congressional disapproval of a National Mediation Board rules change regarding airline and railway union elections under the Railway Labor Act. Motion rejected 43-56: D 3-54; R 40-0; I 0-2. A "nay" was a vote in support of the president's position. Sept. 23, 2010.

240. **S 3628. Campaign Finance Disclosure/Cloture.** Motion to invoke cloture (thus limiting debate) on the motion to proceed to the bill that would require corporations and unions to disclose in their campaign advertising the chief donors who paid for the ad. Motion rejected 59-39: D 57-0; R 0-39; I 2-0. Three-fifths of the total Senate (60) is required to invoke cloture. (Previously, a Reid, D-Nev., motion to reconsider was adopted by unanimous consent.) A "yea" was a vote in support of the president's position. Sept. 23, 2010.

241. **Procedural Motion/Require Attendance.** Reid, D-Nev., motion to instruct the sergeant at arms to request the attendance of absent senators. Motion agreed to 48-25: D 44-0; R 2-25; I 2-0. Sept. 27, 2010.

242. **S 3816. Overseas Taxes/Motion to Proceed.** Motion to invoke cloture (thus limiting debate) on the motion to proceed to the bill that would give U.S. companies a two-year reduction in their share of Social Security payroll taxes for new employees hired to replace workers performing similar duties overseas. It would be offset by repealing various tax breaks for companies that close plants in the United States and move operations overseas. Motion rejected 53-45: D 52-4; R 0-40; I 1-1. Three-fifths of the total Senate (60) is required to invoke cloture. Sept. 28, 2010.

243. **HR 3081. Continuing Appropriations 'Shell'/Cloture.** Motion to invoke cloture (thus limiting debate) on the motion to proceed to the bill that would provide fiscal 2010 appropriations for the State Department and foreign assistance programs. The bill was intended to serve as the legislative vehicle for continuing appropriations for fiscal 2011. Motion agreed to 84-14: D 56-0; R 26-14; I 2-0. Sept. 28, 2010.

244. **S J Res 39. Grandfathered Health Plans/Motion to Proceed.** Enzi, R-Wyo., motion to proceed to consideration of a joint resolution that would provide for congressional disapproval of a rule regarding grandfathering of health insurance plans under the 2010 health care overhaul law. Motion rejected 40-59: D 0-57; R 40-0; I 0-2. A "nay" was a vote in support of the president's position. Sept. 29, 2010.

	238	239	240	241	242	243	244		238	239	240	241	242	243	244
ALABAMA								**MONTANA**							
Shelby	N	Y	N	N	N	N	Y	Baucus	Y	N	Y	Y	N	Y	N
Sessions	N	Y	N	N	N	N	Y	Tester	Y	N	Y	Y	N	Y	N
ALASKA								**NEBRASKA**							
Murkowski	?	?	?	?	?	?	?	Nelson	Y	Y	Y	Y	N	Y	N
Begich	Y	N	Y	Y	Y	Y	N	Johanns	N	Y	N	N	N	Y	Y
ARIZONA								**NEVADA**							
McCain	N	Y	N	N	N	N	Y	Reid	N	N	Y	Y	Y	Y	N
Kyl	N	Y	N	?	N	Y	Y	Ensign	N	Y	N	Y	N	Y	Y
ARKANSAS								**NEW HAMPSHIRE**							
Lincoln	N	Y	Y	?	?	?	N	Gregg	N	Y	N	N	N	Y	Y
Pryor	N	Y	Y	Y	Y	Y	N	Shaheen	Y	N	Y	?	Y	Y	N
CALIFORNIA								**NEW JERSEY**							
Feinstein	Y	N	Y	Y	Y	Y	N	Lautenberg	Y	N	Y	Y	Y	Y	N
Boxer	Y	N	Y	Y	Y	Y	N	Menendez	Y	N	Y	?	Y	Y	N
COLORADO								**NEW MEXICO**							
Udall	Y	N	Y	Y	Y	Y	N	Bingaman	Y	N	Y	Y	Y	Y	N
Bennet	Y	N	Y	Y	Y	Y	N	Udall	Y	N	Y	Y	Y	Y	N
CONNECTICUT								**NEW YORK**							
Dodd	Y	N	Y	?	Y	Y	N	Schumer	Y	N	Y	Y	Y	Y	N
Lieberman	Y	N	Y	N	Y	N	N	Gillibrand	Y	N	Y	Y	Y	Y	N
DELAWARE								**NORTH CAROLINA**							
Carper	Y	N	Y	?	Y	Y	N	**Burr**	N	Y	N	N	N	Y	Y
Kaufman	Y	N	Y	Y	Y	Y	N	Hagan	Y	N	Y	?	Y	Y	N
FLORIDA								**NORTH DAKOTA**							
Nelson	Y	N	Y	?	Y	Y	N	Conrad	Y	N	Y	?	Y	Y	N
LeMieux	N	Y	N	N	N	Y	Y	Dorgan	Y	N	Y	?	Y	Y	N
GEORGIA								**OHIO**							
Chambliss	N	Y	N	?	N	N	Y	**Voinovich**	N	Y	N	N	N	Y	Y
Isakson	N	Y	N	?	N	N	Y	Brown	Y	N	Y	Y	Y	Y	N
HAWAII								**OKLAHOMA**							
Inouye	Y	N	Y	Y	Y	Y	N	**Inhofe**	N	Y	N	N	N	N	Y
Akaka	Y	N	Y	Y	Y	Y	N	**Coburn**	N	Y	N	N	N	N	Y
IDAHO								**OREGON**							
Crapo	N	Y	N	?	N	N	Y	Wyden	Y	N	Y	Y	Y	Y	N
Risch	N	Y	N	?	N	N	Y	Merkley	Y	N	Y	Y	Y	Y	N
ILLINOIS								**PENNSYLVANIA**							
Durbin	Y	N	Y	Y	Y	Y	N	Specter	Y	N	Y	Y	Y	Y	N
Burris	Y	N	Y	Y	Y	Y	N	Casey	Y	N	Y	Y	Y	Y	N
INDIANA								**RHODE ISLAND**							
Lugar	N	Y	N	N	N	Y	Y	Reed	Y	N	Y	Y	Y	Y	N
Bayh	Y	N	Y	?	Y	Y	N	Whitehouse	Y	N	Y	Y	Y	Y	N
IOWA								**SOUTH CAROLINA**							
Grassley	N	Y	N	N	N	Y	Y	**Graham**	N	Y	N	?	N	Y	Y
Harkin	Y	N	Y	Y	Y	Y	N	**DeMint**	N	Y	N	?	N	N	Y
KANSAS								**SOUTH DAKOTA**							
Brownback	N	Y	N	N	N	Y	Y	Johnson	Y	N	Y	Y	Y	Y	N
Roberts	N	Y	N	N	N	Y	Y	**Thune**	N	Y	N	?	N	N	Y
KENTUCKY								**TENNESSEE**							
McConnell	N	Y	N	N	N	Y	Y	**Alexander**	N	Y	N	N	N	Y	Y
Bunning	N	Y	N	?	N	Y	Y	**Corker**	N	Y	N	N	N	Y	Y
LOUISIANA								**TEXAS**							
Landrieu	Y	N	Y	Y	Y	Y	N	**Hutchison**	N	Y	?	?	N	Y	Y
Vitter	N	Y	N	N	N	Y	Y	**Cornyn**	N	Y	N	?	N	N	Y
MAINE								**UTAH**							
Snowe	N	Y	N	N	N	N	Y	**Hatch**	N	Y	N	N	N	Y	Y
Collins	N	Y	N	N	N	N	Y	**Bennett**	N	Y	N	N	N	Y	Y
MARYLAND								**VERMONT**							
Mikulski	Y	N	Y	?	Y	Y	N	Leahy	Y	N	Y	Y	Y	Y	N
Cardin	Y	N	Y	Y	Y	Y	N	*Sanders*	Y	N	Y	Y	Y	Y	N
MASSACHUSETTS								**VIRGINIA**							
Kerry	Y	N	Y	?	Y	Y	N	Webb	Y	N	Y	Y	Y	Y	N
Brown	N	Y	N	Y	N	Y	Y	Warner	Y	N	Y	Y	Y	Y	N
MICHIGAN								**WASHINGTON**							
Levin	Y	N	Y	Y	Y	Y	N	Murray	Y	N	Y	?	Y	Y	N
Stabenow	Y	N	Y	Y	Y	Y	N	Cantwell	Y	N	Y	Y	Y	Y	N
MINNESOTA								**WEST VIRGINIA**							
Klobuchar	Y	N	Y	Y	Y	Y	N	Rockefeller	Y	N	Y	Y	Y	Y	N
Franken	Y	N	Y	Y	Y	Y	N	Goodwin	Y	N	Y	Y	Y	Y	N
MISSISSIPPI								**WISCONSIN**							
Cochran	N	Y	N	N	N	Y	Y	Kohl	Y	N	Y	Y	Y	Y	N
Wicker	N	Y	N	N	N	Y	Y	Feingold	Y	N	Y	Y	Y	Y	N
MISSOURI								**WYOMING**							
Bond	N	Y	N	N	N	Y	Y	**Enzi**	N	Y	N	?	N	N	Y
McCaskill	Y	N	Y	Y	Y	Y	N	**Barrasso**	N	Y	N	N	N	N	Y

KEY   **Republicans**   Democrats   *Independents*

Y Voted for (yea)	X Paired against
# Paired for	− Announced against
+ Announced for	P Voted "present"
N Voted against (nay)	C Voted "present" to avoid possible conflict of interest
	? Did not vote or otherwise make a position known

IN THE SENATE | By Vote Number

245. HR 3081. Continuing Appropriations 'Shell'/Spending Reductions. Thune, R-S.D., amendment to the Inouye, D-Hawaii, substitute amendment. The Thune amendment would provide for a 5 percent reduction in spending, except for defense, homeland security, veterans' programs and other matters adjusted by the substitute. The substitute would provide continuing appropriations through Dec. 3, 2010, for all federal departments and agencies, none of whose fiscal 2011 appropriations bills have been enacted. Rejected 48-51: D 8-49; R 40-0; I 0-2. (By unanimous consent, the Senate agreed to raise the majority requirement for adoption of the Thune amendment to 60 votes. Subsequently, the amendment was withdrawn.) Sept. 29, 2010.

246. HR 3081. Continuing Appropriations 'Shell'/Extension. DeMint, R-S.C., amendment to the Inouye, D-Hawaii, substitute amendment. The DeMint amendment would provide continuing appropriations until Feb. 4, 2011. Rejected 39-60: D 4-53; R 35-5; I 0-2. (By unanimous consent, the Senate agreed to raise the majority requirement for adoption of the DeMint amendment to 60 votes. Subsequently, the amendment was withdrawn.) Sept. 29, 2010.

247. HR 3081. Continuing Appropriations/Passage. Passage of the bill that would provide continuing appropriations through Dec. 3, 2010, for all federal departments and agencies, none of whose fiscal 2011 appropriations bills have been enacted. It includes several spending adjustments, including an increase of $624 million for the National Nuclear Security Administration. It also would extend year-round child nutrition programs and the Federal Emergency Management Agency's pre-disaster mitigation operations. It would allow the District of Columbia to implement its local budget beginning Oct. 1, 2010. Passed 69-30: D 56-1; R 11-29; I 2-0. (Previously, the Inouye, D-Hawaii, substitute was adopted by unanimous consent.) Sept. 29, 2010.

248. H Con Res 321. Adjournment/Adoption. Adoption of the concurrent resolution that would provide for the adjournment of the House until 2 p.m. Monday, Nov. 15, 2010, and the conditional adjournment of the Senate until noon Monday, Nov. 15, 2010. Adopted 54-39: D 52-2; R 1-37; I 1-0. Sept. 29, 2010.

249. S 3772. Wage Discrimination/Cloture. Motion to invoke cloture (thus limiting debate) on the Reid, D-Nev., motion to proceed to the bill that would seek to provide comparable wages for women by requiring that employers show that any pay disparity is job-related and not based on gender. Motion rejected 58-41: D 56-1; R 0-40; I 2-0. Three-fifths of the total Senate (60) is required to invoke cloture. A "yea" was a vote in support of the president's position. Nov. 17, 2010.

250. S 510. Food Safety/Cloture. Motion to invoke cloture (thus limiting debate) on the Reid, D-Nev., motion to proceed to the bill that would overhaul food safety laws and expand Food and Drug Administration enforcement powers. Motion agreed to 74-25: D 56-1; R 16-24; I 2-0. Three-fifths of the total Senate (60) is required to invoke cloture. Nov. 17, 2010.

251. S 510. Food Safety/Motion to Proceed. Reid, D-Nev., motion to proceed to the bill that would overhaul food safety laws and expand Food and Drug Administration enforcement powers. Motion agreed to 57-27: D 51-0; R 4-27; I 2-0. Nov. 18, 2010.

	245	246	247	248	249	250	251
ALABAMA							
Shelby	Y	Y	N	N	N	N	N
Sessions	Y	Y	N	N	N	N	N
ALASKA							
Murkowski	?	?	?	?	?	?	?
Begich	N	N	Y	Y	Y	Y	Y
ARIZONA							
McCain	Y	Y	N	N	N	N	N
Kyl	Y	Y	Y	?	N	N	N
ARKANSAS							
Lincoln	Y	N	Y	N	Y	Y	Y
Pryor	N	N	Y	Y	Y	Y	Y
CALIFORNIA							
Feinstein	N	N	Y	Y	Y	Y	Y
Boxer	N	N	Y	Y	Y	Y	Y
COLORADO							
Udall	Y	Y	Y	Y	Y	Y	Y
Bennet	Y	Y	Y	N	Y	Y	Y
CONNECTICUT							
Dodd	N	N	Y	?	Y	Y	Y
Lieberman	N	N	Y	Y	Y	Y	Y
DELAWARE							
Carper	N	N	Y	?	Y	Y	Y
Coons					Y	Y	Y
FLORIDA							
Nelson	N	N	Y	Y	Y	Y	Y
LeMieux	Y	Y	N	N	N	Y	N
GEORGIA							
Chambliss	Y	Y	N	N	N	N	N
Isakson	Y	Y	N	N	N	N	N
HAWAII							
Inouye	N	N	Y	Y	Y	Y	Y
Akaka	N	N	Y	Y	Y	Y	Y
IDAHO							
Crapo	Y	Y	N	N	N	N	N
Risch	Y	Y	N	N	N	N	?
ILLINOIS							
Durbin	N	N	Y	Y	Y	Y	Y
Burris	N	N	Y	Y	Y	Y	Y
INDIANA							
Lugar	Y	Y	Y	N	N	Y	N
Bayh	Y	Y	Y	Y	Y	Y	?
IOWA							
Grassley	Y	Y	Y	N	N	Y	N
Harkin	N	N	Y	Y	Y	Y	Y
KANSAS							
Brownback	Y	Y	N	N	N	N	N
Roberts	Y	Y	N	N	N	N	N
KENTUCKY							
McConnell	Y	Y	N	N	N	N	N
Bunning	Y	Y	N	N	N	N	-
LOUISIANA							
Landrieu	N	N	Y	Y	Y	Y	Y
Vitter	Y	Y	N	N	N	Y	?
MAINE							
Snowe	Y	Y	N	N	N	Y	N
Collins	Y	N	N	N	N	Y	Y
MARYLAND							
Mikulski	N	N	Y	Y	Y	Y	Y
Cardin	N	N	Y	Y	Y	Y	Y
MASSACHUSETTS							
Kerry	N	N	Y	Y	Y	Y	+
Brown	Y	Y	N	N	N	Y	N
MICHIGAN							
Levin	N	N	Y	Y	Y	Y	Y
Stabenow	N	N	Y	Y	Y	Y	Y
MINNESOTA							
Klobuchar	Y	N	Y	Y	Y	Y	Y
Franken	N	N	Y	Y	Y	Y	Y
MISSISSIPPI							
Cochran	Y	Y	N	N	N	N	N
Wicker	Y	Y	N	N	N	N	N
MISSOURI							
Bond	Y	N	Y	?	N	N	N
McCaskill	Y	Y	Y	Y	Y	Y	Y

	245	246	247	248	249	250	251
MONTANA							
Baucus	N	N	Y	Y	Y	Y	Y
Tester	N	N	Y	Y	Y	Y	Y
NEBRASKA							
Nelson	N	N	Y	Y	N	N	Y
Johanns	Y	Y	Y	N	N	Y	?
NEVADA							
Reid	N	N	Y	Y	Y	Y	Y
Ensign	Y	Y	N	N	N	N	?
NEW HAMPSHIRE							
Gregg	Y	Y	Y	Y	N	Y	?
Shaheen	N	N	Y	Y	Y	Y	Y
NEW JERSEY							
Lautenberg	N	N	Y	Y	Y	Y	Y
Menendez	N	N	Y	Y	Y	Y	?
NEW MEXICO							
Bingaman	N	N	Y	Y	Y	Y	Y
Udall	N	N	Y	Y	Y	Y	Y
NEW YORK							
Schumer	N	N	Y	Y	Y	Y	Y
Gillibrand	N	N	Y	Y	Y	Y	Y
NORTH CAROLINA							
Burr	Y	Y	N	N	N	N	N
Hagan	N	N	Y	Y	Y	Y	Y
NORTH DAKOTA							
Conrad	N	N	Y	Y	Y	Y	Y
Dorgan	N	N	Y	Y	Y	Y	Y
OHIO							
Voinovich	Y	Y	N	N	Y	Y	N
Brown	N	N	Y	Y	Y	Y	Y
OKLAHOMA							
Inhofe	Y	Y	N	N	N	N	N
Coburn	Y	Y	N	N	N	N	N
OREGON							
Wyden	N	N	Y	Y	Y	Y	Y
Merkley	N	N	Y	Y	Y	Y	Y
PENNSYLVANIA							
Specter	N	N	Y	Y	Y	Y	?
Casey	N	N	Y	Y	Y	Y	Y
RHODE ISLAND							
Reed	N	N	Y	Y	Y	Y	Y
Whitehouse	N	N	Y	Y	Y	Y	Y
SOUTH CAROLINA							
Graham	Y	Y	N	N	N	N	N
DeMint	Y	Y	N	N	N	N	?
SOUTH DAKOTA							
Johnson	N	N	Y	Y	Y	Y	Y
Thune	Y	Y	N	N	N	Y	N
TENNESSEE							
Alexander	Y	Y	N	N	Y	Y	-
Corker	Y	Y	N	N	N	Y	N
TEXAS							
Hutchison	Y	Y	N	N	N	N	?
Cornyn	Y	Y	N	N	N	N	N
UTAH							
Hatch	Y	Y	N	N	N	N	N
Bennett	Y	N	Y	N	N	N	N
VERMONT							
Leahy	N	N	Y	Y	Y	Y	Y
Sanders	N	N	Y	?	Y	Y	Y
VIRGINIA							
Webb	Y	N	Y	Y	Y	Y	?
Warner	N	N	Y	Y	Y	Y	Y
WASHINGTON							
Murray	N	N	Y	Y	Y	Y	Y
Cantwell	N	N	Y	Y	Y	Y	Y
WEST VIRGINIA							
Rockefeller	N	N	Y	?	Y	Y	?
Manchin					Y	Y	Y
WISCONSIN							
Kohl	N	N	Y	Y	Y	Y	Y
Feingold	Y	N	N	Y	Y	Y	Y
WYOMING							
Enzi	Y	Y	N	N	N	Y	N
Barrasso	Y	Y	N	N	N	Y	N

KEY   **Republicans**   Democrats   *Independents*

Y Voted for (yea)	X Paired against	C Voted "present" to avoid possible conflict of interest	
# Paired for	- Announced against		
+ Announced for	P Voted "present"	? Did not vote or otherwise make a position known	
N Voted against (nay)			

[1] Sen. Chris Coons, D-Del., was sworn in Nov. 15 to replace fellow Democrat Ted Kaufman, who retired. The first vote for which Coons was eligible was vote 249.

[2] Sen. Joe Manchin III, D-W.Va., was sworn in Nov. 15 to replace fellow Democrat Carte P. Goodwin, who retired. The first vote for which Manchin was eligible was vote 249.

IN THE SENATE | By Vote Number

252. **S 510. Food Safety/Cloture.** Motion to invoke cloture (thus limiting debate) on the Harkin, D-Iowa, substitute amendment that would overhaul food safety laws and expand Food and Drug Administration (FDA) enforcement powers. Motion agreed to 69-26: D 54-0; R 14-26; I 1-0. Three-fifths of the total Senate (60) is required to invoke cloture. (Subsequently, the substitute amendment was adopted by voice vote.) Nov. 29, 2010.

253. **S 510. Food Safety/1099 Information Reporting.** Johanns, R-Neb., motion to suspend Rule 22 to permit the consideration of a Johanns amendment that would repeal an information-reporting requirement for certain vendors to whom businesses pay in excess of $600 in a year, enacted as part of the 2010 health care overhaul. It also would rescind $39 billion in unobligated federal spending. Motion rejected 61-35: D 21-34; R 40-0; I 0-1. A two-thirds majority of senators voting (64 in this case), a quorum being present, is required to suspend Rule 22. Nov. 29, 2010.

254. **S 510. Food Safety/1099 Information Reporting.** Baucus, D-Mont., motion to suspend Rule 22 to permit the consideration of a Baucus amendment that would repeal an information-reporting requirement for certain vendors to whom businesses pay in excess of $600 in a year, enacted as part of the 2010 health care overhaul. Motion rejected 44-53: D 41-15; R 2-38; I 1-0. A two-thirds majority of senators voting (65 in this case), a quorum being present, is required to suspend Rule 22. Nov. 29, 2010.

255. **S 510. Food Safety/Earmarks.** Coburn, R-Okla., motion to suspend Rule 22 to permit the consideration of a Coburn amendment that would establish a point of order against considering legislation containing both earmarks and limited benefits in the tax code, including limited tariff benefits. Motion rejected 39-56: D 7-46; R 32-8; I 0-2. A two-thirds majority of senators voting (64 in this case), a quorum being present, is required to suspend Rule 22. Nov. 30, 2010.

256. **S 510. Food Safety/Coburn Substitute.** Coburn, R-Okla., motion to suspend Rule 22 to permit the consideration of a Coburn substitute amendment that would require the FDA and the Agriculture Department to share information related to products and facilities. It also would require the creation of a strategic plan to update the FDA's health information technology systems to address food safety issues and establish communication systems between the FDA and other agencies. Motion rejected 36-62: D 0-56; R 36-4; I 0-2. A two-thirds majority of senators voting (66 in this case), a quorum being present, is required to suspend Rule 22. Nov. 30, 2010.

257. **S 510. Food Safety/Passage.** Passage of the bill that would overhaul food safety laws and expand FDA enforcement powers. It would give the agency authority to force a company to recall foods believed to be contaminated. It would require registration every two years by operators who import, export, manufacture, process, pack or hold food for consumption in the United States, and it would require inspections of registered domestic facilities on a risk-based schedule. Producers and processors would have to submit information on food items believed to be adulterated or contaminated, and suppliers of imported foods would have to provide certification that the items comply with established food safety requirements. An exemption would be provided for small-scale farms and food processing operations that sell directly to consumers within 275 miles and that average less than $500,000 in annual sales. Passed 73-25: D 56-0; R 15-25; I 2-0. A "yea" was a vote in support of the president's position. Nov. 30, 2010.

* Sen. Mark Steven Kirk, R-Ill., was sworn in Nov. 29, 2010, after winning a special election to replace Democrat Roland W. Burris, who held the seat on an interim basis. The last vote for which Burris was eligible was vote 251; the first vote for which Kirk was eligible was vote 252.

	252	253	254	255	256	257
ALABAMA						
Shelby	N	Y	N	N	Y	N
Sessions	N	Y	N	Y	Y	N
ALASKA						
Murkowski	Y	Y	N	N	Y	Y
Begich	Y	N	Y	N	N	Y
ARIZONA						
McCain	N	Y	N	Y	Y	N
Kyl	N	Y	N	Y	Y	N
ARKANSAS						
Lincoln	Y	Y	N	N	N	Y
Pryor	?	+	N	N	N	Y
CALIFORNIA						
Feinstein	Y	N	Y	N	N	Y
Boxer	Y	N	Y	–	N	Y
COLORADO						
Udall	Y	Y	N	Y	N	Y
Bennet	Y	Y	N	Y	N	Y
CONNECTICUT						
Dodd	Y	N	N	N	N	Y
Lieberman	?	–	+	N	N	Y
DELAWARE						
Carper	Y	N	N	N	N	Y
Coons	Y	N	Y	N	N	Y
FLORIDA						
Nelson	Y	Y	N	N	N	Y
LeMieux	Y	Y	N	Y	Y	Y
GEORGIA						
Chambliss	N	Y	N	Y	Y	N
Isakson	N	Y	N	Y	Y	N
HAWAII						
Inouye	Y	N	Y	N	N	Y
Akaka	Y	N	Y	N	N	Y
IDAHO						
Crapo	N	Y	N	Y	Y	N
Risch	N	Y	N	Y	Y	N
ILLINOIS						
Durbin	Y	N	N	N	N	Y
Kirk*	Y	Y	Y	Y	N	Y
INDIANA						
Lugar	Y	Y	N	N	N	Y
Bayh	Y	Y	Y	N	N	Y
IOWA						
Grassley	Y	Y	Y	Y	Y	Y
Harkin	Y	N	N	N	N	Y
KANSAS						
Brownback	?	?	?	?	?	?
Roberts	N	Y	N	Y	Y	N
KENTUCKY						
McConnell	N	Y	N	Y	Y	N
Bunning	N	Y	N	Y	Y	N
LOUISIANA						
Landrieu	Y	N	Y	N	N	Y
Vitter	Y	Y	N	Y	N	Y
MAINE						
Snowe	Y	Y	Y	N	Y	Y
Collins	Y	Y	N	N	Y	Y
MARYLAND						
Mikulski	Y	N	Y	?	N	Y
Cardin	Y	N	Y	N	N	Y
MASSACHUSETTS						
Kerry	Y	N	Y	N	N	Y
Brown	Y	Y	Y	Y	Y	Y
MICHIGAN						
Levin	Y	N	Y	N	N	Y
Stabenow	Y	Y	Y	N	N	Y
MINNESOTA						
Klobuchar	Y	Y	Y	N	N	Y
Franken	Y	N	Y	N	N	Y
MISSISSIPPI						
Cochran	N	Y	N	N	Y	N
Wicker	N	Y	N	Y	Y	N
MISSOURI						
Bond	N	Y	N	?	?	?
McCaskill	Y	Y	N	Y	N	Y
MONTANA						
Baucus	Y	N	Y	N	N	Y
Tester	+	Y	Y	N	N	Y
NEBRASKA						
Nelson	Y	Y	Y	N	N	Y
Johanns	Y	Y	N	Y	Y	Y
NEVADA						
Reid	Y	N	N	N	N	Y
Ensign	N	Y	N	Y	Y	N
NEW HAMPSHIRE						
Gregg	Y	Y	N	Y	Y	Y
Shaheen	Y	N	Y	?	N	Y
NEW JERSEY						
Lautenberg	Y	N	Y	N	N	Y
Menendez	Y	Y	Y	N	N	Y
NEW MEXICO						
Bingaman	Y	Y	N	N	N	Y
Udall	Y	Y	N	N	N	Y
NEW YORK						
Schumer	Y	N	Y	N	N	Y
Gillibrand	Y	N	Y	N	N	Y
NORTH CAROLINA						
Burr	?	?	?	Y	Y	Y
Hagan	Y	Y	Y	N	N	Y
NORTH DAKOTA						
Conrad	Y	Y	N	N	N	Y
Dorgan	Y	N	Y	N	N	Y
OHIO						
Voinovich	Y	Y	N	N	N	Y
Brown	Y	N	Y	N	N	Y
OKLAHOMA						
Inhofe	N	Y	N	N	Y	N
Coburn	N	Y	N	Y	Y	N
OREGON						
Wyden	Y	N	Y	N	N	Y
Merkley	Y	N	Y	N	N	Y
PENNSYLVANIA						
Specter	Y	N	Y	N	N	Y
Casey	Y	N	Y	N	N	Y
RHODE ISLAND						
Reed	Y	N	Y	N	N	Y
Whitehouse	Y	N	Y	N	N	Y
SOUTH CAROLINA						
Graham	N	Y	N	Y	Y	N
DeMint	N	Y	N	Y	Y	N
SOUTH DAKOTA						
Johnson	Y	N	Y	N	N	Y
Thune	N	Y	N	Y	Y	N
TENNESSEE						
Alexander	Y	Y	N	Y	N	Y
Corker	N	Y	N	Y	Y	N
TEXAS						
Hutchison	N	Y	N	Y	Y	N
Cornyn	N	Y	N	Y	Y	N
UTAH						
Hatch	N	Y	N	N	Y	N
Bennett	N	Y	N	N	Y	N
VERMONT						
Leahy	Y	N	Y	N	N	Y
Sanders	Y	N	Y	N	N	Y
VIRGINIA						
Webb	Y	Y	Y	N	N	Y
Warner	Y	Y	Y	N	N	Y
WASHINGTON						
Murray	Y	N	Y	N	N	Y
Cantwell	Y	Y	Y	N	N	Y
WEST VIRGINIA						
Rockefeller	Y	N	Y	N	N	Y
Manchin	Y	Y	Y	N	N	Y
WISCONSIN						
Kohl	Y	Y	N	N	N	Y
Feingold	Y	Y	N	Y	N	Y
WYOMING						
Enzi	Y	Y	N	Y	Y	Y
Barrasso	N	Y	N	Y	Y	N

KEY   **Republicans**   Democrats   *Independents*

Y Voted for (yea)	X Paired against	C Voted "present" to avoid possible conflict of interest
# Paired for	– Announced against	
+ Announced for	P Voted "present"	? Did not vote or otherwise make a position known
N Voted against (nay)		

IN THE SENATE | By Vote Number

258. **HR 4853. Tax Rates Extensions/Cloture.** Motion to invoke cloture (thus limiting debate) on the Reid, D-Nev., motion to concur in the House amendment to the Senate amendment with a further Baucus, D-Mont., substitute amendment that would make permanent the 2001- and 2003-enacted tax cuts on income up to $200,000 for individuals and $250,000 for married couples filing joint returns. The extensions would include the current lower tax rates for capital gains and dividends, elimination of the "marriage penalty" and an expansion of the increased child tax credit. It also would extend unemployment insurance benefits for 13 months. Motion rejected 53-36: D 52-4; R 0-31; I 1-1. Three-fifths of the total Senate (60) is required to invoke cloture. A "yea" was a vote in support of the president's position. Dec. 4, 2010.

259. **HR 4853. Tax Rates Extensions/Cloture.** Motion to invoke cloture (thus limiting debate) on the Reid, D-Nev., motion to concur in the House amendment to the Senate amendment with a further Schumer, D-N.Y., substitute amendment that would generally make permanent the 2001- and 2003-enacted tax cuts for taxpayers with income under $1 million. Motion rejected 53-37: D 52-4; R 0-32; I 1-1. Three-fifths of the total Senate (60) is required to invoke cloture. Dec. 4, 2010.

260. **Impeachment Trial of Judge Porteous/Motion to Disaggregate.** Adoption of a defense motion that the articles of impeachment brought by the House against Judge G. Thomas Porteous Jr. of the U.S. District Court for the Eastern District of Louisiana were improperly aggregated, notwithstanding Rule 23 of the Senate's impeachment rules prohibiting division of the question in impeachment proceedings. Motion rejected 0-94: D 0-53; R 0-40; I 0-1. Dec. 8, 2010.

261. **Impeachment Trial of Judge Porteous/Improper Relationships With Lawyers.** Conviction by the Senate court of impeachment on Article I, which impeached Judge G. Thomas Porteous Jr. of the U.S. District Court for the Eastern District of Louisiana in relation to taking money from lawyers involved in *Lifemark Hospitals of La. v. Liljeberg Enterprises*, a 1996-2000 case that Porteous oversaw. Convicted (thus removed from the federal bench) 96-0: D 54-0; R 40-0; I 2-0. A two-thirds majority of senators present and voting (64 in this case) is required for conviction in the court of impeachment. Dec. 8, 2010.

262. **Impeachment Trial of Judge Porteous/Bail Bondsmen Gifts.** Conviction by the Senate court of impeachment on Article II of the resolution, which impeached Judge G. Thomas Porteous Jr. of the U.S. District Court for the Eastern District of Louisiana for accepting items of value from bail bondsman Louis M. Marcotte III and his sister Lori Marcotte in exchange for taking official actions that benefited the Marcottes, including setting, reducing and splitting bonds as requested by the Marcottes, and improperly setting aside or expunging felony convictions for two Marcotte employees. Convicted 69-27: D 45-9; R 23-17; I 1-1. A two-thirds majority of senators present and voting (64 in this case) is required for conviction in the court of impeachment. Dec. 8, 2010.

	258	259	260	261	262			258	259	260	261	262
ALABAMA							**MONTANA**					
Shelby	N	N	N	Y	Y		Baucus	Y	Y	N	Y	Y
Sessions	?	?	N	Y	Y		Tester	Y	Y	N	Y	Y
ALASKA							**NEBRASKA**					
Murkowski	N	N	N	Y	N		Nelson	N	Y	N	Y	Y
Begich	Y	Y	N	Y	Y		Johanns	N	N	N	Y	Y
ARIZONA							**NEVADA**					
McCain	N	N	N	Y	Y		Reid	Y	Y	N	Y	N
Kyl	N	N	N	Y	Y		Ensign	N	N	N	Y	N
ARKANSAS							**NEW HAMPSHIRE**					
Lincoln	Y	Y	?	?	?		Gregg	?	?	N	Y	N
Pryor	Y	Y	N	Y	Y		Shaheen	Y	Y	N	Y	Y
CALIFORNIA							**NEW JERSEY**					
Feinstein	Y	Y	N	Y	Y		Lautenberg	Y	Y	N	Y	Y
Boxer	Y	Y	N	Y	Y		Menendez	Y	Y	N	Y	Y
COLORADO							**NEW MEXICO**					
Udall	Y	Y	N	Y	Y		Bingaman	Y	Y	N	Y	Y
Bennet	Y	Y	N	Y	Y		Udall	Y	Y	N	Y	Y
CONNECTICUT							**NEW YORK**					
Dodd	Y	Y	?	?	?		Schumer	Y	Y	N	Y	Y
Lieberman	N	N	N	Y	N		Gillibrand	Y	Y	N	Y	Y
DELAWARE							**NORTH CAROLINA**					
Carper	Y	Y	?	Y	Y		**Burr**	?	?	N	Y	N
Coons	Y	Y	N	Y	Y		Hagan	Y	Y	N	Y	Y
FLORIDA							**NORTH DAKOTA**					
Nelson	Y	Y	N	Y	Y		Conrad	Y	Y	N	Y	Y
LeMieux	N	N	N	Y	N		Dorgan	Y	Y	N	Y	Y
GEORGIA							**OHIO**					
Chambliss	?	?	N	Y	N		**Voinovich**	?	N	N	Y	Y
Isakson	?	?	N	Y	Y		Brown	Y	Y	N	Y	N
HAWAII							**OKLAHOMA**					
Inouye	Y	Y	N	Y	N		**Inhofe**	?	?	N	Y	Y
Akaka	Y	Y	N	Y	N		Coburn	N	N	N	Y	Y
IDAHO							**OREGON**					
Crapo	N	N	N	Y	Y		Wyden	Y	Y	N	Y	Y
Risch	N	N	N	Y	Y		Merkley	Y	Y	N	Y	Y
ILLINOIS							**PENNSYLVANIA**					
Durbin	Y	N	N	Y	Y		Specter	Y	Y	N	Y	Y
Kirk	N	N	?	?	?		Casey	Y	Y	N	Y	Y
INDIANA							**RHODE ISLAND**					
Lugar	N	N	N	Y	Y		Reed	Y	Y	N	Y	N
Bayh	Y	Y	N	Y	Y		Whitehouse	Y	Y	N	Y	N
IOWA							**SOUTH CAROLINA**					
Grassley	N	N	N	Y	Y		**Graham**	N	N	N	Y	N
Harkin	Y	N	N	Y	N		**DeMint**	N	N	N	Y	Y
KANSAS							**SOUTH DAKOTA**					
Brownback	N	N	?	?	?		Johnson	Y	Y	N	Y	Y
Roberts	N	N	N	Y	Y		**Thune**	N	N	N	Y	Y
KENTUCKY							**TENNESSEE**					
McConnell	N	N	N	Y	Y		**Alexander**	N	N	N	Y	N
Bunning	–	–	N	Y	Y		**Corker**	N	N	N	Y	N
LOUISIANA							**TEXAS**					
Landrieu	Y	Y	N	Y	Y		**Hutchison**	?	?	N	Y	N
Vitter	?	?	N	Y	Y		**Cornyn**	–	–	N	Y	N
MAINE							**UTAH**					
Snowe	N	N	N	Y	Y		**Hatch**	N	N	N	Y	N
Collins	N	N	N	Y	N		**Bennett**	N	N	N	Y	N
MARYLAND							**VERMONT**					
Mikulski	Y	Y	N	Y	Y		Leahy	Y	Y	N	Y	Y
Cardin	Y	Y	N	Y	Y		*Sanders*	Y	Y	?	Y	Y
MASSACHUSETTS							**VIRGINIA**					
Kerry	Y	Y	N	Y	Y		Webb	N	Y	N	Y	Y
Brown	N	N	N	Y	N		Warner	Y	Y	N	Y	Y
MICHIGAN							**WASHINGTON**					
Levin	Y	Y	N	Y	Y		Murray	Y	Y	N	Y	Y
Stabenow	Y	Y	N	Y	Y		Cantwell	Y	Y	N	Y	Y
MINNESOTA							**WEST VIRGINIA**					
Klobuchar	Y	Y	N	Y	Y		Rockefeller	Y	N	N	Y	Y
Franken	Y	Y	N	Y	Y		Manchin	N	Y	N	Y	N
MISSISSIPPI							**WISCONSIN**					
Cochran	N	N	N	Y	Y		Kohl	Y	Y	N	Y	Y
Wicker	N	N	N	Y	N		Feingold	N	N	N	Y	Y
MISSOURI							**WYOMING**					
Bond	N	N	N	Y	Y		**Enzi**	N	N	N	Y	Y
McCaskill	Y	Y	N	Y	N		**Barrasso**	N	N	N	Y	Y

KEY   **Republicans**   Democrats   *Independents*

Y Voted for (yea)	X Paired against	C Voted "present" to avoid possible conflict of interest
# Paired for	– Announced against	
+ Announced for	P Voted "present"	? Did not vote or otherwise make a position known
N Voted against (nay)		

IN THE SENATE | By Vote Number

263. **Impeachment Trial of Judge Porteous/False Statements.** Conviction by the Senate court of impeachment on Article III, which impeached Judge G. Thomas Porteous Jr. of the U.S. District Court for the Eastern District of Louisiana for making false statements and representations under penalty of perjury related to his personal bankruptcy filing and repeatedly violating a court order in his bankruptcy case. Convicted 88-8: D 49-5; R 38-2; I 1-1. A two-thirds majority of senators present and voting (64 in this case) is required for conviction in the court of impeachment. Dec. 8, 2010.

264. **Impeachment Trial of Judge Porteous/False Statements.** Conviction by the Senate court of impeachment on Article IV, which impeached Judge G. Thomas Porteous Jr. of the U.S. District Court for the Eastern District of Louisiana for making false statements about his past to both the Senate and the FBI during his Senate confirmation process. Convicted 90-6: D 48-6; R 40-0; I 2-0. A two-thirds majority of senators present and voting (64 in this case) is required for conviction in the court of impeachment. Dec. 8, 2010.

265. **Impeachment Trial of Judge Porteous/Motion to Disqualify.** Reid, D-Nev., motion to disqualify G. Thomas Porteous Jr. of Louisiana from holding future federal office. Motion agreed to 94-2: D 53-1; R 40-0; I 1-1. Dec. 8, 2010.

266. **S 3991. Public Safety Workers Collective Bargaining/Cloture.** Motion to invoke cloture (thus limiting debate) on the Reid, D-Nev., motion to proceed to the bill that would extend bargaining rights to police and firefighters in states that do not allow such public safety workers to join unions. The bill would not apply to certain sheriffs' deputies. Motion rejected 55-43: D 53-3; R 0-40; I 2-0. Three-fifths of the total Senate (60) is required to invoke cloture. Dec. 8, 2010.

267. **S 3985. Social Security Single Payment/Cloture.** Motion to invoke cloture (thus limiting debate) on the Reid, D-Nev., motion to proceed to the bill that would provide one-time payments of $250 to Social Security recipients and others who have not received cost-of-living payments because inflation has not been high enough to trigger such adjustments. Motion rejected 53-45: D 52-4; R 0-40; I 1-1. Three-fifths of the total Senate (60) is required to invoke cloture. A "yea" was a vote in support of the president's position. Dec. 8, 2010.

	263	264	265	266	267			263	264	265	266	267
ALABAMA							**MONTANA**					
Shelby	Y	Y	Y	N	N		Baucus	Y	Y	Y	Y	Y
Sessions	Y	Y	Y	N	N		Tester	Y	Y	Y	Y	Y
ALASKA							**NEBRASKA**					
Murkowski	Y	Y	Y	N	N		Nelson	Y	Y	Y	Y	Y
Begich	Y	Y	Y	Y	Y		Johanns	Y	Y	Y	N	N
ARIZONA							**NEVADA**					
McCain	Y	Y	Y	N	N		Reid	N	N	Y	Y	Y
Kyl	Y	Y	Y	N	N		Ensign	Y	Y	Y	N	N
ARKANSAS							**NEW HAMPSHIRE**					
Lincoln	?	?	?	Y	Y		Gregg	Y	Y	Y	?	?
Pryor	Y	Y	Y	Y	Y		Shaheen	Y	Y	Y	Y	Y
CALIFORNIA							**NEW JERSEY**					
Feinstein	Y	Y	Y	Y	Y		Lautenberg	Y	Y	Y	Y	Y
Boxer	Y	Y	Y	Y	Y		Menendez	Y	Y	Y	Y	Y
COLORADO							**NEW MEXICO**					
Udall	Y	Y	Y	Y	N		Bingaman	Y	Y	N	Y	Y
Bennet	Y	Y	Y	N	Y		Udall	Y	Y	Y	Y	Y
CONNECTICUT							**NEW YORK**					
Dodd	?	?	?	Y	Y		Schumer	Y	Y	Y	Y	Y
Lieberman	N	Y	N	Y	N		Gillibrand	Y	Y	Y	Y	Y
DELAWARE							**NORTH CAROLINA**					
Carper	Y	Y	Y	Y	Y		Burr	Y	Y	Y	N	N
Coons	Y	Y	Y	Y	Y		Hagan	Y	Y	Y	N	N
FLORIDA							**NORTH DAKOTA**					
Nelson	Y	Y	Y	Y	Y		Conrad	Y	Y	Y	Y	Y
LeMieux	Y	Y	Y	N	N		Dorgan	Y	Y	Y	Y	Y
GEORGIA							**OHIO**					
Chambliss	Y	Y	Y	N	N		Voinovich	Y	Y	Y	N	N
Isakson	Y	Y	Y	N	N		Brown	Y	Y	Y	Y	Y
HAWAII							**OKLAHOMA**					
Inouye	Y	Y	Y	Y	Y		Inhofe	Y	Y	Y	N	N
Akaka	N	Y	Y	Y	Y		Coburn	Y	Y	Y	N	N
IDAHO							**OREGON**					
Crapo	Y	Y	Y	N	N		Wyden	Y	Y	Y	Y	Y
Risch	Y	Y	Y	N	N		Merkley	Y	Y	Y	Y	Y
ILLINOIS							**PENNSYLVANIA**					
Durbin	Y	N	Y	Y	Y		Specter	Y	Y	Y	Y	Y
Kirk	?	?	?	N	N		Casey	Y	Y	Y	Y	Y
INDIANA							**RHODE ISLAND**					
Lugar	Y	Y	Y	N	N		Reed	Y	Y	Y	Y	Y
Bayh	Y	Y	Y	Y	Y		Whitehouse	Y	Y	Y	Y	Y
IOWA							**SOUTH CAROLINA**					
Grassley	Y	Y	Y	N	N		Graham	Y	Y	Y	N	N
Harkin	Y	N	Y	Y	Y		DeMint	Y	Y	Y	N	N
KANSAS							**SOUTH DAKOTA**					
Brownback	?	?	?	?	?		Johnson	Y	Y	Y	Y	Y
Roberts	Y	Y	Y	N	N		Thune	Y	Y	Y	N	N
KENTUCKY							**TENNESSEE**					
McConnell	Y	Y	Y	N	N		Alexander	Y	Y	Y	N	N
Bunning	Y	Y	Y	N	N		Corker	Y	Y	Y	N	N
LOUISIANA							**TEXAS**					
Landrieu	Y	Y	Y	Y	Y		Hutchison	Y	Y	Y	N	N
Vitter	Y	Y	Y	N	N		Cornyn	Y	Y	Y	N	N
MAINE							**UTAH**					
Snowe	Y	Y	Y	N	N		Hatch	N	Y	Y	N	N
Collins	Y	Y	Y	N	N		Bennett	Y	Y	Y	N	N
MARYLAND							**VERMONT**					
Mikulski	Y	Y	Y	Y	Y		Leahy	Y	Y	Y	Y	Y
Cardin	Y	N	Y	Y	Y		*Sanders*	Y	Y	Y	Y	Y
MASSACHUSETTS							**VIRGINIA**					
Kerry	Y	Y	Y	Y	Y		Webb	Y	Y	Y	Y	Y
Brown	Y	Y	Y	N	N		Warner	Y	Y	Y	N	N
MICHIGAN							**WASHINGTON**					
Levin	Y	N	Y	Y	Y		Murray	Y	Y	Y	Y	Y
Stabenow	Y	Y	Y	Y	Y		Cantwell	Y	Y	Y	Y	Y
MINNESOTA							**WEST VIRGINIA**					
Klobuchar	Y	Y	Y	Y	Y		Rockefeller	Y	Y	Y	Y	Y
Franken	N	N	Y	Y	Y		Manchin	N	Y	Y	Y	Y
MISSISSIPPI							**WISCONSIN**					
Cochran	Y	Y	Y	N	N		Kohl	Y	Y	Y	Y	Y
Wicker	N	Y	Y	N	N		Feingold	Y	Y	Y	Y	N
MISSOURI							**WYOMING**					
Bond	Y	Y	Y	N	N		Enzi	Y	Y	Y	N	N
McCaskill	N	Y	Y	Y	Y		Barrasso	Y	Y	Y	N	N

KEY   Republicans   Democrats   *Independents*

Y Voted for (yea)	X Paired against	C Voted "present" to avoid possible conflict of interest
# Paired for	– Announced against	
+ Announced for	P Voted "present"	? Did not vote or otherwise make a position known
N Voted against (nay)		

IN THE SENATE | By Vote Number

268. **S 3992. Immigration Policy Revisions/Motion to Table.** Reid, D-Nev., motion to table (kill) the Reid motion to proceed to the bill that would provide legal status and a pathway to citizenship for certain young illegal immigrants who join the military or attend college. Motion agreed to 59-40: D 52-4; R 5-36; I 2-0. Dec. 9, 2010.

269. **HR 847. Sept. 11 Health and Compensation Fund/Cloture.** Motion to invoke cloture (thus limiting debate) on the Reid, D-Nev., motion to proceed to the bill that would create a program to provide medical services and health monitoring for first-responders and others with conditions related to the Sept. 11 attacks and reopen the Sept. 11 Victim Compensation Fund. The bill would be offset with changes to tax-withholding rules for certain payments made by U.S. subsidiaries of foreign corporations. Motion rejected 57-42: D 55-1; R 0-41; I 2-0. Dec. 9, 2010.

270. **S 3454. Fiscal 2011 Defense Authorization/Cloture.** Motion to invoke cloture (thus limiting debate) on the motion to proceed to the bill that would authorize $725.7 billion in discretionary funding for defense programs in fiscal 2011. It also would repeal a 1993 law that codifies the "don't ask, don't tell" policy on military service by openly gay men and women. Motion rejected 57-40: D 54-1; R 1-39; I 2-0. Dec. 9, 2010.

271. **HR 4853. Tax Rates Extensions/Motion to Table.** Reid, D-Nev., motion to table (kill) the Reid motion to refer the House message on a bill that would extend certain tax rates to the Finance Committee with instructions that the bill be reported back with technical changes. Motion agreed to 65-11: D 38-7; R 26-3; I 1-1. Dec. 9, 2010.

	268	269	270	271			268	269	270	271
ALABAMA						**MONTANA**				
Shelby	N	N	N	Y		Baucus	Y	Y	Y	Y
Sessions	N	N	N	Y		Tester	Y	Y	Y	?
ALASKA						**NEBRASKA**				
Murkowski	Y	N	N	Y		Nelson	Y	Y	Y	Y
Begich	Y	Y	Y	?		Johanns	N	N	N	Y
ARIZONA						**NEVADA**				
McCain	N	N	N	Y		Reid	Y	N	Y	Y
Kyl	N	N	N	?		Ensign	N	N	N	N
ARKANSAS						**NEW HAMPSHIRE**				
Lincoln	Y	Y	+	Y		Gregg	N	N	N	?
Pryor	N	Y	Y	Y		Shaheen	Y	Y	Y	Y
CALIFORNIA						**NEW JERSEY**				
Feinstein	Y	Y	Y	Y		Lautenberg	Y	Y	Y	Y
Boxer	Y	Y	Y	?		Menendez	N	Y	Y	N
COLORADO						**NEW MEXICO**				
Udall	Y	Y	Y	N		Bingaman	Y	Y	Y	Y
Bennet	Y	Y	Y	Y		Udall	Y	Y	Y	N
CONNECTICUT						**NEW YORK**				
Dodd	Y	Y	Y	?		Schumer	Y	Y	Y	Y
Lieberman	Y	Y	Y	Y		Gillibrand	Y	Y	Y	Y
DELAWARE						**NORTH CAROLINA**				
Carper	Y	Y	Y	Y		Burr	N	N	N	?
Coons	Y	Y	Y	?		Hagan	Y	Y	Y	Y
FLORIDA						**NORTH DAKOTA**				
Nelson	Y	Y	Y	?		Conrad	Y	Y	Y	Y
LeMieux	N	N	N	?		Dorgan	Y	Y	Y	Y
GEORGIA						**OHIO**				
Chambliss	N	N	N	Y		Voinovich	N	N	N	N
Isakson	N	N	N	Y		Brown	Y	Y	Y	N
HAWAII						**OKLAHOMA**				
Inouye	Y	Y	Y	Y		Inhofe	N	N	N	?
Akaka	Y	Y	Y	Y		Coburn	N	N	N	Y
IDAHO						**OREGON**				
Crapo	Y	N	N	?		Wyden	Y	Y	Y	Y
Risch	Y	N	N	Y		Merkley	N	Y	Y	N
ILLINOIS						**PENNSYLVANIA**				
Durbin	Y	Y	Y	Y		Specter	Y	Y	Y	Y
Kirk	N	N	N	Y		Casey	Y	Y	Y	Y
INDIANA						**RHODE ISLAND**				
Lugar	N	N	N	Y		Reed	Y	Y	Y	Y
Bayh	Y	Y	Y	?		Whitehouse	Y	Y	Y	Y
IOWA						**SOUTH CAROLINA**				
Grassley	N	N	N	Y		Graham	N	N	N	?
Harkin	Y	Y	Y	N		DeMint	N	N	N	N
KANSAS						**SOUTH DAKOTA**				
Brownback	?	?	?	?		Johnson	Y	Y	Y	?
Roberts	N	N	N	Y		Thune	N	N	N	Y
KENTUCKY						**TENNESSEE**				
McConnell	N	N	N	Y		Alexander	N	N	N	+
Bunning	N	N	N	+		Corker	Y	N	N	Y
LOUISIANA						**TEXAS**				
Landrieu	Y	Y	Y	N		Hutchison	N	N	N	?
Vitter	Y	N	N	?		Cornyn	N	N	?	+
MAINE						**UTAH**				
Snowe	N	N	N	Y		Hatch	N	N	N	Y
Collins	N	N	Y	Y		Bennett	N	N	N	Y
MARYLAND						**VERMONT**				
Mikulski	Y	Y	Y	Y		Leahy	Y	Y	Y	Y
Cardin	Y	Y	Y	Y		*Sanders*	Y	Y	N	Y
MASSACHUSETTS						**VIRGINIA**				
Kerry	Y	Y	Y	Y		Webb	Y	Y	Y	?
Brown	N	N	N	Y		Warner	Y	Y	Y	?
MICHIGAN						**WASHINGTON**				
Levin	Y	Y	Y	Y		Murray	Y	Y	Y	Y
Stabenow	Y	Y	Y	Y		Cantwell	Y	Y	Y	Y
MINNESOTA						**WEST VIRGINIA**				
Klobuchar	Y	Y	Y	Y		Rockefeller	Y	Y	Y	Y
Franken	Y	Y	Y	Y		Manchin	Y	Y	N	Y
MISSISSIPPI						**WISCONSIN**				
Cochran	N	N	N	Y		Kohl	Y	Y	Y	Y
Wicker	N	N	N	Y		Feingold	N	Y	Y	?
MISSOURI						**WYOMING**				
Bond	N	N	N	Y		Enzi	N	N	N	Y
McCaskill	Y	Y	Y	Y		Barrasso	N	N	N	Y

KEY	**Republicans**	Democrats	*Independents*		
Y Voted for (yea)		X Paired against		C Voted "present" to avoid possible conflict of interest	
# Paired for		− Announced against			
+ Announced for		P Voted "present"		? Did not vote or otherwise make a position known	
N Voted against (nay)					

IN THE SENATE | By Vote Number

272. **HR 4853. Tax Rates Extensions/Cloture.** Motion to invoke cloture (thus limiting debate) on the Reid, D-Nev., motion to concur in the House amendment to the Senate amendment with a further Reid and McConnell, R-Ky., substitute amendment that would extend the 2001 and 2003 tax cuts for all taxpayers for two years, as well as reinstitute the estate tax at a 35 percent rate on the value of estates in excess of $5 million. It also would continue expanded unemployment insurance benefits for 13 months. Motion agreed to 83-15: D 45-9; R 37-5; I 1-1. Three-fifths of the total Senate (60) is required to invoke cloture. Dec. 13, 2010.

273. **HR 4853. Tax Rates Extensions/Partial Offset.** Coburn, R-Okla., motion to suspend Rule 22 to permit the consideration of a Coburn amendment that would partially offset the cost of the measure by rescinding an assortment of federal appropriations. It also would prohibit payment of unemployment insurance benefits to millionaires. Motion rejected 47-52: D 5-50; R 42-0; I 0-2. A two-thirds majority of senators voting (66 in this case), a quorum being present, is required to suspend Rule 22. Dec. 15, 2010.

274. **HR 4853. Tax Rates Extensions/DeMint Substitute.** DeMint, R-S.C., motion to suspend Rule 22 to permit the consideration of a DeMint substitute amendment that would permanently extend 2001 and 2003 tax rates for all income levels. It also would provide for the permanent higher exemptions from the alternative minimum tax and the permanent repeal of the estate tax. Motion rejected 37-63: D 1-55; R 36-6; I 0-2. A two-thirds majority of senators voting (67 in this case), a quorum being present, is required to suspend Rule 22. Dec. 15, 2010.

275. **HR 4853. Tax Rates Extensions/Sanders Substitute.** Sanders, I-Vt., motion to suspend Rule 22 to permit the consideration of a Sanders amendment that would extend 2001 and 2003 tax rates on most income up to $200,000 for individuals and $250,000 for married couples filing joint returns. It also would set an estate tax at 2009 levels for two years with a 45 percent tax rate on the value of estates in excess of $3.5 million. Motion rejected 43-57: D 42-14; R 0-42; I 1-1. A two-thirds majority of senators voting (67 in this case), a quorum being present, is required to suspend Rule 22. Dec. 15, 2010.

276. **HR 4853. Tax Rates Extensions/Motion to Concur.** Reid, D-Nev., motion to concur in the House amendment to the Senate amendment with a further Reid and McConnell, R-Ky., substitute amendment that would extend the 2001 and 2003 tax cuts for all taxpayers for two years, as well as reinstitute the estate tax at a 35 percent rate on the value of estates in excess of $5 million. It also would continue expanded unemployment insurance benefits for 13 months. Motion agreed to 81-19: D 43-13; R 37-5; I 1-1. A "yea" was a vote in support of the president's position. Dec. 15, 2010.

277. **Treaty Doc 111-5. New START Agreement/Motion to Proceed.** Reid, D-Nev., motion to proceed to executive session to consider the New Strategic Arms Reduction Treaty (Treaty Doc 111-5), also known as New START, which would require the United States and Russia to further reduce their stockpiles of certain nuclear arms. Motion agreed to 66-32: D 55-0; R 9-32; I 2-0. Dec. 15, 2010.

	272	273	274	275	276	277
ALABAMA						
Shelby	Y	Y	Y	N	Y	N
Sessions	N	Y	Y	N	N	N
ALASKA						
Murkowski	Y	Y	N	N	Y	Y
Begich	Y	?	N	Y	Y	Y
ARIZONA						
McCain	Y	Y	Y	N	Y	Y
Kyl	Y	Y	Y	N	Y	N
ARKANSAS						
Lincoln	Y	Y	N	N	Y	Y
Pryor	Y	N	N	N	Y	Y
CALIFORNIA						
Feinstein	Y	N	N	Y	Y	Y
Boxer	Y	N	N	Y	Y	Y
COLORADO						
Udall	N	N	N	N	N	Y
Bennet	Y	N	N	N	Y	Y
CONNECTICUT						
Dodd	Y	N	N	Y	Y	Y
Lieberman	Y	N	N	N	Y	Y
DELAWARE						
Carper	Y	N	N	Y	Y	Y
Coons	Y	N	N	Y	Y	Y
FLORIDA						
Nelson	Y	N	N	N	Y	Y
LeMieux	Y	Y	Y	N	Y	N
GEORGIA						
Chambliss	Y	Y	Y	N	Y	N
Isakson	Y	Y	Y	N	Y	N
HAWAII						
Inouye	Y	N	N	Y	Y	Y
Akaka	Y	N	N	Y	Y	Y
IDAHO						
Crapo	Y	Y	Y	N	Y	N
Risch	Y	Y	Y	N	Y	N
ILLINOIS						
Durbin	Y	N	N	Y	Y	Y
Kirk	Y	Y	N	N	Y	N
INDIANA						
Lugar	Y	Y	Y	N	Y	Y
Bayh	Y	Y	N	N	Y	?
IOWA						
Grassley	Y	Y	Y	N	Y	N
Harkin	Y	N	N	N	Y	Y
KANSAS						
Brownback	Y	Y	Y	N	Y	N
Roberts	Y	Y	Y	N	Y	N
KENTUCKY						
McConnell	Y	Y	Y	N	Y	N
Bunning	Y	Y	Y	N	Y	N
LOUISIANA						
Landrieu	Y	N	N	Y	Y	Y
Vitter	Y	Y	Y	N	Y	N
MAINE						
Snowe	Y	Y	Y	N	Y	Y
Collins	Y	Y	N	N	Y	Y
MARYLAND						
Mikulski	Y	N	N	Y	Y	Y
Cardin	Y	N	N	N	Y	Y
MASSACHUSETTS						
Kerry	Y	N	N	Y	Y	Y
Brown	Y	Y	N	N	Y	Y
MICHIGAN						
Levin	N	N	N	Y	N	Y
Stabenow	Y	N	N	Y	Y	Y
MINNESOTA						
Klobuchar	Y	N	N	Y	Y	Y
Franken	Y	N	N	Y	Y	Y
MISSISSIPPI						
Cochran	Y	Y	Y	N	Y	Y
Wicker	Y	Y	Y	N	Y	N
MISSOURI						
Bond	Y	Y	Y	N	Y	N
McCaskill	Y	Y	N	N	Y	Y
MONTANA						
Baucus	Y	N	N	N	Y	Y
Tester	Y	Y	N	Y	Y	Y
NEBRASKA						
Nelson	Y	N	Y	N	Y	Y
Johanns	Y	Y	Y	N	Y	N
NEVADA						
Reid	Y	N	N	Y	Y	Y
Ensign	N	Y	Y	N	N	N
NEW HAMPSHIRE						
Gregg	Y	Y	Y	N	Y	N
Shaheen	Y	N	N	Y	Y	Y
NEW JERSEY						
Lautenberg	N	N	N	Y	Y	Y
Menendez	Y	N	N	Y	Y	Y
NEW MEXICO						
Bingaman	N	N	N	Y	N	Y
Udall	Y	N	N	Y	Y	Y
NEW YORK						
Schumer	Y	N	N	Y	Y	Y
Gillibrand	N	N	N	Y	N	Y
NORTH CAROLINA						
Burr	Y	Y	Y	N	Y	N
Hagan	N	Y	N	N	N	Y
NORTH DAKOTA						
Conrad	Y	N	N	Y	Y	Y
Dorgan	Y	N	N	Y	N	Y
OHIO						
Voinovich	N	Y	N	N	Y	Y
Brown	N	N	N	Y	Y	Y
OKLAHOMA						
Inhofe	Y	Y	Y	N	Y	N
Coburn	N	Y	Y	N	N	N
OREGON						
Wyden	?	N	N	Y	N	Y
Merkley	?	N	N	Y	N	Y
PENNSYLVANIA						
Specter	Y	N	N	N	Y	Y
Casey	Y	N	N	N	Y	Y
RHODE ISLAND						
Reed	Y	N	N	Y	Y	Y
Whitehouse	Y	N	N	Y	Y	Y
SOUTH CAROLINA						
Graham	Y	Y	Y	N	Y	Y
DeMint	N	Y	N	N	N	N
SOUTH DAKOTA						
Johnson	Y	N	N	Y	Y	Y
Thune	Y	Y	Y	N	Y	N
TENNESSEE						
Alexander	Y	Y	Y	N	Y	N
Corker	Y	Y	Y	N	Y	N
TEXAS						
Hutchison	Y	Y	Y	N	Y	N
Cornyn	Y	Y	Y	N	Y	N
UTAH						
Hatch	Y	Y	Y	N	Y	N
Bennett	Y	Y	Y	N	Y	N
VERMONT						
Leahy	N	N	N	Y	N	Y
Sanders	N	N	N	Y	N	Y
VIRGINIA						
Webb	Y	N	N	N	Y	Y
Warner	Y	N	N	Y	Y	Y
WASHINGTON						
Murray	Y	N	N	Y	Y	Y
Cantwell	Y	N	N	Y	Y	Y
WEST VIRGINIA						
Rockefeller	Y	N	N	Y	Y	Y
Manchin	Y	N	N	N	Y	Y
WISCONSIN						
Kohl	Y	N	N	Y	Y	Y
Feingold	N	N	N	Y	N	Y
WYOMING						
Enzi	Y	Y	Y	N	Y	?
Barrasso	Y	Y	Y	N	Y	N

KEY	**Republicans**	Democrats	*Independents*	
Y	Voted for (yea)	X	Paired against	C Voted "present" to avoid possible conflict of interest
#	Paired for	–	Announced against	
+	Announced for	P	Voted "present"	? Did not vote or otherwise make a position known
N	Voted against (nay)			

IN THE SENATE | By Vote Number

278. **HR 5281. Immigration Policy Revisions/Cloture.** Motion to invoke cloture (thus limiting debate) on the Reid, D-Nev., motion to concur in the House amendment to the third Senate amendment to the bill. The House amendment would allow the Homeland Security Department to grant conditional non-immigrant status to the undocumented children of illegal immigrants if they meet certain requirements, including having been in the United States continuously for more than five years, having been younger than 16 when they entered the country and having been admitted to a U.S. college or university or enlisted in the military. The individual would have to pay a $525 application surcharge and a subsequent fee and could be eligible to apply for legal permanent status after 10 years. Motion rejected 55-41: D 50-5; R 3-36; I 2-0. Three-fifths of the total Senate (60) is required to invoke cloture. A "yea" was a vote in support of the president's position. Dec. 18, 2010.

279. **HR 2965. 'Don't Ask, Don't Tell' Policy Repeal/Cloture.** Motion to invoke cloture (thus limiting debate) on the Reid, D-Nev., motion to concur in the Senate amendment to the bill with a House amendment that would allow for the repeal of the "don't ask, don't tell" policy on military service. Motion agreed to 63-33: D 55-0; R 6-33; I 2-0. Three-fifths of the total Senate (60) is required to invoke cloture. Dec. 18, 2010.

280. **Hollander Nomination/Confirmation.** Confirmation of President Obama's nomination of Ellen Hollander of Maryland to be a judge for the U.S. District Court for the District of Maryland. Confirmed 95-0: D 54-0; R 39-0; I 2-0. A "yea" was a vote in support of the president's position. Dec. 18, 2010.

281. **HR 2965. 'Don't Ask, Don't Tell' Policy Repeal/Motion to Concur.** Reid, D-Nev., motion to concur in the Senate amendment to the bill with a House amendment that would allow for the repeal of the "don't ask, don't tell" policy, which prohibits military service by openly gay men and women, after certain requirements are met, including the submission of a written certification, signed by the president, the secretary of Defense and the chairman of the Joint Chiefs of Staff, that the repeal is consistent with military readiness and effectiveness and that they have considered the recommendations of the Comprehensive Review Working Group and prepared the necessary policies and regulations to implement the repeal. Motion agreed to, thus clearing the bill for the president, 65-31: D 55-0; R 8-31; I 2-0. A "yea" was a vote in support of the president's position. Dec. 18, 2010.

282. **Treaty Doc 111-5. New START Agreement/Preamble.** McCain, R-Ariz., amendment that would strike language from the preamble regarding the relationship between offensive and defensive weapons. Rejected 37-59: D 0-55; R 36-3; I 1-1. Dec. 18, 2010.

283. **Treaty Doc 111-5. New START Agreement/Preamble.** Risch, R-Idaho, amendment that would add language to the preamble regarding the importance of tactical nuclear weapons. Rejected 32-60: D 0-53; R 32-5; I 0-2. Dec. 19, 2010.

284. **Lohier Nomination/Confirmation.** Confirmation of President Obama's nomination of Raymond Joseph Lohier Jr. of New York to be a judge for the 2nd U.S. Circuit Court of Appeals. Confirmed 92-0: D 53-0; R 37-0; I 2-0. A "yea" was a vote in support of the president's position. Dec. 19, 2010.

	278	279	280	281	282	283	284
ALABAMA							
Shelby	N	N	Y	N	Y	Y	Y
Sessions	N	N	Y	N	Y	Y	Y
ALASKA							
Murkowski	Y	Y	Y	Y	Y	Y	Y
Begich	Y	Y	Y	Y	N	N	Y
ARIZONA							
McCain	N	N	Y	N	Y	Y	Y
Kyl	N	N	Y	N	Y	Y	Y
ARKANSAS							
Lincoln	Y	Y	Y	Y	N	N	Y
Pryor	N	Y	Y	Y	N	N	Y
CALIFORNIA							
Feinstein	Y	Y	Y	Y	N	N	Y
Boxer	Y	Y	Y	Y	N	N	Y
COLORADO							
Udall	Y	Y	Y	Y	N	N	Y
Bennet	Y	Y	Y	Y	N	N	Y
CONNECTICUT							
Dodd	Y	Y	Y	Y	N	N	Y
Lieberman	Y	Y	Y	Y	Y	N	Y
DELAWARE							
Carper	Y	Y	Y	Y	N	N	Y
Coons	Y	Y	Y	Y	N	N	Y
FLORIDA							
Nelson	Y	Y	Y	Y	N	N	Y
LeMieux	N	N	Y	N	Y	Y	Y
GEORGIA							
Chambliss	N	N	Y	N	Y	Y	Y
Isakson	N	N	Y	N	Y	?	?
HAWAII							
Inouye	Y	Y	Y	Y	N	N	Y
Akaka	Y	Y	Y	Y	N	N	Y
IDAHO							
Crapo	N	N	Y	N	Y	Y	Y
Risch	N	N	Y	N	Y	Y	Y
ILLINOIS							
Durbin	Y	Y	Y	Y	N	N	Y
Kirk	N	Y	Y	Y	Y	?	?
INDIANA							
Lugar	Y	N	Y	N	N	N	Y
Bayh	Y	Y	Y	Y	N	N	Y
IOWA							
Grassley	N	N	Y	N	Y	Y	Y
Harkin	Y	Y	Y	Y	N	N	Y
KANSAS							
Brownback	N	N	Y	N	Y	Y	Y
Roberts	N	N	Y	N	Y	Y	Y
KENTUCKY							
McConnell	N	N	Y	N	Y	Y	Y
Bunning	–	–	+	–	+	+	+
LOUISIANA							
Landrieu	Y	Y	?	Y	N	N	Y
Vitter	N	N	Y	N	Y	Y	Y
MAINE							
Snowe	N	Y	Y	Y	N	Y	Y
Collins	N	Y	Y	Y	Y	Y	Y
MARYLAND							
Mikulski	Y	Y	Y	Y	N	N	Y
Cardin	Y	Y	Y	Y	N	N	Y
MASSACHUSETTS							
Kerry	Y	Y	Y	Y	N	N	Y
Brown	N	Y	Y	Y	Y	Y	Y
MICHIGAN							
Levin	Y	Y	Y	Y	N	N	Y
Stabenow	Y	Y	Y	Y	N	N	Y
MINNESOTA							
Klobuchar	Y	Y	Y	Y	N	N	Y
Franken	Y	Y	Y	Y	N	N	Y
MISSISSIPPI							
Cochran	N	N	Y	N	Y	Y	Y
Wicker	N	N	Y	N	Y	Y	Y
MISSOURI							
Bond	N	N	Y	N	Y	Y	Y
McCaskill	Y	Y	Y	Y	N	N	Y

	278	279	280	281	282	283	284
MONTANA							
Baucus	N	Y	Y	Y	N	N	Y
Tester	N	Y	Y	Y	N	N	Y
NEBRASKA							
Nelson	N	Y	Y	Y	N	N	Y
Johanns	N	N	Y	N	Y	Y	Y
NEVADA							
Reid	Y	Y	Y	Y	N	N	Y
Ensign	N	N	Y	Y	Y	Y	Y
NEW HAMPSHIRE							
Gregg	?	?	?	?	?	N	Y
Shaheen	Y	Y	Y	Y	N	?	?
NEW JERSEY							
Lautenberg	Y	Y	Y	Y	N	N	Y
Menendez	Y	Y	Y	Y	N	N	Y
NEW MEXICO							
Bingaman	Y	Y	Y	Y	N	N	Y
Udall	Y	Y	Y	Y	N	N	Y
NEW YORK							
Schumer	Y	Y	Y	Y	N	N	Y
Gillibrand	Y	Y	Y	Y	N	N	Y
NORTH CAROLINA							
Burr	N	N	Y	Y	Y	Y	Y
Hagan	N	Y	Y	Y	N	N	Y
NORTH DAKOTA							
Conrad	Y	Y	Y	Y	N	N	Y
Dorgan	Y	Y	Y	Y	N	N	Y
OHIO							
Voinovich	N	Y	Y	Y	N	?	?
Brown	Y	Y	Y	Y	N	N	Y
OKLAHOMA							
Inhofe	N	N	Y	N	Y	Y	Y
Coburn	N	N	Y	N	Y	Y	Y
OREGON							
Wyden	Y	Y	Y	Y	N	?	?
Merkley	Y	Y	Y	Y	N	N	Y
PENNSYLVANIA							
Specter	Y	Y	Y	Y	N	?	?
Casey	Y	Y	Y	Y	N	N	Y
RHODE ISLAND							
Reed	Y	Y	Y	Y	N	N	Y
Whitehouse	Y	Y	Y	Y	N	N	Y
SOUTH CAROLINA							
Graham	N	N	Y	N	Y	Y	Y
DeMint	N	N	Y	N	Y	+	+
SOUTH DAKOTA							
Johnson	Y	Y	Y	Y	N	N	Y
Thune	N	N	Y	N	Y	Y	Y
TENNESSEE							
Alexander	N	N	Y	N	Y	Y	Y
Corker	N	N	Y	N	Y	Y	Y
TEXAS							
Hutchison	N	N	Y	N	Y	Y	Y
Cornyn	N	N	Y	N	Y	Y	Y
UTAH							
Hatch	–	–	+	–	+	Y	Y
Bennett	Y	N	Y	N	N	N	Y
VERMONT							
Leahy	Y	Y	Y	Y	N	N	Y
Sanders	Y	Y	Y	Y	N	N	Y
VIRGINIA							
Webb	Y	Y	Y	Y	N	N	Y
Warner	Y	Y	Y	Y	N	N	Y
WASHINGTON							
Murray	Y	Y	Y	Y	N	N	Y
Cantwell	Y	Y	Y	Y	N	N	Y
WEST VIRGINIA							
Rockefeller	Y	Y	Y	Y	N	N	Y
Manchin	–	–	?	?	?	N	Y
WISCONSIN							
Kohl	Y	Y	Y	Y	N	N	Y
Feingold	Y	Y	Y	Y	N	N	Y
WYOMING							
Enzi	N	N	Y	N	Y	Y	Y
Barrasso	N	N	Y	N	Y	Y	Y

KEY   **Republicans**   Democrats   *Independents*

Y Voted for (yea)	X Paired against	C Voted "present" to avoid possible conflict of interest
# Paired for	– Announced against	
+ Announced for	P Voted "present"	? Did not vote or otherwise make a position known
N Voted against (nay)		

IN THE SENATE | By Vote Number

285. **Treaty Doc 111-5. New START Agreement/Inspections.** Inhofe, R-Okla., amendment to the treaty to require a larger number of inspections and verifications regarding nuclear arsenals. Rejected 33-64: D 0-54; R 33-8; I 0-2. Dec. 20, 2010.

286. **Treaty Doc 111-5. New START Agreement/Delivery Systems.** Thune, R-S.D., amendment to the treaty to increase the number of nuclear delivery systems allowed under the treaty, from 700 to 720. Rejected 33-64: D 0-54; R 33-8; I 0-2. Dec. 20, 2010.

287. **Treaty Doc 111-5. New START Agreement/Tactical Nuclear Weapons.** LeMieux, R-Fla., amendment to the treaty to require the United States and Russia to enter into negotiations on a treaty regarding tactical nuclear weapons. Rejected 35-62: D 0-54; R 35-6; I 0-2. Dec. 20, 2010.

288. **HR 3082. Fiscal 2011 Continuing Appropriations/Cloture.** Motion to invoke cloture (thus limiting debate) on the Reid, D-Nev., motion to concur in the House amendment to the Senate amendment with a further Reid substitute amendment that would continue most appropriations at fiscal 2010-enacted levels through March 4, 2011. Motion agreed to 82-14: D 52-2; R 28-12; I 2-0. Three-fifths of the total Senate (60) is required to invoke cloture. Dec. 21, 2010.

289. **HR 3082. Fiscal 2011 Continuing Appropriations/Motion to Concur.** Reid, D-Nev., motion to concur in the House amendment to the Senate amendment with a further Reid substitute amendment that would continue most appropriations at fiscal 2010-enacted levels through March 4, 2011. The measure would provide an overall annualized spending rate that is $1.16 billion more than fiscal 2010 levels. It would provide additional funding for the Low Income Home Energy Assistance Program and Pell grants. It also would allow the awarding of a Navy contract for shipbuilding of Littoral Combat Ships to multiple suppliers. Motion agreed to 79-16: D 52-2; R 25-14; I 2-0. Dec. 21, 2010.

290. **Pearson Nomination/Confirmation.** Confirmation of President Obama's nomination of Benita Y. Pearson of Ohio to be a judge for the U.S. District Court for the Northern District of Ohio. Confirmed 56-39: D 53-1; R 1-38; I 2-0. A "yea" was a vote in support of the president's position. Dec. 21, 2010.

291. **Martinez Nomination/Confirmation.** Confirmation of President Obama's nomination of William Joseph Martinez of Colorado to be a judge for the U.S. District Court for the District of Colorado. Confirmed 58-37: D 54-0; R 2-37; I 2-0. A "yea" was a vote in support of the president's position. Dec. 21, 2010.

	285	286	287	288	289	290	291
ALABAMA							
Shelby	Y	Y	Y	Y	Y	N	N
Sessions	Y	Y	Y	Y	Y	N	N
ALASKA							
Murkowski	N	N	Y	Y	Y	N	N
Begich	N	N	N	Y	Y	Y	Y
ARIZONA							
McCain	Y	Y	Y	N	N	N	N
Kyl	Y	Y	Y	Y	Y	N	N
ARKANSAS							
Lincoln	N	N	N	Y	Y	Y	Y
Pryor	N	N	N	Y	Y	Y	Y
CALIFORNIA							
Feinstein	N	N	N	Y	Y	Y	Y
Boxer	N	N	N	Y	Y	Y	Y
COLORADO							
Udall	N	N	N	Y	Y	Y	Y
Bennet	N	N	N	Y	Y	Y	Y
CONNECTICUT							
Dodd	N	N	N	Y	Y	Y	Y
Lieberman	N	N	N	Y	Y	Y	Y
DELAWARE							
Carper	N	N	N	Y	Y	Y	Y
Coons	N	N	N	Y	Y	Y	Y
FLORIDA							
Nelson	N	N	N	Y	Y	Y	Y
LeMieux	Y	Y	N	N	N	N	N
GEORGIA							
Chambliss	Y	Y	Y	N	N	N	N
Isakson	N	Y	Y	N	N	N	N
HAWAII							
Inouye	N	N	N	Y	Y	Y	Y
Akaka	N	N	N	Y	Y	Y	Y
IDAHO							
Crapo	Y	Y	Y	N	N	N	N
Risch	Y	Y	Y	N	N	N	N
ILLINOIS							
Durbin	N	N	N	Y	Y	Y	Y
Kirk	Y	Y	Y	Y	Y	N	N
INDIANA							
Lugar	N	N	N	Y	Y	N	N
Bayh	?	?	?	?	?	?	?
IOWA							
Grassley	Y	Y	Y	Y	Y	N	N
Harkin	N	N	N	Y	Y	Y	Y
KANSAS							
Brownback	?	?	?	?	?	?	?
Roberts	Y	Y	Y	Y	Y	N	N
KENTUCKY							
McConnell	Y	Y	Y	Y	Y	N	N
Bunning	Y	Y	Y	Y	Y	N	N
LOUISIANA							
Landrieu	N	N	N	Y	Y	Y	Y
Vitter	Y	Y	Y	N	N	N	N
MAINE							
Snowe	Y	Y	Y	Y	Y	N	N
Collins	Y	N	Y	Y	Y	N	Y
MARYLAND							
Mikulski	N	N	N	Y	Y	Y	Y
Cardin	N	N	N	Y	Y	Y	Y
MASSACHUSETTS							
Kerry	N	N	N	Y	Y	Y	Y
Brown	Y	Y	Y	Y	Y	N	N
MICHIGAN							
Levin	N	N	N	Y	Y	Y	Y
Stabenow	N	N	N	Y	Y	Y	Y
MINNESOTA							
Klobuchar	N	N	N	Y	Y	Y	Y
Franken	N	N	N	Y	Y	Y	Y
MISSISSIPPI							
Cochran	Y	Y	Y	Y	Y	N	N
Wicker	Y	Y	Y	Y	Y	N	N
MISSOURI							
Bond	Y	Y	Y	Y	?	?	?
McCaskill	N	N	N	Y	Y	Y	Y
MONTANA							
Baucus	N	N	N	Y	Y	Y	Y
Tester	N	N	N	Y	Y	Y	Y
NEBRASKA							
Nelson	N	N	N	N	N	N	Y
Johanns	Y	Y	Y	Y	Y	N	N
NEVADA							
Reid	N	N	N	Y	Y	Y	Y
Ensign	Y	Y	Y	Y	Y	N	N
NEW HAMPSHIRE							
Gregg	N	N	N	?	?	?	?
Shaheen	N	N	N	Y	Y	Y	Y
NEW JERSEY							
Lautenberg	N	N	N	Y	Y	Y	Y
Menendez	N	N	N	Y	Y	Y	Y
NEW MEXICO							
Bingaman	N	N	N	Y	Y	Y	Y
Udall	N	N	N	Y	Y	Y	Y
NEW YORK							
Schumer	N	N	N	Y	Y	Y	Y
Gillibrand	N	N	N	Y	Y	Y	Y
NORTH CAROLINA							
Burr	Y	Y	Y	N	N	N	N
Hagan	N	N	N	Y	Y	Y	Y
NORTH DAKOTA							
Conrad	N	N	N	Y	Y	Y	Y
Dorgan	N	N	N	Y	Y	Y	Y
OHIO							
Voinovich	N	N	N	Y	Y	Y	Y
Brown	N	N	N	Y	Y	Y	Y
OKLAHOMA							
Inhofe	Y	Y	Y	N	N	N	N
Coburn	Y	Y	Y	N	N	N	N
OREGON							
Wyden	?	?	?	?	?	?	?
Merkley	N	N	N	Y	Y	Y	Y
PENNSYLVANIA							
Specter	N	N	N	Y	Y	Y	Y
Casey	N	N	N	Y	Y	Y	Y
RHODE ISLAND							
Reed	N	N	N	Y	Y	Y	Y
Whitehouse	N	N	N	Y	Y	Y	Y
SOUTH CAROLINA							
Graham	Y	Y	Y	N	N	N	N
DeMint	Y	Y	Y	N	N	N	N
SOUTH DAKOTA							
Johnson	N	N	N	Y	Y	Y	Y
Thune	Y	Y	Y	Y	Y	N	N
TENNESSEE							
Alexander	N	N	N	Y	Y	Y	Y
Corker	N	N	N	Y	Y	Y	Y
TEXAS							
Hutchison	Y	Y	Y	Y	Y	N	N
Cornyn	Y	Y	Y	Y	Y	N	N
UTAH							
Hatch	Y	Y	Y	N	N	N	N
Bennett	N	N	N	Y	Y	Y	Y
VERMONT							
Leahy	N	N	N	Y	Y	Y	Y
Sanders	N	N	N	Y	Y	Y	Y
VIRGINIA							
Webb	N	N	N	Y	Y	Y	Y
Warner	N	N	N	Y	Y	Y	Y
WASHINGTON							
Murray	N	N	N	Y	Y	Y	Y
Cantwell	N	N	N	Y	Y	Y	Y
WEST VIRGINIA							
Rockefeller	N	N	N	Y	Y	Y	Y
Manchin	N	N	N	Y	Y	Y	Y
WISCONSIN							
Kohl	N	N	N	Y	Y	Y	Y
Feingold	N	N	N	N	N	Y	Y
WYOMING							
Enzi	Y	Y	Y	Y	N	N	N
Barrasso	Y	Y	Y	Y	N	N	N

KEY   **Republicans**   Democrats   *Independents*

Y Voted for (yea)	X Paired against
# Paired for	– Announced against
+ Announced for	P Voted "present"
N Voted against (nay)	

C Voted "present" to avoid possible conflict of interest

? Did not vote or otherwise make a position known

IN THE SENATE | By Vote Number

292. **Treaty Doc 111-5. New START Agreement/Cloture.** Motion to invoke cloture (thus limiting debate) with respect to the New START agreement with Russia that would restrict each country to a maximum of 1,550 deployed nuclear warheads, a cut of about 30 percent. The resolution of ratification would state that the April 2010 unilateral statement by Russia on missile defense does not impose any legal obligation on the United States. Motion agreed to 67-28: D 54-0; R 11-28; I 2-0. Three-fifths of the total Senate (60) is required to invoke cloture. Dec. 21, 2010.

293. **Treaty Doc 111-5. New START Agreement/Rail-Mobile Missiles.** Ensign, R-Nev., amendment to the treaty to clarify the definition of rail-mobile missiles. Rejected 32-63: D 0-54; R 32-7; I 0-2. Dec. 21, 2010.

294. **Treaty Doc 111-5. New START Agreement/Stolen Military Property.** Kerry, D-Mass., motion to table (kill) the Risch, R-Idaho, amendment to the resolution of ratification to require certification that Russia has returned stolen U.S. military property. Motion agreed to 61-32: D 53-0; R 7-31; I 1-1. Dec. 21, 2010.

295. **Treaty Doc 111-5. New START Agreement/Bilateral Commission.** Wicker, R-Miss., amendment to the resolution of ratification to specify that provisions adopted by the Bilateral Consultative Commission affecting substantive rights must be submitted to the Senate. Rejected 34-59: D 0-53; R 34-4; I 0-2. Dec. 21, 2010.

296. **Treaty Doc 111-5. New START Agreement/Sea-Based Missiles.** Kyl, R-Ariz., amendment to the resolution of ratification to require the parties to enter into a legally binding side agreement on nuclear missiles launched from the sea. Rejected 31-62: D 0-53; R 31-7; I 0-2. Dec. 21, 2010.

297. **Treaty Doc 111-5. New START Agreement/Telemetry.** Kyl, R-Ariz., amendment to the resolution of ratification to require a legally binding side agreement on telemetric exchanges for new ballistic missile systems. It also would require agreement on restoring Russian use of shrouds to interfere with the counting of warheads. Rejected 30-63: D 0-53; R 30-8; I 0-2. Dec. 21, 2010.

	292	293	294	295	296	297
ALABAMA						
Shelby	N	Y	N	?	?	?
Sessions	N	Y	N	Y	Y	Y
ALASKA						
Murkowski	Y	N	Y	Y	N	N
Begich	Y	N	Y	?	?	?
ARIZONA						
McCain	N	Y	N	Y	Y	Y
Kyl	N	Y	N	Y	Y	Y
ARKANSAS						
Lincoln	Y	N	Y	N	N	N
Pryor	Y	N	Y	N	N	N
CALIFORNIA						
Feinstein	Y	N	Y	N	N	N
Boxer	Y	N	Y	N	N	N
COLORADO						
Udall	Y	N	Y	N	N	N
Bennet	Y	N	Y	N	N	N
CONNECTICUT						
Dodd	Y	N	Y	N	N	N
Lieberman	Y	N	N	N	N	N
DELAWARE						
Carper	Y	N	Y	N	N	N
Coons	Y	N	Y	N	N	N
FLORIDA						
Nelson	Y	N	Y	N	N	N
LeMieux	N	Y	N	Y	Y	Y
GEORGIA						
Chambliss	N	Y	N	Y	Y	Y
Isakson	Y	Y	N	Y	N	N
HAWAII						
Inouye	Y	N	Y	N	N	N
Akaka	Y	N	Y	N	N	N
IDAHO						
Crapo	N	Y	N	Y	Y	Y
Risch	N	Y	N	Y	Y	Y
ILLINOIS						
Durbin	Y	N	Y	N	N	N
Kirk	N	Y	Y	Y	Y	Y
INDIANA						
Lugar	Y	N	Y	N	N	N
Bayh	?	?	?	?	?	?
IOWA						
Grassley	N	Y	N	Y	N	Y
Harkin	Y	N	Y	N	N	N
KANSAS						
Brownback	?	?	?	?	?	?
Roberts	N	Y	N	Y	Y	Y
KENTUCKY						
McConnell	N	Y	N	Y	Y	Y
Bunning	N	Y	N	Y	Y	Y
LOUISIANA						
Landrieu	Y	N	Y	N	N	N
Vitter	N	Y	N	Y	Y	Y
MAINE						
Snowe	Y	Y	N	Y	Y	Y
Collins	Y	N	Y	Y	Y	N
MARYLAND						
Mikulski	Y	N	Y	N	N	N
Cardin	Y	N	Y	N	N	N
MASSACHUSETTS						
Kerry	Y	N	Y	N	N	N
Brown	Y	Y	N	Y	Y	Y
MICHIGAN						
Levin	Y	N	Y	N	N	N
Stabenow	Y	N	Y	N	N	N
MINNESOTA						
Klobuchar	Y	N	Y	N	N	N
Franken	Y	N	Y	N	N	N
MISSISSIPPI						
Cochran	Y	Y	N	Y	Y	Y
Wicker	N	Y	N	Y	Y	Y
MISSOURI						
Bond	?	?	?	?	?	?
McCaskill	Y	N	Y	N	N	N
MONTANA						
Baucus	Y	N	Y	N	N	N
Tester	Y	N	Y	N	N	N
NEBRASKA						
Nelson	Y	N	Y	N	N	N
Johanns	N	Y	N	Y	Y	Y
NEVADA						
Reid	Y	N	Y	N	N	N
Ensign	N	Y	N	Y	Y	Y
NEW HAMPSHIRE						
Gregg	?	?	?	?	?	?
Shaheen	Y	N	Y	N	N	N
NEW JERSEY						
Lautenberg	Y	N	Y	N	N	N
Menendez	Y	N	Y	N	N	N
NEW MEXICO						
Bingaman	Y	N	Y	N	N	N
Udall	Y	N	Y	N	N	N
NEW YORK						
Schumer	Y	N	Y	N	N	N
Gillibrand	Y	N	?	N	N	N
NORTH CAROLINA						
Burr	N	Y	N	Y	Y	Y
Hagan	Y	N	Y	N	N	N
NORTH DAKOTA						
Conrad	Y	N	Y	N	N	N
Dorgan	Y	N	Y	N	N	N
OHIO						
Voinovich	Y	N	N	N	N	N
Brown	Y	N	Y	N	N	N
OKLAHOMA						
Inhofe	N	Y	N	Y	Y	Y
Coburn	N	Y	?	Y	Y	Y
OREGON						
Wyden	?	?	?	?	?	?
Merkley	Y	N	Y	N	N	N
PENNSYLVANIA						
Specter	Y	N	Y	N	N	N
Casey	Y	N	Y	N	N	N
RHODE ISLAND						
Reed	Y	N	Y	N	N	N
Whitehouse	Y	N	Y	N	N	N
SOUTH CAROLINA						
Graham	N	Y	N	Y	Y	Y
DeMint	N	Y	N	Y	Y	Y
SOUTH DAKOTA						
Johnson	Y	N	Y	N	N	N
Thune	N	Y	N	Y	Y	Y
TENNESSEE						
Alexander	Y	N	Y	Y	N	N
Corker	Y	N	Y	N	N	N
TEXAS						
Hutchison	N	Y	N	Y	Y	Y
Cornyn	N	Y	N	Y	Y	Y
UTAH						
Hatch	N	Y	N	Y	Y	Y
Bennett	Y	N	Y	N	N	N
VERMONT						
Leahy	Y	N	Y	N	N	N
Sanders	Y	N	Y	N	N	N
VIRGINIA						
Webb	Y	N	Y	N	N	N
Warner	Y	N	Y	N	N	N
WASHINGTON						
Murray	Y	N	Y	N	N	N
Cantwell	Y	N	Y	N	N	N
WEST VIRGINIA						
Rockefeller	Y	N	Y	N	N	N
Manchin	Y	N	Y	N	N	N
WISCONSIN						
Kohl	Y	N	Y	N	N	N
Feingold	Y	N	Y	N	N	N
WYOMING						
Enzi	N	Y	N	Y	Y	Y
Barrasso	N	Y	N	Y	Y	Y

KEY   **Republicans**   Democrats   *Independents*

Y Voted for (yea)	**X** Paired against	**C** Voted "present" to avoid possible conflict of interest
# Paired for	**–** Announced against	
+ Announced for	**P** Voted "present"	**?** Did not vote or otherwise make a position known
N Voted against (nay)		

IN THE SENATE | By Vote Number

298. **Treaty Doc 111-5. New START Agreement/Adoption.** Adoption of the resolution of ratification for the New Strategic Arms Reduction Treaty (START) with Russia. The treaty would restrict each country to a maximum of 1,550 deployed nuclear warheads, a cut of about 30 percent. The resolution of ratification would state that the April 2010 unilateral statement by Russia on missile defense does not impose any legal obligation on the United States. Adopted (thus consenting to ratification) 71-26: D 56-0; R 13-26; I 2-0. A two-thirds majority of those present and voting (65 in this case) is required for adoption of resolutions of ratification. A "yea" was a vote in support of the president's position. Dec. 22, 2010.

299. **Murguia Nomination/Confirmation.** Confirmation of President Obama's nomination of Mary Helen Murguia of Arizona to be a judge for the 9th U.S. Circuit Court of Appeals. Confirmed 89-0: D 51-0; R 36-0; I 2-0. A "yea" was a vote in support of the president's position. Dec. 22, 2010.

	298	299			298	299
ALABAMA				**MONTANA**		
Shelby	N	Y		Baucus	Y	Y
Sessions	N	Y		Tester	Y	Y
ALASKA				**NEBRASKA**		
Murkowski	Y	Y		Nelson	Y	Y
Begich	Y	Y		Johanns	Y	Y
ARIZONA				**NEVADA**		
McCain	N	Y		Reid	Y	Y
Kyl	N	Y		Ensign	N	Y
ARKANSAS				**NEW HAMPSHIRE**		
Lincoln	Y	Y		Gregg	Y	Y
Pryor	Y	Y		Shaheen	Y	Y
CALIFORNIA				**NEW JERSEY**		
Feinstein	Y	Y		Lautenberg	Y	Y
Boxer	Y	Y		Menendez	Y	Y
COLORADO				**NEW MEXICO**		
Udall	Y	Y		Bingaman	Y	Y
Bennet	Y	Y		Udall	Y	Y
CONNECTICUT				**NEW YORK**		
Dodd	Y	Y		Schumer	Y	Y
Lieberman	Y	Y		Gillibrand	Y	Y
DELAWARE				**NORTH CAROLINA**		
Carper	Y	Y		Burr	N	Y
Coons	Y	Y		Hagan	Y	Y
FLORIDA				**NORTH DAKOTA**		
Nelson	Y	Y		Conrad	Y	Y
LeMieux	N	Y		Dorgan	Y	Y
GEORGIA				**OHIO**		
Chambliss	N	Y		Voinovich	Y	Y
Isakson	Y	Y		Brown	Y	Y
HAWAII				**OKLAHOMA**		
Inouye	Y	Y		Inhofe	N	Y
Akaka	Y	Y		Coburn	N	Y
IDAHO				**OREGON**		
Crapo	N	Y		Wyden	Y	?
Risch	N	Y		Merkley	Y	Y
ILLINOIS				**PENNSYLVANIA**		
Durbin	Y	Y		Specter	Y	Y
Kirk	N	Y		Casey	Y	Y
INDIANA				**RHODE ISLAND**		
Lugar	Y	Y		Reed	Y	Y
Bayh	Y	Y		Whitehouse	Y	Y
IOWA				**SOUTH CAROLINA**		
Grassley	N	Y		Graham	N	Y
Harkin	Y	?		DeMint	N	Y
KANSAS				**SOUTH DAKOTA**		
Brownback	?	?		Johnson	Y	Y
Roberts	N	?		Thune	N	Y
KENTUCKY				**TENNESSEE**		
McConnell	N	Y		Alexander	Y	?
Bunning	?	?		Corker	Y	Y
LOUISIANA				**TEXAS**		
Landrieu	Y	Y		Hutchison	N	Y
Vitter	N	?		Cornyn	N	Y
MAINE				**UTAH**		
Snowe	Y	Y		Hatch	N	Y
Collins	Y	Y		Bennett	Y	Y
MARYLAND				**VERMONT**		
Mikulski	Y	Y		Leahy	Y	Y
Cardin	Y	Y		*Sanders*	Y	Y
MASSACHUSETTS				**VIRGINIA**		
Kerry	Y	Y		Webb	Y	Y
Brown	Y	Y		Warner	Y	Y
MICHIGAN				**WASHINGTON**		
Levin	Y	Y		Murray	Y	Y
Stabenow	Y	?		Cantwell	Y	Y
MINNESOTA				**WEST VIRGINIA**		
Klobuchar	Y	Y		Rockefeller	Y	Y
Franken	Y	Y		Manchin	Y	Y
MISSISSIPPI				**WISCONSIN**		
Cochran	Y	Y		Kohl	Y	Y
Wicker	N	Y		Feingold	Y	?
MISSOURI				**WYOMING**		
Bond	?	?		Enzi	N	Y
McCaskill	Y	?		Barrasso	N	Y

KEY **Republicans** Democrats *Independents*

Y	Voted for (yea)	X Paired against	C Voted "present" to avoid possible conflict of interest
#	Paired for	− Announced against	
+	Announced for	P Voted "present"	? Did not vote or otherwise make a position known
N	Voted against (nay)		

Senate Roll Call Index by Subject

Appendix I

GENERAL INDEX

General Index